SENIORS'
· · · · ·
DEVOTIONAL BIBLE

PRESENTED
TO

....

BY

....

ON

....

SENIORS'
DEVOTIONAL BIBLE

NEW INTERNATIONAL VERSION

ZondervanPublishingHouse
GRAND RAPIDS, MICHIGAN 49530, U.S.A

You will be pleased to know that a portion of the purchase price of your new NIV Bible has been provided to International Bible Society to help spread the gospel of Jesus Christ around the world!

CONTENTS

INTRODUCTION—
SENIORS' DEVOTIONAL BIBLE

Someone once said, "To know how to grow old is the master work of wisdom, and one of the most difficult chapters in the great art of living." This special edition of the Bible was carefully crafted to highlight God's wisdom for your life, wherever you are in the process of "growing old." It covers issues that are important to you as a fellow traveler with brothers and sisters of all ages, and it covers issues that are especially important to you as an older adult. The NIV Seniors' Devotional Bible provides the full text of God's powerful and enduring Word, plus a year's worth of devotions written by a wide variety of men and women who have insight to share with those who want to "know how to grow old."

The Bible

The NIV Seniors' Devotional Bible features the complete text of the Holy Bible, New International Version. This accurate and readable translation will help you to experience the stories, the people, the truth of the Bible in a fresh way.

Book Introductions

The introduction to each of the 66 books of the Bible highlights that book's practical themes. Each introduction provides helpful background information, as well as practical applications to your daily life.

The Devotions

The devotions are designed to provide provocative and practical commentary on a broad array of issues that touch your life. Many of the devotions will give you something to think about throughout the day. The benefit you receive from your daily reading will be greatly enhanced as you read the passage and verse for the day, as well as the suggested additional Scripture readings.

The devotions follow the days of the week. No matter when you begin your reading, simply turn to a devotion for that day. To proceed to the next reading, look at the bottom of the devotion where you will be directed to the page number for the next devotion.

Each Friday devotion will direct you to a "Weekending," which will provide brief devotional thoughts in poetic form combined with suggested Scripture readings. The end of every "Weekending" will direct you to the following Monday's devotion.

Author Biographies

You may recognize the names of many of the men and women who contributed devotions to the NIV Seniors' Devotional Bible. The author index, found on page 1647, gives information about each author, as well a list of the page numbers where his or her devotions appear.

Subject Index

The subject index on page 1651 gives you a handy way to find devotions that address topics of interest to you. No matter what your circumstances —grandparent or grandparent-in-waiting, retiree or retiree-in-waiting, married or single—the subject index will direct you to a devotion and Scripture passage that will meet your need.

PREFACE

· · · · · · · · · ●●● · · · ·

THE NEW INTERNATIONAL VERSION is a completely new translation of the Holy Bible made by over a hundred scholars working directly from the best available Hebrew, Aramaic and Greek texts. It had its beginning in 1965 when, after several years of exploratory study by committees from the Christian Reformed Church and the National Association of Evangelicals, a group of scholars met at Palos Heights, Illinois, and concurred in the need for a new translation of the Bible in contemporary English. This group, though not made up of official church representatives, was transdenominational. Its conclusion was endorsed by a large number of leaders from many denominations who met in Chicago in 1966.

Responsibility for the new version was delegated by the Palos Heights group to a self-governing body of fifteen, the Committee on Bible Translation, composed for the most part of biblical scholars from colleges, universities and seminaries. In 1967 the New York Bible Society (now the International Bible Society) generously undertook the financial sponsorship of the project—a sponsorship that made it possible to enlist the help of many distinguished scholars. The fact that participants from the United States, Great Britain, Canada, Australia and New Zealand worked together gave the project its international scope. That they were from many denominations—including Anglican, Assemblies of God, Baptist, Brethren, Christian Reformed, Church of Christ, Evangelical Free, Lutheran, Mennonite, Methodist, Nazarene, Presbyterian, Wesleyan and other churches—helped to safeguard the translation from sectarian bias.

How it was made helps to give the New International Version its distinctiveness. The translation of each book was assigned to a team of scholars. Next, one of the Intermediate Editorial Committees revised the initial translation, with constant reference to the Hebrew, Aramaic or Greek. Their work then went to one of the General Editorial Committees, which checked it in detail and made another thorough revision. This revision in turn was carefully reviewed by the Committee on Bible Translation, which made further changes and then released the final version for publication. In this way the entire Bible underwent three revisions, during each of which the translation was examined for its faithfulness to the original languages and for its English style.

All this involved many thousands of hours of research and discussion regarding the meaning of the texts and the precise way of putting them into English. It may well be that no other translation has been made by a more thorough process of review and revision from committee to committee than this one.

From the beginning of the project, the Committee on Bible Translation held to certain goals for the New International Version: that it would be an accurate translation and one that would have clarity and literary quality and so prove suitable for public and private reading, teaching, preaching, memorizing and liturgical use. The Committee also sought to preserve some measure of continuity with the long tradition of translating the Scriptures into English.

In working toward these goals, the translators were united in their commitment to the authority and infallibility of the Bible as God's Word in written form. They believe that it contains the divine answer to the deepest needs of humanity, that it sheds unique light on our path in a dark world, and that it sets forth the way to our eternal well-being.

The first concern of the translators has been the accuracy of the translation and its fidelity to the thought of the biblical writers. They have weighed the significance of the lexical and grammatical details of the Hebrew, Aramaic and Greek texts. At the same time, they have striven for more than a word-for-word translation. Because thought patterns and syntax differ from language to language, faithful communication of the meaning of the writers of the Bible demands frequent modifications in sentence structure and constant regard for the contextual meanings of words.

A sensitive feeling for style does not always accompany scholarship. Accordingly the Committee on Bible Translation submitted the developing version to a number of stylistic consultants. Two of them read every book of both Old and New Testaments twice—once before and once after the last major revision—and made invaluable suggestions. Samples of the translation were tested for clarity and ease of reading by various kinds of people—young and old, highly educated and less well educated, ministers and laymen.

Concern for clear and natural English—that the New International Version should be idiomatic but not idiosyncratic, contemporary but not dated—motivated the translators and consultants. At the same time, they tried to reflect the differing styles of the biblical writers. In view of the international use of English, the translators sought to avoid obvious Americanisms on the one hand and obvious Anglicisms on the other. A British edition reflects the comparatively few differences of significant idiom and of spelling.

As for the traditional pronouns "thou," "thee" and "thine" in reference to the Deity, the translators judged that to use these archaisms (along with the old verb forms such as "doest," "wouldest" and "hadst") would violate accuracy in translation. Neither Hebrew, Aramaic nor Greek uses special pronouns for the persons of the Godhead. A present-day translation is not enhanced by forms that in the time of the King James Version were used in everyday speech, whether referring to God or man.

For the Old Testament the standard Hebrew text, the Masoretic Text as published in the latest editions of *Biblia Hebraica*, was used throughout. The Dead Sea Scrolls contain material bearing on an earlier stage of the Hebrew text. They were consulted, as were the Samaritan Pentateuch and the ancient scribal traditions relating to textual changes. Sometimes a variant Hebrew reading in the margin of the Masoretic Text was followed instead of the text itself. Such instances, being variants within the Masoretic tradition, are not specified by footnotes. In rare cases, words in the consonantal text were divided differently from the way they appear in the Masoretic Text. Footnotes indicate this. The translators also consulted the more important early versions—the Septuagint; Aquila, Symmachus and Theodotion; the Vulgate; the Syriac Peshitta; the Targums; and for the Psalms the *Juxta Hebraica* of Jerome. Readings from these versions were occasionally followed where the Masoretic Text seemed doubtful and where accepted principles of textual criticism showed that one or more of these textual witnesses appeared to provide the correct reading. Such instances are footnoted. Sometimes vowel letters and vowel signs did not, in the judgment of the translators, represent the correct vowels for the original consonantal text. Accordingly some words were read with a different set of vowels. These instances are usually not indicated by footnotes.

The Greek text used in translating the New Testament was an eclectic one. No other piece of ancient literature has such an abundance of manuscript witnesses as does the New Testament. Where existing manuscripts differ, the translators made their choice of readings according to accepted principles of New Testament textual criticism. Footnotes call attention to places where there was uncertainty about what the original text was. The best current printed texts of the Greek New Testament were used.

There is a sense in which the work of translation is never wholly finished. This applies to all great literature and uniquely so to the Bible. In 1973 the New Testament in the New International Version was published. Since then, suggestions for corrections and revisions have been received from various sources. The Committee on Bible Translation carefully considered the suggestions and adopted a number of them. These were incorporated in the first printing of the entire Bible in 1978. Additional revisions were made by the Committee on Bible Translation in 1983 and appear in printings after that date.

As in other ancient documents, the precise meaning of the biblical texts is sometimes uncertain. This is more often the case with the Hebrew and Aramaic texts than with the Greek text. Although archaeological and linguistic discoveries in this century aid in understanding difficult passages, some uncertainties remain. The more significant of these have been called to the reader's attention in the footnotes.

In regard to the divine name YHWH, commonly referred to as the *Tetragrammaton*, the translators adopted the device used in most English versions of rendering that name as "LORD" in capital letters to distinguish it from *Adonai*, another Hebrew word rendered "Lord," for which small letters are used. Wherever the two names stand together in the Old Testament as a compound name of God, they are rendered "Sovereign LORD."

Because for most readers today the phrases "the LORD of hosts" and "God of hosts" have little meaning, this version renders them "the LORD Almighty" and "God Almighty." These renderings convey the sense of the Hebrew, namely, "he who is sovereign over all the 'hosts' (powers) in heaven and on earth, especially over the "hosts" (armies) of Israel." For readers unacquainted with Hebrew this does not make clear the distinction between *Sabaoth* ("hosts" or "Almighty") and *Shaddai* (which can also be translated "Almighty"), but the latter occurs infrequently and is always footnoted. When *Adonai* and *YHWH Sabaoth* occur together, they are rendered "the Lord, the LORD Almighty."

As for other proper nouns, the familiar spellings of the King James Version are generally retained. Names traditionally spelled with "ch," except where it is final, are usually spelled in this translation with "k" or "c," since the biblical languages do not have the sound that "ch" frequently indicates in English—for example, in *chant*. For well-known names such as Zechariah, however, the traditional spelling has been retained. Variation in the spelling of names in the original languages has usually not been indicated. Where a person or place has two or more different names in the Hebrew, Aramaic or Greek texts, the more familiar one has generally been used, with footnotes where needed.

To achieve clarity the translators sometimes supplied words not in the original texts but required by the context. If there was uncertainty about such material, it is enclosed in brackets. Also for the sake of clarity or style, nouns, including some proper nouns, are sometimes substituted for pronouns, and vice versa. And though the Hebrew writers often shifted back and forth between first, second and third personal pronouns without change of antecedent, this translation often makes them uniform, in accordance with English style and without the use of footnotes.

Poetical passages are printed as poetry, that is, with indentation of lines with separate stanzas. These are generally designed to reflect the structure of Hebrew poetry. This poetry is normally characterized by parallelism in balanced lines. Most of the poetry in the Bible is in the Old Testament, and scholars differ regarding the scansion of Hebrew lines. The translators determined the stanza divisions for the most part by analysis of the subject matter. The stanzas therefore serve as poetic paragraphs.

As an aid to the reader, italicized sectional headings are inserted in most of the books. They are not to be regarded as part of the NIV text, are not for oral reading, and are not intended to dictate the interpretation of the sections they head.

The footnotes in this version are of several kinds, most of which need no explanation. Those giving alternative translations begin with "Or" and generally introduce the alternative with the last word preceding it in the text, except when it is a single-word alternative; in poetry quoted in a footnote a slant mark indicates a line division. Footnotes introduced by "Or" do not have uniform significance. In some cases two possible translations were considered to have about equal validity. In other cases, though the translators were convinced that the translation in the text was correct, they judged that another interpretation was possible and of sufficient importance to be represented in a footnote.

In the New Testament, footnotes that refer to uncertainty regarding the original text are introduced by "Some manuscripts" or similar expressions. In the Old Testament, evidence for the reading chosen is given first and evidence for the alternative is added after a semicolon (for example: Septuagint; Hebrew *father*). In such notes the term "Hebrew" refers to the Masoretic Text.

It should be noted that minerals, flora and fauna, architectural details, articles of clothing and jewelry, musical instruments and other articles cannot always be identified with precision. Also measures of capacity in the biblical period are particularly uncertain (see the table of weights and measures following the text).

Like all translations of the Bible, made as they are by imperfect man, this one undoubtedly falls short of its goals. Yet we are grateful to God for the extent to which he has enabled us to realize these goals and for the strength he has given us and our colleagues to complete our task. We offer this version of the Bible to him in whose name and for whose glory it has been made. We pray that it will lead many into a better understanding of the Holy Scriptures and a fuller knowledge of Jesus Christ the incarnate Word, of whom the Scriptures so faithfully testify.

The Committee on Bible Translation

June 1978
(Revised August 1983)

Names of the translators and editors may be secured
from the International Bible Society,
translation sponsors of the New International Version,
1820 Jet Stream Drive, Colorado Springs, Colorado
80921-3696 U.S.A.

OLD TESTAMENT

...T...

his book goes back to the beginning to tell of the first plants and animals, the first man and woman, the first sin, the first news of salvation. It also describes God's dealings with Adam and Eve, Noah, Abraham, Isaac, Jacob and Joseph. As you read Genesis, remember the special promises made to Abraham and rest in the assurance that God keeps his promises to walk alongside you every step of your journey.

GENESIS

The Beginning

1 In the beginning God created the heavens and the earth. ²Now the earth was*a* formless and empty, darkness was over the surface of the deep, and the Spirit of God was hovering over the waters.

³And God said, "Let there be light," and there was light. ⁴God saw that the light was good, and he separated the light from the darkness. ⁵God called the light "day," and the darkness he called "night." And there was evening, and there was morning—the first day.

⁶And God said, "Let there be an expanse between the waters to separate water from water." ⁷So God made the expanse and separated the water under the expanse from the water above it. And it was so. ⁸God called the expanse "sky." And there was evening, and there was morning—the second day.

⁹And God said, "Let the water under the sky be gathered to one place, and let dry ground appear." And it was so. ¹⁰God called the dry ground "land," and the gathered waters he called "seas." And God saw that it was good.

¹¹Then God said, "Let the land produce vegetation: seed-bearing plants and trees on the land that bear fruit with seed in it, according to their various kinds." And it was so. ¹²The land produced vegetation: plants bearing seed according to their kinds and trees

*a*2 Or possibly *became*

bearing fruit with seed in it according to their kinds. And God saw that it was good. ¹³And there was evening, and there was morning—the third day. ¹⁴And God said, "Let there be lights in the expanse of the sky to separate the day from the night, and let them serve as signs to mark seasons and days and years, ¹⁵and let them be lights in the expanse of the sky to give light on the earth." And it was so. ¹⁶God made two great lights—the great-er light to govern the day and the lesser light to govern the night. He also made the stars. ¹⁷God set them in the expanse of the sky to give light on the earth, ¹⁸to govern the day and the night, and to separate light from darkness. And God saw that it was good. ¹⁹And there was evening, and there was morning—the fourth day. ²⁰And God said, "Let the water teem with living creatures, and let birds fly above the earth across

VERSE:	AUTHOR:	PASSAGE:
Genesis 1:1	A.W. Tozer	Genesis 1:1–31

The God We Must See

To regain her lost power the Church must see heaven opened and have a transforming vision of God.

But the God we must see is not the utilitarian God who is having such a run of popularity today, whose chief claim to man's attention is his ability to bring them success in their various undertakings and who for that reason is being cajoled and flattered by everyone who wants a favor. The God we must learn to know is the Majesty in the heavens, God the Father Almighty, Maker of heaven and earth, the only wise God our Savior. He it is that sitteth upon the circle of the earth, who stretcheth out the heavens as a curtain and spreadeth them out as a tent to dwell in, who bringeth out his starry host by number and calleth them all by name through the greatness of his power, who seeth the works of man as vanity, who putteth no confidence in princes and asks no counsel of kings.

ADDITIONAL SCRIPTURE READINGS
Job 37:14–24; Psalm 104

Go to page 5 for your next devotional reading.

the expanse of the sky." ²¹So God created the great creatures of the sea and every living and moving thing with which the water teems, according to their kinds, and every winged bird according to its kind. And God saw that it was good. ²²God blessed them and said, "Be fruitful and increase in number and fill the water in the seas, and let the birds increase on the earth." ²³And there was evening, and there was morning—the fifth day.

²⁴And God said, "Let the land produce living creatures according to their kinds: livestock, creatures that move along the ground, and wild animals, each according to its kind." And it was so. ²⁵God made the wild animals according to their kinds, the livestock according to their kinds, and all the creatures that move along the ground according to their kinds. And God saw that it was good.

²⁶Then God said, "Let us make man in our image, in our likeness, and let them rule over the fish of the sea and the birds of the air, over the livestock, over all the earth,^a and over all the creatures that move along the ground."

²⁷So God created man in his own image,
in the image of God he created him;
male and female he created them.

²⁸God blessed them and said to them, "Be fruitful and increase in number; fill the earth and subdue it. Rule over the fish of the sea and the birds of the air and over every living creature that moves on the ground."

²⁹Then God said, "I give you every seed-bearing plant on the face of the whole earth and every tree that has fruit with seed in it.

They will be yours for food. ³⁰And to all the beasts of the earth and all the birds of the air and all the creatures that move on the ground—everything that has the breath of life in it—I give every green plant for food." And it was so.

³¹God saw all that he had made, and it was very good. And there was evening, and there was morning—the sixth day.

2 Thus the heavens and the earth were completed in all their vast array.

²By the seventh day God had finished the work he had been doing; so on the seventh day he rested^b from all his work. ³And God blessed the seventh day and made it holy, because on it he rested from all the work of creating that he had done.

Adam and Eve

⁴This is the account of the heavens and the earth when they were created.

When the LORD God made the earth and the heavens— ⁵and no shrub of the field had yet appeared on the earth^c and no plant of the field had yet sprung up, for the LORD God had not sent rain on the earth^c and there was no man to work the ground, ⁶but streams^d came up from the earth and watered the whole surface of the ground— ⁷the LORD God formed the man^e from the dust of the ground and breathed into his nostrils the breath of life, and the man became a living being.

⁸Now the LORD God had planted a garden in the east, in Eden; and there he put the man he had formed. ⁹And the LORD God made all kinds of trees grow out of the ground—trees that were pleasing to the eye and good for food. In the middle of the garden

---

^a26 Hebrew; Syriac *all the wild animals*   ^b2 Or *ceased*; also in verse 3   ^c5 Or *land*; also in verse 6   ^d6 Or *mist*   ^e7 The Hebrew for *man (adam)* sounds like and may be related to the Hebrew for *ground (adamah)*; it is also the name *Adam* (see Gen. 2:20).

were the tree of life and the tree of the knowledge of good and evil.

[10]A river watering the garden flowed from Eden; from there it was separated into four headwaters. [11]The name of the first is the Pishon; it winds through the entire land of Havilah, where there is gold. [12](The gold of that land is good; aromatic resin[a] and onyx are also there.) [13]The name of the second river is the Gihon; it winds through the entire land of Cush.[b] [14]The name of the third river is the Tigris; it runs along the east side of Asshur. And the fourth river is the Euphrates.

[15]The LORD God took the man and put him in the Garden of Eden to work it and take care of it. [16]And the LORD God commanded the man, "You are free to eat from any tree in the garden; [17]but you must not eat from the tree of the knowledge of good and evil, for when you eat of it you will surely die."

[18]The LORD God said, "It is not good for the man to be alone. I will make a helper suitable for him."

[19]Now the LORD God had formed out of the ground all the beasts of the field and all the birds of the air. He brought them to the man to see what he would name them; and whatever the man called each living creature, that was its name. [20]So the man gave names to all the livestock, the birds of the air and all the beasts of the field.

But for Adam[c] no suitable helper was found. [21]So the LORD God caused the man to fall into a deep sleep; and while he was sleeping, he took one of the man's ribs[d] and closed up the place with flesh. [22]Then the LORD God made a woman from the rib[e] he had taken out of the man, and he brought her to the man.

[23]The man said,

"This is now bone of my bones
    and flesh of my flesh;
she shall be called 'woman,'[f]
    for she was taken out of man."

[24]For this reason a man will leave his father and mother and be united to his wife, and they will become one flesh.

[25]The man and his wife were both naked, and they felt no shame.

The Fall of Man

3 Now the serpent was more crafty than any of the wild animals the LORD God had made. He said to the woman, "Did God really say, 'You must not eat from any tree in the garden'?"

[2]The woman said to the serpent, "We may eat fruit from the trees in the garden, [3]but God did say, 'You must not eat fruit from the tree that is in the middle of the garden, and you must not touch it, or you will die.' "

[4]"You will not surely die," the serpent said to the woman. [5]"For God knows that when you eat of it your eyes will be opened, and you will be like God, knowing good and evil."

[6]When the woman saw that the fruit of the tree was good for food and pleasing to the eye, and also desirable for gaining wisdom, she took some and ate it. She also gave some to her husband, who was with her, and he ate it. [7]Then the eyes of both of them were opened, and they realized they were naked; so they sewed fig leaves together and made coverings for themselves.

[8]Then the man and his wife heard the sound of the LORD God as he was walking in the garden in the cool of the day, and they hid from the LORD God among the trees of the garden. [9]But the LORD God called to the man, "Where are you?"

[10]He answered, "I heard you in the garden, and I was afraid because I was naked; so I hid."

[11]And he said, "Who told you that you were naked? Have you eaten from the tree that I commanded you not to eat from?"

[12]The man said, "The woman you

---

[a]12 Or good; pearls   [b]13 Possibly southeast Mesopotamia   [c]20 Or the man   [d]21 Or took part of the man's side   [e]22 Or part   [f]23 The Hebrew for woman sounds like the Hebrew for man.

VERSE:	AUTHOR:	PASSAGE:
Genesis 3:8	Andrew Kuyvenhoven	Genesis 3:1–19

The Voice

Apparently it was not unusual for God to come into the garden and talk with Adam and Eve. But on this day everything is different. Yesterday they enjoyed being close to God. Now they are overwhelmed with shame and fear. They cover themselves and they hide from God. Cowardly Adam tries to blame Eve, and Eve blames the serpent.

Sin has radically changed the relationship between God and his creatures. People no longer turn to God as flowers turn to the sun, but they love "darkness instead of light" (John 3:19). When God reveals himself, people cringe with fear. After the Bible's account of the fall, whenever God came to speak with a person, that person trembled—whether he was Isaiah the prophet (Isaiah 6:5) or a shepherd in Bethlehem's field (Luke 2:9). Whenever the glory of the Lord appears, sinners fear for their lives. There is no shelter for our wretchedness when we confront God's blazing holiness.

In their hiding place among the trees, Adam and Eve hear God call, "Where are you?" They are afraid, but God's call is actually the first sign of his grace. God seeks them. They have not been abandoned. From now on, history will be the story of God seeking and calling while people are running and hiding.

"Where are you?" God has not stopped calling. Not yet. If you hear his voice today, do not delay but come.

ADDITIONAL SCRIPTURE READINGS
Ezekiel 34:11–16; Luke 19:1–10
Go to page 15 for your next devotional reading.

put here with me—she gave me some fruit from the tree, and I ate it."

¹³Then the LORD God said to the woman, "What is this you have done?"

The woman said, "The serpent deceived me, and I ate."

¹⁴So the LORD God said to the serpent, "Because you have done this,

"Cursed are you above all the livestock
and all the wild animals!
You will crawl on your belly
and you will eat dust
all the days of your life.
¹⁵And I will put enmity
between you and the woman,
and between your offspring[a]
and hers;
he will crush[b] your head,
and you will strike his heel."

¹⁶To the woman he said,

"I will greatly increase your pains in childbearing;
with pain you will give birth to children.
Your desire will be for your husband,
and he will rule over you."

¹⁷To Adam he said, "Because you listened to your wife and ate from the tree about which I commanded you, 'You must not eat of it,'

"Cursed is the ground because of you;
through painful toil you will eat of it
all the days of your life.
¹⁸It will produce thorns and thistles for you,
and you will eat the plants of the field.
¹⁹By the sweat of your brow
you will eat your food
until you return to the ground,
since from it you were taken;
for dust you are
and to dust you will return."

²⁰Adam[c] named his wife Eve,[d] because she would become the mother of all the living.

²¹The LORD God made garments of skin for Adam and his wife and clothed them. ²²And the LORD God said, "The man has now become like one of us, knowing good and evil. He must not be allowed to reach out his hand and take also from the tree of life and eat, and live forever." ²³So the LORD God banished him from the Garden of Eden to work the ground from which he had been taken. ²⁴After he drove the man out, he placed on the east side[e] of the Garden of Eden cherubim and a flaming sword flashing back and forth to guard the way to the tree of life.

Cain and Abel

4 Adam[c] lay with his wife Eve, and she became pregnant and gave birth to Cain.[f] She said, "With the help of the LORD I have brought forth[g] a man." ²Later she gave birth to his brother Abel.

Now Abel kept flocks, and Cain worked the soil. ³In the course of time Cain brought some of the fruits of the soil as an offering to the LORD. ⁴But Abel brought fat portions from some of the firstborn of his flock. The LORD looked with favor on Abel and his offering, ⁵but on Cain and his offering he did not look with favor. So Cain was very angry, and his face was downcast.

⁶Then the LORD said to Cain, "Why are you angry? Why is your face downcast? ⁷If you do what is right, will you not be accepted? But if you do not do what is right, sin is crouching at your door; it desires to have you, but you must master it."

⁸Now Cain said to his brother Abel, "Let's go out to the field."[h] And while they were in the field, Cain attacked his brother Abel and killed him.

---

a15 Or *seed*   *b15* Or *strike*   *c20,1* Or *The man*   *d20 Eve* probably means *living.*   *e24* Or *placed in front*   *f1 Cain* sounds like the Hebrew for *brought forth* or *acquired.*   *g1* Or *have acquired*   *h8* Samaritan Pentateuch, Septuagint, Vulgate and Syriac; Masoretic Text does not have *"Let's go out to the field."*

⁹Then the LORD said to Cain, "Where is your brother Abel?"

"I don't know," he replied. "Am I my brother's keeper?"

¹⁰The LORD said, "What have you done? Listen! Your brother's blood cries out to me from the ground. ¹¹Now you are under a curse and driven from the ground, which opened its mouth to receive your brother's blood from your hand. ¹²When you work the ground, it will no longer yield its crops for you. You will be a restless wanderer on the earth."

¹³Cain said to the LORD, "My punishment is more than I can bear. ¹⁴Today you are driving me from the land, and I will be hidden from your presence; I will be a restless wanderer on the earth, and whoever finds me will kill me."

¹⁵But the LORD said to him, "Not so*a*; if anyone kills Cain, he will suffer vengeance seven times over." Then the LORD put a mark on Cain so that no one who found him would kill him. ¹⁶So Cain went out from the LORD's presence and lived in the land of Nod,*b* east of Eden.

¹⁷Cain lay with his wife, and she became pregnant and gave birth to Enoch. Cain was then building a city, and he named it after his son Enoch. ¹⁸To Enoch was born Irad, and Irad was the father of Mehujael, and Mehujael was the father of Methushael, and Methushael was the father of Lamech.

¹⁹Lamech married two women, one named Adah and the other Zillah. ²⁰Adah gave birth to Jabal; he was the father of those who live in tents and raise livestock. ²¹His brother's name was Jubal; he was the father of all who play the harp and flute. ²²Zillah also had a son, Tubal-Cain, who forged all kinds of tools out of*c* bronze and iron. Tubal-Cain's sister was Naamah.

²³Lamech said to his wives,

"Adah and Zillah, listen to me;
    wives of Lamech, hear my
        words.
I have killed*d* a man for
        wounding me,
    a young man for injuring me.
²⁴If Cain is avenged seven times,
    then Lamech seventy-seven
        times."

²⁵Adam lay with his wife again, and she gave birth to a son and named him Seth,*e* saying, "God has granted me another child in place of Abel, since Cain killed him." ²⁶Seth also had a son, and he named him Enosh.

At that time men began to call on*f* the name of the LORD.

From Adam to Noah

5 This is the written account of Adam's line.

When God created man, he made him in the likeness of God. ²He created them male and female and blessed them. And when they were created, he called them "man.*g*"

³When Adam had lived 130 years, he had a son in his own likeness, in his own image; and he named him Seth. ⁴After Seth was born, Adam lived 800 years and had other sons and daughters. ⁵Altogether, Adam lived 930 years, and then he died.

⁶When Seth had lived 105 years, he became the father*h* of Enosh. ⁷And after he became the father of Enosh, Seth lived 807 years and had other sons and daughters. ⁸Altogether, Seth lived 912 years, and then he died.

⁹When Enosh had lived 90 years, he became the father of Kenan. ¹⁰And after he became the father of Kenan, Enosh lived 815 years and had other sons and daughters. ¹¹Altogether,

a15 Septuagint, Vulgate and Syriac; Hebrew Very well 12 and 14). c22 Or who instructed all who work in means granted. f26 Or to proclaim g2 Hebrew adam in verses 7-26. b16 Nod means wandering (see verses d23 Or I will kill e25 Seth probably h6 Father may mean ancestor; also

Enosh lived 905 years, and then he died.

¹²When Kenan had lived 70 years, he became the father of Mahalalel. ¹³And after he became the father of Mahalalel, Kenan lived 840 years and had other sons and daughters. ¹⁴Altogether, Kenan lived 910 years, and then he died.

¹⁵When Mahalalel had lived 65 years, he became the father of Jared. ¹⁶And after he became the father of Jared, Mahalalel lived 830 years and had other sons and daughters. ¹⁷Altogether, Mahalalel lived 895 years, and then he died.

¹⁸When Jared had lived 162 years, he became the father of Enoch. ¹⁹And after he became the father of Enoch, Jared lived 800 years and had other sons and daughters. ²⁰Altogether, Jared lived 962 years, and then he died.

²¹When Enoch had lived 65 years, he became the father of Methuselah. ²²And after he became the father of Methuselah, Enoch walked with God 300 years and had other sons and daughters. ²³Altogether, Enoch lived 365 years. ²⁴Enoch walked with God; then he was no more, because God took him away.

²⁵When Methuselah had lived 187 years, he became the father of Lamech. ²⁶And after he became the father of Lamech, Methuselah lived 782 years and had other sons and daughters. ²⁷Altogether, Methuselah lived 969 years, and then he died.

²⁸When Lamech had lived 182 years, he had a son. ²⁹He named him Noah[a] and said, "He will comfort us in the labor and painful toil of our hands caused by the ground the LORD has cursed." ³⁰After Noah was born, Lamech lived 595 years and had other sons and daughters. ³¹Altogether, Lamech lived 777 years, and then he died.

³²After Noah was 500 years old, he became the father of Shem, Ham and Japheth.

The Flood

6 When men began to increase in number on the earth and daughters were born to them, ²the sons of God saw that the daughters of men were beautiful, and they married any of them they chose. ³Then the LORD said, "My Spirit will not contend with[b] man forever, for he is mortal[c]; his days will be a hundred and twenty years."

⁴The Nephilim were on the earth in those days—and also afterward—when the sons of God went to the daughters of men and had children by them. They were the heroes of old, men of renown.

⁵The LORD saw how great man's wickedness on the earth had become, and that every inclination of the thoughts of his heart was only evil all the time. ⁶The LORD was grieved that he had made man on the earth, and his heart was filled with pain. ⁷So the LORD said, "I will wipe mankind, whom I have created, from the face of the earth—men and animals, and creatures that move along the ground, and birds of the air—for I am grieved that I have made them." ⁸But Noah found favor in the eyes of the LORD.

⁹This is the account of Noah.

Noah was a righteous man, blameless among the people of his time, and he walked with God. ¹⁰Noah had three sons: Shem, Ham and Japheth.

¹¹Now the earth was corrupt in God's sight and was full of violence. ¹²God saw how corrupt the earth had become, for all the people on earth had corrupted their ways. ¹³So God said to Noah, "I am going to put an end to all people, for the earth is filled with violence because of them. I am surely going to destroy both them and the earth. ¹⁴So make yourself an ark of cypress[d] wood; make rooms in it and coat it with pitch inside and out. ¹⁵This is how you are to build it: The ark is to be 450 feet long, 75 feet

---

a29 *Noah* sounds like the Hebrew for *comfort.*   *b3* Or *My spirit will not remain in*   *c3* Or *corrupt*   *d14* The meaning of the Hebrew for this word is uncertain.

wide and 45 feet high.[a] [16]Make a roof for it and finish[b] the ark to within 18 inches[c] of the top. Put a door in the side of the ark and make lower, middle and upper decks. [17]I am going to bring floodwaters on the earth to destroy all life under the heavens, every creature that has the breath of life in it. Everything on earth will perish. [18]But I will establish my covenant with you, and you will enter the ark—you and your sons and your wife and your sons' wives with you. [19]You are to bring into the ark two of all living creatures, male and female, to keep them alive with you. [20]Two of every kind of bird, of every kind of animal and of every kind of creature that moves along the ground will come to you to be kept alive. [21]You are to take every kind of food that is to be eaten and store it away as food for you and for them."

[22]Noah did everything just as God commanded him.

7 The LORD then said to Noah, "Go into the ark, you and your whole family, because I have found you righteous in this generation. [2]Take with you seven[d] of every kind of clean animal, a male and its mate, and two of every kind of unclean animal, a male and its mate, [3]and also seven of every kind of bird, male and female, to keep their various kinds alive throughout the earth. [4]Seven days from now I will send rain on the earth for forty days and forty nights, and I will wipe from the face of the earth every living creature I have made."

[5]And Noah did all that the LORD commanded him.

[6]Noah was six hundred years old when the floodwaters came on the earth. [7]And Noah and his sons and his wife and his sons' wives entered the ark to escape the waters of the flood. [8]Pairs of clean and unclean animals, of birds and of all creatures that move along the ground, [9]male and female, came to Noah and entered the ark, as God had commanded Noah. [10]And after the seven days the floodwaters came on the earth.

[11]In the six hundredth year of Noah's life, on the seventeenth day of the second month—on that day all the springs of the great deep burst forth, and the floodgates of the heavens were opened. [12]And rain fell on the earth forty days and forty nights.

[13]On that very day Noah and his sons, Shem, Ham and Japheth, together with his wife and the wives of his three sons, entered the ark. [14]They had with them every wild animal according to its kind, all livestock according to their kinds, every creature that moves along the ground according to its kind and every bird according to its kind, everything with wings. [15]Pairs of all creatures that have the breath of life in them came to Noah and entered the ark. [16]The animals going in were male and female of every living thing, as God had commanded Noah. Then the LORD shut him in.

[17]For forty days the flood kept coming on the earth, and as the waters increased they lifted the ark high above the earth. [18]The waters rose and increased greatly on the earth, and the ark floated on the surface of the water. [19]They rose greatly on the earth, and all the high mountains under the entire heavens were covered. [20]The waters rose and covered the mountains to a depth of more than twenty feet.[e,f] [21]Every living thing that moved on the earth perished—birds, livestock, wild animals, all the creatures that swarm over the earth, and all mankind. [22]Everything on dry land that had the breath of life in its nostrils died. [23]Every living thing on the face of the earth was wiped out; men and animals and the creatures that move along the ground and the birds of the air were wiped from the earth.

---

[a]15 Hebrew *300 cubits long, 50 cubits wide and 30 cubits high* (about 140 meters long, 23 meters wide and 13.5 meters high)   [b]16 Or *Make an opening for light by finishing*   [c]16 Hebrew *a cubit* (about 0.5 meter)   [d]2 Or *seven pairs*; also in verse 3   [e]20 Hebrew *fifteen cubits* (about 6.9 meters)   [f]20 Or *rose more than twenty feet, and the mountains were covered*

Only Noah was left, and those with him in the ark.

²⁴The waters flooded the earth for a hundred and fifty days.

8 But God remembered Noah and all the wild animals and the livestock that were with him in the ark, and he sent a wind over the earth, and the waters receded. ²Now the springs of the deep and the floodgates of the heavens had been closed, and the rain had stopped falling from the sky. ³The water receded steadily from the earth. At the end of the hundred and fifty days the water had gone down, ⁴and on the seventeenth day of the seventh month the ark came to rest on the mountains of Ararat. ⁵The waters continued to recede until the tenth month, and on the first day of the tenth month the tops of the mountains became visible.

⁶After forty days Noah opened the window he had made in the ark ⁷and sent out a raven, and it kept flying back and forth until the water had dried up from the earth. ⁸Then he sent out a dove to see if the water had receded from the surface of the ground. ⁹But the dove could find no place to set its feet because there was water over all the surface of the earth; so it returned to Noah in the ark. He reached out his hand and took the dove and brought it back to himself in the ark. ¹⁰He waited seven more days and again sent out the dove from the ark. ¹¹When the dove returned to him in the evening, there in its beak was a freshly plucked olive leaf! Then Noah knew that the water had receded from the earth. ¹²He waited seven more days and sent the dove out again, but this time it did not return to him.

¹³By the first day of the first month of Noah's six hundred and first year, the water had dried up from the earth. Noah then removed the covering from the ark and saw that the surface of the ground was dry. ¹⁴By the twenty-seventh day of the second month the earth was completely dry.

¹⁵Then God said to Noah, ¹⁶"Come out of the ark, you and your wife and your sons and their wives. ¹⁷Bring out every kind of living creature that is with you—the birds, the animals, and all the creatures that move along the ground—so they can multiply on the earth and be fruitful and increase in number upon it."

¹⁸So Noah came out, together with his sons and his wife and his sons' wives. ¹⁹All the animals and all the creatures that move along the ground and all the birds—everything that moves on the earth—came out of the ark, one kind after another.

²⁰Then Noah built an altar to the LORD and, taking some of all the clean animals and clean birds, he sacrificed burnt offerings on it. ²¹The LORD smelled the pleasing aroma and said in his heart: "Never again will I curse the ground because of man, even though^a every inclination of his heart is evil from childhood. And never again will I destroy all living creatures, as I have done.

²²"As long as the earth endures,
  seedtime and harvest,
  cold and heat,
  summer and winter,
  day and night
  will never cease."

God's Covenant With Noah

9 Then God blessed Noah and his sons, saying to them, "Be fruitful and increase in number and fill the earth. ²The fear and dread of you will fall upon all the beasts of the earth and all the birds of the air, upon every creature that moves along the ground, and upon all the fish of the sea; they are given into your hands. ³Everything that lives and moves will be food for you. Just as I gave you the green plants, I now give you everything.

⁴"But you must not eat meat that has its lifeblood still in it. ⁵And for your lifeblood I will surely demand an accounting. I will demand an ac-

---

^{a}21 Or *man, for*

counting from every animal. And from each man, too, I will demand an accounting for the life of his fellow man.

⁶"Whoever sheds the blood of man,
    by man shall his blood be shed;
for in the image of God
    has God made man.

⁷As for you, be fruitful and increase in number; multiply on the earth and increase upon it."

⁸Then God said to Noah and to his sons with him: ⁹"I now establish my covenant with you and with your descendants after you ¹⁰and with every living creature that was with you—the birds, the livestock and all the wild animals, all those that came out of the ark with you—every living creature on earth. ¹¹I establish my covenant with you: Never again will all life be cut off by the waters of a flood; never again will there be a flood to destroy the earth."

¹²And God said, "This is the sign of the covenant I am making between me and you and every living creature with you, a covenant for all generations to come: ¹³I have set my rainbow in the clouds, and it will be the sign of the covenant between me and the earth. ¹⁴Whenever I bring clouds over the earth and the rainbow appears in the clouds, ¹⁵I will remember my covenant between me and you and all living creatures of every kind. Never again will the waters become a flood to destroy all life. ¹⁶Whenever the rainbow appears in the clouds, I will see it and remember the everlasting covenant between God and all living creatures of every kind on the earth." ¹⁷So God said to Noah, "This is the sign of the covenant I have established between me and all life on the earth."

The Sons of Noah

¹⁸The sons of Noah who came out of the ark were Shem, Ham and Ja-

pheth. (Ham was the father of Canaan.) ¹⁹These were the three sons of Noah, and from them came the people who were scattered over the earth.

²⁰Noah, a man of the soil, proceeded[a] to plant a vineyard. ²¹When he drank some of its wine, he became drunk and lay uncovered inside his tent. ²²Ham, the father of Canaan, saw his father's nakedness and told his two brothers outside. ²³But Shem and Japheth took a garment and laid it across their shoulders; then they walked in backward and covered their father's nakedness. Their faces were turned the other way so that they would not see their father's nakedness.

²⁴When Noah awoke from his wine and found out what his youngest son had done to him, ²⁵he said,

"Cursed be Canaan!
    The lowest of slaves
    will he be to his brothers."

²⁶He also said,

"Blessed be the LORD, the God of
    Shem!
May Canaan be the slave of
    Shem.[b]
²⁷May God extend the territory of
    Japheth[c];
may Japheth live in the tents of
    Shem,
and may Canaan be his[d]
    slave."

²⁸After the flood Noah lived 350 years. ²⁹Altogether, Noah lived 950 years, and then he died.

The Table of Nations

10 This is the account of Shem, Ham and Japheth, Noah's sons, who themselves had sons after the flood.

The Japhethites

²The sons[e] of Japheth:
    Gomer, Magog, Madai, Javan,
    Tubal, Meshech and Tiras.

---

[a]20 Or *soil, was the first*   [b]26 Or *be his slave*   [c]27 *Japheth* sounds like the Hebrew for *extend.*
[d]27 Or *their*   [e]2 *Sons* may mean *descendants* or *successors* or *nations*; also in verses 3, 4, 6, 7, 20-23, 29 and 31.

³The sons of Gomer:
  Ashkenaz, Riphath and Togarmah.
⁴The sons of Javan:
  Elishah, Tarshish, the Kittim
  and the Rodanim.ᵃ ⁵(From
  these the maritime peoples
  spread out into their territories by their clans within their
  nations, each with its own
  language.)

The Hamites

  ⁶The sons of Ham:
    Cush, Mizraim,ᵇ Put and
    Canaan.
  ⁷The sons of Cush:
    Seba, Havilah, Sabtah, Raa-
    mah and Sabteca.
  The sons of Raamah:
    Sheba and Dedan.

⁸Cush was the fatherᶜ of Nimrod,
who grew to be a mighty warrior on
the earth. ⁹He was a mighty hunter
before the LORD; that is why it is said,
"Like Nimrod, a mighty hunter before the LORD." ¹⁰The first centers of
his kingdom were Babylon, Erech,
Akkad and Calneh, inᵈ Shinar.ᵉ
¹¹From that land he went to Assyria,
where he built Nineveh, Rehoboth
Ir,ᶠ Calah ¹²and Resen, which is between Nineveh and Calah; that is the
great city.

¹³Mizraim was the father of
  the Ludites, Anamites, Lehabites, Naphtuhites, ¹⁴Pathru-
  sites, Casluhites (from whom
  the Philistines came) and
  Caphtorites.
¹⁵Canaan was the father of
  Sidon his firstborn,ᵍ and of
  the Hittites, ¹⁶Jebusites, Amorites, Girgashites, ¹⁷Hivites,
  Arkites, Sinites, ¹⁸Arvadites,
  Zemarites and Hamathites.

Later the Canaanite clans scattered
¹⁹and the borders of Canaan reached
from Sidon toward Gerar as far as
Gaza, and then toward Sodom, Gomorrah, Admah and Zeboiim, as far
as Lasha.
²⁰These are the sons of Ham by
their clans and languages, in their territories and nations.

The Semites

²¹Sons were also born to Shem,
whose older brother wasʰ Japheth;
Shem was the ancestor of all the sons
of Eber.

²²The sons of Shem:
  Elam, Asshur, Arphaxad, Lud
  and Aram.
²³The sons of Aram:
  Uz, Hul, Gether and Me-
  shech.ⁱ
²⁴Arphaxad was the father ofʲ
  Shelah,
  and Shelah the father of Eber.
²⁵Two sons were born to Eber:
  One was named Peleg,ᵏ because in his time the earth
  was divided; his brother was
  named Joktan.
²⁶Joktan was the father of
  Almodad, Sheleph, Hazarmaveth, Jerah, ²⁷Hadoram, Uzal,
  Diklah, ²⁸Obal, Abimael, Sheba, ²⁹Ophir, Havilah and Jobab. All these were sons of
  Joktan.

³⁰The region where they lived
stretched from Mesha toward Sephar,
in the eastern hill country.
³¹These are the sons of Shem by
their clans and languages, in their territories and nations.

³²These are the clans of Noah's
sons, according to their lines of descent, within their nations. From these

---

ᵃ4 Some manuscripts of the Masoretic Text and Samaritan Pentateuch (see also Septuagint and
1 Chron. 1:7); most manuscripts of the Masoretic Text *Dodanim*   ᵇ6 That is, Egypt; also in
verse 13   ᶜ8 *Father* may mean *ancestor* or *predecessor* or *founder; also in verses 13, 15, 24 and 26.*
ᵈ10 Or *Erech and Akkad—all of them in*   ᵉ10 That is, Babylonia   ᶠ11 Or *Nineveh with its city
squares*   ᵍ15 Or *of the Sidonians, the foremost*   ʰ21 Or *Shem, the older brother of*   ⁱ23 See
Septuagint and 1 Chron. 1:17; Hebrew *Mash*   ʲ24 Hebrew; Septuagint *father of Cainan, and
Cainan was the father of*   ᵏ25 *Peleg* means *division.*

the nations spread out over the earth after the flood.

The Tower of Babel

11 Now the whole world had one language and a common speech. ²As men moved eastward,ᵃ they found a plain in Shinarᵇ and settled there.

³They said to each other, "Come, let's make bricks and bake them thoroughly." They used brick instead of stone, and tar for mortar. ⁴Then they said, "Come, let us build ourselves a city, with a tower that reaches to the heavens, so that we may make a name for ourselves and not be scattered over the face of the whole earth."

⁵But the LORD came down to see the city and the tower that the men were building. ⁶The LORD said, "If as one people speaking the same language they have begun to do this, then nothing they plan to do will be impossible for them. ⁷Come, let us go down and confuse their language so they will not understand each other."

⁸So the LORD scattered them from there over all the earth, and they stopped building the city. ⁹That is why it was called Babelᶜ—because there the LORD confused the language of the whole world. From there the LORD scattered them over the face of the whole earth.

From Shem to Abram

¹⁰This is the account of Shem.

Two years after the flood, when Shem was 100 years old, he became the fatherᵈ of Arphaxad. ¹¹And after he became the father of Arphaxad, Shem lived 500 years and had other sons and daughters.

¹²When Arphaxad had lived 35 years, he became the father of Shelah. ¹³And after he became the father of Shelah, Arphaxad lived 403 years and had other sons and daughters.ᵉ

¹⁴When Shelah had lived 30 years, he became the father of Eber. ¹⁵And after he became the father of Eber, Shelah lived 403 years and had other sons and daughters.

¹⁶When Eber had lived 34 years, he became the father of Peleg. ¹⁷And after he became the father of Peleg, Eber lived 430 years and had other sons and daughters.

¹⁸When Peleg had lived 30 years, he became the father of Reu. ¹⁹And after he became the father of Reu, Peleg lived 209 years and had other sons and daughters.

²⁰When Reu had lived 32 years, he became the father of Serug. ²¹And after he became the father of Serug, Reu lived 207 years and had other sons and daughters.

²²When Serug had lived 30 years, he became the father of Nahor. ²³And after he became the father of Nahor, Serug lived 200 years and had other sons and daughters.

²⁴When Nahor had lived 29 years, he became the father of Terah. ²⁵And after he became the father of Terah, Nahor lived 119 years and had other sons and daughters.

²⁶After Terah had lived 70 years, he became the father of Abram, Nahor and Haran.

²⁷This is the account of Terah.

Terah became the father of Abram, Nahor and Haran. And Haran became the father of Lot. ²⁸While his father Terah was still alive, Haran died in Ur of the Chaldeans, in the land of his birth. ²⁹Abram and Nahor both married. The name of Abram's wife was Sarai, and the name of Nahor's wife was Milcah; she was the daughter of Haran, the father of both Milcah and Iscah. ³⁰Now Sarai was barren; she had no children.

³¹Terah took his son Abram, his grandson Lot son of Haran, and his daughter-in-law Sarai, the wife of his son Abram, and together they set out from Ur of the Chaldeans to go to Canaan. But when they came to Haran, they settled there.

³²Terah lived 205 years, and he died in Haran.

The Call of Abram

12 The LORD had said to Abram, "Leave your country, your people and your father's household and go to the land I will show you.

²"I will make you into a great
    nation
  and I will bless you;
 I will make your name great,
    and you will be a blessing.
³I will bless those who bless you,
    and whoever curses you I will
        curse;
 and all peoples on earth
    will be blessed through you."

⁴So Abram left, as the LORD had told him; and Lot went with him. Abram was seventy-five years old when he set out from Haran. ⁵He took his wife Sarai, his nephew Lot, all the possessions they had accumulated and the people they had acquired in Haran, and they set out for the land of Canaan, and they arrived there.

⁶Abram traveled through the land as far as the site of the great tree of Moreh at Shechem. At that time the Canaanites were in the land. ⁷The LORD appeared to Abram and said, "To your offspring^a I will give this land." So he built an altar there to the LORD, who had appeared to him.

⁸From there he went on toward the hills east of Bethel and pitched his tent, with Bethel on the west and Ai on the east. There he built an altar to the LORD and called on the name of the LORD. ⁹Then Abram set out and continued toward the Negev.

Abram in Egypt

¹⁰Now there was a famine in the land, and Abram went down to Egypt to live there for a while because the famine was severe. ¹¹As he was about to enter Egypt, he said to his wife Sarai, "I know what a beautiful woman you are. ¹²When the Egyptians see you, they will say, 'This is his wife.' Then they will kill me but will let you live. ¹³Say you are my sister, so that I will be treated well for your sake and my life will be spared because of you."

¹⁴When Abram came to Egypt, the Egyptians saw that she was a very beautiful woman. ¹⁵And when Pharaoh's officials saw her, they praised her to Pharaoh, and she was taken into his palace. ¹⁶He treated Abram well for her sake, and Abram acquired sheep and cattle, male and female donkeys, menservants and maidservants, and camels.

¹⁷But the LORD inflicted serious diseases on Pharaoh and his household because of Abram's wife Sarai. ¹⁸So Pharaoh summoned Abram. "What have you done to me?" he said. "Why didn't you tell me she was your wife? ¹⁹Why did you say, 'She is my sister,' so that I took her to be my wife? Now then, here is your wife. Take her and go!" ²⁰Then Pharaoh gave orders about Abram to his men, and they sent him on his way, with his wife and everything he had.

Abram and Lot Separate

13 So Abram went up from Egypt to the Negev, with his wife and everything he had, and Lot went with him. ²Abram had become very wealthy in livestock and in silver and gold.

³From the Negev he went from place to place until he came to Bethel, to the place between Bethel and Ai where his tent had been earlier ⁴and where he had first built an altar. There Abram called on the name of the LORD.

⁵Now Lot, who was moving about with Abram, also had flocks and herds and tents. ⁶But the land could

^a7 Or *seed*

not support them while they stayed together, for their possessions were so great that they were not able to stay together. ⁷And quarreling arose between Abram's herdsmen and the herdsmen of Lot. The Canaanites and Perizzites were also living in the land at that time.

⁸So Abram said to Lot, "Let's not have any quarreling between you and me, or between your herdsmen and mine, for we are brothers. ⁹Is not the

WEDNESDAY

VERSE:
Genesis 12:2

AUTHOR:
John Timmer

PASSAGE:
Genesis 12:1–9

Beyond Dead-endedness

God promises Abraham that he will become a great nation and that through him and his descendants all people on earth will be blessed. Marvelous! But just a few verses earlier, in Genesis 11, we are told that Abraham's wife Sarah is barren, which makes us wonder what God might possibly have in mind. How can Abraham become a great nation when his wife is barren? Barrenness is dead-endedness, a blind alley. How then can life go on where it has come to an end? God's promise is spoken against the backdrop of barrenness. And we cannot help but wonder: How can God make good on his promise when he chooses such a faulty mechanism as the barrenness of Sarah? There is only one answer. God chooses this route to show that he has power to create new life beyond our dead-endedness . . .

For some people dead-endedness is a sudden process; for others a gradual one. Some people's lives are placed in crisis suddenly; some slowly evolve to the point where the people must finally admit their bankruptcy . . .

We must hear the voice of the risen Jesus say to us, "Come to me, all you who are weary and burdened, and I will give you rest. Experience my resurrecting power, all you who are stuck in dead-endedness."

ADDITIONAL SCRIPTURE READINGS
Ezekiel 37:1–14; Matthew 11:25–30

Go to page 18 for your next devotional reading.

whole land before you? Let's part company. If you go to the left, I'll go to the right; if you go to the right, I'll go to the left."

¹⁰Lot looked up and saw that the whole plain of the Jordan was well watered, like the garden of the LORD, like the land of Egypt, toward Zoar. (This was before the LORD destroyed Sodom and Gomorrah.) ¹¹So Lot chose for himself the whole plain of the Jordan and set out toward the east. The two men parted company: ¹²Abram lived in the land of Canaan, while Lot lived among the cities of the plain and pitched his tents near Sodom. ¹³Now the men of Sodom were wicked and were sinning greatly against the LORD.

¹⁴The LORD said to Abram after Lot had parted from him, "Lift up your eyes from where you are and look north and south, east and west. ¹⁵All the land that you see I will give to you and your offspring*ᵃ* forever. ¹⁶I will make your offspring like the dust of the earth, so that if anyone could count the dust, then your offspring could be counted. ¹⁷Go, walk through the length and breadth of the land, for I am giving it to you."

¹⁸So Abram moved his tents and went to live near the great trees of Mamre at Hebron, where he built an altar to the LORD.

Abram Rescues Lot

14 At this time Amraphel king of Shinar,ᵇ Arioch king of Ellasar, Kedorlaomer king of Elam and Tidal king of Goiim ²went to war against Bera king of Sodom, Birsha king of Gomorrah, Shinab king of Admah, Shemeber king of Zeboiim, and the king of Bela (that is, Zoar). ³All these latter kings joined forces in the Valley of Siddim (the Salt Seaᶜ). ⁴For twelve years they had been subject to Kedorlaomer, but in the thirteenth year they rebelled.

⁵In the fourteenth year, Kedorlao-mer and the kings allied with him went out and defeated the Rephaites in Ashteroth Karnaim, the Zuzites in Ham, the Emites in Shaveh Kiriathaim ⁶and the Horites in the hill country of Seir, as far as El Paran near the desert. ⁷Then they turned back and went to En Mishpat (that is, Kadesh), and they conquered the whole territory of the Amalekites, as well as the Amorites who were living in Hazazon Tamar.

⁸Then the king of Sodom, the king of Gomorrah, the king of Admah, the king of Zeboiim and the king of Bela (that is, Zoar) marched out and drew up their battle lines in the Valley of Siddim ⁹against Kedorlaomer king of Elam, Tidal king of Goiim, Amraphel king of Shinar and Arioch king of Ellasar—four kings against five. ¹⁰Now the Valley of Siddim was full of tar pits, and when the kings of Sodom and Gomorrah fled, some of the men fell into them and the rest fled to the hills. ¹¹The four kings seized all the goods of Sodom and Gomorrah and all their food; then they went away. ¹²They also carried off Abram's nephew Lot and his possessions, since he was living in Sodom.

¹³One who had escaped came and reported this to Abram the Hebrew. Now Abram was living near the great trees of Mamre the Amorite, a brotherᵈ of Eshcol and Aner, all of whom were allied with Abram. ¹⁴When Abram heard that his relative had been taken captive, he called out the 318 trained men born in his household and went in pursuit as far as Dan. ¹⁵During the night Abram divided his men to attack them and he routed them, pursuing them as far as Hobah, north of Damascus. ¹⁶He recovered all the goods and brought back his relative Lot and his possessions, together with the women and the other people.

¹⁷After Abram returned from de-

ᵃ15 Or *seed*; also in verse 16   ᵇ1 That is, Babylonia; also in verse 9   ᶜ3 That is, the Dead Sea   ᵈ13 Or *a relative*; or *an ally*

feating Kedorlaomer and the kings allied with him, the king of Sodom came out to meet him in the Valley of Shaveh (that is, the King's Valley).

[18]Then Melchizedek king of Salem[a] brought out bread and wine. He was priest of God Most High, [19]and he blessed Abram, saying,

"Blessed be Abram by God Most
    High,
  Creator[b] of heaven and earth.
[20]And blessed be[c] God Most High,
  who delivered your enemies
    into your hand."

Then Abram gave him a tenth of everything.

[21]The king of Sodom said to Abram, "Give me the people and keep the goods for yourself."

[22]But Abram said to the king of Sodom, "I have raised my hand to the LORD, God Most High, Creator of heaven and earth, and have taken an oath [23]that I will accept nothing belonging to you, not even a thread or the thong of a sandal, so that you will never be able to say, 'I made Abram rich.' [24]I will accept nothing but what my men have eaten and the share that belongs to the men who went with me—to Aner, Eshcol and Mamre. Let them have their share."

God's Covenant With Abram

15 After this, the word of the LORD came to Abram in a vision:

"Do not be afraid, Abram.
  I am your shield,[d]
  your very great reward.[e]"

[2]But Abram said, "O Sovereign LORD, what can you give me since I remain childless and the one who will inherit[f] my estate is Eliezer of Damascus?" [3]And Abram said, "You have given me no children; so a servant in my household will be my heir."

[4]Then the word of the LORD came to him: "This man will not be your heir, but a son coming from your own body will be your heir." [5]He took him outside and said, "Look up at the heavens and count the stars—if indeed you can count them." Then he said to him, "So shall your offspring be."

[6]Abram believed the LORD, and he credited it to him as righteousness.

[7]He also said to him, "I am the LORD, who brought you out of Ur of the Chaldeans to give you this land to take possession of it."

[8]But Abram said, "O Sovereign LORD, how can I know that I will gain possession of it?"

[9]So the LORD said to him, "Bring me a heifer, a goat and a ram, each three years old, along with a dove and a young pigeon."

[10]Abram brought all these to him, cut them in two and arranged the halves opposite each other; the birds, however, he did not cut in half. [11]Then birds of prey came down on the carcasses, but Abram drove them away.

[12]As the sun was setting, Abram fell into a deep sleep, and a thick and dreadful darkness came over him. [13]Then the LORD said to him, "Know for certain that your descendants will be strangers in a country not their own, and they will be enslaved and mistreated four hundred years. [14]But I will punish the nation they serve as slaves, and afterward they will come out with great possessions. [15]You, however, will go to your fathers in peace and be buried at a good old age. [16]In the fourth generation your descendants will come back here, for the sin of the Amorites has not yet reached its full measure."

[17]When the sun had set and darkness had fallen, a smoking firepot with a blazing torch appeared and passed between the pieces. [18]On that day the LORD made a covenant with

---

a18 That is, Jerusalem   *b19* Or *Possessor*; also in verse 22   *c20* Or *And praise be to*   *d1* Or *sovereign*   *e1* Or *shield; / your reward will be very great*   *f2* The meaning of the Hebrew for this phrase is uncertain.

Abram and said, "To your descendants I give this land, from the river*a* of Egypt to the great river, the Euphrates— [19]the land of the Kenites, Kenizzites, Kadmonites, [20]Hittites, Perizzites, Rephaites, [21]Amorites, Canaanites, Girgashites and Jebusites."

Hagar and Ishmael

16 Now Sarai, Abram's wife, had borne him no children. But she had an Egyptian maidservant named Hagar; [2]so she said to Abram, "The LORD has kept me from having chil-

*a*18 Or *Wadi*

THURSDAY

VERSE: AUTHOR: PASSAGE:
Genesis 15:6   Elisabeth Elliot   Genesis 15:1 — 16:4

The Christian's Safety

God is God. That was the stunning lesson of that most stunning event in my life. Jim's [my husband's] death required me to deny God or believe him, to trust him or to renounce him. The lesson is the same for all of us . . .

If we believe that God is God, our faith is not a deduction from the facts around us. It is not an instinct. It is not inferred from the happy way things work. Faith is a gift from God, and we must respond to him with a decision: The God of the universe has spoken, we believe what he says, and we will obey. We must make a decision that we will hold in the face of all opposition and apparent contradiction.

The powers of hell can never prevail against the soul that takes its stand on God and on his Word. This kind of faith overcomes the world. The world of today must be shown . . . We (you and I) must show them . . . that we love the Father and will do what he says . . .

Letting go of what the world calls safety and surrendering to the Lord is our insurance of fulfillment. Christ knew his Father and offered himself unreservedly into his hands. If we let ourselves be lost for his sake, trusting the same God as Lord of all, we shall find safety where Christ found his, in the bosom of the Father.

ADDITIONAL SCRIPTURE READINGS
Matthew 16:21–28; Matthew 26:36–46

Go to page 22 for your next devotional reading.

dren. Go, sleep with my maidservant; perhaps I can build a family through her."

Abram agreed to what Sarai said. ³So after Abram had been living in Canaan ten years, Sarai his wife took her Egyptian maidservant Hagar and gave her to her husband to be his wife. ⁴He slept with Hagar, and she conceived.

When she knew she was pregnant, she began to despise her mistress. ⁵Then Sarai said to Abram, "You are responsible for the wrong I am suffering. I put my servant in your arms, and now that she knows she is pregnant, she despises me. May the LORD judge between you and me."

⁶"Your servant is in your hands," Abram said. "Do with her whatever you think best." Then Sarai mistreated Hagar; so she fled from her.

⁷The angel of the LORD found Hagar near a spring in the desert; it was the spring that is beside the road to Shur. ⁸And he said, "Hagar, servant of Sarai, where have you come from, and where are you going?"

"I'm running away from my mistress Sarai," she answered.

⁹Then the angel of the LORD told her, "Go back to your mistress and submit to her." ¹⁰The angel added, "I will so increase your descendants that they will be too numerous to count."

¹¹The angel of the LORD also said to her:

"You are now with child
    and you will have a son.
You shall name him Ishmael,ª
    for the LORD has heard of your
        misery.
¹²He will be a wild donkey of a
        man;
    his hand will be against
        everyone
    and everyone's hand against
        him,
and he will live in hostility
    towardᵇ all his brothers."

¹³She gave this name to the LORD who spoke to her: "You are the God who sees me," for she said, "I have now seenᶜ the One who sees me." ¹⁴That is why the well was called Beer Lahai Roiᵈ; it is still there, between Kadesh and Bered.

¹⁵So Hagar bore Abram a son, and Abram gave the name Ishmael to the son she had borne. ¹⁶Abram was eighty-six years old when Hagar bore him Ishmael.

The Covenant of Circumcision

17 When Abram was ninety-nine years old, the LORD appeared to him and said, "I am God Almightyᵉ; walk before me and be blameless. ²I will confirm my covenant between me and you and will greatly increase your numbers."

³Abram fell facedown, and God said to him, ⁴"As for me, this is my covenant with you: You will be the father of many nations. ⁵No longer will you be called Abramᶠ; your name will be Abraham,ᵍ for I have made you a father of many nations. ⁶I will make you very fruitful; I will make nations of you, and kings will come from you. ⁷I will establish my covenant as an everlasting covenant between me and you and your descendants after you for the generations to come, to be your God and the God of your descendants after you. ⁸The whole land of Canaan, where you are now an alien, I will give as an everlasting possession to you and your descendants after you; and I will be their God."

⁹Then God said to Abraham, "As for you, you must keep my covenant, you and your descendants after you for the generations to come. ¹⁰This is my covenant with you and your descendants after you, the covenant you are to keep: Every male among you shall be circumcised. ¹¹You are to undergo circumcision, and it will be the sign of the covenant between me

---

ª11 *Ishmael* means *God hears.*   ᵇ12 Or *live to the east / of*   ᶜ13 Or *seen the back of*   ᵈ14 *Beer Lahai Roi* means *well of the Living One who sees me.*   ᵉ1 Hebrew *El-Shaddai*   ᶠ5 *Abram* means *exalted father.*   ᵍ5 *Abraham* means *father of many.*

and you. ¹²For the generations to come every male among you who is eight days old must be circumcised, including those born in your household or bought with money from a foreigner—those who are not your offspring. ¹³Whether born in your household or bought with your money, they must be circumcised. My covenant in your flesh is to be an everlasting covenant. ¹⁴Any uncircumcised male, who has not been circumcised in the flesh, will be cut off from his people; he has broken my covenant."

¹⁵God also said to Abraham, "As for Sarai your wife, you are no longer to call her Sarai; her name will be Sarah. ¹⁶I will bless her and will surely give you a son by her. I will bless her so that she will be the mother of nations; kings of peoples will come from her."

¹⁷Abraham fell facedown; he laughed and said to himself, "Will a son be born to a man a hundred years old? Will Sarah bear a child at the age of ninety?" ¹⁸And Abraham said to God, "If only Ishmael might live under your blessing!"

¹⁹Then God said, "Yes, but your wife Sarah will bear you a son, and you will call him Isaac.ᵃ I will establish my covenant with him as an everlasting covenant for his descendants after him. ²⁰And as for Ishmael, I have heard you: I will surely bless him; I will make him fruitful and will greatly increase his numbers. He will be the father of twelve rulers, and I will make him into a great nation. ²¹But my covenant I will establish with Isaac, whom Sarah will bear to you by this time next year." ²²When he had finished speaking with Abraham, God went up from him.

²³On that very day Abraham took his son Ishmael and all those born in his household or bought with his money, every male in his household, and circumcised them, as God told him. ²⁴Abraham was ninety-nine

years old when he was circumcised, ²⁵and his son Ishmael was thirteen; ²⁶Abraham and his son Ishmael were both circumcised on that same day. ²⁷And every male in Abraham's household, including those born in his household or bought from a foreigner, was circumcised with him.

The Three Visitors

18 The Lᴏʀᴅ appeared to Abraham near the great trees of Mamre while he was sitting at the entrance to his tent in the heat of the day. ²Abraham looked up and saw three men standing nearby. When he saw them, he hurried from the entrance of his tent to meet them and bowed low to the ground.

³He said, "If I have found favor in your eyes, my lord,ᵇ do not pass your servant by. ⁴Let a little water be brought, and then you may all wash your feet and rest under this tree. ⁵Let me get you something to eat, so you can be refreshed and then go on your way—now that you have come to your servant."

"Very well," they answered, "do as you say."

⁶So Abraham hurried into the tent to Sarah. "Quick," he said, "get three seahsᶜ of fine flour and knead it and bake some bread."

⁷Then he ran to the herd and selected a choice, tender calf and gave it to a servant, who hurried to prepare it. ⁸He then brought some curds and milk and the calf that had been prepared, and set these before them. While they ate, he stood near them under a tree.

⁹"Where is your wife Sarah?" they asked him.

"There, in the tent," he said.

¹⁰Then the Lᴏʀᴅᵈ said, "I will surely return to you about this time next year, and Sarah your wife will have a son."

Now Sarah was listening at the entrance to the tent, which was behind him. ¹¹Abraham and Sarah were al-

---

ᵃ19 *Isaac* means *he laughs.*   ᵇ3 Or *O Lord*   ᶜ6 That is, probably about 20 quarts (about 22 liters)   ᵈ10 Hebrew *Then he*

ready old and well advanced in years, and Sarah was past the age of child-bearing. ¹²So Sarah laughed to herself as she thought, "After I am worn out and my master*a* is old, will I now have this pleasure?"

¹³Then the Lord said to Abraham, "Why did Sarah laugh and say, 'Will I really have a child, now that I am old?' ¹⁴Is anything too hard for the Lord? I will return to you at the appointed time next year and Sarah will have a son."

¹⁵Sarah was afraid, so she lied and said, "I did not laugh."

But he said, "Yes, you did laugh."

Abraham Pleads for Sodom

¹⁶When the men got up to leave, they looked down toward Sodom, and Abraham walked along with them to see them on their way. ¹⁷Then the Lord said, "Shall I hide from Abraham what I am about to do? ¹⁸Abraham will surely become a great and powerful nation, and all nations on earth will be blessed through him. ¹⁹For I have chosen him, so that he will direct his children and his household after him to keep the way of the Lord by doing what is right and just, so that the Lord will bring about for Abraham what he has promised him."

²⁰Then the Lord said, "The outcry against Sodom and Gomorrah is so great and their sin so grievous ²¹that I will go down and see if what they have done is as bad as the outcry that has reached me. If not, I will know."

²²The men turned away and went toward Sodom, but Abraham remained standing before the Lord.*b* ²³Then Abraham approached him and said: "Will you sweep away the righteous with the wicked? ²⁴What if there are fifty righteous people in the city? Will you really sweep it away and not spare*c* the place for the sake of the fifty righteous people in it? ²⁵Far be it from you to do such a thing—to kill the righteous with the wicked, treat-

ing the righteous and the wicked alike. Far be it from you! Will not the Judge*d* of all the earth do right?"

²⁶The Lord said, "If I find fifty righteous people in the city of Sodom, I will spare the whole place for their sake."

²⁷Then Abraham spoke up again: "Now that I have been so bold as to speak to the Lord, though I am nothing but dust and ashes, ²⁸what if the number of the righteous is five less than fifty? Will you destroy the whole city because of five people?"

"If I find forty-five there," he said, "I will not destroy it."

²⁹Once again he spoke to him, "What if only forty are found there?"

He said, "For the sake of forty, I will not do it."

³⁰Then he said, "May the Lord not be angry, but let me speak. What if only thirty can be found there?"

He answered, "I will not do it if I find thirty there."

³¹Abraham said, "Now that I have been so bold as to speak to the Lord, what if only twenty can be found there?"

He said, "For the sake of twenty, I will not destroy it."

³²Then he said, "May the Lord not be angry, but let me speak just once more. What if only ten can be found there?"

He answered, "For the sake of ten, I will not destroy it."

³³When the Lord had finished speaking with Abraham, he left, and Abraham returned home.

Sodom and Gomorrah Destroyed

19 The two angels arrived at Sodom in the evening, and Lot was sitting in the gateway of the city. When he saw them, he got up to meet them and bowed down with his face to the ground. ²"My lords," he said, "please turn aside to your servant's house. You can wash your feet and spend the night and then go on your way early in the morning."

---

*a*12 Or *husband*   *b*22 Masoretic Text; an ancient Hebrew scribal tradition *but the* Lord *remained standing before Abraham*   *c*24 Or *forgive;* also in verse 26   *d*25 Or *Ruler*

"No," they answered, "we will spend the night in the square."

[3]But he insisted so strongly that they did go with him and entered his house. He prepared a meal for them, baking bread without yeast, and they ate. [4]Before they had gone to bed, all the men from every part of the city of Sodom—both young and old—surrounded the house. [5]They called to Lot, "Where are the men who came to you tonight? Bring them

FRIDAY

VERSE:	AUTHOR:	PASSAGE:
Genesis 18:12	John Gilmore	Genesis 18:1–15

You Would Laugh Too

We should be careful not to judge Sarah too critically, for we'd laugh too if we were in her shoes. As a matter of fact, though we're not near 90 and have no chance or need for pregnancy, we laugh at other potential miracles that could happen to us or through us.

Poor health may be the reason some can't continue to serve. But usually it is not the hardening of arteries but the hardening of attitudes that keeps us on the sidelines. Rigidity of programming is one of the perils of senior-hood. We give up on others. We give up on ourselves. Do we not, like Sarah, think we know more than God? However, God is not done with us, though we are done with ourselves . . .

What can *we* do to strengthen the local church, to energize God's prophets, to get the gospel out to an ink-dark society? God can use us in the far-reaching endeavors that we would naturally dismiss.

A volunteer senior force can make a church effective. Many are not too old to sew, to pray, to sing, to usher, to teach. Either we are too bashful to volunteer or too unwilling to try. Why not go out of life maximizing our influence for Christ, instead of sitting around waiting for an escort of heavenly angels?

ADDITIONAL SCRIPTURE READINGS
1 Corinthians 12:1–11; Ephesians 4:1–16

Go to page 25 for your next devotional reading.

out to us so that we can have sex with them."

⁶Lot went outside to meet them and shut the door behind him ⁷and said, "No, my friends. Don't do this wicked thing. ⁸Look, I have two daughters who have never slept with a man. Let me bring them out to you, and you can do what you like with them. But don't do anything to these men, for they have come under the protection of my roof."

⁹"Get out of our way," they replied. And they said, "This fellow came here as an alien, and now he wants to play the judge! We'll treat you worse than them." They kept bringing pressure on Lot and moved forward to break down the door.

¹⁰But the men inside reached out and pulled Lot back into the house and shut the door. ¹¹Then they struck the men who were at the door of the house, young and old, with blindness so that they could not find the door.

¹²The two men said to Lot, "Do you have anyone else here—sons-in-law, sons or daughters, or anyone else in the city who belongs to you? Get them out of here, ¹³because we are going to destroy this place. The outcry to the LORD against its people is so great that he has sent us to destroy it."

¹⁴So Lot went out and spoke to his sons-in-law, who were pledged to marryᵃ his daughters. He said, "Hurry and get out of this place, because the LORD is about to destroy the city!" But his sons-in-law thought he was joking.

¹⁵With the coming of dawn, the angels urged Lot, saying, "Hurry! Take your wife and your two daughters who are here, or you will be swept away when the city is punished."

¹⁶When he hesitated, the men grasped his hand and the hands of his wife and of his two daughters and led them safely out of the city, for the LORD was merciful to them. ¹⁷As soon as they had brought them out, one of

them said, "Flee for your lives! Don't look back, and don't stop anywhere in the plain! Flee to the mountains or you will be swept away!"

¹⁸But Lot said to them, "No, my lords,ᵇ please! ¹⁹Yourᶜ servant has found favor in yourᶜ eyes, and youᶜ have shown great kindness to me in sparing my life. But I can't flee to the mountains; this disaster will overtake me, and I'll die. ²⁰Look, here is a town near enough to run to, and it is small. Let me flee to it—it is very small, isn't it? Then my life will be spared."

²¹He said to him, "Very well, I will grant this request too; I will not overthrow the town you speak of. ²²But flee there quickly, because I cannot do anything until you reach it." (That is why the town was called Zoar.ᵈ)

²³By the time Lot reached Zoar, the sun had risen over the land. ²⁴Then the LORD rained down burning sulfur on Sodom and Gomorrah—from the LORD out of the heavens. ²⁵Thus he overthrew those cities and the entire plain, including all those living in the cities—and also the vegetation in the land. ²⁶But Lot's wife looked back, and she became a pillar of salt.

²⁷Early the next morning Abraham got up and returned to the place where he had stood before the LORD. ²⁸He looked down toward Sodom and Gomorrah, toward all the land of the plain, and he saw dense smoke rising from the land, like smoke from a furnace.

²⁹So when God destroyed the cities of the plain, he remembered Abraham, and he brought Lot out of the catastrophe that overthrew the cities where Lot had lived.

Lot and His Daughters

³⁰Lot and his two daughters left Zoar and settled in the mountains, for he was afraid to stay in Zoar. He and his two daughters lived in a cave. ³¹One day the older daughter said to the younger, "Our father is old, and

---

ᵃ14 Or were married to   ᵇ18 Or No, Lord; or No, my lord   ᶜ19 The Hebrew is singular.
ᵈ22 Zoar means small.

there is no man around here to lie
with us, as is the custom all over the
earth. ³²Let's get our father to drink
wine and then lie with him and preserve our family line through our father."

³³That night they got their father to
drink wine, and the older daughter
went in and lay with him. He was not
aware of it when she lay down or
when she got up.

³⁴The next day the older daughter
said to the younger, "Last night I lay
with my father. Let's get him to drink
wine again tonight, and you go in and
lie with him so we can preserve our
family line through our father." ³⁵So
they got their father to drink wine
that night also, and the younger
daughter went and lay with him.
Again he was not aware of it when
she lay down or when she got up.

³⁶So both of Lot's daughters became pregnant by their father. ³⁷The
older daughter had a son, and she
named him Moab*a*; he is the father
of the Moabites of today. ³⁸The younger daughter also had a son, and she
named him Ben-Ammi*b*; he is the father of the Ammonites of today.

Abraham and Abimelech

20 Now Abraham moved on from
there into the region of the
Negev and lived between Kadesh and
Shur. For a while he stayed in Gerar,
²and there Abraham said of his wife
Sarah, "She is my sister." Then Abimelech king of Gerar sent for Sarah and
took her.

³But God came to Abimelech in a
dream one night and said to him,
"You are as good as dead because of
the woman you have taken; she is a
married woman."

⁴Now Abimelech had not gone
near her, so he said, "Lord, will you
destroy an innocent nation? ⁵Did he
not say to me, 'She is my sister,' and
didn't she also say, 'He is my brother'? I have done this with a clear conscience and clean hands."

⁶Then God said to him in the
dream, "Yes, I know you did this with
a clear conscience, and so I have kept
you from sinning against me. That is
why I did not let you touch her. ⁷Now
return the man's wife, for he is a
prophet, and he will pray for you and
you will live. But if you do not return
her, you may be sure that you and all
yours will die."

⁸Early the next morning Abimelech
summoned all his officials, and when
he told them all that had happened,
they were very much afraid. ⁹Then
Abimelech called Abraham in and
said, "What have you done to us?
How have I wronged you that you
have brought such great guilt upon
me and my kingdom? You have done
things to me that should not be
done." ¹⁰And Abimelech asked Abraham, "What was your reason for doing this?"

¹¹Abraham replied, "I said to myself, 'There is surely no fear of God in
this place, and they will kill me because of my wife.' ¹²Besides, she
really is my sister, the daughter of my
father though not of my mother; and
she became my wife. ¹³And when
God had me wander from my father's
household, I said to her, 'This is how
you can show your love to me: Everywhere we go, say of me, "He is my
brother." ' "

¹⁴Then Abimelech brought sheep
and cattle and male and female slaves
and gave them to Abraham, and he
returned Sarah his wife to him. ¹⁵And
Abimelech said, "My land is before
you; live wherever you like."

¹⁶To Sarah he said, "I am giving
your brother a thousand shekels*c* of
silver. This is to cover the offense
against you before all who are with
you; you are completely vindicated."

¹⁷Then Abraham prayed to God,
and God healed Abimelech, his wife
and his slave girls so they could have
children again, ¹⁸for the LORD had
closed up every womb in Abimelech's

a37 Moab sounds like the Hebrew for *from father.*   *b38* Ben-Ammi means *son of my people.*
c16 That is, about 25 pounds (about 11.5 kilograms)

PASSAGE: Genesis 1:27–31; 2 Corinthians 3:1–18
AUTHOR: Ruth Bell Graham

The Master Artist

As the portrait is unconscious
of the master artist's touch,
unaware of growing beauty,
unaware of changing much,
so you have not guessed His working
in your life throughout each year,
have not seen the growing beauty
have not sensed it, Mother dear.
We have seen and marveled greatly
at the Master Artist's skill,
marveled at the lovely picture
daily growing lovelier still;
watched His brush strokes
change each feature
to a likeness of His face,
till in you we see the Master,
feel His presence, glimpse His grace;
pray the fragrance of His presence
may through you seem doubly sweet,
till your years on earth are ended
and the portrait is complete.

Ruth Bell Graham (written for her mother)

Go to page 28 for your next devotional reading.

household because of Abraham's wife
Sarah.

The Birth of Isaac

21 Now the LORD was gracious to Sarah as he had said, and the LORD did for Sarah what he had promised. ²Sarah became pregnant and bore a son to Abraham in his old age, at the very time God had promised him. ³Abraham gave the name Isaac*a* to the son Sarah bore him. ⁴When his son Isaac was eight days old, Abraham circumcised him, as God commanded him. ⁵Abraham was a hundred years old when his son Isaac was born to him.

⁶Sarah said, "God has brought me laughter, and everyone who hears about this will laugh with me." ⁷And she added, "Who would have said to Abraham that Sarah would nurse children? Yet I have borne him a son in his old age."

Hagar and Ishmael Sent Away

⁸The child grew and was weaned, and on the day Isaac was weaned Abraham held a great feast. ⁹But Sarah saw that the son whom Hagar the Egyptian had borne to Abraham was mocking, ¹⁰and she said to Abraham, "Get rid of that slave woman and her son, for that slave woman's son will never share in the inheritance with my son Isaac."

¹¹The matter distressed Abraham greatly because it concerned his son. ¹²But God said to him, "Do not be so distressed about the boy and your maidservant. Listen to whatever Sarah tells you, because it is through Isaac that your offspring*b* will be reckoned. ¹³I will make the son of the maidservant into a nation also, because he is your offspring."

¹⁴Early the next morning Abraham took some food and a skin of water and gave them to Hagar. He set them on her shoulders and then sent her off with the boy. She went on her way and wandered in the desert of Beersheba.

¹⁵When the water in the skin was gone, she put the boy under one of the bushes. ¹⁶Then she went off and sat down nearby, about a bowshot away, for she thought, "I cannot watch the boy die." And as she sat there nearby, she*c* began to sob.

¹⁷God heard the boy crying, and the angel of God called to Hagar from heaven and said to her, "What is the matter, Hagar? Do not be afraid; God has heard the boy crying as he lies there. ¹⁸Lift the boy up and take him by the hand, for I will make him into a great nation."

¹⁹Then God opened her eyes and she saw a well of water. So she went and filled the skin with water and gave the boy a drink.

²⁰God was with the boy as he grew up. He lived in the desert and became an archer. ²¹While he was living in the Desert of Paran, his mother got a wife for him from Egypt.

The Treaty at Beersheba

²²At that time Abimelech and Phicol the commander of his forces said to Abraham, "God is with you in everything you do. ²³Now swear to me here before God that you will not deal falsely with me or my children or my descendants. Show to me and the country where you are living as an alien the same kindness I have shown to you."

²⁴Abraham said, "I swear it."

²⁵Then Abraham complained to Abimelech about a well of water that Abimelech's servants had seized. ²⁶But Abimelech said, "I don't know who has done this. You did not tell me, and I heard about it only today."

²⁷So Abraham brought sheep and cattle and gave them to Abimelech, and the two men made a treaty. ²⁸Abraham set apart seven ewe lambs from the flock, ²⁹and Abimelech asked Abraham, "What is the meaning of these seven ewe lambs you have set apart by themselves?"

³⁰He replied, "Accept these seven

---

*a*3 *Isaac* means *he laughs.*   *b*12 Or *seed*   *c*16 Hebrew; Septuagint *the child* lambs from my hand as a witness that I dug this well."

³¹So that place was called Beersheba,ᵃ because the two men swore an oath there.

³²After the treaty had been made at Beersheba, Abimelech and Phicol the commander of his forces returned to the land of the Philistines. ³³Abraham planted a tamarisk tree in Beersheba, and there he called upon the name of the Lord, the Eternal God. ³⁴And Abraham stayed in the land of the Philistines for a long time.

Abraham Tested

22 Some time later God tested Abraham. He said to him, "Abraham!"

"Here I am," he replied.

²Then God said, "Take your son, your only son, Isaac, whom you love, and go to the region of Moriah. Sacrifice him there as a burnt offering on one of the mountains I will tell you about.

³Early the next morning Abraham got up and saddled his donkey. He took with him two of his servants and his son Isaac. When he had cut enough wood for the burnt offering, he set out for the place God had told him about. ⁴On the third day Abraham looked up and saw the place in the distance. ⁵He said to his servants, "Stay here with the donkey while I and the boy go over there. We will worship and then we will come back to you."

⁶Abraham took the wood for the burnt offering and placed it on his son Isaac, and he himself carried the fire and the knife. As the two of them went on together, ⁷Isaac spoke up and said to his father Abraham, "Father?"

"Yes, my son?" Abraham replied.

"The fire and wood are here," Isaac said, "but where is the lamb for the burnt offering?"

⁸Abraham answered, "God himself will provide the lamb for the burnt offering, my son." And the two of them went on together.

⁹When they reached the place God had told him about, Abraham built an altar there and arranged the wood on it. He bound his son Isaac and laid him on the altar, on top of the wood. ¹⁰Then he reached out his hand and took the knife to slay his son. ¹¹But the angel of the Lord called out to him from heaven, "Abraham! Abraham!"

"Here I am," he replied.

¹²"Do not lay a hand on the boy," he said. "Do not do anything to him. Now I know that you fear God, because you have not withheld from me your son, your only son."

¹³Abraham looked up and there in a thicket he saw a ramᵇ caught by its horns. He went over and took the ram and sacrificed it as a burnt offering instead of his son. ¹⁴So Abraham called that place The Lord Will Provide. And to this day it is said, "On the mountain of the Lord it will be provided."

¹⁵The angel of the Lord called to Abraham from heaven a second time ¹⁶and said, "I swear by myself, declares the Lord, that because you have done this and have not withheld your son, your only son, ¹⁷I will surely bless you and make your descendants as numerous as the stars in the sky and as the sand on the seashore. Your descendants will take possession of the cities of their enemies, ¹⁸and through your offspringᶜ all nations on earth will be blessed, because you have obeyed me."

¹⁹Then Abraham returned to his servants, and they set off together for Beersheba. And Abraham stayed in Beersheba.

Nahor's Sons

²⁰Some time later Abraham was told, "Milcah is also a mother; she has borne sons to your brother Nahor: ²¹Uz the firstborn, Buz his brother,

Kemuel (the father of Aram), ²²Kesed, Hazo, Pildash, Jidlaph and Bethuel." ²³Bethuel became the father of Rebekah. Milcah bore these eight sons to Abraham's brother Nahor. ²⁴His concubine, whose name was Reumah, also had sons: Tebah, Gaham, Tahash and Maacah.

The Death of Sarah

23 Sarah lived to be a hundred and twenty-seven years old. ²She died at Kiriath Arba (that is, Hebron) in the land of Canaan, and Abraham went to mourn for Sarah and to weep over her.

³Then Abraham rose from beside

VERSE:	AUTHOR:	PASSAGE:
Genesis 22:9	Oswald Chambers	Genesis 22:1–14

Does My Sacrifice Live?

This incident is a picture of the blunder we make in thinking that the final thing God wants of us is the sacrifice of death. What God wants is the sacrifice *through* death, which enables us to do what Jesus did, namely, sacrifice our lives. Not — I am willing to go to death with thee, but — I am willing to be identified with thy death so that I may sacrifice my life to God. We seem to think that God wants us to give up things! God purified Abraham from this blunder, and the same discipline goes on in our lives. God nowhere tells us to give up things for the sake of giving them up. He tells us to give them up for the sake of the only thing worth having, namely, life with himself. It is a question of loosening the bands that hinder the life, and immediately those bands are loosened by identification with the death of Jesus, we enter into a relationship with God whereby we can sacrifice our lives to him.

It is of no value to God to give him your life for death. He wants you to be a *"living* sacrifice," to let him have all your powers that have been saved and sanctified through Jesus. This is the thing that is acceptable to God.

ADDITIONAL SCRIPTURE READINGS
Matthew 16:21–28; Romans 12:1–2

Go to page 61 for your next devotional reading.

his dead wife and spoke to the Hittites.*ᵃ* He said, ⁴"I am an alien and a stranger among you. Sell me some property for a burial site here so I can bury my dead."

⁵The Hittites replied to Abraham, ⁶"Sir, listen to us. You are a mighty prince among us. Bury your dead in the choicest of our tombs. None of us will refuse you his tomb for burying your dead."

⁷Then Abraham rose and bowed down before the people of the land, the Hittites. ⁸He said to them, "If you are willing to let me bury my dead, then listen to me and intercede with Ephron son of Zohar on my behalf ⁹so he will sell me the cave of Machpelah, which belongs to him and is at the end of his field. Ask him to sell it to me for the full price as a burial site among you."

¹⁰Ephron the Hittite was sitting among his people and he replied to Abraham in the hearing of all the Hittites who had come to the gate of his city. ¹¹"No, my lord," he said. "Listen to me; I give*ᵇ* you the field, and I give*ᵇ* you the cave that is in it. I give*ᵇ* it to you in the presence of my people. Bury your dead."

¹²Again Abraham bowed down before the people of the land ¹³and he said to Ephron in their hearing, "Listen to me, if you will. I will pay the price of the field. Accept it from me so I can bury my dead there."

¹⁴Ephron answered Abraham, ¹⁵"Listen to me, my lord; the land is worth four hundred shekels*ᶜ* of silver, but what is that between me and you? Bury your dead."

¹⁶Abraham agreed to Ephron's terms and weighed out for him the price he had named in the hearing of the Hittites: four hundred shekels of silver, according to the weight current among the merchants.

¹⁷So Ephron's field in Machpelah near Mamre—both the field and the cave in it, and all the trees within the borders of the field—was deeded ¹⁸to Abraham as his property in the presence of all the Hittites who had come to the gate of the city. ¹⁹Afterward Abraham buried his wife Sarah in the cave in the field of Machpelah near Mamre (which is at Hebron) in the land of Canaan. ²⁰So the field and the cave in it were deeded to Abraham by the Hittites as a burial site.

Isaac and Rebekah

24 Abraham was now old and well advanced in years, and the LORD had blessed him in every way. ²He said to the chief*ᵈ* servant in his household, the one in charge of all that he had, "Put your hand under my thigh. ³I want you to swear by the LORD, the God of heaven and the God of earth, that you will not get a wife for my son from the daughters of the Canaanites, among whom I am living, ⁴but will go to my country and my own relatives and get a wife for my son Isaac."

⁵The servant asked him, "What if the woman is unwilling to come back with me to this land? Shall I then take your son back to the country you came from?"

⁶"Make sure that you do not take my son back there," Abraham said. ⁷"The LORD, the God of heaven, who brought me out of my father's household and my native land and who spoke to me and promised me on oath, saying, 'To your offspring*ᵉ* I will give this land'—he will send his angel before you so that you can get a wife for my son from there. ⁸If the woman is unwilling to come back with you, then you will be released from this oath of mine. Only do not take my son back there." ⁹So the servant put his hand under the thigh of his master Abraham and swore an oath to him concerning this matter.

¹⁰Then the servant took ten of his master's camels and left, taking with him all kinds of good things from his master. He set out for Aram Nahara-

---

ᵃ3 Or *the sons of Heth;* also in verses 5, 7, 10, 16, 18 and 20   *ᵇ11* Or *sell*   *ᶜ15* That is, about 10 pounds (about 4.5 kilograms)   *ᵈ2* Or *oldest*   *ᵉ7* Or *seed*

im[a] and made his way to the town of Nahor. [11]He had the camels kneel down near the well outside the town; it was toward evening, the time the women go out to draw water.

[12]Then he prayed, "O Lord, God of my master Abraham, give me success today, and show kindness to my master Abraham. [13]See, I am standing beside this spring, and the daughters of the townspeople are coming out to draw water. [14]May it be that when I say to a girl, 'Please let down your jar that I may have a drink,' and she says, 'Drink, and I'll water your camels too'—let her be the one you have chosen for your servant Isaac. By this I will know that you have shown kindness to my master."

[15]Before he had finished praying, Rebekah came out with her jar on her shoulder. She was the daughter of Bethuel son of Milcah, who was the wife of Abraham's brother Nahor. [16]The girl was very beautiful, a virgin; no man had ever lain with her. She went down to the spring, filled her jar and came up again.

[17]The servant hurried to meet her and said, "Please give me a little water from your jar."

[18]"Drink, my lord," she said, and quickly lowered the jar to her hands and gave him a drink.

[19]After she had given him a drink, she said, "I'll draw water for your camels too, until they have finished drinking." [20]So she quickly emptied her jar into the trough, ran back to the well to draw more water, and drew enough for all his camels. [21]Without saying a word, the man watched her closely to learn whether or not the Lord had made his journey successful.

[22]When the camels had finished drinking, the man took out a gold nose ring weighing a beka[b] and two gold bracelets weighing ten shekels.[c] [23]Then he asked, "Whose daughter are you? Please tell me, is there room in your father's house for us to spend the night?"

[24]She answered him, "I am the daughter of Bethuel, the son that Milcah bore to Nahor." [25]And she added, "We have plenty of straw and fodder, as well as room for you to spend the night."

[26]Then the man bowed down and worshiped the Lord, [27]saying, "Praise be to the Lord, the God of my master Abraham, who has not abandoned his kindness and faithfulness to my master. As for me, the Lord has led me on the journey to the house of my master's relatives."

[28]The girl ran and told her mother's household about these things. [29]Now Rebekah had a brother named Laban, and he hurried out to the man at the spring. [30]As soon as he had seen the nose ring, and the bracelets on his sister's arms, and had heard Rebekah tell what the man said to her, he went out to the man and found him standing by the camels near the spring. [31]"Come, you who are blessed by the Lord," he said. "Why are you standing out here? I have prepared the house and a place for the camels."

[32]So the man went to the house, and the camels were unloaded. Straw and fodder were brought for the camels, and water for him and his men to wash their feet. [33]Then food was set before him, but he said, "I will not eat until I have told you what I have to say."

"Then tell us," ⌊Laban⌋ said.

[34]So he said, "I am Abraham's servant. [35]The Lord has blessed my master abundantly, and he has become wealthy. He has given him sheep and cattle, silver and gold, menservants and maidservants, and camels and donkeys. [36]My master's wife Sarah has borne him a son in her[d] old age, and he has given him everything he owns. [37]And my master made me swear an oath, and said, 'You must not get a wife for my son from the daughters of the Canaanites, in whose land I live, [38]but go to my father's

---

[a]10 That is, Northwest Mesopotamia   [b]22 That is, about 1/5 ounce (about 5.5 grams)
[c]22 That is, about 4 ounces (about 110 grams)   [d]36 Or his

family and to my own clan, and get a wife for my son.'

³⁹"Then I asked my master, 'What if the woman will not come back with me?'

⁴⁰"He replied, 'The LORD, before whom I have walked, will send his angel with you and make your journey a success, so that you can get a wife for my son from my own clan and from my father's family. ⁴¹Then, when you go to my clan, you will be released from my oath even if they refuse to give her to you—you will be released from my oath.'

⁴²"When I came to the spring today, I said, 'O LORD, God of my master Abraham, if you will, please grant success to the journey on which I have come. ⁴³See, I am standing beside this spring; if a maiden comes out to draw water and I say to her, "Please let me drink a little water from your jar," ⁴⁴and if she says to me, "Drink, and I'll draw water for your camels too," let her be the one the LORD has chosen for my master's son.'

⁴⁵"Before I finished praying in my heart, Rebekah came out, with her jar on her shoulder. She went down to the spring and drew water, and I said to her, 'Please give me a drink.'

⁴⁶"She quickly lowered her jar from her shoulder and said, 'Drink, and I'll water your camels too.' So I drank, and she watered the camels also.

⁴⁷"I asked her, 'Whose daughter are you?'

"She said, 'The daughter of Bethuel son of Nahor, whom Milcah bore to him.'

"Then I put the ring in her nose and the bracelets on her arms, ⁴⁸and I bowed down and worshiped the LORD. I praised the LORD, the God of my master Abraham, who had led me on the right road to get the granddaughter of my master's brother for his son. ⁴⁹Now if you will show kindness and faithfulness to my master, tell me; and if not, tell me, so I may know which way to turn."

⁵⁰Laban and Bethuel answered, "This is from the LORD; we can say nothing to you one way or the other. ⁵¹Here is Rebekah; take her and go, and let her become the wife of your master's son, as the LORD has directed."

⁵²When Abraham's servant heard what they said, he bowed down to the ground before the LORD. ⁵³Then the servant brought out gold and silver jewelry and articles of clothing and gave them to Rebekah; he also gave costly gifts to her brother and to her mother. ⁵⁴Then he and the men who were with him ate and drank and spent the night there.

When they got up the next morning, he said, "Send me on my way to my master."

⁵⁵But her brother and her mother replied, "Let the girl remain with us ten days or so; then you*ᵃ* may go."

⁵⁶But he said to them, "Do not detain me, now that the LORD has granted success to my journey. Send me on my way so I may go to my master."

⁵⁷Then they said, "Let's call the girl and ask her about it." ⁵⁸So they called Rebekah and asked her, "Will you go with this man?"

"I will go," she said.

⁵⁹So they sent their sister Rebekah on her way, along with her nurse and Abraham's servant and his men. ⁶⁰And they blessed Rebekah and said to her,

"Our sister, may you increase
    to thousands upon thousands;
may your offspring possess
    the gates of their enemies."

⁶¹Then Rebekah and her maids got ready and mounted their camels and went back with the man. So the servant took Rebekah and left.

⁶²Now Isaac had come from Beer Lahai Roi, for he was living in the Negev. ⁶³He went out to the field one evening to meditate,*ᵇ* and as he looked up, he saw camels approaching. ⁶⁴Rebekah also looked up and saw Isaac. She got down from her

---

*ᵃ*55 Or *she*   *ᵇ*63 The meaning of the Hebrew for this word is uncertain.

camel ⁶⁵and asked the servant, "Who is that man in the field coming to meet us?"

"He is my master," the servant answered. So she took her veil and covered herself.

⁶⁶Then the servant told Isaac all he had done. ⁶⁷Isaac brought her into the tent of his mother Sarah, and he married Rebekah. So she became his wife, and he loved her; and Isaac was comforted after his mother's death.

The Death of Abraham

25 Abraham took*a* another wife, whose name was Keturah. ²She bore him Zimran, Jokshan, Medan, Midian, Ishbak and Shuah. ³Jokshan was the father of Sheba and Dedan; the descendants of Dedan were the Asshurites, the Letushites and the Leummites. ⁴The sons of Midian were Ephah, Epher, Hanoch, Abida and Eldaah. All these were descendants of Keturah.

⁵Abraham left everything he owned to Isaac. ⁶But while he was still living, he gave gifts to the sons of his concubines and sent them away from his son Isaac to the land of the east.

⁷Altogether, Abraham lived a hundred and seventy-five years. ⁸Then Abraham breathed his last and died at a good old age, an old man and full of years; and he was gathered to his people. ⁹His sons Isaac and Ishmael buried him in the cave of Machpelah near Mamre, in the field of Ephron son of Zohar the Hittite, ¹⁰the field Abraham had bought from the Hittites.*b* There Abraham was buried with his wife Sarah. ¹¹After Abraham's death, God blessed his son Isaac, who then lived near Beer Lahai Roi.

Ishmael's Sons

¹²This is the account of Abraham's son Ishmael, whom Sarah's maidservant, Hagar the Egyptian, bore to Abraham.

¹³These are the names of the sons of Ishmael, listed in the order of their birth: Nebaioth the firstborn of Ishmael, Kedar, Adbeel, Mibsam, ¹⁴Mishma, Dumah, Massa, ¹⁵Hadad, Tema, Jetur, Naphish and Kedemah. ¹⁶These were the sons of Ishmael, and these are the names of the twelve tribal rulers according to their settlements and camps. ¹⁷Altogether, Ishmael lived a hundred and thirty-seven years. He breathed his last and died, and he was gathered to his people. ¹⁸His descendants settled in the area from Havilah to Shur, near the border of Egypt, as you go toward Asshur. And they lived in hostility toward*c* all their brothers.

Jacob and Esau

¹⁹This is the account of Abraham's son Isaac.

Abraham became the father of Isaac, ²⁰and Isaac was forty years old when he married Rebekah daughter of Bethuel the Aramean from Paddan Aram*d* and sister of Laban the Aramean.

²¹Isaac prayed to the LORD on behalf of his wife, because she was barren. The LORD answered his prayer, and his wife Rebekah became pregnant. ²²The babies jostled each other within her, and she said, "Why is this happening to me?" So she went to inquire of the LORD.

²³The LORD said to her,

"Two nations are in your womb,
 and two peoples from within
  you will be separated;
one people will be stronger than
   the other,
 and the older will serve the
   younger."

²⁴When the time came for her to give birth, there were twin boys in her womb. ²⁵The first to come out was red, and his whole body was like a hairy garment; so they named him Esau.*e* ²⁶After this, his brother came

out, with his hand grasping Esau's heel; so he was named Jacob.[a] Isaac was sixty years old when Rebekah gave birth to them.

27The boys grew up, and Esau became a skillful hunter, a man of the open country, while Jacob was a quiet man, staying among the tents. 28Isaac, who had a taste for wild game, loved Esau, but Rebekah loved Jacob.

29Once when Jacob was cooking some stew, Esau came in from the open country, famished. 30He said to Jacob, "Quick, let me have some of that red stew! I'm famished!" (That is why he was also called Edom.[b])

31Jacob replied, "First sell me your birthright."

32"Look, I am about to die," Esau said. "What good is the birthright to me?"

33But Jacob said, "Swear to me first." So he swore an oath to him, selling his birthright to Jacob.

34Then Jacob gave Esau some bread and some lentil stew. He ate and drank, and then got up and left.

So Esau despised his birthright.

Isaac and Abimelech

26 Now there was a famine in the land—besides the earlier famine of Abraham's time—and Isaac went to Abimelech king of the Philistines in Gerar. 2The LORD appeared to Isaac and said, "Do not go down to Egypt; live in the land where I tell you to live. 3Stay in this land for a while, and I will be with you and will bless you. For to you and your descendants I will give all these lands and will confirm the oath I swore to your father Abraham. 4I will make your descendants as numerous as the stars in the sky and will give them all these lands, and through your offspring[c] all nations on earth will be blessed, 5because Abraham obeyed me and kept my requirements, my commands, my decrees and my laws." 6So Isaac stayed in Gerar.

7When the men of that place asked him about his wife, he said, "She is my sister," because he was afraid to say, "She is my wife." He thought, "The men of this place might kill me on account of Rebekah, because she is beautiful."

8When Isaac had been there a long time, Abimelech king of the Philistines looked down from a window and saw Isaac caressing his wife Rebekah. 9So Abimelech summoned Isaac and said, "She is really your wife! Why did you say, 'She is my sister'?"

Isaac answered him, "Because I thought I might lose my life on account of her."

10Then Abimelech said, "What is this you have done to us? One of the men might well have slept with your wife, and you would have brought guilt upon us."

11So Abimelech gave orders to all the people: "Anyone who molests this man or his wife shall surely be put to death."

12Isaac planted crops in that land and the same year reaped a hundredfold, because the LORD blessed him. 13The man became rich, and his wealth continued to grow until he became very wealthy. 14He had so many flocks and herds and servants that the Philistines envied him. 15So all the wells that his father's servants had dug in the time of his father Abraham, the Philistines stopped up, filling them with earth.

16Then Abimelech said to Isaac, "Move away from us; you have become too powerful for us."

17So Isaac moved away from there and encamped in the Valley of Gerar and settled there. 18Isaac reopened the wells that had been dug in the time of his father Abraham, which the Philistines had stopped up after Abraham died, and he gave them the same names his father had given them.

19Isaac's servants dug in the valley and discovered a well of fresh water there. 20But the herdsmen of Gerar

a26 Jacob means he grasps the heel (figuratively, he deceives).   b30 Edom means red.
c4 Or seed

quarreled with Isaac's herdsmen and said, "The water is ours!" So he named the well Esek,ᵃ because they disputed with him. ²¹Then they dug another well, but they quarreled over that one also; so he named it Sitnah.ᵇ ²²He moved on from there and dug another well, and no one quarreled over it. He named it Rehoboth,ᶜ saying, "Now the LORD has given us room and we will flourish in the land."

²³From there he went up to Beersheba. ²⁴That night the LORD appeared to him and said, "I am the God of your father Abraham. Do not be afraid, for I am with you; I will bless you and will increase the number of your descendants for the sake of my servant Abraham."

²⁵Isaac built an altar there and called on the name of the LORD. There he pitched his tent, and there his servants dug a well.

²⁶Meanwhile, Abimelech had come to him from Gerar, with Ahuzzath his personal adviser and Phicol the commander of his forces. ²⁷Isaac asked them, "Why have you come to me, since you were hostile to me and sent me away?"

²⁸They answered, "We saw clearly that the LORD was with you; so we said, 'There ought to be a sworn agreement between us'—between us and you. Let us make a treaty with you ²⁹that you will do us no harm, just as we did not molest you but always treated you well and sent you away in peace. And now you are blessed by the LORD."

³⁰Isaac then made a feast for them, and they ate and drank. ³¹Early the next morning the men swore an oath to each other. Then Isaac sent them on their way, and they left him in peace.

³²That day Isaac's servants came and told him about the well they had dug. They said, "We've found water!" ³³He called it Shibah,ᵈ and to this day the name of the town has been Beersheba.ᵉ

³⁴When Esau was forty years old, he married Judith daughter of Beeri the Hittite, and also Basemath daughter of Elon the Hittite. ³⁵They were a source of grief to Isaac and Rebekah.

Jacob Gets Isaac's Blessing

27 When Isaac was old and his eyes were so weak that he could no longer see, he called for Esau his older son and said to him, "My son."

"Here I am," he answered.

²Isaac said, "I am now an old man and don't know the day of my death. ³Now then, get your weapons—your quiver and bow—and go out to the open country to hunt some wild game for me. ⁴Prepare me the kind of tasty food I like and bring it to me to eat, so that I may give you my blessing before I die."

⁵Now Rebekah was listening as Isaac spoke to his son Esau. When Esau left for the open country to hunt game and bring it back, ⁶Rebekah said to her son Jacob, "Look, I overheard your father say to your brother Esau, ⁷'Bring me some game and prepare me some tasty food to eat, so that I may give you my blessing in the presence of the LORD before I die.' ⁸Now, my son, listen carefully and do what I tell you: ⁹Go out to the flock and bring me two choice young goats, so I can prepare some tasty food for your father, just the way he likes it. ¹⁰Then take it to your father to eat, so that he may give you his blessing before he dies."

¹¹Jacob said to Rebekah his mother, "But my brother Esau is a hairy man, and I'm a man with smooth skin. ¹²What if my father touches me? I would appear to be tricking him and would bring down a curse on myself rather than a blessing."

¹³His mother said to him, "My son, let the curse fall on me. Just do what I say; go and get them for me."

¹⁴So he went and got them and brought them to his mother, and she

---

prepared some tasty food, just the way his father liked it. ¹⁵Then Rebekah took the best clothes of Esau her older son, which she had in the house, and put them on her younger son Jacob. ¹⁶She also covered his hands and the smooth part of his neck with the goatskins. ¹⁷Then she handed to her son Jacob the tasty food and the bread she had made.

¹⁸He went to his father and said, "My father."

"Yes, my son," he answered. "Who is it?"

¹⁹Jacob said to his father, "I am Esau your firstborn. I have done as you told me. Please sit up and eat some of my game so that you may give me your blessing."

²⁰Isaac asked his son, "How did you find it so quickly, my son?"

"The LORD your God gave me success," he replied.

²¹Then Isaac said to Jacob, "Come near so I can touch you, my son, to know whether you really are my son Esau or not."

²²Jacob went close to his father Isaac, who touched him and said, "The voice is the voice of Jacob, but the hands are the hands of Esau." ²³He did not recognize him, for his hands were hairy like those of his brother Esau; so he blessed him. ²⁴"Are you really my son Esau?" he asked.

"I am," he replied.

²⁵Then he said, "My son, bring me some of your game to eat, so that I may give you my blessing."

Jacob brought it to him and he ate; and he brought some wine and he drank. ²⁶Then his father Isaac said to him, "Come here, my son, and kiss me."

²⁷So he went to him and kissed him. When Isaac caught the smell of his clothes, he blessed him and said,

"Ah, the smell of my son
   is like the smell of a field
   that the LORD has blessed.

²⁸May God give you of heaven's
      dew
   and of earth's richness—
      an abundance of grain and new
         wine.
²⁹May nations serve you
   and peoples bow down to you.
Be lord over your brothers,
   and may the sons of your
      mother bow down to you.
May those who curse you be
      cursed
   and those who bless you be
      blessed."

³⁰After Isaac finished blessing him and Jacob had scarcely left his father's presence, his brother Esau came in from hunting. ³¹He too prepared some tasty food and brought it to his father. Then he said to him, "My father, sit up and eat some of my game, so that you may give me your blessing."

³²His father Isaac asked him, "Who are you?"

"I am your son," he answered, "your firstborn, Esau."

³³Isaac trembled violently and said, "Who was it, then, that hunted game and brought it to me? I ate it just before you came and I blessed him— and indeed he will be blessed!"

³⁴When Esau heard his father's words, he burst out with a loud and bitter cry and said to his father, "Bless me—me too, my father!"

³⁵But he said, "Your brother came deceitfully and took your blessing."

³⁶Esau said, "Isn't he rightly named Jacobᵃ? He has deceived me these two times: He took my birthright, and now he's taken my blessing!" Then he asked, "Haven't you reserved any blessing for me?"

³⁷Isaac answered Esau, "I have made him lord over you and have made all his relatives his servants, and I have sustained him with grain and new wine. So what can I possibly do for you, my son?"

³⁸Esau said to his father, "Do you have only one blessing, my father?

ᵃ36 *Jacob* means *he grasps the heel* (figuratively, *he deceives*).

Bless me too, my father!" Then Esau wept aloud.

³⁹His father Isaac answered him,

"Your dwelling will be
away from the earth's richness,
away from the dew of heaven
above.
⁴⁰You will live by the sword
and you will serve your brother.
But when you grow restless,
you will throw his yoke
from off your neck."

Jacob Flees to Laban

⁴¹Esau held a grudge against Jacob because of the blessing his father had given him. He said to himself, "The days of mourning for my father are near; then I will kill my brother Jacob."

⁴²When Rebekah was told what her older son Esau had said, she sent for her younger son Jacob and said to him, "Your brother Esau is consoling himself with the thought of killing you. ⁴³Now then, my son, do what I say: Flee at once to my brother Laban in Haran. ⁴⁴Stay with him for a while until your brother's fury subsides. ⁴⁵When your brother is no longer angry with you and forgets what you did to him, I'll send word for you to come back from there. Why should I lose both of you in one day?"

⁴⁶Then Rebekah said to Isaac, "I'm disgusted with living because of these Hittite women. If Jacob takes a wife from among the women of this land, from Hittite women like these, my life will not be worth living."

28 So Isaac called for Jacob and blessed[a] him and commanded him: "Do not marry a Canaanite woman. ²Go at once to Paddan Aram,[b] to the house of your mother's father Bethuel. Take a wife for yourself there, from among the daughters of Laban, your mother's brother. ³May God Almighty[c] bless you and make you fruitful and increase your numbers until you be-

come a community of peoples. ⁴May he give you and your descendants the blessing given to Abraham, so that you may take possession of the land where you now live as an alien, the land God gave to Abraham." ⁵Then Isaac sent Jacob on his way, and he went to Paddan Aram, to Laban son of Bethuel the Aramean, the brother of Rebekah, who was the mother of Jacob and Esau.

⁶Now Esau learned that Isaac had blessed Jacob and had sent him to Paddan Aram to take a wife from there, and that when he blessed him he commanded him, "Do not marry a Canaanite woman," ⁷and that Jacob had obeyed his father and mother and had gone to Paddan Aram. ⁸Esau then realized how displeasing the Canaanite women were to his father Isaac; ⁹so he went to Ishmael and married Mahalath, the sister of Nebaioth and daughter of Ishmael son of Abraham, in addition to the wives he already had.

Jacob's Dream at Bethel

¹⁰Jacob left Beersheba and set out for Haran. ¹¹When he reached a certain place, he stopped for the night because the sun had set. Taking one of the stones there, he put it under his head and lay down to sleep. ¹²He had a dream in which he saw a stairway[d] resting on the earth, with its top reaching to heaven, and the angels of God were ascending and descending on it. ¹³There above it[e] stood the LORD, and he said: "I am the LORD, the God of your father Abraham and the God of Isaac. I will give you and your descendants the land on which you are lying. ¹⁴Your descendants will be like the dust of the earth, and you will spread out to the west and to the east, to the north and to the south. All peoples on earth will be blessed through you and your offspring. ¹⁵I am with you and will watch over you wherever you go, and I will bring you back to this land. I will not leave

---

*a*1 Or *greeted*　　*b*2 That is, Northwest Mesopotamia; also in verses 5, 6 and 7　　*c*3 Hebrew *El-Shaddai*　　*d*12 Or *ladder*　　*e*13 Or *There beside him*

you until I have done what I have promised you."

¹⁶When Jacob awoke from his sleep, he thought, "Surely the LORD is in this place, and I was not aware of it." ¹⁷He was afraid and said, "How awesome is this place! This is none other than the house of God; this is the gate of heaven."

¹⁸Early the next morning Jacob took the stone he had placed under his head and set it up as a pillar and poured oil on top of it. ¹⁹He called that place Bethel,ᵃ though the city used to be called Luz.

²⁰Then Jacob made a vow, saying, "If God will be with me and will watch over me on this journey I am taking and will give me food to eat and clothes to wear ²¹so that I return safely to my father's house, then the LORDᵇ will be my God ²²andᶜ this stone that I have set up as a pillar will be God's house, and of all that you give me I will give you a tenth."

Jacob Arrives in Paddan Aram

29 Then Jacob continued on his journey and came to the land of the eastern peoples. ²There he saw a well in the field, with three flocks of sheep lying near it because the flocks were watered from that well. The stone over the mouth of the well was large. ³When all the flocks were gathered there, the shepherds would roll the stone away from the well's mouth and water the sheep. Then they would return the stone to its place over the mouth of the well.

⁴Jacob asked the shepherds, "My brothers, where are you from?"

"We're from Haran," they replied.

⁵He said to them, "Do you know Laban, Nahor's grandson?"

"Yes, we know him," they answered.

⁶Then Jacob asked them, "Is he well?"

"Yes, he is," they said, "and here comes his daughter Rachel with the sheep."

⁷"Look," he said, "the sun is still high; it is not time for the flocks to be gathered. Water the sheep and take them back to pasture."

⁸"We can't," they replied, "until all the flocks are gathered and the stone has been rolled away from the mouth of the well. Then we will water the sheep."

⁹While he was still talking with them, Rachel came with her father's sheep, for she was a shepherdess. ¹⁰When Jacob saw Rachel daughter of Laban, his mother's brother, and Laban's sheep, he went over and rolled the stone away from the mouth of the well and watered his uncle's sheep. ¹¹Then Jacob kissed Rachel and began to weep aloud. ¹²He had told Rachel that he was a relative of her father and a son of Rebekah. So she ran and told her father.

¹³As soon as Laban heard the news about Jacob, his sister's son, he hurried to meet him. He embraced him and kissed him and brought him to his home, and there Jacob told him all these things. ¹⁴Then Laban said to him, "You are my own flesh and blood."

Jacob Marries Leah and Rachel

After Jacob had stayed with him for a whole month, ¹⁵Laban said to him, "Just because you are a relative of mine, should you work for me for nothing? Tell me what your wages should be."

¹⁶Now Laban had two daughters; the name of the older was Leah, and the name of the younger was Rachel. ¹⁷Leah had weakᵈ eyes, but Rachel was lovely in form, and beautiful. ¹⁸Jacob was in love with Rachel and said, "I'll work for you seven years in return for your younger daughter Rachel."

¹⁹Laban said, "It's better that I give her to you than to some other man. Stay here with me." ²⁰So Jacob served seven years to get Rachel, but they

---

ᵃ19 *Bethel* means *house of God.*   ᵇ20,21 Or *Since God . . . father's house, the* LORD   ᶜ21,22 Or *house, and the* LORD *will be my God,* ²²*then*   ᵈ17 Or *delicate*

seemed like only a few days to him because of his love for her.

²¹Then Jacob said to Laban, "Give me my wife. My time is completed, and I want to lie with her."

²²So Laban brought together all the people of the place and gave a feast. ²³But when evening came, he took his daughter Leah and gave her to Jacob, and Jacob lay with her. ²⁴And Laban gave his servant girl Zilpah to his daughter as her maidservant.

²⁵When morning came, there was Leah! So Jacob said to Laban, "What is this you have done to me? I served you for Rachel, didn't I? Why have you deceived me?"

²⁶Laban replied, "It is not our custom here to give the younger daughter in marriage before the older one. ²⁷Finish this daughter's bridal week; then we will give you the younger one also, in return for another seven years of work."

²⁸And Jacob did so. He finished the week with Leah, and then Laban gave him his daughter Rachel to be his wife. ²⁹Laban gave his servant girl Bilhah to his daughter Rachel as her maidservant. ³⁰Jacob lay with Rachel also, and he loved Rachel more than Leah. And he worked for Laban another seven years.

Jacob's Children

³¹When the LORD saw that Leah was not loved, he opened her womb, but Rachel was barren. ³²Leah became pregnant and gave birth to a son. She named him Reuben,ᵃ for she said, "It is because the LORD has seen my misery. Surely my husband will love me now."

³³She conceived again, and when she gave birth to a son she said, "Because the LORD heard that I am not loved, he gave me this one too." So she named him Simeon.ᵇ

³⁴Again she conceived, and when she gave birth to a son she said, "Now at last my husband will become attached to me, because I have borne him three sons." So he was named Levi.ᶜ

³⁵She conceived again, and when she gave birth to a son she said, "This time I will praise the LORD." So she named him Judah.ᵈ Then she stopped having children.

30 When Rachel saw that she was not bearing Jacob any children, she became jealous of her sister. So she said to Jacob, "Give me children, or I'll die!"

²Jacob became angry with her and said, "Am I in the place of God, who has kept you from having children?"

³Then she said, "Here is Bilhah, my maidservant. Sleep with her so that she can bear children for me and that through her I too can build a family."

⁴So she gave him her servant Bilhah as a wife. Jacob slept with her, ⁵and she became pregnant and bore him a son. ⁶Then Rachel said, "God has vindicated me; he has listened to my plea and given me a son." Because of this she named him Dan.ᵉ

⁷Rachel's servant Bilhah conceived again and bore Jacob a second son. ⁸Then Rachel said, "I have had a great struggle with my sister, and I have won." So she named him Naphtali.ᶠ

⁹When Leah saw that she had stopped having children, she took her maidservant Zilpah and gave her to Jacob as a wife. ¹⁰Leah's servant Zilpah bore Jacob a son. ¹¹Then Leah said, "What good fortune!"ᵍ So she named him Gad.ʰ

¹²Leah's servant Zilpah bore Jacob a second son. ¹³Then Leah said, "How happy I am! The women will call me happy." So she named him Asher.ⁱ

¹⁴During wheat harvest, Reuben went out into the fields and found some mandrake plants, which he brought to his mother Leah. Rachel

---

ᵃ32 *Reuben* sounds like the Hebrew for *he has seen my misery*; the name means *see, a son.* ᵇ33 *Simeon* probably means *one who hears.*   ᶜ34 *Levi* sounds like and may be derived from the Hebrew for *attached.*   ᵈ35 *Judah* sounds like and may be derived from the Hebrew for *praise.* ᵉ6 *Dan* here means *he has vindicated.*   ᶠ8 *Naphtali* means *my struggle.*   ᵍ11 Or "A troop is coming!"   ʰ11 *Gad* can mean *good fortune* or *a troop.*   ⁱ13 *Asher* means *happy.*

said to Leah, "Please give me some of your son's mandrakes."

¹⁵But she said to her, "Wasn't it enough that you took away my husband? Will you take my son's mandrakes too?"

"Very well," Rachel said, "he can sleep with you tonight in return for your son's mandrakes."

¹⁶So when Jacob came in from the fields that evening, Leah went out to meet him. "You must sleep with me," she said. "I have hired you with my son's mandrakes." So he slept with her that night.

¹⁷God listened to Leah, and she became pregnant and bore Jacob a fifth son. ¹⁸Then Leah said, "God has rewarded me for giving my maidservant to my husband." So she named him Issachar.ᵃ

¹⁹Leah conceived again and bore Jacob a sixth son. ²⁰Then Leah said, "God has presented me with a precious gift. This time my husband will treat me with honor, because I have borne him six sons." So she named him Zebulun.ᵇ

²¹Some time later she gave birth to a daughter and named her Dinah.

²²Then God remembered Rachel; he listened to her and opened her womb. ²³She became pregnant and gave birth to a son and said, "God has taken away my disgrace." ²⁴She named him Joseph,ᶜ and said, "May the LORD add to me another son."

Jacob's Flocks Increase

²⁵After Rachel gave birth to Joseph, Jacob said to Laban, "Send me on my way so I can go back to my own homeland. ²⁶Give me my wives and children, for whom I have served you, and I will be on my way. You know how much work I've done for you."

²⁷But Laban said to him, "If I have found favor in your eyes, please stay. I have learned by divination thatᵈ the LORD has blessed me because of you." ²⁸He added, "Name your wages, and I will pay them."

²⁹Jacob said to him, "You know how I have worked for you and how your livestock has fared under my care. ³⁰The little you had before I came has increased greatly, and the LORD has blessed you wherever I have been. But now, when may I do something for my own household?"

³¹"What shall I give you?" he asked.

"Don't give me anything," Jacob replied. "But if you will do this one thing for me, I will go on tending your flocks and watching over them: ³²Let me go through all your flocks today and remove from them every speckled or spotted sheep, every dark-colored lamb and every spotted or speckled goat. They will be my wages. ³³And my honesty will testify for me in the future, whenever you check on the wages you have paid me. Any goat in my possession that is not speckled or spotted, or any lamb that is not dark-colored, will be considered stolen."

³⁴"Agreed," said Laban. "Let it be as you have said." ³⁵That same day he removed all the male goats that were streaked or spotted, and all the speckled or spotted female goats (all that had white on them) and all the dark-colored lambs, and he placed them in the care of his sons. ³⁶Then he put a three-day journey between himself and Jacob, while Jacob continued to tend the rest of Laban's flocks.

³⁷Jacob, however, took fresh-cut branches from poplar, almond and plane trees and made white stripes on them by peeling the bark and exposing the white inner wood of the branches. ³⁸Then he placed the peeled branches in all the watering troughs, so that they would be directly in front of the flocks when they came to drink. When the flocks were in heat and came to drink, ³⁹they mated in front of the branches. And they bore young that were streaked or speckled or spotted. ⁴⁰Jacob set apart the young of the flock by themselves, but made the

---

ᵃ18 *Issachar* sounds like the Hebrew for *reward.*   ᵇ20 *Zebulun* probably means *honor.*
ᶜ24 *Joseph* means *may he add.*   ᵈ27 Or possibly *have become rich and*

rest face the streaked and dark-colored animals that belonged to Laban. Thus he made separate flocks for himself and did not put them with Laban's animals. [41]Whenever the stronger females were in heat, Jacob would place the branches in the troughs in front of the animals so they would mate near the branches, [42]but if the animals were weak, he would not place them there. So the weak animals went to Laban and the strong ones to Jacob. [43]In this way the man grew exceedingly prosperous and came to own large flocks, and maidservants and menservants, and camels and donkeys.

Jacob Flees From Laban

31 Jacob heard that Laban's sons were saying, "Jacob has taken everything our father owned and has gained all this wealth from what belonged to our father." [2]And Jacob noticed that Laban's attitude toward him was not what it had been.

[3]Then the LORD said to Jacob, "Go back to the land of your fathers and to your relatives, and I will be with you."

[4]So Jacob sent word to Rachel and Leah to come out to the fields where his flocks were. [5]He said to them, "I see that your father's attitude toward me is not what it was before, but the God of my father has been with me. [6]You know that I've worked for your father with all my strength, [7]yet your father has cheated me by changing my wages ten times. However, God has not allowed him to harm me. [8]If he said, 'The speckled ones will be your wages,' then all the flocks gave birth to speckled young; and if he said, 'The streaked ones will be your wages,' then all the flocks bore streaked young. [9]So God has taken away your father's livestock and has given them to me.

[10]"In breeding season I once had a dream in which I looked up and saw that the male goats mating with the flock were streaked, speckled or spot-ted. [11]The angel of God said to me in the dream, 'Jacob.' I answered, 'Here I am.' [12]And he said, 'Look up and see that all the male goats mating with the flock are streaked, speckled or spotted, for I have seen all that Laban has been doing to you. [13]I am the God of Bethel, where you anointed a pillar and where you made a vow to me. Now leave this land at once and go back to your native land.' "

[14]Then Rachel and Leah replied, "Do we still have any share in the inheritance of our father's estate? [15]Does he not regard us as foreigners? Not only has he sold us, but he has used up what was paid for us. [16]Surely all the wealth that God took away from our father belongs to us and our children. So do whatever God has told you."

[17]Then Jacob put his children and his wives on camels, [18]and he drove all his livestock ahead of him, along with all the goods he had accumulated in Paddan Aram,[a] to go to his father Isaac in the land of Canaan.

[19]When Laban had gone to shear his sheep, Rachel stole her father's household gods. [20]Moreover, Jacob deceived Laban the Aramean by not telling him he was running away. [21]So he fled with all he had, and crossing the River,[b] he headed for the hill country of Gilead.

Laban Pursues Jacob

[22]On the third day Laban was told that Jacob had fled. [23]Taking his relatives with him, he pursued Jacob for seven days and caught up with him in the hill country of Gilead. [24]Then God came to Laban the Aramean in a dream at night and said to him, "Be careful not to say anything to Jacob, either good or bad."

[25]Jacob had pitched his tent in the hill country of Gilead when Laban overtook him, and Laban and his relatives camped there too. [26]Then Laban said to Jacob, "What have you done? You've deceived me, and you've carried off my daughters like captives in

---

[a]18 That is, Northwest Mesopotamia   [b]21 That is, the Euphrates

war. ²⁷Why did you run off secretly and deceive me? Why didn't you tell me, so I could send you away with joy and singing to the music of tambourines and harps? ²⁸You didn't even let me kiss my grandchildren and my daughters good-by. You have done a foolish thing. ²⁹I have the power to harm you; but last night the God of your father said to me, 'Be careful not to say anything to Jacob, either good or bad.' ³⁰Now you have gone off because you longed to return to your father's house. But why did you steal my gods?"

³¹Jacob answered Laban, "I was afraid, because I thought you would take your daughters away from me by force. ³²But if you find anyone who has your gods, he shall not live. In the presence of our relatives, see for yourself whether there is anything of yours here with me; and if so, take it." Now Jacob did not know that Rachel had stolen the gods.

³³So Laban went into Jacob's tent and into Leah's tent and into the tent of the two maidservants, but he found nothing. After he came out of Leah's tent, he entered Rachel's tent. ³⁴Now Rachel had taken the household gods and put them inside her camel's saddle and was sitting on them. Laban searched through everything in the tent but found nothing.

³⁵Rachel said to her father, "Don't be angry, my lord, that I cannot stand up in your presence; I'm having my period." So he searched but could not find the household gods.

³⁶Jacob was angry and took Laban to task. "What is my crime?" he asked Laban. "What sin have I committed that you hunt me down? ³⁷Now that you have searched through all my goods, what have you found that belongs to your household? Put it here in front of your relatives and mine, and let them judge between the two of us.

³⁸"I have been with you for twenty years now. Your sheep and goats have not miscarried, nor have I eaten rams from your flocks. ³⁹I did not bring you animals torn by wild beasts; I bore the loss myself. And you demanded payment from me for whatever was stolen by day or night. ⁴⁰This was my situation: The heat consumed me in the daytime and the cold at night, and sleep fled from my eyes. ⁴¹It was like this for the twenty years I was in your household. I worked for you fourteen years for your two daughters and six years for your flocks, and you changed my wages ten times. ⁴²If the God of my father, the God of Abraham and the Fear of Isaac, had not been with me, you would surely have sent me away empty-handed. But God has seen my hardship and the toil of my hands, and last night he rebuked you."

⁴³Laban answered Jacob, "The women are my daughters, the children are my children, and the flocks are my flocks. All you see is mine. Yet what can I do today about these daughters of mine, or about the children they have borne? ⁴⁴Come now, let's make a covenant, you and I, and let it serve as a witness between us."

⁴⁵So Jacob took a stone and set it up as a pillar. ⁴⁶He said to his relatives, "Gather some stones." So they took stones and piled them in a heap, and they ate there by the heap. ⁴⁷Laban called it Jegar Sahadutha,ᵃ and Jacob called it Galeed.ᵇ

⁴⁸Laban said, "This heap is a witness between you and me today." That is why it was called Galeed. ⁴⁹It was also called Mizpah,ᶜ because he said, "May the LORD keep watch between you and me when we are away from each other. ⁵⁰If you mistreat my daughters or if you take any wives besides my daughters, even though no one is with us, remember that God is a witness between you and me."

⁵¹Laban also said to Jacob, "Here is this heap, and here is this pillar I have set up between you and me. ⁵²This heap is a witness, and this pillar is a

ᵃ47 The Aramaic *Jegar Sahadutha* means *witness heap.* ᵇ47 The Hebrew *Galeed* means *witness heap.* ᶜ49 *Mizpah* means *watchtower.*

witness, that I will not go past this heap to your side to harm you and that you will not go past this heap and pillar to my side to harm me. [53]May the God of Abraham and the God of Nahor, the God of their father, judge between us."

So Jacob took an oath in the name of the Fear of his father Isaac. [54]He offered a sacrifice there in the hill country and invited his relatives to a meal. After they had eaten, they spent the night there.

[55]Early the next morning Laban kissed his grandchildren and his daughters and blessed them. Then he left and returned home.

Jacob Prepares to Meet Esau

32 Jacob also went on his way, and the angels of God met him. [2]When Jacob saw them, he said, "This is the camp of God!" So he named that place Mahanaim.[a]

[3]Jacob sent messengers ahead of him to his brother Esau in the land of Seir, the country of Edom. [4]He instructed them: "This is what you are to say to my master Esau: 'Your servant Jacob says, I have been staying with Laban and have remained there till now. [5]I have cattle and donkeys, sheep and goats, menservants and maidservants. Now I am sending this message to my lord, that I may find favor in your eyes.' "

[6]When the messengers returned to Jacob, they said, "We went to your brother Esau, and now he is coming to meet you, and four hundred men are with him."

[7]In great fear and distress Jacob divided the people who were with him into two groups,[b] and the flocks and herds and camels as well. [8]He thought, "If Esau comes and attacks one group,[c] the group[c] that is left may escape."

[9]Then Jacob prayed, "O God of my father Abraham, God of my father Isaac, O LORD, who said to me, 'Go back to your country and your relatives, and I will make you prosper,' [10]I am unworthy of all the kindness and faithfulness you have shown your servant. I had only my staff when I crossed this Jordan, but now I have become two groups. [11]Save me, I pray, from the hand of my brother Esau, for I am afraid he will come and attack me, and also the mothers with their children. [12]But you have said, 'I will surely make you prosper and will make your descendants like the sand of the sea, which cannot be counted.' "

[13]He spent the night there, and from what he had with him he selected a gift for his brother Esau: [14]two hundred female goats and twenty male goats, two hundred ewes and twenty rams, [15]thirty female camels with their young, forty cows and ten bulls, and twenty female donkeys and ten male donkeys. [16]He put them in the care of his servants, each herd by itself, and said to his servants, "Go ahead of me, and keep some space between the herds."

[17]He instructed the one in the lead: "When my brother Esau meets you and asks, 'To whom do you belong, and where are you going, and who owns all these animals in front of you?' [18]then you are to say, 'They belong to your servant Jacob. They are a gift sent to my lord Esau, and he is coming behind us.' "

[19]He also instructed the second, the third and all the others who followed the herds: "You are to say the same thing to Esau when you meet him. [20]And be sure to say, 'Your servant Jacob is coming behind us.' " For he thought, "I will pacify him with these gifts I am sending on ahead; later, when I see him, perhaps he will receive me." [21]So Jacob's gifts went on ahead of him, but he himself spent the night in the camp.

Jacob Wrestles With God

[22]That night Jacob got up and took his two wives, his two maidservants and his eleven sons and crossed the ford of the Jabbok. [23]After he had sent

---

[a]2 Mahanaim means two camps.   [b]7 Or camps; also in verse 10   [c]8 Or camp

them across the stream, he sent over all his possessions. ²⁴So Jacob was left alone, and a man wrestled with him till daybreak. ²⁵When the man saw that he could not overpower him, he touched the socket of Jacob's hip so that his hip was wrenched as he wrestled with the man. ²⁶Then the man said, "Let me go, for it is daybreak."

But Jacob replied, "I will not let you go unless you bless me."

²⁷The man asked him, "What is your name?"

"Jacob," he answered.

²⁸Then the man said, "Your name will no longer be Jacob, but Israel,ᵃ because you have struggled with God and with men and have overcome."

²⁹Jacob said, "Please tell me your name."

But he replied, "Why do you ask my name?" Then he blessed him there.

³⁰So Jacob called the place Peniel,ᵇ saying, "It is because I saw God face to face, and yet my life was spared."

³¹The sun rose above him as he passed Peniel,ᶜ and he was limping because of his hip. ³²Therefore to this day the Israelites do not eat the tendon attached to the socket of the hip, because the socket of Jacob's hip was touched near the tendon.

Jacob Meets Esau

33 Jacob looked up and there was Esau, coming with his four hundred men; so he divided the children among Leah, Rachel and the two maidservants. ²He put the maidservants and their children in front, Leah and her children next, and Rachel and Joseph in the rear. ³He himself went on ahead and bowed down to the ground seven times as he approached his brother.

⁴But Esau ran to meet Jacob and embraced him; he threw his arms around his neck and kissed him. And they wept. ⁵Then Esau looked up and saw the women and children. "Who are these with you?" he asked.

Jacob answered, "They are the children God has graciously given your servant."

⁶Then the maidservants and their children approached and bowed down. ⁷Next, Leah and her children came and bowed down. Last of all came Joseph and Rachel, and they too bowed down.

⁸Esau asked, "What do you mean by all these droves I met?"

"To find favor in your eyes, my lord," he said.

⁹But Esau said, "I already have plenty, my brother. Keep what you have for yourself."

¹⁰"No, please!" said Jacob. "If I have found favor in your eyes, accept this gift from me. For to see your face is like seeing the face of God, now that you have received me favorably. ¹¹Please accept the present that was brought to you, for God has been gracious to me and I have all I need." And because Jacob insisted, Esau accepted it.

¹²Then Esau said, "Let us be on our way; I'll accompany you."

¹³But Jacob said to him, "My lord knows that the children are tender and that I must care for the ewes and cows that are nursing their young. If they are driven hard just one day, all the animals will die. ¹⁴So let my lord go on ahead of his servant, while I move along slowly at the pace of the droves before me and that of the children, until I come to my lord in Seir."

¹⁵Esau said, "Then let me leave some of my men with you."

"But why do that?" Jacob asked. "Just let me find favor in the eyes of my lord."

¹⁶So that day Esau started on his way back to Seir. ¹⁷Jacob, however, went to Succoth, where he built a place for himself and made shelters for his livestock. That is why the place is called Succoth.ᵈ

¹⁸After Jacob came from Paddan

ᵃ28 *Israel* means *he struggles with God.*   ᵇ30 *Peniel* means *face of God.*   ᶜ31 Hebrew *Penuel,* a variant of *Peniel*   ᵈ17 *Succoth* means *shelters.*

Aram,*a* he arrived safely at the*b* city of Shechem in Canaan and camped within sight of the city. ¹⁹For a hundred pieces of silver,*c* he bought from the sons of Hamor, the father of Shechem, the plot of ground where he pitched his tent. ²⁰There he set up an altar and called it El Elohe Israel.*d*

Dinah and the Shechemites

34 Now Dinah, the daughter Leah had borne to Jacob, went out to visit the women of the land. ²When Shechem son of Hamor the Hivite, the ruler of that area, saw her, he took her and violated her. ³His heart was drawn to Dinah daughter of Jacob, and he loved the girl and spoke tenderly to her. ⁴And Shechem said to his father Hamor, "Get me this girl as my wife."

⁵When Jacob heard that his daughter Dinah had been defiled, his sons were in the fields with his livestock; so he kept quiet about it until they came home.

⁶Then Shechem's father Hamor went out to talk with Jacob. ⁷Now Jacob's sons had come in from the fields as soon as they heard what had happened. They were filled with grief and fury, because Shechem had done a disgraceful thing in*e* Israel by lying with Jacob's daughter—a thing that should not be done.

⁸But Hamor said to them, "My son Shechem has his heart set on your daughter. Please give her to him as his wife. ⁹Intermarry with us; give us your daughters and take our daughters for yourselves. ¹⁰You can settle among us; the land is open to you. Live in it, trade*f* in it, and acquire property in it."

¹¹Then Shechem said to Dinah's father and brothers, "Let me find favor in your eyes, and I will give you whatever you ask. ¹²Make the price for the bride and the gift I am to bring as great as you like, and I'll pay what-

ever you ask me. Only give me the girl as my wife."

¹³Because their sister Dinah had been defiled, Jacob's sons replied deceitfully as they spoke to Shechem and his father Hamor. ¹⁴They said to them, "We can't do such a thing; we can't give our sister to a man who is not circumcised. That would be a disgrace to us. ¹⁵We will give our consent to you on one condition only: that you become like us by circumcising all your males. ¹⁶Then we will give you our daughters and take your daughters for ourselves. We'll settle among you and become one people with you. ¹⁷But if you will not agree to be circumcised, we'll take our sister*g* and go."

¹⁸Their proposal seemed good to Hamor and his son Shechem. ¹⁹The young man, who was the most honored of all his father's household, lost no time in doing what they said, because he was delighted with Jacob's daughter. ²⁰So Hamor and his son Shechem went to the gate of their city to speak to their fellow townsmen. ²¹"These men are friendly toward us," they said. "Let them live in our land and trade in it; the land has plenty of room for them. We can marry their daughters and they can marry ours. ²²But the men will consent to live with us as one people only on the condition that our males be circumcised, as they themselves are. ²³Won't their livestock, their property and all their other animals become ours? So let us give our consent to them, and they will settle among us."

²⁴All the men who went out of the city gate agreed with Hamor and his son Shechem, and every male in the city was circumcised.

²⁵Three days later, while all of them were still in pain, two of Jacob's sons, Simeon and Levi, Dinah's brothers, took their swords and attacked the unsuspecting city, killing every male.

---

a18 That is, Northwest Mesopotamia   *b18* Or *arrived at Shalem, a*   *c19* Hebrew *hundred kesitahs*; a kesitah was a unit of money of unknown weight and value.   *d20* El Elohe Israel can mean *God, the God of Israel* or *mighty is the God of Israel.*   *e7* Or *against*   *f10* Or *move about freely*; also in verse 21   *g17* Hebrew *daughter*

²⁶They put Hamor and his son Shechem to the sword and took Dinah from Shechem's house and left. ²⁷The sons of Jacob came upon the dead bodies and looted the city where^a their sister had been defiled. ²⁸They seized their flocks and herds and donkeys and everything else of theirs in the city and out in the fields. ²⁹They carried off all their wealth and all their women and children, taking as plunder everything in the houses.

³⁰Then Jacob said to Simeon and Levi, "You have brought trouble on me by making me a stench to the Canaanites and Perizzites, the people living in this land. We are few in number, and if they join forces against me and attack me, I and my household will be destroyed."

³¹But they replied, "Should he have treated our sister like a prostitute?"

Jacob Returns to Bethel

35 Then God said to Jacob, "Go up to Bethel and settle there, and build an altar there to God, who appeared to you when you were fleeing from your brother Esau."

²So Jacob said to his household and to all who were with him, "Get rid of the foreign gods you have with you, and purify yourselves and change your clothes. ³Then come, let us go up to Bethel, where I will build an altar to God, who answered me in the day of my distress and who has been with me wherever I have gone." ⁴So they gave Jacob all the foreign gods they had and the rings in their ears, and Jacob buried them under the oak at Shechem. ⁵Then they set out, and the terror of God fell upon the towns all around them so that no one pursued them.

⁶Jacob and all the people with him came to Luz (that is, Bethel) in the land of Canaan. ⁷There he built an altar, and he called the place El Bethel,^b because it was there that God revealed himself to him when he was fleeing from his brother.

⁸Now Deborah, Rebekah's nurse, died and was buried under the oak below Bethel. So it was named Allon Bacuth.^c

⁹After Jacob returned from Paddan Aram,^d God appeared to him again and blessed him. ¹⁰God said to him, "Your name is Jacob,^e but you will no longer be called Jacob; your name will be Israel.^f" So he named him Israel.

¹¹And God said to him, "I am God Almighty^g; be fruitful and increase in number. A nation and a community of nations will come from you, and kings will come from your body. ¹²The land I gave to Abraham and Isaac I also give to you, and I will give this land to your descendants after you." ¹³Then God went up from him at the place where he had talked with him.

¹⁴Jacob set up a stone pillar at the place where God had talked with him, and he poured out a drink offering on it; he also poured oil on it. ¹⁵Jacob called the place where God had talked with him Bethel.^h

The Deaths of Rachel and Isaac

¹⁶Then they moved on from Bethel. While they were still some distance from Ephrath, Rachel began to give birth and had great difficulty. ¹⁷And as she was having great difficulty in childbirth, the midwife said to her, "Don't be afraid, for you have another son." ¹⁸As she breathed her last—for she was dying—she named her son Ben-Oni.ⁱ But his father named him Benjamin.^j

¹⁹So Rachel died and was buried on the way to Ephrath (that is, Bethlehem). ²⁰Over her tomb Jacob set up a pillar, and to this day that pillar marks Rachel's tomb.

---

²¹Israel moved on again and pitched his tent beyond Migdal Eder. ²²While Israel was living in that region, Reuben went in and slept with his father's concubine Bilhah, and Israel heard of it.

Jacob had twelve sons:
²³The sons of Leah:
Reuben the firstborn of Jacob, Simeon, Levi, Judah, Issachar and Zebulun.
²⁴The sons of Rachel:
Joseph and Benjamin.
²⁵The sons of Rachel's maidservant Bilhah:
Dan and Naphtali.
²⁶The sons of Leah's maidservant Zilpah:
Gad and Asher.
These were the sons of Jacob, who were born to him in Paddan Aram.

²⁷Jacob came home to his father Isaac in Mamre, near Kiriath Arba (that is, Hebron), where Abraham and Isaac had stayed. ²⁸Isaac lived a hundred and eighty years. ²⁹Then he breathed his last and died and was gathered to his people, old and full of years. And his sons Esau and Jacob buried him.

Esau's Descendants

36 This is the account of Esau (that is, Edom).

²Esau took his wives from the women of Canaan: Adah daughter of Elon the Hittite, and Oholibamah daughter of Anah and granddaughter of Zibeon the Hivite— ³also Basemath daughter of Ishmael and sister of Nebaioth.

⁴Adah bore Eliphaz to Esau, Basemath bore Reuel, ⁵and Oholibamah bore Jeush, Jalam and Korah. These were the sons of Esau, who were born to him in Canaan.

⁶Esau took his wives and sons and daughters and all the members of his household, as well as his livestock and all his other animals and all the goods he had acquired in Canaan, and moved to a land some distance from his brother Jacob. ⁷Their possessions were too great for them to remain together; the land where they were staying could not support them both because of their livestock. ⁸So Esau (that is, Edom) settled in the hill country of Seir.

⁹This is the account of Esau the father of the Edomites in the hill country of Seir.

¹⁰These are the names of Esau's sons:
Eliphaz, the son of Esau's wife Adah, and Reuel, the son of Esau's wife Basemath.
¹¹The sons of Eliphaz:
Teman, Omar, Zepho, Gatam and Kenaz.
¹²Esau's son Eliphaz also had a concubine named Timna, who bore him Amalek. These were grandsons of Esau's wife Adah.
¹³The sons of Reuel:
Nahath, Zerah, Shammah and Mizzah. These were grandsons of Esau's wife Basemath.
¹⁴The sons of Esau's wife Oholibamah daughter of Anah and granddaughter of Zibeon, whom she bore to Esau:
Jeush, Jalam and Korah.

¹⁵These were the chiefs among Esau's descendants:
The sons of Eliphaz the firstborn of Esau:
Chiefs Teman, Omar, Zepho, Kenaz, ¹⁶Korah,ᵃ Gatam and Amalek. These were the chiefs descended from Eliphaz in Edom; they were grandsons of Adah.
¹⁷The sons of Esau's son Reuel:

ᵃ16 Masoretic Text; Samaritan Pentateuch (see also Gen. 36:11 and 1 Chron. 1:36) does not have Korah.

Chiefs Nahath, Zerah, Shammah and Mizzah. These were the chiefs descended from Reuel in Edom; they were grandsons of Esau's wife Basemath.

¹⁸The sons of Esau's wife Oholibamah:

Chiefs Jeush, Jalam and Korah. These were the chiefs descended from Esau's wife Oholibamah daughter of Anah.

¹⁹These were the sons of Esau (that is, Edom), and these were their chiefs.

²⁰These were the sons of Seir the Horite, who were living in the region:

Lotan, Shobal, Zibeon, Anah, ²¹Dishon, Ezer and Dishan. These sons of Seir in Edom were Horite chiefs.

²²The sons of Lotan:

Hori and Homam.ᵃ Timna was Lotan's sister.

²³The sons of Shobal:

Alvan, Manahath, Ebal, Shepho and Onam.

²⁴The sons of Zibeon:

Aiah and Anah. This is the Anah who discovered the hot springsᵇ in the desert while he was grazing the donkeys of his father Zibeon.

²⁵The children of Anah:

Dishon and Oholibamah daughter of Anah.

²⁶The sons of Dishonᶜ:

Hemdan, Eshban, Ithran and Keran.

²⁷The sons of Ezer:

Bilhan, Zaavan and Akan.

²⁸The sons of Dishan:

Uz and Aran.

²⁹These were the Horite chiefs:

Lotan, Shobal, Zibeon, Anah, ³⁰Dishon, Ezer and Dishan. These were the Horite chiefs, according to their divisions, in the land of Seir.

The Rulers of Edom

³¹These were the kings who reigned in Edom before any Israelite king reignedᵈ:

³²Bela son of Beor became king of Edom. His city was named Dinhabah.

³³When Bela died, Jobab son of Zerah from Bozrah succeeded him as king.

³⁴When Jobab died, Husham from the land of the Temanites succeeded him as king.

³⁵When Husham died, Hadad son of Bedad, who defeated Midian in the country of Moab, succeeded him as king. His city was named Avith.

³⁶When Hadad died, Samlah from Masrekah succeeded him as king.

³⁷When Samlah died, Shaul from Rehoboth on the riverᵉ succeeded him as king.

³⁸When Shaul died, Baal-Hanan son of Acbor succeeded him as king.

³⁹When Baal-Hanan son of Acbor died, Hadadᶠ succeeded him as king. His city was named Pau, and his wife's name was Mehetabel daughter of Matred, the daughter of Me-Zahab.

⁴⁰These were the chiefs descended from Esau, by name, according to their clans and regions:

Timna, Alvah, Jetheth, ⁴¹Oholibamah, Elah, Pinon, ⁴²Kenaz, Teman, Mibzar, ⁴³Magdiel and Iram. These were the chiefs of Edom, according to their settlements in the land they occupied.

This was Esau the father of the Edomites.

ᵃ22 Hebrew *Hemam,* a variant of *Homam* (see 1 Chron. 1:39)   ᵇ24 Vulgate; Syriac *discovered water;* the meaning of the Hebrew for this word is uncertain.   ᶜ26 Hebrew *Dishan,* a variant of *Dishon*   ᵈ31 Or *before an Israelite king reigned over them*   ᵉ37 Possibly the Euphrates   ᶠ39 Many manuscripts of the Masoretic Text, Samaritan Pentateuch and Syriac (see also 1 Chron. 1:50); most manuscripts of the Masoretic Text *Hadar*

Joseph's Dreams

37 Jacob lived in the land where his father had stayed, the land of Canaan.

²This is the account of Jacob.

Joseph, a young man of seventeen, was tending the flocks with his brothers, the sons of Bilhah and the sons of Zilpah, his father's wives, and he brought their father a bad report about them.

³Now Israel loved Joseph more than any of his other sons, because he had been born to him in his old age; and he made a richly ornamented*a* robe for him. ⁴When his brothers saw that their father loved him more than any of them, they hated him and could not speak a kind word to him.

⁵Joseph had a dream, and when he told it to his brothers, they hated him all the more. ⁶He said to them, "Listen to this dream I had: ⁷We were binding sheaves of grain out in the field when suddenly my sheaf rose and stood upright, while your sheaves gathered around mine and bowed down to it."

⁸His brothers said to him, "Do you intend to reign over us? Will you actually rule us?" And they hated him all the more because of his dream and what he had said.

⁹Then he had another dream, and he told it to his brothers. "Listen," he said, "I had another dream, and this time the sun and moon and eleven stars were bowing down to me."

¹⁰When he told his father as well as his brothers, his father rebuked him and said, "What is this dream you had? Will your mother and I and your brothers actually come and bow down to the ground before you?" ¹¹His brothers were jealous of him, but his father kept the matter in mind.

Joseph Sold by His Brothers

¹²Now his brothers had gone to graze their father's flocks near Shechem, ¹³and Israel said to Joseph, "As you know, your brothers are grazing the flocks near Shechem. Come, I am going to send you to them."

"Very well," he replied.

¹⁴So he said to him, "Go and see if all is well with your brothers and with the flocks, and bring word back to me." Then he sent him off from the Valley of Hebron.

When Joseph arrived at Shechem, ¹⁵a man found him wandering around in the fields and asked him, "What are you looking for?"

¹⁶He replied, "I'm looking for my brothers. Can you tell me where they are grazing their flocks?"

¹⁷"They have moved on from here," the man answered. "I heard them say, 'Let's go to Dothan.' "

So Joseph went after his brothers and found them near Dothan. ¹⁸But they saw him in the distance, and before he reached them, they plotted to kill him.

¹⁹"Here comes that dreamer!" they said to each other. ²⁰"Come now, let's kill him and throw him into one of these cisterns and say that a ferocious animal devoured him. Then we'll see what comes of his dreams."

²¹When Reuben heard this, he tried to rescue him from their hands. "Let's not take his life," he said. ²²"Don't shed any blood. Throw him into this cistern here in the desert, but don't lay a hand on him." Reuben said this to rescue him from them and take him back to his father.

²³So when Joseph came to his brothers, they stripped him of his robe—the richly ornamented robe he was wearing— ²⁴and they took him and threw him into the cistern. Now the cistern was empty; there was no water in it.

²⁵As they sat down to eat their meal, they looked up and saw a caravan of Ishmaelites coming from Gilead. Their camels were loaded with spices, balm and myrrh, and they were on their way to take them down to Egypt.

²⁶Judah said to his brothers, "What will we gain if we kill our brother and

---

a3 The meaning of the Hebrew for *richly ornamented* is uncertain; also in verses 23 and 32.

cover up his blood? ²⁷Come, let's sell him to the Ishmaelites and not lay our hands on him; after all, he is our brother, our own flesh and blood." His brothers agreed.

²⁸So when the Midianite merchants came by, his brothers pulled Joseph up out of the cistern and sold him for twenty shekels*a* of silver to the Ishmaelites, who took him to Egypt.

²⁹When Reuben returned to the cistern and saw that Joseph was not there, he tore his clothes. ³⁰He went back to his brothers and said, "The boy isn't there! Where can I turn now?"

³¹Then they got Joseph's robe, slaughtered a goat and dipped the robe in the blood. ³²They took the ornamented robe back to their father and said, "We found this. Examine it to see whether it is your son's robe."

³³He recognized it and said, "It is my son's robe! Some ferocious animal has devoured him. Joseph has surely been torn to pieces."

³⁴Then Jacob tore his clothes, put on sackcloth and mourned for his son many days. ³⁵All his sons and daughters came to comfort him, but he refused to be comforted. "No," he said, "in mourning will I go down to the grave*b* to my son." So his father wept for him.

³⁶Meanwhile, the Midianites*c* sold Joseph in Egypt to Potiphar, one of Pharaoh's officials, the captain of the guard.

Judah and Tamar

38 At that time, Judah left his brothers and went down to stay with a man of Adullam named Hirah. ²There Judah met the daughter of a Canaanite man named Shua. He married her and lay with her; ³she became pregnant and gave birth to a son, who was named Er. ⁴She conceived again and gave birth to a son and named him Onan. ⁵She gave birth to still another son and named him Shelah. It was at Kezib that she gave birth to him.

⁶Judah got a wife for Er, his firstborn, and her name was Tamar. ⁷But Er, Judah's firstborn, was wicked in the Lᴏʀᴅ's sight; so the Lᴏʀᴅ put him to death.

⁸Then Judah said to Onan, "Lie with your brother's wife and fulfill your duty to her as a brother-in-law to produce offspring for your brother." ⁹But Onan knew that the offspring would not be his; so whenever he lay with his brother's wife, he spilled his semen on the ground to keep from producing offspring for his brother. ¹⁰What he did was wicked in the Lᴏʀᴅ's sight; so he put him to death also.

¹¹Judah then said to his daughter-in-law Tamar, "Live as a widow in your father's house until my son Shelah grows up." For he thought, "He may die too, just like his brothers." So Tamar went to live in her father's house.

¹²After a long time Judah's wife, the daughter of Shua, died. When Judah had recovered from his grief, he went up to Timnah, to the men who were shearing his sheep, and his friend Hirah the Adullamite went with him.

¹³When Tamar was told, "Your father-in-law is on his way to Timnah to shear his sheep," ¹⁴she took off her widow's clothes, covered herself with a veil to disguise herself, and then sat down at the entrance to Enaim, which is on the road to Timnah. For she saw that, though Shelah had now grown up, she had not been given to him as his wife.

¹⁵When Judah saw her, he thought she was a prostitute, for she had covered her face. ¹⁶Not realizing that she was his daughter-in-law, he went over to her by the roadside and said, "Come now, let me sleep with you."

"And what will you give me to sleep with you?" she asked.

¹⁷"I'll send you a young goat from my flock," he said.

---

a28 That is, about 8 ounces (about 0.2 kilogram)　　*b35* Hebrew *Sheol*　　*c36* Samaritan Pentateuch, Septuagint, Vulgate and Syriac (see also verse 28); Masoretic Text *Medanites*

"Will you give me something as a pledge until you send it?" she asked. [18]He said, "What pledge should I give you?"

"Your seal and its cord, and the staff in your hand," she answered. So he gave them to her and slept with her, and she became pregnant by him. [19]After she left, she took off her veil and put on her widow's clothes again.

[20]Meanwhile Judah sent the young goat by his friend the Adullamite in order to get his pledge back from the woman, but he did not find her. [21]He asked the men who lived there, "Where is the shrine prostitute who was beside the road at Enaim?"

"There hasn't been any shrine prostitute here," they said.

[22]So he went back to Judah and said, "I didn't find her. Besides, the men who lived there said, 'There hasn't been any shrine prostitute here.'"

[23]Then Judah said, "Let her keep what she has, or we will become a laughingstock. After all, I did send her this young goat, but you didn't find her."

[24]About three months later Judah was told, "Your daughter-in-law Tamar is guilty of prostitution, and as a result she is now pregnant."

Judah said, "Bring her out and have her burned to death!"

[25]As she was being brought out, she sent a message to her father-in-law. "I am pregnant by the man who owns these," she said. And she added, "See if you recognize whose seal and cord and staff these are."

[26]Judah recognized them and said, "She is more righteous than I, since I wouldn't give her to my son Shelah." And he did not sleep with her again.

[27]When the time came for her to give birth, there were twin boys in her womb. [28]As she was giving birth, one of them put out his hand; so the midwife took a scarlet thread and tied it on his wrist and said, "This one came out first." [29]But when he drew back his hand, his brother came out, and she said, "So this is how you have broken out!" And he was named Perez.[a] [30]Then his brother, who had the scarlet thread on his wrist, came out and he was given the name Zerah.[b]

Joseph and Potiphar's Wife

39 Now Joseph had been taken down to Egypt. Potiphar, an Egyptian who was one of Pharaoh's officials, the captain of the guard, bought him from the Ishmaelites who had taken him there.

[2]The LORD was with Joseph and he prospered, and he lived in the house of his Egyptian master. [3]When his master saw that the LORD was with him and that the LORD gave him success in everything he did, [4]Joseph found favor in his eyes and became his attendant. Potiphar put him in charge of his household, and he entrusted to his care everything he owned. [5]From the time he put him in charge of his household and of all that he owned, the LORD blessed the household of the Egyptian because of Joseph. The blessing of the LORD was on everything Potiphar had, both in the house and in the field. [6]So he left in Joseph's care everything he had; with Joseph in charge, he did not concern himself with anything except the food he ate.

Now Joseph was well-built and handsome, [7]and after a while his master's wife took notice of Joseph and said, "Come to bed with me!"

[8]But he refused. "With me in charge," he told her, "my master does not concern himself with anything in the house; everything he owns he has entrusted to my care. [9]No one is greater in this house than I am. My master has withheld nothing from me except you, because you are his wife. How then could I do such a wicked thing and sin against God?" [10]And though she spoke to Joseph day after day, he refused to go to bed with her or even be with her.

[11]One day he went into the house to attend to his duties, and none of the

---

[a]29 *Perez* means *breaking out*.   [b]30 *Zerah* can mean *scarlet* or *brightness*.

household servants was inside. ¹²She caught him by his cloak and said, "Come to bed with me!" But he left his cloak in her hand and ran out of the house.

¹³When she saw that he had left his cloak in her hand and had run out of the house, ¹⁴she called her household servants. "Look," she said to them, "this Hebrew has been brought to us to make sport of us! He came in here to sleep with me, but I screamed. ¹⁵When he heard me scream for help, he left his cloak beside me and ran out of the house."

¹⁶She kept his cloak beside her until his master came home. ¹⁷Then she told him this story: "That Hebrew slave you brought us came to me to make sport of me. ¹⁸But as soon as I screamed for help, he left his cloak beside me and ran out of the house."

¹⁹When his master heard the story his wife told him, saying, "This is how your slave treated me," he burned with anger. ²⁰Joseph's master took him and put him in prison, the place where the king's prisoners were confined.

But while Joseph was there in the prison, ²¹the LORD was with him; he showed him kindness and granted him favor in the eyes of the prison warden. ²²So the warden put Joseph in charge of all those held in the prison, and he was made responsible for all that was done there. ²³The warden paid no attention to anything under Joseph's care, because the LORD was with Joseph and gave him success in whatever he did.

The Cupbearer and the Baker

40 Some time later, the cupbearer and the baker of the king of Egypt offended their master, the king of Egypt. ²Pharaoh was angry with his two officials, the chief cupbearer and the chief baker, ³and put them in custody in the house of the captain of the guard, in the same prison where Joseph was confined. ⁴The captain of the guard assigned them to Joseph, and he attended them.

After they had been in custody for some time, ⁵each of the two men—the cupbearer and the baker of the king of Egypt, who were being held in prison—had a dream the same night, and each dream had a meaning of its own.

⁶When Joseph came to them the next morning, he saw that they were dejected. ⁷So he asked Pharaoh's officials who were in custody with him in his master's house, "Why are your faces so sad today?"

⁸"We both had dreams," they answered, "but there is no one to interpret them."

Then Joseph said to them, "Do not interpretations belong to God? Tell me your dreams."

⁹So the chief cupbearer told Joseph his dream. He said to him, "In my dream I saw a vine in front of me, ¹⁰and on the vine were three branches. As soon as it budded, it blossomed, and its clusters ripened into grapes. ¹¹Pharaoh's cup was in my hand, and I took the grapes, squeezed them into Pharaoh's cup and put the cup in his hand."

¹²"This is what it means," Joseph said to him. "The three branches are three days. ¹³Within three days Pharaoh will lift up your head and restore you to your position, and you will put Pharaoh's cup in his hand, just as you used to do when you were his cupbearer. ¹⁴But when all goes well with you, remember me and show me kindness; mention me to Pharaoh and get me out of this prison. ¹⁵For I was forcibly carried off from the land of the Hebrews, and even here I have done nothing to deserve being put in a dungeon."

¹⁶When the chief baker saw that Joseph had given a favorable interpretation, he said to Joseph, "I too had a dream: On my head were three baskets of bread.ᵃ ¹⁷In the top basket were all kinds of baked goods for Pharaoh, but the birds were eating them out of the basket on my head."

ᵃ16 Or three wicker baskets

18"This is what it means," Joseph said. "The three baskets are three days. 19Within three days Pharaoh will lift off your head and hang you on a tree.*a* And the birds will eat away your flesh."

20Now the third day was Pharaoh's birthday, and he gave a feast for all his officials. He lifted up the heads of the chief cupbearer and the chief baker in the presence of his officials: 21He restored the chief cupbearer to his position, so that he once again put the cup into Pharaoh's hand, 22but he hanged*b* the chief baker, just as Joseph had said to them in his interpretation.

23The chief cupbearer, however, did not remember Joseph; he forgot him.

Pharaoh's Dreams

41 When two full years had passed, Pharaoh had a dream: He was standing by the Nile, 2when out of the river there came up seven cows, sleek and fat, and they grazed among the reeds. 3After them, seven other cows, ugly and gaunt, came up out of the Nile and stood beside those on the riverbank. 4And the cows that were ugly and gaunt ate up the seven sleek, fat cows. Then Pharaoh woke up.

5He fell asleep again and had a second dream: Seven heads of grain, healthy and good, were growing on a single stalk. 6After them, seven other heads of grain sprouted—thin and scorched by the east wind. 7The thin heads of grain swallowed up the seven healthy, full heads. Then Pharaoh woke up; it had been a dream.

8In the morning his mind was troubled, so he sent for all the magicians and wise men of Egypt. Pharaoh told them his dreams, but no one could interpret them for him.

9Then the chief cupbearer said to Pharaoh, "Today I am reminded of my shortcomings. 10Pharaoh was once angry with his servants, and he imprisoned me and the chief baker in the house of the captain of the guard.

11Each of us had a dream the same night, and each dream had a meaning of its own. 12Now a young Hebrew was there with us, a servant of the captain of the guard. We told him our dreams, and he interpreted them for us, giving each man the interpretation of his dream. 13And things turned out exactly as he interpreted them to us: I was restored to my position, and the other man was hanged.*b*"

14So Pharaoh sent for Joseph, and he was quickly brought from the dungeon. When he had shaved and changed his clothes, he came before Pharaoh.

15Pharaoh said to Joseph, "I had a dream, and no one can interpret it. But I have heard it said of you that when you hear a dream you can interpret it."

16"I cannot do it," Joseph replied to Pharaoh, "but God will give Pharaoh the answer he desires."

17Then Pharaoh said to Joseph, "In my dream I was standing on the bank of the Nile, 18when out of the river there came up seven cows, fat and sleek, and they grazed among the reeds. 19After them, seven other cows came up—scrawny and very ugly and lean. I had never seen such ugly cows in all the land of Egypt. 20The lean, ugly cows ate up the seven fat cows that came up first. 21But even after they ate them, no one could tell that they had done so; they looked just as ugly as before. Then I woke up.

22"In my dreams I also saw seven heads of grain, full and good, growing on a single stalk. 23After them, seven other heads sprouted—withered and thin and scorched by the east wind. 24The thin heads of grain swallowed up the seven good heads. I told this to the magicians, but none could explain it to me."

25Then Joseph said to Pharaoh, "The dreams of Pharaoh are one and the same. God has revealed to Pharaoh what he is about to do. 26The seven good cows are seven years, and the

---

*a*19 Or *and impale you on a pole*   *b*22,13 Or *impaled*

seven good heads of grain are seven years; it is one and the same dream. 27The seven lean, ugly cows that came up afterward are seven years, and so are the seven worthless heads of grain scorched by the east wind: They are seven years of famine.

28"It is just as I said to Pharaoh: God has shown Pharaoh what he is about to do. 29Seven years of great abundance are coming throughout the land of Egypt, 30but seven years of famine will follow them. Then all the abundance in Egypt will be forgotten, and the famine will ravage the land. 31The abundance in the land will not be remembered, because the famine that follows it will be so severe. 32The reason the dream was given to Pharaoh in two forms is that the matter has been firmly decided by God, and God will do it soon.

33"And now let Pharaoh look for a discerning and wise man and put him in charge of the land of Egypt. 34Let Pharaoh appoint commissioners over the land to take a fifth of the harvest of Egypt during the seven years of abundance. 35They should collect all the food of these good years that are coming and store up the grain under the authority of Pharaoh, to be kept in the cities for food. 36This food should be held in reserve for the country, to be used during the seven years of famine that will come upon Egypt, so that the country may not be ruined by the famine."

37The plan seemed good to Pharaoh and to all his officials. 38So Pharaoh asked them, "Can we find anyone like this man, one in whom is the spirit of God*a*?"

39Then Pharaoh said to Joseph, "Since God has made all this known to you, there is no one so discerning and wise as you. 40You shall be in charge of my palace, and all my people are to submit to your orders. Only

with respect to the throne will I be greater than you."

Joseph in Charge of Egypt

41So Pharaoh said to Joseph, "I hereby put you in charge of the whole land of Egypt." 42Then Pharaoh took his signet ring from his finger and put it on Joseph's finger. He dressed him in robes of fine linen and put a gold chain around his neck. 43He had him ride in a chariot as his second-in-command,*b* and men shouted before him, "Make way*c*!" Thus he put him in charge of the whole land of Egypt.

44Then Pharaoh said to Joseph, "I am Pharaoh, but without your word no one will lift hand or foot in all Egypt." 45Pharaoh gave Joseph the name Zaphenath-Paneah and gave him Asenath daughter of Potiphera, priest of On,*d* to be his wife. And Joseph went throughout the land of Egypt.

46Joseph was thirty years old when he entered the service of Pharaoh king of Egypt. And Joseph went out from Pharaoh's presence and traveled throughout Egypt. 47During the seven years of abundance the land produced plentifully. 48Joseph collected all the food produced in those seven years of abundance in Egypt and stored it in the cities. In each city he put the food grown in the fields surrounding it. 49Joseph stored up huge quantities of grain, like the sand of the sea; it was so much that he stopped keeping records because it was beyond measure.

50Before the years of famine came, two sons were born to Joseph by Asenath daughter of Potiphera, priest of On. 51Joseph named his firstborn Manasseh*e* and said, "It is because God has made me forget all my trouble and all my father's household." 52The second son he named Ephraim*f* and said, "It is because God has made me fruitful in the land of my suffering."

---

*a*38 Or *of the gods*   *b*43 Or *in the chariot of his second-in-command*; or *in his second chariot*
*c*43 Or *Bow down*   *d*45 That is, Heliopolis; also in verse 50   *e*51 *Manasseh* sounds like and may be derived from the Hebrew for *forget*.   *f*52 *Ephraim* sounds like the Hebrew for *twice fruitful*.

53The seven years of abundance in Egypt came to an end, 54and the seven years of famine began, just as Joseph had said. There was famine in all the other lands, but in the whole land of Egypt there was food. 55When all Egypt began to feel the famine, the people cried to Pharaoh for food. Then Pharaoh told all the Egyptians, "Go to Joseph and do what he tells you."

56When the famine had spread over the whole country, Joseph opened the storehouses and sold grain to the Egyptians, for the famine was severe throughout Egypt. 57And all the countries came to Egypt to buy grain from Joseph, because the famine was severe in all the world.

Joseph's Brothers Go to Egypt

42 When Jacob learned that there was grain in Egypt, he said to his sons, "Why do you just keep looking at each other?" 2He continued, "I have heard that there is grain in Egypt. Go down there and buy some for us, so that we may live and not die."

3Then ten of Joseph's brothers went down to buy grain from Egypt. 4But Jacob did not send Benjamin, Joseph's brother, with the others, because he was afraid that harm might come to him. 5So Israel's sons were among those who went to buy grain, for the famine was in the land of Canaan also.

6Now Joseph was the governor of the land, the one who sold grain to all its people. So when Joseph's brothers arrived, they bowed down to him with their faces to the ground. 7As soon as Joseph saw his brothers, he recognized them, but he pretended to be a stranger and spoke harshly to them. "Where do you come from?" he asked.

"From the land of Canaan," they replied, "to buy food."

8Although Joseph recognized his brothers, they did not recognize him. 9Then he remembered his dreams about them and said to them, "You are spies! You have come to see where our land is unprotected."

10"No, my lord," they answered. "Your servants have come to buy food. 11We are all the sons of one man. Your servants are honest men, not spies."

12"No!" he said to them. "You have come to see where our land is unprotected."

13But they replied, "Your servants were twelve brothers, the sons of one man, who lives in the land of Canaan. The youngest is now with our father, and one is no more."

14Joseph said to them, "It is just as I told you: You are spies! 15And this is how you will be tested: As surely as Pharaoh lives, you will not leave this place unless your youngest brother comes here. 16Send one of your number to get your brother; the rest of you will be kept in prison, so that your words may be tested to see if you are telling the truth. If you are not, then as surely as Pharaoh lives, you are spies!" 17And he put them all in custody for three days.

18On the third day, Joseph said to them, "Do this and you will live, for I fear God: 19If you are honest men, let one of your brothers stay here in prison, while the rest of you go and take grain back for your starving households. 20But you must bring your youngest brother to me, so that your words may be verified and that you may not die." This they proceeded to do.

21They said to one another, "Surely we are being punished because of our brother. We saw how distressed he was when he pleaded with us for his life, but we would not listen; that's why this distress has come upon us."

22Reuben replied, "Didn't I tell you not to sin against the boy? But you wouldn't listen! Now we must give an accounting for his blood." 23They did not realize that Joseph could understand them, since he was using an interpreter.

24He turned away from them and began to weep, but then turned back and spoke to them again. He had Simeon taken from them and bound before their eyes.

²⁵Joseph gave orders to fill their bags with grain, to put each man's silver back in his sack, and to give them provisions for their journey. After this was done for them, ²⁶they loaded their grain on their donkeys and left.

²⁷At the place where they stopped for the night one of them opened his sack to get feed for his donkey, and he saw his silver in the mouth of his sack. ²⁸"My silver has been returned," he said to his brothers. "Here it is in my sack."

Their hearts sank and they turned to each other trembling and said, "What is this that God has done to us?"

²⁹When they came to their father Jacob in the land of Canaan, they told him all that had happened to them. They said, ³⁰"The man who is lord over the land spoke harshly to us and treated us as though we were spying on the land. ³¹But we said to him, 'We are honest men; we are not spies. ³²We were twelve brothers, sons of one father. One is no more, and the youngest is now with our father in Canaan.'

³³"Then the man who is lord over the land said to us, 'This is how I will know whether you are honest men: Leave one of your brothers here with me, and take food for your starving households and go. ³⁴But bring your youngest brother to me so I will know that you are not spies but honest men. Then I will give your brother back to you, and you can trade*ᵃ* in the land.' "

³⁵As they were emptying their sacks, there in each man's sack was his pouch of silver! When they and their father saw the money pouches, they were frightened. ³⁶Their father Jacob said to them, "You have deprived me of my children. Joseph is no more and Simeon is no more, and now you want to take Benjamin. Everything is against me!"

³⁷Then Reuben said to his father,

"You may put both of my sons to death if I do not bring him back to you. Entrust him to my care, and I will bring him back."

³⁸But Jacob said, "My son will not go down there with you; his brother is dead and he is the only one left. If harm comes to him on the journey you are taking, you will bring my gray head down to the grave*ᵇ* in sorrow."

The Second Journey to Egypt

43 Now the famine was still severe in the land. ²So when they had eaten all the grain they had brought from Egypt, their father said to them, "Go back and buy us a little more food."

³But Judah said to him, "The man warned us solemnly, 'You will not see my face again unless your brother is with you.' ⁴If you will send our brother along with us, we will go down and buy food for you. ⁵But if you will not send him, we will not go down, because the man said to us, 'You will not see my face again unless your brother is with you.' "

⁶Israel asked, "Why did you bring this trouble on me by telling the man you had another brother?"

⁷They replied, "The man questioned us closely about ourselves and our family. 'Is your father still living?' he asked us. 'Do you have another brother?' We simply answered his questions. How were we to know he would say, 'Bring your brother down here'?"

⁸Then Judah said to Israel his father, "Send the boy along with me and we will go at once, so that we and you and our children may live and not die. ⁹I myself will guarantee his safety; you can hold me personally responsible for him. If I do not bring him back to you and set him here before you, I will bear the blame before you all my life. ¹⁰As it is, if we had not delayed, we could have gone and returned twice."

¹¹Then their father Israel said to

them, "If it must be, then do this: Put some of the best products of the land in your bags and take them down to the man as a gift—a little balm and a little honey, some spices and myrrh, some pistachio nuts and almonds. ¹²Take double the amount of silver with you, for you must return the silver that was put back into the mouths of your sacks. Perhaps it was a mistake. ¹³Take your brother also and go back to the man at once. ¹⁴And may God Almighty[a] grant you mercy before the man so that he will let your other brother and Benjamin come back with you. As for me, if I am bereaved, I am bereaved."

¹⁵So the men took the gifts and double the amount of silver, and Benjamin also. They hurried down to Egypt and presented themselves to Joseph. ¹⁶When Joseph saw Benjamin with them, he said to the steward of his house, "Take these men to my house, slaughter an animal and prepare dinner; they are to eat with me at noon."

¹⁷The man did as Joseph told him and took the men to Joseph's house. ¹⁸Now the men were frightened when they were taken to his house. They thought, "We were brought here because of the silver that was put back into our sacks the first time. He wants to attack us and overpower us and seize us as slaves and take our donkeys."

¹⁹So they went up to Joseph's steward and spoke to him at the entrance to the house. ²⁰"Please, sir," they said, "we came down here the first time to buy food. ²¹But at the place where we stopped for the night we opened our sacks and each of us found his silver—the exact weight—in the mouth of his sack. So we have brought it back with us. ²²We have also brought additional silver with us to buy food. We don't know who put our silver in our sacks."

²³"It's all right," he said. "Don't be afraid. Your God, the God of your father, has given you treasure in your sacks; I received your silver." Then he brought Simeon out to them.

²⁴The steward took the men into Joseph's house, gave them water to wash their feet and provided fodder for their donkeys. ²⁵They prepared their gifts for Joseph's arrival at noon, because they had heard that they were to eat there.

²⁶When Joseph came home, they presented to him the gifts they had brought into the house, and they bowed down before him to the ground. ²⁷He asked them how they were, and then he said, "How is your aged father you told me about? Is he still living?"

²⁸They replied, "Your servant our father is still alive and well." And they bowed low to pay him honor.

²⁹As he looked about and saw his brother Benjamin, his own mother's son, he asked, "Is this your youngest brother, the one you told me about?" And he said, "God be gracious to you, my son." ³⁰Deeply moved at the sight of his brother, Joseph hurried out and looked for a place to weep. He went into his private room and wept there.

³¹After he had washed his face, he came out and, controlling himself, said, "Serve the food."

³²They served him by himself, the brothers by themselves, and the Egyptians who ate with him by themselves, because Egyptians could not eat with Hebrews, for that is detestable to Egyptians. ³³The men had been seated before him in the order of their ages, from the firstborn to the youngest; and they looked at each other in astonishment. ³⁴When portions were served to them from Joseph's table, Benjamin's portion was five times as much as anyone else's. So they feasted and drank freely with him.

A Silver Cup in a Sack

44 Now Joseph gave these instructions to the steward of his house: "Fill the men's sacks with as much food as they can carry, and put

each man's silver in the mouth of his sack. ²Then put my cup, the silver one, in the mouth of the youngest one's sack, along with the silver for his grain." And he did as Joseph said.

³As morning dawned, the men were sent on their way with their donkeys. ⁴They had not gone far from the city when Joseph said to his steward, "Go after those men at once, and when you catch up with them, say to them, 'Why have you repaid good with evil? ⁵Isn't this the cup my master drinks from and also uses for divination? This is a wicked thing you have done.' "

⁶When he caught up with them, he repeated these words to them. ⁷But they said to him, "Why does my lord say such things? Far be it from your servants to do anything like that! ⁸We even brought back to you from the land of Canaan the silver we found inside the mouths of our sacks. So why would we steal silver or gold from your master's house? ⁹If any of your servants is found to have it, he will die; and the rest of us will become my lord's slaves."

¹⁰"Very well, then," he said, "let it be as you say. Whoever is found to have it will become my slave; the rest of you will be free from blame."

¹¹Each of them quickly lowered his sack to the ground and opened it. ¹²Then the steward proceeded to search, beginning with the oldest and ending with the youngest. And the cup was found in Benjamin's sack. ¹³At this, they tore their clothes. Then they all loaded their donkeys and returned to the city.

¹⁴Joseph was still in the house when Judah and his brothers came in, and they threw themselves to the ground before him. ¹⁵Joseph said to them, "What is this you have done? Don't you know that a man like me can find things out by divination?"

¹⁶"What can we say to my lord?" Judah replied. "What can we say? How can we prove our innocence? God has uncovered your servants'

guilt. We are now my lord's slaves—we ourselves and the one who was found to have the cup."

¹⁷But Joseph said, "Far be it from me to do such a thing! Only the man who was found to have the cup will become my slave. The rest of you, go back to your father in peace."

¹⁸Then Judah went up to him and said: "Please, my lord, let your servant speak a word to my lord. Do not be angry with your servant, though you are equal to Pharaoh himself. ¹⁹My lord asked his servants, 'Do you have a father or a brother?' ²⁰And we answered, 'We have an aged father, and there is a young son born to him in his old age. His brother is dead, and he is the only one of his mother's sons left, and his father loves him.'

²¹"Then you said to your servants, 'Bring him down to me so I can see him for myself.' ²²And we said to my lord, 'The boy cannot leave his father; if he leaves him, his father will die.' ²³But you told your servants, 'Unless your youngest brother comes down with you, you will not see my face again.' ²⁴When we went back to your servant my father, we told him what my lord had said.

²⁵"Then our father said, 'Go back and buy a little more food.' ²⁶But we said, 'We cannot go down. Only if our youngest brother is with us will we go. We cannot see the man's face unless our youngest brother is with us.'

²⁷"Your servant my father said to us, 'You know that my wife bore me two sons. ²⁸One of them went away from me, and I said, "He has surely been torn to pieces." And I have not seen him since. ²⁹If you take this one from me too and harm comes to him, you will bring my gray head down to the graveᵃ in misery.'

³⁰"So now, if the boy is not with us when I go back to your servant my father and if my father, whose life is closely bound up with the boy's life, ³¹sees that the boy isn't there, he will die. Your servants will bring the gray head of our father down to the grave

ᵃ29 Hebrew *Sheol*; also in verse 31

in sorrow. [32]Your servant guaranteed the boy's safety to my father. I said, 'If I do not bring him back to you, I will bear the blame before you, my father, all my life!'

[33]"Now then, please let your servant remain here as my lord's slave in place of the boy, and let the boy return with his brothers. [34]How can I go back to my father if the boy is not with me? No! Do not let me see the misery that would come upon my father."

Joseph Makes Himself Known

45 Then Joseph could no longer control himself before all his attendants, and he cried out, "Have everyone leave my presence!" So there was no one with Joseph when he made himself known to his brothers. [2]And he wept so loudly that the Egyptians heard him, and Pharaoh's household heard about it.

[3]Joseph said to his brothers, "I am Joseph! Is my father still living?" But his brothers were not able to answer him, because they were terrified at his presence.

[4]Then Joseph said to his brothers, "Come close to me." When they had done so, he said, "I am your brother Joseph, the one you sold into Egypt! [5]And now, do not be distressed and do not be angry with yourselves for selling me here, because it was to save lives that God sent me ahead of you. [6]For two years now there has been famine in the land, and for the next five years there will not be plowing and reaping. [7]But God sent me ahead of you to preserve for you a remnant on earth and to save your lives by a great deliverance.[a]

[8]"So then, it was not you who sent me here, but God. He made me father to Pharaoh, lord of his entire household and ruler of all Egypt. [9]Now hurry back to my father and say to him, 'This is what your son Joseph says: God has made me lord of all Egypt. Come down to me; don't delay. [10]You shall live in the region of Goshen and be near me—you, your children and grandchildren, your flocks and herds, and all you have. [11]I will provide for you there, because five years of famine are still to come. Otherwise you and your household and all who belong to you will become destitute.'

[12]"You can see for yourselves, and so can my brother Benjamin, that it is really I who am speaking to you. [13]Tell my father about all the honor accorded me in Egypt and about everything you have seen. And bring my father down here quickly."

[14]Then he threw his arms around his brother Benjamin and wept, and Benjamin embraced him, weeping. [15]And he kissed all his brothers and wept over them. Afterward his brothers talked with him.

[16]When the news reached Pharaoh's palace that Joseph's brothers had come, Pharaoh and all his officials were pleased. [17]Pharaoh said to Joseph, "Tell your brothers, 'Do this: Load your animals and return to the land of Canaan, [18]and bring your father and your families back to me. I will give you the best of the land of Egypt and you can enjoy the fat of the land.'

[19]"You are also directed to tell them, 'Do this: Take some carts from Egypt for your children and your wives, and get your father and come. [20]Never mind about your belongings, because the best of all Egypt will be yours.' "

[21]So the sons of Israel did this. Joseph gave them carts, as Pharaoh had commanded, and he also gave them provisions for their journey. [22]To each of them he gave new clothing, but to Benjamin he gave three hundred shekels[b] of silver and five sets of clothes. [23]And this is what he sent to his father: ten donkeys loaded with the best things of Egypt, and ten female donkeys loaded with grain and bread and other provisions for his

---

[a]7 Or *save you as a great band of survivors*   [b]22 That is, about 7 1/2 pounds (about 3.5 kilograms)

journey. ²⁴Then he sent his brothers away, and as they were leaving he said to them, "Don't quarrel on the way!"

²⁵So they went up out of Egypt and came to their father Jacob in the land of Canaan. ²⁶They told him, "Joseph is still alive! In fact, he is ruler of all Egypt." Jacob was stunned; he did not believe them. ²⁷But when they told him everything Joseph had said to them, and when he saw the carts Joseph had sent to carry him back, the spirit of their father Jacob revived. ²⁸And Israel said, "I'm convinced! My son Joseph is still alive. I will go and see him before I die."

Jacob Goes to Egypt

46 So Israel set out with all that was his, and when he reached Beersheba, he offered sacrifices to the God of his father Isaac.

²And God spoke to Israel in a vision at night and said, "Jacob! Jacob!"

"Here I am," he replied.

³"I am God, the God of your father," he said. "Do not be afraid to go down to Egypt, for I will make you into a great nation there. ⁴I will go down to Egypt with you, and I will surely bring you back again. And Joseph's own hand will close your eyes."

⁵Then Jacob left Beersheba, and Israel's sons took their father Jacob and their children and their wives in the carts that Pharaoh had sent to transport him. ⁶They also took with them their livestock and the possessions they had acquired in Canaan, and Jacob and all his offspring went to Egypt. ⁷He took with him to Egypt his sons and grandsons and his daughters and granddaughters—all his offspring.

⁸These are the names of the sons of Israel (Jacob and his descendants) who went to Egypt:

Reuben the firstborn of Jacob.
⁹The sons of Reuben:
Hanoch, Pallu, Hezron and Carmi.
¹⁰The sons of Simeon:
Jemuel, Jamin, Ohad, Jakin, Zohar and Shaul the son of a Canaanite woman.
¹¹The sons of Levi:
Gershon, Kohath and Merari.
¹²The sons of Judah:
Er, Onan, Shelah, Perez and Zerah (but Er and Onan had died in the land of Canaan).
The sons of Perez:
Hezron and Hamul.
¹³The sons of Issachar:
Tola, Puah,ᵃ Jashubᵇ and Shimron.
¹⁴The sons of Zebulun:
Sered, Elon and Jahleel.
¹⁵These were the sons Leah bore to Jacob in Paddan Aram,ᶜ besides his daughter Dinah. These sons and daughters of his were thirty-three in all.

¹⁶The sons of Gad:
Zephon,ᵈ Haggi, Shuni, Ezbon, Eri, Arodi and Areli.
¹⁷The sons of Asher:
Imnah, Ishvah, Ishvi and Beriah.
Their sister was Serah.
The sons of Beriah:
Heber and Malkiel.
¹⁸These were the children born to Jacob by Zilpah, whom Laban had given to his daughter Leah—sixteen in all.

¹⁹The sons of Jacob's wife Rachel:
Joseph and Benjamin. ²⁰In Egypt, Manasseh and Ephraim were born to Joseph by Asenath daughter of Potiphera, priest of On.ᵉ
²¹The sons of Benjamin:
Bela, Beker, Ashbel, Gera, Naaman, Ehi, Rosh, Muppim, Huppim and Ard.

ᵃ13 Samaritan Pentateuch and Syriac (see also 1 Chron. 7:1); Masoretic Text *Puvah*
ᵇ13 Samaritan Pentateuch and some Septuagint manuscripts (see also Num. 26:24 and 1 Chron. 7:1); Masoretic Text *Iob*   ᶜ15 That is, Northwest Mesopotamia   ᵈ16 Samaritan Pentateuch and Septuagint (see also Num. 26:15); Masoretic Text *Ziphion*   ᵉ20 That is, Heliopolis

²²These were the sons of Rachel who were born to Jacob—fourteen in all.

²³The son of Dan:
Hushim.
²⁴The sons of Naphtali:
Jahziel, Guni, Jezer and Shillem.
²⁵These were the sons born to Jacob by Bilhah, whom Laban had given to his daughter Rachel—seven in all.

²⁶All those who went to Egypt with Jacob—those who were his direct descendants, not counting his sons' wives—numbered sixty-six persons. ²⁷With the two sons[a] who had been born to Joseph in Egypt, the members of Jacob's family, which went to Egypt, were seventy[b] in all.

²⁸Now Jacob sent Judah ahead of him to Joseph to get directions to Goshen. When they arrived in the region of Goshen, ²⁹Joseph had his chariot made ready and went to Goshen to meet his father Israel. As soon as Joseph appeared before him, he threw his arms around his father[c] and wept for a long time.

³⁰Israel said to Joseph, "Now I am ready to die, since I have seen for myself that you are still alive."

³¹Then Joseph said to his brothers and to his father's household, "I will go up and speak to Pharaoh and will say to him, 'My brothers and my father's household, who were living in the land of Canaan, have come to me. ³²The men are shepherds; they tend livestock, and they have brought along their flocks and herds and everything they own.' ³³When Pharaoh calls you in and asks, 'What is your occupation?' ³⁴you should answer, 'Your servants have tended livestock from our boyhood on, just as our fathers did.' Then you will be allowed to settle in the region of Goshen, for all shepherds are detestable to the Egyptians."

47 Joseph went and told Pharaoh, "My father and brothers, with their flocks and herds and everything they own, have come from the land of Canaan and are now in Goshen." ²He chose five of his brothers and presented them before Pharaoh.

³Pharaoh asked the brothers, "What is your occupation?"

"Your servants are shepherds," they replied to Pharaoh, "just as our fathers were." ⁴They also said to him, "We have come to live here awhile, because the famine is severe in Canaan and your servants' flocks have no pasture. So now, please let your servants settle in Goshen."

⁵Pharaoh said to Joseph, "Your father and your brothers have come to you, ⁶and the land of Egypt is before you; settle your father and your brothers in the best part of the land. Let them live in Goshen. And if you know of any among them with special ability, put them in charge of my own livestock."

⁷Then Joseph brought his father Jacob in and presented him before Pharaoh. After Jacob blessed[d] Pharaoh, ⁸Pharaoh asked him, "How old are you?"

⁹And Jacob said to Pharaoh, "The years of my pilgrimage are a hundred and thirty. My years have been few and difficult, and they do not equal the years of the pilgrimage of my fathers." ¹⁰Then Jacob blessed[e] Pharaoh and went out from his presence.

¹¹So Joseph settled his father and his brothers in Egypt and gave them property in the best part of the land, the district of Rameses, as Pharaoh directed. ¹²Joseph also provided his father and his brothers and all his father's household with food, according to the number of their children.

Joseph and the Famine

¹³There was no food, however, in the whole region because the famine was severe; both Egypt and Canaan

---

a27 Hebrew; Septuagint *the nine children* Septuagint (see also Acts 7:14) *seventy-five*   b27 Hebrew (see also Exodus 1:5 and footnote);   c29 Hebrew *around him*   d7 Or *greeted*   e10 Or *said farewell to*

VERSE:
Genesis
47:9

AUTHOR:
François Fénelon

PASSAGE:
Genesis
46:30 — 47:12

We Have a Good Master

We reach a point in life in which we are forced to think about the inevitable end which is approaching, and the older . . . we become the more we find ourselves dwelling on this matter. We might wish that we could put these thoughts out of our minds, but I remind you that God makes use of these thoughts to keep us from being deceived about how brave we are in the face of death. It is good to think seriously about death so that we are kept aware of our human weaknesses, and kept humble in his hands . . .

When we come to these valley experiences, when we are deprived of faith and assurance, there is only one thing to do. We must go straight on through the valley, walking with the Shepherd just as we did before we entered that valley. As we go through, let us deal with any sin which the Lord reveals to us, still walking in the light he gives . . . We must remain peaceful, not pitying ourselves because death is approaching. Instead, let's keep a detached attitude about life, giving it in sacrifice to God and keeping ourselves confidently abandoned to him. When he was dying, Saint Ambrose was asked whether he was not afraid to face God at the judgment. He replied with these unforgettable words, "We have a good Master." We need to remind ourselves of this.

ADDITIONAL SCRIPTURE READINGS
Psalm 23; 2 Timothy 4:6–8

Go to page 66 for your next devotional reading.

wasted away because of the famine. [14]Joseph collected all the money that was to be found in Egypt and Canaan in payment for the grain they were buying, and he brought it to Pharaoh's palace. [15]When the money of the people of Egypt and Canaan was gone, all Egypt came to Joseph and said, "Give us food. Why should we die before your eyes? Our money is used up."

[16]"Then bring your livestock," said Joseph. "I will sell you food in exchange for your livestock, since your money is gone." [17]So they brought their livestock to Joseph, and he gave them food in exchange for their horses, their sheep and goats, their cattle and donkeys. And he brought them through that year with food in exchange for all their livestock.

[18]When that year was over, they came to him the following year and said, "We cannot hide from our lord the fact that since our money is gone and our livestock belongs to you, there is nothing left for our lord except our bodies and our land. [19]Why should we perish before your eyes— we and our land as well? Buy us and our land in exchange for food, and we with our land will be in bondage to Pharaoh. Give us seed so that we may live and not die, and that the land may not become desolate."

[20]So Joseph bought all the land in Egypt for Pharaoh. The Egyptians, one and all, sold their fields, because the famine was too severe for them. The land became Pharaoh's, [21]and Joseph reduced the people to servitude,[a] from one end of Egypt to the other. [22]However, he did not buy the land of the priests, because they received a regular allotment from Pharaoh and had food enough from the allotment Pharaoh gave them. That is why they did not sell their land.

[23]Joseph said to the people, "Now that I have bought you and your land today for Pharaoh, here is seed for you so you can plant the ground.

[24]But when the crop comes in, give a fifth of it to Pharaoh. The other four-fifths you may keep as seed for the fields and as food for yourselves and your households and your children."

[25]"You have saved our lives," they said. "May we find favor in the eyes of our lord; we will be in bondage to Pharaoh."

[26]So Joseph established it as a law concerning land in Egypt—still in force today—that a fifth of the produce belongs to Pharaoh. It was only the land of the priests that did not become Pharaoh's.

[27]Now the Israelites settled in Egypt in the region of Goshen. They acquired property there and were fruitful and increased greatly in number.

[28]Jacob lived in Egypt seventeen years, and the years of his life were a hundred and forty-seven. [29]When the time drew near for Israel to die, he called for his son Joseph and said to him, "If I have found favor in your eyes, put your hand under my thigh and promise that you will show me kindness and faithfulness. Do not bury me in Egypt, [30]but when I rest with my fathers, carry me out of Egypt and bury me where they are buried."

"I will do as you say," he said.

[31]"Swear to me," he said. Then Joseph swore to him, and Israel worshiped as he leaned on the top of his staff.[b]

Manasseh and Ephraim

48 Some time later Joseph was told, "Your father is ill." So he took his two sons Manasseh and Ephraim along with him. [2]When Jacob was told, "Your son Joseph has come to you," Israel rallied his strength and sat up on the bed.

[3]Jacob said to Joseph, "God Almighty[c] appeared to me at Luz in the land of Canaan, and there he blessed me [4]and said to me, 'I am going to make you fruitful and will in-

---

[a]21 Samaritan Pentateuch and Septuagint (see also Vulgate); Masoretic Text *and he moved the people into the cities*   [b]31 Or *Israel bowed down at the head of his bed*   [c]3 Hebrew *El-Shaddai*

crease your numbers. I will make you a community of peoples, and I will give this land as an everlasting possession to your descendants after you.'

⁵"Now then, your two sons born to you in Egypt before I came to you here will be reckoned as mine; Ephraim and Manasseh will be mine, just as Reuben and Simeon are mine. ⁶Any children born to you after them will be yours; in the territory they inherit they will be reckoned under the names of their brothers. ⁷As I was returning from Paddan,ᵃ to my sorrow Rachel died in the land of Canaan while we were still on the way, a little distance from Ephrath. So I buried her there beside the road to Ephrath" (that is, Bethlehem).

⁸When Israel saw the sons of Joseph, he asked, "Who are these?"

⁹"They are the sons God has given me here," Joseph said to his father.

Then Israel said, "Bring them to me so I may bless them."

¹⁰Now Israel's eyes were failing because of old age, and he could hardly see. So Joseph brought his sons close to him, and his father kissed them and embraced them.

¹¹Israel said to Joseph, "I never expected to see your face again, and now God has allowed me to see your children too."

¹²Then Joseph removed them from Israel's knees and bowed down with his face to the ground. ¹³And Joseph took both of them, Ephraim on his right toward Israel's left hand and Manasseh on his left toward Israel's right hand, and brought them close to him. ¹⁴But Israel reached out his right hand and put it on Ephraim's head, though he was the younger, and crossing his arms, he put his left hand on Manasseh's head, even though Manasseh was the firstborn.

¹⁵Then he blessed Joseph and said,

"May the God before whom my
       fathers

Abraham and Isaac walked,
the God who has been my
       shepherd
all my life to this day,
¹⁶the Angel who has delivered me
       from all harm
—may he bless these boys.
May they be called by my name
   and the names of my fathers
       Abraham and Isaac,
and may they increase greatly
   upon the earth."

¹⁷When Joseph saw his father placing his right hand on Ephraim's head he was displeased; so he took hold of his father's hand to move it from Ephraim's head to Manasseh's head. ¹⁸Joseph said to him, "No, my father, this one is the firstborn; put your right hand on his head."

¹⁹But his father refused and said, "I know, my son, I know. He too will become a people, and he too will become great. Nevertheless, his younger brother will be greater than he, and his descendants will become a group of nations." ²⁰He blessed them that day and said,

"In yourᵇ name will Israel
       pronounce this blessing:
   'May God make you like
       Ephraim and Manasseh.' "

So he put Ephraim ahead of Manasseh.

²¹Then Israel said to Joseph, "I am about to die, but God will be with youᶜ and take youᶜ back to the land of yourᶜ fathers. ²²And to you, as one who is over your brothers, I give the ridge of landᵈ I took from the Amorites with my sword and my bow."

Jacob Blesses His Sons

49 Then Jacob called for his sons and said: "Gather around so I can tell you what will happen to you in days to come.

²"Assemble and listen, sons of
       Jacob;
   listen to your father Israel.

ᵃ7 That is, Northwest Mesopotamia   ᵇ20 The Hebrew is singular.   ᶜ21 The Hebrew is plural.   ᵈ22 Or *And to you I give one portion more than to your brothers—the portion*

³"Reuben, you are my firstborn,
  my might, the first sign of my
    strength,
  excelling in honor, excelling in
    power.
⁴Turbulent as the waters, you will
    no longer excel,
  for you went up onto your
    father's bed,
  onto my couch and defiled it.

⁵"Simeon and Levi are brothers—
  their swords*ᵃ* are weapons of
    violence.
⁶Let me not enter their council,
  let me not join their assembly,
for they have killed men in their
    anger
  and hamstrung oxen as they
    pleased.
⁷Cursed be their anger, so fierce,
  and their fury, so cruel!
I will scatter them in Jacob
  and disperse them in Israel.

⁸"Judah,*ᵇ* your brothers will praise
    you;
  your hand will be on the neck
    of your enemies;
  your father's sons will bow
    down to you.
⁹You are a lion's cub, O Judah;
  you return from the prey, my
    son.
Like a lion he crouches and lies
    down,
  like a lioness—who dares to
    rouse him?
¹⁰The scepter will not depart from
    Judah,
  nor the ruler's staff from
    between his feet,
until he comes to whom it
    belongs*ᶜ*
  and the obedience of the nations
    is his.
¹¹He will tether his donkey to a
    vine,
  his colt to the choicest branch;

he will wash his garments in
    wine,
  his robes in the blood of grapes.
¹²His eyes will be darker than wine,
  his teeth whiter than milk.*ᵈ*

¹³"Zebulun will live by the seashore
  and become a haven for ships;
  his border will extend toward
    Sidon.

¹⁴"Issachar is a rawboned*ᵉ* donkey
  lying down between two
    saddlebags.*ᶠ*
¹⁵When he sees how good is his
    resting place
  and how pleasant is his land,
he will bend his shoulder to the
    burden
  and submit to forced labor.

¹⁶"Dan*ᵍ* will provide justice for his
    people
  as one of the tribes of Israel.
¹⁷Dan will be a serpent by the
    roadside,
  a viper along the path,
that bites the horse's heels
  so that its rider tumbles
    backward.

¹⁸"I look for your deliverance,
  O LORD.

¹⁹"Gad*ʰ* will be attacked by a band
    of raiders,
  but he will attack them at their
    heels.

²⁰"Asher's food will be rich;
  he will provide delicacies fit for
    a king.

²¹"Naphtali is a doe set free
  that bears beautiful fawns.*ⁱ*

²²"Joseph is a fruitful vine,
  a fruitful vine near a spring,
  whose branches climb over a
    wall.*ʲ*
²³With bitterness archers attacked
    him;
  they shot at him with hostility.

ᵃ5 The meaning of the Hebrew for this word is uncertain.   *ᵇ8 Judah* sounds like and may be
derived from the Hebrew for *praise.*   *ᶜ10* Or *until Shiloh comes;* or *until he comes to whom tribute
belongs*   *ᵈ12* Or *will be dull from wine, / his teeth white from milk*   *ᵉ14* Or *strong*   *ᶠ14* Or
campfires   *ᵍ16 Dan* here means *he provides justice.*   *ʰ19 Gad* can mean *attack* and *band of
raiders.*   *ⁱ21* Or *free; / he utters beautiful words*   *ʲ22* Or *Joseph is a wild colt, / a wild colt near a
spring, / a wild donkey on a terraced hill*

²⁴But his bow remained steady,
  his strong arms stayed*a* limber,
because of the hand of the Mighty
    One of Jacob,
  because of the Shepherd, the
    Rock of Israel,
²⁵because of your father's God, who
    helps you,
  because of the Almighty,*b* who
    blesses you
with blessings of the heavens
    above,
  blessings of the deep that lies
    below,
  blessings of the breast and
    womb.
²⁶Your father's blessings are greater
  than the blessings of the ancient
    mountains,
  than*c* the bounty of the
    age-old hills.
Let all these rest on the head of
    Joseph,
  on the brow of the prince
    among*d* his brothers.

²⁷"Benjamin is a ravenous wolf;
  in the morning he devours the
    prey,
  in the evening he divides the
    plunder."

²⁸All these are the twelve tribes of
Israel, and this is what their father
said to them when he blessed them,
giving each the blessing appropriate
to him.

The Death of Jacob

²⁹Then he gave them these instructions: "I am about to be gathered to
my people. Bury me with my fathers
in the cave in the field of Ephron the
Hittite, ³⁰the cave in the field of Machpelah, near Mamre in Canaan, which
Abraham bought as a burial place
from Ephron the Hittite, along with
the field. ³¹There Abraham and his
wife Sarah were buried, there Isaac
and his wife Rebekah were buried,
and there I buried Leah. ³²The field

and the cave in it were bought from
the Hittites.*e*"

³³When Jacob had finished giving
instructions to his sons, he drew his
feet up into the bed, breathed his last
and was gathered to his people.

50 Joseph threw himself upon his
  father and wept over him and
kissed him. ²Then Joseph directed the
physicians in his service to embalm
his father Israel. So the physicians
embalmed him, ³taking a full forty
days, for that was the time required
for embalming. And the Egyptians
mourned for him seventy days.

⁴When the days of mourning had
passed, Joseph said to Pharaoh's
court, "If I have found favor in your
eyes, speak to Pharaoh for me. Tell
him, ⁵'My father made me swear an
oath and said, "I am about to die;
bury me in the tomb I dug for myself
in the land of Canaan." Now let me
go up and bury my father; then I will
return.' "

⁶Pharaoh said, "Go up and bury
your father, as he made you swear
to do."

⁷So Joseph went up to bury his father. All Pharaoh's officials accompanied him—the dignitaries of his court
and all the dignitaries of Egypt— ⁸be-
sides all the members of Joseph's
household and his brothers and those
belonging to his father's household.
Only their children and their flocks
and herds were left in Goshen. ⁹Char-
iots and horsemen*f* also went up
with him. It was a very large company.

¹⁰When they reached the threshing
floor of Atad, near the Jordan, they
lamented loudly and bitterly; and
there Joseph observed a seven-day
period of mourning for his father.
¹¹When the Canaanites who lived
there saw the mourning at the threshing floor of Atad, they said, "The
Egyptians are holding a solemn ceremony of mourning." That is why that

*a*23,24 Or *archers will attack . . . will shoot . . . will remain . . . will stay*   *b*25 Hebrew *Shaddai*
*c*26 Or *of my progenitors, / as great as*   *d*26 Or *the one separated from*   *e*32 Or *the sons of Heth*
*f*9 Or *charioteers*

VERSE:	AUTHOR:	PASSAGE:
Genesis 50:20	Charles Stanley	Genesis 50:15–21

Free to Believe

Trusting God to use the circumstantial disappointments in life is difficult. Trusting him to work through people's evil intentions is something else entirely. It is one thing when the church picnic is rained out. It is quite another when a "friend" at work intentionally lies in order to get your job.

When events such as a betrayal occur, a wall of frustration clouds our relationship with God. We ask, "Why didn't you stop this? Didn't you know this was going to happen?" As our frustration turns to doubt, we lose confidence in God's concern and involvement in our lives . . .

To be free from the doubt and resentment we tend to feel toward God when we are intentionally hurt by others, we must focus on the principle stated so clearly by Joseph: "You intended to harm me, but God intended it for good." Through all the rejection and abuse Joseph encountered at the hands of his brothers, God had not abandoned him. Just the opposite was true. Through the intentional mistreatment Joseph experienced, God was working to accomplish his divine plan.

There is a catch. In order for God to turn a negative situation into a positive one, we must remain faithful through the process. Imagine what would have happened if Joseph had allowed himself to grow bitter at God and at his family. This story may not have had such a happy ending. It was Joseph's faithfulness through the process that gave God the freedom to work.

ADDITIONAL SCRIPTURE READINGS
Romans 8:28–39; Philippians 2:12–18

Go to page 71 for your next devotional reading.

place near the Jordan is called Abel Mizraim.[a]

[12]So Jacob's sons did as he had commanded them: [13]They carried him to the land of Canaan and buried him in the cave in the field of Machpelah, near Mamre, which Abraham had bought as a burial place from Ephron the Hittite, along with the field. [14]After burying his father, Joseph returned to Egypt, together with his brothers and all the others who had gone with him to bury his father.

Joseph Reassures His Brothers

[15]When Joseph's brothers saw that their father was dead, they said, "What if Joseph holds a grudge against us and pays us back for all the wrongs we did to him?" [16]So they sent word to Joseph, saying, "Your father left these instructions before he died: [17]'This is what you are to say to Joseph: I ask you to forgive your brothers the sins and the wrongs they committed in treating you so badly.' Now please forgive the sins of the servants of the God of your father." When their message came to him, Joseph wept.

[18]His brothers then came and threw themselves down before him. "We are your slaves," they said.

[19]But Joseph said to them, "Don't be afraid. Am I in the place of God? [20]You intended to harm me, but God intended it for good to accomplish what is now being done, the saving of many lives. [21]So then, don't be afraid. I will provide for you and your children." And he reassured them and spoke kindly to them.

The Death of Joseph

[22]Joseph stayed in Egypt, along with all his father's family. He lived a hundred and ten years [23]and saw the third generation of Ephraim's children. Also the children of Makir son of Manasseh were placed at birth on Joseph's knees.[b]

[24]Then Joseph said to his brothers, "I am about to die. But God will surely come to your aid and take you up out of this land to the land he promised on oath to Abraham, Isaac and Jacob." [25]And Joseph made the sons of Israel swear an oath and said, "God will surely come to your aid, and then you must carry my bones up from this place."

[26]So Joseph died at the age of a hundred and ten. And after they embalmed him, he was placed in a coffin in Egypt.

---

[a]11 Abel Mizraim means mourning of the Egyptians.   [b]23 That is, were counted as his

...**T**... his book recounts the
supernatural rescue of an entire people by
their God. Despite God's intervention and
his gracious guidance, the Israelites seem
unable to remain loyal to him. As you read
Exodus, be encouraged that God responds to
you, as he asks you to trust him as your only
hope and to obey his commands given to
guide you throughout your days on earth.

EXODUS

The Israelites Oppressed

1 These are the names of the sons of Israel who went to Egypt with Jacob, each with his family: ²Reuben, Simeon, Levi and Judah; ³Issachar, Zebulun and Benjamin; ⁴Dan and Naphtali; Gad and Asher. ⁵The descendants of Jacob numbered seventy*ᵃ* in all; Joseph was already in Egypt.

⁶Now Joseph and all his brothers and all that generation died, ⁷but the Israelites were fruitful and multiplied greatly and became exceedingly numerous, so that the land was filled with them.

⁸Then a new king, who did not know about Joseph, came to power in Egypt. ⁹"Look," he said to his people, "the Israelites have become much too numerous for us. ¹⁰Come, we must deal shrewdly with them or they will become even more numerous and, if war breaks out, will join our enemies,

fight against us and leave the country."

¹¹So they put slave masters over them to oppress them with forced labor, and they built Pithom and Rameses as store cities for Pharaoh. ¹²But the more they were oppressed, the more they multiplied and spread; so the Egyptians came to dread the Israelites ¹³and worked them ruthlessly. ¹⁴They made their lives bitter with hard labor in brick and mortar and with all kinds of work in the fields; in all their hard labor the Egyptians used them ruthlessly.

¹⁵The king of Egypt said to the Hebrew midwives, whose names were Shiphrah and Puah, ¹⁶"When you help the Hebrew women in childbirth and observe them on the delivery stool, if it is a boy, kill him; but if it is a girl, let her live." ¹⁷The midwives, however, feared God and did not do what the king of Egypt had told them

---

ᵃ5 Masoretic Text (see also Gen. 46:27); Dead Sea Scrolls and Septuagint (see also Acts 7:14 and note at Gen. 46:27) *seventy-five*

to do; they let the boys live. ¹⁸Then the king of Egypt summoned the midwives and asked them, "Why have you done this? Why have you let the boys live?"

¹⁹The midwives answered Pharaoh, "Hebrew women are not like Egyptian women; they are vigorous and give birth before the midwives arrive."

²⁰So God was kind to the midwives and the people increased and became even more numerous. ²¹And because the midwives feared God, he gave them families of their own.

²²Then Pharaoh gave this order to all his people: "Every boy that is born*ᵃ* you must throw into the Nile, but let every girl live."

The Birth of Moses

2 Now a man of the house of Levi married a Levite woman, ²and she became pregnant and gave birth to a son. When she saw that he was a fine child, she hid him for three months. ³But when she could hide him no longer, she got a papyrus basket for him and coated it with tar and pitch. Then she placed the child in it and put it among the reeds along the bank of the Nile. ⁴His sister stood at a distance to see what would happen to him.

⁵Then Pharaoh's daughter went down to the Nile to bathe, and her attendants were walking along the river bank. She saw the basket among the reeds and sent her slave girl to get it. ⁶She opened it and saw the baby. He was crying, and she felt sorry for him. "This is one of the Hebrew babies," she said.

⁷Then his sister asked Pharaoh's daughter, "Shall I go and get one of the Hebrew women to nurse the baby for you?"

⁸"Yes, go," she answered. And the girl went and got the baby's mother. ⁹Pharaoh's daughter said to her, "Take this baby and nurse him for

me, and I will pay you." So the woman took the baby and nursed him. ¹⁰When the child grew older, she took him to Pharaoh's daughter and he became her son. She named him Moses,*ᵇ* saying, "I drew him out of the water."

Moses Flees to Midian

¹¹One day, after Moses had grown up, he went out to where his own people were and watched them at their hard labor. He saw an Egyptian beating a Hebrew, one of his own people. ¹²Glancing this way and that and seeing no one, he killed the Egyptian and hid him in the sand. ¹³The next day he went out and saw two Hebrews fighting. He asked the one in the wrong, "Why are you hitting your fellow Hebrew?"

¹⁴The man said, "Who made you ruler and judge over us? Are you thinking of killing me as you killed the Egyptian?" Then Moses was afraid and thought, "What I did must have become known."

¹⁵When Pharaoh heard of this, he tried to kill Moses, but Moses fled from Pharaoh and went to live in Midian, where he sat down by a well. ¹⁶Now a priest of Midian had seven daughters, and they came to draw water and fill the troughs to water their father's flock. ¹⁷Some shepherds came along and drove them away, but Moses got up and came to their rescue and watered their flock.

¹⁸When the girls returned to Reuel their father, he asked them, "Why have you returned so early today?"

¹⁹They answered, "An Egyptian rescued us from the shepherds. He even drew water for us and watered the flock."

²⁰"And where is he?" he asked his daughters. "Why did you leave him? Invite him to have something to eat."

²¹Moses agreed to stay with the man, who gave his daughter Zipporah to Moses in marriage. ²²Zipporah gave birth to a son, and Moses named

ᵃ22 Masoretic Text; Samaritan Pentateuch, Septuagint and Targums *born to the Hebrews*
ᵇ10 *Moses* sounds like the Hebrew for *draw out*.

him Gershom,[a] saying, "I have become an alien in a foreign land."

[23]During that long period, the king of Egypt died. The Israelites groaned in their slavery and cried out, and their cry for help because of their slavery went up to God. [24]God heard their groaning and he remembered his covenant with Abraham, with Isaac and with Jacob. [25]So God looked on the Israelites and was concerned about them.

Moses and the Burning Bush

3 Now Moses was tending the flock of Jethro his father-in-law, the priest of Midian, and he led the flock to the far side of the desert and came to Horeb, the mountain of God. [2]There the angel of the LORD appeared to him in flames of fire from within a bush. Moses saw that though the bush was on fire it did not burn up. [3]So Moses thought, "I will go over and see this strange sight—why the bush does not burn up."

[4]When the LORD saw that he had gone over to look, God called to him from within the bush, "Moses! Moses!"

And Moses said, "Here I am."

[5]"Do not come any closer," God said. "Take off your sandals, for the place where you are standing is holy ground." [6]Then he said, "I am the God of your father, the God of Abraham, the God of Isaac and the God of Jacob." At this, Moses hid his face, because he was afraid to look at God.

[7]The LORD said, "I have indeed seen the misery of my people in Egypt. I have heard them crying out because of their slave drivers, and I am concerned about their suffering. [8]So I have come down to rescue them from the hand of the Egyptians and to bring them up out of that land into a good and spacious land, a land flowing with milk and honey—the home of the Canaanites, Hittites, Amorites, Perizzites, Hivites and Jebusites. [9]And

now the cry of the Israelites has reached me, and I have seen the way the Egyptians are oppressing them. [10]So now, go. I am sending you to Pharaoh to bring my people the Israelites out of Egypt."

[11]But Moses said to God, "Who am I, that I should go to Pharaoh and bring the Israelites out of Egypt?"

[12]And God said, "I will be with you. And this will be the sign to you that it is I who have sent you: When you have brought the people out of Egypt, you[b] will worship God on this mountain."

[13]Moses said to God, "Suppose I go to the Israelites and say to them, 'The God of your fathers has sent me to you,' and they ask me, 'What is his name?' Then what shall I tell them?"

[14]God said to Moses, "I AM WHO I AM.[c] This is what you are to say to the Israelites: 'I AM has sent me to you.' "

[15]God also said to Moses, "Say to the Israelites, 'The LORD,[d] the God of your fathers—the God of Abraham, the God of Isaac and the God of Jacob—has sent me to you.' This is my name forever, the name by which I am to be remembered from generation to generation.

[16]"Go, assemble the elders of Israel and say to them, 'The LORD, the God of your fathers—the God of Abraham, Isaac and Jacob—appeared to me and said: I have watched over you and have seen what has been done to you in Egypt. [17]And I have promised to bring you up out of your misery in Egypt into the land of the Canaanites, Hittites, Amorites, Perizzites, Hivites and Jebusites—a land flowing with milk and honey.'

[18]"The elders of Israel will listen to you. Then you and the elders are to go to the king of Egypt and say to him, 'The LORD, the God of the Hebrews, has met with us. Let us take a three-day journey into the desert to offer sacrifices to the LORD our God.'

---

[a]22 *Gershom* sounds like the Hebrew for *an alien there.*   [b]12 The Hebrew is plural.   [c]14 Or *I WILL BE WHAT I WILL BE*   [d]15 The Hebrew for LORD sounds like and may be derived from the Hebrew for *I AM* in verse 14.

¹⁹But I know that the king of Egypt will not let you go unless a mighty hand compels him. ²⁰So I will stretch out my hand and strike the Egyptians with all the wonders that I will perform among them. After that, he will let you go.

²¹"And I will make the Egyptians favorably disposed toward this people, so that when you leave you will not go empty-handed. ²²Every wom-

an is to ask her neighbor and any woman living in her house for articles of silver and gold and for clothing, which you will put on your sons and daughters. And so you will plunder the Egyptians."

Signs for Moses

4 Moses answered, "What if they do not believe me or listen to me

THURSDAY

VERSE:	AUTHOR:	PASSAGE:
Exodus 3:14	F.B. Meyer	Exodus 3:1–14

Our Partnership Is With God

Nothing is more needed today than God's partnership as a realized fact in Christian experience. Many of us may assent to what is written in these lines, and then put it aside, as a dream which is too ethereal to be of practical service. But when the apostle [1 John 1:3] said that "our fellowship [that is, our *partnership*] is with the Father and with his Son, Jesus Christ," it is surely meant that we should enter upon our inheritance. "I AM ... " says our great Partner; "fill in your need, and I will meet your demand, according to the riches of my glory in Christ Jesus." Let us tear out the order-forms from God's service-register, fill them up, and present them for delivery. Not one of them would be dishonored. And if it happened that we had wrongly diagnosed our need, he would erase the demand based on our imperfect knowledge, and substitute what we would ask if we knew. There is nothing more certain than that the more we ask of God, the more pleased he is to do exceeding abundantly beyond all that we ask or think.

ADDITIONAL SCRIPTURE READINGS
John 14:5–14; Ephesians 3:14–21

Go to page 84 for your next devotional reading.

and say, 'The LORD did not appear to you'?"

²Then the LORD said to him, "What is that in your hand?"

"A staff," he replied.

³The LORD said, "Throw it on the ground."

Moses threw it on the ground and it became a snake, and he ran from it. ⁴Then the LORD said to him, "Reach out your hand and take it by the tail." So Moses reached out and took hold of the snake and it turned back into a staff in his hand. ⁵"This," said the LORD, "is so that they may believe that the LORD, the God of their fathers—the God of Abraham, the God of Isaac and the God of Jacob—has appeared to you."

⁶Then the LORD said, "Put your hand inside your cloak." So Moses put his hand into his cloak, and when he took it out, it was leprous,[a] like snow.

⁷"Now put it back into your cloak," he said. So Moses put his hand back into his cloak, and when he took it out, it was restored, like the rest of his flesh.

⁸Then the LORD said, "If they do not believe you or pay attention to the first miraculous sign, they may believe the second. ⁹But if they do not believe these two signs or listen to you, take some water from the Nile and pour it on the dry ground. The water you take from the river will become blood on the ground."

¹⁰Moses said to the LORD, "O Lord, I have never been eloquent, neither in the past nor since you have spoken to your servant. I am slow of speech and tongue."

¹¹The LORD said to him, "Who gave man his mouth? Who makes him deaf or mute? Who gives him sight or makes him blind? Is it not I, the LORD? ¹²Now go; I will help you speak and will teach you what to say."

¹³But Moses said, "O Lord, please send someone else to do it."

¹⁴Then the LORD's anger burned against Moses and he said, "What about your brother, Aaron the Levite? I know he can speak well. He is already on his way to meet you, and his heart will be glad when he sees you. ¹⁵You shall speak to him and put words in his mouth; I will help both of you speak and will teach you what to do. ¹⁶He will speak to the people for you, and it will be as if he were your mouth and as if you were God to him. ¹⁷But take this staff in your hand so you can perform miraculous signs with it."

Moses Returns to Egypt

¹⁸Then Moses went back to Jethro his father-in-law and said to him, "Let me go back to my own people in Egypt to see if any of them are still alive."

Jethro said, "Go, and I wish you well."

¹⁹Now the LORD had said to Moses in Midian, "Go back to Egypt, for all the men who wanted to kill you are dead." ²⁰So Moses took his wife and sons, put them on a donkey and started back to Egypt. And he took the staff of God in his hand.

²¹The LORD said to Moses, "When you return to Egypt, see that you perform before Pharaoh all the wonders I have given you the power to do. But I will harden his heart so that he will not let the people go. ²²Then say to Pharaoh, 'This is what the LORD says: Israel is my firstborn son, ²³and I told you, "Let my son go, so he may worship me." But you refused to let him go; so I will kill your firstborn son.'"

²⁴At a lodging place on the way, the LORD met ⌊Moses⌋[b] and was about to kill him. ²⁵But Zipporah took a flint knife, cut off her son's foreskin and touched ⌊Moses'⌋ feet with it.[c] "Surely you are a bridegroom of blood to me," she said. ²⁶So the LORD let him alone. (At that time she said "bridegroom of blood," referring to circumcision.)

²⁷The LORD said to Aaron, "Go into

---

the desert to meet Moses." So he met Moses at the mountain of God and kissed him. 28Then Moses told Aaron everything the LORD had sent him to say, and also about all the miraculous signs he had commanded him to perform.

29Moses and Aaron brought together all the elders of the Israelites, 30and Aaron told them everything the LORD had said to Moses. He also performed the signs before the people, 31and they believed. And when they heard that the LORD was concerned about them and had seen their misery, they bowed down and worshiped.

Bricks Without Straw

5 Afterward Moses and Aaron went to Pharaoh and said, "This is what the LORD, the God of Israel, says: 'Let my people go, so that they may hold a festival to me in the desert.' "

2Pharaoh said, "Who is the LORD, that I should obey him and let Israel go? I do not know the LORD and I will not let Israel go."

3Then they said, "The God of the Hebrews has met with us. Now let us take a three-day journey into the desert to offer sacrifices to the LORD our God, or he may strike us with plagues or with the sword."

4But the king of Egypt said, "Moses and Aaron, why are you taking the people away from their labor? Get back to your work!" 5Then Pharaoh said, "Look, the people of the land are now numerous, and you are stopping them from working."

6That same day Pharaoh gave this order to the slave drivers and foremen in charge of the people: 7"You are no longer to supply the people with straw for making bricks; let them go and gather their own straw. 8But require them to make the same number of bricks as before; don't reduce the quota. They are lazy; that is why they are crying out, 'Let us go and sacrifice to our God.' 9Make the work harder for the men so that they keep working and pay no attention to lies."

10Then the slave drivers and the foremen went out and said to the people, "This is what Pharaoh says: 'I will not give you any more straw. 11Go and get your own straw wherever you can find it, but your work will not be reduced at all.' " 12So the people scattered all over Egypt to gather stubble to use for straw. 13The slave drivers kept pressing them, saying, "Complete the work required of you for each day, just as when you had straw." 14The Israelite foremen appointed by Pharaoh's slave drivers were beaten and were asked, "Why didn't you meet your quota of bricks yesterday or today, as before?"

15Then the Israelite foremen went and appealed to Pharaoh: "Why have you treated your servants this way? 16Your servants are given no straw, yet we are told, 'Make bricks!' Your servants are being beaten, but the fault is with your own people."

17Pharaoh said, "Lazy, that's what you are—lazy! That is why you keep saying, 'Let us go and sacrifice to the LORD.' 18Now get to work. You will not be given any straw, yet you must produce your full quota of bricks."

19The Israelite foremen realized they were in trouble when they were told, "You are not to reduce the number of bricks required of you for each day." 20When they left Pharaoh, they found Moses and Aaron waiting to meet them, 21and they said, "May the LORD look upon you and judge you! You have made us a stench to Pharaoh and his officials and have put a sword in their hand to kill us."

God Promises Deliverance

22Moses returned to the LORD and said, "O Lord, why have you brought trouble upon this people? Is this why you sent me? 23Ever since I went to Pharaoh to speak in your name, he has brought trouble upon this people, and you have not rescued your people at all."

6 Then the LORD said to Moses, "Now you will see what I will do to Pharaoh: Because of my mighty hand he will let them go; because of

my mighty hand he will drive them out of his country."

²God also said to Moses, "I am the LORD. ³I appeared to Abraham, to Isaac and to Jacob as God Almighty,[a] but by my name the LORD[b] I did not make myself known to them.[c] ⁴I also established my covenant with them to give them the land of Canaan, where they lived as aliens. ⁵Moreover, I have heard the groaning of the Israelites, whom the Egyptians are enslaving, and I have remembered my covenant.

⁶"Therefore, say to the Israelites: 'I am the LORD, and I will bring you out from under the yoke of the Egyptians. I will free you from being slaves to them, and I will redeem you with an outstretched arm and with mighty acts of judgment. ⁷I will take you as my own people, and I will be your God. Then you will know that I am the LORD your God, who brought you out from under the yoke of the Egyptians. ⁸And I will bring you to the land I swore with uplifted hand to give to Abraham, to Isaac and to Jacob. I will give it to you as a possession. I am the LORD.' "

⁹Moses reported this to the Israelites, but they did not listen to him because of their discouragement and cruel bondage.

¹⁰Then the LORD said to Moses, ¹¹"Go, tell Pharaoh king of Egypt to let the Israelites go out of his country."

¹²But Moses said to the LORD, "If the Israelites will not listen to me, why would Pharaoh listen to me, since I speak with faltering lips[d]?"

Family Record of Moses and Aaron

¹³Now the LORD spoke to Moses and Aaron about the Israelites and Pharaoh king of Egypt, and he commanded them to bring the Israelites out of Egypt.

¹⁴These were the heads of their families[e]:

The sons of Reuben the firstborn son of Israel were Hanoch and Pallu, Hezron and Carmi. These were the clans of Reuben.

¹⁵The sons of Simeon were Jemuel, Jamin, Ohad, Jakin, Zohar and Shaul the son of a Canaanite woman. These were the clans of Simeon.

¹⁶These were the names of the sons of Levi according to their records: Gershon, Kohath and Merari. Levi lived 137 years.

¹⁷The sons of Gershon, by clans, were Libni and Shimei.

¹⁸The sons of Kohath were Amram, Izhar, Hebron and Uzziel. Kohath lived 133 years.

¹⁹The sons of Merari were Mahli and Mushi.

These were the clans of Levi according to their records.

²⁰Amram married his father's sister Jochebed, who bore him Aaron and Moses. Amram lived 137 years.

²¹The sons of Izhar were Korah, Nepheg and Zicri.

²²The sons of Uzziel were Mishael, Elzaphan and Sithri.

²³Aaron married Elisheba, daughter of Amminadab and sister of Nahshon, and she bore him Nadab and Abihu, Eleazar and Ithamar.

²⁴The sons of Korah were Assir, Elkanah and Abiasaph. These were the Korahite clans.

²⁵Eleazar son of Aaron married one of the daughters of Putiel, and she bore him Phinehas.

These were the heads of the Levite families, clan by clan.

²⁶It was this same Aaron and Moses to whom the LORD said, "Bring the Israelites out of Egypt by their divisions." ²⁷They were the ones who spoke to Pharaoh king of Egypt about bringing the Israelites out of Egypt. It was the same Moses and Aaron.

---

[a]3 Hebrew El-Shaddai   [b]3 See note at Exodus 3:15.   [c]3 Or Almighty, and by my name the LORD did I not let myself be known to them?   [d]12 Hebrew I am uncircumcised of lips; also in verse 30   [e]14 The Hebrew for families here and in verse 25 refers to units larger than clans.

Aaron to Speak for Moses

²⁸Now when the LORD spoke to Moses in Egypt, ²⁹he said to him, "I am the LORD. Tell Pharaoh king of Egypt everything I tell you."

³⁰But Moses said to the LORD, "Since I speak with faltering lips, why would Pharaoh listen to me?"

7 Then the LORD said to Moses, "See, I have made you like God to Pharaoh, and your brother Aaron will be your prophet. ²You are to say everything I command you, and your brother Aaron is to tell Pharaoh to let the Israelites go out of his country. ³But I will harden Pharaoh's heart, and though I multiply my miraculous signs and wonders in Egypt, ⁴he will not listen to you. Then I will lay my hand on Egypt and with mighty acts of judgment I will bring out my divisions, my people the Israelites. ⁵And the Egyptians will know that I am the LORD when I stretch out my hand against Egypt and bring the Israelites out of it."

⁶Moses and Aaron did just as the LORD commanded them. ⁷Moses was eighty years old and Aaron eighty-three when they spoke to Pharaoh.

Aaron's Staff Becomes a Snake

⁸The LORD said to Moses and Aaron, ⁹"When Pharaoh says to you, 'Perform a miracle,' then say to Aaron, 'Take your staff and throw it down before Pharaoh,' and it will become a snake."

¹⁰So Moses and Aaron went to Pharaoh and did just as the LORD commanded. Aaron threw his staff down in front of Pharaoh and his officials, and it became a snake. ¹¹Pharaoh then summoned wise men and sorcerers, and the Egyptian magicians also did the same things by their secret arts: ¹²Each one threw down his staff and it became a snake. But Aaron's staff swallowed up their staffs. ¹³Yet Pharaoh's heart became hard and he would not listen to them, just as the LORD had said.

The Plague of Blood

¹⁴Then the LORD said to Moses, "Pharaoh's heart is unyielding; he refuses to let the people go. ¹⁵Go to Pharaoh in the morning as he goes out to the water. Wait on the bank of the Nile to meet him, and take in your hand the staff that was changed into a snake. ¹⁶Then say to him, 'The LORD, the God of the Hebrews, has sent me to say to you: Let my people go, so that they may worship me in the desert. But until now you have not listened. ¹⁷This is what the LORD says: By this you will know that I am the LORD: With the staff that is in my hand I will strike the water of the Nile, and it will be changed into blood. ¹⁸The fish in the Nile will die, and the river will stink; the Egyptians will not be able to drink its water.' "

¹⁹The LORD said to Moses, "Tell Aaron, 'Take your staff and stretch out your hand over the waters of Egypt—over the streams and canals, over the ponds and all the reservoirs'—and they will turn to blood. Blood will be everywhere in Egypt, even in the wooden buckets and stone jars."

²⁰Moses and Aaron did just as the LORD had commanded. He raised his staff in the presence of Pharaoh and his officials and struck the water of the Nile, and all the water was changed into blood. ²¹The fish in the Nile died, and the river smelled so bad that the Egyptians could not drink its water. Blood was everywhere in Egypt.

²²But the Egyptian magicians did the same things by their secret arts, and Pharaoh's heart became hard; he would not listen to Moses and Aaron, just as the LORD had said. ²³Instead, he turned and went into his palace, and did not take even this to heart. ²⁴And all the Egyptians dug along the Nile to get drinking water, because they could not drink the water of the river.

The Plague of Frogs

²⁵Seven days passed after the LORD

8 struck the Nile. ¹Then the LORD said to Moses, "Go to Pharaoh and say to him, 'This is what the LORD says: Let my people go, so that they may worship me. ²If you refuse to let them go, I will plague your whole country with frogs. ³The Nile will teem with frogs. They will come up into your palace and your bedroom and onto your bed, into the houses of your officials and on your people, and into your ovens and kneading troughs. ⁴The frogs will go up on you and your people and all your officials.' "

⁵Then the LORD said to Moses, "Tell Aaron, 'Stretch out your hand with your staff over the streams and canals and ponds, and make frogs come up on the land of Egypt.' "

⁶So Aaron stretched out his hand over the waters of Egypt, and the frogs came up and covered the land. ⁷But the magicians did the same things by their secret arts; they also made frogs come up on the land of Egypt.

⁸Pharaoh summoned Moses and Aaron and said, "Pray to the LORD to take the frogs away from me and my people, and I will let your people go to offer sacrifices to the LORD."

⁹Moses said to Pharaoh, "I leave to you the honor of setting the time for me to pray for you and your officials and your people that you and your houses may be rid of the frogs, except for those that remain in the Nile."

¹⁰"Tomorrow," Pharaoh said.

Moses replied, "It will be as you say, so that you may know there is no one like the LORD our God. ¹¹The frogs will leave you and your houses, your officials and your people; they will remain only in the Nile."

¹²After Moses and Aaron left Pharaoh, Moses cried out to the LORD about the frogs he had brought on Pharaoh. ¹³And the LORD did what Moses asked. The frogs died in the houses, in the courtyards and in the fields. ¹⁴They were piled into heaps, and the land reeked of them. ¹⁵But when Pharaoh saw that there was relief, he hardened his heart and would not listen to Moses and Aaron, just as the LORD had said.

The Plague of Gnats

¹⁶Then the LORD said to Moses, "Tell Aaron, 'Stretch out your staff and strike the dust of the ground,' and throughout the land of Egypt the dust will become gnats." ¹⁷They did this, and when Aaron stretched out his hand with the staff and struck the dust of the ground, gnats came upon men and animals. All the dust throughout the land of Egypt became gnats. ¹⁸But when the magicians tried to produce gnats by their secret arts, they could not. And the gnats were on men and animals.

¹⁹The magicians said to Pharaoh, "This is the finger of God." But Pharaoh's heart was hard and he would not listen, just as the LORD had said.

The Plague of Flies

²⁰Then the LORD said to Moses, "Get up early in the morning and confront Pharaoh as he goes to the water and say to him, 'This is what the LORD says: Let my people go, so that they may worship me. ²¹If you do not let my people go, I will send swarms of flies on you and your officials, on your people and into your houses. The houses of the Egyptians will be full of flies, and even the ground where they are.

²²" 'But on that day I will deal differently with the land of Goshen, where my people live; no swarms of flies will be there, so that you will know that I, the LORD, am in this land. ²³I will make a distinction[a] between my people and your people. This miraculous sign will occur tomorrow.' "

²⁴And the LORD did this. Dense swarms of flies poured into Pharaoh's palace and into the houses of his officials, and throughout Egypt the land was ruined by the flies.

²⁵Then Pharaoh summoned Moses

---

a23 Septuagint and Vulgate; Hebrew will put a deliverance

and Aaron and said, "Go, sacrifice to your God here in the land."

²⁶But Moses said, "That would not be right. The sacrifices we offer the LORD our God would be detestable to the Egyptians. And if we offer sacrifices that are detestable in their eyes, will they not stone us? ²⁷We must take a three-day journey into the desert to offer sacrifices to the LORD our God, as he commands us."

²⁸Pharaoh said, "I will let you go to offer sacrifices to the LORD your God in the desert, but you must not go very far. Now pray for me."

²⁹Moses answered, "As soon as I leave you, I will pray to the LORD, and tomorrow the flies will leave Pharaoh and his officials and his people. Only be sure that Pharaoh does not act deceitfully again by not letting the people go to offer sacrifices to the LORD."

³⁰Then Moses left Pharaoh and prayed to the LORD, ³¹and the LORD did what Moses asked: The flies left Pharaoh and his officials and his people; not a fly remained. ³²But this time also Pharaoh hardened his heart and would not let the people go.

The Plague on Livestock

9 Then the LORD said to Moses, "Go to Pharaoh and say to him, 'This is what the LORD, the God of the Hebrews, says: "Let my people go, so that they may worship me." ²If you refuse to let them go and continue to hold them back, ³the hand of the LORD will bring a terrible plague on your livestock in the field—on your horses and donkeys and camels and on your cattle and sheep and goats. ⁴But the LORD will make a distinction between the livestock of Israel and that of Egypt, so that no animal belonging to the Israelites will die.' "

⁵The LORD set a time and said, "Tomorrow the LORD will do this in the land." ⁶And the next day the LORD did it: All the livestock of the Egyptians died, but not one animal belonging to the Israelites died. ⁷Pharaoh sent men to investigate and found that not even

one of the animals of the Israelites had died. Yet his heart was unyielding and he would not let the people go.

The Plague of Boils

⁸Then the LORD said to Moses and Aaron, "Take handfuls of soot from a furnace and have Moses toss it into the air in the presence of Pharaoh. ⁹It will become fine dust over the whole land of Egypt, and festering boils will break out on men and animals throughout the land."

¹⁰So they took soot from a furnace and stood before Pharaoh. Moses tossed it into the air, and festering boils broke out on men and animals. ¹¹The magicians could not stand before Moses because of the boils that were on them and on all the Egyptians. ¹²But the LORD hardened Pharaoh's heart and he would not listen to Moses and Aaron, just as the LORD had said to Moses.

The Plague of Hail

¹³Then the LORD said to Moses, "Get up early in the morning, confront Pharaoh and say to him, 'This is what the LORD, the God of the Hebrews, says: Let my people go, so that they may worship me, ¹⁴or this time I will send the full force of my plagues against you and against your officials and your people, so you may know that there is no one like me in all the earth. ¹⁵For by now I could have stretched out my hand and struck you and your people with a plague that would have wiped you off the earth. ¹⁶But I have raised you up[a] for this very purpose, that I might show you my power and that my name might be proclaimed in all the earth. ¹⁷You still set yourself against my people and will not let them go. ¹⁸Therefore, at this time tomorrow I will send the worst hailstorm that has ever fallen on Egypt, from the day it was founded till now. ¹⁹Give an order now to bring your livestock and everything you have in the field to a place of

---

[a]16 Or *have spared you*

shelter, because the hail will fall on every man and animal that has not been brought in and is still out in the field, and they will die.' "

20Those officials of Pharaoh who feared the word of the LORD hurried to bring their slaves and their livestock inside. 21But those who ignored the word of the LORD left their slaves and livestock in the field.

22Then the LORD said to Moses, "Stretch out your hand toward the sky so that hail will fall all over Egypt—on men and animals and on everything growing in the fields of Egypt." 23When Moses stretched out his staff toward the sky, the LORD sent thunder and hail, and lightning flashed down to the ground. So the LORD rained hail on the land of Egypt; 24hail fell and lightning flashed back and forth. It was the worst storm in all the land of Egypt since it had become a nation. 25Throughout Egypt hail struck everything in the fields—both men and animals; it beat down everything growing in the fields and stripped every tree. 26The only place it did not hail was the land of Goshen, where the Israelites were.

27Then Pharaoh summoned Moses and Aaron. "This time I have sinned," he said to them. "The LORD is in the right, and I and my people are in the wrong. 28Pray to the LORD, for we have had enough thunder and hail. I will let you go; you don't have to stay any longer."

29Moses replied, "When I have gone out of the city, I will spread out my hands in prayer to the LORD. The thunder will stop and there will be no more hail, so you may know that the earth is the LORD's. 30But I know that you and your officials still do not fear the LORD God."

31(The flax and barley were destroyed, since the barley had headed and the flax was in bloom. 32The wheat and spelt, however, were not destroyed, because they ripen later.)

33Then Moses left Pharaoh and went out of the city. He spread out his hands toward the LORD; the thunder and hail stopped, and the rain no

longer poured down on the land. 34When Pharaoh saw that the rain and hail and thunder had stopped, he sinned again: He and his officials hardened their hearts. 35So Pharaoh's heart was hard and he would not let the Israelites go, just as the LORD had said through Moses.

The Plague of Locusts

10 Then the LORD said to Moses, "Go to Pharaoh, for I have hardened his heart and the hearts of his officials so that I may perform these miraculous signs of mine among them 2that you may tell your children and grandchildren how I dealt harshly with the Egyptians and how I performed my signs among them, and that you may know that I am the LORD."

3So Moses and Aaron went to Pharaoh and said to him, "This is what the LORD, the God of the Hebrews, says: 'How long will you refuse to humble yourself before me? Let my people go, so that they may worship me. 4If you refuse to let them go, I will bring locusts into your country tomorrow. 5They will cover the face of the ground so that it cannot be seen. They will devour what little you have left after the hail, including every tree that is growing in your fields. 6They will fill your houses and those of all your officials and all the Egyptians—something neither your fathers nor your forefathers have ever seen from the day they settled in this land till now.' " Then Moses turned and left Pharaoh.

7Pharaoh's officials said to him, "How long will this man be a snare to us? Let the people go, so that they may worship the LORD their God. Do you not yet realize that Egypt is ruined?"

8Then Moses and Aaron were brought back to Pharaoh. "Go, worship the LORD your God," he said. "But just who will be going?"

9Moses answered, "We will go with our young and old, with our sons and daughters, and with our flocks and herds, because we are to celebrate a festival to the LORD."

¹⁰Pharaoh said, "The LORD be with you—if I let you go, along with your women and children! Clearly you are bent on evil.ᵃ ¹¹No! Have only the men go; and worship the LORD, since that's what you have been asking for." Then Moses and Aaron were driven out of Pharaoh's presence.

¹²And the LORD said to Moses, "Stretch out your hand over Egypt so that locusts will swarm over the land and devour everything growing in the fields, everything left by the hail."

¹³So Moses stretched out his staff over Egypt, and the LORD made an east wind blow across the land all that day and all that night. By morning the wind had brought the locusts; ¹⁴they invaded all Egypt and settled down in every area of the country in great numbers. Never before had there been such a plague of locusts, nor will there ever be again. ¹⁵They covered all the ground until it was black. They devoured all that was left after the hail—everything growing in the fields and the fruit on the trees. Nothing green remained on tree or plant in all the land of Egypt.

¹⁶Pharaoh quickly summoned Moses and Aaron and said, "I have sinned against the LORD your God and against you. ¹⁷Now forgive my sin once more and pray to the LORD your God to take this deadly plague away from me."

¹⁸Moses then left Pharaoh and prayed to the LORD. ¹⁹And the LORD changed the wind to a very strong west wind, which caught up the locusts and carried them into the Red Sea.ᵇ Not a locust was left anywhere in Egypt. ²⁰But the LORD hardened Pharaoh's heart, and he would not let the Israelites go.

The Plague of Darkness

²¹Then the LORD said to Moses, "Stretch out your hand toward the sky so that darkness will spread over Egypt—darkness that can be felt."

²²So Moses stretched out his hand toward the sky, and total darkness covered all Egypt for three days. ²³No one could see anyone else or leave his place for three days. Yet all the Israelites had light in the places where they lived.

²⁴Then Pharaoh summoned Moses and said, "Go, worship the LORD. Even your women and children may go with you; only leave your flocks and herds behind."

²⁵But Moses said, "You must allow us to have sacrifices and burnt offerings to present to the LORD our God. ²⁶Our livestock too must go with us; not a hoof is to be left behind. We have to use some of them in worshiping the LORD our God, and until we get there we will not know what we are to use to worship the LORD."

²⁷But the LORD hardened Pharaoh's heart, and he was not willing to let them go. ²⁸Pharaoh said to Moses, "Get out of my sight! Make sure you do not appear before me again! The day you see my face you will die."

²⁹"Just as you say," Moses replied, "I will never appear before you again."

The Plague on the Firstborn

11 Now the LORD had said to Moses, "I will bring one more plague on Pharaoh and on Egypt. After that, he will let you go from here, and when he does, he will drive you out completely. ²Tell the people that men and women alike are to ask their neighbors for articles of silver and gold." ³(The LORD made the Egyptians favorably disposed toward the people, and Moses himself was highly regarded in Egypt by Pharaoh's officials and by the people.)

⁴So Moses said, "This is what the LORD says: 'About midnight I will go throughout Egypt. ⁵Every firstborn son in Egypt will die, from the firstborn son of Pharaoh, who sits on the throne, to the firstborn son of the slave girl, who is at her hand mill, and all the firstborn of the cattle as

---

ᵃ10 Or Be careful, trouble is in store for you!   ᵇ19 Hebrew Yam Suph; that is, Sea of Reeds

well. ⁶There will be loud wailing throughout Egypt—worse than there has ever been or ever will be again. ⁷But among the Israelites not a dog will bark at any man or animal.' Then you will know that the LORD makes a distinction between Egypt and Israel. ⁸All these officials of yours will come to me, bowing down before me and saying, 'Go, you and all the people who follow you!' After that I will leave." Then Moses, hot with anger, left Pharaoh.

⁹The LORD had said to Moses, "Pharaoh will refuse to listen to you—so that my wonders may be multiplied in Egypt." ¹⁰Moses and Aaron performed all these wonders before Pharaoh, but the LORD hardened Pharaoh's heart, and he would not let the Israelites go out of his country.

The Passover

12 The LORD said to Moses and Aaron in Egypt, ²"This month is to be for you the first month, the first month of your year. ³Tell the whole community of Israel that on the tenth day of this month each man is to take a lamb*a* for his family, one for each household. ⁴If any household is too small for a whole lamb, they must share one with their nearest neighbor, having taken into account the number of people there are. You are to determine the amount of lamb needed in accordance with what each person will eat. ⁵The animals you choose must be year-old males without defect, and you may take them from the sheep or the goats. ⁶Take care of them until the fourteenth day of the month, when all the people of the community of Israel must slaughter them at twilight. ⁷Then they are to take some of the blood and put it on the sides and tops of the doorframes of the houses where they eat the lambs. ⁸That same night they are to eat the meat roasted over the fire, along with bitter herbs, and bread made without yeast. ⁹Do not eat the meat raw or cooked in water, but roast it over the fire—head, legs and inner parts. ¹⁰Do not leave any of it till morning; if some is left till morning, you must burn it. ¹¹This is how you are to eat it: with your cloak tucked into your belt, your sandals on your feet and your staff in your hand. Eat it in haste; it is the LORD's Passover.

¹²"On that same night I will pass through Egypt and strike down every firstborn—both men and animals—and I will bring judgment on all the gods of Egypt. I am the LORD. ¹³The blood will be a sign for you on the houses where you are; and when I see the blood, I will pass over you. No destructive plague will touch you when I strike Egypt.

¹⁴"This is a day you are to commemorate; for the generations to come you shall celebrate it as a festival to the LORD—a lasting ordinance. ¹⁵For seven days you are to eat bread made without yeast. On the first day remove the yeast from your houses, for whoever eats anything with yeast in it from the first day through the seventh must be cut off from Israel. ¹⁶On the first day hold a sacred assembly, and another one on the seventh day. Do no work at all on these days, except to prepare food for everyone to eat—that is all you may do.

¹⁷"Celebrate the Feast of Unleavened Bread, because it was on this very day that I brought your divisions out of Egypt. Celebrate this day as a lasting ordinance for the generations to come. ¹⁸In the first month you are to eat bread made without yeast, from the evening of the fourteenth day until the evening of the twenty-first day. ¹⁹For seven days no yeast is to be found in your houses. And whoever eats anything with yeast in it must be cut off from the community of Israel, whether he is an alien or native-born. ²⁰Eat nothing made with yeast. Wherever you live, you must eat unleavened bread."

²¹Then Moses summoned all the elders of Israel and said to them, "Go at

---

*a*3 The Hebrew word can mean *lamb* or *kid*; also in verse 4.

once and select the animals for your families and slaughter the Passover lamb. ²²Take a bunch of hyssop, dip it into the blood in the basin and put some of the blood on the top and on both sides of the doorframe. Not one of you shall go out the door of his house until morning. ²³When the LORD goes through the land to strike down the Egyptians, he will see the blood on the top and sides of the doorframe and will pass over that doorway, and he will not permit the destroyer to enter your houses and strike you down.

²⁴"Obey these instructions as a lasting ordinance for you and your descendants. ²⁵When you enter the land that the LORD will give you as he promised, observe this ceremony. ²⁶And when your children ask you, 'What does this ceremony mean to you?' ²⁷then tell them, 'It is the Passover sacrifice to the LORD, who passed over the houses of the Israelites in Egypt and spared our homes when he struck down the Egyptians.' " Then the people bowed down and worshiped. ²⁸The Israelites did just what the LORD commanded Moses and Aaron.

²⁹At midnight the LORD struck down all the firstborn in Egypt, from the firstborn of Pharaoh, who sat on the throne, to the firstborn of the prisoner, who was in the dungeon, and the firstborn of all the livestock as well. ³⁰Pharaoh and all his officials and all the Egyptians got up during the night, and there was loud wailing in Egypt, for there was not a house without someone dead.

The Exodus

³¹During the night Pharaoh summoned Moses and Aaron and said, "Up! Leave my people, you and the Israelites! Go, worship the LORD as you have requested. ³²Take your flocks and herds, as you have said, and go. And also bless me."

³³The Egyptians urged the people to hurry and leave the country. "For otherwise," they said, "we will all die!" ³⁴So the people took their dough before the yeast was added, and carried it on their shoulders in kneading troughs wrapped in clothing. ³⁵The Israelites did as Moses instructed and asked the Egyptians for articles of silver and gold and for clothing. ³⁶The LORD had made the Egyptians favorably disposed toward the people, and they gave them what they asked for; so they plundered the Egyptians.

³⁷The Israelites journeyed from Rameses to Succoth. There were about six hundred thousand men on foot, besides women and children. ³⁸Many other people went up with them, as well as large droves of livestock, both flocks and herds. ³⁹With the dough they had brought from Egypt, they baked cakes of unleavened bread. The dough was without yeast because they had been driven out of Egypt and did not have time to prepare food for themselves.

⁴⁰Now the length of time the Israelite people lived in Egypt^a was 430 years. ⁴¹At the end of the 430 years, to the very day, all the LORD's divisions left Egypt. ⁴²Because the LORD kept vigil that night to bring them out of Egypt, on this night all the Israelites are to keep vigil to honor the LORD for the generations to come.

Passover Restrictions

⁴³The LORD said to Moses and Aaron, "These are the regulations for the Passover:

"No foreigner is to eat of it. ⁴⁴Any slave you have bought may eat of it after you have circumcised him, ⁴⁵but a temporary resident and a hired worker may not eat of it.

⁴⁶"It must be eaten inside one house; take none of the meat outside the house. Do not break any of the bones. ⁴⁷The whole community of Israel must celebrate it.

⁴⁸"An alien living among you who wants to celebrate the LORD's Passover must have all the males in his household circumcised; then he may take part like one born in the land. No un-

---

^{a}40 Masoretic Text; Samaritan Pentateuch and Septuagint *Egypt and Canaan*

circumcised male may eat of it. ⁴⁹The same law applies to the native-born and to the alien living among you."

⁵⁰All the Israelites did just what the LORD had commanded Moses and Aaron. ⁵¹And on that very day the LORD brought the Israelites out of Egypt by their divisions.

Consecration of the Firstborn

13 The LORD said to Moses, ²"Consecrate to me every firstborn male. The first offspring of every womb among the Israelites belongs to me, whether man or animal."

³Then Moses said to the people, "Commemorate this day, the day you came out of Egypt, out of the land of slavery, because the LORD brought you out of it with a mighty hand. Eat nothing containing yeast. ⁴Today, in the month of Abib, you are leaving. ⁵When the LORD brings you into the land of the Canaanites, Hittites, Amorites, Hivites and Jebusites—the land he swore to your forefathers to give you, a land flowing with milk and honey—you are to observe this ceremony in this month: ⁶For seven days eat bread made without yeast and on the seventh day hold a festival to the LORD. ⁷Eat unleavened bread during those seven days; nothing with yeast in it is to be seen among you, nor shall any yeast be seen anywhere within your borders. ⁸On that day tell your son, 'I do this because of what the LORD did for me when I came out of Egypt.' ⁹This observance will be for you like a sign on your hand and a reminder on your forehead that the law of the LORD is to be on your lips. For the LORD brought you out of Egypt with his mighty hand. ¹⁰You must keep this ordinance at the appointed time year after year.

¹¹"After the LORD brings you into the land of the Canaanites and gives it to you, as he promised on oath to you and your forefathers, ¹²you are to give over to the LORD the first offspring of every womb. All the firstborn males

of your livestock belong to the LORD. ¹³Redeem with a lamb every firstborn donkey, but if you do not redeem it, break its neck. Redeem every firstborn among your sons.

¹⁴"In days to come, when your son asks you, 'What does this mean?' say to him, 'With a mighty hand the LORD brought us out of Egypt, out of the land of slavery. ¹⁵When Pharaoh stubbornly refused to let us go, the LORD killed every firstborn in Egypt, both man and animal. This is why I sacrifice to the LORD the first male offspring of every womb and redeem each of my firstborn sons.' ¹⁶And it will be like a sign on your hand and a symbol on your forehead that the LORD brought us out of Egypt with his mighty hand."

Crossing the Sea

¹⁷When Pharaoh let the people go, God did not lead them on the road through the Philistine country, though that was shorter. For God said, "If they face war, they might change their minds and return to Egypt." ¹⁸So God led the people around by the desert road toward the Red Sea.ᵃ The Israelites went up out of Egypt armed for battle.

¹⁹Moses took the bones of Joseph with him because Joseph had made the sons of Israel swear an oath. He had said, "God will surely come to your aid, and then you must carry my bones up with you from this place."ᵇ

²⁰After leaving Succoth they camped at Etham on the edge of the desert. ²¹By day the LORD went ahead of them in a pillar of cloud to guide them on their way and by night in a pillar of fire to give them light, so that they could travel by day or night. ²²Neither the pillar of cloud by day nor the pillar of fire by night left its place in front of the people.

14 Then the LORD said to Moses, ²"Tell the Israelites to turn back and encamp near Pi Hahiroth, between Migdol and the sea. They are to encamp by the sea, directly opposite

---

ᵃ18 Hebrew *Yam Suph*; that is, Sea of Reeds   ᵇ19 See Gen. 50:25.

Baal Zephon. ³Pharaoh will think, 'The Israelites are wandering around the land in confusion, hemmed in by the desert.' ⁴And I will harden Pharaoh's heart, and he will pursue them. But I will gain glory for myself through Pharaoh and all his army, and the Egyptians will know that I am the LORD." So the Israelites did this.

⁵When the king of Egypt was told that the people had fled, Pharaoh and his officials changed their minds about them and said, "What have we done? We have let the Israelites go and have lost their services!" ⁶So he had his chariot made ready and took his army with him. ⁷He took six hundred of the best chariots, along with all the other chariots of Egypt, with officers over all of them. ⁸The LORD hardened the heart of Pharaoh king of Egypt, so that he pursued the Israelites, who were marching out boldly. ⁹The Egyptians—all Pharaoh's horses and chariots, horsemen*a* and troops—pursued the Israelites and overtook them as they camped by the sea near Pi Hahiroth, opposite Baal Zephon.

¹⁰As Pharaoh approached, the Israelites looked up, and there were the Egyptians, marching after them. They were terrified and cried out to the LORD. ¹¹They said to Moses, "Was it because there were no graves in Egypt that you brought us to the desert to die? What have you done to us by bringing us out of Egypt? ¹²Didn't we say to you in Egypt, 'Leave us alone; let us serve the Egyptians'? It would have been better for us to serve the Egyptians than to die in the desert!"

¹³Moses answered the people, "Do not be afraid. Stand firm and you will see the deliverance the LORD will bring you today. The Egyptians you see today you will never see again. ¹⁴The LORD will fight for you; you need only to be still."

¹⁵Then the LORD said to Moses, "Why are you crying out to me? Tell the Israelites to move on. ¹⁶Raise your staff and stretch out your hand over the sea to divide the water so that the Israelites can go through the sea on dry ground. ¹⁷I will harden the hearts of the Egyptians so that they will go in after them. And I will gain glory through Pharaoh and all his army, through his chariots and his horsemen. ¹⁸The Egyptians will know that I am the LORD when I gain glory through Pharaoh, his chariots and his horsemen."

¹⁹Then the angel of God, who had been traveling in front of Israel's army, withdrew and went behind them. The pillar of cloud also moved from in front and stood behind them, ²⁰coming between the armies of Egypt and Israel. Throughout the night the cloud brought darkness to the one side and light to the other side; so neither went near the other all night long.

²¹Then Moses stretched out his hand over the sea, and all that night the LORD drove the sea back with a strong east wind and turned it into dry land. The waters were divided, ²²and the Israelites went through the sea on dry ground, with a wall of water on their right and on their left.

²³The Egyptians pursued them, and all Pharaoh's horses and chariots and horsemen followed them into the sea. ²⁴During the last watch of the night the LORD looked down from the pillar of fire and cloud at the Egyptian army and threw it into confusion. ²⁵He made the wheels of their chariots come off*b* so that they had difficulty driving. And the Egyptians said, "Let's get away from the Israelites! The LORD is fighting for them against Egypt."

²⁶Then the LORD said to Moses, "Stretch out your hand over the sea so that the waters may flow back over the Egyptians and their chariots and horsemen." ²⁷Moses stretched out his hand over the sea, and at daybreak

---

*a*9 Or *charioteers*; also in verses 17, 18, 23, 26 and 28   *b*25 Or *He jammed the wheels of their chariots* (see Samaritan Pentateuch, Septuagint and Syriac)

the sea went back to its place. The Egyptians were fleeing toward[a] it, and the LORD swept them into the sea. ²⁸The water flowed back and covered the chariots and horsemen—the entire army of Pharaoh that had followed the Israelites into the sea. Not one of them survived.

²⁹But the Israelites went through the sea on dry ground, with a wall of water on their right and on their left. ³⁰That day the LORD saved Israel from the hands of the Egyptians, and Israel saw the Egyptians lying dead on the shore. ³¹And when the Israelites saw the great power the LORD displayed

[a]27 Or *from*

VERSE:	AUTHOR:	PASSAGE:
Exodus 14:16	Joni Eareckson Tada	Exodus 14:10–22

Exchange the Meaning

When God parted the Red Sea, he told Moses to "raise your staff." After the glorious miracle occurred, Moses was careful to refer to it as "the staff of God" [Exodus 17:9]. It was just an ordinary stick of wood, but when the Lord chose it for his tool, the staff took on new ownership and meaning.

God can exchange the tragic meaning behind accidents or injuries for something new and positive. The cross is a good example. What was once a symbol of torture and pain now represents hope and salvation. My wheelchair, which once signified tragedy and confinement, is the very thing that now gives me freedom and mobility.

When God uses for his glory the most ordinary things—such as a staff, or a cross, or a wheelchair—he gives each one unique and special meaning.

What are the symbols of tragedy in your life? A crutch or hearing aid? Where you live? Your appearance or abilities? God can exchange the meaning of the heartbreak for something hopeful and positive. God did it at the cross, and he can do it for you.

ADDITIONAL SCRIPTURE READINGS
John 14:5–14; Colossians 2:6–15

Go to page 87 for your next devotional reading.

against the Egyptians, the people feared the Lord and put their trust in him and in Moses his servant.

The Song of Moses and Miriam

15 Then Moses and the Israelites sang this song to the Lord:

"I will sing to the Lord,
    for he is highly exalted.
The horse and its rider
    he has hurled into the sea.
²The Lord is my strength and my
        song;
    he has become my salvation.
He is my God, and I will praise
        him,
    my father's God, and I will
        exalt him.
³The Lord is a warrior;
    the Lord is his name.
⁴Pharaoh's chariots and his army
    he has hurled into the sea.
The best of Pharaoh's officers
    are drowned in the Red Sea.ᵃ
⁵The deep waters have covered
        them;
    they sank to the depths like a
        stone.

⁶"Your right hand, O Lord,
    was majestic in power.
Your right hand, O Lord,
    shattered the enemy.
⁷In the greatness of your majesty
    you threw down those who
        opposed you.
You unleashed your burning
        anger;
    it consumed them like stubble.
⁸By the blast of your nostrils
    the waters piled up.
The surging waters stood firm like
        a wall;
    the deep waters congealed in
        the heart of the sea.

⁹"The enemy boasted,
    'I will pursue, I will overtake
        them.
I will divide the spoils;
    I will gorge myself on them.
I will draw my sword

and my hand will destroy
        them.'
¹⁰But you blew with your breath,
    and the sea covered them.
They sank like lead
    in the mighty waters.

¹¹"Who among the gods is like you,
        O Lord?
Who is like you—
    majestic in holiness,
    awesome in glory,
        working wonders?
¹²You stretched out your right hand
    and the earth swallowed them.

¹³"In your unfailing love you will
        lead
    the people you have redeemed.
In your strength you will guide
        them
    to your holy dwelling.
¹⁴The nations will hear and tremble;
    anguish will grip the people of
        Philistia.
¹⁵The chiefs of Edom will be
        terrified,
    the leaders of Moab will be
        seized with trembling,
the peopleᵇ of Canaan will melt
        away;
¹⁶   terror and dread will fall upon
        them.
By the power of your arm
    they will be as still as a stone—
until your people pass by, O Lord,
    until the people you boughtᶜ
        pass by.
¹⁷You will bring them in and plant
        them
    on the mountain of your
        inheritance—
the place, O Lord, you made for
        your dwelling,
    the sanctuary, O Lord, your
        hands established.
¹⁸The Lord will reign
    for ever and ever."

¹⁹When Pharaoh's horses, chariots and horsemenᵈ went into the sea, the Lord brought the waters of the sea back over them, but the Israelites

---

ᵃ4 Hebrew *Yam Suph*; that is, Sea of Reeds; also in verse 22   ᵇ15 Or *rulers*   ᶜ16 Or *created*
ᵈ19 Or *charioteers*

walked through the sea on dry ground. ²⁰Then Miriam the prophetess, Aaron's sister, took a tambourine in her hand, and all the women followed her, with tambourines and dancing. ²¹Miriam sang to them:

"Sing to the LORD,
  for he is highly exalted.
The horse and its rider
  he has hurled into the sea."

The Waters of Marah and Elim

²²Then Moses led Israel from the Red Sea and they went into the Desert of Shur. For three days they traveled in the desert without finding water. ²³When they came to Marah, they could not drink its water because it was bitter. (That is why the place is called Marah.ᵃ) ²⁴So the people grumbled against Moses, saying, "What are we to drink?"

²⁵Then Moses cried out to the LORD, and the LORD showed him a piece of wood. He threw it into the water, and the water became sweet.

There the LORD made a decree and a law for them, and there he tested them. ²⁶He said, "If you listen carefully to the voice of the LORD your God and do what is right in his eyes, if you pay attention to his commands and keep all his decrees, I will not bring on you any of the diseases I brought on the Egyptians, for I am the LORD, who heals you."

²⁷Then they came to Elim, where there were twelve springs and seventy palm trees, and they camped there near the water.

Manna and Quail

16 The whole Israelite community set out from Elim and came to the Desert of Sin, which is between Elim and Sinai, on the fifteenth day of the second month after they had come out of Egypt. ²In the desert the whole community grumbled against Moses and Aaron. ³The Israelites said to them, "If only we had died by the LORD's hand in Egypt! There we sat around pots of meat and ate all the food we wanted, but you have brought us out into this desert to starve this entire assembly to death."

⁴Then the LORD said to Moses, "I will rain down bread from heaven for you. The people are to go out each day and gather enough for that day. In this way I will test them and see whether they will follow my instructions. ⁵On the sixth day they are to prepare what they bring in, and that is to be twice as much as they gather on the other days."

⁶So Moses and Aaron said to all the Israelites, "In the evening you will know that it was the LORD who brought you out of Egypt, ⁷and in the morning you will see the glory of the LORD, because he has heard your grumbling against him. Who are we, that you should grumble against us?" ⁸Moses also said, "You will know that it was the LORD when he gives you meat to eat in the evening and all the bread you want in the morning, because he has heard your grumbling against him. Who are we? You are not grumbling against us, but against the LORD."

⁹Then Moses told Aaron, "Say to the entire Israelite community, 'Come before the LORD, for he has heard your grumbling.' "

¹⁰While Aaron was speaking to the whole Israelite community, they looked toward the desert, and there was the glory of the LORD appearing in the cloud.

¹¹The LORD said to Moses, ¹²"I have heard the grumbling of the Israelites. Tell them, 'At twilight you will eat meat, and in the morning you will be filled with bread. Then you will know that I am the LORD your God.' "

¹³That evening quail came and covered the camp, and in the morning there was a layer of dew around the camp. ¹⁴When the dew was gone, thin flakes like frost on the ground appeared on the desert floor. ¹⁵When the Israelites saw it, they said to each oth-

---

ᵃ23 Marah means bitter.

PASSAGE: Exodus 14:13–31; Psalm 31:1–5
AUTHOR: John Henry Newman

The Pillar of the Cloud

Lead, Kindly Light, amid the circling gloom,
    Lead Thou me on!
The night is dark, and I am far from home —
    Lead Thou me on!
Keep Thou my feet; I do not ask to see
The distant scene — one step enough for me.

I was not ever thus, nor prayed that Thou
    Shouldst lead me on!
I loved to choose and see my path; but now
    Lead Thou me on!
I loved the garish day, and, spite of fears,
Pride ruled my will: remember not past years.

So long Thy power hath blest me, sure it still
    Will lead me on,
O'er moor and fen, o'er crag and torrent, till
    The night is gone;
And with the morn those angel faces smile
Which I have loved long since, and lost awhile.

Go to page 90 for your next devotional reading.

er, "What is it?" For they did not know what it was.

Moses said to them, "It is the bread the Lord has given you to eat. ¹⁶This is what the Lord has commanded: 'Each one is to gather as much as he needs. Take an omer[a] for each person you have in your tent.' "

¹⁷The Israelites did as they were told; some gathered much, some little. ¹⁸And when they measured it by the omer, he who gathered much did not have too much, and he who gathered little did not have too little. Each one gathered as much as he needed.

¹⁹Then Moses said to them, "No one is to keep any of it until morning."

²⁰However, some of them paid no attention to Moses; they kept part of it until morning, but it was full of maggots and began to smell. So Moses was angry with them.

²¹Each morning everyone gathered as much as he needed, and when the sun grew hot, it melted away. ²²On the sixth day, they gathered twice as much—two omers[b] for each person—and the leaders of the community came and reported this to Moses. ²³He said to them, "This is what the Lord commanded: 'Tomorrow is to be a day of rest, a holy Sabbath to the Lord. So bake what you want to bake and boil what you want to boil. Save whatever is left and keep it until morning.' "

²⁴So they saved it until morning, as Moses commanded, and it did not stink or get maggots in it. ²⁵"Eat it today," Moses said, "because today is a Sabbath to the Lord. You will not find any of it on the ground today. ²⁶Six days you are to gather it, but on the seventh day, the Sabbath, there will not be any."

²⁷Nevertheless, some of the people went out on the seventh day to gather it, but they found none. ²⁸Then the Lord said to Moses, "How long will you[c] refuse to keep my commands

and my instructions? ²⁹Bear in mind that the Lord has given you the Sabbath; that is why on the sixth day he gives you bread for two days. Everyone is to stay where he is on the seventh day; no one is to go out." ³⁰So the people rested on the seventh day.

³¹The people of Israel called the bread manna.[d] It was white like coriander seed and tasted like wafers made with honey. ³²Moses said, "This is what the Lord has commanded: 'Take an omer of manna and keep it for the generations to come, so they can see the bread I gave you to eat in the desert when I brought you out of Egypt.' "

³³So Moses said to Aaron, "Take a jar and put an omer of manna in it. Then place it before the Lord to be kept for the generations to come."

³⁴As the Lord commanded Moses, Aaron put the manna in front of the Testimony, that it might be kept. ³⁵The Israelites ate manna forty years, until they came to a land that was settled; they ate manna until they reached the border of Canaan.

³⁶(An omer is one tenth of an ephah.)

Water From the Rock

17 The whole Israelite community set out from the Desert of Sin, traveling from place to place as the Lord commanded. They camped at Rephidim, but there was no water for the people to drink. ²So they quarreled with Moses and said, "Give us water to drink."

Moses replied, "Why do you quarrel with me? Why do you put the Lord to the test?"

³But the people were thirsty for water there, and they grumbled against Moses. They said, "Why did you bring us up out of Egypt to make us and our children and livestock die of thirst?"

⁴Then Moses cried out to the Lord,

---

[a]16 That is, probably about 2 quarts (about 2 liters); also in verses 18, 32, 33 and 36   [b]22 That is, probably about 4 quarts (about 4.5 liters)   [c]28 The Hebrew is plural.   [d]31 Manna means What is it? (see verse 15).

"What am I to do with these people? They are almost ready to stone me."

⁵The LORD answered Moses, "Walk on ahead of the people. Take with you some of the elders of Israel and take in your hand the staff with which you struck the Nile, and go. ⁶I will stand there before you by the rock at Horeb. Strike the rock, and water will come out of it for the people to drink." So Moses did this in the sight of the elders of Israel. ⁷And he called the place Massah*ᵃ* and Meribah*ᵇ* because the Israelites quarreled and because they tested the LORD saying, "Is the LORD among us or not?"

The Amalekites Defeated

⁸The Amalekites came and attacked the Israelites at Rephidim. ⁹Moses said to Joshua, "Choose some of our men and go out to fight the Amalekites. Tomorrow I will stand on top of the hill with the staff of God in my hands."

¹⁰So Joshua fought the Amalekites as Moses had ordered, and Moses, Aaron and Hur went to the top of the hill. ¹¹As long as Moses held up his hands, the Israelites were winning, but whenever he lowered his hands, the Amalekites were winning. ¹²When Moses' hands grew tired, they took a stone and put it under him and he sat on it. Aaron and Hur held his hands up—one on one side, one on the other—so that his hands remained steady till sunset. ¹³So Joshua overcame the Amalekite army with the sword.

¹⁴Then the LORD said to Moses, "Write this on a scroll as something to be remembered and make sure that Joshua hears it, because I will completely blot out the memory of Amalek from under heaven."

¹⁵Moses built an altar and called it The LORD is my Banner. ¹⁶He said, "For hands were lifted up to the throne of the LORD. The*ᶜ* LORD will be at war against the Amalekites from generation to generation."

Jethro Visits Moses

18 Now Jethro, the priest of Midian and father-in-law of Moses, heard of everything God had done for Moses and for his people Israel, and how the LORD had brought Israel out of Egypt.

²After Moses had sent away his wife Zipporah, his father-in-law Jethro received her ³and her two sons. One son was named Gershom,*ᵈ* for Moses said, "I have become an alien in a foreign land"; ⁴and the other was named Eliezer,*ᵉ* for he said, "My father's God was my helper; he saved me from the sword of Pharaoh."

⁵Jethro, Moses' father-in-law, together with Moses' sons and wife, came to him in the desert, where he was camped near the mountain of God. ⁶Jethro had sent word to him, "I, your father-in-law Jethro, am coming to you with your wife and her two sons."

⁷So Moses went out to meet his father-in-law and bowed down and kissed him. They greeted each other and then went into the tent. ⁸Moses told his father-in-law about everything the LORD had done to Pharaoh and the Egyptians for Israel's sake and about all the hardships they had met along the way and how the LORD had saved them.

⁹Jethro was delighted to hear about all the good things the LORD had done for Israel in rescuing them from the hand of the Egyptians. ¹⁰He said, "Praise be to the LORD, who rescued you from the hand of the Egyptians and of Pharaoh, and who rescued the people from the hand of the Egyptians. ¹¹Now I know that the LORD is greater than all other gods, for he did this to those who had treated Israel arrogantly." ¹²Then Jethro, Moses' father-in-law, brought a burnt offering and other sacrifices to God, and Aar-

---

ᵃ7 Massah means *testing.*   *ᵇ7 Meribah* means *quarreling.*   *ᶜ16 Or "Because a hand was against the throne of the* LORD, *the* *ᵈ3 Gershom* sounds like the Hebrew for *an alien there.*   *ᵉ4 Eliezer* means *my God is helper.*

VERSE:	AUTHOR:	PASSAGE:
Exodus 17:12	J. Oswald Sanders	Exodus 17:8–16

Weaponless Hands of Prayer

The story of the conflict between Joshua and the Amalekites gives an encouraging parabolic illustration of the joy of intercessory ministry that is open to . . . octogenarians. In the fluctuations of that battle, the key to final victory was not in the hands of Joshua and his army battling in the valley, but in those of Moses and Aaron and Hur—all octogenarians—on the mountaintop. As long as Moses held aloft his staff—symbol of his divinely given authority—the battle swayed in favor of Israel. But when from sheer weariness he allowed it to fall, victory turned to defeat . . .

It proved to be *weaponless hands of prayer* on the mountain rather than the clash of arms in the valley that controlled the tides of battle. When Moses could no longer stand, he sat. When he could no longer hold his hands up, Aaron and Hur on either side held them aloft until victory was complete.

Old as they were, those three were young enough to be God's hidden instruments in victory. *Elderly people can pray*, and prayer is more powerful than arms. Through the ministry of intercession and the exercise of their spiritual authority, those old men strengthened the hands of the younger Joshua and his men who were struggling on the battlefront. Is that not a model for us today?

ADDITIONAL SCRIPTURE READINGS
Romans 12:9–16; James 5:13–18

Go to page 108 for your next devotional reading.

on came with all the elders of Israel to eat bread with Moses' father-in-law in the presence of God.

¹³The next day Moses took his seat to serve as judge for the people, and they stood around him from morning till evening. ¹⁴When his father-in-law saw all that Moses was doing for the people, he said, "What is this you are doing for the people? Why do you alone sit as judge, while all these people stand around you from morning till evening?"

¹⁵Moses answered him, "Because the people come to me to seek God's will. ¹⁶Whenever they have a dispute, it is brought to me, and I decide between the parties and inform them of God's decrees and laws."

¹⁷Moses' father-in-law replied, "What you are doing is not good. ¹⁸You and these people who come to you will only wear yourselves out. The work is too heavy for you; you cannot handle it alone. ¹⁹Listen now to me and I will give you some advice, and may God be with you. You must be the people's representative before God and bring their disputes to him. ²⁰Teach them the decrees and laws, and show them the way to live and the duties they are to perform. ²¹But select capable men from all the people—men who fear God, trustworthy men who hate dishonest gain—and appoint them as officials over thousands, hundreds, fifties and tens. ²²Have them serve as judges for the people at all times, but have them bring every difficult case to you; the simple cases they can decide themselves. That will make your load lighter, because they will share it with you. ²³If you do this and God so commands, you will be able to stand the strain, and all these people will go home satisfied."

²⁴Moses listened to his father-in-law and did everything he said. ²⁵He chose capable men from all Israel and made them leaders of the people, officials over thousands, hundreds, fifties and tens. ²⁶They served as judges for the people at all times. The difficult cases they brought to Moses, but the simple ones they decided themselves.

²⁷Then Moses sent his father-in-law on his way, and Jethro returned to his own country.

At Mount Sinai

19 In the third month after the Israelites left Egypt—on the very day—they came to the Desert of Sinai. ²After they set out from Rephidim, they entered the Desert of Sinai, and Israel camped there in the desert in front of the mountain.

³Then Moses went up to God, and the LORD called to him from the mountain and said, "This is what you are to say to the house of Jacob and what you are to tell the people of Israel: ⁴'You yourselves have seen what I did to Egypt, and how I carried you on eagles' wings and brought you to myself. ⁵Now if you obey me fully and keep my covenant, then out of all nations you will be my treasured possession. Although the whole earth is mine, ⁶youᵃ will be for me a kingdom of priests and a holy nation.' These are the words you are to speak to the Israelites."

⁷So Moses went back and summoned the elders of the people and set before them all the words the LORD had commanded him to speak. ⁸The people all responded together, "We will do everything the LORD has said." So Moses brought their answer back to the LORD.

⁹The LORD said to Moses, "I am going to come to you in a dense cloud, so that the people will hear me speaking with you and will always put their trust in you." Then Moses told the LORD what the people had said.

¹⁰And the LORD said to Moses, "Go to the people and consecrate them today and tomorrow. Have them wash their clothes ¹¹and be ready by the third day, because on that day the LORD will come down on Mount Sinai in the sight of all the people. ¹²Put limits for the people around the

---

ᵃ5,6 Or possession, for the whole earth is mine. 6You

mountain and tell them, 'Be careful that you do not go up the mountain or touch the foot of it. Whoever touches the mountain shall surely be put to death. ¹³He shall surely be stoned or shot with arrows; not a hand is to be laid on him. Whether man or animal, he shall not be permitted to live.' Only when the ram's horn sounds a long blast may they go up to the mountain."

¹⁴After Moses had gone down the mountain to the people, he consecrated them, and they washed their clothes. ¹⁵Then he said to the people, "Prepare yourselves for the third day. Abstain from sexual relations."

¹⁶On the morning of the third day there was thunder and lightning, with a thick cloud over the mountain, and a very loud trumpet blast. Everyone in the camp trembled. ¹⁷Then Moses led the people out of the camp to meet with God, and they stood at the foot of the mountain. ¹⁸Mount Sinai was covered with smoke, because the LORD descended on it in fire. The smoke billowed up from it like smoke from a furnace, the whole mountainᵃ trembled violently, ¹⁹and the sound of the trumpet grew louder and louder. Then Moses spoke and the voice of God answered him.ᵇ

²⁰The LORD descended to the top of Mount Sinai and called Moses to the top of the mountain. So Moses went up ²¹and the LORD said to him, "Go down and warn the people so they do not force their way through to see the LORD and many of them perish. ²²Even the priests, who approach the LORD, must consecrate themselves, or the LORD will break out against them."

²³Moses said to the LORD, "The people cannot come up Mount Sinai, because you yourself warned us, 'Put limits around the mountain and set it apart as holy.' "

²⁴The LORD replied, "Go down and bring Aaron up with you. But the priests and the people must not force their way through to come up to the LORD, or he will break out against them."

²⁵So Moses went down to the people and told them.

The Ten Commandments

20 And God spoke all these words:

²"I am the LORD your God, who brought you out of Egypt, out of the land of slavery.

³"You shall have no other gods beforeᶜ me.

⁴"You shall not make for yourself an idol in the form of anything in heaven above or on the earth beneath or in the waters below. ⁵You shall not bow down to them or worship them; for I, the LORD your God, am a jealous God, punishing the children for the sin of the fathers to the third and fourth generation of those who hate me, ⁶but showing love to a thousand ⌊generations⌋ of those who love me and keep my commandments.

⁷"You shall not misuse the name of the LORD your God, for the LORD will not hold anyone guiltless who misuses his name.

⁸"Remember the Sabbath day by keeping it holy. ⁹Six days you shall labor and do all your work, ¹⁰but the seventh day is a Sabbath to the LORD your God. On it you shall not do any work, neither you, nor your son or daughter, nor your manservant or maidservant, nor your animals, nor the alien within your gates. ¹¹For in six days the LORD made the heavens and the earth, the sea, and all that

---

ᵃ18 Most Hebrew manuscripts; a few Hebrew manuscripts and Septuagint *all the people*
ᵇ19 Or *and God answered him with thunder*   ᶜ3 Or *besides*

is in them, but he rested on the seventh day. Therefore the LORD blessed the Sabbath day and made it holy.

¹²"Honor your father and your mother, so that you may live long in the land the LORD your God is giving you.

¹³"You shall not murder.

¹⁴"You shall not commit adultery.

¹⁵"You shall not steal.

¹⁶"You shall not give false testimony against your neighbor.

¹⁷"You shall not covet your neighbor's house. You shall not covet your neighbor's wife, or his manservant or maidservant, his ox or donkey, or anything that belongs to your neighbor."

¹⁸When the people saw the thunder and lightning and heard the trumpet and saw the mountain in smoke, they trembled with fear. They stayed at a distance ¹⁹and said to Moses, "Speak to us yourself and we will listen. But do not have God speak to us or we will die."

²⁰Moses said to the people, "Do not be afraid. God has come to test you, so that the fear of God will be with you to keep you from sinning."

²¹The people remained at a distance, while Moses approached the thick darkness where God was.

Idols and Altars

²²Then the LORD said to Moses, "Tell the Israelites this: 'You have seen for yourselves that I have spoken to you from heaven: ²³Do not make any gods to be alongside me; do not make for yourselves gods of silver or gods of gold.

²⁴" 'Make an altar of earth for me and sacrifice on it your burnt offerings and fellowship offerings,^a your sheep and goats and your cattle. Wherever I cause my name to be honored, I will come to you and bless

you. ²⁵If you make an altar of stones for me, do not build it with dressed stones, for you will defile it if you use a tool on it. ²⁶And do not go up to my altar on steps, lest your nakedness be exposed on it.'

21 "These are the laws you are to set before them:

Hebrew Servants

²"If you buy a Hebrew servant, he is to serve you for six years. But in the seventh year, he shall go free, without paying anything. ³If he comes alone, he is to go free alone; but if he has a wife when he comes, she is to go with him. ⁴If his master gives him a wife and she bears him sons or daughters, the woman and her children shall belong to her master, and only the man shall go free.

⁵"But if the servant declares, 'I love my master and my wife and children and do not want to go free,' ⁶then his master must take him before the judges.^b He shall take him to the door or the doorpost and pierce his ear with an awl. Then he will be his servant for life.

⁷"If a man sells his daughter as a servant, she is not to go free as menservants do. ⁸If she does not please the master who has selected her for himself,^c he must let her be redeemed. He has no right to sell her to foreigners, because he has broken faith with her. ⁹If he selects her for his son, he must grant her the rights of a daughter. ¹⁰If he marries another woman, he must not deprive the first one of her food, clothing and marital rights. ¹¹If he does not provide her with these three things, she is to go free, without any payment of money.

Personal Injuries

¹²"Anyone who strikes a man and kills him shall surely be put to death. ¹³However, if he does not do it intentionally, but God lets it happen, he is to flee to a place I will designate. ¹⁴But if a man schemes and kills another

^a24 Traditionally *peace offerings*   ^b6 Or *before God*   ^c8 Or *master so that he does not choose her*

man deliberately, take him away from my altar and put him to death.

¹⁵"Anyone who attacks[a] his father or his mother must be put to death.

¹⁶"Anyone who kidnaps another and either sells him or still has him when he is caught must be put to death.

¹⁷"Anyone who curses his father or mother must be put to death.

¹⁸"If men quarrel and one hits the other with a stone or with his fist[b] and he does not die but is confined to bed, ¹⁹the one who struck the blow will not be held responsible if the other gets up and walks around outside with his staff; however, he must pay the injured man for the loss of his time and see that he is completely healed.

²⁰"If a man beats his male or female slave with a rod and the slave dies as a direct result, he must be punished, ²¹but he is not to be punished if the slave gets up after a day or two, since the slave is his property.

²²"If men who are fighting hit a pregnant woman and she gives birth prematurely[c] but there is no serious injury, the offender must be fined whatever the woman's husband demands and the court allows. ²³But if there is serious injury, you are to take life for life, ²⁴eye for eye, tooth for tooth, hand for hand, foot for foot, ²⁵burn for burn, wound for wound, bruise for bruise.

²⁶"If a man hits a manservant or maidservant in the eye and destroys it, he must let the servant go free to compensate for the eye. ²⁷And if he knocks out the tooth of a manservant or maidservant, he must let the servant go free to compensate for the tooth.

²⁸"If a bull gores a man or a woman to death, the bull must be stoned to death, and its meat must not be eaten. But the owner of the bull will not be held responsible. ²⁹If, however, the bull has had the habit of goring and the owner has been warned but has not kept it penned up and it kills a man or woman, the bull must be stoned and the owner also must be put to death. ³⁰However, if payment is demanded of him, he may redeem his life by paying whatever is demanded. ³¹This law also applies if the bull gores a son or daughter. ³²If the bull gores a male or female slave, the owner must pay thirty shekels[d] of silver to the master of the slave, and the bull must be stoned.

³³"If a man uncovers a pit or digs one and fails to cover it and an ox or a donkey falls into it, ³⁴the owner of the pit must pay for the loss; he must pay its owner, and the dead animal will be his.

³⁵"If a man's bull injures the bull of another and it dies, they are to sell the live one and divide both the money and the dead animal equally. ³⁶However, if it was known that the bull had the habit of goring, yet the owner did not keep it penned up, the owner must pay, animal for animal, and the dead animal will be his.

Protection of Property

22 "If a man steals an ox or a sheep and slaughters it or sells it, he must pay back five head of cattle for the ox and four sheep for the sheep.

²"If a thief is caught breaking in and is struck so that he dies, the defender is not guilty of bloodshed; ³but if it happens[e] after sunrise, he is guilty of bloodshed.

"A thief must certainly make restitution, but if he has nothing, he must be sold to pay for his theft.

⁴"If the stolen animal is found alive in his possession—whether ox or donkey or sheep—he must pay back double.

⁵"If a man grazes his livestock in a field or vineyard and lets them stray and they graze in another man's field, he must make restitution from the best of his own field or vineyard.

⁶"If a fire breaks out and spreads

ᵃ15 Or kills   ᵇ18 Or with a tool   ᶜ22 Or she has a miscarriage   ᵈ32 That is, about 12 ounces (about 0.3 kilogram)   ᵉ3 Or if he strikes him into thornbushes so that it burns shocks of grain or standing grain or the whole field, the one who started the fire must make restitution.

⁷"If a man gives his neighbor silver or goods for safekeeping and they are stolen from the neighbor's house, the thief, if he is caught, must pay back double. ⁸But if the thief is not found, the owner of the house must appear before the judges[a] to determine whether he has laid his hands on the other man's property. ⁹In all cases of illegal possession of an ox, a donkey, a sheep, a garment, or any other lost property about which somebody says, 'This is mine,' both parties are to bring their cases before the judges. The one whom the judges declare[b] guilty must pay back double to his neighbor.

¹⁰"If a man gives a donkey, an ox, a sheep or any other animal to his neighbor for safekeeping and it dies or is injured or is taken away while no one is looking, ¹¹the issue between them will be settled by the taking of an oath before the Lord that the neighbor did not lay hands on the other person's property. The owner is to accept this, and no restitution is required. ¹²But if the animal was stolen from the neighbor, he must make restitution to the owner. ¹³If it was torn to pieces by a wild animal, he shall bring in the remains as evidence and he will not be required to pay for the torn animal.

¹⁴"If a man borrows an animal from his neighbor and it is injured or dies while the owner is not present, he must make restitution. ¹⁵But if the owner is with the animal, the borrower will not have to pay. If the animal was hired, the money paid for the hire covers the loss.

Social Responsibility

¹⁶"If a man seduces a virgin who is not pledged to be married and sleeps with her, he must pay the bride-price, and she shall be his wife. ¹⁷If her father absolutely refuses to give her to him, he must still pay the bride-price for virgins.

¹⁸"Do not allow a sorceress to live.

¹⁹"Anyone who has sexual relations with an animal must be put to death.

²⁰"Whoever sacrifices to any god other than the Lord must be destroyed.[c]

²¹"Do not mistreat an alien or oppress him, for you were aliens in Egypt.

²²"Do not take advantage of a widow or an orphan. ²³If you do and they cry out to me, I will certainly hear their cry. ²⁴My anger will be aroused, and I will kill you with the sword; your wives will become widows and your children fatherless.

²⁵"If you lend money to one of my people among you who is needy, do not be like a moneylender; charge him no interest.[d] ²⁶If you take your neighbor's cloak as a pledge, return it to him by sunset, ²⁷because his cloak is the only covering he has for his body. What else will he sleep in? When he cries out to me, I will hear, for I am compassionate.

²⁸"Do not blaspheme God[e] or curse the ruler of your people.

²⁹"Do not hold back offerings from your granaries or your vats.[f]

"You must give me the firstborn of your sons. ³⁰Do the same with your cattle and your sheep. Let them stay with their mothers for seven days, but give them to me on the eighth day.

³¹"You are to be my holy people. So do not eat the meat of an animal torn by wild beasts; throw it to the dogs.

Laws of Justice and Mercy

23 "Do not spread false reports. Do not help a wicked man by being a malicious witness.

²"Do not follow the crowd in doing wrong. When you give testimony in a

---

[a]8 Or *before God*; also in verse 9   [b]9 Or *whom God declares*   [c]20 The Hebrew term refers to the irrevocable giving over of things or persons to the Lord, often by totally destroying them.   [d]25 Or *excessive interest*   [e]28 Or *Do not revile the judges*   [f]29 The meaning of the Hebrew for this phrase is uncertain.

lawsuit, do not pervert justice by siding with the crowd, ³and do not show favoritism to a poor man in his lawsuit.

⁴"If you come across your enemy's ox or donkey wandering off, be sure to take it back to him. ⁵If you see the donkey of someone who hates you fallen down under its load, do not leave it there; be sure you help him with it.

⁶"Do not deny justice to your poor people in their lawsuits. ⁷Have nothing to do with a false charge and do not put an innocent or honest person to death, for I will not acquit the guilty.

⁸"Do not accept a bribe, for a bribe blinds those who see and twists the words of the righteous.

⁹"Do not oppress an alien; you yourselves know how it feels to be aliens, because you were aliens in Egypt.

Sabbath Laws

¹⁰"For six years you are to sow your fields and harvest the crops, ¹¹but during the seventh year let the land lie unplowed and unused. Then the poor among your people may get food from it, and the wild animals may eat what they leave. Do the same with your vineyard and your olive grove.

¹²"Six days do your work, but on the seventh day do not work, so that your ox and your donkey may rest and the slave born in your household, and the alien as well, may be refreshed.

¹³"Be careful to do everything I have said to you. Do not invoke the names of other gods; do not let them be heard on your lips.

The Three Annual Festivals

¹⁴"Three times a year you are to celebrate a festival to me.

¹⁵"Celebrate the Feast of Unleavened Bread; for seven days eat bread made without yeast, as I commanded you. Do this at the appointed time in the month of Abib, for in that month you came out of Egypt.

"No one is to appear before me empty-handed.

¹⁶"Celebrate the Feast of Harvest with the firstfruits of the crops you sow in your field.

"Celebrate the Feast of Ingathering at the end of the year, when you gather in your crops from the field.

¹⁷"Three times a year all the men are to appear before the Sovereign LORD.

¹⁸"Do not offer the blood of a sacrifice to me along with anything containing yeast.

"The fat of my festival offerings must not be kept until morning.

¹⁹"Bring the best of the firstfruits of your soil to the house of the LORD your God.

"Do not cook a young goat in its mother's milk.

God's Angel to Prepare the Way

²⁰"See, I am sending an angel ahead of you to guard you along the way and to bring you to the place I have prepared. ²¹Pay attention to him and listen to what he says. Do not rebel against him; he will not forgive your rebellion, since my Name is in him. ²²If you listen carefully to what he says and do all that I say, I will be an enemy to your enemies and will oppose those who oppose you. ²³My angel will go ahead of you and bring you into the land of the Amorites, Hittites, Perizzites, Canaanites, Hivites and Jebusites, and I will wipe them out. ²⁴Do not bow down before their gods or worship them or follow their practices. You must demolish them and break their sacred stones to pieces. ²⁵Worship the LORD your God, and his blessing will be on your food and water. I will take away sickness from among you, ²⁶and none will miscarry or be barren in your land. I will give you a full life span.

²⁷"I will send my terror ahead of you and throw into confusion every nation you encounter. I will make all your enemies turn their backs and run. ²⁸I will send the hornet ahead of you to drive the Hivites, Canaanites and Hittites out of your way. ²⁹But I

will not drive them out in a single year, because the land would become desolate and the wild animals too numerous for you. ³⁰Little by little I will drive them out before you, until you have increased enough to take possession of the land.

³¹"I will establish your borders from the Red Sea[a] to the Sea of the Philistines,[b] and from the desert to the River.[c] I will hand over to you the people who live in the land and you will drive them out before you. ³²Do not make a covenant with them or with their gods. ³³Do not let them live in your land, or they will cause you to sin against me, because the worship of their gods will certainly be a snare to you."

The Covenant Confirmed

24 Then he said to Moses, "Come up to the LORD, you and Aaron, Nadab and Abihu, and seventy of the elders of Israel. You are to worship at a distance, ²but Moses alone is to approach the LORD; the others must not come near. And the people may not come up with him."

³When Moses went and told the people all the LORD's words and laws, they responded with one voice, "Everything the LORD has said we will do." ⁴Moses then wrote down everything the LORD had said.

He got up early the next morning and built an altar at the foot of the mountain and set up twelve stone pillars representing the twelve tribes of Israel. ⁵Then he sent young Israelite men, and they offered burnt offerings and sacrificed young bulls as fellowship offerings[d] to the LORD. ⁶Moses took half of the blood and put it in bowls, and the other half he sprinkled on the altar. ⁷Then he took the Book of the Covenant and read it to the people. They responded, "We will do everything the LORD has said; we will obey."

⁸Moses then took the blood, sprinkled it on the people and said, "This is the blood of the covenant that the LORD has made with you in accordance with all these words."

⁹Moses and Aaron, Nadab and Abihu, and the seventy elders of Israel went up ¹⁰and saw the God of Israel. Under his feet was something like a pavement made of sapphire,[e] clear as the sky itself. ¹¹But God did not raise his hand against these leaders of the Israelites; they saw God, and they ate and drank.

¹²The LORD said to Moses, "Come up to me on the mountain and stay here, and I will give you the tablets of stone, with the law and commands I have written for their instruction."

¹³Then Moses set out with Joshua his aide, and Moses went up on the mountain of God. ¹⁴He said to the elders, "Wait here for us until we come back to you. Aaron and Hur are with you, and anyone involved in a dispute can go to them."

¹⁵When Moses went up on the mountain, the cloud covered it, ¹⁶and the glory of the LORD settled on Mount Sinai. For six days the cloud covered the mountain, and on the seventh day the LORD called to Moses from within the cloud. ¹⁷To the Israelites the glory of the LORD looked like a consuming fire on top of the mountain. ¹⁸Then Moses entered the cloud as he went on up the mountain. And he stayed on the mountain forty days and forty nights.

Offerings for the Tabernacle

25 The LORD said to Moses, ²"Tell the Israelites to bring me an offering. You are to receive the offering for me from each man whose heart prompts him to give. ³These are the offerings you are to receive from them: gold, silver and bronze; ⁴blue, purple and scarlet yarn and fine linen; goat hair; ⁵ram skins dyed red and hides of sea cows[f]; acacia wood; ⁶olive oil for the light; spices for the anointing oil and for the fragrant incense; ⁷and onyx stones and other gems to be mounted on the ephod and breastpiece.

⁸"Then have them make a sanctuary for me, and I will dwell among them. ⁹Make this tabernacle and all its furnishings exactly like the pattern I will show you.

The Ark

¹⁰"Have them make a chest of acacia wood—two and a half cubits long, a cubit and a half wide, and a cubit and a half high.ᵃ ¹¹Overlay it with pure gold, both inside and out, and make a gold molding around it. ¹²Cast four gold rings for it and fasten them to its four feet, with two rings on one side and two rings on the other. ¹³Then make poles of acacia wood and overlay them with gold. ¹⁴Insert the poles into the rings on the sides of the chest to carry it. ¹⁵The poles are to remain in the rings of this ark; they are not to be removed. ¹⁶Then put in the ark the Testimony, which I will give you.

¹⁷"Make an atonement coverᵇ of pure gold—two and a half cubits long and a cubit and a half wide.ᶜ ¹⁸And make two cherubim out of hammered gold at the ends of the cover. ¹⁹Make one cherub on one end and the second cherub on the other; make the cherubim of one piece with the cover, at the two ends. ²⁰The cherubim are to have their wings spread upward, overshadowing the cover with them. The cherubim are to face each other, looking toward the cover. ²¹Place the cover on top of the ark and put in the ark the Testimony, which I will give you. ²²There, above the cover between the two cherubim that are over the ark of the Testimony, I will meet with you and give you all my commands for the Israelites.

The Table

²³"Make a table of acacia wood—

two cubits long, a cubit wide and a cubit and a half high.ᵈ ²⁴Overlay it with pure gold and make a gold molding around it. ²⁵Also make around it a rim a handbreadthᵉ wide and put a gold molding on the rim. ²⁶Make four gold rings for the table and fasten them to the four corners, where the four legs are. ²⁷The rings are to be close to the rim to hold the poles used in carrying the table. ²⁸Make the poles of acacia wood, overlay them with gold and carry the table with them. ²⁹And make its plates and dishes of pure gold, as well as its pitchers and bowls for the pouring out of offerings. ³⁰Put the bread of the Presence on this table to be before me at all times.

The Lampstand

³¹"Make a lampstand of pure gold and hammer it out, base and shaft; its flowerlike cups, buds and blossoms shall be of one piece with it. ³²Six branches are to extend from the sides of the lampstand—three on one side and three on the other. ³³Three cups shaped like almond flowers with buds and blossoms are to be on one branch, three on the next branch, and the same for all six branches extending from the lampstand. ³⁴And on the lampstand there are to be four cups shaped like almond flowers with buds and blossoms. ³⁵One bud shall be under the first pair of branches extending from the lampstand, a second bud under the second pair, and a third bud under the third pair—six branches in all. ³⁶The buds and branches shall all be of one piece with the lampstand, hammered out of pure gold.

³⁷"Then make its seven lamps and set them up on it so that they light the space in front of it. ³⁸Its wick trimmers and trays are to be of pure gold. ³⁹A talentᶠ of pure gold is to be used for

---

ᵃ10 That is, about 3 3/4 feet (about 1.1 meters) long and 2 1/4 feet (about 0.7 meter) wide and high   ᵇ17 Traditionally *a mercy seat*   ᶜ17 That is, about 3 3/4 feet (about 1.1 meters) long and 2 1/4 feet (about 0.7 meter) wide   ᵈ23 That is, about 3 feet (about 0.9 meter) long and 1 1/2 feet (about 0.5 meter) wide and 2 1/4 feet (about 0.7 meter) high   ᵉ25 That is, about 3 inches (about 8 centimeters)   ᶠ39 That is, about 75 pounds (about 34 kilograms)

the lampstand and all these accessories. ⁴⁰See that you make them according to the pattern shown you on the mountain.

The Tabernacle

26 "Make the tabernacle with ten curtains of finely twisted linen and blue, purple and scarlet yarn, with cherubim worked into them by a skilled craftsman. ²All the curtains are to be the same size—twenty-eight cubits long and four cubits wide.ᵃ ³Join five of the curtains together, and do the same with the other five. ⁴Make loops of blue material along the edge of the end curtain in one set, and do the same with the end curtain in the other set. ⁵Make fifty loops on one curtain and fifty loops on the end curtain of the other set, with the loops opposite each other. ⁶Then make fifty gold clasps and use them to fasten the curtains together so that the tabernacle is a unit.

⁷"Make curtains of goat hair for the tent over the tabernacle—eleven altogether. ⁸All eleven curtains are to be the same size—thirty cubits long and four cubits wide.ᵇ ⁹Join five of the curtains together into one set and the other six into another set. Fold the sixth curtain double at the front of the tent. ¹⁰Make fifty loops along the edge of the end curtain in one set and also along the edge of the end curtain in the other set. ¹¹Then make fifty bronze clasps and put them in the loops to fasten the tent together as a unit. ¹²As for the additional length of the tent curtains, the half curtain that is left over is to hang down at the rear of the tabernacle. ¹³The tent curtains will be a cubitᶜ longer on both sides; what is left will hang over the sides of the tabernacle so as to cover it. ¹⁴Make for the tent a covering of ram skins dyed red, and over that a covering of hides of sea cows.ᵈ

¹⁵"Make upright frames of acacia wood for the tabernacle. ¹⁶Each frame is to be ten cubits long and a cubit and a half wide,ᵉ ¹⁷with two projections set parallel to each other. Make all the frames of the tabernacle in this way. ¹⁸Make twenty frames for the south side of the tabernacle ¹⁹and make forty silver bases to go under them—two bases for each frame, one under each projection. ²⁰For the other side, the north side of the tabernacle, make twenty frames ²¹and forty silver bases—two under each frame. ²²Make six frames for the far end, that is, the west end of the tabernacle, ²³and make two frames for the corners at the far end. ²⁴At these two corners they must be double from the bottom all the way to the top, and fitted into a single ring; both shall be like that. ²⁵So there will be eight frames and sixteen silver bases—two under each frame.

²⁶"Also make crossbars of acacia wood: five for the frames on one side of the tabernacle, ²⁷five for those on the other side, and five for the frames on the west, at the far end of the tabernacle. ²⁸The center crossbar is to extend from end to end at the middle of the frames. ²⁹Overlay the frames with gold and make gold rings to hold the crossbars. Also overlay the crossbars with gold.

³⁰"Set up the tabernacle according to the plan shown you on the mountain.

³¹"Make a curtain of blue, purple and scarlet yarn and finely twisted linen, with cherubim worked into it by a skilled craftsman. ³²Hang it with gold hooks on four posts of acacia wood overlaid with gold and standing on four silver bases. ³³Hang the curtain from the clasps and place the ark of the Testimony behind the curtain. The curtain will separate the Holy Place from the Most Holy Place. ³⁴Put the atonement cover on the ark of the Testimony in the Most Holy

---

ᵃ2 That is, about 42 feet (about 12.5 meters) long and 6 feet (about 1.8 meters) wide   ᵇ8 That is, about 45 feet (about 13.5 meters) long and 6 feet (about 1.8 meters) wide   ᶜ13 That is, about 1 1/2 feet (about 0.5 meter)   ᵈ14 That is, dugongs   ᵉ16 That is, about 15 feet (about 4.5 meters) long and 2 1/4 feet (about 0.7 meter) wide

Place. ³⁵Place the table outside the curtain on the north side of the tabernacle and put the lampstand opposite it on the south side.

³⁶"For the entrance to the tent make a curtain of blue, purple and scarlet yarn and finely twisted linen—the work of an embroiderer. ³⁷Make gold hooks for this curtain and five posts of acacia wood overlaid with gold. And cast five bronze bases for them.

The Altar of Burnt Offering

27 "Build an altar of acacia wood, three cubits*ᵃ* high; it is to be square, five cubits long and five cubits wide.*ᵇ* ²Make a horn at each of the four corners, so that the horns and the altar are of one piece, and overlay the altar with bronze. ³Make all its utensils of bronze—its pots to remove the ashes, and its shovels, sprinkling bowls, meat forks and firepans. ⁴Make a grating for it, a bronze network, and make a bronze ring at each of the four corners of the network. ⁵Put it under the ledge of the altar so that it is halfway up the altar. ⁶Make poles of acacia wood for the altar and overlay them with bronze. ⁷The poles are to be inserted into the rings so they will be on two sides of the altar when it is carried. ⁸Make the altar hollow, out of boards. It is to be made just as you were shown on the mountain.

The Courtyard

⁹"Make a courtyard for the tabernacle. The south side shall be a hundred cubits*ᶜ* long and is to have curtains of finely twisted linen, ¹⁰with twenty posts and twenty bronze bases and with silver hooks and bands on the posts. ¹¹The north side shall also be a hundred cubits long and is to have curtains, with twenty posts and twenty bronze bases and with silver hooks and bands on the posts.

¹²"The west end of the courtyard shall be fifty cubits*ᵈ* wide and have curtains, with ten posts and ten bases. ¹³On the east end, toward the sunrise, the courtyard shall also be fifty cubits wide. ¹⁴Curtains fifteen cubits*ᵉ* long are to be on one side of the entrance, with three posts and three bases, ¹⁵and curtains fifteen cubits long are to be on the other side, with three posts and three bases.

¹⁶"For the entrance to the courtyard, provide a curtain twenty cubits*ᶠ* long, of blue, purple and scarlet yarn and finely twisted linen—the work of an embroiderer—with four posts and four bases. ¹⁷All the posts around the courtyard are to have silver bands and hooks, and bronze bases. ¹⁸The courtyard shall be a hundred cubits long and fifty cubits wide,*ᵍ* with curtains of finely twisted linen five cubits*ʰ* high, and with bronze bases. ¹⁹All the other articles used in the service of the tabernacle, whatever their function, including all the tent pegs for it and those for the courtyard, are to be of bronze.

Oil for the Lampstand

²⁰"Command the Israelites to bring you clear oil of pressed olives for the light so that the lamps may be kept burning. ²¹In the Tent of Meeting, outside the curtain that is in front of the Testimony, Aaron and his sons are to keep the lamps burning before the LORD from evening till morning. This is to be a lasting ordinance among the Israelites for the generations to come.

The Priestly Garments

28 "Have Aaron your brother brought to you from among the Israelites, along with his sons Nadab and Abihu, Eleazar and Ithamar, so they may serve me as priests. ²Make sacred garments for your brother Aaron, to give him dignity

---

ᵃ1 That is, about 4 1/2 feet (about 1.3 meters) long and wide   *ᶜ9* That is, about 150 feet (about 46 meters); also in verse 11   *ᵈ12* That is, about 75 feet (about 23 meters); also in verse 13   *ᵉ14* That is, about 22 1/2 feet (about 6.9 meters); also in verse 15   *ᶠ16* That is, about 30 feet (about 9 meters)   *ᵇ1* That is, about 7 1/2 feet (about 2.3 meters)   *ᵍ18* That is, about 150 feet (about 46 meters) long and 75 feet (about 23 meters) wide   *ʰ18* That is, about 7 1/2 feet (about 2.3 meters)

and honor. ³Tell all the skilled men to whom I have given wisdom in such matters that they are to make garments for Aaron, for his consecration, so he may serve me as priest. ⁴These are the garments they are to make: a breastpiece, an ephod, a robe, a woven tunic, a turban and a sash. They are to make these sacred garments for your brother Aaron and his sons, so they may serve me as priests. ⁵Have them use gold, and blue, purple and scarlet yarn, and fine linen.

The Ephod

⁶"Make the ephod of gold, and of blue, purple and scarlet yarn, and of finely twisted linen—the work of a skilled craftsman. ⁷It is to have two shoulder pieces attached to two of its corners, so it can be fastened. ⁸Its skillfully woven waistband is to be like it—of one piece with the ephod and made with gold, and with blue, purple and scarlet yarn, and with finely twisted linen.

⁹"Take two onyx stones and engrave on them the names of the sons of Israel ¹⁰in the order of their birth—six names on one stone and the remaining six on the other. ¹¹Engrave the names of the sons of Israel on the two stones the way a gem cutter engraves a seal. Then mount the stones in gold filigree settings ¹²and fasten them on the shoulder pieces of the ephod as memorial stones for the sons of Israel. Aaron is to bear the names on his shoulders as a memorial before the Lord. ¹³Make gold filigree settings ¹⁴and two braided chains of pure gold, like a rope, and attach the chains to the settings.

The Breastpiece

¹⁵"Fashion a breastpiece for making decisions—the work of a skilled craftsman. Make it like the ephod: of gold, and of blue, purple and scarlet yarn, and of finely twisted linen. ¹⁶It is to be square—a span[a] long and a span wide—and folded double.

¹⁷Then mount four rows of precious stones on it. In the first row there shall be a ruby, a topaz and a beryl; ¹⁸in the second row a turquoise, a sapphire[b] and an emerald; ¹⁹in the third row a jacinth, an agate and an amethyst; ²⁰in the fourth row a chrysolite, an onyx and a jasper.[c] Mount them in gold filigree settings. ²¹There are to be twelve stones, one for each of the names of the sons of Israel, each engraved like a seal with the name of one of the twelve tribes.

²²"For the breastpiece make braided chains of pure gold, like a rope. ²³Make two gold rings for it and fasten them to two corners of the breastpiece. ²⁴Fasten the two gold chains to the rings at the corners of the breastpiece, ²⁵and the other ends of the chains to the two settings, attaching them to the shoulder pieces of the ephod at the front. ²⁶Make two gold rings and attach them to the other two corners of the breastpiece on the inside edge next to the ephod. ²⁷Make two more gold rings and attach them to the bottom of the shoulder pieces on the front of the ephod, close to the seam just above the waistband of the ephod. ²⁸The rings of the breastpiece are to be tied to the rings of the ephod with blue cord, connecting it to the waistband, so that the breastpiece will not swing out from the ephod.

²⁹"Whenever Aaron enters the Holy Place, he will bear the names of the sons of Israel over his heart on the breastpiece of decision as a continuing memorial before the Lord. ³⁰Also put the Urim and the Thummim in the breastpiece, so they may be over Aaron's heart whenever he enters the presence of the Lord. Thus Aaron will always bear the means of making decisions for the Israelites over his heart before the Lord.

Other Priestly Garments

³¹"Make the robe of the ephod entirely of blue cloth, ³²with an opening for the head in its center. There shall

---

ᵃ16 That is, about 9 inches (about 22 centimeters)   ᵇ18 Or lapis lazuli   ᶜ20 The precise identification of some of these precious stones is uncertain.

be a woven edge like a collar[a] around this opening, so that it will not tear. ³³Make pomegranates of blue, purple and scarlet yarn around the hem of the robe, with gold bells between them. ³⁴The gold bells and the pomegranates are to alternate around the hem of the robe. ³⁵Aaron must wear it when he ministers. The sound of the bells will be heard when he enters the Holy Place before the LORD and when he comes out, so that he will not die.

³⁶"Make a plate of pure gold and engrave on it as on a seal: HOLY TO THE LORD. ³⁷Fasten a blue cord to it to attach it to the turban; it is to be on the front of the turban. ³⁸It will be on Aaron's forehead, and he will bear the guilt involved in the sacred gifts the Israelites consecrate, whatever their gifts may be. It will be on Aaron's forehead continually so that they will be acceptable to the LORD.

³⁹"Weave the tunic of fine linen and make the turban of fine linen. The sash is to be the work of an embroiderer. ⁴⁰Make tunics, sashes and headbands for Aaron's sons, to give them dignity and honor. ⁴¹After you put these clothes on your brother Aaron and his sons, anoint and ordain them. Consecrate them so they may serve me as priests.

⁴²"Make linen undergarments as a covering for the body, reaching from the waist to the thigh. ⁴³Aaron and his sons must wear them whenever they enter the Tent of Meeting or approach the altar to minister in the Holy Place, so that they will not incur guilt and die.

"This is to be a lasting ordinance for Aaron and his descendants.

Consecration of the Priests

29 "This is what you are to do to consecrate them, so they may serve me as priests: Take a young bull and two rams without defect. ²And from fine wheat flour, without yeast, make bread, and cakes mixed with oil, and wafers spread with oil. ³Put them in a basket and present them in it—along with the bull and the two rams. ⁴Then bring Aaron and his sons to the entrance to the Tent of Meeting and wash them with water. ⁵Take the garments and dress Aaron with the tunic, the robe of the ephod, the ephod itself and the breastpiece. Fasten the ephod on him by its skillfully woven waistband. ⁶Put the turban on his head and attach the sacred diadem to the turban. ⁷Take the anointing oil and anoint him by pouring it on his head. ⁸Bring his sons and dress them in tunics ⁹and put headbands on them. Then tie sashes on Aaron and his sons.[b] The priesthood is theirs by a lasting ordinance. In this way you shall ordain Aaron and his sons.

¹⁰"Bring the bull to the front of the Tent of Meeting, and Aaron and his sons shall lay their hands on its head. ¹¹Slaughter it in the LORD's presence at the entrance to the Tent of Meeting. ¹²Take some of the bull's blood and put it on the horns of the altar with your finger, and pour out the rest of it at the base of the altar. ¹³Then take all the fat around the inner parts, the covering of the liver, and both kidneys with the fat on them, and burn them on the altar. ¹⁴But burn the bull's flesh and its hide and its offal outside the camp. It is a sin offering.

¹⁵"Take one of the rams, and Aaron and his sons shall lay their hands on its head. ¹⁶Slaughter it and take the blood and sprinkle it against the altar on all sides. ¹⁷Cut the ram into pieces and wash the inner parts and the legs, putting them with the head and the other pieces. ¹⁸Then burn the entire ram on the altar. It is a burnt offering to the LORD, a pleasing aroma, an offering made to the LORD by fire.

¹⁹"Take the other ram, and Aaron and his sons shall lay their hands on its head. ²⁰Slaughter it, take some of its blood and put it on the lobes of the right ears of Aaron and his sons, on the thumbs of their right hands, and on the big toes of their right feet. Then

---

[a]32 The meaning of the Hebrew for this word is uncertain.   [b]9 Hebrew; Septuagint *on them*

sprinkle blood against the altar on all sides. ²¹And take some of the blood on the altar and some of the anointing oil and sprinkle it on Aaron and his garments and on his sons and their garments. Then he and his sons and their garments will be consecrated.

²²"Take from this ram the fat, the fat tail, the fat around the inner parts, the covering of the liver, both kidneys with the fat on them, and the right thigh. (This is the ram for the ordination.) ²³From the basket of bread made without yeast, which is before the Lord, take a loaf, and a cake made with oil, and a wafer. ²⁴Put all these in the hands of Aaron and his sons and wave them before the Lord as a wave offering. ²⁵Then take them from their hands and burn them on the altar along with the burnt offering for a pleasing aroma to the Lord, an offering made to the Lord by fire. ²⁶After you take the breast of the ram for Aaron's ordination, wave it before the Lord as a wave offering, and it will be your share.

²⁷"Consecrate those parts of the ordination ram that belong to Aaron and his sons: the breast that was waved and the thigh that was presented. ²⁸This is always to be the regular share from the Israelites for Aaron and his sons. It is the contribution the Israelites are to make to the Lord from their fellowship offerings.ᵃ

²⁹"Aaron's sacred garments will belong to his descendants so that they can be anointed and ordained in them. ³⁰The son who succeeds him as priest and comes to the Tent of Meeting to minister in the Holy Place is to wear them seven days.

³¹"Take the ram for the ordination and cook the meat in a sacred place. ³²At the entrance to the Tent of Meeting, Aaron and his sons are to eat the meat of the ram and the bread that is in the basket. ³³They are to eat these offerings by which atonement was made for their ordination and consecration. But no one else may eat them,

because they are sacred. ³⁴And if any of the meat of the ordination ram or any bread is left over till morning, burn it up. It must not be eaten, because it is sacred.

³⁵"Do for Aaron and his sons everything I have commanded you, taking seven days to ordain them. ³⁶Sacrifice a bull each day as a sin offering to make atonement. Purify the altar by making atonement for it, and anoint it to consecrate it. ³⁷For seven days make atonement for the altar and consecrate it. Then the altar will be most holy, and whatever touches it will be holy.

³⁸"This is what you are to offer on the altar regularly each day: two lambs a year old. ³⁹Offer one in the morning and the other at twilight. ⁴⁰With the first lamb offer a tenth of an ephahᵇ of fine flour mixed with a quarter of a hinᶜ of oil from pressed olives, and a quarter of a hin of wine as a drink offering. ⁴¹Sacrifice the other lamb at twilight with the same grain offering and its drink offering as in the morning—a pleasing aroma, an offering made to the Lord by fire.

⁴²"For the generations to come this burnt offering is to be made regularly at the entrance to the Tent of Meeting before the Lord. There I will meet you and speak to you; ⁴³there also I will meet with the Israelites, and the place will be consecrated by my glory.

⁴⁴"So I will consecrate the Tent of Meeting and the altar and will consecrate Aaron and his sons to serve me as priests. ⁴⁵Then I will dwell among the Israelites and be their God. ⁴⁶They will know that I am the Lord their God, who brought them out of Egypt so that I might dwell among them. I am the Lord their God.

The Altar of Incense

30 "Make an altar of acacia wood for burning incense. ²It is to be square, a cubit long and a cubit wide,

---

ᵃ28 Traditionally *peace offerings*   ᵇ40 That is, probably about 2 quarts (about 2 liters)
ᶜ40 That is, probably about 1 quart (about 1 liter)

and two cubits high*a*—its horns of one piece with it. ³Overlay the top and all the sides and the horns with pure gold, and make a gold molding around it. ⁴Make two gold rings for the altar below the molding—two on opposite sides—to hold the poles used to carry it. ⁵Make the poles of acacia wood and overlay them with gold. ⁶Put the altar in front of the curtain that is before the ark of the Testimony—before the atonement cover that is over the Testimony—where I will meet with you.

⁷"Aaron must burn fragrant incense on the altar every morning when he tends the lamps. ⁸He must burn incense again when he lights the lamps at twilight so incense will burn regularly before the LORD for the generations to come. ⁹Do not offer on this altar any other incense or any burnt offering or grain offering, and do not pour a drink offering on it. ¹⁰Once a year Aaron shall make atonement on its horns. This annual atonement must be made with the blood of the atoning sin offering for the generations to come. It is most holy to the LORD."

Atonement Money

¹¹Then the LORD said to Moses, ¹²"When you take a census of the Israelites to count them, each one must pay the LORD a ransom for his life at the time he is counted. Then no plague will come on them when you number them. ¹³Each one who crosses over to those already counted is to give a half shekel,*b* according to the sanctuary shekel, which weighs twenty gerahs. This half shekel is an offering to the LORD. ¹⁴All who cross over, those twenty years old or more, are to give an offering to the LORD. ¹⁵The rich are not to give more than a half shekel and the poor are not to give less when you make the offering to the LORD to atone for your lives. ¹⁶Receive the atonement money from the Israelites

and use it for the service of the Tent of Meeting. It will be a memorial for the Israelites before the LORD, making atonement for your lives."

Basin for Washing

¹⁷Then the LORD said to Moses, ¹⁸"Make a bronze basin, with its bronze stand, for washing. Place it between the Tent of Meeting and the altar, and put water in it. ¹⁹Aaron and his sons are to wash their hands and feet with water from it. ²⁰Whenever they enter the Tent of Meeting, they shall wash with water so that they will not die. Also, when they approach the altar to minister by presenting an offering made to the LORD by fire, ²¹they shall wash their hands and feet so that they will not die. This is to be a lasting ordinance for Aaron and his descendants for the generations to come."

Anointing Oil

²²Then the LORD said to Moses, ²³"Take the following fine spices: 500 shekels*c* of liquid myrrh, half as much (that is, 250 shekels) of fragrant cinnamon, 250 shekels of fragrant cane, ²⁴500 shekels of cassia—all according to the sanctuary shekel—and a hin*d* of olive oil. ²⁵Make these into a sacred anointing oil, a fragrant blend, the work of a perfumer. It will be the sacred anointing oil. ²⁶Then use it to anoint the Tent of Meeting, the ark of the Testimony, ²⁷the table and all its articles, the lampstand and its accessories, the altar of incense, ²⁸the altar of burnt offering and all its utensils, and the basin with its stand. ²⁹You shall consecrate them so they will be most holy, and whatever touches them will be holy.

³⁰"Anoint Aaron and his sons and consecrate them so they may serve me as priests. ³¹Say to the Israelites, 'This is to be my sacred anointing oil for the generations to come. ³²Do not pour it on men's bodies and do not

---

*a*2 That is, about 1 1/2 feet (about 0.5 meter) long and wide and about 3 feet (about 0.9 meter) high   *b*13 That is, about 1/5 ounce (about 6 grams); also in verse 15   *c*23 That is, about 12 1/2 pounds (about 6 kilograms)   *d*24 That is, probably about 4 quarts (about 4 liters)

make any oil with the same formula. It is sacred, and you are to consider it sacred. ³³Whoever makes perfume like it and whoever puts it on anyone other than a priest must be cut off from his people.' "

Incense

³⁴Then the LORD said to Moses, "Take fragrant spices—gum resin, onycha and galbanum—and pure frankincense, all in equal amounts, ³⁵and make a fragrant blend of incense, the work of a perfumer. It is to be salted and pure and sacred. ³⁶Grind some of it to powder and place it in front of the Testimony in the Tent of Meeting, where I will meet with you. It shall be most holy to you. ³⁷Do not make any incense with this formula for yourselves; consider it holy to the LORD. ³⁸Whoever makes any like it to enjoy its fragrance must be cut off from his people."

Bezalel and Oholiab

31 Then the LORD said to Moses, ²"See, I have chosen Bezalel son of Uri, the son of Hur, of the tribe of Judah, ³and I have filled him with the Spirit of God, with skill, ability and knowledge in all kinds of crafts— ⁴to make artistic designs for work in gold, silver and bronze, ⁵to cut and set stones, to work in wood, and to engage in all kinds of craftsmanship. ⁶Moreover, I have appointed Oholiab son of Ahisamach, of the tribe of Dan, to help him. Also I have given skill to all the craftsmen to make everything I have commanded you: ⁷the Tent of Meeting, the ark of the Testimony with the atonement cover on it, and all the other furnishings of the tent— ⁸the table and its articles, the pure gold lampstand and all its accessories, the altar of incense, ⁹the altar of burnt offering and all its utensils, the basin with its stand— ¹⁰and also the woven garments, both the sacred garments for Aaron the priest and the garments for his sons when they serve as priests, ¹¹and the anointing oil and

fragrant incense for the Holy Place. They are to make them just as I commanded you."

The Sabbath

¹²Then the LORD said to Moses, ¹³"Say to the Israelites, 'You must observe my Sabbaths. This will be a sign between me and you for the generations to come, so you may know that I am the LORD, who makes you holy.ᵃ

¹⁴" 'Observe the Sabbath, because it is holy to you. Anyone who desecrates it must be put to death; whoever does any work on that day must be cut off from his people. ¹⁵For six days, work is to be done, but the seventh day is a Sabbath of rest, holy to the LORD. Whoever does any work on the Sabbath day must be put to death. ¹⁶The Israelites are to observe the Sabbath, celebrating it for the generations to come as a lasting covenant. ¹⁷It will be a sign between me and the Israelites forever, for in six days the LORD made the heavens and the earth, and on the seventh day he abstained from work and rested.' "

¹⁸When the LORD finished speaking to Moses on Mount Sinai, he gave him the two tablets of the Testimony, the tablets of stone inscribed by the finger of God.

The Golden Calf

32 When the people saw that Moses was so long in coming down from the mountain, they gathered around Aaron and said, "Come, make us godsᵇ who will go before us. As for this fellow Moses who brought us up out of Egypt, we don't know what has happened to him."

²Aaron answered them, "Take off the gold earrings that your wives, your sons and your daughters are wearing, and bring them to me." ³So all the people took off their earrings and brought them to Aaron. ⁴He took what they handed him and made it into an idol cast in the shape of a calf, fashioning it with a tool. Then

---

ᵃ13 Or *who sanctifies you; or who sets you apart as holy*   ᵇ1 Or *a god*; also in verses 23 and 31

they said, "These are your gods,[a] O Israel, who brought you up out of Egypt."

⁵When Aaron saw this, he built an altar in front of the calf and announced, "Tomorrow there will be a festival to the LORD." ⁶So the next day the people rose early and sacrificed burnt offerings and presented fellowship offerings.[b] Afterward they sat down to eat and drink and got up to indulge in revelry.

⁷Then the LORD said to Moses, "Go down, because your people, whom you brought up out of Egypt, have become corrupt. ⁸They have been quick to turn away from what I commanded them and have made themselves an idol cast in the shape of a calf. They have bowed down to it and sacrificed to it and have said, 'These are your gods, O Israel, who brought you up out of Egypt.'

⁹"I have seen these people," the LORD said to Moses, "and they are a stiff-necked people. ¹⁰Now leave me alone so that my anger may burn against them and that I may destroy them. Then I will make you into a great nation."

¹¹But Moses sought the favor of the LORD his God. "O LORD," he said, "why should your anger burn against your people, whom you brought out of Egypt with great power and a mighty hand? ¹²Why should the Egyptians say, 'It was with evil intent that he brought them out, to kill them in the mountains and to wipe them off the face of the earth'? Turn from your fierce anger; relent and do not bring disaster on your people. ¹³Remember your servants Abraham, Isaac and Israel, to whom you swore by your own self: 'I will make your descendants as numerous as the stars in the sky and I will give your descendants all this land I promised them, and it will be their inheritance forever.' " ¹⁴Then the LORD relented and did not bring on his people the disaster he had threatened.

¹⁵Moses turned and went down the mountain with the two tablets of the Testimony in his hands. They were inscribed on both sides, front and back. ¹⁶The tablets were the work of God; the writing was the writing of God, engraved on the tablets.

¹⁷When Joshua heard the noise of the people shouting, he said to Moses, "There is the sound of war in the camp."

¹⁸Moses replied:

"It is not the sound of victory,
   it is not the sound of defeat;
   it is the sound of singing that I
      hear."

¹⁹When Moses approached the camp and saw the calf and the dancing, his anger burned and he threw the tablets out of his hands, breaking them to pieces at the foot of the mountain. ²⁰And he took the calf they had made and burned it in the fire; then he ground it to powder, scattered it on the water and made the Israelites drink it.

²¹He said to Aaron, "What did these people do to you, that you led them into such great sin?"

²²"Do not be angry, my lord," Aaron answered. "You know how prone these people are to evil. ²³They said to me, 'Make us gods who will go before us. As for this fellow Moses who brought us up out of Egypt, we don't know what has happened to him.' ²⁴So I told them, 'Whoever has any gold jewelry, take it off.' Then they gave me the gold, and I threw it into the fire, and out came this calf'

²⁵Moses saw that the people were running wild and that Aaron had let them get out of control and so become a laughingstock to their enemies. ²⁶So he stood at the entrance to the camp and said, "Whoever is for the LORD, come to me." And all the Levites rallied to him.

²⁷Then he said to them, "This is what the LORD, the God of Israel, says: 'Each man strap a sword to his side. Go back and forth through the camp from one end to the other, each killing

---

a4 Or *This is your god*; also in verse 8   b6 Traditionally *peace offerings*

his brother and friend and neighbor.' " ²⁸The Levites did as Moses commanded, and that day about three thousand of the people died. ²⁹Then Moses said, "You have been set apart to the LORD today, for you were against your own sons and brothers, and he has blessed you this day."

³⁰The next day Moses said to the people, "You have committed a great sin. But now I will go up to the LORD; perhaps I can make atonement for your sin."

³¹So Moses went back to the LORD and said, "Oh, what a great sin these people have committed! They have made themselves gods of gold. ³²But now, please forgive their sin—but if not, then blot me out of the book you have written."

³³The LORD replied to Moses, "Whoever has sinned against me I will blot out of my book. ³⁴Now go, lead the people to the place I spoke of, and my angel will go before you. However, when the time comes for me to punish, I will punish them for their sin."

³⁵And the LORD struck the people with a plague because of what they did with the calf Aaron had made.

33 Then the LORD said to Moses, "Leave this place, you and the people you brought up out of Egypt, and go up to the land I promised on oath to Abraham, Isaac and Jacob, saying, 'I will give it to your descendants.' ²I will send an angel before you and drive out the Canaanites, Amorites, Hittites, Perizzites, Hivites and Jebusites. ³Go up to the land flowing with milk and honey. But I will not go with you, because you are a stiff-necked people and I might destroy you on the way."

⁴When the people heard these distressing words, they began to mourn and no one put on any ornaments. ⁵For the LORD had said to Moses, "Tell the Israelites, 'You are a stiff-necked people. If I were to go with you even for a moment, I might destroy you. Now take off your ornaments and I will decide what to do with you.' " ⁶So the Israelites stripped off their ornaments at Mount Horeb.

The Tent of Meeting

⁷Now Moses used to take a tent and pitch it outside the camp some distance away, calling it the "tent of meeting." Anyone inquiring of the LORD would go to the tent of meeting outside the camp. ⁸And whenever Moses went out to the tent, all the people rose and stood at the entrances to their tents, watching Moses until he entered the tent. ⁹As Moses went into the tent, the pillar of cloud would come down and stay at the entrance, while the LORD spoke with Moses. ¹⁰Whenever the people saw the pillar of cloud standing at the entrance to the tent, they all stood and worshiped, each at the entrance to his tent. ¹¹The LORD would speak to Moses face to face, as a man speaks with his friend. Then Moses would return to the camp, but his young aide Joshua son of Nun did not leave the tent.

Moses and the Glory of the LORD

¹²Moses said to the LORD, "You have been telling me, 'Lead these people,' but you have not let me know whom you will send with me. You have said, 'I know you by name and you have found favor with me.' ¹³If you are pleased with me, teach me your ways so I may know you and continue to find favor with you. Remember that this nation is your people."

¹⁴The LORD replied, "My Presence will go with you, and I will give you rest."

¹⁵Then Moses said to him, "If your Presence does not go with us, do not send us up from here. ¹⁶How will anyone know that you are pleased with me and with your people unless you go with us? What else will distinguish me and your people from all the other people on the face of the earth?"

¹⁷And the LORD said to Moses, "I will do the very thing you have asked, because I am pleased with you and I know you by name."

¹⁸Then Moses said, "Now show me your glory."

¹⁹And the LORD said, "I will cause all my goodness to pass in front of you, and I will proclaim my name, the LORD, in your presence. I will have mercy on whom I will have mercy, and I will have compassion on whom I will have compassion. ²⁰But," he said, "you cannot see my face, for no one may see me and live."

²¹Then the LORD said, "There is a place near me where you may stand on a rock. ²²When my glory passes by, I will put you in a cleft in the rock and cover you with my hand until I have passed by. ²³Then I will remove my hand and you will see my back; but my face must not be seen."

The New Stone Tablets

34 The LORD said to Moses, "Chisel out two stone tablets like the first ones, and I will write on them the words that were on the first tablets, which you broke. ²Be ready in the morning, and then come up on Mount Sinai. Present yourself to me there on top of the mountain. ³No one is to come with you or be seen anywhere on the mountain; not even the flocks and herds may graze in front of the mountain."

⁴So Moses chiseled out two stone tablets like the first ones and went up Mount Sinai early in the morning, as the LORD had commanded him; and

VERSE:	AUTHOR:	PASSAGE:
Exodus 33:11	A.W. Tozer	Exodus 33:7–11

We Are God's Friends

God's love tells us he is friendly and his Word assures us that he is our friend and wants us to be his friends. No man with a trace of humility would first think that he is a friend of God; but the idea did not originate with men. Abraham would never have said, "I am God's friend," but God himself said that Abraham was his friend. The disciples might well have hesitated to claim friendship with Christ, but Christ said to them, "You are my friends." Modesty may demur at so rash a thought, but audacious faith dares to believe the Word and claim friendship with God. We do God more honor by believing what he has said about himself and having the courage to come boldly to the throne of grace than by hiding in self-conscious humility among the trees of the garden.

ADDITIONAL SCRIPTURE READINGS
John 15:9–17; James 2:20–24

Go to page 137 for your next devotional reading.

he carried the two stone tablets in his hands. ⁵Then the LORD came down in the cloud and stood there with him and proclaimed his name, the LORD. ⁶And he passed in front of Moses, proclaiming, "The LORD, the LORD, the compassionate and gracious God, slow to anger, abounding in love and faithfulness, ⁷maintaining love to thousands, and forgiving wickedness, rebellion and sin. Yet he does not leave the guilty unpunished; he punishes the children and their children for the sin of the fathers to the third and fourth generation."

⁸Moses bowed to the ground at once and worshiped. ⁹"O Lord, if I have found favor in your eyes," he said, "then let the Lord go with us. Although this is a stiff-necked people, forgive our wickedness and our sin, and take us as your inheritance."

¹⁰Then the LORD said: "I am making a covenant with you. Before all your people I will do wonders never before done in any nation in all the world. The people you live among will see how awesome is the work that I, the LORD, will do for you. ¹¹Obey what I command you today. I will drive out before you the Amorites, Canaanites, Hittites, Perizzites, Hivites and Jebusites. ¹²Be careful not to make a treaty with those who live in the land where you are going, or they will be a snare among you. ¹³Break down their altars, smash their sacred stones and cut down their Asherah poles.ᵃ ¹⁴Do not worship any other god, for the LORD, whose name is Jealous, is a jealous God.

¹⁵"Be careful not to make a treaty with those who live in the land; for when they prostitute themselves to their gods and sacrifice to them, they will invite you and you will eat their sacrifices. ¹⁶And when you choose some of their daughters as wives for your sons and those daughters prostitute themselves to their gods, they will lead your sons to do the same.

¹⁷"Do not make cast idols.

¹⁸"Celebrate the Feast of Unleav-ened Bread. For seven days eat bread made without yeast, as I commanded you. Do this at the appointed time in the month of Abib, for in that month you came out of Egypt.

¹⁹"The first offspring of every womb belongs to me, including all the firstborn males of your livestock, whether from herd or flock. ²⁰Redeem the firstborn donkey with a lamb, but if you do not redeem it, break its neck. Redeem all your firstborn sons.

"No one is to appear before me empty-handed.

²¹"Six days you shall labor, but on the seventh day you shall rest; even during the plowing season and harvest you must rest.

²²"Celebrate the Feast of Weeks with the firstfruits of the wheat harvest, and the Feast of Ingathering at the turn of the year.ᵇ ²³Three times a year all your men are to appear before the Sovereign LORD, the God of Israel. ²⁴I will drive out nations before you and enlarge your territory, and no one will covet your land when you go up three times each year to appear before the LORD your God.

²⁵"Do not offer the blood of a sacrifice to me along with anything containing yeast, and do not let any of the sacrifice from the Passover Feast remain until morning.

²⁶"Bring the best of the firstfruits of your soil to the house of the LORD your God.

"Do not cook a young goat in its mother's milk."

²⁷Then the LORD said to Moses, "Write down these words, for in accordance with these words I have made a covenant with you and with Israel." ²⁸Moses was there with the LORD forty days and forty nights without eating bread or drinking water. And he wrote on the tablets the words of the covenant—the Ten Commandments.

The Radiant Face of Moses

²⁹When Moses came down from Mount Sinai with the two tablets of

---

ᵃ13 That is, symbols of the goddess Asherah   ᵇ22 That is, in the fall

the Testimony in his hands, he was not aware that his face was radiant because he had spoken with the LORD. [30]When Aaron and all the Israelites saw Moses, his face was radiant, and they were afraid to come near him. [31]But Moses called to them; so Aaron and all the leaders of the community came back to him, and he spoke to them. [32]Afterward all the Israelites came near him, and he gave them all the commands the LORD had given him on Mount Sinai.

[33]When Moses finished speaking to them, he put a veil over his face. [34]But whenever he entered the LORD's presence to speak with him, he removed the veil until he came out. And when he came out and told the Israelites what he had been commanded, [35]they saw that his face was radiant. Then Moses would put the veil back over his face until he went in to speak with the LORD.

Sabbath Regulations

35 Moses assembled the whole Israelite community and said to them, "These are the things the LORD has commanded you to do: [2]For six days, work is to be done, but the seventh day shall be your holy day, a Sabbath of rest to the LORD. Whoever does any work on it must be put to death. [3]Do not light a fire in any of your dwellings on the Sabbath day."

Materials for the Tabernacle

[4]Moses said to the whole Israelite community, "This is what the LORD has commanded: [5]From what you have, take an offering for the LORD. Everyone who is willing is to bring to the LORD an offering of gold, silver and bronze; [6]blue, purple and scarlet yarn and fine linen; goat hair; [7]ram skins dyed red and hides of sea cows[a]; acacia wood; [8]olive oil for the light; spices for the anointing oil and for the fragrant incense; [9]and onyx stones and other gems to be mounted on the ephod and breastpiece.

[10]"All who are skilled among you are to come and make everything the LORD has commanded: [11]the tabernacle with its tent and its covering, clasps, frames, crossbars, posts and bases; [12]the ark with its poles and the atonement cover and the curtain that shields it; [13]the table with its poles and all its articles and the bread of the Presence; [14]the lampstand that is for light with its accessories, lamps and oil for the light; [15]the altar of incense with its poles, the anointing oil and the fragrant incense; the curtain for the doorway at the entrance to the tabernacle; [16]the altar of burnt offering with its bronze grating, its poles and all its utensils; the bronze basin with its stand; [17]the curtains of the courtyard with its posts and bases, and the curtain for the entrance to the courtyard; [18]the tent pegs for the tabernacle and for the courtyard, and their ropes; [19]the woven garments worn for ministering in the sanctuary—both the sacred garments for Aaron the priest and the garments for his sons when they serve as priests."

[20]Then the whole Israelite community withdrew from Moses' presence, [21]and everyone who was willing and whose heart moved him came and brought an offering to the LORD for the work on the Tent of Meeting, for all its service, and for the sacred garments. [22]All who were willing, men and women alike, came and brought gold jewelry of all kinds: brooches, earrings, rings and ornaments. They all presented their gold as a wave offering to the LORD. [23]Everyone who had blue, purple or scarlet yarn or fine linen, or goat hair, ram skins dyed red or hides of sea cows brought them. [24]Those presenting an offering of silver or bronze brought it as an offering to the LORD, and everyone who had acacia wood for any part of the work brought it. [25]Every skilled woman spun with her hands and brought what she had spun—blue, purple or scarlet yarn or fine linen. [26]And all the women who were willing and had the skill spun the goat

---

[a]7 That is, dugongs; also in verse 23

hair. ²⁷The leaders brought onyx stones and other gems to be mounted on the ephod and breastpiece. ²⁸They also brought spices and olive oil for the light and for the anointing oil and for the fragrant incense. ²⁹All the Israelite men and women who were willing brought to the LORD freewill offerings for all the work the LORD through Moses had commanded them to do.

Bezalel and Oholiab

³⁰Then Moses said to the Israelites, "See, the LORD has chosen Bezalel son of Uri, the son of Hur, of the tribe of Judah, ³¹and he has filled him with the Spirit of God, with skill, ability and knowledge in all kinds of crafts—³²to make artistic designs for work in gold, silver and bronze, ³³to cut and set stones, to work in wood and to engage in all kinds of artistic craftsmanship. ³⁴And he has given both him and Oholiab son of Ahisamach, of the tribe of Dan, the ability to teach others. ³⁵He has filled them with skill to do all kinds of work as craftsmen, designers, embroiderers in blue, purple and scarlet yarn and fine linen, and weavers—all of them master **36** craftsmen and designers. ¹So Bezalel, Oholiab and every skilled person to whom the LORD has given skill and ability to know how to carry out all the work of constructing the sanctuary are to do the work just as the Lord has commanded."

²Then Moses summoned Bezalel and Oholiab and every skilled person to whom the LORD had given ability and who was willing to come and do the work. ³They received from Moses all the offerings the Israelites had brought to carry out the work of constructing the sanctuary. And the people continued to bring freewill offerings morning after morning. ⁴So all the skilled craftsmen who were doing all the work on the sanctuary left their work ⁵and said to Moses, "The people are bringing more than enough for

doing the work the LORD commanded to be done."

⁶Then Moses gave an order and they sent this word throughout the camp: "No man or woman is to make anything else as an offering for the sanctuary." And so the people were restrained from bringing more, ⁷because what they already had was more than enough to do all the work.

The Tabernacle

⁸All the skilled men among the workmen made the tabernacle with ten curtains of finely twisted linen and blue, purple and scarlet yarn, with cherubim worked into them by a skilled craftsman. ⁹All the curtains were the same size—twenty-eight cubits long and four cubits wide.ᵃ ¹⁰They joined five of the curtains together and did the same with the other five. ¹¹Then they made loops of blue material along the edge of the end curtain in one set, and the same was done with the end curtain in the other set. ¹²They also made fifty loops on one curtain and fifty loops on the end curtain of the other set, with the loops opposite each other. ¹³Then they made fifty gold clasps and used them to fasten the two sets of curtains together so that the tabernacle was a unit.

¹⁴They made curtains of goat hair for the tent over the tabernacle—eleven altogether. ¹⁵All eleven curtains were the same size—thirty cubits long and four cubits wide.ᵇ ¹⁶They joined five of the curtains into one set and the other six into another set. ¹⁷Then they made fifty loops along the edge of the end curtain in one set and also along the edge of the end curtain in the other set. ¹⁸They made fifty bronze clasps to fasten the tent together as a unit. ¹⁹Then they made for the tent a covering of ram skins dyed red, and over that a covering of hides of sea cows.ᶜ

²⁰They made upright frames of aca-

ᵃ9 That is, about 42 feet (about 12.5 meters) long and 6 feet (about 1.8 meters) wide   ᵇ15 That is, about 45 feet (about 13.5 meters) long and 6 feet (about 1.8 meters) wide   ᶜ19 That is, dugongs

cia wood for the tabernacle. ²¹Each frame was ten cubits long and a cubit and a half wide,ᵃ ²²with two projections set parallel to each other. They made all the frames of the tabernacle in this way. ²³They made twenty frames for the south side of the tabernacle ²⁴and made forty silver bases to go under them—two bases for each frame, one under each projection. ²⁵For the other side, the north side of the tabernacle, they made twenty frames ²⁶and forty silver bases—two under each frame. ²⁷They made six frames for the far end, that is, the west end of the tabernacle, ²⁸and two frames were made for the corners of the tabernacle at the far end. ²⁹At these two corners the frames were double from the bottom all the way to the top and fitted into a single ring; both were made alike. ³⁰So there were eight frames and sixteen silver bases—two under each frame.

³¹They also made crossbars of acacia wood: five for the frames on one side of the tabernacle, ³²five for those on the other side, and five for the frames on the west, at the far end of the tabernacle. ³³They made the center crossbar so that it extended from end to end at the middle of the frames. ³⁴They overlaid the frames with gold and made gold rings to hold the crossbars. They also overlaid the crossbars with gold.

³⁵They made the curtain of blue, purple and scarlet yarn and finely twisted linen, with cherubim worked into it by a skilled craftsman. ³⁶They made four posts of acacia wood for it and overlaid them with gold. They made gold hooks for them and cast their four silver bases. ³⁷For the entrance to the tent they made a curtain of blue, purple and scarlet yarn and finely twisted linen—the work of an embroiderer; ³⁸and they made five posts with hooks for them. They over-

laid the tops of the posts and their bands with gold and made their five bases of bronze.

The Ark

37 Bezalel made the ark of acacia wood—two and a half cubits long, a cubit and a half wide, and a cubit and a half high.ᵇ ²He overlaid it with pure gold, both inside and out, and made a gold molding around it. ³He cast four gold rings for it and fastened them to its four feet, with two rings on one side and two rings on the other. ⁴Then he made poles of acacia wood and overlaid them with gold. ⁵And he inserted the poles into the rings on the sides of the ark to carry it.

⁶He made the atonement cover of pure gold—two and a half cubits long and a cubit and a half wide.ᶜ ⁷Then he made two cherubim out of hammered gold at the ends of the cover. ⁸He made one cherub on one end and the second cherub on the other; at the two ends he made them of one piece with the cover. ⁹The cherubim had their wings spread upward, overshadowing the cover with them. The cherubim faced each other, looking toward the cover.

The Table

¹⁰Theyᵈ made the table of acacia wood—two cubits long, a cubit wide, and a cubit and a half high.ᵉ ¹¹Then they overlaid it with pure gold and made a gold molding around it. ¹²They also made around it a rim a handbreadthᶠ wide and put a gold molding on the rim. ¹³They cast four gold rings for the table and fastened them to the four corners, where the four legs were. ¹⁴The rings were put close to the rim to hold the poles used in carrying the table. ¹⁵The poles for carrying the table were made of acacia wood and were overlaid with

---

ᵃ21 That is, about 15 feet (about 4.5 meters) long and 2 1/4 feet (about 0.7 meter) wide   ᵇ1 That is, about 3 3/4 feet (about 1.1 meters) long and 2 1/4 feet (about 0.7 meter) wide and high   ᶜ6 That is, about 3 3/4 feet (about 1.1 meters) long and 2 1/4 feet (about 0.7 meter) wide   ᵈ10 Or He; also in verses 11-29   ᵉ10 That is, about 3 feet (about 0.9 meter) long, 1 1/2 feet (about 0.5 meter) wide, and 2 1/4 feet (about 0.7 meter) high   ᶠ12 That is, about 3 inches (about 8 centimeters)

gold. ¹⁶And they made from pure gold the articles for the table—its plates and dishes and bowls and its pitchers for the pouring out of drink offerings.

The Lampstand

¹⁷They made the lampstand of pure gold and hammered it out, base and shaft; its flowerlike cups, buds and blossoms were of one piece with it. ¹⁸Six branches extended from the sides of the lampstand—three on one side and three on the other. ¹⁹Three cups shaped like almond flowers with buds and blossoms were on one branch, three on the next branch and the same for all six branches extending from the lampstand. ²⁰And on the lampstand were four cups shaped like almond flowers with buds and blossoms. ²¹One bud was under the first pair of branches extending from the lampstand, a second bud under the second pair, and a third bud under the third pair—six branches in all. ²²The buds and the branches were all of one piece with the lampstand, hammered out of pure gold.

²³They made its seven lamps, as well as its wick trimmers and trays, of pure gold. ²⁴They made the lampstand and all its accessories from one talent[a] of pure gold.

The Altar of Incense

²⁵They made the altar of incense out of acacia wood. It was square, a cubit long and a cubit wide, and two cubits high[b]—its horns of one piece with it. ²⁶They overlaid the top and all the sides and the horns with pure gold, and made a gold molding around it. ²⁷They made two gold rings below the molding—two on opposite sides—to hold the poles used to carry it. ²⁸They made the poles of acacia wood and overlaid them with gold.

²⁹They also made the sacred anoint-ing oil and the pure, fragrant incense—the work of a perfumer.

The Altar of Burnt Offering

38 They[c] built the altar of burnt offering of acacia wood, three cubits[d] high; it was square, five cubits long and five cubits wide.[e] ²They made a horn at each of the four corners, so that the horns and the altar were of one piece, and they overlaid the altar with bronze. ³They made all its utensils of bronze—its pots, shovels, sprinkling bowls, meat forks and firepans. ⁴They made a grating for the altar, a bronze network, to be under its ledge, halfway up the altar. ⁵They cast bronze rings to hold the poles for the four corners of the bronze grating. ⁶They made the poles of acacia wood and overlaid them with bronze. ⁷They inserted the poles into the rings so they would be on the sides of the altar for carrying it. They made it hollow, out of boards.

Basin for Washing

⁸They made the bronze basin and its bronze stand from the mirrors of the women who served at the entrance to the Tent of Meeting.

The Courtyard

⁹Next they made the courtyard. The south side was a hundred cubits[f] long and had curtains of finely twisted linen, ¹⁰with twenty posts and twenty bronze bases, and with silver hooks and bands on the posts. ¹¹The north side was also a hundred cubits long and had twenty posts and twenty bronze bases, with silver hooks and bands on the posts.

¹²The west end was fifty cubits[g] wide and had curtains, with ten posts and ten bases, with silver hooks and bands on the posts. ¹³The east end, toward the sunrise, was also fifty cubits wide. ¹⁴Curtains fifteen cubits[h] long

---

^a24 That is, about 75 pounds (about 34 kilograms)   ^b25 That is, about 1 1/2 feet (about 0.5 meter) long and wide, and about 3 feet (about 0.9 meter) high   ^c1 Or *He*; also in verses 2-9   ^d1 That is, about 4 1/2 feet (about 1.3 meters)   ^e1 That is, about 7 1/2 feet (about 2.3 meters) long and wide   ^f9 That is, about 150 feet (about 46 meters)   ^g12 That is, about 75 feet (about 23 meters)   ^h14 That is, about 22 1/2 feet (about 6.9 meters)

were on one side of the entrance, with three posts and three bases, ¹⁵and curtains fifteen cubits long were on the other side of the entrance to the courtyard, with three posts and three bases. ¹⁶All the curtains around the courtyard were of finely twisted linen. ¹⁷The bases for the posts were bronze. The hooks and bands on the posts were silver, and their tops were overlaid with silver; so all the posts of the courtyard had silver bands.

¹⁸The curtain for the entrance to the courtyard was of blue, purple and scarlet yarn and finely twisted linen—the work of an embroiderer. It was twenty cubits*a* long and, like the curtains of the courtyard, five cubits*b* high, ¹⁹with four posts and four bronze bases. Their hooks and bands were silver, and their tops were overlaid with silver. ²⁰All the tent pegs of the tabernacle and of the surrounding courtyard were bronze.

The Materials Used

²¹These are the amounts of the materials used for the tabernacle, the tabernacle of the Testimony, which were recorded at Moses' command by the Levites under the direction of Ithamar son of Aaron, the priest. ²²(Bezalel son of Uri, the son of Hur, of the tribe of Judah, made everything the LORD commanded Moses; ²³with him was Oholiab son of Ahisamach, of the tribe of Dan—a craftsman and designer, and an embroiderer in blue, purple and scarlet yarn and fine linen.) ²⁴The total amount of the gold from the wave offering used for all the work on the sanctuary was 29 talents and 730 shekels,*c* according to the sanctuary shekel.

²⁵The silver obtained from those of the community who were counted in the census was 100 talents and 1,775 shekels,*d* according to the sanctuary shekel— ²⁶one beka per person, that

is, half a shekel,*e* according to the sanctuary shekel, from everyone who had crossed over to those counted, twenty years old or more, a total of 603,550 men. ²⁷The 100 talents*f* of silver were used to cast the bases for the sanctuary and for the curtain—100 bases from the 100 talents, one talent for each base. ²⁸They used the 1,775 shekels*g* to make the hooks for the posts, to overlay the tops of the posts, and to make their bands.

²⁹The bronze from the wave offering was 70 talents and 2,400 shekels.*h* ³⁰They used it to make the bases for the entrance to the Tent of Meeting, the bronze altar with its bronze grating and all its utensils, ³¹the bases for the surrounding courtyard and those for its entrance and all the tent pegs for the tabernacle and those for the surrounding courtyard.

The Priestly Garments

39 From the blue, purple and scarlet yarn they made woven garments for ministering in the sanctuary. They also made sacred garments for Aaron, as the LORD commanded Moses.

The Ephod

²They*i* made the ephod of gold, and of blue, purple and scarlet yarn, and of finely twisted linen. ³They hammered out thin sheets of gold and cut strands to be worked into the blue, purple and scarlet yarn and fine linen—the work of a skilled craftsman. ⁴They made shoulder pieces for the ephod, which were attached to two of its corners, so it could be fastened. ⁵Its skillfully woven waistband was like it—of one piece with the ephod and made with gold, and with blue, purple and scarlet yarn, and with finely twisted linen, as the LORD commanded Moses.

⁶They mounted the onyx stones in

---

a18 That is, about 30 feet (about 9 meters)   *b18* That is, about 7 1/2 feet (about 2.3 meters)
c24 The weight of the gold was a little over one ton (about 1 metric ton).   *d25* The weight of the silver was a little over 3 3/4 tons (about 3.4 metric tons).   *e26* That is, about 1/5 ounce (about 5.5 grams)   *f27* That is, about 3 3/4 tons (about 3.4 metric tons)   *g28* That is, about 45 pounds (about 20 kilograms)   *h29* The weight of the bronze was about 2 1/2 tons (about 2.4 metric tons).   *i2* Or *He*; also in verses 7, 8 and 22

gold filigree settings and engraved them like a seal with the names of the sons of Israel. [7]Then they fastened them on the shoulder pieces of the ephod as memorial stones for the sons of Israel, as the LORD commanded Moses.

The Breastpiece

[8]They fashioned the breastpiece—the work of a skilled craftsman. They made it like the ephod: of gold, and of blue, purple and scarlet yarn, and of finely twisted linen. [9]It was square—a span[a] long and a span wide—and folded double. [10]Then they mounted four rows of precious stones on it. In the first row there was a ruby, a topaz and a beryl; [11]in the second row a turquoise, a sapphire[b] and an emerald; [12]in the third row a jacinth, an agate and an amethyst; [13]in the fourth row a chrysolite, an onyx and a jasper.[c] They were mounted in gold filigree settings. [14]There were twelve stones, one for each of the names of the sons of Israel, each engraved like a seal with the name of one of the twelve tribes.

[15]For the breastpiece they made braided chains of pure gold, like a rope. [16]They made two gold filigree settings and two gold rings, and fastened the rings to two of the corners of the breastpiece. [17]They fastened the two gold chains to the rings at the corners of the breastpiece, [18]and the other ends of the chains to the two settings, attaching them to the shoulder pieces of the ephod at the front. [19]They made two gold rings and attached them to the other two corners of the breastpiece on the inside edge next to the ephod. [20]Then they made two more gold rings and attached them to the bottom of the shoulder pieces on the front of the ephod, close to the seam just above the waistband of the ephod. [21]They tied the rings of the breastpiece to the rings of the ephod with blue cord, connecting it to the waistband so that the breastpiece would not swing out from the ephod—as the LORD commanded Moses.

Other Priestly Garments

[22]They made the robe of the ephod entirely of blue cloth—the work of a weaver— [23]with an opening in the center of the robe like the opening of a collar,[d] and a band around this opening, so that it would not tear. [24]They made pomegranates of blue, purple and scarlet yarn and finely twisted linen around the hem of the robe. [25]And they made bells of pure gold and attached them around the hem between the pomegranates. [26]The bells and pomegranates alternated around the hem of the robe to be worn for ministering, as the LORD commanded Moses.

[27]For Aaron and his sons, they made tunics of fine linen—the work of a weaver— [28]and the turban of fine linen, the linen headbands and the undergarments of finely twisted linen. [29]The sash was of finely twisted linen and blue, purple and scarlet yarn—the work of an embroiderer—as the LORD commanded Moses.

[30]They made the plate, the sacred diadem, out of pure gold and engraved on it, like an inscription on a seal: HOLY TO THE LORD. [31]Then they fastened a blue cord to it to attach it to the turban, as the LORD commanded Moses.

Moses Inspects the Tabernacle

[32]So all the work on the tabernacle, the Tent of Meeting, was completed. The Israelites did everything just as the LORD commanded Moses. [33]Then they brought the tabernacle to Moses: the tent and all its furnishings, its clasps, frames, crossbars, posts and bases; [34]the covering of ram skins dyed red, the covering of hides of sea cows[e] and the shielding curtain; [35]the ark of the Testimony with its

---

[a]9 That is, about 9 inches (about 22 centimeters)   [b]11 Or *lapis lazuli*   [c]13 The precise identification of some of these precious stones is uncertain.   [d]23 The meaning of the Hebrew for this word is uncertain.   [e]34 That is, dugongs

poles and the atonement cover; ³⁶the table with all its articles and the bread of the Presence; ³⁷the pure gold lampstand with its row of lamps and all its accessories, and the oil for the light; ³⁸the gold altar, the anointing oil, the fragrant incense, and the curtain for the entrance to the tent; ³⁹the bronze altar with its bronze grating, its poles and all its utensils; the basin with its stand; ⁴⁰the curtains of the courtyard with its posts and bases, and the curtain for the entrance to the courtyard; the ropes and tent pegs for the courtyard; all the furnishings for the tabernacle, the Tent of Meeting; ⁴¹and the woven garments worn for ministering in the sanctuary, both the sacred garments for Aaron the priest and the garments for his sons when serving as priests.

⁴²The Israelites had done all the work just as the Lord had commanded Moses. ⁴³Moses inspected the work and saw that they had done it just as the Lord had commanded. So Moses blessed them.

Setting Up the Tabernacle

40 Then the Lord said to Moses: ²"Set up the tabernacle, the Tent of Meeting, on the first day of the first month. ³Place the ark of the Testimony in it and shield the ark with the curtain. ⁴Bring in the table and set out what belongs on it. Then bring in the lampstand and set up its lamps. ⁵Place the gold altar of incense in front of the ark of the Testimony and put the curtain at the entrance to the tabernacle.

⁶"Place the altar of burnt offering in front of the entrance to the tabernacle, the Tent of Meeting; ⁷place the basin between the Tent of Meeting and the altar and put water in it. ⁸Set up the courtyard around it and put the curtain at the entrance to the courtyard.

⁹"Take the anointing oil and anoint the tabernacle and everything in it; consecrate it and all its furnishings, and it will be holy. ¹⁰Then anoint the altar of burnt offering and all its utensils; consecrate the altar, and it will be

most holy. ¹¹Anoint the basin and its stand and consecrate them.

¹²"Bring Aaron and his sons to the entrance to the Tent of Meeting and wash them with water. ¹³Then dress Aaron in the sacred garments, anoint him and consecrate him so he may serve me as priest. ¹⁴Bring his sons and dress them in tunics. ¹⁵Anoint them just as you anointed their father, so they may serve me as priests. Their anointing will be to a priesthood that will continue for all generations to come." ¹⁶Moses did everything just as the Lord commanded him.

¹⁷So the tabernacle was set up on the first day of the first month in the second year. ¹⁸When Moses set up the tabernacle, he put the bases in place, erected the frames, inserted the crossbars and set up the posts. ¹⁹Then he spread the tent over the tabernacle and put the covering over the tent, as the Lord commanded him.

²⁰He took the Testimony and placed it in the ark, attached the poles to the ark and put the atonement cover over it. ²¹Then he brought the ark into the tabernacle and hung the shielding curtain and shielded the ark of the Testimony, as the Lord commanded him.

²²Moses placed the table in the Tent of Meeting on the north side of the tabernacle outside the curtain ²³and set out the bread on it before the Lord, as the Lord commanded him.

²⁴He placed the lampstand in the Tent of Meeting opposite the table on the south side of the tabernacle ²⁵and set up the lamps before the Lord, as the Lord commanded him.

²⁶Moses placed the gold altar in the Tent of Meeting in front of the curtain ²⁷and burned fragrant incense on it, as the Lord commanded him. ²⁸Then he put up the curtain at the entrance to the tabernacle.

²⁹He set the altar of burnt offering near the entrance to the tabernacle, the Tent of Meeting, and offered on it burnt offerings and grain offerings, as the Lord commanded him.

³⁰He placed the basin between the Tent of Meeting and the altar and put

water in it for washing, [31]and Moses and Aaron and his sons used it to wash their hands and feet. [32]They washed whenever they entered the Tent of Meeting or approached the altar, as the LORD commanded Moses.

[33]Then Moses set up the courtyard around the tabernacle and altar and put up the curtain at the entrance to the courtyard. And so Moses finished the work.

The Glory of the LORD

[34]Then the cloud covered the Tent of Meeting, and the glory of the LORD filled the tabernacle. [35]Moses could not enter the Tent of Meeting because the cloud had settled upon it, and the glory of the LORD filled the tabernacle.

[36]In all the travels of the Israelites, whenever the cloud lifted from above the tabernacle, they would set out; [37]but if the cloud did not lift, they did not set out—until the day it lifted. [38]So the cloud of the LORD was over the tabernacle by day, and fire was in the cloud by night, in the sight of all the house of Israel during all their travels.

This book of laws shows God's tender concern for the health, safety and moral purity of his people. As you read Leviticus, look for the principles behind the regulations and take comfort in discovering that God wants to have a personal relationship with you marked by a loving, grateful obedience to his will.

LEVITICUS

The Burnt Offering

1 The LORD called to Moses and spoke to him from the Tent of Meeting. He said, ²"Speak to the Israelites and say to them: 'When any of you brings an offering to the LORD, bring as your offering an animal from either the herd or the flock.

³" 'If the offering is a burnt offering from the herd, he is to offer a male without defect. He must present it at the entrance to the Tent of Meeting so that it*ᵃ* will be acceptable to the LORD. ⁴He is to lay his hand on the head of the burnt offering, and it will be accepted on his behalf to make atonement for him. ⁵He is to slaughter the young bull before the LORD, and then Aaron's sons the priests shall bring the blood and sprinkle it against the altar on all sides at the entrance to the Tent of Meeting. ⁶He is to skin the burnt offering and cut it into pieces. ⁷The sons of Aaron the priest are to put fire on the altar and arrange wood on the fire. ⁸Then Aaron's sons the priests shall arrange the pieces, including the head and the fat, on the burning wood that is on the altar. ⁹He is to wash the inner parts and the legs with water, and the priest is to burn all of it on the altar. It is a burnt offering, an offering made by fire, an aroma pleasing to the LORD.

¹⁰" 'If the offering is a burnt offering from the flock, from either the sheep or the goats, he is to offer a male without defect. ¹¹He is to slaughter it at the north side of the altar before the LORD, and Aaron's sons the priests shall sprinkle its blood against the altar on all sides. ¹²He is to cut it into pieces, and the priest shall arrange them, including the head and the fat, on the burning wood that is on the altar. ¹³He is to wash the inner parts and the legs with water, and the priest is to bring all of it and burn it on the altar. It is a burnt offering, an offering made by fire, an aroma pleasing to the LORD.

¹⁴" 'If the offering to the LORD is a

ᵃ3 Or *he*

burnt offering of birds, he is to offer a dove or a young pigeon. [15]The priest shall bring it to the altar, wring off the head and burn it on the altar; its blood shall be drained out on the side of the altar. [16]He is to remove the crop with its contents[a] and throw it to the east side of the altar, where the ashes are. [17]He shall tear it open by the wings, not severing it completely, and then the priest shall burn it on the wood that is on the fire on the altar. It is a burnt offering, an offering made by fire, an aroma pleasing to the LORD.

The Grain Offering

2 " 'When someone brings a grain offering to the LORD, his offering is to be of fine flour. He is to pour oil on it, put incense on it [2]and take it to Aaron's sons the priests. The priest shall take a handful of the fine flour and oil, together with all the incense, and burn this as a memorial portion on the altar, an offering made by fire, an aroma pleasing to the LORD. [3]The rest of the grain offering belongs to Aaron and his sons; it is a most holy part of the offerings made to the LORD by fire.

[4]" 'If you bring a grain offering baked in an oven, it is to consist of fine flour: cakes made without yeast and mixed with oil, or[b] wafers made without yeast and spread with oil. [5]If your grain offering is prepared on a griddle, it is to be made of fine flour mixed with oil, and without yeast. [6]Crumble it and pour oil on it; it is a grain offering. [7]If your grain offering is cooked in a pan, it is to be made of fine flour and oil. [8]Bring the grain offering made of these things to the LORD; present it to the priest, who shall take it to the altar. [9]He shall take out the memorial portion from the grain offering and burn it on the altar as an offering made by fire, an aroma pleasing to the LORD. [10]The rest of the grain offering belongs to Aaron and his sons; it is a most holy part of the offerings made to the LORD by fire.

[11]" 'Every grain offering you bring to the LORD must be made without yeast, for you are not to burn any yeast or honey in an offering made to the LORD by fire. [12]You may bring them to the LORD as an offering of the firstfruits, but they are not to be offered on the altar as a pleasing aroma. [13]Season all your grain offerings with salt. Do not leave the salt of the covenant of your God out of your grain offerings; add salt to all your offerings.

[14]" 'If you bring a grain offering of firstfruits to the LORD, offer crushed heads of new grain roasted in the fire. [15]Put oil and incense on it; it is a grain offering. [16]The priest shall burn the memorial portion of the crushed grain and the oil, together with all the incense, as an offering made to the LORD by fire.

The Fellowship Offering

3 " 'If someone's offering is a fellowship offering,[c] and he offers an animal from the herd, whether male or female, he is to present before the LORD an animal without defect. [2]He is to lay his hand on the head of his offering and slaughter it at the entrance to the Tent of Meeting. Then Aaron's sons the priests shall sprinkle the blood against the altar on all sides. [3]From the fellowship offering he is to bring a sacrifice made to the LORD by fire: all the fat that covers the inner parts or is connected to them, [4]both kidneys with the fat on them near the loins, and the covering of the liver, which he will remove with the kidneys. [5]Then Aaron's sons are to burn it on the altar on top of the burnt offering that is on the burning wood, as an offering made by fire, an aroma pleasing to the LORD.

[6]" 'If he offers an animal from the flock as a fellowship offering to the LORD, he is to offer a male or female without defect. [7]If he offers a lamb, he is to present it before the LORD. [8]He is to lay his hand on the head of his of-

---

[a]16 Or *crop and the feathers*; the meaning of the Hebrew for this word is uncertain.   [b]4 Or *and*
[c]1 Traditionally *peace offering*; also in verses 3, 6 and 9

fering and slaughter it in front of the Tent of Meeting. Then Aaron's sons shall sprinkle its blood against the altar on all sides. ⁹From the fellowship offering he is to bring a sacrifice made to the LORD by fire: its fat, the entire fat tail cut off close to the backbone, all the fat that covers the inner parts or is connected to them, ¹⁰both kidneys with the fat on them near the loins, and the covering of the liver, which he will remove with the kidneys. ¹¹The priest shall burn them on the altar as food, an offering made to the LORD by fire.

¹²" 'If his offering is a goat, he is to present it before the LORD. ¹³He is to lay his hand on its head and slaughter it in front of the Tent of Meeting. Then Aaron's sons shall sprinkle its blood against the altar on all sides. ¹⁴From what he offers he is to make this offering to the LORD by fire: all the fat that covers the inner parts or is connected to them, ¹⁵both kidneys with the fat on them near the loins, and the covering of the liver, which he will remove with the kidneys. ¹⁶The priest shall burn them on the altar as food, an offering made by fire, a pleasing aroma. All the fat is the LORD's.

¹⁷" 'This is a lasting ordinance for the generations to come, wherever you live: You must not eat any fat or any blood.' "

The Sin Offering

4 The LORD said to Moses, ²"Say to the Israelites: 'When anyone sins unintentionally and does what is forbidden in any of the LORD's commands—

³" 'If the anointed priest sins, bringing guilt on the people, he must bring to the LORD a young bull without defect as a sin offering for the sin he has committed. ⁴He is to present the bull at the entrance to the Tent of Meeting before the LORD. He is to lay his hand on its head and slaughter it before the

LORD. ⁵Then the anointed priest shall take some of the bull's blood and carry it into the Tent of Meeting. ⁶He is to dip his finger into the blood and sprinkle some of it seven times before the LORD, in front of the curtain of the sanctuary. ⁷The priest shall then put some of the blood on the horns of the altar of fragrant incense that is before the LORD in the Tent of Meeting. The rest of the bull's blood he shall pour out at the base of the altar of burnt offering at the entrance to the Tent of Meeting. ⁸He shall remove all the fat from the bull of the sin offering—the fat that covers the inner parts or is connected to them, ⁹both kidneys with the fat on them near the loins, and the covering of the liver, which he will remove with the kidneys— ¹⁰just as the fat is removed from the ox*ᵃ* sacrificed as a fellowship offering.*ᵇ* Then the priest shall burn them on the altar of burnt offering. ¹¹But the hide of the bull and all its flesh, as well as the head and legs, the inner parts and offal— ¹²that is, all the rest of the bull—he must take outside the camp to a place ceremonially clean, where the ashes are thrown, and burn it in a wood fire on the ash heap.

¹³" 'If the whole Israelite community sins unintentionally and does what is forbidden in any of the LORD's commands, even though the community is unaware of the matter, they are guilty. ¹⁴When they become aware of the sin they committed, the assembly must bring a young bull as a sin offering and present it before the Tent of Meeting. ¹⁵The elders of the community are to lay their hands on the bull's head before the LORD, and the bull shall be slaughtered before the LORD. ¹⁶Then the anointed priest is to take some of the bull's blood into the Tent of Meeting. ¹⁷He shall dip his finger into the blood and sprinkle it before the LORD seven times in front of the curtain. ¹⁸He is to put some of the blood on the horns of the altar that is

---

ᵃ10 The Hebrew word can include both male and female.   *ᵇ10* Traditionally *peace offering*; also in verses 26, 31 and 35

before the LORD in the Tent of Meeting. The rest of the blood he shall pour out at the base of the altar of burnt offering at the entrance to the Tent of Meeting. ¹⁹He shall remove all the fat from it and burn it on the altar, ²⁰and do with this bull just as he did with the bull for the sin offering. In this way the priest will make atonement for them, and they will be forgiven. ²¹Then he shall take the bull outside the camp and burn it as he burned the first bull. This is the sin offering for the community.

²²"'When a leader sins unintentionally and does what is forbidden in any of the commands of the LORD his God, he is guilty. ²³When he is made aware of the sin he committed, he must bring as his offering a male goat without defect. ²⁴He is to lay his hand on the goat's head and slaughter it at the place where the burnt offering is slaughtered before the LORD. It is a sin offering. ²⁵Then the priest shall take some of the blood of the sin offering with his finger and put it on the horns of the altar of burnt offering and pour out the rest of the blood at the base of the altar. ²⁶He shall burn all the fat on the altar as he burned the fat of the fellowship offering. In this way the priest will make atonement for the man's sin, and he will be forgiven.

²⁷"'If a member of the community sins unintentionally and does what is forbidden in any of the LORD's commands, he is guilty. ²⁸When he is made aware of the sin he committed, he must bring as his offering for the sin he committed a female goat without defect. ²⁹He is to lay his hand on the head of the sin offering and slaughter it at the place of the burnt offering. ³⁰Then the priest is to take some of the blood with his finger and put it on the horns of the altar of burnt offering and pour out the rest of the blood at the base of the altar. ³¹He shall remove all the fat, just as the fat is removed from the fellowship offering, and the priest shall burn it on the altar as an aroma pleasing to the LORD. In this way the priest will make

atonement for him, and he will be forgiven.

³²"'If he brings a lamb as his sin offering, he is to bring a female without defect. ³³He is to lay his hand on its head and slaughter it for a sin offering at the place where the burnt offering is slaughtered. ³⁴Then the priest shall take some of the blood of the sin offering with his finger and put it on the horns of the altar of burnt offering and pour out the rest of the blood at the base of the altar. ³⁵He shall remove all the fat, just as the fat is removed from the lamb of the fellowship offering, and the priest shall burn it on the altar on top of the offerings made to the LORD by fire. In this way the priest will make atonement for him for the sin he has committed, and he will be forgiven.

5 "'If a person sins because he does not speak up when he hears a public charge to testify regarding something he has seen or learned about, he will be held responsible.

²"'Or if a person touches anything ceremonially unclean—whether the carcasses of unclean wild animals or of unclean livestock or of unclean creatures that move along the ground—even though he is unaware of it, he has become unclean and is guilty.

³"'Or if he touches human uncleanness—anything that would make him unclean—even though he is unaware of it, when he learns of it he will be guilty.

⁴"'Or if a person thoughtlessly takes an oath to do anything, whether good or evil—in any matter one might carelessly swear about—even though he is unaware of it, in any case when he learns of it he will be guilty.

⁵"'When anyone is guilty in any of these ways, he must confess in what way he has sinned ⁶and, as a penalty for the sin he has committed, he must bring to the LORD a female lamb or goat from the flock as a sin offering; and the priest shall make atonement for him for his sin.

7" 'If he cannot afford a lamb, he is to bring two doves or two young pigeons to the LORD as a penalty for his sin—one for a sin offering and the other for a burnt offering. ⁸He is to bring them to the priest, who shall first offer the one for the sin offering. He is to wring its head from its neck, not severing it completely, ⁹and is to sprinkle some of the blood of the sin offering against the side of the altar; the rest of the blood must be drained out at the base of the altar. It is a sin offering. ¹⁰The priest shall then offer the other as a burnt offering in the prescribed way and make atonement for him for the sin he has committed, and he will be forgiven.

¹¹" 'If, however, he cannot afford two doves or two young pigeons, he is to bring as an offering for his sin a tenth of an ephah*ᵃ* of fine flour for a sin offering. He must not put oil or incense on it, because it is a sin offering. ¹²He is to bring it to the priest, who shall take a handful of it as a memorial portion and burn it on the altar on top of the offerings made to the LORD by fire. It is a sin offering. ¹³In this way the priest will make atonement for him for any of these sins he has committed, and he will be forgiven. The rest of the offering will belong to the priest, as in the case of the grain offering.' "

The Guilt Offering

¹⁴The LORD said to Moses: ¹⁵"When a person commits a violation and sins unintentionally in regard to any of the LORD's holy things, he is to bring to the LORD as a penalty a ram from the flock, one without defect and of the proper value in silver, according to the sanctuary shekel.*ᵇ* It is a guilt offering. ¹⁶He must make restitution for what he has failed to do in regard to the holy things, add a fifth of the value to that and give it all to the priest, who will make atonement for him with the ram as a guilt offering, and he will be forgiven.

¹⁷"If a person sins and does what is forbidden in any of the LORD's commands, even though he does not know it, he is guilty and will be held responsible. ¹⁸He is to bring to the priest as a guilt offering a ram from the flock, one without defect and of the proper value. In this way the priest will make atonement for him for the wrong he has committed unintentionally, and he will be forgiven. ¹⁹It is a guilt offering; he has been guilty of*ᶜ* wrongdoing against the LORD."

6 The LORD said to Moses: ²"If anyone sins and is unfaithful to the LORD by deceiving his neighbor about something entrusted to him or left in his care or stolen, or if he cheats him, ³or if he finds lost property and lies about it, or if he swears falsely, or if he commits any such sin that people may do— ⁴when he thus sins and becomes guilty, he must return what he has stolen or taken by extortion, or what was entrusted to him, or the lost property he found, ⁵or whatever it was he swore falsely about. He must make restitution in full, add a fifth of the value to it and give it all to the owner on the day he presents his guilt offering. ⁶And as a penalty he must bring to the priest, that is, to the LORD, his guilt offering, a ram from the flock, one without defect and of the proper value. ⁷In this way the priest will make atonement for him before the LORD, and he will be forgiven for any of these things he did that made him guilty."

The Burnt Offering

⁸The LORD said to Moses: ⁹"Give Aaron and his sons this command: 'These are the regulations for the burnt offering: The burnt offering is to remain on the altar hearth throughout the night, till morning, and the fire must be kept burning on the altar. ¹⁰The priest shall then put on his linen clothes, with linen undergarments next to his body, and shall remove the

---

ᵃ11 That is, probably about 2 quarts (about 2 liters) grams)   *ᶜ19* Or *has made full expiation for his*   *ᵇ15* That is, about 2/5 ounce (about 11.5

ashes of the burnt offering that the fire has consumed on the altar and place them beside the altar. ¹¹Then he is to take off these clothes and put on others, and carry the ashes outside the camp to a place that is ceremonially clean. ¹²The fire on the altar must be kept burning; it must not go out. Every morning the priest is to add firewood and arrange the burnt offering on the fire and burn the fat of the fellowship offerings*a* on it. ¹³The fire must be kept burning on the altar continuously; it must not go out.

The Grain Offering

¹⁴" 'These are the regulations for the grain offering: Aaron's sons are to bring it before the LORD, in front of the altar. ¹⁵The priest is to take a handful of fine flour and oil, together with all the incense on the grain offering, and burn the memorial portion on the altar as an aroma pleasing to the LORD. ¹⁶Aaron and his sons shall eat the rest of it, but it is to be eaten without yeast in a holy place; they are to eat it in the courtyard of the Tent of Meeting. ¹⁷It must not be baked with yeast; I have given it as their share of the offerings made to me by fire. Like the sin offering and the guilt offering, it is most holy. ¹⁸Any male descendant of Aaron may eat it. It is his regular share of the offerings made to the LORD by fire for the generations to come. Whatever touches them will become holy.*b* ' "

¹⁹The LORD also said to Moses, ²⁰"This is the offering Aaron and his sons are to bring to the LORD on the day he*c* is anointed: a tenth of an ephah*d* of fine flour as a regular grain offering, half of it in the morning and half in the evening. ²¹Prepare it with oil on a griddle; bring it well-mixed and present the grain offering broken*e* in pieces as an aroma pleasing to the LORD. ²²The son who is to succeed him as anointed priest shall prepare it. It is the LORD's regular share and is to be burned completely.

²³Every grain offering of a priest shall be burned completely; it must not be eaten."

The Sin Offering

²⁴The LORD said to Moses, ²⁵"Say to Aaron and his sons: 'These are the regulations for the sin offering: The sin offering is to be slaughtered before the LORD in the place the burnt offering is slaughtered; it is most holy. ²⁶The priest who offers it shall eat it; it is to be eaten in a holy place, in the courtyard of the Tent of Meeting. ²⁷Whatever touches any of the flesh will become holy, and if any of the blood is spattered on a garment, you must wash it in a holy place. ²⁸The clay pot the meat is cooked in must be broken; but if it is cooked in a bronze pot, the pot is to be scoured and rinsed with water. ²⁹Any male in a priest's family may eat it; it is most holy. ³⁰But any sin offering whose blood is brought into the Tent of Meeting to make atonement in the Holy Place must not be eaten; it must be burned.

The Guilt Offering

7 " 'These are the regulations for the guilt offering, which is most holy: ²The guilt offering is to be slaughtered in the place where the burnt offering is slaughtered, and its blood is to be sprinkled against the altar on all sides. ³All its fat shall be offered: the fat tail and the fat that covers the inner parts, ⁴both kidneys with the fat on them near the loins, and the covering of the liver, which is to be removed with the kidneys. ⁵The priest shall burn them on the altar as an offering made to the LORD by fire. It is a guilt offering. ⁶Any male in a priest's family may eat it, but it must be eaten in a holy place; it is most holy.

⁷" 'The same law applies to both the sin offering and the guilt offering: They belong to the priest who makes

---

*a*12 Traditionally *peace offerings*   *b*18 Or *Whoever touches them must be holy*; similarly in verse 27   *c*20 Or *each*   *d*20 That is, probably about 2 quarts (about 2 liters)   *e*21 The meaning of the Hebrew for this word is uncertain.

atonement with them. ⁸The priest who offers a burnt offering for anyone may keep its hide for himself. ⁹Every grain offering baked in an oven or cooked in a pan or on a griddle belongs to the priest who offers it, ¹⁰and every grain offering, whether mixed with oil or dry, belongs equally to all the sons of Aaron.

The Fellowship Offering

¹¹ 'These are the regulations for the fellowship offering*ᵃ* a person may present to the Lord:

¹²" 'If he offers it as an expression of thankfulness, then along with this thank offering he is to offer cakes of bread made without yeast and mixed with oil, wafers made without yeast and spread with oil, and cakes of fine flour well-kneaded and mixed with oil. ¹³Along with his fellowship offering of thanksgiving he is to present an offering with cakes of bread made with yeast. ¹⁴He is to bring one of each kind as an offering, a contribution to the Lord; it belongs to the priest who sprinkles the blood of the fellowship offerings. ¹⁵The meat of his fellowship offering of thanksgiving must be eaten on the day it is offered; he must leave none of it till morning.

¹⁶" 'If, however, his offering is the result of a vow or is a freewill offering, the sacrifice shall be eaten on the day he offers it, but anything left over may be eaten on the next day. ¹⁷Any meat of the sacrifice left over till the third day must be burned up. ¹⁸If any meat of the fellowship offering is eaten on the third day, it will not be accepted. It will not be credited to the one who offered it, for it is impure; the person who eats any of it will be held responsible.

¹⁹" 'Meat that touches anything ceremonially unclean must not be eaten; it must be burned up. As for other meat, anyone ceremonially clean may eat it. ²⁰But if anyone who is unclean eats any meat of the fellowship offering belonging to the Lord, that person must be cut off from his people. ²¹If

anyone touches something unclean—whether human uncleanness or an unclean animal or any unclean, detestable thing—and then eats any of the meat of the fellowship offering belonging to the Lord, that person must be cut off from his people.' "

Eating Fat and Blood Forbidden

²²The Lord said to Moses, ²³"Say to the Israelites: 'Do not eat any of the fat of cattle, sheep or goats. ²⁴The fat of an animal found dead or torn by wild animals may be used for any other purpose, but you must not eat it. ²⁵Anyone who eats the fat of an animal from which an offering by fire may be*ᵇ* made to the Lord must be cut off from his people. ²⁶And wherever you live, you must not eat the blood of any bird or animal. ²⁷If anyone eats blood, that person must be cut off from his people.' "

The Priests' Share

²⁸The Lord said to Moses, ²⁹"Say to the Israelites: 'Anyone who brings a fellowship offering to the Lord is to bring part of it as his sacrifice to the Lord. ³⁰With his own hands he is to bring the offering made to the Lord by fire; he is to bring the fat, together with the breast, and wave the breast before the Lord as a wave offering. ³¹The priest shall burn the fat on the altar, but the breast belongs to Aaron and his sons. ³²You are to give the right thigh of your fellowship offerings to the priest as a contribution. ³³The son of Aaron who offers the blood and the fat of the fellowship offering shall have the right thigh as his share. ³⁴From the fellowship offerings of the Israelites, I have taken the breast that is waved and the thigh that is presented and have given them to Aaron the priest and his sons as their regular share from the Israelites.' "

³⁵This is the portion of the offerings made to the Lord by fire that were allotted to Aaron and his sons on the day they were presented to serve the

LORD as priests. ³⁶On the day they were anointed, the LORD commanded that the Israelites give this to them as their regular share for the generations to come.

³⁷These, then, are the regulations for the burnt offering, the grain offering, the sin offering, the guilt offering, the ordination offering and the fellowship offering, ³⁸which the LORD gave Moses on Mount Sinai on the day he commanded the Israelites to bring their offerings to the LORD, in the Desert of Sinai.

The Ordination of Aaron and His Sons

8 The LORD said to Moses, ²"Bring Aaron and his sons, their garments, the anointing oil, the bull for the sin offering, the two rams and the basket containing bread made without yeast, ³and gather the entire assembly at the entrance to the Tent of Meeting." ⁴Moses did as the LORD commanded him, and the assembly gathered at the entrance to the Tent of Meeting.

⁵Moses said to the assembly, "This is what the LORD has commanded to be done." ⁶Then Moses brought Aaron and his sons forward and washed them with water. ⁷He put the tunic on Aaron, tied the sash around him, clothed him with the robe and put the ephod on him. He also tied the ephod to him by its skillfully woven waistband; so it was fastened on him. ⁸He placed the breastpiece on him and put the Urim and Thummim in the breastpiece. ⁹Then he placed the turban on Aaron's head and set the gold plate, the sacred diadem, on the front of it, as the LORD commanded Moses.

¹⁰Then Moses took the anointing oil and anointed the tabernacle and everything in it, and so consecrated them. ¹¹He sprinkled some of the oil on the altar seven times, anointing the altar and all its utensils and the basin with its stand, to consecrate them. ¹²He poured some of the anointing oil on Aaron's head and anointed him to consecrate him. ¹³Then he brought Aaron's sons forward, put tunics on them, tied sashes around them and put headbands on them, as the LORD commanded Moses.

¹⁴He then presented the bull for the sin offering, and Aaron and his sons laid their hands on its head. ¹⁵Moses slaughtered the bull and took some of the blood, and with his finger he put it on all the horns of the altar to purify the altar. He poured out the rest of the blood at the base of the altar. So he consecrated it to make atonement for it. ¹⁶Moses also took all the fat around the inner parts, the covering of the liver, and both kidneys and their fat, and burned it on the altar. ¹⁷But the bull with its hide and its flesh and its offal he burned up outside the camp, as the LORD commanded Moses.

¹⁸He then presented the ram for the burnt offering, and Aaron and his sons laid their hands on its head. ¹⁹Then Moses slaughtered the ram and sprinkled the blood against the altar on all sides. ²⁰He cut the ram into pieces and burned the head, the pieces and the fat. ²¹He washed the inner parts and the legs with water and burned the whole ram on the altar as a burnt offering, a pleasing aroma, an offering made to the LORD by fire, as the LORD commanded Moses.

²²He then presented the other ram, the ram for the ordination, and Aaron and his sons laid their hands on its head. ²³Moses slaughtered the ram and took some of its blood and put it on the lobe of Aaron's right ear, on the thumb of his right hand and on the big toe of his right foot. ²⁴Moses also brought Aaron's sons forward and put some of the blood on the lobes of their right ears, on the thumbs of their right hands and on the big toes of their right feet. Then he sprinkled blood against the altar on all sides. ²⁵He took the fat, the fat tail, all the fat around the inner parts, the covering of the liver, both kidneys and their fat and the right thigh. ²⁶Then from the basket of bread made without yeast, which was before the LORD, he took a cake of bread, and one made with oil, and a wafer; he put

these on the fat portions and on the right thigh. ²⁷He put all these in the hands of Aaron and his sons and waved them before the LORD as a wave offering. ²⁸Then Moses took them from their hands and burned them on the altar on top of the burnt offering as an ordination offering, a pleasing aroma, an offering made to the LORD by fire. ²⁹He also took the breast—Moses' share of the ordination ram—and waved it before the LORD as a wave offering, as the LORD commanded Moses.

³⁰Then Moses took some of the anointing oil and some of the blood from the altar and sprinkled them on Aaron and his garments and on his sons and their garments. So he consecrated Aaron and his garments and his sons and their garments.

³¹Moses then said to Aaron and his sons, "Cook the meat at the entrance to the Tent of Meeting and eat it there with the bread from the basket of ordination offerings, as I commanded, saying,ᵃ 'Aaron and his sons are to eat it.' ³²Then burn up the rest of the meat and the bread. ³³Do not leave the entrance to the Tent of Meeting for seven days, until the days of your ordination are completed, for your ordination will last seven days. ³⁴What has been done today was commanded by the LORD to make atonement for you. ³⁵You must stay at the entrance to the Tent of Meeting day and night for seven days and do what the LORD requires, so you will not die; for that is what I have been commanded." ³⁶So Aaron and his sons did everything the LORD commanded through Moses.

The Priests Begin Their Ministry

9 On the eighth day Moses summoned Aaron and his sons and the elders of Israel. ²He said to Aaron, "Take a bull calf for your sin offering and a ram for your burnt offering, both without defect, and present them before the LORD. ³Then say to the Israelites: 'Take a male goat for a sin offering, a calf and a lamb—both a year old and without defect—for a burnt offering, ⁴and an oxᵇ and a ram for a fellowship offeringᶜ to sacrifice before the LORD, together with a grain offering mixed with oil. For today the LORD will appear to you.' "

⁵They took the things Moses commanded to the front of the Tent of Meeting, and the entire assembly came near and stood before the LORD. ⁶Then Moses said, "This is what the LORD has commanded you to do, so that the glory of the LORD may appear to you."

⁷Moses said to Aaron, "Come to the altar and sacrifice your sin offering and your burnt offering and make atonement for yourself and the people; sacrifice the offering that is for the people and make atonement for them, as the LORD has commanded."

⁸So Aaron came to the altar and slaughtered the calf as a sin offering for himself. ⁹His sons brought the blood to him, and he dipped his finger into the blood and put it on the horns of the altar; the rest of the blood he poured out at the base of the altar. ¹⁰On the altar he burned the fat, the kidneys and the covering of the liver from the sin offering, as the LORD commanded Moses; ¹¹the flesh and the hide he burned up outside the camp.

¹²Then he slaughtered the burnt offering. His sons handed him the blood, and he sprinkled it against the altar on all sides. ¹³They handed him the burnt offering piece by piece, including the head, and he burned them on the altar. ¹⁴He washed the inner parts and the legs and burned them on top of the burnt offering on the altar.

¹⁵Aaron then brought the offering that was for the people. He took the goat for the people's sin offering and slaughtered it and offered it for a sin offering as he did with the first one.

ᵃ31 Or I was commanded: ᵇ4 The Hebrew word can include both male and female; also in verses 18 and 19.   ᶜ4 Traditionally peace offering; also in verses 18 and 22

¹⁶He brought the burnt offering and offered it in the prescribed way. ¹⁷He also brought the grain offering, took a handful of it and burned it on the altar in addition to the morning's burnt offering.

¹⁸He slaughtered the ox and the ram as the fellowship offering for the people. His sons handed him the blood, and he sprinkled it against the altar on all sides. ¹⁹But the fat portions of the ox and the ram—the fat tail, the layer of fat, the kidneys and the covering of the liver— ²⁰these they laid on the breasts, and then Aaron burned the fat on the altar. ²¹Aaron waved the breasts and the right thigh before the LORD as a wave offering, as Moses commanded.

²²Then Aaron lifted his hands toward the people and blessed them. And having sacrificed the sin offering, the burnt offering and the fellowship offering, he stepped down.

²³Moses and Aaron then went into the Tent of Meeting. When they came out, they blessed the people; and the glory of the LORD appeared to all the people. ²⁴Fire came out from the presence of the LORD and consumed the burnt offering and the fat portions on the altar. And when all the people saw it, they shouted for joy and fell facedown.

The Death of Nadab and Abihu

10 Aaron's sons Nadab and Abihu took their censers, put fire in them and added incense; and they offered unauthorized fire before the LORD, contrary to his command. ²So fire came out from the presence of the LORD and consumed them, and they died before the LORD. ³Moses then said to Aaron, "This is what the LORD spoke of when he said:

" 'Among those who approach me
    I will show myself holy;
in the sight of all the people
    I will be honored.' "

Aaron remained silent.

⁴Moses summoned Mishael and El-zaphan, sons of Aaron's uncle Uzziel, and said to them, "Come here; carry your cousins outside the camp, away from the front of the sanctuary." ⁵So they came and carried them, still in their tunics, outside the camp, as Moses ordered.

⁶Then Moses said to Aaron and his sons Eleazar and Ithamar, "Do not let your hair become unkempt,ᵃ and do not tear your clothes, or you will die and the LORD will be angry with the whole community. But your relatives, all the house of Israel, may mourn for those the LORD has destroyed by fire. ⁷Do not leave the entrance to the Tent of Meeting or you will die, because the LORD's anointing oil is on you." So they did as Moses said.

⁸Then the LORD said to Aaron, ⁹"You and your sons are not to drink wine or other fermented drink whenever you go into the Tent of Meeting, or you will die. This is a lasting ordinance for the generations to come. ¹⁰You must distinguish between the holy and the common, between the unclean and the clean, ¹¹and you must teach the Israelites all the decrees the LORD has given them through Moses."

¹²Moses said to Aaron and his remaining sons, Eleazar and Ithamar, "Take the grain offering left over from the offerings made to the LORD by fire and eat it prepared without yeast beside the altar, for it is most holy. ¹³Eat it in a holy place, because it is your share and your sons' share of the offerings made to the LORD by fire; for so I have been commanded. ¹⁴But you and your sons and your daughters may eat the breast that was waved and the thigh that was presented. Eat them in a ceremonially clean place; they have been given to you and your children as your share of the Israelites' fellowship offerings.ᵇ ¹⁵The thigh that was presented and the breast that was waved must be brought with the fat portions of the offerings made by fire, to be waved before the LORD as a wave offering. This will be the regular share for you

---

ᵃ6 Or *Do not uncover your heads*   ᵇ14 Traditionally *peace offerings* and your children, as the LORD has commanded."

16When Moses inquired about the goat of the sin offering and found that it had been burned up, he was angry with Eleazar and Ithamar, Aaron's remaining sons, and asked, 17"Why didn't you eat the sin offering in the sanctuary area? It is most holy; it was given to you to take away the guilt of the community by making atonement for them before the LORD. 18Since its blood was not taken into the Holy Place, you should have eaten the goat in the sanctuary area, as I commanded."

19Aaron replied to Moses, "Today they sacrificed their sin offering and their burnt offering before the LORD, but such things as this have happened to me. Would the LORD have been pleased if I had eaten the sin offering today?" 20When Moses heard this, he was satisfied.

Clean and Unclean Food

11 The LORD said to Moses and Aaron, 2"Say to the Israelites: 'Of all the animals that live on land, these are the ones you may eat: 3You may eat any animal that has a split hoof completely divided and that chews the cud.

4" 'There are some that only chew the cud or only have a split hoof, but you must not eat them. The camel, though it chews the cud, does not have a split hoof; it is ceremonially unclean for you. 5The coney,a though it chews the cud, does not have a split hoof; it is unclean for you. 6The rabbit, though it chews the cud, does not have a split hoof; it is unclean for you. 7And the pig, though it has a split hoof completely divided, does not chew the cud; it is unclean for you. 8You must not eat their meat or touch their carcasses; they are unclean for you.

9" 'Of all the creatures living in the water of the seas and the streams, you may eat any that have fins and scales.

10But all creatures in the seas or streams that do not have fins and scales—whether among all the swarming things or among all the other living creatures in the water—you are to detest. 11And since you are to detest them, you must not eat their meat and you must detest their carcasses. 12Anything living in the water that does not have fins and scales is to be detestable to you.

13" 'These are the birds you are to detest and not eat because they are detestable: the eagle, the vulture, the black vulture, 14the red kite, any kind of black kite, 15any kind of raven, 16the horned owl, the screech owl, the gull, any kind of hawk, 17the little owl, the cormorant, the great owl, 18the white owl, the desert owl, the osprey, 19the stork, any kind of heron, the hoopoe and the bat.b

20" 'All flying insects that walk on all fours are to be detestable to you. 21There are, however, some winged creatures that walk on all fours that you may eat: those that have jointed legs for hopping on the ground. 22Of these you may eat any kind of locust, katydid, cricket or grasshopper. 23But all other winged creatures that have four legs you are to detest.

24" 'You will make yourselves unclean by these; whoever touches their carcasses will be unclean till evening. 25Whoever picks up one of their carcasses must wash his clothes, and he will be unclean till evening.

26" 'Every animal that has a split hoof not completely divided or that does not chew the cud is unclean for you; whoever touches ˻the carcass of˼ any of them will be unclean. 27Of all the animals that walk on all fours, those that walk on their paws are unclean for you; whoever touches their carcasses will be unclean till evening. 28Anyone who picks up their carcasses must wash his clothes, and he will be unclean till evening. They are unclean for you.

29" 'Of the animals that move about

---

a5 That is, the hyrax or rock badger   b19 The precise identification of some of the birds, insects and animals in this chapter is uncertain.

on the ground, these are unclean for you: the weasel, the rat, any kind of great lizard, ³⁰the gecko, the monitor lizard, the wall lizard, the skink and the chameleon. ³¹Of all those that move along the ground, these are unclean for you. Whoever touches them when they are dead will be unclean till evening. ³²When one of them dies and falls on something, that article, whatever its use, will be unclean, whether it is made of wood, cloth, hide or sackcloth. Put it in water; it will be unclean till evening, and then it will be clean. ³³If one of them falls into a clay pot, everything in it will be unclean, and you must break the pot. ³⁴Any food that could be eaten but has water on it from such a pot is unclean, and any liquid that could be drunk from it is unclean. ³⁵Anything that one of their carcasses falls on becomes unclean; an oven or cooking pot must be broken up. They are unclean, and you are to regard them as unclean. ³⁶A spring, however, or a cistern for collecting water remains clean, but anyone who touches one of these carcasses is unclean. ³⁷If a carcass falls on any seeds that are to be planted, they remain clean. ³⁸But if water has been put on the seed and a carcass falls on it, it is unclean for you.

³⁹" 'If an animal that you are allowed to eat dies, anyone who touches the carcass will be unclean till evening. ⁴⁰Anyone who eats some of the carcass must wash his clothes, and he will be unclean till evening. Anyone who picks up the carcass must wash his clothes, and he will be unclean till evening.

⁴¹" 'Every creature that moves about on the ground is detestable; it is not to be eaten. ⁴²You are not to eat any creature that moves about on the ground, whether it moves on its belly or walks on all fours or on many feet; it is detestable. ⁴³Do not defile yourselves by any of these creatures. Do not make yourselves unclean by means of them or be made unclean by them. ⁴⁴I am the LORD your God; con-

secrate yourselves and be holy, because I am holy. Do not make yourselves unclean by any creature that moves about on the ground. ⁴⁵I am the LORD who brought you up out of Egypt to be your God; therefore be holy, because I am holy.

⁴⁶" 'These are the regulations concerning animals, birds, every living thing that moves in the water and every creature that moves about on the ground. ⁴⁷You must distinguish between the unclean and the clean, between living creatures that may be eaten and those that may not be eaten.' "

Purification After Childbirth

12 The LORD said to Moses, ²"Say to the Israelites: 'A woman who becomes pregnant and gives birth to a son will be ceremonially unclean for seven days, just as she is unclean during her monthly period. ³On the eighth day the boy is to be circumcised. ⁴Then the woman must wait thirty-three days to be purified from her bleeding. She must not touch anything sacred or go to the sanctuary until the days of her purification are over. ⁵If she gives birth to a daughter, for two weeks the woman will be unclean, as during her period. Then she must wait sixty-six days to be purified from her bleeding.

⁶" 'When the days of her purification for a son or daughter are over, she is to bring to the priest at the entrance to the Tent of Meeting a year-old lamb for a burnt offering and a young pigeon or a dove for a sin offering. ⁷He shall offer them before the LORD to make atonement for her, and then she will be ceremonially clean from her flow of blood.

" 'These are the regulations for the woman who gives birth to a boy or a girl. ⁸If she cannot afford a lamb, she is to bring two doves or two young pigeons, one for a burnt offering and the other for a sin offering. In this way the priest will make atonement for her, and she will be clean.' "

Regulations About Infectious Skin Diseases

13 The LORD said to Moses and Aaron, ²"When anyone has a swelling or a rash or a bright spot on his skin that may become an infectious skin disease,ᵃ he must be brought to Aaron the priest or to one of his sonsᵇ who is a priest. ³The priest is to examine the sore on his skin, and if the hair in the sore has turned white and the sore appears to be more than skin deep,ᶜ it is an infectious skin disease. When the priest examines him, he shall pronounce him ceremonially unclean. ⁴If the spot on his skin is white but does not appear to be more than skin deep and the hair in it has not turned white, the priest is to put the infected person in isolation for seven days. ⁵On the seventh day the priest is to examine him, and if he sees that the sore is unchanged and has not spread in the skin, he is to keep him in isolation another seven days. ⁶On the seventh day the priest is to examine him again, and if the sore has faded and has not spread in the skin, the priest shall pronounce him clean; it is only a rash. The man must wash his clothes, and he will be clean. ⁷But if the rash does spread in his skin after he has shown himself to the priest to be pronounced clean, he must appear before the priest again. ⁸The priest is to examine him, and if the rash has spread in the skin, he shall pronounce him unclean; it is an infectious disease.

⁹"When anyone has an infectious skin disease, he must be brought to the priest. ¹⁰The priest is to examine him, and if there is a white swelling in the skin that has turned the hair white and if there is raw flesh in the swelling, ¹¹it is a chronic skin disease and the priest shall pronounce him unclean. He is not to put him in isolation, because he is already unclean.

¹²"If the disease breaks out all over his skin and, so far as the priest can see, it covers all the skin of the infected person from head to foot, ¹³the priest is to examine him, and if the disease has covered his whole body, he shall pronounce that person clean. Since it has all turned white, he is clean. ¹⁴But whenever raw flesh appears on him, he will be unclean. ¹⁵When the priest sees the raw flesh, he shall pronounce him unclean. The raw flesh is unclean; he has an infectious disease. ¹⁶Should the raw flesh change and turn white, he must go to the priest. ¹⁷The priest is to examine him, and if the sores have turned white, the priest shall pronounce the infected person clean; then he will be clean.

¹⁸"When someone has a boil on his skin and it heals, ¹⁹and in the place where the boil was, a white swelling or reddish-white spot appears, he must present himself to the priest. ²⁰The priest is to examine it, and if it appears to be more than skin deep and the hair in it has turned white, the priest shall pronounce him unclean. It is an infectious skin disease that has broken out where the boil was. ²¹But if, when the priest examines it, there is no white hair in it and it is not more than skin deep and has faded, then the priest is to put him in isolation for seven days. ²²If it is spreading in the skin, the priest shall pronounce him unclean; it is infectious. ²³But if the spot is unchanged and has not spread, it is only a scar from the boil, and the priest shall pronounce him clean.

²⁴"When someone has a burn on his skin and a reddish-white or white spot appears in the raw flesh of the burn, ²⁵the priest is to examine the spot, and if the hair in it has turned white, and it appears to be more than skin deep, it is an infectious disease that has broken out in the burn. The priest shall pronounce him unclean; it is an infectious skin disease. ²⁶But if

ᵃ2 Traditionally *leprosy*; the Hebrew word was used for various diseases affecting the skin—not necessarily leprosy; also elsewhere in this chapter.   ᵇ2 Or *descendants*   ᶜ3 Or *be lower than the rest of the skin*; also elsewhere in this chapter

the priest examines it and there is no white hair in the spot and if it is not more than skin deep and has faded, then the priest is to put him in isolation for seven days. [27]On the seventh day the priest is to examine him, and if it is spreading in the skin, the priest shall pronounce him unclean; it is an infectious skin disease. [28]If, however, the spot is unchanged and has not spread in the skin but has faded, it is a swelling from the burn, and the priest shall pronounce him clean; it is only a scar from the burn.

[29]"If a man or woman has a sore on the head or on the chin, [30]the priest is to examine the sore, and if it appears to be more than skin deep and the hair in it is yellow and thin, the priest shall pronounce that person unclean; it is an itch, an infectious disease of the head or chin. [31]But if, when the priest examines this kind of sore, it does not seem to be more than skin deep and there is no black hair in it, then the priest is to put the infected person in isolation for seven days. [32]On the seventh day the priest is to examine the sore, and if the itch has not spread and there is no yellow hair in it and it does not appear to be more than skin deep, [33]he must be shaved except for the diseased area, and the priest is to keep him in isolation another seven days. [34]On the seventh day the priest is to examine the itch, and if it has not spread in the skin and appears to be no more than skin deep, the priest shall pronounce him clean. He must wash his clothes, and he will be clean. [35]But if the itch does spread in the skin after he is pronounced clean, [36]the priest is to examine him, and if the itch has spread in the skin, the priest does not need to look for yellow hair; the person is unclean. [37]If, however, in his judgment it is unchanged and black hair has grown in it, the itch is healed. He is clean, and the priest shall pronounce him clean.

[38]"When a man or woman has white spots on the skin, [39]the priest is to examine them, and if the spots are dull white, it is a harmless rash that has broken out on the skin; that person is clean.

[40]"When a man has lost his hair and is bald, he is clean. [41]If he has lost his hair from the front of his scalp and has a bald forehead, he is clean. [42]But if he has a reddish-white sore on his bald head or forehead, it is an infectious disease breaking out on his head or forehead. [43]The priest is to examine him, and if the swollen sore on his head or forehead is reddish-white like an infectious skin disease, [44]the man is diseased and is unclean. The priest shall pronounce him unclean because of the sore on his head.

[45]"The person with such an infectious disease must wear torn clothes, let his hair be unkempt,[a] cover the lower part of his face and cry out, 'Unclean! Unclean!' [46]As long as he has the infection he remains unclean. He must live alone; he must live outside the camp.

Regulations About Mildew

[47]"If any clothing is contaminated with mildew—any woolen or linen clothing, [48]any woven or knitted material of linen or wool, any leather or anything made of leather— [49]and if the contamination in the clothing, or leather, or woven or knitted material, or any leather article, is greenish or reddish, it is a spreading mildew and must be shown to the priest. [50]The priest is to examine the mildew and isolate the affected article for seven days. [51]On the seventh day he is to examine it, and if the mildew has spread in the clothing, or the woven or knitted material, or the leather, whatever its use, it is a destructive mildew; the article is unclean. [52]He must burn up the clothing, or the woven or knitted material of wool or linen, or any leather article that has the contamination in it, because the mildew is destructive; the article must be burned up.

[53]"But if, when the priest examines it, the mildew has not spread in the

[a]45 Or *clothes, uncover his head*

clothing, or the woven or knitted material, or the leather article, ⁵⁴he shall order that the contaminated article be washed. Then he is to isolate it for another seven days. ⁵⁵After the affected article has been washed, the priest is to examine it, and if the mildew has not changed its appearance, even though it has not spread, it is unclean. Burn it with fire, whether the mildew has affected one side or the other. ⁵⁶If, when the priest examines it, the mildew has faded after the article has been washed, he is to tear the contaminated part out of the clothing, or the leather, or the woven or knitted material. ⁵⁷But if it reappears in the clothing, or in the woven or knitted material, or in the leather article, it is spreading, and whatever has the mildew must be burned with fire. ⁵⁸The clothing, or the woven or knitted material, or any leather article that has been washed and is rid of the mildew, must be washed again, and it will be clean."

⁵⁹These are the regulations concerning contamination by mildew in woolen or linen clothing, woven or knitted material, or any leather article, for pronouncing them clean or unclean.

Cleansing From Infectious Skin Diseases

14 The LORD said to Moses, ²"These are the regulations for the diseased person at the time of his ceremonial cleansing, when he is brought to the priest: ³The priest is to go outside the camp and examine him. If the person has been healed of his infectious skin disease,ᵃ ⁴the priest shall order that two live clean birds and some cedar wood, scarlet yarn and hyssop be brought for the one to be cleansed. ⁵Then the priest shall order that one of the birds be killed over fresh water in a clay pot. ⁶He is then to take the live bird and dip it, together with the cedar wood, the scarlet yarn and the hyssop, into the blood of the bird that was killed over the fresh water. ⁷Seven times he shall sprinkle the one to be cleansed of the infectious disease and pronounce him clean. Then he is to release the live bird in the open fields.

⁸"The person to be cleansed must wash his clothes, shave off all his hair and bathe with water; then he will be ceremonially clean. After this he may come into the camp, but he must stay outside his tent for seven days. ⁹On the seventh day he must shave off all his hair; he must shave his head, his beard, his eyebrows and the rest of his hair. He must wash his clothes and bathe himself with water, and he will be clean.

¹⁰"On the eighth day he must bring two male lambs and one ewe lamb a year old, each without defect, along with three-tenths of an ephahᵇ of fine flour mixed with oil for a grain offering, and one logᶜ of oil. ¹¹The priest who pronounces him clean shall present both the one to be cleansed and his offerings before the LORD at the entrance to the Tent of Meeting.

¹²"Then the priest is to take one of the male lambs and offer it as a guilt offering, along with the log of oil; he shall wave them before the LORD as a wave offering. ¹³He is to slaughter the lamb in the holy place where the sin offering and the burnt offering are slaughtered. Like the sin offering, the guilt offering belongs to the priest; it is most holy. ¹⁴The priest is to take some of the blood of the guilt offering and put it on the lobe of the right ear of the one to be cleansed, on the thumb of his right hand and on the big toe of his right foot. ¹⁵The priest shall then take some of the log of oil, pour it in the palm of his own left hand, ¹⁶dip his right forefinger into the oil in his palm, and with his finger

---

ᵃ3 Traditionally *leprosy*; the Hebrew word was used for various diseases affecting the skin—not necessarily leprosy; also elsewhere in this chapter.   ᵇ10 That is, probably about 6 quarts (about 6.5 liters)   ᶜ10 That is, probably about 2/3 pint (about 0.3 liter); also in verses 12, 15, 21 and 24

sprinkle some of it before the LORD seven times. [17]The priest is to put some of the oil remaining in his palm on the lobe of the right ear of the one to be cleansed, on the thumb of his right hand and on the big toe of his right foot, on top of the blood of the guilt offering. [18]The rest of the oil in his palm the priest shall put on the head of the one to be cleansed and make atonement for him before the LORD.

[19]"Then the priest is to sacrifice the sin offering and make atonement for the one to be cleansed from his uncleanness. After that, the priest shall slaughter the burnt offering [20]and offer it on the altar, together with the grain offering, and make atonement for him, and he will be clean.

[21]"If, however, he is poor and cannot afford these, he must take one male lamb as a guilt offering to be waved to make atonement for him, together with a tenth of an ephah[a] of fine flour mixed with oil for a grain offering, a log of oil, [22]and two doves or two young pigeons, which he can afford, one for a sin offering and the other for a burnt offering.

[23]"On the eighth day he must bring them for his cleansing to the priest at the entrance to the Tent of Meeting, before the LORD. [24]The priest is to take the lamb for the guilt offering, together with the log of oil, and wave them before the LORD as a wave offering. [25]He shall slaughter the lamb for the guilt offering and take some of its blood and put it on the lobe of the right ear of the one to be cleansed, on the thumb of his right hand and on the big toe of his right foot. [26]The priest is to pour some of the oil into the palm of his own left hand, [27]and with his right forefinger sprinkle some of the oil from his palm seven times before the LORD. [28]Some of the oil in his palm he is to put on the same places he put the blood of the guilt offering—on the lobe of the right ear of the one to be cleansed, on

the thumb of his right hand and on the big toe of his right foot. [29]The rest of the oil in his palm the priest shall put on the head of the one to be cleansed, to make atonement for him before the LORD. [30]Then he shall sacrifice the doves or the young pigeons, which the person can afford, [31]one[b] as a sin offering and the other as a burnt offering, together with the grain offering. In this way the priest will make atonement before the LORD on behalf of the one to be cleansed."

[32]These are the regulations for anyone who has an infectious skin disease and who cannot afford the regular offerings for his cleansing.

Cleansing From Mildew

[33]The LORD said to Moses and Aaron, [34]"When you enter the land of Canaan, which I am giving you as your possession, and I put a spreading mildew in a house in that land, [35]the owner of the house must go and tell the priest, 'I have seen something that looks like mildew in my house.' [36]The priest is to order the house to be emptied before he goes in to examine the mildew, so that nothing in the house will be pronounced unclean. After this the priest is to go in and inspect the house. [37]He is to examine the mildew on the walls, and if it has greenish or reddish depressions that appear to be deeper than the surface of the wall, [38]the priest shall go out the doorway of the house and close it up for seven days. [39]On the seventh day the priest shall return to inspect the house. If the mildew has spread on the walls, [40]he is to order that the contaminated stones be torn out and thrown into an unclean place outside the town. [41]He must have all the inside walls of the house scraped and the material that is scraped off dumped into an unclean place outside the town. [42]Then they are to take other stones to replace these and take new clay and plaster the house.

[43]"If the mildew reappears in the

---

[a]21 That is, probably about 2 quarts (about 2 liters) [b]31 Septuagint and Syriac; Hebrew [31]such as the person can afford, one

house after the stones have been torn out and the house scraped and plastered, ⁴⁴the priest is to go and examine it and, if the mildew has spread in the house, it is a destructive mildew; the house is unclean. ⁴⁵It must be torn down—its stones, timbers and all the plaster—and taken out of the town to an unclean place.

⁴⁶"Anyone who goes into the house while it is closed up will be unclean till evening. ⁴⁷Anyone who sleeps or eats in the house must wash his clothes.

⁴⁸"But if the priest comes to examine it and the mildew has not spread after the house has been plastered, he shall pronounce the house clean, because the mildew is gone. ⁴⁹To purify the house he is to take two birds and some cedar wood, scarlet yarn and hyssop. ⁵⁰He shall kill one of the birds over fresh water in a clay pot. ⁵¹Then he is to take the cedar wood, the hyssop, the scarlet yarn and the live bird, dip them into the blood of the dead bird and the fresh water, and sprinkle the house seven times. ⁵²He shall purify the house with the bird's blood, the fresh water, the live bird, the cedar wood, the hyssop and the scarlet yarn. ⁵³Then he is to release the live bird in the open fields outside the town. In this way he will make atonement for the house, and it will be clean."

⁵⁴These are the regulations for any infectious skin disease, for an itch, ⁵⁵for mildew in clothing or in a house, ⁵⁶and for a swelling, a rash or a bright spot, ⁵⁷to determine when something is clean or unclean.

These are the regulations for infectious skin diseases and mildew.

Discharges Causing Uncleanness

15 The Lord said to Moses and Aaron, ²"Speak to the Israelites and say to them: 'When any man has a bodily discharge, the discharge is unclean. ³Whether it continues flowing from his body or is blocked, it will make him unclean. This is how his discharge will bring about uncleanness:

⁴" 'Any bed the man with a discharge lies on will be unclean, and anything he sits on will be unclean. ⁵Anyone who touches his bed must wash his clothes and bathe with water, and he will be unclean till evening. ⁶Whoever sits on anything that the man with a discharge sat on must wash his clothes and bathe with water, and he will be unclean till evening.

⁷" 'Whoever touches the man who has a discharge must wash his clothes and bathe with water, and he will be unclean till evening.

⁸" 'If the man with the discharge spits on someone who is clean, that person must wash his clothes and bathe with water, and he will be unclean till evening.

⁹" 'Everything the man sits on when riding will be unclean, ¹⁰and whoever touches any of the things that were under him will be unclean till evening; whoever picks up those things must wash his clothes and bathe with water, and he will be unclean till evening.

¹¹" 'Anyone the man with a discharge touches without rinsing his hands with water must wash his clothes and bathe with water, and he will be unclean till evening.

¹²" 'A clay pot that the man touches must be broken, and any wooden article is to be rinsed with water.

¹³" 'When a man is cleansed from his discharge, he is to count off seven days for his ceremonial cleansing; he must wash his clothes and bathe himself with fresh water, and he will be clean. ¹⁴On the eighth day he must take two doves or two young pigeons and come before the Lord to the entrance to the Tent of Meeting and give them to the priest. ¹⁵The priest is to sacrifice them, the one for a sin offering and the other for a burnt offering. In this way he will make atonement before the Lord for the man because of his discharge.

¹⁶" 'When a man has an emission of semen, he must bathe his whole body with water, and he will be unclean till evening. ¹⁷Any clothing or leather

that has semen on it must be washed with water, and it will be unclean till evening. ¹⁸When a man lies with a woman and there is an emission of semen, both must bathe with water, and they will be unclean till evening.

¹⁹" 'When a woman has her regular flow of blood, the impurity of her monthly period will last seven days, and anyone who touches her will be unclean till evening.

²⁰" 'Anything she lies on during her period will be unclean, and anything she sits on will be unclean. ²¹Whoever touches her bed must wash his clothes and bathe with water, and he will be unclean till evening. ²²Whoever touches anything she sits on must wash his clothes and bathe with water, and he will be unclean till evening. ²³Whether it is the bed or anything she was sitting on, when anyone touches it, he will be unclean till evening.

²⁴" 'If a man lies with her and her monthly flow touches him, he will be unclean for seven days; any bed he lies on will be unclean.

²⁵" 'When a woman has a discharge of blood for many days at a time other than her monthly period or has a discharge that continues beyond her period, she will be unclean as long as she has the discharge, just as in the days of her period. ²⁶Any bed she lies on while her discharge continues will be unclean, as is her bed during her monthly period, and anything she sits on will be unclean, as during her period. ²⁷Whoever touches them will be unclean; he must wash his clothes and bathe with water, and he will be unclean till evening.

²⁸" 'When she is cleansed from her discharge, she must count off seven days, and after that she will be ceremonially clean. ²⁹On the eighth day she must take two doves or two young pigeons and bring them to the priest at the entrance to the Tent of Meeting. ³⁰The priest is to sacrifice one for a sin offering and the other for a burnt offering. In this way he will make atonement for her before the LORD for the uncleanness of her discharge.

³¹" 'You must keep the Israelites separate from things that make them unclean, so they will not die in their uncleanness for defiling my dwelling place,ᵃ which is among them.' "

³²These are the regulations for a man with a discharge, for anyone made unclean by an emission of semen, ³³for a woman in her monthly period, for a man or a woman with a discharge, and for a man who lies with a woman who is ceremonially unclean.

The Day of Atonement

16 The LORD spoke to Moses after the death of the two sons of Aaron who died when they approached the LORD. ²The LORD said to Moses: "Tell your brother Aaron not to come whenever he chooses into the Most Holy Place behind the curtain in front of the atonement cover on the ark, or else he will die, because I appear in the cloud over the atonement cover.

³"This is how Aaron is to enter the sanctuary area: with a young bull for a sin offering and a ram for a burnt offering. ⁴He is to put on the sacred linen tunic, with linen undergarments next to his body; he is to tie the linen sash around him and put on the linen turban. These are sacred garments; so he must bathe himself with water before he puts them on. ⁵From the Israelite community he is to take two male goats for a sin offering and a ram for a burnt offering.

⁶"Aaron is to offer the bull for his own sin offering to make atonement for himself and his household. ⁷Then he is to take the two goats and present them before the LORD at the entrance to the Tent of Meeting. ⁸He is to cast lots for the two goats—one lot for the LORD and the other for the scapegoat.ᵇ ⁹Aaron shall bring the goat whose lot falls to the LORD and sacrifice it for a sin offering. ¹⁰But the goat

---

ᵃ31 Or *my tabernacle*   ᵇ8 That is, the goat of removal; Hebrew *azazel*; also in verses 10 and 26

chosen by lot as the scapegoat shall be presented alive before the LORD to be used for making atonement by sending it into the desert as a scapegoat.

11"Aaron shall bring the bull for his own sin offering to make atonement for himself and his household, and he is to slaughter the bull for his own sin offering. 12He is to take a censer full of burning coals from the altar before the LORD and two handfuls of finely ground fragrant incense and take them behind the curtain. 13He is to put the incense on the fire before the LORD, and the smoke of the incense will conceal the atonement cover above the Testimony, so that he will not die. 14He is to take some of the bull's blood and with his finger sprinkle it on the front of the atonement cover; then he shall sprinkle some of it with his finger seven times before the atonement cover.

15"He shall then slaughter the goat for the sin offering for the people and take its blood behind the curtain and do with it as he did with the bull's blood: He shall sprinkle it on the atonement cover and in front of it. 16In this way he will make atonement for the Most Holy Place because of the uncleanness and rebellion of the Israelites, whatever their sins have been. He is to do the same for the Tent of Meeting, which is among them in the midst of their uncleanness. 17No one is to be in the Tent of Meeting from the time Aaron goes in to make atonement in the Most Holy Place until he comes out, having made atonement for himself, his household and the whole community of Israel.

18"Then he shall come out to the altar that is before the LORD and make atonement for it. He shall take some of the bull's blood and some of the goat's blood and put it on all the horns of the altar. 19He shall sprinkle some of the blood on it with his finger seven times to cleanse it and to consecrate it from the uncleanness of the Israelites.

20"When Aaron has finished making atonement for the Most Holy Place, the Tent of Meeting and the altar, he shall bring forward the live goat. 21He is to lay both hands on the head of the live goat and confess over it all the wickedness and rebellion of the Israelites—all their sins—and put them on the goat's head. He shall send the goat away into the desert in the care of a man appointed for the task. 22The goat will carry on itself all their sins to a solitary place; and the man shall release it in the desert.

23"Then Aaron is to go into the Tent of Meeting and take off the linen garments he put on before he entered the Most Holy Place, and he is to leave them there. 24He shall bathe himself with water in a holy place and put on his regular garments. Then he shall come out and sacrifice the burnt offering for himself and the burnt offering for the people, to make atonement for himself and for the people. 25He shall also burn the fat of the sin offering on the altar.

26"The man who releases the goat as a scapegoat must wash his clothes and bathe himself with water; afterward he may come into the camp. 27The bull and the goat for the sin offerings, whose blood was brought into the Most Holy Place to make atonement, must be taken outside the camp; their hides, flesh and offal are to be burned up. 28The man who burns them must wash his clothes and bathe himself with water; afterward he may come into the camp.

29"This is to be a lasting ordinance for you: On the tenth day of the seventh month you must deny yourselves*a* and not do any work— whether native-born or an alien living among you— 30because on this day atonement will be made for you, to cleanse you. Then, before the LORD, you will be clean from all your sins. 31It is a sabbath of rest, and you must deny yourselves; it is a lasting ordinance. 32The priest who is anointed and ordained to succeed his father as high priest is to make atonement. He

---

a29 Or *must fast*; also in verse 31

VERSE: AUTHOR: PASSAGE:
Leviticus 16:10   John F. MacArthur, Jr.   Leviticus 16:6–22

Infinite Forgiveness

On Israel's Day of Atonement (Yom Kippur), the high priest selected two goats. One was sacrificed, the other set free. Before releasing the second goat, the high priest symbolically placed the sins of the people on it by laying his hands on its head. This "scapegoat" was then taken a great distance from camp and released — never to return again . . .

In Christ, God canceled your debt and pardoned your transgressions, and he did so "in accordance with the riches of God's grace that he lavished on [you]" (Ephesians 1:7–8). That means you have infinite forgiveness, because God's grace is infinite. You cannot sin beyond God's grace, because where sin abounds, grace superabounds (Romans 5:20).

God delights in lavishing his grace upon you. Such grace is overflowing and cannot be contained. You are forgiven for every sin — past, present and future. You will never be condemned by God or separated from him (Romans 8:1–2,31–39). Even when you fail, God doesn't hold your sins against you. Christ bore them all so that you might know the joy and peace that freedom from sin and guilt brings.

Let the reality of God's grace fill your heart with joy and assurance. Let the responsibility of glorifying him fill you with awe and reverence. Let this day be a sacrifice of praise and service to him.

ADDITIONAL SCRIPTURE READINGS
Romans 5:12–21; Ephesians 1:3–14
Go to page 141 for your next devotional reading.

is to put on the sacred linen garments
[33]and make atonement for the Most
Holy Place, for the Tent of Meeting
and the altar, and for the priests and
all the people of the community.

[34]"This is to be a lasting ordinance
for you: Atonement is to be made
once a year for all the sins of the Israelites."

And it was done, as the Lord commanded Moses.

Eating Blood Forbidden

17 The Lord said to Moses,
[2]"Speak to Aaron and his sons
and to all the Israelites and say to
them: 'This is what the Lord has commanded: [3]Any Israelite who sacrifices
an ox,[a] a lamb or a goat in the camp
or outside of it [4]instead of bringing it
to the entrance to the Tent of Meeting
to present it as an offering to the Lord
in front of the tabernacle of the
Lord—that man shall be considered
guilty of bloodshed; he has shed
blood and must be cut off from his
people. [5]This is so the Israelites will
bring to the Lord the sacrifices they
are now making in the open fields.
They must bring them to the priest,
that is, to the Lord, at the entrance to
the Tent of Meeting and sacrifice
them as fellowship offerings.[b] [6]The
priest is to sprinkle the blood against
the altar of the Lord at the entrance to
the Tent of Meeting and burn the fat
as an aroma pleasing to the Lord.
[7]They must no longer offer any of
their sacrifices to the goat idols[c] to
whom they prostitute themselves.
This is to be a lasting ordinance for
them and for the generations to
come.'

[8]"Say to them: 'Any Israelite or any
alien living among them who offers a
burnt offering or sacrifice [9]and does
not bring it to the entrance to the Tent
of Meeting to sacrifice it to the Lord—
that man must be cut off from his
people.

[10]" 'Any Israelite or any alien living
among them who eats any blood—I
will set my face against that person
who eats blood and will cut him off
from his people. [11]For the life of a
creature is in the blood, and I have
given it to you to make atonement for
yourselves on the altar; it is the blood
that makes atonement for one's life.
[12]Therefore I say to the Israelites,
"None of you may eat blood, nor may
an alien living among you eat blood."

[13]" 'Any Israelite or any alien living
among you who hunts any animal or
bird that may be eaten must drain out
the blood and cover it with earth,
[14]because the life of every creature is
its blood. That is why I have said to
the Israelites, "You must not eat the
blood of any creature, because the life
of every creature is its blood; anyone
who eats it must be cut off."

[15]" 'Anyone, whether native-born
or alien, who eats anything found
dead or torn by wild animals must
wash his clothes and bathe with water, and he will be ceremonially unclean till evening; then he will be
clean. [16]But if he does not wash his
clothes and bathe himself, he will be
held responsible.' "

Unlawful Sexual Relations

18 The Lord said to Moses,
[2]"Speak to the Israelites and
say to them: 'I am the Lord your God.
[3]You must not do as they do in Egypt,
where you used to live, and you must
not do as they do in the land of Canaan, where I am bringing you. Do
not follow their practices. [4]You must
obey my laws and be careful to follow
my decrees. I am the Lord your God.
[5]Keep my decrees and laws, for the
man who obeys them will live by
them. I am the Lord.

[6]" 'No one is to approach any close
relative to have sexual relations. I am
the Lord.

[7]" 'Do not dishonor your father by
having sexual relations with your
mother. She is your mother; do not
have relations with her.

[8]" 'Do not have sexual relations

with your father's wife; that would dishonor your father.

⁹" 'Do not have sexual relations with your sister, either your father's daughter or your mother's daughter, whether she was born in the same home or elsewhere.

¹⁰" 'Do not have sexual relations with your son's daughter or your daughter's daughter; that would dishonor you.

¹¹" 'Do not have sexual relations with the daughter of your father's wife, born to your father; she is your sister.

¹²" 'Do not have sexual relations with your father's sister; she is your father's close relative.

¹³" 'Do not have sexual relations with your mother's sister, because she is your mother's close relative.

¹⁴" 'Do not dishonor your father's brother by approaching his wife to have sexual relations; she is your aunt.

¹⁵" 'Do not have sexual relations with your daughter-in-law. She is your son's wife; do not have relations with her.

¹⁶" 'Do not have sexual relations with your brother's wife; that would dishonor your brother.

¹⁷" 'Do not have sexual relations with both a woman and her daughter. Do not have sexual relations with either her son's daughter or her daughter's daughter; they are her close relatives. That is wickedness.

¹⁸" 'Do not take your wife's sister as a rival wife and have sexual relations with her while your wife is living.

¹⁹" 'Do not approach a woman to have sexual relations during the uncleanness of her monthly period.

²⁰" 'Do not have sexual relations with your neighbor's wife and defile yourself with her.

²¹" 'Do not give any of your children to be sacrificed[a] to Molech, for you must not profane the name of your God. I am the LORD.

²²" 'Do not lie with a man as one lies with a woman; that is detestable.

²³" 'Do not have sexual relations with an animal and defile yourself with it. A woman must not present herself to an animal to have sexual relations with it; that is a perversion.

²⁴" 'Do not defile yourselves in any of these ways, because this is how the nations that I am going to drive out before you became defiled. ²⁵Even the land was defiled; so I punished it for its sin, and the land vomited out its inhabitants. ²⁶But you must keep my decrees and my laws. The native-born and the aliens living among you must not do any of these detestable things, ²⁷for all these things were done by the people who lived in the land before you, and the land became defiled. ²⁸And if you defile the land, it will vomit you out as it vomited out the nations that were before you.

²⁹" 'Everyone who does any of these detestable things—such persons must be cut off from their people. ³⁰Keep my requirements and do not follow any of the detestable customs that were practiced before you came and do not defile yourselves with them. I am the LORD your God.' "

Various Laws

19 The LORD said to Moses, ²"Speak to the entire assembly of Israel and say to them: 'Be holy because I, the LORD your God, am holy.

³" 'Each of you must respect his mother and father, and you must observe my Sabbaths. I am the LORD your God.

⁴" 'Do not turn to idols or make gods of cast metal for yourselves. I am the LORD your God.

⁵" 'When you sacrifice a fellowship offering[b] to the LORD, sacrifice it in such a way that it will be accepted on your behalf. ⁶It shall be eaten on the day you sacrifice it or on the next day; anything left over until the third day must be burned up. ⁷If any of it is eaten on the third day, it is impure and will not be accepted. ⁸Whoever eats it will be held responsible because he has desecrated what is holy to the

---

a21 Or *to be passed through ⌞the fire⌟*   *b5* Traditionally *peace offering*

LORD; that person must be cut off from his people.

⁹" 'When you reap the harvest of your land, do not reap to the very edges of your field or gather the gleanings of your harvest. ¹⁰Do not go over your vineyard a second time or pick up the grapes that have fallen. Leave them for the poor and the alien. I am the LORD your God.

¹¹" 'Do not steal.

" 'Do not lie.

" 'Do not deceive one another.

¹²" 'Do not swear falsely by my name and so profane the name of your God. I am the LORD.

¹³" 'Do not defraud your neighbor or rob him.

" 'Do not hold back the wages of a hired man overnight.

¹⁴" 'Do not curse the deaf or put a stumbling block in front of the blind, but fear your God. I am the LORD.

¹⁵" 'Do not pervert justice; do not show partiality to the poor or favoritism to the great, but judge your neighbor fairly.

¹⁶" 'Do not go about spreading slander among your people.

" 'Do not do anything that endangers your neighbor's life. I am the LORD.

¹⁷" 'Do not hate your brother in your heart. Rebuke your neighbor frankly so you will not share in his guilt.

¹⁸" 'Do not seek revenge or bear a grudge against one of your people, but love your neighbor as yourself. I am the LORD.

¹⁹" 'Keep my decrees.

" 'Do not mate different kinds of animals.

" 'Do not plant your field with two kinds of seed.

" 'Do not wear clothing woven of two kinds of material.

²⁰" 'If a man sleeps with a woman who is a slave girl promised to another man but who has not been ransomed or given her freedom, there must be due punishment. Yet they are not to be put to death, because she

had not been freed. ²¹The man, however, must bring a ram to the entrance to the Tent of Meeting for a guilt offering to the LORD. ²²With the ram of the guilt offering the priest is to make atonement for him before the LORD for the sin he has committed, and his sin will be forgiven.

²³" 'When you enter the land and plant any kind of fruit tree, regard its fruit as forbidden.ᵃ For three years you are to consider it forbiddenᵃ; it must not be eaten. ²⁴In the fourth year all its fruit will be holy, an offering of praise to the LORD. ²⁵But in the fifth year you may eat its fruit. In this way your harvest will be increased. I am the LORD your God.

²⁶" 'Do not eat any meat with the blood still in it.

" 'Do not practice divination or sorcery.

²⁷" 'Do not cut the hair at the sides of your head or clip off the edges of your beard.

²⁸" 'Do not cut your bodies for the dead or put tattoo marks on yourselves. I am the LORD.

²⁹" 'Do not degrade your daughter by making her a prostitute, or the land will turn to prostitution and be filled with wickedness.

³⁰" 'Observe my Sabbaths and have reverence for my sanctuary. I am the LORD.

³¹" 'Do not turn to mediums or seek out spiritists, for you will be defiled by them. I am the LORD your God.

³²" 'Rise in the presence of the aged, show respect for the elderly and revere your God. I am the LORD.

³³" 'When an alien lives with you in your land, do not mistreat him. ³⁴The alien living with you must be treated as one of your native-born. Love him as yourself, for you were aliens in Egypt. I am the LORD your God.

³⁵" 'Do not use dishonest standards when measuring length, weight or quantity. ³⁶Use honest scales and honest weights, an honest ephahᵇ and

---

ᵃ23 Hebrew *uncircumcised*   ᵇ36 An ephah was a dry measure.

VERSE:	AUTHOR:	PASSAGE:
Leviticus 19:15	William L. Coleman	Leviticus 19:9–18

The Favoritism Trap

There are a number of Christian values which could help us stay away from the favoritism trap. They are extremely important and well worth the effort to put them into operation.

First, *recognize that every child is a gift from God.* The child who graduates from Harvard is no more a gift from God than the daughter who works at the Quik Shop. The child who attends church is not more special than the one who never does. That isn't the way we naturally feel, but in God's economy every child is special. That includes the two-year-old and the forty-two-year-old . . .

Second, *impartiality is basic.* None of us is permitted to favor the athlete, the cheerleader or the valedictorian. All are of equal value by Biblical standards. Nor can we show partiality to the slow learner, the sick or the poor. They are not better than anyone else either. All of us are of equal value . . . We are important because God created us in his image and Jesus Christ died for us . . .

Third, *God does not show favoritism.* Often Christians must think exactly opposite of the world around them. Whether or not others show partiality to certain children, that option still does not belong to us. There is a godly wisdom that takes the Christian to higher and better standards. That wisdom helps us handle all of our children as equals.

ADDITIONAL SCRIPTURE READINGS
1 Corinthians 12:12–26; James 2:1–13
Go to page 152 for your next devotional reading.

an honest hin.[a] I am the Lord your God, who brought you out of Egypt.

37" 'Keep all my decrees and all my laws and follow them. I am the Lord.' "

Punishments for Sin

20 The Lord said to Moses, 2"Say to the Israelites: 'Any Israelite or any alien living in Israel who gives[b] any of his children to Molech must be put to death. The people of the community are to stone him. 3I will set my face against that man and I will cut him off from his people; for by giving his children to Molech, he has defiled my sanctuary and profaned my holy name. 4If the people of the community close their eyes when that man gives one of his children to Molech and they fail to put him to death, 5I will set my face against that man and his family and will cut off from their people both him and all who follow him in prostituting themselves to Molech.

6" 'I will set my face against the person who turns to mediums and spiritists to prostitute himself by following them, and I will cut him off from his people.

7" 'Consecrate yourselves and be holy, because I am the Lord your God. 8Keep my decrees and follow them. I am the Lord, who makes you holy.[c]

9" 'If anyone curses his father or mother, he must be put to death. He has cursed his father or his mother, and his blood will be on his own head.

10" 'If a man commits adultery with another man's wife—with the wife of his neighbor—both the adulterer and the adulteress must be put to death.

11" 'If a man sleeps with his father's wife, he has dishonored his father. Both the man and the woman must be put to death; their blood will be on their own heads.

12" 'If a man sleeps with his daughter-in-law, both of them must be put to death. What they have done is a perversion; their blood will be on their own heads.

13" 'If a man lies with a man as one lies with a woman, both of them have done what is detestable. They must be put to death; their blood will be on their own heads.

14" 'If a man marries both a woman and her mother, it is wicked. Both he and they must be burned in the fire, so that no wickedness will be among you.

15" 'If a man has sexual relations with an animal, he must be put to death, and you must kill the animal.

16" 'If a woman approaches an animal to have sexual relations with it, kill both the woman and the animal. They must be put to death; their blood will be on their own heads.

17" 'If a man marries his sister, the daughter of either his father or his mother, and they have sexual relations, it is a disgrace. They must be cut off before the eyes of their people. He has dishonored his sister and will be held responsible.

18" 'If a man lies with a woman during her monthly period and has sexual relations with her, he has exposed the source of her flow, and she has also uncovered it. Both of them must be cut off from their people.

19" 'Do not have sexual relations with the sister of either your mother or your father, for that would dishonor a close relative; both of you would be held responsible.

20" 'If a man sleeps with his aunt, he has dishonored his uncle. They will be held responsible; they will die childless.

21" 'If a man marries his brother's wife, it is an act of impurity; he has dishonored his brother. They will be childless.

22" 'Keep all my decrees and laws and follow them, so that the land where I am bringing you to live may not vomit you out. 23You must not live according to the customs of the nations I am going to drive out before

---

a36 A hin was a liquid measure.   b2 Or *sacrifices*; also in verses 3 and 4   c8 Or *who sanctifies you*; or *who sets you apart as holy*

you. Because they did all these things, I abhorred them. 24But I said to you, "You will possess their land; I will give it to you as an inheritance, a land flowing with milk and honey." I am the LORD your God, who has set you apart from the nations.

25" 'You must therefore make a distinction between clean and unclean animals and between unclean and clean birds. Do not defile yourselves by any animal or bird or anything that moves along the ground—those which I have set apart as unclean for you. 26You are to be holy to me[a] because I, the LORD, am holy, and I have set you apart from the nations to be my own.

27" 'A man or woman who is a medium or spiritist among you must be put to death. You are to stone them; their blood will be on their own heads.' "

Rules for Priests

21 The LORD said to Moses, "Speak to the priests, the sons of Aaron, and say to them: 'A priest must not make himself ceremonially unclean for any of his people who die, 2except for a close relative, such as his mother or father, his son or daughter, his brother, 3or an unmarried sister who is dependent on him since she has no husband—for her he may make himself unclean. 4He must not make himself unclean for people related to him by marriage,[b] and so defile himself.

5" 'Priests must not shave their heads or shave off the edges of their beards or cut their bodies. 6They must be holy to their God and must not profane the name of their God. Because they present the offerings made to the LORD by fire, the food of their God, they are to be holy.

7" 'They must not marry women defiled by prostitution or divorced from their husbands, because priests are holy to their God. 8Regard them

as holy, because they offer up the food of your God. Consider them holy, because I the LORD am holy—I who make you holy.[c]

9" 'If a priest's daughter defiles herself by becoming a prostitute, she disgraces her father; she must be burned in the fire.

10" 'The high priest, the one among his brothers who has had the anointing oil poured on his head and who has been ordained to wear the priestly garments, must not let his hair become unkempt[d] or tear his clothes. 11He must not enter a place where there is a dead body. He must not make himself unclean, even for his father or mother, 12nor leave the sanctuary of his God or desecrate it, because he has been dedicated by the anointing oil of his God. I am the LORD.

13" 'The woman he marries must be a virgin. 14He must not marry a widow, a divorced woman, or a woman defiled by prostitution, but only a virgin from his own people, 15so he will not defile his offspring among his people. I am the LORD, who makes him holy.[e] ' "

16The LORD said to Moses, 17"Say to Aaron: 'For the generations to come none of your descendants who has a defect may come near to offer the food of his God. 18No man who has any defect may come near: no man who is blind or lame, disfigured or deformed; 19no man with a crippled foot or hand, 20or who is hunchbacked or dwarfed, or who has any eye defect, or who has festering or running sores or damaged testicles. 21No descendant of Aaron the priest who has any defect is to come near to present the offerings made to the LORD by fire. He has a defect; he must not come near to offer the food of his God. 22He may eat the most holy food of his God, as well as the holy food; 23yet because of his defect, he must not go near the curtain or approach the altar, and so desecrate my sanctu-

---

[a]26 Or be my holy ones who set you apart as holy him apart as holy   [b]4 Or unclean as a leader among his people   [c]8 Or who sanctify you; or   [d]10 Or not uncover his head   [e]15 Or who sanctifies him; or who sets

ary. I am the LORD, who makes them holy.[a]' "

²⁴So Moses told this to Aaron and his sons and to all the Israelites.

22 The LORD said to Moses, ²"Tell Aaron and his sons to treat with respect the sacred offerings the Israelites consecrate to me, so they will not profane my holy name. I am the LORD.

³"Say to them: 'For the generations to come, if any of your descendants is ceremonially unclean and yet comes near the sacred offerings that the Israelites consecrate to the LORD, that person must be cut off from my presence. I am the LORD.

⁴" 'If a descendant of Aaron has an infectious skin disease[b] or a bodily discharge, he may not eat the sacred offerings until he is cleansed. He will also be unclean if he touches something defiled by a corpse or by anyone who has an emission of semen, ⁵or if he touches any crawling thing that makes him unclean, or any person who makes him unclean, whatever the uncleanness may be. ⁶The one who touches any such thing will be unclean till evening. He must not eat any of the sacred offerings unless he has bathed himself with water. ⁷When the sun goes down, he will be clean, and after that he may eat the sacred offerings, for they are his food. ⁸He must not eat anything found dead or torn by wild animals, and so become unclean through it. I am the LORD.

⁹" 'The priests are to keep my requirements so that they do not become guilty and die for treating them with contempt. I am the LORD, who makes them holy.[c]

¹⁰" 'No one outside a priest's family may eat the sacred offering, nor may the guest of a priest or his hired worker eat it. ¹¹But if a priest buys a slave with money, or if a slave is born in his household, that slave may eat his food. ¹²If a priest's daughter marries anyone other than a priest, she may not eat any of the sacred contributions. ¹³But if a priest's daughter becomes a widow or is divorced, yet has no children, and she returns to live in her father's house as in her youth, she may eat of her father's food. No unauthorized person, however, may eat any of it.

¹⁴" 'If anyone eats a sacred offering by mistake, he must make restitution to the priest for the offering and add a fifth of the value to it. ¹⁵The priests must not desecrate the sacred offerings the Israelites present to the LORD ¹⁶by allowing them to eat the sacred offerings and so bring upon them guilt requiring payment. I am the LORD, who makes them holy.' "

Unacceptable Sacrifices

¹⁷The LORD said to Moses, ¹⁸"Speak to Aaron and his sons and to all the Israelites and say to them: 'If any of you—either an Israelite or an alien living in Israel—presents a gift for a burnt offering to the LORD, either to fulfill a vow or as a freewill offering, ¹⁹you must present a male without defect from the cattle, sheep or goats in order that it may be accepted on your behalf. ²⁰Do not bring anything with a defect, because it will not be accepted on your behalf. ²¹When anyone brings from the herd or flock a fellowship offering[d] to the LORD to fulfill a special vow or as a freewill offering, it must be without defect or blemish to be acceptable. ²²Do not offer to the LORD the blind, the injured or the maimed, or anything with warts or festering or running sores. Do not place any of these on the altar as an offering made to the LORD by fire. ²³You may, however, present as a freewill offering an ox[e] or a sheep that is deformed or stunted, but it will not be accepted in fulfillment of a vow. ²⁴You must not offer to the LORD

---

[a]23 Or *who sanctifies them*; or *who sets them apart as holy*   [b]4 Traditionally *leprosy*; the Hebrew word was used for various diseases affecting the skin—not necessarily leprosy.   [c]9 Or *who sanctifies them*; or *who sets them apart as holy*; also in verse 16   [d]21 Traditionally *peace offering*   [e]23 The Hebrew word can include both male and female.

an animal whose testicles are bruised, crushed, torn or cut. You must not do this in your own land, ²⁵and you must not accept such animals from the hand of a foreigner and offer them as the food of your God. They will not be accepted on your behalf, because they are deformed and have defects.' "

²⁶The LORD said to Moses, ²⁷"When a calf, a lamb or a goat is born, it is to remain with its mother for seven days. From the eighth day on, it will be acceptable as an offering made to the LORD by fire. ²⁸Do not slaughter a cow or a sheep and its young on the same day.

²⁹"When you sacrifice a thank offering to the LORD, sacrifice it in such a way that it will be accepted on your behalf. ³⁰It must be eaten that same day; leave none of it till morning. I am the LORD.

³¹"Keep my commands and follow them. I am the LORD. ³²Do not profane my holy name. I must be acknowledged as holy by the Israelites. I am the LORD, who makes*a* you holy*b* ³³and who brought you out of Egypt to be your God. I am the LORD."

23 The LORD said to Moses, ²"Speak to the Israelites and say to them: 'These are my appointed feasts, the appointed feasts of the LORD, which you are to proclaim as sacred assemblies.

The Sabbath

³" 'There are six days when you may work, but the seventh day is a Sabbath of rest, a day of sacred assembly. You are not to do any work; wherever you live, it is a Sabbath to the LORD.

The Passover and Unleavened Bread

⁴" 'These are the LORD's appointed feasts, the sacred assemblies you are to proclaim at their appointed times: ⁵The LORD's Passover begins at twilight on the fourteenth day of the first month. ⁶On the fifteenth day of that month the LORD's Feast of Unleavened Bread begins; for seven days you must eat bread made without yeast. ⁷On the first day hold a sacred assembly and do no regular work. ⁸For seven days present an offering made to the LORD by fire. And on the seventh day hold a sacred assembly and do no regular work.' "

Firstfruits

⁹The LORD said to Moses, ¹⁰"Speak to the Israelites and say to them: 'When you enter the land I am going to give you and you reap its harvest, bring to the priest a sheaf of the first grain you harvest. ¹¹He is to wave the sheaf before the LORD so it will be accepted on your behalf; the priest is to wave it on the day after the Sabbath. ¹²On the day you wave the sheaf, you must sacrifice as a burnt offering to the LORD a lamb a year old without defect, ¹³together with its grain offering of two-tenths of an ephah*c* of fine flour mixed with oil—an offering made to the LORD by fire, a pleasing aroma—and its drink offering of a quarter of a hin*d* of wine. ¹⁴You must not eat any bread, or roasted or new grain, until the very day you bring this offering to your God. This is to be a lasting ordinance for the generations to come, wherever you live.

Feast of Weeks

¹⁵" 'From the day after the Sabbath, the day you brought the sheaf of the wave offering, count off seven full weeks. ¹⁶Count off fifty days up to the day after the seventh Sabbath, and then present an offering of new grain to the LORD. ¹⁷From wherever you live, bring two loaves made of two-tenths of an ephah of fine flour, baked with yeast, as a wave offering of firstfruits to the LORD. ¹⁸Present with this bread seven male lambs, each a year old and without defect, one young bull and

---

*a*32 Or *made*   *b*32 Or *who sanctifies you; or who sets you apart as holy*   *c*13 That is, probably about 4 quarts (about 4.5 liters); also in verse 17   *d*13 That is, probably about 1 quart (about 1 liter)

two rams. They will be a burnt offering to the Lord, together with their grain offerings and drink offerings—an offering made by fire, an aroma pleasing to the Lord. ¹⁹Then sacrifice one male goat for a sin offering and two lambs, each a year old, for a fellowship offering.ᵃ ²⁰The priest is to wave the two lambs before the Lord as a wave offering, together with the bread of the firstfruits. They are a sacred offering to the Lord for the priest. ²¹On that same day you are to proclaim a sacred assembly and do no regular work. This is to be a lasting ordinance for the generations to come, wherever you live.

²²" 'When you reap the harvest of your land, do not reap to the very edges of your field or gather the gleanings of your harvest. Leave them for the poor and the alien. I am the Lord your God.' "

Feast of Trumpets

²³The Lord said to Moses, ²⁴"Say to the Israelites: 'On the first day of the seventh month you are to have a day of rest, a sacred assembly commemorated with trumpet blasts. ²⁵Do no regular work, but present an offering made to the Lord by fire.' "

Day of Atonement

²⁶The Lord said to Moses, ²⁷"The tenth day of this seventh month is the Day of Atonement. Hold a sacred assembly and deny yourselves,ᵇ and present an offering made to the Lord by fire. ²⁸Do no work on that day, because it is the Day of Atonement, when atonement is made for you before the Lord your God. ²⁹Anyone who does not deny himself on that day must be cut off from his people. ³⁰I will destroy from among his people anyone who does any work on that day. ³¹You shall do no work at all. This is to be a lasting ordinance for the generations to come, wherever you live. ³²It is a sabbath of rest for you, and you must deny yourselves.

From the evening of the ninth day of the month until the following evening you are to observe your sabbath."

Feast of Tabernacles

³³The Lord said to Moses, ³⁴"Say to the Israelites: 'On the fifteenth day of the seventh month the Lord's Feast of Tabernacles begins, and it lasts for seven days. ³⁵The first day is a sacred assembly; do no regular work. ³⁶For seven days present offerings made to the Lord by fire, and on the eighth day hold a sacred assembly and present an offering made to the Lord by fire. It is the closing assembly; do no regular work.

³⁷(" 'These are the Lord's appointed feasts, which you are to proclaim as sacred assemblies for bringing offerings made to the Lord by fire—the burnt offerings and grain offerings, sacrifices and drink offerings required for each day. ³⁸These offerings are in addition to those for the Lord's Sabbaths andᶜ in addition to your gifts and whatever you have vowed and all the freewill offerings you give to the Lord.)

³⁹" 'So beginning with the fifteenth day of the seventh month, after you have gathered the crops of the land, celebrate the festival to the Lord for seven days; the first day is a day of rest, and the eighth day also is a day of rest. ⁴⁰On the first day you are to take choice fruit from the trees, and palm fronds, leafy branches and poplars, and rejoice before the Lord your God for seven days. ⁴¹Celebrate this as a festival to the Lord for seven days each year. This is to be a lasting ordinance for the generations to come; celebrate it in the seventh month. ⁴²Live in booths for seven days: All native-born Israelites are to live in booths ⁴³so your descendants will know that I had the Israelites live in booths when I brought them out of Egypt. I am the Lord your God.' "

⁴⁴So Moses announced to the Israelites the appointed feasts of the Lord.

ᵃ19 Traditionally *peace offering*   ᵇ27 Or *and fast*; also in verses 29 and 32   ᶜ38 Or *These feasts are in addition to the Lord's Sabbaths, and these offerings are*

Oil and Bread Set Before the LORD

24 The LORD said to Moses, [2]"Command the Israelites to bring you clear oil of pressed olives for the light so that the lamps may be kept burning continually. [3]Outside the curtain of the Testimony in the Tent of Meeting, Aaron is to tend the lamps before the LORD from evening till morning, continually. This is to be a lasting ordinance for the generations to come. [4]The lamps on the pure gold lampstand before the LORD must be tended continually.

[5]"Take fine flour and bake twelve loaves of bread, using two-tenths of an ephah[a] for each loaf. [6]Set them in two rows, six in each row, on the table of pure gold before the LORD. [7]Along each row put some pure incense as a memorial portion to represent the bread and to be an offering made to the LORD by fire. [8]This bread is to be set out before the LORD regularly, Sabbath after Sabbath, on behalf of the Israelites, as a lasting covenant. [9]It belongs to Aaron and his sons, who are to eat it in a holy place, because it is a most holy part of their regular share of the offerings made to the LORD by fire."

A Blasphemer Stoned

[10]Now the son of an Israelite mother and an Egyptian father went out among the Israelites, and a fight broke out in the camp between him and an Israelite. [11]The son of the Israelite woman blasphemed the Name with a curse; so they brought him to Moses. (His mother's name was Shelomith, the daughter of Dibri the Danite.) [12]They put him in custody until the will of the LORD should be made clear to them.

[13]Then the LORD said to Moses: [14]"Take the blasphemer outside the camp. All those who heard him are to lay their hands on his head, and the entire assembly is to stone him. [15]Say to the Israelites: 'If anyone curses his God, he will be held responsible; [16]anyone who blasphemes the name of the LORD must be put to death. The entire assembly must stone him. Whether an alien or native-born, when he blasphemes the Name, he must be put to death.

[17]" 'If anyone takes the life of a human being, he must be put to death. [18]Anyone who takes the life of someone's animal must make restitution—life for life. [19]If anyone injures his neighbor, whatever he has done must be done to him: [20]fracture for fracture, eye for eye, tooth for tooth. As he has injured the other, so he is to be injured. [21]Whoever kills an animal must make restitution, but whoever kills a man must be put to death. [22]You are to have the same law for the alien and the native-born. I am the LORD your God.' "

[23]Then Moses spoke to the Israelites, and they took the blasphemer outside the camp and stoned him. The Israelites did as the LORD commanded Moses.

The Sabbath Year

25 The LORD said to Moses on Mount Sinai, [2]"Speak to the Israelites and say to them: 'When you enter the land I am going to give you, the land itself must observe a sabbath to the LORD. [3]For six years sow your fields, and for six years prune your vineyards and gather their crops. [4]But in the seventh year the land is to have a sabbath of rest, a sabbath to the LORD. Do not sow your fields or prune your vineyards. [5]Do not reap what grows of itself or harvest the grapes of your untended vines. The land is to have a year of rest. [6]Whatever the land yields during the sabbath year will be food for you—for yourself, your manservant and maidservant, and the hired worker and temporary resident who live among you, [7]as well as for your livestock and the wild animals in your land. Whatever the land produces may be eaten.

[a]5 That is, probably about 4 quarts (about 4.5 liters)

The Year of Jubilee

⁸" 'Count off seven sabbaths of years—seven times seven years—so that the seven sabbaths of years amount to a period of forty-nine years. ⁹Then have the trumpet sounded everywhere on the tenth day of the seventh month; on the Day of Atonement sound the trumpet throughout your land. ¹⁰Consecrate the fiftieth year and proclaim liberty throughout the land to all its inhabitants. It shall be a jubilee for you; each one of you is to return to his family property and each to his own clan. ¹¹The fiftieth year shall be a jubilee for you; do not sow and do not reap what grows of itself or harvest the untended vines. ¹²For it is a jubilee and is to be holy for you; eat only what is taken directly from the fields.

¹³" 'In this Year of Jubilee everyone is to return to his own property.

¹⁴" 'If you sell land to one of your countrymen or buy any from him, do not take advantage of each other. ¹⁵You are to buy from your countryman on the basis of the number of years since the Jubilee. And he is to sell to you on the basis of the number of years left for harvesting crops. ¹⁶When the years are many, you are to increase the price, and when the years are few, you are to decrease the price, because what he is really selling you is the number of crops. ¹⁷Do not take advantage of each other, but fear your God. I am the LORD your God.

¹⁸" 'Follow my decrees and be careful to obey my laws, and you will live safely in the land. ¹⁹Then the land will yield its fruit, and you will eat your fill and live there in safety. ²⁰You may ask, "What will we eat in the seventh year if we do not plant or harvest our crops?" ²¹I will send you such a blessing in the sixth year that the land will yield enough for three years. ²²While you plant during the eighth year, you will eat from the old crop and will continue to eat from it until the harvest of the ninth year comes in.

²³" 'The land must not be sold permanently, because the land is mine and you are but aliens and my tenants. ²⁴Throughout the country that you hold as a possession, you must provide for the redemption of the land.

²⁵" 'If one of your countrymen becomes poor and sells some of his property, his nearest relative is to come and redeem what his countryman has sold. ²⁶If, however, a man has no one to redeem it for him but he himself prospers and acquires sufficient means to redeem it, ²⁷he is to determine the value for the years since he sold it and refund the balance to the man to whom he sold it; he can then go back to his own property. ²⁸But if he does not acquire the means to repay him, what he sold will remain in the possession of the buyer until the Year of Jubilee. It will be returned in the Jubilee, and he can then go back to his property.

²⁹" 'If a man sells a house in a walled city, he retains the right of redemption a full year after its sale. During that time he may redeem it. ³⁰If it is not redeemed before a full year has passed, the house in the walled city shall belong permanently to the buyer and his descendants. It is not to be returned in the Jubilee. ³¹But houses in villages without walls around them are to be considered as open country. They can be redeemed, and they are to be returned in the Jubilee.

³²" 'The Levites always have the right to redeem their houses in the Levitical towns, which they possess. ³³So the property of the Levites is redeemable—that is, a house sold in any town they hold—and is to be returned in the Jubilee, because the houses in the towns of the Levites are their property among the Israelites. ³⁴But the pastureland belonging to their towns must not be sold; it is their permanent possession.

³⁵" 'If one of your countrymen becomes poor and is unable to support himself among you, help him as you would an alien or a temporary resident, so he can continue to live among you. ³⁶Do not take interest of

any kind*a* from him, but fear your God, so that your countryman may continue to live among you. ³⁷You must not lend him money at interest or sell him food at a profit. ³⁸I am the LORD your God, who brought you out of Egypt to give you the land of Canaan and to be your God.

³⁹" 'If one of your countrymen becomes poor among you and sells himself to you, do not make him work as a slave. ⁴⁰He is to be treated as a hired worker or a temporary resident among you; he is to work for you until the Year of Jubilee. ⁴¹Then he and his children are to be released, and he will go back to his own clan and to the property of his forefathers. ⁴²Because the Israelites are my servants, whom I brought out of Egypt, they must not be sold as slaves. ⁴³Do not rule over them ruthlessly, but fear your God.

⁴⁴" 'Your male and female slaves are to come from the nations around you; from them you may buy slaves. ⁴⁵You may also buy some of the temporary residents living among you and members of their clans born in your country, and they will become your property. ⁴⁶You can will them to your children as inherited property and can make them slaves for life, but you must not rule over your fellow Israelites ruthlessly.

⁴⁷" 'If an alien or a temporary resident among you becomes rich and one of your countrymen becomes poor and sells himself to the alien living among you or to a member of the alien's clan, ⁴⁸he retains the right of redemption after he has sold himself. One of his relatives may redeem him: ⁴⁹An uncle or a cousin or any blood relative in his clan may redeem him. Or if he prospers, he may redeem himself. ⁵⁰He and his buyer are to count the time from the year he sold himself up to the Year of Jubilee. The price for his release is to be based on the rate paid to a hired man for that number of years. ⁵¹If many years remain, he must pay for his redemption

a larger share of the price paid for him. ⁵²If only a few years remain until the Year of Jubilee, he is to compute that and pay for his redemption accordingly. ⁵³He is to be treated as a man hired from year to year; you must see to it that his owner does not rule over him ruthlessly.

⁵⁴" 'Even if he is not redeemed in any of these ways, he and his children are to be released in the Year of Jubilee, ⁵⁵for the Israelites belong to me as servants. They are my servants, whom I brought out of Egypt. I am the LORD your God.

Reward for Obedience

26 " 'Do not make idols or set up an image or a sacred stone for yourselves, and do not place a carved stone in your land to bow down before it. I am the LORD your God.

²" 'Observe my Sabbaths and have reverence for my sanctuary. I am the LORD.

³" 'If you follow my decrees and are careful to obey my commands, ⁴I will send you rain in its season, and the ground will yield its crops and the trees of the field their fruit. ⁵Your threshing will continue until grape harvest and the grape harvest will continue until planting, and you will eat all the food you want and live in safety in your land.

⁶" 'I will grant peace in the land, and you will lie down and no one will make you afraid. I will remove savage beasts from the land, and the sword will not pass through your country. ⁷You will pursue your enemies, and they will fall by the sword before you. ⁸Five of you will chase a hundred, and a hundred of you will chase ten thousand, and your enemies will fall by the sword before you.

⁹" 'I will look on you with favor and make you fruitful and increase your numbers, and I will keep my covenant with you. ¹⁰You will still be eating last year's harvest when you will have to move it out to make room for the new. ¹¹I will put my dwelling

---

a36 Or take excessive interest; similarly in verse 37

place[a] among you, and I will not abhor you. [12]I will walk among you and be your God, and you will be my people. [13]I am the LORD your God, who brought you out of Egypt so that you would no longer be slaves to the Egyptians; I broke the bars of your yoke and enabled you to walk with heads held high.

Punishment for Disobedience

[14]" 'But if you will not listen to me and carry out all these commands, [15]and if you reject my decrees and abhor my laws and fail to carry out all my commands and so violate my covenant, [16]then I will do this to you: I will bring upon you sudden terror, wasting diseases and fever that will destroy your sight and drain away your life. You will plant seed in vain, because your enemies will eat it. [17]I will set my face against you so that you will be defeated by your enemies; those who hate you will rule over you, and you will flee even when no one is pursuing you.

[18]" 'If after all this you will not listen to me, I will punish you for your sins seven times over. [19]I will break down your stubborn pride and make the sky above you like iron and the ground beneath you like bronze. [20]Your strength will be spent in vain, because your soil will not yield its crops, nor will the trees of the land yield their fruit.

[21]" 'If you remain hostile toward me and refuse to listen to me, I will multiply your afflictions seven times over, as your sins deserve. [22]I will send wild animals against you, and they will rob you of your children, destroy your cattle and make you so few in number that your roads will be deserted.

[23]" 'If in spite of these things you do not accept my correction but continue to be hostile toward me, [24]I myself will be hostile toward you and will afflict you for your sins seven times over. [25]And I will bring the sword upon you to avenge the break-

ing of the covenant. When you withdraw into your cities, I will send a plague among you, and you will be given into enemy hands. [26]When I cut off your supply of bread, ten women will be able to bake your bread in one oven, and they will dole out the bread by weight. You will eat, but you will not be satisfied.

[27]" 'If in spite of this you still do not listen to me but continue to be hostile toward me, [28]then in my anger I will be hostile toward you, and I myself will punish you for your sins seven times over. [29]You will eat the flesh of your sons and the flesh of your daughters. [30]I will destroy your high places, cut down your incense altars and pile your dead bodies on the lifeless forms of your idols, and I will abhor you. [31]I will turn your cities into ruins and lay waste your sanctuaries, and I will take no delight in the pleasing aroma of your offerings. [32]I will lay waste the land, so that your enemies who live there will be appalled. [33]I will scatter you among the nations and will draw out my sword and pursue you. Your land will be laid waste, and your cities will lie in ruins. [34]Then the land will enjoy its sabbath years all the time that it lies desolate and you are in the country of your enemies; then the land will rest and enjoy its sabbaths. [35]All the time that it lies desolate, the land will have the rest it did not have during the sabbaths you lived in it.

[36]" 'As for those of you who are left, I will make their hearts so fearful in the lands of their enemies that the sound of a windblown leaf will put them to flight. They will run as though fleeing from the sword, and they will fall, even though no one is pursuing them. [37]They will stumble over one another as though fleeing from the sword, even though no one is pursuing them. So you will not be able to stand before your enemies. [38]You will perish among the nations; the land of your enemies will devour you. [39]Those of you who are left will

a11 Or my tabernacle

waste away in the lands of their enemies because of their sins; also because of their fathers' sins they will
waste away.

^{40}" 'But if they will confess their
sins and the sins of their fathers—
their treachery against me and their
hostility toward me, ^{41}which made
me hostile toward them so that I sent
them into the land of their enemies—
then when their uncircumcised hearts
are humbled and they pay for their
sin, ^{42}I will remember my covenant
with Jacob and my covenant with
Isaac and my covenant with Abraham, and I will remember the land.
^{43}For the land will be deserted by
them and will enjoy its sabbaths
while it lies desolate without them.
They will pay for their sins because
they rejected my laws and abhorred
my decrees. ^{44}Yet in spite of this,
when they are in the land of their enemies, I will not reject them or abhor
them so as to destroy them completely, breaking my covenant with them. I
am the LORD their God. ^{45}But for their
sake I will remember the covenant
with their ancestors whom I brought
out of Egypt in the sight of the nations to be their God. I am the LORD.' "

^{46}These are the decrees, the laws
and the regulations that the LORD established on Mount Sinai between
himself and the Israelites through
Moses.

Redeeming What Is the LORD's

27 The LORD said to Moses,
^{2}"Speak to the Israelites and
say to them: 'If anyone makes a special vow to dedicate persons to the
LORD by giving equivalent values, ^{3}set
the value of a male between the ages
of twenty and sixty at fifty shekels^a
of silver, according to the sanctuary
shekel^b; ^{4}and if it is a female, set her
value at thirty shekels.^{c} ^{5}If it is a person between the ages of five and

twenty, set the value of a male at
twenty shekels^d and of a female at
ten shekels.^{e} ^{6}If it is a person between one month and five years, set
the value of a male at five shekels^f of
silver and that of a female at three
shekels^g of silver. ^{7}If it is a person
sixty years old or more, set the value
of a male at fifteen shekels^h and of a
female at ten shekels. ^{8}If anyone making the vow is too poor to pay the
specified amount, he is to present the
person to the priest, who will set
the value for him according to what
the man making the vow can afford.

^{9}" 'If what he vowed is an animal
that is acceptable as an offering to the
LORD, such an animal given to the
LORD becomes holy. ^{10}He must not exchange it or substitute a good one for
a bad one, or a bad one for a good
one; if he should substitute one animal for another, both it and the substitute become holy. ^{11}If what he
vowed is a ceremonially unclean animal—one that is not acceptable as an
offering to the LORD—the animal must
be presented to the priest, ^{12}who will
judge its quality as good or bad.
Whatever value the priest then sets,
that is what it will be. ^{13}If the owner
wishes to redeem the animal, he must
add a fifth to its value.

^{14}" 'If a man dedicates his house as
something holy to the LORD, the priest
will judge its quality as good or bad.
Whatever value the priest then sets,
so it will remain. ^{15}If the man who
dedicates his house redeems it, he
must add a fifth to its value, and the
house will again become his.

^{16}" 'If a man dedicates to the LORD
part of his family land, its value is to
be set according to the amount of
seed required for it—fifty shekels of
silver to a homer^i of barley seed. ^{17}If
he dedicates his field during the Year
of Jubilee, the value that has been set
remains. ^{18}But if he dedicates his field

^{a}3 That is, about 1 1/4 pounds (about 0.6 kilogram); also in verse 16 ^{b}3 That is, about 2/5
ounce (about 11.5 grams); also in verse 25 ^{c}4 That is, about 12 ounces (about 0.3 kilogram)
^{d}5 That is, about 8 ounces (about 0.2 kilogram) ^{e}5 That is, about 4 ounces (about 110 grams);
also in verse 7 ^{f}6 That is, about 2 ounces (about 55 grams) ^{g}6 That is, about 1 1/4 ounces
(about 35 grams) ^{h}7 That is, about 6 ounces (about 170 grams) ^{i}16 That is, probably
about 6 bushels (about 220 liters)

VERSE:	AUTHOR:	PASSAGE:
Leviticus 27:30	D. James Kennedy	Leviticus 27:28–34

Who Is the Master?

There are many people who think they have overcome the world when they have simply gained a large chunk of it . . .

I think of a man who started out well . . . He was tithing his income regularly, and God blessed him in doing that, and he became more and more prosperous. Then one day the man went to Peter Marshall, the famous chaplain of the United States Senate, and said, "Dr. Marshall, I have a problem. I have been tithing for some time. It wasn't too bad when I was making twenty thousand dollars a year. I could afford to give the two thousand. But, you see, doctor, now I am making five hundred thousand dollars a year and there is just no way I can afford to give away fifty thousand dollars a year."

Dr. Marshall said, "Yes, sir. I see that you do have a problem. I think we ought to pray about it. Is that all right?"

The man agreed, so Dr. Marshall bowed his head and said, "Dear Lord, this man has a problem, and I pray that you will help him. Lord, reduce his salary back to the place where he can afford to tithe."

The man was so startled he let out a yelp. "No, Dr. Marshall, that's not what I meant!" But the point was made very well. Who is the master, and who is he that overcomes the world? We are to have mastery over things, not to let things have mastery over us.

- - - - - - - - - - - - - - ● ● - - - - - - - - - - - - - - -

ADDITIONAL SCRIPTURE READINGS
Malachi 3:6–15; 1 John 5:1–5

Go to page 160 for your next devotional reading.

after the Jubilee, the priest will deter-mine the value according to the num-ber of years that remain until the next Year of Jubilee, and its set value will be reduced. ¹⁹If the man who dedi-cates the field wishes to redeem it, he must add a fifth to its value, and the field will again become his. ²⁰If, how-ever, he does not redeem the field, or if he has sold it to someone else, it can never be redeemed. ²¹When the field is released in the Jubilee, it will be-come holy, like a field devoted to the LORD; it will become the property of the priests.ᵃ

²²" 'If a man dedicates to the LORD a field he has bought, which is not part of his family land, ²³the priest will de-termine its value up to the Year of Ju-bilee, and the man must pay its value on that day as something holy to the LORD. ²⁴In the Year of Jubilee the field will revert to the person from whom he bought it, the one whose land it was. ²⁵Every value is to be set accord-ing to the sanctuary shekel, twenty gerahs to the shekel.

²⁶" 'No one, however, may dedicate the firstborn of an animal, since the firstborn already belongs to the LORD; whether an oxᵇ or a sheep, it is the LORD's. ²⁷If it is one of the unclean ani-mals, he may buy it back at its set val-ue, adding a fifth of the value to it. If he does not redeem it, it is to be sold at its set value.

²⁸" 'But nothing that a man owns and devotesᶜ to the LORD—whether man or animal or family land—may be sold or redeemed; everything so devoted is most holy to the LORD.

²⁹" 'No person devoted to destruc-tionᵈ may be ransomed; he must be put to death.

³⁰" 'A tithe of everything from the land, whether grain from the soil or fruit from the trees, belongs to the LORD; it is holy to the LORD. ³¹If a man redeems any of his tithe, he must add a fifth of the value to it. ³²The entire tithe of the herd and flock—every tenth animal that passes under the shepherd's rod—will be holy to the LORD. ³³He must not pick out the good from the bad or make any substitu-tion. If he does make a substitution, both the animal and its substitute become holy and cannot be re-deemed.' "

³⁴These are the commands the LORD gave Moses on Mount Sinai for the Israelites.

ᵃ21 Or priest   ᵇ26 The Hebrew word can include both male and female.   ᶜ28 The Hebrew term refers to the irrevocable giving over of things or persons to the LORD.   ᵈ29 The Hebrew term refers to the irrevocable giving over of things or persons to the LORD, often by totally destroying them.

Although human failure and rebellion darken the stories told in this book, God's patience and mercy pierce through the gloom to bring comfort to those who turn from their sin toward him. As you read Numbers, rejoice in God's love and care in your life in spite of your sins. No matter how many times you fail him, he waits to welcome you back into his arms.

NUMBERS

The Census

1 The LORD spoke to Moses in the Tent of Meeting in the Desert of Sinai on the first day of the second month of the second year after the Israelites came out of Egypt. He said: ²"Take a census of the whole Israelite community by their clans and families, listing every man by name, one by one. ³You and Aaron are to number by their divisions all the men in Israel twenty years old or more who are able to serve in the army. ⁴One man from each tribe, each the head of his family, is to help you. ⁵These are the names of the men who are to assist you:

from Reuben, Elizur son of Shedeur;
⁶from Simeon, Shelumiel son of Zurishaddai;
⁷from Judah, Nahshon son of Amminadab;
⁸from Issachar, Nethanel son of Zuar;

⁹from Zebulun, Eliab son of Helon;
¹⁰from the sons of Joseph:
from Ephraim, Elishama son of Ammihud;
from Manasseh, Gamaliel son of Pedahzur;
¹¹from Benjamin, Abidan son of Gideoni;
¹²from Dan, Ahiezer son of Ammishaddai;
¹³from Asher, Pagiel son of Ocran;
¹⁴from Gad, Eliasaph son of Deuel;
¹⁵from Naphtali, Ahira son of Enan."

¹⁶These were the men appointed from the community, the leaders of their ancestral tribes. They were the heads of the clans of Israel.

¹⁷Moses and Aaron took these men whose names had been given, ¹⁸and they called the whole community together on the first day of the second month. The people indicated their ancestry by their clans and families, and

the men twenty years old or more were listed by name, one by one, [19]as the LORD commanded Moses. And so he counted them in the Desert of Sinai:

[20]From the descendants of Reuben the firstborn son of Israel:

All the men twenty years old or more who were able to serve in the army were listed by name, one by one, according to the records of their clans and families. [21]The number from the tribe of Reuben was 46,500.

[22]From the descendants of Simeon:

All the men twenty years old or more who were able to serve in the army were counted and listed by name, one by one, according to the records of their clans and families. [23]The number from the tribe of Simeon was 59,300.

[24]From the descendants of Gad:

All the men twenty years old or more who were able to serve in the army were listed by name, according to the records of their clans and families. [25]The number from the tribe of Gad was 45,650.

[26]From the descendants of Judah:

All the men twenty years old or more who were able to serve in the army were listed by name, according to the records of their clans and families. [27]The number from the tribe of Judah was 74,600.

[28]From the descendants of Issachar:

All the men twenty years old or more who were able to serve in the army were listed by name, according to the records of their clans and families. [29]The number from the tribe of Issachar was 54,400.

[30]From the descendants of Zebulun:

All the men twenty years old or more who were able to serve in the army were listed by name, according to the records of their clans and families. [31]The number from the tribe of Zebulun was 57,400.

[32]From the sons of Joseph:

From the descendants of Ephraim:

All the men twenty years old or more who were able to serve in the army were listed by name, according to the records of their clans and families. [33]The number from the tribe of Ephraim was 40,500.

[34]From the descendants of Manasseh:

All the men twenty years old or more who were able to serve in the army were listed by name, according to the records of their clans and families. [35]The number from the tribe of Manasseh was 32,200.

[36]From the descendants of Benjamin:

All the men twenty years old or more who were able to serve in the army were listed by name, according to the records of their clans and families. [37]The number from the tribe of Benjamin was 35,400.

[38]From the descendants of Dan:

All the men twenty years old or more who were able to serve in the army were listed by name, according to the records of their clans and families. [39]The number from the tribe of Dan was 62,700.

[40]From the descendants of Asher:

All the men twenty years old or more who were able to serve in the army were listed by name, according to the records of their clans and families. [41]The number from the tribe of Asher was 41,500.

[42]From the descendants of Naphtali:

All the men twenty years old

or more who were able to serve in the army were listed by name, according to the records of their clans and families. [43]The number from the tribe of Naphtali was 53,400.

[44]These were the men counted by Moses and Aaron and the twelve leaders of Israel, each one representing his family. [45]All the Israelites twenty years old or more who were able to serve in Israel's army were counted according to their families. [46]The total number was 603,550.

[47]The families of the tribe of Levi, however, were not counted along with the others. [48]The LORD had said to Moses: [49]"You must not count the tribe of Levi or include them in the census of the other Israelites. [50]Instead, appoint the Levites to be in charge of the tabernacle of the Testimony—over all its furnishings and everything belonging to it. They are to carry the tabernacle and all its furnishings; they are to take care of it and encamp around it. [51]Whenever the tabernacle is to move, the Levites are to take it down, and whenever the tabernacle is to be set up, the Levites shall do it. Anyone else who goes near it shall be put to death. [52]The Israelites are to set up their tents by divisions, each man in his own camp under his own standard. [53]The Levites, however, are to set up their tents around the tabernacle of the Testimony so that wrath will not fall on the Israelite community. The Levites are to be responsible for the care of the tabernacle of the Testimony."

[54]The Israelites did all this just as the LORD commanded Moses.

The Arrangement of the Tribal Camps

2 The LORD said to Moses and Aaron: [2]"The Israelites are to camp around the Tent of Meeting some distance from it, each man under his standard with the banners of his family."

[3]On the east, toward the sunrise, the divisions of the camp of Judah are to encamp under their standard. The leader of the people of Judah is Nahshon son of Amminadab. [4]His division numbers 74,600.

[5]The tribe of Issachar will camp next to them. The leader of the people of Issachar is Nethanel son of Zuar. [6]His division numbers 54,400.

[7]The tribe of Zebulun will be next. The leader of the people of Zebulun is Eliab son of Helon. [8]His division numbers 57,400.

[9]All the men assigned to the camp of Judah, according to their divisions, number 186,400. They will set out first.

[10]On the south will be the divisions of the camp of Reuben under their standard. The leader of the people of Reuben is Elizur son of Shedeur. [11]His division numbers 46,500.

[12]The tribe of Simeon will camp next to them. The leader of the people of Simeon is Shelumiel son of Zurishaddai. [13]His division numbers 59,300.

[14]The tribe of Gad will be next. The leader of the people of Gad is Eliasaph son of Deuel.[a] [15]His division numbers 45,650.

[16]All the men assigned to the camp of Reuben, according to their divisions, number 151,450. They will set out second.

[17]Then the Tent of Meeting and the camp of the Levites will set out in the middle of the camps. They will set out in the same order as they encamp, each in his own place under his standard.

[18]On the west will be the divisions of the camp of Ephraim un-

---

[a]14 Many manuscripts of the Masoretic Text, Samaritan Pentateuch and Vulgate (see also Num. 1:14); most manuscripts of the Masoretic Text *Reuel*

der their standard. The leader of the people of Ephraim is Elishama son of Ammihud. [19]His division numbers 40,500.

[20]The tribe of Manasseh will be next to them. The leader of the people of Manasseh is Gamaliel son of Pedahzur. [21]His division numbers 32,200.

[22]The tribe of Benjamin will be next. The leader of the people of Benjamin is Abidan son of Gideoni. [23]His division numbers 35,400.

[24]All the men assigned to the camp of Ephraim, according to their divisions, number 108,100. They will set out third.

[25]On the north will be the divisions of the camp of Dan, under their standard. The leader of the people of Dan is Ahiezer son of Ammishaddai. [26]His division numbers 62,700.

[27]The tribe of Asher will camp next to them. The leader of the people of Asher is Pagiel son of Ocran. [28]His division numbers 41,500.

[29]The tribe of Naphtali will be next. The leader of the people of Naphtali is Ahira son of Enan. [30]His division numbers 53,400.

[31]All the men assigned to the camp of Dan number 157,600. They will set out last, under their standards.

[32]These are the Israelites, counted according to their families. All those in the camps, by their divisions, number 603,550. [33]The Levites, however, were not counted along with the other Israelites, as the LORD commanded Moses.

[34]So the Israelites did everything the LORD commanded Moses; that is the way they encamped under their standards, and that is the way they set out, each with his clan and family.

The Levites

3 This is the account of the family of Aaron and Moses at the time the LORD talked with Moses on Mount Sinai.

[2]The names of the sons of Aaron were Nadab the firstborn and Abihu, Eleazar and Ithamar. [3]Those were the names of Aaron's sons, the anointed priests, who were ordained to serve as priests. [4]Nadab and Abihu, however, fell dead before the LORD when they made an offering with unauthorized fire before him in the Desert of Sinai. They had no sons; so only Eleazar and Ithamar served as priests during the lifetime of their father Aaron.

[5]The LORD said to Moses, [6]"Bring the tribe of Levi and present them to Aaron the priest to assist him. [7]They are to perform duties for him and for the whole community at the Tent of Meeting by doing the work of the tabernacle. [8]They are to take care of all the furnishings of the Tent of Meeting, fulfilling the obligations of the Israelites by doing the work of the tabernacle. [9]Give the Levites to Aaron and his sons; they are the Israelites who are to be given wholly to him.[a] [10]Appoint Aaron and his sons to serve as priests; anyone else who approaches the sanctuary must be put to death."

[11]The LORD also said to Moses, [12]"I have taken the Levites from among the Israelites in place of the first male offspring of every Israelite woman. The Levites are mine, [13]for all the firstborn are mine. When I struck down all the firstborn in Egypt, I set apart for myself every firstborn in Israel, whether man or animal. They are to be mine. I am the LORD."

[14]The LORD said to Moses in the Desert of Sinai, [15]"Count the Levites by their families and clans. Count every male a month old or more." [16]So Moses counted them, as he was commanded by the word of the LORD.

---

[a]9 Most manuscripts of the Masoretic Text; some manuscripts of the Masoretic Text, Samaritan Pentateuch and Septuagint (see also Num. 8:16) to me

¹⁷These were the names of the
sons of Levi:
  Gershon, Kohath and Merari.
¹⁸These were the names of the
Gershonite clans:
  Libni and Shimei.
¹⁹The Kohathite clans:
  Amram, Izhar, Hebron and
  Uzziel.
²⁰The Merarite clans:
  Mahli and Mushi.
These were the Levite clans, ac-
cording to their families.

²¹To Gershon belonged the clans of
the Libnites and Shimeites; these were
the Gershonite clans. ²²The number of
all the males a month old or more
who were counted was 7,500. ²³The
Gershonite clans were to camp on the
west, behind the tabernacle. ²⁴The
leader of the families of the Gershonites was Eliasaph son of Lael. ²⁵At the
Tent of Meeting the Gershonites were
responsible for the care of the tabernacle and tent, its coverings, the curtain at the entrance to the Tent of
Meeting, ²⁶the curtains of the courtyard, the curtain at the entrance to the
courtyard surrounding the tabernacle
and altar, and the ropes—and everything related to their use.

²⁷To Kohath belonged the clans of
the Amramites, Izharites, Hebronites
and Uzzielites; these were the Kohathite clans. ²⁸The number of all the
males a month old or more was
8,600.ᵃ The Kohathites were responsible for the care of the sanctuary.
²⁹The Kohathite clans were to camp
on the south side of the tabernacle.
³⁰The leader of the families of the Kohathite clans was Elizaphan son of
Uzziel. ³¹They were responsible for
the care of the ark, the table, the lampstand, the altars, the articles of the
sanctuary used in ministering, the
curtain, and everything related to
their use. ³²The chief leader of the Levites was Eleazar son of Aaron, the
priest. He was appointed over those

who were responsible for the care of
the sanctuary.

³³To Merari belonged the clans of
the Mahlites and the Mushites; these
were the Merarite clans. ³⁴The number of all the males a month old or
more who were counted was 6,200.
³⁵The leader of the families of the Merarite clans was Zuriel son of Abihail;
they were to camp on the north side
of the tabernacle. ³⁶The Merarites
were appointed to take care of the
frames of the tabernacle, its crossbars,
posts, bases, all its equipment, and
everything related to their use, ³⁷as
well as the posts of the surrounding
courtyard with their bases, tent pegs
and ropes.

³⁸Moses and Aaron and his sons
were to camp to the east of the tabernacle, toward the sunrise, in front of
the Tent of Meeting. They were responsible for the care of the sanctuary
on behalf of the Israelites. Anyone
else who approached the sanctuary
was to be put to death.

³⁹The total number of Levites
counted at the LORD's command by
Moses and Aaron according to their
clans, including every male a month
old or more, was 22,000.

⁴⁰The LORD said to Moses, "Count
all the firstborn Israelite males who
are a month old or more and make a
list of their names. ⁴¹Take the Levites
for me in place of all the firstborn of
the Israelites, and the livestock of the
Levites in place of all the firstborn of
the livestock of the Israelites. I am the
LORD."
⁴²So Moses counted all the firstborn
of the Israelites, as the LORD commanded him. ⁴³The total number of
firstborn males a month old or more,
listed by name, was 22,273.
⁴⁴The LORD also said to Moses,
⁴⁵"Take the Levites in place of all the
firstborn of Israel, and the livestock of
the Levites in place of their livestock.

ᵃ28 Hebrew; some Septuagint manuscripts 8,300

The Levites are to be mine. I am the LORD. 46To redeem the 273 firstborn Israelites who exceed the number of the Levites, 47collect five shekels[a] for each one, according to the sanctuary shekel, which weighs twenty gerahs. 48Give the money for the redemption of the additional Israelites to Aaron and his sons."

49So Moses collected the redemption money from those who exceeded the number redeemed by the Levites. 50From the firstborn of the Israelites he collected silver weighing 1,365 shekels,[b] according to the sanctuary shekel. 51Moses gave the redemption money to Aaron and his sons, as he was commanded by the word of the LORD.

The Kohathites

4 The LORD said to Moses and Aaron: 2"Take a census of the Kohathite branch of the Levites by their clans and families. 3Count all the men from thirty to fifty years of age who come to serve in the work in the Tent of Meeting.

4"This is the work of the Kohathites in the Tent of Meeting: the care of the most holy things. 5When the camp is to move, Aaron and his sons are to go in and take down the shielding curtain and cover the ark of the Testimony with it. 6Then they are to cover this with hides of sea cows,[c] spread a cloth of solid blue over that and put the poles in place.

7"Over the table of the Presence they are to spread a blue cloth and put on it the plates, dishes and bowls, and the jars for drink offerings; the bread that is continually there is to remain on it. 8Over these they are to spread a scarlet cloth, cover that with hides of sea cows and put its poles in place.

9"They are to take a blue cloth and cover the lampstand that is for light, together with its lamps, its wick trimmers and trays, and all its jars for the oil used to supply it. 10Then they are to wrap it and all its accessories in a covering of hides of sea cows and put it on a carrying frame.

11"Over the gold altar they are to spread a blue cloth and cover that with hides of sea cows and put its poles in place.

12"They are to take all the articles used for ministering in the sanctuary, wrap them in a blue cloth, cover that with hides of sea cows and put them on a carrying frame.

13"They are to remove the ashes from the bronze altar and spread a purple cloth over it. 14Then they are to place on it all the utensils used for ministering at the altar, including the firepans, meat forks, shovels and sprinkling bowls. Over it they are to spread a covering of hides of sea cows and put its poles in place.

15"After Aaron and his sons have finished covering the holy furnishings and all the holy articles, and when the camp is ready to move, the Kohathites are to come to do the carrying. But they must not touch the holy things or they will die. The Kohathites are to carry those things that are in the Tent of Meeting.

16"Eleazar son of Aaron, the priest, is to have charge of the oil for the light, the fragrant incense, the regular grain offering and the anointing oil. He is to be in charge of the entire tabernacle and everything in it, including its holy furnishings and articles."

17The LORD said to Moses and Aaron, 18"See that the Kohathite tribal clans are not cut off from the Levites. 19So that they may live and not die when they come near the most holy things, do this for them: Aaron and his sons are to go into the sanctuary and assign to each man his work and what he is to carry. 20But the Kohathites must not go in to look at the holy things, even for a moment, or they will die."

The Gershonites

21The LORD said to Moses, 22"Take a

---

[a]47 That is, about 2 ounces (about 55 grams)   [b]50 That is, about 35 pounds (about 15.5 kilograms)   [c]6 That is, dugongs; also in verses 8, 10, 11, 12, 14 and 25

PASSAGE: Exodus 19:1–8; Isaiah 6:1–8

AUTHOR: Frances R. Havergal

Take My Life and Let It Be

Take my life and let it be
　　Consecrated, Lord, to thee;
Take my hands and let them move
　　At the impulse of thy love,
　　At the impulse of thy love.

Take my feet and let them be
　　Swift and beautiful for thee;
Take my voice and let me sing
　　Always, only, for my King,
　　Always, only, for my King.

Take my love — my God I pour
　　At thy feet its treasure store;
Take myself — and I will be
　　Ever, only, all for thee,
　　Ever, only, all for thee.

Go to page 169 for your next devotional reading.

census also of the Gershonites by their families and clans. ²³Count all the men from thirty to fifty years of age who come to serve in the work at the Tent of Meeting.

²⁴"This is the service of the Gershonite clans as they work and carry burdens: ²⁵They are to carry the curtains of the tabernacle, the Tent of Meeting, its covering and the outer covering of hides of sea cows, the curtains for the entrance to the Tent of Meeting, ²⁶the curtains of the courtyard surrounding the tabernacle and altar, the curtain for the entrance, the ropes and all the equipment used in its service. The Gershonites are to do all that needs to be done with these things. ²⁷All their service, whether carrying or doing other work, is to be done under the direction of Aaron and his sons. You shall assign to them as their responsibility all they are to carry. ²⁸This is the service of the Gershonite clans at the Tent of Meeting. Their duties are to be under the direction of Ithamar son of Aaron, the priest.

The Merarites

²⁹"Count the Merarites by their clans and families. ³⁰Count all the men from thirty to fifty years of age who come to serve in the work at the Tent of Meeting. ³¹This is their duty as they perform service at the Tent of Meeting: to carry the frames of the tabernacle, its crossbars, posts and bases, ³²as well as the posts of the surrounding courtyard with their bases, tent pegs, ropes, all their equipment and everything related to their use. Assign to each man the specific things he is to carry. ³³This is the service of the Merarite clans as they work at the Tent of Meeting under the direction of Ithamar son of Aaron, the priest."

The Numbering of the Levite Clans

³⁴Moses, Aaron and the leaders of the community counted the Kohathites by their clans and families. ³⁵All

the men from thirty to fifty years of age who came to serve in the work in the Tent of Meeting, ³⁶counted by clans, were 2,750. ³⁷This was the total of all those in the Kohathite clans who served in the Tent of Meeting. Moses and Aaron counted them according to the LORD's command through Moses.

³⁸The Gershonites were counted by their clans and families. ³⁹All the men from thirty to fifty years of age who came to serve in the work at the Tent of Meeting, ⁴⁰counted by their clans and families, were 2,630. ⁴¹This was the total of those in the Gershonite clans who served at the Tent of Meeting. Moses and Aaron counted them according to the LORD's command.

⁴²The Merarites were counted by their clans and families. ⁴³All the men from thirty to fifty years of age who came to serve in the work at the Tent of Meeting, ⁴⁴counted by their clans, were 3,200. ⁴⁵This was the total of those in the Merarite clans. Moses and Aaron counted them according to the LORD's command through Moses.

⁴⁶So Moses, Aaron and the leaders of Israel counted all the Levites by their clans and families. ⁴⁷All the men from thirty to fifty years of age who came to do the work of serving and carrying the Tent of Meeting ⁴⁸numbered 8,580. ⁴⁹At the LORD's command through Moses, each was assigned his work and told what to carry.

Thus they were counted, as the LORD commanded Moses.

The Purity of the Camp

5 The LORD said to Moses, ²"Command the Israelites to send away from the camp anyone who has an infectious skin disease[a] or a discharge of any kind, or who is ceremonially unclean because of a dead body. ³Send away male and female alike; send them outside the camp so they will not defile their camp, where I dwell among them." ⁴The Israelites did this; they sent them outside the

---

[a]2 Traditionally *leprosy*; the Hebrew word was used for various diseases affecting the skin—not necessarily leprosy.

camp. They did just as the LORD had instructed Moses.

Restitution for Wrongs

5The LORD said to Moses, **6**"Say to the Israelites: 'When a man or woman wrongs another in any way*a* and so is unfaithful to the LORD, that person is guilty **7**and must confess the sin he has committed. He must make full restitution for his wrong, add one fifth to it and give it all to the person he has wronged. **8**But if that person has no close relative to whom restitution can be made for the wrong, the restitution belongs to the LORD and must be given to the priest, along with the ram with which atonement is made for him. **9**All the sacred contributions the Israelites bring to a priest will belong to him. **10**Each man's sacred gifts are his own, but what he gives to the priest will belong to the priest.' "

The Test for an Unfaithful Wife

11Then the LORD said to Moses, **12**"Speak to the Israelites and say to them: 'If a man's wife goes astray and is unfaithful to him **13**by sleeping with another man, and this is hidden from her husband and her impurity is undetected (since there is no witness against her and she has not been caught in the act), **14**and if feelings of jealousy come over her husband and he suspects his wife and she is impure—or if he is jealous and suspects her even though she is not impure— **15**then he is to take his wife to the priest. He must also take an offering of a tenth of an ephah*b* of barley flour on her behalf. He must not pour oil on it or put incense on it, because it is a grain offering for jealousy, a reminder offering to draw attention to guilt.

16" 'The priest shall bring her and have her stand before the LORD. **17**Then he shall take some holy water

in a clay jar and put some dust from the tabernacle floor into the water. **18**After the priest has had the woman stand before the LORD, he shall loosen her hair and place in her hands the reminder offering, the grain offering for jealousy, while he himself holds the bitter water that brings a curse. **19**Then the priest shall put the woman under oath and say to her, "If no other man has slept with you and you have not gone astray and become impure while married to your husband, may this bitter water that brings a curse not harm you. **20**But if you have gone astray while married to your husband and you have defiled yourself by sleeping with a man other than your husband"— **21**here the priest is to put the woman under this curse of the oath—"may the LORD cause your people to curse and denounce you when he causes your thigh to waste away and your abdomen to swell.*c* **22**May this water that brings a curse enter your body so that your abdomen swells and your thigh wastes away.*d* "

" 'Then the woman is to say, "Amen. So be it."

23" 'The priest is to write these curses on a scroll and then wash them off into the bitter water. **24**He shall have the woman drink the bitter water that brings a curse, and this water will enter her and cause bitter suffering. **25**The priest is to take from her hands the grain offering for jealousy, wave it before the LORD and bring it to the altar. **26**The priest is then to take a handful of the grain offering as a memorial offering and burn it on the altar; after that, he is to have the woman drink the water. **27**If she has defiled herself and been unfaithful to her husband, then when she is made to drink the water that brings a curse, it will go into her and cause bitter suffering; her abdomen will swell and her thigh waste away,*e* and she will

a6 Or woman commits any wrong common to mankind   *b15 That is, probably about 2 quarts (about 2 liters)*   *c21 Or causes you to have a miscarrying womb and barrenness*   *d22 Or body and cause you to be barren and have a miscarrying womb*   *e27 Or suffering; she will have barrenness and a miscarrying womb*

become accursed among her people. [28]If, however, the woman has not defiled herself and is free from impurity, she will be cleared of guilt and will be able to have children.

[29]" 'This, then, is the law of jealousy when a woman goes astray and defiles herself while married to her husband, [30]or when feelings of jealousy come over a man because he suspects his wife. The priest is to have her stand before the LORD and is to apply this entire law to her. [31]The husband will be innocent of any wrongdoing, but the woman will bear the consequences of her sin.' "

The Nazirite

6 The LORD said to Moses, [2]"Speak to the Israelites and say to them: 'If a man or woman wants to make a special vow, a vow of separation to the LORD as a Nazirite, [3]he must abstain from wine and other fermented drink and must not drink vinegar made from wine or from other fermented drink. He must not drink grape juice or eat grapes or raisins. [4]As long as he is a Nazirite, he must not eat anything that comes from the grapevine, not even the seeds or skins.

[5]" 'During the entire period of his vow of separation no razor may be used on his head. He must be holy until the period of his separation to the LORD is over; he must let the hair of his head grow long. [6]Throughout the period of his separation to the LORD he must not go near a dead body. [7]Even if his own father or mother or brother or sister dies, he must not make himself ceremonially unclean on account of them, because the symbol of his separation to God is on his head. [8]Throughout the period of his separation he is consecrated to the LORD.

[9]" 'If someone dies suddenly in his presence, thus defiling the hair he has dedicated, he must shave his head on the day of his cleansing—the seventh day. [10]Then on the eighth day he must bring two doves or two young pigeons to the priest at the entrance to the Tent of Meeting. [11]The priest is to offer one as a sin offering and the other as a burnt offering to make atonement for him because he sinned by being in the presence of the dead body. That same day he is to consecrate his head. [12]He must dedicate himself to the LORD for the period of his separation and must bring a year-old male lamb as a guilt offering. The previous days do not count, because he became defiled during his separation.

[13]" 'Now this is the law for the Nazirite when the period of his separation is over. He is to be brought to the entrance to the Tent of Meeting. [14]There he is to present his offerings to the LORD: a year-old male lamb without defect for a burnt offering, a year-old ewe lamb without defect for a sin offering, a ram without defect for a fellowship offering,[a] [15]together with their grain offerings and drink offerings, and a basket of bread made without yeast—cakes made of fine flour mixed with oil, and wafers spread with oil.

[16]" 'The priest is to present them before the LORD and make the sin offering and the burnt offering. [17]He is to present the basket of unleavened bread and is to sacrifice the ram as a fellowship offering to the LORD, together with its grain offering and drink offering.

[18]" 'Then at the entrance to the Tent of Meeting, the Nazirite must shave off the hair that he dedicated. He is to take the hair and put it in the fire that is under the sacrifice of the fellowship offering.

[19]" 'After the Nazirite has shaved off the hair of his dedication, the priest is to place in his hands a boiled shoulder of the ram, and a cake and a wafer from the basket, both made without yeast. [20]The priest shall then wave them before the LORD as a wave offering; they are holy and belong to the priest, together with the breast

---

[a]14 Traditionally *peace offering*; also in verses 17 and 18

that was waved and the thigh that was presented. After that, the Nazirite may drink wine.

21" 'This is the law of the Nazirite who vows his offering to the LORD in accordance with his separation, in addition to whatever else he can afford. He must fulfill the vow he has made, according to the law of the Nazirite.' "

The Priestly Blessing

22The LORD said to Moses, 23"Tell Aaron and his sons, 'This is how you are to bless the Israelites. Say to them:

24" ' "The LORD bless you
    and keep you;
25the LORD make his face shine upon
        you
    and be gracious to you;
26the LORD turn his face toward you
    and give you peace." '

27"So they will put my name on the Israelites, and I will bless them."

Offerings at the Dedication of the Tabernacle

7 When Moses finished setting up the tabernacle, he anointed it and consecrated it and all its furnishings. He also anointed and consecrated the altar and all its utensils. 2Then the leaders of Israel, the heads of families who were the tribal leaders in charge of those who were counted, made offerings. 3They brought as their gifts before the LORD six covered carts and twelve oxen—an ox from each leader and a cart from every two. These they presented before the tabernacle.

4The LORD said to Moses, 5"Accept these from them, that they may be used in the work at the Tent of Meeting. Give them to the Levites as each man's work requires."

6So Moses took the carts and oxen and gave them to the Levites. 7He gave two carts and four oxen to the Gershonites, as their work required, 8and he gave four carts and eight oxen to the Merarites, as their work required. They were all under the direction of Ithamar son of Aaron, the priest. 9But Moses did not give any to the Kohathites, because they were to carry on their shoulders the holy things, for which they were responsible.

10When the altar was anointed, the leaders brought their offerings for its dedication and presented them before the altar. 11For the LORD had said to Moses, "Each day one leader is to bring his offering for the dedication of the altar."

12The one who brought his offering on the first day was Nahshon son of Amminadab of the tribe of Judah.

13His offering was one silver plate weighing a hundred and thirty shekels,a and one silver sprinkling bowl weighing seventy shekels,b both according to the sanctuary shekel, each filled with fine flour mixed with oil as a grain offering; 14one gold dish weighing ten shekels,c filled with incense; 15one young bull, one ram and one male lamb a year old, for a burnt offering; 16one male goat for a sin offering; 17and two oxen, five rams, five male goats and five male lambs a year old, to be sacrificed as a fellowship offering.d This was the offering of Nahshon son of Amminadab.

18On the second day Nethanel son of Zuar, the leader of Issachar, brought his offering.

19The offering he brought was one silver plate weighing a hundred and thirty shekels, and one silver sprinkling bowl weighing seventy shekels, both according to the sanctuary shekel, each filled with fine flour mixed with oil as a grain offering; 20one gold dish weighing ten shekels, filled

---

a13 That is, about 3 1/4 pounds (about 1.5 kilograms); also elsewhere in this chapter
b13 That is, about 1 3/4 pounds (about 0.8 kilogram); also elsewhere in this chapter   c14 That is, about 4 ounces (about 110 grams); also elsewhere in this chapter   d17 Traditionally *peace offering*; also elsewhere in this chapter

with incense; ²¹one young bull, one ram and one male lamb a year old, for a burnt offering; ²²one male goat for a sin offering; ²³and two oxen, five rams, five male goats and five male lambs a year old, to be sacrificed as a fellowship offering. This was the offering of Nethanel son of Zuar.

²⁴On the third day, Eliab son of Helon, the leader of the people of Zebulun, brought his offering.

²⁵His offering was one silver plate weighing a hundred and thirty shekels, and one silver sprinkling bowl weighing seventy shekels, both according to the sanctuary shekel, each filled with fine flour mixed with oil as a grain offering; ²⁶one gold dish weighing ten shekels, filled with incense; ²⁷one young bull, one ram and one male lamb a year old, for a burnt offering; ²⁸one male goat for a sin offering; ²⁹and two oxen, five rams, five male goats and five male lambs a year old, to be sacrificed as a fellowship offering. This was the offering of Eliab son of Helon.

³⁰On the fourth day Elizur son of Shedeur, the leader of the people of Reuben, brought his offering.

³¹His offering was one silver plate weighing a hundred and thirty shekels, and one silver sprinkling bowl weighing seventy shekels, both according to the sanctuary shekel, each filled with fine flour mixed with oil as a grain offering; ³²one gold dish weighing ten shekels, filled with incense; ³³one young bull, one ram and one male lamb a year old, for a burnt offering; ³⁴one male goat for a sin offering; ³⁵and two oxen, five rams, five male goats and five male lambs a year old, to be sacrificed as a fellowship offering. This was the offering of Elizur son of Shedeur.

³⁶On the fifth day Shelumiel son of Zurishaddai, the leader of the people of Simeon, brought his offering.

³⁷His offering was one silver plate weighing a hundred and thirty shekels, and one silver sprinkling bowl weighing seventy shekels, both according to the sanctuary shekel, each filled with fine flour mixed with oil as a grain offering; ³⁸one gold dish weighing ten shekels, filled with incense; ³⁹one young bull, one ram and one male lamb a year old, for a burnt offering; ⁴⁰one male goat for a sin offering; ⁴¹and two oxen, five rams, five male goats and five male lambs a year old, to be sacrificed as a fellowship offering. This was the offering of Shelumiel son of Zurishaddai.

⁴²On the sixth day Eliasaph son of Deuel, the leader of the people of Gad, brought his offering.

⁴³His offering was one silver plate weighing a hundred and thirty shekels, and one silver sprinkling bowl weighing seventy shekels, both according to the sanctuary shekel, each filled with fine flour mixed with oil as a grain offering; ⁴⁴one gold dish weighing ten shekels, filled with incense; ⁴⁵one young bull, one ram and one male lamb a year old, for a burnt offering; ⁴⁶one male goat for a sin offering; ⁴⁷and two oxen, five rams, five male goats and five male lambs a year old, to be sacrificed as a fellowship offering. This was the offering of Eliasaph son of Deuel.

⁴⁸On the seventh day Elishama son of Ammihud, the leader of the people of Ephraim, brought his offering.

⁴⁹His offering was one silver plate weighing a hundred and thirty shekels, and one silver sprinkling bowl weighing seventy shekels, both according to the sanctuary shekel, each filled with fine flour mixed with oil as a grain offering; ⁵⁰one gold dish

weighing ten shekels, filled with incense; ⁵¹one young bull, one ram and one male lamb a year old, for a burnt offering; ⁵²one male goat for a sin offering; ⁵³and two oxen, five rams, five male goats and five male lambs a year old, to be sacrificed as a fellowship offering. This was the offering of Elishama son of Ammihud.

⁵⁴On the eighth day Gamaliel son of Pedahzur, the leader of the people of Manasseh, brought his offering.

⁵⁵His offering was one silver plate weighing a hundred and thirty shekels, and one silver sprinkling bowl weighing seventy shekels, both according to the sanctuary shekel, each filled with fine flour mixed with oil as a grain offering; ⁵⁶one gold dish weighing ten shekels, filled with incense; ⁵⁷one young bull, one ram and one male lamb a year old, for a burnt offering; ⁵⁸one male goat for a sin offering; ⁵⁹and two oxen, five rams, five male goats and five male lambs a year old, to be sacrificed as a fellowship offering. This was the offering of Gamaliel son of Pedahzur.

⁶⁰On the ninth day Abidan son of Gideoni, the leader of the people of Benjamin, brought his offering.

⁶¹His offering was one silver plate weighing a hundred and thirty shekels, and one silver sprinkling bowl weighing seventy shekels, both according to the sanctuary shekel, each filled with fine flour mixed with oil as a grain offering; ⁶²one gold dish weighing ten shekels, filled with incense; ⁶³one young bull, one ram and one male lamb a year old, for a burnt offering; ⁶⁴one male goat for a sin offering; ⁶⁵and two oxen, five rams, five male goats and five male lambs a year old, to be sacrificed as a fel-

lowship offering. This was the offering of Abidan son of Gideoni.

⁶⁶On the tenth day Ahiezer son of Ammishaddai, the leader of the people of Dan, brought his offering.

⁶⁷His offering was one silver plate weighing a hundred and thirty shekels, and one silver sprinkling bowl weighing seventy shekels, both according to the sanctuary shekel, each filled with fine flour mixed with oil as a grain offering; ⁶⁸one gold dish weighing ten shekels, filled with incense; ⁶⁹one young bull, one ram and one male lamb a year old, for a burnt offering; ⁷⁰one male goat for a sin offering; ⁷¹and two oxen, five rams, five male goats and five male lambs a year old, to be sacrificed as a fellowship offering. This was the offering of Ahiezer son of Ammishaddai.

⁷²On the eleventh day Pagiel son of Ocran, the leader of the people of Asher, brought his offering.

⁷³His offering was one silver plate weighing a hundred and thirty shekels, and one silver sprinkling bowl weighing seventy shekels, both according to the sanctuary shekel, each filled with fine flour mixed with oil as a grain offering; ⁷⁴one gold dish weighing ten shekels, filled with incense; ⁷⁵one young bull, one ram and one male lamb a year old, for a burnt offering; ⁷⁶one male goat for a sin offering; ⁷⁷and two oxen, five rams, five male goats and five male lambs a year old, to be sacrificed as a fellowship offering. This was the offering of Pagiel son of Ocran.

⁷⁸On the twelfth day Ahira son of Enan, the leader of the people of Naphtali, brought his offering.

⁷⁹His offering was one silver plate weighing a hundred and thirty shekels, and one silver

sprinkling bowl weighing seventy shekels, both according to the sanctuary shekel, each filled with fine flour mixed with oil as a grain offering; [80]one gold dish weighing ten shekels, filled with incense; [81]one young bull, one ram and one male lamb a year old, for a burnt offering; [82]one male goat for a sin offering; [83]and two oxen, five rams, five male goats and five male lambs a year old, to be sacrificed as a fellowship offering. This was the offering of Ahira son of Enan.

[84]These were the offerings of the Israelite leaders for the dedication of the altar when it was anointed: twelve silver plates, twelve silver sprinkling bowls and twelve gold dishes. [85]Each silver plate weighed a hundred and thirty shekels, and each sprinkling bowl seventy shekels. Altogether, the silver dishes weighed two thousand four hundred shekels,[a] according to the sanctuary shekel. [86]The twelve gold dishes filled with incense weighed ten shekels each, according to the sanctuary shekel. Altogether, the gold dishes weighed a hundred and twenty shekels.[b] [87]The total number of animals for the burnt offering came to twelve young bulls, twelve rams and twelve male lambs a year old, together with their grain offering. Twelve male goats were used for the sin offering. [88]The total number of animals for the sacrifice of the fellowship offering came to twenty-four oxen, sixty rams, sixty male goats and sixty male lambs a year old. These were the offerings for the dedication of the altar after it was anointed.

[89]When Moses entered the Tent of Meeting to speak with the LORD, he heard the voice speaking to him from between the two cherubim above the atonement cover on the ark of the Testimony. And he spoke with him.

Setting Up the Lamps

8 The LORD said to Moses, [2]"Speak to Aaron and say to him, 'When you set up the seven lamps, they are to light the area in front of the lampstand.' "

[3]Aaron did so; he set up the lamps so that they faced forward on the lampstand, just as the LORD commanded Moses. [4]This is how the lampstand was made: It was made of hammered gold—from its base to its blossoms. The lampstand was made exactly like the pattern the LORD had shown Moses.

The Setting Apart of the Levites

[5]The LORD said to Moses: [6]"Take the Levites from among the other Israelites and make them ceremonially clean. [7]To purify them, do this: Sprinkle the water of cleansing on them; then have them shave their whole bodies and wash their clothes, and so purify themselves. [8]Have them take a young bull with its grain offering of fine flour mixed with oil; then you are to take a second young bull for a sin offering. [9]Bring the Levites to the front of the Tent of Meeting and assemble the whole Israelite community. [10]You are to bring the Levites before the LORD, and the Israelites are to lay their hands on them. [11]Aaron is to present the Levites before the LORD as a wave offering from the Israelites, so that they may be ready to do the work of the LORD.

[12]"After the Levites lay their hands on the heads of the bulls, use the one for a sin offering to the LORD and the other for a burnt offering, to make atonement for the Levites. [13]Have the Levites stand in front of Aaron and his sons and then present them as a wave offering to the LORD. [14]In this way you are to set the Levites apart from the other Israelites, and the Levites will be mine.

[15]"After you have purified the Levites and presented them as a wave

---

[a]85 That is, about 60 pounds (about 28 kilograms)   [b]86 That is, about 3 pounds (about 1.4 kilograms)

offering, they are to come to do their work at the Tent of Meeting. ¹⁶They are the Israelites who are to be given wholly to me. I have taken them as my own in place of the firstborn, the first male offspring from every Israelite woman. ¹⁷Every firstborn male in Israel, whether man or animal, is mine. When I struck down all the firstborn in Egypt, I set them apart for myself. ¹⁸And I have taken the Levites in place of all the firstborn sons in Israel. ¹⁹Of all the Israelites, I have given the Levites as gifts to Aaron and his sons to do the work at the Tent of Meeting on behalf of the Israelites and to make atonement for them so that no plague will strike the Israelites when they go near the sanctuary."

²⁰Moses, Aaron and the whole Israelite community did with the Levites just as the LORD commanded Moses. ²¹The Levites purified themselves and washed their clothes. Then Aaron presented them as a wave offering before the LORD and made atonement for them to purify them. ²²After that, the Levites came to do their work at the Tent of Meeting under the supervision of Aaron and his sons. They did with the Levites just as the LORD commanded Moses.

²³The LORD said to Moses, ²⁴"This applies to the Levites: Men twenty-five years old or more shall come to take part in the work at the Tent of Meeting, ²⁵but at the age of fifty, they must retire from their regular service and work no longer. ²⁶They may assist their brothers in performing their duties at the Tent of Meeting, but they themselves must not do the work. This, then, is how you are to assign the responsibilities of the Levites."

The Passover

9 The LORD spoke to Moses in the Desert of Sinai in the first month of the second year after they came out of Egypt. He said, ²"Have the Israelites celebrate the Passover at the appointed time. ³Celebrate it at the appointed time, at twilight on the fourteenth day of this month, in ac-

cordance with all its rules and regulations."

⁴So Moses told the Israelites to celebrate the Passover, ⁵and they did so in the Desert of Sinai at twilight on the fourteenth day of the first month. The Israelites did everything just as the LORD commanded Moses.

⁶But some of them could not celebrate the Passover on that day because they were ceremonially unclean on account of a dead body. So they came to Moses and Aaron that same day ⁷and said to Moses, "We have become unclean because of a dead body, but why should we be kept from presenting the LORD's offering with the other Israelites at the appointed time?"

⁸Moses answered them, "Wait until I find out what the LORD commands concerning you."

⁹Then the LORD said to Moses, ¹⁰"Tell the Israelites: 'When any of you or your descendants are unclean because of a dead body or are away on a journey, they may still celebrate the LORD's Passover. ¹¹They are to celebrate it on the fourteenth day of the second month at twilight. They are to eat the lamb, together with unleavened bread and bitter herbs. ¹²They must not leave any of it till morning or break any of its bones. When they celebrate the Passover, they must follow all the regulations. ¹³But if a man who is ceremonially clean and not on a journey fails to celebrate the Passover, that person must be cut off from his people because he did not present the LORD's offering at the appointed time. That man will bear the consequences of his sin.

¹⁴" 'An alien living among you who wants to celebrate the LORD's Passover must do so in accordance with its rules and regulations. You must have the same regulations for the alien and the native-born.' "

The Cloud Above the Tabernacle

¹⁵On the day the tabernacle, the Tent of the Testimony, was set up, the cloud covered it. From evening till morning the cloud above the taberna-

cle looked like fire. ¹⁶That is how it continued to be; the cloud covered it, and at night it looked like fire. ¹⁷Whenever the cloud lifted from above the Tent, the Israelites set out; wherever the cloud settled, the Israelites encamped. ¹⁸At the LORD's command the Israelites set out, and at his command they encamped. As long as the cloud stayed over the tabernacle, they remained in camp. ¹⁹When the cloud remained over the tabernacle a long time, the Israelites obeyed the LORD's order and did not set out. ²⁰Sometimes the cloud was over the tabernacle only a few days; at the LORD's command they would encamp, and then at his command they would set out. ²¹Sometimes the cloud stayed only from evening till morning, and when it lifted in the morning, they set out. Whether by day or by night,

MONDAY

VERSE: AUTHOR: PASSAGE:
Numbers 8:25   Richard L. Morgan   Numbers 8:5–26

Redirected, Not Retired

The word *retirement* can be misleading. For some, retirement connotes a stop sign or a rocking chair. Perhaps the word *redirection* is a better one. That means a new beginning for the best 20 years of our life.

The Levites retired from active ministry at age 50, but that did not mean complete inactivity. They began "second careers" in assisting, advising, ministering to their fellow Levites in the Tent of Meeting. Their retirement seems to have included becoming teachers and advisers to the younger men.

Perhaps we should stop using the word *retirement* with its often negative connotations, and use instead the concept of *freedom*. Freedom to read, to interact socially, to change one's life-style, to find new priorities . . .

Retirement is redirection. In retirement we may *do* a bit less so that we can *be* who we are. We may slow down, but we can be as active and involved as we ever were. Retirement is just another station on life's journey as we change gears and move on.

ADDITIONAL SCRIPTURE READINGS
Galatians 5:1–15; 1 Peter 4:7–11

Go to page 176 for your next devotional reading.

whenever the cloud lifted, they set out. ²²Whether the cloud stayed over the tabernacle for two days or a month or a year, the Israelites would remain in camp and not set out; but when it lifted, they would set out. ²³At the LORD's command they encamped, and at the LORD's command they set out. They obeyed the LORD's order, in accordance with his command through Moses.

The Silver Trumpets

10 The LORD said to Moses: ²"Make two trumpets of hammered silver, and use them for calling the community together and for having the camps set out. ³When both are sounded, the whole community is to assemble before you at the entrance to the Tent of Meeting. ⁴If only one is sounded, the leaders—the heads of the clans of Israel—are to assemble before you. ⁵When a trumpet blast is sounded, the tribes camping on the east are to set out. ⁶At the sounding of a second blast, the camps on the south are to set out. The blast will be the signal for setting out. ⁷To gather the assembly, blow the trumpets, but not with the same signal.

⁸"The sons of Aaron, the priests, are to blow the trumpets. This is to be a lasting ordinance for you and the generations to come. ⁹When you go into battle in your own land against an enemy who is oppressing you, sound a blast on the trumpets. Then you will be remembered by the LORD your God and rescued from your enemies. ¹⁰Also at your times of rejoicing—your appointed feasts and New Moon festivals—you are to sound the trumpets over your burnt offerings and fellowship offerings,ᵃ and they will be a memorial for you before your God. I am the LORD your God."

The Israelites Leave Sinai

¹¹On the twentieth day of the second month of the second year, the cloud lifted from above the tabernacle of the Testimony. ¹²Then the Israelites

set out from the Desert of Sinai and traveled from place to place until the cloud came to rest in the Desert of Paran. ¹³They set out, this first time, at the LORD's command through Moses.

¹⁴The divisions of the camp of Judah went first, under their standard. Nahshon son of Amminadab was in command. ¹⁵Nethanel son of Zuar was over the division of the tribe of Issachar, ¹⁶and Eliab son of Helon was over the division of the tribe of Zebulun. ¹⁷Then the tabernacle was taken down, and the Gershonites and Merarites, who carried it, set out.

¹⁸The divisions of the camp of Reuben went next, under their standard. Elizur son of Shedeur was in command. ¹⁹Shelumiel son of Zurishaddai was over the division of the tribe of Simeon, ²⁰and Eliasaph son of Deuel was over the division of the tribe of Gad. ²¹Then the Kohathites set out, carrying the holy things. The tabernacle was to be set up before they arrived.

²²The divisions of the camp of Ephraim went next, under their standard. Elishama son of Ammihud was in command. ²³Gamaliel son of Pedahzur was over the division of the tribe of Manasseh, ²⁴and Abidan son of Gideoni was over the division of the tribe of Benjamin.

²⁵Finally, as the rear guard for all the units, the divisions of the camp of Dan set out, under their standard. Ahiezer son of Ammishaddai was in command. ²⁶Pagiel son of Ocran was over the division of the tribe of Asher, ²⁷and Ahira son of Enan was over the division of the tribe of Naphtali. ²⁸This was the order of march for the Israelite divisions as they set out.

²⁹Now Moses said to Hobab son of Reuel the Midianite, Moses' father-in-law, "We are setting out for the place about which the LORD said, 'I will give it to you.' Come with us and we will treat you well, for the LORD has promised good things to Israel."

³⁰He answered, "No, I will not go; I

ᵃ10 Traditionally *peace offerings*

am going back to my own land and my own people."

³¹But Moses said, "Please do not leave us. You know where we should camp in the desert, and you can be our eyes. ³²If you come with us, we will share with you whatever good things the LORD gives us."

³³So they set out from the mountain of the LORD and traveled for three days. The ark of the covenant of the LORD went before them during those three days to find them a place to rest. ³⁴The cloud of the LORD was over them by day when they set out from the camp.

³⁵Whenever the ark set out, Moses said,

"Rise up, O LORD!
    May your enemies be scattered;
    may your foes flee before you."

³⁶Whenever it came to rest, he said,

"Return, O LORD,
    to the countless thousands of
        Israel."

Fire From the LORD

11 Now the people complained about their hardships in the hearing of the LORD, and when he heard them his anger was aroused. Then fire from the LORD burned among them and consumed some of the outskirts of the camp. ²When the people cried out to Moses, he prayed to the LORD and the fire died down. ³So that place was called Taberah,ᵃ because fire from the LORD had burned among them.

Quail From the LORD

⁴The rabble with them began to crave other food, and again the Israelites started wailing and said, "If only we had meat to eat! ⁵We remember the fish we ate in Egypt at no cost— also the cucumbers, melons, leeks, onions and garlic. ⁶But now we have lost our appetite; we never see anything but this manna!"

⁷The manna was like coriander seed and looked like resin. ⁸The people went around gathering it, and then ground it in a handmill or crushed it in a mortar. They cooked it in a pot or made it into cakes. And it tasted like something made with olive oil. ⁹When the dew settled on the camp at night, the manna also came down.

¹⁰Moses heard the people of every family wailing, each at the entrance to his tent. The LORD became exceedingly angry, and Moses was troubled. ¹¹He asked the LORD, "Why have you brought this trouble on your servant? What have I done to displease you that you put the burden of all these people on me? ¹²Did I conceive all these people? Did I give them birth? Why do you tell me to carry them in my arms, as a nurse carries an infant, to the land you promised on oath to their forefathers? ¹³Where can I get meat for all these people? They keep wailing to me, 'Give us meat to eat!' ¹⁴I cannot carry all these people by myself; the burden is too heavy for me. ¹⁵If this is how you are going to treat me, put me to death right now— if I have found favor in your eyes— and do not let me face my own ruin."

¹⁶The LORD said to Moses: "Bring me seventy of Israel's elders who are known to you as leaders and officials among the people. Have them come to the Tent of Meeting, that they may stand there with you. ¹⁷I will come down and speak with you there, and I will take of the Spirit that is on you and put the Spirit on them. They will help you carry the burden of the people so that you will not have to carry it alone.

¹⁸"Tell the people: 'Consecrate yourselves in preparation for tomorrow, when you will eat meat. The LORD heard you when you wailed, "If only we had meat to eat! We were better off in Egypt!" Now the LORD will give you meat, and you will eat it. ¹⁹You will not eat it for just one day, or two days, or five, ten or twenty days, ²⁰but for a whole month—un-

ᵃ3 *Taberah* means *burning.*

til it comes out of your nostrils and you loathe it—because you have rejected the LORD, who is among you, and have wailed before him, saying, "Why did we ever leave Egypt?" ' "

²¹But Moses said, "Here I am among six hundred thousand men on foot, and you say, 'I will give them meat to eat for a whole month!' ²²Would they have enough if flocks and herds were slaughtered for them? Would they have enough if all the fish in the sea were caught for them?"

²³The LORD answered Moses, "Is the LORD's arm too short? You will now see whether or not what I say will come true for you."

²⁴So Moses went out and told the people what the LORD had said. He brought together seventy of their elders and had them stand around the Tent. ²⁵Then the LORD came down in the cloud and spoke with him, and he took of the Spirit that was on him and put the Spirit on the seventy elders. When the Spirit rested on them, they prophesied, but they did not do so again.ᵃ

²⁶However, two men, whose names were Eldad and Medad, had remained in the camp. They were listed among the elders, but did not go out to the Tent. Yet the Spirit also rested on them, and they prophesied in the camp. ²⁷A young man ran and told Moses, "Eldad and Medad are prophesying in the camp."

²⁸Joshua son of Nun, who had been Moses' aide since youth, spoke up and said, "Moses, my lord, stop them!"

²⁹But Moses replied, "Are you jealous for my sake? I wish that all the LORD's people were prophets and that the LORD would put his Spirit on them!" ³⁰Then Moses and the elders of Israel returned to the camp.

³¹Now a wind went out from the LORD and drove quail in from the sea. It brought themᵇ down all around the camp to about three feetᶜ above the ground, as far as a day's walk in any direction. ³²All that day and night and all the next day the people went out and gathered quail. No one gathered less than ten homers.ᵈ Then they spread them out all around the camp. ³³But while the meat was still between their teeth and before it could be consumed, the anger of the LORD burned against the people, and he struck them with a severe plague. ³⁴Therefore the place was named Kibroth Hattaavah,ᵉ because there they buried the people who had craved other food.

³⁵From Kibroth Hattaavah the people traveled to Hazeroth and stayed there.

Miriam and Aaron Oppose Moses

12 Miriam and Aaron began to talk against Moses because of his Cushite wife, for he had married a Cushite. ²"Has the LORD spoken only through Moses?" they asked. "Hasn't he also spoken through us?" And the LORD heard this.

³(Now Moses was a very humble man, more humble than anyone else on the face of the earth.)

⁴At once the LORD said to Moses, Aaron and Miriam, "Come out to the Tent of Meeting, all three of you." So the three of them came out. ⁵Then the LORD came down in a pillar of cloud; he stood at the entrance to the Tent and summoned Aaron and Miriam. When both of them stepped forward, ⁶he said, "Listen to my words:

"When a prophet of the LORD is
    among you,
  I reveal myself to him in
      visions,
  I speak to him in dreams.
⁷But this is not true of my servant
      Moses;
  he is faithful in all my house.
⁸With him I speak face to face,
  clearly and not in riddles;
  he sees the form of the LORD.
Why then were you not afraid

ᵃ25 Or prophesied and continued to do so   ᵇ31 Or They flew   ᶜ31 Hebrew two cubits (about 1 meter)   ᵈ32 That is, probably about 60 bushels (about 2.2 kiloliters)   ᵉ34 Kibroth Hattaavah means graves of craving.

to speak against my servant Moses?"

⁹The anger of the LORD burned against them, and he left them.

¹⁰When the cloud lifted from above the Tent, there stood Miriam—leprous,ᵃ like snow. Aaron turned toward her and saw that she had leprosy; ¹¹and he said to Moses, "Please, my lord, do not hold against us the sin we have so foolishly committed. ¹²Do not let her be like a stillborn infant coming from its mother's womb with its flesh half eaten away."

¹³So Moses cried out to the LORD, "O God, please heal her!"

¹⁴The LORD replied to Moses, "If her father had spit in her face, would she not have been in disgrace for seven days? Confine her outside the camp for seven days; after that she can be brought back." ¹⁵So Miriam was confined outside the camp for seven days, and the people did not move on till she was brought back.

¹⁶After that, the people left Hazeroth and encamped in the Desert of Paran.

Exploring Canaan

13 The LORD said to Moses, ²"Send some men to explore the land of Canaan, which I am giving to the Israelites. From each ancestral tribe send one of its leaders."

³So at the LORD's command Moses sent them out from the Desert of Paran. All of them were leaders of the Israelites. ⁴These are their names:

from the tribe of Reuben, Shammua son of Zaccur;
⁵from the tribe of Simeon, Shaphat son of Hori;
⁶from the tribe of Judah, Caleb son of Jephunneh;
⁷from the tribe of Issachar, Igal son of Joseph;
⁸from the tribe of Ephraim, Hoshea son of Nun;
⁹from the tribe of Benjamin, Palti son of Raphu;
¹⁰from the tribe of Zebulun, Gaddiel son of Sodi;
¹¹from the tribe of Manasseh (a tribe of Joseph), Gaddi son of Susi;
¹²from the tribe of Dan, Ammiel son of Gemalli;
¹³from the tribe of Asher, Sethur son of Michael;
¹⁴from the tribe of Naphtali, Nahbi son of Vophsi;
¹⁵from the tribe of Gad, Geuel son of Maki.

¹⁶These are the names of the men Moses sent to explore the land. (Moses gave Hoshea son of Nun the name Joshua.)

¹⁷When Moses sent them to explore Canaan, he said, "Go up through the Negev and on into the hill country. ¹⁸See what the land is like and whether the people who live there are strong or weak, few or many. ¹⁹What kind of land do they live in? Is it good or bad? What kind of towns do they live in? Are they unwalled or fortified? ²⁰How is the soil? Is it fertile or poor? Are there trees on it or not? Do your best to bring back some of the fruit of the land." (It was the season for the first ripe grapes.)

²¹So they went up and explored the land from the Desert of Zin as far as Rehob, toward Leboᵇ Hamath. ²²They went up through the Negev and came to Hebron, where Ahiman, Sheshai and Talmai, the descendants of Anak, lived. (Hebron had been built seven years before Zoan in Egypt.) ²³When they reached the Valley of Eshcol,ᶜ they cut off a branch bearing a single cluster of grapes. Two of them carried it on a pole between them, along with some pomegranates and figs. ²⁴That place was called the Valley of Eshcol because of the cluster of grapes the Israelites cut off there. ²⁵At the end of forty days they returned from exploring the land.

ᵃ10 The Hebrew word was used for various diseases affecting the skin—not necessarily leprosy.   ᵇ21 Or toward the entrance to   ᶜ23 Eshcol means cluster; also in verse 24.

Report on the Exploration

26They came back to Moses and Aaron and the whole Israelite community at Kadesh in the Desert of Paran. There they reported to them and to the whole assembly and showed them the fruit of the land. 27They gave Moses this account: "We went into the land to which you sent us, and it does flow with milk and honey! Here is its fruit. 28But the people who live there are powerful, and the cities are fortified and very large. We even saw descendants of Anak there. 29The Amalekites live in the Negev; the Hittites, Jebusites and Amorites live in the hill country; and the Canaanites live near the sea and along the Jordan."

30Then Caleb silenced the people before Moses and said, "We should go up and take possession of the land, for we can certainly do it."

31But the men who had gone up with him said, "We can't attack those people; they are stronger than we are." 32And they spread among the Israelites a bad report about the land they had explored. They said, "The land we explored devours those living in it. All the people we saw there are of great size. 33We saw the Nephilim there (the descendants of Anak come from the Nephilim). We seemed like grasshoppers in our own eyes, and we looked the same to them."

The People Rebel

14 That night all the people of the community raised their voices and wept aloud. 2All the Israelites grumbled against Moses and Aaron, and the whole assembly said to them, "If only we had died in Egypt! Or in this desert! 3Why is the Lord bringing us to this land only to let us fall by the sword? Our wives and children will be taken as plunder. Wouldn't it be better for us to go back to Egypt?" 4And they said to each other, "We should choose a leader and go back to Egypt."

5Then Moses and Aaron fell facedown in front of the whole Israelite assembly gathered there. 6Joshua son of Nun and Caleb son of Jephunneh, who were among those who had explored the land, tore their clothes 7and said to the entire Israelite assembly, "The land we passed through and explored is exceedingly good. 8If the Lord is pleased with us, he will lead us into that land, a land flowing with milk and honey, and will give it to us. 9Only do not rebel against the Lord. And do not be afraid of the people of the land, because we will swallow them up. Their protection is gone, but the Lord is with us. Do not be afraid of them."

10But the whole assembly talked about stoning them. Then the glory of the Lord appeared at the Tent of Meeting to all the Israelites. 11The Lord said to Moses, "How long will these people treat me with contempt? How long will they refuse to believe in me, in spite of all the miraculous signs I have performed among them? 12I will strike them down with a plague and destroy them, but I will make you into a nation greater and stronger than they."

13Moses said to the Lord, "Then the Egyptians will hear about it! By your power you brought these people up from among them. 14And they will tell the inhabitants of this land about it. They have already heard that you, O Lord, are with these people and that you, O Lord, have been seen face to face, that your cloud stays over them, and that you go before them in a pillar of cloud by day and a pillar of fire by night. 15If you put these people to death all at one time, the nations who have heard this report about you will say, 16'The Lord was not able to bring these people into the land he promised them on oath; so he slaughtered them in the desert.'

17"Now may the Lord's strength be displayed, just as you have declared: 18'The Lord is slow to anger, abounding in love and forgiving sin and rebellion. Yet he does not leave the guilty unpunished; he punishes the children for the sin of the fathers to the third and fourth generation.' 19In accordance with your great love, forgive the sin of these people, just as you have pardoned them from the time they left Egypt until now."

²⁰The LORD replied, "I have forgiven them, as you asked. ²¹Nevertheless, as surely as I live and as surely as the glory of the LORD fills the whole earth, ²²not one of the men who saw my glory and the miraculous signs I performed in Egypt and in the desert but who disobeyed me and tested me ten times— ²³not one of them will ever see the land I promised on oath to their forefathers. No one who has treated me with contempt will ever see it. ²⁴But because my servant Caleb has a different spirit and follows me wholeheartedly, I will bring him into the land he went to, and his descendants will inherit it. ²⁵Since the Amalekites and Canaanites are living in the valleys, turn back tomorrow and set out toward the desert along the route to the Red Sea.*"

²⁶The LORD said to Moses and Aaron: ²⁷"How long will this wicked community grumble against me? I have heard the complaints of these grumbling Israelites. ²⁸So tell them, 'As surely as I live, declares the LORD, I will do to you the very things I heard you say: ²⁹In this desert your bodies will fall—every one of you twenty years old or more who was counted in the census and who has grumbled against me. ³⁰Not one of you will enter the land I swore with uplifted hand to make your home, except Caleb son of Jephunneh and Joshua son of Nun. ³¹As for your children that you said would be taken as plunder, I will bring them in to enjoy the land you have rejected. ³²But you—your bodies will fall in this desert. ³³Your children will be shepherds here for forty years, suffering for your unfaithfulness, until the last of your bodies lies in the desert. ³⁴For forty years—one year for each of the forty days you explored the land— you will suffer for your sins and know what it is like to have me against you.' ³⁵I, the LORD, have spo-

ken, and I will surely do these things to this whole wicked community, which has banded together against me. They will meet their end in this desert; here they will die."

³⁶So the men Moses had sent to explore the land, who returned and made the whole community grumble against him by spreading a bad report about it— ³⁷these men responsible for spreading the bad report about the land were struck down and died of a plague before the LORD. ³⁸Of the men who went to explore the land, only Joshua son of Nun and Caleb son of Jephunneh survived.

³⁹When Moses reported this to all the Israelites, they mourned bitterly. ⁴⁰Early the next morning they went up toward the high hill country. "We have sinned," they said. "We will go up to the place the LORD promised."

⁴¹But Moses said, "Why are you disobeying the LORD's command? This will not succeed! ⁴²Do not go up, because the LORD is not with you. You will be defeated by your enemies, ⁴³for the Amalekites and Canaanites will face you there. Because you have turned away from the LORD, he will not be with you and you will fall by the sword."

⁴⁴Nevertheless, in their presumption they went up toward the high hill country, though neither Moses nor the ark of the LORD's covenant moved from the camp. ⁴⁵Then the Amalekites and Canaanites who lived in that hill country came down and attacked them and beat them down all the way to Hormah.

Supplementary Offerings

15 The LORD said to Moses, ²"Speak to the Israelites and say to them: 'After you enter the land I am giving you as a home ³and you present to the LORD offerings made by fire, from the herd or the flock, as an aroma pleasing to the LORD—whether burnt offerings or sacrifices, for special vows or freewill offerings or festival offerings— ⁴then the one who

---

*25 Hebrew *Yam Suph*; that is, Sea of Reeds

VERSE:
Numbers 14:24

AUTHOR:
J. Oswald Sanders

PASSAGE:
Numbers 14:1–38

The Best Is Yet to Be

Caleb is an endless source of encouragement and inspiration. The message of his life is "the best is yet to be." He never ceased growing because his devotion to God never weakened . . .

What was the secret that enabled Caleb to succeed while the younger Israelites failed? It was enshrined in seven words: "I followed the LORD my God wholeheartedly" (Joshua 14:8). "I followed the LORD my God wholeheartedly," Caleb was able to testify with a clear conscience. This was just sober statement, not proud boasting—a plain statement of an undeflected aim.

"You have followed the LORD my God wholeheartedly," Moses was able to add in testimony (Joshua 14:9) . . . But the most astounding testimony comes from God himself: "My servant Caleb has a different spirit and follows me wholeheartedly" (Numbers 14:24). What higher eulogy could have been made?

The conclusion is plain and the lesson for us obvious. Caleb subdued and dispossessed his enemies, giants and all, because he followed the Lord wholeheartedly. He entertained no divided loyalties. Throughout his life there was consistent obedience to light received . . .

Do we find our title much larger than the spiritual territory we actually occupy and enjoy? In our lives are there still enemies that refuse to budge, giants who laugh at our puny efforts to dislodge them? . . .

It could be that we have failed in appropriating our inheritance. Or there could be some inner reservation, something that short-circuits spiritual power and saps vitality. Caleb's secret is open to us. Complete victory comes from restful confidence and unreserved obedience.

ADDITIONAL SCRIPTURE READINGS
Joshua 14:6–15; 1 Peter 1:3–9

Go to page 185 for your next devotional reading.

brings his offering shall present to the LORD a grain offering of a tenth of an ephah*a* of fine flour mixed with a quarter of a hin*b* of oil. ⁵With each lamb for the burnt offering or the sacrifice, prepare a quarter of a hin of wine as a drink offering.

⁶" 'With a ram prepare a grain offering of two-tenths of an ephah*c* of fine flour mixed with a third of a hin*d* of oil, ⁷and a third of a hin of wine as a drink offering. Offer it as an aroma pleasing to the LORD.

⁸" 'When you prepare a young bull as a burnt offering or sacrifice, for a special vow or a fellowship offering*e* to the LORD, ⁹bring with the bull a grain offering of three-tenths of an ephah*f* of fine flour mixed with half a hin*g* of oil. ¹⁰Also bring half a hin of wine as a drink offering. It will be an offering made by fire, an aroma pleasing to the LORD. ¹¹Each bull or ram, each lamb or young goat, is to be prepared in this manner. ¹²Do this for each one, for as many as you prepare.

¹³" 'Everyone who is native-born must do these things in this way when he brings an offering made by fire as an aroma pleasing to the LORD. ¹⁴For the generations to come, whenever an alien or anyone else living among you presents an offering made by fire as an aroma pleasing to the LORD, he must do exactly as you do. ¹⁵The community is to have the same rules for you and for the alien living among you; this is a lasting ordinance for the generations to come. You and the alien shall be the same before the LORD: ¹⁶The same laws and regulations will apply both to you and to the alien living among you.' "

¹⁷The LORD said to Moses, ¹⁸"Speak to the Israelites and say to them: 'When you enter the land to which I am taking you ¹⁹and you eat the food of the land, present a portion as an offering to the LORD. ²⁰Present a cake from the first of your ground meal and present it as an offering from the threshing floor. ²¹Throughout the generations to come you are to give this offering to the LORD from the first of your ground meal.

Offerings for Unintentional Sins

²²" 'Now if you unintentionally fail to keep any of these commands the LORD gave Moses— ²³any of the LORD's commands to you through him, from the day the LORD gave them and continuing through the generations to come— ²⁴and if this is done unintentionally without the community being aware of it, then the whole community is to offer a young bull for a burnt offering as an aroma pleasing to the LORD, along with its prescribed grain offering and drink offering, and a male goat for a sin offering. ²⁵The priest is to make atonement for the whole Israelite community, and they will be forgiven, for it was not intentional and they have brought to the LORD for their wrong an offering made by fire and a sin offering. ²⁶The whole Israelite community and the aliens living among them will be forgiven, because all the people were involved in the unintentional wrong.

²⁷" 'But if just one person sins unintentionally, he must bring a year-old female goat for a sin offering. ²⁸The priest is to make atonement before the LORD for the one who erred by sinning unintentionally, and when atonement has been made for him, he will be forgiven. ²⁹One and the same law applies to everyone who sins unintentionally, whether he is a native-born Israelite or an alien.

³⁰" 'But anyone who sins defiantly, whether native-born or alien, blasphemes the LORD, and that person must be cut off from his people. ³¹Because he has despised the LORD's word and broken his commands, that

---

a4 That is, probably about 2 quarts (about 2 liters)   *b4* That is, probably about 1 quart (about 1 liter); also in verse 5   *c6* That is, probably about 4 quarts (about 4.5 liters)   *d6* That is, probably about 1 1/4 quarts (about 1.2 liters); also in verse 7   *e8* Traditionally *peace offering*   *f9* That is, probably about 6 quarts (about 6.5 liters)   *g9* That is, probably about 2 quarts (about 2 liters); also in verse 10

person must surely be cut off; his guilt remains on him.' "

The Sabbath-Breaker Put to Death

[32]While the Israelites were in the desert, a man was found gathering wood on the Sabbath day. [33]Those who found him gathering wood brought him to Moses and Aaron and the whole assembly, [34]and they kept him in custody, because it was not clear what should be done to him. [35]Then the LORD said to Moses, "The man must die. The whole assembly must stone him outside the camp." [36]So the assembly took him outside the camp and stoned him to death, as the LORD commanded Moses.

Tassels on Garments

[37]The LORD said to Moses, [38]"Speak to the Israelites and say to them: 'Throughout the generations to come you are to make tassels on the corners of your garments, with a blue cord on each tassel. [39]You will have these tassels to look at and so you will remember all the commands of the LORD, that you may obey them and not prostitute yourselves by going after the lusts of your own hearts and eyes. [40]Then you will remember to obey all my commands and will be consecrated to your God. [41]I am the LORD your God, who brought you out of Egypt to be your God. I am the LORD your God.' "

Korah, Dathan and Abiram

16 Korah son of Izhar, the son of Kohath, the son of Levi, and certain Reubenites—Dathan and Abiram, sons of Eliab, and On son of Peleth—became insolent[a] [2]and rose up against Moses. With them were 250 Israelite men, well-known community leaders who had been appointed members of the council. [3]They came as a group to oppose Moses and Aaron and said to them, "You have gone too far! The whole community is holy, every one of them, and the LORD is with them. Why then do you set yourselves above the LORD's assembly?"

[4]When Moses heard this, he fell facedown. [5]Then he said to Korah and all his followers: "In the morning the LORD will show who belongs to him and who is holy, and he will have that person come near him. The man he chooses he will cause to come near him. [6]You, Korah, and all your followers are to do this: Take censers [7]and tomorrow put fire and incense in them before the LORD. The man the LORD chooses will be the one who is holy. You Levites have gone too far!"

[8]Moses also said to Korah, "Now listen, you Levites! [9]Isn't it enough for you that the God of Israel has separated you from the rest of the Israelite community and brought you near himself to do the work at the LORD's tabernacle and to stand before the community and minister to them? [10]He has brought you and all your fellow Levites near himself, but now you are trying to get the priesthood too. [11]It is against the LORD that you and all your followers have banded together. Who is Aaron that you should grumble against him?"

[12]Then Moses summoned Dathan and Abiram, the sons of Eliab. But they said, "We will not come! [13]Isn't it enough that you have brought us up out of a land flowing with milk and honey to kill us in the desert? And now you also want to lord it over us? [14]Moreover, you haven't brought us into a land flowing with milk and honey or given us an inheritance of fields and vineyards. Will you gouge out the eyes of[b] these men? No, we will not come!"

[15]Then Moses became very angry and said to the LORD, "Do not accept their offering. I have not taken so much as a donkey from them, nor have I wronged any of them."

[16]Moses said to Korah, "You and all your followers are to appear before the LORD tomorrow—you and they and Aaron. [17]Each man is to take his censer and put incense in it—250 cen-

---

[a]1 Or *Peleth—took ⌞men⌟*   [b]14 Or *you make slaves of*; or *you deceive*

sers in all—and present it before the Lord. You and Aaron are to present your censers also." ¹⁸So each man took his censer, put fire and incense in it, and stood with Moses and Aaron at the entrance to the Tent of Meeting. ¹⁹When Korah had gathered all his followers in opposition to them at the entrance to the Tent of Meeting, the glory of the Lord appeared to the entire assembly. ²⁰The Lord said to Moses and Aaron, ²¹"Separate yourselves from this assembly so I can put an end to them at once."

²²But Moses and Aaron fell facedown and cried out, "O God, God of the spirits of all mankind, will you be angry with the entire assembly when only one man sins?"

²³Then the Lord said to Moses, ²⁴"Say to the assembly, 'Move away from the tents of Korah, Dathan and Abiram.' "

²⁵Moses got up and went to Dathan and Abiram, and the elders of Israel followed him. ²⁶He warned the assembly, "Move back from the tents of these wicked men! Do not touch anything belonging to them, or you will be swept away because of all their sins." ²⁷So they moved away from the tents of Korah, Dathan and Abiram. Dathan and Abiram had come out and were standing with their wives, children and little ones at the entrances to their tents.

²⁸Then Moses said, "This is how you will know that the Lord has sent me to do all these things and that it was not my idea: ²⁹If these men die a natural death and experience only what usually happens to men, then the Lord has not sent me. ³⁰But if the Lord brings about something totally new, and the earth opens its mouth and swallows them, with everything that belongs to them, and they go down alive into the grave,ᵃ then you will know that these men have treated the Lord with contempt."

³¹As soon as he finished saying all this, the ground under them split apart ³²and the earth opened its mouth and swallowed them, with their households and all Korah's men and all their possessions. ³³They went down alive into the grave, with everything they owned; the earth closed over them, and they perished and were gone from the community. ³⁴At their cries, all the Israelites around them fled, shouting, "The earth is going to swallow us too!"

³⁵And fire came out from the Lord and consumed the 250 men who were offering the incense.

³⁶The Lord said to Moses, ³⁷"Tell Eleazar son of Aaron, the priest, to take the censers out of the smoldering remains and scatter the coals some distance away, for the censers are holy— ³⁸the censers of the men who sinned at the cost of their lives. Hammer the censers into sheets to overlay the altar, for they were presented before the Lord and have become holy. Let them be a sign to the Israelites."

³⁹So Eleazar the priest collected the bronze censers brought by those who had been burned up, and he had them hammered out to overlay the altar, ⁴⁰as the Lord directed him through Moses. This was to remind the Israelites that no one except a descendant of Aaron should come to burn incense before the Lord, or he would become like Korah and his followers.

⁴¹The next day the whole Israelite community grumbled against Moses and Aaron. "You have killed the Lord's people," they said.

⁴²But when the assembly gathered in opposition to Moses and Aaron and turned toward the Tent of Meeting, suddenly the cloud covered it and the glory of the Lord appeared. ⁴³Then Moses and Aaron went to the front of the Tent of Meeting, ⁴⁴and the Lord said to Moses, ⁴⁵"Get away from this assembly so I can put an end to them at once." And they fell facedown.

⁴⁶Then Moses said to Aaron, "Take your censer and put incense in it, along with fire from the altar, and hurry to the assembly to make atone-

ᵃ30 Hebrew *Sheol*; also in verse 33

ment for them. Wrath has come out from the LORD; the plague has started." ⁴⁷So Aaron did as Moses said, and ran into the midst of the assembly. The plague had already started among the people, but Aaron offered the incense and made atonement for them. ⁴⁸He stood between the living and the dead, and the plague stopped. ⁴⁹But 14,700 people died from the plague, in addition to those who had died because of Korah. ⁵⁰Then Aaron returned to Moses at the entrance to the Tent of Meeting, for the plague had stopped.

The Budding of Aaron's Staff

17 The LORD said to Moses, ²"Speak to the Israelites and get twelve staffs from them, one from the leader of each of their ancestral tribes. Write the name of each man on his staff. ³On the staff of Levi write Aaron's name, for there must be one staff for the head of each ancestral tribe. ⁴Place them in the Tent of Meeting in front of the Testimony, where I meet with you. ⁵The staff belonging to the man I choose will sprout, and I will rid myself of this constant grumbling against you by the Israelites."

⁶So Moses spoke to the Israelites, and their leaders gave him twelve staffs, one for the leader of each of their ancestral tribes, and Aaron's staff was among them. ⁷Moses placed the staffs before the LORD in the Tent of the Testimony.

⁸The next day Moses entered the Tent of the Testimony and saw that Aaron's staff, which represented the house of Levi, had not only sprouted but had budded, blossomed and produced almonds. ⁹Then Moses brought out all the staffs from the LORD's presence to all the Israelites. They looked at them, and each man took his own staff.

¹⁰The LORD said to Moses, "Put back Aaron's staff in front of the Testimony, to be kept as a sign to the rebellious. This will put an end to their grumbling against me, so that they will not die." ¹¹Moses did just as the LORD commanded him.

¹²The Israelites said to Moses, "We will die! We are lost, we are all lost! ¹³Anyone who even comes near the tabernacle of the LORD will die. Are we all going to die?"

Duties of Priests and Levites

18 The LORD said to Aaron, "You, your sons and your father's family are to bear the responsibility for offenses against the sanctuary, and you and your sons alone are to bear the responsibility for offenses against the priesthood. ²Bring your fellow Levites from your ancestral tribe to join you and assist you when you and your sons minister before the Tent of the Testimony. ³They are to be responsible to you and are to perform all the duties of the Tent, but they must not go near the furnishings of the sanctuary or the altar, or both they and you will die. ⁴They are to join you and be responsible for the care of the Tent of Meeting—all the work at the Tent—and no one else may come near where you are.

⁵"You are to be responsible for the care of the sanctuary and the altar, so that wrath will not fall on the Israelites again. ⁶I myself have selected your fellow Levites from among the Israelites as a gift to you, dedicated to the LORD to do the work at the Tent of Meeting. ⁷But only you and your sons may serve as priests in connection with everything at the altar and inside the curtain. I am giving you the service of the priesthood as a gift. Anyone else who comes near the sanctuary must be put to death."

Offerings for Priests and Levites

⁸Then the LORD said to Aaron, "I myself have put you in charge of the offerings presented to me; all the holy offerings the Israelites give me I give to you and your sons as your portion and regular share. ⁹You are to have the part of the most holy offerings that is kept from the fire. From all the gifts they bring me as most holy offerings, whether grain or sin or guilt offerings, that part belongs to you and your sons. ¹⁰Eat it as something most

holy; every male shall eat it. You must regard it as holy.

¹¹"This also is yours: whatever is set aside from the gifts of all the wave offerings of the Israelites. I give this to you and your sons and daughters as your regular share. Everyone in your household who is ceremonially clean may eat it.

¹²"I give you all the finest olive oil and all the finest new wine and grain they give the LORD as the firstfruits of their harvest. ¹³All the land's first-fruits that they bring to the LORD will be yours. Everyone in your household who is ceremonially clean may eat it. ¹⁴"Everything in Israel that is de-voted*a* to the LORD is yours. ¹⁵The first offspring of every womb, both man and animal, that is offered to the LORD is yours. But you must redeem every firstborn son and every first-born male of unclean animals. ¹⁶When they are a month old, you must re-deem them at the redemption price set at five shekels*b* of silver, accord-ing to the sanctuary shekel, which weighs twenty gerahs.

¹⁷"But you must not redeem the firstborn of an ox, a sheep or a goat; they are holy. Sprinkle their blood on the altar and burn their fat as an offer-ing made by fire, an aroma pleasing to the LORD. ¹⁸Their meat is to be yours, just as the breast of the wave offering and the right thigh are yours. ¹⁹Whatever is set aside from the holy offerings the Israelites present to the LORD I give to you and your sons and daughters as your regular share. It is an everlasting covenant of salt before the LORD for both you and your off-spring."

²⁰The LORD said to Aaron, "You will have no inheritance in their land, nor will you have any share among them; I am your share and your inheritance among the Israelites.

²¹"I give to the Levites all the tithes in Israel as their inheritance in return for the work they do while serving at the Tent of Meeting. ²²From now on

the Israelites must not go near the Tent of Meeting, or they will bear the consequences of their sin and will die. ²³It is the Levites who are to do the work at the Tent of Meeting and bear the responsibility for offenses against it. This is a lasting ordinance for the generations to come. They will re-ceive no inheritance among the Israel-ites. ²⁴Instead, I give to the Levites as their inheritance the tithes that the Is-raelites present as an offering to the LORD. That is why I said concerning them: 'They will have no inheritance among the Israelites.' "

²⁵The LORD said to Moses, ²⁶"Speak to the Levites and say to them: 'When you receive from the Israelites the tithe I give you as your inheritance, you must present a tenth of that tithe as the LORD's offering. ²⁷Your offering will be reckoned to you as grain from the threshing floor or juice from the winepress. ²⁸In this way you also will present an offering to the LORD from all the tithes you receive from the Is-raelites. From these tithes you must give the LORD's portion to Aaron the priest. ²⁹You must present as the LORD's portion the best and holiest part of everything given to you.'

³⁰"Say to the Levites: 'When you present the best part, it will be reck-oned to you as the product of the threshing floor or the winepress. ³¹You and your households may eat the rest of it anywhere, for it is your wages for your work at the Tent of Meeting. ³²By presenting the best part of it you will not be guilty in this mat-ter; then you will not defile the holy offerings of the Israelites, and you will not die.' "

The Water of Cleansing

19 The LORD said to Moses and Aaron: ²"This is a requirement of the law that the LORD has com-manded: Tell the Israelites to bring you a red heifer without defect or blemish and that has never been un-der a yoke. ³Give it to Eleazar the

---

a14 The Hebrew term refers to the irrevocable giving over of things or persons to the LORD.
b16 That is, about 2 ounces (about 55 grams)

priest; it is to be taken outside the camp and slaughtered in his presence. ⁴Then Eleazar the priest is to take some of its blood on his finger and sprinkle it seven times toward the front of the Tent of Meeting. ⁵While he watches, the heifer is to be burned—its hide, flesh, blood and offal. ⁶The priest is to take some cedar wood, hyssop and scarlet wool and throw them onto the burning heifer. ⁷After that, the priest must wash his clothes and bathe himself with water. He may then come into the camp, but he will be ceremonially unclean till evening. ⁸The man who burns it must also wash his clothes and bathe with water, and he too will be unclean till evening.

⁹"A man who is clean shall gather up the ashes of the heifer and put them in a ceremonially clean place outside the camp. They shall be kept by the Israelite community for use in the water of cleansing; it is for purification from sin. ¹⁰The man who gathers up the ashes of the heifer must also wash his clothes, and he too will be unclean till evening. This will be a lasting ordinance both for the Israelites and for the aliens living among them.

¹¹"Whoever touches the dead body of anyone will be unclean for seven days. ¹²He must purify himself with the water on the third day and on the seventh day; then he will be clean. But if he does not purify himself on the third and seventh days, he will not be clean. ¹³Whoever touches the dead body of anyone and fails to purify himself defiles the LORD's tabernacle. That person must be cut off from Israel. Because the water of cleansing has not been sprinkled on him, he is unclean; his uncleanness remains on him.

¹⁴"This is the law that applies when a person dies in a tent: Anyone who enters the tent and anyone who is in it will be unclean for seven days, ¹⁵and every open container without a lid fastened on it will be unclean.

¹⁶"Anyone out in the open who touches someone who has been killed with a sword or someone who has died a natural death, or anyone who touches a human bone or a grave, will be unclean for seven days.

¹⁷"For the unclean person, put some ashes from the burned purification offering into a jar and pour fresh water over them. ¹⁸Then a man who is ceremonially clean is to take some hyssop, dip it in the water and sprinkle the tent and all the furnishings and the people who were there. He must also sprinkle anyone who has touched a human bone or a grave or someone who has been killed or someone who has died a natural death. ¹⁹The man who is clean is to sprinkle the unclean person on the third and seventh days, and on the seventh day he is to purify him. The person being cleansed must wash his clothes and bathe with water, and that evening he will be clean. ²⁰But if a person who is unclean does not purify himself, he must be cut off from the community, because he has defiled the sanctuary of the LORD. The water of cleansing has not been sprinkled on him, and he is unclean. ²¹This is a lasting ordinance for them.

"The man who sprinkles the water of cleansing must also wash his clothes, and anyone who touches the water of cleansing will be unclean till evening. ²²Anything that an unclean person touches becomes unclean, and anyone who touches it becomes unclean till evening."

Water From the Rock

20 In the first month the whole Israelite community arrived at the Desert of Zin, and they stayed at Kadesh. There Miriam died and was buried.

²Now there was no water for the community, and the people gathered in opposition to Moses and Aaron. ³They quarreled with Moses and said, "If only we had died when our brothers fell dead before the LORD! ⁴Why did you bring the LORD's community into this desert, that we and our livestock should die here? ⁵Why did you bring us up out of Egypt to this terri-

ble place? It has no grain or figs, grapevines or pomegranates. And there is no water to drink!"

⁶Moses and Aaron went from the assembly to the entrance to the Tent of Meeting and fell facedown, and the glory of the LORD appeared to them. ⁷The LORD said to Moses, ⁸"Take the staff, and you and your brother Aaron gather the assembly together. Speak to that rock before their eyes and it will pour out its water. You will bring water out of the rock for the community so they and their livestock can drink."

⁹So Moses took the staff from the LORD's presence, just as he commanded him. ¹⁰He and Aaron gathered the assembly together in front of the rock and Moses said to them, "Listen, you rebels, must we bring you water out of this rock?" ¹¹Then Moses raised his arm and struck the rock twice with his staff. Water gushed out, and the community and their livestock drank.

¹²But the LORD said to Moses and Aaron, "Because you did not trust in me enough to honor me as holy in the sight of the Israelites, you will not bring this community into the land I give them."

¹³These were the waters of Meribah,ᵃ where the Israelites quarreled with the LORD and where he showed himself holy among them.

Edom Denies Israel Passage

¹⁴Moses sent messengers from Kadesh to the king of Edom, saying:

"This is what your brother Israel says: You know about all the hardships that have come upon us. ¹⁵Our forefathers went down into Egypt, and we lived there many years. The Egyptians mistreated us and our fathers, ¹⁶but when we cried out to the LORD, he heard our cry and sent an angel and brought us out of Egypt.

"Now we are here at Kadesh, a town on the edge of your territory. ¹⁷Please let us pass through

your country. We will not go through any field or vineyard, or drink water from any well. We will travel along the king's highway and not turn to the right or to the left until we have passed through your territory."

¹⁸But Edom answered:

"You may not pass through here; if you try, we will march out and attack you with the sword."

¹⁹The Israelites replied:

"We will go along the main road, and if we or our livestock drink any of your water, we will pay for it. We only want to pass through on foot—nothing else."

²⁰Again they answered:

"You may not pass through."

Then Edom came out against them with a large and powerful army. ²¹Since Edom refused to let them go through their territory, Israel turned away from them.

The Death of Aaron

²²The whole Israelite community set out from Kadesh and came to Mount Hor. ²³At Mount Hor, near the border of Edom, the LORD said to Moses and Aaron, ²⁴"Aaron will be gathered to his people. He will not enter the land I give the Israelites, because both of you rebelled against my command at the waters of Meribah. ²⁵Get Aaron and his son Eleazar and take them up Mount Hor. ²⁶Remove Aaron's garments and put them on his son Eleazar, for Aaron will be gathered to his people; he will die there."

²⁷Moses did as the LORD commanded: They went up Mount Hor in the sight of the whole community. ²⁸Moses removed Aaron's garments and put them on his son Eleazar. And Aaron died there on top of the mountain. Then Moses and Eleazar came down from the mountain, ²⁹and when

---

ᵃ13 *Meribah* means *quarreling.*

the whole community learned that Aaron had died, the entire house of Israel mourned for him thirty days.

Arad Destroyed

21 When the Canaanite king of Arad, who lived in the Negev, heard that Israel was coming along the road to Atharim, he attacked the Israelites and captured some of them. ²Then Israel made this vow to the LORD: "If you will deliver these people into our hands, we will totally destroy*a* their cities." ³The LORD listened to Israel's plea and gave the Canaanites over to them. They completely destroyed them and their towns; so the place was named Hormah.*b*

The Bronze Snake

⁴They traveled from Mount Hor along the route to the Red Sea,*c* to go around Edom. But the people grew impatient on the way; ⁵they spoke against God and against Moses, and said, "Why have you brought us up out of Egypt to die in the desert? There is no bread! There is no water! And we detest this miserable food!"

⁶Then the LORD sent venomous snakes among them; they bit the people and many Israelites died. ⁷The people came to Moses and said, "We sinned when we spoke against the LORD and against you. Pray that the LORD will take the snakes away from us." So Moses prayed for the people.

⁸The LORD said to Moses, "Make a snake and put it up on a pole; anyone who is bitten can look at it and live." ⁹So Moses made a bronze snake and put it up on a pole. Then when anyone was bitten by a snake and looked at the bronze snake, he lived.

The Journey to Moab

¹⁰The Israelites moved on and camped at Oboth. ¹¹Then they set out from Oboth and camped in Iye Aba-

rim, in the desert that faces Moab toward the sunrise. ¹²From there they moved on and camped in the Zered Valley. ¹³They set out from there and camped alongside the Arnon, which is in the desert extending into Amorite territory. The Arnon is the border of Moab, between Moab and the Amorites. ¹⁴That is why the Book of the Wars of the LORD says:

> ". . . Waheb in Suphah*d* and the
>   ravines,
>   the Arnon ¹⁵and*e* the slopes of
>   the ravines
> that lead to the site of Ar
>   and lie along the border of
>   Moab."

¹⁶From there they continued on to Beer, the well where the LORD said to Moses, "Gather the people together and I will give them water."

¹⁷Then Israel sang this song:

> "Spring up, O well!
>   Sing about it,
> ¹⁸about the well that the princes
>   dug,
>   that the nobles of the people
>   sank—
>   the nobles with scepters and
>   staffs."

Then they went from the desert to Mattanah, ¹⁹from Mattanah to Nahaliel, from Nahaliel to Bamoth, ²⁰and from Bamoth to the valley in Moab where the top of Pisgah overlooks the wasteland.

Defeat of Sihon and Og

²¹Israel sent messengers to say to Sihon king of the Amorites:

> ²²"Let us pass through your country. We will not turn aside into any field or vineyard, or drink water from any well. We will travel along the king's highway until we have passed through your territory."

---

a2 The Hebrew term refers to the irrevocable giving over of things or persons to the LORD, often by totally destroying them; also in verse 3.   *b3* *Hormah* means *destruction*.   *c4* Hebrew *Yam Suph*; that is, Sea of Reeds   *d14* The meaning of the Hebrew for this phrase is uncertain.   *e14,15* Or *"I have been given from Suphah and the ravines / of the Arnon* ¹⁵*to*

²³But Sihon would not let Israel pass through his territory. He mustered his entire army and marched out into the desert against Israel. When he reached Jahaz, he fought with Israel. ²⁴Israel, however, put him to the sword and took over his land from the Arnon to the Jabbok, but only as far as the Ammonites, because their border was fortified. ²⁵Israel captured all the cities of the Amorites and occupied them, including Heshbon and all its surrounding settlements. ²⁶Heshbon was the city of Sihon king of the Amorites, who had fought against the former king of Moab and had taken from him all his land as far as the Arnon.

VERSE:
Numbers 21:8

AUTHOR:
Dirk R. Buursma

PASSAGE:
Numbers 21:4–9

Look at It, And Live

It's one of the most incredible stories in the Bible. A people sick and tired of wandering around in the desert, hot and irritable and impatient—a people prone to complain bitterly, a people who made God so angry that he sent poisonous snakes among them to punish them.

No, this story of rebellion really isn't so incredible. Nor is God's response to their acknowledgment of their sin so hard to believe—God proves over and over again his faithfulness in the face of our faithlessness.

Read on—"Make a snake and put it up on a pole; anyone who is bitten can look at it and live." The animal that brought destruction now pictures life graciously given back. What a miraculous, glorious provision!

But it really does get even more incredible. All of us who are incurably sick, all of us who are dying, can fix our eyes on another pole—a cross where God's Son stretched out his arms—and live. John records the grace-filled words of Jesus: "Just as Moses lifted up the snake in the desert, so the Son of Man must be lifted up, that everyone who believes in him may have eternal life" (John 3:14–15).

ADDITIONAL SCRIPTURE READINGS
John 3:1–21; John 12:20–36

Go to page 211 for your next devotional reading.

²⁷That is why the poets say:

"Come to Heshbon and let it be
    rebuilt;
let Sihon's city be restored.

²⁸"Fire went out from Heshbon,
    a blaze from the city of Sihon.
It consumed Ar of Moab,
    the citizens of Arnon's heights.
²⁹Woe to you, O Moab!
    You are destroyed, O people of
    Chemosh!
He has given up his sons as
    fugitives
and his daughters as captives
to Sihon king of the Amorites.

³⁰"But we have overthrown them;
    Heshbon is destroyed all the
    way to Dibon.
We have demolished them as far
    as Nophah,
which extends to Medeba."

³¹So Israel settled in the land of the Amorites.

³²After Moses had sent spies to Jazer, the Israelites captured its surrounding settlements and drove out the Amorites who were there. ³³Then they turned and went up along the road toward Bashan, and Og king of Bashan and his whole army marched out to meet them in battle at Edrei.

³⁴The Lord said to Moses, "Do not be afraid of him, for I have handed him over to you, with his whole army and his land. Do to him what you did to Sihon king of the Amorites, who reigned in Heshbon."

³⁵So they struck him down, together with his sons and his whole army, leaving them no survivors. And they took possession of his land.

Balak Summons Balaam

22 Then the Israelites traveled to the plains of Moab and camped along the Jordan across from Jericho.ᵃ

²Now Balak son of Zippor saw all that Israel had done to the Amorites, ³and Moab was terrified because there

were so many people. Indeed, Moab was filled with dread because of the Israelites.

⁴The Moabites said to the elders of Midian, "This horde is going to lick up everything around us, as an ox licks up the grass of the field."

So Balak son of Zippor, who was king of Moab at that time, ⁵sent messengers to summon Balaam son of Beor, who was at Pethor, near the River,ᵇ in his native land. Balak said:

"A people has come out of Egypt; they cover the face of the land and have settled next to me. ⁶Now come and put a curse on these people, because they are too powerful for me. Perhaps then I will be able to defeat them and drive them out of the country. For I know that those you bless are blessed, and those you curse are cursed."

⁷The elders of Moab and Midian left, taking with them the fee for divination. When they came to Balaam, they told him what Balak had said.

⁸"Spend the night here," Balaam said to them, "and I will bring you back the answer the Lord gives me." So the Moabite princes stayed with him.

⁹God came to Balaam and asked, "Who are these men with you?"

¹⁰Balaam said to God, "Balak son of Zippor, king of Moab, sent me this message: ¹¹'A people that has come out of Egypt covers the face of the land. Now come and put a curse on them for me. Perhaps then I will be able to fight them and drive them away.'"

¹²But God said to Balaam, "Do not go with them. You must not put a curse on those people, because they are blessed."

¹³The next morning Balaam got up and said to Balak's princes, "Go back to your own country, for the Lord has refused to let me go with you."

¹⁴So the Moabite princes returned

ᵃ1 Hebrew *Jordan of Jericho*; possibly an ancient name for the Jordan River   ᵇ5 That is, the Euphrates to Balak and said, "Balaam refused to come with us."

¹⁵Then Balak sent other princes, more numerous and more distinguished than the first. ¹⁶They came to Balaam and said:

"This is what Balak son of Zippor says: Do not let anything keep you from coming to me, ¹⁷because I will reward you handsomely and do whatever you say. Come and put a curse on these people for me."

¹⁸But Balaam answered them, "Even if Balak gave me his palace filled with silver and gold, I could not do anything great or small to go beyond the command of the LORD my God. ¹⁹Now stay here tonight as the others did, and I will find out what else the LORD will tell me."

²⁰That night God came to Balaam and said, "Since these men have come to summon you, go with them, but do only what I tell you."

Balaam's Donkey

²¹Balaam got up in the morning, saddled his donkey and went with the princes of Moab. ²²But God was very angry when he went, and the angel of the LORD stood in the road to oppose him. Balaam was riding on his donkey, and his two servants were with him. ²³When the donkey saw the angel of the LORD standing in the road with a drawn sword in his hand, she turned off the road into a field. Balaam beat her to get her back on the road.

²⁴Then the angel of the LORD stood in a narrow path between two vineyards, with walls on both sides. ²⁵When the donkey saw the angel of the LORD, she pressed close to the wall, crushing Balaam's foot against it. So he beat her again.

²⁶Then the angel of the LORD moved on ahead and stood in a narrow place where there was no room to turn, either to the right or to the left. ²⁷When the donkey saw the angel of the LORD,

she lay down under Balaam, and he was angry and beat her with his staff. ²⁸Then the LORD opened the donkey's mouth, and she said to Balaam, "What have I done to you to make you beat me these three times?"

²⁹Balaam answered the donkey, "You have made a fool of me! If I had a sword in my hand, I would kill you right now."

³⁰The donkey said to Balaam, "Am I not your own donkey, which you have always ridden, to this day? Have I been in the habit of doing this to you?"

"No," he said.

³¹Then the LORD opened Balaam's eyes, and he saw the angel of the LORD standing in the road with his sword drawn. So he bowed low and fell facedown.

³²The angel of the LORD asked him, "Why have you beaten your donkey these three times? I have come here to oppose you because your path is a reckless one before me.ᵃ ³³The donkey saw me and turned away from me these three times. If she had not turned away, I would certainly have killed you by now, but I would have spared her."

³⁴Balaam said to the angel of the LORD, "I have sinned. I did not realize you were standing in the road to oppose me. Now if you are displeased, I will go back."

³⁵The angel of the LORD said to Balaam, "Go with the men, but speak only what I tell you." So Balaam went with the princes of Balak.

³⁶When Balak heard that Balaam was coming, he went out to meet him at the Moabite town on the Arnon border, at the edge of his territory. ³⁷Balak said to Balaam, "Did I not send you an urgent summons? Why didn't you come to me? Am I really not able to reward you?"

³⁸"Well, I have come to you now," Balaam replied. "But can I say just anything? I must speak only what God puts in my mouth."

³⁹Then Balaam went with Balak to

ᵃ32 The meaning of the Hebrew for this clause is uncertain.

Kiriath Huzoth. ⁴⁰Balak sacrificed cattle and sheep, and gave some to Balaam and the princes who were with him. ⁴¹The next morning Balak took Balaam up to Bamoth Baal, and from there he saw part of the people.

Balaam's First Oracle

23 Balaam said, "Build me seven altars here, and prepare seven bulls and seven rams for me." ²Balak did as Balaam said, and the two of them offered a bull and a ram on each altar.

³Then Balaam said to Balak, "Stay here beside your offering while I go aside. Perhaps the LORD will come to meet with me. Whatever he reveals to me I will tell you." Then he went off to a barren height.

⁴God met with him, and Balaam said, "I have prepared seven altars, and on each altar I have offered a bull and a ram."

⁵The LORD put a message in Balaam's mouth and said, "Go back to Balak and give him this message."

⁶So he went back to him and found him standing beside his offering, with all the princes of Moab. ⁷Then Balaam uttered his oracle:

"Balak brought me from Aram,
    the king of Moab from the
        eastern mountains.
'Come,' he said, 'curse Jacob for
    me;
    come, denounce Israel.'
⁸How can I curse
    those whom God has not
        cursed?
  How can I denounce
    those whom the LORD has not
        denounced?
⁹From the rocky peaks I see them,
    from the heights I view them.
  I see a people who live apart
    and do not consider themselves
        one of the nations.
¹⁰Who can count the dust of Jacob
    or number the fourth part of
        Israel?

Let me die the death of the
    righteous,
    and may my end be like theirs!"

¹¹Balak said to Balaam, "What have you done to me? I brought you to curse my enemies, but you have done nothing but bless them!"

¹²He answered, "Must I not speak what the LORD puts in my mouth?"

Balaam's Second Oracle

¹³Then Balak said to him, "Come with me to another place where you can see them; you will see only a part but not all of them. And from there, curse them for me." ¹⁴So he took him to the field of Zophim on the top of Pisgah, and there he built seven altars and offered a bull and a ram on each altar.

¹⁵Balaam said to Balak, "Stay here beside your offering while I meet with him over there."

¹⁶The LORD met with Balaam and put a message in his mouth and said, "Go back to Balak and give him this message."

¹⁷So he went to him and found him standing beside his offering, with the princes of Moab. Balak asked him, "What did the LORD say?"

¹⁸Then he uttered his oracle:

"Arise, Balak, and listen;
    hear me, son of Zippor.
¹⁹God is not a man, that he should
    lie,
    nor a son of man, that he
        should change his mind.
  Does he speak and then not act?
    Does he promise and not fulfill?
²⁰I have received a command to
    bless;
    he has blessed, and I cannot
        change it.

²¹"No misfortune is seen in Jacob,
    no misery observed in Israel.ᵃ
  The LORD their God is with them;
    the shout of the King is among
        them.
²²God brought them out of Egypt;

ᵃ21 Or *He has not looked on Jacob's offenses / or on the wrongs found in Israel.*

they have the strength of a wild
  ox.
²³There is no sorcery against Jacob,
  no divination against Israel.
It will now be said of Jacob
  and of Israel, 'See what God has
    done!'
²⁴The people rise like a lioness;
  they rouse themselves like a
    lion
that does not rest till he devours
  his prey
  and drinks the blood of his
    victims."

²⁵Then Balak said to Balaam, "Neither curse them at all nor bless them at all!"

²⁶Balaam answered, "Did I not tell you I must do whatever the LORD says?"

Balaam's Third Oracle

²⁷Then Balak said to Balaam, "Come, let me take you to another place. Perhaps it will please God to let you curse them for me from there." ²⁸And Balak took Balaam to the top of Peor, overlooking the wasteland.

²⁹Balaam said, "Build me seven altars here, and prepare seven bulls and seven rams for me." ³⁰Balak did as Balaam had said, and offered a bull and a ram on each altar.

24 Now when Balaam saw that it pleased the LORD to bless Israel, he did not resort to sorcery as at other times, but turned his face toward the desert. ²When Balaam looked out and saw Israel encamped tribe by tribe, the Spirit of God came upon him ³and he uttered his oracle:

"The oracle of Balaam son of Beor,
  the oracle of one whose eye sees
    clearly,
⁴the oracle of one who hears the
    words of God,
  who sees a vision from the
    Almighty,ᵃ
  who falls prostrate, and whose
    eyes are opened:

⁵"How beautiful are your tents,
  O Jacob,
  your dwelling places, O Israel!

⁶"Like valleys they spread out,
  like gardens beside a river,
like aloes planted by the LORD,
  like cedars beside the waters.
⁷Water will flow from their
    buckets;
  their seed will have abundant
    water.

"Their king will be greater than
    Agag;
  their kingdom will be exalted.

⁸"God brought them out of Egypt;
  they have the strength of a wild
    ox.
They devour hostile nations
  and break their bones in pieces;
  with their arrows they pierce
    them.
⁹Like a lion they crouch and lie
    down,
  like a lioness—who dares to
    rouse them?

"May those who bless you be
    blessed
  and those who curse you be
    cursed!"

¹⁰Then Balak's anger burned against Balaam. He struck his hands together and said to him, "I summoned you to curse my enemies, but you have blessed them these three times. ¹¹Now leave at once and go home! I said I would reward you handsomely, but the LORD has kept you from being rewarded."

¹²Balaam answered Balak, "Did I not tell the messengers you sent me, ¹³'Even if Balak gave me his palace filled with silver and gold, I could not do anything of my own accord, good or bad, to go beyond the command of the LORD—and I must say only what the LORD says'? ¹⁴Now I am going back to my people, but come, let me warn you of what this people will do to your people in days to come."

ᵃ4 Hebrew *Shaddai*; also in verse 16

Balaam's Fourth Oracle

¹⁵Then he uttered his oracle:

"The oracle of Balaam son of Beor,
  the oracle of one whose eye sees
  clearly,
¹⁶the oracle of one who hears the
  words of God,
who has knowledge from the
  Most High,
who sees a vision from the
  Almighty,
who falls prostrate, and whose
  eyes are opened:

¹⁷"I see him, but not now;
  I behold him, but not near.
A star will come out of Jacob;
  a scepter will rise out of Israel.
He will crush the foreheads of
  Moab,
  the skulls*a* of*b* all the sons of
  Sheth.*c*
¹⁸Edom will be conquered;
  Seir, his enemy, will be
  conquered,
but Israel will grow strong.
¹⁹A ruler will come out of Jacob
  and destroy the survivors of the
  city."

Balaam's Final Oracles

²⁰Then Balaam saw Amalek and uttered his oracle:

"Amalek was first among the
  nations,
  but he will come to ruin at
  last."

²¹Then he saw the Kenites and uttered his oracle:

"Your dwelling place is secure,
  your nest is set in a rock;
²²yet you Kenites will be destroyed
  when Asshur takes you
  captive."

²³Then he uttered his oracle:

"Ah, who can live when God does
  this?*d*

²⁴ Ships will come from the shores
    of Kittim;
  they will subdue Asshur and Eber,
    but they too will come to ruin."

²⁵Then Balaam got up and returned
home and Balak went his own way.

Moab Seduces Israel

25 While Israel was staying in
Shittim, the men began to indulge in sexual immorality with Moabite women, ²who invited them to
the sacrifices to their gods. The people
ate and bowed down before these
gods. ³So Israel joined in worshiping
the Baal of Peor. And the LORD's anger
burned against them.

⁴The LORD said to Moses, "Take all
the leaders of these people, kill them
and expose them in broad daylight
before the LORD, so that the LORD's
fierce anger may turn away from Israel."

⁵So Moses said to Israel's judges,
"Each of you must put to death those
of your men who have joined in worshiping the Baal of Peor."

⁶Then an Israelite man brought to
his family a Midianite woman right
before the eyes of Moses and the
whole assembly of Israel while they
were weeping at the entrance to the
Tent of Meeting. ⁷When Phinehas son
of Eleazar, the son of Aaron, the
priest, saw this, he left the assembly,
took a spear in his hand ⁸and followed the Israelite into the tent. He
drove the spear through both of
them—through the Israelite and into
the woman's body. Then the plague
against the Israelites was stopped;
⁹but those who died in the plague
numbered 24,000.

¹⁰The LORD said to Moses, ¹¹"Phinehas son of Eleazar, the son of Aaron,
the priest, has turned my anger away
from the Israelites; for he was as zealous as I am for my honor among
them, so that in my zeal I did not put
an end to them. ¹²Therefore tell him I
am making my covenant of peace

---

*a*17 Samaritan Pentateuch (see also Jer. 48:45); the meaning of the word in the Masoretic Text is
uncertain.   *b*17 Or possibly *Moab, / batter*   *c*17 Or *all the noisy boasters*   *d*23 Masoretic
Text; with a different word division of the Hebrew *A people will gather from the north.*

with him. ¹³He and his descendants will have a covenant of a lasting priesthood, because he was zealous for the honor of his God and made atonement for the Israelites."

¹⁴The name of the Israelite who was killed with the Midianite woman was Zimri son of Salu, the leader of a Simeonite family. ¹⁵And the name of the Midianite woman who was put to death was Cozbi daughter of Zur, a tribal chief of a Midianite family.

¹⁶The Lord said to Moses, ¹⁷"Treat the Midianites as enemies and kill them, ¹⁸because they treated you as enemies when they deceived you in the affair of Peor and their sister Cozbi, the daughter of a Midianite leader, the woman who was killed when the plague came as a result of Peor."

The Second Census

26 After the plague the Lord said to Moses and Eleazar son of Aaron, the priest, ²"Take a census of the whole Israelite community by families—all those twenty years old or more who are able to serve in the army of Israel." ³So on the plains of Moab by the Jordan across from Jericho,ᵃ Moses and Eleazar the priest spoke with them and said, ⁴"Take a census of the men twenty years old or more, as the Lord commanded Moses."

These were the Israelites who came out of Egypt:

⁵The descendants of Reuben, the firstborn son of Israel, were:
through Hanoch, the Hanochite clan;
through Pallu, the Palluite clan;
⁶through Hezron, the Hezronite clan;
through Carmi, the Carmite clan.
⁷These were the clans of Reuben; those numbered were 43,730.
⁸The son of Pallu was Eliab, ⁹and the sons of Eliab were Nemuel, Dathan and Abiram. The same Dathan

and Abiram were the community officials who rebelled against Moses and Aaron and were among Korah's followers when they rebelled against the Lord. ¹⁰The earth opened its mouth and swallowed them along with Korah, whose followers died when the fire devoured the 250 men. And they served as a warning sign. ¹¹The line of Korah, however, did not die out.

¹²The descendants of Simeon by their clans were:
through Nemuel, the Nemuelite clan;
through Jamin, the Jaminite clan;
through Jakin, the Jakinite clan;
¹³through Zerah, the Zerahite clan;
through Shaul, the Shaulite clan.
¹⁴These were the clans of Simeon; there were 22,200 men.

¹⁵The descendants of Gad by their clans were:
through Zephon, the Zephonite clan;
through Haggi, the Haggite clan;
through Shuni, the Shunite clan;
¹⁶through Ozni, the Oznite clan;
through Eri, the Erite clan;
¹⁷through Arodi,ᵇ the Arodite clan;
through Areli, the Arelite clan.
¹⁸These were the clans of Gad; those numbered were 40,500.

¹⁹Er and Onan were sons of Judah, but they died in Canaan. ²⁰The descendants of Judah by their clans were:
through Shelah, the Shelanite clan;
through Perez, the Perezite clan;
through Zerah, the Zerahite clan.
²¹The descendants of Perez were:
through Hezron, the Hezronite clan;
through Hamul, the Hamulite clan.

ᵃ3 Hebrew *Jordan of Jericho*; possibly an ancient name for the Jordan River; also in verse 63
ᵇ17 Samaritan Pentateuch and Syriac (see also Gen. 46:16); Masoretic Text *Arod*

²²These were the clans of Judah; those numbered were 76,500.

²³The descendants of Issachar by their clans were:

through Tola, the Tolaite clan;

through Puah, the Puite[a] clan;

²⁴through Jashub, the Jashubite clan;

through Shimron, the Shimronite clan.

²⁵These were the clans of Issachar; those numbered were 64,300.

²⁶The descendants of Zebulun by their clans were:

through Sered, the Seredite clan;

through Elon, the Elonite clan;

through Jahleel, the Jahleelite clan.

²⁷These were the clans of Zebulun; those numbered were 60,500.

²⁸The descendants of Joseph by their clans through Manasseh and Ephraim were:

²⁹The descendants of Manasseh:

through Makir, the Makirite clan (Makir was the father of Gilead);

through Gilead, the Gileadite clan.

³⁰These were the descendants of Gilead:

through Iezer, the Iezerite clan;

through Helek, the Helekite clan;

³¹through Asriel, the Asrielite clan;

through Shechem, the Shechemite clan;

³²through Shemida, the Shemidaite clan;

through Hepher, the Hepherite clan.

³³(Zelophehad son of Hepher had no sons; he had only daughters, whose names

were Mahlah, Noah, Hoglah, Milcah and Tirzah.)

³⁴These were the clans of Manasseh; those numbered were 52,700.

³⁵These were the descendants of Ephraim by their clans:

through Shuthelah, the Shuthelahite clan;

through Beker, the Bekerite clan;

through Tahan, the Tahanite clan.

³⁶These were the descendants of Shuthelah:

through Eran, the Eranite clan.

³⁷These were the clans of Ephraim; those numbered were 32,500.

These were the descendants of Joseph by their clans.

³⁸The descendants of Benjamin by their clans were:

through Bela, the Belaite clan;

through Ashbel, the Ashbelite clan;

through Ahiram, the Ahiramite clan;

³⁹through Shupham,[b] the Shuphamite clan;

through Hupham, the Huphamite clan.

⁴⁰The descendants of Bela through Ard and Naaman were:

through Ard,[c] the Ardite clan;

through Naaman, the Naamite clan.

⁴¹These were the clans of Benjamin; those numbered were 45,600.

⁴²These were the descendants of Dan by their clans:

through Shuham, the Shuhamite clan.

These were the clans of Dan: ⁴³All of them were Shuhamite clans; and those numbered were 64,400.

---

[a]23 Samaritan Pentateuch, Septuagint, Vulgate and Syriac (see also 1 Chron. 7:1); Masoretic Text *through Puvah, the Punite*   [b]39 A few manuscripts of the Masoretic Text, Samaritan Pentateuch, Vulgate and Syriac (see also Septuagint); most manuscripts of the Masoretic Text *Shephupham*   [c]40 Samaritan Pentateuch and Vulgate (see also Septuagint); Masoretic Text does not have *through Ard.*

⁴⁴The descendants of Asher by their clans were:

through Imnah, the Imnite clan;
through Ishvi, the Ishvite clan;
through Beriah, the Beriite clan;
⁴⁵and through the descendants of Beriah:

through Heber, the Heberite clan;
through Malkiel, the Malkielite clan.

⁴⁶(Asher had a daughter named Serah.)

⁴⁷These were the clans of Asher; those numbered were 53,400.

⁴⁸The descendants of Naphtali by their clans were:

through Jahzeel, the Jahzeelite clan;
through Guni, the Gunite clan;
⁴⁹through Jezer, the Jezerite clan;
through Shillem, the Shillemite clan.

⁵⁰These were the clans of Naphtali; those numbered were 45,400.

⁵¹The total number of the men of Israel was 601,730.

⁵²The LORD said to Moses, ⁵³"The land is to be allotted to them as an inheritance based on the number of names. ⁵⁴To a larger group give a larger inheritance, and to a smaller group a smaller one; each is to receive its inheritance according to the number of those listed. ⁵⁵Be sure that the land is distributed by lot. What each group inherits will be according to the names for its ancestral tribe. ⁵⁶Each inheritance is to be distributed by lot among the larger and smaller groups."

⁵⁷These were the Levites who were counted by their clans:

through Gershon, the Gershonite clan;
through Kohath, the Kohathite clan;
through Merari, the Merarite clan.

⁵⁸These also were Levite clans:

the Libnite clan,
the Hebronite clan,
the Mahlite clan,
the Mushite clan,
the Korahite clan.

(Kohath was the forefather of Amram; ⁵⁹the name of Amram's wife was Jochebed, a descendant of Levi, who was born to the Levites*a* in Egypt. To Amram she bore Aaron, Moses and their sister Miriam. ⁶⁰Aaron was the father of Nadab and Abihu, Eleazar and Ithamar. ⁶¹But Nadab and Abihu died when they made an offering before the LORD with unauthorized fire.)

⁶²All the male Levites a month old or more numbered 23,000. They were not counted along with the other Israelites because they received no inheritance among them.

⁶³These are the ones counted by Moses and Eleazar the priest when they counted the Israelites on the plains of Moab by the Jordan across from Jericho. ⁶⁴Not one of them was among those counted by Moses and Aaron the priest when they counted the Israelites in the Desert of Sinai. ⁶⁵For the LORD had told those Israelites they would surely die in the desert, and not one of them was left except Caleb son of Jephunneh and Joshua son of Nun.

Zelophehad's Daughters

27 The daughters of Zelophehad son of Hepher, the son of Gilead, the son of Makir, the son of Manasseh, belonged to the clans of Manasseh son of Joseph. The names of the daughters were Mahlah, Noah, Hoglah, Milcah and Tirzah. They approached ²the entrance to the Tent of Meeting and stood before Moses, Eleazar the priest, the leaders and the whole assembly, and said, ³"Our father died in the desert. He was not among Korah's followers, who banded together against the LORD, but he died for his own sin and left no sons.

---

a59 Or *Jochebed, a daughter of Levi, who was born to Levi*

⁴Why should our father's name disappear from his clan because he had no son? Give us property among our father's relatives."

⁵So Moses brought their case before the Lord ⁶and the Lord said to him, ⁷"What Zelophehad's daughters are saying is right. You must certainly give them property as an inheritance among their father's relatives and turn their father's inheritance over to them.

⁸"Say to the Israelites, 'If a man dies and leaves no son, turn his inheritance over to his daughter. ⁹If he has no daughter, give his inheritance to his brothers. ¹⁰If he has no brothers, give his inheritance to his father's brothers. ¹¹If his father had no brothers, give his inheritance to the nearest relative in his clan, that he may possess it. This is to be a legal requirement for the Israelites, as the Lord commanded Moses.' "

Joshua to Succeed Moses

¹²Then the Lord said to Moses, "Go up this mountain in the Abarim range and see the land I have given the Israelites. ¹³After you have seen it, you too will be gathered to your people, as your brother Aaron was, ¹⁴for when the community rebelled at the waters in the Desert of Zin, both of you disobeyed my command to honor me as holy before their eyes." (These were the waters of Meribah Kadesh, in the Desert of Zin.)

¹⁵Moses said to the Lord, ¹⁶"May the Lord, the God of the spirits of all mankind, appoint a man over this community ¹⁷to go out and come in before them, one who will lead them out and bring them in, so the Lord's people will not be like sheep without a shepherd."

¹⁸So the Lord said to Moses, "Take Joshua son of Nun, a man in whom is the spirit,ᵃ and lay your hand on him. ¹⁹Have him stand before Eleazar the priest and the entire assembly and commission him in their presence.

²⁰Give him some of your authority so the whole Israelite community will obey him. ²¹He is to stand before Eleazar the priest, who will obtain decisions for him by inquiring of the Urim before the Lord. At his command he and the entire community of the Israelites will go out, and at his command they will come in."

²²Moses did as the Lord commanded him. He took Joshua and had him stand before Eleazar the priest and the whole assembly. ²³Then he laid his hands on him and commissioned him, as the Lord instructed through Moses.

Daily Offerings

28 The Lord said to Moses, ²"Give this command to the Israelites and say to them: 'See that you present to me at the appointed time the food for my offerings made by fire, as an aroma pleasing to me.' ³Say to them: 'This is the offering made by fire that you are to present to the Lord: two lambs a year old without defect, as a regular burnt offering each day. ⁴Prepare one lamb in the morning and the other at twilight, ⁵together with a grain offering of a tenth of an ephahᵇ of fine flour mixed with a quarter of a hinᶜ of oil from pressed olives. ⁶This is the regular burnt offering instituted at Mount Sinai as a pleasing aroma, an offering made to the Lord by fire. ⁷The accompanying drink offering is to be a quarter of a hin of fermented drink with each lamb. Pour out the drink offering to the Lord at the sanctuary. ⁸Prepare the second lamb at twilight, along with the same kind of grain offering and drink offering that you prepare in the morning. This is an offering made by fire, an aroma pleasing to the Lord.

Sabbath Offerings

⁹" 'On the Sabbath day, make an offering of two lambs a year old without defect, together with its drink offering and a grain offering of

---

ᵃ18 Or *Spirit*   ᵇ5 That is, probably about 2 quarts (about 2 liters); also in verses 13, 21 and 29
ᶜ5 That is, probably about 1 quart (about 1 liter); also in verses 7 and 14

two-tenths of an ephah[a] of fine flour mixed with oil. [10]This is the burnt offering for every Sabbath, in addition to the regular burnt offering and its drink offering.

Monthly Offerings

[11]" 'On the first of every month, present to the LORD a burnt offering of two young bulls, one ram and seven male lambs a year old, all without defect. [12]With each bull there is to be a grain offering of three-tenths of an ephah[b] of fine flour mixed with oil; with the ram, a grain offering of two-tenths of an ephah of fine flour mixed with oil; [13]and with each lamb, a grain offering of a tenth of an ephah of fine flour mixed with oil. This is for a burnt offering, a pleasing aroma, an offering made to the LORD by fire. [14]With each bull there is to be a drink offering of half a hin[c] of wine; with the ram, a third of a hin[d]; and with each lamb, a quarter of a hin. This is the monthly burnt offering to be made at each new moon during the year. [15]Besides the regular burnt offering with its drink offering, one male goat is to be presented to the LORD as a sin offering.

The Passover

[16]" 'On the fourteenth day of the first month the LORD's Passover is to be held. [17]On the fifteenth day of this month there is to be a festival; for seven days eat bread made without yeast. [18]On the first day hold a sacred assembly and do no regular work. [19]Present to the LORD an offering made by fire, a burnt offering of two young bulls, one ram and seven male lambs a year old, all without defect. [20]With each bull prepare a grain offering of three-tenths of an ephah of fine flour mixed with oil; with the ram, two-tenths; [21]and with each of the seven lambs, one-tenth. [22]Include one male

goat as a sin offering to make atonement for you. [23]Prepare these in addition to the regular morning burnt offering. [24]In this way prepare the food for the offering made by fire every day for seven days as an aroma pleasing to the LORD; it is to be prepared in addition to the regular burnt offering and its drink offering. [25]On the seventh day hold a sacred assembly and do no regular work.

Feast of Weeks

[26]" 'On the day of firstfruits, when you present to the LORD an offering of new grain during the Feast of Weeks, hold a sacred assembly and do no regular work. [27]Present a burnt offering of two young bulls, one ram and seven male lambs a year old as an aroma pleasing to the LORD. [28]With each bull there is to be a grain offering of three-tenths of an ephah of fine flour mixed with oil; with the ram, two-tenths; [29]and with each of the seven lambs, one-tenth. [30]Include one male goat to make atonement for you. [31]Prepare these together with their drink offerings, in addition to the regular burnt offering and its grain offering. Be sure the animals are without defect.

Feast of Trumpets

29 " 'On the first day of the seventh month hold a sacred assembly and do no regular work. It is a day for you to sound the trumpets. [2]As an aroma pleasing to the LORD, prepare a burnt offering of one young bull, one ram and seven male lambs a year old, all without defect. [3]With the bull prepare a grain offering of three-tenths of an ephah[e] of fine flour mixed with oil; with the ram, two-tenths[f]; [4]and with each of the seven lambs, one-tenth.[g] [5]Include one male goat as a sin offering to make atonement for you. [6]These are in addition

---

[a]9 That is, probably about 4 quarts (about 4.5 liters); also in verses 12, 20 and 28   [b]12 That is, probably about 6 quarts (about 6.5 liters); also in verses 20 and 28   [c]14 That is, probably about 2 quarts (about 2 liters)   [d]14 That is, probably about 1 1/4 quarts (about 1.2 liters)   [e]3 That is, probably about 6 quarts (about 6.5 liters); also in verses 9 and 14   [f]3 That is, probably about 4 quarts (about 4.5 liters); also in verses 9 and 14   [g]4 That is, probably about 2 quarts (about 2 liters); also in verses 10 and 15

to the monthly and daily burnt offerings with their grain offerings and drink offerings as specified. They are offerings made to the LORD by fire—a pleasing aroma.

Day of Atonement

7" 'On the tenth day of this seventh month hold a sacred assembly. You must deny yourselves[a] and do no work. 8Present as an aroma pleasing to the LORD a burnt offering of one young bull, one ram and seven male lambs a year old, all without defect. 9With the bull prepare a grain offering of three-tenths of an ephah of fine flour mixed with oil; with the ram, two-tenths; 10and with each of the seven lambs, one-tenth. 11Include one male goat as a sin offering, in addition to the sin offering for atonement and the regular burnt offering with its grain offering, and their drink offerings.

Feast of Tabernacles

12" 'On the fifteenth day of the seventh month, hold a sacred assembly and do no regular work. Celebrate a festival to the LORD for seven days. 13Present an offering made by fire as an aroma pleasing to the LORD, a burnt offering of thirteen young bulls, two rams and fourteen male lambs a year old, all without defect. 14With each of the thirteen bulls prepare a grain offering of three-tenths of an ephah of fine flour mixed with oil; with each of the two rams, two-tenths; 15and with each of the fourteen lambs, one-tenth. 16Include one male goat as a sin offering, in addition to the regular burnt offering with its grain offering and drink offering.

17" 'On the second day prepare twelve young bulls, two rams and fourteen male lambs a year old, all without defect. 18With the bulls, rams and lambs, prepare their grain offerings and drink offerings according to the number specified. 19Include one male goat as a sin offering, in addition to the regular burnt offering with

its grain offering, and their drink offerings.

20" 'On the third day prepare eleven bulls, two rams and fourteen male lambs a year old, all without defect. 21With the bulls, rams and lambs, prepare their grain offerings and drink offerings according to the number specified. 22Include one male goat as a sin offering, in addition to the regular burnt offering with its grain offering and drink offering.

23" 'On the fourth day prepare ten bulls, two rams and fourteen male lambs a year old, all without defect. 24With the bulls, rams and lambs, prepare their grain offerings and drink offerings according to the number specified. 25Include one male goat as a sin offering, in addition to the regular burnt offering with its grain offering and drink offering.

26" 'On the fifth day prepare nine bulls, two rams and fourteen male lambs a year old, all without defect. 27With the bulls, rams and lambs, prepare their grain offerings and drink offerings according to the number specified. 28Include one male goat as a sin offering, in addition to the regular burnt offering with its grain offering and drink offering.

29" 'On the sixth day prepare eight bulls, two rams and fourteen male lambs a year old, all without defect. 30With the bulls, rams and lambs, prepare their grain offerings and drink offerings according to the number specified. 31Include one male goat as a sin offering, in addition to the regular burnt offering with its grain offering and drink offering.

32" 'On the seventh day prepare seven bulls, two rams and fourteen male lambs a year old, all without defect. 33With the bulls, rams and lambs, prepare their grain offerings and drink offerings according to the number specified. 34Include one male goat as a sin offering, in addition to the regular burnt offering with its grain offering and drink offering.

35" 'On the eighth day hold an as-

a7 Or must fast

sembly and do no regular work. ³⁶Present an offering made by fire as an aroma pleasing to the Lord, a burnt offering of one bull, one ram and seven male lambs a year old, all without defect. ³⁷With the bull, the ram and the lambs, prepare their grain offerings and drink offerings according to the number specified. ³⁸Include one male goat as a sin offering, in addition to the regular burnt offering with its grain offering and drink offering.

³⁹" 'In addition to what you vow and your freewill offerings, prepare these for the Lord at your appointed feasts: your burnt offerings, grain offerings, drink offerings and fellowship offerings.*' "

⁴⁰Moses told the Israelites all that the Lord commanded him.

Vows

30 Moses said to the heads of the tribes of Israel: "This is what the Lord commands: ²When a man makes a vow to the Lord or takes an oath to obligate himself by a pledge, he must not break his word but must do everything he said.

³"When a young woman still living in her father's house makes a vow to the Lord or obligates herself by a pledge ⁴and her father hears about her vow or pledge but says nothing to her, then all her vows and every pledge by which she obligated herself will stand. ⁵But if her father forbids her when he hears about it, none of her vows or the pledges by which she obligated herself will stand; the Lord will release her because her father has forbidden her.

⁶"If she marries after she makes a vow or after her lips utter a rash promise by which she obligates herself ⁷and her husband hears about it but says nothing to her, then her vows or the pledges by which she obligated herself will stand. ⁸But if her husband forbids her when he hears about it, he nullifies the vow that obligates her or the rash promise by

which she obligates herself, and the Lord will release her.

⁹"Any vow or obligation taken by a widow or divorced woman will be binding on her.

¹⁰"If a woman living with her husband makes a vow or obligates herself by a pledge under oath ¹¹and her husband hears about it but says nothing to her and does not forbid her, then all her vows or the pledges by which she obligated herself will stand. ¹²But if her husband nullifies them when he hears about them, then none of the vows or pledges that came from her lips will stand. Her husband has nullified them, and the Lord will release her. ¹³Her husband may confirm or nullify any vow she makes or any sworn pledge to deny herself. ¹⁴But if her husband says nothing to her about it from day to day, then he confirms all her vows or the pledges binding on her. He confirms them by saying nothing to her when he hears about them. ¹⁵If, however, he nullifies them some time after he hears about them, then he is responsible for her guilt."

¹⁶These are the regulations the Lord gave Moses concerning relationships between a man and his wife, and between a father and his young daughter still living in his house.

Vengeance on the Midianites

31 The Lord said to Moses, ²"Take vengeance on the Midianites for the Israelites. After that, you will be gathered to your people."

³So Moses said to the people, "Arm some of your men to go to war against the Midianites and to carry out the Lord's vengeance on them. ⁴Send into battle a thousand men from each of the tribes of Israel." ⁵So twelve thousand men armed for battle, a thousand from each tribe, were supplied from the clans of Israel. ⁶Moses sent them into battle, a thousand from each tribe, along with Phinehas son of Eleazar, the priest, who took

---

a39 Traditionally *peace offerings*

with him articles from the sanctuary and the trumpets for signaling.

7They fought against Midian, as the LORD commanded Moses, and killed every man. 8Among their victims were Evi, Rekem, Zur, Hur and Reba—the five kings of Midian. They also killed Balaam son of Beor with the sword. 9The Israelites captured the Midianite women and children and took all the Midianite herds, flocks and goods as plunder. 10They burned all the towns where the Midianites had settled, as well as all their camps. 11They took all the plunder and spoils, including the people and animals, 12and brought the captives, spoils and plunder to Moses and Eleazar the priest and the Israelite assembly at their camp on the plains of Moab, by the Jordan across from Jericho.a

13Moses, Eleazar the priest and all the leaders of the community went to meet them outside the camp. 14Moses was angry with the officers of the army—the commanders of thousands and commanders of hundreds—who returned from the battle.

15"Have you allowed all the women to live?" he asked them. 16"They were the ones who followed Balaam's advice and were the means of turning the Israelites away from the LORD in what happened at Peor, so that a plague struck the LORD's people. 17Now kill all the boys. And kill every woman who has slept with a man, 18but save for yourselves every girl who has never slept with a man.

19"All of you who have killed anyone or touched anyone who was killed must stay outside the camp seven days. On the third and seventh days you must purify yourselves and your captives. 20Purify every garment as well as everything made of leather, goat hair or wood."

21Then Eleazar the priest said to the soldiers who had gone into battle, "This is the requirement of the law that the LORD gave Moses: 22Gold, silver, bronze, iron, tin, lead 23and any-

thing else that can withstand fire must be put through the fire, and then it will be clean. But it must also be purified with the water of cleansing. And whatever cannot withstand fire must be put through that water. 24On the seventh day wash your clothes and you will be clean. Then you may come into the camp."

Dividing the Spoils

25The LORD said to Moses, 26"You and Eleazar the priest and the family heads of the community are to count all the people and animals that were captured. 27Divide the spoils between the soldiers who took part in the battle and the rest of the community. 28From the soldiers who fought in the battle, set apart as tribute for the LORD one out of every five hundred, whether persons, cattle, donkeys, sheep or goats. 29Take this tribute from their half share and give it to Eleazar the priest as the LORD's part. 30From the Israelites' half, select one out of every fifty, whether persons, cattle, donkeys, sheep, goats or other animals. Give them to the Levites, who are responsible for the care of the LORD's tabernacle." 31So Moses and Eleazar the priest did as the LORD commanded Moses.

32The plunder remaining from the spoils that the soldiers took was 675,000 sheep, 3372,000 cattle, 3461,000 donkeys 35and 32,000 women who had never slept with a man.

36The half share of those who fought in the battle was:

337,500 sheep, 37of which the tribute for the LORD was 675;
3836,000 cattle, of which the tribute for the LORD was 72;
3930,500 donkeys, of which the tribute for the LORD was 61;
4016,000 people, of which the tribute for the LORD was 32.

41Moses gave the tribute to Eleazar the priest as the LORD's part, as the LORD commanded Moses.

42The half belonging to the Israel-

a12 Hebrew Jordan of Jericho; possibly an ancient name for the Jordan River

ites, which Moses set apart from that of the fighting men— ⁴³the community's half—was 337,500 sheep, ⁴⁴36,000 cattle, ⁴⁵30,500 donkeys ⁴⁶and 16,000 people. ⁴⁷From the Israelites' half, Moses selected one out of every fifty persons and animals, as the LORD commanded him, and gave them to the Levites, who were responsible for the care of the LORD's tabernacle.

⁴⁸Then the officers who were over the units of the army—the commanders of thousands and commanders of hundreds—went to Moses ⁴⁹and said to him, "Your servants have counted the soldiers under our command, and not one is missing. ⁵⁰So we have brought as an offering to the LORD the gold articles each of us acquired—armlets, bracelets, signet rings, earrings and necklaces—to make atonement for ourselves before the LORD."

⁵¹Moses and Eleazar the priest accepted from them the gold—all the crafted articles. ⁵²All the gold from the commanders of thousands and commanders of hundreds that Moses and Eleazar presented as a gift to the LORD weighed 16,750 shekels.ᵃ ⁵³Each soldier had taken plunder for himself. ⁵⁴Moses and Eleazar the priest accepted the gold from the commanders of thousands and commanders of hundreds and brought it into the Tent of Meeting as a memorial for the Israelites before the LORD.

The Transjordan Tribes

32 The Reubenites and Gadites, who had very large herds and flocks, saw that the lands of Jazer and Gilead were suitable for livestock. ²So they came to Moses and Eleazar the priest and to the leaders of the community, and said, ³"Ataroth, Dibon, Jazer, Nimrah, Heshbon, Elealeh, Sebam, Nebo and Beon— ⁴the land the LORD subdued before the people of Israel—are suitable for livestock, and your servants have livestock. ⁵If we have found favor in your eyes," they said, "let this land be given to your servants as our possession. Do not make us cross the Jordan."

⁶Moses said to the Gadites and Reubenites, "Shall your countrymen go to war while you sit here? ⁷Why do you discourage the Israelites from going over into the land the LORD has given them? ⁸This is what your fathers did when I sent them from Kadesh Barnea to look over the land. ⁹After they went up to the Valley of Eshcol and viewed the land, they discouraged the Israelites from entering the land the LORD had given them. ¹⁰The LORD's anger was aroused that day and he swore this oath: ¹¹'Because they have not followed me wholeheartedly, not one of the men twenty years old or more who came up out of Egypt will see the land I promised on oath to Abraham, Isaac and Jacob— ¹²not one except Caleb son of Jephunneh the Kenizzite and Joshua son of Nun, for they followed the LORD wholeheartedly.' ¹³The LORD's anger burned against Israel and he made them wander in the desert forty years, until the whole generation of those who had done evil in his sight was gone.

¹⁴"And here you are, a brood of sinners, standing in the place of your fathers and making the LORD even more angry with Israel. ¹⁵If you turn away from following him, he will again leave all this people in the desert, and you will be the cause of their destruction."

¹⁶Then they came up to him and said, "We would like to build pens here for our livestock and cities for our women and children. ¹⁷But we are ready to arm ourselves and go ahead of the Israelites until we have brought them to their place. Meanwhile our women and children will live in fortified cities, for protection from the inhabitants of the land. ¹⁸We will not return to our homes until every Israelite has received his inheritance. ¹⁹We will not receive any inheritance with them on the other side of the Jordan, because our inheritance has

---

ᵃ52 That is, about 420 pounds (about 190 kilograms)

come to us on the east side of the Jordan."

²⁰Then Moses said to them, "If you will do this—if you will arm yourselves before the Lord for battle, ²¹and if all of you will go armed over the Jordan before the Lord until he has driven his enemies out before him— ²²then when the land is subdued before the Lord, you may return and be free from your obligation to the Lord and to Israel. And this land will be your possession before the Lord.

²³"But if you fail to do this, you will be sinning against the Lord; and you may be sure that your sin will find you out. ²⁴Build cities for your women and children, and pens for your flocks, but do what you have promised."

²⁵The Gadites and Reubenites said to Moses, "We your servants will do as our lord commands. ²⁶Our children and wives, our flocks and herds will remain here in the cities of Gilead. ²⁷But your servants, every man armed for battle, will cross over to fight before the Lord, just as our lord says."

²⁸Then Moses gave orders about them to Eleazar the priest and Joshua son of Nun and to the family heads of the Israelite tribes. ²⁹He said to them, "If the Gadites and Reubenites, every man armed for battle, cross over the Jordan with you before the Lord, then when the land is subdued before you, give them the land of Gilead as their possession. ³⁰But if they do not cross over with you armed, they must accept their possession with you in Canaan."

³¹The Gadites and Reubenites answered, "Your servants will do what the Lord has said. ³²We will cross over before the Lord into Canaan armed, but the property we inherit will be on this side of the Jordan."

³³Then Moses gave to the Gadites, the Reubenites and the half-tribe of Manasseh son of Joseph the kingdom of Sihon king of the Amorites and the kingdom of Og king of Bashan—the whole land with its cities and the territory around them.

³⁴The Gadites built up Dibon, Ataroth, Aroer, ³⁵Atroth Shophan, Jazer, Jogbehah, ³⁶Beth Nimrah and Beth Haran as fortified cities, and built pens for their flocks. ³⁷And the Reubenites rebuilt Heshbon, Elealeh and Kiriathaim, ³⁸as well as Nebo and Baal Meon (these names were changed) and Sibmah. They gave names to the cities they rebuilt.

³⁹The descendants of Makir son of Manasseh went to Gilead, captured it and drove out the Amorites who were there. ⁴⁰So Moses gave Gilead to the Makirites, the descendants of Manasseh, and they settled there. ⁴¹Jair, a descendant of Manasseh, captured their settlements and called them Havvoth Jair.ᵃ ⁴²And Nobah captured Kenath and its surrounding settlements and called it Nobah after himself.

Stages in Israel's Journey

33 Here are the stages in the journey of the Israelites when they came out of Egypt by divisions under the leadership of Moses and Aaron. ²At the Lord's command Moses recorded the stages in their journey. This is their journey by stages:

³The Israelites set out from Rameses on the fifteenth day of the first month, the day after the Passover. They marched out boldly in full view of all the Egyptians, ⁴who were burying all their firstborn, whom the Lord had struck down among them; for the Lord had brought judgment on their gods.

⁵The Israelites left Rameses and camped at Succoth.

⁶They left Succoth and camped at Etham, on the edge of the desert.

⁷They left Etham, turned back to Pi Hahiroth, to the east of Baal Zephon, and camped near Migdol.

[8]They left Pi Hahiroth[a] and passed through the sea into the desert, and when they had traveled for three days in the Desert of Etham, they camped at Marah.

[9]They left Marah and went to Elim, where there were twelve springs and seventy palm trees, and they camped there.

[10]They left Elim and camped by the Red Sea.[b]

[11]They left the Red Sea and camped in the Desert of Sin.

[12]They left the Desert of Sin and camped at Dophkah.

[13]They left Dophkah and camped at Alush.

[14]They left Alush and camped at Rephidim, where there was no water for the people to drink.

[15]They left Rephidim and camped in the Desert of Sinai.

[16]They left the Desert of Sinai and camped at Kibroth Hattaavah.

[17]They left Kibroth Hattaavah and camped at Hazeroth.

[18]They left Hazeroth and camped at Rithmah.

[19]They left Rithmah and camped at Rimmon Perez.

[20]They left Rimmon Perez and camped at Libnah.

[21]They left Libnah and camped at Rissah.

[22]They left Rissah and camped at Kehelathah.

[23]They left Kehelathah and camped at Mount Shepher.

[24]They left Mount Shepher and camped at Haradah.

[25]They left Haradah and camped at Makheloth.

[26]They left Makheloth and camped at Tahath.

[27]They left Tahath and camped at Terah.

[28]They left Terah and camped at Mithcah.

[29]They left Mithcah and camped at Hashmonah.

[30]They left Hashmonah and camped at Moseroth.

[31]They left Moseroth and camped at Bene Jaakan.

[32]They left Bene Jaakan and camped at Hor Haggidgad.

[33]They left Hor Haggidgad and camped at Jotbathah.

[34]They left Jotbathah and camped at Abronah.

[35]They left Abronah and camped at Ezion Geber.

[36]They left Ezion Geber and camped at Kadesh, in the Desert of Zin.

[37]They left Kadesh and camped at Mount Hor, on the border of Edom. [38]At the LORD's command Aaron the priest went up Mount Hor, where he died on the first day of the fifth month of the fortieth year after the Israelites came out of Egypt. [39]Aaron was a hundred and twenty-three years old when he died on Mount Hor.

[40]The Canaanite king of Arad, who lived in the Negev of Canaan, heard that the Israelites were coming.

[41]They left Mount Hor and camped at Zalmonah.

[42]They left Zalmonah and camped at Punon.

[43]They left Punon and camped at Oboth.

[44]They left Oboth and camped at Iye Abarim, on the border of Moab.

[45]They left Iyim[c] and camped at Dibon Gad.

[46]They left Dibon Gad and camped at Almon Diblathaim.

[47]They left Almon Diblathaim and camped in the mountains of Abarim, near Nebo.

[48]They left the mountains of Abarim and camped on the plains of Moab by the Jordan

---

[a]8 Many manuscripts of the Masoretic Text, Samaritan Pentateuch and Vulgate; most manuscripts of the Masoretic Text *left from before Hahiroth*   [b]10 Hebrew *Yam Suph*; that is, Sea of Reeds; also in verse 11   [c]45 That is, Iye Abarim

across from Jericho.[a] [49]There on the plains of Moab they camped along the Jordan from Beth Jeshimoth to Abel Shittim.

[50]On the plains of Moab by the Jordan across from Jericho the LORD said to Moses, [51]"Speak to the Israelites and say to them: 'When you cross the Jordan into Canaan, [52]drive out all the inhabitants of the land before you. Destroy all their carved images and their cast idols, and demolish all their high places. [53]Take possession of the land and settle in it, for I have given you the land to possess. [54]Distribute the land by lot, according to your clans. To a larger group give a larger inheritance, and to a smaller group a smaller one. Whatever falls to them by lot will be theirs. Distribute it according to your ancestral tribes.

[55]" 'But if you do not drive out the inhabitants of the land, those you allow to remain will become barbs in your eyes and thorns in your sides. They will give you trouble in the land where you will live. [56]And then I will do to you what I plan to do to them.' "

Boundaries of Canaan

34 The LORD said to Moses, [2]"Command the Israelites and say to them: 'When you enter Canaan, the land that will be allotted to you as an inheritance will have these boundaries:

[3]" 'Your southern side will include some of the Desert of Zin along the border of Edom. On the east, your southern boundary will start from the end of the Salt Sea,[b] [4]cross south of Scorpion[c] Pass, continue on to Zin and go south of Kadesh Barnea. Then it will go to Hazar Addar and over to Azmon, [5]where it will turn, join the Wadi of Egypt and end at the Sea.[d]

[6]" 'Your western boundary will be the coast of the Great Sea. This will be your boundary on the west.

[7]" 'For your northern boundary, run a line from the Great Sea to Mount Hor [8]and from Mount Hor to Lebo[e] Hamath. Then the boundary will go to Zedad, [9]continue to Ziphron and end at Hazar Enan. This will be your boundary on the north.

[10]" 'For your eastern boundary, run a line from Hazar Enan to Shepham. [11]The boundary will go down from Shepham to Riblah on the east side of Ain and continue along the slopes east of the Sea of Kinnereth.[f] [12]Then the boundary will go down along the Jordan and end at the Salt Sea.

" 'This will be your land, with its boundaries on every side.' "

[13]Moses commanded the Israelites: "Assign this land by lot as an inheritance. The LORD has ordered that it be given to the nine and a half tribes, [14]because the families of the tribe of Reuben, the tribe of Gad and the half-tribe of Manasseh have received their inheritance. [15]These two and a half tribes have received their inheritance on the east side of the Jordan of Jericho,[g] toward the sunrise."

[16]The LORD said to Moses, [17]"These are the names of the men who are to assign the land for you as an inheritance: Eleazar the priest and Joshua son of Nun. [18]And appoint one leader from each tribe to help assign the land. [19]These are their names:

Caleb son of Jephunneh,
 from the tribe of Judah;
[20]Shemuel son of Ammihud,
 from the tribe of Simeon;
[21]Elidad son of Kislon,
 from the tribe of Benjamin;
[22]Bukki son of Jogli,
 the leader from the tribe of Dan;
[23]Hanniel son of Ephod,
 the leader from the tribe of Manasseh son of Joseph;
[24]Kemuel son of Shiphtan,

---

a48 Hebrew *Jordan of Jericho*; possibly an ancient name for the Jordan River; also in verse 50   *b3* That is, the Dead Sea; also in verse 12   *c4* Hebrew *Akrabbim*   *d5* That is, the Mediterranean; also in verses 6 and 7   *e8* Or *to the entrance to*   *f11* That is, Galilee   *g15* *Jordan of Jericho* was possibly an ancient name for the Jordan River.

the leader from the tribe of Ephraim son of Joseph; 25Elizaphan son of Parnach, the leader from the tribe of Zebulun; 26Paltiel son of Azzan, the leader from the tribe of Issachar; 27Ahihud son of Shelomi, the leader from the tribe of Asher; 28Pedahel son of Ammihud, the leader from the tribe of Naphtali."

29These are the men the LORD commanded to assign the inheritance to the Israelites in the land of Canaan.

Towns for the Levites

35 On the plains of Moab by the Jordan across from Jericho,a the LORD said to Moses, 2"Command the Israelites to give the Levites towns to live in from the inheritance the Israelites will possess. And give them pasturelands around the towns. 3Then they will have towns to live in and pasturelands for their cattle, flocks and all their other livestock.

4"The pasturelands around the towns that you give the Levites will extend out fifteen hundred feetb from the town wall. 5Outside the town, measure three thousand feetc on the east side, three thousand on the south side, three thousand on the west and three thousand on the north, with the town in the center. They will have this area as pastureland for the towns.

Cities of Refuge

6"Six of the towns you give the Levites will be cities of refuge, to which a person who has killed someone may flee. In addition, give them forty-two other towns. 7In all you must give the Levites forty-eight towns, together with their pasturelands. 8The towns you give the Levites from the land the Israelites possess are to be given in proportion to the inheritance of each

tribe: Take many towns from a tribe that has many, but few from one that has few."

9Then the LORD said to Moses: 10"Speak to the Israelites and say to them: 'When you cross the Jordan into Canaan, 11select some towns to be your cities of refuge, to which a person who has killed someone accidentally may flee. 12They will be places of refuge from the avenger, so that a person accused of murder may not die before he stands trial before the assembly. 13These six towns you give will be your cities of refuge. 14Give three on this side of the Jordan and three in Canaan as cities of refuge. 15These six towns will be a place of refuge for Israelites, aliens and any other people living among them, so that anyone who has killed another accidentally can flee there.

16" 'If a man strikes someone with an iron object so that he dies, he is a murderer; the murderer shall be put to death. 17Or if anyone has a stone in his hand that could kill, and he strikes someone so that he dies, he is a murderer; the murderer shall be put to death. 18Or if anyone has a wooden object in his hand that could kill, and he hits someone so that he dies, he is a murderer; the murderer shall be put to death. 19The avenger of blood shall put the murderer to death; when he meets him, he shall put him to death. 20If anyone with malice aforethought shoves another or throws something at him intentionally so that he dies 21or if in hostility he hits him with his fist so that he dies, that person shall be put to death; he is a murderer. The avenger of blood shall put the murderer to death when he meets him.

22" 'But if without hostility someone suddenly shoves another or throws something at him unintentionally 23or, without seeing him, drops a stone on him that could kill him, and he dies, then since he was not his enemy and he did not intend to harm him, 24the assembly must judge be-

a1 Hebrew *Jordan of Jericho;* possibly an ancient name for the Jordan River   b4 Hebrew *a thousand cubits* (about 450 meters)   c5 Hebrew *two thousand cubits* (about 900 meters)

tween him and the avenger of blood according to these regulations. ²⁵The assembly must protect the one accused of murder from the avenger of blood and send him back to the city of refuge to which he fled. He must stay there until the death of the high priest, who was anointed with the holy oil.

²⁶" 'But if the accused ever goes outside the limits of the city of refuge to which he has fled ²⁷and the avenger of blood finds him outside the city, the avenger of blood may kill the accused without being guilty of murder. ²⁸The accused must stay in his city of refuge until the death of the high priest; only after the death of the high priest may he return to his own property.

²⁹" 'These are to be legal requirements for you throughout the generations to come, wherever you live.

³⁰" 'Anyone who kills a person is to be put to death as a murderer only on the testimony of witnesses. But no one is to be put to death on the testimony of only one witness.

³¹" 'Do not accept a ransom for the life of a murderer, who deserves to die. He must surely be put to death.

³²" 'Do not accept a ransom for anyone who has fled to a city of refuge and so allow him to go back and live on his own land before the death of the high priest.

³³" 'Do not pollute the land where you are. Bloodshed pollutes the land, and atonement cannot be made for the land on which blood has been shed, except by the blood of the one who shed it. ³⁴Do not defile the land where you live and where I dwell, for I, the LORD, dwell among the Israelites.' "

Inheritance of Zelophehad's Daughters

36 The family heads of the clan of Gilead son of Makir, the son of Manasseh, who were from the clans of the descendants of Joseph, came

and spoke before Moses and the leaders, the heads of the Israelite families. ²They said, "When the LORD commanded my lord to give the land as an inheritance to the Israelites by lot, he ordered you to give the inheritance of our brother Zelophehad to his daughters. ³Now suppose they marry men from other Israelite tribes; then their inheritance will be taken from our ancestral inheritance and added to that of the tribe they marry into. And so part of the inheritance allotted to us will be taken away. ⁴When the Year of Jubilee for the Israelites comes, their inheritance will be added to that of the tribe into which they marry, and their property will be taken from the tribal inheritance of our forefathers."

⁵Then at the LORD's command Moses gave this order to the Israelites: "What the tribe of the descendants of Joseph is saying is right. ⁶This is what the LORD commands for Zelophehad's daughters: They may marry anyone they please as long as they marry within the tribal clan of their father. ⁷No inheritance in Israel is to pass from tribe to tribe, for every Israelite shall keep the tribal land inherited from his forefathers. ⁸Every daughter who inherits land in any Israelite tribe must marry someone in her father's tribal clan, so that every Israelite will possess the inheritance of his fathers. ⁹No inheritance may pass from tribe to tribe, for each Israelite tribe is to keep the land it inherits."

¹⁰So Zelophehad's daughters did as the LORD commanded Moses. ¹¹Zelophehad's daughters—Mahlah, Tirzah, Hoglah, Milcah and Noah—married their cousins on their father's side. ¹²They married within the clans of the descendants of Manasseh son of Joseph, and their inheritance remained in their father's clan and tribe.

¹³These are the commands and regulations the LORD gave through Moses to the Israelites on the plains of Moab by the Jordan across from Jericho.^a

---

^a13 Hebrew *Jordan of Jericho*; possibly an ancient name for the Jordan River

T...

his book gives a warm, personal look at the relationship between God, Moses and the Israelites. Moses reminds the people of God's unfailing love and their need to be totally committed to him. As you read Deuteronomy, look back on how God has cared for you throughout your life and commit yourself anew to him as you trust him to care for you all your life long.

DEUTERONOMY

The Command to Leave Horeb

1 These are the words Moses spoke to all Israel in the desert east of the Jordan—that is, in the Arabah—opposite Suph, between Paran and Tophel, Laban, Hazeroth and Dizahab. ²(It takes eleven days to go from Horeb to Kadesh Barnea by the Mount Seir road.)

³In the fortieth year, on the first day of the eleventh month, Moses proclaimed to the Israelites all that the LORD had commanded him concerning them. ⁴This was after he had defeated Sihon king of the Amorites, who reigned in Heshbon, and at Edrei had defeated Og king of Bashan, who reigned in Ashtaroth.

⁵East of the Jordan in the territory of Moab, Moses began to expound this law, saying:

⁶The LORD our God said to us at Horeb, "You have stayed long enough at this mountain. ⁷Break camp and advance into the hill country of the Amorites; go to all the neighboring peoples in the Arabah, in the mountains, in the western foothills, in the Negev and along the coast, to the land of the Canaanites and to Lebanon, as far as the great river, the Euphrates. ⁸See, I have given you this land. Go in and take possession of the land that the LORD swore he would give to your fathers—to Abraham, Isaac and Jacob—and to their descendants after them."

The Appointment of Leaders

⁹At that time I said to you, "You are too heavy a burden for me to carry alone. ¹⁰The LORD your God has increased your numbers so that today you are as many as the stars in the sky. ¹¹May the LORD, the God of your fathers, increase you a thousand times and bless you as he has promised! ¹²But how can I bear your problems and your burdens and your disputes

all by myself? ¹³Choose some wise, understanding and respected men from each of your tribes, and I will set them over you."

¹⁴You answered me, "What you propose to do is good."

¹⁵So I took the leading men of your tribes, wise and respected men, and appointed them to have authority over you—as commanders of thousands, of hundreds, of fifties and of tens and as tribal officials. ¹⁶And I charged your judges at that time: Hear the disputes between your brothers and judge fairly, whether the case is between brother Israelites or between one of them and an alien. ¹⁷Do not show partiality in judging; hear both small and great alike. Do not be afraid of any man, for judgment belongs to God. Bring me any case too hard for you, and I will hear it. ¹⁸And at that time I told you everything you were to do.

Spies Sent Out

¹⁹Then, as the LORD our God commanded us, we set out from Horeb and went toward the hill country of the Amorites through all that vast and dreadful desert that you have seen, and so we reached Kadesh Barnea. ²⁰Then I said to you, "You have reached the hill country of the Amorites, which the LORD our God is giving us. ²¹See, the LORD your God has given you the land. Go up and take possession of it as the LORD, the God of your fathers, told you. Do not be afraid; do not be discouraged."

²²Then all of you came to me and said, "Let us send men ahead to spy out the land for us and bring back a report about the route we are to take and the towns we will come to."

²³The idea seemed good to me; so I selected twelve of you, one man from each tribe. ²⁴They left and went up into the hill country, and came to the Valley of Eshcol and explored it. ²⁵Taking with them some of the fruit of the land, they brought it down to us and reported, "It is a good land that the LORD our God is giving us."

Rebellion Against the LORD

²⁶But you were unwilling to go up; you rebelled against the command of the LORD your God. ²⁷You grumbled in your tents and said, "The LORD hates us; so he brought us out of Egypt to deliver us into the hands of the Amorites to destroy us. ²⁸Where can we go? Our brothers have made us lose heart. They say, 'The people are stronger and taller than we are; the cities are large, with walls up to the sky. We even saw the Anakites there.' "

²⁹Then I said to you, "Do not be terrified; do not be afraid of them. ³⁰The LORD your God, who is going before you, will fight for you, as he did for you in Egypt, before your very eyes, ³¹and in the desert. There you saw how the LORD your God carried you, as a father carries his son, all the way you went until you reached this place."

³²In spite of this, you did not trust in the LORD your God, ³³who went ahead of you on your journey, in fire by night and in a cloud by day, to search out places for you to camp and to show you the way you should go.

³⁴When the LORD heard what you said, he was angry and solemnly swore: ³⁵"Not a man of this evil generation shall see the good land I swore to give your forefathers, ³⁶except Caleb son of Jephunneh. He will see it, and I will give him and his descendants the land he set his feet on, because he followed the LORD wholeheartedly."

³⁷Because of you the LORD became angry with me also and said, "You shall not enter it, either. ³⁸But your assistant, Joshua son of Nun, will enter it. Encourage him, because he will lead Israel to inherit it. ³⁹And the little ones that you said would be taken captive, your children who do not yet know good from bad—they will enter the land. I will give it to them and they will take possession of it. ⁴⁰But as for you, turn around and set out to-

ward the desert along the route to the Red Sea.*"

41Then you replied, "We have sinned against the LORD. We will go up and fight, as the LORD our God commanded us." So every one of you put on his weapons, thinking it easy to go up into the hill country.

42But the LORD said to me, "Tell them, 'Do not go up and fight, because I will not be with you. You will be defeated by your enemies.' "

43So I told you, but you would not listen. You rebelled against the LORD's command and in your arrogance you marched up into the hill country. **44**The Amorites who lived in those hills came out against you; they chased you like a swarm of bees and beat you down from Seir all the way to Hormah. **45**You came back and wept before the LORD, but he paid no attention to your weeping and turned a deaf ear to you. **46**And so you stayed in Kadesh many days—all the time you spent there.

Wanderings in the Desert

2 Then we turned back and set out toward the desert along the route to the Red Sea,* as the LORD had directed me. For a long time we made our way around the hill country of Seir.

2Then the LORD said to me, **3**"You have made your way around this hill country long enough; now turn north. **4**Give the people these orders: 'You are about to pass through the territory of your brothers the descendants of Esau, who live in Seir. They will be afraid of you, but be very careful. **5**Do not provoke them to war, for I will not give you any of their land, not even enough to put your foot on. I have given Esau the hill country of Seir as his own. **6**You are to pay them in silver for the food you eat and the water you drink.' "

7The LORD your God has blessed you in all the work of your hands. He has watched over your journey through this vast desert. These forty years the LORD your God has been with you, and you have not lacked anything.

8So we went on past our brothers the descendants of Esau, who live in Seir. We turned from the Arabah road, which comes up from Elath and Ezion Geber, and traveled along the desert road of Moab.

9Then the LORD said to me, "Do not harass the Moabites or provoke them to war, for I will not give you any part of their land. I have given Ar to the descendants of Lot as a possession."

10(The Emites used to live there—a people strong and numerous, and as tall as the Anakites. **11**Like the Anakites, they too were considered Rephaites, but the Moabites called them Emites. **12**Horites used to live in Seir, but the descendants of Esau drove them out. They destroyed the Horites from before them and settled in their place, just as Israel did in the land the LORD gave them as their possession.)

13And the LORD said, "Now get up and cross the Zered Valley." So we crossed the valley.

14Thirty-eight years passed from the time we left Kadesh Barnea until we crossed the Zered Valley. By then, that entire generation of fighting men had perished from the camp, as the LORD had sworn to them. **15**The LORD's hand was against them until he had completely eliminated them from the camp.

16Now when the last of these fighting men among the people had died, **17**the LORD said to me, **18**"Today you are to pass by the region of Moab at Ar. **19**When you come to the Ammonites, do not harass them or provoke them to war, for I will not give you possession of any land belonging to the Ammonites. I have given it as a possession to the descendants of Lot."

20(That too was considered a land of the Rephaites, who used to live there; but the Ammonites called them Zamzummites. **21**They were a people strong and numerous, and as tall as the Anakites. The LORD destroyed

a40,1 Hebrew Yam Suph; that is, Sea of Reeds

them from before the Ammonites, who drove them out and settled in their place. ²²The LORD had done the same for the descendants of Esau, who lived in Seir, when he destroyed the Horites from before them. They drove them out and have lived in their place to this day. ²³And as for the Avvites who lived in villages as far as Gaza, the Caphtorites coming out from Caphtor*ᵃ* destroyed them and settled in their place.)

Defeat of Sihon King of Heshbon

²⁴"Set out now and cross the Arnon Gorge. See, I have given into your hand Sihon the Amorite, king of Heshbon, and his country. Begin to take possession of it and engage him in battle. ²⁵This very day I will begin to put the terror and fear of you on all the nations under heaven. They will hear reports of you and will tremble and be in anguish because of you."

²⁶From the desert of Kedemoth I sent messengers to Sihon king of Heshbon offering peace and saying, ²⁷"Let us pass through your country. We will stay on the main road; we will not turn aside to the right or to the left. ²⁸Sell us food to eat and water to drink for their price in silver. Only let us pass through on foot— ²⁹as the descendants of Esau, who live in Seir, and the Moabites, who live in Ar, did for us—until we cross the Jordan into the land the LORD our God is giving us." ³⁰But Sihon king of Heshbon refused to let us pass through. For the LORD your God had made his spirit stubborn and his heart obstinate in order to give him into your hands, as he has now done.

³¹The LORD said to me, "See, I have begun to deliver Sihon and his country over to you. Now begin to conquer and possess his land."

³²When Sihon and all his army came out to meet us in battle at Jahaz, ³³the LORD our God delivered him over to us and we struck him down, together with his sons and his whole army. ³⁴At that time we took all his towns and completely destroyed*ᵇ* them—men, women and children. We left no survivors. ³⁵But the livestock and the plunder from the towns we had captured we carried off for ourselves. ³⁶From Aroer on the rim of the Arnon Gorge, and from the town in the gorge, even as far as Gilead, not one town was too strong for us. The LORD our God gave us all of them. ³⁷But in accordance with the command of the LORD our God, you did not encroach on any of the land of the Ammonites, neither the land along the course of the Jabbok nor that around the towns in the hills.

Defeat of Og King of Bashan

3 Next we turned and went up along the road toward Bashan, and Og king of Bashan with his whole army marched out to meet us in battle at Edrei. ²The LORD said to me, "Do not be afraid of him, for I have handed him over to you with his whole army and his land. Do to him what you did to Sihon king of the Amorites, who reigned in Heshbon."

³So the LORD our God also gave into our hands Og king of Bashan and all his army. We struck them down, leaving no survivors. ⁴At that time we took all his cities. There was not one of the sixty cities that we did not take from them—the whole region of Argob, Og's kingdom in Bashan. ⁵All these cities were fortified with high walls and with gates and bars, and there were also a great many unwalled villages. ⁶We completely destroyed*ᵇ* them, as we had done with Sihon king of Heshbon, destroying*ᵇ* every city—men, women and children. ⁷But all the livestock and the plunder from their cities we carried off for ourselves.

⁸So at that time we took from these two kings of the Amorites the territory east of the Jordan, from the Arnon Gorge as far as Mount Hermon. ⁹(Hermon is called Sirion by the Sido-

---

*ᵃ*23 That is, Crete   *ᵇ*34,6 The Hebrew term refers to the irrevocable giving over of things or persons to the LORD, often by totally destroying them.

nians; the Amorites call it Senir.) ¹⁰We took all the towns on the plateau, and all Gilead, and all Bashan as far as Salecah and Edrei, towns of Og's kingdom in Bashan. ¹¹(Only Og king of Bashan was left of the remnant of the Rephaites. His bed*a* was made of iron and was more than thirteen feet long and six feet wide.*b* It is still in Rabbah of the Ammonites.)

Division of the Land

¹²Of the land that we took over at that time, I gave the Reubenites and the Gadites the territory north of Aroer by the Arnon Gorge, including half the hill country of Gilead, together with its towns. ¹³The rest of Gilead and also all of Bashan, the kingdom of Og, I gave to the half tribe of Manasseh. (The whole region of Argob in Bashan used to be known as a land of the Rephaites. ¹⁴Jair, a descendant of Manasseh, took the whole region of Argob as far as the border of the Geshurites and the Maacathites; it was named after him, so that to this day Bashan is called Havvoth Jair.*c*) ¹⁵And I gave Gilead to Makir. ¹⁶But to the Reubenites and the Gadites I gave the territory extending from Gilead down to the Arnon Gorge (the middle of the gorge being the border) and out to the Jabbok River, which is the border of the Ammonites. ¹⁷Its western border was the Jordan in the Arabah, from Kinnereth to the Sea of the Arabah (the Salt Sea*d*), below the slopes of Pisgah.

¹⁸I commanded you at that time: "The LORD your God has given you this land to take possession of it. But all your able-bodied men, armed for battle, must cross over ahead of your brother Israelites. ¹⁹However, your wives, your children and your livestock (I know you have much livestock) may stay in the towns I have given you, ²⁰until the LORD gives rest to your brothers as he has to you, and they too have taken over the land that the LORD your God is giving them, across the Jordan. After that, each of you may go back to the possession I have given you."

Moses Forbidden to Cross the Jordan

²¹At that time I commanded Joshua: "You have seen with your own eyes all that the LORD your God has done to these two kings. The LORD will do the same to all the kingdoms over there where you are going. ²²Do not be afraid of them; the LORD your God himself will fight for you."

²³At that time I pleaded with the LORD: ²⁴"O Sovereign LORD, you have begun to show to your servant your greatness and your strong hand. For what god is there in heaven or on earth who can do the deeds and mighty works you do? ²⁵Let me go over and see the good land beyond the Jordan—that fine hill country and Lebanon."

²⁶But because of you the LORD was angry with me and would not listen to me. "That is enough," the LORD said. "Do not speak to me anymore about this matter. ²⁷Go up to the top of Pisgah and look west and north and south and east. Look at the land with your own eyes, since you are not going to cross this Jordan. ²⁸But commission Joshua, and encourage and strengthen him, for he will lead this people across and will cause them to inherit the land that you will see." ²⁹So we stayed in the valley near Beth Peor.

Obedience Commanded

4 Hear now, O Israel, the decrees and laws I am about to teach you. Follow them so that you may live and may go in and take possession of the land that the LORD, the God of your fathers, is giving you. ²Do not add to what I command you and do not subtract from it, but keep the commands of the LORD your God that I give you.

³You saw with your own eyes what the LORD did at Baal Peor. The LORD

*a*11 Or *sarcophagus*   *b*11 Hebrew *nine cubits long and four cubits wide* (about 4 meters long and 1.8 meters wide)   *c*14 Or *called the settlements of Jair*   *d*17 That is, the Dead Sea

your God destroyed from among you everyone who followed the Baal of Peor, [4]but all of you who held fast to the LORD your God are still alive today.

[5]See, I have taught you decrees and laws as the LORD my God commanded me, so that you may follow them in the land you are entering to take possession of it. [6]Observe them carefully, for this will show your wisdom and understanding to the nations, who will hear about all these decrees and say, "Surely this great nation is a wise and understanding people." [7]What other nation is so great as to have their gods near them the way the LORD our God is near us whenever we pray to him? [8]And what other nation is so great as to have such righteous decrees and laws as this body of laws I am setting before you today?

[9]Only be careful, and watch yourselves closely so that you do not forget the things your eyes have seen or let them slip from your heart as long as you live. Teach them to your children and to their children after them. [10]Remember the day you stood before the LORD your God at Horeb, when he said to me, "Assemble the people before me to hear my words so that they may learn to revere me as long as they live in the land and may teach them to their children." [11]You came near and stood at the foot of the mountain while it blazed with fire to the very heavens, with black clouds and deep darkness. [12]Then the LORD spoke to you out of the fire. You heard the sound of words but saw no form; there was only a voice. [13]He declared to you his covenant, the Ten Commandments, which he commanded you to follow and then wrote them on two stone tablets. [14]And the LORD directed me at that time to teach you the decrees and laws you are to follow in the land that you are crossing the Jordan to possess.

Idolatry Forbidden

[15]You saw no form of any kind the day the LORD spoke to you at Horeb out of the fire. Therefore watch yourselves very carefully, [16]so that you do not become corrupt and make for yourselves an idol, an image of any shape, whether formed like a man or a woman, [17]or like any animal on earth or any bird that flies in the air, [18]or like any creature that moves along the ground or any fish in the waters below. [19]And when you look up to the sky and see the sun, the moon and the stars—all the heavenly array—do not be enticed into bowing down to them and worshiping things the LORD your God has apportioned to all the nations under heaven. [20]But as for you, the LORD took you and brought you out of the iron-smelting furnace, out of Egypt, to be the people of his inheritance, as you now are.

[21]The LORD was angry with me because of you, and he solemnly swore that I would not cross the Jordan and enter the good land the LORD your God is giving you as your inheritance. [22]I will die in this land; I will not cross the Jordan; but you are about to cross over and take possession of that good land. [23]Be careful not to forget the covenant of the LORD your God that he made with you; do not make for yourselves an idol in the form of anything the LORD your God has forbidden. [24]For the LORD your God is a consuming fire, a jealous God.

[25]After you have had children and grandchildren and have lived in the land a long time—if you then become corrupt and make any kind of idol, doing evil in the eyes of the LORD your God and provoking him to anger, [26]I call heaven and earth as witnesses against you this day that you will quickly perish from the land that you are crossing the Jordan to possess. You will not live there long but will certainly be destroyed. [27]The LORD will scatter you among the peoples, and only a few of you will survive among the nations to which the LORD will drive you. [28]There you will worship man-made gods of wood and stone, which cannot see or hear or eat or smell. [29]But if from there you seek the LORD your God, you will find him if you look for him with all your heart

VERSE:	AUTHOR:	PASSAGE:
Deuteronomy 4:9	Don Anderson	Deuteronomy 4:1–14

Sharing Jesus

A vital function of Christian grandparents is to impart spiritual truth to their grandchildren. Grandparents have unique opportunities to share Christ and see the gospel spread among those they love most. Here are six ways you can share Jesus in your family:

1. The rules are simple. Life is always more important than lip, walk than work, conduct than creed. Relational evangelism means I love, serve and stay involved to earn the right to share my faith . . .

2. Let your children and grandchildren really know you. Let yourself be interviewed by family members; make a cassette or videotape of yourself recalling childhood memories, family members and events . . .

3. Take the grandkids to your church with you occasionally . . .

4. Invest in a week for your kids, grandkids and yourself at a Christian family camp . . .

5. Build a good library of Christian videos the grandchildren can watch when they come. Send some home with them for further viewing.

6. If your children object to your sharing your faith with their children, back off. You've bumped into green fruit. Keep praying. Your time will come. Trust God and watch him work.

You probably have plenty of time for these important relationships in your senior years. What you do with it reflects whom you are living for!

ADDITIONAL SCRIPTURE READINGS
Psalm 78:1–8; 1 Peter 3:13–22

Go to page 215 for your next devotional reading.

and with all your soul. ³⁰When you are in distress and all these things have happened to you, then in later days you will return to the LORD your God and obey him. ³¹For the LORD your God is a merciful God; he will not abandon or destroy you or forget the covenant with your forefathers, which he confirmed to them by oath.

The LORD Is God

³²Ask now about the former days, long before your time, from the day God created man on the earth; ask from one end of the heavens to the other. Has anything so great as this ever happened, or has anything like it ever been heard of? ³³Has any other people heard the voice of God[a] speaking out of fire, as you have, and lived? ³⁴Has any god ever tried to take for himself one nation out of another nation, by testings, by miraculous signs and wonders, by war, by a mighty hand and an outstretched arm, or by great and awesome deeds, like all the things the LORD your God did for you in Egypt before your very eyes?

³⁵You were shown these things so that you might know that the LORD is God; besides him there is no other. ³⁶From heaven he made you hear his voice to discipline you. On earth he showed you his great fire, and you heard his words from out of the fire. ³⁷Because he loved your forefathers and chose their descendants after them, he brought you out of Egypt by his Presence and his great strength, ³⁸to drive out before you nations greater and stronger than you and to bring you into their land to give it to you for your inheritance, as it is today.

³⁹Acknowledge and take to heart this day that the LORD is God in heaven above and on the earth below. There is no other. ⁴⁰Keep his decrees and commands, which I am giving you today, so that it may go well with you and your children after you and

that you may live long in the land the LORD your God gives you for all time.

Cities of Refuge

⁴¹Then Moses set aside three cities east of the Jordan, ⁴²to which anyone who had killed a person could flee if he had unintentionally killed his neighbor without malice aforethought. He could flee into one of these cities and save his life. ⁴³The cities were these: Bezer in the desert plateau, for the Reubenites; Ramoth in Gilead, for the Gadites; and Golan in Bashan, for the Manassites.

Introduction to the Law

⁴⁴This is the law Moses set before the Israelites. ⁴⁵These are the stipulations, decrees and laws Moses gave them when they came out of Egypt ⁴⁶and were in the valley near Beth Peor east of the Jordan, in the land of Sihon king of the Amorites, who reigned in Heshbon and was defeated by Moses and the Israelites as they came out of Egypt. ⁴⁷They took possession of his land and the land of Og king of Bashan, the two Amorite kings east of the Jordan. ⁴⁸This land extended from Aroer on the rim of the Arnon Gorge to Mount Siyon[b] (that is, Hermon), ⁴⁹and included all the Arabah east of the Jordan, as far as the Sea of the Arabah,[c] below the slopes of Pisgah.

The Ten Commandments

5 Moses summoned all Israel and said:

Hear, O Israel, the decrees and laws I declare in your hearing today. Learn them and be sure to follow them. ²The LORD our God made a covenant with us at Horeb. ³It was not with our fathers that the LORD made this covenant, but with us, with all of us who are alive here today. ⁴The LORD spoke to you face to face out of the fire on the mountain. ⁵(At that time I stood between the LORD and you to declare to you the word of the LORD, because you were afraid of the

---

[a]33 Or of a god   [b]48 Hebrew; Syriac (see also Deut. 3:9) Sirion   [c]49 That is, the Dead Sea

fire and did not go up the mountain.) And he said:

⁶"I am the LORD your God, who brought you out of Egypt, out of the land of slavery.

⁷"You shall have no other gods before[a] me.

⁸"You shall not make for yourself an idol in the form of anything in heaven above or on the earth beneath or in the waters below. ⁹You shall not bow down to them or worship them; for I, the LORD your God, am a jealous God, punishing the children for the sin of the fathers to the third and fourth generation of those who hate me, ¹⁰but showing love to a thousand ⌐generations⌐ of those who love me and keep my commandments.

¹¹"You shall not misuse the name of the LORD your God, for the LORD will not hold anyone guiltless who misuses his name.

¹²"Observe the Sabbath day by keeping it holy, as the LORD your God has commanded you. ¹³Six days you shall labor and do all your work, ¹⁴but the seventh day is a Sabbath to the LORD your God. On it you shall not do any work, neither you, nor your son or daughter, nor your manservant or maidservant, nor your ox, your donkey or any of your animals, nor the alien within your gates, so that your manservant and maidservant may rest, as you do. ¹⁵Remember that you were slaves in Egypt and that the LORD your God brought you out of there with a mighty hand and an outstretched arm. Therefore the LORD your God has commanded you to observe the Sabbath day.

¹⁶"Honor your father and your mother, as the LORD your God has commanded you, so that you may live long and that it may go well with you in the land the LORD your God is giving you.

¹⁷"You shall not murder.

¹⁸"You shall not commit adultery.

¹⁹"You shall not steal.

²⁰"You shall not give false testimony against your neighbor.

²¹"You shall not covet your neighbor's wife. You shall not set your desire on your neighbor's house or land, his manservant or maidservant, his ox or donkey, or anything that belongs to your neighbor."

²²These are the commandments the LORD proclaimed in a loud voice to your whole assembly there on the mountain from out of the fire, the cloud and the deep darkness; and he added nothing more. Then he wrote them on two stone tablets and gave them to me.

²³When you heard the voice out of the darkness, while the mountain was ablaze with fire, all the leading men of your tribes and your elders came to me. ²⁴And you said, "The LORD our God has shown us his glory and his majesty, and we have heard his voice from the fire. Today we have seen that a man can live even if God speaks with him. ²⁵But now, why should we die? This great fire will consume us, and we will die if we hear the voice of the LORD our God any longer. ²⁶For what mortal man has ever heard the voice of the living God speaking out of fire, as we have, and survived? ²⁷Go near and listen to all that the LORD our God says. Then

---

a7 Or *besides*

tell us whatever the LORD our God tells you. We will listen and obey."

28The LORD heard you when you spoke to me and the LORD said to me, "I have heard what this people said to you. Everything they said was good. 29Oh, that their hearts would be inclined to fear me and keep all my commands always, so that it might go well with them and their children forever!

30"Go, tell them to return to their tents. 31But you stay here with me so that I may give you all the commands, decrees and laws you are to teach them to follow in the land I am giving them to possess."

32So be careful to do what the LORD your God has commanded you; do not turn aside to the right or to the left. 33Walk in all the way that the LORD your God has commanded you, so that you may live and prosper and prolong your days in the land that you will possess.

Love the LORD Your God

6 These are the commands, decrees and laws the LORD your God directed me to teach you to observe in the land that you are crossing the Jordan to possess, 2so that you, your children and their children after them may fear the LORD your God as long as you live by keeping all his decrees and commands that I give you, and so that you may enjoy long life. 3Hear, O Israel, and be careful to obey so that it may go well with you and that you may increase greatly in a land flowing with milk and honey, just as the LORD, the God of your fathers, promised you.

4Hear, O Israel: The LORD our God, the LORD is one.*a* 5Love the LORD your God with all your heart and with all your soul and with all your strength. 6These commandments that I give you today are to be upon your hearts. 7Impress them on your children. Talk about them when you sit at home and

when you walk along the road, when you lie down and when you get up. 8Tie them as symbols on your hands and bind them on your foreheads. 9Write them on the doorframes of your houses and on your gates.

10When the LORD your God brings you into the land he swore to your fathers, to Abraham, Isaac and Jacob, to give you—a land with large, flourishing cities you did not build, 11houses filled with all kinds of good things you did not provide, wells you did not dig, and vineyards and olive groves you did not plant—then when you eat and are satisfied, 12be careful that you do not forget the LORD, who brought you out of Egypt, out of the land of slavery.

13Fear the LORD your God, serve him only and take your oaths in his name. 14Do not follow other gods, the gods of the peoples around you; 15for the LORD your God, who is among you, is a jealous God and his anger will burn against you, and he will destroy you from the face of the land. 16Do not test the LORD your God as you did at Massah. 17Be sure to keep the commands of the LORD your God and the stipulations and decrees he has given you. 18Do what is right and good in the LORD's sight, so that it may go well with you and you may go in and take over the good land that the LORD promised on oath to your forefathers, 19thrusting out all your enemies before you, as the LORD said.

20In the future, when your son asks you, "What is the meaning of the stipulations, decrees and laws the LORD our God has commanded you?" 21tell him: "We were slaves of Pharaoh in Egypt, but the LORD brought us out of Egypt with a mighty hand. 22Before our eyes the LORD sent miraculous signs and wonders—great and terrible—upon Egypt and Pharaoh and his whole household. 23But he brought us out from there to bring us in and give us the land that he promised on oath to our forefathers. 24The

---

a4 Or *The LORD our God is one LORD*; or *The LORD is our God, the LORD is one*; or *The LORD is our God, the LORD alone*

LORD commanded us to obey all these decrees and to fear the LORD our God, so that we might always prosper and be kept alive, as is the case today. ²⁵And if we are careful to obey all this law before the LORD our God, as he has commanded us, that will be our righteousness."

Driving Out the Nations

7 When the LORD your God brings you into the land you are entering

VERSE: AUTHOR: PASSAGE:
Deuteronomy 5:33   Larry Burkett   Deuteronomy 5:23–33

A Total Transfer

A Christian must transfer ownership of every possession to God. That means his money, time, family, material possessions, education, even earning potential for the future. Doing so is essential to experiencing the Spirit-filled life in his finances.

A Christian must realize that there is absolutely no substitute for this step. If you believe that you are the owner of even a single possession, anything affecting that possession will affect your attitude. God will not input his perfect will into our lives unless we first surrender our will to him.

If, however, we make a total transfer of everything to God, he will demonstrate his ability. It is important to understand and accept God's conditions for his control (Deuteronomy 5:32–33). God will keep his promise to provide every need we have through physical, material and spiritual means. It is simple to say, "I make total transfer of everything to God," but it is not simple to do. At first, it is difficult to consistently seek God's will in the area of material things because we are so accustomed to self-management and control.

What a great relief it is to turn our burdens over to him.

ADDITIONAL SCRIPTURE READINGS
Psalm 50:1–15; 1 Peter 5:1–11

Go to page 216 for your next devotional reading.

PASSAGE: Deuteronomy 27:1–8; Hebrews 13:15–16
AUTHOR: George Herbert

The Altar

A broken ALTAR, Lord, thy servant rears,
Made of a heart, and cemented with tears:
Whose parts are as thy hand did frame;
No workman's tool hath touched the same.
A HEART alone
Is such a stone,
As nothing but
Thy power doth cut.
Wherefore each part
Of my hard heart
Meets in this frame,
To praise thy name,
That if I chance to hold my peace,
These stones to praise thee may not cease.
O let thy blessed SACRIFICE be mine,
And sanctify this ALTAR to be thine.

Go to page 218 for your next devotional reading.

to possess and drives out before you many nations—the Hittites, Girgashites, Amorites, Canaanites, Perizzites, Hivites and Jebusites, seven nations larger and stronger than you— [2]and when the LORD your God has delivered them over to you and you have defeated them, then you must destroy them totally.[a] Make no treaty with them, and show them no mercy. [3]Do not intermarry with them. Do not give your daughters to their sons or take their daughters for your sons, [4]for they will turn your sons away from following me to serve other gods, and the LORD's anger will burn against you and will quickly destroy you. [5]This is what you are to do to them: Break down their altars, smash their sacred stones, cut down their Asherah poles[b] and burn their idols in the fire. [6]For you are a people holy to the LORD your God. The LORD your God has chosen you out of all the peoples on the face of the earth to be his people, his treasured possession.

[7]The LORD did not set his affection on you and choose you because you were more numerous than other peoples, for you were the fewest of all peoples. [8]But it was because the LORD loved you and kept the oath he swore to your forefathers that he brought you out with a mighty hand and redeemed you from the land of slavery, from the power of Pharaoh king of Egypt. [9]Know therefore that the LORD your God is God; he is the faithful God, keeping his covenant of love to a thousand generations of those who love him and keep his commands. [10]But

> those who hate him he will repay
>> to their face by destruction;
> he will not be slow to repay to
>> their face those who hate
>> him.

[11]Therefore, take care to follow the commands, decrees and laws I give you today.

[12]If you pay attention to these laws and are careful to follow them, then the LORD your God will keep his covenant of love with you, as he swore to your forefathers. [13]He will love you and bless you and increase your numbers. He will bless the fruit of your womb, the crops of your land—your grain, new wine and oil—the calves of your herds and the lambs of your flocks in the land that he swore to your forefathers to give you. [14]You will be blessed more than any other people; none of your men or women will be childless, nor any of your livestock without young. [15]The LORD will keep you free from every disease. He will not inflict on you the horrible diseases you knew in Egypt, but he will inflict them on all who hate you. [16]You must destroy all the peoples the LORD your God gives over to you. Do not look on them with pity and do not serve their gods, for that will be a snare to you.

[17]You may say to yourselves, "These nations are stronger than we are. How can we drive them out?" [18]But do not be afraid of them; remember well what the LORD your God did to Pharaoh and to all Egypt. [19]You saw with your own eyes the great trials, the miraculous signs and wonders, the mighty hand and outstretched arm, with which the LORD your God brought you out. The LORD your God will do the same to all the peoples you now fear. [20]Moreover, the LORD your God will send the hornet among them until even the survivors who hide from you have perished. [21]Do not be terrified by them, for the LORD your God, who is among you, is a great and awesome God. [22]The LORD your God will drive out those nations before you, little by little. You will not be allowed to eliminate them all at once, or the wild animals will multiply around you. [23]But the LORD your God will deliver them over to you, throwing them into great

---

[a]2 The Hebrew term refers to the irrevocable giving over of things or persons to the LORD, often by totally destroying them; also in verse 26.   [b]5 That is, symbols of the goddess Asherah; here and elsewhere in Deuteronomy

confusion until they are destroyed. [24]He will give their kings into your hand, and you will wipe out their names from under heaven. No one will be able to stand up against you; you will destroy them. [25]The images of their gods you are to burn in the fire. Do not covet the silver and gold on them, and do not take it for yourselves, or you will be ensnared by it, for it is detestable to the LORD your God. [26]Do not bring a detestable thing into your house or you, like it, will be set apart for destruction. Utterly abhor and detest it, for it is set apart for destruction.

Do Not Forget the LORD

8 Be careful to follow every command I am giving you today, so that you may live and increase and may enter and possess the land that

VERSE:	AUTHOR:	PASSAGE:
Deuteronomy 7:6	Leslie E. Moser	Deuteronomy 7:1–9

A Gift for God's Children

When we feel our worth as children of God and firmly believe in our ability to live productively, we acknowledge God. Through our life, we worship him who created our bodies, minds and talents for his service . . .

Self-esteem generally grows stronger with age because, as we grow up, we find meaning and a sense of self through our endeavors. True, a large source of meaning for our life is God himself, but important sources of meaning are the tasks to be done, the children to be reared, the vocations to be pursued . . .

We must sustain a sense of purpose and significance as we grow older. We must not give up the struggle to make a difference in the name of and to the glory of God.

Self-esteem. As a child of God, you can know of his love for you and your worth to him. As an older and wiser person, you can know what to do to protect that sense of self-worth. And it's that healthy sense of self-esteem that will keep you living a meaningful life.

ADDITIONAL SCRIPTURE READINGS
Matthew 6:25–34; 1 Peter 1:9–10

Go to page 220 for your next devotional reading.

the LORD promised on oath to your forefathers. ²Remember how the LORD your God led you all the way in the desert these forty years, to humble you and to test you in order to know what was in your heart, whether or not you would keep his commands. ³He humbled you, causing you to hunger and then feeding you with manna, which neither you nor your fathers had known, to teach you that man does not live on bread alone but on every word that comes from the mouth of the LORD. ⁴Your clothes did not wear out and your feet did not swell during these forty years. ⁵Know then in your heart that as a man disciplines his son, so the LORD your God disciplines you.

⁶Observe the commands of the LORD your God, walking in his ways and revering him. ⁷For the LORD your God is bringing you into a good land—a land with streams and pools of water, with springs flowing in the valleys and hills; ⁸a land with wheat and barley, vines and fig trees, pomegranates, olive oil and honey; ⁹a land where bread will not be scarce and you will lack nothing; a land where the rocks are iron and you can dig copper out of the hills.

¹⁰When you have eaten and are satisfied, praise the LORD your God for the good land he has given you. ¹¹Be careful that you do not forget the LORD your God, failing to observe his commands, his laws and his decrees that I am giving you this day. ¹²Otherwise, when you eat and are satisfied, when you build fine houses and settle down, ¹³and when your herds and flocks grow large and your silver and gold increase and all you have is multiplied, ¹⁴then your heart will become proud and you will forget the LORD your God, who brought you out of Egypt, out of the land of slavery. ¹⁵He led you through the vast and dreadful desert, that thirsty and waterless land, with its venomous snakes and scorpions. He brought you water out of hard rock. ¹⁶He gave you manna to eat in the desert, something your fathers had never known, to humble

and to test you so that in the end it might go well with you. ¹⁷You may say to yourself, "My power and the strength of my hands have produced this wealth for me." ¹⁸But remember the LORD your God, for it is he who gives you the ability to produce wealth, and so confirms his covenant, which he swore to your forefathers, as it is today.

¹⁹If you ever forget the LORD your God and follow other gods and worship and bow down to them, I testify against you today that you will surely be destroyed. ²⁰Like the nations the LORD destroyed before you, so you will be destroyed for not obeying the LORD your God.

Not Because of Israel's Righteousness

9 Hear, O Israel. You are now about to cross the Jordan to go in and dispossess nations greater and stronger than you, with large cities that have walls up to the sky. ²The people are strong and tall—Anakites! You know about them and have heard it said: "Who can stand up against the Anakites?" ³But be assured today that the LORD your God is the one who goes across ahead of you like a devouring fire. He will destroy them; he will subdue them before you. And you will drive them out and annihilate them quickly, as the LORD has promised you.

⁴After the LORD your God has driven them out before you, do not say to yourself, "The LORD has brought me here to take possession of this land because of my righteousness." No, it is on account of the wickedness of these nations that the LORD is going to drive them out before you. ⁵It is not because of your righteousness or your integrity that you are going in to take possession of their land; but on account of the wickedness of these nations, the LORD your God will drive them out before you, to accomplish what he swore to your fathers, to Abraham, Isaac and Jacob. ⁶Understand, then, that it is not because of

VERSE: AUTHOR: PASSAGE:
Deuteronomy 8:2   Author Unknown   Deuteronomy 8:1–20

The Season of Reflection

The evening of life! Yes: life has its sunset hour, its twilight season. The dim eye, the silvered lock and the feeble step indicate that the closing period of earthly existence has arrived. How rapid has been the flight of time! How near must be the approach of eternity!

Evening is the time for reflection . . . "Remember how the LORD your God led you all the way in the desert these forty years." Old age is the most appropriate season for this consideration of the past . . .

Let neither pride nor prejudice hide the real state of things from your eyes. Ask God himself to be your teacher. Make this your prayer: "Search me, O God, and know my heart; test me and know my anxious thoughts. See if there is any offensive way in me, and lead me in the way everlasting" (Psalm 139:23–24).

The retrospect is humbling. Yet it leads to hope, and peace, and salvation. Both to the troubled Christian and the penitent sinner the cheering annunciation of the gospel is: "The blood of Jesus Christ cleanses us from all our sins" . . .

Looking back should be combined with looking forward. The weary pilgrim, who recalls with mingled sorrow and gladness the events that have occurred during his journey, will also think of the rest and the welcome that wait for him in his happy home. The Christian traveler, as evening is closing in around him, loves to let his imagination dwell upon the many rooms in his Father's house, where a place is being prepared for him.

ADDITIONAL SCRIPTURE READINGS
Psalm 139; John 14:1–14

Go to page 236 for your next devotional reading.

your righteousness that the LORD your God is giving you this good land to possess, for you are a stiff-necked people.

The Golden Calf

[7]Remember this and never forget how you provoked the LORD your God to anger in the desert. From the day you left Egypt until you arrived here, you have been rebellious against the LORD. [8]At Horeb you aroused the LORD's wrath so that he was angry enough to destroy you. [9]When I went up on the mountain to receive the tablets of stone, the tablets of the covenant that the LORD had made with you, I stayed on the mountain forty days and forty nights; I ate no bread and drank no water. [10]The LORD gave me two stone tablets inscribed by the finger of God. On them were all the commandments the LORD proclaimed to you on the mountain out of the fire, on the day of the assembly.

[11]At the end of the forty days and forty nights, the LORD gave me the two stone tablets, the tablets of the covenant. [12]Then the LORD told me, "Go down from here at once, because your people whom you brought out of Egypt have become corrupt. They have turned away quickly from what I commanded them and have made a cast idol for themselves."

[13]And the LORD said to me, "I have seen this people, and they are a stiff-necked people indeed! [14]Let me alone, so that I may destroy them and blot out their name from under heaven. And I will make you into a nation stronger and more numerous than they."

[15]So I turned and went down from the mountain while it was ablaze with fire. And the two tablets of the covenant were in my hands.[a] [16]When I looked, I saw that you had sinned against the LORD your God; you had made for yourselves an idol cast in the shape of a calf. You had turned aside quickly from the way that the LORD had commanded you. [17]So I took

the two tablets and threw them out of my hands, breaking them to pieces before your eyes.

[18]Then once again I fell prostrate before the LORD for forty days and forty nights; I ate no bread and drank no water, because of all the sin you had committed, doing what was evil in the LORD's sight and so provoking him to anger. [19]I feared the anger and wrath of the LORD, for he was angry enough with you to destroy you. But again the LORD listened to me. [20]And the LORD was angry enough with Aaron to destroy him, but at that time I prayed for Aaron too. [21]Also I took that sinful thing of yours, the calf you had made, and burned it in the fire. Then I crushed it and ground it to powder as fine as dust and threw the dust into a stream that flowed down the mountain.

[22]You also made the LORD angry at Taberah, at Massah and at Kibroth Hattaavah.

[23]And when the LORD sent you out from Kadesh Barnea, he said, "Go up and take possession of the land I have given you." But you rebelled against the command of the LORD your God. You did not trust him or obey him. [24]You have been rebellious against the LORD ever since I have known you.

[25]I lay prostrate before the LORD those forty days and forty nights because the LORD had said he would destroy you. [26]I prayed to the LORD and said, "O Sovereign LORD, do not destroy your people, your own inheritance that you redeemed by your great power and brought out of Egypt with a mighty hand. [27]Remember your servants Abraham, Isaac and Jacob. Overlook the stubbornness of this people, their wickedness and their sin. [28]Otherwise, the country from which you brought us will say, 'Because the LORD was not able to take them into the land he had promised them, and because he hated them, he brought them out to put them to death in the desert.' [29]But they are your people, your inheritance that

---

[a]15 Or *And I had the two tablets of the covenant with me, one in each hand*

you brought out by your great power and your outstretched arm."

Tablets Like the First Ones

10 At that time the LORD said to me, "Chisel out two stone tablets like the first ones and come up to me on the mountain. Also make a wooden chest.[a] 2I will write on the tablets the words that were on the first tablets, which you broke. Then you are to put them in the chest."

3So I made the ark out of acacia wood and chiseled out two stone tablets like the first ones, and I went up on the mountain with the two tablets in my hands. 4The LORD wrote on these tablets what he had written before, the Ten Commandments he had proclaimed to you on the mountain, out of the fire, on the day of the assembly. And the LORD gave them to me. 5Then I came back down the mountain and put the tablets in the ark I had made, as the LORD commanded me, and they are there now.

6(The Israelites traveled from the wells of the Jaakanites to Moserah. There Aaron died and was buried, and Eleazar his son succeeded him as priest. 7From there they traveled to Gudgodah and on to Jotbathah, a land with streams of water. 8At that time the LORD set apart the tribe of Levi to carry the ark of the covenant of the LORD, to stand before the LORD to minister and to pronounce blessings in his name, as they still do today. 9That is why the Levites have no share or inheritance among their brothers; the LORD is their inheritance, as the LORD your God told them.)

10Now I had stayed on the mountain forty days and nights, as I did the first time, and the LORD listened to me at this time also. It was not his will to destroy you. 11"Go," the LORD said to me, "and lead the people on their way, so that they may enter and possess the land that I swore to their fathers to give them."

Fear the LORD

12And now, O Israel, what does the LORD your God ask of you but to fear the LORD your God, to walk in all his ways, to love him, to serve the LORD your God with all your heart and with all your soul, 13and to observe the LORD's commands and decrees that I am giving you today for your own good?

14To the LORD your God belong the heavens, even the highest heavens, the earth and everything in it. 15Yet the LORD set his affection on your forefathers and loved them, and he chose you, their descendants, above all the nations, as it is today. 16Circumcise your hearts, therefore, and do not be stiff-necked any longer. 17For the LORD your God is God of gods and Lord of lords, the great God, mighty and awesome, who shows no partiality and accepts no bribes. 18He defends the cause of the fatherless and the widow, and loves the alien, giving him food and clothing. 19And you are to love those who are aliens, for you yourselves were aliens in Egypt. 20Fear the LORD your God and serve him. Hold fast to him and take your oaths in his name. 21He is your praise; he is your God, who performed for you those great and awesome wonders you saw with your own eyes. 22Your forefathers who went down into Egypt were seventy in all, and now the LORD your God has made you as numerous as the stars in the sky.

Love and Obey the LORD

11 Love the LORD your God and keep his requirements, his decrees, his laws and his commands always. 2Remember today that your children were not the ones who saw and experienced the discipline of the LORD your God: his majesty, his mighty hand, his outstretched arm; 3the signs he performed and the things he did in the heart of Egypt, both to Pharaoh king of Egypt and to his whole country; 4what he did to the

---

a1 That is, an ark

Egyptian army, to its horses and chariots, how he overwhelmed them with the waters of the Red Sea[a] as they were pursuing you, and how the LORD brought lasting ruin on them. [5]It was not your children who saw what he did for you in the desert until you arrived at this place, [6]and what he did to Dathan and Abiram, sons of Eliab the Reubenite, when the earth opened its mouth right in the middle of all Israel and swallowed them up with their households, their tents and every living thing that belonged to them. [7]But it was your own eyes that saw all these great things the LORD has done.

[8]Observe therefore all the commands I am giving you today, so that you may have the strength to go in and take over the land that you are crossing the Jordan to possess, [9]and so that you may live long in the land that the LORD swore to your forefathers to give to them and their descendants, a land flowing with milk and honey. [10]The land you are entering to take over is not like the land of Egypt, from which you have come, where you planted your seed and irrigated it by foot as in a vegetable garden. [11]But the land you are crossing the Jordan to take possession of is a land of mountains and valleys that drinks rain from heaven. [12]It is a land the LORD your God cares for; the eyes of the LORD your God are continually on it from the beginning of the year to its end.

[13]So if you faithfully obey the commands I am giving you today—to love the LORD your God and to serve him with all your heart and with all your soul— [14]then I will send rain on your land in its season, both autumn and spring rains, so that you may gather in your grain, new wine and oil. [15]I will provide grass in the fields for your cattle, and you will eat and be satisfied.

[16]Be careful, or you will be enticed to turn away and worship other gods and bow down to them. [17]Then the LORD's anger will burn against you, and he will shut the heavens so that it will not rain and the ground will yield no produce, and you will soon perish from the good land the LORD is giving you. [18]Fix these words of mine in your hearts and minds; tie them as symbols on your hands and bind them on your foreheads. [19]Teach them to your children, talking about them when you sit at home and when you walk along the road, when you lie down and when you get up. [20]Write them on the doorframes of your houses and on your gates, [21]so that your days and the days of your children may be many in the land that the LORD swore to give your forefathers, as many as the days that the heavens are above the earth.

[22]If you carefully observe all these commands I am giving you to follow—to love the LORD your God, to walk in all his ways and to hold fast to him— [23]then the LORD will drive out all these nations before you, and you will dispossess nations larger and stronger than you. [24]Every place where you set your foot will be yours: Your territory will extend from the desert to Lebanon, and from the Euphrates River to the western sea.[b] [25]No man will be able to stand against you. The LORD your God, as he promised you, will put the terror and fear of you on the whole land, wherever you go.

[26]See, I am setting before you today a blessing and a curse— [27]the blessing if you obey the commands of the LORD your God that I am giving you today; [28]the curse if you disobey the commands of the LORD your God and turn from the way that I command you today by following other gods, which you have not known. [29]When the LORD your God has brought you into the land you are entering to possess, you are to proclaim on Mount Gerizim the blessings, and on Mount Ebal the curses. [30]As you know, these mountains are across the Jordan, west of the

a4 Hebrew *Yam Suph*; that is, Sea of Reeds   b24 That is, the Mediterranean

road,[a] toward the setting sun, near the great trees of Moreh, in the territory of those Canaanites living in the Arabah in the vicinity of Gilgal. ³¹You are about to cross the Jordan to enter and take possession of the land the LORD your God is giving you. When you have taken it over and are living there, ³²be sure that you obey all the decrees and laws I am setting before you today.

The One Place of Worship

12 These are the decrees and laws you must be careful to follow in the land that the LORD, the God of your fathers, has given you to possess—as long as you live in the land. ²Destroy completely all the places on the high mountains and on the hills and under every spreading tree where the nations you are dispossessing worship their gods. ³Break down their altars, smash their sacred stones and burn their Asherah poles in the fire; cut down the idols of their gods and wipe out their names from those places.

⁴You must not worship the LORD your God in their way. ⁵But you are to seek the place the LORD your God will choose from among all your tribes to put his Name there for his dwelling. To that place you must go; ⁶there bring your burnt offerings and sacrifices, your tithes and special gifts, what you have vowed to give and your freewill offerings, and the firstborn of your herds and flocks. ⁷There, in the presence of the LORD your God, you and your families shall eat and shall rejoice in everything you have put your hand to, because the LORD your God has blessed you.

⁸You are not to do as we do here today, everyone as he sees fit, ⁹since you have not yet reached the resting place and the inheritance the LORD your God is giving you. ¹⁰But you will cross the Jordan and settle in the land the LORD your God is giving you as an inheritance, and he will give you rest from all your enemies around you so

that you will live in safety. ¹¹Then to the place the LORD your God will choose as a dwelling for his Name—there you are to bring everything I command you: your burnt offerings and sacrifices, your tithes and special gifts, and all the choice possessions you have vowed to the LORD. ¹²And there rejoice before the LORD your God, you, your sons and daughters, your menservants and maidservants, and the Levites from your towns, who have no allotment or inheritance of their own. ¹³Be careful not to sacrifice your burnt offerings anywhere you please. ¹⁴Offer them only at the place the LORD will choose in one of your tribes, and there observe everything I command you.

¹⁵Nevertheless, you may slaughter your animals in any of your towns and eat as much of the meat as you want, as if it were gazelle or deer, according to the blessing the LORD your God gives you. Both the ceremonially unclean and the clean may eat it. ¹⁶But you must not eat the blood; pour it out on the ground like water. ¹⁷You must not eat in your own towns the tithe of your grain and new wine and oil, or the firstborn of your herds and flocks, or whatever you have vowed to give, or your freewill offerings or special gifts. ¹⁸Instead, you are to eat them in the presence of the LORD your God at the place the LORD your God will choose—you, your sons and daughters, your menservants and maidservants, and the Levites from your towns—and you are to rejoice before the LORD your God in everything you put your hand to. ¹⁹Be careful not to neglect the Levites as long as you live in your land.

²⁰When the LORD your God has enlarged your territory as he promised you, and you crave meat and say, "I would like some meat," then you may eat as much of it as you want. ²¹If the place where the LORD your God chooses to put his Name is too far away from you, you may slaughter animals from the herds and flocks the

LORD has given you, as I have commanded you, and in your own towns you may eat as much of them as you want. ²²Eat them as you would gazelle or deer. Both the ceremonially unclean and the clean may eat. ²³But be sure you do not eat the blood, because the blood is the life, and you must not eat the life with the meat. ²⁴You must not eat the blood; pour it out on the ground like water. ²⁵Do not eat it, so that it may go well with you and your children after you, because you will be doing what is right in the eyes of the LORD.

²⁶But take your consecrated things and whatever you have vowed to give, and go to the place the LORD will choose. ²⁷Present your burnt offerings on the altar of the LORD your God, both the meat and the blood. The blood of your sacrifices must be poured beside the altar of the LORD your God, but you may eat the meat. ²⁸Be careful to obey all these regulations I am giving you, so that it may always go well with you and your children after you, because you will be doing what is good and right in the eyes of the LORD your God.

²⁹The LORD your God will cut off before you the nations you are about to invade and dispossess. But when you have driven them out and settled in their land, ³⁰and after they have been destroyed before you, be careful not to be ensnared by inquiring about their gods, saying, "How do these nations serve their gods? We will do the same." ³¹You must not worship the LORD your God in their way, because in worshiping their gods, they do all kinds of detestable things the LORD hates. They even burn their sons and daughters in the fire as sacrifices to their gods.

³²See that you do all I command you; do not add to it or take away from it.

Worshiping Other Gods

13 If a prophet, or one who foretells by dreams, appears among you and announces to you a miraculous sign or wonder, ²and if the sign or wonder of which he has spoken takes place, and he says, "Let us follow other gods" (gods you have not known) "and let us worship them," ³you must not listen to the words of that prophet or dreamer. The LORD your God is testing you to find out whether you love him with all your heart and with all your soul. ⁴It is the LORD your God you must follow, and him you must revere. Keep his commands and obey him; serve him and hold fast to him. ⁵That prophet or dreamer must be put to death, because he preached rebellion against the LORD your God, who brought you out of Egypt and redeemed you from the land of slavery; he has tried to turn you from the way the LORD your God commanded you to follow. You must purge the evil from among you.

⁶If your very own brother, or your son or daughter, or the wife you love, or your closest friend secretly entices you, saying, "Let us go and worship other gods" (gods that neither you nor your fathers have known, ⁷gods of the peoples around you, whether near or far, from one end of the land to the other), ⁸do not yield to him or listen to him. Show him no pity. Do not spare him or shield him. ⁹You must certainly put him to death. Your hand must be the first in putting him to death, and then the hands of all the people. ¹⁰Stone him to death, because he tried to turn you away from the LORD your God, who brought you out of Egypt, out of the land of slavery. ¹¹Then all Israel will hear and be afraid, and no one among you will do such an evil thing again.

¹²If you hear it said about one of the towns the LORD your God is giving you to live in ¹³that wicked men have arisen among you and have led the people of their town astray, saying, "Let us go and worship other gods" (gods you have not known), ¹⁴then you must inquire, probe and investigate it thoroughly. And if it is true and it has been proved that this detestable thing has been done among you, ¹⁵you must certainly put to the

sword all who live in that town. Destroy it completely,[a] both its people and its livestock. [16]Gather all the plunder of the town into the middle of the public square and completely burn the town and all its plunder as a whole burnt offering to the LORD your God. It is to remain a ruin forever, never to be rebuilt. [17]None of those condemned things[a] shall be found in your hands, so that the LORD will turn from his fierce anger; he will show you mercy, have compassion on you, and increase your numbers, as he promised on oath to your forefathers, [18]because you obey the LORD your God, keeping all his commands that I am giving you today and doing what is right in his eyes.

Clean and Unclean Food

14 You are the children of the LORD your God. Do not cut yourselves or shave the front of your heads for the dead, [2]for you are a people holy to the LORD your God. Out of all the peoples on the face of the earth, the LORD has chosen you to be his treasured possession.

[3]Do not eat any detestable thing. [4]These are the animals you may eat: the ox, the sheep, the goat, [5]the deer, the gazelle, the roe deer, the wild goat, the ibex, the antelope and the mountain sheep.[b] [6]You may eat any animal that has a split hoof divided in two and that chews the cud. [7]However, of those that chew the cud or that have a split hoof completely divided you may not eat the camel, the rabbit or the coney.[c] Although they chew the cud, they do not have a split hoof; they are ceremonially unclean for you. [8]The pig is also unclean; although it has a split hoof, it does not chew the cud. You are not to eat their meat or touch their carcasses.

[9]Of all the creatures living in the water, you may eat any that has fins and scales. [10]But anything that does not have fins and scales you may not eat; for you it is unclean.

[11]You may eat any clean bird. [12]But these you may not eat: the eagle, the vulture, the black vulture, [13]the red kite, the black kite, any kind of falcon, [14]any kind of raven, [15]the horned owl, the screech owl, the gull, any kind of hawk, [16]the little owl, the great owl, the white owl, [17]the desert owl, the osprey, the cormorant, [18]the stork, any kind of heron, the hoopoe and the bat.

[19]All flying insects that swarm are unclean to you; do not eat them. [20]But any winged creature that is clean you may eat.

[21]Do not eat anything you find already dead. You may give it to an alien living in any of your towns, and he may eat it, or you may sell it to a foreigner. But you are a people holy to the LORD your God.

Do not cook a young goat in its mother's milk.

Tithes

[22]Be sure to set aside a tenth of all that your fields produce each year. [23]Eat the tithe of your grain, new wine and oil, and the firstborn of your herds and flocks in the presence of the LORD your God at the place he will choose as a dwelling for his Name, so that you may learn to revere the LORD your God always. [24]But if that place is too distant and you have been blessed by the LORD your God and cannot carry your tithe (because the place where the LORD will choose to put his Name is so far away), [25]then exchange your tithe for silver, and take the silver with you and go to the place the LORD your God will choose. [26]Use the silver to buy whatever you like: cattle, sheep, wine or other fermented drink, or anything you wish. Then you and your household shall eat there in the presence of the LORD your God and rejoice. [27]And do not neglect the Levites living in your towns, for they

---

[a]15,17 The Hebrew term refers to the irrevocable giving over of things or persons to the LORD, often by totally destroying them.   [b]5 The precise identification of some of the birds and animals in this chapter is uncertain.   [c]7 That is, the hyrax or rock badger

have no allotment or inheritance of their own.

²⁸At the end of every three years, bring all the tithes of that year's produce and store it in your towns, ²⁹so that the Levites (who have no allotment or inheritance of their own) and the aliens, the fatherless and the widows who live in your towns may come and eat and be satisfied, and so that the LORD your God may bless you in all the work of your hands.

The Year for Canceling Debts

15 At the end of every seven years you must cancel debts. ²This is how it is to be done: Every creditor shall cancel the loan he has made to his fellow Israelite. He shall not require payment from his fellow Israelite or brother, because the LORD's time for canceling debts has been proclaimed. ³You may require payment from a foreigner, but you must cancel any debt your brother owes you. ⁴However, there should be no poor among you, for in the land the LORD your God is giving you to possess as your inheritance, he will richly bless you, ⁵if only you fully obey the LORD your God and are careful to follow all these commands I am giving you today. ⁶For the LORD your God will bless you as he has promised, and you will lend to many nations but will borrow from none. You will rule over many nations but none will rule over you.

⁷If there is a poor man among your brothers in any of the towns of the land that the LORD your God is giving you, do not be hardhearted or tightfisted toward your poor brother. ⁸Rather be openhanded and freely lend him whatever he needs. ⁹Be careful not to harbor this wicked thought: "The seventh year, the year for canceling debts, is near," so that you do not show ill will toward your needy brother and give him nothing. He may then appeal to the LORD against you, and you will be found guilty of sin. ¹⁰Give generously to him and do so without a grudging heart; then because of this the LORD your God will bless you in all your work and in

everything you put your hand to. ¹¹There will always be poor people in the land. Therefore I command you to be openhanded toward your brothers and toward the poor and needy in your land.

Freeing Servants

¹²If a fellow Hebrew, a man or a woman, sells himself to you and serves you six years, in the seventh year you must let him go free. ¹³And when you release him, do not send him away empty-handed. ¹⁴Supply him liberally from your flock, your threshing floor and your winepress. Give to him as the LORD your God has blessed you. ¹⁵Remember that you were slaves in Egypt and the LORD your God redeemed you. That is why I give you this command today.

¹⁶But if your servant says to you, "I do not want to leave you," because he loves you and your family and is well off with you, ¹⁷then take an awl and push it through his ear lobe into the door, and he will become your servant for life. Do the same for your maidservant.

¹⁸Do not consider it a hardship to set your servant free, because his service to you these six years has been worth twice as much as that of a hired hand. And the LORD your God will bless you in everything you do.

The Firstborn Animals

¹⁹Set apart for the LORD your God every firstborn male of your herds and flocks. Do not put the firstborn of your oxen to work, and do not shear the firstborn of your sheep. ²⁰Each year you and your family are to eat them in the presence of the LORD your God at the place he will choose. ²¹If an animal has a defect, is lame or blind, or has any serious flaw, you must not sacrifice it to the LORD your God. ²²You are to eat it in your own towns. Both the ceremonially unclean and the clean may eat it, as if it were gazelle or deer. ²³But you must not eat the blood; pour it out on the ground like water.

Passover

16 Observe the month of Abib and celebrate the Passover of the LORD your God, because in the month of Abib he brought you out of Egypt by night. ²Sacrifice as the Passover to the LORD your God an animal from your flock or herd at the place the LORD will choose as a dwelling for his Name. ³Do not eat it with bread made with yeast, but for seven days eat unleavened bread, the bread of affliction, because you left Egypt in haste—so that all the days of your life you may remember the time of your departure from Egypt. ⁴Let no yeast be found in your possession in all your land for seven days. Do not let any of the meat you sacrifice on the evening of the first day remain until morning.

⁵You must not sacrifice the Passover in any town the LORD your God gives you ⁶except in the place he will choose as a dwelling for his Name. There you must sacrifice the Passover in the evening, when the sun goes down, on the anniversary*ᵃ* of your departure from Egypt. ⁷Roast it and eat it at the place the LORD your God will choose. Then in the morning return to your tents. ⁸For six days eat unleavened bread and on the seventh day hold an assembly to the LORD your God and do no work.

Feast of Weeks

⁹Count off seven weeks from the time you begin to put the sickle to the standing grain. ¹⁰Then celebrate the Feast of Weeks to the LORD your God by giving a freewill offering in proportion to the blessings the LORD your God has given you. ¹¹And rejoice before the LORD your God at the place he will choose as a dwelling for his Name—you, your sons and daughters, your menservants and maidservants, the Levites in your towns, and the aliens, the fatherless and the widows living among you. ¹²Remember that you were slaves in Egypt, and follow carefully these decrees.

Feast of Tabernacles

¹³Celebrate the Feast of Tabernacles for seven days after you have gathered the produce of your threshing floor and your winepress. ¹⁴Be joyful at your Feast—you, your sons and daughters, your menservants and maidservants, and the Levites, the aliens, the fatherless and the widows who live in your towns. ¹⁵For seven days celebrate the Feast to the LORD your God at the place the LORD will choose. For the LORD your God will bless you in all your harvest and in all the work of your hands, and your joy will be complete.

¹⁶Three times a year all your men must appear before the LORD your God at the place he will choose: at the Feast of Unleavened Bread, the Feast of Weeks and the Feast of Tabernacles. No man should appear before the LORD empty-handed: ¹⁷Each of you must bring a gift in proportion to the way the LORD your God has blessed you.

Judges

¹⁸Appoint judges and officials for each of your tribes in every town the LORD your God is giving you, and they shall judge the people fairly. ¹⁹Do not pervert justice or show partiality. Do not accept a bribe, for a bribe blinds the eyes of the wise and twists the words of the righteous. ²⁰Follow justice and justice alone, so that you may live and possess the land the LORD your God is giving you.

Worshiping Other Gods

²¹Do not set up any wooden Asherah pole*ᵇ* beside the altar you build to the LORD your God, ²²and do not erect a sacred stone, for these the LORD your God hates.

17 Do not sacrifice to the LORD your God an ox or a sheep that has any defect or flaw in it, for that would be detestable to him.

ᵃ6 Or *down, at the time of day*　　*ᵇ21* Or *Do not plant any tree dedicated to Asherah*

²If a man or woman living among you in one of the towns the Lord gives you is found doing evil in the eyes of the Lord your God in violation of his covenant, ³and contrary to my command has worshiped other gods, bowing down to them or to the sun or the moon or the stars of the sky, ⁴and this has been brought to your attention, then you must investigate it thoroughly. If it is true and it has been proved that this detestable thing has been done in Israel, ⁵take the man or woman who has done this evil deed to your city gate and stone that person to death. ⁶On the testimony of two or three witnesses a man shall be put to death, but no one shall be put to death on the testimony of only one witness. ⁷The hands of the witnesses must be the first in putting him to death, and then the hands of all the people. You must purge the evil from among you.

Law Courts

⁸If cases come before your courts that are too difficult for you to judge—whether bloodshed, lawsuits or assaults—take them to the place the Lord your God will choose. ⁹Go to the priests, who are Levites, and to the judge who is in office at that time. Inquire of them and they will give you the verdict. ¹⁰You must act according to the decisions they give you at the place the Lord will choose. Be careful to do everything they direct you to do. ¹¹Act according to the law they teach you and the decisions they give you. Do not turn aside from what they tell you, to the right or to the left. ¹²The man who shows contempt for the judge or for the priest who stands ministering there to the Lord your God must be put to death. You must purge the evil from Israel. ¹³All the people will hear and be afraid, and will not be contemptuous again.

The King

¹⁴When you enter the land the Lord your God is giving you and have taken possession of it and settled in it, and you say, "Let us set a king over us like all the nations around us," ¹⁵be sure to appoint over you the king the Lord your God chooses. He must be from among your own brothers. Do not place a foreigner over you, one who is not a brother Israelite. ¹⁶The king, moreover, must not acquire great numbers of horses for himself or make the people return to Egypt to get more of them, for the Lord has told you, "You are not to go back that way again." ¹⁷He must not take many wives, or his heart will be led astray. He must not accumulate large amounts of silver and gold.

¹⁸When he takes the throne of his kingdom, he is to write for himself on a scroll a copy of this law, taken from that of the priests, who are Levites. ¹⁹It is to be with him, and he is to read it all the days of his life so that he may learn to revere the Lord his God and follow carefully all the words of this law and these decrees ²⁰and not consider himself better than his brothers and turn from the law to the right or to the left. Then he and his descendants will reign a long time over his kingdom in Israel.

Offerings for Priests and Levites

18 The priests, who are Levites—indeed the whole tribe of Levi—are to have no allotment or inheritance with Israel. They shall live on the offerings made to the Lord by fire, for that is their inheritance. ²They shall have no inheritance among their brothers; the Lord is their inheritance, as he promised them.

³This is the share due the priests from the people who sacrifice a bull or a sheep: the shoulder, the jowls and the inner parts. ⁴You are to give them the firstfruits of your grain, new wine and oil, and the first wool from the shearing of your sheep, ⁵for the Lord your God has chosen them and their descendants out of all your tribes to stand and minister in the Lord's name always.

⁶If a Levite moves from one of your towns anywhere in Israel where he is living, and comes in all earnestness to

the place the LORD will choose, [7]he may minister in the name of the LORD his God like all his fellow Levites who serve there in the presence of the LORD. [8]He is to share equally in their benefits, even though he has received money from the sale of family possessions.

Detestable Practices

[9]When you enter the land the LORD your God is giving you, do not learn to imitate the detestable ways of the nations there. [10]Let no one be found among you who sacrifices his son or daughter in[a] the fire, who practices divination or sorcery, interprets omens, engages in witchcraft, [11]or casts spells, or who is a medium or spiritist or who consults the dead. [12]Anyone who does these things is detestable to the LORD, and because of these detestable practices the LORD your God will drive out those nations before you. [13]You must be blameless before the LORD your God.

The Prophet

[14]The nations you will dispossess listen to those who practice sorcery or divination. But as for you, the LORD your God has not permitted you to do so. [15]The LORD your God will raise up for you a prophet like me from among your own brothers. You must listen to him. [16]For this is what you asked of the LORD your God at Horeb on the day of the assembly when you said, "Let us not hear the voice of the LORD our God nor see this great fire anymore, or we will die."

[17]The LORD said to me: "What they say is good. [18]I will raise up for them a prophet like you from among their brothers; I will put my words in his mouth, and he will tell them everything I command him. [19]If anyone does not listen to my words that the prophet speaks in my name, I myself will call him to account. [20]But a prophet who presumes to speak in my name anything I have not commanded him to say, or a prophet who speaks in the name of other gods, must be put to death."

[21]You may say to yourselves, "How can we know when a message has not been spoken by the LORD?" [22]If what a prophet proclaims in the name of the LORD does not take place or come true, that is a message the LORD has not spoken. That prophet has spoken presumptuously. Do not be afraid of him.

Cities of Refuge

19 When the LORD your God has destroyed the nations whose land he is giving you, and when you have driven them out and settled in their towns and houses, [2]then set aside for yourselves three cities centrally located in the land the LORD your God is giving you to possess. [3]Build roads to them and divide into three parts the land the LORD your God is giving you as an inheritance, so that anyone who kills a man may flee there.

[4]This is the rule concerning the man who kills another and flees there to save his life—one who kills his neighbor unintentionally, without malice aforethought. [5]For instance, a man may go into the forest with his neighbor to cut wood, and as he swings his ax to fell a tree, the head may fly off and hit his neighbor and kill him. That man may flee to one of these cities and save his life. [6]Otherwise, the avenger of blood might pursue him in a rage, overtake him if the distance is too great, and kill him even though he is not deserving of death, since he did it to his neighbor without malice aforethought. [7]This is why I command you to set aside for yourselves three cities.

[8]If the LORD your God enlarges your territory, as he promised on oath to your forefathers, and gives you the whole land he promised them, [9]because you carefully follow all these laws I command you today—to love the LORD your God and to walk always in his ways—then you are to set

---

[a]10 Or *who makes his son or daughter pass through*

aside three more cities. ¹⁰Do this so that innocent blood will not be shed in your land, which the LORD your God is giving you as your inheritance, and so that you will not be guilty of bloodshed.

¹¹But if a man hates his neighbor and lies in wait for him, assaults and kills him, and then flees to one of these cities, ¹²the elders of his town shall send for him, bring him back from the city, and hand him over to the avenger of blood to die. ¹³Show him no pity. You must purge from Israel the guilt of shedding innocent blood, so that it may go well with you.

¹⁴Do not move your neighbor's boundary stone set up by your predecessors in the inheritance you receive in the land the LORD your God is giving you to possess.

Witnesses

¹⁵One witness is not enough to convict a man accused of any crime or offense he may have committed. A matter must be established by the testimony of two or three witnesses.

¹⁶If a malicious witness takes the stand to accuse a man of a crime, ¹⁷the two men involved in the dispute must stand in the presence of the LORD before the priests and the judges who are in office at the time. ¹⁸The judges must make a thorough investigation, and if the witness proves to be a liar, giving false testimony against his brother, ¹⁹then do to him as he intended to do to his brother. You must purge the evil from among you. ²⁰The rest of the people will hear of this and be afraid, and never again will such an evil thing be done among you. ²¹Show no pity: life for life, eye for eye, tooth for tooth, hand for hand, foot for foot.

Going to War

20 When you go to war against your enemies and see horses and chariots and an army greater than yours, do not be afraid of them, because the LORD your God, who brought you up out of Egypt, will be with you. ²When you are about to go into battle, the priest shall come forward and address the army. ³He shall say: "Hear, O Israel, today you are going into battle against your enemies. Do not be fainthearted or afraid; do not be terrified or give way to panic before them. ⁴For the LORD your God is the one who goes with you to fight for you against your enemies to give you victory."

⁵The officers shall say to the army: "Has anyone built a new house and not dedicated it? Let him go home, or he may die in battle and someone else may dedicate it. ⁶Has anyone planted a vineyard and not begun to enjoy it? Let him go home, or he may die in battle and someone else enjoy it. ⁷Has anyone become pledged to a woman and not married her? Let him go home, or he may die in battle and someone else marry her." ⁸Then the officers shall add, "Is any man afraid or fainthearted? Let him go home so that his brothers will not become disheartened too." ⁹When the officers have finished speaking to the army, they shall appoint commanders over it.

¹⁰When you march up to attack a city, make its people an offer of peace. ¹¹If they accept and open their gates, all the people in it shall be subject to forced labor and shall work for you. ¹²If they refuse to make peace and they engage you in battle, lay siege to that city. ¹³When the LORD your God delivers it into your hand, put to the sword all the men in it. ¹⁴As for the women, the children, the livestock and everything else in the city, you may take these as plunder for yourselves. And you may use the plunder the LORD your God gives you from your enemies. ¹⁵This is how you are to treat all the cities that are at a distance from you and do not belong to the nations nearby.

¹⁶However, in the cities of the nations the LORD your God is giving you as an inheritance, do not leave alive anything that breathes. ¹⁷Completely

destroy[a] them—the Hittites, Amorites, Canaanites, Perizzites, Hivites and Jebusites—as the LORD your God has commanded you. [18]Otherwise, they will teach you to follow all the detestable things they do in worshiping their gods, and you will sin against the LORD your God.

[19]When you lay siege to a city for a long time, fighting against it to capture it, do not destroy its trees by putting an ax to them, because you can eat their fruit. Do not cut them down. Are the trees of the field people, that you should besiege them?[b] [20]However, you may cut down trees that you know are not fruit trees and use them to build siege works until the city at war with you falls.

Atonement for an Unsolved Murder

21 If a man is found slain, lying in a field in the land the LORD your God is giving you to possess, and it is not known who killed him, [2]your elders and judges shall go out and measure the distance from the body to the neighboring towns. [3]Then the elders of the town nearest the body shall take a heifer that has never been worked and has never worn a yoke [4]and lead her down to a valley that has not been plowed or planted and where there is a flowing stream. There in the valley they are to break the heifer's neck. [5]The priests, the sons of Levi, shall step forward, for the LORD your God has chosen them to minister and to pronounce blessings in the name of the LORD and to decide all cases of dispute and assault. [6]Then all the elders of the town nearest the body shall wash their hands over the heifer whose neck was broken in the valley, [7]and they shall declare: "Our hands did not shed this blood, nor did our eyes see it done. [8]Accept this atonement for your people Israel, whom you have redeemed, O LORD, and do not hold your people guilty of the blood of an innocent

man." And the bloodshed will be atoned for. [9]So you will purge from yourselves the guilt of shedding innocent blood, since you have done what is right in the eyes of the LORD.

Marrying a Captive Woman

[10]When you go to war against your enemies and the LORD your God delivers them into your hands and you take captives, [11]if you notice among the captives a beautiful woman and are attracted to her, you may take her as your wife. [12]Bring her into your home and have her shave her head, trim her nails [13]and put aside the clothes she was wearing when captured. After she has lived in your house and mourned her father and mother for a full month, then you may go to her and be her husband and she shall be your wife. [14]If you are not pleased with her, let her go wherever she wishes. You must not sell her or treat her as a slave, since you have dishonored her.

The Right of the Firstborn

[15]If a man has two wives, and he loves one but not the other, and both bear him sons but the firstborn is the son of the wife he does not love, [16]when he wills his property to his sons, he must not give the rights of the firstborn to the son of the wife he loves in preference to his actual firstborn, the son of the wife he does not love. [17]He must acknowledge the son of his unloved wife as the firstborn by giving him a double share of all he has. That son is the first sign of his father's strength. The right of the firstborn belongs to him.

A Rebellious Son

[18]If a man has a stubborn and rebellious son who does not obey his father and mother and will not listen to them when they discipline him, [19]his father and mother shall take hold of him and bring him to the elders at the

---

[a]17 The Hebrew term refers to the irrevocable giving over of things or persons to the LORD, often by totally destroying them.   [b]19 Or *down to use in the siege, for the fruit trees are for the benefit of man.*

gate of his town. ²⁰They shall say to the elders, "This son of ours is stubborn and rebellious. He will not obey us. He is a profligate and a drunkard." ²¹Then all the men of his town shall stone him to death. You must purge the evil from among you. All Israel will hear of it and be afraid.

Various Laws

²²If a man guilty of a capital offense is put to death and his body is hung on a tree, ²³you must not leave his body on the tree overnight. Be sure to bury him that same day, because anyone who is hung on a tree is under God's curse. You must not desecrate the land the LORD your God is giving you as an inheritance.

22 If you see your brother's ox or sheep straying, do not ignore it but be sure to take it back to him. ²If the brother does not live near you or if you do not know who he is, take it home with you and keep it until he comes looking for it. Then give it back to him. ³Do the same if you find your brother's donkey or his cloak or anything he loses. Do not ignore it.

⁴If you see your brother's donkey or his ox fallen on the road, do not ignore it. Help him get it to its feet.

⁵A woman must not wear men's clothing, nor a man wear women's clothing, for the LORD your God detests anyone who does this.

⁶If you come across a bird's nest beside the road, either in a tree or on the ground, and the mother is sitting on the young or on the eggs, do not take the mother with the young. ⁷You may take the young, but be sure to let the mother go, so that it may go well with you and you may have a long life.

⁸When you build a new house, make a parapet around your roof so that you may not bring the guilt of bloodshed on your house if someone falls from the roof.

⁹Do not plant two kinds of seed in your vineyard; if you do, not only the crops you plant but also the fruit of the vineyard will be defiled.^a

¹⁰Do not plow with an ox and a donkey yoked together.

¹¹Do not wear clothes of wool and linen woven together.

¹²Make tassels on the four corners of the cloak you wear.

Marriage Violations

¹³If a man takes a wife and, after lying with her, dislikes her ¹⁴and slanders her and gives her a bad name, saying, "I married this woman, but when I approached her, I did not find proof of her virginity," ¹⁵then the girl's father and mother shall bring proof that she was a virgin to the town elders at the gate. ¹⁶The girl's father will say to the elders, "I gave my daughter in marriage to this man, but he dislikes her. ¹⁷Now he has slandered her and said, 'I did not find your daughter to be a virgin.' But here is the proof of my daughter's virginity." Then her parents shall display the cloth before the elders of the town, ¹⁸and the elders shall take the man and punish him. ¹⁹They shall fine him a hundred shekels of silver^b and give them to the girl's father, because this man has given an Israelite virgin a bad name. She shall continue to be his wife; he must not divorce her as long as he lives.

²⁰If, however, the charge is true and no proof of the girl's virginity can be found, ²¹she shall be brought to the door of her father's house and there the men of her town shall stone her to death. She has done a disgraceful thing in Israel by being promiscuous while still in her father's house. You must purge the evil from among you.

²²If a man is found sleeping with another man's wife, both the man who slept with her and the woman must die. You must purge the evil from Israel.

²³If a man happens to meet in a town a virgin pledged to be married and he sleeps with her, ²⁴you shall take both of them to the gate of that town and stone them to death—the girl because she was in a town and

---

^a9 Or *be forfeited to the sanctuary*   ^b19 That is, about 2 1/2 pounds (about 1 kilogram)

did not scream for help, and the man because he violated another man's wife. You must purge the evil from among you.

²⁵But if out in the country a man happens to meet a girl pledged to be married and rapes her, only the man who has done this shall die. ²⁶Do nothing to the girl; she has committed no sin deserving death. This case is like that of someone who attacks and murders his neighbor, ²⁷for the man found the girl out in the country, and though the betrothed girl screamed, there was no one to rescue her.

²⁸If a man happens to meet a virgin who is not pledged to be married and rapes her and they are discovered, ²⁹he shall pay the girl's father fifty shekels of silver.^a He must marry the girl, for he has violated her. He can never divorce her as long as he lives.

³⁰A man is not to marry his father's wife; he must not dishonor his father's bed.

Exclusion From the Assembly

23 No one who has been emasculated by crushing or cutting may enter the assembly of the LORD.

²No one born of a forbidden marriage^b nor any of his descendants may enter the assembly of the LORD, even down to the tenth generation.

³No Ammonite or Moabite or any of his descendants may enter the assembly of the LORD, even down to the tenth generation. ⁴For they did not come to meet you with bread and water on your way when you came out of Egypt, and they hired Balaam son of Beor from Pethor in Aram Naharaim^c to pronounce a curse on you. ⁵However, the LORD your God would not listen to Balaam but turned the curse into a blessing for you, because the LORD your God loves you. ⁶Do not seek a treaty of friendship with them as long as you live.

⁷Do not abhor an Edomite, for he is your brother. Do not abhor an Egyptian, because you lived as an alien in his country. ⁸The third generation of children born to them may enter the assembly of the LORD.

Uncleanness in the Camp

⁹When you are encamped against your enemies, keep away from everything impure. ¹⁰If one of your men is unclean because of a nocturnal emission, he is to go outside the camp and stay there. ¹¹But as evening approaches he is to wash himself, and at sunset he may return to the camp.

¹²Designate a place outside the camp where you can go to relieve yourself. ¹³As part of your equipment have something to dig with, and when you relieve yourself, dig a hole and cover up your excrement. ¹⁴For the LORD your God moves about in your camp to protect you and to deliver your enemies to you. Your camp must be holy, so that he will not see among you anything indecent and turn away from you.

Miscellaneous Laws

¹⁵If a slave has taken refuge with you, do not hand him over to his master. ¹⁶Let him live among you wherever he likes and in whatever town he chooses. Do not oppress him.

¹⁷No Israelite man or woman is to become a shrine prostitute. ¹⁸You must not bring the earnings of a female prostitute or of a male prostitute^d into the house of the LORD your God to pay any vow, because the LORD your God detests them both.

¹⁹Do not charge your brother interest, whether on money or food or anything else that may earn interest. ²⁰You may charge a foreigner interest, but not a brother Israelite, so that the LORD your God may bless you in everything you put your hand to in the land you are entering to possess.

²¹If you make a vow to the LORD your God, do not be slow to pay it, for the LORD your God will certainly demand it of you and you will be guilty of sin. ²²But if you refrain from mak-

---

^a29 That is, about 1 1/4 pounds (about 0.6 kilogram) is, Northwest Mesopotamia   ^d18 Hebrew *of a dog*   ^b2 Or *one of illegitimate birth*   ^c4 That

ing a vow, you will not be guilty. ²³Whatever your lips utter you must be sure to do, because you made your vow freely to the LORD your God with your own mouth.

²⁴If you enter your neighbor's vineyard, you may eat all the grapes you want, but do not put any in your basket. ²⁵If you enter your neighbor's grainfield, you may pick kernels with your hands, but you must not put a sickle to his standing grain.

24 If a man marries a woman who becomes displeasing to him because he finds something indecent about her, and he writes her a certificate of divorce, gives it to her and sends her from his house, ²and if after she leaves his house she becomes the wife of another man, ³and her second husband dislikes her and writes her a certificate of divorce, gives it to her and sends her from his house, or if he dies, ⁴then her first husband, who divorced her, is not allowed to marry her again after she has been defiled. That would be detestable in the eyes of the LORD. Do not bring sin upon the land the LORD your God is giving you as an inheritance.

⁵If a man has recently married, he must not be sent to war or have any other duty laid on him. For one year he is to be free to stay at home and bring happiness to the wife he has married.

⁶Do not take a pair of millstones—not even the upper one—as security for a debt, because that would be taking a man's livelihood as security.

⁷If a man is caught kidnapping one of his brother Israelites and treats him as a slave or sells him, the kidnapper must die. You must purge the evil from among you.

⁸In cases of leprous*a* diseases be very careful to do exactly as the priests, who are Levites, instruct you. You must follow carefully what I have commanded them. ⁹Remember what the LORD your God did to Miriam along the way after you came out of Egypt.

¹⁰When you make a loan of any kind to your neighbor, do not go into his house to get what he is offering as a pledge. ¹¹Stay outside and let the man to whom you are making the loan bring the pledge out to you. ¹²If the man is poor, do not go to sleep with his pledge in your possession. ¹³Return his cloak to him by sunset so that he may sleep in it. Then he will thank you, and it will be regarded as a righteous act in the sight of the LORD your God.

¹⁴Do not take advantage of a hired man who is poor and needy, whether he is a brother Israelite or an alien living in one of your towns. ¹⁵Pay him his wages each day before sunset, because he is poor and is counting on it. Otherwise he may cry to the LORD against you, and you will be guilty of sin.

¹⁶Fathers shall not be put to death for their children, nor children put to death for their fathers; each is to die for his own sin.

¹⁷Do not deprive the alien or the fatherless of justice, or take the cloak of the widow as a pledge. ¹⁸Remember that you were slaves in Egypt and the LORD your God redeemed you from there. That is why I command you to do this.

¹⁹When you are harvesting in your field and you overlook a sheaf, do not go back to get it. Leave it for the alien, the fatherless and the widow, so that the LORD your God may bless you in all the work of your hands. ²⁰When you beat the olives from your trees, do not go over the branches a second time. Leave what remains for the alien, the fatherless and the widow. ²¹When you harvest the grapes in your vineyard, do not go over the vines again. Leave what remains for the alien, the fatherless and the widow. ²²Remember that you were slaves in Egypt. That is why I command you to do this.

25 When men have a dispute, they are to take it to court and the judges will decide the case, ac-

---

a8 The Hebrew word was used for various diseases affecting the skin—not necessarily leprosy.

quitting the innocent and condemning the guilty. ²If the guilty man deserves to be beaten, the judge shall make him lie down and have him flogged in his presence with the number of lashes his crime deserves, ³but he must not give him more than forty lashes. If he is flogged more than that, your brother will be degraded in your eyes.

⁴Do not muzzle an ox while it is treading out the grain.

⁵If brothers are living together and one of them dies without a son, his widow must not marry outside the family. Her husband's brother shall take her and marry her and fulfill the duty of a brother-in-law to her. ⁶The first son she bears shall carry on the name of the dead brother so that his name will not be blotted out from Israel.

⁷However, if a man does not want to marry his brother's wife, she shall go to the elders at the town gate and say, "My husband's brother refuses to carry on his brother's name in Israel. He will not fulfill the duty of a broth-

VERSE: AUTHOR: PASSAGE:
Deuteronomy 24:22   Charles L. Allen   Deuteronomy 24:9–22

We Remember

Remembering keeps you *you*. One of the strengths of life is remembering some very difficult experience and remembering how we survived it. Out of the struggles of our lives have evolved strength, understanding, and more loving persons. We do not need to *live* in our unhappy memories, but occasionally it is good to make a short visit back to those times.

Most important, remembering is our road to faith in God. God is the God of tomorrow just as he is the God of yesterday. We cannot see tomorrow, but we can see yesterday. It truly strengthens our faith as we remember how we were forced to go through some "valley of the shadow" and remember as the psalmist says, "You are with me." Faith faces today and tomorrow but faith is built by the experiences of yesterday.

Most important: we do know that *God still loves us*, in spite of some failures, or shame, or sin of the past.

ADDITIONAL SCRIPTURE READINGS
Psalm 23; Hebrews 13:1–8

Go to page 245 for your next devotional reading.

er-in-law to me." ⁸Then the elders of his town shall summon him and talk to him. If he persists in saying, "I do not want to marry her," ⁹his brother's widow shall go up to him in the presence of the elders, take off one of his sandals, spit in his face and say, "This is what is done to the man who will not build up his brother's family line." ¹⁰That man's line shall be known in Israel as The Family of the Unsandaled.

¹¹If two men are fighting and the wife of one of them comes to rescue her husband from his assailant, and she reaches out and seizes him by his private parts, ¹²you shall cut off her hand. Show her no pity.

¹³Do not have two differing weights in your bag—one heavy, one light. ¹⁴Do not have two differing measures in your house—one large, one small. ¹⁵You must have accurate and honest weights and measures, so that you may live long in the land the LORD your God is giving you. ¹⁶For the LORD your God detests anyone who does these things, anyone who deals dishonestly.

¹⁷Remember what the Amalekites did to you along the way when you came out of Egypt. ¹⁸When you were weary and worn out, they met you on your journey and cut off all who were lagging behind; they had no fear of God. ¹⁹When the LORD your God gives you rest from all the enemies around you in the land he is giving you to possess as an inheritance, you shall blot out the memory of Amalek from under heaven. Do not forget!

Firstfruits and Tithes

26 When you have entered the land the LORD your God is giving you as an inheritance and have taken possession of it and settled in it, ²take some of the firstfruits of all that you produce from the soil of the land the LORD your God is giving you and put them in a basket. Then go to the place the LORD your God will choose as a dwelling for his Name ³and say to the priest in office at the time, "I declare today to the LORD your God

that I have come to the land the LORD swore to our forefathers to give us." ⁴The priest shall take the basket from your hands and set it down in front of the altar of the LORD your God. ⁵Then you shall declare before the LORD your God: "My father was a wandering Aramean, and he went down into Egypt with a few people and lived there and became a great nation, powerful and numerous. ⁶But the Egyptians mistreated us and made us suffer, putting us to hard labor. ⁷Then we cried out to the LORD, the God of our fathers, and the LORD heard our voice and saw our misery, toil and oppression. ⁸So the LORD brought us out of Egypt with a mighty hand and an outstretched arm, with great terror and with miraculous signs and wonders. ⁹He brought us to this place and gave us this land, a land flowing with milk and honey; ¹⁰and now I bring the firstfruits of the soil that you, O LORD, have given me." Place the basket before the LORD your God and bow down before him. ¹¹And you and the Levites and the aliens among you shall rejoice in all the good things the LORD your God has given to you and your household.

¹²When you have finished setting aside a tenth of all your produce in the third year, the year of the tithe, you shall give it to the Levite, the alien, the fatherless and the widow, so that they may eat in your towns and be satisfied. ¹³Then say to the LORD your God: "I have removed from my house the sacred portion and have given it to the Levite, the alien, the fatherless and the widow, according to all you commanded. I have not turned aside from your commands nor have I forgotten any of them. ¹⁴I have not eaten any of the sacred portion while I was in mourning, nor have I removed any of it while I was unclean, nor have I offered any of it to the dead. I have obeyed the LORD my God; I have done everything you commanded me. ¹⁵Look down from heaven, your holy dwelling place, and bless your people Israel and the land you have given us as you prom-

ised on oath to our forefathers, a land flowing with milk and honey."

Follow the Lord's Commands

¹⁶The Lord your God commands you this day to follow these decrees and laws; carefully observe them with all your heart and with all your soul. ¹⁷You have declared this day that the Lord is your God and that you will walk in his ways, that you will keep his decrees, commands and laws, and that you will obey him. ¹⁸And the Lord has declared this day that you are his people, his treasured possession as he promised, and that you are to keep all his commands. ¹⁹He has declared that he will set you in praise, fame and honor high above all the nations he has made and that you will be a people holy to the Lord your God, as he promised.

The Altar on Mount Ebal

27 Moses and the elders of Israel commanded the people: "Keep all these commands that I give you today. ²When you have crossed the Jordan into the land the Lord your God is giving you, set up some large stones and coat them with plaster. ³Write on them all the words of this law when you have crossed over to enter the land the Lord your God is giving you, a land flowing with milk and honey, just as the Lord, the God of your fathers, promised you. ⁴And when you have crossed the Jordan, set up these stones on Mount Ebal, as I command you today, and coat them with plaster. ⁵Build there an altar to the Lord your God, an altar of stones. Do not use any iron tool upon them. ⁶Build the altar of the Lord your God with fieldstones and offer burnt offerings on it to the Lord your God. ⁷Sacrifice fellowship offerings[a] there, eating them and rejoicing in the presence of the Lord your God. ⁸And you shall write very clearly all the words of this law on these stones you have set up."

Curses From Mount Ebal

⁹Then Moses and the priests, who are Levites, said to all Israel, "Be silent, O Israel, and listen! You have now become the people of the Lord your God. ¹⁰Obey the Lord your God and follow his commands and decrees that I give you today."

¹¹On the same day Moses commanded the people:

¹²When you have crossed the Jordan, these tribes shall stand on Mount Gerizim to bless the people: Simeon, Levi, Judah, Issachar, Joseph and Benjamin. ¹³And these tribes shall stand on Mount Ebal to pronounce curses: Reuben, Gad, Asher, Zebulun, Dan and Naphtali.

¹⁴The Levites shall recite to all the people of Israel in a loud voice:

¹⁵"Cursed is the man who carves an image or casts an idol—a thing detestable to the Lord, the work of the craftsman's hands—and sets it up in secret."

Then all the people shall say, "Amen!"

¹⁶"Cursed is the man who dishonors his father or his mother."

Then all the people shall say, "Amen!"

¹⁷"Cursed is the man who moves his neighbor's boundary stone."

Then all the people shall say, "Amen!"

¹⁸"Cursed is the man who leads the blind astray on the road."

Then all the people shall say, "Amen!"

¹⁹"Cursed is the man who withholds justice from the alien, the fatherless or the widow."

Then all the people shall say, "Amen!"

²⁰"Cursed is the man who sleeps with his father's wife, for he dishonors his father's bed."

Then all the people shall say, "Amen!"

²¹"Cursed is the man who has

sexual relations with any animal."

Then all the people shall say,
"Amen!"

²²"Cursed is the man who
sleeps with his sister, the daughter of his father or the daughter
of his mother."

Then all the people shall say,
"Amen!"

²³"Cursed is the man who
sleeps with his mother-in-law."

Then all the people shall say,
"Amen!"

²⁴"Cursed is the man who kills
his neighbor secretly."

Then all the people shall say,
"Amen!"

²⁵"Cursed is the man who accepts a bribe to kill an innocent
person."

Then all the people shall say,
"Amen!"

²⁶"Cursed is the man who
does not uphold the words of
this law by carrying them out."

Then all the people shall say,
"Amen!"

Blessings for Obedience

28 If you fully obey the LORD your
God and carefully follow all
his commands I give you today, the
LORD your God will set you high
above all the nations on earth. ²All
these blessings will come upon you
and accompany you if you obey the
LORD your God:

³You will be blessed in the city
and blessed in the country.

⁴The fruit of your womb will
be blessed, and the crops of your
land and the young of your livestock—the calves of your herds
and the lambs of your flocks.

⁵Your basket and your kneading trough will be blessed.

⁶You will be blessed when you
come in and blessed when you
go out.

⁷The LORD will grant that the enemies who rise up against you will be
defeated before you. They will come

at you from one direction but flee
from you in seven.

⁸The LORD will send a blessing on
your barns and on everything you put
your hand to. The LORD your God will
bless you in the land he is giving you.

⁹The LORD will establish you as his
holy people, as he promised you on
oath, if you keep the commands of the
LORD your God and walk in his ways.
¹⁰Then all the peoples on earth will
see that you are called by the name of
the LORD, and they will fear you. ¹¹The
LORD will grant you abundant prosperity—in the fruit of your womb, the
young of your livestock and the crops
of your ground—in the land he swore
to your forefathers to give you.

¹²The LORD will open the heavens,
the storehouse of his bounty, to send
rain on your land in season and to
bless all the work of your hands. You
will lend to many nations but will
borrow from none. ¹³The LORD will
make you the head, not the tail. If you
pay attention to the commands of the
LORD your God that I give you this
day and carefully follow them, you
will always be at the top, never at the
bottom. ¹⁴Do not turn aside from any
of the commands I give you today, to
the right or to the left, following other
gods and serving them.

Curses for Disobedience

¹⁵However, if you do not obey the
LORD your God and do not carefully
follow all his commands and decrees I
am giving you today, all these curses
will come upon you and overtake
you:

¹⁶You will be cursed in the city
and cursed in the country.

¹⁷Your basket and your kneading trough will be cursed.

¹⁸The fruit of your womb will
be cursed, and the crops of your
land, and the calves of your
herds and the lambs of your
flocks.

¹⁹You will be cursed when you
come in and cursed when you go
out.

²⁰The LORD will send on you curses,

confusion and rebuke in everything you put your hand to, until you are destroyed and come to sudden ruin because of the evil you have done in forsaking him.ᵃ ²¹The Lᴏʀᴅ will plague you with diseases until he has destroyed you from the land you are entering to possess. ²²The Lᴏʀᴅ will strike you with wasting disease, with fever and inflammation, with scorching heat and drought, with blight and mildew, which will plague you until you perish. ²³The sky over your head will be bronze, the ground beneath you iron. ²⁴The Lᴏʀᴅ will turn the rain of your country into dust and powder; it will come down from the skies until you are destroyed.

²⁵The Lᴏʀᴅ will cause you to be defeated before your enemies. You will come at them from one direction but flee from them in seven, and you will become a thing of horror to all the kingdoms on earth. ²⁶Your carcasses will be food for all the birds of the air and the beasts of the earth, and there will be no one to frighten them away. ²⁷The Lᴏʀᴅ will afflict you with the boils of Egypt and with tumors, festering sores and the itch, from which you cannot be cured. ²⁸The Lᴏʀᴅ will afflict you with madness, blindness and confusion of mind. ²⁹At midday you will grope about like a blind man in the dark. You will be unsuccessful in everything you do; day after day you will be oppressed and robbed, with no one to rescue you.

³⁰You will be pledged to be married to a woman, but another will take her and ravish her. You will build a house, but you will not live in it. You will plant a vineyard, but you will not even begin to enjoy its fruit. ³¹Your ox will be slaughtered before your eyes, but you will eat none of it. Your donkey will be forcibly taken from you and will not be returned. Your sheep will be given to your enemies, and no one will rescue them. ³²Your sons and daughters will be given to another nation, and you will wear out your eyes watching for them day after day,

powerless to lift a hand. ³³A people that you do not know will eat what your land and labor produce, and you will have nothing but cruel oppression all your days. ³⁴The sights you see will drive you mad. ³⁵The Lᴏʀᴅ will afflict your knees and legs with painful boils that cannot be cured, spreading from the soles of your feet to the top of your head.

³⁶The Lᴏʀᴅ will drive you and the king you set over you to a nation unknown to you or your fathers. There you will worship other gods, gods of wood and stone. ³⁷You will become a thing of horror and an object of scorn and ridicule to all the nations where the Lᴏʀᴅ will drive you.

³⁸You will sow much seed in the field but you will harvest little, because locusts will devour it. ³⁹You will plant vineyards and cultivate them but you will not drink the wine or gather the grapes, because worms will eat them. ⁴⁰You will have olive trees throughout your country but you will not use the oil, because the olives will drop off. ⁴¹You will have sons and daughters but you will not keep them, because they will go into captivity. ⁴²Swarms of locusts will take over all your trees and the crops of your land.

⁴³The alien who lives among you will rise above you higher and higher, but you will sink lower and lower. ⁴⁴He will lend to you, but you will not lend to him. He will be the head, but you will be the tail.

⁴⁵All these curses will come upon you. They will pursue you and overtake you until you are destroyed, because you did not obey the Lᴏʀᴅ your God and observe the commands and decrees he gave you. ⁴⁶They will be a sign and a wonder to you and your descendants forever. ⁴⁷Because you did not serve the Lᴏʀᴅ your God joyfully and gladly in the time of prosperity, ⁴⁸therefore in hunger and thirst, in nakedness and dire poverty, you will serve the enemies the Lᴏʀᴅ sends against you. He will put an iron

ᵃ20 Hebrew me

yoke on your neck until he has destroyed you.

⁴⁹The LORD will bring a nation against you from far away, from the ends of the earth, like an eagle swooping down, a nation whose language you will not understand, ⁵⁰a fierce-looking nation without respect for the old or pity for the young. ⁵¹They will devour the young of your livestock and the crops of your land until you are destroyed. They will leave you no grain, new wine or oil, nor any calves of your herds or lambs of your flocks until you are ruined. ⁵²They will lay siege to all the cities throughout your land until the high fortified walls in which you trust fall down. They will besiege all the cities throughout the land the LORD your God is giving you.

⁵³Because of the suffering that your enemy will inflict on you during the siege, you will eat the fruit of the womb, the flesh of the sons and daughters the LORD your God has given you. ⁵⁴Even the most gentle and sensitive man among you will have no compassion on his own brother or the wife he loves or his surviving children, ⁵⁵and he will not give to one of them any of the flesh of his children that he is eating. It will be all he has left because of the suffering your enemy will inflict on you during the siege of all your cities. ⁵⁶The most gentle and sensitive woman among you—so sensitive and gentle that she would not venture to touch the ground with the sole of her foot—will begrudge the husband she loves and her own son or daughter ⁵⁷the afterbirth from her womb and the children she bears. For she intends to eat them secretly during the siege and in the distress that your enemy will inflict on you in your cities.

⁵⁸If you do not carefully follow all the words of this law, which are written in this book, and do not revere this glorious and awesome name— the LORD your God— ⁵⁹the LORD will send fearful plagues on you and your descendants, harsh and prolonged disasters, and severe and lingering illnesses. ⁶⁰He will bring upon you all the diseases of Egypt that you dreaded, and they will cling to you. ⁶¹The LORD will also bring on you every kind of sickness and disaster not recorded in this Book of the Law, until you are destroyed. ⁶²You who were as numerous as the stars in the sky will be left but few in number, because you did not obey the LORD your God. ⁶³Just as it pleased the LORD to make you prosper and increase in number, so it will please him to ruin and destroy you. You will be uprooted from the land you are entering to possess.

⁶⁴Then the LORD will scatter you among all nations, from one end of the earth to the other. There you will worship other gods—gods of wood and stone, which neither you nor your fathers have known. ⁶⁵Among those nations you will find no repose, no resting place for the sole of your foot. There the LORD will give you an anxious mind, eyes weary with longing, and a despairing heart. ⁶⁶You will live in constant suspense, filled with dread both night and day, never sure of your life. ⁶⁷In the morning you will say, "If only it were evening!" and in the evening, "If only it were morning!"—because of the terror that will fill your hearts and the sights that your eyes will see. ⁶⁸The LORD will send you back in ships to Egypt on a journey I said you should never make again. There you will offer yourselves for sale to your enemies as male and female slaves, but no one will buy you.

Renewal of the Covenant

29 These are the terms of the covenant the LORD commanded Moses to make with the Israelites in Moab, in addition to the covenant he had made with them at Horeb.

²Moses summoned all the Israelites and said to them:

Your eyes have seen all that the LORD did in Egypt to Pharaoh, to all his officials and to all his land. ³With your own eyes you saw those great trials, those miraculous signs and great wonders. ⁴But to this day the

LORD has not given you a mind that understands or eyes that see or ears that hear. ⁵During the forty years that I led you through the desert, your clothes did not wear out, nor did the sandals on your feet. ⁶You ate no bread and drank no wine or other fermented drink. I did this so that you might know that I am the LORD your God.

⁷When you reached this place, Sihon king of Heshbon and Og king of Bashan came out to fight against us, but we defeated them. ⁸We took their land and gave it as an inheritance to the Reubenites, the Gadites and the half-tribe of Manasseh.

⁹Carefully follow the terms of this covenant, so that you may prosper in everything you do. ¹⁰All of you are standing today in the presence of the LORD your God—your leaders and chief men, your elders and officials, and all the other men of Israel, ¹¹together with your children and your wives, and the aliens living in your camps who chop your wood and carry your water. ¹²You are standing here in order to enter into a covenant with the LORD your God, a covenant the LORD is making with you this day and sealing with an oath, ¹³to confirm you this day as his people, that he may be your God as he promised you and as he swore to your fathers, Abraham, Isaac and Jacob. ¹⁴I am making this covenant, with its oath, not only with you ¹⁵who are standing here with us today in the presence of the LORD our God but also with those who are not here today.

¹⁶You yourselves know how we lived in Egypt and how we passed through the countries on the way here. ¹⁷You saw among them their detestable images and idols of wood and stone, of silver and gold. ¹⁸Make sure there is no man or woman, clan or tribe among you today whose heart turns away from the LORD our God to go and worship the gods of those nations; make sure there is no

root among you that produces such bitter poison.

¹⁹When such a person hears the words of this oath, he invokes a blessing on himself and therefore thinks, "I will be safe, even though I persist in going my own way." This will bring disaster on the watered land as well as the dry.ᵃ ²⁰The LORD will never be willing to forgive him; his wrath and zeal will burn against that man. All the curses written in this book will fall upon him, and the LORD will blot out his name from under heaven. ²¹The LORD will single him out from all the tribes of Israel for disaster, according to all the curses of the covenant written in this Book of the Law.

²²Your children who follow you in later generations and foreigners who come from distant lands will see the calamities that have fallen on the land and the diseases with which the LORD has afflicted it. ²³The whole land will be a burning waste of salt and sulfur—nothing planted, nothing sprouting, no vegetation growing on it. It will be like the destruction of Sodom and Gomorrah, Admah and Zeboiim, which the LORD overthrew in fierce anger. ²⁴All the nations will ask: "Why has the LORD done this to this land? Why this fierce, burning anger?"

²⁵And the answer will be: "It is because this people abandoned the covenant of the LORD, the God of their fathers, the covenant he made with them when he brought them out of Egypt. ²⁶They went off and worshiped other gods and bowed down to them, gods they did not know, gods he had not given them. ²⁷Therefore the LORD's anger burned against this land, so that he brought on it all the curses written in this book. ²⁸In furious anger and in great wrath the LORD uprooted them from their land and thrust them into another land, as it is now."

²⁹The secret things belong to the LORD our God, but the things revealed belong to us and to our children for-

ever, that we may follow all the words of this law.

Prosperity After Turning to the LORD

30 When all these blessings and curses I have set before you come upon you and you take them to heart wherever the LORD your God disperses you among the nations, ²and when you and your children return to the LORD your God and obey him with all your heart and with all your soul according to everything I command you today, ³then the LORD your God will restore your fortunes[a] and have compassion on you and gather you again from all the nations where he scattered you. ⁴Even if you have been banished to the most distant land under the heavens, from there the LORD your God will gather you and bring you back. ⁵He will bring you to the land that belonged to your fathers, and you will take possession of it. He will make you more prosperous and numerous than your fathers. ⁶The LORD your God will circumcise your hearts and the hearts of your descendants, so that you may love him with all your heart and with all your soul, and live. ⁷The LORD your God will put all these curses on your enemies who hate and persecute you. ⁸You will again obey the LORD and follow all his commands I am giving you today. ⁹Then the LORD your God will make you most prosperous in all the work of your hands and in the fruit of your womb, the young of your livestock and the crops of your land. The LORD will again delight in you and make you prosperous, just as he delighted in your fathers, ¹⁰if you obey the LORD your God and keep his commands and decrees that are written in this Book of the Law and turn to the LORD your God with all your heart and with all your soul.

The Offer of Life or Death

¹¹Now what I am commanding you today is not too difficult for you or beyond your reach. ¹²It is not up in heaven, so that you have to ask, "Who will ascend into heaven to get it and proclaim it to us so we may obey it?" ¹³Nor is it beyond the sea, so that you have to ask, "Who will cross the sea to get it and proclaim it to us so we may obey it?" ¹⁴No, the word is very near you; it is in your mouth and in your heart so you may obey it.

¹⁵See, I set before you today life and prosperity, death and destruction. ¹⁶For I command you today to love the LORD your God, to walk in his ways, and to keep his commands, decrees and laws; then you will live and increase, and the LORD your God will bless you in the land you are entering to possess.

¹⁷But if your heart turns away and you are not obedient, and if you are drawn away to bow down to other gods and worship them, ¹⁸I declare to you this day that you will certainly be destroyed. You will not live long in the land you are crossing the Jordan to enter and possess.

¹⁹This day I call heaven and earth as witnesses against you that I have set before you life and death, blessings and curses. Now choose life, so that you and your children may live ²⁰and that you may love the LORD your God, listen to his voice, and hold fast to him. For the LORD is your life, and he will give you many years in the land he swore to give to your fathers, Abraham, Isaac and Jacob.

Joshua to Succeed Moses

31 Then Moses went out and spoke these words to all Israel: ²"I am now a hundred and twenty years old and I am no longer able to lead you. The LORD has said to me, 'You shall not cross the Jordan.' ³The LORD your God himself will cross over ahead of you. He will destroy these nations before you, and you will take possession of their land. Joshua also will cross over ahead of you, as the LORD said. ⁴And the LORD will do to

a3 Or *will bring you back from captivity*

them what he did to Sihon and Og, the kings of the Amorites, whom he destroyed along with their land. ⁵The LORD will deliver them to you, and you must do to them all that I have commanded you. ⁶Be strong and courageous. Do not be afraid or terrified because of them, for the LORD your God goes with you; he will never leave you nor forsake you."

⁷Then Moses summoned Joshua and said to him in the presence of all Israel, "Be strong and courageous, for you must go with this people into the land that the LORD swore to their forefathers to give them, and you must divide it among them as their inheritance. ⁸The LORD himself goes before you and will be with you; he will never leave you nor forsake you. Do not be afraid; do not be discouraged."

The Reading of the Law

⁹So Moses wrote down this law and gave it to the priests, the sons of Levi, who carried the ark of the covenant of the LORD, and to all the elders of Israel. ¹⁰Then Moses commanded them: "At the end of every seven years, in the year for canceling debts, during the Feast of Tabernacles, ¹¹when all Israel comes to appear before the LORD your God at the place he will choose, you shall read this law before them in their hearing. ¹²Assemble the people—men, women and children, and the aliens living in your towns—so they can listen and learn to fear the LORD your God and follow carefully all the words of this law. ¹³Their children, who do not know this law, must hear it and learn to fear the LORD your God as long as you live in the land you are crossing the Jordan to possess."

Israel's Rebellion Predicted

¹⁴The LORD said to Moses, "Now the day of your death is near. Call Joshua and present yourselves at the Tent of Meeting, where I will commission him." So Moses and Joshua came and presented themselves at the Tent of Meeting.

¹⁵Then the LORD appeared at the Tent in a pillar of cloud, and the cloud stood over the entrance to the Tent. ¹⁶And the LORD said to Moses: "You are going to rest with your fathers, and these people will soon prostitute themselves to the foreign gods of the land they are entering. They will forsake me and break the covenant I made with them. ¹⁷On that day I will become angry with them and forsake them; I will hide my face from them, and they will be destroyed. Many disasters and difficulties will come upon them, and on that day they will ask, 'Have not these disasters come upon us because our God is not with us?' ¹⁸And I will certainly hide my face on that day because of all their wickedness in turning to other gods.

¹⁹"Now write down for yourselves this song and teach it to the Israelites and have them sing it, so that it may be a witness for me against them. ²⁰When I have brought them into the land flowing with milk and honey, the land I promised on oath to their forefathers, and when they eat their fill and thrive, they will turn to other gods and worship them, rejecting me and breaking my covenant. ²¹And when many disasters and difficulties come upon them, this song will testify against them, because it will not be forgotten by their descendants. I know what they are disposed to do, even before I bring them into the land I promised them on oath." ²²So Moses wrote down this song that day and taught it to the Israelites.

²³The LORD gave this command to Joshua son of Nun: "Be strong and courageous, for you will bring the Israelites into the land I promised them on oath, and I myself will be with you."

²⁴After Moses finished writing in a book the words of this law from beginning to end, ²⁵he gave this command to the Levites who carried the ark of the covenant of the LORD: ²⁶"Take this Book of the Law and place it beside the ark of the covenant of the LORD your God. There it will remain as a witness against you. ²⁷For I know how rebellious and stiff-

VERSE: AUTHOR: PASSAGE:
Deuteronomy 31:6   Leslie E. Moser   Deuteronomy 31:1–8

Growing Pains

Change and growth usually become more painful as life unfolds. Parents, for instance, pay a high price when they give their last child to the university, to a marriage and to moving far away. Yes, growing forward exacts a price.

But how much greater a price is exacted in refusing to grow! When we fail to let go of the past, we can find no meaning in the present and the enriching experiences of each new day.

Some of life's changes don't fit neatly with the idea of growth. The death of a child, a parent, a spouse; the breakup of a marriage; retirement; moving to less expansive and less expensive living quarters—are these not times for tears? Of course they are, so let the tears flow. But ultimately each of us must ask ourselves the question, "Do I try too hard to hang on to that which was, or do I want to reach out to that which is and might be?"

Our capacity to change and grow will depend on our roots. Are we firmly rooted in the promise of God that he will never leave us? . . . As we let go of the loved ones who pass, the relationships which did not endure, and our disappointments in people and events, we give up our cherished illusions of safety. In return, we gain a greater understanding of self, of God and of eternity.

We can be still and know that God is God (Psalm 46:10); we can know, too, that God "rewards those who earnestly seek him" (Hebrews 11:6).

ADDITIONAL SCRIPTURE READINGS
Joshua 1:1–9; Psalm 46
Go to page 249 for your next devotional reading.

necked you are. If you have been rebellious against the LORD while I am still alive and with you, how much more will you rebel after I die! [28]Assemble before me all the elders of your tribes and all your officials, so that I can speak these words in their hearing and call heaven and earth to testify against them. [29]For I know that after my death you are sure to become utterly corrupt and to turn from the way I have commanded you. In days to come, disaster will fall upon you because you will do evil in the sight of the LORD and provoke him to anger by what your hands have made."

The Song of Moses

[30]And Moses recited the words of this song from beginning to end in the hearing of the whole assembly of Israel:

32 Listen, O heavens, and I will speak;
    hear, O earth, the words of my mouth.
[2]Let my teaching fall like rain
    and my words descend like dew,
  like showers on new grass,
    like abundant rain on tender plants.

[3]I will proclaim the name of the LORD.
    Oh, praise the greatness of our God!
[4]He is the Rock, his works are perfect,
    and all his ways are just.
  A faithful God who does no wrong,
    upright and just is he.

[5]They have acted corruptly toward him;
    to their shame they are no longer his children,
  but a warped and crooked generation.[a]

[6]Is this the way you repay the LORD,
    O foolish and unwise people?
  Is he not your Father, your Creator,[b]
    who made you and formed you?

[7]Remember the days of old;
    consider the generations long past.
  Ask your father and he will tell you,
    your elders, and they will explain to you.
[8]When the Most High gave the nations their inheritance,
    when he divided all mankind,
  he set up boundaries for the peoples
    according to the number of the sons of Israel.[c]
[9]For the LORD's portion is his people,
    Jacob his allotted inheritance.

[10]In a desert land he found him,
    in a barren and howling waste.
  He shielded him and cared for him;
    he guarded him as the apple of his eye,
[11]like an eagle that stirs up its nest
    and hovers over its young,
  that spreads its wings to catch them
    and carries them on its pinions.
[12]The LORD alone led him;
    no foreign god was with him.

[13]He made him ride on the heights of the land
    and fed him with the fruit of the fields.
  He nourished him with honey from the rock,
    and with oil from the flinty crag,
[14]with curds and milk from herd and flock
    and with fattened lambs and goats,
  with choice rams of Bashan

---

[a]5 Or Corrupt are they and not his children, / a generation warped and twisted to their shame   [b]6 Or Father, who bought you   [c]8 Masoretic Text; Dead Sea Scrolls (see also Septuagint) sons of God

and the finest kernels of wheat.
You drank the foaming blood of
     the grape.

¹⁵Jeshurun[a] grew fat and kicked;
     filled with food, he became
          heavy and sleek.
He abandoned the God who made
     him
     and rejected the Rock his
          Savior.
¹⁶They made him jealous with their
     foreign gods
     and angered him with their
          detestable idols.
¹⁷They sacrificed to demons, which
     are not God—
     gods they had not known,
     gods that recently appeared,
     gods your fathers did not fear.
¹⁸You deserted the Rock, who
     fathered you;
     you forgot the God who gave
          you birth.

¹⁹The LORD saw this and rejected
     them
     because he was angered by his
          sons and daughters.
²⁰"I will hide my face from them,"
     he said,
     "and see what their end will be;
for they are a perverse generation,
     children who are unfaithful.
²¹They made me jealous by what is
     no god
     and angered me with their
          worthless idols.
I will make them envious by those
     who are not a people;
     I will make them angry by a
          nation that has no
          understanding.
²²For a fire has been kindled by my
     wrath,
     one that burns to the realm of
          death[b] below.
It will devour the earth and its
     harvests
     and set afire the foundations of
          the mountains.

²³"I will heap calamities upon them

and spend my arrows against
     them.
²⁴I will send wasting famine against
     them,
     consuming pestilence and
          deadly plague;
I will send against them the fangs
     of wild beasts,
     the venom of vipers that glide
          in the dust.
²⁵In the street the sword will make
     them childless;
     in their homes terror will reign.
Young men and young women
     will perish,
     infants and gray-haired men.
²⁶I said I would scatter them
     and blot out their memory from
          mankind,
²⁷but I dreaded the taunt of the
     enemy,
     lest the adversary
          misunderstand
and say, 'Our hand has
     triumphed;
     the LORD has not done all this.' "

²⁸They are a nation without sense,
     there is no discernment in them.
²⁹If only they were wise and would
     understand this
     and discern what their end will
          be!
³⁰How could one man chase a
     thousand,
     or two put ten thousand to
          flight,
unless their Rock had sold them,
     unless the LORD had given them
          up?
³¹For their rock is not like our Rock,
     as even our enemies concede.
³²Their vine comes from the vine of
     Sodom
     and from the fields of
          Gomorrah.
Their grapes are filled with
     poison,
     and their clusters with
          bitterness.
³³Their wine is the venom of
     serpents,
     the deadly poison of cobras.

---

a15 *Jeshurun* means *the upright one,* that is, Israel.   b22 Hebrew *to Sheol*

³⁴"Have I not kept this in reserve
and sealed it in my vaults?
³⁵It is mine to avenge; I will repay.
In due time their foot will slip;
their day of disaster is near
and their doom rushes upon
them."

³⁶The LORD will judge his people
and have compassion on his
servants
when he sees their strength is
gone
and no one is left, slave or free.
³⁷He will say: "Now where are their
gods,
the rock they took refuge in,
³⁸the gods who ate the fat of their
sacrifices
and drank the wine of their
drink offerings?
Let them rise up to help you!
Let them give you shelter!

³⁹"See now that I myself am He!
There is no god besides me.
I put to death and I bring to life,
I have wounded and I will heal,
and no one can deliver out of
my hand.
⁴⁰I lift my hand to heaven and
declare:
As surely as I live forever,
⁴¹when I sharpen my flashing
sword
and my hand grasps it in
judgment,
I will take vengeance on my
adversaries
and repay those who hate me.
⁴²I will make my arrows drunk with
blood,
while my sword devours flesh:
the blood of the slain and the
captives,
the heads of the enemy
leaders."

⁴³Rejoice, O nations, with his
people,[a,b]
for he will avenge the blood of
his servants;

he will take vengeance on his
enemies
and make atonement for his
land and people.

⁴⁴Moses came with Joshua[c] son of
Nun and spoke all the words of this
song in the hearing of the people.
⁴⁵When Moses finished reciting all
these words to all Israel, ⁴⁶he said to
them, "Take to heart all the words I
have solemnly declared to you this
day, so that you may command your
children to obey carefully all the
words of this law. ⁴⁷They are not just
idle words for you—they are your
life. By them you will live long in the
land you are crossing the Jordan to
possess."

Moses to Die on Mount Nebo

⁴⁸On that same day the LORD told
Moses, ⁴⁹"Go up into the Abarim
Range to Mount Nebo in Moab,
across from Jericho, and view Canaan, the land I am giving the Israelites as their own possession. ⁵⁰There
on the mountain that you have
climbed you will die and be gathered
to your people, just as your brother
Aaron died on Mount Hor and was
gathered to his people. ⁵¹This is because both of you broke faith with me
in the presence of the Israelites at the
waters of Meribah Kadesh in the
Desert of Zin and because you did not
uphold my holiness among the Israelites. ⁵²Therefore, you will see the land
only from a distance; you will not enter the land I am giving to the people
of Israel."

Moses Blesses the Tribes

33 This is the blessing that Moses
the man of God pronounced on
the Israelites before his death. ²He
said:

"The LORD came from Sinai
and dawned over them from
Seir;
he shone forth from Mount
Paran.

---

[a]43 Or *Make his people rejoice, O nations*   [b]43 Masoretic Text; Dead Sea Scrolls (see also
Septuagint) *people, / and let all the angels worship him /*   [c]44 Hebrew *Hoshea,* a variant of *Joshua*

He came with[a] myriads of holy
ones
from the south, from his
mountain slopes.[b]
[3]Surely it is you who love the
people;
all the holy ones are in your
hand.
At your feet they all bow down,
and from you receive
instruction,

[4]the law that Moses gave us,
the possession of the assembly
of Jacob.
[5]He was king over Jeshurun[c]
when the leaders of the people
assembled,
along with the tribes of Israel.

[6]"Let Reuben live and not die,
nor[d] his men be few."

[7]And this he said about Judah:

---

[a]2 Or *from*   [b]2 The meaning of the Hebrew for this phrase is uncertain.   [c]5 *Jeshurun* means
the upright one, that is, Israel; also in verse 26.   [d]6 Or *but let*

FRIDAY

VERSE:	AUTHOR:	PASSAGE:
Deuteronomy 33:1	Elizabeth Skoglund	Deuteronomy 33:1–29

It's *Your* Will

Whether a person is 20 or 80, making a will does not
make you die any more than not making a will ensures
that you will live. It simply ensures that after your death
your money goes where you want it to go. Such knowledge helps guard against the feeling of loss of control.

A will is *your* will. It should reflect what you want, not
what your family dictates. It should be prayerfully decided upon, with the primary consideration being the
will of God. As Christians our stewardship of earthly belongings should transcend petty family quarrels. People
who automatically leave all their material goods to their
children may or may not be doing the will of God. For
that matter, neither is it automatically God's will to simply "leave it to the church" . . .

When you make out your will, it should be just
that — your final will, not the will of your family or anyone else except God alone.

ADDITIONAL SCRIPTURE READINGS
Psalm 49; Proverbs 13:20–22
Go to page 252 for your next devotional reading.

"Hear, O Lord, the cry of Judah;
  bring him to his people.
With his own hands he defends
    his cause.
  Oh, be his help against his
    foes!"

⁸About Levi he said:

"Your Thummim and Urim belong
  to the man you favored.
You tested him at Massah;
  you contended with him at the
    waters of Meribah.
⁹He said of his father and mother,
  'I have no regard for them.'
He did not recognize his brothers
  or acknowledge his own
    children,
but he watched over your word
  and guarded your covenant.
¹⁰He teaches your precepts to Jacob
  and your law to Israel.
He offers incense before you
  and whole burnt offerings on
    your altar.
¹¹Bless all his skills, O Lord,
  and be pleased with the work
    of his hands.
Smite the loins of those who rise
    up against him;
  strike his foes till they rise no
    more."

¹²About Benjamin he said:

"Let the beloved of the Lord rest
    secure in him,
  for he shields him all day long,
  and the one the Lord loves rests
    between his shoulders."

¹³About Joseph he said:

"May the Lord bless his land
  with the precious dew from
    heaven above
  and with the deep waters that
    lie below;
¹⁴with the best the sun brings forth
  and the finest the moon can
    yield;
¹⁵with the choicest gifts of the
    ancient mountains

and the fruitfulness of the
  everlasting hills;
¹⁶with the best gifts of the earth and
    its fullness
  and the favor of him who dwelt
    in the burning bush.
Let all these rest on the head of
    Joseph,
  on the brow of the prince
    amongᵃ his brothers.
¹⁷In majesty he is like a firstborn
    bull;
  his horns are the horns of a
    wild ox.
With them he will gore the
    nations,
  even those at the ends of the
    earth.
Such are the ten thousands of
    Ephraim;
  such are the thousands of
    Manasseh."

¹⁸About Zebulun he said:

"Rejoice, Zebulun, in your going
    out,
  and you, Issachar, in your tents.
¹⁹They will summon peoples to the
    mountain
  and there offer sacrifices of
    righteousness;
they will feast on the abundance
    of the seas,
  on the treasures hidden in the
    sand."

²⁰About Gad he said:

"Blessed is he who enlarges Gad's
    domain!
  Gad lives there like a lion,
  tearing at arm or head.
²¹He chose the best land for himself;
  the leader's portion was kept
    for him.
When the heads of the people
    assembled,
  he carried out the Lord's
    righteous will,
  and his judgments concerning
    Israel."

ᵃ16 Or *of the one separated from*

[22]About Dan he said:

"Dan is a lion's cub,
    springing out of Bashan."

[23]About Naphtali he said:

"Naphtali is abounding with the
        favor of the LORD
    and is full of his blessing;
    he will inherit southward to the
        lake."

[24]About Asher he said:

"Most blessed of sons is Asher;
    let him be favored by his
        brothers,
    and let him bathe his feet in oil.
[25]The bolts of your gates will be
        iron and bronze,
    and your strength will equal
        your days.

[26]"There is no one like the God of
        Jeshurun,
    who rides on the heavens to
        help you
    and on the clouds in his
        majesty.
[27]The eternal God is your refuge,
    and underneath are the
        everlasting arms.
He will drive out your enemy
        before you,
    saying, 'Destroy him!'
[28]So Israel will live in safety alone;
    Jacob's spring is secure
in a land of grain and new wine,
    where the heavens drop dew.
[29]Blessed are you, O Israel!
    Who is like you,
    a people saved by the LORD?
He is your shield and helper
    and your glorious sword.
Your enemies will cower before
        you,
    and you will trample down
        their high places.[a]"

The Death of Moses

34 Then Moses climbed Mount Nebo from the plains of Moab to the top of Pisgah, across from Jericho. There the LORD showed him the whole land—from Gilead to Dan, [2]all of Naphtali, the territory of Ephraim and Manasseh, all the land of Judah as far as the western sea,[b] [3]the Negev and the whole region from the Valley of Jericho, the City of Palms, as far as Zoar. [4]Then the LORD said to him, "This is the land I promised on oath to Abraham, Isaac and Jacob when I said, 'I will give it to your descendants.' I have let you see it with your eyes, but you will not cross over into it."

[5]And Moses the servant of the LORD died there in Moab, as the LORD had said. [6]He buried him[c] in Moab, in the valley opposite Beth Peor, but to this day no one knows where his grave is. [7]Moses was a hundred and twenty years old when he died, yet his eyes were not weak nor his strength gone. [8]The Israelites grieved for Moses in the plains of Moab thirty days, until the time of weeping and mourning was over.

[9]Now Joshua son of Nun was filled with the spirit[d] of wisdom because Moses had laid his hands on him. So the Israelites listened to him and did what the LORD had commanded Moses.

[10]Since then, no prophet has risen in Israel like Moses, whom the LORD knew face to face, [11]who did all those miraculous signs and wonders the LORD sent him to do in Egypt—to Pharaoh and to all his officials and to his whole land. [12]For no one has ever shown the mighty power or performed the awesome deeds that Moses did in the sight of all Israel.

---

[a]29 Or *will tread upon their bodies*   [b]2 That is, the Mediterranean   [c]6 Or *He was buried*
[d]9 Or *Spirit*

PASSAGE: Deuteronomy 34:1–12; Joshua 14:6–15
AUTHOR: Henry Wadsworth Longfellow

Age Is Opportunity

It is too late! Ah, nothing is too late
Till the tired heart shall cease to palpitate.
Cato learned Greek at eighty; Sophocles
Wrote his grand Oedipus, and Simonides
Bore off the prize of verse from his compeers
When each had numbered more than fourscore
      years . . .
Chaucer, at Woodstock, with the nightingales,
At sixty wrote the Canterbury Tales;
Goethe at Weimar, toiling to the last,
Completed Faust when eighty years were past . . .
What then? Shall we sit idly down and say
The night hath come; it is no longer day? . . .
For age is opportunity no less
Than youth itself, though in another dress;
And as the evening twilight fades away
The sky is filled with stars invisible by day.

Go to page 254 for your next devotional reading.

Joshua tells how the Israelites defeated their enemies and divided up the promised land. In his infinite mercy, God offered the Israelites a second chance to possess the land after their years of wandering in the desert. As you read this book, give thanks for the new beginning God extends to you and choose to live each day in service to him.

JOSHUA

The LORD Commands Joshua

1 After the death of Moses the servant of the LORD, the LORD said to Joshua son of Nun, Moses' aide: ²"Moses my servant is dead. Now then, you and all these people, get ready to cross the Jordan River into the land I am about to give to them— to the Israelites. ³I will give you every place where you set your foot, as I promised Moses. ⁴Your territory will extend from the desert to Lebanon, and from the great river, the Euphrates—all the Hittite country—to the Great Sea[a] on the west. ⁵No one will be able to stand up against you all the days of your life. As I was with Moses, so I will be with you; I will never leave you nor forsake you.

⁶"Be strong and courageous, because you will lead these people to inherit the land I swore to their forefathers to give them. ⁷Be strong and very courageous. Be careful to obey all the law my servant Moses gave you; do not turn from it to the right or to the left, that you may be successful wherever you go. ⁸Do not let this Book of the Law depart from your mouth; meditate on it day and night, so that you may be careful to do everything written in it. Then you will be prosperous and successful. ⁹Have I not commanded you? Be strong and courageous. Do not be terrified; do not be discouraged, for the LORD your God will be with you wherever you go."

¹⁰So Joshua ordered the officers of the people: ¹¹"Go through the camp and tell the people, 'Get your supplies ready. Three days from now you will cross the Jordan here to go in and take possession of the land the LORD your God is giving you for your own.' "

¹²But to the Reubenites, the Gadites and the half-tribe of Manasseh, Joshua said, ¹³"Remember the command that Moses the servant of the LORD

VERSE:	AUTHOR:	PASSAGE:
Joshua 1:9	Kay Arthur	Joshua 1:1–11

Disappointment's Twin

Discouragement and disappointment are like twins. Open the door to disappointment, and you will find discouragement dashing in right behind. Satan's goal is to weaken you, to dishearten you, to make you lose courage. And once discouragement enters your camp, it seems to be downhill all the way.

That is why God was so careful in his instructions to Joshua as the Israelites prepared to occupy the land that God had given them. They had missed occupying Canaan 40 years earlier because of unbelief at Kadesh Barnea . . .

Some 40 years later, they were preparing to enter the same land and meet the same giants and so God said, not once but three times, "Be strong and courageous!" (Joshua 1:6,7,9) . . .

Joshua knew the results of discouragement. He had been one of those original 12 spies. He and Caleb had torn their clothes, beseeching the children of Israel to walk in faith, to believe God (Numbers 13:30). Yet they would not listen. Word of the giants and the fortified cities had penetrated their line of defense, and discouragement followed, bringing dejection and despair, until they were totally demoralized.

And so what is God's word to you today? It is to be strong and courageous, for your Father, the Lord God Omnipotent, reigns. So stop weeping and rejoice in the God of your salvation, for he is your strength and he will enable you to stand (Habakkuk 3:18–19).

ADDITIONAL SCRIPTURE READINGS
Psalm 18:16–36; Habakkuk 3:16–19

Go to page 260 for your next devotional reading.

gave you: 'The LORD your God is giving you rest and has granted you this land.' ¹⁴Your wives, your children and your livestock may stay in the land that Moses gave you east of the Jordan, but all your fighting men, fully armed, must cross over ahead of your brothers. You are to help your brothers ¹⁵until the LORD gives them rest, as he has done for you, and until they too have taken possession of the land that the LORD your God is giving them. After that, you may go back and occupy your own land, which Moses the servant of the LORD gave you east of the Jordan toward the sunrise."

¹⁶Then they answered Joshua, "Whatever you have commanded us we will do, and wherever you send us we will go. ¹⁷Just as we fully obeyed Moses, so we will obey you. Only may the LORD your God be with you as he was with Moses. ¹⁸Whoever rebels against your word and does not obey your words, whatever you may command them, will be put to death. Only be strong and courageous!"

Rahab and the Spies

2 Then Joshua son of Nun secretly sent two spies from Shittim. "Go, look over the land," he said, "especially Jericho." So they went and entered the house of a prostitute*ᵃ* named Rahab and stayed there.

²The king of Jericho was told, "Look! Some of the Israelites have come here tonight to spy out the land." ³So the king of Jericho sent this message to Rahab: "Bring out the men who came to you and entered your house, because they have come to spy out the whole land."

⁴But the woman had taken the two men and hidden them. She said, "Yes, the men came to me, but I did not know where they had come from. ⁵At dusk, when it was time to close the city gate, the men left. I don't know which way they went. Go after them quickly. You may catch up with them." ⁶(But she had taken them up to the roof and hidden them under the stalks of flax she had laid out on the roof.) ⁷So the men set out in pursuit of the spies on the road that leads to the fords of the Jordan, and as soon as the pursuers had gone out, the gate was shut.

⁸Before the spies lay down for the night, she went up on the roof ⁹and said to them, "I know that the LORD has given this land to you and that a great fear of you has fallen on us, so that all who live in this country are melting in fear because of you. ¹⁰We have heard how the LORD dried up the water of the Red Sea*ᵇ* for you when you came out of Egypt, and what you did to Sihon and Og, the two kings of the Amorites east of the Jordan, whom you completely destroyed.*ᶜ* ¹¹When we heard of it, our hearts melted and everyone's courage failed because of you, for the LORD your God is God in heaven above and on the earth below. ¹²Now then, please swear to me by the LORD that you will show kindness to my family, because I have shown kindness to you. Give me a sure sign ¹³that you will spare the lives of my father and mother, my brothers and sisters, and all who belong to them, and that you will save us from death."

¹⁴"Our lives for your lives!" the men assured her. "If you don't tell what we are doing, we will treat you kindly and faithfully when the LORD gives us the land."

¹⁵So she let them down by a rope through the window, for the house she lived in was part of the city wall. ¹⁶Now she had said to them, "Go to the hills so the pursuers will not find you. Hide yourselves there three days until they return, and then go on your way."

¹⁷The men said to her, "This oath you made us swear will not be binding on us ¹⁸unless, when we enter the

---

ᵃ1 Or possibly *an innkeeper*   *ᵇ10* Hebrew *Yam Suph*; that is, Sea of Reeds   *ᶜ10* The Hebrew term refers to the irrevocable giving over of things or persons to the LORD, often by totally destroying them.

land, you have tied this scarlet cord in the window through which you let us down, and unless you have brought your father and mother, your brothers and all your family into your house. ¹⁹If anyone goes outside your house into the street, his blood will be on his own head; we will not be responsible. As for anyone who is in the house with you, his blood will be on our head if a hand is laid on him. ²⁰But if you tell what we are doing, we will be released from the oath you made us swear."

²¹"Agreed," she replied. "Let it be as you say." So she sent them away and they departed. And she tied the scarlet cord in the window.

²²When they left, they went into the hills and stayed there three days, until the pursuers had searched all along the road and returned without finding them. ²³Then the two men started back. They went down out of the hills, forded the river and came to Joshua son of Nun and told him everything that had happened to them. ²⁴They said to Joshua, "The LORD has surely given the whole land into our hands; all the people are melting in fear because of us."

Crossing the Jordan

3 Early in the morning Joshua and all the Israelites set out from Shittim and went to the Jordan, where they camped before crossing over. ²After three days the officers went throughout the camp, ³giving orders to the people: "When you see the ark of the covenant of the LORD your God, and the priests, who are Levites, carrying it, you are to move out from your positions and follow it. ⁴Then you will know which way to go, since you have never been this way before. But keep a distance of about a thousand yards[a] between you and the ark; do not go near it."

⁵Joshua told the people, "Consecrate yourselves, for tomorrow the LORD will do amazing things among you."

⁶Joshua said to the priests, "Take up the ark of the covenant and pass on ahead of the people." So they took it up and went ahead of them.

⁷And the LORD said to Joshua, "Today I will begin to exalt you in the eyes of all Israel, so they may know that I am with you as I was with Moses. ⁸Tell the priests who carry the ark of the covenant: 'When you reach the edge of the Jordan's waters, go and stand in the river.' "

⁹Joshua said to the Israelites, "Come here and listen to the words of the LORD your God. ¹⁰This is how you will know that the living God is among you and that he will certainly drive out before you the Canaanites, Hittites, Hivites, Perizzites, Girgashites, Amorites and Jebusites. ¹¹See, the ark of the covenant of the Lord of all the earth will go into the Jordan ahead of you. ¹²Now then, choose twelve men from the tribes of Israel, one from each tribe. ¹³And as soon as the priests who carry the ark of the LORD—the Lord of all the earth—set foot in the Jordan, its waters flowing downstream will be cut off and stand up in a heap."

¹⁴So when the people broke camp to cross the Jordan, the priests carrying the ark of the covenant went ahead of them. ¹⁵Now the Jordan is at flood stage all during harvest. Yet as soon as the priests who carried the ark reached the Jordan and their feet touched the water's edge, ¹⁶the water from upstream stopped flowing. It piled up in a heap a great distance away, at a town called Adam in the vicinity of Zarethan, while the water flowing down to the Sea of the Arabah (the Salt Sea [b]) was completely cut off. So the people crossed over opposite Jericho. ¹⁷The priests who carried the ark of the covenant of the LORD stood firm on dry ground in the middle of the Jordan, while all Israel passed by until the whole nation had completed the crossing on dry ground.

---

[a]4 Hebrew *about two thousand cubits* (about 900 meters)   [b]16 That is, the Dead Sea

4 When the whole nation had finished crossing the Jordan, the LORD said to Joshua, 2"Choose twelve men from among the people, one from each tribe, 3and tell them to take up twelve stones from the middle of the Jordan from right where the priests stood and to carry them over with you and put them down at the place where you stay tonight."

4So Joshua called together the twelve men he had appointed from the Israelites, one from each tribe, 5and said to them, "Go over before the ark of the LORD your God into the middle of the Jordan. Each of you is to take up a stone on his shoulder, according to the number of the tribes of the Israelites, 6to serve as a sign among you. In the future, when your children ask you, 'What do these stones mean?' 7tell them that the flow of the Jordan was cut off before the ark of the covenant of the LORD. When it crossed the Jordan, the waters of the Jordan were cut off. These stones are to be a memorial to the people of Israel forever."

8So the Israelites did as Joshua commanded them. They took twelve stones from the middle of the Jordan, according to the number of the tribes of the Israelites, as the LORD had told Joshua; and they carried them over with them to their camp, where they put them down. 9Joshua set up the twelve stones that had been[a] in the middle of the Jordan at the spot where the priests who carried the ark of the covenant had stood. And they are there to this day.

10Now the priests who carried the ark remained standing in the middle of the Jordan until everything the LORD had commanded Joshua was done by the people, just as Moses had directed Joshua. The people hurried over, 11and as soon as all of them had crossed, the ark of the LORD and the priests came to the other side while the people watched. 12The men of Reuben, Gad and the half-tribe of Manasseh crossed over, armed, in front

of the Israelites, as Moses had directed them. 13About forty thousand armed for battle crossed over before the LORD to the plains of Jericho for war.

14That day the LORD exalted Joshua in the sight of all Israel; and they revered him all the days of his life, just as they had revered Moses.

15Then the LORD said to Joshua, 16"Command the priests carrying the ark of the Testimony to come up out of the Jordan."

17So Joshua commanded the priests, "Come up out of the Jordan."

18And the priests came up out of the river carrying the ark of the covenant of the LORD. No sooner had they set their feet on the dry ground than the waters of the Jordan returned to their place and ran at flood stage as before.

19On the tenth day of the first month the people went up from the Jordan and camped at Gilgal on the eastern border of Jericho. 20And Joshua set up at Gilgal the twelve stones they had taken out of the Jordan. 21He said to the Israelites, "In the future when your descendants ask their fathers, 'What do these stones mean?' 22tell them, 'Israel crossed the Jordan on dry ground.' 23For the LORD your God dried up the Jordan before you until you had crossed over. The LORD your God did to the Jordan just what he had done to the Red Sea[b] when he dried it up before us until we had crossed over. 24He did this so that all the peoples of the earth might know that the hand of the LORD is powerful and so that you might always fear the LORD your God."

Circumcision at Gilgal

5 Now when all the Amorite kings west of the Jordan and all the Canaanite kings along the coast heard how the LORD had dried up the Jordan before the Israelites until we had crossed over, their hearts melted and they no longer had the courage to face the Israelites.

---

[a]9 Or Joshua also set up twelve stones   [b]23 Hebrew Yam Suph; that is, Sea of Reeds

²At that time the LORD said to Joshua, "Make flint knives and circumcise the Israelites again." ³So Joshua made flint knives and circumcised the Israelites at Gibeath Haaraloth.ᵃ

⁴Now this is why he did so: All those who came out of Egypt—all the men of military age—died in the desert on the way after leaving Egypt. ⁵All the people that came out had been circumcised, but all the people born in the desert during the journey from Egypt had not. ⁶The Israelites had moved about in the desert forty years until all the men who were of military age when they left Egypt had died, since they had not obeyed the LORD. For the LORD had sworn to them that they would not see the land that he had solemnly promised their fathers to give us, a land flowing with milk and honey. ⁷So he raised up their sons in their place, and these were the ones Joshua circumcised. They were still uncircumcised because they had not been circumcised on the way. ⁸And after the whole nation had been circumcised, they remained where they were in camp until they were healed.

⁹Then the LORD said to Joshua, "Today I have rolled away the reproach of Egypt from you." So the place has been called Gilgalᵇ to this day.

¹⁰On the evening of the fourteenth day of the month, while camped at Gilgal on the plains of Jericho, the Israelites celebrated the Passover. ¹¹The day after the Passover, that very day, they ate some of the produce of the land: unleavened bread and roasted grain. ¹²The manna stopped the day afterᶜ they ate this food from the land; there was no longer any manna for the Israelites, but that year they ate of the produce of Canaan.

The Fall of Jericho

¹³Now when Joshua was near Jericho, he looked up and saw a man standing in front of him with a drawn sword in his hand. Joshua went up to him and asked, "Are you for us or for our enemies?"

¹⁴"Neither," he replied, "but as commander of the army of the LORD I have now come." Then Joshua fell facedown to the ground in reverence, and asked him, "What message does my Lordᵈ have for his servant?"

¹⁵The commander of the LORD's army replied, "Take off your sandals, for the place where you are standing is holy." And Joshua did so.

6 Now Jericho was tightly shut up because of the Israelites. No one went out and no one came in.

²Then the LORD said to Joshua, "See, I have delivered Jericho into your hands, along with its king and its fighting men. ³March around the city once with all the armed men. Do this for six days. ⁴Have seven priests carry trumpets of rams' horns in front of the ark. On the seventh day, march around the city seven times, with the priests blowing the trumpets. ⁵When you hear them sound a long blast on the trumpets, have all the people give a loud shout; then the wall of the city will collapse and the people will go up, every man straight in."

⁶So Joshua son of Nun called the priests and said to them, "Take up the ark of the covenant of the LORD and have seven priests carry trumpets in front of it." ⁷And he ordered the people, "Advance! March around the city, with the armed guard going ahead of the ark of the LORD."

⁸When Joshua had spoken to the people, the seven priests carrying the seven trumpets before the LORD went forward, blowing their trumpets, and the ark of the LORD's covenant followed them. ⁹The armed guard marched ahead of the priests who blew the trumpets, and the rear guard followed the ark. All this time the trumpets were sounding. ¹⁰But Joshua had commanded the people, "Do not give a war cry, do not raise your voices, do not say a word until the

---

ᵃ3 *Gibeath Haaraloth* means *hill of foreskins.*   ᵇ9 *Gilgal* sounds like the Hebrew for *roll.*
ᶜ12 Or *the day*   ᵈ14 Or *lord*

day I tell you to shout. Then shout!" ¹¹So he had the ark of the LORD carried around the city, circling it once. Then the people returned to camp and spent the night there.

¹²Joshua got up early the next morning and the priests took up the ark of the LORD. ¹³The seven priests carrying the seven trumpets went forward, marching before the ark of the LORD and blowing the trumpets. The armed men went ahead of them and the rear guard followed the ark of the LORD, while the trumpets kept sounding. ¹⁴So on the second day they marched around the city once and returned to the camp. They did this for six days.

¹⁵On the seventh day, they got up at daybreak and marched around the city seven times in the same manner, except that on that day they circled the city seven times. ¹⁶The seventh time around, when the priests sounded the trumpet blast, Joshua commanded the people, "Shout! For the LORD has given you the city! ¹⁷The city and all that is in it are to be devoted*a* to the LORD. Only Rahab the prostitute*b* and all who are with her in her house shall be spared, because she hid the spies we sent. ¹⁸But keep away from the devoted things, so that you will not bring about your own destruction by taking any of them. Otherwise you will make the camp of Israel liable to destruction and bring trouble on it. ¹⁹All the silver and gold and the articles of bronze and iron are sacred to the LORD and must go into his treasury."

²⁰When the trumpets sounded, the people shouted, and at the sound of the trumpet, when the people gave a loud shout, the wall collapsed; so every man charged straight in, and they took the city. ²¹They devoted the city to the LORD and destroyed with the sword every living thing in it—men and women, young and old, cattle, sheep and donkeys.

²²Joshua said to the two men who had spied out the land, "Go into the prostitute's house and bring her out and all who belong to her, in accordance with your oath to her." ²³So the young men who had done the spying went in and brought out Rahab, her father and mother and brothers and all who belonged to her. They brought out her entire family and put them in a place outside the camp of Israel.

²⁴Then they burned the whole city and everything in it, but they put the silver and gold and the articles of bronze and iron into the treasury of the LORD's house. ²⁵But Joshua spared Rahab the prostitute, with her family and all who belonged to her, because she hid the men Joshua had sent as spies to Jericho—and she lives among the Israelites to this day.

²⁶At that time Joshua pronounced this solemn oath: "Cursed before the LORD is the man who undertakes to rebuild this city, Jericho:

"At the cost of his firstborn son
    will he lay its foundations;
at the cost of his youngest
    will he set up its gates."

²⁷So the LORD was with Joshua, and his fame spread throughout the land.

Achan's Sin

7 But the Israelites acted unfaithfully in regard to the devoted things*c*; Achan son of Carmi, the son of Zimri,*d* the son of Zerah, of the tribe of Judah, took some of them. So the LORD's anger burned against Israel.

²Now Joshua sent men from Jericho to Ai, which is near Beth Aven to the east of Bethel, and told them, "Go up

---

a17 The Hebrew term refers to the irrevocable giving over of things or persons to the LORD, often by totally destroying them; also in verses 18 and 21.   *b17* Or possibly *innkeeper*; also in verses 22 and 25   *c1* The Hebrew term refers to the irrevocable giving over of things or persons to the LORD, often by totally destroying them; also in verses 11, 12, 13 and 15.   *d1* See Septuagint and 1 Chron. 2:6; Hebrew *Zabdi*; also in verses 17 and 18.

and spy out the region." So the men went up and spied out Ai.

³When they returned to Joshua, they said, "Not all the people will have to go up against Ai. Send two or three thousand men to take it and do not weary all the people, for only a few men are there." ⁴So about three thousand men went up; but they were routed by the men of Ai, ⁵who killed about thirty-six of them. They chased the Israelites from the city gate as far

TUESDAY

VERSE:
Joshua 6:20

AUTHOR:
Dirk R. Buursma

PASSAGE:
Joshua 6:1–25

No Ordinary Plan

You must admit, it was some kind of unorthodox military strategy; march around the city for six days without saying a word, on the seventh day go around seven times, listen for the long blast of the trumpet, and then shout.

Not exactly your commonplace, ordinary procedure of battle. But Joshua heard it in striking fashion from the mouth of the commander of the Lord's army (Joshua 5:14), and he in turn passed it on to the people.

The Israelites followed God's instructions to a tee, even though the whole operation was a venture of faith that involved taking a tremendous risk. In the face of what must have seemed like insurmountable odds, they were relying on God's faithfulness. A nation notorious for its murmuring and complaining obeyed *in silence*. What a testimony to God's power.

Do you today face a personal Jericho—some unconfessed sin, some unanswered prayer for family members or friends, some seemingly hopeless situation? Perhaps God is calling you today to a new "ignoring of the odds," to a new step of faith, to a new risk-taking! The story of God's victory at Jericho rules out any hint of fatalism, which gives up hope because of high walls—because it is God himself who brings down the walls.

ADDITIONAL SCRIPTURE READINGS
Psalm 20; Isaiah 50

Go to page 271 for your next devotional reading.

as the stone quarries[a] and struck them down on the slopes. At this the hearts of the people melted and became like water.

[6]Then Joshua tore his clothes and fell facedown to the ground before the ark of the LORD, remaining there till evening. The elders of Israel did the same, and sprinkled dust on their heads. [7]And Joshua said, "Ah, Sovereign LORD, why did you ever bring this people across the Jordan to deliver us into the hands of the Amorites to destroy us? If only we had been content to stay on the other side of the Jordan! [8]O Lord, what can I say, now that Israel has been routed by its enemies? [9]The Canaanites and the other people of the country will hear about this and they will surround us and wipe out our name from the earth. What then will you do for your own great name?"

[10]The LORD said to Joshua, "Stand up! What are you doing down on your face? [11]Israel has sinned; they have violated my covenant, which I commanded them to keep. They have taken some of the devoted things; they have stolen, they have lied, they have put them with their own possessions. [12]That is why the Israelites cannot stand against their enemies; they turn their backs and run because they have been made liable to destruction. I will not be with you anymore unless you destroy whatever among you is devoted to destruction.

[13]"Go, consecrate the people. Tell them, 'Consecrate yourselves in preparation for tomorrow; for this is what the LORD, the God of Israel, says: That which is devoted is among you, O Israel. You cannot stand against your enemies until you remove it.

[14]"'In the morning, present yourselves tribe by tribe. The tribe that the LORD takes shall come forward clan by clan; the clan that the LORD takes shall come forward family by family; and the family that the LORD takes shall

come forward man by man. [15]He who is caught with the devoted things shall be destroyed by fire, along with all that belongs to him. He has violated the covenant of the LORD and has done a disgraceful thing in Israel!' "

[16]Early the next morning Joshua had Israel come forward by tribes, and Judah was taken. [17]The clans of Judah came forward, and he took the Zerahites. He had the clan of the Zerahites come forward by families, and Zimri was taken. [18]Joshua had his family come forward man by man, and Achan son of Carmi, the son of Zimri, the son of Zerah, of the tribe of Judah, was taken.

[19]Then Joshua said to Achan, "My son, give glory to the LORD,[b] the God of Israel, and give him the praise.[c] Tell me what you have done; do not hide it from me."

[20]Achan replied, "It is true! I have sinned against the LORD, the God of Israel. This is what I have done: [21]When I saw in the plunder a beautiful robe from Babylonia,[d] two hundred shekels[e] of silver and a wedge of gold weighing fifty shekels,[f] I coveted them and took them. They are hidden in the ground inside my tent, with the silver underneath."

[22]So Joshua sent messengers, and they ran to the tent, and there it was, hidden in his tent, with the silver underneath. [23]They took the things from the tent, brought them to Joshua and all the Israelites and spread them out before the LORD.

[24]Then Joshua, together with all Israel, took Achan son of Zerah, the silver, the robe, the gold wedge, his sons and daughters, his cattle, donkeys and sheep, his tent and all that he had, to the Valley of Achor. [25]Joshua said, "Why have you brought this trouble on us? The LORD will bring trouble on you today."

Then all Israel stoned him, and after they had stoned the rest, they burned them. [26]Over Achan they

---

[a]5 Or *as far as Shebarim*   [b]19 A solemn charge to tell the truth   [c]19 Or *and confess to him*
[d]21 Hebrew *Shinar*   [e]21 That is, about 5 pounds (about 2.3 kilograms)   [f]21 That is, about 1 1/4 pounds (about 0.6 kilogram)

heaped up a large pile of rocks, which remains to this day. Then the LORD turned from his fierce anger. Therefore that place has been called the Valley of Achor*a* ever since.

Ai Destroyed

8 Then the LORD said to Joshua, "Do not be afraid; do not be discouraged. Take the whole army with you, and go up and attack Ai. For I have delivered into your hands the king of Ai, his people, his city and his land. ²You shall do to Ai and its king as you did to Jericho and its king, except that you may carry off their plunder and livestock for yourselves. Set an ambush behind the city."

³So Joshua and the whole army moved out to attack Ai. He chose thirty thousand of his best fighting men and sent them out at night ⁴with these orders: "Listen carefully. You are to set an ambush behind the city. Don't go very far from it. All of you be on the alert. ⁵I and all those with me will advance on the city, and when the men come out against us, as they did before, we will flee from them. ⁶They will pursue us until we have lured them away from the city, for they will say, 'They are running away from us as they did before.' So when we flee from them, ⁷you are to rise up from ambush and take the city. The LORD your God will give it into your hand. ⁸When you have taken the city, set it on fire. Do what the LORD has commanded. See to it; you have my orders."

⁹Then Joshua sent them off, and they went to the place of ambush and lay in wait between Bethel and Ai, to the west of Ai—but Joshua spent that night with the people.

¹⁰Early the next morning Joshua mustered his men, and he and the leaders of Israel marched before them to Ai. ¹¹The entire force that was with him marched up and approached the city and arrived in front of it. They set up camp north of Ai, with the valley between them and the city. ¹²Joshua

had taken about five thousand men and set them in ambush between Bethel and Ai, to the west of the city. ¹³They had the soldiers take up their positions—all those in the camp to the north of the city and the ambush to the west of it. That night Joshua went into the valley.

¹⁴When the king of Ai saw this, he and all the men of the city hurried out early in the morning to meet Israel in battle at a certain place overlooking the Arabah. But he did not know that an ambush had been set against him behind the city. ¹⁵Joshua and all Israel let themselves be driven back before them, and they fled toward the desert. ¹⁶All the men of Ai were called to pursue them, and they pursued Joshua and were lured away from the city. ¹⁷Not a man remained in Ai or Bethel who did not go after Israel. They left the city open and went in pursuit of Israel.

¹⁸Then the LORD said to Joshua, "Hold out toward Ai the javelin that is in your hand, for into your hand I will deliver the city." So Joshua held out his javelin toward Ai. ¹⁹As soon as he did this, the men in the ambush rose quickly from their position and rushed forward. They entered the city and captured it and quickly set it on fire.

²⁰The men of Ai looked back and saw the smoke of the city rising against the sky, but they had no chance to escape in any direction, for the Israelites who had been fleeing toward the desert had turned back against their pursuers. ²¹For when Joshua and all Israel saw that the ambush had taken the city and that smoke was going up from the city, they turned around and attacked the men of Ai. ²²The men of the ambush also came out of the city against them, so that they were caught in the middle, with Israelites on both sides. Israel cut them down, leaving them neither survivors nor fugitives. ²³But they took the king of Ai alive and brought him to Joshua.

a26 Achor means *trouble.*

²⁴When Israel had finished killing all the men of Ai in the fields and in the desert where they had chased them, and when every one of them had been put to the sword, all the Israelites returned to Ai and killed those who were in it. ²⁵Twelve thousand men and women fell that day— all the people of Ai. ²⁶For Joshua did not draw back the hand that held out his javelin until he had destroyed*a* all who lived in Ai. ²⁷But Israel did carry off for themselves the livestock and plunder of this city, as the LORD had instructed Joshua.

²⁸So Joshua burned Ai and made it a permanent heap of ruins, a desolate place to this day. ²⁹He hung the king of Ai on a tree and left him there until evening. At sunset, Joshua ordered them to take his body from the tree and throw it down at the entrance of the city gate. And they raised a large pile of rocks over it, which remains to this day.

The Covenant Renewed at Mount Ebal

³⁰Then Joshua built on Mount Ebal an altar to the LORD, the God of Israel, ³¹as Moses the servant of the LORD had commanded the Israelites. He built it according to what is written in the Book of the Law of Moses—an altar of uncut stones, on which no iron tool had been used. On it they offered to the LORD burnt offerings and sacrificed fellowship offerings.*b* ³²There, in the presence of the Israelites, Joshua copied on stones the law of Moses, which he had written. ³³All Israel, aliens and citizens alike, with their elders, officials and judges, were standing on both sides of the ark of the covenant of the LORD, facing those who carried it—the priests, who were Levites. Half of the people stood in front of Mount Gerizim and half of them in front of Mount Ebal, as Moses the servant of the LORD had formerly commanded when he gave instructions to bless the people of Israel.

³⁴Afterward, Joshua read all the words of the law—the blessings and the curses—just as it is written in the Book of the Law. ³⁵There was not a word of all that Moses had commanded that Joshua did not read to the whole assembly of Israel, including the women and children, and the aliens who lived among them.

The Gibeonite Deception

9 Now when all the kings west of the Jordan heard about these things—those in the hill country, in the western foothills, and along the entire coast of the Great Sea*c* as far as Lebanon (the kings of the Hittites, Amorites, Canaanites, Perizzites, Hivites and Jebusites)— ²they came together to make war against Joshua and Israel.

³However, when the people of Gibeon heard what Joshua had done to Jericho and Ai, ⁴they resorted to a ruse: They went as a delegation whose donkeys were loaded*d* with worn-out sacks and old wineskins, cracked and mended. ⁵The men put worn and patched sandals on their feet and wore old clothes. All the bread of their food supply was dry and moldy. ⁶Then they went to Joshua in the camp at Gilgal and said to him and the men of Israel, "We have come from a distant country; make a treaty with us."

⁷The men of Israel said to the Hivites, "But perhaps you live near us. How then can we make a treaty with you?"

⁸"We are your servants," they said to Joshua.

But Joshua asked, "Who are you and where do you come from?"

⁹They answered: "Your servants have come from a very distant country because of the fame of the LORD your God. For we have heard reports

---

a26 The Hebrew term refers to the irrevocable giving over of things or persons to the LORD, often by totally destroying them.   *b31* Traditionally *peace offerings*   *c1* That is, the Mediterranean   *d4* Most Hebrew manuscripts; some Hebrew manuscripts, Vulgate and Syriac (see also Septuagint) *They prepared provisions and loaded their donkeys*

of him: all that he did in Egypt, [10]and all that he did to the two kings of the Amorites east of the Jordan—Sihon king of Heshbon, and Og king of Bashan, who reigned in Ashtaroth. [11]And our elders and all those living in our country said to us, 'Take provisions for your journey; go and meet them and say to them, "We are your servants; make a treaty with us." ' [12]This bread of ours was warm when we packed it at home on the day we left to come to you. But now see how dry and moldy it is. [13]And these wineskins that we filled were new, but see how cracked they are. And our clothes and sandals are worn out by the very long journey."

[14]The men of Israel sampled their provisions but did not inquire of the LORD. [15]Then Joshua made a treaty of peace with them to let them live, and the leaders of the assembly ratified it by oath.

[16]Three days after they made the treaty with the Gibeonites, the Israelites heard that they were neighbors, living near them. [17]So the Israelites set out and on the third day came to their cities: Gibeon, Kephirah, Beeroth and Kiriath Jearim. [18]But the Israelites did not attack them, because the leaders of the assembly had sworn an oath to them by the LORD, the God of Israel.

The whole assembly grumbled against the leaders, [19]but all the leaders answered, "We have given them our oath by the LORD, the God of Israel, and we cannot touch them now. [20]This is what we will do to them: We will let them live, so that wrath will not fall on us for breaking the oath we swore to them." [21]They continued, "Let them live, but let them be woodcutters and water carriers for the entire community." So the leaders' promise to them was kept.

[22]Then Joshua summoned the Gibeonites and said, "Why did you deceive us by saying, 'We live a long way from you,' while actually you live near us? [23]You are now under a curse: You will never cease to serve as woodcutters and water carriers for the house of my God."

[24]They answered Joshua, "Your servants were clearly told how the LORD your God had commanded his servant Moses to give you the whole land and to wipe out all its inhabitants from before you. So we feared for our lives because of you, and that is why we did this. [25]We are now in your hands. Do to us whatever seems good and right to you."

[26]So Joshua saved them from the Israelites, and they did not kill them. [27]That day he made the Gibeonites woodcutters and water carriers for the community and for the altar of the LORD at the place the LORD would choose. And that is what they are to this day.

The Sun Stands Still

10 Now Adoni-Zedek king of Jerusalem heard that Joshua had taken Ai and totally destroyed[a] it, doing to Ai and its king as he had done to Jericho and its king, and that the people of Gibeon had made a treaty of peace with Israel and were living near them. [2]He and his people were very much alarmed at this, because Gibeon was an important city, like one of the royal cities; it was larger than Ai, and all its men were good fighters. [3]So Adoni-Zedek king of Jerusalem appealed to Hoham king of Hebron, Piram king of Jarmuth, Japhia king of Lachish and Debir king of Eglon. [4]"Come up and help me attack Gibeon," he said, "because it has made peace with Joshua and the Israelites."

[5]Then the five kings of the Amorites—the kings of Jerusalem, Hebron, Jarmuth, Lachish and Eglon—joined forces. They moved up with all their troops and took up positions against Gibeon and attacked it.

[6]The Gibeonites then sent word to Joshua in the camp at Gilgal: "Do not abandon your servants. Come up to

---

[a]1 The Hebrew term refers to the irrevocable giving over of things or persons to the LORD, often by totally destroying them; also in verses 28, 35, 37, 39 and 40.

us quickly and save us! Help us, because all the Amorite kings from the hill country have joined forces against us."

⁷So Joshua marched up from Gilgal with his entire army, including all the best fighting men. ⁸The LORD said to Joshua, "Do not be afraid of them; I have given them into your hand. Not one of them will be able to withstand you."

⁹After an all-night march from Gilgal, Joshua took them by surprise. ¹⁰The LORD threw them into confusion before Israel, who defeated them in a great victory at Gibeon. Israel pursued them along the road going up to Beth Horon and cut them down all the way to Azekah and Makkedah. ¹¹As they fled before Israel on the road down from Beth Horon to Azekah, the LORD hurled large hailstones down on them from the sky, and more of them died from the hailstones than were killed by the swords of the Israelites.

¹²On the day the LORD gave the Amorites over to Israel, Joshua said to the LORD in the presence of Israel:

"O sun, stand still over Gibeon,
    O moon, over the Valley of
        Aijalon."
¹³So the sun stood still,
    and the moon stopped,
    till the nation avenged itself
        on*a* its enemies,

as it is written in the Book of Jashar.

The sun stopped in the middle of the sky and delayed going down about a full day. ¹⁴There has never been a day like it before or since, a day when the LORD listened to a man. Surely the LORD was fighting for Israel!

¹⁵Then Joshua returned with all Israel to the camp at Gilgal.

Five Amorite Kings Killed

¹⁶Now the five kings had fled and hidden in the cave at Makkedah. ¹⁷When Joshua was told that the five kings had been found hiding in the cave at Makkedah, ¹⁸he said, "Roll large rocks up to the mouth of the cave, and post some men there to guard it. ¹⁹But don't stop! Pursue your enemies, attack them from the rear and don't let them reach their cities, for the LORD your God has given them into your hand."

²⁰So Joshua and the Israelites destroyed them completely—almost to a man—but the few who were left reached their fortified cities. ²¹The whole army then returned safely to Joshua in the camp at Makkedah, and no one uttered a word against the Israelites.

²²Joshua said, "Open the mouth of the cave and bring those five kings out to me." ²³So they brought the five kings out of the cave—the kings of Jerusalem, Hebron, Jarmuth, Lachish and Eglon. ²⁴When they had brought these kings to Joshua, he summoned all the men of Israel and said to the army commanders who had come with him, "Come here and put your feet on the necks of these kings." So they came forward and placed their feet on their necks.

²⁵Joshua said to them, "Do not be afraid; do not be discouraged. Be strong and courageous. This is what the LORD will do to all the enemies you are going to fight." ²⁶Then Joshua struck and killed the kings and hung them on five trees, and they were left hanging on the trees until evening.

²⁷At sunset Joshua gave the order and they took them down from the trees and threw them into the cave where they had been hiding. At the mouth of the cave they placed large rocks, which are there to this day.

²⁸That day Joshua took Makkedah. He put the city and its king to the sword and totally destroyed everyone in it. He left no survivors. And he did to the king of Makkedah as he had done to the king of Jericho.

Southern Cities Conquered

²⁹Then Joshua and all Israel with him moved on from Makkedah to

---

*a*13 Or *nation triumphed over*

Libnah and attacked it. ³⁰The LORD also gave that city and its king into Israel's hand. The city and everyone in it Joshua put to the sword. He left no survivors there. And he did to its king as he had done to the king of Jericho.

³¹Then Joshua and all Israel with him moved on from Libnah to Lachish; he took up positions against it and attacked it. ³²The LORD handed Lachish over to Israel, and Joshua took it on the second day. The city and everyone in it he put to the sword, just as he had done to Libnah. ³³Meanwhile, Horam king of Gezer had come up to help Lachish, but Joshua defeated him and his army—until no survivors were left.

³⁴Then Joshua and all Israel with him moved on from Lachish to Eglon; they took up positions against it and attacked it. ³⁵They captured it that same day and put it to the sword and totally destroyed everyone in it, just as they had done to Lachish.

³⁶Then Joshua and all Israel with him went up from Eglon to Hebron and attacked it. ³⁷They took the city and put it to the sword, together with its king, its villages and everyone in it. They left no survivors. Just as at Eglon, they totally destroyed it and everyone in it.

³⁸Then Joshua and all Israel with him turned around and attacked Debir. ³⁹They took the city, its king and its villages, and put them to the sword. Everyone in it they totally destroyed. They left no survivors. They did to Debir and its king as they had done to Libnah and its king and to Hebron.

⁴⁰So Joshua subdued the whole region, including the hill country, the Negev, the western foothills and the mountain slopes, together with all their kings. He left no survivors. He totally destroyed all who breathed, just as the LORD, the God of Israel, had commanded. ⁴¹Joshua subdued them from Kadesh Barnea to Gaza and from the whole region of Goshen to Gibeon. ⁴²All these kings and their lands Joshua conquered in one campaign, because the LORD, the God of Israel, fought for Israel.

⁴³Then Joshua returned with all Israel to the camp at Gilgal.

Northern Kings Defeated

11 When Jabin king of Hazor heard of this, he sent word to Jobab king of Madon, to the kings of Shimron and Acshaph, ²and to the northern kings who were in the mountains, in the Arabah south of Kinnereth, in the western foothills and in Naphoth Dor*ᵃ* on the west; ³to the Canaanites in the east and west; to the Amorites, Hittites, Perizzites and Jebusites in the hill country; and to the Hivites below Hermon in the region of Mizpah. ⁴They came out with all their troops and a large number of horses and chariots—a huge army, as numerous as the sand on the seashore. ⁵All these kings joined forces and made camp together at the Waters of Merom, to fight against Israel.

⁶The LORD said to Joshua, "Do not be afraid of them, because by this time tomorrow I will hand all of them over to Israel, slain. You are to hamstring their horses and burn their chariots."

⁷So Joshua and his whole army came against them suddenly at the Waters of Merom and attacked them, ⁸and the LORD gave them into the hand of Israel. They defeated them and pursued them all the way to Greater Sidon, to Misrephoth Maim, and to the Valley of Mizpah on the east, until no survivors were left. ⁹Joshua did to them as the LORD had directed: He hamstrung their horses and burned their chariots.

¹⁰At that time Joshua turned back and captured Hazor and put its king to the sword. (Hazor had been the head of all these kingdoms.) ¹¹Everyone in it they put to the sword. They

---

ᵃ2 Or *in the heights of Dor*

totally destroyed[a] them, not sparing anything that breathed, and he burned up Hazor itself.

[12]Joshua took all these royal cities and their kings and put them to the sword. He totally destroyed them, as Moses the servant of the LORD had commanded. [13]Yet Israel did not burn any of the cities built on their mounds—except Hazor, which Joshua burned. [14]The Israelites carried off for themselves all the plunder and livestock of these cities, but all the people they put to the sword until they completely destroyed them, not sparing anyone that breathed. [15]As the LORD commanded his servant Moses, so Moses commanded Joshua, and Joshua did it; he left nothing undone of all that the LORD commanded Moses.

[16]So Joshua took this entire land: the hill country, all the Negev, the whole region of Goshen, the western foothills, the Arabah and the mountains of Israel with their foothills, [17]from Mount Halak, which rises toward Seir, to Baal Gad in the Valley of Lebanon below Mount Hermon. He captured all their kings and struck them down, putting them to death. [18]Joshua waged war against all these kings for a long time. [19]Except for the Hivites living in Gibeon, not one city made a treaty of peace with the Israelites, who took them all in battle. [20]For it was the LORD himself who hardened their hearts to wage war against Israel, so that he might destroy them totally, exterminating them without mercy, as the LORD had commanded Moses.

[21]At that time Joshua went and destroyed the Anakites from the hill country: from Hebron, Debir and Anab, from all the hill country of Judah, and from all the hill country of Israel. Joshua totally destroyed them and their towns. [22]No Anakites were left in Israelite territory; only in Gaza, Gath and Ashdod did any survive.

[23]So Joshua took the entire land, just as the LORD had directed Moses, and he gave it as an inheritance to Israel according to their tribal divisions.

Then the land had rest from war.

List of Defeated Kings

12 These are the kings of the land whom the Israelites had defeated and whose territory they took over east of the Jordan, from the Arnon Gorge to Mount Hermon, including all the eastern side of the Arabah:

[2]Sihon king of the Amorites,
who reigned in Heshbon. He ruled from Aroer on the rim of the Arnon Gorge—from the middle of the gorge—to the Jabbok River, which is the border of the Ammonites. This included half of Gilead. [3]He also ruled over the eastern Arabah from the Sea of Kinnereth[b] to the Sea of the Arabah (the Salt Sea[c]), to Beth Jeshimoth, and then southward below the slopes of Pisgah.

[4]And the territory of Og king of Bashan,
one of the last of the Rephaites, who reigned in Ashtaroth and Edrei. [5]He ruled over Mount Hermon, Salecah, all of Bashan to the border of the people of Geshur and Maacah, and half of Gilead to the border of Sihon king of Heshbon.

[6]Moses, the servant of the LORD, and the Israelites conquered them. And Moses the servant of the LORD gave their land to the Reubenites, the Gadites and the half-tribe of Manasseh to be their possession.

[7]These are the kings of the land that Joshua and the Israelites conquered on the west side of the Jordan, from Baal Gad in the Valley of Lebanon to Mount Halak, which rises toward Seir (their lands Joshua gave as an inheritance to the tribes of Israel according to their tribal divisions— [8]the hill

---

[a]11 The Hebrew term refers to the irrevocable giving over of things or persons to the LORD, often by totally destroying them; also in verses 12, 20 and 21.   [b]3 That is, Galilee   [c]3 That is, the Dead Sea

country, the western foothills, the Arabah, the mountain slopes, the desert and the Negev—the lands of the Hittites, Amorites, Canaanites, Perizzites, Hivites and Jebusites):

[9] the king of Jericho	one
the king of Ai (near Bethel)	one
[10] the king of Jerusalem	one
the king of Hebron	one
[11] the king of Jarmuth	one
the king of Lachish	one
[12] the king of Eglon	one
the king of Gezer	one
[13] the king of Debir	one
the king of Geder	one
[14] the king of Hormah	one
the king of Arad	one
[15] the king of Libnah	one
the king of Adullam	one
[16] the king of Makkedah	one
the king of Bethel	one
[17] the king of Tappuah	one
the king of Hepher	one
[18] the king of Aphek	one
the king of Lasharon	one
[19] the king of Madon	one
the king of Hazor	one
[20] the king of Shimron Meron	one
the king of Acshaph	one
[21] the king of Taanach	one
the king of Megiddo	one
[22] the king of Kedesh	one
the king of Jokneam in Carmel	one
[23] the king of Dor (in Naphoth Dor[a])	one
the king of Goyim in Gilgal	one
[24] the king of Tirzah	one

thirty-one kings in all.

Land Still to Be Taken

13 When Joshua was old and well advanced in years, the LORD said to him, "You are very old, and there are still very large areas of land to be taken over.

[2] "This is the land that remains: all the regions of the Philistines

and Geshurites: [3] from the Shihor River on the east of Egypt to the territory of Ekron on the north, all of it counted as Canaanite (the territory of the five Philistine rulers in Gaza, Ashdod, Ashkelon, Gath and Ekron—that of the Avvites); [4] from the south, all the land of the Canaanites, from Arah of the Sidonians as far as Aphek, the region of the Amorites, [5] the area of the Gebalites[b]; and all Lebanon to the east, from Baal Gad below Mount Hermon to Lebo[c] Hamath.

[6] "As for all the inhabitants of the mountain regions from Lebanon to Misrephoth Maim, that is, all the Sidonians, I myself will drive them out before the Israelites. Be sure to allocate this land to Israel for an inheritance, as I have instructed you, [7] and divide it as an inheritance among the nine tribes and half of the tribe of Manasseh."

Division of the Land East of the Jordan

[8] The other half of Manasseh,[d] the Reubenites and the Gadites had received the inheritance that Moses had given them east of the Jordan, as he, the servant of the LORD, had assigned it to them.

[9] It extended from Aroer on the rim of the Arnon Gorge, and from the town in the middle of the gorge, and included the whole plateau of Medeba as far as Dibon, [10] and all the towns of Sihon king of the Amorites, who ruled in Heshbon, out to the border of the Ammonites. [11] It also included Gilead, the territory of the people of Geshur and Maacah, all of Mount Hermon and all Bashan as far as Salecah— [12] that is, the whole kingdom of Og in Bashan, who had reigned in Ashtaroth and Edrei and had survived as one of the last of the

---

[a]23 Or *in the heights of Dor*   [b]5 That is, the area of Byblos   [c]5 Or *to the entrance to*
[d]8 Hebrew *With it* (that is, with the other half of Manasseh)

Rephaites. Moses had defeated them and taken over their land. ¹³But the Israelites did not drive out the people of Geshur and Maacah, so they continue to live among the Israelites to this day.

¹⁴But to the tribe of Levi he gave no inheritance, since the offerings made by fire to the LORD, the God of Israel, are their inheritance, as he promised them.

¹⁵This is what Moses had given to the tribe of Reuben, clan by clan:

¹⁶The territory from Aroer on the rim of the Arnon Gorge, and from the town in the middle of the gorge, and the whole plateau past Medeba ¹⁷to Heshbon and all its towns on the plateau, including Dibon, Bamoth Baal, Beth Baal Meon, ¹⁸Jahaz, Kedemoth, Mephaath, ¹⁹Kiriathaim, Sibmah, Zereth Shahar on the hill in the valley, ²⁰Beth Peor, the slopes of Pisgah, and Beth Jeshimoth ²¹—all the towns on the plateau and the entire realm of Sihon king of the Amorites, who ruled at Heshbon. Moses had defeated him and the Midianite chiefs, Evi, Rekem, Zur, Hur and Reba—princes allied with Sihon—who lived in that country. ²²In addition to those slain in battle, the Israelites had put to the sword Balaam son of Beor, who practiced divination. ²³The boundary of the Reubenites was the bank of the Jordan. These towns and their villages were the inheritance of the Reubenites, clan by clan.

²⁴This is what Moses had given to the tribe of Gad, clan by clan:

²⁵The territory of Jazer, all the towns of Gilead and half the Ammonite country as far as Aroer, near Rabbah; ²⁶and from Heshbon to Ramath Mizpah and Betonim, and from Mahanaim to the territory of Debir; ²⁷and in the valley, Beth Haram, Beth Nimrah, Succoth and Zaphon with the rest of the realm of Sihon king of Heshbon (the east side of the Jordan, the territory up to the end of the Sea of Kinnereth^a). ²⁸These towns and their villages were the inheritance of the Gadites, clan by clan.

²⁹This is what Moses had given to the half-tribe of Manasseh, that is, to half the family of the descendants of Manasseh, clan by clan:

³⁰The territory extending from Mahanaim and including all of Bashan, the entire realm of Og king of Bashan—all the settlements of Jair in Bashan, sixty towns, ³¹half of Gilead, and Ashtaroth and Edrei (the royal cities of Og in Bashan). This was for the descendants of Makir son of Manasseh—for half of the sons of Makir, clan by clan.

³²This is the inheritance Moses had given when he was in the plains of Moab across the Jordan east of Jericho. ³³But to the tribe of Levi, Moses had given no inheritance; the LORD, the God of Israel, is their inheritance, as he promised them.

Division of the Land West of the Jordan

14 Now these are the areas the Israelites received as an inheritance in the land of Canaan, which Eleazar the priest, Joshua son of Nun and the heads of the tribal clans of Israel allotted to them. ²Their inheritances were assigned by lot to the nine-and-a-half tribes, as the LORD had commanded through Moses. ³Moses had granted the two-and-a-half tribes their inheritance east of the Jordan but had not granted the Levites an inheritance among the rest, ⁴for the sons of Joseph had become two tribes— Manasseh and Ephraim. The Levites received no share of the land but only

---

*a*27 That is, Galilee

towns to live in, with pasturelands for their flocks and herds. [5]So the Israelites divided the land, just as the LORD had commanded Moses.

Hebron Given to Caleb

[6]Now the men of Judah approached Joshua at Gilgal, and Caleb son of Jephunneh the Kenizzite said to him, "You know what the LORD said to Moses the man of God at Kadesh Barnea about you and me. [7]I was forty years old when Moses the servant of the LORD sent me from Kadesh Barnea to explore the land. And I brought him back a report according to my convictions, [8]but my brothers who went up with me made the hearts of the people melt with fear. I, however, followed the LORD my God wholeheartedly. [9]So on that day Moses swore to me, 'The land on which your feet have walked will be your inheritance and that of your children forever, because you have followed the LORD my God wholeheartedly.'[a]

[10]"Now then, just as the LORD promised, he has kept me alive for forty-five years since the time he said this to Moses, while Israel moved about in the desert. So here I am today, eighty-five years old! [11]I am still as strong today as the day Moses sent me out; I'm just as vigorous to go out to battle now as I was then. [12]Now give me this hill country that the LORD promised me that day. You yourself heard then that the Anakites were there and their cities were large and fortified, but, the LORD helping me, I will drive them out just as he said."

[13]Then Joshua blessed Caleb son of Jephunneh and gave him Hebron as his inheritance. [14]So Hebron has belonged to Caleb son of Jephunneh the Kenizzite ever since, because he followed the LORD, the God of Israel, wholeheartedly. [15](Hebron used to be called Kiriath Arba after Arba, who was the greatest man among the Anakites.)

Then the land had rest from war.

Allotment for Judah

15 The allotment for the tribe of Judah, clan by clan, extended down to the territory of Edom, to the Desert of Zin in the extreme south.

[2]Their southern boundary started from the bay at the southern end of the Salt Sea,[b] [3]crossed south of Scorpion[c] Pass, continued on to Zin and went over to the south of Kadesh Barnea. Then it ran past Hezron up to Addar and curved around to Karka. [4]It then passed along to Azmon and joined the Wadi of Egypt, ending at the sea. This is their[d] southern boundary.

[5]The eastern boundary is the Salt Sea as far as the mouth of the Jordan.

The northern boundary started from the bay of the sea at the mouth of the Jordan, [6]went up to Beth Hoglah and continued north of Beth Arabah to the Stone of Bohan son of Reuben. [7]The boundary then went up to Debir from the Valley of Achor and turned north to Gilgal, which faces the Pass of Adummim south of the gorge. It continued along to the waters of En Shemesh and came out at En Rogel. [8]Then it ran up the Valley of Ben Hinnom along the southern slope of the Jebusite city (that is, Jerusalem). From there it climbed to the top of the hill west of the Hinnom Valley at the northern end of the Valley of Rephaim. [9]From the hilltop the boundary headed toward the spring of the waters of Nephtoah, came out at the towns of Mount Ephron and went down toward Baalah (that is, Kiriath Jearim). [10]Then it curved westward from Baalah to Mount Seir, ran along the northern slope of Mount Jearim (that is, Kesalon), continued down to Beth She-

---

[a]9 Deut. 1:36   [b]2 That is, the Dead Sea; also in verse 5   [c]3 Hebrew *Akrabbim*
[d]4 Hebrew *your*

VERSE:
Joshua 14:8

AUTHOR:
Charles R. Swindoll

PASSAGE:
Joshua 14:6–15

A Fresh Run at Life

I cannot imagine anything more boring and less desirable than being poured into the mold of predictability as I grow older. Few things interest me less than the routine, the norm, the expected, the status quo. Call it the rebel in me, but I simply can't bear plain vanilla when life offers so many other colorful and stimulating flavors. A fresh run at life by an untried route will get my vote every time — in spite of the risk . . .

Life abounds with everyday problems needing transformation into creative projects. Try taking life by the throat and achieve mastery over a few things that have haunted and harassed you long enough. Or — how about a course at a nearby school . . . or a serious study of some subject all on your own. Why not broaden yourself in some *new* way to the greater glory of God.

Remember our old friend, Caleb. He was 85 and still growing when he gripped an uncertain future and put the torch to the bridges behind him. At a time when the ease and comfort of retirement seemed predictable, he fearlessly faced the invincible giants of the mountain. Read Joshua 14. There was no dust on that fella. Every new sunrise introduced another reminder that his body and rocking chair weren't made for each other. While his peers were yawning, Caleb was yearning.

Every one of us was poured into a mold . . . but some are "moldier" than others. If you are determined and work quickly, you can keep the concrete of predictability from setting rock-hard up to your ears.

ADDITIONAL SCRIPTURE READINGS
Numbers 13:26–33; Numbers 14:17–25

Go to page 281 for your next devotional reading.

mesh and crossed to Timnah. ¹¹It went to the northern slope of Ekron, turned toward Shikkeron, passed along to Mount Baalah and reached Jabneel. The boundary ended at the sea.

¹²The western boundary is the coastline of the Great Sea.ᵃ These are the boundaries around the people of Judah by their clans.

¹³In accordance with the LORD's command to him, Joshua gave to Caleb son of Jephunneh a portion in Judah—Kiriath Arba, that is, Hebron. (Arba was the forefather of Anak.) ¹⁴From Hebron Caleb drove out the three Anakites—Sheshai, Ahiman and Talmai—descendants of Anak. ¹⁵From there he marched against the people living in Debir (formerly called Kiriath Sepher). ¹⁶And Caleb said, "I will give my daughter Acsah in marriage to the man who attacks and captures Kiriath Sepher." ¹⁷Othniel son of Kenaz, Caleb's brother, took it; so Caleb gave his daughter Acsah to him in marriage.

¹⁸One day when she came to Othniel, she urged himᵇ to ask her father for a field. When she got off her donkey, Caleb asked her, "What can I do for you?"

¹⁹She replied, "Do me a special favor. Since you have given me land in the Negev, give me also springs of water." So Caleb gave her the upper and lower springs.

²⁰This is the inheritance of the tribe of Judah, clan by clan:

²¹The southernmost towns of the tribe of Judah in the Negev toward the boundary of Edom were:

Kabzeel, Eder, Jagur, ²²Kinah, Dimonah, Adadah, ²³Kedesh, Hazor, Ithnan, ²⁴Ziph, Telem, Bealoth, ²⁵Hazor Hadattah, Kerioth Hezron (that is, Hazor), ²⁶Amam, Shema, Moladah, ²⁷Hazar Gaddah, Heshmon, Beth Pelet, ²⁸Hazar Shual, Beersheba, Biziothiah, ²⁹Baalah, Iim, Ezem, ³⁰Eltolad, Kesil, Hormah, ³¹Ziklag, Madmannah, Sansannah, ³²Lebaoth, Shilhim, Ain and Rimmon—a total of twenty-nine towns and their villages.

³³In the western foothills:

Eshtaol, Zorah, Ashnah, ³⁴Zanoah, En Gannim, Tappuah, Enam, ³⁵Jarmuth, Adullam, Socoh, Azekah, ³⁶Shaaraim, Adithaim and Gederah (or Gederothaim)ᶜ—fourteen towns and their villages.

³⁷Zenan, Hadashah, Migdal Gad, ³⁸Dilean, Mizpah, Joktheel, ³⁹Lachish, Bozkath, Eglon, ⁴⁰Cabbon, Lahmas, Kitlish, ⁴¹Gederoth, Beth Dagon, Naamah and Makkedah—sixteen towns and their villages.

⁴²Libnah, Ether, Ashan, ⁴³Iphtah, Ashnah, Nezib, ⁴⁴Keilah, Aczib and Mareshah—nine towns and their villages.

⁴⁵Ekron, with its surrounding settlements and villages; ⁴⁶west of Ekron, all that were in the vicinity of Ashdod, together with their villages; ⁴⁷Ashdod, its surrounding settlements and villages; and Gaza, its settlements and villages, as far as the Wadi of Egypt and the coastline of the Great Sea.

⁴⁸In the hill country:

Shamir, Jattir, Socoh, ⁴⁹Dannah, Kiriath Sannah (that is, Debir), ⁵⁰Anab, Eshtemoh, Anim, ⁵¹Goshen, Holon and Giloh—eleven towns and their villages.

⁵²Arab, Dumah, Eshan, ⁵³Janim, Beth Tappuah, Aphekah, ⁵⁴Humtah, Kiriath Arba (that is, Hebron) and Zior—nine towns and their villages.

⁵⁵Maon, Carmel, Ziph, Juttah, ⁵⁶Jezreel, Jokdeam, Zanoah, ⁵⁷Kain, Gibeah and Timnah—ten towns and their villages.

ᵃ12 That is, the Mediterranean; also in verse 47   ᵇ18 Hebrew and some Septuagint manuscripts; other Septuagint manuscripts (see also note at Judges 1:14) *Othniel, he urged her* ᶜ36 Or *Gederah and Gederothaim*

⁵⁸Halhul, Beth Zur, Gedor, ⁵⁹Maarath, Beth Anoth and Eltekon—six towns and their villages.

⁶⁰Kiriath Baal (that is, Kiriath Jearim) and Rabbah—two towns and their villages.

⁶¹In the desert:

Beth Arabah, Middin, Secacah, ⁶²Nibshan, the City of Salt and En Gedi—six towns and their villages.

⁶³Judah could not dislodge the Jebusites, who were living in Jerusalem; to this day the Jebusites live there with the people of Judah.

Allotment for Ephraim and Manasseh

16 The allotment for Joseph began at the Jordan of Jericho,ᵃ east of the waters of Jericho, and went up from there through the desert into the hill country of Bethel. ²It went on from Bethel (that is, Luz),ᵇ crossed over to the territory of the Arkites in Ataroth, ³descended westward to the territory of the Japhletites as far as the region of Lower Beth Horon and on to Gezer, ending at the sea.

⁴So Manasseh and Ephraim, the descendants of Joseph, received their inheritance.

⁵This was the territory of Ephraim, clan by clan:

The boundary of their inheritance went from Ataroth Addar in the east to Upper Beth Horon ⁶and continued to the sea. From Micmethath on the north it curved eastward to Taanath Shiloh, passing by it to Janoah on the east. ⁷Then it went down from Janoah to Ataroth and Naarah, touched Jericho and came out at the Jordan. ⁸From Tappuah the border went west to the Kanah Ravine and ended at the sea. This was the inheritance of the tribe of the Ephraimites, clan by clan. ⁹It also included all the towns and their villages that were set aside for the Ephraimites within the inheritance of the Manassites.

¹⁰They did not dislodge the Canaanites living in Gezer; to this day the Canaanites live among the people of Ephraim but are required to do forced labor.

17 This was the allotment for the tribe of Manasseh as Joseph's firstborn, that is, for Makir, Manasseh's firstborn. Makir was the ancestor of the Gileadites, who had received Gilead and Bashan because the Makirites were great soldiers. ²So this allotment was for the rest of the people of Manasseh—the clans of Abiezer, Helek, Asriel, Shechem, Hepher and Shemida. These are the other male descendants of Manasseh son of Joseph by their clans.

³Now Zelophehad son of Hepher, the son of Gilead, the son of Makir, the son of Manasseh, had no sons but only daughters, whose names were Mahlah, Noah, Hoglah, Milcah and Tirzah. ⁴They went to Eleazar the priest, Joshua son of Nun, and the leaders and said, "The LORD commanded Moses to give us an inheritance among our brothers." So Joshua gave them an inheritance along with the brothers of their father, according to the LORD's command. ⁵Manasseh's share consisted of ten tracts of land besides Gilead and Bashan east of the Jordan, ⁶because the daughters of the tribe of Manasseh received an inheritance among the sons. The land of Gilead belonged to the rest of the descendants of Manasseh.

⁷The territory of Manasseh extended from Asher to Micmethath east of Shechem. The boundary ran southward from there to include the people living at En Tappuah. ⁸(Manasseh had the land of Tappuah, but Tappuah itself, on the boundary of Ma-

---

ᵃ1 Jordan of Jericho was possibly an ancient name for the Jordan River.   ᵇ2 Septuagint; Hebrew Bethel to Luz

nasseh, belonged to the Ephraimites.) ⁹Then the boundary
continued south to the Kanah
Ravine. There were towns belonging to Ephraim lying among
the towns of Manasseh, but the
boundary of Manasseh was the
northern side of the ravine and
ended at the sea. ¹⁰On the south
the land belonged to Ephraim,
on the north to Manasseh. The
territory of Manasseh reached
the sea and bordered Asher on
the north and Issachar on the
east.

¹¹Within Issachar and Asher,
Manasseh also had Beth Shan,
Ibleam and the people of Dor,
Endor, Taanach and Megiddo,
together with their surrounding
settlements (the third in the list
is Naphoth*a*).

¹²Yet the Manassites were not able to
occupy these towns, for the Canaanites were determined to live in that
region. ¹³However, when the Israelites grew stronger, they subjected the
Canaanites to forced labor but did not
drive them out completely.

¹⁴The people of Joseph said to Joshua, "Why have you given us only one
allotment and one portion for an inheritance? We are a numerous people
and the LORD has blessed us abundantly."

¹⁵"If you are so numerous," Joshua
answered, "and if the hill country of
Ephraim is too small for you, go up
into the forest and clear land for yourselves there in the land of the Perizzites and Rephaites."

¹⁶The people of Joseph replied,
"The hill country is not enough for us,
and all the Canaanites who live in the
plain have iron chariots, both those in
Beth Shan and its settlements and
those in the Valley of Jezreel."

¹⁷But Joshua said to the house of
Joseph—to Ephraim and Manasseh—
"You are numerous and very powerful. You will have not only one allotment ¹⁸but the forested hill country as
well. Clear it, and its farthest limits

will be yours; though the Canaanites
have iron chariots and though they
are strong, you can drive them out."

Division of the Rest of the Land

18 The whole assembly of the Israelites gathered at Shiloh and
set up the Tent of Meeting there. The
country was brought under their control, ²but there were still seven Israelite tribes who had not yet received
their inheritance.

³So Joshua said to the Israelites:
"How long will you wait before you
begin to take possession of the land
that the LORD, the God of your fathers,
has given you? ⁴Appoint three men
from each tribe. I will send them out
to make a survey of the land and to
write a description of it, according to
the inheritance of each. Then they will
return to me. ⁵You are to divide the
land into seven parts. Judah is to remain in its territory on the south and
the house of Joseph in its territory on
the north. ⁶After you have written descriptions of the seven parts of the
land, bring them here to me and I will
cast lots for you in the presence of the
LORD our God. ⁷The Levites, however,
do not get a portion among you, because the priestly service of the LORD
is their inheritance. And Gad, Reuben
and the half-tribe of Manasseh have
already received their inheritance on
the east side of the Jordan. Moses the
servant of the LORD gave it to them."

⁸As the men started on their way to
map out the land, Joshua instructed
them, "Go and make a survey of the
land and write a description of it.
Then return to me, and I will cast lots
for you here at Shiloh in the presence
of the LORD." ⁹So the men left and
went through the land. They wrote its
description on a scroll, town by town,
in seven parts, and returned to Joshua
in the camp at Shiloh. ¹⁰Joshua then
cast lots for them in Shiloh in the
presence of the LORD, and there he distributed the land to the Israelites according to their tribal divisions.

a11 That is, Naphoth Dor

Allotment for Benjamin

¹¹The lot came up for the tribe of Benjamin, clan by clan. Their allotted territory lay between the tribes of Judah and Joseph:

¹²On the north side their boundary began at the Jordan, passed the northern slope of Jericho and headed west into the hill country, coming out at the desert of Beth Aven. ¹³From there it crossed to the south slope of Luz (that is, Bethel) and went down to Ataroth Addar on the hill south of Lower Beth Horon.

¹⁴From the hill facing Beth Horon on the south the boundary turned south along the western side and came out at Kiriath Baal (that is, Kiriath Jearim), a town of the people of Judah. This was the western side.

¹⁵The southern side began at the outskirts of Kiriath Jearim on the west, and the boundary came out at the spring of the waters of Nephtoah. ¹⁶The boundary went down to the foot of the hill facing the Valley of Ben Hinnom, north of the Valley of Rephaim. It continued down the Hinnom Valley along the southern slope of the Jebusite city and so to En Rogel. ¹⁷It then curved north, went to En Shemesh, continued to Geliloth, which faces the Pass of Adummim, and ran down to the Stone of Bohan son of Reuben. ¹⁸It continued to the northern slope of Beth Arabahᵃ and on down into the Arabah. ¹⁹It then went to the northern slope of Beth Hoglah and came out at the northern bay of the Salt Sea,ᵇ at the mouth of the Jordan in the south. This was the southern boundary.

²⁰The Jordan formed the boundary on the eastern side.

These were the boundaries that marked out the inheritance of the clans of Benjamin on all sides.

²¹The tribe of Benjamin, clan by clan, had the following cities:

Jericho, Beth Hoglah, Emek Keziz, ²²Beth Arabah, Zemaraim, Bethel, ²³Avvim, Parah, Ophrah, ²⁴Kephar Ammoni, Ophni and Geba—twelve towns and their villages.

²⁵Gibeon, Ramah, Beeroth, ²⁶Mizpah, Kephirah, Mozah, ²⁷Rekem, Irpeel, Taralah, ²⁸Zelah, Haeleph, the Jebusite city (that is, Jerusalem), Gibeah and Kiriath—fourteen towns and their villages.

This was the inheritance of Benjamin for its clans.

Allotment for Simeon

19 The second lot came out for the tribe of Simeon, clan by clan. Their inheritance lay within the territory of Judah. ²It included:

Beersheba (or Sheba),ᶜ Moladah, ³Hazar Shual, Balah, Ezem, ⁴Eltolad, Bethul, Hormah, ⁵Ziklag, Beth Marcaboth, Hazar Susah, ⁶Beth Lebaoth and Sharuhen—thirteen towns and their villages;

⁷Ain, Rimmon, Ether and Ashan—four towns and their villages— ⁸and all the villages around these towns as far as Baalath Beer (Ramah in the Negev).

This was the inheritance of the tribe of the Simeonites, clan by clan. ⁹The inheritance of the Simeonites was taken from the share of Judah, because Judah's portion was more than they needed. So the Simeonites received their inheritance within the territory of Judah.

Allotment for Zebulun

¹⁰The third lot came up for Zebulun, clan by clan:

The boundary of their inheritance went as far as Sarid. ¹¹Go-

---

ᵃ18 Septuagint; Hebrew *slope facing the Arabah*   ᵇ19 That is, the Dead Sea   ᶜ2 Or *Beersheba,*
Sheba; 1 Chron. 4:28 does not have *Sheba*.

ing west it ran to Maralah, touched Dabbesheth, and extended to the ravine near Jokneam. ¹²It turned east from Sarid toward the sunrise to the territory of Kisloth Tabor and went on to Daberath and up to Japhia. ¹³Then it continued eastward to Gath Hepher and Eth Kazin; it came out at Rimmon and turned toward Neah. ¹⁴There the boundary went around on the north to Hannathon and ended at the Valley of Iphtah El. ¹⁵Included were Kattath, Nahalal, Shimron, Idalah and Bethlehem. There were twelve towns and their villages.

¹⁶These towns and their villages were the inheritance of Zebulun, clan by clan.

Allotment for Issachar

¹⁷The fourth lot came out for Issachar, clan by clan. ¹⁸Their territory included:

Jezreel, Kesulloth, Shunem, ¹⁹Hapharaim, Shion, Anaharath, ²⁰Rabbith, Kishion, Ebez, ²¹Remeth, En Gannim, En Haddah and Beth Pazzez. ²²The boundary touched Tabor, Shahazumah and Beth Shemesh, and ended at the Jordan. There were sixteen towns and their villages.

²³These towns and their villages were the inheritance of the tribe of Issachar, clan by clan.

Allotment for Asher

²⁴The fifth lot came out for the tribe of Asher, clan by clan. ²⁵Their territory included:

Helkath, Hali, Beten, Acshaph, ²⁶Allammelech, Amad and Mishal. On the west the boundary touched Carmel and Shihor Libnath. ²⁷It then turned east toward Beth Dagon, touched Zebulun and the Valley of Iphtah El, and went north to Beth Emek and Neiel, passing Cabul on the left.

²⁸It went to Abdon,^a Rehob, Hammon and Kanah, as far as Greater Sidon. ²⁹The boundary then turned back toward Ramah and went to the fortified city of Tyre, turned toward Hosah and came out at the sea in the region of Aczib, ³⁰Ummah, Aphek and Rehob. There were twenty-two towns and their villages.

³¹These towns and their villages were the inheritance of the tribe of Asher, clan by clan.

Allotment for Naphtali

³²The sixth lot came out for Naphtali, clan by clan:

³³Their boundary went from Heleph and the large tree in Zaanannim, passing Adami Nekeb and Jabneel to Lakkum and ending at the Jordan. ³⁴The boundary ran west through Aznoth Tabor and came out at Hukkok. It touched Zebulun on the south, Asher on the west and the Jordan^b on the east. ³⁵The fortified cities were Ziddim, Zer, Hammath, Rakkath, Kinnereth, ³⁶Adamah, Ramah, Hazor, ³⁷Kedesh, Edrei, En Hazor, ³⁸Iron, Migdal El, Horem, Beth Anath and Beth Shemesh. There were nineteen towns and their villages.

³⁹These towns and their villages were the inheritance of the tribe of Naphtali, clan by clan.

Allotment for Dan

⁴⁰The seventh lot came out for the tribe of Dan, clan by clan. ⁴¹The territory of their inheritance included:

Zorah, Eshtaol, Ir Shemesh, ⁴²Shaalabbin, Aijalon, Ithlah, ⁴³Elon, Timnah, Ekron, ⁴⁴Eltekeh, Gibbethon, Baalath, ⁴⁵Jehud, Bene Berak, Gath Rimmon, ⁴⁶Me Jarkon and Rakkon, with the area facing Joppa.

⁴⁷(But the Danites had difficulty taking possession of their territory, so they went up and attacked Leshem,

---

^a28 Some Hebrew manuscripts (see also Joshua 21:30); most Hebrew manuscripts *Ebron*
^b34 Septuagint; Hebrew *west, and Judah, the Jordan,*

took it, put it to the sword and occupied it. They settled in Leshem and named it Dan after their forefather.) [48]These towns and their villages were the inheritance of the tribe of Dan, clan by clan.

Allotment for Joshua

[49]When they had finished dividing the land into its allotted portions, the Israelites gave Joshua son of Nun an inheritance among them, [50]as the LORD had commanded. They gave him the town he asked for—Timnath Serah[a] in the hill country of Ephraim. And he built up the town and settled there.

[51]These are the territories that Eleazar the priest, Joshua son of Nun and the heads of the tribal clans of Israel assigned by lot at Shiloh in the presence of the LORD at the entrance to the Tent of Meeting. And so they finished dividing the land.

Cities of Refuge

20 Then the LORD said to Joshua: [2]"Tell the Israelites to designate the cities of refuge, as I instructed you through Moses, [3]so that anyone who kills a person accidentally and unintentionally may flee there and find protection from the avenger of blood.

[4]"When he flees to one of these cities, he is to stand in the entrance of the city gate and state his case before the elders of that city. Then they are to admit him into their city and give him a place to live with them. [5]If the avenger of blood pursues him, they must not surrender the one accused, because he killed his neighbor unintentionally and without malice aforethought. [6]He is to stay in that city until he has stood trial before the assembly and until the death of the high priest who is serving at that time. Then he may go back to his own home in the town from which he fled."

[7]So they set apart Kedesh in Galilee in the hill country of Naphtali, Shechem in the hill country of Ephraim,

and Kiriath Arba (that is, Hebron) in the hill country of Judah. [8]On the east side of the Jordan of Jericho[b] they designated Bezer in the desert on the plateau in the tribe of Reuben, Ramoth in Gilead in the tribe of Gad, and Golan in Bashan in the tribe of Manasseh. [9]Any of the Israelites or any alien living among them who killed someone accidentally could flee to these designated cities and not be killed by the avenger of blood prior to standing trial before the assembly.

Towns for the Levites

21 Now the family heads of the Levites approached Eleazar the priest, Joshua son of Nun, and the heads of the other tribal families of Israel [2]at Shiloh in Canaan and said to them, "The LORD commanded through Moses that you give us towns to live in, with pasturelands for our livestock." [3]So, as the LORD had commanded, the Israelites gave the Levites the following towns and pasturelands out of their own inheritance:

[4]The first lot came out for the Kohathites, clan by clan. The Levites who were descendants of Aaron the priest were allotted thirteen towns from the tribes of Judah, Simeon and Benjamin. [5]The rest of Kohath's descendants were allotted ten towns from the clans of the tribes of Ephraim, Dan and half of Manasseh.

[6]The descendants of Gershon were allotted thirteen towns from the clans of the tribes of Issachar, Asher, Naphtali and the half-tribe of Manasseh in Bashan.

[7]The descendants of Merari, clan by clan, received twelve towns from the tribes of Reuben, Gad and Zebulun.

[8]So the Israelites allotted to the Levites these towns and their pasturelands, as the LORD had commanded through Moses.

[9]From the tribes of Judah and Simeon they allotted the following towns by

---

[a]50 Also known as Timnath Heres (see Judges 2:9) name for the Jordan River.   [b]8 Jordan of Jericho was possibly an ancient

name ¹⁰(these towns were assigned to the descendants of Aaron who were from the Kohathite clans of the Levites, because the first lot fell to them):

¹¹They gave them Kiriath Arba (that is, Hebron), with its surrounding pastureland, in the hill country of Judah. (Arba was the forefather of Anak.) ¹²But the fields and villages around the city they had given to Caleb son of Jephunneh as his possession.

¹³So to the descendants of Aaron the priest they gave Hebron (a city of refuge for one accused of murder), Libnah, ¹⁴Jattir, Eshtemoa, ¹⁵Holon, Debir, ¹⁶Ain, Juttah and Beth Shemesh, together with their pasturelands—nine towns from these two tribes.

¹⁷And from the tribe of Benjamin they gave them Gibeon, Geba, ¹⁸Anathoth and Almon, together with their pasturelands—four towns.

¹⁹All the towns for the priests, the descendants of Aaron, were thirteen, together with their pasturelands.

²⁰The rest of the Kohathite clans of the Levites were allotted towns from the tribe of Ephraim:

²¹In the hill country of Ephraim they were given Shechem (a city of refuge for one accused of murder) and Gezer, ²²Kibzaim and Beth Horon, together with their pasturelands—four towns.

²³Also from the tribe of Dan they received Eltekeh, Gibbethon, ²⁴Aijalon and Gath Rimmon, together with their pasturelands—four towns.

²⁵From half the tribe of Manasseh they received Taanach and Gath Rimmon, together with their pasturelands—two towns.

²⁶All these ten towns and their pasturelands were given to the rest of the Kohathite clans.

²⁷The Levite clans of the Gershonites were given:
from the half-tribe of Manasseh,
Golan in Bashan (a city of refuge for one accused of murder) and Be Eshtarah, together with their pasturelands—two towns;
²⁸from the tribe of Issachar,
Kishion, Daberath, ²⁹Jarmuth and En Gannim, together with their pasturelands—four towns;
³⁰from the tribe of Asher,
Mishal, Abdon, ³¹Helkath and Rehob, together with their pasturelands—four towns;
³²from the tribe of Naphtali,
Kedesh in Galilee (a city of refuge for one accused of murder), Hammoth Dor and Kartan, together with their pasturelands—three towns.
³³All the towns of the Gershonite clans were thirteen, together with their pasturelands.

³⁴The Merarite clans (the rest of the Levites) were given:
from the tribe of Zebulun,
Jokneam, Kartah, ³⁵Dimnah and Nahalal, together with their pasturelands—four towns;
³⁶from the tribe of Reuben,
Bezer, Jahaz, ³⁷Kedemoth and Mephaath, together with their pasturelands—four towns;
³⁸from the tribe of Gad,
Ramoth in Gilead (a city of refuge for one accused of murder), Mahanaim, ³⁹Heshbon and Jazer, together with their pasturelands—four towns in all.
⁴⁰All the towns allotted to the Merarite clans, who were the rest of the Levites, were twelve.

⁴¹The towns of the Levites in the territory held by the Israelites were forty-eight in all, together with their pasturelands. ⁴²Each of these towns had pasturelands surrounding it; this was true for all these towns.

⁴³So the LORD gave Israel all the land he had sworn to give their forefathers, and they took possession of it and settled there. ⁴⁴The LORD gave them rest on every side, just as he had sworn to their forefathers. Not one of their enemies withstood them; the LORD handed all their enemies over to

them. [45]Not one of all the Lord's good promises to the house of Israel failed; every one was fulfilled.

Eastern Tribes Return Home

22 Then Joshua summoned the Reubenites, the Gadites and the half-tribe of Manasseh [2]and said to them, "You have done all that Moses the servant of the Lord commanded, and you have obeyed me in everything I commanded. [3]For a long time now—to this very day—you have not deserted your brothers but have carried out the mission the Lord your God gave you. [4]Now that the Lord your God has given your brothers rest as he promised, return to your homes in the land that Moses the servant of the Lord gave you on the other side of the Jordan. [5]But be very careful to keep the commandment and the law that Moses the servant of the Lord gave you: to love the Lord your God, to walk in all his ways, to obey his commands, to hold fast to him and to serve him with all your heart and all your soul."

[6]Then Joshua blessed them and sent them away, and they went to their homes. [7](To the half-tribe of Manasseh Moses had given land in Bashan, and to the other half of the tribe Joshua gave land on the west side of the Jordan with their brothers.) When Joshua sent them home, he blessed them, [8]saying, "Return to your homes with your great wealth—with large herds of livestock, with silver, gold, bronze and iron, and a great quantity of clothing—and divide with your brothers the plunder from your enemies."

[9]So the Reubenites, the Gadites and the half-tribe of Manasseh left the Israelites at Shiloh in Canaan to return to Gilead, their own land, which they had acquired in accordance with the command of the Lord through Moses.

[10]When they came to Geliloth near the Jordan in the land of Canaan, the Reubenites, the Gadites and the half-tribe of Manasseh built an imposing altar there by the Jordan. [11]And when the Israelites heard that they had built the altar on the border of Canaan at Geliloth near the Jordan on the Israelite side, [12]the whole assembly of Israel gathered at Shiloh to go to war against them.

[13]So the Israelites sent Phinehas son of Eleazar, the priest, to the land of Gilead—to Reuben, Gad and the half-tribe of Manasseh. [14]With him they sent ten of the chief men, one for each of the tribes of Israel, each the head of a family division among the Israelite clans.

[15]When they went to Gilead—to Reuben, Gad and the half-tribe of Manasseh—they said to them: [16]"The whole assembly of the Lord says: 'How could you break faith with the God of Israel like this? How could you turn away from the Lord and build yourselves an altar in rebellion against him now? [17]Was not the sin of Peor enough for us? Up to this very day we have not cleansed ourselves from that sin, even though a plague fell on the community of the Lord! [18]And are you now turning away from the Lord?

" 'If you rebel against the Lord today, tomorrow he will be angry with the whole community of Israel. [19]If the land you possess is defiled, come over to the Lord's land, where the Lord's tabernacle stands, and share the land with us. But do not rebel against the Lord or against us by building an altar for yourselves, other than the altar of the Lord our God. [20]When Achan son of Zerah acted unfaithfully regarding the devoted things,[a] did not wrath come upon the whole community of Israel? He was not the only one who died for his sin.' "

[21]Then Reuben, Gad and the half-tribe of Manasseh replied to the heads of the clans of Israel: [22]"The Mighty One, God, the Lord! The Mighty One, God, the Lord! He knows! And let Is-

---

[a]20 The Hebrew term refers to the irrevocable giving over of things or persons to the Lord, often by totally destroying them.

rael know! If this has been in rebellion or disobedience to the LORD, do not spare us this day. ²³If we have built our own altar to turn away from the LORD and to offer burnt offerings and grain offerings, or to sacrifice fellowship offerings*a* on it, may the LORD himself call us to account.

²⁴"No! We did it for fear that some day your descendants might say to ours, 'What do you have to do with the LORD, the God of Israel? ²⁵The LORD has made the Jordan a boundary between us and you—you Reubenites and Gadites! You have no share in the LORD.' So your descendants might cause ours to stop fearing the LORD.

²⁶"That is why we said, 'Let us get ready and build an altar—but not for burnt offerings or sacrifices.' ²⁷On the contrary, it is to be a witness between us and you and the generations that follow, that we will worship the LORD at his sanctuary with our burnt offerings, sacrifices and fellowship offerings. Then in the future your descendants will not be able to say to ours, 'You have no share in the LORD.'

²⁸"And we said, 'If they ever say this to us, or to our descendants, we will answer: Look at the replica of the LORD's altar, which our fathers built, not for burnt offerings and sacrifices, but as a witness between us and you.'

²⁹"Far be it from us to rebel against the LORD and turn away from him today by building an altar for burnt offerings, grain offerings and sacrifices, other than the altar of the LORD our God that stands before his tabernacle."

³⁰When Phinehas the priest and the leaders of the community—the heads of the clans of the Israelites—heard what Reuben, Gad and Manasseh had to say, they were pleased. ³¹And Phinehas son of Eleazar, the priest, said to Reuben, Gad and Manasseh, "Today we know that the LORD is with us, because you have not acted unfaithfully toward the LORD in this matter. Now you have rescued the Israelites from the LORD's hand."

³²Then Phinehas son of Eleazar, the priest, and the leaders returned to Canaan from their meeting with the Reubenites and Gadites in Gilead and reported to the Israelites. ³³They were glad to hear the report and praised God. And they talked no more about going to war against them to devastate the country where the Reubenites and the Gadites lived.

³⁴And the Reubenites and the Gadites gave the altar this name: A Witness Between Us that the LORD is God.

Joshua's Farewell to the Leaders

23 After a long time had passed and the LORD had given Israel rest from all their enemies around them, Joshua, by then old and well advanced in years, ²summoned all Israel—their elders, leaders, judges and officials—and said to them: "I am old and well advanced in years. ³You yourselves have seen everything the LORD your God has done to all these nations for your sake; it was the LORD your God who fought for you. ⁴Remember how I have allotted as an inheritance for your tribes all the land of the nations that remain—the nations I conquered—between the Jordan and the Great Sea*b* in the west. ⁵The LORD your God himself will drive them out of your way. He will push them out before you, and you will take possession of their land, as the LORD your God promised you.

⁶"Be very strong; be careful to obey all that is written in the Book of the Law of Moses, without turning aside to the right or to the left. ⁷Do not associate with these nations that remain among you; do not invoke the names of their gods or swear by them. You must not serve them or bow down to them. ⁸But you are to hold fast to the LORD your God, as you have until now.

⁹"The LORD has driven out before you great and powerful nations; to this day no one has been able to withstand you. ¹⁰One of you routs a thou-

a23 Traditionally *peace offerings*; also in verse 27   *b4* That is, the Mediterranean

VERSE:	AUTHOR:	PASSAGE:
Joshua 23:14	Sherwood Eliot Wirt	Joshua 23:1–16

To Look Back on Life

By the time we reach retirement age, all of us have accumulated a sizable store of memories — some rich, some not so rich. These memories seem to cling to us; they can be called up at any moment, often without provocation. Pleasant memories are what give zest to life; they are a boon and blessing from heaven to us of the older generation, adding as they do a lovely ingredient to life in retirement.

What about the other kind? Let's face it: We've got them, too . . . Crushing experiences and sour disappointments can happen to us at any time, whether we are young, middle-aged or older . . .

"God has poured out his love into our hearts by the Holy Spirit, whom he has given us" (Romans 5:5). To be filled with the Spirit, therefore, is to be filled with love, and when we are filled with love we have no room in our hearts for the negative thoughts conjured up by bad memories . . .

This love is bound up with and accompanied by joy. Many older people have dwelt so long in the tents of misery they have almost forgotten about joy. But Jesus taught us that love and joy go together. It was for the joy set before him, as well as his love for the world, that he went to the cross . . .

Love is victorious at the cross, and when love is victorious it brings joy. That is what Easter is all about, what Pentecost is all about, what life is all about.

. . . .

ADDITIONAL SCRIPTURE READINGS
John 16:17–28; Romans 5:1–11

Go to page 283 for your next devotional reading.

sand, because the Lord your God fights for you, just as he promised. [11]So be very careful to love the Lord your God.

[12]"But if you turn away and ally yourselves with the survivors of these nations that remain among you and if you intermarry with them and associate with them, [13]then you may be sure that the Lord your God will no longer drive out these nations before you. Instead, they will become snares and traps for you, whips on your backs and thorns in your eyes, until you perish from this good land, which the Lord your God has given you.

[14]"Now I am about to go the way of all the earth. You know with all your heart and soul that not one of all the good promises the Lord your God gave you has failed. Every promise has been fulfilled; not one has failed. [15]But just as every good promise of the Lord your God has come true, so the Lord will bring on you all the evil he has threatened, until he has destroyed you from this good land he has given you. [16]If you violate the covenant of the Lord your God, which he commanded you, and go and serve other gods and bow down to them, the Lord's anger will burn against you, and you will quickly perish from the good land he has given you."

The Covenant Renewed at Shechem

24 Then Joshua assembled all the tribes of Israel at Shechem. He summoned the elders, leaders, judges and officials of Israel, and they presented themselves before God.

[2]Joshua said to all the people, "This is what the Lord, the God of Israel, says: 'Long ago your forefathers, including Terah the father of Abraham and Nahor, lived beyond the River[a] and worshiped other gods. [3]But I took your father Abraham from the land beyond the River and led him throughout Canaan and gave him many descendants. I gave him Isaac,

[4]and to Isaac I gave Jacob and Esau. I assigned the hill country of Seir to Esau, but Jacob and his sons went down to Egypt.

[5]" 'Then I sent Moses and Aaron, and I afflicted the Egyptians by what I did there, and I brought you out. [6]When I brought your fathers out of Egypt, you came to the sea, and the Egyptians pursued them with chariots and horsemen[b] as far as the Red Sea.[c] [7]But they cried to the Lord for help, and he put darkness between you and the Egyptians; he brought the sea over them and covered them. You saw with your own eyes what I did to the Egyptians. Then you lived in the desert for a long time.

[8]" 'I brought you to the land of the Amorites who lived east of the Jordan. They fought against you, but I gave them into your hands. I destroyed them from before you, and you took possession of their land. [9]When Balak son of Zippor, the king of Moab, prepared to fight against Israel, he sent for Balaam son of Beor to put a curse on you. [10]But I would not listen to Balaam, so he blessed you again and again, and I delivered you out of his hand.

[11]" 'Then you crossed the Jordan and came to Jericho. The citizens of Jericho fought against you, as did also the Amorites, Perizzites, Canaanites, Hittites, Girgashites, Hivites and Jebusites, but I gave them into your hands. [12]I sent the hornet ahead of you, which drove them out before you—also the two Amorite kings. You did not do it with your own sword and bow. [13]So I gave you a land on which you did not toil and cities you did not build; and you live in them and eat from vineyards and olive groves that you did not plant.'

[14]"Now fear the Lord and serve him with all faithfulness. Throw away the gods your forefathers worshiped beyond the River and in Egypt, and

---

[a]2 That is, the Euphrates; also in verses 3, 14 and 15   [b]6 Or charioteers   [c]6 Hebrew Yam Suph; that is, Sea of Reeds

serve the LORD. [15]But if serving the LORD seems undesirable to you, then choose for yourselves this day whom you will serve, whether the gods your forefathers served beyond the River, or the gods of the Amorites, in whose land you are living. But as for me and my household, we will serve the LORD."

[16]Then the people answered, "Far be it from us to forsake the LORD to serve other gods! [17]It was the LORD our God himself who brought us and our fathers up out of Egypt, from that land of slavery, and performed those great signs before our eyes. He pro-

tected us on our entire journey and among all the nations through which we traveled. [18]And the LORD drove out before us all the nations, including the Amorites, who lived in the land. We too will serve the LORD, because he is our God."

[19]Joshua said to the people, "You are not able to serve the LORD. He is a holy God; he is a jealous God. He will not forgive your rebellion and your sins. [20]If you forsake the LORD and serve foreign gods, he will turn and bring disaster on you and make an end of you, after he has been good to you."

FRIDAY

VERSE:
Joshua 24:21

AUTHOR:
Paul B. Maves

PASSAGE:
Joshua 24:14–24

Fully Human, Fully Alive

God is holy. We are to be like God, to have in us the mind that was in Christ Jesus. We are called to be some-one as well as to do something.

To be holy is to be "set apart." To be holy is to be committed or to be dedicated to those values that are at the center of all created being. To be holy also means to be "whole" or "healthy." To be holy is to be perfected, to be mature, to become what God intended when he created us.

It is in commitment to God's calling, in allowing ourselves to be set apart for God's ministry, that we are made whole and grow up into that full measure of maturity that was in Christ Jesus. Perhaps instead of using the term aging, we should talk about becoming fully human, living out the life to which we were destined.

ADDITIONAL SCRIPTURE READINGS
Matthew 5:43–48; Ephesians 4:1–16

Go to page 289 for your next devotional reading.

²¹But the people said to Joshua, "No! We will serve the LORD."

²²Then Joshua said, "You are witnesses against yourselves that you have chosen to serve the LORD."

"Yes, we are witnesses," they replied.

²³"Now then," said Joshua, "throw away the foreign gods that are among you and yield your hearts to the LORD, the God of Israel."

²⁴And the people said to Joshua, "We will serve the LORD our God and obey him."

²⁵On that day Joshua made a covenant for the people, and there at Shechem he drew up for them decrees and laws. ²⁶And Joshua recorded these things in the Book of the Law of God. Then he took a large stone and set it up there under the oak near the holy place of the LORD.

²⁷"See!" he said to all the people. "This stone will be a witness against us. It has heard all the words the LORD has said to us. It will be a witness against you if you are untrue to your God."

Buried in the Promised Land

²⁸Then Joshua sent the people away, each to his own inheritance.

²⁹After these things, Joshua son of Nun, the servant of the LORD, died at the age of a hundred and ten. ³⁰And they buried him in the land of his inheritance, at Timnath Serah[a] in the hill country of Ephraim, north of Mount Gaash.

³¹Israel served the LORD throughout the lifetime of Joshua and of the elders who outlived him and who had experienced everything the LORD had done for Israel.

³²And Joseph's bones, which the Israelites had brought up from Egypt, were buried at Shechem in the tract of land that Jacob bought for a hundred pieces of silver[b] from the sons of Hamor, the father of Shechem. This became the inheritance of Joseph's descendants.

³³And Eleazar son of Aaron died and was buried at Gibeah, which had been allotted to his son Phinehas in the hill country of Ephraim.

---

*a*30 Also known as *Timnath Heres* (see Judges 2:9) a unit of money of unknown weight and value.   *b*32 Hebrew *hundred kesitahs*; a kesitah was

Judges recounts a pattern
of repeated behavior among the Israelites:
they worship idols; they suffer at the hands
of enemies; they cry out to God; and God
delivers them through a "judge," or leader.
As you read this book, be aware of your own
bent toward sin, and God's promise to give
you the victory over sin and death when you
seek him in repentance.

JUDGES

Israel Fights the Remaining Canaanites

1 After the death of Joshua, the Israelites asked the LORD, "Who will be the first to go up and fight for us against the Canaanites?"

²The LORD answered, "Judah is to go; I have given the land into their hands."

³Then the men of Judah said to the Simeonites their brothers, "Come up with us into the territory allotted to us, to fight against the Canaanites. We in turn will go with you into yours." So the Simeonites went with them.

⁴When Judah attacked, the LORD gave the Canaanites and Perizzites into their hands and they struck down ten thousand men at Bezek. ⁵It was there that they found Adoni-Bezek and fought against him, putting to rout the Canaanites and Perizzites. ⁶Adoni-Bezek fled, but they chased him and caught him, and cut off his thumbs and big toes.

⁷Then Adoni-Bezek said, "Seventy kings with their thumbs and big toes cut off have picked up scraps under my table. Now God has paid me back for what I did to them." They brought him to Jerusalem, and he died there.

⁸The men of Judah attacked Jerusalem also and took it. They put the city to the sword and set it on fire.

⁹After that, the men of Judah went down to fight against the Canaanites living in the hill country, the Negev and the western foothills. ¹⁰They advanced against the Canaanites living in Hebron (formerly called Kiriath Arba) and defeated Sheshai, Ahiman and Talmai.

¹¹From there they advanced against the people living in Debir (formerly called Kiriath Sepher). ¹²And Caleb said, "I will give my daughter Acsah in marriage to the man who attacks and captures Kiriath Sepher." ¹³Othniel son of Kenaz, Caleb's younger brother, took it; so Caleb gave his daughter Acsah to him in marriage. ¹⁴One day when she came to Othni-

el, she urged him[a] to ask her father for a field. When she got off her donkey, Caleb asked her, "What can I do for you?"

¹⁵She replied, "Do me a special favor. Since you have given me land in the Negev, give me also springs of water." Then Caleb gave her the upper and lower springs.

¹⁶The descendants of Moses' father-in-law, the Kenite, went up from the City of Palms[b] with the men of Judah to live among the people of the Desert of Judah in the Negev near Arad.

¹⁷Then the men of Judah went with the Simeonites their brothers and attacked the Canaanites living in Zephath, and they totally destroyed[c] the city. Therefore it was called Hormah.[d] ¹⁸The men of Judah also took[e] Gaza, Ashkelon and Ekron—each city with its territory.

¹⁹The LORD was with the men of Judah. They took possession of the hill country, but they were unable to drive the people from the plains, because they had iron chariots. ²⁰As Moses had promised, Hebron was given to Caleb, who drove from it the three sons of Anak. ²¹The Benjamites, however, failed to dislodge the Jebusites, who were living in Jerusalem; to this day the Jebusites live there with the Benjamites.

²²Now the house of Joseph attacked Bethel, and the LORD was with them. ²³When they sent men to spy out Bethel (formerly called Luz), ²⁴the spies saw a man coming out of the city and they said to him, "Show us how to get into the city and we will see that you are treated well." ²⁵So he showed them, and they put the city to the sword but spared the man and his whole family. ²⁶He then went to the land of the Hittites, where he built a city and called it Luz, which is its name to this day.

²⁷But Manasseh did not drive out the people of Beth Shan or Taanach or Dor or Ibleam or Megiddo and their surrounding settlements, for the Canaanites were determined to live in that land. ²⁸When Israel became strong, they pressed the Canaanites into forced labor but never drove them out completely. ²⁹Nor did Ephraim drive out the Canaanites living in Gezer, but the Canaanites continued to live there among them. ³⁰Neither did Zebulun drive out the Canaanites living in Kitron or Nahalol, who remained among them; but they did subject them to forced labor. ³¹Nor did Asher drive out those living in Acco or Sidon or Ahlab or Aczib or Helbah or Aphek or Rehob, ³²and because of this the people of Asher lived among the Canaanite inhabitants of the land. ³³Neither did Naphtali drive out those living in Beth Shemesh or Beth Anath; but the Naphtalites too lived among the Canaanite inhabitants of the land, and those living in Beth Shemesh and Beth Anath became forced laborers for them. ³⁴The Amorites confined the Danites to the hill country, not allowing them to come down into the plain. ³⁵And the Amorites were determined also to hold out in Mount Heres, Aijalon and Shaalbim, but when the power of the house of Joseph increased, they too were pressed into forced labor. ³⁶The boundary of the Amorites was from Scorpion[f] Pass to Sela and beyond.

The Angel of the LORD at Bokim

2 The angel of the LORD went up from Gilgal to Bokim and said, "I brought you up out of Egypt and led you into the land that I swore to give to your forefathers. I said, 'I will never break my covenant with you, ²and you shall not make a covenant with the people of this land, but you shall break down their altars.' Yet you have disobeyed me. Why have you done this? ³Now therefore I tell you that I

---

will not drive them out before you; they will be ˻thorns˼ in your sides and their gods will be a snare to you."

⁴When the angel of the LORD had spoken these things to all the Israelites, the people wept aloud, ⁵and they called that place Bokim.ᵃ There they offered sacrifices to the LORD.

Disobedience and Defeat

⁶After Joshua had dismissed the Israelites, they went to take possession of the land, each to his own inheritance. ⁷The people served the LORD throughout the lifetime of Joshua and of the elders who outlived him and who had seen all the great things the LORD had done for Israel.

⁸Joshua son of Nun, the servant of the LORD, died at the age of a hundred and ten. ⁹And they buried him in the land of his inheritance, at Timnath Heresᵇ in the hill country of Ephraim, north of Mount Gaash.

¹⁰After that whole generation had been gathered to their fathers, another generation grew up, who knew neither the LORD nor what he had done for Israel. ¹¹Then the Israelites did evil in the eyes of the LORD and served the Baals. ¹²They forsook the LORD, the God of their fathers, who had brought them out of Egypt. They followed and worshiped various gods of the peoples around them. They provoked the LORD to anger ¹³because they forsook him and served Baal and the Ashtoreths. ¹⁴In his anger against Israel the LORD handed them over to raiders who plundered them. He sold them to their enemies all around, whom they were no longer able to resist. ¹⁵Whenever Israel went out to fight, the hand of the LORD was against them to defeat them, just as he had sworn to them. They were in great distress.

¹⁶Then the LORD raised up judges,ᶜ who saved them out of the hands of these raiders. ¹⁷Yet they would not listen to their judges but prostituted themselves to other gods and worshiped them. Unlike their fathers, they quickly turned from the way in which their fathers had walked, the way of obedience to the LORD's commands. ¹⁸Whenever the LORD raised up a judge for them, he was with the judge and saved them out of the hands of their enemies as long as the judge lived; for the LORD had compassion on them as they groaned under those who oppressed and afflicted them. ¹⁹But when the judge died, the people returned to ways even more corrupt than those of their fathers, following other gods and serving and worshiping them. They refused to give up their evil practices and stubborn ways.

²⁰Therefore the LORD was very angry with Israel and said, "Because this nation has violated the covenant that I laid down for their forefathers and has not listened to me, ²¹I will no longer drive out before them any of the nations Joshua left when he died. ²²I will use them to test Israel and see whether they will keep the way of the LORD and walk in it as their forefathers did." ²³The LORD had allowed those nations to remain; he did not drive them out at once by giving them into the hands of Joshua.

3 These are the nations the LORD left to test all those Israelites who had not experienced any of the wars in Canaan ²(he did this only to teach warfare to the descendants of the Israelites who had not had previous battle experience): ³the five rulers of the Philistines, all the Canaanites, the Sidonians, and the Hivites living in the Lebanon mountains from Mount Baal Hermon to Leboᵈ Hamath. ⁴They were left to test the Israelites to see whether they would obey the LORD's commands, which he had given their forefathers through Moses.

⁵The Israelites lived among the Canaanites, Hittites, Amorites, Perizzites, Hivites and Jebusites. ⁶They took their daughters in marriage and

---

ᵃ5 *Bokim* means *weepers.*   ᵇ9 Also known as *Timnath Serah* (see Joshua 19:50 and 24:30)
ᶜ16 Or *leaders;* similarly in verses 17-19   ᵈ3 Or *to the entrance to*

gave their own daughters to their sons, and served their gods.

Othniel

7The Israelites did evil in the eyes of the LORD; they forgot the LORD their God and served the Baals and the Asherahs. **8**The anger of the LORD burned against Israel so that he sold them into the hands of Cushan-Rishathaim king of Aram Naharaim,*a* to whom the Israelites were subject for eight years. **9**But when they cried out to the LORD, he raised up for them a deliverer, Othniel son of Kenaz, Caleb's younger brother, who saved them. **10**The Spirit of the LORD came upon him, so that he became Israel's judge*b* and went to war. The LORD gave Cushan-Rishathaim king of Aram into the hands of Othniel, who overpowered him. **11**So the land had peace for forty years, until Othniel son of Kenaz died.

Ehud

12Once again the Israelites did evil in the eyes of the LORD, and because they did this evil the LORD gave Eglon king of Moab power over Israel. **13**Getting the Ammonites and Amalekites to join him, Eglon came and attacked Israel, and they took possession of the City of Palms.*c* **14**The Israelites were subject to Eglon king of Moab for eighteen years.

15Again the Israelites cried out to the LORD, and he gave them a deliverer—Ehud, a left-handed man, the son of Gera the Benjamite. The Israelites sent him with tribute to Eglon king of Moab. **16**Now Ehud had made a double-edged sword about a foot and a half*d* long, which he strapped to his right thigh under his clothing. **17**He presented the tribute to Eglon king of Moab, who was a very fat man. **18**After Ehud had presented the tribute, he sent on their way the men who had carried it. **19**At the idols*e* near Gilgal

he himself turned back and said, "I have a secret message for you, O king."

The king said, "Quiet!" And all his attendants left him.

20Ehud then approached him while he was sitting alone in the upper room of his summer palace*f* and said, "I have a message from God for you." As the king rose from his seat, **21**Ehud reached with his left hand, drew the sword from his right thigh and plunged it into the king's belly. **22**Even the handle sank in after the blade, which came out his back. Ehud did not pull the sword out, and the fat closed in over it. **23**Then Ehud went out to the porch*g*; he shut the doors of the upper room behind him and locked them.

24After he had gone, the servants came and found the doors of the upper room locked. They said, "He must be relieving himself in the inner room of the house." **25**They waited to the point of embarrassment, but when he did not open the doors of the room, they took a key and unlocked them. There they saw their lord fallen to the floor, dead.

26While they waited, Ehud got away. He passed by the idols and escaped to Seirah. **27**When he arrived there, he blew a trumpet in the hill country of Ephraim, and the Israelites went down with him from the hills, with him leading them.

28"Follow me," he ordered, "for the LORD has given Moab, your enemy, into your hands." So they followed him down and, taking possession of the fords of the Jordan that led to Moab, they allowed no one to cross over. **29**At that time they struck down about ten thousand Moabites, all vigorous and strong; not a man escaped. **30**That day Moab was made subject to Israel, and the land had peace for eighty years.

PASSAGE: Psalm 71; 2 Corinthians 12:1–10
AUTHOR: Lancelot Andrewes

An Evening Prayer

The day is over, and I give you thanks, O Lord.
Evening is at hand; furnish it with brightness.
Do not forsake me now that my strength is failing;
But bear me, carry me, deliver me, to my old age,
To the time of my white hair.
Stay with me, Lord, for evening is coming,
And the day of this fretful life is far spent.
May your strength be made perfect in my
  weakness.

Go to page 294 for your next devotional reading.

Shamgar

³¹After Ehud came Shamgar son of Anath, who struck down six hundred Philistines with an oxgoad. He too saved Israel.

Deborah

4 After Ehud died, the Israelites once again did evil in the eyes of the LORD. ²So the LORD sold them into the hands of Jabin, a king of Canaan, who reigned in Hazor. The commander of his army was Sisera, who lived in Harosheth Haggoyim. ³Because he had nine hundred iron chariots and had cruelly oppressed the Israelites for twenty years, they cried to the LORD for help.

⁴Deborah, a prophetess, the wife of Lappidoth, was leading*ᵃ* Israel at that time. ⁵She held court under the Palm of Deborah between Ramah and Bethel in the hill country of Ephraim, and the Israelites came to her to have their disputes decided. ⁶She sent for Barak son of Abinoam from Kedesh in Naphtali and said to him, "The LORD, the God of Israel, commands you: 'Go, take with you ten thousand men of Naphtali and Zebulun and lead the way to Mount Tabor. ⁷I will lure Sisera, the commander of Jabin's army, with his chariots and his troops to the Kishon River and give him into your hands.' "

⁸Barak said to her, "If you go with me, I will go; but if you don't go with me, I won't go."

⁹"Very well," Deborah said, "I will go with you. But because of the way you are going about this,*ᵇ* the honor will not be yours, for the LORD will hand Sisera over to a woman." So Deborah went with Barak to Kedesh, ¹⁰where he summoned Zebulun and Naphtali. Ten thousand men followed him, and Deborah also went with him.

¹¹Now Heber the Kenite had left the other Kenites, the descendants of Hobab, Moses' brother-in-law,*ᶜ* and pitched his tent by the great tree in Zaanannim near Kedesh.

¹²When they told Sisera that Barak son of Abinoam had gone up to Mount Tabor, ¹³Sisera gathered together his nine hundred iron chariots and all the men with him, from Harosheth Haggoyim to the Kishon River.

¹⁴Then Deborah said to Barak, "Go! This is the day the LORD has given Sisera into your hands. Has not the LORD gone ahead of you?" So Barak went down Mount Tabor, followed by ten thousand men. ¹⁵At Barak's advance, the LORD routed Sisera and all his chariots and army by the sword, and Sisera abandoned his chariot and fled on foot. ¹⁶But Barak pursued the chariots and army as far as Harosheth Haggoyim. All the troops of Sisera fell by the sword; not a man was left.

¹⁷Sisera, however, fled on foot to the tent of Jael, the wife of Heber the Kenite, because there were friendly relations between Jabin king of Hazor and the clan of Heber the Kenite.

¹⁸Jael went out to meet Sisera and said to him, "Come, my lord, come right in. Don't be afraid." So he entered her tent, and she put a covering over him.

¹⁹"I'm thirsty," he said. "Please give me some water." She opened a skin of milk, gave him a drink, and covered him up.

²⁰"Stand in the doorway of the tent," he told her. "If someone comes by and asks you, 'Is anyone here?' say 'No.' "

²¹But Jael, Heber's wife, picked up a tent peg and a hammer and went quietly to him while he lay fast asleep, exhausted. She drove the peg through his temple into the ground, and he died.

²²Barak came by in pursuit of Sisera, and Jael went out to meet him. "Come," she said, "I will show you the man you're looking for." So he went in with her, and there lay Sisera with the tent peg through his temple—dead.

²³On that day God subdued Jabin,

ᵃ4 Traditionally *judging*   *ᵇ9* Or *But on the expedition you are undertaking*   *ᶜ11* Or *father-in-law*

the Canaanite king, before the Israelites. ²⁴And the hand of the Israelites grew stronger and stronger against Jabin, the Canaanite king, until they destroyed him.

The Song of Deborah

5 On that day Deborah and Barak son of Abinoam sang this song:

²"When the princes in Israel take the lead,
    when the people willingly offer themselves—
    praise the LORD!

³"Hear this, you kings! Listen, you rulers!
    I will sing to*ᵃ* the LORD, I will sing;
    I will make music to*ᵇ* the LORD, the God of Israel.

⁴"O LORD, when you went out from Seir,
    when you marched from the land of Edom,
  the earth shook, the heavens poured,
    the clouds poured down water.
⁵The mountains quaked before the LORD, the One of Sinai,
    before the LORD, the God of Israel.

⁶"In the days of Shamgar son of Anath,
    in the days of Jael, the roads were abandoned;
    travelers took to winding paths.
⁷Village life*ᶜ* in Israel ceased,
    ceased until I,*ᵈ* Deborah, arose,
    arose a mother in Israel.
⁸When they chose new gods,
    war came to the city gates,
  and not a shield or spear was seen
    among forty thousand in Israel.
⁹My heart is with Israel's princes,
    with the willing volunteers among the people.
    Praise the LORD!

¹⁰"You who ride on white donkeys,
    sitting on your saddle blankets,

and you who walk along the road,
  consider ¹¹the voice of the singers*ᵉ* at the watering places.
    They recite the righteous acts of the LORD,
    the righteous acts of his warriors*ᶠ* in Israel.

"Then the people of the LORD went down to the city gates.
¹²'Wake up, wake up, Deborah!
    Wake up, wake up, break out in song!
  Arise, O Barak!
    Take captive your captives, O son of Abinoam.'

¹³"Then the men who were left came down to the nobles;
    the people of the LORD came to me with the mighty.
¹⁴Some came from Ephraim, whose roots were in Amalek;
    Benjamin was with the people who followed you.
  From Makir captains came down,
    from Zebulun those who bear a commander's staff.
¹⁵The princes of Issachar were with Deborah;
    yes, Issachar was with Barak,
    rushing after him into the valley.
  In the districts of Reuben
    there was much searching of heart.
¹⁶Why did you stay among the campfires*ᵍ*
    to hear the whistling for the flocks?
  In the districts of Reuben
    there was much searching of heart.
¹⁷Gilead stayed beyond the Jordan.
    And Dan, why did he linger by the ships?
  Asher remained on the coast
    and stayed in his coves.
¹⁸The people of Zebulun risked their very lives;

---

*ᵃ3 Or of   *ᵇ3 Or / with song I will praise   *ᶜ7 Or Warriors   *ᵈ7 Or you   *ᵉ11 Or archers;
the meaning of the Hebrew for this word is uncertain.   *ᶠ11 Or villagers   *ᵍ16 Or saddlebags

so did Naphtali on the heights
    of the field.

19"Kings came, they fought;
    the kings of Canaan fought
at Taanach by the waters of
        Megiddo,
    but they carried off no silver, no
        plunder.
20From the heavens the stars fought,
    from their courses they fought
        against Sisera.
21The river Kishon swept them
        away,
    the age-old river, the river
        Kishon.
    March on, my soul; be strong!
22Then thundered the horses'
        hoofs—
    galloping, galloping go his
        mighty steeds.
23'Curse Meroz,' said the angel of
        the LORD.
    'Curse its people bitterly,
because they did not come to help
        the LORD,
    to help the LORD against the
        mighty.'

24"Most blessed of women be Jael,
    the wife of Heber the Kenite,
    most blessed of tent-dwelling
        women.
25He asked for water, and she gave
        him milk;
    in a bowl fit for nobles she
        brought him curdled milk.
26Her hand reached for the tent peg,
    her right hand for the
        workman's hammer.
She struck Sisera, she crushed his
        head,
    she shattered and pierced his
        temple.
27At her feet he sank,
    he fell; there he lay.
At her feet he sank, he fell;
    where he sank, there he fell—
        dead.

28"Through the window peered
        Sisera's mother;
    behind the lattice she cried out,
'Why is his chariot so long in
        coming?

Why is the clatter of his chariots
        delayed?'
29The wisest of her ladies answer
        her;
    indeed, she keeps saying to
        herself,
30'Are they not finding and dividing
        the spoils:
    a girl or two for each man,
    colorful garments as plunder for
        Sisera,
    colorful garments embroidered,
    highly embroidered garments
        for my neck—
all this as plunder?'

31"So may all your enemies perish,
        O LORD!
    But may they who love you be
        like the sun
    when it rises in its strength."

Then the land had peace forty
years.

Gideon

6 Again the Israelites did evil in the
    eyes of the LORD, and for seven
years he gave them into the hands of
the Midianites. 2Because the power of
Midian was so oppressive, the Israelites prepared shelters for themselves
in mountain clefts, caves and strongholds. 3Whenever the Israelites planted their crops, the Midianites, Amalekites and other eastern peoples
invaded the country. 4They camped
on the land and ruined the crops all
the way to Gaza and did not spare a
living thing for Israel, neither sheep
nor cattle nor donkeys. 5They came
up with their livestock and their tents
like swarms of locusts. It was impossible to count the men and their camels; they invaded the land to ravage it.
6Midian so impoverished the Israelites that they cried out to the LORD for
help.
    7When the Israelites cried to the
LORD because of Midian, 8he sent them
a prophet, who said, "This is what the
LORD, the God of Israel, says: I
brought you up out of Egypt, out of
the land of slavery. 9I snatched you
from the power of Egypt and from the

hand of all your oppressors. I drove them from before you and gave you their land. ¹⁰I said to you, 'I am the Lord your God; do not worship the gods of the Amorites, in whose land you live.' But you have not listened to me."

¹¹The angel of the Lord came and sat down under the oak in Ophrah that belonged to Joash the Abiezrite, where his son Gideon was threshing wheat in a winepress to keep it from the Midianites. ¹²When the angel of the Lord appeared to Gideon, he said, "The Lord is with you, mighty warrior."

¹³"But sir," Gideon replied, "if the Lord is with us, why has all this happened to us? Where are all his wonders that our fathers told us about when they said, 'Did not the Lord bring us up out of Egypt?' But now the Lord has abandoned us and put us into the hand of Midian."

¹⁴The Lord turned to him and said, "Go in the strength you have and save Israel out of Midian's hand. Am I not sending you?"

¹⁵"But Lord,ᵃ" Gideon asked, "how can I save Israel? My clan is the weakest in Manasseh, and I am the least in my family."

¹⁶The Lord answered, "I will be with you, and you will strike down all the Midianites together."

¹⁷Gideon replied, "If now I have found favor in your eyes, give me a sign that it is really you talking to me. ¹⁸Please do not go away until I come back and bring my offering and set it before you."

And the Lord said, "I will wait until you return."

¹⁹Gideon went in, prepared a young goat, and from an ephahᵇ of flour he made bread without yeast. Putting the meat in a basket and its broth in a pot, he brought them out and offered them to him under the oak.

²⁰The angel of God said to him, "Take the meat and the unleavened bread, place them on this rock, and pour out the broth." And Gideon did so. ²¹With the tip of the staff that was in his hand, the angel of the Lord touched the meat and the unleavened bread. Fire flared from the rock, consuming the meat and the bread. And the angel of the Lord disappeared. ²²When Gideon realized that it was the angel of the Lord, he exclaimed, "Ah, Sovereign Lord! I have seen the angel of the Lord face to face!"

²³But the Lord said to him, "Peace! Do not be afraid. You are not going to die."

²⁴So Gideon built an altar to the Lord there and called it The Lord is Peace. To this day it stands in Ophrah of the Abiezrites.

²⁵That same night the Lord said to him, "Take the second bull from your father's herd, the one seven years old.ᶜ Tear down your father's altar to Baal and cut down the Asherah poleᵈ beside it. ²⁶Then build a proper kind ofᵉ altar to the Lord your God on the top of this height. Using the wood of the Asherah pole that you cut down, offer the secondᶠ bull as a burnt offering."

²⁷So Gideon took ten of his servants and did as the Lord told him. But because he was afraid of his family and the men of the town, he did it at night rather than in the daytime.

²⁸In the morning when the men of the town got up, there was Baal's altar, demolished, with the Asherah pole beside it cut down and the second bull sacrificed on the newly built altar!

²⁹They asked each other, "Who did this?"

When they carefully investigated, they were told, "Gideon son of Joash did it."

³⁰The men of the town demanded of Joash, "Bring out your son. He

ᵃ15 Or sir　ᵇ19 That is, probably about 3/5 bushel (about 22 liters)　ᶜ25 Or Take a full-grown, mature bull from your father's herd　ᵈ25 That is, a symbol of the goddess Asherah; here and elsewhere in Judges　ᵉ26 Or build with layers of stone an　ᶠ26 Or full-grown; also in verse 28

VERSE:	AUTHOR:	PASSAGE:
Judges 6:13	Lloyd John Ogilvie	Judges 6:1–24

Why Has All This Happened?

Gideon's question to the angel expresses how we feel at times: "If the Lord is with us, why has all this happened to us?" Hardly a day goes by that someone doesn't ask me, "If God is love, why does he allow me to have problems?"

God doesn't send problems. There are already enough to go around. The most difficult choice God ever made was to create humankind with free will so we could choose to love and glorify him. We are not marionettes. We know what we did with our freedom: the fall, endless generations of rebellion, a world estranged from its Creator and Lord . . .

God came in Christ to solve our most momentous problem. He reconciled us to himself, defeated the forces of evil, conquered death and sent the risen Christ to be with us forever. So when we accept our salvation and Christ's present power, the biggest problems are behind us. And now, the only problems that can defeat us are those we try to handle on our own. Our challenge is to own the problem by coming to grips with it. Then we must disown the temptation to try to solve it on our own. We'll always have problems; that's life. But the Lord will give us a strategy to solve our problems and strength to endure; that's the abundant life!

ADDITIONAL SCRIPTURE READINGS
Genesis 2:15–17; Ephesians 2:11–22

Go to page 298 for your next devotional reading.

must die, because he has broken down Baal's altar and cut down the Asherah pole beside it."

³¹But Joash replied to the hostile crowd around him, "Are you going to plead Baal's cause? Are you trying to save him? Whoever fights for him shall be put to death by morning! If Baal really is a god, he can defend himself when someone breaks down his altar." ³²So that day they called Gideon "Jerub-Baal,ᵃ" saying, "Let Baal contend with him," because he broke down Baal's altar.

³³Now all the Midianites, Amalekites and other eastern peoples joined forces and crossed over the Jordan and camped in the Valley of Jezreel. ³⁴Then the Spirit of the LORD came upon Gideon, and he blew a trumpet, summoning the Abiezrites to follow him. ³⁵He sent messengers throughout Manasseh, calling them to arms, and also into Asher, Zebulun and Naphtali, so that they too went up to meet them.

³⁶Gideon said to God, "If you will save Israel by my hand as you have promised— ³⁷look, I will place a wool fleece on the threshing floor. If there is dew only on the fleece and all the ground is dry, then I will know that you will save Israel by my hand, as you said." ³⁸And that is what happened. Gideon rose early the next day; he squeezed the fleece and wrung out the dew—a bowlful of water.

³⁹Then Gideon said to God, "Do not be angry with me. Let me make just one more request. Allow me one more test with the fleece. This time make the fleece dry and the ground covered with dew." ⁴⁰That night God did so. Only the fleece was dry; all the ground was covered with dew.

Gideon Defeats the Midianites

7 Early in the morning, Jerub-Baal (that is, Gideon) and all his men camped at the spring of Harod. The camp of Midian was north of them in the valley near the hill of Moreh. ²The

LORD said to Gideon, "You have too many men for me to deliver Midian into their hands. In order that Israel may not boast against me that her own strength has saved her, ³announce now to the people, 'Anyone who trembles with fear may turn back and leave Mount Gilead.' " So twenty-two thousand men left, while ten thousand remained.

⁴But the LORD said to Gideon, "There are still too many men. Take them down to the water, and I will sift them for you there. If I say, 'This one shall go with you,' he shall go; but if I say, 'This one shall not go with you,' he shall not go."

⁵So Gideon took the men down to the water. There the LORD told him, "Separate those who lap the water with their tongues like a dog from those who kneel down to drink." ⁶Three hundred men lapped with their hands to their mouths. All the rest got down on their knees to drink.

⁷The LORD said to Gideon, "With the three hundred men that lapped I will save you and give the Midianites into your hands. Let all the other men go, each to his own place." ⁸So Gideon sent the rest of the Israelites to their tents but kept the three hundred, who took over the provisions and trumpets of the others.

Now the camp of Midian lay below him in the valley. ⁹During that night the LORD said to Gideon, "Get up, go down against the camp, because I am going to give it into your hands. ¹⁰If you are afraid to attack, go down to the camp with your servant Purah ¹¹and listen to what they are saying. Afterward, you will be encouraged to attack the camp." So he and Purah his servant went down to the outposts of the camp. ¹²The Midianites, the Amalekites and all the other eastern peoples had settled in the valley, thick as locusts. Their camels could no more be counted than the sand on the seashore.

¹³Gideon arrived just as a man was telling a friend his dream. "I had a

---

ᵃ32 *Jerub-Baal* means *let Baal contend*.

dream," he was saying. "A round loaf of barley bread came tumbling into the Midianite camp. It struck the tent with such force that the tent overturned and collapsed."

¹⁴His friend responded, "This can be nothing other than the sword of Gideon son of Joash, the Israelite. God has given the Midianites and the whole camp into his hands."

¹⁵When Gideon heard the dream and its interpretation, he worshiped God. He returned to the camp of Israel and called out, "Get up! The LORD has given the Midianite camp into your hands." ¹⁶Dividing the three hundred men into three companies, he placed trumpets and empty jars in the hands of all of them, with torches inside.

¹⁷"Watch me," he told them. "Follow my lead. When I get to the edge of the camp, do exactly as I do. ¹⁸When I and all who are with me blow our trumpets, then from all around the camp blow yours and shout, 'For the LORD and for Gideon.'"

¹⁹Gideon and the hundred men with him reached the edge of the camp at the beginning of the middle watch, just after they had changed the guard. They blew their trumpets and broke the jars that were in their hands. ²⁰The three companies blew the trumpets and smashed the jars. Grasping the torches in their left hands and holding in their right hands the trumpets they were to blow, they shouted, "A sword for the LORD and for Gideon!" ²¹While each man held his position around the camp, all the Midianites ran, crying out as they fled.

²²When the three hundred trumpets sounded, the LORD caused the men throughout the camp to turn on each other with their swords. The army fled to Beth Shittah toward Zererah as far as the border of Abel Meholah near Tabbath. ²³Israelites from Naphtali, Asher and all Manasseh were called out, and they pursued the

Midianites. ²⁴Gideon sent messengers throughout the hill country of Ephraim, saying, "Come down against the Midianites and seize the waters of the Jordan ahead of them as far as Beth Barah."

So all the men of Ephraim were called out and they took the waters of the Jordan as far as Beth Barah. ²⁵They also captured two of the Midianite leaders, Oreb and Zeeb. They killed Oreb at the rock of Oreb, and Zeeb at the winepress of Zeeb. They pursued the Midianites and brought the heads of Oreb and Zeeb to Gideon, who was by the Jordan.

Zebah and Zalmunna

8 Now the Ephraimites asked Gideon, "Why have you treated us like this? Why didn't you call us when you went to fight Midian?" And they criticized him sharply.

²But he answered them, "What have I accomplished compared to you? Aren't the gleanings of Ephraim's grapes better than the full grape harvest of Abiezer? ³God gave Oreb and Zeeb, the Midianite leaders, into your hands. What was I able to do compared to you?" At this, their resentment against him subsided.

⁴Gideon and his three hundred men, exhausted yet keeping up the pursuit, came to the Jordan and crossed it. ⁵He said to the men of Succoth, "Give my troops some bread; they are worn out, and I am still pursuing Zebah and Zalmunna, the kings of Midian."

⁶But the officials of Succoth said, "Do you already have the hands of Zebah and Zalmunna in your possession? Why should we give bread to your troops?"

⁷Then Gideon replied, "Just for that, when the LORD has given Zebah and Zalmunna into my hand, I will tear your flesh with desert thorns and briers."

⁸From there he went up to Peniel[a] and made the same request of them, but they answered as the men of Suc-

---

^a8 Hebrew *Penuel*, a variant of *Peniel*; also in verses 9 and 17

coth had. ⁹So he said to the men of Peniel, "When I return in triumph, I will tear down this tower."

¹⁰Now Zebah and Zalmunna were in Karkor with a force of about fifteen thousand men, all that were left of the armies of the eastern peoples; a hundred and twenty thousand swordsmen had fallen. ¹¹Gideon went up by the route of the nomads east of Nobah and Jogbehah and fell upon the unsuspecting army. ¹²Zebah and Zalmunna, the two kings of Midian, fled, but he pursued them and captured them, routing their entire army.

¹³Gideon son of Joash then returned from the battle by the Pass of Heres. ¹⁴He caught a young man of Succoth and questioned him, and the young man wrote down for him the names of the seventy-seven officials of Succoth, the elders of the town. ¹⁵Then Gideon came and said to the men of Succoth, "Here are Zebah and Zalmunna, about whom you taunted me by saying, 'Do you already have the hands of Zebah and Zalmunna in your possession? Why should we give bread to your exhausted men?' " ¹⁶He took the elders of the town and taught the men of Succoth a lesson by punishing them with desert thorns and briers. ¹⁷He also pulled down the tower of Peniel and killed the men of the town.

¹⁸Then he asked Zebah and Zalmunna, "What kind of men did you kill at Tabor?"

"Men like you," they answered, "each one with the bearing of a prince."

¹⁹Gideon replied, "Those were my brothers, the sons of my own mother. As surely as the LORD lives, if you had spared their lives, I would not kill you." ²⁰Turning to Jether, his oldest son, he said, "Kill them!" But Jether did not draw his sword, because he was only a boy and was afraid.

²¹Zebah and Zalmunna said, "Come, do it yourself. 'As is the man, so is his strength.' " So Gideon stepped forward and killed them, and took the ornaments off their camels' necks.

Gideon's Ephod

²²The Israelites said to Gideon, "Rule over us—you, your son and your grandson—because you have saved us out of the hand of Midian."

²³But Gideon told them, "I will not rule over you, nor will my son rule over you. The LORD will rule over you." ²⁴And he said, "I do have one request, that each of you give me an earring from your share of the plunder." (It was the custom of the Ishmaelites to wear gold earrings.)

²⁵They answered, "We'll be glad to give them." So they spread out a garment, and each man threw a ring from his plunder onto it. ²⁶The weight of the gold rings he asked for came to seventeen hundred shekels,ᵃ not counting the ornaments, the pendants and the purple garments worn by the kings of Midian or the chains that were on their camels' necks. ²⁷Gideon made the gold into an ephod, which he placed in Ophrah, his town. All Israel prostituted themselves by worshiping it there, and it became a snare to Gideon and his family.

Gideon's Death

²⁸Thus Midian was subdued before the Israelites and did not raise its head again. During Gideon's lifetime, the land enjoyed peace forty years.

²⁹Jerub-Baal son of Joash went back home to live. ³⁰He had seventy sons of his own, for he had many wives. ³¹His concubine, who lived in Shechem, also bore him a son, whom he named Abimelech. ³²Gideon son of Joash died at a good old age and was buried in the tomb of his father Joash in Ophrah of the Abiezrites.

³³No sooner had Gideon died than the Israelites again prostituted themselves to the Baals. They set up Baal-Berith as their god and ³⁴did not remember the LORD their God, who had rescued them from the hands of all their enemies on every side. ³⁵They

ᵃ26 That is, about 43 pounds (about 19.5 kilograms)

also failed to show kindness to the family of Jerub-Baal (that is, Gideon) for all the good things he had done for them.

Abimelech

9 Abimelech son of Jerub-Baal went to his mother's brothers in Shechem and said to them and to all his mother's clan, ²"Ask all the citizens of Shechem, 'Which is better for you: to have all seventy of Jerub-Baal's sons rule over you, or just one man?' Remember, I am your flesh and blood."

³When the brothers repeated all this to the citizens of Shechem, they were inclined to follow Abimelech, for they said, "He is our brother."

VERSE:	AUTHOR:	PASSAGE:
Judges 8:32	Elizabeth Skoglund	Judges 8:28–32

An Honor, Not a Curse

Contrary to popular thinking, God never meant old age to be a curse. Nor was the physical process of aging meant to be hidden out of embarrassment by the excessive use of cosmetics or cosmetic surgery. To be old was not meant to be a cause of shame; rather, the Bible presents old age as a state to be desired for oneself and honored by others. Indeed, the only one of the Ten Commandments connected with a promise offers long life as the incentive [Exodus 20:12] . . .

I once heard William F. Buckley, Jr., state something to the effect that, while a love of life is healthy, a veneration of age is idolatry. Consistent with that thought, he observed that Christ would not have died on the cross if he had venerated life. I thought his point was well taken. When the Bible speaks of age as a blessing and even a reward, it encourages a love of life, not its worship . . .

Wrinkles in the face and furrows on the brow can be distinguishing signs of wisdom, to be honored in those who have endured and grown and contributed with their lives, and who now have a distilled reservoir of knowledge to offer those who are still young.

ADDITIONAL SCRIPTURE READINGS
Proverbs 10:27–32; Proverbs 16:31

Go to page 318 for your next devotional reading.

⁴They gave him seventy shekels^a of silver from the temple of Baal-Berith, and Abimelech used it to hire reckless adventurers, who became his followers. ⁵He went to his father's home in Ophrah and on one stone murdered his seventy brothers, the sons of Jerub-Baal. But Jotham, the youngest son of Jerub-Baal, escaped by hiding. ⁶Then all the citizens of Shechem and Beth Millo gathered beside the great tree at the pillar in Shechem to crown Abimelech king.

⁷When Jotham was told about this, he climbed up on the top of Mount Gerizim and shouted to them, "Listen to me, citizens of Shechem, so that God may listen to you. ⁸One day the trees went out to anoint a king for themselves. They said to the olive tree, 'Be our king.'

⁹"But the olive tree answered, 'Should I give up my oil, by which both gods and men are honored, to hold sway over the trees?'

¹⁰"Next, the trees said to the fig tree, 'Come and be our king.'

¹¹"But the fig tree replied, 'Should I give up my fruit, so good and sweet, to hold sway over the trees?'

¹²"Then the trees said to the vine, 'Come and be our king.'

¹³"But the vine answered, 'Should I give up my wine, which cheers both gods and men, to hold sway over the trees?'

¹⁴"Finally all the trees said to the thornbush, 'Come and be our king.'

¹⁵"The thornbush said to the trees, 'If you really want to anoint me king over you, come and take refuge in my shade; but if not, then let fire come out of the thornbush and consume the cedars of Lebanon!'

¹⁶"Now if you have acted honorably and in good faith when you made Abimelech king, and if you have been fair to Jerub-Baal and his family, and if you have treated him as he deserves— ¹⁷and to think that my father fought for you, risked his life to rescue you from the hand of Midian ¹⁸(but today you have revolted against my father's family, murdered his seventy sons on a single stone, and made Abimelech, the son of his slave girl, king over the citizens of Shechem because he is your brother)— ¹⁹if then you have acted honorably and in good faith toward Jerub-Baal and his family today, may Abimelech be your joy, and may you be his, too! ²⁰But if you have not, let fire come out from Abimelech and consume you, citizens of Shechem and Beth Millo, and let fire come out from you, citizens of Shechem and Beth Millo, and consume Abimelech!"

²¹Then Jotham fled, escaping to Beer, and he lived there because he was afraid of his brother Abimelech.

²²After Abimelech had governed Israel three years, ²³God sent an evil spirit between Abimelech and the citizens of Shechem, who acted treacherously against Abimelech. ²⁴God did this in order that the crime against Jerub-Baal's seventy sons, the shedding of their blood, might be avenged on their brother Abimelech and on the citizens of Shechem, who had helped him murder his brothers. ²⁵In opposition to him these citizens of Shechem set men on the hilltops to ambush and rob everyone who passed by, and this was reported to Abimelech.

²⁶Now Gaal son of Ebed moved with his brothers into Shechem, and its citizens put their confidence in him. ²⁷After they had gone out into the fields and gathered the grapes and trodden them, they held a festival in the temple of their god. While they were eating and drinking, they cursed Abimelech. ²⁸Then Gaal son of Ebed said, "Who is Abimelech, and who is Shechem, that we should be subject to him? Isn't he Jerub-Baal's son, and isn't Zebul his deputy? Serve the men of Hamor, Shechem's father! Why should we serve Abimelech? ²⁹If only this people were under my command! Then I would get rid of him. I would

_____
^a4 That is, about 1 3/4 pounds (about 0.8 kilogram)

say to Abimelech, 'Call out your whole army!' "[a]

³⁰When Zebul the governor of the city heard what Gaal son of Ebed said, he was very angry. ³¹Under cover he sent messengers to Abimelech, saying, "Gaal son of Ebed and his brothers have come to Shechem and are stirring up the city against you. ³²Now then, during the night you and your men should come and lie in wait in the fields. ³³In the morning at sunrise, advance against the city. When Gaal and his men come out against you, do whatever your hand finds to do."

³⁴So Abimelech and all his troops set out by night and took up concealed positions near Shechem in four companies. ³⁵Now Gaal son of Ebed had gone out and was standing at the entrance to the city gate just as Abimelech and his soldiers came out from their hiding place.

³⁶When Gaal saw them, he said to Zebul, "Look, people are coming down from the tops of the mountains!"

Zebul replied, "You mistake the shadows of the mountains for men."

³⁷But Gaal spoke up again: "Look, people are coming down from the center of the land, and a company is coming from the direction of the soothsayers' tree."

³⁸Then Zebul said to him, "Where is your big talk now, you who said, 'Who is Abimelech that we should be subject to him?' Aren't these the men you ridiculed? Go out and fight them!"

³⁹So Gaal led out[b] the citizens of Shechem and fought Abimelech. ⁴⁰Abimelech chased him, and many fell wounded in the flight—all the way to the entrance to the gate. ⁴¹Abimelech stayed in Arumah, and Zebul drove Gaal and his brothers out of Shechem.

⁴²The next day the people of Shechem went out to the fields, and this was reported to Abimelech. ⁴³So he took his men, divided them into three companies and set an ambush in the fields. When he saw the people coming out of the city, he rose to attack them. ⁴⁴Abimelech and the companies with him rushed forward to a position at the entrance to the city gate. Then two companies rushed upon those in the fields and struck them down. ⁴⁵All that day Abimelech pressed his attack against the city until he had captured it and killed its people. Then he destroyed the city and scattered salt over it.

⁴⁶On hearing this, the citizens in the tower of Shechem went into the stronghold of the temple of El-Berith. ⁴⁷When Abimelech heard that they had assembled there, ⁴⁸he and all his men went up Mount Zalmon. He took an ax and cut off some branches, which he lifted to his shoulders. He ordered the men with him, "Quick! Do what you have seen me do!" ⁴⁹So all the men cut branches and followed Abimelech. They piled them against the stronghold and set it on fire over the people inside. So all the people in the tower of Shechem, about a thousand men and women, also died.

⁵⁰Next Abimelech went to Thebez and besieged it and captured it. ⁵¹Inside the city, however, was a strong tower, to which all the men and women—all the people of the city—fled. They locked themselves in and climbed up on the tower roof. ⁵²Abimelech went to the tower and stormed it. But as he approached the entrance to the tower to set it on fire, ⁵³a woman dropped an upper millstone on his head and cracked his skull.

⁵⁴Hurriedly he called to his armorbearer, "Draw your sword and kill me, so that they can't say, 'A woman killed him.' " So his servant ran him through, and he died. ⁵⁵When the Israelites saw that Abimelech was dead, they went home.

⁵⁶Thus God repaid the wickedness that Abimelech had done to his father by murdering his seventy brothers.

---

[a]29 Septuagint; Hebrew *him." Then he said to Abimelech, "Call out your whole army!"*   [b]39 Or *Gaal went out in the sight of*

57God also made the men of Shechem pay for all their wickedness. The curse of Jotham son of Jerub-Baal came on them.

Tola

10 After the time of Abimelech a man of Issachar, Tola son of Puah, the son of Dodo, rose to save Israel. He lived in Shamir, in the hill country of Ephraim. 2He led*a* Israel twenty-three years; then he died, and was buried in Shamir.

Jair

3He was followed by Jair of Gilead, who led Israel twenty-two years. 4He had thirty sons, who rode thirty donkeys. They controlled thirty towns in Gilead, which to this day are called Havvoth Jair.*b* 5When Jair died, he was buried in Kamon.

Jephthah

6Again the Israelites did evil in the eyes of the LORD. They served the Baals and the Ashtoreths, and the gods of Aram, the gods of Sidon, the gods of Moab, the gods of the Ammonites and the gods of the Philistines. And because the Israelites forsook the LORD and no longer served him, 7he became angry with them. He sold them into the hands of the Philistines and the Ammonites, 8who that year shattered and crushed them. For eighteen years they oppressed all the Israelites on the east side of the Jordan in Gilead, the land of the Amorites. 9The Ammonites also crossed the Jordan to fight against Judah, Benjamin and the house of Ephraim; and Israel was in great distress. 10Then the Israelites cried out to the LORD, "We have sinned against you, forsaking our God and serving the Baals."

11The LORD replied, "When the Egyptians, the Amorites, the Ammonites, the Philistines, 12the Sidonians, the Amalekites and the Maonites*c* oppressed you and you cried to me for help, did I not save you from their

hands? 13But you have forsaken me and served other gods, so I will no longer save you. 14Go and cry out to the gods you have chosen. Let them save you when you are in trouble!"

15But the Israelites said to the LORD, "We have sinned. Do with us whatever you think best, but please rescue us now." 16Then they got rid of the foreign gods among them and served the LORD. And he could bear Israel's misery no longer.

17When the Ammonites were called to arms and camped in Gilead, the Israelites assembled and camped at Mizpah. 18The leaders of the people of Gilead said to each other, "Whoever will launch the attack against the Ammonites will be the head of all those living in Gilead."

11 Jephthah the Gileadite was a mighty warrior. His father was Gilead; his mother was a prostitute. 2Gilead's wife also bore him sons, and when they were grown up, they drove Jephthah away. "You are not going to get any inheritance in our family," they said, "because you are the son of another woman." 3So Jephthah fled from his brothers and settled in the land of Tob, where a group of adventurers gathered around him and followed him.

4Some time later, when the Ammonites made war on Israel, 5the elders of Gilead went to get Jephthah from the land of Tob. 6"Come," they said, "be our commander, so we can fight the Ammonites."

7Jephthah said to them, "Didn't you hate me and drive me from my father's house? Why do you come to me now, when you're in trouble?"

8The elders of Gilead said to him, "Nevertheless, we are turning to you now; come with us to fight the Ammonites, and you will be our head over all who live in Gilead."

9Jephthah answered, "Suppose you take me back to fight the Ammonites and the LORD gives them to me—will I really be your head?"

---

*a*2 Traditionally *judged*; also in verse 3   *b*4 Or *called the settlements of Jair*   *c*12 Hebrew; some Septuagint manuscripts *Midianites*

[10]The elders of Gilead replied, "The LORD is our witness; we will certainly do as you say." [11]So Jephthah went with the elders of Gilead, and the people made him head and commander over them. And he repeated all his words before the LORD in Mizpah.

[12]Then Jephthah sent messengers to the Ammonite king with the question: "What do you have against us that you have attacked our country?"

[13]The king of the Ammonites answered Jephthah's messengers, "When Israel came up out of Egypt, they took away my land from the Arnon to the Jabbok, all the way to the Jordan. Now give it back peaceably."

[14]Jephthah sent back messengers to the Ammonite king, [15]saying:

"This is what Jephthah says: Israel did not take the land of Moab or the land of the Ammonites. [16]But when they came up out of Egypt, Israel went through the desert to the Red Sea[a] and on to Kadesh. [17]Then Israel sent messengers to the king of Edom, saying, 'Give us permission to go through your country,' but the king of Edom would not listen. They sent also to the king of Moab, and he refused. So Israel stayed at Kadesh.

[18]"Next they traveled through the desert, skirted the lands of Edom and Moab, passed along the eastern side of the country of Moab, and camped on the other side of the Arnon. They did not enter the territory of Moab, for the Arnon was its border.

[19]"Then Israel sent messengers to Sihon king of the Amorites, who ruled in Heshbon, and said to him, 'Let us pass through your country to our own place.' [20]Sihon, however, did not trust Israel[b] to pass through his territory. He mustered all his men and encamped at Jahaz and fought with Israel.

[21]"Then the LORD, the God of Israel, gave Sihon and all his men into Israel's hands, and they defeated them. Israel took over all the land of the Amorites who lived in that country, [22]capturing all of it from the Arnon to the Jabbok and from the desert to the Jordan.

[23]"Now since the LORD, the God of Israel, has driven the Amorites out before his people Israel, what right have you to take it over? [24]Will you not take what your god Chemosh gives you? Likewise, whatever the LORD our God has given us, we will possess. [25]Are you better than Balak son of Zippor, king of Moab? Did he ever quarrel with Israel or fight with them? [26]For three hundred years Israel occupied Heshbon, Aroer, the surrounding settlements and all the towns along the Arnon. Why didn't you retake them during that time? [27]I have not wronged you, but you are doing me wrong by waging war against me. Let the LORD, the Judge,[c] decide the dispute this day between the Israelites and the Ammonites."

[28]The king of Ammon, however, paid no attention to the message Jephthah sent him.

[29]Then the Spirit of the LORD came upon Jephthah. He crossed Gilead and Manasseh, passed through Mizpah of Gilead, and from there he advanced against the Ammonites. [30]And Jephthah made a vow to the LORD: "If you give the Ammonites into my hands, [31]whatever comes out of the door of my house to meet me when I return in triumph from the Ammonites will be the LORD's, and I will sacrifice it as a burnt offering."

[32]Then Jephthah went over to fight

---

[a]16 Hebrew *Yam Suph*; that is, Sea of Reeds   [b]20 Or *however, would not make an agreement for Israel*   [c]27 Or *Ruler*

the Ammonites, and the LORD gave them into his hands. ³³He devastated twenty towns from Aroer to the vicinity of Minnith, as far as Abel Keramim. Thus Israel subdued Ammon.

³⁴When Jephthah returned to his home in Mizpah, who should come out to meet him but his daughter, dancing to the sound of tambourines! She was an only child. Except for her he had neither son nor daughter. ³⁵When he saw her, he tore his clothes and cried, "Oh! My daughter! You have made me miserable and wretched, because I have made a vow to the LORD that I cannot break."

³⁶"My father," she replied, "you have given your word to the LORD. Do to me just as you promised, now that the LORD has avenged you of your enemies, the Ammonites. ³⁷But grant me this one request," she said. "Give me two months to roam the hills and weep with my friends, because I will never marry."

³⁸"You may go," he said. And he let her go for two months. She and the girls went into the hills and wept because she would never marry. ³⁹After the two months, she returned to her father and he did to her as he had vowed. And she was a virgin.

From this comes the Israelite custom ⁴⁰that each year the young women of Israel go out for four days to commemorate the daughter of Jephthah the Gileadite.

Jephthah and Ephraim

12 The men of Ephraim called out their forces, crossed over to Zaphon and said to Jephthah, "Why did you go to fight the Ammonites without calling us to go with you? We're going to burn down your house over your head."

²Jephthah answered, "I and my people were engaged in a great struggle with the Ammonites, and although I called, you didn't save me out of their hands. ³When I saw that you wouldn't help, I took my life in my hands and crossed over to fight

the Ammonites, and the LORD gave me the victory over them. Now why have you come up today to fight me?"

⁴Jephthah then called together the men of Gilead and fought against Ephraim. The Gileadites struck them down because the Ephraimites had said, "You Gileadites are renegades from Ephraim and Manasseh." ⁵The Gileadites captured the fords of the Jordan leading to Ephraim, and whenever a survivor of Ephraim said, "Let me cross over," the men of Gilead asked him, "Are you an Ephraimite?" If he replied, "No," ⁶they said, "All right, say 'Shibboleth.'" If he said, "Sibboleth," because he could not pronounce the word correctly, they seized him and killed him at the fords of the Jordan. Forty-two thousand Ephraimites were killed at that time.

⁷Jephthah led^a Israel six years. Then Jephthah the Gileadite died, and was buried in a town in Gilead.

Ibzan, Elon and Abdon

⁸After him, Ibzan of Bethlehem led Israel. ⁹He had thirty sons and thirty daughters. He gave his daughters away in marriage to those outside his clan, and for his sons he brought in thirty young women as wives from outside his clan. Ibzan led Israel seven years. ¹⁰Then Ibzan died, and was buried in Bethlehem.

¹¹After him, Elon the Zebulunite led Israel ten years. ¹²Then Elon died, and was buried in Aijalon in the land of Zebulun.

¹³After him, Abdon son of Hillel, from Pirathon, led Israel. ¹⁴He had forty sons and thirty grandsons, who rode on seventy donkeys. He led Israel eight years. ¹⁵Then Abdon son of Hillel died, and was buried at Pirathon in Ephraim, in the hill country of the Amalekites.

The Birth of Samson

13 Again the Israelites did evil in the eyes of the LORD, so the

---

^a 7 Traditionally *judged*; also in verses 8-14

LORD delivered them into the hands of the Philistines for forty years.

²A certain man of Zorah, named Manoah, from the clan of the Danites, had a wife who was sterile and remained childless. ³The angel of the LORD appeared to her and said, "You are sterile and childless, but you are going to conceive and have a son. ⁴Now see to it that you drink no wine or other fermented drink and that you do not eat anything unclean, ⁵because you will conceive and give birth to a son. No razor may be used on his head, because the boy is to be a Nazirite, set apart to God from birth, and he will begin the deliverance of Israel from the hands of the Philistines."

⁶Then the woman went to her husband and told him, "A man of God came to me. He looked like an angel of God, very awesome. I didn't ask him where he came from, and he didn't tell me his name. ⁷But he said to me, 'You will conceive and give birth to a son. Now then, drink no wine or other fermented drink and do not eat anything unclean, because the boy will be a Nazirite of God from birth until the day of his death.'"

⁸Then Manoah prayed to the LORD: "O Lord, I beg you, let the man of God you sent to us come again to teach us how to bring up the boy who is to be born."

⁹God heard Manoah, and the angel of God came again to the woman while she was out in the field; but her husband Manoah was not with her. ¹⁰The woman hurried to tell her husband, "He's here! The man who appeared to me the other day!"

¹¹Manoah got up and followed his wife. When he came to the man, he said, "Are you the one who talked to my wife?"

"I am," he said.

¹²So Manoah asked him, "When your words are fulfilled, what is to be the rule for the boy's life and work?"

¹³The angel of the LORD answered, "Your wife must do all that I have told her. ¹⁴She must not eat anything

that comes from the grapevine, nor drink any wine or other fermented drink nor eat anything unclean. She must do everything I have commanded her."

¹⁵Manoah said to the angel of the LORD, "We would like you to stay until we prepare a young goat for you."

¹⁶The angel of the LORD replied, "Even though you detain me, I will not eat any of your food. But if you prepare a burnt offering, offer it to the LORD." (Manoah did not realize that it was the angel of the LORD.)

¹⁷Then Manoah inquired of the angel of the LORD, "What is your name, so that we may honor you when your word comes true?"

¹⁸He replied, "Why do you ask my name? It is beyond understanding.ᵃ" ¹⁹Then Manoah took a young goat, together with the grain offering, and sacrificed it on a rock to the LORD. And the LORD did an amazing thing while Manoah and his wife watched: ²⁰As the flame blazed up from the altar toward heaven, the angel of the LORD ascended in the flame. Seeing this, Manoah and his wife fell with their faces to the ground. ²¹When the angel of the LORD did not show himself again to Manoah and his wife, Manoah realized that it was the angel of the LORD.

²²"We are doomed to die!" he said to his wife. "We have seen God!"

²³But his wife answered, "If the LORD had meant to kill us, he would not have accepted a burnt offering and grain offering from our hands, nor shown us all these things or now told us this."

²⁴The woman gave birth to a boy and named him Samson. He grew and the LORD blessed him, ²⁵and the Spirit of the LORD began to stir him while he was in Mahaneh Dan, between Zorah and Eshtaol.

Samson's Marriage

14 Samson went down to Timnah and saw there a young Philistine woman. ²When he returned, he

---

ᵃ18 Or *is wonderful*

said to his father and mother, "I have seen a Philistine woman in Timnah; now get her for me as my wife."

³His father and mother replied, "Isn't there an acceptable woman among your relatives or among all our people? Must you go to the uncircumcised Philistines to get a wife?"

But Samson said to his father, "Get her for me. She's the right one for me." ⁴(His parents did not know that this was from the LORD, who was seeking an occasion to confront the Philistines; for at that time they were ruling over Israel.) ⁵Samson went down to Timnah together with his father and mother. As they approached the vineyards of Timnah, suddenly a young lion came roaring toward him. ⁶The Spirit of the LORD came upon him in power so that he tore the lion apart with his bare hands as he might have torn a young goat. But he told neither his father nor his mother what he had done. ⁷Then he went down and talked with the woman, and he liked her.

⁸Some time later, when he went back to marry her, he turned aside to look at the lion's carcass. In it was a swarm of bees and some honey, ⁹which he scooped out with his hands and ate as he went along. When he rejoined his parents, he gave them some, and they too ate it. But he did not tell them that he had taken the honey from the lion's carcass.

¹⁰Now his father went down to see the woman. And Samson made a feast there, as was customary for bridegrooms. ¹¹When he appeared, he was given thirty companions.

¹²"Let me tell you a riddle," Samson said to them. "If you can give me the answer within the seven days of the feast, I will give you thirty linen garments and thirty sets of clothes. ¹³If you can't tell me the answer, you must give me thirty linen garments and thirty sets of clothes."

"Tell us your riddle," they said. "Let's hear it."

¹⁴He replied,

"Out of the eater, something to eat;
out of the strong, something sweet."

For three days they could not give the answer.

¹⁵On the fourth[a] day, they said to Samson's wife, "Coax your husband into explaining the riddle for us, or we will burn you and your father's household to death. Did you invite us here to rob us?"

¹⁶Then Samson's wife threw herself on him, sobbing, "You hate me! You don't really love me. You've given my people a riddle, but you haven't told me the answer."

"I haven't even explained it to my father or mother," he replied, "so why should I explain it to you?" ¹⁷She cried the whole seven days of the feast. So on the seventh day he finally told her, because she continued to press him. She in turn explained the riddle to her people.

¹⁸Before sunset on the seventh day the men of the town said to him,

"What is sweeter than honey?
What is stronger than a lion?"

Samson said to them,

"If you had not plowed with my heifer,
you would not have solved my riddle."

¹⁹Then the Spirit of the LORD came upon him in power. He went down to Ashkelon, struck down thirty of their men, stripped them of their belongings and gave their clothes to those who had explained the riddle. Burning with anger, he went up to his father's house. ²⁰And Samson's wife was given to the friend who had attended him at his wedding.

Samson's Vengeance on the Philistines

15 Later on, at the time of wheat harvest, Samson took a young goat and went to visit his wife. He

---

a15 Some Septuagint manuscripts and Syriac; Hebrew *seventh*

said, "I'm going to my wife's room."
But her father would not let him
go in.

²"I was so sure you thoroughly hated her," he said, "that I gave her to
your friend. Isn't her younger sister
more attractive? Take her instead."

³Samson said to them, "This time I
have a right to get even with the Philistines; I will really harm them." ⁴So
he went out and caught three hundred foxes and tied them tail to tail in
pairs. He then fastened a torch to every pair of tails, ⁵lit the torches and let
the foxes loose in the standing grain
of the Philistines. He burned up the
shocks and standing grain, together
with the vineyards and olive groves.

⁶When the Philistines asked, "Who
did this?" they were told, "Samson,
the Timnite's son-in-law, because his
wife was given to his friend."

So the Philistines went up and
burned her and her father to death.
⁷Samson said to them, "Since you've
acted like this, I won't stop until I get
my revenge on you." ⁸He attacked
them viciously and slaughtered many
of them. Then he went down and
stayed in a cave in the rock of Etam.

⁹The Philistines went up and
camped in Judah, spreading out near
Lehi. ¹⁰The men of Judah asked,
"Why have you come to fight us?"

"We have come to take Samson
prisoner," they answered, "to do to
him as he did to us."

¹¹Then three thousand men from
Judah went down to the cave in the
rock of Etam and said to Samson,
"Don't you realize that the Philistines
are rulers over us? What have you
done to us?"

He answered, "I merely did to
them what they did to me."

¹²They said to him, "We've come to
tie you up and hand you over to the
Philistines."

Samson said, "Swear to me that
you won't kill me yourselves."

¹³"Agreed," they answered. "We

will only tie you up and hand you
over to them. We will not kill you."
So they bound him with two new
ropes and led him up from the rock.
¹⁴As he approached Lehi, the Philistines came toward him shouting. The
Spirit of the LORD came upon him in
power. The ropes on his arms became
like charred flax, and the bindings
dropped from his hands. ¹⁵Finding
a fresh jawbone of a donkey, he
grabbed it and struck down a thousand men.

¹⁶Then Samson said,

"With a donkey's jawbone
    I have made donkeys of them.ᵃ
With a donkey's jawbone
    I have killed a thousand men."

¹⁷When he finished speaking, he
threw away the jawbone; and the
place was called Ramath Lehi.ᵇ

¹⁸Because he was very thirsty, he
cried out to the LORD, "You have giv-
en your servant this great victory.
Must I now die of thirst and fall into
the hands of the uncircumcised?"
¹⁹Then God opened up the hollow
place in Lehi, and water came out of
it. When Samson drank, his strength
returned and he revived. So the
spring was called En Hakkore,ᶜ and
it is still there in Lehi.

²⁰Samson ledᵈ Israel for twenty
years in the days of the Philistines.

Samson and Delilah

16 One day Samson went to Gaza,
where he saw a prostitute. He
went in to spend the night with her.
²The people of Gaza were told, "Samson is here!" So they surrounded the
place and lay in wait for him all night
at the city gate. They made no move
during the night, saying, "At dawn
we'll kill him."

³But Samson lay there only until
the middle of the night. Then he got
up and took hold of the doors of the
city gate, together with the two posts,
and tore them loose, bar and all. He

ᵃ16 Or made a heap or two; the Hebrew for donkey sounds like the Hebrew for heap.
ᵇ17 Ramath Lehi means jawbone hill.   ᶜ19 En Hakkore means caller's spring.   ᵈ20 Traditionally judged

lifted them to his shoulders and carried them to the top of the hill that faces Hebron.

[4]Some time later, he fell in love with a woman in the Valley of Sorek whose name was Delilah. [5]The rulers of the Philistines went to her and said, "See if you can lure him into showing you the secret of his great strength and how we can overpower him so we may tie him up and subdue him. Each one of us will give you eleven hundred shekels[a] of silver."

[6]So Delilah said to Samson, "Tell me the secret of your great strength and how you can be tied up and subdued."

[7]Samson answered her, "If anyone ties me with seven fresh thongs[b] that have not been dried, I'll become as weak as any other man."

[8]Then the rulers of the Philistines brought her seven fresh thongs that had not been dried, and she tied him with them. [9]With men hidden in the room, she called to him, "Samson, the Philistines are upon you!" But he snapped the thongs as easily as a piece of string snaps when it comes close to a flame. So the secret of his strength was not discovered.

[10]Then Delilah said to Samson, "You have made a fool of me; you lied to me. Come now, tell me how you can be tied."

[11]He said, "If anyone ties me securely with new ropes that have never been used, I'll become as weak as any other man."

[12]So Delilah took new ropes and tied him with them. Then, with men hidden in the room, she called to him, "Samson, the Philistines are upon you!" But he snapped the ropes off his arms as if they were threads.

[13]Delilah then said to Samson, "Until now, you have been making a fool of me and lying to me. Tell me how you can be tied."

He replied, "If you weave the seven braids of my head into the fabric ⌐on the loom⌐ and tighten it with the pin, I'll become as weak as any other man." So while he was sleeping, Delilah took the seven braids of his head, wove them into the fabric [14]and[c] tightened it with the pin.

Again she called to him, "Samson, the Philistines are upon you!" He awoke from his sleep and pulled up the pin and the loom, with the fabric.

[15]Then she said to him, "How can you say, 'I love you,' when you won't confide in me? This is the third time you have made a fool of me and haven't told me the secret of your great strength." [16]With such nagging she prodded him day after day until he was tired to death.

[17]So he told her everything. "No razor has ever been used on my head," he said, "because I have been a Nazirite set apart to God since birth. If my head were shaved, my strength would leave me, and I would become as weak as any other man."

[18]When Delilah saw that he had told her everything, she sent word to the rulers of the Philistines, "Come back once more; he has told me everything." So the rulers of the Philistines returned with the silver in their hands. [19]Having put him to sleep on her lap, she called a man to shave off the seven braids of his hair, and so began to subdue him.[d] And his strength left him.

[20]Then she called, "Samson, the Philistines are upon you!"

He awoke from his sleep and thought, "I'll go out as before and shake myself free." But he did not know that the LORD had left him.

[21]Then the Philistines seized him, gouged out his eyes and took him down to Gaza. Binding him with bronze shackles, they set him to grinding in the prison. [22]But the hair on his head began to grow again after it had been shaved.

---

[a]5 That is, about 28 pounds (about 13 kilograms)   [b]7 Or *bowstrings*; also in verses 8 and 9
[c]13,14 Some Septuagint manuscripts; Hebrew *"⌐I can⌐ if you weave the seven braids of my head into the fabric ⌐on the loom⌐."* [14]*So she*   [d]19 Hebrew; some Septuagint manuscripts *and he began to weaken*

The Death of Samson

²³Now the rulers of the Philistines assembled to offer a great sacrifice to Dagon their god and to celebrate, saying, "Our god has delivered Samson, our enemy, into our hands."

²⁴When the people saw him, they praised their god, saying,

"Our god has delivered our
         enemy
   into our hands,
the one who laid waste our land
   and multiplied our slain."

²⁵While they were in high spirits, they shouted, "Bring out Samson to entertain us." So they called Samson out of the prison, and he performed for them.

When they stood him among the pillars, ²⁶Samson said to the servant who held his hand, "Put me where I can feel the pillars that support the temple, so that I may lean against them." ²⁷Now the temple was crowded with men and women; all the rulers of the Philistines were there, and on the roof were about three thousand men and women watching Samson perform. ²⁸Then Samson prayed to the LORD, "O Sovereign LORD, remember me. O God, please strengthen me just once more, and let me with one blow get revenge on the Philistines for my two eyes." ²⁹Then Samson reached toward the two central pillars on which the temple stood. Bracing himself against them, his right hand on the one and his left hand on the other, ³⁰Samson said, "Let me die with the Philistines!" Then he pushed with all his might, and down came the temple on the rulers and all the people in it. Thus he killed many more when he died than while he lived.

³¹Then his brothers and his father's whole family went down to get him. They brought him back and buried him between Zorah and Eshtaol in the tomb of Manoah his father. He had led[a] Israel twenty years.

Micah's Idols

17 Now a man named Micah from the hill country of Ephraim ²said to his mother, "The eleven hundred shekels[b] of silver that were taken from you and about which I heard you utter a curse—I have that silver with me; I took it."

Then his mother said, "The LORD bless you, my son!"

³When he returned the eleven hundred shekels of silver to his mother, she said, "I solemnly consecrate my silver to the LORD for my son to make a carved image and a cast idol. I will give it back to you."

⁴So he returned the silver to his mother, and she took two hundred shekels[c] of silver and gave them to a silversmith, who made them into the image and the idol. And they were put in Micah's house.

⁵Now this man Micah had a shrine, and he made an ephod and some idols and installed one of his sons as his priest. ⁶In those days Israel had no king; everyone did as he saw fit.

⁷A young Levite from Bethlehem in Judah, who had been living within the clan of Judah, ⁸left that town in search of some other place to stay. On his way[d] he came to Micah's house in the hill country of Ephraim.

⁹Micah asked him, "Where are you from?"

"I'm a Levite from Bethlehem in Judah," he said, "and I'm looking for a place to stay."

¹⁰Then Micah said to him, "Live with me and be my father and priest, and I'll give you ten shekels[e] of silver a year, your clothes and your food." ¹¹So the Levite agreed to live with him, and the young man was to him like one of his sons. ¹²Then Micah installed the Levite, and the young man became his priest and lived in his house. ¹³And Micah said, "Now I

---

^a31 Traditionally *judged*   ^b2 That is, about 28 pounds (about 13 kilograms)   ^c4 That is, about 5 pounds (about 2.3 kilograms)   ^d8 Or *To carry on his profession*   ^e10 That is, about 4 ounces (about 110 grams)

know that the LORD will be good to me, since this Levite has become my priest."

Danites Settle in Laish

18 In those days Israel had no king.

And in those days the tribe of the Danites was seeking a place of their own where they might settle, because they had not yet come into an inheritance among the tribes of Israel. ²So the Danites sent five warriors from Zorah and Eshtaol to spy out the land and explore it. These men represented all their clans. They told them, "Go, explore the land."

The men entered the hill country of Ephraim and came to the house of Micah, where they spent the night. ³When they were near Micah's house, they recognized the voice of the young Levite; so they turned in there and asked him, "Who brought you here? What are you doing in this place? Why are you here?"

⁴He told them what Micah had done for him, and said, "He has hired me and I am his priest."

⁵Then they said to him, "Please inquire of God to learn whether our journey will be successful."

⁶The priest answered them, "Go in peace. Your journey has the LORD's approval."

⁷So the five men left and came to Laish, where they saw that the people were living in safety, like the Sidonians, unsuspecting and secure. And since their land lacked nothing, they were prosperous.ᵃ Also, they lived a long way from the Sidonians and had no relationship with anyone else.ᵇ

⁸When they returned to Zorah and Eshtaol, their brothers asked them, "How did you find things?"

⁹They answered, "Come on, let's attack them! We have seen that the land is very good. Aren't you going to do something? Don't hesitate to go there and take it over. ¹⁰When you get there, you will find an unsuspecting people and a spacious land that God has put into your hands, a land that lacks nothing whatever."

¹¹Then six hundred men from the clan of the Danites, armed for battle, set out from Zorah and Eshtaol. ¹²On their way they set up camp near Kiriath Jearim in Judah. This is why the place west of Kiriath Jearim is called Mahaneh Danᶜ to this day. ¹³From there they went on to the hill country of Ephraim and came to Micah's house.

¹⁴Then the five men who had spied out the land of Laish said to their brothers, "Do you know that one of these houses has an ephod, other household gods, a carved image and a cast idol? Now you know what to do." ¹⁵So they turned in there and went to the house of the young Levite at Micah's place and greeted him. ¹⁶The six hundred Danites, armed for battle, stood at the entrance to the gate. ¹⁷The five men who had spied out the land went inside and took the carved image, the ephod, the other household gods and the cast idol while the priest and the six hundred armed men stood at the entrance to the gate.

¹⁸When these men went into Micah's house and took the carved image, the ephod, the other household gods and the cast idol, the priest said to them, "What are you doing?"

¹⁹They answered him, "Be quiet! Don't say a word. Come with us, and be our father and priest. Isn't it better that you serve a tribe and clan in Israel as priest rather than just one man's household?" ²⁰Then the priest was glad. He took the ephod, the other household gods and the carved image and went along with the people. ²¹Putting their little children, their livestock and their possessions in front of them, they turned away and left.

²²When they had gone some distance from Micah's house, the men who lived near Micah were called to-

---

ᵃ7 The meaning of the Hebrew for this clause is uncertain.   ᵇ7 Hebrew; some Septuagint manuscripts *with the Arameans*   ᶜ12 *Mahaneh Dan* means *Dan's camp*.

gether and overtook the Danites. ²³As they shouted after them, the Danites turned and said to Micah, "What's the matter with you that you called out your men to fight?"

²⁴He replied, "You took the gods I made, and my priest, and went away. What else do I have? How can you ask, 'What's the matter with you?'"

²⁵The Danites answered, "Don't argue with us, or some hot-tempered men will attack you, and you and your family will lose your lives." ²⁶So the Danites went their way, and Micah, seeing that they were too strong for him, turned around and went back home.

²⁷Then they took what Micah had made, and his priest, and went on to Laish, against a peaceful and unsuspecting people. They attacked them with the sword and burned down their city. ²⁸There was no one to rescue them because they lived a long way from Sidon and had no relationship with anyone else. The city was in a valley near Beth Rehob.

The Danites rebuilt the city and settled there. ²⁹They named it Dan after their forefather Dan, who was born to Israel—though the city used to be called Laish. ³⁰There the Danites set up for themselves the idols, and Jonathan son of Gershom, the son of Moses,ᵃ and his sons were priests for the tribe of Dan until the time of the captivity of the land. ³¹They continued to use the idols Micah had made, all the time the house of God was in Shiloh.

A Levite and His Concubine

19 In those days Israel had no king.

Now a Levite who lived in a remote area in the hill country of Ephraim took a concubine from Bethlehem in Judah. ²But she was unfaithful to him. She left him and went back to her father's house in Bethlehem, Judah. After she had been there four months, ³her husband went to her to persuade her to return. He had with him his servant and two donkeys. She took him into her father's house, and when her father saw him, he gladly welcomed him. ⁴His father-in-law, the girl's father, prevailed upon him to stay; so he remained with him three days, eating and drinking, and sleeping there.

⁵On the fourth day they got up early and he prepared to leave, but the girl's father said to his son-in-law, "Refresh yourself with something to eat; then you can go." ⁶So the two of them sat down to eat and drink together. Afterward the girl's father said, "Please stay tonight and enjoy yourself." ⁷And when the man got up to go, his father-in-law persuaded him, so he stayed there that night. ⁸On the morning of the fifth day, when he rose to go, the girl's father said, "Refresh yourself. Wait till afternoon!" So the two of them ate together.

⁹Then when the man, with his concubine and his servant, got up to leave, his father-in-law, the girl's father, said, "Now look, it's almost evening. Spend the night here; the day is nearly over. Stay and enjoy yourself. Early tomorrow morning you can get up and be on your way home." ¹⁰But, unwilling to stay another night, the man left and went toward Jebus (that is, Jerusalem), with his two saddled donkeys and his concubine.

¹¹When they were near Jebus and the day was almost gone, the servant said to his master, "Come, let's stop at this city of the Jebusites and spend the night."

¹²His master replied, "No. We won't go into an alien city, whose people are not Israelites. We will go on to Gibeah." ¹³He added, "Come, let's try to reach Gibeah or Ramah and spend the night in one of those places." ¹⁴So they went on, and the sun set as they neared Gibeah in Benjamin. ¹⁵There they stopped to spend the night. They went and sat in the

---

ᵃ30 An ancient Hebrew scribal tradition, some Septuagint manuscripts and Vulgate; Masoretic Text *Manasseh*

city square, but no one took them into his home for the night.

¹⁶That evening an old man from the hill country of Ephraim, who was living in Gibeah (the men of the place were Benjamites), came in from his work in the fields. ¹⁷When he looked and saw the traveler in the city square, the old man asked, "Where are you going? Where did you come from?"

¹⁸He answered, "We are on our way from Bethlehem in Judah to a remote area in the hill country of Ephraim where I live. I have been to Bethlehem in Judah and now I am going to the house of the LORD. No one has taken me into his house. ¹⁹We have both straw and fodder for our donkeys and bread and wine for ourselves your servants—me, your maidservant, and the young man with us. We don't need anything."

²⁰"You are welcome at my house," the old man said. "Let me supply whatever you need. Only don't spend the night in the square." ²¹So he took him into his house and fed his donkeys. After they had washed their feet, they had something to eat and drink.

²²While they were enjoying themselves, some of the wicked men of the city surrounded the house. Pounding on the door, they shouted to the old man who owned the house, "Bring out the man who came to your house so we can have sex with him."

²³The owner of the house went outside and said to them, "No, my friends, don't be so vile. Since this man is my guest, don't do this disgraceful thing. ²⁴Look, here is my virgin daughter, and his concubine. I will bring them out to you now, and you can use them and do to them whatever you wish. But to this man, don't do such a disgraceful thing."

²⁵But the men would not listen to him. So the man took his concubine and sent her outside to them, and they raped her and abused her throughout the night, and at dawn they let her go. ²⁶At daybreak the woman went back to the house where her master was staying, fell down at the door and lay there until daylight.

²⁷When her master got up in the morning and opened the door of the house and stepped out to continue on his way, there lay his concubine, fallen in the doorway of the house, with her hands on the threshold. ²⁸He said to her, "Get up; let's go." But there was no answer. Then the man put her on his donkey and set out for home.

²⁹When he reached home, he took a knife and cut up his concubine, limb by limb, into twelve parts and sent them into all the areas of Israel. ³⁰Everyone who saw it said, "Such a thing has never been seen or done, not since the day the Israelites came up out of Egypt. Think about it! Consider it! Tell us what to do!"

Israelites Fight the Benjamites

20 Then all the Israelites from Dan to Beersheba and from the land of Gilead came out as one man and assembled before the LORD in Mizpah. ²The leaders of all the people of the tribes of Israel took their places in the assembly of the people of God, four hundred thousand soldiers armed with swords. ³(The Benjamites heard that the Israelites had gone up to Mizpah.) Then the Israelites said, "Tell us how this awful thing happened."

⁴So the Levite, the husband of the murdered woman, said, "I and my concubine came to Gibeah in Benjamin to spend the night. ⁵During the night the men of Gibeah came after me and surrounded the house, intending to kill me. They raped my concubine, and she died. ⁶I took my concubine, cut her into pieces and sent one piece to each region of Israel's inheritance, because they committed this lewd and disgraceful act in Israel. ⁷Now, all you Israelites, speak up and give your verdict."

⁸All the people rose as one man, saying, "None of us will go home. No, not one of us will return to his house. ⁹But now this is what we'll do to Gibeah: We'll go up against it as the lot directs. ¹⁰We'll take ten men out of every hundred from all the tribes of Is-

rael, and a hundred from a thousand, and a thousand from ten thousand, to get provisions for the army. Then, when the army arrives at Gibeah*a* in Benjamin, it can give them what they deserve for all this vileness done in Israel." **11**So all the men of Israel got together and united as one man against the city.

12The tribes of Israel sent men throughout the tribe of Benjamin, saying, "What about this awful crime that was committed among you? **13**Now surrender those wicked men of Gibeah so that we may put them to death and purge the evil from Israel."

But the Benjamites would not listen to their fellow Israelites. **14**From their towns they came together at Gibeah to fight against the Israelites. **15**At once the Benjamites mobilized twenty-six thousand swordsmen from their towns, in addition to seven hundred chosen men from those living in Gibeah. **16**Among all these soldiers there were seven hundred chosen men who were left-handed, each of whom could sling a stone at a hair and not miss.

17Israel, apart from Benjamin, mustered four hundred thousand swordsmen, all of them fighting men.

18The Israelites went up to Bethel*b* and inquired of God. They said, "Who of us shall go first to fight against the Benjamites?"

The LORD replied, "Judah shall go first."

19The next morning the Israelites got up and pitched camp near Gibeah. **20**The men of Israel went out to fight the Benjamites and took up battle positions against them at Gibeah. **21**The Benjamites came out of Gibeah and cut down twenty-two thousand Israelites on the battlefield that day. **22**But the men of Israel encouraged one another and again took up their positions where they had stationed themselves the first day. **23**The Israelites went up and wept before the LORD until evening, and they inquired of the LORD. They said, "Shall we go up again to battle against the Benjamites, our brothers?"

The LORD answered, "Go up against them."

24Then the Israelites drew near to Benjamin the second day. **25**This time, when the Benjamites came out from Gibeah to oppose them, they cut down another eighteen thousand Israelites, all of them armed with swords.

26Then the Israelites, all the people, went up to Bethel, and there they sat weeping before the LORD. They fasted that day until evening and presented burnt offerings and fellowship offerings*c* to the LORD. **27**And the Israelites inquired of the LORD. (In those days the ark of the covenant of God was there, **28**with Phinehas son of Eleazar, the son of Aaron, ministering before it.) They asked, "Shall we go up again to battle with Benjamin our brother, or not?"

The LORD responded, "Go, for tomorrow I will give them into your hands."

29Then Israel set an ambush around Gibeah. **30**They went up against the Benjamites on the third day and took up positions against Gibeah as they had done before. **31**The Benjamites came out to meet them and were drawn away from the city. They began to inflict casualties on the Israelites as before, so that about thirty men fell in the open field and on the roads—the one leading to Bethel and the other to Gibeah.

32While the Benjamites were saying, "We are defeating them as before," the Israelites were saying, "Let's retreat and draw them away from the city to the roads."

33All the men of Israel moved from their places and took up positions at Baal Tamar, and the Israelite ambush charged out of its place on the west*d* of Gibeah.[a] 34Then ten thousand of Israel's finest men made a frontal attack on Gibeah. The fighting was so heavy that the Benjamites did not realize how near disaster was. 35The LORD defeated Benjamin before Israel, and on that day the Israelites struck down 25,100 Benjamites, all armed with swords. 36Then the Benjamites saw that they were beaten.

Now the men of Israel had given way before Benjamin, because they relied on the ambush they had set near Gibeah. 37The men who had been in ambush made a sudden dash into Gibeah, spread out and put the whole city to the sword. 38The men of Israel had arranged with the ambush that they should send up a great cloud of smoke from the city, 39and then the men of Israel would turn in the battle.

The Benjamites had begun to inflict casualties on the men of Israel (about thirty), and they said, "We are defeating them as in the first battle." 40But when the column of smoke began to rise from the city, the Benjamites turned and saw the smoke of the whole city going up into the sky. 41Then the men of Israel turned on them, and the men of Benjamin were terrified, because they realized that disaster had come upon them. 42So they fled before the Israelites in the direction of the desert, but they could not escape the battle. And the men of Israel who came out of the towns cut them down there. 43They surrounded the Benjamites, chased them and easily[b] overran them in the vicinity of Gibeah on the east. 44Eighteen thousand Benjamites fell, all of them valiant fighters. 45As they turned and fled toward the desert to the rock of Rimmon, the Israelites cut down five thousand men along the roads. They kept pressing after the Benjamites as far as Gidom and struck down two thousand more.

46On that day twenty-five thousand Benjamite swordsmen fell, all of them valiant fighters. 47But six hundred men turned and fled into the desert to the rock of Rimmon, where they stayed four months. 48The men of Israel went back to Benjamin and put all the towns to the sword, including the animals and everything else they found. All the towns they came across they set on fire.

Wives for the Benjamites

21 The men of Israel had taken an oath at Mizpah: "Not one of us will give his daughter in marriage to a Benjamite."

2The people went to Bethel,[c] where they sat before God until evening, raising their voices and weeping bitterly. 3"O LORD, the God of Israel," they cried, "why has this happened to Israel? Why should one tribe be missing from Israel today?"

4Early the next day the people built an altar and presented burnt offerings and fellowship offerings.[d]

5Then the Israelites asked, "Who from all the tribes of Israel has failed to assemble before the LORD?" For they had taken a solemn oath that anyone who failed to assemble before the LORD at Mizpah should certainly be put to death.

6Now the Israelites grieved for their brothers, the Benjamites. "Today one tribe is cut off from Israel," they said. 7"How can we provide wives for those who are left, since we have taken an oath by the LORD not to give them any of our daughters in marriage?" 8Then they asked, "Which one of the tribes of Israel failed to assemble before the LORD at Mizpah?" They discovered that no one from Jabesh Gilead had come to the camp for the assembly. 9For when they counted the people, they found that none of the people of Jabesh Gilead were there.

10So the assembly sent twelve thousand fighting men with instructions to go to Jabesh Gilead and put to the sword those living there, including the women and children. 11"This is

---

a33 Hebrew Geba, a variant of Gibeah uncertain.   b43 The meaning of the Hebrew for this word is   c2 Or to the house of God   d4 Traditionally peace offerings

what you are to do," they said. "Kill every male and every woman who is not a virgin." ¹²They found among the people living in Jabesh Gilead four hundred young women who had never slept with a man, and they took them to the camp at Shiloh in Canaan.

¹³Then the whole assembly sent an offer of peace to the Benjamites at the rock of Rimmon. ¹⁴So the Benjamites returned at that time and were given the women of Jabesh Gilead who had been spared. But there were not enough for all of them.

¹⁵The people grieved for Benjamin, because the LORD had made a gap in the tribes of Israel. ¹⁶And the elders of the assembly said, "With the women of Benjamin destroyed, how shall we provide wives for the men who are left? ¹⁷The Benjamite survivors must have heirs," they said, "so that a tribe of Israel will not be wiped out. ¹⁸We can't give them our daughters as wives, since we Israelites have taken this oath: 'Cursed be anyone who gives a wife to a Benjamite.' ¹⁹But look, there is the annual festival of the LORD in Shiloh, to the north of Bethel, and east of the road that goes from Bethel to Shechem, and to the south of Lebonah."

²⁰So they instructed the Benjamites, saying, "Go and hide in the vineyards ²¹and watch. When the girls of Shiloh come out to join in the dancing, then rush from the vineyards and each of you seize a wife from the girls of Shiloh and go to the land of Benjamin. ²²When their fathers or brothers complain to us, we will say to them, 'Do us a kindness by helping them, because we did not get wives for them during the war, and you are innocent, since you did not give your daughters to them.'"

²³So that is what the Benjamites did. While the girls were dancing, each man caught one and carried her off to be his wife. Then they returned to their inheritance and rebuilt the towns and settled in them.

²⁴At that time the Israelites left that place and went home to their tribes and clans, each to his own inheritance.

²⁵In those days Israel had no king; everyone did as he saw fit.

This book tells the story of two people whose lives are transformed from emptiness to fullness through God's compassionate care. As you read Ruth, celebrate how God works in your life through family members and friends to bring renewal and hope to your days. Rejoice in the way God works through difficult situations to bring you to a new day of peace.

RUTH

Naomi and Ruth

1 In the days when the judges ruled,[a] there was a famine in the land, and a man from Bethlehem in Judah, together with his wife and two sons, went to live for a while in the country of Moab. ²The man's name was Elimelech, his wife's name Naomi, and the names of his two sons were Mahlon and Kilion. They were Ephrathites from Bethlehem, Judah. And they went to Moab and lived there.

³Now Elimelech, Naomi's husband, died, and she was left with her two sons. ⁴They married Moabite women, one named Orpah and the other Ruth. After they had lived there about ten years, ⁵both Mahlon and Kilion also died, and Naomi was left without her two sons and her husband.

⁶When she heard in Moab that the LORD had come to the aid of his people by providing food for them, Naomi and her daughters-in-law prepared to return home from there. ⁷With her two daughters-in-law she left the place where she had been living and set out on the road that would take them back to the land of Judah.

⁸Then Naomi said to her two daughters-in-law, "Go back, each of you, to your mother's home. May the LORD show kindness to you, as you have shown to your dead and to me. ⁹May the LORD grant that each of you will find rest in the home of another husband."

Then she kissed them and they wept aloud ¹⁰and said to her, "We will go back with you to your people."

¹¹But Naomi said, "Return home, my daughters. Why would you come with me? Am I going to have any more sons, who could become your husbands? ¹²Return home, my daughters; I am too old to have another hus-

band. Even if I thought there was still hope for me—even if I had a husband tonight and then gave birth to sons— ¹³would you wait until they grew up? Would you remain unmarried for them? No, my daughters. It is more bitter for me than for you, because the LORD's hand has gone out against me!"

¹⁴At this they wept again. Then Orpah kissed her mother-in-law goodby, but Ruth clung to her.

¹⁵"Look," said Naomi, "your sister-in-law is going back to her people and her gods. Go back with her."

¹⁶But Ruth replied, "Don't urge me to leave you or to turn back from you. Where you go I will go, and where you stay I will stay. Your people will be my people and your God my God. ¹⁷Where you die I will die, and there I will be buried. May the LORD deal with me, be it ever so severely, if anything but death separates you and me." ¹⁸When Naomi realized that Ruth was determined to go with her, she stopped urging her.

¹⁹So the two women went on until they came to Bethlehem. When they arrived in Bethlehem, the whole town was stirred because of them, and the women exclaimed, "Can this be Naomi?"

²⁰"Don't call me Naomi,ᵃ" she told them. "Call me Mara,ᵇ because the Almightyᶜ has made my life very bitter. ²¹I went away full, but the LORD has brought me back empty. Why call me Naomi? The LORD has afflictedᵈ me; the Almighty has brought misfortune upon me."

²²So Naomi returned from Moab accompanied by Ruth the Moabitess, her daughter-in-law, arriving in Bethlehem as the barley harvest was beginning.

Ruth Meets Boaz

2 Now Naomi had a relative on her husband's side, from the clan of Elimelech, a man of standing, whose name was Boaz.

²And Ruth the Moabitess said to Naomi, "Let me go to the fields and pick up the leftover grain behind anyone in whose eyes I find favor."

Naomi said to her, "Go ahead, my daughter." ³So she went out and began to glean in the fields behind the harvesters. As it turned out, she found herself working in a field belonging to Boaz, who was from the clan of Elimelech.

⁴Just then Boaz arrived from Bethlehem and greeted the harvesters, "The LORD be with you!"

"The LORD bless you!" they called back.

⁵Boaz asked the foreman of his harvesters, "Whose young woman is that?"

⁶The foreman replied, "She is the Moabitess who came back from Moab with Naomi. ⁷She said, 'Please let me glean and gather among the sheaves behind the harvesters.' She went into the field and has worked steadily from morning till now, except for a short rest in the shelter."

⁸So Boaz said to Ruth, "My daughter, listen to me. Don't go and glean in another field and don't go away from here. Stay here with my servant girls. ⁹Watch the field where the men are harvesting, and follow along after the girls. I have told the men not to touch you. And whenever you are thirsty, go and get a drink from the water jars the men have filled."

¹⁰At this, she bowed down with her face to the ground. She exclaimed, "Why have I found such favor in your eyes that you notice me—a foreigner?"

¹¹Boaz replied, "I've been told all about what you have done for your mother-in-law since the death of your husband—how you left your father and mother and your homeland and came to live with a people you did not know before. ¹²May the LORD repay you for what you have done. May you be richly rewarded by the LORD,

ᵃ20 Naomi means pleasant; also in verse 21. ᵇ20 Mara means bitter. ᶜ20 Hebrew Shaddai; also in verse 21 ᵈ21 Or has testified against

the God of Israel, under whose wings you have come to take refuge."

¹³"May I continue to find favor in your eyes, my lord," she said. "You have given me comfort and have spoken kindly to your servant—though I do not have the standing of one of your servant girls."

¹⁴At mealtime Boaz said to her, "Come over here. Have some bread and dip it in the wine vinegar."

When she sat down with the harvesters, he offered her some roasted grain. She ate all she wanted and had some left over. ¹⁵As she got up to glean, Boaz gave orders to his men, "Even if she gathers among the sheaves, don't embarrass her. ¹⁶Rather, pull out some stalks for her from the bundles and leave them for her to pick up, and don't rebuke her."

¹⁷So Ruth gleaned in the field until evening. Then she threshed the barley she had gathered, and it amounted to about an ephah.ᵃ ¹⁸She carried it back to town, and her mother-in-law saw how much she had gathered. Ruth also brought out and gave her what she had left over after she had eaten enough.

¹⁹Her mother-in-law asked her, "Where did you glean today? Where did you work? Blessed be the man who took notice of you!"

Then Ruth told her mother-in-law about the one at whose place she had been working. "The name of the man I worked with today is Boaz," she said.

²⁰"The Lord bless him!" Naomi said to her daughter-in-law. "He has not stopped showing his kindness to the living and the dead." She added, "That man is our close relative; he is one of our kinsman-redeemers."

²¹Then Ruth the Moabitess said, "He even said to me, 'Stay with my workers until they finish harvesting all my grain.' "

²²Naomi said to Ruth her daughter-in-law, "It will be good for you, my daughter, to go with his girls, because

in someone else's field you might be harmed."

²³So Ruth stayed close to the servant girls of Boaz to glean until the barley and wheat harvests were finished. And she lived with her mother-in-law.

Ruth and Boaz at the Threshing Floor

3 One day Naomi her mother-in-law said to her, "My daughter, should I not try to find a homeᵇ for you, where you will be well provided for? ²Is not Boaz, with whose servant girls you have been, a kinsman of ours? Tonight he will be winnowing barley on the threshing floor. ³Wash and perfume yourself, and put on your best clothes. Then go down to the threshing floor, but don't let him know you are there until he has finished eating and drinking. ⁴When he lies down, note the place where he is lying. Then go and uncover his feet and lie down. He will tell you what to do."

⁵"I will do whatever you say," Ruth answered. ⁶So she went down to the threshing floor and did everything her mother-in-law told her to do.

⁷When Boaz had finished eating and drinking and was in good spirits, he went over to lie down at the far end of the grain pile. Ruth approached quietly, uncovered his feet and lay down. ⁸In the middle of the night something startled the man, and he turned and discovered a woman lying at his feet.

⁹"Who are you?" he asked.

"I am your servant Ruth," she said. "Spread the corner of your garment over me, since you are a kinsman-redeemer."

¹⁰"The Lord bless you, my daughter," he replied. "This kindness is greater than that which you showed earlier: You have not run after the younger men, whether rich or poor. ¹¹And now, my daughter, don't be afraid. I will do for you all you ask.

ᵃ17 That is, probably about 3/5 bushel (about 22 liters)   ᵇ1 Hebrew find rest (see Ruth 1:9)

All my fellow townsmen know that you are a woman of noble character. ¹²Although it is true that I am near of kin, there is a kinsman-redeemer nearer than I. ¹³Stay here for the night, and in the morning if he wants to redeem, good; let him redeem. But if he is not willing, as surely as the LORD lives I will do it. Lie here until morning."

¹⁴So she lay at his feet until morning, but got up before anyone could be recognized; and he said, "Don't let it be known that a woman came to the threshing floor."

¹⁵He also said, "Bring me the shawl you are wearing and hold it out." When she did so, he poured into it six measures of barley and put it on her. Then he^a went back to town.

¹⁶When Ruth came to her mother-in-law, Naomi asked, "How did it go, my daughter?"

Then she told her everything Boaz had done for her ¹⁷and added, "He gave me these six measures of barley, saying, 'Don't go back to your mother-in-law empty-handed.' "

¹⁸Then Naomi said, "Wait, my daughter, until you find out what happens. For the man will not rest until the matter is settled today."

Boaz Marries Ruth

4 Meanwhile Boaz went up to the town gate and sat there. When the

^{a}15 Most Hebrew manuscripts; many Hebrew manuscripts, Vulgate and Syriac *she*

VERSE:	AUTHOR:	PASSAGE:
Ruth 4:15	Richard L. Morgan	Ruth 4:13–22

Grandchildren Renew Our Lives

There is something special about grandchildren. When Naomi held little Obed in her arms, she not only felt joy over the assured future of her family name; she must have experienced that renewal of life that comes with the birth of a child. No wonder the ancient psalmist prayed, "May you live to see your children's children" (Psalm 128:6). Grandchildren are a wonder. Their antics amuse us; their presence evokes deep and mysterious feelings; they provide a spark of joy in our aging years.

For the laughter of little grandchildren, the way they brighten our days and make our later years so full of joy, we will always be grateful, dear God. Amen.

ADDITIONAL SCRIPTURE READINGS
Psalm 103; Psalm 128

Go to page 323 for your next devotional reading.

kinsman-redeemer he had mentioned came along, Boaz said, "Come over here, my friend, and sit down." So he went over and sat down.

[2]Boaz took ten of the elders of the town and said, "Sit here," and they did so. [3]Then he said to the kinsman-redeemer, "Naomi, who has come back from Moab, is selling the piece of land that belonged to our brother Elimelech. [4]I thought I should bring the matter to your attention and suggest that you buy it in the presence of these seated here and in the presence of the elders of my people. If you will redeem it, do so. But if you[a] will not, tell me, so I will know. For no one has the right to do it except you, and I am next in line."

"I will redeem it," he said.

[5]Then Boaz said, "On the day you buy the land from Naomi and from Ruth the Moabitess, you acquire[b] the dead man's widow, in order to maintain the name of the dead with his property."

[6]At this, the kinsman-redeemer said, "Then I cannot redeem it because I might endanger my own estate. You redeem it yourself. I cannot do it."

[7](Now in earlier times in Israel, for the redemption and transfer of property to become final, one party took off his sandal and gave it to the other. This was the method of legalizing transactions in Israel.)

[8]So the kinsman-redeemer said to Boaz, "Buy it yourself." And he removed his sandal.

[9]Then Boaz announced to the elders and all the people, "Today you are witnesses that I have bought from Naomi all the property of Elimelech, Kilion and Mahlon. [10]I have also acquired Ruth the Moabitess, Mahlon's widow, as my wife, in order to maintain the name of the dead with his property, so that his name will not disappear from among his family or from the town records. Today you are witnesses!"

[11]Then the elders and all those at the gate said, "We are witnesses. May the LORD make the woman who is coming into your home like Rachel and Leah, who together built up the house of Israel. May you have standing in Ephrathah and be famous in Bethlehem. [12]Through the offspring the LORD gives you by this young woman, may your family be like that of Perez, whom Tamar bore to Judah."

The Genealogy of David

[13]So Boaz took Ruth and she became his wife. Then he went to her, and the LORD enabled her to conceive, and she gave birth to a son. [14]The women said to Naomi: "Praise be to the LORD, who this day has not left you without a kinsman-redeemer. May he become famous throughout Israel! [15]He will renew your life and sustain you in your old age. For your daughter-in-law, who loves you and who is better to you than seven sons, has given him birth."

[16]Then Naomi took the child, laid him in her lap and cared for him. [17]The women living there said, "Naomi has a son." And they named him Obed. He was the father of Jesse, the father of David.

[18]This, then, is the family line of Perez:

Perez was the father of Hezron,
[19]Hezron the father of Ram,
Ram the father of Amminadab,
[20]Amminadab the father of Nahshon,
Nahshon the father of Salmon,[c]
[21]Salmon the father of Boaz,
Boaz the father of Obed,
[22]Obed the father of Jesse,
and Jesse the father of David.

---

[a]4 Many Hebrew manuscripts, Septuagint, Vulgate and Syriac; most Hebrew manuscripts *he*
[b]5 Hebrew; Vulgate and Syriac *Naomi, you acquire Ruth the Moabitess,*   [c]20 A few Hebrew manuscripts, some Septuagint manuscripts and Vulgate (see also verse 21 and Septuagint of 1 Chron. 2:11); most Hebrew manuscripts *Salma*

...T...his book covers the lives of Samuel, the last judge, and Saul, the first king of Israel. As you read 1 Samuel, reflect on how powerless you are without God and how powerful you can be when you let God direct your life. Give thanks for the way he has worked and is working in your life and trust that he will bring his work in you to completion.

1 SAMUEL

The Birth of Samuel

1 There was a certain man from Ramathaim, a Zuphite[a] from the hill country of Ephraim, whose name was Elkanah son of Jeroham, the son of Elihu, the son of Tohu, the son of Zuph, an Ephraimite. ²He had two wives; one was called Hannah and the other Peninnah. Peninnah had children, but Hannah had none.

³Year after year this man went up from his town to worship and sacrifice to the LORD Almighty at Shiloh, where Hophni and Phinehas, the two sons of Eli, were priests of the LORD. ⁴Whenever the day came for Elkanah to sacrifice, he would give portions of the meat to his wife Peninnah and to all her sons and daughters. ⁵But to Hannah he gave a double portion because he loved her, and the LORD had closed her womb. ⁶And because the LORD had closed her womb, her rival kept provoking her in order to irritate

her. ⁷This went on year after year. Whenever Hannah went up to the house of the LORD, her rival provoked her till she wept and would not eat. ⁸Elkanah her husband would say to her, "Hannah, why are you weeping? Why don't you eat? Why are you downhearted? Don't I mean more to you than ten sons?"

⁹Once when they had finished eating and drinking in Shiloh, Hannah stood up. Now Eli the priest was sitting on a chair by the doorpost of the LORD's temple.[b] ¹⁰In bitterness of soul Hannah wept much and prayed to the LORD. ¹¹And she made a vow, saying, "O LORD Almighty, if you will only look upon your servant's misery and remember me, and not forget your servant but give her a son, then I will give him to the LORD for all the days of his life, and no razor will ever be used on his head."

¹²As she kept on praying to the LORD, Eli observed her mouth. ¹³Han-

---

a1 Or *from Ramathaim Zuphim*   b9 That is, tabernacle

nah was praying in her heart, and her lips were moving but her voice was not heard. Eli thought she was drunk [14]and said to her, "How long will you keep on getting drunk? Get rid of your wine."

[15]"Not so, my lord," Hannah replied, "I am a woman who is deeply troubled. I have not been drinking wine or beer; I was pouring out my soul to the LORD. [16]Do not take your servant for a wicked woman; I have been praying here out of my great anguish and grief."

[17]Eli answered, "Go in peace, and may the God of Israel grant you what you have asked of him."

[18]She said, "May your servant find favor in your eyes." Then she went her way and ate something, and her face was no longer downcast.

[19]Early the next morning they arose and worshiped before the LORD and then went back to their home at Ramah. Elkanah lay with Hannah his wife, and the LORD remembered her. [20]So in the course of time Hannah conceived and gave birth to a son. She named him Samuel,[a] saying, "Because I asked the LORD for him."

Hannah Dedicates Samuel

[21]When the man Elkanah went up with all his family to offer the annual sacrifice to the LORD and to fulfill his vow, [22]Hannah did not go. She said to her husband, "After the boy is weaned, I will take him and present him before the LORD, and he will live there always."

[23]"Do what seems best to you," Elkanah her husband told her. "Stay here until you have weaned him; only may the LORD make good his[b] word." So the woman stayed at home and nursed her son until she had weaned him. [24]After he was weaned, she took the boy with her, young as he was, along with a three-year-old bull,[c] an ephah[d] of flour and a skin of wine, and brought him to the house of the LORD at Shiloh. [25]When they had slaughtered the bull, they brought the boy to Eli, [26]and she said to him, "As surely as you live, my lord, I am the woman who stood here beside you praying to the LORD. [27]I prayed for this child, and the LORD has granted me what I asked of him. [28]So now I give him to the LORD. For his whole life he will be given over to the LORD." And he worshiped the LORD there.

Hannah's Prayer

2 Then Hannah prayed and said:

"My heart rejoices in the LORD;
    in the LORD my horn[e] is lifted
        high.
My mouth boasts over my
        enemies,
    for I delight in your deliverance.

[2]"There is no one holy[f] like the
        LORD;
    there is no one besides you;
    there is no Rock like our God.

[3]"Do not keep talking so proudly
    or let your mouth speak such
        arrogance,
for the LORD is a God who knows,
    and by him deeds are weighed.

[4]"The bows of the warriors are
        broken,
    but those who stumbled are
        armed with strength.
[5]Those who were full hire
        themselves out for food,
    but those who were hungry
        hunger no more.
She who was barren has borne
        seven children,
    but she who has had many sons
        pines away.

[6]"The LORD brings death and makes
        alive;
    he brings down to the grave[g]
        and raises up.

7The LORD sends poverty and
    wealth;
  he humbles and he exalts.
8He raises the poor from the dust
    and lifts the needy from the ash
      heap;
  he seats them with princes
    and has them inherit a throne of
      honor.

"For the foundations of the earth
    are the LORD's;
  upon them he has set the world.
9He will guard the feet of his
    saints,
  but the wicked will be silenced
    in darkness.

"It is not by strength that one
    prevails;
10   those who oppose the LORD will
    be shattered.
  He will thunder against them
    from heaven;
  the LORD will judge the ends of
    the earth.

"He will give strength to his king
    and exalt the horn of his
      anointed."

11Then Elkanah went home to Ramah, but the boy ministered before
the LORD under Eli the priest.

Eli's Wicked Sons

12Eli's sons were wicked men; they
had no regard for the LORD. 13Now it
was the practice of the priests with
the people that whenever anyone offered a sacrifice and while the meat
was being boiled, the servant of the
priest would come with a three-
pronged fork in his hand. 14He would
plunge it into the pan or kettle or cal-
dron or pot, and the priest would take
for himself whatever the fork brought
up. This is how they treated all the
Israelites who came to Shiloh. 15But
even before the fat was burned, the
servant of the priest would come and
say to the man who was sacrificing,
"Give the priest some meat to roast;
he won't accept boiled meat from
you, but only raw."

16If the man said to him, "Let the
fat be burned up first, and then take
whatever you want," the servant
would then answer, "No, hand it over
now; if you don't, I'll take it by force."
17This sin of the young men was
very great in the LORD's sight, for
they[a] were treating the LORD's offering with contempt.
18But Samuel was ministering before the LORD—a boy wearing a linen
ephod. 19Each year his mother made
him a little robe and took it to him
when she went up with her husband
to offer the annual sacrifice. 20Eli
would bless Elkanah and his wife,
saying, "May the LORD give you children by this woman to take the place
of the one she prayed for and gave to
the LORD." Then they would go home.
21And the LORD was gracious to Hannah; she conceived and gave birth to
three sons and two daughters. Meanwhile, the boy Samuel grew up in the
presence of the LORD.
22Now Eli, who was very old, heard
about everything his sons were doing
to all Israel and how they slept with
the women who served at the entrance to the Tent of Meeting. 23So he
said to them, "Why do you do such
things? I hear from all the people
about these wicked deeds of yours.
24No, my sons; it is not a good report
that I hear spreading among the
LORD's people. 25If a man sins against
another man, God[b] may mediate for
him; but if a man sins against the
LORD, who will intercede for him?"
His sons, however, did not listen to
their father's rebuke, for it was the
LORD's will to put them to death.
26And the boy Samuel continued to
grow in stature and in favor with the
LORD and with men.

Prophecy Against the House of Eli

27Now a man of God came to Eli
and said to him, "This is what the
LORD says: 'Did I not clearly reveal
myself to your father's house when
they were in Egypt under Pharaoh?
28I chose your father out of all the

tribes of Israel to be my priest, to go up to my altar, to burn incense, and to wear an ephod in my presence. I also gave your father's house all the offer- ings made with fire by the Israelites. [a]29Why do you[a] scorn my sacrifice and offering that I prescribed for my dwelling? Why do you honor your

[a]29 The Hebrew is plural.

THURSDAY

VERSE:
1 Samuel 2:22

AUTHOR:
Debra Klingsporn

PASSAGE:
1 Samuel 2:12–26

After Winter Comes Spring

She is in the winter of her life. She now has more gray hair than dark. Her once deep, brown eyes are now slightly cloudy, as if she's looking at her world through an early morning mist . . .

And she grieves the chill of an estranged relationship with one of her children. Blaming herself, she struggles to let go of the "if onlys" and longs for the warmth of reconciliation. She lives with the dull ache of unspoken anger and the sting of love turned dutiful.

Winter's cold is not always cozy and the winter years are not always golden. Yet we each, in our own ways, do the best we can for those we love. Our love is always human, always short of perfection. We, too, will be inadequate stewards of our children's childhoods, incapable of meeting the needs of those we would wish to spare from all of life's hurts and disappointments.

Although I can't offer healing to one who lives in the winter years or bears a wintry heart, I can offer hope. The God of spring's new life, of summer's joy and of autumn's fullness is also the God of winter's chill. Although we never know what lies buried beneath the frozen stillness, we can trust that surely, surely, after winter comes the spring.

ADDITIONAL SCRIPTURE READINGS
Psalm 33:18–22; Hebrews 6:13–20

Go to page 331 for your next devotional reading.

sons more than me by fattening yourselves on the choice parts of every offering made by my people Israel?'

³⁰"Therefore the LORD, the God of Israel, declares: 'I promised that your house and your father's house would minister before me forever.' But now the LORD declares: 'Far be it from me! Those who honor me I will honor, but those who despise me will be disdained. ³¹The time is coming when I will cut short your strength and the strength of your father's house, so that there will not be an old man in your family line ³²and you will see distress in my dwelling. Although good will be done to Israel, in your family line there will never be an old man. ³³Every one of you that I do not cut off from my altar will be spared only to blind your eyes with tears and to grieve your heart, and all your descendants will die in the prime of life.

³⁴" 'And what happens to your two sons, Hophni and Phinehas, will be a sign to you—they will both die on the same day. ³⁵I will raise up for myself a faithful priest, who will do according to what is in my heart and mind. I will firmly establish his house, and he will minister before my anointed one always. ³⁶Then everyone left in your family line will come and bow down before him for a piece of silver and a crust of bread and plead, "Appoint me to some priestly office so I can have food to eat." ' "

The LORD Calls Samuel

3 The boy Samuel ministered before the LORD under Eli. In those days the word of the LORD was rare; there were not many visions.

²One night Eli, whose eyes were becoming so weak that he could barely see, was lying down in his usual place. ³The lamp of God had not yet gone out, and Samuel was lying down in the temple*a* of the LORD, where the ark of God was. ⁴Then the LORD called Samuel.

Samuel answered, "Here I am." ⁵And he ran to Eli and said, "Here I am; you called me."

But Eli said, "I did not call; go back and lie down." So he went and lay down.

⁶Again the LORD called, "Samuel!" And Samuel got up and went to Eli and said, "Here I am; you called me."

"My son," Eli said, "I did not call; go back and lie down."

⁷Now Samuel did not yet know the LORD: The word of the LORD had not yet been revealed to him.

⁸The LORD called Samuel a third time, and Samuel got up and went to Eli and said, "Here I am; you called me."

Then Eli realized that the LORD was calling the boy. ⁹So Eli told Samuel, "Go and lie down, and if he calls you, say, 'Speak, LORD, for your servant is listening.' " So Samuel went and lay down in his place.

¹⁰The LORD came and stood there, calling as at the other times, "Samuel! Samuel!"

Then Samuel said, "Speak, for your servant is listening."

¹¹And the LORD said to Samuel: "See, I am about to do something in Israel that will make the ears of everyone who hears of it tingle. ¹²At that time I will carry out against Eli everything I spoke against his family—from beginning to end. ¹³For I told him that I would judge his family forever because of the sin he knew about; his sons made themselves contemptible,*b* and he failed to restrain them. ¹⁴Therefore, I swore to the house of Eli, 'The guilt of Eli's house will never be atoned for by sacrifice or offering.' "

¹⁵Samuel lay down until morning and then opened the doors of the house of the LORD. He was afraid to tell Eli the vision, ¹⁶but Eli called him and said, "Samuel, my son."

Samuel answered, "Here I am."

¹⁷"What was it he said to you?" Eli asked. "Do not hide it from me. May

---

*a*3 That is, tabernacle   *b*13 Masoretic Text; an ancient Hebrew scribal tradition and Septuagint *sons blasphemed God*

God deal with you, be it ever so severely, if you hide from me anything he told you." ¹⁸So Samuel told him everything, hiding nothing from him. Then Eli said, "He is the LORD; let him do what is good in his eyes."

¹⁹The LORD was with Samuel as he grew up, and he let none of his words fall to the ground. ²⁰And all Israel from Dan to Beersheba recognized that Samuel was attested as a prophet of the LORD. ²¹The LORD continued to appear at Shiloh, and there he revealed himself to Samuel through his word.

4 And Samuel's word came to all Israel.

The Philistines Capture the Ark

Now the Israelites went out to fight against the Philistines. The Israelites camped at Ebenezer, and the Philistines at Aphek. ²The Philistines deployed their forces to meet Israel, and as the battle spread, Israel was defeated by the Philistines, who killed about four thousand of them on the battlefield. ³When the soldiers returned to camp, the elders of Israel asked, "Why did the LORD bring defeat upon us today before the Philistines? Let us bring the ark of the LORD's covenant from Shiloh, so that it*ᵃ* may go with us and save us from the hand of our enemies."

⁴So the people sent men to Shiloh, and they brought back the ark of the covenant of the LORD Almighty, who is enthroned between the cherubim. And Eli's two sons, Hophni and Phinehas, were there with the ark of the covenant of God.

⁵When the ark of the LORD's covenant came into the camp, all Israel raised such a great shout that the ground shook. ⁶Hearing the uproar, the Philistines asked, "What's all this shouting in the Hebrew camp?"

When they learned that the ark of the LORD had come into the camp, ⁷the Philistines were afraid. "A god has come into the camp," they said.

"We're in trouble! Nothing like this has happened before. ⁸Woe to us! Who will deliver us from the hand of these mighty gods? They are the gods who struck the Egyptians with all kinds of plagues in the desert. ⁹Be strong, Philistines! Be men, or you will be subject to the Hebrews, as they have been to you. Be men, and fight!"

¹⁰So the Philistines fought, and the Israelites were defeated and every man fled to his tent. The slaughter was very great; Israel lost thirty thousand foot soldiers. ¹¹The ark of God was captured, and Eli's two sons, Hophni and Phinehas, died.

Death of Eli

¹²That same day a Benjamite ran from the battle line and went to Shiloh, his clothes torn and dust on his head. ¹³When he arrived, there was Eli sitting on his chair by the side of the road, watching, because his heart feared for the ark of God. When the man entered the town and told what had happened, the whole town sent up a cry.

¹⁴Eli heard the outcry and asked, "What is the meaning of this uproar?"

The man hurried over to Eli, ¹⁵who was ninety-eight years old and whose eyes were set so that he could not see. ¹⁶He told Eli, "I have just come from the battle line; I fled from it this very day."

Eli asked, "What happened, my son?"

¹⁷The man who brought the news replied, "Israel fled before the Philistines, and the army has suffered heavy losses. Also your two sons, Hophni and Phinehas, are dead, and the ark of God has been captured."

¹⁸When he mentioned the ark of God, Eli fell backward off his chair by the side of the gate. His neck was broken and he died, for he was an old man and heavy. He had led*ᵇ* Israel forty years.

¹⁹His daughter-in-law, the wife of Phinehas, was pregnant and near the time of delivery. When she heard the

ᵃ3 Or he   ᵇ18 Traditionally judged

news that the ark of God had been captured and that her father-in-law and her husband were dead, she went into labor and gave birth, but was overcome by her labor pains. 20As she was dying, the women attending her said, "Don't despair; you have given birth to a son." But she did not respond or pay any attention.

21She named the boy Ichabod,[a] saying, "The glory has departed from Israel"—because of the capture of the ark of God and the deaths of her father-in-law and her husband. 22She said, "The glory has departed from Israel, for the ark of God has been captured."

The Ark in Ashdod and Ekron

5 After the Philistines had captured the ark of God, they took it from Ebenezer to Ashdod. 2Then they carried the ark into Dagon's temple and set it beside Dagon. 3When the people of Ashdod rose early the next day, there was Dagon, fallen on his face on the ground before the ark of the LORD! They took Dagon and put him back in his place. 4But the following morning when they rose, there was Dagon, fallen on his face on the ground before the ark of the LORD! His head and hands had been broken off and were lying on the threshold; only his body remained. 5That is why to this day neither the priests of Dagon nor any others who enter Dagon's temple at Ashdod step on the threshold.

6The LORD's hand was heavy upon the people of Ashdod and its vicinity; he brought devastation upon them and afflicted them with tumors.[b] 7When the men of Ashdod saw what was happening, they said, "The ark of the god of Israel must not stay here with us, because his hand is heavy upon us and upon Dagon our god." 8So they called together all the rulers of the Philistines and asked them, "What shall we do with the ark of the god of Israel?"

They answered, "Have the ark of the god of Israel moved to Gath." So they moved the ark of the God of Israel.

9But after they had moved it, the LORD's hand was against that city, throwing it into a great panic. He afflicted the people of the city, both young and old, with an outbreak of tumors.[c] 10So they sent the ark of God to Ekron.

As the ark of God was entering Ekron, the people of Ekron cried out, "They have brought the ark of the god of Israel around to us to kill us and our people." 11So they called together all the rulers of the Philistines and said, "Send the ark of the god of Israel away; let it go back to its own place, or it[d] will kill us and our people." For death had filled the city with panic; God's hand was very heavy upon it. 12Those who did not die were afflicted with tumors, and the outcry of the city went up to heaven.

The Ark Returned to Israel

6 When the ark of the LORD had been in Philistine territory seven months, 2the Philistines called for the priests and the diviners and said, "What shall we do with the ark of the LORD? Tell us how we should send it back to its place."

3They answered, "If you return the ark of the god of Israel, do not send it away empty, but by all means send a guilt offering to him. Then you will be healed, and you will know why his hand has not been lifted from you."

4The Philistines asked, "What guilt offering should we send to him?"

They replied, "Five gold tumors and five gold rats, according to the number of the Philistine rulers, because the same plague has struck both you and your rulers. 5Make models of the tumors and of the rats that are destroying the country, and pay honor to Israel's god. Perhaps he will lift his hand from you and your gods and

---

a21 *Ichabod* means *no glory.*   b6 Hebrew; Septuagint and Vulgate *tumors. And rats appeared in their land, and death and destruction were throughout the city*   c9 Or *with tumors in the groin* (see Septuagint)   d11 Or *he*

your land. [6]Why do you harden your hearts as the Egyptians and Pharaoh did? When he[a] treated them harshly, did they not send the Israelites out so they could go on their way?

[7]"Now then, get a new cart ready, with two cows that have calved and have never been yoked. Hitch the cows to the cart, but take their calves away and pen them up. [8]Take the ark of the LORD and put it on the cart, and in a chest beside it put the gold objects you are sending back to him as a guilt offering. Send it on its way, [9]but keep watching it. If it goes up to its own territory, toward Beth Shemesh, then the LORD has brought this great disaster on us. But if it does not, then we will know that it was not his hand that struck us and that it happened to us by chance."

[10]So they did this. They took two such cows and hitched them to the cart and penned up their calves. [11]They placed the ark of the LORD on the cart and along with it the chest containing the gold rats and the models of the tumors. [12]Then the cows went straight up toward Beth Shemesh, keeping on the road and lowing all the way; they did not turn to the right or to the left. The rulers of the Philistines followed them as far as the border of Beth Shemesh.

[13]Now the people of Beth Shemesh were harvesting their wheat in the valley, and when they looked up and saw the ark, they rejoiced at the sight. [14]The cart came to the field of Joshua of Beth Shemesh, and there it stopped beside a large rock. The people chopped up the wood of the cart and sacrificed the cows as a burnt offering to the LORD. [15]The Levites took down the ark of the LORD, together with the chest containing the gold objects, and placed them on the large rock. On that day the people of Beth Shemesh offered burnt offerings and made sacrifices to the LORD. [16]The five rulers of the Philistines saw all this and then returned that same day to Ekron.

[17]These are the gold tumors the Philistines sent as a guilt offering to the LORD—one each for Ashdod, Gaza, Ashkelon, Gath and Ekron. [18]And the number of the gold rats was according to the number of Philistine towns belonging to the five rulers—the fortified towns with their country villages. The large rock, on which[b] they set the ark of the LORD, is a witness to this day in the field of Joshua of Beth Shemesh.

[19]But God struck down some of the men of Beth Shemesh, putting seventy[c] of them to death because they had looked into the ark of the LORD. The people mourned because of the heavy blow the LORD had dealt them, [20]and the men of Beth Shemesh asked, "Who can stand in the presence of the LORD, this holy God? To whom will the ark go up from here?"

[21]Then they sent messengers to the people of Kiriath Jearim, saying, "The Philistines have returned the ark of the LORD. Come down and take it up to your place." [1]So the men of Kiriath Jearim came and took up the ark of the LORD. They took it to Abinadab's house on the hill and consecrated Eleazar his son to guard the ark of the LORD.

Samuel Subdues the Philistines at Mizpah

[2]It was a long time, twenty years in all, that the ark remained at Kiriath Jearim, and all the people of Israel mourned and sought after the LORD. [3]And Samuel said to the whole house of Israel, "If you are returning to the LORD with all your hearts, then rid yourselves of the foreign gods and the Ashtoreths and commit yourselves to the LORD and serve him only, and he will deliver you out of the hand of the Philistines." [4]So the Israelites put away their Baals and Ashtoreths, and served the LORD only.

---

[a]6 That is, God   [b]18 A few Hebrew manuscripts (see also Septuagint); most Hebrew manuscripts *villages as far as Greater Abel, where*   [c]19 A few Hebrew manuscripts; most Hebrew manuscripts and Septuagint 50,070

⁵Then Samuel said, "Assemble all Israel at Mizpah and I will intercede with the Lord for you." ⁶When they had assembled at Mizpah, they drew water and poured it out before the Lord. On that day they fasted and there they confessed, "We have sinned against the Lord." And Samuel was leader*ᵃ* of Israel at Mizpah.

⁷When the Philistines heard that Israel had assembled at Mizpah, the rulers of the Philistines came up to attack them. And when the Israelites heard of it, they were afraid because of the Philistines. ⁸They said to Samuel, "Do not stop crying out to the Lord our God for us, that he may rescue us from the hand of the Philistines." ⁹Then Samuel took a suckling lamb and offered it up as a whole burnt offering to the Lord. He cried out to the Lord on Israel's behalf, and the Lord answered him.

¹⁰While Samuel was sacrificing the burnt offering, the Philistines drew near to engage Israel in battle. But that day the Lord thundered with loud thunder against the Philistines and threw them into such a panic that they were routed before the Israelites. ¹¹The men of Israel rushed out of Mizpah and pursued the Philistines, slaughtering them along the way to a point below Beth Car.

¹²Then Samuel took a stone and set it up between Mizpah and Shen. He named it Ebenezer,*ᵇ* saying, "Thus far has the Lord helped us." ¹³So the Philistines were subdued and did not invade Israelite territory again.

Throughout Samuel's lifetime, the hand of the Lord was against the Philistines. ¹⁴The towns from Ekron to Gath that the Philistines had captured from Israel were restored to her, and Israel delivered the neighboring territory from the power of the Philistines. And there was peace between Israel and the Amorites.

¹⁵Samuel continued as judge over Israel all the days of his life. ¹⁶From year to year he went on a circuit from Bethel to Gilgal to Mizpah, judging Israel in all those places. ¹⁷But he always went back to Ramah, where his home was, and there he also judged Israel. And he built an altar there to the Lord.

Israel Asks for a King

8 When Samuel grew old, he appointed his sons as judges for Israel. ²The name of his firstborn was Joel and the name of his second was Abijah, and they served at Beersheba. ³But his sons did not walk in his ways. They turned aside after dishonest gain and accepted bribes and perverted justice.

⁴So all the elders of Israel gathered together and came to Samuel at Ramah. ⁵They said to him, "You are old, and your sons do not walk in your ways; now appoint a king to lead*ᶜ* us, such as all the other nations have."

⁶But when they said, "Give us a king to lead us," this displeased Samuel; so he prayed to the Lord. ⁷And the Lord told him: "Listen to all that the people are saying to you; it is not you they have rejected, but they have rejected me as their king. ⁸As they have done from the day I brought them up out of Egypt until this day, forsaking me and serving other gods, so they are doing to you. ⁹Now listen to them; but warn them solemnly and let them know what the king who will reign over them will do."

¹⁰Samuel told all the words of the Lord to the people who were asking him for a king. ¹¹He said, "This is what the king who will reign over you will do: He will take your sons and make them serve with his chariots and horses, and they will run in front of his chariots. ¹²Some he will assign to be commanders of thousands and commanders of fifties, and others to plow his ground and reap his harvest, and still others to make weapons of war and equipment for his chariots. ¹³He will take your daughters to be perfumers and cooks

---

ᵃ6 Traditionally *judge;* also in verses 6 and 20   *ᵇ12 Ebenezer* means *stone of help.*   *ᶜ5* Traditionally *judge;* also in

and bakers. [14]He will take the best of your fields and vineyards and olive groves and give them to his attendants. [15]He will take a tenth of your grain and of your vintage and give it to his officials and attendants. [16]Your menservants and maidservants and the best of your cattle[a] and donkeys he will take for his own use. [17]He will take a tenth of your flocks, and you yourselves will become his slaves. [18]When that day comes, you will cry out for relief from the king you have chosen, and the LORD will not answer you in that day."

[19]But the people refused to listen to Samuel. "No!" they said. "We want a king over us. [20]Then we will be like all the other nations, with a king to lead us and to go out before us and fight our battles."

[21]When Samuel heard all that the people said, he repeated it before the LORD. [22]The LORD answered, "Listen to them and give them a king."

Then Samuel said to the men of Israel, "Everyone go back to his town."

Samuel Anoints Saul

9 There was a Benjamite, a man of standing, whose name was Kish son of Abiel, the son of Zeror, the son of Becorath, the son of Aphiah of Benjamin. [2]He had a son named Saul, an impressive young man without equal among the Israelites—a head taller than any of the others.

[3]Now the donkeys belonging to Saul's father Kish were lost, and Kish said to his son Saul, "Take one of the servants with you and go and look for the donkeys." [4]So he passed through the hill country of Ephraim and through the area around Shalisha, but they did not find them. They went on into the district of Shaalim, but the donkeys were not there. Then he passed through the territory of Benjamin, but they did not find them.

[5]When they reached the district of Zuph, Saul said to the servant who was with him, "Come, let's go back, or my father will stop thinking about the donkeys and start worrying about us."

[6]But the servant replied, "Look, in this town there is a man of God; he is highly respected, and everything he says comes true. Let's go there now. Perhaps he will tell us what way to take."

[7]Saul said to his servant, "If we go, what can we give the man? The food in our sacks is gone. We have no gift to take to the man of God. What do we have?"

[8]The servant answered him again. "Look," he said, "I have a quarter of a shekel[b] of silver. I will give it to the man of God so that he will tell us what way to take." [9](Formerly in Israel, if a man went to inquire of God, he would say, "Come, let us go to the seer," because the prophet of today used to be called a seer.)

[10]"Good," Saul said to his servant. "Come, let's go." So they set out for the town where the man of God was.

[11]As they were going up the hill to the town, they met some girls coming out to draw water, and they asked them, "Is the seer here?"

[12]"He is," they answered. "He's ahead of you. Hurry now; he has just come to our town today, for the people have a sacrifice at the high place. [13]As soon as you enter the town, you will find him before he goes up to the high place to eat. The people will not begin eating until he comes, because he must bless the sacrifice; afterward, those who are invited will eat. Go up now; you should find him about this time."

[14]They went up to the town, and as they were entering it, there was Samuel, coming toward them on his way up to the high place.

[15]Now the day before Saul came, the LORD had revealed this to Samuel: [16]"About this time tomorrow I will send you a man from the land of Benjamin. Anoint him leader over my people Israel; he will deliver my people from the hand of the Philistines. I

---

[a]16 Septuagint; Hebrew *young men*   [b]8 That is, about 1/10 ounce (about 3 grams)

have looked upon my people, for their cry has reached me."

¹⁷When Samuel caught sight of Saul, the LORD said to him, "This is the man I spoke to you about; he will govern my people."

¹⁸Saul approached Samuel in the gateway and asked, "Would you please tell me where the seer's house is?"

¹⁹"I am the seer," Samuel replied. "Go up ahead of me to the high place, for today you are to eat with me, and in the morning I will let you go and will tell you all that is in your heart. ²⁰As for the donkeys you lost three days ago, do not worry about them; they have been found. And to whom is all the desire of Israel turned, if not to you and all your father's family?"

²¹Saul answered, "But am I not a Benjamite, from the smallest tribe of Israel, and is not my clan the least of all the clans of the tribe of Benjamin? Why do you say such a thing to me?"

²²Then Samuel brought Saul and his servant into the hall and seated them at the head of those who were invited—about thirty in number. ²³Samuel said to the cook, "Bring the piece of meat I gave you, the one I told you to lay aside."

²⁴So the cook took up the leg with what was on it and set it in front of Saul. Samuel said, "Here is what has been kept for you. Eat, because it was set aside for you for this occasion, from the time I said, 'I have invited guests.' " And Saul dined with Samuel that day.

²⁵After they came down from the high place to the town, Samuel talked with Saul on the roof of his house. ²⁶They rose about daybreak and Samuel called to Saul on the roof, "Get ready, and I will send you on your way." When Saul got ready, he and Samuel went outside together. ²⁷As they were going down to the edge of the town, Samuel said to Saul, "Tell the servant to go on ahead of us"—

and the servant did so—"but you stay here awhile, so that I may give you a message from God."

10 Then Samuel took a flask of oil and poured it on Saul's head and kissed him, saying, "Has not the LORD anointed you leader over his inheritance?ᵃ ²When you leave me today, you will meet two men near Rachel's tomb, at Zelzah on the border of Benjamin. They will say to you, 'The donkeys you set out to look for have been found. And now your father has stopped thinking about them and is worried about you. He is asking, "What shall I do about my son?" '

³"Then you will go on from there until you reach the great tree of Tabor. Three men going up to God at Bethel will meet you there. One will be carrying three young goats, another three loaves of bread, and another a skin of wine. ⁴They will greet you and offer you two loaves of bread, which you will accept from them.

⁵"After that you will go to Gibeah of God, where there is a Philistine outpost. As you approach the town, you will meet a procession of prophets coming down from the high place with lyres, tambourines, flutes and harps being played before them, and they will be prophesying. ⁶The Spirit of the LORD will come upon you in power, and you will prophesy with them; and you will be changed into a different person. ⁷Once these signs are fulfilled, do whatever your hand finds to do, for God is with you.

⁸"Go down ahead of me to Gilgal. I will surely come down to you to sacrifice burnt offerings and fellowship offerings,ᵇ but you must wait seven days until I come to you and tell you what you are to do."

Saul Made King

⁹As Saul turned to leave Samuel, God changed Saul's heart, and all these signs were fulfilled that day. ¹⁰When they arrived at Gibeah, a pro-

---

ᵃ1 Hebrew; Septuagint and Vulgate *over his people Israel? You will reign over the* LORD'*s people and save them from the power of their enemies round about. And this will be a sign to you that the* LORD *has anointed you leader over his inheritance:*   ᵇ8 Traditionally *peace offerings*

cession of prophets met him; the Spirit of God came upon him in power, and he joined in their prophesying. ¹¹When all those who had formerly known him saw him prophesying with the prophets, they asked each other, "What is this that has happened to the son of Kish? Is Saul also among the prophets?"

¹²A man who lived there answered, "And who is their father?" So it became a saying: "Is Saul also among

VERSE:	AUTHOR:	PASSAGE:
1 Samuel 10:6	William L. Coleman	1 Samuel 10:1–9

The God of Change

Change is hard. It can be rewarding, exciting, fulfilling and tons of fun, but it is eventually difficult . . . We are fortunate to have a heavenly Father who is the God of change.

New events, new challenges, new opportunities, new lives are normal with God. The Bible is rich with the word "new" because God is not simply dedicated to the past. It speaks of: new self; new and living way; new creation; new command; new every morning; new growth; new man; new attitude; new teaching; new song; new birth; new spirit; new covenant.

These are just a few. The word *change* doesn't need to be frightening . . . It's true that God's character doesn't change (Malachi 3:6). But God is continuously infusing change into the lives of his people.

Take special note of how God dealt with Saul. Saul was reluctant to believe that God had chosen him king of Israel and hesitant to follow Samuel, but the Scripture simply says, "God changed Saul's heart" (1 Samuel 10:9).

When we try to hold on to the past and wrap ourselves in the security of yesterday, we may miss the great blessing that God has for us today.

ADDITIONAL SCRIPTURE READINGS
Isaiah 43:14–28; Lamentations 3:19–26

Go to page 336 for your next devotional reading.

the prophets?" ¹³After Saul stopped prophesying, he went to the high place.

¹⁴Now Saul's uncle asked him and his servant, "Where have you been?"

"Looking for the donkeys," he said. "But when we saw they were not to be found, we went to Samuel."

¹⁵Saul's uncle said, "Tell me what Samuel said to you."

¹⁶Saul replied, "He assured us that the donkeys had been found." But he did not tell his uncle what Samuel had said about the kingship.

¹⁷Samuel summoned the people of Israel to the LORD at Mizpah ¹⁸and said to them, "This is what the LORD, the God of Israel, says: 'I brought Israel up out of Egypt, and I delivered you from the power of Egypt and all the kingdoms that oppressed you.' ¹⁹But you have now rejected your God, who saves you out of all your calamities and distresses. And you have said, 'No, set a king over us.' So now present yourselves before the LORD by your tribes and clans."

²⁰When Samuel brought all the tribes of Israel near, the tribe of Benjamin was chosen. ²¹Then he brought forward the tribe of Benjamin, clan by clan, and Matri's clan was chosen. Finally Saul son of Kish was chosen. But when they looked for him, he was not to be found. ²²So they inquired further of the LORD, "Has the man come here yet?"

And the LORD said, "Yes, he has hidden himself among the baggage."

²³They ran and brought him out, and as he stood among the people he was a head taller than any of the others. ²⁴Samuel said to all the people, "Do you see the man the LORD has chosen? There is no one like him among all the people."

Then the people shouted, "Long live the king!"

²⁵Samuel explained to the people the regulations of the kingship. He wrote them down on a scroll and deposited it before the LORD. Then Samuel dismissed the people, each to his own home.

²⁶Saul also went to his home in Gib-

eah, accompanied by valiant men whose hearts God had touched. ²⁷But some troublemakers said, "How can this fellow save us?" They despised him and brought him no gifts. But Saul kept silent.

Saul Rescues the City of Jabesh

11 Nahash the Ammonite went up and besieged Jabesh Gilead. And all the men of Jabesh said to him, "Make a treaty with us, and we will be subject to you."

²But Nahash the Ammonite replied, "I will make a treaty with you only on the condition that I gouge out the right eye of every one of you and so bring disgrace on all Israel."

³The elders of Jabesh said to him, "Give us seven days so we can send messengers throughout Israel; if no one comes to rescue us, we will surrender to you."

⁴When the messengers came to Gibeah of Saul and reported these terms to the people, they all wept aloud. ⁵Just then Saul was returning from the fields, behind his oxen, and he asked, "What is wrong with the people? Why are they weeping?" Then they repeated to him what the men of Jabesh had said.

⁶When Saul heard their words, the Spirit of God came upon him in power, and he burned with anger. ⁷He took a pair of oxen, cut them into pieces, and sent the pieces by messengers throughout Israel, proclaiming, "This is what will be done to the oxen of anyone who does not follow Saul and Samuel." Then the terror of the LORD fell on the people, and they turned out as one man. ⁸When Saul mustered them at Bezek, the men of Israel numbered three hundred thousand and the men of Judah thirty thousand.

⁹They told the messengers who had come, "Say to the men of Jabesh Gilead, 'By the time the sun is hot tomorrow, you will be delivered.' " When the messengers went and reported this to the men of Jabesh, they were elated. ¹⁰They said to the Ammonites, "Tomorrow we will surrender to you,

and you can do to us whatever seems good to you."

¹¹The next day Saul separated his men into three divisions; during the last watch of the night they broke into the camp of the Ammonites and slaughtered them until the heat of the day. Those who survived were scattered, so that no two of them were left together.

Saul Confirmed as King

¹²The people then said to Samuel, "Who was it that asked, 'Shall Saul reign over us?' Bring these men to us and we will put them to death."

¹³But Saul said, "No one shall be put to death today, for this day the Lord has rescued Israel."

¹⁴Then Samuel said to the people, "Come, let us go to Gilgal and there reaffirm the kingship." ¹⁵So all the people went to Gilgal and confirmed Saul as king in the presence of the Lord. There they sacrificed fellowship offerings[a] before the Lord, and Saul and all the Israelites held a great celebration.

Samuel's Farewell Speech

12 Samuel said to all Israel, "I have listened to everything you said to me and have set a king over you. ²Now you have a king as your leader. As for me, I am old and gray, and my sons are here with you. I have been your leader from my youth until this day. ³Here I stand. Testify against me in the presence of the Lord and his anointed. Whose ox have I taken? Whose donkey have I taken? Whom have I cheated? Whom have I oppressed? From whose hand have I accepted a bribe to make me shut my eyes? If I have done any of these, I will make it right."

⁴"You have not cheated or oppressed us," they replied. "You have not taken anything from anyone's hand."

⁵Samuel said to them, "The Lord is witness against you, and also his anointed is witness this day, that you have not found anything in my hand."

"He is witness," they said.

⁶Then Samuel said to the people, "It is the Lord who appointed Moses and Aaron and brought your forefathers up out of Egypt. ⁷Now then, stand here, because I am going to confront you with evidence before the Lord as to all the righteous acts performed by the Lord for you and your fathers.

⁸"After Jacob entered Egypt, they cried to the Lord for help, and the Lord sent Moses and Aaron, who brought your forefathers out of Egypt and settled them in this place.

⁹"But they forgot the Lord their God; so he sold them into the hand of Sisera, the commander of the army of Hazor, and into the hands of the Philistines and the king of Moab, who fought against them. ¹⁰They cried out to the Lord and said, 'We have sinned; we have forsaken the Lord and served the Baals and the Ashtoreths. But now deliver us from the hands of our enemies, and we will serve you.' ¹¹Then the Lord sent Jerub-Baal,[b] Barak,[c] Jephthah and Samuel,[d] and he delivered you from the hands of your enemies on every side, so that you lived securely.

¹²"But when you saw that Nahash king of the Ammonites was moving against you, you said to me, 'No, we want a king to rule over us'—even though the Lord your God was your king. ¹³Now here is the king you have chosen, the one you asked for; see, the Lord has set a king over you. ¹⁴If you fear the Lord and serve and obey him and do not rebel against his commands, and if both you and the king who reigns over you follow the Lord your God—good! ¹⁵But if you do not obey the Lord, and if you rebel against his commands, his hand will be against you, as it was against your fathers.

¹⁶"Now then, stand still and see

---

a15 Traditionally *peace offerings*   *b11* Also called *Gideon*   *c11* Some Septuagint manuscripts and Syriac; Hebrew *Bedan*   *d11* Hebrew; some Septuagint manuscripts and Syriac *Samson*

this great thing the LORD is about to do before your eyes! [17]Is it not wheat harvest now? I will call upon the LORD to send thunder and rain. And you will realize what an evil thing you did in the eyes of the LORD when you asked for a king."

[18]Then Samuel called upon the LORD, and that same day the LORD sent thunder and rain. So all the people stood in awe of the LORD and of Samuel.

[19]The people all said to Samuel, "Pray to the LORD your God for your servants so that we will not die, for we have added to all our other sins the evil of asking for a king."

[20]"Do not be afraid," Samuel replied. "You have done all this evil; yet do not turn away from the LORD, but serve the LORD with all your heart. [21]Do not turn away after useless idols. They can do you no good, nor can they rescue you, because they are useless. [22]For the sake of his great name the LORD will not reject his people, because the LORD was pleased to make you his own. [23]As for me, far be it from me that I should sin against the LORD by failing to pray for you. And I will teach you the way that is good and right. [24]But be sure to fear the LORD and serve him faithfully with all your heart; consider what great things he has done for you. [25]Yet if you persist in doing evil, both you and your king will be swept away."

Samuel Rebukes Saul

13 Saul was ⌊thirty⌋[a] years old when he became king, and he reigned over Israel ⌊forty-⌋[b] two years.

[2]Saul[c] chose three thousand men from Israel; two thousand were with him at Micmash and in the hill country of Bethel, and a thousand were with Jonathan at Gibeah in Benjamin. The rest of the men he sent back to their homes.

[3]Jonathan attacked the Philistine outpost at Geba, and the Philistines heard about it. Then Saul had the trumpet blown throughout the land and said, "Let the Hebrews hear!" [4]So all Israel heard the news: "Saul has attacked the Philistine outpost, and now Israel has become a stench to the Philistines." And the people were summoned to join Saul at Gilgal.

[5]The Philistines assembled to fight Israel, with three thousand[d] chariots, six thousand charioteers, and soldiers as numerous as the sand on the seashore. They went up and camped at Micmash, east of Beth Aven. [6]When the men of Israel saw that their situation was critical and that their army was hard pressed, they hid in caves and thickets, among the rocks, and in pits and cisterns. [7]Some Hebrews even crossed the Jordan to the land of Gad and Gilead.

Saul remained at Gilgal, and all the troops with him were quaking with fear. [8]He waited seven days, the time set by Samuel; but Samuel did not come to Gilgal, and Saul's men began to scatter. [9]So he said, "Bring me the burnt offering and the fellowship offerings.[e]" And Saul offered up the burnt offering. [10]Just as he finished making the offering, Samuel arrived, and Saul went out to greet him.

[11]"What have you done?" asked Samuel.

Saul replied, "When I saw that the men were scattering, and that you did not come at the set time, and that the Philistines were assembling at Micmash, [12]I thought, 'Now the Philistines will come down against me at Gilgal, and I have not sought the LORD's favor.' So I felt compelled to offer the burnt offering."

[13]"You acted foolishly," Samuel said. "You have not kept the command the LORD your God gave you; if you had, he would have established your kingdom over Israel for all time.

---

[a]1 A few late manuscripts of the Septuagint; Hebrew does not have *thirty*.   [b]1 See the round number in Acts 13:21; Hebrew does not have *forty-*.   [c]1,2 Or *and when he had reigned over Israel two years,* [2]*he*   [d]5 Some Septuagint manuscripts and Syriac; Hebrew *thirty thousand*   [e]9 Traditionally *peace offerings*

¹⁴But now your kingdom will not endure; the LORD has sought out a man after his own heart and appointed him leader of his people, because you have not kept the LORD's command."

¹⁵Then Samuel left Gilgal*ᵃ* and went up to Gibeah in Benjamin, and Saul counted the men who were with him. They numbered about six hundred.

Israel Without Weapons

¹⁶Saul and his son Jonathan and the men with them were staying in Gibeah*ᵇ* in Benjamin, while the Philistines camped at Micmash. ¹⁷Raiding parties went out from the Philistine camp in three detachments. One turned toward Ophrah in the vicinity of Shual, ¹⁸another toward Beth Horon, and the third toward the borderland overlooking the Valley of Zeboim facing the desert.

¹⁹Not a blacksmith could be found in the whole land of Israel, because the Philistines had said, "Otherwise the Hebrews will make swords or spears!" ²⁰So all Israel went down to the Philistines to have their plowshares, mattocks, axes and sickles*ᶜ* sharpened. ²¹The price was two thirds of a shekel*ᵈ* for sharpening plowshares and mattocks, and a third of a shekel*ᵉ* for sharpening forks and axes and for repointing goads. ²²So on the day of the battle not a soldier with Saul and Jonathan had a sword or spear in his hand; only Saul and his son Jonathan had them.

Jonathan Attacks the Philistines

²³Now a detachment of Philistines had gone out to the pass at Micmash.

14 ¹One day Jonathan son of Saul said to the young man bearing his armor, "Come, let's go over to the Philistine outpost on the other side." But he did not tell his father.

²Saul was staying on the outskirts of Gibeah under a pomegranate tree in Migron. With him were about six hundred men, ³among whom was Ahijah, who was wearing an ephod. He was a son of Ichabod's brother Ahitub son of Phinehas, the son of Eli, the LORD's priest in Shiloh. No one was aware that Jonathan had left.

⁴On each side of the pass that Jonathan intended to cross to reach the Philistine outpost was a cliff; one was called Bozez, and the other Seneh. ⁵One cliff stood to the north toward Micmash, the other to the south toward Geba.

⁶Jonathan said to his young armor-bearer, "Come, let's go over to the outpost of those uncircumcised fellows. Perhaps the LORD will act in our behalf. Nothing can hinder the LORD from saving, whether by many or by few."

⁷"Do all that you have in mind," his armor-bearer said. "Go ahead; I am with you heart and soul."

⁸Jonathan said, "Come, then; we will cross over toward the men and let them see us. ⁹If they say to us, 'Wait there until we come to you,' we will stay where we are and not go up to them. ¹⁰But if they say, 'Come up to us,' we will climb up, because that will be our sign that the LORD has given them into our hands."

¹¹So both of them showed themselves to the Philistine outpost. "Look!" said the Philistines. "The Hebrews are crawling out of the holes they were hiding in." ¹²The men of the outpost shouted to Jonathan and his armor-bearer, "Come up to us and we'll teach you a lesson."

So Jonathan said to his armor-bearer, "Climb up after me; the LORD has given them into the hand of Israel."

¹³Jonathan climbed up, using his hands and feet, with his armor-bearer right behind him. The Philistines fell before Jonathan, and his armor-bearer followed and killed behind him. ¹⁴In that first attack Jonathan and his ar-

---

ᵃ15 Hebrew; Septuagint *Gilgal and went his way; the rest of the people went after Saul to meet the army, and they went out of Gilgal*   *ᵇ16* Two Hebrew manuscripts; most Hebrew manuscripts *Geba,* a variant of *Gibeah*   *ᶜ20* Septuagint; Hebrew *plowshares*   *ᵈ21* Hebrew *pim;* that is, about 1/4 ounce (about 8 grams)   *ᵉ21* That is, about 1/8 ounce (about 4 grams)

PASSAGE: 1 Chronicles 16:7–13; Jeremiah 29:10–14
AUTHOR: Anselm

For Ever Possess You

Grant, Lord, that we may hold to you without
       parting,
Worship you without wearying,
Serve you without failing,
Faithfully seek you,
Happily find you,
And for ever possess you,
The only God,
Blessed, now and for ever.

Let me seek you in my desire,
Let me desire you in my seeking.
Let me find you by loving you,
Let me love you when I find you.

Go to page 340 for your next devotional reading.

mor-bearer killed some twenty men in an area of about half an acre.*a*

Israel Routs the Philistines

15Then panic struck the whole army—those in the camp and field, and those in the outposts and raiding parties—and the ground shook. It was a panic sent by God.*b* **16**Saul's lookouts at Gibeah in Benjamin saw the army melting away in all directions. **17**Then Saul said to the men who were with him, "Muster the forces and see who has left us." When they did, it was Jonathan and his armor-bearer who were not there.

18Saul said to Ahijah, "Bring the ark of God." (At that time it was with the Israelites.)*c* **19**While Saul was talking to the priest, the tumult in the Philistine camp increased more and more. So Saul said to the priest, "Withdraw your hand."

20Then Saul and all his men assembled and went to the battle. They found the Philistines in total confusion, striking each other with their swords. **21**Those Hebrews who had previously been with the Philistines and had gone up with them to their camp went over to the Israelites who were with Saul and Jonathan. **22**When all the Israelites who had hidden in the hill country of Ephraim heard that the Philistines were on the run, they joined the battle in hot pursuit. **23**So the LORD rescued Israel that day, and the battle moved on beyond Beth Aven.

Jonathan Eats Honey

24Now the men of Israel were in distress that day, because Saul had bound the people under an oath, saying, "Cursed be any man who eats food before evening comes, before I have avenged myself on my enemies!" So none of the troops tasted food.

25The entire army*d* entered the woods, and there was honey on the ground. **26**When they went into the woods, they saw the honey oozing out, yet no one put his hand to his mouth, because they feared the oath. **27**But Jonathan had not heard that his father had bound the people with the oath, so he reached out the end of the staff that was in his hand and dipped it into the honeycomb. He raised his hand to his mouth, and his eyes brightened.*e* **28**Then one of the soldiers told him, "Your father bound the army under a strict oath, saying, 'Cursed be any man who eats food today!' That is why the men are faint."

29Jonathan said, "My father has made trouble for the country. See how my eyes brightened*f* when I tasted a little of this honey. **30**How much better it would have been if the men had eaten today some of the plunder they took from their enemies. Would not the slaughter of the Philistines have been even greater?"

31That day, after the Israelites had struck down the Philistines from Micmash to Aijalon, they were exhausted. **32**They pounced on the plunder and, taking sheep, cattle and calves, they butchered them on the ground and ate them, together with the blood. **33**Then someone said to Saul, "Look, the men are sinning against the LORD by eating meat that has blood in it."

"You have broken faith," he said. "Roll a large stone over here at once." **34**Then he said, "Go out among the men and tell them, 'Each of you bring me your cattle and sheep, and slaughter them here and eat them. Do not sin against the LORD by eating meat with blood still in it.'"

So everyone brought his ox that night and slaughtered it there. **35**Then Saul built an altar to the LORD; it was the first time he had done this.

36Saul said, "Let us go down after the Philistines by night and plunder

---

a14 Hebrew half a yoke; a "yoke" was the land plowed by a yoke of oxen in one day.   b15 Or a terrible panic   c18 Hebrew; Septuagint "Bring the ephod." (At that time he wore the ephod before the Israelites.)   d25 Or Now all the people of the land   e27 Or his strength was renewed   f29 Or my strength was renewed

them till dawn, and let us not leave one of them alive."

"Do whatever seems best to you," they replied.

But the priest said, "Let us inquire of God here."

37So Saul asked God, "Shall I go down after the Philistines? Will you give them into Israel's hand?" But God did not answer him that day.

38Saul therefore said, "Come here, all you who are leaders of the army, and let us find out what sin has been committed today. 39As surely as the LORD who rescues Israel lives, even if it lies with my son Jonathan, he must die." But not one of the men said a word.

40Saul then said to all the Israelites, "You stand over there; I and Jonathan my son will stand over here."

"Do what seems best to you," the men replied.

41Then Saul prayed to the LORD, the God of Israel, "Give me the right answer."*a* And Jonathan and Saul were taken by lot, and the men were cleared. 42Saul said, "Cast the lot between me and Jonathan my son." And Jonathan was taken.

43Then Saul said to Jonathan, "Tell me what you have done."

So Jonathan told him, "I merely tasted a little honey with the end of my staff. And now must I die?"

44Saul said, "May God deal with me, be it ever so severely, if you do not die, Jonathan."

45But the men said to Saul, "Should Jonathan die—he who has brought about this great deliverance in Israel? Never! As surely as the LORD lives, not a hair of his head will fall to the ground, for he did this today with God's help." So the men rescued Jonathan, and he was not put to death.

46Then Saul stopped pursuing the Philistines, and they withdrew to their own land.

47After Saul had assumed rule over Israel, he fought against their enemies on every side: Moab, the Ammonites, Edom, the kings*b* of Zobah, and the Philistines. Wherever he turned, he inflicted punishment on them.*c* 48He fought valiantly and defeated the Amalekites, delivering Israel from the hands of those who had plundered them.

Saul's Family

49Saul's sons were Jonathan, Ishvi and Malki-Shua. The name of his older daughter was Merab, and that of the younger was Michal. 50His wife's name was Ahinoam daughter of Ahimaaz. The name of the commander of Saul's army was Abner son of Ner, and Ner was Saul's uncle. 51Saul's father Kish and Abner's father Ner were sons of Abiel.

52All the days of Saul there was bitter war with the Philistines, and whenever Saul saw a mighty or brave man, he took him into his service.

The LORD Rejects Saul as King

15 Samuel said to Saul, "I am the one the LORD sent to anoint you king over his people Israel; so listen now to the message from the LORD. 2This is what the LORD Almighty says: 'I will punish the Amalekites for what they did to Israel when they waylaid them as they came up from Egypt. 3Now go, attack the Amalekites and totally destroy*d* everything that belongs to them. Do not spare them; put to death men and women, children and infants, cattle and sheep, camels and donkeys.' "

4So Saul summoned the men and mustered them at Telaim—two hundred thousand foot soldiers and ten thousand men from Judah. 5Saul went to the city of Amalek and set an ambush in the ravine. 6Then he said to the Kenites, "Go away, leave the Am-

---

*a*41 Hebrew; Septuagint *"Why have you not answered your servant today? If the fault is in me or my son Jonathan, respond with Urim, but if the men of Israel are at fault, respond with Thummim."* *b*47 Masoretic Text; Dead Sea Scrolls and Septuagint *king*   *c*47 Hebrew; Septuagint *he was victorious*   *d*3 The Hebrew term refers to the irrevocable giving over of things or persons to the LORD, often by totally destroying them; also in verses 8, 9, 15, 18, 20 and 21.

alekites so that I do not destroy you along with them; for you showed kindness to all the Israelites when they came up out of Egypt." So the Kenites moved away from the Amalekites.

⁷Then Saul attacked the Amalekites all the way from Havilah to Shur, to the east of Egypt. ⁸He took Agag king of the Amalekites alive, and all his people he totally destroyed with the sword. ⁹But Saul and the army spared Agag and the best of the sheep and cattle, the fat calves*ᵃ* and lambs—everything that was good. These they were unwilling to destroy completely, but everything that was despised and weak they totally destroyed.

¹⁰Then the word of the LORD came to Samuel: ¹¹"I am grieved that I have made Saul king, because he has turned away from me and has not carried out my instructions." Samuel was troubled, and he cried out to the LORD all that night.

¹²Early in the morning Samuel got up and went to meet Saul, but he was told, "Saul has gone to Carmel. There he has set up a monument in his own honor and has turned and gone on down to Gilgal."

¹³When Samuel reached him, Saul said, "The LORD bless you! I have carried out the LORD's instructions."

¹⁴But Samuel said, "What then is this bleating of sheep in my ears? What is this lowing of cattle that I hear?"

¹⁵Saul answered, "The soldiers brought them from the Amalekites; they spared the best of the sheep and cattle to sacrifice to the LORD your God, but we totally destroyed the rest."

¹⁶"Stop!" Samuel said to Saul. "Let me tell you what the LORD said to me last night."

"Tell me," Saul replied.

¹⁷Samuel said, "Although you were once small in your own eyes, did you not become the head of the tribes of Israel? The LORD anointed you king over Israel. ¹⁸And he sent you on a mission, saying, 'Go and completely destroy those wicked people, the Amalekites; make war on them until you have wiped them out.' ¹⁹Why did you not obey the LORD? Why did you pounce on the plunder and do evil in the eyes of the LORD?"

²⁰"But I did obey the LORD," Saul said. "I went on the mission the LORD assigned me. I completely destroyed the Amalekites and brought back Agag their king. ²¹The soldiers took sheep and cattle from the plunder, the best of what was devoted to God, in order to sacrifice them to the LORD your God at Gilgal."

²²But Samuel replied:

"Does the LORD delight in burnt
    offerings and sacrifices
  as much as in obeying the voice
    of the LORD?
To obey is better than sacrifice,
  and to heed is better than the
    fat of rams.
²³For rebellion is like the sin of
    divination,
  and arrogance like the evil of
    idolatry.
Because you have rejected the
    word of the LORD,
  he has rejected you as king."

²⁴Then Saul said to Samuel, "I have sinned. I violated the LORD's command and your instructions. I was afraid of the people and so I gave in to them. ²⁵Now I beg you, forgive my sin and come back with me, so that I may worship the LORD."

²⁶But Samuel said to him, "I will not go back with you. You have rejected the word of the LORD, and the LORD has rejected you as king over Israel!"

²⁷As Samuel turned to leave, Saul caught hold of the hem of his robe, and it tore. ²⁸Samuel said to him, "The LORD has torn the kingdom of Israel from you today and has given it to one of your neighbors—to one better than you. ²⁹He who is the Glory of

---

ᵃ9 Or *the grown bulls;* the meaning of the Hebrew for this phrase is uncertain.

Israel does not lie or change his mind; for he is not a man, that he should change his mind."

30Saul replied, "I have sinned. But please honor me before the elders of my people and before Israel; come back with me, so that I may worship the LORD your God." 31So Samuel went back with Saul, and Saul worshiped the LORD.

32Then Samuel said, "Bring me Agag king of the Amalekites."

Agag came to him confidently,ᵃ thinking, "Surely the bitterness of death is past."

33But Samuel said,

ᵃ32 Or *him trembling, yet*

VERSE:
1 Samuel 15:22

AUTHOR:
Thomas R. Kelly

PASSAGE:
1 Samuel 15:1–23

Holy Obedience

Meister Eckhart wrote: "There are plenty to follow our Lord half-way, but not the other half. They will give up possessions, friends and honors, but it touches them too closely to disown themselves." It is just this astonishing life which is willing to follow him the other half, sincerely to disown itself, this life which intends *complete* obedience, without *any* reservations, that I would propose to you in all humility, in all boldness, in all seriousness. I mean this literally, utterly, completely, and I mean it for you and for me — commit your lives in unreserved obedience to him . . .

To this extraordinary life I call you — or he calls you through me — not as a lovely ideal, a charming pattern to aim at hopefully, but as a serious, concrete program of life, to be lived here and now . . . by you and by me . . . The life that intends to be wholly obedient, wholly submissive, wholly listening, is astonishing in its completeness. Its joys are ravishing, its peace profound, its humility the deepest, its power world-shaking, its love enveloping, its simplicity that of a trusting child.

ADDITIONAL SCRIPTURE READINGS
Psalm 119:57–64; 2 Corinthians 10:1–6

Go to page 342 for your next devotional reading.

"As your sword has made women
  childless,
 so will your mother be childless
  among women."

And Samuel put Agag to death before
the LORD at Gilgal.

34Then Samuel left for Ramah, but
Saul went up to his home in Gibeah of
Saul. 35Until the day Samuel died, he
did not go to see Saul again, though
Samuel mourned for him. And the
LORD was grieved that he had made
Saul king over Israel.

Samuel Anoints David

16 The LORD said to Samuel, "How
long will you mourn for Saul,
since I have rejected him as king over
Israel? Fill your horn with oil and be
on your way; I am sending you to Jesse of Bethlehem. I have chosen one of
his sons to be king."

2But Samuel said, "How can I go?
Saul will hear about it and kill me."

The LORD said, "Take a heifer with
you and say, 'I have come to sacrifice
to the LORD.' 3Invite Jesse to the sacrifice, and I will show you what to do.
You are to anoint for me the one I indicate."

4Samuel did what the LORD said.
When he arrived at Bethlehem, the elders of the town trembled when they
met him. They asked, "Do you come
in peace?"

5Samuel replied, "Yes, in peace; I
have come to sacrifice to the LORD.
Consecrate yourselves and come to
the sacrifice with me." Then he consecrated Jesse and his sons and invited
them to the sacrifice.

6When they arrived, Samuel saw
Eliab and thought, "Surely the LORD's
anointed stands here before the
LORD."

7But the LORD said to Samuel, "Do
not consider his appearance or his
height, for I have rejected him. The
LORD does not look at the things man
looks at. Man looks at the outward

appearance, but the LORD looks at the
heart."

8Then Jesse called Abinadab and
had him pass in front of Samuel. But
Samuel said, "The LORD has not chosen this one either." 9Jesse then had
Shammah pass by, but Samuel said,
"Nor has the LORD chosen this one."
10Jesse had seven of his sons pass before Samuel, but Samuel said to him,
"The LORD has not chosen these." 11So
he asked Jesse, "Are these all the sons
you have?"

"There is still the youngest," Jesse
answered, "but he is tending the
sheep."

Samuel said, "Send for him; we
will not sit downᵃ until he arrives."

12So he sent and had him brought
in. He was ruddy, with a fine appearance and handsome features.

Then the LORD said, "Rise and
anoint him; he is the one."

13So Samuel took the horn of oil
and anointed him in the presence of
his brothers, and from that day on the
Spirit of the LORD came upon David in
power. Samuel then went to Ramah.

David in Saul's Service

14Now the Spirit of the LORD had
departed from Saul, and an evilᵇ
spirit from the LORD tormented him.

15Saul's attendants said to him,
"See, an evil spirit from God is tor-
menting you. 16Let our lord command
his servants here to search for someone who can play the harp. He will
play when the evil spirit from God
comes upon you, and you will feel
better."

17So Saul said to his attendants,
"Find someone who plays well and
bring him to me."

18One of the servants answered, "I
have seen a son of Jesse of Bethlehem
who knows how to play the harp. He
is a brave man and a warrior. He
speaks well and is a fine-looking
man. And the LORD is with him."

19Then Saul sent messengers to Jesse and said, "Send me your son Da-

ᵃ11 Some Septuagint manuscripts; Hebrew not gather around
15, 16 and 23   ᵇ14 Or injurious; also in verses

VERSE:	AUTHOR:	PASSAGE:
1 Samuel 16:7	Charles Stanley	1 Samuel 16:1–13

The Big Picture

Great Bible characters weren't always so great. Moses and Peter had very inauspicious beginnings. David encountered serious obstacles, some of his own making, throughout his life. Gideon started slowly, fared well for a season, and ended with some question marks.

That's significant to me and to you because it reveals some crucial facts about the Christian life that affect our ability to personally embrace God's love.

It tells us that God is as interested in the process as he is in the result. Those who trust in Christ as Savior will arrive safely in heaven. Jesus' performance on the cross settles that issue. This means that the process of becoming like Christ is what God is primarily up to in our short span on earth. This involves failure and success, joy and grief, wisdom and foolishness, peace and turmoil. Certainly, if you were to chart the lives of Moses and David, the graph would resemble a mountain-range silhouette. God wants you to exhibit and express the life of Christ, and that is a lifelong process . . .

If you know God is interested in the process, looks for ultimate progress and sees unlimited potential, you can be liberated to walk and act under the umbrella of his love. God's commitment is for eternity, but he is with you today to help you make the most of each opportunity.

ADDITIONAL SCRIPTURE READINGS
2 Corinthians 4:7–12; Philippians 2:1–11
Go to page 362 for your next devotional reading.

vid, who is with the sheep." ²⁰So Jesse took a donkey loaded with bread, a skin of wine and a young goat and sent them with his son David to Saul.

²¹David came to Saul and entered his service. Saul liked him very much, and David became one of his armor-bearers. ²²Then Saul sent word to Jesse, saying, "Allow David to remain in my service, for I am pleased with him."

²³Whenever the spirit from God came upon Saul, David would take his harp and play. Then relief would come to Saul; he would feel better, and the evil spirit would leave him.

David and Goliath

17 Now the Philistines gathered their forces for war and assembled at Socoh in Judah. They pitched camp at Ephes Dammim, between Socoh and Azekah. ²Saul and the Israelites assembled and camped in the Valley of Elah and drew up their battle line to meet the Philistines. ³The Philistines occupied one hill and the Israelites another, with the valley between them.

⁴A champion named Goliath, who was from Gath, came out of the Philistine camp. He was over nine feet*a* tall. ⁵He had a bronze helmet on his head and wore a coat of scale armor of bronze weighing five thousand shekels*b*; ⁶on his legs he wore bronze greaves, and a bronze javelin was slung on his back. ⁷His spear shaft was like a weaver's rod, and its iron point weighed six hundred shekels.*c* His shield bearer went ahead of him.

⁸Goliath stood and shouted to the ranks of Israel, "Why do you come out and line up for battle? Am I not a Philistine, and are you not the servants of Saul? Choose a man and have him come down to me. ⁹If he is able to fight and kill me, we will become your subjects; but if I overcome him and kill him, you will become our subjects and serve us." ¹⁰Then the

Philistine said, "This day I defy the ranks of Israel! Give me a man and let us fight each other." ¹¹On hearing the Philistine's words, Saul and all the Israelites were dismayed and terrified.

¹²Now David was the son of an Ephrathite named Jesse, who was from Bethlehem in Judah. Jesse had eight sons, and in Saul's time he was old and well advanced in years. ¹³Jesse's three oldest sons had followed Saul to the war: The firstborn was Eliab; the second, Abinadab; and the third, Shammah. ¹⁴David was the youngest. The three oldest followed Saul, ¹⁵but David went back and forth from Saul to tend his father's sheep at Bethlehem.

¹⁶For forty days the Philistine came forward every morning and evening and took his stand.

¹⁷Now Jesse said to his son David, "Take this ephah*d* of roasted grain and these ten loaves of bread for your brothers and hurry to their camp. ¹⁸Take along these ten cheeses to the commander of their unit.*e* See how your brothers are and bring back some assurance*f* from them. ¹⁹They are with Saul and all the men of Israel in the Valley of Elah, fighting against the Philistines."

²⁰Early in the morning David left the flock with a shepherd, loaded up and set out, as Jesse had directed. He reached the camp as the army was going out to its battle positions, shouting the war cry. ²¹Israel and the Philistines were drawing up their lines facing each other. ²²David left his things with the keeper of supplies, ran to the battle lines and greeted his brothers. ²³As he was talking with them, Goliath, the Philistine champion from Gath, stepped out from his lines and shouted his usual defiance, and David heard it. ²⁴When the Israelites saw the man, they all ran from him in great fear.

²⁵Now the Israelites had been saying, "Do you see how this man keeps

---

a4 Hebrew *was six cubits and a span* (about 3 meters)   *b5* That is, about 125 pounds (about 57 kilograms)   *c7* That is, about 15 pounds (about 7 kilograms)   *d17* That is, probably about 3/5 bushel (about 22 liters)   *e18* Hebrew *thousand*   *f18* Or *some token;* or *some pledge of spoils*

coming out? He comes out to defy Israel. The king will give great wealth to the man who kills him. He will also give him his daughter in marriage and will exempt his father's family from taxes in Israel."

26David asked the men standing near him, "What will be done for the man who kills this Philistine and removes this disgrace from Israel? Who is this uncircumcised Philistine that he should defy the armies of the living God?"

27They repeated to him what they had been saying and told him, "This is what will be done for the man who kills him."

28When Eliab, David's oldest brother, heard him speaking with the men, he burned with anger at him and asked, "Why have you come down here? And with whom did you leave those few sheep in the desert? I know how conceited you are and how wicked your heart is; you came down only to watch the battle."

29"Now what have I done?" said David. "Can't I even speak?" 30He then turned away to someone else and brought up the same matter, and the men answered him as before. 31What David said was overheard and reported to Saul, and Saul sent for him.

32David said to Saul, "Let no one lose heart on account of this Philistine; your servant will go and fight him."

33Saul replied, "You are not able to go out against this Philistine and fight him; you are only a boy, and he has been a fighting man from his youth."

34But David said to Saul, "Your servant has been keeping his father's sheep. When a lion or a bear came and carried off a sheep from the flock, 35I went after it, struck it and rescued the sheep from its mouth. When it turned on me, I seized it by its hair, struck it and killed it. 36Your servant has killed both the lion and the bear; this uncircumcised Philistine will be like one of them, because he has defied the armies of the living God. 37The LORD who delivered me from the paw of the lion and the paw of the bear will deliver me from the hand of this Philistine."

Saul said to David, "Go, and the LORD be with you."

38Then Saul dressed David in his own tunic. He put a coat of armor on him and a bronze helmet on his head. 39David fastened on his sword over the tunic and tried walking around, because he was not used to them.

"I cannot go in these," he said to Saul, "because I am not used to them." So he took them off. 40Then he took his staff in his hand, chose five smooth stones from the stream, put them in the pouch of his shepherd's bag and, with his sling in his hand, approached the Philistine.

41Meanwhile, the Philistine, with his shield bearer in front of him, kept coming closer to David. 42He looked David over and saw that he was only a boy, ruddy and handsome, and he despised him. 43He said to David, "Am I a dog, that you come at me with sticks?" And the Philistine cursed David by his gods. 44"Come here," he said, "and I'll give your flesh to the birds of the air and the beasts of the field!"

45David said to the Philistine, "You come against me with sword and spear and javelin, but I come against you in the name of the LORD Almighty, the God of the armies of Israel, whom you have defied. 46This day the LORD will hand you over to me, and I'll strike you down and cut off your head. Today I will give the carcasses of the Philistine army to the birds of the air and the beasts of the earth, and the whole world will know that there is a God in Israel. 47All those gathered here will know that it is not by sword or spear that the LORD saves; for the battle is the LORD's, and he will give all of you into our hands."

48As the Philistine moved closer to attack him, David ran quickly toward the battle line to meet him. 49Reaching into his bag and taking out a stone, he slung it and struck the Philistine on the forehead. The stone sank into his forehead, and he fell facedown on the ground. ⁵⁰So David triumphed over the Philistine with a sling and a stone; without a sword in his hand he struck down the Philistine and killed him.

⁵¹David ran and stood over him. He took hold of the Philistine's sword and drew it from the scabbard. After he killed him, he cut off his head with the sword.

When the Philistines saw that their hero was dead, they turned and ran. ⁵²Then the men of Israel and Judah surged forward with a shout and pursued the Philistines to the entrance of Gath*ᵃ* and to the gates of Ekron. Their dead were strewn along the Shaaraim road to Gath and Ekron. ⁵³When the Israelites returned from chasing the Philistines, they plundered their camp. ⁵⁴David took the Philistine's head and brought it to Jerusalem, and he put the Philistine's weapons in his own tent.

⁵⁵As Saul watched David going out to meet the Philistine, he said to Abner, commander of the army, "Abner, whose son is that young man?"

Abner replied, "As surely as you live, O king, I don't know."

⁵⁶The king said, "Find out whose son this young man is."

⁵⁷As soon as David returned from killing the Philistine, Abner took him and brought him before Saul, with David still holding the Philistine's head.

⁵⁸"Whose son are you, young man?" Saul asked him.

David said, "I am the son of your servant Jesse of Bethlehem."

Saul's Jealousy of David

18 After David had finished talking with Saul, Jonathan became one in spirit with David, and he loved him as himself. ²From that day Saul kept David with him and did not let him return to his father's house. ³And Jonathan made a covenant with David because he loved him as himself.

⁴Jonathan took off the robe he was wearing and gave it to David, along with his tunic, and even his sword, his bow and his belt.

⁵Whatever Saul sent him to do, David did it so successfully*ᵇ* that Saul gave him a high rank in the army. This pleased all the people, and Saul's officers as well.

⁶When the men were returning home after David had killed the Philistine, the women came out from all the towns of Israel to meet King Saul with singing and dancing, with joyful songs and with tambourines and lutes. ⁷As they danced, they sang:

"Saul has slain his thousands,
  and David his tens of
    thousands."

⁸Saul was very angry; this refrain galled him. "They have credited David with tens of thousands," he thought, "but me with only thousands. What more can he get but the kingdom?" ⁹And from that time on Saul kept a jealous eye on David.

¹⁰The next day an evil*ᶜ* spirit from God came forcefully upon Saul. He was prophesying in his house, while David was playing the harp, as he usually did. Saul had a spear in his hand ¹¹and he hurled it, saying to himself, "I'll pin David to the wall." But David eluded him twice.

¹²Saul was afraid of David, because the Lord was with David but had left Saul. ¹³So he sent David away from him and gave him command over a thousand men, and David led the troops in their campaigns. ¹⁴In everything he did he had great success,*ᵈ* because the Lord was with him. ¹⁵When Saul saw how successful*ᵉ* he was, he was afraid of him. ¹⁶But all Israel and Judah loved David, because he led them in their campaigns.

¹⁷Saul said to David, "Here is my older daughter Merab. I will give her to you in marriage; only serve me bravely and fight the battles of the Lord." For Saul said to himself, "I will

---

ᵃ52 Some Septuagint manuscripts; Hebrew *a valley*   *ᵇ5* Or *wisely*   *ᶜ10* Or *injurious*
ᵈ14 Or *he was very wise*   *ᵉ15* Or *wise*

not raise a hand against him. Let the Philistines do that!"

¹⁸But David said to Saul, "Who am I, and what is my family or my father's clan in Israel, that I should become the king's son-in-law?" ¹⁹Soᵃ when the time came for Merab, Saul's daughter, to be given to David, she was given in marriage to Adriel of Meholah.

²⁰Now Saul's daughter Michal was in love with David, and when they told Saul about it, he was pleased. ²¹"I will give her to him," he thought, "so that she may be a snare to him and so that the hand of the Philistines may be against him." So Saul said to David, "Now you have a second opportunity to become my son-in-law."

²²Then Saul ordered his attendants: "Speak to David privately and say, 'Look, the king is pleased with you, and his attendants all like you; now become his son-in-law.'"

²³They repeated these words to David. But David said, "Do you think it is a small matter to become the king's son-in-law? I'm only a poor man and little known."

²⁴When Saul's servants told him what David had said, ²⁵Saul replied, "Say to David, 'The king wants no other price for the bride than a hundred Philistine foreskins, to take revenge on his enemies.'" Saul's plan was to have David fall by the hands of the Philistines.

²⁶When the attendants told David these things, he was pleased to become the king's son-in-law. So before the allotted time elapsed, ²⁷David and his men went out and killed two hundred Philistines. He brought their foreskins and presented the full number to the king so that he might become the king's son-in-law. Then Saul gave him his daughter Michal in marriage.

²⁸When Saul realized that the LORD was with David and that his daughter Michal loved David, ²⁹Saul became still more afraid of him, and he remained his enemy the rest of his days.

³⁰The Philistine commanders continued to go out to battle, and as often as they did, David met with more successᵇ than the rest of Saul's officers, and his name became well known.

Saul Tries to Kill David

19 Saul told his son Jonathan and all the attendants to kill David. But Jonathan was very fond of David ²and warned him, "My father Saul is looking for a chance to kill you. Be on your guard tomorrow morning; go into hiding and stay there. ³I will go out and stand with my father in the field where you are. I'll speak to him about you and will tell you what I find out."

⁴Jonathan spoke well of David to Saul his father and said to him, "Let not the king do wrong to his servant David; he has not wronged you, and what he has done has benefited you greatly. ⁵He took his life in his hands when he killed the Philistine. The LORD won a great victory for all Israel, and you saw it and were glad. Why then would you do wrong to an innocent man like David by killing him for no reason?"

⁶Saul listened to Jonathan and took this oath: "As surely as the LORD lives, David will not be put to death."

⁷So Jonathan called David and told him the whole conversation. He brought him to Saul, and David was with Saul as before.

⁸Once more war broke out, and David went out and fought the Philistines. He struck them with such force that they fled before him.

⁹But an evilᶜ spirit from the LORD came upon Saul as he was sitting in his house with his spear in his hand. While David was playing the harp, ¹⁰Saul tried to pin him to the wall with his spear, but David eluded him as Saul drove the spear into the wall. That night David made good his escape.

¹¹Saul sent men to David's house to watch it and to kill him in the morn-

ᵃ19 Or However,   ᵇ30 Or David acted more wisely   ᶜ9 Or injurious

ing. But Michal, David's wife, warned him, "If you don't run for your life tonight, tomorrow you'll be killed." ¹²So Michal let David down through a window, and he fled and escaped. ¹³Then Michal took an idol[a] and laid it on the bed, covering it with a garment and putting some goats' hair at the head.

¹⁴When Saul sent the men to capture David, Michal said, "He is ill."

¹⁵Then Saul sent the men back to see David and told them, "Bring him up to me in his bed so that I may kill him." ¹⁶But when the men entered, there was the idol in the bed, and at the head was some goats' hair.

¹⁷Saul said to Michal, "Why did you deceive me like this and send my enemy away so that he escaped?"

Michal told him, "He said to me, 'Let me get away. Why should I kill you?'"

¹⁸When David had fled and made his escape, he went to Samuel at Ramah and told him all that Saul had done to him. Then he and Samuel went to Naioth and stayed there. ¹⁹Word came to Saul: "David is in Naioth at Ramah"; ²⁰so he sent men to capture him. But when they saw a group of prophets prophesying, with Samuel standing there as their leader, the Spirit of God came upon Saul's men and they also prophesied. ²¹Saul was told about it, and he sent more men, and they prophesied too. Saul sent men a third time, and they also prophesied. ²²Finally, he himself left for Ramah and went to the great cistern at Secu. And he asked, "Where are Samuel and David?"

"Over in Naioth at Ramah," they said.

²³So Saul went to Naioth at Ramah. But the Spirit of God came even upon him, and he walked along prophesying until he came to Naioth. ²⁴He stripped off his robes and also prophesied in Samuel's presence. He lay that way all that day and night. This is why people say, "Is Saul also among the prophets?"

David and Jonathan

20 Then David fled from Naioth at Ramah and went to Jonathan and asked, "What have I done? What is my crime? How have I wronged your father, that he is trying to take my life?"

²"Never!" Jonathan replied. "You are not going to die! Look, my father doesn't do anything, great or small, without confiding in me. Why would he hide this from me? It's not so!"

³But David took an oath and said, "Your father knows very well that I have found favor in your eyes, and he has said to himself, 'Jonathan must not know this or he will be grieved.' Yet as surely as the LORD lives and as you live, there is only a step between me and death."

⁴Jonathan said to David, "Whatever you want me to do, I'll do for you."

⁵So David said, "Look, tomorrow is the New Moon festival, and I am supposed to dine with the king; but let me go and hide in the field until the evening of the day after tomorrow. ⁶If your father misses me at all, tell him, 'David earnestly asked my permission to hurry to Bethlehem, his hometown, because an annual sacrifice is being made there for his whole clan.' ⁷If he says, 'Very well,' then your servant is safe. But if he loses his temper, you can be sure that he is determined to harm me. ⁸As for you, show kindness to your servant, for you have brought him into a covenant with you before the LORD. If I am guilty, then kill me yourself! Why hand me over to your father?"

⁹"Never!" Jonathan said. "If I had the least inkling that my father was determined to harm you, wouldn't I tell you?"

¹⁰David asked, "Who will tell me if your father answers you harshly?"

¹¹"Come," Jonathan said, "let's go out into the field." So they went there together.

¹²Then Jonathan said to David: "By the LORD, the God of Israel, I will sure-

[a]13 Hebrew *teraphim*; also in verse 16

ly sound out my father by this time the day after tomorrow! If he is favorably disposed toward you, will I not send you word and let you know? ¹³But if my father is inclined to harm you, may the LORD deal with me, be it ever so severely, if I do not let you know and send you away safely. May the LORD be with you as he has been with my father. ¹⁴But show me unfailing kindness like that of the LORD as long as I live, so that I may not be killed, ¹⁵and do not ever cut off your kindness from my family—not even when the LORD has cut off every one of David's enemies from the face of the earth."

¹⁶So Jonathan made a covenant with the house of David, saying, "May the LORD call David's enemies to account." ¹⁷And Jonathan had David reaffirm his oath out of love for him, because he loved him as he loved himself.

¹⁸Then Jonathan said to David: "Tomorrow is the New Moon festival. You will be missed, because your seat will be empty. ¹⁹The day after tomorrow, toward evening, go to the place where you hid when this trouble began, and wait by the stone Ezel. ²⁰I will shoot three arrows to the side of it, as though I were shooting at a target. ²¹Then I will send a boy and say, 'Go, find the arrows.' If I say to him, 'Look, the arrows are on this side of you; bring them here,' then come, because, as surely as the LORD lives, you are safe; there is no danger. ²²But if I say to the boy, 'Look, the arrows are beyond you,' then you must go, because the LORD has sent you away. ²³And about the matter you and I discussed—remember, the LORD is witness between you and me forever."

²⁴So David hid in the field, and when the New Moon festival came, the king sat down to eat. ²⁵He sat in his customary place by the wall, opposite Jonathan,ᵃ and Abner sat next to Saul, but David's place was empty. ²⁶Saul said nothing that day, for he thought, "Something must have hap-

pened to David to make him ceremonially unclean—surely he is unclean." ²⁷But the next day, the second day of the month, David's place was empty again. Then Saul said to his son Jonathan, "Why hasn't the son of Jesse come to the meal, either yesterday or today?"

²⁸Jonathan answered, "David earnestly asked me for permission to go to Bethlehem. ²⁹He said, 'Let me go, because our family is observing a sacrifice in the town and my brother has ordered me to be there. If I have found favor in your eyes, let me get away to see my brothers.' That is why he has not come to the king's table."

³⁰Saul's anger flared up at Jonathan and he said to him, "You son of a perverse and rebellious woman! Don't I know that you have sided with the son of Jesse to your own shame and to the shame of the mother who bore you? ³¹As long as the son of Jesse lives on this earth, neither you nor your kingdom will be established. Now send and bring him to me, for he must die!"

³²"Why should he be put to death? What has he done?" Jonathan asked his father. ³³But Saul hurled his spear at him to kill him. Then Jonathan knew that his father intended to kill David.

³⁴Jonathan got up from the table in fierce anger; on that second day of the month he did not eat, because he was grieved at his father's shameful treatment of David.

³⁵In the morning Jonathan went out to the field for his meeting with David. He had a small boy with him, ³⁶and he said to the boy, "Run and find the arrows I shoot." As the boy ran, he shot an arrow beyond him. ³⁷When the boy came to the place where Jonathan's arrow had fallen, Jonathan called out after him, "Isn't the arrow beyond you?" ³⁸Then he shouted, "Hurry! Go quickly! Don't stop!" The boy picked up the arrow and returned to his master. ³⁹(The boy knew nothing of all this; only Jona-

---

ᵃ25 Septuagint; Hebrew *wall. Jonathan arose*

than and David knew.) ⁴⁰Then Jonathan gave his weapons to the boy and said, "Go, carry them back to town."

⁴¹After the boy had gone, David got up from the south side ⌊of the stone⌋ and bowed down before Jonathan three times, with his face to the ground. Then they kissed each other and wept together—but David wept the most.

⁴²Jonathan said to David, "Go in peace, for we have sworn friendship with each other in the name of the Lord, saying, 'The Lord is witness between you and me, and between your descendants and my descendants forever.' " Then David left, and Jonathan went back to the town.

David at Nob

21 David went to Nob, to Ahimelech the priest. Ahimelech trembled when he met him, and asked, "Why are you alone? Why is no one with you?"

²David answered Ahimelech the priest, "The king charged me with a certain matter and said to me, 'No one is to know anything about your mission and your instructions.' As for my men, I have told them to meet me at a certain place. ³Now then, what do you have on hand? Give me five loaves of bread, or whatever you can find."

⁴But the priest answered David, "I don't have any ordinary bread on hand; however, there is some consecrated bread here—provided the men have kept themselves from women."

⁵David replied, "Indeed women have been kept from us, as usual whenever*a* I set out. The men's things*b* are holy even on missions that are not holy. How much more so today!" ⁶So the priest gave him the consecrated bread, since there was no bread there except the bread of the Presence that had been removed from before the Lord and replaced by hot bread on the day it was taken away.

⁷Now one of Saul's servants was there that day, detained before the Lord; he was Doeg the Edomite, Saul's head shepherd.

⁸David asked Ahimelech, "Don't you have a spear or a sword here? I haven't brought my sword or any other weapon, because the king's business was urgent."

⁹The priest replied, "The sword of Goliath the Philistine, whom you killed in the Valley of Elah, is here; it is wrapped in a cloth behind the ephod. If you want it, take it; there is no sword here but that one."

David said, "There is none like it; give it to me."

David at Gath

¹⁰That day David fled from Saul and went to Achish king of Gath. ¹¹But the servants of Achish said to him, "Isn't this David, the king of the land? Isn't he the one they sing about in their dances:

" 'Saul has slain his thousands,
    and David his tens of
        thousands'?"

¹²David took these words to heart and was very much afraid of Achish king of Gath. ¹³So he pretended to be insane in their presence; and while he was in their hands he acted like a madman, making marks on the doors of the gate and letting saliva run down his beard.

¹⁴Achish said to his servants, "Look at the man! He is insane! Why bring him to me? ¹⁵Am I so short of madmen that you have to bring this fellow here to carry on like this in front of me? Must this man come into my house?"

David at Adullam and Mizpah

22 David left Gath and escaped to the cave of Adullam. When his brothers and his father's household heard about it, they went down to him there. ²All those who were in distress or in debt or discontented gathered around him, and he became their leader. About four hundred men were with him.

---

a5 Or *from us in the past few days since*   *b5* Or *bodies*

³From there David went to Mizpah in Moab and said to the king of Moab, "Would you let my father and mother come and stay with you until I learn what God will do for me?" ⁴So he left them with the king of Moab, and they stayed with him as long as David was in the stronghold.

⁵But the prophet Gad said to David, "Do not stay in the stronghold. Go into the land of Judah." So David left and went to the forest of Hereth.

Saul Kills the Priests of Nob

⁶Now Saul heard that David and his men had been discovered. And Saul, spear in hand, was seated under the tamarisk tree on the hill at Gibeah, with all his officials standing around him. ⁷Saul said to them, "Listen, men of Benjamin! Will the son of Jesse give all of you fields and vineyards? Will he make all of you commanders of thousands and commanders of hundreds? ⁸Is that why you have all conspired against me? No one tells me when my son makes a covenant with the son of Jesse. None of you is concerned about me or tells me that my son has incited my servant to lie in wait for me, as he does today."

⁹But Doeg the Edomite, who was standing with Saul's officials, said, "I saw the son of Jesse come to Ahimelech son of Ahitub at Nob. ¹⁰Ahimelech inquired of the LORD for him; he also gave him provisions and the sword of Goliath the Philistine."

¹¹Then the king sent for the priest Ahimelech son of Ahitub and his father's whole family, who were the priests at Nob, and they all came to the king. ¹²Saul said, "Listen now, son of Ahitub."

"Yes, my lord," he answered.

¹³Saul said to him, "Why have you conspired against me, you and the son of Jesse, giving him bread and a sword and inquiring of God for him, so that he has rebelled against me and lies in wait for me, as he does today?"

¹⁴Ahimelech answered the king, "Who of all your servants is as loyal as David, the king's son-in-law, captain of your bodyguard and highly respected in your household? ¹⁵Was that day the first time I inquired of God for him? Of course not! Let not the king accuse your servant or any of his father's family, for your servant knows nothing at all about this whole affair."

¹⁶But the king said, "You will surely die, Ahimelech, you and your father's whole family."

¹⁷Then the king ordered the guards at his side: "Turn and kill the priests of the LORD, because they too have sided with David. They knew he was fleeing, yet they did not tell me."

But the king's officials were not willing to raise a hand to strike the priests of the LORD.

¹⁸The king then ordered Doeg, "You turn and strike down the priests." So Doeg the Edomite turned and struck them down. That day he killed eighty-five men who wore the linen ephod. ¹⁹He also put to the sword Nob, the town of the priests, with its men and women, its children and infants, and its cattle, donkeys and sheep.

²⁰But Abiathar, a son of Ahimelech son of Ahitub, escaped and fled to join David. ²¹He told David that Saul had killed the priests of the LORD. ²²Then David said to Abiathar: "That day, when Doeg the Edomite was there, I knew he would be sure to tell Saul. I am responsible for the death of your father's whole family. ²³Stay with me; don't be afraid; the man who is seeking your life is seeking mine also. You will be safe with me."

David Saves Keilah

23 When David was told, "Look, the Philistines are fighting against Keilah and are looting the threshing floors," ²he inquired of the LORD, saying, "Shall I go and attack these Philistines?"

The LORD answered him, "Go, attack the Philistines and save Keilah."

³But David's men said to him, "Here in Judah we are afraid. How much more, then, if we go to Keilah against the Philistine forces!"

⁴Once again David inquired of the

LORD, and the LORD answered him, "Go down to Keilah, for I am going to give the Philistines into your hand." [5]So David and his men went to Keilah, fought the Philistines and carried off their livestock. He inflicted heavy losses on the Philistines and saved the people of Keilah. [6](Now Abiathar son of Ahimelech had brought the ephod down with him when he fled to David at Keilah.)

Saul Pursues David

[7]Saul was told that David had gone to Keilah, and he said, "God has handed him over to me, for David has imprisoned himself by entering a town with gates and bars." [8]And Saul called up all his forces for battle, to go down to Keilah to besiege David and his men.

[9]When David learned that Saul was plotting against him, he said to Abiathar the priest, "Bring the ephod." [10]David said, "O LORD, God of Israel, your servant has heard definitely that Saul plans to come to Keilah and destroy the town on account of me. [11]Will the citizens of Keilah surrender me to him? Will Saul come down, as your servant has heard? O LORD, God of Israel, tell your servant."

And the LORD said, "He will."

[12]Again David asked, "Will the citizens of Keilah surrender me and my men to Saul?"

And the LORD said, "They will."

[13]So David and his men, about six hundred in number, left Keilah and kept moving from place to place. When Saul was told that David had escaped from Keilah, he did not go there.

[14]David stayed in the desert strongholds and in the hills of the Desert of Ziph. Day after day Saul searched for him, but God did not give David into his hands.

[15]While David was at Horesh in the Desert of Ziph, he learned that Saul had come out to take his life. [16]And Saul's son Jonathan went to David at Horesh and helped him find strength in God. [17]"Don't be afraid," he said. "My father Saul will not lay a hand on you. You will be king over Israel, and I will be second to you. Even my father Saul knows this." [18]The two of them made a covenant before the LORD. Then Jonathan went home, but David remained at Horesh.

[19]The Ziphites went up to Saul at Gibeah and said, "Is not David hiding among us in the strongholds at Horesh, on the hill of Hakilah, south of Jeshimon? [20]Now, O king, come down whenever it pleases you to do so, and we will be responsible for handing him over to the king."

[21]Saul replied, "The LORD bless you for your concern for me. [22]Go and make further preparation. Find out where David usually goes and who has seen him there. They tell me he is very crafty. [23]Find out about all the hiding places he uses and come back to me with definite information.[a] Then I will go with you; if he is in the area, I will track him down among all the clans of Judah."

[24]So they set out and went to Ziph ahead of Saul. Now David and his men were in the Desert of Maon, in the Arabah south of Jeshimon. [25]Saul and his men began the search, and when David was told about it, he went down to the rock and stayed in the Desert of Maon. When Saul heard this, he went into the Desert of Maon in pursuit of David.

[26]Saul was going along one side of the mountain, and David and his men were on the other side, hurrying to get away from Saul. As Saul and his forces were closing in on David and his men to capture them, [27]a messenger came to Saul, saying, "Come quickly! The Philistines are raiding the land." [28]Then Saul broke off his pursuit of David and went to meet the Philistines. That is why they call this place Sela Hammahlekoth.[b] [29]And David went up from there and lived in the strongholds of En Gedi.

---

[a]23 Or *me at Nacon*   [b]28 *Sela Hammahlekoth* means *rock of parting.*

David Spares Saul's Life

24 After Saul returned from pursuing the Philistines, he was told, "David is in the Desert of En Gedi." ²So Saul took three thousand chosen men from all Israel and set out to look for David and his men near the Crags of the Wild Goats.

³He came to the sheep pens along the way; a cave was there, and Saul went in to relieve himself. David and his men were far back in the cave. ⁴The men said, "This is the day the LORD spoke of when he said*ª* to you, 'I will give your enemy into your hands for you to deal with as you wish.' " Then David crept up unnoticed and cut off a corner of Saul's robe.

⁵Afterward, David was conscience-stricken for having cut off a corner of his robe. ⁶He said to his men, "The LORD forbid that I should do such a thing to my master, the LORD's anointed, or lift my hand against him; for he is the anointed of the LORD." ⁷With these words David rebuked his men and did not allow them to attack Saul. And Saul left the cave and went his way.

⁸Then David went out of the cave and called out to Saul, "My lord the king!" When Saul looked behind him, David bowed down and prostrated himself with his face to the ground. ⁹He said to Saul, "Why do you listen when men say, 'David is bent on harming you'? ¹⁰This day you have seen with your own eyes how the LORD delivered you into my hands in the cave. Some urged me to kill you, but I spared you; I said, 'I will not lift my hand against my master, because he is the LORD's anointed.' ¹¹See, my father, look at this piece of your robe in my hand! I cut off the corner of your robe but did not kill you. Now understand and recognize that I am not guilty of wrongdoing or rebellion. I have not wronged you, but you are hunting me down to take my life. ¹²May the LORD judge between you and me. And may the LORD avenge the wrongs you have done to me, but my hand will not touch you. ¹³As the old saying goes, 'From evildoers come evil deeds,' so my hand will not touch you.

¹⁴"Against whom has the king of Israel come out? Whom are you pursuing? A dead dog? A flea? ¹⁵May the LORD be our judge and decide between us. May he consider my cause and uphold it; may he vindicate me by delivering me from your hand."

¹⁶When David finished saying this, Saul asked, "Is that your voice, David my son?" And he wept aloud. ¹⁷"You are more righteous than I," he said. "You have treated me well, but I have treated you badly. ¹⁸You have just now told me of the good you did to me; the LORD delivered me into your hands, but you did not kill me. ¹⁹When a man finds his enemy, does he let him get away unharmed? May the LORD reward you well for the way you treated me today. ²⁰I know that you will surely be king and that the kingdom of Israel will be established in your hands. ²¹Now swear to me by the LORD that you will not cut off my descendants or wipe out my name from my father's family."

²²So David gave his oath to Saul. Then Saul returned home, but David and his men went up to the stronghold.

David, Nabal and Abigail

25 Now Samuel died, and all Israel assembled and mourned for him; and they buried him at his home in Ramah.

Then David moved down into the Desert of Maon.*ᵇ* ²A certain man in Maon, who had property there at Carmel, was very wealthy. He had a thousand goats and three thousand sheep, which he was shearing in Carmel. ³His name was Nabal and his wife's name was Abigail. She was an intelligent and beautiful woman, but her husband, a Calebite, was surly and mean in his dealings.

ª4 Or *"Today the LORD is saying*   *ᵇ1* Some Septuagint manuscripts; Hebrew *Paran*

⁴While David was in the desert, he heard that Nabal was shearing sheep. ⁵So he sent ten young men and said to them, "Go up to Nabal at Carmel and greet him in my name. ⁶Say to him: 'Long life to you! Good health to you and your household! And good health to all that is yours!

⁷" 'Now I hear that it is sheep-shearing time. When your shepherds were with us, we did not mistreat them, and the whole time they were at Carmel nothing of theirs was missing. ⁸Ask your own servants and they will tell you. Therefore be favorable toward my young men, since we come at a festive time. Please give your servants and your son David whatever you can find for them.' "

⁹When David's men arrived, they gave Nabal this message in David's name. Then they waited.

¹⁰Nabal answered David's servants, "Who is this David? Who is this son of Jesse? Many servants are breaking away from their masters these days. ¹¹Why should I take my bread and water, and the meat I have slaughtered for my shearers, and give it to men coming from who knows where?"

¹²David's men turned around and went back. When they arrived, they reported every word. ¹³David said to his men, "Put on your swords!" So they put on their swords, and David put on his. About four hundred men went up with David, while two hundred stayed with the supplies.

¹⁴One of the servants told Nabal's wife Abigail: "David sent messengers from the desert to give our master his greetings, but he hurled insults at them. ¹⁵Yet these men were very good to us. They did not mistreat us, and the whole time we were out in the fields near them nothing was missing. ¹⁶Night and day they were a wall around us all the time we were herding our sheep near them. ¹⁷Now think it over and see what you can do, because disaster is hanging over our master and his whole household. He is such a wicked man that no one can talk to him."

¹⁸Abigail lost no time. She took two hundred loaves of bread, two skins of wine, five dressed sheep, five seahs[a] of roasted grain, a hundred cakes of raisins and two hundred cakes of pressed figs, and loaded them on donkeys. ¹⁹Then she told her servants, "Go on ahead; I'll follow you." But she did not tell her husband Nabal.

²⁰As she came riding her donkey into a mountain ravine, there were David and his men descending toward her, and she met them. ²¹David had just said, "It's been useless—all my watching over this fellow's property in the desert so that nothing of his was missing. He has paid me back evil for good. ²²May God deal with David,[b] be it ever so severely, if by morning I leave alive one male of all who belong to him!"

²³When Abigail saw David, she quickly got off her donkey and bowed down before David with her face to the ground. ²⁴She fell at his feet and said: "My lord, let the blame be on me alone. Please let your servant speak to you; hear what your servant has to say. ²⁵May my lord pay no attention to that wicked man Nabal. He is just like his name—his name is Fool, and folly goes with him. But as for me, your servant, I did not see the men my master sent.

²⁶"Now since the LORD has kept you, my master, from bloodshed and from avenging yourself with your own hands, as surely as the LORD lives and as you live, may your enemies and all who intend to harm my master be like Nabal. ²⁷And let this gift, which your servant has brought to my master, be given to the men who follow you. ²⁸Please forgive your servant's offense, for the LORD will certainly make a lasting dynasty for my master, because he fights the LORD's battles. Let no wrongdoing be found in you as long as you live. ²⁹Even

---

a18 That is, probably about a bushel (about 37 liters)   *b22* Some Septuagint manuscripts; Hebrew *with David's enemies*

though someone is pursuing you to take your life, the life of my master will be bound securely in the bundle of the living by the LORD your God. But the lives of your enemies he will hurl away as from the pocket of a sling. ³⁰When the LORD has done for my master every good thing he promised concerning him and has appointed him leader over Israel, ³¹my master will not have on his conscience the staggering burden of needless bloodshed or of having avenged himself. And when the LORD has brought my master success, remember your servant."

³²David said to Abigail, "Praise be to the LORD, the God of Israel, who has sent you today to meet me. ³³May you be blessed for your good judgment and for keeping me from bloodshed this day and from avenging myself with my own hands. ³⁴Otherwise, as surely as the LORD, the God of Israel, lives, who has kept me from harming you, if you had not come quickly to meet me, not one male belonging to Nabal would have been left alive by daybreak."

³⁵Then David accepted from her hand what she had brought him and said, "Go home in peace. I have heard your words and granted your request."

³⁶When Abigail went to Nabal, he was in the house holding a banquet like that of a king. He was in high spirits and very drunk. So she told him nothing until daybreak. ³⁷Then in the morning, when Nabal was sober, his wife told him all these things, and his heart failed him and he became like a stone. ³⁸About ten days later, the LORD struck Nabal and he died.

³⁹When David heard that Nabal was dead, he said, "Praise be to the LORD, who has upheld my cause against Nabal for treating me with contempt. He has kept his servant from doing wrong and has brought Nabal's wrongdoing down on his own head."

Then David sent word to Abigail,

asking her to become his wife. ⁴⁰His servants went to Carmel and said to Abigail, "David has sent us to you to take you to become his wife."

⁴¹She bowed down with her face to the ground and said, "Here is your maidservant, ready to serve you and wash the feet of my master's servants." ⁴²Abigail quickly got on a donkey and, attended by her five maids, went with David's messengers and became his wife. ⁴³David had also married Ahinoam of Jezreel, and they both were his wives. ⁴⁴But Saul had given his daughter Michal, David's wife, to Paltiel^a son of Laish, who was from Gallim.

David Again Spares Saul's Life

26 The Ziphites went to Saul at Gibeah and said, "Is not David hiding on the hill of Hakilah, which faces Jeshimon?"

²So Saul went down to the Desert of Ziph, with his three thousand chosen men of Israel, to search there for David. ³Saul made his camp beside the road on the hill of Hakilah facing Jeshimon, but David stayed in the desert. When he saw that Saul had followed him there, ⁴he sent out scouts and learned that Saul had definitely arrived.^b

⁵Then David set out and went to the place where Saul had camped. He saw where Saul and Abner son of Ner, the commander of the army, had lain down. Saul was lying inside the camp, with the army encamped around him.

⁶David then asked Ahimelech the Hittite and Abishai son of Zeruiah, Joab's brother, "Who will go down into the camp with me to Saul?"

"I'll go with you," said Abishai.

⁷So David and Abishai went to the army by night, and there was Saul, lying asleep inside the camp with his spear stuck in the ground near his head. Abner and the soldiers were lying around him.

⁸Abishai said to David, "Today God has delivered your enemy into

---

^a44 Hebrew *Palti*, a variant of *Paltiel*   ^b4 Or *had come to Nacon*

your hands. Now let me pin him to the ground with one thrust of my spear; I won't strike him twice."

⁹But David said to Abishai, "Don't destroy him! Who can lay a hand on the LORD's anointed and be guiltless? ¹⁰As surely as the LORD lives," he said, "the LORD himself will strike him; either his time will come and he will die, or he will go into battle and perish. ¹¹But the LORD forbid that I should lay a hand on the LORD's anointed. Now get the spear and water jug that are near his head, and let's go."

¹²So David took the spear and water jug near Saul's head, and they left. No one saw or knew about it, nor did anyone wake up. They were all sleeping, because the LORD had put them into a deep sleep.

¹³Then David crossed over to the other side and stood on top of the hill some distance away; there was a wide space between them. ¹⁴He called out to the army and to Abner son of Ner, "Aren't you going to answer me, Abner?"

Abner replied, "Who are you who calls to the king?"

¹⁵David said, "You're a man, aren't you? And who is like you in Israel? Why didn't you guard your lord the king? Someone came to destroy your lord the king. ¹⁶What you have done is not good. As surely as the LORD lives, you and your men deserve to die, because you did not guard your master, the LORD's anointed. Look around you. Where are the king's spear and water jug that were near his head?"

¹⁷Saul recognized David's voice and said, "Is that your voice, David my son?"

David replied, "Yes it is, my lord the king." ¹⁸And he added, "Why is my lord pursuing his servant? What have I done, and what wrong am I guilty of? ¹⁹Now let my lord the king listen to his servant's words. If the LORD has incited you against me, then may he accept an offering. If, however, men have done it, may they be cursed before the LORD! They have now driven me from my share in the

LORD's inheritance and have said, 'Go, serve other gods.' ²⁰Now do not let my blood fall to the ground far from the presence of the LORD. The king of Israel has come out to look for a flea—as one hunts a partridge in the mountains."

²¹Then Saul said, "I have sinned. Come back, David my son. Because you considered my life precious today, I will not try to harm you again. Surely I have acted like a fool and have erred greatly."

²²"Here is the king's spear," David answered. "Let one of your young men come over and get it. ²³The LORD rewards every man for his righteousness and faithfulness. The LORD delivered you into my hands today, but I would not lay a hand on the LORD's anointed. ²⁴As surely as I valued your life today, so may the LORD value my life and deliver me from all trouble."

²⁵Then Saul said to David, "May you be blessed, my son David; you will do great things and surely triumph."

So David went on his way, and Saul returned home.

David Among the Philistines

27 But David thought to himself, "One of these days I will be destroyed by the hand of Saul. The best thing I can do is to escape to the land of the Philistines. Then Saul will give up searching for me anywhere in Israel, and I will slip out of his hand."

²So David and the six hundred men with him left and went over to Achish son of Maoch king of Gath. ³David and his men settled in Gath with Achish. Each man had his family with him, and David had his two wives: Ahinoam of Jezreel and Abigail of Carmel, the widow of Nabal. ⁴When Saul was told that David had fled to Gath, he no longer searched for him.

⁵Then David said to Achish, "If I have found favor in your eyes, let a place be assigned to me in one of the country towns, that I may live there. Why should your servant live in the royal city with you?"

⁶So on that day Achish gave him

Ziklag, and it has belonged to the kings of Judah ever since. [7]David lived in Philistine territory a year and four months.

[8]Now David and his men went up and raided the Geshurites, the Girzites and the Amalekites. (From ancient times these peoples had lived in the land extending to Shur and Egypt.) [9]Whenever David attacked an area, he did not leave a man or woman alive, but took sheep and cattle, donkeys and camels, and clothes. Then he returned to Achish.

[10]When Achish asked, "Where did you go raiding today?" David would say, "Against the Negev of Judah" or "Against the Negev of Jerahmeel" or "Against the Negev of the Kenites." [11]He did not leave a man or woman alive to be brought to Gath, for he thought, "They might inform on us and say, 'This is what David did.'" And such was his practice as long as he lived in Philistine territory. [12]Achish trusted David and said to himself, "He has become so odious to his people, the Israelites, that he will be my servant forever."

Saul and the Witch of Endor

28 In those days the Philistines gathered their forces to fight against Israel. Achish said to David, "You must understand that you and your men will accompany me in the army."

[2]David said, "Then you will see for yourself what your servant can do."

Achish replied, "Very well, I will make you my bodyguard for life."

[3]Now Samuel was dead, and all Israel had mourned for him and buried him in his own town of Ramah. Saul had expelled the mediums and spiritists from the land.

[4]The Philistines assembled and came and set up camp at Shunem, while Saul gathered all the Israelites and set up camp at Gilboa. [5]When Saul saw the Philistine army, he was afraid; terror filled his heart. [6]He inquired of the LORD, but the LORD did

not answer him by dreams or Urim or prophets. [7]Saul then said to his attendants, "Find me a woman who is a medium, so I may go and inquire of her."

"There is one in Endor," they said.

[8]So Saul disguised himself, putting on other clothes, and at night he and two men went to the woman. "Consult a spirit for me," he said, "and bring up for me the one I name."

[9]But the woman said to him, "Surely you know what Saul has done. He has cut off the mediums and spiritists from the land. Why have you set a trap for my life to bring about my death?"

[10]Saul swore to her by the LORD, "As surely as the LORD lives, you will not be punished for this."

[11]Then the woman asked, "Whom shall I bring up for you?"

"Bring up Samuel," he said.

[12]When the woman saw Samuel, she cried out at the top of her voice and said to Saul, "Why have you deceived me? You are Saul!"

[13]The king said to her, "Don't be afraid. What do you see?"

The woman said, "I see a spirit[a] coming up out of the ground."

[14]"What does he look like?" he asked.

"An old man wearing a robe is coming up," she said.

Then Saul knew it was Samuel, and he bowed down and prostrated himself with his face to the ground.

[15]Samuel said to Saul, "Why have you disturbed me by bringing me up?"

"I am in great distress," Saul said. "The Philistines are fighting against me, and God has turned away from me. He no longer answers me, either by prophets or by dreams. So I have called on you to tell me what to do."

[16]Samuel said, "Why do you consult me, now that the LORD has turned away from you and become your enemy? [17]The LORD has done what he predicted through me. The LORD has torn the kingdom out of your hands and

---

[a]13 Or *see spirits*; or *see gods*

given it to one of your neighbors—to David. [18]Because you did not obey the LORD or carry out his fierce wrath against the Amalekites, the LORD has done this to you today. [19]The LORD will hand over both Israel and you to the Philistines, and tomorrow you and your sons will be with me. The LORD will also hand over the army of Israel to the Philistines."

[20]Immediately Saul fell full length on the ground, filled with fear because of Samuel's words. His strength was gone, for he had eaten nothing all that day and night.

[21]When the woman came to Saul and saw that he was greatly shaken, she said, "Look, your maidservant has obeyed you. I took my life in my hands and did what you told me to do. [22]Now please listen to your servant and let me give you some food so you may eat and have the strength to go on your way."

[23]He refused and said, "I will not eat."

But his men joined the woman in urging him, and he listened to them. He got up from the ground and sat on the couch.

[24]The woman had a fattened calf at the house, which she butchered at once. She took some flour, kneaded it and baked bread without yeast. [25]Then she set it before Saul and his men, and they ate. That same night they got up and left.

Achish Sends David Back to Ziklag

29 The Philistines gathered all their forces at Aphek, and Israel camped by the spring in Jezreel. [2]As the Philistine rulers marched with their units of hundreds and thousands, David and his men were marching at the rear with Achish. [3]The commanders of the Philistines asked, "What about these Hebrews?"

Achish replied, "Is this not David, who was an officer of Saul king of Israel? He has already been with me for over a year, and from the day he left Saul until now, I have found no fault in him."

[4]But the Philistine commanders were angry with him and said, "Send the man back, that he may return to the place you assigned him. He must not go with us into battle, or he will turn against us during the fighting. How better could he regain his master's favor than by taking the heads of our own men? [5]Isn't this the David they sang about in their dances:

" 'Saul has slain his thousands,
    and David his tens of
        thousands'?"

[6]So Achish called David and said to him, "As surely as the LORD lives, you have been reliable, and I would be pleased to have you serve with me in the army. From the day you came to me until now, I have found no fault in you, but the rulers don't approve of you. [7]Turn back and go in peace; do nothing to displease the Philistine rulers."

[8]"But what have I done?" asked David. "What have you found against your servant from the day I came to you until now? Why can't I go and fight against the enemies of my lord the king?"

[9]Achish answered, "I know that you have been as pleasing in my eyes as an angel of God; nevertheless, the Philistine commanders have said, 'He must not go up with us into battle.' [10]Now get up early, along with your master's servants who have come with you, and leave in the morning as soon as it is light."

[11]So David and his men got up early in the morning to go back to the land of the Philistines, and the Philistines went up to Jezreel.

David Destroys the Amalekites

30 David and his men reached Ziklag on the third day. Now the Amalekites had raided the Negev and Ziklag. They had attacked Ziklag and burned it, [2]and had taken captive the women and all who were in it, both young and old. They killed none of them, but carried them off as they went on their way.

[3]When David and his men came to Ziklag, they found it destroyed by fire

and their wives and sons and daughters taken captive. ⁴So David and his men wept aloud until they had no strength left to weep. ⁵David's two wives had been captured—Ahinoam of Jezreel and Abigail, the widow of Nabal of Carmel. ⁶David was greatly distressed because the men were talking of stoning him; each one was bitter in spirit because of his sons and daughters. But David found strength in the LORD his God.

⁷Then David said to Abiathar the priest, the son of Ahimelech, "Bring me the ephod." Abiathar brought it to him, ⁸and David inquired of the LORD, "Shall I pursue this raiding party? Will I overtake them?"

"Pursue them," he answered. "You will certainly overtake them and succeed in the rescue."

⁹David and the six hundred men with him came to the Besor Ravine, where some stayed behind, ¹⁰for two hundred men were too exhausted to cross the ravine. But David and four hundred men continued the pursuit.

¹¹They found an Egyptian in a field and brought him to David. They gave him water to drink and food to eat—¹²part of a cake of pressed figs and two cakes of raisins. He ate and was revived, for he had not eaten any food or drunk any water for three days and three nights.

¹³David asked him, "To whom do you belong, and where do you come from?"

He said, "I am an Egyptian, the slave of an Amalekite. My master abandoned me when I became ill three days ago. ¹⁴We raided the Negev of the Kerethites and the territory belonging to Judah and the Negev of Caleb. And we burned Ziklag."

¹⁵David asked him, "Can you lead me down to this raiding party?"

He answered, "Swear to me before God that you will not kill me or hand me over to my master, and I will take you down to them."

¹⁶He led David down, and there they were, scattered over the countryside, eating, drinking and reveling because of the great amount of plunder they had taken from the land of the Philistines and from Judah. ¹⁷David fought them from dusk until the evening of the next day, and none of them got away, except four hundred young men who rode off on camels and fled. ¹⁸David recovered everything the Amalekites had taken, including his two wives. ¹⁹Nothing was missing: young or old, boy or girl, plunder or anything else they had taken. David brought everything back. ²⁰He took all the flocks and herds, and his men drove them ahead of the other livestock, saying, "This is David's plunder."

²¹Then David came to the two hundred men who had been too exhausted to follow him and who were left behind at the Besor Ravine. They came out to meet David and the people with him. As David and his men approached, he greeted them. ²²But all the evil men and troublemakers among David's followers said, "Because they did not go out with us, we will not share with them the plunder we recovered. However, each man may take his wife and children and go."

²³David replied, "No, my brothers, you must not do that with what the LORD has given us. He has protected us and handed over to us the forces that came against us. ²⁴Who will listen to what you say? The share of the man who stayed with the supplies is to be the same as that of him who went down to the battle. All will share alike." ²⁵David made this a statute and ordinance for Israel from that day to this.

²⁶When David arrived in Ziklag, he sent some of the plunder to the elders of Judah, who were his friends, saying, "Here is a present for you from the plunder of the LORD's enemies."

²⁷He sent it to those who were in Bethel, Ramoth Negev and Jattir; ²⁸to those in Aroer, Siphmoth, Eshtemoa ²⁹and Racal; to the towns of the Jerahmeelites and the Kenites; ³⁰to those in Hormah, Bor Ashan, Athach ³¹and Hebron; and to those in all the

other places where David and his men had roamed.

Saul Takes His Life

31 Now the Philistines fought against Israel; the Israelites fled before them, and many fell slain on Mount Gilboa. ²The Philistines pressed hard after Saul and his sons, and they killed his sons Jonathan, Abinadab and Malki-Shua. ³The fighting grew fierce around Saul, and when the archers overtook him, they wounded him critically.

⁴Saul said to his armor-bearer, "Draw your sword and run me through, or these uncircumcised fellows will come and run me through and abuse me."

But his armor-bearer was terrified and would not do it; so Saul took his own sword and fell on it. ⁵When the armor-bearer saw that Saul was dead, he too fell on his sword and died with him. ⁶So Saul and his three sons and his armor-bearer and all his men died together that same day.

⁷When the Israelites along the valley and those across the Jordan saw that the Israelite army had fled and that Saul and his sons had died, they abandoned their towns and fled. And the Philistines came and occupied them.

⁸The next day, when the Philistines came to strip the dead, they found Saul and his three sons fallen on Mount Gilboa. ⁹They cut off his head and stripped off his armor, and they sent messengers throughout the land of the Philistines to proclaim the news in the temple of their idols and among their people. ¹⁰They put his armor in the temple of the Ashtoreths and fastened his body to the wall of Beth Shan.

¹¹When the people of Jabesh Gilead heard of what the Philistines had done to Saul, ¹²all their valiant men journeyed through the night to Beth Shan. They took down the bodies of Saul and his sons from the wall of Beth Shan and went to Jabesh, where they burned them. ¹³Then they took their bones and buried them under a tamarisk tree at Jabesh, and they fasted seven days.

This book covers David's reign, his many successes and his striking failures. Despite David's sins of adultery and murder, God remained faithful to him. As you read 2 Samuel, acknowledge your own struggle against sin and sorrow, but also remember that God wants you to lay your failures and sins before him and allow him to bless your life with his acceptance and forgiveness.

2 SAMUEL

David Hears of Saul's Death

1 After the death of Saul, David returned from defeating the Amalekites and stayed in Ziklag two days. ²On the third day a man arrived from Saul's camp, with his clothes torn and with dust on his head. When he came to David, he fell to the ground to pay him honor.

³"Where have you come from?" David asked him.

He answered, "I have escaped from the Israelite camp."

⁴"What happened?" David asked. "Tell me."

He said, "The men fled from the battle. Many of them fell and died. And Saul and his son Jonathan are dead."

⁵Then David said to the young man who brought him the report, "How do you know that Saul and his son Jonathan are dead?"

⁶"I happened to be on Mount Gil-boa," the young man said, "and there was Saul, leaning on his spear, with the chariots and riders almost upon him. ⁷When he turned around and saw me, he called out to me, and I said, 'What can I do?'

⁸"He asked me, 'Who are you?'

" 'An Amalekite,' I answered.

⁹"Then he said to me, 'Stand over me and kill me! I am in the throes of death, but I'm still alive.'

¹⁰"So I stood over him and killed him, because I knew that after he had fallen he could not survive. And I took the crown that was on his head and the band on his arm and have brought them here to my lord."

¹¹Then David and all the men with him took hold of their clothes and tore them. ¹²They mourned and wept and fasted till evening for Saul and his son Jonathan, and for the army of the LORD and the house of Israel, because they had fallen by the sword.

¹³David said to the young man who

brought him the report, "Where are you from?"

"I am the son of an alien, an Amalekite," he answered.

[14]David asked him, "Why were you not afraid to lift your hand to destroy the Lord's anointed?"

[15]Then David called one of his men and said, "Go, strike him down!" So he struck him down, and he died. [16]For David had said to him, "Your blood be on your own head. Your own mouth testified against you when you said, 'I killed the Lord's anointed.' "

David's Lament for Saul and Jonathan

[17]David took up this lament concerning Saul and his son Jonathan, [18]and ordered that the men of Judah be taught this lament of the bow (it is written in the Book of Jashar):

[19]"Your glory, O Israel, lies slain on
      your heights.
   How the mighty have fallen!

[20]"Tell it not in Gath,
      proclaim it not in the streets of
         Ashkelon,
   lest the daughters of the
         Philistines be glad,
   lest the daughters of the
         uncircumcised rejoice.

[21]"O mountains of Gilboa,
   may you have neither dew nor
         rain,
   nor fields that yield offerings ⌊of
         grain⌋.
   For there the shield of the mighty
         was defiled,
      the shield of Saul—no longer
         rubbed with oil.
[22]From the blood of the slain,
      from the flesh of the mighty,
   the bow of Jonathan did not turn
         back,
      the sword of Saul did not
         return unsatisfied.

[23]"Saul and Jonathan—
   in life they were loved and
         gracious,

   and in death they were not
      parted.
   They were swifter than eagles,
      they were stronger than lions.

[24]"O daughters of Israel,
      weep for Saul,
   who clothed you in scarlet and
         finery,
      who adorned your garments
         with ornaments of gold.

[25]"How the mighty have fallen in
         battle!
   Jonathan lies slain on your
         heights.
[26]I grieve for you, Jonathan my
         brother;
      you were very dear to me.
   Your love for me was wonderful,
      more wonderful than that of
         women.

[27]"How the mighty have fallen!
   The weapons of war have
         perished!"

David Anointed King Over Judah

2 In the course of time, David inquired of the Lord. "Shall I go up to one of the towns of Judah?" he asked.

The Lord said, "Go up."

David asked, "Where shall I go?"

"To Hebron," the Lord answered.

[2]So David went up there with his two wives, Ahinoam of Jezreel and Abigail, the widow of Nabal of Carmel. [3]David also took the men who were with him, each with his family, and they settled in Hebron and its towns. [4]Then the men of Judah came to Hebron and there they anointed David king over the house of Judah.

When David was told that it was the men of Jabesh Gilead who had buried Saul, [5]he sent messengers to the men of Jabesh Gilead to say to them, "The Lord bless you for showing this kindness to Saul your master by burying him. [6]May the Lord now show you kindness and faithfulness, and I too will show you the same favor because you have done this. [7]Now then, be strong and brave, for Saul your master is dead, and the

VERSE:	AUTHOR:	PASSAGE:
2 Samuel 1:12	Jean Shaw	2 Samuel 1:1–16

A Time to Mourn

When Jacob heard the story that his son Joseph had been killed, he tore his clothes, put on sackcloth, and mourned many days. David tore his clothes when he heard of Saul's death; he wept and fasted until evening. The ancients had a proper outlet for their grief. Our culture is much more restrictive . . .

Holding our heads high when we want to tear our clothes is one of the hardest things to do in life. The words "Try to be brave, dear" help very little. We want to wail and lament, put on sackcloth and ashes, and show our hurt to the world. But we cannot. We are told to buy a new dress — "Something in a bright color" — and to plunge into a sea of activities "to get our mind off our loss."

Those who have studied death and dying agree that a time of grief is essential and therapeutic. Honest acknowledgment of our feelings helps us to face life again without our loved one. But the time comes when tearing must stop. We must begin mending our lives. God offers all his resources. With David we can say, "You turned my wailing into dancing; you removed my sackcloth and clothed me with joy, that my heart may sing to you and not be silent. O LORD my God, I will give you thanks forever" (Psalm 30:11–12).

ADDITIONAL SCRIPTURE READINGS
Psalm 30; Ecclesiastes 3:1–8
Go to page 384 for your next devotional reading.

house of Judah has anointed me king over them."

War Between the Houses of David and Saul

⁸Meanwhile, Abner son of Ner, the commander of Saul's army, had taken Ish-Bosheth son of Saul and brought him over to Mahanaim. ⁹He made him king over Gilead, Ashuri[a] and Jezreel, and also over Ephraim, Benjamin and all Israel.

¹⁰Ish-Bosheth son of Saul was forty years old when he became king over Israel, and he reigned two years. The house of Judah, however, followed David. ¹¹The length of time David was king in Hebron over the house of Judah was seven years and six months.

¹²Abner son of Ner, together with the men of Ish-Bosheth son of Saul, left Mahanaim and went to Gibeon. ¹³Joab son of Zeruiah and David's men went out and met them at the pool of Gibeon. One group sat down on one side of the pool and one group on the other side.

¹⁴Then Abner said to Joab, "Let's have some of the young men get up and fight hand to hand in front of us."

"All right, let them do it," Joab said.

¹⁵So they stood up and were counted off—twelve men for Benjamin and Ish-Bosheth son of Saul, and twelve for David. ¹⁶Then each man grabbed his opponent by the head and thrust his dagger into his opponent's side, and they fell down together. So that place in Gibeon was called Helkath Hazzurim.[b]

¹⁷The battle that day was very fierce, and Abner and the men of Israel were defeated by David's men.

¹⁸The three sons of Zeruiah were there: Joab, Abishai and Asahel. Now Asahel was as fleet-footed as a wild gazelle. ¹⁹He chased Abner, turning neither to the right nor to the left as he pursued him. ²⁰Abner looked behind him and asked, "Is that you, Asahel?"

"It is," he answered.

²¹Then Abner said to him, "Turn aside to the right or to the left; take on one of the young men and strip him of his weapons." But Asahel would not stop chasing him.

²²Again Abner warned Asahel, "Stop chasing me! Why should I strike you down? How could I look your brother Joab in the face?"

²³But Asahel refused to give up the pursuit; so Abner thrust the butt of his spear into Asahel's stomach, and the spear came out through his back. He fell there and died on the spot. And every man stopped when he came to the place where Asahel had fallen and died.

²⁴But Joab and Abishai pursued Abner, and as the sun was setting, they came to the hill of Ammah, near Giah on the way to the wasteland of Gibeon. ²⁵Then the men of Benjamin rallied behind Abner. They formed themselves into a group and took their stand on top of a hill.

²⁶Abner called out to Joab, "Must the sword devour forever? Don't you realize that this will end in bitterness? How long before you order your men to stop pursuing their brothers?"

²⁷Joab answered, "As surely as God lives, if you had not spoken, the men would have continued the pursuit of their brothers until morning.[c]"

²⁸So Joab blew the trumpet, and all the men came to a halt; they no longer pursued Israel, nor did they fight anymore.

²⁹All that night Abner and his men marched through the Arabah. They crossed the Jordan, continued through the whole Bithron[d] and came to Mahanaim.

³⁰Then Joab returned from pursuing Abner and assembled all his men.

---

[a]9 Or *Asher*   [b]16 *Helkath Hazzurim* means *field of daggers* or *field of hostilities.*   [c]27 Or *spoken this morning, the men would not have taken up the pursuit of their brothers;* or *spoken, the men would have given up the pursuit of their brothers by morning*   [d]29 Or *morning;* or *ravine;* the meaning of the Hebrew for this word is uncertain.

Besides Asahel, nineteen of David's men were found missing. [31]But David's men had killed three hundred and sixty Benjamites who were with Abner. [32]They took Asahel and buried him in his father's tomb at Bethlehem. Then Joab and his men marched all night and arrived at Hebron by daybreak.

3 The war between the house of Saul and the house of David lasted a long time. David grew stronger and stronger, while the house of Saul grew weaker and weaker.

[2]Sons were born to David in Hebron:

His firstborn was Amnon the son of Ahinoam of Jezreel;

[3]his second, Kileab the son of Abigail the widow of Nabal of Carmel;

the third, Absalom the son of Maacah daughter of Talmai king of Geshur;

[4]the fourth, Adonijah the son of Haggith;

the fifth, Shephatiah the son of Abital;

[5]and the sixth, Ithream the son of David's wife Eglah.

These were born to David in Hebron.

Abner Goes Over to David

[6]During the war between the house of Saul and the house of David, Abner had been strengthening his own position in the house of Saul. [7]Now Saul had had a concubine named Rizpah daughter of Aiah. And Ish-Bosheth said to Abner, "Why did you sleep with my father's concubine?"

[8]Abner was very angry because of what Ish-Bosheth said and he answered, "Am I a dog's head—on Judah's side? This very day I am loyal to the house of your father Saul and to his family and friends. I haven't handed you over to David. Yet now you accuse me of an offense involving this woman! [9]May God deal with Abner, be it ever so severely, if I do not do for David what the LORD promised him on oath [10]and transfer the kingdom from the house of Saul and es-

tablish David's throne over Israel and Judah from Dan to Beersheba." [11]Ish-Bosheth did not dare to say another word to Abner, because he was afraid of him.

[12]Then Abner sent messengers on his behalf to say to David, "Whose land is it? Make an agreement with me, and I will help you bring all Israel over to you."

[13]"Good," said David. "I will make an agreement with you. But I demand one thing of you: Do not come into my presence unless you bring Michal daughter of Saul when you come to see me." [14]Then David sent messengers to Ish-Bosheth son of Saul, demanding, "Give me my wife Michal, whom I betrothed to myself for the price of a hundred Philistine foreskins."

[15]So Ish-Bosheth gave orders and had her taken away from her husband Paltiel son of Laish. [16]Her husband, however, went with her, weeping behind her all the way to Bahurim. Then Abner said to him, "Go back home!" So he went back.

[17]Abner conferred with the elders of Israel and said, "For some time you have wanted to make David your king. [18]Now do it! For the LORD promised David, 'By my servant David I will rescue my people Israel from the hand of the Philistines and from the hand of all their enemies.' "

[19]Abner also spoke to the Benjamites in person. Then he went to Hebron to tell David everything that Israel and the whole house of Benjamin wanted to do. [20]When Abner, who had twenty men with him, came to David at Hebron, David prepared a feast for him and his men. [21]Then Abner said to David, "Let me go at once and assemble all Israel for my lord the king, so that they may make a compact with you, and that you may rule over all that your heart desires." So David sent Abner away, and he went in peace.

Joab Murders Abner

[22]Just then David's men and Joab returned from a raid and brought

with them a great deal of plunder. But Abner was no longer with David in Hebron, because David had sent him away, and he had gone in peace. ²³When Joab and all the soldiers with him arrived, he was told that Abner son of Ner had come to the king and that the king had sent him away and that he had gone in peace.

²⁴So Joab went to the king and said, "What have you done? Look, Abner came to you. Why did you let him go? Now he is gone! ²⁵You know Abner son of Ner; he came to deceive you and observe your movements and find out everything you are doing."

²⁶Joab then left David and sent messengers after Abner, and they brought him back from the well of Sirah. But David did not know it. ²⁷Now when Abner returned to Hebron, Joab took him aside into the gateway, as though to speak with him privately. And there, to avenge the blood of his brother Asahel, Joab stabbed him in the stomach, and he died.

²⁸Later, when David heard about this, he said, "I and my kingdom are forever innocent before the LORD concerning the blood of Abner son of Ner. ²⁹May his blood fall upon the head of Joab and upon all his father's house! May Joab's house never be without someone who has a running sore or leprosy*a* or who leans on a crutch or who falls by the sword or who lacks food."

³⁰(Joab and his brother Abishai murdered Abner because he had killed their brother Asahel in the battle at Gibeon.)

³¹Then David said to Joab and all the people with him, "Tear your clothes and put on sackcloth and walk in mourning in front of Abner." King David himself walked behind the bier. ³²They buried Abner in Hebron, and the king wept aloud at Abner's tomb. All the people wept also.

³³The king sang this lament for Abner:

"Should Abner have died as the lawless die?
³⁴ Your hands were not bound,
    your feet were not fettered.
You fell as one falls before wicked men."

And all the people wept over him again.

³⁵Then they all came and urged David to eat something while it was still day; but David took an oath, saying, "May God deal with me, be it ever so severely, if I taste bread or anything else before the sun sets!"

³⁶All the people took note and were pleased; indeed, everything the king did pleased them. ³⁷So on that day all the people and all Israel knew that the king had no part in the murder of Abner son of Ner.

³⁸Then the king said to his men, "Do you not realize that a prince and a great man has fallen in Israel this day? ³⁹And today, though I am the anointed king, I am weak, and these sons of Zeruiah are too strong for me. May the LORD repay the evildoer according to his evil deeds!"

Ish-Bosheth Murdered

4 When Ish-Bosheth son of Saul heard that Abner had died in Hebron, he lost courage, and all Israel became alarmed. ²Now Saul's son had two men who were leaders of raiding bands. One was named Baanah and the other Recab; they were sons of Rimmon the Beerothite from the tribe of Benjamin—Beeroth is considered part of Benjamin, ³because the people of Beeroth fled to Gittaim and have lived there as aliens to this day.

⁴(Jonathan son of Saul had a son who was lame in both feet. He was five years old when the news about Saul and Jonathan came from Jezreel. His nurse picked him up and fled, but as she hurried to leave, he fell and became crippled. His name was Mephibosheth.)

⁵Now Recab and Baanah, the sons of Rimmon the Beerothite, set out for

---

a29 The Hebrew word was used for various diseases affecting the skin—not necessarily leprosy.

the house of Ish-Bosheth, and they arrived there in the heat of the day while he was taking his noonday rest. 6They went into the inner part of the house as if to get some wheat, and they stabbed him in the stomach. Then Recab and his brother Baanah slipped away.

7They had gone into the house while he was lying on the bed in his bedroom. After they stabbed and killed him, they cut off his head. Taking it with them, they traveled all night by way of the Arabah. 8They brought the head of Ish-Bosheth to David at Hebron and said to the king, "Here is the head of Ish-Bosheth son of Saul, your enemy, who tried to take your life. This day the LORD has avenged my lord the king against Saul and his offspring."

9David answered Recab and his brother Baanah, the sons of Rimmon the Beerothite, "As surely as the LORD lives, who has delivered me out of all trouble, 10when a man told me, 'Saul is dead,' and thought he was bringing good news, I seized him and put him to death in Ziklag. That was the reward I gave him for his news! 11How much more—when wicked men have killed an innocent man in his own house and on his own bed—should I not now demand his blood from your hand and rid the earth of you!"

12So David gave an order to his men, and they killed them. They cut off their hands and feet and hung the bodies by the pool in Hebron. But they took the head of Ish-Bosheth and buried it in Abner's tomb at Hebron.

David Becomes King Over Israel

5 All the tribes of Israel came to David at Hebron and said, "We are your own flesh and blood. 2In the past, while Saul was king over us, you were the one who led Israel on their military campaigns. And the LORD said to you, 'You will shepherd my people Israel, and you will become their ruler.' "

3When all the elders of Israel had come to King David at Hebron, the king made a compact with them at Hebron before the LORD, and they anointed David king over Israel.

4David was thirty years old when he became king, and he reigned forty years. 5In Hebron he reigned over Judah seven years and six months, and in Jerusalem he reigned over all Israel and Judah thirty-three years.

David Conquers Jerusalem

6The king and his men marched to Jerusalem to attack the Jebusites, who lived there. The Jebusites said to David, "You will not get in here; even the blind and the lame can ward you off." They thought, "David cannot get in here." 7Nevertheless, David captured the fortress of Zion, the City of David.

8On that day, David said, "Anyone who conquers the Jebusites will have to use the water shaft*a* to reach those 'lame and blind' who are David's enemies.*b*" That is why they say, "The 'blind and lame' will not enter the palace."

9David then took up residence in the fortress and called it the City of David. He built up the area around it, from the supporting terraces*c* inward. 10And he became more and more powerful, because the LORD God Almighty was with him.

11Now Hiram king of Tyre sent messengers to David, along with cedar logs and carpenters and stonemasons, and they built a palace for David. 12And David knew that the LORD had established him as king over Israel and had exalted his kingdom for the sake of his people Israel.

13After he left Hebron, David took more concubines and wives in Jerusalem, and more sons and daughters were born to him. 14These are the names of the children born to him there: Shammua, Shobab, Nathan, Solomon, 15Ibhar, Elishua, Nepheg, Japhia, 16Elishama, Eliada and Eliphelet.

---

*a*8 Or *use scaling hooks*   *b*8 Or *are hated by David*   *c*9 Or *the Millo*

David Defeats the Philistines

17When the Philistines heard that David had been anointed king over Israel, they went up in full force to search for him, but David heard about it and went down to the stronghold. **18**Now the Philistines had come and spread out in the Valley of Rephaim; **19**so David inquired of the Lord, "Shall I go and attack the Philistines? Will you hand them over to me?"

The Lord answered him, "Go, for I will surely hand the Philistines over to you."

20So David went to Baal Perazim, and there he defeated them. He said, "As waters break out, the Lord has broken out against my enemies before me." So that place was called Baal Perazim.*a* **21**The Philistines abandoned their idols there, and David and his men carried them off.

22Once more the Philistines came up and spread out in the Valley of Rephaim; **23**so David inquired of the Lord, and he answered, "Do not go straight up, but circle around behind them and attack them in front of the balsam trees. **24**As soon as you hear the sound of marching in the tops of the balsam trees, move quickly, because that will mean the Lord has gone out in front of you to strike the Philistine army." **25**So David did as the Lord commanded him, and he struck down the Philistines all the way from Gibeon*b* to Gezer.

The Ark Brought to Jerusalem

6 David again brought together out of Israel chosen men, thirty thousand in all. **2**He and all his men set out from Baalah of Judah*c* to bring up from there the ark of God, which is called by the Name,*d* the name of the Lord Almighty, who is enthroned between the cherubim that are on the

ark. **3**They set the ark of God on a new cart and brought it from the house of Abinadab, which was on the hill. Uzzah and Ahio, sons of Abinadab, were guiding the new cart **4**with the ark of God on it,*e* and Ahio was walking in front of it. **5**David and the whole house of Israel were celebrating with all their might before the Lord, with songs*f* and with harps, lyres, tambourines, sistrums and cymbals.

6When they came to the threshing floor of Nacon, Uzzah reached out and took hold of the ark of God, because the oxen stumbled. **7**The Lord's anger burned against Uzzah because of his irreverent act; therefore God struck him down and he died there beside the ark of God.

8Then David was angry because the Lord's wrath had broken out against Uzzah, and to this day that place is called Perez Uzzah.*g*

9David was afraid of the Lord that day and said, "How can the ark of the Lord ever come to me?" **10**He was not willing to take the ark of the Lord to be with him in the City of David. Instead, he took it aside to the house of Obed-Edom the Gittite. **11**The ark of the Lord remained in the house of Obed-Edom the Gittite for three months, and the Lord blessed him and his entire household.

12Now King David was told, "The Lord has blessed the household of Obed-Edom and everything he has, because of the ark of God." So David went down and brought up the ark of God from the house of Obed-Edom to the City of David with rejoicing. **13**When those who were carrying the ark of the Lord had taken six steps, he sacrificed a bull and a fattened calf. **14**David, wearing a linen ephod, danced before the Lord with all his might, **15**while he and the entire house of Israel brought up the ark of the

---

a20 Baal Perazim means *the lord who breaks out.*   *b25* Septuagint (see also 1 Chron. 14:16); Hebrew Geba   *c2* That is, Kiriath Jearim; Hebrew Baale Judah, a variant of Baalah of Judah *d2* Hebrew; Septuagint and Vulgate do not have *the Name.*   *e3,4* Dead Sea Scrolls and some Septuagint manuscripts; Masoretic Text cart *4and they brought it with the ark of God from the house of Abinadab, which was on the hill*   *f5* See Dead Sea Scrolls, Septuagint and 1 Chronicles 13:8; Masoretic Text celebrating before the Lord with all kinds of instruments made of pine.   *g8* Perez Uzzah means outbreak against Uzzah.

LORD with shouts and the sound of trumpets.

¹⁶As the ark of the LORD was entering the City of David, Michal daughter of Saul watched from a window. And when she saw King David leaping and dancing before the LORD, she despised him in her heart.

¹⁷They brought the ark of the LORD and set it in its place inside the tent that David had pitched for it, and David sacrificed burnt offerings and fellowship offerings^a before the LORD. ¹⁸After he had finished sacrificing the burnt offerings and fellowship offerings, he blessed the people in the name of the LORD Almighty. ¹⁹Then he gave a loaf of bread, a cake of dates and a cake of raisins to each person in the whole crowd of Israelites, both men and women. And all the people went to their homes.

²⁰When David returned home to bless his household, Michal daughter of Saul came out to meet him and said, "How the king of Israel has distinguished himself today, disrobing in the sight of the slave girls of his servants as any vulgar fellow would!"

²¹David said to Michal, "It was before the LORD, who chose me rather than your father or anyone from his house when he appointed me ruler over the LORD's people Israel—I will celebrate before the LORD. ²²I will become even more undignified than this, and I will be humiliated in my own eyes. But by these slave girls you spoke of, I will be held in honor."

²³And Michal daughter of Saul had no children to the day of her death.

God's Promise to David

7 After the king was settled in his palace and the LORD had given him rest from all his enemies around him, ²he said to Nathan the prophet, "Here I am, living in a palace of cedar, while the ark of God remains in a tent."

³Nathan replied to the king, "Whatever you have in mind, go ahead and do it, for the LORD is with you."

⁴That night the word of the LORD came to Nathan, saying:

⁵"Go and tell my servant David, 'This is what the LORD says: Are you the one to build me a house to dwell in? ⁶I have not dwelt in a house from the day I brought the Israelites up out of Egypt to this day. I have been moving from place to place with a tent as my dwelling. ⁷Wherever I have moved with all the Israelites, did I ever say to any of their rulers whom I commanded to shepherd my people Israel, "Why have you not built me a house of cedar?"'

⁸"Now then, tell my servant David, 'This is what the LORD Almighty says: I took you from the pasture and from following the flock to be ruler over my people Israel. ⁹I have been with you wherever you have gone, and I have cut off all your enemies from before you. Now I will make your name great, like the names of the greatest men of the earth. ¹⁰And I will provide a place for my people Israel and will plant them so that they can have a home of their own and no longer be disturbed. Wicked people will not oppress them anymore, as they did at the beginning ¹¹and have done ever since the time I appointed leaders^b over my people Israel. I will also give you rest from all your enemies.

" 'The LORD declares to you that the LORD himself will establish a house for you: ¹²When your days are over and you rest with your fathers, I will raise up your offspring to succeed you, who will come from your own body, and I will establish his kingdom. ¹³He is the one who will build a house for my Name, and I will establish the throne of his kingdom forever. ¹⁴I will be

---

^a17 Traditionally *peace offerings*; also in verse 18   ^b11 Traditionally *judges*

his father, and he will be my son. When he does wrong, I will punish him with the rod of men, with floggings inflicted by men. [15]But my love will never be taken away from him, as I took it away from Saul, whom I removed from before you. [16]Your house and your kingdom will endure forever before me[a]; your throne will be established forever.' "

[17]Nathan reported to David all the words of this entire revelation.

David's Prayer

[18]Then King David went in and sat before the LORD, and he said:

"Who am I, O Sovereign LORD, and what is my family, that you have brought me this far? [19]And as if this were not enough in your sight, O Sovereign LORD, you have also spoken about the future of the house of your servant. Is this your usual way of dealing with man, O Sovereign LORD?

[20]"What more can David say to you? For you know your servant, O Sovereign LORD. [21]For the sake of your word and according to your will, you have done this great thing and made it known to your servant.

[22]"How great you are, O Sovereign LORD! There is no one like you, and there is no God but you, as we have heard with our own ears. [23]And who is like your people Israel—the one nation on earth that God went out to redeem as a people for himself, and to make a name for himself, and to perform great and awesome wonders by driving out nations and their gods from before your people, whom you redeemed from Egypt?[b] [24]You have established your people Israel as your very own forever, and you, O LORD, have become their God.

[25]"And now, LORD God, keep forever the promise you have made concerning your servant and his house. Do as you promised, [26]so that your name will be great forever. Then men will say, 'The LORD Almighty is God over Israel!' And the house of your servant David will be established before you.

[27]"O LORD Almighty, God of Israel, you have revealed this to your servant, saying, 'I will build a house for you.' So your servant has found courage to offer you this prayer. [28]O Sovereign LORD, you are God! Your words are trustworthy, and you have promised these good things to your servant. [29]Now be pleased to bless the house of your servant, that it may continue forever in your sight; for you, O Sovereign LORD, have spoken, and with your blessing the house of your servant will be blessed forever."

David's Victories

8 In the course of time, David defeated the Philistines and subdued them, and he took Metheg Ammah from the control of the Philistines.

[2]David also defeated the Moabites. He made them lie down on the ground and measured them off with a length of cord. Every two lengths of them were put to death, and the third length was allowed to live. So the Moabites became subject to David and brought tribute.

[3]Moreover, David fought Hadadezer son of Rehob, king of Zobah, when he went to restore his control along the Euphrates River. [4]David captured a thousand of his chariots,

---

[a]16 Some Hebrew manuscripts and Septuagint; most Hebrew manuscripts *you*   [b]23 See Septuagint and 1 Chron. 17:21; Hebrew *wonders for your land and before your people, whom you redeemed from Egypt, from the nations and their gods.*

seven thousand charioteers*a* and twenty thousand foot soldiers. He hamstrung all but a hundred of the chariot horses.

⁵When the Arameans of Damascus came to help Hadadezer king of Zobah, David struck down twenty-two thousand of them. ⁶He put garrisons in the Aramean kingdom of Damascus, and the Arameans became subject to him and brought tribute. The LORD gave David victory wherever he went.

⁷David took the gold shields that belonged to the officers of Hadadezer and brought them to Jerusalem. ⁸From Tebah*b* and Berothai, towns that belonged to Hadadezer, King David took a great quantity of bronze.

⁹When Tou*c* king of Hamath heard that David had defeated the entire army of Hadadezer, ¹⁰he sent his son Joram*d* to King David to greet him and congratulate him on his victory in battle over Hadadezer, who had been at war with Tou. Joram brought with him articles of silver and gold and bronze.

¹¹King David dedicated these articles to the LORD, as he had done with the silver and gold from all the nations he had subdued: ¹²Edom*e* and Moab, the Ammonites and the Philistines, and Amalek. He also dedicated the plunder taken from Hadadezer son of Rehob, king of Zobah.

¹³And David became famous after he returned from striking down eighteen thousand Edomites*f* in the Valley of Salt.

¹⁴He put garrisons throughout Edom, and all the Edomites became subject to David. The LORD gave David victory wherever he went.

David's Officials

¹⁵David reigned over all Israel, doing what was just and right for all his people. ¹⁶Joab son of Zeruiah was over the army; Jehoshaphat son of Ahilud was recorder; ¹⁷Zadok son of Ahitub and Ahimelech son of Abiathar were priests; Seraiah was secretary; ¹⁸Benaiah son of Jehoiada was over the Kerethites and Pelethites; and David's sons were royal advisers.*g*

David and Mephibosheth

9 David asked, "Is there anyone still left of the house of Saul to whom I can show kindness for Jonathan's sake?"

²Now there was a servant of Saul's household named Ziba. They called him to appear before David, and the king said to him, "Are you Ziba?"

"Your servant," he replied.

³The king asked, "Is there no one still left of the house of Saul to whom I can show God's kindness?"

Ziba answered the king, "There is still a son of Jonathan; he is crippled in both feet."

⁴"Where is he?" the king asked.

Ziba answered, "He is at the house of Makir son of Ammiel in Lo Debar."

⁵So King David had him brought from Lo Debar, from the house of Makir son of Ammiel.

⁶When Mephibosheth son of Jonathan, the son of Saul, came to David, he bowed down to pay him honor.

David said, "Mephibosheth!"

"Your servant," he replied.

⁷"Don't be afraid," David said to him, "for I will surely show you kindness for the sake of your father Jonathan. I will restore to you all the land that belonged to your grandfather Saul, and you will always eat at my table."

⁸Mephibosheth bowed down and said, "What is your servant, that you should notice a dead dog like me?"

⁹Then the king summoned Ziba, Saul's servant, and said to him, "I have given your master's grandson

---

*a*4 Septuagint (see also Dead Sea Scrolls and 1 Chron. 18:4); Masoretic Text *captured seventeen hundred of his charioteers*　　*b*8 See some Septuagint manuscripts (see also 1 Chron. 18:8); Hebrew *Betah.*　　*c*9 Hebrew *Toi,* a variant of *Tou;* also in verse 10　　*d*10 A variant of *Hadoram*　　*e*12 Some Hebrew manuscripts, Septuagint and Syriac (see also 1 Chron. 18:11); most Hebrew manuscripts *Aram*　　*f*13 A few Hebrew manuscripts, Septuagint and Syriac (see also 1 Chron. 18:12); most Hebrew manuscripts *Aram* (that is, Arameans)　　*g*18 Or *were priests*

everything that belonged to Saul and his family. [10]You and your sons and your servants are to farm the land for him and bring in the crops, so that your master's grandson may be provided for. And Mephibosheth, grandson of your master, will always eat at my table." (Now Ziba had fifteen sons and twenty servants.)

[11]Then Ziba said to the king, "Your servant will do whatever my lord the king commands his servant to do." So Mephibosheth ate at David's[a] table like one of the king's sons.

[12]Mephibosheth had a young son named Mica, and all the members of Ziba's household were servants of Mephibosheth. [13]And Mephibosheth lived in Jerusalem, because he always ate at the king's table, and he was crippled in both feet.

David Defeats the Ammonites

10 In the course of time, the king of the Ammonites died, and his son Hanun succeeded him as king. [2]David thought, "I will show kindness to Hanun son of Nahash, just as his father showed kindness to me." So David sent a delegation to express his sympathy to Hanun concerning his father.

When David's men came to the land of the Ammonites, [3]the Ammonite nobles said to Hanun their lord, "Do you think David is honoring your father by sending men to you to express sympathy? Hasn't David sent them to you to explore the city and spy it out and overthrow it?" [4]So Hanun seized David's men, shaved off half of each man's beard, cut off their garments in the middle at the buttocks, and sent them away.

[5]When David was told about this, he sent messengers to meet the men, for they were greatly humiliated. The king said, "Stay at Jericho till your beards have grown, and then come back."

[6]When the Ammonites realized that they had become a stench in David's nostrils, they hired twenty thousand Aramean foot soldiers from Beth Rehob and Zobah, as well as the king of Maacah with a thousand men, and also twelve thousand men from Tob.

[7]On hearing this, David sent Joab out with the entire army of fighting men. [8]The Ammonites came out and drew up in battle formation at the entrance to their city gate, while the Arameans of Zobah and Rehob and the men of Tob and Maacah were by themselves in the open country.

[9]Joab saw that there were battle lines in front of him and behind him; so he selected some of the best troops in Israel and deployed them against the Arameans. [10]He put the rest of the men under the command of Abishai his brother and deployed them against the Ammonites. [11]Joab said, "If the Arameans are too strong for me, then you are to come to my rescue; but if the Ammonites are too strong for you, then I will come to rescue you. [12]Be strong and let us fight bravely for our people and the cities of our God. The LORD will do what is good in his sight."

[13]Then Joab and the troops with him advanced to fight the Arameans, and they fled before him. [14]When the Ammonites saw that the Arameans were fleeing, they fled before Abishai and went inside the city. So Joab returned from fighting the Ammonites and came to Jerusalem.

[15]After the Arameans saw that they had been routed by Israel, they regrouped. [16]Hadadezer had Arameans brought from beyond the River[b]; they went to Helam, with Shobach the commander of Hadadezer's army leading them.

[17]When David was told of this, he gathered all Israel, crossed the Jordan and went to Helam. The Arameans formed their battle lines to meet David and fought against him. [18]But they fled before Israel, and David killed seven hundred of their charioteers and forty thousand of their foot sol-

---

[a]11 Septuagint; Hebrew *my*   [b]16 That is, the Euphrates

diers.[a] He also struck down Shobach the commander of their army, and he died there. 19When all the kings who were vassals of Hadadezer saw that they had been defeated by Israel, they made peace with the Israelites and became subject to them.

So the Arameans were afraid to help the Ammonites anymore.

David and Bathsheba

11 In the spring, at the time when kings go off to war, David sent Joab out with the king's men and the whole Israelite army. They destroyed the Ammonites and besieged Rabbah. But David remained in Jerusalem.

2One evening David got up from his bed and walked around on the roof of the palace. From the roof he saw a woman bathing. The woman was very beautiful, 3and David sent someone to find out about her. The man said, "Isn't this Bathsheba, the daughter of Eliam and the wife of Uriah the Hittite?" 4Then David sent messengers to get her. She came to him, and he slept with her. (She had purified herself from her uncleanness.) Then[b] she went back home. 5The woman conceived and sent word to David, saying, "I am pregnant."

6So David sent this word to Joab: "Send me Uriah the Hittite." And Joab sent him to David. 7When Uriah came to him, David asked him how Joab was, how the soldiers were and how the war was going. 8Then David said to Uriah, "Go down to your house and wash your feet." So Uriah left the palace, and a gift from the king was sent after him. 9But Uriah slept at the entrance to the palace with all his master's servants and did not go down to his house.

10When David was told, "Uriah did not go home," he asked him, "Haven't you just come from a distance? Why didn't you go home?" 11Uriah said to David, "The ark and Israel and Judah are staying in tents, and my master Joab and my lord's men are camped in the open fields. How could I go to my house to eat and drink and lie with my wife? As surely as you live, I will not do such a thing!"

12Then David said to him, "Stay here one more day, and tomorrow I will send you back." So Uriah remained in Jerusalem that day and the next. 13At David's invitation, he ate and drank with him, and David made him drunk. But in the evening Uriah went out to sleep on his mat among his master's servants; he did not go home.

14In the morning David wrote a letter to Joab and sent it with Uriah. 15In it he wrote, "Put Uriah in the front line where the fighting is fiercest. Then withdraw from him so he will be struck down and die."

16So while Joab had the city under siege, he put Uriah at a place where he knew the strongest defenders were. 17When the men of the city came out and fought against Joab, some of the men in David's army fell; moreover, Uriah the Hittite died.

18Joab sent David a full account of the battle. 19He instructed the messenger: "When you have finished giving the king this account of the battle, 20the king's anger may flare up, and he may ask you, 'Why did you get so close to the city to fight? Didn't you know they would shoot arrows from the wall? 21Who killed Abimelech son of Jerub-Besheth[c]? Didn't a woman throw an upper millstone on him from the wall, so that he died in Thebez? Why did you get so close to the wall?' If he asks you this, then say to him, 'Also, your servant Uriah the Hittite is dead.' "

22The messenger set out, and when he arrived he told David everything Joab had sent him to say. 23The messenger said to David, "The men overpowered us and came out against us in the open, but we drove them back to the entrance to the city gate. 24Then

---

a18 Some Septuagint manuscripts (see also 1 Chron. 19:18); Hebrew *horsemen*   *b4* Or *with her.*
When she purified herself from her uncleanness,   *c21* Also known as *Jerub-Baal* (that is, Gideon)

the archers shot arrows at your servants from the wall, and some of the king's men died. Moreover, your servant Uriah the Hittite is dead."

²⁵David told the messenger, "Say this to Joab: 'Don't let this upset you; the sword devours one as well as another. Press the attack against the city and destroy it.' Say this to encourage Joab."

²⁶When Uriah's wife heard that her husband was dead, she mourned for him. ²⁷After the time of mourning was over, David had her brought to his house, and she became his wife and bore him a son. But the thing David had done displeased the LORD.

Nathan Rebukes David

12 The LORD sent Nathan to David. When he came to him, he said, "There were two men in a certain town, one rich and the other poor. ²The rich man had a very large number of sheep and cattle, ³but the poor man had nothing except one little ewe lamb he had bought. He raised it, and it grew up with him and his children. It shared his food, drank from his cup and even slept in his arms. It was like a daughter to him.

⁴"Now a traveler came to the rich man, but the rich man refrained from taking one of his own sheep or cattle to prepare a meal for the traveler who had come to him. Instead, he took the ewe lamb that belonged to the poor man and prepared it for the one who had come to him."

⁵David burned with anger against the man and said to Nathan, "As surely as the LORD lives, the man who did this deserves to die! ⁶He must pay for that lamb four times over, because he did such a thing and had no pity."

⁷Then Nathan said to David, "You are the man! This is what the LORD, the God of Israel, says: 'I anointed you king over Israel, and I delivered you from the hand of Saul. ⁸I gave your master's house to you, and your master's wives into your arms. I gave

you the house of Israel and Judah. And if all this had been too little, I would have given you even more. ⁹Why did you despise the word of the LORD by doing what is evil in his eyes? You struck down Uriah the Hittite with the sword and took his wife to be your own. You killed him with the sword of the Ammonites. ¹⁰Now, therefore, the sword will never depart from your house, because you despised me and took the wife of Uriah the Hittite to be your own.'

¹¹"This is what the LORD says: 'Out of your own household I am going to bring calamity upon you. Before your very eyes I will take your wives and give them to one who is close to you, and he will lie with your wives in broad daylight. ¹²You did it in secret, but I will do this thing in broad daylight before all Israel.' "

¹³Then David said to Nathan, "I have sinned against the LORD."

Nathan replied, "The LORD has taken away your sin. You are not going to die. ¹⁴But because by doing this you have made the enemies of the LORD show utter contempt,ᵃ the son born to you will die."

¹⁵After Nathan had gone home, the LORD struck the child that Uriah's wife had borne to David, and he became ill. ¹⁶David pleaded with God for the child. He fasted and went into his house and spent the nights lying on the ground. ¹⁷The elders of his household stood beside him to get him up from the ground, but he refused, and he would not eat any food with them.

¹⁸On the seventh day the child died. David's servants were afraid to tell him that the child was dead, for they thought, "While the child was still living, we spoke to David but he would not listen to us. How can we tell him the child is dead? He may do something desperate."

¹⁹David noticed that his servants were whispering among themselves and he realized the child was dead. "Is the child dead?" he asked.

ᵃ14 Masoretic Text; an ancient Hebrew scribal tradition *this you have shown utter contempt for the LORD*

"Yes," they replied, "he is dead."

²⁰Then David got up from the ground. After he had washed, put on lotions and changed his clothes, he went into the house of the LORD and worshiped. Then he went to his own house, and at his request they served him food, and he ate.

²¹His servants asked him, "Why are you acting this way? While the child was alive, you fasted and wept, but now that the child is dead, you get up and eat!"

²²He answered, "While the child was still alive, I fasted and wept. I thought, 'Who knows? The LORD may be gracious to me and let the child live.' ²³But now that he is dead, why should I fast? Can I bring him back again? I will go to him, but he will not return to me."

²⁴Then David comforted his wife Bathsheba, and he went to her and lay with her. She gave birth to a son, and they named him Solomon. The LORD loved him; ²⁵and because the LORD loved him, he sent word through Nathan the prophet to name him Jedidiah.ᵃ

²⁶Meanwhile Joab fought against Rabbah of the Ammonites and captured the royal citadel. ²⁷Joab then sent messengers to David, saying, "I have fought against Rabbah and taken its water supply. ²⁸Now muster the rest of the troops and besiege the city and capture it. Otherwise I will take the city, and it will be named after me."

²⁹So David mustered the entire army and went to Rabbah, and attacked and captured it. ³⁰He took the crown from the head of their kingᵇ—its weight was a talentᶜ of gold, and it was set with precious stones—and it was placed on David's head. He took a great quantity of plunder from the city ³¹and brought out the people who were there, consigning them to labor with saws and with iron picks and axes, and he made them work at brickmaking.ᵈ He did this to all the Ammonite towns. Then David and his entire army returned to Jerusalem.

Amnon and Tamar

13 In the course of time, Amnon son of David fell in love with Tamar, the beautiful sister of Absalom son of David.

²Amnon became frustrated to the point of illness on account of his sister Tamar, for she was a virgin, and it seemed impossible for him to do anything to her.

³Now Amnon had a friend named Jonadab son of Shimeah, David's brother. Jonadab was a very shrewd man. ⁴He asked Amnon, "Why do you, the king's son, look so haggard morning after morning? Won't you tell me?"

Amnon said to him, "I'm in love with Tamar, my brother Absalom's sister."

⁵"Go to bed and pretend to be ill," Jonadab said. "When your father comes to see you, say to him, 'I would like my sister Tamar to come and give me something to eat. Let her prepare the food in my sight so I may watch her and then eat it from her hand.' "

⁶So Amnon lay down and pretended to be ill. When the king came to see him, Amnon said to him, "I would like my sister Tamar to come and make some special bread in my sight, so I may eat from her hand."

⁷David sent word to Tamar at the palace: "Go to the house of your brother Amnon and prepare some food for him." ⁸So Tamar went to the house of her brother Amnon, who was lying down. She took some dough, kneaded it, made the bread in his sight and baked it. ⁹Then she took the pan and served him the bread, but he refused to eat.

"Send everyone out of here," Amnon said. So everyone left him. ¹⁰Then Amnon said to Tamar, "Bring the

---

ᵃ25 *Jedidiah* means *loved by the* LORD.   ᵇ30 Or *of Milcom* (that is, Molech)   ᶜ30 That is, about 75 pounds (about 34 kilograms)   ᵈ31 The meaning of the Hebrew for this clause is uncertain.

food here into my bedroom so I may eat from your hand." And Tamar took the bread she had prepared and brought it to her brother Amnon in his bedroom. [11]But when she took it to him to eat, he grabbed her and said, "Come to bed with me, my sister."

[12]"Don't, my brother!" she said to him. "Don't force me. Such a thing should not be done in Israel! Don't do this wicked thing. [13]What about me? Where could I get rid of my disgrace? And what about you? You would be like one of the wicked fools in Israel. Please speak to the king; he will not keep me from being married to you." [14]But he refused to listen to her, and since he was stronger than she, he raped her.

[15]Then Amnon hated her with intense hatred. In fact, he hated her more than he had loved her. Amnon said to her, "Get up and get out!"

[16]"No!" she said to him. "Sending me away would be a greater wrong than what you have already done to me."

But he refused to listen to her. [17]He called his personal servant and said, "Get this woman out of here and bolt the door after her." [18]So his servant put her out and bolted the door after her. She was wearing a richly ornamented[a] robe, for this was the kind of garment the virgin daughters of the king wore. [19]Tamar put ashes on her head and tore the ornamented[b] robe she was wearing. She put her hand on her head and went away, weeping aloud as she went.

[20]Her brother Absalom said to her, "Has that Amnon, your brother, been with you? Be quiet now, my sister; he is your brother. Don't take this thing to heart." And Tamar lived in her brother Absalom's house, a desolate woman.

[21]When King David heard all this, he was furious. [22]Absalom never said a word to Amnon, either good or bad; he hated Amnon because he had disgraced his sister Tamar.

Absalom Kills Amnon

[23]Two years later, when Absalom's sheepshearers were at Baal Hazor near the border of Ephraim, he invited all the king's sons to come there. [24]Absalom went to the king and said, "Your servant has had shearers come. Will the king and his officials please join me?"

[25]"No, my son," the king replied. "All of us should not go; we would only be a burden to you." Although Absalom urged him, he still refused to go, but gave him his blessing.

[26]Then Absalom said, "If not, please let my brother Amnon come with us."

The king asked him, "Why should he go with you?" [27]But Absalom urged him, so he sent with him Amnon and the rest of the king's sons.

[28]Absalom ordered his men, "Listen! When Amnon is in high spirits from drinking wine and I say to you, 'Strike Amnon down,' then kill him. Don't be afraid. Have not I given you this order? Be strong and brave." [29]So Absalom's men did to Amnon what Absalom had ordered. Then all the king's sons got up, mounted their mules and fled.

[30]While they were on their way, the report came to David: "Absalom has struck down all the king's sons; not one of them is left." [31]The king stood up, tore his clothes and lay down on the ground; and all his servants stood by with their clothes torn.

[32]But Jonadab son of Shimeah, David's brother, said, "My lord should not think that they killed all the princes; only Amnon is dead. This has been Absalom's expressed intention ever since the day Amnon raped his sister Tamar. [33]My lord the king should not be concerned about the report that all the king's sons are dead. Only Amnon is dead."

[34]Meanwhile, Absalom had fled.

Now the man standing watch looked up and saw many people on

---

[a]18 The meaning of the Hebrew for this phrase is uncertain.   [b]19 The meaning of the Hebrew for this word is uncertain.

the road west of him, coming down the side of the hill. The watchman went and told the king, "I see men in the direction of Horonaim, on the side of the hill."*a*

35Jonadab said to the king, "See, the king's sons are here; it has happened just as your servant said."

36As he finished speaking, the king's sons came in, wailing loudly. The king, too, and all his servants wept very bitterly.

37Absalom fled and went to Talmai son of Ammihud, the king of Geshur. But King David mourned for his son every day.

38After Absalom fled and went to Geshur, he stayed there three years. 39And the spirit of the king*b* longed to go to Absalom, for he was consoled concerning Amnon's death.

Absalom Returns to Jerusalem

14 Joab son of Zeruiah knew that the king's heart longed for Absalom. 2So Joab sent someone to Tekoa and had a wise woman brought from there. He said to her, "Pretend you are in mourning. Dress in mourning clothes, and don't use any cosmetic lotions. Act like a woman who has spent many days grieving for the dead. 3Then go to the king and speak these words to him." And Joab put the words in her mouth.

4When the woman from Tekoa went*c* to the king, she fell with her face to the ground to pay him honor, and she said, "Help me, O king!"

5The king asked her, "What is troubling you?"

She said, "I am indeed a widow; my husband is dead. 6I your servant had two sons. They got into a fight with each other in the field, and no one was there to separate them. One struck the other and killed him. 7Now the whole clan has risen up against your servant; they say, 'Hand over the one who struck his brother down, so that we may put him to death for the life of his brother whom he killed; then we will get rid of the heir as well.' They would put out the only burning coal I have left, leaving my husband neither name nor descendant on the face of the earth."

8The king said to the woman, "Go home, and I will issue an order in your behalf."

9But the woman from Tekoa said to him, "My lord the king, let the blame rest on me and on my father's family, and let the king and his throne be without guilt."

10The king replied, "If anyone says anything to you, bring him to me, and he will not bother you again."

11She said, "Then let the king invoke the LORD his God to prevent the avenger of blood from adding to the destruction, so that my son will not be destroyed."

"As surely as the LORD lives," he said, "not one hair of your son's head will fall to the ground."

12Then the woman said, "Let your servant speak a word to my lord the king."

"Speak," he replied.

13The woman said, "Why then have you devised a thing like this against the people of God? When the king says this, does he not convict himself, for the king has not brought back his banished son? 14Like water spilled on the ground, which cannot be recovered, so we must die. But God does not take away life; instead, he devises ways so that a banished person may not remain estranged from him.

15"And now I have come to say this to my lord the king because the people have made me afraid. Your servant thought, 'I will speak to the king; perhaps he will do what his servant asks. 16Perhaps the king will agree to deliver his servant from the hand of the man who is trying to cut off both me and my son from the inheritance God gave us.'

17"And now your servant says,

---

a34 Septuagint; Hebrew does not have this sentence.   *b39* Dead Sea Scrolls and some Septuagint manuscripts; Masoretic Text *But ⌊the spirit of⌋ David the king*   *c4* Many Hebrew manuscripts, Septuagint, Vulgate and Syriac; most Hebrew manuscripts *spoke*

'May the word of my lord the king bring me rest, for my lord the king is like an angel of God in discerning good and evil. May the LORD your God be with you.' "

¹⁸Then the king said to the woman, "Do not keep from me the answer to what I am going to ask you."

"Let my lord the king speak," the woman said.

¹⁹The king asked, "Isn't the hand of Joab with you in all this?"

The woman answered, "As surely as you live, my lord the king, no one can turn to the right or to the left from anything my lord the king says. Yes, it was your servant Joab who instructed me to do this and who put all these words into the mouth of your servant. ²⁰Your servant Joab did this to change the present situation. My lord has wisdom like that of an angel of God—he knows everything that happens in the land."

²¹The king said to Joab, "Very well, I will do it. Go, bring back the young man Absalom."

²²Joab fell with his face to the ground to pay him honor, and he blessed the king. Joab said, "Today your servant knows that he has found favor in your eyes, my lord the king, because the king has granted his servant's request."

²³Then Joab went to Geshur and brought Absalom back to Jerusalem. ²⁴But the king said, "He must go to his own house; he must not see my face." So Absalom went to his own house and did not see the face of the king.

²⁵In all Israel there was not a man so highly praised for his handsome appearance as Absalom. From the top of his head to the sole of his foot there was no blemish in him. ²⁶Whenever he cut the hair of his head—he used to cut his hair from time to time when it became too heavy for him—he would weigh it, and its weight was two hundred shekels[a] by the royal standard.

²⁷Three sons and a daughter were born to Absalom. The daughter's name was Tamar, and she became a beautiful woman.

²⁸Absalom lived two years in Jerusalem without seeing the king's face. ²⁹Then Absalom sent for Joab in order to send him to the king, but Joab refused to come to him. So he sent a second time, but he refused to come. ³⁰Then he said to his servants, "Look, Joab's field is next to mine, and he has barley there. Go and set it on fire." So Absalom's servants set the field on fire.

³¹Then Joab did go to Absalom's house and he said to him, "Why have your servants set my field on fire?"

³²Absalom said to Joab, "Look, I sent word to you and said, 'Come here so I can send you to the king to ask, "Why have I come from Geshur? It would be better for me if I were still there!" ' Now then, I want to see the king's face, and if I am guilty of anything, let him put me to death."

³³So Joab went to the king and told him this. Then the king summoned Absalom, and he came in and bowed down with his face to the ground before the king. And the king kissed Absalom.

Absalom's Conspiracy

15 In the course of time, Absalom provided himself with a chariot and horses and with fifty men to run ahead of him. ²He would get up early and stand by the side of the road leading to the city gate. Whenever anyone came with a complaint to be placed before the king for a decision, Absalom would call out to him, "What town are you from?" He would answer, "Your servant is from one of the tribes of Israel." ³Then Absalom would say to him, "Look, your claims are valid and proper, but there is no representative of the king to hear you." ⁴And Absalom would add, "If only I were appointed judge in the land! Then everyone who has a complaint or case could come to me and I would see that he gets justice."

ᵃ26 That is, about 5 pounds (about 2.3 kilograms)

⁵Also, whenever anyone approached him to bow down before him, Absalom would reach out his hand, take hold of him and kiss him. ⁶Absalom behaved in this way toward all the Israelites who came to the king asking for justice, and so he stole the hearts of the men of Israel.

⁷At the end of four*ᵃ* years, Absalom said to the king, "Let me go to Hebron and fulfill a vow I made to the LORD. ⁸While your servant was living at Geshur in Aram, I made this vow: 'If the LORD takes me back to Jerusalem, I will worship the LORD in Hebron.*ᵇ*' "

⁹The king said to him, "Go in peace." So he went to Hebron.

¹⁰Then Absalom sent secret messengers throughout the tribes of Israel to say, "As soon as you hear the sound of the trumpets, then say, 'Absalom is king in Hebron.' " ¹¹Two hundred men from Jerusalem had accompanied Absalom. They had been invited as guests and went quite innocently, knowing nothing about the matter. ¹²While Absalom was offering sacrifices, he also sent for Ahithophel the Gilonite, David's counselor, to come from Giloh, his hometown. And so the conspiracy gained strength, and Absalom's following kept on increasing.

David Flees

¹³A messenger came and told David, "The hearts of the men of Israel are with Absalom."

¹⁴Then David said to all his officials who were with him in Jerusalem, "Come! We must flee, or none of us will escape from Absalom. We must leave immediately, or he will move quickly to overtake us and bring ruin upon us and put the city to the sword."

¹⁵The king's officials answered him, "Your servants are ready to do whatever our lord the king chooses."

¹⁶The king set out, with his entire household following him; but he left ten concubines to take care of the palace. ¹⁷So the king set out, with all the people following him, and they halted at a place some distance away. ¹⁸All his men marched past him, along with all the Kerethites and Pelethites; and all the six hundred Gittites who had accompanied him from Gath marched before the king.

¹⁹The king said to Ittai the Gittite, "Why should you come along with us? Go back and stay with King Absalom. You are a foreigner, an exile from your homeland. ²⁰You came only yesterday. And today shall I make you wander about with us, when I do not know where I am going? Go back, and take your countrymen. May kindness and faithfulness be with you."

²¹But Ittai replied to the king, "As surely as the LORD lives, and as my lord the king lives, wherever my lord the king may be, whether it means life or death, there will your servant be."

²²David said to Ittai, "Go ahead, march on." So Ittai the Gittite marched on with all his men and the families that were with him.

²³The whole countryside wept aloud as all the people passed by. The king also crossed the Kidron Valley, and all the people moved on toward the desert.

²⁴Zadok was there, too, and all the Levites who were with him were carrying the ark of the covenant of God. They set down the ark of God, and Abiathar offered sacrifices*ᶜ* until all the people had finished leaving the city.

²⁵Then the king said to Zadok, "Take the ark of God back into the city. If I find favor in the LORD's eyes, he will bring me back and let me see it and his dwelling place again. ²⁶But if he says, 'I am not pleased with you,' then I am ready; let him do to me whatever seems good to him."

²⁷The king also said to Zadok the priest, "Aren't you a seer? Go back to the city in peace, with your son Ahim-

---

aaz and Jonathan son of Abiathar. You and Abiathar take your two sons with you. ²⁸I will wait at the fords in the desert until word comes from you to inform me." ²⁹So Zadok and Abiathar took the ark of God back to Jerusalem and stayed there.

³⁰But David continued up the Mount of Olives, weeping as he went; his head was covered and he was barefoot. All the people with him covered their heads too and were weeping as they went up. ³¹Now David had been told, "Ahithophel is among the conspirators with Absalom." So David prayed, "O Lord, turn Ahithophel's counsel into foolishness."

³²When David arrived at the summit, where people used to worship God, Hushai the Arkite was there to meet him, his robe torn and dust on his head. ³³David said to him, "If you go with me, you will be a burden to me. ³⁴But if you return to the city and say to Absalom, 'I will be your servant, O king; I was your father's servant in the past, but now I will be your servant,' then you can help me by frustrating Ahithophel's advice. ³⁵Won't the priests Zadok and Abiathar be there with you? Tell them anything you hear in the king's palace. ³⁶Their two sons, Ahimaaz son of Zadok and Jonathan son of Abiathar, are there with them. Send them to me with anything you hear."

³⁷So David's friend Hushai arrived at Jerusalem as Absalom was entering the city.

David and Ziba

16 When David had gone a short distance beyond the summit, there was Ziba, the steward of Mephibosheth, waiting to meet him. He had a string of donkeys saddled and loaded with two hundred loaves of bread, a hundred cakes of raisins, a hundred cakes of figs and a skin of wine.

²The king asked Ziba, "Why have you brought these?"

Ziba answered, "The donkeys are for the king's household to ride on, the bread and fruit are for the men to eat, and the wine is to refresh those who become exhausted in the desert."

³The king then asked, "Where is your master's grandson?"

Ziba said to him, "He is staying in Jerusalem, because he thinks, 'Today the house of Israel will give me back my grandfather's kingdom.' "

⁴Then the king said to Ziba, "All that belonged to Mephibosheth is now yours."

"I humbly bow," Ziba said. "May I find favor in your eyes, my lord the king."

Shimei Curses David

⁵As King David approached Bahurim, a man from the same clan as Saul's family came out from there. His name was Shimei son of Gera, and he cursed as he came out. ⁶He pelted David and all the king's officials with stones, though all the troops and the special guard were on David's right and left. ⁷As he cursed, Shimei said, "Get out, get out, you man of blood, you scoundrel! ⁸The Lord has repaid you for all the blood you shed in the household of Saul, in whose place you have reigned. The Lord has handed the kingdom over to your son Absalom. You have come to ruin because you are a man of blood!"

⁹Then Abishai son of Zeruiah said to the king, "Why should this dead dog curse my lord the king? Let me go over and cut off his head."

¹⁰But the king said, "What do you and I have in common, you sons of Zeruiah? If he is cursing because the Lord said to him, 'Curse David,' who can ask, 'Why do you do this?' "

¹¹David then said to Abishai and all his officials, "My son, who is of my own flesh, is trying to take my life. How much more, then, this Benjamite! Leave him alone; let him curse, for the Lord has told him to. ¹²It may be that the Lord will see my distress and repay me with good for the cursing I am receiving today."

¹³So David and his men continued along the road while Shimei was going along the hillside opposite him, cursing as he went and throwing

stones at him and showering him with dirt. [14]The king and all the people with him arrived at their destination exhausted. And there he refreshed himself.

The Advice of Hushai and Ahithophel

[15]Meanwhile, Absalom and all the men of Israel came to Jerusalem, and Ahithophel was with him. [16]Then Hushai the Arkite, David's friend, went to Absalom and said to him, "Long live the king! Long live the king!"

[17]Absalom asked Hushai, "Is this the love you show your friend? Why didn't you go with your friend?"

[18]Hushai said to Absalom, "No, the one chosen by the LORD, by these people, and by all the men of Israel—his I will be, and I will remain with him. [19]Furthermore, whom should I serve? Should I not serve the son? Just as I served your father, so I will serve you."

[20]Absalom said to Ahithophel, "Give us your advice. What should we do?"

[21]Ahithophel answered, "Lie with your father's concubines whom he left to take care of the palace. Then all Israel will hear that you have made yourself a stench in your father's nostrils, and the hands of everyone with you will be strengthened." [22]So they pitched a tent for Absalom on the roof, and he lay with his father's concubines in the sight of all Israel.

[23]Now in those days the advice Ahithophel gave was like that of one who inquires of God. That was how both David and Absalom regarded all of Ahithophel's advice.

17 Ahithophel said to Absalom, "I would[a] choose twelve thousand men and set out tonight in pursuit of David. [2]I would[b] attack him while he is weary and weak. I would[b] strike him with terror, and then all the people with him will flee. I would[b] strike down only the king [3]and bring all the people back to you.

The death of the man you seek will mean the return of all; all the people will be unharmed." [4]This plan seemed good to Absalom and to all the elders of Israel.

[5]But Absalom said, "Summon also Hushai the Arkite, so we can hear what he has to say." [6]When Hushai came to him, Absalom said, "Ahithophel has given this advice. Should we do what he says? If not, give us your opinion."

[7]Hushai replied to Absalom, "The advice Ahithophel has given is not good this time. [8]You know your father and his men; they are fighters, and as fierce as a wild bear robbed of her cubs. Besides, your father is an experienced fighter; he will not spend the night with the troops. [9]Even now, he is hidden in a cave or some other place. If he should attack your troops first,[c] whoever hears about it will say, 'There has been a slaughter among the troops who follow Absalom.' [10]Then even the bravest soldier, whose heart is like the heart of a lion, will melt with fear, for all Israel knows that your father is a fighter and that those with him are brave.

[11]"So I advise you: Let all Israel, from Dan to Beersheba—as numerous as the sand on the seashore—be gathered to you, with you yourself leading them into battle. [12]Then we will attack him wherever he may be found, and we will fall on him as dew settles on the ground. Neither he nor any of his men will be left alive. [13]If he withdraws into a city, then all Israel will bring ropes to that city, and we will drag it down to the valley until not even a piece of it can be found."

[14]Absalom and all the men of Israel said, "The advice of Hushai the Arkite is better than that of Ahithophel." For the LORD had determined to frustrate the good advice of Ahithophel in order to bring disaster on Absalom.

[15]Hushai told Zadok and Abiathar, the priests, "Ahithophel has advised Absalom and the elders of Israel to do such and such, but I have advised

---

[a]1 Or *Let me*   [b]2 Or *will*   [c]9 Or *When some of the men fall at the first attack*

them to do so and so. ¹⁶Now send a message immediately and tell David, 'Do not spend the night at the fords in the desert; cross over without fail, or the king and all the people with him will be swallowed up.' "

¹⁷Jonathan and Ahimaaz were staying at En Rogel. A servant girl was to go and inform them, and they were to go and tell King David, for they could not risk being seen entering the city. ¹⁸But a young man saw them and told Absalom. So the two of them left quickly and went to the house of a man in Bahurim. He had a well in his courtyard, and they climbed down into it. ¹⁹His wife took a covering and spread it out over the opening of the well and scattered grain over it. No one knew anything about it.

²⁰When Absalom's men came to the woman at the house, they asked, "Where are Ahimaaz and Jonathan?"

The woman answered them, "They crossed over the brook."ᵃ The men searched but found no one, so they returned to Jerusalem.

²¹After the men had gone, the two climbed out of the well and went to inform King David. They said to him, "Set out and cross the river at once; Ahithophel has advised such and such against you." ²²So David and all the people with him set out and crossed the Jordan. By daybreak, no one was left who had not crossed the Jordan.

²³When Ahithophel saw that his advice had not been followed, he saddled his donkey and set out for his house in his hometown. He put his house in order and then hanged himself. So he died and was buried in his father's tomb.

²⁴David went to Mahanaim, and Absalom crossed the Jordan with all the men of Israel. ²⁵Absalom had appointed Amasa over the army in place of Joab. Amasa was the son of a man named Jether,ᵇ an Israeliteᶜ who had married Abigail,ᵈ the daughter of Nahash and sister of Zeruiah the mother of Joab. ²⁶The Israelites and Absalom camped in the land of Gilead.

²⁷When David came to Mahanaim, Shobi son of Nahash from Rabbah of the Ammonites, and Makir son of Ammiel from Lo Debar, and Barzillai the Gileadite from Rogelim ²⁸brought bedding and bowls and articles of pottery. They also brought wheat and barley, flour and roasted grain, beans and lentils,ᵉ ²⁹honey and curds, sheep, and cheese from cows' milk for David and his people to eat. For they said, "The people have become hungry and tired and thirsty in the desert."

Absalom's Death

18 David mustered the men who were with him and appointed over them commanders of thousands and commanders of hundreds. ²David sent the troops out—a third under the command of Joab, a third under Joab's brother Abishai son of Zeruiah, and a third under Ittai the Gittite. The king told the troops, "I myself will surely march out with you."

³But the men said, "You must not go out; if we are forced to flee, they won't care about us. Even if half of us die, they won't care; but you are worth ten thousand of us.ᶠ It would be better now for you to give us support from the city."

⁴The king answered, "I will do whatever seems best to you."

So the king stood beside the gate while all the men marched out in units of hundreds and of thousands. ⁵The king commanded Joab, Abishai and Ittai, "Be gentle with the young man Absalom for my sake." And all the troops heard the king giving or-

---

ᵃ20 Or *"They passed by the sheep pen toward the water."*   ᵇ25 Hebrew *Ithra*, a variant of *Jether*
ᶜ25 Hebrew and some Septuagint manuscripts; other Septuagint manuscripts (see also 1 Chron. 2:17) *Ishmaelite* or *Jezreelite*   ᵈ25 Hebrew *Abigal*, a variant of *Abigail*   ᵉ28 Most Septuagint manuscripts and Syriac; Hebrew *lentils, and roasted grain*   ᶠ3 Two Hebrew manuscripts, some Septuagint manuscripts and Vulgate; most Hebrew manuscripts *care; for now there are ten thousand like us*

ders concerning Absalom to each of the commanders.

⁶The army marched into the field to fight Israel, and the battle took place in the forest of Ephraim. ⁷There the army of Israel was defeated by David's men, and the casualties that day were great—twenty thousand men. ⁸The battle spread out over the whole countryside, and the forest claimed more lives that day than the sword.

⁹Now Absalom happened to meet David's men. He was riding his mule, and as the mule went under the thick branches of a large oak, Absalom's head got caught in the tree. He was left hanging in midair, while the mule he was riding kept on going.

¹⁰When one of the men saw this, he told Joab, "I just saw Absalom hanging in an oak tree."

¹¹Joab said to the man who had told him this, "What! You saw him? Why didn't you strike him to the ground right there? Then I would have had to give you ten shekels[a] of silver and a warrior's belt."

¹²But the man replied, "Even if a thousand shekels[b] were weighed out into my hands, I would not lift my hand against the king's son. In our hearing the king commanded you and Abishai and Ittai, 'Protect the young man Absalom for my sake.[c]' ¹³And if I had put my life in jeopardy[d]—and nothing is hidden from the king—you would have kept your distance from me."

¹⁴Joab said, "I'm not going to wait like this for you." So he took three javelins in his hand and plunged them into Absalom's heart while Absalom was still alive in the oak tree. ¹⁵And ten of Joab's armor-bearers surrounded Absalom, struck him and killed him.

¹⁶Then Joab sounded the trumpet, and the troops stopped pursuing Israel, for Joab halted them. ¹⁷They took Absalom, threw him into a big pit in the forest and piled up a large heap of rocks over him. Meanwhile, all the Israelites fled to their homes.

¹⁸During his lifetime Absalom had taken a pillar and erected it in the King's Valley as a monument to himself, for he thought, "I have no son to carry on the memory of my name." He named the pillar after himself, and it is called Absalom's Monument to this day.

David Mourns

¹⁹Now Ahimaaz son of Zadok said, "Let me run and take the news to the king that the LORD has delivered him from the hand of his enemies."

²⁰"You are not the one to take the news today," Joab told him. "You may take the news another time, but you must not do so today, because the king's son is dead."

²¹Then Joab said to a Cushite, "Go, tell the king what you have seen." The Cushite bowed down before Joab and ran off.

²²Ahimaaz son of Zadok again said to Joab, "Come what may, please let me run behind the Cushite."

But Joab replied, "My son, why do you want to go? You don't have any news that will bring you a reward."

²³He said, "Come what may, I want to run."

So Joab said, "Run!" Then Ahimaaz ran by way of the plain[e] and outran the Cushite.

²⁴While David was sitting between the inner and outer gates, the watchman went up to the roof of the gateway by the wall. As he looked out, he saw a man running alone. ²⁵The watchman called out to the king and reported it.

The king said, "If he is alone, he must have good news." And the man came closer and closer.

²⁶Then the watchman saw another man running, and he called down to

---

a11 That is, about 4 ounces (about 115 grams)   *b12* That is, about 25 pounds (about 11 kilograms)   *c12* A few Hebrew manuscripts, Septuagint, Vulgate and Syriac; most Hebrew manuscripts may be translated *Absalom, whoever you may be.*   *d13* Or *Otherwise, if I had acted treacherously toward him*   *e23* That is, the plain of the Jordan

the gatekeeper, "Look, another man running alone!"

The king said, "He must be bringing good news, too."

27The watchman said, "It seems to me that the first one runs like Ahimaaz son of Zadok."

"He's a good man," the king said. "He comes with good news."

28Then Ahimaaz called out to the king, "All is well!" He bowed down before the king with his face to the ground and said, "Praise be to the LORD your God! He has delivered up the men who lifted their hands against my lord the king."

29The king asked, "Is the young man Absalom safe?"

Ahimaaz answered, "I saw great confusion just as Joab was about to send the king's servant and me, your servant, but I don't know what it was."

30The king said, "Stand aside and wait here." So he stepped aside and stood there.

31Then the Cushite arrived and said, "My lord the king, hear the good news! The LORD has delivered you today from all who rose up against you."

32The king asked the Cushite, "Is the young man Absalom safe?"

The Cushite replied, "May the enemies of my lord the king and all who rise up to harm you be like that young man."

33The king was shaken. He went up to the room over the gateway and wept. As he went, he said: "O my son Absalom! My son, my son Absalom! If only I had died instead of you—O Absalom, my son, my son!"

19 Joab was told, "The king is weeping and mourning for Absalom." 2And for the whole army the victory that day was turned into mourning, because on that day the troops heard it said, "The king is grieving for his son." 3The men stole into the city that day as men steal in who are ashamed when they flee from battle. 4The king covered his face and cried aloud, "O my son Absalom! O Absalom, my son, my son!"

5Then Joab went into the house to the king and said, "Today you have humiliated all your men, who have just saved your life and the lives of your sons and daughters and the lives of your wives and concubines. 6You love those who hate you and hate those who love you. You have made it clear today that the commanders and their men mean nothing to you. I see that you would be pleased if Absalom were alive today and all of us were dead. 7Now go out and encourage your men. I swear by the LORD that if you don't go out, not a man will be left with you by nightfall. This will be worse for you than all the calamities that have come upon you from your youth till now."

8So the king got up and took his seat in the gateway. When the men were told, "The king is sitting in the gateway," they all came before him.

David Returns to Jerusalem

Meanwhile, the Israelites had fled to their homes. 9Throughout the tribes of Israel, the people were all arguing with each other, saying, "The king delivered us from the hand of our enemies; he is the one who rescued us from the hand of the Philistines. But now he has fled the country because of Absalom; 10and Absalom, whom we anointed to rule over us, has died in battle. So why do you say nothing about bringing the king back?"

11King David sent this message to Zadok and Abiathar, the priests: "Ask the elders of Judah, 'Why should you be the last to bring the king back to his palace, since what is being said throughout Israel has reached the king at his quarters? 12You are my brothers, my own flesh and blood. So why should you be the last to bring back the king?' 13And say to Amasa, 'Are you not my own flesh and blood? May God deal with me, be it ever so severely, if from now on you are not the commander of my army in place of Joab.' "

14He won over the hearts of all the men of Judah as though they were one man. They sent word to the king,

VERSE:	AUTHORS:	PASSAGE:
2 Samuel	Raymond Mitsch &	2 Samuel
18:33	Lynn Brookside	18:19 — 19:4

Taking Grief by the Neck

Sometime during the weeks or months following our loss, most of us experience a fleeting instant when we believe we have seen our loved one. It may be in a check-out line or on the street or in the half-light of a movie theater. Wherever we are when it occurs, it cannot help but reawaken our great sorrow. Tears spring to our eyes and we are once again completely and painfully aware that we miss our loved one more than words can ever express. We would give anything to have him or her back. We wrestle with our grief . . .

It's likely that this case of mistaken identity is just one more way we have of reminding ourselves of the reality of our pain. It is far too easy to belittle our pain. We may even have convinced ourselves that our pain is insignificant, our grieving process unnecessary. Then it happens. The back of someone's head, the way he or she walks, sends us scurrying. We rush ahead to catch a glimpse of the person's face, hoping and praying it will be our loved one and we will be able to declare that we have only had a nightmare. Yet we know all the while how fruitless our effort will be . . .

It's in the moments following such an incident that we need to remind ourselves that this time of grief serves a purpose. God created us with an inherent ability to heal, and our grief process is designed to bless us with healing. It is in those moments when we need to take our grief by the neck and shout, "I will not let you go until you bless me!"

ADDITIONAL SCRIPTURE READINGS
Genesis 32:22–32; Isaiah 61:1–7

Go to page 386 for your next devotional reading.

"Return, you and all your men." ¹⁵Then the king returned and went as far as the Jordan.

Now the men of Judah had come to Gilgal to go out and meet the king and bring him across the Jordan. ¹⁶Shimei son of Gera, the Benjamite from Bahurim, hurried down with the men of Judah to meet King David. ¹⁷With him were a thousand Benjamites, along with Ziba, the steward of Saul's household, and his fifteen sons and twenty servants. They rushed to the Jordan, where the king was. ¹⁸They crossed at the ford to take the king's household over and to do whatever he wished.

When Shimei son of Gera crossed the Jordan, he fell prostrate before the king ¹⁹and said to him, "May my lord not hold me guilty. Do not remember how your servant did wrong on the day my lord the king left Jerusalem. May the king put it out of his mind. ²⁰For I your servant know that I have sinned, but today I have come here as the first of the whole house of Joseph to come down and meet my lord the king."

²¹Then Abishai son of Zeruiah said, "Shouldn't Shimei be put to death for this? He cursed the LORD's anointed." ²²David replied, "What do you and I have in common, you sons of Zeruiah? This day you have become my adversaries! Should anyone be put to death in Israel today? Do I not know that today I am king over Israel?" ²³So the king said to Shimei, "You shall not die." And the king promised him on oath.

²⁴Mephibosheth, Saul's grandson, also went down to meet the king. He had not taken care of his feet or trimmed his mustache or washed his clothes from the day the king left until the day he returned safely. ²⁵When he came from Jerusalem to meet the king, the king asked him, "Why didn't you go with me, Mephibosheth?" ²⁶He said, "My lord the king, since I your servant am lame, I said, 'I will have my donkey saddled and will ride on it, so I can go with the king.'

But Ziba my servant betrayed me. ²⁷And he has slandered your servant to my lord the king. My lord the king is like an angel of God; so do whatever pleases you. ²⁸All my grandfather's descendants deserved nothing but death from my lord the king, but you gave your servant a place among those who eat at your table. So what right do I have to make any more appeals to the king?"

²⁹The king said to him, "Why say more? I order you and Ziba to divide the fields." ³⁰Mephibosheth said to the king, "Let him take everything, now that my lord the king has arrived home safely."

³¹Barzillai the Gileadite also came down from Rogelim to cross the Jordan with the king and to send him on his way from there. ³²Now Barzillai was a very old man, eighty years of age. He had provided for the king during his stay in Mahanaim, for he was a very wealthy man. ³³The king said to Barzillai, "Cross over with me and stay with me in Jerusalem, and I will provide for you."

³⁴But Barzillai answered the king, "How many more years will I live, that I should go up to Jerusalem with the king? ³⁵I am now eighty years old. Can I tell the difference between what is good and what is not? Can your servant taste what he eats and drinks? Can I still hear the voices of men and women singers? Why should your servant be an added burden to my lord the king? ³⁶Your servant will cross over the Jordan with the king for a short distance, but why should the king reward me in this way? ³⁷Let your servant return, that I may die in my own town near the tomb of my father and mother. But here is your servant Kimham. Let him cross over with my lord the king. Do for him whatever pleases you."

³⁸The king said, "Kimham shall cross over with me, and I will do for him whatever pleases you. And anything you desire from me I will do for you."

³⁹So all the people crossed the Jor-

VERSE:	AUTHOR:	PASSAGE:
2 Samuel 19:32	John Gilmore	2 Samuel 19:31–39

The Quality of Generosity

Barzillai was a man of wealth. He got rich from the fertile hills, probably as a successful animal husbandman or farmer. Along with wealth came responsibilities, reputation, influence, and possibly a job in local politics. He wanted his money to be used to promote the just cause of David. No expense was spared in getting David restored to his office.

Full support was Barzillai's style. He is a symbol for those many Christians seniors who give generously to God's work. Large bequests and generous gifts from Christian seniors indicate the depth of their feelings, the totality of their dedication, and their determination to keep the causes of Christ not only solvent, but strong. Many Christian seniors reduce their own financial security by making courageous donations for the spread of the gospel.

Today's Barzillais also pitch in, contributing to churches and Christian enterprises by volunteering their expertise. Retired executives, generals and scientists have donated their time, talent and energies to jumpstart stalled Christian enterprises. Many Christian seniors refuse pay for their efforts and consider it an offering of thanks to God for his goodness down through the years.

Praise God for the Barzillais of the modern church.

ADDITIONAL SCRIPTURE READINGS
2 Corinthians 8:1–9; 1 Timothy 6:17–21

Go to page 390 for your next devotional reading.

dan, and then the king crossed over. The king kissed Barzillai and gave him his blessing, and Barzillai returned to his home.

⁴⁰When the king crossed over to Gilgal, Kimham crossed with him. All the troops of Judah and half the troops of Israel had taken the king over.

⁴¹Soon all the men of Israel were coming to the king and saying to him, "Why did our brothers, the men of Judah, steal the king away and bring him and his household across the Jordan, together with all his men?"

⁴²All the men of Judah answered the men of Israel, "We did this because the king is closely related to us. Why are you angry about it? Have we eaten any of the king's provisions? Have we taken anything for ourselves?"

⁴³Then the men of Israel answered the men of Judah, "We have ten shares in the king; and besides, we have a greater claim on David than you have. So why do you treat us with contempt? Were we not the first to speak of bringing back our king?"

But the men of Judah responded even more harshly than the men of Israel.

Sheba Rebels Against David

20 Now a troublemaker named Sheba son of Bicri, a Benjamite, happened to be there. He sounded the trumpet and shouted,

"We have no share in David,
     no part in Jesse's son!
Every man to his tent, O Israel!"

²So all the men of Israel deserted David to follow Sheba son of Bicri. But the men of Judah stayed by their king all the way from the Jordan to Jerusalem.

³When David returned to his palace in Jerusalem, he took the ten concubines he had left to take care of the palace and put them in a house under guard. He provided for them, but did not lie with them. They were kept in confinement till the day of their death, living as widows.

⁴Then the king said to Amasa, "Summon the men of Judah to come to me within three days, and be here yourself." ⁵But when Amasa went to summon Judah, he took longer than the time the king had set for him.

⁶David said to Abishai, "Now Sheba son of Bicri will do us more harm than Absalom did. Take your master's men and pursue him, or he will find fortified cities and escape from us." ⁷So Joab's men and the Kerethites and Pelethites and all the mighty warriors went out under the command of Abishai. They marched out from Jerusalem to pursue Sheba son of Bicri.

⁸While they were at the great rock in Gibeon, Amasa came to meet them. Joab was wearing his military tunic, and strapped over it at his waist was a belt with a dagger in its sheath. As he stepped forward, it dropped out of its sheath.

⁹Joab said to Amasa, "How are you, my brother?" Then Joab took Amasa by the beard with his right hand to kiss him. ¹⁰Amasa was not on his guard against the dagger in Joab's hand, and Joab plunged it into his belly, and his intestines spilled out on the ground. Without being stabbed again, Amasa died. Then Joab and his brother Abishai pursued Sheba son of Bicri.

¹¹One of Joab's men stood beside Amasa and said, "Whoever favors Joab, and whoever is for David, let him follow Joab!" ¹²Amasa lay wallowing in his blood in the middle of the road, and the man saw that all the troops came to a halt there. When he realized that everyone who came up to Amasa stopped, he dragged him from the road into a field and threw a garment over him. ¹³After Amasa had been removed from the road, all the men went on with Joab to pursue Sheba son of Bicri.

¹⁴Sheba passed through all the tribes of Israel to Abel Beth Maacah[a]

ᵃ14 Or *Abel, even Beth Maacah*; also in verse 15

and through the entire region of the Berites, who gathered together and followed him. ¹⁵All the troops with Joab came and besieged Sheba in Abel Beth Maacah. They built a siege ramp up to the city, and it stood against the outer fortifications. While they were battering the wall to bring it down, ¹⁶a wise woman called from the city, "Listen! Listen! Tell Joab to come here so I can speak to him." ¹⁷He went toward her, and she asked, "Are you Joab?"

"I am," he answered.

She said, "Listen to what your servant has to say."

"I'm listening," he said.

¹⁸She continued, "Long ago they used to say, 'Get your answer at Abel,' and that settled it. ¹⁹We are the peaceful and faithful in Israel. You are trying to destroy a city that is a mother in Israel. Why do you want to swallow up the LORD's inheritance?"

²⁰"Far be it from me!" Joab replied, "Far be it from me to swallow up or destroy! ²¹That is not the case. A man named Sheba son of Bicri, from the hill country of Ephraim, has lifted up his hand against the king, against David. Hand over this one man, and I'll withdraw from the city."

The woman said to Joab, "His head will be thrown to you from the wall."

²²Then the woman went to all the people with her wise advice, and they cut off the head of Sheba son of Bicri and threw it to Joab. So he sounded the trumpet, and his men dispersed from the city, each returning to his home. And Joab went back to the king in Jerusalem.

²³Joab was over Israel's entire army; Benaiah son of Jehoiada was over the Kerethites and Pelethites; ²⁴Adoniram[a] was in charge of forced labor; Jehoshaphat son of Ahilud was recorder; ²⁵Sheva was secretary; Zadok and Abiathar were priests; ²⁶and Ira the Jairite was David's priest.

The Gibeonites Avenged

21 During the reign of David, there was a famine for three successive years; so David sought the face of the LORD. The LORD said, "It is on account of Saul and his blood-stained house; it is because he put the Gibeonites to death."

²The king summoned the Gibeonites and spoke to them. (Now the Gibeonites were not a part of Israel but were survivors of the Amorites; the Israelites had sworn to ˌspareˌ them, but Saul in his zeal for Israel and Judah had tried to annihilate them.) ³David asked the Gibeonites, "What shall I do for you? How shall I make amends so that you will bless the LORD's inheritance?"

⁴The Gibeonites answered him, "We have no right to demand silver or gold from Saul or his family, nor do we have the right to put anyone in Israel to death."

"What do you want me to do for you?" David asked.

⁵They answered the king, "As for the man who destroyed us and plotted against us so that we have been decimated and have no place anywhere in Israel, ⁶let seven of his male descendants be given to us to be killed and exposed before the LORD at Gibeah of Saul—the LORD's chosen one."

So the king said, "I will give them to you."

⁷The king spared Mephibosheth son of Jonathan, the son of Saul, because of the oath before the LORD between David and Jonathan son of Saul. ⁸But the king took Armoni and Mephibosheth, the two sons of Aiah's daughter Rizpah, whom she had borne to Saul, together with the five sons of Saul's daughter Merab,[b] whom she had borne to Adriel son of Barzillai the Meholathite. ⁹He handed them over to the Gibeonites, who killed and exposed them on a hill before the LORD. All seven of them fell

---

a24 Some Septuagint manuscripts (see also 1 Kings 4:6 and 5:14); Hebrew *Adoram*   *b8* Two Hebrew manuscripts, some Septuagint manuscripts and Syriac (see also 1 Samuel 18:19); most Hebrew and Septuagint manuscripts *Michal*

together; they were put to death during the first days of the harvest, just as the barley harvest was beginning. [10]Rizpah daughter of Aiah took sackcloth and spread it out for herself on a rock. From the beginning of the harvest till the rain poured down from the heavens on the bodies, she did not let the birds of the air touch them by day or the wild animals by night. [11]When David was told what Aiah's daughter Rizpah, Saul's concubine, had done, [12]he went and took the bones of Saul and his son Jonathan from the citizens of Jabesh Gilead. (They had taken them secretly from the public square at Beth Shan, where the Philistines had hung them after they struck Saul down on Gilboa.) [13]David brought the bones of Saul and his son Jonathan from there, and the bones of those who had been killed and exposed were gathered up. [14]They buried the bones of Saul and his son Jonathan in the tomb of Saul's father Kish, at Zela in Benjamin, and did everything the king commanded. After that, God answered prayer in behalf of the land.

Wars Against the Philistines

[15]Once again there was a battle between the Philistines and Israel. David went down with his men to fight against the Philistines, and he became exhausted. [16]And Ishbi-Benob, one of the descendants of Rapha, whose bronze spearhead weighed three hundred shekels[a] and who was armed with a new ⌊sword⌋, said he would kill David. [17]But Abishai son of Zeruiah came to David's rescue; he struck the Philistine down and killed him. Then David's men swore to him, saying, "Never again will you go out with us to battle, so that the lamp of Israel will not be extinguished."

[18]In the course of time, there was another battle with the Philistines, at Gob. At that time Sibbecai the Hushathite killed Saph, one of the descendants of Rapha. [19]In another battle with the Philistines at Gob, Elhanan son of Jaare-Oregim[b] the Bethlehemite killed Goliath[c] the Gittite, who had a spear with a shaft like a weaver's rod. [20]In still another battle, which took place at Gath, there was a huge man with six fingers on each hand and six toes on each foot—twenty-four in all. He also was descended from Rapha. [21]When he taunted Israel, Jonathan son of Shimeah, David's brother, killed him.

[22]These four were descendants of Rapha in Gath, and they fell at the hands of David and his men.

David's Song of Praise

22 David sang to the LORD the words of this song when the LORD delivered him from the hand of all his enemies and from the hand of Saul. [2]He said:

"The LORD is my rock, my fortress
    and my deliverer;
[3] my God is my rock, in whom I
        take refuge,
    my shield and the horn[d] of my
        salvation.
He is my stronghold, my refuge
        and my savior—
    from violent men you save me.
[4]I call to the LORD, who is worthy
        of praise,
    and I am saved from my
        enemies.

[5]"The waves of death swirled
        about me;
    the torrents of destruction
        overwhelmed me.
[6]The cords of the grave[e] coiled
        around me;
    the snares of death confronted
        me.
[7]In my distress I called to the LORD;
    I called out to my God.

---

[a]16 That is, about 7 1/2 pounds (about 3.5 kilograms)   [b]19 Or son of Jair the weaver   [c]19 Hebrew and Septuagint; 1 Chron. 20:5 son of Jair killed Lahmi the brother of Goliath   [d]3 Horn here symbolizes strength.   [e]6 Hebrew Sheol

PASSAGE: 2 Samuel 22:1–7; Ephesians 6:10–18
AUTHOR: Lady Jane Grey

My Strong Tower

O merciful God, be thou now unto me
a strong tower of defense, I humbly entreat thee.
Give me grace to await thy leisure,
    and patiently to bear what thou doest unto
        me;
    nothing doubting or mistrusting thy
        goodness towards me;
    for thou knowest what is good for me
        better than I do.
Therefore do with me in all things what thou wilt;
    only arm me, I beseech thee, with thine
        armor,
    that I may stand fast;
    above all things, taking home the shield of
        faith;
    praying always that I may refer myself
        wholly to thy will . . .
I am assuredly persuaded
    that all thou doest cannot but be well;
    and unto thee be all honor and glory.
        Amen.

Go to page 393 for your next devotional reading.

From his temple he heard my
voice;
my cry came to his ears.
8"The earth trembled and quaked,
the foundations of the
heavens[a] shook;
they trembled because he was
angry.
9Smoke rose from his nostrils;
consuming fire came from his
mouth,
burning coals blazed out of it.
10He parted the heavens and came
down;
dark clouds were under his feet.
11He mounted the cherubim and
flew;
he soared[b] on the wings of the
wind.
12He made darkness his canopy
around him—
the dark[c] rain clouds of the
sky.
13Out of the brightness of his
presence
bolts of lightning blazed forth.
14The LORD thundered from heaven;
the voice of the Most High
resounded.
15He shot arrows and scattered ˻the
enemies˼,
bolts of lightning and routed
them.
16The valleys of the sea were
exposed
and the foundations of the earth
laid bare
at the rebuke of the LORD,
at the blast of breath from his
nostrils.
17"He reached down from on high
and took hold of me;
he drew me out of deep waters.
18He rescued me from my powerful
enemy,
from my foes, who were too
strong for me.
19They confronted me in the day of
my disaster,

but the LORD was my support.
20He brought me out into a spacious
place;
he rescued me because he
delighted in me.
21"The LORD has dealt with me
according to my
righteousness;
according to the cleanness of
my hands he has rewarded
me.
22For I have kept the ways of the
LORD;
I have not done evil by turning
from my God.
23All his laws are before me;
I have not turned away from
his decrees.
24I have been blameless before him
and have kept myself from sin.
25The LORD has rewarded me
according to my
righteousness,
according to my cleanness[d] in
his sight.
26"To the faithful you show yourself
faithful,
to the blameless you show
yourself blameless,
27to the pure you show yourself
pure,
but to the crooked you show
yourself shrewd.
28You save the humble,
but your eyes are on the
haughty to bring them low.
29You are my lamp, O LORD;
the LORD turns my darkness into
light.
30With your help I can advance
against a troop[e];
with my God I can scale a wall.
31"As for God, his way is perfect;
the word of the LORD is flawless.
He is a shield
for all who take refuge in him.
32For who is God besides the LORD?
And who is the Rock except our
God?

³³It is God who arms me with
     strength[a]
  and makes my way perfect.
³⁴He makes my feet like the feet of
     a deer;
  he enables me to stand on the
     heights.
³⁵He trains my hands for battle;
  my arms can bend a bow of
     bronze.
³⁶You give me your shield of
     victory;
  you stoop down to make me
     great.
³⁷You broaden the path beneath me,
  so that my ankles do not turn.

³⁸"I pursued my enemies and
     crushed them;
  I did not turn back till they
     were destroyed.
³⁹I crushed them completely, and
     they could not rise;
  they fell beneath my feet.
⁴⁰You armed me with strength for
     battle;
  you made my adversaries bow
     at my feet.
⁴¹You made my enemies turn their
     backs in flight,
  and I destroyed my foes.
⁴²They cried for help, but there was
     no one to save them—
  to the LORD, but he did not
     answer.
⁴³I beat them as fine as the dust of
     the earth;
  I pounded and trampled them
     like mud in the streets.

⁴⁴"You have delivered me from the
     attacks of my people;
  you have preserved me as the
     head of nations.
  People I did not know are subject
     to me,
⁴⁵   and foreigners come cringing to
     me;
  as soon as they hear me, they
     obey me.
⁴⁶They all lose heart;

they come trembling[b] from
     their strongholds.

⁴⁷"The LORD lives! Praise be to my
     Rock!
  Exalted be God, the Rock, my
     Savior!
⁴⁸He is the God who avenges me,
  who puts the nations under me,
⁴⁹   who sets me free from my
     enemies.
  You exalted me above my foes;
  from violent men you rescued
     me.
⁵⁰Therefore I will praise you,
     O LORD, among the nations;
  I will sing praises to your name.
⁵¹He gives his king great victories;
  he shows unfailing kindness to
     his anointed,
  to David and his descendants
     forever."

The Last Words of David

23 These are the last words of Da-
     vid:

  "The oracle of David son of Jesse,
  the oracle of the man exalted by
     the Most High,
  the man anointed by the God of
     Jacob,
  Israel's singer of songs[c]:

²"The Spirit of the LORD spoke
     through me;
  his word was on my tongue.
³The God of Israel spoke,
  the Rock of Israel said to me:
  'When one rules over men in
     righteousness,
  when he rules in the fear of
     God,
⁴he is like the light of morning at
     sunrise
  on a cloudless morning,
  like the brightness after rain
  that brings the grass from the
     earth.'
⁵"Is not my house right with God?
  Has he not made with me an
     everlasting covenant,

---

[a]33 Dead Sea Scrolls, some Septuagint manuscripts, Vulgate and Syriac (see also Psalm 18:32);
Masoretic Text *who is my strong refuge*   [b]46 Some Septuagint manuscripts and Vulgate (see
also Psalm 18:45); Masoretic Text *they arm themselves.*   [c]1 Or *Israel's beloved singer*

arranged and secured in every part?
Will he not bring to fruition my salvation
and grant me my every desire?

⁶But evil men are all to be cast aside like thorns,
which are not gathered with the hand.
⁷Whoever touches thorns

MONDAY

VERSE:
2 Samuel 23:4

AUTHOR:
Joni Eareckson Tada

PASSAGE:
2 Samuel 23:1–7

Post-blizzard Promise

Roaring winds, the spray of sleet and snow, dangerous and slippery ice. Remember those storms when you were a child? I sure do. I'd shiver under my quilt, listening to the creaking branches outside my bedroom window. Would the house survive? Would I?

Moaning winds made me feel lonesome . . . Would morning ever come?

Yes, but with it, a different picture. I awoke to soft rays of sun warming my bed covers . . . Quiet called me out of bed and to the window where I gasped at the dazzling white landscape. It was beautiful.

There are days when my soul feels windblown, raw and exposed—times when I'm tossed in a blustery tempest with everything breaking loose. But the God who brings beauty out of blizzards promises to bring peace after the storm. And when the beauty dawns, I hardly remember the fright of that stormy trial.

If you sense storm warnings, hold on to a couple of "winter watch" verses from Scripture. Recall how near and present the Lord really is. Cling to his promise of peace. Remember that joy comes in the morning. Let him cover your fear with his love, like a blanket of snow, soft and gentle.

ADDITIONAL SCRIPTURE READINGS
Psalm 30; Psalm 91

Go to page 411 for your next devotional reading.

uses a tool of iron or the shaft
   of a spear;
they are burned up where they
   lie."

David's Mighty Men

⁸These are the names of David's
mighty men:

Josheb-Basshebeth,ᵃ a Tahkemo-
nite,ᵇ was chief of the Three; he
raised his spear against eight hundred
men, whom he killedᶜ in one encounter.

⁹Next to him was Eleazar son of
Dodai the Ahohite. As one of the
three mighty men, he was with David
when they taunted the Philistines
gathered ⌊at Pas Dammim⌋ᵈ for battle. Then the men of Israel retreated,
¹⁰but he stood his ground and struck
down the Philistines till his hand
grew tired and froze to the sword.
The LORD brought about a great victory that day. The troops returned to Eleazar, but only to strip the dead.

¹¹Next to him was Shammah son of
Agee the Hararite. When the Philistines banded together at a place
where there was a field full of lentils,
Israel's troops fled from them. ¹²But
Shammah took his stand in the middle of the field. He defended it and
struck the Philistines down, and the
LORD brought about a great victory.

¹³During harvest time, three of the
thirty chief men came down to David
at the cave of Adullam, while a band
of Philistines was encamped in the
Valley of Rephaim. ¹⁴At that time David was in the stronghold, and the
Philistine garrison was at Bethlehem.
¹⁵David longed for water and said,
"Oh, that someone would get me a
drink of water from the well near the
gate of Bethlehem!" ¹⁶So the three
mighty men broke through the Philistine lines, drew water from the well
near the gate of Bethlehem and car-

ried it back to David. But he refused
to drink it; instead, he poured it out
before the LORD. ¹⁷"Far be it from me,
O LORD, to do this!" he said. "Is it not
the blood of men who went at the risk
of their lives?" And David would not
drink it.

Such were the exploits of the three
mighty men.

¹⁸Abishai the brother of Joab son of
Zeruiah was chief of the Three.ᵉ He
raised his spear against three hundred men, whom he killed, and so he
became as famous as the Three. ¹⁹Was
he not held in greater honor than the
Three? He became their commander,
even though he was not included
among them.

²⁰Benaiah son of Jehoiada was a
valiant fighter from Kabzeel, who
performed great exploits. He struck
down two of Moab's best men. He
also went down into a pit on a snowy
day and killed a lion. ²¹And he struck
down a huge Egyptian. Although the
Egyptian had a spear in his hand, Benaiah went against him with a club.
He snatched the spear from the Egyptian's hand and killed him with his
own spear. ²²Such were the exploits of
Benaiah son of Jehoiada; he too was
as famous as the three mighty men.
²³He was held in greater honor than
any of the Thirty, but he was not included among the Three. And David
put him in charge of his bodyguard.

²⁴Among the Thirty were:
   Asahel the brother of Joab,
   Elhanan son of Dodo from
      Bethlehem,
²⁵Shammah the Harodite,
   Elika the Harodite,
²⁶Helez the Paltite,
   Ira son of Ikkesh from Tekoa,
²⁷Abiezer from Anathoth,
   Mebunnaiᶠ the Hushathite,
²⁸Zalmon the Ahohite,

ᵃ8 Hebrew; some Septuagint manuscripts suggest *Ish-Bosheth,* that is, *Esh-Baal* (see also 1 Chron.
11:11 *Jashobeam*).   ᵇ8 Probably a variant of *Hacmonite* (see 1 Chron. 11:11)   ᶜ8 Some
Septuagint manuscripts (see also 1 Chron. 11:11); Hebrew and other Septuagint manuscripts
Three; it was Adino the Eznite who killed eight hundred men   ᵈ9 See 1 Chron. 11:13; Hebrew
gathered there.   ᵉ18 Most Hebrew manuscripts (see also 1 Chron. 11:20); two Hebrew
manuscripts and Syriac *Thirty*   ᶠ27 Hebrew; some Septuagint manuscripts (see also 1 Chron.
11:29) *Sibbecai*

Maharai the Netophathite,
²⁹Heled*a* son of Baanah the Netophathite,
Ithai son of Ribai from Gibeah in Benjamin,
³⁰Benaiah the Pirathonite,
Hiddai*b* from the ravines of Gaash,
³¹Abi-Albon the Arbathite,
Azmaveth the Barhumite,
³²Eliahba the Shaalbonite,
the sons of Jashen,
Jonathan ³³son of*c* Shammah the Hararite,
Ahiam son of Sharar*d* the Hararite,
³⁴Eliphelet son of Ahasbai the Maacathite,
Eliam son of Ahithophel the Gilonite,
³⁵Hezro the Carmelite,
Paarai the Arbite,
³⁶Igal son of Nathan from Zobah,
the son of Hagri,*e*
³⁷Zelek the Ammonite,
Naharai the Beerothite, the armor-bearer of Joab son of Zeruiah,
³⁸Ira the Ithrite,
Gareb the Ithrite
³⁹and Uriah the Hittite.
There were thirty-seven in all.

David Counts the Fighting Men

24 Again the anger of the Lord burned against Israel, and he incited David against them, saying, "Go and take a census of Israel and Judah."

²So the king said to Joab and the army commanders*f* with him, "Go throughout the tribes of Israel from Dan to Beersheba and enroll the fighting men, so that I may know how many there are."

³But Joab replied to the king, "May the Lord your God multiply the troops a hundred times over, and may the eyes of my lord the king see it. But why does my lord the king want to do such a thing?"

⁴The king's word, however, overruled Joab and the army commanders; so they left the presence of the king to enroll the fighting men of Israel.

⁵After crossing the Jordan, they camped near Aroer, south of the town in the gorge, and then went through Gad and on to Jazer. ⁶They went to Gilead and the region of Tahtim Hodshi, and on to Dan Jaan and around toward Sidon. ⁷Then they went toward the fortress of Tyre and all the towns of the Hivites and Canaanites. Finally, they went on to Beersheba in the Negev of Judah.

⁸After they had gone through the entire land, they came back to Jerusalem at the end of nine months and twenty days.

⁹Joab reported the number of the fighting men to the king: In Israel there were eight hundred thousand able-bodied men who could handle a sword, and in Judah five hundred thousand.

¹⁰David was conscience-stricken after he had counted the fighting men, and he said to the Lord, "I have sinned greatly in what I have done. Now, O Lord, I beg you, take away the guilt of your servant. I have done a very foolish thing."

¹¹Before David got up the next morning, the word of the Lord had come to Gad the prophet, David's seer: ¹²"Go and tell David, 'This is what the Lord says: I am giving you three options. Choose one of them for me to carry out against you.' "

¹³So Gad went to David and said to him, "Shall there come upon you three*g* years of famine in your land? Or three months of fleeing from your

enemies while they pursue you? Or three days of plague in your land? Now then, think it over and decide how I should answer the one who sent me."

¹⁴David said to Gad, "I am in deep distress. Let us fall into the hands of the LORD, for his mercy is great; but do not let me fall into the hands of men."

¹⁵So the LORD sent a plague on Israel from that morning until the end of the time designated, and seventy thousand of the people from Dan to Beersheba died. ¹⁶When the angel stretched out his hand to destroy Jerusalem, the LORD was grieved because of the calamity and said to the angel who was afflicting the people, "Enough! Withdraw your hand." The angel of the LORD was then at the threshing floor of Araunah the Jebusite.

¹⁷When David saw the angel who was striking down the people, he said to the LORD, "I am the one who has sinned and done wrong. These are but sheep. What have they done? Let your hand fall upon me and my family."

David Builds an Altar

¹⁸On that day Gad went to David and said to him, "Go up and build an altar to the LORD on the threshing floor of Araunah the Jebusite." ¹⁹So David went up, as the LORD had commanded through Gad. ²⁰When Araunah looked and saw the king and his men coming toward him, he went out and bowed down before the king with his face to the ground.

²¹Araunah said, "Why has my lord the king come to his servant?"

"To buy your threshing floor," David answered, "so I can build an altar to the LORD, that the plague on the people may be stopped."

²²Araunah said to David, "Let my lord the king take whatever pleases him and offer it up. Here are oxen for the burnt offering, and here are threshing sledges and ox yokes for the wood. ²³O king, Araunah gives all this to the king." Araunah also said to him, "May the LORD your God accept you."

²⁴But the king replied to Araunah, "No, I insist on paying you for it. I will not sacrifice to the LORD my God burnt offerings that cost me nothing."

So David bought the threshing floor and the oxen and paid fifty shekels*a* of silver for them. ²⁵David built an altar to the LORD there and sacrificed burnt offerings and fellowship offerings.*b* Then the LORD answered prayer in behalf of the land, and the plague on Israel was stopped.

---

*a*24 That is, about 1 1/4 pounds (about 0.6 kilogram)   *b*25 Traditionally *peace offerings*

This book covers the last
days of David, the reign and fall of Solomon,
David's son, and the division of the kingdom
into two nations, Israel and Judah. Look for
the tragic pattern of idol worship begun by
Solomon and continued by most of the kings
after him. As you read 1 Kings, consider
ways you compromise your trust in God,
and turn again to God in wholehearted
obedience.

1 KINGS

Adonijah Sets Himself Up as King

1 When King David was old and
well advanced in years, he could
not keep warm even when they put
covers over him. ²So his servants said
to him, "Let us look for a young virgin to attend the king and take care of
him. She can lie beside him so that
our lord the king may keep warm."

³Then they searched throughout Israel for a beautiful girl and found Abishag, a Shunammite, and brought
her to the king. ⁴The girl was very
beautiful; she took care of the king
and waited on him, but the king had
no intimate relations with her.

⁵Now Adonijah, whose mother was
Haggith, put himself forward and
said, "I will be king." So he got chariots and horses*ᵃ* ready, with fifty men
to run ahead of him. ⁶(His father had
never interfered with him by asking,

"Why do you behave as you do?" He
was also very handsome and was
born next after Absalom.)

⁷Adonijah conferred with Joab son
of Zeruiah and with Abiathar the
priest, and they gave him their support. ⁸But Zadok the priest, Benaiah
son of Jehoiada, Nathan the prophet,
Shimei and Rei*ᵇ* and David's special
guard did not join Adonijah.

⁹Adonijah then sacrificed sheep,
cattle and fattened calves at the Stone
of Zoheleth near En Rogel. He invited
all his brothers, the king's sons, and
all the men of Judah who were royal
officials, ¹⁰but he did not invite Nathan the prophet or Benaiah or the
special guard or his brother Solomon.

¹¹Then Nathan asked Bathsheba,
Solomon's mother, "Have you not
heard that Adonijah, the son of Haggith, has become king without our
lord David's knowing it? ¹²Now then,

ᵃ5 Or charioteers   ᵇ8 Or and his friends

let me advise you how you can save your own life and the life of your son Solomon. ¹³Go in to King David and say to him, 'My lord the king, did you not swear to me your servant: "Surely Solomon your son shall be king after me, and he will sit on my throne"? Why then has Adonijah become king?' ¹⁴While you are still there talking to the king, I will come in and confirm what you have said."

¹⁵So Bathsheba went to see the aged king in his room, where Abishag the Shunammite was attending him. ¹⁶Bathsheba bowed low and knelt before the king.

"What is it you want?" the king asked.

¹⁷She said to him, "My lord, you yourself swore to me your servant by the LORD your God: 'Solomon your son shall be king after me, and he will sit on my throne.' ¹⁸But now Adonijah has become king, and you, my lord the king, do not know about it. ¹⁹He has sacrificed great numbers of cattle, fattened calves, and sheep, and has invited all the king's sons, Abiathar the priest and Joab the commander of the army, but he has not invited Solomon your servant. ²⁰My lord the king, the eyes of all Israel are on you, to learn from you who will sit on the throne of my lord the king after him. ²¹Otherwise, as soon as my lord the king is laid to rest with his fathers, I and my son Solomon will be treated as criminals."

²²While she was still speaking with the king, Nathan the prophet arrived. ²³And they told the king, "Nathan the prophet is here." So he went before the king and bowed with his face to the ground.

²⁴Nathan said, "Have you, my lord the king, declared that Adonijah shall be king after you, and that he will sit on your throne? ²⁵Today he has gone down and sacrificed great numbers of cattle, fattened calves, and sheep. He has invited all the king's sons, the commanders of the army and Abiathar the priest. Right now they are eating and drinking with him and saying, 'Long live King Adonijah!'

²⁶But me your servant, and Zadok the priest, and Benaiah son of Jehoiada, and your servant Solomon he did not invite. ²⁷Is this something my lord the king has done without letting his servants know who should sit on the throne of my lord the king after him?"

David Makes Solomon King

²⁸Then King David said, "Call in Bathsheba." So she came into the king's presence and stood before him. ²⁹The king then took an oath: "As surely as the LORD lives, who has delivered me out of every trouble, ³⁰I will surely carry out today what I swore to you by the LORD, the God of Israel: Solomon your son shall be king after me, and he will sit on my throne in my place."

³¹Then Bathsheba bowed low with her face to the ground and, kneeling before the king, said, "May my lord King David live forever!"

³²King David said, "Call in Zadok the priest, Nathan the prophet and Benaiah son of Jehoiada." When they came before the king, ³³he said to them: "Take your lord's servants with you and set Solomon my son on my own mule and take him down to Gihon. ³⁴There have Zadok the priest and Nathan the prophet anoint him king over Israel. Blow the trumpet and shout, 'Long live King Solomon!' ³⁵Then you are to go up with him, and he is to come and sit on my throne and reign in my place. I have appointed him ruler over Israel and Judah."

³⁶Benaiah son of Jehoiada answered the king, "Amen! May the LORD, the God of my lord the king, so declare it. ³⁷As the LORD was with my lord the king, so may he be with Solomon to make his throne even greater than the throne of my lord King David!"

³⁸So Zadok the priest, Nathan the prophet, Benaiah son of Jehoiada, the Kerethites and the Pelethites went down and put Solomon on King David's mule and escorted him to Gihon. ³⁹Zadok the priest took the horn of oil from the sacred tent and anointed Solomon. Then they sounded the trumpet and all the people shouted,

"Long live King Solomon!" [40]And all the people went up after him, playing flutes and rejoicing greatly, so that the ground shook with the sound.

[41]Adonijah and all the guests who were with him heard it as they were finishing their feast. On hearing the sound of the trumpet, Joab asked, "What's the meaning of all the noise in the city?"

[42]Even as he was speaking, Jonathan son of Abiathar the priest arrived. Adonijah said, "Come in. A worthy man like you must be bringing good news."

[43]"Not at all!" Jonathan answered. "Our lord King David has made Solomon king. [44]The king has sent with him Zadok the priest, Nathan the prophet, Benaiah son of Jehoiada, the Kerethites and the Pelethites, and they have put him on the king's mule, [45]and Zadok the priest and Nathan the prophet have anointed him king at Gihon. From there they have gone up cheering, and the city resounds with it. That's the noise you hear. [46]Moreover, Solomon has taken his seat on the royal throne. [47]Also, the royal officials have come to congratulate our lord King David, saying, 'May your God make Solomon's name more famous than yours and his throne greater than yours!' And the king bowed in worship on his bed [48]and said, 'Praise be to the LORD, the God of Israel, who has allowed my eyes to see a successor on my throne today.' "

[49]At this, all Adonijah's guests rose in alarm and dispersed. [50]But Adonijah, in fear of Solomon, went and took hold of the horns of the altar. [51]Then Solomon was told, "Adonijah is afraid of King Solomon and is clinging to the horns of the altar. He says, 'Let King Solomon swear to me today that he will not put his servant to death with the sword.' "

[52]Solomon replied, "If he shows himself to be a worthy man, not a hair of his head will fall to the ground; but if evil is found in him, he will die." [53]Then King Solomon sent men, and they brought him down from the altar. And Adonijah came and bowed down to King Solomon, and Solomon said, "Go to your home."

David's Charge to Solomon

2 When the time drew near for David to die, he gave a charge to Solomon his son.

[2]"I am about to go the way of all the earth," he said. "So be strong, show yourself a man, [3]and observe what the LORD your God requires: Walk in his ways, and keep his decrees and commands, his laws and requirements, as written in the Law of Moses, so that you may prosper in all you do and wherever you go, [4]and that the LORD may keep his promise to me: 'If your descendants watch how they live, and if they walk faithfully before me with all their heart and soul, you will never fail to have a man on the throne of Israel.'

[5]"Now you yourself know what Joab son of Zeruiah did to me—what he did to the two commanders of Israel's armies, Abner son of Ner and Amasa son of Jether. He killed them, shedding their blood in peacetime as if in battle, and with that blood stained the belt around his waist and the sandals on his feet. [6]Deal with him according to your wisdom, but do not let his gray head go down to the grave[a] in peace.

[7]"But show kindness to the sons of Barzillai of Gilead and let them be among those who eat at your table. They stood by me when I fled from your brother Absalom.

[8]"And remember, you have with you Shimei son of Gera, the Benjamite from Bahurim, who called down bitter curses on me the day I went to Mahanaim. When he came down to meet me at the Jordan, I swore to him by the LORD: 'I will not put you to death by the sword.' [9]But now, do not consider him innocent. You are a man of wisdom; you will know what to do

[a]6 Hebrew *Sheol*; also in verse 9

to him. Bring his gray head down to the grave in blood."

¹⁰Then David rested with his fathers and was buried in the City of David. ¹¹He had reigned forty years over Israel—seven years in Hebron and thirty-three in Jerusalem. ¹²So Solomon sat on the throne of his father David, and his rule was firmly established.

Solomon's Throne Established

¹³Now Adonijah, the son of Haggith, went to Bathsheba, Solomon's mother. Bathsheba asked him, "Do you come peacefully?"

He answered, "Yes, peacefully." ¹⁴Then he added, "I have something to say to you."

"You may say it," she replied.

¹⁵"As you know," he said, "the kingdom was mine. All Israel looked to me as their king. But things changed, and the kingdom has gone to my brother; for it has come to him from the LORD. ¹⁶Now I have one request to make of you. Do not refuse me."

"You may make it," she said.

¹⁷So he continued, "Please ask King Solomon—he will not refuse you—to give me Abishag the Shunammite as my wife."

¹⁸"Very well," Bathsheba replied, "I will speak to the king for you."

¹⁹When Bathsheba went to King Solomon to speak to him for Adonijah, the king stood up to meet her, bowed down to her and sat down on his throne. He had a throne brought for the king's mother, and she sat down at his right hand.

²⁰"I have one small request to make of you," she said. "Do not refuse me."

The king replied, "Make it, my mother; I will not refuse you."

²¹So she said, "Let Abishag the Shunammite be given in marriage to your brother Adonijah."

²²King Solomon answered his mother, "Why do you request Abishag the Shunammite for Adonijah? You might as well request the kingdom for him—after all, he is my older brother—yes, for him and for Abiathar the priest and Joab son of Zeruiah!"

²³Then King Solomon swore by the LORD: "May God deal with me, be it ever so severely, if Adonijah does not pay with his life for this request! ²⁴And now, as surely as the LORD lives—he who has established me securely on the throne of my father David and has founded a dynasty for me as he promised—Adonijah shall be put to death today!" ²⁵So King Solomon gave orders to Benaiah son of Jehoiada, and he struck down Adonijah and he died.

²⁶To Abiathar the priest the king said, "Go back to your fields in Anathoth. You deserve to die, but I will not put you to death now, because you carried the ark of the Sovereign LORD before my father David and shared all my father's hardships." ²⁷So Solomon removed Abiathar from the priesthood of the LORD, fulfilling the word the LORD had spoken at Shiloh about the house of Eli.

²⁸When the news reached Joab, who had conspired with Adonijah though not with Absalom, he fled to the tent of the LORD and took hold of the horns of the altar. ²⁹King Solomon was told that Joab had fled to the tent of the LORD and was beside the altar. Then Solomon ordered Benaiah son of Jehoiada, "Go, strike him down!"

³⁰So Benaiah entered the tent of the LORD and said to Joab, "The king says, 'Come out!' "

But he answered, "No, I will die here."

Benaiah reported to the king, "This is how Joab answered me."

³¹Then the king commanded Benaiah, "Do as he says. Strike him down and bury him, and so clear me and my father's house of the guilt of the innocent blood that Joab shed. ³²The LORD will repay him for the blood he shed, because without the knowledge of my father David he attacked two men and killed them with the sword. Both of them—Abner son of Ner, commander of Israel's army, and Amasa son of Jether, commander of Judah's army—were better men and

more upright than he. ³³May the guilt of their blood rest on the head of Joab and his descendants forever. But on David and his descendants, his house and his throne, may there be the LORD's peace forever."

³⁴So Benaiah son of Jehoiada went up and struck down Joab and killed him, and he was buried on his own land*a* in the desert. ³⁵The king put Benaiah son of Jehoiada over the army in Joab's position and replaced Abiathar with Zadok the priest.

³⁶Then the king sent for Shimei and said to him, "Build yourself a house in Jerusalem and live there, but do not go anywhere else. ³⁷The day you leave and cross the Kidron Valley, you can be sure you will die; your blood will be on your own head."

³⁸Shimei answered the king, "What you say is good. Your servant will do as my lord the king has said." And Shimei stayed in Jerusalem for a long time.

³⁹But three years later, two of Shimei's slaves ran off to Achish son of Maacah, king of Gath, and Shimei was told, "Your slaves are in Gath." ⁴⁰At this, he saddled his donkey and went to Achish at Gath in search of his slaves. So Shimei went away and brought the slaves back from Gath.

⁴¹When Solomon was told that Shimei had gone from Jerusalem to Gath and had returned, ⁴²the king summoned Shimei and said to him, "Did I not make you swear by the LORD and warn you, 'On the day you leave to go anywhere else, you can be sure you will die'? At that time you said to me, 'What you say is good. I will obey.' ⁴³Why then did you not keep your oath to the LORD and obey the command I gave you?"

⁴⁴The king also said to Shimei, "You know in your heart all the wrong you did to my father David. Now the LORD will repay you for your wrongdoing. ⁴⁵But King Solomon will be blessed, and David's throne will remain secure before the LORD forever."

⁴⁶Then the king gave the order to Benaiah son of Jehoiada, and he went out and struck Shimei down and killed him.

The kingdom was now firmly established in Solomon's hands.

Solomon Asks for Wisdom

3 Solomon made an alliance with Pharaoh king of Egypt and married his daughter. He brought her to the City of David until he finished building his palace and the temple of the LORD, and the wall around Jerusalem. ²The people, however, were still sacrificing at the high places, because a temple had not yet been built for the Name of the LORD. ³Solomon showed his love for the LORD by walking according to the statutes of his father David, except that he offered sacrifices and burned incense on the high places.

⁴The king went to Gibeon to offer sacrifices, for that was the most important high place, and Solomon offered a thousand burnt offerings on that altar. ⁵At Gibeon the LORD appeared to Solomon during the night in a dream, and God said, "Ask for whatever you want me to give you."

⁶Solomon answered, "You have shown great kindness to your servant, my father David, because he was faithful to you and righteous and upright in heart. You have continued this great kindness to him and have given him a son to sit on his throne this very day.

⁷"Now, O LORD my God, you have made your servant king in place of my father David. But I am only a little child and do not know how to carry out my duties. ⁸Your servant is here among the people you have chosen, a great people, too numerous to count or number. ⁹So give your servant a discerning heart to govern your people and to distinguish between right and wrong. For who is able to govern this great people of yours?"

¹⁰The Lord was pleased that Solomon had asked for this. ¹¹So God said

a34 Or buried in his tomb

to him, "Since you have asked for this and not for long life or wealth for yourself, nor have asked for the death of your enemies but for discernment in administering justice, ¹²I will do what you have asked. I will give you a wise and discerning heart, so that there will never have been anyone like you, nor will there ever be. ¹³Moreover, I will give you what you have not asked for—both riches and honor—so that in your lifetime you will have no equal among kings. ¹⁴And if you walk in my ways and obey my statutes and commands as David your father did, I will give you a long life." ¹⁵Then Solomon awoke— and he realized it had been a dream.

He returned to Jerusalem, stood before the ark of the Lord's covenant and sacrificed burnt offerings and fellowship offerings.ᵃ Then he gave a feast for all his court.

A Wise Ruling

¹⁶Now two prostitutes came to the king and stood before him. ¹⁷One of them said, "My lord, this woman and I live in the same house. I had a baby while she was there with me. ¹⁸The third day after my child was born, this woman also had a baby. We were alone; there was no one in the house but the two of us.

¹⁹"During the night this woman's son died because she lay on him. ²⁰So she got up in the middle of the night and took my son from my side while I your servant was asleep. She put him by her breast and put her dead son by my breast. ²¹The next morning, I got up to nurse my son—and he was dead! But when I looked at him closely in the morning light, I saw that it wasn't the son I had borne."

²²The other woman said, "No! The living one is my son; the dead one is yours."

But the first one insisted, "No! The dead one is yours; the living one is mine." And so they argued before the king.

²³The king said, "This one says, 'My son is alive and your son is dead,' while that one says, 'No! Your son is dead and mine is alive.' "

²⁴Then the king said, "Bring me a sword." So they brought a sword for the king. ²⁵He then gave an order: "Cut the living child in two and give half to one and half to the other."

²⁶The woman whose son was alive was filled with compassion for her son and said to the king, "Please, my lord, give her the living baby! Don't kill him!"

But the other said, "Neither I nor you shall have him. Cut him in two!"

²⁷Then the king gave his ruling: "Give the living baby to the first woman. Do not kill him; she is his mother."

²⁸When all Israel heard the verdict the king had given, they held the king in awe, because they saw that he had wisdom from God to administer justice.

Solomon's Officials and Governors

4 So King Solomon ruled over all Israel. ²And these were his chief officials:

Azariah son of Zadok—the priest;
³Elihoreph and Ahijah, sons of Shisha—secretaries;
Jehoshaphat son of Ahilud—recorder;
⁴Benaiah son of Jehoiada—commander in chief;
Zadok and Abiathar—priests;
⁵Azariah son of Nathan—in charge of the district officers;
Zabud son of Nathan—a priest and personal adviser to the king;
⁶Ahishar—in charge of the palace;
Adoniram son of Abda—in charge of forced labor.

⁷Solomon also had twelve district governors over all Israel, who supplied provisions for the king and the royal household. Each one had to pro-

ᵃ15 Traditionally *peace offerings*

vide supplies for one month in the year. [8]These are their names:

Ben-Hur—in the hill country of Ephraim;

[9]Ben-Deker—in Makaz, Shaalbim, Beth Shemesh and Elon Bethhanan;

[10]Ben-Hesed—in Arubboth (Socoh and all the land of Hepher were his);

[11]Ben-Abinadab—in Naphoth Dor[a] (he was married to Taphath daughter of Solomon);

[12]Baana son of Ahilud—in Taanach and Megiddo, and in all of Beth Shan next to Zarethan below Jezreel, from Beth Shan to Abel Meholah across to Jokmeam;

[13]Ben-Geber—in Ramoth Gilead (the settlements of Jair son of Manasseh in Gilead were his, as well as the district of Argob in Bashan and its sixty large walled cities with bronze gate bars);

[14]Ahinadab son of Iddo—in Mahanaim;

[15]Ahimaaz—in Naphtali (he had married Basemath daughter of Solomon);

[16]Baana son of Hushai—in Asher and in Aloth;

[17]Jehoshaphat son of Paruah—in Issachar;

[18]Shimei son of Ela—in Benjamin;

[19]Geber son of Uri—in Gilead (the country of Sihon king of the Amorites and the country of Og king of Bashan). He was the only governor over the district.

Solomon's Daily Provisions

[20]The people of Judah and Israel were as numerous as the sand on the seashore; they ate, they drank and they were happy. [21]And Solomon ruled over all the kingdoms from the River[b] to the land of the Philistines, as far as the border of Egypt. These countries brought tribute and were Solomon's subjects all his life.

[22]Solomon's daily provisions were thirty cors[c] of fine flour and sixty cors[d] of meal, [23]ten head of stall-fed cattle, twenty of pasture-fed cattle and a hundred sheep and goats, as well as deer, gazelles, roebucks and choice fowl. [24]For he ruled over all the kingdoms west of the River, from Tiphsah to Gaza, and had peace on all sides. [25]During Solomon's lifetime Judah and Israel, from Dan to Beersheba, lived in safety, each man under his own vine and fig tree.

[26]Solomon had four[e] thousand stalls for chariot horses, and twelve thousand horses.[f]

[27]The district officers, each in his month, supplied provisions for King Solomon and all who came to the king's table. They saw to it that nothing was lacking. [28]They also brought to the proper place their quotas of barley and straw for the chariot horses and the other horses.

Solomon's Wisdom

[29]God gave Solomon wisdom and very great insight, and a breadth of understanding as measureless as the sand on the seashore. [30]Solomon's wisdom was greater than the wisdom of all the men of the East, and greater than all the wisdom of Egypt. [31]He was wiser than any other man, including Ethan the Ezrahite—wiser than Heman, Calcol and Darda, the sons of Mahol. And his fame spread to all the surrounding nations. [32]He spoke three thousand proverbs and his songs numbered a thousand and five. [33]He described plant life, from the cedar of Lebanon to the hyssop that grows out of walls. He also taught about animals and birds, reptiles and fish. [34]Men of all nations came to listen to Solomon's wisdom,

---

[a]11 Or *in the heights of Dor*   [b]21 That is, the Euphrates; also in verse 24   [c]22 That is, probably about 185 bushels (about 6.6 kiloliters)   [d]22 That is, probably about 375 bushels (about 13.2 kiloliters)   [e]26 Some Septuagint manuscripts (see also 2 Chron. 9:25); Hebrew *forty* [f]26 Or *charioteers*

sent by all the kings of the world, who had heard of his wisdom.

Preparations for Building the Temple

5 When Hiram king of Tyre heard that Solomon had been anointed king to succeed his father David, he sent his envoys to Solomon, because he had always been on friendly terms with David. ²Solomon sent back this message to Hiram:

³"You know that because of the wars waged against my father David from all sides, he could not build a temple for the Name of the LORD his God until the LORD put his enemies under his feet. ⁴But now the LORD my God has given me rest on every side, and there is no adversary or disaster. ⁵I intend, therefore, to build a temple for the Name of the LORD my God, as the LORD told my father David, when he said, 'Your son whom I will put on the throne in your place will build the temple for my Name.'

⁶"So give orders that cedars of Lebanon be cut for me. My men will work with yours, and I will pay you for your men whatever wages you set. You know that we have no one so skilled in felling timber as the Sidonians."

⁷When Hiram heard Solomon's message, he was greatly pleased and said, "Praise be to the LORD today, for he has given David a wise son to rule over this great nation."

⁸So Hiram sent word to Solomon:

"I have received the message you sent me and will do all you want in providing the cedar and pine logs. ⁹My men will haul them down from Lebanon to the sea, and I will float them in rafts by sea to the place you specify.

There I will separate them and you can take them away. And you are to grant my wish by providing food for my royal household."

¹⁰In this way Hiram kept Solomon supplied with all the cedar and pine logs he wanted, ¹¹and Solomon gave Hiram twenty thousand cors^a of wheat as food for his household, in addition to twenty thousand baths^{b,c} of pressed olive oil. Solomon continued to do this for Hiram year after year. ¹²The LORD gave Solomon wisdom, just as he had promised him. There were peaceful relations between Hiram and Solomon, and the two of them made a treaty.

¹³King Solomon conscripted laborers from all Israel—thirty thousand men. ¹⁴He sent them off to Lebanon in shifts of ten thousand a month, so that they spent one month in Lebanon and two months at home. Adoniram was in charge of the forced labor. ¹⁵Solomon had seventy thousand carriers and eighty thousand stonecutters in the hills, ¹⁶as well as thirty-three hundred^d foremen who supervised the project and directed the workmen. ¹⁷At the king's command they removed from the quarry large blocks of quality stone to provide a foundation of dressed stone for the temple. ¹⁸The craftsmen of Solomon and Hiram and the men of Gebal^e cut and prepared the timber and stone for the building of the temple.

Solomon Builds the Temple

6 In the four hundred and eightieth^f year after the Israelites had come out of Egypt, in the fourth year of Solomon's reign over Israel, in the month of Ziv, the second month, he began to build the temple of the LORD.

²The temple that King Solomon built for the LORD was sixty cubits

---

$^a11$ That is, probably about 125,000 bushels (about 4,400 kiloliters) $^b11$ Septuagint (see also 2 Chron. 2:10); Hebrew *twenty cors* $^c11$ That is, about 115,000 gallons (about 440 kiloliters) $^d16$ Hebrew; some Septuagint manuscripts (see also 2 Chron. 2:2, 18) *thirty-six hundred* $^e18$ That is, Byblos $^f1$ Hebrew; Septuagint *four hundred and fortieth*

long, twenty wide and thirty high.[a]
[3]The portico at the front of the main hall of the temple extended the width of the temple, that is twenty cubits,[b] and projected ten cubits[c] from the front of the temple. [4]He made narrow clerestory windows in the temple. [5]Against the walls of the main hall and inner sanctuary he built a structure around the building, in which there were side rooms. [6]The lowest floor was five cubits[d] wide, the middle floor six cubits[e] and the third floor seven.[f] He made offset ledges around the outside of the temple so that nothing would be inserted into the temple walls.

[7]In building the temple, only blocks dressed at the quarry were used, and no hammer, chisel or any other iron tool was heard at the temple site while it was being built.

[8]The entrance to the lowest[g] floor was on the south side of the temple; a stairway led up to the middle level and from there to the third. [9]So he built the temple and completed it, roofing it with beams and cedar planks. [10]And he built the side rooms all along the temple. The height of each was five cubits, and they were attached to the temple by beams of cedar.

[11]The word of the LORD came to Solomon: [12]"As for this temple you are building, if you follow my decrees, carry out my regulations and keep all my commands and obey them, I will fulfill through you the promise I gave to David your father. [13]And I will live among the Israelites and will not abandon my people Israel."

[14]So Solomon built the temple and completed it. [15]He lined its interior walls with cedar boards, paneling them from the floor of the temple to the ceiling, and covered the floor of the temple with planks of pine. [16]He partitioned off twenty cubits[b] at the rear of the temple with cedar boards from floor to ceiling to form within the temple an inner sanctuary, the Most Holy Place. [17]The main hall in front of this room was forty cubits[h] long. [18]The inside of the temple was cedar, carved with gourds and open flowers. Everything was cedar; no stone was to be seen.

[19]He prepared the inner sanctuary within the temple to set the ark of the covenant of the LORD there. [20]The inner sanctuary was twenty cubits long, twenty wide and twenty high.[i] He overlaid the inside with pure gold, and he also overlaid the altar of cedar. [21]Solomon covered the inside of the temple with pure gold, and he extended gold chains across the front of the inner sanctuary, which was overlaid with gold. [22]So he overlaid the whole interior with gold. He also overlaid with gold the altar that belonged to the inner sanctuary.

[23]In the inner sanctuary he made a pair of cherubim of olive wood, each ten cubits[c] high. [24]One wing of the first cherub was five cubits long, and the other wing five cubits—ten cubits from wing tip to wing tip. [25]The second cherub also measured ten cubits, for the two cherubim were identical in size and shape. [26]The height of each cherub was ten cubits. [27]He placed the cherubim inside the innermost room of the temple, with their wings spread out. The wing of one cherub touched one wall, while the wing of the other touched the other wall, and their wings touched each other in the middle of the room. [28]He overlaid the cherubim with gold.

[29]On the walls all around the temple, in both the inner and outer rooms, he carved cherubim, palm trees and open flowers. [30]He also covered the floors of both the inner and outer rooms of the temple with gold. [31]For the entrance of the inner sanc-

a2 That is, about 90 feet (about 27 meters) long and 30 feet (about 9 meters) wide and 45 feet (about 13.5 meters) high   b3,16 That is, about 30 feet (about 9 meters)   c3,23 That is, about 15 feet (about 4.5 meters)   d6 That is, about 7 1/2 feet (about 2.3 meters); also in verses 10 and 24   e6 That is, about 9 feet (about 2.7 meters)   f6 That is, about 10 1/2 feet (about 3.1 meters)   g8 Septuagint; Hebrew middle   h17 That is, about 60 feet (about 18 meters) i20 That is, about 30 feet (about 9 meters) long, wide and high

tuary he made doors of olive wood with five-sided jambs. ³²And on the two olive wood doors he carved cherubim, palm trees and open flowers, and overlaid the cherubim and palm trees with beaten gold. ³³In the same way he made four-sided jambs of olive wood for the entrance to the main hall. ³⁴He also made two pine doors, each having two leaves that turned in sockets. ³⁵He carved cherubim, palm trees and open flowers on them and overlaid them with gold hammered evenly over the carvings.

³⁶And he built the inner courtyard of three courses of dressed stone and one course of trimmed cedar beams.

³⁷The foundation of the temple of the LORD was laid in the fourth year, in the month of Ziv. ³⁸In the eleventh year in the month of Bul, the eighth month, the temple was finished in all its details according to its specifications. He had spent seven years building it.

Solomon Builds His Palace

7 It took Solomon thirteen years, however, to complete the construction of his palace. ²He built the Palace of the Forest of Lebanon a hundred cubits long, fifty wide and thirty high,ᵃ with four rows of cedar columns supporting trimmed cedar beams. ³It was roofed with cedar above the beams that rested on the columns—forty-five beams, fifteen to a row. ⁴Its windows were placed high in sets of three, facing each other. ⁵All the doorways had rectangular frames; they were in the front part in sets of three, facing each other.ᵇ

⁶He made a colonnade fifty cubits long and thirty wide.ᶜ In front of it was a portico, and in front of that were pillars and an overhanging roof.

⁷He built the throne hall, the Hall of Justice, where he was to judge, and he covered it with cedar from floor to ceiling.ᵈ ⁸And the palace in which he was to live, set farther back, was similar in design. Solomon also made a palace like this hall for Pharaoh's daughter, whom he had married.

⁹All these structures, from the outside to the great courtyard and from foundation to eaves, were made of blocks of high-grade stone cut to size and trimmed with a saw on their inner and outer faces. ¹⁰The foundations were laid with large stones of good quality, some measuring ten cubitsᵉ and some eight.ᶠ ¹¹Above were high-grade stones, cut to size, and cedar beams. ¹²The great courtyard was surrounded by a wall of three courses of dressed stone and one course of trimmed cedar beams, as was the inner courtyard of the temple of the LORD with its portico.

The Temple's Furnishings

¹³King Solomon sent to Tyre and brought Huram,ᵍ ¹⁴whose mother was a widow from the tribe of Naphtali and whose father was a man of Tyre and a craftsman in bronze. Huram was highly skilled and experienced in all kinds of bronze work. He came to King Solomon and did all the work assigned to him.

¹⁵He cast two bronze pillars, each eighteen cubits high and twelve cubits around,ʰ by line. ¹⁶He also made two capitals of cast bronze to set on the tops of the pillars; each capital was five cubitsⁱ high. ¹⁷A network of interwoven chains festooned the capitals on top of the pillars, seven for each capital. ¹⁸He made pomegranates in two rowsʲ encircling each network to decorate the capitals on

---

ᵃ2 That is, about 150 feet (about 46 meters) long, 75 feet (about 23 meters) wide and 45 feet (about 13.5 meters) high   ᵇ5 The meaning of the Hebrew for this verse is uncertain. ᶜ6 That is, about 75 feet (about 23 meters) long and 45 feet (about 13.5 meters) wide ᵈ7 Vulgate and Syriac; Hebrew *floor*   ᵉ10 That is, about 15 feet (about 4.5 meters)   ᶠ10 That is, about 12 feet (about 3.6 meters)   ᵍ13 Hebrew *Hiram*, a variant of *Huram*; also in verses 40 and 45   ʰ15 That is, about 27 feet (about 8.1 meters) high and 18 feet (about 5.4 meters) around   ⁱ16 That is, about 7 1/2 feet (about 2.3 meters); also in verse 23   ʲ18 Two Hebrew manuscripts and Septuagint; most Hebrew manuscripts *made the pillars, and there were two rows*

top of the pillars.[a] He did the same for each capital. [19]The capitals on top of the pillars in the portico were in the shape of lilies, four cubits[b] high. [20]On the capitals of both pillars, above the bowl-shaped part next to the network, were the two hundred pomegranates in rows all around. [21]He erected the pillars at the portico of the temple. The pillar to the south he named Jakin[c] and the one to the north Boaz.[d] [22]The capitals on top were in the shape of lilies. And so the work on the pillars was completed.

[23]He made the Sea of cast metal, circular in shape, measuring ten cubits[e] from rim to rim and five cubits high. It took a line of thirty cubits[f] to measure around it. [24]Below the rim, gourds encircled it—ten to a cubit. The gourds were cast in two rows in one piece with the Sea.

[25]The Sea stood on twelve bulls, three facing north, three facing west, three facing south and three facing east. The Sea rested on top of them, and their hindquarters were toward the center. [26]It was a handbreadth[g] in thickness, and its rim was like the rim of a cup, like a lily blossom. It held two thousand baths.[h]

[27]He also made ten movable stands of bronze; each was four cubits long, four wide and three high.[i] [28]This is how the stands were made: They had side panels attached to uprights. [29]On the panels between the uprights were lions, bulls and cherubim—and on the uprights as well. Above and below the lions and bulls were wreaths of hammered work. [30]Each stand had four bronze wheels with bronze axles, and each had a basin resting on four supports, cast with wreaths on each side. [31]On the inside of the stand there was an opening that had a circular frame one cubit[j] deep. This opening was round, and with its basework it measured a cubit and a half.[k] Around its opening there was engraving. The panels of the stands were square, not round. [32]The four wheels were under the panels, and the axles of the wheels were attached to the stand. The diameter of each wheel was a cubit and a half. [33]The wheels were made like chariot wheels; the axles, rims, spokes and hubs were all of cast metal.

[34]Each stand had four handles, one on each corner, projecting from the stand. [35]At the top of the stand there was a circular band half a cubit[l] deep. The supports and panels were attached to the top of the stand. [36]He engraved cherubim, lions and palm trees on the surfaces of the supports and on the panels, in every available space, with wreaths all around. [37]This is the way he made the ten stands. They were all cast in the same molds and were identical in size and shape.

[38]He then made ten bronze basins, each holding forty baths[m] and measuring four cubits across, one basin to go on each of the ten stands. [39]He placed five of the stands on the south side of the temple and five on the north. He placed the Sea on the south side, at the southeast corner of the temple. [40]He also made the basins and shovels and sprinkling bowls.

So Huram finished all the work he had undertaken for King Solomon in the temple of the LORD:

[41]the two pillars;
  the two bowl-shaped capitals on top of the pillars;
  the two sets of network decorating the two bowl-shaped capitals on top of the pillars;
[42]the four hundred pomegranates

---

[a]18 Many Hebrew manuscripts and Syriac; most Hebrew manuscripts *pomegranates*   [b]19 That is, about 6 feet (about 1.8 meters); also in verse 38   [c]21 *Jakin* probably means *he establishes.*
[d]21 *Boaz* probably means *in him is strength.*   [e]23 That is, about 15 feet (about 4.5 meters)
[f]23 That is, about 45 feet (about 13.5 meters)   [g]26 That is, about 3 inches (about 8 centimeters)
[h]26 That is, probably about 11,500 gallons (about 44 kiloliters); the Septuagint does not have this sentence.   [i]27 That is, about 6 feet (about 1.8 meters) long and wide and about 4 1/2 feet (about 1.3 meters) high   [j]31 That is, about 1 1/2 feet (about 0.5 meter)   [k]31 That is, about 2 1/4 feet (about 0.7 meter); also in verse 32   [l]35 That is, about 3/4 foot (about 0.2 meter)
[m]38 That is, about 230 gallons (about 880 liters)

for the two sets of network (two rows of pomegranates for each network, decorating the bowl-shaped capitals on top of the pillars);
⁴³the ten stands with their ten basins;
⁴⁴the Sea and the twelve bulls under it;
⁴⁵the pots, shovels and sprinkling bowls.

All these objects that Huram made for King Solomon for the temple of the Lord were of burnished bronze. ⁴⁶The king had them cast in clay molds in the plain of the Jordan between Succoth and Zarethan. ⁴⁷Solomon left all these things unweighed, because there were so many; the weight of the bronze was not determined.

⁴⁸Solomon also made all the furnishings that were in the Lord's temple:

the golden altar;
the golden table on which was the bread of the Presence;
⁴⁹the lampstands of pure gold (five on the right and five on the left, in front of the inner sanctuary);
the gold floral work and lamps and tongs;
⁵⁰the pure gold basins, wick trimmers, sprinkling bowls, dishes and censers;
and the gold sockets for the doors of the innermost room, the Most Holy Place, and also for the doors of the main hall of the temple.

⁵¹When all the work King Solomon had done for the temple of the Lord was finished, he brought in the things his father David had dedicated—the silver and gold and the furnishings—and he placed them in the treasuries of the Lord's temple.

The Ark Brought to the Temple

8 Then King Solomon summoned into his presence at Jerusalem the elders of Israel, all the heads of the tribes and the chiefs of the Israelite families, to bring up the ark of the Lord's covenant from Zion, the City of David. ²All the men of Israel came together to King Solomon at the time of the festival in the month of Ethanim, the seventh month.

³When all the elders of Israel had arrived, the priests took up the ark, ⁴and they brought up the ark of the Lord and the Tent of Meeting and all the sacred furnishings in it. The priests and Levites carried them up, ⁵and King Solomon and the entire assembly of Israel that had gathered about him were before the ark, sacrificing so many sheep and cattle that they could not be recorded or counted.

⁶The priests then brought the ark of the Lord's covenant to its place in the inner sanctuary of the temple, the Most Holy Place, and put it beneath the wings of the cherubim. ⁷The cherubim spread their wings over the place of the ark and overshadowed the ark and its carrying poles. ⁸These poles were so long that their ends could be seen from the Holy Place in front of the inner sanctuary, but not from outside the Holy Place; and they are still there today. ⁹There was nothing in the ark except the two stone tablets that Moses had placed in it at Horeb, where the Lord made a covenant with the Israelites after they came out of Egypt.

¹⁰When the priests withdrew from the Holy Place, the cloud filled the temple of the Lord. ¹¹And the priests could not perform their service because of the cloud, for the glory of the Lord filled his temple.

¹²Then Solomon said, "The Lord has said that he would dwell in a dark cloud; ¹³I have indeed built a magnificent temple for you, a place for you to dwell forever."

¹⁴While the whole assembly of Israel was standing there, the king turned around and blessed them. ¹⁵Then he said:

"Praise be to the Lord, the God of Israel, who with his own hand has fulfilled what he promised with his own mouth to my father David. For he said, 16"Since the day I brought my people Israel out of Egypt, I have not chosen a city in any tribe of Israel to have a temple built for my Name to be there, but I have chosen David to rule my people Israel.'

17"My father David had it in his heart to build a temple for the Name of the LORD, the God of Israel. 18But the LORD said to my father David, 'Because it was in your heart to build a temple for my Name, you did well to have this in your heart. 19Nevertheless, you are not the one to build the temple, but your son, who is your own flesh and blood—he is the one who will build the temple for my Name.'

20"The LORD has kept the promise he made: I have succeeded David my father and now I sit on the throne of Israel, just as the LORD promised, and I have built the temple for the Name of the LORD, the God of Israel. 21I have provided a place there for the ark, in which is the covenant of the LORD that he made with our fathers when he brought them out of Egypt."

Solomon's Prayer of Dedication

22Then Solomon stood before the altar of the LORD in front of the whole assembly of Israel, spread out his hands toward heaven 23and said:

"O LORD, God of Israel, there is no God like you in heaven above or on earth below—you who keep your covenant of love with your servants who continue wholeheartedly in your way. 24You have kept your promise to your servant David my father; with your mouth you have promised and with your hand you have fulfilled it—as it is today. 25"Now LORD, God of Israel, keep for your servant David my

father the promises you made to him when you said, 'You shall never fail to have a man to sit before me on the throne of Israel, if only your sons are careful in all they do to walk before me as you have done.' 26And now, O God of Israel, let your word that you promised your servant David my father come true.

27"But will God really dwell on earth? The heavens, even the highest heaven, cannot contain you. How much less this temple I have built! 28Yet give attention to your servant's prayer and his plea for mercy, O LORD my God. Hear the cry and the prayer that your servant is praying in your presence this day. 29May your eyes be open toward this temple night and day, this place of which you said, 'My Name shall be there,' so that you will hear the prayer your servant prays toward this place. 30Hear the supplication of your servant and of your people Israel when they pray toward this place. Hear from heaven, your dwelling place, and when you hear, forgive.

31"When a man wrongs his neighbor and is required to take an oath and he comes and swears the oath before your altar in this temple, 32then hear from heaven and act. Judge between your servants, condemning the guilty and bringing down on his own head what he has done. Declare the innocent not guilty, and so establish his innocence.

33"When your people Israel have been defeated by an enemy because they have sinned against you, and when they turn back to you and confess your name, praying and making supplication to you in this temple, 34then hear from heaven and forgive the sin of your people Israel and bring them back to the land you gave to their fathers.

35"When the heavens are shut

up and there is no rain because your people have sinned against you, and when they pray toward this place and confess your name and turn from their sin because you have afflicted them, ³⁶then hear from heaven and forgive the sin of your servants, your people Israel. Teach them the right way to live, and send rain on the land you gave your people for an inheritance.

³⁷"When famine or plague comes to the land, or blight or mildew, locusts or grasshoppers, or when an enemy besieges them in any of their cities, whatever disaster or disease may come, ³⁸and when a prayer or plea is made by any of your people Israel—each one aware of the afflictions of his own heart, and spreading out his hands toward this temple— ³⁹then hear from heaven, your dwelling place. Forgive and act; deal with each man according to all he does, since you alone know his heart (for you alone know the hearts of all men), ⁴⁰so that they will fear you all the time they live in the land you gave our fathers.

⁴¹"As for the foreigner who does not belong to your people Israel but has come from a distant land because of your name— ⁴²for men will hear of your great name and your mighty hand and your outstretched arm—when he comes and prays toward this temple, ⁴³then hear from heaven, your dwelling place, and do whatever the foreigner asks of you, so that all the peoples of the earth may know your name and fear you, as do your own people Israel, and may know that this house I have built bears your Name.

⁴⁴"When your people go to war against their enemies, wherever you send them, and when they pray to the LORD toward the city you have chosen and the temple I have built for your Name, ⁴⁵then hear from heaven their prayer and their plea, and uphold their cause.

⁴⁶"When they sin against you—for there is no one who does not sin—and you become angry with them and give them over to the enemy, who takes them captive to his own land, far away or near; ⁴⁷and if they have a change of heart in the land where they are held captive, and repent and plead with you in the land of their conquerors and say, 'We have sinned, we have done wrong, we have acted wickedly'; ⁴⁸and if they turn back to you with all their heart and soul in the land of their enemies who took them captive, and pray to you toward the land you gave their fathers, toward the city you have chosen and the temple I have built for your Name; ⁴⁹then from heaven, your dwelling place, hear their prayer and their plea, and uphold their cause. ⁵⁰And forgive your people, who have sinned against you; forgive all the offenses they have committed against you, and cause their conquerors to show them mercy; ⁵¹for they are your people and your inheritance, whom you brought out of Egypt, out of that iron-smelting furnace.

⁵²"May your eyes be open to your servant's plea and to the plea of your people Israel, and may you listen to them whenever they cry out to you. ⁵³For you singled them out from all the nations of the world to be your own inheritance, just as you declared through your servant Moses when you, O Sovereign LORD, brought our fathers out of Egypt."

⁵⁴When Solomon had finished all these prayers and supplications to the LORD, he rose from before the altar of the LORD, where he had been kneeling with his hands spread out toward heaven. ⁵⁵He stood and blessed the

VERSE:
1 Kings 8:46

AUTHOR:
Arthur H. Becker

PASSAGE:
1 Kings 8:46–53

The Prayer for All Ages

We must be cautious about too romantic a view of elders in the Bible. Most of the historical books of the Old Testament portray the patriarchs Abraham, Jacob, Saul, David and Solomon as demonstrating that observation of Solomon's that "there is no one who does not sin" (1 Kings 8:46). The final years of these men were not always beautiful portraits of "the golden years." The Bible avoids the stereotype of equating old age with virtue. Old and young alike are vulnerable, as was Moses when breaking faith with the Lord in old age (Deuteronomy 32:51). Even the book of Job, which displays considerable respect for age ("Is not wisdom found among the aged? Does not long life bring understanding?" [Job 12:12]), does not equate this with age in any automatic fashion. Elihu's speech (Job 32–37) offers a caution against equating quality with quantity of life; what he does suggest, however, is the importance of giving respect to the elders as individuals. The book of Psalms clearly shows that what makes aging a blessing and a source of wisdom is not longevity but fidelity to God; elders should be wise, but even elders can be taught wisdom (Psalm 105:22). "Teach us to number our days aright, that we may gain a heart of wisdom" is the prayer for all ages (Psalm 90:12).

ADDITIONAL SCRIPTURE READINGS
Psalm 90; James 1:2–8

Go to page 425 for your next devotional reading.

whole assembly of Israel in a loud voice, saying:

⁵⁶"Praise be to the Lord, who has given rest to his people Israel just as he promised. Not one word has failed of all the good promises he gave through his servant Moses. ⁵⁷May the Lord our God be with us as he was with our fathers; may he never leave us nor forsake us. ⁵⁸May he turn our hearts to him, to walk in all his ways and to keep the commands, decrees and regulations he gave our fathers. ⁵⁹And may these words of mine, which I have prayed before the Lord, be near to the Lord our God day and night, that he may uphold the cause of his servant and the cause of his people Israel according to each day's need, ⁶⁰so that all the peoples of the earth may know that the Lord is God and that there is no other. ⁶¹But your hearts must be fully committed to the Lord our God, to live by his decrees and obey his commands, as at this time."

The Dedication of the Temple

⁶²Then the king and all Israel with him offered sacrifices before the Lord. ⁶³Solomon offered a sacrifice of fellowship offeringsᵃ to the Lord: twenty-two thousand cattle and a hundred and twenty thousand sheep and goats. So the king and all the Israelites dedicated the temple of the Lord. ⁶⁴On that same day the king consecrated the middle part of the courtyard in front of the temple of the Lord, and there he offered burnt offerings, grain offerings and the fat of the fellowship offerings, because the bronze altar before the Lord was too small to hold the burnt offerings, the grain offerings and the fat of the fellowship offerings.

⁶⁵So Solomon observed the festival at that time, and all Israel with him—

a vast assembly, people from Leboᵇ Hamath to the Wadi of Egypt. They celebrated it before the Lord our God for seven days and seven days more, fourteen days in all. ⁶⁶On the following day he sent the people away. They blessed the king and then went home, joyful and glad in heart for all the good things the Lord had done for his servant David and his people Israel.

The Lord Appears to Solomon

9 When Solomon had finished building the temple of the Lord and the royal palace, and had achieved all he had desired to do, ²the Lord appeared to him a second time, as he had appeared to him at Gibeon. ³The Lord said to him:

"I have heard the prayer and plea you have made before me; I have consecrated this temple, which you have built, by putting my Name there forever. My eyes and my heart will always be there.

⁴"As for you, if you walk before me in integrity of heart and uprightness, as David your father did, and do all I command and observe my decrees and laws, ⁵I will establish your royal throne over Israel forever, as I promised David your father when I said, 'You shall never fail to have a man on the throne of Israel.'

⁶"But if youᶜ or your sons turn away from me and do not observe the commands and decrees I have given youᶜ and go off to serve other gods and worship them, ⁷then I will cut off Israel from the land I have given them and will reject this temple I have consecrated for my Name. Israel will then become a byword and an object of ridicule among all peoples. ⁸And though this temple is now imposing, all who

pass by will be appalled and will scoff and say, 'Why has the LORD done such a thing to this land and to this temple?' ⁹People will answer, 'Because they have forsaken the LORD their God, who brought their fathers out of Egypt, and have embraced other gods, worshiping and serving them—that is why the LORD brought all this disaster on them.' "

Solomon's Other Activities

¹⁰At the end of twenty years, during which Solomon built these two buildings—the temple of the LORD and the royal palace— ¹¹King Solomon gave twenty towns in Galilee to Hiram king of Tyre, because Hiram had supplied him with all the cedar and pine and gold he wanted. ¹²But when Hiram went from Tyre to see the towns that Solomon had given him, he was not pleased with them. ¹³"What kind of towns are these you have given me, my brother?" he asked. And he called them the Land of Cabul,ᵃ a name they have to this day. ¹⁴Now Hiram had sent to the king 120 talentsᵇ of gold.

¹⁵Here is the account of the forced labor King Solomon conscripted to build the LORD's temple, his own palace, the supporting terraces,ᶜ the wall of Jerusalem, and Hazor, Megiddo and Gezer. ¹⁶(Pharaoh king of Egypt had attacked and captured Gezer. He had set it on fire. He killed its Canaanite inhabitants and then gave it as a wedding gift to his daughter, Solomon's wife. ¹⁷And Solomon rebuilt Gezer.) He built up Lower Beth Horon, ¹⁸Baalath, and Tadmorᵈ in the desert, within his land, ¹⁹as well as all his store cities and the towns for his chariots and for his horsesᵉ— whatever he desired to build in Jeru-

salem, in Lebanon and throughout all the territory he ruled.

²⁰All the people left from the Amorites, Hittites, Perizzites, Hivites and Jebusites (these peoples were not Israelites), ²¹that is, their descendants remaining in the land, whom the Israelites could not exterminateᶠ—these Solomon conscripted for his slave labor force, as it is to this day. ²²But Solomon did not make slaves of any of the Israelites; they were his fighting men, his government officials, his officers, his captains, and the commanders of his chariots and charioteers. ²³They were also the chief officials in charge of Solomon's projects—550 officials supervising the men who did the work.

²⁴After Pharaoh's daughter had come up from the City of David to the palace Solomon had built for her, he constructed the supporting terraces.

²⁵Three times a year Solomon sacrificed burnt offerings and fellowship offeringsᵍ on the altar he had built for the LORD, burning incense before the LORD along with them, and so fulfilled the temple obligations.

²⁶King Solomon also built ships at Ezion Geber, which is near Elath in Edom, on the shore of the Red Sea.ʰ ²⁷And Hiram sent his men—sailors who knew the sea—to serve in the fleet with Solomon's men. ²⁸They sailed to Ophir and brought back 420 talentsⁱ of gold, which they delivered to King Solomon.

The Queen of Sheba Visits Solomon

10 When the queen of Sheba heard about the fame of Solomon and his relation to the name of the LORD, she came to test him with hard questions. ²Arriving at Jerusalem with a very great caravan—with camels carrying spices, large quantities of gold, and precious stones—she came to Solomon and talked with him

---

ᵃ13 *Cabul* sounds like the Hebrew for *good-for-nothing.*   ᵇ14 That is, about 4 1/2 tons (about 4 metric tons)   ᶜ15 Or *the Millo*; also in verse 24   ᵈ18 The Hebrew may also be read *Tamar.* ᵉ19 Or *charioteers*   ᶠ21 The Hebrew term refers to the irrevocable giving over of things or persons to the LORD, often by totally destroying them.   ᵍ25 Traditionally *peace offerings* ʰ26 Hebrew *Yam Suph*; that is, Sea of Reeds   ⁱ28 That is, about 16 tons (about 14.5 metric tons)

about all that she had on her mind. ³Solomon answered all her questions; nothing was too hard for the king to explain to her. ⁴When the queen of Sheba saw all the wisdom of Solomon and the palace he had built, ⁵the food on his table, the seating of his officials, the attending servants in their robes, his cupbearers, and the burnt offerings he made at*ᵃ* the temple of the LORD, she was overwhelmed.

⁶She said to the king, "The report I heard in my own country about your achievements and your wisdom is true. ⁷But I did not believe these things until I came and saw with my own eyes. Indeed, not even half was told me; in wisdom and wealth you have far exceeded the report I heard. ⁸How happy your men must be! How happy your officials, who continually stand before you and hear your wisdom! ⁹Praise be to the LORD your God, who has delighted in you and placed you on the throne of Israel. Because of the LORD's eternal love for Israel, he has made you king, to maintain justice and righteousness."

¹⁰And she gave the king 120 talents*ᵇ* of gold, large quantities of spices, and precious stones. Never again were so many spices brought in as those the queen of Sheba gave to King Solomon.

¹¹(Hiram's ships brought gold from Ophir; and from there they brought great cargoes of almugwood*ᶜ* and precious stones. ¹²The king used the almugwood to make supports for the temple of the LORD and for the royal palace, and to make harps and lyres for the musicians. So much almugwood has never been imported or seen since that day.)

¹³King Solomon gave the queen of Sheba all she desired and asked for, besides what he had given her out of his royal bounty. Then she left and returned with her retinue to her own country.

Solomon's Splendor

¹⁴The weight of the gold that Solomon received yearly was 666 talents,*ᵈ* ¹⁵not including the revenues from merchants and traders and from all the Arabian kings and the governors of the land.

¹⁶King Solomon made two hundred large shields of hammered gold; six hundred bekas*ᵉ* of gold went into each shield. ¹⁷He also made three hundred small shields of hammered gold, with three minas*ᶠ* of gold in each shield. The king put them in the Palace of the Forest of Lebanon.

¹⁸Then the king made a great throne inlaid with ivory and overlaid with fine gold. ¹⁹The throne had six steps, and its back had a rounded top. On both sides of the seat were armrests, with a lion standing beside each of them. ²⁰Twelve lions stood on the six steps, one at either end of each step. Nothing like it had ever been made for any other kingdom. ²¹All King Solomon's goblets were gold, and all the household articles in the Palace of the Forest of Lebanon were pure gold. Nothing was made of silver, because silver was considered of little value in Solomon's days. ²²The king had a fleet of trading ships*ᵍ* at sea along with the ships of Hiram. Once every three years it returned, carrying gold, silver and ivory, and apes and baboons.

²³King Solomon was greater in riches and wisdom than all the other kings of the earth. ²⁴The whole world sought audience with Solomon to hear the wisdom God had put in his heart. ²⁵Year after year, everyone who came brought a gift—articles of silver and gold, robes, weapons and spices, and horses and mules.

²⁶Solomon accumulated chariots and horses; he had fourteen hundred chariots and twelve thousand horses,*ʰ* which he kept in the chariot cities and also with him in Jerusalem.

ᵃ5 Or *the ascent by which he went up to*   *ᵇ10* That is, about 4 1/2 tons (about 4 metric tons) *ᶜ11* Probably a variant of *algumwood*; also in verse 12   *ᵈ14* That is, about 25 tons (about 23 metric tons)   *ᵉ16* That is, about 7 1/2 pounds (about 3.5 kilograms)   *ᶠ17* That is, about 3 3/4 pounds (about 1.7 kilograms)   *ᵍ22* Hebrew *of ships of Tarshish*   *ʰ26* Or *charioteers*

27The king made silver as common in Jerusalem as stones, and cedar as plentiful as sycamore-fig trees in the foothills. 28Solomon's horses were imported from Egypt*a* and from Kue*b*—the royal merchants purchased them from Kue. 29They imported a chariot from Egypt for six hundred shekels*c* of silver, and a horse for a hundred and fifty.*d* They also exported them to all the kings of the Hittites and of the Arameans.

Solomon's Wives

11 King Solomon, however, loved many foreign women besides Pharaoh's daughter—Moabites, Ammonites, Edomites, Sidonians and Hittites. 2They were from nations about which the LORD had told the Israelites, "You must not intermarry with them, because they will surely turn your hearts after their gods." Nevertheless, Solomon held fast to them in love. 3He had seven hundred wives of royal birth and three hundred concubines, and his wives led him astray. 4As Solomon grew old, his wives turned his heart after other gods, and his heart was not fully devoted to the LORD his God, as the heart of David his father had been. 5He followed Ashtoreth the goddess of the Sidonians, and Molech*e* the detestable god of the Ammonites. 6So Solomon did evil in the eyes of the LORD; he did not follow the LORD completely, as David his father had done.

7On a hill east of Jerusalem, Solomon built a high place for Chemosh the detestable god of Moab, and for Molech the detestable god of the Ammonites. 8He did the same for all his foreign wives, who burned incense and offered sacrifices to their gods.

9The LORD became angry with Solomon because his heart had turned away from the LORD, the God of Israel, who had appeared to him twice. 10Although he had forbidden Solomon to follow other gods, Solomon did not

keep the LORD's command. 11So the LORD said to Solomon, "Since this is your attitude and you have not kept my covenant and my decrees, which I commanded you, I will most certainly tear the kingdom away from you and give it to one of your subordinates. 12Nevertheless, for the sake of David your father, I will not do it during your lifetime. I will tear it out of the hand of your son. 13Yet I will not tear the whole kingdom from him, but will give him one tribe for the sake of David my servant and for the sake of Jerusalem, which I have chosen."

Solomon's Adversaries

14Then the LORD raised up against Solomon an adversary, Hadad the Edomite, from the royal line of Edom. 15Earlier when David was fighting with Edom, Joab the commander of the army, who had gone up to bury the dead, had struck down all the men in Edom. 16Joab and all the Israelites stayed there for six months, until they had destroyed all the men in Edom. 17But Hadad, still only a boy, fled to Egypt with some Edomite officials who had served his father. 18They set out from Midian and went to Paran. Then taking men from Paran with them, they went to Egypt, to Pharaoh king of Egypt, who gave Hadad a house and land and provided him with food.

19Pharaoh was so pleased with Hadad that he gave him a sister of his own wife, Queen Tahpenes, in marriage. 20The sister of Tahpenes bore him a son named Genubath, whom Tahpenes brought up in the royal palace. There Genubath lived with Pharaoh's own children.

21While he was in Egypt, Hadad heard that David rested with his fathers and that Joab the commander of the army was also dead. Then Hadad said to Pharaoh, "Let me go, that I may return to my own country."

22"What have you lacked here that

*a*28 Or possibly *Muzur*, a region in Cilicia; also in verse 29   *b*28 Probably *Cilicia*   *c*29 That is, about 15 pounds (about 7 kilograms)   *d*29 That is, about 3 3/4 pounds (about 1.7 kilograms)   *e*5 Hebrew *Milcom*; also in verse 33

you want to go back to your own country?" Pharaoh asked.

"Nothing," Hadad replied, "but do let me go!"

²³And God raised up against Solomon another adversary, Rezon son of Eliada, who had fled from his master, Hadadezer king of Zobah. ²⁴He gathered men around him and became the leader of a band of rebels when David destroyed the forces*ᵃ* ⌐of Zobah⌐; the rebels went to Damascus, where they settled and took control. ²⁵Rezon was Israel's adversary as long as Solomon lived, adding to the trouble caused by Hadad. So Rezon ruled in Aram and was hostile toward Israel.

Jeroboam Rebels Against Solomon

²⁶Also, Jeroboam son of Nebat rebelled against the king. He was one of Solomon's officials, an Ephraimite from Zeredah, and his mother was a widow named Zeruah.

²⁷Here is the account of how he rebelled against the king: Solomon had built the supporting terracesᵇ and had filled in the gap in the wall of the city of David his father. ²⁸Now Jeroboam was a man of standing, and when Solomon saw how well the young man did his work, he put him in charge of the whole labor force of the house of Joseph.

²⁹About that time Jeroboam was going out of Jerusalem, and Ahijah the prophet of Shiloh met him on the way, wearing a new cloak. The two of them were alone out in the country, ³⁰and Ahijah took hold of the new cloak he was wearing and tore it into twelve pieces. ³¹Then he said to Jeroboam, "Take ten pieces for yourself, for this is what the LORD, the God of Israel, says: 'See, I am going to tear the kingdom out of Solomon's hand and give you ten tribes. ³²But for the sake of my servant David and the city of Jerusalem, which I have chosen out of all the tribes of Israel, he will have one tribe. ³³I will do this because theyᶜ have forsaken me and worshiped

Ashtoreth the goddess of the Sidonians, Chemosh the god of the Moabites, and Molech the god of the Ammonites, and have not walked in my ways, nor done what is right in my eyes, nor kept my statutes and laws as David, Solomon's father, did.

³⁴" 'But I will not take the whole kingdom out of Solomon's hand; I have made him ruler all the days of his life for the sake of David my servant, whom I chose and who observed my commands and statutes. ³⁵I will take the kingdom from his son's hands and give you ten tribes. ³⁶I will give one tribe to his son so that David my servant may always have a lamp before me in Jerusalem, the city where I chose to put my Name. ³⁷However, as for you, I will take you, and you will rule over all that your heart desires; you will be king over Israel. ³⁸If you do whatever I command you and walk in my ways and do what is right in my eyes by keeping my statutes and commands, as David my servant did, I will be with you. I will build you a dynasty as enduring as the one I built for David and will give Israel to you. ³⁹I will humble David's descendants because of this, but not forever.' "

⁴⁰Solomon tried to kill Jeroboam, but Jeroboam fled to Egypt, to Shishak the king, and stayed there until Solomon's death.

Solomon's Death

⁴¹As for the other events of Solomon's reign—all he did and the wisdom he displayed—are they not written in the book of the annals of Solomon? ⁴²Solomon reigned in Jerusalem over all Israel forty years. ⁴³Then he rested with his fathers and was buried in the city of David his father. And Rehoboam his son succeeded him as king.

Israel Rebels Against Rehoboam

12 Rehoboam went to Shechem, for all the Israelites had gone

---

*ᵃ*24 Hebrew *destroyed them*   *ᵇ*27 Or *the Millo*   *ᶜ*33 Hebrew; Septuagint, Vulgate and Syriac *because he has* there to make him king. ²When Jeroboam son of Nebat heard this (he was still in Egypt, where he had fled from King Solomon), he returned from[a] Egypt. ³So they sent for Jeroboam, and he and the whole assembly of Israel went to Rehoboam and said to him: ⁴"Your father put a heavy yoke on us, but now lighten the harsh labor and the heavy yoke he put on us, and we will serve you."

⁵Rehoboam answered, "Go away for three days and then come back to me." So the people went away.

⁶Then King Rehoboam consulted the elders who had served his father Solomon during his lifetime. "How would you advise me to answer these people?" he asked.

⁷They replied, "If today you will be a servant to these people and serve them and give them a favorable answer, they will always be your servants."

⁸But Rehoboam rejected the advice the elders gave him and consulted the young men who had grown up with him and were serving him. ⁹He asked them, "What is your advice? How should we answer these people who say to me, 'Lighten the yoke your father put on us'?"

¹⁰The young men who had grown up with him replied, "Tell these people who have said to you, 'Your father put a heavy yoke on us, but make our yoke lighter'—tell them, 'My little finger is thicker than my father's waist. ¹¹My father laid on you a heavy yoke; I will make it even heavier. My father scourged you with whips; I will scourge you with scorpions.' "

¹²Three days later Jeroboam and all the people returned to Rehoboam, as the king had said, "Come back to me in three days." ¹³The king answered the people harshly. Rejecting the advice given him by the elders, ¹⁴he followed the advice of the young men and said, "My father made your yoke heavy; I will make it even heavier. My father scourged you with whips; I

will scourge you with scorpions." ¹⁵So the king did not listen to the people, for this turn of events was from the LORD, to fulfill the word the LORD had spoken to Jeroboam son of Nebat through Ahijah the Shilonite.

¹⁶When all Israel saw that the king refused to listen to them, they answered the king:

"What share do we have in David,
  what part in Jesse's son?
To your tents, O Israel!
  Look after your own house,
    O David!"

So the Israelites went home. ¹⁷But as for the Israelites who were living in the towns of Judah, Rehoboam still ruled over them.

¹⁸King Rehoboam sent out Adoniram,[b] who was in charge of forced labor, but all Israel stoned him to death. King Rehoboam, however, managed to get into his chariot and escape to Jerusalem. ¹⁹So Israel has been in rebellion against the house of David to this day.

²⁰When all the Israelites heard that Jeroboam had returned, they sent and called him to the assembly and made him king over all Israel. Only the tribe of Judah remained loyal to the house of David.

²¹When Rehoboam arrived in Jerusalem, he mustered the whole house of Judah and the tribe of Benjamin—a hundred and eighty thousand fighting men—to make war against the house of Israel and to regain the kingdom for Rehoboam son of Solomon.

²²But this word of God came to Shemaiah the man of God: ²³"Say to Rehoboam son of Solomon king of Judah, to the whole house of Judah and Benjamin, and to the rest of the people, ²⁴'This is what the LORD says: Do not go up to fight against your brothers, the Israelites. Go home, every one of you, for this is my doing.' " So they obeyed the word of the LORD and went home again, as the LORD had ordered.

---

[a]2 Or he remained in 5:14); Hebrew Adoram   [b]18 Some Septuagint manuscripts and Syriac (see also 1 Kings 4:6 and

Golden Calves at Bethel and Dan

²⁵Then Jeroboam fortified Shechem in the hill country of Ephraim and lived there. From there he went out and built up Peniel.^a

²⁶Jeroboam thought to himself, "The kingdom will now likely revert to the house of David. ²⁷If these people go up to offer sacrifices at the temple of the LORD in Jerusalem, they will again give their allegiance to their lord, Rehoboam king of Judah. They will kill me and return to King Rehoboam."

²⁸After seeking advice, the king made two golden calves. He said to the people, "It is too much for you to go up to Jerusalem. Here are your gods, O Israel, who brought you up out of Egypt." ²⁹One he set up in Bethel, and the other in Dan. ³⁰And this thing became a sin; the people went even as far as Dan to worship the one there.

³¹Jeroboam built shrines on high places and appointed priests from all sorts of people, even though they were not Levites. ³²He instituted a festival on the fifteenth day of the eighth month, like the festival held in Judah, and offered sacrifices on the altar. This he did in Bethel, sacrificing to the calves he had made. And at Bethel he also installed priests at the high places he had made. ³³On the fifteenth day of the eighth month, a month of his own choosing, he offered sacrifices on the altar he had built at Bethel. So he instituted the festival for the Israelites and went up to the altar to make offerings.

The Man of God From Judah

13 By the word of the LORD a man of God came from Judah to Bethel, as Jeroboam was standing by the altar to make an offering. ²He cried out against the altar by the word of the LORD: "O altar, altar! This is what the LORD says: 'A son named Josiah will be born to the house of David. On you he will sacrifice the priests of the high places who now make offerings here, and human bones will be burned on you.' " ³That same day the man of God gave a sign: "This is the sign the LORD has declared: The altar will be split apart and the ashes on it will be poured out."

⁴When King Jeroboam heard what the man of God cried out against the altar at Bethel, he stretched out his hand from the altar and said, "Seize him!" But the hand he stretched out toward the man shriveled up, so that he could not pull it back. ⁵Also, the altar was split apart and its ashes poured out according to the sign given by the man of God by the word of the LORD.

⁶Then the king said to the man of God, "Intercede with the LORD your God and pray for me that my hand may be restored." So the man of God interceded with the LORD, and the king's hand was restored and became as it was before.

⁷The king said to the man of God, "Come home with me and have something to eat, and I will give you a gift."

⁸But the man of God answered the king, "Even if you were to give me half your possessions, I would not go with you, nor would I eat bread or drink water here. ⁹For I was commanded by the word of the LORD: 'You must not eat bread or drink water or return by the way you came.' " ¹⁰So he took another road and did not return by the way he had come to Bethel.

¹¹Now there was a certain old prophet living in Bethel, whose sons came and told him all that the man of God had done there that day. They also told their father what he had said to the king. ¹²Their father asked them, "Which way did he go?" And his sons showed him which road the man of God from Judah had taken. ¹³So he said to his sons, "Saddle the donkey for me." And when they had saddled the donkey for him, he mounted it

^a25 Hebrew *Penuel*, a variant of *Peniel*

¹⁴and rode after the man of God. He found him sitting under an oak tree and asked, "Are you the man of God who came from Judah?"

"I am," he replied.

¹⁵So the prophet said to him, "Come home with me and eat."

¹⁶The man of God said, "I cannot turn back and go with you, nor can I eat bread or drink water with you in this place. ¹⁷I have been told by the word of the LORD: 'You must not eat bread or drink water there or return by the way you came.' "

¹⁸The old prophet answered, "I too am a prophet, as you are. And an angel said to me by the word of the LORD: 'Bring him back with you to your house so that he may eat bread and drink water.' " (But he was lying to him.) ¹⁹So the man of God returned with him and ate and drank in his house.

²⁰While they were sitting at the table, the word of the LORD came to the old prophet who had brought him back. ²¹He cried out to the man of God who had come from Judah, "This is what the LORD says: 'You have defied the word of the LORD and have not kept the command the LORD your God gave you. ²²You came back and ate bread and drank water in the place where he told you not to eat or drink. Therefore your body will not be buried in the tomb of your fathers.' "

²³When the man of God had finished eating and drinking, the prophet who had brought him back saddled his donkey for him. ²⁴As he went on his way, a lion met him on the road and killed him, and his body was thrown down on the road, with both the donkey and the lion standing beside it. ²⁵Some people who passed by saw the body thrown down there, with the lion standing beside the body, and they went and reported it in the city where the old prophet lived.

²⁶When the prophet who had brought him back from his journey heard of it, he said, "It is the man of God who defied the word of the LORD.

The LORD has given him over to the lion, which has mauled him and killed him, as the word of the LORD had warned him."

²⁷The prophet said to his sons, "Saddle the donkey for me," and they did so. ²⁸Then he went out and found the body thrown down on the road, with the donkey and the lion standing beside it. The lion had neither eaten the body nor mauled the donkey. ²⁹So the prophet picked up the body of the man of God, laid it on the donkey, and brought it back to his own city to mourn for him and bury him. ³⁰Then he laid the body in his own tomb, and they mourned over him and said, "Oh, my brother!"

³¹After burying him, he said to his sons, "When I die, bury me in the grave where the man of God is buried; lay my bones beside his bones. ³²For the message he declared by the word of the LORD against the altar in Bethel and against all the shrines on the high places in the towns of Samaria will certainly come true."

³³Even after this, Jeroboam did not change his evil ways, but once more appointed priests for the high places from all sorts of people. Anyone who wanted to become a priest he consecrated for the high places. ³⁴This was the sin of the house of Jeroboam that led to its downfall and to its destruction from the face of the earth.

Ahijah's Prophecy Against Jeroboam

14 At that time Abijah son of Jeroboam became ill, ²and Jeroboam said to his wife, "Go, disguise yourself, so you won't be recognized as the wife of Jeroboam. Then go to Shiloh. Ahijah the prophet is there—the one who told me I would be king over this people. ³Take ten loaves of bread with you, some cakes and a jar of honey, and go to him. He will tell you what will happen to the boy." ⁴So Jeroboam's wife did what he said and went to Ahijah's house in Shiloh.

Now Ahijah could not see; his sight was gone because of his age. ⁵But the LORD had told Ahijah, "Jeroboam's wife is coming to ask you about her son, for he is ill, and you are to give her such and such an answer. When she arrives, she will pretend to be someone else."

[6]So when Ahijah heard the sound of her footsteps at the door, he said, "Come in, wife of Jeroboam. Why this pretense? I have been sent to you with bad news. [7]Go, tell Jeroboam that this is what the LORD, the God of Israel, says: 'I raised you up from among the people and made you a leader over my people Israel. [8]I tore the kingdom away from the house of David and gave it to you, but you have not been like my servant David, who kept my commands and followed me with all his heart, doing only what was right in my eyes. [9]You have done more evil than all who lived before you. You have made for yourself other gods, idols made of metal; you have provoked me to anger and thrust me behind your back.

[10]"'Because of this, I am going to bring disaster on the house of Jeroboam. I will cut off from Jeroboam every last male in Israel—slave or free. I will burn up the house of Jeroboam as one burns dung, until it is all gone. [11]Dogs will eat those belonging to Jeroboam who die in the city, and the birds of the air will feed on those who die in the country. The LORD has spoken!'

[12]"As for you, go back home. When you set foot in your city, the boy will die. [13]All Israel will mourn for him and bury him. He is the only one belonging to Jeroboam who will be buried, because he is the only one in the house of Jeroboam in whom the LORD, the God of Israel, has found anything good.

[14]"The LORD will raise up for himself a king over Israel who will cut off the family of Jeroboam. This is the day! What? Yes, even now.[a] [15]And the LORD will strike Israel, so that it will be like a reed swaying in the water. He will uproot Israel from this good land that he gave to their forefa-

thers and scatter them beyond the River,[b] because they provoked the LORD to anger by making Asherah poles.[c] [16]And he will give Israel up because of the sins Jeroboam has committed and has caused Israel to commit."

[17]Then Jeroboam's wife got up and left and went to Tirzah. As soon as she stepped over the threshold of the house, the boy died. [18]They buried him, and all Israel mourned for him, as the LORD had said through his servant the prophet Ahijah.

[19]The other events of Jeroboam's reign, his wars and how he ruled, are written in the book of the annals of the kings of Israel. [20]He reigned for twenty-two years and then rested with his fathers. And Nadab his son succeeded him as king.

Rehoboam King of Judah

[21]Rehoboam son of Solomon was king in Judah. He was forty-one years old when he became king, and he reigned seventeen years in Jerusalem, the city the LORD had chosen out of all the tribes of Israel in which to put his Name. His mother's name was Naamah; she was an Ammonite. [22]Judah did evil in the eyes of the LORD. By the sins they committed they stirred up his jealous anger more than their fathers had done. [23]They also set up for themselves high places, sacred stones and Asherah poles on every high hill and under every spreading tree. [24]There were even male shrine prostitutes in the land; the people engaged in all the detestable practices of the nations the LORD had driven out before the Israelites.

[25]In the fifth year of King Rehoboam, Shishak king of Egypt attacked Jerusalem. [26]He carried off the treasures of the temple of the LORD and the treasures of the royal palace. He took everything, including all the gold shields Solomon had made. [27]So King Rehoboam made bronze shields to replace them and assigned these to

---

[a]14 The meaning of the Hebrew for this sentence is uncertain.   [b]15 That is, the Euphrates
[c]15 That is, symbols of the goddess Asherah; here and elsewhere in 1 Kings

the commanders of the guard on duty at the entrance to the royal palace. ²⁸Whenever the king went to the Lord's temple, the guards bore the shields, and afterward they returned them to the guardroom.

²⁹As for the other events of Rehoboam's reign, and all he did, are they not written in the book of the annals of the kings of Judah? ³⁰There was continual warfare between Rehoboam and Jeroboam. ³¹And Rehoboam rested with his fathers and was buried with them in the City of David. His mother's name was Naamah; she was an Ammonite. And Abijah^a his son succeeded him as king.

Abijah King of Judah

15 In the eighteenth year of the reign of Jeroboam son of Nebat, Abijah^b became king of Judah, ²and he reigned in Jerusalem three years. His mother's name was Maacah daughter of Abishalom.^c

³He committed all the sins his father had done before him; his heart was not fully devoted to the Lord his God, as the heart of David his forefather had been. ⁴Nevertheless, for David's sake the Lord his God gave him a lamp in Jerusalem by raising up a son to succeed him and by making Jerusalem strong. ⁵For David had done what was right in the eyes of the Lord and had not failed to keep any of the Lord's commands all the days of his life—except in the case of Uriah the Hittite.

⁶There was war between Rehoboam^d and Jeroboam throughout ⌊Abijah's⌋ lifetime. ⁷As for the other events of Abijah's reign, and all he did, are they not written in the book of the annals of the kings of Judah? There was war between Abijah and Jeroboam. ⁸And Abijah rested with his fathers and was buried in the City of David.

And Asa his son succeeded him as king.

Asa King of Judah

⁹In the twentieth year of Jeroboam king of Israel, Asa became king of Judah, ¹⁰and he reigned in Jerusalem forty-one years. His grandmother's name was Maacah daughter of Abishalom.

¹¹Asa did what was right in the eyes of the Lord, as his father David had done. ¹²He expelled the male shrine prostitutes from the land and got rid of all the idols his fathers had made. ¹³He even deposed his grandmother Maacah from her position as queen mother, because she had made a repulsive Asherah pole. Asa cut the pole down and burned it in the Kidron Valley. ¹⁴Although he did not remove the high places, Asa's heart was fully committed to the Lord all his life. ¹⁵He brought into the temple of the Lord the silver and gold and the articles that he and his father had dedicated.

¹⁶There was war between Asa and Baasha king of Israel throughout their reigns. ¹⁷Baasha king of Israel went up against Judah and fortified Ramah to prevent anyone from leaving or entering the territory of Asa king of Judah.

¹⁸Asa then took all the silver and gold that was left in the treasuries of the Lord's temple and of his own palace. He entrusted it to his officials and sent them to Ben-Hadad son of Tabrimmon, the son of Hezion, the king of Aram, who was ruling in Damascus. ¹⁹"Let there be a treaty between me and you," he said, "as there was between my father and your father. See, I am sending you a gift of silver and gold. Now break your treaty with Baasha king of Israel so he will withdraw from me."

²⁰Ben-Hadad agreed with King Asa

---

^a31 Some Hebrew manuscripts and Septuagint (see also 2 Chron. 12:16); most Hebrew manuscripts *Abijam*   ^b1 Some Hebrew manuscripts and Septuagint (see also 2 Chron. 12:16); most Hebrew manuscripts *Abijam*; also in verses 7 and 8   ^c2 A variant of *Absalom*; also in verse 10   ^d6 Most Hebrew manuscripts; some Hebrew manuscripts and Syriac *Abijam* (that is, Abijah)

and sent the commanders of his forces against the towns of Israel. He conquered Ijon, Dan, Abel Beth Maacah and all Kinnereth in addition to Naphtali. ²¹When Baasha heard this, he stopped building Ramah and withdrew to Tirzah. ²²Then King Asa issued an order to all Judah—no one was exempt—and they carried away from Ramah the stones and timber Baasha had been using there. With them King Asa built up Geba in Benjamin, and also Mizpah.

²³As for all the other events of Asa's reign, all his achievements, all he did and the cities he built, are they not written in the book of the annals of the kings of Judah? In his old age, however, his feet became diseased. ²⁴Then Asa rested with his fathers and was buried with them in the city of his father David. And Jehoshaphat his son succeeded him as king.

Nadab King of Israel

²⁵Nadab son of Jeroboam became king of Israel in the second year of Asa king of Judah, and he reigned over Israel two years. ²⁶He did evil in the eyes of the Lord, walking in the ways of his father and in his sin, which he had caused Israel to commit.

²⁷Baasha son of Ahijah of the house of Issachar plotted against him, and he struck him down at Gibbethon, a Philistine town, while Nadab and all Israel were besieging it. ²⁸Baasha killed Nadab in the third year of Asa king of Judah and succeeded him as king.

²⁹As soon as he began to reign, he killed Jeroboam's whole family. He did not leave Jeroboam anyone that breathed, but destroyed them all, according to the word of the Lord given through his servant Ahijah the Shilonite— ³⁰because of the sins Jeroboam had committed and had caused Israel to commit, and because he provoked the Lord, the God of Israel, to anger.

³¹As for the other events of Nadab's reign, and all he did, are they not written in the book of the annals of the kings of Israel? ³²There was war between Asa and Baasha king of Israel throughout their reigns.

Baasha King of Israel

³³In the third year of Asa king of Judah, Baasha son of Ahijah became king of all Israel in Tirzah, and he reigned twenty-four years. ³⁴He did evil in the eyes of the Lord, walking in the ways of Jeroboam and in his sin, which he had caused Israel to commit.

16 Then the word of the Lord came to Jehu son of Hanani against Baasha: ²"I lifted you up from the dust and made you leader of my people Israel, but you walked in the ways of Jeroboam and caused my people Israel to sin and to provoke me to anger by their sins. ³So I am about to consume Baasha and his house, and I will make your house like that of Jeroboam son of Nebat. ⁴Dogs will eat those belonging to Baasha who die in the city, and the birds of the air will feed on those who die in the country."

⁵As for the other events of Baasha's reign, what he did and his achievements, are they not written in the book of the annals of the kings of Israel? ⁶Baasha rested with his fathers and was buried in Tirzah. And Elah his son succeeded him as king.

⁷Moreover, the word of the Lord came through the prophet Jehu son of Hanani to Baasha and his house, because of all the evil he had done in the eyes of the Lord, provoking him to anger by the things he did, and becoming like the house of Jeroboam— and also because he destroyed it.

Elah King of Israel

⁸In the twenty-sixth year of Asa king of Judah, Elah son of Baasha became king of Israel, and he reigned in Tirzah two years.

⁹Zimri, one of his officials, who had command of half his chariots, plotted against him. Elah was in Tirzah at the time, getting drunk in the home of Arza, the man in charge of the palace at Tirzah. ¹⁰Zimri came in, struck him down and killed him in the twenty-

seventh year of Asa king of Judah. Then he succeeded him as king.

¹¹As soon as he began to reign and was seated on the throne, he killed off Baasha's whole family. He did not spare a single male, whether relative or friend. ¹²So Zimri destroyed the whole family of Baasha, in accordance with the word of the LORD spoken against Baasha through the prophet Jehu— ¹³because of all the sins Baasha and his son Elah had committed and had caused Israel to commit, so that they provoked the LORD, the God of Israel, to anger by their worthless idols.

¹⁴As for the other events of Elah's reign, and all he did, are they not written in the book of the annals of the kings of Israel?

Zimri King of Israel

¹⁵In the twenty-seventh year of Asa king of Judah, Zimri reigned in Tirzah seven days. The army was encamped near Gibbethon, a Philistine town. ¹⁶When the Israelites in the camp heard that Zimri had plotted against the king and murdered him, they proclaimed Omri, the commander of the army, king over Israel that very day there in the camp. ¹⁷Then Omri and all the Israelites with him withdrew from Gibbethon and laid siege to Tirzah. ¹⁸When Zimri saw that the city was taken, he went into the citadel of the royal palace and set the palace on fire around him. So he died, ¹⁹because of the sins he had committed, doing evil in the eyes of the LORD and walking in the ways of Jeroboam and in the sin he had committed and had caused Israel to commit.

²⁰As for the other events of Zimri's reign, and the rebellion he carried out, are they not written in the book of the annals of the kings of Israel?

Omri King of Israel

²¹Then the people of Israel were split into two factions; half supported Tibni son of Ginath for king, and the other half supported Omri. ²²But Omri's followers proved stronger than those of Tibni son of Ginath. So Tibni died and Omri became king.

²³In the thirty-first year of Asa king of Judah, Omri became king of Israel, and he reigned twelve years, six of them in Tirzah. ²⁴He bought the hill of Samaria from Shemer for two talents[a] of silver and built a city on the hill, calling it Samaria, after Shemer, the name of the former owner of the hill.

²⁵But Omri did evil in the eyes of the LORD and sinned more than all those before him. ²⁶He walked in all the ways of Jeroboam son of Nebat and in his sin, which he had caused Israel to commit, so that they provoked the LORD, the God of Israel, to anger by their worthless idols.

²⁷As for the other events of Omri's reign, what he did and the things he achieved, are they not written in the book of the annals of the kings of Israel? ²⁸Omri rested with his fathers and was buried in Samaria. And Ahab his son succeeded him as king.

Ahab Becomes King of Israel

²⁹In the thirty-eighth year of Asa king of Judah, Ahab son of Omri became king of Israel, and he reigned in Samaria over Israel twenty-two years. ³⁰Ahab son of Omri did more evil in the eyes of the LORD than any of those before him. ³¹He not only considered it trivial to commit the sins of Jeroboam son of Nebat, but he also married Jezebel daughter of Ethbaal king of the Sidonians, and began to serve Baal and worship him. ³²He set up an altar for Baal in the temple of Baal that he built in Samaria. ³³Ahab also made an Asherah pole and did more to provoke the LORD, the God of Israel, to anger than did all the kings of Israel before him.

³⁴In Ahab's time, Hiel of Bethel rebuilt Jericho. He laid its foundations at the cost of his firstborn son Abiram, and he set up its gates at the cost of his youngest son Segub, in accor-

---

^a24 That is, about 150 pounds (about 70 kilograms)

dance with the word of the LORD spoken by Joshua son of Nun.

Elijah Fed by Ravens

17 Now Elijah the Tishbite, from Tishbe[a] in Gilead, said to Ahab, "As the LORD, the God of Israel, lives, whom I serve, there will be neither dew nor rain in the next few years except at my word."

²Then the word of the LORD came to Elijah: ³"Leave here, turn eastward and hide in the Kerith Ravine, east of the Jordan. ⁴You will drink from the brook, and I have ordered the ravens to feed you there."

⁵So he did what the LORD had told him. He went to the Kerith Ravine, east of the Jordan, and stayed there. ⁶The ravens brought him bread and meat in the morning and bread and meat in the evening, and he drank from the brook.

The Widow at Zarephath

⁷Some time later the brook dried up because there had been no rain in the land. ⁸Then the word of the LORD came to him: ⁹"Go at once to Zarephath of Sidon and stay there. I have commanded a widow in that place to supply you with food." ¹⁰So he went to Zarephath. When he came to the town gate, a widow was there gathering sticks. He called to her and asked, "Would you bring me a little water in a jar so I may have a drink?" ¹¹As she was going to get it, he called, "And bring me, please, a piece of bread."

¹²"As surely as the LORD your God lives," she replied, "I don't have any bread—only a handful of flour in a jar and a little oil in a jug. I am gathering a few sticks to take home and make a meal for myself and my son, that we may eat it—and die."

¹³Elijah said to her, "Don't be afraid. Go home and do as you have said. But first make a small cake of bread for me from what you have and bring it to me, and then make something for yourself and your son. ¹⁴For this is what the LORD, the God of Isra-el, says: 'The jar of flour will not be used up and the jug of oil will not run dry until the day the LORD gives rain on the land.' "

¹⁵She went away and did as Elijah had told her. So there was food every day for Elijah and for the woman and her family. ¹⁶For the jar of flour was not used up and the jug of oil did not run dry, in keeping with the word of the LORD spoken by Elijah.

¹⁷Some time later the son of the woman who owned the house became ill. He grew worse and worse, and finally stopped breathing. ¹⁸She said to Elijah, "What do you have against me, man of God? Did you come to remind me of my sin and kill my son?"

¹⁹"Give me your son," Elijah replied. He took him from her arms, carried him to the upper room where he was staying, and laid him on his bed. ²⁰Then he cried out to the LORD, "O LORD my God, have you brought tragedy also upon this widow I am staying with, by causing her son to die?" ²¹Then he stretched himself out on the boy three times and cried to the LORD, "O LORD my God, let this boy's life return to him!"

²²The LORD heard Elijah's cry, and the boy's life returned to him, and he lived. ²³Elijah picked up the child and carried him down from the room into the house. He gave him to his mother and said, "Look, your son is alive!"

²⁴Then the woman said to Elijah, "Now I know that you are a man of God and that the word of the LORD from your mouth is the truth."

Elijah and Obadiah

18 After a long time, in the third year, the word of the LORD came to Elijah: "Go and present yourself to Ahab, and I will send rain on the land." ²So Elijah went to present himself to Ahab.

Now the famine was severe in Samaria, ³and Ahab had summoned Obadiah, who was in charge of his palace. (Obadiah was a devout believ-

---

a1 Or Tishbite, of the settlers

VERSE:
1 Kings 17:15

AUTHOR:
Charles H. Spurgeon

PASSAGE:
1 Kings 17:7–16

A Cure for Worry

A wonderful way to overcome sorrow is to realize, "He cares for me."

Christian, do not discredit your Lord by worrying. Come, throw your burden on him. You are staggering under a load your Father would not feel. What to you is a crushing burden is to him a speck of dust on a scale . . .

Suffering child, be patient. God has not forgotten you. He who feeds the sparrows will furnish your needs (Matthew 6:26). Do not despair. Hope on. Hope forever. Take the weapons of faith against a sea of trouble, and your opposition and distress will end.

There is One who cares for you. His eye is on you. His heart beats with pity for the difficulties you face, and his omnipotent hand will bring you help. The darkest cloud will scatter in showers of mercy. The blackest night will give way to morning. If you are his, he will bind your wounds and heal your broken heart. Don't doubt his grace because of your trials. He loves you as much in times of trouble as in days of happiness.

What a pleasant and quiet life you might have if you left the providing to the God of providence! With a little oil in the jug and a handful of flour in the bin, Elijah overcame the famine. God can do the same for you!

ADDITIONAL SCRIPTURE READINGS
Matthew 6:25–34; 1 Peter 5:5–7

Go to page 429 for your next devotional reading.

er in the LORD. ⁴While Jezebel was killing off the LORD's prophets, Obadiah had taken a hundred prophets and hidden them in two caves, fifty in each, and had supplied them with food and water.) ⁵Ahab had said to Obadiah, "Go through the land to all the springs and valleys. Maybe we can find some grass to keep the horses and mules alive so we will not have to kill any of our animals." ⁶So they divided the land they were to cover, Ahab going in one direction and Obadiah in another.

⁷As Obadiah was walking along, Elijah met him. Obadiah recognized him, bowed down to the ground, and said, "Is it really you, my lord Elijah?"

⁸"Yes," he replied. "Go tell your master, 'Elijah is here.' "

⁹"What have I done wrong," asked Obadiah, "that you are handing your servant over to Ahab to be put to death? ¹⁰As surely as the LORD your God lives, there is not a nation or kingdom where my master has not sent someone to look for you. And whenever a nation or kingdom claimed you were not there, he made them swear they could not find you. ¹¹But now you tell me to go to my master and say, 'Elijah is here.' ¹²I don't know where the Spirit of the LORD may carry you when I leave you. If I go and tell Ahab and he doesn't find you, he will kill me. Yet I your servant have worshiped the LORD since my youth. ¹³Haven't you heard, my lord, what I did while Jezebel was killing the prophets of the LORD? I hid a hundred of the LORD's prophets in two caves, fifty in each, and supplied them with food and water. ¹⁴And now you tell me to go to my master and say, 'Elijah is here.' He will kill me!"

¹⁵Elijah said, "As the LORD Almighty lives, whom I serve, I will surely present myself to Ahab today."

Elijah on Mount Carmel

¹⁶So Obadiah went to meet Ahab and told him, and Ahab went to meet Elijah. ¹⁷When he saw Elijah, he said to him, "Is that you, you troubler of Israel?"

¹⁸"I have not made trouble for Israel," Elijah replied. "But you and your father's family have. You have abandoned the LORD's commands and have followed the Baals. ¹⁹Now summon the people from all over Israel to meet me on Mount Carmel. And bring the four hundred and fifty prophets of Baal and the four hundred prophets of Asherah, who eat at Jezebel's table."

²⁰So Ahab sent word throughout all Israel and assembled the prophets on Mount Carmel. ²¹Elijah went before the people and said, "How long will you waver between two opinions? If the LORD is God, follow him; but if Baal is God, follow him."

But the people said nothing.

²²Then Elijah said to them, "I am the only one of the LORD's prophets left, but Baal has four hundred and fifty prophets. ²³Get two bulls for us. Let them choose one for themselves, and let them cut it into pieces and put it on the wood but not set fire to it. I will prepare the other bull and put it on the wood but not set fire to it. ²⁴Then you call on the name of your god, and I will call on the name of the LORD. The god who answers by fire— he is God."

Then all the people said, "What you say is good."

²⁵Elijah said to the prophets of Baal, "Choose one of the bulls and prepare it first, since there are so many of you. Call on the name of your god, but do not light the fire." ²⁶So they took the bull given them and prepared it.

Then they called on the name of Baal from morning till noon. "O Baal, answer us!" they shouted. But there was no response; no one answered. And they danced around the altar they had made.

²⁷At noon Elijah began to taunt them. "Shout louder!" he said. "Surely he is a god! Perhaps he is deep in thought, or busy, or traveling. Maybe he is sleeping and must be awakened." ²⁸So they shouted louder and slashed themselves with swords and spears, as was their custom, until their blood flowed. ²⁹Midday passed,

and they continued their frantic prophesying until the time for the evening sacrifice. But there was no response, no one answered, no one paid attention.

³⁰Then Elijah said to all the people, "Come here to me." They came to him, and he repaired the altar of the LORD, which was in ruins. ³¹Elijah took twelve stones, one for each of the tribes descended from Jacob, to whom the word of the LORD had come, saying, "Your name shall be Israel." ³²With the stones he built an altar in the name of the LORD, and he dug a trench around it large enough to hold two seahs^a of seed. ³³He arranged the wood, cut the bull into pieces and laid it on the wood. Then he said to them, "Fill four large jars with water and pour it on the offering and on the wood."

³⁴"Do it again," he said, and they did it again.

"Do it a third time," he ordered, and they did it the third time. ³⁵The water ran down around the altar and even filled the trench.

³⁶At the time of sacrifice, the prophet Elijah stepped forward and prayed: "O LORD, God of Abraham, Isaac and Israel, let it be known today that you are God in Israel and that I am your servant and have done all these things at your command. ³⁷Answer me, O LORD, answer me, so these people will know that you, O LORD, are God, and that you are turning their hearts back again."

³⁸Then the fire of the LORD fell and burned up the sacrifice, the wood, the stones and the soil, and also licked up the water in the trench.

³⁹When all the people saw this, they fell prostrate and cried, "The LORD— he is God! The LORD—he is God!"

⁴⁰Then Elijah commanded them, "Seize the prophets of Baal. Don't let anyone get away!" They seized them, and Elijah had them brought down to the Kishon Valley and slaughtered there.

⁴¹And Elijah said to Ahab, "Go, eat and drink, for there is the sound of a heavy rain." ⁴²So Ahab went off to eat and drink, but Elijah climbed to the top of Carmel, bent down to the ground and put his face between his knees.

⁴³"Go and look toward the sea," he told his servant. And he went up and looked.

"There is nothing there," he said.

Seven times Elijah said, "Go back."

⁴⁴The seventh time the servant reported, "A cloud as small as a man's hand is rising from the sea."

So Elijah said, "Go and tell Ahab, 'Hitch up your chariot and go down before the rain stops you.'"

⁴⁵Meanwhile, the sky grew black with clouds, the wind rose, a heavy rain came on and Ahab rode off to Jezreel. ⁴⁶The power of the LORD came upon Elijah and, tucking his cloak into his belt, he ran ahead of Ahab all the way to Jezreel.

Elijah Flees to Horeb

19 Now Ahab told Jezebel everything Elijah had done and how he had killed all the prophets with the sword. ²So Jezebel sent a messenger to Elijah to say, "May the gods deal with me, be it ever so severely, if by this time tomorrow I do not make your life like that of one of them."

³Elijah was afraid^b and ran for his life. When he came to Beersheba in Judah, he left his servant there, ⁴while he himself went a day's journey into the desert. He came to a broom tree, sat down under it and prayed that he might die. "I have had enough, LORD," he said. "Take my life; I am no better than my ancestors." ⁵Then he lay down under the tree and fell asleep.

All at once an angel touched him and said, "Get up and eat." ⁶He looked around, and there by his head was a cake of bread baked over hot coals, and a jar of water. He ate and drank and then lay down again.

⁷The angel of the LORD came back a second time and touched him and said, "Get up and eat, for the journey

is too much for you." ⁸So he got up and ate and drank. Strengthened by that food, he traveled forty days and forty nights until he reached Horeb, the mountain of God. ⁹There he went into a cave and spent the night.

The Lord Appears to Elijah

And the word of the Lord came to him: "What are you doing here, Elijah?"

¹⁰He replied, "I have been very zealous for the Lord God Almighty. The Israelites have rejected your covenant, broken down your altars, and put your prophets to death with the sword. I am the only one left, and now they are trying to kill me too."

¹¹The Lord said, "Go out and stand on the mountain in the presence of the Lord, for the Lord is about to pass by."

Then a great and powerful wind tore the mountains apart and shattered the rocks before the Lord, but the Lord was not in the wind. After the wind there was an earthquake, but the Lord was not in the earthquake. ¹²After the earthquake came a fire, but the Lord was not in the fire. And after the fire came a gentle whisper. ¹³When Elijah heard it, he pulled his cloak over his face and went out and stood at the mouth of the cave.

Then a voice said to him, "What are you doing here, Elijah?"

¹⁴He replied, "I have been very zealous for the Lord God Almighty. The Israelites have rejected your covenant, broken down your altars, and put your prophets to death with the sword. I am the only one left, and now they are trying to kill me too."

¹⁵The Lord said to him, "Go back the way you came, and go to the Desert of Damascus. When you get there, anoint Hazael king over Aram. ¹⁶Also, anoint Jehu son of Nimshi king over Israel, and anoint Elisha son of Shaphat from Abel Meholah to succeed you as prophet. ¹⁷Jehu will put to death any who escape the sword of Hazael, and Elisha will put to death any who escape the sword of Jehu. ¹⁸Yet I reserve seven thousand in Israel—all whose knees have not bowed down to Baal and all whose mouths have not kissed him."

The Call of Elisha

¹⁹So Elijah went from there and found Elisha son of Shaphat. He was plowing with twelve yoke of oxen, and he himself was driving the twelfth pair. Elijah went up to him and threw his cloak around him. ²⁰Elisha then left his oxen and ran after Elijah. "Let me kiss my father and mother good-by," he said, "and then I will come with you."

"Go back," Elijah replied. "What have I done to you?"

²¹So Elisha left him and went back. He took his yoke of oxen and slaughtered them. He burned the plowing equipment to cook the meat and gave it to the people, and they ate. Then he set out to follow Elijah and became his attendant.

Ben-Hadad Attacks Samaria

20 Now Ben-Hadad king of Aram mustered his entire army. Accompanied by thirty-two kings with their horses and chariots, he went up and besieged Samaria and attacked it. ²He sent messengers into the city to Ahab king of Israel, saying, "This is what Ben-Hadad says: ³'Your silver and gold are mine, and the best of your wives and children are mine.'"

⁴The king of Israel answered, "Just as you say, my lord the king. I and all I have are yours."

⁵The messengers came again and said, "This is what Ben-Hadad says: 'I sent to demand your silver and gold, your wives and your children. ⁶But about this time tomorrow I am going to send my officials to search your palace and the houses of your officials. They will seize everything you value and carry it away.'"

⁷The king of Israel summoned all the elders of the land and said to them, "See how this man is looking for trouble! When he sent for my wives and my children, my silver and my gold, I did not refuse him."

⁸The elders and the people all an-

VERSE:	AUTHOR:	PASSAGE:
1 Kings 19:12	Millie Stamm	1 Kings 19:1–18

God's Gentle Whisper

After a great victory, we often experience a letdown, a time of depression. After Elijah's victory at Mount Carmel, Jezebel warned that she would have him killed. Terrified, Elijah fled for his life. Finally, he sat under a broom tree. Filled with self-pity, he prayed, "I have had enough . . . Take my life." He was probably thinking, "Lord, I've been faithful to you, but this is too much. I give up."

He was physically and emotionally exhausted. The Lord knew he needed rest and food. After he was physically refreshed, he continued on his way until he came to a cave, where he retreated. It became a cave of self-pity with an invisible sign over it: Out of Service.

God asked, "What are you doing here, Elijah?" God didn't rebuke or scold him. He loved him just as he was and where he was. But Elijah had his eyes on Jezebel, his circumstances and himself instead of the Lord. He needed a fresh revelation of the Lord and who he was.

God sent the wind, the earthquake and the fire, but the Lord was not in them. They were a mighty demonstration of the power of God, but they didn't reveal the person of God. Finally Elijah heard the still, small voice. It was God's voice of gentle stillness, a whisper of love for Elijah . . .

Today are you in a cave of disappointment? self-pity? failure? heartache? Have you said, "I'm through"? Have you hung up an Out-of-Service sign? God cannot use you hidden in a cave. Listen to him lovingly speaking to you in the gentle whisper of the Word. As you listen, you too are cleansed, refreshed and ready for service.

ADDITIONAL SCRIPTURE READINGS
Psalm 111; 2 Corinthians 12:1–10

Go to page 437 for your next devotional reading.

swered, "Don't listen to him or agree to his demands."

⁹So he replied to Ben-Hadad's messengers, "Tell my lord the king, 'Your servant will do all you demanded the first time, but this demand I cannot meet.'" They left and took the answer back to Ben-Hadad.

¹⁰Then Ben-Hadad sent another message to Ahab: "May the gods deal with me, be it ever so severely, if enough dust remains in Samaria to give each of my men a handful."

¹¹The king of Israel answered, "Tell him: 'One who puts on his armor should not boast like one who takes it off.'"

¹²Ben-Hadad heard this message while he and the kings were drinking in their tents,ᵃ and he ordered his men: "Prepare to attack." So they prepared to attack the city.

Ahab Defeats Ben-Hadad

¹³Meanwhile a prophet came to Ahab king of Israel and announced, "This is what the LORD says: 'Do you see this vast army? I will give it into your hand today, and then you will know that I am the LORD.'"

¹⁴"But who will do this?" asked Ahab.

The prophet replied, "This is what the LORD says: 'The young officers of the provincial commanders will do it.'"

"And who will start the battle?" he asked.

The prophet answered, "You will."

¹⁵So Ahab summoned the young officers of the provincial commanders, 232 men. Then he assembled the rest of the Israelites, 7,000 in all. ¹⁶They set out at noon while Ben-Hadad and the 32 kings allied with him were in their tents getting drunk. ¹⁷The young officers of the provincial commanders went out first.

Now Ben-Hadad had dispatched scouts, who reported, "Men are advancing from Samaria."

¹⁸He said, "If they have come out for peace, take them alive; if they

have come out for war, take them alive."

¹⁹The young officers of the provincial commanders marched out of the city with the army behind them ²⁰and each one struck down his opponent. At that, the Arameans fled, with the Israelites in pursuit. But Ben-Hadad king of Aram escaped on horseback with some of his horsemen. ²¹The king of Israel advanced and overpowered the horses and chariots and inflicted heavy losses on the Arameans.

²²Afterward, the prophet came to the king of Israel and said, "Strengthen your position and see what must be done, because next spring the king of Aram will attack you again."

²³Meanwhile, the officials of the king of Aram advised him, "Their gods are gods of the hills. That is why they were too strong for us. But if we fight them on the plains, surely we will be stronger than they. ²⁴Do this: Remove all the kings from their commands and replace them with other officers. ²⁵You must also raise an army like the one you lost—horse for horse and chariot for chariot—so we can fight Israel on the plains. Then surely we will be stronger than they." He agreed with them and acted accordingly.

²⁶The next spring Ben-Hadad mustered the Arameans and went up to Aphek to fight against Israel. ²⁷When the Israelites were also mustered and given provisions, they marched out to meet them. The Israelites camped opposite them like two small flocks of goats, while the Arameans covered the countryside.

²⁸The man of God came up and told the king of Israel, "This is what the LORD says: 'Because the Arameans think the LORD is a god of the hills and not a god of the valleys, I will deliver this vast army into your hands, and you will know that I am the LORD.'"

²⁹For seven days they camped opposite each other, and on the seventh day the battle was joined. The Israelites inflicted a hundred thousand ca-

---

ᵃ12 Or *in Succoth*; also in verse 16

sualties on the Aramean foot soldiers in one day. ³⁰The rest of them escaped to the city of Aphek, where the wall collapsed on twenty-seven thousand of them. And Ben-Hadad fled to the city and hid in an inner room.

³¹His officials said to him, "Look, we have heard that the kings of the house of Israel are merciful. Let us go to the king of Israel with sackcloth around our waists and ropes around our heads. Perhaps he will spare your life."

³²Wearing sackcloth around their waists and ropes around their heads, they went to the king of Israel and said, "Your servant Ben-Hadad says: 'Please let me live.' "

The king answered, "Is he still alive? He is my brother."

³³The men took this as a good sign and were quick to pick up his word. "Yes, your brother Ben-Hadad!" they said.

"Go and get him," the king said. When Ben-Hadad came out, Ahab had him come up into his chariot.

³⁴"I will return the cities my father took from your father," Ben-Hadad offered. "You may set up your own market areas in Damascus, as my father did in Samaria."

⌊Ahab said,⌋ "On the basis of a treaty I will set you free." So he made a treaty with him, and let him go.

A Prophet Condemns Ahab

³⁵By the word of the LORD one of the sons of the prophets said to his companion, "Strike me with your weapon," but the man refused.

³⁶So the prophet said, "Because you have not obeyed the LORD, as soon as you leave me a lion will kill you." And after the man went away, a lion found him and killed him.

³⁷The prophet found another man and said, "Strike me, please." So the man struck him and wounded him. ³⁸Then the prophet went and stood by the road waiting for the king. He disguised himself with his headband

down over his eyes. ³⁹As the king passed by, the prophet called out to him, "Your servant went into the thick of the battle, and someone came to me with a captive and said, 'Guard this man. If he is missing, it will be your life for his life, or you must pay a talent[a] of silver.' ⁴⁰While your servant was busy here and there, the man disappeared."

"That is your sentence," the king of Israel said. "You have pronounced it yourself."

⁴¹Then the prophet quickly removed the headband from his eyes, and the king of Israel recognized him as one of the prophets. ⁴²He said to the king, "This is what the LORD says: 'You have set free a man I had determined should die.[b] Therefore it is your life for his life, your people for his people.' " ⁴³Sullen and angry, the king of Israel went to his palace in Samaria.

Naboth's Vineyard

21 Some time later there was an incident involving a vineyard belonging to Naboth the Jezreelite. The vineyard was in Jezreel, close to the palace of Ahab king of Samaria. ²Ahab said to Naboth, "Let me have your vineyard to use for a vegetable garden, since it is close to my palace. In exchange I will give you a better vineyard or, if you prefer, I will pay you whatever it is worth."

³But Naboth replied, "The LORD forbid that I should give you the inheritance of my fathers."

⁴So Ahab went home, sullen and angry because Naboth the Jezreelite had said, "I will not give you the inheritance of my fathers." He lay on his bed sulking and refused to eat.

⁵His wife Jezebel came in and asked him, "Why are you so sullen? Why won't you eat?"

⁶He answered her, "Because I said to Naboth the Jezreelite, 'Sell me your vineyard; or if you prefer, I will give you another vineyard in its place.' But

---

[a]39 That is, about 75 pounds (about 34 kilograms)   [b]42 The Hebrew term refers to the irrevocable giving over of things or persons to the LORD, often by totally destroying them.

he said, 'I will not give you my vineyard.' "

⁷Jezebel his wife said, "Is this how you act as king over Israel? Get up and eat! Cheer up. I'll get you the vineyard of Naboth the Jezreelite."

⁸So she wrote letters in Ahab's name, placed his seal on them, and sent them to the elders and nobles who lived in Naboth's city with him. ⁹In those letters she wrote:

"Proclaim a day of fasting and seat Naboth in a prominent place among the people. ¹⁰But seat two scoundrels opposite him and have them testify that he has cursed both God and the king. Then take him out and stone him to death."

¹¹So the elders and nobles who lived in Naboth's city did as Jezebel directed in the letters she had written to them. ¹²They proclaimed a fast and seated Naboth in a prominent place among the people. ¹³Then two scoundrels came and sat opposite him and brought charges against Naboth before the people, saying, "Naboth has cursed both God and the king." So they took him outside the city and stoned him to death. ¹⁴Then they sent word to Jezebel: "Naboth has been stoned and is dead."

¹⁵As soon as Jezebel heard that Naboth had been stoned to death, she said to Ahab, "Get up and take possession of the vineyard of Naboth the Jezreelite that he refused to sell you. He is no longer alive, but dead." ¹⁶When Ahab heard that Naboth was dead, he got up and went down to take possession of Naboth's vineyard.

¹⁷Then the word of the LORD came to Elijah the Tishbite: ¹⁸"Go down to meet Ahab king of Israel, who rules in Samaria. He is now in Naboth's vineyard, where he has gone to take possession of it. ¹⁹Say to him, 'This is what the LORD says: Have you not murdered a man and seized his property?' Then say to him, 'This is what

the LORD says: In the place where dogs licked up Naboth's blood, dogs will lick up your blood—yes, yours!' "

²⁰Ahab said to Elijah, "So you have found me, my enemy!"

"I have found you," he answered, "because you have sold yourself to do evil in the eyes of the LORD. ²¹'I am going to bring disaster on you. I will consume your descendants and cut off from Ahab every last male in Israel—slave or free. ²²I will make your house like that of Jeroboam son of Nebat and that of Baasha son of Ahijah, because you have provoked me to anger and have caused Israel to sin.'

²³"And also concerning Jezebel the LORD says: 'Dogs will devour Jezebel by the wall of ͣ Jezreel.'

²⁴"Dogs will eat those belonging to Ahab who die in the city, and the birds of the air will feed on those who die in the country."

²⁵(There was never a man like Ahab, who sold himself to do evil in the eyes of the LORD, urged on by Jezebel his wife. ²⁶He behaved in the vilest manner by going after idols, like the Amorites the LORD drove out before Israel.)

²⁷When Ahab heard these words, he tore his clothes, put on sackcloth and fasted. He lay in sackcloth and went around meekly.

²⁸Then the word of the LORD came to Elijah the Tishbite: ²⁹"Have you noticed how Ahab has humbled himself before me? Because he has humbled himself, I will not bring this disaster in his day, but I will bring it on his house in the days of his son."

Micaiah Prophesies Against Ahab

22 For three years there was no war between Aram and Israel. ²But in the third year Jehoshaphat king of Judah went down to see the king of Israel. ³The king of Israel had said to his officials, "Don't you know that Ramoth Gilead belongs to us and yet we are doing nothing to retake it from the king of Aram?"

ͣ23 Most Hebrew manuscripts; a few Hebrew manuscripts, Vulgate and Syriac (see also 2 Kings 9:26) *the plot of ground at*

⁴So he asked Jehoshaphat, "Will you go with me to fight against Ramoth Gilead?"

Jehoshaphat replied to the king of Israel, "I am as you are, my people as your people, my horses as your horses." ⁵But Jehoshaphat also said to the king of Israel, "First seek the counsel of the Lord."

⁶So the king of Israel brought together the prophets—about four hundred men—and asked them, "Shall I go to war against Ramoth Gilead, or shall I refrain?"

"Go," they answered, "for the Lord will give it into the king's hand."

⁷But Jehoshaphat asked, "Is there not a prophet of the Lord here whom we can inquire of?"

⁸The king of Israel answered Jehoshaphat, "There is still one man through whom we can inquire of the Lord, but I hate him because he never prophesies anything good about me, but always bad. He is Micaiah son of Imlah."

"The king should not say that," Jehoshaphat replied.

⁹So the king of Israel called one of his officials and said, "Bring Micaiah son of Imlah at once."

¹⁰Dressed in their royal robes, the king of Israel and Jehoshaphat king of Judah were sitting on their thrones at the threshing floor by the entrance of the gate of Samaria, with all the prophets prophesying before them. ¹¹Now Zedekiah son of Kenaanah had made iron horns and he declared, "This is what the Lord says: 'With these you will gore the Arameans until they are destroyed.' "

¹²All the other prophets were prophesying the same thing. "Attack Ramoth Gilead and be victorious," they said, "for the Lord will give it into the king's hand."

¹³The messenger who had gone to summon Micaiah said to him, "Look, as one man the other prophets are predicting success for the king. Let your word agree with theirs, and speak favorably."

¹⁴But Micaiah said, "As surely as the Lord lives, I can tell him only what the Lord tells me."

¹⁵When he arrived, the king asked him, "Micaiah, shall we go to war against Ramoth Gilead, or shall I refrain?"

"Attack and be victorious," he answered, "for the Lord will give it into the king's hand."

¹⁶The king said to him, "How many times must I make you swear to tell me nothing but the truth in the name of the Lord?"

¹⁷Then Micaiah answered, "I saw all Israel scattered on the hills like sheep without a shepherd, and the Lord said, 'These people have no master. Let each one go home in peace.' "

¹⁸The king of Israel said to Jehoshaphat, "Didn't I tell you that he never prophesies anything good about me, but only bad?"

¹⁹Micaiah continued, "Therefore hear the word of the Lord: I saw the Lord sitting on his throne with all the host of heaven standing around him on his right and on his left. ²⁰And the Lord said, 'Who will entice Ahab into attacking Ramoth Gilead and going to his death there?'

"One suggested this, and another that. ²¹Finally, a spirit came forward, stood before the Lord and said, 'I will entice him.'

²²" 'By what means?' the Lord asked.

" 'I will go out and be a lying spirit in the mouths of all his prophets,' he said.

" 'You will succeed in enticing him,' said the Lord. 'Go and do it.'

²³"So now the Lord has put a lying spirit in the mouths of all these prophets of yours. The Lord has decreed disaster for you."

²⁴Then Zedekiah son of Kenaanah went up and slapped Micaiah in the face. "Which way did the spirit from^a the Lord go when he went from me to speak to you?" he asked.

²⁵Micaiah replied, "You will find

ᵃ24 Or *Spirit of*

out on the day you go to hide in an inner room."

²⁶The king of Israel then ordered, "Take Micaiah and send him back to Amon the ruler of the city and to Joash the king's son ²⁷and say, 'This is what the king says: Put this fellow in prison and give him nothing but bread and water until I return safely.' "

²⁸Micaiah declared, "If you ever return safely, the LORD has not spoken through me." Then he added, "Mark my words, all you people!"

Ahab Killed at Ramoth Gilead

²⁹So the king of Israel and Jehoshaphat king of Judah went up to Ramoth Gilead. ³⁰The king of Israel said to Jehoshaphat, "I will enter the battle in disguise, but you wear your royal robes." So the king of Israel disguised himself and went into battle.

³¹Now the king of Aram had ordered his thirty-two chariot commanders, "Do not fight with anyone, small or great, except the king of Israel." ³²When the chariot commanders saw Jehoshaphat, they thought, "Surely this is the king of Israel." So they turned to attack him, but when Jehoshaphat cried out, ³³the chariot commanders saw that he was not the king of Israel and stopped pursuing him.

³⁴But someone drew his bow at random and hit the king of Israel between the sections of his armor. The king told his chariot driver, "Wheel around and get me out of the fighting. I've been wounded." ³⁵All day long the battle raged, and the king was propped up in his chariot facing the Arameans. The blood from his wound ran onto the floor of the chariot, and that evening he died. ³⁶As the sun was setting, a cry spread through the army: "Every man to his town; everyone to his land!"

³⁷So the king died and was brought to Samaria, and they buried him there. ³⁸They washed the chariot at a pool in Samaria (where the prostitutes bathed),ᵃ and the dogs licked up his blood, as the word of the LORD had declared.

³⁹As for the other events of Ahab's reign, including all he did, the palace he built and inlaid with ivory, and the cities he fortified, are they not written in the book of the annals of the kings of Israel? ⁴⁰Ahab rested with his fathers. And Ahaziah his son succeeded him as king.

Jehoshaphat King of Judah

⁴¹Jehoshaphat son of Asa became king of Judah in the fourth year of Ahab king of Israel. ⁴²Jehoshaphat was thirty-five years old when he became king, and he reigned in Jerusalem twenty-five years. His mother's name was Azubah daughter of Shilhi. ⁴³In everything he walked in the ways of his father Asa and did not stray from them; he did what was right in the eyes of the LORD. The high places, however, were not removed, and the people continued to offer sacrifices and burn incense there. ⁴⁴Jehoshaphat was also at peace with the king of Israel.

⁴⁵As for the other events of Jehoshaphat's reign, the things he achieved and his military exploits, are they not written in the book of the annals of the kings of Judah? ⁴⁶He rid the land of the rest of the male shrine prostitutes who remained there even after the reign of his father Asa. ⁴⁷There was then no king in Edom; a deputy ruled.

⁴⁸Now Jehoshaphat built a fleet of trading shipsᵇ to go to Ophir for gold, but they never set sail—they were wrecked at Ezion Geber. ⁴⁹At that time Ahaziah son of Ahab said to Jehoshaphat, "Let my men sail with your men," but Jehoshaphat refused.

⁵⁰Then Jehoshaphat rested with his fathers and was buried with them in the city of David his father. And Jehoram his son succeeded him.

Ahaziah King of Israel

⁵¹Ahaziah son of Ahab became

ᵃ38 Or Samaria and cleaned the weapons   ᵇ48 Hebrew of ships of Tarshish king of Israel in Samaria in the seventeenth year of Jehoshaphat king of Judah, and he reigned over Israel two years. ⁵²He did evil in the eyes of the LORD, because he walked in the ways of his father and mother and in the ways of Jeroboam son of Nebat, who caused Israel to sin. ⁵³He served and worshiped Baal and provoked the LORD, the God of Israel, to anger, just as his father had done.

*T*his book continues the history of Israel and Judah begun in 1 Kings. When kings humbled themselves and followed God's will, the people prospered; when kings led people into idol worship, defeat and destruction eventually resulted. As you read 2 Kings, praise God for his faithful love to you in spite of your sins and respond in turn with your love and commitment.

2 KINGS

The Lord's Judgment on Ahaziah

1 After Ahab's death, Moab rebelled against Israel. ²Now Ahaziah had fallen through the lattice of his upper room in Samaria and injured himself. So he sent messengers, saying to them, "Go and consult Baal-Zebub, the god of Ekron, to see if I will recover from this injury."

³But the angel of the Lord said to Elijah the Tishbite, "Go up and meet the messengers of the king of Samaria and ask them, 'Is it because there is no God in Israel that you are going off to consult Baal-Zebub, the god of Ekron?' ⁴Therefore this is what the Lord says: 'You will not leave the bed you are lying on. You will certainly die!' " So Elijah went.

⁵When the messengers returned to the king, he asked them, "Why have you come back?"

⁶"A man came to meet us," they replied. "And he said to us, 'Go back to the king who sent you and tell him, "This is what the Lord says: Is it because there is no God in Israel that you are sending men to consult Baal-Zebub, the god of Ekron? Therefore you will not leave the bed you are lying on. You will certainly die!" ' "

⁷The king asked them, "What kind of man was it who came to meet you and told you this?"

⁸They replied, "He was a man with a garment of hair and with a leather belt around his waist."

The king said, "That was Elijah the Tishbite."

⁹Then he sent to Elijah a captain with his company of fifty men. The captain went up to Elijah, who was sitting on the top of a hill, and said to him, "Man of God, the king says, 'Come down!' "

¹⁰Elijah answered the captain, "If I am a man of God, may fire come down from heaven and consume you and your fifty men!" Then fire fell from heaven and consumed the captain and his men.

¹¹At this the king sent to Elijah another captain with his fifty men. The captain said to him, "Man of God, this is what the king says, 'Come down at once!'"

¹²"If I am a man of God," Elijah replied, "may fire come down from heaven and consume you and your fifty men!" Then the fire of God fell from heaven and consumed him and his fifty men.

¹³So the king sent a third captain with his fifty men. This third captain went up and fell on his knees before Elijah. "Man of God," he begged, "please have respect for my life and the lives of these fifty men, your servants! ¹⁴See, fire has fallen from heav-

FRIDAY

VERSE:
2 Kings 1:3

AUTHOR:
Andrew Kuyvenhoven

PASSAGE:
2 Kings 1:1–8

Where Do You Turn?

King Ahaziah was the son of Ahab and Jezebel. One day he fell through the lattice of his upper room in his palace ... Ahaziah was badly injured by the fall and feared he would die. A true son of his mother, he asked for an oracle from Baal: Will I live or die? ...

Isn't it terrible that the king of Israel turns to an idol? Especially when a person is sick, he or she should turn to the living God. Illness and accidents don't just happen. We may not blame God for them, but these trial are ultimately intended to make us better people. And the first thing we ought to do in the face of illness and other troubles is turn to the living God.

But Ahaziah didn't. Neither did another king, whom the writer of Chronicles tells about: "Though his disease was severe, even in his illness he did not seek help from the LORD, but only from the physicians" (2 Chronicles 16:12).

Even in his illness he did not seek help from the LORD. We offend God if we don't pray to him. He will not always give us health and happiness, although he can easily do so. But God *will* give us himself. And God is our life.

ADDITIONAL SCRIPTURE READINGS
Acts 14:8–18; 1 Thessalonians 1:4–10

Go to page 441 for your next devotional reading.

en and consumed the first two captains and all their men. But now have respect for my life!"

¹⁵The angel of the LORD said to Elijah, "Go down with him; do not be afraid of him." So Elijah got up and went down with him to the king.

¹⁶He told the king, "This is what the LORD says: Is it because there is no God in Israel for you to consult that you have sent messengers to consult Baal-Zebub, the god of Ekron? Because you have done this, you will never leave the bed you are lying on. You will certainly die!" ¹⁷So he died, according to the word of the LORD that Elijah had spoken.

Because Ahaziah had no son, Joram[a] succeeded him as king in the second year of Jehoram son of Jehoshaphat king of Judah. ¹⁸As for all the other events of Ahaziah's reign, and what he did, are they not written in the book of the annals of the kings of Israel?

Elijah Taken Up to Heaven

2 When the LORD was about to take Elijah up to heaven in a whirlwind, Elijah and Elisha were on their way from Gilgal. ²Elijah said to Elisha, "Stay here; the LORD has sent me to Bethel."

But Elisha said, "As surely as the LORD lives and as you live, I will not leave you." So they went down to Bethel.

³The company of the prophets at Bethel came out to Elisha and asked, "Do you know that the LORD is going to take your master from you today?"

"Yes, I know," Elisha replied, "but do not speak of it."

⁴Then Elijah said to him, "Stay here, Elisha; the LORD has sent me to Jericho."

And he replied, "As surely as the LORD lives and as you live, I will not leave you." So they went to Jericho.

⁵The company of the prophets at Jericho went up to Elisha and asked him, "Do you know that the LORD is going to take your master from you today?"

"Yes, I know," he replied, "but do not speak of it."

⁶Then Elijah said to him, "Stay here; the LORD has sent me to the Jordan."

And he replied, "As surely as the LORD lives and as you live, I will not leave you." So the two of them walked on.

⁷Fifty men of the company of the prophets went and stood at a distance, facing the place where Elijah and Elisha had stopped at the Jordan. ⁸Elijah took his cloak, rolled it up and struck the water with it. The water divided to the right and to the left, and the two of them crossed over on dry ground.

⁹When they had crossed, Elijah said to Elisha, "Tell me, what can I do for you before I am taken from you?"

"Let me inherit a double portion of your spirit," Elisha replied.

¹⁰"You have asked a difficult thing," Elijah said, "yet if you see me when I am taken from you, it will be yours—otherwise not."

¹¹As they were walking along and talking together, suddenly a chariot of fire and horses of fire appeared and separated the two of them, and Elijah went up to heaven in a whirlwind. ¹²Elisha saw this and cried out, "My father! My father! The chariots and horsemen of Israel!" And Elisha saw him no more. Then he took hold of his own clothes and tore them apart.

¹³He picked up the cloak that had fallen from Elijah and went back and stood on the bank of the Jordan. ¹⁴Then he took the cloak that had fallen from him and struck the water with it. "Where now is the LORD, the God of Elijah?" he asked. When he struck the water, it divided to the right and to the left, and he crossed over.

¹⁵The company of the prophets from Jericho, who were watching, said, "The spirit of Elijah is resting on Elisha." And they went to meet him

---

a17 Hebrew Jehoram, a variant of Joram

and bowed to the ground before him.
[16]"Look," they said, "we your servants have fifty able men. Let them go and look for your master. Perhaps the Spirit of the LORD has picked him up and set him down on some mountain or in some valley."

"No," Elisha replied, "do not send them."

[17]But they persisted until he was too ashamed to refuse. So he said, "Send them." And they sent fifty men, who searched for three days but did not find him. [18]When they returned to Elisha, who was staying in Jericho, he said to them, "Didn't I tell you not to go?"

Healing of the Water

[19]The men of the city said to Elisha, "Look, our lord, this town is well situated, as you can see, but the water is bad and the land is unproductive."

[20]"Bring me a new bowl," he said, "and put salt in it." So they brought it to him.

[21]Then he went out to the spring and threw the salt into it, saying, "This is what the LORD says: 'I have healed this water. Never again will it cause death or make the land unproductive.' " [22]And the water has remained wholesome to this day, according to the word Elisha had spoken.

Elisha Is Jeered

[23]From there Elisha went up to Bethel. As he was walking along the road, some youths came out of the town and jeered at him. "Go on up, you baldhead!" they said. "Go on up, you baldhead!" [24]He turned around, looked at them and called down a curse on them in the name of the LORD. Then two bears came out of the woods and mauled forty-two of the youths. [25]And he went on to Mount Carmel and from there returned to Samaria.

Moab Revolts

3 Joram[a] son of Ahab became king of Israel in Samaria in the eighteenth year of Jehoshaphat king of Judah, and he reigned twelve years. [2]He did evil in the eyes of the LORD, but not as his father and mother had done. He got rid of the sacred stone of Baal that his father had made. [3]Nevertheless he clung to the sins of Jeroboam son of Nebat, which he had caused Israel to commit; he did not turn away from them.

[4]Now Mesha king of Moab raised sheep, and he had to supply the king of Israel with a hundred thousand lambs and with the wool of a hundred thousand rams. [5]But after Ahab died, the king of Moab rebelled against the king of Israel. [6]So at that time King Joram set out from Samaria and mobilized all Israel. [7]He also sent this message to Jehoshaphat king of Judah: "The king of Moab has rebelled against me. Will you go with me to fight against Moab?"

"I will go with you," he replied. "I am as you are, my people as your people, my horses as your horses."

[8]"By what route shall we attack?" he asked.

"Through the Desert of Edom," he answered.

[9]So the king of Israel set out with the king of Judah and the king of Edom. After a roundabout march of seven days, the army had no more water for themselves or for the animals with them.

[10]"What!" exclaimed the king of Israel. "Has the LORD called us three kings together only to hand us over to Moab?"

[11]But Jehoshaphat asked, "Is there no prophet of the LORD here, that we may inquire of the LORD through him?"

An officer of the king of Israel answered, "Elisha son of Shaphat is here. He used to pour water on the hands of Elijah.[b]"

---

[a]1 Hebrew *Jehoram*, a variant of *Joram*; also in verse 6　　[b]11 That is, he was Elijah's personal servant.

¹²Jehoshaphat said, "The word of the LORD is with him." So the king of Israel and Jehoshaphat and the king of Edom went down to him.

¹³Elisha said to the king of Israel, "What do we have to do with each other? Go to the prophets of your father and the prophets of your mother."

"No," the king of Israel answered, "because it was the LORD who called us three kings together to hand us over to Moab."

¹⁴Elisha said, "As surely as the LORD Almighty lives, whom I serve, if I did not have respect for the presence of Jehoshaphat king of Judah, I would not look at you or even notice you. ¹⁵But now bring me a harpist."

While the harpist was playing, the hand of the LORD came upon Elisha ¹⁶and he said, "This is what the LORD says: Make this valley full of ditches. ¹⁷For this is what the LORD says: You will see neither wind nor rain, yet this valley will be filled with water, and you, your cattle and your other animals will drink. ¹⁸This is an easy thing in the eyes of the LORD; he will also hand Moab over to you. ¹⁹You will overthrow every fortified city and every major town. You will cut down every good tree, stop up all the springs, and ruin every good field with stones."

²⁰The next morning, about the time for offering the sacrifice, there it was—water flowing from the direction of Edom! And the land was filled with water.

²¹Now all the Moabites had heard that the kings had come to fight against them; so every man, young and old, who could bear arms was called up and stationed on the border. ²²When they got up early in the morning, the sun was shining on the water. To the Moabites across the way, the water looked red—like blood. ²³"That's blood!" they said. "Those kings must have fought and slaughtered each other. Now to the plunder, Moab!"

²⁴But when the Moabites came to the camp of Israel, the Israelites rose up and fought them until they fled. And the Israelites invaded the land and slaughtered the Moabites. ²⁵They destroyed the towns, and each man threw a stone on every good field until it was covered. They stopped up all the springs and cut down every good tree. Only Kir Hareseth was left with its stones in place, but men armed with slings surrounded it and attacked it as well.

²⁶When the king of Moab saw that the battle had gone against him, he took with him seven hundred swordsmen to break through to the king of Edom, but they failed. ²⁷Then he took his firstborn son, who was to succeed him as king, and offered him as a sacrifice on the city wall. The fury against Israel was great; they withdrew and returned to their own land.

The Widow's Oil

4 The wife of a man from the company of the prophets cried out to Elisha, "Your servant my husband is dead, and you know that he revered the LORD. But now his creditor is coming to take my two boys as his slaves."

²Elisha replied to her, "How can I help you? Tell me, what do you have in your house?"

"Your servant has nothing there at all," she said, "except a little oil."

³Elisha said, "Go around and ask all your neighbors for empty jars. Don't ask for just a few. ⁴Then go inside and shut the door behind you and your sons. Pour oil into all the jars, and as each is filled, put it to one side."

⁵She left him and afterward shut the door behind her and her sons. They brought the jars to her and she kept pouring. ⁶When all the jars were full, she said to her son, "Bring me another one."

But he replied, "There is not a jar left." Then the oil stopped flowing.

⁷She went and told the man of God, and he said, "Go, sell the oil and pay your debts. You and your sons can live on what is left."

PASSAGE: Psalm 118:19–29; 2 Thessalonians 2:13–17
AUTHOR: Joseph Bayly

A Psalm of Today

This is the day
the Lord has made.
The Lord?
Today?
Yesterday perhaps
could claim your craft
or hopefully tomorrow
but not today
this disappointing day so filled
with problems
needs
despair and doubt.
This is the day
the Lord has made
and making it
He'll give me strength
and hope
to take me through.
This is the day
the Lord has made
so I'll be glad
and I'll rejoice in it.

Go to page 446 for your next devotional reading.

The Shunammite's Son Restored to Life

⁸One day Elisha went to Shunem. And a well-to-do woman was there, who urged him to stay for a meal. So whenever he came by, he stopped there to eat. ⁹She said to her husband, "I know that this man who often comes our way is a holy man of God. ¹⁰Let's make a small room on the roof and put in it a bed and a table, a chair and a lamp for him. Then he can stay there whenever he comes to us."

¹¹One day when Elisha came, he went up to his room and lay down there. ¹²He said to his servant Gehazi, "Call the Shunammite." So he called her, and she stood before him. ¹³Elisha said to him, "Tell her, 'You have gone to all this trouble for us. Now what can be done for you? Can we speak on your behalf to the king or the commander of the army?'"

She replied, "I have a home among my own people."

¹⁴"What can be done for her?" Elisha asked.

Gehazi said, "Well, she has no son and her husband is old."

¹⁵Then Elisha said, "Call her." So he called her, and she stood in the doorway. ¹⁶"About this time next year," Elisha said, "you will hold a son in your arms."

"No, my lord," she objected. "Don't mislead your servant, O man of God!"

¹⁷But the woman became pregnant, and the next year about that same time she gave birth to a son, just as Elisha had told her.

¹⁸The child grew, and one day he went out to his father, who was with the reapers. ¹⁹"My head! My head!" he said to his father.

His father told a servant, "Carry him to his mother." ²⁰After the servant had lifted him up and carried him to his mother, the boy sat on her lap until noon, and then he died. ²¹She went up and laid him on the bed of the man of God, then shut the door and went out.

²²She called her husband and said, "Please send me one of the servants and a donkey so I can go to the man of God quickly and return."

²³"Why go to him today?" he asked. "It's not the New Moon or the Sabbath."

"It's all right," she said.

²⁴She saddled the donkey and said to her servant, "Lead on; don't slow down for me unless I tell you." ²⁵So she set out and came to the man of God at Mount Carmel.

When he saw her in the distance, the man of God said to his servant Gehazi, "Look! There's the Shunammite! ²⁶Run to meet her and ask her, 'Are you all right? Is your husband all right? Is your child all right?'"

"Everything is all right," she said.

²⁷When she reached the man of God at the mountain, she took hold of his feet. Gehazi came over to push her away, but the man of God said, "Leave her alone! She is in bitter distress, but the Lord has hidden it from me and has not told me why."

²⁸"Did I ask you for a son, my lord?" she said. "Didn't I tell you, 'Don't raise my hopes'?"

²⁹Elisha said to Gehazi, "Tuck your cloak into your belt, take my staff in your hand and run. If you meet anyone, do not greet him, and if anyone greets you, do not answer. Lay my staff on the boy's face."

³⁰But the child's mother said, "As surely as the Lord lives and as you live, I will not leave you." So he got up and followed her.

³¹Gehazi went on ahead and laid the staff on the boy's face, but there was no sound or response. So Gehazi went back to meet Elisha and told him, "The boy has not awakened."

³²When Elisha reached the house, there was the boy lying dead on his couch. ³³He went in, shut the door on the two of them and prayed to the Lord. ³⁴Then he got on the bed and lay upon the boy, mouth to mouth, eyes to eyes, hands to hands. As he stretched himself out upon him, the boy's body grew warm. ³⁵Elisha turned away and walked back and forth in the room and then got on the bed and stretched out upon him once

more. The boy sneezed seven times and opened his eyes.

³⁶Elisha summoned Gehazi and said, "Call the Shunammite." And he did. When she came, he said, "Take your son." ³⁷She came in, fell at his feet and bowed to the ground. Then she took her son and went out.

Death in the Pot

³⁸Elisha returned to Gilgal and there was a famine in that region. While the company of the prophets was meeting with him, he said to his servant, "Put on the large pot and cook some stew for these men."

³⁹One of them went out into the fields to gather herbs and found a wild vine. He gathered some of its gourds and filled the fold of his cloak. When he returned, he cut them up into the pot of stew, though no one knew what they were. ⁴⁰The stew was poured out for the men, but as they began to eat it, they cried out, "O man of God, there is death in the pot!" And they could not eat it.

⁴¹Elisha said, "Get some flour." He put it into the pot and said, "Serve it to the people to eat." And there was nothing harmful in the pot.

Feeding of a Hundred

⁴²A man came from Baal Shalishah, bringing the man of God twenty loaves of barley bread baked from the first ripe grain, along with some heads of new grain. "Give it to the people to eat," Elisha said.

⁴³"How can I set this before a hundred men?" his servant asked.

But Elisha answered, "Give it to the people to eat. For this is what the LORD says: 'They will eat and have some left over.' " ⁴⁴Then he set it before them, and they ate and had some left over, according to the word of the LORD.

Naaman Healed of Leprosy

5 Now Naaman was commander of the army of the king of Aram. He was a great man in the sight of his master and highly regarded, because through him the LORD had given victory to Aram. He was a valiant soldier, but he had leprosy.ᵃ

²Now bands from Aram had gone out and had taken captive a young girl from Israel, and she served Naaman's wife. ³She said to her mistress, "If only my master would see the prophet who is in Samaria! He would cure him of his leprosy."

⁴Naaman went to his master and told him what the girl from Israel had said. ⁵"By all means, go," the king of Aram replied. "I will send a letter to the king of Israel." So Naaman left, taking with him ten talentsᵇ of silver, six thousand shekelsᶜ of gold and ten sets of clothing. ⁶The letter that he took to the king of Israel read: "With this letter I am sending my servant Naaman to you so that you may cure him of his leprosy."

⁷As soon as the king of Israel read the letter, he tore his robes and said, "Am I God? Can I kill and bring back to life? Why does this fellow send someone to me to be cured of his leprosy? See how he is trying to pick a quarrel with me!"

⁸When Elisha the man of God heard that the king of Israel had torn his robes, he sent him this message: "Why have you torn your robes? Have the man come to me and he will know that there is a prophet in Israel." ⁹So Naaman went with his horses and chariots and stopped at the door of Elisha's house. ¹⁰Elisha sent a messenger to say to him, "Go, wash yourself seven times in the Jordan, and your flesh will be restored and you will be cleansed."

¹¹But Naaman went away angry and said, "I thought that he would surely come out to me and stand and call on the name of the LORD his God,

---

ᵃ1 The Hebrew word was used for various diseases affecting the skin—not necessarily leprosy; also in verses 3, 6, 7, 11 and 27.   ᵇ5 That is, about 750 pounds (about 340 kilograms)
ᶜ5 That is, about 150 pounds (about 70 kilograms)

wave his hand over the spot and cure me of my leprosy. ¹²Are not Abana and Pharpar, the rivers of Damascus, better than any of the waters of Israel? Couldn't I wash in them and be cleansed?" So he turned and went off in a rage.

¹³Naaman's servants went to him and said, "My father, if the prophet had told you to do some great thing, would you not have done it? How much more, then, when he tells you, 'Wash and be cleansed'!" ¹⁴So he went down and dipped himself in the Jordan seven times, as the man of God had told him, and his flesh was restored and became clean like that of a young boy.

¹⁵Then Naaman and all his attendants went back to the man of God. He stood before him and said, "Now I know that there is no God in all the world except in Israel. Please accept now a gift from your servant."

¹⁶The prophet answered, "As surely as the LORD lives, whom I serve, I will not accept a thing." And even though Naaman urged him, he refused.

¹⁷"If you will not," said Naaman, "please let me, your servant, be given as much earth as a pair of mules can carry, for your servant will never again make burnt offerings and sacrifices to any other god but the LORD. ¹⁸But may the LORD forgive your servant for this one thing: When my master enters the temple of Rimmon to bow down and he is leaning on my arm and I bow there also—when I bow down in the temple of Rimmon, may the LORD forgive your servant for this."

¹⁹"Go in peace," Elisha said.

After Naaman had traveled some distance, ²⁰Gehazi, the servant of Elisha the man of God, said to himself, "My master was too easy on Naaman, this Aramean, by not accepting from him what he brought. As surely as the LORD lives, I will run after him and get something from him."

²¹So Gehazi hurried after Naaman. When Naaman saw him running toward him, he got down from the chariot to meet him. "Is everything all right?" he asked.

²²"Everything is all right," Gehazi answered. "My master sent me to say, 'Two young men from the company of the prophets have just come to me from the hill country of Ephraim. Please give them a talent[a] of silver and two sets of clothing.' "

²³"By all means, take two talents," said Naaman. He urged Gehazi to accept them, and then tied up the two talents of silver in two bags, with two sets of clothing. He gave them to two of his servants, and they carried them ahead of Gehazi. ²⁴When Gehazi came to the hill, he took the things from the servants and put them away in the house. He sent the men away and they left. ²⁵Then he went in and stood before his master Elisha.

"Where have you been, Gehazi?" Elisha asked.

"Your servant didn't go anywhere," Gehazi answered.

²⁶But Elisha said to him, "Was not my spirit with you when the man got down from his chariot to meet you? Is this the time to take money, or to accept clothes, olive groves, vineyards, flocks, herds, or menservants and maidservants? ²⁷Naaman's leprosy will cling to you and to your descendants forever." Then Gehazi went from Elisha's presence and he was leprous, as white as snow.

An Axhead Floats

6 The company of the prophets said to Elisha, "Look, the place where we meet with you is too small for us. ²Let us go to the Jordan, where each of us can get a pole; and let us build a place there for us to live."

And he said, "Go."

³Then one of them said, "Won't you please come with your servants?"

"I will," Elisha replied. ⁴And he went with them.

They went to the Jordan and began to cut down trees. ⁵As one of them

---

a22 That is, about 75 pounds (about 34 kilograms)

was cutting down a tree, the iron ax-head fell into the water. "Oh, my lord," he cried out, "it was borrowed!"

⁶The man of God asked, "Where did it fall?" When he showed him the place, Elisha cut a stick and threw it there, and made the iron float. ⁷"Lift it out," he said. Then the man reached out his hand and took it.

Elisha Traps Blinded Arameans

⁸Now the king of Aram was at war with Israel. After conferring with his officers, he said, "I will set up my camp in such and such a place."

⁹The man of God sent word to the king of Israel: "Beware of passing that place, because the Arameans are going down there." ¹⁰So the king of Israel checked on the place indicated by the man of God. Time and again Elisha warned the king, so that he was on his guard in such places.

¹¹This enraged the king of Aram. He summoned his officers and demanded of them, "Will you not tell me which of us is on the side of the king of Israel?"

¹²"None of us, my lord the king," said one of his officers, "but Elisha, the prophet who is in Israel, tells the king of Israel the very words you speak in your bedroom."

¹³"Go, find out where he is," the king ordered, "so I can send men and capture him." The report came back: "He is in Dothan." ¹⁴Then he sent horses and chariots and a strong force there. They went by night and surrounded the city.

¹⁵When the servant of the man of God got up and went out early the next morning, an army with horses and chariots had surrounded the city. "Oh, my lord, what shall we do?" the servant asked.

¹⁶"Don't be afraid," the prophet answered. "Those who are with us are more than those who are with them."

¹⁷And Elisha prayed, "O LORD, open his eyes so he may see." Then the LORD opened the servant's eyes, and he looked and saw the hills full of horses and chariots of fire all around Elisha.

¹⁸As the enemy came down toward him, Elisha prayed to the LORD, "Strike these people with blindness." So he struck them with blindness, as Elisha had asked.

¹⁹Elisha told them, "This is not the road and this is not the city. Follow me, and I will lead you to the man you are looking for." And he led them to Samaria.

²⁰After they entered the city, Elisha said, "LORD, open the eyes of these men so they can see." Then the LORD opened their eyes and they looked, and there they were, inside Samaria.

²¹When the king of Israel saw them, he asked Elisha, "Shall I kill them, my father? Shall I kill them?"

²²"Do not kill them," he answered. "Would you kill men you have captured with your own sword or bow? Set food and water before them so that they may eat and drink and then go back to their master." ²³So he prepared a great feast for them, and after they had finished eating and drinking, he sent them away, and they returned to their master. So the bands from Aram stopped raiding Israel's territory.

Famine in Besieged Samaria

²⁴Some time later, Ben-Hadad king of Aram mobilized his entire army and marched up and laid siege to Samaria. ²⁵There was a great famine in the city; the siege lasted so long that a donkey's head sold for eighty shekels[a] of silver, and a quarter of a cab[b] of seed pods[c] for five shekels.[d]

²⁶As the king of Israel was passing by on the wall, a woman cried to him, "Help me, my lord the king!"

²⁷The king replied, "If the LORD

---

a25 That is, about 2 pounds (about 1 kilogram) 0.3 liter)   c25 Or of dove's dung   b25 That is, probably about 1/2 pint (about d25 That is, about 2 ounces (about 55 grams)

VERSE:
2 Kings 6:16

AUTHOR:
Millie Stamm

PASSAGE:
2 Kings 6:8–23

Spiritual Vision

When Ben-Hadad, the Aramean king, was waging war on Israel, his military secrets kept leaking out. Learning that Elisha was responsible, the king sent his soldiers to capture him . . .

One morning Elisha's servant discovered they were completely surrounded by Ben-Hadad's army. Frightened, he hurried to Elisha, saying, "Oh, my lord, what shall we do?"

To his surprise, Elisha did not panic, but was completely undisturbed. Elisha, having spiritual vision, saw the great invisible host of God around them. Elisha said, "Don't be afraid. Those who are with us are more than those who are with them." How ineffective were Ben-Hadad's chances against a man who had the resources of heaven at his disposal . . .

Today we may be facing problems and situations that have no visible solution. We may be looking at our problems with our physical eyes. We may be crying out, "What shall we do?" When our eyes are on our circumstances we panic. When they are on God we are at rest.

We need to let God open our eyes of faith, giving us spiritual vision. By faith our inner eyes can see God's provision for us. "Don't be afraid. Those who are with us are more than those who are with them." We may not see our way out of our problem, but we can trust God to encircle us with his invisible host in the midst of it.

ADDITIONAL SCRIPTURE READINGS
Psalm 55:16–23; 1 John 4:1–6
Go to page 462 for your next devotional reading.

does not help you, where can I get help for you? From the threshing floor? From the winepress?" ²⁸Then he asked her, "What's the matter?"

She answered, "This woman said to me, 'Give up your son so we may eat him today, and tomorrow we'll eat my son.' ²⁹So we cooked my son and ate him. The next day I said to her, 'Give up your son so we may eat him,' but she had hidden him."

³⁰When the king heard the woman's words, he tore his robes. As he went along the wall, the people looked, and there, underneath, he had sackcloth on his body. ³¹He said, "May God deal with me, be it ever so severely, if the head of Elisha son of Shaphat remains on his shoulders today!"

³²Now Elisha was sitting in his house, and the elders were sitting with him. The king sent a messenger ahead, but before he arrived, Elisha said to the elders, "Don't you see how this murderer is sending someone to cut off my head? Look, when the messenger comes, shut the door and hold it shut against him. Is not the sound of his master's footsteps behind him?"

³³While he was still talking to them, the messenger came down to him. And ⌊the king⌋ said, "This disaster is from the LORD. Why should I wait for the LORD any longer?"

7 Elisha said, "Hear the word of the LORD. This is what the LORD says: About this time tomorrow, a seah*ᵃ* of flour will sell for a shekel*ᵇ* and two seahs*ᶜ* of barley for a shekel at the gate of Samaria."

²The officer on whose arm the king was leaning said to the man of God, "Look, even if the LORD should open the floodgates of the heavens, could this happen?"

"You will see it with your own eyes," answered Elisha, "but you will not eat any of it!"

The Siege Lifted

³Now there were four men with leprosy*ᵈ* at the entrance of the city gate. They said to each other, "Why stay here until we die? ⁴If we say, 'We'll go into the city'—the famine is there, and we will die. And if we stay here, we will die. So let's go over to the camp of the Arameans and surrender. If they spare us, we live; if they kill us, then we die."

⁵At dusk they got up and went to the camp of the Arameans. When they reached the edge of the camp, not a man was there, ⁶for the Lord had caused the Arameans to hear the sound of chariots and horses and a great army, so that they said to one another, "Look, the king of Israel has hired the Hittite and Egyptian kings to attack us!" ⁷So they got up and fled in the dusk and abandoned their tents and their horses and donkeys. They left the camp as it was and ran for their lives.

⁸The men who had leprosy reached the edge of the camp and entered one of the tents. They ate and drank, and carried away silver, gold and clothes, and went off and hid them. They returned and entered another tent and took some things from it and hid them also.

⁹Then they said to each other, "We're not doing right. This is a day of good news and we are keeping it to ourselves. If we wait until daylight, punishment will overtake us. Let's go at once and report this to the royal palace."

¹⁰So they went and called out to the city gatekeepers and told them, "We went into the Aramean camp and not a man was there—not a sound of anyone—only tethered horses and donkeys, and the tents left just as they were." ¹¹The gatekeepers shouted the news, and it was reported within the palace.

---

*ᵃ*1 That is, probably about 7 quarts (about 7.3 liters); also in verses 16 and 18   *ᵇ*1 That is, about 2/5 ounce (about 11 grams); also in verses 16 and 18   *ᶜ*1 That is, probably about 13 quarts (about 15 liters); also in verses 16 and 18   *ᵈ*3 The Hebrew word is used for various diseases affecting the skin—not necessarily leprosy; also in verse 8.

¹²The king got up in the night and said to his officers, "I will tell you what the Arameans have done to us. They know we are starving; so they have left the camp to hide in the countryside, thinking, 'They will surely come out, and then we will take them alive and get into the city.' "

¹³One of his officers answered, "Have some men take five of the horses that are left in the city. Their plight will be like that of all the Israelites left here—yes, they will only be like all these Israelites who are doomed. So let us send them to find out what happened."

¹⁴So they selected two chariots with their horses, and the king sent them after the Aramean army. He commanded the drivers, "Go and find out what has happened." ¹⁵They followed them as far as the Jordan, and they found the whole road strewn with the clothing and equipment the Arameans had thrown away in their headlong flight. So the messengers returned and reported to the king. ¹⁶Then the people went out and plundered the camp of the Arameans. So a seah of flour sold for a shekel, and two seahs of barley sold for a shekel, as the LORD had said.

¹⁷Now the king had put the officer on whose arm he leaned in charge of the gate, and the people trampled him in the gateway, and he died, just as the man of God had foretold when the king came down to his house. ¹⁸It happened as the man of God had said to the king: "About this time tomorrow, a seah of flour will sell for a shekel and two seahs of barley for a shekel at the gate of Samaria."

¹⁹The officer had said to the man of God, "Look, even if the LORD should open the floodgates of the heavens, could this happen?" The man of God had replied, "You will see it with your own eyes, but you will not eat any of it!" ²⁰And that is exactly what happened to him, for the people trampled him in the gateway, and he died.

The Shunammite's Land Restored

8 Now Elisha had said to the woman whose son he had restored to life, "Go away with your family and stay for a while wherever you can, because the LORD has decreed a famine in the land that will last seven years." ²The woman proceeded to do as the man of God said. She and her family went away and stayed in the land of the Philistines seven years.

³At the end of the seven years she came back from the land of the Philistines and went to the king to beg for her house and land. ⁴The king was talking to Gehazi, the servant of the man of God, and had said, "Tell me about all the great things Elisha has done." ⁵Just as Gehazi was telling the king how Elisha had restored the dead to life, the woman whose son Elisha had brought back to life came to beg the king for her house and land.

Gehazi said, "This is the woman, my lord the king, and this is her son whom Elisha restored to life." ⁶The king asked the woman about it, and she told him.

Then he assigned an official to her case and said to him, "Give back everything that belonged to her, including all the income from her land from the day she left the country until now."

Hazael Murders Ben-Hadad

⁷Elisha went to Damascus, and Ben-Hadad king of Aram was ill. When the king was told, "The man of God has come all the way up here," ⁸he said to Hazael, "Take a gift with you and go to meet the man of God. Consult the LORD through him; ask him, 'Will I recover from this illness?' "

⁹Hazael went to meet Elisha, taking with him as a gift forty camel-loads of all the finest wares of Damascus. He went in and stood before him, and said, "Your son Ben-Hadad king of Aram has sent me to ask, 'Will I recover from this illness?' "

¹⁰Elisha answered, "Go and say to

him, 'You will certainly recover'; but[a] the LORD has revealed to me that he will in fact die." [11]He stared at him with a fixed gaze until Hazael felt ashamed. Then the man of God began to weep.

[12]"Why is my lord weeping?" asked Hazael.

"Because I know the harm you will do to the Israelites," he answered. "You will set fire to their fortified places, kill their young men with the sword, dash their little children to the ground, and rip open their pregnant women."

[13]Hazael said, "How could your servant, a mere dog, accomplish such a feat?"

"The LORD has shown me that you will become king of Aram," answered Elisha.

[14]Then Hazael left Elisha and returned to his master. When Ben-Hadad asked, "What did Elisha say to you?" Hazael replied, "He told me that you would certainly recover." [15]But the next day he took a thick cloth, soaked it in water and spread it over the king's face, so that he died. Then Hazael succeeded him as king.

Jehoram King of Judah

[16]In the fifth year of Joram son of Ahab king of Israel, when Jehoshaphat was king of Judah, Jehoram son of Jehoshaphat began his reign as king of Judah. [17]He was thirty-two years old when he became king, and he reigned in Jerusalem eight years. [18]He walked in the ways of the kings of Israel, as the house of Ahab had done, for he married a daughter of Ahab. He did evil in the eyes of the LORD. [19]Nevertheless, for the sake of his servant David, the LORD was not willing to destroy Judah. He had promised to maintain a lamp for David and his descendants forever.

[20]In the time of Jehoram, Edom rebelled against Judah and set up its own king. [21]So Jehoram[b] went to Zair with all his chariots. The Edom-

ites surrounded him and his chariot commanders, but he rose up and broke through by night; his army, however, fled back home. [22]To this day Edom has been in rebellion against Judah. Libnah revolted at the same time.

[23]As for the other events of Jehoram's reign, and all he did, are they not written in the book of the annals of the kings of Judah? [24]Jehoram rested with his fathers and was buried with them in the City of David. And Ahaziah his son succeeded him as king.

Ahaziah King of Judah

[25]In the twelfth year of Joram son of Ahab king of Israel, Ahaziah son of Jehoram king of Judah began to reign. [26]Ahaziah was twenty-two years old when he became king, and he reigned in Jerusalem one year. His mother's name was Athaliah, a granddaughter of Omri king of Israel. [27]He walked in the ways of the house of Ahab and did evil in the eyes of the LORD, as the house of Ahab had done, for he was related by marriage to Ahab's family.

[28]Ahaziah went with Joram son of Ahab to war against Hazael king of Aram at Ramoth Gilead. The Arameans wounded Joram; [29]so King Joram returned to Jezreel to recover from the wounds the Arameans had inflicted on him at Ramoth[c] in his battle with Hazael king of Aram.

Then Ahaziah son of Jehoram king of Judah went down to Jezreel to see Joram son of Ahab, because he had been wounded.

Jehu Anointed King of Israel

9 The prophet Elisha summoned a man from the company of the prophets and said to him, "Tuck your cloak into your belt, take this flask of oil with you and go to Ramoth Gilead. [2]When you get there, look for Jehu son of Jehoshaphat, the son of Nimshi. Go to him, get him away from his companions and take him into an in-

---

[a]10 The Hebrew may also be read *Go and say, 'You will certainly not recover,' for.*   [b]21 Hebrew *Joram,* a variant of *Jehoram;* also in verses 23 and 24   [c]29 Hebrew *Ramah,* a variant of *Ramoth*

ner room. ³Then take the flask and pour the oil on his head and declare, 'This is what the LORD says: I anoint you king over Israel.' Then open the door and run; don't delay!"

⁴So the young man, the prophet, went to Ramoth Gilead. ⁵When he arrived, he found the army officers sitting together. "I have a message for you, commander," he said.

"For which of us?" asked Jehu.

"For you, commander," he replied.

⁶Jehu got up and went into the house. Then the prophet poured the oil on Jehu's head and declared, "This is what the LORD, the God of Israel, says: 'I anoint you king over the LORD's people Israel. ⁷You are to destroy the house of Ahab your master, and I will avenge the blood of my servants the prophets and the blood of all the LORD's servants shed by Jezebel. ⁸The whole house of Ahab will perish. I will cut off from Ahab every last male in Israel—slave or free. ⁹I will make the house of Ahab like the house of Jeroboam son of Nebat and like the house of Baasha son of Ahijah. ¹⁰As for Jezebel, dogs will devour her on the plot of ground at Jezreel, and no one will bury her.' " Then he opened the door and ran.

¹¹When Jehu went out to his fellow officers, one of them asked him, "Is everything all right? Why did this madman come to you?"

"You know the man and the sort of things he says," Jehu replied.

¹²"That's not true!" they said. "Tell us."

Jehu said, "Here is what he told me: 'This is what the LORD says: I anoint you king over Israel.' "

¹³They hurried and took their cloaks and spread them under him on the bare steps. Then they blew the trumpet and shouted, "Jehu is king!"

Jehu Kills Joram and Ahaziah

¹⁴So Jehu son of Jehoshaphat, the son of Nimshi, conspired against Joram. (Now Joram and all Israel had been defending Ramoth Gilead against Hazael king of Aram, ¹⁵but King Joram*ᵃ* had returned to Jezreel to recover from the wounds the Arameans had inflicted on him in the battle with Hazael king of Aram.) Jehu said, "If this is the way you feel, don't let anyone slip out of the city to go and tell the news in Jezreel." ¹⁶Then he got into his chariot and rode to Jezreel, because Joram was resting there and Ahaziah king of Judah had gone down to see him.

¹⁷When the lookout standing on the tower in Jezreel saw Jehu's troops approaching, he called out, "I see some troops coming."

"Get a horseman," Joram ordered. "Send him to meet them and ask, 'Do you come in peace?' "

¹⁸The horseman rode off to meet Jehu and said, "This is what the king says: 'Do you come in peace?' "

"What do you have to do with peace?" Jehu replied. "Fall in behind me."

The lookout reported, "The messenger has reached them, but he isn't coming back."

¹⁹So the king sent out a second horseman. When he came to them he said, "This is what the king says: 'Do you come in peace?' "

Jehu replied, "What do you have to do with peace? Fall in behind me."

²⁰The lookout reported, "He has reached them, but he isn't coming back either. The driving is like that of Jehu son of Nimshi—he drives like a madman."

²¹"Hitch up my chariot," Joram ordered. And when it was hitched up, Joram king of Israel and Ahaziah king of Judah rode out, each in his own chariot, to meet Jehu. They met him at the plot of ground that had belonged to Naboth the Jezreelite. ²²When Joram saw Jehu he asked, "Have you come in peace, Jehu?"

"How can there be peace," Jehu replied, "as long as all the idolatry and witchcraft of your mother Jezebel abound?"

²³Joram turned about and fled, call-

<hr>

ᵃ15 Hebrew *Jehoram,* a variant of *Joram;* also in verses 17 and 21-24

ing out to Ahaziah, "Treachery, Ahaziah!"

²⁴Then Jehu drew his bow and shot Joram between the shoulders. The arrow pierced his heart and he slumped down in his chariot. ²⁵Jehu said to Bidkar, his chariot officer, "Pick him up and throw him on the field that belonged to Naboth the Jezreelite. Remember how you and I were riding together in chariots behind Ahab his father when the LORD made this prophecy about him: ²⁶'Yesterday I saw the blood of Naboth and the blood of his sons, declares the LORD, and I will surely make you pay for it on this plot of ground, declares the LORD.'ᵃ Now then, pick him up and throw him on that plot, in accordance with the word of the LORD."

²⁷When Ahaziah king of Judah saw what had happened, he fled up the road to Beth Haggan.ᵇ Jehu chased him, shouting, "Kill him too!" They wounded him in his chariot on the way up to Gur near Ibleam, but he escaped to Megiddo and died there. ²⁸His servants took him by chariot to Jerusalem and buried him with his fathers in his tomb in the City of David. ²⁹(In the eleventh year of Joram son of Ahab, Ahaziah had become king of Judah.)

Jezebel Killed

³⁰Then Jehu went to Jezreel. When Jezebel heard about it, she painted her eyes, arranged her hair and looked out of a window. ³¹As Jehu entered the gate, she asked, "Have you come in peace, Zimri, you murderer of your master?"ᶜ

³²He looked up at the window and called out, "Who is on my side? Who?" Two or three eunuchs looked down at him. ³³"Throw her down!" Jehu said. So they threw her down, and some of her blood spattered the wall and the horses as they trampled her underfoot.

³⁴Jehu went in and ate and drank.

"Take care of that cursed woman," he said, "and bury her, for she was a king's daughter." ³⁵But when they went out to bury her, they found nothing except her skull, her feet and her hands. ³⁶They went back and told Jehu, who said, "This is the word of the LORD that he spoke through his servant Elijah the Tishbite: On the plot of ground at Jezreel dogs will devour Jezebel's flesh.ᵈ ³⁷Jezebel's body will be like refuse on the ground in the plot at Jezreel, so that no one will be able to say, 'This is Jezebel.' "

Ahab's Family Killed

10 Now there were in Samaria seventy sons of the house of Ahab. So Jehu wrote letters and sent them to Samaria: to the officials of Jezreel,ᵉ to the elders and to the guardians of Ahab's children. He said, ²"As soon as this letter reaches you, since your master's sons are with you and you have chariots and horses, a fortified city and weapons, ³choose the best and most worthy of your master's sons and set him on his father's throne. Then fight for your master's house."

⁴But they were terrified and said, "If two kings could not resist him, how can we?"

⁵So the palace administrator, the city governor, the elders and the guardians sent this message to Jehu: "We are your servants and we will do anything you say. We will not appoint anyone as king; you do whatever you think best."

⁶Then Jehu wrote them a second letter, saying, "If you are on my side and will obey me, take the heads of your master's sons and come to me in Jezreel by this time tomorrow."

Now the royal princes, seventy of them, were with the leading men of the city, who were rearing them. ⁷When the letter arrived, these men took the princes and slaughtered all seventy of them. They put their heads

---

ᵃ26 See 1 Kings 21:19.   ᵇ27 Or *fled by way of the garden house*   ᶜ31 Or *"Did Zimri have peace, who murdered his master?"*   ᵈ36 See 1 Kings 21:23.   ᵉ1 Hebrew; some Septuagint manuscripts and Vulgate *of the city*

in baskets and sent them to Jehu in Jezreel. [8]When the messenger arrived, he told Jehu, "They have brought the heads of the princes."

Then Jehu ordered, "Put them in two piles at the entrance of the city gate until morning."

[9]The next morning Jehu went out. He stood before all the people and said, "You are innocent. It was I who conspired against my master and killed him, but who killed all these? [10]Know then, that not a word the LORD has spoken against the house of Ahab will fail. The LORD has done what he promised through his servant Elijah." [11]So Jehu killed everyone in Jezreel who remained of the house of Ahab, as well as all his chief men, his close friends and his priests, leaving him no survivor.

[12]Jehu then set out and went toward Samaria. At Beth Eked of the Shepherds, [13]he met some relatives of Ahaziah king of Judah and asked, "Who are you?"

They said, "We are relatives of Ahaziah, and we have come down to greet the families of the king and of the queen mother."

[14]"Take them alive!" he ordered. So they took them alive and slaughtered them by the well of Beth Eked—forty-two men. He left no survivor.

[15]After he left there, he came upon Jehonadab son of Recab, who was on his way to meet him. Jehu greeted him and said, "Are you in accord with me, as I am with you?"

"I am," Jehonadab answered.

"If so," said Jehu, "give me your hand." So he did, and Jehu helped him up into the chariot. [16]Jehu said, "Come with me and see my zeal for the LORD." Then he had him ride along in his chariot.

[17]When Jehu came to Samaria, he killed all who were left there of Ahab's family; he destroyed them, according to the word of the LORD spoken to Elijah.

Ministers of Baal Killed

[18]Then Jehu brought all the people together and said to them, "Ahab served Baal a little; Jehu will serve him much. [19]Now summon all the prophets of Baal, all his ministers and all his priests. See that no one is missing, because I am going to hold a great sacrifice for Baal. Anyone who fails to come will no longer live." But Jehu was acting deceptively in order to destroy the ministers of Baal.

[20]Jehu said, "Call an assembly in honor of Baal." So they proclaimed it. [21]Then he sent word throughout Israel, and all the ministers of Baal came; not one stayed away. They crowded into the temple of Baal until it was full from one end to the other. [22]And Jehu said to the keeper of the wardrobe, "Bring robes for all the ministers of Baal." So he brought out robes for them.

[23]Then Jehu and Jehonadab son of Recab went into the temple of Baal. Jehu said to the ministers of Baal, "Look around and see that no servants of the LORD are here with you—only ministers of Baal." [24]So they went in to make sacrifices and burnt offerings. Now Jehu had posted eighty men outside with this warning: "If one of you lets any of the men I am placing in your hands escape, it will be your life for his life."

[25]As soon as Jehu had finished making the burnt offering, he ordered the guards and officers: "Go in and kill them; let no one escape." So they cut them down with the sword. The guards and officers threw the bodies out and then entered the inner shrine of the temple of Baal. [26]They brought the sacred stone out of the temple of Baal and burned it. [27]They demolished the sacred stone of Baal and tore down the temple of Baal, and people have used it for a latrine to this day.

[28]So Jehu destroyed Baal worship in Israel. [29]However, he did not turn away from the sins of Jeroboam son of Nebat, which he had caused Israel to commit—the worship of the golden calves at Bethel and Dan.

[30]The LORD said to Jehu, "Because you have done well in accomplishing what is right in my eyes and have

done to the house of Ahab all I had in mind to do, your descendants will sit on the throne of Israel to the fourth generation." ³¹Yet Jehu was not careful to keep the law of the LORD, the God of Israel, with all his heart. He did not turn away from the sins of Jeroboam, which he had caused Israel to commit.

³²In those days the LORD began to reduce the size of Israel. Hazael overpowered the Israelites throughout their territory ³³east of the Jordan in all the land of Gilead (the region of Gad, Reuben and Manasseh), from Aroer by the Arnon Gorge through Gilead to Bashan.

³⁴As for the other events of Jehu's reign, all he did, and all his achievements, are they not written in the book of the annals of the kings of Israel?

³⁵Jehu rested with his fathers and was buried in Samaria. And Jehoahaz his son succeeded him as king. ³⁶The time that Jehu reigned over Israel in Samaria was twenty-eight years.

Athaliah and Joash

11 When Athaliah the mother of Ahaziah saw that her son was dead, she proceeded to destroy the whole royal family. ²But Jehosheba, the daughter of King Jehoram[a] and sister of Ahaziah, took Joash son of Ahaziah and stole him away from among the royal princes, who were about to be murdered. She put him and his nurse in a bedroom to hide him from Athaliah; so he was not killed. ³He remained hidden with his nurse at the temple of the LORD for six years while Athaliah ruled the land.

⁴In the seventh year Jehoiada sent for the commanders of units of a hundred, the Carites and the guards and had them brought to him at the temple of the LORD. He made a covenant with them and put them under oath at the temple of the LORD. Then he showed them the king's son. ⁵He commanded them, saying, "This is

what you are to do: You who are in the three companies that are going on duty on the Sabbath—a third of you guarding the royal palace, ⁶a third at the Sur Gate, and a third at the gate behind the guard, who take turns guarding the temple— ⁷and you who are in the other two companies that normally go off Sabbath duty are all to guard the temple for the king. ⁸Station yourselves around the king, each man with his weapon in his hand. Anyone who approaches your ranks[b] must be put to death. Stay close to the king wherever he goes."

⁹The commanders of units of a hundred did just as Jehoiada the priest ordered. Each one took his men—those who were going on duty on the Sabbath and those who were going off duty—and came to Jehoiada the priest. ¹⁰Then he gave the commanders the spears and shields that had belonged to King David and that were in the temple of the LORD. ¹¹The guards, each with his weapon in his hand, stationed themselves around the king—near the altar and the temple, from the south side to the north side of the temple.

¹²Jehoiada brought out the king's son and put the crown on him; he presented him with a copy of the covenant and proclaimed him king. They anointed him, and the people clapped their hands and shouted, "Long live the king!"

¹³When Athaliah heard the noise made by the guards and the people, she went to the people at the temple of the LORD. ¹⁴She looked and there was the king, standing by the pillar, as the custom was. The officers and the trumpeters were beside the king, and all the people of the land were rejoicing and blowing trumpets. Then Athaliah tore her robes and called out, "Treason! Treason!"

¹⁵Jehoiada the priest ordered the commanders of units of a hundred, who were in charge of the troops: "Bring her out between the ranks[c]

---

[a]2 Hebrew Joram, a variant of Jehoram   [b]8 Or approaches the precincts   [c]15 Or out from the precincts

and put to the sword anyone who follows her." For the priest had said, "She must not be put to death in the temple of the LORD." [16]So they seized her as she reached the place where the horses enter the palace grounds, and there she was put to death.

[17]Jehoiada then made a covenant between the LORD and the king and people that they would be the LORD's people. He also made a covenant between the king and the people. [18]All the people of the land went to the temple of Baal and tore it down. They smashed the altars and idols to pieces and killed Mattan the priest of Baal in front of the altars.

Then Jehoiada the priest posted guards at the temple of the LORD. [19]He took with him the commanders of hundreds, the Carites, the guards and all the people of the land, and together they brought the king down from the temple of the LORD and went into the palace, entering by way of the gate of the guards. The king then took his place on the royal throne, [20]and all the people of the land rejoiced. And the city was quiet, because Athaliah had been slain with the sword at the palace.

[21]Joash[a] was seven years old when he began to reign.

Joash Repairs the Temple

12 In the seventh year of Jehu, Joash[b] became king, and he reigned in Jerusalem forty years. His mother's name was Zibiah; she was from Beersheba. [2]Joash did what was right in the eyes of the LORD all the years Jehoiada the priest instructed him. [3]The high places, however, were not removed; the people continued to offer sacrifices and burn incense there.

[4]Joash said to the priests, "Collect all the money that is brought as sacred offerings to the temple of the LORD—the money collected in the census, the money received from personal vows and the money brought voluntarily to the temple. [5]Let every priest receive the money from one of the treasurers, and let it be used to repair whatever damage is found in the temple."

[6]But by the twenty-third year of King Joash the priests still had not repaired the temple. [7]Therefore King Joash summoned Jehoiada the priest and the other priests and asked them, "Why aren't you repairing the damage done to the temple? Take no more money from your treasurers, but hand it over for repairing the temple." [8]The priests agreed that they would not collect any more money from the people and that they would not repair the temple themselves.

[9]Jehoiada the priest took a chest and bored a hole in its lid. He placed it beside the altar, on the right side as one enters the temple of the LORD. The priests who guarded the entrance put into the chest all the money that was brought to the temple of the LORD. [10]Whenever they saw that there was a large amount of money in the chest, the royal secretary and the high priest came, counted the money that had been brought into the temple of the LORD and put it into bags. [11]When the amount had been determined, they gave the money to the men appointed to supervise the work on the temple. With it they paid those who worked on the temple of the LORD—the carpenters and builders, [12]the masons and stonecutters. They purchased timber and dressed stone for the repair of the temple of the LORD, and met all the other expenses of restoring the temple.

[13]The money brought into the temple was not spent for making silver basins, wick trimmers, sprinkling bowls, trumpets or any other articles of gold or silver for the temple of the LORD; [14]it was paid to the workmen, who used it to repair the temple. [15]They did not require an accounting from those to whom they gave the money to pay the workers, because

---

[a]21 Hebrew *Jehoash*, a variant of *Joash*   [b]1 Hebrew *Jehoash*, a variant of *Joash*; also in verses 2, 4, 6, 7 and 18

they acted with complete honesty. ¹⁶The money from the guilt offerings and sin offerings was not brought into the temple of the LORD; it belonged to the priests.

¹⁷About this time Hazael king of Aram went up and attacked Gath and captured it. Then he turned to attack Jerusalem. ¹⁸But Joash king of Judah took all the sacred objects dedicated by his fathers—Jehoshaphat, Jehoram and Ahaziah, the kings of Judah—and the gifts he himself had dedicated and all the gold found in the treasuries of the temple of the LORD and of the royal palace, and he sent them to Hazael king of Aram, who then withdrew from Jerusalem.

¹⁹As for the other events of the reign of Joash, and all he did, are they not written in the book of the annals of the kings of Judah? ²⁰His officials conspired against him and assassinated him at Beth Millo, on the road down to Silla. ²¹The officials who murdered him were Jozabad son of Shimeath and Jehozabad son of Shomer. He died and was buried with his fathers in the City of David. And Amaziah his son succeeded him as king.

Jehoahaz King of Israel

13 In the twenty-third year of Joash son of Ahaziah king of Judah, Jehoahaz son of Jehu became king of Israel in Samaria, and he reigned seventeen years. ²He did evil in the eyes of the LORD by following the sins of Jeroboam son of Nebat, which he had caused Israel to commit, and he did not turn away from them. ³So the LORD's anger burned against Israel, and for a long time he kept them under the power of Hazael king of Aram and Ben-Hadad his son.

⁴Then Jehoahaz sought the LORD's favor, and the LORD listened to him, for he saw how severely the king of Aram was oppressing Israel. ⁵The LORD provided a deliverer for Israel, and they escaped from the power of Aram. So the Israelites lived in their own homes as they had before. ⁶But they did not turn away from the sins of the house of Jeroboam, which he had caused Israel to commit; they continued in them. Also, the Asherah pole*ᵃ* remained standing in Samaria.

⁷Nothing had been left of the army of Jehoahaz except fifty horsemen, ten chariots and ten thousand foot soldiers, for the king of Aram had destroyed the rest and made them like the dust at threshing time.

⁸As for the other events of the reign of Jehoahaz, all he did and his achievements, are they not written in the book of the annals of the kings of Israel? ⁹Jehoahaz rested with his fathers and was buried in Samaria. And Jehoash*ᵇ* his son succeeded him as king.

Jehoash King of Israel

¹⁰In the thirty-seventh year of Joash king of Judah, Jehoash son of Jehoahaz became king of Israel in Samaria, and he reigned sixteen years. ¹¹He did evil in the eyes of the LORD and did not turn away from any of the sins of Jeroboam son of Nebat, which he had caused Israel to commit; he continued in them.

¹²As for the other events of the reign of Jehoash, all he did and his achievements, including his war against Amaziah king of Judah, are they not written in the book of the annals of the kings of Israel? ¹³Jehoash rested with his fathers, and Jeroboam succeeded him on the throne. Jehoash was buried in Samaria with the kings of Israel.

¹⁴Now Elisha was suffering from the illness from which he died. Jehoash king of Israel went down to see him and wept over him. "My father! My father!" he cried. "The chariots and horsemen of Israel!"

¹⁵Elisha said, "Get a bow and some arrows," and he did so. ¹⁶"Take the bow in your hands," he said to the king of Israel. When he had taken it,

---

ᵃ6 That is, a symbol of the goddess Asherah; here and elsewhere in 2 Kings a variant of *Jehoash*; also in verses 12-14 and 25   *ᵇ9* Hebrew *Joash,*

Elisha put his hands on the king's hands.

¹⁷"Open the east window," he said, and he opened it. "Shoot!" Elisha said, and he shot. "The LORD's arrow of victory, the arrow of victory over Aram!" Elisha declared. "You will completely destroy the Arameans at Aphek."

¹⁸Then he said, "Take the arrows," and the king took them. Elisha told him, "Strike the ground." He struck it three times and stopped. ¹⁹The man of God was angry with him and said, "You should have struck the ground five or six times; then you would have defeated Aram and completely destroyed it. But now you will defeat it only three times."

²⁰Elisha died and was buried.

Now Moabite raiders used to enter the country every spring. ²¹Once while some Israelites were burying a man, suddenly they saw a band of raiders; so they threw the man's body into Elisha's tomb. When the body touched Elisha's bones, the man came to life and stood up on his feet.

²²Hazael king of Aram oppressed Israel throughout the reign of Jehoahaz. ²³But the LORD was gracious to them and had compassion and showed concern for them because of his covenant with Abraham, Isaac and Jacob. To this day he has been unwilling to destroy them or banish them from his presence.

²⁴Hazael king of Aram died, and Ben-Hadad his son succeeded him as king. ²⁵Then Jehoash son of Jehoahaz recaptured from Ben-Hadad son of Hazael the towns he had taken in battle from his father Jehoahaz. Three times Jehoash defeated him, and so he recovered the Israelite towns.

Amaziah King of Judah

14 In the second year of Jehoash[a] son of Jehoahaz king of Israel, Amaziah son of Joash king of Judah began to reign. ²He was twenty-five years old when he became king, and he reigned in Jerusalem twenty-nine years. His mother's name was Jehoaddin; she was from Jerusalem. ³He did what was right in the eyes of the LORD, but not as his father David had done. In everything he followed the example of his father Joash. ⁴The high places, however, were not removed; the people continued to offer sacrifices and burn incense there.

⁵After the kingdom was firmly in his grasp, he executed the officials who had murdered his father the king. ⁶Yet he did not put the sons of the assassins to death, in accordance with what is written in the Book of the Law of Moses where the LORD commanded: "Fathers shall not be put to death for their children, nor children put to death for their fathers; each is to die for his own sins."[b]

⁷He was the one who defeated ten thousand Edomites in the Valley of Salt and captured Sela in battle, calling it Joktheel, the name it has to this day.

⁸Then Amaziah sent messengers to Jehoash son of Jehoahaz, the son of Jehu, king of Israel, with the challenge: "Come, meet me face to face."

⁹But Jehoash king of Israel replied to Amaziah king of Judah: "A thistle in Lebanon sent a message to a cedar in Lebanon, 'Give your daughter to my son in marriage.' Then a wild beast in Lebanon came along and trampled the thistle underfoot. ¹⁰You have indeed defeated Edom and now you are arrogant. Glory in your victory, but stay at home! Why ask for trouble and cause your own downfall and that of Judah also?"

¹¹Amaziah, however, would not listen, so Jehoash king of Israel attacked. He and Amaziah king of Judah faced each other at Beth Shemesh in Judah. ¹²Judah was routed by Israel, and every man fled to his home. ¹³Jehoash king of Israel captured Amaziah king of Judah, the son of Joash, the son of Ahaziah, at Beth Shemesh. Then Jehoash went to Jerusalem and broke down the wall of Jerusalem from the Ephraim Gate to the Corner Gate—a

---

a1 Hebrew *Joash*, a variant of *Jehoash*; also in verses 13, 23 and 27　　*b6* Deut. 24:16

section about six hundred feet long.[a]
[14]He took all the gold and silver and all the articles found in the temple of the LORD and in the treasuries of the royal palace. He also took hostages and returned to Samaria.

[15]As for the other events of the reign of Jehoash, what he did and his achievements, including his war against Amaziah king of Judah, are they not written in the book of the annals of the kings of Israel? [16]Jehoash rested with his fathers and was buried in Samaria with the kings of Israel. And Jeroboam his son succeeded him as king.

[17]Amaziah son of Joash king of Judah lived for fifteen years after the death of Jehoash son of Jehoahaz king of Israel. [18]As for the other events of Amaziah's reign, are they not written in the book of the annals of the kings of Judah?

[19]They conspired against him in Jerusalem, and he fled to Lachish, but they sent men after him to Lachish and killed him there. [20]He was brought back by horse and was buried in Jerusalem with his fathers, in the City of David.

[21]Then all the people of Judah took Azariah,[b] who was sixteen years old, and made him king in place of his father Amaziah. [22]He was the one who rebuilt Elath and restored it to Judah after Amaziah rested with his fathers.

Jeroboam II King of Israel

[23]In the fifteenth year of Amaziah son of Joash king of Judah, Jeroboam son of Jehoash king of Israel became king in Samaria, and he reigned forty-one years. [24]He did evil in the eyes of the LORD and did not turn away from any of the sins of Jeroboam son of Nebat, which he had caused Israel to commit. [25]He was the one who restored the boundaries of Israel from Lebo[c] Hamath to the Sea of the Arabah,[d] in accordance with the word of the LORD, the God of Israel, spoken through his servant Jonah son of Amittai, the prophet from Gath Hepher.

[26]The LORD had seen how bitterly everyone in Israel, whether slave or free, was suffering; there was no one to help them. [27]And since the LORD had not said he would blot out the name of Israel from under heaven, he saved them by the hand of Jeroboam son of Jehoash.

[28]As for the other events of Jeroboam's reign, all he did, and his military achievements, including how he recovered for Israel both Damascus and Hamath, which had belonged to Yaudi,[e] are they not written in the book of the annals of the kings of Israel? [29]Jeroboam rested with his fathers, the kings of Israel. And Zechariah his son succeeded him as king.

Azariah King of Judah

15 In the twenty-seventh year of Jeroboam king of Israel, Azariah son of Amaziah king of Judah began to reign. [2]He was sixteen years old when he became king, and he reigned in Jerusalem fifty-two years. His mother's name was Jecoliah; she was from Jerusalem. [3]He did what was right in the eyes of the LORD, just as his father Amaziah had done. [4]The high places, however, were not removed; the people continued to offer sacrifices and burn incense there.

[5]The LORD afflicted the king with leprosy[f] until the day he died, and he lived in a separate house.[g] Jotham the king's son had charge of the palace and governed the people of the land.

[6]As for the other events of Azariah's reign, and all he did, are they not written in the book of the annals of the kings of Judah? [7]Azariah rested with his fathers and was buried near them in the City of David. And Jotham his son succeeded him as king.

---

[a]13 Hebrew *four hundred cubits* (about 180 meters)   [b]21 Also called *Uzziah*   [c]25 Or *from the entrance to*   [d]25 That is, the Dead Sea   [e]28 Or *Judah*   [f]5 The Hebrew word was used for various diseases affecting the skin—not necessarily leprosy.   [g]5 Or *in a house where he was relieved of responsibility*

Zechariah King of Israel

8In the thirty-eighth year of Azariah king of Judah, Zechariah son of Jeroboam became king of Israel in Samaria, and he reigned six months. **9**He did evil in the eyes of the LORD, as his fathers had done. He did not turn away from the sins of Jeroboam son of Nebat, which he had caused Israel to commit.

10Shallum son of Jabesh conspired against Zechariah. He attacked him in front of the people,*a* assassinated him and succeeded him as king. **11**The other events of Zechariah's reign are written in the book of the annals of the kings of Israel. **12**So the word of the LORD spoken to Jehu was fulfilled: "Your descendants will sit on the throne of Israel to the fourth generation."*b*

Shallum King of Israel

13Shallum son of Jabesh became king in the thirty-ninth year of Uzziah king of Judah, and he reigned in Samaria one month. **14**Then Menahem son of Gadi went from Tirzah up to Samaria. He attacked Shallum son of Jabesh in Samaria, assassinated him and succeeded him as king. **15**The other events of Shallum's reign, and the conspiracy he led, are written in the book of the annals of the kings of Israel.

16At that time Menahem, starting out from Tirzah, attacked Tiphsah and everyone in the city and its vicinity, because they refused to open their gates. He sacked Tiphsah and ripped open all the pregnant women.

Menahem King of Israel

17In the thirty-ninth year of Azariah king of Judah, Menahem son of Gadi became king of Israel, and he reigned in Samaria ten years. **18**He did evil in the eyes of the LORD. During his entire reign he did not turn away from the sins of Jeroboam son of Nebat, which he had caused Israel to commit.

19Then Pul*c* king of Assyria invaded the land, and Menahem gave him a thousand talents*d* of silver to gain his support and strengthen his own hold on the kingdom. **20**Menahem exacted this money from Israel. Every wealthy man had to contribute fifty shekels*e* of silver to be given to the king of Assyria. So the king of Assyria withdrew and stayed in the land no longer.

21As for the other events of Menahem's reign, and all he did, are they not written in the book of the annals of the kings of Israel? **22**Menahem rested with his fathers. And Pekahiah his son succeeded him as king.

Pekahiah King of Israel

23In the fiftieth year of Azariah king of Judah, Pekahiah son of Menahem became king of Israel in Samaria, and he reigned two years. **24**Pekahiah did evil in the eyes of the LORD. He did not turn away from the sins of Jeroboam son of Nebat, which he had caused Israel to commit. **25**One of his chief officers, Pekah son of Remaliah, conspired against him. Taking fifty men of Gilead with him, he assassinated Pekahiah, along with Argob and Arieh, in the citadel of the royal palace at Samaria. So Pekah killed Pekahiah and succeeded him as king.

26The other events of Pekahiah's reign, and all he did, are written in the book of the annals of the kings of Israel.

Pekah King of Israel

27In the fifty-second year of Azariah king of Judah, Pekah son of Remaliah became king of Israel in Samaria, and he reigned twenty years. **28**He did evil in the eyes of the LORD. He did not turn away from the sins of Jeroboam son of Nebat, which he had caused Israel to commit.

29In the time of Pekah king of Israel, Tiglath-Pileser king of Assyria came and took Ijon, Abel Beth Maacah, Ja-

a10 Hebrew; some Septuagint manuscripts *in Ibleam*   *b12* 2 Kings 10:30   *c19* Also called Tiglath-Pileser   *d19* That is, about 37 tons (about 34 metric tons)   *e20* That is, about 1 1/4 pounds (about 0.6 kilogram)

noah, Kedesh and Hazor. He took Gilead and Galilee, including all the land of Naphtali, and deported the people to Assyria. ³⁰Then Hoshea son of Elah conspired against Pekah son of Remaliah. He attacked and assassinated him, and then succeeded him as king in the twentieth year of Jotham son of Uzziah.

³¹As for the other events of Pekah's reign, and all he did, are they not written in the book of the annals of the kings of Israel?

Jotham King of Judah

³²In the second year of Pekah son of Remaliah king of Israel, Jotham son of Uzziah king of Judah began to reign. ³³He was twenty-five years old when he became king, and he reigned in Jerusalem sixteen years. His mother's name was Jerusha daughter of Zadok. ³⁴He did what was right in the eyes of the LORD, just as his father Uzziah had done. ³⁵The high places, however, were not removed; the people continued to offer sacrifices and burn incense there. Jotham rebuilt the Upper Gate of the temple of the LORD.

³⁶As for the other events of Jotham's reign, and what he did, are they not written in the book of the annals of the kings of Judah? ³⁷(In those days the LORD began to send Rezin king of Aram and Pekah son of Remaliah against Judah.) ³⁸Jotham rested with his fathers and was buried with them in the City of David, the city of his father. And Ahaz his son succeeded him as king.

Ahaz King of Judah

16 In the seventeenth year of Pekah son of Remaliah, Ahaz son of Jotham king of Judah began to reign. ²Ahaz was twenty years old when he became king, and he reigned in Jerusalem sixteen years. Unlike David his father, he did not do what was right in the eyes of the LORD his God. ³He walked in the ways of the kings of Israel and even sacrificed his son in*a* the fire, following the detestable

ways of the nations the LORD had driven out before the Israelites. ⁴He offered sacrifices and burned incense at the high places, on the hilltops and under every spreading tree.

⁵Then Rezin king of Aram and Pekah son of Remaliah king of Israel marched up to fight against Jerusalem and besieged Ahaz, but they could not overpower him. ⁶At that time, Rezin king of Aram recovered Elath for Aram by driving out the men of Judah. Edomites then moved into Elath and have lived there to this day.

⁷Ahaz sent messengers to say to Tiglath-Pileser king of Assyria, "I am your servant and vassal. Come up and save me out of the hand of the king of Aram and of the king of Israel, who are attacking me." ⁸And Ahaz took the silver and gold found in the temple of the LORD and in the treasuries of the royal palace and sent it as a gift to the king of Assyria. ⁹The king of Assyria complied by attacking Damascus and capturing it. He deported its inhabitants to Kir and put Rezin to death.

¹⁰Then King Ahaz went to Damascus to meet Tiglath-Pileser king of Assyria. He saw an altar in Damascus and sent to Uriah the priest a sketch of the altar, with detailed plans for its construction. ¹¹So Uriah the priest built an altar in accordance with all the plans that King Ahaz had sent from Damascus and finished it before King Ahaz returned. ¹²When the king came back from Damascus and saw the altar, he approached it and presented offerings*b* on it. ¹³He offered up his burnt offering and grain offering, poured out his drink offering, and sprinkled the blood of his fellowship offerings*c* on the altar. ¹⁴The bronze altar that stood before the LORD he brought from the front of the temple—from between the new altar and the temple of the LORD—and put it on the north side of the new altar. ¹⁵King Ahaz then gave these orders to Uriah the priest: "On the large new altar, offer the morning burnt offering

---

a3 Or *even made his son pass through*   *b12* Or *and went up*   *c13* Traditionally *peace offerings*

and the evening grain offering, the king's burnt offering and his grain offering, and the burnt offering of all the people of the land, and their grain offering and their drink offering. Sprinkle on the altar all the blood of the burnt offerings and sacrifices. But I will use the bronze altar for seeking guidance." [16]And Uriah the priest did just as King Ahaz had ordered.

[17]King Ahaz took away the side panels and removed the basins from the movable stands. He removed the Sea from the bronze bulls that supported it and set it on a stone base. [18]He took away the Sabbath canopy[a] that had been built at the temple and removed the royal entryway outside the temple of the LORD, in deference to the king of Assyria.

[19]As for the other events of the reign of Ahaz, and what he did, are they not written in the book of the annals of the kings of Judah? [20]Ahaz rested with his fathers and was buried with them in the City of David. And Hezekiah his son succeeded him as king.

Hoshea Last King of Israel

17 In the twelfth year of Ahaz king of Judah, Hoshea son of Elah became king of Israel in Samaria, and he reigned nine years. [2]He did evil in the eyes of the LORD, but not like the kings of Israel who preceded him.

[3]Shalmaneser king of Assyria came up to attack Hoshea, who had been Shalmaneser's vassal and had paid him tribute. [4]But the king of Assyria discovered that Hoshea was a traitor, for he had sent envoys to So[b] king of Egypt, and he no longer paid tribute to the king of Assyria, as he had done year by year. Therefore Shalmaneser seized him and put him in prison. [5]The king of Assyria invaded the entire land, marched against Samaria and laid siege to it for three years. [6]In the ninth year of Hoshea, the king of Assyria captured Samaria and deport-

ed the Israelites to Assyria. He settled them in Halah, in Gozan on the Habor River and in the towns of the Medes.

Israel Exiled Because of Sin

[7]All this took place because the Israelites had sinned against the LORD their God, who had brought them up out of Egypt from under the power of Pharaoh king of Egypt. They worshiped other gods [8]and followed the practices of the nations the LORD had driven out before them, as well as the practices that the kings of Israel had introduced. [9]The Israelites secretly did things against the LORD their God that were not right. From watchtower to fortified city they built themselves high places in all their towns. [10]They set up sacred stones and Asherah poles on every high hill and under every spreading tree. [11]At every high place they burned incense, as the nations whom the LORD had driven out before them had done. They did wicked things that provoked the LORD to anger. [12]They worshiped idols, though the LORD had said, "You shall not do this."[c] [13]The LORD warned Israel and Judah through all his prophets and seers: "Turn from your evil ways. Observe my commands and decrees, in accordance with the entire Law that I commanded your fathers to obey and that I delivered to you through my servants the prophets."

[14]But they would not listen and were as stiff-necked as their fathers, who did not trust in the LORD their God. [15]They rejected his decrees and the covenant he had made with their fathers and the warnings he had given them. They followed worthless idols and themselves became worthless. They imitated the nations around them although the LORD had ordered them, "Do not do as they do," and they did the things the LORD had forbidden them to do.

[16]They forsook all the commands of the LORD their God and made for

---

[a]18 Or the dais of his throne (see Septuagint) abbreviation for Osorkon.   [c]12 Exodus 20:4, 5   [b]4 Or to Sais, to the; So is possibly an

themselves two idols cast in the shape of calves, and an Asherah pole. They bowed down to all the starry hosts, and they worshiped Baal. [17]They sacrificed their sons and daughters in[a] the fire. They practiced divination and sorcery and sold themselves to do evil in the eyes of the LORD, provoking him to anger.

[18]So the LORD was very angry with Israel and removed them from his presence. Only the tribe of Judah was left, [19]and even Judah did not keep the commands of the LORD their God. They followed the practices Israel had introduced. [20]Therefore the LORD rejected all the people of Israel; he afflicted them and gave them into the hands of plunderers, until he thrust them from his presence.

[21]When he tore Israel away from the house of David, they made Jeroboam son of Nebat their king. Jeroboam enticed Israel away from following the LORD and caused them to commit a great sin. [22]The Israelites persisted in all the sins of Jeroboam and did not turn away from them [23]until the LORD removed them from his presence, as he had warned through all his servants the prophets. So the people of Israel were taken from their homeland into exile in Assyria, and they are still there.

Samaria Resettled

[24]The king of Assyria brought people from Babylon, Cuthah, Avva, Hamath and Sepharvaim and settled them in the towns of Samaria to replace the Israelites. They took over Samaria and lived in its towns. [25]When they first lived there, they did not worship the LORD; so he sent lions among them and they killed some of the people. [26]It was reported to the king of Assyria: "The people you deported and resettled in the towns of Samaria do not know what the god of that country requires. He has sent lions among them, which are killing them off, because the people do not know what he requires."

[27]Then the king of Assyria gave this order: "Have one of the priests you took captive from Samaria go back to live there and teach the people what the god of the land requires." [28]So one of the priests who had been exiled from Samaria came to live in Bethel and taught them how to worship the LORD.

[29]Nevertheless, each national group made its own gods in the several towns where they settled, and set them up in the shrines the people of Samaria had made at the high places. [30]The men from Babylon made Succoth Benoth, the men from Cuthah made Nergal, and the men from Hamath made Ashima; [31]the Avvites made Nibhaz and Tartak, and the Sepharvites burned their children in the fire as sacrifices to Adrammelech and Anammelech, the gods of Sepharvaim. [32]They worshiped the LORD, but they also appointed all sorts of their own people to officiate for them as priests in the shrines at the high places. [33]They worshiped the LORD, but they also served their own gods in accordance with the customs of the nations from which they had been brought.

[34]To this day they persist in their former practices. They neither worship the LORD nor adhere to the decrees and ordinances, the laws and commands that the LORD gave the descendants of Jacob, whom he named Israel. [35]When the LORD made a covenant with the Israelites, he commanded them: "Do not worship any other gods or bow down to them, serve them or sacrifice to them. [36]But the LORD, who brought you up out of Egypt with mighty power and outstretched arm, is the one you must worship. To him you shall bow down and to him offer sacrifices. [37]You must always be careful to keep the decrees and ordinances, the laws and commands he wrote for you. Do not worship other gods. [38]Do not forget the covenant I have made with you, and do not worship other gods. [39]Rather,

---

a17 Or *They made their sons and daughters pass through*

VERSE:	AUTHOR:	PASSAGE:
2 Kings 17:14	John Killinger	2 Kings 17:7–17

The Panorama of Grace

Maybe part of our homework at the time of transition from late mid-life into retirement is a personal prayer of confession, some word of our own expression in which we admit to God what a botch we have made of things and ask to be shriven in order to turn with healthy minds and hearts to the new business that lies ahead: Would it run something like this?

O God of the ages, in the folds of whose arms lies my only forgiveness, I confess to you my deep inadequacy for the years of serving my calling. I have been proud and stiff-necked, and have gone my own way in solving problems, dealing with other people's needs and declaring the Word. I have spent too little time listening, either to you or to those around me, and now feel despair because I know my own failure better than I know anything else in life. Take away my sin, O God, and heal my brokenness. Repair my life that I may yet glorify your name. Through Jesus Christ, my Lord. Amen.

And God, who hears every prayer of a broken and contrite heart, will forgive our sin and put his Spirit within us, that we may walk in the light and not in the darkness . . .

We need to confess; there is no way around that. We do not get off the hook by letting ourselves off. But, having confessed and had our vision renewed, we are able to see, with new clarity from our new vantage point, how rich is the panorama of grace in our lives!

. . . .

ADDITIONAL SCRIPTURE READINGS
Micah 7:18–20; 1 John 1:5–10

Go to page 499 for your next devotional reading.

worship the LORD your God; it is he who will deliver you from the hand of all your enemies."

⁴⁰They would not listen, however, but persisted in their former practices. ⁴¹Even while these people were worshiping the LORD, they were serving their idols. To this day their children and grandchildren continue to do as their fathers did.

Hezekiah King of Judah

18 In the third year of Hoshea son of Elah king of Israel, Hezekiah son of Ahaz king of Judah began to reign. ²He was twenty-five years old when he became king, and he reigned in Jerusalem twenty-nine years. His mother's name was Abijah*ᵃ* daughter of Zechariah. ³He did what was right in the eyes of the LORD, just as his father David had done. ⁴He removed the high places, smashed the sacred stones and cut down the Asherah poles. He broke into pieces the bronze snake Moses had made, for up to that time the Israelites had been burning incense to it. (It was called*ᵇ* Nehushtan.*ᶜ*)

⁵Hezekiah trusted in the LORD, the God of Israel. There was no one like him among all the kings of Judah, either before him or after him. ⁶He held fast to the LORD and did not cease to follow him; he kept the commands the LORD had given Moses. ⁷And the LORD was with him; he was successful in whatever he undertook. He rebelled against the king of Assyria and did not serve him. ⁸From watchtower to fortified city, he defeated the Philistines, as far as Gaza and its territory.

⁹In King Hezekiah's fourth year, which was the seventh year of Hoshea son of Elah king of Israel, Shalmaneser king of Assyria marched against Samaria and laid siege to it. ¹⁰At the end of three years the Assyrians took it. So Samaria was captured in Hezekiah's sixth year, which was the ninth year of Hoshea king of Israel. ¹¹The king of Assyria deported Israel to Assyria and settled them in Halah, in Gozan on the Habor River and in towns of the Medes. ¹²This happened because they had not obeyed the LORD their God, but had violated his covenant—all that Moses the servant of the LORD commanded. They neither listened to the commands nor carried them out.

¹³In the fourteenth year of King Hezekiah's reign, Sennacherib king of Assyria attacked all the fortified cities of Judah and captured them. ¹⁴So Hezekiah king of Judah sent this message to the king of Assyria at Lachish: "I have done wrong. Withdraw from me, and I will pay whatever you demand of me." The king of Assyria exacted from Hezekiah king of Judah three hundred talents*ᵈ* of silver and thirty talents*ᵉ* of gold. ¹⁵So Hezekiah gave him all the silver that was found in the temple of the LORD and in the treasuries of the royal palace.

¹⁶At this time Hezekiah king of Judah stripped off the gold with which he had covered the doors and doorposts of the temple of the LORD, and gave it to the king of Assyria.

Sennacherib Threatens Jerusalem

¹⁷The king of Assyria sent his supreme commander, his chief officer and his field commander with a large army, from Lachish to King Hezekiah at Jerusalem. They came up to Jerusalem and stopped at the aqueduct of the Upper Pool, on the road to the Washerman's Field. ¹⁸They called for the king; and Eliakim son of Hilkiah the palace administrator, Shebna the secretary, and Joah son of Asaph the recorder went out to them.

¹⁹The field commander said to them, "Tell Hezekiah:

" 'This is what the great king, the king of Assyria, says: On what are you basing this confidence of yours? ²⁰You say you have strategy and military

---

ᵃ2 Hebrew *Abi,* a variant of *Abijah*   *ᵇ4* Or *He called it* Hebrew for *bronze* and *snake* and *unclean thing.*   *ᶜ4 Nehushtan* sounds like the   *ᵈ14* That is, about 11 tons (about 10 metric tons)   *ᵉ14* That is, about 1 ton (about 1 metric ton)

strength—but you speak only empty words. On whom are you depending, that you rebel against me? 21Look now, you are depending on Egypt, that splintered reed of a staff, which pierces a man's hand and wounds him if he leans on it! Such is Pharaoh king of Egypt to all who depend on him. 22And if you say to me, "We are depending on the LORD our God"—isn't he the one whose high places and altars Hezekiah removed, saying to Judah and Jerusalem, "You must worship before this altar in Jerusalem"?

23" 'Come now, make a bargain with my master, the king of Assyria: I will give you two thousand horses—if you can put riders on them! 24How can you repulse one officer of the least of my master's officials, even though you are depending on Egypt for chariots and horsemen*a*? 25Furthermore, have I come to attack and destroy this place without word from the LORD? The LORD himself told me to march against this country and destroy it.' "

26Then Eliakim son of Hilkiah, and Shebna and Joah said to the field commander, "Please speak to your servants in Aramaic, since we understand it. Don't speak to us in Hebrew in the hearing of the people on the wall."

27But the commander replied, "Was it only to your master and you that my master sent me to say these things, and not to the men sitting on the wall—who, like you, will have to eat their own filth and drink their own urine?"

28Then the commander stood and called out in Hebrew: "Hear the word of the great king, the king of Assyria! 29This is what the king says: Do not let Hezekiah deceive you. He cannot deliver you from my hand. 30Do not let

Hezekiah persuade you to trust in the LORD when he says, 'The LORD will surely deliver us; this city will not be given into the hand of the king of Assyria.'

31"Do not listen to Hezekiah. This is what the king of Assyria says: Make peace with me and come out to me. Then every one of you will eat from his own vine and fig tree and drink water from his own cistern, 32until I come and take you to a land like your own, a land of grain and new wine, a land of bread and vineyards, a land of olive trees and honey. Choose life and not death!

"Do not listen to Hezekiah, for he is misleading you when he says, 'The LORD will deliver us.' 33Has the god of any nation ever delivered his land from the hand of the king of Assyria? 34Where are the gods of Hamath and Arpad? Where are the gods of Sepharvaim, Hena and Ivvah? Have they rescued Samaria from my hand? 35Who of all the gods of these countries has been able to save his land from me? How then can the LORD deliver Jerusalem from my hand?"

36But the people remained silent and said nothing in reply, because the king had commanded, "Do not answer him."

37Then Eliakim son of Hilkiah the palace administrator, Shebna the secretary and Joah son of Asaph the recorder went to Hezekiah, with their clothes torn, and told him what the field commander had said.

Jerusalem's Deliverance Foretold

19 When King Hezekiah heard this, he tore his clothes and put on sackcloth and went into the temple of the LORD. 2He sent Eliakim the palace administrator, Shebna the secretary and the leading priests, all wearing sackcloth, to the prophet Isaiah son of Amoz. 3They told him, "This is what Hezekiah says: This day is a day of distress and rebuke and disgrace, as when children come to the point of birth and there is no strength to deliv-

a24 Or charioteers

er them. ⁴It may be that the LORD your God will hear all the words of the field commander, whom his master, the king of Assyria, has sent to ridicule the living God, and that he will rebuke him for the words the LORD your God has heard. Therefore pray for the remnant that still survives."

⁵When King Hezekiah's officials came to Isaiah, ⁶Isaiah said to them, "Tell your master, 'This is what the LORD says: Do not be afraid of what you have heard—those words with which the underlings of the king of Assyria have blasphemed me. ⁷Listen! I am going to put such a spirit in him that when he hears a certain report, he will return to his own country, and there I will have him cut down with the sword.' "

⁸When the field commander heard that the king of Assyria had left Lachish, he withdrew and found the king fighting against Libnah.

⁹Now Sennacherib received a report that Tirhakah, the Cushiteᵃ king ⌊of Egypt⌋, was marching out to fight against him. So he again sent messengers to Hezekiah with this word: ¹⁰"Say to Hezekiah king of Judah: Do not let the god you depend on deceive you when he says, 'Jerusalem will not be handed over to the king of Assyria.' ¹¹Surely you have heard what the kings of Assyria have done to all the countries, destroying them completely. And will you be delivered? ¹²Did the gods of the nations that were destroyed by my forefathers deliver them: the gods of Gozan, Haran, Rezeph and the people of Eden who were in Tel Assar? ¹³Where is the king of Hamath, the king of Arpad, the king of the city of Sepharvaim, or of Hena or Ivvah?"

Hezekiah's Prayer

¹⁴Hezekiah received the letter from the messengers and read it. Then he went up to the temple of the LORD and spread it out before the LORD. ¹⁵And Hezekiah prayed to the LORD: "O LORD, God of Israel, enthroned be-

tween the cherubim, you alone are God over all the kingdoms of the earth. You have made heaven and earth. ¹⁶Give ear, O LORD, and hear; open your eyes, O LORD, and see; listen to the words Sennacherib has sent to insult the living God.

¹⁷"It is true, O LORD, that the Assyrian kings have laid waste these nations and their lands. ¹⁸They have thrown their gods into the fire and destroyed them, for they were not gods but only wood and stone, fashioned by men's hands. ¹⁹Now, O LORD our God, deliver us from his hand, so that all kingdoms on earth may know that you alone, O LORD, are God."

Isaiah Prophesies Sennacherib's Fall

²⁰Then Isaiah son of Amoz sent a message to Hezekiah: "This is what the LORD, the God of Israel, says: I have heard your prayer concerning Sennacherib king of Assyria. ²¹This is the word that the LORD has spoken against him:

" 'The Virgin Daughter of Zion
    despises you and mocks you.
The Daughter of Jerusalem
    tosses her head as you flee.
²²Who is it you have insulted and
        blasphemed?
    Against whom have you raised
        your voice
and lifted your eyes in pride?
    Against the Holy One of Israel!
²³By your messengers
    you have heaped insults on the
        Lord.
And you have said,
    "With my many chariots
I have ascended the heights of the
        mountains,
    the utmost heights of Lebanon.
I have cut down its tallest cedars,
    the choicest of its pines.
I have reached its remotest parts,
    the finest of its forests.
²⁴I have dug wells in foreign lands
    and drunk the water there.
With the soles of my feet

ᵃ9 That is, from the upper Nile region

I have dried up all the streams
    of Egypt."

25" 'Have you not heard?
    Long ago I ordained it.
In days of old I planned it;
    now I have brought it to pass,
that you have turned fortified
        cities
into piles of stone.
26Their people, drained of power,
    are dismayed and put to shame.
They are like plants in the field,
    like tender green shoots,
like grass sprouting on the roof,
    scorched before it grows up.

27" 'But I know where you stay
    and when you come and go
    and how you rage against me.
28Because you rage against me
    and your insolence has reached
        my ears,
I will put my hook in your nose
    and my bit in your mouth,
and I will make you return
    by the way you came.'

29"This will be the sign for you,
O Hezekiah:

"This year you will eat what
        grows by itself,
    and the second year what
        springs from that.
But in the third year sow and
        reap,
    plant vineyards and eat their
        fruit.
30Once more a remnant of the house
        of Judah
    will take root below and bear
        fruit above.
31For out of Jerusalem will come a
        remnant,
    and out of Mount Zion a band
        of survivors.

The zeal of the LORD Almighty will accomplish this.

32"Therefore this is what the LORD
says concerning the king of Assyria:

"He will not enter this city
    or shoot an arrow here.
He will not come before it with
        shield

or build a siege ramp against it.
33By the way that he came he will
        return;
    he will not enter this city,
        declares the LORD.
34I will defend this city and save it,
    for my sake and for the sake of
        David my servant."

35That night the angel of the LORD
went out and put to death a hundred
and eighty-five thousand men in the
Assyrian camp. When the people got
up the next morning—there were all
the dead bodies! 36So Sennacherib
king of Assyria broke camp and withdrew. He returned to Nineveh and
stayed there.

37One day, while he was worshiping in the temple of his god Nisroch,
his sons Adrammelech and Sharezer
cut him down with the sword, and
they escaped to the land of Ararat.
And Esarhaddon his son succeeded
him as king.

Hezekiah's Illness

20 In those days Hezekiah became
ill and was at the point of
death. The prophet Isaiah son of
Amoz went to him and said, "This is
what the LORD says: Put your house in
order, because you are going to die;
you will not recover."

2Hezekiah turned his face to the
wall and prayed to the LORD, 3"Remember, O LORD, how I have walked
before you faithfully and with wholehearted devotion and have done what
is good in your eyes." And Hezekiah
wept bitterly.

4Before Isaiah had left the middle
court, the word of the LORD came to
him: 5"Go back and tell Hezekiah, the
leader of my people, 'This is what the
LORD, the God of your father David,
says: I have heard your prayer and
seen your tears; I will heal you. On
the third day from now you will go
up to the temple of the LORD. 6I will
add fifteen years to your life. And I
will deliver you and this city from the
hand of the king of Assyria. I will defend this city for my sake and for the
sake of my servant David.' "

⁷Then Isaiah said, "Prepare a poultice of figs." They did so and applied it to the boil, and he recovered.

⁸Hezekiah had asked Isaiah, "What will be the sign that the LORD will heal me and that I will go up to the temple of the LORD on the third day from now?"

⁹Isaiah answered, "This is the LORD's sign to you that the LORD will do what he has promised: Shall the shadow go forward ten steps, or shall it go back ten steps?"

¹⁰"It is a simple matter for the shadow to go forward ten steps," said Hezekiah. "Rather, have it go back ten steps."

¹¹Then the prophet Isaiah called upon the LORD, and the LORD made the shadow go back the ten steps it had gone down on the stairway of Ahaz.

Envoys From Babylon

¹²At that time Merodach-Baladan son of Baladan king of Babylon sent Hezekiah letters and a gift, because he had heard of Hezekiah's illness. ¹³Hezekiah received the messengers and showed them all that was in his storehouses—the silver, the gold, the spices and the fine oil—his armory and everything found among his treasures. There was nothing in his palace or in all his kingdom that Hezekiah did not show them.

¹⁴Then Isaiah the prophet went to King Hezekiah and asked, "What did those men say, and where did they come from?"

"From a distant land," Hezekiah replied. "They came from Babylon."

¹⁵The prophet asked, "What did they see in your palace?"

"They saw everything in my palace," Hezekiah said. "There is nothing among my treasures that I did not show them."

¹⁶Then Isaiah said to Hezekiah, "Hear the word of the LORD: ¹⁷The time will surely come when everything in your palace, and all that your fathers have stored up until this day, will be carried off to Babylon. Noth-

ing will be left, says the LORD. ¹⁸And some of your descendants, your own flesh and blood, that will be born to you, will be taken away, and they will become eunuchs in the palace of the king of Babylon."

¹⁹"The word of the LORD you have spoken is good," Hezekiah replied. For he thought, "Will there not be peace and security in my lifetime?"

²⁰As for the other events of Hezekiah's reign, all his achievements and how he made the pool and the tunnel by which he brought water into the city, are they not written in the book of the annals of the kings of Judah? ²¹Hezekiah rested with his fathers. And Manasseh his son succeeded him as king.

Manasseh King of Judah

21 Manasseh was twelve years old when he became king, and he reigned in Jerusalem fifty-five years. His mother's name was Hephzibah. ²He did evil in the eyes of the LORD, following the detestable practices of the nations the LORD had driven out before the Israelites. ³He rebuilt the high places his father Hezekiah had destroyed; he also erected altars to Baal and made an Asherah pole, as Ahab king of Israel had done. He bowed down to all the starry hosts and worshiped them. ⁴He built altars in the temple of the LORD, of which the LORD had said, "In Jerusalem I will put my Name." ⁵In both courts of the temple of the LORD, he built altars to all the starry hosts. ⁶He sacrificed his own son in*a* the fire, practiced sorcery and divination, and consulted mediums and spiritists. He did much evil in the eyes of the LORD, provoking him to anger.

⁷He took the carved Asherah pole he had made and put it in the temple, of which the LORD had said to David and to his son Solomon, "In this temple and in Jerusalem, which I have chosen out of all the tribes of Israel, I will put my Name forever. ⁸I will not again make the feet of the Israelites

a6 Or He made his own son pass through

wander from the land I gave their forefathers, if only they will be careful to do everything I commanded them and will keep the whole Law that my servant Moses gave them." ⁹But the people did not listen. Manasseh led them astray, so that they did more evil than the nations the LORD had destroyed before the Israelites.

¹⁰The LORD said through his servants the prophets: ¹¹"Manasseh king of Judah has committed these detestable sins. He has done more evil than the Amorites who preceded him and has led Judah into sin with his idols. ¹²Therefore this is what the LORD, the God of Israel, says: I am going to bring such disaster on Jerusalem and Judah that the ears of everyone who hears of it will tingle. ¹³I will stretch out over Jerusalem the measuring line used against Samaria and the plumb line used against the house of Ahab. I will wipe out Jerusalem as one wipes a dish, wiping it and turning it upside down. ¹⁴I will forsake the remnant of my inheritance and hand them over to their enemies. They will be looted and plundered by all their foes, ¹⁵because they have done evil in my eyes and have provoked me to anger from the day their forefathers came out of Egypt until this day."

¹⁶Moreover, Manasseh also shed so much innocent blood that he filled Jerusalem from end to end—besides the sin that he had caused Judah to commit, so that they did evil in the eyes of the LORD.

¹⁷As for the other events of Manasseh's reign, and all he did, including the sin he committed, are they not written in the book of the annals of the kings of Judah? ¹⁸Manasseh rested with his fathers and was buried in his palace garden, the garden of Uzza. And Amon his son succeeded him as king.

Amon King of Judah

¹⁹Amon was twenty-two years old when he became king, and he reigned in Jerusalem two years. His mother's name was Meshullemeth daughter of Haruz; she was from Jotbah. ²⁰He did evil in the eyes of the LORD, as his father Manasseh had done. ²¹He walked in all the ways of his father; he worshiped the idols his father had worshiped, and bowed down to them. ²²He forsook the LORD, the God of his fathers, and did not walk in the way of the LORD.

²³Amon's officials conspired against him and assassinated the king in his palace. ²⁴Then the people of the land killed all who had plotted against King Amon, and they made Josiah his son king in his place.

²⁵As for the other events of Amon's reign, and what he did, are they not written in the book of the annals of the kings of Judah? ²⁶He was buried in his grave in the garden of Uzza. And Josiah his son succeeded him as king.

The Book of the Law Found

22 Josiah was eight years old when he became king, and he reigned in Jerusalem thirty-one years. His mother's name was Jedidah daughter of Adaiah; she was from Bozkath. ²He did what was right in the eyes of the LORD and walked in all the ways of his father David, not turning aside to the right or to the left.

³In the eighteenth year of his reign, King Josiah sent the secretary, Shaphan son of Azaliah, the son of Meshullam, to the temple of the LORD. He said: ⁴"Go up to Hilkiah the high priest and have him get ready the money that has been brought into the temple of the LORD, which the doorkeepers have collected from the people. ⁵Have them entrust it to the men appointed to supervise the work on the temple. And have these men pay the workers who repair the temple of the LORD— ⁶the carpenters, the builders and the masons. Also have them purchase timber and dressed stone to repair the temple. ⁷But they need not account for the money entrusted to them, because they are acting faithfully."

⁸Hilkiah the high priest said to Shaphan the secretary, "I have found the Book of the Law in the temple of the

LORD." He gave it to Shaphan, who read it. ⁹Then Shaphan the secretary went to the king and reported to him: "Your officials have paid out the money that was in the temple of the LORD and have entrusted it to the workers and supervisors at the temple." ¹⁰Then Shaphan the secretary informed the king, "Hilkiah the priest has given me a book." And Shaphan read from it in the presence of the king.

¹¹When the king heard the words of the Book of the Law, he tore his robes. ¹²He gave these orders to Hilkiah the priest, Ahikam son of Shaphan, Acbor son of Micaiah, Shaphan the secretary and Asaiah the king's attendant: ¹³"Go and inquire of the LORD for me and for the people and for all Judah about what is written in this book that has been found. Great is the LORD's anger that burns against us because our fathers have not obeyed the words of this book; they have not acted in accordance with all that is written there concerning us."

¹⁴Hilkiah the priest, Ahikam, Acbor, Shaphan and Asaiah went to speak to the prophetess Huldah, who was the wife of Shallum son of Tikvah, the son of Harhas, keeper of the wardrobe. She lived in Jerusalem, in the Second District.

¹⁵She said to them, "This is what the LORD, the God of Israel, says: Tell the man who sent you to me, ¹⁶'This is what the LORD says: I am going to bring disaster on this place and its people, according to everything written in the book the king of Judah has read. ¹⁷Because they have forsaken me and burned incense to other gods and provoked me to anger by all the idols their hands have made,ᵃ my anger will burn against this place and will not be quenched.' ¹⁸Tell the king of Judah, who sent you to inquire of the LORD, 'This is what the LORD, the God of Israel, says concerning the words you heard: ¹⁹Because your heart was responsive and you humbled yourself before the LORD when

you heard what I have spoken against this place and its people, that they would become accursed and laid waste, and because you tore your robes and wept in my presence, I have heard you, declares the LORD. ²⁰Therefore I will gather you to your fathers, and you will be buried in peace. Your eyes will not see all the disaster I am going to bring on this place.' "

So they took her answer back to the king.

Josiah Renews the Covenant

23 Then the king called together all the elders of Judah and Jerusalem. ²He went up to the temple of the LORD with the men of Judah, the people of Jerusalem, the priests and the prophets—all the people from the least to the greatest. He read in their hearing all the words of the Book of the Covenant, which had been found in the temple of the LORD. ³The king stood by the pillar and renewed the covenant in the presence of the LORD—to follow the LORD and keep his commands, regulations and decrees with all his heart and all his soul, thus confirming the words of the covenant written in this book. Then all the people pledged themselves to the covenant.

⁴The king ordered Hilkiah the high priest, the priests next in rank and the doorkeepers to remove from the temple of the LORD all the articles made for Baal and Asherah and all the starry hosts. He burned them outside Jerusalem in the fields of the Kidron Valley and took the ashes to Bethel. ⁵He did away with the pagan priests appointed by the kings of Judah to burn incense on the high places of the towns of Judah and on those around Jerusalem—those who burned incense to Baal, to the sun and moon, to the constellations and to all the starry hosts. ⁶He took the Asherah pole from the temple of the LORD to the Kidron Valley outside Jerusalem and burned it there. He ground it to powder and

---

ᵃ17 Or *by everything they have done*

scattered the dust over the graves of the common people. ⁷He also tore down the quarters of the male shrine prostitutes, which were in the temple of the LORD and where women did weaving for Asherah.

⁸Josiah brought all the priests from the towns of Judah and desecrated the high places, from Geba to Beersheba, where the priests had burned incense. He broke down the shrinesᵃ at the gates—at the entrance to the Gate of Joshua, the city governor, which is on the left of the city gate. ⁹Although the priests of the high places did not serve at the altar of the LORD in Jerusalem, they ate unleavened bread with their fellow priests.

¹⁰He desecrated Topheth, which was in the Valley of Ben Hinnom, so no one could use it to sacrifice his son or daughter inᵇ the fire to Molech. ¹¹He removed from the entrance to the temple of the LORD the horses that the kings of Judah had dedicated to the sun. They were in the court near the room of an official named Nathan-Melech. Josiah then burned the chariots dedicated to the sun.

¹²He pulled down the altars the kings of Judah had erected on the roof near the upper room of Ahaz, and the altars Manasseh had built in the two courts of the temple of the LORD. He removed them from there, smashed them to pieces and threw the rubble into the Kidron Valley. ¹³The king also desecrated the high places that were east of Jerusalem on the south of the Hill of Corruption—the ones Solomon king of Israel had built for Ashtoreth the vile goddess of the Sidonians, for Chemosh the vile god of Moab, and for Molechᶜ the detestable god of the people of Ammon. ¹⁴Josiah smashed the sacred stones and cut down the Asherah poles and covered the sites with human bones.

¹⁵Even the altar at Bethel, the high place made by Jeroboam son of Nebat, who had caused Israel to sin—even that altar and high place he demolished. He burned the high place

and ground it to powder, and burned the Asherah pole also. ¹⁶Then Josiah looked around, and when he saw the tombs that were there on the hillside, he had the bones removed from them and burned on the altar to defile it, in accordance with the word of the LORD proclaimed by the man of God who foretold these things.

¹⁷The king asked, "What is that tombstone I see?"

The men of the city said, "It marks the tomb of the man of God who came from Judah and pronounced against the altar of Bethel the very things you have done to it."

¹⁸"Leave it alone," he said. "Don't let anyone disturb his bones." So they spared his bones and those of the prophet who had come from Samaria.

¹⁹Just as he had done at Bethel, Josiah removed and defiled all the shrines at the high places that the kings of Israel had built in the towns of Samaria that had provoked the LORD to anger. ²⁰Josiah slaughtered all the priests of those high places on the altars and burned human bones on them. Then he went back to Jerusalem.

²¹The king gave this order to all the people: "Celebrate the Passover to the LORD your God, as it is written in this Book of the Covenant." ²²Not since the days of the judges who led Israel, nor throughout the days of the kings of Israel and the kings of Judah, had any such Passover been observed. ²³But in the eighteenth year of King Josiah, this Passover was celebrated to the LORD in Jerusalem.

²⁴Furthermore, Josiah got rid of the mediums and spiritists, the household gods, the idols and all the other detestable things seen in Judah and Jerusalem. This he did to fulfill the requirements of the law written in the book that Hilkiah the priest had discovered in the temple of the LORD. ²⁵Neither before nor after Josiah was there a king like him who turned to the LORD as he did—with all his heart and with all his soul and with all his

strength, in accordance with all the Law of Moses.

²⁶Nevertheless, the LORD did not turn away from the heat of his fierce anger, which burned against Judah because of all that Manasseh had done to provoke him to anger. ²⁷So the LORD said, "I will remove Judah also from my presence as I removed Israel, and I will reject Jerusalem, the city I chose, and this temple, about which I said, 'There shall my Name be.'ᵃ"

²⁸As for the other events of Josiah's reign, and all he did, are they not written in the book of the annals of the kings of Judah?

²⁹While Josiah was king, Pharaoh Neco king of Egypt went up to the Euphrates River to help the king of Assyria. King Josiah marched out to meet him in battle, but Neco faced him and killed him at Megiddo. ³⁰Josiah's servants brought his body in a chariot from Megiddo to Jerusalem and buried him in his own tomb. And the people of the land took Jehoahaz son of Josiah and anointed him and made him king in place of his father.

Jehoahaz King of Judah

³¹Jehoahaz was twenty-three years old when he became king, and he reigned in Jerusalem three months. His mother's name was Hamutal daughter of Jeremiah; she was from Libnah. ³²He did evil in the eyes of the LORD, just as his fathers had done. ³³Pharaoh Neco put him in chains at Riblah in the land of Hamathᵇ so that he might not reign in Jerusalem, and he imposed on Judah a levy of a hundred talentsᶜ of silver and a talentᵈ of gold. ³⁴Pharaoh Neco made Eliakim son of Josiah king in place of his father Josiah and changed Eliakim's name to Jehoiakim. But he took Jehoahaz and carried him off to Egypt, and there he died. ³⁵Jehoiakim paid Pharaoh Neco the silver and gold he demanded. In order to do so,

he taxed the land and exacted the silver and gold from the people of the land according to their assessments.

Jehoiakim King of Judah

³⁶Jehoiakim was twenty-five years old when he became king, and he reigned in Jerusalem eleven years. His mother's name was Zebidah daughter of Pedaiah; she was from Rumah. ³⁷And he did evil in the eyes of the LORD, just as his fathers had done.

24 During Jehoiakim's reign, Nebuchadnezzar king of Babylon invaded the land, and Jehoiakim became his vassal for three years. But then he changed his mind and rebelled against Nebuchadnezzar. ²The LORD sent Babylonian,ᵉ Aramean, Moabite and Ammonite raiders against him. He sent them to destroy Judah, in accordance with the word of the LORD proclaimed by his servants the prophets. ³Surely these things happened to Judah according to the LORD's command, in order to remove them from his presence because of the sins of Manasseh and all he had done, ⁴including the shedding of innocent blood. For he had filled Jerusalem with innocent blood, and the LORD was not willing to forgive.

⁵As for the other events of Jehoiakim's reign, and all he did, are they not written in the book of the annals of the kings of Judah? ⁶Jehoiakim rested with his fathers. And Jehoiachin his son succeeded him as king.

⁷The king of Egypt did not march out from his own country again, because the king of Babylon had taken all his territory, from the Wadi of Egypt to the Euphrates River.

Jehoiachin King of Judah

⁸Jehoiachin was eighteen years old when he became king, and he reigned in Jerusalem three months. His mother's name was Nehushta daughter of Elnathan; she was from Jerusalem.

ᵃ27 1 Kings 8:29   ᵇ33 Hebrew; Septuagint (see also 2 Chron. 36:3) Neco at Riblah in Hamath removed him   ᶜ33 That is, about 3 3/4 tons (about 3.4 metric tons)   ᵈ33 That is, about 75 pounds (about 34 kilograms)   ᵉ2 Or Chaldean

⁹He did evil in the eyes of the LORD, just as his father had done.

¹⁰At that time the officers of Nebuchadnezzar king of Babylon advanced on Jerusalem and laid siege to it, ¹¹and Nebuchadnezzar himself came up to the city while his officers were besieging it. ¹²Jehoiachin king of Judah, his mother, his attendants, his nobles and his officials all surrendered to him.

In the eighth year of the reign of the king of Babylon, he took Jehoiachin prisoner. ¹³As the LORD had declared, Nebuchadnezzar removed all the treasures from the temple of the LORD and from the royal palace, and took away all the gold articles that Solomon king of Israel had made for the temple of the LORD. ¹⁴He carried into exile all Jerusalem: all the officers and fighting men, and all the craftsmen and artisans—a total of ten thousand. Only the poorest people of the land were left.

¹⁵Nebuchadnezzar took Jehoiachin captive to Babylon. He also took from Jerusalem to Babylon the king's mother, his wives, his officials and the leading men of the land. ¹⁶The king of Babylon also deported to Babylon the entire force of seven thousand fighting men, strong and fit for war, and a thousand craftsmen and artisans. ¹⁷He made Mattaniah, Jehoiachin's uncle, king in his place and changed his name to Zedekiah.

Zedekiah King of Judah

¹⁸Zedekiah was twenty-one years old when he became king, and he reigned in Jerusalem eleven years. His mother's name was Hamutal daughter of Jeremiah; she was from Libnah. ¹⁹He did evil in the eyes of the LORD, just as Jehoiakim had done. ²⁰It was because of the LORD's anger that all this happened to Jerusalem and Judah, and in the end he thrust them from his presence.

The Fall of Jerusalem

Now Zedekiah rebelled against the king of Babylon.

25 So in the ninth year of Zedekiah's reign, on the tenth day of the tenth month, Nebuchadnezzar king of Babylon marched against Jerusalem with his whole army. He encamped outside the city and built siege works all around it. ²The city was kept under siege until the eleventh year of King Zedekiah. ³By the ninth day of the ⌊fourth⌋ᵃ month the famine in the city had become so severe that there was no food for the people to eat. ⁴Then the city wall was broken through, and the whole army fled at night through the gate between the two walls near the king's garden, though the Babyloniansᵇ were surrounding the city. They fled toward the Arabah,ᶜ ⁵but the Babylonianᵈ army pursued the king and overtook him in the plains of Jericho. All his soldiers were separated from him and scattered, ⁶and he was captured. He was taken to the king of Babylon at Riblah, where sentence was pronounced on him. ⁷They killed the sons of Zedekiah before his eyes. Then they put out his eyes, bound him with bronze shackles and took him to Babylon.

⁸On the seventh day of the fifth month, in the nineteenth year of Nebuchadnezzar king of Babylon, Nebuzaradan commander of the imperial guard, an official of the king of Babylon, came to Jerusalem. ⁹He set fire to the temple of the LORD, the royal palace and all the houses of Jerusalem. Every important building he burned down. ¹⁰The whole Babylonian army, under the commander of the imperial guard, broke down the walls around Jerusalem. ¹¹Nebuzaradan the commander of the guard carried into exile the people who remained in the city, along with the rest of the populace and those who had gone over to the king of Babylon. ¹²But the com-

---

ᵃ3 See Jer. 52:6.   ᵇ4 Or *Chaldeans*; also in verses 13, 25 and 26   ᶜ4 Or *the Jordan Valley*
ᵈ5 Or *Chaldean*; also in verses 10 and 24

mander left behind some of the poorest people of the land to work the vineyards and fields.

¹³The Babylonians broke up the bronze pillars, the movable stands and the bronze Sea that were at the temple of the LORD and they carried the bronze to Babylon. ¹⁴They also took away the pots, shovels, wick trimmers, dishes and all the bronze articles used in the temple service. ¹⁵The commander of the imperial guard took away the censers and sprinkling bowls—all that were made of pure gold or silver.

¹⁶The bronze from the two pillars, the Sea and the movable stands, which Solomon had made for the temple of the LORD, was more than could be weighed. ¹⁷Each pillar was twenty-seven feet*a* high. The bronze capital on top of one pillar was four and a half feet*b* high and was decorated with a network and pomegranates of bronze all around. The other pillar, with its network, was similar.

¹⁸The commander of the guard took as prisoners Seraiah the chief priest, Zephaniah the priest next in rank and the three doorkeepers. ¹⁹Of those still in the city, he took the officer in charge of the fighting men and five royal advisers. He also took the secretary who was chief officer in charge of conscripting the people of the land and sixty of his men who were found in the city. ²⁰Nebuzaradan the commander took them all and brought them to the king of Babylon at Riblah. ²¹There at Riblah, in the land of Hamath, the king had them executed.

So Judah went into captivity, away from her land.

²²Nebuchadnezzar king of Babylon appointed Gedaliah son of Ahikam, the son of Shaphan, to be over the people he had left behind in Judah. ²³When all the army officers and their men heard that the king of Babylon had appointed Gedaliah as governor, they came to Gedaliah at Mizpah—Ishmael son of Nethaniah, Johanan son of Kareah, Seraiah son of Tanhumeth the Netophathite, Jaazaniah the son of the Maacathite, and their men. ²⁴Gedaliah took an oath to reassure them and their men. "Do not be afraid of the Babylonian officials," he said. "Settle down in the land and serve the king of Babylon, and it will go well with you."

²⁵In the seventh month, however, Ishmael son of Nethaniah, the son of Elishama, who was of royal blood, came with ten men and assassinated Gedaliah and also the men of Judah and the Babylonians who were with him at Mizpah. ²⁶At this, all the people from the least to the greatest, together with the army officers, fled to Egypt for fear of the Babylonians.

Jehoiachin Released

²⁷In the thirty-seventh year of the exile of Jehoiachin king of Judah, in the year Evil-Merodach*c* became king of Babylon, he released Jehoiachin from prison on the twenty-seventh day of the twelfth month. ²⁸He spoke kindly to him and gave him a seat of honor higher than those of the other kings who were with him in Babylon. ²⁹So Jehoiachin put aside his prison clothes and for the rest of his life ate regularly at the king's table. ³⁰Day by day the king gave Jehoiachin a regular allowance as long as he lived.

---

a17 Hebrew *eighteen cubits* (about 8.1 meters)   *b17* Hebrew *three cubits* (about 1.3 meters)
c27 Also called *Amel-Marduk*

*...*A*...fter listing the gene-*
alogies of God's people from Adam to David,
this book describes how David conducted his
administrative and religious affairs. Note
especially David's role in leading Israel to
worship God. As you read 1 Chronicles, take
comfort in knowing that you stand in a long
line of people who belong to God; respond by
worshiping God for who he is and what he's
done in your life.

1 CHRONICLES

Historical Records From Adam to Abraham

To Noah's Sons

1 Adam, Seth, Enosh, [2]Kenan, Mahalalel, Jared, [3]Enoch, Methuselah, Lamech, Noah.

[4]The sons of Noah:[a]
Shem, Ham and Japheth.

The Japhethites

[5]The sons[b] of Japheth:
Gomer, Magog, Madai, Javan, Tubal, Meshech and Tiras.
[6]The sons of Gomer:
Ashkenaz, Riphath[c] and Togarmah.
[7]The sons of Javan:
Elishah, Tarshish, the Kittim and the Rodanim.

The Hamites

[8]The sons of Ham:
Cush, Mizraim,[d] Put and Canaan.
[9]The sons of Cush:
Seba, Havilah, Sabta, Raamah and Sabteca.
The sons of Raamah:
Sheba and Dedan.
[10]Cush was the father[e] of Nimrod, who grew to be a mighty warrior on earth.
[11]Mizraim was the father of the Ludites, Anamites, Lehabites, Naphtuhites, [12]Pathrusites, Casluhites (from whom

---

[a]4 Septuagint; Hebrew does not have *The sons of Noah:* [b]5 *Sons* may mean *descendants* or *successors* or *nations*; also in verses 6-10, 17 and 20. [c]6 Many Hebrew manuscripts and Vulgate (see also Septuagint and Gen. 10:3); most Hebrew manuscripts *Diphath* [d]8 That is, Egypt; also in verse 11 [e]10 *Father* may mean *ancestor* or *predecessor* or *founder*; also in verses 11, 13, 18 and 20.

the Philistines came) and Caphtorites.

¹³Canaan was the father of
Sidon his firstborn,ᵃ and of the Hittites, ¹⁴Jebusites, Amorites, Girgashites, ¹⁵Hivites, Arkites, Sinites, ¹⁶Arvadites, Zemarites and Hamathites.

The Semites

¹⁷The sons of Shem:
Elam, Asshur, Arphaxad, Lud and Aram.
The sons of Aramᵇ:
Uz, Hul, Gether and Meshech.
¹⁸Arphaxad was the father of Shelah,
and Shelah the father of Eber.
¹⁹Two sons were born to Eber:
One was named Peleg,ᶜ because in his time the earth was divided; his brother was named Joktan.
²⁰Joktan was the father of
Almodad, Sheleph, Hazarmaveth, Jerah, ²¹Hadoram, Uzal, Diklah, ²²Obal,ᵈ Abimael, Sheba, ²³Ophir, Havilah and Jobab. All these were sons of Joktan.

²⁴Shem, Arphaxad,ᵉ Shelah,
²⁵Eber, Peleg, Reu,
²⁶Serug, Nahor, Terah
²⁷and Abram (that is, Abraham).

The Family of Abraham

²⁸The sons of Abraham:
Isaac and Ishmael.

Descendants of Hagar

²⁹These were their descendants:
Nebaioth the firstborn of Ishmael, Kedar, Adbeel, Mibsam, ³⁰Mishma, Dumah, Massa, Hadad, Tema, ³¹Jetur,

Naphish and Kedemah. These were the sons of Ishmael.

Descendants of Keturah

³²The sons born to Keturah, Abraham's concubine:
Zimran, Jokshan, Medan, Midian, Ishbak and Shuah.
The sons of Jokshan:
Sheba and Dedan.
³³The sons of Midian:
Ephah, Epher, Hanoch, Abida and Eldaah.
All these were descendants of Keturah.

Descendants of Sarah

³⁴Abraham was the father of Isaac.
The sons of Isaac:
Esau and Israel.

Esau's Sons

³⁵The sons of Esau:
Eliphaz, Reuel, Jeush, Jalam and Korah.
³⁶The sons of Eliphaz:
Teman, Omar, Zepho,ᶠ Gatam and Kenaz;
by Timna: Amalek.ᵍ
³⁷The sons of Reuel:
Nahath, Zerah, Shammah and Mizzah.

The People of Seir in Edom

³⁸The sons of Seir:
Lotan, Shobal, Zibeon, Anah, Dishon, Ezer and Dishan.
³⁹The sons of Lotan:
Hori and Homam. Timna was Lotan's sister.
⁴⁰The sons of Shobal:
Alvan,ʰ Manahath, Ebal, Shepho and Onam.
The sons of Zibeon:
Aiah and Anah.

ᵃ13 Or of the Sidonians, the foremost   ᵇ17 One Hebrew manuscript and some Septuagint manuscripts (see also Gen. 10:23); most Hebrew manuscripts do not have this line.   ᶜ19 Peleg means division.   ᵈ22 Some Hebrew manuscripts and Syriac (see also Gen. 10:28); most Hebrew manuscripts Ebal   ᵉ24 Hebrew; some Septuagint manuscripts Arphaxad, Cainan (see also note at Gen. 11:10)   ᶠ36 Many Hebrew manuscripts, some Septuagint manuscripts and Syriac (see also Gen. 36:11); most Hebrew manuscripts Zephi   ᵍ36 Some Septuagint manuscripts (see also Gen. 36:12); Hebrew Gatam, Kenaz, Timna and Amalek   ʰ40 Many Hebrew manuscripts and some Septuagint manuscripts (see also Gen. 36:23); most Hebrew manuscripts Alian

⁴¹The son of Anah:
   Dishon.
   The sons of Dishon:
   Hemdan,ᵃ   Eshban,   Ithran
   and Keran.
⁴²The sons of Ezer:
   Bilhan, Zaavan and Akan.ᵇ
   The sons of Dishanᶜ:
   Uz and Aran.

The Rulers of Edom

⁴³These were the kings who
reigned in Edom before any Israelite king reignedᵈ:
   Bela son of Beor, whose city
   was named Dinhabah.
⁴⁴When Bela died, Jobab son of
Zerah from Bozrah succeeded
him as king.
⁴⁵When Jobab died, Husham from
the land of the Temanites succeeded him as king.
⁴⁶When Husham died, Hadad son
of Bedad, who defeated Midian in the country of Moab,
succeeded him as king. His
city was named Avith.
⁴⁷When Hadad died, Samlah from
Masrekah succeeded him as
king.
⁴⁸When Samlah died, Shaul from
Rehoboth on the riverᵉ succeeded him as king.
⁴⁹When Shaul died, Baal-Hanan
son of Acbor succeeded him
as king.
⁵⁰When Baal-Hanan died, Hadad
succeeded him as king. His
city was named Pau,ᶠ and
his wife's name was Mehetabel daughter of Matred, the
daughter of Me-Zahab. ⁵¹Ha-
dad also died.

The chiefs of Edom were:
   Timna,   Alvah,   Jetheth,

⁵²Oholibamah,   Elah,   Pinon,
⁵³Kenaz,   Teman,   Mibzar,
⁵⁴Magdiel and Iram. These
were the chiefs of Edom.

Israel's Sons

2 These were the sons of Israel:
   Reuben, Simeon, Levi, Judah,
Issachar, Zebulun, ²Dan, Jo-
seph, Benjamin, Naphtali,
Gad and Asher.

Judah

To Hezron's Sons

³The sons of Judah:
   Er, Onan and Shelah. These
   three were born to him by
   a Canaanite woman, the
   daughter of Shua. Er, Judah's
   firstborn, was wicked in the
   LORD's sight; so the LORD put
   him to death. ⁴Tamar, Judah's
   daughter-in-law, bore him
   Perez and Zerah. Judah had
   five sons in all.

⁵The sons of Perez:
   Hezron and Hamul.
⁶The sons of Zerah:
   Zimri, Ethan, Heman, Calcol
   and Dardaᵍ—five in all.
⁷The son of Carmi:
   Achar,ʰ who brought trouble on Israel by violating the
   ban on taking devoted
   things.ⁱ
⁸The son of Ethan:
   Azariah.
⁹The sons born to Hezron were:
   Jerahmeel, Ram and Caleb.ʲ

From Ram Son of Hezron

¹⁰Ram was the father of

ᵃ41 Many Hebrew manuscripts and some Septuagint manuscripts (see also Gen. 36:26); most
Hebrew manuscripts *Hamran*   ᵇ42 Many Hebrew and Septuagint manuscripts (see also Gen.
36:27); most Hebrew manuscripts *Zaavan, Jaakan*   ᶜ42 Hebrew *Dishon*, a variant of *Dishan*
ᵈ43 Or *before an Israelite king reigned over them*   ᵉ48 Possibly the Euphrates   ᶠ50 Many
Hebrew manuscripts, some Septuagint manuscripts, Vulgate and Syriac (see also Gen. 36:39);
most Hebrew manuscripts *Pai*   ᵍ6 Many Hebrew manuscripts, some Septuagint manuscripts
and Syriac (see also 1 Kings 4:31); most Hebrew manuscripts *Dara*   ʰ7 *Achar* means *trouble*;
Achar is called *Achan* in Joshua.   ⁱ7 The Hebrew term refers to the irrevocable giving over of
things or persons to the LORD, often by totally destroying them.   ʲ9 Hebrew *Kelubai*, a variant
of *Caleb*

Amminadab, and Amminadab the father of Nahshon, the leader of the people of Judah. ¹¹Nahshon was the father of Salmon,ᵃ Salmon the father of Boaz, ¹²Boaz the father of Obed and Obed the father of Jesse.

¹³Jesse was the father of
Eliab his firstborn; the second son was Abinadab, the third Shimea, ¹⁴the fourth Nethanel, the fifth Raddai, ¹⁵the sixth Ozem and the seventh David. ¹⁶Their sisters were Zeruiah and Abigail. Zeruiah's three sons were Abishai, Joab and Asahel. ¹⁷Abigail was the mother of Amasa, whose father was Jether the Ishmaelite.

Caleb Son of Hezron

¹⁸Caleb son of Hezron had children by his wife Azubah (and by Jerioth). These were her sons: Jesher, Shobab and Ardon. ¹⁹When Azubah died, Caleb married Ephrath, who bore him Hur. ²⁰Hur was the father of Uri, and Uri the father of Bezalel.

²¹Later, Hezron lay with the daughter of Makir the father of Gilead (he had married her when he was sixty years old), and she bore him Segub. ²²Segub was the father of Jair, who controlled twenty-three towns in Gilead. ²³(But Geshur and Aram captured Havvoth Jair,ᵇ as well as Kenath with its surrounding settlements—sixty towns.) All these were descendants of Makir the father of Gilead.

²⁴After Hezron died in Caleb Ephrathah, Abijah the wife of Hezron bore him Ashhur the fatherᶜ of Tekoa.

Jerahmeel Son of Hezron

²⁵The sons of Jerahmeel the firstborn of Hezron:
Ram his firstborn, Bunah, Oren, Ozem andᵈ Ahijah. ²⁶Jerahmeel had another wife, whose name was Atarah; she was the mother of Onam.
²⁷The sons of Ram the firstborn of Jerahmeel:
Maaz, Jamin and Eker.
²⁸The sons of Onam:
Shammai and Jada.
The sons of Shammai:
Nadab and Abishur.
²⁹Abishur's wife was named Abihail, who bore him Ahban and Molid.
³⁰The sons of Nadab:
Seled and Appaim. Seled died without children.
³¹The son of Appaim:
Ishi, who was the father of Sheshan.
Sheshan was the father of Ahlai.
³²The sons of Jada, Shammai's brother:
Jether and Jonathan. Jether died without children.
³³The sons of Jonathan:
Peleth and Zaza.
These were the descendants of Jerahmeel.
³⁴Sheshan had no sons—only daughters.
He had an Egyptian servant named Jarha. ³⁵Sheshan gave his daughter in marriage to his servant Jarha, and she bore him Attai.
³⁶Attai was the father of Nathan,
Nathan the father of Zabad,
³⁷Zabad the father of Ephlal,
Ephlal the father of Obed,
³⁸Obed the father of Jehu,
Jehu the father of Azariah,
³⁹Azariah the father of Helez,
Helez the father of Eleasah,
⁴⁰Eleasah the father of Sismai,
Sismai the father of Shallum,

ᵃ11 Septuagint (see also Ruth 4:21); Hebrew *Salma*   ᵇ23 Or *captured the settlements of Jair*
ᶜ24 *Father* may mean *civic leader* or *military leader*; also in verses 42, 45, 49-52 and possibly elsewhere.   ᵈ25 Or *Oren and Ozem, by*

41Shallum the father of Jekamiah,
and Jekamiah the father of Elishama.

The Clans of Caleb

42The sons of Caleb the brother of Jerahmeel:
Mesha his firstborn, who was the father of Ziph, and his son Mareshah,*a* who was the father of Hebron.
43The sons of Hebron:
Korah, Tappuah, Rekem and Shema. **44**Shema was the father of Raham, and Raham the father of Jorkeam. Rekem was the father of Shammai. **45**The son of Shammai was Maon, and Maon was the father of Beth Zur.
46Caleb's concubine Ephah was the mother of Haran, Moza and Gazez. Haran was the father of Gazez.
47The sons of Jahdai:
Regem, Jotham, Geshan, Pelet, Ephah and Shaaph.
48Caleb's concubine Maacah was the mother of Sheber and Tirhanah. **49**She also gave birth to Shaaph the father of Madmannah and to Sheva the father of Macbenah and Gibea. Caleb's daughter was Acsah. **50**These were the descendants of Caleb.

The sons of Hur the firstborn of Ephrathah:
Shobal the father of Kiriath Jearim, **51**Salma the father of Bethlehem, and Hareph the father of Beth Gader.
52The descendants of Shobal the father of Kiriath Jearim were:
Haroeh, half the Manahathites, **53**and the clans of Kiriath Jearim: the Ithrites, Puthites, Shumathites and Mishraites.

From these descended the Zorathites and Eshtaolites.
54The descendants of Salma:
Bethlehem, the Netophathites, Atroth Beth Joab, half the Manahathites, the Zorites, **55**and the clans of scribes*b* who lived at Jabez: the Tirathites, Shimeathites and Sucathites. These are the Kenites who came from Hammath, the father of the house of Recab.*c*

The Sons of David

3 These were the sons of David born to him in Hebron:
The firstborn was Amnon the son of Ahinoam of Jezreel;
the second, Daniel the son of Abigail of Carmel;
2the third, Absalom the son of Maacah daughter of Talmai king of Geshur;
the fourth, Adonijah the son of Haggith;
3the fifth, Shephatiah the son of Abital;
and the sixth, Ithream, by his wife Eglah.
4These six were born to David in Hebron, where he reigned seven years and six months.
David reigned in Jerusalem thirty-three years, **5**and these were the children born to him there:
Shammua,*d* Shobab, Nathan and Solomon. These four were by Bathsheba*e* daughter of Ammiel. **6**There were also Ibhar, Elishua,*f* Eliphelet, **7**Nogah, Nepheg, Japhia, **8**Elishama, Eliada and Eliphelet—nine in all. **9**All these were the sons of David, besides his sons by his concubines. And Tamar was their sister.

---

*a*42 The meaning of the Hebrew for this phrase is uncertain.   *b*55 Or *of the Sopherites*   *c*55 Or *father of Beth Recab*   *d*5 Hebrew *Shimea,* a variant of *Shammua*   *e*5 One Hebrew manuscript and Vulgate (see also Septuagint and 2 Samuel 11:3); most Hebrew manuscripts *Bathshua*   *f*6 Two Hebrew manuscripts (see also 2 Samuel 5:15 and 1 Chron. 14:5); most Hebrew manuscripts *Elishama*

The Kings of Judah

¹⁰Solomon's son was Rehoboam,
  Abijah his son,
  Asa his son,
  Jehoshaphat his son,
¹¹Jehoram*a* his son,
  Ahaziah his son,
  Joash his son,
¹²Amaziah his son,
  Azariah his son,
  Jotham his son,
¹³Ahaz his son,
  Hezekiah his son,
  Manasseh his son,
¹⁴Amon his son,
  Josiah his son.
¹⁵The sons of Josiah:
  Johanan the firstborn,
  Jehoiakim the second son,
  Zedekiah the third,
  Shallum the fourth.
¹⁶The successors of Jehoiakim:
  Jehoiachin*b* his son,
  and Zedekiah.

The Royal Line After the Exile

¹⁷The descendants of Jehoiachin
  the captive:
  Shealtiel his son, ¹⁸Malkiram,
  Pedaiah, Shenazzar, Jekami-
  ah, Hoshama and Nedabiah.
¹⁹The sons of Pedaiah:
  Zerubbabel and Shimei.
  The sons of Zerubbabel:
  Meshullam and Hananiah.
  Shelomith was their sister.
²⁰There were also five others:
  Hashubah, Ohel, Berekiah,
  Hasadiah and Jushab-Hesed.
²¹The descendants of Hananiah:
  Pelatiah and Jeshaiah, and the
  sons of Rephaiah, of Arnan,
  of Obadiah and of Shecaniah.
²²The descendants of Shecaniah:
  Shemaiah and his sons:
  Hattush, Igal, Bariah, Neariah
  and Shaphat—six in all.
²³The sons of Neariah:
  Elioenai, Hizkiah and Azri-
  kam—three in all.

²⁴The sons of Elioenai:
  Hodaviah, Eliashib, Pelaiah,
  Akkub, Johanan, Delaiah and
  Anani—seven in all.

Other Clans of Judah

4 The descendants of Judah:
  Perez, Hezron, Carmi, Hur
  and Shobal.
²Reaiah son of Shobal was the father of Jahath, and Jahath the
  father of Ahumai and Lahad.
  These were the clans of the
  Zorathites.
³These were the sons*c* of Etam:
  Jezreel, Ishma and Idbash.
  Their sister was named Haz-
  zelelponi. ⁴Penuel was the father of Gedor, and Ezer the
  father of Hushah.
  These were the descendants of
  Hur, the firstborn of Ephrathah and father*d* of Bethlehem.
⁵Ashhur the father of Tekoa had
  two wives, Helah and Naarah.
⁶Naarah bore him Ahuzzam, Hepher, Temeni and Haahashta-
  ri. These were the descendants of Naarah.
⁷The sons of Helah:
  Zereth, Zohar, Ethnan, ⁸and
  Koz, who was the father of
  Anub and Hazzobebah and
  of the clans of Aharhel son of
  Harum.

⁹Jabez was more honorable than his
brothers. His mother had named him
Jabez,*e* saying, "I gave birth to him
in pain." ¹⁰Jabez cried out to the God
of Israel, "Oh, that you would bless
me and enlarge my territory! Let your
hand be with me, and keep me from
harm so that I will be free from pain."
And God granted his request.

¹¹Kelub, Shuhah's brother, was
  the father of Mehir, who was
  the father of Eshton. ¹²Eshton

---

*a*11 Hebrew *Joram*, a variant of *Jehoram*   *b*16 Hebrew *Jeconiah*, a variant of *Jehoiachin*; also in
verse 17   *c*3 Some Septuagint manuscripts (see also Vulgate); Hebrew *father*   *d*4 *Father* may
mean *civic leader* or *military leader*; also in verses 12, 14, 17, 18 and possibly elsewhere.
*e*9 *Jabez* sounds like the Hebrew for *pain*.

was the father of Beth Rapha, Paseah and Tehinnah the father of Ir Nahash.[a] These were the men of Recah.

¹³The sons of Kenaz:
Othniel and Seraiah.
The sons of Othniel:
Hathath and Meonothai.[b]
¹⁴Meonothai was the father of Ophrah.
Seraiah was the father of Joab, the father of Ge Harashim.[c] It was called this because its people were craftsmen.
¹⁵The sons of Caleb son of Jephunneh:
Iru, Elah and Naam.
The son of Elah:
Kenaz.
¹⁶The sons of Jehallelel:
Ziph, Ziphah, Tiria and Asarel.
¹⁷The sons of Ezrah:
Jether, Mered, Epher and Jalon. One of Mered's wives gave birth to Miriam, Shammai and Ishbah the father of Eshtemoa. ¹⁸(His Judean wife gave birth to Jered the father of Gedor, Heber the father of Soco, and Jekuthiel the father of Zanoah.) These were the children of Pharaoh's daughter Bithiah, whom Mered had married.
¹⁹The sons of Hodiah's wife, the sister of Naham:
the father of Keilah the Garmite, and Eshtemoa the Maacathite.
²⁰The sons of Shimon:
Amnon, Rinnah, Ben-Hanan and Tilon.
The descendants of Ishi:
Zoheth and Ben-Zoheth.
²¹The sons of Shelah son of Judah:
Er the father of Lecah, Laadah the father of Mareshah and the clans of the linen workers at Beth Ashbea, ²²Jokim, the men of Cozeba, and Joash

and Saraph, who ruled in Moab and Jashubi Lehem. (These records are from ancient times.) ²³They were the potters who lived at Netaim and Gederah; they stayed there and worked for the king.

Simeon

²⁴The descendants of Simeon:
Nemuel, Jamin, Jarib, Zerah and Shaul;
²⁵Shallum was Shaul's son, Mibsam his son and Mishma his son.
²⁶The descendants of Mishma:
Hammuel his son, Zaccur his son and Shimei his son.
²⁷Shimei had sixteen sons and six daughters, but his brothers did not have many children; so their entire clan did not become as numerous as the people of Judah. ²⁸They lived in Beersheba, Moladah, Hazar Shual, ²⁹Bilhah, Ezem, Tolad, ³⁰Bethuel, Hormah, Ziklag, ³¹Beth Marcaboth, Hazar Susim, Beth Biri and Shaaraim. These were their towns until the reign of David. ³²Their surrounding villages were Etam, Ain, Rimmon, Token and Ashan—five towns— ³³and all the villages around these towns as far as Baalath.[d] These were their settlements. And they kept a genealogical record.

³⁴Meshobab, Jamlech, Joshah son of Amaziah, ³⁵Joel, Jehu son of Joshibiah, the son of Seraiah, the son of Asiel, ³⁶also Elioenai, Jaakobah, Jeshohaiah, Asaiah, Adiel, Jesimiel, Benaiah, ³⁷and Ziza son of Shiphi, the son of Allon, the son of Jedaiah, the son of Shimri, the son of Shemaiah.

³⁸The men listed above by name were leaders of their clans. Their families increased greatly, ³⁹and they went to the outskirts of Gedor to the east of the valley in search of pasture

---

[a]12 Or of the city of Nahash   [b]13 Some Septuagint manuscripts and Vulgate; Hebrew does not have and Meonothai.   [c]14 Ge Harashim means valley of craftsmen.   [d]33 Some Septuagint manuscripts (see also Joshua 19:8); Hebrew Baal

for their flocks. ⁴⁰They found rich, good pasture, and the land was spacious, peaceful and quiet. Some Hamites had lived there formerly.

⁴¹The men whose names were listed came in the days of Hezekiah king of Judah. They attacked the Hamites in their dwellings and also the Meunites who were there and completely destroyed*a* them, as is evident to this day. Then they settled in their place, because there was pasture for their flocks. ⁴²And five hundred of these Simeonites, led by Pelatiah, Neariah, Rephaiah and Uzziel, the sons of Ishi, invaded the hill country of Seir. ⁴³They killed the remaining Amalekites who had escaped, and they have lived there to this day.

Reuben

5 The sons of Reuben the firstborn of Israel (he was the firstborn, but when he defiled his father's marriage bed, his rights as firstborn were given to the sons of Joseph son of Israel; so he could not be listed in the genealogical record in accordance with his birthright, ²and though Judah was the strongest of his brothers and a ruler came from him, the rights of the firstborn belonged to Joseph)— ³the sons of Reuben the firstborn of Israel:

Hanoch, Pallu, Hezron and Carmi.

⁴The descendants of Joel:
Shemaiah his son, Gog his son,
Shimei his son, ⁵Micah his son,
Reaiah his son, Baal his son,
⁶and Beerah his son, whom Tiglath-Pileser*b* king of Assyria took into exile. Beerah was a leader of the Reubenites.

⁷Their relatives by clans, listed according to their genealogical records:
Jeiel the chief, Zechariah, ⁸and Bela son of Azaz, the son

of Shema, the son of Joel. They settled in the area from Aroer to Nebo and Baal Meon. ⁹To the east they occupied the land up to the edge of the desert that extends to the Euphrates River, because their livestock had increased in Gilead.

¹⁰During Saul's reign they waged war against the Hagrites, who were defeated at their hands; they occupied the dwellings of the Hagrites throughout the entire region east of Gilead.

Gad

¹¹The Gadites lived next to them in Bashan, as far as Salecah:
¹²Joel was the chief, Shapham the second, then Janai and Shaphat, in Bashan.
¹³Their relatives, by families, were:
Michael, Meshullam, Sheba, Jorai, Jacan, Zia and Eber— seven in all.
¹⁴These were the sons of Abihail son of Huri, the son of Jaroah, the son of Gilead, the son of Michael, the son of Jeshishai, the son of Jahdo, the son of Buz.
¹⁵Ahi son of Abdiel, the son of Guni, was head of their family.
¹⁶The Gadites lived in Gilead, in Bashan and its outlying villages, and on all the pasturelands of Sharon as far as they extended.
¹⁷All these were entered in the genealogical records during the reigns of Jotham king of Judah and Jeroboam king of Israel.

¹⁸The Reubenites, the Gadites and the half-tribe of Manasseh had 44,760 men ready for military service—able-bodied men who could handle shield and sword, who could use a bow, and who were trained for battle. ¹⁹They

---

a41 The Hebrew term refers to the irrevocable giving over of things or persons to the LORD, often by totally destroying them.   *b6* Hebrew *Tilgath-Pilneser*, a variant of *Tiglath-Pileser*; also in verse 26

waged war against the Hagrites, Jetur, Naphish and Nodab. ²⁰They were helped in fighting them, and God handed the Hagrites and all their allies over to them, because they cried out to him during the battle. He answered their prayers, because they trusted in him. ²¹They seized the livestock of the Hagrites—fifty thousand camels, two hundred fifty thousand sheep and two thousand donkeys. They also took one hundred thousand people captive, ²²and many others fell slain, because the battle was God's. And they occupied the land until the exile.

The Half-Tribe of Manasseh

²³The people of the half-tribe of Manasseh were numerous; they settled in the land from Bashan to Baal Hermon, that is, to Senir (Mount Hermon).

²⁴These were the heads of their families: Epher, Ishi, Eliel, Azriel, Jeremiah, Hodaviah and Jahdiel. They were brave warriors, famous men, and heads of their families. ²⁵But they were unfaithful to the God of their fathers and prostituted themselves to the gods of the peoples of the land, whom God had destroyed before them. ²⁶So the God of Israel stirred up the spirit of Pul king of Assyria (that is, Tiglath-Pileser king of Assyria), who took the Reubenites, the Gadites and the half-tribe of Manasseh into exile. He took them to Halah, Habor, Hara and the river of Gozan, where they are to this day.

Levi

6 The sons of Levi:
Gershon, Kohath and Merari.
²The sons of Kohath:
Amram, Izhar, Hebron and Uzziel.
³The children of Amram:
Aaron, Moses and Miriam.
The sons of Aaron:
Nadab, Abihu, Eleazar and Ithamar.

⁴Eleazar was the father of Phinehas,
Phinehas the father of Abishua,
⁵Abishua the father of Bukki,
Bukki the father of Uzzi,
⁶Uzzi the father of Zerahiah,
Zerahiah the father of Meraioth,
⁷Meraioth the father of Amariah,
Amariah the father of Ahitub,
⁸Ahitub the father of Zadok,
Zadok the father of Ahimaaz,
⁹Ahimaaz the father of Azariah,
Azariah the father of Johanan,
¹⁰Johanan the father of Azariah (it was he who served as priest in the temple Solomon built in Jerusalem),
¹¹Azariah the father of Amariah,
Amariah the father of Ahitub,
¹²Ahitub the father of Zadok,
Zadok the father of Shallum,
¹³Shallum the father of Hilkiah,
Hilkiah the father of Azariah,
¹⁴Azariah the father of Seraiah,
and Seraiah the father of Jehozadak.

¹⁵Jehozadak was deported when the LORD sent Judah and Jerusalem into exile by the hand of Nebuchadnezzar.

¹⁶The sons of Levi:
Gershon,ᵃ Kohath and Merari.
¹⁷These are the names of the sons of Gershon:
Libni and Shimei.
¹⁸The sons of Kohath:
Amram, Izhar, Hebron and Uzziel.
¹⁹The sons of Merari:
Mahli and Mushi.
These are the clans of the Levites listed according to their fathers:
²⁰Of Gershon:
Libni his son, Jehath his son,

ᵃ16 Hebrew *Gershom*, a variant of *Gershon*; also in verses 17, 20, 43, 62 and 71

Zimmah his son, ²¹Joah his
son,
Iddo his son, Zerah his son
and Jeatherai his son.
²²The descendants of Kohath:
Amminadab his son, Korah
his son,
Assir his son, ²³Elkanah his
son,
Ebiasaph his son, Assir his
son,
²⁴Tahath his son, Uriel his son,
Uzziah his son and Shaul his
son.
²⁵The descendants of Elkanah:
Amasai, Ahimoth,
²⁶Elkanah his son,ᵃ Zophai his
son,
Nahath his son, ²⁷Eliab his
son,
Jeroham his son, Elkanah his
son
and Samuel his son.ᵇ
²⁸The sons of Samuel:
Joelᶜ the firstborn
and Abijah the second son.
²⁹The descendants of Merari:
Mahli, Libni his son,
Shimei his son, Uzzah his
son,
³⁰Shimea his son, Haggiah his
son
and Asaiah his son.

The Temple Musicians

³¹These are the men David put in
charge of the music in the house of
the LORD after the ark came to rest
there. ³²They ministered with music
before the tabernacle, the Tent of
Meeting, until Solomon built the temple of the LORD in Jerusalem. They
performed their duties according to
the regulations laid down for them.
³³Here are the men who served, together with their sons:
From the Kohathites:
Heman, the musician,

the son of Joel, the son of
Samuel,
³⁴the son of Elkanah, the son of
Jeroham,
the son of Eliel, the son of
Toah,
³⁵the son of Zuph, the son of
Elkanah,
the son of Mahath, the son of
Amasai,
³⁶the son of Elkanah, the son of
Joel,
the son of Azariah, the son of
Zephaniah,
³⁷the son of Tahath, the son of
Assir,
the son of Ebiasaph, the son
of Korah,
³⁸the son of Izhar, the son of
Kohath,
the son of Levi, the son of Israel;
³⁹and Heman's associate Asaph,
who served at his right hand:
Asaph son of Berekiah, the
son of Shimea,
⁴⁰the son of Michael, the son of
Baaseiah,ᵈ
the son of Malkijah, ⁴¹the son
of Ethni,
the son of Zerah, the son of
Adaiah,
⁴²the son of Ethan, the son of
Zimmah,
the son of Shimei, ⁴³the son of
Jahath,
the son of Gershon, the son of
Levi;
⁴⁴and from their associates, the
Merarites, at his left hand:
Ethan son of Kishi, the son of
Abdi,
the son of Malluch, ⁴⁵the son
of Hashabiah,
the son of Amaziah, the son
of Hilkiah,
⁴⁶the son of Amzi, the son of
Bani,

ᵃ26 Some Hebrew manuscripts, Septuagint and Syriac; most Hebrew manuscripts *Ahimoth* ²⁶*and
Elkanah. The sons of Elkanah:*   ᵇ27 Some Septuagint manuscripts (see also 1 Samuel 1:19,20 and
1 Chron. 6:33,34); Hebrew does not have *and Samuel his son.*   ᶜ28 Some Septuagint manuscripts
and Syriac (see also 1 Samuel 8:2 and 1 Chron. 6:33); Hebrew does not have *Joel.*   ᵈ40 Most
Hebrew manuscripts; some Hebrew manuscripts, one Septuagint manuscript and Syriac *Maaseiah*

the son of Shemer, [47]the son
of Mahli,
the son of Mushi, the son of
Merari,
the son of Levi.

[48]Their fellow Levites were assigned to all the other duties of the tabernacle, the house of God. [49]But Aaron and his descendants were the ones who presented offerings on the altar of burnt offering and on the altar of incense in connection with all that was done in the Most Holy Place, making atonement for Israel, in accordance with all that Moses the servant of God had commanded.

[50]These were the descendants of
Aaron:
Eleazar his son, Phinehas his
son,
Abishua his son, [51]Bukki his
son,
Uzzi his son, Zerahiah his
son,
[52]Meraioth his son, Amariah
his son,
Ahitub his son, [53]Zadok his
son
and Ahimaaz his son.

[54]These were the locations of their settlements allotted as their territory (they were assigned to the descendants of Aaron who were from the Kohathite clan, because the first lot was for them): [55]They were given Hebron in Judah with its surrounding pasturelands. [56]But the fields and villages around the city were given to Caleb son of Jephunneh. [57]So the descendants of Aaron were given Hebron (a city of refuge), and Libnah,[a] Jattir, Eshtemoa, [58]Hilen, Debir, [59]Ashan, Juttah[b] and Beth Shemesh, together with their pasturelands. [60]And from the tribe of Benjamin they were given Gibeon,[c] Geba, Alemeth and Anathoth, together with their pasturelands.

These towns, which were distributed among the Kohathite clans, were thirteen in all. [61]The rest of Kohath's descendants were allotted ten towns from the clans of half the tribe of Manasseh.

[62]The descendants of Gershon, clan by clan, were allotted thirteen towns from the tribes of Issachar, Asher and Naphtali, and from the part of the tribe of Manasseh that is in Bashan.

[63]The descendants of Merari, clan by clan, were allotted twelve towns from the tribes of Reuben, Gad and Zebulun.

[64]So the Israelites gave the Levites these towns and their pasturelands. [65]From the tribes of Judah, Simeon and Benjamin they allotted the previously named towns.

[66]Some of the Kohathite clans were given as their territory towns from the tribe of Ephraim.

[67]In the hill country of Ephraim they were given Shechem (a city of refuge), and Gezer,[d] [68]Jokmeam, Beth Horon, [69]Aijalon and Gath Rimmon, together with their pasturelands.

[70]And from half the tribe of Manasseh the Israelites gave Aner and Bileam, together with their pasturelands, to the rest of the Kohathite clans.

[71]The Gershonites received the following:
From the clan of the half-tribe of Manasseh
they received Golan in Bashan and also Ashtaroth, together with their pasturelands;
[72]from the tribe of Issachar
they received Kedesh, Daberath, [73]Ramoth and Anem, together with their pasturelands;
[74]from the tribe of Asher
they received Mashal, Abdon, [75]Hukok and Rehob, together with their pasturelands;

---

[a]57 See Joshua 21:13; Hebrew given the cities of refuge: Hebron, Libnah.   [b]59 Syriac (see also Septuagint and Joshua 21:16); Hebrew does not have Juttah.   [c]60 See Joshua 21:17; Hebrew does not have Gibeon.   [d]67 See Joshua 21:21; Hebrew given the cities of refuge: Shechem, Gezer.

[76]and from the tribe of Naphtali they received Kedesh in Galilee, Hammon and Kiriathaim, together with their pasturelands.

[77]The Merarites (the rest of the Levites) received the following:
From the tribe of Zebulun they received Jokneam, Kartah,[a] Rimmono and Tabor, together with their pasturelands;
[78]from the tribe of Reuben across the Jordan east of Jericho they received Bezer in the desert, Jahzah, [79]Kedemoth and Mephaath, together with their pasturelands;
[80]and from the tribe of Gad they received Ramoth in Gilead, Mahanaim, [81]Heshbon and Jazer, together with their pasturelands.

Issachar

7 The sons of Issachar:
Tola, Puah, Jashub and Shimron—four in all.
[2]The sons of Tola:
Uzzi, Rephaiah, Jeriel, Jahmai, Ibsam and Samuel—heads of their families. During the reign of David, the descendants of Tola listed as fighting men in their genealogy numbered 22,600.
[3]The son of Uzzi:
Izrahiah.
The sons of Izrahiah:
Michael, Obadiah, Joel and Isshiah. All five of them were chiefs. [4]According to their family genealogy, they had 36,000 men ready for battle, for they had many wives and children.
[5]The relatives who were fighting men belonging to all the clans of Issachar, as listed in their genealogy, were 87,000 in all.

Benjamin

[6]Three sons of Benjamin:
Bela, Beker and Jediael.
[7]The sons of Bela:
Ezbon, Uzzi, Uzziel, Jerimoth and Iri, heads of families—five in all. Their genealogical record listed 22,034 fighting men.
[8]The sons of Beker:
Zemirah, Joash, Eliezer, Elioenai, Omri, Jeremoth, Abijah, Anathoth and Alemeth. All these were the sons of Beker. [9]Their genealogical record listed the heads of families and 20,200 fighting men.
[10]The son of Jediael:
Bilhan.
The sons of Bilhan:
Jeush, Benjamin, Ehud, Kenaanah, Zethan, Tarshish and Ahishahar. [11]All these sons of Jediael were heads of families. There were 17,200 fighting men ready to go out to war.
[12]The Shuppites and Huppites were the descendants of Ir, and the Hushites the descendants of Aher.

Naphtali

[13]The sons of Naphtali:
Jahziel, Guni, Jezer and Shillem[b]—the descendants of Bilhah.

Manasseh

[14]The descendants of Manasseh:
Asriel was his descendant through his Aramean concubine. She gave birth to Makir the father of Gilead. [15]Makir took a wife from among the Huppites and Shuppites. His sister's name was Maacah.
Another descendant was named Zelophehad, who had only daughters.
[16]Makir's wife Maacah gave

birth to a son and named him Peresh. His brother was named Sheresh, and his sons were Ulam and Rakem.

¹⁷The son of Ulam:

Bedan.

These were the sons of Gilead son of Makir, the son of Manasseh. ¹⁸His sister Hammoleketh gave birth to Ishhod, Abiezer and Mahlah.

¹⁹The sons of Shemida were:

Ahian, Shechem, Likhi and Aniam.

Ephraim

²⁰The descendants of Ephraim:

Shuthelah, Bered his son,
Tahath his son, Eleadah his son,
Tahath his son, ²¹Zabad his son
and Shuthelah his son.

Ezer and Elead were killed by the native-born men of Gath, when they went down to seize their livestock. ²²Their father Ephraim mourned for them many days, and his relatives came to comfort him. ²³Then he lay with his wife again, and she became pregnant and gave birth to a son. He named him Beriah,ᵃ because there had been misfortune in his family. ²⁴His daughter was Sheerah, who built Lower and Upper Beth Horon as well as Uzzen Sheerah.

²⁵Rephah was his son, Resheph his son,ᵇ
Telah his son, Tahan his son,
²⁶Ladan his son, Ammihud his son,
Elishama his son, ²⁷Nun his son
and Joshua his son.

²⁸Their lands and settlements included Bethel and its surrounding villages, Naaran to the east, Gezer and its villages to the west, and Shechem and its villages all the way to Ayyah

and its villages. ²⁹Along the borders of Manasseh were Beth Shan, Taanach, Megiddo and Dor, together with their villages. The descendants of Joseph son of Israel lived in these towns.

Asher

³⁰The sons of Asher:

Imnah, Ishvah, Ishvi and Beriah. Their sister was Serah.

³¹The sons of Beriah:

Heber and Malkiel, who was the father of Birzaith.

³²Heber was the father of Japhlet, Shomer and Hotham and of their sister Shua.

³³The sons of Japhlet:

Pasach, Bimhal and Ashvath. These were Japhlet's sons.

³⁴The sons of Shomer:

Ahi, Rohgah,ᶜ Hubbah and Aram.

³⁵The sons of his brother Helem:

Zophah, Imna, Shelesh and Amal.

³⁶The sons of Zophah:

Suah, Harnepher, Shual, Beri, Imrah, ³⁷Bezer, Hod, Shamma, Shilshah, Ithranᵈ and Beera.

³⁸The sons of Jether:

Jephunneh, Pispah and Ara.

³⁹The sons of Ulla:

Arah, Hanniel and Rizia.

⁴⁰All these were descendants of Asher—heads of families, choice men, brave warriors and outstanding leaders. The number of men ready for battle, as listed in their genealogy, was 26,000.

The Genealogy of Saul the Benjamite

8 Benjamin was the father of Bela his firstborn,

Ashbel the second son, Aharah the third,
²Nohah the fourth and Rapha the fifth.

³The sons of Bela were:

ᵃ23 *Beriah* sounds like the Hebrew for *misfortune.*   ᵇ25 Some Septuagint manuscripts; Hebrew does not have *his son.*   ᶜ34 Or *of his brother Shomer: Rohgah*   ᵈ37 Possibly a variant of *Jether*

Addar, Gera, Abihud,[a] [4]Abishua, Naaman, Ahoah, [5]Gera, Shephuphan and Huram.

[6]These were the descendants of Ehud, who were heads of families of those living in Geba and were deported to Manahath:

[7]Naaman, Ahijah, and Gera, who deported them and who was the father of Uzza and Ahihud.

[8]Sons were born to Shaharaim in Moab after he had divorced his wives Hushim and Baara. [9]By his wife Hodesh he had Jobab, Zibia, Mesha, Malcam, [10]Jeuz, Sakia and Mirmah. These were his sons, heads of families. [11]By Hushim he had Abitub and Elpaal.

[12]The sons of Elpaal:

Eber, Misham, Shemed (who built Ono and Lod with its surrounding villages), [13]and Beriah and Shema, who were heads of families of those living in Aijalon and who drove out the inhabitants of Gath.

[14]Ahio, Shashak, Jeremoth, [15]Zebadiah, Arad, Eder, [16]Michael, Ishpah and Joha were the sons of Beriah.

[17]Zebadiah, Meshullam, Hizki, Heber, [18]Ishmerai, Izliah and Jobab were the sons of Elpaal.

[19]Jakim, Zicri, Zabdi, [20]Elienai, Zillethai, Eliel, [21]Adaiah, Beraiah and Shimrath were the sons of Shimei.

[22]Ishpan, Eber, Eliel, [23]Abdon, Zicri, Hanan, [24]Hananiah, Elam, Anthothijah, [25]Iphdeiah and Penuel were the sons of Shashak.

[26]Shamsherai, Shehariah, Athaliah, [27]Jaareshiah, Elijah and Zicri were the sons of Jeroham.

[28]All these were heads of families, chiefs as listed in their genealogy, and they lived in Jerusalem.

[29]Jeiel[b] the father[c] of Gibeon lived in Gibeon.

His wife's name was Maacah, [30]and his firstborn son was Abdon, followed by Zur, Kish, Baal, Ner,[d] Nadab, [31]Gedor, Ahio, Zeker [32]and Mikloth, who was the father of Shimeah. They too lived near their relatives in Jerusalem.

[33]Ner was the father of Kish, Kish the father of Saul, and Saul the father of Jonathan, Malki-Shua, Abinadab and Esh-Baal.[e]

[34]The son of Jonathan:

Merib-Baal,[f] who was the father of Micah.

[35]The sons of Micah:

Pithon, Melech, Tarea and Ahaz.

[36]Ahaz was the father of Jehoaddah, Jehoaddah was the father of Alemeth, Azmaveth and Zimri, and Zimri was the father of Moza. [37]Moza was the father of Binea; Raphah was his son, Eleasah his son and Azel his son.

[38]Azel had six sons, and these were their names:

Azrikam, Bokeru, Ishmael, Sheariah, Obadiah and Hanan. All these were the sons of Azel.

[39]The sons of his brother Eshek:

Ulam his firstborn, Jeush the second son and Eliphelet the third. [40]The sons of Ulam were brave warriors who could handle the bow. They had many sons and grandsons—150 in all.

All these were the descendants of Benjamin.

[a]3 Or Gera the father of Ehud   [b]29 Some Septuagint manuscripts (see also 1 Chron. 9:35); Hebrew does not have Jeiel.   [c]29 Father may mean civic leader or military leader.   [d]30 Some Septuagint manuscripts (see also 1 Chron. 9:36); Hebrew does not have Ner.   [e]33 Also known as Ish-Bosheth   [f]34 Also known as Mephibosheth

9 All Israel was listed in the genealogies recorded in the book of the kings of Israel.

The People in Jerusalem

The people of Judah were taken captive to Babylon because of their unfaithfulness. 2Now the first to resettle on their own property in their own towns were some Israelites, priests, Levites and temple servants.

3Those from Judah, from Benjamin, and from Ephraim and Manasseh who lived in Jerusalem were:

4Uthai son of Ammihud, the son of Omri, the son of Imri, the son of Bani, a descendant of Perez son of Judah.

5Of the Shilonites:

Asaiah the firstborn and his sons.

6Of the Zerahites:

Jeuel.

The people from Judah numbered 690.

7Of the Benjamites:

Sallu son of Meshullam, the son of Hodaviah, the son of Hassenuah;

8Ibneiah son of Jeroham; Elah son of Uzzi, the son of Micri; and Meshullam son of Shephatiah, the son of Reuel, the son of Ibnijah.

9The people from Benjamin, as listed in their genealogy, numbered 956. All these men were heads of their families.

10Of the priests:

Jedaiah; Jehoiarib; Jakin;

11Azariah son of Hilkiah, the son of Meshullam, the son of Zadok, the son of Meraioth, the son of Ahitub, the official in charge of the house of God;

12Adaiah son of Jeroham, the son of Pashhur, the son of Malkijah; and Maasai son of Adiel, the son of Jahzerah, the son of Meshullam, the son of Meshillemith, the son of Immer.

13The priests, who were heads of families, numbered 1,760. They were able men, responsible for ministering in the house of God.

14Of the Levites:

Shemaiah son of Hasshub, the son of Azrikam, the son of Hashabiah, a Merarite; 15Bakbakkar, Heresh, Galal and Mattaniah son of Mica, the son of Zicri, the son of Asaph; 16Obadiah son of Shemaiah, the son of Galal, the son of Jeduthun; and Berekiah son of Asa, the son of Elkanah, who lived in the villages of the Netophathites.

17The gatekeepers:

Shallum, Akkub, Talmon, Ahiman and their brothers, Shallum their chief 18being stationed at the King's Gate on the east, up to the present time. These were the gatekeepers belonging to the camp of the Levites. 19Shallum son of Kore, the son of Ebiasaph, the son of Korah, and his fellow gatekeepers from his family (the Korahites) were responsible for guarding the thresholds of the Tent*a* just as their fathers had been responsible for guarding the entrance to the dwelling of the LORD. 20In earlier times Phinehas son of Eleazar was in charge of the gatekeepers, and the LORD was with him. 21Zechariah son of Meshelemiah was the gatekeeper at the entrance to the Tent of Meeting.

22Altogether, those chosen to be gatekeepers at the thresholds numbered 212. They were registered by genealogy in their villages. The gatekeepers had been assigned to their positions of trust by David and Samuel the seer. 23They and their descendants were in charge of guarding the gates of the house of the LORD—the

---

a19 That is, the temple; also in verses 21 and 23

house called the Tent. ²⁴The gatekeepers were on the four sides: east, west, north and south. ²⁵Their brothers in their villages had to come from time to time and share their duties for seven-day periods. ²⁶But the four principal gatekeepers, who were Levites, were entrusted with the responsibility for the rooms and treasuries in the house of God. ²⁷They would spend the night stationed around the house of God, because they had to guard it; and they had charge of the key for opening it each morning.

²⁸Some of them were in charge of the articles used in the temple service; they counted them when they were brought in and when they were taken out. ²⁹Others were assigned to take care of the furnishings and all the other articles of the sanctuary, as well as the flour and wine, and the oil, incense and spices. ³⁰But some of the priests took care of mixing the spices. ³¹A Levite named Mattithiah, the firstborn son of Shallum the Korahite, was entrusted with the responsibility for baking the offering bread. ³²Some of their Kohathite brothers were in charge of preparing for every Sabbath the bread set out on the table.

³³Those who were musicians, heads of Levite families, stayed in the rooms of the temple and were exempt from other duties because they were responsible for the work day and night. ³⁴All these were heads of Levite families, chiefs as listed in their genealogy, and they lived in Jerusalem.

The Genealogy of Saul

³⁵Jeiel the father*ᵃ* of Gibeon lived in Gibeon.

His wife's name was Maacah, ³⁶and his firstborn son was Abdon, followed by Zur, Kish, Baal, Ner, Nadab, ³⁷Gedor, Ahio, Zechariah and Mikloth. ³⁸Mikloth was the father of Shimeam. They too

lived near their relatives in Jerusalem.

³⁹Ner was the father of Kish, Kish the father of Saul, and Saul the father of Jonathan, Malki-Shua, Abinadab and Esh-Baal.*ᵇ*

⁴⁰The son of Jonathan:
Merib-Baal,*ᶜ* who was the father of Micah.

⁴¹The sons of Micah:
Pithon, Melech, Tahrea and Ahaz.*ᵈ*

⁴²Ahaz was the father of Jadah, Jadah*ᵉ* was the father of Alemeth, Azmaveth and Zimri, and Zimri was the father of Moza. ⁴³Moza was the father of Binea; Rephaiah was his son, Eleasah his son and Azel his son.

⁴⁴Azel had six sons, and these were their names:
Azrikam, Bokeru, Ishmael, Sheariah, Obadiah and Hanan. These were the sons of Azel.

Saul Takes His Life

10 Now the Philistines fought against Israel; the Israelites fled before them, and many fell slain on Mount Gilboa. ²The Philistines pressed hard after Saul and his sons, and they killed his sons Jonathan, Abinadab and Malki-Shua. ³The fighting grew fierce around Saul, and when the archers overtook him, they wounded him.

⁴Saul said to his armor-bearer, "Draw your sword and run me through, or these uncircumcised fellows will come and abuse me."

But his armor-bearer was terrified and would not do it; so Saul took his own sword and fell on it. ⁵When the armor-bearer saw that Saul was dead, he too fell on his sword and died. ⁶So Saul and his three sons died, and all his house died together.

ᵃ35 *Father* may mean *civic leader* or *military leader.*   *ᵇ39* Also known as *Ish-Bosheth*   *ᶜ40* Also known as *Mephibosheth*   *ᵈ41* Vulgate and Syriac (see also Septuagint and 1 Chron. 8:35); Hebrew does not have *and Ahaz.*   *ᵉ42* Some Hebrew manuscripts and Septuagint (see also 1 Chron. 8:36); most Hebrew manuscripts *Jarah, Jarah*

⁷When all the Israelites in the valley saw that the army had fled and that Saul and his sons had died, they abandoned their towns and fled. And the Philistines came and occupied them.

⁸The next day, when the Philistines came to strip the dead, they found Saul and his sons fallen on Mount Gilboa. ⁹They stripped him and took his head and his armor, and sent messengers throughout the land of the Philistines to proclaim the news among their idols and their people. ¹⁰They put his armor in the temple of their gods and hung up his head in the temple of Dagon.

¹¹When all the inhabitants of Jabesh Gilead heard of everything the Philistines had done to Saul, ¹²all their valiant men went and took the bodies of Saul and his sons and brought them to Jabesh. Then they buried their bones under the great tree in Jabesh, and they fasted seven days.

¹³Saul died because he was unfaithful to the Lord; he did not keep the word of the Lord and even consulted a medium for guidance, ¹⁴and did not inquire of the Lord. So the Lord put him to death and turned the kingdom over to David son of Jesse.

David Becomes King Over Israel

11 All Israel came together to David at Hebron and said, "We are your own flesh and blood. ²In the past, even while Saul was king, you were the one who led Israel on their military campaigns. And the Lord your God said to you, 'You will shepherd my people Israel, and you will become their ruler.' "

³When all the elders of Israel had come to King David at Hebron, he made a compact with them at Hebron before the Lord, and they anointed David king over Israel, as the Lord had promised through Samuel.

David Conquers Jerusalem

⁴David and all the Israelites marched to Jerusalem (that is, Jebus). The Jebusites who lived there ⁵said to David, "You will not get in here." Nevertheless, David captured the fortress of Zion, the City of David.

⁶David had said, "Whoever leads the attack on the Jebusites will become commander-in-chief." Joab son of Zeruiah went up first, and so he received the command.

⁷David then took up residence in the fortress, and so it was called the City of David. ⁸He built up the city around it, from the supporting terraces[a] to the surrounding wall, while Joab restored the rest of the city. ⁹And David became more and more powerful, because the Lord Almighty was with him.

David's Mighty Men

¹⁰These were the chiefs of David's mighty men—they, together with all Israel, gave his kingship strong support to extend it over the whole land, as the Lord had promised— ¹¹this is the list of David's mighty men:

Jashobeam,[b] a Hacmonite, was chief of the officers[c]; he raised his spear against three hundred men, whom he killed in one encounter.

¹²Next to him was Eleazar son of Dodai the Ahohite, one of the three mighty men. ¹³He was with David at Pas Dammim when the Philistines gathered there for battle. At a place where there was a field full of barley, the troops fled from the Philistines. ¹⁴But they took their stand in the middle of the field. They defended it and struck the Philistines down, and the Lord brought about a great victory.

¹⁵Three of the thirty chiefs came down to David to the rock at the cave of Adullam, while a band of Philistines was encamped in the Valley of Rephaim. ¹⁶At that time David was in the stronghold, and the Philistine garrison was at Bethlehem. ¹⁷David longed for water and said, "Oh, that someone would get me a drink of water from the well near the gate of

---

a8 Or *the Millo*   *b11* Possibly a variant of *Jashob-Baal*   *c11* Or *Thirty*; some Septuagint manuscripts *Three* (see also 2 Samuel 23:8)

Bethlehem!" ¹⁸So the Three broke through the Philistine lines, drew water from the well near the gate of Bethlehem and carried it back to David. But he refused to drink it; instead, he poured it out before the LORD. ¹⁹"God forbid that I should do this!" he said. "Should I drink the blood of these men who went at the risk of their lives?" Because they risked their lives to bring it back, David would not drink it.

Such were the exploits of the three mighty men.

²⁰Abishai the brother of Joab was chief of the Three. He raised his spear against three hundred men, whom he killed, and so he became as famous as the Three. ²¹He was doubly honored above the Three and became their commander, even though he was not included among them.

²²Benaiah son of Jehoiada was a valiant fighter from Kabzeel, who performed great exploits. He struck down two of Moab's best men. He also went down into a pit on a snowy day and killed a lion. ²³And he struck down an Egyptian who was seven and a half feet[a] tall. Although the Egyptian had a spear like a weaver's rod in his hand, Benaiah went against him with a club. He snatched the spear from the Egyptian's hand and killed him with his own spear. ²⁴Such were the exploits of Benaiah son of Jehoiada; he too was as famous as the three mighty men. ²⁵He was held in greater honor than any of the Thirty, but he was not included among the Three. And David put him in charge of his bodyguard.

²⁶The mighty men were:

Asahel the brother of Joab,
Elhanan son of Dodo from Bethlehem,
²⁷Shammoth the Harorite,
Helez the Pelonite,
²⁸Ira son of Ikkesh from Tekoa,
Abiezer from Anathoth,
²⁹Sibbecai the Hushathite,
Ilai the Ahohite,
³⁰Maharai the Netophathite,
Heled son of Baanah the Netophathite,
³¹Ithai son of Ribai from Gibeah in Benjamin,
Benaiah the Pirathonite,
³²Hurai from the ravines of Gaash,
Abiel the Arbathite,
³³Azmaveth the Baharumite,
Eliahba the Shaalbonite,
³⁴the sons of Hashem the Gizonite,
Jonathan son of Shagee the Hararite,
³⁵Ahiam son of Sacar the Hararite,
Eliphal son of Ur,
³⁶Hepher the Mekerathite,
Ahijah the Pelonite,
³⁷Hezro the Carmelite,
Naarai son of Ezbai,
³⁸Joel the brother of Nathan,
Mibhar son of Hagri,
³⁹Zelek the Ammonite,
Naharai the Berothite, the armor-bearer of Joab son of Zeruiah,
⁴⁰Ira the Ithrite,
Gareb the Ithrite,
⁴¹Uriah the Hittite,
Zabad son of Ahlai,
⁴²Adina son of Shiza the Reubenite, who was chief of the Reubenites, and the thirty with him,
⁴³Hanan son of Maacah,
Joshaphat the Mithnite,
⁴⁴Uzzia the Ashterathite,
Shama and Jeiel the sons of Hotham the Aroerite,
⁴⁵Jediael son of Shimri,
his brother Joha the Tizite,
⁴⁶Eliel the Mahavite,
Jeribai and Joshaviah the sons of Elnaam,
Ithmah the Moabite,
⁴⁷Eliel, Obed and Jaasiel the Mezobaite.

Warriors Join David

12 These were the men who came to David at Ziklag, while he

---

a23 Hebrew *five cubits* (about 2.3 meters)

was banished from the presence of Saul son of Kish (they were among the warriors who helped him in battle; [2]they were armed with bows and were able to shoot arrows or to sling stones right-handed or left-handed; they were kinsmen of Saul from the tribe of Benjamin):

[3]Ahiezer their chief and Joash the sons of Shemaah the Gibeathite; Jeziel and Pelet the sons of Azmaveth; Beracah, Jehu the Anathothite, [4]and Ishmaiah the Gibeonite, a mighty man among the Thirty, who was a leader of the Thirty; Jeremiah, Jahaziel, Johanan, Jozabad the Gederathite, [5]Eluzai, Jerimoth, Bealiah, Shemariah and Shephatiah the Haruphite; [6]Elkanah, Isshiah, Azarel, Joezer and Jashobeam the Korahites; [7]and Joelah and Zebadiah the sons of Jeroham from Gedor.

[8]Some Gadites defected to David at his stronghold in the desert. They were brave warriors, ready for battle and able to handle the shield and spear. Their faces were the faces of lions, and they were as swift as gazelles in the mountains.
[9]Ezer was the chief,
Obadiah the second in command, Eliab the third,
[10]Mishmannah the fourth, Jeremiah the fifth,
[11]Attai the sixth, Eliel the seventh,
[12]Johanan the eighth, Elzabad the ninth,
[13]Jeremiah the tenth and Macbannai the eleventh.
[14]These Gadites were army commanders; the least was a match for a hundred, and the greatest for a thousand. [15]It was they who crossed the Jordan in the first month when it was overflowing all its banks, and they put to flight everyone living in the valleys, to the east and to the west.
[16]Other Benjamites and some men from Judah also came to David in his stronghold. [17]David went out to meet them and said to them, "If you have come to me in peace, to help me, I am ready to have you unite with me. But if you have come to betray me to my enemies when my hands are free from violence, may the God of our fathers see it and judge you."
[18]Then the Spirit came upon Amasai, chief of the Thirty, and he said:

"We are yours, O David!
We are with you, O son of Jesse!
Success, success to you,
and success to those who help you,
for your God will help you."

So David received them and made them leaders of his raiding bands.
[19]Some of the men of Manasseh defected to David when he went with the Philistines to fight against Saul. (He and his men did not help the Philistines because, after consultation, their rulers sent him away. They said, "It will cost us our heads if he deserts to his master Saul.") [20]When David went to Ziklag, these were the men of Manasseh who defected to him: Adnah, Jozabad, Jediael, Michael, Jozabad, Elihu and Zillethai, leaders of units of a thousand in Manasseh. [21]They helped David against raiding bands, for all of them were brave warriors, and they were commanders in his army. [22]Day after day men came to help David, until he had a great army, like the army of God.[a]

Others Join David at Hebron

[23]These are the numbers of the men armed for battle who came to David at Hebron to turn Saul's kingdom over to him, as the LORD had said:
[24]men of Judah, carrying shield and spear—6,800 armed for battle;
[25]men of Simeon, warriors ready for battle—7,100;
[26]men of Levi—4,600, [27]including Jehoiada, leader of the family of Aaron, with 3,700 men, [28]and Zadok, a brave young

[a]22 Or *a great and mighty army*

warrior, with 22 officers from his family;

²⁹men of Benjamin, Saul's kinsmen—3,000, most of whom had remained loyal to Saul's house until then;

³⁰men of Ephraim, brave warriors, famous in their own clans—20,800;

³¹men of half the tribe of Manasseh, designated by name to come and make David king—18,000;

³²men of Issachar, who understood the times and knew what Israel should do—200 chiefs, with all their relatives under their command;

³³men of Zebulun, experienced soldiers prepared for battle with every type of weapon, to help David with undivided loyalty—50,000;

³⁴men of Naphtali—1,000 officers, together with 37,000 men carrying shields and spears;

³⁵men of Dan, ready for battle—28,600;

³⁶men of Asher, experienced soldiers prepared for battle—40,000;

³⁷and from east of the Jordan, men of Reuben, Gad and the half-tribe of Manasseh, armed with every type of weapon—120,000.

³⁸All these were fighting men who volunteered to serve in the ranks. They came to Hebron fully determined to make David king over all Israel. All the rest of the Israelites were also of one mind to make David king. ³⁹The men spent three days there with David, eating and drinking, for their families had supplied provisions for them. ⁴⁰Also, their neighbors from as far away as Issachar, Zebulun and Naphtali came bringing food on donkeys, camels, mules and oxen. There were plentiful supplies of flour, fig cakes, raisin cakes, wine, oil, cattle and sheep, for there was joy in Israel.

Bringing Back the Ark

13 David conferred with each of his officers, the commanders of thousands and commanders of hundreds. ²He then said to the whole assembly of Israel, "If it seems good to you and if it is the will of the LORD our God, let us send word far and wide to the rest of our brothers throughout the territories of Israel, and also to the priests and Levites who are with them in their towns and pasturelands, to come and join us. ³Let us bring the ark of our God back to us, for we did not inquire of[a] it[b] during the reign of Saul." ⁴The whole assembly agreed to do this, because it seemed right to all the people.

⁵So David assembled all the Israelites, from the Shihor River in Egypt to Lebo[c] Hamath, to bring the ark of God from Kiriath Jearim. ⁶David and all the Israelites with him went to Baalah of Judah (Kiriath Jearim) to bring up from there the ark of God the LORD, who is enthroned between the cherubim—the ark that is called by the Name.

⁷They moved the ark of God from Abinadab's house on a new cart, with Uzzah and Ahio guiding it. ⁸David and all the Israelites were celebrating with all their might before God, with songs and with harps, lyres, tambourines, cymbals and trumpets.

⁹When they came to the threshing floor of Kidon, Uzzah reached out his hand to steady the ark, because the oxen stumbled. ¹⁰The LORD's anger burned against Uzzah, and he struck him down because he had put his hand on the ark. So he died there before God.

¹¹Then David was angry because the LORD's wrath had broken out against Uzzah, and to this day that place is called Perez Uzzah.[d]

¹²David was afraid of God that day and asked, "How can I ever bring the

---

[a]3 Or we neglected   [b]3 Or him   [c]5 Or to the entrance to   [d]11 Perez Uzzah means outbreak against Uzzah.

ark of God to me?" [13]He did not take the ark to be with him in the City of David. Instead, he took it aside to the house of Obed-Edom the Gittite. [14]The ark of God remained with the family of Obed-Edom in his house for three months, and the LORD blessed his household and everything he had.

David's House and Family

14 Now Hiram king of Tyre sent messengers to David, along with cedar logs, stonemasons and carpenters to build a palace for him. [2]And David knew that the LORD had established him as king over Israel and that his kingdom had been highly exalted for the sake of his people Israel.

[3]In Jerusalem David took more wives and became the father of more sons and daughters. [4]These are the names of the children born to him there: Shammua, Shobab, Nathan, Solomon, [5]Ibhar, Elishua, Elpelet, [6]Nogah, Nepheg, Japhia, [7]Elishama, Beeliada[a] and Eliphelet.

David Defeats the Philistines

[8]When the Philistines heard that David had been anointed king over all Israel, they went up in full force to search for him, but David heard about it and went out to meet them. [9]Now the Philistines had come and raided the Valley of Rephaim; [10]so David inquired of God: "Shall I go and attack the Philistines? Will you hand them over to me?"

The LORD answered him, "Go, I will hand them over to you."

[11]So David and his men went up to Baal Perazim, and there he defeated them. He said, "As waters break out, God has broken out against my enemies by my hand." So that place was called Baal Perazim.[b] [12]The Philistines had abandoned their gods there, and David gave orders to burn them in the fire.

[13]Once more the Philistines raided the valley; [14]so David inquired of God

again, and God answered him, "Do not go straight up, but circle around them and attack them in front of the balsam trees. [15]As soon as you hear the sound of marching in the tops of the balsam trees, move out to battle, because that will mean God has gone out in front of you to strike the Philistine army." [16]So David did as God commanded him, and they struck down the Philistine army, all the way from Gibeon to Gezer.

[17]So David's fame spread throughout every land, and the LORD made all the nations fear him.

The Ark Brought to Jerusalem

15 After David had constructed buildings for himself in the City of David, he prepared a place for the ark of God and pitched a tent for it. [2]Then David said, "No one but the Levites may carry the ark of God, because the LORD chose them to carry the ark of the LORD and to minister before him forever."

[3]David assembled all Israel in Jerusalem to bring up the ark of the LORD to the place he had prepared for it. [4]He called together the descendants of Aaron and the Levites:

[5]From the descendants of Kohath,
Uriel the leader and 120 relatives;
[6]from the descendants of Merari,
Asaiah the leader and 220 relatives;
[7]from the descendants of Gershon,[c]
Joel the leader and 130 relatives;
[8]from the descendants of Elizaphan,
Shemaiah the leader and 200 relatives;
[9]from the descendants of Hebron,
Eliel the leader and 80 relatives;
[10]from the descendants of Uzziel,

---

[a]7 A variant of *Eliada*   [b]11 *Baal Perazim* means *the lord who breaks out*.   [c]7 Hebrew *Gershom*, a variant of *Gershon*

Amminadab the leader and 112 relatives.

¹¹Then David summoned Zadok and Abiathar the priests, and Uriel, Asaiah, Joel, Shemaiah, Eliel and Amminadab the Levites. ¹²He said to them, "You are the heads of the Levitical families; you and your fellow Levites are to consecrate yourselves and bring up the ark of the LORD, the God of Israel, to the place I have prepared for it. ¹³It was because you, the Levites, did not bring it up the first time that the LORD our God broke out in anger against us. We did not inquire of him about how to do it in the prescribed way." ¹⁴So the priests and Levites consecrated themselves in order to bring up the ark of the LORD, the God of Israel. ¹⁵And the Levites carried the ark of God with the poles on their shoulders, as Moses had commanded in accordance with the word of the LORD.

¹⁶David told the leaders of the Levites to appoint their brothers as singers to sing joyful songs, accompanied by musical instruments: lyres, harps and cymbals.

¹⁷So the Levites appointed Heman son of Joel; from his brothers, Asaph son of Berekiah; and from their brothers the Merarites, Ethan son of Kushaiah; ¹⁸and with them their brothers next in rank: Zechariah,ᵃ Jaaziel, Shemiramoth, Jehiel, Unni, Eliab, Benaiah, Maaseiah, Mattithiah, Eliphelehu, Mikneiah, Obed-Edom and Jeiel,ᵇ the gatekeepers.

¹⁹The musicians Heman, Asaph and Ethan were to sound the bronze cymbals; ²⁰Zechariah, Aziel, Shemiramoth, Jehiel, Unni, Eliab, Maaseiah and Benaiah were to play the lyres according to alamoth,ᶜ ²¹and Mattithiah, Eliphelehu, Mikneiah, Obed-Edom, Jeiel and Azaziah were to play the harps, directing according to sheminith.ᶜ ²²Kenaniah the head Levite was in charge of the singing; that

was his responsibility because he was skillful at it.

²³Berekiah and Elkanah were to be doorkeepers for the ark. ²⁴Shebaniah, Joshaphat, Nethanel, Amasai, Zechariah, Benaiah and Eliezer the priests were to blow trumpets before the ark of God. Obed-Edom and Jehiah were also to be doorkeepers for the ark.

²⁵So David and the elders of Israel and the commanders of units of a thousand went to bring up the ark of the covenant of the LORD from the house of Obed-Edom, with rejoicing. ²⁶Because God had helped the Levites who were carrying the ark of the covenant of the LORD, seven bulls and seven rams were sacrificed. ²⁷Now David was clothed in a robe of fine linen, as were all the Levites who were carrying the ark, and as were the singers, and Kenaniah, who was in charge of the singing of the choirs. David also wore a linen ephod. ²⁸So all Israel brought up the ark of the covenant of the LORD with shouts, with the sounding of rams' horns and trumpets, and of cymbals, and the playing of lyres and harps.

²⁹As the ark of the covenant of the LORD was entering the City of David, Michal daughter of Saul watched from a window. And when she saw King David dancing and celebrating, she despised him in her heart.

16 They brought the ark of God and set it inside the tent that David had pitched for it, and they presented burnt offerings and fellowship offeringsᵈ before God. ²After David had finished sacrificing the burnt offerings and fellowship offerings, he blessed the people in the name of the LORD. ³Then he gave a loaf of bread, a cake of dates and a cake of raisins to each Israelite man and woman.

⁴He appointed some of the Levites to minister before the ark of the LORD, to make petition, to give thanks, and

---

ᵃ18 Three Hebrew manuscripts and most Septuagint manuscripts (see also verse 20 and 1 Chron. 16:5); most Hebrew manuscripts Zechariah son and or Zechariah, Ben and   ᵇ18 Hebrew; Septuagint (see also verse 21) Jeiel and Azaziah   ᶜ20,21 Probably a musical term   ᵈ1 Traditionally peace offerings; also in verse 2

to praise the LORD, the God of Israel: ⁵Asaph was the chief, Zechariah second, then Jeiel, Shemiramoth, Jehiel, Mattithiah, Eliab, Benaiah, Obed-Edom and Jeiel. They were to play the lyres and harps, Asaph was to sound the cymbals, ⁶and Benaiah and Jahaziel the priests were to blow the trumpets regularly before the ark of the covenant of God.

David's Psalm of Thanks

⁷That day David first committed to Asaph and his associates this psalm of thanks to the LORD:

⁸Give thanks to the LORD, call on
       his name;
   make known among the nations
       what he has done.
⁹Sing to him, sing praise to him;
   tell of all his wonderful acts.
¹⁰Glory in his holy name;
   let the hearts of those who seek
       the LORD rejoice.
¹¹Look to the LORD and his strength;
   seek his face always.
¹²Remember the wonders he has
       done,
   his miracles, and the judgments
       he pronounced,
¹³O descendants of Israel his
       servant,
   O sons of Jacob, his chosen
       ones.

¹⁴He is the LORD our God;
   his judgments are in all the
       earth.
¹⁵He remembersᵃ his covenant
       forever,
   the word he commanded, for a
       thousand generations,
¹⁶the covenant he made with
       Abraham,
   the oath he swore to Isaac.
¹⁷He confirmed it to Jacob as a
       decree,
   to Israel as an everlasting
       covenant:

¹⁸"To you I will give the land of
       Canaan
   as the portion you will inherit."

¹⁹When they were but few in
       number,
   few indeed, and strangers in it,
²⁰theyᵇ wandered from nation to
       nation,
   from one kingdom to another.
²¹He allowed no man to oppress
       them;
   for their sake he rebuked kings:
²²"Do not touch my anointed ones;
   do my prophets no harm."

²³Sing to the LORD, all the earth;
   proclaim his salvation day after
       day.
²⁴Declare his glory among the
       nations,
   his marvelous deeds among all
       peoples.
²⁵For great is the LORD and most
       worthy of praise;
   he is to be feared above all
       gods.
²⁶For all the gods of the nations are
       idols,
   but the LORD made the heavens.
²⁷Splendor and majesty are before
       him;
   strength and joy in his dwelling
       place.
²⁸Ascribe to the LORD, O families of
       nations,
   ascribe to the LORD glory and
       strength,
²⁹   ascribe to the LORD the glory
       due his name.
   Bring an offering and come before
       him;
   worship the LORD in the
       splendor of hisᶜ holiness.
³⁰Tremble before him, all the earth!
   The world is firmly established;
       it cannot be moved.
³¹Let the heavens rejoice, let the
       earth be glad;
   let them say among the nations,
       "The LORD reigns!"

ᵃ15 Some Septuagint manuscripts (see also Psalm 105:8); Hebrew *Remember*   ᵇ18-20 One Hebrew manuscript, Septuagint and Vulgate (see also Psalm 105:12); most Hebrew manuscripts *inherit, | ¹⁹though you are but few in number, | few indeed, and strangers in it." | ²⁰They*   ᶜ29 Or *LORD with the splendor of*

³²Let the sea resound, and all that is
    in it;
  let the fields be jubilant, and
    everything in them!
³³Then the trees of the forest will
    sing,
  they will sing for joy before the
    LORD,
  for he comes to judge the earth.

³⁴Give thanks to the LORD, for he is
    good;
  his love endures forever.
³⁵Cry out, "Save us, O God our
    Savior;
  gather us and deliver us from
    the nations,
  that we may give thanks to your
    holy name,
  that we may glory in your
    praise."
³⁶Praise be to the LORD, the God of
    Israel,
  from everlasting to everlasting.

Then all the people said "Amen" and
"Praise the LORD."

³⁷David left Asaph and his associates before the ark of the covenant of the LORD to minister there regularly, according to each day's requirements. ³⁸He also left Obed-Edom and his sixty-eight associates to minister with them. Obed-Edom son of Jeduthun, and also Hosah, were gatekeepers.

³⁹David left Zadok the priest and his fellow priests before the tabernacle of the LORD at the high place in Gibeon ⁴⁰to present burnt offerings to the LORD on the altar of burnt offering regularly, morning and evening, in accordance with everything written in the Law of the LORD, which he had given Israel. ⁴¹With them were Heman and Jeduthun and the rest of those chosen and designated by name to give thanks to the LORD, "for his love endures forever." ⁴²Heman and Jeduthun were responsible for the sounding of the trumpets and cymbals and for the playing of the other instruments for sacred song. The sons

of Jeduthun were stationed at the gate.
⁴³Then all the people left, each for his own home, and David returned home to bless his family.

God's Promise to David

17 After David was settled in his palace, he said to Nathan the prophet, "Here I am, living in a palace of cedar, while the ark of the covenant of the LORD is under a tent."

²Nathan replied to David, "Whatever you have in mind, do it, for God is with you."

³That night the word of God came to Nathan, saying:

⁴"Go and tell my servant David, 'This is what the LORD says: You are not the one to build me a house to dwell in. ⁵I have not dwelt in a house from the day I brought Israel up out of Egypt to this day. I have moved from one tent site to another, from one dwelling place to another. ⁶Wherever I have moved with all the Israelites, did I ever say to any of their leaders*a* whom I commanded to shepherd my people, "Why have you not built me a house of cedar?" '

⁷"Now then, tell my servant David, 'This is what the LORD Almighty says: I took you from the pasture and from following the flock, to be ruler over my people Israel. ⁸I have been with you wherever you have gone, and I have cut off all your enemies from before you. Now I will make your name like the names of the greatest men of the earth. ⁹And I will provide a place for my people Israel and will plant them so that they can have a home of their own and no longer be disturbed. Wicked people will not oppress them anymore, as they did at the beginning ¹⁰and have done ever since the time I appointed leaders over my peo-

a6 Traditionally judges; also in verse 10

ple Israel. I will also subdue all your enemies.

" 'I declare to you that the LORD will build a house for you: ¹¹When your days are over and you go to be with your fathers, I will raise up your offspring to succeed you, one of your own sons, and I will establish his kingdom. ¹²He is the one who will build a house for me, and I will establish his throne forever. ¹³I will be his father, and he will be my son. I will never take my love away from him, as I took it away from your predecessor. ¹⁴I will set him over my house and my kingdom forever; his throne will be established forever.' "

¹⁵Nathan reported to David all the words of this entire revelation.

David's Prayer

¹⁶Then King David went in and sat before the LORD, and he said:

"Who am I, O LORD God, and what is my family, that you have brought me this far? ¹⁷And as if this were not enough in your sight, O God, you have spoken about the future of the house of your servant. You have looked on me as though I were the most exalted of men, O LORD God.

¹⁸"What more can David say to you for honoring your servant? For you know your servant, ¹⁹O LORD. For the sake of your servant and according to your will, you have done this great thing and made known all these great promises.

²⁰"There is no one like you, O LORD, and there is no God but you, as we have heard with our own ears. ²¹And who is like your people Israel—the one nation on earth whose God went out to redeem a people for himself, and to make a name for yourself, and to perform great and awesome wonders by driving out nations from before your people, whom you redeemed from Egypt?

²²You made your people Israel your very own forever, and you, O LORD, have become their God.

²³"And now, LORD, let the promise you have made concerning your servant and his house be established forever. Do as you promised, ²⁴so that it will be established and that your name will be great forever. Then men will say, 'The LORD Almighty, the God over Israel, is Israel's God!' And the house of your servant David will be established before you.

²⁵"You, my God, have revealed to your servant that you will build a house for him. So your servant has found courage to pray to you. ²⁶O LORD, you are God! You have promised these good things to your servant. ²⁷Now you have been pleased to bless the house of your servant, that it may continue forever in your sight; for you, O LORD, have blessed it, and it will be blessed forever."

David's Victories

18 In the course of time, David defeated the Philistines and subdued them, and he took Gath and its surrounding villages from the control of the Philistines.

²David also defeated the Moabites, and they became subject to him and brought tribute.

³Moreover, David fought Hadadezer king of Zobah, as far as Hamath, when he went to establish his control along the Euphrates River. ⁴David captured a thousand of his chariots, seven thousand charioteers and twenty thousand foot soldiers. He hamstrung all but a hundred of the chariot horses.

⁵When the Arameans of Damascus came to help Hadadezer king of Zobah, David struck down twenty-two thousand of them. ⁶He put garrisons in the Aramean kingdom of Damascus, and the Arameans became subject to him and brought tribute. The

LORD gave David victory everywhere he went.

[7]David took the gold shields carried by the officers of Hadadezer and brought them to Jerusalem. [8]From Tebah[a] and Cun, towns that belonged to Hadadezer, David took a great quantity of bronze, which Solomon used to make the bronze Sea, the pillars and various bronze articles.

[9]When Tou king of Hamath heard that David had defeated the entire army of Hadadezer king of Zobah, [10]he sent his son Hadoram to King David to greet him and congratulate him on his victory in battle over Had-

[a]8 Hebrew *Tibhath*, a variant of *Tebah*

VERSE:	AUTHOR:	PASSAGE:
1 Chronicles 17:19	Lloyd John Ogilvie	1 Chronicles 17:16–27

Entrusted Greatness

Louis XIV was very specific in his will about the way he wanted his funeral to be conducted. The cathedral was to be dimly lit with only one large candle placed next to his golden coffin. The king wanted a spectacular funeral that drew attention to *his* greatness . . .

Bishop Massilon was appointed to give the eulogy. The large congregation waited in hushed silence. The bishop walked to the casket and gave his very brief eulogy — not to Louis but to God. He reached up to the candle and snuffed it out and said, "Only God is great!"

When we focus on the greatness of our Lord and accept his blessings, our true greatness results. It is his greatness in us. All we can do is yield to the greatness he wants to be in us. Then when something great happens through us, we give him the glory. That was King David's secret to receiving silent strength . . .

Whatever greatness we have is what God produces in us. Nothing will deny us of the greatness he wants for us faster than trying to be great on our own.

ADDITIONAL SCRIPTURE READINGS
Psalm 145; Mark 10:35–45

Go to page 505 for your next devotional reading.

adezer, who had been at war with Tou. Hadoram brought all kinds of articles of gold and silver and bronze.

¹¹King David dedicated these articles to the LORD, as he had done with the silver and gold he had taken from all these nations: Edom and Moab, the Ammonites and the Philistines, and Amalek.

¹²Abishai son of Zeruiah struck down eighteen thousand Edomites in the Valley of Salt. ¹³He put garrisons in Edom, and all the Edomites became subject to David. The LORD gave David victory everywhere he went.

David's Officials

¹⁴David reigned over all Israel, doing what was just and right for all his people. ¹⁵Joab son of Zeruiah was over the army; Jehoshaphat son of Ahilud was recorder; ¹⁶Zadok son of Ahitub and Ahimelech*ᵃ* son of Abiathar were priests; Shavsha was secretary; ¹⁷Benaiah son of Jehoiada was over the Kerethites and Pelethites; and David's sons were chief officials at the king's side.

The Battle Against the Ammonites

19 In the course of time, Nahash king of the Ammonites died, and his son succeeded him as king. ²David thought, "I will show kindness to Hanun son of Nahash, because his father showed kindness to me." So David sent a delegation to express his sympathy to Hanun concerning his father.

When David's men came to Hanun in the land of the Ammonites to express sympathy to him, ³the Ammonite nobles said to Hanun, "Do you think David is honoring your father by sending men to you to express sympathy? Haven't his men come to you to explore and spy out the country and overthrow it?" ⁴So Hanun seized David's men, shaved them, cut off their garments in the middle at the buttocks, and sent them away.

⁵When someone came and told David about the men, he sent messengers to meet them, for they were greatly humiliated. The king said, "Stay at Jericho till your beards have grown, and then come back."

⁶When the Ammonites realized that they had become a stench in David's nostrils, Hanun and the Ammonites sent a thousand talentsᵇ of silver to hire chariots and charioteers from Aram Naharaim,ᶜ Aram Maacah and Zobah. ⁷They hired thirty-two thousand chariots and charioteers, as well as the king of Maacah with his troops, who came and camped near Medeba, while the Ammonites were mustered from their towns and moved out for battle.

⁸On hearing this, David sent Joab out with the entire army of fighting men. ⁹The Ammonites came out and drew up in battle formation at the entrance to their city, while the kings who had come were by themselves in the open country.

¹⁰Joab saw that there were battle lines in front of him and behind him; so he selected some of the best troops in Israel and deployed them against the Arameans. ¹¹He put the rest of the men under the command of Abishai his brother, and they were deployed against the Ammonites. ¹²Joab said, "If the Arameans are too strong for me, then you are to rescue me; but if the Ammonites are too strong for you, then I will rescue you. ¹³Be strong and let us fight bravely for our people and the cities of our God. The LORD will do what is good in his sight."

¹⁴Then Joab and the troops with him advanced to fight the Arameans, and they fled before him. ¹⁵When the Ammonites saw that the Arameans were fleeing, they too fled before his brother Abishai and went inside the city. So Joab went back to Jerusalem.

¹⁶After the Arameans saw that they had been routed by Israel, they sent messengers and had Arameans

---

ᵃ16 Some Hebrew manuscripts, Vulgate and Syriac (see also 2 Samuel 8:17); most Hebrew manuscripts *Abimelech*   *ᵇ6* That is, about 37 tons (about 34 metric tons)   *ᶜ6* That is, Northwest Mesopotamia

brought from beyond the River,ᵃ with Shophach the commander of Hadadezer's army leading them.

¹⁷When David was told of this, he gathered all Israel and crossed the Jordan; he advanced against them and formed his battle lines opposite them. David formed his lines to meet the Arameans in battle, and they fought against him. ¹⁸But they fled before Israel, and David killed seven thousand of their charioteers and forty thousand of their foot soldiers. He also killed Shophach the commander of their army.

¹⁹When the vassals of Hadadezer saw that they had been defeated by Israel, they made peace with David and became subject to him.

So the Arameans were not willing to help the Ammonites anymore.

The Capture of Rabbah

20 In the spring, at the time when kings go off to war, Joab led out the armed forces. He laid waste the land of the Ammonites and went to Rabbah and besieged it, but David remained in Jerusalem. Joab attacked Rabbah and left it in ruins. ²David took the crown from the head of their kingᵇ—its weight was found to be a talentᶜ of gold, and it was set with precious stones—and it was placed on David's head. He took a great quantity of plunder from the city ³and brought out the people who were there, consigning them to labor with saws and with iron picks and axes. David did this to all the Ammonite towns. Then David and his entire army returned to Jerusalem.

War With the Philistines

⁴In the course of time, war broke out with the Philistines, at Gezer. At that time Sibbecai the Hushathite killed Sippai, one of the descendants of the Rephaites, and the Philistines were subjugated.

⁵In another battle with the Philistines, Elhanan son of Jair killed Lahmi the brother of Goliath the Gittite, who had a spear with a shaft like a weaver's rod.

⁶In still another battle, which took place at Gath, there was a huge man with six fingers on each hand and six toes on each foot—twenty-four in all. He also was descended from Rapha. ⁷When he taunted Israel, Jonathan son of Shimea, David's brother, killed him.

⁸These were descendants of Rapha in Gath, and they fell at the hands of David and his men.

David Numbers the Fighting Men

21 Satan rose up against Israel and incited David to take a census of Israel. ²So David said to Joab and the commanders of the troops, "Go and count the Israelites from Beersheba to Dan. Then report back to me so that I may know how many there are."

³But Joab replied, "May the LORD multiply his troops a hundred times over. My lord the king, are they not all my lord's subjects? Why does my lord want to do this? Why should he bring guilt on Israel?"

⁴The king's word, however, overruled Joab; so Joab left and went throughout Israel and then came back to Jerusalem. ⁵Joab reported the number of the fighting men to David: In all Israel there were one million one hundred thousand men who could handle a sword, including four hundred and seventy thousand in Judah.

⁶But Joab did not include Levi and Benjamin in the numbering, because the king's command was repulsive to him. ⁷This command was also evil in the sight of God; so he punished Israel.

⁸Then David said to God, "I have sinned greatly by doing this. Now, I beg you, take away the guilt of your servant. I have done a very foolish thing."

⁹The LORD said to Gad, David's seer, ¹⁰"Go and tell David, 'This is

---

ᵃ16 That is, the Euphrates (about 34 kilograms)   ᵇ2 Or of Milcom, that is, Molech   ᶜ2 That is, about 75 pounds

what the LORD says: I am giving you three options. Choose one of them for me to carry out against you.' "

¹¹So Gad went to David and said to him, "This is what the LORD says: 'Take your choice: ¹²three years of famine, three months of being swept away*a* before your enemies, with their swords overtaking you, or three days of the sword of the LORD—days of plague in the land, with the angel of the LORD ravaging every part of Israel.' Now then, decide how I should answer the one who sent me."

¹³David said to Gad, "I am in deep distress. Let me fall into the hands of the LORD, for his mercy is very great; but do not let me fall into the hands of men."

¹⁴So the LORD sent a plague on Israel, and seventy thousand men of Israel fell dead. ¹⁵And God sent an angel to destroy Jerusalem. But as the angel was doing so, the LORD saw it and was grieved because of the calamity and said to the angel who was destroying the people, "Enough! Withdraw your hand." The angel of the LORD was then standing at the threshing floor of Araunah*b* the Jebusite.

¹⁶David looked up and saw the angel of the LORD standing between heaven and earth, with a drawn sword in his hand extended over Jerusalem. Then David and the elders, clothed in sackcloth, fell facedown.

¹⁷David said to God, "Was it not I who ordered the fighting men to be counted? I am the one who has sinned and done wrong. These are but sheep. What have they done? O LORD my God, let your hand fall upon me and my family, but do not let this plague remain on your people."

¹⁸Then the angel of the LORD ordered Gad to tell David to go up and build an altar to the LORD on the threshing floor of Araunah the Jebusite. ¹⁹So David went up in obedience to the word that Gad had spoken in the name of the LORD.

²⁰While Araunah was threshing wheat, he turned and saw the angel; his four sons who were with him hid themselves. ²¹Then David approached, and when Araunah looked and saw him, he left the threshing floor and bowed down before David with his face to the ground.

²²David said to him, "Let me have the site of your threshing floor so I can build an altar to the LORD, that the plague on the people may be stopped. Sell it to me at the full price."

²³Araunah said to David, "Take it! Let my lord the king do whatever pleases him. Look, I will give the oxen for the burnt offerings, the threshing sledges for the wood, and the wheat for the grain offering. I will give all this."

²⁴But King David replied to Araunah, "No, I insist on paying the full price. I will not take for the LORD what is yours, or sacrifice a burnt offering that costs me nothing."

²⁵So David paid Araunah six hundred shekels*c* of gold for the site. ²⁶David built an altar to the LORD there and sacrificed burnt offerings and fellowship offerings.*d* He called on the LORD, and the LORD answered him with fire from heaven on the altar of burnt offering.

²⁷Then the LORD spoke to the angel, and he put his sword back into its sheath. ²⁸At that time, when David saw that the LORD had answered him on the threshing floor of Araunah the Jebusite, he offered sacrifices there. ²⁹The tabernacle of the LORD, which Moses had made in the desert, and the altar of burnt offering were at that time on the high place at Gibeon. ³⁰But David could not go before it to inquire of God, because he was afraid of the sword of the angel of the LORD.

22 Then David said, "The house of the LORD God is to be here, and also the altar of burnt offering for Israel."

---

*a*12 Hebrew; Septuagint and Vulgate (see also 2 Samuel 24:13) *of fleeing*   *b*15 Hebrew *Ornan*, a variant of *Araunah*; also in verses 18-28   *c*25 That is, about 15 pounds (about 7 kilograms)   *d*26 Traditionally *peace offerings*

Preparations for the Temple

[2]So David gave orders to assemble the aliens living in Israel, and from among them he appointed stonecutters to prepare dressed stone for building the house of God. [3]He provided a large amount of iron to make nails for the doors of the gateways and for the fittings, and more bronze than could be weighed. [4]He also provided more cedar logs than could be counted, for the Sidonians and Tyrians had brought large numbers of them to David.

[5]David said, "My son Solomon is young and inexperienced, and the house to be built for the LORD should be of great magnificence and fame and splendor in the sight of all the nations. Therefore I will make preparations for it." So David made extensive preparations before his death.

[6]Then he called for his son Solomon and charged him to build a house for the LORD, the God of Israel. [7]David said to Solomon: "My son, I had it in my heart to build a house for the Name of the LORD my God. [8]But this word of the LORD came to me: 'You have shed much blood and have fought many wars. You are not to build a house for my Name, because you have shed much blood on the earth in my sight. [9]But you will have a son who will be a man of peace and rest, and I will give him rest from all his enemies on every side. His name will be Solomon,[a] and I will grant Israel peace and quiet during his reign. [10]He is the one who will build a house for my Name. He will be my son, and I will be his father. And I will establish the throne of his kingdom over Israel forever.'

[11]"Now, my son, the LORD be with you, and may you have success and build the house of the LORD your God, as he said you would. [12]May the LORD give you discretion and understanding when he puts you in command over Israel, so that you may keep the law of the LORD your God. [13]Then you will have success if you are careful to observe the decrees and laws that the LORD gave Moses for Israel. Be strong and courageous. Do not be afraid or discouraged.

[14]"I have taken great pains to provide for the temple of the LORD a hundred thousand talents[b] of gold, a million talents[c] of silver, quantities of bronze and iron too great to be weighed, and wood and stone. And you may add to them. [15]You have many workmen: stonecutters, masons and carpenters, as well as men skilled in every kind of work [16]in gold and silver, bronze and iron—craftsmen beyond number. Now begin the work, and the LORD be with you."

[17]Then David ordered all the leaders of Israel to help his son Solomon. [18]He said to them, "Is not the LORD your God with you? And has he not granted you rest on every side? For he has handed the inhabitants of the land over to me, and the land is subject to the LORD and to his people. [19]Now devote your heart and soul to seeking the LORD your God. Begin to build the sanctuary of the LORD God, so that you may bring the ark of the covenant of the LORD and the sacred articles belonging to God into the temple that will be built for the Name of the LORD."

The Levites

23 When David was old and full of years, he made his son Solomon king over Israel.

[2]He also gathered together all the leaders of Israel, as well as the priests and Levites. [3]The Levites thirty years old or more were counted, and the total number of men was thirty-eight thousand. [4]David said, "Of these, twenty-four thousand are to supervise the work of the temple of the LORD and six thousand are to be officials and judges. [5]Four thousand are to be gatekeepers and four thousand are to praise the LORD with the musi-

---

[a]9 *Solomon* sounds like and may be derived from the Hebrew for *peace.*   [b]14 That is, about 3,750 tons (about 3,450 metric tons)   [c]14 That is, about 37,500 tons (about 34,500 metric tons)

cal instruments I have provided for that purpose."

⁶David divided the Levites into groups corresponding to the sons of Levi: Gershon, Kohath and Merari.

Gershonites

⁷Belonging to the Gershonites:
    Ladan and Shimei.
⁸The sons of Ladan:
    Jehiel the first, Zetham and Joel—three in all.
⁹The sons of Shimei:
    Shelomoth, Haziel and Haran—three in all.
    These were the heads of the families of Ladan.
¹⁰And the sons of Shimei:
    Jahath, Ziza,ᵃ Jeush and Beriah.
    These were the sons of Shimei—four in all.
¹¹Jahath was the first and Ziza the second, but Jeush and Beriah did not have many sons; so they were counted as one family with one assignment.

Kohathites

¹²The sons of Kohath:
    Amram, Izhar, Hebron and Uzziel—four in all.
¹³The sons of Amram:
    Aaron and Moses.
    Aaron was set apart, he and his descendants forever, to consecrate the most holy things, to offer sacrifices before the LORD, to minister before him and to pronounce blessings in his name forever.
¹⁴The sons of Moses the man of God were counted as part of the tribe of Levi.
¹⁵The sons of Moses:
    Gershom and Eliezer.
¹⁶The descendants of Gershom:
    Shubael was the first.
¹⁷The descendants of Eliezer:
    Rehabiah was the first.
    Eliezer had no other sons, but the sons of Rehabiah were very numerous.
¹⁸The sons of Izhar:
    Shelomith was the first.
¹⁹The sons of Hebron:
    Jeriah the first, Amariah the second, Jahaziel the third and Jekameam the fourth.
²⁰The sons of Uzziel:
    Micah the first and Isshiah the second.

Merarites

²¹The sons of Merari:
    Mahli and Mushi.
    The sons of Mahli:
    Eleazar and Kish.
²²Eleazar died without having sons: he had only daughters. Their cousins, the sons of Kish, married them.
²³The sons of Mushi:
    Mahli, Eder and Jerimoth—three in all.

²⁴These were the descendants of Levi by their families—the heads of families as they were registered under their names and counted individually, that is, the workers twenty years old or more who served in the temple of the LORD. ²⁵For David had said, "Since the LORD, the God of Israel, has granted rest to his people and has come to dwell in Jerusalem forever, ²⁶the Levites no longer need to carry the tabernacle or any of the articles used in its service." ²⁷According to the last instructions of David, the Levites were counted from those twenty years old or more.

²⁸The duty of the Levites was to help Aaron's descendants in the service of the temple of the LORD: to be in charge of the courtyards, the side rooms, the purification of all sacred things and the performance of other duties at the house of God. ²⁹They were in charge of the bread set out on the table, the flour for the grain offerings, the unleavened wafers, the baking and the mixing, and all measure-

ᵃ10 One Hebrew manuscript, Septuagint and Vulgate (see also verse 11); most Hebrew manuscripts *Zina*

ments of quantity and size. ³⁰They were also to stand every morning to thank and praise the Lord. They were to do the same in the evening ³¹and whenever burnt offerings were presented to the Lord on Sabbaths and at New Moon festivals and at appointed feasts. They were to serve before the Lord regularly in the proper number and in the way prescribed for them.

³²And so the Levites carried out their responsibilities for the Tent of Meeting, for the Holy Place and, under their brothers the descendants of Aaron, for the service of the temple of the Lord.

The Divisions of Priests

24 These were the divisions of the sons of Aaron:

VERSE:
1 Chronicles
23:30

AUTHOR:
Robert H. Schuller

PASSAGE:
1 Chronicles
23:28–31

A New Day

At the end of every day, the last thing I do is to have a prayer. "Father in heaven, Jesus Christ, I've sinned again today." And I try to think of what my sins are specifically. I confess. I ask God to forgive me. I know he does. He died on the cross for me . . .

Now, that's the first thing I pray for. Then I pray for his Spirit to come and fill my life. I know he does, so I sleep peacefully. If I wake up very, very early it's because I'm enthused and excited about things I can do for God. Then I begin the day with this prayer: "Father in heaven, this morning is a brand new day! Filled with bright new opportunities!" Isn't that exciting!

If you begin your day that way and if you end your day that way, chances are that in between you're going to have a lot of positive emotions, because the Holy Spirit of God will come into your life, guide you, lead you and direct you. You're going to get involved, and that means you're going to get excited, and it also means you'll become enthused! And that means energy!

ADDITIONAL SCRIPTURE READINGS
Isaiah 42:5–9; Ephesians 4:20–24

Go to page 509 for your next devotional reading.

The sons of Aaron were Nadab, Abihu, Eleazar and Ithamar. ²But Nadab and Abihu died before their father did, and they had no sons; so Eleazar and Ithamar served as the priests. ³With the help of Zadok a descendant of Eleazar and Ahimelech a descendant of Ithamar, David separated them into divisions for their appointed order of ministering. ⁴A larger number of leaders were found among Eleazar's descendants than among Ithamar's, and they were divided accordingly: sixteen heads of families from Eleazar's descendants and eight heads of families from Ithamar's descendants. ⁵They divided them impartially by drawing lots, for there were officials of the sanctuary and officials of God among the descendants of both Eleazar and Ithamar.

⁶The scribe Shemaiah son of Nethanel, a Levite, recorded their names in the presence of the king and of the officials: Zadok the priest, Ahimelech son of Abiathar and the heads of families of the priests and of the Levites— one family being taken from Eleazar and then one from Ithamar.

⁷The first lot fell to Jehoiarib,
  the second to Jedaiah,
⁸the third to Harim,
  the fourth to Seorim,
⁹the fifth to Malkijah,
  the sixth to Mijamin,
¹⁰the seventh to Hakkoz,
  the eighth to Abijah,
¹¹the ninth to Jeshua,
  the tenth to Shecaniah,
¹²the eleventh to Eliashib,
  the twelfth to Jakim,
¹³the thirteenth to Huppah,
  the fourteenth to Jeshebeab,
¹⁴the fifteenth to Bilgah,
  the sixteenth to Immer,
¹⁵the seventeenth to Hezir,
  the eighteenth to Happizzez,
¹⁶the nineteenth to Pethahiah,
  the twentieth to Jehezkel,
¹⁷the twenty-first to Jakin,

  the twenty-second to Gamul,
¹⁸the twenty-third to Delaiah
  and the twenty-fourth to Maaziah.

¹⁹This was their appointed order of ministering when they entered the temple of the LORD, according to the regulations prescribed for them by their forefather Aaron, as the LORD, the God of Israel, had commanded him.

The Rest of the Levites

²⁰As for the rest of the descendants of Levi:
  from the sons of Amram: Shubael;
  from the sons of Shubael: Jehdeiah.
²¹As for Rehabiah, from his sons:
  Isshiah was the first.
²²From the Izharites: Shelomoth;
  from the sons of Shelomoth: Jahath.
²³The sons of Hebron: Jeriah the first,ᵃ Amariah the second, Jahaziel the third and Jekameam the fourth.
²⁴The son of Uzziel: Micah;
  from the sons of Micah: Shamir.
²⁵The brother of Micah: Isshiah;
  from the sons of Isshiah: Zechariah.
²⁶The sons of Merari: Mahli and Mushi.
  The son of Jaaziah: Beno.
²⁷The sons of Merari:
  from Jaaziah: Beno, Shoham, Zaccur and Ibri.
²⁸From Mahli: Eleazar, who had no sons.
²⁹From Kish: the son of Kish: Jerahmeel.
³⁰And the sons of Mushi: Mahli, Eder and Jerimoth.

These were the Levites, according to their families. ³¹They also cast lots, just as their brothers the descendants of Aaron did, in the presence of King

---

ᵃ23 Two Hebrew manuscripts and some Septuagint manuscripts (see also 1 Chron. 23:19); most Hebrew manuscripts *The sons of Jeriah:*

David and of Zadok, Ahimelech, and the heads of families of the priests and of the Levites. The families of the oldest brother were treated the same as those of the youngest.

The Singers

25 David, together with the commanders of the army, set apart some of the sons of Asaph, Heman and Jeduthun for the ministry of prophesying, accompanied by harps, lyres and cymbals. Here is the list of the men who performed this service:

[2]From the sons of Asaph:
Zaccur, Joseph, Nethaniah and Asarelah. The sons of Asaph were under the supervision of Asaph, who prophesied under the king's supervision.
[3]As for Jeduthun, from his sons:
Gedaliah, Zeri, Jeshaiah, Shimei,[a] Hashabiah and Mattithiah, six in all, under the supervision of their father Jeduthun, who prophesied, using the harp in thanking and praising the LORD.
[4]As for Heman, from his sons:
Bukkiah, Mattaniah, Uzziel, Shubael and Jerimoth; Hananiah, Hanani, Eliathah, Giddalti and Romamti-Ezer; Joshbekashah, Mallothi, Hothir and Mahazioth.
[5]All these were sons of Heman the king's seer. They were given him through the promises of God to exalt him.[b] God gave Heman fourteen sons and three daughters.

[6]All these men were under the supervision of their fathers for the music of the temple of the LORD, with cymbals, lyres and harps, for the ministry at the house of God. Asaph, Jeduthun and Heman were under the supervision of the king. [7]Along with their relatives—all of them trained and skilled in music for the LORD—

they numbered 288. [8]Young and old alike, teacher as well as student, cast lots for their duties.

[9]The first lot, which was for Asaph, fell to Joseph,
    his sons and relatives,[c]   12[d]
the second to Gedaliah,
    he and his relatives and sons,   12
[10]the third to Zaccur,
    his sons and relatives,   12
[11]the fourth to Izri,[e]
    his sons and relatives,   12
[12]the fifth to Nethaniah,
    his sons and relatives,   12
[13]the sixth to Bukkiah,
    his sons and relatives,   12
[14]the seventh to Jesarelah,[f]
    his sons and relatives,   12
[15]the eighth to Jeshaiah,
    his sons and relatives,   12
[16]the ninth to Mattaniah,
    his sons and relatives,   12
[17]the tenth to Shimei,
    his sons and relatives,   12
[18]the eleventh to Azarel,[g]
    his sons and relatives,   12
[19]the twelfth to Hashabiah,
    his sons and relatives,   12
[20]the thirteenth to Shubael,
    his sons and relatives,   12
[21]the fourteenth to Mattithiah,
    his sons and relatives,   12
[22]the fifteenth to Jerimoth,
    his sons and relatives,   12
[23]the sixteenth to Hananiah,
    his sons and relatives,   12
[24]the seventeenth to Joshbekashah,
    his sons and relatives,   12
[25]the eighteenth to Hanani,
    his sons and relatives,   12
[26]the nineteenth to Mallothi,
    his sons and relatives,   12
[27]the twentieth to Eliathah,
    his sons and relatives,   12
[28]the twenty-first to Hothir,
    his sons and relatives,   12

---

[a]3 One Hebrew manuscript and some Septuagint manuscripts (see also verse 17); most Hebrew manuscripts do not have *Shimei*.   [b]5 Hebrew *exalt the horn*   [c]9 See Septuagint; Hebrew does not have *his sons and relatives*.   [d]9 See the total in verse 7; Hebrew does not have *twelve*.   [e]11 A variant of *Zeri*   [f]14 A variant of *Asarelah*   [g]18 A variant of *Uzziel*

²⁹the twenty-second to Giddalti,

his sons and relatives,   12

³⁰the twenty-third to Mahazioth,

his sons and relatives,   12

³¹the twenty-fourth to Romamti-Ezer,

his sons and relatives,   12

The Gatekeepers

26 The divisions of the gatekeepers:

From the Korahites: Meshelemiah son of Kore, one of the sons of Asaph.

²Meshelemiah had sons:

Zechariah the firstborn,

Jediael the second,

Zebadiah the third,

Jathniel the fourth,

³Elam the fifth,

Jehohanan the sixth

and Eliehoenai the seventh.

⁴Obed-Edom also had sons:

Shemaiah the firstborn,

Jehozabad the second,

Joah the third,

Sacar the fourth,

Nethanel the fifth,

⁵Ammiel the sixth,

Issachar the seventh

and Peullethai the eighth.

(For God had blessed Obed-Edom.)

⁶His son Shemaiah also had sons, who were leaders in their father's family because they were very capable men. ⁷The sons of Shemaiah: Othni, Rephael, Obed and Elzabad; his relatives Elihu and Semakiah were also able men. ⁸All these were descendants of Obed-Edom; they and their sons and their relatives were capable men with the strength to do the work—descendants of Obed-Edom, 62 in all.

⁹Meshelemiah had sons and relatives, who were able men— 18 in all.

¹⁰Hosah the Merarite had sons: Shimri the first (although he was not the firstborn, his father had appointed him the first), ¹¹Hilkiah the second, Tabaliah the third and Zechariah the fourth. The sons and relatives of Hosah were 13 in all.

¹²These divisions of the gatekeepers, through their chief men, had duties for ministering in the temple of the LORD, just as their relatives had. ¹³Lots were cast for each gate, according to their families, young and old alike.

¹⁴The lot for the East Gate fell to Shelemiah.[a] Then lots were cast for his son Zechariah, a wise counselor, and the lot for the North Gate fell to him. ¹⁵The lot for the South Gate fell to Obed-Edom, and the lot for the storehouse fell to his sons. ¹⁶The lots for the West Gate and the Shalleketh Gate on the upper road fell to Shuppim and Hosah.

Guard was alongside of guard: ¹⁷There were six Levites a day on the east, four a day on the north, four a day on the south and two at a time at the storehouse. ¹⁸As for the court to the west, there were four at the road and two at the court itself.

¹⁹These were the divisions of the gatekeepers who were descendants of Korah and Merari.

The Treasurers and Other Officials

²⁰Their fellow Levites were[b] in charge of the treasuries of the house of God and the treasuries for the dedicated things.

²¹The descendants of Ladan, who were Gershonites through Ladan and who were heads of families belonging to Ladan the Gershonite, were Jehieli, ²²the sons of Jehieli, Zetham and his brother Joel. They were in charge of the treasuries of the temple of the LORD.

---

*a*14 A variant of *Meshelemiah*   *b*20 Septuagint; Hebrew *As for the Levites, Ahijah was*

²³From the Amramites, the Izharites, the Hebronites and the Uzzielites:

²⁴Shubael, a descendant of Gershom son of Moses, was the officer in charge of the treasuries. ²⁵His relatives through Eliezer: Rehabiah his son, Jeshaiah his son, Joram his son, Zicri his son and Shelomith his son. ²⁶Shelomith and his relatives were in charge of all the treasuries for the things dedicated by King David, by the heads of families who were the commanders of thousands and commanders of hundreds, and by the other army commanders. ²⁷Some of the plunder taken in battle they dedicated for the repair of the temple of the LORD. ²⁸And everything dedicated by Samuel the seer and by Saul son of Kish, Abner son of

FRIDAY

VERSE:	AUTHOR:	PASSAGE:
1 Chronicles 26:27	Mrs. Charles E. Cowman	1 Chronicles 26:24–28

Plunder Taken in Battle

Spiritual force is stored in the depths of our being, through the very pain which we cannot understand.

Some day we shall find that the "plunder" we have won from our trials was just preparing us to become true "Great Hearts" in the *Pilgrim's Progress,* and to lead our fellow pilgrims triumphantly through trial to the city of the King.

But let us never forget that the source of helping other people must be victorious suffering. The whining, murmuring pang never does anybody any good.

Paul did not carry a cemetery with him, but a chorus of victorious praise; and the harder the trial, the more he trusted and rejoiced, shouting from the very altar of sacrifice. He said, "But even if I am being poured out like a drink offering on the sacrifice and service coming from your faith, I am glad and rejoice with all of you" (Philippians 2:17). Lord, help me this day to draw strength from all that comes to me!

ADDITIONAL SCRIPTURE READINGS
2 Corinthians 4:7–18; Philippians 2:12–18
Go to page 512 for your next devotional reading.

Ner and Joab son of Zeruiah, and all the other dedicated things were in the care of Shelomith and his relatives.
²⁹From the Izharites: Kenaniah and his sons were assigned duties away from the temple, as officials and judges over Israel.
³⁰From the Hebronites: Hashabiah and his relatives—seventeen hundred able men—were responsible in Israel west of the Jordan for all the work of the Lᴏʀᴅ and for the king's service. ³¹As for the Hebronites, Jeriah was their chief according to the genealogical records of their families. In the fortieth year of David's reign a search was made in the records, and capable men among the Hebronites were found at Jazer in Gilead. ³²Jeriah had twenty-seven hundred relatives, who were able men and heads of families, and King David put them in charge of the Reubenites, the Gadites and the half-tribe of Manasseh for every matter pertaining to God and for the affairs of the king.

Army Divisions

27 This is the list of the Israelites—heads of families, commanders of thousands and commanders of hundreds, and their officers, who served the king in all that concerned the army divisions that were on duty month by month throughout the year. Each division consisted of 24,000 men.

²In charge of the first division, for the first month, was Jashobeam son of Zabdiel. There were 24,000 men in his division. ³He was a descendant of Perez and chief of all the army officers for the first month.
⁴In charge of the division for the second month was Dodai the Aho-

hite; Mikloth was the leader of his division. There were 24,000 men in his division.
⁵The third army commander, for the third month, was Benaiah son of Jehoiada the priest. He was chief and there were 24,000 men in his division. ⁶This was the Benaiah who was a mighty man among the Thirty and was over the Thirty. His son Ammizabad was in charge of his division.
⁷The fourth, for the fourth month, was Asahel the brother of Joab; his son Zebadiah was his successor. There were 24,000 men in his division.
⁸The fifth, for the fifth month, was the commander Shamhuth the Izrahite. There were 24,000 men in his division.
⁹The sixth, for the sixth month, was Ira the son of Ikkesh the Tekoite. There were 24,000 men in his division.
¹⁰The seventh, for the seventh month, was Helez the Pelonite, an Ephraimite. There were 24,000 men in his division.
¹¹The eighth, for the eighth month, was Sibbecai the Hushathite, a Zerahite. There were 24,000 men in his division.
¹²The ninth, for the ninth month, was Abiezer the Anathothite, a Benjamite. There were 24,000 men in his division.
¹³The tenth, for the tenth month, was Maharai the Netophathite, a Zerahite. There were 24,000 men in his division.
¹⁴The eleventh, for the eleventh month, was Benaiah the Pirathonite, an Ephraimite. There were 24,000 men in his division.
¹⁵The twelfth, for the twelfth month, was Heldai the Netophathite, from the family of Othniel. There were 24,000 men in his division.

Officers of the Tribes

¹⁶The officers over the tribes of Israel:

1 CHRONICLES 27–28

17over Levi: Hashabiah son of Kemuel;

over Aaron: Zadok;

18over Judah: Elihu, a brother of David;

over Issachar: Omri son of Michael;

19over Zebulun: Ishmaiah son of Obadiah;

over Naphtali: Jerimoth son of Azriel;

20over the Ephraimites: Hoshea son of Azaziah;

over half the tribe of Manasseh: Joel son of Pedaiah;

21over the half-tribe of Manasseh in Gilead: Iddo son of Zechariah;

over Benjamin: Jaasiel son of Abner;

22over Dan: Azarel son of Jeroham.

These were the officers over the tribes of Israel.

23David did not take the number of the men twenty years old or less, because the LORD had promised to make Israel as numerous as the stars in the sky. 24Joab son of Zeruiah began to count the men but did not finish. Wrath came on Israel on account of this numbering, and the number was not entered in the book*a* of the annals of King David.

The King's Overseers

25Azmaveth son of Adiel was in charge of the royal storehouses.

Jonathan son of Uzziah was in charge of the storehouses in the outlying districts, in the towns, the villages and the watchtowers.

26Ezri son of Kelub was in charge of the field workers who farmed the land.

27Shimei the Ramathite was in charge of the vineyards.

Zabdi the Shiphmite was in charge

of the produce of the vineyards for the wine vats.

28Baal-Hanan the Gederite was in charge of the olive and sycamore-fig trees in the western foothills.

Joash was in charge of the supplies of olive oil.

29Shitrai the Sharonite was in charge of the herds grazing in Sharon.

Shaphat son of Adlai was in charge of the herds in the valleys.

30Obil the Ishmaelite was in charge of the camels.

Jehdeiah the Meronothite was in charge of the donkeys.

31Jaziz the Hagrite was in charge of the flocks.

All these were the officials in charge of King David's property.

32Jonathan, David's uncle, was a counselor, a man of insight and a scribe. Jehiel son of Hacmoni took care of the king's sons.

33Ahithophel was the king's counselor.

Hushai the Arkite was the king's friend. 34Ahithophel was succeeded by Jehoiada son of Benaiah and by Abiathar.

Joab was the commander of the royal army.

David's Plans for the Temple

28 David summoned all the officials of Israel to assemble at Jerusalem: the officers over the tribes, the commanders of the divisions in the service of the king, the commanders of thousands and commanders of hundreds, and the officials in charge of all the property and livestock belonging to the king and his sons, together with the palace officials, the mighty men and all the brave warriors.

2King David rose to his feet and said: "Listen to me, my brothers and my people. I had it in my heart to build a house as a place of rest for the ark of the covenant of the LORD, for the footstool of our God, and I made plans to build it. 3But God said to me,

---

a24 Septuagint; Hebrew number

PASSAGE: 2 Corinthians 3:7 — 4:6; Ephesians 4:17 — 5:2
AUTHOR: Luci Shaw

... More and More

... I find myself coinciding
with myself. I meet me coming
and going and when I think of me,
there I am, quite often. I'm getting hard
to escape; I used to be hard to find.

What irony, when I have been everywhere,
my life spread so wide — flung, taut, like a single
bedsheet stretched to cover the whole world.
Thinned to transparency, a bubble bursting.
Stalled, a wave too spent to conquer the beach.

Now, though, it's like double vision — when
your eyes finally get it right, and pull
the split image into one. I see myself mirrored,
clean at all my edges, even the hairs around my
                    head
in focus, the sun blazing them into a halo.

Go to page 515 for your next devotional reading.

'You are not to build a house for my Name, because you are a warrior and have shed blood.'

⁴"Yet the LORD, the God of Israel, chose me from my whole family to be king over Israel forever. He chose Judah as leader, and from the house of Judah he chose my family, and from my father's sons he was pleased to make me king over all Israel. ⁵Of all my sons—and the LORD has given me many—he has chosen my son Solomon to sit on the throne of the kingdom of the LORD over Israel. ⁶He said to me: 'Solomon your son is the one who will build my house and my courts, for I have chosen him to be my son, and I will be his father. ⁷I will establish his kingdom forever if he is unswerving in carrying out my commands and laws, as is being done at this time.'

⁸"So now I charge you in the sight of all Israel and of the assembly of the LORD, and in the hearing of our God: Be careful to follow all the commands of the LORD your God, that you may possess this good land and pass it on as an inheritance to your descendants forever.

⁹"And you, my son Solomon, acknowledge the God of your father, and serve him with wholehearted devotion and with a willing mind, for the LORD searches every heart and understands every motive behind the thoughts. If you seek him, he will be found by you; but if you forsake him, he will reject you forever. ¹⁰Consider now, for the LORD has chosen you to build a temple as a sanctuary. Be strong and do the work."

¹¹Then David gave his son Solomon the plans for the portico of the temple, its buildings, its storerooms, its upper parts, its inner rooms and the place of atonement. ¹²He gave him the plans of all that the Spirit had put in his mind for the courts of the temple of the LORD and all the surrounding rooms, for the treasuries of the temple of God and for the treasuries for the dedicated things. ¹³He gave him instructions for the divisions of the priests and Levites, and for all the work of serving in the temple of the LORD, as well as for all the articles to be used in its service. ¹⁴He designated the weight of gold for all the gold articles to be used in various kinds of service, and the weight of silver for all the silver articles to be used in various kinds of service: ¹⁵the weight of gold for the gold lampstands and their lamps, with the weight for each lampstand and its lamps; and the weight of silver for each silver lampstand and its lamps, according to the use of each lampstand; ¹⁶the weight of gold for each table for consecrated bread; the weight of silver for the silver tables; ¹⁷the weight of pure gold for the forks, sprinkling bowls and pitchers; the weight of gold for each gold dish; the weight of silver for each silver dish; ¹⁸and the weight of the refined gold for the altar of incense. He also gave him the plan for the chariot, that is, the cherubim of gold that spread their wings and shelter the ark of the covenant of the LORD.

¹⁹"All this," David said, "I have in writing from the hand of the LORD upon me, and he gave me understanding in all the details of the plan."

²⁰David also said to Solomon his son, "Be strong and courageous, and do the work. Do not be afraid or discouraged, for the LORD God, my God, is with you. He will not fail you or forsake you until all the work for the service of the temple of the LORD is finished. ²¹The divisions of the priests and Levites are ready for all the work on the temple of God, and every willing man skilled in any craft will help you in all the work. The officials and all the people will obey your every command."

Gifts for Building the Temple

29 Then King David said to the whole assembly: "My son Solomon, the one whom God has chosen, is young and inexperienced. The task is great, because this palatial structure is not for man but for the LORD God. ²With all my resources I have provided for the temple of my God—gold for the gold work, silver for the silver, bronze for the bronze, iron for the iron and wood for the wood, as well as onyx for the settings, turquoise,[a] stones of various colors, and all kinds of fine stone and marble—all of these in large quantities. ³Besides, in my devotion to the temple of my God I now give my personal treasures of gold and silver for the temple of my God, over and above everything I have provided for this holy temple: ⁴three thousand talents[b] of gold (gold of Ophir) and seven thousand talents[c] of refined silver, for the overlaying of the walls of the buildings, ⁵for the gold work and the silver work, and for all the work to be done by the craftsmen. Now, who is willing to consecrate himself today to the LORD?"

⁶Then the leaders of families, the officers of the tribes of Israel, the commanders of thousands and commanders of hundreds, and the officials in charge of the king's work gave willingly. ⁷They gave toward the work on the temple of God five thousand talents[d] and ten thousand darics[e] of gold, ten thousand talents[f] of silver, eighteen thousand talents[g] of bronze and a hundred thousand talents[h] of iron. ⁸Any who had precious stones gave them to the treasury of the temple of the LORD in the custody of Jehiel the Gershonite. ⁹The people rejoiced at the willing response of their leaders, for they had given freely and wholeheartedly to the LORD. David the king also rejoiced greatly.

David's Prayer

¹⁰David praised the LORD in the presence of the whole assembly, saying,

"Praise be to you, O LORD,
    God of our father Israel,
    from everlasting to everlasting.

¹¹Yours, O LORD, is the greatness
    and the power
    and the glory and the majesty
    and the splendor,
    for everything in heaven and
        earth is yours.
Yours, O LORD, is the kingdom;
    you are exalted as head over all.
¹²Wealth and honor come from you;
    you are the ruler of all things.
In your hands are strength and
        power
    to exalt and give strength to all.
¹³Now, our God, we give you
        thanks,
    and praise your glorious name.

¹⁴"But who am I, and who are my people, that we should be able to give as generously as this? Everything comes from you, and we have given you only what comes from your hand. ¹⁵We are aliens and strangers in your sight, as were all our forefathers. Our days on earth are like a shadow, without hope. ¹⁶O LORD our God, as for all this abundance that we have provided for building you a temple for your Holy Name, it comes from your hand, and all of it belongs to you. ¹⁷I know, my God, that you test the heart and are pleased with integrity. All these things have I given willingly and with honest intent. And now I have seen with joy how willingly your people who are here have given to you. ¹⁸O LORD, God of our fathers Abraham, Isaac and Israel, keep this desire in the hearts of your people forever, and keep their hearts loyal to you. ¹⁹And give my son Solomon the wholehearted devotion to keep your commands, requirements and decrees and to do everything to build the palatial structure for which I have provided."

²⁰Then David said to the whole assembly, "Praise the LORD your God." So they all praised the LORD, the God

---

a2 The meaning of the Hebrew for this word is uncertain.   b4 That is, about 110 tons (about 100 metric tons)   c4 That is, about 260 tons (about 240 metric tons)   d7 That is, about 190 tons (about 170 metric tons)   e7 That is, about 185 pounds (about 84 kilograms)   f7 That is, about 375 tons (about 345 metric tons)   g7 That is, about 675 tons (about 610 metric tons)   h7 That is, about 3,750 tons (about 3,450 metric tons)

of their fathers; they bowed low and fell prostrate before the LORD and the king.

Solomon Acknowledged as King

²¹The next day they made sacrifices to the LORD and presented burnt offerings to him: a thousand bulls, a thousand rams and a thousand male lambs, together with their drink offerings, and other sacrifices in abundance for all Israel. ²²They ate and

VERSE:
1 Chronicles 29:10

AUTHOR:
John Gilmore

PASSAGE:
1 Chronicles 29:10–20

A Senior Who Applauded God

David, sweet singer of Israel and its king for 40 years, died at 70, "having enjoyed long life, wealth and honor" (1 Chronicles 29:28). The last ten years of his life, however, were not a cakewalk. Indeed, it was a rough decade. He sustained the revolt of Absalom, his son, a three-year famine after his return to power, then the usurpation of his other son, Adonijah.

David could have moaned and complained to the sky. But in the last decade of his life, he did not hang up his harp. He still wrote a significant number of psalms — between 63 and 80. David's faith was severely tested in his senior years. But his trust in God showed a titanium tenacity . . .

In his better moments, especially his final hours, King David played to the audience of God. His praise was the result of learning to know and please God . . .

God multiplies years and provides extended life. Life is able to rise above mere existence when the Lord is central in our thinking, the One to whom we give all praise. David left life vigorously praising God. Do we begin and end our days with prime attention to the Lord? May David inspire us to praise the Lord with effort and enjoyment.

ADDITIONAL SCRIPTURE READINGS
2 Samuel 22:26–51; Psalm 138

Go to page 522 for your next devotional reading.

drank with great joy in the presence of the LORD that day.

Then they acknowledged Solomon son of David as king a second time, anointing him before the LORD to be ruler and Zadok to be priest. ²³So Solomon sat on the throne of the LORD as king in place of his father David. He prospered and all Israel obeyed him. ²⁴All the officers and mighty men, as well as all of King David's sons, pledged their submission to King Solomon.

²⁵The LORD highly exalted Solomon in the sight of all Israel and bestowed on him royal splendor such as no king over Israel ever had before.

The Death of David

²⁶David son of Jesse was king over all Israel. ²⁷He ruled over Israel forty years—seven in Hebron and thirty-three in Jerusalem. ²⁸He died at a good old age, having enjoyed long life, wealth and honor. His son Solomon succeeded him as king.

²⁹As for the events of King David's reign, from beginning to end, they are written in the records of Samuel the seer, the records of Nathan the prophet and the records of Gad the seer, ³⁰together with the details of his reign and power, and the circumstances that surrounded him and Israel and the kingdoms of all the other lands.

This book continues the history of God's people begun in 1 Chronicles, concentrating exclusively on the nation of Judah. Note God's powerful presence in his people's lives; even when they are carried off into captivity he holds on to them. As you read 2 Chronicles, rest in God's promise that even when life unravels, he still has a purpose for you. He loves you and he wants to bring you safely home.

2 CHRONICLES

Solomon Asks for Wisdom

1 Solomon son of David established himself firmly over his kingdom, for the LORD his God was with him and made him exceedingly great.

²Then Solomon spoke to all Israel— to the commanders of thousands and commanders of hundreds, to the judges and to all the leaders in Israel, the heads of families— ³and Solomon and the whole assembly went to the high place at Gibeon, for God's Tent of Meeting was there, which Moses the LORD's servant had made in the desert. ⁴Now David had brought up the ark of God from Kiriath Jearim to the place he had prepared for it, because he had pitched a tent for it in Jerusalem. ⁵But the bronze altar that Bezalel son of Uri, the son of Hur, had made was in Gibeon in front of the tabernacle of the LORD; so Solomon and the assembly inquired of him there. ⁶Solomon went up to the bronze altar before the LORD in the Tent of Meeting and offered a thousand burnt offerings on it.

⁷That night God appeared to Solomon and said to him, "Ask for whatever you want me to give you."

⁸Solomon answered God, "You have shown great kindness to David my father and have made me king in his place. ⁹Now, LORD God, let your promise to my father David be confirmed, for you have made me king over a people who are as numerous as the dust of the earth. ¹⁰Give me wisdom and knowledge, that I may lead this people, for who is able to govern this great people of yours?"

¹¹God said to Solomon, "Since this is your heart's desire and you have not asked for wealth, riches or honor, nor for the death of your enemies, and since you have not asked for a long life but for wisdom and knowledge to govern my people over whom I have made you king, ¹²therefore wis-

dom and knowledge will be given you. And I will also give you wealth, riches and honor, such as no king who was before you ever had and none after you will have."

¹³Then Solomon went to Jerusalem from the high place at Gibeon, from before the Tent of Meeting. And he reigned over Israel.

¹⁴Solomon accumulated chariots and horses; he had fourteen hundred chariots and twelve thousand horses,ᵃ which he kept in the chariot cities and also with him in Jerusalem. ¹⁵The king made silver and gold as common in Jerusalem as stones, and cedar as plentiful as sycamore-fig trees in the foothills. ¹⁶Solomon's horses were imported from Egyptᵇ and from Kueᶜ—the royal merchants purchased them from Kue. ¹⁷They imported a chariot from Egypt for six hundred shekelsᵈ of silver, and a horse for a hundred and fifty.ᵉ They also exported them to all the kings of the Hittites and of the Arameans.

Preparations for Building the Temple

2 Solomon gave orders to build a temple for the Name of the LORD and a royal palace for himself. ²He conscripted seventy thousand men as carriers and eighty thousand as stonecutters in the hills and thirty-six hundred as foremen over them.

³Solomon sent this message to Hiramᶠ king of Tyre:

"Send me cedar logs as you did for my father David when you sent him cedar to build a palace to live in. ⁴Now I am about to build a temple for the Name of the LORD my God and to dedicate it to him for burning fragrant incense before him, for setting out the consecrated bread regularly, and for making burnt offerings every morning and evening and on Sabbaths and New Moons and at the appointed feasts of the LORD our God. This is a lasting ordinance for Israel.

⁵"The temple I am going to build will be great, because our God is greater than all other gods. ⁶But who is able to build a temple for him, since the heavens, even the highest heavens, cannot contain him? Who then am I to build a temple for him, except as a place to burn sacrifices before him?

⁷"Send me, therefore, a man skilled to work in gold and silver, bronze and iron, and in purple, crimson and blue yarn, and experienced in the art of engraving, to work in Judah and Jerusalem with my skilled craftsmen, whom my father David provided.

⁸"Send me also cedar, pine and algumᵍ logs from Lebanon, for I know that your men are skilled in cutting timber there. My men will work with yours ⁹to provide me with plenty of lumber, because the temple I build must be large and magnificent. ¹⁰I will give your servants, the woodsmen who cut the timber, twenty thousand corsʰ of ground wheat, twenty thousand cors of barley, twenty thousand bathsⁱ of wine and twenty thousand baths of olive oil."

¹¹Hiram king of Tyre replied by letter to Solomon:

"Because the LORD loves his people, he has made you their king."

¹²And Hiram added:

ᵃ14 Or *charioteers*   ᵇ16 Or possibly *Muzur,* a region in Cilicia; also in verse 17
ᶜ16 Probably Cilicia   ᵈ17 That is, about 15 pounds (about 7 kilograms)   ᵉ17 That is, about 3 3/4 pounds (about 1.7 kilograms)   ᶠ3 Hebrew *Huram,* a variant of *Hiram;* also in verses 11 and 12   ᵍ8 Probably a variant of *almug;* possibly juniper   ʰ10 That is, probably about 125,000 bushels (about 4,400 kiloliters)   ⁱ10 That is, probably about 115,000 gallons (about 440 kiloliters)

"Praise be to the LORD, the God of Israel, who made heaven and earth! He has given King David a wise son, endowed with intelligence and discernment, who will build a temple for the LORD and a palace for himself.

13"I am sending you Huram-Abi, a man of great skill, 14whose mother was from Dan and whose father was from Tyre. He is trained to work in gold and silver, bronze and iron, stone and wood, and with purple and blue and crimson yarn and fine linen. He is experienced in all kinds of engraving and can execute any design given to him. He will work with your craftsmen and with those of my lord, David your father.

15"Now let my lord send his servants the wheat and barley and the olive oil and wine he promised, 16and we will cut all the logs from Lebanon that you need and will float them in rafts by sea down to Joppa. You can then take them up to Jerusalem."

17Solomon took a census of all the aliens who were in Israel, after the census his father David had taken; and they were found to be 153,600. 18He assigned 70,000 of them to be carriers and 80,000 to be stonecutters in the hills, with 3,600 foremen over them to keep the people working.

Solomon Builds the Temple

3 Then Solomon began to build the temple of the LORD in Jerusalem on Mount Moriah, where the LORD had appeared to his father David. It was on the threshing floor of Araunah[a] the Jebusite, the place provided by David. 2He began building on the second day of the second month in the fourth year of his reign.

3The foundation Solomon laid for building the temple of God was sixty cubits long and twenty cubits wide[b] (using the cubit of the old standard). 4The portico at the front of the temple was twenty cubits[c] long across the width of the building and twenty cubits[d] high.

He overlaid the inside with pure gold. 5He paneled the main hall with pine and covered it with fine gold and decorated it with palm tree and chain designs. 6He adorned the temple with precious stones. And the gold he used was gold of Parvaim. 7He overlaid the ceiling beams, doorframes, walls and doors of the temple with gold, and he carved cherubim on the walls.

8He built the Most Holy Place, its length corresponding to the width of the temple—twenty cubits long and twenty cubits wide. He overlaid the inside with six hundred talents[e] of fine gold. 9The gold nails weighed fifty shekels.[f] He also overlaid the upper parts with gold.

10In the Most Holy Place he made a pair of sculptured cherubim and overlaid them with gold. 11The total wingspan of the cherubim was twenty cubits. One wing of the first cherub was five cubits[g] long and touched the temple wall, while its other wing, also five cubits long, touched the wing of the other cherub. 12Similarly one wing of the second cherub was five cubits long and touched the other temple wall, and its other wing, also five cubits long, touched the wing of the first cherub. 13The wings of these cherubim extended twenty cubits. They stood on their feet, facing the main hall.[h]

14He made the curtain of blue, purple and crimson yarn and fine linen, with cherubim worked into it.

15In the front of the temple he made two pillars, which ⌊together⌋ were

---

a1 Hebrew *Ornan*, a variant of *Araunah*   b3 That is, about 90 feet (about 27 meters) long and 30 feet (about 9 meters) wide   c4 That is, about 30 feet (about 9 meters); also in verses 8, 11 and 13   d4 Some Septuagint and Syriac manuscripts; Hebrew *and a hundred and twenty*
e8 That is, about 23 tons (about 21 metric tons)   f9 That is, about 1 1/4 pounds (about 0.6 kilogram)   g11 That is, about 7 1/2 feet (about 2.3 meters); also in verse 15   h13 Or *facing inward*

thirty-five cubits[a] long, each with a capital on top measuring five cubits. [16]He made interwoven chains[b] and put them on top of the pillars. He also made a hundred pomegranates and attached them to the chains. [17]He erected the pillars in the front of the temple, one to the south and one to the north. The one to the south he named Jakin[c] and the one to the north Boaz.[d]

The Temple's Furnishings

4 He made a bronze altar twenty cubits long, twenty cubits wide and ten cubits high.[e] [2]He made the Sea of cast metal, circular in shape, measuring ten cubits from rim to rim and five cubits[f] high. It took a line of thirty cubits[g] to measure around it. [3]Below the rim, figures of bulls encircled it—ten to a cubit.[h] The bulls were cast in two rows in one piece with the Sea.

[4]The Sea stood on twelve bulls, three facing north, three facing west, three facing south and three facing east. The Sea rested on top of them, and their hindquarters were toward the center. [5]It was a handbreadth[i] in thickness, and its rim was like the rim of a cup, like a lily blossom. It held three thousand baths.[j]

[6]He then made ten basins for washing and placed five on the south side and five on the north. In them the things to be used for the burnt offerings were rinsed, but the Sea was to be used by the priests for washing.

[7]He made ten gold lampstands according to the specifications for them and placed them in the temple, five on the south side and five on the north.

[8]He made ten tables and placed them in the temple, five on the south side and five on the north. He also made a hundred gold sprinkling bowls.

[9]He made the courtyard of the priests, and the large court and the doors for the court, and overlaid the doors with bronze. [10]He placed the Sea on the south side, at the southeast corner.

[11]He also made the pots and shovels and sprinkling bowls.

So Huram finished the work he had undertaken for King Solomon in the temple of God:

[12]the two pillars;
 the two bowl-shaped capitals on top of the pillars;
 the two sets of network decorating the two bowl-shaped capitals on top of the pillars;
[13]the four hundred pomegranates for the two sets of network (two rows of pomegranates for each network, decorating the bowl-shaped capitals on top of the pillars);
[14]the stands with their basins;
[15]the Sea and the twelve bulls under it;
[16]the pots, shovels, meat forks and all related articles.

All the objects that Huram-Abi made for King Solomon for the temple of the LORD were of polished bronze. [17]The king had them cast in clay molds in the plain of the Jordan between Succoth and Zarethan.[k] [18]All these things that Solomon made amounted to so much that the weight of the bronze was not determined.

[19]Solomon also made all the furnishings that were in God's temple:

 the golden altar;
 the tables on which was the bread of the Presence;
[20]the lampstands of pure gold with their lamps, to burn in

---

[a]15 That is, about 52 feet (about 16 meters)   [b]16 Or possibly *made chains in the inner sanctuary*; the meaning of the Hebrew for this phrase is uncertain.   [c]17 *Jakin* probably means *he establishes.*   [d]17 *Boaz* probably means *in him is strength.*   [e]1 That is, about 30 feet (about 9 meters) long and wide, and about 15 feet (about 4.5 meters) high   [f]2 That is, about 7 1/2 feet (about 2.3 meters)   [g]2 That is, about 45 feet (about 13.5 meters)   [h]3 That is, about 1 1/2 feet (about 0.5 meter)   [i]5 That is, about 3 inches (about 8 centimeters)   [j]5 That is, about 17,500 gallons (about 66 kiloliters)   [k]17 Hebrew *Zeredatha*, a variant of *Zarethan*

front of the inner sanctuary as prescribed;
²¹the gold floral work and lamps and tongs (they were solid gold);
²²the pure gold wick trimmers, sprinkling bowls, dishes and censers; and the gold doors of the temple: the inner doors to the Most Holy Place and the doors of the main hall.

5 When all the work Solomon had done for the temple of the LORD was finished, he brought in the things his father David had dedicated—the silver and gold and all the furnishings—and he placed them in the treasuries of God's temple.

The Ark Brought to the Temple

²Then Solomon summoned to Jerusalem the elders of Israel, all the heads of the tribes and the chiefs of the Israelite families, to bring up the ark of the LORD's covenant from Zion, the City of David. ³And all the men of Israel came together to the king at the time of the festival in the seventh month.

⁴When all the elders of Israel had arrived, the Levites took up the ark, ⁵and they brought up the ark and the Tent of Meeting and all the sacred furnishings in it. The priests, who were Levites, carried them up; ⁶and King Solomon and the entire assembly of Israel that had gathered about him were before the ark, sacrificing so many sheep and cattle that they could not be recorded or counted.

⁷The priests then brought the ark of the LORD's covenant to its place in the inner sanctuary of the temple, the Most Holy Place, and put it beneath the wings of the cherubim. ⁸The cherubim spread their wings over the place of the ark and covered the ark and its carrying poles. ⁹These poles were so long that their ends, extending from the ark, could be seen from in front of the inner sanctuary, but not from outside the Holy Place; and they are still there today. ¹⁰There was nothing in the ark except the two tablets that Moses had placed in it at Horeb, where the LORD made a covenant with the Israelites after they came out of Egypt.

¹¹The priests then withdrew from the Holy Place. All the priests who were there had consecrated themselves, regardless of their divisions. ¹²All the Levites who were musicians—Asaph, Heman, Jeduthun and their sons and relatives—stood on the east side of the altar, dressed in fine linen and playing cymbals, harps and lyres. They were accompanied by 120 priests sounding trumpets. ¹³The trumpeters and singers joined in unison, as with one voice, to give praise and thanks to the LORD. Accompanied by trumpets, cymbals and other instruments, they raised their voices in praise to the LORD and sang:

"He is good;
    his love endures forever."

Then the temple of the LORD was filled with a cloud, ¹⁴and the priests could not perform their service because of the cloud, for the glory of the LORD filled the temple of God.

6 Then Solomon said, "The LORD has said that he would dwell in a dark cloud; ²I have built a magnificent temple for you, a place for you to dwell forever."

³While the whole assembly of Israel was standing there, the king turned around and blessed them. ⁴Then he said:

"Praise be to the LORD, the God of Israel, who with his hands has fulfilled what he promised with his mouth to my father David. For he said, ⁵'Since the day I brought my people out of Egypt, I have not chosen a city in any tribe of Israel to have a temple built for my Name to be there, nor have I chosen anyone to be the leader over my people Israel. ⁶But now I have chosen Jerusalem for my Name to be there, and I have chosen David to rule my people Israel.'

⁷"My father David had it in

VERSE:	AUTHOR:	PASSAGE:
2 Chronicles 5:14	Verlyn D. Verbrugge	2 Chronicles 5:2–14

Engulfed in God's Glory

Don't you wish you had been there? Thousands of people press forward when the ark is brought into the temple. Hundreds of professional musicians are ready to sing. The orchestra is huge, the trumpet section alone numbers 120. Conductor Asaph ascends the podium and raises his hand. A mass choir begins to praise the Lord with full gusto. Can you hear it? Israel's "Praise Festival."

What happens then? The glory of the Lord fills the temple. The sanctuary becomes so brilliant that the priests can't even enter it to light the sacrifices. No problem. God does it himself—with fire from heaven (2 Chronicles 7:1).

When God's people put the ark in the center of their worship, they become engulfed in God's glory. When they sing praises for the goodness and love of God, they see his splendor filling the temple.

Wouldn't it be great to see the shining glory of God today? You can! For Jesus is the glory of God in human flesh (John 1:14). Like the ark, he symbolizes God's presence. And you are the temple in which God dwells (Ephesians 2:22).

The more we put Jesus in the center of our lives, the more God makes his glory appear in us. The more we sing about the goodness and love of God, the more radiant our faces become. The more we love other people the way Jesus loves them, the more others will say, "Now I know what the face of God is like."

ADDITIONAL SCRIPTURE READINGS
John 17:20–24; 2 Corinthians 3:7–18

Go to page 538 for your next devotional reading.

his heart to build a temple for the Name of the LORD, the God of Israel. [8]But the LORD said to my father David, 'Because it was in your heart to build a temple for my Name, you did well to have this in your heart. [9]Nevertheless, you are not the one to build the temple, but your son, who is your own flesh and blood—he is the one who will build the temple for my Name.'

[10]"The LORD has kept the promise he made. I have succeeded David my father and now I sit on the throne of Israel, just as the LORD promised, and I have built the temple for the Name of the LORD, the God of Israel. [11]There I have placed the ark, in which is the covenant of the LORD that he made with the people of Israel."

Solomon's Prayer of Dedication

[12]Then Solomon stood before the altar of the LORD in front of the whole assembly of Israel and spread out his hands. [13]Now he had made a bronze platform, five cubits[a] long, five cubits wide and three cubits[b] high, and had placed it in the center of the outer court. He stood on the platform and then knelt down before the whole assembly of Israel and spread out his hands toward heaven. [14]He said:

"O LORD, God of Israel, there is no God like you in heaven or on earth—you who keep your covenant of love with your servants who continue wholeheartedly in your way. [15]You have kept your promise to your servant David my father; with your mouth you have promised and with your hand you have fulfilled it—as it is today.

[16]"Now LORD, God of Israel, keep for your servant David my father the promises you made to

him when you said, 'You shall never fail to have a man to sit before me on the throne of Israel, if only your sons are careful in all they do to walk before me according to my law, as you have done.' [17]And now, O LORD, God of Israel, let your word that you promised your servant David come true.

[18]"But will God really dwell on earth with men? The heavens, even the highest heavens, cannot contain you. How much less this temple I have built! [19]Yet give attention to your servant's prayer and his plea for mercy, O LORD my God. Hear the cry and the prayer that your servant is praying in your presence. [20]May your eyes be open toward this temple day and night, this place of which you said you would put your Name there. May you hear the prayer your servant prays toward this place. [21]Hear the supplications of your servant and of your people Israel when they pray toward this place. Hear from heaven, your dwelling place; and when you hear, forgive.

[22]"When a man wrongs his neighbor and is required to take an oath and he comes and swears the oath before your altar in this temple, [23]then hear from heaven and act. Judge between your servants, repaying the guilty by bringing down on his own head what he has done. Declare the innocent not guilty and so establish his innocence.

[24]"When your people Israel have been defeated by an enemy because they have sinned against you and when they turn back and confess your name, praying and making supplication before you in this temple, [25]then hear

---

[a]13 That is, about 7 1/2 feet (about 2.3 meters) meters)

[b]13 That is, about 4 1/2 feet (about 1.3

from heaven and forgive the sin of your people Israel and bring them back to the land you gave to them and their fathers.

²⁶"When the heavens are shut up and there is no rain because your people have sinned against you, and when they pray toward this place and confess your name and turn from their sin because you have afflicted them, ²⁷then hear from heaven and forgive the sin of your servants, your people Israel. Teach them the right way to live, and send rain on the land you gave your people for an inheritance.

²⁸"When famine or plague comes to the land, or blight or mildew, locusts or grasshoppers, or when enemies besiege them in any of their cities, whatever disaster or disease may come, ²⁹and when a prayer or plea is made by any of your people Israel—each one aware of his afflictions and pains, and spreading out his hands toward this temple— ³⁰then hear from heaven, your dwelling place. Forgive, and deal with each man according to all he does, since you know his heart (for you alone know the hearts of men), ³¹so that they will fear you and walk in your ways all the time they live in the land you gave our fathers.

³²"As for the foreigner who does not belong to your people Israel but has come from a distant land because of your great name and your mighty hand and your outstretched arm—when he comes and prays toward this temple, ³³then hear from heaven, your dwelling place, and do whatever the foreigner asks of you, so that all the peoples of the earth may know your name and fear you, as do your own people Israel, and may know that this house I have built bears your Name.

³⁴"When your people go to war against their enemies, wherever you send them, and when they pray to you toward this city you have chosen and the temple I have built for your Name, ³⁵then hear from heaven their prayer and their plea, and uphold their cause.

³⁶"When they sin against you—for there is no one who does not sin—and you become angry with them and give them over to the enemy, who takes them captive to a land far away or near; ³⁷and if they have a change of heart in the land where they are held captive, and repent and plead with you in the land of their captivity and say, 'We have sinned, we have done wrong and acted wickedly'; ³⁸and if they turn back to you with all their heart and soul in the land of their captivity where they were taken, and pray toward the land you gave their fathers, toward the city you have chosen and toward the temple I have built for your Name; ³⁹then from heaven, your dwelling place, hear their prayer and their pleas, and uphold their cause. And forgive your people, who have sinned against you.

⁴⁰"Now, my God, may your eyes be open and your ears attentive to the prayers offered in this place.

⁴¹"Now arise, O Lord God, and
come to your resting
place,
you and the ark of your
might.
May your priests, O Lord
God, be clothed with
salvation,
may your saints rejoice in
your goodness.
⁴²O Lord God, do not reject
your anointed one.
Remember the great love
promised to David
your servant."

The Dedication of the Temple

7 When Solomon finished praying, fire came down from heaven and consumed the burnt offering and the sacrifices, and the glory of the LORD filled the temple. ²The priests could not enter the temple of the LORD because the glory of the LORD filled it. ³When all the Israelites saw the fire coming down and the glory of the LORD above the temple, they knelt on the pavement with their faces to the ground, and they worshiped and gave thanks to the LORD, saying,

"He is good;
    his love endures forever."

⁴Then the king and all the people offered sacrifices before the LORD. ⁵And King Solomon offered a sacrifice of twenty-two thousand head of cattle and a hundred and twenty thousand sheep and goats. So the king and all the people dedicated the temple of God. ⁶The priests took their positions, as did the Levites with the LORD's musical instruments, which King David had made for praising the LORD and which were used when he gave thanks, saying, "His love endures forever." Opposite the Levites, the priests blew their trumpets, and all the Israelites were standing.

⁷Solomon consecrated the middle part of the courtyard in front of the temple of the LORD, and there he offered burnt offerings and the fat of the fellowship offerings,ᵃ because the bronze altar he had made could not hold the burnt offerings, the grain offerings and the fat portions.

⁸So Solomon observed the festival at that time for seven days, and all Israel with him—a vast assembly, people from Leboᵇ Hamath to the Wadi of Egypt. ⁹On the eighth day they held an assembly, for they had celebrated the dedication of the altar for seven days and the festival for seven days more. ¹⁰On the twenty-third day of the seventh month he sent the people to their homes, joyful and glad in heart for the good things the LORD had done for David and Solomon and for his people Israel.

The LORD Appears to Solomon

¹¹When Solomon had finished the temple of the LORD and the royal palace, and had succeeded in carrying out all he had in mind to do in the temple of the LORD and in his own palace, ¹²the LORD appeared to him at night and said:

"I have heard your prayer and have chosen this place for myself as a temple for sacrifices.

¹³"When I shut up the heavens so that there is no rain, or command locusts to devour the land or send a plague among my people, ¹⁴if my people, who are called by my name, will humble themselves and pray and seek my face and turn from their wicked ways, then will I hear from heaven and will forgive their sin and will heal their land. ¹⁵Now my eyes will be open and my ears attentive to the prayers offered in this place. ¹⁶I have chosen and consecrated this temple so that my Name may be there forever. My eyes and my heart will always be there.

¹⁷"As for you, if you walk before me as David your father did, and do all I command, and observe my decrees and laws, ¹⁸I will establish your royal throne, as I covenanted with David your father when I said, 'You shall never fail to have a man to rule over Israel.'

¹⁹"But if youᶜ turn away and forsake the decrees and commands I have given youᶜ and go off to serve other gods and worship them, ²⁰then I will uproot Israel from my land, which I have given them, and will reject this temple I have consecrated for my Name. I will make it a byword and an object of ridicule

---

ᵃ7 Traditionally *peace offerings*   ᵇ8 Or *from the entrance to*   ᶜ19 The Hebrew is plural.

among all peoples. 21And though this temple is now so imposing, all who pass by will be appalled and say, 'Why has the Lord done such a thing to this land and to this temple?' 22People will answer, 'Because they have forsaken the Lord, the God of their fathers, who brought them out of Egypt, and have embraced other gods, worshiping and serving them—that is why he brought all this disaster on them.' "

Solomon's Other Activities

8 At the end of twenty years, during which Solomon built the temple of the Lord and his own palace, 2Solomon rebuilt the villages that Hiram*a* had given him, and settled Israelites in them. 3Solomon then went to Hamath Zobah and captured it. 4He also built up Tadmor in the desert and all the store cities he had built in Hamath. 5He rebuilt Upper Beth Horon and Lower Beth Horon as fortified cities, with walls and with gates and bars, 6as well as Baalath and all his store cities, and all the cities for his chariots and for his horses*b*—whatever he desired to build in Jerusalem, in Lebanon and throughout all the territory he ruled.

7All the people left from the Hittites, Amorites, Perizzites, Hivites and Jebusites (these peoples were not Israelites), 8that is, their descendants remaining in the land, whom the Israelites had not destroyed—these Solomon conscripted for his slave labor force, as it is to this day. 9But Solomon did not make slaves of the Israelites for his work; they were his fighting men, commanders of his captains, and commanders of his chariots and charioteers. 10They were also King Solomon's chief officials—two hundred and fifty officials supervising the men.

11Solomon brought Pharaoh's daughter up from the City of David to the palace he had built for her, for he said, "My wife must not live in the palace of David king of Israel, because the places the ark of the Lord has entered are holy."

12On the altar of the Lord that he had built in front of the portico, Solomon sacrificed burnt offerings to the Lord, 13according to the daily requirement for offerings commanded by Moses for Sabbaths, New Moons and the three annual feasts—the Feast of Unleavened Bread, the Feast of Weeks and the Feast of Tabernacles. 14In keeping with the ordinance of his father David, he appointed the divisions of the priests for their duties, and the Levites to lead the praise and to assist the priests according to each day's requirement. He also appointed the gatekeepers by divisions for the various gates, because this was what David the man of God had ordered. 15They did not deviate from the king's commands to the priests or to the Levites in any matter, including that of the treasuries.

16All Solomon's work was carried out, from the day the foundation of the temple of the Lord was laid until its completion. So the temple of the Lord was finished.

17Then Solomon went to Ezion Geber and Elath on the coast of Edom. 18And Hiram sent him ships commanded by his own officers, men who knew the sea. These, with Solomon's men, sailed to Ophir and brought back four hundred and fifty talents*c* of gold, which they delivered to King Solomon.

The Queen of Sheba Visits Solomon

9 When the queen of Sheba heard of Solomon's fame, she came to Jerusalem to test him with hard questions. Arriving with a very great caravan—with camels carrying spices, large quantities of gold, and precious stones—she came to Solomon and talked with him about all she had on her mind. 2Solomon answered all her

---

a2 Hebrew *Huram*, a variant of *Hiram*; also in verse 18   *b6* Or *charioteers*   *c18* That is, about 17 tons (about 16 metric tons)

questions; nothing was too hard for him to explain to her. ³When the queen of Sheba saw the wisdom of Solomon, as well as the palace he had built, ⁴the food on his table, the seating of his officials, the attending servants in their robes, the cupbearers in their robes and the burnt offerings he made at^a the temple of the LORD, she was overwhelmed.

⁵She said to the king, "The report I heard in my own country about your achievements and your wisdom is true. ⁶But I did not believe what they said until I came and saw with my own eyes. Indeed, not even half the greatness of your wisdom was told me; you have far exceeded the report I heard. ⁷How happy your men must be! How happy your officials, who continually stand before you and hear your wisdom! ⁸Praise be to the LORD your God, who has delighted in you and placed you on his throne as king to rule for the LORD your God. Because of the love of your God for Israel and his desire to uphold them forever, he has made you king over them, to maintain justice and righteousness."

⁹Then she gave the king 120 talents^b of gold, large quantities of spices, and precious stones. There had never been such spices as those the queen of Sheba gave to King Solomon.

¹⁰(The men of Hiram and the men of Solomon brought gold from Ophir; they also brought algumwood^c and precious stones. ¹¹The king used the algumwood to make steps for the temple of the LORD and for the royal palace, and to make harps and lyres for the musicians. Nothing like them had ever been seen in Judah.)

¹²King Solomon gave the queen of Sheba all she desired and asked for; he gave her more than she had brought to him. Then she left and re-turned with her retinue to her own country.

Solomon's Splendor

¹³The weight of the gold that Solomon received yearly was 666 talents,^{d} ¹⁴not including the revenues brought in by merchants and traders. Also all the kings of Arabia and the governors of the land brought gold and silver to Solomon.

¹⁵King Solomon made two hundred large shields of hammered gold; six hundred bekas^e of hammered gold went into each shield. ¹⁶He also made three hundred small shields of hammered gold, with three hundred bekas^f of gold in each shield. The king put them in the Palace of the Forest of Lebanon.

¹⁷Then the king made a great throne inlaid with ivory and overlaid with pure gold. ¹⁸The throne had six steps, and a footstool of gold was attached to it. On both sides of the seat were armrests, with a lion standing beside each of them. ¹⁹Twelve lions stood on the six steps, one at either end of each step. Nothing like it had ever been made for any other kingdom. ²⁰All King Solomon's goblets were gold, and all the household articles in the Palace of the Forest of Lebanon were pure gold. Nothing was made of silver, because silver was considered of little value in Solomon's day. ²¹The king had a fleet of trading ships^g manned by Hiram's^h men. Once every three years it returned, carrying gold, silver and ivory, and apes and baboons.

²²King Solomon was greater in riches and wisdom than all the other kings of the earth. ²³All the kings of the earth sought audience with Solomon to hear the wisdom God had put in his heart. ²⁴Year after year, everyone who came brought a gift—articles of silver and gold, and robes,

---

^{a}4 Or *the ascent by which he went up to* ^{b}9 That is, about 4 1/2 tons (about 4 metric tons)
^{c}10 Probably a variant of *almugwood* ^{d}13 That is, about 25 tons (about 23 metric tons)
^{e}15 That is, about 7 1/2 pounds (about 3.5 kilograms) ^{f}16 That is, about 3 3/4 pounds (about 1.7 kilograms) ^{g}21 Hebrew *of ships that could go to Tarshish* ^{h}21 Hebrew *Huram,* a variant of *Hiram*

weapons and spices, and horses and mules. ²⁵Solomon had four thousand stalls for horses and chariots, and twelve thousand horses,ᵃ which he kept in the chariot cities and also with him in Jerusalem. ²⁶He ruled over all the kings from the Riverᵇ to the land of the Philistines, as far as the border of Egypt. ²⁷The king made silver as common in Jerusalem as stones, and cedar as plentiful as sycamore-fig trees in the foothills. ²⁸Solomon's horses were imported from Egyptᶜ and from all other countries.

Solomon's Death

²⁹As for the other events of Solomon's reign, from beginning to end, are they not written in the records of Nathan the prophet, in the prophecy of Ahijah the Shilonite and in the visions of Iddo the seer concerning Jeroboam son of Nebat? ³⁰Solomon reigned in Jerusalem over all Israel forty years. ³¹Then he rested with his fathers and was buried in the city of David his father. And Rehoboam his son succeeded him as king.

Israel Rebels Against Rehoboam

10 Rehoboam went to Shechem, for all the Israelites had gone there to make him king. ²When Jeroboam son of Nebat heard this (he was in Egypt, where he had fled from King Solomon), he returned from Egypt. ³So they sent for Jeroboam, and he and all Israel went to Rehoboam and said to him: ⁴"Your father put a heavy yoke on us, but now lighten the harsh labor and the heavy yoke he put on us, and we will serve you."

⁵Rehoboam answered, "Come back to me in three days." So the people went away.

⁶Then King Rehoboam consulted the elders who had served his father Solomon during his lifetime. "How would you advise me to answer these people?" he asked.

⁷They replied, "If you will be kind to these people and please them and give them a favorable answer, they will always be your servants."

⁸But Rehoboam rejected the advice the elders gave him and consulted the young men who had grown up with him and were serving him. ⁹He asked them, "What is your advice? How should we answer these people who say to me, 'Lighten the yoke your father put on us'?"

¹⁰The young men who had grown up with him replied, "Tell the people who have said to you, 'Your father put a heavy yoke on us, but make our yoke lighter'—tell them, 'My little finger is thicker than my father's waist. ¹¹My father laid on you a heavy yoke; I will make it even heavier. My father scourged you with whips; I will scourge you with scorpions.' "

¹²Three days later Jeroboam and all the people returned to Rehoboam, as the king had said, "Come back to me in three days." ¹³The king answered them harshly. Rejecting the advice of the elders, ¹⁴he followed the advice of the young men and said, "My father made your yoke heavy; I will make it even heavier. My father scourged you with whips; I will scourge you with scorpions." ¹⁵So the king did not listen to the people, for this turn of events was from God, to fulfill the word the LORD had spoken to Jeroboam son of Nebat through Ahijah the Shilonite.

¹⁶When all Israel saw that the king refused to listen to them, they answered the king:

"What share do we have in David,
  what part in Jesse's son?
To your tents, O Israel!
  Look after your own house,
    O David!"

So all the Israelites went home. ¹⁷But as for the Israelites who were living in the towns of Judah, Rehoboam still ruled over them.

¹⁸King Rehoboam sent out Adoniram,ᵈ who was in charge of forced

---

ᵃ25 Or charioteers   ᵇ26 That is, the Euphrates   ᶜ28 Or possibly Muzur, a region in Cilicia
ᵈ18 Hebrew Hadoram, a variant of Adoniram

labor, but the Israelites stoned him to death. King Rehoboam, however, managed to get into his chariot and escape to Jerusalem. ¹⁹So Israel has been in rebellion against the house of David to this day.

11 When Rehoboam arrived in Jerusalem, he mustered the house of Judah and Benjamin—a hundred and eighty thousand fighting men—to make war against Israel and to regain the kingdom for Rehoboam.

²But this word of the LORD came to Shemaiah the man of God: ³"Say to Rehoboam son of Solomon king of Judah and to all the Israelites in Judah and Benjamin, ⁴'This is what the LORD says: Do not go up to fight against your brothers. Go home, every one of you, for this is my doing.'" So they obeyed the words of the LORD and turned back from marching against Jeroboam.

Rehoboam Fortifies Judah

⁵Rehoboam lived in Jerusalem and built up towns for defense in Judah: ⁶Bethlehem, Etam, Tekoa, ⁷Beth Zur, Soco, Adullam, ⁸Gath, Mareshah, Ziph, ⁹Adoraim, Lachish, Azekah, ¹⁰Zorah, Aijalon and Hebron. These were fortified cities in Judah and Benjamin. ¹¹He strengthened their defenses and put commanders in them, with supplies of food, olive oil and wine. ¹²He put shields and spears in all the cities, and made them very strong. So Judah and Benjamin were his.

¹³The priests and Levites from all their districts throughout Israel sided with him. ¹⁴The Levites even abandoned their pasturelands and property, and came to Judah and Jerusalem because Jeroboam and his sons had rejected them as priests of the LORD. ¹⁵And he appointed his own priests for the high places and for the goat and calf idols he had made. ¹⁶Those from every tribe of Israel who set their hearts on seeking the LORD, the God of Israel, followed the Levites to Jerusalem to offer sacrifices to the LORD, the God of their fathers. ¹⁷They strengthened the kingdom of Judah and supported Rehoboam son of Solomon three years, walking in the ways of David and Solomon during this time.

Rehoboam's Family

¹⁸Rehoboam married Mahalath, who was the daughter of David's son Jerimoth and of Abihail, the daughter of Jesse's son Eliab. ¹⁹She bore him sons: Jeush, Shemariah and Zaham. ²⁰Then he married Maacah daughter of Absalom, who bore him Abijah, Attai, Ziza and Shelomith. ²¹Rehoboam loved Maacah daughter of Absalom more than any of his other wives and concubines. In all, he had eighteen wives and sixty concubines, twenty-eight sons and sixty daughters.

²²Rehoboam appointed Abijah son of Maacah to be the chief prince among his brothers, in order to make him king. ²³He acted wisely, dispersing some of his sons throughout the districts of Judah and Benjamin, and to all the fortified cities. He gave them abundant provisions and took many wives for them.

Shishak Attacks Jerusalem

12 After Rehoboam's position as king was established and he had become strong, he and all Israel[a] with him abandoned the law of the LORD. ²Because they had been unfaithful to the LORD, Shishak king of Egypt attacked Jerusalem in the fifth year of King Rehoboam. ³With twelve hundred chariots and sixty thousand horsemen and the innumerable troops of Libyans, Sukkites and Cushites[b] that came with him from Egypt, ⁴he captured the fortified cities of Judah and came as far as Jerusalem.

⁵Then the prophet Shemaiah came to Rehoboam and to the leaders of Judah who had assembled in Jerusalem for fear of Shishak, and he said to them, "This is what the LORD says,

a1 That is, Judah, as frequently in 2 Chronicles   b3 That is, people from the upper Nile region

'You have abandoned me; therefore, I now abandon you to Shishak.' "

6The leaders of Israel and the king humbled themselves and said, "The LORD is just."

7When the LORD saw that they humbled themselves, this word of the LORD came to Shemaiah: "Since they have humbled themselves, I will not destroy them but will soon give them deliverance. My wrath will not be poured out on Jerusalem through Shishak. 8They will, however, become subject to him, so that they may learn the difference between serving me and serving the kings of other lands."

9When Shishak king of Egypt attacked Jerusalem, he carried off the treasures of the temple of the LORD and the treasures of the royal palace. He took everything, including the gold shields Solomon had made. 10So King Rehoboam made bronze shields to replace them and assigned these to the commanders of the guard on duty at the entrance to the royal palace. 11Whenever the king went to the LORD's temple, the guards went with him, bearing the shields, and afterward they returned them to the guardroom.

12Because Rehoboam humbled himself, the LORD's anger turned from him, and he was not totally destroyed. Indeed, there was some good in Judah.

13King Rehoboam established himself firmly in Jerusalem and continued as king. He was forty-one years old when he became king, and he reigned seventeen years in Jerusalem, the city the LORD had chosen out of all the tribes of Israel in which to put his Name. His mother's name was Naamah; she was an Ammonite. 14He did evil because he had not set his heart on seeking the LORD.

15As for the events of Rehoboam's reign, from beginning to end, are they not written in the records of Shemaiah the prophet and of Iddo the seer that deal with genealogies? There was

continual warfare between Rehoboam and Jeroboam. 16Rehoboam rested with his fathers and was buried in the City of David. And Abijah his son succeeded him as king.

Abijah King of Judah

13 In the eighteenth year of the reign of Jeroboam, Abijah became king of Judah, 2and he reigned in Jerusalem three years. His mother's name was Maacah,a a daughterb of Uriel of Gibeah.

There was war between Abijah and Jeroboam. 3Abijah went into battle with a force of four hundred thousand able fighting men, and Jeroboam drew up a battle line against him with eight hundred thousand able troops.

4Abijah stood on Mount Zemaraim, in the hill country of Ephraim, and said, "Jeroboam and all Israel, listen to me! 5Don't you know that the LORD, the God of Israel, has given the kingship of Israel to David and his descendants forever by a covenant of salt? 6Yet Jeroboam son of Nebat, an official of Solomon son of David, rebelled against his master. 7Some worthless scoundrels gathered around him and opposed Rehoboam son of Solomon when he was young and indecisive and not strong enough to resist them.

8"And now you plan to resist the kingdom of the LORD, which is in the hands of David's descendants. You are indeed a vast army and have with you the golden calves that Jeroboam made to be your gods. 9But didn't you drive out the priests of the LORD, the sons of Aaron, and the Levites, and make priests of your own as the peoples of other lands do? Whoever comes to consecrate himself with a young bull and seven rams may become a priest of what are not gods.

10"As for us, the LORD is our God, and we have not forsaken him. The priests who serve the LORD are sons of Aaron, and the Levites assist them. 11Every morning and evening they present burnt offerings and fragrant

---

a2 Most Septuagint manuscripts and Syriac (see also 2 Chron. 11:20 and 1 Kings 15:2); Hebrew Micaiah   b2 Or granddaughter

incense to the LORD. They set out the bread on the ceremonially clean table and light the lamps on the gold lampstand every evening. We are observing the requirements of the LORD our God. But you have forsaken him. [12]God is with us; he is our leader. His priests with their trumpets will sound the battle cry against you. Men of Israel, do not fight against the LORD, the God of your fathers, for you will not succeed."

[13]Now Jeroboam had sent troops around to the rear, so that while he was in front of Judah the ambush was behind them. [14]Judah turned and saw that they were being attacked at both front and rear. Then they cried out to the LORD. The priests blew their trumpets [15]and the men of Judah raised the battle cry. At the sound of their battle cry, God routed Jeroboam and all Israel before Abijah and Judah. [16]The Israelites fled before Judah, and God delivered them into their hands. [17]Abijah and his men inflicted heavy losses on them, so that there were five hundred thousand casualties among Israel's able men. [18]The men of Israel were subdued on that occasion, and the men of Judah were victorious because they relied on the LORD, the God of their fathers.

[19]Abijah pursued Jeroboam and took from him the towns of Bethel, Jeshanah and Ephron, with their surrounding villages. [20]Jeroboam did not regain power during the time of Abijah. And the LORD struck him down and he died.

[21]But Abijah grew in strength. He married fourteen wives and had twenty-two sons and sixteen daughters.

[22]The other events of Abijah's reign, what he did and what he said, are written in the annotations of the prophet Iddo.

14 And Abijah rested with his fathers and was buried in the City of David. Asa his son succeeded him as king, and in his days the country was at peace for ten years.

Asa King of Judah

[2]Asa did what was good and right in the eyes of the LORD his God. [3]He removed the foreign altars and the high places, smashed the sacred stones and cut down the Asherah poles.[a] [4]He commanded Judah to seek the LORD, the God of their fathers, and to obey his laws and commands. [5]He removed the high places and incense altars in every town in Judah, and the kingdom was at peace under him. [6]He built up the fortified cities of Judah, since the land was at peace. No one was at war with him during those years, for the LORD gave him rest.

[7]"Let us build up these towns," he said to Judah, "and put walls around them, with towers, gates and bars. The land is still ours, because we have sought the LORD our God; we sought him and he has given us rest on every side." So they built and prospered.

[8]Asa had an army of three hundred thousand men from Judah, equipped with large shields and with spears, and two hundred and eighty thousand from Benjamin, armed with small shields and with bows. All these were brave fighting men.

[9]Zerah the Cushite marched out against them with a vast army[b] and three hundred chariots, and came as far as Mareshah. [10]Asa went out to meet him, and they took up battle positions in the Valley of Zephathah near Mareshah.

[11]Then Asa called to the LORD his God and said, "LORD, there is no one like you to help the powerless against the mighty. Help us, O LORD our God, for we rely on you, and in your name we have come against this vast army. O LORD, you are our God; do not let man prevail against you."

[12]The LORD struck down the Cushites before Asa and Judah. The Cushites fled, [13]and Asa and his army pur-

---

[a]3 That is, symbols of the goddess Asherah; here and elsewhere in 2 Chronicles   [b]9 Hebrew *with an army of a thousand thousands* or *with an army of thousands upon thousands*

sued them as far as Gerar. Such a great number of Cushites fell that they could not recover; they were crushed before the Lord and his forces. The men of Judah carried off a large amount of plunder. ¹⁴They destroyed all the villages around Gerar, for the terror of the Lord had fallen upon them. They plundered all these villages, since there was much booty there. ¹⁵They also attacked the camps of the herdsmen and carried off droves of sheep and goats and camels. Then they returned to Jerusalem.

Asa's Reform

15 The Spirit of God came upon Azariah son of Oded. ²He went out to meet Asa and said to him, "Listen to me, Asa and all Judah and Benjamin. The Lord is with you when you are with him. If you seek him, he will be found by you, but if you forsake him, he will forsake you. ³For a long time Israel was without the true God, without a priest to teach and without the law. ⁴But in their distress they turned to the Lord, the God of Israel, and sought him, and he was found by them. ⁵In those days it was not safe to travel about, for all the inhabitants of the lands were in great turmoil. ⁶One nation was being crushed by another and one city by another, because God was troubling them with every kind of distress. ⁷But as for you, be strong and do not give up, for your work will be rewarded."

⁸When Asa heard these words and the prophecy of Azariah son of[a] Oded the prophet, he took courage. He removed the detestable idols from the whole land of Judah and Benjamin and from the towns he had captured in the hills of Ephraim. He repaired the altar of the Lord that was in front of the portico of the Lord's temple.

⁹Then he assembled all Judah and Benjamin and the people from Ephraim, Manasseh and Simeon who had settled among them, for large numbers had come over to him from Israel when they saw that the Lord his God was with him.

¹⁰They assembled at Jerusalem in the third month of the fifteenth year of Asa's reign. ¹¹At that time they sacrificed to the Lord seven hundred head of cattle and seven thousand sheep and goats from the plunder they had brought back. ¹²They entered into a covenant to seek the Lord, the God of their fathers, with all their heart and soul. ¹³All who would not seek the Lord, the God of Israel, were to be put to death, whether small or great, man or woman. ¹⁴They took an oath to the Lord with loud acclamation, with shouting and with trumpets and horns. ¹⁵All Judah rejoiced about the oath because they had sworn it wholeheartedly. They sought God eagerly, and he was found by them. So the Lord gave them rest on every side.

¹⁶King Asa also deposed his grandmother Maacah from her position as queen mother, because she had made a repulsive Asherah pole. Asa cut the pole down, broke it up and burned it in the Kidron Valley. ¹⁷Although he did not remove the high places from Israel, Asa's heart was fully committed ⌊to the Lord⌋ all his life. ¹⁸He brought into the temple of God the silver and gold and the articles that he and his father had dedicated.

¹⁹There was no more war until the thirty-fifth year of Asa's reign.

Asa's Last Years

16 In the thirty-sixth year of Asa's reign Baasha king of Israel went up against Judah and fortified Ramah to prevent anyone from leaving or entering the territory of Asa king of Judah.

²Asa then took the silver and gold out of the treasuries of the Lord's temple and of his own palace and sent it to Ben-Hadad king of Aram, who was ruling in Damascus. ³"Let there be a treaty between me and you," he said, "as there was between my father and your father. See, I am sending you sil-

---

a 8 Vulgate and Syriac (see also Septuagint and verse 1); Hebrew does not have *Azariah son of.*

ver and gold. Now break your treaty with Baasha king of Israel so he will withdraw from me."

⁴Ben-Hadad agreed with King Asa and sent the commanders of his forces against the towns of Israel. They conquered Ijon, Dan, Abel Maim*ᵃ* and all the store cities of Naphtali. ⁵When Baasha heard this, he stopped building Ramah and abandoned his work. ⁶Then King Asa brought all the men of Judah, and they carried away from Ramah the stones and timber Baasha had been using. With them he built up Geba and Mizpah.

⁷At that time Hanani the seer came to Asa king of Judah and said to him: "Because you relied on the king of Aram and not on the LORD your God, the army of the king of Aram has escaped from your hand. ⁸Were not the Cushites*ᵇ* and Libyans a mighty army with great numbers of chariots and horsemen*ᶜ*? Yet when you relied on the LORD, he delivered them into your hand. ⁹For the eyes of the LORD range throughout the earth to strengthen those whose hearts are fully committed to him. You have done a foolish thing, and from now on you will be at war."

¹⁰Asa was angry with the seer because of this; he was so enraged that he put him in prison. At the same time Asa brutally oppressed some of the people.

¹¹The events of Asa's reign, from beginning to end, are written in the book of the kings of Judah and Israel. ¹²In the thirty-ninth year of his reign Asa was afflicted with a disease in his feet. Though his disease was severe, even in his illness he did not seek help from the LORD, but only from the physicians. ¹³Then in the forty-first year of his reign Asa died and rested with his fathers. ¹⁴They buried him in the tomb that he had cut out for himself in the City of David. They laid him on a bier covered with spices and various blended perfumes, and they made a huge fire in his honor.

Jehoshaphat King of Judah

17 Jehoshaphat his son succeeded him as king and strengthened himself against Israel. ²He stationed troops in all the fortified cities of Judah and put garrisons in Judah and in the towns of Ephraim that his father Asa had captured.

³The LORD was with Jehoshaphat because in his early years he walked in the ways his father David had followed. He did not consult the Baals ⁴but sought the God of his father and followed his commands rather than the practices of Israel. ⁵The LORD established the kingdom under his control; and all Judah brought gifts to Jehoshaphat, so that he had great wealth and honor. ⁶His heart was devoted to the ways of the LORD; furthermore, he removed the high places and the Asherah poles from Judah.

⁷In the third year of his reign he sent his officials Ben-Hail, Obadiah, Zechariah, Nethanel and Micaiah to teach in the towns of Judah. ⁸With them were certain Levites—Shemaiah, Nethaniah, Zebadiah, Asahel, Shemiramoth, Jehonathan, Adonijah, Tobijah and Tob-Adonijah—and the priests Elishama and Jehoram. ⁹They taught throughout Judah, taking with them the Book of the Law of the LORD; they went around to all the towns of Judah and taught the people.

¹⁰The fear of the LORD fell on all the kingdoms of the lands surrounding Judah, so that they did not make war with Jehoshaphat. ¹¹Some Philistines brought Jehoshaphat gifts and silver as tribute, and the Arabs brought him flocks: seven thousand seven hundred rams and seven thousand seven hundred goats.

¹²Jehoshaphat became more and more powerful; he built forts and store cities in Judah ¹³and had large supplies in the towns of Judah. He also kept experienced fighting men in Jerusalem. ¹⁴Their enrollment by families was as follows:

ᵃ4 Also known as *Abel Beth Maacah* *ᵇ8* That is, people from the upper Nile region *ᶜ8* Or *charioteers*

From Judah, commanders of units of 1,000:

Adnah the commander, with 300,000 fighting men;

[15]next, Jehohanan the commander, with 280,000;

[16]next, Amasiah son of Zicri, who volunteered himself for the service of the LORD, with 200,000.

[17]From Benjamin:

Eliada, a valiant soldier, with 200,000 men armed with bows and shields;

[18]next, Jehozabad, with 180,000 men armed for battle.

[19]These were the men who served the king, besides those he stationed in the fortified cities throughout Judah.

Micaiah Prophesies Against Ahab

18 Now Jehoshaphat had great wealth and honor, and he allied himself with Ahab by marriage. [2]Some years later he went down to visit Ahab in Samaria. Ahab slaughtered many sheep and cattle for him and the people with him and urged him to attack Ramoth Gilead. [3]Ahab king of Israel asked Jehoshaphat king of Judah, "Will you go with me against Ramoth Gilead?"

Jehoshaphat replied, "I am as you are, and my people as your people; we will join you in the war." [4]But Jehoshaphat also said to the king of Israel, "First seek the counsel of the LORD."

[5]So the king of Israel brought together the prophets—four hundred men—and asked them, "Shall we go to war against Ramoth Gilead, or shall I refrain?"

"Go," they answered, "for God will give it into the king's hand."

[6]But Jehoshaphat asked, "Is there not a prophet of the LORD here whom we can inquire of?"

[7]The king of Israel answered Jehoshaphat, "There is still one man through whom we can inquire of the LORD, but I hate him because he never prophesies anything good about me, but always bad. He is Micaiah son of Imlah."

"The king should not say that," Jehoshaphat replied.

[8]So the king of Israel called one of his officials and said, "Bring Micaiah son of Imlah at once."

[9]Dressed in their royal robes, the king of Israel and Jehoshaphat king of Judah were sitting on their thrones at the threshing floor by the entrance to the gate of Samaria, with all the prophets prophesying before them. [10]Now Zedekiah son of Kenaanah had made iron horns, and he declared, "This is what the LORD says: 'With these you will gore the Arameans until they are destroyed.'"

[11]All the other prophets were prophesying the same thing. "Attack Ramoth Gilead and be victorious," they said, "for the LORD will give it into the king's hand."

[12]The messenger who had gone to summon Micaiah said to him, "Look, as one man the other prophets are predicting success for the king. Let your word agree with theirs, and speak favorably."

[13]But Micaiah said, "As surely as the LORD lives, I can tell him only what my God says."

[14]When he arrived, the king asked him, "Micaiah, shall we go to war against Ramoth Gilead, or shall I refrain?"

"Attack and be victorious," he answered, "for they will be given into your hand."

[15]The king said to him, "How many times must I make you swear to tell me nothing but the truth in the name of the LORD?"

[16]Then Micaiah answered, "I saw all Israel scattered on the hills like sheep without a shepherd, and the LORD said, 'These people have no master. Let each one go home in peace.'"

[17]The king of Israel said to Jehoshaphat, "Didn't I tell you that he never prophesies anything good about me, but only bad?"

[18]Micaiah continued, "Therefore hear the word of the LORD: I saw the LORD sitting on his throne with all the

host of heaven standing on his right and on his left. ¹⁹And the LORD said, 'Who will entice Ahab king of Israel into attacking Ramoth Gilead and going to his death there?'

"One suggested this, and another that. ²⁰Finally, a spirit came forward, stood before the LORD and said, 'I will entice him.'

" 'By what means?' the LORD asked.

²¹" 'I will go and be a lying spirit in the mouths of all his prophets,' he said.

" 'You will succeed in enticing him,' said the LORD. 'Go and do it.'

²²"So now the LORD has put a lying spirit in the mouths of these prophets of yours. The LORD has decreed disaster for you."

²³Then Zedekiah son of Kenaanah went up and slapped Micaiah in the face. "Which way did the spirit from*ᵃ* the LORD go when he went from me to speak to you?" he asked.

²⁴Micaiah replied, "You will find out on the day you go to hide in an inner room."

²⁵The king of Israel then ordered, "Take Micaiah and send him back to Amon the ruler of the city and to Joash the king's son, ²⁶and say, 'This is what the king says: Put this fellow in prison and give him nothing but bread and water until I return safely.' "

²⁷Micaiah declared, "If you ever return safely, the LORD has not spoken through me." Then he added, "Mark my words, all you people!"

Ahab Killed at Ramoth Gilead

²⁸So the king of Israel and Jehoshaphat king of Judah went up to Ramoth Gilead. ²⁹The king of Israel said to Jehoshaphat, "I will enter the battle in disguise, but you wear your royal robes." So the king of Israel disguised himself and went into battle.

³⁰Now the king of Aram had ordered his chariot commanders, "Do not fight with anyone, small or great, except the king of Israel." ³¹When the chariot commanders saw Jehosha-

phat, they thought, "This is the king of Israel." So they turned to attack him, but Jehoshaphat cried out, and the LORD helped him. God drew them away from him, ³²for when the chariot commanders saw that he was not the king of Israel, they stopped pursuing him.

³³But someone drew his bow at random and hit the king of Israel between the sections of his armor. The king told the chariot driver, "Wheel around and get me out of the fighting. I've been wounded." ³⁴All day long the battle raged, and the king of Israel propped himself up in his chariot facing the Arameans until evening. Then at sunset he died.

19 When Jehoshaphat king of Judah returned safely to his palace in Jerusalem, ²Jehu the seer, the son of Hanani, went out to meet him and said to the king, "Should you help the wicked and love*ᵇ* those who hate the LORD? Because of this, the wrath of the LORD is upon you. ³There is, however, some good in you, for you have rid the land of the Asherah poles and have set your heart on seeking God."

Jehoshaphat Appoints Judges

⁴Jehoshaphat lived in Jerusalem, and he went out again among the people from Beersheba to the hill country of Ephraim and turned them back to the LORD, the God of their fathers. ⁵He appointed judges in the land, in each of the fortified cities of Judah. ⁶He told them, "Consider carefully what you do, because you are not judging for man but for the LORD, who is with you whenever you give a verdict. ⁷Now let the fear of the LORD be upon you. Judge carefully, for with the LORD our God there is no injustice or partiality or bribery."

⁸In Jerusalem also, Jehoshaphat appointed some of the Levites, priests and heads of Israelite families to administer the law of the LORD and to settle disputes. And they lived in Jerusalem. ⁹He gave them these orders:

ᵃ23 Or *Spirit of*   *ᵇ2* Or *and make alliances with*

"You must serve faithfully and wholeheartedly in the fear of the LORD. ¹⁰In every case that comes before you from your fellow countrymen who live in the cities—whether bloodshed or other concerns of the law, commands, decrees or ordinances—you are to warn them not to sin against the LORD; otherwise his wrath will come on you and your brothers. Do this, and you will not sin.

¹¹"Amariah the chief priest will be over you in any matter concerning the LORD, and Zebadiah son of Ishmael, the leader of the tribe of Judah, will be over you in any matter concerning the king, and the Levites will serve as officials before you. Act with courage, and may the LORD be with those who do well."

Jehoshaphat Defeats Moab and Ammon

20 After this, the Moabites and Ammonites with some of the Meunites[a] came to make war on Jehoshaphat.

²Some men came and told Jehoshaphat, "A vast army is coming against you from Edom,[b] from the other side of the Sea.[c] It is already in Hazazon Tamar" (that is, En Gedi). ³Alarmed, Jehoshaphat resolved to inquire of the LORD, and he proclaimed a fast for all Judah. ⁴The people of Judah came together to seek help from the LORD; indeed, they came from every town in Judah to seek him.

⁵Then Jehoshaphat stood up in the assembly of Judah and Jerusalem at the temple of the LORD in the front of the new courtyard ⁶and said:

"O LORD, God of our fathers, are you not the God who is in heaven? You rule over all the kingdoms of the nations. Power and might are in your hand, and no one can withstand you. ⁷O our God, did you not drive out the inhabitants of this land

before your people Israel and give it forever to the descendants of Abraham your friend? ⁸They have lived in it and have built in it a sanctuary for your Name, saying, ⁹'If calamity comes upon us, whether the sword of judgment, or plague or famine, we will stand in your presence before this temple that bears your Name and will cry out to you in our distress, and you will hear us and save us.'

¹⁰"But now here are men from Ammon, Moab and Mount Seir, whose territory you would not allow Israel to invade when they came from Egypt; so they turned away from them and did not destroy them. ¹¹See how they are repaying us by coming to drive us out of the possession you gave us as an inheritance. ¹²O our God, will you not judge them? For we have no power to face this vast army that is attacking us. We do not know what to do, but our eyes are upon you."

¹³All the men of Judah, with their wives and children and little ones, stood there before the LORD.

¹⁴Then the Spirit of the LORD came upon Jahaziel son of Zechariah, the son of Benaiah, the son of Jeiel, the son of Mattaniah, a Levite and descendant of Asaph, as he stood in the assembly.

¹⁵He said: "Listen, King Jehoshaphat and all who live in Judah and Jerusalem! This is what the LORD says to you: 'Do not be afraid or discouraged because of this vast army. For the battle is not yours, but God's. ¹⁶Tomorrow march down against them. They will be climbing up by the Pass of Ziz, and you will find them at the end of the gorge in the Desert of Jeruel. ¹⁷You will not have to fight this battle. Take up your positions; stand firm and see the deliverance the LORD will give you, O Judah and Jerusalem.

---

a1 Some Septuagint manuscripts; Hebrew Ammonites   *b2 One Hebrew manuscript; most*
Hebrew manuscripts, Septuagint and Vulgate *Aram*   *c2 That is, the Dead Sea*

Do not be afraid; do not be discouraged. Go out to face them tomorrow, and the LORD will be with you.' "
[18]Jehoshaphat bowed with his face to the ground, and all the people of Judah and Jerusalem fell down in worship before the LORD. [19]Then some Levites from the Kohathites and Korahites stood up and praised the LORD, the God of Israel, with very loud voice.

[20]Early in the morning they left for the Desert of Tekoa. As they set out, Jehoshaphat stood and said, "Listen to me, Judah and people of Jerusalem! Have faith in the LORD your God and you will be upheld; have faith in his prophets and you will be successful." [21]After consulting the people, Jehoshaphat appointed men to sing to the LORD and to praise him for the splendor of his[a] holiness as they went out at the head of the army, saying:

"Give thanks to the LORD,
    for his love endures forever."

[22]As they began to sing and praise, the LORD set ambushes against the men of Ammon and Moab and Mount Seir who were invading Judah, and they were defeated. [23]The men of Ammon and Moab rose up against the men from Mount Seir to destroy and annihilate them. After they finished slaughtering the men from Seir, they helped to destroy one another.

[24]When the men of Judah came to the place that overlooks the desert and looked toward the vast army, they saw only dead bodies lying on the ground; no one had escaped. [25]So Jehoshaphat and his men went to carry off their plunder, and they found among them a great amount of equipment and clothing[b] and also articles of value—more than they could take away. There was so much plunder that it took three days to collect it. [26]On the fourth day they assembled in the Valley of Beracah, where they praised the LORD. This is why it is called the Valley of Beracah[c] to this day.

[27]Then, led by Jehoshaphat, all the men of Judah and Jerusalem returned joyfully to Jerusalem, for the LORD had given them cause to rejoice over their enemies. [28]They entered Jerusalem and went to the temple of the LORD with harps and lutes and trumpets.

[29]The fear of God came upon all the kingdoms of the countries when they heard how the LORD had fought against the enemies of Israel. [30]And the kingdom of Jehoshaphat was at peace, for his God had given him rest on every side.

The End of Jehoshaphat's Reign

[31]So Jehoshaphat reigned over Judah. He was thirty-five years old when he became king of Judah, and he reigned in Jerusalem twenty-five years. His mother's name was Azubah daughter of Shilhi. [32]He walked in the ways of his father Asa and did not stray from them; he did what was right in the eyes of the LORD. [33]The high places, however, were not removed, and the people still had not set their hearts on the God of their fathers.

[34]The other events of Jehoshaphat's reign, from beginning to end, are written in the annals of Jehu son of Hanani, which are recorded in the book of the kings of Israel.

[35]Later, Jehoshaphat king of Judah made an alliance with Ahaziah king of Israel, who was guilty of wickedness. [36]He agreed with him to construct a fleet of trading ships.[d] After these were built at Ezion Geber, [37]Eliezer son of Dodavahu of Mareshah prophesied against Jehoshaphat, saying, "Because you have made an alliance with Ahaziah, the LORD will destroy what you have made." The ships were wrecked and were not able to set sail to trade.[e]

21 Then Jehoshaphat rested with his fathers and was buried

---

[a]21 Or *him with the splendor of*   [b]25 Some Hebrew manuscripts and Vulgate; most Hebrew manuscripts *corpses*   [c]26 *Beracah* means *praise.*   [d]36 Hebrew *of ships that could go to Tarshish*
[e]37 Hebrew *sail for Tarshish*

with them in the City of David. And Jehoram his son succeeded him as king. ²Jehoram's brothers, the sons of Jehoshaphat, were Azariah, Jehiel, Zechariah, Azariahu, Michael and Shephatiah. All these were sons of Jehoshaphat king of Israel.ᵃ ³Their father had given them many gifts of sil-

ver and gold and articles of value, as well as fortified cities in Judah, but he had given the kingdom to Jehoram because he was his firstborn son.

Jehoram King of Judah

⁴When Jehoram established himself firmly over his father's kingdom, he

ᵃ2 That is, Judah, as frequently in 2 Chronicles

VERSE:	AUTHOR:	PASSAGE:
2 Chronicles 20:22	Mrs. Charles E. Cowman	2 Chronicles 20:15–23

The Power of Praise

Oh, that we could reason less about our troubles, and sing and praise more! There are thousands of things that we wear as shackles which we might use as instruments with music in them, if we only knew how.

Those people who ponder, and meditate, and weigh the affairs of life, and study the mysterious developments of God's providence, and wonder why they should be burdened and thwarted and hampered—how different and how much more joyful would be their lives, if, instead of forever indulging in self-revolving and inward thinking, they would take their experiences, day by day, and lift them up and praise God for them.

We can sing our cares away easier than we can reason them away. Sing in the morning. The birds are the earliest to sing, and birds are more without care than anything else that I know of. Sing at evening. Singing is the last thing that robins do. When they have done their daily work, when they have flown their last flight and picked up their last morsel of food, then on a topmost twig, they sing one song of praise.

ADDITIONAL SCRIPTURE READINGS
Psalm 147:1–11; Ephesians 5:15–20
Go to page 549 for your next devotional reading.

put all his brothers to the sword along with some of the princes of Israel. ⁵Jehoram was thirty-two years old when he became king, and he reigned in Jerusalem eight years. ⁶He walked in the ways of the kings of Israel, as the house of Ahab had done, for he married a daughter of Ahab. He did evil in the eyes of the LORD. ⁷Nevertheless, because of the covenant the LORD had made with David, the LORD was not willing to destroy the house of David. He had promised to maintain a lamp for him and his descendants forever.

⁸In the time of Jehoram, Edom rebelled against Judah and set up its own king. ⁹So Jehoram went there with his officers and all his chariots. The Edomites surrounded him and his chariot commanders, but he rose up and broke through by night. ¹⁰To this day Edom has been in rebellion against Judah.

Libnah revolted at the same time, because Jehoram had forsaken the LORD, the God of his fathers. ¹¹He had also built high places on the hills of Judah and had caused the people of Jerusalem to prostitute themselves and had led Judah astray.

¹²Jehoram received a letter from Elijah the prophet, which said:

"This is what the LORD, the God of your father David, says: 'You have not walked in the ways of your father Jehoshaphat or of Asa king of Judah. ¹³But you have walked in the ways of the kings of Israel, and you have led Judah and the people of Jerusalem to prostitute themselves, just as the house of Ahab did. You have also murdered your own brothers, members of your father's house, men who were better than you. ¹⁴So now the LORD is about to strike your people, your sons, your wives and everything that is yours, with a heavy blow. ¹⁵You yourself will be very ill with a lingering disease of the bowels, until the disease causes your bowels to come out.' "

¹⁶The LORD aroused against Jehoram the hostility of the Philistines and of the Arabs who lived near the Cushites. ¹⁷They attacked Judah, invaded it and carried off all the goods found in the king's palace, together with his sons and wives. Not a son was left to him except Ahaziah,ᵃ the youngest.

¹⁸After all this, the LORD afflicted Jehoram with an incurable disease of the bowels. ¹⁹In the course of time, at the end of the second year, his bowels came out because of the disease, and he died in great pain. His people made no fire in his honor, as they had for his fathers.

²⁰Jehoram was thirty-two years old when he became king, and he reigned in Jerusalem eight years. He passed away, to no one's regret, and was buried in the City of David, but not in the tombs of the kings.

Ahaziah King of Judah

22 The people of Jerusalem made Ahaziah, Jehoram's youngest son, king in his place, since the raiders, who came with the Arabs into the camp, had killed all the older sons. So Ahaziah son of Jehoram king of Judah began to reign.

²Ahaziah was twenty-twoᵇ years old when he became king, and he reigned in Jerusalem one year. His mother's name was Athaliah, a granddaughter of Omri.

³He too walked in the ways of the house of Ahab, for his mother encouraged him in doing wrong. ⁴He did evil in the eyes of the LORD, as the house of Ahab had done, for after his father's death they became his advisers, to his undoing. ⁵He also followed their counsel when he went with Joramᶜ son of Ahab king of Israel to war against Hazael king of Aram at Ramoth Gilead. The Arameans wounded Joram; ⁶so he returned to

---

ᵃ17 Hebrew *Jehoahaz*, a variant of *Ahaziah* (see also 2 Kings 8:26); Hebrew *forty-two*   ᵇ2 Some Septuagint manuscripts and Syriac (see   ᶜ5 Hebrew *Jehoram*, a variant of *Joram*; also in verses 6 and 7

Jezreel to recover from the wounds they had inflicted on him at Ramoth[a] in his battle with Hazael king of Aram.

Then Ahaziah[b] son of Jehoram king of Judah went down to Jezreel to see Joram son of Ahab because he had been wounded.

⁷Through Ahaziah's visit to Joram, God brought about Ahaziah's downfall. When Ahaziah arrived, he went out with Joram to meet Jehu son of Nimshi, whom the Lord had anointed to destroy the house of Ahab. ⁸While Jehu was executing judgment on the house of Ahab, he found the princes of Judah and the sons of Ahaziah's relatives, who had been attending Ahaziah, and he killed them. ⁹He then went in search of Ahaziah, and his men captured him while he was hiding in Samaria. He was brought to Jehu and put to death. They buried him, for they said, "He was a son of Jehoshaphat, who sought the Lord with all his heart." So there was no one in the house of Ahaziah powerful enough to retain the kingdom.

Athaliah and Joash

¹⁰When Athaliah the mother of Ahaziah saw that her son was dead, she proceeded to destroy the whole royal family of the house of Judah. ¹¹But Jehosheba,[c] the daughter of King Jehoram, took Joash son of Ahaziah and stole him away from among the royal princes who were about to be murdered and put him and his nurse in a bedroom. Because Jehosheba,[c] the daughter of King Jehoram and wife of the priest Jehoiada, was Ahaziah's sister, she hid the child from Athaliah so she could not kill him. ¹²He remained hidden with them at the temple of God for six years while Athaliah ruled the land.

23 In the seventh year Jehoiada showed his strength. He made a covenant with the commanders of units of a hundred: Azariah son of Jeroham, Ishmael son of Jehohanan, Azariah son of Obed, Maaseiah son of Adaiah, and Elishaphat son of Zicri. ²They went throughout Judah and gathered the Levites and the heads of Israelite families from all the towns. When they came to Jerusalem, ³the whole assembly made a covenant with the king at the temple of God.

Jehoiada said to them, "The king's son shall reign, as the Lord promised concerning the descendants of David. ⁴Now this is what you are to do: A third of you priests and Levites who are going on duty on the Sabbath are to keep watch at the doors, ⁵a third of you at the royal palace and a third at the Foundation Gate, and all the other men are to be in the courtyards of the temple of the Lord. ⁶No one is to enter the temple of the Lord except the priests and Levites on duty; they may enter because they are consecrated, but all the other men are to guard what the Lord has assigned to them.[d] ⁷The Levites are to station themselves around the king, each man with his weapons in his hand. Anyone who enters the temple must be put to death. Stay close to the king wherever he goes."

⁸The Levites and all the men of Judah did just as Jehoiada the priest ordered. Each one took his men—those who were going on duty on the Sabbath and those who were going off duty—for Jehoiada the priest had not released any of the divisions. ⁹Then he gave the commanders of units of a hundred the spears and the large and small shields that had belonged to King David and that were in the temple of God. ¹⁰He stationed all the men, each with his weapon in his hand, around the king—near the altar and the temple, from the south side to the north side of the temple.

¹¹Jehoiada and his sons brought out the king's son and put the crown on him; they presented him with a copy of the covenant and proclaimed him

king. They anointed him and shouted, "Long live the king!"

¹²When Athaliah heard the noise of the people running and cheering the king, she went to them at the temple of the LORD. ¹³She looked, and there was the king, standing by his pillar at the entrance. The officers and the trumpeters were beside the king, and all the people of the land were rejoicing and blowing trumpets, and singers with musical instruments were leading the praises. Then Athaliah tore her robes and shouted, "Treason! Treason!"

¹⁴Jehoiada the priest sent out the commanders of units of a hundred, who were in charge of the troops, and said to them: "Bring her out between the ranks*a* and put to the sword anyone who follows her." For the priest had said, "Do not put her to death at the temple of the LORD." ¹⁵So they seized her as she reached the entrance of the Horse Gate on the palace grounds, and there they put her to death.

¹⁶Jehoiada then made a covenant that he and the people and the king*b* would be the LORD's people. ¹⁷All the people went to the temple of Baal and tore it down. They smashed the altars and idols and killed Mattan the priest of Baal in front of the altars.

¹⁸Then Jehoiada placed the oversight of the temple of the LORD in the hands of the priests, who were Levites, to whom David had made assignments in the temple, to present the burnt offerings of the LORD as written in the Law of Moses, with rejoicing and singing, as David had ordered. ¹⁹He also stationed doorkeepers at the gates of the LORD's temple so that no one who was in any way unclean might enter.

²⁰He took with him the commanders of hundreds, the nobles, the rulers of the people and all the people of the land and brought the king down from the temple of the LORD. They went into the palace through the Upper Gate and seated the king on the royal throne, ²¹and all the people of the land rejoiced. And the city was quiet, because Athaliah had been slain with the sword.

Joash Repairs the Temple

24 Joash was seven years old when he became king, and he reigned in Jerusalem forty years. His mother's name was Zibiah; she was from Beersheba. ²Joash did what was right in the eyes of the LORD all the years of Jehoiada the priest. ³Jehoiada chose two wives for him, and he had sons and daughters.

⁴Some time later Joash decided to restore the temple of the LORD. ⁵He called together the priests and Levites and said to them, "Go to the towns of Judah and collect the money due annually from all Israel, to repair the temple of your God. Do it now." But the Levites did not act at once.

⁶Therefore the king summoned Jehoiada the chief priest and said to him, "Why haven't you required the Levites to bring in from Judah and Jerusalem the tax imposed by Moses the servant of the LORD and by the assembly of Israel for the Tent of the Testimony?"

⁷Now the sons of that wicked woman Athaliah had broken into the temple of God and had used even its sacred objects for the Baals.

⁸At the king's command, a chest was made and placed outside, at the gate of the temple of the LORD. ⁹A proclamation was then issued in Judah and Jerusalem that they should bring to the LORD the tax that Moses the servant of God had required of Israel in the desert. ¹⁰All the officials and all the people brought their contributions gladly, dropping them into the chest until it was full. ¹¹Whenever the chest was brought in by the Levites to the king's officials and they saw that there was a large amount of money, the royal secretary and the officer of the chief priest would come

---

a14 Or *out from the precincts they* (see 2 Kings 11:17)   *b16* Or *covenant between ⌞the LORD⌟ and the people and the king that*

and empty the chest and carry it back to its place. They did this regularly and collected a great amount of money. ¹²The king and Jehoiada gave it to the men who carried out the work required for the temple of the LORD. They hired masons and carpenters to restore the LORD's temple, and also workers in iron and bronze to repair the temple.

¹³The men in charge of the work were diligent, and the repairs progressed under them. They rebuilt the temple of God according to its original design and reinforced it. ¹⁴When they had finished, they brought the rest of the money to the king and Jehoiada, and with it were made articles for the LORD's temple: articles for the service and for the burnt offerings, and also dishes and other objects of gold and silver. As long as Jehoiada lived, burnt offerings were presented continually in the temple of the LORD.

¹⁵Now Jehoiada was old and full of years, and he died at the age of a hundred and thirty. ¹⁶He was buried with the kings in the City of David, because of the good he had done in Israel for God and his temple.

The Wickedness of Joash

¹⁷After the death of Jehoiada, the officials of Judah came and paid homage to the king, and he listened to them. ¹⁸They abandoned the temple of the LORD, the God of their fathers, and worshiped Asherah poles and idols. Because of their guilt, God's anger came upon Judah and Jerusalem. ¹⁹Although the LORD sent prophets to the people to bring them back to him, and though they testified against them, they would not listen.

²⁰Then the Spirit of God came upon Zechariah son of Jehoiada the priest. He stood before the people and said, "This is what God says: 'Why do you disobey the LORD's commands? You will not prosper. Because you have forsaken the LORD, he has forsaken you.'"

²¹But they plotted against him, and by order of the king they stoned him to death in the courtyard of the LORD's temple. ²²King Joash did not remember the kindness Zechariah's father Jehoiada had shown him but killed his son, who said as he lay dying, "May the LORD see this and call you to account."

²³At the turn of the year,[a] the army of Aram marched against Joash; it invaded Judah and Jerusalem and killed all the leaders of the people. They sent all the plunder to their king in Damascus. ²⁴Although the Aramean army had come with only a few men, the LORD delivered into their hands a much larger army. Because Judah had forsaken the LORD, the God of their fathers, judgment was executed on Joash. ²⁵When the Arameans withdrew, they left Joash severely wounded. His officials conspired against him for murdering the son of Jehoiada the priest, and they killed him in his bed. So he died and was buried in the City of David, but not in the tombs of the kings.

²⁶Those who conspired against him were Zabad,[b] son of Shimeath an Ammonite woman, and Jehozabad, son of Shimrith[c] a Moabite woman. ²⁷The account of his sons, the many prophecies about him, and the record of the restoration of the temple of God are written in the annotations on the book of the kings. And Amaziah his son succeeded him as king.

Amaziah King of Judah

25 Amaziah was twenty-five years old when he became king, and he reigned in Jerusalem twenty-nine years. His mother's name was Jehoaddin[d]; she was from Jerusalem. ²He did what was right in the eyes of the LORD, but not wholeheartedly. ³After the kingdom was firmly in his control, he executed the officials who had murdered his father the king. ⁴Yet he did not put their sons to death, but acted in accordance with

---

a23 Probably in the spring   b26 A variant of *Jozabad*   c26 A variant of *Shomer*
d1 Hebrew *Jehoaddan*, a variant of *Jehoaddin*

what is written in the Law, in the Book of Moses, where the LORD commanded: "Fathers shall not be put to death for their children, nor children put to death for their fathers; each is to die for his own sins."[a]

[5]Amaziah called the people of Judah together and assigned them according to their families to commanders of thousands and commanders of hundreds for all Judah and Benjamin. He then mustered those twenty years old or more and found that there were three hundred thousand men ready for military service, able to handle the spear and shield. [6]He also hired a hundred thousand fighting men from Israel for a hundred talents[b] of silver.

[7]But a man of God came to him and said, "O king, these troops from Israel must not march with you, for the LORD is not with Israel—not with any of the people of Ephraim. [8]Even if you go and fight courageously in battle, God will overthrow you before the enemy, for God has the power to help or to overthrow."

[9]Amaziah asked the man of God, "But what about the hundred talents I paid for these Israelite troops?"

The man of God replied, "The LORD can give you much more than that."

[10]So Amaziah dismissed the troops who had come to him from Ephraim and sent them home. They were furious with Judah and left for home in a great rage.

[11]Amaziah then marshaled his strength and led his army to the Valley of Salt, where he killed ten thousand men of Seir. [12]The army of Judah also captured ten thousand men alive, took them to the top of a cliff and threw them down so that all were dashed to pieces.

[13]Meanwhile the troops that Amaziah had sent back and had not allowed to take part in the war raided Judean towns from Samaria to Beth Horon. They killed three thousand people and carried off great quantities of plunder.

[14]When Amaziah returned from slaughtering the Edomites, he brought back the gods of the people of Seir. He set them up as his own gods, bowed down to them and burned sacrifices to them. [15]The anger of the LORD burned against Amaziah, and he sent a prophet to him, who said, "Why do you consult this people's gods, which could not save their own people from your hand?"

[16]While he was still speaking, the king said to him, "Have we appointed you an adviser to the king? Stop! Why be struck down?"

So the prophet stopped but said, "I know that God has determined to destroy you, because you have done this and have not listened to my counsel."

[17]After Amaziah king of Judah consulted his advisers, he sent this challenge to Jehoash[c] son of Jehoahaz, the son of Jehu, king of Israel: "Come, meet me face to face."

[18]But Jehoash king of Israel replied to Amaziah king of Judah: "A thistle in Lebanon sent a message to a cedar in Lebanon, 'Give your daughter to my son in marriage.' Then a wild beast in Lebanon came along and trampled the thistle underfoot. [19]You say to yourself that you have defeated Edom, and now you are arrogant and proud. But stay at home! Why ask for trouble and cause your own downfall and that of Judah also?"

[20]Amaziah, however, would not listen, for God so worked that he might hand them over to ⌊Jehoash⌋, because they sought the gods of Edom. [21]So Jehoash king of Israel attacked. He and Amaziah king of Judah faced each other at Beth Shemesh in Judah. [22]Judah was routed by Israel, and every man fled to his home. [23]Jehoash king of Israel captured Amaziah king of Judah, the son of Joash, the son of Ahaziah,[d] at Beth Shemesh. Then Jehoash brought him to Jerusalem and

---

[a]4 Deut. 24:16   [b]6 That is, about 3 3/4 tons (about 3.4 metric tons); also in verse 9
[c]17 Hebrew *Joash*, a variant of *Jehoash*; also in verses 18, 21, 23 and 25   [d]23 Hebrew *Jehoahaz*, a variant of *Ahaziah*

broke down the wall of Jerusalem from the Ephraim Gate to the Corner Gate—a section about six hundred feet[a] long. ²⁴He took all the gold and silver and all the articles found in the temple of God that had been in the care of Obed-Edom, together with the palace treasures and the hostages, and returned to Samaria.

²⁵Amaziah son of Joash king of Judah lived for fifteen years after the death of Jehoash son of Jehoahaz king of Israel. ²⁶As for the other events of Amaziah's reign, from beginning to end, are they not written in the book of the kings of Judah and Israel? ²⁷From the time that Amaziah turned away from following the LORD, they conspired against him in Jerusalem and he fled to Lachish, but they sent men after him to Lachish and killed him there. ²⁸He was brought back by horse and was buried with his fathers in the City of Judah.

Uzziah King of Judah

26 Then all the people of Judah took Uzziah,[b] who was sixteen years old, and made him king in place of his father Amaziah. ²He was the one who rebuilt Elath and restored it to Judah after Amaziah rested with his fathers.

³Uzziah was sixteen years old when he became king, and he reigned in Jerusalem fifty-two years. His mother's name was Jecoliah; she was from Jerusalem. ⁴He did what was right in the eyes of the LORD, just as his father Amaziah had done. ⁵He sought God during the days of Zechariah, who instructed him in the fear[c] of God. As long as he sought the LORD, God gave him success.

⁶He went to war against the Philistines and broke down the walls of Gath, Jabneh and Ashdod. He then rebuilt towns near Ashdod and elsewhere among the Philistines. ⁷God helped him against the Philistines and against the Arabs who lived in Gur Baal and against the Meunites. ⁸The

Ammonites brought tribute to Uzziah, and his fame spread as far as the border of Egypt, because he had become very powerful.

⁹Uzziah built towers in Jerusalem at the Corner Gate, at the Valley Gate and at the angle of the wall, and he fortified them. ¹⁰He also built towers in the desert and dug many cisterns, because he had much livestock in the foothills and in the plain. He had people working his fields and vineyards in the hills and in the fertile lands, for he loved the soil.

¹¹Uzziah had a well-trained army, ready to go out by divisions according to their numbers as mustered by Jeiel the secretary and Maaseiah the officer under the direction of Hananiah, one of the royal officials. ¹²The total number of family leaders over the fighting men was 2,600. ¹³Under their command was an army of 307,500 men trained for war, a powerful force to support the king against his enemies. ¹⁴Uzziah provided shields, spears, helmets, coats of armor, bows and slingstones for the entire army. ¹⁵In Jerusalem he made machines designed by skillful men for use on the towers and on the corner defenses to shoot arrows and hurl large stones. His fame spread far and wide, for he was greatly helped until he became powerful.

¹⁶But after Uzziah became powerful, his pride led to his downfall. He was unfaithful to the LORD his God, and entered the temple of the LORD to burn incense on the altar of incense. ¹⁷Azariah the priest with eighty other courageous priests of the LORD followed him in. ¹⁸They confronted him and said, "It is not right for you, Uzziah, to burn incense to the LORD. That is for the priests, the descendants of Aaron, who have been consecrated to burn incense. Leave the sanctuary, for you have been unfaithful; and you will not be honored by the LORD God."

¹⁹Uzziah, who had a censer in his

---

a23 Hebrew *four hundred cubits* (about 180 meters)   *b1* Also called *Azariah*   *c5* Many Hebrew manuscripts, Septuagint and Syriac; other Hebrew manuscripts *vision*

hand ready to burn incense, became angry. While he was raging at the priests in their presence before the incense altar in the LORD's temple, leprosy[a] broke out on his forehead. [20]When Azariah the chief priest and all the other priests looked at him, they saw that he had leprosy on his forehead, so they hurried him out. Indeed, he himself was eager to leave, because the LORD had afflicted him.

[21]King Uzziah had leprosy until the day he died. He lived in a separate house[b]—leprous, and excluded from the temple of the LORD. Jotham his son had charge of the palace and governed the people of the land.

[22]The other events of Uzziah's reign, from beginning to end, are recorded by the prophet Isaiah son of Amoz. [23]Uzziah rested with his fathers and was buried near them in a field for burial that belonged to the kings, for people said, "He had leprosy." And Jotham his son succeeded him as king.

Jotham King of Judah

27 Jotham was twenty-five years old when he became king, and he reigned in Jerusalem sixteen years. His mother's name was Jerusha daughter of Zadok. [2]He did what was right in the eyes of the LORD, just as his father Uzziah had done, but unlike him he did not enter the temple of the LORD. The people, however, continued their corrupt practices. [3]Jotham rebuilt the Upper Gate of the temple of the LORD and did extensive work on the wall at the hill of Ophel. [4]He built towns in the Judean hills and forts and towers in the wooded areas.

[5]Jotham made war on the king of the Ammonites and conquered them. That year the Ammonites paid him a hundred talents[c] of silver, ten thousand cors[d] of wheat and ten thousand cors of barley. The Ammonites

brought him the same amount also in the second and third years.

[6]Jotham grew powerful because he walked steadfastly before the LORD his God.

[7]The other events of Jotham's reign, including all his wars and the other things he did, are written in the book of the kings of Israel and Judah. [8]He was twenty-five years old when he became king, and he reigned in Jerusalem sixteen years. [9]Jotham rested with his fathers and was buried in the City of David. And Ahaz his son succeeded him as king.

Ahaz King of Judah

28 Ahaz was twenty years old when he became king, and he reigned in Jerusalem sixteen years. Unlike David his father, he did not do what was right in the eyes of the LORD. [2]He walked in the ways of the kings of Israel and also made cast idols for worshiping the Baals. [3]He burned sacrifices in the Valley of Ben Hinnom and sacrificed his sons in the fire, following the detestable ways of the nations the LORD had driven out before the Israelites. [4]He offered sacrifices and burned incense at the high places, on the hilltops and under every spreading tree.

[5]Therefore the LORD his God handed him over to the king of Aram. The Arameans defeated him and took many of his people as prisoners and brought them to Damascus.

He was also given into the hands of the king of Israel, who inflicted heavy casualties on him. [6]In one day Pekah son of Remaliah killed a hundred and twenty thousand soldiers in Judah—because Judah had forsaken the LORD, the God of their fathers. [7]Zicri, an Ephraimite warrior, killed Maaseiah the king's son, Azrikam the officer in charge of the palace, and Elkanah, second to the king. [8]The Israelites took captive from their kinsmen two

---

[a]19 The Hebrew word was used for various diseases affecting the skin—not necessarily leprosy; also in verses 20, 21 and 23.   [b]21 Or *in a house where he was relieved of responsibilities*
[c]5 That is, about 3 3/4 tons (about 3.4 metric tons)   [d]5 That is, probably about 62,000 bushels (about 2,200 kiloliters)

hundred thousand wives, sons and daughters. They also took a great deal of plunder, which they carried back to Samaria.

⁹But a prophet of the LORD named Oded was there, and he went out to meet the army when it returned to Samaria. He said to them, "Because the LORD, the God of your fathers, was angry with Judah, he gave them into your hand. But you have slaughtered them in a rage that reaches to heaven. ¹⁰And now you intend to make the men and women of Judah and Jerusalem your slaves. But aren't you also guilty of sins against the LORD your God? ¹¹Now listen to me! Send back your fellow countrymen you have taken as prisoners, for the LORD's fierce anger rests on you."

¹²Then some of the leaders in Ephraim—Azariah son of Jehohanan, Berekiah son of Meshillemoth, Jehizkiah son of Shallum, and Amasa son of Hadlai—confronted those who were arriving from the war. ¹³"You must not bring those prisoners here," they said, "or we will be guilty before the LORD. Do you intend to add to our sin and guilt? For our guilt is already great, and his fierce anger rests on Israel."

¹⁴So the soldiers gave up the prisoners and plunder in the presence of the officials and all the assembly. ¹⁵The men designated by name took the prisoners, and from the plunder they clothed all who were naked. They provided them with clothes and sandals, food and drink, and healing balm. All those who were weak they put on donkeys. So they took them back to their fellow countrymen at Jericho, the City of Palms, and returned to Samaria.

¹⁶At that time King Ahaz sent to the kingᵃ of Assyria for help. ¹⁷The Edomites had again come and attacked Judah and carried away prisoners, ¹⁸while the Philistines had raided towns in the foothills and in the

Negev of Judah. They captured and occupied Beth Shemesh, Aijalon and Gederoth, as well as Soco, Timnah and Gimzo, with their surrounding villages. ¹⁹The LORD had humbled Judah because of Ahaz king of Israel,ᵇ for he had promoted wickedness in Judah and had been most unfaithful to the LORD. ²⁰Tiglath-Pileserᶜ king of Assyria came to him, but he gave him trouble instead of help. ²¹Ahaz took some of the things from the temple of the LORD and from the royal palace and from the princes and presented them to the king of Assyria, but that did not help him.

²²In his time of trouble King Ahaz became even more unfaithful to the LORD. ²³He offered sacrifices to the gods of Damascus, who had defeated him; for he thought, "Since the gods of the kings of Aram have helped them, I will sacrifice to them so they will help me." But they were his downfall and the downfall of all Israel.

²⁴Ahaz gathered together the furnishings from the temple of God and took them away.ᵈ He shut the doors of the LORD's temple and set up altars at every street corner in Jerusalem. ²⁵In every town in Judah he built high places to burn sacrifices to other gods and provoked the LORD, the God of his fathers, to anger.

²⁶The other events of his reign and all his ways, from beginning to end, are written in the book of the kings of Judah and Israel. ²⁷Ahaz rested with his fathers and was buried in the city of Jerusalem, but he was not placed in the tombs of the kings of Israel. And Hezekiah his son succeeded him as king.

Hezekiah Purifies the Temple

29 Hezekiah was twenty-five years old when he became king, and he reigned in Jerusalem twenty-nine years. His mother's name was Abijah daughter of Zechariah.

ᵃ16 One Hebrew manuscript, Septuagint and Vulgate (see also 2 Kings 16:7); most Hebrew manuscripts *kings*   ᵇ19 That is, Judah, as frequently in 2 Chronicles   ᶜ20 Hebrew *Tilgath-Pilneser*, a variant of *Tiglath-Pileser*   ᵈ24 Or *and cut them up*

²He did what was right in the eyes of the LORD, just as his father David had done.

³In the first month of the first year of his reign, he opened the doors of the temple of the LORD and repaired them. ⁴He brought in the priests and the Levites, assembled them in the square on the east side ⁵and said: "Listen to me, Levites! Consecrate yourselves now and consecrate the temple of the LORD, the God of your fathers. Remove all defilement from the sanctuary. ⁶Our fathers were unfaithful; they did evil in the eyes of the LORD our God and forsook him. They turned their faces away from the LORD's dwelling place and turned their backs on him. ⁷They also shut the doors of the portico and put out the lamps. They did not burn incense or present any burnt offerings at the sanctuary to the God of Israel. ⁸Therefore, the anger of the LORD has fallen on Judah and Jerusalem; he has made them an object of dread and horror and scorn, as you can see with your own eyes. ⁹This is why our fathers have fallen by the sword and why our sons and daughters and our wives are in captivity. ¹⁰Now I intend to make a covenant with the LORD, the God of Israel, so that his fierce anger will turn away from us. ¹¹My sons, do not be negligent now, for the LORD has chosen you to stand before him and serve him, to minister before him and to burn incense."

¹²Then these Levites set to work:
   from the Kohathites,
      Mahath son of Amasai and Joel son of Azariah;
   from the Merarites,
      Kish son of Abdi and Azariah son of Jehallel;
   from the Gershonites,
      Joah son of Zimmah and Eden son of Joah;
¹³from the descendants of Elizaphan,
      Shimri and Jeiel;
   from the descendants of Asaph,
      Zechariah and Mattaniah;
¹⁴from the descendants of Heman,
      Jehiel and Shimei;

   from the descendants of Jeduthun,
      Shemaiah and Uzziel.

¹⁵When they had assembled their brothers and consecrated themselves, they went in to purify the temple of the LORD, as the king had ordered, following the word of the LORD. ¹⁶The priests went into the sanctuary of the LORD to purify it. They brought out to the courtyard of the LORD's temple everything unclean that they found in the temple of the LORD. The Levites took it and carried it out to the Kidron Valley. ¹⁷They began the consecration on the first day of the first month, and by the eighth day of the month they reached the portico of the LORD. For eight more days they consecrated the temple of the LORD itself, finishing on the sixteenth day of the first month.

¹⁸Then they went in to King Hezekiah and reported: "We have purified the entire temple of the LORD, the altar of burnt offering with all its utensils, and the table for setting out the consecrated bread, with all its articles. ¹⁹We have prepared and consecrated all the articles that King Ahaz removed in his unfaithfulness while he was king. They are now in front of the LORD's altar."

²⁰Early the next morning King Hezekiah gathered the city officials together and went up to the temple of the LORD. ²¹They brought seven bulls, seven rams, seven male lambs and seven male goats as a sin offering for the kingdom, for the sanctuary and for Judah. The king commanded the priests, the descendants of Aaron, to offer these on the altar of the LORD. ²²So they slaughtered the bulls, and the priests took the blood and sprinkled it on the altar; next they slaughtered the rams and sprinkled their blood on the altar; then they slaughtered the lambs and sprinkled their blood on the altar. ²³The goats for the sin offering were brought before the king and the assembly, and they laid their hands on them. ²⁴The priests then slaughtered the goats and presented their blood on the altar for a sin offering to atone for all Israel, be-

cause the king had ordered the burnt offering and the sin offering for all Israel.

²⁵He stationed the Levites in the temple of the LORD with cymbals, harps and lyres in the way prescribed by David and Gad the king's seer and Nathan the prophet; this was commanded by the LORD through his prophets. ²⁶So the Levites stood ready with David's instruments, and the priests with their trumpets.

²⁷Hezekiah gave the order to sacrifice the burnt offering on the altar. As the offering began, singing to the LORD began also, accompanied by trumpets and the instruments of David king of Israel. ²⁸The whole assembly bowed in worship, while the singers sang and the trumpeters played. All this continued until the sacrifice of the burnt offering was completed.

²⁹When the offerings were finished, the king and everyone present with him knelt down and worshiped. ³⁰King Hezekiah and his officials ordered the Levites to praise the LORD with the words of David and of Asaph the seer. So they sang praises with gladness and bowed their heads and worshiped.

³¹Then Hezekiah said, "You have now dedicated yourselves to the LORD. Come and bring sacrifices and thank offerings to the temple of the LORD." So the assembly brought sacrifices and thank offerings, and all whose hearts were willing brought burnt offerings.

³²The number of burnt offerings the assembly brought was seventy bulls, a hundred rams and two hundred male lambs—all of them for burnt offerings to the LORD. ³³The animals consecrated as sacrifices amounted to six hundred bulls and three thousand sheep and goats. ³⁴The priests, however, were too few to skin all the burnt offerings; so their kinsmen the Levites helped them until the task was finished and until other priests had been consecrated, for the Levites had been more conscientious in con-

secrating themselves than the priests had been. ³⁵There were burnt offerings in abundance, together with the fat of the fellowship offerings[a] and the drink offerings that accompanied the burnt offerings.

So the service of the temple of the LORD was reestablished. ³⁶Hezekiah and all the people rejoiced at what God had brought about for his people, because it was done so quickly.

Hezekiah Celebrates the Passover

30 Hezekiah sent word to all Israel and Judah and also wrote letters to Ephraim and Manasseh, inviting them to come to the temple of the LORD in Jerusalem and celebrate the Passover to the LORD, the God of Israel. ²The king and his officials and the whole assembly in Jerusalem decided to celebrate the Passover in the second month. ³They had not been able to celebrate it at the regular time because not enough priests had consecrated themselves and the people had not assembled in Jerusalem. ⁴The plan seemed right both to the king and to the whole assembly. ⁵They decided to send a proclamation throughout Israel, from Beersheba to Dan, calling the people to come to Jerusalem and celebrate the Passover to the LORD, the God of Israel. It had not been celebrated in large numbers according to what was written.

⁶At the king's command, couriers went throughout Israel and Judah with letters from the king and from his officials, which read:

"People of Israel, return to the LORD, the God of Abraham, Isaac and Israel, that he may return to you who are left, who have escaped from the hand of the kings of Assyria. ⁷Do not be like your fathers and brothers, who were unfaithful to the LORD, the God of their fathers, so that he made them an object of horror, as you see. ⁸Do not be stiff-necked, as your fathers were; submit to the

---

ᵃ35 Traditionally *peace offerings*

THURSDAY

VERSE:
2 Chronicles
29:27

AUTHOR:
Lloyd John Ogilvie

PASSAGE:
2 Chronicles
29:25–31

Sacrifice, Trumpets and Song

When Hezekiah became king, he instituted sweeping reforms and purified the temple that had fallen into misuse. The day of reinstituting worship in the temple was a momentous day . . . At the altar the sacrifice for sin was offered. And at the moment the sacrifice began, the trumpets were sounded and all the people broke into a song of praise.

There are strategic times in our lives like that. They come when we must place our sacrifice on the altar. But since the ultimate sacrifice was made for us on Calvary, our sacrifice is the surrender of our lives. That sacrifice often becomes very specific as we commit our plans, projects and programs to the Lord. Often what we want to do for the Lord gets mixed up with our own egos and willfulness. Then there comes a time when we must give up our control and self-serving efforts. The same thing is true of our hopes and dreams for people. We sometimes forget they belong to God and not to us.

When we place our cherished extensions of our self on the altar, there's a trumpet blast in heaven and all the company of heaven bursts into song. We've turned over our control and now we can live with freedom. The Lord's will be done! He knows what is best. And once the sacrifice of relinquishment is made, the Lord is able to multiply what we have been holding tightly. Have you heard the trumpets and song today?

ADDITIONAL SCRIPTURE READINGS
Romans 12:1–8; Galatians 5:1–6

Go to page 563 for your next devotional reading.

LORD. Come to the sanctuary, which he has consecrated forever. Serve the LORD your God, so that his fierce anger will turn away from you. ⁹If you return to the LORD, then your brothers and your children will be shown compassion by their captors and will come back to this land, for the LORD your God is gracious and compassionate. He will not turn his face from you if you return to him."

¹⁰The couriers went from town to town in Ephraim and Manasseh, as far as Zebulun, but the people scorned and ridiculed them. ¹¹Nevertheless, some men of Asher, Manasseh and Zebulun humbled themselves and went to Jerusalem. ¹²Also in Judah the hand of God was on the people to give them unity of mind to carry out what the king and his officials had ordered, following the word of the LORD.

¹³A very large crowd of people assembled in Jerusalem to celebrate the Feast of Unleavened Bread in the second month. ¹⁴They removed the altars in Jerusalem and cleared away the incense altars and threw them into the Kidron Valley.

¹⁵They slaughtered the Passover lamb on the fourteenth day of the second month. The priests and the Levites were ashamed and consecrated themselves and brought burnt offerings to the temple of the LORD. ¹⁶Then they took up their regular positions as prescribed in the Law of Moses the man of God. The priests sprinkled the blood handed to them by the Levites. ¹⁷Since many in the crowd had not consecrated themselves, the Levites had to kill the Passover lambs for all those who were not ceremonially clean and could not consecrate ⌊their lambs⌋ to the LORD. ¹⁸Although most of the many people who came from Ephraim, Manasseh, Issachar and Zebulun had not purified themselves, yet they ate the Passover, contrary to what was written. But Hezekiah prayed for them, saying, "May the LORD, who is good, pardon everyone ¹⁹who sets his heart on seeking God— the LORD, the God of his fathers— even if he is not clean according to the rules of the sanctuary." ²⁰And the LORD heard Hezekiah and healed the people.

²¹The Israelites who were present in Jerusalem celebrated the Feast of Unleavened Bread for seven days with great rejoicing, while the Levites and priests sang to the LORD every day, accompanied by the LORD's instruments of praise.ᵃ

²²Hezekiah spoke encouragingly to all the Levites, who showed good understanding of the service of the LORD. For the seven days they ate their assigned portion and offered fellowship offeringsᵇ and praised the LORD, the God of their fathers.

²³The whole assembly then agreed to celebrate the festival seven more days; so for another seven days they celebrated joyfully. ²⁴Hezekiah king of Judah provided a thousand bulls and seven thousand sheep and goats for the assembly, and the officials provided them with a thousand bulls and ten thousand sheep and goats. A great number of priests consecrated themselves. ²⁵The entire assembly of Judah rejoiced, along with the priests and Levites and all who had assembled from Israel, including the aliens who had come from Israel and those who lived in Judah. ²⁶There was great joy in Jerusalem, for since the days of Solomon son of David king of Israel there had been nothing like this in Jerusalem. ²⁷The priests and the Levites stood to bless the people, and God heard them, for their prayer reached heaven, his holy dwelling place.

31 When all this had ended, the Israelites who were there went out to the towns of Judah, smashed the sacred stones and cut down the Asherah poles. They destroyed the

---

ᵃ21 Or *priests praised the LORD every day with resounding instruments belonging to the LORD*
ᵇ22 Traditionally *peace offerings*

high places and the altars throughout Judah and Benjamin and in Ephraim and Manasseh. After they had destroyed all of them, the Israelites returned to their own towns and to their own property.

Contributions for Worship

²Hezekiah assigned the priests and Levites to divisions—each of them according to their duties as priests or Levites—to offer burnt offerings and fellowship offerings,ª to minister, to give thanks and to sing praises at the gates of the LORD's dwelling. ³The king contributed from his own possessions for the morning and evening burnt offerings and for the burnt offerings on the Sabbaths, New Moons and appointed feasts as written in the Law of the LORD. ⁴He ordered the people living in Jerusalem to give the portion due the priests and Levites so they could devote themselves to the Law of the LORD. ⁵As soon as the order went out, the Israelites generously gave the firstfruits of their grain, new wine, oil and honey and all that the fields produced. They brought a great amount, a tithe of everything. ⁶The men of Israel and Judah who lived in the towns of Judah also brought a tithe of their herds and flocks and a tithe of the holy things dedicated to the LORD their God, and they piled them in heaps. ⁷They began doing this in the third month and finished in the seventh month. ⁸When Hezekiah and his officials came and saw the heaps, they praised the LORD and blessed his people Israel.

⁹Hezekiah asked the priests and Levites about the heaps; ¹⁰and Azariah the chief priest, from the family of Zadok, answered, "Since the people began to bring their contributions to the temple of the LORD, we have had enough to eat and plenty to spare, because the LORD has blessed his people, and this great amount is left over."

¹¹Hezekiah gave orders to prepare storerooms in the temple of the LORD, and this was done. ¹²Then they faithfully brought in the contributions, tithes and dedicated gifts. Conaniah, a Levite, was in charge of these things, and his brother Shimei was next in rank. ¹³Jehiel, Azaziah, Nahath, Asahel, Jerimoth, Jozabad, Eliel, Ismakiah, Mahath and Benaiah were supervisors under Conaniah and Shimei his brother, by appointment of King Hezekiah and Azariah the official in charge of the temple of God.

¹⁴Kore son of Imnah the Levite, keeper of the East Gate, was in charge of the freewill offerings given to God, distributing the contributions made to the LORD and also the consecrated gifts. ¹⁵Eden, Miniamin, Jeshua, Shemaiah, Amariah and Shecaniah assisted him faithfully in the towns of the priests, distributing to their fellow priests according to their divisions, old and young alike.

¹⁶In addition, they distributed to the males three years old or more whose names were in the genealogical records—all who would enter the temple of the LORD to perform the daily duties of their various tasks, according to their responsibilities and their divisions. ¹⁷And they distributed to the priests enrolled by their families in the genealogical records and likewise to the Levites twenty years old or more, according to their responsibilities and their divisions. ¹⁸They included all the little ones, the wives, and the sons and daughters of the whole community listed in these genealogical records. For they were faithful in consecrating themselves.

¹⁹As for the priests, the descendants of Aaron, who lived on the farm lands around their towns or in any other towns, men were designated by name to distribute portions to every male among them and to all who were recorded in the genealogies of the Levites.

²⁰This is what Hezekiah did throughout Judah, doing what was good and right and faithful before the LORD his God. ²¹In everything that he undertook in the service of God's

---

ª2 Traditionally *peace offerings*

temple and in obedience to the law and the commands, he sought his God and worked wholeheartedly. And so he prospered.

Sennacherib Threatens Jerusalem

32 After all that Hezekiah had so faithfully done, Sennacherib king of Assyria came and invaded Judah. He laid siege to the fortified cities, thinking to conquer them for himself. ²When Hezekiah saw that Sennacherib had come and that he intended to make war on Jerusalem, ³he consulted with his officials and military staff about blocking off the water from the springs outside the city, and they helped him. ⁴A large force of men assembled, and they blocked all the springs and the stream that flowed through the land. "Why should the kings*ᵃ* of Assyria come and find plenty of water?" they said. ⁵Then he worked hard repairing all the broken sections of the wall and building towers on it. He built another wall outside that one and reinforced the supporting terraces*ᵇ* of the City of David. He also made large numbers of weapons and shields.

⁶He appointed military officers over the people and assembled them before him in the square at the city gate and encouraged them with these words: ⁷"Be strong and courageous. Do not be afraid or discouraged because of the king of Assyria and the vast army with him, for there is a greater power with us than with him. ⁸With him is only the arm of flesh, but with us is the LORD our God to help us and to fight our battles." And the people gained confidence from what Hezekiah the king of Judah said.

⁹Later, when Sennacherib king of Assyria and all his forces were laying siege to Lachish, he sent his officers to Jerusalem with this message for Hezekiah king of Judah and for all the people of Judah who were there:

¹⁰"This is what Sennacherib king of Assyria says: On what are you basing your confidence, that you remain in Jerusalem under siege? ¹¹When Hezekiah says, 'The LORD our God will save us from the hand of the king of Assyria,' he is misleading you, to let you die of hunger and thirst. ¹²Did not Hezekiah himself remove this god's high places and altars, saying to Judah and Jerusalem, 'You must worship before one altar and burn sacrifices on it'?

¹³"Do you not know what I and my fathers have done to all the peoples of the other lands? Were the gods of those nations ever able to deliver their land from my hand? ¹⁴Who of all the gods of these nations that my fathers destroyed has been able to save his people from me? How then can your god deliver you from my hand? ¹⁵Now do not let Hezekiah deceive you and mislead you like this. Do not believe him, for no god of any nation or kingdom has been able to deliver his people from my hand or the hand of my fathers. How much less will your god deliver you from my hand!"

¹⁶Sennacherib's officers spoke further against the LORD God and against his servant Hezekiah. ¹⁷The king also wrote letters insulting the LORD, the God of Israel, and saying this against him: "Just as the gods of the peoples of the other lands did not rescue their people from my hand, so the god of Hezekiah will not rescue his people from my hand." ¹⁸Then they called out in Hebrew to the people of Jerusalem who were on the wall, to terrify them and make them afraid in order to capture the city. ¹⁹They spoke about the God of Jerusalem as they did about the gods of the other peoples of the world—the work of men's hands.

²⁰King Hezekiah and the prophet Isaiah son of Amoz cried out in

---

*ᵃ*4 Hebrew; Septuagint and Syriac *king*   *ᵇ*5 Or *the Millo* prayer to heaven about this. ²¹And the LORD sent an angel, who annihilated all the fighting men and the leaders and officers in the camp of the Assyrian king. So he withdrew to his own land in disgrace. And when he went into the temple of his god, some of his sons cut him down with the sword.

²²So the LORD saved Hezekiah and the people of Jerusalem from the hand of Sennacherib king of Assyria and from the hand of all others. He took care of them*ᵃ* on every side. ²³Many brought offerings to Jerusalem for the LORD and valuable gifts for Hezekiah king of Judah. From then on he was highly regarded by all the nations.

Hezekiah's Pride, Success and Death

²⁴In those days Hezekiah became ill and was at the point of death. He prayed to the LORD, who answered him and gave him a miraculous sign. ²⁵But Hezekiah's heart was proud and he did not respond to the kindness shown him; therefore the LORD's wrath was on him and on Judah and Jerusalem. ²⁶Then Hezekiah repented of the pride of his heart, as did the people of Jerusalem; therefore the LORD's wrath did not come upon them during the days of Hezekiah.

²⁷Hezekiah had very great riches and honor, and he made treasuries for his silver and gold and for his precious stones, spices, shields and all kinds of valuables. ²⁸He also made buildings to store the harvest of grain, new wine and oil; and he made stalls for various kinds of cattle, and pens for the flocks. ²⁹He built villages and acquired great numbers of flocks and herds, for God had given him very great riches. ³⁰It was Hezekiah who blocked the upper outlet of the Gihon spring and channeled the water down to the west side of the City of David. He succeeded in everything he undertook. ³¹But when envoys were sent by the rulers

of Babylon to ask him about the miraculous sign that had occurred in the land, God left him to test him and to know everything that was in his heart.

³²The other events of Hezekiah's reign and his acts of devotion are written in the vision of the prophet Isaiah son of Amoz in the book of the kings of Judah and Israel. ³³Hezekiah rested with his fathers and was buried on the hill where the tombs of David's descendants are. All Judah and the people of Jerusalem honored him when he died. And Manasseh his son succeeded him as king.

Manasseh King of Judah

33 Manasseh was twelve years old when he became king, and he reigned in Jerusalem fifty-five years. ²He did evil in the eyes of the LORD, following the detestable practices of the nations the LORD had driven out before the Israelites. ³He rebuilt the high places his father Hezekiah had demolished; he also erected altars to the Baals and made Asherah poles. He bowed down to all the starry hosts and worshiped them. ⁴He built altars in the temple of the LORD, of which the LORD had said, "My Name will remain in Jerusalem forever." ⁵In both courts of the temple of the LORD, he built altars to all the starry hosts. ⁶He sacrificed his sons in*ᵇ* the fire in the Valley of Ben Hinnom, practiced sorcery, divination and witchcraft, and consulted mediums and spiritists. He did much evil in the eyes of the LORD, provoking him to anger.

⁷He took the carved image he had made and put it in God's temple, of which God had said to David and to his son Solomon, "In this temple and in Jerusalem, which I have chosen out of all the tribes of Israel, I will put my Name forever. ⁸I will not again make the feet of the Israelites leave the land I assigned to your forefathers, if only they will be careful to do everything I commanded them concerning all the

---

*ᵃ*22 Hebrew; Septuagint and Vulgate *He gave them rest*   *ᵇ*6 Or *He made his sons pass through*

laws, decrees and ordinances given through Moses." ⁹But Manasseh led Judah and the people of Jerusalem astray, so that they did more evil than the nations the Lord had destroyed before the Israelites.

¹⁰The Lord spoke to Manasseh and his people, but they paid no attention. ¹¹So the Lord brought against them the army commanders of the king of Assyria, who took Manasseh prisoner, put a hook in his nose, bound him with bronze shackles and took him to Babylon. ¹²In his distress he sought the favor of the Lord his God and humbled himself greatly before the God of his fathers. ¹³And when he prayed to him, the Lord was moved by his entreaty and listened to his plea; so he brought him back to Jerusalem and to his kingdom. Then Manasseh knew that the Lord is God.

¹⁴Afterward he rebuilt the outer wall of the City of David, west of the Gihon spring in the valley, as far as the entrance of the Fish Gate and encircling the hill of Ophel; he also made it much higher. He stationed military commanders in all the fortified cities in Judah.

¹⁵He got rid of the foreign gods and removed the image from the temple of the Lord, as well as all the altars he had built on the temple hill and in Jerusalem; and he threw them out of the city. ¹⁶Then he restored the altar of the Lord and sacrificed fellowship offerings[a] and thank offerings on it, and told Judah to serve the Lord, the God of Israel. ¹⁷The people, however, continued to sacrifice at the high places, but only to the Lord their God.

¹⁸The other events of Manasseh's reign, including his prayer to his God and the words the seers spoke to him in the name of the Lord, the God of Israel, are written in the annals of the kings of Israel.[b] ¹⁹His prayer and how God was moved by his entreaty, as well as all his sins and unfaithfulness, and the sites where he built high places and set up Asherah poles and idols before he humbled himself—all are written in the records of the seers.[c] ²⁰Manasseh rested with his fathers and was buried in his palace. And Amon his son succeeded him as king.

Amon King of Judah

²¹Amon was twenty-two years old when he became king, and he reigned in Jerusalem two years. ²²He did evil in the eyes of the Lord, as his father Manasseh had done. Amon worshiped and offered sacrifices to all the idols Manasseh had made. ²³But unlike his father Manasseh, he did not humble himself before the Lord; Amon increased his guilt.

²⁴Amon's officials conspired against him and assassinated him in his palace. ²⁵Then the people of the land killed all who had plotted against King Amon, and they made Josiah his son king in his place.

Josiah's Reforms

34 Josiah was eight years old when he became king, and he reigned in Jerusalem thirty-one years. ²He did what was right in the eyes of the Lord and walked in the ways of his father David, not turning aside to the right or to the left.

³In the eighth year of his reign, while he was still young, he began to seek the God of his father David. In his twelfth year he began to purge Judah and Jerusalem of high places, Asherah poles, carved idols and cast images. ⁴Under his direction the altars of the Baals were torn down; he cut to pieces the incense altars that were above them, and smashed the Asherah poles, the idols and the images. These he broke to pieces and scattered over the graves of those who had sacrificed to them. ⁵He burned the bones of the priests on their altars, and so he purged Judah and Jerusalem. ⁶In the towns of Manasseh, Ephraim and Simeon, as far as Naphtali, and in the ruins around them, ⁷he tore down the

---

a16 Traditionally *peace offerings*   *b18* That is, Judah, as frequently in 2 Chronicles   *c19* One Hebrew manuscript and Septuagint; most Hebrew manuscripts *of Hozai*

altars and the Asherah poles and crushed the idols to powder and cut to pieces all the incense altars throughout Israel. Then he went back to Jerusalem.

[8]In the eighteenth year of Josiah's reign, to purify the land and the temple, he sent Shaphan son of Azaliah and Maaseiah the ruler of the city, with Joah son of Joahaz, the recorder, to repair the temple of the LORD his God.

[9]They went to Hilkiah the high priest and gave him the money that had been brought into the temple of God, which the Levites who were the doorkeepers had collected from the people of Manasseh, Ephraim and the entire remnant of Israel and from all the people of Judah and Benjamin and the inhabitants of Jerusalem. [10]Then they entrusted it to the men appointed to supervise the work on the LORD's temple. These men paid the workers who repaired and restored the temple. [11]They also gave money to the carpenters and builders to purchase dressed stone, and timber for joists and beams for the buildings that the kings of Judah had allowed to fall into ruin.

[12]The men did the work faithfully. Over them to direct them were Jahath and Obadiah, Levites descended from Merari, and Zechariah and Meshullam, descended from Kohath. The Levites—all who were skilled in playing musical instruments— [13]had charge of the laborers and supervised all the workers from job to job. Some of the Levites were secretaries, scribes and doorkeepers.

The Book of the Law Found

[14]While they were bringing out the money that had been taken into the temple of the LORD, Hilkiah the priest found the Book of the Law of the LORD that had been given through Moses. [15]Hilkiah said to Shaphan the secretary, "I have found the Book of the Law in the temple of the LORD." He gave it to Shaphan.

[16]Then Shaphan took the book to the king and reported to him: "Your officials are doing everything that has been committed to them. [17]They have paid out the money that was in the temple of the LORD and have entrusted it to the supervisors and workers." [18]Then Shaphan the secretary informed the king, "Hilkiah the priest has given me a book." And Shaphan read from it in the presence of the king.

[19]When the king heard the words of the Law, he tore his robes. [20]He gave these orders to Hilkiah, Ahikam son of Shaphan, Abdon son of Micah,[a] Shaphan the secretary and Asaiah the king's attendant: [21]"Go and inquire of the LORD for me and for the remnant in Israel and Judah about what is written in this book that has been found. Great is the LORD's anger that is poured out on us because our fathers have not kept the word of the LORD; they have not acted in accordance with all that is written in this book."

[22]Hilkiah and those the king had sent with him[b] went to speak to the prophetess Huldah, who was the wife of Shallum son of Tokhath,[c] the son of Hasrah,[d] keeper of the wardrobe. She lived in Jerusalem, in the Second District.

[23]She said to them, "This is what the LORD, the God of Israel, says: Tell the man who sent you to me, [24]'This is what the LORD says: I am going to bring disaster on this place and its people—all the curses written in the book that has been read in the presence of the king of Judah. [25]Because they have forsaken me and burned incense to other gods and provoked me to anger by all that their hands have made,[e] my anger will be poured out on this place and will not be quenched.' [26]Tell the king of Judah, who sent you to inquire of the LORD,

---

[a]20 Also called *Acbor son of Micaiah*   [b]22 One Hebrew manuscript, Vulgate and Syriac; most Hebrew manuscripts do not have *had sent with him*.   [c]22 Also called *Tikvah*   [d]22 Also called *Harhas*   [e]25 Or *by everything they have done*

'This is what the LORD, the God of Israel, says concerning the words you heard: ²⁷Because your heart was responsive and you humbled yourself before God when you heard what he spoke against this place and its people, and because you humbled yourself before me and tore your robes and wept in my presence, I have heard you, declares the LORD. ²⁸Now I will gather you to your fathers, and you will be buried in peace. Your eyes will not see all the disaster I am going to bring on this place and on those who live here.' "

So they took her answer back to the king.

²⁹Then the king called together all the elders of Judah and Jerusalem. ³⁰He went up to the temple of the LORD with the men of Judah, the people of Jerusalem, the priests and the Levites—all the people from the least to the greatest. He read in their hearing all the words of the Book of the Covenant, which had been found in the temple of the LORD. ³¹The king stood by his pillar and renewed the covenant in the presence of the LORD—to follow the LORD and keep his commands, regulations and decrees with all his heart and all his soul, and to obey the words of the covenant written in this book.

³²Then he had everyone in Jerusalem and Benjamin pledge themselves to it; the people of Jerusalem did this in accordance with the covenant of God, the God of their fathers.

³³Josiah removed all the detestable idols from all the territory belonging to the Israelites, and he had all who were present in Israel serve the LORD their God. As long as he lived, they did not fail to follow the LORD, the God of their fathers.

Josiah Celebrates the Passover

35 Josiah celebrated the Passover to the LORD in Jerusalem, and the Passover lamb was slaughtered on the fourteenth day of the first month. ²He appointed the priests to their duties and encouraged them in the service of the LORD's temple. ³He said to the Levites, who instructed all Israel and who had been consecrated to the LORD: "Put the sacred ark in the temple that Solomon son of David king of Israel built. It is not to be carried about on your shoulders. Now serve the LORD your God and his people Israel. ⁴Prepare yourselves by families in your divisions, according to the directions written by David king of Israel and by his son Solomon.

⁵"Stand in the holy place with a group of Levites for each subdivision of the families of your fellow countrymen, the lay people. ⁶Slaughter the Passover lambs, consecrate yourselves and prepare ⌞the lambs⌟ for your fellow countrymen, doing what the LORD commanded through Moses."

⁷Josiah provided for all the lay people who were there a total of thirty thousand sheep and goats for the Passover offerings, and also three thousand cattle—all from the king's own possessions.

⁸His officials also contributed voluntarily to the people and the priests and Levites. Hilkiah, Zechariah and Jehiel, the administrators of God's temple, gave the priests twenty-six hundred Passover offerings and three hundred cattle. ⁹Also Conaniah along with Shemaiah and Nethanel, his brothers, and Hashabiah, Jeiel and Jozabad, the leaders of the Levites, provided five thousand Passover offerings and five hundred head of cattle for the Levites.

¹⁰The service was arranged and the priests stood in their places with the Levites in their divisions as the king had ordered. ¹¹The Passover lambs were slaughtered, and the priests sprinkled the blood handed to them while the Levites skinned the animals. ¹²They set aside the burnt offerings to give them to the subdivisions of the families of the people to offer to the LORD, as is written in the Book of Moses. They did the same with the cattle. ¹³They roasted the Passover animals over the fire as prescribed, and boiled the holy offerings in pots, caldrons and pans and served them quickly to

all the people. ¹⁴After this, they made preparations for themselves and for the priests, because the priests, the descendants of Aaron, were sacrificing the burnt offerings and the fat portions until nightfall. So the Levites made preparations for themselves and for the Aaronic priests.

¹⁵The musicians, the descendants of Asaph, were in the places prescribed by David, Asaph, Heman and Jeduthun the king's seer. The gatekeepers at each gate did not need to leave their posts, because their fellow Levites made the preparations for them.

¹⁶So at that time the entire service of the LORD was carried out for the celebration of the Passover and the offering of burnt offerings on the altar of the LORD, as King Josiah had ordered. ¹⁷The Israelites who were present celebrated the Passover at that time and observed the Feast of Unleavened Bread for seven days. ¹⁸The Passover had not been observed like this in Israel since the days of the prophet Samuel; and none of the kings of Israel had ever celebrated such a Passover as did Josiah, with the priests, the Levites and all Judah and Israel who were there with the people of Jerusalem. ¹⁹This Passover was celebrated in the eighteenth year of Josiah's reign.

The Death of Josiah

²⁰After all this, when Josiah had set the temple in order, Neco king of Egypt went up to fight at Carchemish on the Euphrates, and Josiah marched out to meet him in battle. ²¹But Neco sent messengers to him, saying, "What quarrel is there between you and me, O king of Judah? It is not you I am attacking at this time, but the house with which I am at war. God has told me to hurry; so stop opposing God, who is with me, or he will destroy you."

²²Josiah, however, would not turn away from him, but disguised himself to engage him in battle. He would not listen to what Neco had said at God's command but went to fight him on the plain of Megiddo.

²³Archers shot King Josiah, and he told his officers, "Take me away; I am badly wounded." ²⁴So they took him out of his chariot, put him in the other chariot he had and brought him to Jerusalem, where he died. He was buried in the tombs of his fathers, and all Judah and Jerusalem mourned for him.

²⁵Jeremiah composed laments for Josiah, and to this day all the men and women singers commemorate Josiah in the laments. These became a tradition in Israel and are written in the Laments.

²⁶The other events of Josiah's reign and his acts of devotion, according to what is written in the Law of the LORD— ²⁷all the events, from beginning to end, are written in the book of the kings of Israel and Judah.

36

¹And the people of the land took Jehoahaz son of Josiah and made him king in Jerusalem in place of his father.

Jehoahaz King of Judah

²Jehoahaz*a* was twenty-three years old when he became king, and he reigned in Jerusalem three months. ³The king of Egypt dethroned him in Jerusalem and imposed on Judah a levy of a hundred talents*b* of silver and a talent*c* of gold. ⁴The king of Egypt made Eliakim, a brother of Jehoahaz, king over Judah and Jerusalem and changed Eliakim's name to Jehoiakim. But Neco took Eliakim's brother Jehoahaz and carried him off to Egypt.

Jehoiakim King of Judah

⁵Jehoiakim was twenty-five years old when he became king, and he reigned in Jerusalem eleven years. He did evil in the eyes of the LORD his God. ⁶Nebuchadnezzar king of Babylon attacked him and bound him with bronze shackles to take him to Babylon. ⁷Nebuchadnezzar also took

---

*a*2 Hebrew *Joahaz,* a variant of *Jehoahaz;* also in verse 4   *b*3 That is, about 3 3/4 tons (about 3.4 metric tons)   *c*3 That is, about 75 pounds (about 34 kilograms)

to Babylon articles from the temple of the LORD and put them in his temple[a] there.

[8]The other events of Jehoiakim's reign, the detestable things he did and all that was found against him, are written in the book of the kings of Israel and Judah. And Jehoiachin his son succeeded him as king.

Jehoiachin King of Judah

[9]Jehoiachin was eighteen[b] years old when he became king, and he reigned in Jerusalem three months and ten days. He did evil in the eyes of the LORD. [10]In the spring, King Nebuchadnezzar sent for him and brought him to Babylon, together with articles of value from the temple of the LORD, and he made Jehoiachin's uncle,[c] Zedekiah, king over Judah and Jerusalem.

Zedekiah King of Judah

[11]Zedekiah was twenty-one years old when he became king, and he reigned in Jerusalem eleven years. [12]He did evil in the eyes of the LORD his God and did not humble himself before Jeremiah the prophet, who spoke the word of the LORD. [13]He also rebelled against King Nebuchadnezzar, who had made him take an oath in God's name. He became stiff-necked and hardened his heart and would not turn to the LORD, the God of Israel. [14]Furthermore, all the leaders of the priests and the people became more and more unfaithful, following all the detestable practices of the nations and defiling the temple of the LORD, which he had consecrated in Jerusalem.

The Fall of Jerusalem

[15]The LORD, the God of their fathers, sent word to them through his messengers again and again, because he had pity on his people and on his dwelling place. [16]But they mocked God's messengers, despised his words and scoffed at his prophets until the wrath of the LORD was aroused against his people and there was no remedy. [17]He brought up against them the king of the Babylonians,[d] who killed their young men with the sword in the sanctuary, and spared neither young man nor young woman, old man or aged. God handed all of them over to Nebuchadnezzar. [18]He carried to Babylon all the articles from the temple of God, both large and small, and the treasures of the LORD's temple and the treasures of the king and his officials. [19]They set fire to God's temple and broke down the wall of Jerusalem; they burned all the palaces and destroyed everything of value there.

[20]He carried into exile to Babylon the remnant, who escaped from the sword, and they became servants to him and his sons until the kingdom of Persia came to power. [21]The land enjoyed its sabbath rests; all the time of its desolation it rested, until the seventy years were completed in fulfillment of the word of the LORD spoken by Jeremiah.

[22]In the first year of Cyrus king of Persia, in order to fulfill the word of the LORD spoken by Jeremiah, the LORD moved the heart of Cyrus king of Persia to make a proclamation throughout his realm and to put it in writing:

[23]"This is what Cyrus king of Persia says:

" 'The LORD, the God of heaven, has given me all the kingdoms of the earth and he has appointed me to build a temple for him at Jerusalem in Judah. Anyone of his people among you— may the LORD his God be with him, and let him go up.' "

---

a7 Or *palace*   *b9* One Hebrew manuscript, some Septuagint manuscripts and Syriac (see also 2 Kings 24:8); most Hebrew manuscripts *eight*   *c10* Hebrew *brother*, that is, relative (see 2 Kings 24:17)   *d17* Or *Chaldeans*

...E...

zra writes about the return of two groups of exiles from Babylon to the promised land. He gives God the credit for working through various rulers and circumstances to bring God's people home. As you read this book, take heart that the God of faithfulness always gives you a second chance to trust and follow him. He will give you what you need to make your life count for him.

EZRA

Cyrus Helps the Exiles to Return

1 In the first year of Cyrus king of Persia, in order to fulfill the word of the LORD spoken by Jeremiah, the LORD moved the heart of Cyrus king of Persia to make a proclamation throughout his realm and to put it in writing:

2"This is what Cyrus king of Persia says:

" 'The LORD, the God of heaven, has given me all the kingdoms of the earth and he has appointed me to build a temple for him at Jerusalem in Judah. 3Anyone of his people among you— may his God be with him, and let him go up to Jerusalem in Judah and build the temple of the LORD, the God of Israel, the God who is in Jerusalem. 4And the people of any place where survivors may now be living are to provide him with silver and gold, with goods and livestock, and with freewill offerings for the temple of God in Jerusalem.' "

5Then the family heads of Judah and Benjamin, and the priests and Levites—everyone whose heart God had moved—prepared to go up and build the house of the LORD in Jerusalem. 6All their neighbors assisted them with articles of silver and gold, with goods and livestock, and with valuable gifts, in addition to all the freewill offerings. 7Moreover, King Cyrus brought out the articles belonging to the temple of the LORD, which Nebuchadnezzar had carried away from Jerusalem and had placed in the temple of his god.[a] 8Cyrus king of Persia had them brought by Mithre-

a7 Or gods

dath the treasurer, who counted them out to Sheshbazzar the prince of Judah.

⁹This was the inventory:

gold dishes	30
silver dishes	1,000
silver pans*a*	29
¹⁰gold bowls	30
matching silver bowls	410
other articles	1,000

¹¹In all, there were 5,400 articles of gold and of silver. Sheshbazzar brought all these along when the exiles came up from Babylon to Jerusalem.

The List of the Exiles Who Returned

2 Now these are the people of the province who came up from the captivity of the exiles, whom Nebuchadnezzar king of Babylon had taken captive to Babylon (they returned to Jerusalem and Judah, each to his own town, ²in company with Zerubbabel, Jeshua, Nehemiah, Seraiah, Reelaiah, Mordecai, Bilshan, Mispar, Bigvai, Rehum and Baanah):

The list of the men of the people of Israel:

³the descendants of Parosh	2,172
⁴of Shephatiah	372
⁵of Arah	775
⁶of Pahath-Moab (through the line of Jeshua and Joab)	2,812
⁷of Elam	1,254
⁸of Zattu	945
⁹of Zaccai	760
¹⁰of Bani	642
¹¹of Bebai	623
¹²of Azgad	1,222
¹³of Adonikam	666
¹⁴of Bigvai	2,056
¹⁵of Adin	454
¹⁶of Ater (through Hezekiah)	98
¹⁷of Bezai	323
¹⁸of Jorah	112
¹⁹of Hashum	223
²⁰of Gibbar	95
²¹the men of Bethlehem	123
²²of Netophah	56
²³of Anathoth	128
²⁴of Azmaveth	42
²⁵of Kiriath Jearim,*b* Kephirah and Beeroth	743
²⁶of Ramah and Geba	621
²⁷of Micmash	122
²⁸of Bethel and Ai	223
²⁹of Nebo	52
³⁰of Magbish	156
³¹of the other Elam	1,254
³²of Harim	320
³³of Lod, Hadid and Ono	725
³⁴of Jericho	345
³⁵of Senaah	3,630

³⁶The priests:

the descendants of Jedaiah (through the family of Jeshua)	973
³⁷of Immer	1,052
³⁸of Pashhur	1,247
³⁹of Harim	1,017

⁴⁰The Levites:

the descendants of Jeshua and Kadmiel (through the line of Hodaviah)	74

⁴¹The singers:

the descendants of Asaph	128

⁴²The gatekeepers of the temple:

the descendants of Shallum, Ater, Talmon, Akkub, Hatita and Shobai	139

⁴³The temple servants:

the descendants of Ziha, Hasupha, Tabbaoth, ⁴⁴Keros, Siaha, Padon, ⁴⁵Lebanah, Hagabah, Akkub, ⁴⁶Hagab, Shalmai, Hanan, ⁴⁷Giddel, Gahar, Reaiah, ⁴⁸Rezin, Nekoda, Gazzam, ⁴⁹Uzza, Paseah, Besai,

*a*9 The meaning of the Hebrew for this word is uncertain. *b*25 See Septuagint (see also Neh. 7:29); Hebrew *Kiriath Arim*.

⁵⁰Asnah, Meunim,
Nephussim,
⁵¹Bakbuk, Hakupha, Harhur,
⁵²Bazluth, Mehida, Harsha,
⁵³Barkos, Sisera, Temah,
⁵⁴Neziah and Hatipha

⁵⁵The descendants of the servants of Solomon:

the descendants of
Sotai, Hassophereth,
Peruda,
⁵⁶Jaala, Darkon, Giddel,
⁵⁷Shephatiah, Hattil,
Pokereth-Hazzebaim and
Ami

⁵⁸The temple servants and
the descendants of the
servants of Solomon   392

⁵⁹The following came up from the towns of Tel Melah, Tel Harsha, Kerub, Addon and Immer, but they could not show that their families were descended from Israel:

⁶⁰The descendants of
Delaiah, Tobiah and
Nekoda   652

⁶¹And from among the priests:

The descendants of
Hobaiah, Hakkoz and
Barzillai (a man who had
married a daughter of
Barzillai the Gileadite and
was called by that name).

⁶²These searched for their family records, but they could not find them and so were excluded from the priesthood as unclean. ⁶³The governor ordered them not to eat any of the most sacred food until there was a priest ministering with the Urim and Thummim.

⁶⁴The whole company numbered 42,360, ⁶⁵besides their 7,337 menservants and maidservants; and they also had 200 men and women singers. ⁶⁶They had

736 horses, 245 mules, ⁶⁷435 camels and 6,720 donkeys.

⁶⁸When they arrived at the house of the Lord in Jerusalem, some of the heads of the families gave freewill offerings toward the rebuilding of the house of God on its site. ⁶⁹According to their ability they gave to the treasury for this work 61,000 drachmas[a] of gold, 5,000 minas[b] of silver and 100 priestly garments.

⁷⁰The priests, the Levites, the singers, the gatekeepers and the temple servants settled in their own towns, along with some of the other people, and the rest of the Israelites settled in their towns.

Rebuilding the Altar

3 When the seventh month came and the Israelites had settled in their towns, the people assembled as one man in Jerusalem. ²Then Jeshua son of Jozadak and his fellow priests and Zerubbabel son of Shealtiel and his associates began to build the altar of the God of Israel to sacrifice burnt offerings on it, in accordance with what is written in the Law of Moses the man of God. ³Despite their fear of the peoples around them, they built the altar on its foundation and sacrificed burnt offerings on it to the Lord, both the morning and evening sacrifices. ⁴Then in accordance with what is written, they celebrated the Feast of Tabernacles with the required number of burnt offerings prescribed for each day. ⁵After that, they presented the regular burnt offerings, the New Moon sacrifices and the sacrifices for all the appointed sacred feasts of the Lord, as well as those brought as freewill offerings to the Lord. ⁶On the first day of the seventh month they began to offer burnt offerings to the Lord, though the foundation of the Lord's temple had not yet been laid.

Rebuilding the Temple

⁷Then they gave money to the ma-

ᵃ69 That is, about 1,100 pounds (about 500 kilograms) metric tons)   ᵇ69 That is, about 3 tons (about 2.9

sons and carpenters, and gave food and drink and oil to the people of Sidon and Tyre, so that they would bring cedar logs by sea from Lebanon to Joppa, as authorized by Cyrus king of Persia.

[8]In the second month of the second year after their arrival at the house of God in Jerusalem, Zerubbabel son of Shealtiel, Jeshua son of Jozadak and the rest of their brothers (the priests and the Levites and all who had returned from the captivity to Jerusalem) began the work, appointing Levites twenty years of age and older to supervise the building of the house of the LORD. [9]Jeshua and his sons and brothers and Kadmiel and his sons (descendants of Hodaviah[a]) and the sons of Henadad and their sons and brothers—all Levites—joined together in supervising those working on the house of God.

[10]When the builders laid the foundation of the temple of the LORD, the priests in their vestments and with trumpets, and the Levites (the sons of Asaph) with cymbals, took their places to praise the LORD, as prescribed by David king of Israel. [11]With praise and thanksgiving they sang to the LORD:

"He is good;
　his love to Israel endures
　　forever."

And all the people gave a great shout of praise to the LORD, because the foundation of the house of the LORD was laid. [12]But many of the older priests and Levites and family heads, who had seen the former temple, wept aloud when they saw the foundation of this temple being laid, while many others shouted for joy. [13]No one could distinguish the sound of the shouts of joy from the sound of weeping, because the people made so much noise. And the sound was heard far away.

Opposition to the Rebuilding

4 When the enemies of Judah and Benjamin heard that the exiles were building a temple for the LORD, the God of Israel, [2]they came to Zerubbabel and to the heads of the families and said, "Let us help you build because, like you, we seek your God and have been sacrificing to him since the time of Esarhaddon king of Assyria, who brought us here."

[3]But Zerubbabel, Jeshua and the rest of the heads of the families of Israel answered, "You have no part with us in building a temple to our God. We alone will build it for the LORD, the God of Israel, as King Cyrus, the king of Persia, commanded us."

[4]Then the peoples around them set out to discourage the people of Judah and make them afraid to go on building.[b] [5]They hired counselors to work against them and frustrate their plans during the entire reign of Cyrus king of Persia and down to the reign of Darius king of Persia.

Later Opposition Under Xerxes and Artaxerxes

[6]At the beginning of the reign of Xerxes,[c] they lodged an accusation against the people of Judah and Jerusalem.

[7]And in the days of Artaxerxes king of Persia, Bishlam, Mithredath, Tabeel and the rest of his associates wrote a letter to Artaxerxes. The letter was written in Aramaic script and in the Aramaic language.[d,e]

[8]Rehum the commanding officer and Shimshai the secretary wrote a letter against Jerusalem to Artaxerxes the king as follows:

[9]Rehum the commanding officer and Shimshai the secretary, together with the rest of their associates—the judges and officials

---

[a]9 Hebrew *Yehudah*, probably a variant of *Hodaviah*　　　[b]4 Or *and troubled them as they built*
[c]6 Hebrew *Ahasuerus*, a variant of Xerxes' Persian name　　　[d]7 Or *written in Aramaic and*
translated　　　[e]7 The text of Ezra 4:8—6:18 is in Aramaic.

over the men from Tripolis, Persia,[a] Erech and Babylon, the Elamites of Susa, [10]and the other people whom the great and honorable Ashurbanipal[b] deported and settled in the city of Samaria and elsewhere in Trans-Euphrates.

[11](This is a copy of the letter they sent him.)

To King Artaxerxes,

From your servants, the men of Trans-Euphrates:

[12]The king should know that

[a]9 Or officials, magistrates and governors over the men from Ashurbanipal   [b]10 Aramaic Osnappar, a variant of

FRIDAY

VERSE:
Ezra 3:12

AUTHOR:
Leslie E. Moser

PASSAGE:
Ezra 3:7–13

Growing in Joy

Growing older brings with it many problems. Some of us have failing health, some have broken families, and almost all experience body aches, heartaches, or both. Adversity should never be the glue that holds us in relationship with the Lord. On the other hand, adversity should never separate us from the love of God nor from our joy in the Lord.

Is your joy in the Lord waning? Are you allowing despair about your aging to get between you and the Lord? If your answer to either question is yes, then you would do well to say, "Get behind me, Satan!" (Matthew 16:23). This command applies whether you feel that Satan is a personal demon intruding in your life or if you think of your own personal weaknesses as an evil force. As you move through life toward heavenly fellowship with the Lord, your joy should become more and more full, even if your joy must sometimes be clouded by a film of physical or mental pain. And be aware that Satan will do what he can to minimize the joy the Lord would have you experience.

ADDITIONAL SCRIPTURE READINGS
Psalm 126; John 16:17–28

Go to page 571 for your next devotional reading.

the Jews who came up to us from you have gone to Jerusalem and are rebuilding that rebellious and wicked city. They are restoring the walls and repairing the foundations.

[13]Furthermore, the king should know that if this city is built and its walls are restored, no more taxes, tribute or duty will be paid, and the royal revenues will suffer. [14]Now since we are under obligation to the palace and it is not proper for us to see the king dishonored, we are sending this message to inform the king, [15]so that a search may be made in the archives of your predecessors. In these records you will find that this city is a rebellious city, troublesome to kings and provinces, a place of rebellion from ancient times. That is why this city was destroyed. [16]We inform the king that if this city is built and its walls are restored, you will be left with nothing in Trans-Euphrates.

[17]The king sent this reply:

To Rehum the commanding officer, Shimshai the secretary and the rest of their associates living in Samaria and elsewhere in Trans-Euphrates:

Greetings.

[18]The letter you sent us has been read and translated in my presence. [19]I issued an order and a search was made, and it was found that this city has a long history of revolt against kings and has been a place of rebellion and sedition. [20]Jerusalem has had powerful kings ruling over the whole of Trans-Euphrates, and taxes, tribute and duty were paid to them. [21]Now issue an order to these men to stop work, so that this city will not be rebuilt until I so order. [22]Be careful not to neglect this matter. Why let this threat grow, to the detriment of the royal interests?

[23]As soon as the copy of the letter of King Artaxerxes was read to Rehum and Shimshai the secretary and their associates, they went immediately to the Jews in Jerusalem and compelled them by force to stop.

[24]Thus the work on the house of God in Jerusalem came to a standstill until the second year of the reign of Darius king of Persia.

Tattenai's Letter to Darius

5 Now Haggai the prophet and Zechariah the prophet, a descendant of Iddo, prophesied to the Jews in Judah and Jerusalem in the name of the God of Israel, who was over them. [2]Then Zerubbabel son of Shealtiel and Jeshua son of Jozadak set to work to rebuild the house of God in Jerusalem. And the prophets of God were with them, helping them.

[3]At that time Tattenai, governor of Trans-Euphrates, and Shethar-Bozenai and their associates went to them and asked, "Who authorized you to rebuild this temple and restore this structure?" [4]They also asked, "What are the names of the men constructing this building?"[a] [5]But the eye of their God was watching over the elders of the Jews, and they were not stopped until a report could go to Darius and his written reply be received.

[6]This is a copy of the letter that Tattenai, governor of Trans-Euphrates, and Shethar-Bozenai and their associates, the officials of Trans-Euphrates, sent to King Darius. [7]The report they sent him read as follows:

To King Darius:

Cordial greetings.

[8]The king should know that we went to the district of Judah, to the temple of the great God. The people are building it with

large stones and placing the timbers in the walls. The work is being carried on with diligence and is making rapid progress under their direction.

[9] We questioned the elders and asked them, "Who authorized you to rebuild this temple and restore this structure?" [10] We also asked them their names, so that we could write down the names of their leaders for your information.

[11] This is the answer they gave us:

"We are the servants of the God of heaven and earth, and we are rebuilding the temple that was built many years ago, one that a great king of Israel built and finished. [12] But because our fathers angered the God of heaven, he handed them over to Nebuchadnezzar the Chaldean, king of Babylon, who destroyed this temple and deported the people to Babylon.

[13] "However, in the first year of Cyrus king of Babylon, King Cyrus issued a decree to rebuild this house of God. [14] He even removed from the temple[a] of Babylon the gold and silver articles of the house of God, which Nebuchadnezzar had taken from the temple in Jerusalem and brought to the temple[a] in Babylon.

"Then King Cyrus gave them to a man named Sheshbazzar, whom he had appointed governor, [15] and he told him, 'Take these articles and go and deposit them in the temple in Jerusalem. And rebuild the house of God on its site.' [16] So this Sheshbazzar came and laid the foundations of the house of God in Jerusalem. From that day to the present it has been under construction but is not yet finished."

[17] Now if it pleases the king, let a search be made in the royal archives of Babylon to see if King Cyrus did in fact issue a decree to rebuild this house of God in Jerusalem. Then let the king send us his decision in this matter.

The Decree of Darius

6 King Darius then issued an order, and they searched in the archives stored in the treasury at Babylon. [2] A scroll was found in the citadel of Ecbatana in the province of Media, and this was written on it:

Memorandum:

[3] In the first year of King Cyrus, the king issued a decree concerning the temple of God in Jerusalem:

Let the temple be rebuilt as a place to present sacrifices, and let its foundations be laid. It is to be ninety feet[b] high and ninety feet wide, [4] with three courses of large stones and one of timbers. The costs are to be paid by the royal treasury. [5] Also, the gold and silver articles of the house of God, which Nebuchadnezzar took from the temple in Jerusalem and brought to Babylon, are to be returned to their places in the temple in Jerusalem; they are to be deposited in the house of God.

[6] Now then, Tattenai, governor of Trans-Euphrates, and Shethar-Bozenai and you, their fellow officials of that province, stay away from there. [7] Do not interfere with the work on this temple of God. Let the governor of the Jews and the Jewish elders rebuild this house of God on its site.

[8] Moreover, I hereby decree what you are to do for these elders of the Jews in the construction of this house of God:
The expenses of these men are

---

[a]14 Or palace   [b]3 Aramaic sixty cubits (about 27 meters)

to be fully paid out of the royal treasury, from the revenues of Trans-Euphrates, so that the work will not stop. ⁹Whatever is needed—young bulls, rams, male lambs for burnt offerings to the God of heaven, and wheat, salt, wine and oil, as requested by the priests in Jerusalem—must be given them daily without fail, ¹⁰so that they may offer sacrifices pleasing to the God of heaven and pray for the well-being of the king and his sons.

¹¹Furthermore, I decree that if anyone changes this edict, a beam is to be pulled from his house and he is to be lifted up and impaled on it. And for this crime his house is to be made a pile of rubble. ¹²May God, who has caused his Name to dwell there, overthrow any king or people who lifts a hand to change this decree or to destroy this temple in Jerusalem.

I Darius have decreed it. Let it be carried out with diligence.

Completion and Dedication of the Temple

¹³Then, because of the decree King Darius had sent, Tattenai, governor of Trans-Euphrates, and Shethar-Bozenai and their associates carried it out with diligence. ¹⁴So the elders of the Jews continued to build and prosper under the preaching of Haggai the prophet and Zechariah, a descendant of Iddo. They finished building the temple according to the command of the God of Israel and the decrees of Cyrus, Darius and Artaxerxes, kings of Persia. ¹⁵The temple was completed on the third day of the month Adar, in the sixth year of the reign of King Darius.

¹⁶Then the people of Israel—the priests, the Levites and the rest of the exiles—celebrated the dedication of the house of God with joy. ¹⁷For the dedication of this house of God they offered a hundred bulls, two hundred rams, four hundred male lambs and,

as a sin offering for all Israel, twelve male goats, one for each of the tribes of Israel. ¹⁸And they installed the priests in their divisions and the Levites in their groups for the service of God at Jerusalem, according to what is written in the Book of Moses.

The Passover

¹⁹On the fourteenth day of the first month, the exiles celebrated the Passover. ²⁰The priests and Levites had purified themselves and were all ceremonially clean. The Levites slaughtered the Passover lamb for all the exiles, for their brothers the priests and for themselves. ²¹So the Israelites who had returned from the exile ate it, together with all who had separated themselves from the unclean practices of their Gentile neighbors in order to seek the LORD, the God of Israel. ²²For seven days they celebrated with joy the Feast of Unleavened Bread, because the LORD had filled them with joy by changing the attitude of the king of Assyria, so that he assisted them in the work on the house of God, the God of Israel.

Ezra Comes to Jerusalem

7 After these things, during the reign of Artaxerxes king of Persia, Ezra son of Seraiah, the son of Azariah, the son of Hilkiah, ²the son of Shallum, the son of Zadok, the son of Ahitub, ³the son of Amariah, the son of Azariah, the son of Meraioth, ⁴the son of Zerahiah, the son of Uzzi, the son of Bukki, ⁵the son of Abishua, the son of Phinehas, the son of Eleazar, the son of Aaron the chief priest— ⁶this Ezra came up from Babylon. He was a teacher well versed in the Law of Moses, which the LORD, the God of Israel, had given. The king had granted him everything he asked, for the hand of the LORD his God was on him. ⁷Some of the Israelites, including priests, Levites, singers, gatekeepers and temple servants, also came up to Jerusalem in the seventh year of King Artaxerxes.

⁸Ezra arrived in Jerusalem in the fifth month of the seventh year of the

king. ⁹He had begun his journey from Babylon on the first day of the first month, and he arrived in Jerusalem on the first day of the fifth month, for the gracious hand of his God was on him. ¹⁰For Ezra had devoted himself to the study and observance of the Law of the LORD, and to teaching its decrees and laws in Israel.

King Artaxerxes' Letter to Ezra

¹¹This is a copy of the letter King Artaxerxes had given to Ezra the priest and teacher, a man learned in matters concerning the commands and decrees of the LORD for Israel:

¹²ᵃArtaxerxes, king of kings,

To Ezra the priest, a teacher of the Law of the God of heaven:

Greetings.

¹³Now I decree that any of the Israelites in my kingdom, including priests and Levites, who wish to go to Jerusalem with you, may go. ¹⁴You are sent by the king and his seven advisers to inquire about Judah and Jerusalem with regard to the Law of your God, which is in your hand. ¹⁵Moreover, you are to take with you the silver and gold that the king and his advisers have freely given to the God of Israel, whose dwelling is in Jerusalem, ¹⁶together with all the silver and gold you may obtain from the province of Babylon, as well as the freewill offerings of the people and priests for the temple of their God in Jerusalem. ¹⁷With this money be sure to buy bulls, rams and male lambs, together with their grain offerings and drink offerings, and sacrifice them on the altar of the temple of your God in Jerusalem.

¹⁸You and your brother Jews may then do whatever seems best with the rest of the silver and gold, in accordance with the will of your God. ¹⁹Deliver to the God of Jerusalem all the articles entrusted to you for worship in the temple of your God. ²⁰And anything else needed for the temple of your God that you may have occasion to supply, you may provide from the royal treasury.

²¹Now I, King Artaxerxes, order all the treasurers of Trans-Euphrates to provide with diligence whatever Ezra the priest, a teacher of the Law of the God of heaven, may ask of you— ²²up to a hundred talentsᵇ of silver, a hundred corsᶜ of wheat, a hundred bathsᵈ of wine, a hundred bathsᵈ of olive oil, and salt without limit. ²³Whatever the God of heaven has prescribed, let it be done with diligence for the temple of the God of heaven. Why should there be wrath against the realm of the king and of his sons? ²⁴You are also to know that you have no authority to impose taxes, tribute or duty on any of the priests, Levites, singers, gatekeepers, temple servants or other workers at this house of God.

²⁵And you, Ezra, in accordance with the wisdom of your God, which you possess, appoint magistrates and judges to administer justice to all the people of Trans-Euphrates—all who know the laws of your God. And you are to teach any who do not know them. ²⁶Whoever does not obey the law of your God and the law of the king must surely be punished by death, banishment, confiscation of property, or imprisonment.

²⁷Praise be to the LORD, the God of our fathers, who has put it into the king's heart to bring honor to the house of the LORD in Jerusalem in this

---

ᵃ12 The text of Ezra 7:12-26 is in Aramaic.   ᵇ22 That is, about 3 3/4 tons (about 3.4 metric tons)   ᶜ22 That is, probably about 600 bushels (about 22 kiloliters)   ᵈ22 That is, probably about 600 gallons (about 2.2 kiloliters)

way 28and who has extended his good favor to me before the king and his advisers and all the king's powerful officials. Because the hand of the LORD my God was on me, I took courage and gathered leading men from Israel to go up with me.

List of the Family Heads Returning With Ezra

8 These are the family heads and those registered with them who came up with me from Babylon during the reign of King Artaxerxes:

2of the descendants of Phinehas, Gershom;
   of the descendants of Ithamar, Daniel;
   of the descendants of David, Hattush 3of the descendants of Shecaniah;

   of the descendants of Parosh, Zechariah, and with him were registered 150 men;
4of the descendants of Pahath-Moab, Eliehoenai son of Zerahiah, and with him 200 men;
5of the descendants of Zattu,a Shecaniah son of Jahaziel, and with him 300 men;
6of the descendants of Adin, Ebed son of Jonathan, and with him 50 men;
7of the descendants of Elam, Jeshaiah son of Athaliah, and with him 70 men;
8of the descendants of Shephatiah, Zebadiah son of Michael, and with him 80 men;
9of the descendants of Joab, Obadiah son of Jehiel, and with him 218 men;
10of the descendants of Bani,b Shelomith son of Josiphiah, and with him 160 men;
11of the descendants of Bebai, Zechariah son of Bebai, and with him 28 men;
12of the descendants of Azgad, Johanan son of Hakkatan, and with him 110 men;

13of the descendants of Adonikam, the last ones, whose names were Eliphelet, Jeuel and Shemaiah, and with them 60 men;
14of the descendants of Bigvai, Uthai and Zaccur, and with them 70 men.

The Return to Jerusalem

15I assembled them at the canal that flows toward Ahava, and we camped there three days. When I checked among the people and the priests, I found no Levites there. 16So I summoned Eliezer, Ariel, Shemaiah, Elnathan, Jarib, Elnathan, Nathan, Zechariah and Meshullam, who were leaders, and Joiarib and Elnathan, who were men of learning, 17and I sent them to Iddo, the leader in Casiphia. I told them what to say to Iddo and his kinsmen, the temple servants in Casiphia, so that they might bring attendants to us for the house of our God. 18Because the gracious hand of our God was on us, they brought us Sherebiah, a capable man, from the descendants of Mahli son of Levi, the son of Israel, and Sherebiah's sons and brothers, 18 men; 19and Hashabiah, together with Jeshaiah from the descendants of Merari, and his brothers and nephews, 20 men. 20They also brought 220 of the temple servants—a body that David and the officials had established to assist the Levites. All were registered by name.

21There, by the Ahava Canal, I proclaimed a fast, so that we might humble ourselves before our God and ask him for a safe journey for us and our children, with all our possessions. 22I was ashamed to ask the king for soldiers and horsemen to protect us from enemies on the road, because we had told the king, "The gracious hand of our God is on everyone who looks to him, but his great anger is against all who forsake him." 23So we fasted and petitioned our God about this, and he answered our prayer.

---

a5 Some Septuagint manuscripts (also 1 Esdras 8:32); Hebrew does not have Zattu.　　b10 Some Septuagint manuscripts (also 1 Esdras 8:36); Hebrew does not have Bani.

²⁴Then I set apart twelve of the leading priests, together with Sherebiah, Hashabiah and ten of their brothers, ²⁵and I weighed out to them the offering of silver and gold and the articles that the king, his advisers, his officials and all Israel present there had donated for the house of our God. ²⁶I weighed out to them 650 talents*a* of silver, silver articles weighing 100 talents,*b* 100 talents*b* of gold, ²⁷20 bowls of gold valued at 1,000 darics,*c* and two fine articles of polished bronze, as precious as gold.

²⁸I said to them, "You as well as these articles are consecrated to the LORD. The silver and gold are a freewill offering to the LORD, the God of your fathers. ²⁹Guard them carefully until you weigh them out in the chambers of the house of the LORD in Jerusalem before the leading priests and the Levites and the family heads of Israel." ³⁰Then the priests and Levites received the silver and gold and sacred articles that had been weighed out to be taken to the house of our God in Jerusalem.

³¹On the twelfth day of the first month we set out from the Ahava Canal to go to Jerusalem. The hand of our God was on us, and he protected us from enemies and bandits along the way. ³²So we arrived in Jerusalem, where we rested three days.

³³On the fourth day, in the house of our God, we weighed out the silver and gold and the sacred articles into the hands of Meremoth son of Uriah, the priest. Eleazar son of Phinehas was with him, and so were the Levites Jozabad son of Jeshua and Noadiah son of Binnui. ³⁴Everything was accounted for by number and weight, and the entire weight was recorded at that time.

³⁵Then the exiles who had returned from captivity sacrificed burnt offerings to the God of Israel: twelve bulls for all Israel, ninety-six rams, seventy-seven male lambs and, as a sin offering, twelve male goats. All this was a burnt offering to the LORD. ³⁶They also delivered the king's orders to the royal satraps and to the governors of Trans-Euphrates, who then gave assistance to the people and to the house of God.

Ezra's Prayer About Intermarriage

9 After these things had been done, the leaders came to me and said, "The people of Israel, including the priests and the Levites, have not kept themselves separate from the neighboring peoples with their detestable practices, like those of the Canaanites, Hittites, Perizzites, Jebusites, Ammonites, Moabites, Egyptians and Amorites. ²They have taken some of their daughters as wives for themselves and their sons, and have mingled the holy race with the peoples around them. And the leaders and officials have led the way in this unfaithfulness."

³When I heard this, I tore my tunic and cloak, pulled hair from my head and beard and sat down appalled. ⁴Then everyone who trembled at the words of the God of Israel gathered around me because of this unfaithfulness of the exiles. And I sat there appalled until the evening sacrifice.

⁵Then, at the evening sacrifice, I rose from my self-abasement, with my tunic and cloak torn, and fell on my knees with my hands spread out to the LORD my God ⁶and prayed:

"O my God, I am too ashamed and disgraced to lift up my face to you, my God, because our sins are higher than our heads and our guilt has reached to the heavens. ⁷From the days of our forefathers until now, our guilt has been great. Because of our sins, we and our kings and our priests have been subjected to the sword and captivity, to pillage and humiliation at the hand of foreign kings, as it is today.

⁸"But now, for a brief moment,

---

a26 That is, about 25 tons (about 22 metric tons)   *b26* That is, about 3 3/4 tons (about 3.4 metric tons)   *c27* That is, about 19 pounds (about 8.5 kilograms) the LORD our God has been gracious in leaving us a remnant and giving us a firm place in his sanctuary, and so our God gives light to our eyes and a little relief in our bondage. [9]Though we are slaves, our God has not deserted us in our bondage. He has shown us kindness in the sight of the kings of Persia: He has granted us new life to rebuild the house of our God and repair its ruins, and he has given us a wall of protection in Judah and Jerusalem.

[10]"But now, O our God, what can we say after this? For we have disregarded the commands [11]you gave through your servants the prophets when you said: 'The land you are entering to possess is a land polluted by the corruption of its peoples. By their detestable practices they have filled it with their impurity from one end to the other. [12]Therefore, do not give your daughters in marriage to their sons or take their daughters for your sons. Do not seek a treaty of friendship with them at any time, that you may be strong and eat the good things of the land and leave it to your children as an everlasting inheritance.'

[13]"What has happened to us is a result of our evil deeds and our great guilt, and yet, our God, you have punished us less than our sins have deserved and have given us a remnant like this. [14]Shall we again break your commands and intermarry with the peoples who commit such detestable practices? Would you not be angry enough with us to destroy us, leaving us no remnant or survivor? [15]O LORD, God of Israel, you are righteous! We are left this day as a remnant. Here we are before you in our guilt, though because of it not one of us can stand in your presence."

The People's Confession of Sin

10 While Ezra was praying and confessing, weeping and throwing himself down before the house of God, a large crowd of Israelites—men, women and children—gathered around him. They too wept bitterly. [2]Then Shecaniah son of Jehiel, one of the descendants of Elam, said to Ezra, "We have been unfaithful to our God by marrying foreign women from the peoples around us. But in spite of this, there is still hope for Israel. [3]Now let us make a covenant before our God to send away all these women and their children, in accordance with the counsel of my lord and of those who fear the commands of our God. Let it be done according to the Law. [4]Rise up; this matter is in your hands. We will support you, so take courage and do it."

[5]So Ezra rose up and put the leading priests and Levites and all Israel under oath to do what had been suggested. And they took the oath. [6]Then Ezra withdrew from before the house of God and went to the room of Jehohanan son of Eliashib. While he was there, he ate no food and drank no water, because he continued to mourn over the unfaithfulness of the exiles.

[7]A proclamation was then issued throughout Judah and Jerusalem for all the exiles to assemble in Jerusalem. [8]Anyone who failed to appear within three days would forfeit all his property, in accordance with the decision of the officials and elders, and would himself be expelled from the assembly of the exiles.

[9]Within the three days, all the men of Judah and Benjamin had gathered in Jerusalem. And on the twentieth day of the ninth month, all the people were sitting in the square before the house of God, greatly distressed by the occasion and because of the rain. [10]Then Ezra the priest stood up and said to them, "You have been unfaithful; you have married foreign women, adding to Israel's guilt. [11]Now make confession to the LORD, the God of your fathers, and do his will. Separate

PASSAGE: 1 Corinthians 1:26–31; 2 Corinthians 12:21–30
AUTHOR: Author Unknown

My Prayer Is Answered

I asked for strength that I might achieve;
    I was made weak that I might obey.
I asked for health that I might do greater things;
    I was given infirmity that I might do better
        things.
I asked for riches that I might be happy;
    I was given poverty that I might be wise.
I asked for power that I might have the praise of
    men;
    I was given weakness that I might feel the
        need of God.
I asked for all things that I might enjoy life;
    I was given life that I might enjoy all things.
I have received nothing I asked for, all that
    I hoped for.
My prayer is answered.

Go to page 579 for your next devotional reading.

yourselves from the peoples around you and from your foreign wives."

¹²The whole assembly responded with a loud voice: "You are right! We must do as you say. ¹³But there are many people here and it is the rainy season; so we cannot stand outside. Besides, this matter cannot be taken care of in a day or two, because we have sinned greatly in this thing. ¹⁴Let our officials act for the whole assembly. Then let everyone in our towns who has married a foreign woman come at a set time, along with the elders and judges of each town, until the fierce anger of our God in this matter is turned away from us." ¹⁵Only Jonathan son of Asahel and Jahzeiah son of Tikvah, supported by Meshullam and Shabbethai the Levite, opposed this.

¹⁶So the exiles did as was proposed. Ezra the priest selected men who were family heads, one from each family division, and all of them designated by name. On the first day of the tenth month they sat down to investigate the cases, ¹⁷and by the first day of the first month they finished dealing with all the men who had married foreign women.

Those Guilty of Intermarriage

¹⁸Among the descendants of the priests, the following had married foreign women:

From the descendants of Jeshua son of Jozadak, and his brothers: Maaseiah, Eliezer, Jarib and Gedaliah. ¹⁹(They all gave their hands in pledge to put away their wives, and for their guilt they each presented a ram from the flock as a guilt offering.)

²⁰From the descendants of Immer:
Hanani and Zebadiah.

²¹From the descendants of Harim:
Maaseiah, Elijah, Shemaiah, Jehiel and Uzziah.

²²From the descendants of Pashhur:

Elioenai, Maaseiah, Ishmael, Nethanel, Jozabad and Elasah.

²³Among the Levites:

Jozabad, Shimei, Kelaiah (that is, Kelita), Pethahiah, Judah and Eliezer.

²⁴From the singers:
Eliashib.
From the gatekeepers:
Shallum, Telem and Uri.

²⁵And among the other Israelites:

From the descendants of Parosh:
Ramiah, Izziah, Malkijah, Mijamin, Eleazar, Malkijah and Benaiah.

²⁶From the descendants of Elam:
Mattaniah, Zechariah, Jehiel, Abdi, Jeremoth and Elijah.

²⁷From the descendants of Zattu:
Elioenai, Eliashib, Mattaniah, Jeremoth, Zabad and Aziza.

²⁸From the descendants of Bebai:
Jehohanan, Hananiah, Zabbai and Athlai.

²⁹From the descendants of Bani:
Meshullam, Malluch, Adaiah, Jashub, Sheal and Jeremoth.

³⁰From the descendants of Pahath-Moab:
Adna, Kelal, Benaiah, Maaseiah, Mattaniah, Bezalel, Binnui and Manasseh.

³¹From the descendants of Harim:
Eliezer, Ishijah, Malkijah, Shemaiah, Shimeon, ³²Benjamin, Malluch and Shemariah.

³³From the descendants of Hashum:
Mattenai, Mattattah, Zabad, Eliphelet, Jeremai, Manasseh and Shimei.

³⁴From the descendants of Bani:
Maadai, Amram, Uel, ³⁵Benaiah, Bedeiah, Keluhi, ³⁶Vaniah, Meremoth, Eliashib, ³⁷Mattaniah, Mattenai and Jaasu.

³⁸From the descendants of Binnui:ᵃ

ᵃ37,38 See Septuagint (also 1 Esdras 9:34); Hebrew *Jaasu* ³⁸*and Bani and Binnui,*

Shimei, [39]Shelemiah, Nathan, Adaiah, [40]Macnadebai, Shashai, Sharai, [41]Azarel, Shelemiah, Shemariah, [42]Shallum, Amariah and Joseph. [43]From the descendants of Nebo:

Jeiel, Mattithiah, Zabad, Zebina, Jaddai, Joel and Benaiah.

[44]All these had married foreign women, and some of them had children by these wives.[a]

*...T...*his book recounts Nehemiah's time as governor of Judah when the Jews were returning from Babylon. Using savvy leadership skills, a servant attitude, hard work and reliance on God in prayer, he completed the rebuilding of the walls of Jerusalem in 52 days. As you read this book, catch the vision of serving God, whatever your age or situation in life may be. God will use you as you tap into his abundant power.

NEHEMIAH

Nehemiah's Prayer

1 The words of Nehemiah son of Hacaliah:

In the month of Kislev in the twentieth year, while I was in the citadel of Susa, ²Hanani, one of my brothers, came from Judah with some other men, and I questioned them about the Jewish remnant that survived the exile, and also about Jerusalem.

³They said to me, "Those who survived the exile and are back in the province are in great trouble and disgrace. The wall of Jerusalem is broken down, and its gates have been burned with fire."

⁴When I heard these things, I sat down and wept. For some days I mourned and fasted and prayed before the God of heaven. ⁵Then I said:

"O Lᴏʀᴅ, God of heaven, the great and awesome God, who keeps his covenant of love with those who love him and obey his commands, ⁶let your ear be attentive and your eyes open to hear the prayer your servant is praying before you day and night for your servants, the people of Israel. I confess the sins we Israelites, including myself and my father's house, have committed against you. ⁷We have acted very wickedly toward you. We have not obeyed the commands, decrees and laws you gave your servant Moses.

⁸"Remember the instruction you gave your servant Moses, saying, 'If you are unfaithful, I will scatter you among the nations, ⁹but if you return to me and obey my commands, then even if your exiled people are at the farthest horizon, I will gather them from there and bring them to the place I have chosen as a dwelling for my Name.'

¹⁰"They are your servants and your people, whom you redeemed by your great strength and your mighty hand. ¹¹O Lord, let your ear be attentive to the prayer of this your servant and to the prayer of your servants who delight in revering your name. Give your servant success today by granting him favor in the presence of this man."

I was cupbearer to the king.

Artaxerxes Sends Nehemiah to Jerusalem

2 In the month of Nisan in the twentieth year of King Artaxerxes, when wine was brought for him, I took the wine and gave it to the king. I had not been sad in his presence before; ²so the king asked me, "Why does your face look so sad when you are not ill? This can be nothing but sadness of heart."

I was very much afraid, ³but I said to the king, "May the king live forever! Why should my face not look sad when the city where my fathers are buried lies in ruins, and its gates have been destroyed by fire?"

⁴The king said to me, "What is it you want?"

Then I prayed to the God of heaven, ⁵and I answered the king, "If it pleases the king and if your servant has found favor in his sight, let him send me to the city in Judah where my fathers are buried so that I can rebuild it."

⁶Then the king, with the queen sitting beside him, asked me, "How long will your journey take, and when will you get back?" It pleased the king to send me; so I set a time.

⁷I also said to him, "If it pleases the king, may I have letters to the governors of Trans-Euphrates, so that they will provide me safe-conduct until I arrive in Judah? ⁸And may I have a letter to Asaph, keeper of the king's forest, so he will give me timber to make beams for the gates of the citadel by the temple and for the city wall and for the residence I will occupy?" And because the gracious hand of my God was upon me, the king granted my requests. ⁹So I went to the governors of Trans-Euphrates and gave them the king's letters. The king had also sent army officers and cavalry with me.

¹⁰When Sanballat the Horonite and Tobiah the Ammonite official heard about this, they were very much disturbed that someone had come to promote the welfare of the Israelites.

Nehemiah Inspects Jerusalem's Walls

¹¹I went to Jerusalem, and after staying there three days ¹²I set out during the night with a few men. I had not told anyone what my God had put in my heart to do for Jerusalem. There were no mounts with me except the one I was riding on.

¹³By night I went out through the Valley Gate toward the Jackal[a] Well and the Dung Gate, examining the walls of Jerusalem, which had been broken down, and its gates, which had been destroyed by fire. ¹⁴Then I moved on toward the Fountain Gate and the King's Pool, but there was not enough room for my mount to get through; ¹⁵so I went up the valley by night, examining the wall. Finally, I turned back and reentered through the Valley Gate. ¹⁶The officials did not know where I had gone or what I was doing, because as yet I had said nothing to the Jews or the priests or nobles or officials or any others who would be doing the work.

¹⁷Then I said to them, "You see the trouble we are in: Jerusalem lies in ruins, and its gates have been burned with fire. Come, let us rebuild the wall of Jerusalem, and we will no longer be in disgrace." ¹⁸I also told them about the gracious hand of my God upon me and what the king had said to me.

a13 Or Serpent or Fig

They replied, "Let us start rebuilding." So they began this good work.

[19]But when Sanballat the Horonite, Tobiah the Ammonite official and Geshem the Arab heard about it, they mocked and ridiculed us. "What is this you are doing?" they asked. "Are you rebelling against the king?"

[20]I answered them by saying, "The God of heaven will give us success. We his servants will start rebuilding, but as for you, you have no share in Jerusalem or any claim or historic right to it."

Builders of the Wall

3 Eliashib the high priest and his fellow priests went to work and rebuilt the Sheep Gate. They dedicated it and set its doors in place, building as far as the Tower of the Hundred, which they dedicated, and as far as the Tower of Hananel. [2]The men of Jericho built the adjoining section, and Zaccur son of Imri built next to them.

[3]The Fish Gate was rebuilt by the sons of Hassenaah. They laid its beams and put its doors and bolts and bars in place. [4]Meremoth son of Uriah, the son of Hakkoz, repaired the next section. Next to him Meshullam son of Berekiah, the son of Meshezabel, made repairs, and next to him Zadok son of Baana also made repairs. [5]The next section was repaired by the men of Tekoa, but their nobles would not put their shoulders to the work under their supervisors.[a]

[6]The Jeshanah[b] Gate was repaired by Joiada son of Paseah and Meshullam son of Besodeiah. They laid its beams and put its doors and bolts and bars in place. [7]Next to them, repairs were made by men from Gibeon and Mizpah—Melatiah of Gibeon and Jadon of Meronoth—places under the authority of the governor of TransEuphrates. [8]Uzziel son of Harhaiah, one of the goldsmiths, repaired the next section; and Hananiah, one of the perfume-makers, made repairs next to that. They restored[c] Jerusalem as far as the Broad Wall. [9]Rephaiah son of Hur, ruler of a half-district of Jerusalem, repaired the next section. [10]Adjoining this, Jedaiah son of Harumaph made repairs opposite his house, and Hattush son of Hashabneiah made repairs next to him. [11]Malkijah son of Harim and Hasshub son of PahathMoab repaired another section and the Tower of the Ovens. [12]Shallum son of Hallohesh, ruler of a half-district of Jerusalem, repaired the next section with the help of his daughters.

[13]The Valley Gate was repaired by Hanun and the residents of Zanoah. They rebuilt it and put its doors and bolts and bars in place. They also repaired five hundred yards[d] of the wall as far as the Dung Gate.

[14]The Dung Gate was repaired by Malkijah son of Recab, ruler of the district of Beth Hakkerem. He rebuilt it and put its doors and bolts and bars in place.

[15]The Fountain Gate was repaired by Shallun son of Col-Hozeh, ruler of the district of Mizpah. He rebuilt it, roofing it over and putting its doors and bolts and bars in place. He also repaired the wall of the Pool of Siloam,[e] by the King's Garden, as far as the steps going down from the City of David. [16]Beyond him, Nehemiah son of Azbuk, ruler of a half-district of Beth Zur, made repairs up to a point opposite the tombs[f] of David, as far as the artificial pool and the House of the Heroes.

[17]Next to him, the repairs were made by the Levites under Rehum son of Bani. Beside him, Hashabiah, ruler of half the district of Keilah, carried out repairs for his district. [18]Next to him, the repairs were made by their countrymen under Binnui[g] son of

---

[a]5 Or their Lord or the governor   [b]6 Or Old   [c]8 Or They left out part of   [d]13 Hebrew a thousand cubits (about 450 meters)   [e]15 Hebrew Shelah, a variant of Shiloah, that is, Siloam   [f]16 Hebrew; Septuagint, some Vulgate manuscripts and Syriac tomb   [g]18 Two Hebrew manuscripts and Syriac (see also Septuagint and verse 24); most Hebrew manuscripts Bavvai

Henadad, ruler of the other half-district of Keilah. [19]Next to him, Ezer son of Jeshua, ruler of Mizpah, repaired another section, from a point facing the ascent to the armory as far as the angle. [20]Next to him, Baruch son of Zabbai zealously repaired another section, from the angle to the entrance of the house of Eliashib the high priest. [21]Next to him, Meremoth son of Uriah, the son of Hakkoz, repaired another section, from the entrance of Eliashib's house to the end of it.

[22]The repairs next to him were made by the priests from the surrounding region. [23]Beyond them, Benjamin and Hasshub made repairs in front of their house; and next to them, Azariah son of Maaseiah, the son of Ananiah, made repairs beside his house. [24]Next to him, Binnui son of Henadad repaired another section, from Azariah's house to the angle and the corner, [25]and Palal son of Uzai worked opposite the angle and the tower projecting from the upper palace near the court of the guard. Next to him, Pedaiah son of Parosh [26]and the temple servants living on the hill of Ophel made repairs up to a point opposite the Water Gate toward the east and the projecting tower. [27]Next to them, the men of Tekoa repaired another section, from the great projecting tower to the wall of Ophel.

[28]Above the Horse Gate, the priests made repairs, each in front of his own house. [29]Next to them, Zadok son of Immer made repairs opposite his house. Next to him, Shemaiah son of Shecaniah, the guard at the East Gate, made repairs. [30]Next to him, Hananiah son of Shelemiah, and Hanun, the sixth son of Zalaph, repaired another section. Next to them, Meshullam son of Berekiah made repairs opposite his living quarters. [31]Next to him, Malkijah, one of the goldsmiths, made repairs as far as the house of the temple servants and the merchants, opposite the Inspection Gate, and as far as the room above the corner; [32]and between

the room above the corner and the Sheep Gate the goldsmiths and merchants made repairs.

Opposition to the Rebuilding

4 When Sanballat heard that we were rebuilding the wall, he became angry and was greatly incensed. He ridiculed the Jews, [2]and in the presence of his associates and the army of Samaria, he said, "What are those feeble Jews doing? Will they restore their wall? Will they offer sacrifices? Will they finish in a day? Can they bring the stones back to life from those heaps of rubble—burned as they are?"

[3]Tobiah the Ammonite, who was at his side, said, "What they are building—if even a fox climbed up on it, he would break down their wall of stones!"

[4]Hear us, O our God, for we are despised. Turn their insults back on their own heads. Give them over as plunder in a land of captivity. [5]Do not cover up their guilt or blot out their sins from your sight, for they have thrown insults in the face of[a] the builders.

[6]So we rebuilt the wall till all of it reached half its height, for the people worked with all their heart.

[7]But when Sanballat, Tobiah, the Arabs, the Ammonites and the men of Ashdod heard that the repairs to Jerusalem's walls had gone ahead and that the gaps were being closed, they were very angry. [8]They all plotted together to come and fight against Jerusalem and stir up trouble against it. [9]But we prayed to our God and posted a guard day and night to meet this threat.

[10]Meanwhile, the people in Judah said, "The strength of the laborers is giving out, and there is so much rubble that we cannot rebuild the wall."

[11]Also our enemies said, "Before they know it or see us, we will be right there among them and will

---

[a]5 Or *have provoked you to anger before*

kill them and put an end to the work."

¹²Then the Jews who lived near them came and told us ten times over, "Wherever you turn, they will attack us."

¹³Therefore I stationed some of the people behind the lowest points of the wall at the exposed places, posting them by families, with their swords, spears and bows. ¹⁴After I looked things over, I stood up and said to the nobles, the officials and the rest of the people, "Don't be afraid of them. Remember the Lord, who is great and awesome, and fight for your brothers, your sons and your daughters, your wives and your homes."

¹⁵When our enemies heard that we were aware of their plot and that God had frustrated it, we all returned to the wall, each to his own work.

¹⁶From that day on, half of my men did the work, while the other half were equipped with spears, shields, bows and armor. The officers posted themselves behind all the people of Judah ¹⁷who were building the wall. Those who carried materials did their work with one hand and held a weapon in the other, ¹⁸and each of the builders wore his sword at his side as he worked. But the man who sounded the trumpet stayed with me.

¹⁹Then I said to the nobles, the officials and the rest of the people, "The work is extensive and spread out, and we are widely separated from each other along the wall. ²⁰Wherever you hear the sound of the trumpet, join us there. Our God will fight for us!"

²¹So we continued the work with half the men holding spears, from the first light of dawn till the stars came out. ²²At that time I also said to the people, "Have every man and his helper stay inside Jerusalem at night, so they can serve us as guards by night and workmen by day." ²³Neither I nor my brothers nor my men nor the guards with me took off our clothes; each had his weapon, even when he went for water.ᵃ

Nehemiah Helps the Poor

5 Now the men and their wives raised a great outcry against their Jewish brothers. ²Some were saying, "We and our sons and daughters are numerous; in order for us to eat and stay alive, we must get grain."

³Others were saying, "We are mortgaging our fields, our vineyards and our homes to get grain during the famine."

⁴Still others were saying, "We have had to borrow money to pay the king's tax on our fields and vineyards. ⁵Although we are of the same flesh and blood as our countrymen and though our sons are as good as theirs, yet we have to subject our sons and daughters to slavery. Some of our daughters have already been enslaved, but we are powerless, because our fields and our vineyards belong to others."

⁶When I heard their outcry and these charges, I was very angry. ⁷I pondered them in my mind and then accused the nobles and officials. I told them, "You are exacting usury from your own countrymen!" So I called together a large meeting to deal with them ⁸and said: "As far as possible, we have bought back our Jewish brothers who were sold to the Gentiles. Now you are selling your brothers, only for them to be sold back to us!" They kept quiet, because they could find nothing to say.

⁹So I continued, "What you are doing is not right. Shouldn't you walk in the fear of our God to avoid the reproach of our Gentile enemies? ¹⁰I and my brothers and my men are also lending the people money and grain. But let the exacting of usury stop! ¹¹Give back to them immediately their fields, vineyards, olive groves and houses, and also the usury you are charging them—the hundredth part of the money, grain, new wine and oil."

¹²"We will give it back," they said. "And we will not demand anything

---

ᵃ23 The meaning of the Hebrew for this clause is uncertain.

more from them. We will do as you say."

Then I summoned the priests and made the nobles and officials take an oath to do what they had promised. [13]I also shook out the folds of my robe and said, "In this way may God shake out of his house and possessions every man who does not keep this promise. So may such a man be shaken out and emptied!"

At this the whole assembly said, "Amen," and praised the LORD. And the people did as they had promised.

[14]Moreover, from the twentieth year of King Artaxerxes, when I was

MONDAY

VERSE:
Nehemiah 4:18

AUTHOR:
Jill Briscoe

PASSAGE:
Nehemiah 4:12–23

The Man With the Trumpet

Nehemiah undoubtedly rejoiced in the companionship of the man with the trumpet. How glad he must have been for the man's presence during those dark and dangerous days as they kept watch over God's family together. I am sure the man with the trumpet brought Nehemiah great consolation. This type of heavenly companionship is one of the evidences of the Spirit's indwelling — an inner assurance, deeper than emotion, that convinces us we are never alone — even when humanly speaking we are!

Furthermore, when the man with the trumpet comes to us, we find that he is not only company, but *good* company. He brings with him a sense of stability as he inhabits our souls, and we find we are "content with what [we] have, because God has said, 'Never will I leave you; never will I forsake you'" (Hebrews 13:5).

So the person who wonders if he or she has ever received the Holy Spirit in the first place has to ask this question: "What do I know of this constant Helper who has the ability to touch the raw edges of my inner hurts and whisper that healing is on the way? Do I really know what it is to be content with what I have or what I have not because I have him?"

ADDITIONAL SCRIPTURE READINGS
John 14:15–27; Romans 8:1–17

Go to page 581 for your next devotional reading.

appointed to be their governor in the land of Judah, until his thirty-second year—twelve years—neither I nor my brothers ate the food allotted to the governor. ¹⁵But the earlier governors—those preceding me—placed a heavy burden on the people and took forty shekels[a] of silver from them in addition to food and wine. Their assistants also lorded it over the people. But out of reverence for God I did not act like that. ¹⁶Instead, I devoted myself to the work on this wall. All my men were assembled there for the work; we[b] did not acquire any land.

¹⁷Furthermore, a hundred and fifty Jews and officials ate at my table, as well as those who came to us from the surrounding nations. ¹⁸Each day one ox, six choice sheep and some poultry were prepared for me, and every ten days an abundant supply of wine of all kinds. In spite of all this, I never demanded the food allotted to the governor, because the demands were heavy on these people.

¹⁹Remember me with favor, O my God, for all I have done for these people.

Further Opposition to the Rebuilding

6 When word came to Sanballat, Tobiah, Geshem the Arab and the rest of our enemies that I had rebuilt the wall and not a gap was left in it— though up to that time I had not set the doors in the gates— ²Sanballat and Geshem sent me this message: "Come, let us meet together in one of the villages[c] on the plain of Ono."

But they were scheming to harm me; ³so I sent messengers to them with this reply: "I am carrying on a great project and cannot go down. Why should the work stop while I leave it and go down to you?" ⁴Four times they sent me the same message, and each time I gave them the same answer.

⁵Then, the fifth time, Sanballat sent his aide to me with the same message, and in his hand was an unsealed letter ⁶in which was written:

"It is reported among the nations—and Geshem[d] says it is true—that you and the Jews are plotting to revolt, and therefore you are building the wall. Moreover, according to these reports you are about to become their king ⁷and have even appointed prophets to make this proclamation about you in Jerusalem: 'There is a king in Judah!' Now this report will get back to the king; so come, let us confer together."

⁸I sent him this reply: "Nothing like what you are saying is happening; you are just making it up out of your head."

⁹They were all trying to frighten us, thinking, "Their hands will get too weak for the work, and it will not be completed."

⌊But I prayed,⌋ "Now strengthen my hands."

¹⁰One day I went to the house of Shemaiah son of Delaiah, the son of Mehetabel, who was shut in at his home. He said, "Let us meet in the house of God, inside the temple, and let us close the temple doors, because men are coming to kill you—by night they are coming to kill you."

¹¹But I said, "Should a man like me run away? Or should one like me go into the temple to save his life? I will not go!" ¹²I realized that God had not sent him, but that he had prophesied against me because Tobiah and Sanballat had hired him. ¹³He had been hired to intimidate me so that I would commit a sin by doing this, and then they would give me a bad name to discredit me.

¹⁴Remember Tobiah and Sanballat, O my God, because of what they have done; remember also the prophetess Noadiah and the rest of the prophets

---

a15 That is, about 1 pound (about 0.5 kilogram)   b16 Most Hebrew manuscripts; some
Hebrew manuscripts, Septuagint, Vulgate and Syriac I   c2 Or in Kephirim   d6 Hebrew
Gashmu, a variant of Geshem

VERSE:	AUTHOR:	PASSAGE:
Nehemiah 6:9	Cornelis Gilhuis	Nehemiah 6:1–9

The School of Preparation

Work as long as it is day, as long as it is possible . . . You are no longer 40 or 50 years old. Gradually work should, if at all possible, become a little less. But you ought always to set yourself a task until it is no longer possible. Even then the work of prayer remains as a task. People who always just "sit there doing nothing," as I sometimes observe in some rest homes, are aging rapidly—if not physically, then spiritually. One can always find a task, certainly, if he does not set his goals too high and does not allow money to play too large a role.

Isn't there something to occupy you at home, in the family, in the church, at the neighbor's, among acquaintances who are ill, in the community? Isn't there something for which you can begin to care—even if it may seem insignificant at first?

And then, you should enter your so-called period of retirement as a new *phase of life*, as a new school of learning with new assignments. That period is not just an appendix to your previous life, but the *determining end-phase*. If the Lord grants you the life of a retired person, you must see this as an opportunity, a school of learning.

Look at your retirement and the days of your old age as a school for the aged which prepares you for the eternal life that awaits you.

ADDITIONAL SCRIPTURE READINGS
Psalm 90; 1 Corinthians 15:50–58

Go to page 585 for your next devotional reading.

who have been trying to intimidate me.

The Completion of the Wall

15So the wall was completed on the
twenty-fifth of Elul, in fifty-two days.
16When all our enemies heard about
this, all the surrounding nations were
afraid and lost their self-confidence,
because they realized that this work
had been done with the help of our
God.

17Also, in those days the nobles of
Judah were sending many letters to
Tobiah, and replies from Tobiah kept
coming to them. 18For many in Judah
were under oath to him, since he was
son-in-law to Shecaniah son of Arah,
and his son Jehohanan had married
the daughter of Meshullam son of
Berekiah. 19Moreover, they kept reporting to me his good deeds and
then telling him what I said. And Tobiah sent letters to intimidate me.

7 After the wall had been rebuilt
and I had set the doors in place,
the gatekeepers and the singers and
the Levites were appointed. 2I put in
charge of Jerusalem my brother Hanani, along with[a] Hananiah the commander of the citadel, because he was
a man of integrity and feared God
more than most men do. 3I said to
them, "The gates of Jerusalem are not
to be opened until the sun is hot.
While the gatekeepers are still on
duty, have them shut the doors and
bar them. Also appoint residents of
Jerusalem as guards, some at their
posts and some near their own
houses."

The List of the Exiles Who
Returned

4Now the city was large and spacious, but there were few people in it,
and the houses had not yet been rebuilt. 5So my God put it into my heart
to assemble the nobles, the officials
and the common people for registration by families. I found the genealogical record of those who had been the

first to return. This is what I found
written there:

6These are the people of the
province who came up from the
captivity of the exiles whom
Nebuchadnezzar king of Babylon had taken captive (they returned to Jerusalem and Judah,
each to his own town, 7in company with Zerubbabel, Jeshua, Nehemiah, Azariah, Raamiah, Na-
hamani, Mordecai, Bilshan,
Mispereth, Bigvai, Nehum and
Baanah):

The list of the men of Israel:

8the descendants of	
Parosh	2,172
9of Shephatiah	372
10of Arah	652
11of Pahath-Moab	
(through the line of	
Jeshua and Joab)	2,818
12of Elam	1,254
13of Zattu	845
14of Zaccai	760
15of Binnui	648
16of Bebai	628
17of Azgad	2,322
18of Adonikam	667
19of Bigvai	2,067
20of Adin	655
21of Ater (through	
Hezekiah)	98
22of Hashum	328
23of Bezai	324
24of Hariph	112
25of Gibeon	95
26the men of Bethlehem and	
Netophah	188
27of Anathoth	128
28of Beth Azmaveth	42
29of Kiriath Jearim,	
Kephirah and Beeroth	743
30of Ramah and Geba	621
31of Micmash	122
32of Bethel and Ai	123
33of the other Nebo	52
34of the other Elam	1,254
35of Harim	320
36of Jericho	345

a2 Or Hanani, that is,

³⁷of Lod, Hadid and
Ono   721
³⁸of Senaah   3,930

³⁹The priests:

the descendants of
Jedaiah (through the
family of Jeshua)   973
⁴⁰of Immer   1,052
⁴¹of Pashhur   1,247
⁴²of Harim   1,017

⁴³The Levites:

the descendants of Jeshua
(through Kadmiel
through the line of
Hodaviah)   74

⁴⁴The singers:

the descendants of Asaph   148

⁴⁵The gatekeepers:

the descendants of
Shallum, Ater, Talmon,
Akkub, Hatita and
Shobai   138

⁴⁶The temple servants:

the descendants of
Ziha, Hasupha, Tabbaoth,
⁴⁷Keros, Sia, Padon,
⁴⁸Lebana, Hagaba, Shalmai,
⁴⁹Hanan, Giddel, Gahar,
⁵⁰Reaiah, Rezin, Nekoda,
⁵¹Gazzam, Uzza, Paseah,
⁵²Besai, Meunim, Nephussim,
⁵³Bakbuk, Hakupha, Harhur,
⁵⁴Bazluth, Mehida, Harsha,
⁵⁵Barkos, Sisera, Temah,
⁵⁶Neziah and Hatipha

⁵⁷The descendants of the servants
of Solomon:

the descendants of
Sotai, Sophereth, Perida,
⁵⁸Jaala, Darkon, Giddel,
⁵⁹Shephatiah, Hattil,
Pokereth-Hazzebaim and
Amon

⁶⁰The temple servants and
the descendants of the
servants of Solomon   392

⁶¹The following came up from
the towns of Tel Melah, Tel Harsha,
Kerub, Addon and Immer,
but they could not show that
their families were descended
from Israel:

⁶²the descendants of
Delaiah, Tobiah and
Nekoda   642

⁶³And from among the priests:

the descendants of
Hobaiah, Hakkoz and
Barzillai (a man who had
married a daughter of
Barzillai the Gileadite and
was called by that name).
⁶⁴These searched for their family
records, but they could not
find them and so were excluded
from the priesthood as unclean.
⁶⁵The governor, therefore, ordered
them not to eat any of the
most sacred food until there
should be a priest ministering
with the Urim and Thummim.

⁶⁶The whole company numbered
42,360, ⁶⁷besides their
7,337 menservants and maidservants;
and they also had 245 men
and women singers. ⁶⁸There
were 736 horses, 245 mules,^a
⁶⁹435 camels and 6,720 donkeys.

⁷⁰Some of the heads of the
families contributed to the work.
The governor gave to the treasury
1,000 drachmas^b of gold,
50 bowls and 530 garments for
priests. ⁷¹Some of the heads of
the families gave to the treasury
for the work 20,000 drachmas^c
of gold and 2,200 minas^d of
silver. ⁷²The total given by the
rest of the people was 20,000
drachmas of gold, 2,000 minas^e

a68 Some Hebrew manuscripts (see also Ezra 2:66); most Hebrew manuscripts do not have this
verse.   *b70* That is, about 19 pounds (about 8.5 kilograms)   *c71* That is, about 375 pounds
(about 170 kilograms); also in verse 72   *d71* That is, about 1 1/3 tons (about 1.2 metric tons)
e72 That is, about 1 1/4 tons (about 1.1 metric tons)

of silver and 67 garments for priests.

73The priests, the Levites, the gatekeepers, the singers and the temple servants, along with certain of the people and the rest of the Israelites, settled in their own towns.

Ezra Reads the Law

When the seventh month came and the Israelites had settled in their 8 towns, 1all the people assembled as one man in the square before the Water Gate. They told Ezra the scribe to bring out the Book of the Law of Moses, which the LORD had commanded for Israel.

2So on the first day of the seventh month Ezra the priest brought the Law before the assembly, which was made up of men and women and all who were able to understand. 3He read it aloud from daybreak till noon as he faced the square before the Water Gate in the presence of the men, women and others who could understand. And all the people listened attentively to the Book of the Law.

4Ezra the scribe stood on a high wooden platform built for the occasion. Beside him on his right stood Mattithiah, Shema, Anaiah, Uriah, Hilkiah and Maaseiah; and on his left were Pedaiah, Mishael, Malkijah, Hashum, Hashbaddanah, Zechariah and Meshullam.

5Ezra opened the book. All the people could see him because he was standing above them; and as he opened it, the people all stood up. 6Ezra praised the LORD, the great God; and all the people lifted their hands and responded, "Amen! Amen!" Then they bowed down and worshiped the LORD with their faces to the ground.

7The Levites—Jeshua, Bani, Sherebiah, Jamin, Akkub, Shabbethai, Hodiah, Maaseiah, Kelita, Azariah, Jozabad, Hanan and Pelaiah—instructed the people in the Law while the people were standing there. 8They read

from the Book of the Law of God, making it clear[a] and giving the meaning so that the people could understand what was being read.

9Then Nehemiah the governor, Ezra the priest and scribe, and the Levites who were instructing the people said to them all, "This day is sacred to the LORD your God. Do not mourn or weep." For all the people had been weeping as they listened to the words of the Law.

10Nehemiah said, "Go and enjoy choice food and sweet drinks, and send some to those who have nothing prepared. This day is sacred to our Lord. Do not grieve, for the joy of the LORD is your strength."

11The Levites calmed all the people, saying, "Be still, for this is a sacred day. Do not grieve."

12Then all the people went away to eat and drink, to send portions of food and to celebrate with great joy, because they now understood the words that had been made known to them.

13On the second day of the month, the heads of all the families, along with the priests and the Levites, gathered around Ezra the scribe to give attention to the words of the Law. 14They found written in the Law, which the LORD had commanded through Moses, that the Israelites were to live in booths during the feast of the seventh month 15and that they should proclaim this word and spread it throughout their towns and in Jerusalem: "Go out into the hill country and bring back branches from olive and wild olive trees, and from myrtles, palms and shade trees, to make booths"—as it is written.[b]

16So the people went out and brought back branches and built themselves booths on their own roofs, in their courtyards, in the courts of the house of God and in the square by the Water Gate and the one by the Gate of Ephraim. 17The whole company that had returned from exile built booths and lived in them. From the

---

a8 Or God, translating it   b15 See Lev. 23:37-40.

days of Joshua son of Nun until that day, the Israelites had not celebrated it like this. And their joy was very great.

¹⁸Day after day, from the first day to the last, Ezra read from the Book of the Law of God. They celebrated the feast for seven days, and on the eighth day, in accordance with the regulation, there was an assembly.

The Israelites Confess Their Sins

9 On the twenty-fourth day of the same month, the Israelites gathered together, fasting and wearing sackcloth and having dust on their

WEDNESDAY

VERSE:
Nehemiah 8:10

AUTHOR:
Charles H. Spurgeon

PASSAGE:
Nehemiah 8:1–12

A Delight and a Joy

Delight in God's service is a sign of his acceptance. Those who serve God with a sad face because what they are doing is unpleasant are not serving him. They are bringing a form of homage, but life is absent.

God does not require slaves to grace his throne. He is Lord of the empire of love and his servants dress in robes of joy. The angels of God serve with songs, not with groans. Just a murmur or a sigh would be mutiny because obedience that is not voluntary is disobedience. The Lord looks at the heart, and if we were forced to serve, he would reject our offering. Service coupled with joy is heart service, and heart service is true service . . .

"The joy of the LORD is your strength" (Nehemiah 8:10). Joy removes difficulties. Joy is to our service as oil is to the wheels of a railroad car. Without oil the axle grows hot and accidents occur. If there is no holy joy to oil our wheels, our spirit will soon be clogged with weariness . . .

Let me ask you a question. Do you serve the Lord with joy? Then show the people of the world, who think our religion is slavery, that serving God is a delight and a joy.

ADDITIONAL SCRIPTURE READINGS
Psalm 100; Philippians 4:4–7

Go to page 599 for your next devotional reading.

heads. ²Those of Israelite descent had separated themselves from all foreigners. They stood in their places and confessed their sins and the wickedness of their fathers. ³They stood where they were and read from the Book of the Law of the LORD their God for a quarter of the day, and spent another quarter in confession and in worshiping the LORD their God. ⁴Standing on the stairs were the Levites—Jeshua, Bani, Kadmiel, Shebaniah, Bunni, Sherebiah, Bani and Kenani—who called with loud voices to the LORD their God. ⁵And the Levites—Jeshua, Kadmiel, Bani, Hashabneiah, Sherebiah, Hodiah, Shebaniah and Pethahiah—said: "Stand up and praise the LORD your God, who is from everlasting to everlasting.ᵃ"

"Blessed be your glorious name, and may it be exalted above all blessing and praise. ⁶You alone are the LORD. You made the heavens, even the highest heavens, and all their starry host, the earth and all that is on it, the seas and all that is in them. You give life to everything, and the multitudes of heaven worship you.

⁷"You are the LORD God, who chose Abram and brought him out of Ur of the Chaldeans and named him Abraham. ⁸You found his heart faithful to you, and you made a covenant with him to give to his descendants the land of the Canaanites, Hittites, Amorites, Perizzites, Jebusites and Girgashites. You have kept your promise because you are righteous.

⁹"You saw the suffering of our forefathers in Egypt; you heard their cry at the Red Sea.ᵇ ¹⁰You sent miraculous signs and wonders against Pharaoh, against all his officials and all the people of his land, for you knew how arrogantly the Egyptians treated them. You made a name for yourself, which remains to this day. ¹¹You divided the sea before them, so that they passed through it on dry ground, but you hurled their pursuers into the depths, like a stone into mighty waters. ¹²By day you led them with a pillar of cloud, and by night with a pillar of fire to give them light on the way they were to take.

¹³"You came down on Mount Sinai; you spoke to them from heaven. You gave them regulations and laws that are just and right, and decrees and commands that are good. ¹⁴You made known to them your holy Sabbath and gave them commands, decrees and laws through your servant Moses. ¹⁵In their hunger you gave them bread from heaven and in their thirst you brought them water from the rock; you told them to go in and take possession of the land you had sworn with uplifted hand to give them.

¹⁶"But they, our forefathers, became arrogant and stiffnecked, and did not obey your commands. ¹⁷They refused to listen and failed to remember the miracles you performed among them. They became stiff-necked and in their rebellion appointed a leader in order to return to their slavery. But you are a forgiving God, gracious and compassionate, slow to anger and abounding in love. Therefore you did not desert them, ¹⁸even when they cast for themselves an image of a calf and said, 'This is your god, who brought you up out of Egypt,' or when they committed awful blasphemies.

¹⁹"Because of your great compassion you did not abandon them in the desert. By day the pillar of cloud did not cease to guide them on their path, nor the pillar of fire by night to shine on

---

ᵃ5 Or *God for ever and ever*   ᵇ9 Hebrew *Yam Suph*; that is, Sea of Reeds

the way they were to take. ²⁰You gave your good Spirit to instruct them. You did not withhold your manna from their mouths, and you gave them water for their thirst. ²¹For forty years you sustained them in the desert; they lacked nothing, their clothes did not wear out nor did their feet become swollen.

²²"You gave them kingdoms and nations, allotting to them even the remotest frontiers. They took over the country of Sihon^a king of Heshbon and the country of Og king of Bashan. ²³You made their sons as numerous as the stars in the sky, and you brought them into the land that you told their fathers to enter and possess. ²⁴Their sons went in and took possession of the land. You subdued before them the Canaanites, who lived in the land; you handed the Canaanites over to them, along with their kings and the peoples of the land, to deal with them as they pleased. ²⁵They captured fortified cities and fertile land; they took possession of houses filled with all kinds of good things, wells already dug, vineyards, olive groves and fruit trees in abundance. They ate to the full and were well-nourished; they reveled in your great goodness.

²⁶"But they were disobedient and rebelled against you; they put your law behind their backs. They killed your prophets, who had admonished them in order to turn them back to you; they committed awful blasphemies. ²⁷So you handed them over to their enemies, who oppressed them. But when they were oppressed they cried out to you. From heaven you heard them, and in your great compassion you gave them deliverers, who rescued them from the hand of their enemies.

²⁸"But as soon as they were at rest, they again did what was evil in your sight. Then you abandoned them to the hand of their enemies so that they ruled over them. And when they cried out to you again, you heard from heaven, and in your compassion you delivered them time after time.

²⁹"You warned them to return to your law, but they became arrogant and disobeyed your commands. They sinned against your ordinances, by which a man will live if he obeys them. Stubbornly they turned their backs on you, became stiff-necked and refused to listen. ³⁰For many years you were patient with them. By your Spirit you admonished them through your prophets. Yet they paid no attention, so you handed them over to the neighboring peoples. ³¹But in your great mercy you did not put an end to them or abandon them, for you are a gracious and merciful God.

³²"Now therefore, O our God, the great, mighty and awesome God, who keeps his covenant of love, do not let all this hardship seem trifling in your eyes—the hardship that has come upon us, upon our kings and leaders, upon our priests and prophets, upon our fathers and all your people, from the days of the kings of Assyria until today. ³³In all that has happened to us, you have been just; you have acted faithfully, while we did wrong. ³⁴Our kings, our leaders, our priests and our fathers did not follow your law; they did not pay attention to your commands or the warnings you gave them. ³⁵Even while they were in their kingdom, enjoying your great

---

^a22 One Hebrew manuscript and Septuagint; most Hebrew manuscripts Sihon, that is, the country of the

goodness to them in the spacious and fertile land you gave them, they did not serve you or turn from their evil ways.

³⁶"But see, we are slaves today, slaves in the land you gave our forefathers so they could eat its fruit and the other good things it produces. ³⁷Because of our sins, its abundant harvest goes to the kings you have placed over us. They rule over our bodies and our cattle as they please. We are in great distress.

The Agreement of the People

³⁸"In view of all this, we are making a binding agreement, putting it in writing, and our leaders, our Levites and our priests are affixing their seals to it."

10 Those who sealed it were:

Nehemiah the governor, the son of Hacaliah.

Zedekiah, ²Seraiah, Azariah, Jeremiah,
³Pashhur, Amariah, Malkijah,
⁴Hattush, Shebaniah, Malluch,
⁵Harim, Meremoth, Obadiah,
⁶Daniel, Ginnethon, Baruch,
⁷Meshullam, Abijah, Mijamin,
⁸Maaziah, Bilgai and Shemaiah.
These were the priests.

⁹The Levites:

Jeshua son of Azaniah, Binnui of the sons of Henadad, Kadmiel,
¹⁰and their associates: Shebaniah, Hodiah, Kelita, Pelaiah, Hanan,
¹¹Mica, Rehob, Hashabiah,
¹²Zaccur, Sherebiah, Shebaniah,
¹³Hodiah, Bani and Beninu.

¹⁴The leaders of the people:

Parosh, Pahath-Moab, Elam, Zattu, Bani,
¹⁵Bunni, Azgad, Bebai,
¹⁶Adonijah, Bigvai, Adin,
¹⁷Ater, Hezekiah, Azzur,
¹⁸Hodiah, Hashum, Bezai,
¹⁹Hariph, Anathoth, Nebai,
²⁰Magpiash, Meshullam, Hezir,
²¹Meshezabel, Zadok, Jaddua,
²²Pelatiah, Hanan, Anaiah,
²³Hoshea, Hananiah, Hasshub,
²⁴Hallohesh, Pilha, Shobek,
²⁵Rehum, Hashabnah, Maaseiah,
²⁶Ahiah, Hanan, Anan,
²⁷Malluch, Harim and Baanah.

²⁸"The rest of the people—priests, Levites, gatekeepers, singers, temple servants and all who separated themselves from the neighboring peoples for the sake of the Law of God, together with their wives and all their sons and daughters who are able to understand— ²⁹all these now join their brothers the nobles, and bind themselves with a curse and an oath to follow the Law of God given through Moses the servant of God and to obey carefully all the commands, regulations and decrees of the Lord our Lord.

³⁰"We promise not to give our daughters in marriage to the peoples around us or take their daughters for our sons.

³¹"When the neighboring peoples bring merchandise or grain to sell on the Sabbath, we will not buy from them on the Sabbath or on any holy day. Every seventh year we will forgo working the land and will cancel all debts.

³²"We assume the responsibility for carrying out the commands to give a third of a shekel*a* each year for the service of the house of our God: ³³for the bread set out on the table; for the regular grain offerings and burnt offerings; for the offerings on the Sabbaths, New Moon festivals and appointed feasts; for the holy offerings; for sin offerings to make atonement for Israel; and for all the duties of the house of our God.

*a32 That is, about 1/8 ounce (about 4 grams)

³⁴"We—the priests, the Levites and the people—have cast lots to determine when each of our families is to bring to the house of our God at set times each year a contribution of wood to burn on the altar of the LORD our God, as it is written in the Law.

³⁵"We also assume responsibility for bringing to the house of the LORD each year the first-fruits of our crops and of every fruit tree.

³⁶"As it is also written in the Law, we will bring the firstborn of our sons and of our cattle, of our herds and of our flocks to the house of our God, to the priests ministering there.

³⁷"Moreover, we will bring to the storerooms of the house of our God, to the priests, the first of our ground meal, of our ∟grain⌐ offerings, of the fruit of all our trees and of our new wine and oil. And we will bring a tithe of our crops to the Levites, for it is the Levites who collect the tithes in all the towns where we work. ³⁸A priest descended from Aaron is to accompany the Levites when they receive the tithes, and the Levites are to bring a tenth of the tithes up to the house of our God, to the storerooms of the treasury. ³⁹The people of Israel, including the Levites, are to bring their contributions of grain, new wine and oil to the storerooms where the articles for the sanctuary are kept and where the ministering priests, the gatekeepers and the singers stay.

"We will not neglect the house of our God."

The New Residents of Jerusalem

11 Now the leaders of the people settled in Jerusalem, and the rest of the people cast lots to bring one out of every ten to live in Jerusalem, the holy city, while the remaining nine were to stay in their own towns. ²The people commended all the men who volunteered to live in Jerusalem.

³These are the provincial leaders who settled in Jerusalem (now some Israelites, priests, Levites, temple servants and descendants of Solomon's servants lived in the towns of Judah, each on his own property in the various towns, ⁴while other people from both Judah and Benjamin lived in Jerusalem):

From the descendants of Judah:

Athaiah son of Uzziah, the son of Zechariah, the son of Amariah, the son of Shephatiah, the son of Mahalalel, a descendant of Perez; ⁵and Maaseiah son of Baruch, the son of Col-Hozeh, the son of Hazaiah, the son of Adaiah, the son of Joiarib, the son of Zechariah, a descendant of Shelah. ⁶The descendants of Perez who lived in Jerusalem totaled 468 able men.

⁷From the descendants of Benjamin:

Sallu son of Meshullam, the son of Joed, the son of Pedaiah, the son of Kolaiah, the son of Maaseiah, the son of Ithiel, the son of Jeshaiah, ⁸and his followers, Gabbai and Sallai—928 men. ⁹Joel son of Zicri was their chief officer, and Judah son of Hassenuah was over the Second District of the city.

¹⁰From the priests:

Jedaiah; the son of Joiarib; Jakin; ¹¹Seraiah son of Hilkiah, the son of Meshullam, the son of Zadok, the son of Meraioth, the son of Ahitub, supervisor in the house of God, ¹²and their associates, who carried on work for the temple—822 men; Adaiah son of Jeroham, the son of Pelaliah, the son of Amzi, the son of Zechariah, the son of Pashhur, the son of Malkijah, ¹³and his associates, who were heads of families—242 men; Amashsai son of Azarel, the son of Ahzai, the son of Meshillemoth, the son of Immer, [14]and his[a] associates, who were able men—128. Their chief officer was Zabdiel son of Haggedolim.

[15]From the Levites:

Shemaiah son of Hasshub, the son of Azrikam, the son of Hashabiah, the son of Bunni; [16]Shabbethai and Jozabad, two of the heads of the Levites, who had charge of the outside work of the house of God; [17]Mattaniah son of Mica, the son of Zabdi, the son of Asaph, the director who led in thanksgiving and prayer; Bakbukiah, second among his associates; and Abda son of Shammua, the son of Galal, the son of Jeduthun. [18]The Levites in the holy city totaled 284.

[19]The gatekeepers:

Akkub, Talmon and their associates, who kept watch at the gates—172 men.

[20]The rest of the Israelites, with the priests and Levites, were in all the towns of Judah, each on his ancestral property.

[21]The temple servants lived on the hill of Ophel, and Ziha and Gishpa were in charge of them.

[22]The chief officer of the Levites in Jerusalem was Uzzi son of Bani, the son of Hashabiah, the son of Mattaniah, the son of Mica. Uzzi was one of Asaph's descendants, who were the singers responsible for the service of the house of God. [23]The singers were under the king's orders, which regulated their daily activity.

[24]Pethahiah son of Meshezabel, one of the descendants of Zerah son of Judah, was the king's agent in all affairs relating to the people.

[25]As for the villages with their fields, some of the people of Judah lived in Kiriath Arba and its surrounding settlements, in Dibon and its settlements, in Jekabzeel and its villages, [26]in Jeshua, in Moladah, in Beth Pelet, [27]in Hazar Shual, in Beersheba and its settlements, [28]in Ziklag, in Meconah and its settlements, [29]in En Rimmon, in Zorah, in Jarmuth, [30]Zanoah, Adullam and their villages, in Lachish and its fields, and in Azekah and its settlements. So they were living all the way from Beersheba to the Valley of Hinnom.

[31]The descendants of the Benjamites from Geba lived in Micmash, Aija, Bethel and its settlements, [32]in Anathoth, Nob and Ananiah, [33]in Hazor, Ramah and Gittaim, [34]in Hadid, Zeboim and Neballat, [35]in Lod and Ono, and in the Valley of the Craftsmen.

[36]Some of the divisions of the Levites of Judah settled in Benjamin.

Priests and Levites

12 These were the priests and Levites who returned with Zerubbabel son of Shealtiel and with Jeshua:

Seraiah, Jeremiah, Ezra,
[2]Amariah, Malluch, Hattush,
[3]Shecaniah, Rehum, Meremoth,
[4]Iddo, Ginnethon,[b] Abijah,
[5]Mijamin,[c] Moadiah, Bilgah,
[6]Shemaiah, Joiarib, Jedaiah,
[7]Sallu, Amok, Hilkiah and Jedaiah.

These were the leaders of the priests and their associates in the days of Jeshua.

[8]The Levites were Jeshua, Binnui, Kadmiel, Sherebiah, Judah, and also Mattaniah, who, together with his associates, was in charge of the songs of thanksgiving. [9]Bakbukiah and Unni, their associates, stood opposite them in the services.

[10]Jeshua was the father of Joiakim, Joiakim the father of Eliashib, Eliashib the father of Joiada, [11]Joiada the father of Jonathan, and Jonathan the father of Jaddua.

[12]In the days of Joiakim, these were the heads of the priestly families:

---

[a]14 Most Septuagint manuscripts; Hebrew *their* (see also Neh. 12:16); most Hebrew manuscripts *Ginnethoi*   [b]4 Many Hebrew manuscripts and Vulgate (see also Neh. 12:16); most Hebrew manuscripts *Ginnethoi*   [c]5 A variant of *Miniamin*

of Seraiah's family, Meraiah;
of Jeremiah's, Hananiah;
13of Ezra's, Meshullam;
of Amariah's, Jehohanan;
14of Malluch's, Jonathan;
of Shecaniah's,^a Joseph;
15of Harim's, Adna;
of Meremoth's,^b Helkai;
16of Iddo's, Zechariah;
of Ginnethon's, Meshullam;
17of Abijah's, Zicri;
of Miniamin's and of Moadiah's, Piltai;
18of Bilgah's, Shammua;
of Shemaiah's, Jehonathan;
19of Joiarib's, Mattenai;
of Jedaiah's, Uzzi;
20of Sallu's, Kallai;
of Amok's, Eber;
21of Hilkiah's, Hashabiah;
of Jedaiah's, Nethanel.

22The family heads of the Levites in the days of Eliashib, Joiada, Johanan and Jaddua, as well as those of the priests, were recorded in the reign of Darius the Persian. 23The family heads among the descendants of Levi up to the time of Johanan son of Eliashib were recorded in the book of the annals. 24And the leaders of the Levites were Hashabiah, Sherebiah, Jeshua son of Kadmiel, and their associates, who stood opposite them to give praise and thanksgiving, one section responding to the other, as prescribed by David the man of God.

25Mattaniah, Bakbukiah, Obadiah, Meshullam, Talmon and Akkub were gatekeepers who guarded the storerooms at the gates. 26They served in the days of Joiakim son of Jeshua, the son of Jozadak, and in the days of Nehemiah the governor and of Ezra the priest and scribe.

Dedication of the Wall of Jerusalem

27At the dedication of the wall of Jerusalem, the Levites were sought out from where they lived and were brought to Jerusalem to celebrate joyfully the dedication with songs of thanksgiving and with the music of cymbals, harps and lyres. 28The singers also were brought together from the region around Jerusalem—from the villages of the Netophathites, 29from Beth Gilgal, and from the area of Geba and Azmaveth, for the singers had built villages for themselves around Jerusalem. 30When the priests and Levites had purified themselves ceremonially, they purified the people, the gates and the wall.

31I had the leaders of Judah go up on top^c of the wall. I also assigned two large choirs to give thanks. One was to proceed on top^d of the wall to the right, toward the Dung Gate. 32Hoshaiah and half the leaders of Judah followed them, 33along with Azariah, Ezra, Meshullam, 34Judah, Benjamin, Shemaiah, Jeremiah, 35as well as some priests with trumpets, and also Zechariah son of Jonathan, the son of Shemaiah, the son of Mattaniah, the son of Micaiah, the son of Zaccur, the son of Asaph, 36and his associates—Shemaiah, Azarel, Milalai, Gilalai, Maai, Nethanel, Judah and Hanani—with musical instruments ∟ prescribed by⌟ David the man of God. Ezra the scribe led the procession. 37At the Fountain Gate they continued directly up the steps of the City of David on the ascent to the wall and passed above the house of David to the Water Gate on the east.

38The second choir proceeded in the opposite direction. I followed them on top^e of the wall, together with half the people—past the Tower of the Ovens to the Broad Wall, 39over the Gate of Ephraim, the Jeshanah^f Gate, the Fish Gate, the Tower of Hananel and the Tower of the Hundred, as far as the Sheep Gate. At the Gate of the Guard they stopped.

40The two choirs that gave thanks then took their places in the house of God; so did I, together with half the

---

^a14 Very many Hebrew manuscripts, some Septuagint manuscripts and Syriac (see also Neh. 12:3); most Hebrew manuscripts *Shebaniah's*   ^b15 Some Septuagint manuscripts (see also Neh. 12:3); Hebrew *Meraioth's*   ^c31 Or *go alongside*   ^d31 Or *proceed alongside*   ^e38 Or *them* alongside   ^f39 Or *Old*

officials, [41]as well as the priests—Eliakim, Maaseiah, Miniamin, Micaiah, Elioenai, Zechariah and Hananiah with their trumpets— [42]and also Maaseiah, Shemaiah, Eleazar, Uzzi, Jehohanan, Malkijah, Elam and Ezer. The choirs sang under the direction of Jezrahiah. [43]And on that day they offered great sacrifices, rejoicing because God had given them great joy. The women and children also rejoiced. The sound of rejoicing in Jerusalem could be heard far away.

[44]At that time men were appointed to be in charge of the storerooms for the contributions, firstfruits and tithes. From the fields around the towns they were to bring into the storerooms the portions required by the Law for the priests and the Levites, for Judah was pleased with the ministering priests and Levites. [45]They performed the service of their God and the service of purification, as did also the singers and gatekeepers, according to the commands of David and his son Solomon. [46]For long ago, in the days of David and Asaph, there had been directors for the singers and for the songs of praise and thanksgiving to God. [47]So in the days of Zerubbabel and of Nehemiah, all Israel contributed the daily portions for the singers and gatekeepers. They also set aside the portion for the other Levites, and the Levites set aside the portion for the descendants of Aaron.

Nehemiah's Final Reforms

13 On that day the Book of Moses was read aloud in the hearing of the people and there it was found written that no Ammonite or Moabite should ever be admitted into the assembly of God, [2]because they had not met the Israelites with food and water but had hired Balaam to call a curse down on them. (Our God, however, turned the curse into a blessing.) [3]When the people heard this law, they excluded from Israel all who were of foreign descent.

[4]Before this, Eliashib the priest had been put in charge of the storerooms of the house of our God. He was closely associated with Tobiah, [5]and he had provided him with a large room formerly used to store the grain offerings and incense and temple articles, and also the tithes of grain, new wine and oil prescribed for the Levites, singers and gatekeepers, as well as the contributions for the priests.

[6]But while all this was going on, I was not in Jerusalem, for in the thirty-second year of Artaxerxes king of Babylon I had returned to the king. Some time later I asked his permission [7]and came back to Jerusalem. Here I learned about the evil thing Eliashib had done in providing Tobiah a room in the courts of the house of God. [8]I was greatly displeased and threw all Tobiah's household goods out of the room. [9]I gave orders to purify the rooms, and then I put back into them the equipment of the house of God, with the grain offerings and the incense.

[10]I also learned that the portions assigned to the Levites had not been given to them, and that all the Levites and singers responsible for the service had gone back to their own fields. [11]So I rebuked the officials and asked them, "Why is the house of God neglected?" Then I called them together and stationed them at their posts.

[12]All Judah brought the tithes of grain, new wine and oil into the storerooms. [13]I put Shelemiah the priest, Zadok the scribe, and a Levite named Pedaiah in charge of the storerooms and made Hanan son of Zaccur, the son of Mattaniah, their assistant, because these men were considered trustworthy. They were made responsible for distributing the supplies to their brothers.

[14]Remember me for this, O my God, and do not blot out what I have so faithfully done for the house of my God and its services.

[15]In those days I saw men in Judah treading winepresses on the Sabbath and bringing in grain and loading it on donkeys, together with wine, grapes, figs and all other kinds of loads. And they were bringing all this

into Jerusalem on the Sabbath. Therefore I warned them against selling food on that day. ¹⁶Men from Tyre who lived in Jerusalem were bringing in fish and all kinds of merchandise and selling them in Jerusalem on the Sabbath to the people of Judah. ¹⁷I rebuked the nobles of Judah and said to them, "What is this wicked thing you are doing—desecrating the Sabbath day? ¹⁸Didn't your forefathers do the same things, so that our God brought all this calamity upon us and upon this city? Now you are stirring up more wrath against Israel by desecrating the Sabbath."

¹⁹When evening shadows fell on the gates of Jerusalem before the Sabbath, I ordered the doors to be shut and not opened until the Sabbath was over. I stationed some of my own men at the gates so that no load could be brought in on the Sabbath day. ²⁰Once or twice the merchants and sellers of all kinds of goods spent the night outside Jerusalem. ²¹But I warned them and said, "Why do you spend the night by the wall? If you do this again, I will lay hands on you." From that time on they no longer came on the Sabbath. ²²Then I commanded the Levites to purify themselves and go and guard the gates in order to keep the Sabbath day holy.

Remember me for this also, O my God, and show mercy to me according to your great love.

²³Moreover, in those days I saw men of Judah who had married women from Ashdod, Ammon and Moab. ²⁴Half of their children spoke the language of Ashdod or the language of one of the other peoples, and did not know how to speak the language of Judah. ²⁵I rebuked them and called curses down on them. I beat some of the men and pulled out their hair. I made them take an oath in God's name and said: "You are not to give your daughters in marriage to their sons, nor are you to take their daughters in marriage for your sons or for yourselves. ²⁶Was it not because of marriages like these that Solomon king of Israel sinned? Among the many nations there was no king like him. He was loved by his God, and God made him king over all Israel, but even he was led into sin by foreign women. ²⁷Must we hear now that you too are doing all this terrible wickedness and are being unfaithful to our God by marrying foreign women?"

²⁸One of the sons of Joiada son of Eliashib the high priest was son-in-law to Sanballat the Horonite. And I drove him away from me.

²⁹Remember them, O my God, because they defiled the priestly office and the covenant of the priesthood and of the Levites.

³⁰So I purified the priests and the Levites of everything foreign, and assigned them duties, each to his own task. ³¹I also made provision for contributions of wood at designated times, and for the firstfruits.

Remember me with favor, O my God.

*E*sther records God's remarkable, providential care of his exiled people when their enemies threatened to destroy them. Although God's name is never mentioned in the book, he is in control throughout, directing circumstances and working through Esther. As you read this book, look back and observe how God's hand led you every step of the way, and claim his leading for your present and your future.

ESTHER

Queen Vashti Deposed

1 This is what happened during the time of Xerxes,[a] the Xerxes who ruled over 127 provinces stretching from India to Cush[b]: ²At that time King Xerxes reigned from his royal throne in the citadel of Susa, ³and in the third year of his reign he gave a banquet for all his nobles and officials. The military leaders of Persia and Media, the princes, and the nobles of the provinces were present.

⁴For a full 180 days he displayed the vast wealth of his kingdom and the splendor and glory of his majesty. ⁵When these days were over, the king gave a banquet, lasting seven days, in the enclosed garden of the king's palace, for all the people from the least to the greatest, who were in the citadel of Susa. ⁶The garden had hangings of white and blue linen, fastened with cords of white linen and purple material to silver rings on marble pillars. There were couches of gold and silver on a mosaic pavement of porphyry, marble, mother-of-pearl and other costly stones. ⁷Wine was served in goblets of gold, each one different from the other, and the royal wine was abundant, in keeping with the king's liberality. ⁸By the king's command each guest was allowed to drink in his own way, for the king instructed all the wine stewards to serve each man what he wished.

⁹Queen Vashti also gave a banquet for the women in the royal palace of King Xerxes.

¹⁰On the seventh day, when King

a1 Hebrew *Ahasuerus*, a variant of Xerxes' Persian name; here and throughout Esther   b1 That is, the upper Nile region

Xerxes was in high spirits from wine, he commanded the seven eunuchs who served him—Mehuman, Biztha, Harbona, Bigtha, Abagtha, Zethar and Carcas— [11]to bring before him Queen Vashti, wearing her royal crown, in order to display her beauty to the people and nobles, for she was lovely to look at. [12]But when the attendants delivered the king's command, Queen Vashti refused to come. Then the king became furious and burned with anger.

[13]Since it was customary for the king to consult experts in matters of law and justice, he spoke with the wise men who understood the times [14]and were closest to the king—Carshena, Shethar, Admatha, Tarshish, Meres, Marsena and Memucan, the seven nobles of Persia and Media who had special access to the king and were highest in the kingdom.

[15]"According to law, what must be done to Queen Vashti?" he asked. "She has not obeyed the command of King Xerxes that the eunuchs have taken to her."

[16]Then Memucan replied in the presence of the king and the nobles, "Queen Vashti has done wrong, not only against the king but also against all the nobles and the peoples of all the provinces of King Xerxes. [17]For the queen's conduct will become known to all the women, and so they will despise their husbands and say, 'King Xerxes commanded Queen Vashti to be brought before him, but she would not come.' [18]This very day the Persian and Median women of the nobility who have heard about the queen's conduct will respond to all the king's nobles in the same way. There will be no end of disrespect and discord.

[19]"Therefore, if it pleases the king, let him issue a royal decree and let it be written in the laws of Persia and Media, which cannot be repealed, that Vashti is never again to enter the presence of King Xerxes. Also let the king give her royal position to someone else who is better than she. [20]Then when the king's edict is proclaimed throughout all his vast realm, all the women will respect their husbands, from the least to the greatest."

[21]The king and his nobles were pleased with this advice, so the king did as Memucan proposed. [22]He sent dispatches to all parts of the kingdom, to each province in its own script and to each people in its own language, proclaiming in each people's tongue that every man should be ruler over his own household.

Esther Made Queen

2 Later when the anger of King Xerxes had subsided, he remembered Vashti and what she had done and what he had decreed about her. [2]Then the king's personal attendants proposed, "Let a search be made for beautiful young virgins for the king. [3]Let the king appoint commissioners in every province of his realm to bring all these beautiful girls into the harem at the citadel of Susa. Let them be placed under the care of Hegai, the king's eunuch, who is in charge of the women; and let beauty treatments be given to them. [4]Then let the girl who pleases the king be queen instead of Vashti." This advice appealed to the king, and he followed it.

[5]Now there was in the citadel of Susa a Jew of the tribe of Benjamin, named Mordecai son of Jair, the son of Shimei, the son of Kish, [6]who had been carried into exile from Jerusalem by Nebuchadnezzar king of Babylon, among those taken captive with Jehoiachin[a] king of Judah. [7]Mordecai had a cousin named Hadassah, whom he had brought up because she had neither father nor mother. This girl, who was also known as Esther, was lovely in form and features, and Mordecai had taken her as his own daughter when her father and mother died.

[8]When the king's order and edict had been proclaimed, many girls were brought to the citadel of Susa and put under the care of Hegai. Es-

ther also was taken to the king's palace and entrusted to Hegai, who had charge of the harem. 9The girl pleased him and won his favor. Immediately he provided her with her beauty treatments and special food. He assigned to her seven maids selected from the king's palace and moved her and her maids into the best place in the harem.

10Esther had not revealed her nationality and family background, because Mordecai had forbidden her to do so. 11Every day he walked back and forth near the courtyard of the harem to find out how Esther was and what was happening to her.

12Before a girl's turn came to go in to King Xerxes, she had to complete twelve months of beauty treatments prescribed for the women, six months with oil of myrrh and six with perfumes and cosmetics. 13And this is how she would go to the king: Anything she wanted was given her to take with her from the harem to the king's palace. 14In the evening she would go there and in the morning return to another part of the harem to the care of Shaashgaz, the king's eunuch who was in charge of the concubines. She would not return to the king unless he was pleased with her and summoned her by name.

15When the turn came for Esther (the girl Mordecai had adopted, the daughter of his uncle Abihail) to go to the king, she asked for nothing other than what Hegai, the king's eunuch who was in charge of the harem, suggested. And Esther won the favor of everyone who saw her. 16She was taken to King Xerxes in the royal residence in the tenth month, the month of Tebeth, in the seventh year of his reign.

17Now the king was attracted to Esther more than to any of the other women, and she won his favor and approval more than any of the other virgins. So he set a royal crown on her head and made her queen instead of Vashti. 18And the king gave a great banquet, Esther's banquet, for all his nobles and officials. He proclaimed a holiday throughout the provinces and distributed gifts with royal liberality.

Mordecai Uncovers a Conspiracy

19When the virgins were assembled a second time, Mordecai was sitting at the king's gate. 20But Esther had kept secret her family background and nationality just as Mordecai had told her to do, for she continued to follow Mordecai's instructions as she had done when he was bringing her up.

21During the time Mordecai was sitting at the king's gate, Bigthana*a* and Teresh, two of the king's officers who guarded the doorway, became angry and conspired to assassinate King Xerxes. 22But Mordecai found out about the plot and told Queen Esther, who in turn reported it to the king, giving credit to Mordecai. 23And when the report was investigated and found to be true, the two officials were hanged on a gallows.*b* All this was recorded in the book of the annals in the presence of the king.

Haman's Plot to Destroy the Jews

3 After these events, King Xerxes honored Haman son of Hammedatha, the Agagite, elevating him and giving him a seat of honor higher than that of all the other nobles. 2All the royal officials at the king's gate knelt down and paid honor to Haman, for the king had commanded this concerning him. But Mordecai would not kneel down or pay him honor.

3Then the royal officials at the king's gate asked Mordecai, "Why do you disobey the king's command?" 4Day after day they spoke to him but he refused to comply. Therefore they told Haman about it to see whether Mordecai's behavior would be tolerated, for he had told them he was a Jew.

5When Haman saw that Mordecai

---

*a*21 Hebrew *Bigthan,* a variant of *Bigthana* elsewhere in Esther   *b*23 Or *were hung* (or *impaled*) *on poles;* similarly would not kneel down or pay him honor, he was enraged. ⁶Yet having learned who Mordecai's people were, he scorned the idea of killing only Mordecai. Instead Haman looked for a way to destroy all Mordecai's people, the Jews, throughout the whole kingdom of Xerxes.

⁷In the twelfth year of King Xerxes, in the first month, the month of Nisan, they cast the *pur* (that is, the lot) in the presence of Haman to select a day and month. And the lot fell on*ᵃ* the twelfth month, the month of Adar.

⁸Then Haman said to King Xerxes, "There is a certain people dispersed and scattered among the peoples in all the provinces of your kingdom whose customs are different from those of all other people and who do not obey the king's laws; it is not in the king's best interest to tolerate them. ⁹If it pleases the king, let a decree be issued to destroy them, and I will put ten thousand talents*ᵇ* of silver into the royal treasury for the men who carry out this business."

¹⁰So the king took his signet ring from his finger and gave it to Haman son of Hammedatha, the Agagite, the enemy of the Jews. ¹¹"Keep the money," the king said to Haman, "and do with the people as you please."

¹²Then on the thirteenth day of the first month the royal secretaries were summoned. They wrote out in the script of each province and in the language of each people all Haman's orders to the king's satraps, the governors of the various provinces and the nobles of the various peoples. These were written in the name of King Xerxes himself and sealed with his own ring. ¹³Dispatches were sent by couriers to all the king's provinces with the order to destroy, kill and annihilate all the Jews—young and old, women and little children—on a single day, the thirteenth day of the twelfth month, the month of Adar, and to plunder their goods. ¹⁴A copy of the text of the edict was to be issued as law in every province and made known to the people of every nationality so they would be ready for that day.

¹⁵Spurred on by the king's command, the couriers went out, and the edict was issued in the citadel of Susa. The king and Haman sat down to drink, but the city of Susa was bewildered.

Mordecai Persuades Esther to Help

4 When Mordecai learned of all that had been done, he tore his clothes, put on sackcloth and ashes, and went out into the city, wailing loudly and bitterly. ²But he went only as far as the king's gate, because no one clothed in sackcloth was allowed to enter it. ³In every province to which the edict and order of the king came, there was great mourning among the Jews, with fasting, weeping and wailing. Many lay in sackcloth and ashes.

⁴When Esther's maids and eunuchs came and told her about Mordecai, she was in great distress. She sent clothes for him to put on instead of his sackcloth, but he would not accept them. ⁵Then Esther summoned Hathach, one of the king's eunuchs assigned to attend her, and ordered him to find out what was troubling Mordecai and why.

⁶So Hathach went out to Mordecai in the open square of the city in front of the king's gate. ⁷Mordecai told him everything that had happened to him, including the exact amount of money Haman had promised to pay into the royal treasury for the destruction of the Jews. ⁸He also gave him a copy of the text of the edict for their annihilation, which had been published in Susa, to show to Esther and explain it to her, and he told him to urge her to go into the king's presence to beg for mercy and plead with him for her people.

⁹Hathach went back and reported

to Esther what Mordecai had said. ¹⁰Then she instructed him to say to Mordecai, ¹¹"All the king's officials and the people of the royal provinces know that for any man or woman who approaches the king in the inner court without being summoned the king has but one law: that he be put to death. The only exception to this is for the king to extend the gold scepter to him and spare his life. But thirty days have passed since I was called to go to the king."

¹²When Esther's words were reported to Mordecai, ¹³he sent back this answer: "Do not think that because you are in the king's house you alone of all the Jews will escape. ¹⁴For if you remain silent at this time, relief and deliverance for the Jews will arise from another place, but you and your father's family will perish. And who knows but that you have come to royal position for such a time as this?"

¹⁵Then Esther sent this reply to Mordecai: ¹⁶"Go, gather together all the Jews who are in Susa, and fast for me. Do not eat or drink for three days, night or day. I and my maids will fast as you do. When this is done, I will go to the king, even though it is against the law. And if I perish, I perish."

¹⁷So Mordecai went away and carried out all of Esther's instructions.

Esther's Request to the King

5 On the third day Esther put on her royal robes and stood in the inner court of the palace, in front of the king's hall. The king was sitting on his royal throne in the hall, facing the entrance. ²When he saw Queen Esther standing in the court, he was pleased with her and held out to her the gold scepter that was in his hand. So Esther approached and touched the tip of the scepter.

³Then the king asked, "What is it, Queen Esther? What is your request? Even up to half the kingdom, it will be given you."

⁴"If it pleases the king," replied Esther, "let the king, together with Ha-man, come today to a banquet I have prepared for him."

⁵"Bring Haman at once," the king said, "so that we may do what Esther asks."

So the king and Haman went to the banquet Esther had prepared. ⁶As they were drinking wine, the king again asked Esther, "Now what is your petition? It will be given you. And what is your request? Even up to half the kingdom, it will be granted."

⁷Esther replied, "My petition and my request is this: ⁸If the king regards me with favor and if it pleases the king to grant my petition and fulfill my request, let the king and Haman come tomorrow to the banquet I will prepare for them. Then I will answer the king's question."

Haman's Rage Against Mordecai

⁹Haman went out that day happy and in high spirits. But when he saw Mordecai at the king's gate and observed that he neither rose nor showed fear in his presence, he was filled with rage against Mordecai. ¹⁰Nevertheless, Haman restrained himself and went home.

Calling together his friends and Zeresh, his wife, ¹¹Haman boasted to them about his vast wealth, his many sons, and all the ways the king had honored him and how he had elevated him above the other nobles and officials. ¹²"And that's not all," Haman added. "I'm the only person Queen Esther invited to accompany the king to the banquet she gave. And she has invited me along with the king tomorrow. ¹³But all this gives me no satisfaction as long as I see that Jew Mordecai sitting at the king's gate."

¹⁴His wife Zeresh and all his friends said to him, "Have a gallows built, seventy-five feet[a] high, and ask the king in the morning to have Mordecai hanged on it. Then go with the king to the dinner and be happy." This suggestion delighted Haman, and he had the gallows built.

[a]14 Hebrew *fifty cubits* (about 23 meters)

VERSE:	AUTHOR:	PASSAGE:
Esther 4:14	Jill Briscoe	Esther 4:9–16

How to Be a Light

When a human star that is cold and dead, just a lump of material, chooses to look to the Son, then he or she begins to shine with that reflected glory! . . .

Esther literally means "star," and she had every intention of being a star! She believed the plan of God was to redeem lost mankind and that that divine plan concerned her nation Israel . . .

From this special people, the bright Morning Star, the Messiah himself, would come . . . Esther literally staked her life on these bright and enduring promises, and she trusted even when she lived in "such a time as this"—"such a time as this" being possibly one of the blackest and darkest periods of her nation's history . . .

She must have wondered so often about the plan of God and his promises. But this we know, she staked her life on the providence of God that would enable him to keep his promises concerning his plan.

What happens to us when we find ourselves in the middle of dark situations? Do we believe the things that are happening to us are accidental? Do we seek to change our circumstances, or do we accept them with a fatalistic attitude? *Can* we change our circumstances, or should we even try?

Sometimes we *can* change things, and we *must* try. That is why we are there! At other times, having tried, we find we cannot alter anything, nor can we escape, and so we must allow those situations to change us and we must accept the privilege of shining there.

. . . .

ADDITIONAL SCRIPTURE READINGS
Psalm 145:13b–21; Isaiah 60:1–3

Go to page 601 for your next devotional reading.

Mordecai Honored

6 That night the king could not sleep; so he ordered the book of the chronicles, the record of his reign, to be brought in and read to him. ²It was found recorded there that Mordecai had exposed Bigthana and Teresh, two of the king's officers who guarded the doorway, who had conspired to assassinate King Xerxes.

³"What honor and recognition has Mordecai received for this?" the king asked.

"Nothing has been done for him," his attendants answered.

⁴The king said, "Who is in the court?" Now Haman had just entered the outer court of the palace to speak to the king about hanging Mordecai on the gallows he had erected for him.

⁵His attendants answered, "Haman is standing in the court."

"Bring him in," the king ordered.

⁶When Haman entered, the king asked him, "What should be done for the man the king delights to honor?"

Now Haman thought to himself, "Who is there that the king would rather honor than me?" ⁷So he answered the king, "For the man the king delights to honor, ⁸have them bring a royal robe the king has worn and a horse the king has ridden, one with a royal crest placed on its head. ⁹Then let the robe and horse be entrusted to one of the king's most noble princes. Let them robe the man the king delights to honor, and lead him on the horse through the city streets, proclaiming before him, 'This is what is done for the man the king delights to honor!' "

¹⁰"Go at once," the king commanded Haman. "Get the robe and the horse and do just as you have suggested for Mordecai the Jew, who sits at the king's gate. Do not neglect anything you have recommended."

¹¹So Haman got the robe and the horse. He robed Mordecai, and led him on horseback through the city streets, proclaiming before him, "This is what is done for the man the king delights to honor!"

¹²Afterward Mordecai returned to the king's gate. But Haman rushed home, with his head covered in grief, ¹³and told Zeresh his wife and all his friends everything that had happened to him.

His advisers and his wife Zeresh said to him, "Since Mordecai, before whom your downfall has started, is of Jewish origin, you cannot stand against him—you will surely come to ruin!" ¹⁴While they were still talking with him, the king's eunuchs arrived and hurried Haman away to the banquet Esther had prepared.

Haman Hanged

7 So the king and Haman went to dine with Queen Esther, ²and as they were drinking wine on that second day, the king again asked, "Queen Esther, what is your petition? It will be given you. What is your request? Even up to half the kingdom, it will be granted."

³Then Queen Esther answered, "If I have found favor with you, O king, and if it pleases your majesty, grant me my life—this is my petition. And spare my people—this is my request. ⁴For I and my people have been sold for destruction and slaughter and annihilation. If we had merely been sold as male and female slaves, I would have kept quiet, because no such distress would justify disturbing the king.[a]"

⁵King Xerxes asked Queen Esther, "Who is he? Where is the man who has dared to do such a thing?"

⁶Esther said, "The adversary and enemy is this vile Haman."

Then Haman was terrified before the king and queen. ⁷The king got up in a rage, left his wine and went out into the palace garden. But Haman, realizing that the king had already

---

a4 Or quiet, but the compensation our adversary offers cannot be compared with the loss the king would suffer

decided his fate, stayed behind to beg Queen Esther for his life.

[8]Just as the king returned from the palace garden to the banquet hall, Haman was falling on the couch where Esther was reclining.

The king exclaimed, "Will he even molest the queen while she is with me in the house?"

As soon as the word left the king's mouth, they covered Haman's face. [9]Then Harbona, one of the eunuchs attending the king, said, "A gallows seventy-five feet[a] high stands by Haman's house. He had it made for Mordecai, who spoke up to help the king."

The king said, "Hang him on it!" [10]So they hanged Haman on the gallows he had prepared for Mordecai. Then the king's fury subsided.

The King's Edict in Behalf of the Jews

8 That same day King Xerxes gave Queen Esther the estate of Haman, the enemy of the Jews. And Mordecai came into the presence of the king, for Esther had told how he was related to her. [2]The king took off

[a]9 Hebrew *fifty cubits* (about 23 meters)

VERSE:
Esther 6:1

AUTHOR:
Barbara Deane

PASSAGE:
Esther 6:1–14

God's Night School

More than half of all people over 65 complain about insomnia, but few recognize it as a spiritual opportunity ...

Being alone with God in the middle of the night, when all the daytime distractions are far away, can give us the opportunity to do some of the important spiritual work of the later years. It may be the cleansing of unconfessed sins of the past, forgiving others and asking forgiveness for ourselves, or bringing to mind those with whom we need to seek reconciliation and healing of relationships. It may be learning to simply "be" with him, bathing ourselves in the light of his love.

There is much more to prayer than most of us have ever dreamed possible, and now we have great volumes of time to learn it.

ADDITIONAL SCRIPTURE READINGS
Psalm 32; Colossians 3:12–17

Go to page 603 for your next devotional reading.

his signet ring, which he had reclaimed from Haman, and presented it to Mordecai. And Esther appointed him over Haman's estate.

³Esther again pleaded with the king, falling at his feet and weeping. She begged him to put an end to the evil plan of Haman the Agagite, which he had devised against the Jews. ⁴Then the king extended the gold scepter to Esther and she arose and stood before him.

⁵"If it pleases the king," she said, "and if he regards me with favor and thinks it the right thing to do, and if he is pleased with me, let an order be written overruling the dispatches that Haman son of Hammedatha, the Agagite, devised and wrote to destroy the Jews in all the king's provinces. ⁶For how can I bear to see disaster fall on my people? How can I bear to see the destruction of my family?"

⁷King Xerxes replied to Queen Esther and to Mordecai the Jew, "Because Haman attacked the Jews, I have given his estate to Esther, and they have hanged him on the gallows. ⁸Now write another decree in the king's name in behalf of the Jews as seems best to you, and seal it with the king's signet ring—for no document written in the king's name and sealed with his ring can be revoked."

⁹At once the royal secretaries were summoned—on the twenty-third day of the third month, the month of Sivan. They wrote out all Mordecai's orders to the Jews, and to the satraps, governors and nobles of the 127 provinces stretching from India to Cush.ᵃ These orders were written in the script of each province and the language of each people and also to the Jews in their own script and language. ¹⁰Mordecai wrote in the name of King Xerxes, sealed the dispatches with the king's signet ring, and sent them by mounted couriers, who rode fast horses especially bred for the king.

¹¹The king's edict granted the Jews in every city the right to assemble and protect themselves; to destroy, kill and annihilate any armed force of any nationality or province that might attack them and their women and children; and to plunder the property of their enemies. ¹²The day appointed for the Jews to do this in all the provinces of King Xerxes was the thirteenth day of the twelfth month, the month of Adar. ¹³A copy of the text of the edict was to be issued as law in every province and made known to the people of every nationality so that the Jews would be ready on that day to avenge themselves on their enemies.

¹⁴The couriers, riding the royal horses, raced out, spurred on by the king's command. And the edict was also issued in the citadel of Susa.

¹⁵Mordecai left the king's presence wearing royal garments of blue and white, a large crown of gold and a purple robe of fine linen. And the city of Susa held a joyous celebration. ¹⁶For the Jews it was a time of happiness and joy, gladness and honor. ¹⁷In every province and in every city, wherever the edict of the king went, there was joy and gladness among the Jews, with feasting and celebrating. And many people of other nationalities became Jews because fear of the Jews had seized them.

Triumph of the Jews

9 On the thirteenth day of the twelfth month, the month of Adar, the edict commanded by the king was to be carried out. On this day the enemies of the Jews had hoped to overpower them, but now the tables were turned and the Jews got the upper hand over those who hated them. ²The Jews assembled in their cities in all the provinces of King Xerxes to attack those seeking their destruction. No one could stand against them, because the people of all the other nationalities were afraid of them. ³And all the nobles of the provinces, the satraps, the governors and the king's administrators helped

---

ᵃ9 That is, the upper Nile region

PASSAGE: Psalm 61; Isaiah 43:14–21
AUTHOR: John Newton

The Lord Will Provide

Though troubles assail us, and dangers afright,
Though friends should all fail us, and foes all unite,
Yet one thing secures us, whatever betide,
The promise assures us, "the Lord will provide."
The birds, without garner or storehouse, are fed;
From them let us learn to trust God for our bread:
His saints what is fitting shall ne'er be denied
So long as 'tis written, "the Lord will provide."
When Satan assails us to stop up our path,
And courage all fails us, we triumph by faith.
He cannot take from us, though oft he has tried,
This heart-cheering promise, "the Lord will
          provide."
No strength of our own, and no goodness we
          claim;
Yet, since we have known of the Savior's great
          Name,
In this our strong tower for safety we hide:
The Lord is our power, "the Lord will provide."

Go to page 607 for your next devotional reading.

the Jews, because fear of Mordecai had seized them. ⁴Mordecai was prominent in the palace; his reputation spread throughout the provinces, and he became more and more powerful.

⁵The Jews struck down all their enemies with the sword, killing and destroying them, and they did what they pleased to those who hated them. ⁶In the citadel of Susa, the Jews killed and destroyed five hundred men. ⁷They also killed Parshandatha, Dalphon, Aspatha, ⁸Poratha, Adalia, Aridatha, ⁹Parmashta, Arisai, Aridai and Vaizatha, ¹⁰the ten sons of Haman son of Hammedatha, the enemy of the Jews. But they did not lay their hands on the plunder.

¹¹The number of those slain in the citadel of Susa was reported to the king that same day. ¹²The king said to Queen Esther, "The Jews have killed and destroyed five hundred men and the ten sons of Haman in the citadel of Susa. What have they done in the rest of the king's provinces? Now what is your petition? It will be given you. What is your request? It will also be granted."

¹³"If it pleases the king," Esther answered, "give the Jews in Susa permission to carry out this day's edict tomorrow also, and let Haman's ten sons be hanged on gallows."

¹⁴So the king commanded that this be done. An edict was issued in Susa, and they hanged the ten sons of Haman. ¹⁵The Jews in Susa came together on the fourteenth day of the month of Adar, and they put to death in Susa three hundred men, but they did not lay their hands on the plunder.

¹⁶Meanwhile, the remainder of the Jews who were in the king's provinces also assembled to protect themselves and get relief from their enemies. They killed seventy-five thousand of them but did not lay their hands on the plunder. ¹⁷This happened on the thirteenth day of the month of Adar, and on the fourteenth they rested and made it a day of feasting and joy.

Purim Celebrated

¹⁸The Jews in Susa, however, had assembled on the thirteenth and fourteenth, and then on the fifteenth they rested and made it a day of feasting and joy.

¹⁹That is why rural Jews—those living in villages—observe the fourteenth of the month of Adar as a day of joy and feasting, a day for giving presents to each other.

²⁰Mordecai recorded these events, and he sent letters to all the Jews throughout the provinces of King Xerxes, near and far, ²¹to have them celebrate annually the fourteenth and fifteenth days of the month of Adar ²²as the time when the Jews got relief from their enemies, and as the month when their sorrow was turned into joy and their mourning into a day of celebration. He wrote them to observe the days as days of feasting and joy and giving presents of food to one another and gifts to the poor.

²³So the Jews agreed to continue the celebration they had begun, doing what Mordecai had written to them. ²⁴For Haman son of Hammedatha, the Agagite, the enemy of all the Jews, had plotted against the Jews to destroy them and had cast the *pur* (that is, the lot) for their ruin and destruction. ²⁵But when the plot came to the king's attention,ᵃ he issued written orders that the evil scheme Haman had devised against the Jews should come back onto his own head, and that he and his sons should be hanged on the gallows. ²⁶(Therefore these days were called Purim, from the word *pur*.) Because of everything written in this letter and because of what they had seen and what had happened to them, ²⁷the Jews took it upon themselves to establish the custom that they and their descendants and all who join them should without fail observe these two days every year, in the way prescribed and at the

ᵃ25 Or *when Esther came before the king*

time appointed. ²⁸These days should be remembered and observed in every generation by every family, and in every province and in every city. And these days of Purim should never cease to be celebrated by the Jews, nor should the memory of them die out among their descendants.

²⁹So Queen Esther, daughter of Abihail, along with Mordecai the Jew, wrote with full authority to confirm this second letter concerning Purim. ³⁰And Mordecai sent letters to all the Jews in the 127 provinces of the kingdom of Xerxes—words of goodwill and assurance— ³¹to establish these days of Purim at their designated times, as Mordecai the Jew and Queen Esther had decreed for them, and as they had established for themselves and their descendants in regard to their times of fasting and lamentation. ³²Esther's decree confirmed these regulations about Purim, and it was written down in the records.

The Greatness of Mordecai

10 King Xerxes imposed tribute throughout the empire, to its distant shores. ²And all his acts of power and might, together with a full account of the greatness of Mordecai to which the king had raised him, are they not written in the book of the annals of the kings of Media and Persia? ³Mordecai the Jew was second in rank to King Xerxes, preeminent among the Jews, and held in high esteem by his many fellow Jews, because he worked for the good of his people and spoke up for the welfare of all the Jews.

This ancient account addresses the persistent question, "Why do bad things happen to good people?" Job struggles in vain to identify a reason for his suffering, yet maintains his innocence and his faith in God. In the end God declares his awesome power and his unfailing love. As you read this book, remember that even though you don't have answers to all your questions about suffering, God is still in control.

JOB

Prologue

1 In the land of Uz there lived a man whose name was Job. This man was blameless and upright; he feared God and shunned evil. ²He had seven sons and three daughters, ³and he owned seven thousand sheep, three thousand camels, five hundred yoke of oxen and five hundred donkeys, and had a large number of servants. He was the greatest man among all the people of the East.

⁴His sons used to take turns holding feasts in their homes, and they would invite their three sisters to eat and drink with them. ⁵When a period of feasting had run its course, Job would send and have them purified. Early in the morning he would sacrifice a burnt offering for each of them, thinking, "Perhaps my children have sinned and cursed God in their hearts." This was Job's regular custom.

Job's First Test

⁶One day the angels[a] came to present themselves before the LORD, and Satan[b] also came with them. ⁷The LORD said to Satan, "Where have you come from?"

Satan answered the LORD, "From roaming through the earth and going back and forth in it."

⁸Then the LORD said to Satan, "Have you considered my servant Job? There is no one on earth like him; he is blameless and upright, a man who fears God and shuns evil."

⁹"Does Job fear God for nothing?" Satan replied. ¹⁰"Have you not put a hedge around him and his household

---

a 6 Hebrew *the sons of God*   *b 6* Satan *means* accuser.

and everything he has? You have blessed the work of his hands, so that his flocks and herds are spread throughout the land. ¹¹But stretch out your hand and strike everything he has, and he will surely curse you to your face."

¹²The LORD said to Satan, "Very well, then, everything he has is in your hands, but on the man himself do not lay a finger."

Then Satan went out from the presence of the LORD.

¹³One day when Job's sons and daughters were feasting and drinking wine at the oldest brother's house, ¹⁴a messenger came to Job and said, "The oxen were plowing and the donkeys

VERSE:	AUTHOR:	PASSAGE:
Job 1:9	Charles H. Spurgeon	Job 1:6–22

The Reward

There are people who love God only because he prospers them . . . They love the table but not the host. They love the cupboard but not the master of the house.

True Christians expect their reward in the next life and anticipate enduring adversity in this life. The promise of the old covenant was prosperity, but the promise of the new covenant is adversity. Remember Christ's words: "Every branch that does bear fruit he prunes so that it will be even more fruitful" (John 15:2).

"What!" you say. "That is a terrible promise." Yet this affliction yields such precious results that the Christian who goes through it learns to rejoice in trials. This evening rejoice in the blessed assurance that as trials increase so does his grace.

Let me promise you this, child of God, you will be no stranger to the rod. Sooner or later every bar of gold must pass through the fire. Do not worry. Rejoice. Such fruitful days are ahead that you will forget this world and be ready for heaven. You will be delivered from clinging to the present to looking forward to eternal things soon to be revealed.

ADDITIONAL SCRIPTURE READINGS
John 15:1–8; 1 Peter 1:3–9

Go to page 609 for your next devotional reading.

were grazing nearby, ¹⁵and the Sabeans attacked and carried them off. They put the servants to the sword, and I am the only one who has escaped to tell you!"

¹⁶While he was still speaking, another messenger came and said, "The fire of God fell from the sky and burned up the sheep and the servants, and I am the only one who has escaped to tell you!"

¹⁷While he was still speaking, another messenger came and said, "The Chaldeans formed three raiding parties and swept down on your camels and carried them off. They put the servants to the sword, and I am the only one who has escaped to tell you!"

¹⁸While he was still speaking, yet another messenger came and said, "Your sons and daughters were feasting and drinking wine at the oldest brother's house, ¹⁹when suddenly a mighty wind swept in from the desert and struck the four corners of the house. It collapsed on them and they are dead, and I am the only one who has escaped to tell you!"

²⁰At this, Job got up and tore his robe and shaved his head. Then he fell to the ground in worship ²¹and said:

"Naked I came from my mother's
    womb,
  and naked I will depart.ᵃ
The LORD gave and the LORD has
    taken away;
  may the name of the LORD be
    praised."

²²In all this, Job did not sin by charging God with wrongdoing.

Job's Second Test

2 On another day the angelsᵇ came to present themselves before the LORD, and Satan also came with them to present himself before him. ²And the LORD said to Satan, "Where have you come from?"

Satan answered the LORD, "From roaming through the earth and going back and forth in it."

³Then the LORD said to Satan, "Have you considered my servant Job? There is no one on earth like him; he is blameless and upright, a man who fears God and shuns evil. And he still maintains his integrity, though you incited me against him to ruin him without any reason."

⁴"Skin for skin!" Satan replied. "A man will give all he has for his own life. ⁵But stretch out your hand and strike his flesh and bones, and he will surely curse you to your face."

⁶The LORD said to Satan, "Very well, then, he is in your hands; but you must spare his life."

⁷So Satan went out from the presence of the LORD and afflicted Job with painful sores from the soles of his feet to the top of his head. ⁸Then Job took a piece of broken pottery and scraped himself with it as he sat among the ashes.

⁹His wife said to him, "Are you still holding on to your integrity? Curse God and die!"

¹⁰He replied, "You are talking like a foolishᶜ woman. Shall we accept good from God, and not trouble?"

In all this, Job did not sin in what he said.

Job's Three Friends

¹¹When Job's three friends, Eliphaz the Temanite, Bildad the Shuhite and Zophar the Naamathite, heard about all the troubles that had come upon him, they set out from their homes and met together by agreement to go and sympathize with him and comfort him. ¹²When they saw him from a distance, they could hardly recognize him; they began to weep aloud, and they tore their robes and sprinkled dust on their heads. ¹³Then they sat on the ground with him for seven days and seven nights. No one said a word to him, because they saw how great his suffering was.

ᵃ21 Or *will return there*   ᵇ1 Hebrew *the sons of God*   ᶜ10 The Hebrew word rendered *foolish* denotes moral deficiency.

VERSE:	AUTHOR:	PASSAGE:
Job 2:13	Joseph Bayly	Job 2:11–13

He Just Sat Beside Me

What do we say when we talk to the grieving person? We are most likely to be helpful with an economy of words. In our contacts with people at death as at other times, it is easy to say too much, to talk when we ought to listen . . .

Sensitivity in the presence of grief should usually make us more silent, more listening.

"I'm sorry," is honest; "I know how you feel," is usually not—even though you may have experienced the death of a person who had the same familial relationship to you as the deceased person had to the grieving one . . .

Don't try to "prove" anything to a survivor. An arm about the shoulder, a firm grip of the hand, a kiss: these are the proofs grief needs, not logical reasoning.

I was sitting, torn by grief. Someone came and talked to me of God's dealings, of why it happened, of hope beyond the grave. He talked constantly, he said things I knew were true.

I was unmoved, except to wish he'd go away. He finally did.

Another came and sat beside me. He didn't talk. He didn't ask leading questions. He just sat beside me for an hour and more, listened when I said something, answered briefly, prayed simply, left.

I was moved. I was comforted. I hated to see him go.

ADDITIONAL SCRIPTURE READINGS
2 Corinthians 1:3–7; 1 Peter 3:8–12

Go to page 620 for your next devotional reading.

Job Speaks

3 After this, Job opened his mouth and cursed the day of his birth. ²He said:

³"May the day of my birth perish,
  and the night it was said, 'A
  boy is born!'
⁴That day—may it turn to
  darkness;
  may God above not care about
  it;
  may no light shine upon it.
⁵May darkness and deep shadow*a*
  claim it once more;
  may a cloud settle over it;
  may blackness overwhelm its
  light.
⁶That night—may thick darkness
  seize it;
  may it not be included among
  the days of the year
  nor be entered in any of the
  months.
⁷May that night be barren;
  may no shout of joy be heard in
  it.
⁸May those who curse days*b* curse
  that day,
  those who are ready to rouse
  Leviathan.
⁹May its morning stars become
  dark;
  may it wait for daylight in vain
  and not see the first rays of
  dawn,
¹⁰for it did not shut the doors of the
  womb on me
  to hide trouble from my eyes.

¹¹"Why did I not perish at birth,
  and die as I came from the
  womb?
¹²Why were there knees to receive
  me
  and breasts that I might be
  nursed?
¹³For now I would be lying down in
  peace;
  I would be asleep and at rest
¹⁴with kings and counselors of the
  earth,

who built for themselves places
  now lying in ruins,
¹⁵with rulers who had gold,
  who filled their houses with
  silver.
¹⁶Or why was I not hidden in the
  ground like a stillborn
  child,
  like an infant who never saw
  the light of day?
¹⁷There the wicked cease from
  turmoil,
  and there the weary are at rest.
¹⁸Captives also enjoy their ease;
  they no longer hear the slave
  driver's shout.
¹⁹The small and the great are there,
  and the slave is freed from his
  master.

²⁰"Why is light given to those in
  misery,
  and life to the bitter of soul,
²¹to those who long for death that
  does not come,
  who search for it more than for
  hidden treasure,
²²who are filled with gladness
  and rejoice when they reach the
  grave?
²³Why is life given to a man
  whose way is hidden,
  whom God has hedged in?
²⁴For sighing comes to me instead
  of food;
  my groans pour out like water.
²⁵What I feared has come upon me;
  what I dreaded has happened to
  me.
²⁶I have no peace, no quietness;
  I have no rest, but only
  turmoil."

Eliphaz

4 Then Eliphaz the Temanite replied:

²"If someone ventures a word with
  you, will you be impatient?
  But who can keep from
  speaking?
³Think how you have instructed
  many,

---

*a*5 Or *and the shadow of death*   *b*8 Or *the sea*

how you have strengthened
  feeble hands.
⁴Your words have supported those
    who stumbled;
  you have strengthened faltering
    knees.
⁵But now trouble comes to you,
    and you are discouraged;
  it strikes you, and you are
    dismayed.
⁶Should not your piety be your
    confidence
  and your blameless ways your
    hope?

⁷"Consider now: Who, being
    innocent, has ever
    perished?
  Where were the upright ever
    destroyed?
⁸As I have observed, those who
    plow evil
  and those who sow trouble reap
    it.
⁹At the breath of God they are
    destroyed;
  at the blast of his anger they
    perish.
¹⁰The lions may roar and growl,
  yet the teeth of the great lions
    are broken.
¹¹The lion perishes for lack of prey,
  and the cubs of the lioness are
    scattered.

¹²"A word was secretly brought to
    me,
  my ears caught a whisper of it.
¹³Amid disquieting dreams in the
    night,
  when deep sleep falls on men,
¹⁴fear and trembling seized me
  and made all my bones shake.
¹⁵A spirit glided past my face,
  and the hair on my body stood
    on end.
¹⁶It stopped,
  but I could not tell what it was.
  A form stood before my eyes,
  and I heard a hushed voice:
¹⁷'Can a mortal be more righteous
    than God?
  Can a man be more pure than
    his Maker?

¹⁸If God places no trust in his
    servants,
  if he charges his angels with
    error,
¹⁹how much more those who live in
    houses of clay,
  whose foundations are in the
    dust,
  who are crushed more readily
    than a moth!
²⁰Between dawn and dusk they are
    broken to pieces;
  unnoticed, they perish forever.
²¹Are not the cords of their tent
    pulled up,
  so that they die without
    wisdom?'ᵃ

5 "Call if you will, but who will
    answer you?
  To which of the holy ones will
    you turn?
²Resentment kills a fool,
  and envy slays the simple.
³I myself have seen a fool taking
    root,
  but suddenly his house was
    cursed.
⁴His children are far from safety,
  crushed in court without a
    defender.
⁵The hungry consume his harvest,
  taking it even from among
    thorns,
  and the thirsty pant after his
    wealth.
⁶For hardship does not spring from
    the soil,
  nor does trouble sprout from
    the ground.
⁷Yet man is born to trouble
  as surely as sparks fly upward.

⁸"But if it were I, I would appeal to
    God;
  I would lay my cause before
    him.
⁹He performs wonders that cannot
    be fathomed,
  miracles that cannot be counted.
¹⁰He bestows rain on the earth;
  he sends water upon the
    countryside.

ᵃ21 Some interpreters end the quotation after verse 17.

11The lowly he sets on high,
   and those who mourn are lifted
     to safety.
12He thwarts the plans of the
   crafty,
   so that their hands achieve
     no success.
13He catches the wise in their
   craftiness,
   and the schemes of the wily are
     swept away.
14Darkness comes upon them in the
   daytime;
   at noon they grope as in the
     night.
15He saves the needy from the
   sword in their mouth;
   he saves them from the clutches
     of the powerful.
16So the poor have hope,
   and injustice shuts its mouth.

17"Blessed is the man whom God
   corrects;
   so do not despise the discipline
     of the Almighty.*a*
18For he wounds, but he also binds
   up;
   he injures, but his hands also
     heal.
19From six calamities he will rescue
   you;
   in seven no harm will befall
     you.
20In famine he will ransom you
   from death,
   and in battle from the stroke of
     the sword.
21You will be protected from the
   lash of the tongue,
   and need not fear when
     destruction comes.
22You will laugh at destruction and
   famine,
   and need not fear the beasts of
     the earth.
23For you will have a covenant with
   the stones of the field,
   and the wild animals will be at
     peace with you.
24You will know that your tent is
   secure;

you will take stock of your
   property and find nothing
     missing.
25You will know that your children
   will be many,
   and your descendants like the
     grass of the earth.
26You will come to the grave in full
   vigor,
   like sheaves gathered in season.

27"We have examined this, and it is
   true.
   So hear it and apply it to
     yourself."

Job

6 Then Job replied:

2"If only my anguish could be
   weighed
   and all my misery be placed on
     the scales!
3It would surely outweigh the sand
   of the seas—
   no wonder my words have been
     impetuous.
4The arrows of the Almighty are in
   me,
   my spirit drinks in their poison;
   God's terrors are marshaled
     against me.
5Does a wild donkey bray when it
   has grass,
   or an ox bellow when it has
     fodder?
6Is tasteless food eaten without salt,
   or is there flavor in the white of
     an egg*b*?
7I refuse to touch it;
   such food makes me ill.

8"Oh, that I might have my
   request,
   that God would grant what I
     hope for,
9that God would be willing to
   crush me,
   to let loose his hand and cut me
     off!
10Then I would still have this
   consolation—
   my joy in unrelenting pain—

---

*a*17 Hebrew *Shaddai*; here and throughout Job
is uncertain.

*b*6 The meaning of the Hebrew for this phrase

that I had not denied the words
  of the Holy One.

¹¹"What strength do I have, that I
    should still hope?
  What prospects, that I should be
    patient?
¹²Do I have the strength of stone?
  Is my flesh bronze?
¹³Do I have any power to help
    myself,
  now that success has been
    driven from me?

¹⁴"A despairing man should have
    the devotion of his friends,
  even though he forsakes the
    fear of the Almighty.
¹⁵But my brothers are as
    undependable as
    intermittent streams,
  as the streams that overflow
¹⁶when darkened by thawing ice
  and swollen with melting snow,
¹⁷but that cease to flow in the dry
    season,
  and in the heat vanish from
    their channels.
¹⁸Caravans turn aside from their
    routes;
  they go up into the wasteland
    and perish.
¹⁹The caravans of Tema look for
    water,
  the traveling merchants of
    Sheba look in hope.
²⁰They are distressed, because they
    had been confident;
  they arrive there, only to be
    disappointed.
²¹Now you too have proved to be of
    no help;
  you see something dreadful and
    are afraid.
²²Have I ever said, 'Give something
    on my behalf,
  pay a ransom for me from your
    wealth,
²³deliver me from the hand of the
    enemy,
  ransom me from the clutches of
    the ruthless'?
²⁴"Teach me, and I will be quiet;

show me where I have been
  wrong.
²⁵How painful are honest words!
  But what do your arguments
    prove?
²⁶Do you mean to correct what I
    say,
  and treat the words of a
    despairing man as wind?
²⁷You would even cast lots for the
    fatherless
  and barter away your friend.

²⁸"But now be so kind as to look at
    me.
  Would I lie to your face?
²⁹Relent, do not be unjust;
  reconsider, for my integrity is at
    stake.ᵃ
³⁰Is there any wickedness on my
    lips?
  Can my mouth not discern
    malice?

7 "Does not man have hard
    service on earth?
  Are not his days like those of a
    hired man?
²Like a slave longing for the
    evening shadows,
  or a hired man waiting eagerly
    for his wages,
³so I have been allotted months of
    futility,
  and nights of misery have been
    assigned to me.
⁴When I lie down I think, 'How
    long before I get up?'
  The night drags on, and I toss
    till dawn.
⁵My body is clothed with worms
    and scabs,
  my skin is broken and festering.

⁶"My days are swifter than a
    weaver's shuttle,
  and they come to an end
    without hope.
⁷Remember, O God, that my life is
    but a breath;
  my eyes will never see
    happiness again.
⁸The eye that now sees me will see
    me no longer;

ᵃ29 Or *my righteousness still stands*

you will look for me, but I will
  be no more.
⁹As a cloud vanishes and is gone,
  so he who goes down to the
    grave*ª* does not return.
¹⁰He will never come to his house
  again;
  his place will know him no
    more.

¹¹"Therefore I will not keep silent;
  I will speak out in the anguish
    of my spirit,
  I will complain in the bitterness
    of my soul.
¹²Am I the sea, or the monster of
  the deep,
  that you put me under guard?
¹³When I think my bed will comfort
  me
  and my couch will ease my
    complaint,
¹⁴even then you frighten me with
  dreams
  and terrify me with visions,
¹⁵so that I prefer strangling and
  death,
  rather than this body of mine.
¹⁶I despise my life; I would not live
  forever.
  Let me alone; my days have no
    meaning.

¹⁷"What is man that you make so
  much of him,
  that you give him so much
    attention,
¹⁸that you examine him every
  morning
  and test him every moment?
¹⁹Will you never look away from
  me,
  or let me alone even for an
    instant?
²⁰If I have sinned, what have I done
  to you,
  O watcher of men?
  Why have you made me your
    target?
  Have I become a burden to
    you?*ᵇ*
²¹Why do you not pardon my
  offenses

and forgive my sins?
For I will soon lie down in the
  dust;
  you will search for me, but I
    will be no more."

Bildad

8 Then Bildad the Shuhite replied:

²"How long will you say such
  things?
  Your words are a blustering
    wind.
³Does God pervert justice?
  Does the Almighty pervert what
    is right?
⁴When your children sinned
  against him,
  he gave them over to the
    penalty of their sin.
⁵But if you will look to God
  and plead with the Almighty,
⁶if you are pure and upright,
  even now he will rouse himself
    on your behalf
  and restore you to your rightful
    place.
⁷Your beginnings will seem
  humble,
  so prosperous will your future
    be.

⁸"Ask the former generations
  and find out what their fathers
    learned,
⁹for we were born only yesterday
  and know nothing,
  and our days on earth are but a
    shadow.
¹⁰Will they not instruct you and tell
  you?
  Will they not bring forth words
    from their understanding?
¹¹Can papyrus grow tall where
  there is no marsh?
  Can reeds thrive without water?
¹²While still growing and uncut,
  they wither more quickly than
    grass.
¹³Such is the destiny of all who
  forget God;

*ª*9 Hebrew *Sheol*   *ᵇ*20 A few manuscripts of the Masoretic Text, an ancient Hebrew scribal tradition and Septuagint; most manuscripts of the Masoretic Text *I have become a burden to myself.*

so perishes the hope of the
        godless.
¹⁴What he trusts in is fragile*ᵃ*;
    what he relies on is a spider's
        web.
¹⁵He leans on his web, but it gives
        way;
    he clings to it, but it does not
        hold.
¹⁶He is like a well-watered plant in
        the sunshine,
    spreading its shoots over the
        garden;
¹⁷it entwines its roots around a pile
        of rocks
    and looks for a place among the
        stones.
¹⁸But when it is torn from its spot,
    that place disowns it and says,
        'I never saw you.'
¹⁹Surely its life withers away,
    andᵇ from the soil other plants
        grow.

²⁰"Surely God does not reject a
        blameless man
    or strengthen the hands of
        evildoers.
²¹He will yet fill your mouth with
        laughter
    and your lips with shouts of
        joy.
²²Your enemies will be clothed in
        shame,
    and the tents of the wicked will
        be no more."

Job

9 Then Job replied:

²"Indeed, I know that this is true.
    But how can a mortal be
        righteous before God?
³Though one wished to dispute
        with him,
    he could not answer him one
        time out of a thousand.
⁴His wisdom is profound, his
        power is vast.
    Who has resisted him and come
        out unscathed?

⁵He moves mountains without their
        knowing it
    and overturns them in his
        anger.
⁶He shakes the earth from its place
    and makes its pillars tremble.
⁷He speaks to the sun and it does
        not shine;
    he seals off the light of the
        stars.
⁸He alone stretches out the heavens
    and treads on the waves of the
        sea.
⁹He is the Maker of the Bear and
        Orion,
    the Pleiades and the
        constellations of the south.
¹⁰He performs wonders that cannot
        be fathomed,
    miracles that cannot be counted.
¹¹When he passes me, I cannot see
        him;
    when he goes by, I cannot
        perceive him.
¹²If he snatches away, who can stop
        him?
    Who can say to him, 'What are
        you doing?'
¹³God does not restrain his anger;
    even the cohorts of Rahab
        cowered at his feet.

¹⁴"How then can I dispute with
        him?
    How can I find words to argue
        with him?
¹⁵Though I were innocent, I could
        not answer him;
    I could only plead with my
        Judge for mercy.
¹⁶Even if I summoned him and he
        responded,
    I do not believe he would give
        me a hearing.
¹⁷He would crush me with a storm
    and multiply my wounds for no
        reason.
¹⁸He would not let me regain my
        breath
    but would overwhelm me with
        misery.

ᵃ14 The meaning of the Hebrew for this word is uncertain.   ᵇ19 Or *Surely all the joy it has / is that*

¹⁹If it is a matter of strength, he is
        mighty!
    And if it is a matter of justice,
        who will summon him*?
²⁰Even if I were innocent, my
        mouth would condemn me;
    if I were blameless, it would
        pronounce me guilty.
²¹"Although I am blameless,
    I have no concern for myself;
    I despise my own life.
²²It is all the same; that is why I
        say,
    'He destroys both the blameless
        and the wicked.'
²³When a scourge brings sudden
        death,
    he mocks the despair of the
        innocent.
²⁴When a land falls into the hands
        of the wicked,
    he blindfolds its judges.
    If it is not he, then who is it?

²⁵"My days are swifter than a
        runner;
    they fly away without a glimpse
        of joy.
²⁶They skim past like boats of
        papyrus,
    like eagles swooping down on
        their prey.
²⁷If I say, 'I will forget my
        complaint,
    I will change my expression,
        and smile,'
²⁸I still dread all my sufferings,
    for I know you will not hold
        me innocent.
²⁹Since I am already found guilty,
    why should I struggle in vain?
³⁰Even if I washed myself with
        soap*
    and my hands with washing
        soda,
³¹you would plunge me into a slime
        pit
    so that even my clothes would
        detest me.

³²"He is not a man like me that I
        might answer him,

that we might confront each
        other in court.
³³If only there were someone to
        arbitrate between us,
    to lay his hand upon us both,
³⁴someone to remove God's rod
        from me,
    so that his terror would frighte
        me no more.
³⁵Then I would speak up without
        fear of him,
    but as it now stands with me, I
        cannot.

10 "I loathe my very life;
        therefore I will give free rein
        to my complaint
    and speak out in the bitterness
        of my soul.
²I will say to God: Do not condem
        me,
    but tell me what charges you
        have against me.
³Does it please you to oppress me,
    to spurn the work of your
        hands,
    while you smile on the scheme
        of the wicked?
⁴Do you have eyes of flesh?
    Do you see as a mortal sees?
⁵Are your days like those of a
        mortal
    or your years like those of a
        man,
⁶that you must search out my
        faults
    and probe after my sin—
⁷though you know that I am not
        guilty
    and that no one can rescue me
        from your hand?

⁸"Your hands shaped me and mad
        me.
    Will you now turn and destroy
        me?
⁹Remember that you molded me
        like clay.
    Will you now turn me to dust
        again?
¹⁰Did you not pour me out like mil
    and curdle me like cheese,
¹¹clothe me with skin and flesh

*19 See Septuagint; Hebrew *me*.   *30 Or *snow*

and knit me together with
   bones and sinews?
¹²You gave me life and showed me
   kindness,
   and in your providence watched
      over my spirit.

¹³"But this is what you concealed in
      your heart,
   and I know that this was in
      your mind:
¹⁴If I sinned, you would be
      watching me
   and would not let my offense
      go unpunished.
¹⁵If I am guilty—woe to me!
   Even if I am innocent, I cannot
      lift my head,
   for I am full of shame
   and drowned in* my affliction.
¹⁶If I hold my head high, you stalk
      me like a lion
   and again display your
      awesome power against
      me.
¹⁷You bring new witnesses against
      me
   and increase your anger toward
      me;
   your forces come against me
      wave upon wave.

¹⁸"Why then did you bring me out
      of the womb?
   I wish I had died before any
      eye saw me.
¹⁹If only I had never come into
      being,
   or had been carried straight
      from the womb to the
      grave!
²⁰Are not my few days almost over?
   Turn away from me so I can
      have a moment's joy
²¹before I go to the place of no
      return,
   to the land of gloom and deep
      shadow,*
²²to the land of deepest night,
   of deep shadow and disorder,
   where even the light is like
      darkness."

Zophar

11 Then Zophar the Naamathite
      replied:

²"Are all these words to go
      unanswered?
   Is this talker to be vindicated?
³Will your idle talk reduce men to
      silence?
   Will no one rebuke you when
      you mock?
⁴You say to God, 'My beliefs are
      flawless
   and I am pure in your sight.'
⁵Oh, how I wish that God would
      speak,
   that he would open his lips
      against you
⁶and disclose to you the secrets of
      wisdom,
   for true wisdom has two sides.
   Know this: God has even
      forgotten some of your sin.

⁷"Can you fathom the mysteries of
      God?
   Can you probe the limits of the
      Almighty?
⁸They are higher than the
      heavens—what can you
      do?
   They are deeper than the depths
      of the grave*—what can
      you know?
⁹Their measure is longer than the
      earth
   and wider than the sea.

¹⁰"If he comes along and confines
      you in prison
   and convenes a court, who can
      oppose him?
¹¹Surely he recognizes deceitful
      men;
   and when he sees evil, does he
      not take note?
¹²But a witless man can no more
      become wise
   than a wild donkey's colt can be
      born a man.*

¹³"Yet if you devote your heart to
      him

---

*a15 Or *and aware of*   *b21 Or *and the shadow of death;* also in verse 22   *c8 Hebrew *than Sheol*
*d12 Or *wild donkey can be born tame*

and stretch out your hands to
  him,
¹⁴if you put away the sin that is in
    your hand
  and allow no evil to dwell in
    your tent,
¹⁵then you will lift up your face
    without shame;
  you will stand firm and without
    fear.
¹⁶You will surely forget your
    trouble,
  recalling it only as waters gone
    by.
¹⁷Life will be brighter than
    noonday,
  and darkness will become like
    morning.
¹⁸You will be secure, because there
    is hope;
  you will look about you and
    take your rest in safety.
¹⁹You will lie down, with no one to
    make you afraid,
  and many will court your favor.
²⁰But the eyes of the wicked will
    fail,
  and escape will elude them;
    their hope will become a dying
    gasp."

Job

12 Then Job replied:

²"Doubtless you are the people,
  and wisdom will die with you!
³But I have a mind as well as you;
  I am not inferior to you.
  Who does not know all these
    things?

⁴"I have become a laughingstock to
    my friends,
  though I called upon God and
    he answered—
  a mere laughingstock, though
    righteous and blameless!
⁵Men at ease have contempt for
    misfortune
  as the fate of those whose feet
    are slipping.
⁶The tents of marauders are
    undisturbed,

and those who provoke God are
    secure—
  those who carry their god in
    their hands.^a

⁷"But ask the animals, and they
    will teach you,
  or the birds of the air, and they
    will tell you;
⁸or speak to the earth, and it will
    teach you,
  or let the fish of the sea inform
    you.
⁹Which of all these does not know
  that the hand of the LORD has
    done this?
¹⁰In his hand is the life of every
    creature
  and the breath of all mankind.
¹¹Does not the ear test words
  as the tongue tastes food?
¹²Is not wisdom found among the
    aged?
  Does not long life bring
    understanding?

¹³"To God belong wisdom and
    power;
  counsel and understanding are
    his.
¹⁴What he tears down cannot be
    rebuilt;
  the man he imprisons cannot be
    released.
¹⁵If he holds back the waters, there
    is drought;
  if he lets them loose, they
    devastate the land.
¹⁶To him belong strength and
    victory;
  both deceived and deceiver are
    his.
¹⁷He leads counselors away stripped
  and makes fools of judges.
¹⁸He takes off the shackles put on
    by kings
  and ties a loincloth^b around
    their waist.
¹⁹He leads priests away stripped
  and overthrows men long
    established.
²⁰He silences the lips of trusted
    advisers

---

^a6 Or *secure | in what God's hand brings them*　　　^b18 Or *shackles of kings | and ties a belt*

and takes away the discernment
of elders.
²¹He pours contempt on nobles
and disarms the mighty.
²²He reveals the deep things of
darkness
and brings deep shadows into
the light.
²³He makes nations great, and
destroys them;
he enlarges nations, and
disperses them.
²⁴He deprives the leaders of the
earth of their reason;
he sends them wandering
through a trackless waste.
²⁵They grope in darkness with no
light;
he makes them stagger like
drunkards.

13 "My eyes have seen all this,
my ears have heard and
understood it.
²What you know, I also know;
I am not inferior to you.
³But I desire to speak to the
Almighty
and to argue my case with God.
⁴You, however, smear me with lies;
you are worthless physicians, all
of you!
⁵If only you would be altogether
silent!
For you, that would be wisdom.
⁶Hear now my argument;
listen to the plea of my lips.
⁷Will you speak wickedly on God's
behalf?
Will you speak deceitfully for
him?
⁸Will you show him partiality?
Will you argue the case for
God?
⁹Would it turn out well if he
examined you?
Could you deceive him as you
might deceive men?
¹⁰He would surely rebuke you
if you secretly showed
partiality.
¹¹Would not his splendor terrify
you?

Would not the dread of him fall
on you?
¹²Your maxims are proverbs of
ashes;
your defenses are defenses of
clay.

¹³"Keep silent and let me speak;
then let come to me what may.
¹⁴Why do I put myself in jeopardy
and take my life in my hands?
¹⁵Though he slay me, yet will I
hope in him;
I will surely[a] defend my ways
to his face.
¹⁶Indeed, this will turn out for my
deliverance,
for no godless man would dare
come before him!
¹⁷Listen carefully to my words;
let your ears take in what I
say.
¹⁸Now that I have prepared my
case,
I know I will be vindicated.
¹⁹Can anyone bring charges against
me?
If so, I will be silent and die.

²⁰"Only grant me these two things,
O God,
and then I will not hide from
you:
²¹Withdraw your hand far from me,
and stop frightening me with
your terrors.
²²Then summon me and I will
answer,
or let me speak, and you reply.
²³How many wrongs and sins have
I committed?
Show me my offense and my
sin.
²⁴Why do you hide your face
and consider me your enemy?
²⁵Will you torment a windblown
leaf?
Will you chase after dry chaff?
²⁶For you write down bitter things
against me
and make me inherit the sins of
my youth.
²⁷You fasten my feet in shackles;

a15 Or *He will surely slay me; I have no hope —* / *yet I will*

you keep close watch on all my
  paths
by putting marks on the soles of
  my feet.

28"So man wastes away like
    something rotten,
  like a garment eaten by moths.

14 "Man born of woman
    is of few days and full of
    trouble.
2He springs up like a flower and
    withers away;
  like a fleeting shadow, he does
    not endure.

VERSE:	AUTHOR:	PASSAGE:
Job 13:15	J. Oswald Sanders	Job 13:1–19

The Bitter and the Sweet

Faith grows only as it is tested, and old age is one of the crucibles in which the testing takes place. It is through the dark experiences of life rather than in its lightsome joys that our faith rises to new heights. Such experiences will develop in us a more restful confidence in our heavenly Father's love and providential care . . .

With advancing years there comes maturing wisdom, a wisdom that develops only with age. Such wisdom cannot be gleaned from textbooks. No college course can provide it. It must be hammered out, often painfully, on the anvil of real-life experience. In our old age we have the privilege of sharing with others our dearly bought discoveries.

We can with Job, for example, experience the joy of mastering the art of accepting the bitter with the sweet. In the midst of his holocaust of trouble Job's wife urged him to "curse God and die" (Job 2:9) and thus escape further trials. Job's magnificent acceptance of the will of God not only silenced her, but also vindicated God's confidence in him and defeated the devil. It provided succeeding generations with a glowing example of unquestioning confidence in a God whom Job knew to be absolutely trustworthy.

ADDITIONAL SCRIPTURE READINGS
Psalm 25; Isaiah 12

Go to page 622 for your next devotional reading.

³Do you fix your eye on such a
    one?
  Will you bring him[a] before
      you for judgment?
⁴Who can bring what is pure from
    the impure?
  No one!
⁵Man's days are determined;
  you have decreed the number
      of his months
  and have set limits he cannot
      exceed.
⁶So look away from him and let
    him alone,
  till he has put in his time like a
      hired man.

⁷"At least there is hope for a tree:
  If it is cut down, it will sprout
      again,
  and its new shoots will not fail.
⁸Its roots may grow old in the
      ground
  and its stump die in the soil,
⁹yet at the scent of water it will
      bud
  and put forth shoots like a
      plant.
¹⁰But man dies and is laid low;
  he breathes his last and is no
      more.
¹¹As water disappears from the sea
  or a riverbed becomes parched
      and dry,
¹²so man lies down and does not
      rise;
  till the heavens are no more,
      men will not awake
  or be roused from their sleep.

¹³"If only you would hide me in the
      grave[b]
  and conceal me till your anger
      has passed!
  If only you would set me a time
  and then remember me!
¹⁴If a man dies, will he live again?
  All the days of my hard service
  I will wait for my renewal[c] to
      come.
¹⁵You will call and I will answer
      you;
  you will long for the creature
      your hands have made.

¹⁶Surely then you will count my
      steps
  but not keep track of my sin.
¹⁷My offenses will be sealed up in a
      bag;
  you will cover over my sin.

¹⁸"But as a mountain erodes and
      crumbles
  and as a rock is moved from its
      place,
¹⁹as water wears away stones
  and torrents wash away the
      soil,
  so you destroy man's hope.
²⁰You overpower him once for all,
      and he is gone;
  you change his countenance and
      send him away.
²¹If his sons are honored, he does
      not know it;
  if they are brought low, he does
      not see it.
²²He feels but the pain of his own
      body
  and mourns only for himself."

Eliphaz

15 Then Eliphaz the Temanite re-
         plied:

²"Would a wise man answer with
      empty notions
  or fill his belly with the hot east
      wind?
³Would he argue with useless
      words,
  with speeches that have no
      value?
⁴But you even undermine piety
  and hinder devotion to God.
⁵Your sin prompts your mouth;
  you adopt the tongue of the
      crafty.
⁶Your own mouth condemns you,
      not mine;
  your own lips testify against
      you.

⁷"Are you the first man ever born?
  Were you brought forth before
      the hills?
⁸Do you listen in on God's council?

Do you limit wisdom to
yourself?
⁹What do you know that we do not
know?
What insights do you have that
we do not have?
¹⁰The gray-haired and the aged are
on our side,
men even older than your
father.

¹¹Are God's consolations not
enough for you,
words spoken gently to you?
¹²Why has your heart carried you
away,
and why do your eyes flash,
¹³so that you vent your rage against
God
and pour out such words from
your mouth?

VERSE:
Job 14:5

AUTHOR:
Billy Graham

PASSAGE:
Job 14:1–22

Time and Eternity

Life is like a shadow, like a fleeting cloud moving across
the face of the sun. David said, "We are aliens and
strangers in your sight" (1 Chronicles 29:15). The world
is not our permanent home, it is only temporary . . .

When English patriot Sir William Russell went to the
scaffold in 1683, he took his watch out of his pocket and
handed it to the physician who attended him in his
death. "Would you kindly take my timepiece?" he asked.
"I have no use for it. I am now dealing with eternity" . . .

How different would today be if you knew it would be
your last one on earth before meeting God face to face?
We should strive to live every day as if it was our last,
for one day it will be!

The Bible teaches that God knows the exact moment
when each person is to die (Job 14:5). There are appointed bounds beyond which we cannot pass. And I am
convinced that when a man or woman is prepared to die,
he or she is also prepared to live. The primary goal in
life, therefore, should be to prepare for death. Everything else is secondary.

ADDITIONAL SCRIPTURE READINGS
Psalm 39; Psalm 90

Go to page 648 for your next devotional reading.

¹⁴"What is man, that he could be
    pure,
  or one born of woman, that he
    could be righteous?
¹⁵If God places no trust in his holy
    ones,
  if even the heavens are not pure
    in his eyes,
¹⁶how much less man, who is vile
    and corrupt,
  who drinks up evil like water!

¹⁷"Listen to me and I will explain to
    you;
  let me tell you what I have
    seen,
¹⁸what wise men have declared,
  hiding nothing received from
    their fathers
¹⁹(to whom alone the land was
    given
  when no alien passed among
    them):
²⁰All his days the wicked man
    suffers torment,
  the ruthless through all the
    years stored up for him.
²¹Terrifying sounds fill his ears;
  when all seems well, marauders
    attack him.
²²He despairs of escaping the
    darkness;
  he is marked for the sword.
²³He wanders about—food for
    vultures[a];
  he knows the day of darkness is
    at hand.
²⁴Distress and anguish fill him with
    terror;
  they overwhelm him, like a
    king poised to attack,
²⁵because he shakes his fist at God
  and vaunts himself against the
    Almighty,
²⁶defiantly charging against him
  with a thick, strong shield.

²⁷"Though his face is covered with
    fat
  and his waist bulges with flesh,
²⁸he will inhabit ruined towns
  and houses where no one lives,
  houses crumbling to rubble.

²⁹He will no longer be rich and his
    wealth will not endure,
  nor will his possessions spread
    over the land.
³⁰He will not escape the darkness;
  a flame will wither his shoots,
  and the breath of God's mouth
    will carry him away.
³¹Let him not deceive himself by
    trusting what is worthless,
  for he will get nothing in
    return.
³²Before his time he will be paid in
    full,
  and his branches will not
    flourish.
³³He will be like a vine stripped of
    its unripe grapes,
  like an olive tree shedding its
    blossoms.
³⁴For the company of the godless
    will be barren,
  and fire will consume the tents
    of those who love bribes.
³⁵They conceive trouble and give
    birth to evil;
  their womb fashions deceit."

Job

16
Then Job replied:
²"I have heard many things like
    these;
  miserable comforters are you
    all!
³Will your long-winded speeches
    never end?
  What ails you that you keep on
    arguing?
⁴I also could speak like you,
  if you were in my place;
  I could make fine speeches against
    you
  and shake my head at you.
⁵But my mouth would encourage
    you;
  comfort from my lips would
    bring you relief.

⁶"Yet if I speak, my pain is not
    relieved;
  and if I refrain, it does not go
    away.

[a]23 Or *about, looking for food*

7Surely, O God, you have worn me
out;
   you have devastated my entire
     household.
8You have bound me—and it has
     become a witness;
   my gauntness rises up and
     testifies against me.
9God assails me and tears me in
     his anger
   and gnashes his teeth at me;
   my opponent fastens on me his
     piercing eyes.
10Men open their mouths to jeer at
     me;
   they strike my cheek in scorn
   and unite together against me.
11God has turned me over to evil
     men
   and thrown me into the clutches
     of the wicked.
12All was well with me, but he
     shattered me;
   he seized me by the neck and
     crushed me.
He has made me his target;
13   his archers surround me.
Without pity, he pierces my
     kidneys
   and spills my gall on the
     ground.
14Again and again he bursts upon
     me;
   he rushes at me like a warrior.

15"I have sewed sackcloth over my
     skin
   and buried my brow in the
     dust.
16My face is red with weeping,
   deep shadows ring my eyes;
17yet my hands have been free of
     violence
   and my prayer is pure.

18"O earth, do not cover my blood;
   may my cry never be laid to
     rest!
19Even now my witness is in
     heaven;
   my advocate is on high.
20My intercessor is my friend*a*
   as my eyes pour out tears to
     God;

21on behalf of a man he pleads with
     God
   as a man pleads for his friend.

22"Only a few years will pass
   before I go on the journey of no
     return.

17 1My spirit is broken,
    my days are cut short,
the grave awaits me.
2Surely mockers surround me;
   my eyes must dwell on their
     hostility.

3"Give me, O God, the pledge you
     demand.
   Who else will put up security
     for me?
4You have closed their minds to
     understanding;
   therefore you will not let them
     triumph.
5If a man denounces his friends for
     reward,
   the eyes of his children will fail.

6"God has made me a byword to
     everyone,
   a man in whose face people
     spit.
7My eyes have grown dim with
     grief;
   my whole frame is but a
     shadow.
8Upright men are appalled at this;
   the innocent are aroused against
     the ungodly.
9Nevertheless, the righteous will
     hold to their ways,
   and those with clean hands will
     grow stronger.

10"But come on, all of you, try
     again!
   I will not find a wise man
     among you.
11My days have passed, my plans
     are shattered,
   and so are the desires of my
     heart.
12These men turn night into day;
   in the face of darkness they say,
     'Light is near.'
13If the only home I hope for is the
     grave,*b*

---

*a*20 Or *My friends treat me with scorn*   *b*13 Hebrew *Sheol*

if I spread out my bed in
darkness,
¹⁴if I say to corruption, 'You are my
father,'
and to the worm, 'My mother'
or 'My sister,'
¹⁵where then is my hope?
Who can see any hope for me?
¹⁶Will it go down to the gates of
death*ᵃ*?
Will we descend together into
the dust?"

Bildad

18 Then Bildad the Shuhite replied:

²"When will you end these
speeches?
Be sensible, and then we can
talk.
³Why are we regarded as cattle
and considered stupid in your
sight?
⁴You who tear yourself to pieces in
your anger,
is the earth to be abandoned for
your sake?
Or must the rocks be moved
from their place?

⁵"The lamp of the wicked is
snuffed out;
the flame of his fire stops
burning.
⁶The light in his tent becomes dark;
the lamp beside him goes out.
⁷The vigor of his step is weakened;
his own schemes throw him
down.
⁸His feet thrust him into a net
and he wanders into its mesh.
⁹A trap seizes him by the heel;
a snare holds him fast.
¹⁰A noose is hidden for him on the
ground;
a trap lies in his path.
¹¹Terrors startle him on every side
and dog his every step.
¹²Calamity is hungry for him;
disaster is ready for him when
he falls.
¹³It eats away parts of his skin;

death's firstborn devours his
limbs.
¹⁴He is torn from the security of his
tent
and marched off to the king of
terrors.
¹⁵Fire resides*ᵇ* in his tent;
burning sulfur is scattered over
his dwelling.
¹⁶His roots dry up below
and his branches wither above.
¹⁷The memory of him perishes from
the earth;
he has no name in the land.
¹⁸He is driven from light into
darkness
and is banished from the world.
¹⁹He has no offspring or
descendants among his
people,
no survivor where once he
lived.
²⁰Men of the west are appalled at
his fate;
men of the east are seized with
horror.
²¹Surely such is the dwelling of an
evil man;
such is the place of one who
knows not God."

Job

19 Then Job replied:

²"How long will you torment me
and crush me with words?
³Ten times now you have
reproached me;
shamelessly you attack me.
⁴If it is true that I have gone astray,
my error remains my concern
alone.
⁵If indeed you would exalt
yourselves above me
and use my humiliation against
me,
⁶then know that God has wronged
me
and drawn his net around me.

⁷"Though I cry, 'I've been
wronged!' I get no
response;

---

*ᵃ*16 Hebrew *Sheol*   *ᵇ*15 Or *Nothing he had remains*

though I call for help, there is
   no justice.
⁸He has blocked my way so I
   cannot pass;
   he has shrouded my paths in
      darkness.
⁹He has stripped me of my honor
   and removed the crown from
      my head.
¹⁰He tears me down on every side
   till I am gone;
   he uproots my hope like a tree.
¹¹His anger burns against me;
   he counts me among his
      enemies.
¹²His troops advance in force;
   they build a siege ramp against
      me
   and encamp around my tent.

¹³"He has alienated my brothers
   from me;
   my acquaintances are
      completely estranged from
      me.
¹⁴My kinsmen have gone away;
   my friends have forgotten me.
¹⁵My guests and my maidservants
      count me a stranger;
   they look upon me as an alien.
¹⁶I summon my servant, but he does
      not answer,
   though I beg him with my own
      mouth.
¹⁷My breath is offensive to my wife;
   I am loathsome to my own
      brothers.
¹⁸Even the little boys scorn me;
   when I appear, they ridicule
      me.
¹⁹All my intimate friends detest me;
   those I love have turned against
      me.
²⁰I am nothing but skin and bones;
   I have escaped with only the
      skin of my teeth.ᵃ

²¹"Have pity on me, my friends,
      have pity,
   for the hand of God has struck
      me.

²²Why do you pursue me as God
      does?
   Will you never get enough of
      my flesh?

²³"Oh, that my words were
      recorded,
   that they were written on a
      scroll,
²⁴that they were inscribed with an
      iron tool onᵇ lead,
   or engraved in rock forever!
²⁵I know that my Redeemerᶜ lives,
   and that in the end he will
      stand upon the earth.ᵈ
²⁶And after my skin has been
      destroyed,
   yetᵉ inᶠ my flesh I will see
      God;
²⁷I myself will see him
   with my own eyes—I, and not
      another.
   How my heart yearns within
      me!

²⁸"If you say, 'How we will hound
      him,
   since the root of the trouble lies
      in him,'ᵍ
²⁹you should fear the sword
      yourselves;
   for wrath will bring punishment
      by the sword,
   and then you will know that
      there is judgment.ʰ"

Zophar

20 Then Zophar the Naamathite
      replied:

²"My troubled thoughts prompt me
      to answer
   because I am greatly disturbed.
³I hear a rebuke that dishonors me,
   and my understanding inspires
      me to reply.

⁴"Surely you know how it has been
      from of old,
   ever since manⁱ was placed on
      the earth,

ᵃ20 Or *only my gums*   ᵇ24 Or *and*   ᶜ25 Or *defender*   ᵈ25 Or *upon my grave*   ᵉ26 Or
And after I awake, / though this ˌbodyˌ has been destroyed, / then   ᶠ26 Or / *apart from*
ᵍ28 Many Hebrew manuscripts, Septuagint and Vulgate; most Hebrew manuscripts *me*
ʰ29 Or / *that you may come to know the Almighty*   ⁱ4 Or *Adam*

⁵that the mirth of the wicked is
    brief,
  the joy of the godless lasts but a
    moment.
⁶Though his pride reaches to the
    heavens
  and his head touches the
    clouds,
⁷he will perish forever, like his
    own dung;
  those who have seen him will
    say, 'Where is he?'
⁸Like a dream he flies away, no
    more to be found,
  banished like a vision of the
    night.
⁹The eye that saw him will not see
    him again;
  his place will look on him no
    more.
¹⁰His children must make amends
    to the poor;
  his own hands must give back
    his wealth.
¹¹The youthful vigor that fills his
    bones
  will lie with him in the dust.

¹²"Though evil is sweet in his
    mouth
  and he hides it under his
    tongue,
¹³though he cannot bear to let it go
  and keeps it in his mouth,
¹⁴yet his food will turn sour in his
    stomach;
  it will become the venom of
    serpents within him.
¹⁵He will spit out the riches he
    swallowed;
  God will make his stomach
    vomit them up.
¹⁶He will suck the poison of
    serpents;
  the fangs of an adder will kill
    him.
¹⁷He will not enjoy the streams,
  the rivers flowing with honey
    and cream.
¹⁸What he toiled for he must give
    back uneaten;
  he will not enjoy the profit from
    his trading.

¹⁹For he has oppressed the poor and
    left them destitute;
  he has seized houses he did not
    build.
²⁰"Surely he will have no respite
    from his craving;
  he cannot save himself by his
    treasure.
²¹Nothing is left for him to devour;
  his prosperity will not endure.
²²In the midst of his plenty, distress
    will overtake him;
  the full force of misery will
    come upon him.
²³When he has filled his belly,
  God will vent his burning anger
    against him
  and rain down his blows upon
    him.
²⁴Though he flees from an iron
    weapon,
  a bronze-tipped arrow pierces
    him.
²⁵He pulls it out of his back,
  the gleaming point out of his
    liver.
  Terrors will come over him;
²⁶ total darkness lies in wait for
    his treasures.
  A fire unfanned will consume him
  and devour what is left in his
    tent.
²⁷The heavens will expose his guilt;
  the earth will rise up against
    him.
²⁸A flood will carry off his house,
  rushing waters*a* on the day of
    God's wrath.
²⁹Such is the fate God allots the
    wicked,
  the heritage appointed for them
    by God."

Job

21 Then Job replied:
²"Listen carefully to my words;
  let this be the consolation you
    give me.
³Bear with me while I speak,
  and after I have spoken, mock
    on.

a28 Or The possessions in his house will be carried off, / washed away

4"Is my complaint directed to man?
   Why should I not be impatient?
5Look at me and be astonished;
   clap your hand over your
      mouth.
6When I think about this, I am
      terrified;
   trembling seizes my body.
7Why do the wicked live on,
   growing old and increasing in
      power?
8They see their children established
      around them,
   their offspring before their eyes.
9Their homes are safe and free
      from fear;
   the rod of God is not upon
      them.
10Their bulls never fail to breed;
   their cows calve and do not
      miscarry.
11They send forth their children as a
      flock;
   their little ones dance about.
12They sing to the music of
      tambourine and harp;
   they make merry to the sound
      of the flute.
13They spend their years in
      prosperity
   and go down to the grave*a* in
      peace.*b*
14Yet they say to God, 'Leave us
      alone!
   We have no desire to know
      your ways.
15Who is the Almighty, that we
      should serve him?
   What would we gain by
      praying to him?'
16But their prosperity is not in their
      own hands,
   so I stand aloof from the
      counsel of the wicked.

17"Yet how often is the lamp of the
      wicked snuffed out?
   How often does calamity come
      upon them,
   the fate God allots in his anger?
18How often are they like straw
      before the wind,

like chaff swept away by a
      gale?
19It is said, 'God stores up a man's
      punishment for his sons.'
   Let him repay the man himself,
      so that he will know it!
20Let his own eyes see his
      destruction;
   let him drink of the wrath of
      the Almighty.*c*
21For what does he care about the
      family he leaves behind
   when his allotted months come
      to an end?

22"Can anyone teach knowledge to
      God,
   since he judges even the
      highest?
23One man dies in full vigor,
   completely secure and at ease,
24his body*d* well nourished,
   his bones rich with marrow.
25Another man dies in bitterness of
      soul,
   never having enjoyed anything
      good.
26Side by side they lie in the dust,
   and worms cover them both.

27"I know full well what you are
      thinking,
   the schemes by which you
      would wrong me.
28You say, 'Where now is the great
      man's house,
   the tents where wicked men
      lived?'
29Have you never questioned those
      who travel?
   Have you paid no regard to
      their accounts—
30that the evil man is spared from
      the day of calamity,
   that he is delivered from*e* the
      day of wrath?
31Who denounces his conduct to his
      face?
   Who repays him for what he
      has done?
32He is carried to the grave,

*a*13 Hebrew *Sheol*   *b*13 Or *in an instant*   *c*17-20 Verses 17 and 18 may be taken as
exclamations and 19 and 20 as declarations.   *d*24 The meaning of the Hebrew for this word is
uncertain.   *e*30 Or *man is reserved for the day of calamity, / that he is brought forth to*

and watch is kept over his
   tomb.
³³The soil in the valley is sweet to
   him;
   all men follow after him,
   and a countless throng goes^a
   before him.

³⁴"So how can you console me with
   your nonsense?
   Nothing is left of your answers
   but falsehood!"

Eliphaz

22 Then Eliphaz the Temanite replied:

²"Can a man be of benefit to God?
   Can even a wise man benefit
   him?
³What pleasure would it give the
   Almighty if you were
   righteous?
   What would he gain if your
   ways were blameless?

⁴"Is it for your piety that he
   rebukes you
   and brings charges against you?
⁵Is not your wickedness great?
   Are not your sins endless?
⁶You demanded security from your
   brothers for no reason;
   you stripped men of their
   clothing, leaving them
   naked.
⁷You gave no water to the weary
   and you withheld food from the
   hungry,
⁸though you were a powerful man,
   owning land—
   an honored man, living on it.
⁹And you sent widows away
   empty-handed
   and broke the strength of the
   fatherless.
¹⁰That is why snares are all around
   you,
   why sudden peril terrifies you,
¹¹why it is so dark you cannot see,
   and why a flood of water
   covers you.

¹²"Is not God in the heights of
   heaven?
   And see how lofty are the
   highest stars!
¹³Yet you say, 'What does God
   know?
   Does he judge through such
   darkness?
¹⁴Thick clouds veil him, so he does
   not see us
   as he goes about in the vaulted
   heavens.'
¹⁵Will you keep to the old path
   that evil men have trod?
¹⁶They were carried off before their
   time,
   their foundations washed away
   by a flood.
¹⁷They said to God, 'Leave us alone!
   What can the Almighty do to
   us?'
¹⁸Yet it was he who filled their
   houses with good things,
   so I stand aloof from the
   counsel of the wicked.

¹⁹"The righteous see their ruin and
   rejoice;
   the innocent mock them, saying,
²⁰'Surely our foes are destroyed,
   and fire devours their wealth.'

²¹"Submit to God and be at peace
   with him;
   in this way prosperity will come
   to you.
²²Accept instruction from his mouth
   and lay up his words in your
   heart.
²³If you return to the Almighty, you
   will be restored:
   If you remove wickedness far
   from your tent
²⁴and assign your nuggets to the
   dust,
   your gold of Ophir to the rocks
   in the ravines,
²⁵then the Almighty will be your
   gold,
   the choicest silver for you.
²⁶Surely then you will find delight
   in the Almighty
   and will lift up your face to
   God.

^a33 Or / *as a countless throng went*

²⁷You will pray to him, and he will
  hear you,
  and you will fulfill your vows.
²⁸What you decide on will be done,
  and light will shine on your
  ways.
²⁹When men are brought low and
  you say, 'Lift them up!'
  then he will save the downcast.
³⁰He will deliver even one who is
  not innocent,
  who will be delivered through
  the cleanness of your
  hands."

Job

23 Then Job replied:

²"Even today my complaint is
  bitter;
  his hand*ᵃ* is heavy in spite of*ᵇ*
  my groaning.
³If only I knew where to find him;
  if only I could go to his
  dwelling!
⁴I would state my case before him
  and fill my mouth with
  arguments.
⁵I would find out what he would
  answer me,
  and consider what he would
  say.
⁶Would he oppose me with great
  power?
  No, he would not press charges
  against me.
⁷There an upright man could
  present his case before him,
  and I would be delivered
  forever from my judge.

⁸"But if I go to the east, he is not
  there;
  if I go to the west, I do not find
  him.
⁹When he is at work in the north, I
  do not see him;
  when he turns to the south, I
  catch no glimpse of him.
¹⁰But he knows the way that I take;
  when he has tested me, I will
  come forth as gold.

¹¹My feet have closely followed his
  steps;
  I have kept to his way without
  turning aside.
¹²I have not departed from the
  commands of his lips;
  I have treasured the words of
  his mouth more than my
  daily bread.

¹³"But he stands alone, and who can
  oppose him?
  He does whatever he pleases.
¹⁴He carries out his decree against
  me,
  and many such plans he still
  has in store.
¹⁵That is why I am terrified before
  him;
  when I think of all this, I fear
  him.
¹⁶God has made my heart faint;
  the Almighty has terrified me.
¹⁷Yet I am not silenced by the
  darkness,
  by the thick darkness that
  covers my face.

24 "Why does the Almighty not
  set times for judgment?
  Why must those who know him
  look in vain for such days?
²Men move boundary stones;
  they pasture flocks they have
  stolen.
³They drive away the orphan's
  donkey
  and take the widow's ox in
  pledge.
⁴They thrust the needy from the
  path
  and force all the poor of the
  land into hiding.
⁵Like wild donkeys in the desert,
  the poor go about their labor of
  foraging food;
  the wasteland provides food for
  their children.
⁶They gather fodder in the fields
  and glean in the vineyards of
  the wicked.
⁷Lacking clothes, they spend the
  night naked;

ᵃ2 Septuagint and Syriac; Hebrew / the hand on me   ᵇ2 Or heavy on me in

they have nothing to cover
    themselves in the cold.
⁸They are drenched by mountain
    rains
    and hug the rocks for lack of
        shelter.
⁹The fatherless child is snatched
    from the breast;
    the infant of the poor is seized
        for a debt.
¹⁰Lacking clothes, they go about
    naked;
    they carry the sheaves, but still
        go hungry.
¹¹They crush olives among the
    terraces*a*;
    they tread the winepresses, yet
        suffer thirst.
¹²The groans of the dying rise from
    the city,
    and the souls of the wounded
        cry out for help.
    But God charges no one with
        wrongdoing.

¹³"There are those who rebel against
    the light,
    who do not know its ways
    or stay in its paths.
¹⁴When daylight is gone, the
    murderer rises up
    and kills the poor and needy;
    in the night he steals forth like
        a thief.
¹⁵The eye of the adulterer watches
    for dusk;
    he thinks, 'No eye will see me,'
    and he keeps his face concealed.
¹⁶In the dark, men break into
    houses,
    but by day they shut themselves
        in;
    they want nothing to do with
        the light.
¹⁷For all of them, deep darkness is
    their morning*b*;
    they make friends with the
        terrors of darkness.*c*

¹⁸"Yet they are foam on the surface
    of the water;

their portion of the land is
    cursed,
    so that no one goes to the
        vineyards.
¹⁹As heat and drought snatch away
    the melted snow,
    so the grave*d* snatches away
        those who have sinned.
²⁰The womb forgets them,
    the worm feasts on them;
    evil men are no longer
        remembered
    but are broken like a tree.
²¹They prey on the barren and
    childless woman,
    and to the widow show no
        kindness.
²²But God drags away the mighty
    by his power;
    though they become established,
        they have no assurance of
        life.
²³He may let them rest in a feeling
    of security,
    but his eyes are on their ways.
²⁴For a little while they are exalted,
    and then they are gone;
    they are brought low and
        gathered up like all others;
    they are cut off like heads of
        grain.

²⁵"If this is not so, who can prove
    me false
    and reduce my words to
        nothing?"

Bildad

25 Then Bildad the Shuhite re-
    plied:

²"Dominion and awe belong to
    God;
    he establishes order in the
        heights of heaven.
³Can his forces be numbered?
    Upon whom does his light not
        rise?
⁴How then can a man be righteous
    before God?
    How can one born of woman be
        pure?

---

*a*11 Or *olives between the millstones;* the meaning of the Hebrew for this word is uncertain.
*b*17 Or *them, their morning is like the shadow of death*   *c*17 Or *of the shadow of death*
*d*19 Hebrew *Sheol*

⁵If even the moon is not bright
    and the stars are not pure in his
        eyes,
⁶how much less man, who is but a
        maggot—
    a son of man, who is only a
        worm!"

Job

26 Then Job replied:

²"How you have helped the
        powerless!
    How you have saved the arm
        that is feeble!
³What advice you have offered to
        one without wisdom!
    And what great insight you
        have displayed!
⁴Who has helped you utter these
        words?
    And whose spirit spoke from
        your mouth?

⁵"The dead are in deep anguish,
    those beneath the waters and all
        that live in them.
⁶Death*a* is naked before God;
    Destruction*b* lies uncovered.
⁷He spreads out the northern
        ⌊skies⌋ over empty space;
    he suspends the earth over
        nothing.
⁸He wraps up the waters in his
        clouds,
    yet the clouds do not burst
        under their weight.
⁹He covers the face of the full
        moon,
    spreading his clouds over it.
¹⁰He marks out the horizon on the
        face of the waters
    for a boundary between light
        and darkness.
¹¹The pillars of the heavens quake,
    aghast at his rebuke.
¹²By his power he churned up the
        sea;
    by his wisdom he cut Rahab to
        pieces.
¹³By his breath the skies became
        fair;

his hand pierced the gliding
        serpent.
¹⁴And these are but the outer fringe
        of his works;
    how faint the whisper we hear
        of him!
    Who then can understand the
        thunder of his power?"

27 And Job continued his dis-
        course:

²"As surely as God lives, who has
        denied me justice,
    the Almighty, who has made
        me taste bitterness of soul,
³as long as I have life within me,
    the breath of God in my
        nostrils,
⁴my lips will not speak wickedness,
    and my tongue will utter no
        deceit.
⁵I will never admit you are in the
        right;
    till I die, I will not deny my
        integrity.
⁶I will maintain my righteousness
        and never let go of it;
    my conscience will not reproach
        me as long as I live.

⁷"May my enemies be like the
        wicked,
    my adversaries like the unjust!
⁸For what hope has the godless
        when he is cut off,
    when God takes away his life?
⁹Does God listen to his cry
    when distress comes upon him?
¹⁰Will he find delight in the
        Almighty?
    Will he call upon God at all
        times?

¹¹"I will teach you about the power
        of God;
    the ways of the Almighty I will
        not conceal.
¹²You have all seen this yourselves.
    Why then this meaningless talk?

¹³"Here is the fate God allots to the
        wicked,

the heritage a ruthless man
  receives from the
  Almighty:
¹⁴However many his children, their
  fate is the sword;
  his offspring will never have
  enough to eat.
¹⁵The plague will bury those who
  survive him,
  and their widows will not weep
  for them.
¹⁶Though he heaps up silver like
  dust
  and clothes like piles of clay,
¹⁷what he lays up the righteous will
  wear,
  and the innocent will divide his
  silver.
¹⁸The house he builds is like a
  moth's cocoon,
  like a hut made by a watchman.
¹⁹He lies down wealthy, but will do
  so no more;
  when he opens his eyes, all is
  gone.
²⁰Terrors overtake him like a flood;
  a tempest snatches him away in
  the night.
²¹The east wind carries him off, and
  he is gone;
  it sweeps him out of his place.
²²It hurls itself against him without
  mercy
  as he flees headlong from its
  power.
²³It claps its hands in derision
  and hisses him out of his place.

28 "There is a mine for silver
     and a place where gold is
  refined.
²Iron is taken from the earth,
  and copper is smelted from ore.
³Man puts an end to the darkness;
  he searches the farthest recesses
  for ore in the blackest darkness.
⁴Far from where people dwell he
  cuts a shaft,
  in places forgotten by the foot
  of man;
  far from men he dangles and
  sways.
⁵The earth, from which food comes,

is transformed below as by fire;
⁶sapphires*ᵃ* come from its rocks,
  and its dust contains nuggets of
  gold.
⁷No bird of prey knows that
  hidden path,
  no falcon's eye has seen it.
⁸Proud beasts do not set foot on it,
  and no lion prowls there.
⁹Man's hand assaults the flinty
  rock
  and lays bare the roots of the
  mountains.
¹⁰He tunnels through the rock;
  his eyes see all its treasures.
¹¹He searches*ᵇ* the sources of the
  rivers
  and brings hidden things to
  light.
¹²"But where can wisdom be found?
  Where does understanding
  dwell?
¹³Man does not comprehend its
  worth;
  it cannot be found in the land
  of the living.
¹⁴The deep says, 'It is not in me';
  the sea says, 'It is not with me.'
¹⁵It cannot be bought with the finest
  gold,
  nor can its price be weighed in
  silver.
¹⁶It cannot be bought with the gold
  of Ophir,
  with precious onyx or
  sapphires.
¹⁷Neither gold nor crystal can
  compare with it,
  nor can it be had for jewels of
  gold.
¹⁸Coral and jasper are not worthy of
  mention;
  the price of wisdom is beyond
  rubies.
¹⁹The topaz of Cush cannot compare
  with it;
  it cannot be bought with pure
  gold.
²⁰"Where then does wisdom come
  from?
  Where does understanding
  dwell?

²¹It is hidden from the eyes of every
living thing,
  concealed even from the birds
of the air.
²²Destruction^a and Death say,
  'Only a rumor of it has reached
our ears.'
²³God understands the way to it
  and he alone knows where it
dwells,
²⁴for he views the ends of the earth
  and sees everything under the
heavens.
²⁵When he established the force of
the wind
  and measured out the waters,
²⁶when he made a decree for the
rain
  and a path for the
thunderstorm,
²⁷then he looked at wisdom and
appraised it;
  he confirmed it and tested it.
²⁸And he said to man,
  'The fear of the Lord—that is
wisdom,
  and to shun evil is
understanding.' "

29 Job continued his discourse:

²"How I long for the months gone
by,
  for the days when God watched
over me,
³when his lamp shone upon my
head
  and by his light I walked
through darkness!
⁴Oh, for the days when I was in
my prime,
  when God's intimate friendship
blessed my house,
⁵when the Almighty was still with
me
  and my children were around
me,
⁶when my path was drenched with
cream
  and the rock poured out for me
streams of olive oil.

⁷"When I went to the gate of the
city

and took my seat in the public
square,
⁸the young men saw me and
stepped aside
  and the old men rose to their
feet;
⁹the chief men refrained from
speaking
  and covered their mouths with
their hands;
¹⁰the voices of the nobles were
hushed,
  and their tongues stuck to the
roof of their mouths.
¹¹Whoever heard me spoke well of
me,
  and those who saw me
commended me,
¹²because I rescued the poor who
cried for help,
  and the fatherless who had
none to assist him.
¹³The man who was dying blessed
me;
  I made the widow's heart sing.
¹⁴I put on righteousness as my
clothing;
  justice was my robe and my
turban.
¹⁵I was eyes to the blind
  and feet to the lame.
¹⁶I was a father to the needy;
  I took up the case of the
stranger.
¹⁷I broke the fangs of the wicked
  and snatched the victims from
their teeth.

¹⁸"I thought, 'I will die in my own
house,
  my days as numerous as the
grains of sand.
¹⁹My roots will reach to the water,
  and the dew will lie all night on
my branches.
²⁰My glory will remain fresh in me,
  the bow ever new in my hand.'

²¹"Men listened to me expectantly,
  waiting in silence for my
counsel.
²²After I had spoken, they spoke no
more;

my words fell gently on their
ears.
²³They waited for me as for showers
and drank in my words as the
spring rain.
²⁴When I smiled at them, they
scarcely believed it;
the light of my face was
precious to them.ᵃ
²⁵I chose the way for them and sat
as their chief;
I dwelt as a king among his
troops;
I was like one who comforts
mourners.

30
"But now they mock me,
men younger than I,
whose fathers I would have
disdained
to put with my sheep dogs.
²Of what use was the strength of
their hands to me,
since their vigor had gone from
them?
³Haggard from want and hunger,
they roamedᵇ the parched land
in desolate wastelands at night.
⁴In the brush they gathered salt
herbs,
and their foodᶜ was the root of
the broom tree.
⁵They were banished from their
fellow men,
shouted at as if they were
thieves.
⁶They were forced to live in the
dry stream beds,
among the rocks and in holes in
the ground.
⁷They brayed among the bushes
and huddled in the
undergrowth.
⁸A base and nameless brood,
they were driven out of the
land.

⁹"And now their sons mock me in
song;
I have become a byword among
them.

¹⁰They detest me and keep their
distance;
they do not hesitate to spit in
my face.
¹¹Now that God has unstrung my
bow and afflicted me,
they throw off restraint in my
presence.
¹²On my right the tribeᵈ attacks;
they lay snares for my feet,
they build their siege ramps
against me.
¹³They break up my road;
they succeed in destroying
me—
without anyone's helping
them.ᵉ
¹⁴They advance as through a gaping
breach;
amid the ruins they come
rolling in.
¹⁵Terrors overwhelm me;
my dignity is driven away as by
the wind,
my safety vanishes like a cloud.

¹⁶"And now my life ebbs away;
days of suffering grip me.
¹⁷Night pierces my bones;
my gnawing pains never rest.
¹⁸In his great power ⌊God⌋ becomes
like clothing to meᶠ;
he binds me like the neck of my
garment.
¹⁹He throws me into the mud,
and I am reduced to dust and
ashes.

²⁰"I cry out to you, O God, but you
do not answer;
I stand up, but you merely look
at me.
²¹You turn on me ruthlessly;
with the might of your hand
you attack me.
²²You snatch me up and drive me
before the wind;
you toss me about in the storm.
²³I know you will bring me down to
death,
to the place appointed for all
the living.

ᵃ24 The meaning of the Hebrew for this clause is uncertain.
ᵈ12 The meaning of the Hebrew for this word is uncertain.
⌊they say⌋.   ᶠ18 Hebrew; Septuagint ⌊God⌋ grasps my clothing
ᵇ3 Or gnawed   ᶜ4 Or fuel
ᵉ13 Or me. / 'No one can help him,'

²⁴"Surely no one lays a hand on a
     broken man
   when he cries for help in his
     distress.
²⁵Have I not wept for those in
     trouble?
   Has not my soul grieved for the
     poor?
²⁶Yet when I hoped for good, evil
     came;
   when I looked for light, then
     came darkness.
²⁷The churning inside me never
     stops;
   days of suffering confront me.
²⁸I go about blackened, but not by
     the sun;
   I stand up in the assembly and
     cry for help.
²⁹I have become a brother of jackals,
   a companion of owls.
³⁰My skin grows black and peels;
   my body burns with fever.
³¹My harp is tuned to mourning,
   and my flute to the sound of
     wailing.

31

"I made a covenant with my
     eyes
   not to look lustfully at a girl.
²For what is man's lot from God
     above,
   his heritage from the Almighty
     on high?
³Is it not ruin for the wicked,
   disaster for those who do
     wrong?
⁴Does he not see my ways
   and count my every step?

⁵"If I have walked in falsehood
   or my foot has hurried after
     deceit—
⁶let God weigh me in honest scales
   and he will know that I am
     blameless—
⁷if my steps have turned from the
     path,
   if my heart has been led by my
     eyes,
   or if my hands have been
     defiled,

⁸then may others eat what I have
     sown,
   and may my crops be uprooted.

⁹"If my heart has been enticed by a
     woman,
   or if I have lurked at my
     neighbor's door,
¹⁰then may my wife grind another
     man's grain,
   and may other men sleep with
     her.
¹¹For that would have been
     shameful,
   a sin to be judged.
¹²It is a fire that burns to
     Destruction[a];
   it would have uprooted my
     harvest.

¹³"If I have denied justice to my
     menservants and
     maidservants
   when they had a grievance
     against me,
¹⁴what will I do when God
     confronts me?
   What will I answer when called
     to account?
¹⁵Did not he who made me in the
     womb make them?
   Did not the same one form us
     both within our mothers?

¹⁶"If I have denied the desires of the
     poor
   or let the eyes of the widow
     grow weary,
¹⁷if I have kept my bread to myself,
   not sharing it with the
     fatherless—
¹⁸but from my youth I reared him
     as would a father,
   and from my birth I guided the
     widow—
¹⁹if I have seen anyone perishing for
     lack of clothing,
   or a needy man without a
     garment,
²⁰and his heart did not bless me
   for warming him with the fleece
     from my sheep,
²¹if I have raised my hand against
     the fatherless,

___

a12 Hebrew *Abaddon*

knowing that I had influence in
     court,
²²then let my arm fall from the
     shoulder,
   let it be broken off at the joint.
²³For I dreaded destruction from
     God,
   and for fear of his splendor I
     could not do such things.

²⁴"If I have put my trust in gold
   or said to pure gold, 'You are
     my security,'
²⁵if I have rejoiced over my great
     wealth,
   the fortune my hands had
     gained,
²⁶if I have regarded the sun in its
     radiance
   or the moon moving in
     splendor,
²⁷so that my heart was secretly
     enticed
   and my hand offered them a
     kiss of homage,
²⁸then these also would be sins to
     be judged,
   for I would have been
     unfaithful to God on high.

²⁹"If I have rejoiced at my enemy's
     misfortune
   or gloated over the trouble that
     came to him—
³⁰I have not allowed my mouth to
     sin
   by invoking a curse against his
     life—
³¹if the men of my household have
     never said,
   'Who has not had his fill of
     Job's meat?'—
³²but no stranger had to spend the
     night in the street,
   for my door was always open
     to the traveler—
³³if I have concealed my sin as men
     do,ᵃ
   by hiding my guilt in my heart
³⁴because I so feared the crowd
   and so dreaded the contempt of
     the clans

that I kept silent and would not
     go outside

³⁵("Oh, that I had someone to hear
     me!
   I sign now my defense—let the
     Almighty answer me;
   let my accuser put his
     indictment in writing.
³⁶Surely I would wear it on my
     shoulder,
   I would put it on like a crown.
³⁷I would give him an account of
     my every step;
   like a prince I would approach
     him.)—

³⁸"if my land cries out against me
   and all its furrows are wet with
     tears,
³⁹if I have devoured its yield
     without payment
   or broken the spirit of its
     tenants,
⁴⁰then let briers come up instead of
     wheat
   and weeds instead of barley."

The words of Job are ended.

Elihu

32 So these three men stopped answering Job, because he was
righteous in his own eyes. ²But Elihu
son of Barakel the Buzite, of the family of Ram, became very angry with
Job for justifying himself rather than
God. ³He was also angry with the
three friends, because they had found
no way to refute Job, and yet had condemned him.ᵇ ⁴Now Elihu had waited before speaking to Job because
they were older than he. ⁵But when he
saw that the three men had nothing
more to say, his anger was aroused.
⁶So Elihu son of Barakel the Buzite
said:

   "I am young in years,
     and you are old;
   that is why I was fearful,
     not daring to tell you what I
       know.

ᵃ33 Or as Adam did   ᵇ3 Masoretic Text; an ancient Hebrew scribal tradition Job, and so had
condemned God

7I thought, 'Age should speak;
        advanced years should teach
        wisdom.'
8But it is the spirit[a] in a man,
        the breath of the Almighty, that
        gives him understanding.
9It is not only the old[b] who are
        wise,
        not only the aged who
        understand what is right.

10"Therefore I say: Listen to me;
        I too will tell you what I know.
11I waited while you spoke,
        I listened to your reasoning;
        while you were searching for
        words,
12   I gave you my full attention.
        But not one of you has proved Job
        wrong;
        none of you has answered his
        arguments.
13Do not say, 'We have found
        wisdom;
        let God refute him, not man.'
14But Job has not marshaled his
        words against me,
        and I will not answer him with
        your arguments.

15"They are dismayed and have no
        more to say;
        words have failed them.
16Must I wait, now that they are
        silent,
        now that they stand there with
        no reply?
17I too will have my say;
        I too will tell what I know.
18For I am full of words,
        and the spirit within me
        compels me;
19inside I am like bottled-up wine,
        like new wineskins ready to
        burst.
20I must speak and find relief;
        I must open my lips and reply.
21I will show partiality to no one,
        nor will I flatter any man;
22for if I were skilled in flattery,
        my Maker would soon take me
        away.

33 "But now, Job, listen to my
        words;
        pay attention to everything I
        say.
2I am about to open my mouth;
        my words are on the tip of my
        tongue.
3My words come from an upright
        heart;
        my lips sincerely speak what I
        know.
4The Spirit of God has made me;
        the breath of the Almighty gives
        me life.
5Answer me then, if you can;
        prepare yourself and confront
        me.
6I am just like you before God;
        I too have been taken from clay.
7No fear of me should alarm you,
        nor should my hand be heavy
        upon you.

8"But you have said in my
        hearing—
        I heard the very words—
9'I am pure and without sin;
        I am clean and free from guilt.
10Yet God has found fault with me;
        he considers me his enemy.
11He fastens my feet in shackles;
        he keeps close watch on all my
        paths.'

12"But I tell you, in this you are not
        right,
        for God is greater than man.
13Why do you complain to him
        that he answers none of man's
        words[c]?
14For God does speak—now one
        way, now another—
        though man may not perceive
        it.
15In a dream, in a vision of the
        night,
        when deep sleep falls on men
        as they slumber in their beds,
16he may speak in their ears
        and terrify them with warnings,
17to turn man from wrongdoing
        and keep him from pride,
18to preserve his soul from the pit,[d]

---

a8 Or *Spirit*; also in verse 18   b9 Or *many*; or *great*   c13 Or *that he does not answer for any of his actions*   d18 Or *preserve him from the grave*

his life from perishing by the
    sword.^a
¹⁹Or a man may be chastened on a
    bed of pain
  with constant distress in his
    bones,
²⁰so that his very being finds food
    repulsive
  and his soul loathes the choicest
    meal.
²¹His flesh wastes away to nothing,
  and his bones, once hidden,
    now stick out.
²²His soul draws near to the pit,^b
  and his life to the messengers of
    death.^c

²³"Yet if there is an angel on his
    side
  as a mediator, one out of a
    thousand,
  to tell a man what is right for
    him,
²⁴to be gracious to him and say,
  'Spare him from going down to
    the pit^d;
  I have found a ransom for
    him'—
²⁵then his flesh is renewed like a
    child's;
  it is restored as in the days of
    his youth.
²⁶He prays to God and finds favor
    with him,
  he sees God's face and shouts
    for joy;
  he is restored by God to his
    righteous state.
²⁷Then he comes to men and says,
  'I sinned, and perverted what
    was right,
  but I did not get what I
    deserved.
²⁸He redeemed my soul from going
    down to the pit,^e
  and I will live to enjoy the
    light.'

²⁹"God does all these things to a
    man—
  twice, even three times—

³⁰to turn back his soul from the
    pit,^f
  that the light of life may shine
    on him.

³¹"Pay attention, Job, and listen to
    me;
  be silent, and I will speak.
³²If you have anything to say,
    answer me;
  speak up, for I want you to be
    cleared.
³³But if not, then listen to me;
  be silent, and I will teach you
    wisdom."

34 Then Elihu said:
²"Hear my words, you wise men;
  listen to me, you men of
    learning.
³For the ear tests words
  as the tongue tastes food.
⁴Let us discern for ourselves what
    is right;
  let us learn together what is
    good.

⁵"Job says, 'I am innocent,
  but God denies me justice.
⁶Although I am right,
  I am considered a liar;
  although I am guiltless,
  his arrow inflicts an incurable
    wound.'
⁷What man is like Job,
  who drinks scorn like water?
⁸He keeps company with evildoers;
  he associates with wicked men.
⁹For he says, 'It profits a man
    nothing
  when he tries to please God.'

¹⁰"So listen to me, you men of
    understanding.
  Far be it from God to do evil,
  from the Almighty to do wrong.
¹¹He repays a man for what he has
    done;
  he brings upon him what his
    conduct deserves.
¹²It is unthinkable that God would
    do wrong,

that the Almighty would
    pervert justice.
¹³Who appointed him over the
    earth?
    Who put him in charge of the
       whole world?
¹⁴If it were his intention
    and he withdrew his spirit*a*
       and breath,
¹⁵all mankind would perish together
    and man would return to the
       dust.

¹⁶"If you have understanding, hear
    this;
    listen to what I say.
¹⁷Can he who hates justice govern?
    Will you condemn the just and
       mighty One?
¹⁸Is he not the One who says to
       kings, 'You are worthless,'
    and to nobles, 'You are wicked,'
¹⁹who shows no partiality to princes
    and does not favor the rich over
       the poor,
    for they are all the work of his
       hands?
²⁰They die in an instant, in the
       middle of the night;
    the people are shaken and they
       pass away;
    the mighty are removed without
       human hand.

²¹"His eyes are on the ways of men;
    he sees their every step.
²²There is no dark place, no deep
       shadow,
    where evildoers can hide.
²³God has no need to examine men
       further,
    that they should come before
       him for judgment.
²⁴Without inquiry he shatters the
       mighty
    and sets up others in their
       place.
²⁵Because he takes note of their
       deeds,
    he overthrows them in the night
       and they are crushed.
²⁶He punishes them for their
       wickedness
    where everyone can see them,

²⁷because they turned from
       following him
    and had no regard for any of
       his ways.
²⁸They caused the cry of the poor to
       come before him,
    so that he heard the cry of the
       needy.
²⁹But if he remains silent, who can
       condemn him?
    If he hides his face, who can see
       him?
    Yet he is over man and nation
       alike,
30   to keep a godless man from
       ruling,
    from laying snares for the
       people.

³¹"Suppose a man says to God,
    'I am guilty but will offend no
       more.
³²Teach me what I cannot see;
    if I have done wrong, I will not
       do so again.'
³³Should God then reward you on
       your terms,
    when you refuse to repent?
    You must decide, not I;
    so tell me what you know.

³⁴"Men of understanding declare,
    wise men who hear me say to
       me,
³⁵'Job speaks without knowledge;
    his words lack insight.'
³⁶Oh, that Job might be tested to the
       utmost
    for answering like a wicked
       man!
³⁷To his sin he adds rebellion;
    scornfully he claps his hands
       among us
    and multiplies his words
       against God."

35 Then Elihu said:

²"Do you think this is just?
    You say, 'I will be cleared by
       God.'*b*
³Yet you ask him, 'What profit is it
       to me,*c*

---

a14 Or *Spirit*   *b2* Or *My righteousness is more than God's*   *c3* Or *you*

and what do I gain by not
    sinning?'

⁴"I would like to reply to you
    and to your friends with you.
⁵Look up at the heavens and see;
    gaze at the clouds so high
      above you.
⁶If you sin, how does that affect
    him?
    If your sins are many, what
      does that do to him?
⁷If you are righteous, what do you
    give to him,
    or what does he receive from
      your hand?
⁸Your wickedness affects only a
    man like yourself,
    and your righteousness only the
      sons of men.

⁹"Men cry out under a load of
    oppression;
    they plead for relief from the
      arm of the powerful.
¹⁰But no one says, 'Where is God
    my Maker,
    who gives songs in the night,
¹¹who teaches more to us than to[a]
    the beasts of the earth
    and makes us wiser than[b] the
      birds of the air?'
¹²He does not answer when men
    cry out
    because of the arrogance of the
      wicked.
¹³Indeed, God does not listen to
    their empty plea;
    the Almighty pays no attention
      to it.
¹⁴How much less, then, will he
    listen
    when you say that you do not
      see him,
    that your case is before him
    and you must wait for him,
¹⁵and further, that his anger never
    punishes
    and he does not take the least
      notice of wickedness.[c]
¹⁶So Job opens his mouth with
    empty talk;

without knowledge he
    multiplies words."

36 Elihu continued:

²"Bear with me a little longer and I
    will show you
    that there is more to be said in
      God's behalf.
³I get my knowledge from afar;
    I will ascribe justice to my
      Maker.
⁴Be assured that my words are not
    false;
    one perfect in knowledge is
      with you.

⁵"God is mighty, but does not
    despise men;
    he is mighty, and firm in his
      purpose.
⁶He does not keep the wicked alive
    but gives the afflicted their
      rights.
⁷He does not take his eyes off the
    righteous;
    he enthrones them with kings
    and exalts them forever.
⁸But if men are bound in chains,
    held fast by cords of affliction,
⁹he tells them what they have
    done—
    that they have sinned
      arrogantly.
¹⁰He makes them listen to correction
    and commands them to repent
      of their evil.
¹¹If they obey and serve him,
    they will spend the rest of their
      days in prosperity
    and their years in contentment.
¹²But if they do not listen,
    they will perish by the sword[d]
    and die without knowledge.

¹³"The godless in heart harbor
    resentment;
    even when he fetters them, they
      do not cry for help.
¹⁴They die in their youth,
    among male prostitutes of the
      shrines.

---

a11 Or *teaches us by*   *b11* Or *us wise by*   *c15* Symmachus, Theodotion and Vulgate; the
meaning of the Hebrew for this word is uncertain.   *d12* Or *will cross the River*

¹⁵But those who suffer he delivers
    in their suffering;
  he speaks to them in their
    affliction.

¹⁶"He is wooing you from the jaws
    of distress
  to a spacious place free from
    restriction,
  to the comfort of your table
    laden with choice food.
¹⁷But now you are laden with the
    judgment due the wicked;
  judgment and justice have taken
    hold of you.
¹⁸Be careful that no one entices you
    by riches;
  do not let a large bribe turn you
    aside.
¹⁹Would your wealth
    or even all your mighty efforts
  sustain you so you would not
    be in distress?
²⁰Do not long for the night,
  to drag people away from their
    homes.ᵃ
²¹Beware of turning to evil,
  which you seem to prefer to
    affliction.

²²"God is exalted in his power.
  Who is a teacher like him?
²³Who has prescribed his ways for
    him,
  or said to him, 'You have done
    wrong'?
²⁴Remember to extol his work,
  which men have praised in
    song.
²⁵All mankind has seen it;
  men gaze on it from afar.
²⁶How great is God—beyond our
    understanding!
  The number of his years is past
    finding out.

²⁷"He draws up the drops of water,
  which distill as rain to the
    streamsᵇ;
²⁸the clouds pour down their
    moisture
  and abundant showers fall on
    mankind.

²⁹Who can understand how he
    spreads out the clouds,
  how he thunders from his
    pavilion?
³⁰See how he scatters his lightning
    about him,
  bathing the depths of the sea.
³¹This is the way he governsᶜ the
    nations
  and provides food in
    abundance.
³²He fills his hands with lightning
  and commands it to strike its
    mark.
³³His thunder announces the
    coming storm;
  even the cattle make known its
    approach.ᵈ

37 "At this my heart pounds
    and leaps from its place.
²Listen! Listen to the roar of his
    voice,
  to the rumbling that comes from
    his mouth.
³He unleashes his lightning beneath
    the whole heaven
  and sends it to the ends of the
    earth.
⁴After that comes the sound of his
    roar;
  he thunders with his majestic
    voice.
  When his voice resounds,
    he holds nothing back.
⁵God's voice thunders in marvelous
    ways;
  he does great things beyond our
    understanding.
⁶He says to the snow, 'Fall on the
    earth,'
  and to the rain shower, 'Be a
    mighty downpour.'
⁷So that all men he has made may
    know his work,
  he stops every man from his
    labor.ᵉ
⁸The animals take cover;
  they remain in their dens.
⁹The tempest comes out from its
    chamber,

the cold from the driving
winds.
¹⁰The breath of God produces ice,
and the broad waters become
frozen.
¹¹He loads the clouds with
moisture;
he scatters his lightning through
them.
¹²At his direction they swirl around
over the face of the whole earth
to do whatever he commands
them.
¹³He brings the clouds to punish
men,
or to water his earth*a* and
show his love.

¹⁴"Listen to this, Job;
stop and consider God's
wonders.
¹⁵Do you know how God controls
the clouds
and makes his lightning flash?
¹⁶Do you know how the clouds
hang poised,
those wonders of him who is
perfect in knowledge?
¹⁷You who swelter in your clothes
when the land lies hushed
under the south wind,
¹⁸can you join him in spreading out
the skies,
hard as a mirror of cast bronze?

¹⁹"Tell us what we should say to
him;
we cannot draw up our case
because of our darkness.
²⁰Should he be told that I want to
speak?
Would any man ask to be
swallowed up?
²¹Now no one can look at the sun,
bright as it is in the skies
after the wind has swept them
clean.
²²Out of the north he comes in
golden splendor;
God comes in awesome majesty.
²³The Almighty is beyond our reach
and exalted in power;

in his justice and great
righteousness, he does not
oppress.
²⁴Therefore, men revere him,
for does he not have regard for
all the wise in heart?*b*"

The LORD Speaks

38 Then the LORD answered Job
out of the storm. He said:

²"Who is this that darkens my
counsel
with words without knowledge?
³Brace yourself like a man;
I will question you,
and you shall answer me.

⁴"Where were you when I laid the
earth's foundation?
Tell me, if you understand.
⁵Who marked off its dimensions?
Surely you know!
Who stretched a measuring line
across it?
⁶On what were its footings set,
or who laid its cornerstone—
⁷while the morning stars sang
together
and all the angels*c* shouted for
joy?

⁸"Who shut up the sea behind
doors
when it burst forth from the
womb,
⁹when I made the clouds its
garment
and wrapped it in thick
darkness,
¹⁰when I fixed limits for it
and set its doors and bars in
place,
¹¹when I said, 'This far you may
come and no farther;
here is where your proud waves
halt'?

¹²"Have you ever given orders to
the morning,
or shown the dawn its place,
¹³that it might take the earth by the
edges
and shake the wicked out of it?

a13 Or *to favor them*   *b24* Or *for he does not have regard for any who think they are wise.*
c7 Hebrew *the sons of God*

¹⁴The earth takes shape like clay
        under a seal;
    its features stand out like those
        of a garment.
¹⁵The wicked are denied their light,
    and their upraised arm is
        broken.

¹⁶"Have you journeyed to the
        springs of the sea
    or walked in the recesses of the
        deep?
¹⁷Have the gates of death been
        shown to you?
    Have you seen the gates of the
        shadow of death ͬ?
¹⁸Have you comprehended the vast
        expanses of the earth?
    Tell me, if you know all this.

¹⁹"What is the way to the abode of
        light?
    And where does darkness
        reside?
²⁰Can you take them to their places?
    Do you know the paths to their
        dwellings?
²¹Surely you know, for you were
        already born!
    You have lived so many years!

²²"Have you entered the
        storehouses of the snow
    or seen the storehouses of the
        hail,
²³which I reserve for times of
        trouble,
    for days of war and battle?
²⁴What is the way to the place
        where the lightning is
        dispersed,
    or the place where the east
        winds are scattered over
        the earth?
²⁵Who cuts a channel for the
        torrents of rain,
    and a path for the
        thunderstorm,
²⁶to water a land where no man
        lives,
    a desert with no one in it,
²⁷to satisfy a desolate wasteland
    and make it sprout with grass?

²⁸Does the rain have a father?
    Who fathers the drops of dew?
²⁹From whose womb comes the ice?
    Who gives birth to the frost
        from the heavens
³⁰when the waters become hard as
        stone,
    when the surface of the deep is
        frozen?

³¹"Can you bind the beautiful ᵇ
        Pleiades?
    Can you loose the cords of
        Orion?
³²Can you bring forth the
        constellations in their
        seasons ͨ
    or lead out the Bear ͩ with its
        cubs?
³³Do you know the laws of the
        heavens?
    Can you set up ⌐God's ͤ⌐
        dominion over the earth?

³⁴"Can you raise your voice to the
        clouds
    and cover yourself with a flood
        of water?
³⁵Do you send the lightning bolts
        on their way?
    Do they report to you, 'Here we
        are'?
³⁶Who endowed the heart ͦ with
        wisdom
    or gave understanding to the
        mind ͦ?
³⁷Who has the wisdom to count the
        clouds?
    Who can tip over the water jars
        of the heavens
³⁸when the dust becomes hard
    and the clods of earth stick
        together?

³⁹"Do you hunt the prey for the
        lioness
    and satisfy the hunger of the
        lions
⁴⁰when they crouch in their dens
    or lie in wait in a thicket?
⁴¹Who provides food for the raven
    when its young cry out to God

ᵃ17 Or gates of deep shadows   ᵇ31 Or the twinkling; or the chains of the   ͨ32 Or the morning
star in its season   ͩ32 Or out Leo   ͤ33 Or his; or their   ͦ36 The meaning of the Hebrew
for this word is uncertain.

and wander about for lack of food?

39

"Do you know when the mountain goats give birth?
Do you watch when the doe bears her fawn?
²Do you count the months till they bear?
Do you know the time they give birth?
³They crouch down and bring forth their young;
their labor pains are ended.
⁴Their young thrive and grow strong in the wilds;
they leave and do not return.

⁵"Who let the wild donkey go free?
Who untied his ropes?
⁶I gave him the wasteland as his home,
the salt flats as his habitat.
⁷He laughs at the commotion in the town;
he does not hear a driver's shout.
⁸He ranges the hills for his pasture
and searches for any green thing.

⁹"Will the wild ox consent to serve you?
Will he stay by your manger at night?
¹⁰Can you hold him to the furrow with a harness?
Will he till the valleys behind you?
¹¹Will you rely on him for his great strength?
Will you leave your heavy work to him?
¹²Can you trust him to bring in your grain
and gather it to your threshing floor?

¹³"The wings of the ostrich flap joyfully,
but they cannot compare with the pinions and feathers of the stork.
¹⁴She lays her eggs on the ground and lets them warm in the sand,
¹⁵unmindful that a foot may crush them,
that some wild animal may trample them.
¹⁶She treats her young harshly, as if they were not hers;
she cares not that her labor was in vain,
¹⁷for God did not endow her with wisdom
or give her a share of good sense.
¹⁸Yet when she spreads her feathers to run,
she laughs at horse and rider.

¹⁹"Do you give the horse his strength
or clothe his neck with a flowing mane?
²⁰Do you make him leap like a locust,
striking terror with his proud snorting?
²¹He paws fiercely, rejoicing in his strength,
and charges into the fray.
²²He laughs at fear, afraid of nothing;
he does not shy away from the sword.
²³The quiver rattles against his side,
along with the flashing spear and lance.
²⁴In frenzied excitement he eats up the ground;
he cannot stand still when the trumpet sounds.
²⁵At the blast of the trumpet he snorts, 'Aha!'
He catches the scent of battle from afar,
the shout of commanders and the battle cry.

²⁶"Does the hawk take flight by your wisdom
and spread his wings toward the south?
²⁷Does the eagle soar at your command
and build his nest on high?
²⁸He dwells on a cliff and stays there at night;
a rocky crag is his stronghold.
²⁹From there he seeks out his food;
his eyes detect it from afar.
³⁰His young ones feast on blood,

and where the slain are, there is he."

40 The LORD said to Job:

2"Will the one who contends with
   the Almighty correct him?
Let him who accuses God
   answer him!"

3Then Job answered the LORD:

4"I am unworthy—how can I reply
   to you?
I put my hand over my mouth.
5I spoke once, but I have no
   answer—
twice, but I will say no more."

6Then the LORD spoke to Job out of
the storm:

7"Brace yourself like a man;
   I will question you,
   and you shall answer me.

8"Would you discredit my justice?
   Would you condemn me to
      justify yourself?
9Do you have an arm like God's,
   and can your voice thunder like
      his?
10Then adorn yourself with glory
      and splendor,
   and clothe yourself in honor
      and majesty.
11Unleash the fury of your wrath,
   look at every proud man and
      bring him low,
12look at every proud man and
      humble him,
   crush the wicked where they
      stand.
13Bury them all in the dust together;
   shroud their faces in the grave.
14Then I myself will admit to you
   that your own right hand can
      save you.

15"Look at the behemoth,[a]
   which I made along with you
   and which feeds on grass like
      an ox.
16What strength he has in his loins,

what power in the muscles of
   his belly!
17His tail[b] sways like a cedar;
   the sinews of his thighs are
      close-knit.
18His bones are tubes of bronze,
   his limbs like rods of iron.
19He ranks first among the works of
      God,
   yet his Maker can approach him
      with his sword.
20The hills bring him their produce,
   and all the wild animals play
      nearby.
21Under the lotus plants he lies,
   hidden among the reeds in the
      marsh.
22The lotuses conceal him in their
      shadow;
   the poplars by the stream
      surround him.
23When the river rages, he is not
      alarmed;
   he is secure, though the Jordan
      should surge against his
      mouth.
24Can anyone capture him by the
      eyes,[c]
   or trap him and pierce his nose?

41 "Can you pull in the
      leviathan[d] with a fishhook
   or tie down his tongue with a
      rope?
2Can you put a cord through his
      nose
   or pierce his jaw with a hook?
3Will he keep begging you for
      mercy?
   Will he speak to you with
      gentle words?
4Will he make an agreement with
      you
   for you to take him as your
      slave for life?
5Can you make a pet of him like a
      bird
   or put him on a leash for your
      girls?
6Will traders barter for him?
   Will they divide him up among
      the merchants?

---

a15 Possibly the hippopotamus or the elephant   b17 Possibly trunk   c24 Or *by a water hole*
d1 Possibly the crocodile

⁷Can you fill his hide with
    harpoons
  or his head with fishing spears?
⁸If you lay a hand on him,
  you will remember the struggle
    and never do it again!
⁹Any hope of subduing him is
    false;
  the mere sight of him is
    overpowering.
¹⁰No one is fierce enough to rouse
    him.
  Who then is able to stand
    against me?
¹¹Who has a claim against me that I
    must pay?
  Everything under heaven
    belongs to me.

¹²"I will not fail to speak of his
    limbs,
  his strength and his graceful
    form.
¹³Who can strip off his outer coat?
  Who would approach him with
    a bridle?
¹⁴Who dares open the doors of his
    mouth,
    ringed about with his fearsome
      teeth?
¹⁵His back has*a* rows of shields
    tightly sealed together;
¹⁶each is so close to the next
    that no air can pass between.
¹⁷They are joined fast to one
      another;
    they cling together and cannot
      be parted.
¹⁸His snorting throws out flashes of
      light;
    his eyes are like the rays of
      dawn.
¹⁹Firebrands stream from his mouth;
    sparks of fire shoot out.
²⁰Smoke pours from his nostrils
    as from a boiling pot over a fire
      of reeds.
²¹His breath sets coals ablaze,
    and flames dart from his mouth.
²²Strength resides in his neck;
    dismay goes before him.
²³The folds of his flesh are tightly
    joined;

they are firm and immovable.
²⁴His chest is hard as rock,
  hard as a lower millstone.
²⁵When he rises up, the mighty are
    terrified;
  they retreat before his thrashing.
²⁶The sword that reaches him has
    no effect,
  nor does the spear or the dart
    or the javelin.
²⁷Iron he treats like straw
  and bronze like rotten wood.
²⁸Arrows do not make him flee;
  slingstones are like chaff to him.
²⁹A club seems to him but a piece
    of straw;
  he laughs at the rattling of the
    lance.
³⁰His undersides are jagged
    potsherds,
  leaving a trail in the mud like a
    threshing sledge.
³¹He makes the depths churn like a
    boiling caldron
  and stirs up the sea like a pot of
    ointment.
³²Behind him he leaves a glistening
    wake;
  one would think the deep had
    white hair.
³³Nothing on earth is his equal—
  a creature without fear.
³⁴He looks down on all that are
    haughty;
  he is king over all that are
    proud."

Job

42

Then Job replied to the Lord:
²"I know that you can do all
    things;
  no plan of yours can be
    thwarted.
³⌊You asked,⌋ 'Who is this that
    obscures my counsel
    without knowledge?'
  Surely I spoke of things I did
    not understand,
  things too wonderful for me to
    know.

---

*a*15 Or *His pride is his*

VERSE:	AUTHOR:	PASSAGE:
Job 42:3	Charles R. Swindoll	Job 42:1–6

I Rest My Case

Job could write about wounds . . . He could describe intense inner suffering in the first person because of his own sea of pain . . .

How could anyone handle such a series of grief-laden ordeals so calmly [see Job 1–2]? Think of the aftermath: bankruptcy, pain, ten fresh graves . . . the loneliness of those empty rooms. Yet we read that he worshiped God, he did not sin, nor did he blame his Maker.

Well, why didn't he? How could he ward off the bitterness or ignore thoughts of suicide? At the risk of oversimplifying the situation, I suggest three basic answers:

First, *Job claimed God's loving sovereignty.* He sincerely believed that the Lord who gave had every right to take away (Job 1:21). Stated in his own words, "Shall we accept good from God, and not trouble" (Job 2:10) He looked *up,* claiming his Lord's right to rule over his life.

Second, *he counted on the promise of resurrection.* Do you remember his immortal words: "I know that my Redeemer lives . . . I myself will see him" (Job 19:25,27). He looked *ahead,* counting on his Lord's promise to make all things bright and beautiful in the life beyond . . . Job endured today by envisioning tomorrow.

Third, *he confessed his own lack of understanding* . . . Listen to his admission of this fact: "Surely I spoke of things I did not understand" (Job 42:3) He looked *within,* confessing his inability to put it all together. Resting his case with the righteous Judge, Job did not feel compelled to answer all the questions or unravel all the burning riddles. God would judge. The Judge would be right.

ADDITIONAL SCRIPTURE READINGS
Isaiah 40:12–31; Isaiah 55:6–9

Go to page 651 for your next devotional reading.

⁴ᴸ"You said,ᴶ 'Listen now, and I
will speak;
I will question you,
and you shall answer me.'
⁵My ears had heard of you
but now my eyes have seen
you.
⁶Therefore I despise myself
and repent in dust and ashes."

Epilogue

⁷After the LORD had said these
things to Job, he said to Eliphaz the
Temanite, "I am angry with you and
your two friends, because you have
not spoken of me what is right, as my
servant Job has. ⁸So now take seven
bulls and seven rams and go to my
servant Job and sacrifice a burnt offering for yourselves. My servant
Job will pray for you, and I will accept his prayer and not deal with you
according to your folly. You have not
spoken of me what is right, as my servant Job has." ⁹So Eliphaz the Temanite, Bildad the Shuhite and Zophar the
Naamathite did what the LORD told
them; and the LORD accepted Job's
prayer.

¹⁰After Job had prayed for his
friends, the LORD made him prosperous again and gave him twice as
much as he had before. ¹¹All his
brothers and sisters and everyone
who had known him before came and
ate with him in his house. They comforted and consoled him over all the
trouble the LORD had brought upon
him, and each one gave him a piece of
silverᵃ and a gold ring.
¹²The LORD blessed the latter part of
Job's life more than the first. He had
fourteen thousand sheep, six thousand camels, a thousand yoke of oxen
and a thousand donkeys. ¹³And he
also had seven sons and three daughters. ¹⁴The first daughter he named Je-
mimah, the second Keziah and the
third Keren-Happuch. ¹⁵Nowhere in
all the land were there found women
as beautiful as Job's daughters, and
their father granted them an inheritance along with their brothers.
¹⁶After this, Job lived a hundred
and forty years; he saw his children
and their children to the fourth generation. ¹⁷And so he died, old and full of
years.

ᵃ11 Hebrew *him a kesitah*; a kesitah was a unit of money of unknown weight and value.

This collection of psalms, many of which were written by David, expresses a wide range of human emotion—joy, love, excitement, compassion, anger, frustration, grief, depression. As you read this book, remember that accepting your feelings is part of accepting yourself. Whatever your need, your loving God welcomes your honest expression and your childlike trust in him.

PSALMS

BOOK I
Psalms 1–41

Psalm 1

¹Blessed is the man
 who does not walk in the
  counsel of the wicked
or stand in the way of sinners
 or sit in the seat of mockers.
²But his delight is in the law of the
  LORD,
 and on his law he meditates
  day and night.
³He is like a tree planted by
  streams of water,
 which yields its fruit in season
and whose leaf does not wither.
 Whatever he does prospers.

⁴Not so the wicked!
 They are like chaff
  that the wind blows away.
⁵Therefore the wicked will not
  stand in the judgment,

nor sinners in the assembly of
  the righteous.

⁶For the LORD watches over the way
  of the righteous,
 but the way of the wicked will
  perish.

Psalm 2

¹Why do the nations conspire*ᵃ*
 and the peoples plot in vain?
²The kings of the earth take their
  stand
 and the rulers gather together
against the LORD
 and against his Anointed One.*ᵇ*
³"Let us break their chains," they
  say,
 "and throw off their fetters."

⁴The One enthroned in heaven
  laughs;
 the Lord scoffs at them.
⁵Then he rebukes them in his anger

*ᵃ*1 Hebrew; Septuagint *rage*   *ᵇ*2 Or *anointed one*

PASSAGE: Psalm 1; Proverbs 3:1–6
AUTHOR: Robert Browning

Grow Old Along With Me

Grow old along with me!
   The best is yet to be,
The last of life, for which the first was made:
    Our times are in His hand
    Who saith, "A whole I planned,
Youth shows but half; trust God, see all, nor be
    afraid."

Go to page 656 for your next devotional reading.

and terrifies them in his wrath,
saying,
6"I have installed my King*a*
on Zion, my holy hill."

7I will proclaim the decree of the
LORD:

He said to me, "You are my
Son*b*;
today I have become your
Father.*c*
8Ask of me,
and I will make the nations
your inheritance,
the ends of the earth your
possession.
9You will rule them with an iron
scepter*d*;
you will dash them to pieces
like pottery."

10Therefore, you kings, be wise;
be warned, you rulers of the
earth.
11Serve the LORD with fear
and rejoice with trembling.
12Kiss the Son, lest he be angry
and you be destroyed in your
way,
for his wrath can flare up in a
moment.
Blessed are all who take refuge
in him.

Psalm 3

A psalm of David. When he fled from
his son Absalom.

1O LORD, how many are my foes!
How many rise up against me!
2Many are saying of me,
"God will not deliver him."
*Selah*e

3But you are a shield around me,
O LORD;
you bestow glory on me and
lift*f* up my head.
4To the LORD I cry aloud,
and he answers me from his
holy hill.   *Selah*

5I lie down and sleep;
I wake again, because the LORD
sustains me.
6I will not fear the tens of
thousands
drawn up against me on every
side.

7Arise, O LORD!
Deliver me, O my God!
Strike all my enemies on the jaw;
break the teeth of the wicked.

8From the LORD comes deliverance.
May your blessing be on your
people.   *Selah*

Psalm 4

For the director of music. With
stringed instruments. A psalm
of David.

1Answer me when I call to you,
O my righteous God.
Give me relief from my distress;
be merciful to me and hear my
prayer.

2How long, O men, will you turn
my glory into shame*g*?
How long will you love
delusions and seek false
gods*h*?   *Selah*
3Know that the LORD has set apart
the godly for himself;
the LORD will hear when I call to
him.

4In your anger do not sin;
when you are on your beds,
search your hearts and be silent.
Selah
5Offer right sacrifices
and trust in the LORD.

6Many are asking, "Who can show
us any good?"
Let the light of your face shine
upon us, O LORD.
7You have filled my heart with
greater joy

---

*a*6 Or *king*   *b*7 Or *son*; also in verse 12   *c*7 Or *have begotten you*   *d*9 Or *will break them
with a rod of iron*   *e*2 A word of uncertain meaning, occurring frequently in the Psalms;
possibly a musical term   *f*3 Or LORD, / *my Glorious One, who lifts*   *g*2 Or *you dishonor my
Glorious One*   *h*2 Or *seek lies*

than when their grain and new
wine abound.
⁸I will lie down and sleep in peace,
    for you alone, O LORD,
    make me dwell in safety.

Psalm 5

*For the director of music. For flutes.
A psalm of David.*

¹Give ear to my words, O LORD,
    consider my sighing.
²Listen to my cry for help,
    my King and my God,
    for to you I pray.
³In the morning, O LORD, you hear
        my voice;
    in the morning I lay my
        requests before you
    and wait in expectation.

⁴You are not a God who takes
        pleasure in evil;
    with you the wicked cannot
        dwell.
⁵The arrogant cannot stand in your
        presence;
    you hate all who do wrong.
⁶You destroy those who tell lies;
    bloodthirsty and deceitful men
        the LORD abhors.

⁷But I, by your great mercy,
    will come into your house;
    in reverence will I bow down
        toward your holy temple.
⁸Lead me, O LORD, in your
        righteousness
    because of my enemies—
    make straight your way before
        me.

⁹Not a word from their mouth can
        be trusted;
    their heart is filled with
        destruction.
Their throat is an open grave;
    with their tongue they speak
        deceit.
¹⁰Declare them guilty, O God!
    Let their intrigues be their
        downfall.
Banish them for their many sins,

for they have rebelled against
    you.

¹¹But let all who take refuge in you
        be glad;
    let them ever sing for joy.
Spread your protection over them,
    that those who love your name
        may rejoice in you.
¹²For surely, O LORD, you bless the
        righteous;
    you surround them with your
        favor as with a shield.

Psalm 6

*For the director of music. With
stringed instruments. According to
sheminith.ᵃ A psalm of David.*

¹O LORD, do not rebuke me in your
        anger
    or discipline me in your wrath.
²Be merciful to me, LORD, for I am
        faint;
    O LORD, heal me, for my bones
        are in agony.
³My soul is in anguish.
    How long, O LORD, how long?

⁴Turn, O LORD, and deliver me;
    save me because of your
        unfailing love.
⁵No one remembers you when he
        is dead.
    Who praises you from the
        graveᵇ?

⁶I am worn out from groaning;
    all night long I flood my bed
        with weeping
    and drench my couch with
        tears.
⁷My eyes grow weak with sorrow;
    they fail because of all my foes.

⁸Away from me, all you who do
        evil,
    for the LORD has heard my
        weeping.
⁹The LORD has heard my cry for
        mercy;
    the LORD accepts my prayer.
¹⁰All my enemies will be ashamed
        and dismayed;

ᵃTitle: Probably a musical term   ᵇ5 Hebrew *Sheol*

they will turn back in sudden
disgrace.

Psalm 7

A *shiggaion*[a] of David, which he
sang to the LORD concerning Cush,
a Benjamite.

¹O LORD my God, I take refuge in
    you;
  save and deliver me from all
    who pursue me,
²or they will tear me like a lion
  and rip me to pieces with no
    one to rescue me.

³O LORD my God, if I have done
    this
  and there is guilt on my
    hands—
⁴if I have done evil to him who is
    at peace with me
  or without cause have robbed
    my foe—
⁵then let my enemy pursue and
    overtake me;
  let him trample my life to the
    ground
  and make me sleep in the dust.
                 Selah

⁶Arise, O LORD, in your anger;
  rise up against the rage of my
    enemies.
  Awake, my God; decree justice.
⁷Let the assembled peoples gather
    around you.
  Rule over them from on high;
⁸ let the LORD judge the peoples.
  Judge me, O LORD, according to
    my righteousness,
    according to my integrity,
      O Most High.
⁹O righteous God,
  who searches minds and hearts,
  bring to an end the violence of the
    wicked
  and make the righteous secure.

¹⁰My shield[b] is God Most High,
  who saves the upright in heart.
¹¹God is a righteous judge,

a God who expresses his wrath
    every day.
¹²If he does not relent,
  he[c] will sharpen his sword;
  he will bend and string his
    bow.
¹³He has prepared his deadly
    weapons;
  he makes ready his flaming
    arrows.

¹⁴He who is pregnant with evil
  and conceives trouble gives
    birth to disillusionment.
¹⁵He who digs a hole and scoops it
    out
  falls into the pit he has made.
¹⁶The trouble he causes recoils on
    himself;
  his violence comes down on his
    own head.

¹⁷I will give thanks to the LORD
    because of his
    righteousness
  and will sing praise to the name
    of the LORD Most High.

Psalm 8

For the director of music. According
to *gittith*.[d] A psalm of David.

¹O LORD, our Lord,
  how majestic is your name in
    all the earth!

You have set your glory
  above the heavens.
²From the lips of children and
    infants
  you have ordained praise[e]
because of your enemies,
  to silence the foe and the
    avenger.

³When I consider your heavens,
  the work of your fingers,
the moon and the stars,
  which you have set in place,
⁴what is man that you are mindful
    of him,
  the son of man that you care for
    him?

---

*a*Title: Probably a literary or musical term   *b*10 Or *sovereign*   *c*12 Or *If a man does not*
repent, / God   *d*Title: Probably a musical term   *e*2 Or *strength*

[5]You made him a little lower than
  the heavenly beings[a]
and crowned him with glory
  and honor.

[6]You made him ruler over the
  works of your hands;
you put everything under his
  feet:
[7]all flocks and herds,
  and the beasts of the field,
[8]the birds of the air,
  and the fish of the sea,
all that swim the paths of the
  seas.

[9]O Lord, our Lord,
  how majestic is your name in
  all the earth!

Psalm 9[b]

For the director of music. To ⌊the
tune of⌋ "The Death of the Son."
A psalm of David.

[1]I will praise you, O Lord, with all
  my heart;
I will tell of all your wonders.
[2]I will be glad and rejoice in you;
I will sing praise to your name,
  O Most High.

[3]My enemies turn back;
  they stumble and perish before
  you.
[4]For you have upheld my right and
  my cause;
you have sat on your throne,
  judging righteously.
[5]You have rebuked the nations and
  destroyed the wicked;
you have blotted out their name
  for ever and ever.
[6]Endless ruin has overtaken the
  enemy,
you have uprooted their cities;
even the memory of them has
  perished.

[7]The Lord reigns forever;
  he has established his throne for
  judgment.

[8]He will judge the world in
  righteousness;
he will govern the peoples with
  justice.
[9]The Lord is a refuge for the
  oppressed,
a stronghold in times of trouble.
[10]Those who know your name will
  trust in you,
for you, Lord, have never
  forsaken those who seek
  you.

[11]Sing praises to the Lord,
  enthroned in Zion;
proclaim among the nations
  what he has done.
[12]For he who avenges blood
  remembers;
he does not ignore the cry of
  the afflicted.

[13]O Lord, see how my enemies
  persecute me!
Have mercy and lift me up
  from the gates of death,
[14]that I may declare your praises
  in the gates of the Daughter of
  Zion
and there rejoice in your
  salvation.
[15]The nations have fallen into the
  pit they have dug;
their feet are caught in the net
  they have hidden.
[16]The Lord is known by his justice;
  the wicked are ensnared by the
  work of their hands.
                    Higgaion.[c] Selah
[17]The wicked return to the grave,[d]
  all the nations that forget God.
[18]But the needy will not always be
  forgotten,
nor the hope of the afflicted
  ever perish.

[19]Arise, O Lord, let not man
  triumph;
let the nations be judged in
  your presence.
[20]Strike them with terror, O Lord;
  let the nations know they are
  but men.   *Selah*

[a]5 Or *than God*   [b]Psalms 9 and 10 may have been originally a single acrostic poem, the
stanzas of which begin with the successive letters of the Hebrew alphabet. In the Septuagint they
constitute one psalm.   [c]16 Or *Meditation;* possibly a musical notation   [d]17 Hebrew *Sheol*

VERSE:
Psalm 8:4

AUTHOR:
Billy Graham

PASSAGE:
Psalm 8:1–9

God Values Us

A certain rich man died and the question was asked at his funeral, "How much did he leave?" "He left it all," came the reply.

Often, I hear someone introduced this way: "This is Bob and he works for . . . " as if where a person works determines his or her value. I have noticed that it is usually only the well-to-do or those who are thought of as "successful" who are introduced this way.

Yet God does not judge us by success. He loves each person the same because your value and mine does not come from what we do or have, the clothes we wear, the house in which we live, or the type of car we drive. Our value comes from the fact that God made us and Christ died for us. And so, whether we have things or not, we are just as valuable to God.

God gave all that he had—his Son, the Lord Jesus Christ—because he valued us so highly, even when we did not value him. Since God thought this much of us, shouldn't we show that we value him by putting him first in all that we do—our family life, our business life, our spiritual life? . . .

The actual value of an object is that which is placed on it by the owner or buyer. God has shown the value he has placed on you by sending his Son to redeem you.

ADDITIONAL SCRIPTURE READINGS
2 Corinthians 8:1–9; Titus 2:11–14

Go to page 665 for your next devotional reading.

Psalm 10[a]

[1]Why, O Lord, do you stand far
off?
  Why do you hide yourself in
    times of trouble?

[2]In his arrogance the wicked man
    hunts down the weak,
  who are caught in the schemes
    he devises.
[3]He boasts of the cravings of his
    heart;
  he blesses the greedy and
    reviles the Lord.
[4]In his pride the wicked does not
    seek him;
  in all his thoughts there is no
    room for God.
[5]His ways are always prosperous;
  he is haughty and your laws are
    far from him;
  he sneers at all his enemies.
[6]He says to himself, "Nothing will
    shake me;
  I'll always be happy and never
    have trouble."
[7]His mouth is full of curses and
    lies and threats;
  trouble and evil are under his
    tongue.
[8]He lies in wait near the villages;
  from ambush he murders the
    innocent,
  watching in secret for his
    victims.
[9]He lies in wait like a lion in cover;
  he lies in wait to catch the
    helpless;
  he catches the helpless and
    drags them off in his net.
[10]His victims are crushed, they
    collapse;
  they fall under his strength.
[11]He says to himself, "God has
    forgotten;
  he covers his face and never
    sees."

[12]Arise, Lord! Lift up your hand,
    O God.
  Do not forget the helpless.

[13]Why does the wicked man revile
    God?
  Why does he say to himself,
    "He won't call me to account"?
[14]But you, O God, do see trouble
    and grief;
  you consider it to take it in
    hand.
The victim commits himself to
    you;
  you are the helper of the
    fatherless.
[15]Break the arm of the wicked and
    evil man;
  call him to account for his
    wickedness
  that would not be found out.

[16]The Lord is King for ever and
    ever;
  the nations will perish from his
    land.
[17]You hear, O Lord, the desire of
    the afflicted;
  you encourage them, and you
    listen to their cry,
[18]defending the fatherless and the
    oppressed,
  in order that man, who is of the
    earth, may terrify no more.

Psalm 11

For the director of music. Of David.

[1]In the Lord I take refuge.
  How then can you say to me:
  "Flee like a bird to your
    mountain.
[2]For look, the wicked bend their
    bows;
  they set their arrows against the
    strings
to shoot from the shadows
  at the upright in heart.
[3]When the foundations are being
    destroyed,
  what can the righteous do[b]?"

[4]The Lord is in his holy temple;
  the Lord is on his heavenly
    throne.

---

[a]Psalms 9 and 10 may have been originally a single acrostic poem, the stanzas of which begin
with the successive letters of the Hebrew alphabet. In the Septuagint they constitute one psalm.
[b]3 Or *what is the Righteous One doing*

He observes the sons of men;
  his eyes examine them.
5The LORD examines the righteous,
  but the wicked*a* and those who
    love violence
  his soul hates.
6On the wicked he will rain
  fiery coals and burning sulfur;
  a scorching wind will be their
    lot.

7For the LORD is righteous,
  he loves justice;
  upright men will see his face.

Psalm 12

For the director of music. According
to *sheminith.b* A psalm of David.

1Help, LORD, for the godly are no
  more;
  the faithful have vanished from
    among men.
2Everyone lies to his neighbor;
  their flattering lips speak with
    deception.

3May the LORD cut off all flattering
  lips
  and every boastful tongue
4that says, "We will triumph with
  our tongues;
  we own our lips*c*—who is our
    master?"

5"Because of the oppression of the
  weak
  and the groaning of the needy,
I will now arise," says the LORD.
  "I will protect them from those
    who malign them."
6And the words of the LORD are
  flawless,
  like silver refined in a furnace
    of clay,
  purified seven times.

7O LORD, you will keep us safe
  and protect us from such people
    forever.
8The wicked freely strut about
  when what is vile is honored
    among men.

Psalm 13

For the director of music. A psalm
of David.

1How long, O LORD? Will you
  forget me forever?
  How long will you hide your
    face from me?
2How long must I wrestle with my
  thoughts
  and every day have sorrow in
    my heart?
  How long will my enemy
    triumph over me?

3Look on me and answer, O LORD
  my God.
  Give light to my eyes, or I will
    sleep in death;
4my enemy will say, "I have
  overcome him,"
  and my foes will rejoice when I
    fall.

5But I trust in your unfailing love;
  my heart rejoices in your
    salvation.
6I will sing to the LORD,
  for he has been good to me.

Psalm 14

For the director of music. Of David.

1The fool*d* says in his heart,
  "There is no God."
They are corrupt, their deeds are
  vile;
  there is no one who does good.

2The LORD looks down from heaven
  on the sons of men
to see if there are any who
  understand,
  any who seek God.
3All have turned aside,
  they have together become
    corrupt;
there is no one who does good,
  not even one.

4Will evildoers never learn—

---

a5 Or The LORD, the Righteous One, examines the wicked, /   *bTitle: Probably a musical term*
c4 Or / our lips are our plowshares   *d1 The Hebrew words rendered fool in Psalms denote one*
who is morally deficient.

those who devour my people as
    men eat bread
and who do not call on the
    LORD?
⁵There they are, overwhelmed with
    dread,
    for God is present in the
        company of the righteous.
⁶You evildoers frustrate the plans
    of the poor,
    but the LORD is their refuge.

⁷Oh, that salvation for Israel would
    come out of Zion!
When the LORD restores the
    fortunes of his people,
    let Jacob rejoice and Israel be
        glad!

Psalm 15

A psalm of David.

¹LORD, who may dwell in your
    sanctuary?
    Who may live on your holy
        hill?

²He whose walk is blameless
    and who does what is
        righteous,
who speaks the truth from his
    heart
³   and has no slander on his
        tongue,
who does his neighbor no wrong
    and casts no slur on his
        fellowman,
⁴who despises a vile man
    but honors those who fear the
        LORD,
who keeps his oath
    even when it hurts,
⁵who lends his money without
    usury
    and does not accept a bribe
        against the innocent.

He who does these things
    will never be shaken.

Psalm 16

A miktam[a] of David.

¹Keep me safe, O God,
    for in you I take refuge.

²I said to the LORD, "You are my
    Lord;
    apart from you I have no good
        thing."
³As for the saints who are in the
    land,
    they are the glorious ones in
        whom is all my delight.[b]
⁴The sorrows of those will increase
    who run after other gods.
I will not pour out their libations
    of blood
    or take up their names on my
        lips.

⁵LORD, you have assigned me my
    portion and my cup;
    you have made my lot secure.
⁶The boundary lines have fallen for
    me in pleasant places;
    surely I have a delightful
        inheritance.

⁷I will praise the LORD, who
    counsels me;
    even at night my heart instructs
        me.
⁸I have set the LORD always before
    me.
    Because he is at my right hand,
    I will not be shaken.

⁹Therefore my heart is glad and my
    tongue rejoices;
    my body also will rest secure,
¹⁰because you will not abandon me
    to the grave,[c]
    nor will you let your Holy
        One[d] see decay.
¹¹You have made[e] known to me
    the path of life;
    you will fill me with joy in your
        presence,
    with eternal pleasures at your
        right hand.

---

[a]Title: Probably a literary or musical term
and the nobles in whom all delight, I said: [c]10 Hebrew *Sheol*   [b]3 Or *As for the pagan priests who are in the land /*
[e]11 Or *You will make*   [d]10 Or *your faithful one*

Psalm 17

A prayer of David.

[1] Hear, O Lord, my righteous plea;
    listen to my cry.
Give ear to my prayer—
    it does not rise from deceitful
        lips.
[2] May my vindication come from
        you;
    may your eyes see what is right.

[3] Though you probe my heart and
        examine me at night,
    though you test me, you will
        find nothing;
    I have resolved that my mouth
        will not sin.
[4] As for the deeds of men—
        by the word of your lips
    I have kept myself
        from the ways of the violent.
[5] My steps have held to your paths;
    my feet have not slipped.

[6] I call on you, O God, for you will
        answer me;
    give ear to me and hear my
        prayer.
[7] Show the wonder of your great
        love,
    you who save by your right
        hand
    those who take refuge in you
        from their foes.
[8] Keep me as the apple of your eye;
    hide me in the shadow of your
        wings
[9] from the wicked who assail me,
    from my mortal enemies who
        surround me.

[10] They close up their callous hearts,
    and their mouths speak with
        arrogance.
[11] They have tracked me down, they
        now surround me,
    with eyes alert, to throw me to
        the ground.
[12] They are like a lion hungry for
        prey,
    like a great lion crouching in
        cover.

[13] Rise up, O Lord, confront them,
        bring them down;
    rescue me from the wicked by
        your sword.
[14] O Lord, by your hand save me
        from such men,
    from men of this world whose
        reward is in this life.

You still the hunger of those you
        cherish;
    their sons have plenty,
    and they store up wealth for
        their children.
[15] And I—in righteousness I will see
        your face;
    when I awake, I will be satisfied
        with seeing your likeness.

Psalm 18

*For the director of music. Of David
the servant of the Lord. He sang to
the Lord the words of this song when
the Lord delivered him from the hand
of all his enemies and from the hand
of Saul. He said:*

[1] I love you, O Lord, my strength.

[2] The Lord is my rock, my fortress
        and my deliverer;
    my God is my rock, in whom I
        take refuge.
    He is my shield and the horn[a]
        of my salvation, my
        stronghold.
[3] I call to the Lord, who is worthy
        of praise,
    and I am saved from my
        enemies.

[4] The cords of death entangled me;
    the torrents of destruction
        overwhelmed me.
[5] The cords of the grave[b] coiled
        around me;
    the snares of death confronted
        me.
[6] In my distress I called to the Lord;
    I cried to my God for help.
From his temple he heard my
        voice;
    my cry came before him, into
        his ears.

---

a2 Horn here symbolizes strength.   *b5 Hebrew Sheol*

⁷The earth trembled and quaked,
  and the foundations of the
    mountains shook;
  they trembled because he was
    angry.
⁸Smoke rose from his nostrils;
  consuming fire came from his
    mouth,
  burning coals blazed out of it.
⁹He parted the heavens and came
    down;
  dark clouds were under his feet.
¹⁰He mounted the cherubim and
    flew;
  he soared on the wings of the
    wind.
¹¹He made darkness his covering,
    his canopy around him—
  the dark rain clouds of the sky.
¹²Out of the brightness of his
    presence clouds advanced,
  with hailstones and bolts of
    lightning.
¹³The LORD thundered from heaven;
  the voice of the Most High
    resounded.ᵃ
¹⁴He shot his arrows and scattered
    ˻the enemies˼,
  great bolts of lightning and
    routed them.
¹⁵The valleys of the sea were
    exposed
  and the foundations of the earth
    laid bare
  at your rebuke, O LORD,
  at the blast of breath from your
    nostrils.

¹⁶He reached down from on high
    and took hold of me;
  he drew me out of deep waters.
¹⁷He rescued me from my powerful
    enemy,
  from my foes, who were too
    strong for me.
¹⁸They confronted me in the day of
    my disaster,
  but the LORD was my support.
¹⁹He brought me out into a spacious
    place;
  he rescued me because he
    delighted in me.

²⁰The LORD has dealt with me
    according to my
    righteousness;
  according to the cleanness of
    my hands he has rewarded
    me.
²¹For I have kept the ways of the
    LORD;
  I have not done evil by turning
    from my God.
²²All his laws are before me;
  I have not turned away from
    his decrees.
²³I have been blameless before him
  and have kept myself from sin.
²⁴The LORD has rewarded me
    according to my
    righteousness,
  according to the cleanness of
    my hands in his sight.

²⁵To the faithful you show yourself
    faithful,
  to the blameless you show
    yourself blameless,
²⁶to the pure you show yourself
    pure,
  but to the crooked you show
    yourself shrewd.
²⁷You save the humble
  but bring low those whose eyes
    are haughty.
²⁸You, O LORD, keep my lamp
    burning;
  my God turns my darkness into
    light.
²⁹With your help I can advance
    against a troopᵇ;
  with my God I can scale a wall.

³⁰As for God, his way is perfect;
  the word of the LORD is flawless.
He is a shield
  for all who take refuge in him.
³¹For who is God besides the LORD?
  And who is the Rock except our
    God?
³²It is God who arms me with
    strength
  and makes my way perfect.
³³He makes my feet like the feet of
    a deer;

ᵃ13 Some Hebrew manuscripts and Septuagint (see also 2 Samuel 22:14); most Hebrew
manuscripts *resounded, / amid hailstones and bolts of lightning*   ᵇ29 Or *can run through a barricade*

he enables me to stand on the
heights.
34He trains my hands for battle;
my arms can bend a bow of
bronze.
35You give me your shield of
victory,
and your right hand sustains
me;
you stoop down to make me
great.
36You broaden the path beneath me,
so that my ankles do not turn.

37I pursued my enemies and
overtook them;
I did not turn back till they
were destroyed.
38I crushed them so that they could
not rise;
they fell beneath my feet.
39You armed me with strength for
battle;
you made my adversaries bow
at my feet.
40You made my enemies turn their
backs in flight,
and I destroyed my foes.
41They cried for help, but there was
no one to save them—
to the Lord, but he did not
answer.
42I beat them as fine as dust borne
on the wind;
I poured them out like mud in
the streets.

43You have delivered me from the
attacks of the people;
you have made me the head of
nations;
people I did not know are
subject to me.
44As soon as they hear me, they
obey me;
foreigners cringe before me.
45They all lose heart;
they come trembling from their
strongholds.

46The Lord lives! Praise be to my
Rock!
Exalted be God my Savior!

47He is the God who avenges me,
who subdues nations under me,
48　who saves me from my
enemies.
You exalted me above my foes;
from violent men you rescued
me.
49Therefore I will praise you among
the nations, O Lord;
I will sing praises to your name.
50He gives his king great victories;
he shows unfailing kindness to
his anointed,
to David and his descendants
forever.

Psalm 19

For the director of music. A psalm
of David.

1The heavens declare the glory of
God;
the skies proclaim the work of
his hands.
2Day after day they pour forth
speech;
night after night they display
knowledge.
3There is no speech or language
where their voice is not
heard.a
4Their voiceb goes out into all the
earth,
their words to the ends of the
world.

In the heavens he has pitched a
tent for the sun,
5　which is like a bridegroom
coming forth from his
pavilion,
like a champion rejoicing to run
his course.
6It rises at one end of the heavens
and makes its circuit to the
other;
nothing is hidden from its heat.

7The law of the Lord is perfect,
reviving the soul.
The statutes of the Lord are
trustworthy,

a3 Or *They have no speech, there are no words; / no sound is heard from them*　b4 Septuagint,
Jerome and Syriac; Hebrew *line*

making wise the simple.
⁸The precepts of the Lord are right,
    giving joy to the heart.
The commands of the Lord are
        radiant,
    giving light to the eyes.
⁹The fear of the Lord is pure,
    enduring forever.
The ordinances of the Lord are
        sure
and altogether righteous.
¹⁰They are more precious than gold,
    than much pure gold;
they are sweeter than honey,
    than honey from the comb.
¹¹By them is your servant warned;
    in keeping them there is great
        reward.

¹²Who can discern his errors?
    Forgive my hidden faults.
¹³Keep your servant also from
        willful sins;
    may they not rule over me.
Then will I be blameless,
    innocent of great transgression.

¹⁴May the words of my mouth and
        the meditation of my heart
be pleasing in your sight,
O Lord, my Rock and my
        Redeemer.

Psalm 20

*For the director of music. A psalm
of David.*

¹May the Lord answer you when
    you are in distress;
may the name of the God of
    Jacob protect you.
²May he send you help from the
        sanctuary
and grant you support from
        Zion.
³May he remember all your
        sacrifices
and accept your burnt offerings.   *Selah*
⁴May he give you the desire of
        your heart
and make all your plans
        succeed.

⁵We will shout for joy when you
    are victorious
and will lift up our banners in
    the name of our God.
May the Lord grant all your
    requests.

⁶Now I know that the Lord saves
    his anointed;
he answers him from his holy
        heaven
with the saving power of his
        right hand.
⁷Some trust in chariots and some in
        horses,
but we trust in the name of the
        Lord our God.
⁸They are brought to their knees
        and fall,
but we rise up and stand firm.

⁹O Lord, save the king!
    Answer[a] us when we call!

Psalm 21

*For the director of music. A psalm
of David.*

¹O Lord, the king rejoices in your
        strength.
How great is his joy in the
        victories you give!
²You have granted him the desire
        of his heart
and have not withheld the
        request of his lips.   *Selah*
³You welcomed him with rich
        blessings
and placed a crown of pure
        gold on his head.
⁴He asked you for life, and you
        gave it to him—
length of days, for ever and
        ever.
⁵Through the victories you gave,
    his glory is great;
you have bestowed on him
    splendor and majesty.
⁶Surely you have granted him
    eternal blessings
and made him glad with the joy
    of your presence.
⁷For the king trusts in the Lord;

---

a9 Or save! | O King, answer

through the unfailing love of
the Most High
he will not be shaken.

8Your hand will lay hold on all
your enemies;
your right hand will seize your
foes.
9At the time of your appearing
you will make them like a fiery
furnace.
In his wrath the LORD will swallow
them up,
and his fire will consume them.
10You will destroy their descendants
from the earth,
their posterity from mankind.
11Though they plot evil against you
and devise wicked schemes,
they cannot succeed;
12for you will make them turn their
backs
when you aim at them with
drawn bow.

13Be exalted, O LORD, in your
strength;
we will sing and praise your
might.

Psalm 22

For the director of music. To ˻the
tune of˼ "The Doe of the Morning."
A psalm of David.

1My God, my God, why have you
forsaken me?
Why are you so far from saving
me,
so far from the words of my
groaning?
2O my God, I cry out by day, but
you do not answer,
by night, and am not silent.

3Yet you are enthroned as the Holy
One;
you are the praise of Israel.a
4In you our fathers put their trust;
they trusted and you delivered
them.
5They cried to you and were saved;

in you they trusted and were
not disappointed.

6But I am a worm and not a man,
scorned by men and despised
by the people.
7All who see me mock me;
they hurl insults, shaking their
heads:
8"He trusts in the LORD;
let the LORD rescue him.
Let him deliver him,
since he delights in him."

9Yet you brought me out of the
womb;
you made me trust in you
even at my mother's breast.
10From birth I was cast upon you;
from my mother's womb you
have been my God.
11Do not be far from me,
for trouble is near
and there is no one to help.

12Many bulls surround me;
strong bulls of Bashan encircle
me.
13Roaring lions tearing their prey
open their mouths wide against
me.
14I am poured out like water,
and all my bones are out of
joint.
My heart has turned to wax;
it has melted away within me.
15My strength is dried up like a
potsherd,
and my tongue sticks to the
roof of my mouth;
you lay meb in the dust of
death.
16Dogs have surrounded me;
a band of evil men has encircled
me,
they have piercedc my hands
and my feet.
17I can count all my bones;
people stare and gloat over me.
18They divide my garments among
them
and cast lots for my clothing.
19But you, O LORD, be not far off;

---

a3 Or Yet you are holy, / enthroned on the praises of Israel   b15 Or / I am laid   c16 Some
Hebrew manuscripts, Septuagint and Syriac; most Hebrew manuscripts / like the lion,

TUESDAY

VERSE:
Psalm 21:7

AUTHOR:
Charles Stanley

PASSAGE:
Psalm 21:1–13

Unfailing Love

The steadfast love of God never changes, is never diminished by my behavior, is never quenched by my indifference or even rebellion. The loyal, covenant-keeping love of Christ is ever fresh, ever healing, ever faithful, ever sufficient.

Since God's love for you is unfailing and unchanging, you need not be unsettled. "For the king trusts in the LORD; through the unfailing love of the Most High he will not be shaken" (Psalm 21:7). Those were the words of David, whose life was constantly in peril. His safety and stability rested securely in God's remarkable love for him, and so do yours . . .

Each morning, think upon God's unfailing love, how it is expressed to you, its immensity, its power, its nature. Let God satisfy you with the sure knowledge that he has set his love upon you and will never turn it away. The more frequently you ponder God's boundless love, the more joyful you will become. The more joyful you are, the more exciting is your walk with Jesus and the more dynamic is your faith.

The unfailing, steadfast love of Christ for you is your anchor for every storm, sustaining you, keeping you, upholding you. It satisfies the deepest longing of your heart.

ADDITIONAL SCRIPTURE READINGS
Psalm 90:13–17; Romans 8:28–39

Go to page 667 for your next devotional reading.

O my Strength, come quickly to
    help me.
²⁰Deliver my life from the sword,
    my precious life from the power
      of the dogs.
²¹Rescue me from the mouth of the
    lions;
    save[a] me from the horns of the
      wild oxen.

²²I will declare your name to my
    brothers;
    in the congregation I will praise
      you.
²³You who fear the LORD, praise
    him!
    All you descendants of Jacob,
      honor him!
    Revere him, all you descendants
      of Israel!
²⁴For he has not despised or
    disdained
    the suffering of the afflicted
      one;
he has not hidden his face from
    him
    but has listened to his cry for
      help.

²⁵From you comes the theme of my
    praise in the great
      assembly;
    before those who fear you[b]
      will I fulfill my vows.
²⁶The poor will eat and be satisfied;
    they who seek the LORD will
      praise him—
    may your hearts live forever!
²⁷All the ends of the earth
    will remember and turn to the
      LORD,
and all the families of the nations
    will bow down before him,
²⁸for dominion belongs to the LORD
    and he rules over the nations.

²⁹All the rich of the earth will feast
    and worship;
    all who go down to the dust
      will kneel before him—
    those who cannot keep
      themselves alive.
³⁰Posterity will serve him;

future generations will be told
    about the Lord.
³¹They will proclaim his
    righteousness
    to a people yet unborn—
    for he has done it.

Psalm 23

A psalm of David.

¹The LORD is my shepherd, I shall
    not be in want.
² He makes me lie down in green
    pastures,
he leads me beside quiet waters,
³ he restores my soul.
He guides me in paths of
    righteousness
    for his name's sake.
⁴Even though I walk
    through the valley of the
      shadow of death,[c]
I will fear no evil,
    for you are with me;
your rod and your staff,
    they comfort me.

⁵You prepare a table before me
    in the presence of my enemies.
You anoint my head with oil;
    my cup overflows.
⁶Surely goodness and love will
    follow me
    all the days of my life,
and I will dwell in the house of
    the LORD
    forever.

Psalm 24

Of David. A psalm.

¹The earth is the LORD's, and
    everything in it,
    the world, and all who live
      in it;
²for he founded it upon the seas
    and established it upon the
      waters.

³Who may ascend the hill of the
    LORD?

---

^a21 Or / *you have heard*   ^b25 Hebrew *him*   ^c4 Or *through the darkest valley*

VERSE:
Psalm 23:6

AUTHOR:
W. Phillip Keller

PASSAGE:
Psalm 23:1–6

Do I Leave a Blessing?

God's goodness and mercy and compassion to me are new every day. And my assurance is lodged in these aspects of his character. My trust is in his love for me as his own. My serenity has as its basis an implicit, unshakable reliance on his ability to do the right thing, the best thing in any given situation.

This to me is the *supreme* portrait of my Shepherd. Continually there flows out to me his goodness and his mercy, which, even though I do not deserve them, come unremittingly from their source of supply—his own great heart of love . . .

It is then proper to ask myself, "Is this outflow of goodness and love for me to stop and stagnate in my life? Is there no way in which it can pass on through me to benefit others?"

There is a positive, practical aspect in which my life in turn should be one whereby goodness and love follow in my footsteps for the well-being of others. Just as God's goodness and love flow to me all the days of my life, so goodness and love should follow me, should be left behind me, as a legacy to others, wherever I may go . . .

Sometimes it is profitable to ask ourselves such simple questions as: "Do I leave behind peace in lives—or turmoil? Do I leave behind forgiveness—or bitterness? Do I leave behind contentment—or conflict? Do I leave behind flowers of joy—or frustration? Do I leave behind love—or rancor?"

ADDITIONAL SCRIPTURE READINGS
Psalm 71:14–18; Titus 2:1–5

Go to page 669 for your next devotional reading.

Who may stand in his holy
place?
⁴He who has clean hands and a
pure heart,
who does not lift up his soul to
an idol
or swear by what is false.ᵃ
⁵He will receive blessing from the
LORD
and vindication from God his
Savior.
⁶Such is the generation of those
who seek him,
who seek your face, O God of
Jacob.ᵇ   *Selah*

⁷Lift up your heads, O you gates;
be lifted up, you ancient doors,
that the King of glory may
come in.
⁸Who is this King of glory?
The LORD strong and mighty,
the LORD mighty in battle.
⁹Lift up your heads, O you gates;
lift them up, you ancient doors,
that the King of glory may
come in.
¹⁰Who is he, this King of glory?
The LORD Almighty—
he is the King of glory.   *Selah*

Psalm 25ᶜ

Of David.

¹To you, O LORD, I lift up my soul;
²   in you I trust, O my God.
Do not let me be put to shame,
nor let my enemies triumph
over me.
³No one whose hope is in you
will ever be put to shame,
but they will be put to shame
who are treacherous without
excuse.

⁴Show me your ways, O LORD,
teach me your paths;
⁵guide me in your truth and teach
me,
for you are God my Savior,

and my hope is in you all day
long.
⁶Remember, O LORD, your great
mercy and love,
for they are from of old.
⁷Remember not the sins of my
youth
and my rebellious ways;
according to your love remember
me,
for you are good, O LORD.

⁸Good and upright is the LORD;
therefore he instructs sinners in
his ways.
⁹He guides the humble in what is
right
and teaches them his way.
¹⁰All the ways of the LORD are
loving and faithful
for those who keep the
demands of his covenant.
¹¹For the sake of your name,
O LORD,
forgive my iniquity, though it is
great.
¹²Who, then, is the man that fears
the LORD?
He will instruct him in the way
chosen for him.
¹³He will spend his days in
prosperity,
and his descendants will inherit
the land.
¹⁴The LORD confides in those who
fear him;
he makes his covenant known
to them.
¹⁵My eyes are ever on the LORD,
for only he will release my feet
from the snare.

¹⁶Turn to me and be gracious to me,
for I am lonely and afflicted.
¹⁷The troubles of my heart have
multiplied;
free me from my anguish.
¹⁸Look upon my affliction and my
distress
and take away all my sins.
¹⁹See how my enemies have
increased

ᵃ4 Or *swear falsely*   ᵇ6 Two Hebrew manuscripts and Syriac (see also Septuagint); most
Hebrew manuscripts *face, Jacob*   ᶜThis psalm is an acrostic poem, the verses of which begin
with the successive letters of the Hebrew alphabet.

and how fiercely they hate me!
²⁰Guard my life and rescue me;
    let me not be put to shame,
    for I take refuge in you.
²¹May integrity and uprightness
        protect me,
    because my hope is in you.

²²Redeem Israel, O God,
    from all their troubles!

Psalm 26

Of David.

¹Vindicate me, O LORD,
    for I have led a blameless life;

I have trusted in the LORD
    without wavering.
²Test me, O LORD, and try me,
    examine my heart and my
        mind;
³for your love is ever before me,
    and I walk continually in your
        truth.
⁴I do not sit with deceitful men,
    nor do I consort with
        hypocrites;
⁵I abhor the assembly of evildoers
    and refuse to sit with the
        wicked.
⁶I wash my hands in innocence,
    and go about your altar,
        O LORD,

VERSE:	AUTHOR:	PASSAGE:
Psalm 25:14	Oswald Chambers	Psalm 25:1–22

Secret Sorrows, Secret Joys

What is the sign of a friend? That he tells you secret sorrows? No, that he tells you secret joys. Many will confide to you their secret sorrows, but the last mark of intimacy is to confide secret joys. Have we ever let God tell us any of his joys, or are we telling God our secrets so continually that we leave no room for him to talk to us? At the beginning of our Christian life we are full of requests to God, then we find that God wants to get us into relationship with himself, to get us in touch with his purposes. Are we so wedded to Jesus Christ's idea of prayer — "Your will be done" — that we catch the secrets of God? The things that make God dear to us are not so much his great big blessings as the tiny things, because they show his amazing intimacy with us; he knows every detail of our individual lives.

ADDITIONAL SCRIPTURE READINGS
2 Chronicles 6:28–31; Psalm 139:1–12

Go to page 673 for your next devotional reading.

⁷proclaiming aloud your praise
    and telling of all your
        wonderful deeds.
⁸I love the house where you live,
    O Lord,
    the place where your glory
        dwells.

⁹Do not take away my soul along
        with sinners,
    my life with bloodthirsty men,
¹⁰in whose hands are wicked
        schemes,
    whose right hands are full of
        bribes.
¹¹But I lead a blameless life;
    redeem me and be merciful to
        me.

¹²My feet stand on level ground;
    in the great assembly I will
        praise the Lord.

Psalm 27

Of David.

¹The Lord is my light and my
        salvation—
    whom shall I fear?
    The Lord is the stronghold of my
        life—
    of whom shall I be afraid?
²When evil men advance against
        me
    to devour my flesh,ᵃ
    when my enemies and my foes
        attack me,
        they will stumble and fall.
³Though an army besiege me,
    my heart will not fear;
    though war break out against me,
        even then will I be confident.

⁴One thing I ask of the Lord,
    this is what I seek:
    that I may dwell in the house of
        the Lord
    all the days of my life,
    to gaze upon the beauty of the
        Lord
    and to seek him in his temple.
⁵For in the day of trouble

he will keep me safe in his
        dwelling;
    he will hide me in the shelter of
        his tabernacle
    and set me high upon a rock.
⁶Then my head will be exalted
    above the enemies who
        surround me;
    at his tabernacle will I sacrifice
        with shouts of joy;
    I will sing and make music to
        the Lord.

⁷Hear my voice when I call,
    O Lord;
    be merciful to me and answer
        me.
⁸My heart says of you, "Seek hisᵇ
        face!"
    Your face, Lord, I will seek.
⁹Do not hide your face from me,
    do not turn your servant away
        in anger;
    you have been my helper.
    Do not reject me or forsake me,
        O God my Savior.
¹⁰Though my father and mother
        forsake me,
    the Lord will receive me.
¹¹Teach me your way, O Lord;
    lead me in a straight path
    because of my oppressors.
¹²Do not turn me over to the desire
        of my foes,
    for false witnesses rise up
        against me,
    breathing out violence.

¹³I am still confident of this:
    I will see the goodness of the
        Lord
    in the land of the living.
¹⁴Wait for the Lord;
    be strong and take heart
    and wait for the Lord.

Psalm 28

Of David.

¹To you I call, O Lord my Rock;
    do not turn a deaf ear to me.
    For if you remain silent,

ᵃ2 Or to slander me   ᵇ8 Or To you, O my heart, he has said, "Seek my

I will be like those who have
  gone down to the pit.
²Hear my cry for mercy
  as I call to you for help,
as I lift up my hands
  toward your Most Holy Place.

³Do not drag me away with the
    wicked,
  with those who do evil,
who speak cordially with their
    neighbors
  but harbor malice in their
    hearts.
⁴Repay them for their deeds
  and for their evil work;
repay them for what their hands
    have done
  and bring back upon them what
    they deserve.
⁵Since they show no regard for the
    works of the LORD
  and what his hands have done,
he will tear them down
  and never build them up again.

⁶Praise be to the LORD,
  for he has heard my cry for
    mercy.
⁷The LORD is my strength and my
    shield;
  my heart trusts in him, and I
    am helped.
My heart leaps for joy
  and I will give thanks to him in
    song.

⁸The LORD is the strength of his
    people,
  a fortress of salvation for his
    anointed one.
⁹Save your people and bless your
    inheritance;
  be their shepherd and carry
    them forever.

Psalm 29

A psalm of David.

¹Ascribe to the LORD, O mighty
    ones,
  ascribe to the LORD glory and
    strength.
²Ascribe to the LORD the glory due
    his name;
  worship the LORD in the
    splendor of his^a holiness.
³The voice of the LORD is over the
    waters;
  the God of glory thunders,
  the LORD thunders over the
    mighty waters.
⁴The voice of the LORD is powerful;
  the voice of the LORD is majestic.
⁵The voice of the LORD breaks the
    cedars;
  the LORD breaks in pieces the
    cedars of Lebanon.
⁶He makes Lebanon skip like a calf,
  Sirion^b like a young wild ox.
⁷The voice of the LORD strikes
  with flashes of lightning.
⁸The voice of the LORD shakes the
    desert;
  the LORD shakes the Desert of
    Kadesh.
⁹The voice of the LORD twists the
    oaks^c
  and strips the forests bare.
And in his temple all cry, "Glory!"

¹⁰The LORD sits^d enthroned over the
    flood;
  the LORD is enthroned as King
    forever.
¹¹The LORD gives strength to his
    people;
  the LORD blesses his people with
    peace.

Psalm 30

A psalm. A song. For the dedication
  of the temple.^{e} Of David.

¹I will exalt you, O LORD,
  for you lifted me out of the
    depths
  and did not let my enemies
    gloat over me.
²O LORD my God, I called to you
    for help
  and you healed me.
³O LORD, you brought me up from
    the grave^f;

---

^{a}2 Or LORD with the splendor of ^{b}6 That is, Mount Hermon ^{c}9 Or LORD makes the deer give
birth ^{d}10 Or sat ^{e}Title: Or palace ^{f}3 Hebrew Sheol

you spared me from going
    down into the pit.

4Sing to the LORD, you saints of his;
    praise his holy name.
5For his anger lasts only a moment,
    but his favor lasts a lifetime;
weeping may remain for a night,
    but rejoicing comes in the
        morning.

6When I felt secure, I said,
    "I will never be shaken."
7O LORD, when you favored me,
    you made my mountain*a* stand
        firm;
but when you hid your face,
    I was dismayed.

8To you, O LORD, I called;
    to the Lord I cried for mercy:
9"What gain is there in my
        destruction,*b*
    in my going down into the pit?
Will the dust praise you?
    Will it proclaim your
        faithfulness?
10Hear, O LORD, and be merciful to
        me;
    O LORD, be my help."

11You turned my wailing into
        dancing;
    you removed my sackcloth and
        clothed me with joy,
12that my heart may sing to you
        and not be silent.
    O LORD my God, I will give you
        thanks forever.

Psalm 31

For the director of music. A psalm
of David.

1In you, O LORD, I have taken
        refuge;
    let me never be put to shame;
    deliver me in your
        righteousness.
2Turn your ear to me,
    come quickly to my rescue;
be my rock of refuge,
    a strong fortress to save me.

3Since you are my rock and my
        fortress,
    for the sake of your name lead
        and guide me.
4Free me from the trap that is set
        for me,
    for you are my refuge.
5Into your hands I commit my
        spirit;
    redeem me, O LORD, the God of
        truth.

6I hate those who cling to
        worthless idols;
    I trust in the LORD.
7I will be glad and rejoice in your
        love,
    for you saw my affliction
    and knew the anguish of my
        soul.
8You have not handed me over to
        the enemy
    but have set my feet in a
        spacious place.

9Be merciful to me, O LORD, for I
        am in distress;
    my eyes grow weak with
        sorrow,
    my soul and my body with
        grief.
10My life is consumed by anguish
    and my years by groaning;
my strength fails because of my
        affliction,*c*
    and my bones grow weak.
11Because of all my enemies,
    I am the utter contempt of my
        neighbors;
I am a dread to my friends—
    those who see me on the street
        flee from me.
12I am forgotten by them as though
        I were dead;
    I have become like broken
        pottery.
13For I hear the slander of many;
    there is terror on every side;
they conspire against me
    and plot to take my life.

14But I trust in you, O LORD;
    I say, "You are my God."

---

a7 Or *hill country*   b9 Or *there if I am silenced*   c10 Or *guilt*

¹⁵My times are in your hands;
  deliver me from my enemies
  and from those who pursue me.
¹⁶Let your face shine on your
    servant;
  save me in your unfailing love.
¹⁷Let me not be put to shame,
    O LORD,
  for I have cried out to you;

but let the wicked be put to
    shame
  and lie silent in the grave.ᵃ
¹⁸Let their lying lips be silenced,
  for with pride and contempt
  they speak arrogantly against
    the righteous.

¹⁹How great is your goodness,

ᵃ17 Hebrew *Sheol*

VERSE: AUTHOR: PASSAGE:
Psalm 31:10   Charles L. Allen   Psalm 31:1–16

Are You Lonely Today?

Loneliness is a fact of life. Nature created people for relationships. It is normal for all creatures, including humans, to reach out beyond themselves.

We sometimes feel that only aging people are lonely.
The fact is all people feel loneliness. Loneliness comes
when we feel separated or that something is missing . . .
Keep in mind:

1. It is good to admit it when we feel lonely—at least,
do not hide it from yourself.

2. Sometimes you need to express your feelings of loneliness—cry, talk out loud to yourself, talk with someone
about it, such as a neighbor, friend, counselor or pastor.

3. Check to see when you feel lonely. Fatigue, lack of
exercise or poor diet are some of the instigators of loneliness.

4. Remember that our spiritual life is closely associated
with whether or not we feel lonely. A sense of the presence of God is of supreme importance. If we can transform our loneliness into solitude, we then have time and
space for God.

ADDITIONAL SCRIPTURE READINGS
Joshua 31:1–8; Psalm 25

Go to page 675 for your next devotional reading.

which you have stored up for
those who fear you,
which you bestow in the sight of
men
on those who take refuge in
you.
20In the shelter of your presence
you hide them
from the intrigues of men;
in your dwelling you keep them
safe
from accusing tongues.

21Praise be to the LORD,
for he showed his wonderful
love to me
when I was in a besieged city.
22In my alarm I said,
"I am cut off from your sight!"
Yet you heard my cry for mercy
when I called to you for help.

23Love the LORD, all his saints!
The LORD preserves the faithful,
but the proud he pays back in
full.
24Be strong and take heart,
all you who hope in the LORD.

Psalm 32

Of David. A *maskil.*[a]

1Blessed is he
whose transgressions are
forgiven,
whose sins are covered.
2Blessed is the man
whose sin the LORD does not
count against him
and in whose spirit is no deceit.

3When I kept silent,
my bones wasted away
through my groaning all day
long.
4For day and night
your hand was heavy upon me;
my strength was sapped
as in the heat of summer.   *Selah*
5Then I acknowledged my sin to
you
and did not cover up my
iniquity.

I said, "I will confess
my transgressions to the
LORD"—
and you forgave
the guilt of my sin.   *Selah*

6Therefore let everyone who is
godly pray to you
while you may be found;
surely when the mighty waters
rise,
they will not reach him.
7You are my hiding place;
you will protect me from
trouble
and surround me with songs of
deliverance.   *Selah*

8I will instruct you and teach you
in the way you should go;
I will counsel you and watch
over you.
9Do not be like the horse or the
mule,
which have no understanding
but must be controlled by bit and
bridle
or they will not come to you.
10Many are the woes of the wicked,
but the LORD's unfailing love
surrounds the man who trusts
in him.

11Rejoice in the LORD and be glad,
you righteous;
sing, all you who are upright in
heart!

Psalm 33

1Sing joyfully to the LORD, you
righteous;
it is fitting for the upright to
praise him.
2Praise the LORD with the harp;
make music to him on the
ten-stringed lyre.
3Sing to him a new song;
play skillfully, and shout for
joy.

4For the word of the LORD is right
and true;
he is faithful in all he does.

aTitle: Probably a literary or musical term

PASSAGE: Psalm 32; Psalm 142
AUTHOR: Dietrich Bonhoeffer

Help Me to Pray

O God, early in the morning I cry to you.
Help me to pray,
    and to concentrate my thoughts on you:
I cannot do this alone.

In me there is darkness,
But with you there is light;
I am lonely,
    but you do not leave me;
I am feeble in heart,
    but with you there is help;
I am restless,
    but with you there is peace.
In me there is bitterness,
    but with you there is patience;
I do not understand your ways,
    but you know the way for me.

Restore me to liberty,
And enable me so to live now
    that I may answer before you and before me.
Lord, whatever this day may bring,
Your name be praised.

Go to page 678 for your next devotional reading.

⁵The LORD loves righteousness and justice;
the earth is full of his unfailing love.

⁶By the word of the LORD were the heavens made,
their starry host by the breath of his mouth.
⁷He gathers the waters of the sea into jars*a*;
he puts the deep into storehouses.
⁸Let all the earth fear the LORD;
let all the people of the world revere him.
⁹For he spoke, and it came to be;
he commanded, and it stood firm.
¹⁰The LORD foils the plans of the nations;
he thwarts the purposes of the peoples.
¹¹But the plans of the LORD stand firm forever,
the purposes of his heart through all generations.

¹²Blessed is the nation whose God is the LORD,
the people he chose for his inheritance.
¹³From heaven the LORD looks down and sees all mankind;
¹⁴from his dwelling place he watches
all who live on earth—
¹⁵he who forms the hearts of all,
who considers everything they do.

¹⁶No king is saved by the size of his army;
no warrior escapes by his great strength.
¹⁷A horse is a vain hope for deliverance;
despite all its great strength it cannot save.
¹⁸But the eyes of the LORD are on those who fear him,
on those whose hope is in his unfailing love,

¹⁹to deliver them from death
and keep them alive in famine.

²⁰We wait in hope for the LORD;
he is our help and our shield.
²¹In him our hearts rejoice,
for we trust in his holy name.
²²May your unfailing love rest upon us, O LORD,
even as we put our hope in you.

Psalm 34*b*

Of David. When he pretended to be insane before Abimelech, who drove him away, and he left.

¹I will extol the LORD at all times;
his praise will always be on my lips.
²My soul will boast in the LORD;
let the afflicted hear and rejoice.
³Glorify the LORD with me;
let us exalt his name together.

⁴I sought the LORD, and he answered me;
he delivered me from all my fears.
⁵Those who look to him are radiant;
their faces are never covered with shame.
⁶This poor man called, and the LORD heard him;
he saved him out of all his troubles.
⁷The angel of the LORD encamps around those who fear him,
and he delivers them.

⁸Taste and see that the LORD is good;
blessed is the man who takes refuge in him.
⁹Fear the LORD, you his saints,
for those who fear him lack nothing.
¹⁰The lions may grow weak and hungry,
but those who seek the LORD lack no good thing.

---

*a*7 Or *sea as into a heap*   *b*This psalm is an acrostic poem, the verses of which begin with the successive letters of the Hebrew alphabet.

¹¹Come, my children, listen to me;
    I will teach you the fear of the
      LORD.
¹²Whoever of you loves life
    and desires to see many good
      days,
¹³keep your tongue from evil
    and your lips from speaking
      lies.
¹⁴Turn from evil and do good;
    seek peace and pursue it.

¹⁵The eyes of the LORD are on the
      righteous
    and his ears are attentive to
      their cry;
¹⁶the face of the LORD is against
      those who do evil,
    to cut off the memory of them
      from the earth.

¹⁷The righteous cry out, and the
      LORD hears them;
    he delivers them from all their
      troubles.
¹⁸The LORD is close to the
      brokenhearted
    and saves those who are
      crushed in spirit.

¹⁹A righteous man may have many
      troubles,
    but the LORD delivers him from
      them all;
²⁰he protects all his bones,
    not one of them will be broken.

²¹Evil will slay the wicked;
    the foes of the righteous will be
      condemned.
²²The LORD redeems his servants;
    no one will be condemned who
      takes refuge in him.

Psalm 35

Of David.

¹Contend, O LORD, with those who
      contend with me;
    fight against those who fight
      against me.
²Take up shield and buckler;
    arise and come to my aid.
³Brandish spear and javelin*ᵃ*

against those who pursue me.
Say to my soul,
    "I am your salvation."

⁴May those who seek my life
    be disgraced and put to shame;
may those who plot my ruin
    be turned back in dismay.
⁵May they be like chaff before the
      wind,
    with the angel of the LORD
      driving them away;
⁶may their path be dark and
      slippery,
    with the angel of the LORD
      pursuing them.
⁷Since they hid their net for me
      without cause
    and without cause dug a pit for
      me,
⁸may ruin overtake them by
      surprise—
    may the net they hid entangle
      them,
    may they fall into the pit, to
      their ruin.
⁹Then my soul will rejoice in the
      LORD
    and delight in his salvation.
¹⁰My whole being will exclaim,
    "Who is like you, O LORD?
You rescue the poor from those
      too strong for them,
    the poor and needy from those
      who rob them."

¹¹Ruthless witnesses come forward;
    they question me on things I
      know nothing about.
¹²They repay me evil for good
    and leave my soul forlorn.
¹³Yet when they were ill, I put on
      sackcloth
    and humbled myself with
      fasting.
When my prayers returned to me
      unanswered,
¹⁴   I went about mourning
    as though for my friend or
      brother.
I bowed my head in grief
    as though weeping for my
      mother.

ᵃ3 Or *and block the way*

VERSE:	AUTHOR:	PASSAGE:
Psalm 34:2	Jean Shaw	Psalm 34:1–22

The Hope of the Afflicted

"Liberty and justice for all" is not a reality. Many people have neither the strength, tenacity nor money to fight the wickedness that curtails their personal liberty. Since wickedness also exists in the place of judgment—the court system itself is not immune to corruption—the effects of crime run the gamut from frustration to annoyance to sheer terror and eventual physical assault. Older people are especially vulnerable.

All of this does not go unnoticed by God. He promises that the righteous and the wicked will be brought to judgment. Whatever may go amiss in the legal process down here, we are all going to have our day in God's court. Like Job, we may cry out, "Why does the Almighty not set times for judgment? Why must those who know him look in vain for such days?" (Job 24:1). God answers through David. "The LORD is known by his justice; the wicked are ensnared by the work of their hands. The wicked return to the grave, all the nations that forget God. But the needy will not always be forgotten, nor the hope of the afflicted ever perish" (Psalm 9:16–18).

Our timing for retribution may not agree with God's, but we have the assurance that "there will be a time" (Ecclesiastes 3:17). Meanwhile we can find patience and strength in prayer, both for ourselves and those with the responsibility to protect us.

ADDITIONAL SCRIPTURE READINGS
Psalm 9; Isaiah 49:8–18

Go to page 688 for your next devotional reading.

¹⁵But when I stumbled, they
  gathered in glee;
  attackers gathered against me
  when I was unaware.
  They slandered me without
  ceasing.
¹⁶Like the ungodly they maliciously
  mocked*;
  they gnashed their teeth at me.
¹⁷O Lord, how long will you look
  on?
  Rescue my life from their
  ravages,
  my precious life from these
  lions.
¹⁸I will give you thanks in the great
  assembly;
  among throngs of people I will
  praise you.

¹⁹Let not those gloat over me
  who are my enemies without
  cause;
  let not those who hate me without
  reason
  maliciously wink the eye.
²⁰They do not speak peaceably,
  but devise false accusations
  against those who live quietly
  in the land.
²¹They gape at me and say, "Aha!
  Aha!
  With our own eyes we have
  seen it."

²²O LORD, you have seen this; be not
  silent.
  Do not be far from me, O Lord.
²³Awake, and rise to my defense!
  Contend for me, my God and
  Lord.
²⁴Vindicate me in your
  righteousness, O LORD my
  God;
  do not let them gloat over me.
²⁵Do not let them think, "Aha, just
  what we wanted!"
  or say, "We have swallowed
  him up."

²⁶May all who gloat over my
  distress
  be put to shame and confusion;

may all who exalt themselves over
  me
  be clothed with shame and
  disgrace.
²⁷May those who delight in my
  vindication
  shout for joy and gladness;
  may they always say, "The LORD
  be exalted,
  who delights in the well-being
  of his servant."
²⁸My tongue will speak of your
  righteousness
  and of your praises all day
  long.

Psalm 36

For the director of music. Of David
the servant of the LORD.

¹An oracle is within my heart
  concerning the sinfulness of the
  wicked:*
There is no fear of God
  before his eyes.
²For in his own eyes he flatters
  himself
  too much to detect or hate his
  sin.
³The words of his mouth are
  wicked and deceitful;
  he has ceased to be wise and to
  do good.
⁴Even on his bed he plots evil;
  he commits himself to a sinful
  course
  and does not reject what is
  wrong.

⁵Your love, O LORD, reaches to the
  heavens,
  your faithfulness to the skies.
⁶Your righteousness is like the
  mighty mountains,
  your justice like the great deep.
O LORD, you preserve both man
  and beast.
⁷ How priceless is your unfailing
  love!
Both high and low among men
  find* refuge in the shadow of
  your wings.

---

*16 Septuagint; Hebrew may mean *ungodly circle of mockers.*   *1 Or *heart: | Sin proceeds from the wicked.*   *7 Or *love, O God! | Men find*; or *love! | Both heavenly beings and men | find*

⁸They feast on the abundance of
    your house;
  you give them drink from your
    river of delights.
⁹For with you is the fountain of
    life;
  in your light we see light.

¹⁰Continue your love to those who
    know you,
  your righteousness to the
    upright in heart.
¹¹May the foot of the proud not
    come against me,
  nor the hand of the wicked
    drive me away.
¹²See how the evildoers lie fallen—
  thrown down, not able to rise!

Psalm 37*ᵃ*

Of David.

¹Do not fret because of evil men
  or be envious of those who do
    wrong;
²for like the grass they will soon
    wither,
  like green plants they will soon
    die away.

³Trust in the LORD and do good;
  dwell in the land and enjoy safe
    pasture.
⁴Delight yourself in the LORD
  and he will give you the desires
    of your heart.

⁵Commit your way to the LORD;
  trust in him and he will do this:
⁶He will make your righteousness
    shine like the dawn,
  the justice of your cause like the
    noonday sun.

⁷Be still before the LORD and wait
    patiently for him;
  do not fret when men succeed
    in their ways,
  when they carry out their
    wicked schemes.

⁸Refrain from anger and turn from
    wrath;

do not fret—it leads only to
    evil.
⁹For evil men will be cut off,
  but those who hope in the LORD
    will inherit the land.

¹⁰A little while, and the wicked will
    be no more;
  though you look for them, they
    will not be found.
¹¹But the meek will inherit the land
  and enjoy great peace.

¹²The wicked plot against the
    righteous
  and gnash their teeth at them;
¹³but the Lord laughs at the wicked
  for he knows their day is
    coming.

¹⁴The wicked draw the sword
  and bend the bow
to bring down the poor and
    needy,
  to slay those whose ways are
    upright.
¹⁵But their swords will pierce their
    own hearts,
  and their bows will be broken.

¹⁶Better the little that the righteous
    have
  than the wealth of many
    wicked;
¹⁷for the power of the wicked will
    be broken,
  but the LORD upholds the
    righteous.

¹⁸The days of the blameless are
    known to the LORD,
  and their inheritance will
    endure forever.
¹⁹In times of disaster they will not
    wither;
  in days of famine they will
    enjoy plenty.

²⁰But the wicked will perish:
  The LORD's enemies will be like
    the beauty of the fields,
  they will vanish—vanish like
    smoke.

---

*ᵃ*This psalm is an acrostic poem, the stanzas of which begin with the successive letters of the
Hebrew alphabet.

²¹The wicked borrow and do not
  repay,
    but the righteous give
      generously;
²²those the LORD blesses will inherit
  the land,
    but those he curses will be cut
      off.

²³If the LORD delights in a man's
  way,
    he makes his steps firm;
²⁴though he stumble, he will not
  fall,
    for the LORD upholds him with
      his hand.

²⁵I was young and now I am old,
    yet I have never seen the
      righteous forsaken
  or their children begging bread.
²⁶They are always generous and
  lend freely;
    their children will be blessed.

²⁷Turn from evil and do good;
    then you will dwell in the land
      forever.
²⁸For the LORD loves the just
    and will not forsake his faithful
      ones.

They will be protected forever,
    but the offspring of the wicked
      will be cut off;
²⁹the righteous will inherit the land
    and dwell in it forever.

³⁰The mouth of the righteous man
  utters wisdom,
    and his tongue speaks what is
      just.
³¹The law of his God is in his heart;
    his feet do not slip.

³²The wicked lie in wait for the
  righteous,
    seeking their very lives;
³³but the LORD will not leave them
  in their power
    or let them be condemned when
      brought to trial.

³⁴Wait for the LORD
    and keep his way.

He will exalt you to inherit the
  land;
    when the wicked are cut off,
      you will see it.

³⁵I have seen a wicked and ruthless
  man
    flourishing like a green tree in
      its native soil,
³⁶but he soon passed away and was
  no more;
    though I looked for him, he
      could not be found.

³⁷Consider the blameless, observe
  the upright;
    there is a future[a] for the man
      of peace.
³⁸But all sinners will be destroyed;
    the future[b] of the wicked will
      be cut off.

³⁹The salvation of the righteous
    comes from the LORD;
  he is their stronghold in time of
    trouble.
⁴⁰The LORD helps them and delivers
  them;
    he delivers them from the
      wicked and saves them,
  because they take refuge in him.

Psalm 38

A psalm of David. A petition.

¹O LORD, do not rebuke me in your
  anger
    or discipline me in your wrath.
²For your arrows have pierced me,
    and your hand has come down
      upon me.
³Because of your wrath there is no
  health in my body;
    my bones have no soundness
      because of my sin.
⁴My guilt has overwhelmed me
    like a burden too heavy to bear.

⁵My wounds fester and are
  loathsome
    because of my sinful folly.

ᵃ37 Or there will be posterity   ᵇ38 Or posterity

⁶I am bowed down and brought
    very low;
  all day long I go about
    mourning.
⁷My back is filled with searing
    pain;
  there is no health in my body.
⁸I am feeble and utterly crushed;
  I groan in anguish of heart.

⁹All my longings lie open before
    you, O Lord;
  my sighing is not hidden from
    you.
¹⁰My heart pounds, my strength
    fails me;
  even the light has gone from
    my eyes.
¹¹My friends and companions avoid
    me because of my wounds;
  my neighbors stay far away.
¹²Those who seek my life set their
    traps,
  those who would harm me talk
    of my ruin;
  all day long they plot deception.

¹³I am like a deaf man, who cannot
    hear,
  like a mute, who cannot open
    his mouth;
¹⁴I have become like a man who
    does not hear,
  whose mouth can offer no
    reply.
¹⁵I wait for you, O Lord;
  you will answer, O Lord my
    God.
¹⁶For I said, "Do not let them gloat
  or exalt themselves over me
    when my foot slips."

¹⁷For I am about to fall,
  and my pain is ever with me.
¹⁸I confess my iniquity;
  I am troubled by my sin.
¹⁹Many are those who are my
    vigorous enemies;
  those who hate me without
    reason are numerous.
²⁰Those who repay my good with
    evil
  slander me when I pursue what
    is good.

²¹O Lord, do not forsake me;
  be not far from me, O my God.

²²Come quickly to help me,
  O Lord my Savior.

Psalm 39

For the director of music. For
Jeduthun. A psalm of David.

¹I said, "I will watch my ways
  and keep my tongue from sin;
  I will put a muzzle on my mouth
    as long as the wicked are in my
      presence."
²But when I was silent and still,
  not even saying anything good,
    my anguish increased.
³My heart grew hot within me,
  and as I meditated, the fire
    burned;
  then I spoke with my tongue:

⁴"Show me, O Lord, my life's end
  and the number of my days;
  let me know how fleeting is my
    life.
⁵You have made my days a mere
    handbreadth;
  the span of my years is as
    nothing before you.
  Each man's life is but a breath.
                                    Selah
⁶Man is a mere phantom as he
    goes to and fro:
  He bustles about, but only in
    vain;
  he heaps up wealth, not
    knowing who will get it.

⁷"But now, Lord, what do I look
    for?
  My hope is in you.
⁸Save me from all my
    transgressions;
  do not make me the scorn of
    fools.
⁹I was silent; I would not open my
    mouth,
  for you are the one who has
    done this.
¹⁰Remove your scourge from me;
  I am overcome by the blow of
    your hand.
¹¹You rebuke and discipline men for
    their sin;

you consume their wealth like a
    moth—
each man is but a breath.   *Selah*

[12]"Hear my prayer, O LORD,
    listen to my cry for help;
    be not deaf to my weeping.
For I dwell with you as an alien,
    a stranger, as all my fathers
        were.
[13]Look away from me, that I may
        rejoice again
    before I depart and am no
        more."

Psalm 40

For the director of music. Of David.
A psalm.

[1]I waited patiently for the LORD;
    he turned to me and heard my
        cry.
[2]He lifted me out of the slimy pit,
    out of the mud and mire;
he set my feet on a rock
    and gave me a firm place to
        stand.
[3]He put a new song in my mouth,
    a hymn of praise to our God.
Many will see and fear
    and put their trust in the LORD.

[4]Blessed is the man
    who makes the LORD his trust,
who does not look to the proud,
    to those who turn aside to false
        gods.[a]
[5]Many, O LORD my God,
    are the wonders you have done.
The things you planned for us
    no one can recount to you;
were I to speak and tell of them,
    they would be too many to
        declare.

[6]Sacrifice and offering you did not
        desire,
    but my ears you have
        pierced[b,c];
burnt offerings and sin offerings

you did not require.
[7]Then I said, "Here I am, I have
        come—
    it is written about me in the
        scroll.[d]
[8]I desire to do your will, O my
        God;
    your law is within my heart."

[9]I proclaim righteousness in the
        great assembly;
    I do not seal my lips,
    as you know, O LORD.
[10]I do not hide your righteousness
        in my heart;
    I speak of your faithfulness and
        salvation.
I do not conceal your love and
        your truth
    from the great assembly.

[11]Do not withhold your mercy from
        me, O LORD;
    may your love and your truth
        always protect me.
[12]For troubles without number
        surround me;
    my sins have overtaken me, and
        I cannot see.
They are more than the hairs of
        my head,
    and my heart fails within me.

[13]Be pleased, O LORD, to save me;
    O LORD, come quickly to help
        me.
[14]May all who seek to take my life
    be put to shame and confusion;
may all who desire my ruin
    be turned back in disgrace.
[15]May those who say to me, "Aha!
        Aha!"
    be appalled at their own shame.
[16]But may all who seek you
    rejoice and be glad in you;
may those who love your
        salvation always say,
    "The LORD be exalted!"

[17]Yet I am poor and needy;
    may the Lord think of me.
You are my help and my
        deliverer;
    O my God, do not delay.

---

[a]4 Or *to falsehood*   [b]6 Hebrew; Septuagint *but a body you have prepared for me* (see also
Symmachus and Theodotion)   [c]6 Or *opened*   [d]7 Or *come | with the scroll written for me*

Psalm 41

For the director of music. A psalm
of David.

[1]Blessed is he who has regard for
the weak;
    the LORD delivers him in times
of trouble.
[2]The LORD will protect him and
preserve his life;
    he will bless him in the land
    and not surrender him to the
desire of his foes.
[3]The LORD will sustain him on his
sickbed
    and restore him from his bed of
illness.

[4]I said, "O LORD, have mercy on
me;
    heal me, for I have sinned
against you."
[5]My enemies say of me in malice,
    "When will he die and his name
perish?"
[6]Whenever one comes to see me,
    he speaks falsely, while his
heart gathers slander;
    then he goes out and spreads it
abroad.

[7]All my enemies whisper together
against me;
    they imagine the worst for me,
saying,
[8]"A vile disease has beset him;
    he will never get up from the
place where he lies."
[9]Even my close friend, whom I
trusted,
    he who shared my bread,
    has lifted up his heel against
me.

[10]But you, O LORD, have mercy on
me;
    raise me up, that I may repay
them.
[11]I know that you are pleased with
me,
    for my enemy does not triumph
over me.

[12]In my integrity you uphold me
    and set me in your presence
forever.

[13]Praise be to the LORD, the God of
Israel,
    from everlasting to everlasting.
    Amen and Amen.

BOOK II

Psalms 42–72

Psalm 42[a]

For the director of music. A *maskil*[b]
of the Sons of Korah.

[1]As the deer pants for streams of
water,
    so my soul pants for you,
    O God.
[2]My soul thirsts for God, for the
living God.
    When can I go and meet with
God?
[3]My tears have been my food
day and night,
    while men say to me all day long,
    "Where is your God?"
[4]These things I remember
as I pour out my soul:
    how I used to go with the
multitude,
    leading the procession to the
house of God,
with shouts of joy and
thanksgiving
    among the festive throng.

[5]Why are you downcast, O my
soul?
    Why so disturbed within me?
Put your hope in God,
    for I will yet praise him,
    my Savior and [6]my God.

My[c] soul is downcast within me;
    therefore I will remember you
from the land of the Jordan,
    the heights of Hermon—from
Mount Mizar.
[7]Deep calls to deep

---

[a]In many Hebrew manuscripts Psalms 42 and 43 constitute one psalm.   [b]Title: Probably a
literary or musical term   [c]5,6 A few Hebrew manuscripts, Septuagint and Syriac; most
Hebrew manuscripts *praise him for his saving help. / 6O my God, my*

in the roar of your waterfalls;
all your waves and breakers
have swept over me.

[8]By day the LORD directs his love,
    at night his song is with me—
    a prayer to the God of my life.

[9]I say to God my Rock,
    "Why have you forgotten me?
Why must I go about mourning,
    oppressed by the enemy?"
[10]My bones suffer mortal agony
    as my foes taunt me,
saying to me all day long,
    "Where is your God?"

[11]Why are you downcast, O my
        soul?
    Why so disturbed within me?
Put your hope in God,
    for I will yet praise him,
    my Savior and my God.

Psalm 43[a]

[1]Vindicate me, O God,
    and plead my cause against an
        ungodly nation;
    rescue me from deceitful and
        wicked men.
[2]You are God my stronghold.
    Why have you rejected me?
Why must I go about mourning,
    oppressed by the enemy?
[3]Send forth your light and your
        truth,
    let them guide me;
let them bring me to your holy
        mountain,
    to the place where you dwell.
[4]Then will I go to the altar of God,
    to God, my joy and my delight.
I will praise you with the harp,
    O God, my God.

[5]Why are you downcast, O my
        soul?
    Why so disturbed within me?
Put your hope in God,
    for I will yet praise him,
    my Savior and my God.

Psalm 44

For the director of music. Of the Sons
    of Korah. A *maskil*.[b]

[1]We have heard with our ears,
        O God;
    our fathers have told us
what you did in their days,
    in days long ago.
[2]With your hand you drove out the
        nations
    and planted our fathers;
you crushed the peoples
    and made our fathers flourish.
[3]It was not by their sword that
        they won the land,
    nor did their arm bring them
        victory;
it was your right hand, your arm,
    and the light of your face, for
        you loved them.

[4]You are my King and my God,
    who decrees[c] victories for
        Jacob.
[5]Through you we push back our
        enemies;
    through your name we trample
        our foes.
[6]I do not trust in my bow,
    my sword does not bring me
        victory;
[7]but you give us victory over our
        enemies,
    you put our adversaries to
        shame.
[8]In God we make our boast all day
        long,
    and we will praise your name
        forever.   *Selah*

[9]But now you have rejected and
        humbled us;
    you no longer go out with our
        armies.
[10]You made us retreat before the
        enemy,
    and our adversaries have
        plundered us.
[11]You gave us up to be devoured
        like sheep

---

[a]In many Hebrew manuscripts Psalms 42 and 43 constitute one psalm.   [b]Title: Probably a
literary or musical term   [c]4 Septuagint, Aquila and Syriac; Hebrew *King, O God; / command*

and have scattered us among
    the nations.
¹²You sold your people for a
    pittance,
    gaining nothing from their sale.

¹³You have made us a reproach to
    our neighbors,
    the scorn and derision of those
      around us.
¹⁴You have made us a byword
    among the nations;
    the peoples shake their heads at
      us.
¹⁵My disgrace is before me all day
    long,
    and my face is covered with
      shame
¹⁶at the taunts of those who
      reproach and revile me,
    because of the enemy, who is
      bent on revenge.

¹⁷All this happened to us,
    though we had not forgotten
      you
    or been false to your covenant.
¹⁸Our hearts had not turned back;
    our feet had not strayed from
      your path.
¹⁹But you crushed us and made us
    a haunt for jackals
    and covered us over with deep
      darkness.

²⁰If we had forgotten the name of
    our God
    or spread out our hands to a
      foreign god,
²¹would not God have discovered it,
    since he knows the secrets of
      the heart?
²²Yet for your sake we face death all
    day long;
    we are considered as sheep to
      be slaughtered.

²³Awake, O Lord! Why do you
    sleep?
    Rouse yourself! Do not reject us
      forever.
²⁴Why do you hide your face
    and forget our misery and
      oppression?

²⁵We are brought down to the dust;
    our bodies cling to the ground.
²⁶Rise up and help us;
    redeem us because of your
      unfailing love.

Psalm 45

For the director of music. To ⌊the
tune of⌋ "Lilies." Of the Sons of
Korah. A *maskil*.ᵃ A wedding song.

¹My heart is stirred by a noble
    theme
    as I recite my verses for the
      king;
    my tongue is the pen of a
      skillful writer.

²You are the most excellent of men
    and your lips have been
      anointed with grace,
    since God has blessed you
      forever.
³Gird your sword upon your side,
    O mighty one;
    clothe yourself with splendor
      and majesty.
⁴In your majesty ride forth
    victoriously
    in behalf of truth, humility and
      righteousness;
    let your right hand display
      awesome deeds.
⁵Let your sharp arrows pierce the
    hearts of the king's
      enemies;
    let the nations fall beneath your
      feet.
⁶Your throne, O God, will last for
    ever and ever;
    a scepter of justice will be the
      scepter of your kingdom.
⁷You love righteousness and hate
    wickedness;
    therefore God, your God, has
      set you above your
      companions
    by anointing you with the oil of
      joy.
⁸All your robes are fragrant with
    myrrh and aloes and
      cassia;

ᵃTitle: Probably a literary or musical term

from palaces adorned with
ivory
the music of the strings makes
you glad.
⁹Daughters of kings are among
your honored women;
at your right hand is the royal
bride in gold of Ophir.

¹⁰Listen, O daughter, consider and
give ear:
Forget your people and your
father's house.
¹¹The king is enthralled by your
beauty;
honor him, for he is your lord.
¹²The Daughter of Tyre will come
with a gift,ᵃ
men of wealth will seek your
favor.

¹³All glorious is the princess within
⌞her chamber⌟;
her gown is interwoven with
gold.
¹⁴In embroidered garments she is
led to the king;
her virgin companions follow
her
and are brought to you.
¹⁵They are led in with joy and
gladness;
they enter the palace of the
king.

¹⁶Your sons will take the place of
your fathers;
you will make them princes
throughout the land.
¹⁷I will perpetuate your memory
through all generations;
therefore the nations will praise
you for ever and ever.

Psalm 46

For the director of music. Of the Sons
of Korah. According to *alamoth.*ᵇ
A song.

¹God is our refuge and strength,
an ever-present help in trouble.
²Therefore we will not fear, though
the earth give way

and the mountains fall into the
heart of the sea,
³though its waters roar and foam
and the mountains quake with
their surging.   *Selah*

⁴There is a river whose streams
make glad the city of God,
the holy place where the Most
High dwells.
⁵God is within her, she will not
fall;
God will help her at break of
day.
⁶Nations are in uproar, kingdoms
fall;
he lifts his voice, the earth
melts.

⁷The LORD Almighty is with us;
the God of Jacob is our fortress.
Selah

⁸Come and see the works of the
LORD,
the desolations he has brought
on the earth.
⁹He makes wars cease to the ends
of the earth;
he breaks the bow and shatters
the spear,
he burns the shieldsᶜ with fire.
¹⁰"Be still, and know that I am God;
I will be exalted among the
nations,
I will be exalted in the earth."

¹¹The LORD Almighty is with us;
the God of Jacob is our fortress.
Selah

Psalm 47

For the director of music. Of the Sons
of Korah. A psalm.

¹Clap your hands, all you nations;
shout to God with cries of joy.
²How awesome is the LORD Most
High,
the great King over all the
earth!
³He subdued nations under us,
peoples under our feet.
⁴He chose our inheritance for us,

ᵃ12 Or *A Tyrian robe is among the gifts*   ᵇTitle: Probably a musical term   ᶜ9 Or *chariots*

the pride of Jacob, whom he
   loved.   *Selah*

⁵God has ascended amid shouts of
   joy,
   the LORD amid the sounding of
      trumpets.

⁶Sing praises to God, sing praises;
   sing praises to our King, sing
      praises.

⁷For God is the King of all the
   earth;
   sing to him a psalm*ᵃ* of praise.

ᵃ7 Or *a maskil* (probably a literary or musical term)

VERSE:	AUTHORS:	PASSAGE:
Psalm 46:10	Winfield Arn & Charles Arn	Psalm 46:1–11

When Change Happens to You

We can expect change. Change is sometimes welcome, sometimes dreaded. But healthy senior adults realize that it is inevitable . . .

We may not know *why*, but we do know this: an optimistic, forward-looking, courageous attitude toward the future is the secret to dealing with change. By contrast, when people begin looking backward to their life before the change, it is the beginning of the end . . .

Keep searching for the good. Do you see the cup half-full or half-empty? People who see the cup half-full are able to handle change much better. They have a positive mental attitude. The apostle Paul, as we saw earlier, believed that "in all things God works for the good of those who love him, who have been called according to his purpose" (Romans 8:28). Work on developing an outlook on life that says, "The best is yet to come" . . .

I urge you to look at the changes that happen and ask, *Can I see the possibilities and opportunities in my new situation?* Those people who live long and love it search out the riches made possible by change.

ADDITIONAL SCRIPTURE READINGS
Jeremiah 29:10–14; 2 Timothy 1:3–12

Go to page 692 for your next devotional reading.

⁸God reigns over the nations;
God is seated on his holy
throne.
⁹The nobles of the nations assemble
as the people of the God of
Abraham,
for the kings*a* of the earth belong
to God;
he is greatly exalted.

Psalm 48

*A song. A psalm of the Sons
of Korah.*

¹Great is the LORD, and most
worthy of praise,
in the city of our God, his holy
mountain.
²It is beautiful in its loftiness,
the joy of the whole earth.
Like the utmost heights of
Zaphon*b* is Mount Zion,
the*c* city of the Great King.
³God is in her citadels;
he has shown himself to be her
fortress.

⁴When the kings joined forces,
when they advanced together,
⁵they saw ˌherˌ and were
astounded;
they fled in terror.
⁶Trembling seized them there,
pain like that of a woman in
labor.
⁷You destroyed them like ships of
Tarshish
shattered by an east wind.

⁸As we have heard,
so have we seen
in the city of the LORD Almighty,
in the city of our God:
God makes her secure forever.
Selah

⁹Within your temple, O God,
we meditate on your unfailing
love.
¹⁰Like your name, O God,

your praise reaches to the ends
of the earth;
your right hand is filled with
righteousness.
¹¹Mount Zion rejoices,
the villages of Judah are glad
because of your judgments.

¹²Walk about Zion, go around her,
count her towers,
¹³consider well her ramparts,
view her citadels,
that you may tell of them to the
next generation.
¹⁴For this God is our God for ever
and ever;
he will be our guide even to the
end.

Psalm 49

*For the director of music. Of the Sons
of Korah. A psalm.*

¹Hear this, all you peoples;
listen, all who live in this world,
²both low and high,
rich and poor alike:
³My mouth will speak words of
wisdom;
the utterance from my heart
will give understanding.
⁴I will turn my ear to a proverb;
with the harp I will expound
my riddle:

⁵Why should I fear when evil days
come,
when wicked deceivers
surround me—
⁶those who trust in their wealth
and boast of their great riches?
⁷No man can redeem the life of
another
or give to God a ransom for
him—
⁸the ransom for a life is costly,
no payment is ever enough—
⁹that he should live on forever
and not see decay.
¹⁰For all can see that wise men die;

*a9 Or shields   b2 Zaphon can refer to a sacred mountain or the direction north.
c2 Or earth, / Mount Zion, on the northern side / of the*

the foolish and the senseless
    alike perish
and leave their wealth to others.
¹¹Their tombs will remain their
    houses^a forever,
  their dwellings for endless
    generations,
  though they had^b named lands
    after themselves.

¹²But man, despite his riches, does
    not endure;
  he is^c like the beasts that
    perish.

¹³This is the fate of those who trust
    in themselves,
  and of their followers, who
    approve their sayings. *Selah*
¹⁴Like sheep they are destined for
    the grave,^d
  and death will feed on them.
The upright will rule over them in
    the morning;
  their forms will decay in the
    grave,^d
  far from their princely
    mansions.
¹⁵But God will redeem my life^e
    from the grave;
  he will surely take me to
    himself.   *Selah*

¹⁶Do not be overawed when a man
    grows rich,
  when the splendor of his house
    increases;
¹⁷for he will take nothing with him
    when he dies,
  his splendor will not descend
    with him.
¹⁸Though while he lived he counted
    himself blessed—
  and men praise you when you
    prosper—
¹⁹he will join the generation of his
    fathers,
  who will never see the light ⌐of
    life⌐.

²⁰A man who has riches without
    understanding
  is like the beasts that perish.

Psalm 50

A psalm of Asaph.

¹The Mighty One, God, the LORD,
  speaks and summons the earth
  from the rising of the sun to the
    place where it sets.
²From Zion, perfect in beauty,
  God shines forth.
³Our God comes and will not be
    silent;
  a fire devours before him,
  and around him a tempest
    rages.
⁴He summons the heavens above,
  and the earth, that he may
    judge his people:
⁵"Gather to me my consecrated
    ones,
  who made a covenant with me
    by sacrifice."
⁶And the heavens proclaim his
    righteousness,
  for God himself is judge.   *Selah*

⁷"Hear, O my people, and I will
    speak,
  O Israel, and I will testify
    against you:
  I am God, your God.
⁸I do not rebuke you for your
    sacrifices
  or your burnt offerings, which
    are ever before me.
⁹I have no need of a bull from your
    stall
  or of goats from your pens,
¹⁰for every animal of the forest is
    mine,
  and the cattle on a thousand
    hills.
¹¹I know every bird in the
    mountains,
  and the creatures of the field
    are mine.
¹²If I were hungry I would not tell
    you,
  for the world is mine, and all
    that is in it.
¹³Do I eat the flesh of bulls
  or drink the blood of goats?

---

a11 Septuagint and Syriac; Hebrew *In their thoughts their houses will remain*   *b11* Or / *for they
have*   *c12* Hebrew; Septuagint and Syriac read verse 12 the same as verse 20.   *d14* Hebrew
Sheol; also in verse 15   *e15* Or *soul*

¹⁴Sacrifice thank offerings to God,
　　fulfill your vows to the Most
　　High,
¹⁵and call upon me in the day of
　　trouble;
　　I will deliver you, and you will
　　honor me."

¹⁶But to the wicked, God says:

"What right have you to recite my
　　laws
　　or take my covenant on your
　　lips?
¹⁷You hate my instruction
　　and cast my words behind you.
¹⁸When you see a thief, you join
　　with him;
　　you throw in your lot with
　　adulterers.
¹⁹You use your mouth for evil
　　and harness your tongue to
　　deceit.
²⁰You speak continually against
　　your brother
　　and slander your own mother's
　　son.
²¹These things you have done and I
　　kept silent;
　　you thought I was altogether^a
　　like you.
But I will rebuke you
　　and accuse you to your face.

²²"Consider this, you who forget
　　God,
　　or I will tear you to pieces, with
　　none to rescue:
²³He who sacrifices thank offerings
　　honors me,
　　and he prepares the way
　　so that I may show him^b the
　　salvation of God."

Psalm 51

For the director of music. A psalm of
David. When the prophet Nathan
came to him after David had
committed adultery with Bathsheba.

¹Have mercy on me, O God,
　　according to your unfailing
　　love;

according to your great
　　compassion
　　blot out my transgressions.
²Wash away all my iniquity
　　and cleanse me from my
　　sin.

³For I know my transgressions,
　　and my sin is always before
　　me.
⁴Against you, you only, have I
　　sinned
　　and done what is evil in your
　　sight,
　　so that you are proved right when
　　you speak
　　and justified when you judge.
⁵Surely I was sinful at birth,
　　sinful from the time my mother
　　conceived me.
⁶Surely you desire truth in the
　　inner parts^c;
　　you teach^d me wisdom in the
　　inmost place.

⁷Cleanse me with hyssop, and I
　　will be clean;
　　wash me, and I will be whiter
　　than snow.
⁸Let me hear joy and gladness;
　　let the bones you have crushed
　　rejoice.
⁹Hide your face from my sins
　　and blot out all my iniquity.

¹⁰Create in me a pure heart, O God,
　　and renew a steadfast spirit
　　within me.
¹¹Do not cast me from your
　　presence
　　or take your Holy Spirit from
　　me.
¹²Restore to me the joy of your
　　salvation
　　and grant me a willing spirit, to
　　sustain me.

¹³Then I will teach transgressors
　　your ways,
　　and sinners will turn back to
　　you.
¹⁴Save me from bloodguilt, O God,

^a21 Or *thought the 'I* AM' *was*　　　^b23 Or *and to him who considers his way / I will show*　　　^c6 The
meaning of the Hebrew for this phrase is uncertain.　　　^d6 Or *you desired . . . ; / you taught*

the God who saves me,
and my tongue will sing of
your righteousness.
15O Lord, open my lips,
and my mouth will declare your
praise.
16You do not delight in sacrifice, or
I would bring it;
you do not take pleasure in
burnt offerings.
17The sacrifices of God are[a] a
broken spirit;

a17 Or *My sacrifice, O God, is*

a broken and contrite heart,
O God, you will not despise.

18In your good pleasure make Zion
prosper;
build up the walls of Jerusalem.
19Then there will be righteous
sacrifices,
whole burnt offerings to delight
you;
then bulls will be offered on
your altar.

VERSE:	AUTHOR:	PASSAGE:
Psalm 51:1	John Knox	Psalm 51:1–12

Can I Forgive Myself?

Why should the sins and follies of years long past seem, as I look back on them, so grievous, so very grievous —burdening my conscience in sleepless hours and often haunting my dreams? Why, I ask myself, should it be so? It is not because I distrust the forgiveness of God. His grace, to which I owe all that is good in my life, is surely sufficient to cover all that is evil. No, it is because I cannot forgive myself. I used to pray with the psalmist: "Remember not the sins of my youth and my rebellious ways" (Psalm 25:7). Now I am more strongly and deeply moved also to forget them. I say with the great congregation: "Forgive us our debts, as we also have forgiven our debtors" (Matthew 6:12). But I have learned in these later years that, hard as it sometimes is to forgive another, it is often far easier than to forgive oneself.

ADDITIONAL SCRIPTURE READINGS
Isaiah 33:20–24; Micah 7:18–20

Go to page 699 for your next devotional reading.

Psalm 52

For the director of music. A *maskil*[a] of David. When Doeg the Edomite had gone to Saul and told him: "David has gone to the house of Ahimelech."

[1]Why do you boast of evil, you mighty man?
Why do you boast all day long,
you who are a disgrace in the eyes of God?
[2]Your tongue plots destruction;
it is like a sharpened razor,
you who practice deceit.
[3]You love evil rather than good,
falsehood rather than speaking the truth.   *Selah*
[4]You love every harmful word,
O you deceitful tongue!

[5]Surely God will bring you down to everlasting ruin:
He will snatch you up and tear you from your tent;
he will uproot you from the land of the living.   *Selah*
[6]The righteous will see and fear;
they will laugh at him, saying,
[7]"Here now is the man
who did not make God his stronghold
but trusted in his great wealth
and grew strong by destroying others!"

[8]But I am like an olive tree
flourishing in the house of God;
I trust in God's unfailing love
for ever and ever.
[9]I will praise you forever for what you have done;
in your name I will hope, for your name is good.
I will praise you in the presence of your saints.

Psalm 53

For the director of music. According to *mahalath*.[b] A *maskil*[a] of David.

[1]The fool says in his heart,
"There is no God."

They are corrupt, and their ways are vile;
there is no one who does good.

[2]God looks down from heaven on the sons of men
to see if there are any who understand,
any who seek God.
[3]Everyone has turned away,
they have together become corrupt;
there is no one who does good,
not even one.

[4]Will the evildoers never learn—
those who devour my people as men eat bread
and who do not call on God?
[5]There they were, overwhelmed with dread,
where there was nothing to dread.
God scattered the bones of those who attacked you;
you put them to shame, for God despised them.

[6]Oh, that salvation for Israel would come out of Zion!
When God restores the fortunes of his people,
let Jacob rejoice and Israel be glad!

Psalm 54

For the director of music. With stringed instruments. A *maskil*[a] of David. When the Ziphites had gone to Saul and said, "Is not David hiding among us?"

[1]Save me, O God, by your name;
vindicate me by your might.
[2]Hear my prayer, O God;
listen to the words of my mouth.

[3]Strangers are attacking me;
ruthless men seek my life—
men without regard for God.
                              Selah

---

[a]Title: Probably a literary or musical term   [b]Title: Probably a musical term

4Surely God is my help;
   the Lord is the one who
      sustains me.

5Let evil recoil on those who
   slander me;
   in your faithfulness destroy
      them.

6I will sacrifice a freewill offering
   to you;
   I will praise your name, O Lord,
   for it is good.
7For he has delivered me from all
   my troubles,
   and my eyes have looked in
      triumph on my foes.

Psalm 55

For the director of music. With
stringed instruments. A *maskil*[a]
of David.

1Listen to my prayer, O God,
   do not ignore my plea;
2 hear me and answer me.
My thoughts trouble me and I am
      distraught
3 at the voice of the enemy,
   at the stares of the wicked;
for they bring down suffering
      upon me
   and revile me in their anger.

4My heart is in anguish within me;
   the terrors of death assail me.
5Fear and trembling have beset me;
   horror has overwhelmed me.
6I said, "Oh, that I had the wings
   of a dove!
   I would fly away and be at
      rest—
7I would flee far away
   and stay in the desert;   *Selah*
8I would hurry to my place of
      shelter,
   far from the tempest and
      storm."

9Confuse the wicked, O Lord,
   confound their speech,
   for I see violence and strife in
      the city.

10Day and night they prowl about
   on its walls;
   malice and abuse are within it.
11Destructive forces are at work in
   the city;
   threats and lies never leave its
      streets.

12If an enemy were insulting me,
   I could endure it;
if a foe were raising himself
      against me,
   I could hide from him.
13But it is you, a man like myself,
   my companion, my close friend,
14with whom I once enjoyed sweet
      fellowship
   as we walked with the throng
      at the house of God.

15Let death take my enemies by
      surprise;
   let them go down alive to the
      grave,[b]
   for evil finds lodging among
      them.

16But I call to God,
   and the Lord saves me.
17Evening, morning and noon
   I cry out in distress,
   and he hears my voice.
18He ransoms me unharmed
   from the battle waged against
      me,
   even though many oppose me.
19God, who is enthroned forever,
   will hear them and afflict
      them—   *Selah*
men who never change their ways
   and have no fear of God.

20My companion attacks his friends;
   he violates his covenant.
21His speech is smooth as butter,
   yet war is in his heart;
his words are more soothing than
      oil,
   yet they are drawn swords.

22Cast your cares on the Lord
   and he will sustain you;
   he will never let the righteous
      fall.

---

[a]Title: Probably a literary or musical term   [b]15 Hebrew *Sheol*

²³But you, O God, will bring down
      the wicked
   into the pit of corruption;
bloodthirsty and deceitful men
   will not live out half their days.

But as for me, I trust in you.

Psalm 56

For the director of music. To ⌊the
tune of⌋ "A Dove on Distant Oaks."
Of David. A *miktam*.ᵃ When the
Philistines had seized him in Gath.

¹Be merciful to me, O God, for men
      hotly pursue me;
   all day long they press their
      attack.
²My slanderers pursue me all day
      long;
   many are attacking me in their
      pride.

³When I am afraid,
   I will trust in you.
⁴In God, whose word I praise,
   in God I trust; I will not be
      afraid.
   What can mortal man do to me?

⁵All day long they twist my words;
   they are always plotting to
      harm me.
⁶They conspire, they lurk,
   they watch my steps,
   eager to take my life.

⁷On no account let them escape;
   in your anger, O God, bring
      down the nations.
⁸Record my lament;
   list my tears on your scrollᵇ—
   are they not in your record?

⁹Then my enemies will turn back
   when I call for help.
   By this I will know that God is
      for me.
¹⁰In God, whose word I praise,
   in the LORD, whose word I
      praise—
¹¹in God I trust; I will not be afraid.
   What can man do to me?

¹²I am under vows to you, O God;
   I will present my thank
      offerings to you.
¹³For you have delivered meᶜ from
      death
   and my feet from stumbling,
that I may walk before God
   in the light of life.ᵈ

Psalm 57

For the director of music. ⌊To the
tune of⌋ "Do Not Destroy." Of David.
A *miktam*.ᵃ When he had fled from
Saul into the cave.

¹Have mercy on me, O God, have
      mercy on me,
   for in you my soul takes refuge.
   I will take refuge in the shadow of
      your wings
   until the disaster has passed.

²I cry out to God Most High,
   to God, who fulfills ⌊his
      purpose⌋ for me.
³He sends from heaven and saves
      me,
   rebuking those who hotly
      pursue me;   *Selah*
   God sends his love and his
      faithfulness.

⁴I am in the midst of lions;
   I lie among ravenous beasts—
men whose teeth are spears and
      arrows,
   whose tongues are sharp
      swords.

⁵Be exalted, O God, above the
      heavens;
   let your glory be over all the
      earth.

⁶They spread a net for my feet—
   I was bowed down in distress.
They dug a pit in my path—
   but they have fallen into it
      themselves.   *Selah*

⁷My heart is steadfast, O God,
   my heart is steadfast;

ᵃTitle: Probably a literary or musical term   ᵇ8 Or / *put my tears in your wineskin*   ᶜ13 Or
my soul   ᵈ13 Or *the land of the living*

I will sing and make music.
⁸Awake, my soul!
  Awake, harp and lyre!
  I will awaken the dawn.

⁹I will praise you, O Lord, among
    the nations;
  I will sing of you among the
    peoples.
¹⁰For great is your love, reaching to
    the heavens;
  your faithfulness reaches to the
    skies.

¹¹Be exalted, O God, above the
    heavens;
  let your glory be over all the
    earth.

Psalm 58

For the director of music. ⌐To the
tune of⌐ "Do Not Destroy." Of David.
A *miktam.*ᵃ

¹Do you rulers indeed speak justly?
  Do you judge uprightly among
    men?
²No, in your heart you devise
    injustice,
  and your hands mete out
    violence on the earth.
³Even from birth the wicked go
    astray;
  from the womb they are
    wayward and speak lies.
⁴Their venom is like the venom of
    a snake,
  like that of a cobra that has
    stopped its ears,
⁵that will not heed the tune of the
    charmer,
  however skillful the enchanter
    may be.

⁶Break the teeth in their mouths,
    O God;
  tear out, O LORD, the fangs of
    the lions!
⁷Let them vanish like water that
    flows away;

when they draw the bow, let
    their arrows be blunted.
⁸Like a slug melting away as it
    moves along,
  like a stillborn child, may they
    not see the sun.

⁹Before your pots can feel ⌐the heat
    of⌐ the thorns—
  whether they be green or dry—
    the wicked will be swept
    away.ᵇ

¹⁰The righteous will be glad when
    they are avenged,
  when they bathe their feet in
    the blood of the wicked.
¹¹Then men will say,
  "Surely the righteous still are
    rewarded;
  surely there is a God who
    judges the earth."

Psalm 59

For the director of music. ⌐To the
tune of⌐ "Do Not Destroy." Of David.
A *miktam.*ᵃ When Saul had sent men
to watch David's house in order to
kill him.

¹Deliver me from my enemies,
    O God;
  protect me from those who rise
    up against me.
²Deliver me from evildoers
  and save me from bloodthirsty
    men.

³See how they lie in wait for me!
  Fierce men conspire against me
  for no offense or sin of mine,
    O LORD.
⁴I have done no wrong, yet they
    are ready to attack me.
  Arise to help me; look on my
    plight!
⁵O LORD God Almighty, the God of
    Israel,
  rouse yourself to punish all the
    nations;
  show no mercy to wicked
    traitors.   *Selah*

ᵃTitle: Probably a literary or musical term
uncertain.

ᵇ9 The meaning of the Hebrew for this verse is

⁶They return at evening,
 snarling like dogs,
 and prowl about the city.
⁷See what they spew from their
     mouths—
 they spew out swords from
     their lips,
 and they say, "Who can hear
     us?"
⁸But you, O LORD, laugh at them;
 you scoff at all those nations.

⁹O my Strength, I watch for you;
 you, O God, are my fortress,
 ¹⁰my loving God.

God will go before me
 and will let me gloat over those
     who slander me.
¹¹But do not kill them, O Lord our
     shield,ᵃ
 or my people will forget.
In your might make them wander
     about,
 and bring them down.
¹²For the sins of their mouths,
 for the words of their lips,
 let them be caught in their
     pride.
For the curses and lies they utter,
¹³ consume them in wrath,
 consume them till they are no
     more.
Then it will be known to the ends
     of the earth
 that God rules over Jacob.   *Selah*

¹⁴They return at evening,
 snarling like dogs,
 and prowl about the city.
¹⁵They wander about for food
 and howl if not satisfied.
¹⁶But I will sing of your strength,
 in the morning I will sing of
     your love;
 for you are my fortress,
 my refuge in times of trouble.

¹⁷O my Strength, I sing praise to
     you;
 you, O God, are my fortress, my
     loving God.

Psalm 60

For the director of music. To ⌐the
tune of⌐ "The Lily of the Covenant."
A *miktam*ᵇ of David. For teaching.
When he fought Aram Naharaimᶜ
and Aram Zobah,ᵈ and when
Joab returned and struck down
twelve thousand Edomites in the
Valley of Salt.

¹You have rejected us, O God, and
     burst forth upon us;
 you have been angry—now
     restore us!
²You have shaken the land and
     torn it open;
 mend its fractures, for it is
     quaking.
³You have shown your people
     desperate times;
 you have given us wine that
     makes us stagger.

⁴But for those who fear you, you
     have raised a banner
 to be unfurled against the bow.
                              Selah

⁵Save us and help us with your
     right hand,
 that those you love may be
     delivered.
⁶God has spoken from his
     sanctuary:
 "In triumph I will parcel out
     Shechem
 and measure off the Valley of
     Succoth.
⁷Gilead is mine, and Manasseh is
     mine;
 Ephraim is my helmet,
 Judah my scepter.
⁸Moab is my washbasin,
 upon Edom I toss my sandal;
 over Philistia I shout in
     triumph."

⁹Who will bring me to the fortified
     city?
 Who will lead me to Edom?
¹⁰Is it not you, O God, you who
     have rejected us
 and no longer go out with our
     armies?

ᵃ11 Or *sovereign*   ᵇTitle: Probably a literary or musical term   ᶜTitle: That is, Arameans of
Northwest Mesopotamia   ᵈTitle: That is, Arameans of central Syria

¹¹Give us aid against the enemy,
    for the help of man is worthless.
¹²With God we will gain the victory,
    and he will trample down our
        enemies.

Psalm 61

For the director of music. With
stringed instruments. Of David.

¹Hear my cry, O God;
    listen to my prayer.

²From the ends of the earth I call
        to you,
    I call as my heart grows faint;
    lead me to the rock that is
        higher than I.
³For you have been my refuge,
    a strong tower against the foe.

⁴I long to dwell in your tent
        forever
    and take refuge in the shelter of
        your wings.   Selah
⁵For you have heard my vows,
        O God;
    you have given me the heritage
        of those who fear your
        name.

⁶Increase the days of the king's life,
    his years for many generations.
⁷May he be enthroned in God's
        presence forever;
    appoint your love and
        faithfulness to protect him.

⁸Then will I ever sing praise to
        your name
    and fulfill my vows day after
        day.

Psalm 62

For the director of music. For
Jeduthun. A psalm of David.

¹My soul finds rest in God alone;
    my salvation comes from him.
²He alone is my rock and my
        salvation;
    he is my fortress, I will never be
        shaken.

³How long will you assault a man?
    Would all of you throw him
        down—
    this leaning wall, this tottering
        fence?
⁴They fully intend to topple him
        from his lofty place;
    they take delight in lies.
    With their mouths they bless,
        but in their hearts they curse.
                                    Selah

⁵Find rest, O my soul, in God
        alone;
    my hope comes from him.
⁶He alone is my rock and my
        salvation;
    he is my fortress, I will not be
        shaken.
⁷My salvation and my honor
        depend on God[a];
    he is my mighty rock, my
        refuge.
⁸Trust in him at all times,
        O people;
    pour out your hearts to him,
        for God is our refuge.   Selah

⁹Lowborn men are but a breath,
    the highborn are but a lie;
    if weighed on a balance, they are
        nothing;
    together they are only a breath.
¹⁰Do not trust in extortion
    or take pride in stolen goods;
    though your riches increase,
        do not set your heart on them.

¹¹One thing God has spoken,
    two things have I heard:
    that you, O God, are strong,
¹²   and that you, O Lord, are
        loving.
    Surely you will reward each
        person
    according to what he has done.

Psalm 63

A psalm of David. When he was in
the Desert of Judah.

¹O God, you are my God,
    earnestly I seek you;
    my soul thirsts for you,

a7 Or / God Most High is my salvation and my honor

VERSE:	AUTHOR:	PASSAGE:
Psalm 62:1	Ted Engstrom	Psalm 62:1–12

Make Your Life a Symphony

The psalmist uses the term *selah* to indicate a pause in the reading of the psalter while music plays. Music uses a symbol called a rest at certain locations on the score. There is no music in the rest but, as John Rusken pointed out, "there's the making of music in it." Retired persons are in a good position to take advantage of that rest to make their lives a symphony.

God introduced leisure when he created the world in six days and rested on the seventh. What do you think of when you think of leisure time? A quiet stroll on the beach; a thirty-foot Air Stream trailer behind your car as you travel to the North Woods? Playing croquet in the back yard? Warming your toes beside your fireplace on a cold winter night?

The term *leisure* comes from the Latin *licere*, meaning to be permitted. We will not experience leisure until we give ourselves permission . . .

To enjoy your free time to the utmost, regard it as an opportunity to look anew at yourself and your life, to come closer to the meaning of your life in relation to the world around you, to continue to grow personally, emotionally and spiritually. Ideally, your emphasis in retirement should be on *learning* to live rather than *earning* a living.

ADDITIONAL SCRIPTURE READINGS
Isaiah 30:15–18; Hebrews 4:1–11
Go to page 707 for your next devotional reading.

my body longs for you,
in a dry and weary land
    where there is no water.

2I have seen you in the sanctuary
    and beheld your power and
        your glory.
3Because your love is better than
        life,
    my lips will glorify you.
4I will praise you as long as I live,
    and in your name I will lift up
        my hands.
5My soul will be satisfied as with
        the richest of foods;
    with singing lips my mouth will
        praise you.

6On my bed I remember you;
    I think of you through the
        watches of the night.
7Because you are my help,
    I sing in the shadow of your
        wings.
8My soul clings to you;
    your right hand upholds me.

9They who seek my life will be
        destroyed;
    they will go down to the depths
        of the earth.
10They will be given over to the
        sword
    and become food for jackals.

11But the king will rejoice in God;
    all who swear by God's name
        will praise him,
    while the mouths of liars will
        be silenced.

Psalm 64

For the director of music. A psalm
of David.

1Hear me, O God, as I voice my
        complaint;
    protect my life from the threat
        of the enemy.
2Hide me from the conspiracy of
        the wicked,
    from that noisy crowd of
        evildoers.

3They sharpen their tongues like
        swords
    and aim their words like deadly
        arrows.
4They shoot from ambush at the
        innocent man;
    they shoot at him suddenly,
        without fear.

5They encourage each other in evil
        plans,
    they talk about hiding their
        snares;
    they say, "Who will see
        them[a]?"
6They plot injustice and say,
    "We have devised a perfect
        plan!"
    Surely the mind and heart of
        man are cunning.

7But God will shoot them with
        arrows;
    suddenly they will be struck
        down.
8He will turn their own tongues
        against them
    and bring them to ruin;
    all who see them will shake
        their heads in scorn.

9All mankind will fear;
    they will proclaim the works of
        God
    and ponder what he has done.
10Let the righteous rejoice in the
        LORD
    and take refuge in him;
    let all the upright in heart
        praise him!

Psalm 65

For the director of music. A psalm
of David. A song.

1Praise awaits[b] you, O God, in
        Zion;
    to you our vows will be
        fulfilled.
2O you who hear prayer,
    to you all men will come.
3When we were overwhelmed by
        sins,

---

a5 Or us   b1 Or befits; the meaning of the Hebrew for this word is uncertain.

you forgave[a] our
transgressions.
4Blessed are those you choose
and bring near to live in your
courts!
We are filled with the good things
of your house,
of your holy temple.

5You answer us with awesome
deeds of righteousness,
O God our Savior,
the hope of all the ends of the
earth
and of the farthest seas,
6who formed the mountains by
your power,
having armed yourself with
strength,
7who stilled the roaring of the seas,
the roaring of their waves,
and the turmoil of the nations.
8Those living far away fear your
wonders;
where morning dawns and
evening fades
you call forth songs of joy.

9You care for the land and water it;
you enrich it abundantly.
The streams of God are filled with
water
to provide the people with
grain,
for so you have ordained it.[b]
10You drench its furrows
and level its ridges;
you soften it with showers
and bless its crops.
11You crown the year with your
bounty,
and your carts overflow with
abundance.
12The grasslands of the desert
overflow;
the hills are clothed with
gladness.
13The meadows are covered with
flocks
and the valleys are mantled
with grain;
they shout for joy and sing.

Psalm 66

For the director of music. A song.
A psalm.

1Shout with joy to God, all the
earth!
2 Sing the glory of his name;
make his praise glorious!
3Say to God, "How awesome are
your deeds!
So great is your power
that your enemies cringe before
you.
4All the earth bows down to you;
they sing praise to you,
they sing praise to your name."
Selah

5Come and see what God has done,
how awesome his works in
man's behalf!
6He turned the sea into dry land,
they passed through the waters
on foot—
come, let us rejoice in him.
7He rules forever by his power,
his eyes watch the nations—
let not the rebellious rise up
against him.   *Selah*

8Praise our God, O peoples,
let the sound of his praise be
heard;
9he has preserved our lives
and kept our feet from slipping.
10For you, O God, tested us;
you refined us like silver.
11You brought us into prison
and laid burdens on our backs.
12You let men ride over our heads;
we went through fire and
water,
but you brought us to a place of
abundance.

13I will come to your temple with
burnt offerings
and fulfill my vows to you—
14vows my lips promised and my
mouth spoke
when I was in trouble.

a3 Or *made atonement for*   b9 Or *for that is how you prepare the land*

¹⁵I will sacrifice fat animals to you
and an offering of rams;
I will offer bulls and goats.
Selah

¹⁶Come and listen, all you who fear
God;
let me tell you what he has
done for me.
¹⁷I cried out to him with my mouth;
his praise was on my tongue.
¹⁸If I had cherished sin in my heart,
the Lord would not have
listened;
¹⁹but God has surely listened
and heard my voice in prayer.
²⁰Praise be to God,
who has not rejected my prayer
or withheld his love from me!

Psalm 67

For the director of music. With
stringed instruments. A psalm.
A song.

¹May God be gracious to us and
bless us
and make his face shine upon
us,   *Selah*
²that your ways may be known on
earth,
your salvation among all
nations.

³May the peoples praise you,
O God;
may all the peoples praise you.
⁴May the nations be glad and sing
for joy,
for you rule the peoples justly
and guide the nations of the
earth.   *Selah*
⁵May the peoples praise you,
O God;
may all the peoples praise you.

⁶Then the land will yield its
harvest,
and God, our God, will bless us.
⁷God will bless us,
and all the ends of the earth
will fear him.

Psalm 68

For the director of music. Of David.
A psalm. A song.

¹May God arise, may his enemies
be scattered;
may his foes flee before him.
²As smoke is blown away by the
wind,
may you blow them away;
as wax melts before the fire,
may the wicked perish before
God.
³But may the righteous be glad
and rejoice before God;
may they be happy and joyful.

⁴Sing to God, sing praise to his
name,
extol him who rides on the
clouds^a—
his name is the LORD—
and rejoice before him.
⁵A father to the fatherless, a
defender of widows,
is God in his holy dwelling.
⁶God sets the lonely in families,^b
he leads forth the prisoners
with singing;
but the rebellious live in a
sun-scorched land.

⁷When you went out before your
people, O God,
when you marched through the
wasteland,   *Selah*
⁸the earth shook,
the heavens poured down rain,
before God, the One of Sinai,
before God, the God of Israel.
⁹You gave abundant showers,
O God;
you refreshed your weary
inheritance.
¹⁰Your people settled in it,
and from your bounty, O God,
you provided for the poor.

¹¹The Lord announced the word,
and great was the company of
those who proclaimed it:
¹²"Kings and armies flee in haste;
in the camps men divide the
plunder.

a4 Or / prepare the way for him who rides through the deserts   b6 Or the desolate in a homeland

¹³Even while you sleep among the
    campfires,^a
  the wings of ⌐my⌐ dove are
    sheathed with silver,
    its feathers with shining gold."
¹⁴When the Almighty^b scattered
    the kings in the land,
  it was like snow fallen on
    Zalmon.

¹⁵The mountains of Bashan are
    majestic mountains;
  rugged are the mountains of
    Bashan.
¹⁶Why gaze in envy, O rugged
    mountains,
  at the mountain where God
    chooses to reign,
  where the LORD himself will
    dwell forever?
¹⁷The chariots of God are tens of
    thousands
  and thousands of thousands;
  the Lord ⌐has come⌐ from Sinai
    into his sanctuary.
¹⁸When you ascended on high,
  you led captives in your train;
  you received gifts from men,
  even from^c the rebellious—
    that you,^d O LORD God, might
    dwell there.

¹⁹Praise be to the Lord, to God our
    Savior,
  who daily bears our burdens.
                                    Selah
²⁰Our God is a God who saves;
  from the Sovereign LORD comes
    escape from death.

²¹Surely God will crush the heads of
    his enemies,
  the hairy crowns of those who
    go on in their sins.
²²The Lord says, "I will bring them
    from Bashan;
  I will bring them from the
    depths of the sea,
²³that you may plunge your feet in
    the blood of your foes,
  while the tongues of your dogs
    have their share."

²⁴Your procession has come into
    view, O God,
  the procession of my God and
    King into the sanctuary.
²⁵In front are the singers, after them
    the musicians;
  with them are the maidens
    playing tambourines.
²⁶Praise God in the great
    congregation;
  praise the LORD in the assembly
    of Israel.
²⁷There is the little tribe of
    Benjamin, leading them,
  there the great throng of
    Judah's princes,
  and there the princes of
    Zebulun and of Naphtali.

²⁸Summon your power, O God^e;
  show us your strength, O God,
    as you have done before.
²⁹Because of your temple at
    Jerusalem
  kings will bring you gifts.
³⁰Rebuke the beast among the reeds,
  the herd of bulls among the
    calves of the nations.
  Humbled, may it bring bars of
    silver.
  Scatter the nations who delight
    in war.
³¹Envoys will come from Egypt;
  Cush^f will submit herself to
    God.

³²Sing to God, O kingdoms of the
    earth,
  sing praise to the Lord,   *Selah*
³³to him who rides the ancient skies
    above,
  who thunders with mighty
    voice.
³⁴Proclaim the power of God,
  whose majesty is over Israel,
  whose power is in the skies.
³⁵You are awesome, O God, in your
    sanctuary;
  the God of Israel gives power
    and strength to his people.

Praise be to God!

---

^a13 Or *saddlebags*   ^b14 Hebrew *Shaddai*   ^c18 Or *gifts for men, / even*   ^d18 Or *they*
^e28 Many Hebrew manuscripts, Septuagint and Syriac; most Hebrew manuscripts *Your God has
summoned power for you*   ^f31 That is, the upper Nile region

Psalm 69

*For the director of music. To the
tune of, "Lilies." Of David.*

¹Save me, O God,
  for the waters have come up to
    my neck.
²I sink in the miry depths,
  where there is no foothold.
I have come into the deep waters;
  the floods engulf me.
³I am worn out calling for help;
  my throat is parched.
My eyes fail,
  looking for my God.
⁴Those who hate me without
    reason
    outnumber the hairs of my
      head;
many are my enemies without
    cause,
  those who seek to destroy me.
I am forced to restore
  what I did not steal.

⁵You know my folly, O God;
  my guilt is not hidden from
    you.

⁶May those who hope in you
  not be disgraced because of me,
  O Lord, the Lᴏʀᴅ Almighty;
may those who seek you
  not be put to shame because of
    me,
  O God of Israel.
⁷For I endure scorn for your sake,
  and shame covers my face.
⁸I am a stranger to my brothers,
  an alien to my own mother's
    sons;
⁹for zeal for your house consumes
    me,
  and the insults of those who
    insult you fall on me.
¹⁰When I weep and fast,
  I must endure scorn;
¹¹when I put on sackcloth,
  people make sport of me.
¹²Those who sit at the gate mock
    me,
  and I am the song of the
    drunkards.

¹³But I pray to you, O Lᴏʀᴅ,
  in the time of your favor;
in your great love, O God,
  answer me with your sure
    salvation.
¹⁴Rescue me from the mire,
  do not let me sink;
deliver me from those who hate
    me,
  from the deep waters.
¹⁵Do not let the floodwaters engulf
    me
  or the depths swallow me up
  or the pit close its mouth over
    me.
¹⁶Answer me, O Lᴏʀᴅ, out of the
    goodness of your love;
  in your great mercy turn to me.
¹⁷Do not hide your face from your
    servant;
  answer me quickly, for I am in
    trouble.
¹⁸Come near and rescue me;
  redeem me because of my foes.

¹⁹You know how I am scorned,
  disgraced and shamed;
  all my enemies are before you.
²⁰Scorn has broken my heart
  and has left me helpless;
I looked for sympathy, but there
    was none,
  for comforters, but I found
    none.
²¹They put gall in my food
  and gave me vinegar for my
    thirst.

²²May the table set before them
    become a snare;
  may it become retribution and[a]
    a trap.
²³May their eyes be darkened so
    they cannot see,
  and their backs be bent forever.
²⁴Pour out your wrath on them;
  let your fierce anger overtake
    them.
²⁵May their place be deserted;
  let there be no one to dwell in
    their tents.
²⁶For they persecute those you
    wound

---

a22 Or snare / and their fellowship become

and talk about the pain of those
  you hurt.
²⁷Charge them with crime upon
    crime;
  do not let them share in your
    salvation.
²⁸May they be blotted out of the
    book of life
  and not be listed with the
    righteous.

²⁹I am in pain and distress;
  may your salvation, O God,
    protect me.

³⁰I will praise God's name in song
  and glorify him with
    thanksgiving.
³¹This will please the LORD more
    than an ox,
  more than a bull with its horns
    and hoofs.
³²The poor will see and be glad—
  you who seek God, may your
    hearts live!
³³The LORD hears the needy
  and does not despise his captive
    people.

³⁴Let heaven and earth praise him,
  the seas and all that move in
    them,
³⁵for God will save Zion
  and rebuild the cities of Judah.
  Then people will settle there and
    possess it;
³⁶ the children of his servants will
    inherit it,
  and those who love his name
    will dwell there.

Psalm 70

For the director of music. Of David.
A petition.

¹Hasten, O God, to save me;
  O LORD, come quickly to help
    me.
²May those who seek my life
  be put to shame and confusion;
  may all who desire my ruin
  be turned back in disgrace.
³May those who say to me, "Aha!
    Aha!"

turn back because of their
    shame.
⁴But may all who seek you
  rejoice and be glad in you;
  may those who love your
    salvation always say,
  "Let God be exalted!"

⁵Yet I am poor and needy;
  come quickly to me, O God.
  You are my help and my
    deliverer;
  O LORD, do not delay.

Psalm 71

¹In you, O LORD, I have taken
    refuge;
  let me never be put to shame.
²Rescue me and deliver me in your
    righteousness;
  turn your ear to me and save
    me.
³Be my rock of refuge,
  to which I can always go;
  give the command to save me,
  for you are my rock and my
    fortress.
⁴Deliver me, O my God, from the
    hand of the wicked,
  from the grasp of evil and cruel
    men.

⁵For you have been my hope,
  O Sovereign LORD,
  my confidence since my youth.
⁶From birth I have relied on you;
  you brought me forth from my
    mother's womb.
  I will ever praise you.
⁷I have become like a portent to
    many,
  but you are my strong refuge.
⁸My mouth is filled with your
    praise,
  declaring your splendor all day
    long.

⁹Do not cast me away when I am
    old;
  do not forsake me when my
    strength is gone.
¹⁰For my enemies speak against me;
  those who wait to kill me
    conspire together.
¹¹They say, "God has forsaken him;
  pursue him and seize him,

for no one will rescue him."
¹²Be not far from me, O God;
  come quickly, O my God, to
    help me.
¹³May my accusers perish in shame;
  may those who want to harm
    me
  be covered with scorn and
    disgrace.

¹⁴But as for me, I will always have
    hope;
  I will praise you more and
    more.
¹⁵My mouth will tell of your
    righteousness,
  of your salvation all day long,
  though I know not its measure.
¹⁶I will come and proclaim your
    mighty acts, O Sovereign
    Lord;
  I will proclaim your
    righteousness, yours alone.
¹⁷Since my youth, O God, you have
    taught me,
  and to this day I declare your
    marvelous deeds.
¹⁸Even when I am old and gray,
  do not forsake me, O God,
  till I declare your power to the
    next generation,
  your might to all who are to
    come.

¹⁹Your righteousness reaches to the
    skies, O God,
  you who have done great
    things.
  Who, O God, is like you?
²⁰Though you have made me see
    troubles, many and bitter,
  you will restore my life again;
  from the depths of the earth
  you will again bring me up.
²¹You will increase my honor
  and comfort me once again.

²²I will praise you with the harp
  for your faithfulness, O my
    God;
  I will sing praise to you with the
    lyre,
  O Holy One of Israel.

²³My lips will shout for joy
  when I sing praise to you—
  I, whom you have redeemed.
²⁴My tongue will tell of your
    righteous acts
  all day long,
  for those who wanted to harm me
  have been put to shame and
    confusion.

Psalm 72

Of Solomon.

¹Endow the king with your justice,
    O God,
  the royal son with your
    righteousness.
²He will[a] judge your people in
    righteousness,
  your afflicted ones with justice.
³The mountains will bring
    prosperity to the people,
  the hills the fruit of
    righteousness.
⁴He will defend the afflicted among
    the people
  and save the children of the
    needy;
  he will crush the oppressor.

⁵He will endure[b] as long as the
    sun,
  as long as the moon, through all
    generations.
⁶He will be like rain falling on a
    mown field,
  like showers watering the earth.
⁷In his days the righteous will
    flourish;
  prosperity will abound till the
    moon is no more.

⁸He will rule from sea to sea
  and from the River[c] to the
    ends of the earth.[d]
⁹The desert tribes will bow before
    him
  and his enemies will lick the
    dust.
¹⁰The kings of Tarshish and of
    distant shores
  will bring tribute to him;

---

a2 Or *May he*; similarly in verses 3-11 and 17   b5 Septuagint; Hebrew *You will be feared*
c8 That is, the Euphrates   d8 Or *the end of the land*

the kings of Sheba and Seba
will present him gifts.
¹¹All kings will bow down to him
and all nations will serve him.

¹²For he will deliver the needy who
cry out,
the afflicted who have no one to
help.
¹³He will take pity on the weak and
the needy
and save the needy from death.

¹⁴He will rescue them from
oppression and violence,
for precious is their blood in his
sight.

¹⁵Long may he live!
May gold from Sheba be given
him.
May people ever pray for him
and bless him all day long.
¹⁶Let grain abound throughout the
land;

FRIDAY

VERSE:
Psalm 71:6

AUTHOR:
Henri J.M. Nouwen

PASSAGE:
Psalm 71:1–24

Darkness, or Light?

Is aging a way to the darkness or a way to the light? It is
not given to anyone to make a final judgment, since the
answer can only be brought forth from the center of our
being. No one can decide for anyone else how his or her
aging shall or should be. It belongs to the greatness of
men and women that the meaning of their existence escapes the power of calculations and predictions. Ultimately, it can only be discovered and affirmed in the
freedom of the heart. There we are able to decide between segregation and unity, between desolation and
hope, between loss of self and a new recreating vision . . .

Aging is one of the most essential human processes,
one that can be denied only with great harm. Every man
and woman who has discovered or rediscovered his or
her own aging has a unique opportunity to enrich the
quality of his or her own life and that of every fellow human being.

ADDITIONAL SCRIPTURE READINGS
Psalm 90; Proverbs 4:20–27

Go to page 710 for your next devotional reading.

on the tops of the hills may it
    sway.
Let its fruit flourish like Lebanon;
    let it thrive like the grass of the
        field.
¹⁷May his name endure forever;
    may it continue as long as the
        sun.

All nations will be blessed
    through him,
and they will call him blessed.

¹⁸Praise be to the Lord God, the
    God of Israel,
who alone does marvelous
    deeds.
¹⁹Praise be to his glorious name
    forever;
may the whole earth be filled
    with his glory.
        Amen and Amen.

²⁰This concludes the prayers of
    David son of Jesse.

BOOK III
Psalms 73–89

Psalm 73

A psalm of Asaph.

¹Surely God is good to Israel,
    to those who are pure in heart.

²But as for me, my feet had almost
    slipped;
    I had nearly lost my foothold.
³For I envied the arrogant
    when I saw the prosperity of
        the wicked.

⁴They have no struggles;
    their bodies are healthy and
        strong.^a
⁵They are free from the burdens
    common to man;
    they are not plagued by human
        ills.
⁶Therefore pride is their necklace;

they clothe themselves with
    violence.
⁷From their callous hearts comes
    iniquity^b;
    the evil conceits of their minds
        know no limits.
⁸They scoff, and speak with malice;
    in their arrogance they threaten
        oppression.
⁹Their mouths lay claim to heaven,
    and their tongues take
        possession of the earth.
¹⁰Therefore their people turn to
    them
    and drink up waters in
        abundance.^c
¹¹They say, "How can God know?
    Does the Most High have
        knowledge?"

¹²This is what the wicked are like—
    always carefree, they increase in
        wealth.

¹³Surely in vain have I kept my
    heart pure;
    in vain have I washed my
        hands in innocence.
¹⁴All day long I have been plagued;
    I have been punished every
        morning.

¹⁵If I had said, "I will speak thus,"
    I would have betrayed your
        children.
¹⁶When I tried to understand all
    this,
    it was oppressive to me
¹⁷till I entered the sanctuary of God;
    then I understood their final
        destiny.

¹⁸Surely you place them on slippery
    ground;
    you cast them down to ruin.
¹⁹How suddenly are they destroyed,
    completely swept away by
        terrors!
²⁰As a dream when one awakes,
    so when you arise, O Lord,
    you will despise them as
        fantasies.

²¹When my heart was grieved

---

^a4 With a different word division of the Hebrew; Masoretic Text *struggles at their death; | their
bodies are healthy*   ^b7 Syriac (see also Septuagint); Hebrew *Their eyes bulge with fat*   ^c10 The
meaning of the Hebrew for this verse is uncertain.

and my spirit embittered,
²²I was senseless and ignorant;
    I was a brute beast before you.

²³Yet I am always with you;
    you hold me by my right hand.
²⁴You guide me with your counsel,
    and afterward you will take me
        into glory.
²⁵Whom have I in heaven but you?
    And earth has nothing I desire
        besides you.
²⁶My flesh and my heart may fail,
    but God is the strength of my
        heart
    and my portion forever.

²⁷Those who are far from you will
        perish;
    you destroy all who are
        unfaithful to you.
²⁸But as for me, it is good to be
        near God.
    I have made the Sovereign LORD
        my refuge;
    I will tell of all your deeds.

Psalm 74

A *maskil*ᵃ of Asaph.

¹Why have you rejected us forever,
        O God?
    Why does your anger smolder
        against the sheep of your
        pasture?
²Remember the people you
        purchased of old,
    the tribe of your inheritance,
        whom you redeemed—
    Mount Zion, where you dwelt.
³Turn your steps toward these
        everlasting ruins,
    all this destruction the enemy
        has brought on the
        sanctuary.

⁴Your foes roared in the place
        where you met with us;
    they set up their standards as
        signs.
⁵They behaved like men wielding
        axes
    to cut through a thicket of trees.

⁶They smashed all the carved
        paneling
    with their axes and hatchets.
⁷They burned your sanctuary to the
        ground;
    they defiled the dwelling place
        of your Name.
⁸They said in their hearts, "We will
        crush them completely!"
    They burned every place where
        God was worshiped in the
        land.
⁹We are given no miraculous signs;
    no prophets are left,
    and none of us knows how long
        this will be.

¹⁰How long will the enemy mock
        you, O God?
    Will the foe revile your name
        forever?
¹¹Why do you hold back your hand,
        your right hand?
    Take it from the folds of your
        garment and destroy them!

¹²But you, O God, are my king from
        of old;
    you bring salvation upon the
        earth.
¹³It was you who split open the sea
        by your power;
    you broke the heads of the
        monster in the waters.
¹⁴It was you who crushed the heads
        of Leviathan
    and gave him as food to the
        creatures of the desert.
¹⁵It was you who opened up
        springs and streams;
    you dried up the ever flowing
        rivers.
¹⁶The day is yours, and yours also
        the night;
    you established the sun and
        moon.
¹⁷It was you who set all the
        boundaries of the earth;
    you made both summer and
        winter.

¹⁸Remember how the enemy has
        mocked you, O LORD,

ᵃTitle: Probably a literary or musical term

PASSAGE: Psalm 73:23–28; Isaiah 42:1–9
AUTHOR: Author Unknown

Alone, But Never Alone

I live alone, dear Lord,
Stay by my side.
In all my daily needs,
Be thou my guide.

And when I'm feeling low,
Or in despair,
Lift up my heart,
And help me in my prayer.

I live alone, dear Lord,
Yet have no fear,
Because I feel your presence,
Ever near.
Amen.

Go to page 714 for your next devotional reading.

how foolish people have reviled
    your name.
¹⁹Do not hand over the life of your
    dove to wild beasts;
  do not forget the lives of your
    afflicted people forever.
²⁰Have regard for your covenant,
  because haunts of violence fill
    the dark places of the land.
²¹Do not let the oppressed retreat in
    disgrace;
  may the poor and needy praise
    your name.

²²Rise up, O God, and defend your
    cause;
  remember how fools mock you
    all day long.
²³Do not ignore the clamor of your
    adversaries,
  the uproar of your enemies,
    which rises continually.

Psalm 75

For the director of music. ⌊To the
tune of⌋ "Do Not Destroy." A psalm
of Asaph. A song.

¹We give thanks to you, O God,
  we give thanks, for your Name
    is near;
  men tell of your wonderful
    deeds.

²You say, "I choose the appointed
    time;
  it is I who judge uprightly.
³When the earth and all its people
    quake,
  it is I who hold its pillars firm.
                  Selah
⁴To the arrogant I say, 'Boast no
    more,'
  and to the wicked, 'Do not lift
    up your horns.
⁵Do not lift your horns against
    heaven;
  do not speak with outstretched
    neck.' "

⁶No one from the east or the west
  or from the desert can exalt a
    man.
⁷But it is God who judges:

He brings one down, he exalts
    another.
⁸In the hand of the LORD is a cup
  full of foaming wine mixed with
    spices;
  he pours it out, and all the wicked
    of the earth
  drink it down to its very dregs.

⁹As for me, I will declare this
    forever;
  I will sing praise to the God of
    Jacob.
¹⁰I will cut off the horns of all the
    wicked,
  but the horns of the righteous
    will be lifted up.

Psalm 76

For the director of music. With
stringed instruments. A psalm of
Asaph. A song.

¹In Judah God is known;
  his name is great in Israel.
²His tent is in Salem,
  his dwelling place in Zion.
³There he broke the flashing
    arrows,
  the shields and the swords, the
    weapons of war.   *Selah*

⁴You are resplendent with light,
  more majestic than mountains
    rich with game.
⁵Valiant men lie plundered,
  they sleep their last sleep;
  not one of the warriors
    can lift his hands.
⁶At your rebuke, O God of Jacob,
  both horse and chariot lie still.
⁷You alone are to be feared.
  Who can stand before you when
    you are angry?
⁸From heaven you pronounced
    judgment,
  and the land feared and was
    quiet—
⁹when you, O God, rose up to
    judge,
  to save all the afflicted of the
    land.   *Selah*
¹⁰Surely your wrath against men
  brings you praise,

and the survivors of your wrath
  are restrained.[a]
[11]Make vows to the LORD your God
    and fulfill them;
  let all the neighboring lands
  bring gifts to the One to be
    feared.
[12]He breaks the spirit of rulers;
  he is feared by the kings of the
    earth.

Psalm 77

For the director of music. For
Jeduthun. Of Asaph. A psalm.

[1]I cried out to God for help;
  I cried out to God to hear me.
[2]When I was in distress, I sought
    the Lord;
  at night I stretched out untiring
    hands
  and my soul refused to be
    comforted.

[3]I remembered you, O God, and I
    groaned;
  I mused, and my spirit grew
    faint.   Selah
[4]You kept my eyes from closing;
  I was too troubled to speak.
[5]I thought about the former days,
  the years of long ago;
[6]I remembered my songs in the
    night.
  My heart mused and my spirit
    inquired:

[7]"Will the Lord reject forever?
  Will he never show his favor
    again?
[8]Has his unfailing love vanished
    forever?
  Has his promise failed for all
    time?
[9]Has God forgotten to be merciful?
  Has he in anger withheld his
    compassion?"   Selah

[10]Then I thought, "To this I will
    appeal:
  the years of the right hand of
    the Most High."

[11]I will remember the deeds of the
    LORD;
  yes, I will remember your
    miracles of long ago.
[12]I will meditate on all your works
  and consider all your mighty
    deeds.

[13]Your ways, O God, are holy.
  What god is so great as our
    God?
[14]You are the God who performs
    miracles;
  you display your power among
    the peoples.
[15]With your mighty arm you
    redeemed your people,
  the descendants of Jacob and
    Joseph.   Selah

[16]The waters saw you, O God,
  the waters saw you and
    writhed;
  the very depths were convulsed.
[17]The clouds poured down water,
  the skies resounded with
    thunder;
  your arrows flashed back and
    forth.
[18]Your thunder was heard in the
    whirlwind,
  your lightning lit up the world;
  the earth trembled and quaked.
[19]Your path led through the sea,
  your way through the mighty
    waters,
  though your footprints were not
    seen.

[20]You led your people like a flock
  by the hand of Moses and
    Aaron.

Psalm 78

A maskil[b] of Asaph.

[1]O my people, hear my teaching;
  listen to the words of my
    mouth.
[2]I will open my mouth in parables,
  I will utter hidden things,
    things from of old—
[3]what we have heard and known,

---

[a]10 Or Surely the wrath of men brings you praise, / and with the remainder of wrath you arm yourself
[b]Title: Probably a literary or musical term

what our fathers have told us.
⁴We will not hide them from their
children;
we will tell the next generation
the praiseworthy deeds of the
LORD,
his power, and the wonders he
has done.
⁵He decreed statutes for Jacob
and established the law in
Israel,
which he commanded our
forefathers
to teach their children,
⁶so the next generation would
know them,
even the children yet to be
born,
and they in turn would tell
their children.
⁷Then they would put their trust in
God
and would not forget his deeds
but would keep his commands.
⁸They would not be like their
forefathers—
a stubborn and rebellious
generation,
whose hearts were not loyal to
God,
whose spirits were not faithful
to him.
⁹The men of Ephraim, though
armed with bows,
turned back on the day of
battle;
¹⁰they did not keep God's covenant
and refused to live by his law.
¹¹They forgot what he had done,
the wonders he had shown
them.
¹²He did miracles in the sight of
their fathers
in the land of Egypt, in the
region of Zoan.
¹³He divided the sea and led them
through;
he made the water stand firm
like a wall.
¹⁴He guided them with the cloud by
day
and with light from the fire all
night.

¹⁵He split the rocks in the desert
and gave them water as
abundant as the seas;
¹⁶he brought streams out of a rocky
crag
and made water flow down like
rivers.
¹⁷But they continued to sin against
him,
rebelling in the desert against
the Most High.
¹⁸They willfully put God to the test
by demanding the food they
craved.
¹⁹They spoke against God, saying,
"Can God spread a table in the
desert?
²⁰When he struck the rock, water
gushed out,
and streams flowed abundantly.
But can he also give us food?
Can he supply meat for his
people?"
²¹When the LORD heard them, he
was very angry;
his fire broke out against Jacob,
and his wrath rose against
Israel,
²²for they did not believe in God
or trust in his deliverance.
²³Yet he gave a command to the
skies above
and opened the doors of the
heavens;
²⁴he rained down manna for the
people to eat,
he gave them the grain of
heaven.
²⁵Men ate the bread of angels;
he sent them all the food they
could eat.
²⁶He let loose the east wind from
the heavens
and led forth the south wind by
his power.
²⁷He rained meat down on them
like dust,
flying birds like sand on the
seashore.
²⁸He made them come down inside
their camp,
all around their tents.

VERSE:
Psalm 78:4

AUTHOR:
Charles R. Swindoll

PASSAGE:
Psalm 78:1–8

Like a Massive Tree

Grandparents' favorite gesture is open arms and their favorite question is, "What do you wanna do?" and their favorite words are "I love you, honey." They don't look for mistakes and failures; they forgive them ... They don't skip pages when they read to you ... nor do they say "hurry up" when you want to see how far you can make the rock skip across the lake. They'll even stop and lick an ice cream cone with ya.

But best of all, when you want to talk, they want to listen. Long, loud lectures are out ... It's funny, but you somehow get the impression that things like money and possessions and clothes aren't nearly as important as *you*. And getting somewhere on time isn't half as significant as enjoying the trip.

Isn't God good? Generation after generation he provides a fresh set of grandparents, an ever-present counterculture in our busy world ... They've made enough errors to understand that perfectionism is a harsh taskmaster and that self-imposed guilt is a hardened killer. They could be superb instructors, but their best lessons are caught, not taught. Their Christianity is seasoned, filtered through the tight weave of realism, heartache, loss and compromise. Jesus is not only their Lord, he's their Friend and longtime Counselor. Like a massive tree, they provide needed shade, they add beauty to the landscape and they don't mind being used. They're there. Even if not much is happening, they are there.

ADDITIONAL SCRIPTURE READINGS
Psalm 22:22–31; Psalm 145

Go to page 725 for your next devotional reading.

²⁹They ate till they had more than
    enough,
  for he had given them what
    they craved.
³⁰But before they turned from the
    food they craved,
  even while it was still in their
    mouths,
³¹God's anger rose against them;
  he put to death the sturdiest
    among them,
  cutting down the young men of
    Israel.

³²In spite of all this, they kept on
    sinning;
  in spite of his wonders, they
    did not believe.
³³So he ended their days in futility
  and their years in terror.
³⁴Whenever God slew them, they
    would seek him;
  they eagerly turned to him
    again.
³⁵They remembered that God was
    their Rock,
  that God Most High was their
    Redeemer.
³⁶But then they would flatter him
    with their mouths,
  lying to him with their tongues;
³⁷their hearts were not loyal to him,
  they were not faithful to his
    covenant.
³⁸Yet he was merciful;
  he forgave their iniquities
  and did not destroy them.
  Time after time he restrained his
    anger
  and did not stir up his full
    wrath.
³⁹He remembered that they were
    but flesh,
  a passing breeze that does not
    return.

⁴⁰How often they rebelled against
    him in the desert
  and grieved him in the
    wasteland!
⁴¹Again and again they put God to
    the test;
  they vexed the Holy One of
    Israel.
⁴²They did not remember his
    power—

the day he redeemed them from
    the oppressor,
⁴³the day he displayed his
    miraculous signs in Egypt,
  his wonders in the region of
    Zoan.
⁴⁴He turned their rivers to blood;
  they could not drink from their
    streams.
⁴⁵He sent swarms of flies that
    devoured them,
  and frogs that devastated them.
⁴⁶He gave their crops to the
    grasshopper,
  their produce to the locust.
⁴⁷He destroyed their vines with
    hail
  and their sycamore-figs with
    sleet.
⁴⁸He gave over their cattle to the
    hail,
  their livestock to bolts of
    lightning.
⁴⁹He unleashed against them his hot
    anger,
  his wrath, indignation and
    hostility—
  a band of destroying angels.
⁵⁰He prepared a path for his anger;
  he did not spare them from
    death
  but gave them over to the
    plague.
⁵¹He struck down all the firstborn of
    Egypt,
  the firstfruits of manhood in the
    tents of Ham.
⁵²But he brought his people out like
    a flock;
  he led them like sheep through
    the desert.
⁵³He guided them safely, so they
    were unafraid;
  but the sea engulfed their
    enemies.
⁵⁴Thus he brought them to the
    border of his holy land,
  to the hill country his right
    hand had taken.
⁵⁵He drove out nations before them
  and allotted their lands to them
    as an inheritance;
  he settled the tribes of Israel in
    their homes.

56But they put God to the test
    and rebelled against the Most
        High;
    they did not keep his statutes.
57Like their fathers they were
        disloyal and faithless,
    as unreliable as a faulty bow.
58They angered him with their high
        places;
    they aroused his jealousy with
        their idols.
59When God heard them, he was
        very angry;
    he rejected Israel completely.
60He abandoned the tabernacle of
        Shiloh,
    the tent he had set up among
        men.
61He sent ˻the ark of˼ his might into
        captivity,
    his splendor into the hands of
        the enemy.
62He gave his people over to the
        sword;
    he was very angry with his
        inheritance.
63Fire consumed their young men,
    and their maidens had no
        wedding songs;
64their priests were put to the
        sword,
    and their widows could not
        weep.

65Then the Lord awoke as from
        sleep,
    as a man wakes from the stupor
        of wine.
66He beat back his enemies;
    he put them to everlasting
        shame.
67Then he rejected the tents of
        Joseph,
    he did not choose the tribe of
        Ephraim;
68but he chose the tribe of Judah,
    Mount Zion, which he loved.
69He built his sanctuary like the
        heights,
    like the earth that he established
        forever.
70He chose David his servant
    and took him from the sheep
        pens;

71from tending the sheep he brought
        him
    to be the shepherd of his people
        Jacob,
    of Israel his inheritance.
72And David shepherded them with
        integrity of heart;
    with skillful hands he led them.

Psalm 79

A psalm of Asaph.

1O God, the nations have invaded
        your inheritance;
    they have defiled your holy
        temple,
    they have reduced Jerusalem to
        rubble.
2They have given the dead bodies
        of your servants
    as food to the birds of the air,
    the flesh of your saints to the
        beasts of the earth.
3They have poured out blood like
        water
    all around Jerusalem,
    and there is no one to bury the
        dead.
4We are objects of reproach to our
        neighbors,
    of scorn and derision to those
        around us.

5How long, O LORD? Will you be
        angry forever?
    How long will your jealousy
        burn like fire?
6Pour out your wrath on the
        nations
    that do not acknowledge you,
on the kingdoms
    that do not call on your name;
7for they have devoured Jacob
    and destroyed his homeland.
8Do not hold against us the sins of
        the fathers;
    may your mercy come quickly
        to meet us,
    for we are in desperate need.

9Help us, O God our Savior,
    for the glory of your name;

deliver us and forgive our sins
for your name's sake.
¹⁰Why should the nations say,
"Where is their God?"
Before our eyes, make known
among the nations
that you avenge the outpoured
blood of your servants.
¹¹May the groans of the prisoners
come before you;
by the strength of your arm
preserve those condemned to
die.

¹²Pay back into the laps of our
neighbors seven times
the reproach they have hurled
at you, O Lord.
¹³Then we your people, the sheep of
your pasture,
will praise you forever;
from generation to generation
we will recount your praise.

Psalm 80

For the director of music. To ⌊the
tune of⌋ "The Lilies of the Covenant."
Of Asaph. A psalm.

¹Hear us, O Shepherd of Israel,
you who lead Joseph like a
flock;
you who sit enthroned between
the cherubim, shine forth
² before Ephraim, Benjamin and
Manasseh.
Awaken your might;
come and save us.

³Restore us, O God;
make your face shine upon us,
that we may be saved.

⁴O LORD God Almighty,
how long will your anger
smolder
against the prayers of your
people?
⁵You have fed them with the bread
of tears;
you have made them drink
tears by the bowlful.

⁶You have made us a source of
contention to our
neighbors,
and our enemies mock us.

⁷Restore us, O God Almighty;
make your face shine upon us,
that we may be saved.

⁸You brought a vine out of Egypt;
you drove out the nations and
planted it.
⁹You cleared the ground for it,
and it took root and filled the
land.
¹⁰The mountains were covered with
its shade,
the mighty cedars with its
branches.
¹¹It sent out its boughs to the Sea,ᵃ
its shoots as far as the River.ᵇ

¹²Why have you broken down its
walls
so that all who pass by pick its
grapes?
¹³Boars from the forest ravage it
and the creatures of the field
feed on it.
¹⁴Return to us, O God Almighty!
Look down from heaven and
see!
Watch over this vine,
15   the root your right hand has
planted,
the sonᶜ you have raised up
for yourself.

¹⁶Your vine is cut down, it is
burned with fire;
at your rebuke your people
perish.
¹⁷Let your hand rest on the man at
your right hand,
the son of man you have raised
up for yourself.
¹⁸Then we will not turn away from
you;
revive us, and we will call on
your name.

¹⁹Restore us, O LORD God Almighty;
make your face shine upon us,
that we may be saved.

ᵃ11 Probably the Mediterranean   ᵇ11 That is, the Euphrates   ᶜ15 Or *branch*

Psalm 81

For the director of music. According
to *gittith.*^a Of Asaph.

¹Sing for joy to God our strength;
    shout aloud to the God of
        Jacob!
²Begin the music, strike the
        tambourine,
    play the melodious harp and
        lyre.

³Sound the ram's horn at the New
        Moon,
    and when the moon is full, on
        the day of our Feast;
⁴this is a decree for Israel,
    an ordinance of the God of
        Jacob.
⁵He established it as a statute for
        Joseph
    when he went out against
        Egypt,
    where we heard a language we
        did not understand.^b

⁶He says, "I removed the burden
        from their shoulders;
    their hands were set free from
        the basket.
⁷In your distress you called and I
        rescued you,
    I answered you out of a
        thundercloud;
    I tested you at the waters of
        Meribah.   *Selah*

⁸"Hear, O my people, and I will
        warn you—
    if you would but listen to me,
        O Israel!
⁹You shall have no foreign god
        among you;
    you shall not bow down to an
        alien god.
¹⁰I am the LORD your God,
    who brought you up out of
        Egypt.
    Open wide your mouth and I
        will fill it.

¹¹"But my people would not listen
        to me;

Israel would not submit to me.
¹²So I gave them over to their
        stubborn hearts
    to follow their own devices.

¹³"If my people would but listen to
        me,
    if Israel would follow my ways,
¹⁴how quickly would I subdue their
        enemies
    and turn my hand against their
        foes!
¹⁵Those who hate the LORD would
        cringe before him,
    and their punishment would
        last forever.
¹⁶But you would be fed with the
        finest of wheat;
    with honey from the rock I
        would satisfy you."

Psalm 82

A psalm of Asaph.

¹God presides in the great
        assembly;
    he gives judgment among the
        "gods":

²"How long will you^c defend the
        unjust
    and show partiality to the
        wicked?   *Selah*
³Defend the cause of the weak and
        fatherless;
    maintain the rights of the poor
        and oppressed.
⁴Rescue the weak and needy;
    deliver them from the hand of
        the wicked.

⁵"They know nothing, they
        understand nothing.
    They walk about in darkness;
    all the foundations of the earth
        are shaken.

⁶"I said, 'You are "gods";
    you are all sons of the Most
        High.'
⁷But you will die like mere men;
    you will fall like every other
        ruler."

---

^aTitle: Probably a musical term   ^b5 Or / *and we heard a voice we had not known*   ^c2 The
Hebrew is plural.

⁸Rise up, O God, judge the earth,
    for all the nations are your
        inheritance.

Psalm 83

A song. A psalm of Asaph.

¹O God, do not keep silent;
    be not quiet, O God, be not still.
²See how your enemies are astir,
    how your foes rear their heads.
³With cunning they conspire
        against your people;
    they plot against those you
        cherish.
⁴"Come," they say, "let us destroy
        them as a nation,
    that the name of Israel be
        remembered no more."

⁵With one mind they plot together;
    they form an alliance against
        you—
⁶the tents of Edom and the
        Ishmaelites,
    of Moab and the Hagrites,
⁷Gebal,ᵃ Ammon and Amalek,
    Philistia, with the people of
        Tyre.
⁸Even Assyria has joined them
    to lend strength to the
        descendants of Lot.   *Selah*

⁹Do to them as you did to Midian,
    as you did to Sisera and Jabin
        at the river Kishon,
¹⁰who perished at Endor
    and became like refuse on the
        ground.
¹¹Make their nobles like Oreb and
        Zeeb,
    all their princes like Zebah and
        Zalmunna,
¹²who said, "Let us take possession
    of the pasturelands of God."

¹³Make them like tumbleweed,
        O my God,
    like chaff before the wind.
¹⁴As fire consumes the forest
    or a flame sets the mountains
        ablaze,
¹⁵so pursue them with your tempest

and terrify them with your
        storm.
¹⁶Cover their faces with shame
    so that men will seek your
        name, O LORD.

¹⁷May they ever be ashamed and
        dismayed;
    may they perish in disgrace.
¹⁸Let them know that you, whose
        name is the LORD—
    that you alone are the Most
        High over all the earth.

Psalm 84

*For the director of music. According
to* gittith.ᵇ *Of the Sons of Korah.
A psalm.*

¹How lovely is your dwelling
        place,
    O LORD Almighty!
²My soul yearns, even faints,
    for the courts of the LORD;
my heart and my flesh cry out
    for the living God.

³Even the sparrow has found a
        home,
    and the swallow a nest for
        herself,
    where she may have her
        young—
a place near your altar,
    O LORD Almighty, my King and
        my God.
⁴Blessed are those who dwell in
        your house;
    they are ever praising you. *Selah*

⁵Blessed are those whose strength
        is in you,
    who have set their hearts on
        pilgrimage.
⁶As they pass through the Valley of
        Baca,
    they make it a place of springs;
    the autumn rains also cover it
        with pools.ᶜ
⁷They go from strength to strength,
    till each appears before God in
        Zion.

ᵃ7 That is, Byblos   ᵇTitle: Probably a musical term   ᶜ6 Or *blessings*

⁸Hear my prayer, O LORD God
        Almighty;
    listen to me, O God of Jacob.
                                    Selah
⁹Look upon our shield,ᵃ O God;
    look with favor on your
        anointed one.

¹⁰Better is one day in your courts
        than a thousand elsewhere;
    I would rather be a doorkeeper in
        the house of my God
    than dwell in the tents of the
        wicked.
¹¹For the LORD God is a sun and
        shield;
    the LORD bestows favor and
        honor;
    no good thing does he withhold
        from those whose walk is
        blameless.

¹²O LORD Almighty,
    blessed is the man who trusts in
        you.

Psalm 85

*For the director of music. Of the Sons
    of Korah. A psalm.*

¹You showed favor to your land,
        O LORD;
    you restored the fortunes of
        Jacob.
²You forgave the iniquity of your
        people
    and covered all their sins.   *Selah*
³You set aside all your wrath
    and turned from your fierce
        anger.

⁴Restore us again, O God our
        Savior,
    and put away your displeasure
        toward us.
⁵Will you be angry with us
        forever?
    Will you prolong your anger
        through all generations?
⁶Will you not revive us again,
    that your people may rejoice in
        you?

⁷Show us your unfailing love,
        O LORD,
    and grant us your salvation.

⁸I will listen to what God the LORD
        will say;
    he promises peace to his people,
        his saints—
    but let them not return to folly.
⁹Surely his salvation is near those
        who fear him,
    that his glory may dwell in our
        land.

¹⁰Love and faithfulness meet
        together;
    righteousness and peace kiss
        each other.
¹¹Faithfulness springs forth from the
        earth,
    and righteousness looks down
        from heaven.
¹²The LORD will indeed give what is
        good,
    and our land will yield its
        harvest.
¹³Righteousness goes before him
    and prepares the way for his
        steps.

Psalm 86

A prayer of David.

¹Hear, O LORD, and answer me,
    for I am poor and needy.
²Guard my life, for I am devoted to
        you.
    You are my God; save your
        servant
    who trusts in you.
³Have mercy on me, O Lord,
    for I call to you all day long.
⁴Bring joy to your servant,
    for to you, O Lord,
    I lift up my soul.

⁵You are forgiving and good,
        O Lord,
    abounding in love to all who
        call to you.

ᵃ9 Or *sovereign*

⁶Hear my prayer, O Lᴏʀᴅ;
  listen to my cry for mercy.
⁷In the day of my trouble I will call
    to you,
  for you will answer me.

⁸Among the gods there is none like
    you, O Lord;
  no deeds can compare with
    yours.
⁹All the nations you have made
  will come and worship before
    you, O Lord;
  they will bring glory to your
    name.
¹⁰For you are great and do
    marvelous deeds;
  you alone are God.

¹¹Teach me your way, O Lᴏʀᴅ,
  and I will walk in your truth;
give me an undivided heart,
  that I may fear your name.
¹²I will praise you, O Lord my God,
    with all my heart;
  I will glorify your name forever.
¹³For great is your love toward me;
  you have delivered me from the
    depths of the grave.ᵃ

¹⁴The arrogant are attacking me,
    O God;
  a band of ruthless men seeks
    my life—
  men without regard for you.
¹⁵But you, O Lord, are a
    compassionate and
    gracious God,
  slow to anger, abounding in
    love and faithfulness.
¹⁶Turn to me and have mercy on
    me;
  grant your strength to your
    servant
  and save the son of your
    maidservant.ᵇ
¹⁷Give me a sign of your goodness,
  that my enemies may see it and
    be put to shame,
  for you, O Lᴏʀᴅ, have helped
    me and comforted me.

Psalm 87

*Of the Sons of Korah. A psalm.
A song.*

¹He has set his foundation on the
    holy mountain;
² the Lᴏʀᴅ loves the gates of Zion
  more than all the dwellings of
    Jacob.
³Glorious things are said of you,
    O city of God: *Selah*
⁴"I will record Rahabᶜ and
    Babylon
  among those who acknowledge
    me—
  Philistia too, and Tyre, along with
    Cushᵈ—
  and will say, 'Thisᵉ one was
    born in Zion.' "
⁵Indeed, of Zion it will be said,
  "This one and that one were
    born in her,
  and the Most High himself will
    establish her."
⁶The Lᴏʀᴅ will write in the register
    of the peoples:
  "This one was born in Zion."
                                Selah
⁷As they make music they will
    sing,
  "All my fountains are in you."

Psalm 88

*A song. A psalm of the Sons of
Korah. For the director of music.
According to mahalath leannoth.ᶠ A
maskilᵍ of Heman the Ezrahite.*

¹O Lᴏʀᴅ, the God who saves me,
  day and night I cry out before
    you.
²May my prayer come before you;
  turn your ear to my cry.

³For my soul is full of trouble
  and my life draws near the
    grave.ᵃ
⁴I am counted among those who go
    down to the pit;

ᵃ13,3 Hebrew *Sheol*   ᵇ16 Or *save your faithful son*   ᶜ4 A poetic name for Egypt   ᵈ4 That
is, the upper Nile region   ᵉ4 Or *"O Rahab and Babylon, / Philistia, Tyre and Cush, / I will record
concerning those who acknowledge me: / 'This*   ᶠTitle: Possibly a tune, "The Suffering of
Affliction"   ᵍTitle: Probably a literary or musical term

I am like a man without
     strength.
⁵I am set apart with the dead,
     like the slain who lie in the
          grave,
whom you remember no more,
     who are cut off from your care.

⁶You have put me in the lowest pit,
     in the darkest depths.
⁷Your wrath lies heavily upon me;
     you have overwhelmed me with
          all your waves.   *Selah*
⁸You have taken from me my
          closest friends
     and have made me repulsive to
          them.
I am confined and cannot escape;
⁹   my eyes are dim with grief.

I call to you, O LORD, every day;
     I spread out my hands to you.
¹⁰Do you show your wonders to the
          dead?
     Do those who are dead rise up
          and praise you?   *Selah*
¹¹Is your love declared in the grave,
     your faithfulness in
          Destruction*ª*?
¹²Are your wonders known in the
          place of darkness,
     or your righteous deeds in the
          land of oblivion?

¹³But I cry to you for help, O LORD;
     in the morning my prayer
          comes before you.
¹⁴Why, O LORD, do you reject me
     and hide your face from me?

¹⁵From my youth I have been
          afflicted and close to death;
     I have suffered your terrors and
          am in despair.
¹⁶Your wrath has swept over me;
     your terrors have destroyed me.
¹⁷All day long they surround me
          like a flood;
     they have completely engulfed
          me.
¹⁸You have taken my companions
          and loved ones from me;
     the darkness is my closest
          friend.

Psalm 89

A *maskil*ᵇ of Ethan the Ezrahite.

¹I will sing of the LORD's great love
          forever;
     with my mouth I will make
          your faithfulness known
          through all generations.
²I will declare that your love stands
          firm forever,
     that you established your
          faithfulness in heaven
          itself.

³You said, "I have made a
          covenant with my chosen
          one,
     I have sworn to David my
          servant,
⁴'I will establish your line forever
     and make your throne firm
          through all generations.' "
                              Selah

⁵The heavens praise your wonders,
          O LORD,
     your faithfulness too, in the
          assembly of the holy ones.
⁶For who in the skies above can
          compare with the LORD?
     Who is like the LORD among the
          heavenly beings?
⁷In the council of the holy ones
          God is greatly feared;
     he is more awesome than all
          who surround him.
⁸O LORD God Almighty, who is like
          you?
     You are mighty, O LORD, and
          your faithfulness surrounds
          you.

⁹You rule over the surging sea;
     when its waves mount up, you
          still them.
¹⁰You crushed Rahab like one of the
          slain;
     with your strong arm you
          scattered your enemies.
¹¹The heavens are yours, and yours
          also the earth;
     you founded the world and all
          that is in it.

a11 Hebrew *Abaddon*   *b*Title: Probably a literary or musical term

¹²You created the north and the
      south;
   Tabor and Hermon sing for joy
      at your name.
¹³Your arm is endued with power;
   your hand is strong, your right
      hand exalted.

¹⁴Righteousness and justice are the
      foundation of your throne;
   love and faithfulness go before
      you.
¹⁵Blessed are those who have
      learned to acclaim you,
   who walk in the light of your
      presence, O Lord.
¹⁶They rejoice in your name all day
      long;
   they exult in your
      righteousness.
¹⁷For you are their glory and
      strength,
   and by your favor you exalt our
      horn.ᵃ
¹⁸Indeed, our shieldᵇ belongs to
      the Lord,
   our king to the Holy One of
      Israel.

¹⁹Once you spoke in a vision,
   to your faithful people you said:
   "I have bestowed strength on a
      warrior;
   I have exalted a young man
      from among the people.
²⁰I have found David my servant;
   with my sacred oil I have
      anointed him.
²¹My hand will sustain him;
   surely my arm will strengthen
      him.
²²No enemy will subject him to
      tribute;
   no wicked man will oppress
      him.
²³I will crush his foes before him
   and strike down his adversaries.
²⁴My faithful love will be with him,
   and through my name his
      hornᶜ will be exalted.

²⁵I will set his hand over the sea,
   his right hand over the rivers.
²⁶He will call out to me, 'You are
      my Father,
   my God, the Rock my Savior.'
²⁷I will also appoint him my
      firstborn,
   the most exalted of the kings of
      the earth.
²⁸I will maintain my love to him
      forever,
   and my covenant with him will
      never fail.
²⁹I will establish his line forever,
   his throne as long as the
      heavens endure.

³⁰"If his sons forsake my law
   and do not follow my statutes,
³¹if they violate my decrees
   and fail to keep my commands,
³²I will punish their sin with the
      rod,
   their iniquity with flogging;
³³but I will not take my love from
      him,
   nor will I ever betray my
      faithfulness.
³⁴I will not violate my covenant
   or alter what my lips have
      uttered.
³⁵Once for all, I have sworn by my
      holiness—
   and I will not lie to David—
³⁶that his line will continue forever
   and his throne endure before
      me like the sun;
³⁷it will be established forever like
      the moon,
   the faithful witness in the sky."
                              Selah

³⁸But you have rejected, you have
      spurned,
   you have been very angry with
      your anointed one.
³⁹You have renounced the covenant
      with your servant
   and have defiled his crown in
      the dust.

ᵃ17 *Horn* here symbolizes strong one.   ᵇ18 Or *sovereign*   ᶜ24 *Horn* here symbolizes
strength.

⁴⁰You have broken through all his
        walls
    and reduced his strongholds to
        ruins.
⁴¹All who pass by have plundered
        him;
    he has become the scorn of his
        neighbors.
⁴²You have exalted the right hand
        of his foes;
    you have made all his enemies
        rejoice.
⁴³You have turned back the edge of
        his sword
    and have not supported him in
        battle.
⁴⁴You have put an end to his
        splendor
    and cast his throne to the
        ground.
⁴⁵You have cut short the days of his
        youth;
    you have covered him with a
        mantle of shame.   *Selah*

⁴⁶How long, O Lᴏʀᴅ? Will you hide
        yourself forever?
    How long will your wrath burn
        like fire?
⁴⁷Remember how fleeting is my life.
    For what futility you have
        created all men!
⁴⁸What man can live and not see
        death,
    or save himself from the power
        of the grave*ᵃ*?   *Selah*
⁴⁹O Lord, where is your former
        great love,
    which in your faithfulness you
        swore to David?
⁵⁰Remember, Lord, how your
        servant has*ᵇ* been mocked,
    how I bear in my heart the
        taunts of all the nations,
⁵¹the taunts with which your
        enemies have mocked,
        O Lᴏʀᴅ,
    with which they have mocked
        every step of your anointed
        one.

⁵²Praise be to the Lᴏʀᴅ forever!
    Amen and Amen.

BOOK IV
Psalms 90–106

Psalm 90

A prayer of Moses the man of God.

¹Lord, you have been our dwelling
        place
    throughout all generations.
²Before the mountains were born
    or you brought forth the earth
        and the world,
    from everlasting to everlasting
        you are God.

³You turn men back to dust,
    saying, "Return to dust, O sons
        of men."
⁴For a thousand years in your sight
    are like a day that has just gone
        by,
    or like a watch in the night.
⁵You sweep men away in the sleep
        of death;
    they are like the new grass of
        the morning—
⁶though in the morning it springs
        up new,
    by evening it is dry and
        withered.

⁷We are consumed by your anger
    and terrified by your
        indignation.
⁸You have set our iniquities before
        you,
    our secret sins in the light of
        your presence.
⁹All our days pass away under
        your wrath;
    we finish our years with a
        moan.
¹⁰The length of our days is seventy
        years—
    or eighty, if we have the
        strength;
    yet their span*ᶜ* is but trouble and
        sorrow,
    for they quickly pass, and we
        fly away.

¹¹Who knows the power of your
        anger?

ᵃ48 Hebrew *Sheol*   *ᵇ50* Or *your servants have*   *ᶜ10* Or *yet the best of them*

For your wrath is as great as
the fear that is due you.
¹²Teach us to number our days
aright,
that we may gain a heart of
wisdom.
¹³Relent, O Lᴏʀᴅ! How long will it
be?

Have compassion on your
servants.
¹⁴Satisfy us in the morning with
your unfailing love,
that we may sing for joy and be
glad all our days.
¹⁵Make us glad for as many days as
you have afflicted us,

TUESDAY

VERSE:
Psalm 90:1

AUTHOR:
John Gilmore

PASSAGE:
Psalm 90:1–17

Making God Our Home

Moses prodded his people as he prayed with them.
"Lord, you have always been our home." We, too, discover God as our home when we can unburden ourselves before him.

Too many times prayers are not conversations with
God, but the dropping off of a want list at his front door.
Then we speed off to someone else. Or we knock but are
unwilling to meet God when he opens the door.

Notice in Psalm 90 that Moses didn't drop off his requests and then hurry off. For the first 11 verses of the
psalm Moses was occupied with God's *person*. It was only
in verses 12–17 that he engaged in petitioning God and
in making requests. That's what it means to settle down
with God, to make God our spiritual home.

In other words, we make God our home when we un-
pack our private feelings. We make him our reference
point. His standards become the criteria of the way we
live instead of our using the world's standards to judge
God. Making God our home means we are willing to
spend time with him, to "let our hair down" and allow
him to speak with us.

ADDITIONAL SCRIPTURE READINGS
1 Corinthians 3:16–17; Ephesians 2:19–22
Go to page 727 for your next devotional reading.

for as many years as we have
seen trouble.
¹⁶May your deeds be shown to your
servants,
your splendor to their children.

¹⁷May the favor*a* of the Lord our
God rest upon us;
establish the work of our hands
for us—
yes, establish the work of our
hands.

Psalm 91

¹He who dwells in the shelter of
the Most High
will rest in the shadow of the
Almighty.*b*
²I will say*c* of the LORD, "He is my
refuge and my fortress,
my God, in whom I trust."

³Surely he will save you from the
fowler's snare
and from the deadly pestilence.
⁴He will cover you with his
feathers,
and under his wings you will
find refuge;
his faithfulness will be your
shield and rampart.
⁵You will not fear the terror of
night,
nor the arrow that flies by day,
⁶nor the pestilence that stalks in the
darkness,
nor the plague that destroys at
midday.
⁷A thousand may fall at your side,
ten thousand at your right
hand,
but it will not come near you.
⁸You will only observe with your
eyes
and see the punishment of the
wicked.

⁹If you make the Most High your
dwelling—
even the LORD, who is my
refuge—
¹⁰then no harm will befall you,

no disaster will come near your
tent.
¹¹For he will command his angels
concerning you
to guard you in all your ways;
¹²they will lift you up in their
hands,
so that you will not strike your
foot against a stone.
¹³You will tread upon the lion and
the cobra;
you will trample the great lion
and the serpent.

¹⁴"Because he loves me," says the
LORD, "I will rescue him;
I will protect him, for he
acknowledges my name.
¹⁵He will call upon me, and I will
answer him;
I will be with him in trouble,
I will deliver him and honor
him.
¹⁶With long life will I satisfy him
and show him my salvation."

Psalm 92

*A psalm. A song. For the
Sabbath day.*

¹It is good to praise the LORD
and make music to your name,
O Most High,
²to proclaim your love in the
morning
and your faithfulness at night,
³to the music of the ten-stringed
lyre
and the melody of the harp.

⁴For you make me glad by your
deeds, O LORD;
I sing for joy at the works of
your hands.
⁵How great are your works,
O LORD,
how profound your thoughts!
⁶The senseless man does not know,
fools do not understand,
⁷that though the wicked spring up
like grass
and all evildoers flourish,

a17 Or beauty   *b1 Hebrew Shaddai*   *c2 Or He says*

they will be forever destroyed.

⁸But you, O LORD, are exalted
    forever.

⁹For surely your enemies, O LORD,
    surely your enemies will perish;
    all evildoers will be scattered.
¹⁰You have exalted my horn*a* like
    that of a wild ox;
    fine oils have been poured upon
    me.
¹¹My eyes have seen the defeat of
    my adversaries;

my ears have heard the rout of
    my wicked foes.

¹²The righteous will flourish like a
    palm tree,
    they will grow like a cedar of
    Lebanon;
¹³planted in the house of the LORD,
    they will flourish in the courts
    of our God.
¹⁴They will still bear fruit in old
    age,
    they will stay fresh and green,

a10 Horn here symbolizes strength.

VERSE:	AUTHOR:	PASSAGE:
Psalm 92:14	Ronald Geschwendt	Psalm 92:1–15

They Will Stay Fresh and Green

Productivity, service and stewardship need to be a part of life until our death. As the psalmist says, we need to stay "fresh and green" (Psalm 92:14).

It is true, of course, that when we reach our senior years we begin to experience the effects of aging. Blood pressure begins to rise. As you drive your car it appears that the people on the freeway are all younger. The aging process cannot be denied. Death is inevitable. But it is prepared for even as we live. And all that we have been in the earlier years matures and flowers in older age. The Christian senior citizen understands grace better than in earlier years; hence, the seasoned years have all the potential for happiness and service in our lives, even if they are on a different playing field. And this is no deterrent to well-being and servanthood. Growing older brings opportunity for the integration of life, accumulated knowledge and discernment.

ADDITIONAL SCRIPTURE READINGS
John 15:1–8; Philippians 1:3–11

Go to page 732 for your next devotional reading.

[15]proclaiming, "The LORD is upright;
    he is my Rock, and there is no
        wickedness in him."

Psalm 93

[1]The LORD reigns, he is robed in
    majesty;
    the LORD is robed in majesty
        and is armed with strength.
The world is firmly established;
    it cannot be moved.
[2]Your throne was established long
    ago;
    you are from all eternity.

[3]The seas have lifted up, O LORD,
    the seas have lifted up their
        voice;
    the seas have lifted up their
        pounding waves.
[4]Mightier than the thunder of the
    great waters,
    mightier than the breakers of
        the sea—
    the LORD on high is mighty.
[5]Your statutes stand firm;
    holiness adorns your house
        for endless days, O LORD.

Psalm 94

[1]O LORD, the God who avenges,
    O God who avenges, shine
        forth.
[2]Rise up, O Judge of the earth;
    pay back to the proud what
        they deserve.
[3]How long will the wicked,
    O LORD,
    how long will the wicked be
        jubilant?

[4]They pour out arrogant words;
    all the evildoers are full of
        boasting.
[5]They crush your people, O LORD;
    they oppress your inheritance.
[6]They slay the widow and the
    alien;
    they murder the fatherless.
[7]They say, "The LORD does not see;
    the God of Jacob pays no heed."

[8]Take heed, you senseless ones
    among the people;

you fools, when will you
    become wise?
[9]Does he who implanted the ear
    not hear?
Does he who formed the eye
    not see?
[10]Does he who disciplines nations
    not punish?
Does he who teaches man lack
    knowledge?
[11]The LORD knows the thoughts of
    man;
    he knows that they are futile.

[12]Blessed is the man you discipline,
    O LORD,
    the man you teach from your
        law;
[13]you grant him relief from days of
    trouble,
    till a pit is dug for the wicked.
[14]For the LORD will not reject his
    people;
    he will never forsake his
        inheritance.
[15]Judgment will again be founded
    on righteousness,
    and all the upright in heart will
        follow it.

[16]Who will rise up for me against
    the wicked?
Who will take a stand for me
    against evildoers?
[17]Unless the LORD had given me
    help,
    I would soon have dwelt in the
        silence of death.
[18]When I said, "My foot is
    slipping,"
    your love, O LORD, supported
        me.
[19]When anxiety was great within
    me,
    your consolation brought joy to
        my soul.

[20]Can a corrupt throne be allied
    with you—
    one that brings on misery by its
        decrees?
[21]They band together against the
    righteous
    and condemn the innocent to
        death.

²²But the LORD has become my
    fortress,
    and my God the rock in whom
        I take refuge.
²³He will repay them for their sins
    and destroy them for their
        wickedness;
    the LORD our God will destroy
        them.

Psalm 95

¹Come, let us sing for joy to the
    LORD;
    let us shout aloud to the Rock
        of our salvation.
²Let us come before him with
        thanksgiving
    and extol him with music and
        song.

³For the LORD is the great God,
    the great King above all gods.
⁴In his hand are the depths of the
        earth,
    and the mountain peaks belong
        to him.
⁵The sea is his, for he made it,
    and his hands formed the dry
        land.

⁶Come, let us bow down in
        worship,
    let us kneel before the LORD our
        Maker;
⁷for he is our God
    and we are the people of his
        pasture,
    the flock under his care.

Today, if you hear his voice,
⁸   do not harden your hearts as
        you did at Meribah,ᵃ
    as you did that day at Massahᵇ
        in the desert,
⁹where your fathers tested and
        tried me,
    though they had seen what I
        did.
¹⁰For forty years I was angry with
        that generation;
    I said, "They are a people
        whose hearts go astray,
    and they have not known my
        ways."

¹¹So I declared on oath in my anger,
    "They shall never enter my
        rest."

Psalm 96

¹Sing to the LORD a new song;
    sing to the LORD, all the earth.
²Sing to the LORD, praise his name;
    proclaim his salvation day after
        day.
³Declare his glory among the
        nations,
    his marvelous deeds among all
        peoples.

⁴For great is the LORD and most
        worthy of praise;
    he is to be feared above all
        gods.
⁵For all the gods of the nations are
        idols,
    but the LORD made the heavens.
⁶Splendor and majesty are before
        him;
    strength and glory are in his
        sanctuary.

⁷Ascribe to the LORD, O families of
        nations,
    ascribe to the LORD glory and
        strength.
⁸Ascribe to the LORD the glory due
        his name;
    bring an offering and come into
        his courts.
⁹Worship the LORD in the splendor
        of hisᶜ holiness;
    tremble before him, all the
        earth.

¹⁰Say among the nations, "The LORD
        reigns."
    The world is firmly established,
        it cannot be moved;
    he will judge the peoples with
        equity.
¹¹Let the heavens rejoice, let the
        earth be glad;
    let the sea resound, and all that
        is in it;
¹²   let the fields be jubilant, and
        everything in them.
    Then all the trees of the forest will
        sing for joy;

ᵃ8 *Meribah* means *quarreling.*   ᵇ8 *Massah* means *testing.*   ᶜ9 Or LORD *with the splendor of*

¹³ they will sing before the LORD,
    for he comes,
  he comes to judge the earth.
He will judge the world in
    righteousness
  and the peoples in his truth.

Psalm 97

¹The LORD reigns, let the earth be
    glad;
  let the distant shores rejoice.

²Clouds and thick darkness
    surround him;
  righteousness and justice are the
    foundation of his throne.
³Fire goes before him
  and consumes his foes on every
    side.
⁴His lightning lights up the world;
  the earth sees and trembles.
⁵The mountains melt like wax
    before the LORD,
  before the Lord of all the earth.
⁶The heavens proclaim his
    righteousness,
  and all the peoples see his
    glory.

⁷All who worship images are put
    to shame,
  those who boast in idols—
  worship him, all you gods!

⁸Zion hears and rejoices
  and the villages of Judah are
    glad
  because of your judgments,
    O LORD.
⁹For you, O LORD, are the Most
    High over all the earth;
  you are exalted far above all
    gods.

¹⁰Let those who love the LORD hate
    evil,
  for he guards the lives of his
    faithful ones
  and delivers them from the
    hand of the wicked.
¹¹Light is shed upon the righteous
  and joy on the upright in heart.
¹²Rejoice in the LORD, you who are
    righteous,
  and praise his holy name.

Psalm 98

A psalm.

¹Sing to the LORD a new song,
  for he has done marvelous
    things;
  his right hand and his holy arm
  have worked salvation for him.
²The LORD has made his salvation
    known
  and revealed his righteousness
    to the nations.
³He has remembered his love
  and his faithfulness to the house
    of Israel;
  all the ends of the earth have seen
    the salvation of our God.

⁴Shout for joy to the LORD, all the
    earth,
  burst into jubilant song with
    music;
⁵make music to the LORD with the
    harp,
  with the harp and the sound of
    singing,
⁶with trumpets and the blast of the
    ram's horn—
  shout for joy before the LORD,
    the King.

⁷Let the sea resound, and
    everything in it,
  the world, and all who live in
    it.
⁸Let the rivers clap their hands,
  let the mountains sing together
    for joy;
⁹let them sing before the LORD,
  for he comes to judge the earth.
He will judge the world in
    righteousness
  and the peoples with equity.

Psalm 99

¹The LORD reigns,
  let the nations tremble;
  he sits enthroned between the
    cherubim,
  let the earth shake.
²Great is the LORD in Zion;
  he is exalted over all the
    nations.

³Let them praise your great and
    awesome name—
    he is holy.

⁴The King is mighty, he loves
    justice—
    you have established equity;
  in Jacob you have done
    what is just and right.
⁵Exalt the LORD our God
    and worship at his footstool;
    he is holy.

⁶Moses and Aaron were among his
    priests,
    Samuel was among those who
    called on his name;
  they called on the LORD
    and he answered them.
⁷He spoke to them from the pillar
    of cloud;
    they kept his statutes and the
    decrees he gave them.

⁸O LORD our God,
    you answered them;
  you were to Israel*a* a forgiving
    God,
    though you punished their
    misdeeds.*b*
⁹Exalt the LORD our God
    and worship at his holy
    mountain,
    for the LORD our God is holy.

Psalm 100

A psalm. For giving thanks.

¹Shout for joy to the LORD, all the
    earth.
²   Worship the LORD with
    gladness;
    come before him with joyful
    songs.
³Know that the LORD is God.
    It is he who made us, and we
    are his*c*;
    we are his people, the sheep of
    his pasture.

⁴Enter his gates with thanksgiving
    and his courts with praise;
    give thanks to him and praise
    his name.

⁵For the LORD is good and his love
    endures forever;
    his faithfulness continues
    through all generations.

Psalm 101

Of David. A psalm.

¹I will sing of your love and
    justice;
    to you, O LORD, I will sing
    praise.
²I will be careful to lead a
    blameless life—
    when will you come to me?

I will walk in my house
    with blameless heart.
³I will set before my eyes
    no vile thing.

The deeds of faithless men I hate;
    they will not cling to me.
⁴Men of perverse heart shall be far
    from me;
    I will have nothing to do with
    evil.

⁵Whoever slanders his neighbor in
    secret,
    him will I put to silence;
  whoever has haughty eyes and a
    proud heart,
    him will I not endure.

⁶My eyes will be on the faithful in
    the land,
    that they may dwell with me;
  he whose walk is blameless
    will minister to me.

⁷No one who practices deceit
    will dwell in my house;
  no one who speaks falsely
    will stand in my presence.

⁸Every morning I will put to
    silence
    all the wicked in the land;
  I will cut off every evildoer
    from the city of the LORD.

---

*a*8 Hebrew *them*   *b*8 Or / *an avenger of the wrongs done to them*   *c*3 Or *and not we ourselves*

VERSE: AUTHOR: PASSAGE:
Psalm 101:3   Jean Shaw   Psalm 101:1–8

A Time to Give Up Searching

The story is told of a man who was walking down the street one day when he spied a dollar bill in the gutter. He spent the next 20 years of his life walking with his head down, hoping for a similar piece of good fortune. He missed seeing the trees bud in the spring, the geese flying south, the sun set. His back grew so humped he couldn't lift his head. He saw a lot of gutters, but he never again found a dollar bill.

Life is marked by occasional surprises — small but bright blessings that give us an unexpected lift. We would like to go back and live them over again, but we cannot. Time has wrought changes . . .

We can spend the last decades of our life searching for a duplicate of some earlier experience. We can even contrive people and events to fit a bygone mold. We load our children with guilt if they don't keep Christmas the way we did 40 years ago. We resist our minister's attempt to change the worship service. If we could only recapture those particular moments when life was so intensely sweet!

There is a time to give up searching. What is lost is lost. We must be alert for the delights that today will bring.

ADDITIONAL SCRIPTURE READINGS
Ecclesiastes 3:1–11; Isaiah 43:14–21
Go to page 736 for your next devotional reading.

Psalm 102

A prayer of an afflicted man. When
he is faint and pours out his lament
before the LORD.

¹Hear my prayer, O LORD;
    let my cry for help come to you.
²Do not hide your face from me
    when I am in distress.
Turn your ear to me;
    when I call, answer me quickly.

³For my days vanish like smoke;
    my bones burn like glowing
      embers.
⁴My heart is blighted and withered
    like grass;
    I forget to eat my food.
⁵Because of my loud groaning
    I am reduced to skin and bones.
⁶I am like a desert owl,
    like an owl among the ruins.
⁷I lie awake; I have become
    like a bird alone on a roof.
⁸All day long my enemies taunt
    me;
    those who rail against me use
      my name as a curse.
⁹For I eat ashes as my food
    and mingle my drink with tears
¹⁰because of your great wrath,
    for you have taken me up and
      thrown me aside.
¹¹My days are like the evening
    shadow;
    I wither away like grass.

¹²But you, O LORD, sit enthroned
    forever;
    your renown endures through
      all generations.
¹³You will arise and have
    compassion on Zion,
    for it is time to show favor to
      her;
    the appointed time has come.
¹⁴For her stones are dear to your
    servants;
    her very dust moves them to
      pity.

¹⁵The nations will fear the name of
    the LORD,
    all the kings of the earth will
      revere your glory.
¹⁶For the LORD will rebuild Zion
    and appear in his glory.
¹⁷He will respond to the prayer of
    the destitute;
    he will not despise their plea.

¹⁸Let this be written for a future
    generation,
    that a people not yet created
      may praise the LORD:
¹⁹"The LORD looked down from his
    sanctuary on high,
    from heaven he viewed the
      earth,
²⁰to hear the groans of the prisoners
    and release those condemned to
      death."
²¹So the name of the LORD will be
    declared in Zion
    and his praise in Jerusalem
²²when the peoples and the
    kingdoms
    assemble to worship the LORD.

²³In the course of my life[a] he broke
    my strength;
    he cut short my days.
²⁴So I said:
    "Do not take me away, O my
      God, in the midst of my
      days;
    your years go on through all
      generations.
²⁵In the beginning you laid the
    foundations of the earth,
    and the heavens are the work of
      your hands.
²⁶They will perish, but you remain;
    they will all wear out like a
      garment.
Like clothing you will change
    them
    and they will be discarded.
²⁷But you remain the same,
    and your years will never end.
²⁸The children of your servants will
    live in your presence;
    their descendants will be
      established before you."

ᵃ23 Or By his power

Psalm 103

Of David.

¹Praise the LORD, O my soul;
   all my inmost being, praise his
      holy name.
²Praise the LORD, O my soul,
   and forget not all his benefits—
³who forgives all your sins
   and heals all your diseases,
⁴who redeems your life from the
      pit
   and crowns you with love and
      compassion,
⁵who satisfies your desires with
      good things
   so that your youth is renewed
      like the eagle's.

⁶The LORD works righteousness
   and justice for all the oppressed.

⁷He made known his ways to
      Moses,
   his deeds to the people of Israel:
⁸The LORD is compassionate and
      gracious,
   slow to anger, abounding in
      love.
⁹He will not always accuse,
   nor will he harbor his anger
      forever;
¹⁰he does not treat us as our sins
      deserve
   or repay us according to our
      iniquities.
¹¹For as high as the heavens are
      above the earth,
   so great is his love for those
      who fear him;
¹²as far as the east is from the west,
   so far has he removed our
      transgressions from us.
¹³As a father has compassion on his
      children,
   so the LORD has compassion on
      those who fear him;
¹⁴for he knows how we are formed,
   he remembers that we are dust.
¹⁵As for man, his days are like
      grass,
   he flourishes like a flower of the
      field;

¹⁶the wind blows over it and it is
      gone,
   and its place remembers it no
      more.
¹⁷But from everlasting to everlasting
   the LORD's love is with those
      who fear him,
   and his righteousness with their
      children's children—
¹⁸with those who keep his covenant
   and remember to obey his
      precepts.

¹⁹The LORD has established his
      throne in heaven,
   and his kingdom rules over all.

²⁰Praise the LORD, you his angels,
   you mighty ones who do his
      bidding,
   who obey his word.
²¹Praise the LORD, all his heavenly
      hosts,
   you his servants who do his
      will.
²²Praise the LORD, all his works
   everywhere in his dominion.

Praise the LORD, O my soul.

Psalm 104

¹Praise the LORD, O my soul.

O LORD my God, you are very
      great;
   you are clothed with splendor
      and majesty.
²He wraps himself in light as with
      a garment;
   he stretches out the heavens like
      a tent
³   and lays the beams of his upper
      chambers on their waters.
He makes the clouds his chariot
   and rides on the wings of the
      wind.
⁴He makes winds his messengers,ᵃ
   flames of fire his servants.

⁵He set the earth on its
      foundations;
   it can never be moved.
⁶You covered it with the deep as
      with a garment;

ᵃ4 Or *angels*

the waters stood above the
mountains.
⁷But at your rebuke the waters
fled,
at the sound of your thunder
they took to flight;
⁸they flowed over the mountains,
they went down into the
valleys,
to the place you assigned for
them.
⁹You set a boundary they cannot
cross;
never again will they cover the
earth.

¹⁰He makes springs pour water into
the ravines;
it flows between the mountains.
¹¹They give water to all the beasts
of the field;
the wild donkeys quench their
thirst.
¹²The birds of the air nest by the
waters;
they sing among the branches.
¹³He waters the mountains from his
upper chambers;
the earth is satisfied by the fruit
of his work.
¹⁴He makes grass grow for the
cattle,
and plants for man to
cultivate—
bringing forth food from the
earth:
¹⁵wine that gladdens the heart of
man,
oil to make his face shine,
and bread that sustains his
heart.
¹⁶The trees of the LORD are well
watered,
the cedars of Lebanon that he
planted.
¹⁷There the birds make their nests;
the stork has its home in the
pine trees.
¹⁸The high mountains belong to the
wild goats;
the crags are a refuge for the
coneys.ᵃ

¹⁹The moon marks off the seasons,
and the sun knows when to go
down.
²⁰You bring darkness, it becomes
night,
and all the beasts of the forest
prowl.
²¹The lions roar for their prey
and seek their food from God.
²²The sun rises, and they steal
away;
they return and lie down in
their dens.
²³Then man goes out to his work,
to his labor until evening.

²⁴How many are your works,
O LORD!
In wisdom you made them all;
the earth is full of your
creatures.
²⁵There is the sea, vast and
spacious,
teeming with creatures beyond
number—
living things both large and
small.
²⁶There the ships go to and fro,
and the leviathan, which you
formed to frolic there.

²⁷These all look to you
to give them their food at the
proper time.
²⁸When you give it to them,
they gather it up;
when you open your hand,
they are satisfied with good
things.
²⁹When you hide your face,
they are terrified;
when you take away their breath,
they die and return to the dust.
³⁰When you send your Spirit,
they are created,
and you renew the face of the
earth.

³¹May the glory of the LORD endure
forever;
may the LORD rejoice in his
works—

ᵃ18 That is, the hyrax or rock badger

³²he who looks at the earth, and it
trembles,
who touches the mountains, and
they smoke.

³³I will sing to the LORD all my
life;
I will sing praise to my God
as long as I live.

³⁴May my meditation be pleasing to
him,
as I rejoice in the LORD.
³⁵But may sinners vanish from the
earth
and the wicked be no more.

Praise the LORD, O my soul.

Praise the LORD.ᵃ

ᵃ35 Hebrew *Hallelu Yah*; in the Septuagint this line stands at the beginning of Psalm 105.

VERSE:	AUTHOR:	PASSAGE:
Psalm 104:31	A.W. Tozer	Psalm 104:1–35

Objects of His Delight

God enjoys his creation. The apostle John says frankly
that God's purpose in creation was his own pleasure.
God is happy in his love for all that he has made. We
cannot miss the feeling of pleasure in God's delighted
references to his handiwork. Psalm 104 is a divinely inspired nature poem almost rhapsodic in its happiness,
and the delight of God is felt throughout it. "May the
glory of the LORD endure forever; may the LORD rejoice
in his works" (Psalm 104:31).

The Lord takes peculiar pleasure in his saints. Many
think of God as far removed, gloomy and mightily displeased with everything, gazing down in a mood of fixed
apathy upon a world in which he has long ago lost interest; but this is to think erroneously. True, God hates sin
and can never look with pleasure upon iniquity, but
where men seek to do God's will he responds in genuine
affection. Christ in his atonement has removed the bar to
the divine fellowship. Now in Christ all believing souls
are objects of God's delight.

ADDITIONAL SCRIPTURE READINGS
Psalm 36:5–9; Zephaniah 3:14–20

Go to page 741 for your next devotional reading.

Psalm 105

¹Give thanks to the LORD, call on
    his name;
  make known among the nations
    what he has done.
²Sing to him, sing praise to him;
  tell of all his wonderful acts.
³Glory in his holy name;
  let the hearts of those who seek
    the LORD rejoice.
⁴Look to the LORD and his strength;
  seek his face always.

⁵Remember the wonders he has
    done,
  his miracles, and the judgments
    he pronounced,
⁶O descendants of Abraham his
    servant,
  O sons of Jacob, his chosen
    ones.
⁷He is the LORD our God;
  his judgments are in all the
    earth.

⁸He remembers his covenant
    forever,
  the word he commanded, for a
    thousand generations,
⁹the covenant he made with
    Abraham,
  the oath he swore to Isaac.
¹⁰He confirmed it to Jacob as a
    decree,
  to Israel as an everlasting
    covenant:
¹¹"To you I will give the land of
    Canaan
  as the portion you will inherit."

¹²When they were but few in
    number,
  few indeed, and strangers in it,
¹³they wandered from nation to
    nation,
  from one kingdom to another.
¹⁴He allowed no one to oppress
    them;
  for their sake he rebuked kings:
¹⁵"Do not touch my anointed ones;
  do my prophets no harm."

¹⁶He called down famine on the
    land
  and destroyed all their supplies
    of food;
¹⁷and he sent a man before them—
  Joseph, sold as a slave.
¹⁸They bruised his feet with
    shackles,
  his neck was put in irons,
¹⁹till what he foretold came to pass,
  till the word of the LORD proved
    him true.
²⁰The king sent and released him,
  the ruler of peoples set him
    free.
²¹He made him master of his
    household,
  ruler over all he possessed,
²²to instruct his princes as he
    pleased
  and teach his elders wisdom.

²³Then Israel entered Egypt;
  Jacob lived as an alien in the
    land of Ham.
²⁴The LORD made his people very
    fruitful;
  he made them too numerous for
    their foes,
²⁵whose hearts he turned to hate his
    people,
  to conspire against his servants.
²⁶He sent Moses his servant,
  and Aaron, whom he had
    chosen.
²⁷They performed his miraculous
    signs among them,
  his wonders in the land of
    Ham.
²⁸He sent darkness and made the
    land dark—
  for had they not rebelled
    against his words?
²⁹He turned their waters into blood,
  causing their fish to die.
³⁰Their land teemed with frogs,
  which went up into the
    bedrooms of their rulers.
³¹He spoke, and there came swarms
    of flies,
  and gnats throughout their
    country.
³²He turned their rain into hail,
  with lightning throughout their
    land;
³³he struck down their vines and fig
    trees
  and shattered the trees of their
    country.

³⁴He spoke, and the locusts came,
   grasshoppers without number;
³⁵they ate up every green thing in
      their land,
   ate up the produce of their soil.
³⁶Then he struck down all the
      firstborn in their land,
   the firstfruits of all their
      manhood.

³⁷He brought out Israel, laden with
      silver and gold,
   and from among their tribes no
      one faltered.
³⁸Egypt was glad when they left,
   because dread of Israel had
      fallen on them.
³⁹He spread out a cloud as a
      covering,
   and a fire to give light at night.
⁴⁰They asked, and he brought them
      quail
   and satisfied them with the
      bread of heaven.
⁴¹He opened the rock, and water
      gushed out;
   like a river it flowed in the
      desert.

⁴²For he remembered his holy
      promise
   given to his servant Abraham.
⁴³He brought out his people with
      rejoicing,
   his chosen ones with shouts of
      joy;
⁴⁴he gave them the lands of the
      nations,
   and they fell heir to what others
      had toiled for—
⁴⁵that they might keep his precepts
   and observe his laws.

   Praise the LORD.ᵃ

Psalm 106

¹Praise the LORD.ᵇ

   Give thanks to the LORD, for he is
      good;
   his love endures forever.
²Who can proclaim the mighty acts
      of the LORD

or fully declare his praise?
³Blessed are they who maintain
      justice,
   who constantly do what is right.
⁴Remember me, O LORD, when you
      show favor to your people,
   come to my aid when you save
      them,
⁵that I may enjoy the prosperity of
      your chosen ones,
   that I may share in the joy of
      your nation
   and join your inheritance in
      giving praise.

⁶We have sinned, even as our
      fathers did;
   we have done wrong and acted
      wickedly.
⁷When our fathers were in Egypt,
   they gave no thought to your
      miracles;
   they did not remember your many
      kindnesses,
   and they rebelled by the sea,
      the Red Sea.ᶜ
⁸Yet he saved them for his name's
      sake,
   to make his mighty power
      known.
⁹He rebuked the Red Sea, and it
      dried up;
   he led them through the depths
      as through a desert.
¹⁰He saved them from the hand of
      the foe;
   from the hand of the enemy he
      redeemed them.
¹¹The waters covered their
      adversaries;
   not one of them survived.
¹²Then they believed his promises
   and sang his praise.

¹³But they soon forgot what he had
      done
   and did not wait for his
      counsel.
¹⁴In the desert they gave in to their
      craving;
   in the wasteland they put God
      to the test.

ᵃ45 Hebrew Hallelu Yah   ᵇ1 Hebrew Hallelu Yah; also in verse 48   ᶜ7 Hebrew Yam Suph;
that is, Sea of Reeds; also in verses 9 and 22

¹⁵So he gave them what they asked
    for,
    but sent a wasting disease upon
        them.

¹⁶In the camp they grew envious of
        Moses
    and of Aaron, who was
        consecrated to the LORD.
¹⁷The earth opened up and
        swallowed Dathan;
    it buried the company of
        Abiram.
¹⁸Fire blazed among their followers;
    a flame consumed the wicked.

¹⁹At Horeb they made a calf
    and worshiped an idol cast
        from metal.
²⁰They exchanged their Glory
    for an image of a bull, which
        eats grass.
²¹They forgot the God who saved
        them,
    who had done great things in
        Egypt,
²²miracles in the land of Ham
    and awesome deeds by the Red
        Sea.
²³So he said he would destroy
        them—
    had not Moses, his chosen one,
    stood in the breach before him
    to keep his wrath from
        destroying them.

²⁴Then they despised the pleasant
        land;
    they did not believe his
        promise.
²⁵They grumbled in their tents
    and did not obey the LORD.
²⁶So he swore to them with uplifted
        hand
    that he would make them fall in
        the desert,
²⁷make their descendants fall among
        the nations
    and scatter them throughout the
        lands.

²⁸They yoked themselves to the Baal
        of Peor
    and ate sacrifices offered to
        lifeless gods;

²⁹they provoked the LORD to anger
        by their wicked deeds,
    and a plague broke out among
        them.
³⁰But Phinehas stood up and
        intervened,
    and the plague was checked.
³¹This was credited to him as
        righteousness
    for endless generations to come.

³²By the waters of Meribah they
        angered the LORD,
    and trouble came to Moses
        because of them;
³³for they rebelled against the Spirit
        of God,
    and rash words came from
        Moses' lips.^a

³⁴They did not destroy the peoples
    as the LORD had commanded
        them,
³⁵but they mingled with the nations
    and adopted their customs.
³⁶They worshiped their idols,
    which became a snare to them.
³⁷They sacrificed their sons
    and their daughters to demons.
³⁸They shed innocent blood,
    the blood of their sons and
        daughters,
    whom they sacrificed to the idols
        of Canaan,
    and the land was desecrated by
        their blood.
³⁹They defiled themselves by what
        they did;
    by their deeds they prostituted
        themselves.

⁴⁰Therefore the LORD was angry with
        his people
    and abhorred his inheritance.
⁴¹He handed them over to the
        nations,
    and their foes ruled over them.
⁴²Their enemies oppressed them
    and subjected them to their
        power.
⁴³Many times he delivered them,
    but they were bent on rebellion
    and they wasted away in their
        sin.

^a33 Or *against his spirit, / and rash words came from his lips*

⁴⁴But he took note of their distress
   when he heard their cry;
⁴⁵for their sake he remembered his
      covenant
   and out of his great love he
      relented.
⁴⁶He caused them to be pitied
   by all who held them captive.

⁴⁷Save us, O LORD our God,
   and gather us from the nations,
that we may give thanks to your
      holy name
   and glory in your praise.

⁴⁸Praise be to the LORD, the God of
      Israel,
   from everlasting to everlasting.
Let all the people say, "Amen!"

Praise the LORD.

BOOK V

Psalms 107–150

Psalm 107

¹Give thanks to the LORD, for he is
      good;
   his love endures forever.
²Let the redeemed of the LORD say
      this—
   those he redeemed from the
      hand of the foe,
³those he gathered from the lands,
   from east and west, from north
      and south.*ᵃ*

⁴Some wandered in desert
      wastelands,
   finding no way to a city where
      they could settle.
⁵They were hungry and thirsty,
   and their lives ebbed away.
⁶Then they cried out to the LORD in
      their trouble,
   and he delivered them from
      their distress.
⁷He led them by a straight way
   to a city where they could
      settle.
⁸Let them give thanks to the LORD
   for his unfailing love
   and his wonderful deeds for
      men,

⁹for he satisfies the thirsty
   and fills the hungry with good
      things.

¹⁰Some sat in darkness and the
      deepest gloom,
   prisoners suffering in iron
      chains,
¹¹for they had rebelled against the
      words of God
   and despised the counsel of the
      Most High.
¹²So he subjected them to bitter
      labor;
   they stumbled, and there was
      no one to help.
¹³Then they cried to the LORD in
      their trouble,
   and he saved them from their
      distress.
¹⁴He brought them out of darkness
      and the deepest gloom
   and broke away their chains.
¹⁵Let them give thanks to the LORD
   for his unfailing love
   and his wonderful deeds for
      men,
¹⁶for he breaks down gates of
      bronze
   and cuts through bars of iron.

¹⁷Some became fools through their
      rebellious ways
   and suffered affliction because
      of their iniquities.
¹⁸They loathed all food
   and drew near the gates of
      death.
¹⁹Then they cried to the LORD in
      their trouble,
   and he saved them from their
      distress.
²⁰He sent forth his word and healed
      them;
   he rescued them from the grave.
²¹Let them give thanks to the LORD
   for his unfailing love
   and his wonderful deeds for
      men.
²²Let them sacrifice thank offerings
   and tell of his works with songs
      of joy.

ᵃ3 Hebrew north and the sea

A Psalm of Forgetfulness

Lord
I'm becoming forgetful
names words
ideas
whether I did this or that.
Remind me Lord
of my memory.
Keep me sharp.
But if it ever
comes to that
let me forget
everything
except
Jesus loves me
this I know
for the Bible
tells me so
and
others love me
even if I forget
everything
including their names.

Go to page 749 for your next devotional reading.

²³Others went out on the sea in
    ships;
they were merchants on the
    mighty waters.
²⁴They saw the works of the LORD,
    his wonderful deeds in the
    deep.
²⁵For he spoke and stirred up a
    tempest
that lifted high the waves.
²⁶They mounted up to the heavens
    and went down to the
    depths;
in their peril their courage
    melted away.
²⁷They reeled and staggered like
    drunken men;
they were at their wits' end.
²⁸Then they cried out to the LORD in
    their trouble,
and he brought them out of
    their distress.
²⁹He stilled the storm to a whisper;
    the waves of the sea were
    hushed.
³⁰They were glad when it grew
    calm,
and he guided them to their
    desired haven.
³¹Let them give thanks to the LORD
    for his unfailing love
and his wonderful deeds for
    men.
³²Let them exalt him in the
    assembly of the people
and praise him in the council of
    the elders.

³³He turned rivers into a desert,
    flowing springs into thirsty
    ground,
³⁴and fruitful land into a salt waste,
    because of the wickedness of
    those who lived there.
³⁵He turned the desert into pools of
    water
and the parched ground into
    flowing springs;
³⁶there he brought the hungry to
    live,
and they founded a city where
    they could settle.
³⁷They sowed fields and planted
    vineyards
that yielded a fruitful harvest;

³⁸he blessed them, and their
    numbers greatly increased,
and he did not let their herds
    diminish.

³⁹Then their numbers decreased,
    and they were humbled
by oppression, calamity and
    sorrow;
⁴⁰he who pours contempt on nobles
    made them wander in a
    trackless waste.
⁴¹But he lifted the needy out of their
    affliction
and increased their families like
    flocks.
⁴²The upright see and rejoice,
    but all the wicked shut their
    mouths.

⁴³Whoever is wise, let him heed
    these things
and consider the great love of
    the LORD.

Psalm 108

A song. A psalm of David.

¹My heart is steadfast, O God;
    I will sing and make music with
    all my soul.
²Awake, harp and lyre!
    I will awaken the dawn.
³I will praise you, O LORD, among
    the nations;
I will sing of you among the
    peoples.
⁴For great is your love, higher than
    the heavens;
your faithfulness reaches to the
    skies.
⁵Be exalted, O God, above the
    heavens,
and let your glory be over all
    the earth.

⁶Save us and help us with your
    right hand,
that those you love may be
    delivered.
⁷God has spoken from his
    sanctuary:
    "In triumph I will parcel out
    Shechem

and measure off the Valley of
    Succoth.
⁸Gilead is mine, Manasseh is mine;
    Ephraim is my helmet,
    Judah my scepter.
⁹Moab is my washbasin,
    upon Edom I toss my sandal;
    over Philistia I shout in
        triumph."

¹⁰Who will bring me to the fortified
        city?
    Who will lead me to Edom?
¹¹Is it not you, O God, you who
        have rejected us
    and no longer go out with our
        armies?
¹²Give us aid against the enemy,
    for the help of man is worthless.
¹³With God we will gain the victory,
    and he will trample down our
        enemies.

Psalm 109

For the director of music. Of David.
A psalm.

¹O God, whom I praise,
    do not remain silent,
²for wicked and deceitful men
    have opened their mouths
        against me;
    they have spoken against me
        with lying tongues.
³With words of hatred they
        surround me;
    they attack me without cause.
⁴In return for my friendship they
        accuse me,
    but I am a man of prayer.
⁵They repay me evil for good,
    and hatred for my friendship.

⁶Appoint*ᵃ* an evil man*ᵇ* to
        oppose him;
    let an accuser*ᶜ* stand at his
        right hand.
⁷When he is tried, let him be found
        guilty,
    and may his prayers condemn
        him.
⁸May his days be few;

may another take his place of
    leadership.
⁹May his children be fatherless
    and his wife a widow.
¹⁰May his children be wandering
        beggars;
    may they be driven*ᵈ* from their
        ruined homes.
¹¹May a creditor seize all he has;
    may strangers plunder the fruits
        of his labor.
¹²May no one extend kindness to
        him
    or take pity on his fatherless
        children.
¹³May his descendants be cut off,
    their names blotted out from
        the next generation.
¹⁴May the iniquity of his fathers be
        remembered before the
        LORD;
    may the sin of his mother never
        be blotted out.
¹⁵May their sins always remain
        before the LORD,
    that he may cut off the memory
        of them from the earth.

¹⁶For he never thought of doing a
        kindness,
    but hounded to death the poor
    and the needy and the
        brokenhearted.
¹⁷He loved to pronounce a curse—
    may it*ᵉ* come on him;
    he found no pleasure in
        blessing—
    may it be*ᶠ* far from him.
¹⁸He wore cursing as his garment;
    it entered into his body like
        water,
    into his bones like oil.
¹⁹May it be like a cloak wrapped
        about him,
    like a belt tied forever around
        him.
²⁰May this be the LORD's payment to
        my accusers,
    to those who speak evil of me.
²¹But you, O Sovereign LORD,

ᵃ6 Or ⌊*They say:*⌋ *"Appoint* (with quotation marks at the end of verse 19)   *ᵇ6* Or *the Evil One*
ᶜ6 Or *let Satan*   *ᵈ10* Septuagint; Hebrew *sought*   *ᵉ17* Or *curse, / and it has*   *ᶠ17* Or
blessing, / and it is

deal well with me for your
  name's sake;
out of the goodness of your
  love, deliver me.
²²For I am poor and needy,
  and my heart is wounded
    within me.
²³I fade away like an evening
  shadow;
  I am shaken off like a locust.
²⁴My knees give way from fasting;
  my body is thin and gaunt.
²⁵I am an object of scorn to my
  accusers;
  when they see me, they shake
    their heads.

²⁶Help me, O LORD my God;
  save me in accordance with
    your love.
²⁷Let them know that it is your
  hand,
  that you, O LORD, have done it.
²⁸They may curse, but you will
  bless;
  when they attack they will be
    put to shame,
  but your servant will rejoice.
²⁹My accusers will be clothed with
  disgrace
  and wrapped in shame as in a
    cloak.

³⁰With my mouth I will greatly
  extol the LORD;
  in the great throng I will praise
    him.
³¹For he stands at the right hand of
  the needy one,
  to save his life from those who
    condemn him.

Psalm 110

Of David. A psalm.

¹The LORD says to my Lord:
  "Sit at my right hand
until I make your enemies
  a footstool for your feet."

²The LORD will extend your mighty
  scepter from Zion;

you will rule in the midst of
  your enemies.
³Your troops will be willing
  on your day of battle.
Arrayed in holy majesty,
  from the womb of the dawn
you will receive the dew of
  your youth.ᵃ

⁴The LORD has sworn
  and will not change his mind:
"You are a priest forever,
  in the order of Melchizedek."

⁵The Lord is at your right hand;
  he will crush kings on the day
    of his wrath.
⁶He will judge the nations, heaping
  up the dead
  and crushing the rulers of the
    whole earth.
⁷He will drink from a brook beside
  the wayᵇ;
  therefore he will lift up his
    head.

Psalm 111ᶜ

¹Praise the LORD.ᵈ

I will extol the LORD with all my
  heart
  in the council of the upright
  and in the assembly.

²Great are the works of the LORD;
  they are pondered by all who
    delight in them.
³Glorious and majestic are his
  deeds,
  and his righteousness endures
    forever.
⁴He has caused his wonders to be
  remembered;
  the LORD is gracious and
    compassionate.
⁵He provides food for those who
  fear him;
  he remembers his covenant
    forever.
⁶He has shown his people the
  power of his works,
  giving them the lands of other
    nations.

ᵃ3 Or / your young men will come to you like the dew   ᵇ7 Or / The One who grants succession will
set him in authority   ᶜThis psalm is an acrostic poem, the lines of which begin with the
successive letters of the Hebrew alphabet.   ᵈ1 Hebrew Hallelu Yah

⁷The works of his hands are
     faithful and just;
all his precepts are trustworthy.
⁸They are steadfast for ever and
     ever,
done in faithfulness and
     uprightness.
⁹He provided redemption for his
     people;
he ordained his covenant
     forever—
holy and awesome is his name.

¹⁰The fear of the Lord is the
     beginning of wisdom;
all who follow his precepts have
     good understanding.
To him belongs eternal praise.

Psalm 112ᵃ

¹Praise the Lord.ᵇ

Blessed is the man who fears the
     Lord,
who finds great delight in his
     commands.

²His children will be mighty in the
     land;
the generation of the upright
     will be blessed.
³Wealth and riches are in his
     house,
and his righteousness endures
     forever.
⁴Even in darkness light dawns for
     the upright,
for the gracious and
     compassionate and
     righteous man.ᶜ
⁵Good will come to him who is
     generous and lends freely,
who conducts his affairs with
     justice.
⁶Surely he will never be shaken;
a righteous man will be
     remembered forever.
⁷He will have no fear of bad news;
his heart is steadfast, trusting in
     the Lord.

⁸His heart is secure, he will have
     no fear;
in the end he will look in
     triumph on his foes.
⁹He has scattered abroad his gifts
     to the poor,
his righteousness endures
     forever;
his hornᵈ will be lifted high in
     honor.

¹⁰The wicked man will see and be
     vexed,
he will gnash his teeth and
     waste away;
the longings of the wicked will
     come to nothing.

Psalm 113

¹Praise the Lord.ᵉ

Praise, O servants of the Lord,
praise the name of the Lord.
²Let the name of the Lord be
     praised,
both now and forevermore.
³From the rising of the sun to the
     place where it sets,
the name of the Lord is to be
     praised.

⁴The Lord is exalted over all the
     nations,
his glory above the heavens.
⁵Who is like the Lord our God,
the One who sits enthroned on
     high,
⁶who stoops down to look
on the heavens and the earth?

⁷He raises the poor from the dust
and lifts the needy from the ash
     heap;
⁸he seats them with princes,
with the princes of their people.
⁹He settles the barren woman in
     her home
as a happy mother of children.

Praise the Lord.

ᵃThis psalm is an acrostic poem, the lines of which begin with the successive letters of the
Hebrew alphabet.   ᵇ1 Hebrew Hallelu Yah   ᶜ4 Or / for ⸤the Lord⸥ is gracious and
compassionate and righteous   ᵈ9 Horn here symbolizes dignity.   ᵉ1 Hebrew Hallelu Yah; also
in verse 9

Psalm 114

¹When Israel came out of Egypt,
   the house of Jacob from a
      people of foreign tongue,
²Judah became God's sanctuary,
   Israel his dominion.

³The sea looked and fled,
   the Jordan turned back;
⁴the mountains skipped like rams,
   the hills like lambs.

⁵Why was it, O sea, that you fled,
   O Jordan, that you turned back,
⁶you mountains, that you skipped
      like rams,
   you hills, like lambs?

⁷Tremble, O earth, at the presence
      of the Lord,
   at the presence of the God of
      Jacob,
⁸who turned the rock into a pool,
   the hard rock into springs of
      water.

Psalm 115

¹Not to us, O LORD, not to us
   but to your name be the glory,
   because of your love and
      faithfulness.

²Why do the nations say,
   "Where is their God?"
³Our God is in heaven;
   he does whatever pleases him.
⁴But their idols are silver and gold,
   made by the hands of men.
⁵They have mouths, but cannot
      speak,
   eyes, but they cannot see;
⁶they have ears, but cannot hear,
   noses, but they cannot smell;
⁷they have hands, but cannot feel,
   feet, but they cannot walk;
   nor can they utter a sound with
      their throats.
⁸Those who make them will be like
      them,
   and so will all who trust in
      them.

⁹O house of Israel, trust in the
   LORD—

   he is their help and shield.
¹⁰O house of Aaron, trust in the
   LORD—
   he is their help and shield.
¹¹You who fear him, trust in the
   LORD—
   he is their help and shield.

¹²The LORD remembers us and will
      bless us:
   He will bless the house of
      Israel,
   he will bless the house of
      Aaron,
¹³he will bless those who fear the
   LORD—
   small and great alike.

¹⁴May the LORD make you increase,
   both you and your children.
¹⁵May you be blessed by the LORD,
   the Maker of heaven and earth.

¹⁶The highest heavens belong to the
   LORD,
   but the earth he has given to
      man.
¹⁷It is not the dead who praise the
   LORD,
   those who go down to silence;
¹⁸it is we who extol the LORD,
   both now and forevermore.

Praise the LORD.ᵃ

Psalm 116

¹I love the LORD, for he heard my
      voice;
   he heard my cry for mercy.
²Because he turned his ear to me,
   I will call on him as long as I
      live.

³The cords of death entangled me,
   the anguish of the graveᵇ came
      upon me;
   I was overcome by trouble and
      sorrow.
⁴Then I called on the name of the
   LORD:
   "O LORD, save me!"

⁵The LORD is gracious and
      righteous;
   our God is full of compassion.

ᵃ18 Hebrew *Hallelu Yah*   ᵇ3 Hebrew *Sheol*

⁶The LORD protects the
  simplehearted;
    when I was in great need, he
      saved me.

⁷Be at rest once more, O my soul,
  for the LORD has been good to
    you.

⁸For you, O LORD, have delivered
  my soul from death,
    my eyes from tears,
    my feet from stumbling,
⁹that I may walk before the LORD
  in the land of the living.
¹⁰I believed; therefore*ᵃ* I said,
  "I am greatly afflicted."
¹¹And in my dismay I said,
  "All men are liars."

¹²How can I repay the LORD
  for all his goodness to me?
¹³I will lift up the cup of salvation
  and call on the name of the
    LORD.
¹⁴I will fulfill my vows to the LORD
  in the presence of all his people.

¹⁵Precious in the sight of the LORD
  is the death of his saints.
¹⁶O LORD, truly I am your servant;
  I am your servant, the son of
    your maidservant*ᵇ*;
    you have freed me from my
      chains.

¹⁷I will sacrifice a thank offering to
  you
    and call on the name of the
      LORD.
¹⁸I will fulfill my vows to the LORD
  in the presence of all his people,
¹⁹in the courts of the house of the
  LORD—
    in your midst, O Jerusalem.

Praise the LORD.*ᶜ*

Psalm 117

¹Praise the LORD, all you nations;
  extol him, all you peoples.
²For great is his love toward us,
  and the faithfulness of the LORD
    endures forever.

Praise the LORD.*ᶜ*

Psalm 118

¹Give thanks to the LORD, for he is
  good;
    his love endures forever.

²Let Israel say:
  "His love endures forever."
³Let the house of Aaron say:
  "His love endures forever."
⁴Let those who fear the LORD say:
  "His love endures forever."

⁵In my anguish I cried to the LORD,
  and he answered by setting me
    free.
⁶The LORD is with me; I will not be
  afraid.
    What can man do to me?
⁷The LORD is with me; he is my
  helper.
    I will look in triumph on my
      enemies.

⁸It is better to take refuge in the
  LORD
    than to trust in man.
⁹It is better to take refuge in the
  LORD
    than to trust in princes.

¹⁰All the nations surrounded me,
  but in the name of the LORD I
    cut them off.
¹¹They surrounded me on every
  side,
    but in the name of the LORD I
      cut them off.
¹²They swarmed around me like
  bees,
    but they died out as quickly as
      burning thorns;
    in the name of the LORD I cut
      them off.

¹³I was pushed back and about to
  fall,
    but the LORD helped me.
¹⁴The LORD is my strength and my
  song;
    he has become my salvation.

¹⁵Shouts of joy and victory

---

*ᵃ*10 Or *believed even when*   *ᵇ*16 Or *servant, your faithful son*   *ᶜ*19,2 Hebrew *Hallelu Yah*

resound in the tents of the
righteous:
"The LORD's right hand has done
mighty things!

16 The LORD's right hand is lifted
high;
the LORD's right hand has done
mighty things!"

17I will not die but live,
and will proclaim what the LORD
has done.
18The LORD has chastened me
severely,
but he has not given me over to
death.

19Open for me the gates of
righteousness;
I will enter and give thanks to
the LORD.
20This is the gate of the LORD
through which the righteous
may enter.
21I will give you thanks, for you
answered me;
you have become my salvation.

22The stone the builders rejected
has become the capstone;
23the LORD has done this,
and it is marvelous in our eyes.
24This is the day the LORD has made;
let us rejoice and be glad in it.

25O LORD, save us;
O LORD, grant us success.
26Blessed is he who comes in the
name of the LORD.
From the house of the LORD we
bless you.a
27The LORD is God,
and he has made his light shine
upon us.
With boughs in hand, join in the
festal procession
upb to the horns of the altar.

28You are my God, and I will give
you thanks;
you are my God, and I will
exalt you.

29Give thanks to the LORD, for he is
good;
his love endures forever.

Psalm 119c

א Aleph

1Blessed are they whose ways are
blameless,
who walk according to the law
of the LORD.
2Blessed are they who keep his
statutes
and seek him with all their
heart.
3They do nothing wrong;
they walk in his ways.
4You have laid down precepts
that are to be fully obeyed.
5Oh, that my ways were steadfast
in obeying your decrees!
6Then I would not be put to shame
when I consider all your
commands.
7I will praise you with an upright
heart
as I learn your righteous laws.
8I will obey your decrees;
do not utterly forsake me.

ב Beth

9How can a young man keep his
way pure?
By living according to your
word.
10I seek you with all my heart;
do not let me stray from your
commands.
11I have hidden your word in my
heart
that I might not sin against you.
12Praise be to you, O LORD;
teach me your decrees.
13With my lips I recount
all the laws that come from
your mouth.
14I rejoice in following your statutes
as one rejoices in great riches.
15I meditate on your precepts
and consider your ways.

---

a26 The Hebrew is plural.   b27 Or *Bind the festal sacrifice with ropes / and take it*   cThis
psalm is an acrostic poem; the verses of each stanza begin with the same letter of the Hebrew
alphabet.

VERSE:	AUTHOR:	PASSAGE:
Psalm 118:24	Lewis B. Smedes	Psalm 118:19–29

The Gift of Joy

You and I were created for joy, and if we miss it, we miss the reason for our existence! More, the reason Jesus Christ lived and died on earth was to restore us to the joy we have lost ... So we can safely believe that when we think about joy we are at the edge of life's deepest secret. We are not talking about emotional frills and psychic indulgences; we are talking about the discovery of all-rightness in the essence of life ...

An ancient verse-maker invites us to do what we were created for and what we truly want to do: "This is the day the LORD has made; let us rejoice and be glad in it." Surely the old poet speaks the language of human longing.

So what is our problem? The problem is that we have such a ridiculously hard job doing the very thing we were created and redeemed for. Kierkegaard put it something like this: Most of us spend our lives building mansions for ourselves and when we finish we choose to live in the doghouse ...

At another time and another place, another man, Jesus, came and spoke to us of many things. When he was about to leave he said, "I have told you this so that my joy may be in you and that your joy may be complete" (John 15:11). And now his Spirit comes to us with the power to believe that joy is our birthright because the Lord has made this day for us. When we have power to *accept* our day as his gift, we have entered our mansion of joy and discovered one more way that it can be all right even when everything is sadly wrong.

ADDITIONAL SCRIPTURE READINGS
John 15:9–17; John 16:19–24

Go to page 754 for your next devotional reading.

¹⁶I delight in your decrees;
I will not neglect your word.

ג   **Gimel**

¹⁷Do good to your servant, and I
will live;
I will obey your word.
¹⁸Open my eyes that I may see
wonderful things in your law.
¹⁹I am a stranger on earth;
do not hide your commands
from me.
²⁰My soul is consumed with longing
for your laws at all times.
²¹You rebuke the arrogant, who are
cursed
and who stray from your
commands.
²²Remove from me scorn and
contempt,
for I keep your statutes.
²³Though rulers sit together and
slander me,
your servant will meditate on
your decrees.
²⁴Your statutes are my delight;
they are my counselors.

ד   **Daleth**

²⁵I am laid low in the dust;
preserve my life according to
your word.
²⁶I recounted my ways and you
answered me;
teach me your decrees.
²⁷Let me understand the teaching of
your precepts;
then I will meditate on your
wonders.
²⁸My soul is weary with sorrow;
strengthen me according to your
word.
²⁹Keep me from deceitful ways;
be gracious to me through your
law.
³⁰I have chosen the way of truth;
I have set my heart on your
laws.
³¹I hold fast to your statutes,
O Lord;
do not let me be put to shame.

³²I run in the path of your
commands,
for you have set my heart free.

ה   **He**

³³Teach me, O Lord, to follow your
decrees;
then I will keep them to the end.
³⁴Give me understanding, and I will
keep your law
and obey it with all my heart.
³⁵Direct me in the path of your
commands,
for there I find delight.
³⁶Turn my heart toward your
statutes
and not toward selfish gain.
³⁷Turn my eyes away from
worthless things;
preserve my life according to
your word.ᵃ
³⁸Fulfill your promise to your
servant,
so that you may be feared.
³⁹Take away the disgrace I dread,
for your laws are good.
⁴⁰How I long for your precepts!
Preserve my life in your
righteousness.

ו   **Waw**

⁴¹May your unfailing love come to
me, O Lord,
your salvation according to
your promise;
⁴²then I will answer the one who
taunts me,
for I trust in your word.
⁴³Do not snatch the word of truth
from my mouth,
for I have put my hope in your
laws.
⁴⁴I will always obey your law,
for ever and ever.
⁴⁵I will walk about in freedom,
for I have sought out your
precepts.
⁴⁶I will speak of your statutes before
kings
and will not be put to shame,
⁴⁷for I delight in your commands
because I love them.

ᵃ37 Two manuscripts of the Masoretic Text and Dead Sea Scrolls; most manuscripts of the
Masoretic Text *life in your way*

⁴⁸I lift up my hands to*a* your
    commands, which I love,
    and I meditate on your decrees.

ז   Zayin

⁴⁹Remember your word to your
    servant,
    for you have given me hope.
⁵⁰My comfort in my suffering is
    this:
    Your promise preserves my life.
⁵¹The arrogant mock me without
    restraint,
    but I do not turn from your
    law.
⁵²I remember your ancient laws,
    O Lord,
    and I find comfort in them.
⁵³Indignation grips me because of
    the wicked,
    who have forsaken your law.
⁵⁴Your decrees are the theme of my
    song
    wherever I lodge.
⁵⁵In the night I remember your
    name, O Lord,
    and I will keep your law.
⁵⁶This has been my practice:
    I obey your precepts.

ח   Heth

⁵⁷You are my portion, O Lord;
    I have promised to obey your
    words.
⁵⁸I have sought your face with all
    my heart;
    be gracious to me according to
    your promise.
⁵⁹I have considered my ways
    and have turned my steps to
    your statutes.
⁶⁰I will hasten and not delay
    to obey your commands.
⁶¹Though the wicked bind me with
    ropes,
    I will not forget your law.
⁶²At midnight I rise to give you
    thanks
    for your righteous laws.
⁶³I am a friend to all who fear you,
    to all who follow your precepts.

⁶⁴The earth is filled with your love,
    O Lord;
    teach me your decrees.

ט   Teth

⁶⁵Do good to your servant
    according to your word,
    O Lord.
⁶⁶Teach me knowledge and good
    judgment,
    for I believe in your commands.
⁶⁷Before I was afflicted I went
    astray,
    but now I obey your word.
⁶⁸You are good, and what you do is
    good;
    teach me your decrees.
⁶⁹Though the arrogant have
    smeared me with lies,
    I keep your precepts with all
    my heart.
⁷⁰Their hearts are callous and
    unfeeling,
    but I delight in your law.
⁷¹It was good for me to be afflicted
    so that I might learn your
    decrees.
⁷²The law from your mouth is more
    precious to me
    than thousands of pieces of
    silver and gold.

י   Yodh

⁷³Your hands made me and formed
    me;
    give me understanding to learn
    your commands.
⁷⁴May those who fear you rejoice
    when they see me,
    for I have put my hope in your
    word.
⁷⁵I know, O Lord, that your laws
    are righteous,
    and in faithfulness you have
    afflicted me.
⁷⁶May your unfailing love be my
    comfort,
    according to your promise to
    your servant.
⁷⁷Let your compassion come to me
    that I may live,
    for your law is my delight.

a48 Or *for*

[78]May the arrogant be put to shame
for wronging me without
cause;
but I will meditate on your
precepts.
[79]May those who fear you turn to
me,
those who understand your
statutes.
[80]May my heart be blameless
toward your decrees,
that I may not be put to shame.

כ Kaph

[81]My soul faints with longing for
your salvation,
but I have put my hope in your
word.
[82]My eyes fail, looking for your
promise;
I say, "When will you comfort
me?"
[83]Though I am like a wineskin in
the smoke,
I do not forget your decrees.
[84]How long must your servant
wait?
When will you punish my
persecutors?
[85]The arrogant dig pitfalls for me,
contrary to your law.
[86]All your commands are
trustworthy;
help me, for men persecute me
without cause.
[87]They almost wiped me from the
earth,
but I have not forsaken your
precepts.
[88]Preserve my life according to your
love,
and I will obey the statutes of
your mouth.

ל Lamedh

[89]Your word, O Lord, is eternal;
it stands firm in the heavens.
[90]Your faithfulness continues
through all generations;
you established the earth, and it
endures.
[91]Your laws endure to this day,
for all things serve you.
[92]If your law had not been my
delight,

I would have perished in my
affliction.
[93]I will never forget your precepts,
for by them you have preserved
my life.
[94]Save me, for I am yours;
I have sought out your precepts.
[95]The wicked are waiting to destroy
me,
but I will ponder your statutes.
[96]To all perfection I see a limit;
but your commands are
boundless.

מ Mem

[97]Oh, how I love your law!
I meditate on it all day long.
[98]Your commands make me wiser
than my enemies,
for they are ever with me.
[99]I have more insight than all my
teachers,
for I meditate on your statutes.
[100]I have more understanding than
the elders,
for I obey your precepts.
[101]I have kept my feet from every
evil path
so that I might obey your word.
[102]I have not departed from your
laws,
for you yourself have taught
me.
[103]How sweet are your words to
my taste,
sweeter than honey to my
mouth!
[104]I gain understanding from your
precepts;
therefore I hate every wrong
path.

נ Nun

[105]Your word is a lamp to my feet
and a light for my path.
[106]I have taken an oath and
confirmed it,
that I will follow your righteous
laws.
[107]I have suffered much;
preserve my life, O Lord,
according to your word.
[108]Accept, O Lord, the willing
praise of my mouth,
and teach me your laws.

[109]Though I constantly take my life
in my hands,
I will not forget your law.
[110]The wicked have set a snare
for me,
but I have not strayed from
your precepts.
[111]Your statutes are my heritage
forever;
they are the joy of my heart.
[112]My heart is set on keeping your
decrees
to the very end.

ס Samekh

[113]I hate double-minded men,
but I love your law.
[114]You are my refuge and my
shield;
I have put my hope in your
word.
[115]Away from me, you evildoers,
that I may keep the commands
of my God!
[116]Sustain me according to your
promise, and I will live;
do not let my hopes be dashed.
[117]Uphold me, and I will be
delivered;
I will always have regard for
your decrees.
[118]You reject all who stray from
your decrees,
for their deceitfulness is in vain.
[119]All the wicked of the earth you
discard like dross;
therefore I love your statutes.
[120]My flesh trembles in fear of you;
I stand in awe of your laws.

ע Ayin

[121]I have done what is righteous
and just;
do not leave me to my
oppressors.
[122]Ensure your servant's well-being;
let not the arrogant oppress me.
[123]My eyes fail, looking for your
salvation,
looking for your righteous
promise.
[124]Deal with your servant according
to your love
and teach me your decrees.

[125]I am your servant; give me
discernment
that I may understand your
statutes.
[126]It is time for you to act, O LORD;
your law is being broken.
[127]Because I love your commands
more than gold, more than pure
gold,
[128]and because I consider all your
precepts right,
I hate every wrong path.

פ Pe

[129]Your statutes are wonderful;
therefore I obey them.
[130]The unfolding of your words
gives light;
it gives understanding to the
simple.
[131]I open my mouth and pant,
longing for your commands.
[132]Turn to me and have mercy
on me,
as you always do to those who
love your name.
[133]Direct my footsteps according to
your word;
let no sin rule over me.
[134]Redeem me from the oppression
of men,
that I may obey your precepts.
[135]Make your face shine upon your
servant
and teach me your decrees.
[136]Streams of tears flow from my
eyes,
for your law is not obeyed.

צ Tsadhe

[137]Righteous are you, O LORD,
and your laws are right.
[138]The statutes you have laid down
are righteous;
they are fully trustworthy.
[139]My zeal wears me out,
for my enemies ignore your
words.
[140]Your promises have been
thoroughly tested,
and your servant loves them.
[141]Though I am lowly and despised,
I do not forget your precepts.
[142]Your righteousness is everlasting

and your law is true.
143Trouble and distress have come
     upon me,
but your commands are my
     delight.
144Your statutes are forever right;

give me understanding that I
     may live.

ק   Qoph

145I call with all my heart; answer
     me, O LORD,

VERSE:	AUTHOR:	PASSAGE:
Psalm 119:105	Gigi Graham Tchividjian	Psalm 119:97–112

The Never-Failing Source

When Daddy's mother was in her late eighties, I went to visit her in the hospital. A short time before my visit, her doctor had come into the room and described her condition to her—which was very serious. After he had spoken, she was so upset she couldn't even speak. When the doctor was momentarily called out of the room, my grandmother instinctively turned to her Lord, whom she had known for so many years, for comfort and strength. A Bible verse she had put to memory many years before came to her mind and gave her the needed courage and assurance for her stay in the hospital.

The Word of God is a living Word . . . Psalm 119 says that the Word cleanses, strengthens, delights, teaches, saves, comforts, directs and gives understanding. What a resource!

I am so grateful that I was taught early to use this resource. To draw strength from it, to use it in seeking direction and guidance, to employ it in times of discouragement, disappointment and loneliness . . .

For whatever life holds for you and your family in the coming days, weave the unfailing fabric of God's Word through your heart and mind. It will hold strong, even if the rest of life unravels.

ADDITIONAL SCRIPTURE READINGS
Isaiah 55:10–13; 2 Timothy 3:10–17

Go to page 757 for your next devotional reading.

and I will obey your decrees.
¹⁴⁶I call out to you; save me
and I will keep your statutes.
¹⁴⁷I rise before dawn and cry for
help;
I have put my hope in your
word.
¹⁴⁸My eyes stay open through the
watches of the night,
that I may meditate on your
promises.
¹⁴⁹Hear my voice in accordance
with your love;
preserve my life, O Lord,
according to your laws.
¹⁵⁰Those who devise wicked
schemes are near,
but they are far from your law.
¹⁵¹Yet you are near, O Lord,
and all your commands are
true.
¹⁵²Long ago I learned from your
statutes
that you established them to last
forever.

ר Resh

¹⁵³Look upon my suffering and
deliver me,
for I have not forgotten your
law.
¹⁵⁴Defend my cause and
redeem me;
preserve my life according to
your promise.
¹⁵⁵Salvation is far from the wicked,
for they do not seek out your
decrees.
¹⁵⁶Your compassion is great,
O Lord;
preserve my life according to
your laws.
¹⁵⁷Many are the foes who
persecute me,
but I have not turned from your
statutes.
¹⁵⁸I look on the faithless with
loathing,
for they do not obey your word.
¹⁵⁹See how I love your precepts;
preserve my life, O Lord,
according to your love.
¹⁶⁰All your words are true;
all your righteous laws are
eternal.

ש Sin and Shin

¹⁶¹Rulers persecute me without
cause,
but my heart trembles at your
word.
¹⁶²I rejoice in your promise
like one who finds great spoil.
¹⁶³I hate and abhor falsehood
but I love your law.
¹⁶⁴Seven times a day I praise you
for your righteous laws.
¹⁶⁵Great peace have they who love
your law,
and nothing can make them
stumble.
¹⁶⁶I wait for your salvation, O Lord,
and I follow your commands.
¹⁶⁷I obey your statutes,
for I love them greatly.
¹⁶⁸I obey your precepts and your
statutes,
for all my ways are known to
you.

ת Taw

¹⁶⁹May my cry come before you,
O Lord;
give me understanding
according to your word.
¹⁷⁰May my supplication come
before you;
deliver me according to your
promise.
¹⁷¹May my lips overflow with
praise,
for you teach me your decrees.
¹⁷²May my tongue sing of your
word,
for all your commands are
righteous.
¹⁷³May your hand be ready to
help me,
for I have chosen your precepts.
¹⁷⁴I long for your salvation, O Lord,
and your law is my delight.
¹⁷⁵Let me live that I may praise
you,
and may your laws sustain
me.
¹⁷⁶I have strayed like a lost sheep.
Seek your servant,
for I have not forgotten your
commands.

Psalm 120

A song of ascents.

[1]I call on the LORD in my distress,
    and he answers me.
[2]Save me, O LORD, from lying
        lips
    and from deceitful tongues.

[3]What will he do to you,
    and what more besides,
        O deceitful tongue?
[4]He will punish you with a
        warrior's sharp arrows,
    with burning coals of the broom
        tree.

[5]Woe to me that I dwell in
        Meshech,
    that I live among the tents of
        Kedar!
[6]Too long have I lived
    among those who hate peace.
[7]I am a man of peace;
    but when I speak, they are for
        war.

Psalm 121

A song of ascents.

[1]I lift up my eyes to the hills—
    where does my help come
        from?
[2]My help comes from the LORD,
    the Maker of heaven and earth.

[3]He will not let your foot slip—
    he who watches over you will
        not slumber;
[4]indeed, he who watches over
        Israel
    will neither slumber nor sleep.

[5]The LORD watches over you—
    the LORD is your shade at your
        right hand;
[6]the sun will not harm you by
        day,
    nor the moon by night.

[7]The LORD will keep you from all
        harm—
    he will watch over your life;

[8]the LORD will watch over your
        coming and going
    both now and forevermore.

Psalm 122

A song of ascents. Of David.

[1]I rejoiced with those who said to
        me,
    "Let us go to the house of the
        LORD."
[2]Our feet are standing
    in your gates, O Jerusalem.

[3]Jerusalem is built like a city
    that is closely compacted
        together.
[4]That is where the tribes go up,
    the tribes of the LORD,
  to praise the name of the LORD
    according to the statute given to
        Israel.
[5]There the thrones for judgment
        stand,
    the thrones of the house of
        David.

[6]Pray for the peace of Jerusalem:
    "May those who love you be
        secure.
[7]May there be peace within your
        walls
    and security within your
        citadels."
[8]For the sake of my brothers and
        friends,
    I will say, "Peace be within
        you."
[9]For the sake of the house of the
        LORD our God,
    I will seek your prosperity.

Psalm 123

A song of ascents.

[1]I lift up my eyes to you,
    to you whose throne is in
        heaven.
[2]As the eyes of slaves look to the
        hand of their master,
    as the eyes of a maid look to
        the hand of her mistress,
  so our eyes look to the LORD our
        God,

till he shows us his mercy.

³Have mercy on us, O LORD, have
    mercy on us,
for we have endured much
    contempt.
⁴We have endured much ridicule
    from the proud,
much contempt from the
    arrogant.

Psalm 124

A song of ascents. Of David.

¹If the LORD had not been on our
    side—
    let Israel say—
²if the LORD had not been on our
    side
    when men attacked us,

VERSE: AUTHOR: PASSAGE:
Psalm 121:2   William L. Coleman   Psalm 121:1–8

The Great Watchman

A large part of our Christian faith consists of giving our
fears to God. He gives us hope in the middle of a changing, trying situation . . . We need the stability and reas-
surance which the Scriptures can offer.

1. Commit our grown children to God. Look at Acts
20:32 . . . What a magnificent blessing Paul bestowed on
the people he cared for. Since they couldn't stay together,
Paul committed them into the safekeeping of the God he
served. Our children are in his hands and not ours.

2. Ask God to watch over them. It is not that we have
washed our hands of them but rather that we have called
for a first-class security guard, our heavenly Father. Our
children are not orphaned but rather are protected by
the ultimate Parent.

We won't be able to watch over them every hour or
hide in the attic of their lives. But the Great Watchman
will be there. Every time a parent prays for a grown
child, he or she clings to that promise and hope . . .

Type up Psalm 121:5–8 and paste it on your bathroom
mirror. Every time you think of your children, claim
these verses.

ADDITIONAL SCRIPTURE READINGS
Psalm 145:17–21; Acts 20:25–38

Go to page 759 for your next devotional reading.

³when their anger flared against us,
     they would have swallowed us
          alive;
⁴the flood would have engulfed us,
     the torrent would have swept
          over us,
⁵the raging waters
     would have swept us away.

⁶Praise be to the LORD,
     who has not let us be torn by
          their teeth.
⁷We have escaped like a bird
     out of the fowler's snare;
the snare has been broken,
     and we have escaped.
⁸Our help is in the name of the
          LORD,
     the Maker of heaven and earth.

Psalm 125

A song of ascents.

¹Those who trust in the LORD are
     like Mount Zion,
     which cannot be shaken but
          endures forever.
²As the mountains surround
          Jerusalem,
     so the LORD surrounds his
          people
     both now and forevermore.

³The scepter of the wicked will not
          remain
     over the land allotted to the
          righteous,
for then the righteous might use
     their hands to do evil.

⁴Do good, O LORD, to those who
     are good,
     to those who are upright in
          heart.
⁵But those who turn to crooked
          ways
     the LORD will banish with the
          evildoers.

     Peace be upon Israel.

Psalm 126

A song of ascents.

¹When the LORD brought back the
     captives to[a] Zion,
     we were like men who
          dreamed.[b]
²Our mouths were filled with
          laughter,
     our tongues with songs of joy.
Then it was said among the
          nations,
     "The LORD has done great things
          for them."
³The LORD has done great things for
          us,
     and we are filled with joy.

⁴Restore our fortunes,[c] O LORD,
     like streams in the Negev.
⁵Those who sow in tears
     will reap with songs of joy.
⁶He who goes out weeping,
     carrying seed to sow,
will return with songs of joy,
     carrying sheaves with him.

Psalm 127

A song of ascents. Of Solomon.

¹Unless the LORD builds the house,
     its builders labor in vain.
Unless the LORD watches over the
          city,
     the watchmen stand guard in
          vain.
²In vain you rise early
     and stay up late,
toiling for food to eat—
     for he grants sleep to[d] those he
          loves.

³Sons are a heritage from the LORD,
     children a reward from him.
⁴Like arrows in the hands of a
          warrior
     are sons born in one's youth.
⁵Blessed is the man
     whose quiver is full of them.
They will not be put to shame
     when they contend with their
          enemies in the gate.

---

*a*1 Or LORD *restored the fortunes of*   *b*1 Or *men restored to health*   *c*4 Or *Bring back our captives*
*d*2 Or *eat— / for while they sleep he provides for*

Psalm 128

A song of ascents.

¹Blessed are all who fear the LORD,
who walk in his ways.
²You will eat the fruit of your labor;
blessings and prosperity will be
yours.

³Your wife will be like a fruitful
vine
within your house;
your sons will be like olive
shoots
around your table.
⁴Thus is the man blessed
who fears the LORD.

THURSDAY

VERSE:
Psalm 130:4

AUTHOR:
Jacob D. Eppinga

PASSAGE:
Psalm 130:1–8

Missed Opportunities

The loss of opportunity.

We had planned to do so much, but now it is too late. There are other things we ought to have done (Romans 7). We have committed sins of omission and commission, and we cannot reverse the clock to erase them.

We all have these regrets, and we must seek forgiveness where it can be found (Psalm 130:4). But it is good to know that while we left so much undone, Jesus did not. For us he cried on the cross, "It is finished" (John 19:30). Therefore, we can have the assurance, as Paul says, that he who began a good work in us will carry it to completion (Philippians 1:6), even though we feel we could have done and should have done so much more for him . . .

We missed opportunities in the past. There was that cup of cold water we didn't bring. Some of us stood at the grave of a loved one and thought of things we should have said and done; now it is too late . . . But there is one matter for which it is not too late, whatever our age, and that is to accept Christ as our Savior and Lord, if we have not done so. For even if we are a hundred, now is still the day of salvation.

ADDITIONAL SCRIPTURE READINGS
Psalm 103:1–18; 1 Corinthians 1:4–9

Go to page 761 for your next devotional reading.

⁵May the LORD bless you from Zion
  all the days of your life;
may you see the prosperity of
    Jerusalem,
6 and may you live to see your
    children's children.

Peace be upon Israel.

Psalm 129

A song of ascents.

¹They have greatly oppressed me
    from my youth—
  let Israel say—
²they have greatly oppressed me
    from my youth,
  but they have not gained the
    victory over me.
³Plowmen have plowed my back
  and made their furrows long.
⁴But the LORD is righteous;
  he has cut me free from the
    cords of the wicked.

⁵May all who hate Zion
  be turned back in shame.
⁶May they be like grass on the roof,
  which withers before it can
    grow;
⁷with it the reaper cannot fill his
    hands,
  nor the one who gathers fill his
    arms.
⁸May those who pass by not say,
  "The blessing of the LORD be
    upon you;
  we bless you in the name of the
    LORD."

Psalm 130

A song of ascents.

¹Out of the depths I cry to you,
    O LORD;
2 O Lord, hear my voice.
  Let your ears be attentive
  to my cry for mercy.

³If you, O LORD, kept a record of
    sins,
  O Lord, who could stand?

⁴But with you there is forgiveness;
  therefore you are feared.

⁵I wait for the LORD, my soul waits,
  and in his word I put my hope.
⁶My soul waits for the Lord
  more than watchmen wait for
    the morning,
  more than watchmen wait for
    the morning.

⁷O Israel, put your hope in the
    LORD,
  for with the LORD is unfailing
    love
  and with him is full
    redemption.
⁸He himself will redeem Israel
  from all their sins.

Psalm 131

A song of ascents. Of David.

¹My heart is not proud, O LORD,
  my eyes are not haughty;
  I do not concern myself with great
    matters
  or things too wonderful for me.
²But I have stilled and quieted my
    soul;
  like a weaned child with its
    mother,
  like a weaned child is my soul
    within me.

³O Israel, put your hope in the
    LORD
  both now and forevermore.

Psalm 132

A song of ascents.

¹O LORD, remember David
  and all the hardships he
    endured.
²He swore an oath to the LORD
  and made a vow to the Mighty
    One of Jacob:
³"I will not enter my house
  or go to my bed—
⁴I will allow no sleep to my eyes,
  no slumber to my eyelids,

⁵till I find a place for the Lᴏʀᴅ,
  a dwelling for the Mighty One
    of Jacob."

⁶We heard it in Ephrathah,
  we came upon it in the fields of
    Jaar*ᵃ*:*ᵇ*
⁷"Let us go to his dwelling place;

let us worship at his footstool—
⁸arise, O Lᴏʀᴅ, and come to your
    resting place,
  you and the ark of your
    might.
⁹May your priests be clothed
    with righteousness;
  may your saints sing for joy."

ᵃ6 That is, Kiriath Jearim   *ᵇ6* Or *heard of it in Ephrathah, / we found it in the fields of Jaar.* (And
no quotes around verses 7-9)

VERSE:	AUTHOR:	PASSAGE:
Psalm 131:2	Kathryn Hillen	Psalm 131:1–3

Slow Down

I remember when we rode along country roads in a Model T Ford back when people were not in such a hurry. The roads were not the current-day straight, smooth ribbons of concrete. And the cars wouldn't travel as fast as our modern ones do. We had time to stop for cattails when dad took us on Sunday-afternoon drives. We enjoyed the scenery, slow motion. We took time to pick wild berries and flowers along the way. I loved it!

If it's a sign of old age to admit to a longing for a slower pace, then I am getting old. Too often we get to our destination and wonder if it was worth the trouble. We don't spend even our leisure time "leisurely" anymore!

I need to slow down. And I'm asking the Lord to help me do it. I want to move slowly enough to be aware of all the joys he has hidden for me. I want to slow down enough to grow as he wants me to grow. I want to be quiet enough to hear his voice. I need his wisdom to know how to spend my time and how to order my days.

ADDITIONAL SCRIPTURE READINGS
Psalm 116; Isaiah 30:15–18

Go to page 764 for your next devotional reading.

¹⁰For the sake of David your
servant,
do not reject your anointed one.

¹¹The LORD swore an oath to David,
a sure oath that he will not
revoke:
"One of your own descendants
I will place on your throne—
¹²if your sons keep my covenant
and the statutes I teach them,
then their sons will sit
on your throne for ever and
ever."

¹³For the LORD has chosen Zion,
he has desired it for his
dwelling:
¹⁴"This is my resting place for ever
and ever;
here I will sit enthroned, for I
have desired it—
¹⁵I will bless her with abundant
provisions;
her poor will I satisfy with
food.
¹⁶I will clothe her priests with
salvation,
and her saints will ever sing for
joy.
¹⁷"Here I will make a horn[a] grow
for David
and set up a lamp for my
anointed one.
¹⁸I will clothe his enemies with
shame,
but the crown on his head will
be resplendent."

Psalm 133

A song of ascents. Of David.

¹How good and pleasant it is
when brothers live together in
unity!
²It is like precious oil poured on
the head,
running down on the beard,
running down on Aaron's beard,
down upon the collar of his
robes.

³It is as if the dew of Hermon
were falling on Mount Zion.
For there the LORD bestows his
blessing,
even life forevermore.

Psalm 134

A song of ascents.

¹Praise the LORD, all you servants of
the LORD
who minister by night in the
house of the LORD.
²Lift up your hands in the
sanctuary
and praise the LORD.

³May the LORD, the Maker of
heaven and earth,
bless you from Zion.

Psalm 135

¹Praise the LORD.[b]

Praise the name of the LORD;
praise him, you servants of the
LORD,
²you who minister in the house of
the LORD,
in the courts of the house of our
God.

³Praise the LORD, for the LORD is
good;
sing praise to his name, for that
is pleasant.
⁴For the LORD has chosen Jacob to
be his own,
Israel to be his treasured
possession.

⁵I know that the LORD is great,
that our Lord is greater than all
gods.
⁶The LORD does whatever pleases
him,
in the heavens and on the earth,
in the seas and all their depths.
⁷He makes clouds rise from the
ends of the earth;
he sends lightning with the rain

---

a17 *Horn* here symbolizes strong one, that is, king.
and 21   b1 Hebrew *Hallelu Yah*; also in verses 3

and brings out the wind from
his storehouses.

8He struck down the firstborn of
Egypt,
the firstborn of men and
animals.
9He sent his signs and wonders
into your midst, O Egypt,
against Pharaoh and all his
servants.
10He struck down many nations
and killed mighty kings—
11Sihon king of the Amorites,
Og king of Bashan
and all the kings of Canaan—
12and he gave their land as an
inheritance,
an inheritance to his people
Israel.

13Your name, O LORD, endures
forever,
your renown, O LORD, through
all generations.
14For the LORD will vindicate his
people
and have compassion on his
servants.

15The idols of the nations are silver
and gold,
made by the hands of men.
16They have mouths, but cannot
speak,
eyes, but they cannot see;
17they have ears, but cannot hear,
nor is there breath in their
mouths.
18Those who make them will be like
them,
and so will all who trust in
them.

19O house of Israel, praise the LORD;
O house of Aaron, praise the
LORD;
20O house of Levi, praise the LORD;
you who fear him, praise the
LORD.
21Praise be to the LORD from Zion,
to him who dwells in Jerusalem.

Praise the LORD.

Psalm 136

1Give thanks to the LORD, for he is
good.
His love endures forever.
2Give thanks to the God of gods.
His love endures forever.
3Give thanks to the Lord of lords:
His love endures forever.

4to him who alone does great
wonders,
His love endures forever.
5who by his understanding made
the heavens,
His love endures forever.
6who spread out the earth upon
the waters,
His love endures forever.
7who made the great lights—
His love endures forever.
8the sun to govern the day,
His love endures forever.
9the moon and stars to govern the
night;
His love endures forever.

10to him who struck down the
firstborn of Egypt
His love endures forever.
11and brought Israel out from
among them
His love endures forever.
12with a mighty hand and
outstretched arm;
His love endures forever.
13to him who divided the Red Sea[a]
asunder
His love endures forever.
14and brought Israel through the
midst of it,
His love endures forever.
15but swept Pharaoh and his army
into the Red Sea;
His love endures forever.

16to him who led his people
through the desert,
His love endures forever.
17who struck down great kings,
His love endures forever.

---

[a]13 Hebrew *Yam Suph*; that is, Sea of Reeds; also in verse 15

PASSAGE: Psalm 138; Jeremiah 29:10–14
AUTHOR: Frances J. Roberts

Eternal Purposes

Hold thou fast, for lo, I am with thee;
Stand thou still, for I am thy God.
Be thou quiet before Me,
For I have arranged all things for thee
according to My good will,
yea, according to Mine eternal purposes.

For I have purposes and plans and desires
which reach far beyond thy present view.
Thou seest as it were the immediate situation,
but My thoughts for thee,
and My planning for thee
embraces eternity.
Yea, thou art in My hand.
Rest there, and leave all else to Me.

Go to page 767 for your next devotional reading.

¹⁸and killed mighty kings—
> *His love endures forever.*
¹⁹Sihon king of the Amorites
> *His love endures forever.*
²⁰and Og king of Bashan—
> *His love endures forever.*
²¹and gave their land as an
> inheritance,
> *His love endures forever.*
²²an inheritance to his servant Israel;
> *His love endures forever.*

²³to the One who remembered us in
> our low estate
> *His love endures forever.*
²⁴and freed us from our enemies,
> *His love endures forever.*
²⁵and who gives food to every
> creature.
> *His love endures forever.*

²⁶Give thanks to the God of heaven.
> *His love endures forever.*

Psalm 137

¹By the rivers of Babylon we sat
> and wept
> when we remembered Zion.
²There on the poplars
> we hung our harps,
³for there our captors asked us for
> songs,
> our tormentors demanded songs
> of joy;
> they said, "Sing us one of the
> songs of Zion!"

⁴How can we sing the songs of the
> LORD
> while in a foreign land?
⁵If I forget you, O Jerusalem,
> may my right hand forget ⌐its
> skill⌐.
⁶May my tongue cling to the roof
> of my mouth
> if I do not remember you,
> if I do not consider Jerusalem
> my highest joy.

⁷Remember, O LORD, what the
> Edomites did
> on the day Jerusalem fell.
> "Tear it down," they cried,
> "tear it down to its
> foundations!"

⁸O Daughter of Babylon, doomed
> to destruction,
> happy is he who repays you
> for what you have done to
> us—
⁹he who seizes your infants
> and dashes them against the
> rocks.

Psalm 138

Of David.

¹I will praise you, O LORD, with all
> my heart;
> before the "gods" I will sing
> your praise.
²I will bow down toward your
> holy temple
> and will praise your name
> for your love and your
> faithfulness,
for you have exalted above all
> things
> your name and your word.
³When I called, you answered me;
> you made me bold and
> stouthearted.

⁴May all the kings of the earth
> praise you, O LORD,
> when they hear the words of
> your mouth.
⁵May they sing of the ways of the
> LORD,
> for the glory of the LORD is
> great.

⁶Though the LORD is on high, he
> looks upon the lowly,
> but the proud he knows from
> afar.
⁷Though I walk in the midst of
> trouble,
> you preserve my life;
you stretch out your hand against
> the anger of my foes,
> with your right hand you save
> me.
⁸The LORD will fulfill ⌐his purpose⌐
> for me;
> your love, O LORD, endures
> forever—
> do not abandon the works of
> your hands.

Psalm 139

For the director of music. Of David.
A psalm.

¹O Lᴏʀᴅ, you have searched me
    and you know me.
²You know when I sit and when I
    rise;
  you perceive my thoughts from
    afar.
³You discern my going out and my
    lying down;
  you are familiar with all my
    ways.
⁴Before a word is on my tongue
  you know it completely,
        O Lᴏʀᴅ.

⁵You hem me in—behind and
    before;
  you have laid your hand upon
    me.
⁶Such knowledge is too wonderful
    for me,
  too lofty for me to attain.

⁷Where can I go from your Spirit?
  Where can I flee from your
    presence?
⁸If I go up to the heavens, you are
    there;
  if I make my bed in the
    depths,ᵃ you are there.
⁹If I rise on the wings of the dawn,
  if I settle on the far side of the
    sea,
¹⁰even there your hand will guide
    me,
  your right hand will hold me
    fast.

¹¹If I say, "Surely the darkness will
    hide me
  and the light become night
    around me,"
¹²even the darkness will not be
    dark to you;
  the night will shine like the
    day,
  for darkness is as light to
    you.

¹³For you created my inmost being;
  you knit me together in my
    mother's womb.
¹⁴I praise you because I am fearfully
    and wonderfully made;
  your works are wonderful,
  I know that full well.
¹⁵My frame was not hidden from
    you
  when I was made in the secret
    place.
  When I was woven together in the
    depths of the earth,
¹⁶ your eyes saw my unformed
    body.
  All the days ordained for me
  were written in your book
  before one of them came to be.

¹⁷How precious toᵇ me are your
    thoughts, O God!
  How vast is the sum of them!
¹⁸Were I to count them,
  they would outnumber the
    grains of sand.
  When I awake,
  I am still with you.

¹⁹If only you would slay the
    wicked, O God!
  Away from me, you
    bloodthirsty men!
²⁰They speak of you with evil
    intent;
  your adversaries misuse your
    name.
²¹Do I not hate those who hate you,
        O Lᴏʀᴅ,
  and abhor those who rise up
    against you?
²²I have nothing but hatred for
    them;
  I count them my enemies.

²³Search me, O God, and know my
    heart;
  test me and know my anxious
    thoughts.
²⁴See if there is any offensive way
    in me,
  and lead me in the way
    everlasting.

ᵃ8 Hebrew *Sheol*   ᵇ17 Or *concerning*

VERSE:
Psalm 139:14

AUTHOR:
Joni Eareckson Tada

PASSAGE:
Psalm 139:1–18

The Enemy's Strategy

This morning I was having a rough start getting out of bed. My paralysis was giving me fits. I shook my head and growled, "This body is a pain . . . I hate it."

Why was that so awful? Because the Enemy has a deep hatred of my flesh and blood and all I was doing was agreeing with him. He gets a charge when I bad-mouth my body. And he would like to get you to do the same.

Why? Because your body, even underneath wrinkles or fat, and despite the ravages of illness or old age, is made in the image of God. Your heart, mind, hands and feet are stamped with the imprint of the Creator. Little wonder that the devil wants you to be ashamed of your body!

This morning I had, once again, to plug my ears against the lies of the tempter and remember that I am "fearfully and wonderfully made." I rehearsed the old, familiar truth that God has a plan for this flesh and blood of mine. That's why the devil considers my body a threat — he understands that when I yield to God my body, albeit paralyzed, my feet and hands are powerful weapons against his forces of darkness.

The devil is only a fallen angel. He is a deceiver. He is doomed for destruction. And until then, he has one goal in mind: your spiritual defeat, emotional malignment and physical frustration. If he tries to get you to agree with him today . . . don't.

ADDITIONAL SCRIPTURE READINGS
Ephesians 6:10–18; Colossians 2:6–15

Go to page 777 for your next devotional reading.

Psalm 140

For the director of music. A psalm
of David.

¹Rescue me, O LORD, from evil men;
  protect me from men of
    violence,
²who devise evil plans in their
    hearts
  and stir up war every day.
³They make their tongues as sharp
    as a serpent's;
  the poison of vipers is on their
    lips.   Selah

⁴Keep me, O LORD, from the hands
    of the wicked;
  protect me from men of
    violence
  who plan to trip my feet.
⁵Proud men have hidden a snare
    for me;
  they have spread out the cords
    of their net
  and have set traps for me along
    my path.   Selah

⁶O LORD, I say to you, "You are my
    God."
  Hear, O LORD, my cry for mercy.
⁷O Sovereign LORD, my strong
    deliverer,
  who shields my head in the day
    of battle—
⁸do not grant the wicked their
    desires, O LORD;
  do not let their plans succeed,
  or they will become proud.
                          Selah

⁹Let the heads of those who
    surround me
  be covered with the trouble
    their lips have caused.
¹⁰Let burning coals fall upon them;
  may they be thrown into the
    fire,
  into miry pits, never to rise.
¹¹Let slanderers not be established
    in the land;
  may disaster hunt down men of
    violence.

¹²I know that the LORD secures
    justice for the poor
  and upholds the cause of the
    needy.
¹³Surely the righteous will praise
    your name
  and the upright will live before
    you.

Psalm 141

A psalm of David.

¹O LORD, I call to you; come quickly
    to me.
  Hear my voice when I call to
    you.
²May my prayer be set before you
    like incense;
  may the lifting up of my hands
    be like the evening
    sacrifice.

³Set a guard over my mouth,
    O LORD;
  keep watch over the door of my
    lips.
⁴Let not my heart be drawn to
    what is evil,
  to take part in wicked deeds
  with men who are evildoers;
  let me not eat of their delicacies.

⁵Let a righteous man[a] strike me—
    it is a kindness;
  let him rebuke me—it is oil on
    my head.
  My head will not refuse it.

Yet my prayer is ever against the
    deeds of evildoers;
⁶   their rulers will be thrown
    down from the cliffs,
  and the wicked will learn that
    my words were well
    spoken.
⁷They will say, "As one plows
    and breaks up the earth,
  so our bones have been
    scattered at the mouth of
    the grave.[b]"

⁸But my eyes are fixed on you,
    O Sovereign LORD;

a5 Or Let the Righteous One   b7 Hebrew Sheol

in you I take refuge—do not
 give me over to death.
[9]Keep me from the snares they
  have laid for me,
 from the traps set by evildoers.
[10]Let the wicked fall into their own
  nets,
 while I pass by in safety.

Psalm 142

*A maskil[a] of David. When he was in
the cave. A prayer.*

[1]I cry aloud to the LORD;
 I lift up my voice to the LORD
  for mercy.
[2]I pour out my complaint before
  him;
 before him I tell my trouble.

[3]When my spirit grows faint within
  me,
 it is you who know my way.
In the path where I walk
 men have hidden a snare for
  me.
[4]Look to my right and see;
 no one is concerned for me.
I have no refuge;
 no one cares for my life.

[5]I cry to you, O LORD;
 I say, "You are my refuge,
 my portion in the land of the
  living."
[6]Listen to my cry,
 for I am in desperate need;
rescue me from those who pursue
  me,
 for they are too strong for me.
[7]Set me free from my prison,
 that I may praise your name.

Then the righteous will gather
  about me
 because of your goodness to
  me.

Psalm 143

A psalm of David.

[1]O LORD, hear my prayer,
 listen to my cry for mercy;

in your faithfulness and
  righteousness
 come to my relief.
[2]Do not bring your servant into
  judgment,
 for no one living is righteous
  before you.

[3]The enemy pursues me,
 he crushes me to the ground;
he makes me dwell in darkness
 like those long dead.
[4]So my spirit grows faint within
  me;
 my heart within me is
  dismayed.

[5]I remember the days of long
  ago;
 I meditate on all your works
and consider what your hands
  have done.
[6]I spread out my hands to you;
 my soul thirsts for you like a
  parched land.   *Selah*

[7]Answer me quickly, O LORD;
 my spirit fails.
Do not hide your face from me
 or I will be like those who go
  down to the pit.
[8]Let the morning bring me word of
  your unfailing love,
 for I have put my trust in you.
Show me the way I should go,
 for to you I lift up my soul.
[9]Rescue me from my enemies,
  O LORD,
 for I hide myself in you.
[10]Teach me to do your will,
 for you are my God;
may your good Spirit
 lead me on level ground.

[11]For your name's sake, O LORD,
  preserve my life;
 in your righteousness, bring me
  out of trouble.
[12]In your unfailing love, silence my
  enemies;
 destroy all my foes,
 for I am your servant.

---

[a]Title: Probably a literary or musical term

Psalm 144

Of David.

¹Praise be to the LORD my Rock,
  who trains my hands for war,
  my fingers for battle.
²He is my loving God and my
    fortress,
  my stronghold and my
    deliverer,
  my shield, in whom I take refuge,
  who subdues peoples[a] under
    me.

³O LORD, what is man that you care
    for him,
  the son of man that you think
    of him?
⁴Man is like a breath;
  his days are like a fleeting
    shadow.

⁵Part your heavens, O LORD, and
    come down;
  touch the mountains, so that
    they smoke.
⁶Send forth lightning and scatter
    ⌊the enemies⌋;
  shoot your arrows and rout
    them.
⁷Reach down your hand from on
    high;
  deliver me and rescue me
 from the mighty waters,
  from the hands of foreigners
⁸whose mouths are full of lies,
  whose right hands are deceitful.

⁹I will sing a new song to you,
    O God;
  on the ten-stringed lyre I will
    make music to you,
¹⁰to the One who gives victory to
    kings,
  who delivers his servant David
    from the deadly sword.

¹¹Deliver me and rescue me
  from the hands of foreigners
whose mouths are full of lies,
  whose right hands are deceitful.

¹²Then our sons in their youth
  will be like well-nurtured
    plants,
and our daughters will be like
    pillars
  carved to adorn a palace.
¹³Our barns will be filled
  with every kind of provision.
Our sheep will increase by
    thousands,
  by tens of thousands in our
    fields;
¹⁴ our oxen will draw heavy
    loads.[b]
There will be no breaching of
    walls,
  no going into captivity,
  no cry of distress in our streets.

¹⁵Blessed are the people of whom
    this is true;
  blessed are the people whose
    God is the LORD.

Psalm 145[c]

A psalm of praise. Of David.

¹I will exalt you, my God the King;
  I will praise your name for ever
    and ever.
²Every day I will praise you
  and extol your name for ever
    and ever.

³Great is the LORD and most worthy
    of praise;
  his greatness no one can
    fathom.
⁴One generation will commend
    your works to another;
  they will tell of your mighty
    acts.
⁵They will speak of the glorious
    splendor of your majesty,
  and I will meditate on your
    wonderful works.[d]

---

[a]2 Many manuscripts of the Masoretic Text, Dead Sea Scrolls, Aquila, Jerome and Syriac; most manuscripts of the Masoretic Text *subdues my people*   [b]14 Or *our chieftains will be firmly established*   [c]This psalm is an acrostic poem, the verses of which (including verse 13b) begin with the successive letters of the Hebrew alphabet.   [d]5 Dead Sea Scrolls and Syriac (see also Septuagint); Masoretic Text *On the glorious splendor of your majesty / and on your wonderful works I will meditate*

⁶They will tell of the power of your
  awesome works,
  and I will proclaim your great
    deeds.
⁷They will celebrate your abundant
    goodness
  and joyfully sing of your
    righteousness.

⁸The LORD is gracious and
    compassionate,
  slow to anger and rich in love.
⁹The LORD is good to all;
  he has compassion on all he has
    made.
¹⁰All you have made will praise
    you, O LORD;
  your saints will extol you.
¹¹They will tell of the glory of your
    kingdom
  and speak of your might,
¹²so that all men may know of your
    mighty acts
  and the glorious splendor of
    your kingdom.
¹³Your kingdom is an everlasting
    kingdom,
  and your dominion endures
    through all generations.

The LORD is faithful to all his
    promises
  and loving toward all he has
    made.ᵃ
¹⁴The LORD upholds all those who
    fall
  and lifts up all who are bowed
    down.
¹⁵The eyes of all look to you,
  and you give them their food at
    the proper time.
¹⁶You open your hand
  and satisfy the desires of every
    living thing.

¹⁷The LORD is righteous in all his
    ways
  and loving toward all he has
    made.
¹⁸The LORD is near to all who call on
    him,
  to all who call on him in truth.

¹⁹He fulfills the desires of those
    who fear him;
  he hears their cry and saves
    them.
²⁰The LORD watches over all who
    love him,
  but all the wicked he will
    destroy.

²¹My mouth will speak in praise of
    the LORD.
  Let every creature praise his
    holy name
  for ever and ever.

Psalm 146

¹Praise the LORD.ᵇ

Praise the LORD, O my soul.
² I will praise the LORD all my life;
  I will sing praise to my God as
    long as I live.

³Do not put your trust in princes,
  in mortal men, who cannot
    save.
⁴When their spirit departs, they
    return to the ground;
  on that very day their plans
    come to nothing.

⁵Blessed is he whose help is the
    God of Jacob,
  whose hope is in the LORD his
    God,
⁶the Maker of heaven and earth,
  the sea, and everything in
    them—
  the LORD, who remains faithful
    forever.
⁷He upholds the cause of the
    oppressed
  and gives food to the hungry.
The LORD sets prisoners free,
⁸ the LORD gives sight to the
    blind,
  the LORD lifts up those who are
    bowed down,
  the LORD loves the righteous.
⁹The LORD watches over the alien
  and sustains the fatherless and
    the widow,

ᵃ13 One manuscript of the Masoretic Text, Dead Sea Scrolls and Syriac (see also Septuagint);
most manuscripts of the Masoretic Text do not have the last two lines of verse 13.   ᵇ1 Hebrew
Hallelu Yah; also in verse 10

but he frustrates the ways of the
wicked.

¹⁰The Lord reigns forever,
your God, O Zion, for all
generations.

Praise the Lord.

Psalm 147

¹Praise the Lord.ᵃ

How good it is to sing praises to
our God,
how pleasant and fitting to
praise him!

²The Lord builds up Jerusalem;
he gathers the exiles of Israel.
³He heals the brokenhearted
and binds up their wounds.
⁴He determines the number of the
stars
and calls them each by name.
⁵Great is our Lord and mighty in
power;
his understanding has no limit.
⁶The Lord sustains the humble
but casts the wicked to the
ground.

⁷Sing to the Lord with
thanksgiving;
make music to our God on the
harp.
⁸He covers the sky with clouds;
he supplies the earth with rain
and makes grass grow on the
hills.
⁹He provides food for the cattle
and for the young ravens when
they call.

¹⁰His pleasure is not in the strength
of the horse,
nor his delight in the legs of a
man;
¹¹the Lord delights in those who
fear him,
who put their hope in his
unfailing love.

¹²Extol the Lord, O Jerusalem;
praise your God, O Zion,

¹³for he strengthens the bars of your
gates
and blesses your people within
you.
¹⁴He grants peace to your borders
and satisfies you with the finest
of wheat.

¹⁵He sends his command to the
earth;
his word runs swiftly.
¹⁶He spreads the snow like wool
and scatters the frost like ashes.
¹⁷He hurls down his hail like
pebbles.
Who can withstand his icy
blast?
¹⁸He sends his word and melts
them;
he stirs up his breezes, and the
waters flow.

¹⁹He has revealed his word to Jacob,
his laws and decrees to Israel.
²⁰He has done this for no other
nation;
they do not know his laws.

Praise the Lord.

Psalm 148

¹Praise the Lord.ᵇ

Praise the Lord from the heavens,
praise him in the heights above.
²Praise him, all his angels,
praise him, all his heavenly
hosts.
³Praise him, sun and moon,
praise him, all you shining
stars.
⁴Praise him, you highest heavens
and you waters above the skies.
⁵Let them praise the name of the
Lord,
for he commanded and they
were created.
⁶He set them in place for ever and
ever;
he gave a decree that will never
pass away.

⁷Praise the Lord from the earth,
you great sea creatures and all
ocean depths,

ᵃ1 Hebrew *Hallelu Yah*; also in verse 20   ᵇ1 Hebrew *Hallelu Yah*; also in verse 14

[8]lightning and hail, snow and
    clouds, ˙
stormy winds that do his
    bidding,
[9]you mountains and all hills,
    fruit trees and all cedars,
[10]wild animals and all cattle,
    small creatures and flying birds,
[11]kings of the earth and all nations,
    you princes and all rulers on
    earth,
[12]young men and maidens,
    old men and children.

[13]Let them praise the name of the
    LORD,
for his name alone is exalted;
his splendor is above the earth
    and the heavens.
[14]He has raised up for his people a
    horn,[a]
the praise of all his saints,
of Israel, the people close to his
    heart.

Praise the LORD.

Psalm 149

[1]Praise the LORD.[b]

Sing to the LORD a new song,
    his praise in the assembly of the
    saints.

[2]Let Israel rejoice in their Maker;
    let the people of Zion be glad in
    their King.
[3]Let them praise his name with
    dancing
and make music to him with
    tambourine and harp.
[4]For the LORD takes delight in his
    people;
he crowns the humble with
    salvation.

[5]Let the saints rejoice in this honor
    and sing for joy on their beds.

[6]May the praise of God be in their
    mouths
and a double-edged sword in
    their hands,
[7]to inflict vengeance on the nations
    and punishment on the peoples,
[8]to bind their kings with fetters,
    their nobles with shackles of
    iron,
[9]to carry out the sentence written
    against them.
This is the glory of all his
    saints.

Praise the LORD.

Psalm 150

[1]Praise the LORD.[c]

Praise God in his sanctuary;
    praise him in his mighty
    heavens.
[2]Praise him for his acts of power;
    praise him for his surpassing
    greatness.
[3]Praise him with the sounding of
    the trumpet,
praise him with the harp and
    lyre,
[4]praise him with tambourine and
    dancing,
praise him with the strings and
    flute,
[5]praise him with the clash of
    cymbals,
praise him with resounding
    cymbals.

[6]Let everything that has breath
    praise the LORD.

Praise the LORD.

---

[a]14 *Horn* here symbolizes strong one, that is, king.
[c]1 Hebrew *Hallelu Yah*; also in verse 6

[b]1 Hebrew *Hallelu Yah*; also in verse 9

...**T**...his collection of sayings
by Solomon and others urges people to seek
wisdom from God. Proverbs offers practical
spiritual counsel on issues ranging from
managing money to making choices to finding the right friends. As you read this book,
look for those nuggets of wisdom that have
special relevance to your situation in life.

PROVERBS

Prologue: Purpose and Theme

1 The proverbs of Solomon son of
David, king of Israel:

²for attaining wisdom and
discipline;
for understanding words of
insight;
³for acquiring a disciplined and
prudent life,
doing what is right and just and
fair;
⁴for giving prudence to the simple,
knowledge and discretion to the
young—
⁵let the wise listen and add to their
learning,
and let the discerning get
guidance—
⁶for understanding proverbs and
parables,
the sayings and riddles of the
wise.

⁷The fear of the LORD is the
beginning of knowledge,
but fools*a* despise wisdom and
discipline.

Exhortations to Embrace Wisdom

Warning Against Enticement

⁸Listen, my son, to your father's
instruction
and do not forsake your
mother's teaching.
⁹They will be a garland to grace
your head
and a chain to adorn your neck.

¹⁰My son, if sinners entice you,
do not give in to them.
¹¹If they say, "Come along with us;
let's lie in wait for someone's
blood,
let's waylay some harmless
soul;
¹²let's swallow them alive, like the
grave,*b*
and whole, like those who go
down to the pit;

---

*a*7 The Hebrew words rendered *fool* in Proverbs, and often elsewhere in the Old Testament,
denote one who is morally deficient.   *b*12 Hebrew *Sheol*

¹³we will get all sorts of valuable
    things
    and fill our houses with
        plunder;
¹⁴throw in your lot with us,
    and we will share a common
        purse"—
¹⁵my son, do not go along with
    them,
    do not set foot on their paths;
¹⁶for their feet rush into sin,
    they are swift to shed blood.
¹⁷How useless to spread a net
    in full view of all the birds!
¹⁸These men lie in wait for their
    own blood;
    they waylay only themselves!
¹⁹Such is the end of all who go after
    ill-gotten gain;
    it takes away the lives of those
        who get it.

Warning Against Rejecting Wisdom

²⁰Wisdom calls aloud in the street,
    she raises her voice in the
        public squares;
²¹at the head of the noisy streets*ᵃ*
    she cries out,
    in the gateways of the city she
        makes her speech:

²²"How long will you simple ones*ᵇ*
    love your simple ways?
    How long will mockers delight
        in mockery
    and fools hate knowledge?
²³If you had responded to my
    rebuke,
    I would have poured out my
        heart to you
    and made my thoughts known
        to you.
²⁴But since you rejected me when I
    called
    and no one gave heed when I
        stretched out my hand,
²⁵since you ignored all my advice
    and would not accept my
        rebuke,
²⁶I in turn will laugh at your
    disaster;

I will mock when calamity
    overtakes you—
²⁷when calamity overtakes you like
    a storm,
    when disaster sweeps over you
        like a whirlwind,
    when distress and trouble
        overwhelm you.

²⁸"Then they will call to me but I
    will not answer;
    they will look for me but will
        not find me.
²⁹Since they hated knowledge
    and did not choose to fear the
        LORD,
³⁰since they would not accept my
    advice
    and spurned my rebuke,
³¹they will eat the fruit of their
    ways
    and be filled with the fruit of
        their schemes.
³²For the waywardness of the
    simple will kill them,
    and the complacency of fools
        will destroy them;
³³but whoever listens to me will live
    in safety
    and be at ease, without fear of
        harm."

Moral Benefits of Wisdom

2 My son, if you accept my words
    and store up my commands
        within you,
²turning your ear to wisdom
    and applying your heart to
        understanding,
³and if you call out for insight
    and cry aloud for
        understanding,
⁴and if you look for it as for silver
    and search for it as for hidden
        treasure,
⁵then you will understand the fear
    of the LORD
    and find the knowledge of God.
⁶For the LORD gives wisdom,
    and from his mouth come
        knowledge and
        understanding.

---

*ᵃ*21 Hebrew; Septuagint / *on the tops of the walls*   *ᵇ*22 The Hebrew word rendered *simple* in
Proverbs generally denotes one without moral direction and inclined to evil.

7He holds victory in store for the
upright,
he is a shield to those whose
walk is blameless,
8for he guards the course of the
just
and protects the way of his
faithful ones.

9Then you will understand what is
right and just
and fair—every good path.
10For wisdom will enter your heart,
and knowledge will be pleasant
to your soul.
11Discretion will protect you,
and understanding will guard
you.

12Wisdom will save you from the
ways of wicked men,
from men whose words are
perverse,
13who leave the straight paths
to walk in dark ways,
14who delight in doing wrong
and rejoice in the perverseness
of evil,
15whose paths are crooked
and who are devious in their
ways.

16It will save you also from the
adulteress,
from the wayward wife with
her seductive words,
17who has left the partner of her
youth
and ignored the covenant she
made before God.a
18For her house leads down to
death
and her paths to the spirits of
the dead.
19None who go to her return
or attain the paths of life.

20Thus you will walk in the ways of
good men
and keep to the paths of the
righteous.
21For the upright will live in the
land,

and the blameless will remain
in it;
22but the wicked will be cut off
from the land,
and the unfaithful will be torn
from it.

Further Benefits of Wisdom

3 My son, do not forget my
teaching,
but keep my commands in your
heart,
2for they will prolong your life
many years
and bring you prosperity.

3Let love and faithfulness never
leave you;
bind them around your neck,
write them on the tablet of your
heart.
4Then you will win favor and a
good name
in the sight of God and man.

5Trust in the LORD with all your
heart
and lean not on your own
understanding;
6in all your ways acknowledge
him,
and he will make your paths
straight.b

7Do not be wise in your own eyes;
fear the LORD and shun evil.
8This will bring health to your
body
and nourishment to your bones.

9Honor the LORD with your wealth,
with the firstfruits of all your
crops;
10then your barns will be filled to
overflowing,
and your vats will brim over
with new wine.

11My son, do not despise the LORD's
discipline
and do not resent his rebuke,
12because the LORD disciplines those
he loves,

---

a17 Or covenant of her God   b6 Or will direct your paths

as a father[a] the son he delights in.

[13]Blessed is the man who finds wisdom,

the man who gains understanding,

[14]for she is more profitable than silver
and yields better returns than gold.

[a]12 Hebrew; Septuagint / *and he punishes*

TUESDAY

VERSE:
Proverbs 2:6

AUTHOR:
Barbara Deane

PASSAGE:
Proverbs 2:1–11

Getting and Sharing Wisdom

The freedom of the retirement adventure gives us an opportunity for one of the greatest tasks of advancing years: getting and sharing wisdom. Wisdom is not something that comes automatically with age. (We all know people who are old but *not* wise.) According to the book of Proverbs, it's a gift from God. It's not based on intellectual ability; even simple people can be wise. It's more of an ability to see the big picture. A sense of proportion. Knowing your own limitations. Knowing what's important in life, and what's trivial.

Many older people confuse wisdom with knowledge and experience. Because they've been around longer and have encountered the same problems in the past, they think younger people should take their advice and avoid making the same mistakes they did. But giving unasked-for advice is the very opposite of wisdom! The wise thing is knowing when to speak and when to keep silent.

As difficult as it is to define, we all know wisdom when we see it. Older people who have it don't have to *do* anything. You just want to "hang out" with them, be near them, bask in their glow. Becoming that kind of attractive old person is well worth giving up some of the things we valued in our youth.

ADDITIONAL SCRIPTURE READINGS
Proverbs 3:13–18; James 3:13–18
Go to page 778 for your next devotional reading.

¹⁵She is more precious than rubies;
　nothing you desire can compare
　　with her.
¹⁶Long life is in her right hand;
　in her left hand are riches and
　　honor.

¹⁷Her ways are pleasant ways,
　and all her paths are peace.
¹⁸She is a tree of life to those who
　embrace her;
　those who lay hold of her will
　be blessed.

WEDNESDAY

VERSE:	AUTHOR:	PASSAGE:
Proverbs 3:5	A.W. Tozer	Proverbs 3:1–10

Trust Him in the Dark

God constantly encourages us to trust him in the dark. "I will give you the treasures of darkness, riches stored in secret places, so that you may know that I am the LORD, the God of Israel, who summons you by name" (Isaiah 45:3).

It is heartening to learn how many of God's mighty deeds were done in secret, away from the prying eyes of men or angels. When God created the heavens and the earth, darkness was upon the face of the deep. When the eternal Son became flesh, he was carried for a time in the darkness of the sweet virgin's womb. When he died for the life of the world, it was in the darkness, seen by no one at the last. When he arose from the dead, it was "very early in the morning" (Luke 24:1). No one saw him rise. It is as if God were saying, "What I am is all that need matter to you, for there lie your hope and your peace. I will do what I will do, and it will all come to light at last, but how I do it is my secret. Trust me, and be not afraid."

With the goodness of God to desire our highest welfare, the wisdom of God to plan it and the power of God to achieve it, what do we lack? Surely we are the most favored of all creatures.

ADDITIONAL SCRIPTURE READINGS
Isaiah 42:10–17; Micah 7:8–13

Go to page 781 for your next devotional reading.

19By wisdom the LORD laid the
earth's foundations,
   by understanding he set the
   heavens in place;
20by his knowledge the deeps were
divided,
   and the clouds let drop the
   dew.

21My son, preserve sound judgment
and discernment,
   do not let them out of your
   sight;
22they will be life for you,
   an ornament to grace your neck.
23Then you will go on your way in
safety,
   and your foot will not stumble;
24when you lie down, you will not
be afraid;
   when you lie down, your sleep
   will be sweet.
25Have no fear of sudden disaster
   or of the ruin that overtakes the
   wicked,
26for the LORD will be your
confidence
   and will keep your foot from
   being snared.

27Do not withhold good from those
who deserve it,
   when it is in your power to act.
28Do not say to your neighbor,
   "Come back later; I'll give it
   tomorrow"—
   when you now have it with
   you.
29Do not plot harm against your
neighbor,
   who lives trustfully near you.
30Do not accuse a man for no
reason—
   when he has done you no
   harm.
31Do not envy a violent man
   or choose any of his ways,
32for the LORD detests a perverse
man
   but takes the upright into his
   confidence.

33The LORD's curse is on the house
of the wicked,
   but he blesses the home of the
   righteous.
34He mocks proud mockers
   but gives grace to the humble.
35The wise inherit honor,
   but fools he holds up to shame.

Wisdom Is Supreme

4 Listen, my sons, to a father's
instruction;
   pay attention and gain
   understanding.
2I give you sound learning,
   so do not forsake my teaching.
3When I was a boy in my father's
house,
   still tender, and an only child of
   my mother,
4he taught me and said,
   "Lay hold of my words with all
   your heart;
   keep my commands and you
   will live.
5Get wisdom, get understanding;
   do not forget my words or
   swerve from them.
6Do not forsake wisdom, and she
will protect you;
   love her, and she will watch
   over you.
7Wisdom is supreme; therefore get
wisdom.
   Though it cost all you have,a
   get understanding.
8Esteem her, and she will exalt
you;
   embrace her, and she will honor
   you.
9She will set a garland of grace on
your head
   and present you with a crown
   of splendor."

10Listen, my son, accept what I say,
   and the years of your life will
   be many.
11I guide you in the way of wisdom
   and lead you along straight
   paths.

a7 Or Whatever else you get

¹²When you walk, your steps will
    not be hampered;
  when you run, you will not
    stumble.
¹³Hold on to instruction, do not let
    it go;
  guard it well, for it is your life.
¹⁴Do not set foot on the path of the
    wicked
  or walk in the way of evil men.
¹⁵Avoid it, do not travel on it;
  turn from it and go on your
    way.
¹⁶For they cannot sleep till they do
    evil;
  they are robbed of slumber till
    they make someone fall.
¹⁷They eat the bread of wickedness
  and drink the wine of violence.

¹⁸The path of the righteous is like
    the first gleam of dawn,
  shining ever brighter till the full
    light of day.
¹⁹But the way of the wicked is like
    deep darkness;
  they do not know what makes
    them stumble.

²⁰My son, pay attention to what I
    say;
  listen closely to my words.
²¹Do not let them out of your sight,
  keep them within your heart;
²²for they are life to those who find
    them
  and health to a man's whole
    body.
²³Above all else, guard your heart,
  for it is the wellspring of life.
²⁴Put away perversity from your
    mouth;
  keep corrupt talk far from your
    lips.
²⁵Let your eyes look straight ahead,
  fix your gaze directly before
    you.
²⁶Make level*ᵃ* paths for your feet
  and take only ways that are
    firm.
²⁷Do not swerve to the right or the
    left;
  keep your foot from evil.

Warning Against Adultery

5 My son, pay attention to my
    wisdom,
  listen well to my words of
    insight,
²that you may maintain discretion
  and your lips may preserve
    knowledge.
³For the lips of an adulteress drip
    honey,
  and her speech is smoother than
    oil;
⁴but in the end she is bitter as gall,
  sharp as a double-edged sword.
⁵Her feet go down to death;
  her steps lead straight to the
    grave.*ᵇ*
⁶She gives no thought to the way
    of life;
  her paths are crooked, but she
    knows it not.

⁷Now then, my sons, listen to
    me;
  do not turn aside from what
    I say.
⁸Keep to a path far from her,
  do not go near the door of her
    house,
⁹lest you give your best strength to
    others
  and your years to one who is
    cruel,
¹⁰lest strangers feast on your wealth
  and your toil enrich another
    man's house.
¹¹At the end of your life you will
    groan,
  when your flesh and body are
    spent.
¹²You will say, "How I hated
    discipline!
  How my heart spurned
    correction!
¹³I would not obey my teachers
  or listen to my instructors.
¹⁴I have come to the brink of utter
    ruin
  in the midst of the whole
    assembly."

ᵃ26 Or Consider the   ᵇ5 Hebrew Sheol

¹⁵Drink water from your own cistern,
    running water from your own
    well.
¹⁶Should your springs overflow in
    the streets,
    your streams of water in the
    public squares?
¹⁷Let them be yours alone,
    never to be shared with
    strangers.

¹⁸May your fountain be blessed,
    and may you rejoice in the wife
    of your youth.
¹⁹A loving doe, a graceful deer—
    may her breasts satisfy you
    always,
    may you ever be captivated by
    her love.
²⁰Why be captivated, my son, by an
    adulteress?

THURSDAY

VERSE: AUTHOR: PASSAGE:
Proverbs 4:23   Carole Mayhall   Proverbs 4:20–27

Fill My Emptiness

Create in me, Lord . . . a pure heart, yes. But Father,
even more. Create in me . . . (out of nothing for that's
what *creation* means) an expectant heart . . . May I stand
on tiptoe waiting each moment in joyous anticipation for
what *you* are going to do! Create in me an enthusiastic
heart — "en theo" — meaning "in God," God in me, filled
to overflowing with you, Lord! Create in me a laughing
heart — one that sees the serendipities of an autumn leaf
and mist upon the mountains and hears the chuckle of a
child. Create in me a heart of integrity — to be *real*, not to
talk above my walk, not to try to *impress*. Create in me a
caring heart — tender toward the hurts and happenings
of others, more concerned with their needs than with my
own. Create in me an attentive heart — able to hear your
whisper, and moment by moment listen to your voice.
Create in me a contented heart — at peace with the circumstances of life. Create in me a hungry heart — longing
to love you more, desiring your Word, reaching . . .
stretching . . . for more of you. Creator Lord, *create in me.*
Amen.

ADDITIONAL SCRIPTURE READINGS
Psalm 51:10–17; Ezekiel 36:24–32

Go to page 787 for your next devotional reading.

Why embrace the bosom of
 another man's wife?

21For a man's ways are in full view
 of the LORD,
 and he examines all his paths.
22The evil deeds of a wicked man
 ensnare him;
 the cords of his sin hold him
  fast.
23He will die for lack of discipline,
 led astray by his own great
  folly.

Warnings Against Folly

6 My son, if you have put up
 security for your neighbor,
 if you have struck hands in
  pledge for another,
2if you have been trapped by what
 you said,
 ensnared by the words of your
  mouth,
3then do this, my son, to free
 yourself,
 since you have fallen into your
  neighbor's hands:
 Go and humble yourself;
 press your plea with your
  neighbor!
4Allow no sleep to your eyes,
 no slumber to your eyelids.
5Free yourself, like a gazelle from
 the hand of the hunter,
 like a bird from the snare of the
  fowler.

6Go to the ant, you sluggard;
 consider its ways and be wise!
7It has no commander,
 no overseer or ruler,
8yet it stores its provisions in
 summer
 and gathers its food at harvest.

9How long will you lie there, you
 sluggard?
 When will you get up from
  your sleep?
10A little sleep, a little slumber,
 a little folding of the hands to
  rest—
11and poverty will come on you like
 a bandit

and scarcity like an armed
 man.[a]

12A scoundrel and villain,
 who goes about with a corrupt
  mouth,
13 who winks with his eye,
 signals with his feet
 and motions with his fingers,
14 who plots evil with deceit in his
  heart—
 he always stirs up dissension.
15Therefore disaster will overtake
 him in an instant;
 he will suddenly be destroyed—
  without remedy.

16There are six things the LORD
 hates,
 seven that are detestable to him:
17 haughty eyes,
 a lying tongue,
 hands that shed innocent
  blood,
18 a heart that devises wicked
  schemes,
 feet that are quick to rush
  into evil,
19 a false witness who pours out
  lies
 and a man who stirs up
  dissension among brothers.

Warning Against Adultery

20My son, keep your father's
 commands
 and do not forsake your
  mother's teaching.
21Bind them upon your heart
 forever;
 fasten them around your neck.
22When you walk, they will guide
 you;
 when you sleep, they will watch
  over you;
 when you awake, they will
  speak to you.
23For these commands are a lamp,
 this teaching is a light,
 and the corrections of discipline
 are the way to life,
24keeping you from the immoral
 woman,

a11 Or like a vagrant / and scarcity like a beggar

from the smooth tongue of the
wayward wife.
²⁵Do not lust in your heart after her
beauty
or let her captivate you with her
eyes,
²⁶for the prostitute reduces you to a
loaf of bread,
and the adulteress preys upon
your very life.
²⁷Can a man scoop fire into his lap
without his clothes being
burned?
²⁸Can a man walk on hot coals
without his feet being scorched?
²⁹So is he who sleeps with another
man's wife;
no one who touches her will go
unpunished.

³⁰Men do not despise a thief if he
steals
to satisfy his hunger when he is
starving.
³¹Yet if he is caught, he must pay
sevenfold,
though it costs him all the
wealth of his house.
³²But a man who commits adultery
lacks judgment;
whoever does so destroys
himself.
³³Blows and disgrace are his lot,
and his shame will never be
wiped away;
³⁴for jealousy arouses a husband's
fury,
and he will show no mercy
when he takes revenge.
³⁵He will not accept any
compensation;
he will refuse the bribe,
however great it is.

Warning Against the Adulteress

7 My son, keep my words
and store up my commands
within you.
²Keep my commands and you will
live;
guard my teachings as the apple
of your eye.
³Bind them on your fingers;

write them on the tablet of your
heart.
⁴Say to wisdom, "You are my
sister,"
and call understanding your
kinsman;
⁵they will keep you from the
adulteress,
from the wayward wife with
her seductive words.

⁶At the window of my house
I looked out through the lattice.
⁷I saw among the simple,
I noticed among the young
men,
a youth who lacked judgment.
⁸He was going down the street
near her corner,
walking along in the direction
of her house
⁹at twilight, as the day was fading,
as the dark of night set in.

¹⁰Then out came a woman to meet
him,
dressed like a prostitute and
with crafty intent.
¹¹(She is loud and defiant,
her feet never stay at home;
¹²now in the street, now in the
squares,
at every corner she lurks.)
¹³She took hold of him and kissed
him
and with a brazen face she said:

¹⁴"I have fellowship offerings[a] at
home;
today I fulfilled my vows.
¹⁵So I came out to meet you;
I looked for you and have
found you!
¹⁶I have covered my bed
with colored linens from Egypt.
¹⁷I have perfumed my bed
with myrrh, aloes and
cinnamon.
¹⁸Come, let's drink deep of love till
morning;
let's enjoy ourselves with love!
¹⁹My husband is not at home;
he has gone on a long journey.

ª14 Traditionally *peace offerings*

²⁰He took his purse filled with
　money
　　and will not be home till full
　　　moon."

²¹With persuasive words she led
　him astray;
　　she seduced him with her
　　　smooth talk.
²²All at once he followed her
　like an ox going to the
　　slaughter,
　like a deer*a* stepping into a
　　noose*b*
²³　till an arrow pierces his liver,
　like a bird darting into a snare,
　　little knowing it will cost him
　　　his life.

²⁴Now then, my sons, listen to me;
　pay attention to what I say.
²⁵Do not let your heart turn to her
　ways
　　or stray into her paths.
²⁶Many are the victims she has
　brought down;
　　her slain are a mighty throng.
²⁷Her house is a highway to the
　grave,*c*
　　leading down to the chambers
　　　of death.

Wisdom's Call

8 Does not wisdom call out?
　　Does not understanding raise
　　　her voice?
²On the heights along the way,
　where the paths meet, she takes
　　her stand;
³beside the gates leading into the
　city,
　　at the entrances, she cries aloud:
⁴"To you, O men, I call out;
　I raise my voice to all mankind.
⁵You who are simple, gain
　prudence;
　　you who are foolish, gain
　　　understanding.
⁶Listen, for I have worthy things to
　say;
　　I open my lips to speak what is
　　　right.

⁷My mouth speaks what is true,
　for my lips detest wickedness.
⁸All the words of my mouth are
　just;
　　none of them is crooked or
　　　perverse.
⁹To the discerning all of them are
　right;
　　they are faultless to those who
　　　have knowledge.
¹⁰Choose my instruction instead of
　silver,
　　knowledge rather than choice
　　　gold,
¹¹for wisdom is more precious than
　rubies,
　　and nothing you desire can
　　　compare with her.

¹²"I, wisdom, dwell together with
　prudence;
　　I possess knowledge and
　　　discretion.
¹³To fear the LORD is to hate evil;
　I hate pride and arrogance,
　　evil behavior and perverse
　　　speech.
¹⁴Counsel and sound judgment are
　mine;
　　I have understanding and
　　　power.
¹⁵By me kings reign
　and rulers make laws that are
　　just;
¹⁶by me princes govern,
　and all nobles who rule on
　　earth.*d*
¹⁷I love those who love me,
　and those who seek me find
　　me.
¹⁸With me are riches and honor,
　enduring wealth and prosperity.
¹⁹My fruit is better than fine gold;
　what I yield surpasses choice
　　silver.
²⁰I walk in the way of
　righteousness,
　　along the paths of justice,
²¹bestowing wealth on those who
　love me
　　and making their treasuries full.

---

a22 Syriac (see also Septuagint); Hebrew *fool*　　*b22* The meaning of the Hebrew for this line is
uncertain.　　*c27* Hebrew *Sheol*　　*d16* Many Hebrew manuscripts and Septuagint; most
Hebrew manuscripts *and nobles—all righteous rulers*

²²"The LORD brought me forth as the
  first of his works,^{a,b}
before his deeds of old;
²³I was appointed^c from eternity,
  from the beginning, before the
    world began.
²⁴When there were no oceans, I was
  given birth,
when there were no springs
  abounding with water;
²⁵before the mountains were settled
  in place,
before the hills, I was given
  birth,
²⁶before he made the earth or its
  fields
or any of the dust of the world.
²⁷I was there when he set the
  heavens in place,
when he marked out the
  horizon on the face of the
    deep,
²⁸when he established the clouds
  above
and fixed securely the fountains
  of the deep,
²⁹when he gave the sea its boundary
so the waters would not
  overstep his command,
and when he marked out the
  foundations of the earth.
³⁰ Then I was the craftsman at his
  side.
I was filled with delight day after
  day,
rejoicing always in his presence,
³¹rejoicing in his whole world
and delighting in mankind.

³²"Now then, my sons, listen to me;
blessed are those who keep my
  ways.
³³Listen to my instruction and be
  wise;
do not ignore it.
³⁴Blessed is the man who listens to
  me,
watching daily at my doors,
  waiting at my doorway.
³⁵For whoever finds me finds life
and receives favor from the
  LORD.

³⁶But whoever fails to find me
  harms himself;
all who hate me love death."

Invitations of Wisdom and of Folly

9 Wisdom has built her house;
  she has hewn out its seven
    pillars.
²She has prepared her meat and
  mixed her wine;
she has also set her table.
³She has sent out her maids, and
  she calls
from the highest point of the
  city.
⁴"Let all who are simple come in
  here!"
she says to those who lack
  judgment.
⁵"Come, eat my food
and drink the wine I have
  mixed.
⁶Leave your simple ways and you
  will live;
walk in the way of
  understanding.

⁷"Whoever corrects a mocker
  invites insult;
whoever rebukes a wicked man
  incurs abuse.
⁸Do not rebuke a mocker or he will
  hate you;
rebuke a wise man and he will
  love you.
⁹Instruct a wise man and he will be
  wiser still;
teach a righteous man and he
  will add to his learning.

¹⁰"The fear of the LORD is the
  beginning of wisdom,
and knowledge of the Holy One
  is understanding.
¹¹For through me your days will be
  many,
and years will be added to your
  life.
¹²If you are wise, your wisdom will
  reward you;
if you are a mocker, you alone
  will suffer."

^a22 Or *way;* or *dominion*   ^b22 Or *The* LORD *possessed me at the beginning of his work;* or *The* LORD
brought me forth at the beginning of his work   ^c23 Or *fashioned*

¹³The woman Folly is loud;
  she is undisciplined and
    without knowledge.
¹⁴She sits at the door of her house,
  on a seat at the highest point of
    the city,
¹⁵calling out to those who pass by,
  who go straight on their way.
¹⁶"Let all who are simple come in
    here!"
  she says to those who lack
    judgment.
¹⁷"Stolen water is sweet;
  food eaten in secret is
    delicious!"
¹⁸But little do they know that the
    dead are there,
  that her guests are in the depths
    of the grave.ᵃ

Proverbs of Solomon

10 The proverbs of Solomon:

A wise son brings joy to his
    father,
  but a foolish son grief to his
    mother.

²Ill-gotten treasures are of no
    value,
  but righteousness delivers from
    death.

³The Lord does not let the
    righteous go hungry
  but he thwarts the craving of
    the wicked.

⁴Lazy hands make a man poor,
  but diligent hands bring wealth.

⁵He who gathers crops in summer
    is a wise son,
  but he who sleeps during
    harvest is a disgraceful son.

⁶Blessings crown the head of the
    righteous,
  but violence overwhelms the
    mouth of the wicked.ᵇ

⁷The memory of the righteous will
    be a blessing,
  but the name of the wicked will
    rot.

⁸The wise in heart accept
    commands,
  but a chattering fool comes to
    ruin.

⁹The man of integrity walks
    securely,
  but he who takes crooked paths
    will be found out.

¹⁰He who winks maliciously causes
    grief,
  and a chattering fool comes to
    ruin.

¹¹The mouth of the righteous is a
    fountain of life,
  but violence overwhelms the
    mouth of the wicked.

¹²Hatred stirs up dissension,
  but love covers over all wrongs.

¹³Wisdom is found on the lips of
    the discerning,
  but a rod is for the back of him
    who lacks judgment.

¹⁴Wise men store up knowledge,
  but the mouth of a fool invites
    ruin.

¹⁵The wealth of the rich is their
    fortified city,
  but poverty is the ruin of the
    poor.

¹⁶The wages of the righteous bring
    them life,
  but the income of the wicked
    brings them punishment.

¹⁷He who heeds discipline shows
    the way to life,
  but whoever ignores correction
    leads others astray.

¹⁸He who conceals his hatred has
    lying lips,
  and whoever spreads slander is
    a fool.

¹⁹When words are many, sin is not
    absent,
  but he who holds his tongue is
    wise.

²⁰The tongue of the righteous is
    choice silver,

ᵃ18 Hebrew *Sheol*   ᵇ6 Or *but the mouth of the wicked conceals violence*; also in verse 11

but the heart of the wicked is of little value.

²¹The lips of the righteous nourish many,
but fools die for lack of judgment.

²²The blessing of the LORD brings wealth,
and he adds no trouble to it.

²³A fool finds pleasure in evil conduct,

VERSE:
Proverbs 10:19

AUTHORS:
Jan Stoop &
Betty Southard

PASSAGE:
Proverbs 10:18–21

A Good Listener

Jumping in with good advice is our natural reaction to any problem our grandchildren have. But resisting the urge to shower them with the benefit of our great wisdom is the sign of a good listener.

By taking the time to listen for feelings and echo back what we hear, we enable our grandchildren to see and understand more clearly what is going on in their lives. This helps them learn to take the steps necessary toward solving their own problems. By asking questions, you show them you are really attentive to what they are saying. Because this is a compliment to your grandchildren, their response is likely to come more readily.

Some of us are especially tempted to overwhelm our grandchildren with spiritual and Scriptural answers, many of which can come across as frustratingly pat to them. Instead of listening to what the kids are saying, we spend our time watching for an opening where we can jump in and present our own point of view. There's nothing wrong with sharing your point of view and your wisdom. It's an important part of teaching—if you wait for your grandchildren to ask for it and if you have listened enough to earn the right to share it.

ADDITIONAL SCRIPTURE READINGS
Proverbs 17:27–28; Ecclesiastes 3:1–11
Go to page 791 for your next devotional reading.

but a man of understanding
delights in wisdom.

²⁴What the wicked dreads will
overtake him;
what the righteous desire will
be granted.

²⁵When the storm has swept by, the
wicked are gone,
but the righteous stand firm
forever.

²⁶As vinegar to the teeth and smoke
to the eyes,
so is a sluggard to those who
send him.

²⁷The fear of the LORD adds length
to life,
but the years of the wicked are
cut short.

²⁸The prospect of the righteous is
joy,
but the hopes of the wicked
come to nothing.

²⁹The way of the LORD is a refuge
for the righteous,
but it is the ruin of those who
do evil.

³⁰The righteous will never be
uprooted,
but the wicked will not remain
in the land.

³¹The mouth of the righteous brings
forth wisdom,
but a perverse tongue will be
cut out.

³²The lips of the righteous know
what is fitting,
but the mouth of the wicked
only what is perverse.

11 The LORD abhors dishonest
scales,
but accurate weights are his
delight.

²When pride comes, then comes
disgrace,
but with humility comes
wisdom.

³The integrity of the upright guides
them,
but the unfaithful are destroyed
by their duplicity.

⁴Wealth is worthless in the day of
wrath,
but righteousness delivers from
death.

⁵The righteousness of the blameless
makes a straight way for
them,
but the wicked are brought
down by their own
wickedness.

⁶The righteousness of the upright
delivers them,
but the unfaithful are trapped
by evil desires.

⁷When a wicked man dies, his
hope perishes;
all he expected from his power
comes to nothing.

⁸The righteous man is rescued from
trouble,
and it comes on the wicked
instead.

⁹With his mouth the godless
destroys his neighbor,
but through knowledge the
righteous escape.

¹⁰When the righteous prosper, the
city rejoices;
when the wicked perish, there
are shouts of joy.

¹¹Through the blessing of the
upright a city is exalted,
but by the mouth of the wicked
it is destroyed.

¹²A man who lacks judgment
derides his neighbor,
but a man of understanding
holds his tongue.

¹³A gossip betrays a confidence,
but a trustworthy man keeps a
secret.

¹⁴For lack of guidance a nation falls,
but many advisers make victory
sure.

¹⁵He who puts up security for
another will surely suffer,

but whoever refuses to strike
hands in pledge is safe.

[16]A kindhearted woman gains
    respect,
but ruthless men gain only
    wealth.

[17]A kind man benefits himself,
but a cruel man brings trouble
    on himself.

[18]The wicked man earns deceptive
    wages,
but he who sows righteousness
    reaps a sure reward.

[19]The truly righteous man attains
    life,
but he who pursues evil goes to
    his death.

[20]The LORD detests men of perverse
    heart
but he delights in those whose
    ways are blameless.

[21]Be sure of this: The wicked will
    not go unpunished,
but those who are righteous will
    go free.

[22]Like a gold ring in a pig's snout
is a beautiful woman who
    shows no discretion.

[23]The desire of the righteous ends
    only in good,
but the hope of the wicked only
    in wrath.

[24]One man gives freely, yet gains
    even more;
another withholds unduly, but
    comes to poverty.

[25]A generous man will prosper;
he who refreshes others will
    himself be refreshed.

[26]People curse the man who hoards
    grain,
but blessing crowns him who is
    willing to sell.

[27]He who seeks good finds
    goodwill,
but evil comes to him who
    searches for it.

[28]Whoever trusts in his riches will
    fall,
but the righteous will thrive like
    a green leaf.

[29]He who brings trouble on his
    family will inherit only
    wind,
and the fool will be servant to
    the wise.

[30]The fruit of the righteous is a tree
    of life,
and he who wins souls is wise.

[31]If the righteous receive their due
    on earth,
how much more the ungodly
    and the sinner!

12 Whoever loves discipline
loves knowledge,
but he who hates correction is
    stupid.

[2]A good man obtains favor from
    the LORD,
but the LORD condemns a crafty
    man.

[3]A man cannot be established
    through wickedness,
but the righteous cannot be
    uprooted.

[4]A wife of noble character is her
    husband's crown,
but a disgraceful wife is like
    decay in his bones.

[5]The plans of the righteous are just,
but the advice of the wicked is
    deceitful.

[6]The words of the wicked lie in
    wait for blood,
but the speech of the upright
    rescues them.

[7]Wicked men are overthrown and
    are no more,
but the house of the righteous
    stands firm.

[8]A man is praised according to his
    wisdom,
but men with warped minds are
    despised.

[9]Better to be a nobody and yet
    have a servant

than pretend to be somebody
and have no food.

¹⁰A righteous man cares for the
needs of his animal,
but the kindest acts of the
wicked are cruel.

¹¹He who works his land will have
abundant food,
but he who chases fantasies
lacks judgment.

¹²The wicked desire the plunder of
evil men,
but the root of the righteous
flourishes.

¹³An evil man is trapped by his
sinful talk,
but a righteous man escapes
trouble.

¹⁴From the fruit of his lips a man is
filled with good things
as surely as the work of his
hands rewards him.

¹⁵The way of a fool seems right to
him,
but a wise man listens to
advice.

¹⁶A fool shows his annoyance at
once,
but a prudent man overlooks an
insult.

¹⁷A truthful witness gives honest
testimony,
but a false witness tells lies.

¹⁸Reckless words pierce like a
sword,
but the tongue of the wise
brings healing.

¹⁹Truthful lips endure forever,
but a lying tongue lasts only a
moment.

²⁰There is deceit in the hearts of
those who plot evil,
but joy for those who promote
peace.

²¹No harm befalls the righteous,

but the wicked have their fill of
trouble.

²²The Lord detests lying lips,
but he delights in men who are
truthful.

²³A prudent man keeps his
knowledge to himself,
but the heart of fools blurts out
folly.

²⁴Diligent hands will rule,
but laziness ends in slave labor.

²⁵An anxious heart weighs a man
down,
but a kind word cheers him up.

²⁶A righteous man is cautious in
friendship,ᵃ
but the way of the wicked leads
them astray.

²⁷The lazy man does not roastᵇ his
game,
but the diligent man prizes his
possessions.

²⁸In the way of righteousness there
is life;
along that path is immortality.

13 A wise son heeds his father's
instruction,
but a mocker does not listen to
rebuke.

²From the fruit of his lips a man
enjoys good things,
but the unfaithful have a
craving for violence.

³He who guards his lips guards his
life,
but he who speaks rashly will
come to ruin.

⁴The sluggard craves and gets
nothing,
but the desires of the diligent
are fully satisfied.

⁵The righteous hate what is false,
but the wicked bring shame and
disgrace.

ᵃ26 Or *man is a guide to his neighbor*   ᵇ27 The meaning of the Hebrew for this word is
uncertain.

PASSAGE: Ephesians 3:14–20; 1 John 3:1–3
AUTHOR: Ralph Spaulding Cushman

Sheer Joy

Oh the sheer joy of it!
   Living with thee,
God of the universe,
   Lord of a tree,
Maker of mountains,
   Lover of me!

Oh, the sheer joy of it!
   Breathing thy air;
Morning is dawning,
   Gone every care,
All the world's singing,
   "God's everywhere."

Oh the sheer joy of it!
   Ever to be
Living in glory,
   Living with thee,
Lord of Tomorrow,
   Lover of me!

Go to page 795 for your next devotional reading.

⁶Righteousness guards the man of
    integrity,
  but wickedness overthrows the
    sinner.

⁷One man pretends to be rich, yet
    has nothing;
  another pretends to be poor, yet
    has great wealth.

⁸A man's riches may ransom his
    life,
  but a poor man hears no threat.

⁹The light of the righteous shines
    brightly,
  but the lamp of the wicked is
    snuffed out.

¹⁰Pride only breeds quarrels,
  but wisdom is found in those
    who take advice.

¹¹Dishonest money dwindles away,
  but he who gathers money little
    by little makes it grow.

¹²Hope deferred makes the heart
    sick,
  but a longing fulfilled is a tree
    of life.

¹³He who scorns instruction will
    pay for it,
  but he who respects a command
    is rewarded.

¹⁴The teaching of the wise is a
    fountain of life,
  turning a man from the snares
    of death.

¹⁵Good understanding wins favor,
  but the way of the unfaithful is
    hard.ᵃ

¹⁶Every prudent man acts out of
    knowledge,
  but a fool exposes his folly.

¹⁷A wicked messenger falls into
    trouble,
  but a trustworthy envoy brings
    healing.

¹⁸He who ignores discipline comes
    to poverty and shame,
  but whoever heeds correction is
    honored.

¹⁹A longing fulfilled is sweet to the
    soul,
  but fools detest turning from
    evil.

²⁰He who walks with the wise
    grows wise,
  but a companion of fools suffers
    harm.

²¹Misfortune pursues the sinner,
  but prosperity is the reward of
    the righteous.

²²A good man leaves an inheritance
    for his children's children,
  but a sinner's wealth is stored
    up for the righteous.

²³A poor man's field may produce
    abundant food,
  but injustice sweeps it away.

²⁴He who spares the rod hates his
    son,
  but he who loves him is careful
    to discipline him.

²⁵The righteous eat to their hearts'
    content,
  but the stomach of the wicked
    goes hungry.

14 The wise woman builds her
    house,
  but with her own hands the
    foolish one tears hers
    down.

²He whose walk is upright fears
    the LORD,
  but he whose ways are devious
    despises him.

³A fool's talk brings a rod to his
    back,
  but the lips of the wise protect
    them.

⁴Where there are no oxen, the
    manger is empty,
  but from the strength of an ox
    comes an abundant
    harvest.

⁵A truthful witness does not
    deceive,

ᵃ15 Or unfaithful does not endure

but a false witness pours out
    lies.

⁶The mocker seeks wisdom and
        finds none,
    but knowledge comes easily to
        the discerning.

⁷Stay away from a foolish man,
    for you will not find knowledge
        on his lips.

⁸The wisdom of the prudent is to
        give thought to their ways,
    but the folly of fools is
        deception.

⁹Fools mock at making amends for
        sin,
    but goodwill is found among
        the upright.

¹⁰Each heart knows its own
        bitterness,
    and no one else can share its
        joy.

¹¹The house of the wicked will be
        destroyed,
    but the tent of the upright will
        flourish.

¹²There is a way that seems right to
        a man,
    but in the end it leads to death.

¹³Even in laughter the heart may
        ache,
    and joy may end in grief.

¹⁴The faithless will be fully repaid
        for their ways,
    and the good man rewarded for
        his.

¹⁵A simple man believes anything,
    but a prudent man gives
        thought to his steps.

¹⁶A wise man fears the LORD and
        shuns evil,
    but a fool is hotheaded and
        reckless.

¹⁷A quick-tempered man does
        foolish things,
    and a crafty man is hated.

¹⁸The simple inherit folly,

but the prudent are crowned
    with knowledge.

¹⁹Evil men will bow down in the
        presence of the good,
    and the wicked at the gates of
        the righteous.

²⁰The poor are shunned even by
        their neighbors,
    but the rich have many friends.

²¹He who despises his neighbor
        sins,
    but blessed is he who is kind to
        the needy.

²²Do not those who plot evil go
        astray?
    But those who plan what is
        good find*ᵃ* love and
        faithfulness.

²³All hard work brings a profit,
    but mere talk leads only to
        poverty.

²⁴The wealth of the wise is their
        crown,
    but the folly of fools yields
        folly.

²⁵A truthful witness saves lives,
    but a false witness is deceitful.

²⁶He who fears the LORD has a
        secure fortress,
    and for his children it will be a
        refuge.

²⁷The fear of the LORD is a fountain
        of life,
    turning a man from the snares
        of death.

²⁸A large population is a king's
        glory,
    but without subjects a prince is
        ruined.

²⁹A patient man has great
        understanding,
    but a quick-tempered man
        displays folly.

³⁰A heart at peace gives life to the
        body,
    but envy rots the bones.

ᵃ22 Or *show*

³¹He who oppresses the poor shows
　　contempt for their Maker,
　but whoever is kind to the
　　needy honors God.

³²When calamity comes, the wicked
　　are brought down,
　but even in death the righteous
　　have a refuge.

³³Wisdom reposes in the heart of
　　the discerning
　and even among fools she lets
　　herself be known.ᵃ

³⁴Righteousness exalts a nation,
　but sin is a disgrace to any
　　people.

³⁵A king delights in a wise servant,
　but a shameful servant incurs
　　his wrath.

15 A gentle answer turns away
　　wrath,
　but a harsh word stirs up anger.

²The tongue of the wise commends
　　knowledge,
　but the mouth of the fool
　　gushes folly.

³The eyes of the LORD are
　　everywhere,
　keeping watch on the wicked
　　and the good.

⁴The tongue that brings healing is a
　　tree of life,
　but a deceitful tongue crushes
　　the spirit.

⁵A fool spurns his father's
　　discipline,
　but whoever heeds correction
　　shows prudence.

⁶The house of the righteous
　　contains great treasure,
　but the income of the wicked
　　brings them trouble.

⁷The lips of the wise spread
　　knowledge;
　not so the hearts of fools.

⁸The LORD detests the sacrifice of
　　the wicked,
　but the prayer of the upright
　　pleases him.

⁹The LORD detests the way of the
　　wicked
　but he loves those who pursue
　　righteousness.

¹⁰Stern discipline awaits him who
　　leaves the path;
　he who hates correction will
　　die.

¹¹Death and Destructionᵇ lie open
　　before the LORD—
　how much more the hearts of
　　men!

¹²A mocker resents correction;
　he will not consult the wise.

¹³A happy heart makes the face
　　cheerful,
　but heartache crushes the spirit.

¹⁴The discerning heart seeks
　　knowledge,
　but the mouth of a fool feeds on
　　folly.

¹⁵All the days of the oppressed are
　　wretched,
　but the cheerful heart has a
　　continual feast.

¹⁶Better a little with the fear of the
　　LORD
　than great wealth with turmoil.

¹⁷Better a meal of vegetables where
　　there is love
　than a fattened calf with hatred.

¹⁸A hot-tempered man stirs up
　　dissension,
　but a patient man calms a
　　quarrel.

¹⁹The way of the sluggard is
　　blocked with thorns,
　but the path of the upright is a
　　highway.

²⁰A wise son brings joy to his
　　father,
　but a foolish man despises his
　　mother.

ᵃ33 Hebrew; Septuagint and Syriac / *but in the heart of fools she is not known*   ᵇ11 Hebrew *Sheol and Abaddon*

VERSE:
Proverbs 15:13

AUTHOR:
Martin A. Janis

PASSAGE:
Proverbs 15:13–30

Give Us a Happy Heart

May you and I, as senior citizens, always comport ourselves in such a way as to assure that passersby will say, with admiration and respect, "There goes a senior citizen," or better yet, "a seasoned citizen."

May we make our retirement period a time of self-renewal, a new plateau of life dedicated to God, our fellowman and our communities.

Let us live a healthy life so as to set an example for other seniors, leading to increased life span for those who follow.

May we always be of good cheer, being sure to smile, give a friendly greeting to others, whether a senior citizen or not, and pass a sincere compliment when possible.

Let us make learning and growing an integral part of our retirement lives; and never stop dreaming, for dreams mean believing in the future.

Let us make good use of our experience, knowledge and wisdom, for others as well as for ourselves.

Let us be active and stay active to the very end, remembering that, even when disabled, it is not what we have lost but what we have left that counts.

Even though we are senior citizens and part of a group, let us remain individuals and express that individualism, within the bounds of society's rules.

May we be ever creative in living our retirement lives, so as to make the last part of our lives the best part.

ADDITIONAL SCRIPTURE READINGS
Psalm 71; Isaiah 46:3–4

Go to page 798 for your next devotional reading.

21Folly delights a man who lacks
  judgment,
  but a man of understanding
  keeps a straight course.

22Plans fail for lack of counsel,
  but with many advisers they
  succeed.

23A man finds joy in giving an apt
  reply—
  and how good is a timely word!

24The path of life leads upward for
  the wise
  to keep him from going down
  to the grave.ᵃ

25The LORD tears down the proud
  man's house
  but he keeps the widow's
  boundaries intact.

26The LORD detests the thoughts of
  the wicked,
  but those of the pure are
  pleasing to him.

27A greedy man brings trouble to
  his family,
  but he who hates bribes will
  live.

28The heart of the righteous weighs
  its answers,
  but the mouth of the wicked
  gushes evil.

29The LORD is far from the wicked
  but he hears the prayer of the
  righteous.

30A cheerful look brings joy to the
  heart,
  and good news gives health to
  the bones.

31He who listens to a life-giving
  rebuke
  will be at home among the
  wise.

32He who ignores discipline
  despises himself,
  but whoever heeds correction
  gains understanding.

33The fear of the LORD teaches a man
  wisdom,ᵇ

and humility comes before
  honor.

16 To man belong the plans of
  the heart,
  but from the LORD comes the
  reply of the tongue.

2All a man's ways seem innocent to
  him,
  but motives are weighed by the
  LORD.

3Commit to the LORD whatever you
  do,
  and your plans will succeed.

4The LORD works out everything for
  his own ends—
  even the wicked for a day of
  disaster.

5The LORD detests all the proud of
  heart.
  Be sure of this: They will not go
  unpunished.

6Through love and faithfulness sin
  is atoned for;
  through the fear of the LORD a
  man avoids evil.

7When a man's ways are pleasing
  to the LORD,
  he makes even his enemies live
  at peace with him.

8Better a little with righteousness
  than much gain with injustice.

9In his heart a man plans his
  course,
  but the LORD determines his
  steps.

10The lips of a king speak as an
  oracle,
  and his mouth should not
  betray justice.

11Honest scales and balances are
  from the LORD;
  all the weights in the bag are of
  his making.

12Kings detest wrongdoing,
  for a throne is established
  through righteousness.

ᵃ24 Hebrew *Sheol*　　ᵇ33 Or *Wisdom teaches the fear of the* LORD

¹³Kings take pleasure in honest lips;
  they value a man who speaks
    the truth.

¹⁴A king's wrath is a messenger of
    death,
  but a wise man will appease it.

¹⁵When a king's face brightens, it
    means life;
  his favor is like a rain cloud in
    spring.

¹⁶How much better to get wisdom
    than gold,
  to choose understanding rather
    than silver!

¹⁷The highway of the upright avoids
    evil;
  he who guards his way guards
    his life.

¹⁸Pride goes before destruction,
  a haughty spirit before a fall.

¹⁹Better to be lowly in spirit and
    among the oppressed
  than to share plunder with the
    proud.

²⁰Whoever gives heed to instruction
    prospers,
  and blessed is he who trusts in
    the Lord.

²¹The wise in heart are called
    discerning,
  and pleasant words promote
    instruction.ᵃ

²²Understanding is a fountain of life
    to those who have it,
  but folly brings punishment to
    fools.

²³A wise man's heart guides his
    mouth,
  and his lips promote
    instruction.ᵇ

²⁴Pleasant words are a honeycomb,
  sweet to the soul and healing to
    the bones.

²⁵There is a way that seems right to
    a man,
  but in the end it leads to death.

²⁶The laborer's appetite works for
    him;
  his hunger drives him on.

²⁷A scoundrel plots evil,
  and his speech is like a
    scorching fire.

²⁸A perverse man stirs up
    dissension,
  and a gossip separates close
    friends.

²⁹A violent man entices his neighbor
  and leads him down a path that
    is not good.

³⁰He who winks with his eye is
    plotting perversity;
  he who purses his lips is bent
    on evil.

³¹Gray hair is a crown of splendor;
  it is attained by a righteous life.

³²Better a patient man than a
    warrior,
  a man who controls his temper
    than one who takes a city.

³³The lot is cast into the lap,
  but its every decision is from
    the Lord.

17 Better a dry crust with peace
    and quiet
  than a house full of feasting,ᶜ
    with strife.

²A wise servant will rule over a
    disgraceful son,
  and will share the inheritance as
    one of the brothers.

³The crucible for silver and the
    furnace for gold,
  but the Lord tests the heart.

⁴A wicked man listens to evil lips;
  a liar pays attention to a
    malicious tongue.

⁵He who mocks the poor shows
    contempt for their Maker;
  whoever gloats over disaster
    will not go unpunished.

ᵃ21 Or words make a man persuasive   ᵇ23 Or mouth / and makes his lips persuasive   ᶜ1 Hebrew
sacrifices

⁶Children's children are a crown to
the aged,
and parents are the pride of
their children.

⁷Arrogant*a* lips are unsuited to a
fool—

how much worse lying lips
to a ruler!

⁸A bribe is a charm to the one
who gives it;
wherever he turns, he
succeeds.

a7 Or Eloquent

TUESDAY

VERSE: AUTHOR: PASSAGE:
Proverbs 16:31   Author Unknown   Proverbs 16:20–31

A Prayer for the Aging

Lord, you know better than I myself know that I am
growing older and will some day be old. Keep me from
being talkative and particularly from the fatal habit of
thinking that I must say something on every subject and
on every occasion. Release me from craving to straighten
out everybody's affairs. Make me thoughtful but not
moody; helpful but not bossy. With my vast store of wisdom, it seems a pity not to use it all, but you know,
Lord, that I want a few friends at the end. Keep my
mind from the recital of endless details—give me wings
to come to the point. I ask for grace enough to listen to
the tales of others' pain. But seal my lips on my own
aches and pains—they are increasing, and my love of re-
hearsing them is becoming sweeter as the years go by . . .

I dare not ask for improved memory but for a growing
humility and a lessening cocksureness when my memory
seems to clash with the memories of others. Teach me
the glorious lesson that occasionally it is possible that I
may be mistaken . . . Give me the ability to see good
things in unexpected places, and talents in unexpected
people. And give me, O Lord, the grace to tell them so.

ADDITIONAL SCRIPTURE READINGS
Philippians 2:1–11; 1 Peter 5:1–11
Go to page 799 for your next devotional reading.

VERSE:	AUTHOR:	PASSAGE:
Proverbs 17:6	Verlyn D. Verbrugge	Proverbs 17:1–6

A Grandparent's Crown

Crowns! Kings wear crowns as a sign of authority (2 Samuel 1:10). Athletes wear crowns as a sign of victory (1 Corinthians 9:25). And grandparents wear crowns too.

Grandparents? What kind of a crown do they wear? The crown of grandparents is their grandchildren (Proverbs 17:6)!

In what way are grandchildren the crown of the elderly? In Bible times it was the exception rather than the rule for a man or woman to live to see the second generation. Too many wars, diseases and famines took lives at a relatively young age. To be able to see one's grandchildren was a sign of a special blessing from God. It was like being crowned by God; it meant being a winner with the Lord.

It's common today, though, isn't it? Many "middle-aged" people are grandparents and many elderly have great-grandchildren and even great-great-grandchildren. But don't ever take that for granted! Every grandchild born yet today signifies God's special love. It means God is faithful to his promises. It means God is restraining the destructive forces of war, epidemic and famine. It means God is blessing us today with extended life spans. If you are grandparents, thank God for that blessing. And don't forget to enjoy your grandchildren as your crown!

ADDITIONAL SCRIPTURE READINGS
Genesis 48:1–11; Psalm 128

Go to page 803 for your next devotional reading.

⁹He who covers over an offense
     promotes love,
  but whoever repeats the matter
     separates close friends.

¹⁰A rebuke impresses a man of
     discernment
  more than a hundred lashes a
     fool.

¹¹An evil man is bent only on
     rebellion;
  a merciless official will be sent
     against him.

¹²Better to meet a bear robbed of
     her cubs
  than a fool in his folly.

¹³If a man pays back evil for good,
  evil will never leave his house.

¹⁴Starting a quarrel is like breaching
     a dam;
  so drop the matter before a
     dispute breaks out.

¹⁵Acquitting the guilty and
     condemning the innocent—
  the LORD detests them both.

¹⁶Of what use is money in the hand
     of a fool,
  since he has no desire to get
     wisdom?

¹⁷A friend loves at all times,
  and a brother is born for
     adversity.

¹⁸A man lacking in judgment strikes
     hands in pledge
  and puts up security for his
     neighbor.

¹⁹He who loves a quarrel loves sin;
  he who builds a high gate
     invites destruction.

²⁰A man of perverse heart does not
     prosper;
  he whose tongue is deceitful
     falls into trouble.

²¹To have a fool for a son brings
     grief;
  there is no joy for the father of
     a fool.

²²A cheerful heart is good medicine,
  but a crushed spirit dries up the
     bones.

²³A wicked man accepts a bribe in
     secret
  to pervert the course of justice.

²⁴A discerning man keeps wisdom
     in view,
  but a fool's eyes wander to the
     ends of the earth.

²⁵A foolish son brings grief to his
     father
  and bitterness to the one who
     bore him.

²⁶It is not good to punish an
     innocent man,
  or to flog officials for their
     integrity.

²⁷A man of knowledge uses words
     with restraint,
  and a man of understanding is
     even-tempered.

²⁸Even a fool is thought wise if he
     keeps silent,
  and discerning if he holds his
     tongue.

18 An unfriendly man pursues
         selfish ends;
  he defies all sound judgment.

²A fool finds no pleasure in
     understanding
  but delights in airing his own
     opinions.

³When wickedness comes, so does
     contempt,
  and with shame comes disgrace.

⁴The words of a man's mouth are
     deep waters,
  but the fountain of wisdom is a
     bubbling brook.

⁵It is not good to be partial to the
     wicked
  or to deprive the innocent of
     justice.

⁶A fool's lips bring him strife,
  and his mouth invites a beating.

⁷A fool's mouth is his undoing,
  and his lips are a snare to his
     soul.

[8]The words of a gossip are like choice morsels;
  they go down to a man's inmost parts.

[9]One who is slack in his work
  is brother to one who destroys.

[10]The name of the LORD is a strong tower;
  the righteous run to it and are safe.

[11]The wealth of the rich is their fortified city;
  they imagine it an unscalable wall.

[12]Before his downfall a man's heart is proud,
  but humility comes before honor.

[13]He who answers before listening—
  that is his folly and his shame.

[14]A man's spirit sustains him in sickness,
  but a crushed spirit who can bear?

[15]The heart of the discerning acquires knowledge;
  the ears of the wise seek it out.

[16]A gift opens the way for the giver
  and ushers him into the presence of the great.

[17]The first to present his case seems right,
  till another comes forward and questions him.

[18]Casting the lot settles disputes
  and keeps strong opponents apart.

[19]An offended brother is more unyielding than a fortified city,
  and disputes are like the barred gates of a citadel.

[20]From the fruit of his mouth a man's stomach is filled;
  with the harvest from his lips he is satisfied.

[21]The tongue has the power of life and death,
  and those who love it will eat its fruit.

[22]He who finds a wife finds what is good
  and receives favor from the LORD.

[23]A poor man pleads for mercy,
  but a rich man answers harshly.

[24]A man of many companions may come to ruin,
  but there is a friend who sticks closer than a brother.

19 Better a poor man whose walk is blameless
  than a fool whose lips are perverse.

[2]It is not good to have zeal without knowledge,
  nor to be hasty and miss the way.

[3]A man's own folly ruins his life,
  yet his heart rages against the LORD.

[4]Wealth brings many friends,
  but a poor man's friend deserts him.

[5]A false witness will not go unpunished,
  and he who pours out lies will not go free.

[6]Many curry favor with a ruler,
  and everyone is the friend of a man who gives gifts.

[7]A poor man is shunned by all his relatives—
  how much more do his friends avoid him!
Though he pursues them with pleading,
  they are nowhere to be found.[a]

[8]He who gets wisdom loves his own soul;
  he who cherishes understanding prospers.

---

[a]7 The meaning of the Hebrew for this sentence is uncertain.

⁹A false witness will not go
    unpunished,
  and he who pours out lies will
    perish.

¹⁰It is not fitting for a fool to live in
    luxury—
  how much worse for a slave to
    rule over princes!

¹¹A man's wisdom gives him
    patience;
  it is to his glory to overlook an
    offense.

¹²A king's rage is like the roar of a
    lion,
  but his favor is like dew on the
    grass.

¹³A foolish son is his father's ruin,
  and a quarrelsome wife is like a
    constant dripping.

¹⁴Houses and wealth are inherited
    from parents,
  but a prudent wife is from the
    LORD.

¹⁵Laziness brings on deep sleep,
  and the shiftless man goes
    hungry.

¹⁶He who obeys instructions guards
    his life,
  but he who is contemptuous of
    his ways will die.

¹⁷He who is kind to the poor lends
    to the LORD,
  and he will reward him for
    what he has done.

¹⁸Discipline your son, for in that
    there is hope;
  do not be a willing party to his
    death.

¹⁹A hot-tempered man must pay the
    penalty;
  if you rescue him, you will have
    to do it again.

²⁰Listen to advice and accept
    instruction,
  and in the end you will be
    wise.

²¹Many are the plans in a man's
    heart,
  but it is the LORD's purpose that
    prevails.

²²What a man desires is unfailing
    love[a];
  better to be poor than a liar.

²³The fear of the LORD leads to
    life:
  Then one rests content,
    untouched by trouble.

²⁴The sluggard buries his hand in
    the dish;
  he will not even bring it back to
    his mouth!

²⁵Flog a mocker, and the simple will
    learn prudence;
  rebuke a discerning man, and
    he will gain knowledge.

²⁶He who robs his father and drives
    out his mother
  is a son who brings shame and
    disgrace.

²⁷Stop listening to instruction, my
    son,
  and you will stray from the
    words of knowledge.

²⁸A corrupt witness mocks at justice,
  and the mouth of the wicked
    gulps down evil.

²⁹Penalties are prepared for
    mockers,
  and beatings for the backs of
    fools.

20 Wine is a mocker and beer a
    brawler;
  whoever is led astray by them
    is not wise.

²A king's wrath is like the roar of a
    lion;
  he who angers him forfeits his
    life.

³It is to a man's honor to avoid
    strife,
  but every fool is quick to
    quarrel.

a22 Or A man's greed is his shame

⁴A sluggard does not plow in
    season;
  so at harvest time he looks but
    finds nothing.

⁵The purposes of a man's heart are
    deep waters,
  but a man of understanding
    draws them out.

⁶Many a man claims to have
    unfailing love,

but a faithful man who can
    find?

⁷The righteous man leads a
    blameless life;
  blessed are his children after
    him.

⁸When a king sits on his throne to
    judge,
  he winnows out all evil with his
    eyes.

THURSDAY

VERSE: AUTHOR: PASSAGE:
Proverbs 19:17   Charles R. Swindoll   Proverbs 19:16–17

Expanding the Bookends

Are you successful? If you are a giver, the answer is yes. And you don't give in just one area—you give generously, you give liberally, you give in a variety of ways . . . It isn't just giving to our families or just giving to the person who is personally attracted to us or to whom we are attracted. It's giving broadly. It's expanding the bookends of our lives so that we gain a vision of the limitless field in front of us . . .

This does not mean we will be free from calamity or misfortune . . . We have no idea what calamity, need or unfortunate event may occur. Nevertheless, we give. We leave the results with our God. Take a quick glance at a proverb Solomon wrote: "He who is kind to the poor lends to the LORD, and he will reward him for what he has done" (Proverbs 19:17).

The Lord says, in effect, "I will take the responsibility of repaying you. Since you are actually lending to me and you are using him as the object of your giving, remember it is I who will repay the good deed." God has a great memory. Trust him not to forget that promise.

ADDITIONAL SCRIPTURE READINGS
Proverbs 3:1–10; Malachi 3:1–15

Go to page 805 for your next devotional reading.

⁹Who can say, "I have kept my
    heart pure;
    I am clean and without sin"?

¹⁰Differing weights and differing
    measures—
    the LORD detests them both.

¹¹Even a child is known by his
    actions,
    by whether his conduct is pure
    and right.

¹²Ears that hear and eyes that see—
    the LORD has made them both.

¹³Do not love sleep or you will
    grow poor;
    stay awake and you will have
    food to spare.

¹⁴"It's no good, it's no good!" says
    the buyer;
    then off he goes and boasts
    about his purchase.

¹⁵Gold there is, and rubies in
    abundance,
    but lips that speak knowledge
    are a rare jewel.

¹⁶Take the garment of one who puts
    up security for a stranger;
    hold it in pledge if he does it
    for a wayward woman.

¹⁷Food gained by fraud tastes sweet
    to a man,
    but he ends up with a mouth
    full of gravel.

¹⁸Make plans by seeking advice;
    if you wage war, obtain
    guidance.

¹⁹A gossip betrays a confidence;
    so avoid a man who talks too
    much.

²⁰If a man curses his father or
    mother,
    his lamp will be snuffed out in
    pitch darkness.

²¹An inheritance quickly gained at
    the beginning
    will not be blessed at the end.

²²Do not say, "I'll pay you back for
    this wrong!"
    Wait for the LORD, and he will
    deliver you.

²³The LORD detests differing weights,
    and dishonest scales do not
    please him.

²⁴A man's steps are directed by the
    LORD.
    How then can anyone
    understand his own way?

²⁵It is a trap for a man to dedicate
    something rashly
    and only later to consider his
    vows.

²⁶A wise king winnows out the
    wicked;
    he drives the threshing wheel
    over them.

²⁷The lamp of the LORD searches the
    spirit of a man[a];
    it searches out his inmost being.

²⁸Love and faithfulness keep a king
    safe;
    through love his throne is made
    secure.

²⁹The glory of young men is their
    strength,
    gray hair the splendor of the
    old.

³⁰Blows and wounds cleanse away
    evil,
    and beatings purge the inmost
    being.

21 The king's heart is in the
    hand of the LORD;
    he directs it like a watercourse
    wherever he pleases.

²All a man's ways seem right to
    him,
    but the LORD weighs the heart.

³To do what is right and just
    is more acceptable to the LORD
    than sacrifice.

⁴Haughty eyes and a proud heart,
    the lamp of the wicked, are sin!

---

a27 Or The spirit of man is the LORD's lamp

5The plans of the diligent lead to
   profit
   as surely as haste leads to
   poverty.

6A fortune made by a lying
   tongue
   is a fleeting vapor and a
   deadly snare.*a*

*a*6 Some Hebrew manuscripts, Septuagint and Vulgate; most Hebrew manuscripts *vapor for those who seek death*

FRIDAY

VERSE:	AUTHOR:	PASSAGE:
Proverbs 20:29	Jacob D. Eppinga	Proverbs 20:27–29

The Splendor of the Old

Proverbs 20:29 tells us that the glory of young men is their strength . . . but the verse goes on to say that gray hairs are the splendor of the old. And the splendor of the old is equal to the glory of the young. Only the old know something about God's patience. Only the old know something about God's long-suffering nature. That God had dealt with Jacob for 130 years was a miracle of grace. That God allows us to be here threescore-years-and-ten or fourscore years is also a miracle of grace. It is a miracle of love that God takes time to hone us. It is a miracle of mercy that he gives us time so we may grow in grace and in the knowledge of his Son (2 Peter 3:18).

These are the beliefs that can shine forth from the eyes of older Christians. Hanging on my study wall is that famous picture of an aged man saying grace. His gnarled hands are folded in prayer over a piece of bread and a glass of water. His old face is filled with that splendor of which Solomon writes and which comes to the devout Christian as the years mount and the skin wrinkles.

Time takes its toll. But it can also bring with it a deeper peace with God. For this to happen we need to mature in spirit.

ADDITIONAL SCRIPTURE READINGS
Colossians 1:3–14; 2 Peter 3:14–18

Go to page 810 for your next devotional reading.

⁷The violence of the wicked will
    drag them away,
  for they refuse to do what is
    right.

⁸The way of the guilty is devious,
  but the conduct of the innocent
    is upright.

⁹Better to live on a corner of the
    roof
  than share a house with a
    quarrelsome wife.

¹⁰The wicked man craves evil;
  his neighbor gets no mercy
    from him.

¹¹When a mocker is punished, the
    simple gain wisdom;
  when a wise man is instructed,
    he gets knowledge.

¹²The Righteous One^a takes note of
    the house of the wicked
  and brings the wicked to ruin.

¹³If a man shuts his ears to the cry
    of the poor,
  he too will cry out and not be
    answered.

¹⁴A gift given in secret soothes
    anger,
  and a bribe concealed in the
    cloak pacifies great wrath.

¹⁵When justice is done, it brings joy
    to the righteous
  but terror to evildoers.

¹⁶A man who strays from the path
    of understanding
  comes to rest in the company of
    the dead.

¹⁷He who loves pleasure will
    become poor;
  whoever loves wine and oil will
    never be rich.

¹⁸The wicked become a ransom for
    the righteous,
  and the unfaithful for the
    upright.

¹⁹Better to live in a desert

than with a quarrelsome and
    ill-tempered wife.

²⁰In the house of the wise are stores
    of choice food and oil,
  but a foolish man devours all he
    has.

²¹He who pursues righteousness
    and love
  finds life, prosperity^b and
    honor.

²²A wise man attacks the city of the
    mighty
  and pulls down the stronghold
    in which they trust.

²³He who guards his mouth and his
    tongue
  keeps himself from calamity.

²⁴The proud and arrogant man—
    "Mocker" is his name;
  he behaves with overweening
    pride.

²⁵The sluggard's craving will be the
    death of him,
  because his hands refuse to
    work.

²⁶All day long he craves for more,
  but the righteous give without
    sparing.

²⁷The sacrifice of the wicked is
    detestable—
  how much more so when
    brought with evil intent!

²⁸A false witness will perish,
  and whoever listens to him will
    be destroyed forever.^c

²⁹A wicked man puts up a bold
    front,
  but an upright man gives
    thought to his ways.

³⁰There is no wisdom, no insight, no
    plan
  that can succeed against the
    Lord.

³¹The horse is made ready for the
    day of battle,
  but victory rests with the Lord.

---

^a12 Or *The righteous man*   ^b21 Or *righteousness*   ^c28 Or / *but the words of an obedient man will*
live on

22
A good name is more
desirable than great riches;
to be esteemed is better than
silver or gold.

²Rich and poor have this in
common:
The LORD is the Maker of them
all.

³A prudent man sees danger and
takes refuge,
but the simple keep going and
suffer for it.

⁴Humility and the fear of the LORD
bring wealth and honor and life.

⁵In the paths of the wicked lie
thorns and snares,
but he who guards his soul
stays far from them.

⁶Train*a* a child in the way he
should go,
and when he is old he will not
turn from it.

⁷The rich rule over the poor,
and the borrower is servant to
the lender.

⁸He who sows wickedness reaps
trouble,
and the rod of his fury will be
destroyed.

⁹A generous man will himself be
blessed,
for he shares his food with the
poor.

¹⁰Drive out the mocker, and out
goes strife;
quarrels and insults are ended.

¹¹He who loves a pure heart and
whose speech is gracious
will have the king for his friend.

¹²The eyes of the LORD keep watch
over knowledge,
but he frustrates the words of
the unfaithful.

¹³The sluggard says, "There is a lion
outside!"
or, "I will be murdered in the
streets!"

¹⁴The mouth of an adulteress is a
deep pit;
he who is under the LORD's
wrath will fall into it.

¹⁵Folly is bound up in the heart of a
child,
but the rod of discipline will
drive it far from him.

¹⁶He who oppresses the poor to
increase his wealth
and he who gives gifts to the
rich—both come to
poverty.

Sayings of the Wise

¹⁷Pay attention and listen to the
sayings of the wise;
apply your heart to what I
teach,
¹⁸for it is pleasing when you keep
them in your heart
and have all of them ready on
your lips.
¹⁹So that your trust may be in the
LORD,
I teach you today, even you.
²⁰Have I not written thirty*b* sayings
for you,
sayings of counsel and
knowledge,
²¹teaching you true and reliable
words,
so that you can give sound
answers
to him who sent you?

²²Do not exploit the poor because
they are poor
and do not crush the needy in
court,
²³for the LORD will take up their case
and will plunder those who
plunder them.

²⁴Do not make friends with a
hot-tempered man,
do not associate with one easily
angered,
²⁵or you may learn his ways
and get yourself ensnared.

*a*6 Or *Start*   *b*20 Or *not formerly written; or not written excellent*

²⁶Do not be a man who strikes
hands in pledge
or puts up security for debts;
²⁷if you lack the means to pay,
your very bed will be snatched
from under you.

²⁸Do not move an ancient boundary
stone
set up by your forefathers.

²⁹Do you see a man skilled in his
work?
He will serve before kings;
he will not serve before obscure
men.

23 When you sit to dine with a
ruler,
note well what*ᵃ* is before you,
²and put a knife to your throat
if you are given to gluttony.
³Do not crave his delicacies,
for that food is deceptive.

⁴Do not wear yourself out to get
rich;
have the wisdom to show
restraint.
⁵Cast but a glance at riches, and
they are gone,
for they will surely sprout
wings
and fly off to the sky like an
eagle.

⁶Do not eat the food of a stingy
man,
do not crave his delicacies;
⁷for he is the kind of man
who is always thinking about
the cost.*ᵇ*
"Eat and drink," he says to you,
but his heart is not with you.
⁸You will vomit up the little you
have eaten
and will have wasted your
compliments.

⁹Do not speak to a fool,
for he will scorn the wisdom of
your words.

¹⁰Do not move an ancient boundary
stone

or encroach on the fields of the
fatherless,
¹¹for their Defender is strong;
he will take up their case
against you.

¹²Apply your heart to instruction
and your ears to words of
knowledge.

¹³Do not withhold discipline from a
child;
if you punish him with the rod,
he will not die.
¹⁴Punish him with the rod
and save his soul from death.*ᶜ*

¹⁵My son, if your heart is wise,
then my heart will be glad;
¹⁶my inmost being will rejoice
when your lips speak what is
right.

¹⁷Do not let your heart envy
sinners,
but always be zealous for the
fear of the LORD.
¹⁸There is surely a future hope for
you,
and your hope will not be cut
off.

¹⁹Listen, my son, and be wise,
and keep your heart on the
right path.
²⁰Do not join those who drink too
much wine
or gorge themselves on meat,
²¹for drunkards and gluttons
become poor,
and drowsiness clothes them in
rags.

²²Listen to your father, who gave
you life,
and do not despise your mother
when she is old.
²³Buy the truth and do not sell it;
get wisdom, discipline and
understanding.
²⁴The father of a righteous man has
great joy;
he who has a wise son delights
in him.

ᵃ1 Or *who*   *ᵇ7* Or *for as he thinks within himself, / so he is;* or *for as he puts on a feast, / so he is*
ᶜ14 Hebrew *Sheol*

²⁵May your father and mother be
  glad;
    may she who gave you birth
      rejoice!

²⁶My son, give me your heart
    and let your eyes keep to my
      ways,
²⁷for a prostitute is a deep pit
    and a wayward wife is a
      narrow well.
²⁸Like a bandit she lies in wait,
    and multiplies the unfaithful
      among men.

²⁹Who has woe? Who has sorrow?
    Who has strife? Who has
      complaints?
    Who has needless bruises? Who
      has bloodshot eyes?
³⁰Those who linger over wine,
    who go to sample bowls of
      mixed wine.
³¹Do not gaze at wine when it is
      red,
    when it sparkles in the cup,
    when it goes down smoothly!
³²In the end it bites like a snake
    and poisons like a viper.
³³Your eyes will see strange sights
    and your mind imagine
      confusing things.
³⁴You will be like one sleeping on
      the high seas,
    lying on top of the rigging.
³⁵"They hit me," you will say, "but
      I'm not hurt!
    They beat me, but I don't feel it!
  When will I wake up
    so I can find another drink?"

24 Do not envy wicked men,
    do not desire their company;
²for their hearts plot violence,
    and their lips talk about making
      trouble.

³By wisdom a house is built,
    and through understanding it is
      established;
⁴through knowledge its rooms are
      filled
    with rare and beautiful
      treasures.

⁵A wise man has great power,

and a man of knowledge
    increases strength;
⁶for waging war you need
      guidance,
    and for victory many advisers.

⁷Wisdom is too high for a fool;
    in the assembly at the gate he
      has nothing to say.

⁸He who plots evil
    will be known as a schemer.
⁹The schemes of folly are sin,
    and men detest a mocker.

¹⁰If you falter in times of trouble,
    how small is your strength!

¹¹Rescue those being led away to
      death;
    hold back those staggering
      toward slaughter.
¹²If you say, "But we knew nothing
      about this,"
    does not he who weighs the
      heart perceive it?
  Does not he who guards your life
      know it?
  Will he not repay each person
      according to what he has
      done?

¹³Eat honey, my son, for it is good;
    honey from the comb is sweet
      to your taste.
¹⁴Know also that wisdom is sweet
      to your soul;
    if you find it, there is a future
      hope for you,
    and your hope will not be cut
      off.

¹⁵Do not lie in wait like an outlaw
      against a righteous man's
      house,
    do not raid his dwelling place;
¹⁶for though a righteous man falls
      seven times, he rises again,
    but the wicked are brought
      down by calamity.

¹⁷Do not gloat when your enemy
      falls;
    when he stumbles, do not let
      your heart rejoice,
¹⁸or the Lord will see and
      disapprove

PASSAGE: Lamentations 3:19–25; Revelation 21:1–5
AUTHOR: Annie Johnson Flint

New Every Morning

Yea, "new every morning," though we may awake,
Our hearts with old sorrow beginning to ache;
With old work unfinished when night stayed our
       hand,
With new duties waiting, unknown and unplanned;
With old care still pressing, to fret and to vex,
With new problems rising, our minds to perplex
In ways long familiar, in paths yet untrod,
Oh, new every morning the mercies of God!
His faithfulness fails not; it meets each new day
New guidance for every new step of the way;
New grace for new trials, new trust for old fears,
New patience for bearing the wrongs of the years,
New strength for new burdens, new courage for
       old,
New faith for whatever the day may unfold;
As fresh for each need as the dew on the sod;
Oh, new every morning the mercies of God!

Go to page 815 for your next devotional reading.

and turn his wrath away from
him.

¹⁹Do not fret because of evil men
or be envious of the wicked,
²⁰for the evil man has no future
hope,
and the lamp of the wicked will
be snuffed out.

²¹Fear the LORD and the king, my
son,
and do not join with the
rebellious,
²²for those two will send sudden
destruction upon them,
and who knows what calamities
they can bring?

Further Sayings of the Wise

²³These also are sayings of the wise:

To show partiality in judging is
not good:
²⁴Whoever says to the guilty, "You
are innocent"—
peoples will curse him and
nations denounce him.
²⁵But it will go well with those who
convict the guilty,
and rich blessing will come
upon them.

²⁶An honest answer
is like a kiss on the lips.

²⁷Finish your outdoor work
and get your fields ready;
after that, build your house.

²⁸Do not testify against your
neighbor without cause,
or use your lips to deceive.
²⁹Do not say, "I'll do to him as he
has done to me;
I'll pay that man back for what
he did."

³⁰I went past the field of the
sluggard,
past the vineyard of the man
who lacks judgment;
³¹thorns had come up everywhere,
the ground was covered with
weeds,

and the stone wall was in ruins.
³²I applied my heart to what I
observed
and learned a lesson from what
I saw:
³³A little sleep, a little slumber,
a little folding of the hands to
rest—
³⁴and poverty will come on you like
a bandit
and scarcity like an armed
man.^a

More Proverbs of Solomon

25 These are more proverbs of
Solomon, copied by the men of
Hezekiah king of Judah:

²It is the glory of God to conceal a
matter;
to search out a matter is the
glory of kings.

³As the heavens are high and the
earth is deep,
so the hearts of kings are
unsearchable.

⁴Remove the dross from the silver,
and out comes material for^b
the silversmith;
⁵remove the wicked from the king's
presence,
and his throne will be
established through
righteousness.

⁶Do not exalt yourself in the king's
presence,
and do not claim a place among
great men;
⁷it is better for him to say to you,
"Come up here,"
than for him to humiliate you
before a nobleman.

What you have seen with your
eyes
⁸ do not bring^c hastily to court,
for what will you do in the end
if your neighbor puts you to
shame?

---

^a34 Or *like a vagrant / and scarcity like a beggar
on whom you had set your eyes. / ⁸Do not go*   ^b4 Or *comes a vessel from*   ^c7,8 Or *nobleman /*

⁹If you argue your case with a
  neighbor,
   do not betray another man's
    confidence,
¹⁰or he who hears it may shame you
   and you will never lose your
    bad reputation.

¹¹A word aptly spoken
   is like apples of gold in settings
    of silver.

¹²Like an earring of gold or an
  ornament of fine gold
   is a wise man's rebuke to a
    listening ear.

¹³Like the coolness of snow at
  harvest time
   is a trustworthy messenger to
    those who send him;
   he refreshes the spirit of his
    masters.

¹⁴Like clouds and wind without rain
   is a man who boasts of gifts he
    does not give.

¹⁵Through patience a ruler can be
  persuaded,
   and a gentle tongue can break a
    bone.

¹⁶If you find honey, eat just
  enough—
   too much of it, and you will
    vomit.

¹⁷Seldom set foot in your neighbor's
  house—
   too much of you, and he will
    hate you.

¹⁸Like a club or a sword or a sharp
  arrow
   is the man who gives false
    testimony against his
     neighbor.

¹⁹Like a bad tooth or a lame foot
   is reliance on the unfaithful in
    times of trouble.

²⁰Like one who takes away a
  garment on a cold day,
   or like vinegar poured on soda,
   is one who sings songs to a
    heavy heart.

²¹If your enemy is hungry, give him
  food to eat;

if he is thirsty, give him water
    to drink.
²²In doing this, you will heap
  burning coals on his head,
   and the LORD will reward you.

²³As a north wind brings rain,
   so a sly tongue brings angry
    looks.

²⁴Better to live on a corner of the
  roof
   than share a house with a
    quarrelsome wife.

²⁵Like cold water to a weary soul
   is good news from a distant
    land.

²⁶Like a muddied spring or a
  polluted well
   is a righteous man who gives
    way to the wicked.

²⁷It is not good to eat too much
  honey,
   nor is it honorable to seek one's
    own honor.

²⁸Like a city whose walls are broken
  down
   is a man who lacks self-control.

26 Like snow in summer or rain
   in harvest,
   honor is not fitting for a fool.

²Like a fluttering sparrow or a
  darting swallow,
   an undeserved curse does not
    come to rest.

³A whip for the horse, a halter for
  the donkey,
   and a rod for the backs of fools!

⁴Do not answer a fool according to
  his folly,
   or you will be like him yourself.

⁵Answer a fool according to his
  folly,
   or he will be wise in his own
    eyes.

⁶Like cutting off one's feet or
  drinking violence
   is the sending of a message by
    the hand of a fool.

⁷Like a lame man's legs that hang
    limp
  is a proverb in the mouth of a
    fool.

⁸Like tying a stone in a sling
  is the giving of honor to a fool.

⁹Like a thornbush in a drunkard's
    hand
  is a proverb in the mouth of a
    fool.

¹⁰Like an archer who wounds at
    random
  is he who hires a fool or any
    passer-by.

¹¹As a dog returns to its vomit,
  so a fool repeats his folly.

¹²Do you see a man wise in his own
    eyes?
  There is more hope for a fool
    than for him.

¹³The sluggard says, "There is a lion
    in the road,
  a fierce lion roaming the
    streets!"

¹⁴As a door turns on its hinges,
  so a sluggard turns on his bed.

¹⁵The sluggard buries his hand in
    the dish;
  he is too lazy to bring it back to
    his mouth.

¹⁶The sluggard is wiser in his own
    eyes
  than seven men who answer
    discreetly.

¹⁷Like one who seizes a dog by the
    ears
  is a passer-by who meddles in a
    quarrel not his own.

¹⁸Like a madman shooting
    firebrands or deadly arrows
¹⁹is a man who deceives his
    neighbor
  and says, "I was only joking!"

²⁰Without wood a fire goes out;
  without gossip a quarrel dies
    down.

²¹As charcoal to embers and as
    wood to fire,
  so is a quarrelsome man for
    kindling strife.

²²The words of a gossip are like
    choice morsels;
  they go down to a man's inmost
    parts.

²³Like a coating of glaze[a] over
    earthenware
  are fervent lips with an evil
    heart.

²⁴A malicious man disguises himself
    with his lips,
  but in his heart he harbors
    deceit.

²⁵Though his speech is charming, do
    not believe him,
  for seven abominations fill his
    heart.

²⁶His malice may be concealed by
    deception,
  but his wickedness will be
    exposed in the assembly.

²⁷If a man digs a pit, he will fall
    into it;
  if a man rolls a stone, it will roll
    back on him.

²⁸A lying tongue hates those it
    hurts,
  and a flattering mouth works
    ruin.

27 Do not boast about tomorrow,
    for you do not know what a
    day may bring forth.

²Let another praise you, and not
    your own mouth;
  someone else, and not your own
    lips.

³Stone is heavy and sand a burden,
  but provocation by a fool is
    heavier than both.

⁴Anger is cruel and fury
    overwhelming,
  but who can stand before
    jealousy?

⁵Better is open rebuke
  than hidden love.

---

a 23 With a different word division of the Hebrew; Masoretic Text *of silver dross*

6Wounds from a friend can be
    trusted,
  but an enemy multiplies kisses.

7He who is full loathes honey,
  but to the hungry even what is
    bitter tastes sweet.

8Like a bird that strays from its
    nest
  is a man who strays from his
    home.

9Perfume and incense bring joy to
    the heart,
  and the pleasantness of one's
    friend springs from his
    earnest counsel.

10Do not forsake your friend and
    the friend of your father,
  and do not go to your brother's
    house when disaster strikes
    you—
  better a neighbor nearby than a
    brother far away.

11Be wise, my son, and bring joy to
    my heart;
  then I can answer anyone who
    treats me with contempt.

12The prudent see danger and take
    refuge,
  but the simple keep going and
    suffer for it.

13Take the garment of one who puts
    up security for a stranger;
  hold it in pledge if he does it
    for a wayward woman.

14If a man loudly blesses his
    neighbor early in the
    morning,
  it will be taken as a curse.

15A quarrelsome wife is like
  a constant dripping on a rainy
    day;
16restraining her is like restraining
    the wind
  or grasping oil with the hand.

17As iron sharpens iron,
  so one man sharpens another.

18He who tends a fig tree will eat its
    fruit,
  and he who looks after his
    master will be honored.

19As water reflects a face,
  so a man's heart reflects the
    man.

20Death and Destruction[a] are never
    satisfied,
  and neither are the eyes of man.

21The crucible for silver and the
    furnace for gold,
  but man is tested by the praise
    he receives.

22Though you grind a fool in a
    mortar,
  grinding him like grain with a
    pestle,
  you will not remove his folly
    from him.

23Be sure you know the condition of
    your flocks,
  give careful attention to your
    herds;
24for riches do not endure forever,
  and a crown is not secure for all
    generations.
25When the hay is removed and
    new growth appears
  and the grass from the hills is
    gathered in,
26the lambs will provide you with
    clothing,
  and the goats with the price of
    a field.
27You will have plenty of goats'
    milk
  to feed you and your family
  and to nourish your servant
    girls.

28 The wicked man flees though
    no one pursues,
  but the righteous are as bold as
    a lion.

2When a country is rebellious, it
    has many rulers,
  but a man of understanding and
    knowledge maintains
    order.

a20 Hebrew *Sheol and Abaddon*

VERSE:
Proverbs 27:20

AUTHOR:
Jerry Bridges

PASSAGE:
Proverbs 27:17–21

Hungry Eyes

Solomon tells us that the eyes of man are never satisfied (Proverbs 27:20). One more lustful look or one more piece of pie never satisfies. In fact, quite the opposite takes place. Every time we say yes to temptation, we make it harder to say no the next time.

We must recognize that we have developed habit patterns of sin. We have developed the habit of shading the facts a little bit when it is to our advantage. We have developed the habit of giving in to the inertia that refuses to let us get up in the morning. These habits must be broken, but they never will till we make a basic commitment to a life of holiness without exceptions . . .

Jonathan Edwards, one of the great preachers of early American history, used to make resolutions. One of his was, "Resolved, never to do anything which I would be afraid to do if it were the last hour of my life." Dare we 20th-century Christians make such a resolution? Are we willing to commit ourselves to the practice of holiness without exceptions. There is no point of praying for victory over temptation if we are not willing to make a commitment to say no to it.

It is only by learning to deny temptation that we will ever put to death the misdeeds of the body. Learning this is usually a slow and painful process, fraught with much failure. Our old desires and our sinful habits are not easily dislodged. To break them requires persistence, often in the face of little success. But this is the path we must tread, painful though it may be.

ADDITIONAL SCRIPTURE READINGS
1 Corinthians 10:1–13; 1 John 2:1–6

Go to page 824 for your next devotional reading.

³A ruler^a who oppresses the poor
   is like a driving rain that leaves
      no crops.

⁴Those who forsake the law praise
      the wicked,
   but those who keep the law
      resist them.

⁵Evil men do not understand
      justice,
   but those who seek the LORD
      understand it fully.

⁶Better a poor man whose walk is
      blameless
   than a rich man whose ways are
      perverse.

⁷He who keeps the law is a
      discerning son,
   but a companion of gluttons
      disgraces his father.

⁸He who increases his wealth by
      exorbitant interest
   amasses it for another, who will
      be kind to the poor.

⁹If anyone turns a deaf ear to the
      law,
   even his prayers are detestable.

¹⁰He who leads the upright along
      an evil path
   will fall into his own trap,
   but the blameless will receive a
      good inheritance.

¹¹A rich man may be wise in his
      own eyes,
   but a poor man who has
      discernment sees through
      him.

¹²When the righteous triumph, there
      is great elation;
   but when the wicked rise to
      power, men go into hiding.

¹³He who conceals his sins does not
      prosper,
   but whoever confesses and
      renounces them finds
      mercy.

¹⁴Blessed is the man who always
      fears the LORD,

but he who hardens his heart
   falls into trouble.

¹⁵Like a roaring lion or a charging
      bear
   is a wicked man ruling over a
      helpless people.

¹⁶A tyrannical ruler lacks judgment,
   but he who hates ill-gotten gain
      will enjoy a long life.

¹⁷A man tormented by the guilt of
      murder
   will be a fugitive till death;
   let no one support him.

¹⁸He whose walk is blameless is
      kept safe,
   but he whose ways are perverse
      will suddenly fall.

¹⁹He who works his land will have
      abundant food,
   but the one who chases
      fantasies will have his fill
      of poverty.

²⁰A faithful man will be richly
      blessed,
   but one eager to get rich will
      not go unpunished.

²¹To show partiality is not good—
   yet a man will do wrong for a
      piece of bread.

²²A stingy man is eager to get rich
   and is unaware that poverty
      awaits him.

²³He who rebukes a man will in the
      end gain more favor
   than he who has a flattering
      tongue.

²⁴He who robs his father or mother
   and says, "It's not wrong"—
   he is partner to him who
      destroys.

²⁵A greedy man stirs up dissension,
   but he who trusts in the LORD
      will prosper.

²⁶He who trusts in himself is a fool,
   but he who walks in wisdom is
      kept safe.

²⁷He who gives to the poor will lack
    nothing,
  but he who closes his eyes to
    them receives many curses.

²⁸When the wicked rise to power,
    people go into hiding;
  but when the wicked perish, the
    righteous thrive.

29 A man who remains
    stiff-necked after many
    rebukes
  will suddenly be destroyed—
    without remedy.

²When the righteous thrive, the
    people rejoice;
  when the wicked rule, the
    people groan.

³A man who loves wisdom brings
    joy to his father,
  but a companion of prostitutes
    squanders his wealth.

⁴By justice a king gives a country
    stability,
  but one who is greedy for
    bribes tears it down.

⁵Whoever flatters his neighbor
  is spreading a net for his feet.

⁶An evil man is snared by his own
    sin,
  but a righteous one can sing
    and be glad.

⁷The righteous care about justice
    for the poor,
  but the wicked have no such
    concern.

⁸Mockers stir up a city,
  but wise men turn away anger.

⁹If a wise man goes to court with a
    fool,
  the fool rages and scoffs, and
    there is no peace.

¹⁰Bloodthirsty men hate a man of
    integrity
  and seek to kill the upright.

¹¹A fool gives full vent to his anger,
  but a wise man keeps himself
    under control.

¹²If a ruler listens to lies,
  all his officials become wicked.

¹³The poor man and the oppressor
    have this in common:
  The Lord gives sight to the eyes
    of both.

¹⁴If a king judges the poor with
    fairness,
  his throne will always be
    secure.

¹⁵The rod of correction imparts
    wisdom,
  but a child left to himself
    disgraces his mother.

¹⁶When the wicked thrive, so does
    sin,
  but the righteous will see their
    downfall.

¹⁷Discipline your son, and he will
    give you peace;
  he will bring delight to your
    soul.

¹⁸Where there is no revelation, the
    people cast off restraint;
  but blessed is he who keeps the
    law.

¹⁹A servant cannot be corrected by
    mere words;
  though he understands, he will
    not respond.

²⁰Do you see a man who speaks in
    haste?
  There is more hope for a fool
    than for him.

²¹If a man pampers his servant from
    youth,
  he will bring grief*ᵃ* in the end.

²²An angry man stirs up dissension,
  and a hot-tempered one
    commits many sins.

²³A man's pride brings him low,
  but a man of lowly spirit gains
    honor.

²⁴The accomplice of a thief is his
    own enemy;
  he is put under oath and dare
    not testify.

ᵃ21 The meaning of the Hebrew for this word is uncertain.

²⁵Fear of man will prove to be a
　　snare,
　　but whoever trusts in the LORD
　　　is kept safe.
²⁶Many seek an audience with a
　　ruler,
　　but it is from the LORD that man
　　　gets justice.
²⁷The righteous detest the dishonest;
　　the wicked detest the upright.

Sayings of Agur

30 The sayings of Agur son of Jakeh—an oracle[a]:

This man declared to Ithiel,
　to Ithiel and to Ucal:[b]

²"I am the most ignorant of men;
　I do not have a man's
　　understanding.
³I have not learned wisdom,
　nor have I knowledge of the
　　Holy One.
⁴Who has gone up to heaven and
　come down?
　Who has gathered up the wind
　　in the hollow of his hands?
　Who has wrapped up the waters
　　in his cloak?
　Who has established all the
　　ends of the earth?
　What is his name, and the name
　　of his son?
　Tell me if you know!

⁵"Every word of God is flawless;
　he is a shield to those who take
　　refuge in him.
⁶Do not add to his words,
　or he will rebuke you and
　　prove you a liar.

⁷"Two things I ask of you, O LORD;
　do not refuse me before I die:
⁸Keep falsehood and lies far from
　me;
　give me neither poverty nor
　　riches,
　but give me only my daily
　　bread.

⁹Otherwise, I may have too much
　and disown you
　and say, 'Who is the LORD?'
　Or I may become poor and steal,
　and so dishonor the name of
　　my God.

¹⁰"Do not slander a servant to his
　master,
　or he will curse you, and you
　　will pay for it.

¹¹"There are those who curse their
　fathers
　and do not bless their mothers;
¹²those who are pure in their own
　eyes
　and yet are not cleansed of their
　　filth;
¹³those whose eyes are ever so
　haughty,
　whose glances are so disdainful;
¹⁴those whose teeth are swords
　and whose jaws are set with
　　knives
　to devour the poor from the earth,
　the needy from among
　　mankind.

¹⁵"The leech has two daughters.
　'Give! Give!' they cry.

　"There are three things that are
　　never satisfied,
　four that never say, 'Enough!':
¹⁶the grave,[c] the barren womb,
　land, which is never satisfied
　　with water,
　and fire, which never says,
　　'Enough!'

¹⁷"The eye that mocks a father,
　that scorns obedience to a
　　mother,
　will be pecked out by the ravens
　　of the valley,
　will be eaten by the vultures.

¹⁸"There are three things that are
　　too amazing for me,
　four that I do not understand:
¹⁹the way of an eagle in the sky,
　the way of a snake on a rock,
　the way of a ship on the high
　　seas,

---

[a]1 Or *Jakeh of Massa*   [b]1 Masoretic Text; with a different word division of the Hebrew *declared,*
"*I am weary, O God; | I am weary, O God, and faint.*   [c]16 Hebrew *Sheol*

and the way of a man with a
   maiden.

²⁰"This is the way of an adulteress:
   She eats and wipes her mouth
   and says, 'I've done nothing
      wrong.'

²¹"Under three things the earth
      trembles,
   under four it cannot bear up:
²²a servant who becomes king,
   a fool who is full of food,
²³an unloved woman who is
      married,
   and a maidservant who
      displaces her mistress.

²⁴"Four things on earth are small,
   yet they are extremely wise:
²⁵Ants are creatures of little
      strength,
   yet they store up their food in
      the summer;
²⁶coneys^a are creatures of little
      power,
   yet they make their home in the
      crags;
²⁷locusts have no king,
   yet they advance together in
      ranks;
²⁸a lizard can be caught with the
      hand,
   yet it is found in kings' palaces.

²⁹"There are three things that are
      stately in their stride,
   four that move with stately
      bearing:
³⁰a lion, mighty among beasts,
   who retreats before nothing;
³¹a strutting rooster, a he-goat,
   and a king with his army
      around him.^b

³²"If you have played the fool and
      exalted yourself,
   or if you have planned evil,
   clap your hand over your
      mouth!
³³For as churning the milk produces
      butter,
   and as twisting the nose
      produces blood,

so stirring up anger produces
   strife."

Sayings of King Lemuel

31 The sayings of King Lemuel—
      an oracle^c his mother taught
him:

²"O my son, O son of my womb,
   O son of my vows,^d
³do not spend your strength on
      women,
   your vigor on those who ruin
      kings.

⁴"It is not for kings, O Lemuel—
   not for kings to drink wine,
   not for rulers to crave beer,
⁵lest they drink and forget what
      the law decrees,
   and deprive all the oppressed of
      their rights.
⁶Give beer to those who are
      perishing,
   wine to those who are in
      anguish;
⁷let them drink and forget their
      poverty
   and remember their misery no
      more.

⁸"Speak up for those who cannot
      speak for themselves,
   for the rights of all who are
      destitute.
⁹Speak up and judge fairly;
   defend the rights of the poor
      and needy."

Epilogue: The Wife of Noble Character

^{10e}A wife of noble character who
      can find?
   She is worth far more than
      rubies.
¹¹Her husband has full confidence
      in her
   and lacks nothing of value.
¹²She brings him good, not harm,
   all the days of her life.

¹³She selects wool and flax
and works with eager hands.
¹⁴She is like the merchant ships,
bringing her food from afar.
¹⁵She gets up while it is still dark;
she provides food for her family
and portions for her servant
girls.
¹⁶She considers a field and buys
it;
out of her earnings she plants
a vineyard.
¹⁷She sets about her work
vigorously;
her arms are strong for her
tasks.
¹⁸She sees that her trading is
profitable,
and her lamp does not go out at
night.
¹⁹In her hand she holds the distaff
and grasps the spindle with her
fingers.
²⁰She opens her arms to the poor
and extends her hands to the
needy.
²¹When it snows, she has no fear for
her household;
for all of them are clothed in
scarlet.
²²She makes coverings for her bed;
she is clothed in fine linen and
purple.

²³Her husband is respected at the
city gate,
where he takes his seat among
the elders of the land.
²⁴She makes linen garments and
sells them,
and supplies the merchants
with sashes.
²⁵She is clothed with strength and
dignity;
she can laugh at the days to
come.
²⁶She speaks with wisdom,
and faithful instruction is on her
tongue.
²⁷She watches over the affairs of her
household
and does not eat the bread of
idleness.
²⁸Her children arise and call her
blessed;
her husband also, and he
praises her:
²⁹"Many women do noble things,
but you surpass them all."
³⁰Charm is deceptive, and beauty is
fleeting;
but a woman who fears the
LORD is to be praised.
³¹Give her the reward she has
earned,
and let her works bring her
praise at the city gate.

*...*T*...*he Teacher, a king in
Jerusalem, faces the deep and perplexing issues of life head on—showing the futility of
so many of life's pursuits, looking at suffering and struggling to find meaning, and in
the end pointing to a solution. As you read
this book, think about how your power to live
a meaningful life comes not from you, but
from God, and recommit to finding your
life's purpose in living for God.

ECCLESIASTES

Everything Is Meaningless

1 The words of the Teacher,*a* son of David, king in Jerusalem:

2"Meaningless! Meaningless!"
   says the Teacher.
"Utterly meaningless!
   Everything is meaningless."

3What does man gain from all his
      labor
   at which he toils under the sun?
4Generations come and generations
      go,
   but the earth remains forever.
5The sun rises and the sun sets,
   and hurries back to where it
      rises.
6The wind blows to the south
   and turns to the north;
round and round it goes,
   ever returning on its course.
7All streams flow into the sea,
   yet the sea is never full.
To the place the streams come
      from,
   there they return again.
8All things are wearisome,
   more than one can say.
The eye never has enough of
      seeing,
   nor the ear its fill of hearing.
9What has been will be again,
   what has been done will be
      done again;
   there is nothing new under the
      sun.
10Is there anything of which one can
      say,
   "Look! This is something new"?
It was here already, long ago;
   it was here before our time.
11There is no remembrance of men
      of old,
   and even those who are yet to
      come

a1 Or *leader of the assembly*; also in verses 2 and 12

will not be remembered
by those who follow.

Wisdom Is Meaningless

¹²I, the Teacher, was king over Israel in Jerusalem. ¹³I devoted myself to study and to explore by wisdom all that is done under heaven. What a heavy burden God has laid on men! ¹⁴I have seen all the things that are done under the sun; all of them are meaningless, a chasing after the wind.

¹⁵What is twisted cannot be
straightened;
what is lacking cannot be
counted.

¹⁶I thought to myself, "Look, I have grown and increased in wisdom more than anyone who has ruled over Jerusalem before me; I have experienced much of wisdom and knowledge." ¹⁷Then I applied myself to the understanding of wisdom, and also of madness and folly, but I learned that this, too, is a chasing after the wind.

¹⁸For with much wisdom comes
much sorrow;
the more knowledge, the more
grief.

Pleasures Are Meaningless

2 I thought in my heart, "Come now, I will test you with pleasure to find out what is good." But that also proved to be meaningless. ²"Laughter," I said, "is foolish. And what does pleasure accomplish?" ³I tried cheering myself with wine, and embracing folly—my mind still guiding me with wisdom. I wanted to see what was worthwhile for men to do under heaven during the few days of their lives. ⁴I undertook great projects: I built houses for myself and planted vineyards. ⁵I made gardens and parks and planted all kinds of fruit trees in them. ⁶I made reservoirs to water groves of flourishing trees. ⁷I bought male and female slaves and had other slaves who were born in my house. I

also owned more herds and flocks than anyone in Jerusalem before me. ⁸I amassed silver and gold for myself, and the treasure of kings and provinces. I acquired men and women singers, and a harem[a] as well—the delights of the heart of man. ⁹I became greater by far than anyone in Jerusalem before me. In all this my wisdom stayed with me.

¹⁰I denied myself nothing my eyes
desired;
I refused my heart no pleasure.
My heart took delight in all my
work,
and this was the reward for all
my labor.
¹¹Yet when I surveyed all that my
hands had done
and what I had toiled to
achieve,
everything was meaningless, a
chasing after the wind;
nothing was gained under the
sun.

Wisdom and Folly Are Meaningless

¹²Then I turned my thoughts to
consider wisdom,
and also madness and folly.
What more can the king's
successor do
than what has already been
done?
¹³I saw that wisdom is better than
folly,
just as light is better than
darkness.
¹⁴The wise man has eyes in his
head,
while the fool walks in the
darkness;
but I came to realize
that the same fate overtakes
them both.

¹⁵Then I thought in my heart,

"The fate of the fool will overtake
me also.
What then do I gain by being
wise?"
I said in my heart,

"This too is meaningless."
¹⁶For the wise man, like the fool,
    will not be long
        remembered;
    in days to come both will be
        forgotten.
Like the fool, the wise man too
    must die!

Toil Is Meaningless

¹⁷So I hated life, because the work that is done under the sun was grievous to me. All of it is meaningless, a chasing after the wind. ¹⁸I hated all the things I had toiled for under the sun, because I must leave them to the one who comes after me. ¹⁹And who knows whether he will be a wise man or a fool? Yet he will have control over all the work into which I have poured my effort and skill under the sun. This too is meaningless. ²⁰So my heart began to despair over all my toilsome labor under the sun. ²¹For a man may do his work with wisdom, knowledge and skill, and then he must leave all he owns to someone who has not worked for it. This too is meaningless and a great misfortune. ²²What does a man get for all the toil and anxious striving with which he labors under the sun? ²³All his days his work is pain and grief; even at night his mind does not rest. This too is meaningless.

²⁴A man can do nothing better than to eat and drink and find satisfaction in his work. This too, I see, is from the hand of God, ²⁵for without him, who can eat or find enjoyment? ²⁶To the man who pleases him, God gives wisdom, knowledge and happiness, but to the sinner he gives the task of gathering and storing up wealth to hand it over to the one who pleases God. This too is meaningless, a chasing after the wind.

A Time for Everything

3 There is a time for everything,
    and a season for every activity
        under heaven:

² a time to be born and a time to
    die,
a time to plant and a time to
    uproot,
³ a time to kill and a time to heal,
a time to tear down and a time
    to build,
⁴ a time to weep and a time to
    laugh,
a time to mourn and a time to
    dance,
⁵ a time to scatter stones and a
    time to gather them,
a time to embrace and a time to
    refrain,
⁶ a time to search and a time to
    give up,
a time to keep and a time to
    throw away,
⁷ a time to tear and a time to
    mend,
a time to be silent and a time to
    speak,
⁸ a time to love and a time to
    hate,
a time for war and a time for
    peace.

⁹What does the worker gain from his toil? ¹⁰I have seen the burden God has laid on men. ¹¹He has made everything beautiful in its time. He has also set eternity in the hearts of men; yet they cannot fathom what God has done from beginning to end. ¹²I know that there is nothing better for men than to be happy and do good while they live. ¹³That everyone may eat and drink, and find satisfaction in all his toil—this is the gift of God. ¹⁴I know that everything God does will endure forever; nothing can be added to it and nothing taken from it. God does it so that men will revere him.

¹⁵Whatever is has already been,
    and what will be has been
        before;
    and God will call the past to
        account.ᵃ

¹⁶And I saw something else under the sun:

ᵃ15 Or *God calls back the past*

VERSE:
Ecclesiastes 3:11

AUTHOR:
Jacob D. Eppinga

PASSAGE:
Ecclesiastes 3:1–15

The Good Old Days

"The good old days" can also be understood more literally to mean the good days now that we are old. Age brings perspective and ripeness . . .

Many centuries ago the Lord said that "as long as the earth endures, seedtime and harvest, cold and heat, summer and winter, day and night will never cease" (Genesis 8:22). Those of us who have been around for awhile can testify to the truth of these words. We have seen many seasons come and go in their order and in yearly cycles. All have their own kind of beauty and appeal.

There is spectacular spring. How exciting to see nature come to life. Spring-time green is like no other green. But summer is lovely too . . . Summer means long, lazy days, open windows, sunshine, soft rain and lingering light at eventide. But fall, when nature's brush paints splashes of color on its forests, is gorgeous as well. Exciting spring, wonderful summer, spectacular fall. And then there is winter . . . What is so lovely as a winter-scape, sun glistening on freshly fallen snow? Truly, when it comes to the seasons, God has made each one beautiful in its time. As are the seasons of the years, so are the seasons of life. Here, too, are spring, summer, fall and winter. The winter of life has rewards and beauties particularly its own . . .

Because God made everything beautiful in its time, we must try to find the sweetness in our lives just as we try to find the sweetness in our food. Instead of waiting only for the joy of heaven, we should give thanks for the joy in our Lord, which we have even now. We should not waste the sunshine. As for the shadows of our winter's day, they will fade when brought into the presence of the One who is our light.

ADDITIONAL SCRIPTURE READINGS
Psalm 27; John 1:1–18

Go to page 827 for your next devotional reading.

In the place of judgment—
wickedness was there,
in the place of justice—
wickedness was there.

[17]I thought in my heart,

"God will bring to judgment
both the righteous and the
wicked,
for there will be a time for every
activity,
a time for every deed."

[18]I also thought, "As for men, God
tests them so that they may see that
they are like the animals. [19]Man's fate
is like that of the animals; the same
fate awaits them both: As one dies,
so dies the other. All have the same
breath[a]; man has no advantage over
the animal. Everything is meaningless. [20]All go to the same place; all
come from dust, and to dust all return. [21]Who knows if the spirit of man
rises upward and if the spirit of the
animal[b] goes down into the earth?"
[22]So I saw that there is nothing better for a man than to enjoy his work,
because that is his lot. For who can
bring him to see what will happen after him?

Oppression, Toil, Friendlessness

4 Again I looked and saw all the
oppression that was taking place
under the sun:

I saw the tears of the oppressed—
and they have no comforter;
power was on the side of their
oppressors—
and they have no comforter.
[2]And I declared that the dead,
who had already died,
are happier than the living,
who are still alive.
[3]But better than both
is he who has not yet been,
who has not seen the evil
that is done under the sun.

[4]And I saw that all labor and all
achievement spring from man's envy

of his neighbor. This too is meaningless, a chasing after the wind.

[5]The fool folds his hands
and ruins himself.
[6]Better one handful with
tranquillity
than two handfuls with toil
and chasing after the wind.

[7]Again I saw something meaningless under the sun:

[8]There was a man all alone;
he had neither son nor brother.
There was no end to his toil,
yet his eyes were not content
with his wealth.
"For whom am I toiling," he
asked,
"and why am I depriving
myself of enjoyment?"
This too is meaningless—
a miserable business!

[9]Two are better than one,
because they have a good
return for their work:
[10]If one falls down,
his friend can help him up.
But pity the man who falls
and has no one to help him up!
[11]Also, if two lie down together,
they will keep warm.
But how can one keep warm
alone?
[12]Though one may be overpowered,
two can defend themselves.
A cord of three strands is not
quickly broken.

Advancement Is Meaningless

[13]Better a poor but wise youth than
an old but foolish king who no longer
knows how to take warning. [14]The
youth may have come from prison to
the kingship, or he may have been
born in poverty within his kingdom.
[15]I saw that all who lived and walked
under the sun followed the youth, the
king's successor. [16]There was no end
to all the people who were before
them. But those who came later were
not pleased with the successor. This

---

[a]19 Or spirit
which   [b]21 Or Who knows the spirit of man, which rises upward, or the spirit of the animal,

too is meaningless, a chasing after the wind.

Stand in Awe of God

5 Guard your steps when you go to the house of God. Go near to listen rather than to offer the sacrifice of fools, who do not know that they do wrong.

2Do not be quick with your mouth,
   do not be hasty in your heart
     to utter anything before God.
God is in heaven
   and you are on earth,
   so let your words be few.
3As a dream comes when there are
     many cares,
   so the speech of a fool when
     there are many words.

4When you make a vow to God, do not delay in fulfilling it. He has no pleasure in fools; fulfill your vow. 5It is better not to vow than to make a vow and not fulfill it. 6Do not let your mouth lead you into sin. And do not protest to the ⌊temple⌋ messenger, "My vow was a mistake." Why should God be angry at what you say and destroy the work of your hands? 7Much dreaming and many words are meaningless. Therefore stand in awe of God.

Riches Are Meaningless

8If you see the poor oppressed in a district, and justice and rights denied, do not be surprised at such things; for one official is eyed by a higher one, and over them both are others higher still. 9The increase from the land is taken by all; the king himself profits from the fields.

10Whoever loves money never has
     money enough;
   whoever loves wealth is never
     satisfied with his income.
This too is meaningless.

11As goods increase,
   so do those who consume them.
And what benefit are they to the
     owner
   except to feast his eyes on
     them?

12The sleep of a laborer is sweet,
   whether he eats little or much,
but the abundance of a rich man
   permits him no sleep.

13I have seen a grievous evil under the sun:

wealth hoarded to the harm of its
     owner,
14   or wealth lost through some
     misfortune,
so that when he has a son
   there is nothing left for him.
15Naked a man comes from his
     mother's womb,
   and as he comes, so he departs.
He takes nothing from his labor
   that he can carry in his hand.

16This too is a grievous evil:

As a man comes, so he departs,
   and what does he gain,
   since he toils for the wind?
17All his days he eats in darkness,
   with great frustration, affliction
     and anger.

18Then I realized that it is good and proper for a man to eat and drink, and to find satisfaction in his toilsome labor under the sun during the few days of life God has given him—for this is his lot. 19Moreover, when God gives any man wealth and possessions, and enables him to enjoy them, to accept his lot and be happy in his work—this is a gift of God. 20He seldom reflects on the days of his life, because God keeps him occupied with gladness of heart.

6 I have seen another evil under the sun, and it weighs heavily on men: 2God gives a man wealth, possessions and honor, so that he lacks nothing his heart desires, but God does not enable him to enjoy them, and a stranger enjoys them instead. This is meaningless, a grievous evil.

3A man may have a hundred children and live many years; yet no matter how long he lives, if he cannot enjoy his prosperity and does not receive proper burial, I say that a stillborn child is better off than he. 4It comes without meaning, it departs in

VERSE: AUTHOR: PASSAGE:
Ecclesiastes 5:2   Richard J. Foster   Ecclesiastes 5:1–7

The Sacrifice of Fools

In Ecclesiastes we read, "Go near to listen rather than to offer the sacrifice of fools" (Ecclesiastes 5:1). The sacrifice of fools is humanly initiated religious talk. The preacher continued, "Do not be quick with your mouth, do not be hasty in your heart to offer anything before God. God is in heaven and you are on earth, so let your words be few" (Ecclesiastes 5:2).

When Jesus took Peter, James and John up to the mountain and was transfigured before them, Moses and Elijah appeared and carried on a conversation with Jesus. The Greek text goes on to say, "And *answering*, Peter said to them . . . if you wish, I will put up three shelters" (Matthew 17:4). That is so telling. No one was even speaking to Peter. He was offering the sacrifice of fools . . .

One reason we can hardly bear to remain silent is that it makes us feel so helpless. We are so accustomed to relying upon words to manage and control others. If we are silent who will take control? God will take control; but we will never let him take control until we trust him. Silence is intimately related to trust . . .

The tongue is a thermometer; it tells us our spiritual temperature. It is also a thermostat; it controls our spiritual temperature. Control of the tongue can mean everything. Have we been set free so that we can hold our tongue?

ADDITIONAL SCRIPTURE READINGS
Proverbs 10:18–20; James 3:1–12
Go to page 828 for your next devotional reading.

darkness, and in darkness its name is shrouded. ⁵Though it never saw the sun or knew anything, it has more rest than does that man— ⁶even if he lives a thousand years twice over but fails to enjoy his prosperity. Do not all go to the same place?

⁷All man's efforts are for his
        mouth,
    yet his appetite is never
        satisfied.
⁸What advantage has a wise man
        over a fool?
  What does a poor man gain
    by knowing how to conduct
        himself before others?
⁹Better what the eye sees

than the roving of the appetite.
This too is meaningless,
    a chasing after the wind.

¹⁰Whatever exists has already been
        named,
    and what man is has been
        known;
    no man can contend
        with one who is stronger than
            he.
¹¹The more the words,
    the less the meaning,
    and how does that profit
        anyone?

¹²For who knows what is good for a man in life, during the few and meaningless days he passes through like a

THURSDAY

VERSE: AUTHOR: PASSAGE:
Ecclesiastes 6:2   Walter Wangerin, Jr.   Ecclesiastes 6:1–6

The Question

The question, my children, is not *whether* you will suffer but *how* you will suffer. For either you will take the world's terms as your own and give as good as you get—an eye for an eye, spit for spite, pain in equal measure—

Either, I say, you will rage like the world to save yourself, feeling justified in any counterattack and changing nothing whatever beneath the sun—

Or you will find in unearned suffering an opportunity of the spirit. This is a hard saying, I know. But it is not impossible. The presence of Christ in you can translate suffering into a ladder—a Jacob's ladder with four rungs up toward redemption and four rungs down that holiness might enter the world again.

ADDITIONAL SCRIPTURE READINGS
Genesis 28:10–22; 2 Corinthians 1:3–7

Go to page 830 for your next devotional reading.

shadow? Who can tell him what will happen under the sun after he is gone?

Wisdom

7 A good name is better than fine perfume,
    and the day of death better than the day of birth.
²It is better to go to a house of mourning
    than to go to a house of feasting,
for death is the destiny of every man;
    the living should take this to heart.
³Sorrow is better than laughter,
    because a sad face is good for the heart.
⁴The heart of the wise is in the house of mourning,
    but the heart of fools is in the house of pleasure.
⁵It is better to heed a wise man's rebuke
    than to listen to the song of fools.
⁶Like the crackling of thorns under the pot,
    so is the laughter of fools.
    This too is meaningless.

⁷Extortion turns a wise man into a fool,
    and a bribe corrupts the heart.

⁸The end of a matter is better than its beginning,
    and patience is better than pride.
⁹Do not be quickly provoked in your spirit,
    for anger resides in the lap of fools.

¹⁰Do not say, "Why were the old days better than these?"
    For it is not wise to ask such questions.

¹¹Wisdom, like an inheritance, is a good thing
    and benefits those who see the sun.

¹²Wisdom is a shelter
    as money is a shelter,
but the advantage of knowledge is this:
    that wisdom preserves the life of its possessor.

¹³Consider what God has done:

Who can straighten
    what he has made crooked?
¹⁴When times are good, be happy;
    but when times are bad, consider:
God has made the one
    as well as the other.
Therefore, a man cannot discover anything about his future.

¹⁵In this meaningless life of mine I have seen both of these:

a righteous man perishing in his righteousness,
    and a wicked man living long in his wickedness.
¹⁶Do not be overrighteous,
    neither be overwise—
    why destroy yourself?
¹⁷Do not be overwicked,
    and do not be a fool—
    why die before your time?
¹⁸It is good to grasp the one
    and not let go of the other.
The man who fears God will avoid all ⌐extremes⌐.ᵃ

¹⁹Wisdom makes one wise man more powerful
    than ten rulers in a city.

²⁰There is not a righteous man on earth
    who does what is right and never sins.

²¹Do not pay attention to every word people say,
    or you may hear your servant cursing you—
²²for you know in your heart
    that many times you yourself have cursed others.

²³All this I tested by wisdom and I said,

ᵃ18 Or *will follow them both*

VERSE:
Ecclesiastes 7:11

AUTHOR:
Sherwood Eliot Wirt

PASSAGE:
Ecclesiastes 7:1–12

If You Want Wisdom

Wisdom! What is it anyway? . . . Now that I am older, I do have a definition: *Wisdom is knowing how to live* . . .

To those who would like a reputation for wisdom in old age, I have set down some suggestions.

If you want wisdom . . .

1. go for it. (What can you lose?)

2. repent. Wisdom begins with the fear of the Lord. Turn about face. Despise sin. Stop fouling your nest. Make restitution.

3. believe on the Lord Jesus Christ. There's no other way to be saved.

4. be filled with the Spirit. Remember; the Holy Spirit is love. He is also wisdom.

5. love everybody. Help everyone you can. Put yourself last . . .

6. live with God. Talk to him every day about everything and everybody.

7. let God talk to you through his Word. Read the Bible regularly.

8. talk up Jesus. We never get too old to do that.

9. never dispense advice gratuitously. Wait until it is asked for . . .

10. relax . . . Smile. Enjoy life. That's what God put you here to do. I was 60 years old before I discovered in the Bible that God created us for his enjoyment and ours; that his wisdom is composed of love, joy and peace; and that he delights to give us pleasure.

And finally, if you want wisdom . . . look for a big day coming.

ADDITIONAL SCRIPTURE READINGS
Job 28:12–28; Proverbs 9:1–12

Go to page 833 for your next devotional reading.

"I am determined to be wise"—
  but this was beyond me.
24Whatever wisdom may be,
  it is far off and most
    profound—
  who can discover it?
25So I turned my mind to
    understand,
  to investigate and to search out
    wisdom and the scheme of
    things
  and to understand the stupidity of
    wickedness
  and the madness of folly.

26I find more bitter than death
  the woman who is a snare,
  whose heart is a trap
  and whose hands are chains.
The man who pleases God will
    escape her,
  but the sinner she will ensnare.

27"Look," says the Teacher,[a] "this
is what I have discovered:

"Adding one thing to another to
    discover the scheme of
    things—
28   while I was still searching
    but not finding—
I found one ⌊upright⌋ man among
    a thousand,
  but not one ⌊upright⌋ woman
    among them all.
29This only have I found:
  God made mankind upright,
  but men have gone in search of
    many schemes."

8 Who is like the wise man?
  Who knows the explanation of
    things?
Wisdom brightens a man's face
  and changes its hard
    appearance.

Obey the King

2Obey the king's command, I say,
because you took an oath before God.
3Do not be in a hurry to leave the
king's presence. Do not stand up for a
bad cause, for he will do whatever he
pleases. 4Since a king's word is supreme, who can say to him, "What
are you doing?"

5Whoever obeys his command will
    come to no harm,
  and the wise heart will know
    the proper time and
    procedure.
6For there is a proper time and
    procedure for every matter,
  though a man's misery weighs
    heavily upon him.

7Since no man knows the future,
  who can tell him what is to
    come?
8No man has power over the wind
    to contain it[b];
  so no one has power over the
    day of his death.
As no one is discharged in time of
    war,
  so wickedness will not release
    those who practice it.

9All this I saw, as I applied my
mind to everything done under the
sun. There is a time when a man lords
it over others to his own[c] hurt.
10Then too, I saw the wicked buried—
those who used to come and go from
the holy place and receive praise[d] in
the city where they did this. This too
is meaningless.

11When the sentence for a crime is
not quickly carried out, the hearts of
the people are filled with schemes to
do wrong. 12Although a wicked man
commits a hundred crimes and still
lives a long time, I know that it will
go better with God-fearing men, who
are reverent before God. 13Yet because
the wicked do not fear God, it will not
go well with them, and their days will
not lengthen like a shadow.

14There is something else meaningless that occurs on earth: righteous
men who get what the wicked deserve, and wicked men who get what
the righteous deserve. This too, I say,
is meaningless. 15So I commend the
enjoyment of life, because nothing is
better for a man under the sun than to

---

a27 Or leader of the assembly   b8 Or over his spirit to retain it   c9 Or to their   d10 Some
Hebrew manuscripts and Septuagint (Aquila); most Hebrew manuscripts and are forgotten

eat and drink and be glad. Then joy will accompany him in his work all the days of the life God has given him under the sun.

16When I applied my mind to know wisdom and to observe man's labor on earth—his eyes not seeing sleep day or night— 17then I saw all that God has done. No one can comprehend what goes on under the sun. Despite all his efforts to search it out, man cannot discover its meaning. Even if a wise man claims he knows, he cannot really comprehend it.

A Common Destiny for All

9 So I reflected on all this and concluded that the righteous and the wise and what they do are in God's hands, but no man knows whether love or hate awaits him. 2All share a common destiny—the righteous and the wicked, the good and the bad,[a] the clean and the unclean, those who offer sacrifices and those who do not.

As it is with the good man,
    so with the sinner;
as it is with those who take oaths,
    so with those who are afraid to
    take them.

3This is the evil in everything that happens under the sun: The same destiny overtakes all. The hearts of men, moreover, are full of evil and there is madness in their hearts while they live, and afterward they join the dead. 4Anyone who is among the living has hope[b]—even a live dog is better off than a dead lion!

5For the living know that they will
    die,
    but the dead know nothing;
they have no further reward,
    and even the memory of them
    is forgotten.
6Their love, their hate
    and their jealousy have long
    since vanished;
never again will they have a part

in anything that happens under the sun.

7Go, eat your food with gladness, and drink your wine with a joyful heart, for it is now that God favors what you do. 8Always be clothed in white, and always anoint your head with oil. 9Enjoy life with your wife, whom you love, all the days of this meaningless life that God has given you under the sun— all your meaningless days. For this is your lot in life and in your toilsome labor under the sun. 10Whatever your hand finds to do, do it with all your might, for in the grave,[c] where you are going, there is neither working nor planning nor knowledge nor wisdom.

11I have seen something else under the sun:

The race is not to the swift
    or the battle to the strong,
nor does food come to the wise
    or wealth to the brilliant
    or favor to the learned;
but time and chance happen to
    them all.

12Moreover, no man knows when his hour will come:

As fish are caught in a cruel net,
    or birds are taken in a snare,
so men are trapped by evil times
    that fall unexpectedly upon
    them.

Wisdom Better Than Folly

13I also saw under the sun this example of wisdom that greatly impressed me: 14There was once a small city with only a few people in it. And a powerful king came against it, surrounded it and built huge siegeworks against it. 15Now there lived in that city a man poor but wise, and he saved the city by his wisdom. But nobody remembered that poor man. 16So I said, "Wisdom is better than strength." But the poor man's wis-

---

a2 Septuagint (Aquila), Vulgate and Syriac; Hebrew does not have and the bad.   b4 Or What then is to be chosen? With all who live, there is hope   c10 Hebrew Sheol

PASSAGE: Psalm 92; Philippians 1:3–11
AUTHOR: Alfred Tennyson

And Not to Yield

Old age hath yet his honor and his toil;
Death closes all: but something ere the end,
Some work of noble note may yet be done . . .
Though much is taken, much abides; and though
We are not now that strength which in old days
Moved earth and heaven, that which we are, we are.
One equal temper of heroic hearts,
Made weak by time and fate, but strong in will
To strive, to seek, to find, and not to yield.

Go to page 835 for your next devotional reading.

dom is despised, and his words are no longer heeded.

¹⁷The quiet words of the wise are
more to be heeded
than the shouts of a ruler of
fools.
¹⁸Wisdom is better than weapons of
war,
but one sinner destroys much
good.

10 As dead flies give perfume a
bad smell,
so a little folly outweighs
wisdom and honor.
²The heart of the wise inclines to
the right,
but the heart of the fool to the
left.
³Even as he walks along the road,
the fool lacks sense
and shows everyone how stupid
he is.
⁴If a ruler's anger rises against you,
do not leave your post;
calmness can lay great errors to
rest.

⁵There is an evil I have seen under
the sun,
the sort of error that arises from
a ruler:
⁶Fools are put in many high
positions,
while the rich occupy the low
ones.
⁷I have seen slaves on horseback,
while princes go on foot like
slaves.

⁸Whoever digs a pit may fall into
it;
whoever breaks through a wall
may be bitten by a snake.
⁹Whoever quarries stones may be
injured by them;
whoever splits logs may be
endangered by them.

¹⁰If the ax is dull
and its edge unsharpened,
more strength is needed
but skill will bring success.

¹¹If a snake bites before it is
charmed,
there is no profit for the
charmer.

¹²Words from a wise man's mouth
are gracious,
but a fool is consumed by his
own lips.
¹³At the beginning his words are
folly;
at the end they are wicked
madness—
¹⁴ and the fool multiplies words.

No one knows what is coming—
who can tell him what will
happen after him?

¹⁵A fool's work wearies him;
he does not know the way to
town.

¹⁶Woe to you, O land whose king
was a servant[a]
and whose princes feast in the
morning.
¹⁷Blessed are you, O land whose
king is of noble birth
and whose princes eat at a
proper time—
for strength and not for
drunkenness.

¹⁸If a man is lazy, the rafters sag;
if his hands are idle, the house
leaks.

¹⁹A feast is made for laughter,
and wine makes life merry,
but money is the answer for
everything.

²⁰Do not revile the king even in
your thoughts,
or curse the rich in your
bedroom,
because a bird of the air may
carry your words,
and a bird on the wing may
report what you say.

Bread Upon the Waters

11 Cast your bread upon the
waters,

---

[a]16 Or *king is a child*

VERSE:	AUTHOR:	PASSAGE:
Ecclesiastes 11:6	Charles R. Swindoll	Ecclesiastes 11:1–6

Trusting God, Regardless

"Sow your seed in the morning, and at evening let not your hands be idle." That means that in the evening of your life, don't look for a place to hide out. As you sowed in the morning, press on in the evening. Don't look for a "Do Not Disturb" sign to hang on the door knob of your life. Resist saying, "Leave me alone; I'm retired; I've paid my dues."

The only way we can do this — the only way we can come to terms with reality — is by trusting God, *regardless*. No ifs, ands, buts or howevers. If I am a farmer and God allows a flood to come and wash away my crops or God chooses to give me the beautiful seasonal rains and a bumper crop, I trust him and I give him praise. If I am in industry or some profession and someone throws me a curve and God allows my whole world to be reversed, I trust him and I give him praise. I take life as it occurs. I don't waste time in the pit of doubt. Nor do I worry over crop failures and strikeouts.

We can't wait for conditions to be perfect. Nor can we wait for things to be free of all risks — absolutely free, absolutely safe. Instead of protecting ourselves, we have to release ourselves. Instead of hoarding, we are to give and invest. Instead of drifting, we are to pursue life. Instead of doubting, we are to courageously trust.

ADDITIONAL SCRIPTURE READINGS
Job 13:13–19; Habakkuk 3:16–19

Go to page 837 for your next devotional reading.

for after many days you will
find it again.
[2]Give portions to seven, yes to
eight,
for you do not know what
disaster may come upon
the land.

[3]If clouds are full of water,
they pour rain upon the earth.
Whether a tree falls to the south
or to the north,
in the place where it falls, there
will it lie.
[4]Whoever watches the wind will
not plant;
whoever looks at the clouds will
not reap.

[5]As you do not know the path of
the wind,
or how the body is formed[a] in
a mother's womb,
so you cannot understand the
work of God,
the Maker of all things.

[6]Sow your seed in the morning,
and at evening let not your
hands be idle,
for you do not know which will
succeed,
whether this or that,
or whether both will do equally
well.

Remember Your Creator While Young

[7]Light is sweet,
and it pleases the eyes to see
the sun.
[8]However many years a man may
live,
let him enjoy them all.
But let him remember the days of
darkness,
for they will be many.
Everything to come is
meaningless.

[9]Be happy, young man, while you
are young,
and let your heart give you joy
in the days of your youth.
Follow the ways of your heart
and whatever your eyes see,
but know that for all these things
God will bring you to
judgment.
[10]So then, banish anxiety from your
heart
and cast off the troubles of your
body,
for youth and vigor are
meaningless.

12 Remember your Creator
in the days of your youth,
before the days of trouble come
and the years approach when
you will say,
"I find no pleasure in them"—
[2]before the sun and the light
and the moon and the stars
grow dark,
and the clouds return after the
rain;
[3]when the keepers of the house
tremble,
and the strong men stoop,
when the grinders cease because
they are few,
and those looking through the
windows grow dim;
[4]when the doors to the street are
closed
and the sound of grinding
fades;
when men rise up at the sound of
birds,
but all their songs grow faint;
[5]when men are afraid of heights
and of dangers in the streets;
when the almond tree blossoms
and the grasshopper drags
himself along
and desire no longer is stirred.
Then man goes to his eternal
home
and mourners go about the
streets.

[6]Remember him—before the silver
cord is severed,
or the golden bowl is broken;

[a]5 Or *know how life* (or *the spirit*) / *enters the body being formed*

before the pitcher is shattered at
the spring,
or the wheel broken at the well,
[7]and the dust returns to the ground
it came from,
and the spirit returns to God
who gave it.

[8]"Meaningless! Meaningless!" says
the Teacher.[a]
"Everything is meaningless!"

The Conclusion of the Matter

[9]Not only was the Teacher wise,
but also he imparted knowledge to

[a]8 Or *the leader of the assembly*; also in verses 9 and 10

TUESDAY

VERSE:
Ecclesiastes 12:5

AUTHOR:
Jacob D. Eppinga

PASSAGE:
Ecclesiastes 12:1–8

Warts and All

The Bible is not blind to the ravages of time on our
physical bodies. Indeed, it speaks in wonderment of a
Moses whose eyes were not weak nor his strength gone
despite his age (Deuteronomy 34:7). At the same time
the Bible is an honest book. It depicts us, warts and all,
not only spiritually but physically too. Ecclesiastes 12
looks life full in the face and states black on white what
happens to our bodies when we become old.

But there is another side. The Bible is never simplistic.
If it speaks to us about predestination, it turns the coin
over and speaks of human responsibility. It shows us
that we are saved by faith and not by works so that no
one can boast (Ephesians 2:8–9). But it turns this coin
over as well to show us that faith without works is dead
(James 2:17).

The Bible deals similarly with the subject of age. If it
says on one page that old age is the "pits" (one man's explanation of Ecclesiastes 12), it tells us on another how
beautiful old age can be (Proverbs 16:31). These are not
contradictions but truths—all of which must be understood in the light of each other.

ADDITIONAL SCRIPTURE READINGS
Deuteronomy 34:1–8; Psalm 92

Go to page 841 for your next devotional reading.

the people. He pondered and searched out and set in order many proverbs. [10]The Teacher searched to find just the right words, and what he wrote was upright and true.

[11]The words of the wise are like goads, their collected sayings like firmly embedded nails—given by one Shepherd. [12]Be warned, my son, of anything in addition to them.

Of making many books there is no end, and much study wearies the body.

[13]Now all has been heard;
  here is the conclusion of the
    matter:
Fear God and keep his
    commandments,
  for this is the whole ⌐duty⌐
    of man.
[14]For God will bring every deed
    into judgment,
  including every hidden
    thing,
  whether it is good or
    evil.

...**M**...*any people wonder*
why a beautifully sensuous love poem is in-
cluded in the Bible. Some suggest it is a pic-
ture of God's unconditional love, while others
find in it a joyous celebration of the beauty,
the power and the exclusiveness of sexual
love. As you read this book, rejoice in God's
gift of love and sexuality and reflect on the
intimacies of God's love for you.

SONG OF SONGS

1 Solomon's Song of Songs.

Beloved[a]

²Let him kiss me with the kisses of
his mouth—
for your love is more delightful
than wine.
³Pleasing is the fragrance of your
perfumes;
your name is like perfume
poured out.
No wonder the maidens love
you!
⁴Take me away with you—let us
hurry!
Let the king bring me into his
chambers.

Friends

We rejoice and delight in you[b];
we will praise your love more
than wine.

Beloved

How right they are to adore you!

⁵Dark am I, yet lovely,
O daughters of Jerusalem,
dark like the tents of Kedar,
like the tent curtains of
Solomon.[c]
⁶Do not stare at me because I am
dark,
because I am darkened by the
sun.
My mother's sons were angry
with me
and made me take care of the
vineyards;
my own vineyard I have
neglected.
⁷Tell me, you whom I love, where
you graze your flock
and where you rest your sheep
at midday.

---

[a]Primarily on the basis of the gender of the Hebrew pronouns used, male and female speakers
are indicated in the margins by the captions *Lover* and *Beloved* respectively. The words of others
are marked *Friends*. In some instances the divisions and their captions are debatable.   [b]4 The
Hebrew is masculine singular.   [c]5 Or *Salma*

Why should I be like a veiled
    woman
  beside the flocks of your
    friends?

Friends
8If you do not know, most
    beautiful of women,
  follow the tracks of the sheep
and graze your young goats
  by the tents of the shepherds.

Lover
9I liken you, my darling, to a mare
    harnessed to one of the chariots
    of Pharaoh.
10Your cheeks are beautiful with
    earrings,
  your neck with strings of jewels.
11We will make you earrings of
    gold,
  studded with silver.

Beloved
12While the king was at his table,
  my perfume spread its
    fragrance.
13My lover is to me a sachet of
    myrrh
  resting between my breasts.
14My lover is to me a cluster of
    henna blossoms
  from the vineyards of En Gedi.

Lover
15How beautiful you are, my
    darling!
  Oh, how beautiful!
  Your eyes are doves.

Beloved
16How handsome you are, my lover!
  Oh, how charming!
  And our bed is verdant.

Lover
17The beams of our house are
    cedars;
  our rafters are firs.

*Beloved*a
2 I am a roseb of Sharon,
    a lily of the valleys.

Lover
2Like a lily among thorns
  is my darling among the
    maidens.

Beloved
3Like an apple tree among the trees
    of the forest
  is my lover among the young
    men.
I delight to sit in his shade,
  and his fruit is sweet to my
    taste.
4He has taken me to the banquet
    hall,
  and his banner over me is love.
5Strengthen me with raisins,
  refresh me with apples,
  for I am faint with love.
6His left arm is under my head,
  and his right arm embraces me.
7Daughters of Jerusalem, I charge
    you
  by the gazelles and by the does
    of the field:
Do not arouse or awaken love
  until it so desires.

8Listen! My lover!
  Look! Here he comes,
leaping across the mountains,
  bounding over the hills.
9My lover is like a gazelle or a
    young stag.
  Look! There he stands behind
    our wall,
gazing through the windows,
  peering through the lattice.
10My lover spoke and said to me,
  "Arise, my darling,
  my beautiful one, and come
    with me.
11See! The winter is past;
  the rains are over and gone.
12Flowers appear on the earth;
  the season of singing has come,
the cooing of doves
  is heard in our land.
13The fig tree forms its early fruit;
  the blossoming vines spread
    their fragrance.
Arise, come, my darling;

a1 Or *Lover*   b1 Possibly a member of the crocus family

my beautiful one, come with
    me."

Lover

¹⁴My dove in the clefts of the rock,
    in the hiding places on the
        mountainside,
    show me your face,
        let me hear your voice;
for your voice is sweet,
        and your face is lovely.

¹⁵Catch for us the foxes,
        the little foxes
    that ruin the vineyards,
        our vineyards that are in bloom.

Beloved

¹⁶My lover is mine and I am his;
        he browses among the lilies.
¹⁷Until the day breaks
        and the shadows flee,
    turn, my lover,

VERSE:	AUTHOR:	PASSAGE:
Song of Songs 2:12	Robert H. Schuller	Song of Songs 2:8–13

Seasons of the Soul

There are seasons in life and there are seasons of the soul—the springtime when faith is born; the summer when faith matures; the reaping and harvesting in the fall; and the dark time, the winter, when you walk over frozen ground and you're sure nothing will ever grow again. I don't know of a single Christian who, in his pilgrimage, could testify that his faith enjoyed springtime always. Everyone has the wintertime of the soul.

Get acquainted with your emotional cycles. Make no decisions in a low time. Make no commitments in a low season. When you're in winter, be calm, be quiet and wait. The mood of strength will return!

The low times that come are generally very natural, very providential. They are planned for you to calm down, slow down, refill, rethink, regroup, realign, get a new perspective, take another check of your values, recheck your goals, and before you know it, winter is passed. Spring returns with a new aspect of your faith reborn.

ADDITIONAL SCRIPTURE READINGS
Psalm 1; Isaiah 30:15–18
Go to page 846 for your next devotional reading.

and be like a gazelle
or like a young stag
  on the rugged hills.[a]

3 All night long on my bed
  I looked for the one my heart
    loves;
  I looked for him but did not
    find him.
[2]I will get up now and go about
    the city,
  through its streets and squares;
I will search for the one my heart
    loves.
  So I looked for him but did not
    find him.
[3]The watchmen found me
  as they made their rounds in
    the city.
  "Have you seen the one my
    heart loves?"
[4]Scarcely had I passed them
  when I found the one my heart
    loves.
I held him and would not let him
    go
  till I had brought him to my
    mother's house,
  to the room of the one who
    conceived me.
[5]Daughters of Jerusalem, I charge
    you
  by the gazelles and by the does
    of the field:
Do not arouse or awaken love
  until it so desires.

[6]Who is this coming up from the
    desert
  like a column of smoke,
perfumed with myrrh and incense
  made from all the spices of the
    merchant?
[7]Look! It is Solomon's carriage,
  escorted by sixty warriors,
  the noblest of Israel,
[8]all of them wearing the sword,
  all experienced in battle,
each with his sword at his side,
  prepared for the terrors of the
    night.
[9]King Solomon made for himself
  the carriage;

he made it of wood from
  Lebanon.
[10]Its posts he made of silver,
  its base of gold.
Its seat was upholstered with
    purple,
  its interior lovingly inlaid
    by[b] the daughters of Jerusalem.
[11]Come out, you daughters of Zion,
  and look at King Solomon
    wearing the crown,
  the crown with which his
    mother crowned him
on the day of his wedding,
  the day his heart rejoiced.

Lover

4 How beautiful you are, my
    darling!
  Oh, how beautiful!
  Your eyes behind your veil are
    doves.
Your hair is like a flock of goats
  descending from Mount Gilead.
[2]Your teeth are like a flock of
    sheep just shorn,
  coming up from the washing.
Each has its twin;
  not one of them is alone.
[3]Your lips are like a scarlet ribbon;
  your mouth is lovely.
Your temples behind your veil
  are like the halves of a
    pomegranate.
[4]Your neck is like the tower of
    David,
  built with elegance[c];
on it hang a thousand shields,
  all of them shields of warriors.
[5]Your two breasts are like two
    fawns,
  like twin fawns of a gazelle
  that browse among the lilies.
[6]Until the day breaks
  and the shadows flee,
I will go to the mountain of myrrh
  and to the hill of incense.
[7]All beautiful you are, my darling;
  there is no flaw in you.

[8]Come with me from Lebanon, my
    bride,

---

[a]17 Or *the hills of Bether*   [b]10 Or *its inlaid interior a gift of love / from*   [c]4 The meaning of the
Hebrew for this word is uncertain.

come with me from Lebanon.
Descend from the crest of Amana,
  from the top of Senir, the
    summit of Hermon,
from the lions' dens
  and the mountain haunts of the
    leopards.
⁹You have stolen my heart, my
  sister, my bride;
  you have stolen my heart
with one glance of your eyes,
  with one jewel of your necklace.
¹⁰How delightful is your love, my
  sister, my bride!
  How much more pleasing is
    your love than wine,
and the fragrance of your
    perfume than any spice!
¹¹Your lips drop sweetness as the
  honeycomb, my bride;
  milk and honey are under your
    tongue.
The fragrance of your garments
  is like that of Lebanon.
¹²You are a garden locked up, my
  sister, my bride;
  you are a spring enclosed, a
    sealed fountain.
¹³Your plants are an orchard of
  pomegranates
  with choice fruits,
  with henna and nard,
14 nard and saffron,
  calamus and cinnamon,
  with every kind of incense tree,
  with myrrh and aloes
  and all the finest spices.
¹⁵You are*ᵃ* a garden fountain,
  a well of flowing water
  streaming down from Lebanon.

Beloved

¹⁶Awake, north wind,
  and come, south wind!
Blow on my garden,
  that its fragrance may spread
    abroad.
Let my lover come into his garden
  and taste its choice fruits.

Lover

5 I have come into my garden, my
  sister, my bride;

I have gathered my myrrh with
  my spice.
I have eaten my honeycomb and
  my honey;
I have drunk my wine and my
  milk.

Friends

Eat, O friends, and drink;
  drink your fill, O lovers.

Beloved

²I slept but my heart was awake.
  Listen! My lover is knocking:
"Open to me, my sister, my
    darling,
  my dove, my flawless one.
My head is drenched with dew,
  my hair with the dampness of
    the night."
³I have taken off my robe—
  must I put it on again?
I have washed my feet—
  must I soil them again?
⁴My lover thrust his hand through
  the latch-opening;
  my heart began to pound for
    him.
⁵I arose to open for my lover,
  and my hands dripped with
    myrrh,
  my fingers with flowing myrrh,
  on the handles of the lock.
⁶I opened for my lover,
  but my lover had left; he was
    gone.
  My heart sank at his
    departure.*ᵇ*
I looked for him but did not find
    him.
  I called him but he did not
    answer.
⁷The watchmen found me
  as they made their rounds in
    the city.
They beat me, they bruised me;
  they took away my cloak,
  those watchmen of the walls!
⁸O daughters of Jerusalem, I charge
    you—
  if you find my lover,
what will you tell him?
  Tell him I am faint with love.

ᵃ15 Or *I am* (spoken by the *Beloved*)   *ᵇ6* Or *heart had gone out to him when he spoke*

Friends

⁹How is your beloved better than
    others,
    most beautiful of women?
How is your beloved better than
    others,
    that you charge us so?

Beloved

¹⁰My lover is radiant and ruddy,
    outstanding among ten
    thousand.
¹¹His head is purest gold;
    his hair is wavy
    and black as a raven.
¹²His eyes are like doves
    by the water streams,
    washed in milk,
    mounted like jewels.
¹³His cheeks are like beds of spice
    yielding perfume.
His lips are like lilies
    dripping with myrrh.
¹⁴His arms are rods of gold
    set with chrysolite.
His body is like polished ivory
    decorated with sapphires.[a]
¹⁵His legs are pillars of marble
    set on bases of pure gold.
His appearance is like Lebanon,
    choice as its cedars.
¹⁶His mouth is sweetness itself;
    he is altogether lovely.
This is my lover, this my friend,
    O daughters of Jerusalem.

Friends

6 Where has your lover gone,
    most beautiful of women?
Which way did your lover turn,
    that we may look for him with
    you?

Beloved

²My lover has gone down to his
    garden,
    to the beds of spices,
to browse in the gardens
    and to gather lilies.

³I am my lover's and my lover is
    mine;
    he browses among the lilies.

Lover

⁴You are beautiful, my darling, as
    Tirzah,
    lovely as Jerusalem,
    majestic as troops with banners.
⁵Turn your eyes from me;
    they overwhelm me.
Your hair is like a flock of goats
    descending from Gilead.
⁶Your teeth are like a flock of
    sheep
    coming up from the washing.
Each has its twin,
    not one of them is alone.
⁷Your temples behind your veil
    are like the halves of a
    pomegranate.
⁸Sixty queens there may be,
    and eighty concubines,
    and virgins beyond number;
⁹but my dove, my perfect one, is
    unique,
    the only daughter of her
    mother,
    the favorite of the one who bore
    her.
The maidens saw her and called
    her blessed;
    the queens and concubines
    praised her.

Friends

¹⁰Who is this that appears like the
    dawn,
    fair as the moon, bright as the
    sun,
    majestic as the stars in
    procession?

Lover

¹¹I went down to the grove of nut
    trees
    to look at the new growth in
    the valley,
to see if the vines had budded
    or the pomegranates were in
    bloom.

a14 Or lapis lazuli

¹²Before I realized it,
   my desire set me among the
      royal chariots of my
      people.*ᵃ*

Friends

¹³Come back, come back,
      O Shulammite;
   come back, come back, that we
      may gaze on you!

Lover

Why would you gaze on the
      Shulammite
   as on the dance of Mahanaim?

7 How beautiful your sandaled
      feet,
   O prince's daughter!
Your graceful legs are like jewels,
   the work of a craftsman's
      hands.
²Your navel is a rounded goblet
   that never lacks blended wine.
Your waist is a mound of wheat
   encircled by lilies.
³Your breasts are like two fawns,
   twins of a gazelle.
⁴Your neck is like an ivory tower.
Your eyes are the pools of
      Heshbon
   by the gate of Bath Rabbim.
Your nose is like the tower of
      Lebanon
   looking toward Damascus.
⁵Your head crowns you like Mount
      Carmel.
   Your hair is like royal tapestry;
   the king is held captive by its
      tresses.
⁶How beautiful you are and how
      pleasing,
   O love, with your delights!
⁷Your stature is like that of the
      palm,
   and your breasts like clusters of
      fruit.
⁸I said, "I will climb the palm tree;
   I will take hold of its fruit."
May your breasts be like the
      clusters of the vine,

the fragrance of your breath like
      apples,
⁹ and your mouth like the best
      wine.

Beloved

May the wine go straight to my
      lover,
   flowing gently over lips and
      teeth.*ᵇ*
¹⁰I belong to my lover,
   and his desire is for me.
¹¹Come, my lover, let us go to the
      countryside,
   let us spend the night in the
      villages.*ᶜ*
¹²Let us go early to the vineyards
   to see if the vines have budded,
   if their blossoms have opened,
   and if the pomegranates are in
      bloom—
   there I will give you my love.
¹³The mandrakes send out their
      fragrance,
   and at our door is every
      delicacy,
   both new and old,
   that I have stored up for you,
      my lover.

8 If only you were to me like a
      brother,
   who was nursed at my mother's
      breasts!
Then, if I found you outside,
   I would kiss you,
   and no one would despise me.
²I would lead you
   and bring you to my mother's
      house—
   she who has taught me.
I would give you spiced wine to
      drink,
   the nectar of my pomegranates.
³His left arm is under my head
   and his right arm embraces
      me.
⁴Daughters of Jerusalem, I charge
      you:
Do not arouse or awaken love
   until it so desires.

ᵃ12 Or among the chariots of Amminadab; or among the chariots of the people of the prince
ᵇ9 Septuagint, Aquila, Vulgate and Syriac; Hebrew lips of sleepers   ᶜ11 Or henna bushes

VERSE:	AUTHOR:	PASSAGE:
Song of Songs 8:6	Don Anderson	Song of Songs 8:5b–7

Go for the Gold

Having a love affair with one's own wife or husband takes time ... and should encompass a lifetime. In the language of running, marriage is not a fast sprint, started by a shotgun and ended in a spurt. Its participants shouldn't plan on crossing the finish line until decades after the race begins ...

Reaching 50 years of marriage is a noteworthy, newsworthy achievement. Why don't we, as a society, treat it as such? We give distinguished medals of honor, purple hearts, stars, ribbons and stripes to our battlefield heroes. Our Olympic athletes compete for the gold, the silver and the bronze. Yet all our couples who make it to the 50-year mark get is a picture in the paper and a letter from the President. I'd like to see us do more; in fact, let's launch an all-out campaign to encourage husbands and wives to go for the gold.

We can begin with the printed and spoken word. I've read hundreds of sports stories telling of athletes who overcame tremendous handicaps to achieve glorious successes. I've heard countless war stories outlining the courageous acts of soldiers in combat. But where are the stories of the husbands and wives who manage to clear the hurdles and survive the fires and trials of a half-century of life together? ...

What a treasure a life filled with the memories of 50 years must be! The couples who make it to 50-plus are worthy of our sincere honor. And those who commit themselves to going for the gold should be encouraged as they run the race together.

ADDITIONAL SCRIPTURE READINGS
Isaiah 40:28–31; Ephesians 5:22–33

Go to page 853 for your next devotional reading.

Friends

⁵Who is this coming up from the
desert
leaning on her lover?

Beloved

Under the apple tree I roused you;
there your mother conceived
you,
there she who was in labor gave
you birth.
⁶Place me like a seal over your
heart,
like a seal on your arm;
for love is as strong as death,
its jealousy*ᵃ* unyielding as the
grave.*ᵇ*
It burns like blazing fire,
like a mighty flame.*ᶜ*
⁷Many waters cannot quench love;
rivers cannot wash it away.
If one were to give
all the wealth of his house for
love,
it*ᵈ* would be utterly scorned.

Friends

⁸We have a young sister,
and her breasts are not yet
grown.
What shall we do for our sister
for the day she is spoken for?
⁹If she is a wall,

we will build towers of silver
on her.
If she is a door,
we will enclose her with panels
of cedar.

Beloved

¹⁰I am a wall,
and my breasts are like towers.
Thus I have become in his eyes
like one bringing contentment.
¹¹Solomon had a vineyard in Baal
Hamon;
he let out his vineyard to
tenants.
Each was to bring for its fruit
a thousand shekels*ᵉ* of silver.
¹²But my own vineyard is mine to
give;
the thousand shekels are for
you, O Solomon,
and two hundred*ᶠ* are for
those who tend its fruit.

Lover

¹³You who dwell in the gardens
with friends in attendance,
let me hear your voice!

Beloved

¹⁴Come away, my lover,
and be like a gazelle
or like a young stag
on the spice-laden mountains.

ᵃ6 Or *ardor*   *ᵇ6* Hebrew *Sheol*   *ᶜ6* Or / *like the very flame of the* Lᴏʀᴅ   *ᵈ7* Or *he*
ᵉ11 That is, about 25 pounds (about 11.5 kilograms); also in verse 12   *ᶠ12* That is, about 5
pounds (about 2.3 kilograms)

*...T...*he prophet Isaiah
preached repentance and salvation to the inhabitants of Judah from about 740 B.C. to
681 B.C. Using vivid language, Isaiah describes both the justice and forgiveness of
God. As you read this book, be honest with
yourself about the sin that mars your life,
and thank God for the restoration he is now
bringing about in you as you submit to his
tender touch.

ISAIAH

1 The vision concerning Judah and Jerusalem that Isaiah son of Amoz saw during the reigns of Uzziah, Jotham, Ahaz and Hezekiah, kings of Judah.

A Rebellious Nation

²Hear, O heavens! Listen, O earth!
  For the LORD has spoken:
"I reared children and brought
    them up,
  but they have rebelled against
    me.
³The ox knows his master,
  the donkey his owner's manger,
but Israel does not know,
  my people do not understand."

⁴Ah, sinful nation,
  a people loaded with guilt,
a brood of evildoers,
  children given to corruption!
They have forsaken the LORD;
  they have spurned the Holy
    One of Israel
and turned their backs on him.

⁵Why should you be beaten
    anymore?
  Why do you persist in
    rebellion?
Your whole head is injured,
  your whole heart afflicted.
⁶From the sole of your foot to the
    top of your head
  there is no soundness—
only wounds and welts
  and open sores,
not cleansed or bandaged
  or soothed with oil.

⁷Your country is desolate,
  your cities burned with fire;
your fields are being stripped by
    foreigners
  right before you,
  laid waste as when overthrown
    by strangers.
⁸The Daughter of Zion is left
  like a shelter in a vineyard,

like a hut in a field of melons,
  like a city under siege.
⁹Unless the LORD Almighty
    had left us some survivors,
we would have become like
    Sodom,
  we would have been like
    Gomorrah.

¹⁰Hear the word of the LORD,
    you rulers of Sodom;
listen to the law of our God,
    you people of Gomorrah!
¹¹"The multitude of your
      sacrifices—
  what are they to me?" says the
    LORD.
"I have more than enough of
      burnt offerings,
  of rams and the fat of fattened
    animals;
I have no pleasure
  in the blood of bulls and lambs
    and goats.
¹²When you come to appear before
    me,
  who has asked this of you,
  this trampling of my courts?
¹³Stop bringing meaningless
      offerings!
  Your incense is detestable to
    me.
New Moons, Sabbaths and
      convocations—
  I cannot bear your evil
    assemblies.
¹⁴Your New Moon festivals and
      your appointed feasts
my soul hates.
They have become a burden to
    me;
  I am weary of bearing them.
¹⁵When you spread out your hands
    in prayer,
  I will hide my eyes from you;
even if you offer many prayers,
  I will not listen.
Your hands are full of blood;
¹⁶   wash and make yourselves
      clean.
Take your evil deeds
  out of my sight!

Stop doing wrong,
¹⁷   learn to do right!
Seek justice,
    encourage the oppressed.ᵃ
Defend the cause of the fatherless,
    plead the case of the widow.

¹⁸"Come now, let us reason
      together,"
    says the LORD.
"Though your sins are like scarlet,
    they shall be as white as snow;
though they are red as crimson,
    they shall be like wool.
¹⁹If you are willing and obedient,
    you will eat the best from the
      land;
²⁰but if you resist and rebel,
    you will be devoured by the
      sword."
        For the mouth of the LORD
          has spoken.

²¹See how the faithful city
    has become a harlot!
She once was full of justice;
    righteousness used to dwell in
      her—
  but now murderers!
²²Your silver has become dross,
    your choice wine is diluted with
      water.
²³Your rulers are rebels,
    companions of thieves;
they all love bribes
    and chase after gifts.
They do not defend the cause of
      the fatherless;
  the widow's case does not come
    before them.
²⁴Therefore the Lord, the LORD
      Almighty,
    the Mighty One of Israel,
      declares:
"Ah, I will get relief from my foes
    and avenge myself on my
      enemies.
²⁵I will turn my hand against you;
    I will thoroughly purge away
      your dross
  and remove all your impurities.
²⁶I will restore your judges as in
    days of old,

ᵃ17 Or / rebuke the oppressor

your counselors as at the
  beginning.
Afterward you will be called
  the City of Righteousness,
  the Faithful City."

27Zion will be redeemed with
    justice,
  her penitent ones with
    righteousness.
28But rebels and sinners will both be
    broken,
  and those who forsake the LORD
    will perish.

29"You will be ashamed because of
    the sacred oaks
  in which you have delighted;
you will be disgraced because of
    the gardens
  that you have chosen.
30You will be like an oak with
    fading leaves,
  like a garden without water.
31The mighty man will become
    tinder
  and his work a spark;
both will burn together,
  with no one to quench the fire."

The Mountain of the LORD

2 This is what Isaiah son of Amoz
   saw concerning Judah and Jerusalem:

  2In the last days

the mountain of the LORD's temple
    will be established
  as chief among the mountains;
it will be raised above the hills,
  and all nations will stream to it.

  3Many peoples will come and say,

"Come, let us go up to the
    mountain of the LORD,
  to the house of the God of
    Jacob.
He will teach us his ways,
  so that we may walk in his
    paths."
The law will go out from Zion,
  the word of the LORD from
    Jerusalem.
  4He will judge between the nations

and will settle disputes for
    many peoples.
They will beat their swords into
    plowshares
  and their spears into pruning
    hooks.
Nation will not take up sword
    against nation,
  nor will they train for war
    anymore.

  5Come, O house of Jacob,
    let us walk in the light of the
      LORD.

The Day of the LORD

  6You have abandoned your people,
    the house of Jacob.
They are full of superstitions from
    the East;
  they practice divination like the
    Philistines
  and clasp hands with pagans.
  7Their land is full of silver and
    gold;
  there is no end to their
    treasures.
Their land is full of horses;
  there is no end to their chariots.
  8Their land is full of idols;
  they bow down to the work of
    their hands,
  to what their fingers have
    made.
  9So man will be brought low
  and mankind humbled—
  do not forgive them.*a*

  10Go into the rocks,
    hide in the ground
  from dread of the LORD
    and the splendor of his majesty!
  11The eyes of the arrogant man will
    be humbled
  and the pride of men brought
    low;
  the LORD alone will be exalted in
    that day.

  12The LORD Almighty has a day in
    store
  for all the proud and lofty,
  for all that is exalted
  (and they will be humbled),

a9 Or not raise them up

¹³for all the cedars of Lebanon, tall
and lofty,
and all the oaks of Bashan,
¹⁴for all the towering mountains
and all the high hills,
¹⁵for every lofty tower
and every fortified wall,
¹⁶for every trading ship[a]
and every stately vessel.
¹⁷The arrogance of man will be
brought low
and the pride of men humbled;
the LORD alone will be exalted in
that day,
¹⁸   and the idols will totally
disappear.

¹⁹Men will flee to caves in the rocks
and to holes in the ground
from dread of the LORD
and the splendor of his majesty,
when he rises to shake the
earth.
²⁰In that day men will throw away
to the rodents and bats
their idols of silver and idols of
gold,
which they made to worship.
²¹They will flee to caverns in the
rocks
and to the overhanging crags
from dread of the LORD
and the splendor of his majesty,
when he rises to shake the
earth.

²²Stop trusting in man,
who has but a breath in his
nostrils.
Of what account is he?

Judgment on Jerusalem and Judah

3 See now, the Lord,
the LORD Almighty,
is about to take from Jerusalem
and Judah
both supply and support:
all supplies of food and all
supplies of water,
²   the hero and warrior,
the judge and prophet,
the soothsayer and elder,
³the captain of fifty and man of
rank,

the counselor, skilled craftsman
and clever enchanter.
⁴I will make boys their officials;
mere children will govern them.
⁵People will oppress each other—
man against man, neighbor
against neighbor.
The young will rise up against the
old,
the base against the honorable.
⁶A man will seize one of his
brothers
at his father's home, and say,
"You have a cloak, you be our
leader;
take charge of this heap of
ruins!"
⁷But in that day he will cry out,
"I have no remedy.
I have no food or clothing in my
house;
do not make me the leader of
the people."

⁸Jerusalem staggers,
Judah is falling;
their words and deeds are against
the LORD,
defying his glorious presence.
⁹The look on their faces testifies
against them;
they parade their sin like
Sodom;
they do not hide it.
Woe to them!
They have brought disaster
upon themselves.

¹⁰Tell the righteous it will be well
with them,
for they will enjoy the fruit of
their deeds.
¹¹Woe to the wicked! Disaster is
upon them!
They will be paid back for what
their hands have done.

¹²Youths oppress my people,
women rule over them.
O my people, your guides lead
you astray;
they turn you from the path.

¹³The LORD takes his place in court;

---

[a]16 Hebrew *every ship of Tarshish*

he rises to judge the people.
¹⁴The LORD enters into judgment
   against the elders and leaders of
      his people:
   "It is you who have ruined my
      vineyard;
   the plunder from the poor is in
      your houses.
¹⁵What do you mean by crushing
      my people
   and grinding the faces of the
      poor?"
                     declares the Lord,
            the LORD Almighty.

¹⁶The LORD says,
   "The women of Zion are
      haughty,
   walking along with outstretched
      necks,
   flirting with their eyes,
   tripping along with mincing steps,
   with ornaments jingling on their
      ankles.
¹⁷Therefore the Lord will bring
      sores on the heads of the
      women of Zion;
   the LORD will make their scalps
      bald."

¹⁸In that day the Lord will snatch
away their finery: the bangles and
headbands and crescent necklaces,
¹⁹the earrings and bracelets and veils,
²⁰the headdresses and ankle chains
and sashes, the perfume bottles and
charms, ²¹the signet rings and nose
rings, ²²the fine robes and the capes
and cloaks, the purses ²³and mirrors,
and the linen garments and tiaras and
shawls.

²⁴Instead of fragrance there will be a
      stench;
   instead of a sash, a rope;
   instead of well-dressed hair,
      baldness;
   instead of fine clothing,
      sackcloth;
   instead of beauty, branding.
²⁵Your men will fall by the sword,
   your warriors in battle.
²⁶The gates of Zion will lament and
      mourn;

destitute, she will sit on the
   ground.

4 In that day seven women
   will take hold of one man
and say, "We will eat our own
   food
   and provide our own clothes;
only let us be called by your
   name.
   Take away our disgrace!"

The Branch of the LORD

²In that day the Branch of the LORD
will be beautiful and glorious, and the
fruit of the land will be the pride and
glory of the survivors in Israel. ³Those
who are left in Zion, who remain in
Jerusalem, will be called holy, all who
are recorded among the living in Jerusalem. ⁴The Lord will wash away the
filth of the women of Zion; he will
cleanse the bloodstains from Jerusalem by a spirit*a* of judgment and a
spirit*a* of fire. ⁵Then the LORD will
create over all of Mount Zion and
over those who assemble there a
cloud of smoke by day and a glow of
flaming fire by night; over all the glory will be a canopy. ⁶It will be a shelter and shade from the heat of the
day, and a refuge and hiding place
from the storm and rain.

The Song of the Vineyard

5 I will sing for the one I love
   a song about his vineyard:
   My loved one had a vineyard
      on a fertile hillside.
²He dug it up and cleared it of
      stones
   and planted it with the choicest
      vines.
   He built a watchtower in it
      and cut out a winepress as well.
   Then he looked for a crop of good
      grapes,
   but it yielded only bad fruit.

³"Now you dwellers in Jerusalem
      and men of Judah,
   judge between me and my
      vineyard.

a4 Or the Spirit

VERSE:
Isaiah 5:2

AUTHOR:
Gigi Graham Tchividjian

PASSAGE:
Isaiah 5:1–7

The Clearing

The rotten stumps and moldy leaves of unpleasant memories, unconfessed sin or musty guilt hidden beneath the debris . . .

The heavy, dead logs of burdens and problems that I try to lug around in my own strength . . .

The undesirable saplings and undergrowth that seem so small and insignificant — like spending habits, TV programs or reading material — yet could grow into serious problems if left unpruned and untrimmed . . .

The mildew of a complaining spirit or negative attitude that puts an unhealthy dampness on my disposition and dims the joy of those around me.

All of these things keep the positive, the worthy, the beautiful from growing. They choke, hide and bury the deep beauty. They keep the Son from reaching much of my life and allow mold and musty unpleasantness to blight my heart and relationships.

I have often tried to clear the yard of my life alone . . . But I soon grew weary and gave up. I had neither the will, the strength nor the proper tools. But when I humbly called for help and allowed the Lord Jesus to weed, cut and prune the undergrowth and debris, I have been amazed at the hidden beauty: a deeper relationship with the Gardener; a stronger sense of serenity and peace; a sharper focus on the important things in life, the things of eternal value.

ADDITIONAL SCRIPTURE READINGS
John 15:1–17; Philippians 4:4–9

Go to page 863 for your next devotional reading.

⁴What more could have been done
  for my vineyard
  than I have done for it?
When I looked for good grapes,
  why did it yield only bad?
⁵Now I will tell you
  what I am going to do to my
    vineyard:
I will take away its hedge,
  and it will be destroyed;
I will break down its wall,
  and it will be trampled.
⁶I will make it a wasteland,
  neither pruned nor cultivated,
  and briers and thorns will grow
    there.
I will command the clouds
  not to rain on it."

⁷The vineyard of the LORD
    Almighty
  is the house of Israel,
and the men of Judah
  are the garden of his delight.
And he looked for justice, but saw
    bloodshed;
  for righteousness, but heard
    cries of distress.

Woes and Judgments

⁸Woe to you who add house to
    house
  and join field to field
till no space is left
  and you live alone in the land.

⁹The LORD Almighty has declared in
my hearing:

"Surely the great houses will
    become desolate,
  the fine mansions left without
    occupants.
¹⁰A ten-acreᵃ vineyard will
    produce only a bathᵇ of
    wine,
  a homerᶜ of seed only an
    ephahᵈ of grain."

¹¹Woe to those who rise early in the
    morning
  to run after their drinks,
who stay up late at night
  till they are inflamed with wine.
¹²They have harps and lyres at their
    banquets,
  tambourines and flutes and
    wine,
but they have no regard for the
    deeds of the LORD,
  no respect for the work of his
    hands.
¹³Therefore my people will go into
    exile
  for lack of understanding;
their men of rank will die of
    hunger
  and their masses will be
    parched with thirst.
¹⁴Therefore the graveᵉ enlarges its
    appetite
  and opens its mouth without
    limit;
into it will descend their nobles
    and masses
  with all their brawlers and
    revelers.
¹⁵So man will be brought low
  and mankind humbled,
  the eyes of the arrogant
    humbled.
¹⁶But the LORD Almighty will be
    exalted by his justice,
  and the holy God will show
    himself holy by his
    righteousness.
¹⁷Then sheep will graze as in their
    own pasture;
  lambs will feedᶠ among the
    ruins of the rich.

¹⁸Woe to those who draw sin along
    with cords of deceit,
  and wickedness as with cart
    ropes,
¹⁹to those who say, "Let God hurry,
  let him hasten his work
  so we may see it.
Let it approach,
  let the plan of the Holy One of
    Israel come,
  so we may know it."

ᵃ10 Hebrew *ten-yoke*, that is, the land plowed by 10 yoke of oxen in one day   ᵇ10 That is,
probably about 6 gallons (about 22 liters)   ᶜ10 That is, probably about 6 bushels (about 220
liters)   ᵈ10 That is, probably about 3/5 bushel (about 22 liters)   ᵉ14 Hebrew *Sheol*
ᶠ17 Septuagint; Hebrew / *strangers will eat*

²⁰Woe to those who call evil good
   and good evil,
who put darkness for light
   and light for darkness,
who put bitter for sweet
   and sweet for bitter.

²¹Woe to those who are wise in
      their own eyes
   and clever in their own sight.

²²Woe to those who are heroes at
      drinking wine
   and champions at mixing
      drinks,
²³who acquit the guilty for a bribe,
   but deny justice to the innocent.
²⁴Therefore, as tongues of fire lick
      up straw
   and as dry grass sinks down in
      the flames,
so their roots will decay
   and their flowers blow away
      like dust;
for they have rejected the law of
      the Lord Almighty
   and spurned the word of the
      Holy One of Israel.
²⁵Therefore the Lord's anger burns
      against his people;
   his hand is raised and he strikes
      them down.
The mountains shake,
   and the dead bodies are like
      refuse in the streets.

Yet for all this, his anger is not
      turned away,
   his hand is still upraised.

²⁶He lifts up a banner for the
      distant nations,
   he whistles for those at the ends
      of the earth.
Here they come,
   swiftly and speedily!
²⁷Not one of them grows tired or
      stumbles,
   not one slumbers or sleeps;
not a belt is loosened at the waist,
   not a sandal thong is broken.
²⁸Their arrows are sharp,
   all their bows are strung;
their horses' hoofs seem like flint,
   their chariot wheels like a
      whirlwind.
²⁹Their roar is like that of the lion,

they roar like young lions;
they growl as they seize their prey
   and carry it off with no one to
      rescue.
³⁰In that day they will roar over it
   like the roaring of the sea.
And if one looks at the land,
   he will see darkness and
      distress;
   even the light will be darkened
      by the clouds.

Isaiah's Commission

6 In the year that King Uzziah died,
I saw the Lord seated on a throne,
high and exalted, and the train of his
robe filled the temple. ²Above him
were seraphs, each with six wings:
With two wings they covered their
faces, with two they covered their
feet, and with two they were flying.
³And they were calling to one another:

"Holy, holy, holy is the Lord
      Almighty;
   the whole earth is full of his
      glory."

⁴At the sound of their voices the doorposts and thresholds shook and the
temple was filled with smoke.
⁵"Woe to me!" I cried. "I am ruined! For I am a man of unclean lips,
and I live among a people of unclean
lips, and my eyes have seen the King,
the Lord Almighty."
⁶Then one of the seraphs flew to me
with a live coal in his hand, which he
had taken with tongs from the altar.
⁷With it he touched my mouth and
said, "See, this has touched your lips;
your guilt is taken away and your sin
atoned for."
⁸Then I heard the voice of the Lord
saying, "Whom shall I send? And
who will go for us?"
   And I said, "Here am I. Send me!"
⁹He said, "Go and tell this people:

" 'Be ever hearing, but never
      understanding;
   be ever seeing, but never
      perceiving.'
¹⁰Make the heart of this people
      calloused;

make their ears dull
and close their eyes.ᵃ
Otherwise they might see with
their eyes,
hear with their ears,
understand with their hearts,
and turn and be healed."

¹¹Then I said, "For how long,
O Lord?"
And he answered:

"Until the cities lie ruined
and without inhabitant,
until the houses are left deserted
and the fields ruined and
ravaged,
¹²until the LORD has sent everyone
far away
and the land is utterly forsaken.
¹³And though a tenth remains in the
land,
it will again be laid waste.
But as the terebinth and oak
leave stumps when they are cut
down,
so the holy seed will be the
stump in the land."

The Sign of Immanuel

7 When Ahaz son of Jotham, the
son of Uzziah, was king of Judah,
King Rezin of Aram and Pekah son of
Remaliah king of Israel marched up
to fight against Jerusalem, but they
could not overpower it.

²Now the house of David was told,
"Aram has allied itself withᵇ Ephraim"; so the hearts of Ahaz and his
people were shaken, as the trees of
the forest are shaken by the wind.

³Then the LORD said to Isaiah, "Go
out, you and your son Shear-Jashub,ᶜ to meet Ahaz at the end of the
aqueduct of the Upper Pool, on the
road to the Washerman's Field. ⁴Say
to him, 'Be careful, keep calm and
don't be afraid. Do not lose heart because of these two smoldering stubs
of firewood—because of the fierce an-

ger of Rezin and Aram and of the son
of Remaliah. ⁵Aram, Ephraim and
Remaliah's son have plotted your
ruin, saying, ⁶"Let us invade Judah;
let us tear it apart and divide it
among ourselves, and make the son
of Tabeel king over it." ⁷Yet this is
what the Sovereign LORD says:

" 'It will not take place,
it will not happen,
⁸for the head of Aram is Damascus,
and the head of Damascus is
only Rezin.
Within sixty-five years
Ephraim will be too shattered to
be a people.
⁹The head of Ephraim is Samaria,
and the head of Samaria is only
Remaliah's son.
If you do not stand firm in your
faith,
you will not stand at all.' "

¹⁰Again the LORD spoke to Ahaz,
¹¹"Ask the LORD your God for a sign,
whether in the deepest depths or in
the highest heights."

¹²But Ahaz said, "I will not ask; I
will not put the LORD to the test."

¹³Then Isaiah said, "Hear now, you
house of David! Is it not enough to try
the patience of men? Will you try the
patience of my God also? ¹⁴Therefore
the Lord himself will give youᵈ a
sign: The virgin will be with child and
will give birth to a son, andᵉ will call
him Immanuel.ᶠ ¹⁵He will eat curds
and honey when he knows enough to
reject the wrong and choose the right.
¹⁶But before the boy knows enough to
reject the wrong and choose the right,
the land of the two kings you dread
will be laid waste. ¹⁷The LORD will
bring on you and on your people and
on the house of your father a time unlike any since Ephraim broke away
from Judah—he will bring the king of
Assyria."

¹⁸In that day the LORD will whistle

ᵃ9,10 Hebrew; Septuagint 'You will be ever hearing, but never understanding; / you will be ever seeing,
but never perceiving.' / ¹⁰This people's heart has become calloused; / they hardly hear with their ears, /
and they have closed their eyes   ᵇ2 Or has set up camp in   ᶜ3 Shear-Jashub means a remnant will
return.   ᵈ14 The Hebrew is plural.   ᵉ14 Masoretic Text; Dead Sea Scrolls and he or and they
ᶠ14 Immanuel means God with us.

for flies from the distant streams of Egypt and for bees from the land of Assyria. ¹⁹They will all come and settle in the steep ravines and in the crevices in the rocks, on all the thornbushes and at all the water holes. ²⁰In that day the Lord will use a razor hired from beyond the River*—the king of Assyria—to shave your head and the hair of your legs, and to take off your beards also. ²¹In that day, a man will keep alive a young cow and two goats. ²²And because of the abundance of the milk they give, he will have curds to eat. All who remain in the land will eat curds and honey. ²³In that day, in every place where there were a thousand vines worth a thousand silver shekels,*b* there will be only briers and thorns. ²⁴Men will go there with bow and arrow, for the land will be covered with briers and thorns. ²⁵As for all the hills once cultivated by the hoe, you will no longer go there for fear of the briers and thorns; they will become places where cattle are turned loose and where sheep run.

Assyria, the Lord's Instrument

8 The Lord said to me, "Take a large scroll and write on it with an ordinary pen: Maher-Shalal-Hash-Baz.*c* ²And I will call in Uriah the priest and Zechariah son of Jeberekiah as reliable witnesses for me."

³Then I went to the prophetess, and she conceived and gave birth to a son. And the Lord said to me, "Name him Maher-Shalal-Hash-Baz. ⁴Before the boy knows how to say 'My father' or 'My mother,' the wealth of Damascus and the plunder of Samaria will be carried off by the king of Assyria."

⁵The Lord spoke to me again:

⁶"Because this people has rejected
  the gently flowing waters of
    Shiloah
and rejoices over Rezin
  and the son of Remaliah,

⁷therefore the Lord is about to
  bring against them
the mighty floodwaters of the
  River*a*—
the king of Assyria with all his
  pomp.
It will overflow all its channels,
  run over all its banks
⁸and sweep on into Judah, swirling
  over it,
  passing through it and reaching
    up to the neck.
Its outspread wings will cover the
  breadth of your land,
  O Immanuel*d*!"

⁹Raise the war cry,*e* you nations,
  and be shattered!
  Listen, all you distant lands.
Prepare for battle, and be
  shattered!
  Prepare for battle, and be
    shattered!
¹⁰Devise your strategy, but it will be
  thwarted;
  propose your plan, but it will
    not stand,
for God is with us.*f*

Fear God

¹¹The Lord spoke to me with his strong hand upon me, warning me not to follow the way of this people. He said:

¹²"Do not call conspiracy
  everything that these people call
    conspiracy*g*;
do not fear what they fear,
  and do not dread it.
¹³The Lord Almighty is the one you
  are to regard as holy,
he is the one you are to fear,
  he is the one you are to dread,
¹⁴and he will be a sanctuary;
  but for both houses of Israel he
    will be
a stone that causes men to
  stumble
  and a rock that makes them fall.

*a20,7 That is, the Euphrates   b23 That is, about 25 pounds (about 11.5 kilograms)
c1 Maher-Shalal-Hash-Baz means quick to the plunder, swift to the spoil; also in verse 3.
d8 Immanuel means God with us.   e9 Or Do your worst   f10 Hebrew Immanuel
g12 Or Do not call for a treaty / every time these people call for a treaty*

And for the people of Jerusalem
    he will be
  a trap and a snare.
15Many of them will stumble;
    they will fall and be broken,
    they will be snared and
        captured."

16Bind up the testimony
    and seal up the law among my
        disciples.
17I will wait for the Lord,
    who is hiding his face from the
        house of Jacob.
  I will put my trust in him.

18Here am I, and the children the
Lord has given me. We are signs and
symbols in Israel from the Lord Almighty, who dwells on Mount Zion.
19When men tell you to consult mediums and spiritists, who whisper
and mutter, should not a people inquire of their God? Why consult the
dead on behalf of the living? 20To the
law and to the testimony! If they do
not speak according to this word,
they have no light of dawn. 21Dis-
tressed and hungry, they will roam
through the land; when they are famished, they will become enraged and,
looking upward, will curse their king
and their God. 22Then they will look
toward the earth and see only distress
and darkness and fearful gloom, and
they will be thrust into utter darkness.

To Us a Child Is Born

9 Nevertheless, there will be no
  more gloom for those who were
in distress. In the past he humbled the
land of Zebulun and the land of
Naphtali, but in the future he will
honor Galilee of the Gentiles, by the
way of the sea, along the Jordan—

2The people walking in darkness
    have seen a great light;
  on those living in the land of the
        shadow of death[a]
  a light has dawned.
3You have enlarged the nation
    and increased their joy;
  they rejoice before you

as people rejoice at the harvest,
as men rejoice
  when dividing the plunder.
4For as in the day of Midian's
        defeat,
  you have shattered
the yoke that burdens them,
  the bar across their shoulders,
  the rod of their oppressor.
5Every warrior's boot used in battle
  and every garment rolled in
        blood
will be destined for burning,
  will be fuel for the fire.
6For to us a child is born,
  to us a son is given,
  and the government will be on
        his shoulders.
And he will be called
  Wonderful Counselor,[b] Mighty
        God,
  Everlasting Father, Prince of
        Peace.
7Of the increase of his government
        and peace
  there will be no end.
He will reign on David's throne
  and over his kingdom,
establishing and upholding it
  with justice and righteousness
  from that time on and forever.
The zeal of the Lord Almighty
  will accomplish this.

The Lord's Anger Against Israel

8The Lord has sent a message
        against Jacob;
  it will fall on Israel.
9All the people will know it—
  Ephraim and the inhabitants of
        Samaria—
  who say with pride
  and arrogance of heart,
10"The bricks have fallen down,
  but we will rebuild with
        dressed stone;
the fig trees have been felled,
  but we will replace them with
        cedars."
11But the Lord has strengthened
        Rezin's foes against them
  and has spurred their enemies
        on.

a2 Or *land of darkness*   b6 Or *Wonderful, Counselor*

¹²Arameans from the east and
    Philistines from the west
have devoured Israel with open
    mouth.

Yet for all this, his anger is not
    turned away,
    his hand is still upraised.

¹³But the people have not returned
    to him who struck them,
    nor have they sought the LORD
    Almighty.
¹⁴So the LORD will cut off from Israel
    both head and tail,
    both palm branch and reed in a
    single day;
¹⁵the elders and prominent men are
    the head,
    the prophets who teach lies are
    the tail.
¹⁶Those who guide this people
    mislead them,
    and those who are guided are
    led astray.
¹⁷Therefore the Lord will take no
    pleasure in the young men,
    nor will he pity the fatherless
    and widows,
for everyone is ungodly and
    wicked,
    every mouth speaks vileness.

Yet for all this, his anger is not
    turned away,
    his hand is still upraised.

¹⁸Surely wickedness burns like a
    fire;
    it consumes briers and thorns,
it sets the forest thickets ablaze,
    so that it rolls upward in a
    column of smoke.
¹⁹By the wrath of the LORD Almighty
    the land will be scorched
and the people will be fuel for the
    fire;
    no one will spare his brother.
²⁰On the right they will devour,
    but still be hungry;
on the left they will eat,
    but not be satisfied.
Each will feed on the flesh of his
    own offspringᵃ:

²¹ Manasseh will feed on Ephraim,
    and Ephraim on Manasseh;
together they will turn against
    Judah.

Yet for all this, his anger is not
    turned away,
    his hand is still upraised.

10 Woe to those who make
    unjust laws,
    to those who issue oppressive
    decrees,
²to deprive the poor of their rights
    and withhold justice from the
    oppressed of my people,
making widows their prey
    and robbing the fatherless.
³What will you do on the day of
    reckoning,
    when disaster comes from afar?
To whom will you run for help?
    Where will you leave your
    riches?
⁴Nothing will remain but to cringe
    among the captives
    or fall among the slain.

Yet for all this, his anger is not
    turned away,
    his hand is still upraised.

God's Judgment on Assyria

⁵"Woe to the Assyrian, the rod of
    my anger,
    in whose hand is the club of my
    wrath!
⁶I send him against a godless
    nation,
    I dispatch him against a people
    who anger me,
to seize loot and snatch plunder,
    and to trample them down like
    mud in the streets.
⁷But this is not what he intends,
    this is not what he has in mind;
his purpose is to destroy,
    to put an end to many nations.
⁸'Are not my commanders all
    kings?' he says.
⁹ 'Has not Calno fared like
    Carchemish?
Is not Hamath like Arpad,
    and Samaria like Damascus?

ᵃ20 Or arm

¹⁰As my hand seized the kingdoms
    of the idols,
  kingdoms whose images
      excelled those of Jerusalem
      and Samaria—
¹¹shall I not deal with Jerusalem
    and her images
  as I dealt with Samaria and her
    idols?' "

¹²When the Lord has finished all his
work against Mount Zion and Jerusalem, he will say, "I will punish the
king of Assyria for the willful pride of
his heart and the haughty look in his
eyes. ¹³For he says:

" 'By the strength of my hand I
    have done this,
  and by my wisdom, because I
    have understanding.
I removed the boundaries of
    nations,
  I plundered their treasures;
  like a mighty one I subdued*a*
    their kings.
¹⁴As one reaches into a nest,
  so my hand reached for the
    wealth of the nations;
as men gather abandoned eggs,
  so I gathered all the countries;
not one flapped a wing,
  or opened its mouth to chirp.' "

¹⁵Does the ax raise itself above him
    who swings it,
  or the saw boast against him
    who uses it?
As if a rod were to wield him
    who lifts it up,
  or a club brandish him who is
    not wood!
¹⁶Therefore, the Lord, the LORD
    Almighty,
  will send a wasting disease
    upon his sturdy warriors;
under his pomp a fire will be
    kindled
like a blazing flame.
¹⁷The Light of Israel will become a
    fire,
  their Holy One a flame;
in a single day it will burn and
    consume

his thorns and his briers.
¹⁸The splendor of his forests and
    fertile fields
it will completely destroy,
  as when a sick man wastes
    away.
¹⁹And the remaining trees of his
    forests will be so few
that a child could write them
    down.

The Remnant of Israel

²⁰In that day the remnant of Israel,
  the survivors of the house of
    Jacob,
will no longer rely on him
  who struck them down
but will truly rely on the LORD,
  the Holy One of Israel.
²¹A remnant will return,*b* a
    remnant of Jacob
  will return to the Mighty God.
²²Though your people, O Israel, be
    like the sand by the sea,
  only a remnant will return.
Destruction has been decreed,
  overwhelming and righteous.
²³The Lord, the LORD Almighty, will
    carry out
  the destruction decreed upon
    the whole land.

²⁴Therefore, this is what the Lord,
the LORD Almighty, says:

"O my people who live in Zion,
  do not be afraid of the
    Assyrians,
who beat you with a rod
  and lift up a club against you,
    as Egypt did.
²⁵Very soon my anger against you
    will end
  and my wrath will be directed
    to their destruction."

²⁶The LORD Almighty will lash them
    with a whip,
  as when he struck down Midian
    at the rock of Oreb;
and he will raise his staff over the
    waters,
  as he did in Egypt.

---

a13 Or / *I subdued the mighty,*   *b21* Hebrew *shear-jashub*; also in verse 22

²⁷In that day their burden will be
　　lifted from your shoulders,
　　their yoke from your neck;
　the yoke will be broken
　　because you have grown so
　　　fat.^a

²⁸They enter Aiath;
　　they pass through Migron;
　　they store supplies at Micmash.
²⁹They go over the pass, and say,
　　"We will camp overnight at
　　　Geba."
　Ramah trembles;
　　Gibeah of Saul flees.
³⁰Cry out, O Daughter of Gallim!
　Listen, O Laishah!
　Poor Anathoth!
³¹Madmenah is in flight;
　the people of Gebim take cover.
³²This day they will halt at Nob;
　　they will shake their fist
　at the mount of the Daughter of
　　　Zion,
　　at the hill of Jerusalem.

³³See, the Lord, the Lord Almighty,
　will lop off the boughs with
　　great power.
　The lofty trees will be felled,
　　the tall ones will be brought
　　　low.
³⁴He will cut down the forest
　　thickets with an ax;
　Lebanon will fall before the
　　Mighty One.

The Branch From Jesse

11 A shoot will come up from
　　the stump of Jesse;
　from his roots a Branch will
　　bear fruit.
²The Spirit of the Lord will rest on
　　him—
　the Spirit of wisdom and of
　　understanding,
　the Spirit of counsel and of
　　power,
　the Spirit of knowledge and of
　　the fear of the Lord—
³and he will delight in the fear of
　　the Lord.

He will not judge by what he sees
　　with his eyes,
　or decide by what he hears with
　　his ears;
⁴but with righteousness he will
　　judge the needy,
　with justice he will give
　　decisions for the poor of
　　the earth.
He will strike the earth with the
　　rod of his mouth;
　with the breath of his lips he
　　will slay the wicked.
⁵Righteousness will be his belt
　　and faithfulness the sash around
　　his waist.

⁶The wolf will live with the lamb,
　the leopard will lie down with
　　the goat,
　the calf and the lion and the
　　yearling^b together;
　and a little child will lead them.
⁷The cow will feed with the bear,
　　their young will lie down
　　together,
　and the lion will eat straw like
　　the ox.
⁸The infant will play near the hole
　　of the cobra,
　and the young child put his
　　hand into the viper's nest.
⁹They will neither harm nor
　　destroy
　on all my holy mountain,
　for the earth will be full of the
　　knowledge of the Lord
　as the waters cover the sea.

¹⁰In that day the Root of Jesse will
stand as a banner for the peoples;
the nations will rally to him, and his
place of rest will be glorious. ¹¹In that
day the Lord will reach out his hand
a second time to reclaim the remnant
that is left of his people from Assyria, from Lower Egypt, from Up-
per Egypt,^c from Cush,^d from Elam,
from Babylonia,^e from Hamath and
from the islands of the sea.

¹²He will raise a banner for the
　　nations

---

^a27 Hebrew; Septuagint *broken / from your shoulders*　　^b6 Hebrew; Septuagint *lion will feed*
^c11 Hebrew *from Pathros*　　^d11 That is, the upper Nile region　　^e11 Hebrew *Shinar*

and gather the exiles of Israel;
he will assemble the scattered
people of Judah
from the four quarters of the
earth.
¹³Ephraim's jealousy will vanish,
and Judah's enemies[a] will be
cut off;
Ephraim will not be jealous of
Judah,
nor Judah hostile toward
Ephraim.
¹⁴They will swoop down on the
slopes of Philistia to the
west;
together they will plunder the
people to the east.
They will lay hands on Edom and
Moab,
and the Ammonites will be
subject to them.
¹⁵The LORD will dry up
the gulf of the Egyptian sea;
with a scorching wind he will
sweep his hand
over the Euphrates River.[b]
He will break it up into seven
streams
so that men can cross over in
sandals.
¹⁶There will be a highway for the
remnant of his people
that is left from Assyria,
as there was for Israel
when they came up from Egypt.

Songs of Praise

12 In that day you will say:

"I will praise you, O LORD.
Although you were angry with
me,
your anger has turned away
and you have comforted me.
²Surely God is my salvation;
I will trust and not be afraid.
The LORD, the LORD, is my strength
and my song;
he has become my salvation."
³With joy you will draw water
from the wells of salvation.

⁴In that day you will say:

"Give thanks to the LORD, call on
his name;
make known among the nations
what he has done,
and proclaim that his name is
exalted.
⁵Sing to the LORD, for he has done
glorious things;
let this be known to all the
world.
⁶Shout aloud and sing for joy,
people of Zion,
for great is the Holy One of
Israel among you."

A Prophecy Against Babylon

13 An oracle concerning Babylon
that Isaiah son of Amoz saw:

²Raise a banner on a bare hilltop,
shout to them;
beckon to them
to enter the gates of the nobles.
³I have commanded my holy ones;
I have summoned my warriors
to carry out my wrath—
those who rejoice in my
triumph.

⁴Listen, a noise on the mountains,
like that of a great multitude!
Listen, an uproar among the
kingdoms,
like nations massing together!
The LORD Almighty is mustering
an army for war.
⁵They come from faraway lands,
from the ends of the heavens—
the LORD and the weapons of his
wrath—
to destroy the whole country.

⁶Wail, for the day of the LORD is
near;
it will come like destruction
from the Almighty.[c]
⁷Because of this, all hands will go
limp,
every man's heart will melt.
⁸Terror will seize them,
pain and anguish will grip
them;
they will writhe like a woman
in labor.

a13 Or hostility   b15 Hebrew the River   c6 Hebrew Shaddai

PASSAGE: Isaiah 6; Matthew 25:31–46
AUTHOR: Robert H. Schuller

I Offer My Life

I offer my life to you, Jesus Christ, for you to live
    in me and through me.
Here is my face — shine from it.
Here are my ears — hear the cry of hurting persons
    through them.
Here are my eyes — see the faces of those who need
    your blessing and bless them with the
        healing look
    that radiates from you, my Lord, through
        my eyes.
Here is my tongue — speak through it!
Speak words of encouragement! Affirmation!
Here, O Lord, are my hands — use them to touch,
    stroke, hold, lift and steady another human
        being.
Here, O Lord, are my feet — walk where you want
        me to go.
    And may those who follow me be following
        Jesus Christ.

Go to page 878 for your next devotional reading.

They will look aghast at each
    other,
  their faces aflame.

⁹See, the day of the LORD is coming
  —a cruel day, with wrath and
    fierce anger—
to make the land desolate
  and destroy the sinners within
    it.
¹⁰The stars of heaven and their
    constellations
  will not show their light.
The rising sun will be darkened
  and the moon will not give its
    light.
¹¹I will punish the world for its evil,
  the wicked for their sins.
I will put an end to the arrogance
    of the haughty
  and will humble the pride of
    the ruthless.
¹²I will make man scarcer than pure
    gold,
  more rare than the gold of
    Ophir.
¹³Therefore I will make the heavens
    tremble;
  and the earth will shake from
    its place
at the wrath of the LORD Almighty,
  in the day of his burning anger.

¹⁴Like a hunted gazelle,
  like sheep without a shepherd,
each will return to his own
    people,
  each will flee to his native land.
¹⁵Whoever is captured will be thrust
    through;
  all who are caught will fall by
    the sword.
¹⁶Their infants will be dashed to
    pieces before their eyes;
  their houses will be looted and
    their wives ravished.

¹⁷See, I will stir up against them the
    Medes,
  who do not care for silver
  and have no delight in gold.
¹⁸Their bows will strike down the
    young men;

they will have no mercy on
    infants
  nor will they look with
    compassion on children.
¹⁹Babylon, the jewel of kingdoms,
  the glory of the Babylonians'ᵃ
    pride,
will be overthrown by God
  like Sodom and Gomorrah.
²⁰She will never be inhabited
  or lived in through all
    generations;
no Arab will pitch his tent there,
  no shepherd will rest his flocks
    there.
²¹But desert creatures will lie there,
  jackals will fill her houses;
there the owls will dwell,
  and there the wild goats will
    leap about.
²²Hyenas will howl in her
    strongholds,
  jackals in her luxurious palaces.
Her time is at hand,
  and her days will not be
    prolonged.

14 The LORD will have
      compassion on Jacob;
  once again he will choose Israel
  and will settle them in their
    own land.
Aliens will join them
  and unite with the house of
    Jacob.
²Nations will take them
  and bring them to their own
    place.
And the house of Israel will
    possess the nations
  as menservants and
    maidservants in the LORD's
    land.
They will make captives of their
    captors
  and rule over their oppressors.

³On the day the LORD gives you relief from suffering and turmoil and
cruel bondage, ⁴you will take up this
taunt against the king of Babylon:

How the oppressor has come to an
    end!

ᵃ19 Or Chaldeans'

How his fury[a] has ended!
⁵The LORD has broken the rod of
    the wicked,
    the scepter of the rulers,
⁶which in anger struck down
    peoples
    with unceasing blows,
and in fury subdued nations
    with relentless aggression.
⁷All the lands are at rest and at
    peace;
    they break into singing.
⁸Even the pine trees and the cedars
    of Lebanon
    exult over you and say,
"Now that you have been laid
    low,
    no woodsman comes to cut us
    down."

⁹The grave[b] below is all astir
    to meet you at your coming;
it rouses the spirits of the
    departed to greet you—
    all those who were leaders in
    the world;
it makes them rise from their
    thrones—
    all those who were kings over
    the nations.
¹⁰They will all respond,
    they will say to you,
"You also have become weak, as
    we are;
    you have become like us."
¹¹All your pomp has been brought
    down to the grave,
    along with the noise of your
    harps;
maggots are spread out beneath
    you
    and worms cover you.

¹²How you have fallen from heaven,
    O morning star, son of the
    dawn!
You have been cast down to the
    earth,
    you who once laid low the
    nations!
¹³You said in your heart,
    "I will ascend to heaven;
I will raise my throne

    above the stars of God;
I will sit enthroned on the mount
    of assembly,
    on the utmost heights of the
    sacred mountain.[c]
¹⁴I will ascend above the tops of the
    clouds;
    I will make myself like the Most
    High."
¹⁵But you are brought down to the
    grave,
    to the depths of the pit.

¹⁶Those who see you stare at you,
    they ponder your fate:
"Is this the man who shook the
    earth
    and made kingdoms tremble,
¹⁷the man who made the world a
    desert,
    who overthrew its cities
    and would not let his captives
    go home?"

¹⁸All the kings of the nations lie in
    state,
    each in his own tomb.
¹⁹But you are cast out of your tomb
    like a rejected branch;
you are covered with the slain,
    with those pierced by the
    sword,
    those who descend to the stones
    of the pit.
Like a corpse trampled underfoot,
²⁰   you will not join them in burial,
for you have destroyed your land
    and killed your people.

The offspring of the wicked
    will never be mentioned again.
²¹Prepare a place to slaughter his
    sons
    for the sins of their forefathers;
they are not to rise to inherit the
    land
    and cover the earth with their
    cities.

²²"I will rise up against them,"
    declares the LORD Almighty.
"I will cut off from Babylon her
    name and survivors,

---

a4 Dead Sea Scrolls, Septuagint and Syriac; the meaning of the word in the Masoretic Text is
uncertain.   *b9* Hebrew *Sheol*; also in verses 11 and 15   *c13* Or *the north*; Hebrew *Zaphon*

her offspring and descendants,"
          declares the LORD.
23"I will turn her into a place for
    owls
  and into swampland;
I will sweep her with the broom
    of destruction,"
  declares the LORD Almighty.

A Prophecy Against Assyria

24The LORD Almighty has sworn,

"Surely, as I have planned, so it
    will be,
  and as I have purposed, so it
    will stand.
25I will crush the Assyrian in my
    land;
  on my mountains I will trample
    him down.
His yoke will be taken from my
    people,
  and his burden removed from
    their shoulders."

26This is the plan determined for the
    whole world;
  this is the hand stretched out
    over all nations.
27For the LORD Almighty has
    purposed, and who can
    thwart him?
  His hand is stretched out, and
    who can turn it back?

A Prophecy Against the Philistines

28This oracle came in the year King
Ahaz died:

29Do not rejoice, all you Philistines,
  that the rod that struck you is
    broken;
  from the root of that snake will
    spring up a viper,
    its fruit will be a darting,
    venomous serpent.
30The poorest of the poor will find
    pasture,
  and the needy will lie down in
    safety.
But your root I will destroy by
    famine;
  it will slay your survivors.

31Wail, O gate! Howl, O city!
  Melt away, all you Philistines!

A cloud of smoke comes from the
    north,
  and there is not a straggler in
    its ranks.
32What answer shall be given
  to the envoys of that nation?
"The LORD has established Zion,
  and in her his afflicted people
    will find refuge."

A Prophecy Against Moab

15 An oracle concerning Moab:

Ar in Moab is ruined,
  destroyed in a night!
Kir in Moab is ruined,
  destroyed in a night!
2Dibon goes up to its temple,
  to its high places to weep;
Moab wails over Nebo and
    Medeba.
Every head is shaved
  and every beard cut off.
3In the streets they wear sackcloth;
  on the roofs and in the public
    squares
they all wail,
  prostrate with weeping.
4Heshbon and Elealeh cry out,
  their voices are heard all the
    way to Jahaz.
Therefore the armed men of Moab
    cry out,
  and their hearts are faint.

5My heart cries out over Moab;
  her fugitives flee as far as Zoar,
  as far as Eglath Shelishiyah.
They go up the way to Luhith,
  weeping as they go;
on the road to Horonaim
  they lament their destruction.
6The waters of Nimrim are dried
    up
  and the grass is withered;
the vegetation is gone
  and nothing green is left.
7So the wealth they have acquired
    and stored up
  they carry away over the Ravine
    of the Poplars.
8Their outcry echoes along the
    border of Moab;
  their wailing reaches as far as
    Eglaim,

their lamentation as far as Beer
    Elim.
⁹Dimon's[a] waters are full of
    blood,
but I will bring still more upon
    Dimon[a]—
a lion upon the fugitives of Moab
and upon those who remain in
    the land.

16 Send lambs as tribute
    to the ruler of the land,
from Sela, across the desert,
    to the mount of the Daughter of
    Zion.
²Like fluttering birds
    pushed from the nest,
so are the women of Moab
    at the fords of the Arnon.

³"Give us counsel,
    render a decision.
Make your shadow like night—
    at high noon.
Hide the fugitives,
    do not betray the refugees.
⁴Let the Moabite fugitives stay with
    you;
    be their shelter from the
    destroyer."

The oppressor will come to an
    end,
    and destruction will cease;
the aggressor will vanish from
    the land.
⁵In love a throne will be
    established;
    in faithfulness a man will sit on
    it—
    one from the house[b] of
    David—
one who in judging seeks justice
and speeds the cause of
    righteousness.

⁶We have heard of Moab's pride—
    her overweening pride and
    conceit,
her pride and her insolence—
    but her boasts are empty.
⁷Therefore the Moabites wail,

they wail together for Moab.
Lament and grieve
    for the men[c] of Kir Hareseth.
⁸The fields of Heshbon wither,
    the vines of Sibmah also.
The rulers of the nations
    have trampled down the
    choicest vines,
which once reached Jazer
    and spread toward the desert.
Their shoots spread out
    and went as far as the sea.
⁹So I weep, as Jazer weeps,
    for the vines of Sibmah.
O Heshbon, O Elealeh,
    I drench you with tears!
The shouts of joy over your
    ripened fruit
    and over your harvests have
    been stilled.
¹⁰Joy and gladness are taken away
    from the orchards;
    no one sings or shouts in the
    vineyards;
no one treads out wine at the
    presses,
    for I have put an end to the
    shouting.
¹¹My heart laments for Moab like a
    harp,
    my inmost being for Kir
    Hareseth.
¹²When Moab appears at her high
    place,
    she only wears herself out;
when she goes to her shrine to
    pray,
    it is to no avail.

¹³This is the word the LORD has already spoken concerning Moab. ¹⁴But
now the LORD says: "Within three
years, as a servant bound by contract
would count them, Moab's splendor
and all her many people will be despised, and her survivors will be very
few and feeble."

An Oracle Against Damascus

17 An oracle concerning Damas-
    cus:

[a]9 Masoretic Text; Dead Sea Scrolls, some Septuagint manuscripts and Vulgate Dibon
[b]5 Hebrew tent   [c]7 Or "raisin cakes," a wordplay

"See, Damascus will no longer be
    a city
  but will become a heap of ruins.
²The cities of Aroer will be
    deserted
  and left to flocks, which will lie
    down,
  with no one to make them
    afraid.
³The fortified city will disappear
    from Ephraim,
  and royal power from
    Damascus;
the remnant of Aram will be
like the glory of the Israelites,"
              declares the LORD
              Almighty.

⁴"In that day the glory of Jacob
    will fade;
  the fat of his body will waste
    away.
⁵It will be as when a reaper gathers
    the standing grain
  and harvests the grain with his
    arm—
as when a man gleans heads of
    grain
  in the Valley of Rephaim.
⁶Yet some gleanings will remain,
  as when an olive tree is beaten,
leaving two or three olives on the
    topmost branches,
  four or five on the fruitful
    boughs,"
         declares the LORD, the God
              of Israel.

⁷In that day men will look to their
    Maker
  and turn their eyes to the Holy
    One of Israel.
⁸They will not look to the altars,
    the work of their hands,
  and they will have no regard for
    the Asherah poles[a]
  and the incense altars their
    fingers have made.

⁹In that day their strong cities,
which they left because of the Israelites, will be like places abandoned to
thickets and undergrowth. And all
will be desolation.

¹⁰You have forgotten God your
    Savior;
  you have not remembered the
    Rock, your fortress.
Therefore, though you set out the
    finest plants
  and plant imported vines,
¹¹though on the day you set them
    out, you make them grow,
  and on the morning when you
    plant them, you bring them
    to bud,
yet the harvest will be as nothing
  in the day of disease and
    incurable pain.

¹²Oh, the raging of many nations—
  they rage like the raging sea!
Oh, the uproar of the peoples—
  they roar like the roaring of
    great waters!
¹³Although the peoples roar like the
    roar of surging waters,
  when he rebukes them they flee
    far away,
driven before the wind like chaff
    on the hills,
  like tumbleweed before a gale.
¹⁴In the evening, sudden terror!
  Before the morning, they are
    gone!
This is the portion of those who
    loot us,
  the lot of those who plunder us.

A Prophecy Against Cush

18 Woe to the land of whirring
    wings[b]
  along the rivers of Cush,[c]
²which sends envoys by sea
  in papyrus boats over the water.

Go, swift messengers,
to a people tall and
    smooth-skinned,
  to a people feared far and wide,
an aggressive nation of strange
    speech,
  whose land is divided by rivers.

³All you people of the world,

---

[a]8 That is, symbols of the goddess Asherah region   [b]1 Or of locusts   [c]1 That is, the upper Nile

you who live on the earth,
when a banner is raised on the
    mountains,
  you will see it,
and when a trumpet sounds,
  you will hear it.
⁴This is what the LORD says to me:
  "I will remain quiet and will
      look on from my dwelling
      place,
  like shimmering heat in the
      sunshine,
    like a cloud of dew in the heat
      of harvest."
⁵For, before the harvest, when the
      blossom is gone
  and the flower becomes a
      ripening grape,
he will cut off the shoots with
      pruning knives,
  and cut down and take away
      the spreading branches.
⁶They will all be left to the
      mountain birds of prey
  and to the wild animals;
the birds will feed on them all
      summer,
  the wild animals all winter.

⁷At that time gifts will be brought
to the LORD Almighty

  from a people tall and
      smooth-skinned,
  from a people feared far and
      wide,
an aggressive nation of strange
      speech,
  whose land is divided by
      rivers—

the gifts will be brought to Mount
Zion, the place of the Name of the
LORD Almighty.

A Prophecy About Egypt

19 An oracle concerning Egypt:

  See, the LORD rides on a swift
      cloud
  and is coming to Egypt.
  The idols of Egypt tremble before
      him,
  and the hearts of the Egyptians
      melt within them.

²"I will stir up Egyptian against
      Egyptian—
  brother will fight against
      brother,
  neighbor against neighbor,
  city against city,
  kingdom against kingdom.
³The Egyptians will lose heart,
  and I will bring their plans to
      nothing;
they will consult the idols and the
      spirits of the dead,
  the mediums and the spiritists.
⁴I will hand the Egyptians over
  to the power of a cruel master,
and a fierce king will rule over
      them,"
  declares the Lord, the LORD
      Almighty.

⁵The waters of the river will dry
      up,
  and the riverbed will be
      parched and dry.
⁶The canals will stink;
  the streams of Egypt will
      dwindle and dry up.
The reeds and rushes will wither,
⁷   also the plants along the Nile,
  at the mouth of the river.
Every sown field along the Nile
  will become parched, will blow
      away and be no more.
⁸The fishermen will groan and
      lament,
  all who cast hooks into the Nile;
those who throw nets on the
      water
  will pine away.
⁹Those who work with combed flax
      will despair,
  the weavers of fine linen will
      lose hope.
¹⁰The workers in cloth will be
      dejected,
  and all the wage earners will be
      sick at heart.

¹¹The officials of Zoan are nothing
      but fools;
  the wise counselors of Pharaoh
      give senseless advice.
How can you say to Pharaoh,
  "I am one of the wise men,
  a disciple of the ancient kings"?

¹²Where are your wise men now?
  Let them show you and make
    known
what the Lᴏʀᴅ Almighty
  has planned against Egypt.
¹³The officials of Zoan have become
    fools,
  the leaders of Memphis[a] are
    deceived;
the cornerstones of her peoples
  have led Egypt astray.
¹⁴The Lᴏʀᴅ has poured into them
  a spirit of dizziness;
they make Egypt stagger in all
    that she does,
  as a drunkard staggers around
    in his vomit.
¹⁵There is nothing Egypt can do—
  head or tail, palm branch or
    reed.

¹⁶In that day the Egyptians will be
like women. They will shudder with
fear at the uplifted hand that the Lᴏʀᴅ
Almighty raises against them. ¹⁷And
the land of Judah will bring terror to
the Egyptians; everyone to whom Judah is mentioned will be terrified, because of what the Lᴏʀᴅ Almighty is
planning against them.
¹⁸In that day five cities in Egypt
will speak the language of Canaan
and swear allegiance to the Lᴏʀᴅ Almighty. One of them will be called the
City of Destruction.[b]
¹⁹In that day there will be an altar
to the Lᴏʀᴅ in the heart of Egypt, and
a monument to the Lᴏʀᴅ at its border.
²⁰It will be a sign and witness to the
Lᴏʀᴅ Almighty in the land of Egypt.
When they cry out to the Lᴏʀᴅ because of their oppressors, he will send
them a savior and defender, and he
will rescue them. ²¹So the Lᴏʀᴅ will
make himself known to the Egyptians, and in that day they will
acknowledge the Lᴏʀᴅ. They will
worship with sacrifices and grain
offerings; they will make vows to
the Lᴏʀᴅ and keep them. ²²The Lᴏʀᴅ
will strike Egypt with a plague; he
will strike them and heal them. They

will turn to the Lᴏʀᴅ, and he will respond to their pleas and heal them.
²³In that day there will be a highway from Egypt to Assyria. The Assyrians will go to Egypt and the
Egyptians to Assyria. The Egyptians
and Assyrians will worship together.
²⁴In that day Israel will be the third,
along with Egypt and Assyria, a
blessing on the earth. ²⁵The Lᴏʀᴅ
Almighty will bless them, saying,
"Blessed be Egypt my people, Assyria
my handiwork, and Israel my inheritance."

A Prophecy Against Egypt and Cush

20 In the year that the supreme
commander, sent by Sargon
king of Assyria, came to Ashdod and
attacked and captured it— ²at that
time the Lᴏʀᴅ spoke through Isaiah
son of Amoz. He said to him, "Take
off the sackcloth from your body and
the sandals from your feet." And he
did so, going around stripped and
barefoot.
³Then the Lᴏʀᴅ said, "Just as my
servant Isaiah has gone stripped and
barefoot for three years, as a sign and
portent against Egypt and Cush,[c] ⁴so
the king of Assyria will lead away
stripped and barefoot the Egyptian
captives and Cushite exiles, young
and old, with buttocks bared—to
Egypt's shame. ⁵Those who trusted in
Cush and boasted in Egypt will be
afraid and put to shame. ⁶In that day
the people who live on this coast will
say, 'See what has happened to those
we relied on, those we fled to for help
and deliverance from the king of Assyria! How then can we escape?' "

A Prophecy Against Babylon

21 An oracle concerning the
Desert by the Sea:

Like whirlwinds sweeping
  through the southland,

---

a13 Hebrew *Noph*   *b18* Most manuscripts of the Masoretic Text; some manuscripts of the
Masoretic Text, Dead Sea Scrolls and Vulgate *City of the Sun* (that is, Heliopolis)   *c3* That is,
the upper Nile region; also in verse 5

an invader comes from the
        desert,
from a land of terror.

²A dire vision has been shown to
        me:
The traitor betrays, the looter
        takes loot.
Elam, attack! Media, lay siege!
        I will bring to an end all the
        groaning she caused.

³At this my body is racked with
        pain,
pangs seize me, like those of a
        woman in labor;
I am staggered by what I hear,
        I am bewildered by what I see.
⁴My heart falters,
        fear makes me tremble;
the twilight I longed for
        has become a horror to me.

⁵They set the tables,
        they spread the rugs,
        they eat, they drink!
Get up, you officers,
        oil the shields!

⁶This is what the Lord says to me:

"Go, post a lookout
        and have him report what he
        sees.
⁷When he sees chariots
        with teams of horses,
riders on donkeys
        or riders on camels,
let him be alert,
        fully alert."

⁸And the lookout*a* shouted,

"Day after day, my lord, I stand
        on the watchtower;
every night I stay at my post.
⁹Look, here comes a man in a
        chariot
with a team of horses.
And he gives back the answer:
        'Babylon has fallen, has fallen!
All the images of its gods
        lie shattered on the ground!' "

¹⁰O my people, crushed on the
        threshing floor,

I tell you what I have heard
from the Lord Almighty,
from the God of Israel.

A Prophecy Against Edom

¹¹An oracle concerning Dumah*b*:

Someone calls to me from Seir,
        "Watchman, what is left of the
        night?
Watchman, what is left of the
        night?"
¹²The watchman replies,
        "Morning is coming, but also
        the night.
If you would ask, then ask;
        and come back yet again."

A Prophecy Against Arabia

¹³An oracle concerning Arabia:

You caravans of Dedanites,
        who camp in the thickets of
        Arabia,
¹⁴ bring water for the thirsty;
you who live in Tema,
        bring food for the fugitives.
¹⁵They flee from the sword,
        from the drawn sword,
from the bent bow
        and from the heat of battle.

¹⁶This is what the Lord says to me:
"Within one year, as a servant bound
by contract would count it, all the
pomp of Kedar will come to an end.
¹⁷The survivors of the bowmen, the
warriors of Kedar, will be few." The
Lord, the God of Israel, has spoken.

A Prophecy About Jerusalem

22 An oracle concerning the Valley of Vision:

What troubles you now,
        that you have all gone up on
        the roofs,
²O town full of commotion,
        O city of tumult and revelry?
Your slain were not killed by the
        sword,
        nor did they die in battle.
³All your leaders have fled
        together;

---

a8 Dead Sea Scrolls and Syriac; Masoretic Text *A lion*   *b11 Dumah* means *silence* or *stillness*, a
wordplay on *Edom*.

they have been captured
　　without using the bow.
All you who were caught were
　　taken prisoner together,
having fled while the enemy
　　was still far away.
⁴Therefore I said, "Turn away from
　　me;
　　let me weep bitterly.
Do not try to console me
　　over the destruction of my
　　people."

⁵The Lord, the LORD Almighty, has
　　a day
of tumult and trampling and
　　terror
　　in the Valley of Vision,
a day of battering down walls
　　and of crying out to the
　　mountains.
⁶Elam takes up the quiver,
　　with her charioteers and horses;
Kir uncovers the shield.
⁷Your choicest valleys are full of
　　chariots,
　　and horsemen are posted at the
　　city gates;
⁸　the defenses of Judah are
　　stripped away.

And you looked in that day
　　to the weapons in the Palace of
　　the Forest;
⁹you saw that the City of David
　　had many breaches in its
　　defenses;
you stored up water
　　in the Lower Pool.
¹⁰You counted the buildings in
　　Jerusalem
and tore down houses to
　　strengthen the wall.
¹¹You built a reservoir between the
　　two walls
　　for the water of the Old Pool,
but you did not look to the One
　　who made it,
　　or have regard for the One who
　　planned it long ago.

¹²The Lord, the LORD Almighty,
　　called you on that day
to weep and to wail,
　　to tear out your hair and put on
　　sackcloth.

¹³But see, there is joy and revelry,
　　slaughtering of cattle and killing
　　of sheep,
　　eating of meat and drinking of
　　wine!
"Let us eat and drink," you say,
　　"for tomorrow we die!"

¹⁴The LORD Almighty has revealed
this in my hearing: "Till your dying
day this sin will not be atoned for,"
says the Lord, the LORD Almighty.

¹⁵This is what the Lord, the LORD
Almighty, says:

"Go, say to this steward,
　　to Shebna, who is in charge of
　　the palace:
¹⁶What are you doing here and who
　　gave you permission
　　to cut out a grave for yourself
　　here,
hewing your grave on the height
　　and chiseling your resting place
　　in the rock?

¹⁷"Beware, the LORD is about to take
　　firm hold of you
　　and hurl you away, O you
　　mighty man.
¹⁸He will roll you up tightly like a
　　ball
　　and throw you into a large
　　country.
There you will die
　　and there your splendid
　　chariots will remain—
you disgrace to your master's
　　house!
¹⁹I will depose you from your office,
　　and you will be ousted from
　　your position.

²⁰"In that day I will summon my
servant, Eliakim son of Hilkiah. ²¹I
will clothe him with your robe and
fasten your sash around him and
hand your authority over to him. He
will be a father to those who live in
Jerusalem and to the house of Judah.
²²I will place on his shoulder the key
to the house of David; what he opens
no one can shut, and what he shuts no
one can open. ²³I will drive him like a
peg into a firm place; he will be a

seat[a] of honor for the house of his father. [24]All the glory of his family will hang on him: its offspring and offshoots—all its lesser vessels, from the bowls to all the jars.

[25]"In that day," declares the LORD Almighty, "the peg driven into the firm place will give way; it will be sheared off and will fall, and the load hanging on it will be cut down." The LORD has spoken.

A Prophecy About Tyre

23
An oracle concerning Tyre:

Wail, O ships of Tarshish!
    For Tyre is destroyed
    and left without house or
        harbor.
From the land of Cyprus[b]
    word has come to them.

[2]Be silent, you people of the island
    and you merchants of Sidon,
    whom the seafarers have
        enriched.
[3]On the great waters
    came the grain of the Shihor;
the harvest of the Nile[c] was the
        revenue of Tyre,
    and she became the marketplace
        of the nations.

[4]Be ashamed, O Sidon, and you,
        O fortress of the sea,
    for the sea has spoken:
"I have neither been in labor nor
        given birth;
    I have neither reared sons nor
        brought up daughters."
[5]When word comes to Egypt,
    they will be in anguish at the
        report from Tyre.

[6]Cross over to Tarshish;
    wail, you people of the island.
[7]Is this your city of revelry,
    the old, old city,
whose feet have taken her
    to settle in far-off lands?
[8]Who planned this against Tyre,

the bestower of crowns,
    whose merchants are princes,
    whose traders are renowned in
        the earth?
[9]The LORD Almighty planned it,
    to bring low the pride of all
        glory
    and to humble all who are
        renowned on the earth.

[10]Till[d] your land as along the Nile,
    O Daughter of Tarshish,
    for you no longer have a
        harbor.
[11]The LORD has stretched out his
        hand over the sea
    and made its kingdoms tremble.
He has given an order concerning
        Phoenicia[e]
    that her fortresses be destroyed.
[12]He said, "No more of your
        reveling,
    O Virgin Daughter of Sidon,
        now crushed!

"Up, cross over to Cyprus[b];
    even there you will find no
        rest."
[13]Look at the land of the
        Babylonians,[f]
    this people that is now of no
        account!
The Assyrians have made it
    a place for desert creatures;
they raised up their siege towers,
    they stripped its fortresses bare
    and turned it into a ruin.

[14]Wail, you ships of Tarshish;
    your fortress is destroyed!

[15]At that time Tyre will be forgotten for seventy years, the span of a king's life. But at the end of these seventy years, it will happen to Tyre as in the song of the prostitute:

[16]"Take up a harp, walk through
        the city,
    O prostitute forgotten;
    play the harp well, sing many a
        song,

---

[a]23 Or *throne*   [b]1,12 Hebrew *Kittim*   [c]2,3 Masoretic Text; one Dead Sea Scroll *Sidon, | who cross over the sea; | your envoys* [3]*are on the great waters. | The grain of the Shihor, | the harvest of the Nile,*   [d]10 Dead Sea Scrolls and some Septuagint manuscripts; Masoretic Text *Go through*   [e]11 Hebrew *Canaan*   [f]13 Or *Chaldeans*

so that you will be
  remembered."

¹⁷At the end of seventy years, the
LORD will deal with Tyre. She will return to her hire as a prostitute and
will ply her trade with all the kingdoms on the face of the earth. ¹⁸Yet
her profit and her earnings will be set
apart for the LORD; they will not be
stored up or hoarded. Her profits will
go to those who live before the LORD,
for abundant food and fine clothes.

The LORD's Devastation of the Earth

24 See, the LORD is going to lay
      waste the earth
  and devastate it;
he will ruin its face
  and scatter its inhabitants—
²it will be the same
  for priest as for people,
  for master as for servant,
  for mistress as for maid,
  for seller as for buyer,
  for borrower as for lender,
  for debtor as for creditor.
³The earth will be completely laid
      waste
  and totally plundered.
              The LORD has spoken
                    this word.

⁴The earth dries up and withers,
  the world languishes and
      withers,
  the exalted of the earth
      languish.
⁵The earth is defiled by its people;
  they have disobeyed the laws,
violated the statutes
  and broken the everlasting
      covenant.
⁶Therefore a curse consumes the
      earth;
  its people must bear their guilt.
Therefore earth's inhabitants are
      burned up,
  and very few are left.
⁷The new wine dries up and the
      vine withers;
  all the merrymakers groan.
⁸The gaiety of the tambourines is
      stilled,
  the noise of the revelers has
      stopped,

the joyful harp is silent.
⁹No longer do they drink wine
      with a song;
  the beer is bitter to its drinkers.
¹⁰The ruined city lies desolate;
  the entrance to every house is
      barred.
¹¹In the streets they cry out for
      wine;
  all joy turns to gloom,
  all gaiety is banished from the
      earth.
¹²The city is left in ruins,
  its gate is battered to pieces.
¹³So will it be on the earth
  and among the nations,
as when an olive tree is beaten,
  or as when gleanings are left
      after the grape harvest.

¹⁴They raise their voices, they shout
      for joy;
  from the west they acclaim the
      LORD's majesty.
¹⁵Therefore in the east give glory to
      the LORD;
  exalt the name of the LORD, the
      God of Israel,
  in the islands of the sea.
¹⁶From the ends of the earth we
      hear singing:
  "Glory to the Righteous One."

But I said, "I waste away, I waste
      away!
  Woe to me!
The treacherous betray!
  With treachery the treacherous
      betray!"
¹⁷Terror and pit and snare await
      you,
  O people of the earth.
¹⁸Whoever flees at the sound of
      terror
  will fall into a pit;
whoever climbs out of the pit
  will be caught in a snare.

The floodgates of the heavens are
      opened,
  the foundations of the earth
      shake.
¹⁹The earth is broken up,
  the earth is split asunder,
  the earth is thoroughly shaken.
²⁰The earth reels like a drunkard,

it sways like a hut in the wind;
so heavy upon it is the guilt of its
rebellion
that it falls—never to rise again.

²¹In that day the LORD will punish
the powers in the heavens
above
and the kings on the earth
below.
²²They will be herded together
like prisoners bound in a
dungeon;
they will be shut up in prison
and be punished^a after many
days.
²³The moon will be abashed, the
sun ashamed;
for the LORD Almighty will reign
on Mount Zion and in Jerusalem,
and before its elders, gloriously.

Praise to the LORD

25 O LORD, you are my God;
I will exalt you and praise
your name,
for in perfect faithfulness
you have done marvelous
things,
things planned long ago.
²You have made the city a heap of
rubble,
the fortified town a ruin,
the foreigners' stronghold a city
no more;
it will never be rebuilt.
³Therefore strong peoples will
honor you;
cities of ruthless nations will
revere you.
⁴You have been a refuge for the
poor,
a refuge for the needy in his
distress,
a shelter from the storm
and a shade from the heat.
For the breath of the ruthless
is like a storm driving against a
wall
⁵   and like the heat of the desert.
You silence the uproar of
foreigners;

as heat is reduced by the
shadow of a cloud,
so the song of the ruthless is
stilled.

⁶On this mountain the LORD
Almighty will prepare
a feast of rich food for all
peoples,
a banquet of aged wine—
the best of meats and the finest
of wines.
⁷On this mountain he will destroy
the shroud that enfolds all
peoples,
the sheet that covers all nations;
⁸   he will swallow up death
forever.
The Sovereign LORD will wipe
away the tears
from all faces;
he will remove the disgrace of his
people
from all the earth.
The LORD has spoken.

⁹In that day they will say,

"Surely this is our God;
we trusted in him, and he saved
us.
This is the LORD, we trusted in
him;
let us rejoice and be glad in his
salvation."

¹⁰The hand of the LORD will rest on
this mountain;
but Moab will be trampled
under him
as straw is trampled down in
the manure.
¹¹They will spread out their hands
in it,
as a swimmer spreads out his
hands to swim.
God will bring down their pride
despite the cleverness^b of their
hands.
¹²He will bring down your high
fortified walls
and lay them low;
he will bring them down to the
ground,
to the very dust.

^a22 Or *released*   ^b11 The meaning of the Hebrew for this word is uncertain.

A Song of Praise

26 In that day this song will be sung in the land of Judah:

We have a strong city;
  God makes salvation
    its walls and ramparts.
²Open the gates
  that the righteous nation may
    enter,
  the nation that keeps faith.
³You will keep in perfect peace
  him whose mind is steadfast,
  because he trusts in you.
⁴Trust in the LORD forever,
  for the LORD, the LORD, is the
    Rock eternal.
⁵He humbles those who dwell on
    high,
  he lays the lofty city low;
he levels it to the ground
  and casts it down to the dust.
⁶Feet trample it down—
  the feet of the oppressed,
  the footsteps of the poor.

⁷The path of the righteous is level;
  O upright One, you make the
    way of the righteous
    smooth.
⁸Yes, LORD, walking in the way of
    your laws,ᵃ
  we wait for you;
your name and renown
  are the desire of our hearts.
⁹My soul yearns for you in the
    night;
  in the morning my spirit longs
    for you.
When your judgments come upon
    the earth,
  the people of the world learn
    righteousness.
¹⁰Though grace is shown to the
    wicked,
  they do not learn righteousness;
even in a land of uprightness they
    go on doing evil
  and regard not the majesty of
    the LORD.
¹¹O LORD, your hand is lifted high,
  but they do not see it.

Let them see your zeal for your
    people and be put to
    shame;
  let the fire reserved for your
    enemies consume them.

¹²LORD, you establish peace for us;
  all that we have accomplished
    you have done for us.
¹³O LORD, our God, other lords
    besides you have ruled
    over us,
  but your name alone do we
    honor.
¹⁴They are now dead, they live no
    more;
  those departed spirits do not
    rise.
You punished them and brought
    them to ruin;
  you wiped out all memory of
    them.
¹⁵You have enlarged the nation,
    O LORD;
  you have enlarged the nation.
You have gained glory for
    yourself;
  you have extended all the
    borders of the land.

¹⁶LORD, they came to you in their
    distress;
  when you disciplined them,
  they could barely whisper a
    prayer.ᵇ
¹⁷As a woman with child and about
    to give birth
  writhes and cries out in her
    pain,
so were we in your presence,
    O LORD.
¹⁸We were with child, we writhed
    in pain,
  but we gave birth to wind.
We have not brought salvation to
    the earth;
  we have not given birth to
    people of the world.

¹⁹But your dead will live;
  their bodies will rise.
You who dwell in the dust,
  wake up and shout for joy.

ᵃ8 Or *judgments*   ᵇ16 The meaning of the Hebrew for this clause is uncertain.

Your dew is like the dew of the
    morning;
  the earth will give birth to her
    dead.

²⁰Go, my people, enter your rooms
    and shut the doors behind you;
  hide yourselves for a little while
    until his wrath has passed by.
²¹See, the LORD is coming out of his
    dwelling
  to punish the people of the
    earth for their sins.
The earth will disclose the blood
    shed upon her;
  she will conceal her slain no
    longer.

Deliverance of Israel

27 In that day,

  the LORD will punish with his
    sword,
  his fierce, great and powerful
    sword,
Leviathan the gliding serpent,
  Leviathan the coiling serpent;
he will slay the monster of the sea.

²In that day—

"Sing about a fruitful vineyard:
³ I, the LORD, watch over it;
   I water it continually.
 I guard it day and night
   so that no one may harm it.
⁴ I am not angry.
 If only there were briers and
   thorns confronting me!
   I would march against them in
     battle;
   I would set them all on fire.
⁵Or else let them come to me for
   refuge;
   let them make peace with me,
   yes, let them make peace with
     me."

⁶In days to come Jacob will take
   root,
   Israel will bud and blossom
   and fill all the world with fruit.

⁷Has ⌊the LORD⌋ struck her

as he struck down those who
    struck her?
Has she been killed
  as those were killed who killed
    her?
⁸By warfare*a* and exile you
    contend with her—
  with his fierce blast he drives
    her out,
  as on a day the east wind
    blows.
⁹By this, then, will Jacob's guilt be
    atoned for,
  and this will be the full fruitage
    of the removal of his sin:
When he makes all the altar stones
  to be like chalk stones crushed
    to pieces,
  no Asherah poles*b* or incense
    altars
  will be left standing.
¹⁰The fortified city stands desolate,
  an abandoned settlement,
    forsaken like the desert;
there the calves graze,
  there they lie down;
  they strip its branches bare.
¹¹When its twigs are dry, they are
    broken off
  and women come and make
    fires with them.
For this is a people without
    understanding;
  so their Maker has no
    compassion on them,
  and their Creator shows them
    no favor.

¹²In that day the LORD will thresh
from the flowing Euphrates*c* to the
Wadi of Egypt, and you, O Israelites,
will be gathered up one by one. ¹³And
in that day a great trumpet will
sound. Those who were perishing in
Assyria and those who were exiled in
Egypt will come and worship the
LORD on the holy mountain in Jerusalem.

Woe to Ephraim

28 Woe to that wreath, the pride
    of Ephraim's drunkards,

---

*a*8 See Septuagint; the meaning of the Hebrew for this word is uncertain.   *b*9 That is, symbols
of the goddess Asherah   *c*12 Hebrew *River*

VERSE:
Isaiah 26:19

AUTHOR:
F.B. Meyer

PASSAGE:
Isaiah 26:12–21

The Dew of the Morning

This cheery summons to wake up and shout is addressed to those who dwell in the dust! The world is filled with them—those who dwell in the dark cells of disappointed love and faith, or who have failed in their life's purpose, or who, like Bartimaeus [Mark 10:46], are blind and reduced to beggary ...

It may be that you have lost all sense of God's nearness and love—not because of any known sin, but through physical weakness, mental exhaustion, or the loneliness of sorrow and suffering. It may be that you have been seeking him *without*, whilst he is *within* ...

It may be that you are perplexed by the mystery of unanswered prayer ... No answer comes back from the Infinite, and your prayers seem like vessels lost at sea.

It may be that your life has not realized its early ideals. As the years go forward, they carry us into disillusionment and heartbreak. Life has its prizes and rewards, but they are not for us.

To all such we pass on Isaiah's words: "Wake up and shout for joy. Your dew is like the dew of the morning" (Isaiah 26:19). The dew is used here of the grace and love of God. Instead of *dust* there will be *dew*, which steals so gently and silently over the earth. The more dry and sapless a patch is, the more tenderly does the dew caress it!

ADDITIONAL SCRIPTURE READINGS
Psalm 118:13–21; Hosea 14:4–9

Go to page 880 for your next devotional reading.

to the fading flower, his
glorious beauty,
set on the head of a fertile
valley—
to that city, the pride of those
laid low by wine!
²See, the Lord has one who is
powerful and strong.
Like a hailstorm and a
destructive wind,
like a driving rain and a flooding
downpour,
he will throw it forcefully to the
ground.
³That wreath, the pride of
Ephraim's drunkards,
will be trampled underfoot.
⁴That fading flower, his glorious
beauty,
set on the head of a fertile
valley,
will be like a fig ripe before
harvest—
as soon as someone sees it and
takes it in his hand,
he swallows it.

⁵In that day the LORD Almighty
will be a glorious crown,
a beautiful wreath
for the remnant of his people.
⁶He will be a spirit of justice
to him who sits in judgment,
a source of strength
to those who turn back the
battle at the gate.

⁷And these also stagger from wine
and reel from beer:
Priests and prophets stagger from
beer
and are befuddled with wine;
they reel from beer,
they stagger when seeing
visions,
they stumble when rendering
decisions.
⁸All the tables are covered with
vomit
and there is not a spot without
filth.

⁹"Who is it he is trying to teach?

To whom is he explaining his
message?
To children weaned from their
milk,
to those just taken from the
breast?
¹⁰For it is:

Do and do, do and do,
rule on rule, rule on rule*ᵃ*;
a little here, a little there."

¹¹Very well then, with foreign lips
and strange tongues
God will speak to this people,
¹²to whom he said,
"This is the resting place, let the
weary rest";
and, "This is the place of
repose"—
but they would not listen.
¹³So then, the word of the LORD to
them will become:

Do and do, do and do,
rule on rule, rule on rule;
a little here, a little there—
so that they will go and fall
backward,
be injured and snared and
captured.

¹⁴Therefore hear the word of the
LORD, you scoffers
who rule this people in
Jerusalem.
¹⁵You boast, "We have entered into
a covenant with death,
with the grave*ᵇ* we have made
an agreement.
When an overwhelming scourge
sweeps by,
it cannot touch us,
for we have made a lie our refuge
and falsehood*ᶜ* our hiding
place."

¹⁶So this is what the Sovereign LORD
says:

"See, I lay a stone in Zion,
a tested stone,
a precious cornerstone for a sure
foundation;

ᵃ10 Hebrew / *sav lasav sav lasav* / *kav lakav kav lakav* (possibly meaningless sounds; perhaps a
mimicking of the prophet's words); also in verse 13   *ᵇ15* Hebrew *Sheol*; also in verse 18
ᶜ15 Or *false gods*

the one who trusts will never be
   dismayed.
¹⁷I will make justice the measuring
   line
   and righteousness the plumb
      line;
   hail will sweep away your refuge,
      the lie,
   and water will overflow your
      hiding place.

¹⁸Your covenant with death will be
   annulled;
   your agreement with the grave
      will not stand.
When the overwhelming scourge
   sweeps by,
   you will be beaten down by
      it.
¹⁹As often as it comes it will carry
   you away;

VERSE:	AUTHOR:	PASSAGE:
Isaiah 28:16	Jean Shaw	Isaiah 28:5–19

A Precious Cornerstone

When you're 25, patience is changing a toddler's training pants. At 65, patience is waiting for a 40-year-old daughter to accept Christ as her Lord and Savior. Only from the vantage point of old age can we see the result of our having to wait. The first baby, the move halfway across the country, the new job, the medical breakthrough, the special friend — all came later than we expected. Now we have an expanded though still incomplete understanding of God's grand design. To quote one of our family maxims: "Hindsight is always 20/20."

These are verses of encouragement. Whatever the trial of faith, never despond. "So this is what the Sovereign LORD says: 'See, I lay a stone in Zion, a tested stone, a precious cornerstone for a sure foundation; the one who trusts will never be dismayed' " (Isaiah 28:16). The precious cornerstone is Christ, of greater value than the whole world. In him are all the promises of God. The person who believes these promises and rests on them with a fixed heart will find peace within the will of God.

ADDITIONAL SCRIPTURE READINGS
Romans 10:1–13; 1 Peter 2:4–8

Go to page 887 for your next devotional reading.

morning after morning, by day
and by night,
it will sweep through."

The understanding of this message
will bring sheer terror.
²⁰The bed is too short to stretch out
on,
the blanket too narrow to wrap
around you.
²¹The LORD will rise up as he did at
Mount Perazim,
he will rouse himself as in the
Valley of Gibeon—
to do his work, his strange work,
and perform his task, his alien
task.
²²Now stop your mocking,
or your chains will become
heavier;
the Lord, the LORD Almighty, has
told me
of the destruction decreed
against the whole land.

²³Listen and hear my voice;
pay attention and hear what I
say.
²⁴When a farmer plows for planting,
does he plow continually?
Does he keep on breaking up
and harrowing the soil?
²⁵When he has leveled the surface,
does he not sow caraway and
scatter cummin?
Does he not plant wheat in its
place,ᵃ
barley in its plot,ᵃ
and spelt in its field?
²⁶His God instructs him
and teaches him the right way.

²⁷Caraway is not threshed with a
sledge,
nor is a cartwheel rolled over
cummin;
caraway is beaten out with a rod,
and cummin with a stick.
²⁸Grain must be ground to make
bread;
so one does not go on threshing
it forever.

Though he drives the wheels of
his threshing cart over it,
his horses do not grind it.
²⁹All this also comes from the LORD
Almighty,
wonderful in counsel and
magnificent in wisdom.

Woe to David's City

29 Woe to you, Ariel, Ariel,
the city where David settled!
Add year to year
and let your cycle of festivals go
on.
²Yet I will besiege Ariel;
she will mourn and lament,
she will be to me like an altar
hearth.ᵇ
³I will encamp against you all
around;
I will encircle you with towers
and set up my siege works
against you.
⁴Brought low, you will speak from
the ground;
your speech will mumble out of
the dust.
Your voice will come ghostlike
from the earth;
out of the dust your speech will
whisper.

⁵But your many enemies will
become like fine dust,
the ruthless hordes like blown
chaff.
Suddenly, in an instant,
⁶   the LORD Almighty will come
with thunder and earthquake and
great noise,
with windstorm and tempest
and flames of a devouring
fire.
⁷Then the hordes of all the nations
that fight against Ariel,
that attack her and her fortress
and besiege her,
will be as it is with a dream,
with a vision in the night—
⁸as when a hungry man dreams
that he is eating,

ᵃ25 The meaning of the Hebrew for this word is uncertain.   ᵇ2 The Hebrew for *altar hearth*
sounds like the Hebrew for *Ariel*.

but he awakens, and his hunger
    remains;
as when a thirsty man dreams that
    he is drinking,
but he awakens faint, with his
    thirst unquenched.
So will it be with the hordes of all
    the nations
that fight against Mount Zion.

⁹Be stunned and amazed,
    blind yourselves and be
        sightless;
be drunk, but not from wine,
    stagger, but not from beer.
¹⁰The Lord has brought over you a
        deep sleep:
    He has sealed your eyes (the
        prophets);
    he has covered your heads (the
        seers).

¹¹For you this whole vision is nothing but words sealed in a scroll. And
if you give the scroll to someone who
can read, and say to him, "Read this,
please," he will answer, "I can't; it is
sealed." ¹²Or if you give the scroll to
someone who cannot read, and say,
"Read this, please," he will answer, "I
don't know how to read."

¹³The Lord says:

"These people come near to me
    with their mouth
and honor me with their lips,
    but their hearts are far from me.
Their worship of me
    is made up only of rules taught
        by men.ᵃ
¹⁴Therefore once more I will
        astound these people
    with wonder upon wonder;
the wisdom of the wise will
        perish,
    the intelligence of the intelligent
        will vanish."
¹⁵Woe to those who go to great
        depths
    to hide their plans from the
        Lord,
who do their work in darkness
    and think,

"Who sees us? Who will
    know?"
¹⁶You turn things upside down,
    as if the potter were thought to
        be like the clay!
Shall what is formed say to him
    who formed it,
    "He did not make me"?
Can the pot say of the potter,
    "He knows nothing"?

¹⁷In a very short time, will not
        Lebanon be turned into a
        fertile field
    and the fertile field seem like a
        forest?
¹⁸In that day the deaf will hear the
        words of the scroll,
    and out of gloom and darkness
    the eyes of the blind will see.
¹⁹Once more the humble will rejoice
        in the Lord;
    the needy will rejoice in the
        Holy One of Israel.
²⁰The ruthless will vanish,
    the mockers will disappear,
    and all who have an eye for evil
        will be cut down—
²¹those who with a word make a
        man out to be guilty,
    who ensnare the defender in
        court
    and with false testimony
        deprive the innocent of
        justice.

²²Therefore this is what the Lord,
who redeemed Abraham, says to the
house of Jacob:

"No longer will Jacob be ashamed;
    no longer will their faces grow
        pale.
²³When they see among them their
        children,
    the work of my hands,
they will keep my name holy;
    they will acknowledge the
        holiness of the Holy One of
        Jacob,
    and will stand in awe of the
        God of Israel.
²⁴Those who are wayward in spirit
    will gain understanding;

ᵃ13 Hebrew; Septuagint *They worship me in vain; / their teachings are but rules taught by men*

those who complain will accept
    instruction."

Woe to the Obstinate Nation

30 "Woe to the obstinate
        children,"
    declares the LORD,
    "to those who carry out plans that
        are not mine,
    forming an alliance, but not by
        my Spirit,
    heaping sin upon sin;
²who go down to Egypt
    without consulting me;
who look for help to Pharaoh's
        protection,
    to Egypt's shade for refuge.
³But Pharaoh's protection will be to
        your shame,
    Egypt's shade will bring you
        disgrace.
⁴Though they have officials in Zoan
    and their envoys have arrived
        in Hanes,
⁵everyone will be put to shame
    because of a people useless to
        them,
who bring neither help nor
        advantage,
    but only shame and disgrace."

⁶An oracle concerning the animals
of the Negev:

Through a land of hardship and
        distress,
    of lions and lionesses,
    of adders and darting snakes,
the envoys carry their riches on
        donkeys' backs,
    their treasures on the humps of
        camels,
to that unprofitable nation,
⁷   to Egypt, whose help is utterly
        useless.
Therefore I call her
    Rahab the Do-Nothing.

⁸Go now, write it on a tablet for
        them,
    inscribe it on a scroll,
that for the days to come
    it may be an everlasting
        witness.
⁹These are rebellious people,
    deceitful children,

children unwilling to listen to
        the LORD's instruction.
¹⁰They say to the seers,
    "See no more visions!"
and to the prophets,
    "Give us no more visions of
        what is right!
Tell us pleasant things,
    prophesy illusions.
¹¹Leave this way,
    get off this path,
and stop confronting us
    with the Holy One of Israel!"

¹²Therefore, this is what the Holy
One of Israel says:

"Because you have rejected this
        message,
    relied on oppression
    and depended on deceit,
¹³this sin will become for you
    like a high wall, cracked and
        bulging,
    that collapses suddenly, in an
        instant.
¹⁴It will break in pieces like pottery,
    shattered so mercilessly
that among its pieces not a
        fragment will be found
    for taking coals from a hearth
    or scooping water out of a
        cistern."

¹⁵This is what the Sovereign LORD,
the Holy One of Israel, says:

"In repentance and rest is your
        salvation,
    in quietness and trust is your
        strength,
    but you would have none of it.
¹⁶You said, 'No, we will flee on
        horses.'
    Therefore you will flee!
You said, 'We will ride off on
        swift horses.'
    Therefore your pursuers will be
        swift!
¹⁷A thousand will flee
    at the threat of one;
at the threat of five
    you will all flee away,
till you are left
    like a flagstaff on a
        mountaintop,
    like a banner on a hill."

[18]Yet the LORD longs to be gracious
to you;
he rises to show you
compassion.
For the LORD is a God of justice.
Blessed are all who wait for
him!

[19]O people of Zion, who live in Jerusalem, you will weep no more. How gracious he will be when you cry for help! As soon as he hears, he will answer you. [20]Although the Lord gives you the bread of adversity and the water of affliction, your teachers will be hidden no more; with your own eyes you will see them. [21]Whether you turn to the right or to the left, your ears will hear a voice behind you, saying, "This is the way; walk in it." [22]Then you will defile your idols overlaid with silver and your images covered with gold; you will throw them away like a menstrual cloth and say to them, "Away with you!"

[23]He will also send you rain for the seed you sow in the ground, and the food that comes from the land will be rich and plentiful. In that day your cattle will graze in broad meadows. [24]The oxen and donkeys that work the soil will eat fodder and mash, spread out with fork and shovel. [25]In the day of great slaughter, when the towers fall, streams of water will flow on every high mountain and every lofty hill. [26]The moon will shine like the sun, and the sunlight will be seven times brighter, like the light of seven full days, when the LORD binds up the bruises of his people and heals the wounds he inflicted.

[27]See, the Name of the LORD comes
from afar,
with burning anger and dense
clouds of smoke;
his lips are full of wrath,
and his tongue is a consuming
fire.
[28]His breath is like a rushing
torrent,
rising up to the neck.
He shakes the nations in the sieve
of destruction;

he places in the jaws of the
peoples
a bit that leads them astray.
[29]And you will sing
as on the night you celebrate a
holy festival;
your hearts will rejoice
as when people go up with
flutes
to the mountain of the LORD,
to the Rock of Israel.
[30]The LORD will cause men to hear
his majestic voice
and will make them see his arm
coming down
with raging anger and consuming
fire,
with cloudburst, thunderstorm
and hail.
[31]The voice of the LORD will shatter
Assyria;
with his scepter he will strike
them down.
[32]Every stroke the LORD lays on
them
with his punishing rod
will be to the music of
tambourines and harps,
as he fights them in battle with
the blows of his arm.
[33]Topheth has long been prepared;
it has been made ready for the
king.
Its fire pit has been made deep
and wide,
with an abundance of fire and
wood;
the breath of the LORD,
like a stream of burning sulfur,
sets it ablaze.

Woe to Those Who Rely on Egypt

31 Woe to those who go down to
Egypt for help,
who rely on horses,
who trust in the multitude of their
chariots
and in the great strength of
their horsemen,
but do not look to the Holy One
of Israel,
or seek help from the LORD.
[2]Yet he too is wise and can bring
disaster;

he does not take back his
    words.
He will rise up against the house
    of the wicked,
    against those who help
      evildoers.
³But the Egyptians are men and
    not God;
    their horses are flesh and not
      spirit.
When the LORD stretches out his
    hand,
    he who helps will stumble,
    he who is helped will fall;
    both will perish together.

⁴This is what the LORD says to me:

"As a lion growls,
    a great lion over his prey—
and though a whole band of
    shepherds
    is called together against him,
he is not frightened by their
    shouts
    or disturbed by their clamor—
so the LORD Almighty will come
    down
    to do battle on Mount Zion and
      on its heights.
⁵Like birds hovering overhead,
    the LORD Almighty will shield
      Jerusalem;
    he will shield it and deliver it,
    he will 'pass over' it and will
      rescue it."

⁶Return to him you have so greatly
revolted against, O Israelites. ⁷For in
that day every one of you will reject
the idols of silver and gold your sinful
hands have made.

⁸"Assyria will fall by a sword that
    is not of man;
    a sword, not of mortals, will
      devour them.
They will flee before the sword
    and their young men will be
      put to forced labor.
⁹Their stronghold will fall because
    of terror;
    at sight of the battle standard
      their commanders will
      panic,"

declares the LORD,
    whose fire is in Zion,
    whose furnace is in Jerusalem.

The Kingdom of Righteousness

32 See, a king will reign in
      righteousness
    and rulers will rule with justice.
²Each man will be like a shelter
    from the wind
    and a refuge from the storm,
like streams of water in the desert
    and the shadow of a great rock
      in a thirsty land.

³Then the eyes of those who see
    will no longer be closed,
    and the ears of those who hear
      will listen.
⁴The mind of the rash will know
    and understand,
    and the stammering tongue will
      be fluent and clear.
⁵No longer will the fool be called
    noble
    nor the scoundrel be highly
      respected.
⁶For the fool speaks folly,
    his mind is busy with evil:
He practices ungodliness
    and spreads error concerning
      the LORD;
the hungry he leaves empty
    and from the thirsty he
      withholds water.
⁷The scoundrel's methods are
    wicked,
    he makes up evil schemes
to destroy the poor with lies,
    even when the plea of the
      needy is just.
⁸But the noble man makes noble
    plans,
    and by noble deeds he stands.

The Women of Jerusalem

⁹You women who are so
    complacent,
    rise up and listen to me;
you daughters who feel secure,
    hear what I have to say!
¹⁰In little more than a year

you who feel secure will
tremble;
the grape harvest will fail,
and the harvest of fruit will not
come.
¹¹Tremble, you complacent women;
shudder, you daughters who
feel secure!
Strip off your clothes,
put sackcloth around your
waists.
¹²Beat your breasts for the pleasant
fields,
for the fruitful vines
¹³and for the land of my people,
a land overgrown with thorns
and briers—
yes, mourn for all houses of
merriment
and for this city of revelry.
¹⁴The fortress will be abandoned,
the noisy city deserted;
citadel and watchtower will
become a wasteland
forever,
the delight of donkeys, a
pasture for flocks,
¹⁵till the Spirit is poured upon us
from on high,
and the desert becomes a fertile
field,
and the fertile field seems like a
forest.
¹⁶Justice will dwell in the desert
and righteousness live in the
fertile field.
¹⁷The fruit of righteousness will be
peace;
the effect of righteousness will
be quietness and
confidence forever.
¹⁸My people will live in peaceful
dwelling places,
in secure homes,
in undisturbed places of rest.
¹⁹Though hail flattens the forest
and the city is leveled
completely,
²⁰how blessed you will be,
sowing your seed by every
stream,
and letting your cattle and
donkeys range free.

Distress and Help

33 Woe to you, O destroyer,
you who have not been
destroyed!
Woe to you, O traitor,
you who have not been
betrayed!
When you stop destroying,
you will be destroyed;
when you stop betraying,
you will be betrayed.

²O LORD, be gracious to us;
we long for you.
Be our strength every morning,
our salvation in time of distress.
³At the thunder of your voice, the
peoples flee;
when you rise up, the nations
scatter.
⁴Your plunder, O nations, is
harvested as by young
locusts;
like a swarm of locusts men
pounce on it.

⁵The LORD is exalted, for he dwells
on high;
he will fill Zion with justice and
righteousness.
⁶He will be the sure foundation for
your times,
a rich store of salvation and
wisdom and knowledge;
the fear of the LORD is the key to
this treasure.ᵃ

⁷Look, their brave men cry aloud
in the streets;
the envoys of peace weep
bitterly.
⁸The highways are deserted,
no travelers are on the roads.
The treaty is broken,
its witnessesᵇ are despised,
no one is respected.
⁹The land mournsᶜ and wastes
away,
Lebanon is ashamed and
withers;
Sharon is like the Arabah,
and Bashan and Carmel drop
their leaves.

ᵃ6 Or is a treasure from him   ᵇ8 Dead Sea Scrolls; Masoretic Text / the cities   ᶜ9 Or dries up

VERSE:	AUTHOR:	PASSAGE:
Isaiah 32:17	Charles R. Swindoll	Isaiah 32:9–20

Quietness

Quietness. Oh, how I love it . . . how I need it . . . I cannot be the man I should be without times of quietness. Stillness is an essential part of our growing deeper as we grow older . . .

I am desperately concerned that we slow down and quiet down and gear down our lives so that intermittently each week we carve out time for quietness, solitude, thought, prayer, meditation and soul-searching. Oh, how much agitation will begin to fade away, how insignificant petty differences will seem, how big God will become and how small our troubles will appear! Security, peace and confidence will move right on in.

This is what Isaiah, the prophet, meant when he wrote: "The fruit of righteousness will be peace; the effect of righteousness will be quietness and confidence forever. My people will live in peaceful dwelling places, in secure homes, in undisturbed places of rest" (Isaiah 32:17–18).

You know something? That still, small voice will never shout. God's methods don't change because we are so noisy and busy. He is longing for your attention, your undivided and full attention. He wants to talk with you in times of quietness (with the TV *off*) about your need for understanding, love, compassion, patience, self-control, a calm spirit, genuine humility . . . and wisdom. But he won't run to catch up. He will wait and wait until you finally sit in silence and listen.

ADDITIONAL SCRIPTURE READINGS
Psalm 46; Psalm 131
Go to page 889 for your next devotional reading.

¹⁰"Now will I arise," says the LORD.
    "Now will I be exalted;
    now will I be lifted up.
¹¹You conceive chaff,
    you give birth to straw;
    your breath is a fire that
        consumes you.
¹²The peoples will be burned as if to
        lime;
    like cut thornbushes they will
        be set ablaze."

¹³You who are far away, hear what
        I have done;
    you who are near, acknowledge
        my power!
¹⁴The sinners in Zion are terrified;
    trembling grips the godless:
"Who of us can dwell with the
        consuming fire?
    Who of us can dwell with
        everlasting burning?"
¹⁵He who walks righteously
    and speaks what is right,
who rejects gain from extortion
    and keeps his hand from
        accepting bribes,
who stops his ears against plots of
        murder
    and shuts his eyes against
        contemplating evil—
¹⁶this is the man who will dwell on
        the heights,
    whose refuge will be the
        mountain fortress.
His bread will be supplied,
    and water will not fail him.

¹⁷Your eyes will see the king in his
        beauty
    and view a land that stretches
        afar.
¹⁸In your thoughts you will ponder
        the former terror:
    "Where is that chief officer?
    Where is the one who took the
        revenue?
    Where is the officer in charge of
        the towers?"
¹⁹You will see those arrogant people
        no more,
    those people of an obscure
        speech,

with their strange,
    incomprehensible tongue.

²⁰Look upon Zion, the city of our
        festivals;
    your eyes will see Jerusalem,
    a peaceful abode, a tent that
        will not be moved;
    its stakes will never be pulled up,
        nor any of its ropes broken.
²¹There the LORD will be our Mighty
        One.
    It will be like a place of broad
        rivers and streams.
No galley with oars will ride
        them,
    no mighty ship will sail them.
²²For the LORD is our judge,
    the LORD is our lawgiver,
    the LORD is our king;
    it is he who will save us.

²³Your rigging hangs loose:
    The mast is not held secure,
    the sail is not spread.
Then an abundance of spoils will
        be divided
    and even the lame will carry off
        plunder.
²⁴No one living in Zion will say, "I
        am ill";
    and the sins of those who dwell
        there will be forgiven.

Judgment Against the Nations

34 Come near, you nations, and
        listen;
    pay attention, you peoples!
Let the earth hear, and all that is
        in it,
    the world, and all that comes
        out of it!
²The LORD is angry with all nations;
    his wrath is upon all their
        armies.
He will totally destroy[a] them,
    he will give them over to
        slaughter.
³Their slain will be thrown out,
    their dead bodies will send up a
        stench;

---

*a*2 The Hebrew term refers to the irrevocable giving over of things or persons to the LORD, often
by totally destroying them; also in verse 5.

the mountains will be soaked
  with their blood.
⁴All the stars of the heavens will be
    dissolved
  and the sky rolled up like a
    scroll;
  all the starry host will fall

like withered leaves from the
  vine,
like shriveled figs from the fig
  tree.

⁵My sword has drunk its fill in the
  heavens;

VERSE:
Isaiah 33:24

AUTHOR:
Jacob D. Eppinga

PASSAGE:
Isaiah 33:20–24

The Last Enemy

Within us are intimations of eternity that are verified by Scripture. Paul said, "For to me, to live is Christ and to die is gain" (Philippians 1:21). "No one living in Zion will say, 'I am ill'; and the sins of those who dwell there will be forgiven" (Isaiah 33:24) ... The Bible contains many more references to the life everlasting.

Before we can reach the other shore, however, we need to go through the valley of the shadow of death. It is important to notice that the Bible does not describe it as a mountaintop experience. It is a valley. The Bible is a realistic book. In 1 Corinthians 15:26 death is described as the last enemy. It is understandable, therefore, that many of us approach it with a measure of apprehension ...

Surely, we may trust that the Lord will take us by the hand and lead us through the valley of the shadow. When we are apprehensive, it may help to know we are not alone. John Bunyan, in *Pilgrim's Progress*, tells us that when Christian's wife received a letter saying she would die, she stepped calmly into the river of death without fear. But when Christian made the same journey, he was almost overcome. Even so, both reached the other side. We may be assured that "he will be our guide even to the end" (Psalm 48:14).

ADDITIONAL SCRIPTURE READINGS
Deuteronomy 31:1–8; Psalm 48
Go to page 898 for your next devotional reading.

see, it descends in judgment on
    Edom,
  the people I have totally
    destroyed.
6The sword of the LORD is bathed
    in blood,
  it is covered with fat—
the blood of lambs and goats,
  fat from the kidneys of rams.
For the LORD has a sacrifice in
    Bozrah
  and a great slaughter in Edom.
7And the wild oxen will fall with
    them,
  the bull calves and the great
    bulls.
Their land will be drenched with
    blood,
  and the dust will be soaked
    with fat.

8For the LORD has a day of
    vengeance,
  a year of retribution, to uphold
    Zion's cause.
9Edom's streams will be turned
    into pitch,
  her dust into burning sulfur;
  her land will become blazing
    pitch!
10It will not be quenched night and
    day;
  its smoke will rise forever.
From generation to generation it
    will lie desolate;
  no one will ever pass through it
    again.
11The desert owl[a] and screech
    owl[a] will possess it;
  the great owl[a] and the raven
    will nest there.
God will stretch out over Edom
  the measuring line of chaos
  and the plumb line of
    desolation.
12Her nobles will have nothing there
    to be called a kingdom,
  all her princes will vanish away.
13Thorns will overrun her citadels,
  nettles and brambles her
    strongholds.
She will become a haunt for
  jackals,

a home for owls.
14Desert creatures will meet with
    hyenas,
  and wild goats will bleat to
    each other;
there the night creatures will also
    repose
  and find for themselves places
    of rest.
15The owl will nest there and lay
    eggs,
  she will hatch them, and care
    for her young under the
    shadow of her wings;
there also the falcons will gather,
  each with its mate.

16Look in the scroll of the LORD and
read:

None of these will be missing,
  not one will lack her mate.
For it is his mouth that has given
    the order,
  and his Spirit will gather them
    together.
17He allots their portions;
  his hand distributes them by
    measure.
They will possess it forever
  and dwell there from generation
    to generation.

Joy of the Redeemed

35 The desert and the parched
      land will be glad;
  the wilderness will rejoice and
    blossom.
Like the crocus, 2it will burst into
    bloom;
  it will rejoice greatly and shout
    for joy.
The glory of Lebanon will be
    given to it,
  the splendor of Carmel and
    Sharon;
they will see the glory of the LORD,
  the splendor of our God.

3Strengthen the feeble hands,
  steady the knees that give way;
4say to those with fearful hearts,
  "Be strong, do not fear;
  your God will come,

---

a11 The precise identification of these birds is uncertain.

he will come with vengeance;
with divine retribution
   he will come to save you."

⁵Then will the eyes of the blind be
      opened
   and the ears of the deaf
      unstopped.
⁶Then will the lame leap like a
      deer,
   and the mute tongue shout for
      joy.
Water will gush forth in the
      wilderness
   and streams in the desert.
⁷The burning sand will become a
      pool,
   the thirsty ground bubbling
      springs.
In the haunts where jackals once
      lay,
   grass and reeds and papyrus
      will grow.

⁸And a highway will be there;
   it will be called the Way of
      Holiness.
The unclean will not journey on it;
   it will be for those who walk in
      that Way;
   wicked fools will not go about
      on it.ᵃ
⁹No lion will be there,
   nor will any ferocious beast get
      up on it;
   they will not be found there.
But only the redeemed will walk
      there,
10   and the ransomed of the LORD
      will return.
They will enter Zion with singing;
   everlasting joy will crown their
      heads.
Gladness and joy will overtake
      them,
   and sorrow and sighing will
      flee away.

Sennacherib Threatens Jerusalem

36 In the fourteenth year of King
Hezekiah's reign, Sennacherib
king of Assyria attacked all the fortified cities of Judah and captured

them. ²Then the king of Assyria sent
his field commander with a large
army from Lachish to King Hezekiah
at Jerusalem. When the commander
stopped at the aqueduct of the Upper
Pool, on the road to the Washerman's
Field, ³Eliakim son of Hilkiah the palace administrator, Shebna the secretary, and Joah son of Asaph the recorder went out to him.

⁴The field commander said to them,
"Tell Hezekiah,

" 'This is what the great king,
the king of Assyria, says: On
what are you basing this confidence of yours? ⁵You say you
have strategy and military
strength—but you speak only
empty words. On whom are you
depending, that you rebel
against me? ⁶Look now, you are
depending on Egypt, that splintered reed of a staff, which
pierces a man's hand and
wounds him if he leans on it!
Such is Pharaoh king of Egypt to
all who depend on him. ⁷And if
you say to me, "We are depending on the LORD our God"—isn't
he the one whose high places
and altars Hezekiah removed,
saying to Judah and Jerusalem,
"You must worship before this
altar"?

⁸" 'Come now, make a bargain
with my master, the king of Assyria: I will give you two thousand horses—if you can put riders on them! ⁹How then can you
repulse one officer of the least
of my master's officials, even
though you are depending on
Egypt for chariots and horsemen? ¹⁰Furthermore, have I
come to attack and destroy this
land without the LORD? The LORD
himself told me to march against
this country and destroy it.' "

¹¹Then Eliakim, Shebna and Joah
said to the field commander, "Please

ᵃ8 Or / the simple will not stray from it

speak to your servants in Aramaic, since we understand it. Don't speak to us in Hebrew in the hearing of the people on the wall."

¹²But the commander replied, "Was it only to your master and you that my master sent me to say these things, and not to the men sitting on the wall—who, like you, will have to eat their own filth and drink their own urine?"

¹³Then the commander stood and called out in Hebrew, "Hear the words of the great king, the king of Assyria! ¹⁴This is what the king says: Do not let Hezekiah deceive you. He cannot deliver you! ¹⁵Do not let Hezekiah persuade you to trust in the LORD when he says, 'The LORD will surely deliver us; this city will not be given into the hand of the king of Assyria.'

¹⁶"Do not listen to Hezekiah. This is what the king of Assyria says: Make peace with me and come out to me. Then every one of you will eat from his own vine and fig tree and drink water from his own cistern, ¹⁷until I come and take you to a land like your own—a land of grain and new wine, a land of bread and vineyards.

¹⁸"Do not let Hezekiah mislead you when he says, 'The LORD will deliver us.' Has the god of any nation ever delivered his land from the hand of the king of Assyria? ¹⁹Where are the gods of Hamath and Arpad? Where are the gods of Sepharvaim? Have they rescued Samaria from my hand? ²⁰Who of all the gods of these countries has been able to save his land from me? How then can the LORD deliver Jerusalem from my hand?"

²¹But the people remained silent and said nothing in reply, because the king had commanded, "Do not answer him."

²²Then Eliakim son of Hilkiah the palace administrator, Shebna the secretary, and Joah son of Asaph the recorder went to Hezekiah, with their clothes torn, and told him what the field commander had said.

Jerusalem's Deliverance Foretold

37 When King Hezekiah heard this, he tore his clothes and put on sackcloth and went into the temple of the LORD. ²He sent Eliakim the palace administrator, Shebna the secretary, and the leading priests, all wearing sackcloth, to the prophet Isaiah son of Amoz. ³They told him, "This is what Hezekiah says: This day is a day of distress and rebuke and disgrace, as when children come to the point of birth and there is no strength to deliver them. ⁴It may be that the LORD your God will hear the words of the field commander, whom his master, the king of Assyria, has sent to ridicule the living God, and that he will rebuke him for the words the LORD your God has heard. Therefore pray for the remnant that still survives."

⁵When King Hezekiah's officials came to Isaiah, ⁶Isaiah said to them, "Tell your master, 'This is what the LORD says: Do not be afraid of what you have heard—those words with which the underlings of the king of Assyria have blasphemed me. ⁷Listen! I am going to put a spirit in him so that when he hears a certain report, he will return to his own country, and there I will have him cut down with the sword.' "

⁸When the field commander heard that the king of Assyria had left Lachish, he withdrew and found the king fighting against Libnah.

⁹Now Sennacherib received a report that Tirhakah, the Cushite[a] king ⌊of Egypt⌋, was marching out to fight against him. When he heard it, he sent messengers to Hezekiah with this word: ¹⁰"Say to Hezekiah king of Judah: Do not let the god you depend on deceive you when he says, 'Jerusalem will not be handed over to the king of Assyria.' ¹¹Surely you have heard what the kings of Assyria have done to all the countries, destroying them completely. And will you be delivered? ¹²Did the gods of the nations that were destroyed by my forefa-

---

a9 That is, from the upper Nile region

thers deliver them—the gods of Gozan, Haran, Rezeph and the people of Eden who were in Tel Assar? [13]Where is the king of Hamath, the king of Arpad, the king of the city of Sepharvaim, or of Hena or Ivvah?"

Hezekiah's Prayer

[14]Hezekiah received the letter from the messengers and read it. Then he went up to the temple of the LORD and spread it out before the LORD. [15]And Hezekiah prayed to the LORD: [16]"O LORD Almighty, God of Israel, enthroned between the cherubim, you alone are God over all the kingdoms of the earth. You have made heaven and earth. [17]Give ear, O LORD, and hear; open your eyes, O LORD, and see; listen to all the words Sennacherib has sent to insult the living God.

[18]"It is true, O LORD, that the Assyrian kings have laid waste all these peoples and their lands. [19]They have thrown their gods into the fire and destroyed them, for they were not gods but only wood and stone, fashioned by human hands. [20]Now, O LORD our God, deliver us from his hand, so that all kingdoms on earth may know that you alone, O LORD, are God.[a]"

Sennacherib's Fall

[21]Then Isaiah son of Amoz sent a message to Hezekiah: "This is what the LORD, the God of Israel, says: Because you have prayed to me concerning Sennacherib king of Assyria, [22]this is the word the LORD has spoken against him:

"The Virgin Daughter of Zion
    despises and mocks you.
The Daughter of Jerusalem
    tosses her head as you flee.
[23]Who is it you have insulted and
    blasphemed?
    Against whom have you raised
        your voice

and lifted your eyes in pride?
    Against the Holy One of Israel!
[24]By your messengers
    you have heaped insults on the
        Lord.
And you have said,
    'With my many chariots
I have ascended the heights of the
    mountains,
    the utmost heights of Lebanon.
I have cut down its tallest cedars,
    the choicest of its pines.
I have reached its remotest
    heights,
    the finest of its forests.
[25]I have dug wells in foreign lands[b]
    and drunk the water there.
With the soles of my feet
    I have dried up all the streams
        of Egypt.'

[26]"Have you not heard?
    Long ago I ordained it.
In days of old I planned it;
    now I have brought it to pass,
that you have turned fortified
    cities
    into piles of stone.
[27]Their people, drained of power,
    are dismayed and put to shame.
They are like plants in the field,
    like tender green shoots,
like grass sprouting on the roof,
    scorched[c] before it grows up.

[28]"But I know where you stay
    and when you come and go
    and how you rage against me.
[29]Because you rage against me
    and because your insolence has
        reached my ears,
I will put my hook in your nose
    and my bit in your mouth,
and I will make you return
    by the way you came.

[30]"This will be the sign for you, O Hezekiah:

"This year you will eat what
    grows by itself,

---

[a]20 Dead Sea Scrolls (see also 2 Kings 19:19); Masoretic Text *alone are the* LORD   [b]25 Dead Sea Scrolls (see also 2 Kings 19:24); Masoretic Text does not have *in foreign lands.*   [c]27 Some manuscripts of the Masoretic Text, Dead Sea Scrolls and some Septuagint manuscripts (see also 2 Kings 19:26); most manuscripts of the Masoretic Text *roof / and terraced fields*

and the second year what
   springs from that.
But in the third year sow and
   reap,
   plant vineyards and eat their
     fruit.
³¹Once more a remnant of the house
   of Judah
   will take root below and bear
     fruit above.
³²For out of Jerusalem will come a
   remnant,
   and out of Mount Zion a band
     of survivors.
The zeal of the LORD Almighty
   will accomplish this.

³³"Therefore this is what the LORD
says concerning the king of Assyria:

"He will not enter this city
   or shoot an arrow here.
He will not come before it with
   shield
   or build a siege ramp against it.
³⁴By the way that he came he will
     return;
   he will not enter this city,"
         declares the LORD.
³⁵"I will defend this city and save it,
   for my sake and for the sake of
     David my servant!"

³⁶Then the angel of the LORD went
out and put to death a hundred and
eighty-five thousand men in the Assyrian camp. When the people got up
the next morning—there were all the
dead bodies! ³⁷So Sennacherib king of
Assyria broke camp and withdrew.
He returned to Nineveh and stayed
there.

³⁸One day, while he was worshiping in the temple of his god Nisroch,
his sons Adrammelech and Sharezer
cut him down with the sword, and
they escaped to the land of Ararat.
And Esarhaddon his son succeeded
him as king.

Hezekiah's Illness

38 In those days Hezekiah became
ill and was at the point of

death. The prophet Isaiah son of
Amoz went to him and said, "This is
what the LORD says: Put your house in
order, because you are going to die;
you will not recover."

²Hezekiah turned his face to the
wall and prayed to the LORD, ³"Remember, O LORD, how I have walked
before you faithfully and with wholehearted devotion and have done what
is good in your eyes." And Hezekiah
wept bitterly.

⁴Then the word of the LORD came to
Isaiah: ⁵"Go and tell Hezekiah, 'This
is what the LORD, the God of your father David, says: I have heard your
prayer and seen your tears; I will add
fifteen years to your life. ⁶And I will
deliver you and this city from the
hand of the king of Assyria. I will defend this city.

⁷" 'This is the LORD's sign to you
that the LORD will do what he has
promised: ⁸I will make the shadow
cast by the sun go back the ten steps
it has gone down on the stairway of
Ahaz.' " So the sunlight went back the
ten steps it had gone down.

⁹A writing of Hezekiah king of Judah after his illness and recovery:

¹⁰I said, "In the prime of my life
   must I go through the gates of
     death*ᵃ*
   and be robbed of the rest of my
     years?"
¹¹I said, "I will not again see the
     LORD,
   the LORD, in the land of the
     living;
   no longer will I look on mankind,
   or be with those who now
     dwell in this world.*ᵇ*
¹²Like a shepherd's tent my house
   has been pulled down and
     taken from me.
Like a weaver I have rolled up my
     life,
   and he has cut me off from the
     loom;
   day and night you made an end
     of me.

ᵃ10 Hebrew *Sheol*   *ᵇ11* A few Hebrew manuscripts; most Hebrew manuscripts *in the place of
cessation*

¹³I waited patiently till dawn,
  but like a lion he broke all my
    bones;
  day and night you made an end
    of me.
¹⁴I cried like a swift or thrush,
  I moaned like a mourning dove.
My eyes grew weak as I looked to
    the heavens.
  I am troubled; O Lord, come to
    my aid!"

¹⁵But what can I say?
  He has spoken to me, and he
    himself has done this.
I will walk humbly all my years
  because of this anguish of my
    soul.
¹⁶Lord, by such things men live;
  and my spirit finds life in them
    too.
You restored me to health
  and let me live.
¹⁷Surely it was for my benefit
  that I suffered such anguish.
In your love you kept me
  from the pit of destruction;
you have put all my sins
  behind your back.
¹⁸For the grave[a] cannot praise you,
  death cannot sing your praise;
  those who go down to the pit
    cannot hope for your
      faithfulness.
¹⁹The living, the living—they praise
    you,
  as I am doing today;
fathers tell their children
  about your faithfulness.

²⁰The Lord will save me,
  and we will sing with stringed
    instruments
all the days of our lives
  in the temple of the Lord.

²¹Isaiah had said, "Prepare a poultice of figs and apply it to the boil, and he will recover."

²²Hezekiah had asked, "What will be the sign that I will go up to the temple of the Lord?"

Envoys From Babylon

39 At that time Merodach-Baladan son of Baladan king of Babylon sent Hezekiah letters and a gift, because he had heard of his illness and recovery. ²Hezekiah received the envoys gladly and showed them what was in his storehouses— the silver, the gold, the spices, the fine oil, his entire armory and everything found among his treasures. There was nothing in his palace or in all his kingdom that Hezekiah did not show them.

³Then Isaiah the prophet went to King Hezekiah and asked, "What did those men say, and where did they come from?"

"From a distant land," Hezekiah replied. "They came to me from Babylon."

⁴The prophet asked, "What did they see in your palace?"

"They saw everything in my palace," Hezekiah said. "There is nothing among my treasures that I did not show them."

⁵Then Isaiah said to Hezekiah, "Hear the word of the Lord Almighty: ⁶The time will surely come when everything in your palace, and all that your fathers have stored up until this day, will be carried off to Babylon. Nothing will be left, says the Lord. ⁷And some of your descendants, your own flesh and blood who will be born to you, will be taken away, and they will become eunuchs in the palace of the king of Babylon."

⁸"The word of the Lord you have spoken is good," Hezekiah replied. For he thought, "There will be peace and security in my lifetime."

Comfort for God's People

40 Comfort, comfort my people, says your God.
²Speak tenderly to Jerusalem,
  and proclaim to her
that her hard service has been
    completed,
  that her sin has been paid for,

<hr>

[a]18 Hebrew *Sheol*

that she has received from the
Lord's hand
double for all her sins.

³A voice of one calling:
"In the desert prepare
the way for the Lord[a];
make straight in the wilderness
a highway for our God.[b]
⁴Every valley shall be raised up,
every mountain and hill made
low;
the rough ground shall become
level,
the rugged places a plain.
⁵And the glory of the Lord will be
revealed,
and all mankind together will
see it.
For the mouth of the Lord
has spoken."

⁶A voice says, "Cry out."
And I said, "What shall I cry?"

"All men are like grass,
and all their glory is like the
flowers of the field.
⁷The grass withers and the flowers
fall,
because the breath of the Lord
blows on them.
Surely the people are grass.
⁸The grass withers and the flowers
fall,
but the word of our God stands
forever."

⁹You who bring good tidings to
Zion,
go up on a high mountain.
You who bring good tidings to
Jerusalem,[c]
lift up your voice with a shout,
lift it up, do not be afraid;
say to the towns of Judah,
"Here is your God!"
¹⁰See, the Sovereign Lord comes
with power,
and his arm rules for him.
See, his reward is with him,
and his recompense
accompanies him.

¹¹He tends his flock like a shepherd:
He gathers the lambs in his
arms
and carries them close to his heart;
he gently leads those that have
young.

¹²Who has measured the waters in
the hollow of his hand,
or with the breadth of his hand
marked off the heavens?
Who has held the dust of the
earth in a basket,
or weighed the mountains on
the scales
and the hills in a balance?
¹³Who has understood the mind[d]
of the Lord,
or instructed him as his
counselor?
¹⁴Whom did the Lord consult to
enlighten him,
and who taught him the right
way?
Who was it that taught him
knowledge
or showed him the path of
understanding?

¹⁵Surely the nations are like a drop
in a bucket;
they are regarded as dust on
the scales;
he weighs the islands as though
they were fine dust.
¹⁶Lebanon is not sufficient for altar
fires,
nor its animals enough for
burnt offerings.
¹⁷Before him all the nations are as
nothing;
they are regarded by him as
worthless
and less than nothing.

¹⁸To whom, then, will you compare
God?
What image will you compare
him to?
¹⁹As for an idol, a craftsman casts it,
and a goldsmith overlays it
with gold
and fashions silver chains for it.

---

a3 Or A voice of one calling in the desert: | "Prepare the way for the Lord   b3 Hebrew; Septuagint
make straight the paths of our God   c9 Or O Zion, bringer of good tidings, | go up on a high
mountain. | O Jerusalem, bringer of good tidings   d13 Or Spirit; or spirit

²⁰A man too poor to present such
an offering
selects wood that will not rot.
He looks for a skilled craftsman
to set up an idol that will not
topple.

²¹Do you not know?
Have you not heard?
Has it not been told you from the
beginning?
Have you not understood since
the earth was founded?
²²He sits enthroned above the circle
of the earth,
and its people are like
grasshoppers.
He stretches out the heavens like a
canopy,
and spreads them out like a tent
to live in.
²³He brings princes to naught
and reduces the rulers of this
world to nothing.
²⁴No sooner are they planted,
no sooner are they sown,
no sooner do they take root in
the ground,
than he blows on them and they
wither,
and a whirlwind sweeps them
away like chaff.

²⁵"To whom will you compare me?
Or who is my equal?" says the
Holy One.
²⁶Lift your eyes and look to the
heavens:
Who created all these?
He who brings out the starry host
one by one,
and calls them each by name.
Because of his great power and
mighty strength,
not one of them is missing.

²⁷Why do you say, O Jacob,
and complain, O Israel,
"My way is hidden from the LORD;
my cause is disregarded by my
God"?
²⁸Do you not know?
Have you not heard?
The LORD is the everlasting God,
the Creator of the ends of the
earth.
He will not grow tired or weary,
and his understanding no one
can fathom.
²⁹He gives strength to the weary
and increases the power of the
weak.
³⁰Even youths grow tired and
weary,
and young men stumble and
fall;
³¹but those who hope in the LORD
will renew their strength.
They will soar on wings like
eagles;
they will run and not grow
weary,
they will walk and not be faint.

The Helper of Israel

41 "Be silent before me, you
islands!
Let the nations renew their
strength!
Let them come forward and speak;
let us meet together at the place
of judgment.

²"Who has stirred up one from the
east,
calling him in righteousness to
his service[a]?
He hands nations over to him
and subdues kings before him.
He turns them to dust with his
sword,
to windblown chaff with his
bow.
³He pursues them and moves on
unscathed,
by a path his feet have not
traveled before.
⁴Who has done this and carried it
through,
calling forth the generations
from the beginning?
I, the LORD—with the first of them
and with the last—I am he."

⁵The islands have seen it and fear;
the ends of the earth tremble.
They approach and come forward;
⁶   each helps the other

ᵃ2 Or / whom victory meets at every step

VERSE:
Isaiah 40:28

AUTHOR:
John Timmer

PASSAGE:
Isaiah 40:25–31

When There's No Place to Run

God's power may come in the form of ecstasy, through the experience of mounting up with wings like eagles . . .

But it is not the only form God's power can take . . . Isaiah says that God's strength can also take the form of energy to do a job or to solve a problem or get on with some task. "They will run and not grow weary." This is another way in which to experience God's power. Our faith can motivate us and empower us to get busy with a project that needs doing . . .

Fortunately Isaiah describes still another form that God's power can assume; namely, endurance — the strength to walk and not tire. In some ways this may look like the least desirable of the three forms of divine strength. For who wants to be slowed down to a walk, just barely above consciousness level . . .

The hardest challenges in life come, not at the point of our soaring or of our running, but at the point of our weakness and helplessness, in times when we find it hard to keep going. And there are more of those times in the Christian's life than there are times of soaring and running. In times when there is no occasion to soar and no place to run, the promise of strength to walk and not be faint, minor though it may seem, becomes of major importance.

ADDITIONAL SCRIPTURE READINGS
2 Corinthians 4:7–18; 2 Corinthians 12:7–10

Go to page 900 for your next devotional reading.

and says to his brother, "Be
strong!"
⁷The craftsman encourages the
goldsmith,
and he who smooths with the
hammer
spurs on him who strikes the
anvil.
He says of the welding, "It is
good."
He nails down the idol so it
will not topple.

⁸"But you, O Israel, my servant,
Jacob, whom I have chosen,
you descendants of Abraham
my friend,
⁹I took you from the ends of the
earth,
from its farthest corners I called
you.
I said, 'You are my servant';
I have chosen you and have not
rejected you.
¹⁰So do not fear, for I am with you;
do not be dismayed, for I am
your God.
I will strengthen you and help
you;
I will uphold you with my
righteous right hand.

¹¹"All who rage against you
will surely be ashamed and
disgraced;
those who oppose you
will be as nothing and perish.
¹²Though you search for your
enemies,
you will not find them.
Those who wage war against you
will be as nothing at all.
¹³For I am the LORD, your God,
who takes hold of your right
hand
and says to you, Do not fear;
I will help you.
¹⁴Do not be afraid, O worm Jacob,
O little Israel,
for I myself will help you,"
declares the LORD,
your Redeemer, the Holy One
of Israel.
¹⁵"See, I will make you into a
threshing sledge,

new and sharp, with many
teeth.
You will thresh the mountains and
crush them,
and reduce the hills to chaff.
¹⁶You will winnow them, the wind
will pick them up,
and a gale will blow them
away.
But you will rejoice in the LORD
and glory in the Holy One of
Israel.

¹⁷"The poor and needy search for
water,
but there is none;
their tongues are parched with
thirst.
But I the LORD will answer them;
I, the God of Israel, will not
forsake them.
¹⁸I will make rivers flow on barren
heights,
and springs within the valleys.
I will turn the desert into pools of
water,
and the parched ground into
springs.
¹⁹I will put in the desert
the cedar and the acacia, the
myrtle and the olive.
I will set pines in the wasteland,
the fir and the cypress together,
²⁰so that people may see and know,
may consider and understand,
that the hand of the LORD has
done this,
that the Holy One of Israel has
created it.

²¹"Present your case," says the LORD.
"Set forth your arguments,"
says Jacob's King.
²²"Bring in ⌐ your idols⌐ to tell us
what is going to happen.
Tell us what the former things
were,
so that we may consider them
and know their final outcome.
Or declare to us the things to
come,
23   tell us what the future holds,
so we may know that you are
gods.
Do something, whether good or
bad,

PASSAGE: Isaiah 41:8–16; Isaiah 43:1–13
AUTHOR: Author Unknown

Do Not Fear

Fear not, I am with you; O be not dismayed,
For I am your God and will still give you aid;
I'll strengthen you, help you, and cause you to
    stand,
Upheld by my righteous, omnipotent hand.

When through the deep waters I call you to go,
The rivers of sorrow shall not overflow,
For I will be with you in trouble to bless,
And sanctify to you your deepest distress.

When through fiery trials your pathway shall lie,
My grace, all-sufficient, shall be your supply;
The flame shall not hurt you; I only design
Your dross to consume and your gold to refine.

E'en down to old age all my people shall prove
My sovereign, eternal, unchangeable love;
And then, when grey hairs shall their temples
    adorn,
Like lambs they shall still in my bosom be borne.

Go to page 902 for your next devotional reading.

so that we will be dismayed
  and filled with fear.
24But you are less than nothing
  and your works are utterly
    worthless;
  he who chooses you is
    detestable.

25"I have stirred up one from the
    north, and he comes—
  one from the rising sun who
    calls on my name.
He treads on rulers as if they were
    mortar,
  as if he were a potter treading
    the clay.
26Who told of this from the
    beginning, so we could
    know,
  or beforehand, so we could say,
    'He was right'?
No one told of this,
  no one foretold it,
  no one heard any words from
    you.
27I was the first to tell Zion, 'Look,
    here they are!'
  I gave to Jerusalem a messenger
    of good tidings.
28I look but there is no one—
  no one among them to give
    counsel,
  no one to give answer when I
    ask them.
29See, they are all false!
  Their deeds amount to nothing;
  their images are but wind and
    confusion.

The Servant of the LORD

42 "Here is my servant, whom I
    uphold,
  my chosen one in whom I
    delight;
  I will put my Spirit on him
  and he will bring justice to the
    nations.
2He will not shout or cry out,
  or raise his voice in the streets.
3A bruised reed he will not break,
  and a smoldering wick he will
    not snuff out.
In faithfulness he will bring forth
  justice;

4 he will not falter or be
    discouraged
till he establishes justice on earth.
  In his law the islands will put
    their hope."

5This is what God the LORD says—
  he who created the heavens and
    stretched them out,
  who spread out the earth and
    all that comes out of it,
  who gives breath to its people,
  and life to those who walk on
    it:
6"I, the LORD, have called you in
    righteousness;
  I will take hold of your hand.
I will keep you and will make you
  to be a covenant for the people
  and a light for the Gentiles,
7to open eyes that are blind,
  to free captives from prison
  and to release from the
    dungeon those who sit in
    darkness.

8"I am the LORD; that is my name!
  I will not give my glory to
    another
  or my praise to idols.
9See, the former things have taken
    place,
  and new things I declare;
  before they spring into being
  I announce them to you."

Song of Praise to the LORD

10Sing to the LORD a new song,
  his praise from the ends of the
    earth,
you who go down to the sea, and
    all that is in it,
  you islands, and all who live in
    them.
11Let the desert and its towns raise
    their voices;
  let the settlements where Kedar
    lives rejoice.
Let the people of Sela sing for joy;
  let them shout from the
    mountaintops.
12Let them give glory to the LORD
  and proclaim his praise in the
    islands.
13The LORD will march out like a
    mighty man,

VERSE:	AUTHOR:	PASSAGE:
Isaiah 42:3	Brennan Manning	Isaiah 42:1–9

God Loves Even Me

It is one thing to feel loved by God when our life is together and all our support systems are in place. Then self-acceptance is relatively easy. We may even claim that we are coming to like ourselves. When we are strong, on top, in control, and as the Celts say, "in fine form," a sense of security crystallizes.

But what happens when life falls through the cracks? What happens when we sin and fail, when our dreams shatter, when our investments crash, when we are regarded with suspicion? What happens when we come face to face with the human condition? . . .

God calls us to stop hiding and come openly to him. God is the father who ran to his prodigal son when he came limping home. God weeps over us when shame and self-hatred immobilize us . . .

God loves who we really are—whether we like it or not. God calls us, as he did Adam [Genesis 3:8], to come out of hiding. No amount of spiritual makeup can render us more presentable to him . . .

"Come to me *now*," Jesus says. "Acknowledge and accept who I want to be for you: a Savior of boundless compassion, infinite patience, unbearable forgiveness and love that keeps no score of wrongs. Quit projecting onto me your own feelings about yourself. At this moment your life is a bruised reed and I will not crush it, a smoldering wick and I will not quench it. *You are in a safe place.*"

ADDITIONAL SCRIPTURE READINGS
Jeremiah 31:1–14; Matthew 11:25–30
Go to page 905 for your next devotional reading.

like a warrior he will stir up his
zeal;
with a shout he will raise the
battle cry
and will triumph over his
enemies.
¹⁴"For a long time I have kept
silent,
I have been quiet and held
myself back.
But now, like a woman in
childbirth,
I cry out, I gasp and pant.
¹⁵I will lay waste the mountains and
hills
and dry up all their vegetation;
I will turn rivers into islands
and dry up the pools.
¹⁶I will lead the blind by ways they
have not known,
along unfamiliar paths I will
guide them;
I will turn the darkness into light
before them
and make the rough places
smooth.
These are the things I will do;
I will not forsake them.
¹⁷But those who trust in idols,
who say to images, 'You are our
gods,'
will be turned back in utter
shame.

Israel Blind and Deaf

¹⁸"Hear, you deaf;
look, you blind, and see!
¹⁹Who is blind but my servant,
and deaf like the messenger I
send?
Who is blind like the one
committed to me,
blind like the servant of the
LORD?
²⁰You have seen many things, but
have paid no attention;
your ears are open, but you
hear nothing."
²¹It pleased the LORD
for the sake of his righteousness
to make his law great and
glorious.

²²But this is a people plundered and
looted,
all of them trapped in pits
or hidden away in prisons.
They have become plunder,
with no one to rescue them;
they have been made loot,
with no one to say, "Send them
back."

²³Which of you will listen to this
or pay close attention in time to
come?
²⁴Who handed Jacob over to become
loot,
and Israel to the plunderers?
Was it not the LORD,
against whom we have sinned?
For they would not follow his
ways;
they did not obey his law.
²⁵So he poured out on them his
burning anger,
the violence of war.
It enveloped them in flames, yet
they did not understand;
it consumed them, but they did
not take it to heart.

Israel's Only Savior

43 But now, this is what the
LORD says—
he who created you, O Jacob,
he who formed you, O Israel:
"Fear not, for I have redeemed
you;
I have summoned you by name;
you are mine.
²When you pass through the
waters,
I will be with you;
and when you pass through the
rivers,
they will not sweep over you.
When you walk through the fire,
you will not be burned;
the flames will not set you
ablaze.
³For I am the LORD, your God,
the Holy One of Israel, your
Savior;
I give Egypt for your ransom,
Cushᵃ and Seba in your stead.

ᵃ3 That is, the upper Nile region

⁴Since you are precious and
    honored in my sight,
    and because I love you,
I will give men in exchange for
    you,
    and people in exchange for your
    life.
⁵Do not be afraid, for I am with
    you;
    I will bring your children from
    the east
    and gather you from the west.
⁶I will say to the north, 'Give them
    up!'
    and to the south, 'Do not hold
    them back.'
Bring my sons from afar
    and my daughters from the
    ends of the earth—
⁷everyone who is called by my
    name,
    whom I created for my glory,
    whom I formed and made."

⁸Lead out those who have eyes but
    are blind,
    who have ears but are deaf.
⁹All the nations gather together
    and the peoples assemble.
Which of them foretold this
    and proclaimed to us the former
    things?
Let them bring in their witnesses
    to prove they were right,
    so that others may hear and
    say, "It is true."
¹⁰"You are my witnesses," declares
    the LORD,
    "and my servant whom I have
    chosen,
so that you may know and believe
    me
    and understand that I am he.
Before me no god was formed,
    nor will there be one after me.
¹¹I, even I, am the LORD,
    and apart from me there is no
    savior.
¹²I have revealed and saved and
    proclaimed—
    I, and not some foreign god
    among you.

You are my witnesses," declares
    the LORD, "that I am God.
¹³ Yes, and from ancient days I am
    he.
No one can deliver out of my
    hand.
    When I act, who can reverse
    it?"

God's Mercy and Israel's Unfaithfulness

¹⁴This is what the LORD says—
    your Redeemer, the Holy One
    of Israel:
"For your sake I will send to
    Babylon
    and bring down as fugitives all
    the Babylonians,ᵃ
    in the ships in which they took
    pride.
¹⁵I am the LORD, your Holy One,
    Israel's Creator, your King."

¹⁶This is what the LORD says—
    he who made a way through
    the sea,
    a path through the mighty
    waters,
¹⁷who drew out the chariots and
    horses,
    the army and reinforcements
    together,
    and they lay there, never to rise
    again,
    extinguished, snuffed out like a
    wick:
¹⁸"Forget the former things;
    do not dwell on the past.
¹⁹See, I am doing a new thing!
    Now it springs up; do you not
    perceive it?
I am making a way in the desert
    and streams in the wasteland.
²⁰The wild animals honor me,
    the jackals and the owls,
because I provide water in the
    desert
    and streams in the wasteland,
to give drink to my people, my
    chosen,
²¹ the people I formed for myself
    that they may proclaim my
    praise.

ᵃ14 Or Chaldeans

VERSE:
Isaiah 43:19

AUTHOR:
Max Lucado

PASSAGE:
Isaiah 43:14–21

A New Thing

It's hard to see things grow old. The town in which I grew up is growing old. I was there recently. Some of the buildings are boarded up. Some of the houses are torn down. Some of my teachers are retired; some are buried . . .

My mother still lives in the same house. You couldn't pay her to move. The house that seemed so big when I was a boy now feels tiny. On the wall are pictures of Mom in her youth — her hair autumn-brown, her face irresistibly beautiful. I see her now — still healthy, still vivacious, but with wrinkles, graying hair, slower step. Would that I could wave the wand and make everything new again . . . but I can't.

I can't. But God can. "He restores my soul," wrote the shepherd [Psalm 23:3]. He doesn't reform; he restores. He doesn't camouflage the old; he restores the new. The Master Builder will pull out the original plan and restore it. He will restore the vigor. He will restore the energy. He will restore the hope. He will restore the soul.

When you see how this world grows stooped and weary and then read of a home where everything is made new [see Revelation 21], tell me, doesn't that make you want to go home? What would you give in exchange for a home like that? Would you really rather have a few possessions on earth than eternal possessions in heaven? Would you really choose a life of slavery to passion over a life of freedom? . . . "Great," said Jesus, "is your reward in heaven" [Matthew 5:12]. He must have smiled when he said that line. His eyes must have danced, and his hand must have pointed skyward. For he should know. It was his idea. It was his home.

ADDITIONAL SCRIPTURE READINGS
Psalm 23; Revelation 21:1–5

Go to page 911 for your next devotional reading.

²²"Yet you have not called upon me,
  O Jacob,
 you have not wearied
  yourselves for me, O Israel.
²³You have not brought me sheep
  for burnt offerings,
 nor honored me with your
  sacrifices.
 I have not burdened you with
  grain offerings
 nor wearied you with demands
  for incense.
²⁴You have not bought any fragrant
  calamus for me,
 or lavished on me the fat of
  your sacrifices.
 But you have burdened me with
  your sins
 and wearied me with your
  offenses.

²⁵"I, even I, am he who blots out
  your transgressions, for my own
  sake,
 and remembers your sins no
  more.
²⁶Review the past for me,
 let us argue the matter together;
  state the case for your
  innocence.
²⁷Your first father sinned;
 your spokesmen rebelled
  against me.
²⁸So I will disgrace the dignitaries of
  your temple,
 and I will consign Jacob to
  destruction^a
 and Israel to scorn.

Israel the Chosen

44 "But now listen, O Jacob, my
  servant,
 Israel, whom I have chosen.
²This is what the LORD says—
 he who made you, who formed
  you in the womb,
 and who will help you:
 Do not be afraid, O Jacob, my
  servant,
 Jeshurun, whom I have chosen.
³For I will pour water on the
  thirsty land,

and streams on the dry ground;
 I will pour out my Spirit on your
  offspring,
 and my blessing on your
  descendants.
⁴They will spring up like grass in a
  meadow,
 like poplar trees by flowing
  streams.
⁵One will say, 'I belong to the
  LORD';
 another will call himself by the
  name of Jacob;
 still another will write on his
  hand, 'The LORD's,'
 and will take the name Israel.

The LORD, Not Idols

⁶"This is what the LORD says—
 Israel's King and Redeemer, the
  LORD Almighty:
 I am the first and I am the last;
 apart from me there is no God.
⁷Who then is like me? Let him
  proclaim it.
 Let him declare and lay out
  before me
 what has happened since I
  established my ancient
  people,
 and what is yet to come—
 yes, let him foretell what will
  come.
⁸Do not tremble, do not be afraid.
 Did I not proclaim this and
  foretell it long ago?
 You are my witnesses. Is there any
  God besides me?
 No, there is no other Rock; I
  know not one."

⁹All who make idols are nothing,
 and the things they treasure are
  worthless.
 Those who would speak up for
  them are blind;
 they are ignorant, to their own
  shame.
¹⁰Who shapes a god and casts an
  idol,
 which can profit him nothing?

---

^a28 The Hebrew term refers to the irrevocable giving over of things or persons to the LORD, often
by totally destroying them.

¹¹He and his kind will be put to
    shame;
  craftsmen are nothing but men.
Let them all come together and
    take their stand;
  they will be brought down to
    terror and infamy.

¹²The blacksmith takes a tool
  and works with it in the coals;
he shapes an idol with hammers,
  he forges it with the might of
    his arm.
He gets hungry and loses his
    strength;
  he drinks no water and grows
    faint.
¹³The carpenter measures with a
    line
  and makes an outline with a
    marker;
he roughs it out with chisels
  and marks it with compasses.
He shapes it in the form of man,
  of man in all his glory,
  that it may dwell in a shrine.
¹⁴He cut down cedars,
  or perhaps took a cypress or
    oak.
He let it grow among the trees of
    the forest,
  or planted a pine, and the rain
    made it grow.
¹⁵It is man's fuel for burning;
  some of it he takes and warms
    himself,
  he kindles a fire and bakes
    bread.
But he also fashions a god and
    worships it;
  he makes an idol and bows
    down to it.
¹⁶Half of the wood he burns in the
    fire;
  over it he prepares his meal,
  he roasts his meat and eats his
    fill.
He also warms himself and says,
  "Ah! I am warm; I see the fire."
¹⁷From the rest he makes a god, his
    idol;
  he bows down to it and
    worships.
He prays to it and says,
  "Save me; you are my god."

¹⁸They know nothing, they
    understand nothing;
  their eyes are plastered over so
    they cannot see,
  and their minds closed so they
    cannot understand.
¹⁹No one stops to think,
  no one has the knowledge or
    understanding to say,
"Half of it I used for fuel;
  I even baked bread over its
    coals,
  I roasted meat and I ate.
Shall I make a detestable thing
    from what is left?
  Shall I bow down to a block of
    wood?"
²⁰He feeds on ashes, a deluded
    heart misleads him;
  he cannot save himself, or say,
  "Is not this thing in my right
    hand a lie?"

²¹"Remember these things, O Jacob,
  for you are my servant,
    O Israel.
I have made you, you are my
    servant;
  O Israel, I will not forget you.
²²I have swept away your offenses
    like a cloud,
  your sins like the morning mist.
Return to me,
  for I have redeemed you."

²³Sing for joy, O heavens, for the
    LORD has done this;
  shout aloud, O earth beneath.
Burst into song, you mountains,
  you forests and all your trees,
for the LORD has redeemed Jacob,
  he displays his glory in Israel.

Jerusalem to Be Inhabited

²⁴"This is what the LORD says—
  your Redeemer, who formed
    you in the womb:

I am the LORD,
  who has made all things,
  who alone stretched out the
    heavens,
  who spread out the earth by
    myself,

²⁵who foils the signs of false
    prophets

and makes fools of diviners,
who overthrows the learning of
　　the wise
and turns it into nonsense,
²⁶who carries out the words of his
　　servants
　and fulfills the predictions of
　　his messengers,

who says of Jerusalem, 'It shall be
　　inhabited,'
　of the towns of Judah, 'They
　　shall be built,'
　and of their ruins, 'I will restore
　　them,'
²⁷who says to the watery deep, 'Be
　　dry,
　and I will dry up your streams,'
²⁸who says of Cyrus, 'He is my
　　shepherd
　and will accomplish all that I
　　please;
　he will say of Jerusalem, "Let it
　　be rebuilt,"
　and of the temple, "Let its
　　foundations be laid." '

45 "This is what the Lord says to
　　his anointed,
　to Cyrus, whose right hand I
　　take hold of
　to subdue nations before him
　　and to strip kings of their
　　armor,
　to open doors before him
　　so that gates will not be shut:
²I will go before you
　　and will level the mountains*ᵃ*;
　I will break down gates of bronze
　　and cut through bars of iron.
³I will give you the treasures of
　　darkness,
　　riches stored in secret places,
　so that you may know that I am
　　the Lord,
　　the God of Israel, who
　　summons you by name.
⁴For the sake of Jacob my servant,
　of Israel my chosen,
　I summon you by name
　　and bestow on you a title of
　　honor,

though you do not acknowledge
　me.
⁵I am the Lord, and there is no
　other;
　apart from me there is no God.
　I will strengthen you,
　　though you have not
　　acknowledged me,
⁶so that from the rising of the sun
　　to the place of its setting
　men may know there is none
　　besides me.
　I am the Lord, and there is no
　other.
⁷I form the light and create
　　darkness,
　　I bring prosperity and create
　　disaster;
　I, the Lord, do all these things.

⁸"You heavens above, rain down
　　righteousness;
　　let the clouds shower it down.
　Let the earth open wide,
　　let salvation spring up,
　let righteousness grow with it;
　　I, the Lord, have created it.

⁹"Woe to him who quarrels with
　　his Maker,
　　to him who is but a potsherd
　　among the potsherds on
　　the ground.
　Does the clay say to the potter,
　　'What are you making?'
　Does your work say,
　　'He has no hands'?
¹⁰Woe to him who says to his
　　father,
　　'What have you begotten?'
　or to his mother,
　　'What have you brought to
　　birth?'

¹¹"This is what the Lord says—
　　the Holy One of Israel, and its
　　Maker:
　Concerning things to come,
　　do you question me about my
　　children,
　　or give me orders about the
　　work of my hands?
¹²It is I who made the earth
　　and created mankind upon it.

ᵃ2 Dead Sea Scrolls and Septuagint; the meaning of the word in the Masoretic Text is uncertain.

My own hands stretched out the
    heavens;
  I marshaled their starry hosts.
[13]I will raise up Cyrus[a] in my
    righteousness:
  I will make all his ways
    straight.
He will rebuild my city
  and set my exiles free,
but not for a price or reward,
  says the LORD Almighty."

[14]This is what the LORD says:

"The products of Egypt and the
    merchandise of Cush,[b]
  and those tall Sabeans—
they will come over to you
  and will be yours;
they will trudge behind you,
  coming over to you in chains.
They will bow down before you
  and plead with you, saying,
'Surely God is with you, and there
    is no other;
  there is no other god.' "

[15]Truly you are a God who hides
    himself,
  O God and Savior of Israel.
[16]All the makers of idols will be put
    to shame and disgraced;
  they will go off into disgrace
    together.
[17]But Israel will be saved by the
    LORD
  with an everlasting salvation;
you will never be put to shame or
    disgraced,
  to ages everlasting.

[18]For this is what the LORD says—
he who created the heavens,
  he is God;
he who fashioned and made the
    earth,
  he founded it;
he did not create it to be empty,
  but formed it to be inhabited—
he says:
"I am the LORD,
  and there is no other.
[19]I have not spoken in secret,
  from somewhere in a land of
    darkness;

I have not said to Jacob's
    descendants,
  'Seek me in vain.'
I, the LORD, speak the truth;
  I declare what is right.

[20]"Gather together and come;
  assemble, you fugitives from the
    nations.
Ignorant are those who carry
    about idols of wood,
  who pray to gods that cannot
    save.
[21]Declare what is to be, present it—
  let them take counsel together.
Who foretold this long ago,
  who declared it from the distant
    past?
Was it not I, the LORD?
  And there is no God apart from
    me,
a righteous God and a Savior;
  there is none but me.

[22]"Turn to me and be saved,
  all you ends of the earth;
for I am God, and there is no
    other.
[23]By myself I have sworn,
  my mouth has uttered in all
    integrity
  a word that will not be revoked:
Before me every knee will bow;
  by me every tongue will swear.
[24]They will say of me, 'In the LORD
    alone
  are righteousness and
    strength.' "
All who have raged against him
  will come to him and be put to
    shame.
[25]But in the LORD all the descendants
    of Israel
  will be found righteous and will
    exult.

Gods of Babylon

46 Bel bows down, Nebo stoops
    low;
  their idols are borne by beasts
    of burden.[c]
The images that are carried about
    are burdensome,
  a burden for the weary.

---

[a]13 Hebrew *him*   [b]14 That is, the upper Nile region   [c]1 Or *are but beasts and cattle*

²They stoop and bow down
    together;
  unable to rescue the burden,
  they themselves go off into
      captivity.

³"Listen to me, O house of Jacob,
  all you who remain of the
      house of Israel,
you whom I have upheld since
    you were conceived,
  and have carried since your
      birth.
⁴Even to your old age and gray
    hairs
  I am he, I am he who will
    sustain you.
I have made you and I will carry
    you;
  I will sustain you and I will
    rescue you.

⁵"To whom will you compare me
    or count me equal?
  To whom will you liken me that
      we may be compared?
⁶Some pour out gold from their
    bags
  and weigh out silver on the
    scales;
they hire a goldsmith to make it
    into a god,
  and they bow down and
    worship it.
⁷They lift it to their shoulders and
    carry it;
  they set it up in its place, and
    there it stands.
From that spot it cannot move.
Though one cries out to it, it does
    not answer;
  it cannot save him from his
    troubles.

⁸"Remember this, fix it in mind,
  take it to heart, you rebels.
⁹Remember the former things,
    those of long ago;
  I am God, and there is no other;
  I am God, and there is none like
    me.
¹⁰I make known the end from the
    beginning,

from ancient times, what is still
    to come.
I say: My purpose will stand,
  and I will do all that I please.
¹¹From the east I summon a bird of
    prey;
  from a far-off land, a man to
    fulfill my purpose.
What I have said, that will I bring
    about;
  what I have planned, that will I
    do.
¹²Listen to me, you
    stubborn-hearted,
  you who are far from
    righteousness.
¹³I am bringing my righteousness
    near,
  it is not far away;
  and my salvation will not be
    delayed.
I will grant salvation to Zion,
  my splendor to Israel.

The Fall of Babylon

47 "Go down, sit in the dust,
    Virgin Daughter of Babylon;
sit on the ground without a
    throne,
  Daughter of the Babylonians.ᵃ
No more will you be called
  tender or delicate.
²Take millstones and grind flour;
  take off your veil.
Lift up your skirts, bare your legs,
  and wade through the streams.
³Your nakedness will be exposed
  and your shame uncovered.
I will take vengeance;
  I will spare no one."

⁴Our Redeemer—the LORD
    Almighty is his name—
  is the Holy One of Israel.

⁵"Sit in silence, go into darkness,
    Daughter of the Babylonians;
no more will you be called
  queen of kingdoms.
⁶I was angry with my people
  and desecrated my inheritance;
I gave them into your hand,
  and you showed them no
    mercy.

ᵃ1 Or *Chaldeans*; also in verse 5

VERSE: AUTHOR: PASSAGE:
Isaiah 46:4   Joni Eareckson Tada   Isaiah 46:1–13

Signed, Sealed, Delivered

Warren Wiersbe once said, "Nothing is harder to heal than a broken heart shattered by experiences that seem so meaningless. But God's people don't live on explanations; God's people live on his promises."

A grocery list of Biblical reasons explaining the whys and wherefores behind suffering doesn't always help when you're hurting. What does help are the promises of God. Even though God's promises are usually devoid of standard explanations and don't always detail the blueprint behind his plan, they *do* point to the loving character of our good and kind Lord.

Take Isaiah 46:4. Even for someone bent over with old age and arthritis, God's explanation is simple and powerful: "I am he who will sustain you." God wants us to understand that he alone is the source of help and hope. God owes us no explanations. He did enough explaining on the cross to show that his love is sufficient to meet every need.

Look again at our verse for the day. In one short sentence, God promises that he will rescue, carry and sustain you. How? At least six times God uses the personal pronoun to point to himself. His promises are signed, sealed and delivered on the basis of who he is. And he is faithful. He is loving. He rescues you and carries you. It's a promise.

ADDITIONAL SCRIPTURE READINGS
Psalm 18:16–36; Psalm 61
Go to page 920 for your next devotional reading.

Even on the aged
  you laid a very heavy yoke.
[7]You said, 'I will continue
    forever—
    the eternal queen!'
But you did not consider these
    things
  or reflect on what might
    happen.

[8]"Now then, listen, you wanton
    creature,
  lounging in your security
and saying to yourself,
  'I am, and there is none besides
    me.
I will never be a widow
  or suffer the loss of children.'
[9]Both of these will overtake you
  in a moment, on a single day:
    loss of children and
    widowhood.
They will come upon you in full
    measure,
  in spite of your many sorceries
  and all your potent spells.
[10]You have trusted in your
    wickedness
  and have said, 'No one sees
    me.'
Your wisdom and knowledge
    mislead you
  when you say to yourself,
  'I am, and there is none besides
    me.'
[11]Disaster will come upon you,
  and you will not know how to
    conjure it away.
A calamity will fall upon you
  that you cannot ward off with a
    ransom;
a catastrophe you cannot foresee
  will suddenly come upon you.

[12]"Keep on, then, with your magic
    spells
  and with your many sorceries,
  which you have labored at since
    childhood.
Perhaps you will succeed,
  perhaps you will cause terror.
[13]All the counsel you have received
  has only worn you out!
Let your astrologers come
    forward,

those stargazers who make
    predictions month by
    month,
  let them save you from what is
    coming upon you.
[14]Surely they are like stubble;
  the fire will burn them up.
They cannot even save themselves
  from the power of the flame.
Here are no coals to warm
    anyone;
  here is no fire to sit by.
[15]That is all they can do for you—
  these you have labored with
  and trafficked with since
    childhood.
Each of them goes on in his error;
  there is not one that can save
    you.

Stubborn Israel

48 "Listen to this, O house of
    Jacob,
  you who are called by the name
    of Israel
  and come from the line of
    Judah,
you who take oaths in the name
    of the Lord
  and invoke the God of Israel—
  but not in truth or
    righteousness—
[2]you who call yourselves citizens of
    the holy city
  and rely on the God of Israel—
  the Lord Almighty is his name:
[3]I foretold the former things long
    ago,
  my mouth announced them and
    I made them known;
  then suddenly I acted, and they
    came to pass.
[4]For I knew how stubborn you
    were;
  the sinews of your neck were
    iron,
  your forehead was bronze.
[5]Therefore I told you these things
    long ago;
  before they happened I
    announced them to you
so that you could not say,
  'My idols did them;
  my wooden image and metal
    god ordained them.'

⁶You have heard these things; look
      at them all.
   Will you not admit them?

"From now on I will tell you of
      new things,
   of hidden things unknown to
      you.
⁷They are created now, and not
      long ago;
   you have not heard of them
      before today.
So you cannot say,
   'Yes, I knew of them.'
⁸You have neither heard nor
      understood;
   from of old your ear has not
      been open.
Well do I know how treacherous
      you are;
   you were called a rebel from
      birth.
⁹For my own name's sake I delay
      my wrath;
   for the sake of my praise I hold
      it back from you,
   so as not to cut you off.
¹⁰See, I have refined you, though
      not as silver;
   I have tested you in the furnace
      of affliction.
¹¹For my own sake, for my own
      sake, I do this.
   How can I let myself be
      defamed?
   I will not yield my glory to
      another.

Israel Freed

¹²"Listen to me, O Jacob,
   Israel, whom I have called:
I am he;
   I am the first and I am the last.
¹³My own hand laid the foundations
      of the earth,
   and my right hand spread out
      the heavens;
when I summon them,
   they all stand up together.

¹⁴"Come together, all of you, and
      listen:
   Which of ⌊the idols⌋ has foretold
      these things?

The LORD's chosen ally
   will carry out his purpose
      against Babylon;
   his arm will be against the
      Babylonians.ᵃ
¹⁵I, even I, have spoken;
   yes, I have called him.
I will bring him,
   and he will succeed in his
      mission.

¹⁶"Come near me and listen to this:

"From the first announcement I
      have not spoken in secret;
   at the time it happens, I am
      there."

And now the Sovereign LORD has
      sent me,
   with his Spirit.

¹⁷This is what the LORD says—
   your Redeemer, the Holy One
      of Israel:
"I am the LORD your God,
   who teaches you what is best
      for you,
   who directs you in the way you
      should go.
¹⁸If only you had paid attention to
      my commands,
   your peace would have been
      like a river,
   your righteousness like the
      waves of the sea.
¹⁹Your descendants would have
      been like the sand,
   your children like its
      numberless grains;
their name would never be cut off
   nor destroyed from before me."

²⁰Leave Babylon,
   flee from the Babylonians!
Announce this with shouts of joy
   and proclaim it.
Send it out to the ends of the
      earth;
   say, "The LORD has redeemed
      his servant Jacob."
²¹They did not thirst when he led
      them through the deserts;
   he made water flow for them
      from the rock;

ᵃ14 Or Chaldeans; also in verse 20

he split the rock
  and water gushed out.

²²"There is no peace," says the LORD,
  "for the wicked."

The Servant of the LORD

49 Listen to me, you islands;
  hear this, you distant nations:
Before I was born the LORD called
  me;
  from my birth he has made
    mention of my name.
²He made my mouth like a
    sharpened sword,
  in the shadow of his hand he
    hid me;
he made me into a polished arrow
  and concealed me in his quiver.
³He said to me, "You are my
    servant,
  Israel, in whom I will display
    my splendor."
⁴But I said, "I have labored to no
    purpose;
  I have spent my strength in
    vain and for nothing.
Yet what is due me is in the
    LORD's hand,
  and my reward is with my
    God."

⁵And now the LORD says—
  he who formed me in the womb
    to be his servant
to bring Jacob back to him
  and gather Israel to himself,
for I am honored in the eyes of
    the LORD
  and my God has been my
    strength—
⁶he says:
  "It is too small a thing for you to
    be my servant
  to restore the tribes of Jacob
  and bring back those of Israel I
    have kept.
I will also make you a light for
    the Gentiles,
  that you may bring my
    salvation to the ends of the
    earth."

⁷This is what the LORD says—

the Redeemer and Holy One of
  Israel—
to him who was despised and
    abhorred by the nation,
  to the servant of rulers:
"Kings will see you and rise up,
  princes will see and bow down,
because of the LORD, who is
    faithful,
  the Holy One of Israel, who has
    chosen you."

Restoration of Israel

⁸This is what the LORD says:

"In the time of my favor I will
    answer you,
  and in the day of salvation I
    will help you;
I will keep you and will make you
    to be a covenant for the people,
to restore the land
  and to reassign its desolate
    inheritances,
⁹to say to the captives, 'Come out,'
  and to those in darkness, 'Be
    free!'

"They will feed beside the roads
  and find pasture on every
    barren hill.
¹⁰They will neither hunger nor
    thirst,
  nor will the desert heat or the
    sun beat upon them.
He who has compassion on them
    will guide them
  and lead them beside springs of
    water.
¹¹I will turn all my mountains into
    roads,
  and my highways will be raised
    up.
¹²See, they will come from afar—
  some from the north, some from
    the west,
  some from the region of
    Aswan.ᵃ"

¹³Shout for joy, O heavens;
  rejoice, O earth;
  burst into song, O mountains!
For the LORD comforts his people

ᵃ12 Dead Sea Scrolls; Masoretic Text *Sinim*

and will have compassion on
his afflicted ones.

¹⁴But Zion said, "The LORD has
forsaken me,
the Lord has forgotten me."

¹⁵"Can a mother forget the baby at
her breast
and have no compassion on the
child she has borne?
Though she may forget,
I will not forget you!
¹⁶See, I have engraved you on the
palms of my hands;
your walls are ever before me.
¹⁷Your sons hasten back,
and those who laid you waste
depart from you.
¹⁸Lift up your eyes and look
around;
all your sons gather and come
to you.
As surely as I live," declares the
LORD,
"you will wear them all as
ornaments;
you will put them on, like a
bride.

¹⁹"Though you were ruined and
made desolate
and your land laid waste,
now you will be too small for
your people,
and those who devoured you
will be far away.
²⁰The children born during your
bereavement
will yet say in your hearing,
'This place is too small for us;
give us more space to live in.'
²¹Then you will say in your heart,
'Who bore me these?
I was bereaved and barren;
I was exiled and rejected.
Who brought these up?
I was left all alone,
but these—where have they
come from?' "

²²This is what the Sovereign LORD
says:

"See, I will beckon to the Gentiles,
I will lift up my banner to the
peoples;
they will bring your sons in their
arms
and carry your daughters on
their shoulders.
²³Kings will be your foster fathers,
and their queens your nursing
mothers.
They will bow down before you
with their faces to the
ground;
they will lick the dust at your
feet.
Then you will know that I am the
LORD;
those who hope in me will not
be disappointed."

²⁴Can plunder be taken from
warriors,
or captives rescued from the
fierce*a*?

²⁵But this is what the LORD says:

"Yes, captives will be taken from
warriors,
and plunder retrieved from the
fierce;
I will contend with those who
contend with you,
and your children I will save.
²⁶I will make your oppressors eat
their own flesh;
they will be drunk on their own
blood, as with wine.
Then all mankind will know
that I, the LORD, am your Savior,
your Redeemer, the Mighty One
of Jacob."

Israel's Sin and the Servant's Obedience

50 This is what the LORD says:

"Where is your mother's certificate
of divorce
with which I sent her away?
Or to which of my creditors
did I sell you?

---

*a*24 Dead Sea Scrolls, Vulgate and Syriac (see also Septuagint and verse 25); Masoretic Text *righteous*

Because of your sins you were
    sold;
    because of your transgressions
        your mother was sent
        away.
²When I came, why was there no
    one?
    When I called, why was there
        no one to answer?
Was my arm too short to ransom
    you?
    Do I lack the strength to rescue
        you?
By a mere rebuke I dry up the sea,
    I turn rivers into a desert;
their fish rot for lack of water
    and die of thirst.
³I clothe the sky with darkness
    and make sackcloth its
        covering."

⁴The Sovereign LORD has given me
    an instructed tongue,
    to know the word that sustains
        the weary.
He wakens me morning by
    morning,
    wakens my ear to listen like one
        being taught.
⁵The Sovereign LORD has opened
    my ears,
    and I have not been rebellious;
    I have not drawn back.
⁶I offered my back to those who
    beat me,
    my cheeks to those who pulled
        out my beard;
I did not hide my face
    from mocking and spitting.
⁷Because the Sovereign LORD helps
    me,
    I will not be disgraced.
Therefore have I set my face like
    flint,
    and I know I will not be put to
        shame.
⁸He who vindicates me is near.
    Who then will bring charges
        against me?
    Let us face each other!
Who is my accuser?
    Let him confront me!
⁹It is the Sovereign LORD who helps
    me.

Who is he that will condemn
    me?
They will all wear out like a
    garment;
    the moths will eat them up.

¹⁰Who among you fears the LORD
    and obeys the word of his
        servant?
Let him who walks in the dark,
    who has no light,
trust in the name of the LORD
    and rely on his God.
¹¹But now, all you who light fires
    and provide yourselves with
        flaming torches,
go, walk in the light of your fires
    and of the torches you have set
        ablaze.
This is what you shall receive
    from my hand:
    You will lie down in torment.

Everlasting Salvation for Zion

51 "Listen to me, you who
    pursue righteousness
    and who seek the LORD:
Look to the rock from which you
    were cut
    and to the quarry from which
        you were hewn;
²look to Abraham, your father,
    and to Sarah, who gave you
        birth.
When I called him he was but
    one,
    and I blessed him and made
        him many.
³The LORD will surely comfort Zion
    and will look with compassion
        on all her ruins;
he will make her deserts like
    Eden,
    her wastelands like the garden
        of the LORD.
Joy and gladness will be found in
    her,
    thanksgiving and the sound of
        singing.

⁴"Listen to me, my people;
    hear me, my nation:
The law will go out from me;
    my justice will become a light
        to the nations.

⁵My righteousness draws near
    speedily,
  my salvation is on the way,
  and my arm will bring justice to
      the nations.
The islands will look to me
  and wait in hope for my arm.
⁶Lift up your eyes to the heavens,
  look at the earth beneath;
the heavens will vanish like
    smoke,
  the earth will wear out like a
      garment
  and its inhabitants die like flies.
But my salvation will last forever,
  my righteousness will never fail.

⁷"Hear me, you who know what is
    right,
  you people who have my law in
      your hearts:
Do not fear the reproach of men
  or be terrified by their insults.
⁸For the moth will eat them up like
    a garment;
  the worm will devour them like
      wool.
But my righteousness will last
    forever,
  my salvation through all
      generations."

⁹Awake, awake! Clothe yourself
    with strength,
  O arm of the LORD;
awake, as in days gone by,
  as in generations of old.
Was it not you who cut Rahab to
    pieces,
  who pierced that monster
      through?
¹⁰Was it not you who dried up the
    sea,
  the waters of the great deep,
who made a road in the depths of
    the sea
  so that the redeemed might
      cross over?
¹¹The ransomed of the LORD will
    return.
  They will enter Zion with
      singing;
  everlasting joy will crown their
      heads.
Gladness and joy will overtake
    them,

and sorrow and sighing will
    flee away.

¹²"I, even I, am he who comforts
    you.
Who are you that you fear
    mortal men,
  the sons of men, who are but
      grass,
¹³that you forget the LORD your
    Maker,
  who stretched out the heavens
  and laid the foundations of the
      earth,
that you live in constant terror
    every day
  because of the wrath of the
      oppressor,
  who is bent on destruction?
For where is the wrath of the
    oppressor?
¹⁴ The cowering prisoners will
      soon be set free;
  they will not die in their dungeon,
  nor will they lack bread.
¹⁵For I am the LORD your God,
  who churns up the sea so that
      its waves roar—
  the LORD Almighty is his name.
¹⁶I have put my words in your
    mouth
  and covered you with the
      shadow of my hand—
I who set the heavens in place,
  who laid the foundations of the
      earth,
  and who say to Zion, 'You are
      my people.' "

The Cup of the LORD's Wrath

¹⁷Awake, awake!
  Rise up, O Jerusalem,
you who have drunk from the
    hand of the LORD
  the cup of his wrath,
you who have drained to its dregs
  the goblet that makes men
      stagger.
¹⁸Of all the sons she bore
  there was none to guide her;
of all the sons she reared
  there was none to take her by
      the hand.
¹⁹These double calamities have
    come upon you—

who can comfort you?—
ruin and destruction, famine and
sword—
who can*a* console you?
²⁰Your sons have fainted;
they lie at the head of every
street,
like antelope caught in a net.
They are filled with the wrath of
the LORD
and the rebuke of your God.

²¹Therefore hear this, you afflicted
one,
made drunk, but not with wine.
²²This is what your Sovereign LORD
says,
your God, who defends his
people:
"See, I have taken out of your
hand
the cup that made you stagger;
from that cup, the goblet of my
wrath,
you will never drink again.
²³I will put it into the hands of your
tormentors,
who said to you,
'Fall prostrate that we may walk
over you.'
And you made your back like the
ground,
like a street to be walked over."

52 Awake, awake, O Zion,
clothe yourself with strength.
Put on your garments of splendor,
O Jerusalem, the holy city.
The uncircumcised and defiled
will not enter you again.
²Shake off your dust;
rise up, sit enthroned,
O Jerusalem.
Free yourself from the chains on
your neck,
O captive Daughter of Zion.

³For this is what the LORD says:

"You were sold for nothing,
and without money you will be
redeemed."

⁴For this is what the Sovereign LORD
says:

"At first my people went down to
Egypt to live;
lately, Assyria has oppressed
them.

⁵"And now what do I have here?"
declares the LORD.

"For my people have been taken
away for nothing,
and those who rule them
mock,*b*"
declares the LORD.

"And all day long
my name is constantly
blasphemed.
⁶Therefore my people will know
my name;
therefore in that day they will
know
that it is I who foretold it.
Yes, it is I."

⁷How beautiful on the mountains
are the feet of those who bring
good news,
who proclaim peace,
who bring good tidings,
who proclaim salvation,
who say to Zion,
"Your God reigns!"
⁸Listen! Your watchmen lift up
their voices;
together they shout for joy.
When the LORD returns to Zion,
they will see it with their own
eyes.
⁹Burst into songs of joy together,
you ruins of Jerusalem,
for the LORD has comforted his
people,
he has redeemed Jerusalem.
¹⁰The LORD will lay bare his holy
arm
in the sight of all the nations,
and all the ends of the earth will
see
the salvation of our God.

¹¹Depart, depart, go out from there!
Touch no unclean thing!

a19 Dead Sea Scrolls, Septuagint, Vulgate and Syriac; Masoretic Text / *how can I*   *b5* Dead Sea
Scrolls and Vulgate; Masoretic Text *wail*

Come out from it and be pure,
you who carry the vessels of the
LORD.
[12]But you will not leave in haste
or go in flight;
for the LORD will go before you,
the God of Israel will be your
rear guard.

The Suffering and Glory
of the Servant

[13]See, my servant will act wisely[a];
he will be raised and lifted up
and highly exalted.
[14]Just as there were many who were
appalled at him[b]—
his appearance was so
disfigured beyond that of
any man
and his form marred beyond
human likeness—
[15]so will he sprinkle many
nations,[c]
and kings will shut their
mouths because of him.
For what they were not told, they
will see,
and what they have not heard,
they will understand.

53 Who has believed our
message
and to whom has the arm of the
LORD been revealed?
[2]He grew up before him like a
tender shoot,
and like a root out of dry
ground.
He had no beauty or majesty to
attract us to him,
nothing in his appearance that
we should desire him.
[3]He was despised and rejected by
men,
a man of sorrows, and familiar
with suffering.
Like one from whom men hide
their faces
he was despised, and we
esteemed him not.

[4]Surely he took up our infirmities
and carried our sorrows,
yet we considered him stricken by
God,
smitten by him, and afflicted.
[5]But he was pierced for our
transgressions,
he was crushed for our
iniquities;
the punishment that brought us
peace was upon him,
and by his wounds we are
healed.
[6]We all, like sheep, have gone
astray,
each of us has turned to his
own way;
and the LORD has laid on him
the iniquity of us all.

[7]He was oppressed and afflicted,
yet he did not open his mouth;
he was led like a lamb to the
slaughter,
and as a sheep before her
shearers is silent,
so he did not open his mouth.
[8]By oppression[d] and judgment he
was taken away.
And who can speak of his
descendants?
For he was cut off from the land
of the living;
for the transgression of my
people he was stricken.[e]
[9]He was assigned a grave with the
wicked,
and with the rich in his death,
though he had done no violence,
nor was any deceit in his
mouth.

[10]Yet it was the LORD's will to crush
him and cause him to
suffer,
and though the LORD makes[f]
his life a guilt offering,
he will see his offspring and
prolong his days,
and the will of the LORD will
prosper in his hand.

---

[a]13 Or *will prosper*   [b]14 Hebrew *you*   [c]15 Hebrew; Septuagint *so will many nations marvel at him*   [d]8 Or *From arrest*   [e]8 Or *away. / Yet who of his generation considered / that he was cut off from the land of the living / for the transgression of my people, / to whom the blow was due?*   [f]10 Hebrew *though you make*

11After the suffering of his soul,
   he will see the light ⌊of life⌋[a]
   and be satisfied[b];
by his knowledge[c] my righteous
   servant will justify many,
   and he will bear their iniquities.
12Therefore I will give him a portion
   among the great,[d]
and he will divide the spoils
   with the strong,[e]
because he poured out his life
   unto death,
and was numbered with the
   transgressors.

For he bore the sin of many,
   and made intercession for the
   transgressors.

The Future Glory of Zion

54 "Sing, O barren woman,
   you who never bore a child;
burst into song, shout for joy,
   you who were never in labor;
because more are the children of
   the desolate woman
than of her who has a
   husband,"
                      says the LORD.

---

[a]11 Dead Sea Scrolls (see also Septuagint); Masoretic Text does not have *the light ⌊of life⌋.*
[b]11 Or (with Masoretic Text) 11*He will see the result of the suffering of his soul / and be satisfied*
[c]11 Or *by knowledge of him*   [d]12 Or *many*   [e]12 Or *numerous*

THURSDAY

VERSE: AUTHOR: PASSAGE:
Isaiah 53:6   R.A. Torrey   Isaiah 53:1–12

The Sunlight of God's Favor

If you are this moment troubled about any sin that you have ever committed, either in the past or in the present, just look at Jesus on the cross; believe what God tells you about him, that this sin which troubles you was laid upon him (Isaiah 53:6).

Thank God that the sin is all settled, be full of gratitude to Jesus, who bore it in your place, and trouble about it no more. It is an act of base ingratitude to God to brood over sins that he in his infinite love has canceled. Keep looking at Christ on the cross and walk always in the sunlight of God's favor. This favor of God has been purchased for you at great cost. Gratitude demands that you should always believe in it and walk in the light of it.

ADDITIONAL SCRIPTURE READINGS
John 1:1–18; 1 Peter 2:18–25

Go to page 934 for your next devotional reading.

²"Enlarge the place of your tent,
   stretch your tent curtains wide,
   do not hold back;
lengthen your cords,
   strengthen your stakes.
³For you will spread out to the
   right and to the left;
   your descendants will
     dispossess nations
   and settle in their desolate
     cities.

⁴"Do not be afraid; you will not
   suffer shame.
   Do not fear disgrace; you will
     not be humiliated.
You will forget the shame of your
   youth
   and remember no more the
     reproach of your
     widowhood.
⁵For your Maker is your
     husband—
   the LORD Almighty is his
     name—
the Holy One of Israel is your
   Redeemer;
   he is called the God of all the
     earth.
⁶The LORD will call you back
   as if you were a wife deserted
     and distressed in spirit—
a wife who married young,
   only to be rejected," says your
     God.
⁷"For a brief moment I abandoned
   you,
   but with deep compassion I will
     bring you back.
⁸In a surge of anger
   I hid my face from you for a
     moment,
but with everlasting kindness
   I will have compassion on you,"
   says the LORD your Redeemer.

⁹"To me this is like the days of
     Noah,
   when I swore that the waters of
     Noah would never again
     cover the earth.
So now I have sworn not to be
   angry with you,

   never to rebuke you again.
¹⁰Though the mountains be shaken
   and the hills be removed,
   yet my unfailing love for you will
     not be shaken
   nor my covenant of peace be
     removed,"
   says the LORD, who has
     compassion on you.

¹¹"O afflicted city, lashed by storms
   and not comforted,
   I will build you with stones of
     turquoise,^a
   your foundations with
     sapphires.^b
¹²I will make your battlements of
     rubies,
   your gates of sparkling jewels,
   and all your walls of precious
     stones.
¹³All your sons will be taught by
     the LORD,
   and great will be your
     children's peace.
¹⁴In righteousness you will be
   established:
Tyranny will be far from you;
   you will have nothing to fear.
Terror will be far removed;
   it will not come near you.
¹⁵If anyone does attack you, it will
   not be my doing;
   whoever attacks you will
     surrender to you.

¹⁶"See, it is I who created the
     blacksmith
   who fans the coals into flame
   and forges a weapon fit for its
     work.
And it is I who have created the
     destroyer to work havoc;
¹⁷   no weapon forged against you
     will prevail,
   and you will refute every
     tongue that accuses you.
This is the heritage of the servants
   of the LORD,
   and this is their vindication
     from me,"
          declares the LORD.

---

^a11 The meaning of the Hebrew for this word is uncertain.   ^b11 Or *lapis lazuli*

Invitation to the Thirsty

55 "Come, all you who are
thirsty,
come to the waters;
and you who have no money,
come, buy and eat!
Come, buy wine and milk
without money and without
cost.
²Why spend money on what is not
bread,
and your labor on what does
not satisfy?
Listen, listen to me, and eat what
is good,
and your soul will delight in
the richest of fare.
³Give ear and come to me;
hear me, that your soul may
live.
I will make an everlasting
covenant with you,
my faithful love promised to
David.
⁴See, I have made him a witness to
the peoples,
a leader and commander of the
peoples.
⁵Surely you will summon nations
you know not,
and nations that do not know
you will hasten to you,
because of the LORD your God,
the Holy One of Israel,
for he has endowed you with
splendor."

⁶Seek the LORD while he may be
found;
call on him while he is near.
⁷Let the wicked forsake his way
and the evil man his thoughts.
Let him turn to the LORD, and he
will have mercy on him,
and to our God, for he will
freely pardon.

⁸"For my thoughts are not your
thoughts,
neither are your ways my
ways,"
declares the LORD.
⁹"As the heavens are higher than
the earth,
so are my ways higher than
your ways
and my thoughts than your
thoughts.
¹⁰As the rain and the snow
come down from heaven,
and do not return to it
without watering the earth
and making it bud and flourish,
so that it yields seed for the
sower and bread for the
eater,
¹¹so is my word that goes out from
my mouth:
It will not return to me empty,
but will accomplish what I desire
and achieve the purpose for
which I sent it.
¹²You will go out in joy
and be led forth in peace;
the mountains and hills
will burst into song before you,
and all the trees of the field
will clap their hands.
¹³Instead of the thornbush will grow
the pine tree,
and instead of briers the myrtle
will grow.
This will be for the LORD's renown,
for an everlasting sign,
which will not be destroyed."

Salvation for Others

56 This is what the LORD says:

"Maintain justice
and do what is right,
for my salvation is close at hand
and my righteousness will soon
be revealed.
²Blessed is the man who does this,
the man who holds it fast,
who keeps the Sabbath without
desecrating it,
and keeps his hand from doing
any evil."

³Let no foreigner who has bound
himself to the LORD say,
"The LORD will surely exclude
me from his people."
And let not any eunuch complain,
"I am only a dry tree."

⁴For this is what the LORD says:

"To the eunuchs who keep my
    Sabbaths,
who choose what pleases me
    and hold fast to my covenant—
⁵to them I will give within my
    temple and its walls
a memorial and a name
    better than sons and daughters;
I will give them an everlasting
    name
that will not be cut off.
⁶And foreigners who bind
    themselves to the LORD
    to serve him,
to love the name of the LORD,
    and to worship him,
all who keep the Sabbath without
    desecrating it
and who hold fast to my
    covenant—
⁷these I will bring to my holy
    mountain
and give them joy in my house
    of prayer.
Their burnt offerings and sacrifices
    will be accepted on my altar;
for my house will be called
    a house of prayer for all
    nations."
⁸The Sovereign LORD declares—
    he who gathers the exiles of
    Israel:
"I will gather still others to them
    besides those already gathered."

God's Accusation Against
the Wicked

⁹Come, all you beasts of the field,
    come and devour, all you beasts
    of the forest!
¹⁰Israel's watchmen are blind,
    they all lack knowledge;
they are all mute dogs,
    they cannot bark;
they lie around and dream,
    they love to sleep.
¹¹They are dogs with mighty
    appetites;
    they never have enough.
They are shepherds who lack
    understanding;
they all turn to their own way,
    each seeks his own gain.

¹²"Come," each one cries, "let me
    get wine!
Let us drink our fill of beer!
And tomorrow will be like today,
    or even far better."

57 The righteous perish,
    and no one ponders it in his
    heart;
devout men are taken away,
    and no one understands
that the righteous are taken away
    to be spared from evil.
²Those who walk uprightly
    enter into peace;
    they find rest as they lie in
    death.

³"But you—come here, you sons of
    a sorceress,
    you offspring of adulterers and
    prostitutes!
⁴Whom are you mocking?
    At whom do you sneer
    and stick out your tongue?
Are you not a brood of rebels,
    the offspring of liars?
⁵You burn with lust among the
    oaks
    and under every spreading tree;
you sacrifice your children in the
    ravines
    and under the overhanging
    crags.
⁶⌊The idols⌋ among the smooth
    stones of the ravines are
    your portion;
    they, they are your lot.
Yes, to them you have poured out
    drink offerings
    and offered grain offerings.
In the light of these things,
    should I relent?
⁷You have made your bed on a
    high and lofty hill;
    there you went up to offer your
    sacrifices.
⁸Behind your doors and your
    doorposts
    you have put your pagan
    symbols.
Forsaking me, you uncovered your
    bed,
    you climbed into it and opened
    it wide;

you made a pact with those whose
beds you love,
and you looked on their
nakedness.
[9]You went to Molech[a] with olive
oil
and increased your perfumes.
You sent your ambassadors[b] far
away;
you descended to the grave[c]
itself!
[10]You were wearied by all your
ways,
but you would not say, 'It is
hopeless.'
You found renewal of your
strength,
and so you did not faint.
[11]"Whom have you so dreaded and
feared
that you have been false to me,
and have neither remembered me
nor pondered this in your
hearts?
Is it not because I have long been
silent
that you do not fear me?
[12]I will expose your righteousness
and your works,
and they will not benefit you.
[13]When you cry out for help,
let your collection ⌊of idols⌋ save
you!
The wind will carry all of them
off,
a mere breath will blow them
away.
But the man who makes me his
refuge
will inherit the land
and possess my holy
mountain."

Comfort for the Contrite

[14]And it will be said:

"Build up, build up, prepare the
road!
Remove the obstacles out of the
way of my people."
[15]For this is what the high and lofty
One says—

he who lives forever, whose
name is holy:
"I live in a high and holy place,
but also with him who is
contrite and lowly in spirit,
to revive the spirit of the lowly
and to revive the heart of the
contrite.
[16]I will not accuse forever,
nor will I always be angry,
for then the spirit of man would
grow faint before me—
the breath of man that I have
created.
[17]I was enraged by his sinful greed;
I punished him, and hid my
face in anger,
yet he kept on in his willful
ways.
[18]I have seen his ways, but I will
heal him;
I will guide him and restore
comfort to him,
[19]   creating praise on the lips of the
mourners in Israel.
Peace, peace, to those far and
near,"
says the LORD. "And I will heal
them."
[20]But the wicked are like the tossing
sea,
which cannot rest,
whose waves cast up mire and
mud.
[21]"There is no peace," says my God,
"for the wicked."

True Fasting

58 "Shout it aloud, do not hold
back.
Raise your voice like a trumpet.
Declare to my people their
rebellion
and to the house of Jacob their
sins.
[2]For day after day they seek me
out;
they seem eager to know my
ways,
as if they were a nation that does
what is right
and has not forsaken the
commands of its God.

---

[a]9 Or *to the king*   [b]9 Or *idols*   [c]9 Hebrew *Sheol*

They ask me for just decisions
    and seem eager for God to
        come near them.
³'Why have we fasted,' they say,
    'and you have not seen it?
Why have we humbled ourselves,
    and you have not noticed?'

"Yet on the day of your fasting,
    you do as you please
and exploit all your workers.
⁴Your fasting ends in quarreling
    and strife,
    and in striking each other with
        wicked fists.
You cannot fast as you do today
    and expect your voice to be
        heard on high.
⁵Is this the kind of fast I have
    chosen,
    only a day for a man to humble
        himself?
Is it only for bowing one's head
    like a reed
    and for lying on sackcloth and
        ashes?
Is that what you call a fast,
    a day acceptable to the LORD?

⁶"Is not this the kind of fasting I
    have chosen:
to loose the chains of injustice
    and untie the cords of the yoke,
to set the oppressed free
    and break every yoke?
⁷Is it not to share your food with
    the hungry
    and to provide the poor
        wanderer with shelter—
when you see the naked, to clothe
    him,
    and not to turn away from your
        own flesh and blood?
⁸Then your light will break forth
    like the dawn,
    and your healing will quickly
        appear;
then your righteousness*ᵃ* will go
    before you,
    and the glory of the LORD will
        be your rear guard.

⁹Then you will call, and the LORD
    will answer;
    you will cry for help, and he
        will say: Here am I.

"If you do away with the yoke of
    oppression,
    with the pointing finger and
        malicious talk,
¹⁰and if you spend yourselves in
    behalf of the hungry
    and satisfy the needs of the
        oppressed,
then your light will rise in the
    darkness,
    and your night will become like
        the noonday.
¹¹The LORD will guide you always;
    he will satisfy your needs in a
        sun-scorched land
    and will strengthen your frame.
You will be like a well-watered
    garden,
    like a spring whose waters
        never fail.
¹²Your people will rebuild the
    ancient ruins
    and will raise up the age-old
        foundations;
you will be called Repairer of
    Broken Walls,
    Restorer of Streets with
        Dwellings.

¹³"If you keep your feet from
    breaking the Sabbath
    and from doing as you please
        on my holy day,
if you call the Sabbath a delight
    and the LORD's holy day
        honorable,
and if you honor it by not going
    your own way
    and not doing as you please or
        speaking idle words,
¹⁴then you will find your joy in the
    LORD,
    and I will cause you to ride on
        the heights of the land
    and to feast on the inheritance
        of your father Jacob."
        The mouth of the LORD
            has spoken.

ᵃ8 Or *your righteous One*

Sin, Confession and Redemption

59 Surely the arm of the LORD is
not too short to save,
nor his ear too dull to hear.
²But your iniquities have separated
you from your God;
your sins have hidden his face
from you,
so that he will not hear.
³For your hands are stained with
blood,
your fingers with guilt.
Your lips have spoken lies,
and your tongue mutters
wicked things.
⁴No one calls for justice;
no one pleads his case with
integrity.
They rely on empty arguments
and speak lies;
they conceive trouble and give
birth to evil.
⁵They hatch the eggs of vipers
and spin a spider's web.
Whoever eats their eggs will die,
and when one is broken, an
adder is hatched.
⁶Their cobwebs are useless for
clothing;
they cannot cover themselves
with what they make.
Their deeds are evil deeds,
and acts of violence are in their
hands.
⁷Their feet rush into sin;
they are swift to shed innocent
blood.
Their thoughts are evil thoughts;
ruin and destruction mark their
ways.
⁸The way of peace they do not
know;
there is no justice in their paths.
They have turned them into
crooked roads;
no one who walks in them will
know peace.

⁹So justice is far from us,
and righteousness does not
reach us.
We look for light, but all is
darkness;
for brightness, but we walk in
deep shadows.

¹⁰Like the blind we grope along the
wall,
feeling our way like men
without eyes.
At midday we stumble as if it
were twilight;
among the strong, we are like
the dead.
¹¹We all growl like bears;
we moan mournfully like doves.
We look for justice, but find none;
for deliverance, but it is far
away.

¹²For our offenses are many in your
sight,
and our sins testify against us.
Our offenses are ever with us,
and we acknowledge our
iniquities:
¹³rebellion and treachery against the
LORD,
turning our backs on our God,
fomenting oppression and revolt,
uttering lies our hearts have
conceived.
¹⁴So justice is driven back,
and righteousness stands at a
distance;
truth has stumbled in the streets,
honesty cannot enter.
¹⁵Truth is nowhere to be found,
and whoever shuns evil
becomes a prey.

The LORD looked and was
displeased
that there was no justice.
¹⁶He saw that there was no one,
he was appalled that there was
no one to intervene;
so his own arm worked salvation
for him,
and his own righteousness
sustained him.
¹⁷He put on righteousness as his
breastplate,
and the helmet of salvation on
his head;
he put on the garments of
vengeance
and wrapped himself in zeal as
in a cloak.
¹⁸According to what they have
done,
so will he repay

wrath to his enemies
and retribution to his foes;
he will repay the islands their
due.
¹⁹From the west, men will fear the
name of the LORD,
and from the rising of the sun,
they will revere his glory.
For he will come like a pent-up
flood
that the breath of the LORD
drives along.ᵃ

²⁰"The Redeemer will come to Zion,
to those in Jacob who repent of
their sins,"
declares the LORD.

²¹"As for me, this is my covenant
with them," says the LORD. "My Spirit,
who is on you, and my words that I
have put in your mouth will not depart from your mouth, or from the
mouths of your children, or from the
mouths of their descendants from this
time on and forever," says the LORD.

The Glory of Zion

60 "Arise, shine, for your light
has come,
and the glory of the LORD rises
upon you.
²See, darkness covers the earth
and thick darkness is over the
peoples,
but the LORD rises upon you
and his glory appears over you.
³Nations will come to your light,
and kings to the brightness of
your dawn.

⁴"Lift up your eyes and look about
you:
All assemble and come to you;
your sons come from afar,
and your daughters are carried
on the arm.
⁵Then you will look and be radiant,
your heart will throb and swell
with joy;
the wealth on the seas will be
brought to you,

to you the riches of the nations
will come.
⁶Herds of camels will cover your
land,
young camels of Midian and
Ephah.
And all from Sheba will come,
bearing gold and incense
and proclaiming the praise of
the LORD.
⁷All Kedar's flocks will be gathered
to you,
the rams of Nebaioth will serve
you;
they will be accepted as offerings
on my altar,
and I will adorn my glorious
temple.

⁸"Who are these that fly along like
clouds,
like doves to their nests?
⁹Surely the islands look to me;
in the lead are the ships of
Tarshish,ᵇ
bringing your sons from afar,
with their silver and gold,
to the honor of the LORD your
God,
the Holy One of Israel,
for he has endowed you with
splendor.

¹⁰"Foreigners will rebuild your
walls,
and their kings will serve you.
Though in anger I struck you,
in favor I will show you
compassion.
¹¹Your gates will always stand
open,
they will never be shut, day or
night,
so that men may bring you the
wealth of the nations—
their kings led in triumphal
procession.
¹²For the nation or kingdom that
will not serve you will
perish;
it will be utterly ruined.

ᵃ19 Or *When the enemy comes in like a flood, / the Spirit of the* LORD *will put him to flight*   ᵇ9 Or
the trading ships

¹³"The glory of Lebanon will come
 to you,
 the pine, the fir and the cypress
  together,
to adorn the place of my
  sanctuary;
 and I will glorify the place of
  my feet.
¹⁴The sons of your oppressors will
  come bowing before you;
 all who despise you will bow
  down at your feet
and will call you the City of the
  LORD,
 Zion of the Holy One of Israel.

¹⁵"Although you have been forsaken
  and hated,
 with no one traveling through,
I will make you the everlasting
  pride
 and the joy of all generations.
¹⁶You will drink the milk of nations
 and be nursed at royal breasts.
Then you will know that I, the
  LORD, am your Savior,
 your Redeemer, the Mighty One
  of Jacob.
¹⁷Instead of bronze I will bring you
  gold,
 and silver in place of iron.
Instead of wood I will bring you
  bronze,
 and iron in place of stones.
I will make peace your governor
 and righteousness your ruler.
¹⁸No longer will violence be heard
  in your land,
 nor ruin or destruction within
  your borders,
but you will call your walls
  Salvation
 and your gates Praise.
¹⁹The sun will no more be your
  light by day,
 nor will the brightness of the
  moon shine on you,
for the LORD will be your
  everlasting light,
 and your God will be your
  glory.
²⁰Your sun will never set again,

and your moon will wane no
  more;
 the LORD will be your everlasting
  light,
 and your days of sorrow will
  end.
²¹Then will all your people be
  righteous
 and they will possess the land
  forever.
They are the shoot I have planted,
 the work of my hands,
 for the display of my splendor.
²²The least of you will become a
  thousand,
 the smallest a mighty nation.
I am the LORD;
 in its time I will do this
  swiftly."

The Year of the LORD's Favor

61 The Spirit of the Sovereign
  LORD is on me,
 because the LORD has anointed
  me
 to preach good news to the
  poor.
He has sent me to bind up the
  brokenhearted,
 to proclaim freedom for the
  captives
 and release from darkness for
  the prisoners,ᵃ
²to proclaim the year of the LORD's
  favor
 and the day of vengeance of our
  God,
to comfort all who mourn,
³ and provide for those who
  grieve in Zion—
to bestow on them a crown of
  beauty
 instead of ashes,
the oil of gladness
 instead of mourning,
and a garment of praise
 instead of a spirit of despair.
They will be called oaks of
  righteousness,
 a planting of the LORD
 for the display of his splendor.

⁴They will rebuild the ancient ruins

ᵃ1 Hebrew; Septuagint *the blind*

and restore the places long
    devastated;
they will renew the ruined cities
    that have been devastated for
    generations.
5Aliens will shepherd your flocks;
    foreigners will work your fields
    and vineyards.
6And you will be called priests of
    the LORD,
    you will be named ministers of
    our God.
You will feed on the wealth of
    nations,
    and in their riches you will
    boast.

7Instead of their shame
    my people will receive a double
    portion,
and instead of disgrace
    they will rejoice in their
    inheritance;
and so they will inherit a double
    portion in their land,
    and everlasting joy will be
    theirs.

8"For I, the LORD, love justice;
    I hate robbery and iniquity.
In my faithfulness I will reward
    them
    and make an everlasting
    covenant with them.
9Their descendants will be known
    among the nations
    and their offspring among the
    peoples.
All who see them will
    acknowledge
    that they are a people the LORD
    has blessed."

10I delight greatly in the LORD;
    my soul rejoices in my God.
For he has clothed me with
    garments of salvation
    and arrayed me in a robe of
    righteousness,
as a bridegroom adorns his head
    like a priest,
    and as a bride adorns herself
    with her jewels.

11For as the soil makes the sprout
    come up
    and a garden causes seeds to
    grow,
so the Sovereign LORD will make
    righteousness and praise
spring up before all nations.

Zion's New Name

62 For Zion's sake I will not
    keep silent,
    for Jerusalem's sake I will not
    remain quiet,
till her righteousness shines out
    like the dawn,
    her salvation like a blazing
    torch.
2The nations will see your
    righteousness,
    and all kings your glory;
you will be called by a new name
    that the mouth of the LORD will
    bestow.
3You will be a crown of splendor
    in the LORD's hand,
    a royal diadem in the hand of
    your God.
4No longer will they call you
    Deserted,
    or name your land Desolate.
But you will be called
    Hephzibah,ᵃ
    and your land Beulahᵇ;
for the LORD will take delight in
    you,
    and your land will be married.
5As a young man marries a
    maiden,
    so will your sonsᶜ marry you;
as a bridegroom rejoices over his
    bride,
    so will your God rejoice over
    you.

6I have posted watchmen on your
    walls, O Jerusalem;
    they will never be silent day or
    night.
You who call on the LORD,
    give yourselves no rest,
7and give him no rest till he
    establishes Jerusalem

ᵃ4 *Hephzibah* means *my delight is in her.*   ᵇ4 *Beulah* means *married.*   ᶜ5 Or *Builder*

and makes her the praise of the
earth.

⁸The Lᴏʀᴅ has sworn by his right
hand
and by his mighty arm:
"Never again will I give your
grain
as food for your enemies,
and never again will foreigners
drink the new wine
for which you have toiled;
⁹but those who harvest it will eat it
and praise the Lᴏʀᴅ,
and those who gather the grapes
will drink it
in the courts of my sanctuary."

¹⁰Pass through, pass through the
gates!
Prepare the way for the people.
Build up, build up the highway!
Remove the stones.
Raise a banner for the nations.

¹¹The Lᴏʀᴅ has made proclamation
to the ends of the earth:
"Say to the Daughter of Zion,
'See, your Savior comes!
See, his reward is with him,
and his recompense
accompanies him.' "
¹²They will be called the Holy
People,
the Redeemed of the Lᴏʀᴅ;
and you will be called Sought
After,
the City No Longer Deserted.

God's Day of Vengeance and Redemption

63 Who is this coming from
Edom,
from Bozrah, with his garments
stained crimson?
Who is this, robed in splendor,
striding forward in the
greatness of his strength?

"It is I, speaking in righteousness,
mighty to save."

²Why are your garments red,
like those of one treading the
winepress?

³"I have trodden the winepress
alone;
from the nations no one was
with me.
I trampled them in my anger
and trod them down in my
wrath;
their blood spattered my
garments,
and I stained all my clothing.
⁴For the day of vengeance was in
my heart,
and the year of my redemption
has come.
⁵I looked, but there was no one to
help,
I was appalled that no one gave
support;
so my own arm worked salvation
for me,
and my own wrath sustained
me.
⁶I trampled the nations in my
anger;
in my wrath I made them
drunk
and poured their blood on the
ground."

Praise and Prayer

⁷I will tell of the kindnesses of the
Lᴏʀᴅ,
the deeds for which he is to be
praised,
according to all the Lᴏʀᴅ has
done for us—
yes, the many good things he has
done
for the house of Israel,
according to his compassion
and many kindnesses.
⁸He said, "Surely they are my
people,
sons who will not be false to
me";
and so he became their Savior.
⁹In all their distress he too was
distressed,
and the angel of his presence
saved them.
In his love and mercy he
redeemed them;
he lifted them up and carried
them
all the days of old.

[10]Yet they rebelled
  and grieved his Holy Spirit.
So he turned and became their
    enemy
  and he himself fought against
    them.

[11]Then his people recalled[a] the
    days of old,
  the days of Moses and his
    people—
where is he who brought them
    through the sea,
  with the shepherd of his flock?
Where is he who set
  his Holy Spirit among them,
[12]who sent his glorious arm of
    power
  to be at Moses' right hand,
who divided the waters before
    them,
  to gain for himself everlasting
    renown,
[13]who led them through the depths?
Like a horse in open country,
  they did not stumble;
[14]like cattle that go down to the
    plain,
  they were given rest by the
    Spirit of the LORD.
This is how you guided your
    people
  to make for yourself a glorious
    name.

[15]Look down from heaven and see
  from your lofty throne, holy
    and glorious.
Where are your zeal and your
    might?
  Your tenderness and
    compassion are withheld
    from us.
[16]But you are our Father,
  though Abraham does not know
    us
or Israel acknowledge us;
  you, O LORD, are our Father,
  our Redeemer from of old is
    your name.
[17]Why, O LORD, do you make us
  wander from your ways

and harden our hearts so we do
  not revere you?
Return for the sake of your
    servants,
  the tribes that are your
    inheritance.
[18]For a little while your people
    possessed your holy place,
  but now our enemies have
    trampled down your
    sanctuary.
[19]We are yours from of old;
  but you have not ruled over
    them,
  they have not been called by
    your name.[b]

64 Oh, that you would rend the
    heavens and come down,
  that the mountains would
    tremble before you!
[2]As when fire sets twigs ablaze
  and causes water to boil,
come down to make your name
    known to your enemies
  and cause the nations to quake
    before you!
[3]For when you did awesome things
    that we did not expect,
  you came down, and the
    mountains trembled before
    you.
[4]Since ancient times no one has
    heard,
  no ear has perceived,
no eye has seen any God besides
    you,
  who acts on behalf of those who
    wait for him.
[5]You come to the help of those
    who gladly do right,
  who remember your ways.
But when we continued to sin
    against them,
  you were angry.
How then can we be saved?
[6]All of us have become like one
    who is unclean,
  and all our righteous acts are
    like filthy rags;
we all shrivel up like a leaf,

<hr>

[a]11 Or But may he recall
your name   [b]19 Or We are like those you have never ruled, / like those never called by

and like the wind our sins
  sweep us away.
⁷No one calls on your name
  or strives to lay hold of you;
for you have hidden your face
    from us
  and made us waste away
    because of our sins.

⁸Yet, O LORD, you are our Father.
  We are the clay, you are the
    potter;
  we are all the work of your
    hand.
⁹Do not be angry beyond measure,
    O LORD;
  do not remember our sins
    forever.
Oh, look upon us, we pray,
  for we are all your people.
¹⁰Your sacred cities have become a
    desert;
  even Zion is a desert, Jerusalem
    a desolation.
¹¹Our holy and glorious temple,
    where our fathers praised
    you,
  has been burned with fire,
  and all that we treasured lies in
    ruins.
¹²After all this, O LORD, will you
    hold yourself back?
  Will you keep silent and punish
    us beyond measure?

Judgment and Salvation

65 "I revealed myself to those
      who did not ask for me;
  I was found by those who did
    not seek me.
To a nation that did not call on
    my name,
  I said, 'Here am I, here am I.'
²All day long I have held out my
    hands
  to an obstinate people,
who walk in ways not good,
  pursuing their own
    imaginations—
³a people who continually provoke
    me
  to my very face,
offering sacrifices in gardens
  and burning incense on altars of
    brick;

⁴who sit among the graves
  and spend their nights keeping
    secret vigil;
who eat the flesh of pigs,
  and whose pots hold broth of
    unclean meat;
⁵who say, 'Keep away; don't come
    near me,
  for I am too sacred for you!'
Such people are smoke in my
    nostrils,
  a fire that keeps burning all
    day.

⁶"See, it stands written before me:
  I will not keep silent but will
    pay back in full;
  I will pay it back into their
    laps—
⁷both your sins and the sins of
    your fathers,"
  says the LORD.
"Because they burned sacrifices on
    the mountains
  and defied me on the hills,
I will measure into their laps
  the full payment for their
    former deeds."

⁸This is what the LORD says:

"As when juice is still found in a
    cluster of grapes
  and men say, 'Don't destroy it,
    there is yet some good in it,'
so will I do in behalf of my
    servants;
  I will not destroy them all.
⁹I will bring forth descendants
    from Jacob,
  and from Judah those who will
    possess my mountains;
my chosen people will inherit
    them,
  and there will my servants live.
¹⁰Sharon will become a pasture for
    flocks,
  and the Valley of Achor a
    resting place for herds,
  for my people who seek me.

¹¹"But as for you who forsake the
    LORD
  and forget my holy mountain,
who spread a table for Fortune
  and fill bowls of mixed wine for
    Destiny,

¹²I will destine you for the sword,
　　and you will all bend down for
　　　the slaughter;
　for I called but you did not
　　　answer,
　　I spoke but you did not listen.
　You did evil in my sight
　　and chose what displeases me."

¹³Therefore this is what the Sovereign LORD says:

　"My servants will eat,
　　but you will go hungry;
　my servants will drink,
　　but you will go thirsty;
　my servants will rejoice,
　　but you will be put to shame.
¹⁴My servants will sing
　　out of the joy of their hearts,
　but you will cry out
　　from anguish of heart
　　and wail in brokenness of spirit.
¹⁵You will leave your name
　　to my chosen ones as a curse;
　the Sovereign LORD will put you to
　　　death,
　　but to his servants he will give
　　　another name.
¹⁶Whoever invokes a blessing in the
　　　land
　will do so by the God of truth;
　he who takes an oath in the land
　　will swear by the God of truth.
　For the past troubles will be
　　　forgotten
　　and hidden from my eyes.

New Heavens and a New Earth

¹⁷"Behold, I will create
　　new heavens and a new earth.
　The former things will not be
　　　remembered,
　　nor will they come to mind.
¹⁸But be glad and rejoice forever
　　in what I will create,
　for I will create Jerusalem to be a
　　　delight
　　and its people a joy.
¹⁹I will rejoice over Jerusalem
　　and take delight in my people;
　the sound of weeping and of
　　　crying
　　will be heard in it no more.

²⁰"Never again will there be in it
　　an infant who lives but a few
　　　days,
　or an old man who does not
　　live out his years;
　he who dies at a hundred
　　will be thought a mere youth;
　he who fails to reachᵃ a hundred
　　will be considered accursed.
²¹They will build houses and dwell
　　　in them;
　they will plant vineyards and
　　eat their fruit.
²²No longer will they build houses
　　and others live in them,
　or plant and others eat.
　For as the days of a tree,
　　so will be the days of my
　　　people;
　my chosen ones will long enjoy
　　the works of their hands.
²³They will not toil in vain
　　or bear children doomed to
　　　misfortune;
　for they will be a people blessed
　　　by the LORD,
　　they and their descendants with
　　　them.
²⁴Before they call I will answer;
　　while they are still speaking I
　　　will hear.
²⁵The wolf and the lamb will feed
　　　together,
　　and the lion will eat straw like
　　　the ox,
　but dust will be the serpent's
　　　food.
　They will neither harm nor
　　　destroy
　　on all my holy mountain,"
　　　　　　　　　　says the LORD.

Judgment and Hope

66 This is what the LORD says:

　"Heaven is my throne,
　　and the earth is my footstool.
　Where is the house you will build
　　　for me?
　　Where will my resting place be?
²Has not my hand made all these
　　　things,

ᵃ20 Or / the sinner who reaches

VERSE:
Isaiah 65:18

AUTHOR:
Elisabeth Elliot

PASSAGE:
Isaiah 65:17–25

Seeing the Unseen

I don't mind getting old. Before the day began this morning I was looking out at starlight on a still, wintry sea. A little song we used to sing at camp came to mind — "Just one day nearer Home." That idea thrills me. I can understand why people who have nothing much to look forward to try frantically and futilely to hang on to the past — to youth and all that ...

Let's be honest. Old age entails suffering. I'm acutely aware of this now as I watch my mother, once so alive and alert and quick, now so quiet and confused and slow ... We see the preview of "coming attractions," ourselves in her shoes, and ponder what this interval means in terms of the glory of God in an old woman.

It would be terrifying if it weren't for something that ought to make the Christian's attitude toward aging utterly distinct from the rest. *We know it is not for nothing* (see Ephesians 1:9–10).

In the meantime, we look at what's happening — limitations of hearing, seeing, moving, digesting, remembering; distortions of countenance, figure and perspective. If that's all we could see, we'd certainly want a face-lift or something.

But we're on a pilgrim road. It's rough and steep, and it winds uphill to the very end. We can lift up our eyes and see the unseen: a celestial city, a light, a welcome and an ineffable face. We shall behold him. We shall be like him. And that makes a difference in how we go about aging.

ADDITIONAL SCRIPTURE READINGS
2 Corinthians 4:16–18; Revelation 22:1–6

Go to page 938 for your next devotional reading.

and so they came into being?"
declares the Lord.

"This is the one I esteem:
  he who is humble and contrite
    in spirit,
  and trembles at my word.
³But whoever sacrifices a bull
  is like one who kills a man,
and whoever offers a lamb,
  like one who breaks a dog's
    neck;
whoever makes a grain offering
  is like one who presents pig's
    blood,
and whoever burns memorial
    incense,
  like one who worships an idol.
They have chosen their own ways,
  and their souls delight in their
    abominations;
⁴so I also will choose harsh
    treatment for them
  and will bring upon them what
    they dread.
For when I called, no one
    answered,
  when I spoke, no one listened.
They did evil in my sight
  and chose what displeases me."

⁵Hear the word of the Lord,
  you who tremble at his word:
"Your brothers who hate you,
  and exclude you because of my
    name, have said,
'Let the Lord be glorified,
  that we may see your joy!'
Yet they will be put to shame.
⁶Hear that uproar from the city,
  hear that noise from the temple!
It is the sound of the Lord
  repaying his enemies all they
    deserve.

⁷"Before she goes into labor,
  she gives birth;
before the pains come upon her,
  she delivers a son.
⁸Who has ever heard of such a
    thing?
  Who has ever seen such things?
Can a country be born in a day
  or a nation be brought forth in
    a moment?
Yet no sooner is Zion in labor

than she gives birth to her
    children.
⁹Do I bring to the moment of birth
  and not give delivery?" says the
    Lord.
"Do I close up the womb
  when I bring to delivery?" says
    your God.
¹⁰"Rejoice with Jerusalem and be
    glad for her,
  all you who love her;
rejoice greatly with her,
  all you who mourn over her.
¹¹For you will nurse and be satisfied
  at her comforting breasts;
you will drink deeply
  and delight in her overflowing
    abundance."

¹²For this is what the Lord says:

"I will extend peace to her like a
    river,
  and the wealth of nations like a
    flooding stream;
you will nurse and be carried on
    her arm
  and dandled on her knees.
¹³As a mother comforts her child,
  so will I comfort you;
  and you will be comforted over
    Jerusalem."

¹⁴When you see this, your heart will
    rejoice
  and you will flourish like grass;
the hand of the Lord will be made
    known to his servants,
  but his fury will be shown to
    his foes.
¹⁵See, the Lord is coming with fire,
  and his chariots are like a
    whirlwind;
he will bring down his anger with
    fury,
  and his rebuke with flames of
    fire.
¹⁶For with fire and with his sword
  the Lord will execute judgment
    upon all men,
  and many will be those slain by
    the Lord.

¹⁷"Those who consecrate and purify themselves to go into the gardens,

following the one in the midst of[a] those who eat the flesh of pigs and rats and other abominable things— they will meet their end together," declares the LORD.

[18]"And I, because of their actions and their imaginations, am about to come[b] and gather all nations and tongues, and they will come and see my glory.

[19]"I will set a sign among them, and I will send some of those who survive to the nations—to Tarshish, to the Libyans[c] and Lydians (famous as archers), to Tubal and Greece, and to the distant islands that have not heard of my fame or seen my glory. They will proclaim my glory among the nations. [20]And they will bring all your brothers, from all the nations, to my holy mountain in Jerusalem as an offering to the LORD—on horses, in chariots and wagons, and on mules and camels," says the LORD. "They will bring them, as the Israelites bring their grain offerings, to the temple of the LORD in ceremonially clean vessels. [21]And I will select some of them also to be priests and Levites," says the LORD.

[22]"As the new heavens and the new earth that I make will endure before me," declares the LORD, "so will your name and descendants endure. [23]From one New Moon to another and from one Sabbath to another, all mankind will come and bow down before me," says the LORD. [24]"And they will go out and look upon the dead bodies of those who rebelled against me; their worm will not die, nor will their fire be quenched, and they will be loathsome to all mankind."

---

[a]17 Or *gardens behind one of your temples, and is uncertain.*   [b]18 The meaning of the Hebrew for this clause   [c]19 Some Septuagint manuscripts *Put* (Libyans); Hebrew *Pul*

..."J"...
eremiah prophesied in the
kingdom of Judah as Jerusalem was being
destroyed and the people carried off into exile. Intermingled with Jeremiah's words of
warning are words of hope about Judah's
future restoration. As you read this book,
watch for Jeremiah's encouragement for you;
the last word is not death but life—life in
Jesus Christ, life that will never end.

JEREMIAH

1 The words of Jeremiah son of Hil-kiah, one of the priests at Ana-thoth in the territory of Benjamin. ²The word of the LORD came to him in the thirteenth year of the reign of Josi-ah son of Amon king of Judah, ³and through the reign of Jehoiakim son of Josiah king of Judah, down to the fifth month of the eleventh year of Zedeki-ah son of Josiah king of Judah, when the people of Jerusalem went into ex-ile.

The Call of Jeremiah

⁴The word of the LORD came to me, saying,

⁵"Before I formed you in the womb
    I knew^a you,
before you were born I set you
    apart;
I appointed you as a prophet to
    the nations."

⁶"Ah, Sovereign LORD," I said, "I do

not know how to speak; I am only a child."

⁷But the LORD said to me, "Do not say, 'I am only a child.' You must go to everyone I send you to and say whatever I command you. ⁸Do not be afraid of them, for I am with you and will rescue you," declares the LORD.

⁹Then the LORD reached out his hand and touched my mouth and said to me, "Now, I have put my words in your mouth. ¹⁰See, today I appoint you over nations and king-doms to uproot and tear down, to de-stroy and overthrow, to build and to plant."

¹¹The word of the LORD came to me: "What do you see, Jeremiah?"

"I see the branch of an almond tree," I replied.

¹²The LORD said to me, "You have seen correctly, for I am watching^b to see that my word is fulfilled."

¹³The word of the LORD came to me again: "What do you see?"

---

^a5 Or *chose*   ^b12 The Hebrew for *watching* sounds like the Hebrew for *almond tree*.

PASSAGE: Jeremiah 9:23–24; Philippians 3:7–11
AUTHOR: Author Unknown

The Greatest of All

My greatest loss, to lose my soul.
My greatest gain, Christ as my Savior.
My greatest object, to glorify God.
My greatest prize, a crown of glory.
My greatest work, to win souls for Christ.
My greatest joy, the joy of God's salvation.
My greatest inheritance, heaven and its glories.
My greatest neglect, the neglect of so great
    salvation.
My greatest crime, to reject Christ the only Savior.
My greatest privilege, power to become a child of
    God.
My greatest bargain, to lose all things to win
    Christ.
My greatest profit, godliness in this life and that to
    come.
My greatest peace, the peace that passeth
    understanding.
My greatest knowledge, to know God and Jesus
    Christ
    whom he hath sent.

Go to page 941 for your next devotional reading.

"I see a boiling pot, tilting away from the north," I answered.

¹⁴The LORD said to me, "From the north disaster will be poured out on all who live in the land. ¹⁵I am about to summon all the peoples of the northern kingdoms," declares the LORD.

"Their kings will come and set up
    their thrones
in the entrance of the gates of
    Jerusalem;
they will come against all her
    surrounding walls
and against all the towns of
    Judah.
¹⁶I will pronounce my judgments on
    my people
because of their wickedness in
    forsaking me,
in burning incense to other gods
and in worshiping what their
    hands have made.

¹⁷"Get yourself ready! Stand up and say to them whatever I command you. Do not be terrified by them, or I will terrify you before them. ¹⁸Today I have made you a fortified city, an iron pillar and a bronze wall to stand against the whole land—against the kings of Judah, its officials, its priests and the people of the land. ¹⁹They will fight against you but will not overcome you, for I am with you and will rescue you," declares the LORD.

Israel Forsakes God

2 The word of the LORD came to me: ²"Go and proclaim in the hearing of Jerusalem:

" 'I remember the devotion of
    your youth,
how as a bride you loved me
and followed me through the
    desert,
through a land not sown.
³Israel was holy to the LORD,
    the firstfruits of his harvest;
all who devoured her were held
    guilty,

and disaster overtook them,' "
            declares the LORD.

⁴Hear the word of the LORD,
    O house of Jacob,
all you clans of the house of
    Israel.

⁵This is what the LORD says:

"What fault did your fathers find
    in me,
that they strayed so far from
    me?
They followed worthless idols
and became worthless
    themselves.
⁶They did not ask, 'Where is the
    LORD,
who brought us up out of
    Egypt
and led us through the barren
    wilderness,
through a land of deserts and
    rifts,
a land of drought and darkness,ᵃ
a land where no one travels and
    no one lives?'
⁷I brought you into a fertile land
to eat its fruit and rich produce.
But you came and defiled my land
and made my inheritance
    detestable.
⁸The priests did not ask,
    'Where is the LORD?'
Those who deal with the law did
    not know me;
the leaders rebelled against me.
The prophets prophesied by Baal,
following worthless idols.

⁹"Therefore I bring charges against
    you again,"
            declares the LORD.
"And I will bring charges
    against your children's
    children.
¹⁰Cross over to the coasts of
    Kittimᵇ and look,
send to Kedarᶜ and observe
    closely;
see if there has ever been
    anything like this:

ᵃ6 Or and the shadow of death   ᵇ10 That is, Cyprus and western coastlands   ᶜ10 The home
of Bedouin tribes in the Syro-Arabian desert

¹¹Has a nation ever changed its
    gods?
  (Yet they are not gods at all.)
But my people have exchanged
    their^a Glory
  for worthless idols.
¹²Be appalled at this, O heavens,
  and shudder with great horror,"
               declares the LORD.
¹³"My people have committed two
    sins:
They have forsaken me,
  the spring of living water,
and have dug their own cisterns,
  broken cisterns that cannot hold
    water.
¹⁴Is Israel a servant, a slave by
    birth?
Why then has he become
    plunder?
¹⁵Lions have roared;
  they have growled at him.
They have laid waste his land;
  his towns are burned and
    deserted.
¹⁶Also, the men of Memphis^b and
    Tahpanhes
  have shaved the crown of your
    head.^c
¹⁷Have you not brought this on
    yourselves
  by forsaking the LORD your God
  when he led you in the way?
¹⁸Now why go to Egypt
  to drink water from the
    Shihor^d?
And why go to Assyria
  to drink water from the
    River^e?
¹⁹Your wickedness will punish you;
  your backsliding will rebuke
    you.
Consider then and realize
  how evil and bitter it is for you
  when you forsake the LORD your
    God
  and have no awe of me,"
             declares the Lord,
        the LORD Almighty.

²⁰"Long ago you broke off your
    yoke

and tore off your bonds;
  you said, 'I will not serve you!'
Indeed, on every high hill
  and under every spreading tree
  you lay down as a prostitute.
²¹I had planted you like a choice
    vine
  of sound and reliable stock.
How then did you turn against
    me
  into a corrupt, wild vine?
²²Although you wash yourself with
    soda
  and use an abundance of soap,
  the stain of your guilt is still
    before me,"
          declares the Sovereign
               LORD.
²³"How can you say, 'I am not
    defiled;
  I have not run after the Baals'?
See how you behaved in the
    valley;
  consider what you have done.
You are a swift she-camel
  running here and there,
²⁴a wild donkey accustomed to the
    desert,
  sniffing the wind in her
    craving—
  in her heat who can restrain
    her?
Any males that pursue her need
    not tire themselves;
  at mating time they will find
    her.
²⁵Do not run until your feet are bare
  and your throat is dry.
But you said, 'It's no use!
  I love foreign gods,
  and I must go after them.'

²⁶"As a thief is disgraced when he
    is caught,
  so the house of Israel is
    disgraced—
  they, their kings and their officials,
  their priests and their prophets.
²⁷They say to wood, 'You are my
    father,'
  and to stone, 'You gave me
    birth.'

---

^a11 Masoretic Text; an ancient Hebrew scribal tradition *my
cracked your skull*   ^d18 That is, a branch of the Nile   ^b16 Hebrew *Noph*   ^c16 Or *have*
  ^e18 That is, the Euphrates

They have turned their backs to
me
and not their faces;
yet when they are in trouble, they
say,
'Come and save us!'
28Where then are the gods you
made for yourselves?
Let them come if they can save
you

when you are in trouble!
For you have as many gods
as you have towns, O Judah.

29"Why do you bring charges
against me?
You have all rebelled against
me,"

                                     declares the LORD.
30"In vain I punished your people;

VERSE: AUTHOR: PASSAGE:
Jeremiah 2:13   Joni Eareckson Tada   Jeremiah 2:9–19

Cisterns and Springs

Jesus said that rivers of living water would flow out of
the lives of those who believe in him. His living water
would brim over from the wellspring of the Spirit within
us, quenching our thirst and touching the parched lives
of those around us. The life of the Lord Jesus is a constantly flowing stream, a river even, keeping us fresh,
filled and satisfied.

We stop the flow, however, when we try to reservoir
God's spring of living water in our lives. We become cisterns — holding tanks for past victories or other people's
ideas. At that point we have forsaken the spring of living
water. We have tried to store that which cannot be
saved, we have tried to keep that which must keep flowing. The result? Our lives lack freshness and freedom,
and we become stagnant pools reflecting old experiences
and tired testimonies.

God says that these cisterns of our own making will
break. What we try to save, we will lose. The warning is
clear: Throw out the broken cisterns and get in the flow
of God's spring of living water.

ADDITIONAL SCRIPTURE READINGS
John 4:1–14; John 7:37–43
Go to page 955 for your next devotional reading.

they did not respond to
    correction.
Your sword has devoured your
    prophets
    like a ravening lion.

³¹"You of this generation, consider
the word of the Lord:

"Have I been a desert to Israel
    or a land of great darkness?
Why do my people say, 'We are
    free to roam;
    we will come to you no more'?
³²Does a maiden forget her jewelry,
    a bride her wedding ornaments?
Yet my people have forgotten me,
    days without number.
³³How skilled you are at pursuing
    love!
    Even the worst of women can
        learn from your ways.
³⁴On your clothes men find
    the lifeblood of the innocent
        poor,
    though you did not catch them
        breaking in.
Yet in spite of all this
³⁵ you say, 'I am innocent;
    he is not angry with me.'
But I will pass judgment on you
    because you say, 'I have not
        sinned.'
³⁶Why do you go about so much,
    changing your ways?
You will be disappointed by Egypt
    as you were by Assyria.
³⁷You will also leave that place
    with your hands on your head,
for the Lord has rejected those you
    trust;
    you will not be helped by them.

3 "If a man divorces his wife
    and she leaves him and marries
        another man,
should he return to her again?
    Would not the land be
        completely defiled?
But you have lived as a prostitute
    with many lovers—
    would you now return to me?"
                declares the Lord.

²"Look up to the barren heights
    and see.
Is there any place where you
    have not been ravished?
By the roadside you sat waiting
    for lovers,
    sat like a nomad*ᵃ* in the desert.
You have defiled the land
    with your prostitution and
        wickedness.
³Therefore the showers have been
    withheld,
    and no spring rains have fallen.
Yet you have the brazen look of a
    prostitute;
    you refuse to blush with shame.
⁴Have you not just called to me:
    'My Father, my friend from my
        youth,
⁵will you always be angry?
    Will your wrath continue
        forever?'
This is how you talk,
    but you do all the evil you
        can."

Unfaithful Israel

⁶During the reign of King Josiah,
the Lord said to me, "Have you seen
what faithless Israel has done? She
has gone up on every high hill and
under every spreading tree and has
committed adultery there. ⁷I thought
that after she had done all this she
would return to me but she did not,
and her unfaithful sister Judah saw it.
⁸I gave faithless Israel her certificate
of divorce and sent her away because
of all her adulteries. Yet I saw that her
unfaithful sister Judah had no fear;
she also went out and committed
adultery. ⁹Because Israel's immorality
mattered so little to her, she defiled
the land and committed adultery with
stone and wood. ¹⁰In spite of all this,
her unfaithful sister Judah did not return to me with all her heart, but only
in pretense," declares the Lord.

¹¹The Lord said to me, "Faithless Israel is more righteous than unfaithful
Judah. ¹²Go, proclaim this message toward the north:

ᵃ2 Or an Arab

" 'Return, faithless Israel,' declares
    the Lord,
'I will frown on you no longer,
  for I am merciful,' declares the
    Lord,
'I will not be angry forever.
13Only acknowledge your guilt—
  you have rebelled against the
    Lord your God,
you have scattered your favors to
    foreign gods
  under every spreading tree,
  and have not obeyed me,' "
              declares the Lord.

14"Return, faithless people," declares the Lord, "for I am your husband. I will choose you—one from a town and two from a clan—and bring you to Zion. 15Then I will give you shepherds after my own heart, who will lead you with knowledge and understanding. 16In those days, when your numbers have increased greatly in the land," declares the Lord, "men will no longer say, 'The ark of the covenant of the Lord.' It will never enter their minds or be remembered; it will not be missed, nor will another one be made. 17At that time they will call Jerusalem The Throne of the Lord, and all nations will gather in Jerusalem to honor the name of the Lord. No longer will they follow the stubbornness of their evil hearts. 18In those days the house of Judah will join the house of Israel, and together they will come from a northern land to the land I gave your forefathers as an inheritance.

19"I myself said,

" 'How gladly would I treat you
    like sons
  and give you a desirable land,
  the most beautiful inheritance of
    any nation.'
I thought you would call me
    'Father'
  and not turn away from
    following me.
20But like a woman unfaithful to her
    husband,
  so you have been unfaithful to
    me, O house of Israel,"
              declares the Lord.

21A cry is heard on the barren
    heights,
  the weeping and pleading of the
    people of Israel,
because they have perverted their
    ways
  and have forgotten the Lord
    their God.

22"Return, faithless people;
  I will cure you of backsliding."

"Yes, we will come to you,
  for you are the Lord our God.
23Surely the ⌐idolatrous⌐ commotion
    on the hills
  and mountains is a deception;
surely in the Lord our God
  is the salvation of Israel.
24From our youth shameful gods
    have consumed
  the fruits of our fathers' labor—
their flocks and herds,
  their sons and daughters.
25Let us lie down in our shame,
  and let our disgrace cover us.
We have sinned against the Lord
    our God,
  both we and our fathers;
from our youth till this day
  we have not obeyed the Lord
    our God."

4 "If you will return, O Israel,
  return to me,"
              declares the Lord.
"If you put your detestable idols
    out of my sight
  and no longer go astray,
2and if in a truthful, just and
    righteous way
  you swear, 'As surely as the
    Lord lives,'
then the nations will be blessed by
    him
  and in him they will glory."

3This is what the Lord says to the men of Judah and to Jerusalem:

"Break up your unplowed ground
  and do not sow among thorns.
4Circumcise yourselves to the Lord,
  circumcise your hearts,
  you men of Judah and people of
    Jerusalem,

or my wrath will break out and
burn like fire
because of the evil you have
done—
burn with no one to quench it.

Disaster From the North

⁵"Announce in Judah and proclaim
in Jerusalem and say:
'Sound the trumpet throughout
the land!'
Cry aloud and say:
'Gather together!
Let us flee to the fortified cities!'
⁶Raise the signal to go to Zion!
Flee for safety without delay!
For I am bringing disaster from
the north,
even terrible destruction."

⁷A lion has come out of his lair;
a destroyer of nations has set
out.
He has left his place
to lay waste your land.
Your towns will lie in ruins
without inhabitant.
⁸So put on sackcloth,
lament and wail,
for the fierce anger of the LORD
has not turned away from us.

⁹"In that day," declares the LORD,
"the king and the officials will
lose heart,
the priests will be horrified,
and the prophets will be
appalled."

¹⁰Then I said, "Ah, Sovereign LORD,
how completely you have deceived
this people and Jerusalem by saying,
'You will have peace,' when the
sword is at our throats."

¹¹At that time this people and Jerusalem will be told, "A scorching wind
from the barren heights in the desert
blows toward my people, but not to
winnow or cleanse; ¹²a wind too
strong for that comes from me.ᵃ
Now I pronounce my judgments
against them."

¹³Look! He advances like the clouds,

his chariots come like a
whirlwind,
his horses are swifter than eagles.
Woe to us! We are ruined!
¹⁴O Jerusalem, wash the evil from
your heart and be saved.
How long will you harbor
wicked thoughts?
¹⁵A voice is announcing from Dan,
proclaiming disaster from the
hills of Ephraim.
¹⁶"Tell this to the nations,
proclaim it to Jerusalem:
'A besieging army is coming from
a distant land,
raising a war cry against the
cities of Judah.
¹⁷They surround her like men
guarding a field,
because she has rebelled against
me,' "
declares the LORD.
¹⁸"Your own conduct and actions
have brought this upon you.
This is your punishment.
How bitter it is!
How it pierces to the heart!"

¹⁹Oh, my anguish, my anguish!
I writhe in pain.
Oh, the agony of my heart!
My heart pounds within me,
I cannot keep silent.
For I have heard the sound of the
trumpet;
I have heard the battle cry.
²⁰Disaster follows disaster;
the whole land lies in ruins.
In an instant my tents are
destroyed,
my shelter in a moment.
²¹How long must I see the battle
standard
and hear the sound of the
trumpet?

²²"My people are fools;
they do not know me.
They are senseless children;
they have no understanding.
They are skilled in doing evil;
they know not how to do
good."

ᵃ12 Or comes at my command

²³I looked at the earth,
and it was formless and empty;
and at the heavens,
and their light was gone.
²⁴I looked at the mountains,
and they were quaking;
all the hills were swaying.
²⁵I looked, and there were no
people;
every bird in the sky had flown
away.
²⁶I looked, and the fruitful land was
a desert;
all its towns lay in ruins
before the LORD, before his fierce
anger.

²⁷This is what the LORD says:

"The whole land will be ruined,
though I will not destroy it
completely.
²⁸Therefore the earth will mourn
and the heavens above grow
dark,
because I have spoken and will
not relent,
I have decided and will not
turn back."

²⁹At the sound of horsemen and
archers
every town takes to flight.
Some go into the thickets;
some climb up among the rocks.
All the towns are deserted;
no one lives in them.

³⁰What are you doing, O devastated
one?
Why dress yourself in scarlet
and put on jewels of gold?
Why shade your eyes with paint?
You adorn yourself in vain.
Your lovers despise you;
they seek your life.

³¹I hear a cry as of a woman in
labor,
a groan as of one bearing her
first child—
the cry of the Daughter of Zion
gasping for breath,
stretching out her hands and
saying,
"Alas! I am fainting;

my life is given over to
murderers."

Not One Is Upright

5 "Go up and down the streets of
Jerusalem,
look around and consider,
search through her squares.
If you can find but one person
who deals honestly and seeks
the truth,
I will forgive this city.
²Although they say, 'As surely as
the LORD lives,'
still they are swearing falsely."

³O LORD, do not your eyes look for
truth?
You struck them, but they felt
no pain;
you crushed them, but they
refused correction.
They made their faces harder than
stone
and refused to repent.
⁴I thought, "These are only the
poor;
they are foolish,
for they do not know the way of
the LORD,
the requirements of their God.
⁵So I will go to the leaders
and speak to them;
surely they know the way of the
LORD,
the requirements of their God."
But with one accord they too had
broken off the yoke
and torn off the bonds.
⁶Therefore a lion from the forest
will attack them,
a wolf from the desert will
ravage them,
a leopard will lie in wait near
their towns
to tear to pieces any who
venture out,
for their rebellion is great
and their backslidings many.

⁷"Why should I forgive you?
Your children have forsaken me
and sworn by gods that are not
gods.
I supplied all their needs,
yet they committed adultery

and thronged to the houses of
    prostitutes.
⁸They are well-fed, lusty stallions,
    each neighing for another man's
        wife.
⁹Should I not punish them for
        this?"
    declares the LORD.
"Should I not avenge myself
    on such a nation as this?

¹⁰"Go through her vineyards and
        ravage them,
    but do not destroy them
        completely.
Strip off her branches,
    for these people do not belong
        to the LORD.
¹¹The house of Israel and the house
        of Judah
    have been utterly unfaithful to
        me,"
                    declares the LORD.

¹²They have lied about the LORD;
    they said, "He will do nothing!
No harm will come to us;
    we will never see sword or
        famine.
¹³The prophets are but wind
    and the word is not in them;
    so let what they say be done to
        them."

¹⁴Therefore this is what the LORD
God Almighty says:

"Because the people have spoken
        these words,
    I will make my words in your
        mouth a fire
    and these people the wood it
        consumes.
¹⁵O house of Israel," declares the
        LORD,
    "I am bringing a distant nation
        against you—
an ancient and enduring nation,
    a people whose language you
        do not know,
    whose speech you do not
        understand.
¹⁶Their quivers are like an open
        grave;
    all of them are mighty warriors.
¹⁷They will devour your harvests
        and food,

devour your sons and
        daughters;
they will devour your flocks and
        herds,
    devour your vines and fig trees.
With the sword they will destroy
    the fortified cities in which you
        trust.

¹⁸"Yet even in those days," declares
the LORD, "I will not destroy you completely. ¹⁹And when the people ask,
'Why has the LORD our God done all
this to us?' you will tell them, 'As you
have forsaken me and served foreign
gods in your own land, so now you
will serve foreigners in a land not
your own.'

²⁰"Announce this to the house of
        Jacob
    and proclaim it in Judah:
²¹Hear this, you foolish and
        senseless people,
    who have eyes but do not see,
    who have ears but do not hear:
²²Should you not fear me?" declares
        the LORD.
    "Should you not tremble in my
        presence?
I made the sand a boundary for
        the sea,
    an everlasting barrier it cannot
        cross.
The waves may roll, but they
        cannot prevail;
    they may roar, but they cannot
        cross it.
²³But these people have stubborn
        and rebellious hearts;
    they have turned aside and
        gone away.
²⁴They do not say to themselves,
    'Let us fear the LORD our God,
who gives autumn and spring
        rains in season,
    who assures us of the regular
        weeks of harvest.'
²⁵Your wrongdoings have kept these
        away;
    your sins have deprived you of
        good.

²⁶"Among my people are wicked
        men

who lie in wait like men who
snare birds
and like those who set traps to
catch men.
27Like cages full of birds,
their houses are full of deceit;
they have become rich and
powerful
28 and have grown fat and sleek.
Their evil deeds have no limit;
they do not plead the case of
the fatherless to win it,
they do not defend the rights of
the poor.
29Should I not punish them for
this?"
declares the LORD.
"Should I not avenge myself
on such a nation as this?

30"A horrible and shocking thing
has happened in the land:
31The prophets prophesy lies,
the priests rule by their own
authority,
and my people love it this way.
But what will you do in the
end?

Jerusalem Under Siege

6 "Flee for safety, people of
Benjamin!
Flee from Jerusalem!
Sound the trumpet in Tekoa!
Raise the signal over Beth
Hakkerem!
For disaster looms out of the
north,
even terrible destruction.
2I will destroy the Daughter of
Zion,
so beautiful and delicate.
3Shepherds with their flocks will
come against her;
they will pitch their tents
around her,
each tending his own portion."

4"Prepare for battle against her!
Arise, let us attack at noon!
But, alas, the daylight is fading,
and the shadows of evening
grow long.

5So arise, let us attack at night
and destroy her fortresses!"

6This is what the LORD Almighty
says:

"Cut down the trees
and build siege ramps against
Jerusalem.
This city must be punished;
it is filled with oppression.
7As a well pours out its water,
so she pours out her
wickedness.
Violence and destruction resound
in her;
her sickness and wounds are
ever before me.
8Take warning, O Jerusalem,
or I will turn away from you
and make your land desolate
so no one can live in it."

9This is what the LORD Almighty
says:

"Let them glean the remnant of
Israel
as thoroughly as a vine;
pass your hand over the branches
again,
like one gathering grapes."

10To whom can I speak and give
warning?
Who will listen to me?
Their ears are closed[a]
so they cannot hear.
The word of the LORD is offensive
to them;
they find no pleasure in it.
11But I am full of the wrath of the
LORD,
and I cannot hold it in.

"Pour it out on the children in the
street
and on the young men gathered
together;
both husband and wife will be
caught in it,
and the old, those weighed
down with years.
12Their houses will be turned over
to others,

a10 Hebrew *uncircumcised*

together with their fields and
　　their wives,
when I stretch out my hand
　　against those who live in the
　　　land,"
　　　　　　　　declares the LORD.
¹³"From the least to the greatest,
　　all are greedy for gain;
prophets and priests alike,
　　all practice deceit.
¹⁴They dress the wound of my
　　people
　　as though it were not serious.
'Peace, peace,' they say,
　　when there is no peace.
¹⁵Are they ashamed of their
　　loathsome conduct?
No, they have no shame at all;
　　they do not even know how to
　　　blush.
So they will fall among the fallen;
　　they will be brought down
　　　when I punish them,"
　　　　　　　　says the LORD.

¹⁶This is what the LORD says:

"Stand at the crossroads and look;
　　ask for the ancient paths,
ask where the good way is, and
　　walk in it,
　　and you will find rest for your
　　　souls.
　　But you said, 'We will not walk
　　　in it.'
¹⁷I appointed watchmen over you
　　and said,
　　'Listen to the sound of the
　　　trumpet!'
　　But you said, 'We will not
　　　listen.'
¹⁸Therefore hear, O nations;
　　observe, O witnesses,
　　what will happen to them.
¹⁹Hear, O earth:
I am bringing disaster on this
　　people,
　　the fruit of their schemes,
because they have not listened to
　　my words
and have rejected my law.
²⁰What do I care about incense from
　　Sheba
　　or sweet calamus from a distant
　　　land?

Your burnt offerings are not
　　acceptable;
　　your sacrifices do not please
　　　me."

²¹Therefore this is what the LORD
says:

"I will put obstacles before this
　　people.
　　Fathers and sons alike will
　　　stumble over them;
　　neighbors and friends will
　　　perish."

²²This is what the LORD says:

"Look, an army is coming
　　from the land of the north;
a great nation is being stirred up
　　from the ends of the earth.
²³They are armed with bow and
　　spear;
　　they are cruel and show no
　　　mercy.
They sound like the roaring sea
　　as they ride on their horses;
they come like men in battle
　　formation
　　to attack you, O Daughter of
　　　Zion."

²⁴We have heard reports about
　　them,
　　and our hands hang limp.
Anguish has gripped us,
　　pain like that of a woman in
　　　labor.
²⁵Do not go out to the fields
　　or walk on the roads,
for the enemy has a sword,
　　and there is terror on every
　　　side.
²⁶O my people, put on sackcloth
　　and roll in ashes;
mourn with bitter wailing
　　as for an only son,
for suddenly the destroyer
　　will come upon us.

²⁷"I have made you a tester of
　　metals
　　and my people the ore,
that you may observe
　　and test their ways.
²⁸They are all hardened rebels,
　　going about to slander.
They are bronze and iron;

they all act corruptly.
²⁹The bellows blow fiercely
    to burn away the lead with fire,
but the refining goes on in vain;
    the wicked are not purged out.
³⁰They are called rejected silver,
    because the LORD has rejected
    them."

False Religion Worthless

7 This is the word that came to Jeremiah from the LORD: ²"Stand at the gate of the LORD's house and there proclaim this message:

" 'Hear the word of the LORD, all you people of Judah who come through these gates to worship the LORD. ³This is what the LORD Almighty, the God of Israel, says: Reform your ways and your actions, and I will let you live in this place. ⁴Do not trust in deceptive words and say, "This is the temple of the LORD, the temple of the LORD, the temple of the LORD!" ⁵If you really change your ways and your actions and deal with each other justly, ⁶if you do not oppress the alien, the fatherless or the widow and do not shed innocent blood in this place, and if you do not follow other gods to your own harm, ⁷then I will let you live in this place, in the land I gave your forefathers for ever and ever. ⁸But look, you are trusting in deceptive words that are worthless.

⁹" 'Will you steal and murder, commit adultery and perjury,ª burn incense to Baal and follow other gods you have not known, ¹⁰and then come and stand before me in this house, which bears my Name, and say, "We are safe"—safe to do all these detestable things? ¹¹Has this house, which bears my Name, become a den of robbers to you? But I have been watching! declares the LORD.

¹²" 'Go now to the place in Shiloh where I first made a dwelling for my Name, and see what I did to it because of the wickedness of my people Israel. ¹³While you were doing all these things, declares the LORD, I spoke to you again and again, but you did not listen; I called you, but you did not answer. ¹⁴Therefore, what I did to Shiloh I will now do to the house that bears my Name, the temple you trust in, the place I gave to you and your fathers. ¹⁵I will thrust you from my presence, just as I did all your brothers, the people of Ephraim.'

¹⁶"So do not pray for this people nor offer any plea or petition for them; do not plead with me, for I will not listen to you. ¹⁷Do you not see what they are doing in the towns of Judah and in the streets of Jerusalem? ¹⁸The children gather wood, the fathers light the fire, and the women knead the dough and make cakes of bread for the Queen of Heaven. They pour out drink offerings to other gods to provoke me to anger. ¹⁹But am I the one they are provoking? declares the LORD. Are they not rather harming themselves, to their own shame?

²⁰" 'Therefore this is what the Sovereign LORD says: My anger and my wrath will be poured out on this place, on man and beast, on the trees of the field and on the fruit of the ground, and it will burn and not be quenched.

²¹" 'This is what the LORD Almighty, the God of Israel, says: Go ahead, add your burnt offerings to your other sacrifices and eat the meat yourselves! ²²For when I brought your forefathers out of Egypt and spoke to them, I did not just give them commands about burnt offerings and sacrifices, ²³but I gave them this command: Obey me, and I will be your God and you will be my people. Walk in all the ways I command you, that it may go well with you. ²⁴But they did not listen or pay attention; instead, they followed the stubborn inclinations of their evil hearts. They went backward and not forward. ²⁵From the time your forefathers left Egypt until now, day after day, again and again I sent you my servants the prophets. ²⁶But they did not listen to me or pay attention. They

---

ª9 Or and swear by false gods

were stiff-necked and did more evil than their forefathers.'

²⁷"When you tell them all this, they will not listen to you; when you call to them, they will not answer. ²⁸Therefore say to them, 'This is the nation that has not obeyed the LORD its God or responded to correction. Truth has perished; it has vanished from their lips. ²⁹Cut off your hair and throw it away; take up a lament on the barren heights, for the LORD has rejected and abandoned this generation that is under his wrath.

The Valley of Slaughter

³⁰" 'The people of Judah have done evil in my eyes, declares the LORD. They have set up their detestable idols in the house that bears my Name and have defiled it. ³¹They have built the high places of Topheth in the Valley of Ben Hinnom to burn their sons and daughters in the fire— something I did not command, nor did it enter my mind. ³²So beware, the days are coming, declares the LORD, when people will no longer call it Topheth or the Valley of Ben Hinnom, but the Valley of Slaughter, for they will bury the dead in Topheth until there is no more room. ³³Then the carcasses of this people will become food for the birds of the air and the beasts of the earth, and there will be no one to frighten them away. ³⁴I will bring an end to the sounds of joy and gladness and to the voices of bride and bridegroom in the towns of Judah and the streets of Jerusalem, for the land will become desolate.

8 " 'At that time, declares the LORD, the bones of the kings and officials of Judah, the bones of the priests and prophets, and the bones of the people of Jerusalem will be removed from their graves. ²They will be exposed to the sun and the moon and all the stars of the heavens, which they have loved and served and which they have followed and consulted and worshiped. They will not be gathered up or buried, but will be like refuse lying on the ground. ³Wherever I banish them, all the survivors of this

evil nation will prefer death to life, declares the LORD Almighty.'

Sin and Punishment

⁴"Say to them, 'This is what the LORD says:

" 'When men fall down, do they
  not get up?
When a man turns away, does
  he not return?
⁵Why then have these people
  turned away?
Why does Jerusalem always
  turn away?
They cling to deceit;
  they refuse to return.
⁶I have listened attentively,
  but they do not say what is
  right.
No one repents of his wickedness,
  saying, "What have I done?"
Each pursues his own course
  like a horse charging into battle.
⁷Even the stork in the sky
  knows her appointed seasons,
and the dove, the swift and the
  thrush
  observe the time of their
  migration.
But my people do not know
  the requirements of the LORD.

⁸" 'How can you say, "We are
  wise,
  for we have the law of the
  LORD,"
when actually the lying pen of the
  scribes
  has handled it falsely?
⁹The wise will be put to shame;
  they will be dismayed and
  trapped.
Since they have rejected the word
  of the LORD,
  what kind of wisdom do they
  have?
¹⁰Therefore I will give their wives to
  other men
  and their fields to new owners.
From the least to the greatest,
  all are greedy for gain;
prophets and priests alike,
  all practice deceit.
¹¹They dress the wound of my
  people

as though it were not serious.
"Peace, peace," they say,
    when there is no peace.
¹²Are they ashamed of their
        loathsome conduct?
    No, they have no shame at all;
    they do not even know how to
        blush.
So they will fall among the fallen;
    they will be brought down
        when they are punished,
                    says the LORD.

¹³" 'I will take away their harvest,
            declares the LORD.
    There will be no grapes on the
        vine.
    There will be no figs on the tree,
        and their leaves will wither.
    What I have given them
        will be taken from them.ᵃ' "

¹⁴"Why are we sitting here?
    Gather together!
    Let us flee to the fortified cities
        and perish there!
    For the LORD our God has doomed
        us to perish
        and given us poisoned water to
            drink,
        because we have sinned against
            him.
¹⁵We hoped for peace
    but no good has come,
    for a time of healing
    but there was only terror.
¹⁶The snorting of the enemy's horses
    is heard from Dan;
    at the neighing of their stallions
        the whole land trembles.
    They have come to devour
        the land and everything in it,
        the city and all who live there."

¹⁷"See, I will send venomous snakes
            among you,
    vipers that cannot be charmed,
    and they will bite you,"
            declares the LORD.

¹⁸O my Comforterᵇ in sorrow,
    my heart is faint within me.
¹⁹Listen to the cry of my people

from a land far away:
    "Is the LORD not in Zion?
    Is her King no longer there?"

"Why have they provoked me to
        anger with their images,
    with their worthless foreign
        idols?"

²⁰"The harvest is past,
    the summer has ended,
    and we are not saved."

²¹Since my people are crushed, I am
        crushed;
    I mourn, and horror grips me.
²²Is there no balm in Gilead?
    Is there no physician there?
    Why then is there no healing
        for the wound of my people?

9 ¹Oh, that my head were a spring
        of water
    and my eyes a fountain of tears!
    I would weep day and night
        for the slain of my people.
²Oh, that I had in the desert
    a lodging place for travelers,
    so that I might leave my people
        and go away from them;
    for they are all adulterers,
        a crowd of unfaithful people.

³"They make ready their tongue
        like a bow, to shoot lies;
    it is not by truth
        that they triumphᶜ in the land.
    They go from one sin to another;
        they do not acknowledge me,"
                    declares the LORD.
⁴"Beware of your friends;
    do not trust your brothers.
    For every brother is a deceiver,ᵈ
        and every friend a slanderer.
⁵Friend deceives friend,
    and no one speaks the truth.
    They have taught their tongues to
        lie;
    they weary themselves with
        sinning.
⁶Youᵉ live in the midst of
        deception;

ᵃ13 The meaning of the Hebrew for this sentence is uncertain.   ᵇ18 The meaning of the
Hebrew for this word is uncertain.   ᶜ3 Or lies; / they are not valiant for truth   ᵈ4 Or a
deceiving Jacob   ᵉ6 That is, Jeremiah (the Hebrew is singular)

in their deceit they refuse to
acknowledge me,"
    declares the Lord.

7Therefore this is what the Lord Almighty says:

"See, I will refine and test them,
    for what else can I do
    because of the sin of my
        people?
8Their tongue is a deadly arrow;
    it speaks with deceit.
With his mouth each speaks
        cordially to his neighbor,
    but in his heart he sets a trap
        for him.
9Should I not punish them for
        this?"
    declares the Lord.
"Should I not avenge myself
    on such a nation as this?"

10I will weep and wail for the
        mountains
    and take up a lament
        concerning the desert
        pastures.
They are desolate and untraveled,
    and the lowing of cattle is not
        heard.
The birds of the air have fled
    and the animals are gone.

11"I will make Jerusalem a heap of
        ruins,
    a haunt of jackals;
and I will lay waste the towns of
        Judah
    so no one can live there."

12What man is wise enough to understand this? Who has been instructed by the Lord and can explain it? Why has the land been ruined and laid waste like a desert that no one can cross?
13The Lord said, "It is because they have forsaken my law, which I set before them; they have not obeyed me or followed my law. 14Instead, they have followed the stubbornness of their hearts; they have followed the Baals, as their fathers taught them." 15Therefore, this is what the Lord Almighty, the God of Israel, says: "See, I will make this people eat bitter food

and drink poisoned water. 16I will scatter them among nations that neither they nor their fathers have known, and I will pursue them with the sword until I have destroyed them."

17This is what the Lord Almighty says:

"Consider now! Call for the
        wailing women to come;
    send for the most skillful of
        them.
18Let them come quickly
    and wail over us
till our eyes overflow with tears
    and water streams from our
        eyelids.
19The sound of wailing is heard
        from Zion:
    'How ruined we are!
    How great is our shame!
We must leave our land
    because our houses are in
        ruins.' "

20Now, O women, hear the word of
        the Lord;
    open your ears to the words of
        his mouth.
Teach your daughters how to
        wail;
    teach one another a lament.
21Death has climbed in through our
        windows
    and has entered our fortresses;
it has cut off the children from the
        streets
    and the young men from the
        public squares.

22Say, "This is what the Lord declares:

" 'The dead bodies of men will lie
    like refuse on the open field,
like cut grain behind the reaper,
    with no one to gather them.' "

23This is what the Lord says:

"Let not the wise man boast of his
        wisdom
    or the strong man boast of his
        strength
    or the rich man boast of his
        riches,

²⁴but let him who boasts boast
about this:
that he understands and knows
me,
that I am the LORD, who exercises
kindness,
justice and righteousness on
earth,
for in these I delight,"
declares the LORD.

²⁵"The days are coming," declares
the LORD, "when I will punish all who
are circumcised only in the flesh—
²⁶Egypt, Judah, Edom, Ammon, Moab
and all who live in the desert in distant places.ᵃ For all these nations are
really uncircumcised, and even the
whole house of Israel is uncircumcised in heart."

God and Idols

10 Hear what the LORD says to
you, O house of Israel. ²This is
what the LORD says:

"Do not learn the ways of the
nations
or be terrified by signs in the
sky,
though the nations are terrified
by them.
³For the customs of the peoples are
worthless;
they cut a tree out of the forest,
and a craftsman shapes it with
his chisel.
⁴They adorn it with silver and
gold;
they fasten it with hammer and
nails
so it will not totter.
⁵Like a scarecrow in a melon patch,
their idols cannot speak;
they must be carried
because they cannot walk.
Do not fear them;
they can do no harm
nor can they do any good."

⁶No one is like you, O LORD;
you are great,
and your name is mighty in
power.

⁷Who should not revere you,
O King of the nations?
This is your due.
Among all the wise men of the
nations
and in all their kingdoms,
there is no one like you.
⁸They are all senseless and foolish;
they are taught by worthless
wooden idols.
⁹Hammered silver is brought from
Tarshish
and gold from Uphaz.
What the craftsman and goldsmith
have made
is then dressed in blue and
purple—
all made by skilled workers.
¹⁰But the LORD is the true God;
he is the living God, the eternal
King.
When he is angry, the earth
trembles;
the nations cannot endure his
wrath.

¹¹"Tell them this: 'These gods, who
did not make the heavens and the
earth, will perish from the earth and
from under the heavens.' "ᵇ

¹²But God made the earth by his
power;
he founded the world by his
wisdom
and stretched out the heavens
by his understanding.
¹³When he thunders, the waters in
the heavens roar;
he makes clouds rise from the
ends of the earth.
He sends lightning with the rain
and brings out the wind from
his storehouses.

¹⁴Everyone is senseless and without
knowledge;
every goldsmith is shamed by
his idols.
His images are a fraud;
they have no breath in them.
¹⁵They are worthless, the objects of
mockery;

ᵃ26 Or *desert and who clip the hair by their foreheads*   ᵇ11 The text of this verse is in Aramaic.

when their judgment comes,
they will perish.
16He who is the Portion of Jacob is
not like these,
for he is the Maker of all things,
including Israel, the tribe of his
inheritance—
the LORD Almighty is his name.

Coming Destruction

17Gather up your belongings to
leave the land,
you who live under siege.
18For this is what the LORD says:
"At this time I will hurl out
those who live in this land;
I will bring distress on them
so that they may be captured."

19Woe to me because of my injury!
My wound is incurable!
Yet I said to myself,
"This is my sickness, and I must
endure it."
20My tent is destroyed;
all its ropes are snapped.
My sons are gone from me and
are no more;
no one is left now to pitch my
tent
or to set up my shelter.
21The shepherds are senseless
and do not inquire of the LORD;
so they do not prosper
and all their flock is scattered.
22Listen! The report is coming—
a great commotion from the
land of the north!
It will make the towns of Judah
desolate,
a haunt of jackals.

Jeremiah's Prayer

23I know, O LORD, that a man's life
is not his own;
it is not for man to direct his
steps.
24Correct me, LORD, but only with
justice—
not in your anger,
lest you reduce me to nothing.
25Pour out your wrath on the
nations
that do not acknowledge you,

on the peoples who do not call
on your name.
For they have devoured Jacob;
they have devoured him
completely
and destroyed his homeland.

The Covenant Is Broken

11 This is the word that came to
Jeremiah from the LORD: 2"Listen to the terms of this covenant and
tell them to the people of Judah and
to those who live in Jerusalem. 3Tell
them that this is what the LORD, the
God of Israel, says: 'Cursed is the man
who does not obey the terms of this
covenant— 4the terms I commanded
your forefathers when I brought them
out of Egypt, out of the iron-smelting
furnace.' I said, 'Obey me and do everything I command you, and you
will be my people, and I will be your
God. 5Then I will fulfill the oath I
swore to your forefathers, to give
them a land flowing with milk and
honey'—the land you possess today."

I answered, "Amen, LORD."

6The LORD said to me, "Proclaim all
these words in the towns of Judah
and in the streets of Jerusalem: 'Listen
to the terms of this covenant and follow them. 7From the time I brought
your forefathers up from Egypt until
today, I warned them again and
again, saying, "Obey me." 8But they
did not listen or pay attention; instead, they followed the stubbornness
of their evil hearts. So I brought on
them all the curses of the covenant I
had commanded them to follow but
that they did not keep.' "

9Then the LORD said to me, "There
is a conspiracy among the people of
Judah and those who live in Jerusalem. 10They have returned to the sins
of their forefathers, who refused to
listen to my words. They have followed other gods to serve them. Both
the house of Israel and the house of
Judah have broken the covenant I
made with their forefathers. 11Therefore this is what the LORD says: 'I will
bring on them a disaster they cannot
escape. Although they cry out to me, I
will not listen to them. 12The towns of

Judah and the people of Jerusalem will go and cry out to the gods to whom they burn incense, but they will not help them at all when disaster strikes. ¹³You have as many gods as you have towns, O Judah; and the altars you have set up to burn incense to that shameful god Baal are as many as the streets of Jerusalem.'

¹⁴"Do not pray for this people nor offer any plea or petition for them, because I will not listen when they call to me in the time of their distress.

¹⁵"What is my beloved doing in my
    temple
    as she works out her evil
        schemes with many?

TUESDAY

VERSE:	AUTHOR:	PASSAGE:
Jeremiah 11:5	F. B. Meyer	Jeremiah 11:1–8

The Soul's Amen

Jeremiah was conscious of the special current of divine energy that was passing into and through his soul. The word had come to him "from the LORD," and he felt it as a burning fire that he could not contain. He must needs give vent to it, but when it has passed his lips, and he has time carefully to consider it, he answers the divine message by saying—"So be it, Lord!"

The soul's affirmation. Let us guard against mistake. It is not always possible to say "Amen"—Yes—to God in tones of triumph and ecstasy. Sometimes our response is choked with sobs that cannot be stifled, and soaked with tears that cannot be repressed . . . These words may be read by some who suffer year after year constant pain, by those whose earthly life is tossed upon the sea of anxiety, over which billows of care and turmoil perpetually roll . . .

Dare to say "Amen" to God's providential dealings. Say it, though heart and flesh fail . . . "What you do not know now, you will know hereafter" is the assurance of our Guide. Dare to trust him, and in the strength of that trust to say, "Amen, O Lord."

ADDITIONAL SCRIPTURE READINGS
Psalm 37:1–7; Matthew 26:36–46

Go to page 961 for your next devotional reading.

Can consecrated meat avert
␣your punishment␣?
When you engage in your
wickedness,
then you rejoice.*"

¹⁶The LORD called you a thriving
olive tree
with fruit beautiful in form.
But with the roar of a mighty
storm
he will set it on fire,
and its branches will be broken.

¹⁷The LORD Almighty, who planted
you, has decreed disaster for you, because the house of Israel and the
house of Judah have done evil and
provoked me to anger by burning incense to Baal.

Plot Against Jeremiah

¹⁸Because the LORD revealed their
plot to me, I knew it, for at that time
he showed me what they were doing.
¹⁹I had been like a gentle lamb led to
the slaughter; I did not realize that
they had plotted against me, saying,

"Let us destroy the tree and its
fruit;
let us cut him off from the land
of the living,
that his name be remembered
no more."

²⁰But, O LORD Almighty, you who
judge righteously
and test the heart and mind,
let me see your vengeance upon
them,
for to you I have committed my
cause.

²¹"Therefore this is what the LORD
says about the men of Anathoth who
are seeking your life and saying, 'Do
not prophesy in the name of the LORD
or you will die by our hands'—
²²therefore this is what the LORD Almighty says: 'I will punish them.
Their young men will die by the
sword, their sons and daughters by
famine. ²³Not even a remnant will be
left to them, because I will bring di-

saster on the men of Anathoth in the
year of their punishment.' "

Jeremiah's Complaint

12 You are always righteous,
O LORD,
when I bring a case before you.
Yet I would speak with you about
your justice:
Why does the way of the
wicked prosper?
Why do all the faithless live at
ease?
²You have planted them, and they
have taken root;
they grow and bear fruit.
You are always on their lips
but far from their hearts.
³Yet you know me, O LORD;
you see me and test my
thoughts about you.
Drag them off like sheep to be
butchered!
Set them apart for the day of
slaughter!
⁴How long will the land lie
parched*
and the grass in every field be
withered?
Because those who live in it are
wicked,
the animals and birds have
perished.
Moreover, the people are saying,
"He will not see what happens
to us."

God's Answer

⁵"If you have raced with men on
foot
and they have worn you out,
how can you compete with
horses?
If you stumble in safe country,*
how will you manage in the
thickets by* the Jordan?
⁶Your brothers, your own family—
even they have betrayed you;
they have raised a loud cry
against you.
Do not trust them,
though they speak well of you.

---

*15 Or *Could consecrated meat avert your punishment? | Then you would rejoice*   *4 Or *land mourn*
*5 Or *If you put your trust in a land of safety*   *5 Or *the flooding of*

7"I will forsake my house,
  abandon my inheritance;
I will give the one I love
  into the hands of her enemies.
8My inheritance has become to me
  like a lion in the forest.
She roars at me;
  therefore I hate her.
9Has not my inheritance become to
    me
  like a speckled bird of prey
  that other birds of prey
    surround and attack?
Go and gather all the wild beasts;
  bring them to devour.
10Many shepherds will ruin my
    vineyard
  and trample down my field;
they will turn my pleasant field
  into a desolate wasteland.
11It will be made a wasteland,
  parched and desolate before me;
the whole land will be laid waste
  because there is no one who
    cares.
12Over all the barren heights in the
    desert
  destroyers will swarm,
for the sword of the LORD will
    devour
  from one end of the land to the
    other;
  no one will be safe.
13They will sow wheat but reap
    thorns;
  they will wear themselves out
    but gain nothing.
So bear the shame of your harvest
  because of the LORD's fierce
    anger."

14This is what the LORD says: "As
for all my wicked neighbors who
seize the inheritance I gave my people
Israel, I will uproot them from their
lands and I will uproot the house of
Judah from among them. 15But after I
uproot them, I will again have compassion and will bring each of them
back to his own inheritance and his
own country. 16And if they learn well
the ways of my people and swear by
my name, saying, 'As surely as the

LORD lives'—even as they once taught
my people to swear by Baal—then
they will be established among my
people. 17But if any nation does not
listen, I will completely uproot and
destroy it," declares the LORD.

A Linen Belt

13 This is what the LORD said to
me: "Go and buy a linen belt
and put it around your waist, but do
not let it touch water." 2So I bought a
belt, as the LORD directed, and put it
around my waist.

3Then the word of the LORD came to
me a second time: 4"Take the belt you
bought and are wearing around your
waist, and go now to Perath[a] and
hide it there in a crevice in the rocks."
5So I went and hid it at Perath, as the
LORD told me.

6Many days later the LORD said to
me, "Go now to Perath and get the
belt I told you to hide there." 7So I
went to Perath and dug up the belt
and took it from the place where I had
hidden it, but now it was ruined and
completely useless.

8Then the word of the LORD came to
me: 9"This is what the LORD says: 'In
the same way I will ruin the pride of
Judah and the great pride of Jerusalem. 10These wicked people, who refuse to listen to my words, who follow the stubbornness of their hearts
and go after other gods to serve and
worship them, will be like this belt—
completely useless! 11For as a belt is
bound around a man's waist, so I
bound the whole house of Israel and
the whole house of Judah to me,' declares the LORD, 'to be my people for
my renown and praise and honor. But
they have not listened.'

Wineskins

12"Say to them: 'This is what the
LORD, the God of Israel, says: Every
wineskin should be filled with wine.'
And if they say to you, 'Don't we
know that every wineskin should be
filled with wine?' 13then tell them,
'This is what the LORD says: I am go-

---

a4 Or possibly *the Euphrates*; also in verses 5-7

ing to fill with drunkenness all who live in this land, including the kings who sit on David's throne, the priests, the prophets and all those living in Jerusalem. ¹⁴I will smash them one against the other, fathers and sons alike, declares the LORD. I will allow no pity or mercy or compassion to keep me from destroying them.' "

Threat of Captivity

¹⁵Hear and pay attention,
  do not be arrogant,
  for the LORD has spoken.
¹⁶Give glory to the LORD your God
  before he brings the darkness,
before your feet stumble
  on the darkening hills.
  You hope for light,
  but he will turn it to thick
    darkness
  and change it to deep gloom.
¹⁷But if you do not listen,
  I will weep in secret
  because of your pride;
my eyes will weep bitterly,
  overflowing with tears,
  because the LORD's flock will be
    taken captive.

¹⁸Say to the king and to the queen
    mother,
  "Come down from your
    thrones,
  for your glorious crowns
  will fall from your heads."
¹⁹The cities in the Negev will be
    shut up,
  and there will be no one to
    open them.
All Judah will be carried into
    exile,
  carried completely away.

²⁰Lift up your eyes and see
  those who are coming from the
    north.
  Where is the flock that was
    entrusted to you,
  the sheep of which you
    boasted?
²¹What will you say when ˌthe
  LORDˌ sets over you

those you cultivated as your
    special allies?
Will not pain grip you
  like that of a woman in labor?
²²And if you ask yourself,
  "Why has this happened to
    me?"—
it is because of your many sins
  that your skirts have been torn
    off
  and your body mistreated.
²³Can the Ethiopian*a* change his
    skin
  or the leopard its spots?
Neither can you do good
  who are accustomed to doing
    evil.

²⁴"I will scatter you like chaff
  driven by the desert wind.
²⁵This is your lot,
  the portion I have decreed for
    you,"
                    declares the LORD,
  "because you have forgotten me
  and trusted in false gods.
²⁶I will pull up your skirts over
    your face
  that your shame may be seen—
²⁷your adulteries and lustful
    neighings,
  your shameless prostitution!
I have seen your detestable acts
  on the hills and in the fields.
Woe to you, O Jerusalem!
  How long will you be unclean?"

Drought, Famine, Sword

14 This is the word of the LORD to Jeremiah concerning the drought:

²"Judah mourns,
  her cities languish;
they wail for the land,
  and a cry goes up from
    Jerusalem.
³The nobles send their servants for
    water;
  they go to the cisterns
  but find no water.
They return with their jars
    unfilled;
  dismayed and despairing,

---

*a*23 Hebrew *Cushite* (probably a person from the upper Nile region)

they cover their heads.
⁴The ground is cracked
   because there is no rain in the
      land;
the farmers are dismayed
   and cover their heads.
⁵Even the doe in the field
   deserts her newborn fawn
   because there is no grass.
⁶Wild donkeys stand on the barren
      heights
   and pant like jackals;
their eyesight fails
   for lack of pasture."

⁷Although our sins testify against
      us,
   O Lord, do something for the
      sake of your name.
For our backsliding is great;
   we have sinned against you.
⁸O Hope of Israel,
   its Savior in times of distress,
why are you like a stranger in the
      land,
   like a traveler who stays only a
      night?
⁹Why are you like a man taken by
      surprise,
   like a warrior powerless to
      save?
You are among us, O Lord,
   and we bear your name;
   do not forsake us!

¹⁰This is what the Lord says about
this people:

"They greatly love to wander;
   they do not restrain their feet.
So the Lord does not accept them;
   he will now remember their
      wickedness
   and punish them for their sins."

¹¹Then the Lord said to me, "Do not
pray for the well-being of this people.
¹²Although they fast, I will not listen
to their cry; though they offer burnt
offerings and grain offerings, I will
not accept them. Instead, I will destroy them with the sword, famine
and plague."
¹³But I said, "Ah, Sovereign Lord,
the prophets keep telling them, 'You

will not see the sword or suffer famine. Indeed, I will give you lasting
peace in this place.' "
¹⁴Then the Lord said to me, "The
prophets are prophesying lies in my
name. I have not sent them or appointed them or spoken to them.
They are prophesying to you false visions, divinations, idolatries[a] and
the delusions of their own minds.
¹⁵Therefore, this is what the Lord says
about the prophets who are prophesying in my name: I did not send
them, yet they are saying, 'No sword
or famine will touch this land.' Those
same prophets will perish by sword
and famine. ¹⁶And the people they are
prophesying to will be thrown out
into the streets of Jerusalem because
of the famine and sword. There will
be no one to bury them or their wives,
their sons or their daughters. I will
pour out on them the calamity they
deserve.

¹⁷"Speak this word to them:

" 'Let my eyes overflow with tears
   night and day without ceasing;
for my virgin daughter—my
      people—
   has suffered a grievous wound,
   a crushing blow.
¹⁸If I go into the country,
   I see those slain by the sword;
if I go into the city,
   I see the ravages of famine.
Both prophet and priest
   have gone to a land they know
      not.' "

¹⁹Have you rejected Judah
      completely?
   Do you despise Zion?
Why have you afflicted us
   so that we cannot be healed?
We hoped for peace
   but no good has come,
for a time of healing
   but there is only terror.
²⁰O Lord, we acknowledge our
      wickedness
   and the guilt of our fathers;

ª14 Or *visions, worthless divinations*

we have indeed sinned against
you.
²¹For the sake of your name do not
despise us;
do not dishonor your glorious
throne.
Remember your covenant with us
and do not break it.
²²Do any of the worthless idols of
the nations bring rain?
Do the skies themselves send
down showers?
No, it is you, O LORD our God.
Therefore our hope is in you,
for you are the one who does
all this.

15 Then the LORD said to me:
"Even if Moses and Samuel
were to stand before me, my heart
would not go out to this people. Send
them away from my presence! Let
them go! ²And if they ask you, 'Where
shall we go?' tell them, 'This is what
the LORD says:

" 'Those destined for death, to
death;
those for the sword, to the sword;
those for starvation, to starvation;
those for captivity, to captivity.'

³"I will send four kinds of destroyers against them," declares the LORD,
"the sword to kill and the dogs to
drag away and the birds of the air and
the beasts of the earth to devour and
destroy. ⁴I will make them abhorrent
to all the kingdoms of the earth because of what Manasseh son of Hezekiah king of Judah did in Jerusalem.

⁵"Who will have pity on you,
O Jerusalem?
Who will mourn for you?
Who will stop to ask how you
are?
⁶You have rejected me," declares
the LORD.
"You keep on backsliding.
So I will lay hands on you and
destroy you;
I can no longer show
compassion.

⁷I will winnow them with a
winnowing fork
at the city gates of the land.
I will bring bereavement and
destruction on my people,
for they have not changed their
ways.
⁸I will make their widows more
numerous
than the sand of the sea.
At midday I will bring a destroyer
against the mothers of their
young men;
suddenly I will bring down on
them
anguish and terror.
⁹The mother of seven will grow
faint
and breathe her last.
Her sun will set while it is still
day;
she will be disgraced and
humiliated.
I will put the survivors to the
sword
before their enemies,"
declares the LORD.

¹⁰Alas, my mother, that you gave
me birth,
a man with whom the whole
land strives and contends!
I have neither lent nor borrowed,
yet everyone curses me.

¹¹The LORD said,

"Surely I will deliver you for a
good purpose;
surely I will make your enemies
plead with you
in times of disaster and times of
distress.

¹²"Can a man break iron—
iron from the north—or bronze?
¹³Your wealth and your treasures
I will give as plunder, without
charge,
because of all your sins
throughout your country.
¹⁴I will enslave you to your enemies
inᵃ a land you do not know,

ᵃ14 Some Hebrew manuscripts, Septuagint and Syriac (see also Jer. 17:4); most Hebrew
manuscripts *I will cause your enemies to bring you* / *into*

for my anger will kindle a fire
that will burn against you."

¹⁵You understand, O Lord;
remember me and care for me.
Avenge me on my persecutors.
You are long-suffering—do not
take me away;
think of how I suffer reproach
for your sake.
¹⁶When your words came, I ate
them;
they were my joy and my
heart's delight,
for I bear your name,
O Lord God Almighty.
¹⁷I never sat in the company of
revelers,
never made merry with them;
I sat alone because your hand was
on me
and you had filled me with
indignation.
¹⁸Why is my pain unending

WEDNESDAY

VERSE:
Jeremiah 15:16

AUTHOR:
Margaret Clarkson

PASSAGE:
Jeremiah 15:16–21

Precious Name

Throughout the Scriptures, God revealed himself to his people in the names by which he chose to be called. His character, his nature, his will, his faithfulness, his might, his honor, his renown, his glory, his grace, his love — all that he is in himself and in his attributes was disclosed by his name. His name was varied from time to time, as he had occasion to reveal himself to his people in different capacities; over 200 titles are used in the Scriptures. A list of his names should have a prominent place in the armory of every Christian and the appropriate name be invoked in any time of need . . .

God has set his name upon every believer in the Lord Jesus Christ, so that we, too, rest enclosed in God's faithfulness to his own name. "I bear your name, O Lord God Almighty" (Jeremiah 15:16). "You are among us, O Lord, and we bear your name" (Jeremiah 14:9). What a refuge and strength is the name of our God! Shall we not, then, learn to live in its power?

ADDITIONAL SCRIPTURE READINGS
Exodus 3:12–15; Psalm 113

Go to page 965 for your next devotional reading.

and my wound grievous and
   incurable?
Will you be to me like a deceptive
      brook,
   like a spring that fails?

¹⁹Therefore this is what the LORD
says:

"If you repent, I will restore you
   that you may serve me;
if you utter worthy, not worthless,
      words,
   you will be my spokesman.
Let this people turn to you,
   but you must not turn to them.
²⁰I will make you a wall to this
      people,
   a fortified wall of bronze;
they will fight against you
   but will not overcome you,
for I am with you
   to rescue and save you,"
             declares the LORD.
²¹"I will save you from the hands of
      the wicked
   and redeem you from the grasp
      of the cruel."

Day of Disaster

16 Then the word of the LORD
came to me: ²"You must not
marry and have sons or daughters in
this place." ³For this is what the LORD
says about the sons and daughters
born in this land and about the wom-
en who are their mothers and the men
who are their fathers: ⁴"They will die
of deadly diseases. They will not be
mourned or buried but will be like refuse lying on the ground. They will
perish by sword and famine, and
their dead bodies will become food
for the birds of the air and the beasts
of the earth."

⁵For this is what the LORD says: "Do
not enter a house where there is a funeral meal; do not go to mourn or
show sympathy, because I have withdrawn my blessing, my love and my
pity from this people," declares the
LORD. ⁶"Both high and low will die in
this land. They will not be buried or
mourned, and no one will cut himself
or shave his head for them. ⁷No one
will offer food to comfort those who

mourn for the dead—not even for a
father or a mother—nor will anyone
give them a drink to console them.

⁸"And do not enter a house where
there is feasting and sit down to eat
and drink. ⁹For this is what the LORD
Almighty, the God of Israel, says: Before your eyes and in your days I will
bring an end to the sounds of joy and
gladness and to the voices of bride
and bridegroom in this place.

¹⁰"When you tell these people all
this and they ask you, 'Why has the
LORD decreed such a great disaster
against us? What wrong have we
done? What sin have we committed
against the LORD our God?' ¹¹then say
to them, 'It is because your fathers
forsook me,' declares the LORD, 'and
followed other gods and served and
worshiped them. They forsook me
and did not keep my law. ¹²But you
have behaved more wickedly than
your fathers. See how each of you is
following the stubbornness of his evil
heart instead of obeying me. ¹³So I
will throw you out of this land into a
land neither you nor your fathers
have known, and there you will serve
other gods day and night, for I will
show you no favor.'

¹⁴"However, the days are coming,"
declares the LORD, "when men will no
longer say, 'As surely as the LORD
lives, who brought the Israelites up
out of Egypt,' ¹⁵but they will say, 'As
surely as the LORD lives, who brought
the Israelites up out of the land of the
north and out of all the countries
where he had banished them.' For I
will restore them to the land I gave
their forefathers.

¹⁶"But now I will send for many
fishermen," declares the LORD, "and
they will catch them. After that I will
send for many hunters, and they will
hunt them down on every mountain
and hill and from the crevices of the
rocks. ¹⁷My eyes are on all their ways;
they are not hidden from me, nor is
their sin concealed from my eyes. ¹⁸I
will repay them double for their wickedness and their sin, because they
have defiled my land with the lifeless
forms of their vile images and have

filled my inheritance with their detestable idols."

¹⁹O Lord, my strength and my fortress,
  my refuge in time of distress,
to you the nations will come
  from the ends of the earth and say,
"Our fathers possessed nothing but false gods,
  worthless idols that did them no good.
²⁰Do men make their own gods?
  Yes, but they are not gods!"

²¹"Therefore I will teach them—
  this time I will teach them
  my power and might.
Then they will know
  that my name is the Lord.

17 "Judah's sin is engraved with an iron tool,
  inscribed with a flint point,
on the tablets of their hearts
  and on the horns of their altars.
²Even their children remember
  their altars and Asherah poles^a
beside the spreading trees
  and on the high hills.
³My mountain in the land
  and your^b wealth and all your treasures
I will give away as plunder,
  together with your high places,
  because of sin throughout your country.
⁴Through your own fault you will lose
  the inheritance I gave you.
I will enslave you to your enemies
  in a land you do not know,
for you have kindled my anger,
  and it will burn forever."

⁵This is what the Lord says:

"Cursed is the one who trusts in man,
  who depends on flesh for his strength
  and whose heart turns away from the Lord.

⁶He will be like a bush in the wastelands;
  he will not see prosperity when it comes.
He will dwell in the parched places of the desert,
  in a salt land where no one lives.

⁷"But blessed is the man who trusts in the Lord,
  whose confidence is in him.
⁸He will be like a tree planted by the water
  that sends out its roots by the stream.
It does not fear when heat comes;
  its leaves are always green.
It has no worries in a year of drought
  and never fails to bear fruit."

⁹The heart is deceitful above all things
  and beyond cure.
  Who can understand it?

¹⁰"I the Lord search the heart
  and examine the mind,
to reward a man according to his conduct,
  according to what his deeds deserve."

¹¹Like a partridge that hatches eggs it did not lay
  is the man who gains riches by unjust means.
When his life is half gone, they will desert him,
  and in the end he will prove to be a fool.

¹²A glorious throne, exalted from the beginning,
  is the place of our sanctuary.
¹³O Lord, the hope of Israel,
  all who forsake you will be put to shame.
Those who turn away from you
  will be written in the dust
because they have forsaken the Lord,
  the spring of living water.

---

^a2 That is, symbols of the goddess Asherah of the land. / Your   ^b2,3 Or hills / ³and the mountains

¹⁴Heal me, O Lord, and I will be
    healed;
  save me and I will be saved,
    for you are the one I praise.
¹⁵They keep saying to me,
  "Where is the word of the Lord?
    Let it now be fulfilled!"
¹⁶I have not run away from being
    your shepherd;
  you know I have not desired
    the day of despair.
  What passes my lips is open
    before you.
¹⁷Do not be a terror to me;
  you are my refuge in the day of
    disaster.
¹⁸Let my persecutors be put to
    shame,
  but keep me from shame;
  let them be terrified,
  but keep me from terror.
  Bring on them the day of disaster;
    destroy them with double
      destruction.

Keeping the Sabbath Holy

¹⁹This is what the Lord said to me:
"Go and stand at the gate of the people, through which the kings of Judah
go in and out; stand also at all the
other gates of Jerusalem. ²⁰Say to
them, 'Hear the word of the Lord, O
kings of Judah and all people of Judah and everyone living in Jerusalem
who come through these gates. ²¹This
is what the Lord says: Be careful not
to carry a load on the Sabbath day or
bring it through the gates of Jerusa-
lem. ²²Do not bring a load out of your
houses or do any work on the Sab-
bath, but keep the Sabbath day holy,
as I commanded your forefathers.
²³Yet they did not listen or pay atten-
tion; they were stiff-necked and
would not listen or respond to discipline. ²⁴But if you are careful to obey
me, declares the Lord, and bring no
load through the gates of this city on
the Sabbath, but keep the Sabbath day
holy by not doing any work on it,
²⁵then kings who sit on David's
throne will come through the gates of
this city with their officials. They and
their officials will come riding in

chariots and on horses, accompanied
by the men of Judah and those living
in Jerusalem, and this city will be inhabited forever. ²⁶People will come
from the towns of Judah and the villages around Jerusalem, from the territory of Benjamin and the western
foothills, from the hill country and the
Negev, bringing burnt offerings and
sacrifices, grain offerings, incense and
thank offerings to the house of the
Lord. ²⁷But if you do not obey me to
keep the Sabbath day holy by not carrying any load as you come through
the gates of Jerusalem on the Sabbath
day, then I will kindle an unquenchable fire in the gates of Jerusalem that
will consume her fortresses.' "

At the Potter's House

18 This is the word that came to
    Jeremiah from the Lord: ²"Go
down to the potter's house, and there
I will give you my message." ³So I
went down to the potter's house, and
I saw him working at the wheel. ⁴But
the pot he was shaping from the clay
was marred in his hands; so the potter
formed it into another pot, shaping it
as seemed best to him.

⁵Then the word of the Lord came to
me: ⁶"O house of Israel, can I not do
with you as this potter does?" declares the Lord. "Like clay in the hand
of the potter, so are you in my hand,
O house of Israel. ⁷If at any time I announce that a nation or kingdom is
to be uprooted, torn down and destroyed, ⁸and if that nation I warned
repents of its evil, then I will relent
and not inflict on it the disaster I had
planned. ⁹And if at another time I announce that a nation or kingdom is to
be built up and planted, ¹⁰and if it
does evil in my sight and does not
obey me, then I will reconsider the
good I had intended to do for it.

¹¹"Now therefore say to the people
of Judah and those living in Jerusalem, 'This is what the Lord says:
Look! I am preparing a disaster for
you and devising a plan against you.
So turn from your evil ways, each one
of you, and reform your ways and
your actions.' ¹²But they will reply,

'It's no use. We will continue with our own plans; each of us will follow the stubbornness of his evil heart.' "

[13]Therefore this is what the LORD says:

"Inquire among the nations:
 Who has ever heard anything
  like this?

A most horrible thing has been
  done
 by Virgin Israel.
[14]Does the snow of Lebanon
  ever vanish from its rocky
   slopes?
 Do its cool waters from distant
  sources
  ever cease to flow?[a]

[a]14 The meaning of the Hebrew for this sentence is uncertain.

VERSE: Jeremiah 18:6 **AUTHOR:** J. Oswald Sanders **PASSAGE:** Jeremiah 18:1–10

Clay in the Potter's Hand

Although we may be advanced in years, the heavenly Potter has not yet put the finishing touches to our lives. There are still glorious possibilities ahead. The past was not better than the future can yet be.

When the beautiful ornament the potter was fashioning of clay collapsed under his hand, he might well have thrown the recalcitrant clay on the scrap heap, and taken a fresh lump that would be more responsive to his molding touch. But he did not do so. Instead, "the potter formed it into another pot, shaping it as seemed best to him" (Jeremiah 18:4).

Even when we have thwarted the purpose of the divine Potter in our lives, he does not despair of us and cast us aside . . .

The reworked vessel may not be as beautiful as the one the heavenly Potter originally planned, but it can still become "an instrument for noble purposes, made holy, useful to the Master and prepared to do any good work" (2 Timothy 2:21). The divine Potter is undiscourageable.

ADDITIONAL SCRIPTURE READINGS
Romans 9:14–29; Ephesians 2:1–10

Go to page 979 for your next devotional reading.

¹⁵Yet my people have forgotten me;
    they burn incense to worthless
        idols,
which made them stumble in their
        ways
    and in the ancient paths.
They made them walk in bypaths
    and on roads not built up.
¹⁶Their land will be laid waste,
    an object of lasting scorn;
all who pass by will be appalled
    and will shake their heads.
¹⁷Like a wind from the east,
    I will scatter them before their
        enemies;
I will show them my back and not
        my face
    in the day of their disaster."

¹⁸They said, "Come, let's make
plans against Jeremiah; for the teaching of the law by the priest will not be
lost, nor will counsel from the wise,
nor the word from the prophets. So
come, let's attack him with our
tongues and pay no attention to anything he says."

¹⁹Listen to me, O LORD;
    hear what my accusers are
        saying!
²⁰Should good be repaid with evil?
    Yet they have dug a pit for me.
Remember that I stood before you
    and spoke in their behalf
    to turn your wrath away from
        them.
²¹So give their children over to
        famine;
    hand them over to the power of
        the sword.
Let their wives be made childless
        and widows;
    let their men be put to death,
    their young men slain by the
        sword in battle.
²²Let a cry be heard from their
        houses
    when you suddenly bring
        invaders against them,
for they have dug a pit to capture
        me
    and have hidden snares for my
        feet.

²³But you know, O LORD,
    all their plots to kill me.
Do not forgive their crimes
    or blot out their sins from your
        sight.
Let them be overthrown before
        you;
    deal with them in the time of
        your anger.

19 This is what the LORD says: "Go and buy a clay jar from a potter. Take along some of the elders of
the people and of the priests ²and go
out to the Valley of Ben Hinnom, near
the entrance of the Potsherd Gate.
There proclaim the words I tell you,
³and say, 'Hear the word of the LORD,
O kings of Judah and people of Jerusalem. This is what the LORD Almighty, the God of Israel, says: Listen! I am going to bring a disaster on
this place that will make the ears of
everyone who hears of it tingle. ⁴For
they have forsaken me and made this
a place of foreign gods; they have
burned sacrifices in it to gods that neither they nor their fathers nor the
kings of Judah ever knew, and they
have filled this place with the blood
of the innocent. ⁵They have built the
high places of Baal to burn their sons
in the fire as offerings to Baal—something I did not command or mention,
nor did it enter my mind. ⁶So beware,
the days are coming, declares the
LORD, when people will no longer
call this place Topheth or the Valley
of Ben Hinnom, but the Valley of
Slaughter.

⁷"'In this place I will ruin*ᵃ* the
plans of Judah and Jerusalem. I will
make them fall by the sword before
their enemies, at the hands of those
who seek their lives, and I will give
their carcasses as food to the birds of
the air and the beasts of the earth. ⁸I
will devastate this city and make it an
object of scorn; all who pass by will be
appalled and will scoff because of all
its wounds. ⁹I will make them eat the
flesh of their sons and daughters, and
they will eat one another's flesh dur-

ᵃ7 The Hebrew for *ruin* sounds like the Hebrew for *jar* (see verses 1 and 10).

ing the stress of the siege imposed on them by the enemies who seek their lives.'

¹⁰"Then break the jar while those who go with you are watching, ¹¹and say to them, 'This is what the LORD Almighty says: I will smash this nation and this city just as this potter's jar is smashed and cannot be repaired. They will bury the dead in Topheth until there is no more room. ¹²This is what I will do to this place and to those who live here, declares the LORD. I will make this city like Topheth. ¹³The houses in Jerusalem and those of the kings of Judah will be defiled like this place, Topheth—all the houses where they burned incense on the roofs to all the starry hosts and poured out drink offerings to other gods.' "

¹⁴Jeremiah then returned from Topheth, where the LORD had sent him to prophesy, and stood in the court of the LORD's temple and said to all the people, ¹⁵"This is what the LORD Almighty, the God of Israel, says: 'Listen! I am going to bring on this city and the villages around it every disaster I pronounced against them, because they were stiff-necked and would not listen to my words.' "

Jeremiah and Pashhur

20 When the priest Pashhur son of Immer, the chief officer in the temple of the LORD, heard Jeremiah prophesying these things, ²he had Jeremiah the prophet beaten and put in the stocks at the Upper Gate of Benjamin at the LORD's temple. ³The next day, when Pashhur released him from the stocks, Jeremiah said to him, "The LORD's name for you is not Pashhur, but Magor-Missabib.ᵃ ⁴For this is what the LORD says: 'I will make you a terror to yourself and to all your friends; with your own eyes you will see them fall by the sword of their enemies. I will hand all Judah over to the king of Babylon, who will carry them away to Babylon or put them to the sword. ⁵I will hand over to their

enemies all the wealth of this city—all its products, all its valuables and all the treasures of the kings of Judah. They will take it away as plunder and carry it off to Babylon. ⁶And you, Pashhur, and all who live in your house will go into exile to Babylon. There you will die and be buried, you and all your friends to whom you have prophesied lies.' "

Jeremiah's Complaint

⁷O LORD, you deceivedᵇ me, and I was deceivedᵇ;
   you overpowered me and prevailed.
I am ridiculed all day long;
   everyone mocks me.
⁸Whenever I speak, I cry out proclaiming violence and destruction.
So the word of the LORD has brought me
   insult and reproach all day long.
⁹But if I say, "I will not mention him
   or speak any more in his name,"
his word is in my heart like a fire,
   a fire shut up in my bones.
I am weary of holding it in;
   indeed, I cannot.
¹⁰I hear many whispering,
   "Terror on every side!
   Report him! Let's report him!"
All my friends
   are waiting for me to slip, saying,
"Perhaps he will be deceived;
   then we will prevail over him
   and take our revenge on him."

¹¹But the LORD is with me like a mighty warrior;
   so my persecutors will stumble and not prevail.
They will fail and be thoroughly disgraced;
   their dishonor will never be forgotten.
¹²O LORD Almighty, you who examine the righteous

─────────────

ᵃ3 *Magor-Missabib* means *terror on every side.*   ᵇ7 Or *persuaded*

and probe the heart and mind,
  let me see your vengeance upon
    them,
  for to you I have committed my
    cause.

13Sing to the LORD!
  Give praise to the LORD!
He rescues the life of the needy
  from the hands of the wicked.

14Cursed be the day I was born!
  May the day my mother bore
    me not be blessed!
15Cursed be the man who brought
    my father the news,
  who made him very glad,
    saying,
  "A child is born to you—a
    son!"
16May that man be like the towns
    the LORD overthrew without
    pity.
  May he hear wailing in the
    morning,
  a battle cry at noon.
17For he did not kill me in the
    womb,
  with my mother as my grave,
    her womb enlarged forever.
18Why did I ever come out of the
    womb
  to see trouble and sorrow
    and to end my days in shame?

God Rejects Zedekiah's Request

21 The word came to Jeremiah
from the LORD when King Zedekiah sent to him Pashhur son of Malkijah and the priest Zephaniah son of
Maaseiah. They said: 2"Inquire now
of the LORD for us because Nebuchadnezzar*a* king of Babylon is attacking
us. Perhaps the LORD will perform
wonders for us as in times past so that
he will withdraw from us."

3But Jeremiah answered them, "Tell
Zedekiah, 4'This is what the LORD, the
God of Israel, says: I am about to turn
against you the weapons of war that
are in your hands, which you are using to fight the king of Babylon and
the Babylonians*b* who are outside

the wall besieging you. And I will
gather them inside this city. 5I myself
will fight against you with an outstretched hand and a mighty arm in
anger and fury and great wrath. 6I
will strike down those who live in this
city—both men and animals—and
they will die of a terrible plague. 7Af-
ter that, declares the LORD, I will hand
over Zedekiah king of Judah, his officials and the people in this city who
survive the plague, sword and famine, to Nebuchadnezzar king of Babylon and to their enemies who seek
their lives. He will put them to the
sword; he will show them no mercy
or pity or compassion.'

8"Furthermore, tell the people,
'This is what the LORD says: See, I am
setting before you the way of life and
the way of death. 9Whoever stays in
this city will die by the sword, famine
or plague. But whoever goes out and
surrenders to the Babylonians who
are besieging you will live; he will escape with his life. 10I have determined
to do this city harm and not good, declares the LORD. It will be given into
the hands of the king of Babylon, and
he will destroy it with fire.'

11"Moreover, say to the royal house
of Judah, 'Hear the word of the LORD;
12O house of David, this is what the
LORD says:

" 'Administer justice every
    morning;
  rescue from the hand of his
    oppressor
  the one who has been robbed,
or my wrath will break out and
    burn like fire
  because of the evil you have
    done—
  burn with no one to quench it.
13I am against you, ⌞Jerusalem,⌟
  you who live above this valley
    on the rocky plateau,
        declares the LORD—
you who say, "Who can come
    against us?
  Who can enter our refuge?"

---

*a*2 Hebrew *Nebuchadrezzar*, of which *Nebuchadnezzar* is a variant; here and often in Jeremiah and
Ezekiel   *b*4 Or *Chaldeans*; also in verse 9

¹⁴I will punish you as your deeds
       deserve,
                  declares the LORD.
I will kindle a fire in your forests
   that will consume everything
       around you.' "

Judgment Against Evil Kings

22 This is what the LORD says: "Go
down to the palace of the king
of Judah and proclaim this message
there: ²'Hear the word of the LORD, O
king of Judah, you who sit on David's
throne—you, your officials and your
people who come through these
gates. ³This is what the LORD says: Do
what is just and right. Rescue from
the hand of his oppressor the one
who has been robbed. Do no wrong
or violence to the alien, the fatherless
or the widow, and do not shed innocent blood in this place. ⁴For if you
are careful to carry out these commands, then kings who sit on David's
throne will come through the gates of
this palace, riding in chariots and on
horses, accompanied by their officials
and their people. ⁵But if you do not
obey these commands, declares the
LORD, I swear by myself that this palace will become a ruin.' "

⁶For this is what the LORD says
about the palace of the king of Judah:

"Though you are like Gilead to
       me,
   like the summit of Lebanon,
I will surely make you like a
       desert,
   like towns not inhabited.
⁷I will send destroyers against you,
   each man with his weapons,
and they will cut up your fine
       cedar beams
   and throw them into the fire.

⁸"People from many nations will
pass by this city and will ask one another, 'Why has the LORD done such a
thing to this great city?' ⁹And the answer will be: 'Because they have forsaken the covenant of the LORD their
God and have worshiped and served
other gods.' "

¹⁰Do not weep for the dead ⌊king⌋
   or mourn his loss;
rather, weep bitterly for him
   who is exiled,
because he will never return
   nor see his native land again.

¹¹For this is what the LORD says about
Shallum[a] son of Josiah, who succeeded his father as king of Judah but
has gone from this place: "He will
never return. ¹²He will die in the place
where they have led him captive; he
will not see this land again."

¹³"Woe to him who builds his
       palace by unrighteousness,
   his upper rooms by injustice,
making his countrymen work for
       nothing,
   not paying them for their labor.
¹⁴He says, 'I will build myself a
       great palace
   with spacious upper rooms.'
So he makes large windows in it,
   panels it with cedar
   and decorates it in red.

¹⁵"Does it make you a king
   to have more and more cedar?
Did not your father have food and
       drink?
   He did what was right and just,
   so all went well with him.
¹⁶He defended the cause of the poor
       and needy,
   and so all went well.
Is that not what it means to know
       me?"
   declares the LORD.
¹⁷"But your eyes and your heart
   are set only on dishonest gain,
on shedding innocent blood
   and on oppression and
       extortion."

¹⁸Therefore this is what the LORD says
about Jehoiakim son of Josiah king of
Judah:

"They will not mourn for him:
   'Alas, my brother! Alas, my
       sister!'
They will not mourn for him:

ᵃ11 Also called *Jehoahaz*

'Alas, my master! Alas, his
    splendor!'
¹⁹He will have the burial of a
    donkey—
    dragged away and thrown
    outside the gates of Jerusalem."

²⁰"Go up to Lebanon and cry out,
    let your voice be heard in
    Bashan,
    cry out from Abarim,
    for all your allies are crushed.
²¹I warned you when you felt
    secure,
    but you said, 'I will not listen!'
This has been your way from your
    youth;
    you have not obeyed me.
²²The wind will drive all your
    shepherds away,
    and your allies will go into
    exile.
Then you will be ashamed and
    disgraced
    because of all your wickedness.
²³You who live in 'Lebanon,ᵃ'
    who are nestled in cedar
    buildings,
how you will groan when pangs
    come upon you,
    pain like that of a woman in
    labor!

²⁴"As surely as I live," declares the
LORD, "even if you, Jehoiachinᵇ son
of Jehoiakim king of Judah, were a
signet ring on my right hand, I would
still pull you off. ²⁵I will hand you
over to those who seek your life,
those you fear—to Nebuchadnezzar
king of Babylon and to the Babyloni-
ans.ᶜ ²⁶I will hurl you and the mother who gave you birth into another
country, where neither of you was
born, and there you both will die.
²⁷You will never come back to the
land you long to return to."

²⁸Is this man Jehoiachin a despised,
    broken pot,
    an object no one wants?
Why will he and his children be
    hurled out,

cast into a land they do not
    know?
²⁹O land, land, land,
    hear the word of the LORD!
³⁰This is what the LORD says:
    "Record this man as if childless,
    a man who will not prosper in
        his lifetime,
for none of his offspring will
    prosper,
    none will sit on the throne of
        David
    or rule anymore in Judah."

The Righteous Branch

23 "Woe to the shepherds who are
destroying and scattering the
sheep of my pasture!" declares the
LORD. ²Therefore this is what the LORD,
the God of Israel, says to the shepherds who tend my people: "Because
you have scattered my flock and driv-
en them away and have not bestowed
care on them, I will bestow punishment on you for the evil you have
done," declares the LORD. ³"I myself
will gather the remnant of my flock
out of all the countries where I have
driven them and will bring them back
to their pasture, where they will be
fruitful and increase in number. ⁴I
will place shepherds over them who
will tend them, and they will no longer be afraid or terrified, nor will any
be missing," declares the LORD.

⁵"The days are coming," declares
    the LORD,
    "when I will raise up to
        Davidᵈ a righteous
        Branch,
    a King who will reign wisely
    and do what is just and right in
        the land.
⁶In his days Judah will be saved
    and Israel will live in safety.
This is the name by which he will
    be called:
    The LORD Our Righteousness.

⁷"So then, the days are coming," declares the LORD, "when people will no
longer say, 'As surely as the LORD

ᵃ23 That is, the palace in Jerusalem (see 1 Kings 7:2)   ᵇ24 Hebrew *Coniah*, a variant of
Jehoiachin; also in verse 28   ᶜ25 Or *Chaldeans*   ᵈ5 Or *up from David's line*

lives, who brought the Israelites up out of Egypt,' 8but they will say, 'As surely as the LORD lives, who brought the descendants of Israel up out of the land of the north and out of all the countries where he had banished them.' Then they will live in their own land."

Lying Prophets

9Concerning the prophets:

My heart is broken within me;
    all my bones tremble.
I am like a drunken man,
    like a man overcome by wine,
because of the LORD
    and his holy words.
10The land is full of adulterers;
    because of the curse*a* the land
        lies parched*b*
    and the pastures in the desert
        are withered.
The ⌐prophets⌐ follow an evil
        course
    and use their power unjustly.

11"Both prophet and priest are
        godless;
    even in my temple I find their
        wickedness,"
                    declares the LORD.
12"Therefore their path will become
        slippery;
    they will be banished to
        darkness
    and there they will fall.
I will bring disaster on them
    in the year they are punished,"
                    declares the LORD.

13"Among the prophets of Samaria
    I saw this repulsive thing:
They prophesied by Baal
    and led my people Israel astray.
14And among the prophets of
        Jerusalem
    I have seen something horrible:
They commit adultery and live
        a lie.
They strengthen the hands of
        evildoers,
    so that no one turns from his
        wickedness.

They are all like Sodom to me;
    the people of Jerusalem are like
        Gomorrah."

15Therefore, this is what the LORD Almighty says concerning the prophets:

"I will make them eat bitter food
    and drink poisoned water,
because from the prophets of
        Jerusalem
    ungodliness has spread
        throughout the land."

16This is what the LORD Almighty says:

"Do not listen to what the
        prophets are prophesying
        to you;
    they fill you with false hopes.
They speak visions from their own
        minds,
    not from the mouth of the LORD.
17They keep saying to those who
        despise me,
    'The LORD says: You will have
        peace.'
And to all who follow the
        stubbornness of their hearts
    they say, 'No harm will come to
        you.'
18But which of them has stood in
        the council of the LORD
    to see or to hear his word?
Who has listened and heard his
        word?
19See, the storm of the LORD
    will burst out in wrath,
a whirlwind swirling down
    on the heads of the wicked.
20The anger of the LORD will not
        turn back
    until he fully accomplishes
        the purposes of his heart.
In days to come
    you will understand it clearly.
21I did not send these prophets,
    yet they have run with their
        message;
I did not speak to them,
    yet they have prophesied.
22But if they had stood in my
        council,

---

*a*10 Or *because of these things*   *b*10 Or *land mourns*

they would have proclaimed my
    words to my people
and would have turned them from
    their evil ways
    and from their evil deeds.

23"Am I only a God nearby,"
                    declares the LORD,
    "and not a God far away?
24Can anyone hide in secret places
    so that I cannot see him?"
                    declares the LORD.
    "Do not I fill heaven and
        earth?"
                    declares the LORD.

25"I have heard what the prophets
say who prophesy lies in my name.
They say, 'I had a dream! I had a
dream!' 26How long will this continue
in the hearts of these lying prophets,
who prophesy the delusions of their
own minds? 27They think the dreams
they tell one another will make my
people forget my name, just as their
fathers forgot my name through Baal
worship. 28Let the prophet who has a
dream tell his dream, but let the one
who has my word speak it faithfully.
For what has straw to do with grain?"
declares the LORD. 29"Is not my word
like fire," declares the LORD, "and like
a hammer that breaks a rock in
pieces?

30"Therefore," declares the LORD, "I
am against the prophets who steal
from one another words supposedly
from me. 31Yes," declares the LORD, "I
am against the prophets who wag
their own tongues and yet declare,
'The LORD declares.' 32Indeed, I am
against those who prophesy false
dreams," declares the LORD. "They tell
them and lead my people astray with
their reckless lies, yet I did not send
or appoint them. They do not benefit
these people in the least," declares the
LORD.

False Oracles and False Prophets

33"When these people, or a prophet
or a priest, ask you, 'What is the oracle[a] of the LORD?' say to them, 'What
oracle?[b] I will forsake you, declares
the LORD.' 34If a prophet or a priest or
anyone else claims, 'This is the oracle
of the LORD,' I will punish that man
and his household. 35This is what each
of you keeps on saying to his friend
or relative: 'What is the LORD's answer?' or 'What has the LORD spoken?'
36But you must not mention 'the oracle of the LORD' again, because every
man's own word becomes his oracle
and so you distort the words of the
living God, the LORD Almighty, our
God. 37This is what you keep saying
to a prophet: 'What is the LORD's answer to you?' or 'What has the LORD
spoken?' 38Although you claim, 'This
is the oracle of the LORD,' this is what
the LORD says: You used the words,
'This is the oracle of the LORD,' even
though I told you that you must not
claim, 'This is the oracle of the LORD.'
39Therefore, I will surely forget you
and cast you out of my presence
along with the city I gave to you
and your fathers. 40I will bring upon
you everlasting disgrace—everlasting
shame that will not be forgotten."

Two Baskets of Figs

24 After Jehoiachin[c] son of Jehoiakim king of Judah and the officials, the craftsmen and the artisans
of Judah were carried into exile from
Jerusalem to Babylon by Nebuchadnezzar king of Babylon, the LORD
showed me two baskets of figs placed
in front of the temple of the LORD.
2One basket had very good figs, like
those that ripen early; the other basket had very poor figs, so bad they
could not be eaten.

3Then the LORD asked me, "What do
you see, Jeremiah?"

"Figs," I answered. "The good ones
are very good, but the poor ones are
so bad they cannot be eaten."

4Then the word of the LORD came to
me: 5"This is what the LORD, the God
of Israel, says: 'Like these good figs, I

---

a33 Or burden (see Septuagint and Vulgate)   b33 Hebrew; Septuagint and Vulgate 'You are the
burden. (The Hebrew for oracle and burden is the same.)   c1 Hebrew Jeconiah, a variant of
Jehoiachin

regard as good the exiles from Judah, whom I sent away from this place to the land of the Babylonians.*a *6My eyes will watch over them for their good, and I will bring them back to this land. I will build them up and not tear them down; I will plant them and not uproot them. 7I will give them a heart to know me, that I am the LORD. They will be my people, and I will be their God, for they will return to me with all their heart.

8" 'But like the poor figs, which are so bad they cannot be eaten,' says the LORD, 'so will I deal with Zedekiah king of Judah, his officials and the survivors from Jerusalem, whether they remain in this land or live in Egypt. 9I will make them abhorrent and an offense to all the kingdoms of the earth, a reproach and a byword, an object of ridicule and cursing, wherever I banish them. 10I will send the sword, famine and plague against them until they are destroyed from the land I gave to them and their fathers.' "

Seventy Years of Captivity

25 The word came to Jeremiah concerning all the people of Judah in the fourth year of Jehoiakim son of Josiah king of Judah, which was the first year of Nebuchadnezzar king of Babylon. 2So Jeremiah the prophet said to all the people of Judah and to all those living in Jerusalem: 3For twenty-three years—from the thirteenth year of Josiah son of Amon king of Judah until this very day—the word of the LORD has come to me and I have spoken to you again and again, but you have not listened.

4And though the LORD has sent all his servants the prophets to you again and again, you have not listened or paid any attention. 5They said, "Turn now, each of you, from your evil ways and your evil practices, and you can stay in the land the LORD gave to you and your fathers for ever and ever. 6Do not follow other gods to serve and worship them; do not provoke me to anger with what your hands have made. Then I will not harm you."

7"But you did not listen to me," declares the LORD, "and you have provoked me with what your hands have made, and you have brought harm to yourselves."

8Therefore the LORD Almighty says this: "Because you have not listened to my words, 9I will summon all the peoples of the north and my servant Nebuchadnezzar king of Babylon," declares the LORD, "and I will bring them against this land and its inhabitants and against all the surrounding nations. I will completely destroy*b them and make them an object of horror and scorn, and an everlasting ruin. 10I will banish from them the sounds of joy and gladness, the voices of bride and bridegroom, the sound of millstones and the light of the lamp. 11This whole country will become a desolate wasteland, and these nations will serve the king of Babylon seventy years.

12"But when the seventy years are fulfilled, I will punish the king of Babylon and his nation, the land of the Babylonians,*a for their guilt," declares the LORD, "and will make it desolate forever. 13I will bring upon that land all the things I have spoken against it, all that are written in this book and prophesied by Jeremiah against all the nations. 14They themselves will be enslaved by many nations and great kings; I will repay them according to their deeds and the work of their hands."

The Cup of God's Wrath

15This is what the LORD, the God of Israel, said to me: "Take from my hand this cup filled with the wine of my wrath and make all the nations to whom I send you drink it. 16When they drink it, they will stagger and go mad because of the sword I will send among them."

---

a5,12 Or *Chaldeans*   *b9* The Hebrew term refers to the irrevocable giving over of things or persons to the LORD, often by totally destroying them.

¹⁷So I took the cup from the LORD's hand and made all the nations to whom he sent me drink it: ¹⁸Jerusalem and the towns of Judah, its kings and officials, to make them a ruin and an object of horror and scorn and cursing, as they are today; ¹⁹Pharaoh king of Egypt, his attendants, his officials and all his people, ²⁰and all the foreign people there; all the kings of Uz; all the kings of the Philistines (those of Ashkelon, Gaza, Ekron, and the people left at Ashdod); ²¹Edom, Moab and Ammon; ²²all the kings of Tyre and Sidon; the kings of the coastlands across the sea; ²³Dedan, Tema, Buz and all who are in distant places*a*; ²⁴all the kings of Arabia and all the kings of the foreign people who live in the desert; ²⁵all the kings of Zimri, Elam and Media; ²⁶and all the kings of the north, near and far, one after the other—all the kingdoms on the face of the earth. And after all of them, the king of Sheshach*b* will drink it too.

²⁷"Then tell them, 'This is what the LORD Almighty, the God of Israel, says: Drink, get drunk and vomit, and fall to rise no more because of the sword I will send among you.' ²⁸But if they refuse to take the cup from your hand and drink, tell them, 'This is what the LORD Almighty says: You must drink it! ²⁹See, I am beginning to bring disaster on the city that bears my Name, and will you indeed go unpunished? You will not go unpunished, for I am calling down a sword upon all who live on the earth, declares the LORD Almighty.'

³⁰"Now prophesy all these words against them and say to them:

" 'The LORD will roar from on
      high;
   he will thunder from his holy
      dwelling
   and roar mightily against his
      land.
He will shout like those who tread
      the grapes,

shout against all who live on
      the earth.
³¹The tumult will resound to the
      ends of the earth,
   for the LORD will bring charges
      against the nations;
he will bring judgment on all
      mankind
   and put the wicked to the
      sword,' "
                        declares the LORD.

³²This is what the LORD Almighty says:

"Look! Disaster is spreading
      from nation to nation;
a mighty storm is rising
      from the ends of the earth."

³³At that time those slain by the LORD will be everywhere—from one end of the earth to the other. They will not be mourned or gathered up or buried, but will be like refuse lying on the ground.

³⁴Weep and wail, you shepherds;
   roll in the dust, you leaders of
      the flock.
For your time to be slaughtered
      has come;
   you will fall and be shattered
      like fine pottery.
³⁵The shepherds will have nowhere
      to flee,
   the leaders of the flock no place
      to escape.
³⁶Hear the cry of the shepherds,
   the wailing of the leaders of the
      flock,
   for the LORD is destroying their
      pasture.
³⁷The peaceful meadows will be laid
      waste
   because of the fierce anger of
      the LORD.
³⁸Like a lion he will leave his lair,
   and their land will become
      desolate
because of the sword*c* of the
      oppressor

---

a23 Or *who clip the hair by their foreheads*   *b26* Sheshach *is a cryptogram for Babylon.*
c38 Some Hebrew manuscripts and Septuagint (see also Jer. 46:16 and 50:16); most Hebrew manuscripts *anger*

and because of the LORD's fierce anger.

Jeremiah Threatened With Death

26 Early in the reign of Jehoiakim son of Josiah king of Judah, this word came from the LORD: ²"This is what the LORD says: Stand in the courtyard of the LORD's house and speak to all the people of the towns of Judah who come to worship in the house of the LORD. Tell them everything I command you; do not omit a word. ³Perhaps they will listen and each will turn from his evil way. Then I will relent and not bring on them the disaster I was planning because of the evil they have done. ⁴Say to them, 'This is what the LORD says: If you do not listen to me and follow my law, which I have set before you, ⁵and if you do not listen to the words of my servants the prophets, whom I have sent to you again and again (though you have not listened), ⁶then I will make this house like Shiloh and this city an object of cursing among all the nations of the earth.' "

⁷The priests, the prophets and all the people heard Jeremiah speak these words in the house of the LORD. ⁸But as soon as Jeremiah finished telling all the people everything the LORD had commanded him to say, the priests, the prophets and all the people seized him and said, "You must die! ⁹Why do you prophesy in the LORD's name that this house will be like Shiloh and this city will be desolate and deserted?" And all the people crowded around Jeremiah in the house of the LORD.

¹⁰When the officials of Judah heard about these things, they went up from the royal palace to the house of the LORD and took their places at the entrance of the New Gate of the LORD's house. ¹¹Then the priests and the prophets said to the officials and all the people, "This man should be sentenced to death because he has prophesied against this city. You have heard it with your own ears!"

¹²Then Jeremiah said to all the officials and all the people: "The LORD sent me to prophesy against this house and this city all the things you have heard. ¹³Now reform your ways and your actions and obey the LORD your God. Then the LORD will relent and not bring the disaster he has pronounced against you. ¹⁴As for me, I am in your hands; do with me whatever you think is good and right. ¹⁵Be assured, however, that if you put me to death, you will bring the guilt of innocent blood on yourselves and on this city and on those who live in it, for in truth the LORD has sent me to you to speak all these words in your hearing."

¹⁶Then the officials and all the people said to the priests and the prophets, "This man should not be sentenced to death! He has spoken to us in the name of the LORD our God."

¹⁷Some of the elders of the land stepped forward and said to the entire assembly of people, ¹⁸"Micah of Moresheth prophesied in the days of Hezekiah king of Judah. He told all the people of Judah, 'This is what the LORD Almighty says:

" 'Zion will be plowed like a field,
   Jerusalem will become a heap of rubble,
   the temple hill a mound
      overgrown with thickets.'ᵃ

¹⁹"Did Hezekiah king of Judah or anyone else in Judah put him to death? Did not Hezekiah fear the LORD and seek his favor? And did not the LORD relent, so that he did not bring the disaster he pronounced against them? We are about to bring a terrible disaster on ourselves!"

²⁰(Now Uriah son of Shemaiah from Kiriath Jearim was another man who prophesied in the name of the LORD; he prophesied the same things against this city and this land as Jeremiah did. ²¹When King Jehoiakim and all his officers and officials heard his words, the king sought to put him to death. But Uriah heard of it and fled

---

ᵃ18 Micah 3:12

in fear to Egypt. [22]King Jehoiakim, however, sent Elnathan son of Acbor to Egypt, along with some other men. [23]They brought Uriah out of Egypt and took him to King Jehoiakim, who had him struck down with a sword and his body thrown into the burial place of the common people.)

[24]Furthermore, Ahikam son of Shaphan supported Jeremiah, and so he was not handed over to the people to be put to death.

Judah to Serve Nebuchadnezzar

27 Early in the reign of Zedekiah[a] son of Josiah king of Judah, this word came to Jeremiah from the LORD: [2]This is what the LORD said to me: "Make a yoke out of straps and crossbars and put it on your neck. [3]Then send word to the kings of Edom, Moab, Ammon, Tyre and Sidon through the envoys who have come to Jerusalem to Zedekiah king of Judah. [4]Give them a message for their masters and say, 'This is what the LORD Almighty, the God of Israel, says: "Tell this to your masters: [5]With my great power and outstretched arm I made the earth and its people and the animals that are on it, and I give it to anyone I please. [6]Now I will hand all your countries over to my servant Nebuchadnezzar king of Babylon; I will make even the wild animals subject to him. [7]All nations will serve him and his son and his grandson until the time for his land comes; then many nations and great kings will subjugate him.

[8]" 'If, however, any nation or kingdom will not serve Nebuchadnezzar king of Babylon or bow its neck under his yoke, I will punish that nation with the sword, famine and plague, declares the LORD, until I destroy it by his hand. [9]So do not listen to your prophets, your diviners, your interpreters of dreams, your mediums or your sorcerers who tell you, 'You will not serve the king of Bab-

ylon.' [10]They prophesy lies to you that will only serve to remove you far from your lands; I will banish you and you will perish. [11]But if any nation will bow its neck under the yoke of the king of Babylon and serve him, I will let that nation remain in its own land to till it and to live there, declares the LORD." ' "

[12]I gave the same message to Zedekiah king of Judah. I said, "Bow your neck under the yoke of the king of Babylon; serve him and his people, and you will live. [13]Why will you and your people die by the sword, famine and plague with which the LORD has threatened any nation that will not serve the king of Babylon? [14]Do not listen to the words of the prophets who say to you, 'You will not serve the king of Babylon,' for they are prophesying lies to you. [15]'I have not sent them,' declares the LORD. 'They are prophesying lies in my name. Therefore, I will banish you and you will perish, both you and the prophets who prophesy to you.' "

[16]Then I said to the priests and all these people, "This is what the LORD says: Do not listen to the prophets who say, 'Very soon now the articles from the LORD's house will be brought back from Babylon.' They are prophesying lies to you. [17]Do not listen to them. Serve the king of Babylon, and you will live. Why should this city become a ruin? [18]If they are prophets and have the word of the LORD, let them plead with the LORD Almighty that the furnishings remaining in the house of the LORD and in the palace of the king of Judah and in Jerusalem not be taken to Babylon. [19]For this is what the LORD Almighty says about the pillars, the Sea, the movable stands and the other furnishings that are left in this city, [20]which Nebuchadnezzar king of Babylon did not take away when he carried Jehoiachin[b] son of Jehoiakim king of Judah into exile from Jerusalem to Babylon,

---

[a]1 A few Hebrew manuscripts and Syriac (see also Jer. 27:3, 12 and 28:1); most Hebrew manuscripts *Jehoiakim* (Most Septuagint manuscripts do not have this verse.)   [b]20 Hebrew *Jeconiah*, a variant of *Jehoiachin*

along with all the nobles of Judah and Jerusalem— ²¹yes, this is what the LORD Almighty, the God of Israel, says about the things that are left in the house of the LORD and in the palace of the king of Judah and in Jerusalem: ²²They will be taken to Babylon and there they will remain until the day I come for them,' declares the LORD. 'Then I will bring them back and restore them to this place.' "

The False Prophet Hananiah

28 In the fifth month of that same year, the fourth year, early in the reign of Zedekiah king of Judah, the prophet Hananiah son of Azzur, who was from Gibeon, said to me in the house of the LORD in the presence of the priests and all the people: ²"This is what the LORD Almighty, the God of Israel, says: 'I will break the yoke of the king of Babylon. ³Within two years I will bring back to this place all the articles of the LORD's house that Nebuchadnezzar king of Babylon removed from here and took to Babylon. ⁴I will also bring back to this place Jehoiachin*a* son of Jehoiakim king of Judah and all the other exiles from Judah who went to Babylon,' declares the LORD, 'for I will break the yoke of the king of Babylon.' "

⁵Then the prophet Jeremiah replied to the prophet Hananiah before the priests and all the people who were standing in the house of the LORD. ⁶He said, "Amen! May the LORD do so! May the LORD fulfill the words you have prophesied by bringing the articles of the LORD's house and all the exiles back to this place from Babylon. ⁷Nevertheless, listen to what I have to say in your hearing and in the hearing of all the people: ⁸From early times the prophets who preceded you and me have prophesied war, disaster and plague against many countries and great kingdoms. ⁹But the prophet who prophesies peace will be recognized as one truly sent by the LORD only if his prediction comes true."

¹⁰Then the prophet Hananiah took the yoke off the neck of the prophet Jeremiah and broke it, ¹¹and he said before all the people, "This is what the LORD says: 'In the same way will I break the yoke of Nebuchadnezzar king of Babylon off the neck of all the nations within two years.' " At this, the prophet Jeremiah went on his way.

¹²Shortly after the prophet Hananiah had broken the yoke off the neck of the prophet Jeremiah, the word of the LORD came to Jeremiah: ¹³"Go and tell Hananiah, 'This is what the LORD says: You have broken a wooden yoke, but in its place you will get a yoke of iron. ¹⁴This is what the LORD Almighty, the God of Israel, says: I will put an iron yoke on the necks of all these nations to make them serve Nebuchadnezzar king of Babylon, and they will serve him. I will even give him control over the wild animals.' "

¹⁵Then the prophet Jeremiah said to Hananiah the prophet, "Listen, Hananiah! The LORD has not sent you, yet you have persuaded this nation to trust in lies. ¹⁶Therefore, this is what the LORD says: 'I am about to remove you from the face of the earth. This very year you are going to die, because you have preached rebellion against the LORD.' "

¹⁷In the seventh month of that same year, Hananiah the prophet died.

A Letter to the Exiles

29 This is the text of the letter that the prophet Jeremiah sent from Jerusalem to the surviving elders among the exiles and to the priests, the prophets and all the other people Nebuchadnezzar had carried into exile from Jerusalem to Babylon. ²(This was after King Jehoiachin*a* and the queen mother, the court officials and the leaders of Judah and Jerusalem, the craftsmen and the artisans had gone into exile from Jerusalem.) ³He entrusted the letter to Elasah son of Shaphan and to Gemariah son of Hilkiah, whom Zedekiah king of Judah

a4,2 Hebrew Jeconiah, a variant of Jehoiachin

sent to King Nebuchadnezzar in Babylon. It said:

⁴This is what the LORD Almighty, the God of Israel, says to all those I carried into exile from Jerusalem to Babylon: ⁵"Build houses and settle down; plant gardens and eat what they produce. ⁶Marry and have sons and daughters; find wives for your sons and give your daughters in marriage, so that they too may have sons and daughters. Increase in number there; do not decrease. ⁷Also, seek the peace and prosperity of the city to which I have carried you into exile. Pray to the LORD for it, because if it prospers, you too will prosper." ⁸Yes, this is what the LORD Almighty, the God of Israel, says: "Do not let the prophets and diviners among you deceive you. Do not listen to the dreams you encourage them to have. ⁹They are prophesying lies to you in my name. I have not sent them," declares the LORD.

¹⁰This is what the LORD says: "When seventy years are completed for Babylon, I will come to you and fulfill my gracious promise to bring you back to this place. ¹¹For I know the plans I have for you," declares the LORD, "plans to prosper you and not to harm you, plans to give you hope and a future. ¹²Then you will call upon me and come and pray to me, and I will listen to you. ¹³You will seek me and find me when you seek me with all your heart. ¹⁴I will be found by you," declares the LORD, "and will bring you back from captivity.ᵃ I will gather you from all the nations and places where I have banished you," declares the LORD, "and will bring you back to the place from which I carried you into exile."

¹⁵You may say, "The LORD has raised up prophets for us in Babylon," ¹⁶but this is what the LORD says about the king who sits on David's throne and all the people who remain in this city, your countrymen who did not go with you into exile— ¹⁷yes, this is what the LORD Almighty says: "I will send the sword, famine and plague against them and I will make them like poor figs that are so bad they cannot be eaten. ¹⁸I will pursue them with the sword, famine and plague and will make them abhorrent to all the kingdoms of the earth and an object of cursing and horror, of scorn and reproach, among all the nations where I drive them. ¹⁹For they have not listened to my words," declares the LORD, "words that I sent to them again and again by my servants the prophets. And you exiles have not listened either," declares the LORD.

²⁰Therefore, hear the word of the LORD, all you exiles whom I have sent away from Jerusalem to Babylon. ²¹This is what the LORD Almighty, the God of Israel, says about Ahab son of Kolaiah and Zedekiah son of Maaseiah, who are prophesying lies to you in my name: "I will hand them over to Nebuchadnezzar king of Babylon, and he will put them to death before your very eyes. ²²Because of them, all the exiles from Judah who are in Babylon will use this curse: 'The LORD treat you like Zedekiah and Ahab, whom the king of Babylon burned in the fire.' ²³For they have done outrageous things in Israel; they have committed adultery with their neighbors' wives and in my name have spoken lies, which I did not tell them to do. I know it and am a witness to it," declares the LORD.

ᵃ14 Or *will restore your fortunes*

Message to Shemaiah

²⁴Tell Shemaiah the Nehelamite, ²⁵"This is what the LORD Almighty, the God of Israel, says: You sent letters in your own name to all the people in Jerusalem, to Zephaniah son of Maaseiah the priest, and to all the other priests. You said to Zephaniah, ²⁶'The LORD has appointed you priest in place of Jehoiada to be in charge of the house of the LORD; you should put any madman who acts like a prophet into the stocks and neck-irons. ²⁷So why have you not reprimanded Jere-

FRIDAY

VERSE:
Jeremiah 29:13

AUTHOR:
R.A. Torrey

PASSAGE:
Jeremiah 29:4–14

Seek Him With All Your Heart

Prayer will promote our personal piety, our individual holiness, our individual growth into the likeness of our Lord and Savior Jesus Christ as almost nothing else, as nothing else but the study of the Word of God; and these two things, prayer and study of the Word of God, always go hand-in-hand, for there is not true prayer without study of the Word of God, and there is no true study of the Word of God without prayer.

Other things being equal, your growth and mine into the likeness of our Lord and Savior Jesus Christ will be in exact proportion to the time and to *the heart* we put into prayer. I put it in that way because there are many who put a great deal of time into praying but they put so little heart into their praying that they do very little praying in the long time they spend at it; while there are others who perhaps may not put so much time into praying but who put so much heart into their praying that they accomplish vastly more by their praying in a short time than the others accomplish by their praying a long time. God himself has told us, "You will seek me and find me when you seek me with all your heart" (Jeremiah 29:13).

ADDITIONAL SCRIPTURE READINGS
Isaiah 55:6–13; Matthew 7:7–12

Go to page 990 for your next devotional reading.

miah from Anathoth, who poses as a prophet among you? ²⁸He has sent this message to us in Babylon: It will be a long time. Therefore build houses and settle down; plant gardens and eat what they produce.' "

²⁹Zephaniah the priest, however, read the letter to Jeremiah the prophet. ³⁰Then the word of the LORD came to Jeremiah: ³¹"Send this message to all the exiles: 'This is what the LORD says about Shemaiah the Nehelamite: Because Shemaiah has prophesied to you, even though I did not send him, and has led you to believe a lie, ³²this is what the LORD says: I will surely punish Shemaiah the Nehelamite and his descendants. He will have no one left among this people, nor will he see the good things I will do for my people, declares the LORD, because he has preached rebellion against me.' "

Restoration of Israel

30 This is the word that came to Jeremiah from the LORD: ²"This is what the LORD, the God of Israel, says: 'Write in a book all the words I have spoken to you. ³The days are coming,' declares the LORD, 'when I will bring my people Israel and Judah back from captivity[a] and restore them to the land I gave their forefathers to possess,' says the LORD."

⁴These are the words the LORD spoke concerning Israel and Judah: ⁵"This is what the LORD says:

" 'Cries of fear are heard—
    terror, not peace.
⁶Ask and see:
    Can a man bear children?
Then why do I see every strong
        man
    with his hands on his stomach
        like a woman in labor,
    every face turned deathly pale?
⁷How awful that day will be!
    None will be like it.
It will be a time of trouble for
        Jacob,
    but he will be saved out of it.

⁸" 'In that day,' declares the LORD
        Almighty,
    'I will break the yoke off their
        necks
and will tear off their bonds;
    no longer will foreigners
        enslave them.
⁹Instead, they will serve the LORD
        their God
    and David their king,
    whom I will raise up for them.

¹⁰" 'So do not fear, O Jacob my
        servant;
    do not be dismayed, O Israel,'
                declares the LORD.
'I will surely save you out of a
        distant place,
    your descendants from the land
        of their exile.
Jacob will again have peace and
        security,
    and no one will make him
        afraid.
¹¹I am with you and will save you,'
    declares the LORD.
'Though I completely destroy all
        the nations
    among which I scatter you,
    I will not completely destroy
        you.
I will discipline you but only with
        justice;
    I will not let you go entirely
        unpunished.'

¹²"This is what the LORD says:

" 'Your wound is incurable,
    your injury beyond healing.
¹³There is no one to plead your
        cause,
    no remedy for your sore,
    no healing for you.
¹⁴All your allies have forgotten you;
    they care nothing for you.
I have struck you as an enemy
        would
    and punished you as would the
        cruel,
because your guilt is so great
    and your sins so many.
¹⁵Why do you cry out over your
        wound,

---

a3 Or will restore the fortunes of my people Israel and Judah

your pain that has no cure?
Because of your great guilt and
many sins
I have done these things to you.

16" 'But all who devour you will be
devoured;
all your enemies will go into
exile.
Those who plunder you will be
plundered;
all who make spoil of you I will
despoil.
17But I will restore you to health
and heal your wounds,'
declares the LORD,
'because you are called an outcast,
Zion for whom no one cares.'

18"This is what the LORD says:

" 'I will restore the fortunes of
Jacob's tents
and have compassion on his
dwellings;
the city will be rebuilt on her
ruins,
and the palace will stand in its
proper place.
19From them will come songs of
thanksgiving
and the sound of rejoicing.
I will add to their numbers,
and they will not be decreased;
I will bring them honor,
and they will not be disdained.
20Their children will be as in days
of old,
and their community will be
established before me;
I will punish all who oppress
them.
21Their leader will be one of their
own;
their ruler will arise from
among them.
I will bring him near and he will
come close to me,
for who is he who will devote
himself
to be close to me?'
declares the LORD.
22" 'So you will be my people,
and I will be your God.' "

23See, the storm of the LORD
will burst out in wrath,
a driving wind swirling down
on the heads of the wicked.
24The fierce anger of the LORD will
not turn back
until he fully accomplishes
the purposes of his heart.
In days to come
you will understand this.

31 "At that time," declares the
LORD, "I will be the God of all
the clans of Israel, and they will be
my people."
2This is what the LORD says:

"The people who survive the
sword
will find favor in the desert;
I will come to give rest to
Israel."

3The LORD appeared to us in the
past,[a] saying:

"I have loved you with an
everlasting love;
I have drawn you with
loving-kindness.
4I will build you up again
and you will be rebuilt,
O Virgin Israel.
Again you will take up your
tambourines
and go out to dance with the
joyful.
5Again you will plant vineyards
on the hills of Samaria;
the farmers will plant them
and enjoy their fruit.
6There will be a day when
watchmen cry out
on the hills of Ephraim,
'Come, let us go up to Zion,
to the LORD our God.' "

7This is what the LORD says:

"Sing with joy for Jacob;
shout for the foremost of the
nations.
Make your praises heard, and say,
'O LORD, save your people,
the remnant of Israel.'

a3 Or LORD has appeared to us from afar

⁸See, I will bring them from the
    land of the north
  and gather them from the ends
    of the earth.
Among them will be the blind and
    the lame,
  expectant mothers and women
    in labor;
  a great throng will return.
⁹They will come with weeping;
  they will pray as I bring them
    back.
I will lead them beside streams of
    water
  on a level path where they will
    not stumble,
because I am Israel's father,
  and Ephraim is my firstborn
    son.

¹⁰"Hear the word of the LORD,
    O nations;
  proclaim it in distant coastlands:
'He who scattered Israel will
    gather them
  and will watch over his flock
    like a shepherd.'
¹¹For the LORD will ransom Jacob
  and redeem them from the
    hand of those stronger than
    they.
¹²They will come and shout for joy
    on the heights of Zion;
  they will rejoice in the bounty
    of the LORD—
the grain, the new wine and the
    oil,
  the young of the flocks and
    herds.
They will be like a well-watered
    garden,
  and they will sorrow no more.
¹³Then maidens will dance and be
    glad,
  young men and old as well.
I will turn their mourning into
    gladness;
  I will give them comfort and joy
    instead of sorrow.
¹⁴I will satisfy the priests with
    abundance,
  and my people will be filled
    with my bounty,"
               declares the LORD.

¹⁵This is what the LORD says:

"A voice is heard in Ramah,
  mourning and great weeping,
Rachel weeping for her children
  and refusing to be comforted,
  because her children are no
    more."

¹⁶This is what the LORD says:

"Restrain your voice from
    weeping
  and your eyes from tears,
for your work will be rewarded,"
             declares the LORD.
"They will return from the land
    of the enemy.
¹⁷So there is hope for your future,"
             declares the LORD.
"Your children will return to
    their own land.

¹⁸"I have surely heard Ephraim's
    moaning:
'You disciplined me like an
    unruly calf,
  and I have been disciplined.
Restore me, and I will return,
  because you are the LORD my
    God.
¹⁹After I strayed,
  I repented;
after I came to understand,
  I beat my breast.
I was ashamed and humiliated
  because I bore the disgrace of
    my youth.'
²⁰Is not Ephraim my dear son,
  the child in whom I delight?
Though I often speak against him,
  I still remember him.
Therefore my heart yearns for
    him;
  I have great compassion for
    him,"
             declares the LORD.

²¹"Set up road signs;
  put up guideposts.
Take note of the highway,
  the road that you take.
Return, O Virgin Israel,
  return to your towns.
²²How long will you wander,
  O unfaithful daughter?
The LORD will create a new thing
    on earth—

a woman will surround[a] a man."

²³This is what the LORD Almighty, the God of Israel, says: "When I bring them back from captivity,[b] the people in the land of Judah and in its towns will once again use these words: 'The LORD bless you, O righteous dwelling, O sacred mountain.' ²⁴People will live together in Judah and all its towns—farmers and those who move about with their flocks. ²⁵I will refresh the weary and satisfy the faint."

²⁶At this I awoke and looked around. My sleep had been pleasant to me.

²⁷"The days are coming," declares the LORD, "when I will plant the house of Israel and the house of Judah with the offspring of men and of animals. ²⁸Just as I watched over them to uproot and tear down, and to overthrow, destroy and bring disaster, so I will watch over them to build and to plant," declares the LORD. ²⁹"In those days people will no longer say,

'The fathers have eaten sour grapes,
    and the children's teeth are set on edge.'

³⁰Instead, everyone will die for his own sin; whoever eats sour grapes—his own teeth will be set on edge.

³¹"The time is coming," declares the LORD,
    "when I will make a new covenant
with the house of Israel
    and with the house of Judah.
³²It will not be like the covenant
    I made with their forefathers
when I took them by the hand
    to lead them out of Egypt,
because they broke my covenant,
    though I was a husband to[c]
    them,[d]"
                    declares the LORD.
³³"This is the covenant I will make
    with the house of Israel

after that time," declares the LORD.
"I will put my law in their minds
    and write it on their hearts.
I will be their God,
    and they will be my people.
³⁴No longer will a man teach his neighbor,
    or a man his brother, saying,
    'Know the LORD,'
because they will all know me,
    from the least of them to the greatest,"
                    declares the LORD.
"For I will forgive their wickedness
    and will remember their sins no more."

³⁵This is what the LORD says,

he who appoints the sun
    to shine by day,
who decrees the moon and stars
    to shine by night,
who stirs up the sea
    so that its waves roar—
    the LORD Almighty is his name:
³⁶"Only if these decrees vanish from my sight,"
    declares the LORD,
"will the descendants of Israel ever cease
    to be a nation before me."

³⁷This is what the LORD says:

"Only if the heavens above can be measured
    and the foundations of the earth below be searched out
will I reject all the descendants of Israel
    because of all they have done,"
                    declares the LORD.

³⁸"The days are coming," declares the LORD, "when this city will be rebuilt for me from the Tower of Hananel to the Corner Gate. ³⁹The measuring line will stretch from there straight to the hill of Gareb and then turn to Goah. ⁴⁰The whole valley where dead bodies and ashes are

a22 Or will go about ⌊seeking⌋; or will protect   b23 Or I restore their fortunes   c32 Hebrew;
Septuagint and Syriac / and I turned away from   d32 Or was their master

thrown, and all the terraces out to the Kidron Valley on the east as far as the corner of the Horse Gate, will be holy to the LORD. The city will never again be uprooted or demolished."

Jeremiah Buys a Field

32 This is the word that came to Jeremiah from the LORD in the tenth year of Zedekiah king of Judah, which was the eighteenth year of Nebuchadnezzar. ²The army of the king of Babylon was then besieging Jerusalem, and Jeremiah the prophet was confined in the courtyard of the guard in the royal palace of Judah.

³Now Zedekiah king of Judah had imprisoned him there, saying, "Why do you prophesy as you do? You say, 'This is what the LORD says: I am about to hand this city over to the king of Babylon, and he will capture it. ⁴Zedekiah king of Judah will not escape out of the hands of the Babylonians[a] but will certainly be handed over to the king of Babylon, and will speak with him face to face and see him with his own eyes. ⁵He will take Zedekiah to Babylon, where he will remain until I deal with him, declares the LORD. If you fight against the Babylonians, you will not succeed.' "

⁶Jeremiah said, "The word of the LORD came to me: ⁷Hanamel son of Shallum your uncle is going to come to you and say, 'Buy my field at Anathoth, because as nearest relative it is your right and duty to buy it.'

⁸"Then, just as the LORD had said, my cousin Hanamel came to me in the courtyard of the guard and said, 'Buy my field at Anathoth in the territory of Benjamin. Since it is your right to redeem it and possess it, buy it for yourself.'

"I knew that this was the word of the LORD; ⁹so I bought the field at Anathoth from my cousin Hanamel and weighed out for him seventeen shekels[b] of silver. ¹⁰I signed and sealed the deed, had it witnessed, and weighed out the silver on the scales.

¹¹I took the deed of purchase—the sealed copy containing the terms and conditions, as well as the unsealed copy— ¹²and I gave this deed to Baruch son of Neriah, the son of Mahseiah, in the presence of my cousin Hanamel and of the witnesses who had signed the deed and of all the Jews sitting in the courtyard of the guard.

¹³"In their presence I gave Baruch these instructions: ¹⁴'This is what the LORD Almighty, the God of Israel, says: Take these documents, both the sealed and unsealed copies of the deed of purchase, and put them in a clay jar so they will last a long time. ¹⁵For this is what the LORD Almighty, the God of Israel, says: Houses, fields and vineyards will again be bought in this land.'

¹⁶"After I had given the deed of purchase to Baruch son of Neriah, I prayed to the LORD:

¹⁷"Ah, Sovereign LORD, you have made the heavens and the earth by your great power and outstretched arm. Nothing is too hard for you. ¹⁸You show love to thousands but bring the punishment for the fathers' sins into the laps of their children after them. O great and powerful God, whose name is the LORD Almighty, ¹⁹great are your purposes and mighty are your deeds. Your eyes are open to all the ways of men; you reward everyone according to his conduct and as his deeds deserve. ²⁰You performed miraculous signs and wonders in Egypt and have continued them to this day, both in Israel and among all mankind, and have gained the renown that is still yours. ²¹You brought your people Israel out of Egypt with signs and wonders, by a mighty hand and an outstretched arm and with great terror. ²²You gave them this land you had sworn to

---

a4 Or Chaldeans; also in verses 5, 24, 25, 28, 29 and 43   *b9 That is, about 7 ounces (about 200 grams)*

give their forefathers, a land flowing with milk and honey. ²³They came in and took possession of it, but they did not obey you or follow your law; they did not do what you commanded them to do. So you brought all this disaster upon them.

²⁴"See how the siege ramps are built up to take the city. Because of the sword, famine and plague, the city will be handed over to the Babylonians who are attacking it. What you said has happened, as you now see. ²⁵And though the city will be handed over to the Babylonians, you, O Sovereign LORD, say to me, 'Buy the field with silver and have the transaction witnessed.'"

²⁶Then the word of the LORD came to Jeremiah: ²⁷"I am the LORD, the God of all mankind. Is anything too hard for me? ²⁸Therefore, this is what the LORD says: I am about to hand this city over to the Babylonians and to Nebuchadnezzar king of Babylon, who will capture it. ²⁹The Babylonians who are attacking this city will come in and set it on fire; they will burn it down, along with the houses where the people provoked me to anger by burning incense on the roofs to Baal and by pouring out drink offerings to other gods.

³⁰"The people of Israel and Judah have done nothing but evil in my sight from their youth; indeed, the people of Israel have done nothing but provoke me with what their hands have made, declares the LORD. ³¹From the day it was built until now, this city has so aroused my anger and wrath that I must remove it from my sight. ³²The people of Israel and Judah have provoked me by all the evil they have done—they, their kings and officials, their priests and prophets, the men of Judah and the people of Jerusalem. ³³They turned their backs to

me and not their faces; though I taught them again and again, they would not listen or respond to discipline. ³⁴They set up their abominable idols in the house that bears my Name and defiled it. ³⁵They built high places for Baal in the Valley of Ben Hinnom to sacrifice their sons and daughters*a* to Molech, though I never commanded, nor did it enter my mind, that they should do such a detestable thing and so make Judah sin.

³⁶"You are saying about this city, 'By the sword, famine and plague it will be handed over to the king of Babylon'; but this is what the LORD, the God of Israel, says: ³⁷I will surely gather them from all the lands where I banish them in my furious anger and great wrath; I will bring them back to this place and let them live in safety. ³⁸They will be my people, and I will be their God. ³⁹I will give them singleness of heart and action, so that they will always fear me for their own good and the good of their children after them. ⁴⁰I will make an everlasting covenant with them: I will never stop doing good to them, and I will inspire them to fear me, so that they will never turn away from me. ⁴¹I will rejoice in doing them good and will assuredly plant them in this land with all my heart and soul.

⁴²"This is what the LORD says: As I have brought all this great calamity on this people, so I will give them all the prosperity I have promised them. ⁴³Once more fields will be bought in this land of which you say, 'It is a desolate waste, without men or animals, for it has been handed over to the Babylonians.' ⁴⁴Fields will be bought for silver, and deeds will be signed, sealed and witnessed in the territory of Benjamin, in the villages around Jerusalem, in the towns of Judah and in the towns of the hill country, of the western foothills and of the Negev, because I will restore their fortunes,*b* declares the LORD."

---

a35 Or *to make their sons and daughters pass through ⌐the fire⌐/captivity*   *b44* Or *will bring them back from*

Promise of Restoration

33 While Jeremiah was still confined in the courtyard of the guard, the word of the LORD came to him a second time: ²"This is what the LORD says, he who made the earth, the LORD who formed it and established it—the LORD is his name: ³'Call to me and I will answer you and tell you great and unsearchable things you do not know.' ⁴For this is what the LORD, the God of Israel, says about the houses in this city and the royal palaces of Judah that have been torn down to be used against the siege ramps and the sword ⁵in the fight with the Babylonians*: 'They will be filled with the dead bodies of the men I will slay in my anger and wrath. I will hide my face from this city because of all its wickedness.

⁶" 'Nevertheless, I will bring health and healing to it; I will heal my people and will let them enjoy abundant peace and security. ⁷I will bring Judah and Israel back from captivity* and will rebuild them as they were before. ⁸I will cleanse them from all the sin they have committed against me and will forgive all their sins of rebellion against me. ⁹Then this city will bring me renown, joy, praise and honor before all nations on earth that hear of all the good things I do for it; and they will be in awe and will tremble at the abundant prosperity and peace I provide for it.'

¹⁰"This is what the LORD says: 'You say about this place, "It is a desolate waste, without men or animals." Yet in the towns of Judah and the streets of Jerusalem that are deserted, inhabited by neither men nor animals, there will be heard once more ¹¹the sounds of joy and gladness, the voices of bride and bridegroom, and the voices of those who bring thank offerings to the house of the LORD, saying,

"Give thanks to the LORD
    Almighty,
  for the LORD is good;
    his love endures forever."

For I will restore the fortunes of the land as they were before,' says the LORD.

¹²"This is what the LORD Almighty says: 'In this place, desolate and without men or animals—in all its towns there will again be pastures for shepherds to rest their flocks. ¹³In the towns of the hill country, of the western foothills and of the Negev, in the territory of Benjamin, in the villages around Jerusalem and in the towns of Judah, flocks will again pass under the hand of the one who counts them,' says the LORD.

¹⁴" 'The days are coming,' declares the LORD, 'when I will fulfill the gracious promise I made to the house of Israel and to the house of Judah.

¹⁵" 'In those days and at that time
    I will make a righteous Branch
      sprout from David's line;
    he will do what is just and right
      in the land.
¹⁶In those days Judah will be saved
    and Jerusalem will live in
      safety.
  This is the name by which it*
      will be called:
    The LORD Our Righteousness.'

¹⁷For this is what the LORD says: 'David will never fail to have a man to sit on the throne of the house of Israel, ¹⁸nor will the priests, who are Levites, ever fail to have a man to stand before me continually to offer burnt offerings, to burn grain offerings and to present sacrifices.' "

¹⁹The word of the LORD came to Jeremiah: ²⁰"This is what the LORD says: 'If you can break my covenant with the day and my covenant with the night, so that day and night no longer come at their appointed time, ²¹then my covenant with David my servant—and my covenant with the Levites who are priests ministering before me—can be broken and David will no longer have a descendant to reign on his throne. ²²I will make the descendants of David my servant and the Levites who minister before me as

---

a5 Or Chaldeans   *b7 Or will restore the fortunes of Judah and Israel*   *c16 Or he*

countless as the stars of the sky and as measureless as the sand on the sea-shore.' "

²³The word of the LORD came to Jeremiah: ²⁴"Have you not noticed that these people are saying, 'The LORD has rejected the two kingdoms[a] he chose'? So they despise my people and no longer regard them as a nation. ²⁵This is what the LORD says: 'If I have not established my covenant with day and night and the fixed laws of heaven and earth, ²⁶then I will reject the descendants of Jacob and David my servant and will not choose one of his sons to rule over the descendants of Abraham, Isaac and Jacob. For I will restore their fortunes[b] and have compassion on them.' "

Warning to Zedekiah

34 While Nebuchadnezzar king of Babylon and all his army and all the kingdoms and peoples in the empire he ruled were fighting against Jerusalem and all its surrounding towns, this word came to Jeremiah from the LORD: ²"This is what the LORD, the God of Israel, says: Go to Zedekiah king of Judah and tell him, 'This is what the LORD says: I am about to hand this city over to the king of Babylon, and he will burn it down. ³You will not escape from his grasp but will surely be captured and handed over to him. You will see the king of Babylon with your own eyes, and he will speak with you face to face. And you will go to Babylon.

⁴" 'Yet hear the promise of the LORD, O Zedekiah king of Judah. This is what the LORD says concerning you: You will not die by the sword; ⁵you will die peacefully. As people made a funeral fire in honor of your fathers, the former kings who preceded you, so they will make a fire in your honor and lament, "Alas, O master!" I myself make this promise, declares the LORD.' "

⁶Then Jeremiah the prophet told all this to Zedekiah king of Judah, in Je-rusalem, ⁷while the army of the king of Babylon was fighting against Jerusalem and the other cities of Judah that were still holding out—Lachish and Azekah. These were the only fortified cities left in Judah.

Freedom for Slaves

⁸The word came to Jeremiah from the LORD after King Zedekiah had made a covenant with all the people in Jerusalem to proclaim freedom for the slaves. ⁹Everyone was to free his Hebrew slaves, both male and female; no one was to hold a fellow Jew in bondage. ¹⁰So all the officials and people who entered into this covenant agreed that they would free their male and female slaves and no longer hold them in bondage. They agreed, and set them free. ¹¹But afterward they changed their minds and took back the slaves they had freed and en-slaved them again.

¹²Then the word of the LORD came to Jeremiah: ¹³"This is what the LORD, the God of Israel, says: I made a covenant with your forefathers when I brought them out of Egypt, out of the land of slavery. I said, ¹⁴'Every seventh year each of you must free any fellow Hebrew who has sold himself to you. After he has served you six years, you must let him go free.'[c] Your fathers, however, did not listen to me or pay attention to me. ¹⁵Recently you repented and did what is right in my sight: Each of you proclaimed freedom to his countrymen. You even made a covenant before me in the house that bears my Name. ¹⁶But now you have turned around and profaned my name; each of you has taken back the male and female slaves you had set free to go where they wished. You have forced them to become your slaves again.

¹⁷"Therefore, this is what the LORD says: You have not obeyed me; you have not proclaimed freedom for your fellow countrymen. So I now proclaim 'freedom' for you, declares the LORD—'freedom' to fall by the

---

[a]24 Or *families*   [b]26 Or *will bring them back from captivity*   [c]14 Deut. 15:12

sword, plague and famine. I will make you abhorrent to all the kingdoms of the earth. ¹⁸The men who have violated my covenant and have not fulfilled the terms of the covenant they made before me, I will treat like the calf they cut in two and then walked between its pieces. ¹⁹The leaders of Judah and Jerusalem, the court officials, the priests and all the people of the land who walked between the pieces of the calf, ²⁰I will hand over to their enemies who seek their lives. Their dead bodies will become food for the birds of the air and the beasts of the earth.

²¹"I will hand Zedekiah king of Judah and his officials over to their enemies who seek their lives, to the army of the king of Babylon, which has withdrawn from you. ²²I am going to give the order, declares the LORD, and I will bring them back to this city. They will fight against it, take it and burn it down. And I will lay waste the towns of Judah so no one can live there."

The Recabites

35 This is the word that came to Jeremiah from the LORD during the reign of Jehoiakim son of Josiah king of Judah: ²"Go to the Recabite family and invite them to come to one of the side rooms of the house of the LORD and give them wine to drink."

³So I went to get Jaazaniah son of Jeremiah, the son of Habazziniah, and his brothers and all his sons—the whole family of the Recabites. ⁴I brought them into the house of the LORD, into the room of the sons of Hanan son of Igdaliah the man of God. It was next to the room of the officials, which was over that of Maaseiah son of Shallum the doorkeeper. ⁵Then I set bowls full of wine and some cups before the men of the Recabite family and said to them, "Drink some wine."

⁶But they replied, "We do not drink wine, because our forefather Jonadab son of Recab gave us this command: 'Neither you nor your descendants must ever drink wine. ⁷Also you must never build houses, sow seed or plant vineyards; you must never have any of these things, but must always live in tents. Then you will live a long time in the land where you are nomads.' ⁸We have obeyed everything our forefather Jonadab son of Recab commanded us. Neither we nor our wives nor our sons and daughters have ever drunk wine ⁹or built houses to live in or had vineyards, fields or crops. ¹⁰We have lived in tents and have fully obeyed everything our forefather Jonadab commanded us. ¹¹But when Nebuchadnezzar king of Babylon invaded this land, we said, 'Come, we must go to Jerusalem to escape the Babylonian*a* and Aramean armies.' So we have remained in Jerusalem."

¹²Then the word of the LORD came to Jeremiah, saying: ¹³"This is what the LORD Almighty, the God of Israel, says: Go and tell the men of Judah and the people of Jerusalem, 'Will you not learn a lesson and obey my words?' declares the LORD. ¹⁴'Jonadab son of Recab ordered his sons not to drink wine and this command has been kept. To this day they do not drink wine, because they obey their forefather's command. But I have spoken to you again and again, yet you have not obeyed me. ¹⁵Again and again I sent all my servants the prophets to you. They said, "Each of you must turn from your wicked ways and reform your actions; do not follow other gods to serve them. Then you will live in the land I have given to you and your fathers." But you have not paid attention or listened to me. ¹⁶The descendants of Jonadab son of Recab have carried out the command their forefather gave them, but these people have not obeyed me.'

¹⁷"Therefore, this is what the LORD God Almighty, the God of Israel, says: 'Listen! I am going to bring on Judah and on everyone living in Jerusalem every disaster I pronounced against them. I spoke to them, but

a11 Or Chaldean

they did not listen; I called to them, but they did not answer.' "

¹⁸Then Jeremiah said to the family of the Recabites, "This is what the LORD Almighty, the God of Israel, says: 'You have obeyed the command of your forefather Jonadab and have followed all his instructions and have done everything he ordered.' ¹⁹Therefore, this is what the LORD Almighty, the God of Israel, says: 'Jonadab son of Recab will never fail to have a man to serve me.' "

Jehoiakim Burns Jeremiah's Scroll

36 In the fourth year of Jehoiakim son of Josiah king of Judah, this word came to Jeremiah from the LORD: ²"Take a scroll and write on it all the words I have spoken to you concerning Israel, Judah and all the other nations from the time I began speaking to you in the reign of Josiah till now. ³Perhaps when the people of Judah hear about every disaster I plan to inflict on them, each of them will turn from his wicked way; then I will forgive their wickedness and their sin."

⁴So Jeremiah called Baruch son of Neriah, and while Jeremiah dictated all the words the LORD had spoken to him, Baruch wrote them on the scroll. ⁵Then Jeremiah told Baruch, "I am restricted; I cannot go to the LORD's temple. ⁶So you go to the house of the LORD on a day of fasting and read to the people from the scroll the words of the LORD that you wrote as I dictated. Read them to all the people of Judah who come in from their towns. ⁷Perhaps they will bring their petition before the LORD, and each will turn from his wicked ways, for the anger and wrath pronounced against this people by the LORD are great."

⁸Baruch son of Neriah did everything Jeremiah the prophet told him to do; at the LORD's temple he read the words of the LORD from the scroll. ⁹In the ninth month of the fifth year of Jehoiakim son of Josiah king of Judah, a time of fasting before the LORD was proclaimed for all the people in Jerusalem and those who had come from the towns of Judah. ¹⁰From the room of Gemariah son of Shaphan the secretary, which was in the upper courtyard at the entrance of the New Gate of the temple, Baruch read to all the people at the LORD's temple the words of Jeremiah from the scroll.

¹¹When Micaiah son of Gemariah, the son of Shaphan, heard all the words of the LORD from the scroll, ¹²he went down to the secretary's room in the royal palace, where all the officials were sitting: Elishama the secretary, Delaiah son of Shemaiah, Elnathan son of Acbor, Gemariah son of Shaphan, Zedekiah son of Hananiah, and all the other officials. ¹³After Micaiah told them everything he had heard Baruch read to the people from the scroll, ¹⁴all the officials sent Jehudi son of Nethaniah, the son of Shelemiah, the son of Cushi, to say to Baruch, "Bring the scroll from which you have read to the people and come." So Baruch son of Neriah went to them with the scroll in his hand. ¹⁵They said to him, "Sit down, please, and read it to us."

So Baruch read it to them. ¹⁶When they heard all these words, they looked at each other in fear and said to Baruch, "We must report all these words to the king." ¹⁷Then they asked Baruch, "Tell us, how did you come to write all this? Did Jeremiah dictate it?"

¹⁸"Yes," Baruch replied, "he dictated all these words to me, and I wrote them in ink on the scroll."

¹⁹Then the officials said to Baruch, "You and Jeremiah, go and hide. Don't let anyone know where you are."

²⁰After they put the scroll in the room of Elishama the secretary, they went to the king in the courtyard and reported everything to him. ²¹The king sent Jehudi to get the scroll, and Jehudi brought it from the room of Elishama the secretary and read it to the king and all the officials standing beside him. ²²It was the ninth month and the king was sitting in the winter apartment, with a fire burning in the

PASSAGE: Isaiah 40:25–31; Jeremiah 31:31–34
AUTHOR: George Matheson

Back Across the Years

O to go back across the years long vanished,
To have the words unsaid, the deeds undone;
The errors canceled, the deep shadows banished
In the glad sense of a new world begun.
To be a little child, whose page of story
Is yet undimmed, unblotted by a stain;
And in the sunrise of primeval glory
To know that life has had its start again.

I may go back across the years long vanished,
I may resume my childhood, Lord, in Thee,
When in the shadow of Thy cross, is banished
All other shadows that encompass me.
And o'er the road that now is dark and dreary,
This soul, made buoyant by the strength of rest,
Shall walk untired, shall run and not be weary
To bear the blessing that has made it blest.

Go to page 995 for your next devotional reading.

firepot in front of him. ²³Whenever Jehudi had read three or four columns of the scroll, the king cut them off with a scribe's knife and threw them into the firepot, until the entire scroll was burned in the fire. ²⁴The king and all his attendants who heard all these words showed no fear, nor did they tear their clothes. ²⁵Even though Elnathan, Delaiah and Gemariah urged the king not to burn the scroll, he would not listen to them. ²⁶Instead, the king commanded Jerahmeel, a son of the king, Seraiah son of Azriel and Shelemiah son of Abdeel to arrest Baruch the scribe and Jeremiah the prophet. But the LORD had hidden them.

²⁷After the king burned the scroll containing the words that Baruch had written at Jeremiah's dictation, the word of the LORD came to Jeremiah: ²⁸"Take another scroll and write on it all the words that were on the first scroll, which Jehoiakim king of Judah burned up. ²⁹Also tell Jehoiakim king of Judah, 'This is what the LORD says: You burned that scroll and said, "Why did you write on it that the king of Babylon would certainly come and destroy this land and cut off both men and animals from it?" ³⁰Therefore, this is what the LORD says about Jehoiakim king of Judah: He will have no one to sit on the throne of David; his body will be thrown out and exposed to the heat by day and the frost by night. ³¹I will punish him and his children and his attendants for their wickedness; I will bring on them and those living in Jerusalem and the people of Judah every disaster I pronounced against them, because they have not listened.' "

³²So Jeremiah took another scroll and gave it to the scribe Baruch son of Neriah, and as Jeremiah dictated, Baruch wrote on it all the words of the scroll that Jehoiakim king of Judah had burned in the fire. And many similar words were added to them.

Jeremiah in Prison

37 Zedekiah son of Josiah was made king of Judah by Nebuchadnezzar king of Babylon; he reigned in place of Jehoiachin[a] son of Jehoiakim. ²Neither he nor his attendants nor the people of the land paid any attention to the words the LORD had spoken through Jeremiah the prophet.

³King Zedekiah, however, sent Jehucal son of Shelemiah with the priest Zephaniah son of Maaseiah to Jeremiah the prophet with this message: "Please pray to the LORD our God for us."

⁴Now Jeremiah was free to come and go among the people, for he had not yet been put in prison. ⁵Pharaoh's army had marched out of Egypt, and when the Babylonians[b] who were besieging Jerusalem heard the report about them, they withdrew from Jerusalem.

⁶Then the word of the LORD came to Jeremiah the prophet: ⁷"This is what the LORD, the God of Israel, says: Tell the king of Judah, who sent you to inquire of me, 'Pharaoh's army, which has marched out to support you, will go back to its own land, to Egypt. ⁸Then the Babylonians will return and attack this city; they will capture it and burn it down.'

⁹"This is what the LORD says: Do not deceive yourselves, thinking, 'The Babylonians will surely leave us.' They will not! ¹⁰Even if you were to defeat the entire Babylonian[c] army that is attacking you and only wounded men were left in their tents, they would come out and burn this city down."

¹¹After the Babylonian army had withdrawn from Jerusalem because of Pharaoh's army, ¹²Jeremiah started to leave the city to go to the territory of Benjamin to get his share of the property among the people there. ¹³But when he reached the Benjamin Gate, the captain of the guard, whose name

---

*a*1 Hebrew *Coniah*, a variant of *Jehoiachin*   *b*5 Or *Chaldeans*; also in verses 8, 9, 13 and 14
*c*10 Or *Chaldean*; also in verse 11

was Irijah son of Shelemiah, the son of Hananiah, arrested him and said, "You are deserting to the Babylonians!"

[14]"That's not true!" Jeremiah said. "I am not deserting to the Babylonians." But Irijah would not listen to him; instead, he arrested Jeremiah and brought him to the officials. [15]They were angry with Jeremiah and had him beaten and imprisoned in the house of Jonathan the secretary, which they had made into a prison.

[16]Jeremiah was put into a vaulted cell in a dungeon, where he remained a long time. [17]Then King Zedekiah sent for him and had him brought to the palace, where he asked him privately, "Is there any word from the LORD?"

"Yes," Jeremiah replied, "you will be handed over to the king of Babylon."

[18]Then Jeremiah said to King Zedekiah, "What crime have I committed against you or your officials or this people, that you have put me in prison? [19]Where are your prophets who prophesied to you, 'The king of Babylon will not attack you or this land'? [20]But now, my lord the king, please listen. Let me bring my petition before you: Do not send me back to the house of Jonathan the secretary, or I will die there."

[21]King Zedekiah then gave orders for Jeremiah to be placed in the courtyard of the guard and given bread from the street of the bakers each day until all the bread in the city was gone. So Jeremiah remained in the courtyard of the guard.

Jeremiah Thrown Into a Cistern

38 Shephatiah son of Mattan, Gedaliah son of Pashhur, Jehucal[a] son of Shelemiah, and Pashhur son of Malkijah heard what Jeremiah was telling all the people when he said, [2]"This is what the LORD says: 'Whoever stays in this city will die by the sword, famine or plague, but whoever goes over to the Babylonians[b] will live. He will escape with his life; he will live.' [3]And this is what the LORD says: 'This city will certainly be handed over to the army of the king of Babylon, who will capture it.'"

[4]Then the officials said to the king, "This man should be put to death. He is discouraging the soldiers who are left in this city, as well as all the people, by the things he is saying to them. This man is not seeking the good of these people but their ruin."

[5]"He is in your hands," King Zedekiah answered. "The king can do nothing to oppose you."

[6]So they took Jeremiah and put him into the cistern of Malkijah, the king's son, which was in the courtyard of the guard. They lowered Jeremiah by ropes into the cistern; it had no water in it, only mud, and Jeremiah sank down into the mud.

[7]But Ebed-Melech, a Cushite,[c] an official[d] in the royal palace, heard that they had put Jeremiah into the cistern. While the king was sitting in the Benjamin Gate, [8]Ebed-Melech went out of the palace and said to him, [9]"My lord the king, these men have acted wickedly in all they have done to Jeremiah the prophet. They have thrown him into a cistern, where he will starve to death when there is no longer any bread in the city."

[10]Then the king commanded Ebed-Melech the Cushite, "Take thirty men from here with you and lift Jeremiah the prophet out of the cistern before he dies."

[11]So Ebed-Melech took the men with him and went to a room under the treasury in the palace. He took some old rags and worn-out clothes from there and let them down with ropes to Jeremiah in the cistern. [12]Ebed-Melech the Cushite said to Jeremiah, "Put these old rags and worn-out clothes under your arms to pad the ropes." Jeremiah did so, [13]and they pulled him up with the ropes

---

a1 Hebrew *Jucal,* a variant of *Jehucal*   b2 Or *Chaldeans;* also in verses 18, 19 and 23
c7 Probably from the upper Nile region   d7 Or *a eunuch*

and lifted him out of the cistern. And Jeremiah remained in the courtyard of the guard.

Zedekiah Questions Jeremiah Again

¹⁴Then King Zedekiah sent for Jeremiah the prophet and had him brought to the third entrance to the temple of the LORD. "I am going to ask you something," the king said to Jeremiah. "Do not hide anything from me."

¹⁵Jeremiah said to Zedekiah, "If I give you an answer, will you not kill me? Even if I did give you counsel, you would not listen to me."

¹⁶But King Zedekiah swore this oath secretly to Jeremiah: "As surely as the LORD lives, who has given us breath, I will neither kill you nor hand you over to those who are seeking your life."

¹⁷Then Jeremiah said to Zedekiah, "This is what the LORD God Almighty, the God of Israel, says: 'If you surrender to the officers of the king of Babylon, your life will be spared and this city will not be burned down; you and your family will live. ¹⁸But if you will not surrender to the officers of the king of Babylon, this city will be handed over to the Babylonians and they will burn it down; you yourself will not escape from their hands.' "

¹⁹King Zedekiah said to Jeremiah, "I am afraid of the Jews who have gone over to the Babylonians, for the Babylonians may hand me over to them and they will mistreat me."

²⁰"They will not hand you over," Jeremiah replied. "Obey the LORD by doing what I tell you. Then it will go well with you, and your life will be spared. ²¹But if you refuse to surrender, this is what the LORD has revealed to me: ²²All the women left in the palace of the king of Judah will be brought out to the officials of the king of Babylon. Those women will say to you:

" 'They misled you and overcame you—

those trusted friends of yours. Your feet are sunk in the mud; your friends have deserted you.'

²³"All your wives and children will be brought out to the Babylonians. You yourself will not escape from their hands but will be captured by the king of Babylon; and this city will[a] be burned down."

²⁴Then Zedekiah said to Jeremiah, "Do not let anyone know about this conversation, or you may die. ²⁵If the officials hear that I talked with you, and they come to you and say, 'Tell us what you said to the king and what the king said to you; do not hide it from us or we will kill you,' ²⁶then tell them, 'I was pleading with the king not to send me back to Jonathan's house to die there.' "

²⁷All the officials did come to Jeremiah and question him, and he told them everything the king had ordered him to say. So they said no more to him, for no one had heard his conversation with the king.

²⁸And Jeremiah remained in the courtyard of the guard until the day Jerusalem was captured.

The Fall of Jerusalem

39 This is how Jerusalem was taken: ¹In the ninth year of Zedekiah king of Judah, in the tenth month, Nebuchadnezzar king of Babylon marched against Jerusalem with his whole army and laid siege to it. ²And on the ninth day of the fourth month of Zedekiah's eleventh year, the city wall was broken through. ³Then all the officials of the king of Babylon came and took seats in the Middle Gate: Nergal-Sharezer of Samgar, Nebo-Sarsekim[b] a chief officer, Nergal-Sharezer a high official and all the other officials of the king of Babylon. ⁴When Zedekiah king of Judah and all the soldiers saw them, they fled; they left the city at night by way of the king's garden, through the

---

a23 Or *and you will cause this city to*   *b3* Or *Nergal-Sharezer, Samgar-Nebo, Sarsekim*

gate between the two walls, and headed toward the Arabah.[a]

[5]But the Babylonian[b] army pursued them and overtook Zedekiah in the plains of Jericho. They captured him and took him to Nebuchadnezzar king of Babylon at Riblah in the land of Hamath, where he pronounced sentence on him. [6]There at Riblah the king of Babylon slaughtered the sons of Zedekiah before his eyes and also killed all the nobles of Judah. [7]Then he put out Zedekiah's eyes and bound him with bronze shackles to take him to Babylon.[c]

[8]The Babylonians[c] set fire to the royal palace and the houses of the people and broke down the walls of Jerusalem. [9]Nebuzaradan commander of the imperial guard carried into exile to Babylon the people who remained in the city, along with those who had gone over to him, and the rest of the people. [10]But Nebuzaradan the commander of the guard left behind in the land of Judah some of the poor people, who owned nothing; and at that time he gave them vineyards and fields.

[11]Now Nebuchadnezzar king of Babylon had given these orders about Jeremiah through Nebuzaradan commander of the imperial guard: [12]"Take him and look after him; don't harm him but do for him whatever he asks." [13]So Nebuzaradan the commander of the guard, Nebushazban a chief officer, Nergal-Sharezer a high official and all the other officers of the king of Babylon [14]sent and had Jeremiah taken out of the courtyard of the guard. They turned him over to Gedaliah son of Ahikam, the son of Shaphan, to take him back to his home. So he remained among his own people.

[15]While Jeremiah had been confined in the courtyard of the guard, the word of the LORD came to him: [16]"Go and tell Ebed-Melech the Cushite, 'This is what the LORD Almighty, the God of Israel, says: I am about to fulfill my words against this city

through disaster, not prosperity. At that time they will be fulfilled before your eyes. [17]But I will rescue you on that day, declares the LORD; you will not be handed over to those you fear. [18]I will save you; you will not fall by the sword but will escape with your life, because you trust in me, declares the LORD.' "

Jeremiah Freed

40 The word came to Jeremiah from the LORD after Nebuzaradan commander of the imperial guard had released him at Ramah. He had found Jeremiah bound in chains among all the captives from Jerusalem and Judah who were being carried into exile to Babylon. [2]When the commander of the guard found Jeremiah, he said to him, "The LORD your God decreed this disaster for this place. [3]And now the LORD has brought it about; he has done just as he said he would. All this happened because you people sinned against the LORD and did not obey him. [4]But today I am freeing you from the chains on your wrists. Come with me to Babylon, if you like, and I will look after you; but if you do not want to, then don't come. Look, the whole country lies before you; go wherever you please." [5]However, before Jeremiah turned to go,[d] Nebuzaradan added, "Go back to Gedaliah son of Ahikam, the son of Shaphan, whom the king of Babylon has appointed over the towns of Judah, and live with him among the people, or go anywhere else you please."

Then the commander gave him provisions and a present and let him go. [6]So Jeremiah went to Gedaliah son of Ahikam at Mizpah and stayed with him among the people who were left behind in the land.

Gedaliah Assassinated

[7]When all the army officers and their men who were still in the open country heard that the king of Babylon had appointed Gedaliah son of

---

[a]4 Or *the Jordan Valley*   [b]5 Or *Chaldean*   [c]8 Or *Chaldeans*   [d]5 Or *Jeremiah answered*

VERSE:
Jeremiah 40:6

AUTHOR:
Eugene H. Peterson

PASSAGE:
Jeremiah 40:1–6

The Place of God's Promise

Jeremiah is singled out, his chains are cut off him and Nebuzaradan presents him with a choice. He can go to Babylon with the promise of special treatment — no chains, no deprivation, protective custody (so that he will never again have to endure the abuse of his fellow citizens) and a special allowance from the king. Or he can stay in Jerusalem, the city he has lived in and labored for all his life . . .

Life in Jerusalem would be starting over: in a brutal environment with the scantiest of resources, human and material, in the midst of a wrecked city with a few poor people who weren't even worth being made prisoners! Not, it would seem, a very happy prospect at age 65.

Life in Babylon would be an easy retirement: honored by the Babylonian court, protected by a Babylonian bodyguard, living on a Babylonian pension. Jeremiah was ready for retirement and he deserved it . . .

But Jeremiah wasn't ready for retirement. He wasn't tired of living by faith. He was used to starting over with nothing. He had been doing it for a long time. He had long since quit calculating his chances by counting his resources; his habit was to expect God's grace, "new every morning" . . .

Jeremiah's choice that day at Ramah is the characteristic action of his life. He chose to be where God commanded, at the center of God's action, at the place of God's promise . . . Jeremiah chose to live by faith.

ADDITIONAL SCRIPTURE READINGS
Romans 1:16–17; Hebrews 11:1–16

Go to page 1019 for your next devotional reading.

Ahikam as governor over the land and had put him in charge of the men, women and children who were the poorest in the land and who had not been carried into exile to Babylon, **8**they came to Gedaliah at Mizpah—Ishmael son of Nethaniah, Johanan and Jonathan the sons of Kareah, Seraiah son of Tanhumeth, the sons of Ephai the Netophathite, and Jaazaniah[a] the son of the Maacathite, and their men. **9**Gedaliah son of Ahikam, the son of Shaphan, took an oath to reassure them and their men. "Do not be afraid to serve the Babylonians,[b]" he said. "Settle down in the land and serve the king of Babylon, and it will go well with you. **10**I myself will stay at Mizpah to represent you before the Babylonians who come to us, but you are to harvest the wine, summer fruit and oil, and put them in your storage jars, and live in the towns you have taken over."

11When all the Jews in Moab, Ammon, Edom and all the other countries heard that the king of Babylon had left a remnant in Judah and had appointed Gedaliah son of Ahikam, the son of Shaphan, as governor over them, **12**they all came back to the land of Judah, to Gedaliah at Mizpah, from all the countries where they had been scattered. And they harvested an abundance of wine and summer fruit.

13Johanan son of Kareah and all the army officers still in the open country came to Gedaliah at Mizpah **14**and said to him, "Don't you know that Baalis king of the Ammonites has sent Ishmael son of Nethaniah to take your life?" But Gedaliah son of Ahikam did not believe them.

15Then Johanan son of Kareah said privately to Gedaliah in Mizpah, "Let me go and kill Ishmael son of Nethaniah, and no one will know it. Why should he take your life and cause all the Jews who are gathered around you to be scattered and the remnant of Judah to perish?"

16But Gedaliah son of Ahikam said to Johanan son of Kareah, "Don't do such a thing! What you are saying about Ishmael is not true."

41 In the seventh month Ishmael son of Nethaniah, the son of Elishama, who was of royal blood and had been one of the king's officers, came with ten men to Gedaliah son of Ahikam at Mizpah. While they were eating together there, **2**Ishmael son of Nethaniah and the ten men who were with him got up and struck down Gedaliah son of Ahikam, the son of Shaphan, with the sword, killing the one whom the king of Babylon had appointed as governor over the land. **3**Ishmael also killed all the Jews who were with Gedaliah at Mizpah, as well as the Babylonian[c] soldiers who were there.

4The day after Gedaliah's assassination, before anyone knew about it, **5**eighty men who had shaved off their beards, torn their clothes and cut themselves came from Shechem, Shiloh and Samaria, bringing grain offerings and incense with them to the house of the LORD. **6**Ishmael son of Nethaniah went out from Mizpah to meet them, weeping as he went. When he met them, he said, "Come to Gedaliah son of Ahikam." **7**When they went into the city, Ishmael son of Nethaniah and the men who were with him slaughtered them and threw them into a cistern. **8**But ten of them said to Ishmael, "Don't kill us! We have wheat and barley, oil and honey, hidden in a field." So he let them alone and did not kill them with the others. **9**Now the cistern where he threw all the bodies of the men he had killed along with Gedaliah was the one King Asa had made as part of his defense against Baasha king of Israel. Ishmael son of Nethaniah filled it with the dead.

10Ishmael made captives of all the rest of the people who were in Mizpah—the king's daughters along with all the others who were left there, over whom Nebuzaradan command-

a8 Hebrew *Jezaniah,* a variant of *Jaazaniah*   *b9* Or *Chaldeans;* also in verse 10   *c3* Or *Chaldean*

er of the imperial guard had appointed Gedaliah son of Ahikam. Ishmael son of Nethaniah took them captive and set out to cross over to the Ammonites.

¹¹When Johanan son of Kareah and all the army officers who were with him heard about all the crimes Ishmael son of Nethaniah had committed, ¹²they took all their men and went to fight Ishmael son of Nethaniah. They caught up with him near the great pool in Gibeon. ¹³When all the people Ishmael had with him saw Johanan son of Kareah and the army officers who were with him, they were glad. ¹⁴All the people Ishmael had taken captive at Mizpah turned and went over to Johanan son of Kareah. ¹⁵But Ishmael son of Nethaniah and eight of his men escaped from Johanan and fled to the Ammonites.

Flight to Egypt

¹⁶Then Johanan son of Kareah and all the army officers who were with him led away all the survivors from Mizpah whom he had recovered from Ishmael son of Nethaniah after he had assassinated Gedaliah son of Ahikam: the soldiers, women, children and court officials he had brought from Gibeon. ¹⁷And they went on, stopping at Geruth Kimham near Bethlehem on their way to Egypt ¹⁸to escape the Babylonians.ᵃ They were afraid of them because Ishmael son of Nethaniah had killed Gedaliah son of Ahikam, whom the king of Babylon had appointed as governor over the land.

42 Then all the army officers, including Johanan son of Kareah and Jezaniahᵇ son of Hoshaiah, and all the people from the least to the greatest approached ²Jeremiah the prophet and said to him, "Please hear our petition and pray to the LORD your God for this entire remnant. For as you now see, though we were once many, now only a few are left. ³Pray that the LORD your God will tell us where we should go and what we should do."

⁴"I have heard you," replied Jeremiah the prophet. "I will certainly pray to the LORD your God as you have requested; I will tell you everything the LORD says and will keep nothing back from you." ⁵Then they said to Jeremiah, "May the LORD be a true and faithful witness against us if we do not act in accordance with everything the LORD your God sends you to tell us. ⁶Whether it is favorable or unfavorable, we will obey the LORD our God, to whom we are sending you, so that it will go well with us, for we will obey the LORD our God."

⁷Ten days later the word of the LORD came to Jeremiah. ⁸So he called together Johanan son of Kareah and all the army officers who were with him and all the people from the least to the greatest. ⁹He said to them, "This is what the LORD, the God of Israel, to whom you sent me to present your petition, says: ¹⁰'If you stay in this land, I will build you up and not tear you down; I will plant you and not uproot you, for I am grieved over the disaster I have inflicted on you. ¹¹Do not be afraid of the king of Babylon, whom you now fear. Do not be afraid of him, declares the LORD, for I am with you and will save you and deliver you from his hands. ¹²I will show you compassion so that he will have compassion on you and restore you to your land.'

¹³"However, if you say, 'We will not stay in this land,' and so disobey the LORD your God, ¹⁴and if you say, 'No, we will go and live in Egypt, where we will not see war or hear the trumpet or be hungry for bread,' ¹⁵then hear the word of the LORD, O remnant of Judah. This is what the LORD Almighty, the God of Israel, says: 'If you are determined to go to Egypt and you do go to settle there, ¹⁶then the sword you fear will overtake you there, and the famine you dread will follow you into Egypt, and there you will die. ¹⁷Indeed, all who are determined to go to Egypt to set-

ᵃ18 Or Chaldeans   ᵇ1 Hebrew; Septuagint (see also 43:2) Azariah

tle there will die by the sword, famine and plague; not one of them will survive or escape the disaster I will bring on them.' [18]This is what the LORD Almighty, the God of Israel, says: 'As my anger and wrath have been poured out on those who lived in Jerusalem, so will my wrath be poured out on you when you go to Egypt. You will be an object of cursing and horror, of condemnation and reproach; you will never see this place again.'

[19]"O remnant of Judah, the LORD has told you, 'Do not go to Egypt.' Be sure of this: I warn you today [20]that you made a fatal mistake[a] when you sent me to the LORD your God and said, 'Pray to the LORD our God for us; tell us everything he says and we will do it.' [21]I have told you today, but you still have not obeyed the LORD your God in all he sent me to tell you. [22]So now, be sure of this: You will die by the sword, famine and plague in the place where you want to go to settle."

43 When Jeremiah finished telling the people all the words of the LORD their God—everything the LORD had sent him to tell them— [2]Azariah son of Hoshaiah and Johanan son of Kareah and all the arrogant men said to Jeremiah, "You are lying! The LORD our God has not sent you to say, 'You must not go to Egypt to settle there.' [3]But Baruch son of Neriah is inciting you against us to hand us over to the Babylonians,[b] so they may kill us or carry us into exile to Babylon."

[4]So Johanan son of Kareah and all the army officers and all the people disobeyed the LORD's command to stay in the land of Judah. [5]Instead, Johanan son of Kareah and all the army officers led away all the remnant of Judah who had come back to live in the land of Judah from all the nations where they had been scattered. [6]They also led away all the men, women and children and the king's daughters whom Nebuzaradan commander of the imperial guard had left with Ged-

aliah son of Ahikam, the son of Shaphan, and Jeremiah the prophet and Baruch son of Neriah. [7]So they entered Egypt in disobedience to the LORD and went as far as Tahpanhes.

[8]In Tahpanhes the word of the LORD came to Jeremiah: [9]"While the Jews are watching, take some large stones with you and bury them in clay in the brick pavement at the entrance to Pharaoh's palace in Tahpanhes. [10]Then say to them, 'This is what the LORD Almighty, the God of Israel, says: I will send for my servant Nebuchadnezzar king of Babylon, and I will set his throne over these stones I have buried here; he will spread his royal canopy above them. [11]He will come and attack Egypt, bringing death to those destined for death, captivity to those destined for captivity, and the sword to those destined for the sword. [12]He[c] will set fire to the temples of the gods of Egypt; he will burn their temples and take their gods captive. As a shepherd wraps his garment around him, so will he wrap Egypt around himself and depart from there unscathed. [13]There in the temple of the sun[d] in Egypt he will demolish the sacred pillars and will burn down the temples of the gods of Egypt.' "

Disaster Because of Idolatry

44 This word came to Jeremiah concerning all the Jews living in Lower Egypt—in Migdol, Tahpanhes and Memphis[e]—and in Upper Egypt[f]: [2]"This is what the LORD Almighty, the God of Israel, says: You saw the great disaster I brought on Jerusalem and on all the towns of Judah. Today they lie deserted and in ruins [3]because of the evil they have done. They provoked me to anger by burning incense and by worshiping other gods that neither they nor you nor your fathers ever knew. [4]Again and again I sent my servants the prophets, who said, 'Do not do this detestable thing that I hate!' [5]But they

---

[a]20 Or *you erred in your hearts*   [b]3 Or *Chaldeans*   [c]12 Or *I*   [d]13 Or *in Heliopolis*
[e]1 Hebrew *Noph*   [f]1 Hebrew *in Pathros*

did not listen or pay attention; they did not turn from their wickedness or stop burning incense to other gods. ⁶Therefore, my fierce anger was poured out; it raged against the towns of Judah and the streets of Jerusalem and made them the desolate ruins they are today.

⁷"Now this is what the LORD God Almighty, the God of Israel, says: Why bring such great disaster on yourselves by cutting off from Judah the men and women, the children and infants, and so leave yourselves without a remnant? ⁸Why provoke me to anger with what your hands have made, burning incense to other gods in Egypt, where you have come to live? You will destroy yourselves and make yourselves an object of cursing and reproach among all the nations on earth. ⁹Have you forgotten the wickedness committed by your fathers and by the kings and queens of Judah and the wickedness committed by you and your wives in the land of Judah and the streets of Jerusalem? ¹⁰To this day they have not humbled themselves or shown reverence, nor have they followed my law and the decrees I set before you and your fathers.

¹¹"Therefore, this is what the LORD Almighty, the God of Israel, says: I am determined to bring disaster on you and to destroy all Judah. ¹²I will take away the remnant of Judah who were determined to go to Egypt to settle there. They will all perish in Egypt; they will fall by the sword or die from famine. From the least to the greatest, they will die by sword or famine. They will become an object of cursing and horror, of condemnation and reproach. ¹³I will punish those who live in Egypt with the sword, famine and plague, as I punished Jerusalem. ¹⁴None of the remnant of Judah who have gone to live in Egypt will escape or survive to return to the land of Judah, to which they long to return and live; none will return except a few fugitives."

¹⁵Then all the men who knew that their wives were burning incense to other gods, along with all the women who were present—a large assembly—and all the people living in Lower and Upper Egypt,^a said to Jeremiah, ¹⁶"We will not listen to the message you have spoken to us in the name of the LORD! ¹⁷We will certainly do everything we said we would: We will burn incense to the Queen of Heaven and will pour out drink offerings to her just as we and our fathers, our kings and our officials did in the towns of Judah and in the streets of Jerusalem. At that time we had plenty of food and were well off and suffered no harm. ¹⁸But ever since we stopped burning incense to the Queen of Heaven and pouring out drink offerings to her, we have had nothing and have been perishing by sword and famine."

¹⁹The women added, "When we burned incense to the Queen of Heaven and poured out drink offerings to her, did not our husbands know that we were making cakes like her image and pouring out drink offerings to her?"

²⁰Then Jeremiah said to all the people, both men and women, who were answering him, ²¹"Did not the LORD remember and think about the incense burned in the towns of Judah and the streets of Jerusalem by you and your fathers, your kings and your officials and the people of the land? ²²When the LORD could no longer endure your wicked actions and the detestable things you did, your land became an object of cursing and a desolate waste without inhabitants, as it is today. ²³Because you have burned incense and have sinned against the LORD and have not obeyed him or followed his law or his decrees or his stipulations, this disaster has come upon you, as you now see."

²⁴Then Jeremiah said to all the people, including the women, "Hear the word of the LORD, all you people of Judah in Egypt. ²⁵This is what the

^a15 Hebrew *in Egypt and Pathros*

LORD Almighty, the God of Israel, says: You and your wives have shown by your actions what you promised when you said, 'We will certainly carry out the vows we made to burn incense and pour out drink offerings to the Queen of Heaven.'

"Go ahead then, do what you promised! Keep your vows! ²⁶But hear the word of the LORD, all Jews living in Egypt: 'I swear by my great name,' says the LORD, 'that no one from Judah living anywhere in Egypt will ever again invoke my name or swear, "As surely as the Sovereign LORD lives." ²⁷For I am watching over them for harm, not for good; the Jews in Egypt will perish by sword and famine until they are all destroyed. ²⁸Those who escape the sword and return to the land of Judah from Egypt will be very few. Then the whole remnant of Judah who came to live in Egypt will know whose word will stand—mine or theirs.

²⁹" 'This will be the sign to you that I will punish you in this place,' declares the LORD, 'so that you will know that my threats of harm against you will surely stand.' ³⁰This is what the LORD says: 'I am going to hand Pharaoh Hophra king of Egypt over to his enemies who seek his life, just as I handed Zedekiah king of Judah over to Nebuchadnezzar king of Babylon, the enemy who was seeking his life.' "

A Message to Baruch

45 This is what Jeremiah the prophet told Baruch son of Neriah in the fourth year of Jehoiakim son of Josiah king of Judah, after Baruch had written on a scroll the words Jeremiah was then dictating: ²"This is what the LORD, the God of Israel, says to you, Baruch: ³You said, 'Woe to me! The LORD has added sorrow to my pain; I am worn out with groaning and find no rest.' "

⁴The LORD said, "Say this to him: 'This is what the LORD says: I will overthrow what I have built and uproot what I have planted, throughout the land. ⁵Should you then seek great things for yourself? Seek them not.

For I will bring disaster on all people, declares the LORD, but wherever you go I will let you escape with your life.' "

A Message About Egypt

46 This is the word of the LORD that came to Jeremiah the prophet concerning the nations:

²Concerning Egypt:

This is the message against the army of Pharaoh Neco king of Egypt, which was defeated at Carchemish on the Euphrates River by Nebuchadnezzar king of Babylon in the fourth year of Jehoiakim son of Josiah king of Judah:

³"Prepare your shields, both large
    and small,
    and march out for battle!
⁴Harness the horses,
    mount the steeds!
Take your positions
    with helmets on!
Polish your spears,
    put on your armor!
⁵What do I see?
    They are terrified,
they are retreating,
    their warriors are defeated.
They flee in haste
    without looking back,
    and there is terror on every
        side,"
                    declares the LORD.
⁶"The swift cannot flee
    nor the strong escape.
In the north by the River
        Euphrates
    they stumble and fall.

⁷"Who is this that rises like the
        Nile,
    like rivers of surging waters?
⁸Egypt rises like the Nile,
    like rivers of surging waters.
She says, 'I will rise and cover the
        earth;
    I will destroy cities and their
        people.'
⁹Charge, O horses!
    Drive furiously, O charioteers!
March on, O warriors—

men of Cush[a] and Put who
    carry shields,
men of Lydia who draw the
    bow.
10But that day belongs to the Lord,
    the LORD Almighty—
a day of vengeance, for
    vengeance on his foes.
The sword will devour till it is
    satisfied,
    till it has quenched its thirst
      with blood.
For the Lord, the LORD Almighty,
    will offer sacrifice
in the land of the north by the
    River Euphrates.

11"Go up to Gilead and get balm,
    O Virgin Daughter of Egypt.
But you multiply remedies in
    vain;
    there is no healing for you.
12The nations will hear of your
    shame;
    your cries will fill the earth.
One warrior will stumble over
    another;
    both will fall down together."

13This is the message the LORD
spoke to Jeremiah the prophet about
the coming of Nebuchadnezzar king
of Babylon to attack Egypt:

14"Announce this in Egypt, and
    proclaim it in Migdol;
proclaim it also in Memphis[b]
    and Tahpanhes:
'Take your positions and get
    ready,
    for the sword devours those
      around you.'
15Why will your warriors be laid
    low?
    They cannot stand, for the LORD
      will push them down.
16They will stumble repeatedly;
    they will fall over each other.
They will say, 'Get up, let us go
    back
    to our own people and our
      native lands,
    away from the sword of the
      oppressor.'

17There they will exclaim,
    'Pharaoh king of Egypt is only a
      loud noise;
    he has missed his opportunity.'

18"As surely as I live," declares the
    King,
    whose name is the LORD
      Almighty,
"one will come who is like Tabor
    among the mountains,
    like Carmel by the sea.
19Pack your belongings for exile,
    you who live in Egypt,
for Memphis will be laid waste
    and lie in ruins without
      inhabitant.

20"Egypt is a beautiful heifer,
    but a gadfly is coming
    against her from the north.
21The mercenaries in her ranks
    are like fattened calves.
They too will turn and flee
    together,
    they will not stand their
      ground,
for the day of disaster is coming
    upon them,
    the time for them to be
      punished.
22Egypt will hiss like a fleeing
    serpent
    as the enemy advances in force;
they will come against her with
    axes,
    like men who cut down trees.
23They will chop down her forest,"
               declares the LORD,
    "dense though it be.
They are more numerous than
    locusts,
    they cannot be counted.
24The Daughter of Egypt will be put
    to shame,
    handed over to the people of
      the north."

25The LORD Almighty, the God of Israel, says: "I am about to bring punishment on Amon god of Thebes,[c]
on Pharaoh, on Egypt and her gods
and her kings, and on those who rely
on Pharaoh. 26I will hand them over to

those who seek their lives, to Nebuchadnezzar king of Babylon and his officers. Later, however, Egypt will be inhabited as in times past," declares the LORD.

²⁷"Do not fear, O Jacob my servant;
    do not be dismayed, O Israel.
I will surely save you out of a
        distant place,
    your descendants from the land
        of their exile.
Jacob will again have peace and
        security,
    and no one will make him
        afraid.
²⁸Do not fear, O Jacob my servant,
    for I am with you," declares the
        LORD.
"Though I completely destroy all
        the nations
    among which I scatter you,
    I will not completely destroy
        you.
I will discipline you but only with
        justice;
    I will not let you go entirely
        unpunished."

A Message About the Philistines

47 This is the word of the LORD that came to Jeremiah the prophet concerning the Philistines before Pharaoh attacked Gaza:

²This is what the LORD says:

"See how the waters are rising in
        the north;
    they will become an
        overflowing torrent.
They will overflow the land and
        everything in it,
    the towns and those who live in
        them.
The people will cry out;
    all who dwell in the land will
        wail
³at the sound of the hoofs of
        galloping steeds,
    at the noise of enemy chariots
    and the rumble of their wheels.

Fathers will not turn to help their
        children;
    their hands will hang limp.
⁴For the day has come
    to destroy all the Philistines
and to cut off all survivors
    who could help Tyre and Sidon.
The LORD is about to destroy the
        Philistines,
    the remnant from the coasts of
        Caphtor.ᵃ
⁵Gaza will shave her head in
        mourning;
    Ashkelon will be silenced.
O remnant on the plain,
    how long will you cut
        yourselves?

⁶" 'Ah, sword of the LORD,' ⌐you
        cry,⌐
    'how long till you rest?
Return to your scabbard;
    cease and be still.'
⁷But how can it rest
    when the LORD has commanded
        it,
when he has ordered it
    to attack Ashkelon and the
        coast?"

A Message About Moab

48 Concerning Moab:

This is what the LORD Almighty, the God of Israel, says:

"Woe to Nebo, for it will be
        ruined.
    Kiriathaim will be disgraced
        and captured;
    the strongholdᵇ will be
        disgraced and shattered.
²Moab will be praised no more;
    in Heshbonᶜ men will plot her
        downfall:
    'Come, let us put an end to that
        nation.'
You too, O Madmen,ᵈ will be
        silenced;
    the sword will pursue you.
³Listen to the cries from Horonaim,
    cries of great havoc and
        destruction.

ᵃ4 That is, Crete   ᵇ1 Or / Misgab   ᶜ2 The Hebrew for Heshbon sounds like the Hebrew for plot.   ᵈ2 The name of the Moabite town Madmen sounds like the Hebrew for be silenced.

⁴Moab will be broken;
  her little ones will cry out.*ᵃ*
⁵They go up the way to Luhith,
  weeping bitterly as they go;
on the road down to Horonaim
  anguished cries over the
    destruction are heard.
⁶Flee! Run for your lives;
  become like a bush*ᵇ* in the
    desert.
⁷Since you trust in your deeds and
    riches,
  you too will be taken captive,
and Chemosh will go into exile,
  together with his priests and
    officials.
⁸The destroyer will come against
    every town,
  and not a town will escape.
The valley will be ruined
  and the plateau destroyed,
  because the LORD has spoken.
⁹Put salt on Moab,
  for she will be laid waste*ᶜ*;
her towns will become desolate,
  with no one to live in them.

¹⁰"A curse on him who is lax in
    doing the LORD's work!
  A curse on him who keeps his
    sword from bloodshed!

¹¹"Moab has been at rest from
    youth,
  like wine left on its dregs,
not poured from one jar to
    another—
  she has not gone into exile.
So she tastes as she did,
  and her aroma is unchanged.
¹²But days are coming,"
  declares the LORD,
"when I will send men who pour
    from jars,
  and they will pour her out;
they will empty her jars
  and smash her jugs.
¹³Then Moab will be ashamed of
    Chemosh,
  as the house of Israel was
    ashamed
  when they trusted in Bethel.

¹⁴"How can you say, 'We are
    warriors,
  men valiant in battle'?
¹⁵Moab will be destroyed and her
    towns invaded;
  her finest young men will go
    down in the slaughter,"
  declares the King, whose name
    is the LORD Almighty.
¹⁶"The fall of Moab is at hand;
  her calamity will come quickly.
¹⁷Mourn for her, all who live
    around her,
  all who know her fame;
say, 'How broken is the mighty
    scepter,
  how broken the glorious staff!'

¹⁸"Come down from your glory
  and sit on the parched ground,
  O inhabitants of the Daughter
    of Dibon,
for he who destroys Moab
  will come up against you
  and ruin your fortified cities.
¹⁹Stand by the road and watch,
  you who live in Aroer.
Ask the man fleeing and the
    woman escaping,
  ask them, 'What has happened?'
²⁰Moab is disgraced, for she is
    shattered.
  Wail and cry out!
Announce by the Arnon
  that Moab is destroyed.
²¹Judgment has come to the
    plateau—
  to Holon, Jahzah and Mephaath,
²² to Dibon, Nebo and Beth
    Diblathaim,
²³ to Kiriathaim, Beth Gamul and
    Beth Meon,
²⁴ to Kerioth and Bozrah—
  to all the towns of Moab, far
    and near.
²⁵Moab's horn*ᵈ* is cut off;
  her arm is broken,"
            declares the LORD.

²⁶"Make her drunk,
  for she has defied the LORD.
Let Moab wallow in her vomit;
  let her be an object of ridicule.

ᵃ4 Hebrew; Septuagint / *proclaim it to Zoar*   *ᵇ6* Or *like Aroer*   *ᶜ9* Or *Give wings to Moab, / for she will fly away*   *ᵈ25* Horn here symbolizes strength.

27Was not Israel the object of your
        ridicule?
    Was she caught among thieves,
    that you shake your head in scorn
        whenever you speak of her?
28Abandon your towns and dwell
        among the rocks,
    you who live in Moab.
    Be like a dove that makes its nest
        at the mouth of a cave.

29"We have heard of Moab's
        pride—
    her overweening pride and
        conceit,
    her pride and arrogance
        and the haughtiness of her
            heart.
30I know her insolence but it is
        futile,"
                        declares the LORD,
    "and her boasts accomplish
        nothing.
31Therefore I wail over Moab,
    for all Moab I cry out,
    I moan for the men of Kir
        Hareseth.
32I weep for you, as Jazer weeps,
    O vines of Sibmah.
    Your branches spread as far as the
        sea;
        they reached as far as the sea of
            Jazer.
    The destroyer has fallen
        on your ripened fruit and
            grapes.
33Joy and gladness are gone
    from the orchards and fields of
        Moab.
    I have stopped the flow of wine
        from the presses;
        no one treads them with shouts
            of joy.
    Although there are shouts,
        they are not shouts of joy.

34"The sound of their cry rises
    from Heshbon to Elealeh and
        Jahaz,
    from Zoar as far as Horonaim and
        Eglath Shelishiyah,
    for even the waters of Nimrim
        are dried up.
35In Moab I will put an end

to those who make offerings on
        the high places
    and burn incense to their gods,"
                        declares the LORD.
36"So my heart laments for Moab
        like a flute;
    it laments like a flute for the
        men of Kir Hareseth.
    The wealth they acquired is
        gone.
37Every head is shaved
    and every beard cut off;
    every hand is slashed
        and every waist is covered with
            sackcloth.
38On all the roofs in Moab
    and in the public squares
    there is nothing but mourning,
        for I have broken Moab
        like a jar that no one wants,"
                        declares the LORD.
39"How shattered she is! How they
        wail!
    How Moab turns her back in
        shame!
    Moab has become an object of
        ridicule,
        an object of horror to all those
            around her."

40This is what the LORD says:

"Look! An eagle is swooping
        down,
    spreading its wings over Moab.
41Kerioth*a* will be captured
    and the strongholds taken.
    In that day the hearts of Moab's
        warriors
        will be like the heart of a
            woman in labor.
42Moab will be destroyed as a
        nation
    because she defied the LORD.
43Terror and pit and snare await
        you,
    O people of Moab,"
                        declares the LORD.
44"Whoever flees from the terror
    will fall into a pit,
    whoever climbs out of the pit
        will be caught in a snare;
    for I will bring upon Moab

a41 Or The cities

the year of her punishment,"
                            declares the Lord.

⁴⁵"In the shadow of Heshbon
      the fugitives stand helpless,
   for a fire has gone out from
         Heshbon,
      a blaze from the midst of Sihon;
   it burns the foreheads of Moab,
      the skulls of the noisy boasters.
⁴⁶Woe to you, O Moab!
      The people of Chemosh are
         destroyed;
   your sons are taken into exile
      and your daughters into
         captivity.

⁴⁷"Yet I will restore the fortunes of
         Moab
   in days to come,"
                     declares the Lord.

Here ends the judgment on Moab.

A Message About Ammon

49 Concerning the Ammonites:

   This is what the Lord says:

   "Has Israel no sons?
      Has she no heirs?
   Why then has Molech*ᵃ* taken
         possession of Gad?
      Why do his people live in its
         towns?
²But the days are coming,"
      declares the Lord,
   "when I will sound the battle cry
      against Rabbah of the
         Ammonites;
   it will become a mound of ruins,
      and its surrounding villages will
         be set on fire.
   Then Israel will drive out
      those who drove her out,"
                        says the Lord.
³"Wail, O Heshbon, for Ai is
         destroyed!
      Cry out, O inhabitants of
         Rabbah!
   Put on sackcloth and mourn;
      rush here and there inside the
         walls,
   for Molech will go into exile,

together with his priests and
      officials.
⁴Why do you boast of your valleys,
      boast of your valleys so fruitful?
   O unfaithful daughter,
      you trust in your riches and
         say,
      'Who will attack me?'
⁵I will bring terror on you
      from all those around you,"
                        declares the Lord,
                           the Lord Almighty.
   "Every one of you will be driven
         away,
      and no one will gather the
         fugitives.

⁶"Yet afterward, I will restore the
         fortunes of the
         Ammonites,"
                        declares the Lord.

A Message About Edom

⁷Concerning Edom:

   This is what the Lord Almighty
says:

   "Is there no longer wisdom in
         Teman?
      Has counsel perished from the
         prudent?
      Has their wisdom decayed?
⁸Turn and flee, hide in deep caves,
      you who live in Dedan,
   for I will bring disaster on Esau
      at the time I punish him.
⁹If grape pickers came to you,
      would they not leave a few
         grapes?
   If thieves came during the night,
      would they not steal only as
         much as they wanted?
¹⁰But I will strip Esau bare;
      I will uncover his hiding places,
   so that he cannot conceal
         himself.
   His children, relatives and
         neighbors will perish,
      and he will be no more.
¹¹Leave your orphans; I will protect
         their lives.
      Your widows too can trust in
         me."

ᵃ1 Or *their king*; Hebrew *malcam*; also in verse 3

¹²This is what the LORD says: "If those who do not deserve to drink the cup must drink it, why should you go unpunished? You will not go unpunished, but must drink it. ¹³I swear by myself," declares the LORD, "that Bozrah will become a ruin and an object of horror, of reproach and of cursing; and all its towns will be in ruins forever."

¹⁴I have heard a message from the
LORD:
An envoy was sent to the
nations to say,
"Assemble yourselves to attack it!
Rise up for battle!"

¹⁵"Now I will make you small
among the nations,
despised among men.
¹⁶The terror you inspire
and the pride of your heart
have deceived you,
you who live in the clefts of the
rocks,
who occupy the heights of the
hill.
Though you build your nest as
high as the eagle's,
from there I will bring you
down,"
declares the LORD.
¹⁷"Edom will become an object of
horror;
all who pass by will be appalled
and will scoff
because of all its wounds.
¹⁸As Sodom and Gomorrah were
overthrown,
along with their neighboring
towns,"
says the LORD,
"so no one will live there;
no man will dwell in it.

¹⁹"Like a lion coming up from
Jordan's thickets
to a rich pastureland,
I will chase Edom from its land in
an instant.
Who is the chosen one I will
appoint for this?
Who is like me and who can
challenge me?
And what shepherd can stand
against me?"
²⁰Therefore, hear what the LORD has
planned against Edom,
what he has purposed against
those who live in Teman:
The young of the flock will be
dragged away;
he will completely destroy their
pasture because of them.
²¹At the sound of their fall the earth
will tremble;
their cry will resound to the
Red Sea.ᵃ
²²Look! An eagle will soar and
swoop down,
spreading its wings over
Bozrah.
In that day the hearts of Edom's
warriors
will be like the heart of a
woman in labor.

A Message About Damascus

²³Concerning Damascus:

"Hamath and Arpad are
dismayed,
for they have heard bad news.
They are disheartened,
troubled likeᵇ the restless sea.
²⁴Damascus has become feeble,
she has turned to flee
and panic has gripped her;
anguish and pain have seized her,
pain like that of a woman in
labor.
²⁵Why has the city of renown not
been abandoned,
the town in which I delight?
²⁶Surely, her young men will fall in
the streets;
all her soldiers will be silenced
in that day,"
declares the LORD
Almighty.
²⁷"I will set fire to the walls of
Damascus;
it will consume the fortresses of
Ben-Hadad."

ᵃ21 Hebrew *Yam Suph*; that is, Sea of Reeds   ᵇ23 Hebrew *on* or *by*

A Message About Kedar and Hazor

²⁸Concerning Kedar and the kingdoms of Hazor, which Nebuchadnezzar king of Babylon attacked:

This is what the LORD says:

"Arise, and attack Kedar
    and destroy the people of the
        East.
²⁹Their tents and their flocks will be
        taken;
    their shelters will be carried off
        with all their goods and camels.
Men will shout to them,
    'Terror on every side!'

³⁰"Flee quickly away!
    Stay in deep caves, you who
        live in Hazor,"
            declares the LORD.
"Nebuchadnezzar king of Babylon
        has plotted against you;
    he has devised a plan against
        you.

³¹"Arise and attack a nation at ease,
    which lives in confidence,"
            declares the LORD,
"a nation that has neither gates
        nor bars;
    its people live alone.
³²Their camels will become plunder,
    and their large herds will be
        booty.
I will scatter to the winds those
        who are in distant places^a
    and will bring disaster on them
        from every side,"
            declares the LORD.
³³"Hazor will become a haunt of
        jackals,
    a desolate place forever.
No one will live there;
    no man will dwell in it."

A Message About Elam

³⁴This is the word of the LORD that came to Jeremiah the prophet concerning Elam, early in the reign of Zedekiah king of Judah:

³⁵This is what the LORD Almighty says:

"See, I will break the bow of
        Elam,
    the mainstay of their might.
³⁶I will bring against Elam the four
        winds
    from the four quarters of the
        heavens;
I will scatter them to the four
        winds,
    and there will not be a nation
    where Elam's exiles do not go.
³⁷I will shatter Elam before their
        foes,
    before those who seek their
        lives;
I will bring disaster upon them,
    even my fierce anger,"
            declares the LORD.
"I will pursue them with the
        sword
    until I have made an end of
        them.
³⁸I will set my throne in Elam
    and destroy her king and
        officials,"
            declares the LORD.

³⁹"Yet I will restore the fortunes of
        Elam
    in days to come,"
            declares the LORD.

A Message About Babylon

50 This is the word the LORD spoke through Jeremiah the prophet concerning Babylon and the land of the Babylonians^b:

²"Announce and proclaim among
        the nations,
    lift up a banner and proclaim it;
    keep nothing back, but say,
'Babylon will be captured;
    Bel will be put to shame,
    Marduk filled with terror.
Her images will be put to shame
    and her idols filled with terror.'
³A nation from the north will
        attack her
    and lay waste her land.
No one will live in it;
    both men and animals will flee
        away.

---

^{a}32 Or *who clip the hair by their foreheads* ^{b}1 Or *Chaldeans*; also in verses 8, 25, 35 and 45

⁴"In those days, at that time,"
   declares the LORD,
"the people of Israel and the
         people of Judah together
   will go in tears to seek the LORD
      their God.
⁵They will ask the way to Zion
   and turn their faces toward it.
They will come and bind
         themselves to the LORD
   in an everlasting covenant
   that will not be forgotten.

⁶"My people have been lost sheep;
   their shepherds have led them
      astray
   and caused them to roam on the
      mountains.
They wandered over mountain
      and hill
   and forgot their own resting
      place.
⁷Whoever found them devoured
      them;
   their enemies said, 'We are not
      guilty,
for they sinned against the LORD,
      their true pasture,
   the LORD, the hope of their
      fathers.'

⁸"Flee out of Babylon;
   leave the land of the
         Babylonians,
   and be like the goats that lead
      the flock.
⁹For I will stir up and bring against
      Babylon
   an alliance of great nations from
      the land of the north.
They will take up their positions
      against her,
   and from the north she will be
      captured.
Their arrows will be like skilled
      warriors
   who do not return
      empty-handed.
¹⁰So Babyloniaᵃ will be plundered;
   all who plunder her will have
      their fill,"
                  declares the LORD.

¹¹"Because you rejoice and are glad,

you who pillage my inheritance,
because you frolic like a heifer
         threshing grain
   and neigh like stallions,
¹²your mother will be greatly
         ashamed;
   she who gave you birth will be
      disgraced.
She will be the least of the
         nations—
   a wilderness, a dry land, a
      desert.
¹³Because of the LORD's anger she
      will not be inhabited
   but will be completely desolate.
All who pass Babylon will be
      horrified and scoff
   because of all her wounds.

¹⁴"Take up your positions around
         Babylon,
   all you who draw the bow.
Shoot at her! Spare no arrows,
   for she has sinned against the
      LORD.
¹⁵Shout against her on every side!
   She surrenders, her towers fall,
   her walls are torn down.
Since this is the vengeance of the
      LORD,
   take vengeance on her;
   do to her as she has done to
      others.
¹⁶Cut off from Babylon the sower,
   and the reaper with his sickle at
      harvest.
Because of the sword of the
         oppressor
   let everyone return to his own
      people,
   let everyone flee to his own
      land.

¹⁷"Israel is a scattered flock
   that lions have chased away.
The first to devour him
   was the king of Assyria;
the last to crush his bones
   was Nebuchadnezzar king of
      Babylon."

¹⁸Therefore this is what the LORD
Almighty, the God of Israel, says:

ᵃ10 Or *Chaldea*

"I will punish the king of Babylon
  and his land
as I punished the king of
  Assyria.
19But I will bring Israel back to his
  own pasture
and he will graze on Carmel
  and Bashan;
his appetite will be satisfied
  on the hills of Ephraim and
  Gilead.
20In those days, at that time,"
  declares the LORD,
"search will be made for Israel's
  guilt,
  but there will be none,
and for the sins of Judah,
  but none will be found,
for I will forgive the remnant I
  spare.

21"Attack the land of Merathaim
  and those who live in Pekod.
Pursue, kill and completely
  destroy[a] them,"
             declares the LORD.
"Do everything I have
  commanded you.
22The noise of battle is in the land,
  the noise of great destruction!
23How broken and shattered
  is the hammer of the whole
  earth!
How desolate is Babylon
  among the nations!
24I set a trap for you, O Babylon,
  and you were caught before you
  knew it;
you were found and captured
  because you opposed the LORD.
25The LORD has opened his arsenal
  and brought out the weapons of
  his wrath,
for the Sovereign LORD Almighty
  has work to do
  in the land of the Babylonians.
26Come against her from afar.
  Break open her granaries;
  pile her up like heaps of grain.
Completely destroy her
  and leave her no remnant.
27Kill all her young bulls;

let them go down to the
  slaughter!
Woe to them! For their day has
  come,
  the time for them to be
  punished.
28Listen to the fugitives and
  refugees from Babylon
  declaring in Zion
how the LORD our God has taken
  vengeance,
  vengeance for his temple.

29"Summon archers against Babylon,
  all those who draw the bow.
Encamp all around her;
  let no one escape.
Repay her for her deeds;
  do to her as she has done.
For she has defied the LORD,
  the Holy One of Israel.
30Therefore, her young men will fall
  in the streets;
  all her soldiers will be silenced
  in that day,"
             declares the LORD.
31"See, I am against you, O arrogant
  one,"
  declares the Lord, the LORD
  Almighty,
"for your day has come,
  the time for you to be punished.
32The arrogant one will stumble and
  fall
  and no one will help her up;
I will kindle a fire in her towns
  that will consume all who are
  around her."

33This is what the LORD Almighty
says:

"The people of Israel are
  oppressed,
  and the people of Judah as well.
All their captors hold them fast,
  refusing to let them go.
34Yet their Redeemer is strong;
  the LORD Almighty is his name.
He will vigorously defend their
  cause
  so that he may bring rest to
  their land,

---

[a]21 The Hebrew term refers to the irrevocable giving over of things or persons to the LORD, often
by totally destroying them; also in verse 26.

but unrest to those who live in
Babylon.

35"A sword against the
Babylonians!"
declares the LORD—
"against those who live in Babylon
and against her officials and
wise men!
36A sword against her false
prophets!
They will become fools.
A sword against her warriors!
They will be filled with terror.
37A sword against her horses and
chariots
and all the foreigners in her
ranks!
They will become women.
A sword against her treasures!
They will be plundered.
38A drought on*a* her waters!
They will dry up.
For it is a land of idols,
idols that will go mad with
terror.

39"So desert creatures and hyenas
will live there,
and there the owl will dwell.
It will never again be inhabited
or lived in from generation to
generation.
40As God overthrew Sodom and
Gomorrah
along with their neighboring
towns,"
declares the LORD,
"so no one will live there;
no man will dwell in it.

41"Look! An army is coming from
the north;
a great nation and many kings
are being stirred up from the
ends of the earth.
42They are armed with bows and
spears;
they are cruel and without
mercy.
They sound like the roaring sea
as they ride on their horses;

they come like men in battle
formation
to attack you, O Daughter of
Babylon.
43The king of Babylon has heard
reports about them,
and his hands hang limp.
Anguish has gripped him,
pain like that of a woman in
labor.
44Like a lion coming up from
Jordan's thickets
to a rich pastureland,
I will chase Babylon from its land
in an instant.
Who is the chosen one I will
appoint for this?
Who is like me and who can
challenge me?
And what shepherd can stand
against me?"
45Therefore, hear what the LORD has
planned against Babylon,
what he has purposed against
the land of the
Babylonians:
The young of the flock will be
dragged away;
he will completely destroy their
pasture because of them.
46At the sound of Babylon's capture
the earth will tremble;
its cry will resound among the
nations.

51 This is what the LORD says:
"See, I will stir up the spirit of a
destroyer
against Babylon and the people
of Leb Kamai.*b*
2I will send foreigners to Babylon
to winnow her and to devastate
her land;
they will oppose her on every side
in the day of her disaster.
3Let not the archer string his bow,
nor let him put on his armor.
Do not spare her young men;
completely destroy*c* her army.

---

*a*38 Or *A sword against*   *b*1 *Leb Kamai* is a cryptogram for Chaldea, that is, Babylonia.
*c*3 The Hebrew term refers to the irrevocable giving over of things or persons to the LORD, often
by totally destroying them.

⁴They will fall down slain in
  Babylon,ᵃ
 fatally wounded in her streets.
⁵For Israel and Judah have not
  been forsaken
 by their God, the LORD
  Almighty,
though their landᵇ is full of guilt
 before the Holy One of Israel.

⁶"Flee from Babylon!
  Run for your lives!
  Do not be destroyed because of
   her sins.
 It is time for the LORD's vengeance;
  he will pay her what she
   deserves.
⁷Babylon was a gold cup in the
  LORD's hand;
 she made the whole earth
  drunk.
 The nations drank her wine;
  therefore they have now gone
   mad.
⁸Babylon will suddenly fall and be
  broken.
  Wail over her!
 Get balm for her pain;
  perhaps she can be healed.

⁹" 'We would have healed Babylon,
  but she cannot be healed;
 let us leave her and each go to his
  own land,
  for her judgment reaches to the
   skies,
  it rises as high as the clouds.'

¹⁰" 'The LORD has vindicated us;
  come, let us tell in Zion
 what the LORD our God has
  done.'

¹¹"Sharpen the arrows,
  take up the shields!
 The LORD has stirred up the kings
  of the Medes,
 because his purpose is to
  destroy Babylon.
 The LORD will take vengeance,
  vengeance for his temple.
¹²Lift up a banner against the walls
  of Babylon!
  Reinforce the guard,
 station the watchmen,

  prepare an ambush!
 The LORD will carry out his
  purpose,
  his decree against the people of
   Babylon.
¹³You who live by many waters
  and are rich in treasures,
 your end has come,
  the time for you to be cut off.
¹⁴The LORD Almighty has sworn by
  himself:
 I will surely fill you with men,
  as with a swarm of locusts,
 and they will shout in triumph
  over you.

¹⁵"He made the earth by his power;
  he founded the world by his
   wisdom
 and stretched out the heavens
  by his understanding.
¹⁶When he thunders, the waters in
  the heavens roar;
 he makes clouds rise from the
  ends of the earth.
 He sends lightning with the rain
  and brings out the wind from
   his storehouses.

¹⁷"Every man is senseless and
  without knowledge;
 every goldsmith is shamed by
  his idols.
 His images are a fraud;
  they have no breath in them.
¹⁸They are worthless, the objects of
  mockery;
 when their judgment comes,
  they will perish.
¹⁹He who is the Portion of Jacob is
  not like these,
 for he is the Maker of all things,
 including the tribe of his
  inheritance—
 the LORD Almighty is his name.

²⁰"You are my war club,
  my weapon for battle—
 with you I shatter nations,
  with you I destroy kingdoms,
²¹with you I shatter horse and rider,
  with you I shatter chariot and
   driver,

ᵃ4 Or Chaldea   ᵇ5 Or / and the land ⌐of the Babylonians⌐

²²with you I shatter man and
    woman,
  with you I shatter old man and
    youth,
  with you I shatter young man
    and maiden,
²³with you I shatter shepherd and
    flock,
  with you I shatter farmer and
    oxen,
  with you I shatter governors
    and officials.

²⁴"Before your eyes I will repay
Babylon and all who live in Babyloniaᵃ for all the wrong they have
done in Zion," declares the LORD.

²⁵"I am against you, O destroying
    mountain,
  you who destroy the whole
    earth,"
                declares the LORD.
"I will stretch out my hand
    against you,
  roll you off the cliffs,
  and make you a burned-out
    mountain.
²⁶No rock will be taken from you
    for a cornerstone,
  nor any stone for a foundation,
  for you will be desolate
    forever,"
                declares the LORD.

²⁷"Lift up a banner in the land!
  Blow the trumpet among the
    nations!
Prepare the nations for battle
    against her;
  summon against her these
    kingdoms:
    Ararat, Minni and Ashkenaz.
Appoint a commander against her;
  send up horses like a swarm of
    locusts.
²⁸Prepare the nations for battle
    against her—
  the kings of the Medes,
  their governors and all their
    officials,
  and all the countries they rule.
²⁹The land trembles and writhes,

for the LORD's purposes against
    Babylon stand—
to lay waste the land of Babylon
  so that no one will live there.
³⁰Babylon's warriors have stopped
    fighting;
  they remain in their
    strongholds.
Their strength is exhausted;
  they have become like women.
Her dwellings are set on fire;
  the bars of her gates are broken.
³¹One courier follows another
  and messenger follows
    messenger
to announce to the king of
    Babylon
  that his entire city is captured,
³²the river crossings seized,
  the marshes set on fire,
  and the soldiers terrified."

³³This is what the LORD Almighty,
the God of Israel, says:

"The Daughter of Babylon is like a
    threshing floor
  at the time it is trampled;
  the time to harvest her will
    soon come."

³⁴"Nebuchadnezzar king of Babylon
    has devoured us,
  he has thrown us into
    confusion,
  he has made us an empty jar.
Like a serpent he has swallowed
    us
  and filled his stomach with our
    delicacies,
  and then has spewed us out.
³⁵May the violence done to our
    fleshᵇ be upon Babylon,"
  say the inhabitants of Zion.
"May our blood be on those who
    live in Babylonia,"
  says Jerusalem.

³⁶Therefore, this is what the LORD
says:

"See, I will defend your cause
    and avenge you;
I will dry up her sea
  and make her springs dry.

ᵃ24 Or *Chaldea*; also in verse 35   ᵇ35 Or *done to us and to our children*

³⁷Babylon will be a heap of ruins,
    a haunt of jackals,
an object of horror and scorn,
    a place where no one lives.
³⁸Her people all roar like young
    lions,
    they growl like lion cubs.
³⁹But while they are aroused,
    I will set out a feast for them
    and make them drunk,
so that they shout with laughter—
    then sleep forever and not
    awake,"
                declares the LORD.
⁴⁰"I will bring them down
    like lambs to the slaughter,
    like rams and goats.

⁴¹"How Sheshach*a* will be
    captured,
    the boast of the whole earth
    seized!
What a horror Babylon will be
    among the nations!
⁴²The sea will rise over Babylon;
    its roaring waves will cover her.
⁴³Her towns will be desolate,
    a dry and desert land,
a land where no one lives,
    through which no man travels.
⁴⁴I will punish Bel in Babylon
    and make him spew out what
    he has swallowed.
The nations will no longer stream
    to him.
    And the wall of Babylon will
    fall.

⁴⁵"Come out of her, my people!
    Run for your lives!
    Run from the fierce anger of the
    LORD.
⁴⁶Do not lose heart or be afraid
    when rumors are heard in the
    land;
one rumor comes this year,
    another the next,
    rumors of violence in the land
    and of ruler against ruler.
⁴⁷For the time will surely come
    when I will punish the idols of
    Babylon;
her whole land will be disgraced

and her slain will all lie fallen
    within her.
⁴⁸Then heaven and earth and all
    that is in them
    will shout for joy over Babylon,
for out of the north
    destroyers will attack her,"
                declares the LORD.

⁴⁹"Babylon must fall because of
    Israel's slain,
just as the slain in all the earth
    have fallen because of Babylon.
⁵⁰You who have escaped the sword,
    leave and do not linger!
Remember the LORD in a distant
    land,
    and think on Jerusalem."

⁵¹"We are disgraced,
    for we have been insulted
    and shame covers our faces,
because foreigners have entered
    the holy places of the LORD's
    house."

⁵²"But days are coming," declares
    the LORD,
    "when I will punish her idols,
and throughout her land
    the wounded will groan.
⁵³Even if Babylon reaches the sky
    and fortifies her lofty
    stronghold,
    I will send destroyers against
    her,"
                declares the LORD.

⁵⁴"The sound of a cry comes from
    Babylon,
    the sound of great destruction
from the land of the
    Babylonians.*b*
⁵⁵The LORD will destroy Babylon;
    he will silence her noisy din.
Waves ⌊of enemies⌋ will rage like
    great waters;
    the roar of their voices will
    resound.
⁵⁶A destroyer will come against
    Babylon;
    her warriors will be captured,
    and their bows will be broken.
For the LORD is a God of
    retribution;

---

a41 Sheshach is a cryptogram for Babylon.   *b54* Or Chaldeans

he will repay in full.
⁵⁷I will make her officials and wise
　　men drunk,
　her governors, officers and
　　warriors as well;
　they will sleep forever and not
　　awake,"
　declares the King, whose name
　　is the Lord Almighty.

⁵⁸This is what the Lord Almighty
says:

"Babylon's thick wall will be
　　leveled
　and her high gates set on fire;
　the peoples exhaust themselves for
　　nothing,
　the nations' labor is only fuel
　　for the flames."

⁵⁹This is the message Jeremiah gave
to the staff officer Seraiah son of Neriah, the son of Mahseiah, when he
went to Babylon with Zedekiah king
of Judah in the fourth year of his
reign. ⁶⁰Jeremiah had written on a
scroll about all the disasters that
would come upon Babylon—all that
had been recorded concerning Babylon. ⁶¹He said to Seraiah, "When you
get to Babylon, see that you read all
these words aloud. ⁶²Then say,
'O Lord, you have said you will destroy this place, so that neither man
nor animal will live in it; it will be
desolate forever.' ⁶³When you finish
reading this scroll, tie a stone to it and
throw it into the Euphrates. ⁶⁴Then
say, 'So will Babylon sink to rise no
more because of the disaster I will
bring upon her. And her people will
fall.' "

The words of Jeremiah end here.

The Fall of Jerusalem

52 Zedekiah was twenty-one
　　 years old when he became
king, and he reigned in Jerusalem
eleven years. His mother's name was
Hamutal daughter of Jeremiah; she
was from Libnah. ²He did evil in the
eyes of the Lord, just as Jehoiakim
had done. ³It was because of the

Lord's anger that all this happened to
Jerusalem and Judah, and in the end
he thrust them from his presence.
　Now Zedekiah rebelled against the
king of Babylon.
　⁴So in the ninth year of Zedekiah's
reign, on the tenth day of the tenth
month, Nebuchadnezzar king of Babylon marched against Jerusalem with
his whole army. They camped outside
the city and built siege works all
around it. ⁵The city was kept under
siege until the eleventh year of King
Zedekiah.
　⁶By the ninth day of the fourth
month the famine in the city had become so severe that there was no food
for the people to eat. ⁷Then the city
wall was broken through, and the
whole army fled. They left the city at
night through the gate between the
two walls near the king's garden,
though the Babylonians[a] were surrounding the city. They fled toward
the Arabah,[b] ⁸but the Babylonian[c]
army pursued King Zedekiah and
overtook him in the plains of Jericho.
All his soldiers were separated from
him and scattered, ⁹and he was captured.
　He was taken to the king of Babylon at Riblah in the land of Hamath,
where he pronounced sentence on
him. ¹⁰There at Riblah the king of Babylon slaughtered the sons of Zedekiah
before his eyes; he also killed all the
officials of Judah. ¹¹Then he put out
Zedekiah's eyes, bound him with
bronze shackles and took him to Babylon, where he put him in prison till
the day of his death.
　¹²On the tenth day of the fifth
month, in the nineteenth year of Nebuchadnezzar king of Babylon, Nebuzaradan commander of the imperial
guard, who served the king of Babylon, came to Jerusalem. ¹³He set fire
to the temple of the Lord, the royal
palace and all the houses of Jerusalem. Every important building he
burned down. ¹⁴The whole Babylonian army under the commander of the
imperial guard broke down all the

---

a7 Or *Chaldeans*; also in verse 17　　b7 Or *the Jordan Valley*　　c8 Or *Chaldean*; also in verse 14 walls around Jerusalem. ¹⁵Nebuzaradan the commander of the guard carried into exile some of the poorest people and those who remained in the city, along with the rest of the craftsmen*ᵃ* and those who had gone over to the king of Babylon. ¹⁶But Nebuzaradan left behind the rest of the poorest people of the land to work the vineyards and fields.

¹⁷The Babylonians broke up the bronze pillars, the movable stands and the bronze Sea that were at the temple of the LORD and they carried all the bronze to Babylon. ¹⁸They also took away the pots, shovels, wick trimmers, sprinkling bowls, dishes and all the bronze articles used in the temple service. ¹⁹The commander of the imperial guard took away the basins, censers, sprinkling bowls, pots, lampstands, dishes and bowls used for drink offerings—all that were made of pure gold or silver.

²⁰The bronze from the two pillars, the Sea and the twelve bronze bulls under it, and the movable stands, which King Solomon had made for the temple of the LORD, was more than could be weighed. ²¹Each of the pillars was eighteen cubits high and twelve cubits in circumference*ᵇ*; each was four fingers thick, and hollow. ²²The bronze capital on top of the one pillar was five cubits*ᶜ* high and was decorated with a network and pomegranates of bronze all around. The other pillar, with its pomegranates, was similar. ²³There were ninety-six pomegranates on the sides; the total number of pomegranates above the surrounding network was a hundred.

²⁴The commander of the guard took as prisoners Seraiah the chief priest, Zephaniah the priest next in rank and the three doorkeepers. ²⁵Of those still in the city, he took the officer in charge of the fighting men, and seven royal advisers. He also took the secretary who was chief officer in charge of conscripting the people of the land and sixty of his men who were found in the city. ²⁶Nebuzaradan the commander took them all and brought them to the king of Babylon at Riblah. ²⁷There at Riblah, in the land of Hamath, the king had them executed.

So Judah went into captivity, away from her land. ²⁸This is the number of the people Nebuchadnezzar carried into exile:

> in the seventh year, 3,023 Jews;
> ²⁹in Nebuchadnezzar's eighteenth year,
> 832 people from Jerusalem;
> ³⁰in his twenty-third year,
> 745 Jews taken into exile by Nebuzaradan the commander of the imperial guard.

There were 4,600 people in all.

Jehoiachin Released

³¹In the thirty-seventh year of the exile of Jehoiachin king of Judah, in the year Evil-Merodach*ᵈ* became king of Babylon, he released Jehoiachin king of Judah and freed him from prison on the twenty-fifth day of the twelfth month. ³²He spoke kindly to him and gave him a seat of honor higher than those of the other kings who were with him in Babylon. ³³So Jehoiachin put aside his prison clothes and for the rest of his life ate regularly at the king's table. ³⁴Day by day the king of Babylon gave Jehoiachin a regular allowance as long as he lived, till the day of his death.

ᵃ15 Or *populace*   *ᵇ21* That is, about 27 feet (about 8.1 meters) high and 18 feet (about 5.4 meters) in circumference   *ᶜ22* That is, about 7 1/2 feet (about 2.3 meters)   *ᵈ31* Also called *Amel-Marduk*

*L*amentations is for you
if you've ever experienced a significant loss.
Jeremiah laments the intense suffering of
God's people and the utter devastation of
Jerusalem. As you read this book, thank God
for his comforting presence in your situation
of suffering and grief. God knows how you
feel, and he promises to renew his compas-
sion for you every morning.

LAMENTATIONS

1 *a* How deserted lies the city,
    once so full of people!
How like a widow is she,
    who once was great among the
        nations!
She who was queen among the
        provinces
    has now become a slave.

²Bitterly she weeps at night,
    tears are upon her cheeks.
Among all her lovers
    there is none to comfort her.
All her friends have betrayed her;
    they have become her enemies.

³After affliction and harsh labor,
    Judah has gone into exile.
She dwells among the nations;
    she finds no resting place.
All who pursue her have
        overtaken her
    in the midst of her distress.

⁴The roads to Zion mourn,

for no one comes to her
    appointed feasts.
All her gateways are desolate,
    her priests groan,
her maidens grieve,
    and she is in bitter anguish.

⁵Her foes have become her masters;
    her enemies are at ease.
The LORD has brought her grief
    because of her many sins.
Her children have gone into exile,
    captive before the foe.

⁶All the splendor has departed
    from the Daughter of Zion.
Her princes are like deer
    that find no pasture;
in weakness they have fled
    before the pursuer.

⁷In the days of her affliction and
        wandering
    Jerusalem remembers all the
        treasures

*a*This chapter is an acrostic poem, the verses of which begin with the successive letters of the Hebrew alphabet.

that were hers in days of old.
When her people fell into enemy
    hands,
  there was no one to help her.
Her enemies looked at her
  and laughed at her destruction.

⁸Jerusalem has sinned greatly
  and so has become unclean.
All who honored her despise her,
  for they have seen her
      nakedness;
she herself groans
  and turns away.

⁹Her filthiness clung to her skirts;
  she did not consider her future.
Her fall was astounding;
  . there was none to comfort her.
"Look, O LORD, on my affliction,
  for the enemy has triumphed."

¹⁰The enemy laid hands
  on all her treasures;
she saw pagan nations
  enter her sanctuary—
those you had forbidden
  to enter your assembly.

¹¹All her people groan
  as they search for bread;
they barter their treasures for food
  to keep themselves alive.
"Look, O LORD, and consider,
  for I am despised."

¹²"Is it nothing to you, all you who
      pass by?
  Look around and see.
Is any suffering like my suffering
  that was inflicted on me,
that the LORD brought on me
  in the day of his fierce anger?

¹³"From on high he sent fire,
  sent it down into my bones.
He spread a net for my feet
  and turned me back.
He made me desolate,
  faint all the day long.

¹⁴"My sins have been bound into a
      yoke*a*;
  by his hands they were woven
      together.

They have come upon my neck
  and the Lord has sapped my
      strength.
He has handed me over
  to those I cannot withstand.

¹⁵"The Lord has rejected
  all the warriors in my midst;
he has summoned an army against
      me
  to*b* crush my young men.
In his winepress the Lord has
      trampled
  the Virgin Daughter of Judah.

¹⁶"This is why I weep
  and my eyes overflow with
      tears.
No one is near to comfort me,
  no one to restore my spirit.
My children are destitute
  because the enemy has
      prevailed."

¹⁷Zion stretches out her hands,
  but there is no one to comfort
      her.
The LORD has decreed for Jacob
  that his neighbors become his
      foes;
Jerusalem has become
  an unclean thing among them.

¹⁸"The LORD is righteous,
  yet I rebelled against his
      command.
Listen, all you peoples;
  look upon my suffering.
My young men and maidens
  have gone into exile.

¹⁹"I called to my allies
  but they betrayed me.
My priests and my elders
  perished in the city
while they searched for food
  to keep themselves alive.

²⁰"See, O LORD, how distressed I am!
  I am in torment within,
and in my heart I am disturbed,
  for I have been most rebellious.
Outside, the sword bereaves;
  inside, there is only death.

---

*a*14 Most Hebrew manuscripts; Septuagint *He kept watch over my sins*   *b*15 Or *has set a time for
me / when he will*

²¹"People have heard my groaning,
  but there is no one to comfort
    me.
All my enemies have heard of my
    distress;
  they rejoice at what you have
    done.
May you bring the day you have
    announced
  so they may become like me.

²²"Let all their wickedness come
    before you;
  deal with them
as you have dealt with me
  because of all my sins.
My groans are many
  and my heart is faint."

2 ^aHow the Lord has covered the
        Daughter of Zion
    with the cloud of his anger^b!
He has hurled down the splendor
    of Israel
  from heaven to earth;
he has not remembered his
    footstool
  in the day of his anger.

²Without pity the Lord has
    swallowed up
  all the dwellings of Jacob;
in his wrath he has torn down
    the strongholds of the Daughter
      of Judah.
He has brought her kingdom and
    its princes
  down to the ground in
    dishonor.

³In fierce anger he has cut off
  every horn^c of Israel.
He has withdrawn his right hand
  at the approach of the enemy.
He has burned in Jacob like a
    flaming fire
  that consumes everything
    around it.

⁴Like an enemy he has strung his
    bow;
  his right hand is ready.

Like a foe he has slain
  all who were pleasing to the
    eye;
he has poured out his wrath like
    fire
  on the tent of the Daughter of
    Zion.

⁵The Lord is like an enemy;
  he has swallowed up Israel.
He has swallowed up all her
    palaces
  and destroyed her strongholds.
He has multiplied mourning and
    lamentation
  for the Daughter of Judah.

⁶He has laid waste his dwelling
    like a garden;
  he has destroyed his place of
    meeting.
The LORD has made Zion forget
  her appointed feasts and her
    Sabbaths;
in his fierce anger he has spurned
  both king and priest.

⁷The Lord has rejected his altar
  and abandoned his sanctuary.
He has handed over to the enemy
  the walls of her palaces;
they have raised a shout in the
    house of the LORD
  as on the day of an appointed
    feast.

⁸The LORD determined to tear down
  the wall around the Daughter of
    Zion.
He stretched out a measuring line
  and did not withhold his hand
    from destroying.
He made ramparts and walls
    lament;
  together they wasted away.

⁹Her gates have sunk into the
    ground;
  their bars he has broken and
    destroyed.
Her king and her princes are
    exiled among the nations,
  the law is no more,

^aThis chapter is an acrostic poem, the verses of which begin with the successive letters of the
Hebrew alphabet.   ^b1 Or *How the Lord in his anger / has treated the Daughter of Zion with
contempt*   ^c3 Or / *all the strength;* or *every king; horn* here symbolizes strength.

VERSE:	AUTHOR:	PASSAGE:
Lamentations 1:16	Charles R. Swindoll	Lamentations 1:1–22

When Words Fail, Tears Flow

Tears have a language all their own. In some mysterious way, our complex inner-communication system knows when to admit its verbal limitations . . . and the tears come . . .

Most often they appear when our soul is overwhelmed with feelings that words cannot describe.

Our tears may flow during the singing of a great, majestic hymn, or when we are alone, lost in some vivid memory or wrestling in prayer . . .

A teardrop on earth summons the King of Heaven. Rather than being ashamed or disappointed, the Lord takes note of our inner friction when hard times are oiled by tears. He turns these situations into moments of tenderness; he never forgets those crises in our lives where tears were shed (Psalm 56:8) . . .

"The weeping prophet" became Jeremiah's nickname and even though he didn't always have the words to describe his feelings, he was never at a loss to communicate his convictions. You could always count on Jeremiah to bury his head in his hands and sob aloud.

Strange that this man was selected by God to be his personal spokesman at the most critical time in Israel's history. Seems like an unlikely choice — unless you value tears as God does.

. . . .

ADDITIONAL SCRIPTURE READINGS
Psalm 56; Luke 7:36–50

Go to page 1023 for your next devotional reading.

and her prophets no longer find
  visions from the LORD.

¹⁰The elders of the Daughter of Zion
    sit on the ground in silence;
  they have sprinkled dust on their
      heads
    and put on sackcloth.
  The young women of Jerusalem
    have bowed their heads to the
      ground.

¹¹My eyes fail from weeping,
    I am in torment within,
  my heart is poured out on the
      ground
    because my people are
      destroyed,
  because children and infants faint
    in the streets of the city.

¹²They say to their mothers,
    "Where is bread and wine?"
  as they faint like wounded men
    in the streets of the city,
  as their lives ebb away
    in their mothers' arms.

¹³What can I say for you?
    With what can I compare you,
    O Daughter of Jerusalem?
  To what can I liken you,
    that I may comfort you,
    O Virgin Daughter of Zion?
  Your wound is as deep as the sea.
    Who can heal you?

¹⁴The visions of your prophets
    were false and worthless;
  they did not expose your sin
    to ward off your captivity.
  The oracles they gave you
    were false and misleading.

¹⁵All who pass your way
    clap their hands at you;
  they scoff and shake their heads
    at the Daughter of Jerusalem:
  "Is this the city that was called
    the perfection of beauty,
    the joy of the whole earth?"

¹⁶All your enemies open their
      mouths
    wide against you;

they scoff and gnash their teeth
    and say, "We have swallowed
      her up.
  This is the day we have waited
      for;
    we have lived to see it."

¹⁷The LORD has done what he
      planned;
  he has fulfilled his word,
    which he decreed long ago.
  He has overthrown you without
      pity,
  he has let the enemy gloat over
      you,
  he has exalted the horn*a* of
      your foes.

¹⁸The hearts of the people
    cry out to the Lord.
  O wall of the Daughter of Zion,
    let your tears flow like a river
      day and night;
  give yourself no relief,
    your eyes no rest.

¹⁹Arise, cry out in the night,
    as the watches of the night
      begin;
  pour out your heart like water
    in the presence of the Lord.
  Lift up your hands to him
    for the lives of your children,
  who faint from hunger
    at the head of every street.

²⁰"Look, O LORD, and consider:
    Whom have you ever treated
      like this?
  Should women eat their offspring,
    the children they have cared
      for?
  Should priest and prophet be
      killed
    in the sanctuary of the Lord?

²¹"Young and old lie together
    in the dust of the streets;
  my young men and maidens
    have fallen by the sword.
  You have slain them in the day of
      your anger;
    you have slaughtered them
      without pity.

a17 Horn here symbolizes strength.

²²"As you summon to a feast day,
  so you summoned against me
    terrors on every side.
In the day of the LORD's anger
  no one escaped or survived;
those I cared for and reared,
  my enemy has destroyed."

3ᵃ I am the man who has seen
      affliction
  by the rod of his wrath.
²He has driven me away and made
    me walk
  in darkness rather than light;
³indeed, he has turned his hand
    against me
  again and again, all day long.

⁴He has made my skin and my
    flesh grow old
  and has broken my bones.
⁵He has besieged me and
    surrounded me
  with bitterness and hardship.
⁶He has made me dwell in
    darkness
  like those long dead.

⁷He has walled me in so I cannot
    escape;
  he has weighed me down with
    chains.
⁸Even when I call out or cry for
    help,
  he shuts out my prayer.
⁹He has barred my way with
    blocks of stone;
  he has made my paths crooked.

¹⁰Like a bear lying in wait,
  like a lion in hiding,
¹¹he dragged me from the path and
    mangled me
  and left me without help.
¹²He drew his bow
  and made me the target for his
    arrows.

¹³He pierced my heart
  with arrows from his quiver.
¹⁴I became the laughingstock of all
  my people;

they mock me in song all day
  long.
¹⁵He has filled me with bitter herbs
  and sated me with gall.

¹⁶He has broken my teeth with
    gravel;
  he has trampled me in the dust.
¹⁷I have been deprived of peace;
  I have forgotten what prosperity
    is.
¹⁸So I say, "My splendor is gone
  and all that I had hoped from
    the LORD."

¹⁹I remember my affliction and my
    wandering,
  the bitterness and the gall.
²⁰I well remember them,
  and my soul is downcast within
    me.
²¹Yet this I call to mind
  and therefore I have hope:

²²Because of the LORD's great love
    we are not consumed,
  for his compassions never fail.
²³They are new every morning;
  great is your faithfulness.
²⁴I say to myself, "The LORD is my
    portion;
  therefore I will wait for him."

²⁵The LORD is good to those whose
    hope is in him,
  to the one who seeks him;
²⁶it is good to wait quietly
  for the salvation of the LORD.
²⁷It is good for a man to bear the
    yoke
  while he is young.

²⁸Let him sit alone in silence,
  for the LORD has laid it on him.
²⁹Let him bury his face in the
    dust—
  there may yet be hope.
³⁰Let him offer his cheek to one
  who would strike him,
  and let him be filled with
    disgrace.

ᵃThis chapter is an acrostic poem; the verses of each stanza begin with the successive letters of
the Hebrew alphabet, and the verses within each stanza begin with the same letter.

³¹For men are not cast off
   by the Lord forever.
³²Though he brings grief, he will
   show compassion,
   so great is his unfailing love.
³³For he does not willingly bring
   affliction
   or grief to the children of men.

³⁴To crush underfoot
   all prisoners in the land,
³⁵to deny a man his rights
   before the Most High,
³⁶to deprive a man of justice—
   would not the Lord see such
   things?

³⁷Who can speak and have it
   happen
   if the Lord has not decreed it?
³⁸Is it not from the mouth of the
   Most High
   that both calamities and good
   things come?
³⁹Why should any living man
   complain
   when punished for his sins?

⁴⁰Let us examine our ways and test
   them,
   and let us return to the Lord.
⁴¹Let us lift up our hearts and our
   hands
   to God in heaven, and say:
⁴²"We have sinned and rebelled
   and you have not forgiven.

⁴³"You have covered yourself with
   anger and pursued us;
   you have slain without pity.
⁴⁴You have covered yourself with a
   cloud
   so that no prayer can get
   through.
⁴⁵You have made us scum and
   refuse
   among the nations.

⁴⁶"All our enemies have opened
   their mouths
   wide against us.
⁴⁷We have suffered terror and
   pitfalls,
   ruin and destruction."
⁴⁸Streams of tears flow from my
   eyes

because my people are
   destroyed.

⁴⁹My eyes will flow unceasingly,
   without relief,
⁵⁰until the Lord looks down
   from heaven and sees.
⁵¹What I see brings grief to my soul
   because of all the women of my
   city.

⁵²Those who were my enemies
   without cause
   hunted me like a bird.
⁵³They tried to end my life in a pit
   and threw stones at me;
⁵⁴the waters closed over my head,
   and I thought I was about to be
   cut off.

⁵⁵I called on your name, O Lord,
   from the depths of the pit.
⁵⁶You heard my plea: "Do not close
   your ears
   to my cry for relief."
⁵⁷You came near when I called you,
   and you said, "Do not fear."

⁵⁸O Lord, you took up my case;
   you redeemed my life.
⁵⁹You have seen, O Lord, the wrong
   done to me.
   Uphold my cause!
⁶⁰You have seen the depth of their
   vengeance,
   all their plots against me.

⁶¹O Lord, you have heard their
   insults,
   all their plots against me—
⁶²what my enemies whisper and
   mutter
   against me all day long.
⁶³Look at them! Sitting or standing,
   they mock me in their songs.

⁶⁴Pay them back what they deserve,
   O Lord,
   for what their hands have done.
⁶⁵Put a veil over their hearts,
   and may your curse be on
   them!
⁶⁶Pursue them in anger and destroy
   them
   from under the heavens of the
   Lord.

VERSE:
Lamentations
3:22

AUTHOR:
Dirk R. Buursma

PASSAGE:
Lamentations
3:19–33

New Every Morning

The pastor's eyes swept over the congregation. In just a moment the worship service would begin. Over there a young man with two kids — in shock because his wife has left him and filed for divorce. Over there the elderly man who doesn't feel very useful anymore, who mourns the loss of an energy and health long departed. And beside him the parents whose grief is as chronic as their daughter's disability.

Yes, you'll find them in every church — and outside the walls of a church. Common, ordinary, everyday people. People with breaking, aching hearts. People who have at least one thing in common: tears, rivers of tears. Can you feel their sorrow? Can you taste their grief? Can you see their despair?

The pastor closed his eyes and breathed a prayer. "Lord, these people desperately need a word of hope. So many of them feel so forsaken, so alone, so hopeless. They need to feel that somehow everything's going to be all right, even when walls are crashing in all around them."

In the middle of a book of tears and overwhelming grief, at a time when you'd least expect it, are some of the most hopeful words ever written: "Yet this I call to mind and therefore I have hope: Because of the LORD's great love we are not consumed, for his compassions never fail. They are new every morning; great is your faithfulness" (Lamentations 3:21–23).

. . . .

ADDITIONAL SCRIPTURE READINGS
Psalm 13; Psalm 130

Go to page 1029 for your next devotional reading.

4

^aHow the gold has lost its luster,
 the fine gold become dull!
The sacred gems are scattered
 at the head of every street.

²How the precious sons of Zion,
 once worth their weight in gold,
are now considered as pots of
  clay,
 the work of a potter's hands!

³Even jackals offer their breasts
 to nurse their young,
but my people have become
  heartless
 like ostriches in the desert.

⁴Because of thirst the infant's
  tongue
 sticks to the roof of its mouth;
the children beg for bread,
 but no one gives it to them.

⁵Those who once ate delicacies
 are destitute in the streets.
Those nurtured in purple
 now lie on ash heaps.

⁶The punishment of my people
 is greater than that of Sodom,
which was overthrown in a
  moment
 without a hand turned to help
  her.

⁷Their princes were brighter than
  snow
 and whiter than milk,
their bodies more ruddy than
  rubies,
 their appearance like
  sapphires.^b

⁸But now they are blacker than
  soot;
 they are not recognized in the
  streets.
Their skin has shriveled on their
  bones;
 it has become as dry as a stick.

⁹Those killed by the sword are
  better off
 than those who die of famine;

racked with hunger, they waste
  away
 for lack of food from the field.

¹⁰With their own hands
  compassionate women
 have cooked their own children,
who became their food
 when my people were
  destroyed.

¹¹The LORD has given full vent to his
  wrath;
 he has poured out his fierce
  anger.
He kindled a fire in Zion
 that consumed her foundations.

¹²The kings of the earth did not
  believe,
 nor did any of the world's
  people,
that enemies and foes could enter
 the gates of Jerusalem.

¹³But it happened because of the
  sins of her prophets
 and the iniquities of her priests,
who shed within her
 the blood of the righteous.

¹⁴Now they grope through the
  streets
 like men who are blind.
They are so defiled with blood
 that no one dares to touch their
  garments.

¹⁵"Go away! You are unclean!" men
  cry to them.
 "Away! Away! Don't touch us!"
When they flee and wander about,
 people among the nations say,
 "They can stay here no longer."

¹⁶The LORD himself has scattered
  them;
 he no longer watches over
  them.
The priests are shown no honor,
 the elders no favor.

¹⁷Moreover, our eyes failed,
 looking in vain for help;
from our towers we watched

^aThis chapter is an acrostic poem, the verses of which begin with the successive letters of the
Hebrew alphabet. ^b7 Or *lapis lazuli*

for a nation that could not save
us.

¹⁸Men stalked us at every step,
so we could not walk in our
streets.
Our end was near, our days were
numbered,
for our end had come.

¹⁹Our pursuers were swifter
than eagles in the sky;
they chased us over the mountains
and lay in wait for us in the
desert.

²⁰The LORD's anointed, our very life
breath,
was caught in their traps.
We thought that under his
shadow
we would live among the
nations.

²¹Rejoice and be glad, O Daughter
of Edom,
you who live in the land of Uz.
But to you also the cup will be
passed;
you will be drunk and stripped
naked.

²²O Daughter of Zion, your
punishment will end;
he will not prolong your exile.
But, O Daughter of Edom, he will
punish your sin
and expose your wickedness.

5 Remember, O LORD, what has
happened to us;
look, and see our disgrace.
²Our inheritance has been turned
over to aliens,
our homes to foreigners.
³We have become orphans and
fatherless,
our mothers like widows.
⁴We must buy the water we drink;
our wood can be had only at a
price.
⁵Those who pursue us are at our
heels;
we are weary and find no rest.

⁶We submitted to Egypt and
Assyria
to get enough bread.
⁷Our fathers sinned and are no
more,
and we bear their punishment.
⁸Slaves rule over us,
and there is none to free us
from their hands.
⁹We get our bread at the risk of
our lives
because of the sword in the
desert.
¹⁰Our skin is hot as an oven,
feverish from hunger.
¹¹Women have been ravished in
Zion,
and virgins in the towns of
Judah.
¹²Princes have been hung up by
their hands;
elders are shown no respect.
¹³Young men toil at the millstones;
boys stagger under loads of
wood.
¹⁴The elders are gone from the city
gate;
the young men have stopped
their music.
¹⁵Joy is gone from our hearts;
our dancing has turned to
mourning.
¹⁶The crown has fallen from our
head.
Woe to us, for we have sinned!
¹⁷Because of this our hearts are
faint,
because of these things our eyes
grow dim
¹⁸for Mount Zion, which lies
desolate,
with jackals prowling over it.

¹⁹You, O LORD, reign forever;
your throne endures from
generation to generation.
²⁰Why do you always forget us?
Why do you forsake us so long?
²¹Restore us to yourself, O LORD,
that we may return;
renew our days as of old
²²unless you have utterly rejected us
and are angry with us beyond
measure.

*L*iving among the exiles in Babylon, Ezekiel uses words, visions and solo "mini-dramas" to urge the people to renew their commitment to God. He explains that God desires a relationship with his people wherever they are. As you read this book, be encouraged that God wants to show himself to you in unlikely places or situations; he invites you to draw close and rest in his love.

EZEKIEL

The Living Creatures and the Glory of the LORD

1 In the*a* thirtieth year, in the fourth month on the fifth day, while I was among the exiles by the Kebar River, the heavens were opened and I saw visions of God.

²On the fifth of the month—it was the fifth year of the exile of King Jehoiachin— ³the word of the LORD came to Ezekiel the priest, the son of Buzi,*b* by the Kebar River in the land of the Babylonians.*c* There the hand of the LORD was upon him.

⁴I looked, and I saw a windstorm coming out of the north—an immense cloud with flashing lightning and surrounded by brilliant light. The center of the fire looked like glowing metal, ⁵and in the fire was what looked like four living creatures. In appearance their form was that of a man, ⁶but each of them had four faces and four wings. ⁷Their legs were straight; their feet were like those of a calf and gleamed like burnished bronze. ⁸Under their wings on their four sides they had the hands of a man. All four of them had faces and wings, ⁹and their wings touched one another. Each one went straight ahead; they did not turn as they moved.

¹⁰Their faces looked like this: Each of the four had the face of a man, and on the right side each had the face of a lion, and on the left the face of an ox; each also had the face of an eagle. ¹¹Such were their faces. Their wings were spread out upward; each had two wings, one touching the wing of another creature on either side, and two wings covering its body. ¹²Each one went straight ahead. Wherever the spirit would go, they would go, without turning as they went. ¹³The appearance of the living creatures was like burning coals of fire or like torches. Fire moved back and forth

*a*1 Or ⌐my⌐   *b*3 Or *Ezekiel son of Buzi the priest*   *c*3 Or *Chaldeans* among the creatures; it was bright, and lightning flashed out of it. ¹⁴The creatures sped back and forth like flashes of lightning.

¹⁵As I looked at the living creatures, I saw a wheel on the ground beside each creature with its four faces. ¹⁶This was the appearance and structure of the wheels: They sparkled like chrysolite, and all four looked alike. Each appeared to be made like a wheel intersecting a wheel. ¹⁷As they moved, they would go in any one of the four directions the creatures faced; the wheels did not turn about[a] as the creatures went. ¹⁸Their rims were high and awesome, and all four rims were full of eyes all around.

¹⁹When the living creatures moved, the wheels beside them moved; and when the living creatures rose from the ground, the wheels also rose. ²⁰Wherever the spirit would go, they would go, and the wheels would rise along with them, because the spirit of the living creatures was in the wheels. ²¹When the creatures moved, they also moved; when the creatures stood still, they also stood still; and when the creatures rose from the ground, the wheels rose along with them, because the spirit of the living creatures was in the wheels.

²²Spread out above the heads of the living creatures was what looked like an expanse, sparkling like ice, and awesome. ²³Under the expanse their wings were stretched out one toward the other, and each had two wings covering its body. ²⁴When the creatures moved, I heard the sound of their wings, like the roar of rushing waters, like the voice of the Almighty,[b] like the tumult of an army. When they stood still, they lowered their wings.

²⁵Then there came a voice from above the expanse over their heads as they stood with lowered wings. ²⁶Above the expanse over their heads was what looked like a throne of sapphire,[c] and high above on the throne was a figure like that of a man. ²⁷I saw that from what appeared to be his waist up he looked like glowing metal, as if full of fire, and that from there down he looked like fire; and brilliant light surrounded him. ²⁸Like the appearance of a rainbow in the clouds on a rainy day, so was the radiance around him.

This was the appearance of the likeness of the glory of the LORD. When I saw it, I fell facedown, and I heard the voice of one speaking.

Ezekiel's Call

2 He said to me, "Son of man, stand up on your feet and I will speak to you." ²As he spoke, the Spirit came into me and raised me to my feet, and I heard him speaking to me.

³He said: "Son of man, I am sending you to the Israelites, to a rebellious nation that has rebelled against me; they and their fathers have been in revolt against me to this very day. ⁴The people to whom I am sending you are obstinate and stubborn. Say to them, 'This is what the Sovereign LORD says.' ⁵And whether they listen or fail to listen—for they are a rebellious house—they will know that a prophet has been among them. ⁶And you, son of man, do not be afraid of them or their words. Do not be afraid, though briers and thorns are all around you and you live among scorpions. Do not be afraid of what they say or terrified by them, though they are a rebellious house. ⁷You must speak my words to them, whether they listen or fail to listen, for they are rebellious. ⁸But you, son of man, listen to what I say to you. Do not rebel like that rebellious house; open your mouth and eat what I give you."

⁹Then I looked, and I saw a hand stretched out to me. In it was a scroll, ¹⁰which he unrolled before me. On both sides of it were written words of lament and mourning and woe.

3 And he said to me, "Son of man, eat what is before you, eat this

---

[a]17 Or aside   [b]24 Hebrew Shaddai   [c]26 Or lapis lazuli

scroll; then go and speak to the house of Israel." ²So I opened my mouth, and he gave me the scroll to eat.

³Then he said to me, "Son of man, eat this scroll I am giving you and fill your stomach with it." So I ate it, and it tasted as sweet as honey in my mouth.

⁴He then said to me: "Son of man, go now to the house of Israel and speak my words to them. ⁵You are not being sent to a people of obscure speech and difficult language, but to the house of Israel— ⁶not to many peoples of obscure speech and difficult language, whose words you cannot understand. Surely if I had sent you to them, they would have listened to you. ⁷But the house of Israel is not willing to listen to you because they are not willing to listen to me, for the whole house of Israel is hardened and obstinate. ⁸But I will make you as unyielding and hardened as they are. ⁹I will make your forehead like the hardest stone, harder than flint. Do not be afraid of them or terrified by them, though they are a rebellious house."

¹⁰And he said to me, "Son of man, listen carefully and take to heart all the words I speak to you. ¹¹Go now to your countrymen in exile and speak to them. Say to them, 'This is what the Sovereign LORD says,' whether they listen or fail to listen."

¹²Then the Spirit lifted me up, and I heard behind me a loud rumbling sound—May the glory of the LORD be praised in his dwelling place!— ¹³the sound of the wings of the living creatures brushing against each other and the sound of the wheels beside them, a loud rumbling sound. ¹⁴The Spirit then lifted me up and took me away, and I went in bitterness and in the anger of my spirit, with the strong hand of the LORD upon me. ¹⁵I came to the exiles who lived at Tel Abib near the Kebar River. And there, where they were living, I sat among them for seven days—overwhelmed.

Warning to Israel

¹⁶At the end of seven days the word of the LORD came to me: ¹⁷"Son of man, I have made you a watchman for the house of Israel; so hear the word I speak and give them warning from me. ¹⁸When I say to a wicked man, 'You will surely die,' and you do not warn him or speak out to dissuade him from his evil ways in order to save his life, that wicked man will die for*a* his sin, and I will hold you accountable for his blood. ¹⁹But if you do warn the wicked man and he does not turn from his wickedness or from his evil ways, he will die for his sin; but you will have saved yourself.

²⁰"Again, when a righteous man turns from his righteousness and does evil, and I put a stumbling block before him, he will die. Since you did not warn him, he will die for his sin. The righteous things he did will not be remembered, and I will hold you accountable for his blood. ²¹But if you do warn the righteous man not to sin and he does not sin, he will surely live because he took warning, and you will have saved yourself."

²²The hand of the LORD was upon me there, and he said to me, "Get up and go out to the plain, and there I will speak to you." ²³So I got up and went out to the plain. And the glory of the LORD was standing there, like the glory I had seen by the Kebar River, and I fell facedown.

²⁴Then the Spirit came into me and raised me to my feet. He spoke to me and said: "Go, shut yourself inside your house. ²⁵And you, son of man, they will tie with ropes; you will be bound so that you cannot go out among the people. ²⁶I will make your tongue stick to the roof of your mouth so that you will be silent and unable to rebuke them, though they are a rebellious house. ²⁷But when I speak to you, I will open your mouth and you shall say to them, 'This is what the Sovereign LORD says.' Whoever will listen let him listen, and whoever will

---

a18 Or *in*; also in verses 19 and 20

VERSE:	AUTHOR:	PASSAGE:
Ezekiel 3:3	Stuart Briscoe	Ezekiel 2:1 — 3:3

Thou Shalt Not Nibble

The Lord made it quite clear to Ezekiel that he intended the scroll to be completely eaten. Not nibbled like a frothy dessert or avoided like something hazardous to health, but eaten with or without enthusiasm.

When it comes to feeding on the Word, people tend to agree with the Lord that they cannot live by bread alone. But then they try to show how much living they can do on as little word from the Lord as possible. They diet the heavy things of God out of their menu. They avoid the nutritious things that need chewing ...

The assimilation of the Word needs to be strongly emphasized in this day and age. Digesting food so thoroughly that it is assimilated by the body and being of a person requires time and the balanced function of a healthy body. So it is with the Word the Lord has for his people. Time taken to read it, mark it, learn it and inwardly digest it is time that needs to be as carefully planned into the daily lifestyle of the believer as time for work and rest ...

When the believer carefully regulates his intake of truth and assiduously trusts and obeys what the truth puts into him, then the miracle of digestion takes place and the food changes from being a lump in the mouth to strength in the muscles, blood in the veins and energy in the brain. To be motivated and strengthened daily by the truth assimilated is one of the basic requirements for normal spiritual health.

ADDITIONAL SCRIPTURE READINGS
Psalm 119:105–112; 2 Timothy 3:10–17
Go to page 1037 for your next devotional reading.

refuse let him refuse; for they are a rebellious house.

Siege of Jerusalem Symbolized

4 "Now, son of man, take a clay tablet, put it in front of you and draw the city of Jerusalem on it. ²Then lay siege to it: Erect siege works against it, build a ramp up to it, set up camps against it and put battering rams around it. ³Then take an iron pan, place it as an iron wall between you and the city and turn your face toward it. It will be under siege, and you shall besiege it. This will be a sign to the house of Israel.

⁴"Then lie on your left side and put the sin of the house of Israel upon yourself.ᵃ You are to bear their sin for the number of days you lie on your side. ⁵I have assigned you the same number of days as the years of their sin. So for 390 days you will bear the sin of the house of Israel.

⁶"After you have finished this, lie down again, this time on your right side, and bear the sin of the house of Judah. I have assigned you 40 days, a day for each year. ⁷Turn your face toward the siege of Jerusalem and with bared arm prophesy against her. ⁸I will tie you up with ropes so that you cannot turn from one side to the other until you have finished the days of your siege.

⁹"Take wheat and barley, beans and lentils, millet and spelt; put them in a storage jar and use them to make bread for yourself. You are to eat it during the 390 days you lie on your side. ¹⁰Weigh out twenty shekelsᵇ of food to eat each day and eat it at set times. ¹¹Also measure out a sixth of a hinᶜ of water and drink it at set times. ¹²Eat the food as you would a barley cake; bake it in the sight of the people, using human excrement for fuel." ¹³The Lord said, "In this way the people of Israel will eat defiled food among the nations where I will drive them."

¹⁴Then I said, "Not so, Sovereign Lord! I have never defiled myself. From my youth until now I have never eaten anything found dead or torn by wild animals. No unclean meat has ever entered my mouth."

¹⁵"Very well," he said, "I will let you bake your bread over cow manure instead of human excrement."

¹⁶He then said to me: "Son of man, I will cut off the supply of food in Jerusalem. The people will eat rationed food in anxiety and drink rationed water in despair, ¹⁷for food and water will be scarce. They will be appalled at the sight of each other and will waste away because ofᵈ their sin.

5 "Now, son of man, take a sharp sword and use it as a barber's razor to shave your head and your beard. Then take a set of scales and divide up the hair. ²When the days of your siege come to an end, burn a third of the hair with fire inside the city. Take a third and strike it with the sword all around the city. And scatter a third to the wind. For I will pursue them with drawn sword. ³But take a few strands of hair and tuck them away in the folds of your garment. ⁴Again, take a few of these and throw them into the fire and burn them up. A fire will spread from there to the whole house of Israel.

⁵"This is what the Sovereign Lord says: This is Jerusalem, which I have set in the center of the nations, with countries all around her. ⁶Yet in her wickedness she has rebelled against my laws and decrees more than the nations and countries around her. She has rejected my laws and has not followed my decrees.

⁷"Therefore this is what the Sovereign Lord says: You have been more unruly than the nations around you and have not followed my decrees or kept my laws. You have not evenᵉ conformed to the standards of the nations around you.

ᵃ4 Or *your side*   ᵇ10 That is, about 8 ounces (about 0.2 kilogram)   ᶜ11 That is, about 2/3 quart (about 0.6 liter)   ᵈ17 Or *away in*   ᵉ7 Most Hebrew manuscripts; some Hebrew manuscripts and Syriac *You have*

⁸"Therefore this is what the Sovereign LORD says: I myself am against you, Jerusalem, and I will inflict punishment on you in the sight of the nations. ⁹Because of all your detestable idols, I will do to you what I have never done before and will never do again. ¹⁰Therefore in your midst fathers will eat their children, and children will eat their fathers. I will inflict punishment on you and will scatter all your survivors to the winds. ¹¹Therefore as surely as I live, declares the Sovereign LORD, because you have defiled my sanctuary with all your vile images and detestable practices, I myself will withdraw my favor; I will not look on you with pity or spare you. ¹²A third of your people will die of the plague or perish by famine inside you; a third will fall by the sword outside your walls; and a third I will scatter to the winds and pursue with drawn sword.

¹³"Then my anger will cease and my wrath against them will subside, and I will be avenged. And when I have spent my wrath upon them, they will know that I the LORD have spoken in my zeal.

¹⁴"I will make you a ruin and a reproach among the nations around you, in the sight of all who pass by. ¹⁵You will be a reproach and a taunt, a warning and an object of horror to the nations around you when I inflict punishment on you in anger and in wrath and with stinging rebuke. I the LORD have spoken. ¹⁶When I shoot at you with my deadly and destructive arrows of famine, I will shoot to destroy you. I will bring more and more famine upon you and cut off your supply of food. ¹⁷I will send famine and wild beasts against you, and they will leave you childless. Plague and bloodshed will sweep through you, and I will bring the sword against you. I the LORD have spoken."

A Prophecy Against the Mountains of Israel

6 The word of the LORD came to me: ²"Son of man, set your face against the mountains of Israel; prophesy against them ³and say: 'O mountains of Israel, hear the word of the Sovereign LORD. This is what the Sovereign LORD says to the mountains and hills, to the ravines and valleys: I am about to bring a sword against you, and I will destroy your high places. ⁴Your altars will be demolished and your incense altars will be smashed; and I will slay your people in front of your idols. ⁵I will lay the dead bodies of the Israelites in front of their idols, and I will scatter your bones around your altars. ⁶Wherever you live, the towns will be laid waste and the high places demolished, so that your altars will be laid waste and devastated, your idols smashed and ruined, your incense altars broken down, and what you have made wiped out. ⁷Your people will fall slain among you, and you will know that I am the LORD.

⁸" 'But I will spare some, for some of you will escape the sword when you are scattered among the lands and nations. ⁹Then in the nations where they have been carried captive, those who escape will remember me—how I have been grieved by their adulterous hearts, which have turned away from me, and by their eyes, which have lusted after their idols. They will loathe themselves for the evil they have done and for all their detestable practices. ¹⁰And they will know that I am the LORD; I did not threaten in vain to bring this calamity on them.

¹¹" 'This is what the Sovereign LORD says: Strike your hands together and stamp your feet and cry out "Alas!" because of all the wicked and detestable practices of the house of Israel, for they will fall by the sword, famine and plague. ¹²He that is far away will die of the plague, and he that is near will fall by the sword, and he that survives and is spared will die of famine. So will I spend my wrath upon them. ¹³And they will know that I am the LORD, when their people lie slain among their idols around their altars, on every high hill and on all the

mountaintops, under every spreading tree and every leafy oak—places where they offered fragrant incense to all their idols. ¹⁴And I will stretch out my hand against them and make the land a desolate waste from the desert to Diblah*ᵃ*—wherever they live. Then they will know that I am the LORD.'"

The End Has Come

7 The word of the LORD came to me: ²"Son of man, this is what the Sovereign LORD says to the land of Israel: The end! The end has come upon the four corners of the land. ³The end is now upon you and I will unleash my anger against you. I will judge you according to your conduct and repay you for all your detestable practices. ⁴I will not look on you with pity or spare you; I will surely repay you for your conduct and the detestable practices among you. Then you will know that I am the LORD.

⁵"This is what the Sovereign LORD says: Disaster! An unheard-of*ᵇ* disaster is coming. ⁶The end has come! The end has come! It has roused itself against you. It has come! ⁷Doom has come upon you—you who dwell in the land. The time has come, the day is near; there is panic, not joy, upon the mountains. ⁸I am about to pour out my wrath on you and spend my anger against you; I will judge you according to your conduct and repay you for all your detestable practices. ⁹I will not look on you with pity or spare you; I will repay you in accordance with your conduct and the detestable practices among you. Then you will know that it is I the LORD who strikes the blow.

¹⁰"The day is here! It has come! Doom has burst forth, the rod has budded, arrogance has blossomed! ¹¹Violence has grown into*ᶜ* a rod to punish wickedness; none of the people will be left, none of that crowd—no wealth, nothing of value. ¹²The

time has come, the day has arrived. Let not the buyer rejoice nor the seller grieve, for wrath is upon the whole crowd. ¹³The seller will not recover the land he has sold as long as both of them live, for the vision concerning the whole crowd will not be reversed. Because of their sins, not one of them will preserve his life. ¹⁴Though they blow the trumpet and get everything ready, no one will go into battle, for my wrath is upon the whole crowd.

¹⁵"Outside is the sword, inside are plague and famine; those in the country will die by the sword, and those in the city will be devoured by famine and plague. ¹⁶All who survive and escape will be in the mountains, moaning like doves of the valleys, each because of his sins. ¹⁷Every hand will go limp, and every knee will become as weak as water. ¹⁸They will put on sackcloth and be clothed with terror. Their faces will be covered with shame and their heads will be shaved. ¹⁹They will throw their silver into the streets, and their gold will be an unclean thing. Their silver and gold will not be able to save them in the day of the LORD's wrath. They will not satisfy their hunger or fill their stomachs with it, for it has made them stumble into sin. ²⁰They were proud of their beautiful jewelry and used it to make their detestable idols and vile images. Therefore I will turn these into an unclean thing for them. ²¹I will hand it all over as plunder to foreigners and as loot to the wicked of the earth, and they will defile it. ²²I will turn my face away from them, and they will desecrate my treasured place; robbers will enter it and desecrate it.

²³"Prepare chains, because the land is full of bloodshed and the city is full of violence. ²⁴I will bring the most wicked of the nations to take possession of their houses; I will put an end to the pride of the mighty, and their sanctuaries will be desecrated. ²⁵When terror comes, they will seek

---

ᵃ14 Most Hebrew manuscripts; a few Hebrew manuscripts *Riblah*   *ᵇ5* Most Hebrew
manuscripts; some Hebrew manuscripts and Syriac *Disaster after*   *ᶜ11* Or *The violent one*
has become

peace, but there will be none. ²⁶Calamity upon calamity will come, and rumor upon rumor. They will try to get a vision from the prophet; the teaching of the law by the priest will be lost, as will the counsel of the elders. ²⁷The king will mourn, the prince will be clothed with despair, and the hands of the people of the land will tremble. I will deal with them according to their conduct, and by their own standards I will judge them. Then they will know that I am the Lord."

Idolatry in the Temple

8 In the sixth year, in the sixth month on the fifth day, while I was sitting in my house and the elders of Judah were sitting before me, the hand of the Sovereign Lord came upon me there. ²I looked, and I saw a figure like that of a man.^a From what appeared to be his waist down he was like fire, and from there up his appearance was as bright as glowing metal. ³He stretched out what looked like a hand and took me by the hair of my head. The Spirit lifted me up between earth and heaven and in visions of God he took me to Jerusalem, to the entrance to the north gate of the inner court, where the idol that provokes to jealousy stood. ⁴And there before me was the glory of the God of Israel, as in the vision I had seen in the plain.

⁵Then he said to me, "Son of man, look toward the north." So I looked, and in the entrance north of the gate of the altar I saw this idol of jealousy.

⁶And he said to me, "Son of man, do you see what they are doing—the utterly detestable things the house of Israel is doing here, things that will drive me far from my sanctuary? But you will see things that are even more detestable."

⁷Then he brought me to the entrance to the court. I looked, and I saw a hole in the wall. ⁸He said to me, "Son of man, now dig into the wall." So I dug into the wall and saw a doorway there.

⁹And he said to me, "Go in and see the wicked and detestable things they are doing here." ¹⁰So I went in and looked, and I saw portrayed all over the walls all kinds of crawling things and detestable animals and all the idols of the house of Israel. ¹¹In front of them stood seventy elders of the house of Israel, and Jaazaniah son of Shaphan was standing among them. Each had a censer in his hand, and a fragrant cloud of incense was rising.

¹²He said to me, "Son of man, have you seen what the elders of the house of Israel are doing in the darkness, each at the shrine of his own idol? They say, 'The Lord does not see us; the Lord has forsaken the land.'" ¹³Again, he said, "You will see them doing things that are even more detestable."

¹⁴Then he brought me to the entrance to the north gate of the house of the Lord, and I saw women sitting there, mourning for Tammuz. ¹⁵He said to me, "Do you see this, son of man? You will see things that are even more detestable than this."

¹⁶He then brought me into the inner court of the house of the Lord, and there at the entrance to the temple, between the portico and the altar, were about twenty-five men. With their backs toward the temple of the Lord and their faces toward the east, they were bowing down to the sun in the east.

¹⁷He said to me, "Have you seen this, son of man? Is it a trivial matter for the house of Judah to do the detestable things they are doing here? Must they also fill the land with violence and continually provoke me to anger? Look at them putting the branch to their nose! ¹⁸Therefore I will deal with them in anger; I will not look on them with pity or spare them. Although they shout in my ears, I will not listen to them."

^a2 Or *saw a fiery figure*

Idolaters Killed

9 Then I heard him call out in a loud voice, "Bring the guards of the city here, each with a weapon in his hand." ²And I saw six men coming from the direction of the upper gate, which faces north, each with a deadly weapon in his hand. With them was a man clothed in linen who had a writing kit at his side. They came in and stood beside the bronze altar.

³Now the glory of the God of Israel went up from above the cherubim, where it had been, and moved to the threshold of the temple. Then the LORD called to the man clothed in linen who had the writing kit at his side ⁴and said to him, "Go throughout the city of Jerusalem and put a mark on the foreheads of those who grieve and lament over all the detestable things that are done in it."

⁵As I listened, he said to the others, "Follow him through the city and kill, without showing pity or compassion. ⁶Slaughter old men, young men and maidens, women and children, but do not touch anyone who has the mark. Begin at my sanctuary." So they began with the elders who were in front of the temple.

⁷Then he said to them, "Defile the temple and fill the courts with the slain. Go!" So they went out and began killing throughout the city. ⁸While they were killing and I was left alone, I fell facedown, crying out, "Ah, Sovereign LORD! Are you going to destroy the entire remnant of Israel in this outpouring of your wrath on Jerusalem?"

⁹He answered me, "The sin of the house of Israel and Judah is exceedingly great; the land is full of bloodshed and the city is full of injustice. They say, 'The LORD has forsaken the land; the LORD does not see.' ¹⁰So I will not look on them with pity or spare them, but I will bring down on their own heads what they have done."

¹¹Then the man in linen with the writing kit at his side brought back word, saying, "I have done as you commanded."

The Glory Departs From the Temple

10 I looked, and I saw the likeness of a throne of sapphire[a] above the expanse that was over the heads of the cherubim. ²The LORD said to the man clothed in linen, "Go in among the wheels beneath the cherubim. Fill your hands with burning coals from among the cherubim and scatter them over the city." And as I watched, he went in.

³Now the cherubim were standing on the south side of the temple when the man went in, and a cloud filled the inner court. ⁴Then the glory of the LORD rose from above the cherubim and moved to the threshold of the temple. The cloud filled the temple, and the court was full of the radiance of the glory of the LORD. ⁵The sound of the wings of the cherubim could be heard as far away as the outer court, like the voice of God Almighty[b] when he speaks.

⁶When the LORD commanded the man in linen, "Take fire from among the wheels, from among the cherubim," the man went in and stood beside a wheel. ⁷Then one of the cherubim reached out his hand to the fire that was among them. He took up some of it and put it into the hands of the man in linen, who took it and went out. ⁸(Under the wings of the cherubim could be seen what looked like the hands of a man.)

⁹I looked, and I saw beside the cherubim four wheels, one beside each of the cherubim; the wheels sparkled like chrysolite. ¹⁰As for their appearance, the four of them looked alike; each was like a wheel intersecting a wheel. ¹¹As they moved, they would go in any one of the four directions the cherubim faced; the wheels did not turn about[c] as the cherubim went. The cherubim went in whatever direction the head faced, without

---

a1 Or *lapis lazuli*   *b5* Hebrew *El-Shaddai*   *c11* Or *aside*

turning as they went. ¹²Their entire bodies, including their backs, their hands and their wings, were completely full of eyes, as were their four wheels. ¹³I heard the wheels being called "the whirling wheels." ¹⁴Each of the cherubim had four faces: One face was that of a cherub, the second the face of a man, the third the face of a lion, and the fourth the face of an eagle.

¹⁵Then the cherubim rose upward. These were the living creatures I had seen by the Kebar River. ¹⁶When the cherubim moved, the wheels beside them moved; and when the cherubim spread their wings to rise from the ground, the wheels did not leave their side. ¹⁷When the cherubim stood still, they also stood still; and when the cherubim rose, they rose with them, because the spirit of the living creatures was in them.

¹⁸Then the glory of the LORD departed from over the threshold of the temple and stopped above the cherubim. ¹⁹While I watched, the cherubim spread their wings and rose from the ground, and as they went, the wheels went with them. They stopped at the entrance to the east gate of the LORD's house, and the glory of the God of Israel was above them.

²⁰These were the living creatures I had seen beneath the God of Israel by the Kebar River, and I realized that they were cherubim. ²¹Each had four faces and four wings, and under their wings was what looked like the hands of a man. ²²Their faces had the same appearance as those I had seen by the Kebar River. Each one went straight ahead.

Judgment on Israel's Leaders

11 Then the Spirit lifted me up and brought me to the gate of the house of the LORD that faces east. There at the entrance to the gate were twenty-five men, and I saw among them Jaazaniah son of Azzur and Pelatiah son of Benaiah, leaders of the people. ²The LORD said to me, "Son of man, these are the men who are plotting evil and giving wicked advice in this city. ³They say, 'Will it not soon be time to build houses?[a] This city is a cooking pot, and we are the meat.' ⁴Therefore prophesy against them; prophesy, son of man."

⁵Then the Spirit of the LORD came upon me, and he told me to say: "This is what the LORD says: That is what you are saying, O house of Israel, but I know what is going through your mind. ⁶You have killed many people in this city and filled its streets with the dead.

⁷"Therefore this is what the Sovereign LORD says: The bodies you have thrown there are the meat and this city is the pot, but I will drive you out of it. ⁸You fear the sword, and the sword is what I will bring against you, declares the Sovereign LORD. ⁹I will drive you out of the city and hand you over to foreigners and inflict punishment on you. ¹⁰You will fall by the sword, and I will execute judgment on you at the borders of Israel. Then you will know that I am the LORD. ¹¹This city will not be a pot for you, nor will you be the meat in it; I will execute judgment on you at the borders of Israel. ¹²And you will know that I am the LORD, for you have not followed my decrees or kept my laws but have conformed to the standards of the nations around you."

¹³Now as I was prophesying, Pelatiah son of Benaiah died. Then I fell facedown and cried out in a loud voice, "Ah, Sovereign LORD! Will you completely destroy the remnant of Israel?"

¹⁴The word of the LORD came to me: ¹⁵"Son of man, your brothers—your brothers who are your blood relatives[b] and the whole house of Israel—are those of whom the people of Jerusalem have said, 'They are[c] far away from the LORD; this land was given to us as our possession.'

---

[a]3 Or *This is not the time to build houses.*   [b]15 Or *are in exile with you* (see Septuagint and Syriac)   [c]15 Or *those to whom the people of Jerusalem have said, 'Stay*

Promised Return of Israel

¹⁶"Therefore say: 'This is what the Sovereign LORD says: Although I sent them far away among the nations and scattered them among the countries, yet for a little while I have been a sanctuary for them in the countries where they have gone.'

¹⁷"Therefore say: 'This is what the Sovereign LORD says: I will gather you from the nations and bring you back from the countries where you have been scattered, and I will give you back the land of Israel again.'

¹⁸"They will return to it and remove all its vile images and detestable idols. ¹⁹I will give them an undivided heart and put a new spirit in them; I will remove from them their heart of stone and give them a heart of flesh. ²⁰Then they will follow my decrees and be careful to keep my laws. They will be my people, and I will be their God. ²¹But as for those whose hearts are devoted to their vile images and detestable idols, I will bring down on their own heads what they have done, declares the Sovereign LORD."

²²Then the cherubim, with the wheels beside them, spread their wings, and the glory of the God of Israel was above them. ²³The glory of the LORD went up from within the city and stopped above the mountain east of it. ²⁴The Spirit lifted me up and brought me to the exiles in Babylonia*a* in the vision given by the Spirit of God.

Then the vision I had seen went up from me, ²⁵and I told the exiles everything the LORD had shown me.

The Exile Symbolized

12 The word of the LORD came to me: ²"Son of man, you are living among a rebellious people. They have eyes to see but do not see and ears to hear but do not hear, for they are a rebellious people.

³"Therefore, son of man, pack your belongings for exile and in the day-time, as they watch, set out and go from where you are to another place. Perhaps they will understand, though they are a rebellious house. ⁴During the daytime, while they watch, bring out your belongings packed for exile. Then in the evening, while they are watching, go out like those who go into exile. ⁵While they watch, dig through the wall and take your belongings out through it. ⁶Put them on your shoulder as they are watching and carry them out at dusk. Cover your face so that you cannot see the land, for I have made you a sign to the house of Israel."

⁷So I did as I was commanded. During the day I brought out my things packed for exile. Then in the evening I dug through the wall with my hands. I took my belongings out at dusk, carrying them on my shoulders while they watched.

⁸In the morning the word of the LORD came to me: ⁹"Son of man, did not that rebellious house of Israel ask you, 'What are you doing?'

¹⁰"Say to them, 'This is what the Sovereign LORD says: This oracle concerns the prince in Jerusalem and the whole house of Israel who are there.' ¹¹Say to them, 'I am a sign to you.'

"As I have done, so it will be done to them. They will go into exile as captives.

¹²"The prince among them will put his things on his shoulder at dusk and leave, and a hole will be dug in the wall for him to go through. He will cover his face so that he cannot see the land. ¹³I will spread my net for him, and he will be caught in my snare; I will bring him to Babylonia, the land of the Chaldeans, but he will not see it, and there he will die. ¹⁴I will scatter to the winds all those around him—his staff and all his troops—and I will pursue them with drawn sword.

¹⁵"They will know that I am the LORD, when I disperse them among the nations and scatter them through the countries. ¹⁶But I will spare a few

of them from the sword, famine and plague, so that in the nations where they go they may acknowledge all their detestable practices. Then they will know that I am the LORD."

17 The word of the LORD came to me: 18 "Son of man, tremble as you eat your food, and shudder in fear as you drink your water. 19 Say to the people of the land: 'This is what the Sovereign LORD says about those living in Jerusalem and in the land of Israel: They will eat their food in anxiety and drink their water in despair, for their

FRIDAY

VERSE:	AUTHOR:	PASSAGE:
Ezekiel 11:19	Stuart Briscoe	Ezekiel 11:16–21

New Hearts for Old

The Lord went on to say what all the world needs to hear: "The problem with my people, Ezekiel, is a heart problem. They need new, warm and tender hearts toward me in the place of those hard, cold hearts that beat in their puffed-out chests and drive them on in their senseless independence and rebellion. I will give new hearts to those who will let me. I will change their inner attitudes and mold their desires to my desires. Their interests and their aspirations will be revolutionized and I will restore my people to a life of service and worship through an inner revolution of loving obedience" . . .

The principle is unchanging and indeed unchangeable. Sin brings judgment; independence bears the fruit of disintegration. Rebellion turns people from God and God from people. No external antidote is available to remedy the ills of any individual or society that knows only outright rebellion and independence from and hostility to the eternal God.

A new heart is needed and God is in the heart transplant business. He specializes in taking the cold, unregenerate heart and infusing into it the life of his Spirit, the reality of his love and the warmth of his presence.

ADDITIONAL SCRIPTURE READINGS
Ezekiel 37:1–14; Romans 8:1–17

Go to page 1054 for your next devotional reading.

land will be stripped of everything in it because of the violence of all who live there. ²⁰The inhabited towns will be laid waste and the land will be desolate. Then you will know that I am the Lord.' "

²¹The word of the Lord came to me: ²²"Son of man, what is this proverb you have in the land of Israel: 'The days go by and every vision comes to nothing'? ²³Say to them, 'This is what the Sovereign Lord says: I am going to put an end to this proverb, and they will no longer quote it in Israel.' Say to them, 'The days are near when every vision will be fulfilled. ²⁴For there will be no more false visions or flattering divinations among the people of Israel. ²⁵But I the Lord will speak what I will, and it shall be fulfilled without delay. For in your days, you rebellious house, I will fulfill whatever I say, declares the Sovereign Lord.' "

²⁶The word of the Lord came to me: ²⁷"Son of man, the house of Israel is saying, 'The vision he sees is for many years from now, and he prophesies about the distant future.'

²⁸"Therefore say to them, 'This is what the Sovereign Lord says: None of my words will be delayed any longer; whatever I say will be fulfilled, declares the Sovereign Lord.' "

False Prophets Condemned

13 The word of the Lord came to me: ²"Son of man, prophesy against the prophets of Israel who are now prophesying. Say to those who prophesy out of their own imagination: 'Hear the word of the Lord! ³This is what the Sovereign Lord says: Woe to the foolish*ᵃ* prophets who follow their own spirit and have seen nothing! ⁴Your prophets, O Israel, are like jackals among ruins. ⁵You have not gone up to the breaks in the wall to repair it for the house of Israel so that it will stand firm in the battle on the day of the Lord. ⁶Their visions are false and their divinations a lie. They say, "The Lord declares," when the Lord has not sent them; yet they expect their words to be fulfilled. ⁷Have you not seen false visions and uttered lying divinations when you say, "The Lord declares," though I have not spoken?

⁸" 'Therefore this is what the Sovereign Lord says: Because of your false words and lying visions, I am against you, declares the Sovereign Lord. ⁹My hand will be against the prophets who see false visions and utter lying divinations. They will not belong to the council of my people or be listed in the records of the house of Israel, nor will they enter the land of Israel. Then you will know that I am the Sovereign Lord.

¹⁰" 'Because they lead my people astray, saying, "Peace," when there is no peace, and because, when a flimsy wall is built, they cover it with whitewash, ¹¹therefore tell those who cover it with whitewash that it is going to fall. Rain will come in torrents, and I will send hailstones hurtling down, and violent winds will burst forth. ¹²When the wall collapses, will people not ask you, "Where is the whitewash you covered it with?"

¹³" 'Therefore this is what the Sovereign Lord says: In my wrath I will unleash a violent wind, and in my anger hailstones and torrents of rain will fall with destructive fury. ¹⁴I will tear down the wall you have covered with whitewash and will level it to the ground so that its foundation will be laid bare. When it*ᵇ* falls, you will be destroyed in it; and you will know that I am the Lord. ¹⁵So I will spend my wrath against the wall and against those who covered it with whitewash. I will say to you, "The wall is gone and so are those who whitewashed it, ¹⁶those prophets of Israel who prophesied to Jerusalem and saw visions of peace for her when there was no peace, declares the Sovereign Lord." '

¹⁷"Now, son of man, set your face against the daughters of your people who prophesy out of their own imagination. Prophesy against them ¹⁸and

---

ᵃ3 Or *wicked*   *ᵇ14* Or *the city*

say, 'This is what the Sovereign LORD says: Woe to the women who sew magic charms on all their wrists and make veils of various lengths for their heads in order to ensnare people. Will you ensnare the lives of my people but preserve your own? ¹⁹You have profaned me among my people for a few handfuls of barley and scraps of bread. By lying to my people, who listen to lies, you have killed those who should not have died and have spared those who should not live.

²⁰" 'Therefore this is what the Sovereign LORD says: I am against your magic charms with which you ensnare people like birds and I will tear them from your arms; I will set free the people that you ensnare like birds. ²¹I will tear off your veils and save my people from your hands, and they will no longer fall prey to your power. Then you will know that I am the LORD. ²²Because you disheartened the righteous with your lies, when I had brought them no grief, and because you encouraged the wicked not to turn from their evil ways and so save their lives, ²³therefore you will no longer see false visions or practice divination. I will save my people from your hands. And then you will know that I am the LORD.' "

Idolaters Condemned

14 Some of the elders of Israel came to me and sat down in front of me. ²Then the word of the LORD came to me: ³"Son of man, these men have set up idols in their hearts and put wicked stumbling blocks before their faces. Should I let them inquire of me at all? ⁴Therefore speak to them and tell them, 'This is what the Sovereign LORD says: When any Israelite sets up idols in his heart and puts a wicked stumbling block before his face and then goes to a prophet, I the LORD will answer him myself in keeping with his great idolatry. ⁵I will do this to recapture the hearts of the people of Israel, who have all deserted me for their idols.'

⁶"Therefore say to the house of Israel, 'This is what the Sovereign LORD says: Repent! Turn from your idols and renounce all your detestable practices!

⁷" 'When any Israelite or any alien living in Israel separates himself from me and sets up idols in his heart and puts a wicked stumbling block before his face and then goes to a prophet to inquire of me, I the LORD will answer him myself. ⁸I will set my face against that man and make him an example and a byword. I will cut him off from my people. Then you will know that I am the LORD.

⁹" 'And if the prophet is enticed to utter a prophecy, I the LORD have enticed that prophet, and I will stretch out my hand against him and destroy him from among my people Israel. ¹⁰They will bear their guilt—the prophet will be as guilty as the one who consults him. ¹¹Then the people of Israel will no longer stray from me, nor will they defile themselves anymore with all their sins. They will be my people, and I will be their God, declares the Sovereign LORD.' "

Judgment Inescapable

¹²The word of the LORD came to me: ¹³"Son of man, if a country sins against me by being unfaithful and I stretch out my hand against it to cut off its food supply and send famine upon it and kill its men and their animals, ¹⁴even if these three men—Noah, Daniel[a] and Job—were in it, they could save only themselves by their righteousness, declares the Sovereign LORD.

¹⁵"Or if I send wild beasts through that country and they leave it childless and it becomes desolate so that no one can pass through it because of the beasts, ¹⁶as surely as I live, declares the Sovereign LORD, even if these three men were in it, they could not save their own sons or daughters.

---

[a]14 Or *Danel*; the Hebrew spelling may suggest a person other than the prophet Daniel; also in verse 20.

They alone would be saved, but the land would be desolate.

¹⁷"Or if I bring a sword against that country and say, 'Let the sword pass throughout the land,' and I kill its men and their animals, ¹⁸as surely as I live, declares the Sovereign LORD, even if these three men were in it, they could not save their own sons or daughters. They alone would be saved.

¹⁹"Or if I send a plague into that land and pour out my wrath upon it through bloodshed, killing its men and their animals, ²⁰as surely as I live, declares the Sovereign LORD, even if Noah, Daniel and Job were in it, they could save neither son nor daughter. They would save only themselves by their righteousness.

²¹"For this is what the Sovereign LORD says: How much worse will it be when I send against Jerusalem my four dreadful judgments—sword and famine and wild beasts and plague—to kill its men and their animals! ²²Yet there will be some survivors—sons and daughters who will be brought out of it. They will come to you, and when you see their conduct and their actions, you will be consoled regarding the disaster I have brought upon Jerusalem—every disaster I have brought upon it. ²³You will be consoled when you see their conduct and their actions, for you will know that I have done nothing in it without cause, declares the Sovereign LORD."

Jerusalem, A Useless Vine

15 The word of the LORD came to me: ²"Son of man, how is the wood of a vine better than that of a branch on any of the trees in the forest? ³Is wood ever taken from it to make anything useful? Do they make pegs from it to hang things on? ⁴And after it is thrown on the fire as fuel and the fire burns both ends and chars the middle, is it then useful for anything? ⁵If it was not useful for anything when it was whole, how

much less can it be made into something useful when the fire has burned it and it is charred?

⁶"Therefore this is what the Sovereign LORD says: As I have given the wood of the vine among the trees of the forest as fuel for the fire, so will I treat the people living in Jerusalem. ⁷I will set my face against them. Although they have come out of the fire, the fire will yet consume them. And when I set my face against them, you will know that I am the LORD. ⁸I will make the land desolate because they have been unfaithful, declares the Sovereign LORD."

An Allegory of Unfaithful Jerusalem

16 The word of the LORD came to me: ²"Son of man, confront Jerusalem with her detestable practices ³and say, 'This is what the Sovereign LORD says to Jerusalem: Your ancestry and birth were in the land of the Canaanites; your father was an Amorite and your mother a Hittite. ⁴On the day you were born your cord was not cut, nor were you washed with water to make you clean, nor were you rubbed with salt or wrapped in cloths. ⁵No one looked on you with pity or had compassion enough to do any of these things for you. Rather, you were thrown out into the open field, for on the day you were born you were despised.

⁶" 'Then I passed by and saw you kicking about in your blood, and as you lay there in your blood I said to you, "Live!"^a ⁷I made you grow like a plant of the field. You grew up and developed and became the most beautiful of jewels.^b Your breasts were formed and your hair grew, you who were naked and bare.

⁸" 'Later I passed by, and when I looked at you and saw that you were old enough for love, I spread the corner of my garment over you and covered your nakedness. I gave you my solemn oath and entered into a cov-

---

^a6 A few Hebrew manuscripts, Septuagint and Syriac; most Hebrew manuscripts *"Live!" And as you lay there in your blood I said to you, "Live!"*   ^b7 Or *became mature*

enant with you, declares the Sovereign LORD, and you became mine.

9" 'I bathed[a] you with water and washed the blood from you and put ointments on you. [10]I clothed you with an embroidered dress and put leather sandals on you. I dressed you in fine linen and covered you with costly garments. [11]I adorned you with jewelry: I put bracelets on your arms and a necklace around your neck, [12]and I put a ring on your nose, earrings on your ears and a beautiful crown on your head. [13]So you were adorned with gold and silver; your clothes were of fine linen and costly fabric and embroidered cloth. Your food was fine flour, honey and olive oil. You became very beautiful and rose to be a queen. [14]And your fame spread among the nations on account of your beauty, because the splendor I had given you made your beauty perfect, declares the Sovereign LORD.

[15]" 'But you trusted in your beauty and used your fame to become a prostitute. You lavished your favors on anyone who passed by and your beauty became his.[b] [16]You took some of your garments to make gaudy high places, where you carried on your prostitution. Such things should not happen, nor should they ever occur. [17]You also took the fine jewelry I gave you, the jewelry made of my gold and silver, and you made for yourself male idols and engaged in prostitution with them. [18]And you took your embroidered clothes to put on them, and you offered my oil and incense before them. [19]Also the food I provided for you—the fine flour, olive oil and honey I gave you to eat—you offered as fragrant incense before them. That is what happened, declares the Sovereign LORD.

[20]" 'And you took your sons and daughters whom you bore to me and sacrificed them as food to the idols. Was your prostitution not enough? [21]You slaughtered my children and sacrificed them[c] to the idols. [22]In all your detestable practices and your prostitution you did not remember the days of your youth, when you were naked and bare, kicking about in your blood.

[23]" 'Woe! Woe to you, declares the Sovereign LORD. In addition to all your other wickedness, [24]you built a mound for yourself and made a lofty shrine in every public square. [25]At the head of every street you built your lofty shrines and degraded your beauty, offering your body with increasing promiscuity to anyone who passed by. [26]You engaged in prostitution with the Egyptians, your lustful neighbors, and provoked me to anger with your increasing promiscuity. [27]So I stretched out my hand against you and reduced your territory; I gave you over to the greed of your enemies, the daughters of the Philistines, who were shocked by your lewd conduct. [28]You engaged in prostitution with the Assyrians too, because you were insatiable; and even after that, you still were not satisfied. [29]Then you increased your promiscuity to include Babylonia,[d] a land of merchants, but even with this you were not satisfied.

[30]" 'How weak-willed you are, declares the Sovereign LORD, when you do all these things, acting like a brazen prostitute! [31]When you built your mounds at the head of every street and made your lofty shrines in every public square, you were unlike a prostitute, because you scorned payment.

[32]" 'You adulterous wife! You prefer strangers to your own husband! [33]Every prostitute receives a fee, but you give gifts to all your lovers, bribing them to come to you from everywhere for your illicit favors. [34]So in your prostitution you are the opposite of others; no one runs after you for your favors. You are the very oppo-

---

[a]9 Or I had bathed   [b]15 Most Hebrew manuscripts; one Hebrew manuscript (see some Septuagint manuscripts) by. Such a thing should not happen   [c]21 Or and made them pass through ˻the fire˼   [d]29 Or Chaldea

site, for you give payment and none is given to you.

³⁵" 'Therefore, you prostitute, hear the word of the LORD! ³⁶This is what the Sovereign LORD says: Because you poured out your wealth*ᵃ* and exposed your nakedness in your promiscuity with your lovers, and because of all your detestable idols, and because you gave them your children's blood, ³⁷therefore I am going to gather all your lovers, with whom you found pleasure, those you loved as well as those you hated. I will gather them against you from all around and will strip you in front of them, and they will see all your nakedness. ³⁸I will sentence you to the punishment of women who commit adultery and who shed blood; I will bring upon you the blood vengeance of my wrath and jealous anger. ³⁹Then I will hand you over to your lovers, and they will tear down your mounds and destroy your lofty shrines. They will strip you of your clothes and take your fine jewelry and leave you naked and bare. ⁴⁰They will bring a mob against you, who will stone you and hack you to pieces with their swords. ⁴¹They will burn down your houses and inflict punishment on you in the sight of many women. I will put a stop to your prostitution, and you will no longer pay your lovers. ⁴²Then my wrath against you will subside and my jealous anger will turn away from you; I will be calm and no longer angry.

⁴³" 'Because you did not remember the days of your youth but enraged me with all these things, I will surely bring down on your head what you have done, declares the Sovereign LORD. Did you not add lewdness to all your other detestable practices?

⁴⁴" 'Everyone who quotes proverbs will quote this proverb about you: "Like mother, like daughter." ⁴⁵You are a true daughter of your mother, who despised her husband and her children; and you are a true sister of your sisters, who despised their husbands and their children. Your mother was a Hittite and your father an Amorite. ⁴⁶Your older sister was Samaria, who lived to the north of you with her daughters; and your younger sister, who lived to the south of you with her daughters, was Sodom. ⁴⁷You not only walked in their ways and copied their detestable practices, but in all your ways you soon became more depraved than they. ⁴⁸As surely as I live, declares the Sovereign LORD, your sister Sodom and her daughters never did what you and your daughters have done.

⁴⁹" 'Now this was the sin of your sister Sodom: She and her daughters were arrogant, overfed and unconcerned; they did not help the poor and needy. ⁵⁰They were haughty and did detestable things before me. Therefore I did away with them as you have seen. ⁵¹Samaria did not commit half the sins you did. You have done more detestable things than they, and have made your sisters seem righteous by all these things you have done. ⁵²Bear your disgrace, for you have furnished some justification for your sisters. Because your sins were more vile than theirs, they appear more righteous than you. So then, be ashamed and bear your disgrace, for you have made your sisters appear righteous.

⁵³" 'However, I will restore the fortunes of Sodom and her daughters and of Samaria and her daughters, and your fortunes along with them, ⁵⁴so that you may bear your disgrace and be ashamed of all you have done in giving them comfort. ⁵⁵And your sisters, Sodom with her daughters and Samaria with her daughters, will return to what they were before; and you and your daughters will return to what you were before. ⁵⁶You would not even mention your sister Sodom in the day of your pride, ⁵⁷before your wickedness was uncovered. Even so, you are now scorned by the daugh-

ᵃ36 Or lust

ters of Edom[a] and all her neighbors and the daughters of the Philistines—all those around you who despise you. [58]You will bear the consequences of your lewdness and your detestable practices, declares the LORD.

[59]" 'This is what the Sovereign LORD says: I will deal with you as you deserve, because you have despised my oath by breaking the covenant. [60]Yet I will remember the covenant I made with you in the days of your youth, and I will establish an everlasting covenant with you. [61]Then you will remember your ways and be ashamed when you receive your sisters, both those who are older than you and those who are younger. I will give them to you as daughters, but not on the basis of my covenant with you. [62]So I will establish my covenant with you, and you will know that I am the LORD. [63]Then, when I make atonement for you for all you have done, you will remember and be ashamed and never again open your mouth because of your humiliation, declares the Sovereign LORD.' "

Two Eagles and a Vine

17 The word of the LORD came to me: [2]"Son of man, set forth an allegory and tell the house of Israel a parable. [3]Say to them, 'This is what the Sovereign LORD says: A great eagle with powerful wings, long feathers and full plumage of varied colors came to Lebanon. Taking hold of the top of a cedar, [4]he broke off its topmost shoot and carried it away to a land of merchants, where he planted it in a city of traders.

[5]" 'He took some of the seed of your land and put it in fertile soil. He planted it like a willow by abundant water, [6]and it sprouted and became a low, spreading vine. Its branches turned toward him, but its roots remained under it. So it became a vine and produced branches and put out leafy boughs.

[7]" 'But there was another great eagle with powerful wings and full plumage. The vine now sent out its roots toward him from the plot where it was planted and stretched out its branches to him for water. [8]It had been planted in good soil by abundant water so that it would produce branches, bear fruit and become a splendid vine.'

[9]"Say to them, 'This is what the Sovereign LORD says: Will it thrive? Will it not be uprooted and stripped of its fruit so that it withers? All its new growth will wither. It will not take a strong arm or many people to pull it up by the roots. [10]Even if it is transplanted, will it thrive? Will it not wither completely when the east wind strikes it—wither away in the plot where it grew?' "

[11]Then the word of the LORD came to me: [12]"Say to this rebellious house, 'Do you not know what these things mean?' Say to them: 'The king of Babylon went to Jerusalem and carried off her king and her nobles, bringing them back with him to Babylon. [13]Then he took a member of the royal family and made a treaty with him, putting him under oath. He also carried away the leading men of the land, [14]so that the kingdom would be brought low, unable to rise again, surviving only by keeping his treaty. [15]But the king rebelled against him by sending his envoys to Egypt to get horses and a large army. Will he succeed? Will he who does such things escape? Will he break the treaty and yet escape?

[16]" 'As surely as I live, declares the Sovereign LORD, he shall die in Babylon, in the land of the king who put him on the throne, whose oath he despised and whose treaty he broke. [17]Pharaoh with his mighty army and great horde will be of no help to him in war, when ramps are built and siege works erected to destroy many lives. [18]He despised the oath by breaking the covenant. Because he had given his hand in pledge and yet

---

[a]57 Many Hebrew manuscripts and Syriac; most Hebrew manuscripts, Septuagint and Vulgate *Aram*

did all these things, he shall not escape.

¹⁹" 'Therefore this is what the Sovereign LORD says: As surely as I live, I will bring down on his head my oath that he despised and my covenant that he broke. ²⁰I will spread my net for him, and he will be caught in my snare. I will bring him to Babylon and execute judgment upon him there because he was unfaithful to me. ²¹All his fleeing troops will fall by the sword, and the survivors will be scattered to the winds. Then you will know that I the LORD have spoken.

²²" 'This is what the Sovereign LORD says: I myself will take a shoot from the very top of a cedar and plant it; I will break off a tender sprig from its topmost shoots and plant it on a high and lofty mountain. ²³On the mountain heights of Israel I will plant it; it will produce branches and bear fruit and become a splendid cedar. Birds of every kind will nest in it; they will find shelter in the shade of its branches. ²⁴All the trees of the field will know that I the LORD bring down the tall tree and make the low tree grow tall. I dry up the green tree and make the dry tree flourish.

" 'I the LORD have spoken, and I will do it.' "

The Soul Who Sins Will Die

18 The word of the LORD came to me: ²"What do you people mean by quoting this proverb about the land of Israel:

" 'The fathers eat sour grapes,
    and the children's teeth are set
        on edge'?

³"As surely as I live, declares the Sovereign LORD, you will no longer quote this proverb in Israel. ⁴For every living soul belongs to me, the father as well as the son—both alike belong to me. The soul who sins is the one who will die.

⁵"Suppose there is a righteous man who does what is just and right.

⁶He does not eat at the mountain shrines
    or look to the idols of the house
        of Israel.
He does not defile his neighbor's
    wife
    or lie with a woman during her
        period.
⁷He does not oppress anyone,
    but returns what he took in
        pledge for a loan.
He does not commit robbery
    but gives his food to the hungry
    and provides clothing for the
        naked.
⁸He does not lend at usury
    or take excessive interest.ᵃ
He withholds his hand from doing
    wrong
    and judges fairly between man
        and man.
⁹He follows my decrees
    and faithfully keeps my laws.
That man is righteous;
    he will surely live,
                declares the Sovereign
                    LORD.

¹⁰"Suppose he has a violent son, who sheds blood or does any of these other thingsᵇ ¹¹(though the father has done none of them):

"He eats at the mountain shrines.
He defiles his neighbor's wife.
¹²He oppresses the poor and needy.
He commits robbery.
He does not return what he took
        in pledge.
He looks to the idols.
He does detestable things.
¹³He lends at usury and takes
        excessive interest.

Will such a man live? He will not! Because he has done all these detestable things, he will surely be put to death and his blood will be on his own head.

¹⁴"But suppose this son has a son who sees all the sins his father commits, and though he sees them, he does not do such things:

ᵃ8 Or take interest; similarly in verses 13 and 17   ᵇ10 Or things to a brother

¹⁵"He does not eat at the mountain
      shrines
    or look to the idols of the house
      of Israel.
  He does not defile his neighbor's
      wife.
¹⁶He does not oppress anyone
    or require a pledge for a loan.
  He does not commit robbery
    but gives his food to the hungry
    and provides clothing for the
      naked.
¹⁷He withholds his hand from sin^a
    and takes no usury or excessive
      interest.
  He keeps my laws and follows my
      decrees.

He will not die for his father's sin; he
will surely live. ¹⁸But his father will
die for his own sin, because he practiced extortion, robbed his brother
and did what was wrong among his
people.

¹⁹"Yet you ask, 'Why does the son
not share the guilt of his father?' Since
the son has done what is just and
right and has been careful to keep all
my decrees, he will surely live. ²⁰The
soul who sins is the one who will die.
The son will not share the guilt of the
father, nor will the father share the
guilt of the son. The righteousness of
the righteous man will be credited to
him, and the wickedness of the wicked will be charged against him.

²¹"But if a wicked man turns away
from all the sins he has committed
and keeps all my decrees and does
what is just and right, he will surely
live; he will not die. ²²None of the offenses he has committed will be remembered against him. Because of
the righteous things he has done, he
will live. ²³Do I take any pleasure in
the death of the wicked? declares the
Sovereign LORD. Rather, am I not
pleased when they turn from their
ways and live?

²⁴"But if a righteous man turns
from his righteousness and commits
sin and does the same detestable
things the wicked man does, will he

live? None of the righteous things he
has done will be remembered. Because of the unfaithfulness he is
guilty of and because of the sins he
has committed, he will die.

²⁵"Yet you say, 'The way of the
Lord is not just.' Hear, O house of Israel: Is my way unjust? Is it not your
ways that are unjust? ²⁶If a righteous
man turns from his righteousness and
commits sin, he will die for it; because
of the sin he has committed he will
die. ²⁷But if a wicked man turns away
from the wickedness he has commit-
ted and does what is just and right, he
will save his life. ²⁸Because he considers all the offenses he has committed
and turns away from them, he will
surely live; he will not die. ²⁹Yet the
house of Israel says, 'The way of the
Lord is not just.' Are my ways unjust,
O house of Israel? Is it not your ways
that are unjust?

³⁰"Therefore, O house of Israel, I
will judge you, each one according to
his ways, declares the Sovereign LORD.
Repent! Turn away from all your offenses; then sin will not be your
downfall. ³¹Rid yourselves of all the
offenses you have committed, and get
a new heart and a new spirit. Why
will you die, O house of Israel? ³²For I
take no pleasure in the death of any-
one, declares the Sovereign LORD. Repent and live!

A Lament for Israel's Princes

19 "Take up a lament concerning
      the princes of Israel ²and say:

  " 'What a lioness was your mother
      among the lions!
  She lay down among the young
      lions
    and reared her cubs.
³She brought up one of her cubs,
    and he became a strong lion.
  He learned to tear the prey
    and he devoured men.
⁴The nations heard about him,
    and he was trapped in their pit.
  They led him with hooks
    to the land of Egypt.

^a17 Septuagint (see also verse 8); Hebrew *from the poor*

⁵" 'When she saw her hope
      unfulfilled,
   her expectation gone,
she took another of her cubs
   and made him a strong lion.
⁶He prowled among the lions,
   for he was now a strong lion.
He learned to tear the prey
   and he devoured men.
⁷He broke down^a their
      strongholds
   and devastated their towns.
The land and all who were in it
   were terrified by his roaring.
⁸Then the nations came against
      him,
   those from regions round about.
They spread their net for him,
   and he was trapped in their pit.
⁹With hooks they pulled him into a
      cage
   and brought him to the king of
      Babylon.
They put him in prison,
   so his roar was heard no longer
   on the mountains of Israel.

¹⁰" 'Your mother was like a vine in
      your vineyard^b
   planted by the water;
it was fruitful and full of branches
   because of abundant water.
¹¹Its branches were strong,
   fit for a ruler's scepter.
It towered high
   above the thick foliage,
conspicuous for its height
   and for its many branches.
¹²But it was uprooted in fury
   and thrown to the ground.
The east wind made it shrivel,
   it was stripped of its fruit;
its strong branches withered
   and fire consumed them.
¹³Now it is planted in the desert,
   in a dry and thirsty land.
¹⁴Fire spread from one of its main^c
      branches
   and consumed its fruit.
No strong branch is left on it
   fit for a ruler's scepter.'

This is a lament and is to be used as a lament."

Rebellious Israel

20 In the seventh year, in the fifth month on the tenth day, some of the elders of Israel came to inquire of the LORD, and they sat down in front of me.

²Then the word of the LORD came to me: ³"Son of man, speak to the elders of Israel and say to them, 'This is what the Sovereign LORD says: Have you come to inquire of me? As surely as I live, I will not let you inquire of me, declares the Sovereign LORD.'

⁴"Will you judge them? Will you judge them, son of man? Then confront them with the detestable practices of their fathers ⁵and say to them: 'This is what the Sovereign LORD says: On the day I chose Israel, I swore with uplifted hand to the descendants of the house of Jacob and revealed myself to them in Egypt. With uplifted hand I said to them, "I am the LORD your God." ⁶On that day I swore to them that I would bring them out of Egypt into a land I had searched out for them, a land flowing with milk and honey, the most beautiful of all lands. ⁷And I said to them, "Each of you, get rid of the vile images you have set your eyes on, and do not defile yourselves with the idols of Egypt. I am the LORD your God."

⁸" 'But they rebelled against me and would not listen to me; they did not get rid of the vile images they had set their eyes on, nor did they forsake the idols of Egypt. So I said I would pour out my wrath on them and spend my anger against them in Egypt. ⁹But for the sake of my name I did what would keep it from being profaned in the eyes of the nations they lived among and in whose sight I had revealed myself to the Israelites by bringing them out of Egypt. ¹⁰Therefore I led them out of Egypt and brought them into the desert. ¹¹I gave them my decrees and made

---

^a7 Targum (see Septuagint); Hebrew *He knew* manuscripts *your blood*   ^c14 Or *from under its*   ^b10 Two Hebrew manuscripts; most Hebrew

known to them my laws, for the man who obeys them will live by them. ¹²Also I gave them my Sabbaths as a sign between us, so they would know that I the Lᴏʀᴅ made them holy.

¹³" 'Yet the people of Israel rebelled against me in the desert. They did not follow my decrees but rejected my laws—although the man who obeys them will live by them—and they utterly desecrated my Sabbaths. So I said I would pour out my wrath on them and destroy them in the desert. ¹⁴But for the sake of my name I did what would keep it from being profaned in the eyes of the nations in whose sight I had brought them out. ¹⁵Also with uplifted hand I swore to them in the desert that I would not bring them into the land I had given them—a land flowing with milk and honey, most beautiful of all lands— ¹⁶because they rejected my laws and did not follow my decrees and desecrated my Sabbaths. For their hearts were devoted to their idols. ¹⁷Yet I looked on them with pity and did not destroy them or put an end to them in the desert. ¹⁸I said to their children in the desert, "Do not follow the statutes of your fathers or keep their laws or defile yourselves with their idols. ¹⁹I am the Lᴏʀᴅ your God; follow my decrees and be careful to keep my laws. ²⁰Keep my Sabbaths holy, that they may be a sign between us. Then you will know that I am the Lᴏʀᴅ your God."

²¹" 'But the children rebelled against me: They did not follow my decrees, they were not careful to keep my laws—although the man who obeys them will live by them—and they desecrated my Sabbaths. So I said I would pour out my wrath on them and spend my anger against them in the desert. ²²But I withheld my hand, and for the sake of my name I did what would keep it from being profaned in the eyes of the nations in whose sight I had brought them out. ²³Also with uplifted hand I

swore to them in the desert that I would disperse them among the nations and scatter them through the countries, ²⁴because they had not obeyed my laws but had rejected my decrees and desecrated my Sabbaths, and their eyes ⌊lusted⌋ after their fathers' idols. ²⁵I also gave them over to statutes that were not good and laws they could not live by; ²⁶I let them become defiled through their gifts—the sacrifice of every firstborn*a*—that I might fill them with horror so they would know that I am the Lᴏʀᴅ.'

²⁷"Therefore, son of man, speak to the people of Israel and say to them, 'This is what the Sovereign Lᴏʀᴅ says: In this also your fathers blasphemed me by forsaking me: ²⁸When I brought them into the land I had sworn to give them and they saw any high hill or any leafy tree, there they offered their sacrifices, made offerings that provoked me to anger, presented their fragrant incense and poured out their drink offerings. ²⁹Then I said to them: What is this high place you go to?' " (It is called Bamah*b* to this day.)

Judgment and Restoration

³⁰"Therefore say to the house of Israel: 'This is what the Sovereign Lᴏʀᴅ says: Will you defile yourselves the way your fathers did and lust after their vile images? ³¹When you offer your gifts—the sacrifice of your sons in*c* the fire—you continue to defile yourselves with all your idols to this day. Am I to let you inquire of me, O house of Israel? As surely as I live, declares the Sovereign Lᴏʀᴅ, I will not let you inquire of me.

³²" 'You say, "We want to be like the nations, like the peoples of the world, who serve wood and stone." But what you have in mind will never happen. ³³As surely as I live, declares the Sovereign Lᴏʀᴅ, I will rule over you with a mighty hand and an outstretched arm and with outpoured wrath. ³⁴I will bring you from the na-

---

a26 Or —*making every firstborn pass through* ⌊*the fire*⌋   *b29* Bamah *means* high place.
c31 Or —*making your sons pass through*

tions and gather you from the countries where you have been scattered—with a mighty hand and an outstretched arm and with outpoured wrath. [35]I will bring you into the desert of the nations and there, face to face, I will execute judgment upon you. [36]As I judged your fathers in the desert of the land of Egypt, so I will judge you, declares the Sovereign LORD. [37]I will take note of you as you pass under my rod, and I will bring you into the bond of the covenant. [38]I will purge you of those who revolt and rebel against me. Although I will bring them out of the land where they are living, yet they will not enter the land of Israel. Then you will know that I am the LORD.

[39]" 'As for you, O house of Israel, this is what the Sovereign LORD says: Go and serve your idols, every one of you! But afterward you will surely listen to me and no longer profane my holy name with your gifts and idols. [40]For on my holy mountain, the high mountain of Israel, declares the Sovereign LORD, there in the land the entire house of Israel will serve me, and there I will accept them. There I will require your offerings and your choice gifts,[a] along with all your holy sacrifices. [41]I will accept you as fragrant incense when I bring you out from the nations and gather you from the countries where you have been scattered, and I will show myself holy among you in the sight of the nations. [42]Then you will know that I am the LORD, when I bring you into the land of Israel, the land I had sworn with uplifted hand to give to your fathers. [43]There you will remember your conduct and all the actions by which you have defiled yourselves, and you will loathe yourselves for all the evil you have done. [44]You will know that I am the LORD, when I deal with you for my name's sake and not according to your evil ways and your corrupt practices, O house of Israel, declares the Sovereign LORD.' "

Prophecy Against the South

[45]The word of the LORD came to me: [46]"Son of man, set your face toward the south; preach against the south and prophesy against the forest of the southland. [47]Say to the southern forest: 'Hear the word of the LORD. This is what the Sovereign LORD says: I am about to set fire to you, and it will consume all your trees, both green and dry. The blazing flame will not be quenched, and every face from south to north will be scorched by it. [48]Everyone will see that I the LORD have kindled it; it will not be quenched.' "

[49]Then I said, "Ah, Sovereign LORD! They are saying of me, 'Isn't he just telling parables?' "

Babylon, God's Sword of Judgment

21 The word of the LORD came to me: [2]"Son of man, set your face against Jerusalem and preach against the sanctuary. Prophesy against the land of Israel [3]and say to her: 'This is what the LORD says: I am against you. I will draw my sword from its scabbard and cut off from you both the righteous and the wicked. [4]Because I am going to cut off the righteous and the wicked, my sword will be unsheathed against everyone from south to north. [5]Then all people will know that I the LORD have drawn my sword from its scabbard; it will not return again.'

[6]"Therefore groan, son of man! Groan before them with broken heart and bitter grief. [7]And when they ask you, 'Why are you groaning?' you shall say, 'Because of the news that is coming. Every heart will melt and every hand go limp; every spirit will become faint and every knee become as weak as water.' It is coming! It will surely take place, declares the Sovereign LORD."

[8]The word of the LORD came to me: [9]"Son of man, prophesy and say, 'This is what the Lord says:

" 'A sword, a sword,
    sharpened and polished—

---

[a]40 Or and the gifts of your firstfruits

¹⁰sharpened for the slaughter,
    polished to flash like lightning!

" 'Shall we rejoice in the scepter of
my son ⌊Judah⌋? The sword despises
every such stick.

¹¹" 'The sword is appointed to be
        polished,
    to be grasped with the hand;
  it is sharpened and polished,
    made ready for the hand of the
        slayer.
¹²Cry out and wail, son of man,
    for it is against my people;
  it is against all the princes of
        Israel.
  They are thrown to the sword
    along with my people.
  Therefore beat your breast.

¹³" 'Testing will surely come. And
what if the scepter ⌊of Judah⌋, which
the sword despises, does not continue? declares the Sovereign LORD.'

¹⁴"So then, son of man, prophesy
    and strike your hands together.
  Let the sword strike twice,
    even three times.
  It is a sword for slaughter—
    a sword for great slaughter,
    closing in on them from every
        side.
¹⁵So that hearts may melt
    and the fallen be many,
  I have stationed the sword for
        slaughter*ᵃ*
    at all their gates.
  Oh! It is made to flash like
        lightning,
    it is grasped for slaughter.
¹⁶O sword, slash to the right,
    then to the left,
    wherever your blade is turned.
¹⁷I too will strike my hands
        together,
    and my wrath will subside.
  I the LORD have spoken."

¹⁸The word of the LORD came to me:
¹⁹"Son of man, mark out two roads for
the sword of the king of Babylon to
take, both starting from the same
country. Make a signpost where the
road branches off to the city. ²⁰Mark
out one road for the sword to come
against Rabbah of the Ammonites
and another against Judah and fortified Jerusalem. ²¹For the king of Babylon will stop at the fork in the road,
at the junction of the two roads, to
seek an omen: He will cast lots with
arrows, he will consult his idols, he
will examine the liver. ²²Into his right
hand will come the lot for Jerusalem,
where he is to set up battering rams,
to give the command to slaughter, to
sound the battle cry, to set battering
rams against the gates, to build a
ramp and to erect siege works. ²³It
will seem like a false omen to those
who have sworn allegiance to him,
but he will remind them of their guilt
and take them captive.

²⁴"Therefore this is what the Sovereign LORD says: 'Because you people
have brought to mind your guilt by
your open rebellion, revealing your
sins in all that you do—because you
have done this, you will be taken captive.

²⁵" 'O profane and wicked prince of
Israel, whose day has come, whose
time of punishment has reached its
climax, ²⁶this is what the Sovereign
LORD says: Take off the turban, remove the crown. It will not be as it
was: The lowly will be exalted and
the exalted will be brought low. ²⁷A
ruin! A ruin! I will make it a ruin! It
will not be restored until he comes to
whom it rightfully belongs; to him I
will give it.'

²⁸"And you, son of man, prophesy
and say, 'This is what the Sovereign
LORD says about the Ammonites and
their insults:

" 'A sword, a sword,
    drawn for the slaughter,
  polished to consume
    and to flash like lightning!
²⁹Despite false visions concerning
        you
    and lying divinations about
        you,
  it will be laid on the necks

ᵃ15 Septuagint; the meaning of the Hebrew for this word is uncertain.

of the wicked who are to be
     slain,
whose day has come,
     whose time of punishment has
          reached its climax.
³⁰Return the sword to its scabbard.
     In the place where you were
          created,
     in the land of your ancestry,
          I will judge you.
³¹I will pour out my wrath upon
          you
     and breathe out my fiery anger
          against you;
     I will hand you over to brutal
          men,
     men skilled in destruction.
³²You will be fuel for the fire,
     your blood will be shed in your
          land,
     you will be remembered no more;
     for I the LORD have spoken.' "

Jerusalem's Sins

22 The word of the LORD came to
     me: ²"Son of man, will you
judge her? Will you judge this city of
bloodshed? Then confront her with all
her detestable practices ³and say:
'This is what the Sovereign LORD says:
O city that brings on herself doom by
shedding blood in her midst and defiles herself by making idols, ⁴you
have become guilty because of the
blood you have shed and have become defiled by the idols you have
made. You have brought your days to
a close, and the end of your years has
come. Therefore I will make you an
object of scorn to the nations and a
laughingstock to all the countries.
⁵Those who are near and those who
are far away will mock you, O infa-
mous city, full of turmoil.

⁶" 'See how each of the princes of
Israel who are in you uses his power
to shed blood. ⁷In you they have treated father and mother with contempt;
in you they have oppressed the alien
and mistreated the fatherless and the
widow. ⁸You have despised my holy
things and desecrated my Sabbaths.
⁹In you are slanderous men bent on

shedding blood; in you are those who
eat at the mountain shrines and commit lewd acts. ¹⁰In you are those who
dishonor their fathers' bed; in you are
those who violate women during
their period, when they are ceremonially unclean. ¹¹In you one man commits a detestable offense with his
neighbor's wife, another shamefully
defiles his daughter-in-law, and another violates his sister, his own father's daughter. ¹²In you men accept
bribes to shed blood; you take usury
and excessive interest[a] and make unjust gain from your neighbors by extortion. And you have forgotten me,
declares the Sovereign LORD.

¹³" 'I will surely strike my hands together at the unjust gain you have
made and at the blood you have shed
in your midst. ¹⁴Will your courage endure or your hands be strong in the
day I deal with you? I the LORD have
spoken, and I will do it. ¹⁵I will disperse you among the nations and
scatter you through the countries; and
I will put an end to your uncleanness.
¹⁶When you have been defiled[b] in
the eyes of the nations, you will know
that I am the LORD.' "

¹⁷Then the word of the LORD came
to me: ¹⁸"Son of man, the house of Israel has become dross to me; all of
them are the copper, tin, iron and lead
left inside a furnace. They are but the
dross of silver. ¹⁹Therefore this is
what the Sovereign LORD says: 'Because you have all become dross, I
will gather you into Jerusalem. ²⁰As
men gather silver, copper, iron, lead
and tin into a furnace to melt it with a
fiery blast, so will I gather you in my
anger and my wrath and put you inside the city and melt you. ²¹I will
gather you and I will blow on you
with my fiery wrath, and you will be
melted inside her. ²²As silver is melted in a furnace, so you will be melted
inside her, and you will know that I
the LORD have poured out my wrath
upon you.' "

²³Again the word of the LORD came
to me: ²⁴"Son of man, say to the land,

ᵃ12 Or *usury and interest*   ᵇ16 Or *When I have allotted you your inheritance*

'You are a land that has had no rain or showers[a] in the day of wrath.' ²⁵There is a conspiracy of her princes[b] within her like a roaring lion tearing its prey; they devour people, take treasures and precious things and make many widows within her. ²⁶Her priests do violence to my law and profane my holy things; they do not distinguish between the holy and the common; they teach that there is no difference between the unclean and the clean; and they shut their eyes to the keeping of my Sabbaths, so that I am profaned among them. ²⁷Her officials within her are like wolves tearing their prey; they shed blood and kill people to make unjust gain. ²⁸Her prophets whitewash these deeds for them by false visions and lying divinations. They say, 'This is what the Sovereign LORD says'—when the LORD has not spoken. ²⁹The people of the land practice extortion and commit robbery; they oppress the poor and needy and mistreat the alien, denying them justice.

³⁰"I looked for a man among them who would build up the wall and stand before me in the gap on behalf of the land so I would not have to destroy it, but I found none. ³¹So I will pour out my wrath on them and consume them with my fiery anger, bringing down on their own heads all they have done, declares the Sovereign LORD."

Two Adulterous Sisters

23 The word of the LORD came to me: ²"Son of man, there were two women, daughters of the same mother. ³They became prostitutes in Egypt, engaging in prostitution from their youth. In that land their breasts were fondled and their virgin bosoms caressed. ⁴The older was named Oholah, and her sister was Oholibah. They were mine and gave birth to sons and daughters. Oholah is Samaria, and Oholibah is Jerusalem.

⁵"Oholah engaged in prostitution while she was still mine; and she lusted after her lovers, the Assyrians—warriors ⁶clothed in blue, governors and commanders, all of them handsome young men, and mounted horsemen. ⁷She gave herself as a prostitute to all the elite of the Assyrians and defiled herself with all the idols of everyone she lusted after. ⁸She did not give up the prostitution she began in Egypt, when during her youth men slept with her, caressed her virgin bosom and poured out their lust upon her.

⁹"Therefore I handed her over to her lovers, the Assyrians, for whom she lusted. ¹⁰They stripped her naked, took away her sons and daughters and killed her with the sword. She became a byword among women, and punishment was inflicted on her.

¹¹"Her sister Oholibah saw this, yet in her lust and prostitution she was more depraved than her sister. ¹²She too lusted after the Assyrians—governors and commanders, warriors in full dress, mounted horsemen, all handsome young men. ¹³I saw that she too defiled herself; both of them went the same way.

¹⁴"But she carried her prostitution still further. She saw men portrayed on a wall, figures of Chaldeans[c] portrayed in red, ¹⁵with belts around their waists and flowing turbans on their heads; all of them looked like Babylonian chariot officers, natives of Chaldea.[d] ¹⁶As soon as she saw them, she lusted after them and sent messengers to them in Chaldea. ¹⁷Then the Babylonians came to her, to the bed of love, and in their lust they defiled her. After she had been defiled by them, she turned away from them in disgust. ¹⁸When she carried on her prostitution openly and exposed her nakedness, I turned away from her in disgust, just as I had turned away from her sister. ¹⁹Yet she became more and more promiscuous as she recalled the days of her youth, when she was a prostitute in Egypt.

²⁰There she lusted after her lovers, whose genitals were like those of donkeys and whose emission was like that of horses. ²¹So you longed for the lewdness of your youth, when in Egypt your bosom was caressed and your young breasts fondled.ᵃ

²²"Therefore, Oholibah, this is what the Sovereign Lord says: I will stir up your lovers against you, those you turned away from in disgust, and I will bring them against you from every side— ²³the Babylonians and all the Chaldeans, the men of Pekod and Shoa and Koa, and all the Assyrians with them, handsome young men, all of them governors and commanders, chariot officers and men of high rank, all mounted on horses. ²⁴They will come against you with weapons,ᵇ chariots and wagons and with a throng of people; they will take up positions against you on every side with large and small shields and with helmets. I will turn you over to them for punishment, and they will punish you according to their standards. ²⁵I will direct my jealous anger against you, and they will deal with you in fury. They will cut off your noses and your ears, and those of you who are left will fall by the sword. They will take away your sons and daughters, and those of you who are left will be consumed by fire. ²⁶They will also strip you of your clothes and take your fine jewelry. ²⁷So I will put a stop to the lewdness and prostitution you began in Egypt. You will not look on these things with longing or remember Egypt anymore.

²⁸"For this is what the Sovereign Lord says: I am about to hand you over to those you hate, to those you turned away from in disgust. ²⁹They will deal with you in hatred and take away everything you have worked for. They will leave you naked and bare, and the shame of your prostitution will be exposed. Your lewdness and promiscuity ³⁰have brought this

upon you, because you lusted after the nations and defiled yourself with their idols. ³¹You have gone the way of your sister; so I will put her cup into your hand.

³²"This is what the Sovereign Lord says:

"You will drink your sister's cup,
    a cup large and deep;
it will bring scorn and derision,
    for it holds so much.
³³You will be filled with
        drunkenness and sorrow,
    the cup of ruin and desolation,
    the cup of your sister Samaria.
³⁴You will drink it and drain it dry;
    you will dash it to pieces
    and tear your breasts.

I have spoken, declares the Sovereign Lord.

³⁵"Therefore this is what the Sovereign Lord says: Since you have forgotten me and thrust me behind your back, you must bear the consequences of your lewdness and prostitution."

³⁶The Lord said to me: "Son of man, will you judge Oholah and Oholibah? Then confront them with their detestable practices, ³⁷for they have committed adultery and blood is on their hands. They committed adultery with their idols; they even sacrificed their children, whom they bore to me,ᶜ as food for them. ³⁸They have also done this to me: At that same time they defiled my sanctuary and desecrated my Sabbaths. ³⁹On the very day they sacrificed their children to their idols, they entered my sanctuary and desecrated it. That is what they did in my house.

⁴⁰"They even sent messengers for men who came from far away, and when they arrived you bathed yourself for them, painted your eyes and put on your jewelry. ⁴¹You sat on an elegant couch, with a table spread before it on which you had placed the incense and oil that belonged to me.

⁴²"The noise of a carefree crowd

ᵃ21 Syriac (see also verse 3); Hebrew *caressed because of your young breasts*   ᵇ24 The meaning of the Hebrew for this word is uncertain.   ᶜ37 Or *even made the children they bore to me pass through ⌐the fire⌐*

was around her; Sabeans[a] were brought from the desert along with men from the rabble, and they put bracelets on the arms of the woman and her sister and beautiful crowns on their heads. 43Then I said about the one worn out by adultery, 'Now let them use her as a prostitute, for that is all she is.' 44And they slept with her. As men sleep with a prostitute, so they slept with those lewd women, Oholah and Oholibah. 45But righteous men will sentence them to the punishment of women who commit adultery and shed blood, because they are adulterous and blood is on their hands.

46"This is what the Sovereign LORD says: Bring a mob against them and give them over to terror and plunder. 47The mob will stone them and cut them down with their swords; they will kill their sons and daughters and burn down their houses.

48"So I will put an end to lewdness in the land, that all women may take warning and not imitate you. 49You will suffer the penalty for your lewdness and bear the consequences of your sins of idolatry. Then you will know that I am the Sovereign LORD."

The Cooking Pot

24 In the ninth year, in the tenth month on the tenth day, the word of the LORD came to me: 2"Son of man, record this date, this very date, because the king of Babylon has laid siege to Jerusalem this very day. 3Tell this rebellious house a parable and say to them: 'This is what the Sovereign LORD says:

" 'Put on the cooking pot; put it on
    and pour water into it.
4Put into it the pieces of meat,
    all the choice pieces—the leg
        and the shoulder.
Fill it with the best of these bones;
5 take the pick of the flock.
Pile wood beneath it for the bones;

bring it to a boil
    and cook the bones in it.

6" 'For this is what the Sovereign LORD says:

" 'Woe to the city of bloodshed,
    to the pot now encrusted,
    whose deposit will not go away!
Empty it piece by piece
    without casting lots for them.

7" 'For the blood she shed is in her midst:
    She poured it on the bare rock;
she did not pour it on the ground,
    where the dust would cover it.
8To stir up wrath and take revenge
    I put her blood on the bare rock,
    so that it would not be covered.

9" 'Therefore this is what the Sovereign LORD says:

" 'Woe to the city of bloodshed!
    I, too, will pile the wood high.
10So heap on the wood
    and kindle the fire.
Cook the meat well,
    mixing in the spices;
    and let the bones be charred.
11Then set the empty pot on the coals
    till it becomes hot and its copper glows
so its impurities may be melted
    and its deposit burned away.
12It has frustrated all efforts;
    its heavy deposit has not been removed,
    not even by fire.

13" 'Now your impurity is lewdness. Because I tried to cleanse you but you would not be cleansed from your impurity, you will not be clean again until my wrath against you has subsided.

14" 'I the LORD have spoken. The time has come for me to act. I will not hold back; I will not have pity, nor will I relent. You will be judged according to your conduct and your actions, declares the Sovereign LORD.' "

a42 Or drunkards

PASSAGE: Ezekiel 11:16–21; Ezekiel 36:24–32
AUTHOR: John Donne

Batter My Heart

Batter my heart, three-personed God, for you
As yet but knock, breathe, shine, and seek to mend;
That I may rise, and stand, o'erthrow me, and bend
Your force, to break, blow, burn, and make me new.
I, like an usurped town, to another due,
Labour to admit you, but oh, to no end;
Reason, your viceroy in me, me should defend,
But is captived, and proves weak or untrue.
Yet dearly I love you, and would be lovèd fain,
But am betrothed unto your enemy;
Divorce me, untie or break that knot again;
Take me to you, imprison me, for I
Except you enthrall me, never shall be free,
Nor ever chaste, except you ravish me.

Go to page 1069 for your next devotional reading.

Ezekiel's Wife Dies

[15]The word of the LORD came to me: [16]"Son of man, with one blow I am about to take away from you the delight of your eyes. Yet do not lament or weep or shed any tears. [17]Groan quietly; do not mourn for the dead. Keep your turban fastened and your sandals on your feet; do not cover the lower part of your face or eat the customary food ⌊of mourners⌋."

[18]So I spoke to the people in the morning, and in the evening my wife died. The next morning I did as I had been commanded.

[19]Then the people asked me, "Won't you tell us what these things have to do with us?"

[20]So I said to them, "The word of the LORD came to me: [21]Say to the house of Israel, 'This is what the Sovereign LORD says: I am about to desecrate my sanctuary—the stronghold in which you take pride, the delight of your eyes, the object of your affection. The sons and daughters you left behind will fall by the sword. [22]And you will do as I have done. You will not cover the lower part of your face or eat the customary food ⌊of mourners⌋. [23]You will keep your turbans on your heads and your sandals on your feet. You will not mourn or weep but will waste away because of[a] your sins and groan among yourselves. [24]Ezekiel will be a sign to you; you will do just as he has done. When this happens, you will know that I am the Sovereign LORD.'

[25]"And you, son of man, on the day I take away their stronghold, their joy and glory, the delight of their eyes, their heart's desire, and their sons and daughters as well— [26]on that day a fugitive will come to tell you the news. [27]At that time your mouth will be opened; you will speak with him and will no longer be silent. So you will be a sign to them, and they will know that I am the LORD."

A Prophecy Against Ammon

25 The word of the LORD came to me: [2]"Son of man, set your face against the Ammonites and prophesy against them. [3]Say to them, 'Hear the word of the Sovereign LORD. This is what the Sovereign LORD says: Because you said "Aha!" over my sanctuary when it was desecrated and over the land of Israel when it was laid waste and over the people of Judah when they went into exile, [4]therefore I am going to give you to the people of the East as a possession. They will set up their camps and pitch their tents among you; they will eat your fruit and drink your milk. [5]I will turn Rabbah into a pasture for camels and Ammon into a resting place for sheep. Then you will know that I am the LORD. [6]For this is what the Sovereign LORD says: Because you have clapped your hands and stamped your feet, rejoicing with all the malice of your heart against the land of Israel, [7]therefore I will stretch out my hand against you and give you as plunder to the nations. I will cut you off from the nations and exterminate you from the countries. I will destroy you, and you will know that I am the LORD.'"

A Prophecy Against Moab

[8]"This is what the Sovereign LORD says: 'Because Moab and Seir said, "Look, the house of Judah has become like all the other nations," [9]therefore I will expose the flank of Moab, beginning at its frontier towns—Beth Jeshimoth, Baal Meon and Kiriathaim—the glory of that land. [10]I will give Moab along with the Ammonites to the people of the East as a possession, so that the Ammonites will not be remembered among the nations; [11]and I will inflict punishment on Moab. Then they will know that I am the LORD.'"

A Prophecy Against Edom

[12]"This is what the Sovereign LORD says: 'Because Edom took revenge on

the house of Judah and became very guilty by doing so, [13]therefore this is what the Sovereign LORD says: I will stretch out my hand against Edom and kill its men and their animals. I will lay it waste, and from Teman to Dedan they will fall by the sword. [14]I will take vengeance on Edom by the hand of my people Israel, and they will deal with Edom in accordance with my anger and my wrath; they will know my vengeance, declares the Sovereign LORD.' "

A Prophecy Against Philistia

[15]"This is what the Sovereign LORD says: 'Because the Philistines acted in vengeance and took revenge with malice in their hearts, and with ancient hostility sought to destroy Judah, [16]therefore this is what the Sovereign LORD says: I am about to stretch out my hand against the Philistines, and I will cut off the Kerethites and destroy those remaining along the coast. [17]I will carry out great vengeance on them and punish them in my wrath. Then they will know that I am the LORD, when I take vengeance on them.' "

A Prophecy Against Tyre

26 In the eleventh year, on the first day of the month, the word of the LORD came to me: [2]"Son of man, because Tyre has said of Jerusalem, 'Aha! The gate to the nations is broken, and its doors have swung open to me; now that she lies in ruins I will prosper,' [3]therefore this is what the Sovereign LORD says: I am against you, O Tyre, and I will bring many nations against you, like the sea casting up its waves. [4]They will destroy the walls of Tyre and pull down her towers; I will scrape away her rubble and make her a bare rock. [5]Out in the sea she will become a place to spread fishnets, for I have spoken, declares the Sovereign LORD. She will become plunder for the nations, [6]and her settlements on the mainland will be rav-

aged by the sword. Then they will know that I am the LORD.

[7]"For this is what the Sovereign LORD says: From the north I am going to bring against Tyre Nebuchadnezzar[a] king of Babylon, king of kings, with horses and chariots, with horsemen and a great army. [8]He will ravage your settlements on the mainland with the sword; he will set up siege works against you, build a ramp up to your walls and raise his shields against you. [9]He will direct the blows of his battering rams against your walls and demolish your towers with his weapons. [10]His horses will be so many that they will cover you with dust. Your walls will tremble at the noise of the war horses, wagons and chariots when he enters your gates as men enter a city whose walls have been broken through. [11]The hoofs of his horses will trample all your streets; he will kill your people with the sword, and your strong pillars will fall to the ground. [12]They will plunder your wealth and loot your merchandise; they will break down your walls and demolish your fine houses and throw your stones, timber and rubble into the sea. [13]I will put an end to your noisy songs, and the music of your harps will be heard no more. [14]I will make you a bare rock, and you will become a place to spread fishnets. You will never be rebuilt, for I the LORD have spoken, declares the Sovereign LORD.

[15]"This is what the Sovereign LORD says to Tyre: Will not the coastlands tremble at the sound of your fall, when the wounded groan and the slaughter takes place in you? [16]Then all the princes of the coast will step down from their thrones and lay aside their robes and take off their embroidered garments. Clothed with terror, they will sit on the ground, trembling every moment, appalled at you. [17]Then they will take up a lament concerning you and say to you:

---

[a]7 Hebrew *Nebuchadrezzar*, of which *Nebuchadnezzar* is a variant; here and often in Ezekiel and Jeremiah

" 'How you are destroyed, O city
    of renown,
  peopled by men of the sea!
You were a power on the seas,
  you and your citizens;
  you put your terror
    on all who lived there.
¹⁸Now the coastlands tremble
  on the day of your fall;
the islands in the sea
  are terrified at your collapse.'

¹⁹"This is what the Sovereign LORD
says: When I make you a desolate
city, like cities no longer inhabited,
and when I bring the ocean depths
over you and its vast waters cover
you, ²⁰then I will bring you down
with those who go down to the pit, to
the people of long ago. I will make
you dwell in the earth below, as in
ancient ruins, with those who go
down to the pit, and you will not return or take your place[a] in the land
of the living. ²¹I will bring you to a
horrible end and you will be no more.
You will be sought, but you will never again be found, declares the Sovereign LORD."

A Lament for Tyre

27 The word of the LORD came to
me: ²"Son of man, take up a lament concerning Tyre. ³Say to Tyre,
situated at the gateway to the sea,
merchant of peoples on many coasts,
'This is what the Sovereign LORD says:

" 'You say, O Tyre,
  "I am perfect in beauty."
⁴Your domain was on the high
    seas;
  your builders brought your
    beauty to perfection.
⁵They made all your timbers
  of pine trees from Senir[b];
they took a cedar from Lebanon
  to make a mast for you.
⁶Of oaks from Bashan
  they made your oars;
of cypress wood[c] from the coasts
  of Cyprus[d]

they made your deck, inlaid
    with ivory.
⁷Fine embroidered linen from
    Egypt was your sail
  and served as your banner;
your awnings were of blue and
    purple
  from the coasts of Elishah.
⁸Men of Sidon and Arvad were
    your oarsmen;
  your skilled men, O Tyre, were
    aboard as your seamen.
⁹Veteran craftsmen of Gebal[e] were
    on board
  as shipwrights to caulk your
    seams.
All the ships of the sea and their
    sailors
  came alongside to trade for
    your wares.

¹⁰" 'Men of Persia, Lydia and Put
    served as soldiers in your army.
They hung their shields and
    helmets on your walls,
  bringing you splendor.
¹¹Men of Arvad and Helech
  manned your walls on every
    side;
men of Gammad
  were in your towers.
They hung their shields around
    your walls;
  they brought your beauty to
    perfection.

¹²" 'Tarshish did business with you
because of your great wealth of
goods; they exchanged silver, iron, tin
and lead for your merchandise.
¹³" 'Greece, Tubal and Meshech
traded with you; they exchanged
slaves and articles of bronze for your
wares.
¹⁴" 'Men of Beth Togarmah ex-
changed work horses, war horses and
mules for your merchandise.
¹⁵" 'The men of Rhodes[f] traded
with you, and many coastlands were
your customers; they paid you with
ivory tusks and ebony.

---

a20 Septuagint; Hebrew *return, and I will give glory*   *b5* That is, Hermon   *c6* Targum; the
Masoretic Text has a different division of the consonants.   *d6* Hebrew *Kittim*   *e9* That is,
Byblos   *f15* Septuagint; Hebrew *Dedan*

¹⁶" 'Aram*ᵃ* did business with you because of your many products; they exchanged turquoise, purple fabric, embroidered work, fine linen, coral and rubies for your merchandise.

¹⁷" 'Judah and Israel traded with you; they exchanged wheat from Minnith and confections,*ᵇ* honey, oil and balm for your wares.

¹⁸" 'Damascus, because of your many products and great wealth of goods, did business with you in wine from Helbon and wool from Zahar.

¹⁹" 'Danites and Greeks from Uzal bought your merchandise; they exchanged wrought iron, cassia and calamus for your wares.

²⁰" 'Dedan traded in saddle blankets with you.

²¹" 'Arabia and all the princes of Kedar were your customers; they did business with you in lambs, rams and goats.

²²" 'The merchants of Sheba and Raamah traded with you; for your merchandise they exchanged the finest of all kinds of spices and precious stones, and gold.

²³" 'Haran, Canneh and Eden and merchants of Sheba, Asshur and Kilmad traded with you. ²⁴In your marketplace they traded with you beautiful garments, blue fabric, embroidered work and multicolored rugs with cords twisted and tightly knotted.

²⁵" 'The ships of Tarshish serve
as carriers for your wares.
You are filled with heavy cargo
in the heart of the sea.
²⁶Your oarsmen take you
out to the high seas.
But the east wind will break you
to pieces
in the heart of the sea.
²⁷Your wealth, merchandise and
wares,
your mariners, seamen and
shipwrights,
your merchants and all your
soldiers,

and everyone else on board
will sink into the heart of the sea
on the day of your shipwreck.
²⁸The shorelands will quake
when your seamen cry out.
²⁹All who handle the oars
will abandon their ships;
the mariners and all the seamen
will stand on the shore.
³⁰They will raise their voice
and cry bitterly over you;
they will sprinkle dust on their
heads
and roll in ashes.
³¹They will shave their heads
because of you
and will put on sackcloth.
They will weep over you with
anguish of soul
and with bitter mourning.
³²As they wail and mourn over you,
they will take up a lament
concerning you:
"Who was ever silenced like Tyre,
surrounded by the sea?"
³³When your merchandise went out
on the seas,
you satisfied many nations;
with your great wealth and your
wares
you enriched the kings of the
earth.
³⁴Now you are shattered by the sea
in the depths of the waters;
your wares and all your company
have gone down with you.
³⁵All who live in the coastlands
are appalled at you;
their kings shudder with horror
and their faces are distorted
with fear.
³⁶The merchants among the nations
hiss at you;
you have come to a horrible
end
and will be no more.' "

A Prophecy Against the King of Tyre

28 The word of the Lord came to me: ²"Son of man, say to the

ᵃ16 Most Hebrew manuscripts; some Hebrew manuscripts and Syriac *Edom*   *ᵇ17* The meaning of the Hebrew for this word is uncertain.

ruler of Tyre, 'This is what the Sovereign LORD says:

" 'In the pride of your heart
   you say, "I am a god;
I sit on the throne of a god
   in the heart of the seas."
But you are a man and not a god,
   though you think you are as
      wise as a god.
³Are you wiser than Daniel[a]?
   Is no secret hidden from you?
⁴By your wisdom and
      understanding
   you have gained wealth for
      yourself
and amassed gold and silver
   in your treasuries.
⁵By your great skill in trading
   you have increased your wealth,
and because of your wealth
   your heart has grown proud.

⁶" 'Therefore this is what the Sovereign LORD says:

" 'Because you think you are wise,
   as wise as a god,
⁷I am going to bring foreigners
      against you,
   the most ruthless of nations;
they will draw their swords
      against your beauty and
         wisdom
   and pierce your shining
      splendor.
⁸They will bring you down to the
      pit,
   and you will die a violent death
      in the heart of the seas.
⁹Will you then say, "I am a god,"
   in the presence of those who
      kill you?
You will be but a man, not a god,
   in the hands of those who slay
      you.
¹⁰You will die the death of the
      uncircumcised
   at the hands of foreigners.

I have spoken, declares the Sovereign LORD.' "

¹¹The word of the LORD came to me:

¹²"Son of man, take up a lament concerning the king of Tyre and say to him: 'This is what the Sovereign LORD says:

" 'You were the model of
      perfection,
   full of wisdom and perfect in
      beauty.
¹³You were in Eden,
   the garden of God;
every precious stone adorned you:
   ruby, topaz and emerald,
   chrysolite, onyx and jasper,
   sapphire,[b] turquoise and
      beryl.[c]
Your settings and mountings[d]
   were made of gold;
on the day you were created
   they were prepared.
¹⁴You were anointed as a guardian
      cherub,
   for so I ordained you.
You were on the holy mount of
      God;
   you walked among the fiery
      stones.
¹⁵You were blameless in your ways
   from the day you were created
   till wickedness was found in
      you.
¹⁶Through your widespread trade
   you were filled with violence,
   and you sinned.
So I drove you in disgrace from
      the mount of God,
   and I expelled you, O guardian
      cherub,
   from among the fiery stones.
¹⁷Your heart became proud
   on account of your beauty,
and you corrupted your wisdom
   because of your splendor.
So I threw you to the earth;
   I made a spectacle of you before
      kings.
¹⁸By your many sins and dishonest
      trade
   you have desecrated your
      sanctuaries.
So I made a fire come out from
      you,

ᵃ3 Or *Danel*; the Hebrew spelling may suggest a person other than the prophet Daniel.
ᵇ13 Or *lapis lazuli*   ᶜ13 The precise identification of some of these precious stones is uncertain.
ᵈ13 The meaning of the Hebrew for this phrase is uncertain.

and it consumed you,
and I reduced you to ashes on the
        ground
    in the sight of all who were
        watching.
¹⁹All the nations who knew you
    are appalled at you;
    you have come to a horrible end
        and will be no more.' "

A Prophecy Against Sidon

²⁰The word of the LORD came to me:
²¹"Son of man, set your face against
Sidon; prophesy against her ²²and
say: 'This is what the Sovereign LORD
says:

" 'I am against you, O Sidon,
    and I will gain glory within
        you.
They will know that I am the
    LORD,
    when I inflict punishment on
        her
    and show myself holy within
        her.
²³I will send a plague upon her
    and make blood flow in her
        streets.
The slain will fall within her,
    with the sword against her on
        every side.
Then they will know that I am the
    LORD.

²⁴" 'No longer will the people of Israel have malicious neighbors who
are painful briers and sharp thorns.
Then they will know that I am the
Sovereign LORD.
²⁵" 'This is what the Sovereign LORD
says: When I gather the people of Israel from the nations where they have
been scattered, I will show myself
holy among them in the sight of the
nations. Then they will live in their
own land, which I gave to my servant
Jacob. ²⁶They will live there in safety
and will build houses and plant vineyards; they will live in safety when I
inflict punishment on all their neighbors who maligned them. Then they
will know that I am the LORD their
God.' "

A Prophecy Against Egypt

29 In the tenth year, in the tenth
month on the twelfth day, the
word of the LORD came to me: ²"Son of
man, set your face against Pharaoh
king of Egypt and prophesy against
him and against all Egypt. ³Speak to
him and say: 'This is what the Sovereign LORD says:

" 'I am against you, Pharaoh king
    of Egypt,
    you great monster lying among
        your streams.
You say, "The Nile is mine;
    I made it for myself."
⁴But I will put hooks in your jaws
    and make the fish of your
        streams stick to your
        scales.
I will pull you out from among
    your streams,
    with all the fish sticking to your
        scales.
⁵I will leave you in the desert,
    you and all the fish of your
        streams.
You will fall on the open field
    and not be gathered or picked
        up.
I will give you as food
    to the beasts of the earth and
        the birds of the air.

⁶Then all who live in Egypt will know
that I am the LORD.

" 'You have been a staff of reed for
the house of Israel. ⁷When they
grasped you with their hands, you
splintered and you tore open their
shoulders; when they leaned on you,
you broke and their backs were
wrenched.ᵃ

⁸" 'Therefore this is what the Sovereign LORD says: I will bring a sword
against you and kill your men and
their animals. ⁹Egypt will become a
desolate wasteland. Then they will
know that I am the LORD.

" 'Because you said, "The Nile is
mine; I made it," ¹⁰therefore I am
against you and against your streams,
and I will make the land of Egypt a

ᵃ7 Syriac (see also Septuagint and Vulgate); Hebrew *and you caused their backs to stand* ruin and a desolate waste from Migdol to Aswan, as far as the border of Cush.ᵃ ¹¹No foot of man or animal will pass through it; no one will live there for forty years. ¹²I will make the land of Egypt desolate among devastated lands, and her cities will lie desolate forty years among ruined cities. And I will disperse the Egyptians among the nations and scatter them through the countries.

¹³" 'Yet this is what the Sovereign Lord says: At the end of forty years I will gather the Egyptians from the nations where they were scattered. ¹⁴I will bring them back from captivity and return them to Upper Egypt,ᵇ the land of their ancestry. There they will be a lowly kingdom. ¹⁵It will be the lowliest of kingdoms and will never again exalt itself above the other nations. I will make it so weak that it will never again rule over the nations. ¹⁶Egypt will no longer be a source of confidence for the people of Israel but will be a reminder of their sin in turning to her for help. Then they will know that I am the Sovereign Lord.' "

¹⁷In the twenty-seventh year, in the first month on the first day, the word of the Lord came to me: ¹⁸"Son of man, Nebuchadnezzar king of Babylon drove his army in a hard campaign against Tyre; every head was rubbed bare and every shoulder made raw. Yet he and his army got no reward from the campaign he led against Tyre. ¹⁹Therefore this is what the Sovereign Lord says: I am going to give Egypt to Nebuchadnezzar king of Babylon, and he will carry off its wealth. He will loot and plunder the land as pay for his army. ²⁰I have given him Egypt as a reward for his efforts because he and his army did it for me, declares the Sovereign Lord.

²¹"On that day I will make a hornᶜ grow for the house of Israel, and I will open your mouth among them. Then they will know that I am the Lord."

A Lament for Egypt

30 The word of the Lord came to me: ²"Son of man, prophesy and say: 'This is what the Sovereign Lord says:

" 'Wail and say,
  "Alas for that day!"
³For the day is near,
  the day of the Lord is near—
a day of clouds,
  a time of doom for the nations.
⁴A sword will come against Egypt,
  and anguish will come upon
    Cush.ᵈ
When the slain fall in Egypt,
  her wealth will be carried away
  and her foundations torn down.

⁵Cush and Put, Lydia and all Arabia, Libyaᵉ and the people of the covenant land will fall by the sword along with Egypt.

⁶" 'This is what the Lord says:

" 'The allies of Egypt will fall
  and her proud strength will fail.
From Migdol to Aswan
  they will fall by the sword
    within her,
        declares the Sovereign
            Lord.
⁷" 'They will be desolate
  among desolate lands,
and their cities will lie
  among ruined cities.
⁸Then they will know that I am the
    Lord,
  when I set fire to Egypt
  and all her helpers are crushed.

⁹" 'On that day messengers will go out from me in ships to frighten Cush out of her complacency. Anguish will take hold of them on the day of Egypt's doom, for it is sure to come.

¹⁰" 'This is what the Sovereign Lord says:

" 'I will put an end to the hordes
    of Egypt
  by the hand of Nebuchadnezzar
    king of Babylon.

¹¹He and his army—the most
       ruthless of nations—
   will be brought in to destroy
       the land.
They will draw their swords
       against Egypt
   and fill the land with the slain.
¹²I will dry up the streams of the
       Nile
   and sell the land to evil men;
by the hand of foreigners
   I will lay waste the land and
       everything in it.

I the LORD have spoken.

   ¹³" 'This is what the Sovereign LORD
says:

" 'I will destroy the idols
   and put an end to the images in
       Memphis.ᵃ
No longer will there be a prince in
       Egypt,
   and I will spread fear
       throughout the land.
¹⁴I will lay waste Upper Egypt,ᵇ
   set fire to Zoan
   and inflict punishment on
       Thebes.ᶜ
¹⁵I will pour out my wrath on
       Pelusium,ᵈ
   the stronghold of Egypt,
   and cut off the hordes of
       Thebes.
¹⁶I will set fire to Egypt;
   Pelusium will writhe in agony.
Thebes will be taken by storm;
   Memphis will be in constant
       distress.
¹⁷The young men of Heliopolisᵉ
       and Bubastisᶠ
   will fall by the sword,
   and the cities themselves will go
       into captivity.
¹⁸Dark will be the day at Tahpanhes
   when I break the yoke of Egypt;
   there her proud strength will
       come to an end.
She will be covered with clouds,
   and her villages will go into
       captivity.

¹⁹So I will inflict punishment on
       Egypt,
   and they will know that I am
       the LORD.' "

   ²⁰In the eleventh year, in the first
month on the seventh day, the word
of the LORD came to me: ²¹"Son of
man, I have broken the arm of Pharaoh king of Egypt. It has not been
bound up for healing or put in a
splint so as to become strong enough
to hold a sword. ²²Therefore this is
what the Sovereign LORD says: I am
against Pharaoh king of Egypt. I will
break both his arms, the good arm as
well as the broken one, and make the
sword fall from his hand. ²³I will disperse the Egyptians among the nations and scatter them through the
countries. ²⁴I will strengthen the arms
of the king of Babylon and put my
sword in his hand, but I will break the
arms of Pharaoh, and he will groan
before him like a mortally wounded
man. ²⁵I will strengthen the arms of
the king of Babylon, but the arms of
Pharaoh will fall limp. Then they will
know that I am the LORD, when I put
my sword into the hand of the king of
Babylon and he brandishes it against
Egypt. ²⁶I will disperse the Egyptians
among the nations and scatter them
through the countries. Then they will
know that I am the LORD."

A Cedar in Lebanon

31 In the eleventh year, in the
       third month on the first day,
the word of the LORD came to me:
²"Son of man, say to Pharaoh king of
Egypt and to his hordes:

" 'Who can be compared with you
       in majesty?
³Consider Assyria, once a cedar in
       Lebanon,
   with beautiful branches
       overshadowing the forest;
it towered on high,
   its top above the thick foliage.
⁴The waters nourished it,

ᵃ13 Hebrew *Noph*; also in verse 16   ᵇ14 Hebrew *waste Pathros*   ᶜ14 Hebrew *No*; also in
verses 15 and 16   ᵈ15 Hebrew *Sin*; also in verse 16   ᵉ17 Hebrew *Awen* (or *On*)
ᶠ17 Hebrew *Pi Beseth*

deep springs made it grow tall;
  their streams flowed
    all around its base
  and sent their channels
    to all the trees of the field.
⁵So it towered higher
    than all the trees of the field;
  its boughs increased
    and its branches grew long,
      spreading because of abundant
        waters.
⁶All the birds of the air
    nested in its boughs,
  all the beasts of the field
    gave birth under its branches;
  all the great nations
    lived in its shade.
⁷It was majestic in beauty,
    with its spreading boughs,
  for its roots went down
    to abundant waters.
⁸The cedars in the garden of God
    could not rival it,
  nor could the pine trees
    equal its boughs,
  nor could the plane trees
    compare with its branches—
  no tree in the garden of God
    could match its beauty.
⁹I made it beautiful
    with abundant branches,
  the envy of all the trees of Eden
    in the garden of God.

¹⁰" 'Therefore this is what the Sovereign LORD says: Because it towered on high, lifting its top above the thick foliage, and because it was proud of its height, ¹¹I handed it over to the ruler of the nations, for him to deal with according to its wickedness. I cast it aside, ¹²and the most ruthless of foreign nations cut it down and left it. Its boughs fell on the mountains and in all the valleys; its branches lay broken in all the ravines of the land. All the nations of the earth came out from under its shade and left it. ¹³All the birds of the air settled on the fallen tree, and all the beasts of the field were among its branches. ¹⁴Therefore no other trees by the waters are ever to tower proudly on high, lifting their

tops above the thick foliage. No other trees so well-watered are ever to reach such a height; they are all destined for death, for the earth below, among mortal men, with those who go down to the pit.

¹⁵" 'This is what the Sovereign LORD says: On the day it was brought down to the grave*a* I covered the deep springs with mourning for it; I held back its streams, and its abundant waters were restrained. Because of it I clothed Lebanon with gloom, and all the trees of the field withered away. ¹⁶I made the nations tremble at the sound of its fall when I brought it down to the grave with those who go down to the pit. Then all the trees of Eden, the choicest and best of Lebanon, all the trees that were well-watered, were consoled in the earth below. ¹⁷Those who lived in its shade, its allies among the nations, had also gone down to the grave with it, joining those killed by the sword.

¹⁸" 'Which of the trees of Eden can be compared with you in splendor and majesty? Yet you, too, will be brought down with the trees of Eden to the earth below; you will lie among the uncircumcised, with those killed by the sword.

" 'This is Pharaoh and all his hordes, declares the Sovereign LORD.' "

A Lament for Pharaoh

32 In the twelfth year, in the twelfth month on the first day, the word of the LORD came to me: ²"Son of man, take up a lament concerning Pharaoh king of Egypt and say to him:

" 'You are like a lion among the
    nations;
  you are like a monster in the
    seas
  thrashing about in your streams,
    churning the water with your
      feet
    and muddying the streams.

---

*a*15 Hebrew *Sheol*; also in verses 16 and 17

³" 'This is what the Sovereign Lord says:

" 'With a great throng of people
    I will cast my net over you,
    and they will haul you up in
        my net.
⁴I will throw you on the land
    and hurl you on the open field.
I will let all the birds of the air
        settle on you
    and all the beasts of the earth
        gorge themselves on you.
⁵I will spread your flesh on the
        mountains
    and fill the valleys with your
        remains.
⁶I will drench the land with your
        flowing blood
    all the way to the mountains,
    and the ravines will be filled
        with your flesh.
⁷When I snuff you out, I will cover
        the heavens
    and darken their stars;
I will cover the sun with a cloud,
    and the moon will not give its
        light.
⁸All the shining lights in the
        heavens
    I will darken over you;
I will bring darkness over your
        land,
            declares the Sovereign
                Lord.
⁹I will trouble the hearts of many
        peoples
    when I bring about your
        destruction among the
        nations,
    amongᵃ lands you have not
        known.
¹⁰I will cause many peoples to be
        appalled at you,
    and their kings will shudder
        with horror because of you
    when I brandish my sword
        before them.
On the day of your downfall
    each of them will tremble
    every moment for his life.

¹¹" 'For this is what the Sovereign
Lord says:

" 'The sword of the king of
        Babylon
    will come against you.
¹²I will cause your hordes to fall
    by the swords of mighty men—
    the most ruthless of all nations.
They will shatter the pride of
        Egypt,
    and all her hordes will be
        overthrown.
¹³I will destroy all her cattle
    from beside abundant waters
no longer to be stirred by the foot
        of man
    or muddied by the hoofs of
        cattle.
¹⁴Then I will let her waters settle
    and make her streams flow like
        oil,
            declares the Sovereign
                Lord.
¹⁵When I make Egypt desolate
    and strip the land of everything
        in it,
    when I strike down all who live
        there,
    then they will know that I am
        the Lord.'

¹⁶"This is the lament they will chant for her. The daughters of the nations will chant it; for Egypt and all her hordes they will chant it, declares the Sovereign Lord."

¹⁷In the twelfth year, on the fifteenth day of the month, the word of the Lord came to me: ¹⁸"Son of man, wail for the hordes of Egypt and consign to the earth below both her and the daughters of mighty nations, with those who go down to the pit. ¹⁹Say to them, 'Are you more favored than others? Go down and be laid among the uncircumcised.' ²⁰They will fall among those killed by the sword. The sword is drawn; let her be dragged off with all her hordes. ²¹From within the graveᵇ the mighty leaders will say of Egypt and her allies, 'They

---

ᵃ9 Hebrew; Septuagint *bring you into captivity among the nations, | to*   ᵇ21 Hebrew *Sheol*; also in
verse 27

have come down and they lie with the uncircumcised, with those killed by the sword.'

²²"Assyria is there with her whole army; she is surrounded by the graves of all her slain, all who have fallen by the sword. ²³Their graves are in the depths of the pit and her army lies around her grave. All who had spread terror in the land of the living are slain, fallen by the sword.

²⁴"Elam is there, with all her hordes around her grave. All of them are slain, fallen by the sword. All who had spread terror in the land of the living went down uncircumcised to the earth below. They bear their shame with those who go down to the pit. ²⁵A bed is made for her among the slain, with all her hordes around her grave. All of them are uncircumcised, killed by the sword. Because their terror had spread in the land of the living, they bear their shame with those who go down to the pit; they are laid among the slain.

²⁶"Meshech and Tubal are there, with all their hordes around their graves. All of them are uncircumcised, killed by the sword because they spread their terror in the land of the living. ²⁷Do they not lie with the other uncircumcised warriors who have fallen, who went down to the grave with their weapons of war, whose swords were placed under their heads? The punishment for their sins rested on their bones, though the terror of these warriors had stalked through the land of the living.

²⁸"You too, O Pharaoh, will be broken and will lie among the uncircumcised, with those killed by the sword.

²⁹"Edom is there, her kings and all her princes; despite their power, they are laid with those killed by the sword. They lie with the uncircumcised, with those who go down to the pit.

³⁰"All the princes of the north and all the Sidonians are there; they went down with the slain in disgrace despite the terror caused by their power.

They lie uncircumcised with those killed by the sword and bear their shame with those who go down to the pit.

³¹"Pharaoh—he and all his army—will see them and he will be consoled for all his hordes that were killed by the sword, declares the Sovereign LORD. ³²Although I had him spread terror in the land of the living, Pharaoh and all his hordes will be laid among the uncircumcised, with those killed by the sword, declares the Sovereign LORD."

Ezekiel a Watchman

33 The word of the LORD came to me: ²"Son of man, speak to your countrymen and say to them: 'When I bring the sword against a land, and the people of the land choose one of their men and make him their watchman, ³and he sees the sword coming against the land and blows the trumpet to warn the people, ⁴then if anyone hears the trumpet but does not take warning and the sword comes and takes his life, his blood will be on his own head. ⁵Since he heard the sound of the trumpet but did not take warning, his blood will be on his own head. If he had taken warning, he would have saved himself. ⁶But if the watchman sees the sword coming and does not blow the trumpet to warn the people and the sword comes and takes the life of one of them, that man will be taken away because of his sin, but I will hold the watchman accountable for his blood.'

⁷"Son of man, I have made you a watchman for the house of Israel; so hear the word I speak and give them warning from me. ⁸When I say to the wicked, 'O wicked man, you will surely die,' and you do not speak out to dissuade him from his ways, that wicked man will die for^a his sin, and I will hold you accountable for his blood. ⁹But if you do warn the wicked man to turn from his ways and he

---

^a8 Or in; also in verse 9

does not do so, he will die for his sin, but you will have saved yourself.

¹⁰"Son of man, say to the house of Israel, 'This is what you are saying: "Our offenses and sins weigh us down, and we are wasting away because of*ᵃ* them. How then can we live?" ' ¹¹Say to them, 'As surely as I live, declares the Sovereign Lord, I take no pleasure in the death of the wicked, but rather that they turn from their ways and live. Turn! Turn from your evil ways! Why will you die, O house of Israel?'

¹²"Therefore, son of man, say to your countrymen, 'The righteousness of the righteous man will not save him when he disobeys, and the wickedness of the wicked man will not cause him to fall when he turns from it. The righteous man, if he sins, will not be allowed to live because of his former righteousness.' ¹³If I tell the righteous man that he will surely live, but then he trusts in his righteousness and does evil, none of the righteous things he has done will be remembered; he will die for the evil he has done. ¹⁴And if I say to the wicked man, 'You will surely die,' but he then turns away from his sin and does what is just and right— ¹⁵if he gives back what he took in pledge for a loan, returns what he has stolen, follows the decrees that give life, and does no evil, he will surely live; he will not die. ¹⁶None of the sins he has committed will be remembered against him. He has done what is just and right; he will surely live.

¹⁷"Yet your countrymen say, 'The way of the Lord is not just.' But it is their way that is not just. ¹⁸If a righteous man turns from his righteousness and does evil, he will die for it. ¹⁹And if a wicked man turns away from his wickedness and does what is just and right, he will live by doing so. ²⁰Yet, O house of Israel, you say, 'The way of the Lord is not just.' But I will judge each of you according to his own ways."

Jerusalem's Fall Explained

²¹In the twelfth year of our exile, in the tenth month on the fifth day, a man who had escaped from Jerusalem came to me and said, "The city has fallen!" ²²Now the evening before the man arrived, the hand of the Lord was upon me, and he opened my mouth before the man came to me in the morning. So my mouth was opened and I was no longer silent.

²³Then the word of the Lord came to me: ²⁴"Son of man, the people living in those ruins in the land of Israel are saying, 'Abraham was only one man, yet he possessed the land. But we are many; surely the land has been given to us as our possession.' ²⁵Therefore say to them, 'This is what the Sovereign Lord says: Since you eat meat with the blood still in it and look to your idols and shed blood, should you then possess the land? ²⁶You rely on your sword, you do detestable things, and each of you defiles his neighbor's wife. Should you then possess the land?'

²⁷"Say this to them: 'This is what the Sovereign Lord says: As surely as I live, those who are left in the ruins will fall by the sword, those out in the country I will give to the wild animals to be devoured, and those in strongholds and caves will die of a plague. ²⁸I will make the land a desolate waste, and her proud strength will come to an end, and the mountains of Israel will become desolate so that no one will cross them. ²⁹Then they will know that I am the Lord, when I have made the land a desolate waste because of all the detestable things they have done.'

³⁰"As for you, son of man, your countrymen are talking together about you by the walls and at the doors of the houses, saying to each other, 'Come and hear the message that has come from the Lord.' ³¹My people come to you, as they usually do, and sit before you to listen to your words, but they do not put them into

---

ᵃ10 Or away in

practice. With their mouths they express devotion, but their hearts are greedy for unjust gain. ³²Indeed, to them you are nothing more than one who sings love songs with a beautiful voice and plays an instrument well, for they hear your words but do not put them into practice.

³³"When all this comes true—and it surely will—then they will know that a prophet has been among them."

Shepherds and Sheep

34 The word of the LORD came to me: ²"Son of man, prophesy against the shepherds of Israel; prophesy and say to them: 'This is what the Sovereign LORD says: Woe to the shepherds of Israel who only take care of themselves! Should not shepherds take care of the flock? ³You eat the curds, clothe yourselves with the wool and slaughter the choice animals, but you do not take care of the flock. ⁴You have not strengthened the weak or healed the sick or bound up the injured. You have not brought back the strays or searched for the lost. You have ruled them harshly and brutally. ⁵So they were scattered because there was no shepherd, and when they were scattered they became food for all the wild animals. ⁶My sheep wandered over all the mountains and on every high hill. They were scattered over the whole earth, and no one searched or looked for them.

⁷" 'Therefore, you shepherds, hear the word of the LORD: ⁸As surely as I live, declares the Sovereign LORD, because my flock lacks a shepherd and so has been plundered and has become food for all the wild animals, and because my shepherds did not search for my flock but cared for themselves rather than for my flock, ⁹therefore, O shepherds, hear the word of the LORD: ¹⁰This is what the Sovereign LORD says: I am against the shepherds and will hold them accountable for my flock. I will remove them from tending the flock so that the shepherds can no longer feed themselves. I will rescue my flock

from their mouths, and it will no longer be food for them.

¹¹" 'For this is what the Sovereign LORD says: I myself will search for my sheep and look after them. ¹²As a shepherd looks after his scattered flock when he is with them, so will I look after my sheep. I will rescue them from all the places where they were scattered on a day of clouds and darkness. ¹³I will bring them out from the nations and gather them from the countries, and I will bring them into their own land. I will pasture them on the mountains of Israel, in the ravines and in all the settlements in the land. ¹⁴I will tend them in a good pasture, and the mountain heights of Israel will be their grazing land. There they will lie down in good grazing land, and there they will feed in a rich pasture on the mountains of Israel. ¹⁵I myself will tend my sheep and have them lie down, declares the Sovereign LORD. ¹⁶I will search for the lost and bring back the strays. I will bind up the injured and strengthen the weak, but the sleek and the strong I will destroy. I will shepherd the flock with justice.

¹⁷" 'As for you, my flock, this is what the Sovereign LORD says: I will judge between one sheep and another, and between rams and goats. ¹⁸Is it not enough for you to feed on the good pasture? Must you also trample the rest of your pasture with your feet? Is it not enough for you to drink clear water? Must you also muddy the rest with your feet? ¹⁹Must my flock feed on what you have trampled and drink what you have muddied with your feet?

²⁰" 'Therefore this is what the Sovereign LORD says to them: See, I myself will judge between the fat sheep and the lean sheep. ²¹Because you shove with flank and shoulder, butting all the weak sheep with your horns until you have driven them away, ²²I will save my flock, and they will no longer be plundered. I will judge between one sheep and another. ²³I will place over them one shepherd, my servant David, and he will

tend them; he will tend them and be their shepherd. ²⁴I the LORD will be their God, and my servant David will be prince among them. I the LORD have spoken.

²⁵" 'I will make a covenant of peace with them and rid the land of wild beasts so that they may live in the desert and sleep in the forests in safety. ²⁶I will bless them and the places surrounding my hill.ᵃ I will send down showers in season; there will be showers of blessing. ²⁷The trees of the field will yield their fruit and the ground will yield its crops; the people will be secure in their land. They will know that I am the LORD, when I break the bars of their yoke and rescue them from the hands of those who enslaved them. ²⁸They will no longer be plundered by the nations, nor will wild animals devour them. They will live in safety, and no one will make them afraid. ²⁹I will provide for them a land renowned for its crops, and they will no longer be victims of famine in the land or bear the scorn of the nations. ³⁰Then they will know that I, the LORD their God, am with them and that they, the house of Israel, are my people, declares the Sovereign LORD. ³¹You my sheep, the sheep of my pasture, are people, and I am your God, declares the Sovereign LORD.' "

A Prophecy Against Edom

35 The word of the LORD came to me: ²"Son of man, set your face against Mount Seir; prophesy against it ³and say: 'This is what the Sovereign LORD says: I am against you, Mount Seir, and I will stretch out my hand against you and make you a desolate waste. ⁴I will turn your towns into ruins and you will be desolate. Then you will know that I am the LORD.

⁵" 'Because you harbored an ancient hostility and delivered the Israelites over to the sword at the time of their calamity, the time their punishment reached its climax, ⁶therefore as

surely as I live, declares the Sovereign LORD, I will give you over to bloodshed and it will pursue you. Since you did not hate bloodshed, bloodshed will pursue you. ⁷I will make Mount Seir a desolate waste and cut off from it all who come and go. ⁸I will fill your mountains with the slain; those killed by the sword will fall on your hills and in your valleys and in all your ravines. ⁹I will make you desolate forever; your towns will not be inhabited. Then you will know that I am the LORD.

¹⁰" 'Because you have said, "These two nations and countries will be ours and we will take possession of them," even though I the LORD was there, ¹¹therefore as surely as I live, declares the Sovereign LORD, I will treat you in accordance with the anger and jealousy you showed in your hatred of them and I will make myself known among them when I judge you. ¹²Then you will know that I the LORD have heard all the contemptible things you have said against the mountains of Israel. You said, "They have been laid waste and have been given over to us to devour." ¹³You boasted against me and spoke against me without restraint, and I heard it. ¹⁴This is what the Sovereign LORD says: While the whole earth rejoices, I will make you desolate. ¹⁵Because you rejoiced when the inheritance of the house of Israel became desolate, that is how I will treat you. You will be desolate, O Mount Seir, you and all of Edom. Then they will know that I am the LORD.' "

A Prophecy to the Mountains of Israel

36 "Son of man, prophesy to the mountains of Israel and say, 'O mountains of Israel, hear the word of the LORD. ²This is what the Sovereign LORD says: The enemy said of you, "Aha! The ancient heights have become our possession." ' ³Therefore prophesy and say, 'This is what the

---

ᵃ26 Or I will make them and the places surrounding my hill a blessing

Sovereign LORD says: Because they ravaged and hounded you from every side so that you became the possession of the rest of the nations and the object of people's malicious talk and slander, ⁴therefore, O mountains of Israel, hear the word of the Sovereign LORD: This is what the Sovereign LORD says to the mountains and hills, to the ravines and valleys, to the desolate ruins and the deserted towns that have been plundered and ridiculed by the rest of the nations around you— ⁵this is what the Sovereign LORD says: In my burning zeal I have spoken against the rest of the nations, and against all Edom, for with glee and with malice in their hearts they made my land their own possession so that they might plunder its pastureland.' ⁶Therefore prophesy concerning the land of Israel and say to

VERSE:
Ezekiel 35:10

AUTHOR:
Charles H. Spurgeon

PASSAGE:
Ezekiel 35:1–15

The Lord Is There

It is our good works that Satan attacks. A saint never had a virtue or a grace that was not the target of hellish bullets. Whether it was bright sparkling hope, or warm fervent love, or all-enduring patience, or flaming zeal, the old enemy of everything that is good has tried to destroy it. The only reason anything virtuous or lovely survives is because "the Lord is there."

And if the Lord is with us through life we will also have confidence through death. When we come to die, we will find that "the Lord is there." When the waves are most turbulent, the water cold and the time passed away, we shall touch bottom and know that it is good because our feet will stand on the Rock of Ages.

From the beginning of our Christian life to the end, the only reason we do not perish is because "the Lord is there." Only if the God of everlasting love could change and let his elect perish would the church be destroyed. But that cannot happen because it is written: *Yahweh Shammah*, the Lord is there.

ADDITIONAL SCRIPTURE READINGS
2 Samuel 22:1–7; Romans 8:28–39

Go to page 1090 for your next devotional reading.

the mountains and hills, to the ravines and valleys: 'This is what the Sovereign LORD says: I speak in my jealous wrath because you have suffered the scorn of the nations. 7Therefore this is what the Sovereign LORD says: I swear with uplifted hand that the nations around you will also suffer scorn.

8" 'But you, O mountains of Israel, will produce branches and fruit for my people Israel, for they will soon come home. 9I am concerned for you and will look on you with favor; you will be plowed and sown, 10and I will multiply the number of people upon you, even the whole house of Israel. The towns will be inhabited and the ruins rebuilt. 11I will increase the number of men and animals upon you, and they will be fruitful and become numerous. I will settle people on you as in the past and will make you prosper more than before. Then you will know that I am the LORD. 12I will cause people, my people Israel, to walk upon you. They will possess you, and you will be their inheritance; you will never again deprive them of their children.

13" 'This is what the Sovereign LORD says: Because people say to you, "You devour men and deprive your nation of its children," 14therefore you will no longer devour men or make your nation childless, declares the Sovereign LORD. 15No longer will I make you hear the taunts of the nations, and no longer will you suffer the scorn of the peoples or cause your nation to fall, declares the Sovereign LORD.' "

16Again the word of the LORD came to me: 17"Son of man, when the people of Israel were living in their own land, they defiled it by their conduct and their actions. Their conduct was like a woman's monthly uncleanness in my sight. 18So I poured out my wrath on them because they had shed blood in the land and because they had defiled it with their idols. 19I dispersed them among the nations, and they were scattered through the countries; I judged them according to their conduct and their actions. 20And wherever they went among the nations they profaned my holy name, for it was said of them, 'These are the LORD's people, and yet they had to leave his land.' 21I had concern for my holy name, which the house of Israel profaned among the nations where they had gone.

22"Therefore say to the house of Israel, 'This is what the Sovereign LORD says: It is not for your sake, O house of Israel, that I am going to do these things, but for the sake of my holy name, which you have profaned among the nations where you have gone. 23I will show the holiness of my great name, which has been profaned among the nations, the name you have profaned among them. Then the nations will know that I am the LORD, declares the Sovereign LORD, when I show myself holy through you before their eyes.

24" 'For I will take you out of the nations; I will gather you from all the countries and bring you back into your own land. 25I will sprinkle clean water on you, and you will be clean; I will cleanse you from all your impurities and from all your idols. 26I will give you a new heart and put a new spirit in you; I will remove from you your heart of stone and give you a heart of flesh. 27And I will put my Spirit in you and move you to follow my decrees and be careful to keep my laws. 28You will live in the land I gave your forefathers; you will be my people, and I will be your God. 29I will save you from all your uncleanness. I will call for the grain and make it plentiful and will not bring famine upon you. 30I will increase the fruit of the trees and the crops of the field, so that you will no longer suffer disgrace among the nations because of famine. 31Then you will remember your evil ways and wicked deeds, and you will loathe yourselves for your sins and detestable practices. 32I want you to know that I am not doing this for your sake, declares the Sovereign LORD. Be ashamed and disgraced for your conduct, O house of Israel!

³³" 'This is what the Sovereign LORD says: On the day I cleanse you from all your sins, I will resettle your towns, and the ruins will be rebuilt. ³⁴The desolate land will be cultivated instead of lying desolate in the sight of all who pass through it. ³⁵They will say, "This land that was laid waste has become like the garden of Eden; the cities that were lying in ruins, desolate and destroyed, are now fortified and inhabited." ³⁶Then the nations around you that remain will know that I the LORD have rebuilt what was destroyed and have replanted what was desolate. I the LORD have spoken, and I will do it.'

³⁷"This is what the Sovereign LORD says: Once again I will yield to the plea of the house of Israel and do this for them: I will make their people as numerous as sheep, ³⁸as numerous as the flocks for offerings at Jerusalem during her appointed feasts. So will the ruined cities be filled with flocks of people. Then they will know that I am the LORD."

The Valley of Dry Bones

37 The hand of the LORD was upon me, and he brought me out by the Spirit of the LORD and set me in the middle of a valley; it was full of bones. ²He led me back and forth among them, and I saw a great many bones on the floor of the valley, bones that were very dry. ³He asked me, "Son of man, can these bones live?"

I said, "O Sovereign LORD, you alone know."

⁴Then he said to me, "Prophesy to these bones and say to them, 'Dry bones, hear the word of the LORD! ⁵This is what the Sovereign LORD says to these bones: I will make breath*ᵃ* enter you, and you will come to life. ⁶I will attach tendons to you and make flesh come upon you and cover you with skin; I will put breath in you, and you will come to life. Then you will know that I am the LORD.' "

⁷So I prophesied as I was commanded. And as I was prophesying,

there was a noise, a rattling sound, and the bones came together, bone to bone. ⁸I looked, and tendons and flesh appeared on them and skin covered them, but there was no breath in them.

⁹Then he said to me, "Prophesy to the breath; prophesy, son of man, and say to it, 'This is what the Sovereign LORD says: Come from the four winds, O breath, and breathe into these slain, that they may live.' " ¹⁰So I prophesied as he commanded me, and breath entered them; they came to life and stood up on their feet—a vast army.

¹¹Then he said to me: "Son of man, these bones are the whole house of Israel. They say, 'Our bones are dried up and our hope is gone; we are cut off.' ¹²Therefore prophesy and say to them: 'This is what the Sovereign LORD says: O my people, I am going to open your graves and bring you up from them; I will bring you back to the land of Israel. ¹³Then you, my people, will know that I am the LORD, when I open your graves and bring you up from them. ¹⁴I will put my Spirit in you and you will live, and I will settle you in your own land. Then you will know that I the LORD have spoken, and I have done it, declares the LORD.' "

One Nation Under One King

¹⁵The word of the LORD came to me: ¹⁶"Son of man, take a stick of wood and write on it, 'Belonging to Judah and the Israelites associated with him.' Then take another stick of wood, and write on it, 'Ephraim's stick, belonging to Joseph and all the house of Israel associated with him.' ¹⁷Join them together into one stick so that they will become one in your hand.

¹⁸"When your countrymen ask you, 'Won't you tell us what you mean by this?' ¹⁹say to them, 'This is what the Sovereign LORD says: I am going to take the stick of Joseph—which is in Ephraim's hand—and of the Israelite

ᵃ5 The Hebrew for this word can also mean wind or spirit (see verses 6-14).

tribes associated with him, and join it to Judah's stick, making them a single stick of wood, and they will become one in my hand.' ²⁰Hold before their eyes the sticks you have written on ²¹and say to them, 'This is what the Sovereign LORD says: I will take the Israelites out of the nations where they have gone. I will gather them from all around and bring them back into their own land. ²²I will make them one nation in the land, on the mountains of Israel. There will be one king over all of them and they will never again be two nations or be divided into two kingdoms. ²³They will no longer defile themselves with their idols and vile images or with any of their offenses, for I will save them from all their sinful backsliding,^a and I will cleanse them. They will be my people, and I will be their God.

²⁴" 'My servant David will be king over them, and they will all have one shepherd. They will follow my laws and be careful to keep my decrees. ²⁵They will live in the land I gave to my servant Jacob, the land where your fathers lived. They and their children and their children's children will live there forever, and David my servant will be their prince forever. ²⁶I will make a covenant of peace with them; it will be an everlasting covenant. I will establish them and increase their numbers, and I will put my sanctuary among them forever. ²⁷My dwelling place will be with them; I will be their God, and they will be my people. ²⁸Then the nations will know that I the LORD make Israel holy, when my sanctuary is among them forever.' "

A Prophecy Against Gog

38 The word of the LORD came to me: ²"Son of man, set your face against Gog, of the land of Magog, the chief prince of^b Meshech and Tubal; prophesy against him ³and say: 'This is what the Sovereign LORD says: I am against you, O Gog, chief prince of^c Meshech and Tubal. ⁴I will turn you around, put hooks in your jaws and bring you out with your whole army—your horses, your horsemen fully armed, and a great horde with large and small shields, all of them brandishing their swords. ⁵Persia, Cush^d and Put will be with them, all with shields and helmets, ⁶also Gomer with all its troops, and Beth Togarmah from the far north with all its troops—the many nations with you.

⁷" 'Get ready; be prepared, you and all the hordes gathered about you, and take command of them. ⁸After many days you will be called to arms. In future years you will invade a land that has recovered from war, whose people were gathered from many nations to the mountains of Israel, which had long been desolate. They had been brought out from the nations, and now all of them live in safety. ⁹You and all your troops and the many nations with you will go up, advancing like a storm; you will be like a cloud covering the land.

¹⁰" 'This is what the Sovereign LORD says: On that day thoughts will come into your mind and you will devise an evil scheme. ¹¹You will say, "I will invade a land of unwalled villages; I will attack a peaceful and unsuspecting people—all of them living without walls and without gates and bars. ¹²I will plunder and loot and turn my hand against the resettled ruins and the people gathered from the nations, rich in livestock and goods, living at the center of the land." ¹³Sheba and Dedan and the merchants of Tarshish and all her villages^e will say to you, "Have you come to plunder? Have you gathered your hordes to loot, to carry off silver and gold, to take away livestock and goods and to seize much plunder?" '

¹⁴"Therefore, son of man, prophesy and say to Gog: 'This is what the Sovereign LORD says: In that day, when

---

^a23 Many Hebrew manuscripts (see also Septuagint); most Hebrew manuscripts *all their dwelling places where they sinned* ^b2 Or *the prince of Rosh,* ^c3 Or *Gog, prince of Rosh,* ^d5 That is, the upper Nile region ^e13 Or *her strong lions*

my people Israel are living in safety, will you not take notice of it? ¹⁵You will come from your place in the far north, you and many nations with you, all of them riding on horses, a great horde, a mighty army. ¹⁶You will advance against my people Israel like a cloud that covers the land. In days to come, O Gog, I will bring you against my land, so that the nations may know me when I show myself holy through you before their eyes.

¹⁷" 'This is what the Sovereign Lord says: Are you not the one I spoke of in former days by my servants the prophets of Israel? At that time they prophesied for years that I would bring you against them. ¹⁸This is what will happen in that day: When Gog attacks the land of Israel, my hot anger will be aroused, declares the Sovereign Lord. ¹⁹In my zeal and fiery wrath I declare that at that time there shall be a great earthquake in the land of Israel. ²⁰The fish of the sea, the birds of the air, the beasts of the field, every creature that moves along the ground, and all the people on the face of the earth will tremble at my presence. The mountains will be overturned, the cliffs will crumble and every wall will fall to the ground. ²¹I will summon a sword against Gog on all my mountains, declares the Sovereign Lord. Every man's sword will be against his brother. ²²I will execute judgment upon him with plague and bloodshed; I will pour down torrents of rain, hailstones and burning sulfur on him and on his troops and on the many nations with him. ²³And so I will show my greatness and my holiness, and I will make myself known in the sight of many nations. Then they will know that I am the Lord.'

39 "Son of man, prophesy against Gog and say: 'This is what the Sovereign Lord says: I am against you, O Gog, chief prince of[a] Meshech and Tubal. ²I will turn you around and drag you along. I will bring you from the far north and send

you against the mountains of Israel. ³Then I will strike your bow from your left hand and make your arrows drop from your right hand. ⁴On the mountains of Israel you will fall, you and all your troops and the nations with you. I will give you as food to all kinds of carrion birds and to the wild animals. ⁵You will fall in the open field, for I have spoken, declares the Sovereign Lord. ⁶I will send fire on Magog and on those who live in safety in the coastlands, and they will know that I am the Lord.

⁷" 'I will make known my holy name among my people Israel. I will no longer let my holy name be profaned, and the nations will know that I the Lord am the Holy One in Israel. ⁸It is coming! It will surely take place, declares the Sovereign Lord. This is the day I have spoken of.

⁹" 'Then those who live in the towns of Israel will go out and use the weapons for fuel and burn them up— the small and large shields, the bows and arrows, the war clubs and spears. For seven years they will use them for fuel. ¹⁰They will not need to gather wood from the fields or cut it from the forests, because they will use the weapons for fuel. And they will plunder those who plundered them and loot those who looted them, declares the Sovereign Lord.

¹¹" 'On that day I will give Gog a burial place in Israel, in the valley of those who travel east toward[b] the Sea.[c] It will block the way of travelers, because Gog and all his hordes will be buried there. So it will be called the Valley of Hamon Gog.[d]

¹²" 'For seven months the house of Israel will be burying them in order to cleanse the land. ¹³All the people of the land will bury them, and the day I am glorified will be a memorable day for them, declares the Sovereign Lord.

¹⁴" 'Men will be regularly employed to cleanse the land. Some will go throughout the land and, in addi-

---

a1 Or *Gog, prince of Rosh,*   b11 Or *of*   c11 That is, the Dead Sea   d11 *Hamon Gog* means *hordes of Gog.*

tion to them, others will bury those that remain on the ground. At the end of the seven months they will begin their search. ¹⁵As they go through the land and one of them sees a human bone, he will set up a marker beside it until the gravediggers have buried it in the Valley of Hamon Gog. ¹⁶(Also a town called Hamonah*a* will be there.) And so they will cleanse the land.'

¹⁷"Son of man, this is what the Sovereign LORD says: Call out to every kind of bird and all the wild animals: 'Assemble and come together from all around to the sacrifice I am preparing for you, the great sacrifice on the mountains of Israel. There you will eat flesh and drink blood. ¹⁸You will eat the flesh of mighty men and drink the blood of the princes of the earth as if they were rams and lambs, goats and bulls—all of them fattened animals from Bashan. ¹⁹At the sacrifice I am preparing for you, you will eat fat till you are glutted and drink blood till you are drunk. ²⁰At my table you will eat your fill of horses and riders, mighty men and soldiers of every kind,' declares the Sovereign LORD.

²¹"I will display my glory among the nations, and all the nations will see the punishment I inflict and the hand I lay upon them. ²²From that day forward the house of Israel will know that I am the LORD their God. ²³And the nations will know that the people of Israel went into exile for their sin, because they were unfaithful to me. So I hid my face from them and handed them over to their enemies, and they all fell by the sword. ²⁴I dealt with them according to their uncleanness and their offenses, and I hid my face from them.

²⁵"Therefore this is what the Sovereign LORD says: I will now bring Jacob back from captivity*b* and will have compassion on all the people of Israel, and I will be zealous for my holy name. ²⁶They will forget their shame and all the unfaithfulness they

showed toward me when they lived in safety in their land with no one to make them afraid. ²⁷When I have brought them back from the nations and have gathered them from the countries of their enemies, I will show myself holy through them in the sight of many nations. ²⁸Then they will know that I am the LORD their God, for though I sent them into exile among the nations, I will gather them to their own land, not leaving any behind. ²⁹I will no longer hide my face from them, for I will pour out my Spirit on the house of Israel, declares the Sovereign LORD."

The New Temple Area

40 In the twenty-fifth year of our exile, at the beginning of the year, on the tenth of the month, in the fourteenth year after the fall of the city—on that very day the hand of the LORD was upon me and he took me there. ²In visions of God he took me to the land of Israel and set me on a very high mountain, on whose south side were some buildings that looked like a city. ³He took me there, and I saw a man whose appearance was like bronze; he was standing in the gateway with a linen cord and a measuring rod in his hand. ⁴The man said to me, "Son of man, look with your eyes and hear with your ears and pay attention to everything I am going to show you, for that is why you have been brought here. Tell the house of Israel everything you see."

The East Gate to the Outer Court

⁵I saw a wall completely surrounding the temple area. The length of the measuring rod in the man's hand was six long cubits, each of which was a cubit*c* and a handbreadth.*d* He measured the wall; it was one measuring rod thick and one rod high. ⁶Then he went to the gate facing east. He climbed its steps and measured the threshold of the gate; it was

---

a16 *Hamonah* means *horde.*   *b25* Or *now restore the fortunes of Jacob*   *c5* The common cubit was about 1 1/2 feet (about 0.5 meter).   *d5* That is, about 3 inches (about 8 centimeters)

one rod deep.*a* ⁷The alcoves for the guards were one rod long and one rod wide, and the projecting walls between the alcoves were five cubits thick. And the threshold of the gate next to the portico facing the temple was one rod deep.

⁸Then he measured the portico of the gateway; ⁹it*b* was eight cubits deep and its jambs were two cubits thick. The portico of the gateway faced the temple.

¹⁰Inside the east gate were three alcoves on each side; the three had the same measurements, and the faces of the projecting walls on each side had the same measurements. ¹¹Then he measured the width of the entrance to the gateway; it was ten cubits and its length was thirteen cubits. ¹²In front of each alcove was a wall one cubit high, and the alcoves were six cubits square. ¹³Then he measured the gateway from the top of the rear wall of one alcove to the top of the opposite one; the distance was twenty-five cubits from one parapet opening to the opposite one. ¹⁴He measured along the faces of the projecting walls all around the inside of the gateway— sixty cubits. The measurement was up to the portico*c* facing the courtyard.*d* ¹⁵The distance from the entrance of the gateway to the far end of its portico was fifty cubits. ¹⁶The alcoves and the projecting walls inside the gateway were surmounted by narrow parapet openings all around, as was the portico; the openings all around faced inward. The faces of the projecting walls were decorated with palm trees.

The Outer Court

¹⁷Then he brought me into the outer court. There I saw some rooms and a pavement that had been constructed all around the court; there were thirty rooms along the pavement. ¹⁸It abutted the sides of the gateways and was as wide as they were long; this was the lower pavement. ¹⁹Then he measured the distance from the inside of the lower gateway to the outside of the inner court; it was a hundred cubits on the east side as well as on the north.

The North Gate

²⁰Then he measured the length and width of the gate facing north, leading into the outer court. ²¹Its alcoves—three on each side—its projecting walls and its portico had the same measurements as those of the first gateway. It was fifty cubits long and twenty-five cubits wide. ²²Its openings, its portico and its palm tree decorations had the same measurements as those of the gate facing east. Seven steps led up to it, with its portico opposite them. ²³There was a gate to the inner court facing the north gate, just as there was on the east. He measured from one gate to the opposite one; it was a hundred cubits.

The South Gate

²⁴Then he led me to the south side and I saw a gate facing south. He measured its jambs and its portico, and they had the same measurements as the others. ²⁵The gateway and its portico had narrow openings all around, like the openings of the others. It was fifty cubits long and twenty-five cubits wide. ²⁶Seven steps led up to it, with its portico opposite them; it had palm tree decorations on the faces of the projecting walls on each side. ²⁷The inner court also had a gate facing south, and he measured from this gate to the outer gate on the south side; it was a hundred cubits.

Gates to the Inner Court

²⁸Then he brought me into the inner court through the south gate, and he measured the south gate; it had the same measurements as the others.

---

a6 Septuagint; Hebrew *deep, the first threshold, one rod deep*   *b8,9* Many Hebrew manuscripts, Septuagint, Vulgate and Syriac; most Hebrew manuscripts *gateway facing the temple; it was one rod deep. 9Then he measured the portico of the gateway; it*   *c14* Septuagint; Hebrew *projecting wall*
d14 The meaning of the Hebrew for this verse is uncertain.

²⁹Its alcoves, its projecting walls and its portico had the same measurements as the others. The gateway and its portico had openings all around. It was fifty cubits long and twenty-five cubits wide. ³⁰(The porticoes of the gateways around the inner court were twenty-five cubits wide and five cubits deep.) ³¹Its portico faced the outer court; palm trees decorated its jambs, and eight steps led up to it.

³²Then he brought me to the inner court on the east side, and he measured the gateway; it had the same measurements as the others. ³³Its alcoves, its projecting walls and its portico had the same measurements as the others. The gateway and its portico had openings all around. It was fifty cubits long and twenty-five cubits wide. ³⁴Its portico faced the outer court; palm trees decorated the jambs on either side, and eight steps led up to it.

³⁵Then he brought me to the north gate and measured it. It had the same measurements as the others, ³⁶as did its alcoves, its projecting walls and its portico, and it had openings all around. It was fifty cubits long and twenty-five cubits wide. ³⁷Its portico*a* faced the outer court; palm trees decorated the jambs on either side, and eight steps led up to it.

The Rooms for Preparing Sacrifices

³⁸A room with a doorway was by the portico in each of the inner gateways, where the burnt offerings were washed. ³⁹In the portico of the gateway were two tables on each side, on which the burnt offerings, sin offerings and guilt offerings were slaughtered. ⁴⁰By the outside wall of the portico of the gateway, near the steps at the entrance to the north gateway were two tables, and on the other side of the steps were two tables. ⁴¹So there were four tables on one side of the gateway and four on the other— eight tables in all—on which the sacrifices were slaughtered. ⁴²There were also four tables of dressed stone for the burnt offerings, each a cubit and a half long, a cubit and a half wide and a cubit high. On them were placed the utensils for slaughtering the burnt offerings and the other sacrifices. ⁴³And double-pronged hooks, each a handbreadth long, were attached to the wall all around. The tables were for the flesh of the offerings.

Rooms for the Priests

⁴⁴Outside the inner gate, within the inner court, were two rooms, one*b* at the side of the north gate and facing south, and another at the side of the south*c* gate and facing north. ⁴⁵He said to me, "The room facing south is for the priests who have charge of the temple, ⁴⁶and the room facing north is for the priests who have charge of the altar. These are the sons of Zadok, who are the only Levites who may draw near to the LORD to minister before him."

⁴⁷Then he measured the court: It was square—a hundred cubits long and a hundred cubits wide. And the altar was in front of the temple.

The Temple

⁴⁸He brought me to the portico of the temple and measured the jambs of the portico; they were five cubits wide on either side. The width of the entrance was fourteen cubits and its projecting walls were*d* three cubits wide on either side. ⁴⁹The portico was twenty cubits wide, and twelve*e* cubits from front to back. It was reached by a flight of stairs,*f* and there were pillars on each side of the jambs.

41 Then the man brought me to the outer sanctuary and measured the jambs; the width of the jambs was six cubits*g* on each side.*h*

a37 Septuagint (see also verses 31 and 34); Hebrew *jambs*   *b44* Septuagint; Hebrew *were rooms for singers, which were*   *c44* Septuagint; Hebrew *east*   *d48* Septuagint; Hebrew *entrance was*   *e49* Septuagint; Hebrew *eleven*   *f49* Hebrew; Septuagint *Ten steps led up to it*   *g1* The common cubit was about 1 1/2 feet (about 0.5 meter).   *h1* One Hebrew manuscript and Septuagint; most Hebrew manuscripts *side, the width of the tent*

²The entrance was ten cubits wide, and the projecting walls on each side of it were five cubits wide. He also measured the outer sanctuary; it was forty cubits long and twenty cubits wide.

³Then he went into the inner sanctuary and measured the jambs of the entrance; each was two cubits wide. The entrance was six cubits wide, and the projecting walls on each side of it were seven cubits wide. ⁴And he measured the length of the inner sanctuary; it was twenty cubits, and its width was twenty cubits across the end of the outer sanctuary. He said to me, "This is the Most Holy Place."

⁵Then he measured the wall of the temple; it was six cubits thick, and each side room around the temple was four cubits wide. ⁶The side rooms were on three levels, one above another, thirty on each level. There were ledges all around the wall of the temple to serve as supports for the side rooms, so that the supports were not inserted into the wall of the temple. ⁷The side rooms all around the temple were wider at each successive level. The structure surrounding the temple was built in ascending stages, so that the rooms widened as one went upward. A stairway went up from the lowest floor to the top floor through the middle floor.

⁸I saw that the temple had a raised base all around it, forming the foundation of the side rooms. It was the length of the rod, six long cubits. ⁹The outer wall of the side rooms was five cubits thick. The open area between the side rooms of the temple ¹⁰and the ⌊priests'⌋ rooms was twenty cubits wide all around the temple. ¹¹There were entrances to the side rooms from the open area, one on the north and another on the south; and the base adjoining the open area was five cubits wide all around.

¹²The building facing the temple courtyard on the west side was seventy cubits wide. The wall of the building was five cubits thick all around, and its length was ninety cubits.

¹³Then he measured the temple; it was a hundred cubits long, and the temple courtyard and the building with its walls were also a hundred cubits long. ¹⁴The width of the temple courtyard on the east, including the front of the temple, was a hundred cubits.

¹⁵Then he measured the length of the building facing the courtyard at the rear of the temple, including its galleries on each side; it was a hundred cubits.

The outer sanctuary, the inner sanctuary and the portico facing the court, ¹⁶as well as the thresholds and the narrow windows and galleries around the three of them—everything beyond and including the threshold was covered with wood. The floor, the wall up to the windows, and the windows were covered. ¹⁷In the space above the outside of the entrance to the inner sanctuary and on the walls at regular intervals all around the inner and outer sanctuary ¹⁸were carved cherubim and palm trees. Palm trees alternated with cherubim. Each cherub had two faces: ¹⁹the face of a man toward the palm tree on one side and the face of a lion toward the palm tree on the other. They were carved all around the whole temple. ²⁰From the floor to the area above the entrance, cherubim and palm trees were carved on the wall of the outer sanctuary.

²¹The outer sanctuary had a rectangular doorframe, and the one at the front of the Most Holy Place was similar. ²²There was a wooden altar three cubits high and two cubits square*ᵃ*; its corners, its base*ᵇ* and its sides were of wood. The man said to me, "This is the table that is before the LORD." ²³Both the outer sanctuary and the Most Holy Place had double doors— ²⁴Each door had two leaves— two hinged leaves for each door. ²⁵And on the doors of the outer sanctuary were carved cherubim and

---

ᵃ22 Septuagint; Hebrew *long*   *ᵇ22* Septuagint; Hebrew *length*

palm trees like those carved on the walls, and there was a wooden overhang on the front of the portico. ²⁶On the sidewalls of the portico were narrow windows with palm trees carved on each side. The side rooms of the temple also had overhangs.

Rooms for the Priests

42 Then the man led me northward into the outer court and brought me to the rooms opposite the temple courtyard and opposite the outer wall on the north side. ²The building whose door faced north was a hundred cubits*a* long and fifty cubits wide. ³Both in the section twenty cubits from the inner court and in the section opposite the pavement of the outer court, gallery faced gallery at the three levels. ⁴In front of the rooms was an inner passageway ten cubits wide and a hundred cubits*b* long. Their doors were on the north. ⁵Now the upper rooms were narrower, for the galleries took more space from them than from the rooms on the lower and middle floors of the building. ⁶The rooms on the third floor had no pillars, as the courts had; so they were smaller in floor space than those on the lower and middle floors. ⁷There was an outer wall parallel to the rooms and the outer court; it extended in front of the rooms for fifty cubits. ⁸While the row of rooms on the side next to the outer court was fifty cubits long, the row on the side nearest the sanctuary was a hundred cubits long. ⁹The lower rooms had an entrance on the east side as one enters them from the outer court.

¹⁰On the south side*c* along the length of the wall of the outer court, adjoining the temple courtyard and opposite the outer wall, were rooms ¹¹with a passageway in front of them. These were like the rooms on the north; they had the same length and width, with similar exits and dimen-

sions. Similar to the doorways on the north ¹²were the doorways of the rooms on the south. There was a doorway at the beginning of the passageway that was parallel to the corresponding wall extending eastward, by which one enters the rooms.

¹³Then he said to me, "The north and south rooms facing the temple courtyard are the priests' rooms, where the priests who approach the Lᴏʀᴅ will eat the most holy offerings. There they will put the most holy offerings—the grain offerings, the sin offerings and the guilt offerings—for the place is holy. ¹⁴Once the priests enter the holy precincts, they are not to go into the outer court until they leave behind the garments in which they minister, for these are holy. They are to put on other clothes before they go near the places that are for the people."

¹⁵When he had finished measuring what was inside the temple area, he led me out by the east gate and measured the area all around: ¹⁶He measured the east side with the measuring rod; it was five hundred cubits.*d* ¹⁷He measured the north side; it was five hundred cubits*e* by the measuring rod. ¹⁸He measured the south side; it was five hundred cubits by the measuring rod. ¹⁹Then he turned to the west side and measured; it was five hundred cubits by the measuring rod. ²⁰So he measured the area on all four sides. It had a wall around it, five hundred cubits long and five hundred cubits wide, to separate the holy from the common.

The Glory Returns to the Temple

43 Then the man brought me to the gate facing east, ²and I saw the glory of the God of Israel coming from the east. His voice was like the roar of rushing waters, and the land was radiant with his glory. ³The vision I saw was like the vision I had

---

*a*2 The common cubit was about 1 1/2 feet (about 0.5 meter).   *b*4 Septuagint and Syriac; Hebrew *and one cubit*   *c*10 Septuagint; Hebrew *Eastward*   *d*16 See Septuagint of verse 17; Hebrew *rods*; also in verses 18 and 19.   *e*17 Septuagint; Hebrew *rods*

seen when he[a] came to destroy the city and like the visions I had seen by the Kebar River, and I fell facedown. [4]The glory of the LORD entered the temple through the gate facing east. [5]Then the Spirit lifted me up and brought me into the inner court, and the glory of the LORD filled the temple.

[6]While the man was standing beside me, I heard someone speaking to me from inside the temple. [7]He said: "Son of man, this is the place of my throne and the place for the soles of my feet. This is where I will live among the Israelites forever. The house of Israel will never again defile my holy name—neither they nor their kings—by their prostitution[b] and the lifeless idols[c] of their kings at their high places. [8]When they placed their threshold next to my threshold and their doorposts beside my doorposts, with only a wall between me and them, they defiled my holy name by their detestable practices. So I destroyed them in my anger. [9]Now let them put away from me their prostitution and the lifeless idols of their kings, and I will live among them forever.

[10]"Son of man, describe the temple to the people of Israel, that they may be ashamed of their sins. Let them consider the plan, [11]and if they are ashamed of all they have done, make known to them the design of the temple—its arrangement, its exits and entrances—its whole design and all its regulations[d] and laws. Write these down before them so that they may be faithful to its design and follow all its regulations.

[12]"This is the law of the temple: All the surrounding area on top of the mountain will be most holy. Such is the law of the temple.

The Altar

[13]"These are the measurements of the altar in long cubits, that cubit being a cubit[e] and a handbreadth[f]: Its gutter is a cubit deep and a cubit wide, with a rim of one span[g] around the edge. And this is the height of the altar: [14]From the gutter on the ground up to the lower ledge it is two cubits high and a cubit wide, and from the smaller ledge up to the larger ledge it is four cubits high and a cubit wide. [15]The altar hearth is four cubits high, and four horns project upward from the hearth. [16]The altar hearth is square, twelve cubits long and twelve cubits wide. [17]The upper ledge also is square, fourteen cubits long and fourteen cubits wide, with a rim of half a cubit and a gutter of a cubit all around. The steps of the altar face east."

[18]Then he said to me, "Son of man, this is what the Sovereign LORD says: These will be the regulations for sacrificing burnt offerings and sprinkling blood upon the altar when it is built: [19]You are to give a young bull as a sin offering to the priests, who are Levites, of the family of Zadok, who come near to minister before me, declares the Sovereign LORD. [20]You are to take some of its blood and put it on the four horns of the altar and on the four corners of the upper ledge and all around the rim, and so purify the altar and make atonement for it. [21]You are to take the bull for the sin offering and burn it in the designated part of the temple area outside the sanctuary.

[22]"On the second day you are to offer a male goat without defect for a sin offering, and the altar is to be purified as it was purified with the bull. [23]When you have finished purifying it, you are to offer a young bull and a ram from the flock, both without defect. [24]You are to offer them before the LORD, and the priests are to sprinkle salt on them and sac-

---

[a]3 Some Hebrew manuscripts and Vulgate; most Hebrew manuscripts *I*   [b]7 Or *their spiritual adultery*; also in verse 9   [c]7 Or *the corpses*; also in verse 9   [d]11 Some Hebrew manuscripts and Septuagint; most Hebrew manuscripts *regulations and its whole design*   [e]13 The common cubit was about 1 1/2 feet (about 0.5 meter).   [f]13 That is, about 3 inches (about 8 centimeters)   [g]13 That is, about 9 inches (about 22 centimeters)

rifice them as a burnt offering to the LORD.

²⁵"For seven days you are to provide a male goat daily for a sin offering; you are also to provide a young bull and a ram from the flock, both without defect. ²⁶For seven days they are to make atonement for the altar and cleanse it; thus they will dedicate it. ²⁷At the end of these days, from the eighth day on, the priests are to present your burnt offerings and fellowship offerings^a on the altar. Then I will accept you, declares the Sovereign LORD."

The Prince, the Levites, the Priests

44 Then the man brought me back to the outer gate of the sanctuary, the one facing east, and it was shut. ²The LORD said to me, "This gate is to remain shut. It must not be opened; no one may enter through it. It is to remain shut because the LORD, the God of Israel, has entered through it. ³The prince himself is the only one who may sit inside the gateway to eat in the presence of the LORD. He is to enter by way of the portico of the gateway and go out the same way."

⁴Then the man brought me by way of the north gate to the front of the temple. I looked and saw the glory of the LORD filling the temple of the LORD, and I fell facedown.

⁵The LORD said to me, "Son of man, look carefully, listen closely and give attention to everything I tell you concerning all the regulations regarding the temple of the LORD. Give attention to the entrance of the temple and all the exits of the sanctuary. ⁶Say to the rebellious house of Israel, 'This is what the Sovereign LORD says: Enough of your detestable practices, O house of Israel! ⁷In addition to all your other detestable practices, you brought foreigners uncircumcised in heart and flesh into my sanctuary, desecrating my temple while you offered me food, fat and blood, and you broke my covenant. ⁸Instead of carrying out your duty in regard to my holy things, you put others in charge of my sanctuary. ⁹This is what the Sovereign LORD says: No foreigner uncircumcised in heart and flesh is to enter my sanctuary, not even the foreigners who live among the Israelites.

¹⁰" 'The Levites who went far from me when Israel went astray and who wandered from me after their idols must bear the consequences of their sin. ¹¹They may serve in my sanctuary, having charge of the gates of the temple and serving in it; they may slaughter the burnt offerings and sacrifices for the people and stand before the people and serve them. ¹²But because they served them in the presence of their idols and made the house of Israel fall into sin, therefore I have sworn with uplifted hand that they must bear the consequences of their sin, declares the Sovereign LORD. ¹³They are not to come near to serve me as priests or come near any of my holy things or my most holy offerings; they must bear the shame of their detestable practices. ¹⁴Yet I will put them in charge of the duties of the temple and all the work that is to be done in it.

¹⁵" 'But the priests, who are Levites and descendants of Zadok and who faithfully carried out the duties of my sanctuary when the Israelites went astray from me, are to come near to minister before me; they are to stand before me to offer sacrifices of fat and blood, declares the Sovereign LORD. ¹⁶They alone are to enter my sanctuary; they alone are to come near my table to minister before me and perform my service.

¹⁷" 'When they enter the gates of the inner court, they are to wear linen clothes; they must not wear any woolen garment while ministering at the gates of the inner court or inside the temple. ¹⁸They are to wear linen turbans on their heads and linen undergarments around their waists. They must not wear anything that makes them perspire. ¹⁹When they go out into the outer court where the people

are, they are to take off the clothes they have been ministering in and are to leave them in the sacred rooms, and put on other clothes, so that they do not consecrate the people by means of their garments.

20" 'They must not shave their heads or let their hair grow long, but they are to keep the hair of their heads trimmed. 21No priest is to drink wine when he enters the inner court. 22They must not marry widows or divorced women; they may marry only virgins of Israelite descent or widows of priests. 23They are to teach my people the difference between the holy and the common and show them how to distinguish between the unclean and the clean.

24" 'In any dispute, the priests are to serve as judges and decide it according to my ordinances. They are to keep my laws and my decrees for all my appointed feasts, and they are to keep my Sabbaths holy.

25" 'A priest must not defile himself by going near a dead person; however, if the dead person was his father or mother, son or daughter, brother or unmarried sister, then he may defile himself. 26After he is cleansed, he must wait seven days. 27On the day he goes into the inner court of the sanctuary to minister in the sanctuary, he is to offer a sin offering for himself, declares the Sovereign LORD.

28" 'I am to be the only inheritance the priests have. You are to give them no possession in Israel; I will be their possession. 29They will eat the grain offerings, the sin offerings and the guilt offerings; and everything in Israel devoted[a] to the LORD will belong to them. 30The best of all the firstfruits and of all your special gifts will belong to the priests. You are to give them the first portion of your ground meal so that a blessing may rest on your household. 31The priests must

not eat anything, bird or animal, found dead or torn by wild animals.

Division of the Land

45 " 'When you allot the land as an inheritance, you are to present to the LORD a portion of the land as a sacred district, 25,000 cubits long and 20,000[b] cubits wide; the entire area will be holy. 2Of this, a section 500 cubits square is to be for the sanctuary, with 50 cubits around it for open land. 3In the sacred district, measure off a section 25,000 cubits[c] long and 10,000 cubits[d] wide. In it will be the sanctuary, the Most Holy Place. 4It will be the sacred portion of the land for the priests, who minister in the sanctuary and who draw near to minister before the LORD. It will be a place for their houses as well as a holy place for the sanctuary. 5An area 25,000 cubits long and 10,000 cubits wide will belong to the Levites, who serve in the temple, as their possession for towns to live in.[e]

6" 'You are to give the city as its property an area 5,000 cubits wide and 25,000 cubits long, adjoining the sacred portion; it will belong to the whole house of Israel.

7" 'The prince will have the land bordering each side of the area formed by the sacred district and the property of the city. It will extend westward from the west side and eastward from the east side, running lengthwise from the western to the eastern border parallel to one of the tribal portions. 8This land will be his possession in Israel. And my princes will no longer oppress my people but will allow the house of Israel to possess the land according to their tribes.

9" 'This is what the Sovereign LORD says: You have gone far enough, O princes of Israel! Give up your violence and oppression and do what is just and right. Stop dispossessing my people, declares the Sovereign LORD.

---

[a]29 The Hebrew term refers to the irrevocable giving over of things or persons to the LORD.   [b]1 Septuagint (see also verses 3 and 5 and 48:9); Hebrew 10,000   [c]3 That is, about 7 miles (about 12 kilometers)   [d]3 That is, about 3 miles (about 5 kilometers)   [e]5 Septuagint; Hebrew temple; they will have as their possession 20 rooms

¹⁰You are to use accurate scales, an accurate ephah[a] and an accurate bath.[b] ¹¹The ephah and the bath are to be the same size, the bath containing a tenth of a homer[c] and the ephah a tenth of a homer; the homer is to be the standard measure for both. ¹²The shekel[d] is to consist of twenty gerahs. Twenty shekels plus twenty-five shekels plus fifteen shekels equal one mina.[e]

Offerings and Holy Days

¹³" 'This is the special gift you are to offer: a sixth of an ephah from each homer of wheat and a sixth of an ephah from each homer of barley. ¹⁴The prescribed portion of oil, measured by the bath, is a tenth of a bath from each cor (which consists of ten baths or one homer, for ten baths are equivalent to a homer). ¹⁵Also one sheep is to be taken from every flock of two hundred from the well-watered pastures of Israel. These will be used for the grain offerings, burnt offerings and fellowship offerings[f] to make atonement for the people, declares the Sovereign LORD. ¹⁶All the people of the land will participate in this special gift for the use of the prince in Israel. ¹⁷It will be the duty of the prince to provide the burnt offerings, grain offerings and drink offerings at the festivals, the New Moons and the Sabbaths—at all the appointed feasts of the house of Israel. He will provide the sin offerings, grain offerings, burnt offerings and fellowship offerings to make atonement for the house of Israel.

¹⁸" 'This is what the Sovereign LORD says: In the first month on the first day you are to take a young bull without defect and purify the sanctuary. ¹⁹The priest is to take some of the blood of the sin offering and put it on the doorposts of the temple, on the four corners of the upper ledge of the altar and on the gateposts of the inner court. ²⁰You are to do the same on the seventh day of the month for anyone who sins unintentionally or through ignorance; so you are to make atonement for the temple.

²¹" 'In the first month on the fourteenth day you are to observe the Passover, a feast lasting seven days, during which you shall eat bread made without yeast. ²²On that day the prince is to provide a bull as a sin offering for himself and for all the people of the land. ²³Every day during the seven days of the Feast he is to provide seven bulls and seven rams without defect as a burnt offering to the LORD, and a male goat for a sin offering. ²⁴He is to provide as a grain offering an ephah for each bull and an ephah for each ram, along with a hin[g] of oil for each ephah.

²⁵" 'During the seven days of the Feast, which begins in the seventh month on the fifteenth day, he is to make the same provision for sin offerings, burnt offerings, grain offerings and oil.

46 " 'This is what the Sovereign LORD says: The gate of the inner court facing east is to be shut on the six working days, but on the Sabbath day and on the day of the New Moon it is to be opened. ²The prince is to enter from the outside through the portico of the gateway and stand by the gatepost. The priests are to sacrifice his burnt offering and his fellowship offerings.[h] He is to worship at the threshold of the gateway and then go out, but the gate will not be shut until evening. ³On the Sabbaths and New Moons the people of the land are to worship in the presence of the LORD at the entrance to that gateway. ⁴The burnt offering the prince brings to the LORD on the Sabbath day is to be six male lambs and a ram, all without defect. ⁵The grain offering given with

---

ᵃ10 An ephah was a dry measure.   ᵇ10 A bath was a liquid measure.   ᶜ11 A homer was a dry measure.   ᵈ12 A shekel weighed about 2/5 ounce (about 11.5 grams).   ᵉ12 That is, 60 shekels; the common mina was 50 shekels.   ᶠ15 Traditionally *peace offerings*; also in verse 17   ᵍ24 That is, probably about 4 quarts (about 4 liters)   ʰ2 Traditionally *peace offerings*; also in verse 12

the ram is to be an ephah,ᵃ and the grain offering with the lambs is to be as much as he pleases, along with a hinᵇ of oil for each ephah. ⁶On the day of the New Moon he is to offer a young bull, six lambs and a ram, all without defect. ⁷He is to provide as a grain offering one ephah with the bull, one ephah with the ram, and with the lambs as much as he wants to give, along with a hin of oil with each ephah. ⁸When the prince enters, he is to go in through the portico of the gateway, and he is to come out the same way.

⁹" 'When the people of the land come before the Lᴏʀᴅ at the appointed feasts, whoever enters by the north gate to worship is to go out the south gate; and whoever enters by the south gate is to go out the north gate. No one is to return through the gate by which he entered, but each is to go out the opposite gate. ¹⁰The prince is to be among them, going in when they go in and going out when they go out.

¹¹" 'At the festivals and the appointed feasts, the grain offering is to be an ephah with a bull, an ephah with a ram, and with the lambs as much as one pleases, along with a hin of oil for each ephah. ¹²When the prince provides a freewill offering to the Lᴏʀᴅ—whether a burnt offering or fellowship offerings—the gate facing east is to be opened for him. He shall offer his burnt offering or his fellowship offerings as he does on the Sabbath day. Then he shall go out, and after he has gone out, the gate will be shut.

¹³" 'Every day you are to provide a year-old lamb without defect for a burnt offering to the Lᴏʀᴅ; morning by morning you shall provide it. ¹⁴You are also to provide with it morning by morning a grain offering, consisting of a sixth of an ephah with a third of a hin of oil to moisten the flour. The presenting of this grain offering to the Lᴏʀᴅ is a lasting ordinance. ¹⁵So the lamb and the grain offering and the oil shall be provided morning by morning for a regular burnt offering.

¹⁶" 'This is what the Sovereign Lᴏʀᴅ says: If the prince makes a gift from his inheritance to one of his sons, it will also belong to his descendants; it is to be their property by inheritance. ¹⁷If, however, he makes a gift from his inheritance to one of his servants, the servant may keep it until the year of freedom; then it will revert to the prince. His inheritance belongs to his sons only; it is theirs. ¹⁸The prince must not take any of the inheritance of the people, driving them off their property. He is to give his sons their inheritance out of his own property, so that none of my people will be separated from his property.' "

¹⁹Then the man brought me through the entrance at the side of the gate to the sacred rooms facing north, which belonged to the priests, and showed me a place at the western end. ²⁰He said to me, "This is the place where the priests will cook the guilt offering and the sin offering and bake the grain offering, to avoid bringing them into the outer court and consecrating the people."

²¹He then brought me to the outer court and led me around to its four corners, and I saw in each corner another court. ²²In the four corners of the outer court were enclosedᶜ courts, forty cubits long and thirty cubits wide; each of the courts in the four corners was the same size. ²³Around the inside of each of the four courts was a ledge of stone, with places for fire built all around under the ledge. ²⁴He said to me, "These are the kitchens where those who minister at the temple will cook the sacrifices of the people."

The River From the Temple

47 The man brought me back to the entrance of the temple, and I saw water coming out from under

ᵃ5 That is, probably about 3/5 bushel (about 22 liters)   ᵇ5 That is, probably about 4 quarts (about 4 liters)   ᶜ22 The meaning of the Hebrew for this word is uncertain.

the threshold of the temple toward the east (for the temple faced east). The water was coming down from under the south side of the temple, south of the altar. ²He then brought me out through the north gate and led me around the outside to the outer gate facing east, and the water was flowing from the south side.

³As the man went eastward with a measuring line in his hand, he measured off a thousand cubits[a] and then led me through water that was ankle-deep. ⁴He measured off another thousand cubits and led me through water that was knee-deep. He measured off another thousand and led me through water that was up to the waist. ⁵He measured off another thousand, but now it was a river that I could not cross, because the water had risen and was deep enough to swim in—a river that no one could cross. ⁶He asked me, "Son of man, do you see this?"

Then he led me back to the bank of the river. ⁷When I arrived there, I saw a great number of trees on each side of the river. ⁸He said to me, "This water flows toward the eastern region and goes down into the Arabah,[b] where it enters the Sea.[c] When it empties into the Sea,[c] the water there becomes fresh. ⁹Swarms of living creatures will live wherever the river flows. There will be large numbers of fish, because this water flows there and makes the salt water fresh; so where the river flows everything will live. ¹⁰Fishermen will stand along the shore; from En Gedi to En Eglaim there will be places for spreading nets. The fish will be of many kinds—like the fish of the Great Sea.[d] ¹¹But the swamps and marshes will not become fresh; they will be left for salt. ¹²Fruit trees of all kinds will grow on both banks of the river. Their leaves will not wither, nor will their fruit

fail. Every month they will bear, because the water from the sanctuary flows to them. Their fruit will serve for food and their leaves for healing."

The Boundaries of the Land

¹³This is what the Sovereign LORD says: "These are the boundaries by which you are to divide the land for an inheritance among the twelve tribes of Israel, with two portions for Joseph. ¹⁴You are to divide it equally among them. Because I swore with uplifted hand to give it to your forefathers, this land will become your inheritance.

¹⁵"This is to be the boundary of the land:

"On the north side it will run from the Great Sea by the Hethlon road past Lebo[e] Hamath to Zedad, ¹⁶Berothah[f] and Sibraim (which lies on the border between Damascus and Hamath), as far as Hazer Hatticon, which is on the border of Hauran. ¹⁷The boundary will extend from the sea to Hazar Enan,[g] along the northern border of Damascus, with the border of Hamath to the north. This will be the north boundary. ¹⁸"On the east side the boundary will run between Hauran and Damascus, along the Jordan between Gilead and the land of Israel, to the eastern sea and as far as Tamar.[h] This will be the east boundary. ¹⁹"On the south side it will run from Tamar as far as the waters of Meribah Kadesh, then along the Wadi ⌊of Egypt⌋ to the Great Sea. This will be the south boundary. ²⁰"On the west side, the Great Sea will be the boundary to a point opposite Lebo[i] Hamath. This will be the west boundary.

²¹"You are to distribute this land

---

[a]3 That is, about 1,500 feet (about 450 meters)   [b]8 Or the Jordan Valley   [c]8 That is, the Dead Sea   [d]10 That is, the Mediterranean; also in verses 15, 19 and 20   [e]15 Or past the entrance to   [f]15,16 See Septuagint and Ezekiel 48:1; Hebrew road to go into Zedad, ¹⁶Hamath, Berothah   [g]17 Hebrew Enon, a variant of Enan   [h]18 Septuagint and Syriac; Hebrew Israel. You will measure to the eastern sea   [i]20 Or opposite the entrance to

among yourselves according to the tribes of Israel. [22]You are to allot it as an inheritance for yourselves and for the aliens who have settled among you and who have children. You are to consider them as native-born Israelites; along with you they are to be allotted an inheritance among the tribes of Israel. [23]In whatever tribe the alien settles, there you are to give him his inheritance," declares the Sovereign LORD.

The Division of the Land

48 "These are the tribes, listed by name: At the northern frontier, Dan will have one portion; it will follow the Hethlon road to Lebo[a] Hamath; Hazar Enan and the northern border of Damascus next to Hamath will be part of its border from the east side to the west side.

[2]"Asher will have one portion; it will border the territory of Dan from east to west.

[3]"Naphtali will have one portion; it will border the territory of Asher from east to west.

[4]"Manasseh will have one portion; it will border the territory of Naphtali from east to west.

[5]"Ephraim will have one portion; it will border the territory of Manasseh from east to west.

[6]"Reuben will have one portion; it will border the territory of Ephraim from east to west.

[7]"Judah will have one portion; it will border the territory of Reuben from east to west.

[8]"Bordering the territory of Judah from east to west will be the portion you are to present as a special gift. It will be 25,000 cubits[b] wide, and its length from east to west will equal one of the tribal portions; the sanctuary will be in the center of it.

[9]"The special portion you are to offer to the LORD will be 25,000 cubits long and 10,000 cubits[c] wide. [10]This will be the sacred portion for the priests. It will be 25,000 cubits long on

the north side, 10,000 cubits wide on the west side, 10,000 cubits wide on the east side and 25,000 cubits long on the south side. In the center of it will be the sanctuary of the LORD. [11]This will be for the consecrated priests, the Zadokites, who were faithful in serving me and did not go astray as the Levites did when the Israelites went astray. [12]It will be a special gift to them from the sacred portion of the land, a most holy portion, bordering the territory of the Levites.

[13]"Alongside the territory of the priests, the Levites will have an allotment 25,000 cubits long and 10,000 cubits wide. Its total length will be 25,000 cubits and its width 10,000 cubits. [14]They must not sell or exchange any of it. This is the best of the land and must not pass into other hands, because it is holy to the LORD.

[15]"The remaining area, 5,000 cubits wide and 25,000 cubits long, will be for the common use of the city, for houses and for pastureland. The city will be in the center of it [16]and will have these measurements: the north side 4,500 cubits, the south side 4,500 cubits, the east side 4,500 cubits, and the west side 4,500 cubits. [17]The pastureland for the city will be 250 cubits on the north, 250 cubits on the south, 250 cubits on the east, and 250 cubits on the west. [18]What remains of the area, bordering on the sacred portion and running the length of it, will be 10,000 cubits on the east side and 10,000 cubits on the west side. Its produce will supply food for the workers of the city. [19]The workers from the city who farm it will come from all the tribes of Israel. [20]The entire portion will be a square, 25,000 cubits on each side. As a special gift you will set aside the sacred portion, along with the property of the city.

[21]"What remains on both sides of the area formed by the sacred portion and the city property will belong to the prince. It will extend eastward from the 25,000 cubits of the sacred

---

[a]1 Or *to the entrance to*   [b]8 That is, about 7 miles (about 12 kilometers)   [c]9 That is, about 3 miles (about 5 kilometers)

portion to the eastern border, and westward from the 25,000 cubits to the western border. Both these areas running the length of the tribal portions will belong to the prince, and the sacred portion with the temple sanctuary will be in the center of them. ²²So the property of the Levites and the property of the city will lie in the center of the area that belongs to the prince. The area belonging to the prince will lie between the border of Judah and the border of Benjamin.

²³"As for the rest of the tribes: Benjamin will have one portion; it will extend from the east side to the west side.

²⁴"Simeon will have one portion; it will border the territory of Benjamin from east to west.

²⁵"Issachar will have one portion; it will border the territory of Simeon from east to west.

²⁶"Zebulun will have one portion; it will border the territory of Issachar from east to west.

²⁷"Gad will have one portion; it will border the territory of Zebulun from east to west.

²⁸"The southern boundary of Gad will run south from Tamar to the waters of Meribah Kadesh, then along the Wadi ⌊of Egypt⌋ to the Great Sea.ᵃ

²⁹"This is the land you are to allot as an inheritance to the tribes of Israel, and these will be their portions," declares the Sovereign LORD.

The Gates of the City

³⁰"These will be the exits of the city: Beginning on the north side, which is 4,500 cubits long, ³¹the gates of city will be named after the tribes of Israel. The three gates on the north side will be the gate of Reuben, the gate of Judah and the gate of Levi.

³²"On the east side, which is 4,500 cubits long, will be three gates: the gate of Joseph, the gate of Benjamin and the gate of Dan.

³³"On the south side, which measures 4,500 cubits, will be three gates: the gate of Simeon, the gate of Issachar and the gate of Zebulun.

³⁴"On the west side, which is 4,500 cubits long, will be three gates: the gate of Gad, the gate of Asher and the gate of Naphtali.

³⁵"The distance all around will be 18,000 cubits.

"And the name of the city from that time on will be:

THE LORD IS THERE."

ᵃ28 That is, the Mediterranean

W...

riting from Babylon during the time of the exile, Daniel tells of God's miraculous power to protect those who belong to him. God gave Daniel and his friends the ability to stand firm and to serve effectively in a hostile environment. As you read this book, rejoice in God's power to work in your life and his promise never to desert you. In that power and in that promise, you will find peace, no matter what.

DANIEL

Daniel's Training in Babylon

1 In the third year of the reign of Jehoiakim king of Judah, Nebuchadnezzar king of Babylon came to Jerusalem and besieged it. ²And the Lord delivered Jehoiakim king of Judah into his hand, along with some of the articles from the temple of God. These he carried off to the temple of his god in Babylonia*ᵃ* and put in the treasure house of his god.

³Then the king ordered Ashpenaz, chief of his court officials, to bring in some of the Israelites from the royal family and the nobility— ⁴young men without any physical defect, handsome, showing aptitude for every kind of learning, well informed, quick to understand, and qualified to serve in the king's palace. He was to teach them the language and literature of the Babylonians.*ᵇ* ⁵The king assigned them a daily amount of food and wine from the king's table. They were to be trained for three years, and after that they were to enter the king's service.

⁶Among these were some from Judah: Daniel, Hananiah, Mishael and Azariah. ⁷The chief official gave them new names: to Daniel, the name Belteshazzar; to Hananiah, Shadrach; to Mishael, Meshach; and to Azariah, Abednego.

⁸But Daniel resolved not to defile himself with the royal food and wine, and he asked the chief official for permission not to defile himself this way. ⁹Now God had caused the official to show favor and sympathy to Daniel, ¹⁰but the official told Daniel, "I am afraid of my lord the king, who has assigned your*ᶜ* food and drink. Why should he see you looking worse than

---

*ᵃ*2 Hebrew *Shinar*   *ᵇ*4 Or *Chaldeans*   *ᶜ*10 The Hebrew for *your* and *you* in this verse is plural.

the other young men your age? The king would then have my head because of you."

[11]Daniel then said to the guard whom the chief official had appointed over Daniel, Hananiah, Mishael and Azariah, [12]"Please test your servants for ten days: Give us nothing but vegetables to eat and water to drink. [13]Then compare our appearance with that of the young men who eat the royal food, and treat your servants in accordance with what you see." [14]So he agreed to this and tested them for ten days.

[15]At the end of the ten days they looked healthier and better nourished than any of the young men who ate the royal food. [16]So the guard took away their choice food and the wine they were to drink and gave them vegetables instead.

[17]To these four young men God gave knowledge and understanding of all kinds of literature and learning. And Daniel could understand visions and dreams of all kinds.

[18]At the end of the time set by the king to bring them in, the chief official presented them to Nebuchadnezzar. [19]The king talked with them, and he found none equal to Daniel, Hananiah, Mishael and Azariah; so they entered the king's service. [20]In every matter of wisdom and understanding about which the king questioned them, he found them ten times better than all the magicians and enchanters in his whole kingdom.

[21]And Daniel remained there until the first year of King Cyrus.

Nebuchadnezzar's Dream

2 In the second year of his reign, Nebuchadnezzar had dreams; his mind was troubled and he could not sleep. [2]So the king summoned the magicians, enchanters, sorcerers and astrologers[a] to tell him what he had dreamed. When they came in and stood before the king, [3]he said to

them, "I have had a dream that troubles me and I want to know what it means.[b]"

[4]Then the astrologers answered the king in Aramaic,[c] "O king, live forever! Tell your servants the dream, and we will interpret it."

[5]The king replied to the astrologers, "This is what I have firmly decided: If you do not tell me what my dream was and interpret it, I will have you cut into pieces and your houses turned into piles of rubble. [6]But if you tell me the dream and explain it, you will receive from me gifts and rewards and great honor. So tell me the dream and interpret it for me."

[7]Once more they replied, "Let the king tell his servants the dream, and we will interpret it."

[8]Then the king answered, "I am certain that you are trying to gain time, because you realize that this is what I have firmly decided: [9]If you do not tell me the dream, there is just one penalty for you. You have conspired to tell me misleading and wicked things, hoping the situation will change. So then, tell me the dream, and I will know that you can interpret it for me."

[10]The astrologers answered the king, "There is not a man on earth who can do what the king asks! No king, however great and mighty, has ever asked such a thing of any magician or enchanter or astrologer. [11]What the king asks is too difficult. No one can reveal it to the king except the gods, and they do not live among men."

[12]This made the king so angry and furious that he ordered the execution of all the wise men of Babylon. [13]So the decree was issued to put the wise men to death, and men were sent to look for Daniel and his friends to put them to death.

[14]When Arioch, the commander of the king's guard, had gone out to put to death the wise men of Babylon, Daniel spoke to him with wisdom

---

[a]2 Or *Chaldeans*; also in verses 4, 5 and 10   [b]3 Or *was*   [c]4 The text from here through chapter 7 is in Aramaic.

and tact. ¹⁵He asked the king's officer, "Why did the king issue such a harsh decree?" Arioch then explained the matter to Daniel. ¹⁶At this, Daniel went in to the king and asked for time, so that he might interpret the dream for him.

¹⁷Then Daniel returned to his house and explained the matter to his friends Hananiah, Mishael and Azariah. ¹⁸He urged them to plead for mercy from the God of heaven concerning this mystery, so that he and his friends might not be executed with the rest of the wise men of Babylon. ¹⁹During the night the mystery was revealed to Daniel in a vision. Then Daniel praised the God of heaven ²⁰and said:

"Praise be to the name of God for
        ever and ever;
    wisdom and power are his.
²¹He changes times and seasons;
    he sets up kings and deposes
        them.
He gives wisdom to the wise
    and knowledge to the
        discerning.
²²He reveals deep and hidden
        things;
    he knows what lies in darkness,
    and light dwells with him.
²³I thank and praise you, O God of
    my fathers:
    You have given me wisdom and
        power,
you have made known to me
        what we asked of you,
    you have made known to us the
        dream of the king."

Daniel Interprets the Dream

²⁴Then Daniel went to Arioch, whom the king had appointed to execute the wise men of Babylon, and said to him, "Do not execute the wise men of Babylon. Take me to the king, and I will interpret his dream for him."

²⁵Arioch took Daniel to the king at once and said, "I have found a man among the exiles from Judah who can tell the king what his dream means."

²⁶The king asked Daniel (also called Belteshazzar), "Are you able to tell me what I saw in my dream and interpret it?"

²⁷Daniel replied, "No wise man, enchanter, magician or diviner can explain to the king the mystery he has asked about, ²⁸but there is a God in heaven who reveals mysteries. He has shown King Nebuchadnezzar what will happen in days to come. Your dream and the visions that passed through your mind as you lay on your bed are these:

²⁹"As you were lying there, O king, your mind turned to things to come, and the revealer of mysteries showed you what is going to happen. ³⁰As for me, this mystery has been revealed to me, not because I have greater wisdom than other living men, but so that you, O king, may know the interpretation and that you may understand what went through your mind.

³¹"You looked, O king, and there before you stood a large statue—an enormous, dazzling statue, awesome in appearance. ³²The head of the statue was made of pure gold, its chest and arms of silver, its belly and thighs of bronze, ³³its legs of iron, its feet partly of iron and partly of baked clay. ³⁴While you were watching, a rock was cut out, but not by human hands. It struck the statue on its feet of iron and clay and smashed them. ³⁵Then the iron, the clay, the bronze, the silver and the gold were broken to pieces at the same time and became like chaff on a threshing floor in the summer. The wind swept them away without leaving a trace. But the rock that struck the statue became a huge mountain and filled the whole earth.

³⁶"This was the dream, and now we will interpret it to the king. ³⁷You, O king, are the king of kings. The God of heaven has given you dominion and power and might and glory; ³⁸in your hands he has placed mankind and the beasts of the field and the birds of the air. Wherever they live, he has made you ruler over them all. You are that head of gold. ³⁹"After you, another kingdom will rise, inferior to yours. Next, a third

VERSE:
Daniel 2:21

AUTHOR:
Sherwood Eliot Wirt

PASSAGE:
Daniel 2:1–23

. . . .

The Gift of Time

Scripture teaches that, humanly speaking, time is nothing else than a gift of God, a precious package of life sent to us by our heavenly Father, individually gift-wrapped and with our name on it . . .

The great boon of retirement is that we "have time." If we don't we are in big trouble. Workaholics who boast they are "busier now than before they retired" are poor risks at best. They labor under the delusion that they are indispensable, which may point to a serious ego problem. Old age was not given to us by God to perpetuate the struggle for existence, and it is a global tragedy that for survival millions of elderly are forced to do just that. Retirement is actually intended to give us the time that never seemed to be ours when we were younger. For our purposes let us assume that you do have that time, that for you the daily rush has subsided somewhat and you can now occasionally gaze at the drifting clouds and smell the hyacinths.

What a wonderful gift this is! Time for our grandchildren. Time for prayer. Time to read the great books. Time to visit old friends. Time to think, to reflect, to love and laugh and listen to music. Time to exercise. Time to work on our own projects. Time to calibrate our spiritual compasses and get the priorities of life in proper order.

. . . .

ADDITIONAL SCRIPTURE READINGS
Ecclesiastes 3:1–14; 2 Corinthians 6:1–2

Go to page 1093 for your next devotional reading.

kingdom, one of bronze, will rule over the whole earth. [40]Finally, there will be a fourth kingdom, strong as iron—for iron breaks and smashes everything—and as iron breaks things to pieces, so it will crush and break all the others. [41]Just as you saw that the feet and toes were partly of baked clay and partly of iron, so this will be a divided kingdom; yet it will have some of the strength of iron in it, even as you saw iron mixed with clay. [42]As the toes were partly iron and partly clay, so this kingdom will be partly strong and partly brittle. [43]And just as you saw the iron mixed with baked clay, so the people will be a mixture and will not remain united, any more than iron mixes with clay.

[44]"In the time of those kings, the God of heaven will set up a kingdom that will never be destroyed, nor will it be left to another people. It will crush all those kingdoms and bring them to an end, but it will itself endure forever. [45]This is the meaning of the vision of the rock cut out of a mountain, but not by human hands— a rock that broke the iron, the bronze, the clay, the silver and the gold to pieces.

"The great God has shown the king what will take place in the future. The dream is true and the interpretation is trustworthy."

[46]Then King Nebuchadnezzar fell prostrate before Daniel and paid him honor and ordered that an offering and incense be presented to him. [47]The king said to Daniel, "Surely your God is the God of gods and the Lord of kings and a revealer of mysteries, for you were able to reveal this mystery."

[48]Then the king placed Daniel in a high position and lavished many gifts on him. He made him ruler over the entire province of Babylon and placed him in charge of all its wise men. [49]Moreover, at Daniel's request the king appointed Shadrach, Meshach and Abednego administrators over the province of Babylon, while Daniel himself remained at the royal court.

The Image of Gold and the Fiery Furnace

3 King Nebuchadnezzar made an image of gold, ninety feet high and nine feet[a] wide, and set it up on the plain of Dura in the province of Babylon. [2]He then summoned the satraps, prefects, governors, advisers, treasurers, judges, magistrates and all the other provincial officials to come to the dedication of the image he had set up. [3]So the satraps, prefects, governors, advisers, treasurers, judges, magistrates and all the other provincial officials assembled for the dedication of the image that King Nebuchadnezzar had set up, and they stood before it.

[4]Then the herald loudly proclaimed, "This is what you are commanded to do, O peoples, nations and men of every language: [5]As soon as you hear the sound of the horn, flute, zither, lyre, harp, pipes and all kinds of music, you must fall down and worship the image of gold that King Nebuchadnezzar has set up. [6]Whoever does not fall down and worship will immediately be thrown into a blazing furnace."

[7]Therefore, as soon as they heard the sound of the horn, flute, zither, lyre, harp and all kinds of music, all the peoples, nations and men of every language fell down and worshiped the image of gold that King Nebuchadnezzar had set up.

[8]At this time some astrologers[b] came forward and denounced the Jews. [9]They said to King Nebuchadnezzar, "O king, live forever! [10]You have issued a decree, O king, that everyone who hears the sound of the horn, flute, zither, lyre, harp, pipes and all kinds of music must fall down and worship the image of gold, [11]and that whoever does not fall down and worship will be thrown into a blazing furnace. [12]But there are some Jews

---

[a]1 Aramaic *sixty cubits high and six cubits wide* (about 27 meters high and 2.7 meters wide)
[b]8 Or *Chaldeans*

whom you have set over the affairs of the province of Babylon—Shadrach, Meshach and Abednego—who pay no attention to you, O king. They neither serve your gods nor worship the image of gold you have set up."

¹³Furious with rage, Nebuchadnezzar summoned Shadrach, Meshach and Abednego. So these men were brought before the king, ¹⁴and Nebuchadnezzar said to them, "Is it true, Shadrach, Meshach and Abednego, that you do not serve my gods or worship the image of gold I have set up? ¹⁵Now when you hear the sound of the horn, flute, zither, lyre, harp, pipes and all kinds of music, if you are ready to fall down and worship the image I made, very good. But if you do not worship it, you will be thrown immediately into a blazing furnace. Then what god will be able to rescue you from my hand?"

¹⁶Shadrach, Meshach and Abednego replied to the king, "O Nebuchadnezzar, we do not need to defend ourselves before you in this matter. ¹⁷If we are thrown into the blazing furnace, the God we serve is able to save us from it, and he will rescue us from your hand, O king. ¹⁸But even if he does not, we want you to know, O king, that we will not serve your gods or worship the image of gold you have set up."

¹⁹Then Nebuchadnezzar was furious with Shadrach, Meshach and Abednego, and his attitude toward them changed. He ordered the furnace heated seven times hotter than usual ²⁰and commanded some of the strongest soldiers in his army to tie up Shadrach, Meshach and Abednego and throw them into the blazing furnace. ²¹So these men, wearing their robes, trousers, turbans and other clothes, were bound and thrown into the blazing furnace. ²²The king's command was so urgent and the furnace so hot that the flames of the fire killed the soldiers who took up Shadrach, Meshach and Abednego, ²³and these three men, firmly tied, fell into the blazing furnace.

²⁴Then King Nebuchadnezzar leaped to his feet in amazement and asked his advisers, "Weren't there three men that we tied up and threw into the fire?"

They replied, "Certainly, O king."

²⁵He said, "Look! I see four men walking around in the fire, unbound and unharmed, and the fourth looks like a son of the gods."

²⁶Nebuchadnezzar then approached the opening of the blazing furnace and shouted, "Shadrach, Meshach and Abednego, servants of the Most High God, come out! Come here!"

So Shadrach, Meshach and Abednego came out of the fire, ²⁷and the satraps, prefects, governors and royal advisers crowded around them. They saw that the fire had not harmed their bodies, nor was a hair of their heads singed; their robes were not scorched, and there was no smell of fire on them.

²⁸Then Nebuchadnezzar said, "Praise be to the God of Shadrach, Meshach and Abednego, who has sent his angel and rescued his servants! They trusted in him and defied the king's command and were willing to give up their lives rather than serve or worship any god except their own God. ²⁹Therefore I decree that the people of any nation or language who say anything against the God of Shadrach, Meshach and Abednego be cut into pieces and their houses be turned into piles of rubble, for no other god can save in this way."

³⁰Then the king promoted Shadrach, Meshach and Abednego in the province of Babylon.

Nebuchadnezzar's Dream of a Tree

4 King Nebuchadnezzar,

To the peoples, nations and men of every language, who live in all the world:

May you prosper greatly!

²It is my pleasure to tell you about the miraculous signs and wonders that the Most High God has performed for me.

VERSE:	AUTHOR:	PASSAGE:
Daniel 3:25	Joni Eareckson Tada	Daniel 3:16–28

Reflections in the Furnace

At one time or another, all of us have felt the flames of the refiner's fire. No matter how we balk at the idea, God has promised to refine his children.

To refine, says Webster, is "to make fine or pure; free from impurities, dross, alloy or sediment . . . to free from imperfection, coarseness, crudeness, etc." A refiner's fire, of course, is supposed to improve whatever commodity goes into it . . .

But how many of us go through the refiner's fire and come out the other end looking like . . . charcoal? Or rusty iron. Or smoking ashes. Often when we come through a period of suffering, we want to make sure that everybody knows all the sad and sordid details. The thing of beauty that God wanted to create by sending us into the flames becomes tarnished by our complaints and woebegone expressions.

Be honest. If you've had one of those days when you feel as if you've been dragged through the refiner's fire, how do you show it? By boasting about your trials? If you do, I'm afraid people are going to smell smoke. Your testimony may end up tarnished. Even scorched.

There's a better way. Let's offer sincere, wholehearted praise to God as we walk through the refiner's fire. Perhaps those who pause to peer into our furnace will see the Son of God walking with us, as he did with Shadrach, Meshach and Abednego.

ADDITIONAL SCRIPTURE READINGS
Psalm 66:8–20; 1 Peter 1:3–9
Go to page 1104 for your next devotional reading.

³How great are his signs,
    how mighty his wonders!
His kingdom is an eternal
    kingdom;
  his dominion endures from
    generation to
    generation.

⁴I, Nebuchadnezzar, was at home in my palace, contented and prosperous. ⁵I had a dream that made me afraid. As I was lying in my bed, the images and visions that passed through my mind terrified me. ⁶So I commanded that all the wise men of Babylon be brought before me to interpret the dream for me. ⁷When the magicians, enchanters, astrologers*a* and diviners came, I told them the dream, but they could not interpret it for me. ⁸Finally, Daniel came into my presence and I told him the dream. (He is called Belteshazzar, after the name of my god, and the spirit of the holy gods is in him.)

⁹I said, "Belteshazzar, chief of the magicians, I know that the spirit of the holy gods is in you, and no mystery is too difficult for you. Here is my dream; interpret it for me. ¹⁰These are the visions I saw while lying in my bed: I looked, and there before me stood a tree in the middle of the land. Its height was enormous. ¹¹The tree grew large and strong and its top touched the sky; it was visible to the ends of the earth. ¹²Its leaves were beautiful, its fruit abundant, and on it was food for all. Under it the beasts of the field found shelter, and the birds of the air lived in its branches; from it every creature was fed.

¹³"In the visions I saw while lying in my bed, I looked, and there before me was a messenger,*b* a holy one, coming down from heaven. ¹⁴He called in a loud voice: 'Cut down the tree and trim off its branches; strip off its leaves and scatter its fruit. Let the animals flee from under it and the birds from its branches. ¹⁵But let the stump and its roots, bound with iron and bronze, remain in the ground, in the grass of the field.

" 'Let him be drenched with the dew of heaven, and let him live with the animals among the plants of the earth. ¹⁶Let his mind be changed from that of a man and let him be given the mind of an animal, till seven times*c* pass by for him.

¹⁷" 'The decision is announced by messengers, the holy ones declare the verdict, so that the living may know that the Most High is sovereign over the kingdoms of men and gives them to anyone he wishes and sets over them the lowliest of men.'

¹⁸"This is the dream that I, King Nebuchadnezzar, had. Now, Belteshazzar, tell me what it means, for none of the wise men in my kingdom can interpret it for me. But you can, because the spirit of the holy gods is in you."

Daniel Interprets the Dream

¹⁹Then Daniel (also called Belteshazzar) was greatly perplexed for a time, and his thoughts terrified him. So the king said, "Belteshazzar, do not let the dream or its meaning alarm you."

Belteshazzar answered, "My lord, if only the dream applied to your enemies and its meaning to your adversaries! ²⁰The tree you saw, which grew large and strong, with its top touching the sky, visible to the whole earth, ²¹with beautiful leaves and abundant fruit, providing food for all, giving shelter to the beasts of the

---

*a*7 Or *Chaldeans*   *b*13 Or *watchman*; also in verses 17 and 23   *c*16 Or *years*; also in verses 23, 25 and 32

field, and having nesting places in its branches for the birds of the air— 22you, O king, are that tree! You have become great and strong; your greatness has grown until it reaches the sky, and your dominion extends to distant parts of the earth.

23"You, O king, saw a messenger, a holy one, coming down from heaven and saying, 'Cut down the tree and destroy it, but leave the stump, bound with iron and bronze, in the grass of the field, while its roots remain in the ground. Let him be drenched with the dew of heaven; let him live like the wild animals, until seven times pass by for him.'

24"This is the interpretation, O king, and this is the decree the Most High has issued against my lord the king: 25You will be driven away from people and will live with the wild animals; you will eat grass like cattle and be drenched with the dew of heaven. Seven times will pass by for you until you acknowledge that the Most High is sovereign over the kingdoms of men and gives them to anyone he wishes. 26The command to leave the stump of the tree with its roots means that your kingdom will be restored to you when you acknowledge that Heaven rules. 27Therefore, O king, be pleased to accept my advice: Renounce your sins by doing what is right, and your wickedness by being kind to the oppressed. It may be that then your prosperity will continue."

The Dream Is Fulfilled

28All this happened to King Nebuchadnezzar. 29Twelve months later, as the king was walking on the roof of the royal palace of Babylon, 30he said, "Is not this the great Babylon I have built as the royal residence, by my mighty power and for the glory of my majesty?"

31The words were still on his lips when a voice came from heaven, "This is what is decreed for you, King Nebuchadnezzar: Your royal authority has been taken from you. 32You will be driven away from people and will live with the wild animals; you will eat grass like cattle. Seven times will pass by for you until you acknowledge that the Most High is sovereign over the kingdoms of men and gives them to anyone he wishes."

33Immediately what had been said about Nebuchadnezzar was fulfilled. He was driven away from people and ate grass like cattle. His body was drenched with the dew of heaven until his hair grew like the feathers of an eagle and his nails like the claws of a bird.

34At the end of that time, I, Nebuchadnezzar, raised my eyes toward heaven, and my sanity was restored. Then I praised the Most High; I honored and glorified him who lives forever.

His dominion is an eternal
      dominion;
   his kingdom endures from
      generation to generation.
35All the peoples of the earth
   are regarded as nothing.
He does as he pleases
   with the powers of heaven
   and the peoples of the earth.
No one can hold back his hand
   or say to him: "What have you
      done?"

36At the same time that my sanity was restored, my honor and splendor were returned to me for the glory of my kingdom. My advisers and nobles sought me out, and I was restored to my throne and became even greater than before. 37Now I, Nebuchadnezzar, praise and exalt and glorify the King of heaven, because everything he does is right and all his ways are just. And those who walk in pride he is able to humble.

The Writing on the Wall

5 King Belshazzar gave a great banquet for a thousand of his nobles and drank wine with them. [2]While Belshazzar was drinking his wine, he gave orders to bring in the gold and silver goblets that Nebuchadnezzar his father[a] had taken from the temple in Jerusalem, so that the king and his nobles, his wives and his concubines might drink from them. [3]So they brought in the gold goblets that had been taken from the temple of God in Jerusalem, and the king and his nobles, his wives and his concubines drank from them. [4]As they drank the wine, they praised the gods of gold and silver, of bronze, iron, wood and stone.

[5]Suddenly the fingers of a human hand appeared and wrote on the plaster of the wall, near the lampstand in the royal palace. The king watched the hand as it wrote. [6]His face turned pale and he was so frightened that his knees knocked together and his legs gave way.

[7]The king called out for the enchanters, astrologers[b] and diviners to be brought and said to these wise men of Babylon, "Whoever reads this writing and tells me what it means will be clothed in purple and have a gold chain placed around his neck, and he will be made the third highest ruler in the kingdom."

[8]Then all the king's wise men came in, but they could not read the writing or tell the king what it meant. [9]So King Belshazzar became even more terrified and his face grew more pale. His nobles were baffled.

[10]The queen,[c] hearing the voices of the king and his nobles, came into the banquet hall. "O king, live forever!" she said. "Don't be alarmed! Don't look so pale! [11]There is a man in your kingdom who has the spirit of the holy gods in him. In the time of your father he was found to have insight and intelligence and wisdom like that of the gods. King Nebuchadnezzar your father—your father the king, I say—appointed him chief of the magicians, enchanters, astrologers and diviners. [12]This man Daniel, whom the king called Belteshazzar, was found to have a keen mind and knowledge and understanding, and also the ability to interpret dreams, explain riddles and solve difficult problems. Call for Daniel, and he will tell you what the writing means."

[13]So Daniel was brought before the king, and the king said to him, "Are you Daniel, one of the exiles my father the king brought from Judah? [14]I have heard that the spirit of the gods is in you and that you have insight, intelligence and outstanding wisdom. [15]The wise men and enchanters were brought before me to read this writing and tell me what it means, but they could not explain it. [16]Now I have heard that you are able to give interpretations and to solve difficult problems. If you can read this writing and tell me what it means, you will be clothed in purple and have a gold chain placed around your neck, and you will be made the third highest ruler in the kingdom."

[17]Then Daniel answered the king, "You may keep your gifts for yourself and give your rewards to someone else. Nevertheless, I will read the writing for the king and tell him what it means.

[18]"O king, the Most High God gave your father Nebuchadnezzar sovereignty and greatness and glory and splendor. [19]Because of the high position he gave him, all the peoples and nations and men of every language dreaded and feared him. Those the king wanted to put to death, he put to death; those he wanted to spare, he spared; those he wanted to promote, he promoted; and those he wanted to humble, he humbled. [20]But when his heart became arrogant and hardened

---

*a*2 Or *ancestor;* or *predecessor;* also in verses 11, 13 and 18   *b*7 Or *Chaldeans;* also in verse 11
*c*10 Or *queen mother*

with pride, he was deposed from his royal throne and stripped of his glory. ²¹He was driven away from people and given the mind of an animal; he lived with the wild donkeys and ate grass like cattle; and his body was drenched with the dew of heaven, until he acknowledged that the Most High God is sovereign over the kingdoms of men and sets over them anyone he wishes.

²²"But you his son,[a] O Belshazzar, have not humbled yourself, though you knew all this. ²³Instead, you have set yourself up against the Lord of heaven. You had the goblets from his temple brought to you, and you and your nobles, your wives and your concubines drank wine from them. You praised the gods of silver and gold, of bronze, iron, wood and stone, which cannot see or hear or understand. But you did not honor the God who holds in his hand your life and all your ways. ²⁴Therefore he sent the hand that wrote the inscription.

²⁵"This is the inscription that was written:

MENE, MENE, TEKEL, PARSIN[b]

²⁶"This is what these words mean:

Mene[c]: God has numbered the days of your reign and brought it to an end.
²⁷*Tekel*[d]: You have been weighed on the scales and found wanting.
²⁸*Peres*[e]: Your kingdom is divided and given to the Medes and Persians."

²⁹Then at Belshazzar's command, Daniel was clothed in purple, a gold chain was placed around his neck, and he was proclaimed the third highest ruler in the kingdom.

³⁰That very night Belshazzar, king of the Babylonians,[f] was slain, ³¹and Darius the Mede took over the kingdom, at the age of sixty-two.

Daniel in the Den of Lions

6 It pleased Darius to appoint 120 satraps to rule throughout the kingdom, ²with three administrators over them, one of whom was Daniel. The satraps were made accountable to them so that the king might not suffer loss. ³Now Daniel so distinguished himself among the administrators and the satraps by his exceptional qualities that the king planned to set him over the whole kingdom. ⁴At this, the administrators and the satraps tried to find grounds for charges against Daniel in his conduct of government affairs, but they were unable to do so. They could find no corruption in him, because he was trustworthy and neither corrupt nor negligent. ⁵Finally these men said, "We will never find any basis for charges against this man Daniel unless it has something to do with the law of his God."

⁶So the administrators and the satraps went as a group to the king and said: "O King Darius, live forever! ⁷The royal administrators, prefects, satraps, advisers and governors have all agreed that the king should issue an edict and enforce the decree that anyone who prays to any god or man during the next thirty days, except to you, O king, shall be thrown into the lions' den. ⁸Now, O king, issue the decree and put it in writing so that it cannot be altered—in accordance with the laws of the Medes and Persians, which cannot be repealed." ⁹So King Darius put the decree in writing.

¹⁰Now when Daniel learned that the decree had been published, he went home to his upstairs room where the windows opened toward Jerusalem. Three times a day he got down on his knees and prayed, giving thanks to his God, just as he had done before. ¹¹Then these men went

---

[a]22 Or *descendant*; or *successor*   [b]25 Aramaic UPARSIN (that is, *AND PARSIN*)   [c]26 *Mene* can mean *numbered* or *mina* (a unit of money).   [d]27 *Tekel* can mean *weighed* or *shekel*.
[e]28 *Peres* (the singular of *Parsin*) can mean *divided* or *Persia* or *a half mina* or *a half shekel*.
[f]30 Or *Chaldeans*

as a group and found Daniel praying and asking God for help. ¹²So they went to the king and spoke to him about his royal decree: "Did you not publish a decree that during the next thirty days anyone who prays to any god or man except to you, O king, would be thrown into the lions' den?"

The king answered, "The decree stands—in accordance with the laws of the Medes and Persians, which cannot be repealed."

¹³Then they said to the king, "Daniel, who is one of the exiles from Judah, pays no attention to you, O king, or to the decree you put in writing. He still prays three times a day." ¹⁴When the king heard this, he was greatly distressed; he was determined to rescue Daniel and made every effort until sundown to save him.

¹⁵Then the men went as a group to the king and said to him, "Remember, O king, that according to the law of the Medes and Persians no decree or edict that the king issues can be changed."

¹⁶So the king gave the order, and they brought Daniel and threw him into the lions' den. The king said to Daniel, "May your God, whom you serve continually, rescue you!"

¹⁷A stone was brought and placed over the mouth of the den, and the king sealed it with his own signet ring and with the rings of his nobles, so that Daniel's situation might not be changed. ¹⁸Then the king returned to his palace and spent the night without eating and without any entertainment being brought to him. And he could not sleep.

¹⁹At the first light of dawn, the king got up and hurried to the lions' den. ²⁰When he came near the den, he called to Daniel in an anguished voice, "Daniel, servant of the living God, has your God, whom you serve continually, been able to rescue you from the lions?"

²¹Daniel answered, "O king, live forever! ²²My God sent his angel, and he shut the mouths of the lions. They

have not hurt me, because I was found innocent in his sight. Nor have I ever done any wrong before you, O king."

²³The king was overjoyed and gave orders to lift Daniel out of the den. And when Daniel was lifted from the den, no wound was found on him, because he had trusted in his God.

²⁴At the king's command, the men who had falsely accused Daniel were brought in and thrown into the lions' den, along with their wives and children. And before they reached the floor of the den, the lions overpowered them and crushed all their bones.

²⁵Then King Darius wrote to all the peoples, nations and men of every language throughout the land:

"May you prosper greatly!

²⁶"I issue a decree that in every part of my kingdom people must fear and reverence the God of Daniel.

"For he is the living God
  and he endures forever;
his kingdom will not be
      destroyed,
  his dominion will never end.
²⁷He rescues and he saves;
  he performs signs and wonders
  in the heavens and on the earth.
He has rescued Daniel
  from the power of the lions."

²⁸So Daniel prospered during the reign of Darius and the reign of Cyrus[a] the Persian.

Daniel's Dream of Four Beasts

7 In the first year of Belshazzar king of Babylon, Daniel had a dream, and visions passed through his mind as he was lying on his bed. He wrote down the substance of his dream.

²Daniel said: "In my vision at night I looked, and there before me were the four winds of heaven churning up the great sea. ³Four great beasts, each different from the others, came up out of the sea.

ᵃ28 Or Darius, that is, the reign of Cyrus

⁴"The first was like a lion, and it had the wings of an eagle. I watched until its wings were torn off and it was lifted from the ground so that it stood on two feet like a man, and the heart of a man was given to it.

⁵"And there before me was a second beast, which looked like a bear. It was raised up on one of its sides, and it had three ribs in its mouth between its teeth. It was told, 'Get up and eat your fill of flesh!'

⁶"After that, I looked, and there before me was another beast, one that looked like a leopard. And on its back it had four wings like those of a bird. This beast had four heads, and it was given authority to rule.

⁷"After that, in my vision at night I looked, and there before me was a fourth beast—terrifying and frightening and very powerful. It had large iron teeth; it crushed and devoured its victims and trampled underfoot whatever was left. It was different from all the former beasts, and it had ten horns.

⁸"While I was thinking about the horns, there before me was another horn, a little one, which came up among them; and three of the first horns were uprooted before it. This horn had eyes like the eyes of a man and a mouth that spoke boastfully.

⁹"As I looked,

"thrones were set in place,
    and the Ancient of Days took
        his seat.
His clothing was as white as
        snow;
    the hair of his head was white
        like wool.
His throne was flaming with fire,
    and its wheels were all ablaze.
¹⁰A river of fire was flowing,
    coming out from before him.
Thousands upon thousands
        attended him;
    ten thousand times ten
        thousand stood before him.
The court was seated,
    and the books were opened.

¹¹"Then I continued to watch because of the boastful words the horn was speaking. I kept looking until the beast was slain and its body destroyed and thrown into the blazing fire. ¹²(The other beasts had been stripped of their authority, but were allowed to live for a period of time.)

¹³"In my vision at night I looked, and there before me was one like a son of man, coming with the clouds of heaven. He approached the Ancient of Days and was led into his presence. ¹⁴He was given authority, glory and sovereign power; all peoples, nations and men of every language worshiped him. His dominion is an everlasting dominion that will not pass away, and his kingdom is one that will never be destroyed.

The Interpretation of the Dream

¹⁵"I, Daniel, was troubled in spirit, and the visions that passed through my mind disturbed me. ¹⁶I approached one of those standing there and asked him the true meaning of all this.

"So he told me and gave me the interpretation of these things: ¹⁷'The four great beasts are four kingdoms that will rise from the earth. ¹⁸But the saints of the Most High will receive the kingdom and will possess it forever—yes, for ever and ever.'

¹⁹"Then I wanted to know the true meaning of the fourth beast, which was different from all the others and most terrifying, with its iron teeth and bronze claws—the beast that crushed and devoured its victims and trampled underfoot whatever was left. ²⁰I also wanted to know about the ten horns on its head and about the other horn that came up, before which three of them fell—the horn that looked more imposing than the others and that had eyes and a mouth that spoke boastfully. ²¹As I watched, this horn was waging war against the saints and defeating them, ²²until the Ancient of Days came and pronounced judgment in favor of the saints of the Most High, and the time came when they possessed the kingdom.

²³"He gave me this explanation: 'The fourth beast is a fourth kingdom

that will appear on earth. It will be different from all the other kingdoms and will devour the whole earth, trampling it down and crushing it. ²⁴The ten horns are ten kings who will come from this kingdom. After them another king will arise, different from the earlier ones; he will subdue three kings. ²⁵He will speak against the Most High and oppress his saints and try to change the set times and the laws. The saints will be handed over to him for a time, times and half a time.*

²⁶" 'But the court will sit, and his power will be taken away and completely destroyed forever. ²⁷Then the sovereignty, power and greatness of the kingdoms under the whole heaven will be handed over to the saints, the people of the Most High. His kingdom will be an everlasting kingdom, and all rulers will worship and obey him.'

²⁸"This is the end of the matter. I, Daniel, was deeply troubled by my thoughts, and my face turned pale, but I kept the matter to myself."

Daniel's Vision of a Ram and a Goat

8 In the third year of King Belshazzar's reign, I, Daniel, had a vision, after the one that had already appeared to me. ²In my vision I saw myself in the citadel of Susa in the province of Elam; in the vision I was beside the Ulai Canal. ³I looked up, and there before me was a ram with two horns, standing beside the canal, and the horns were long. One of the horns was longer than the other but grew up later. ⁴I watched the ram as he charged toward the west and the north and the south. No animal could stand against him, and none could rescue from his power. He did as he pleased and became great.

⁵As I was thinking about this, suddenly a goat with a prominent horn between his eyes came from the west, crossing the whole earth without touching the ground. ⁶He came toward the two-horned ram I had seen standing beside the canal and charged at him in great rage. ⁷I saw him attack the ram furiously, striking the ram and shattering his two horns. The ram was powerless to stand against him; the goat knocked him to the ground and trampled on him, and none could rescue the ram from his power. ⁸The goat became very great, but at the height of his power his large horn was broken off, and in its place four prominent horns grew up toward the four winds of heaven.

⁹Out of one of them came another horn, which started small but grew in power to the south and to the east and toward the Beautiful Land. ¹⁰It grew until it reached the host of the heavens, and it threw some of the starry host down to the earth and trampled on them. ¹¹It set itself up to be as great as the Prince of the host; it took away the daily sacrifice from him, and the place of his sanctuary was brought low. ¹²Because of rebellion, the host ⌊of the saints⌋^b and the daily sacrifice were given over to it. It prospered in everything it did, and truth was thrown to the ground.

¹³Then I heard a holy one speaking, and another holy one said to him, "How long will it take for the vision to be fulfilled—the vision concerning the daily sacrifice, the rebellion that causes desolation, and the surrender of the sanctuary and of the host that will be trampled underfoot?"

¹⁴He said to me, "It will take 2,300 evenings and mornings; then the sanctuary will be reconsecrated."

The Interpretation of the Vision

¹⁵While I, Daniel, was watching the vision and trying to understand it, there before me stood one who looked like a man. ¹⁶And I heard a man's voice from the Ulai calling, "Gabriel, tell this man the meaning of the vision."

¹⁷As he came near the place where I was standing, I was terrified and fell

---

^a25 Or *for a year, two years and half a year*   ^b12 Or *rebellion, the armies*

prostrate. "Son of man," he said to me, "understand that the vision concerns the time of the end."

¹⁸While he was speaking to me, I was in a deep sleep, with my face to the ground. Then he touched me and raised me to my feet.

¹⁹He said: "I am going to tell you what will happen later in the time of wrath, because the vision concerns the appointed time of the end.ᵃ ²⁰The two-horned ram that you saw represents the kings of Media and Persia. ²¹The shaggy goat is the king of Greece, and the large horn between his eyes is the first king. ²²The four horns that replaced the one that was broken off represent four kingdoms that will emerge from his nation but will not have the same power.

²³"In the latter part of their reign, when rebels have become completely wicked, a stern-faced king, a master of intrigue, will arise. ²⁴He will become very strong, but not by his own power. He will cause astounding devastation and will succeed in whatever he does. He will destroy the mighty men and the holy people. ²⁵He will cause deceit to prosper, and he will consider himself superior. When they feel secure, he will destroy many and take his stand against the Prince of princes. Yet he will be destroyed, but not by human power.

²⁶"The vision of the evenings and mornings that has been given you is true, but seal up the vision, for it concerns the distant future."

²⁷I, Daniel, was exhausted and lay ill for several days. Then I got up and went about the king's business. I was appalled by the vision; it was beyond understanding.

Daniel's Prayer

9 In the first year of Darius son of Xerxesᵇ (a Mede by descent), who was made ruler over the Babylonianᶜ kingdom— ²in the first year of his reign, I, Daniel, understood from the Scriptures, according to the word of the LORD given to Jeremiah the prophet, that the desolation of Jerusalem would last seventy years. ³So I turned to the Lord God and pleaded with him in prayer and petition, in fasting, and in sackcloth and ashes.

⁴I prayed to the LORD my God and confessed:

"O Lord, the great and awesome God, who keeps his covenant of love with all who love him and obey his commands, ⁵we have sinned and done wrong. We have been wicked and have rebelled; we have turned away from your commands and laws. ⁶We have not listened to your servants the prophets, who spoke in your name to our kings, our princes and our fathers, and to all the people of the land.

⁷"Lord, you are righteous, but this day we are covered with shame—the men of Judah and people of Jerusalem and all Israel, both near and far, in all the countries where you have scattered us because of our unfaithfulness to you. ⁸O LORD, we and our kings, our princes and our fathers are covered with shame because we have sinned against you. ⁹The Lord our God is merciful and forgiving, even though we have rebelled against him; ¹⁰we have not obeyed the LORD our God or kept the laws he gave us through his servants the prophets. ¹¹All Israel has transgressed your law and turned away, refusing to obey you.

"Therefore the curses and sworn judgments written in the Law of Moses, the servant of God, have been poured out on us, because we have sinned against you. ¹²You have fulfilled the words spoken against us and against our rulers by bringing upon us great disaster. Under the whole heaven nothing has ever been done like what has

---

ᵃ19 Or *because the end will be at the appointed time*   ᵇ1 Hebrew *Ahasuerus*   ᶜ1 Or *Chaldean*

been done to Jerusalem. ¹³Just as it is written in the Law of Moses, all this disaster has come upon us, yet we have not sought the favor of the LORD our God by turning from our sins and giving attention to your truth. ¹⁴The LORD did not hesitate to bring the disaster upon us, for the LORD our God is righteous in everything he does; yet we have not obeyed him.

¹⁵"Now, O Lord our God, who brought your people out of Egypt with a mighty hand and who made for yourself a name that endures to this day, we have sinned, we have done wrong. ¹⁶O Lord, in keeping with all your righteous acts, turn away your anger and your wrath from Jerusalem, your city, your holy hill. Our sins and the iniquities of our fathers have made Jerusalem and your people an object of scorn to all those around us.

¹⁷"Now, our God, hear the prayers and petitions of your servant. For your sake, O Lord, look with favor on your desolate sanctuary. ¹⁸Give ear, O God, and hear; open your eyes and see the desolation of the city that bears your Name. We do not make requests of you because we are righteous, but because of your great mercy. ¹⁹O Lord, listen! O Lord, forgive! O Lord, hear and act! For your sake, O my God, do not delay, because your city and your people bear your Name."

The Seventy "Sevens"

²⁰While I was speaking and praying, confessing my sin and the sin of my people Israel and making my request to the LORD my God for his holy hill— ²¹while I was still in prayer, Ga-briel, the man I had seen in the earlier vision, came to me in swift flight about the time of the evening sacrifice. ²²He instructed me and said to me, "Daniel, I have now come to give you insight and understanding. ²³As soon as you began to pray, an answer was given, which I have come to tell you, for you are highly esteemed. Therefore, consider the message and understand the vision:

²⁴"Seventy 'sevens'^a are decreed for your people and your holy city to finish^b transgression, to put an end to sin, to atone for wickedness, to bring in everlasting righteousness, to seal up vision and prophecy and to anoint the most holy.^c

²⁵"Know and understand this: From the issuing of the decree^d to restore and rebuild Jerusalem until the Anointed One,^e the ruler, comes, there will be seven 'sevens,' and sixty-two 'sevens.' It will be rebuilt with streets and a trench, but in times of trouble. ²⁶After the sixty-two 'sevens,' the Anointed One will be cut off and will have nothing.^f The people of the ruler who will come will destroy the city and the sanctuary. The end will come like a flood: War will continue until the end, and desolations have been decreed. ²⁷He will confirm a covenant with many for one 'seven.'^g In the middle of the 'seven'^g he will put an end to sacrifice and offering. And on a wing ⌊of the temple⌋ he will set up an abomination that causes desolation, until the end that is decreed is poured out on him.^h"ⁱ

Daniel's Vision of a Man

10 In the third year of Cyrus king of Persia, a revelation was given to Daniel (who was called Belteshazzar). Its message was true and it concerned a great war.^j The understanding of the message came to him in a vision.

^a24 Or 'weeks'; also in verses 25 and 26   ^b24 Or restrain   ^c24 Or Most Holy Place; or most holy One   ^d25 Or word   ^e25 Or an anointed one; also in verse 26   ^f26 Or off and will have no one; or off, but not for himself   ^g27 Or 'week'   ^h27 Or it   ⁱ27 Or And one who causes desolation will come upon the pinnacle of the abominable ⌊temple⌋, until the end that is decreed is poured out on the desolated ⌊city⌋   ^j1 Or true and burdensome

[2]At that time I, Daniel, mourned for three weeks. [3]I ate no choice food; no meat or wine touched my lips; and I used no lotions at all until the three weeks were over.

[4]On the twenty-fourth day of the first month, as I was standing on the bank of the great river, the Tigris, [5]I looked up and there before me was a man dressed in linen, with a belt of the finest gold around his waist. [6]His body was like chrysolite, his face like lightning, his eyes like flaming torches, his arms and legs like the gleam of burnished bronze, and his voice like the sound of a multitude.

[7]I, Daniel, was the only one who saw the vision; the men with me did not see it, but such terror overwhelmed them that they fled and hid themselves. [8]So I was left alone, gazing at this great vision; I had no strength left, my face turned deathly pale and I was helpless. [9]Then I heard him speaking, and as I listened to him, I fell into a deep sleep, my face to the ground.

[10]A hand touched me and set me trembling on my hands and knees. [11]He said, "Daniel, you who are highly esteemed, consider carefully the words I am about to speak to you, and stand up, for I have now been sent to you." And when he said this to me, I stood up trembling.

[12]Then he continued, "Do not be afraid, Daniel. Since the first day that you set your mind to gain understanding and to humble yourself before your God, your words were heard, and I have come in response to them. [13]But the prince of the Persian kingdom resisted me twenty-one days. Then Michael, one of the chief princes, came to help me, because I was detained there with the king of Persia. [14]Now I have come to explain to you what will happen to your people in the future, for the vision concerns a time yet to come."

[15]While he was saying this to me, I bowed with my face toward the ground and was speechless. [16]Then one who looked like a man[a] touched my lips, and I opened my mouth and began to speak. I said to the one standing before me, "I am overcome with anguish because of the vision, my lord, and I am helpless. [17]How can I, your servant, talk with you, my lord? My strength is gone and I can hardly breathe."

[18]Again the one who looked like a man touched me and gave me strength. [19]"Do not be afraid, O man highly esteemed," he said. "Peace! Be strong now; be strong."

When he spoke to me, I was strengthened and said, "Speak, my lord, since you have given me strength."

[20]So he said, "Do you know why I have come to you? Soon I will return to fight against the prince of Persia, and when I go, the prince of Greece will come; [21]but first I will tell you what is written in the Book of Truth. (No one supports me against them except Michael, your prince.

11 [1]And in the first year of Darius the Mede, I took my stand to support and protect him.)

The Kings of the South and the North

[2]"Now then, I tell you the truth: Three more kings will appear in Persia, and then a fourth, who will be far richer than all the others. When he has gained power by his wealth, he will stir up everyone against the kingdom of Greece. [3]Then a mighty king will appear, who will rule with great power and do as he pleases. [4]After he has appeared, his empire will be broken up and parceled out toward the four winds of heaven. It will not go to his descendants, nor will it have the power he exercised, because his empire will be uprooted and given to others.

[5]"The king of the South will become strong, but one of his commanders will become even stronger

---

[a]16 Most manuscripts of the Masoretic Text; one manuscript of the Masoretic Text, Dead Sea Scrolls and Septuagint *Then something that looked like a man's hand*

VERSE:	AUTHOR:	PASSAGE:
Daniel 10:13	Gien Karssen	Daniel 10:1 — 11:1

Earthly Prayer . . . Heavenly Battles

Daniel was in great distress concerning the future of his people, which had been revealed to him in a vision. He wrestled with his God for three weeks and ate no food, but heaven seemed to be deaf to his petition . . .

Then a heavenly messenger appeared, saying, "Since the first day that you set your mind to gain understanding and to humble yourself before your God, your words were heard, and I have come in response to them. But the prince of the Persian kingdom resisted me twenty-one days" (Daniel 10:12–13). Satan, an opposer of God and thus an opposer of prayer, had held up the answer.

Daniel, feeling weak and helpless, had nearly collapsed when he saw the messenger. But the man's words gave Daniel new strength and peace.

The New Testament speaks clearly about the fight behind the scenes, the struggle in the heavenly realms (Ephesians 6:10–18). Supernatural powers of evil are more active in our time than ever. Now, as in the past, they can be conquered only by prayer . . .

If answers to our prayers are not forthcoming, then Daniel's experience can encourage us because it revealed what happens between God and Satan when people pray. This should give us perseverance at times when everything seems to be against us. It should encourage us not to give up.

ADDITIONAL SCRIPTURE READINGS
Luke 18:1–8; Ephesians 6:10–18

Go to page 1110 for your next devotional reading.

than he and will rule his own kingdom with great power. [6]After some years, they will become allies. The daughter of the king of the South will go to the king of the North to make an alliance, but she will not retain her power, and he and his power[a] will not last. In those days she will be handed over, together with her royal escort and her father[b] and the one who supported her.

[7]"One from her family line will arise to take her place. He will attack the forces of the king of the North and enter his fortress; he will fight against them and be victorious. [8]He will also seize their gods, their metal images and their valuable articles of silver and gold and carry them off to Egypt. For some years he will leave the king of the North alone. [9]Then the king of the North will invade the realm of the king of the South but will retreat to his own country. [10]His sons will prepare for war and assemble a great army, which will sweep on like an irresistible flood and carry the battle as far as his fortress.

[11]"Then the king of the South will march out in a rage and fight against the king of the North, who will raise a large army, but it will be defeated. [12]When the army is carried off, the king of the South will be filled with pride and will slaughter many thousands, yet he will not remain triumphant. [13]For the king of the North will muster another army, larger than the first; and after several years, he will advance with a huge army fully equipped.

[14]"In those times many will rise against the king of the South. The violent men among your own people will rebel in fulfillment of the vision, but without success. [15]Then the king of the North will come and build up siege ramps and will capture a fortified city. The forces of the South will be powerless to resist; even their best troops will not have the strength to stand. [16]The invader will do as he pleases; no one will be able to stand

against him. He will establish himself in the Beautiful Land and will have the power to destroy it. [17]He will determine to come with the might of his entire kingdom and will make an alliance with the king of the South. And he will give him a daughter in marriage in order to overthrow the kingdom, but his plans[c] will not succeed or help him. [18]Then he will turn his attention to the coastlands and will take many of them, but a commander will put an end to his insolence and will turn his insolence back upon him. [19]After this, he will turn back toward the fortresses of his own country but will stumble and fall, to be seen no more.

[20]"His successor will send out a tax collector to maintain the royal splendor. In a few years, however, he will be destroyed, yet not in anger or in battle.

[21]"He will be succeeded by a contemptible person who has not been given the honor of royalty. He will invade the kingdom when its people feel secure, and he will seize it through intrigue. [22]Then an overwhelming army will be swept away before him; both it and a prince of the covenant will be destroyed. [23]After coming to an agreement with him, he will act deceitfully, and with only a few people he will rise to power. [24]When the richest provinces feel secure, he will invade them and will achieve what neither his fathers nor his forefathers did. He will distribute plunder, loot and wealth among his followers. He will plot the overthrow of fortresses—but only for a time.

[25]"With a large army he will stir up his strength and courage against the king of the South. The king of the South will wage war with a large and very powerful army, but he will not be able to stand because of the plots devised against him. [26]Those who eat from the king's provisions will try to destroy him; his army will be swept away, and many will fall in battle. [27]The two kings, with their hearts

---

[a]6 Or offspring   [b]6 Or child (see Vulgate and Syriac)   [c]17 Or but she

bent on evil, will sit at the same table and lie to each other, but to no avail, because an end will still come at the appointed time. 28The king of the North will return to his own country with great wealth, but his heart will be set against the holy covenant. He will take action against it and then return to his own country.

29"At the appointed time he will invade the South again, but this time the outcome will be different from what it was before. 30Ships of the western coastlands[a] will oppose him, and he will lose heart. Then he will turn back and vent his fury against the holy covenant. He will return and show favor to those who forsake the holy covenant.

31"His armed forces will rise up to desecrate the temple fortress and will abolish the daily sacrifice. Then they will set up the abomination that causes desolation. 32With flattery he will corrupt those who have violated the covenant, but the people who know their God will firmly resist him.

33"Those who are wise will instruct many, though for a time they will fall by the sword or be burned or captured or plundered. 34When they fall, they will receive a little help, and many who are not sincere will join them. 35Some of the wise will stumble, so that they may be refined, purified and made spotless until the time of the end, for it will still come at the appointed time.

The King Who Exalts Himself

36"The king will do as he pleases. He will exalt and magnify himself above every god and will say unheard-of things against the God of gods. He will be successful until the time of wrath is completed, for what has been determined must take place. 37He will show no regard for the gods of his fathers or for the one desired by women, nor will he regard any god, but will exalt himself above them all. 38Instead of them, he will honor a god

of fortresses; a god unknown to his fathers he will honor with gold and silver, with precious stones and costly gifts. 39He will attack the mightiest fortresses with the help of a foreign god and will greatly honor those who acknowledge him. He will make them rulers over many people and will distribute the land at a price.[b]

40"At the time of the end the king of the South will engage him in battle, and the king of the North will storm out against him with chariots and cavalry and a great fleet of ships. He will invade many countries and sweep through them like a flood. 41He will also invade the Beautiful Land. Many countries will fall, but Edom, Moab and the leaders of Ammon will be delivered from his hand. 42He will extend his power over many countries; Egypt will not escape. 43He will gain control of the treasures of gold and silver and all the riches of Egypt, with the Libyans and Nubians in submission. 44But reports from the east and the north will alarm him, and he will set out in a great rage to destroy and annihilate many. 45He will pitch his royal tents between the seas at[c] the beautiful holy mountain. Yet he will come to his end, and no one will help him.

The End Times

12 "At that time Michael, the great prince who protects your people, will arise. There will be a time of distress such as has not happened from the beginning of nations until then. But at that time your people—everyone whose name is found written in the book—will be delivered. 2Multitudes who sleep in the dust of the earth will awake: some to everlasting life, others to shame and everlasting contempt. 3Those who are wise[d] will shine like the brightness of the heavens, and those who lead many to righteousness, like the stars for ever and ever. 4But you, Daniel, close up and seal the words of the

scroll until the time of the end. Many will go here and there to increase knowledge."

⁵Then I, Daniel, looked, and there before me stood two others, one on this bank of the river and one on the opposite bank. ⁶One of them said to the man clothed in linen, who was above the waters of the river, "How long will it be before these astonishing things are fulfilled?"

⁷The man clothed in linen, who was above the waters of the river, lifted his right hand and his left hand toward heaven, and I heard him swear by him who lives forever, saying, "It will be for a time, times and half a time.ᵃ When the power of the holy people has been finally broken, all these things will be completed."

⁸I heard, but I did not understand. So I asked, "My lord, what will the outcome of all this be?"

⁹He replied, "Go your way, Daniel, because the words are closed up and sealed until the time of the end. ¹⁰Many will be purified, made spotless and refined, but the wicked will continue to be wicked. None of the wicked will understand, but those who are wise will understand.

¹¹"From the time that the daily sacrifice is abolished and the abomination that causes desolation is set up, there will be 1,290 days. ¹²Blessed is the one who waits for and reaches the end of the 1,335 days.

¹³"As for you, go your way till the end. You will rest, and then at the end of the days you will rise to receive your allotted inheritance."

ᵃ7 Or *a year, two years and half a year*

*H*osea served as a
prophet in the northern kingdom of Israel
just before it was defeated by the Assyrians
in the eighth century B.C. The story of Hosea
and his wife Gomer illustrates God's love for
his people even when their sins have broken
his heart. As you read this book, take comfort
in knowing that God's love and healing are
available to you, regardless of how difficult
your past may have been.

HOSEA

1 The word of the LORD that came to Hosea son of Beeri during the reigns of Uzziah, Jotham, Ahaz and Hezekiah, kings of Judah, and during the reign of Jeroboam son of Jehoash*a* king of Israel:

Hosea's Wife and Children

²When the LORD began to speak through Hosea, the LORD said to him, "Go, take to yourself an adulterous wife and children of unfaithfulness, because the land is guilty of the vilest adultery in departing from the LORD." ³So he married Gomer daughter of Diblaim, and she conceived and bore him a son.

⁴Then the LORD said to Hosea, "Call him Jezreel, because I will soon punish the house of Jehu for the massacre at Jezreel, and I will put an end to the kingdom of Israel. ⁵In that day I will break Israel's bow in the Valley of Jezreel."

⁶Gomer conceived again and gave birth to a daughter. Then the LORD said to Hosea, "Call her Lo-Ruhamah,*b* for I will no longer show love to the house of Israel, that I should at all forgive them. ⁷Yet I will show love to the house of Judah; and I will save them—not by bow, sword or battle, or by horses and horsemen, but by the LORD their God."

⁸After she had weaned Lo-Ruhamah, Gomer had another son. ⁹Then the LORD said, "Call him Lo-Ammi,*c* for you are not my people, and I am not your God.

¹⁰"Yet the Israelites will be like the sand on the seashore, which cannot be measured or counted. In the place where it was said to them, 'You are not my people,' they will be called

---

*a*1 Hebrew *Joash,* a variant of *Jehoash*   *b*6 *Lo-Ruhamah* means *not loved.*   *c*9 *Lo-Ammi* means *not my people.*

'sons of the living God.' [11]The people of Judah and the people of Israel will be reunited, and they will appoint one leader and will come up out of the land, for great will be the day of Jezreel.

2 "Say of your brothers, 'My people,' and of your sisters, 'My loved one.'

Israel Punished and Restored

[2]"Rebuke your mother, rebuke her,
for she is not my wife,
and I am not her husband.
Let her remove the adulterous
look from her face
and the unfaithfulness from
between her breasts.
[3]Otherwise I will strip her naked
and make her as bare as on the
day she was born;
I will make her like a desert,
turn her into a parched land,
and slay her with thirst.
[4]I will not show my love to her
children,
because they are the children of
adultery.
[5]Their mother has been unfaithful
and has conceived them in
disgrace.
She said, 'I will go after my
lovers,
who give me my food and my
water,
my wool and my linen, my oil
and my drink.'
[6]Therefore I will block her path
with thornbushes;
I will wall her in so that she
cannot find her way.
[7]She will chase after her lovers but
not catch them;
she will look for them but not
find them.
Then she will say,
'I will go back to my husband
as at first,
for then I was better off than
now.'
[8]She has not acknowledged that I
was the one

who gave her the grain, the
new wine and oil,
who lavished on her the silver and
gold—
which they used for Baal.
[9]Therefore I will take away my
grain when it ripens,
and my new wine when it is
ready.
I will take back my wool and my
linen,
intended to cover her
nakedness.
[10]So now I will expose her lewdness
before the eyes of her lovers;
no one will take her out of my
hands.
[11]I will stop all her celebrations:
her yearly festivals, her New
Moons,
her Sabbath days—all her
appointed feasts.
[12]I will ruin her vines and her fig
trees,
which she said were her pay
from her lovers;
I will make them a thicket,
and wild animals will devour
them.
[13]I will punish her for the days
she burned incense to the Baals;
she decked herself with rings and
jewelry,
and went after her lovers,
but me she forgot,"
                         declares the Lord.

[14]"Therefore I am now going to
allure her;
I will lead her into the desert
and speak tenderly to her.
[15]There I will give her back her
vineyards,
and will make the Valley of
Achor[a] a door of hope.
There she will sing[b] as in the
days of her youth,
as in the day she came up out
of Egypt.
[16]"In that day," declares the Lord,
"you will call me 'my husband';

---

[a]15 Achor means *trouble*.   [b]15 Or *respond*

you will no longer call me 'my
master.ᵃ'
17I will remove the names of the
Baals from her lips;

no longer will their names be
invoked.
18In that day I will make a covenant
for them

ᵃ16 Hebrew *baal*

VERSE:	AUTHOR:	PASSAGE:
Hosea 2:15	F.B. Meyer	Hosea 2:14–23

The Door of Hope

The Valley of Achor is the emblem of defeat, failure and the fainting heart ... Is there a single life without its Valley of Achor? ...

Each Valley of Achor has had its door of hope. Sin has reigned unto death, but the grace of God has reigned unto eternal life. Through our sins we have learned, as never before, to appreciate God's forgiveness; through our failures we have been taught our own weakness, and led to magnify the grace which is made perfect in weakness.

Out of such experiences comes the song — "She will sing as in the days of her youth." You say that the spring and gladness of life are gone forever. You insist that you must go mourning all your days, and that life will only bring added grief. But God says that you *will* sing! Though the summer is gone, there will be a second — an Indian summer, even mellower than the first. God wants to give you a new revelation of his love, to draw you into his tenderest friendship and fellowship, to lift you into the life of victory and satisfaction. And when all these things come to pass, and they may begin today as you return to him, you will find that he has put a new song into your mouth, even praise unto our God.

ADDITIONAL SCRIPTURE READINGS
Psalm 40; Isaiah 61:1–7

Go to page 1115 for your next devotional reading.

with the beasts of the field and
the birds of the air
and the creatures that move
along the ground.
Bow and sword and battle
I will abolish from the land,
so that all may lie down in
safety.
19I will betroth you to me forever;
I will betroth you in[a]
righteousness and justice,
in[b] love and compassion.
20I will betroth you in faithfulness,
and you will acknowledge the
LORD.

21"In that day I will respond,"
declares the LORD—
"I will respond to the skies,
and they will respond to the
earth;
22and the earth will respond to the
grain,
the new wine and oil,
and they will respond to
Jezreel.[c]
23I will plant her for myself in the
land;
I will show my love to the one I
called 'Not my loved
one.[d]'
I will say to those called 'Not my
people,[e]' 'You are my
people';
and they will say, 'You are my
God.' "

Hosea's Reconciliation With His Wife

3 The LORD said to me, "Go, show
your love to your wife again,
though she is loved by another and is
an adulteress. Love her as the LORD
loves the Israelites, though they turn
to other gods and love the sacred raisin cakes."

2So I bought her for fifteen shekels[f] of silver and about a homer and
a lethek[g] of barley. 3Then I told her,
"You are to live with[h] me many
days; you must not be a prostitute or

be intimate with any man, and I will
live with[h] you."

4For the Israelites will live many
days without king or prince, without
sacrifice or sacred stones, without
ephod or idol. 5Afterward the Israelites will return and seek the LORD their
God and David their king. They will
come trembling to the LORD and to his
blessings in the last days.

The Charge Against Israel

4 Hear the word of the LORD, you
Israelites,
because the LORD has a charge
to bring
against you who live in the
land:
"There is no faithfulness, no love,
no acknowledgment of God in
the land.
2There is only cursing,[i] lying and
murder,
stealing and adultery;
they break all bounds,
and bloodshed follows
bloodshed.
3Because of this the land mourns,[j]
and all who live in it waste
away;
the beasts of the field and the
birds of the air
and the fish of the sea are
dying.

4"But let no man bring a charge,
let no man accuse another,
for your people are like those
who bring charges against a
priest.
5You stumble day and night,
and the prophets stumble with
you.
So I will destroy your mother—
6 my people are destroyed from
lack of knowledge.

"Because you have rejected
knowledge,
I also reject you as my priests;

---

a19 Or with; also in verse 20   b19 Or with   c22 Jezreel means God plants.   d23 Hebrew
Lo-Ruhamah   e23 Hebrew Lo-Ammi   f2 That is, about 6 ounces (about 170 grams)
g2 That is, probably about 10 bushels (about 330 liters)   h3 Or wait for   i2 That is, to
pronounce a curse upon   j3 Or dries up

because you have ignored the law
    of your God,
  I also will ignore your children.
⁷The more the priests increased,
    the more they sinned against
      me;
  they exchanged[a] their[b] Glory
    for something disgraceful.
⁸They feed on the sins of my
      people
  and relish their wickedness.
⁹And it will be: Like people, like
    priests.
  I will punish both of them for
    their ways
  and repay them for their deeds.

¹⁰"They will eat but not have
      enough;
  they will engage in prostitution
    but not increase,
  because they have deserted the
    LORD
  to give themselves ¹¹to
    prostitution,
  to old wine and new,
    which take away the
      understanding ¹²of my
    people.
  They consult a wooden idol
    and are answered by a stick of
      wood.
  A spirit of prostitution leads them
    astray;
  they are unfaithful to their God.
¹³They sacrifice on the
      mountaintops
    and burn offerings on the hills,
  under oak, poplar and terebinth,
    where the shade is pleasant.
  Therefore your daughters turn to
    prostitution
    and your daughters-in-law to
      adultery.

¹⁴"I will not punish your daughters
    when they turn to prostitution,
  nor your daughters-in-law
    when they commit adultery,
  because the men themselves
    consort with harlots

and sacrifice with shrine
    prostitutes—
  a people without understanding
    will come to ruin!
¹⁵"Though you commit adultery,
    O Israel,
  let not Judah become guilty.

"Do not go to Gilgal;
  do not go up to Beth Aven.[c]
  And do not swear, 'As surely as
    the LORD lives!'
¹⁶The Israelites are stubborn,
    like a stubborn heifer.
  How then can the LORD pasture
      them
  like lambs in a meadow?
¹⁷Ephraim is joined to idols;
    leave him alone!
¹⁸Even when their drinks are gone,
    they continue their prostitution;
  their rulers dearly love
    shameful ways.
¹⁹A whirlwind will sweep them
      away,
  and their sacrifices will bring
    them shame.

Judgment Against Israel

5 "Hear this, you priests!
  Pay attention, you Israelites!
  Listen, O royal house!
    This judgment is against you:
  You have been a snare at Mizpah,
    a net spread out on Tabor.
²The rebels are deep in slaughter.
    I will discipline all of them.
³I know all about Ephraim;
    Israel is not hidden from me.
  Ephraim, you have now turned to
      prostitution;
    Israel is corrupt.

⁴"Their deeds do not permit them
    to return to their God.
  A spirit of prostitution is in their
      heart;
    they do not acknowledge the
      LORD.
⁵Israel's arrogance testifies against
    them;

---

a7 Syriac and an ancient Hebrew scribal tradition; Masoretic Text *I will exchange*   *b7* Masoretic
Text; an ancient Hebrew scribal tradition *my*   *c15 Beth Aven* means *house of wickedness* (a name
for Bethel, which means *house of God*).

the Israelites, even Ephraim,
  stumble in their sin;
Judah also stumbles with them.
⁶When they go with their flocks
    and herds
  to seek the LORD,
  they will not find him;
    he has withdrawn himself from
      them.
⁷They are unfaithful to the LORD;
  they give birth to illegitimate
    children.
Now their New Moon festivals
  will devour them and their
    fields.

⁸"Sound the trumpet in Gibeah,
  the horn in Ramah.
Raise the battle cry in Beth
    Aven*a*;
  lead on, O Benjamin.
⁹Ephraim will be laid waste
  on the day of reckoning.
Among the tribes of Israel
  I proclaim what is certain.
¹⁰Judah's leaders are like those
  who move boundary stones.
I will pour out my wrath on them
  like a flood of water.
¹¹Ephraim is oppressed,
    trampled in judgment,
    intent on pursuing idols.*b*
¹²I am like a moth to Ephraim,
  like rot to the people of Judah.

¹³"When Ephraim saw his sickness,
  and Judah his sores,
then Ephraim turned to Assyria,
  and sent to the great king for
    help.
But he is not able to cure you,
  not able to heal your sores.
¹⁴For I will be like a lion to
    Ephraim,
  like a great lion to Judah.
I will tear them to pieces and go
    away;
  I will carry them off, with no
    one to rescue them.
¹⁵Then I will go back to my place
  until they admit their guilt.
And they will seek my face;

in their misery they will
  earnestly seek me."

Israel Unrepentant

6 "Come, let us return to the LORD.
  He has torn us to pieces
    but he will heal us;
  he has injured us
    but he will bind up our
      wounds.
²After two days he will revive us;
  on the third day he will restore
    us,
  that we may live in his
    presence.
³Let us acknowledge the LORD;
  let us press on to acknowledge
    him.
As surely as the sun rises,
  he will appear;
he will come to us like the winter
    rains,
  like the spring rains that water
    the earth."

⁴"What can I do with you,
    Ephraim?
What can I do with you, Judah?
Your love is like the morning mist,
  like the early dew that
    disappears.
⁵Therefore I cut you in pieces with
    my prophets,
  I killed you with the words of
    my mouth;
  my judgments flashed like
    lightning upon you.
⁶For I desire mercy, not sacrifice,
  and acknowledgment of God
    rather than burnt offerings.
⁷Like Adam,*c* they have broken
    the covenant—
  they were unfaithful to me
    there.
⁸Gilead is a city of wicked men,
  stained with footprints of blood.
⁹As marauders lie in ambush for a
    man,
  so do bands of priests;
they murder on the road to
    Shechem,
  committing shameful crimes.

---

a8 Beth Aven means *house of wickedness* (a name for Bethel, which means *house of God*).
b11 The meaning of the Hebrew for this word is uncertain.   *c7* Or *As at Adam;* or *Like men*

¹⁰I have seen a horrible thing
   in the house of Israel.
There Ephraim is given to
     prostitution
   and Israel is defiled.

¹¹"Also for you, Judah,
   a harvest is appointed.

"Whenever I would restore the
     fortunes of my people,

7 ¹whenever I would heal Israel,
   the sins of Ephraim are exposed
   and the crimes of Samaria
     revealed.
They practice deceit,
   thieves break into houses,
   bandits rob in the streets;
²but they do not realize
   that I remember all their evil
     deeds.
Their sins engulf them;
   they are always before me.

³"They delight the king with their
     wickedness,
   the princes with their lies.
⁴They are all adulterers,
   burning like an oven
whose fire the baker need not stir
   from the kneading of the dough
     till it rises.
⁵On the day of the festival of our
     king
   the princes become inflamed
     with wine,
   and he joins hands with the
     mockers.
⁶Their hearts are like an oven;
   they approach him with
     intrigue.
Their passion smolders all night;
   in the morning it blazes like a
     flaming fire.
⁷All of them are hot as an oven;
   they devour their rulers.
All their kings fall,
   and none of them calls on me.

⁸"Ephraim mixes with the nations;
   Ephraim is a flat cake not
     turned over.
⁹Foreigners sap his strength,
   but he does not realize it.
His hair is sprinkled with gray,

but he does not notice.
¹⁰Israel's arrogance testifies against
     him,
   but despite all this
he does not return to the LORD his
     God
   or search for him.

¹¹"Ephraim is like a dove,
   easily deceived and senseless—
now calling to Egypt,
   now turning to Assyria.
¹²When they go, I will throw my
     net over them;
   I will pull them down like birds
     of the air.
When I hear them flocking
     together,
   I will catch them.
¹³Woe to them,
   because they have strayed from
     me!
Destruction to them,
   because they have rebelled
     against me!
I long to redeem them
   but they speak lies against me.
¹⁴They do not cry out to me from
     their hearts
   but wail upon their beds.
They gather together[a] for grain
     and new wine
   but turn away from me.
¹⁵I trained them and strengthened
     them,
   but they plot evil against me.
¹⁶They do not turn to the Most
     High;
   they are like a faulty bow.
Their leaders will fall by the
     sword
   because of their insolent words.
For this they will be ridiculed
   in the land of Egypt.

Israel to Reap the Whirlwind

8 "Put the trumpet to your lips!
   An eagle is over the house of
     the LORD
because the people have broken
     my covenant
   and rebelled against my law.
²Israel cries out to me,

---

^a14 Most Hebrew manuscripts; some Hebrew manuscripts and Septuagint *They slash themselves*

PASSAGE: Psalm 118; Hosea 11:1–11
AUTHOR: Christina Rossetti

O Lord Seek Us

O Lord seek us, O Lord find us
In Thy patient care,
Be Thy love before, behind us,
Round us everywhere.
Lest the god of this world blind us,
Lest he bait a snare,
Lest he forge a chain to bind us,
Lest he speak us fair,
Turn not from us, call to mind us,
Find, embrace us, hear.
Be Thy love before, behind us,
Round us everywhere.

Go to page 1119 for your next devotional reading.

'O our God, we acknowledge
      you!'
³But Israel has rejected what is
      good;
   an enemy will pursue him.
⁴They set up kings without my
      consent;
   they choose princes without my
      approval.
With their silver and gold
   they make idols for themselves
   to their own destruction.
⁵Throw out your calf-idol,
      O Samaria!
My anger burns against them.
How long will they be incapable
      of purity?
⁶ They are from Israel!
This calf—a craftsman has made
      it;
   it is not God.
It will be broken in pieces,
   that calf of Samaria.

⁷"They sow the wind
   and reap the whirlwind.
The stalk has no head;
   it will produce no flour.
Were it to yield grain,
   foreigners would swallow it up.
⁸Israel is swallowed up;
   now she is among the nations
   like a worthless thing.
⁹For they have gone up to Assyria
   like a wild donkey wandering
      alone.
   Ephraim has sold herself to
      lovers.
¹⁰Although they have sold
      themselves among the
      nations,
   I will now gather them together.
They will begin to waste away
   under the oppression of the
      mighty king.

¹¹"Though Ephraim built many
      altars for sin offerings,
   these have become altars for
      sinning.
¹²I wrote for them the many things
      of my law,
   but they regarded them as
      something alien.

¹³They offer sacrifices given to me
   and they eat the meat,
   but the LORD is not pleased with
      them.
Now he will remember their
      wickedness
   and punish their sins:
   They will return to Egypt.
¹⁴Israel has forgotten his Maker
   and built palaces;
   Judah has fortified many towns.
But I will send fire upon their
      cities
   that will consume their
      fortresses."

Punishment for Israel

9 Do not rejoice, O Israel;
   do not be jubilant like the other
      nations.
For you have been unfaithful to
      your God;
   you love the wages of a
      prostitute
   at every threshing floor.
²Threshing floors and winepresses
   will not feed the people;
   the new wine will fail them.
³They will not remain in the LORD's
      land;
   Ephraim will return to Egypt
   and eat unclean[a] food in
      Assyria.
⁴They will not pour out wine
      offerings to the LORD,
   nor will their sacrifices please
      him.
Such sacrifices will be to them like
      the bread of mourners;
   all who eat them will be
      unclean.
This food will be for themselves;
   it will not come into the temple
      of the LORD.

⁵What will you do on the day of
      your appointed feasts,
   on the festival days of the LORD?
⁶Even if they escape from
      destruction,
   Egypt will gather them,
   and Memphis will bury them.

Their treasures of silver will be
  taken over by briers,
  and thorns will overrun their
    tents.
7The days of punishment are
    coming,
  the days of reckoning are at
    hand.
  Let Israel know this.
Because your sins are so many
  and your hostility so great,
the prophet is considered a fool,
  the inspired man a maniac.
8The prophet, along with my God,
  is the watchman over
    Ephraim,a
yet snares await him on all his
    paths,
  and hostility in the house of his
    God.
9They have sunk deep into
    corruption,
  as in the days of Gibeah.
God will remember their
    wickedness
  and punish them for their sins.

10"When I found Israel,
  it was like finding grapes in the
    desert;
when I saw your fathers,
  it was like seeing the early fruit
    on the fig tree.
But when they came to Baal Peor,
  they consecrated themselves to
    that shameful idol
and became as vile as the thing
    they loved.
11Ephraim's glory will fly away like
    a bird—
  no birth, no pregnancy, no
    conception.
12Even if they rear children,
  I will bereave them of every
    one.
Woe to them
  when I turn away from them!
13I have seen Ephraim, like Tyre,
  planted in a pleasant place.
But Ephraim will bring out
  their children to the slayer."

14Give them, O LORD—

what will you give them?
Give them wombs that miscarry
  and breasts that are dry.

15"Because of all their wickedness in
    Gilgal,
  I hated them there.
Because of their sinful deeds,
  I will drive them out of my
    house.
I will no longer love them;
  all their leaders are rebellious.
16Ephraim is blighted,
  their root is withered,
  they yield no fruit.
Even if they bear children,
  I will slay their cherished
    offspring."

17My God will reject them
  because they have not obeyed
    him;
  they will be wanderers among
    the nations.

10 Israel was a spreading vine;
    he brought forth fruit for
      himself.
As his fruit increased,
  he built more altars;
as his land prospered,
  he adorned his sacred stones.
2Their heart is deceitful,
  and now they must bear their
    guilt.
The LORD will demolish their altars
  and destroy their sacred stones.

3Then they will say, "We have no
    king
  because we did not revere the
    LORD.
But even if we had a king,
  what could he do for us?"
4They make many promises,
  take false oaths
  and make agreements;
therefore lawsuits spring up
  like poisonous weeds in a
    plowed field.
5The people who live in Samaria
    fear
  for the calf-idol of Beth Aven.b
Its people will mourn over it,

---

a8 Or The prophet is the watchman over Ephraim, / the people of my God
house of wickedness (a name for Bethel, which means house of God).   b5 Beth Aven means

and so will its idolatrous
   priests,
those who had rejoiced over its
   splendor,
   because it is taken from them
      into exile.
⁶It will be carried to Assyria
   as tribute for the great king.
Ephraim will be disgraced;
   Israel will be ashamed of its
      wooden idols.ᵃ
⁷Samaria and its king will float
   away
   like a twig on the surface of the
      waters.
⁸The high places of wickednessᵇ
   will be destroyed—
   it is the sin of Israel.
Thorns and thistles will grow up
   and cover their altars.
Then they will say to the
      mountains, "Cover us!"
   and to the hills, "Fall on us!"

⁹"Since the days of Gibeah, you
   have sinned, O Israel,
   and there you have remained.ᶜ
Did not war overtake
   the evildoers in Gibeah?
¹⁰When I please, I will punish them;
   nations will be gathered against
      them
   to put them in bonds for their
      double sin.
¹¹Ephraim is a trained heifer
   that loves to thresh;
so I will put a yoke
   on her fair neck.
I will drive Ephraim,
   Judah must plow,
   and Jacob must break up the
      ground.
¹²Sow for yourselves righteousness,
   reap the fruit of unfailing love,
and break up your unplowed
      ground;
   for it is time to seek the LORD,
until he comes
   and showers righteousness on
      you.
¹³But you have planted wickedness,
   you have reaped evil,

   you have eaten the fruit of
      deception.
Because you have depended on
   your own strength
   and on your many warriors,
¹⁴the roar of battle will rise against
   your people,
   so that all your fortresses will
      be devastated—
as Shalman devastated Beth Arbel
   on the day of battle,
when mothers were dashed to
   the ground with their
      children.
¹⁵Thus will it happen to you,
   O Bethel,
   because your wickedness is
      great.
When that day dawns,
   the king of Israel will be
      completely destroyed.

God's Love for Israel

11 "When Israel was a child, I
      loved him,
   and out of Egypt I called my
      son.
²But the more Iᵈ called Israel,
   the further they went from
      me.ᵉ
They sacrificed to the Baals
   and they burned incense to
      images.
³It was I who taught Ephraim to
      walk,
   taking them by the arms;
but they did not realize
   it was I who healed them.
⁴I led them with cords of human
      kindness,
   with ties of love;
I lifted the yoke from their neck
   and bent down to feed them.

⁵"Will they not return to Egypt
   and will not Assyria rule over
      them
   because they refuse to repent?
⁶Swords will flash in their cities,
   will destroy the bars of their
      gates
   and put an end to their plans.

ᵃ6 Or *its counsel*   ᵇ8 Hebrew *aven*, a reference to Beth Aven (a derogatory name for Bethel)
ᶜ9 Or *there a stand was taken*   ᵈ2 Some Septuagint manuscripts; Hebrew *they*
ᵉ2 Septuagint; Hebrew *them*

⁷My people are determined to turn
    from me.
  Even if they call to the Most
    High,
  he will by no means exalt them.

⁸"How can I give you up,
    Ephraim?
  How can I hand you over,
    Israel?
How can I treat you like Admah?
  How can I make you like
    Zeboiim?
My heart is changed within me;

  all my compassion is aroused.
⁹I will not carry out my fierce
    anger,
  nor will I turn and devastate
    Ephraim.
For I am God, and not man—
  the Holy One among you.
  I will not come in wrath.ᵃ
¹⁰They will follow the LORD;
  he will roar like a lion.
When he roars,
  his children will come trembling
    from the west.

ᵃ9 Or *come against any city*

VERSE:	AUTHOR:	PASSAGE:
Hosea 11:4	Tim Stafford	Hosea 11:1–11

The Heart of the Story

In Scripture, God's love is the center of the universe; he breathes life into ours. It is from him that we get life each day, not from ourselves. Because of that, our losses and our successes are relatively less important. They matter, but they are not final and irreversible. They are not the heart of the story: Christ's life, death and resurrection are.

If Christ's resurrection is central, the ultimate loss of old age—death—is not the end of life, but a crucial turning point. After death, and only after, comes judgment, when the true meaning of each life is made clear—when all the meanings and loose endings of our brief story on earth are sorted out. After death comes glory, glory reflected from God himself. This is the Biblical faith. It offers the only way I know to find meaning and hope.

ADDITIONAL SCRIPTURE READINGS
1 Corinthians 15:12–28; Ephesians 2:1–10

Go to page 1124 for your next devotional reading.

¹¹They will come trembling
    like birds from Egypt,
    like doves from Assyria.
I will settle them in their homes,"
    declares the Lord.

Israel's Sin

¹²Ephraim has surrounded me with
    lies,
    the house of Israel with deceit.
And Judah is unruly against God,
    even against the faithful Holy
    One.

12

¹Ephraim feeds on the wind;
    he pursues the east wind all
    day
and multiplies lies and violence.
He makes a treaty with Assyria
    and sends olive oil to Egypt.
²The Lord has a charge to bring
    against Judah;
    he will punish Jacob[a]
       according to his ways
    and repay him according to his
       deeds.
³In the womb he grasped his
    brother's heel;
    as a man he struggled with
    God.
⁴He struggled with the angel and
    overcame him;
    he wept and begged for his
    favor.
He found him at Bethel
    and talked with him there—
⁵the Lord God Almighty,
    the Lord is his name of renown!
⁶But you must return to your God;
    maintain love and justice,
    and wait for your God always.

⁷The merchant uses dishonest
    scales;
    he loves to defraud.
⁸Ephraim boasts,
    "I am very rich; I have become
    wealthy.
With all my wealth they will not
    find in me
    any iniquity or sin."

⁹"I am the Lord your God,

   ⌊who brought you⌋ out of[b]
    Egypt;
I will make you live in tents
    again,
    as in the days of your
    appointed feasts.
¹⁰I spoke to the prophets,
    gave them many visions
    and told parables through
    them."

¹¹Is Gilead wicked?
    Its people are worthless!
Do they sacrifice bulls in Gilgal?
    Their altars will be like piles of
    stones
    on a plowed field.
¹²Jacob fled to the country of
    Aram[c];
    Israel served to get a wife,
    and to pay for her he tended
    sheep.
¹³The Lord used a prophet to bring
    Israel up from Egypt,
    by a prophet he cared for him.
¹⁴But Ephraim has bitterly provoked
    him to anger;
    his Lord will leave upon him
       the guilt of his bloodshed
    and will repay him for his
    contempt.

The Lord's Anger Against Israel

13

When Ephraim spoke, men
    trembled;
    he was exalted in Israel.
But he became guilty of Baal
    worship and died.
²Now they sin more and more;
    they make idols for themselves
    from their silver,
cleverly fashioned images,
    all of them the work of
    craftsmen.
It is said of these people,
    "They offer human sacrifice
    and kiss[d] the calf-idols."
³Therefore they will be like the
    morning mist,
    like the early dew that
    disappears,

---

[a]2 *Jacob* means *he grasps the heel* (figuratively, *he deceives*).   [b]9 Or *God* / *ever since you were in*   [c]12 That is, Northwest Mesopotamia   [d]2 Or *"Men who sacrifice* / *kiss*

like chaff swirling from a
threshing floor,
like smoke escaping through a
window.

⁴"But I am the LORD your God,
⌐who brought you⌐ out of*ᵃ*
Egypt.
You shall acknowledge no God
but me,
no Savior except me.
⁵I cared for you in the desert,
in the land of burning heat.
⁶When I fed them, they were
satisfied;
when they were satisfied, they
became proud;
then they forgot me.
⁷So I will come upon them like a
lion,
like a leopard I will lurk by the
path.
⁸Like a bear robbed of her cubs,
I will attack them and rip them
open.
Like a lion I will devour them;
a wild animal will tear them
apart.

⁹"You are destroyed, O Israel,
because you are against me,
against your helper.
¹⁰Where is your king, that he may
save you?
Where are your rulers in all
your towns,
of whom you said,
'Give me a king and princes'?
¹¹So in my anger I gave you a king,
and in my wrath I took him
away.
¹²The guilt of Ephraim is stored up,
his sins are kept on record.
¹³Pains as of a woman in childbirth
come to him,
but he is a child without
wisdom;
when the time arrives,
he does not come to the
opening of the womb.

¹⁴"I will ransom them from the
power of the grave*ᵇ*;

I will redeem them from death.
Where, O death, are your plagues?
Where, O grave,*ᵇ* is your
destruction?

"I will have no compassion,
¹⁵   even though he thrives among
his brothers.
An east wind from the LORD will
come,
blowing in from the desert;
his spring will fail
and his well dry up.
His storehouse will be plundered
of all its treasures.
¹⁶The people of Samaria must bear
their guilt,
because they have rebelled
against their God.
They will fall by the sword;
their little ones will be dashed
to the ground,
their pregnant women ripped
open."

Repentance to Bring Blessing

14 Return, O Israel, to the LORD
your God.
Your sins have been your
downfall!
²Take words with you
and return to the LORD.
Say to him:
"Forgive all our sins
and receive us graciously,
that we may offer the fruit of
our lips.*ᶜ*
³Assyria cannot save us;
we will not mount war-horses.
We will never again say 'Our
gods'
to what our own hands have
made,
for in you the fatherless find
compassion."

⁴"I will heal their waywardness
and love them freely,
for my anger has turned away
from them.
⁵I will be like the dew to Israel;
he will blossom like a lily.

ᵃ4 Or God / ever since you were in   *ᵇ14 Hebrew Sheol*   *ᶜ2 Or offer our lips as sacrifices of bulls*

Like a cedar of Lebanon
  he will send down his roots;
6 his young shoots will grow.
His splendor will be like an olive
    tree,
  his fragrance like a cedar of
    Lebanon.
7Men will dwell again in his shade.
  He will flourish like the grain.
He will blossom like a vine,
  and his fame will be like the
    wine from Lebanon.
8O Ephraim, what more have I*a* to
    do with idols?

I will answer him and care for
  him.
I am like a green pine tree;
  your fruitfulness comes from
    me."

9Who is wise? He will realize these
  things.
Who is discerning? He will
  understand them.
The ways of the LORD are right;
  the righteous walk in them,
  but the rebellious stumble in
    them.

---

*a*8 Or *What more has Ephraim*

*J*oel uses the occasion of
a famine to describe what happens to people
who try to live apart from God and his will.
Eventually they lose everything and starve.
As you read this book, examine your heart's
commitment and if necessary confess before
God and open yourself up to a fresh infusion
of the Spirit's power.

JOEL

1 The word of the Lord that came to Joel son of Pethuel.

An Invasion of Locusts

²Hear this, you elders;
 listen, all who live in the land.
 Has anything like this ever
  happened in your days
 or in the days of your
  forefathers?
³Tell it to your children,
 and let your children tell it to
  their children,
 and their children to the next
  generation.
⁴What the locust swarm has left
 the great locusts have eaten;
what the great locusts have left
 the young locusts have eaten;
what the young locusts have left
 other locusts*ᵃ* have eaten.

⁵Wake up, you drunkards, and
  weep!
 Wail, all you drinkers of wine;
wail because of the new wine,

for it has been snatched from
  your lips.
⁶A nation has invaded my land,
 powerful and without number;
it has the teeth of a lion,
 the fangs of a lioness.
⁷It has laid waste my vines
 and ruined my fig trees.
It has stripped off their bark
 and thrown it away,
 leaving their branches white.

⁸Mourn like a virgin*ᵇ* in sackcloth
 grieving for the husband*ᶜ* of
  her youth.
⁹Grain offerings and drink
  offerings
 are cut off from the house of
  the Lord.
The priests are in mourning,
 those who minister before the
  Lord.
¹⁰The fields are ruined,
 the ground is dried up*ᵈ*;
 the grain is destroyed,
 the new wine is dried up,

ᵃ4 The precise meaning of the four Hebrew words used here for locusts is uncertain. *ᵇ8* Or *young woman* *ᶜ8* Or *betrothed* *ᵈ10* Or *ground mourns*

VERSE:	AUTHOR:	PASSAGE:
Joel 1:4	J. Oswald Sanders	Joel 1:1–4

Can I Begin Again?

When we were younger, most of us who are Christians earnestly sought to discover God's plan for our lives, especially when we came to the crossroads of career and marriage. Are we equally diligent in seeking his plan for our old age, or are we just drifting along with no definite aim or goal?

With more time to review the past, it is not difficult to become discouraged as we recall opportunities missed; a lessening of zeal in God's service; a mediocre prayer life; or perhaps actual sins of which we have reason to be ashamed. It is at such moments of introspection that we need to turn our eyes outward and upward to our loving and understanding Father. What balm a verse like Romans 5:20 can bring! "But where sin increased, grace increased all the more."

The wonderful thing about God's abundant grace and favor is that it is never too late to discover and follow God's plan for the remainder of our lives, never too late to make a new start, even if we have missed his plan up till the present time.

To his disillusioned compatriots, the prophet Joel brought an inspiring message of hope—the hope of a new beginning. God delights in giving his failing children a chance to begin again . . . "I will repay you for the years the locusts have eaten" (Joel 2:25).

ADDITIONAL SCRIPTURE READINGS
Psalm 80; Hosea 11:1–11

Go to page 1128 for your next devotional reading.

the oil fails.
¹¹Despair, you farmers,
    wail, you vine growers;
grieve for the wheat and the
    barley,
    because the harvest of the field
    is destroyed.
¹²The vine is dried up
    and the fig tree is withered;
the pomegranate, the palm and
    the apple tree—
all the trees of the field—are
    dried up.
Surely the joy of mankind
    is withered away.

A Call to Repentance

¹³Put on sackcloth, O priests, and
    mourn;
    wail, you who minister before
    the altar.
Come, spend the night in
    sackcloth,
    you who minister before my
    God;
for the grain offerings and drink
    offerings
    are withheld from the house of
    your God.
¹⁴Declare a holy fast;
    call a sacred assembly.
Summon the elders
    and all who live in the land
to the house of the LORD your
    God,
    and cry out to the LORD.

¹⁵Alas for that day!
    For the day of the LORD is near;
    it will come like destruction
    from the Almighty.ᵃ

¹⁶Has not the food been cut off
    before our very eyes—
joy and gladness
    from the house of our God?
¹⁷The seeds are shriveled
    beneath the clods.ᵇ
The storehouses are in ruins,
    the granaries have been broken
    down,
    for the grain has dried up.
¹⁸How the cattle moan!
    The herds mill about

because they have no pasture;
    even the flocks of sheep are
    suffering.

¹⁹To you, O LORD, I call,
    for fire has devoured the open
    pastures
    and flames have burned up all
    the trees of the field.
²⁰Even the wild animals pant for
    you;
    the streams of water have dried
    up
    and fire has devoured the open
    pastures.

An Army of Locusts

2 Blow the trumpet in Zion;
    sound the alarm on my holy
    hill.
Let all who live in the land
    tremble,
    for the day of the LORD is
    coming.
It is close at hand—
² a day of darkness and gloom,
    a day of clouds and blackness.
Like dawn spreading across the
    mountains
    a large and mighty army comes,
such as never was of old
    nor ever will be in ages to
    come.

³Before them fire devours,
    behind them a flame blazes.
Before them the land is like the
    garden of Eden,
    behind them, a desert waste—
    nothing escapes them.
⁴They have the appearance of
    horses;
    they gallop along like cavalry.
⁵With a noise like that of chariots
    they leap over the
    mountaintops,
like a crackling fire consuming
    stubble,
    like a mighty army drawn up
    for battle.

⁶At the sight of them, nations are
    in anguish;
    every face turns pale.

ᵃ15 Hebrew *Shaddai*   ᵇ17 The meaning of the Hebrew for this word is uncertain.

⁷They charge like warriors;
    they scale walls like soldiers.
They all march in line,
    not swerving from their course.
⁸They do not jostle each other;
    each marches straight ahead.
They plunge through defenses
    without breaking ranks.
⁹They rush upon the city;
    they run along the wall.
They climb into the houses;
    like thieves they enter through
      the windows.

¹⁰Before them the earth shakes,
    the sky trembles,
the sun and moon are darkened,
    and the stars no longer shine.
¹¹The LORD thunders
    at the head of his army;
his forces are beyond number,
    and mighty are those who obey
      his command.
The day of the LORD is great;
    it is dreadful.
    Who can endure it?

Rend Your Heart

¹²"Even now," declares the LORD,
    "return to me with all your
      heart,
with fasting and weeping and
      mourning."

¹³Rend your heart
    and not your garments.
Return to the LORD your God,
    for he is gracious and
      compassionate,
slow to anger and abounding in
      love,
    and he relents from sending
      calamity.
¹⁴Who knows? He may turn and
      have pity
    and leave behind a blessing—
grain offerings and drink offerings
    for the LORD your God.

¹⁵Blow the trumpet in Zion,
    declare a holy fast,
    call a sacred assembly.
¹⁶Gather the people,

consecrate the assembly;
    bring together the elders,
    gather the children,
    those nursing at the breast.
Let the bridegroom leave his room
    and the bride her chamber.
¹⁷Let the priests, who minister
    before the LORD,
weep between the temple porch
    and the altar.
Let them say, "Spare your people,
    O LORD.
Do not make your inheritance
    an object of scorn,
a byword among the nations.
Why should they say among the
      peoples,
'Where is their God?' "

The LORD's Answer

¹⁸Then the LORD will be jealous for
    his land
    and take pity on his people.

¹⁹The LORD will reply[a] to them:

"I am sending you grain, new
    wine and oil,
    enough to satisfy you fully;
never again will I make you
    an object of scorn to the nations.

²⁰"I will drive the northern army far
    from you,
    pushing it into a parched and
      barren land,
with its front columns going into
    the eastern sea[b]
and those in the rear into the
    western sea.[c]
And its stench will go up;
    its smell will rise."

Surely he has done great things.[d]
²¹   Be not afraid, O land;
    be glad and rejoice.
Surely the LORD has done great
    things.
²²   Be not afraid, O wild animals,
    for the open pastures are
      becoming green.
The trees are bearing their fruit;
    the fig tree and the vine yield
      their riches.

---

a18,19 Or LORD was jealous . . . / and took pity . . . / 19The LORD replied   *b20 That is, the Dead Sea*
c20 That is, the Mediterranean   *d20 Or rise. / Surely it has done great things."*

²³Be glad, O people of Zion,
rejoice in the LORD your God,
for he has given you
the autumn rains in
righteousness.^a
He sends you abundant showers,
both autumn and spring rains,
as before.
²⁴The threshing floors will be filled
with grain;
the vats will overflow with new
wine and oil.

²⁵"I will repay you for the years the
locusts have eaten—
the great locust and the young
locust,
the other locusts and the locust
swarm^b—
my great army that I sent among
you.
²⁶You will have plenty to eat, until
you are full,
and you will praise the name of
the LORD your God,
who has worked wonders for
you;
never again will my people be
shamed.
²⁷Then you will know that I am in
Israel,
that I am the LORD your God,
and that there is no other;
never again will my people be
shamed.

The Day of the LORD

²⁸"And afterward,
I will pour out my Spirit on all
people.
Your sons and daughters will
prophesy,
your old men will dream
dreams,
your young men will see
visions.
²⁹Even on my servants, both men
and women,
I will pour out my Spirit in
those days.
³⁰I will show wonders in the
heavens

and on the earth,
blood and fire and billows of
smoke.
³¹The sun will be turned to
darkness
and the moon to blood
before the coming of the great
and dreadful day of the
LORD.
³²And everyone who calls
on the name of the LORD will be
saved;
for on Mount Zion and in
Jerusalem
there will be deliverance,
as the LORD has said,
among the survivors
whom the LORD calls.

The Nations Judged

3 "In those days and at that time,
when I restore the fortunes of
Judah and Jerusalem,
²I will gather all nations
and bring them down to the
Valley of Jehoshaphat.^c
There I will enter into judgment
against them
concerning my inheritance, my
people Israel,
for they scattered my people
among the nations
and divided up my land.
³They cast lots for my people
and traded boys for prostitutes;
they sold girls for wine
that they might drink.

⁴"Now what have you against me,
O Tyre and Sidon and all you regions
of Philistia? Are you repaying me for
something I have done? If you are
paying me back, I will swiftly and
speedily return on your own heads
what you have done. ⁵For you took
my silver and my gold and carried off
my finest treasures to your temples.
⁶You sold the people of Judah and Je-
rusalem to the Greeks, that you might
send them far from their homeland.
⁷"See, I am going to rouse them out
of the places to which you sold them,

---

^a23 Or / the teacher for righteousness:
used here for locusts is uncertain.   ^b25 The precise meaning of the four Hebrew words
^c2 Jehoshaphat means the LORD judges; also in verse 12.

VERSE: Joel 2:28	AUTHOR: Dirk R. Buursma	PASSAGE: Joel 2:28–32

Old Men Will Dream Dreams

Simple, ordinary people. Ordinary housewives. Ordinary businessmen. Ordinary retirees. You—and me. Waiting for wholeness. Pursuing peace. Hunting for hope.

"I will pour out my Spirit on all people" (Joel 2:28). Yes, Lord, pour it out. Pour it out on us ordinary people who sense that something's missing—that in spite of trying so hard to follow Jesus, the wholeness isn't there. We're broken, Lord. We need your Spirit to let loose a stream of power within us that will lead us beyond the anxieties and fears that paralyze us, that will pound through the dam of fatigue and despair and faded hope and dreams and a thousand other things that impede us—to bring us to a new life, a new day!

And then it happens! The Spirit comes! Our faith —that faith so often shaken to its roots by the mysteries of life and death, that faith—now purified, restored! The Spirit is there, and once more we dare to dream dreams.

And the Spirit is there—compelling us to stretch out our hands to other seekers. We must tell them that there is hope for the hopeless, that those who feel they have nothing left to dream about can receive God's awesome gift of purpose, of joy, that those who doubt whether there is a future worth staying alive for can have true hope that will not disappoint them.

ADDITIONAL SCRIPTURE READINGS
Acts 2:1–21; Romans 5:1–5

Go to page 1138 for your next devotional reading.

and I will return on your own heads what you have done. ⁸I will sell your sons and daughters to the people of Judah, and they will sell them to the Sabeans, a nation far away." The LORD has spoken.

⁹Proclaim this among the nations:
  Prepare for war!
Rouse the warriors!
  Let all the fighting men draw
    near and attack.
¹⁰Beat your plowshares into swords
  and your pruning hooks into
    spears.
Let the weakling say,
  "I am strong!"
¹¹Come quickly, all you nations
    from every side,
  and assemble there.

Bring down your warriors,
  O LORD!

¹²"Let the nations be roused;
  let them advance into the Valley
    of Jehoshaphat,
for there I will sit
  to judge all the nations on every
    side.
¹³Swing the sickle,
  for the harvest is ripe.
Come, trample the grapes,
  for the winepress is full
  and the vats overflow—
so great is their wickedness!"

¹⁴Multitudes, multitudes
  in the valley of decision!
For the day of the LORD is near
  in the valley of decision.
¹⁵The sun and moon will be
    darkened,

and the stars no longer shine.
¹⁶The LORD will roar from Zion
  and thunder from Jerusalem;
  the earth and the sky will
    tremble.
But the LORD will be a refuge for
    his people,
  a stronghold for the people of
    Israel.

Blessings for God's People

¹⁷"Then you will know that I, the
    LORD your God,
  dwell in Zion, my holy hill.
Jerusalem will be holy;
  never again will foreigners
    invade her.

¹⁸"In that day the mountains will
    drip new wine,
  and the hills will flow with
    milk;
  all the ravines of Judah will run
    with water.
A fountain will flow out of the
    LORD's house
  and will water the valley of
    acacias.ᵃ
¹⁹But Egypt will be desolate,
  Edom a desert waste,
because of violence done to the
    people of Judah,
  in whose land they shed
    innocent blood.
²⁰Judah will be inhabited forever
  and Jerusalem through all
    generations.
²¹Their bloodguilt, which I have not
    pardoned,
  I will pardon."

The LORD dwells in Zion!

ᵃ18 Or Valley of Shittim

Amos prophesied during the reign of Jeroboam II (2 Kings 14:23–29), a time of prosperity for some but extreme poverty for others. He reprimands those who oppress the poor and warns that they will be brought to justice. As you read this book, review your own attitudes and actions toward the weak and the poor, and take comfort in your own situations of weakness that God cares about you.

AMOS

1 The words of Amos, one of the shepherds of Tekoa—what he saw concerning Israel two years before the earthquake, when Uzziah was king of Judah and Jeroboam son of Jehoash[a] was king of Israel.
²He said:

"The LORD roars from Zion
and thunders from Jerusalem;
the pastures of the shepherds dry up,[b]
and the top of Carmel withers."

Judgment on Israel's Neighbors

³This is what the LORD says:

"For three sins of Damascus,
even for four, I will not turn back ⌞my wrath⌟.
Because she threshed Gilead
with sledges having iron teeth,

⁴I will send fire upon the house of Hazael
that will consume the fortresses of Ben-Hadad.
⁵I will break down the gate of Damascus;
I will destroy the king who is in[c] the Valley of Aven[d]
and the one who holds the scepter in Beth Eden.
The people of Aram will go into exile to Kir,"

says the LORD.

⁶This is what the LORD says:

"For three sins of Gaza,
even for four, I will not turn back ⌞my wrath⌟.
Because she took captive whole communities
and sold them to Edom,

---

a1 Hebrew *Joash*, a variant of *Jehoash*   b2 Or *shepherds mourn*   c5 Or *the inhabitants of*
d5 *Aven* means *wickedness*.

7I will send fire upon the walls of
    Gaza
  that will consume her fortresses.
8I will destroy the king^a of
    Ashdod
  and the one who holds the
    scepter in Ashkelon.
I will turn my hand against Ekron,
  till the last of the Philistines is
    dead,"
            says the Sovereign Lord.

9This is what the Lord says:

"For three sins of Tyre,
  even for four, I will not turn
    back ˻my wrath˼.
Because she sold whole
    communities of captives to
    Edom,
  disregarding a treaty of
    brotherhood,
10I will send fire upon the walls of
    Tyre
  that will consume her
    fortresses."

11This is what the Lord says:

"For three sins of Edom,
  even for four, I will not turn
    back ˻my wrath˼.
Because he pursued his brother
    with a sword,
  stifling all compassion,^b
because his anger raged
    continually
  and his fury flamed unchecked,
12I will send fire upon Teman
  that will consume the fortresses
    of Bozrah."

13This is what the Lord says:

"For three sins of Ammon,
  even for four, I will not turn
    back ˻my wrath˼.
Because he ripped open the
    pregnant women of Gilead
  in order to extend his borders,
14I will set fire to the walls of
    Rabbah
  that will consume her fortresses
amid war cries on the day of
    battle,

amid violent winds on a stormy
    day.
15Her king^c will go into exile,
  he and his officials together,"
            says the Lord.

2 This is what the Lord says:

"For three sins of Moab,
  even for four, I will not turn
    back ˻my wrath˼.
Because he burned, as if to lime,
  the bones of Edom's king,
2I will send fire upon Moab
  that will consume the fortresses
    of Kerioth.^d
Moab will go down in great
    tumult
  amid war cries and the blast of
    the trumpet.
3I will destroy her ruler
  and kill all her officials with
    him,"
            says the Lord.

4This is what the Lord says:

"For three sins of Judah,
  even for four, I will not turn
    back ˻my wrath˼.
Because they have rejected the law
    of the Lord
  and have not kept his decrees,
because they have been led astray
    by false gods,^e
  the gods^f their ancestors
    followed,
5I will send fire upon Judah
  that will consume the fortresses
    of Jerusalem."

Judgment on Israel

6This is what the Lord says:

"For three sins of Israel,
  even for four, I will not turn
    back ˻my wrath˼.
They sell the righteous for silver,
  and the needy for a pair of
    sandals.
7They trample on the heads of the
    poor
  as upon the dust of the ground

^a8 Or inhabitants   ^b11 Or sword / and destroyed his allies   ^c15 Or / Molech; Hebrew malcam
^d2 Or of her cities   ^e4 Or by lies   ^f4 Or lies

and deny justice to the
  oppressed.
Father and son use the same girl
  and so profane my holy name.
[8]They lie down beside every altar
  on garments taken in pledge.
In the house of their god
  they drink wine taken as fines.

[9]"I destroyed the Amorite before
  them,
    though he was tall as the cedars
    and strong as the oaks.
I destroyed his fruit above
  and his roots below.

[10]"I brought you up out of Egypt,
  and I led you forty years in the
    desert
  to give you the land of the
    Amorites.
[11]I also raised up prophets from
    among your sons
  and Nazirites from among your
    young men.
Is this not true, people of Israel?"
                  declares the LORD.
[12]"But you made the Nazirites drink
    wine
  and commanded the prophets
    not to prophesy.

[13]"Now then, I will crush you
  as a cart crushes when loaded
    with grain.
[14]The swift will not escape,
  the strong will not muster their
    strength,
  and the warrior will not save
    his life.
[15]The archer will not stand his
    ground,
  the fleet-footed soldier will not
    get away,
  and the horseman will not save
    his life.
[16]Even the bravest warriors
  will flee naked on that day,"
                  declares the LORD.

Witnesses Summoned Against Israel

3 Hear this word the LORD has
  spoken against you, O people of
Israel—against the whole family I
brought up out of Egypt:

[2]"You only have I chosen

of all the families of the earth;
therefore I will punish you
  for all your sins."

[3]Do two walk together
  unless they have agreed to do
    so?
[4]Does a lion roar in the thicket
  when he has no prey?
Does he growl in his den
  when he has caught nothing?
[5]Does a bird fall into a trap on the
    ground
  where no snare has been set?
Does a trap spring up from the
    earth
  when there is nothing to catch?
[6]When a trumpet sounds in a city,
  do not the people tremble?
When disaster comes to a city,
  has not the LORD caused it?

[7]Surely the Sovereign LORD does
    nothing
  without revealing his plan
  to his servants the prophets.

[8]The lion has roared—
  who will not fear?
The Sovereign LORD has spoken—
  who can but prophesy?

[9]Proclaim to the fortresses of
    Ashdod
  and to the fortresses of Egypt:
"Assemble yourselves on the
    mountains of Samaria;
  see the great unrest within her
  and the oppression among her
    people."

[10]"They do not know how to do
    right," declares the LORD,
  "who hoard plunder and loot in
    their fortresses."

[11]Therefore this is what the Sovereign LORD says:

"An enemy will overrun the land;
  he will pull down your
    strongholds
  and plunder your fortresses."

[12]This is what the LORD says:

"As a shepherd saves from the
  lion's mouth

only two leg bones or a piece of
    an ear,
so will the Israelites be saved,
those who sit in Samaria
    on the edge of their beds
    and in Damascus on their
      couches.ᵃ"

¹³"Hear this and testify against the
house of Jacob," declares the Lord,
the Lord God Almighty.

¹⁴"On the day I punish Israel for
    her sins,
    I will destroy the altars of
      Bethel;
the horns of the altar will be cut
      off
    and fall to the ground.
¹⁵I will tear down the winter house
    along with the summer house;
the houses adorned with ivory
      will be destroyed
    and the mansions will be
      demolished,"
            declares the Lord.

Israel Has Not Returned to God

4 Hear this word, you cows of
     Bashan on Mount Samaria,
you women who oppress the
      poor and crush the needy
and say to your husbands,
     "Bring us some drinks!"
²The Sovereign Lord has sworn by
    his holiness:
"The time will surely come
when you will be taken away with
     hooks,
    the last of you with fishhooks.
³You will each go straight out
    through breaks in the wall,
    and you will be cast out toward
      Harmon,ᵇ"
           declares the Lord.
⁴"Go to Bethel and sin;
    go to Gilgal and sin yet more.
Bring your sacrifices every
      morning,
    your tithes every three years.ᶜ
⁵Burn leavened bread as a thank
    offering

and brag about your freewill
      offerings—
boast about them, you Israelites,
    for this is what you love to do,"
        declares the Sovereign
           Lord.

⁶"I gave you empty stomachsᵈ in
     every city
and lack of bread in every
     town,
yet you have not returned to
     me,"
          declares the Lord.

⁷"I also withheld rain from you
    when the harvest was still three
      months away.
I sent rain on one town,
    but withheld it from another.
One field had rain;
    another had none and dried up.
⁸People staggered from town to
     town for water
but did not get enough to drink,
    yet you have not returned to
     me,"
          declares the Lord.

⁹"Many times I struck your
     gardens and vineyards,
I struck them with blight and
     mildew.
Locusts devoured your fig and
     olive trees,
yet you have not returned to
     me,"
          declares the Lord.

¹⁰"I sent plagues among you
    as I did to Egypt.
I killed your young men with the
     sword,
    along with your captured
      horses.
I filled your nostrils with the
     stench of your camps,
yet you have not returned to
     me,"
          declares the Lord.

¹¹"I overthrew some of you
    as Iᵉ overthrew Sodom and
      Gomorrah.

ᵃ12 The meaning of the Hebrew for this line is uncertain.   ᵇ3 Masoretic Text; with a different
word division of the Hebrew (see Septuagint) *out, O mountain of oppression*   ᶜ4 Or *tithes on the
third day*   ᵈ6 Hebrew *you cleanness of teeth*   ᵉ11 Hebrew *God*

You were like a burning stick
        snatched from the fire,
    yet you have not returned to
        me,"
                    declares the LORD.

12"Therefore this is what I will do to
        you, Israel,
    and because I will do this to
        you,
    prepare to meet your God,
        O Israel."

13He who forms the mountains,
    creates the wind,
    and reveals his thoughts to
        man,
    he who turns dawn to darkness,
    and treads the high places of
        the earth—
    the LORD God Almighty is his
        name.

A Lament and Call to Repentance

5 Hear this word, O house of Israel,
    this lament I take up concerning
you:

2"Fallen is Virgin Israel,
    never to rise again,
    deserted in her own land,
    with no one to lift her up."

3This is what the Sovereign LORD
says:

"The city that marches out a
        thousand strong for Israel
    will have only a hundred left;
    the town that marches out a
        hundred strong
    will have only ten left."

4This is what the LORD says to the
house of Israel:

"Seek me and live;
 5   do not seek Bethel,
    do not go to Gilgal,
    do not journey to Beersheba.
    For Gilgal will surely go into exile,
    and Bethel will be reduced to
        nothing.a"
6Seek the LORD and live,
    or he will sweep through the
        house of Joseph like a fire;

it will devour,
    and Bethel will have no one to
        quench it.

7You who turn justice into
        bitterness
    and cast righteousness to the
        ground
8(he who made the Pleiades and
        Orion,
    who turns blackness into dawn
    and darkens day into night,
    who calls for the waters of the sea
    and pours them out over the
        face of the land—
    the LORD is his name—
9he flashes destruction on the
        stronghold
    and brings the fortified city to
        ruin),
10you hate the one who reproves in
        court
    and despise him who tells the
        truth.

11You trample on the poor
    and force him to give you grain.
    Therefore, though you have built
        stone mansions,
    you will not live in them;
    though you have planted lush
        vineyards,
    you will not drink their wine.
12For I know how many are your
        offenses
    and how great your sins.

You oppress the righteous and
        take bribes
    and you deprive the poor of
        justice in the courts.
13Therefore the prudent man keeps
        quiet in such times,
    for the times are evil.

14Seek good, not evil,
    that you may live.
    Then the LORD God Almighty will
        be with you,
    just as you say he is.
15Hate evil, love good;
    maintain justice in the courts.
    Perhaps the LORD God Almighty
        will have mercy
    on the remnant of Joseph.

a5 Or grief; or wickedness; Hebrew aven, a reference to Beth Aven (a derogatory name for Bethel)

¹⁶Therefore this is what the Lord, the LORD God Almighty, says:

"There will be wailing in all the
        streets
    and cries of anguish in every
        public square.
The farmers will be summoned to
        weep
    and the mourners to wail.
¹⁷There will be wailing in all the
        vineyards,
    for I will pass through your
        midst,"
                    says the LORD.

The Day of the LORD

¹⁸Woe to you who long
    for the day of the LORD!
Why do you long for the day of
        the LORD?
    That day will be darkness, not
        light.
¹⁹It will be as though a man fled
        from a lion
    only to meet a bear,
as though he entered his house
    and rested his hand on the wall
    only to have a snake bite him.
²⁰Will not the day of the LORD be
        darkness, not light—
    pitch-dark, without a ray of
        brightness?

²¹"I hate, I despise your religious
        feasts;
    I cannot stand your assemblies.
²²Even though you bring me burnt
        offerings and grain
        offerings,
    I will not accept them.
Though you bring choice
        fellowship offerings,^a
    I will have no regard for them.
²³Away with the noise of your
        songs!
    I will not listen to the music of
        your harps.
²⁴But let justice roll on like a river,
    righteousness like a
        never-failing stream!

²⁵"Did you bring me sacrifices and
        offerings
    forty years in the desert,
        O house of Israel?
²⁶You have lifted up the shrine of
        your king,
    the pedestal of your idols,
    the star of your god^b—
    which you made for yourselves.
²⁷Therefore I will send you into
        exile beyond Damascus,"
    says the LORD, whose name is
        God Almighty.

Woe to the Complacent

6 Woe to you who are complacent
        in Zion,
    and to you who feel secure on
        Mount Samaria,
you notable men of the foremost
        nation,
    to whom the people of Israel
        come!
²Go to Calneh and look at it;
    go from there to great Hamath,
    and then go down to Gath in
        Philistia.
Are they better off than your two
        kingdoms?
    Is their land larger than yours?
³You put off the evil day
    and bring near a reign of terror.
⁴You lie on beds inlaid with ivory
    and lounge on your couches.
You dine on choice lambs
    and fattened calves.
⁵You strum away on your harps
        like David
    and improvise on musical
        instruments.
⁶You drink wine by the bowlful
    and use the finest lotions,
    but you do not grieve over the
        ruin of Joseph.
⁷Therefore you will be among the
        first to go into exile;
    your feasting and lounging will
        end.

The LORD Abhors the Pride of Israel

⁸The Sovereign LORD has sworn by

---

^a22 Traditionally *peace offerings*   ^b26 Or *lifted up Sakkuth your king / and Kaiwan your idols, /
your star-gods;* Septuagint *lifted up the shrine of Molech / and the star of your god Rephan, / their idols*

himself—the Lord God Almighty declares:

"I abhor the pride of Jacob
  and detest his fortresses;
I will deliver up the city
  and everything in it."

⁹If ten men are left in one house, they too will die. ¹⁰And if a relative who is to burn the bodies comes to carry them out of the house and asks anyone still hiding there, "Is anyone with you?" and he says, "No," then he will say, "Hush! We must not mention the name of the Lord."

¹¹For the Lord has given the
    command,
  and he will smash the great
    house into pieces
  and the small house into bits.

¹²Do horses run on the rocky crags?
    Does one plow there with oxen?
  But you have turned justice into
    poison
  and the fruit of righteousness
    into bitterness—
¹³you who rejoice in the conquest of
    Lo Debar[a]
  and say, "Did we not take
    Karnaim[b] by our own
    strength?"

¹⁴For the Lord God Almighty
    declares,
  "I will stir up a nation against
    you, O house of Israel,
  that will oppress you all the way
    from Lebo[c] Hamath to the
    valley of the Arabah."

Locusts, Fire and a Plumb Line

7 This is what the Sovereign Lord showed me: He was preparing swarms of locusts after the king's share had been harvested and just as the second crop was coming up. ²When they had stripped the land clean, I cried out, "Sovereign Lord, forgive! How can Jacob survive? He is so small!"

³So the Lord relented.

"This will not happen," the Lord said.

⁴This is what the Sovereign Lord showed me: The Sovereign Lord was calling for judgment by fire; it dried up the great deep and devoured the land. ⁵Then I cried out, "Sovereign Lord, I beg you, stop! How can Jacob survive? He is so small!"

⁶So the Lord relented.

"This will not happen either," the Sovereign Lord said.

⁷This is what he showed me: The Lord was standing by a wall that had been built true to plumb, with a plumb line in his hand. ⁸And the Lord asked me, "What do you see, Amos?"

"A plumb line," I replied.

Then the Lord said, "Look, I am setting a plumb line among my people Israel; I will spare them no longer.

⁹"The high places of Isaac will be
    destroyed
  and the sanctuaries of Israel will
    be ruined;
  with my sword I will rise
    against the house of
    Jeroboam."

Amos and Amaziah

¹⁰Then Amaziah the priest of Bethel sent a message to Jeroboam king of Israel: "Amos is raising a conspiracy against you in the very heart of Israel. The land cannot bear all his words. ¹¹For this is what Amos is saying:

" 'Jeroboam will die by the sword,
  and Israel will surely go into
    exile,
  away from their native land.' "

¹²Then Amaziah said to Amos, "Get out, you seer! Go back to the land of Judah. Earn your bread there and do your prophesying there. ¹³Don't prophesy anymore at Bethel, because this is the king's sanctuary and the temple of the kingdom."

¹⁴Amos answered Amaziah, "I was neither a prophet nor a prophet's son, but I was a shepherd, and I also took

care of sycamore-fig trees. ¹⁵But the LORD took me from tending the flock and said to me, 'Go, prophesy to my people Israel.' ¹⁶Now then, hear the word of the LORD. You say,

" 'Do not prophesy against Israel,
    and stop preaching against the
        house of Isaac.'

¹⁷"Therefore this is what the LORD says:

" 'Your wife will become a
        prostitute in the city,
    and your sons and daughters
        will fall by the sword.
Your land will be measured and
        divided up,
    and you yourself will die in a
        pagan* country.
And Israel will certainly go into
        exile,
    away from their native land.' "

A Basket of Ripe Fruit

8 This is what the Sovereign LORD showed me: a basket of ripe fruit. ²"What do you see, Amos?" he asked.

"A basket of ripe fruit," I answered.

Then the LORD said to me, "The time is ripe for my people Israel; I will spare them no longer.

³"In that day," declares the Sovereign LORD, "the songs in the temple will turn to wailing.ᵇ Many, many bodies—flung everywhere! Silence!"

⁴Hear this, you who trample the needy
    and do away with the poor of
        the land,

⁵saying,

"When will the New Moon be
        over
    that we may sell grain,
and the Sabbath be ended
    that we may market wheat?"—
skimping the measure,
    boosting the price
    and cheating with dishonest
        scales,
⁶buying the poor with silver

and the needy for a pair of
        sandals,
    selling even the sweepings with
        the wheat.

⁷The LORD has sworn by the Pride of Jacob: "I will never forget anything they have done.

⁸"Will not the land tremble for this,
    and all who live in it mourn?
The whole land will rise like the
        Nile;
    it will be stirred up and then
        sink
    like the river of Egypt.

⁹"In that day," declares the Sovereign LORD,

"I will make the sun go down at
        noon
    and darken the earth in broad
        daylight.
¹⁰I will turn your religious feasts
        into mourning
    and all your singing into
        weeping.
I will make all of you wear
        sackcloth
    and shave your heads.
I will make that time like
        mourning for an only son
    and the end of it like a bitter
        day.

¹¹"The days are coming," declares
        the Sovereign LORD,
    "when I will send a famine
        through the land—
not a famine of food or a thirst for
        water,
    but a famine of hearing the
        words of the LORD.
¹²Men will stagger from sea to sea
    and wander from north to east,
searching for the word of the
        LORD,
    but they will not find it.

¹³"In that day

"the lovely young women and
        strong young men
    will faint because of thirst.

ᵃ17 Hebrew an unclean   ᵇ3 Or "the temple singers will wail

14They who swear by the shame[a]
    of Samaria,
or say, 'As surely as your god
    lives, O Dan,'
or, 'As surely as the god[b] of
    Beersheba lives'—

they will fall,
    never to rise again."

Israel to Be Destroyed

9 I saw the Lord standing by the altar, and he said:

[a]14 Or *by Ashima; or by the idol*   [b]14 Or *power*

THURSDAY

VERSE:	AUTHOR:	PASSAGE:
Amos 8:11	Dirk R. Buursma	Amos 8:1–14

Famine

A famine of hearing the words of the Lord?

"Lord, Lord—things are tough in my life right now. I need a word of hope." "Lord, Lord—I've got this big decision to make. I need a word of guidance."

No answer. Dead silence. All communication between God and his people broken down. An eerie stillness—the kind that sends chills up and down the spine.

Can you imagine? A famine of hearing the words of the Lord! People starving because they don't hear a word from the Lord.

Lord, don't let it happen to us! We admit that so often we take the Bible for granted, that we don't dig into it the way we should, that we don't declare its life-changing truths the way we should. We acknowledge that for some of us it lies tucked away, nice and clean in its leather cover, on our coffee tables—forgotten. Put within us a burning desire to listen to you and to your Word. Let us be prepared, *now*, while there is still time, to listen when you speak, to know your purpose for our lives and to rediscover the freshness, the power of your life-giving, life-transforming Word.

ADDITIONAL SCRIPTURE READINGS
Nehemiah 8:1–12; Hebrews 4:12–13

Go to page 1142 for your next devotional reading.

"Strike the tops of the pillars
so that the thresholds shake.
Bring them down on the heads of
all the people;
those who are left I will kill
with the sword.
Not one will get away,
none will escape.
²Though they dig down to the
depths of the grave,ᵃ
from there my hand will take
them.
Though they climb up to the
heavens,
from there I will bring them
down.
³Though they hide themselves on
the top of Carmel,
there I will hunt them down
and seize them.
Though they hide from me at the
bottom of the sea,
there I will command the
serpent to bite them.
⁴Though they are driven into exile
by their enemies,
there I will command the sword
to slay them.
I will fix my eyes upon them
for evil and not for good."

⁵The Lord, the LORD Almighty,
he who touches the earth and it
melts,
and all who live in it mourn—
the whole land rises like the Nile,
then sinks like the river of
Egypt—
⁶he who builds his lofty palaceᵇ in
the heavens
and sets its foundationᶜ on the
earth,
who calls for the waters of the sea
and pours them out over the
face of the land—
the LORD is his name.

⁷"Are not you Israelites
the same to me as the
Cushitesᵈ?"
declares the LORD.

"Did I not bring Israel up from
Egypt,
the Philistines from Caphtorᵉ
and the Arameans from Kir?

⁸"Surely the eyes of the Sovereign
LORD
are on the sinful kingdom.
I will destroy it
from the face of the earth—
yet I will not totally destroy
the house of Jacob,"
declares the LORD.
⁹"For I will give the command,
and I will shake the house of
Israel
among all the nations
as grain is shaken in a sieve,
and not a pebble will reach the
ground.
¹⁰All the sinners among my people
will die by the sword,
all those who say,
'Disaster will not overtake or
meet us.'

Israel's Restoration

¹¹"In that day I will restore
David's fallen tent.
I will repair its broken places,
restore its ruins,
and build it as it used to be,
¹²so that they may possess the
remnant of Edom
and all the nations that bear my
name,ᶠ"
declares the LORD,
who will do these things.

¹³"The days are coming," declares
the LORD,

"when the reaper will be
overtaken by the plowman
and the planter by the one
treading grapes.
New wine will drip from the
mountains
and flow from all the hills.

ᵃ2 Hebrew to Sheol   ᵇ6 The meaning of the Hebrew for this phrase is uncertain.   ᶜ6 The meaning of the Hebrew for this word is uncertain.   ᵈ7 That is, people from the upper Nile region   ᵉ7 That is, Crete   ᶠ12 Hebrew; Septuagint so that the remnant of men / and all the nations that bear my name may seek ⌞the Lord⌟

14I will bring back my exiled[a]
    people Israel;
  they will rebuild the ruined
    cities and live in them.
They will plant vineyards and
    drink their wine;
  they will make gardens and eat
    their fruit.

15I will plant Israel in their own
    land,
never again to be uprooted
from the land I have given
    them,"

      says the LORD your God.

...T...he short message of Obadiah is about pride. Obadiah reminds the people of Edom that God is in control of the world and urges them to surrender their lives to him. As you read this book, let go of any pride that might be keeping you from obeying God completely, and take comfort from God's assurance that no one can fight against his people and hope to win in the end.

OBADIAH

¹The vision of Obadiah.

This is what the Sovereign LORD says about Edom—

We have heard a message from
    the LORD:
  An envoy was sent to the
      nations to say,
  "Rise, and let us go against her for
      battle"—

²"See, I will make you small
    among the nations;
  you will be utterly despised.
³The pride of your heart has
    deceived you,
  you who live in the clefts of the
      rocks[a]
  and make your home on the
      heights,
you who say to yourself,
  'Who can bring me down to the
      ground?'

⁴Though you soar like the eagle
  and make your nest among the
      stars,
  from there I will bring you
      down,"
                      declares the LORD.
⁵"If thieves came to you,
  if robbers in the night—
Oh, what a disaster awaits you—
  would they not steal only as
      much as they wanted?
If grape pickers came to you,
  would they not leave a few
      grapes?
⁶But how Esau will be ransacked,
  his hidden treasures pillaged!
⁷All your allies will force you to
      the border;
  your friends will deceive and
      overpower you;
  those who eat your bread will set
      a trap for you,[b]
  but you will not detect it.

a3 Or of Sela   b7 The meaning of the Hebrew for this clause is uncertain.

⁸"In that day," declares the
    LORD,
"will I not destroy the wise
    men of Edom,
men of understanding in the
    mountains of Esau?

⁹Your warriors, O Teman, will be
    terrified,
and everyone in Esau's
    mountains
will be cut down in the
    slaughter.

VERSE:	AUTHOR:	PASSAGE:
Obadiah 15	Kevin G. Harney	Obadiah 15–21

Fire in Our Hearts

When we understand divine judgment and the justice of our Lord, our view of God is more balanced. We live in the dynamic tension of experiencing the compassion and love of Yahweh and also acknowledging his coming wrath on sin.

When we reflect on God's judgment and realize what we have been saved from, our hearts break forth in praise and our lips declare the depth of God's grace. When we get a glimpse of the nature of God's wrath and judgment, we begin to understand the price Jesus paid on the cross to set us free from sin and condemnation. Looking judgment squarely in the face and knowing we have been forgiven bring praise and adoration for our God's amazing grace revealed in Jesus Christ.

Finally, and possibly most important, a clear view of divine judgment brings a sober understanding of the need to proclaim the gospel to all people. If we ignore the reality of judgment, wrath and hell, our hearts may grow cold and we can become complacent in our efforts to share the message of forgiveness in Jesus Christ. When we live with a vivid image of the reality of divine judgment, a fire burns in our hearts to share the gospel with family, friends, neighbors and even our enemies.

ADDITIONAL SCRIPTURE READINGS
Psalm 96; Romans 2:1–11

Go to page 1145 for your next devotional reading.

¹⁰Because of the violence against
    your brother Jacob,
you will be covered with
    shame;
you will be destroyed forever.
¹¹On the day you stood aloof
    while strangers carried off his
        wealth
    and foreigners entered his gates
    and cast lots for Jerusalem,
    you were like one of them.
¹²You should not look down on
        your brother
    in the day of his misfortune,
nor rejoice over the people of
        Judah
    in the day of their destruction,
nor boast so much
    in the day of their trouble.
¹³You should not march through the
        gates of my people
    in the day of their disaster,
nor look down on them in their
        calamity
    in the day of their disaster,
nor seize their wealth
    in the day of their disaster.
¹⁴You should not wait at the
        crossroads
    to cut down their fugitives,
nor hand over their survivors
    in the day of their trouble.

¹⁵"The day of the LORD is near
    for all nations.
As you have done, it will be done
        to you;
    your deeds will return upon
        your own head.
¹⁶Just as you drank on my holy hill,
    so all the nations will drink
        continually;

they will drink and drink
    and be as if they had never
        been.
¹⁷But on Mount Zion will be
        deliverance;
    it will be holy,
and the house of Jacob
    will possess its inheritance.
¹⁸The house of Jacob will be a fire
    and the house of Joseph a
        flame;
the house of Esau will be stubble,
    and they will set it on fire and
        consume it.
There will be no survivors
    from the house of Esau."
                The LORD has spoken.

¹⁹People from the Negev will
        occupy
    the mountains of Esau,
and people from the foothills will
        possess
    the land of the Philistines.
They will occupy the fields of
        Ephraim and Samaria,
    and Benjamin will possess
        Gilead.
²⁰This company of Israelite exiles
        who are in Canaan
    will possess ⌊the land⌋ as far as
        Zarephath;
the exiles from Jerusalem who are
        in Sepharad
    will possess the towns of the
        Negev.
²¹Deliverers will go up on[a] Mount
        Zion
    to govern the mountains of
        Esau.
    And the kingdom will be the
        LORD's.

ª21 Or from

...**W**... hen God sent him to warn the people of Nineveh, Jonah ran in the opposite direction. But God used a storm and a great fish to give Jonah a second chance. As you read this book, marvel in God's compassion for all people and the extraordinary lengths to which he will go to get your attention. Find peace today, knowing that God loves you with an undying love and pours out his compassion on you.

JONAH

Jonah Flees From the Lord

1 The word of the Lord came to Jonah son of Amittai: ²"Go to the great city of Nineveh and preach against it, because its wickedness has come up before me."

³But Jonah ran away from the Lord and headed for Tarshish. He went down to Joppa, where he found a ship bound for that port. After paying the fare, he went aboard and sailed for Tarshish to flee from the Lord.

⁴Then the Lord sent a great wind on the sea, and such a violent storm arose that the ship threatened to break up. ⁵All the sailors were afraid and each cried out to his own god. And they threw the cargo into the sea to lighten the ship.

But Jonah had gone below deck, where he lay down and fell into a deep sleep. ⁶The captain went to him and said, "How can you sleep? Get up and call on your god! Maybe he

will take notice of us, and we will not perish."

⁷Then the sailors said to each other, "Come, let us cast lots to find out who is responsible for this calamity." They cast lots and the lot fell on Jonah.

⁸So they asked him, "Tell us, who is responsible for making all this trouble for us? What do you do? Where do you come from? What is your country? From what people are you?"

⁹He answered, "I am a Hebrew and I worship the Lord, the God of heaven, who made the sea and the land."

¹⁰This terrified them and they asked, "What have you done?" (They knew he was running away from the Lord, because he had already told them so.)

¹¹The sea was getting rougher and rougher. So they asked him, "What should we do to you to make the sea calm down for us?"

¹²"Pick me up and throw me into the sea," he replied, "and it will be-

PASSAGE: Ezekiel 34:11–16; Luke 19:1–10
AUTHOR: Augustine

Late Have I Loved You

Late have I loved you, O beauty so ancient and so new. Late have I loved you! You were within me while I have gone outside to seek you. Unlovely myself, I rushed towards all those lovely things you had made. And always you were with me, and I was not with you.

All these beauties kept me far from you — although they would not have existed at all unless they had their being in you.

You called,
 you cried,
  you shattered my deafness.
You sparkled,
 you blazed,
  you drove away my blindness.

You shed your fragrance, and I drew in my breath, and I pant for you. I tasted and now I hunger and thirst. You touched me, and now I burn with longing for your peace.

Go to page 1147 for your next devotional reading.

come calm. I know that it is my fault that this great storm has come upon you."

¹³Instead, the men did their best to row back to land. But they could not, for the sea grew even wilder than before. ¹⁴Then they cried to the LORD, "O LORD, please do not let us die for taking this man's life. Do not hold us accountable for killing an innocent man, for you, O LORD, have done as you pleased." ¹⁵Then they took Jonah and threw him overboard, and the raging sea grew calm. ¹⁶At this the men greatly feared the LORD, and they offered a sacrifice to the LORD and made vows to him.

¹⁷But the LORD provided a great fish to swallow Jonah, and Jonah was inside the fish three days and three nights.

Jonah's Prayer

2 From inside the fish Jonah prayed to the LORD his God. ²He said:

"In my distress I called to the
    LORD,
  and he answered me.
From the depths of the grave[a] I
    called for help,
  and you listened to my cry.
³You hurled me into the deep,
  into the very heart of the seas,
  and the currents swirled about
    me;
all your waves and breakers
    swept over me.
⁴I said, 'I have been banished
    from your sight;
  yet I will look again
  toward your holy temple.'
⁵The engulfing waters threatened
    me,[b]
  the deep surrounded me;
  seaweed was wrapped around
    my head.
⁶To the roots of the mountains I
    sank down;
  the earth beneath barred me in
    forever.

But you brought my life up from
    the pit,
  O LORD my God.

⁷"When my life was ebbing away,
  I remembered you, LORD,
and my prayer rose to you,
  to your holy temple.

⁸"Those who cling to worthless
    idols
  forfeit the grace that could be
    theirs.
⁹But I, with a song of thanksgiving,
  will sacrifice to you.
What I have vowed I will make
    good.
  Salvation comes from the LORD."

¹⁰And the LORD commanded the fish, and it vomited Jonah onto dry land.

Jonah Goes to Nineveh

3 Then the word of the LORD came to Jonah a second time: ²"Go to the great city of Nineveh and proclaim to it the message I give you."

³Jonah obeyed the word of the LORD and went to Nineveh. Now Nineveh was a very important city—a visit required three days. ⁴On the first day, Jonah started into the city. He proclaimed: "Forty more days and Nineveh will be overturned." ⁵The Ninevites believed God. They declared a fast, and all of them, from the greatest to the least, put on sackcloth.

⁶When the news reached the king of Nineveh, he rose from his throne, took off his royal robes, covered himself with sackcloth and sat down in the dust. ⁷Then he issued a proclamation in Nineveh:

"By the decree of the king and his nobles:

Do not let any man or beast, herd or flock, taste anything; do not let them eat or drink. ⁸But let man and beast be covered with sackcloth. Let everyone call urgently on God. Let them give up their evil ways and their vio-

---

ᵃ2 Hebrew *Sheol*　　ᵇ5 Or *waters were at my throat*

VERSE: AUTHOR: PASSAGE:
Jonah 2:2   Joni Eareckson Tada   Jonah 2:1–10

Beating the Waves

I've always loved the ocean. I treasure special memories of camping ... The waves would come in over a long sandbar, breaking up to seven feet high, spilling creamy surf over acres of sand. Now, to a child of six or seven those waves looked pretty high. When I saw them coming, my first inclination was to swim the other way. But that was a mistake, because the rolling, foaming surf would toss you every which way ...

No, I learned young the best thing to do when those waves swelled was to swim fast *toward* them and dive *under* them before they had a chance to break on top of you ...

Waves of crisis or difficulty roll in from the horizon and threaten to break over my life. They seem so high, so insurmountable. My first inclination is to run the other way from those frightening problems. But I've learned that there is no fast escape ...

Jonah learned that lesson in a tough college course called Obedience 101. When he tried to run from the clear challenge God had laid before him, life became exceedingly complicated. In the inhospitable confines of a fish's belly, the reluctant prophet reflected on his attempted escape (see Jonah 2:3,5).

Jonah would agree with me that the best way to beat those waves of trials and tough challenges is to *face* them. Head on ... And when by God's grace I come through it all? Oh, the relief of knowing that problem is behind me. With God's help, I've beaten it. What an invigorating feeling!

ADDITIONAL SCRIPTURE READINGS
Proverbs 18:10; James 4:7–8

Go to page 1149 for your next devotional reading.

lence. ⁹Who knows? God may yet relent and with compassion turn from his fierce anger so that we will not perish."

¹⁰When God saw what they did and how they turned from their evil ways, he had compassion and did not bring upon them the destruction he had threatened.

Jonah's Anger at the LORD's Compassion

4 But Jonah was greatly displeased and became angry. ²He prayed to the LORD, "O LORD, is this not what I said when I was still at home? That is why I was so quick to flee to Tarshish. I knew that you are a gracious and compassionate God, slow to anger and abounding in love, a God who relents from sending calamity. ³Now, O LORD, take away my life, for it is better for me to die than to live."

⁴But the LORD replied, "Have you any right to be angry?"

⁵Jonah went out and sat down at a place east of the city. There he made himself a shelter, sat in its shade and waited to see what would happen to the city. ⁶Then the LORD God provided a vine and made it grow up over Jonah to give shade for his head to ease his discomfort, and Jonah was very happy about the vine. ⁷But at dawn the next day God provided a worm, which chewed the vine so that it withered. ⁸When the sun rose, God provided a scorching east wind, and the sun blazed on Jonah's head so that he grew faint. He wanted to die, and said, "It would be better for me to die than to live."

⁹But God said to Jonah, "Do you have a right to be angry about the vine?"

"I do," he said. "I am angry enough to die."

¹⁰But the LORD said, "You have been concerned about this vine, though you did not tend it or make it grow. It sprang up overnight and died overnight. ¹¹But Nineveh has more than a hundred and twenty thousand people who cannot tell their right hand from their left, and many cattle as well. Should I not be concerned about that great city?"

VERSE:	AUTHOR:	PASSAGE:
Jonah 4:2	Lewis B. Smedes	Jonah 4:1–11

God's Way With Us

What we see in God's way with Nineveh is a parable of God's way with human history, his way with sinful people, his way with us . . .

Compassion moves God to put up with things awhile longer for the sake of people. God puts up with loose ends, with hardness of people's hearts, with worlds full of wrongness, always to give people a chance to come back to him . . . Compassion is the power not to foreclose on the future . . .

God's compassionate patience is also the answer to our personal impatience . . . We should not give up too quickly when everything goes wrong. We should not give up too quickly on our troubled marriage. We should not give up too quickly on our troubled children. We should not give up too quickly on our troubled selves . . .

The conclusion of the matter is that God gives us grace to imitate his patience. He gives us a choice. Will we be the Jonahs of the world who demand instant and violent solutions to our problems? Or will we let God take his time, and let him show us, in his way, that we do not have to foreclose on the future, let him show us that it can get to be all right tomorrow even though everything seems incredibly wrong today. When he does, he will make it feel all right *with us* beginning today, even if we have to wait for the rest.

ADDITIONAL SCRIPTURE READINGS
Psalm 103; 2 Peter 3:1–13

Go to page 1156 for your next devotional reading.

Micah reported God's message during the time of Kings Jotham and Ahaz (2 Chronicles 27–28). He cried out against Judah's sins, insisting that God wants justice in society. But he also inspired hope by announcing the coming of a Messiah and his kingdom of peace. As you read this book, examine your commitments to justice; remember that God is still active and he will not allow sin to hinder his purpose.

MICAH

1 The word of the LORD that came to Micah of Moresheth during the reigns of Jotham, Ahaz and Hezekiah, kings of Judah—the vision he saw concerning Samaria and Jerusalem.

²Hear, O peoples, all of you,
    listen, O earth and all who are
        in it,
that the Sovereign LORD may
        witness against you,
    the Lord from his holy temple.

Judgment Against Samaria and Jerusalem

³Look! The LORD is coming from his
        dwelling place;
    he comes down and treads the
        high places of the earth.
⁴The mountains melt beneath
        him
    and the valleys split apart,
    like wax before the fire,
    like water rushing down a
        slope.
⁵All this is because of Jacob's
        transgression,
    because of the sins of the house
        of Israel.
What is Jacob's transgression?
    Is it not Samaria?
What is Judah's high place?
    Is it not Jerusalem?

⁶"Therefore I will make Samaria a
        heap of rubble,
    a place for planting vineyards.
I will pour her stones into the
        valley
    and lay bare her foundations.
⁷All her idols will be broken to
        pieces;
    all her temple gifts will be
        burned with fire;
    I will destroy all her images.
Since she gathered her gifts from
        the wages of prostitutes,
    as the wages of prostitutes they
        will again be used."

Weeping and Mourning

8Because of this I will weep and
    wail;
  I will go about barefoot and
    naked.
I will howl like a jackal
  and moan like an owl.
9For her wound is incurable;
  it has come to Judah.
It*a* has reached the very gate of
    my people,
  even to Jerusalem itself.
10Tell it not in Gath*b*;
  weep not at all.*c*
In Beth Ophrah*d*
  roll in the dust.
11Pass on in nakedness and shame,
  you who live in Shaphir.*e*
Those who live in Zaanan*f*
  will not come out.
Beth Ezel is in mourning;
  its protection is taken from
    you.
12Those who live in Maroth*g*
    writhe in pain,
  waiting for relief,
because disaster has come from
    the Lord,
  even to the gate of Jerusalem.
13You who live in Lachish,*h*
  harness the team to the chariot.
You were the beginning of sin
  to the Daughter of Zion,
for the transgressions of Israel
  were found in you.
14Therefore you will give parting
    gifts
  to Moresheth Gath.
The town of Aczib*i* will prove
    deceptive
  to the kings of Israel.
15I will bring a conqueror against
    you
  who live in Mareshah.*j*
He who is the glory of Israel
  will come to Adullam.
16Shave your heads in mourning
  for the children in whom you
    delight;

make yourselves as bald as the
    vulture,
  for they will go from you into
    exile.

Man's Plans and God's

2 Woe to those who plan iniquity,
  to those who plot evil on their
    beds!
At morning's light they carry it
    out
  because it is in their power to
    do it.
2They covet fields and seize them,
  and houses, and take them.
They defraud a man of his home,
  a fellowman of his inheritance.

3Therefore, the Lord says:

"I am planning disaster against
    this people,
  from which you cannot save
    yourselves.
You will no longer walk proudly,
  for it will be a time of calamity.
4In that day men will ridicule you;
  they will taunt you with this
    mournful song:
'We are utterly ruined;
  my people's possession is
    divided up.
He takes it from me!
  He assigns our fields to
    traitors.' "

5Therefore you will have no one in
    the assembly of the Lord
  to divide the land by lot.

False Prophets

6"Do not prophesy," their prophets
    say.
  "Do not prophesy about these
    things;
  disgrace will not overtake us."
7Should it be said, O house of
    Jacob:
  "Is the Spirit of the Lord angry?
  Does he do such things?"

---

*a*9 Or *He*   *b*10 *Gath* sounds like the Hebrew for *tell*.   *c*10 Hebrew; Septuagint may suggest
not in Acco. The Hebrew for *in Acco* sounds like the Hebrew for *weep*.   *d*10 *Beth Ophrah* means
house of dust.   *e*11 *Shaphir* means *pleasant*.   *f*11 *Zaanan* sounds like the Hebrew for *come out*.
*g*12 *Maroth* sounds like the Hebrew for *bitter*.   *h*13 *Lachish* sounds like the Hebrew for *team*.
*i*14 *Aczib* means *deception*.   *j*15 *Mareshah* sounds like the Hebrew for *conqueror*.

"Do not my words do good
    to him whose ways are upright?
8Lately my people have risen up
    like an enemy.
You strip off the rich robe
    from those who pass by without
      a care,
    like men returning from battle.
9You drive the women of my
      people
    from their pleasant homes.
You take away my blessing
    from their children forever.
10Get up, go away!
    For this is not your resting
      place,
because it is defiled,
    it is ruined, beyond all remedy.
11If a liar and deceiver comes and
      says,
    'I will prophesy for you plenty
      of wine and beer,'
    he would be just the prophet
      for this people!

Deliverance Promised

12"I will surely gather all of you,
    O Jacob;
    I will surely bring together the
      remnant of Israel.
I will bring them together like
      sheep in a pen,
    like a flock in its pasture;
    the place will throng with
      people.
13One who breaks open the way
      will go up before them;
    they will break through the gate
      and go out.
Their king will pass through
      before them,
    the LORD at their head."

Leaders and Prophets Rebuked

3 Then I said,

"Listen, you leaders of Jacob,
    you rulers of the house of
      Israel.
Should you not know justice,
2   you who hate good and love
      evil;
who tear the skin from my people
    and the flesh from their bones;
3who eat my people's flesh,

strip off their skin
    and break their bones in pieces;
who chop them up like meat for
      the pan,
    like flesh for the pot?"

4Then they will cry out to the LORD,
    but he will not answer them.
At that time he will hide his face
      from them
    because of the evil they have
      done.

5This is what the LORD says:

"As for the prophets
    who lead my people astray,
if one feeds them,
    they proclaim 'peace';
if he does not,
    they prepare to wage war
      against him.
6Therefore night will come over
      you, without visions,
    and darkness, without
      divination.
The sun will set for the prophets,
    and the day will go dark for
      them.
7The seers will be ashamed
    and the diviners disgraced.
They will all cover their faces
    because there is no answer from
      God."

8But as for me, I am filled with
      power,
    with the Spirit of the LORD,
    and with justice and might,
to declare to Jacob his
      transgression,
    to Israel his sin.
9Hear this, you leaders of the
      house of Jacob,
    you rulers of the house of
      Israel,
who despise justice
    and distort all that is right;
10who build Zion with bloodshed,
    and Jerusalem with wickedness.
11Her leaders judge for a bribe,
    her priests teach for a price,
    and her prophets tell fortunes
      for money.
Yet they lean upon the LORD and
      say,
    "Is not the LORD among us?

No disaster will come upon us."
¹²Therefore because of you,
    Zion will be plowed like a field,
Jerusalem will become a heap of
        rubble,
    the temple hill a mound
        overgrown with thickets.

The Mountain of the LORD

4 In the last days

the mountain of the LORD's temple
    will be established
    as chief among the mountains;
it will be raised above the hills,
    and peoples will stream to it.

²Many nations will come and say,

"Come, let us go up to the
        mountain of the LORD,
    to the house of the God of
        Jacob.
He will teach us his ways,
    so that we may walk in his
        paths."
The law will go out from Zion,
    the word of the LORD from
        Jerusalem.
³He will judge between many
        peoples
    and will settle disputes for
        strong nations far and
        wide.
They will beat their swords into
        plowshares
    and their spears into pruning
        hooks.
Nation will not take up sword
        against nation,
    nor will they train for war
        anymore.
⁴Every man will sit under his own
        vine
    and under his own fig tree,
and no one will make them afraid,
    for the LORD Almighty has
        spoken.
⁵All the nations may walk
    in the name of their gods;
we will walk in the name of the
        LORD
    our God for ever and ever.

The LORD's Plan

⁶"In that day," declares the LORD,

"I will gather the lame;
    I will assemble the exiles
    and those I have brought to
        grief.
⁷I will make the lame a remnant,
    those driven away a strong
        nation.
The LORD will rule over them in
        Mount Zion
    from that day and forever.
⁸As for you, O watchtower of the
        flock,
    O strongholdᵃ of the Daughter
        of Zion,
the former dominion will be
        restored to you;
    kingship will come to the
        Daughter of Jerusalem."

⁹Why do you now cry aloud—
    have you no king?
Has your counselor perished,
    that pain seizes you like that of
        a woman in labor?
¹⁰Writhe in agony, O Daughter of
        Zion,
    like a woman in labor,
for now you must leave the city
    to camp in the open field.
You will go to Babylon;
    there you will be rescued.
There the LORD will redeem you
    out of the hand of your
        enemies.

¹¹But now many nations
    are gathered against you.
They say, "Let her be defiled,
    let our eyes gloat over Zion!"
¹²But they do not know
    the thoughts of the LORD;
they do not understand his plan,
    he who gathers them like
        sheaves to the threshing
        floor.

¹³"Rise and thresh, O Daughter of
        Zion,
    for I will give you horns of iron;
I will give you hoofs of bronze

ᵃ8 Or hill

and you will break to pieces
    many nations."

You will devote their ill-gotten
    gains to the LORD,
  their wealth to the Lord of all
    the earth.

A Promised Ruler From Bethlehem

5 Marshal your troops, O city of
    troops,[a]
  for a siege is laid against us.
They will strike Israel's ruler
  on the cheek with a rod.

2"But you, Bethlehem Ephrathah,
    though you are small among
    the clans[b] of Judah,
out of you will come for me
  one who will be ruler over
    Israel,
  whose origins[c] are from of old,
  from ancient times.[d]"

3Therefore Israel will be abandoned
  until the time when she who is
    in labor gives birth
and the rest of his brothers return
  to join the Israelites.

4He will stand and shepherd his
    flock
  in the strength of the LORD,
  in the majesty of the name of
    the LORD his God.
And they will live securely, for
    then his greatness
  will reach to the ends of the
    earth.
5   And he will be their peace.

Deliverance and Destruction

When the Assyrian invades our
    land
  and marches through our
    fortresses,
we will raise against him seven
    shepherds,
  even eight leaders of men.
6They will rule[e] the land of
    Assyria with the sword,
  the land of Nimrod with drawn
    sword.[f]

He will deliver us from the
    Assyrian
  when he invades our land
  and marches into our borders.

7The remnant of Jacob will be
  in the midst of many peoples
like dew from the LORD,
  like showers on the grass,
which do not wait for man
  or linger for mankind.
8The remnant of Jacob will be
    among the nations,
  in the midst of many peoples,
like a lion among the beasts of the
    forest,
  like a young lion among flocks
    of sheep,
which mauls and mangles as it
    goes,
  and no one can rescue.
9Your hand will be lifted up in
    triumph over your
    enemies,
  and all your foes will be
    destroyed.

10"In that day," declares the LORD,

"I will destroy your horses from
    among you
  and demolish your chariots.
11I will destroy the cities of your
    land
  and tear down all your
    strongholds.
12I will destroy your witchcraft
  and you will no longer cast
    spells.
13I will destroy your carved images
  and your sacred stones from
    among you;
you will no longer bow down
  to the work of your hands.
14I will uproot from among you
    your Asherah poles[g]
  and demolish your cities.
15I will take vengeance in anger and
    wrath
  upon the nations that have not
    obeyed me."

The Lord's Case Against Israel

6 Listen to what the Lord says:

"Stand up, plead your case before
the mountains;
let the hills hear what you have
to say.
²Hear, O mountains, the Lord's
accusation;
listen, you everlasting
foundations of the earth.
For the Lord has a case against his
people;
he is lodging a charge against
Israel.

³"My people, what have I done to
you?
How have I burdened you?
Answer me.
⁴I brought you up out of Egypt
and redeemed you from the
land of slavery.
I sent Moses to lead you,
also Aaron and Miriam.
⁵My people, remember
what Balak king of Moab
counseled
and what Balaam son of Beor
answered.
Remember ⌊your journey⌋ from
Shittim to Gilgal,
that you may know the
righteous acts of the Lord."

⁶With what shall I come before the
Lord
and bow down before the
exalted God?
Shall I come before him with
burnt offerings,
with calves a year old?
⁷Will the Lord be pleased with
thousands of rams,
with ten thousand rivers of oil?
Shall I offer my firstborn for my
transgression,
the fruit of my body for the sin
of my soul?
⁸He has showed you, O man, what
is good.

And what does the Lord require
of you?
To act justly and to love mercy
and to walk humbly with your
God.

Israel's Guilt and Punishment

⁹Listen! The Lord is calling to the
city—
and to fear your name is
wisdom—
"Heed the rod and the One who
appointed it.ᵃ
¹⁰Am I still to forget, O wicked
house,
your ill-gotten treasures
and the short ephah,ᵇ which is
accursed?
¹¹Shall I acquit a man with
dishonest scales,
with a bag of false weights?
¹²Her rich men are violent;
her people are liars
and their tongues speak
deceitfully.
¹³Therefore, I have begun to destroy
you,
to ruin you because of your
sins.
¹⁴You will eat but not be satisfied;
your stomach will still be
empty.ᶜ
You will store up but save
nothing,
because what you save I will
give to the sword.
¹⁵You will plant but not harvest;
you will press olives but not
use the oil on yourselves,
you will crush grapes but not
drink the wine.
¹⁶You have observed the statutes of
Omri
and all the practices of Ahab's
house,
and you have followed their
traditions.
Therefore I will give you over to
ruin
and your people to derision;

ᵃ9 The meaning of the Hebrew for this line is uncertain.   ᵇ10 An ephah was a dry measure.
ᶜ14 The meaning of the Hebrew for this word is uncertain.

you will bear the scorn of the
nations.ᵃ"

Israel's Misery

7 What misery is mine!
I am like one who gathers
summer fruit
at the gleaning of the vineyard;
there is no cluster of grapes to eat,
none of the early figs that I
crave.
²The godly have been swept from
the land;
not one upright man remains.
All men lie in wait to shed blood;

each hunts his brother with a
net.
³Both hands are skilled in doing
evil;
the ruler demands gifts,
the judge accepts bribes,
the powerful dictate what they
desire—
they all conspire together.
⁴The best of them is like a brier,
the most upright worse than a
thorn hedge.
The day of your watchmen has
come,
the day God visits you.

ᵃ16 Septuagint; Hebrew *scorn due my people*

WEDNESDAY

VERSE:	AUTHOR:	PASSAGE:
Micah 6:8	Oswald Chambers	Micah 6:1–8

To Walk Humbly

Humility is not an ideal. It is the unconscious result of
living in right relationship to God, centered in him. The
conscious eye of a humble person is not on his service,
but on his Savior . . .

We will be humble if the center of our affection is
God's honor. Our humility will never be understood by
someone who is not Christ-centered; but Christ will
know the source of our attitude.

Jesus Christ did not lift up humility as an ideal. He
lived it. When we serve others only for the sake of
Christ's glory, and not for the purpose of being appreciated by them, we will be humble as he is.

Purge all pride, O God, from my heart and mind. Fill
me with the humility of your holiness.

ADDITIONAL SCRIPTURE READINGS
Matthew 18:1–4; Philippians 2:1–11

Go to page 1158 for your next devotional reading.

Now is the time of their
   confusion.
⁵Do not trust a neighbor;
   put no confidence in a friend.
Even with her who lies in your
   embrace
be careful of your words.
⁶For a son dishonors his father,
   a daughter rises up against her
      mother,
a daughter-in-law against her
   mother-in-law—
a man's enemies are the
   members of his own
   household.

⁷But as for me, I watch in hope for
   the LORD,
I wait for God my Savior;
   my God will hear me.

Israel Will Rise

⁸Do not gloat over me, my enemy!
   Though I have fallen, I will rise.
Though I sit in darkness,
   the LORD will be my light.
⁹Because I have sinned against him,
   I will bear the LORD's wrath,
until he pleads my case
   and establishes my right.
He will bring me out into the
   light;
   I will see his righteousness.
¹⁰Then my enemy will see it
   and will be covered with
      shame,
she who said to me,
   "Where is the LORD your God?"
My eyes will see her downfall;
   even now she will be trampled
      underfoot
like mire in the streets.

¹¹The day for building your walls
   will come,
   the day for extending your
      boundaries.
¹²In that day people will come to
   you
   from Assyria and the cities of
      Egypt,
even from Egypt to the Euphrates

and from sea to sea
   and from mountain to
      mountain.
¹³The earth will become desolate
   because of its inhabitants,
   as the result of their deeds.

Prayer and Praise

¹⁴Shepherd your people with your
   staff,
   the flock of your inheritance,
which lives by itself in a forest,
   in fertile pasturelands.ᵃ
Let them feed in Bashan and
   Gilead
as in days long ago.

¹⁵"As in the days when you came
   out of Egypt,
   I will show them my wonders."
¹⁶Nations will see and be ashamed,
   deprived of all their power.
They will lay their hands on their
   mouths
   and their ears will become deaf.
¹⁷They will lick dust like a snake,
   like creatures that crawl on the
      ground.
They will come trembling out of
   their dens;
   they will turn in fear to the
      LORD our God
   and will be afraid of you.
¹⁸Who is a God like you,
   who pardons sin and forgives
      the transgression
of the remnant of his
   inheritance?
You do not stay angry forever
   but delight to show mercy.
¹⁹You will again have compassion
   on us;
   you will tread our sins
      underfoot
   and hurl all our iniquities into
      the depths of the sea.
²⁰You will be true to Jacob,
   and show mercy to Abraham,
as you pledged on oath to our
   fathers
in days long ago.

ᵃ14 Or *in the middle of Carmel*

VERSE: AUTHOR: PASSAGE:
Micah 7:18   Warren W. Wiersbe   Micah 7:14–20

How to Live With Yourself

Living with others can be a problem, but sometimes living with ourselves may be a greater problem. In fact, if we cannot live with ourselves, it's doubtful whether others can live with us, either. What is the secret of getting along with yourself? Do you have to live with regrets and self-condemnation? Of course not. Your faith in Jesus Christ can make you into the kind of person you really want to live with . . .

I don't know what it is that may be robbing you of your personal peace and satisfaction. There may be something in your life right now that is making it difficult for you to live with yourself. Perhaps it is regret —you feel you have wronged a loved one, or that you didn't do what you were supposed to do. Perhaps it is sin, and the past is haunting you. Perhaps you are weeping over lost opportunities, and you are wondering how different life would have been if only—if only. Maybe you have failed somewhere along the line, and that failure stabs you in the heart every time you think of it.

I have good news for you: Jesus Christ knows all about these problems and wants to solve them for you . . . You see, when you turn yourself over to him, he completely washes away your past—every sin, every mistake, every foolish act. In fact, he promises to forget our past and never hold it against us.

ADDITIONAL SCRIPTURE READINGS
Psalm 103:1–13; Hebrews 10:1–18

Go to page 1160 for your next devotional reading.

*N*ahum, who prophe-
sied against the cruel nation of Assyria, reminded God's people that God is in control
of history and will not allow evil to persist
forever. As you read this book, be comforted
(Nahum means "comfort") that God balances
his holy anger with mercy and love.

NAHUM

1 An oracle concerning Nineveh. The book of the vision of Nahum the Elkoshite.

The LORD's Anger Against Nineveh

²The LORD is a jealous and
    avenging God;
  the LORD takes vengeance and is
    filled with wrath.
The LORD takes vengeance on his
    foes
  and maintains his wrath against
    his enemies.
³The LORD is slow to anger and
    great in power;
  the LORD will not leave the
    guilty unpunished.
His way is in the whirlwind and
    the storm,
  and clouds are the dust of his
    feet.
⁴He rebukes the sea and dries it
    up;
  he makes all the rivers run dry.
Bashan and Carmel wither
  and the blossoms of Lebanon
    fade.

⁵The mountains quake before him
  and the hills melt away.
The earth trembles at his presence,
  the world and all who live in it.
⁶Who can withstand his
    indignation?
  Who can endure his fierce
    anger?
His wrath is poured out like fire;
  the rocks are shattered before
    him.

⁷The LORD is good,
  a refuge in times of trouble.
He cares for those who trust in
    him,
⁸ but with an overwhelming flood
he will make an end of ⌞Nineveh⌟;
  he will pursue his foes into
    darkness.

⁹Whatever they plot against the
    LORD
  he[a] will bring to an end;
  trouble will not come a second
    time.
¹⁰They will be entangled among
    thorns
  and drunk from their wine;

*a*9 Or *What do you foes plot against the* LORD? / *He*

they will be consumed like dry
    stubble.*a*
¹¹From you, ⌐O Nineveh,⌐ has one
    come forth
who plots evil against the LORD
and counsels wickedness.

¹²This is what the LORD says:

"Although they have allies and are
    numerous,
they will be cut off and pass
    away.

Although I have afflicted you,
    ⌐O Judah,⌐
I will afflict you no more.
¹³Now I will break their yoke from
    your neck
and tear your shackles away."

¹⁴The LORD has given a command
    concerning you, ⌐Nineveh⌐:
"You will have no descendants
    to bear your name.
I will destroy the carved images
    and cast idols

a10 The meaning of the Hebrew for this verse is uncertain.

FRIDAY

VERSE:	AUTHOR:	PASSAGE:
Nahum 1:7	Millie Stamm	Nahum 1:2–8

The Lord Is Good

Trouble is universal. No one escapes it. You may be experiencing it today . . . But what do we do about it? We
can worry, panic, be fearful and feel sorry for ourselves,
or we can commit our trouble to the Lord, trusting him
to take us through it.

The prophet Nahum's declaration is reassuring. First,
he says, "The LORD is good." He is good for he is God.
As God, he has custom-designed a plan for our lives. He
works in our trouble so that good will come out of it . . .

Not only does he transform trouble into good, but he
becomes a stronghold for us in the time of our trouble.
He becomes our place of security and safety—a strong
refuge. "The name of the LORD is a strong tower; the
righteous run to it and are safe" (Proverbs 18:10).

God is a stronghold to those who trust him. He will
never fail you, forsake you or forget you.

ADDITIONAL SCRIPTURE READINGS
Psalm 18:1–6; Romans 8:28–39

Go to page 1164 for your next devotional reading.

that are in the temple of your
    gods.
I will prepare your grave,
    for you are vile."

¹⁵Look, there on the mountains,
    the feet of one who brings good
        news,
    who proclaims peace!
Celebrate your festivals, O Judah,
    and fulfill your vows.
No more will the wicked invade
        you;
    they will be completely
        destroyed.

Nineveh to Fall

2 An attacker advances against
    you, ⌊Nineveh⌋.
Guard the fortress,
    watch the road,
    brace yourselves,
    marshal all your strength!

²The LORD will restore the splendor
        of Jacob
    like the splendor of Israel,
though destroyers have laid them
        waste
    and have ruined their vines.

³The shields of his soldiers are red;
    the warriors are clad in scarlet.
The metal on the chariots flashes
    on the day they are made
        ready;
    the spears of pine are
        brandished.ᵃ
⁴The chariots storm through the
        streets,
    rushing back and forth through
        the squares.
They look like flaming torches;
    they dart about like lightning.

⁵He summons his picked troops,
    yet they stumble on their way.
They dash to the city wall;
    the protective shield is put in
        place.
⁶The river gates are thrown open
    and the palace collapses.
⁷It is decreedᵇ that ⌊the city⌋
    be exiled and carried away.

Its slave girls moan like doves
    and beat upon their breasts.
⁸Nineveh is like a pool,
    and its water is draining away.
"Stop! Stop!" they cry,
    but no one turns back.
⁹Plunder the silver!
    Plunder the gold!
The supply is endless,
    the wealth from all its treasures!
¹⁰She is pillaged, plundered,
        stripped!
    Hearts melt, knees give way,
    bodies tremble, every face
        grows pale.

¹¹Where now is the lions' den,
    the place where they fed their
        young,
where the lion and lioness went,
    and the cubs, with nothing to
        fear?
¹²The lion killed enough for his
        cubs
    and strangled the prey for his
        mate,
filling his lairs with the kill
    and his dens with the prey.

¹³"I am against you,"
    declares the LORD Almighty.
"I will burn up your chariots in
        smoke,
    and the sword will devour your
        young lions.
I will leave you no prey on the
        earth.
The voices of your messengers
    will no longer be heard."

Woe to Nineveh

3 Woe to the city of blood,
    full of lies,
full of plunder,
    never without victims!
²The crack of whips,
    the clatter of wheels,
galloping horses
    and jolting chariots!
³Charging cavalry,
    flashing swords
    and glittering spears!
Many casualties,

ᵃ3 Hebrew; Septuagint and Syriac / the horsemen rush to and fro   ᵇ7 The meaning of the
Hebrew for this word is uncertain.

piles of dead,
bodies without number,
   people stumbling over the
     corpses—
⁴all because of the wanton lust of a
   harlot,
   alluring, the mistress of
     sorceries,
who enslaved nations by her
     prostitution
   and peoples by her witchcraft.

⁵"I am against you," declares the
     LORD Almighty.
   "I will lift your skirts over your
     face.
I will show the nations your
     nakedness
   and the kingdoms your shame.
⁶I will pelt you with filth,
   I will treat you with contempt
   and make you a spectacle.
⁷All who see you will flee from
     you and say,
   'Nineveh is in ruins—who will
     mourn for her?'
   Where can I find anyone to
     comfort you?"

⁸Are you better than Thebes,ᵃ
   situated on the Nile,
   with water around her?
The river was her defense,
   the waters her wall.
⁹Cushᵇ and Egypt were her
     boundless strength;
   Put and Libya were among her
     allies.
¹⁰Yet she was taken captive
   and went into exile.
   Her infants were dashed to pieces
   at the head of every street.
Lots were cast for her nobles,
   and all her great men were put
     in chains.
¹¹You too will become drunk;
   you will go into hiding
   and seek refuge from the
     enemy.

¹²All your fortresses are like fig
     trees
   with their first ripe fruit;
when they are shaken,
   the figs fall into the mouth of
     the eater.
¹³Look at your troops—
   they are all women!
The gates of your land
   are wide open to your enemies;
   fire has consumed their bars.

¹⁴Draw water for the siege,
   strengthen your defenses!
Work the clay,
   tread the mortar,
   repair the brickwork!
¹⁵There the fire will devour you;
   the sword will cut you down
   and, like grasshoppers, consume
     you.
Multiply like grasshoppers,
   multiply like locusts!
¹⁶You have increased the number of
     your merchants
   till they are more than the stars
     of the sky,
but like locusts they strip the land
   and then fly away.
¹⁷Your guards are like locusts,
   your officials like swarms of
     locusts
   that settle in the walls on a cold
     day—
but when the sun appears they fly
     away,
   and no one knows where.

¹⁸O king of Assyria, your
     shepherdsᶜ slumber;
   your nobles lie down to rest.
Your people are scattered on the
     mountains
   with no one to gather them.
¹⁹Nothing can heal your wound;
   your injury is fatal.
Everyone who hears the news
     about you
   claps his hands at your fall,
for who has not felt
   your endless cruelty?

ᵃ8 Hebrew *No Amon*   ᵇ9 That is, the upper Nile region   ᶜ18 Or *rulers*

Habakkuk served in
Judah while the Babylonian empire was
threatening to overrun the country (2 Chronicles 35:20—36:8). He asked the same question many ask today: Why does God allow
evil to go unchecked? As you read this book,
come to the conclusion that you can trust
God no matter how bleak or confusing the
present circumstances appear to be. God is
in control!

HABAKKUK

1 The oracle that Habakkuk the prophet received.

Habakkuk's Complaint

²How long, O LORD, must I call for
help,
   but you do not listen?
Or cry out to you, "Violence!"
   but you do not save?
³Why do you make me look at
injustice?
   Why do you tolerate wrong?
Destruction and violence are
before me;
   there is strife, and conflict
abounds.
⁴Therefore the law is paralyzed,
   and justice never prevails.
The wicked hem in the righteous,
   so that justice is perverted.

The LORD's Answer

⁵"Look at the nations and watch—
   and be utterly amazed.
For I am going to do something in
your days
   that you would not believe,
   even if you were told.
⁶I am raising up the Babylonians,ᵃ
   that ruthless and impetuous
people,
who sweep across the whole earth
   to seize dwelling places not
their own.
⁷They are a feared and dreaded
people;
   they are a law to themselves
   and promote their own honor.
⁸Their horses are swifter than
leopards,
   fiercer than wolves at dusk.
Their cavalry gallops headlong;
   their horsemen come from afar.
They fly like a vulture swooping
to devour;
⁹   they all come bent on violence.

ᵃ6 Or Chaldeans

PASSAGE: Psalm 142; Ephesians 2:1–10
AUTHOR: John Newton

. . . .

Amazing Grace

Amazing grace! (how sweet the sound!)
    That sav'd a wretch like me!
I once was lost, but now am found,
    Was blind, but now I see.

'Twas grace that taught my heart to fear,
    And grace my fears reliev'd;
How precious did that grace appear,
    The hour I first believ'd.

Through many danger, toils and snares,
    I have already come;
'Tis grace has brought me safe thus far,
    And grace will lead me home.

The Lord has promis'd good to me,
    His word my hope secures;
He will my shield and portion be,
    As long as life endures.

The earth shall soon dissolve like snow,
    The sun forbear to shine;
But God, who call'd me here below,
    Will be for ever mine.

. . . .

Go to page 1167 for your next devotional reading.

Their hordes*a* advance like a
  desert wind
and gather prisoners like sand.
¹⁰They deride kings
  and scoff at rulers.
They laugh at all fortified cities;
  they build earthen ramps and
  capture them.
¹¹Then they sweep past like the
  wind and go on—
guilty men, whose own strength
  is their god."

Habakkuk's Second Complaint

¹²O LORD, are you not from
  everlasting?
My God, my Holy One, we will
  not die.
O LORD, you have appointed them
  to execute judgment;
O Rock, you have ordained
  them to punish.
¹³Your eyes are too pure to look on
  evil;
  you cannot tolerate wrong.
Why then do you tolerate the
  treacherous?
  Why are you silent while the
  wicked
swallow up those more
  righteous than themselves?
¹⁴You have made men like fish in
  the sea,
  like sea creatures that have no
  ruler.
¹⁵The wicked foe pulls all of them
  up with hooks,
  he catches them in his net,
he gathers them up in his dragnet;
  and so he rejoices and is glad.
¹⁶Therefore he sacrifices to his net
  and burns incense to his
  dragnet,
for by his net he lives in luxury
  and enjoys the choicest food.
¹⁷Is he to keep on emptying his net,
  destroying nations without
  mercy?

2 I will stand at my watch
  and station myself on the
  ramparts;

I will look to see what he will say
  to me,
and what answer I am to give
  to this complaint.*b*

The LORD's Answer

²Then the LORD replied:

"Write down the revelation
  and make it plain on tablets
  so that a herald*c* may run with
  it.
³For the revelation awaits an
  appointed time;
  it speaks of the end
  and will not prove false.
Though it linger, wait for it;
  it*d* will certainly come and will
  not delay.

⁴"See, he is puffed up;
  his desires are not upright—
  but the righteous will live by
  his faith*e*—
⁵indeed, wine betrays him;
  he is arrogant and never at rest.
Because he is as greedy as the
  grave*f*
  and like death is never satisfied,
he gathers to himself all the
  nations
  and takes captive all the
  peoples.

⁶"Will not all of them taunt him
with ridicule and scorn, saying,

" 'Woe to him who piles up stolen
  goods
  and makes himself wealthy by
  extortion!
How long must this go on?'
⁷Will not your debtors*g* suddenly
  arise?
Will they not wake up and
  make you tremble?
Then you will become their
  victim.
⁸Because you have plundered
  many nations,
  the peoples who are left will
  plunder you.
For you have shed man's blood;

---

*a9 The meaning of the Hebrew for this word is uncertain.   b1 Or and what to answer when I
am rebuked   c2 Or so that whoever reads it   d3 Or Though he linger, wait for him; / he
e4 Or faithfulness   f5 Hebrew Sheol   g7 Or creditors*

you have destroyed lands and
    cities and everyone in
    them.

9"Woe to him who builds his realm
        by unjust gain
    to set his nest on high,
    to escape the clutches of ruin!
10You have plotted the ruin of many
        peoples,
    shaming your own house and
        forfeiting your life.
11The stones of the wall will cry out,
    and the beams of the woodwork
        will echo it.

12"Woe to him who builds a city
        with bloodshed
    and establishes a town by
        crime!
13Has not the Lord Almighty
        determined
    that the people's labor is only
        fuel for the fire,
    that the nations exhaust
        themselves for nothing?
14For the earth will be filled with
        the knowledge of the glory
        of the Lord,
    as the waters cover the sea.

15"Woe to him who gives drink to
        his neighbors,
    pouring it from the wineskin till
        they are drunk,
    so that he can gaze on their
        naked bodies.
16You will be filled with shame
        instead of glory.
    Now it is your turn! Drink and
        be exposedᵃ!
The cup from the Lord's right
        hand is coming around to
        you,
    and disgrace will cover your
        glory.
17The violence you have done to
        Lebanon will overwhelm
        you,
    and your destruction of animals
        will terrify you.
For you have shed man's blood;

you have destroyed lands and
    cities and everyone in
    them.

18"Of what value is an idol, since a
        man has carved it?
    Or an image that teaches lies?
For he who makes it trusts in his
        own creation;
    he makes idols that cannot
        speak.
19Woe to him who says to wood,
        'Come to life!'
    Or to lifeless stone, 'Wake up!'
Can it give guidance?
    It is covered with gold and
        silver;
    there is no breath in it.
20But the Lord is in his holy temple;
    let all the earth be silent before
        him."

Habakkuk's Prayer

3 A prayer of Habakkuk the proph-
    et. On shigionoth.ᵇ

2Lord, I have heard of your fame;
    I stand in awe of your deeds,
        O Lord.
Renew them in our day,
    in our time make them known;
    in wrath remember mercy.

3God came from Teman,
    the Holy One from Mount
        Paran.   Selahᶜ
His glory covered the heavens
    and his praise filled the earth.
4His splendor was like the sunrise;
    rays flashed from his hand,
    where his power was hidden.
5Plague went before him;
    pestilence followed his steps.
6He stood, and shook the earth;
    he looked, and made the
        nations tremble.
The ancient mountains crumbled
    and the age-old hills collapsed.
    His ways are eternal.
7I saw the tents of Cushan in
        distress,
    the dwellings of Midian in
        anguish.

ᵃ16 Masoretic Text; Dead Sea Scrolls, Aquila, Vulgate and Syriac (see also Septuagint) and stagger
ᵇ1 Probably a literary or musical term   ᶜ3 A word of uncertain meaning; possibly a musical
term; also in verses 9 and 13

VERSE:
Habakkuk 3:2

AUTHOR:
Warren W. Wiersbe

PASSAGE:
Habakkuk 3:1–19

Sighing into Singing

Habakkuk is a changed man! Instead of complaining, he is praising the Lord. God turns sighing into singing if we (like Habakkuk) take time to wait before him in prayer and listen to his Word.

First, the prophet prays (3:2) ... Habakkuk is simply asking the Lord to keep on working. He knows that there will be wrath and judgment, but he prays that God will remember mercy too.

Then the prophet ponders (3:3–16) ... Habakkuk knew that God had worked in the past, and therefore he could trust him to work in the present and future ...

Finally, the prophet praises (3:17–19). These verses represent one of the greatest confessions of faith found in the Bible. Habakkuk knew that he had no strength of his own, but that God could give him the strength he would need to go through the trials that lay ahead. "He makes my feet like the feet of a deer, he enables me to go on the heights" (3:19).

How much more this ought to mean to us. Habakkuk looked through the fog and mist and wondered at God's program, but in Christ we *know* God's plans for this age (Ephesians 1:8–10; 3:1–21) ...

Habakkuk shows us how to deal with life's problems: (1) admit them honestly; (2) talk to God about them; (3) wait quietly before him in prayer and meditation on the Word; (4) when he speaks, listen and obey.

- -

ADDITIONAL SCRIPTURE READINGS
Ephesians 3:1–21; Philippians 4:10–20

Go to page 1172 for your next devotional reading.

⁸Were you angry with the rivers,
    O LORD?
  Was your wrath against the
    streams?
Did you rage against the sea
  when you rode with your
    horses
  and your victorious chariots?
⁹You uncovered your bow,
  you called for many arrows.
                              Selah

 You split the earth with rivers;
¹⁰ the mountains saw you and
     writhed.
  Torrents of water swept by;
    the deep roared
    and lifted its waves on high.

¹¹Sun and moon stood still in the
     heavens
  at the glint of your flying
    arrows,
  at the lightning of your flashing
    spear.
¹²In wrath you strode through the
     earth
  and in anger you threshed the
    nations.
¹³You came out to deliver your
     people,
  to save your anointed one.
  You crushed the leader of the land
    of wickedness,
  you stripped him from head to
    foot.   *Selah*
¹⁴With his own spear you pierced
     his head

when his warriors stormed out
  to scatter us,
gloating as though about to
  devour
  the wretched who were in
    hiding.
¹⁵You trampled the sea with your
     horses,
  churning the great waters.

¹⁶I heard and my heart pounded,
  my lips quivered at the sound;
decay crept into my bones,
  and my legs trembled.
Yet I will wait patiently for the
  day of calamity
  to come on the nation invading
    us.
¹⁷Though the fig tree does not bud
  and there are no grapes on the
    vines,
though the olive crop fails
  and the fields produce no food,
though there are no sheep in the
    pen
  and no cattle in the stalls,
¹⁸yet I will rejoice in the LORD,
  I will be joyful in God my
    Savior.

¹⁹The Sovereign LORD is my
    strength;
  he makes my feet like the feet
    of a deer,
  he enables me to go on the
    heights.

For the director of music. On my
  stringed instruments.

Zephaniah, who prophesied before Josiah's reforms (2 Chronicles 34:1–13), spoke of a coming day of the Lord. But the prophet also promised healing and restoration to those who would humble themselves. As you read this book, thank God that he is working in your life to a point where you can trust him with your future, confident that he will lead you safely home.

ZEPHANIAH

1 The word of the LORD that came to Zephaniah son of Cushi, the son of Gedaliah, the son of Amariah, the son of Hezekiah, during the reign of Josiah son of Amon king of Judah:

Warning of Coming Destruction

²"I will sweep away everything
from the face of the earth,"
declares the LORD.
³"I will sweep away both men and
animals;
I will sweep away the birds of
the air
and the fish of the sea.
The wicked will have only heaps
of rubble*a*
when I cut off man from the
face of the earth,"
declares the LORD.

Against Judah

⁴"I will stretch out my hand
against Judah

and against all who live in
Jerusalem.
I will cut off from this place every
remnant of Baal,
the names of the pagan and the
idolatrous priests—
⁵those who bow down on the roofs
to worship the starry host,
those who bow down and swear
by the LORD
and who also swear by
Molech,*b*
⁶those who turn back from
following the LORD
and neither seek the LORD nor
inquire of him.
⁷Be silent before the Sovereign
LORD,
for the day of the LORD is near.
The LORD has prepared a sacrifice;
he has consecrated those he has
invited.
⁸On the day of the LORD's sacrifice
I will punish the princes
and the king's sons

---

*a3 The meaning of the Hebrew for this line is uncertain.   *b5 Hebrew *Malcam*, that is, Milcom

and all those clad
  in foreign clothes.
⁹On that day I will punish
  all who avoid stepping on the
    threshold,ª
who fill the temple of their gods
  with violence and deceit.

¹⁰"On that day," declares the LORD,
  "a cry will go up from the Fish
    Gate,
  wailing from the New Quarter,
  and a loud crash from the hills.
¹¹Wail, you who live in the market
    districtᵇ;
  all your merchants will be
    wiped out,
  all who trade withᶜ silver will
    be ruined.
¹²At that time I will search
    Jerusalem with lamps
  and punish those who are
    complacent,
  who are like wine left on its
    dregs,
  who think, 'The LORD will do
    nothing,
  either good or bad.'
¹³Their wealth will be plundered,
  their houses demolished.
They will build houses
  but not live in them;
they will plant vineyards
  but not drink the wine.

The Great Day of the LORD

¹⁴"The great day of the LORD is
    near—
  near and coming quickly.
  Listen! The cry on the day of the
    LORD will be bitter,
  the shouting of the warrior
    there.
¹⁵That day will be a day of wrath,
  a day of distress and anguish,
a day of trouble and ruin,
  a day of darkness and gloom,
  a day of clouds and blackness,
¹⁶a day of trumpet and battle cry
  against the fortified cities
  and against the corner towers.

¹⁷I will bring distress on the people
  and they will walk like blind
    men,
  because they have sinned
    against the LORD.
Their blood will be poured out
  like dust
  and their entrails like filth.
¹⁸Neither their silver nor their gold
  will be able to save them
  on the day of the LORD's wrath.
In the fire of his jealousy
  the whole world will be
    consumed,
for he will make a sudden end
  of all who live in the earth."

2 Gather together, gather together,
  O shameful nation,
²before the appointed time arrives
  and that day sweeps on like
    chaff,
before the fierce anger of the LORD
  comes upon you,
  before the day of the LORD's
    wrath comes upon you.
³Seek the LORD, all you humble of
    the land,
  you who do what he
    commands.
Seek righteousness, seek humility;
  perhaps you will be sheltered
  on the day of the LORD's anger.

Against Philistia

⁴Gaza will be abandoned
  and Ashkelon left in ruins.
At midday Ashdod will be
    emptied
  and Ekron uprooted.
⁵Woe to you who live by the sea,
  O Kerethite people;
the word of the LORD is against
    you,
  O Canaan, land of the
    Philistines.

"I will destroy you,
  and none will be left."

⁶The land by the sea, where the
    Kerethitesᵈ dwell,

will be a place for shepherds
 and sheep pens.
⁷It will belong to the remnant of
   the house of Judah;
 there they will find pasture.
In the evening they will lie down
   in the houses of Ashkelon.
The Lord their God will care for
   them;
 he will restore their fortunes.^a

Against Moab and Ammon

⁸"I have heard the insults of Moab
   and the taunts of the
   Ammonites,
who insulted my people
 and made threats against their
   land.
⁹Therefore, as surely as I live,"
   declares the Lord Almighty, the
   God of Israel,
 "surely Moab will become like
   Sodom,
   the Ammonites like
   Gomorrah—
a place of weeds and salt pits,
 a wasteland forever.
The remnant of my people will
   plunder them;
 the survivors of my nation will
   inherit their land."

¹⁰This is what they will get in
   return for their pride,
 for insulting and mocking the
   people of the Lord
   Almighty.
¹¹The Lord will be awesome to them
 when he destroys all the gods
   of the land.
The nations on every shore will
   worship him,
 every one in its own land.

Against Cush

¹²"You too, O Cushites,^b
 will be slain by my sword."

Against Assyria

¹³He will stretch out his hand
   against the north
 and destroy Assyria,
leaving Nineveh utterly desolate

and dry as the desert.
¹⁴Flocks and herds will lie down
   there,
 creatures of every kind.
The desert owl and the screech
   owl
 will roost on her columns.
Their calls will echo through the
   windows,
 rubble will be in the doorways,
 the beams of cedar will be
   exposed.
¹⁵This is the carefree city
 that lived in safety.
She said to herself,
 "I am, and there is none besides
   me."
What a ruin she has become,
 a lair for wild beasts!
All who pass by her scoff
 and shake their fists.

The Future of Jerusalem

3 Woe to the city of oppressors,
   rebellious and defiled!
²She obeys no one,
 she accepts no correction.
She does not trust in the Lord,
 she does not draw near to her
   God.
³Her officials are roaring lions,
 her rulers are evening wolves,
 who leave nothing for the
   morning.
⁴Her prophets are arrogant;
 they are treacherous men.
Her priests profane the sanctuary
 and do violence to the law.
⁵The Lord within her is righteous;
 he does no wrong.
Morning by morning he dispenses
   his justice,
 and every new day he does not
   fail,
 yet the unrighteous know no
   shame.

⁶"I have cut off nations;
 their strongholds are
   demolished.
I have left their streets deserted,
 with no one passing through.

---

^a7 Or *will bring back their captives*   ^b12 That is, people from the upper Nile region

Their cities are destroyed;
  no one will be left—no one at
    all.
⁷I said to the city,
  'Surely you will fear me
  and accept correction!'

Then her dwelling would not be
  cut off,
  nor all my punishments come
    upon her.
But they were still eager
  to act corruptly in all they did.

TUESDAY

VERSE: AUTHOR: PASSAGE:
Zephaniah 3:17   Lloyd John Ogilvie   Zephaniah 3:14–20

Silent Strength

Strength is an inside secret. It comes from the Lord's Spirit in the well of our inner being. Because his strength is limitless, our wells need never be empty. His strength is constantly surging up to give us exactly what we need in every moment.

Zephaniah gives the secret of lasting strength. It is received in silent receptive communion with the Lord: "Be silent before the Sovereign LORD" (Zephaniah 1:7). What we discover in our silence becomes the source of our strength. Note the glorious progression in Zephaniah 3:17. First, the Lord takes great delight in you. In spite of all our failures, he has chosen to be our God and to cherish us. Think of it! God and all the company of heaven take delight in us! This gives us the confidence of silent strength. We belong to God—he's redeemed us in Christ and placed his Spirit in us. He'll never give up on us.

Alone with him, next the Lord quiets us with his love. The unqualified, indefatigable love of the Lord gives us silent confidence, security and peace. There's no need to prove ourselves or blow our own horns. We can live with calm, winsome joy. And knowing that the Lord rejoices over us frees us to rejoice in him.

ADDITIONAL SCRIPTURE READINGS
Isaiah 61:10–11; Jeremiah 32:36–41

Go to page 1175 for your next devotional reading.

⁸Therefore wait for me," declares
    the Lord,
  "for the day I will stand up to
    testify.ᵃ
I have decided to assemble the
    nations,
  to gather the kingdoms
and to pour out my wrath on
    them—
  all my fierce anger.
The whole world will be
    consumed
  by the fire of my jealous anger.

⁹"Then will I purify the lips of the
    peoples,
  that all of them may call on the
    name of the Lord
  and serve him shoulder to
    shoulder.
¹⁰From beyond the rivers of Cushᵇ
  my worshipers, my scattered
    people,
  will bring me offerings.
¹¹On that day you will not be put to
    shame
  for all the wrongs you have
    done to me,
because I will remove from this
    city
  those who rejoice in their pride.
Never again will you be haughty
  on my holy hill.
¹²But I will leave within you
  the meek and humble,
  who trust in the name of the
    Lord.
¹³The remnant of Israel will do no
    wrong;
  they will speak no lies,
  nor will deceit be found in their
    mouths.
They will eat and lie down
  and no one will make them
    afraid."

¹⁴Sing, O Daughter of Zion;

shout aloud, O Israel!
Be glad and rejoice with all your
    heart,
  O Daughter of Jerusalem!
¹⁵The Lord has taken away your
    punishment,
  he has turned back your enemy.
The Lord, the King of Israel, is
    with you;
  never again will you fear any
    harm.
¹⁶On that day they will say to
    Jerusalem,
  "Do not fear, O Zion;
  do not let your hands hang
    limp.
¹⁷The Lord your God is with you,
  he is mighty to save.
He will take great delight in you,
  he will quiet you with his love,
  he will rejoice over you with
    singing."

¹⁸"The sorrows for the appointed
    feasts
  I will remove from you;
  they are a burden and a
    reproach to you.ᶜ
¹⁹At that time I will deal
  with all who oppressed you;
I will rescue the lame
  and gather those who have been
    scattered.
I will give them praise and honor
  in every land where they were
    put to shame.
²⁰At that time I will gather you;
  at that time I will bring you
    home.
I will give you honor and praise
  among all the peoples of the
    earth
when I restore your fortunesᵈ
  before your very eyes,"
                says the Lord.

ᵃ8 Septuagint and Syriac; Hebrew *will rise up to plunder*   ᵇ10 That is, the upper Nile region
ᶜ18 Or *"I will gather you who mourn for the appointed feasts; / your reproach is a burden to you*
ᵈ20 Or *I bring back your captives*

This prophet proclaimed God's message to the Jews who had returned from exile (Ezra 4:24–5:2). The people had built elegant homes but God's temple still lay in ruins. As you read this book, look for any signs of complacency in your life and ask God to reveal to you a time and a place where you can serve him. He wants you to bear fruit for him, wherever you are.

HAGGAI

A Call to Build the House of the LORD

1 In the second year of King Darius, on the first day of the sixth month, the word of the LORD came through the prophet Haggai to Zerubbabel son of Shealtiel, governor of Judah, and to Joshua[a] son of Jehozadak, the high priest:

2 This is what the LORD Almighty says: "These people say, 'The time has not yet come for the LORD's house to be built.' "

3 Then the word of the LORD came through the prophet Haggai: 4 "Is it a time for you yourselves to be living in your paneled houses, while this house remains a ruin?"

5 Now this is what the LORD Almighty says: "Give careful thought to your ways. 6 You have planted much, but have harvested little. You eat, but never have enough. You drink, but never have your fill. You put on clothes, but are not warm. You earn wages, only to put them in a purse with holes in it."

7 This is what the LORD Almighty says: "Give careful thought to your ways. 8 Go up into the mountains and bring down timber and build the house, so that I may take pleasure in it and be honored," says the LORD. 9 "You expected much, but see, it turned out to be little. What you brought home, I blew away. Why?" declares the LORD Almighty. "Because of my house, which remains a ruin, while each of you is busy with his own house. 10 Therefore, because of you the heavens have withheld their dew and the earth its crops. 11 I called for a drought on the fields and the mountains, on the grain, the new wine, the oil and whatever the ground produces, on men and cattle, and on the labor of your hands."

a1 A variant of *Jeshua*; here and elsewhere in Haggai

¹²Then Zerubbabel son of Shealtiel, Joshua son of Jehozadak, the high priest, and the whole remnant of the people obeyed the voice of the LORD their God and the message of the prophet Haggai, because the LORD their God had sent him. And the people feared the LORD.

¹³Then Haggai, the LORD's messenger, gave this message of the LORD to the people: "I am with you," declares the LORD. ¹⁴So the LORD stirred up the spirit of Zerubbabel son of Shealtiel, governor of Judah, and the spirit of Joshua son of Jehozadak, the high priest, and the spirit of the whole remnant of the people. They came and began to work on the house of the LORD Almighty, their God, ¹⁵on the twenty-fourth day of the sixth month in the second year of King Darius.

VERSE:	AUTHOR:	PASSAGE:
Haggai 1:8	Sherwood Eliot Wirt	Haggai 1:1–15

Go, Build the House

Once we have grasped the significance and importance of having a vision of what God wants for our lives as we grow older, we are to wait for a call from God — unless, of course, we already have one. This call will come to us personally and may well summon us to an immediate, distinct and particular field of endeavor . . .

If you see a need and can do something about it and it lines up with the vision God has given you for serving him, you have a call . . . To recognize a need, and be able to meet that need, is a situation that can take place anywhere. God opens the door, and that's it: you are off and running . . .

Here, then, is a top-of-the-line solution to what sociology insists on calling "the problem of the aging." The solution is this: Find your calling! It may come to you in prayer or Bible study; it may emerge from daily circumstances; it may come as a result of great and sudden need; it may even come through your own vocational skills and interests. Find it! Listen for it!

ADDITIONAL SCRIPTURE READINGS
Ephesians 4:1–16; Hebrews 3:1–6

Go to page 1180 for your next devotional reading.

The Promised Glory of the New House

2 On the twenty-first day of the seventh month, the word of the LORD came through the prophet Haggai: [2]"Speak to Zerubbabel son of Shealtiel, governor of Judah, to Joshua son of Jehozadak, the high priest, and to the remnant of the people. Ask them, [3]'Who of you is left who saw this house in its former glory? How does it look to you now? Does it not seem to you like nothing? [4]But now be strong, O Zerubbabel,' declares the LORD. 'Be strong, O Joshua son of Jehozadak, the high priest. Be strong, all you people of the land,' declares the LORD, 'and work. For I am with you,' declares the LORD Almighty. [5]'This is what I covenanted with you when you came out of Egypt. And my Spirit remains among you. Do not fear.'

[6]"This is what the LORD Almighty says: 'In a little while I will once more shake the heavens and the earth, the sea and the dry land. [7]I will shake all nations, and the desired of all nations will come, and I will fill this house with glory,' says the LORD Almighty. [8]'The silver is mine and the gold is mine,' declares the LORD Almighty. [9]'The glory of this present house will be greater than the glory of the former house,' says the LORD Almighty. 'And in this place I will grant peace,' declares the LORD Almighty."

Blessings for a Defiled People

[10]On the twenty-fourth day of the ninth month, in the second year of Darius, the word of the LORD came to the prophet Haggai: [11]"This is what the LORD Almighty says: 'Ask the priests what the law says: [12]If a person carries consecrated meat in the fold of his garment, and that fold touches some bread or stew, some wine, oil or other food, does it become consecrated?'"

The priests answered, "No."

[13]Then Haggai said, "If a person defiled by contact with a dead body touches one of these things, does it become defiled?"

"Yes," the priests replied, "it becomes defiled."

[14]Then Haggai said, " 'So it is with this people and this nation in my sight,' declares the LORD. 'Whatever they do and whatever they offer there is defiled.

[15]" 'Now give careful thought to this from this day on[a]—consider how things were before one stone was laid on another in the LORD's temple. [16]When anyone came to a heap of twenty measures, there were only ten. When anyone went to a wine vat to draw fifty measures, there were only twenty. [17]I struck all the work of your hands with blight, mildew and hail, yet you did not turn to me,' declares the LORD. [18]'From this day on, from this twenty-fourth day of the ninth month, give careful thought to the day when the foundation of the LORD's temple was laid. Give careful thought: [19]Is there yet any seed left in the barn? Until now, the vine and the fig tree, the pomegranate and the olive tree have not borne fruit.

" 'From this day on I will bless you.' "

Zerubbabel the LORD's Signet Ring

[20]The word of the LORD came to Haggai a second time on the twenty-fourth day of the month: [21]"Tell Zerubbabel governor of Judah that I will shake the heavens and the earth. [22]I will overturn royal thrones and shatter the power of the foreign kingdoms. I will overthrow chariots and their drivers; horses and their riders will fall, each by the sword of his brother.

[23]" 'On that day,' declares the LORD Almighty, 'I will take you, my servant Zerubbabel son of Shealtiel,' declares the LORD, 'and I will make you like my signet ring, for I have chosen you,' declares the LORD Almighty."

[a]15 Or *to the days past*

Zechariah wrote words
of encouragement and motivation to returning exiles who were rebuilding the temple in
Jerusalem. Zechariah described a series of
visions that portray God's control over history and provide a glimpse of the Messiah's
coming kingdom. As you read this book, take
courage in the power of God at work in your
life, giving you strength to persevere.

ZECHARIAH

A Call to Return to the LORD

1 In the eighth month of the second year of Darius, the word of the LORD came to the prophet Zechariah son of Berekiah, the son of Iddo:

²"The LORD was very angry with your forefathers. ³Therefore tell the people: This is what the LORD Almighty says: 'Return to me,' declares the LORD Almighty, 'and I will return to you,' says the LORD Almighty. ⁴Do not be like your forefathers, to whom the earlier prophets proclaimed: This is what the LORD Almighty says: 'Turn from your evil ways and your evil practices.' But they would not listen or pay attention to me, declares the LORD. ⁵Where are your forefathers now? And the prophets, do they live forever? ⁶But did not my words and my decrees, which I commanded my servants the prophets, overtake your forefathers?

"Then they repented and said, 'The LORD Almighty has done to us what

our ways and practices deserve, just as he determined to do.' "

The Man Among the Myrtle Trees

⁷On the twenty-fourth day of the eleventh month, the month of Shebat, in the second year of Darius, the word of the LORD came to the prophet Zechariah son of Berekiah, the son of Iddo.

⁸During the night I had a vision—and there before me was a man riding a red horse! He was standing among the myrtle trees in a ravine. Behind him were red, brown and white horses.

⁹I asked, "What are these, my lord?"

The angel who was talking with me answered, "I will show you what they are."

¹⁰Then the man standing among the myrtle trees explained, "They are the ones the LORD has sent to go throughout the earth."

¹¹And they reported to the angel of

the LORD, who was standing among the myrtle trees, "We have gone throughout the earth and found the whole world at rest and in peace."

¹²Then the angel of the LORD said, "LORD Almighty, how long will you withhold mercy from Jerusalem and from the towns of Judah, which you have been angry with these seventy years?" ¹³So the LORD spoke kind and comforting words to the angel who talked with me.

¹⁴Then the angel who was speaking to me said, "Proclaim this word: This is what the LORD Almighty says: 'I am very jealous for Jerusalem and Zion, ¹⁵but I am very angry with the nations that feel secure. I was only a little angry, but they added to the calamity.'

¹⁶"Therefore, this is what the LORD says: 'I will return to Jerusalem with mercy, and there my house will be rebuilt. And the measuring line will be stretched out over Jerusalem,' declares the LORD Almighty.

¹⁷"Proclaim further: This is what the LORD Almighty says: 'My towns will again overflow with prosperity, and the LORD will again comfort Zion and choose Jerusalem.' "

Four Horns and Four Craftsmen

¹⁸Then I looked up—and there before me were four horns! ¹⁹I asked the angel who was speaking to me, "What are these?"

He answered me, "These are the horns that scattered Judah, Israel and Jerusalem."

²⁰Then the LORD showed me four craftsmen. ²¹I asked, "What are these coming to do?"

He answered, "These are the horns that scattered Judah so that no one could raise his head, but the craftsmen have come to terrify them and throw down these horns of the nations who lifted up their horns against the land of Judah to scatter its people."

A Man With a Measuring Line

2 Then I looked up—and there before me was a man with a measuring line in his hand! ²I asked, "Where are you going?"

He answered me, "To measure Jerusalem, to find out how wide and how long it is."

³Then the angel who was speaking to me left, and another angel came to meet him ⁴and said to him: "Run, tell that young man, 'Jerusalem will be a city without walls because of the great number of men and livestock in it. ⁵And I myself will be a wall of fire around it,' declares the LORD, 'and I will be its glory within.'

⁶"Come! Come! Flee from the land of the north," declares the LORD, "for I have scattered you to the four winds of heaven," declares the LORD.

⁷"Come, O Zion! Escape, you who live in the Daughter of Babylon!" ⁸For this is what the LORD Almighty says: "After he has honored me and has sent me against the nations that have plundered you—for whoever touches you touches the apple of his eye— ⁹I will surely raise my hand against them so that their slaves will plunder them.ᵃ Then you will know that the LORD Almighty has sent me.

¹⁰"Shout and be glad, O Daughter of Zion. For I am coming, and I will live among you," declares the LORD. ¹¹"Many nations will be joined with the LORD in that day and will become my people. I will live among you and you will know that the LORD Almighty has sent me to you. ¹²The LORD will inherit Judah as his portion in the holy land and will again choose Jerusalem. ¹³Be still before the LORD, all mankind, because he has roused himself from his holy dwelling."

Clean Garments for the High Priest

3 Then he showed me Joshuaᵇ the high priest standing before the angel of the LORD, and Satanᶜ standing at his right side to accuse him.

ᵃ8,9 Or *says after . . . eye: 9"I . . . plunder them."* Zechariah   ᶜ1 *Satan* means *accuser.*   ᵇ1 A variant of *Jeshua;* here and elsewhere in

²The Lord said to Satan, "The Lord rebuke you, Satan! The Lord, who has chosen Jerusalem, rebuke you! Is not this man a burning stick snatched from the fire?"

³Now Joshua was dressed in filthy clothes as he stood before the angel. ⁴The angel said to those who were standing before him, "Take off his filthy clothes."

Then he said to Joshua, "See, I have taken away your sin, and I will put rich garments on you."

⁵Then I said, "Put a clean turban on his head." So they put a clean turban on his head and clothed him, while the angel of the Lord stood by.

⁶The angel of the Lord gave this charge to Joshua: ⁷"This is what the Lord Almighty says: 'If you will walk in my ways and keep my requirements, then you will govern my house and have charge of my courts, and I will give you a place among these standing here.

⁸" 'Listen, O high priest Joshua and your associates seated before you, who are men symbolic of things to come: I am going to bring my servant, the Branch. ⁹See, the stone I have set in front of Joshua! There are seven eyes*ᵃ* on that one stone, and I will engrave an inscription on it,' says the Lord Almighty, 'and I will remove the sin of this land in a single day.

¹⁰" 'In that day each of you will invite his neighbor to sit under his vine and fig tree,' declares the Lord Almighty."

The Gold Lampstand and the Two Olive Trees

4 Then the angel who talked with me returned and wakened me, as a man is wakened from his sleep. ²He asked me, "What do you see?"

I answered, "I see a solid gold lampstand with a bowl at the top and seven lights on it, with seven channels to the lights. ³Also there are two olive trees by it, one on the right of the bowl and the other on its left."

⁴I asked the angel who talked with me, "What are these, my lord?"

⁵He answered, "Do you not know what these are?"

"No, my lord," I replied.

⁶So he said to me, "This is the word of the Lord to Zerubbabel: 'Not by might nor by power, but by my Spirit,' says the Lord Almighty.

⁷"What*ᵇ* are you, O mighty mountain? Before Zerubbabel you will become level ground. Then he will bring out the capstone to shouts of 'God bless it! God bless it!' "

⁸Then the word of the Lord came to me: ⁹"The hands of Zerubbabel have laid the foundation of this temple; his hands will also complete it. Then you will know that the Lord Almighty has sent me to you.

¹⁰"Who despises the day of small things? Men will rejoice when they see the plumb line in the hand of Zerubbabel.

"(These seven are the eyes of the Lord, which range throughout the earth.)"

¹¹Then I asked the angel, "What are these two olive trees on the right and the left of the lampstand?"

¹²Again I asked him, "What are these two olive branches beside the two gold pipes that pour out golden oil?"

¹³He replied, "Do you not know what these are?"

"No, my lord," I said.

¹⁴So he said, "These are the two who are anointed to*ᶜ* serve the Lord of all the earth."

The Flying Scroll

5 I looked again—and there before me was a flying scroll!

²He asked me, "What do you see?"

I answered, "I see a flying scroll, thirty feet long and fifteen feet wide.*ᵈ*

³And he said to me, "This is the curse that is going out over the whole land; for according to what it says on one side, every thief will be banished,

---

ᵃ9 Or *facets*   *ᵇ7* Or *Who*   *ᶜ14* Or *two who bring oil and*   *ᵈ2* Hebrew *twenty cubits long and ten cubits wide* (about 9 meters long and 4.5 meters wide)

VERSE: AUTHOR: PASSAGE:
Zechariah 4:6   Jean Vanier   Zechariah 4:1–14

Not by Might

We must go through winters of suffering, through times when prayer is hard and people no longer attract us, but spring is not far away. A death in the family, a failure in work, a sickness which brings a new way of life, an unfaithful friend, all these are wounds to the heart which take us into a period of darkness. This darkness is important. We must learn to be strong and peaceful in darkness, not fighting it, but waiting . . .

So it is with the Spirit of Jesus. His first call is a call of peace and quietness, and we go forth with great rejoicing. But then he wants us to grow strong in our love and our faith. He wants us to grow in a love which is never shaken (Romans 8:35–39).

To be able to say this, we have to go through the strengthening times, which are the times of winter. We have to discover the role of sacrifice, the role of suffering, the role of the offering . . .

It is those who offer themselves in sacrifice who can be close to the suffering ones of the universe. That is why old age is important. It is a time of quiet contemplation, a time of offering. It can be a life of unchanging prayer, resting in the presence of God, accepting the wounds of fatigue and age and perhaps rejection and humiliation, for the wounded of the world . . .

We will pass through the winter of suffering to the kingdom of God and rebirth. We can begin to sense them already, as the peace of the Spirit comes into our hearts, quelling bitterness and recreating hope. We sense the light which is a tiny sign of what we are called to live in the glory of the wedding feast of eternity.

ADDITIONAL SCRIPTURE READINGS
Psalm 18:27–50; Romans 8:28–39

Go to page 1192 for your next devotional reading.

and according to what it says on the other, everyone who swears falsely will be banished. ⁴The Lord Almighty declares, 'I will send it out, and it will enter the house of the thief and the house of him who swears falsely by my name. It will remain in his house and destroy it, both its timbers and its stones.' "

The Woman in a Basket

⁵Then the angel who was speaking to me came forward and said to me, "Look up and see what this is that is appearing."

⁶I asked, "What is it?"

He replied, "It is a measuring basket.ᵃ" And he added, "This is the iniquityᵇ of the people throughout the land."

⁷Then the cover of lead was raised, and there in the basket sat a woman! ⁸He said, "This is wickedness," and he pushed her back into the basket and pushed the lead cover down over its mouth.

⁹Then I looked up—and there before me were two women, with the wind in their wings! They had wings like those of a stork, and they lifted up the basket between heaven and earth.

¹⁰"Where are they taking the basket?" I asked the angel who was speaking to me.

¹¹He replied, "To the country of Babyloniaᶜ to build a house for it. When it is ready, the basket will be set there in its place."

Four Chariots

6 I looked up again—and there before me were four chariots coming out from between two mountains—mountains of bronze! ²The first chariot had red horses, the second black, ³the third white, and the fourth dappled—all of them powerful. ⁴I asked the angel who was speaking to me, "What are these, my lord?"

⁵The angel answered me, "These are the four spiritsᵈ of heaven, going out from standing in the presence of the Lord of the whole world. ⁶The one with the black horses is going toward the north country, the one with the white horses toward the west,ᵉ and the one with the dappled horses toward the south."

⁷When the powerful horses went out, they were straining to go throughout the earth. And he said, "Go throughout the earth!" So they went throughout the earth.

⁸Then he called to me, "Look, those going toward the north country have given my Spiritᶠ rest in the land of the north."

A Crown for Joshua

⁹The word of the Lord came to me: ¹⁰"Take ⌊silver and gold⌋ from the exiles Heldai, Tobijah and Jedaiah, who have arrived from Babylon. Go the same day to the house of Josiah son of Zephaniah. ¹¹Take the silver and gold and make a crown, and set it on the head of the high priest, Joshua son of Jehozadak. ¹²Tell him this is what the Lord Almighty says: 'Here is the man whose name is the Branch, and he will branch out from his place and build the temple of the Lord. ¹³It is he who will build the temple of the Lord, and he will be clothed with majesty and will sit and rule on his throne. And he will be a priest on his throne. And there will be harmony between the two.' ¹⁴The crown will be given to Heldai,ᵍ Tobijah, Jedaiah and Henʰ son of Zephaniah as a memorial in the temple of the Lord. ¹⁵Those who are far away will come and help to build the temple of the Lord, and you will know that the Lord Almighty has sent me to you. This will happen if you diligently obey the Lord your God."

ᵃ6 Hebrew an ephah; also in verses 7-11   ᵇ6 Or appearance   ᶜ11 Hebrew Shinar   ᵈ5 Or winds   ᵉ6 Or horses after them   ᶠ8 Or spirit   ᵍ14 Syriac; Hebrew Helem   ʰ14 Or and the gracious one, the

Justice and Mercy, Not Fasting

7 In the fourth year of King Darius, the word of the LORD came to Zechariah on the fourth day of the ninth month, the month of Kislev. ²The people of Bethel had sent Sharezer and Regem-Melech, together with their men, to entreat the LORD ³by asking the priests of the house of the LORD Almighty and the prophets, "Should I mourn and fast in the fifth month, as I have done for so many years?"

⁴Then the word of the LORD Almighty came to me: ⁵"Ask all the people of the land and the priests, 'When you fasted and mourned in the fifth and seventh months for the past seventy years, was it really for me that you fasted? ⁶And when you were eating and drinking, were you not just feasting for yourselves? ⁷Are these not the words the LORD proclaimed through the earlier prophets when Jerusalem and its surrounding towns were at rest and prosperous, and the Negev and the western foothills were settled?' "

⁸And the word of the LORD came again to Zechariah: ⁹"This is what the LORD Almighty says: 'Administer true justice; show mercy and compassion to one another. ¹⁰Do not oppress the widow or the fatherless, the alien or the poor. In your hearts do not think evil of each other.'

¹¹"But they refused to pay attention; stubbornly they turned their backs and stopped up their ears. ¹²They made their hearts as hard as flint and would not listen to the law or to the words that the LORD Almighty had sent by his Spirit through the earlier prophets. So the LORD Almighty was very angry.

¹³" 'When I called, they did not listen; so when they called, I would not listen,' says the LORD Almighty. ¹⁴'I scattered them with a whirlwind among all the nations, where they were strangers. The land was left so desolate behind them that no one could come or go. This is how they made the pleasant land desolate.' "

The LORD Promises to Bless Jerusalem

8 Again the word of the LORD Almighty came to me. ²This is what the LORD Almighty says: "I am very jealous for Zion; I am burning with jealousy for her."

³This is what the LORD says: "I will return to Zion and dwell in Jerusalem. Then Jerusalem will be called the City of Truth, and the mountain of the LORD Almighty will be called the Holy Mountain."

⁴This is what the LORD Almighty says: "Once again men and women of ripe old age will sit in the streets of Jerusalem, each with cane in hand because of his age. ⁵The city streets will be filled with boys and girls playing there."

⁶This is what the LORD Almighty says: "It may seem marvelous to the remnant of this people at that time, but will it seem marvelous to me?" declares the LORD Almighty.

⁷This is what the LORD Almighty says: "I will save my people from the countries of the east and the west. ⁸I will bring them back to live in Jerusalem; they will be my people, and I will be faithful and righteous to them as their God."

⁹This is what the LORD Almighty says: "You who now hear these words spoken by the prophets who were there when the foundation was laid for the house of the LORD Almighty, let your hands be strong so that the temple may be built. ¹⁰Before that time there were no wages for man or beast. No one could go about his business safely because of his enemy, for I had turned every man against his neighbor. ¹¹But now I will not deal with the remnant of this people as I did in the past," declares the LORD Almighty.

¹²"The seed will grow well, the vine will yield its fruit, the ground will produce its crops, and the heavens will drop their dew. I will give all these things as an inheritance to the remnant of this people. ¹³As you have been an object of cursing among the

nations, O Judah and Israel, so will I save you, and you will be a blessing. Do not be afraid, but let your hands be strong."

¹⁴This is what the LORD Almighty says: "Just as I had determined to bring disaster upon you and showed no pity when your fathers angered me," says the LORD Almighty, ¹⁵"so now I have determined to do good again to Jerusalem and Judah. Do not be afraid. ¹⁶These are the things you are to do: Speak the truth to each other, and render true and sound judgment in your courts; ¹⁷do not plot evil against your neighbor, and do not love to swear falsely. I hate all this," declares the LORD.

¹⁸Again the word of the LORD Almighty came to me. ¹⁹This is what the LORD Almighty says: "The fasts of the fourth, fifth, seventh and tenth months will become joyful and glad occasions and happy festivals for Judah. Therefore love truth and peace."

²⁰This is what the LORD Almighty says: "Many peoples and the inhabitants of many cities will yet come, ²¹and the inhabitants of one city will go to another and say, 'Let us go at once to entreat the LORD and seek the LORD Almighty. I myself am going.' ²²And many peoples and powerful nations will come to Jerusalem to seek the LORD Almighty and to entreat him."

²³This is what the LORD Almighty says: "In those days ten men from all languages and nations will take firm hold of one Jew by the hem of his robe and say, 'Let us go with you, because we have heard that God is with you.'"

Judgment on Israel's Enemies

An Oracle

9 The word of the LORD is against the land of Hadrach and will rest upon Damascus— for the eyes of men and all the tribes of Israel

are on the LORD—[a]
²and upon Hamath too, which
    borders on it,
and upon Tyre and Sidon,
    though they are very
    skillful.
³Tyre has built herself a
    stronghold;
she has heaped up silver like
    dust,
and gold like the dirt of the
    streets.
⁴But the Lord will take away her
    possessions
and destroy her power on the
    sea,
and she will be consumed by
    fire.
⁵Ashkelon will see it and fear;
    Gaza will writhe in agony,
and Ekron too, for her hope will
    wither.
Gaza will lose her king
    and Ashkelon will be deserted.
⁶Foreigners will occupy Ashdod,
    and I will cut off the pride of
    the Philistines.
⁷I will take the blood from their
    mouths,
the forbidden food from
    between their teeth.
Those who are left will belong to
    our God
and become leaders in Judah,
and Ekron will be like the
    Jebusites.
⁸But I will defend my house
    against marauding forces.
Never again will an oppressor
    overrun my people,
for now I am keeping watch.

The Coming of Zion's King

⁹Rejoice greatly, O Daughter of
    Zion!
    Shout, Daughter of Jerusalem!
See, your king[b] comes to you,
    righteous and having salvation,
    gentle and riding on a donkey,
    on a colt, the foal of a donkey.
¹⁰I will take away the chariots from
    Ephraim

---

[a]1 Or Damascus. / For the eye of the LORD is on all mankind, / as well as on the tribes of Israel,
[b]9 Or King

and the war-horses from
  Jerusalem,
and the battle bow will be
  broken.
He will proclaim peace to the
  nations.
His rule will extend from sea to
  sea
and from the River*a* to the
  ends of the earth.*b*
¹¹As for you, because of the blood
  of my covenant with you,
I will free your prisoners from
  the waterless pit.
¹²Return to your fortress,
    O prisoners of hope;
even now I announce that I will
  restore twice as much to
  you.
¹³I will bend Judah as I bend my
  bow
and fill it with Ephraim.
I will rouse your sons, O Zion,
  against your sons, O Greece,
  and make you like a warrior's
  sword.

The LORD Will Appear

¹⁴Then the LORD will appear over
  them;
    his arrow will flash like
    lightning.
The Sovereign LORD will sound the
  trumpet;
    he will march in the storms of
    the south,
¹⁵ and the LORD Almighty will
  shield them.
They will destroy
  and overcome with slingstones.
They will drink and roar as with
  wine;
    they will be full like a bowl
    used for sprinkling*c* the
    corners of the altar.
¹⁶The LORD their God will save them
  on that day
    as the flock of his people.
They will sparkle in his land
  like jewels in a crown.
¹⁷How attractive and beautiful they
  will be!

Grain will make the young men
  thrive,
and new wine the young
  women.

The LORD Will Care for Judah

10 Ask the LORD for rain in the
  springtime;
it is the LORD who makes the
  storm clouds.
He gives showers of rain to men,
  and plants of the field to
  everyone.
²The idols speak deceit,
  diviners see visions that lie;
they tell dreams that are false,
  they give comfort in vain.
Therefore the people wander like
  sheep
    oppressed for lack of a
    shepherd.

³"My anger burns against the
  shepherds,
  and I will punish the leaders;
for the LORD Almighty will care
  for his flock, the house of
  Judah,
    and make them like a proud
    horse in battle.
⁴From Judah will come the
  cornerstone,
  from him the tent peg,
  from him the battle bow,
  from him every ruler.
⁵Together they*d* will be like
  mighty men
    trampling the muddy streets in
    battle.
Because the LORD is with them,
  they will fight and overthrow
  the horsemen.
⁶"I will strengthen the house of
  Judah
  and save the house of Joseph.
I will restore them
  because I have compassion on
  them.
They will be as though
  I had not rejected them,
for I am the LORD their God
  and I will answer them.

---

a10 That is, the Euphrates   *b10* Or *the end of the land*   *c15* Or *bowl,* / *like*   *d4,5* Or *ruler,*
all of them together. / *5They*

⁷The Ephraimites will become like
  mighty men,
  and their hearts will be glad as
    with wine.
Their children will see it and be
    joyful;
  their hearts will rejoice in the
    LORD.
⁸I will signal for them
  and gather them in.
Surely I will redeem them;
  they will be as numerous as
    before.
⁹Though I scatter them among the
    peoples,
  yet in distant lands they will
    remember me.
They and their children will
    survive,
  and they will return.
¹⁰I will bring them back from Egypt
  and gather them from Assyria.
I will bring them to Gilead and
    Lebanon,
  and there will not be room
    enough for them.
¹¹They will pass through the sea of
    trouble;
  the surging sea will be subdued
  and all the depths of the Nile
    will dry up.
Assyria's pride will be brought
    down
  and Egypt's scepter will pass
    away.
¹²I will strengthen them in the LORD
  and in his name they will
    walk,"

                    declares the LORD.

11 Open your doors, O Lebanon,
  so that fire may devour your
    cedars!
²Wail, O pine tree, for the cedar
    has fallen;
  the stately trees are ruined!
Wail, oaks of Bashan;
  the dense forest has been cut
    down!
³Listen to the wail of the
    shepherds;
  their rich pastures are
    destroyed!
Listen to the roar of the lions;

the lush thicket of the Jordan is
    ruined!

Two Shepherds

⁴This is what the LORD my God
says: "Pasture the flock marked for
slaughter. ⁵Their buyers slaughter
them and go unpunished. Those who
sell them say, 'Praise the LORD, I am
rich!' Their own shepherds do not
spare them. ⁶For I will no longer have
pity on the people of the land," declares the LORD. "I will hand everyone
over to his neighbor and his king.
They will oppress the land, and I will
not rescue them from their hands."

⁷So I pastured the flock marked for
slaughter, particularly the oppressed
of the flock. Then I took two staffs
and called one Favor and the other
Union, and I pastured the flock. ⁸In
one month I got rid of the three shepherds.

The flock detested me, and I grew
weary of them ⁹and said, "I will not
be your shepherd. Let the dying die,
and the perishing perish. Let those
who are left eat one another's flesh."

¹⁰Then I took my staff called Favor
and broke it, revoking the covenant I
had made with all the nations. ¹¹It
was revoked on that day, and so the
afflicted of the flock who were watching me knew it was the word of the
LORD.

¹²I told them, "If you think it best,
give me my pay; but if not, keep it."
So they paid me thirty pieces of silver.

¹³And the LORD said to me, "Throw
it to the potter"—the handsome price
at which they priced me! So I took the
thirty pieces of silver and threw them
into the house of the LORD to the potter.

¹⁴Then I broke my second staff
called Union, breaking the brotherhood between Judah and Israel.

¹⁵Then the LORD said to me, "Take
again the equipment of a foolish shepherd. ¹⁶For I am going to raise up a
shepherd over the land who will not
care for the lost, or seek the young, or
heal the injured, or feed the healthy,
but will eat the meat of the choice
sheep, tearing off their hoofs.

¹⁷"Woe to the worthless shepherd,
   who deserts the flock!
 May the sword strike his arm and
   his right eye!
 May his arm be completely
   withered,
   his right eye totally blinded!"

Jerusalem's Enemies to Be Destroyed

An Oracle

12 This is the word of the Lord concerning Israel. The Lord, who stretches out the heavens, who lays the foundation of the earth, and who forms the spirit of man within him, declares: ²"I am going to make Jerusalem a cup that sends all the surrounding peoples reeling. Judah will be besieged as well as Jerusalem. ³On that day, when all the nations of the earth are gathered against her, I will make Jerusalem an immovable rock for all the nations. All who try to move it will injure themselves. ⁴On that day I will strike every horse with panic and its rider with madness," declares the Lord. "I will keep a watchful eye over the house of Judah, but I will blind all the horses of the nations. ⁵Then the leaders of Judah will say in their hearts, 'The people of Jerusalem are strong, because the Lord Almighty is their God.'

⁶"On that day I will make the leaders of Judah like a firepot in a woodpile, like a flaming torch among sheaves. They will consume right and left all the surrounding peoples, but Jerusalem will remain intact in her place.

⁷"The Lord will save the dwellings of Judah first, so that the honor of the house of David and of Jerusalem's inhabitants may not be greater than that of Judah. ⁸On that day the Lord will shield those who live in Jerusalem, so that the feeblest among them will be like David, and the house of David will be like God, like the Angel of the Lord going before them. ⁹On that day

I will set out to destroy all the nations that attack Jerusalem.

Mourning for the One They Pierced

¹⁰"And I will pour out on the house of David and the inhabitants of Jerusalem a spirit[a] of grace and supplication. They will look on[b] me, the one they have pierced, and they will mourn for him as one mourns for an only child, and grieve bitterly for him as one grieves for a firstborn son. ¹¹On that day the weeping in Jerusalem will be great, like the weeping of Hadad Rimmon in the plain of Megiddo. ¹²The land will mourn, each clan by itself, with their wives by themselves: the clan of the house of David and their wives, the clan of the house of Nathan and their wives, ¹³the clan of the house of Levi and their wives, the clan of Shimei and their wives, ¹⁴and all the rest of the clans and their wives.

Cleansing From Sin

13 "On that day a fountain will be opened to the house of David and the inhabitants of Jerusalem, to cleanse them from sin and impurity.

²"On that day, I will banish the names of the idols from the land, and they will be remembered no more," declares the Lord Almighty. "I will remove both the prophets and the spirit of impurity from the land. ³And if anyone still prophesies, his father and mother, to whom he was born, will say to him, 'You must die, because you have told lies in the Lord's name.' When he prophesies, his own parents will stab him.

⁴"On that day every prophet will be ashamed of his prophetic vision. He will not put on a prophet's garment of hair in order to deceive. ⁵He will say, 'I am not a prophet. I am a farmer; the land has been my livelihood since my youth.[c]' ⁶If someone asks him, 'What are these wounds on your body[d]?' he will answer, 'The

---

a10 Or the Spirit   b10 Or to   c5 Or farmer; a man sold me in my youth   d6 Or wounds between your hands

wounds I was given at the house of my friends.'

The Shepherd Struck, the Sheep Scattered

⁷"Awake, O sword, against my
    shepherd,
  against the man who is close to
    me!"
  declares the LORD Almighty.
"Strike the shepherd,
  and the sheep will be scattered,
  and I will turn my hand against
    the little ones.
⁸In the whole land," declares the
    LORD,
  "two-thirds will be struck down
    and perish;
  yet one-third will be left in it.
⁹This third I will bring into the fire;
  I will refine them like silver
  and test them like gold.
They will call on my name
  and I will answer them;
I will say, 'They are my people,'
  and they will say, 'The LORD is
    our God.' "

The LORD Comes and Reigns

14 A day of the LORD is coming when your plunder will be divided among you.
²I will gather all the nations to Jerusalem to fight against it; the city will be captured, the houses ransacked, and the women raped. Half of the city will go into exile, but the rest of the people will not be taken from the city. ³Then the LORD will go out and fight against those nations, as he fights in the day of battle. ⁴On that day his feet will stand on the Mount of Olives, east of Jerusalem, and the Mount of Olives will be split in two from east to west, forming a great valley, with half of the mountain moving north and half moving south. ⁵You will flee by my mountain valley, for it will extend to Azel. You will flee as you fled from the earthquake*a* in the days of Uzziah king of Judah. Then

the LORD my God will come, and all the holy ones with him.

⁶On that day there will be no light, no cold or frost. ⁷It will be a unique day, without daytime or nighttime—a day known to the LORD. When evening comes, there will be light.

⁸On that day living water will flow out from Jerusalem, half to the eastern sea*b* and half to the western sea,*c* in summer and in winter.

⁹The LORD will be king over the whole earth. On that day there will be one LORD, and his name the only name.

¹⁰The whole land, from Geba to Rimmon, south of Jerusalem, will become like the Arabah. But Jerusalem will be raised up and remain in its place, from the Benjamin Gate to the site of the First Gate, to the Corner Gate, and from the Tower of Hananel to the royal winepresses. ¹¹It will be inhabited; never again will it be destroyed. Jerusalem will be secure.

¹²This is the plague with which the LORD will strike all the nations that fought against Jerusalem: Their flesh will rot while they are still standing on their feet, their eyes will rot in their sockets, and their tongues will rot in their mouths. ¹³On that day men will be stricken by the LORD with great panic. Each man will seize the hand of another, and they will attack each other. ¹⁴Judah too will fight at Jerusalem. The wealth of all the surrounding nations will be collected—great quantities of gold and silver and clothing. ¹⁵A similar plague will strike the horses and mules, the camels and donkeys, and all the animals in those camps.

¹⁶Then the survivors from all the nations that have attacked Jerusalem will go up year after year to worship the King, the LORD Almighty, and to celebrate the Feast of Tabernacles. ¹⁷If any of the peoples of the earth do not go up to Jerusalem to worship the King, the LORD Almighty, they will have no rain. ¹⁸If the Egyptian people

---

a5 Or *⁵My mountain valley will be blocked and will extend to Azel. It will be blocked as it was blocked because of the earthquake*   *b8* That is, the Dead Sea   *c8* That is, the Mediterranean

do not go up and take part, they will have no rain. The Lord[a] will bring on them the plague he inflicts on the nations that do not go up to celebrate the Feast of Tabernacles. ¹⁹This will be the punishment of Egypt and the punishment of all the nations that do not go up to celebrate the Feast of Tabernacles.

²⁰On that day HOLY TO THE LORD will be inscribed on the bells of the horses, and the cooking pots in the Lord's house will be like the sacred bowls in front of the altar. ²¹Every pot in Jerusalem and Judah will be holy to the Lord Almighty, and all who come to sacrifice will take some of the pots and cook in them. And on that day there will no longer be a Canaanite[b] in the house of the Lord Almighty.

a18 Or part, then the Lord   b21 Or merchant

Malachi prophesied during the conditions described in Nehemiah 13. He called the complacent and indifferent to renew their relationship with God. As you read this book, examine your own commitment, and surrender yourself to that relentlessly tender and accepting love of God that will never let you go. Gripped by his love, you will be set free to respond in grateful and loving obedience.

MALACHI

1 An oracle: The word of the LORD to Israel through Malachi.[a]

Jacob Loved, Esau Hated

2"I have loved you," says the LORD.

"But you ask, 'How have you loved us?'

"Was not Esau Jacob's brother?" the LORD says. "Yet I have loved Jacob, 3but Esau I have hated, and I have turned his mountains into a wasteland and left his inheritance to the desert jackals."

4Edom may say, "Though we have been crushed, we will rebuild the ruins."

But this is what the LORD Almighty says: "They may build, but I will demolish. They will be called the Wicked Land, a people always under the wrath of the LORD. 5You will see it with your own eyes and say, 'Great is the LORD—even beyond the borders of Israel!'

Blemished Sacrifices

6"A son honors his father, and a servant his master. If I am a father, where is the honor due me? If I am a master, where is the respect due me?" says the LORD Almighty. "It is you, O priests, who show contempt for my name.

"But you ask, 'How have we shown contempt for your name?'

7"You place defiled food on my altar.

"But you ask, 'How have we defiled you?'

"By saying that the LORD's table is contemptible. 8When you bring blind animals for sacrifice, is that not wrong? When you sacrifice crippled or diseased animals, is that not wrong? Try offering them to your governor! Would he be pleased with you? Would he accept you?" says the LORD Almighty.

9"Now implore God to be gracious to us. With such offerings from your hands, will he accept you?"—says the LORD Almighty.

10"Oh, that one of you would shut the temple doors, so that you would not light useless fires on my altar! I am not pleased with you," says the LORD Almighty, "and I will accept no offering from your hands. 11My name will be great among the nations, from the rising to the setting of the sun. In every place incense and pure offerings will be brought to my name, because my name will be great among the nations," says the LORD Almighty.

12"But you profane it by saying of the Lord's table, 'It is defiled,' and of its food, 'It is contemptible.' 13And you say, 'What a burden!' and you sniff at it contemptuously," says the LORD Almighty.

"When you bring injured, crippled or diseased animals and offer them as sacrifices, should I accept them from your hands?" says the LORD. 14"Cursed is the cheat who has an acceptable male in his flock and vows to give it, but then sacrifices a blemished animal to the Lord. For I am a great king," says the LORD Almighty, "and my name is to be feared among the nations.

Admonition for the Priests

2 "And now this admonition is for you, O priests. 2If you do not listen, and if you do not set your heart to honor my name," says the LORD Almighty, "I will send a curse upon you, and I will curse your blessings. Yes, I have already cursed them, because you have not set your heart to honor me.

3"Because of you I will rebuke[a] your descendants[b]; I will spread on your faces the offal from your festival sacrifices, and you will be carried off with it. 4And you will know that I have sent you this admonition so that my covenant with Levi may continue," says the LORD Almighty. 5"My covenant was with him, a covenant of life and peace, and I gave them to him; this called for reverence and he revered me and stood in awe of my name. 6True instruction was in his mouth and nothing false was found on his lips. He walked with me in peace and uprightness, and turned many from sin.

7"For the lips of a priest ought to preserve knowledge, and from his mouth men should seek instruction—because he is the messenger of the LORD Almighty. 8But you have turned from the way and by your teaching have caused many to stumble; you have violated the covenant with Levi," says the LORD Almighty. 9"So I have caused you to be despised and humiliated before all the people, because you have not followed my ways but have shown partiality in matters of the law."

Judah Unfaithful

10Have we not all one Father[c]? Did not one God create us? Why do we profane the covenant of our fathers by breaking faith with one another?

11Judah has broken faith. A detestable thing has been committed in Israel and in Jerusalem: Judah has desecrated the sanctuary the LORD loves, by marrying the daughter of a foreign god. 12As for the man who does this, whoever he may be, may the LORD cut him off from the tents of Jacob[d]— even though he brings offerings to the LORD Almighty.

13Another thing you do: You flood the LORD's altar with tears. You weep and wail because he no longer pays attention to your offerings or accepts them with pleasure from your hands. 14You ask, "Why?" It is because the LORD is acting as the witness between you and the wife of your youth, because you have broken faith with her,

---

a3 Or cut off (see Septuagint)   b3 Or will blight your grain   c10 Or father   d12 Or 12May the LORD cut off from the tents of Jacob anyone who gives testimony in behalf of the man who does this

though she is your partner, the wife of your marriage covenant.

¹⁵Has not ⌞the Lord⌟ made them one? In flesh and spirit they are his. And why one? Because he was seeking godly offspring.ª So guard yourself in your spirit, and do not break faith with the wife of your youth.

¹⁶"I hate divorce," says the Lord God of Israel, "and I hate a man's covering himselfᵇ with violence as well as with his garment," says the Lord Almighty.

So guard yourself in your spirit, and do not break faith.

The Day of Judgment

¹⁷You have wearied the Lord with your words.

"How have we wearied him?" you ask.

By saying, "All who do evil are good in the eyes of the Lord, and he is pleased with them" or "Where is the God of justice?"

3 "See, I will send my messenger, who will prepare the way before me. Then suddenly the Lord you are seeking will come to his temple; the messenger of the covenant, whom you desire, will come," says the Lord Almighty.

²But who can endure the day of his coming? Who can stand when he appears? For he will be like a refiner's fire or a launderer's soap. ³He will sit as a refiner and purifier of silver; he will purify the Levites and refine them like gold and silver. Then the Lord will have men who will bring offerings in righteousness, ⁴and the offerings of Judah and Jerusalem will be acceptable to the Lord, as in days gone by, as in former years.

⁵"So I will come near to you for judgment. I will be quick to testify against sorcerers, adulterers and perjurers, against those who defraud laborers of their wages, who oppress the widows and the fatherless, and deprive aliens of justice, but do not fear me," says the Lord Almighty.

Robbing God

⁶"I the Lord do not change. So you, O descendants of Jacob, are not destroyed. ⁷Ever since the time of your forefathers you have turned away from my decrees and have not kept them. Return to me, and I will return to you," says the Lord Almighty.

"But you ask, 'How are we to return?'

⁸"Will a man rob God? Yet you rob me.

"But you ask, 'How do we rob you?'

"In tithes and offerings. ⁹You are under a curse—the whole nation of you—because you are robbing me. ¹⁰Bring the whole tithe into the storehouse, that there may be food in my house. Test me in this," says the Lord Almighty, "and see if I will not throw open the floodgates of heaven and pour out so much blessing that you will not have room enough for it. ¹¹I will prevent pests from devouring your crops, and the vines in your fields will not cast their fruit," says the Lord Almighty. ¹²"Then all the nations will call you blessed, for yours will be a delightful land," says the Lord Almighty.

¹³"You have said harsh things against me," says the Lord.

"Yet you ask, 'What have we said against you?'

¹⁴"You have said, 'It is futile to serve God. What did we gain by carrying out his requirements and going about like mourners before the Lord Almighty? ¹⁵But now we call the arrogant blessed. Certainly the evildoers prosper, and even those who challenge God escape.'"

¹⁶Then those who feared the Lord talked with each other, and the Lord listened and heard. A scroll of remembrance was written in his presence concerning those who feared the Lord and honored his name.

¹⁷"They will be mine," says the Lord Almighty, "in the day when I

ª15 Or ¹⁵But the one ⌞who is our father⌟ did not do this, not as long as life remained in him. And what was he seeking? An offspring from God   ᵇ16 Or his wife

VERSE:	AUTHOR:	PASSAGE:
Malachi 3:16	John Killinger	Malachi 3:6–18

Rehearsal Theology

Retirement is a time of rethinking and transition and re-ordering of life ... Retirement is a great time to learn about rehearsal theology, if one has never understood it before. It is a time for retrospection, for looking back across the hills and valleys of one's own existence and noting where the Almighty God has intervened in one's path, lifting a burden here and introducing a surprise there ... We need to trace our journey — write our auto-biography as it were — and realize how wonderful the God of the covenant has been ...

Rehearsal theology. God has been with us *here* and *here* and *here*. That is for retirement, isn't it? And more.

In retirement, we have more time to be with him. To practice the Presence. To experience the indwelling Spirit. To be in touch with God ...

I read a beautiful little story somewhere about a boy and an old man sitting on a dock in the late afternoon, fishing. They talked about many things — why sunsets are red, why the rain falls, why the seasons change, what life is like. Finally the boy looked up at the old man ... and asked, "Does anybody ever see God?" "Son," said the old man, looking across the blue waters, "it's getting so I hardly see anything else." That's it, isn't it? That's the way retirement ought to be.

ADDITIONAL SCRIPTURE READINGS
Deuteronomy 8:1–9; Isaiah 46

Go to page 1194 for your next devotional reading.

make up my treasured possession.[a] I will spare them, just as in compassion a man spares his son who serves him. ¹⁸And you will again see the distinction between the righteous and the wicked, between those who serve God and those who do not.

The Day of the LORD

4 "Surely the day is coming; it will burn like a furnace. All the arrogant and every evildoer will be stubble, and that day that is coming will set them on fire," says the LORD Almighty. "Not a root or a branch will be left to them. ²But for you who revere my name, the sun of righteousness will rise with healing in its wings. And you will go out and leap like calves released from the stall. ³Then you will trample down the wicked; they will be ashes under the soles of your feet on the day when I do these things," says the LORD Almighty.

⁴"Remember the law of my servant Moses, the decrees and laws I gave him at Horeb for all Israel.

⁵"See, I will send you the prophet Elijah before that great and dreadful day of the LORD comes. ⁶He will turn the hearts of the fathers to their children, and the hearts of the children to their fathers; or else I will come and strike the land with a curse."

---

[a]17 Or *Almighty, "my treasured possession, in the day when I act*

PASSAGE: Romans 4:1–25; Ephesians 1:3–14
AUTHOR: Thomas Olivers

The God of Abraham

The God of Abraham praise,
　　Who reigns enthroned above,
Ancient of everlasting days,
　　And God of love.
The Lord! Great I AM!
　　By earth and heaven confessed;
I bow and bless the sacred Name
　　For ever blessed.

The God of Abraham praise,
　　Whose all-sufficient grace
Shall guide me all my happy days
　　In all my ways.
He is my faithful Friend,
　　He is my gracious God;
And he shall save me to the end
　　Through Jesus' blood.

He by Himself hath sworn,
　　I on His oath depend:
I shall, on eagles' wings upborne,
　　To heaven ascend;
I shall behold His face,
　　I shall His power adore,
And sing the wonders of His grace
　　For evermore.

Go to page 1201 for your next devotional reading.

NEW TESTAMENT

Matthew, in the first of four Gospels, tells about Jesus' life, death and resurrection. His primary purpose is to show how Jesus fulfilled God's promises from the Old Testament. As you read this book, thank God for keeping his promises to you and be ready to tell others about the difference he's made and continues to make in your life.

MATTHEW

The Genealogy of Jesus

1 A record of the genealogy of Jesus Christ the son of David, the son of Abraham:

²Abraham was the father of Isaac,
Isaac the father of Jacob,
Jacob the father of Judah and his brothers,
³Judah the father of Perez and Zerah, whose mother was Tamar,
Perez the father of Hezron,
Hezron the father of Ram,
⁴Ram the father of Amminadab,
Amminadab the father of Nahshon,
Nahshon the father of Salmon,
⁵Salmon the father of Boaz, whose mother was Rahab,
Boaz the father of Obed, whose mother was Ruth,
Obed the father of Jesse,
⁶and Jesse the father of King David.

David was the father of Solomon, whose mother had been Uriah's wife,
⁷Solomon the father of Rehoboam,
Rehoboam the father of Abijah,
Abijah the father of Asa,
⁸Asa the father of Jehoshaphat,
Jehoshaphat the father of Jehoram,
Jehoram the father of Uzziah,
⁹Uzziah the father of Jotham,
Jotham the father of Ahaz,
Ahaz the father of Hezekiah,
¹⁰Hezekiah the father of Manasseh,
Manasseh the father of Amon,
Amon the father of Josiah,
¹¹and Josiah the father of Jeconiah[a] and his brothers at the time of the exile to Babylon.

a11 That is, Jehoiachin; also in verse 12

12After the exile to Babylon:
Jeconiah was the father of She-altiel,
Shealtiel the father of Zerub-babel,
13Zerubbabel the father of Abiud,
Abiud the father of Eliakim,
Eliakim the father of Azor,
14Azor the father of Zadok,
Zadok the father of Akim,
Akim the father of Eliud,
15Eliud the father of Eleazar,
Eleazar the father of Matthan,
Matthan the father of Jacob,
16and Jacob the father of Joseph,
the husband of Mary, of whom was born Jesus, who is called Christ.

17Thus there were fourteen generations in all from Abraham to David, fourteen from David to the exile to Babylon, and fourteen from the exile to the Christ.[a]

The Birth of Jesus Christ

18This is how the birth of Jesus Christ came about: His mother Mary was pledged to be married to Joseph, but before they came together, she was found to be with child through the Holy Spirit. 19Because Joseph her husband was a righteous man and did not want to expose her to public disgrace, he had in mind to divorce her quietly.

20But after he had considered this, an angel of the Lord appeared to him in a dream and said, "Joseph son of David, do not be afraid to take Mary home as your wife, because what is conceived in her is from the Holy Spirit. 21She will give birth to a son, and you are to give him the name Jesus,[b] because he will save his people from their sins."

22All this took place to fulfill what the Lord had said through the prophet: 23"The virgin will be with child and will give birth to a son, and they will call him Immanuel"[c]—which means, "God with us."

24When Joseph woke up, he did what the angel of the Lord had commanded him and took Mary home as his wife. 25But he had no union with her until she gave birth to a son. And he gave him the name Jesus.

The Visit of the Magi

2 After Jesus was born in Bethlehem in Judea, during the time of King Herod, Magi[d] from the east came to Jerusalem 2and asked, "Where is the one who has been born king of the Jews? We saw his star in the east[e] and have come to worship him."

3When King Herod heard this he was disturbed, and all Jerusalem with him. 4When he had called together all the people's chief priests and teachers of the law, he asked them where the Christ[f] was to be born. 5"In Bethlehem in Judea," they replied, "for this is what the prophet has written:

6" 'But you, Bethlehem, in the land of Judah,
are by no means least among the rulers of Judah;
for out of you will come a ruler who will be the shepherd of my people Israel.'[g]"

7Then Herod called the Magi secretly and found out from them the exact time the star had appeared. 8He sent them to Bethlehem and said, "Go and make a careful search for the child. As soon as you find him, report to me, so that I too may go and worship him."

9After they had heard the king, they went on their way, and the star they had seen in the east[h] went ahead of them until it stopped over the place where the child was. 10When they saw the star, they were overjoyed. 11On coming to the house, they saw the child with his mother Mary,

a17 Or Messiah. "The Christ" (Greek) and "the Messiah" (Hebrew) both mean "the Anointed One."   b21 Jesus is the Greek form of Joshua, which means the LORD saves.   c23 Isaiah 7:14
d1 Traditionally Wise Men   e2 Or star when it rose   f4 Or Messiah   g6 Micah 5:2
h9 Or seen when it rose

and they bowed down and worshiped him. Then they opened their treasures and presented him with gifts of gold and of incense and of myrrh. ¹²And having been warned in a dream not to go back to Herod, they returned to their country by another route.

The Escape to Egypt

¹³When they had gone, an angel of the Lord appeared to Joseph in a dream. "Get up," he said, "take the child and his mother and escape to Egypt. Stay there until I tell you, for Herod is going to search for the child to kill him."

¹⁴So he got up, took the child and his mother during the night and left for Egypt, ¹⁵where he stayed until the death of Herod. And so was fulfilled what the Lord had said through the prophet: "Out of Egypt I called my son."ᵃ

¹⁶When Herod realized that he had been outwitted by the Magi, he was furious, and he gave orders to kill all the boys in Bethlehem and its vicinity who were two years old and under, in accordance with the time he had learned from the Magi. ¹⁷Then what was said through the prophet Jeremiah was fulfilled:

¹⁸"A voice is heard in Ramah,
    weeping and great mourning,
Rachel weeping for her children
    and refusing to be comforted,
because they are no more."ᵇ

The Return to Nazareth

¹⁹After Herod died, an angel of the Lord appeared in a dream to Joseph in Egypt ²⁰and said, "Get up, take the child and his mother and go to the land of Israel, for those who were trying to take the child's life are dead."

²¹So he got up, took the child and his mother and went to the land of Israel. ²²But when he heard that Archelaus was reigning in Judea in place of his father Herod, he was afraid to go there. Having been warned in a dream, he withdrew to the district of Galilee, ²³and he went and lived in a town called Nazareth. So was fulfilled what was said through the prophets: "He will be called a Nazarene."

John the Baptist Prepares the Way

3 In those days John the Baptist came, preaching in the Desert of Judea ²and saying, "Repent, for the kingdom of heaven is near." ³This is he who was spoken of through the prophet Isaiah:

"A voice of one calling in the
    desert,
'Prepare the way for the Lord,
    make straight paths for
        him.' "ᶜ

⁴John's clothes were made of camel's hair, and he had a leather belt around his waist. His food was locusts and wild honey. ⁵People went out to him from Jerusalem and all Judea and the whole region of the Jordan. ⁶Confessing their sins, they were baptized by him in the Jordan River.

⁷But when he saw many of the Pharisees and Sadducees coming to where he was baptizing, he said to them: "You brood of vipers! Who warned you to flee from the coming wrath? ⁸Produce fruit in keeping with repentance. ⁹And do not think you can say to yourselves, 'We have Abraham as our father.' I tell you that out of these stones God can raise up children for Abraham. ¹⁰The ax is already at the root of the trees, and every tree that does not produce good fruit will be cut down and thrown into the fire.

¹¹"I baptize you withᵈ water for repentance. But after me will come one who is more powerful than I, whose sandals I am not fit to carry. He will baptize you with the Holy Spirit and with fire. ¹²His winnowing fork is in his hand, and he will clear his threshing floor, gathering his wheat into the barn and burning up the chaff with unquenchable fire."

ᵃ15 Hosea 11:1   ᵇ18 Jer. 31:15   ᶜ3 Isaiah 40:3   ᵈ11 Or in

The Baptism of Jesus

[13]Then Jesus came from Galilee to the Jordan to be baptized by John. [14]But John tried to deter him, saying, "I need to be baptized by you, and do you come to me?"

[15]Jesus replied, "Let it be so now; it is proper for us to do this to fulfill all righteousness." Then John consented.

[16]As soon as Jesus was baptized, he went up out of the water. At that moment heaven was opened, and he saw the Spirit of God descending like a dove and lighting on him. [17]And a voice from heaven said, "This is my Son, whom I love; with him I am well pleased."

The Temptation of Jesus

4 Then Jesus was led by the Spirit into the desert to be tempted by the devil. [2]After fasting forty days and forty nights, he was hungry. [3]The tempter came to him and said, "If you are the Son of God, tell these stones to become bread."

[4]Jesus answered, "It is written: 'Man does not live on bread alone, but on every word that comes from the mouth of God.'[a]"

[5]Then the devil took him to the holy city and had him stand on the highest point of the temple. [6]"If you are the Son of God," he said, "throw yourself down. For it is written:

" 'He will command his angels
    concerning you,
  and they will lift you up in
    their hands,
so that you will not strike your
    foot against a stone.'[b]"

[7]Jesus answered him, "It is also written: 'Do not put the Lord your God to the test.'[c]"

[8]Again, the devil took him to a very high mountain and showed him all the kingdoms of the world and their splendor. [9]"All this I will give you," he said, "if you will bow down and worship me."

[10]Jesus said to him, "Away from me, Satan! For it is written: 'Worship the Lord your God, and serve him only.'[d]"

[11]Then the devil left him, and angels came and attended him.

Jesus Begins to Preach

[12]When Jesus heard that John had been put in prison, he returned to Galilee. [13]Leaving Nazareth, he went and lived in Capernaum, which was by the lake in the area of Zebulun and Naphtali— [14]to fulfill what was said through the prophet Isaiah:

[15]"Land of Zebulun and land of
      Naphtali,
   the way to the sea, along the
      Jordan,
   Galilee of the Gentiles—
[16]the people living in darkness
   have seen a great light;
 on those living in the land of the
      shadow of death
   a light has dawned."[e]

[17]From that time on Jesus began to preach, "Repent, for the kingdom of heaven is near."

The Calling of the First Disciples

[18]As Jesus was walking beside the Sea of Galilee, he saw two brothers, Simon called Peter and his brother Andrew. They were casting a net into the lake, for they were fishermen. [19]"Come, follow me," Jesus said, "and I will make you fishers of men." [20]At once they left their nets and followed him.

[21]Going on from there, he saw two other brothers, James son of Zebedee and his brother John. They were in a boat with their father Zebedee, preparing their nets. Jesus called them, [22]and immediately they left the boat and their father and followed him.

Jesus Heals the Sick

[23]Jesus went throughout Galilee, teaching in their synagogues, preaching the good news of the kingdom, and healing every disease and sick-

---

[a]4 Deut. 8:3   [b]6 Psalm 91:11,12   [c]7 Deut. 6:16   [d]10 Deut. 6:13   [e]16 Isaiah 9:1,2

ness among the people. ²⁴News about him spread all over Syria, and people brought to him all who were ill with various diseases, those suffering severe pain, the demon-possessed, those having seizures, and the paralyzed, and he healed them. ²⁵Large crowds from Galilee, the Decapolis,ᵃ Jerusalem, Judea and the region across the Jordan followed him.

The Beatitudes

5 Now when he saw the crowds, he went up on a mountainside and sat down. His disciples came to him, ²and he began to teach them, saying:

ᵃ25 That is, the Ten Cities

VERSE:
Matthew 4:1

AUTHOR:
Charles H. Spurgeon

PASSAGE:
Matthew 4:1–11

Watchful in All Seasons

When Satan tempts us, his sparks fall on kindling, but when Satan tempted Christ, his sparks fell on water. If the devil struck when there were no results, how much harder will he work on the flammable material of our hearts. Even if you become greatly sanctified by the Holy Spirit, that great dog of hell will bark at you.

In this world we expect temptation. Even seclusion will not keep us from the tempter. Jesus Christ was led away from human society and into a wilderness where he was tempted by the devil.

Do you think that only the worldly-minded have dreadful and blasphemous temptations? Spiritual people also endure this, and those in the holiest position may suffer the darkest of temptations . . .

If you can tell me when God will permit a Christian to lay aside the armor, I will tell you when Satan will stop tempting. Like the old knights at war, we must sleep with our helmet and breastplate buckled on. The archdeceiver will seize our unguarded moments to make us his prey. May the Lord keep us watchful in all seasons.

ADDITIONAL SCRIPTURE READINGS
Matthew 26:36–46; Hebrews 2:5–18

Go to page 1202 for your next devotional reading.

VERSE:	AUTHOR:	PASSAGE:
Matthew 5:3	Max Lucado	Matthew 5:1–12

A Sacred Delight

How do you change your heart? Jesus gave the plan on the mountain. Back away from the beatitudes once more and view them in sequence.

The first step is an admission of poverty: "Blessed are the poor in spirit." God's gladness is not received by those who earn it, but by those who admit they *don't* deserve it . . .

The second step is sorrow: "Blessed are those who mourn." Joy comes to those who are sincerely sorry for their sin. We discover gladness when we leave the prison of pride and repent of our rebellion.

Sorrow is followed by meekness. The meek are those who are willing to be used by God. Amazed that God would save them, they are just as surprised that God could use them . . .

The result of the first three steps? Hunger. Never have you seen anything like what is happening! You admit sin—you get saved. You confess weakness—you receive strength. You say you are sorry—you find forgiveness. It's a zany, unpredictable path, full, of pleasant encounters . . .

Then comes mercy. The more you receive, the more you give. You find it easier to give grace because you realize you have been given so much . . .

For the first time in your life, you have found a permanent joy, a joy that is not dependent upon your whims and actions. It's a joy from God, a joy no one can take away from you. A sacred delight is placed in your heart. It is sacred because only God can grant it. It is a delight because you would never expect it.

ADDITIONAL SCRIPTURE READINGS
Psalm 4; John 15:1–17

Go to page 1205 for your next devotional reading.

³"Blessed are the poor in spirit,
  for theirs is the kingdom of
    heaven.
⁴Blessed are those who mourn,
  for they will be comforted.
⁵Blessed are the meek,
  for they will inherit the earth.
⁶Blessed are those who hunger and
    thirst for righteousness,
  for they will be filled.
⁷Blessed are the merciful,
  for they will be shown mercy.
⁸Blessed are the pure in heart,
  for they will see God.
⁹Blessed are the peacemakers,
  for they will be called sons of
    God.
¹⁰Blessed are those who are
    persecuted because of
    righteousness,
  for theirs is the kingdom of
    heaven.

¹¹"Blessed are you when people insult you, persecute you and falsely say all kinds of evil against you because of me. ¹²Rejoice and be glad, because great is your reward in heaven, for in the same way they persecuted the prophets who were before you.

Salt and Light

¹³"You are the salt of the earth. But if the salt loses its saltiness, how can it be made salty again? It is no longer good for anything, except to be thrown out and trampled by men.

¹⁴"You are the light of the world. A city on a hill cannot be hidden. ¹⁵Neither do people light a lamp and put it under a bowl. Instead they put it on its stand, and it gives light to everyone in the house. ¹⁶In the same way, let your light shine before men, that they may see your good deeds and praise your Father in heaven.

The Fulfillment of the Law

¹⁷"Do not think that I have come to abolish the Law or the Prophets; I have not come to abolish them but to fulfill them. ¹⁸I tell you the truth, until heaven and earth disappear, not the smallest letter, not the least stroke of a pen, will by any means disappear from the Law until everything is accomplished. ¹⁹Anyone who breaks one of the least of these commandments and teaches others to do the same will be called least in the kingdom of heaven, but whoever practices and teaches these commands will be called great in the kingdom of heaven. ²⁰For I tell you that unless your righteousness surpasses that of the Pharisees and the teachers of the law, you will certainly not enter the kingdom of heaven.

Murder

²¹"You have heard that it was said to the people long ago, 'Do not murder,ᵃ and anyone who murders will be subject to judgment.' ²²But I tell you that anyone who is angry with his brotherᵇ will be subject to judgment. Again, anyone who says to his brother, 'Raca,'ᶜ is answerable to the Sanhedrin. But anyone who says, 'You fool!' will be in danger of the fire of hell.

²³"Therefore, if you are offering your gift at the altar and there remember that your brother has something against you, ²⁴leave your gift there in front of the altar. First go and be reconciled to your brother; then come and offer your gift.

²⁵"Settle matters quickly with your adversary who is taking you to court. Do it while you are still with him on the way, or he may hand you over to the judge, and the judge may hand you over to the officer, and you may be thrown into prison. ²⁶I tell you the truth, you will not get out until you have paid the last penny.ᵈ

Adultery

²⁷"You have heard that it was said, 'Do not commit adultery.'ᵉ ²⁸But I tell you that anyone who looks at a woman lustfully has already committed adultery with her in his heart. ²⁹If

ᵃ21 Exodus 20:13   ᵇ22 Some manuscripts brother without cause   ᶜ22 An Aramaic term of contempt   ᵈ26 Greek kodrantes   ᵉ27 Exodus 20:14

your right eye causes you to sin, gouge it out and throw it away. It is better for you to lose one part of your body than for your whole body to be thrown into hell. 30And if your right hand causes you to sin, cut it off and throw it away. It is better for you to lose one part of your body than for your whole body to go into hell.

Divorce

31"It has been said, 'Anyone who divorces his wife must give her a certificate of divorce.'*a* 32But I tell you that anyone who divorces his wife, except for marital unfaithfulness, causes her to become an adulteress, and anyone who marries the divorced woman commits adultery.

Oaths

33"Again, you have heard that it was said to the people long ago, 'Do not break your oath, but keep the oaths you have made to the Lord.' 34But I tell you, Do not swear at all: either by heaven, for it is God's throne; 35or by the earth, for it is his footstool; or by Jerusalem, for it is the city of the Great King. 36And do not swear by your head, for you cannot make even one hair white or black. 37Simply let your 'Yes' be 'Yes,' and your 'No,' 'No'; anything beyond this comes from the evil one.

An Eye for an Eye

38"You have heard that it was said, 'Eye for eye, and tooth for tooth.'*b* 39But I tell you, Do not resist an evil person. If someone strikes you on the right cheek, turn to him the other also. 40And if someone wants to sue you and take your tunic, let him have your cloak as well. 41If someone forces you to go one mile, go with him two miles. 42Give to the one who asks you, and do not turn away from the one who wants to borrow from you.

Love for Enemies

43"You have heard that it was said,

'Love your neighbor*c* and hate your enemy.' 44But I tell you: Love your enemies*d* and pray for those who persecute you, 45that you may be sons of your Father in heaven. He causes his sun to rise on the evil and the good, and sends rain on the righteous and the unrighteous. 46If you love those who love you, what reward will you get? Are not even the tax collectors doing that? 47And if you greet only your brothers, what are you doing more than others? Do not even pagans do that? 48Be perfect, therefore, as your heavenly Father is perfect.

Giving to the Needy

6 "Be careful not to do your 'acts of righteousness' before men, to be seen by them. If you do, you will have no reward from your Father in heaven.

2"So when you give to the needy, do not announce it with trumpets, as the hypocrites do in the synagogues and on the streets, to be honored by men. I tell you the truth, they have received their reward in full. 3But when you give to the needy, do not let your left hand know what your right hand is doing, 4so that your giving may be in secret. Then your Father, who sees what is done in secret, will reward you.

Prayer

5"And when you pray, do not be like the hypocrites, for they love to pray standing in the synagogues and on the street corners to be seen by men. I tell you the truth, they have received their reward in full. 6But when you pray, go into your room, close the door and pray to your Father, who is unseen. Then your Father, who sees what is done in secret, will reward you. 7And when you pray, do not keep on babbling like pagans, for they think they will be heard because of their many words. 8Do

---

a31 Deut. 24:1   *b38* Exodus 21:24; Lev. 24:20; Deut. 19:21   *c43* Lev. 19:18   *d44* Some late manuscripts *enemies, bless those who curse you, do good to those who hate you*

not be like them, for your Father knows what you need before you ask him.

9"This, then, is how you should pray:

" 'Our Father in heaven,
hallowed be your name,

10your kingdom come,
  your will be done
    on earth as it is in heaven.
11Give us today our daily bread.
12Forgive us our debts,
    as we also have forgiven our
      debtors.
13And lead us not into temptation,

VERSE: AUTHOR: PASSAGE:
Matthew 5:44   Lewis B. Smedes   Matthew 5:43–48

But I Tell You . . .

We have seen the unpredictable, outrageous and creative thing we do when we forgive another human being.

We reverse the flow of seemingly irreversible history . . . of our own history . . . We reverse the flow of pain that began in the past when someone hurt us, a flow that filters into our present to wound our memory and poison our future. We heal ourselves.

It is utterly *unpredictable*; no one could suspect, in the nature of things, in the natural cause and effect of things, that anyone should ever forgive . . .

It is *outrageous*. When we do it we commit an outrage against the strict morality that will not rest with anything short of an even score.

It is *creative*: when we forgive we come as close as any human being can to the essentially divine act of creation. For we create a new act of beginning out of past pain that never had a right to exist in the first place. We create healing for the future by changing a past that had no possibility in it for anything but sickness and death.

When we forgive we ride the crest of love's cosmic wave; we walk in stride with God. And we heal the hurt we never deserved.

ADDITIONAL SCRIPTURE READINGS
Matthew 18:21–35; Colossians 3:12–17

Go to page 1207 for your next devotional reading.

but deliver us from the evil one.*a*'

14For if you forgive men when they sin against you, your heavenly Father will also forgive you. 15But if you do not forgive men their sins, your Father will not forgive your sins.

Fasting

16"When you fast, do not look somber as the hypocrites do, for they disfigure their faces to show men they are fasting. I tell you the truth, they have received their reward in full. 17But when you fast, put oil on your head and wash your face, 18so that it will not be obvious to men that you are fasting, but only to your Father, who is unseen; and your Father, who sees what is done in secret, will reward you.

Treasures in Heaven

19"Do not store up for yourselves treasures on earth, where moth and rust destroy, and where thieves break in and steal. 20But store up for yourselves treasures in heaven, where moth and rust do not destroy, and where thieves do not break in and steal. 21For where your treasure is, there your heart will be also.

22"The eye is the lamp of the body. If your eyes are good, your whole body will be full of light. 23But if your eyes are bad, your whole body will be full of darkness. If then the light within you is darkness, how great is that darkness!

24"No one can serve two masters. Either he will hate the one and love the other, or he will be devoted to the one and despise the other. You cannot serve both God and Money.

Do Not Worry

25"Therefore I tell you, do not worry about your life, what you will eat or drink; or about your body, what you will wear. Is not life more important than food, and the body more im-portant than clothes? 26Look at the birds of the air; they do not sow or reap or store away in barns, and yet your heavenly Father feeds them. Are you not much more valuable than they? 27Who of you by worrying can add a single hour to his life*b*?

28"And why do you worry about clothes? See how the lilies of the field grow. They do not labor or spin. 29Yet I tell you that not even Solomon in all his splendor was dressed like one of these. 30If that is how God clothes the grass of the field, which is here today and tomorrow is thrown into the fire, will he not much more clothe you, O you of little faith? 31So do not worry, saying, 'What shall we eat?' or 'What shall we drink?' or 'What shall we wear?' 32For the pagans run after all these things, and your heavenly Father knows that you need them. 33But seek first his kingdom and his righteousness, and all these things will be given to you as well. 34Therefore do not worry about tomorrow, for tomorrow will worry about itself. Each day has enough trouble of its own.

Judging Others

7 "Do not judge, or you too will be judged. 2For in the same way you judge others, you will be judged, and with the measure you use, it will be measured to you.

3"Why do you look at the speck of sawdust in your brother's eye and pay no attention to the plank in your own eye? 4How can you say to your brother, 'Let me take the speck out of your eye,' when all the time there is a plank in your own eye? 5You hypocrite, first take the plank out of your own eye, and then you will see clearly to remove the speck from your brother's eye.

6"Do not give dogs what is sacred; do not throw your pearls to pigs. If you do, they may trample them under their feet, and then turn and tear you to pieces.

---

*a*13 Or *from evil*; some late manuscripts *one, | for yours is the kingdom and the power and the glory forever. Amen.*   *b*27 Or *single cubit to his height*

VERSE:
Matthew 6:33

AUTHOR:
Henri J.M. Nouwen

PASSAGE:
Matthew 6:25–34

Seek First His Kingdom

Jesus does not respond to our worry-filled way of living by saying that we should not be so busy with worldly affairs. He does not try to pull us away from the many events, activities and people that make up our lives. He does not tell us that what we do is unimportant, valueless or useless . . .

Jesus' response to our worry-filled lives is quite different. He asks us to shift the point of gravity, to relocate the center of our attention, to change our priorities. Jesus wants us to move from the "many things" to the "one necessary thing." It is important for us to realize that Jesus in no way wants us to leave our many-faceted world. Rather, he wants us to live in it, but firmly rooted in the center of all things . . .

What is this center? Jesus calls it the kingdom, the kingdom of his Father. For us of the twentieth century, this may not have much meaning. Kings and kingdoms do not play an important role in our daily life. But only when we understand Jesus' words as an urgent call to make the life of God's Spirit our priority can we see better what is at stake. A heart set on the Father's kingdom is also a heart set on the spiritual life. To set our hearts on the kingdom therefore means to make the life of the Spirit within and among us the center of all we think, say or do.

ADDITIONAL SCRIPTURE READINGS
Psalm 27; Luke 10:38–42

Go to page 1214 for your next devotional reading.

Ask, Seek, Knock

⁷"Ask and it will be given to you; seek and you will find; knock and the door will be opened to you. ⁸For everyone who asks receives; he who seeks finds; and to him who knocks, the door will be opened.

⁹"Which of you, if his son asks for bread, will give him a stone? ¹⁰Or if he asks for a fish, will give him a snake? ¹¹If you, then, though you are evil, know how to give good gifts to your children, how much more will your Father in heaven give good gifts to those who ask him! ¹²So in everything, do to others what you would have them do to you, for this sums up the Law and the Prophets.

The Narrow and Wide Gates

¹³"Enter through the narrow gate. For wide is the gate and broad is the road that leads to destruction, and many enter through it. ¹⁴But small is the gate and narrow the road that leads to life, and only a few find it.

A Tree and Its Fruit

¹⁵"Watch out for false prophets. They come to you in sheep's clothing, but inwardly they are ferocious wolves. ¹⁶By their fruit you will recognize them. Do people pick grapes from thornbushes, or figs from thistles? ¹⁷Likewise every good tree bears good fruit, but a bad tree bears bad fruit. ¹⁸A good tree cannot bear bad fruit, and a bad tree cannot bear good fruit. ¹⁹Every tree that does not bear good fruit is cut down and thrown into the fire. ²⁰Thus, by their fruit you will recognize them.

²¹"Not everyone who says to me, 'Lord, Lord,' will enter the kingdom of heaven, but only he who does the will of my Father who is in heaven. ²²Many will say to me on that day, 'Lord, Lord, did we not prophesy in your name, and in your name drive out demons and perform many miracles?' ²³Then I will tell them plainly, 'I

never knew you. Away from me, you evildoers!'

The Wise and Foolish Builders

²⁴"Therefore everyone who hears these words of mine and puts them into practice is like a wise man who built his house on the rock. ²⁵The rain came down, the streams rose, and the winds blew and beat against that house; yet it did not fall, because it had its foundation on the rock. ²⁶But everyone who hears these words of mine and does not put them into practice is like a foolish man who built his house on sand. ²⁷The rain came down, the streams rose, and the winds blew and beat against that house, and it fell with a great crash."

²⁸When Jesus had finished saying these things, the crowds were amazed at his teaching, ²⁹because he taught as one who had authority, and not as their teachers of the law.

The Man With Leprosy

8 When he came down from the mountainside, large crowds followed him. ²A man with leprosy[a] came and knelt before him and said, "Lord, if you are willing, you can make me clean."

³Jesus reached out his hand and touched the man. "I am willing," he said. "Be clean!" Immediately he was cured[b] of his leprosy. ⁴Then Jesus said to him, "See that you don't tell anyone. But go, show yourself to the priest and offer the gift Moses commanded, as a testimony to them."

The Faith of the Centurion

⁵When Jesus had entered Capernaum, a centurion came to him, asking for help. ⁶"Lord," he said, "my servant lies at home paralyzed and in terrible suffering."

⁷Jesus said to him, "I will go and heal him."

⁸The centurion replied, "Lord, I do not deserve to have you come under

a2 The Greek word was used for various diseases affecting the skin—not necessarily leprosy.
b3 Greek made clean

my roof. But just say the word, and my servant will be healed. ⁹For I myself am a man under authority, with soldiers under me. I tell this one, 'Go,' and he goes; and that one, 'Come,' and he comes. I say to my servant, 'Do this,' and he does it."

¹⁰When Jesus heard this, he was astonished and said to those following him, "I tell you the truth, I have not found anyone in Israel with such great faith. ¹¹I say to you that many will come from the east and the west, and will take their places at the feast with Abraham, Isaac and Jacob in the kingdom of heaven. ¹²But the subjects of the kingdom will be thrown outside, into the darkness, where there will be weeping and gnashing of teeth."

¹³Then Jesus said to the centurion, "Go! It will be done just as you believed it would." And his servant was healed at that very hour.

Jesus Heals Many

¹⁴When Jesus came into Peter's house, he saw Peter's mother-in-law lying in bed with a fever. ¹⁵He touched her hand and the fever left her, and she got up and began to wait on him.

¹⁶When evening came, many who were demon-possessed were brought to him, and he drove out the spirits with a word and healed all the sick. ¹⁷This was to fulfill what was spoken through the prophet Isaiah:

"He took up our infirmities
and carried our diseases."ᵃ

The Cost of Following Jesus

¹⁸When Jesus saw the crowd around him, he gave orders to cross to the other side of the lake. ¹⁹Then a teacher of the law came to him and said, "Teacher, I will follow you wherever you go."

²⁰Jesus replied, "Foxes have holes and birds of the air have nests, but the Son of Man has no place to lay his head."

²¹Another disciple said to him, "Lord, first let me go and bury my father."

²²But Jesus told him, "Follow me, and let the dead bury their own dead."

Jesus Calms the Storm

²³Then he got into the boat and his disciples followed him. ²⁴Without warning, a furious storm came up on the lake, so that the waves swept over the boat. But Jesus was sleeping. ²⁵The disciples went and woke him, saying, "Lord, save us! We're going to drown!"

²⁶He replied, "You of little faith, why are you so afraid?" Then he got up and rebuked the winds and the waves, and it was completely calm.

²⁷The men were amazed and asked, "What kind of man is this? Even the winds and the waves obey him!"

The Healing of Two Demon-possessed Men

²⁸When he arrived at the other side in the region of the Gadarenes,ᵇ two demon-possessed men coming from the tombs met him. They were so violent that no one could pass that way. ²⁹"What do you want with us, Son of God?" they shouted. "Have you come here to torture us before the appointed time?"

³⁰Some distance from them a large herd of pigs was feeding. ³¹The demons begged Jesus, "If you drive us out, send us into the herd of pigs."

³²He said to them, "Go!" So they came out and went into the pigs, and the whole herd rushed down the steep bank into the lake and died in the water. ³³Those tending the pigs ran off, went into the town and reported all this, including what had happened to the demon-possessed men. ³⁴Then the whole town went out to meet Jesus. And when they saw him, they pleaded with him to leave their region.

ᵃ17 Isaiah 53:4   ᵇ28 Some manuscripts *Gergesenes*; others *Gerasenes*

Jesus Heals a Paralytic

9 Jesus stepped into a boat, crossed over and came to his own town. [2]Some men brought to him a paralytic, lying on a mat. When Jesus saw their faith, he said to the paralytic, "Take heart, son; your sins are forgiven."

[3]At this, some of the teachers of the law said to themselves, "This fellow is blaspheming!"

[4]Knowing their thoughts, Jesus said, "Why do you entertain evil thoughts in your hearts? [5]Which is easier: to say, 'Your sins are forgiven,' or to say, 'Get up and walk'? [6]But so that you may know that the Son of Man has authority on earth to forgive sins. . . ." Then he said to the paralytic, "Get up, take your mat and go home." [7]And the man got up and went home. [8]When the crowd saw this, they were filled with awe; and they praised God, who had given such authority to men.

The Calling of Matthew

[9]As Jesus went on from there, he saw a man named Matthew sitting at the tax collector's booth. "Follow me," he told him, and Matthew got up and followed him.

[10]While Jesus was having dinner at Matthew's house, many tax collectors and "sinners" came and ate with him and his disciples. [11]When the Pharisees saw this, they asked his disciples, "Why does your teacher eat with tax collectors and 'sinners'?"

[12]On hearing this, Jesus said, "It is not the healthy who need a doctor, but the sick. [13]But go and learn what this means: 'I desire mercy, not sacrifice.'[a] For I have not come to call the righteous, but sinners."

Jesus Questioned About Fasting

[14]Then John's disciples came and asked him, "How is it that we and the Pharisees fast, but your disciples do not fast?"

[15]Jesus answered, "How can the guests of the bridegroom mourn while he is with them? The time will come when the bridegroom will be taken from them; then they will fast.

[16]"No one sews a patch of unshrunk cloth on an old garment, for the patch will pull away from the garment, making the tear worse. [17]Neither do men pour new wine into old wineskins. If they do, the skins will burst, the wine will run out and the wineskins will be ruined. No, they pour new wine into new wineskins, and both are preserved."

A Dead Girl and a Sick Woman

[18]While he was saying this, a ruler came and knelt before him and said, "My daughter has just died. But come and put your hand on her, and she will live." [19]Jesus got up and went with him, and so did his disciples.

[20]Just then a woman who had been subject to bleeding for twelve years came up behind him and touched the edge of his cloak. [21]She said to herself, "If I only touch his cloak, I will be healed."

[22]Jesus turned and saw her. "Take heart, daughter," he said, "your faith has healed you." And the woman was healed from that moment.

[23]When Jesus entered the ruler's house and saw the flute players and the noisy crowd, [24]he said, "Go away. The girl is not dead but asleep." But they laughed at him. [25]After the crowd had been put outside, he went in and took the girl by the hand, and she got up. [26]News of this spread through all that region.

Jesus Heals the Blind and Mute

[27]As Jesus went on from there, two blind men followed him, calling out, "Have mercy on us, Son of David!"

[28]When he had gone indoors, the blind men came to him, and he asked them, "Do you believe that I am able to do this?"

"Yes, Lord," they replied.

[29]Then he touched their eyes and said, "According to your faith will it

[a]13 Hosea 6:6

be done to you"; [30]and their sight was restored. Jesus warned them sternly, "See that no one knows about this." [31]But they went out and spread the news about him all over that region.

[32]While they were going out, a man who was demon-possessed and could not talk was brought to Jesus. [33]And when the demon was driven out, the man who had been mute spoke. The crowd was amazed and said, "Nothing like this has ever been seen in Israel."

[34]But the Pharisees said, "It is by the prince of demons that he drives out demons."

The Workers Are Few

[35]Jesus went through all the towns and villages, teaching in their synagogues, preaching the good news of the kingdom and healing every disease and sickness. [36]When he saw the crowds, he had compassion on them, because they were harassed and helpless, like sheep without a shepherd. [37]Then he said to his disciples, "The harvest is plentiful but the workers are few. [38]Ask the Lord of the harvest, therefore, to send out workers into his harvest field."

Jesus Sends Out the Twelve

10 He called his twelve disciples to him and gave them authority to drive out evil[a] spirits and to heal every disease and sickness.

[2]These are the names of the twelve apostles: first, Simon (who is called Peter) and his brother Andrew; James son of Zebedee, and his brother John; [3]Philip and Bartholomew; Thomas and Matthew the tax collector; James son of Alphaeus, and Thaddaeus; [4]Simon the Zealot and Judas Iscariot, who betrayed him.

[5]These twelve Jesus sent out with the following instructions: "Do not go among the Gentiles or enter any town of the Samaritans. [6]Go rather to the lost sheep of Israel. [7]As you go, preach this message: 'The kingdom of

heaven is near.' [8]Heal the sick, raise the dead, cleanse those who have leprosy,[b] drive out demons. Freely you have received, freely give. [9]Do not take along any gold or silver or copper in your belts; [10]take no bag for the journey, or extra tunic, or sandals or a staff; for the worker is worth his keep.

[11]"Whatever town or village you enter, search for some worthy person there and stay at his house until you leave. [12]As you enter the home, give it your greeting. [13]If the home is deserving, let your peace rest on it; if it is not, let your peace return to you. [14]If anyone will not welcome you or listen to your words, shake the dust off your feet when you leave that home or town. [15]I tell you the truth, it will be more bearable for Sodom and Gomorrah on the day of judgment than for that town. [16]I am sending you out like sheep among wolves. Therefore be as shrewd as snakes and as innocent as doves.

[17]"Be on your guard against men; they will hand you over to the local councils and flog you in their synagogues. [18]On my account you will be brought before governors and kings as witnesses to them and to the Gentiles. [19]But when they arrest you, do not worry about what to say or how to say it. At that time you will be given what to say, [20]for it will not be you speaking, but the Spirit of your Father speaking through you.

[21]"Brother will betray brother to death, and a father his child; children will rebel against their parents and have them put to death. [22]All men will hate you because of me, but he who stands firm to the end will be saved. [23]When you are persecuted in one place, flee to another. I tell you the truth, you will not finish going through the cities of Israel before the Son of Man comes.

[24]"A student is not above his teacher, nor a servant above his master. [25]It is enough for the student to be like his teacher, and the servant like his mas-

---

[a]1 Greek *unclean*   [b]8 The Greek word was used for various diseases affecting the skin—not necessarily leprosy.

ter. If the head of the house has been called Beelzebub,*a* how much more the members of his household!

26"So do not be afraid of them. There is nothing concealed that will not be disclosed, or hidden that will not be made known. 27What I tell you in the dark, speak in the daylight; what is whispered in your ear, proclaim from the roofs. 28Do not be afraid of those who kill the body but cannot kill the soul. Rather, be afraid of the One who can destroy both soul and body in hell. 29Are not two sparrows sold for a penny*b*? Yet not one of them will fall to the ground apart from the will of your Father. 30And even the very hairs of your head are all numbered. 31So don't be afraid; you are worth more than many sparrows.

32"Whoever acknowledges me before men, I will also acknowledge him before my Father in heaven. 33But whoever disowns me before men, I will disown him before my Father in heaven.

34"Do not suppose that I have come to bring peace to the earth. I did not come to bring peace, but a sword. 35For I have come to turn

" 'a man against his father,
    a daughter against her mother,
a daughter-in-law against her
        mother-in-law—
36   a man's enemies will be the
        members of his own
        household.'*c*

37"Anyone who loves his father or mother more than me is not worthy of me; anyone who loves his son or daughter more than me is not worthy of me; 38and anyone who does not take his cross and follow me is not worthy of me. 39Whoever finds his life will lose it, and whoever loses his life for my sake will find it.

40"He who receives you receives me, and he who receives me receives the one who sent me. 41Anyone who

receives a prophet because he is a prophet will receive a prophet's reward, and anyone who receives a righteous man because he is a righteous man will receive a righteous man's reward. 42And if anyone gives even a cup of cold water to one of these little ones because he is my disciple, I tell you the truth, he will certainly not lose his reward."

Jesus and John the Baptist

11 After Jesus had finished instructing his twelve disciples, he went on from there to teach and preach in the towns of Galilee.*d*

2When John heard in prison what Christ was doing, he sent his disciples 3to ask him, "Are you the one who was to come, or should we expect someone else?"

4Jesus replied, "Go back and report to John what you hear and see: 5The blind receive sight, the lame walk, those who have leprosy*e* are cured, the deaf hear, the dead are raised, and the good news is preached to the poor. 6Blessed is the man who does not fall away on account of me."

7As John's disciples were leaving, Jesus began to speak to the crowd about John: "What did you go out into the desert to see? A reed swayed by the wind? 8If not, what did you go out to see? A man dressed in fine clothes? No, those who wear fine clothes are in kings' palaces. 9Then what did you go out to see? A prophet? Yes, I tell you, and more than a prophet. 10This is the one about whom it is written:

" 'I will send my messenger ahead
        of you,
    who will prepare your way
        before you.'*f*

11I tell you the truth: Among those born of women there has not risen anyone greater than John the Baptist; yet he who is least in the kingdom of heaven is greater than he. 12From the

---

*a*25 Greek *Beezeboul* or *Beelzeboul*   *b*29 Greek *an assarion*   *c*36 Micah 7:6   *d*1 Greek *in their towns*   *e*5 The Greek word was used for various diseases affecting the skin—not necessarily leprosy.   *f*10 Mal. 3:1

days of John the Baptist until now, the kingdom of heaven has been forcefully advancing, and forceful men lay hold of it. [13]For all the Prophets and the Law prophesied until John. [14]And if you are willing to accept it, he is the Elijah who was to come. [15]He who has ears, let him hear.

[16]"To what can I compare this generation? They are like children sitting in the marketplaces and calling out to others:

[17]" 'We played the flute for you,
    and you did not dance;
  we sang a dirge,
    and you did not mourn.'

[18]For John came neither eating nor drinking, and they say, 'He has a demon.' [19]The Son of Man came eating and drinking, and they say, 'Here is a glutton and a drunkard, a friend of tax collectors and "sinners." ' But wisdom is proved right by her actions."

Woe on Unrepentant Cities

[20]Then Jesus began to denounce the cities in which most of his miracles had been performed, because they did not repent. [21]"Woe to you, Korazin! Woe to you, Bethsaida! If the miracles that were performed in you had been performed in Tyre and Sidon, they would have repented long ago in sackcloth and ashes. [22]But I tell you, it will be more bearable for Tyre and Sidon on the day of judgment than for you. [23]And you, Capernaum, will you be lifted up to the skies? No, you will go down to the depths.[a] If the miracles that were performed in you had been performed in Sodom, it would have remained to this day. [24]But I tell you that it will be more bearable for Sodom on the day of judgment than for you."

Rest for the Weary

[25]At that time Jesus said, "I praise you, Father, Lord of heaven and earth, because you have hidden these things from the wise and learned, and revealed them to little children. [26]Yes, Father, for this was your good pleasure.

[27]"All things have been committed to me by my Father. No one knows the Son except the Father, and no one knows the Father except the Son and those to whom the Son chooses to reveal him.

[28]"Come to me, all you who are weary and burdened, and I will give you rest. [29]Take my yoke upon you and learn from me, for I am gentle and humble in heart, and you will find rest for your souls. [30]For my yoke is easy and my burden is light."

Lord of the Sabbath

12 At that time Jesus went through the grainfields on the Sabbath. His disciples were hungry and began to pick some heads of grain and eat them. [2]When the Pharisees saw this, they said to him, "Look! Your disciples are doing what is unlawful on the Sabbath."

[3]He answered, "Haven't you read what David did when he and his companions were hungry? [4]He entered the house of God, and he and his companions ate the consecrated bread—which was not lawful for them to do, but only for the priests. [5]Or haven't you read in the Law that on the Sabbath the priests in the temple desecrate the day and yet are innocent? [6]I tell you that one[b] greater than the temple is here. [7]If you had known what these words mean, 'I desire mercy, not sacrifice,'[c] you would not have condemned the innocent. [8]For the Son of Man is Lord of the Sabbath."

[9]Going on from that place, he went into their synagogue, [10]and a man with a shriveled hand was there. Looking for a reason to accuse Jesus, they asked him, "Is it lawful to heal on the Sabbath?"

[11]He said to them, "If any of you has a sheep and it falls into a pit on the Sabbath, will you not take hold of it and lift it out? [12]How much more valuable is a man than a sheep! There-

---

[a]23 Greek *Hades*   [b]6 Or *something*; also in verses 41 and 42   [c]7 Hosea 6:6

fore it is lawful to do good on the Sabbath."

¹³Then he said to the man, "Stretch
out your hand." So he stretched it out
and it was completely restored, just as
sound as the other. ¹⁴But the Pharisees
went out and plotted how they might
kill Jesus.

God's Chosen Servant

¹⁵Aware of this, Jesus withdrew
from that place. Many followed him,
and he healed all their sick, ¹⁶warning
them not to tell who he was. ¹⁷This
was to fulfill what was spoken
through the prophet Isaiah:

VERSE:	AUTHOR:	PASSAGE:
Matthew 11:30	Hannah Whitall Smith	Matthew 11:25–30

He Will Give You Rest

I knew a Christian lady who had a very heavy temporal
burden ... One day, when it seemed especially heavy,
she noticed lying on the table near her a little tract called
"Hannah's Faith." Attracted by the title, she picked it up
and began to read it, little knowing, however, that it was
to create a revolution in her whole experience. The story
was of a poor woman who had been carried triumphantly through a life of unusual sorrow. She was giving
the history of her life to a kind visitor on one occasion,
and at the close the visitor said feelingly, "Oh, Hannah, I
do not see how you could bear so much sorrow!" "I did
not bear it," was the quick reply; "the Lord bore it for
me." "Yes," said the visitor, "that is the right way. We
must take our troubles to the Lord." "Yes," replied Hannah, "but we must do more than that: we must *leave* them
there. Most people take their burdens to him, but they
bring them away with them again, and are just as worried and unhappy as ever. But I take mine and I leave
them with him, and come away and forget them. If the
worry comes back, I take it to him again; and I do this
over and over, until at last I just forget I have any worries, and am at perfect rest."

ADDITIONAL SCRIPTURE READINGS
Isaiah 30:15–18; 1 Peter 5:1–11

Go to page 1218 for your next devotional reading.

[18]"Here is my servant whom I have
    chosen,
  the one I love, in whom I
    delight;
  I will put my Spirit on him,
    and he will proclaim justice to
    the nations.
[19]He will not quarrel or cry out;
  no one will hear his voice in the
    streets.
[20]A bruised reed he will not break,
  and a smoldering wick he will
    not snuff out,
  till he leads justice to victory.
[21] In his name the nations will put
    their hope." [a]

Jesus and Beelzebub

[22]Then they brought him a demon-possessed man who was blind and mute, and Jesus healed him, so that he could both talk and see. [23]All the people were astonished and said, "Could this be the Son of David?"

[24]But when the Pharisees heard this, they said, "It is only by Beelzebub,[b] the prince of demons, that this fellow drives out demons."

[25]Jesus knew their thoughts and said to them, "Every kingdom divided against itself will be ruined, and every city or household divided against itself will not stand. [26]If Satan drives out Satan, he is divided against himself. How then can his kingdom stand? [27]And if I drive out demons by Beelzebub, by whom do your people drive them out? So then, they will be your judges. [28]But if I drive out demons by the Spirit of God, then the kingdom of God has come upon you.

[29]"Or again, how can anyone enter a strong man's house and carry off his possessions unless he first ties up the strong man? Then he can rob his house.

[30]"He who is not with me is against me, and he who does not gather with me scatters. [31]And so I tell you, every sin and blasphemy will be forgiven men, but the blasphemy against the Spirit will not be forgiven. [32]Anyone who speaks a word against the Son of Man will be forgiven, but anyone who speaks against the Holy Spirit will not be forgiven, either in this age or in the age to come.

[33]"Make a tree good and its fruit will be good, or make a tree bad and its fruit will be bad, for a tree is recognized by its fruit. [34]You brood of vipers, how can you who are evil say anything good? For out of the overflow of the heart the mouth speaks. [35]The good man brings good things out of the good stored up in him, and the evil man brings evil things out of the evil stored up in him. [36]But I tell you that men will have to give account on the day of judgment for every careless word they have spoken. [37]For by your words you will be acquitted, and by your words you will be condemned."

The Sign of Jonah

[38]Then some of the Pharisees and teachers of the law said to him, "Teacher, we want to see a miraculous sign from you."

[39]He answered, "A wicked and adulterous generation asks for a miraculous sign! But none will be given it except the sign of the prophet Jonah. [40]For as Jonah was three days and three nights in the belly of a huge fish, so the Son of Man will be three days and three nights in the heart of the earth. [41]The men of Nineveh will stand up at the judgment with this generation and condemn it; for they repented at the preaching of Jonah, and now one[c] greater than Jonah is here. [42]The Queen of the South will rise at the judgment with this generation and condemn it; for she came from the ends of the earth to listen to Solomon's wisdom, and now one greater than Solomon is here.

[43]"When an evil[d] spirit comes out of a man, it goes through arid places seeking rest and does not find it. [44]Then it says, 'I will return to the house I left.' When it arrives, it finds

---

[a]21 Isaiah 42:1-4   [b]24 Greek *Beezeboul* or *Beelzeboul*; also in verse 27   [c]41 Or *something*; also
in verse 42   [d]43 Greek *unclean*

the house unoccupied, swept clean and put in order. ⁴⁵Then it goes and takes with it seven other spirits more wicked than itself, and they go in and live there. And the final condition of that man is worse than the first. That is how it will be with this wicked generation."

Jesus' Mother and Brothers

⁴⁶While Jesus was still talking to the crowd, his mother and brothers stood outside, wanting to speak to him. ⁴⁷Someone told him, "Your mother and brothers are standing outside, wanting to speak to you."ᵃ ⁴⁸He replied to him, "Who is my mother, and who are my brothers?" ⁴⁹Pointing to his disciples, he said, "Here are my mother and my brothers. ⁵⁰For whoever does the will of my Father in heaven is my brother and sister and mother."

The Parable of the Sower

13 That same day Jesus went out of the house and sat by the lake. ²Such large crowds gathered around him that he got into a boat and sat in it, while all the people stood on the shore. ³Then he told them many things in parables, saying: "A farmer went out to sow his seed. ⁴As he was scattering the seed, some fell along the path, and the birds came and ate it up. ⁵Some fell on rocky places, where it did not have much soil. It sprang up quickly, because the soil was shallow. ⁶But when the sun came up, the plants were scorched, and they withered because they had no root. ⁷Other seed fell among thorns, which grew up and choked the plants. ⁸Still other seed fell on good soil, where it produced a crop— a hundred, sixty or thirty times what was sown. ⁹He who has ears, let him hear."

¹⁰The disciples came to him and asked, "Why do you speak to the people in parables?"

¹¹He replied, "The knowledge of the secrets of the kingdom of heaven has been given to you, but not to them. ¹²Whoever has will be given more, and he will have an abundance. Whoever does not have, even what he has will be taken from him. ¹³This is why I speak to them in parables:

"Though seeing, they do not see;
though hearing, they do not
hear or understand.

¹⁴In them is fulfilled the prophecy of Isaiah:

" 'You will be ever hearing but
never understanding;
you will be ever seeing but
never perceiving.
¹⁵For this people's heart has become
calloused;
they hardly hear with their ears,
and they have closed their eyes.
Otherwise they might see with
their eyes,
hear with their ears,
understand with their hearts
and turn, and I would heal
them.'ᵇ

¹⁶But blessed are your eyes because they see, and your ears because they hear. ¹⁷For I tell you the truth, many prophets and righteous men longed to see what you see but did not see it, and to hear what you hear but did not hear it.

¹⁸"Listen then to what the parable of the sower means: ¹⁹When anyone hears the message about the kingdom and does not understand it, the evil one comes and snatches away what was sown in his heart. This is the seed sown along the path. ²⁰The one who received the seed that fell on rocky places is the man who hears the word and at once receives it with joy. ²¹But since he has no root, he lasts only a short time. When trouble or persecution comes because of the word, he quickly falls away. ²²The one who received the seed that fell among the thorns is the man who hears the word, but the worries of this life and the deceitfulness of wealth choke it, making it unfruitful. ²³But the one

---

ᵃ47 Some manuscripts do not have verse 47.　　ᵇ15 Isaiah 6:9,10

who received the seed that fell on good soil is the man who hears the word and understands it. He produces a crop, yielding a hundred, sixty or thirty times what was sown."

The Parable of the Weeds

24Jesus told them another parable: "The kingdom of heaven is like a man who sowed good seed in his field. 25But while everyone was sleeping, his enemy came and sowed weeds among the wheat, and went away. 26When the wheat sprouted and formed heads, then the weeds also appeared.

27"The owner's servants came to him and said, 'Sir, didn't you sow good seed in your field? Where then did the weeds come from?'

28" 'An enemy did this,' he replied.

"The servants asked him, 'Do you want us to go and pull them up?'

29" 'No,' he answered, 'because while you are pulling the weeds, you may root up the wheat with them. 30Let both grow together until the harvest. At that time I will tell the harvesters: First collect the weeds and tie them in bundles to be burned; then gather the wheat and bring it into my barn.' "

The Parables of the Mustard Seed and the Yeast

31He told them another parable: "The kingdom of heaven is like a mustard seed, which a man took and planted in his field. 32Though it is the smallest of all your seeds, yet when it grows, it is the largest of garden plants and becomes a tree, so that the birds of the air come and perch in its branches."

33He told them still another parable: "The kingdom of heaven is like yeast that a woman took and mixed into a large amount*a* of flour until it worked all through the dough."

34Jesus spoke all these things to the crowd in parables; he did not say anything to them without using a para-

ble. 35So was fulfilled what was spoken through the prophet:

"I will open my mouth in parables,
I will utter things hidden since the creation of the world."*b*

The Parable of the Weeds Explained

36Then he left the crowd and went into the house. His disciples came to him and said, "Explain to us the parable of the weeds in the field."

37He answered, "The one who sowed the good seed is the Son of Man. 38The field is the world, and the good seed stands for the sons of the kingdom. The weeds are the sons of the evil one, 39and the enemy who sows them is the devil. The harvest is the end of the age, and the harvesters are angels.

40"As the weeds are pulled up and burned in the fire, so it will be at the end of the age. 41The Son of Man will send out his angels, and they will weed out of his kingdom everything that causes sin and all who do evil. 42They will throw them into the fiery furnace, where there will be weeping and gnashing of teeth. 43Then the righteous will shine like the sun in the kingdom of their Father. He who has ears, let him hear.

The Parables of the Hidden Treasure and the Pearl

44"The kingdom of heaven is like treasure hidden in a field. When a man found it, he hid it again, and then in his joy went and sold all he had and bought that field.

45"Again, the kingdom of heaven is like a merchant looking for fine pearls. 46When he found one of great value, he went away and sold everything he had and bought it.

The Parable of the Net

47"Once again, the kingdom of heaven is like a net that was let down into the lake and caught all kinds of

a33 Greek *three satas* (probably about 1/2 bushel or 22 liters)   *b35* Psalm 78:2

PASSAGE: Matthew 5:3–12; Luke 6:20–23
AUTHOR: Author Unknown

. . . . ● . . . .

Beatitudes on Aging

Blessed are those who *understand*
  my faltering step
  and weakened *hand*.

Blessed are those who know
  that my ears *today*
  must strain to catch the things they *say*.

Blessed are those with a friendly *smile*
  who just stop by to visit a *while*.

Blessed are those who never *say*
  "You have already told that story twice *today*."

Blessed are those who make it *known*
  that I am loved, respected and not *alone*.

Blessed are those who through love and care
  ease the *days*
  of my journey home in so many *ways*.

. . . . ● . . . .

Go to page 1221 for your next devotional reading.

fish. ⁴⁸When it was full, the fishermen pulled it up on the shore. Then they sat down and collected the good fish in baskets, but threw the bad away. ⁴⁹This is how it will be at the end of the age. The angels will come and separate the wicked from the righteous ⁵⁰and throw them into the fiery furnace, where there will be weeping and gnashing of teeth.

⁵¹"Have you understood all these things?" Jesus asked.

"Yes," they replied.

⁵²He said to them, "Therefore every teacher of the law who has been instructed about the kingdom of heaven is like the owner of a house who brings out of his storeroom new treasures as well as old."

A Prophet Without Honor

⁵³When Jesus had finished these parables, he moved on from there. ⁵⁴Coming to his hometown, he began teaching the people in their synagogue, and they were amazed. "Where did this man get this wisdom and these miraculous powers?" they asked. ⁵⁵"Isn't this the carpenter's son? Isn't his mother's name Mary, and aren't his brothers James, Joseph, Simon and Judas? ⁵⁶Aren't all his sisters with us? Where then did this man get all these things?" ⁵⁷And they took offense at him.

But Jesus said to them, "Only in his hometown and in his own house is a prophet without honor."

⁵⁸And he did not do many miracles there because of their lack of faith.

John the Baptist Beheaded

14 At that time Herod the tetrarch heard the reports about Jesus, ²and he said to his attendants, "This is John the Baptist; he has risen from the dead! That is why miraculous powers are at work in him."

³Now Herod had arrested John and bound him and put him in prison because of Herodias, his brother Philip's wife, ⁴for John had been saying to him: "It is not lawful for you to have her." ⁵Herod wanted to kill John, but he was afraid of the people, because they considered him a prophet.

⁶On Herod's birthday the daughter of Herodias danced for them and pleased Herod so much ⁷that he promised with an oath to give her whatever she asked. ⁸Prompted by her mother, she said, "Give me here on a platter the head of John the Baptist." ⁹The king was distressed, but because of his oaths and his dinner guests, he ordered that her request be granted ¹⁰and had John beheaded in the prison. ¹¹His head was brought in on a platter and given to the girl, who carried it to her mother. ¹²John's disciples came and took his body and buried it. Then they went and told Jesus.

Jesus Feeds the Five Thousand

¹³When Jesus heard what had happened, he withdrew by boat privately to a solitary place. Hearing of this, the crowds followed him on foot from the towns. ¹⁴When Jesus landed and saw a large crowd, he had compassion on them and healed their sick.

¹⁵As evening approached, the disciples came to him and said, "This is a remote place, and it's already getting late. Send the crowds away, so they can go to the villages and buy themselves some food."

¹⁶Jesus replied, "They do not need to go away. You give them something to eat."

¹⁷"We have here only five loaves of bread and two fish," they answered.

¹⁸"Bring them here to me," he said. ¹⁹And he directed the people to sit down on the grass. Taking the five loaves and the two fish and looking up to heaven, he gave thanks and broke the loaves. Then he gave them to the disciples, and the disciples gave them to the people. ²⁰They all ate and were satisfied, and the disciples picked up twelve basketfuls of broken pieces that were left over. ²¹The number of those who ate was about five thousand men, besides women and children.

Jesus Walks on the Water

²²Immediately Jesus made the disci-

ples get into the boat and go on ahead of him to the other side, while he dismissed the crowd. ²³After he had dismissed them, he went up on a mountainside by himself to pray. When evening came, he was there alone, ²⁴but the boat was already a considerable distance*ᵃ* from land, buffeted by the waves because the wind was against it.

²⁵During the fourth watch of the night Jesus went out to them, walking on the lake. ²⁶When the disciples saw him walking on the lake, they were terrified. "It's a ghost," they said, and cried out in fear.

²⁷But Jesus immediately said to them: "Take courage! It is I. Don't be afraid."

²⁸"Lord, if it's you," Peter replied, "tell me to come to you on the water."

²⁹"Come," he said.

Then Peter got down out of the boat, walked on the water and came toward Jesus. ³⁰But when he saw the wind, he was afraid and, beginning to sink, cried out, "Lord, save me!"

³¹Immediately Jesus reached out his hand and caught him. "You of little faith," he said, "why did you doubt?"

³²And when they climbed into the boat, the wind died down. ³³Then those who were in the boat worshiped him, saying, "Truly you are the Son of God."

³⁴When they had crossed over, they landed at Gennesaret. ³⁵And when the men of that place recognized Jesus, they sent word to all the surrounding country. People brought all their sick to him ³⁶and begged him to let the sick just touch the edge of his cloak, and all who touched him were healed.

Clean and Unclean

15 Then some Pharisees and teachers of the law came to Jesus from Jerusalem and asked, ²"Why do your disciples break the tradition of the elders? They don't wash their hands before they eat!"

³Jesus replied, "And why do you break the command of God for the sake of your tradition? ⁴For God said, 'Honor your father and mother'*ᵇ* and 'Anyone who curses his father or mother must be put to death.'*ᶜ* ⁵But you say that if a man says to his father or mother, 'Whatever help you might otherwise have received from me is a gift devoted to God,' ⁶he is not to 'honor his father'*ᵈ*' with it. Thus you nullify the word of God for the sake of your tradition. ⁷You hypocrites! Isaiah was right when he prophesied about you:

⁸" 'These people honor me with
        their lips,
    but their hearts are far from me.
⁹They worship me in vain;
    their teachings are but rules
        taught by men.'*ᵉ*"

¹⁰Jesus called the crowd to him and said, "Listen and understand. ¹¹What goes into a man's mouth does not make him 'unclean,' but what comes out of his mouth, that is what makes him 'unclean.' "

¹²Then the disciples came to him and asked, "Do you know that the Pharisees were offended when they heard this?"

¹³He replied, "Every plant that my heavenly Father has not planted will be pulled up by the roots. ¹⁴Leave them; they are blind guides.*ᶠ* If a blind man leads a blind man, both will fall into a pit."

¹⁵Peter said, "Explain the parable to us."

¹⁶"Are you still so dull?" Jesus asked them. ¹⁷"Don't you see that whatever enters the mouth goes into the stomach and then out of the body? ¹⁸But the things that come out of the mouth come from the heart, and these make a man 'unclean.' ¹⁹For out of the heart come evil thoughts, murder, adultery, sexual immorality,

---

ᵃ24 Greek *many stadia*   *ᵇ4* Exodus 20:12; Deut. 5:16   *ᶜ4* Exodus 21:17; Lev. 20:9
ᵈ6 Some manuscripts *father or his mother*   *ᵉ9* Isaiah 29:13   *ᶠ14* Some manuscripts *guides of the blind*

VERSE:
Matthew 14:31

AUTHOR:
Max Lucado

PASSAGE:
Matthew 14:22–36

Fear That Becomes Faith

Faith is often the child of fear. Fear propelled Peter out of the boat. He'd ridden these waves before. He knew what these storms could do ... And he wanted out ...

"Lord, if it's you," Peter says, "tell me to come to you on the water." Peter is not testing Jesus; he is pleading with Jesus. Stepping onto a stormy sea is not a move of logic; it is a move of desperation.

Peter grabs the edge of the boat. Throws out a leg ... follows with the other. Several steps are taken. It's as if an invisible ridge of rocks runs beneath his feet. At the end of the ridge is the glowing face of a never-say-die friend.

We do the same, don't we? We come to Christ in an hour of deep need. We abandon the boat of good works ... We realize, like Peter, that spanning the gap between us and Jesus is a feat too great for our feet. So we beg for help. Hear his voice. And step out in fear, hoping that our little faith will be enough ...

Some of us, unlike Peter, never look back. Others of us, like Peter, feel the wind and are afraid. Maybe we face the wind of pride: "I'm not such a bad sinner after all. Look at what I can do." Perhaps we face the wind of legalism: "I know that Jesus is doing part of this, but I have to do the rest." Most of us, though, face the wind of doubt: "I'm too bad for God to treat me this well. I don't deserve such a rescue."

And downward we plunge ... With our heads barely above the water, we have to make a decision ... We know Peter's choice: "Beginning to sink, [he] cried out, 'Lord, save me!' Immediately Jesus reached out his hand and caught him."

ADDITIONAL SCRIPTURE READINGS
Psalm 56; 1 John 4:13–18

Go to page 1224 for your next devotional reading.

theft, false testimony, slander. [20]These are what make a man 'unclean'; but eating with unwashed hands does not make him 'unclean.' "

The Faith of the Canaanite Woman

[21]Leaving that place, Jesus withdrew to the region of Tyre and Sidon. [22]A Canaanite woman from that vicinity came to him, crying out, "Lord, Son of David, have mercy on me! My daughter is suffering terribly from demon-possession."

[23]Jesus did not answer a word. So his disciples came to him and urged him, "Send her away, for she keeps crying out after us."

[24]He answered, "I was sent only to the lost sheep of Israel."

[25]The woman came and knelt before him. "Lord, help me!" she said.

[26]He replied, "It is not right to take the children's bread and toss it to their dogs."

[27]"Yes, Lord," she said, "but even the dogs eat the crumbs that fall from their masters' table."

[28]Then Jesus answered, "Woman, you have great faith! Your request is granted." And her daughter was healed from that very hour.

Jesus Feeds the Four Thousand

[29]Jesus left there and went along the Sea of Galilee. Then he went up on a mountainside and sat down. [30]Great crowds came to him, bringing the lame, the blind, the crippled, the mute and many others, and laid them at his feet; and he healed them. [31]The people were amazed when they saw the mute speaking, the crippled made well, the lame walking and the blind seeing. And they praised the God of Israel.

[32]Jesus called his disciples to him and said, "I have compassion for these people; they have already been with me three days and have nothing to eat. I do not want to send them away hungry, or they may collapse on the way."

[33]His disciples answered, "Where could we get enough bread in this remote place to feed such a crowd?"

[34]"How many loaves do you have?" Jesus asked.

"Seven," they replied, "and a few small fish."

[35]He told the crowd to sit down on the ground. [36]Then he took the seven loaves and the fish, and when he had given thanks, he broke them and gave them to the disciples, and they in turn to the people. [37]They all ate and were satisfied. Afterward the disciples picked up seven basketfuls of broken pieces that were left over. [38]The number of those who ate was four thousand, besides women and children. [39]After Jesus had sent the crowd away, he got into the boat and went to the vicinity of Magadan.

The Demand for a Sign

16 The Pharisees and Sadducees came to Jesus and tested him by asking him to show them a sign from heaven.

[2]He replied,[a] "When evening comes, you say, 'It will be fair weather, for the sky is red,' [3]and in the morning, 'Today it will be stormy, for the sky is red and overcast.' You know how to interpret the appearance of the sky, but you cannot interpret the signs of the times. [4]A wicked and adulterous generation looks for a miraculous sign, but none will be given it except the sign of Jonah." Jesus then left them and went away.

The Yeast of the Pharisees and Sadducees

[5]When they went across the lake, the disciples forgot to take bread. [6]"Be careful," Jesus said to them. "Be on your guard against the yeast of the Pharisees and Sadducees."

[7]They discussed this among themselves and said, "It is because we didn't bring any bread."

[8]Aware of their discussion, Jesus asked, "You of little faith, why are you talking among yourselves about

---

[a]2 Some early manuscripts do not have the rest of verse 2 and all of verse 3.

having no bread? ⁹Do you still not understand? Don't you remember the five loaves for the five thousand, and how many basketfuls you gathered? ¹⁰Or the seven loaves for the four thousand, and how many basketfuls you gathered? ¹¹How is it you don't understand that I was not talking to you about bread? But be on your guard against the yeast of the Pharisees and Sadducees." ¹²Then they understood that he was not telling them to guard against the yeast used in bread, but against the teaching of the Pharisees and Sadducees.

Peter's Confession of Christ

¹³When Jesus came to the region of Caesarea Philippi, he asked his disciples, "Who do people say the Son of Man is?"

¹⁴They replied, "Some say John the Baptist; others say Elijah; and still others, Jeremiah or one of the prophets."

¹⁵"But what about you?" he asked. "Who do you say I am?"

¹⁶Simon Peter answered, "You are the Christ,ᵃ the Son of the living God."

¹⁷Jesus replied, "Blessed are you, Simon son of Jonah, for this was not revealed to you by man, but by my Father in heaven. ¹⁸And I tell you that you are Peter,ᵇ and on this rock I will build my church, and the gates of Hadesᶜ will not overcome it.ᵈ ¹⁹I will give you the keys of the kingdom of heaven; whatever you bind on earth will beᵉ bound in heaven, and whatever you loose on earth will beᵉ loosed in heaven." ²⁰Then he warned his disciples not to tell anyone that he was the Christ.

Jesus Predicts His Death

²¹From that time on Jesus began to explain to his disciples that he must go to Jerusalem and suffer many things at the hands of the elders, chief priests and teachers of the law, and that he must be killed and on the third day be raised to life.

²²Peter took him aside and began to rebuke him. "Never, Lord!" he said. "This shall never happen to you!"

²³Jesus turned and said to Peter, "Get behind me, Satan! You are a stumbling block to me; you do not have in mind the things of God, but the things of men."

²⁴Then Jesus said to his disciples, "If anyone would come after me, he must deny himself and take up his cross and follow me. ²⁵For whoever wants to save his lifeᶠ will lose it, but whoever loses his life for me will find it. ²⁶What good will it be for a man if he gains the whole world, yet forfeits his soul? Or what can a man give in exchange for his soul? ²⁷For the Son of Man is going to come in his Father's glory with his angels, and then he will reward each person according to what he has done. ²⁸I tell you the truth, some who are standing here will not taste death before they see the Son of Man coming in his kingdom."

The Transfiguration

17 After six days Jesus took with him Peter, James and John the brother of James, and led them up a high mountain by themselves. ²There he was transfigured before them. His face shone like the sun, and his clothes became as white as the light. ³Just then there appeared before them Moses and Elijah, talking with Jesus.

⁴Peter said to Jesus, "Lord, it is good for us to be here. If you wish, I will put up three shelters—one for you, one for Moses and one for Elijah."

⁵While he was still speaking, a bright cloud enveloped them, and a voice from the cloud said, "This is my Son, whom I love; with him I am well pleased. Listen to him!"

⁶When the disciples heard this, they fell facedown to the ground, ter-

---

ᵃ16 Or *Messiah*; also in verse 20   ᵇ18 *Peter* means *rock.*   ᶜ18 Or *hell*   ᵈ18 Or *not prove stronger than it*   ᵉ19 Or *have been*   ᶠ25 The Greek word means either *life* or *soul*; also in verse 26.

| VERSE: | AUTHOR: | PASSAGE: |
| Matthew 16:25 | Charles Colson | Matthew 16:21–28 |

Losing Your Life

During a visit to Australia, I was interviewed by a well-known radio host. As the program drew to a close, he posed one last question, "Mr. Colson, you are an unusual person. You have conquered the pinnacles of secular success. The goals most people strive their whole lives for, you have achieved—only to see it all collapse as you fell from the White House to prison. But now you're out, leading a new life as a Christian. It's like having lived two lives. How would you sum up the meaning of those two lives?"

I glanced at the clock. Only 20 seconds remained in the live broadcast. Then in a flash the "short" answer came. "If my life stands for anything," I said quickly, "it is the truth of the teaching of Jesus Christ, 'whoever wants to save his life will lose it, but whoever loses his life for me will find it. What good will it be for a man if he gains the whole world, yet forfeits his soul?'" . . .

Certainly those words do embody a staggering paradox. But in my life I've experienced the truth of those words.

I had spent my first 40 years seeking the whole world, to the neglect of my soul. But what I couldn't find in my quest for power and success—true security and meaning—I discovered in prison where all worldly props had been stripped away. And by God's grace, I lost my life that I might find true life in Christ.

ADDITIONAL SCRIPTURE READINGS
Matthew 10:32–42; John 12:20–33

Go to page 1226 for your next devotional reading.

rified. **7**But Jesus came and touched them. "Get up," he said. "Don't be afraid." **8**When they looked up, they saw no one except Jesus.

9As they were coming down the mountain, Jesus instructed them, "Don't tell anyone what you have seen, until the Son of Man has been raised from the dead."

10The disciples asked him, "Why then do the teachers of the law say that Elijah must come first?"

11Jesus replied, "To be sure, Elijah comes and will restore all things. **12**But I tell you, Elijah has already come, and they did not recognize him, but have done to him everything they wished. In the same way the Son of Man is going to suffer at their hands." **13**Then the disciples understood that he was talking to them about John the Baptist.

The Healing of a Boy With a Demon

14When they came to the crowd, a man approached Jesus and knelt before him. **15**"Lord, have mercy on my son," he said. "He has seizures and is suffering greatly. He often falls into the fire or into the water. **16**I brought him to your disciples, but they could not heal him."

17"O unbelieving and perverse generation," Jesus replied, "how long shall I stay with you? How long shall I put up with you? Bring the boy here to me." **18**Jesus rebuked the demon, and it came out of the boy, and he was healed from that moment.

19Then the disciples came to Jesus in private and asked, "Why couldn't we drive it out?"

20He replied, "Because you have so little faith. I tell you the truth, if you have faith as small as a mustard seed, you can say to this mountain, 'Move from here to there' and it will move. Nothing will be impossible for you.*a*"

22When they came together in Galilee, he said to them, "The Son of Man is going to be betrayed into the hands of men. **23**They will kill him, and on the third day he will be raised to life." And the disciples were filled with grief.

The Temple Tax

24After Jesus and his disciples arrived in Capernaum, the collectors of the two-drachma tax came to Peter and asked, "Doesn't your teacher pay the temple tax*b*?"

25"Yes, he does," he replied.

When Peter came into the house, Jesus was the first to speak. "What do you think, Simon?" he asked. "From whom do the kings of the earth collect duty and taxes—from their own sons or from others?"

26"From others," Peter answered.

"Then the sons are exempt," Jesus said to him. **27**"But so that we may not offend them, go to the lake and throw out your line. Take the first fish you catch; open its mouth and you will find a four-drachma coin. Take it and give it to them for my tax and yours."

The Greatest in the Kingdom of Heaven

18 At that time the disciples came to Jesus and asked, "Who is the greatest in the kingdom of heaven?"

2He called a little child and had him stand among them. **3**And he said: "I tell you the truth, unless you change and become like little children, you will never enter the kingdom of heaven. **4**Therefore, whoever humbles himself like this child is the greatest in the kingdom of heaven.

5"And whoever welcomes a little child like this in my name welcomes me. **6**But if anyone causes one of these little ones who believe in me to sin, it would be better for him to have a large millstone hung around his neck and to be drowned in the depths of the sea.

7"Woe to the world because of the things that cause people to sin! Such

a20 Some manuscripts you. 21But this kind does not go out except by prayer and fasting.
b24 Greek the two drachmas

things must come, but woe to the man through whom they come! ⁸If your hand or your foot causes you to sin, cut it off and throw it away. It is better for you to enter life maimed or crippled than to have two hands or two feet and be thrown into eternal fire. ⁹And if your eye causes you to sin, gouge it out and throw it away. It is better for you to enter life with one eye than to have two eyes and be thrown into the fire of hell.

The Parable of the Lost Sheep

¹⁰"See that you do not look down on one of these little ones. For I tell you that their angels in heaven always see the face of my Father in heaven.ᵃ

¹²"What do you think? If a man owns a hundred sheep, and one of them wanders away, will he not leave the ninety-nine on the hills and go to look for the one that wandered off? ¹³And if he finds it, I tell you the

ᵃ10 Some manuscripts *heaven.* ¹¹*The Son of Man came to save what was lost.*

VERSE:	AUTHOR:	PASSAGE:
Matthew 18:3	John Knox	Matthew 18:1–6

Like Little Children

I am looking at a picture received yesterday of my latest grandchild—a picture taken the very day of his birth. I have many happy and grateful thoughts as I gaze at it, but beneath them all is a wonderment amounting to awe . . .

Here he is, this little man, every feature and organ intact and in place, the intricately balanced whole perfectly adapted to his intricately complicated new environment. In the wildest flight of fancy can we conceive of a miracle more miraculous than this? And yet no less amazing and inexplicable, no less wonderful is every common thing in our common life; and we should be able to see it so if we were able to keep this baby's fresh, new eyes . . .

God reveals to babes what is hidden from the wise and prudent and that only to the extent we are able to turn, and become like little children, is it given us to see the kingdom of God.

ADDITIONAL SCRIPTURE READINGS
Matthew 11:25–30; Mark 10:13–16

Go to page 1228 for your next devotional reading.

truth, he is happier about that one sheep than about the ninety-nine that did not wander off. ¹⁴In the same way your Father in heaven is not willing that any of these little ones should be lost.

A Brother Who Sins Against You

¹⁵"If your brother sins against you,ᵃ go and show him his fault, just between the two of you. If he listens to you, you have won your brother over. ¹⁶But if he will not listen, take one or two others along, so that 'every matter may be established by the testimony of two or three witnesses.'ᵇ ¹⁷If he refuses to listen to them, tell it to the church; and if he refuses to listen even to the church, treat him as you would a pagan or a tax collector.

¹⁸"I tell you the truth, whatever you bind on earth will beᶜ bound in heaven, and whatever you loose on earth will beᶜ loosed in heaven.

¹⁹"Again, I tell you that if two of you on earth agree about anything you ask for, it will be done for you by my Father in heaven. ²⁰For where two or three come together in my name, there am I with them."

The Parable of the Unmerciful Servant

²¹Then Peter came to Jesus and asked, "Lord, how many times shall I forgive my brother when he sins against me? Up to seven times?"

²²Jesus answered, "I tell you, not seven times, but seventy-seven times.ᵈ

²³"Therefore, the kingdom of heaven is like a king who wanted to settle accounts with his servants. ²⁴As he began the settlement, a man who owed him ten thousand talentsᵉ was brought to him. ²⁵Since he was not able to pay, the master ordered that he and his wife and his children and all that he had be sold to repay the debt.

²⁶"The servant fell on his knees be-

fore him. 'Be patient with me,' he begged, 'and I will pay back everything.' ²⁷The servant's master took pity on him, canceled the debt and let him go.

²⁸"But when that servant went out, he found one of his fellow servants who owed him a hundred denarii.ᶠ He grabbed him and began to choke him. 'Pay back what you owe me!' he demanded.

²⁹"His fellow servant fell to his knees and begged him, 'Be patient with me, and I will pay you back.'

³⁰"But he refused. Instead, he went off and had the man thrown into prison until he could pay the debt. ³¹When the other servants saw what had happened, they were greatly distressed and went and told their master everything that had happened.

³²"Then the master called the servant in. 'You wicked servant,' he said, 'I canceled all that debt of yours because you begged me to. ³³Shouldn't you have had mercy on your fellow servant just as I had on you?' ³⁴In anger his master turned him over to the jailers to be tortured, until he should pay back all he owed.

³⁵"This is how my heavenly Father will treat each of you unless you forgive your brother from your heart."

Divorce

19 When Jesus had finished saying these things, he left Galilee and went into the region of Judea to the other side of the Jordan. ²Large crowds followed him, and he healed them there.

³Some Pharisees came to him to test him. They asked, "Is it lawful for a man to divorce his wife for any and every reason?"

⁴"Haven't you read," he replied, "that at the beginning the Creator 'made them male and female,'ᵍ ⁵and said, 'For this reason a man will leave his father and mother and be united to his wife, and the two will become

ᵃ15 Some manuscripts do not have against you.   ᵇ16 Deut. 19:15   ᶜ18 Or have been
ᵈ22 Or seventy times seven   ᵉ24 That is, millions of dollars   ᶠ28 That is, a few dollars
ᵍ4 Gen. 1:27

one flesh'[a]? [6]So they are no longer two, but one. Therefore what God has joined together, let man not separate."

[7]"Why then," they asked, "did Moses command that a man give his wife a certificate of divorce and send her away?"

[8]Jesus replied, "Moses permitted you to divorce your wives because your hearts were hard. But it was not this way from the beginning. [9]I tell you that anyone who divorces his wife, except for marital unfaithfulness, and marries another woman commits adultery."

[10]The disciples said to him, "If this is the situation between a husband and wife, it is better not to marry."

[a]5 Gen. 2:24

THURSDAY

VERSE:	AUTHOR:	PASSAGE:
Matthew 18:22	Ben Patterson	Matthew 18:21–35

Bad News . . . or Good?

Peter once asked Jesus how many times he should forgive one who had sinned against him. Suggesting a possible statute of limitations, he asked, "Up to seven times?" Jesus answered, "I tell you, not seven times, but seventy-seven times" (Matthew 18:21–22). Jesus was not expanding the outside limits of forgiveness, he was exploding them! He was saying we should always forgive, times without number. At first that is bad news, of a sort. It tells me I must keep on forgiving the nuisance who repeatedly offends me. But underneath it is unimaginably good news — it tells me that is how often God forgives me! He simply doesn't give up on me. His promises will not fail because of my failures . . .

As we trust a God as merciful and as faithful as this — who will not hold our sins against us, but who will hold us up against our sins — even the memory of our sins can become a cause for joy. We can be filled with hope as we wait for God's promise because we know our sins will not cancel his promise.

ADDITIONAL SCRIPTURE READINGS
Psalm 103; Ephesians 4:25 — 5:2

Go to page 1238 for your next devotional reading.

¹¹Jesus replied, "Not everyone can accept this word, but only those to whom it has been given. ¹²For some are eunuchs because they were born that way; others were made that way by men; and others have renounced marriage^a because of the kingdom of heaven. The one who can accept this should accept it."

The Little Children and Jesus

¹³Then little children were brought to Jesus for him to place his hands on them and pray for them. But the disciples rebuked those who brought them.

¹⁴Jesus said, "Let the little children come to me, and do not hinder them, for the kingdom of heaven belongs to such as these." ¹⁵When he had placed his hands on them, he went on from there.

The Rich Young Man

¹⁶Now a man came up to Jesus and asked, "Teacher, what good thing must I do to get eternal life?"

¹⁷"Why do you ask me about what is good?" Jesus replied. "There is only One who is good. If you want to enter life, obey the commandments."

¹⁸"Which ones?" the man inquired.

Jesus replied, " 'Do not murder, do not commit adultery, do not steal, do not give false testimony, ¹⁹honor your father and mother,'^b and 'love your neighbor as yourself.'^c"

²⁰"All these I have kept," the young man said. "What do I still lack?"

²¹Jesus answered, "If you want to be perfect, go, sell your possessions and give to the poor, and you will have treasure in heaven. Then come, follow me."

²²When the young man heard this, he went away sad, because he had great wealth.

²³Then Jesus said to his disciples, "I tell you the truth, it is hard for a rich man to enter the kingdom of heaven. ²⁴Again I tell you, it is easier for a camel to go through the eye of a nee-

dle than for a rich man to enter the kingdom of God."

²⁵When the disciples heard this, they were greatly astonished and asked, "Who then can be saved?"

²⁶Jesus looked at them and said, "With man this is impossible, but with God all things are possible."

²⁷Peter answered him, "We have left everything to follow you! What then will there be for us?"

²⁸Jesus said to them, "I tell you the truth, at the renewal of all things, when the Son of Man sits on his glorious throne, you who have followed me will also sit on twelve thrones, judging the twelve tribes of Israel. ²⁹And everyone who has left houses or brothers or sisters or father or mother^d or children or fields for my sake will receive a hundred times as much and will inherit eternal life. ³⁰But many who are first will be last, and many who are last will be first.

The Parable of the Workers in the Vineyard

20 "For the kingdom of heaven is like a landowner who went out early in the morning to hire men to work in his vineyard. ²He agreed to pay them a denarius for the day and sent them into his vineyard.

³"About the third hour he went out and saw others standing in the marketplace doing nothing. ⁴He told them, 'You also go and work in my vineyard, and I will pay you whatever is right.' ⁵So they went.

"He went out again about the sixth hour and the ninth hour and did the same thing. ⁶About the eleventh hour he went out and found still others standing around. He asked them, 'Why have you been standing here all day long doing nothing?'

⁷" 'Because no one has hired us,' they answered.

"He said to them, 'You also go and work in my vineyard.'

⁸"When evening came, the owner of the vineyard said to his foreman,

---

^a12 Or *have made themselves eunuchs*   ^b19 Exodus 20:12-16; Deut. 5:16-20   ^c19 Lev. 19:18
^d29 Some manuscripts *mother or wife*

'Call the workers and pay them their wages, beginning with the last ones hired and going on to the first.'

⁹"The workers who were hired about the eleventh hour came and each received a denarius. ¹⁰So when those came who were hired first, they expected to receive more. But each one of them also received a denarius. ¹¹When they received it, they began to grumble against the landowner. ¹²'These men who were hired last worked only one hour,' they said, 'and you have made them equal to us who have borne the burden of the work and the heat of the day.'

¹³"But he answered one of them, 'Friend, I am not being unfair to you. Didn't you agree to work for a denarius? ¹⁴Take your pay and go. I want to give the man who was hired last the same as I gave you. ¹⁵Don't I have the right to do what I want with my own money? Or are you envious because I am generous?'

¹⁶"So the last will be first, and the first will be last."

Jesus Again Predicts His Death

¹⁷Now as Jesus was going up to Jerusalem, he took the twelve disciples aside and said to them, ¹⁸"We are going up to Jerusalem, and the Son of Man will be betrayed to the chief priests and the teachers of the law. They will condemn him to death ¹⁹and will turn him over to the Gentiles to be mocked and flogged and crucified. On the third day he will be raised to life!"

A Mother's Request

²⁰Then the mother of Zebedee's sons came to Jesus with her sons and, kneeling down, asked a favor of him.

²¹"What is it you want?" he asked.

She said, "Grant that one of these two sons of mine may sit at your right and the other at your left in your kingdom."

²²"You don't know what you are asking," Jesus said to them. "Can you drink the cup I am going to drink?"

"We can," they answered.

²³Jesus said to them, "You will indeed drink from my cup, but to sit at my right or left is not for me to grant. These places belong to those for whom they have been prepared by my Father."

²⁴When the ten heard about this, they were indignant with the two brothers. ²⁵Jesus called them together and said, "You know that the rulers of the Gentiles lord it over them, and their high officials exercise authority over them. ²⁶Not so with you. Instead, whoever wants to become great among you must be your servant, ²⁷and whoever wants to be first must be your slave— ²⁸just as the Son of Man did not come to be served, but to serve, and to give his life as a ransom for many."

Two Blind Men Receive Sight

²⁹As Jesus and his disciples were leaving Jericho, a large crowd followed him. ³⁰Two blind men were sitting by the roadside, and when they heard that Jesus was going by, they shouted, "Lord, Son of David, have mercy on us!"

³¹The crowd rebuked them and told them to be quiet, but they shouted all the louder, "Lord, Son of David, have mercy on us!"

³²Jesus stopped and called them. "What do you want me to do for you?" he asked.

³³"Lord," they answered, "we want our sight."

³⁴Jesus had compassion on them and touched their eyes. Immediately they received their sight and followed him.

The Triumphal Entry

21 As they approached Jerusalem and came to Bethphage on the Mount of Olives, Jesus sent two disciples, ²saying to them, "Go to the village ahead of you, and at once you will find a donkey tied there, with her colt by her. Untie them and bring them to me. ³If anyone says anything to you, tell him that the Lord needs them, and he will send them right away."

[4]This took place to fulfill what was spoken through the prophet:

[5]"Say to the Daughter of Zion,
    'See, your king comes to you,
gentle and riding on a donkey,
    on a colt, the foal of a
        donkey.' "[a]

[6]The disciples went and did as Jesus had instructed them. [7]They brought the donkey and the colt, placed their cloaks on them, and Jesus sat on them. [8]A very large crowd spread their cloaks on the road, while others cut branches from the trees and spread them on the road. [9]The crowds that went ahead of him and those that followed shouted,

"Hosanna[b] to the Son of David!"

"Blessed is he who comes in the
    name of the Lord!"[c]

"Hosanna[b] in the highest!"

[10]When Jesus entered Jerusalem, the whole city was stirred and asked, "Who is this?"

[11]The crowds answered, "This is Jesus, the prophet from Nazareth in Galilee."

Jesus at the Temple

[12]Jesus entered the temple area and drove out all who were buying and selling there. He overturned the tables of the money changers and the benches of those selling doves. [13]"It is written," he said to them, " 'My house will be called a house of prayer,'[d] but you are making it a 'den of robbers.'[e]"

[14]The blind and the lame came to him at the temple, and he healed them. [15]But when the chief priests and the teachers of the law saw the wonderful things he did and the children shouting in the temple area, "Hosanna to the Son of David," they were indignant.

[16]"Do you hear what these children are saying?" they asked him.

"Yes," replied Jesus, "have you never read,

" 'From the lips of children and
        infants
    you have ordained praise'[f]?"

[17]And he left them and went out of the city to Bethany, where he spent the night.

The Fig Tree Withers

[18]Early in the morning, as he was on his way back to the city, he was hungry. [19]Seeing a fig tree by the road, he went up to it but found nothing on it except leaves. Then he said to it, "May you never bear fruit again!" Immediately the tree withered.

[20]When the disciples saw this, they were amazed. "How did the fig tree wither so quickly?" they asked.

[21]Jesus replied, "I tell you the truth, if you have faith and do not doubt, not only can you do what was done to the fig tree, but also you can say to this mountain, 'Go, throw yourself into the sea,' and it will be done. [22]If you believe, you will receive whatever you ask for in prayer."

The Authority of Jesus Questioned

[23]Jesus entered the temple courts, and, while he was teaching, the chief priests and the elders of the people came to him. "By what authority are you doing these things?" they asked. "And who gave you this authority?"

[24]Jesus replied, "I will also ask you one question. If you answer me, I will tell you by what authority I am doing these things. [25]John's baptism—where did it come from? Was it from heaven, or from men?"

They discussed it among themselves and said, "If we say, 'From heaven,' he will ask, 'Then why didn't you believe him?' [26]But if we say, 'From men'—we are afraid of the people, for they all hold that John was a prophet."

---

[a]5 Zech. 9:9   [b]9 A Hebrew expression meaning "Save!" which became an exclamation of praise; also in verse 15   [c]9 Psalm 118:26   [d]13 Isaiah 56:7   [e]13 Jer. 7:11   [f]16 Psalm 8:2

²⁷So they answered Jesus, "We don't know."

Then he said, "Neither will I tell you by what authority I am doing these things.

The Parable of the Two Sons

²⁸"What do you think? There was a man who had two sons. He went to the first and said, 'Son, go and work today in the vineyard.'

²⁹" 'I will not,' he answered, but later he changed his mind and went.

³⁰"Then the father went to the other son and said the same thing. He answered, 'I will, sir,' but he did not go.

³¹"Which of the two did what his father wanted?"

"The first," they answered.

Jesus said to them, "I tell you the truth, the tax collectors and the prostitutes are entering the kingdom of God ahead of you. ³²For John came to you to show you the way of righteousness, and you did not believe him, but the tax collectors and the prostitutes did. And even after you saw this, you did not repent and believe him.

The Parable of the Tenants

³³"Listen to another parable: There was a landowner who planted a vineyard. He put a wall around it, dug a winepress in it and built a watchtower. Then he rented the vineyard to some farmers and went away on a journey. ³⁴When the harvest time approached, he sent his servants to the tenants to collect his fruit.

³⁵"The tenants seized his servants; they beat one, killed another, and stoned a third. ³⁶Then he sent other servants to them, more than the first time, and the tenants treated them the same way. ³⁷Last of all, he sent his son to them. 'They will respect my son,' he said.

³⁸"But when the tenants saw the son, they said to each other, 'This is the heir. Come, let's kill him and take his inheritance.' ³⁹So they took him and threw him out of the vineyard and killed him.

⁴⁰"Therefore, when the owner of the vineyard comes, what will he do to those tenants?"

⁴¹"He will bring those wretches to a wretched end," they replied, "and he will rent the vineyard to other tenants, who will give him his share of the crop at harvest time."

⁴²Jesus said to them, "Have you never read in the Scriptures:

" 'The stone the builders rejected
    has become the capstone[a];
the Lord has done this,
    and it is marvelous in our
        eyes'[b]?

⁴³"Therefore I tell you that the kingdom of God will be taken away from you and given to a people who will produce its fruit. ⁴⁴He who falls on this stone will be broken to pieces, but he on whom it falls will be crushed."[c]

⁴⁵When the chief priests and the Pharisees heard Jesus' parables, they knew he was talking about them. ⁴⁶They looked for a way to arrest him, but they were afraid of the crowd because the people held that he was a prophet.

The Parable of the Wedding Banquet

22 Jesus spoke to them again in parables, saying: ²"The kingdom of heaven is like a king who prepared a wedding banquet for his son. ³He sent his servants to those who had been invited to the banquet to tell them to come, but they refused to come.

⁴"Then he sent some more servants and said, 'Tell those who have been invited that I have prepared my dinner: My oxen and fattened cattle have been butchered, and everything is ready. Come to the wedding banquet.'

⁵"But they paid no attention and went off—one to his field, another to his business. ⁶The rest seized his servants, mistreated them and killed

---

a42 Or cornerstone   b42 Psalm 118:22,23   c44 Some manuscripts do not have verse 44.

them. [7]The king was enraged. He sent his army and destroyed those murderers and burned their city.

[8]"Then he said to his servants, 'The wedding banquet is ready, but those I invited did not deserve to come. [9]Go to the street corners and invite to the banquet anyone you find.' [10]So the servants went out into the streets and gathered all the people they could find, both good and bad, and the wedding hall was filled with guests.

[11]"But when the king came in to see the guests, he noticed a man there who was not wearing wedding clothes. [12]'Friend,' he asked, 'how did you get in here without wedding clothes?' The man was speechless.

[13]"Then the king told the attendants, 'Tie him hand and foot, and throw him outside, into the darkness, where there will be weeping and gnashing of teeth.'

[14]"For many are invited, but few are chosen."

Paying Taxes to Caesar

[15]Then the Pharisees went out and laid plans to trap him in his words. [16]They sent their disciples to him along with the Herodians. "Teacher," they said, "we know you are a man of integrity and that you teach the way of God in accordance with the truth. You aren't swayed by men, because you pay no attention to who they are. [17]Tell us then, what is your opinion? Is it right to pay taxes to Caesar or not?"

[18]But Jesus, knowing their evil intent, said, "You hypocrites, why are you trying to trap me? [19]Show me the coin used for paying the tax." They brought him a denarius, [20]and he asked them, "Whose portrait is this? And whose inscription?"

[21]"Caesar's," they replied.

Then he said to them, "Give to Caesar what is Caesar's, and to God what is God's."

[22]When they heard this, they were amazed. So they left him and went away.

Marriage at the Resurrection

[23]That same day the Sadducees, who say there is no resurrection, came to him with a question. [24]"Teacher," they said, "Moses told us that if a man dies without having children, his brother must marry the widow and have children for him. [25]Now there were seven brothers among us. The first one married and died, and since he had no children, he left his wife to his brother. [26]The same thing happened to the second and third brother, right on down to the seventh. [27]Finally, the woman died. [28]Now then, at the resurrection, whose wife will she be of the seven, since all of them were married to her?"

[29]Jesus replied, "You are in error because you do not know the Scriptures or the power of God. [30]At the resurrection people will neither marry nor be given in marriage; they will be like the angels in heaven. [31]But about the resurrection of the dead— have you not read what God said to you, [32]'I am the God of Abraham, the God of Isaac, and the God of Jacob'[a]? He is not the God of the dead but of the living."

[33]When the crowds heard this, they were astonished at his teaching.

The Greatest Commandment

[34]Hearing that Jesus had silenced the Sadducees, the Pharisees got together. [35]One of them, an expert in the law, tested him with this question: [36]"Teacher, which is the greatest commandment in the Law?"

[37]Jesus replied: " 'Love the Lord your God with all your heart and with all your soul and with all your mind.'[b] [38]This is the first and greatest commandment. [39]And the second is like it: 'Love your neighbor as yourself.'[c] [40]All the Law and the Prophets hang on these two commandments."

Whose Son Is the Christ?

[41]While the Pharisees were gathered together, Jesus asked them,

[a]32 Exodus 3:6   [b]37 Deut. 6:5   [c]39 Lev. 19:18

⁴²"What do you think about the Christ[a]? Whose son is he?"

"The son of David," they replied.

⁴³He said to them, "How is it then that David, speaking by the Spirit, calls him 'Lord'? For he says,

⁴⁴" 'The Lord said to my Lord:
  "Sit at my right hand
  until I put your enemies
    under your feet." ' [b]

⁴⁵If then David calls him 'Lord,' how can he be his son?" ⁴⁶No one could say a word in reply, and from that day on no one dared to ask him any more questions.

Seven Woes

23 Then Jesus said to the crowds and to his disciples: ²"The teachers of the law and the Pharisees sit in Moses' seat. ³So you must obey them and do everything they tell you. But do not do what they do, for they do not practice what they preach. ⁴They tie up heavy loads and put them on men's shoulders, but they themselves are not willing to lift a finger to move them.

⁵"Everything they do is done for men to see: They make their phylacteries[c] wide and the tassels on their garments long; ⁶they love the place of honor at banquets and the most important seats in the synagogues; ⁷they love to be greeted in the marketplaces and to have men call them 'Rabbi.'

⁸"But you are not to be called 'Rabbi,' for you have only one Master and you are all brothers. ⁹And do not call anyone on earth 'father,' for you have one Father, and he is in heaven. ¹⁰Nor are you to be called 'teacher,' for you have one Teacher, the Christ.[a] ¹¹The greatest among you will be your servant. ¹²For whoever exalts himself will be humbled, and whoever humbles himself will be exalted.

¹³"Woe to you, teachers of the law and Pharisees, you hypocrites! You shut the kingdom of heaven in men's faces. You yourselves do not enter, nor will you let those enter who are trying to.[d]

¹⁵"Woe to you, teachers of the law and Pharisees, you hypocrites! You travel over land and sea to win a single convert, and when he becomes one, you make him twice as much a son of hell as you are.

¹⁶"Woe to you, blind guides! You say, 'If anyone swears by the temple, it means nothing; but if anyone swears by the gold of the temple, he is bound by his oath.' ¹⁷You blind fools! Which is greater: the gold, or the temple that makes the gold sacred? ¹⁸You also say, 'If anyone swears by the altar, it means nothing; but if anyone swears by the gift on it, he is bound by his oath.' ¹⁹You blind men! Which is greater: the gift, or the altar that makes the gift sacred? ²⁰Therefore, he who swears by the altar swears by it and by everything on it. ²¹And he who swears by the temple swears by it and by the one who dwells in it. ²²And he who swears by heaven swears by God's throne and by the one who sits on it.

²³"Woe to you, teachers of the law and Pharisees, you hypocrites! You give a tenth of your spices—mint, dill and cummin. But you have neglected the more important matters of the law—justice, mercy and faithfulness. You should have practiced the latter, without neglecting the former. ²⁴You blind guides! You strain out a gnat but swallow a camel.

²⁵"Woe to you, teachers of the law and Pharisees, you hypocrites! You clean the outside of the cup and dish, but inside they are full of greed and self-indulgence. ²⁶Blind Pharisee! First clean the inside of the cup and dish, and then the outside also will be clean.

²⁷"Woe to you, teachers of the law and Pharisees, you hypocrites! You

---

a42,10 Or Messiah   b44 Psalm 110:1   c5 That is, boxes containing Scripture verses, worn on forehead and arm   d13 Some manuscripts to. ¹⁴Woe to you, teachers of the law and Pharisees, you hypocrites! You devour widows' houses and for a show make lengthy prayers. Therefore you will be punished more severely.

are like whitewashed tombs, which look beautiful on the outside but on the inside are full of dead men's bones and everything unclean. ²⁸In the same way, on the outside you appear to people as righteous but on the inside you are full of hypocrisy and wickedness.

²⁹"Woe to you, teachers of the law and Pharisees, you hypocrites! You build tombs for the prophets and decorate the graves of the righteous. ³⁰And you say, 'If we had lived in the days of our forefathers, we would not have taken part with them in shedding the blood of the prophets.' ³¹So you testify against yourselves that you are the descendants of those who murdered the prophets. ³²Fill up, then, the measure of the sin of your forefathers!

³³"You snakes! You brood of vipers! How will you escape being condemned to hell? ³⁴Therefore I am sending you prophets and wise men and teachers. Some of them you will kill and crucify; others you will flog in your synagogues and pursue from town to town. ³⁵And so upon you will come all the righteous blood that has been shed on earth, from the blood of righteous Abel to the blood of Zechariah son of Berekiah, whom you murdered between the temple and the altar. ³⁶I tell you the truth, all this will come upon this generation.

³⁷"O Jerusalem, Jerusalem, you who kill the prophets and stone those sent to you, how often I have longed to gather your children together, as a hen gathers her chicks under her wings, but you were not willing. ³⁸Look, your house is left to you desolate. ³⁹For I tell you, you will not see me again until you say, 'Blessed is he who comes in the name of the Lord.'ᵃ"

Signs of the End of the Age

24 Jesus left the temple and was walking away when his disciples came up to him to call his attention to its buildings. ²"Do you see all

these things?" he asked. "I tell you the truth, not one stone here will be left on another; every one will be thrown down."

³As Jesus was sitting on the Mount of Olives, the disciples came to him privately. "Tell us," they said, "when will this happen, and what will be the sign of your coming and of the end of the age?"

⁴Jesus answered: "Watch out that no one deceives you. ⁵For many will come in my name, claiming, 'I am the Christ,ᵇ' and will deceive many. ⁶You will hear of wars and rumors of wars, but see to it that you are not alarmed. Such things must happen, but the end is still to come. ⁷Nation will rise against nation, and kingdom against kingdom. There will be famines and earthquakes in various places. ⁸All these are the beginning of birth pains.

⁹"Then you will be handed over to be persecuted and put to death, and you will be hated by all nations because of me. ¹⁰At that time many will turn away from the faith and will betray and hate each other, ¹¹and many false prophets will appear and deceive many people. ¹²Because of the increase of wickedness, the love of most will grow cold, ¹³but he who stands firm to the end will be saved. ¹⁴And this gospel of the kingdom will be preached in the whole world as a testimony to all nations, and then the end will come.

¹⁵"So when you see standing in the holy place 'the abomination that causes desolation,'ᶜ spoken of through the prophet Daniel—let the reader understand— ¹⁶then let those who are in Judea flee to the mountains. ¹⁷Let no one on the roof of his house go down to take anything out of the house. ¹⁸Let no one in the field go back to get his cloak. ¹⁹How dreadful it will be in those days for pregnant women and nursing mothers! ²⁰Pray that your flight will not take place in winter or on the Sabbath. ²¹For then there will be great distress,

---

ᵃ39 Psalm 118:26   ᵇ5 Or *Messiah*; also in verse 23   ᶜ15 Daniel 9:27; 11:31; 12:11

unequaled from the beginning of the world until now—and never to be equaled again. ²²If those days had not been cut short, no one would survive, but for the sake of the elect those days will be shortened. ²³At that time if anyone says to you, 'Look, here is the Christ!' or, 'There he is!' do not believe it. ²⁴For false Christs and false prophets will appear and perform great signs and miracles to deceive even the elect—if that were possible. ²⁵See, I have told you ahead of time.

²⁶"So if anyone tells you, 'There he is, out in the desert,' do not go out; or, 'Here he is, in the inner rooms,' do not believe it. ²⁷For as lightning that comes from the east is visible even in the west, so will be the coming of the Son of Man. ²⁸Wherever there is a carcass, there the vultures will gather.

²⁹"Immediately after the distress of those days

" 'the sun will be darkened,
   and the moon will not give its
      light;
the stars will fall from the sky,
   and the heavenly bodies will be
      shaken.'[a]

³⁰"At that time the sign of the Son of Man will appear in the sky, and all the nations of the earth will mourn. They will see the Son of Man coming on the clouds of the sky, with power and great glory. ³¹And he will send his angels with a loud trumpet call, and they will gather his elect from the four winds, from one end of the heavens to the other.

³²"Now learn this lesson from the fig tree: As soon as its twigs get tender and its leaves come out, you know that summer is near. ³³Even so, when you see all these things, you know that it[b] is near, right at the door. ³⁴I tell you the truth, this generation[c] will certainly not pass away until all these things have happened. ³⁵Heaven and earth will pass away, but my words will never pass away.

The Day and Hour Unknown

³⁶"No one knows about that day or hour, not even the angels in heaven, nor the Son,[d] but only the Father. ³⁷As it was in the days of Noah, so it will be at the coming of the Son of Man. ³⁸For in the days before the flood, people were eating and drinking, marrying and giving in marriage, up to the day Noah entered the ark; ³⁹and they knew nothing about what would happen until the flood came and took them all away. That is how it will be at the coming of the Son of Man. ⁴⁰Two men will be in the field; one will be taken and the other left. ⁴¹Two women will be grinding with a hand mill; one will be taken and the other left.

⁴²"Therefore keep watch, because you do not know on what day your Lord will come. ⁴³But understand this: If the owner of the house had known at what time of night the thief was coming, he would have kept watch and would not have let his house be broken into. ⁴⁴So you also must be ready, because the Son of Man will come at an hour when you do not expect him.

⁴⁵"Who then is the faithful and wise servant, whom the master has put in charge of the servants in his household to give them their food at the proper time? ⁴⁶It will be good for that servant whose master finds him doing so when he returns. ⁴⁷I tell you the truth, he will put him in charge of all his possessions. ⁴⁸But suppose that servant is wicked and says to himself, 'My master is staying away a long time,' ⁴⁹and he then begins to beat his fellow servants and to eat and drink with drunkards. ⁵⁰The master of that servant will come on a day when he does not expect him and at an hour he is not aware of. ⁵¹He will cut him to pieces and assign him a place with the hypocrites, where there will be weeping and gnashing of teeth.

---

[a]29 Isaiah 13:10; 34:4   [b]33 Or he   [c]34 Or race   [d]36 Some manuscripts do not have nor the Son.

The Parable of the Ten Virgins

25 "At that time the kingdom of heaven will be like ten virgins who took their lamps and went out to meet the bridegroom. ²Five of them were foolish and five were wise. ³The foolish ones took their lamps but did not take any oil with them. ⁴The wise, however, took oil in jars along with their lamps. ⁵The bridegroom was a long time in coming, and they all became drowsy and fell asleep.

⁶"At midnight the cry rang out: 'Here's the bridegroom! Come out to meet him!'

⁷"Then all the virgins woke up and trimmed their lamps. ⁸The foolish ones said to the wise, 'Give us some of your oil; our lamps are going out.'

⁹"'No,' they replied, 'there may not be enough for both us and you. Instead, go to those who sell oil and buy some for yourselves.'

¹⁰"But while they were on their way to buy the oil, the bridegroom arrived. The virgins who were ready went in with him to the wedding banquet. And the door was shut.

¹¹"Later the others also came. 'Sir! Sir!' they said. 'Open the door for us!'

¹²"But he replied, 'I tell you the truth, I don't know you.'

¹³"Therefore keep watch, because you do not know the day or the hour.

The Parable of the Talents

¹⁴"Again, it will be like a man going on a journey, who called his servants and entrusted his property to them. ¹⁵To one he gave five talents[a] of money, to another two talents, and to another one talent, each according to his ability. Then he went on his journey. ¹⁶The man who had received the five talents went at once and put his money to work and gained five more. ¹⁷So also, the one with the two talents gained two more. ¹⁸But the man who had received the one talent went off, dug a hole in the ground and hid his master's money.

¹⁹"After a long time the master of those servants returned and settled accounts with them. ²⁰The man who had received the five talents brought the other five. 'Master,' he said, 'you entrusted me with five talents. See, I have gained five more.'

²¹"His master replied, 'Well done, good and faithful servant! You have been faithful with a few things; I will put you in charge of many things. Come and share your master's happiness!'

²²"The man with the two talents also came. 'Master,' he said, 'you entrusted me with two talents; see, I have gained two more.'

²³"His master replied, 'Well done, good and faithful servant! You have been faithful with a few things; I will put you in charge of many things. Come and share your master's happiness!'

²⁴"Then the man who had received the one talent came. 'Master,' he said, 'I knew that you are a hard man, harvesting where you have not sown and gathering where you have not scattered seed. ²⁵So I was afraid and went out and hid your talent in the ground. See, here is what belongs to you.'

²⁶"His master replied, 'You wicked, lazy servant! So you knew that I harvest where I have not sown and gather where I have not scattered seed? ²⁷Well then, you should have put my money on deposit with the bankers, so that when I returned I would have received it back with interest.

²⁸"'Take the talent from him and give it to the one who has the ten talents. ²⁹For everyone who has will be given more, and he will have an abundance. Whoever does not have, even what he has will be taken from him. ³⁰And throw that worthless servant outside, into the darkness, where there will be weeping and gnashing of teeth.'

The Sheep and the Goats

³¹"When the Son of Man comes in his glory, and all the angels with him, he will sit on his throne in heavenly

---

[a]15 A talent was worth more than a thousand dollars.

VERSE:
Matthew 25:23

AUTHOR:
Richard L. Morgan

PASSAGE:
Matthew 25:14–30

Well Done, Faithful Servant!

The two-talent person was commended for his faithfulness, not his brilliance. He received the same reward as the five-talent person. Every one of us has unique talents and gifts in old age. The question is: Will we use them or lose them? Retirement presents an unparalleled opportunity to develop latent talents. Some of the greatest works in the arts, literature and other fields have come from persons past 70 years of age.

It is easier to grow old if we are neither bored nor boring. Projects are vital to our mental health, and there is no limit to realizing our potential. In our later years we have more time to expand our horizons because we are set free from certain routines and rituals.

The problem is often with us. We are locked in a room with open doors. We try to blame our boredom on outside forces, but the issue is within us. If we take the time to look inward, we may be surprised at our own creativity and ingenuity. Who knows? We may even experience a rebirth of creativity in later years—and amaze ourselves with our newfound gifts.

Generous Provider of all good gifts, rekindle within us latent and buried talents so often neglected in earlier life. May we find in older age the creative person you always knew us to be.

ADDITIONAL SCRIPTURE READINGS
Romans 12:3–8; 2 Timothy 1:3–7
Go to page 1242 for your next devotional reading.

glory. ³²All the nations will be gathered before him, and he will separate the people one from another as a shepherd separates the sheep from the goats. ³³He will put the sheep on his right and the goats on his left.

³⁴"Then the King will say to those on his right, 'Come, you who are blessed by my Father; take your inheritance, the kingdom prepared for you since the creation of the world. ³⁵For I was hungry and you gave me something to eat, I was thirsty and you gave me something to drink, I was a stranger and you invited me in, ³⁶I needed clothes and you clothed me, I was sick and you looked after me, I was in prison and you came to visit me.'

³⁷"Then the righteous will answer him, 'Lord, when did we see you hungry and feed you, or thirsty and give you something to drink? ³⁸When did we see you a stranger and invite you in, or needing clothes and clothe you? ³⁹When did we see you sick or in prison and go to visit you?'

⁴⁰"The King will reply, 'I tell you the truth, whatever you did for one of the least of these brothers of mine, you did for me.'

⁴¹"Then he will say to those on his left, 'Depart from me, you who are cursed, into the eternal fire prepared for the devil and his angels. ⁴²For I was hungry and you gave me nothing to eat, I was thirsty and you gave me nothing to drink, ⁴³I was a stranger and you did not invite me in, I needed clothes and you did not clothe me, I was sick and in prison and you did not look after me.'

⁴⁴"They also will answer, 'Lord, when did we see you hungry or thirsty or a stranger or needing clothes or sick or in prison, and did not help you?'

⁴⁵"He will reply, 'I tell you the truth, whatever you did not do for one of the least of these, you did not do for me.'

⁴⁶"Then they will go away to eternal punishment, but the righteous to eternal life."

The Plot Against Jesus

26 When Jesus had finished saying all these things, he said to his disciples, ²"As you know, the Passover is two days away—and the Son of Man will be handed over to be crucified."

³Then the chief priests and the elders of the people assembled in the palace of the high priest, whose name was Caiaphas, ⁴and they plotted to arrest Jesus in some sly way and kill him. ⁵"But not during the Feast," they said, "or there may be a riot among the people."

Jesus Anointed at Bethany

⁶While Jesus was in Bethany in the home of a man known as Simon the Leper, ⁷a woman came to him with an alabaster jar of very expensive perfume, which she poured on his head as he was reclining at the table.

⁸When the disciples saw this, they were indignant. "Why this waste?" they asked. ⁹"This perfume could have been sold at a high price and the money given to the poor."

¹⁰Aware of this, Jesus said to them, "Why are you bothering this woman? She has done a beautiful thing to me. ¹¹The poor you will always have with you, but you will not always have me. ¹²When she poured this perfume on my body, she did it to prepare me for burial. ¹³I tell you the truth, wherever this gospel is preached throughout the world, what she has done will also be told, in memory of her."

Judas Agrees to Betray Jesus

¹⁴Then one of the Twelve—the one called Judas Iscariot—went to the chief priests ¹⁵and asked, "What are you willing to give me if I hand him over to you?" So they counted out for him thirty silver coins. ¹⁶From then on Judas watched for an opportunity to hand him over.

The Lord's Supper

¹⁷On the first day of the Feast of Unleavened Bread, the disciples came to Jesus and asked, "Where do you

want us to make preparations for you to eat the Passover?"

18He replied, "Go into the city to a certain man and tell him, 'The Teacher says: My appointed time is near. I am going to celebrate the Passover with my disciples at your house.' " 19So the disciples did as Jesus had directed them and prepared the Passover.

20When evening came, Jesus was reclining at the table with the Twelve. 21And while they were eating, he said, "I tell you the truth, one of you will betray me."

22They were very sad and began to say to him one after the other, "Surely not I, Lord?"

23Jesus replied, "The one who has dipped his hand into the bowl with me will betray me. 24The Son of Man will go just as it is written about him. But woe to that man who betrays the Son of Man! It would be better for him if he had not been born."

25Then Judas, the one who would betray him, said, "Surely not I, Rabbi?"

Jesus answered, "Yes, it is you."a

26While they were eating, Jesus took bread, gave thanks and broke it, and gave it to his disciples, saying, "Take and eat; this is my body."

27Then he took the cup, gave thanks and offered it to them, saying, "Drink from it, all of you. 28This is my blood of theb covenant, which is poured out for many for the forgiveness of sins. 29I tell you, I will not drink of this fruit of the vine from now on until that day when I drink it anew with you in my Father's kingdom."

30When they had sung a hymn, they went out to the Mount of Olives.

Jesus Predicts Peter's Denial

31Then Jesus told them, "This very night you will all fall away on account of me, for it is written:

" 'I will strike the shepherd,
    and the sheep of the flock will
      be scattered.'c

32But after I have risen, I will go ahead of you into Galilee."

33Peter replied, "Even if all fall away on account of you, I never will."

34"I tell you the truth," Jesus answered, "this very night, before the rooster crows, you will disown me three times."

35But Peter declared, "Even if I have to die with you, I will never disown you." And all the other disciples said the same.

Gethsemane

36Then Jesus went with his disciples to a place called Gethsemane, and he said to them, "Sit here while I go over there and pray." 37He took Peter and the two sons of Zebedee along with him, and he began to be sorrowful and troubled. 38Then he said to them, "My soul is overwhelmed with sorrow to the point of death. Stay here and keep watch with me."

39Going a little farther, he fell with his face to the ground and prayed, "My Father, if it is possible, may this cup be taken from me. Yet not as I will, but as you will."

40Then he returned to his disciples and found them sleeping. "Could you men not keep watch with me for one hour?" he asked Peter. 41"Watch and pray so that you will not fall into temptation. The spirit is willing, but the body is weak."

42He went away a second time and prayed, "My Father, if it is not possible for this cup to be taken away unless I drink it, may your will be done."

43When he came back, he again found them sleeping, because their eyes were heavy. 44So he left them and went away once more and prayed the third time, saying the same thing.

45Then he returned to the disciples and said to them, "Are you still sleeping and resting? Look, the hour is near, and the Son of Man is betrayed

---

a25 Or "You yourself have said it"   b28 Some manuscripts the new   c31 Zech. 13:7

into the hands of sinners. ⁴⁶Rise, let us go! Here comes my betrayer!"

Jesus Arrested

⁴⁷While he was still speaking, Judas, one of the Twelve, arrived. With him was a large crowd armed with swords and clubs, sent from the chief priests and the elders of the people. ⁴⁸Now the betrayer had arranged a signal with them: "The one I kiss is the man; arrest him." ⁴⁹Going at once to Jesus, Judas said, "Greetings, Rabbi!" and kissed him.

⁵⁰Jesus replied, "Friend, do what you came for."ᵃ

Then the men stepped forward, seized Jesus and arrested him. ⁵¹With that, one of Jesus' companions reached for his sword, drew it out and struck the servant of the high priest, cutting off his ear.

⁵²"Put your sword back in its place," Jesus said to him, "for all who draw the sword will die by the sword. ⁵³Do you think I cannot call on my Father, and he will at once put at my disposal more than twelve legions of angels? ⁵⁴But how then would the Scriptures be fulfilled that say it must happen in this way?"

⁵⁵At that time Jesus said to the crowd, "Am I leading a rebellion, that you have come out with swords and clubs to capture me? Every day I sat in the temple courts teaching, and you did not arrest me. ⁵⁶But this has all taken place that the writings of the prophets might be fulfilled." Then all the disciples deserted him and fled.

Before the Sanhedrin

⁵⁷Those who had arrested Jesus took him to Caiaphas, the high priest, where the teachers of the law and the elders had assembled. ⁵⁸But Peter followed him at a distance, right up to the courtyard of the high priest. He entered and sat down with the guards to see the outcome.

⁵⁹The chief priests and the whole Sanhedrin were looking for false evidence against Jesus so that they could put him to death. ⁶⁰But they did not find any, though many false witnesses came forward.

Finally two came forward ⁶¹and declared, "This fellow said, 'I am able to destroy the temple of God and rebuild it in three days.'"

⁶²Then the high priest stood up and said to Jesus, "Are you not going to answer? What is this testimony that these men are bringing against you?" ⁶³But Jesus remained silent.

The high priest said to him, "I charge you under oath by the living God: Tell us if you are the Christ,ᵇ the Son of God."

⁶⁴"Yes, it is as you say," Jesus replied. "But I say to all of you: In the future you will see the Son of Man sitting at the right hand of the Mighty One and coming on the clouds of heaven."

⁶⁵Then the high priest tore his clothes and said, "He has spoken blasphemy! Why do we need any more witnesses? Look, now you have heard the blasphemy. ⁶⁶What do you think?"

"He is worthy of death," they answered.

⁶⁷Then they spit in his face and struck him with their fists. Others slapped him ⁶⁸and said, "Prophesy to us, Christ. Who hit you?"

Peter Disowns Jesus

⁶⁹Now Peter was sitting out in the courtyard, and a servant girl came to him. "You also were with Jesus of Galilee," she said.

⁷⁰But he denied it before them all. "I don't know what you're talking about," he said.

⁷¹Then he went out to the gateway, where another girl saw him and said to the people there, "This fellow was with Jesus of Nazareth."

⁷²He denied it again, with an oath: "I don't know the man!"

⁷³After a little while, those standing there went up to Peter and said, "Surely you are one of them, for your accent gives you away."

ᵃ50 Or *"Friend, why have you come?"*   ᵇ63 Or *Messiah*; also in verse 68

PASSAGE: Romans 5:1–11; Titus 3:3–8
AUTHOR: Hannah Whitall Smith

Jesus Saves Me Now

Perhaps no four words in the language have more meaning in them than the following, which I would have you repeat over and over with your voice and with your soul, emphasizing each time a different word:

Jesus saves me now.—It is he.
Jesus *saves* me now.—It is his work to save.
Jesus saves *me* now.—I am the one to be saved.
Jesus saves me *now* . . . Trust him as your living
   Savior.

Go to page 1245 for your next devotional reading.

[74]Then he began to call down curses on himself and he swore to them, "I don't know the man!"

Immediately a rooster crowed. [75]Then Peter remembered the word Jesus had spoken: "Before the rooster crows, you will disown me three times." And he went outside and wept bitterly.

Judas Hangs Himself

27 Early in the morning, all the chief priests and the elders of the people came to the decision to put Jesus to death. [2]They bound him, led him away and handed him over to Pilate, the governor.

[3]When Judas, who had betrayed him, saw that Jesus was condemned, he was seized with remorse and returned the thirty silver coins to the chief priests and the elders. [4]"I have sinned," he said, "for I have betrayed innocent blood."

"What is that to us?" they replied. "That's your responsibility."

[5]So Judas threw the money into the temple and left. Then he went away and hanged himself.

[6]The chief priests picked up the coins and said, "It is against the law to put this into the treasury, since it is blood money." [7]So they decided to use the money to buy the potter's field as a burial place for foreigners. [8]That is why it has been called the Field of Blood to this day. [9]Then what was spoken by Jeremiah the prophet was fulfilled: "They took the thirty silver coins, the price set on him by the people of Israel, [10]and they used them to buy the potter's field, as the Lord commanded me."[a]

Jesus Before Pilate

[11]Meanwhile Jesus stood before the governor, and the governor asked him, "Are you the king of the Jews?"

"Yes, it is as you say," Jesus replied.

[12]When he was accused by the chief priests and the elders, he gave no answer. [13]Then Pilate asked him, "Don't you hear the testimony they are bringing against you?" [14]But Jesus made no reply, not even to a single charge—to the great amazement of the governor.

[15]Now it was the governor's custom at the Feast to release a prisoner chosen by the crowd. [16]At that time they had a notorious prisoner, called Barabbas. [17]So when the crowd had gathered, Pilate asked them, "Which one do you want me to release to you: Barabbas, or Jesus who is called Christ?" [18]For he knew it was out of envy that they had handed Jesus over to him.

[19]While Pilate was sitting on the judge's seat, his wife sent him this message: "Don't have anything to do with that innocent man, for I have suffered a great deal today in a dream because of him."

[20]But the chief priests and the elders persuaded the crowd to ask for Barabbas and to have Jesus executed.

[21]"Which of the two do you want me to release to you?" asked the governor.

"Barabbas," they answered.

[22]"What shall I do, then, with Jesus who is called Christ?" Pilate asked.

They all answered, "Crucify him!"

[23]"Why? What crime has he committed?" asked Pilate.

But they shouted all the louder, "Crucify him!"

[24]When Pilate saw that he was getting nowhere, but that instead an uproar was starting, he took water and washed his hands in front of the crowd. "I am innocent of this man's blood," he said. "It is your responsibility!"

[25]All the people answered, "Let his blood be on us and on our children!"

[26]Then he released Barabbas to them. But he had Jesus flogged, and handed him over to be crucified.

The Soldiers Mock Jesus

[27]Then the governor's soldiers took Jesus into the Praetorium and gathered the whole company of soldiers

[a]10 See Zech. 11:12,13; Jer. 19:1-13; 32:6-9.

around him. 28They stripped him and put a scarlet robe on him, 29and then twisted together a crown of thorns and set it on his head. They put a staff in his right hand and knelt in front of him and mocked him. "Hail, king of the Jews!" they said. 30They spit on him, and took the staff and struck him on the head again and again. 31After they had mocked him, they took off the robe and put his own clothes on him. Then they led him away to crucify him.

The Crucifixion

32As they were going out, they met a man from Cyrene, named Simon, and they forced him to carry the cross. 33They came to a place called Golgotha (which means The Place of the Skull). 34There they offered Jesus wine to drink, mixed with gall; but after tasting it, he refused to drink it. 35When they had crucified him, they divided up his clothes by casting lots.ᵃ 36And sitting down, they kept watch over him there. 37Above his head they placed the written charge against him: THIS IS JESUS, THE KING OF THE JEWS. 38Two robbers were crucified with him, one on his right and one on his left. 39Those who passed by hurled insults at him, shaking their heads 40and saying, "You who are going to destroy the temple and build it in three days, save yourself! Come down from the cross, if you are the Son of God!"

41In the same way the chief priests, the teachers of the law and the elders mocked him. 42"He saved others," they said, "but he can't save himself! He's the King of Israel! Let him come down now from the cross, and we will believe in him. 43He trusts in God. Let God rescue him now if he wants him, for he said, 'I am the Son of God.' " 44In the same way the robbers who were crucified with him also heaped insults on him.

The Death of Jesus

45From the sixth hour until the ninth hour darkness came over all the land. 46About the ninth hour Jesus cried out in a loud voice, *"Eloi, Eloi,ᵇ lama sabachthani?"*—which means, "My God, my God, why have you forsaken me?"ᶜ 47When some of those standing there heard this, they said, "He's calling Elijah."

48Immediately one of them ran and got a sponge. He filled it with wine vinegar, put it on a stick, and offered it to Jesus to drink. 49The rest said, "Now leave him alone. Let's see if Elijah comes to save him."

50And when Jesus had cried out again in a loud voice, he gave up his spirit.

51At that moment the curtain of the temple was torn in two from top to bottom. The earth shook and the rocks split. 52The tombs broke open and the bodies of many holy people who had died were raised to life. 53They came out of the tombs, and after Jesus' resurrection they went into the holy city and appeared to many people.

54When the centurion and those with him who were guarding Jesus saw the earthquake and all that had happened, they were terrified, and exclaimed, "Surely he was the Sonᵈ of God!"

55Many women were there, watching from a distance. They had followed Jesus from Galilee to care for his needs. 56Among them were Mary Magdalene, Mary the mother of James and Joses, and the mother of Zebedee's sons.

The Burial of Jesus

57As evening approached, there came a rich man from Arimathea, named Joseph, who had himself become a disciple of Jesus. 58Going to Pilate, he asked for Jesus' body, and Pilate ordered that it be given to him.

ᵃ35 A few late manuscripts *lots that the word spoken by the prophet might be fulfilled: "They divided my garments among themselves and cast lots for my clothing"* (Psalm 22:18)   ᵇ46 Some manuscripts *Eli, Eli*   ᶜ46 Psalm 22:1   ᵈ54 Or *a son*

VERSE:
Matthew 28:20

AUTHOR:
Bruce Larson

PASSAGE:
Matthew 28:1–20

Facing the Future

Both the now and the future come together with our belief in God, who raised his Son from the dead and who has promised that because he lives, we too shall live. In committing one's life to that Lord who lives now and forever, our fear of the future changes into hope. Whether that hope is fulfilled in this life or the next, we aim for the most grand and glorious design that we can comprehend, being copartners with God in the redemption of his world.

But the Resurrection on that first Easter morning inspired a good deal of fear ... As we contemplate that Resurrection, even 2,000 years later, it continues to be fearful. If Jesus is not raised from the dead, the future holds little hope, and we ought to be fearful. If it is true, then there are consequences not just eternal, but immediate ...

The future is always uncertain, and it's meant to be. That ingredient adds excitement to life, calls forth our potential and stretches our aspiration. In one sense, conquering our fear of the future is the key to overcoming a good many of our other fears ...

Compounding a good many of our fears, especially those of illness, pain and death, is the nagging certainty that we will have to go through them alone. That's the point at which our faith is most pertinent. We *can* trust God, not just in his grand design for our lives and the eventual happy ending to the story, but in his promise that we will have a companion in every circumstance, however fearful. Jesus' last words to his disciples ... were "Surely I am with you always, to the very end of the age." To the end of our lives, to the end of time, we are not alone, and we can "fear not."

ADDITIONAL SCRIPTURE READINGS
Romans 8:28–39; 1 Corinthians 15:12–28
Go to page 1250 for your next devotional reading.

⁵⁹Joseph took the body, wrapped it in a clean linen cloth, ⁶⁰and placed it in his own new tomb that he had cut out of the rock. He rolled a big stone in front of the entrance to the tomb and went away. ⁶¹Mary Magdalene and the other Mary were sitting there opposite the tomb.

The Guard at the Tomb

⁶²The next day, the one after Preparation Day, the chief priests and the Pharisees went to Pilate. ⁶³"Sir," they said, "we remember that while he was still alive that deceiver said, 'After three days I will rise again.' ⁶⁴So give the order for the tomb to be made secure until the third day. Otherwise, his disciples may come and steal the body and tell the people that he has been raised from the dead. This last deception will be worse than the first."

⁶⁵"Take a guard," Pilate answered. "Go, make the tomb as secure as you know how." ⁶⁶So they went and made the tomb secure by putting a seal on the stone and posting the guard.

The Resurrection

28 After the Sabbath, at dawn on the first day of the week, Mary Magdalene and the other Mary went to look at the tomb.

²There was a violent earthquake, for an angel of the Lord came down from heaven and, going to the tomb, rolled back the stone and sat on it. ³His appearance was like lightning, and his clothes were white as snow. ⁴The guards were so afraid of him that they shook and became like dead men.

⁵The angel said to the women, "Do not be afraid, for I know that you are looking for Jesus, who was crucified. ⁶He is not here; he has risen, just as he said. Come and see the place where he lay. ⁷Then go quickly and tell his disciples: 'He has risen from the dead and is going ahead of you into Galilee. There you will see him.' Now I have told you."

⁸So the women hurried away from the tomb, afraid yet filled with joy, and ran to tell his disciples. ⁹Suddenly Jesus met them. "Greetings," he said. They came to him, clasped his feet and worshiped him. ¹⁰Then Jesus said to them, "Do not be afraid. Go and tell my brothers to go to Galilee; there they will see me."

The Guards' Report

¹¹While the women were on their way, some of the guards went into the city and reported to the chief priests everything that had happened. ¹²When the chief priests had met with the elders and devised a plan, they gave the soldiers a large sum of money, ¹³telling them, "You are to say, 'His disciples came during the night and stole him away while we were asleep.' ¹⁴If this report gets to the governor, we will satisfy him and keep you out of trouble." ¹⁵So the soldiers took the money and did as they were instructed. And this story has been widely circulated among the Jews to this very day.

The Great Commission

¹⁶Then the eleven disciples went to Galilee, to the mountain where Jesus had told them to go. ¹⁷When they saw him, they worshiped him; but some doubted. ¹⁸Then Jesus came to them and said, "All authority in heaven and on earth has been given to me. ¹⁹Therefore go and make disciples of all nations, baptizing them in*a* the name of the Father and of the Son and of the Holy Spirit, ²⁰and teaching them to obey everything I have commanded you. And surely I am with you always, to the very end of the age."

---

a19 Or *into;* see Acts 8:16; 19:5; Romans 6:3; 1 Cor. 1:13; 10:2 and Gal. 3:27.

... **M** *ark uses a fast-paced style to highlight the ministry, death and resurrection of Jesus Christ, the Son of God. Nearly half of his Gospel deals with the final week of Jesus' life, ending with the death and resurrection. As you read this book, strive to learn from Jesus' example of a life full of purpose and emotion, and ask God to give you the power to live it out.*

MARK

John the Baptist Prepares the Way

1 The beginning of the gospel about Jesus Christ, the Son of God.*a*

²It is written in Isaiah the prophet:

"I will send my messenger ahead
    of you,
  who will prepare your
      way"*b*—
³"a voice of one calling in the
      desert,
  'Prepare the way for the Lord,
    make straight paths for
        him.' "*c*

⁴And so John came, baptizing in the desert region and preaching a baptism of repentance for the forgiveness of sins. ⁵The whole Judean countryside and all the people of Jerusalem went out to him. Confessing their sins, they were baptized by him in the Jordan River. ⁶John wore clothing made of camel's hair, with a leather belt around his waist, and he ate locusts and wild honey. ⁷And this was his message: "After me will come one more powerful than I, the thongs of whose sandals I am not worthy to stoop down and untie. ⁸I baptize you with*d* water, but he will baptize you with the Holy Spirit."

The Baptism and Temptation of Jesus

⁹At that time Jesus came from Nazareth in Galilee and was baptized by John in the Jordan. ¹⁰As Jesus was coming up out of the water, he saw heaven being torn open and the Spirit descending on him like a dove. ¹¹And a voice came from heaven: "You are my Son, whom I love; with you I am well pleased."

¹²At once the Spirit sent him out into the desert, ¹³and he was in the desert forty days, being tempted by

---

*a1 Some manuscripts do not have *the Son of God*.   *b2 Mal. 3:1   *c3 Isaiah 40:3   *d8 Or *in*

Satan. He was with the wild animals, and angels attended him.

The Calling of the First Disciples

¹⁴After John was put in prison, Jesus went into Galilee, proclaiming the good news of God. ¹⁵"The time has come," he said. "The kingdom of God is near. Repent and believe the good news!"

¹⁶As Jesus walked beside the Sea of Galilee, he saw Simon and his brother Andrew casting a net into the lake, for they were fishermen. ¹⁷"Come, follow me," Jesus said, "and I will make you fishers of men." ¹⁸At once they left their nets and followed him.

¹⁹When he had gone a little farther, he saw James son of Zebedee and his brother John in a boat, preparing their nets. ²⁰Without delay he called them, and they left their father Zebedee in the boat with the hired men and followed him.

Jesus Drives Out an Evil Spirit

²¹They went to Capernaum, and when the Sabbath came, Jesus went into the synagogue and began to teach. ²²The people were amazed at his teaching, because he taught them as one who had authority, not as the teachers of the law. ²³Just then a man in their synagogue who was possessed by an evil*ᵃ* spirit cried out, ²⁴"What do you want with us, Jesus of Nazareth? Have you come to destroy us? I know who you are—the Holy One of God!"

²⁵"Be quiet!" said Jesus sternly. "Come out of him!" ²⁶The evil spirit shook the man violently and came out of him with a shriek.

²⁷The people were all so amazed that they asked each other, "What is this? A new teaching—and with authority! He even gives orders to evil spirits and they obey him." ²⁸News about him spread quickly over the whole region of Galilee.

Jesus Heals Many

²⁹As soon as they left the synagogue, they went with James and John to the home of Simon and Andrew. ³⁰Simon's mother-in-law was in bed with a fever, and they told Jesus about her. ³¹So he went to her, took her hand and helped her up. The fever left her and she began to wait on them.

³²That evening after sunset the people brought to Jesus all the sick and demon-possessed. ³³The whole town gathered at the door, ³⁴and Jesus healed many who had various diseases. He also drove out many demons, but he would not let the demons speak because they knew who he was.

Jesus Prays in a Solitary Place

³⁵Very early in the morning, while it was still dark, Jesus got up, left the house and went off to a solitary place, where he prayed. ³⁶Simon and his companions went to look for him, ³⁷and when they found him, they exclaimed: "Everyone is looking for you!"

³⁸Jesus replied, "Let us go somewhere else—to the nearby villages—so I can preach there also. That is why I have come." ³⁹So he traveled throughout Galilee, preaching in their synagogues and driving out demons.

A Man With Leprosy

⁴⁰A man with leprosy*ᵇ* came to him and begged him on his knees, "If you are willing, you can make me clean."

⁴¹Filled with compassion, Jesus reached out his hand and touched the man. "I am willing," he said. "Be clean!" ⁴²Immediately the leprosy left him and he was cured.

⁴³Jesus sent him away at once with a strong warning: ⁴⁴"See that you don't tell this to anyone. But go, show yourself to the priest and offer the sacrifices that Moses commanded for

ᵃ23 Greek *unclean*; also in verses 26 and 27   *ᵇ40* The Greek word was used for various diseases affecting the skin—not necessarily leprosy.

your cleansing, as a testimony to them." ⁴⁵Instead he went out and began to talk freely, spreading the news. As a result, Jesus could no longer enter a town openly but stayed outside in lonely places. Yet the people still came to him from everywhere.

Jesus Heals a Paralytic

2 A few days later, when Jesus again entered Capernaum, the people heard that he had come home. ²So many gathered that there was no room left, not even outside the door, and he preached the word to them. ³Some men came, bringing to him a paralytic, carried by four of them. ⁴Since they could not get him to Jesus because of the crowd, they made an opening in the roof above Jesus and, after digging through it, lowered the mat the paralyzed man was lying on. ⁵When Jesus saw their faith, he said to the paralytic, "Son, your sins are forgiven."

⁶Now some teachers of the law were sitting there, thinking to themselves, ⁷"Why does this fellow talk like that? He's blaspheming! Who can forgive sins but God alone?"

⁸Immediately Jesus knew in his spirit that this was what they were thinking in their hearts, and he said to them, "Why are you thinking these things? ⁹Which is easier: to say to the paralytic, 'Your sins are forgiven,' or to say, 'Get up, take your mat and walk'? ¹⁰But that you may know that the Son of Man has authority on earth to forgive sins . . . ." He said to the paralytic, ¹¹"I tell you, get up, take your mat and go home." ¹²He got up, took his mat and walked out in full view of them all. This amazed everyone and they praised God, saying, "We have never seen anything like this!"

The Calling of Levi

¹³Once again Jesus went out beside the lake. A large crowd came to him, and he began to teach them. ¹⁴As he walked along, he saw Levi son of Alphaeus sitting at the tax col-

lector's booth. "Follow me," Jesus told him, and Levi got up and followed him.

¹⁵While Jesus was having dinner at Levi's house, many tax collectors and "sinners" were eating with him and his disciples, for there were many who followed him. ¹⁶When the teachers of the law who were Pharisees saw him eating with the "sinners" and tax collectors, they asked his disciples: "Why does he eat with tax collectors and 'sinners'?"

¹⁷On hearing this, Jesus said to them, "It is not the healthy who need a doctor, but the sick. I have not come to call the righteous, but sinners."

Jesus Questioned About Fasting

¹⁸Now John's disciples and the Pharisees were fasting. Some people came and asked Jesus, "How is it that John's disciples and the disciples of the Pharisees are fasting, but yours are not?"

¹⁹Jesus answered, "How can the guests of the bridegroom fast while he is with them? They cannot, so long as they have him with them. ²⁰But the time will come when the bridegroom will be taken from them, and on that day they will fast.

²¹"No one sews a patch of unshrunk cloth on an old garment. If he does, the new piece will pull away from the old, making the tear worse. ²²And no one pours new wine into old wineskins. If he does, the wine will burst the skins, and both the wine and the wineskins will be ruined. No, he pours new wine into new wineskins."

Lord of the Sabbath

²³One Sabbath Jesus was going through the grainfields, and as his disciples walked along, they began to pick some heads of grain. ²⁴The Pharisees said to him, "Look, why are they doing what is unlawful on the Sabbath?"

²⁵He answered, "Have you never read what David did when he and his companions were hungry and in

VERSE:	AUTHOR:	PASSAGE:
Mark 2:17	Jean Vanier	Mark 2:13–17

The Gentle Healer

Jesus is the healer, the One who comes to bring me life and liberate me from myself. He comes to heal me from my egoism, from my aggressiveness. He comes to heal me from my anguish . . .

When we become conscious of our own poverty, our lack of fidelity, our fears; when we become conscious that we need our Liberator, then Jesus will reveal himself to us as the quiet and gentle Healer, drawing us from a world of darkness to a world of light, from a world of death to a world of life.

He is the Healer who loves, the Healer who in all the tenderness of his being seeks to come into us. He does not want us to be frightened of him . . . The heart of Jesus is the heart of a lover. When he calls people forth, it is not because he has something for them to do as workers, but because he loves them. When he calls people to become followers, it's not just the mission that he has for them, but something much deeper. It is the call of a person who loves and says, "Walk with me for I love you. You are precious in my eyes. Fear not" . . .

This is the call of Jesus throughout our lives — "Come, follow me." But it is the call of a lover. "Come, if you follow me you will find liberty. Come" . . . Jesus does not impose; he does not try to hold people back. He does not even try to mitigate what he has said, blunting it with compromise. He doesn't put water into the wine and dilute his message. Like all lovers, he is patient and calls forth. This is the word of Jesus: "Come, I do not impose. But come, follow me. Let me touch your inner being, heal the scars of hardness, egoism and cowardice, and call you forth to life and liberation."

ADDITIONAL SCRIPTURE READINGS
Psalm 103; Hosea 11:1–4

Go to page 1260 for your next devotional reading.

need? ²⁶In the days of Abiathar the high priest, he entered the house of God and ate the consecrated bread, which is lawful only for priests to eat. And he also gave some to his companions."

²⁷Then he said to them, "The Sabbath was made for man, not man for the Sabbath. ²⁸So the Son of Man is Lord even of the Sabbath."

3 Another time he went into the synagogue, and a man with a shriveled hand was there. ²Some of them were looking for a reason to accuse Jesus, so they watched him closely to see if he would heal him on the Sabbath. ³Jesus said to the man with the shriveled hand, "Stand up in front of everyone."

⁴Then Jesus asked them, "Which is lawful on the Sabbath: to do good or to do evil, to save life or to kill?" But they remained silent. ⁵He looked around at them in anger and, deeply distressed at their stubborn hearts, said to the man, "Stretch out your hand." He stretched it out, and his hand was completely restored. ⁶Then the Pharisees went out and began to plot with the Herodians how they might kill Jesus.

Crowds Follow Jesus

⁷Jesus withdrew with his disciples to the lake, and a large crowd from Galilee followed. ⁸When they heard all he was doing, many people came to him from Judea, Jerusalem, Idumea, and the regions across the Jordan and around Tyre and Sidon. ⁹Because of the crowd he told his disciples to have a small boat ready for him, to keep the people from crowding him. ¹⁰For he had healed many, so that those with diseases were pushing forward to touch him. ¹¹Whenever the evil^a spirits saw him, they fell down before him and cried out, "You are the Son of God." ¹²But he gave them strict orders not to tell who he was.

The Appointing of the Twelve Apostles

¹³Jesus went up on a mountainside and called to him those he wanted, and they came to him. ¹⁴He appointed twelve—designating them apostles^b—that they might be with him and that he might send them out to preach ¹⁵and to have authority to drive out demons. ¹⁶These are the twelve he appointed: Simon (to whom he gave the name Peter); ¹⁷James son of Zebedee and his brother John (to them he gave the name Boanerges, which means Sons of Thunder); ¹⁸Andrew, Philip, Bartholomew, Matthew, Thomas, James son of Alphaeus, Thaddaeus, Simon the Zealot ¹⁹and Judas Iscariot, who betrayed him.

Jesus and Beelzebub

²⁰Then Jesus entered a house, and again a crowd gathered, so that he and his disciples were not even able to eat. ²¹When his family heard about this, they went to take charge of him, for they said, "He is out of his mind."

²²And the teachers of the law who came down from Jerusalem said, "He is possessed by Beelzebub^c! By the prince of demons he is driving out demons."

²³So Jesus called them and spoke to them in parables: "How can Satan drive out Satan? ²⁴If a kingdom is divided against itself, that kingdom cannot stand. ²⁵If a house is divided against itself, that house cannot stand. ²⁶And if Satan opposes himself and is divided, he cannot stand; his end has come. ²⁷In fact, no one can enter a strong man's house and carry off his possessions unless he first ties up the strong man. Then he can rob his house. ²⁸I tell you the truth, all the sins and blasphemies of men will be forgiven them. ²⁹But whoever blasphemes against the Holy Spirit will never be forgiven; he is guilty of an eternal sin."

---

^a11 Greek *unclean*; also in verse 30   ^b14 Some manuscripts do not have *designating them apostles.*   ^c22 Greek *Beezeboul* or *Beelzeboul*

³⁰He said this because they were saying, "He has an evil spirit."

Jesus' Mother and Brothers

³¹Then Jesus' mother and brothers arrived. Standing outside, they sent someone in to call him. ³²A crowd was sitting around him, and they told him, "Your mother and brothers are outside looking for you."

³³"Who are my mother and my brothers?" he asked.

³⁴Then he looked at those seated in a circle around him and said, "Here are my mother and my brothers! ³⁵Whoever does God's will is my brother and sister and mother."

The Parable of the Sower

4 Again Jesus began to teach by the lake. The crowd that gathered around him was so large that he got into a boat and sat in it out on the lake, while all the people were along the shore at the water's edge. ²He taught them many things by parables, and in his teaching said: ³"Listen! A farmer went out to sow his seed. ⁴As he was scattering the seed, some fell along the path, and the birds came and ate it up. ⁵Some fell on rocky places, where it did not have much soil. It sprang up quickly, because the soil was shallow. ⁶But when the sun came up, the plants were scorched, and they withered because they had no root. ⁷Other seed fell among thorns, which grew up and choked the plants, so that they did not bear grain. ⁸Still other seed fell on good soil. It came up, grew and produced a crop, multiplying thirty, sixty, or even a hundred times."

⁹Then Jesus said, "He who has ears to hear, let him hear."

¹⁰When he was alone, the Twelve and the others around him asked him about the parables. ¹¹He told them, "The secret of the kingdom of God has been given to you. But to those on the outside everything is said in parables ¹²so that,

" 'they may be ever seeing but
      never perceiving,
   and ever hearing but never
      understanding;
   otherwise they might turn and be
      forgiven!' ᵃ "

¹³Then Jesus said to them, "Don't you understand this parable? How then will you understand any parable? ¹⁴The farmer sows the word. ¹⁵Some people are like seed along the path, where the word is sown. As soon as they hear it, Satan comes and takes away the word that was sown in them. ¹⁶Others, like seed sown on rocky places, hear the word and at once receive it with joy. ¹⁷But since they have no root, they last only a short time. When trouble or persecution comes because of the word, they quickly fall away. ¹⁸Still others, like seed sown among thorns, hear the word; ¹⁹but the worries of this life, the deceitfulness of wealth and the desires for other things come in and choke the word, making it unfruitful. ²⁰Others, like seed sown on good soil, hear the word, accept it, and produce a crop—thirty, sixty or even a hundred times what was sown."

A Lamp on a Stand

²¹He said to them, "Do you bring in a lamp to put it under a bowl or a bed? Instead, don't you put it on its stand? ²²For whatever is hidden is meant to be disclosed, and whatever is concealed is meant to be brought out into the open. ²³If anyone has ears to hear, let him hear."

²⁴"Consider carefully what you hear," he continued. "With the measure you use, it will be measured to you—and even more. ²⁵Whoever has will be given more; whoever does not have, even what he has will be taken from him."

The Parable of the Growing Seed

²⁶He also said, "This is what the kingdom of God is like. A man scatters seed on the ground. ²⁷Night and

ᵃ12 Isaiah 6:9,10

day, whether he sleeps or gets up, the seed sprouts and grows, though he does not know how. [28]All by itself the soil produces grain—first the stalk, then the head, then the full kernel in the head. [29]As soon as the grain is ripe, he puts the sickle to it, because the harvest has come."

The Parable of the Mustard Seed

[30]Again he said, "What shall we say the kingdom of God is like, or what parable shall we use to describe it? [31]It is like a mustard seed, which is the smallest seed you plant in the ground. [32]Yet when planted, it grows and becomes the largest of all garden plants, with such big branches that the birds of the air can perch in its shade."

[33]With many similar parables Jesus spoke the word to them, as much as they could understand. [34]He did not say anything to them without using a parable. But when he was alone with his own disciples, he explained everything.

Jesus Calms the Storm

[35]That day when evening came, he said to his disciples, "Let us go over to the other side." [36]Leaving the crowd behind, they took him along, just as he was, in the boat. There were also other boats with him. [37]A furious squall came up, and the waves broke over the boat, so that it was nearly swamped. [38]Jesus was in the stern, sleeping on a cushion. The disciples woke him and said to him, "Teacher, don't you care if we drown?"

[39]He got up, rebuked the wind and said to the waves, "Quiet! Be still!" Then the wind died down and it was completely calm.

[40]He said to his disciples, "Why are you so afraid? Do you still have no faith?"

[41]They were terrified and asked each other, "Who is this? Even the wind and the waves obey him!"

The Healing of a Demon-possessed Man

5 They went across the lake to the region of the Gerasenes.[a] [2]When Jesus got out of the boat, a man with an evil[b] spirit came from the tombs to meet him. [3]This man lived in the tombs, and no one could bind him any more, not even with a chain. [4]For he had often been chained hand and foot, but he tore the chains apart and broke the irons on his feet. No one was strong enough to subdue him. [5]Night and day among the tombs and in the hills he would cry out and cut himself with stones.

[6]When he saw Jesus from a distance, he ran and fell on his knees in front of him. [7]He shouted at the top of his voice, "What do you want with me, Jesus, Son of the Most High God? Swear to God that you won't torture me!" [8]For Jesus had said to him, "Come out of this man, you evil spirit!"

[9]Then Jesus asked him, "What is your name?"

"My name is Legion," he replied, "for we are many." [10]And he begged Jesus again and again not to send them out of the area.

[11]A large herd of pigs was feeding on the nearby hillside. [12]The demons begged Jesus, "Send us among the pigs; allow us to go into them." [13]He gave them permission, and the evil spirits came out and went into the pigs. The herd, about two thousand in number, rushed down the steep bank into the lake and were drowned.

[14]Those tending the pigs ran off and reported this in the town and countryside, and the people went out to see what had happened. [15]When they came to Jesus, they saw the man who had been possessed by the legion of demons, sitting there, dressed and in his right mind; and they were afraid. [16]Those who had seen it told the people what had happened to the demon-possessed man—and told

---

[a]1 Some manuscripts Gadarenes; other manuscripts Gergesenes   [b]2 Greek unclean; also in verses 8 and 13

about the pigs as well. ¹⁷Then the people began to plead with Jesus to leave their region.

¹⁸As Jesus was getting into the boat, the man who had been demon-possessed begged to go with him. ¹⁹Jesus did not let him, but said, "Go home to your family and tell them how much the Lord has done for you, and how he has had mercy on you." ²⁰So the man went away and began to tell in the Decapolis*a* how much Jesus had done for him. And all the people were amazed.

A Dead Girl and a Sick Woman

²¹When Jesus had again crossed over by boat to the other side of the lake, a large crowd gathered around him while he was by the lake. ²²Then one of the synagogue rulers, named Jairus, came there. Seeing Jesus, he fell at his feet ²³and pleaded earnestly with him, "My little daughter is dying. Please come and put your hands on her so that she will be healed and live." ²⁴So Jesus went with him.

A large crowd followed and pressed around him. ²⁵And a woman was there who had been subject to bleeding for twelve years. ²⁶She had suffered a great deal under the care of many doctors and had spent all she had, yet instead of getting better she grew worse. ²⁷When she heard about Jesus, she came up behind him in the crowd and touched his cloak, ²⁸because she thought, "If I just touch his clothes, I will be healed." ²⁹Immediately her bleeding stopped and she felt in her body that she was freed from her suffering.

³⁰At once Jesus realized that power had gone out from him. He turned around in the crowd and asked, "Who touched my clothes?"

³¹"You see the people crowding against you," his disciples answered, "and yet you can ask, 'Who touched me?'"

³²But Jesus kept looking around to see who had done it. ³³Then the woman, knowing what had happened to her, came and fell at his feet and, trembling with fear, told him the whole truth. ³⁴He said to her, "Daughter, your faith has healed you. Go in peace and be freed from your suffering."

³⁵While Jesus was still speaking, some men came from the house of Jairus, the synagogue ruler. "Your daughter is dead," they said. "Why bother the teacher any more?"

³⁶Ignoring what they said, Jesus told the synagogue ruler, "Don't be afraid; just believe."

³⁷He did not let anyone follow him except Peter, James and John the brother of James. ³⁸When they came to the home of the synagogue ruler, Jesus saw a commotion, with people crying and wailing loudly. ³⁹He went in and said to them, "Why all this commotion and wailing? The child is not dead but asleep." ⁴⁰But they laughed at him.

After he put them all out, he took the child's father and mother and the disciples who were with him, and went in where the child was. ⁴¹He took her by the hand and said to her, "Talitha koum!" (which means, "Little girl, I say to you, get up!"). ⁴²Immediately the girl stood up and walked around (she was twelve years old). At this they were completely astonished. ⁴³He gave strict orders not to let anyone know about this, and told them to give her something to eat.

A Prophet Without Honor

6 Jesus left there and went to his hometown, accompanied by his disciples. ²When the Sabbath came, he began to teach in the synagogue, and many who heard him were amazed.

"Where did this man get these things?" they asked. "What's this wisdom that has been given him, that he even does miracles! ³Isn't this the carpenter? Isn't this Mary's son and the brother of James, Joseph,*b* Judas and Simon? Aren't his sisters here with us?" And they took offense at him.

⁴Jesus said to them, "Only in his

---

a20 That is, the Ten Cities   *b3* Greek *Joses,* a variant of *Joseph* hometown, among his relatives and in his own house is a prophet without honor." ⁵He could not do any miracles there, except lay his hands on a few sick people and heal them. ⁶And he was amazed at their lack of faith.

Jesus Sends Out the Twelve

Then Jesus went around teaching from village to village. ⁷Calling the Twelve to him, he sent them out two by two and gave them authority over evil[a] spirits.

⁸These were his instructions: "Take nothing for the journey except a staff—no bread, no bag, no money in your belts. ⁹Wear sandals but not an extra tunic. ¹⁰Whenever you enter a house, stay there until you leave that town. ¹¹And if any place will not welcome you or listen to you, shake the dust off your feet when you leave, as a testimony against them."

¹²They went out and preached that people should repent. ¹³They drove out many demons and anointed many sick people with oil and healed them.

John the Baptist Beheaded

¹⁴King Herod heard about this, for Jesus' name had become well known. Some were saying,[b] "John the Baptist has been raised from the dead, and that is why miraculous powers are at work in him."

¹⁵Others said, "He is Elijah."

And still others claimed, "He is a prophet, like one of the prophets of long ago."

¹⁶But when Herod heard this, he said, "John, the man I beheaded, has been raised from the dead!"

¹⁷For Herod himself had given orders to have John arrested, and he had him bound and put in prison. He did this because of Herodias, his brother Philip's wife, whom he had married. ¹⁸For John had been saying to Herod, "It is not lawful for you to have your brother's wife." ¹⁹So Herodias nursed a grudge against John and wanted to kill him. But she was

not able to, ²⁰because Herod feared John and protected him, knowing him to be a righteous and holy man. When Herod heard John, he was greatly puzzled[c]; yet he liked to listen to him.

²¹Finally the opportune time came. On his birthday Herod gave a banquet for his high officials and military commanders and the leading men of Galilee. ²²When the daughter of Herodias came in and danced, she pleased Herod and his dinner guests.

The king said to the girl, "Ask me for anything you want, and I'll give it to you." ²³And he promised her with an oath, "Whatever you ask I will give you, up to half my kingdom."

²⁴She went out and said to her mother, "What shall I ask for?"

"The head of John the Baptist," she answered.

²⁵At once the girl hurried in to the king with the request: "I want you to give me right now the head of John the Baptist on a platter."

²⁶The king was greatly distressed, but because of his oaths and his dinner guests, he did not want to refuse her. ²⁷So he immediately sent an executioner with orders to bring John's head. The man went, beheaded John in the prison, ²⁸and brought back his head on a platter. He presented it to the girl, and she gave it to her mother. ²⁹On hearing of this, John's disciples came and took his body and laid it in a tomb.

Jesus Feeds the Five Thousand

³⁰The apostles gathered around Jesus and reported to him all they had done and taught. ³¹Then, because so many people were coming and going that they did not even have a chance to eat, he said to them, "Come with me by yourselves to a quiet place and get some rest."

³²So they went away by themselves in a boat to a solitary place. ³³But many who saw them leaving recognized them and ran on foot from all

[a]7 Greek unclean [b]14 Some early manuscripts He was saying [c]20 Some early manuscripts he did many things

the towns and got there ahead of them. [34]When Jesus landed and saw a large crowd, he had compassion on them, because they were like sheep without a shepherd. So he began teaching them many things.

[35]By this time it was late in the day, so his disciples came to him. "This is a remote place," they said, "and it's already very late. [36]Send the people away so they can go to the surrounding countryside and villages and buy themselves something to eat."

[37]But he answered, "You give them something to eat."

They said to him, "That would take eight months of a man's wages[a]! Are we to go and spend that much on bread and give it to them to eat?"

[38]"How many loaves do you have?" he asked. "Go and see."

When they found out, they said, "Five—and two fish."

[39]Then Jesus directed them to have all the people sit down in groups on the green grass. [40]So they sat down in groups of hundreds and fifties. [41]Taking the five loaves and the two fish and looking up to heaven, he gave thanks and broke the loaves. Then he gave them to his disciples to set before the people. He also divided the two fish among them all. [42]They all ate and were satisfied, [43]and the disciples picked up twelve basketfuls of broken pieces of bread and fish. [44]The number of the men who had eaten was five thousand.

Jesus Walks on the Water

[45]Immediately Jesus made his disciples get into the boat and go on ahead of him to Bethsaida, while he dismissed the crowd. [46]After leaving them, he went up on a mountainside to pray.

[47]When evening came, the boat was in the middle of the lake, and he was alone on land. [48]He saw the disciples straining at the oars, because the wind was against them. About the fourth watch of the night he went out

to them, walking on the lake. He was about to pass by them, [49]but when they saw him walking on the lake, they thought he was a ghost. They cried out, [50]because they all saw him and were terrified.

Immediately he spoke to them and said, "Take courage! It is I. Don't be afraid." [51]Then he climbed into the boat with them, and the wind died down. They were completely amazed, [52]for they had not understood about the loaves; their hearts were hardened.

[53]When they had crossed over, they landed at Gennesaret and anchored there. [54]As soon as they got out of the boat, people recognized Jesus. [55]They ran throughout that whole region and carried the sick on mats to wherever they heard he was. [56]And wherever he went—into villages, towns or countryside—they placed the sick in the marketplaces. They begged him to let them touch even the edge of his cloak, and all who touched him were healed.

Clean and Unclean

7 The Pharisees and some of the teachers of the law who had come from Jerusalem gathered around Jesus and [2]saw some of his disciples eating food with hands that were "unclean," that is, unwashed. [3](The Pharisees and all the Jews do not eat unless they give their hands a ceremonial washing, holding to the tradition of the elders. [4]When they come from the marketplace they do not eat unless they wash. And they observe many other traditions, such as the washing of cups, pitchers and kettles.[b])

[5]So the Pharisees and teachers of the law asked Jesus, "Why don't your disciples live according to the tradition of the elders instead of eating their food with 'unclean' hands?"

[6]He replied, "Isaiah was right when he prophesied about you hypocrites; as it is written:

---

[a]37 Greek take two hundred denarii   [b]4 Some early manuscripts pitchers, kettles and dining couches

" 'These people honor me with
    their lips,
but their hearts are far from me.
[7]They worship me in vain;
    their teachings are but rules
    taught by men.'[a]

[8]You have let go of the commands of
God and are holding on to the traditions of men."

[9]And he said to them: "You have a
fine way of setting aside the commands of God in order to observe[b]
your own traditions! [10]For Moses
said, 'Honor your father and your
mother,'[c] and, 'Anyone who curses
his father or mother must be put to
death.'[d] [11]But you say that if a man
says to his father or mother: 'Whatever help you might otherwise have
received from me is Corban' (that is, a
gift devoted to God), [12]then you no
longer let him do anything for his father or mother. [13]Thus you nullify the
word of God by your tradition that
you have handed down. And you do
many things like that."

[14]Again Jesus called the crowd to
him and said, "Listen to me, everyone, and understand this. [15]Nothing
outside a man can make him 'unclean' by going into him. Rather, it is
what comes out of a man that makes
him 'unclean.'[e]"

[17]After he had left the crowd and
entered the house, his disciples asked
him about this parable. [18]"Are you so
dull?" he asked. "Don't you see that
nothing that enters a man from the
outside can make him 'unclean'? [19]For
it doesn't go into his heart but into his
stomach, and then out of his body."
(In saying this, Jesus declared all
foods "clean.")

[20]He went on: "What comes out of
a man is what makes him 'unclean.'
[21]For from within, out of men's hearts,
come evil thoughts, sexual immorality, theft, murder, adultery, [22]greed,
malice, deceit, lewdness, envy, slan-

der, arrogance and folly. [23]All these
evils come from inside and make a
man 'unclean.' "

The Faith of a Syrophoenician Woman

[24]Jesus left that place and went to
the vicinity of Tyre.[f] He entered a
house and did not want anyone to
know it; yet he could not keep his
presence secret. [25]In fact, as soon as
she heard about him, a woman whose
little daughter was possessed by an
evil[g] spirit came and fell at his feet.
[26]The woman was a Greek, born in
Syrian Phoenicia. She begged Jesus to
drive the demon out of her daughter.

[27]"First let the children eat all they
want," he told her, "for it is not right
to take the children's bread and toss it
to their dogs."

[28]"Yes, Lord," she replied, "but
even the dogs under the table eat the
children's crumbs."

[29]Then he told her, "For such a reply, you may go; the demon has left
your daughter."

[30]She went home and found her
child lying on the bed, and the demon
gone.

The Healing of a Deaf and Mute Man

[31]Then Jesus left the vicinity of Tyre
and went through Sidon, down to the
Sea of Galilee and into the region of
the Decapolis.[h] [32]There some people
brought to him a man who was deaf
and could hardly talk, and they
begged him to place his hand on the
man.

[33]After he took him aside, away
from the crowd, Jesus put his fingers
into the man's ears. Then he spit and
touched the man's tongue. [34]He
looked up to heaven and with a deep
sigh said to him, *"Ephphatha!"* (which
means, "Be opened!"). [35]At this, the
man's ears were opened, his tongue

[a]6,7 Isaiah 29:13   [b]9 Some manuscripts *set up*   [c]10 Exodus 20:12; Deut. 5:16
[d]10 Exodus 21:17; Lev. 20:9   [e]15 Some early manuscripts *'unclean.'* [16]*If anyone has ears to hear,*
let him hear.   [f]24 Many early manuscripts *Tyre and Sidon*   [g]25 Greek *unclean*   [h]31 That
is, the Ten Cities

was loosened and he began to speak plainly.

36Jesus commanded them not to tell anyone. But the more he did so, the more they kept talking about it. 37People were overwhelmed with amazement. "He has done everything well," they said. "He even makes the deaf hear and the mute speak."

Jesus Feeds the Four Thousand

8 During those days another large crowd gathered. Since they had nothing to eat, Jesus called his disciples to him and said, 2"I have compassion for these people; they have already been with me three days and have nothing to eat. 3If I send them home hungry, they will collapse on the way, because some of them have come a long distance."

4His disciples answered, "But where in this remote place can anyone get enough bread to feed them?"

5"How many loaves do you have?" Jesus asked.

"Seven," they replied.

6He told the crowd to sit down on the ground. When he had taken the seven loaves and given thanks, he broke them and gave them to his disciples to set before the people, and they did so. 7They had a few small fish as well; he gave thanks for them also and told the disciples to distribute them. 8The people ate and were satisfied. Afterward the disciples picked up seven basketfuls of broken pieces that were left over. 9About four thousand men were present. And having sent them away, 10he got into the boat with his disciples and went to the region of Dalmanutha.

11The Pharisees came and began to question Jesus. To test him, they asked him for a sign from heaven. 12He sighed deeply and said, "Why does this generation ask for a miraculous sign? I tell you the truth, no sign will be given to it." 13Then he left them, got back into the boat and crossed to the other side.

The Yeast of the Pharisees and Herod

14The disciples had forgotten to bring bread, except for one loaf they had with them in the boat. 15"Be careful," Jesus warned them. "Watch out for the yeast of the Pharisees and that of Herod."

16They discussed this with one another and said, "It is because we have no bread."

17Aware of their discussion, Jesus asked them: "Why are you talking about having no bread? Do you still not see or understand? Are your hearts hardened? 18Do you have eyes but fail to see, and ears but fail to hear? And don't you remember? 19When I broke the five loaves for the five thousand, how many basketfuls of pieces did you pick up?"

"Twelve," they replied.

20"And when I broke the seven loaves for the four thousand, how many basketfuls of pieces did you pick up?"

They answered, "Seven."

21He said to them, "Do you still not understand?"

The Healing of a Blind Man at Bethsaida

22They came to Bethsaida, and some people brought a blind man and begged Jesus to touch him. 23He took the blind man by the hand and led him outside the village. When he had spit on the man's eyes and put his hands on him, Jesus asked, "Do you see anything?"

24He looked up and said, "I see people; they look like trees walking around."

25Once more Jesus put his hands on the man's eyes. Then his eyes were opened, his sight was restored, and he saw everything clearly. 26Jesus sent him home, saying, "Don't go into the village.a"

Peter's Confession of Christ

27Jesus and his disciples went on to

---

a26 Some manuscripts *Don't go and tell anyone in the village*

the villages around Caesarea Philippi. On the way he asked them, "Who do people say I am?"

²⁸They replied, "Some say John the Baptist; others say Elijah; and still others, one of the prophets."

²⁹"But what about you?" he asked. "Who do you say I am?"

Peter answered, "You are the Christ.ᵃ"

³⁰Jesus warned them not to tell anyone about him.

Jesus Predicts His Death

³¹He then began to teach them that the Son of Man must suffer many things and be rejected by the elders, chief priests and teachers of the law, and that he must be killed and after three days rise again. ³²He spoke plainly about this, and Peter took him aside and began to rebuke him.

³³But when Jesus turned and looked at his disciples, he rebuked Peter. "Get behind me, Satan!" he said. "You do not have in mind the things of God, but the things of men."

³⁴Then he called the crowd to him along with his disciples and said: "If anyone would come after me, he must deny himself and take up his cross and follow me. ³⁵For whoever wants to save his lifeᵇ will lose it, but whoever loses his life for me and for the gospel will save it. ³⁶What good is it for a man to gain the whole world, yet forfeit his soul? ³⁷Or what can a man give in exchange for his soul? ³⁸If anyone is ashamed of me and my words in this adulterous and sinful generation, the Son of Man will be ashamed of him when he comes in his Father's glory with the holy angels."

9 And he said to them, "I tell you the truth, some who are standing here will not taste death before they see the kingdom of God come with power."

The Transfiguration

²After six days Jesus took Peter, James and John with him and led

them up a high mountain, where they were all alone. There he was transfigured before them. ³His clothes became dazzling white, whiter than anyone in the world could bleach them. ⁴And there appeared before them Elijah and Moses, who were talking with Jesus.

⁵Peter said to Jesus, "Rabbi, it is good for us to be here. Let us put up three shelters—one for you, one for Moses and one for Elijah." ⁶(He did not know what to say, they were so frightened.)

⁷Then a cloud appeared and enveloped them, and a voice came from the cloud: "This is my Son, whom I love. Listen to him!"

⁸Suddenly, when they looked around, they no longer saw anyone with them except Jesus.

⁹As they were coming down the mountain, Jesus gave them orders not to tell anyone what they had seen until the Son of Man had risen from the dead. ¹⁰They kept the matter to themselves, discussing what "rising from the dead" meant.

¹¹And they asked him, "Why do the teachers of the law say that Elijah must come first?"

¹²Jesus replied, "To be sure, Elijah does come first, and restores all things. Why then is it written that the Son of Man must suffer much and be rejected? ¹³But I tell you, Elijah has come, and they have done to him everything they wished, just as it is written about him."

The Healing of a Boy With an Evil Spirit

¹⁴When they came to the other disciples, they saw a large crowd around them and the teachers of the law arguing with them. ¹⁵As soon as all the people saw Jesus, they were overwhelmed with wonder and ran to greet him.

¹⁶"What are you arguing with them about?" he asked.

¹⁷A man in the crowd answered,

ᵃ29 Or Messiah. "The Christ" (Greek) and "the Messiah" (Hebrew) both mean "the Anointed One."   ᵇ35 The Greek word means either life or soul; also in verse 36.

"Teacher, I brought you my son, who is possessed by a spirit that has robbed him of speech. ¹⁸Whenever it seizes him, it throws him to the ground. He foams at the mouth, gnashes his teeth and becomes rigid. I asked your disciples to drive out the spirit, but they could not."

¹⁹"O unbelieving generation," Jesus replied, "how long shall I stay with you? How long shall I put up with you? Bring the boy to me."

²⁰So they brought him. When the spirit saw Jesus, it immediately threw the boy into a convulsion. He fell to the ground and rolled around, foaming at the mouth.

²¹Jesus asked the boy's father, "How long has he been like this?"

"From childhood," he answered.

VERSE:
Mark 8:36

AUTHOR:
J. Oswald Sanders

PASSAGE:
Mark 8:31–38

Finding Value in God's Eyes

There is a great degree of truth in the old adage that one is just as old as he feels. Someone once maintained that most people over 70 are secretly young, disguised in an old skin. The aging and old do not think of themselves as old. Underneath that aging skin and body, they feel as young as ever. Old age is a relative term, and most feel younger than their official age.

While the aging process is largely beyond their control, it must be admitted that many of the problems of the elderly are self-inflicted and could be solved, in measure at least, if they were resolutely attacked. There are some, for example, who feel they are of little social significance—no one needs or wants them. But often it is their own negative attitude toward themselves that prevents their being needed and wanted. To correct that, a new mind-set is demanded. In the Biblical view, no one is insignificant and valueless. Did not our Lord say that to gain the whole world at the cost of one's soul would be a bad bargain (Mark 8:36)? We should learn to view the potential of our lives as God views it.

ADDITIONAL SCRIPTURE READINGS
Luke 12:1–12; 1 Peter 2:4–10

Go to page 1262 for your next devotional reading.

²²"It has often thrown him into fire or water to kill him. But if you can do anything, take pity on us and help us."

²³" 'If you can'?" said Jesus. "Everything is possible for him who believes."

²⁴Immediately the boy's father exclaimed, "I do believe; help me overcome my unbelief!"

²⁵When Jesus saw that a crowd was running to the scene, he rebuked the evil[a] spirit. "You deaf and mute spirit," he said, "I command you, come out of him and never enter him again."

²⁶The spirit shrieked, convulsed him violently and came out. The boy looked so much like a corpse that many said, "He's dead." ²⁷But Jesus took him by the hand and lifted him to his feet, and he stood up.

²⁸After Jesus had gone indoors, his disciples asked him privately, "Why couldn't we drive it out?"

²⁹He replied, "This kind can come out only by prayer.[b]"

³⁰They left that place and passed through Galilee. Jesus did not want anyone to know where they were, ³¹because he was teaching his disciples. He said to them, "The Son of Man is going to be betrayed into the hands of men. They will kill him, and after three days he will rise." ³²But they did not understand what he meant and were afraid to ask him about it.

Who Is the Greatest?

³³They came to Capernaum. When he was in the house, he asked them, "What were you arguing about on the road?" ³⁴But they kept quiet because on the way they had argued about who was the greatest.

³⁵Sitting down, Jesus called the Twelve and said, "If anyone wants to be first, he must be the very last, and the servant of all."

³⁶He took a little child and had him stand among them. Taking him in his arms, he said to them, ³⁷"Whoever welcomes one of these little children in my name welcomes me; and whoever welcomes me does not welcome me but the one who sent me."

Whoever Is Not Against Us Is for Us

³⁸"Teacher," said John, "we saw a man driving out demons in your name and we told him to stop, because he was not one of us."

³⁹"Do not stop him," Jesus said. "No one who does a miracle in my name can in the next moment say anything bad about me, ⁴⁰for whoever is not against us is for us. ⁴¹I tell you the truth, anyone who gives you a cup of water in my name because you belong to Christ will certainly not lose his reward.

Causing to Sin

⁴²"And if anyone causes one of these little ones who believe in me to sin, it would be better for him to be thrown into the sea with a large millstone tied around his neck. ⁴³If your hand causes you to sin, cut it off. It is better for you to enter life maimed than with two hands to go into hell, where the fire never goes out.[c] ⁴⁵And if your foot causes you to sin, cut it off. It is better for you to enter life crippled than to have two feet and be thrown into hell.[d] ⁴⁷And if your eye causes you to sin, pluck it out. It is better for you to enter the kingdom of God with one eye than to have two eyes and be thrown into hell, ⁴⁸where

" 'their worm does not die,
and the fire is not quenched.'[e]

⁴⁹Everyone will be salted with fire.

⁵⁰"Salt is good, but if it loses its saltiness, how can you make it salty

---

^a25 Greek *unclean*   ^b29 Some manuscripts *prayer and fasting*   ^c43 Some manuscripts *out,* ⁴⁴where / " 'their worm does not die, / and the fire is not quenched.'   ^d45 Some manuscripts *hell,* ⁴⁶where / " 'their worm does not die, / and the fire is not quenched.'   ^e48 Isaiah 66:24

again? Have salt in yourselves, and be at peace with each other."

Divorce

10 Jesus then left that place and went into the region of Judea and across the Jordan. Again crowds of people came to him, and as was his custom, he taught them.

²Some Pharisees came and tested him by asking, "Is it lawful for a man to divorce his wife?"

³"What did Moses command you?" he replied.

⁴They said, "Moses permitted a man to write a certificate of divorce and send her away."

⁵"It was because your hearts were hard that Moses wrote you this law,"

THURSDAY

VERSE:
Mark 9:41

AUTHOR:
Herbert VanderLugt

PASSAGE:
Mark 9:33–41

A Cup of Water

The realization that we are here to glorify God is assuring to believers who have been faithful to the Lord but have never achieved great success in the eyes of their peers. It helps them recognize that some of the little things they did because they loved the Savior were important to God, met his approval and will be rewarded. Jesus said that a person who gives a cup of water in his name "will certainly not lose his reward" (Mark 9:41). Though we thought little of them, our kind words and loving deeds pleased God and glorified him. Through them we fulfilled, at least in part, the purpose for which he created us.

This awareness should also work as a challenge. It provides us with an incentive for the development of personal holiness and the "fruit of the Spirit." Peter was addressing old and young alike when he wrote, "But just as he who called you is holy, so be holy in all you do; for it is written: 'Be holy, because I am holy' " (1 Peter 1:15–16).

The autumn season of life is a beautiful time to glorify God by growing the fruit of the Spirit.

ADDITIONAL SCRIPTURE READINGS
John 15:1–17; Galatians 5:16–26

Go to page 1271 for your next devotional reading.

Jesus replied. ⁶"But at the beginning of creation God 'made them male and female.'ᵃ ⁷For this reason a man will leave his father and mother and be united to his wife,ᵇ ⁸and the two will become one flesh.'ᶜ So they are no longer two, but one. ⁹Therefore what God has joined together, let man not separate."

¹⁰When they were in the house again, the disciples asked Jesus about this. ¹¹He answered, "Anyone who divorces his wife and marries another woman commits adultery against her. ¹²And if she divorces her husband and marries another man, she commits adultery."

The Little Children and Jesus

¹³People were bringing little children to Jesus to have him touch them, but the disciples rebuked them. ¹⁴When Jesus saw this, he was indignant. He said to them, "Let the little children come to me, and do not hinder them, for the kingdom of God belongs to such as these. ¹⁵I tell you the truth, anyone who will not receive the kingdom of God like a little child will never enter it." ¹⁶And he took the children in his arms, put his hands on them and blessed them.

The Rich Young Man

¹⁷As Jesus started on his way, a man ran up to him and fell on his knees before him. "Good teacher," he asked, "what must I do to inherit eternal life?"

¹⁸"Why do you call me good?" Jesus answered. "No one is good—except God alone. ¹⁹You know the commandments: 'Do not murder, do not commit adultery, do not steal, do not give false testimony, do not defraud, honor your father and mother.'ᵈ

²⁰"Teacher," he declared, "all these I have kept since I was a boy."

²¹Jesus looked at him and loved him. "One thing you lack," he said. "Go, sell everything you have and give to the poor, and you will have treasure in heaven. Then come, follow me."

²²At this the man's face fell. He went away sad, because he had great wealth.

²³Jesus looked around and said to his disciples, "How hard it is for the rich to enter the kingdom of God!"

²⁴The disciples were amazed at his words. But Jesus said again, "Children, how hard it isᵉ to enter the kingdom of God! ²⁵It is easier for a camel to go through the eye of a needle than for a rich man to enter the kingdom of God."

²⁶The disciples were even more amazed, and said to each other, "Who then can be saved?"

²⁷Jesus looked at them and said, "With man this is impossible, but not with God; all things are possible with God."

²⁸Peter said to him, "We have left everything to follow you!"

²⁹"I tell you the truth," Jesus replied, "no one who has left home or brothers or sisters or mother or father or children or fields for me and the gospel ³⁰will fail to receive a hundred times as much in this present age (homes, brothers, sisters, mothers, children and fields—and with them, persecutions) and in the age to come, eternal life. ³¹But many who are first will be last, and the last first."

Jesus Again Predicts His Death

³²They were on their way up to Jerusalem, with Jesus leading the way, and the disciples were astonished, while those who followed were afraid. Again he took the Twelve aside and told them what was going to happen to him. ³³"We are going up to Jerusalem," he said, "and the Son of Man will be betrayed to the chief priests and teachers of the law. They will condemn him to death and will hand him over to the Gentiles, ³⁴who will mock him and spit on him, flog

ᵃ6 Gen. 1:27   ᵇ7 Some early manuscripts do not have *and be united to his wife.*   ᶜ8 Gen. 2:24
ᵈ19 Exodus 20:12-16; Deut. 5:16-20   ᵉ24 Some manuscripts *is for those who trust in riches*

him and kill him. Three days later he will rise."

The Request of James and John

³⁵Then James and John, the sons of Zebedee, came to him. "Teacher," they said, "we want you to do for us whatever we ask."

³⁶"What do you want me to do for you?" he asked.

³⁷They replied, "Let one of us sit at your right and the other at your left in your glory."

³⁸"You don't know what you are asking," Jesus said. "Can you drink the cup I drink or be baptized with the baptism I am baptized with?"

³⁹"We can," they answered.

Jesus said to them, "You will drink the cup I drink and be baptized with the baptism I am baptized with, ⁴⁰but to sit at my right or left is not for me to grant. These places belong to those for whom they have been prepared."

⁴¹When the ten heard about this, they became indignant with James and John. ⁴²Jesus called them together and said, "You know that those who are regarded as rulers of the Gentiles lord it over them, and their high officials exercise authority over them. ⁴³Not so with you. Instead, whoever wants to become great among you must be your servant, ⁴⁴and whoever wants to be first must be slave of all. ⁴⁵For even the Son of Man did not come to be served, but to serve, and to give his life as a ransom for many."

Blind Bartimaeus Receives His Sight

⁴⁶Then they came to Jericho. As Jesus and his disciples, together with a large crowd, were leaving the city, a blind man, Bartimaeus (that is, the Son of Timaeus), was sitting by the roadside begging. ⁴⁷When he heard that it was Jesus of Nazareth, he began to shout, "Jesus, Son of David, have mercy on me!"

⁴⁸Many rebuked him and told him to be quiet, but he shouted all the more, "Son of David, have mercy on me!"

⁴⁹Jesus stopped and said, "Call him."

So they called to the blind man, "Cheer up! On your feet! He's calling you." ⁵⁰Throwing his cloak aside, he jumped to his feet and came to Jesus.

⁵¹"What do you want me to do for you?" Jesus asked him.

The blind man said, "Rabbi, I want to see."

⁵²"Go," said Jesus, "your faith has healed you." Immediately he received his sight and followed Jesus along the road.

The Triumphal Entry

11 As they approached Jerusalem and came to Bethphage and Bethany at the Mount of Olives, Jesus sent two of his disciples, ²saying to them, "Go to the village ahead of you, and just as you enter it, you will find a colt tied there, which no one has ever ridden. Untie it and bring it here. ³If anyone asks you, 'Why are you doing this?' tell him, 'The Lord needs it and will send it back here shortly.' "

⁴They went and found a colt outside in the street, tied at a doorway. As they untied it, ⁵some people standing there asked, "What are you doing, untying that colt?" ⁶They answered as Jesus had told them to, and the people let them go. ⁷When they brought the colt to Jesus and threw their cloaks over it, he sat on it. ⁸Many people spread their cloaks on the road, while others spread branches they had cut in the fields. ⁹Those who went ahead and those who followed shouted,

"Hosanna!ᵃ"

"Blessed is he who comes in the name of the Lord!"ᵇ

¹⁰"Blessed is the coming kingdom of our father David!"

"Hosanna in the highest!"

ᵃ9 A Hebrew expression meaning "Save!" which became an exclamation of praise; also in verse 10   ᵇ9 Psalm 118:25,26

¹¹Jesus entered Jerusalem and went to the temple. He looked around at everything, but since it was already late, he went out to Bethany with the Twelve.

Jesus Clears the Temple

¹²The next day as they were leaving Bethany, Jesus was hungry. ¹³Seeing in the distance a fig tree in leaf, he went to find out if it had any fruit. When he reached it, he found nothing but leaves, because it was not the season for figs. ¹⁴Then he said to the tree, "May no one ever eat fruit from you again." And his disciples heard him say it.

¹⁵On reaching Jerusalem, Jesus entered the temple area and began driving out those who were buying and selling there. He overturned the tables of the money changers and the benches of those selling doves, ¹⁶and would not allow anyone to carry merchandise through the temple courts. ¹⁷And as he taught them, he said, "Is it not written:

" 'My house will be called
    a house of prayer for all
         nations'ᵃ?

But you have made it 'a den of robbers.'ᵇ"

¹⁸The chief priests and the teachers of the law heard this and began looking for a way to kill him, for they feared him, because the whole crowd was amazed at his teaching.

¹⁹When evening came, theyᶜ went out of the city.

The Withered Fig Tree

²⁰In the morning, as they went along, they saw the fig tree withered from the roots. ²¹Peter remembered and said to Jesus, "Rabbi, look! The fig tree you cursed has withered!"

²²"Haveᵈ faith in God," Jesus answered. ²³"I tell you the truth, if anyone says to this mountain, 'Go, throw yourself into the sea,' and does not doubt in his heart but believes that what he says will happen, it will be done for him. ²⁴Therefore I tell you, whatever you ask for in prayer, believe that you have received it, and it will be yours. ²⁵And when you stand praying, if you hold anything against anyone, forgive him, so that your Father in heaven may forgive you your sins.ᵉ"

The Authority of Jesus Questioned

²⁷They arrived again in Jerusalem, and while Jesus was walking in the temple courts, the chief priests, the teachers of the law and the elders came to him. ²⁸"By what authority are you doing these things?" they asked. "And who gave you authority to do this?"

²⁹Jesus replied, "I will ask you one question. Answer me, and I will tell you by what authority I am doing these things. ³⁰John's baptism—was it from heaven, or from men? Tell me!"

³¹They discussed it among themselves and said, "If we say, 'From heaven,' he will ask, 'Then why didn't you believe him?' ³²But if we say, 'From men' ...." (They feared the people, for everyone held that John really was a prophet.)

³³So they answered Jesus, "We don't know."

Jesus said, "Neither will I tell you by what authority I am doing these things."

The Parable of the Tenants

12 He then began to speak to them in parables: "A man planted a vineyard. He put a wall around it, dug a pit for the winepress and built a watchtower. Then he rented the vineyard to some farmers and went away on a journey. ²At harvest time he sent a servant to the tenants to collect from them some of the fruit of the vineyard. ³But they seized him, beat him and sent him away empty-handed. ⁴Then he sent another ser-

ᵃ17 Isaiah 56:7   ᵇ17 Jer. 7:11   ᶜ19 Some early manuscripts he   ᵈ22 Some early manuscripts If you have   ᵉ25 Some manuscripts sins. ²⁶But if you do not forgive, neither will your Father who is in heaven forgive your sins.

vant to them; they struck this man on the head and treated him shamefully. 5He sent still another, and that one they killed. He sent many others; some of them they beat, others they killed.

6"He had one left to send, a son, whom he loved. He sent him last of all, saying, 'They will respect my son.'

7"But the tenants said to one another, 'This is the heir. Come, let's kill him, and the inheritance will be ours.' 8So they took him and killed him, and threw him out of the vineyard.

9"What then will the owner of the vineyard do? He will come and kill those tenants and give the vineyard to others. 10Haven't you read this scripture:

" 'The stone the builders rejected
　　has become the capstone*a*;
11the Lord has done this,
　　and it is marvelous in our
　　　　eyes'*b*?"

12Then they looked for a way to arrest him because they knew he had spoken the parable against them. But they were afraid of the crowd; so they left him and went away.

Paying Taxes to Caesar

13Later they sent some of the Pharisees and Herodians to Jesus to catch him in his words. 14They came to him and said, "Teacher, we know you are a man of integrity. You aren't swayed by men, because you pay no attention to who they are; but you teach the way of God in accordance with the truth. Is it right to pay taxes to Caesar or not? 15Should we pay or shouldn't we?"

But Jesus knew their hypocrisy. "Why are you trying to trap me?" he asked. "Bring me a denarius and let me look at it." 16They brought the coin, and he asked them, "Whose portrait is this? And whose inscription?"

"Caesar's," they replied.

17Then Jesus said to them, "Give to Caesar what is Caesar's and to God what is God's."

And they were amazed at him.

Marriage at the Resurrection

18Then the Sadducees, who say there is no resurrection, came to him with a question. 19"Teacher," they said, "Moses wrote for us that if a man's brother dies and leaves a wife but no children, the man must marry the widow and have children for his brother. 20Now there were seven brothers. The first one married and died without leaving any children. 21The second one married the widow, but he also died, leaving no child. It was the same with the third. 22In fact, none of the seven left any children. Last of all, the woman died too. 23At the resurrection*c* whose wife will she be, since the seven were married to her?"

24Jesus replied, "Are you not in error because you do not know the Scriptures or the power of God? 25When the dead rise, they will neither marry nor be given in marriage; they will be like the angels in heaven. 26Now about the dead rising—have you not read in the book of Moses, in the account of the bush, how God said to him, 'I am the God of Abraham, the God of Isaac, and the God of Jacob'*d*? 27He is not the God of the dead, but of the living. You are badly mistaken!"

The Greatest Commandment

28One of the teachers of the law came and heard them debating. Noticing that Jesus had given them a good answer, he asked him, "Of all the commandments, which is the most important?"

29"The most important one," answered Jesus, "is this: 'Hear, O Israel, the Lord our God, the Lord is one.*e* 30Love the Lord your God with all your heart and with all your soul and with all your mind and with all your strength.'*f* 31The second is this: 'Love

---

*a*10 Or *cornerstone*　　*b*11 Psalm 118:22,23　　*c*23 Some manuscripts *resurrection, when men rise from the dead,*　　*d*26 Exodus 3:6　　*e*29 Or *the Lord our God is one Lord*　　*f*30 Deut. 6:4,5

your neighbor as yourself.'[a] There is no commandment greater than these."

[32]"Well said, teacher," the man replied. "You are right in saying that God is one and there is no other but him. [33]To love him with all your heart, with all your understanding and with all your strength, and to love your neighbor as yourself is more important than all burnt offerings and sacrifices."

[34]When Jesus saw that he had answered wisely, he said to him, "You are not far from the kingdom of God." And from then on no one dared ask him any more questions.

Whose Son Is the Christ?

[35]While Jesus was teaching in the temple courts, he asked, "How is it that the teachers of the law say that the Christ[b] is the son of David? [36]David himself, speaking by the Holy Spirit, declared:

" 'The Lord said to my Lord:
  "Sit at my right hand
until I put your enemies
  under your feet." '[c]

[37]David himself calls him 'Lord.' How then can he be his son?"

The large crowd listened to him with delight.

[38]As he taught, Jesus said, "Watch out for the teachers of the law. They like to walk around in flowing robes and be greeted in the marketplaces, [39]and have the most important seats in the synagogues and the places of honor at banquets. [40]They devour widows' houses and for a show make lengthy prayers. Such men will be punished most severely."

The Widow's Offering

[41]Jesus sat down opposite the place where the offerings were put and watched the crowd putting their money into the temple treasury. Many rich people threw in large amounts. [42]But a poor widow came and put in two very small copper coins,[d] worth only a fraction of a penny.[e]

[43]Calling his disciples to him, Jesus said, "I tell you the truth, this poor widow has put more into the treasury than all the others. [44]They all gave out of their wealth; but she, out of her poverty, put in everything—all she had to live on."

Signs of the End of the Age

13 As he was leaving the temple, one of his disciples said to him, "Look, Teacher! What massive stones! What magnificent buildings!"

[2]"Do you see all these great buildings?" replied Jesus. "Not one stone here will be left on another; every one will be thrown down."

[3]As Jesus was sitting on the Mount of Olives opposite the temple, Peter, James, John and Andrew asked him privately, [4]"Tell us, when will these things happen? And what will be the sign that they are all about to be fulfilled?"

[5]Jesus said to them: "Watch out that no one deceives you. [6]Many will come in my name, claiming, 'I am he,' and will deceive many. [7]When you hear of wars and rumors of wars, do not be alarmed. Such things must happen, but the end is still to come. [8]Nation will rise against nation, and kingdom against kingdom. There will be earthquakes in various places, and famines. These are the beginning of birth pains.

[9]"You must be on your guard. You will be handed over to the local councils and flogged in the synagogues. On account of me you will stand before governors and kings as witnesses to them. [10]And the gospel must first be preached to all nations. [11]Whenever you are arrested and brought to trial, do not worry beforehand about what to say. Just say whatever is given you at the time, for it is not you speaking, but the Holy Spirit.

[12]"Brother will betray brother to

---

[a]31 Lev. 19:18   [b]35 Or Messiah   [c]36 Psalm 110:1   [d]42 Greek two lepta   [e]42 Greek kodrantes

death, and a father his child. Children will rebel against their parents and have them put to death. [13]All men will hate you because of me, but he who stands firm to the end will be saved.

[14]"When you see 'the abomination that causes desolation'[a] standing where it[b] does not belong—let the reader understand—then let those who are in Judea flee to the mountains. [15]Let no one on the roof of his house go down or enter the house to take anything out. [16]Let no one in the field go back to get his cloak. [17]How dreadful it will be in those days for pregnant women and nursing mothers! [18]Pray that this will not take place in winter, [19]because those will be days of distress unequaled from the beginning, when God created the world, until now—and never to be equaled again. [20]If the Lord had not cut short those days, no one would survive. But for the sake of the elect, whom he has chosen, he has shortened them. [21]At that time if anyone says to you, 'Look, here is the Christ[c]!' or, 'Look, there he is!' do not believe it. [22]For false Christs and false prophets will appear and perform signs and miracles to deceive the elect—if that were possible. [23]So be on your guard; I have told you everything ahead of time.

[24]"But in those days, following that distress,

" 'the sun will be darkened,
    and the moon will not give its light;
[25]the stars will fall from the sky,
    and the heavenly bodies will be shaken.'[d]

[26]"At that time men will see the Son of Man coming in clouds with great power and glory. [27]And he will send his angels and gather his elect from the four winds, from the ends of the earth to the ends of the heavens.

[28]"Now learn this lesson from the fig tree: As soon as its twigs get tender and its leaves come out, you know that summer is near. [29]Even so, when you see these things happening, you know that it is near, right at the door. [30]I tell you the truth, this generation[e] will certainly not pass away until all these things have happened. [31]Heaven and earth will pass away, but my words will never pass away.

The Day and Hour Unknown

[32]"No one knows about that day or hour, not even the angels in heaven, nor the Son, but only the Father. [33]Be on guard! Be alert[f]! You do not know when that time will come. [34]It's like a man going away: He leaves his house and puts his servants in charge, each with his assigned task, and tells the one at the door to keep watch.

[35]"Therefore keep watch because you do not know when the owner of the house will come back—whether in the evening, or at midnight, or when the rooster crows, or at dawn. [36]If he comes suddenly, do not let him find you sleeping. [37]What I say to you, I say to everyone: 'Watch!' "

Jesus Anointed at Bethany

14 Now the Passover and the Feast of Unleavened Bread were only two days away, and the chief priests and the teachers of the law were looking for some sly way to arrest Jesus and kill him. [2]"But not during the Feast," they said, "or the people may riot."

[3]While he was in Bethany, reclining at the table in the home of a man known as Simon the Leper, a woman came with an alabaster jar of very expensive perfume, made of pure nard. She broke the jar and poured the perfume on his head.

[4]Some of those present were saying indignantly to one another, "Why this waste of perfume? [5]It could have been sold for more than a year's wages[g] and the money given to the poor." And they rebuked her harshly.

---

[a]14 Daniel 9:27; 11:31; 12:11   [b]14 Or *he*; also in verse 29   [c]21 Or *Messiah*
[d]25 Isaiah 13:10; 34:4   [e]30 Or *race*   [f]33 Some manuscripts *alert and pray*   [g]5 Greek *than three hundred denarii*

⁶"Leave her alone," said Jesus. "Why are you bothering her? She has done a beautiful thing to me. ⁷The poor you will always have with you, and you can help them any time you want. But you will not always have me. ⁸She did what she could. She poured perfume on my body beforehand to prepare for my burial. ⁹I tell you the truth, wherever the gospel is preached throughout the world, what she has done will also be told, in memory of her."

¹⁰Then Judas Iscariot, one of the Twelve, went to the chief priests to betray Jesus to them. ¹¹They were delighted to hear this and promised to give him money. So he watched for an opportunity to hand him over.

The Lord's Supper

¹²On the first day of the Feast of Unleavened Bread, when it was customary to sacrifice the Passover lamb, Jesus' disciples asked him, "Where do you want us to go and make preparations for you to eat the Passover?"

¹³So he sent two of his disciples, telling them, "Go into the city, and a man carrying a jar of water will meet you. Follow him. ¹⁴Say to the owner of the house he enters, 'The Teacher asks: Where is my guest room, where I may eat the Passover with my disciples?' ¹⁵He will show you a large upper room, furnished and ready. Make preparations for us there."

¹⁶The disciples left, went into the city and found things just as Jesus had told them. So they prepared the Passover.

¹⁷When evening came, Jesus arrived with the Twelve. ¹⁸While they were reclining at the table eating, he said, "I tell you the truth, one of you will betray me—one who is eating with me."

¹⁹They were saddened, and one by one they said to him, "Surely not I?"

²⁰"It is one of the Twelve," he replied, "one who dips bread into the bowl with me. ²¹The Son of Man will go just as it is written about him. But woe to that man who betrays the Son of Man! It would be better for him if he had not been born."

²²While they were eating, Jesus took bread, gave thanks and broke it, and gave it to his disciples, saying, "Take it; this is my body."

²³Then he took the cup, gave thanks and offered it to them, and they all drank from it.

²⁴"This is my blood of theᵃ covenant, which is poured out for many," he said to them. ²⁵"I tell you the truth, I will not drink again of the fruit of the vine until that day when I drink it anew in the kingdom of God."

²⁶When they had sung a hymn, they went out to the Mount of Olives.

Jesus Predicts Peter's Denial

²⁷"You will all fall away," Jesus told them, "for it is written:

" 'I will strike the shepherd,
    and the sheep will be
        scattered.'ᵇ

²⁸But after I have risen, I will go ahead of you into Galilee."

²⁹Peter declared, "Even if all fall away, I will not."

³⁰"I tell you the truth," Jesus answered, "today—yes, tonight—before the rooster crows twiceᶜ you yourself will disown me three times."

³¹But Peter insisted emphatically, "Even if I have to die with you, I will never disown you." And all the others said the same.

Gethsemane

³²They went to a place called Gethsemane, and Jesus said to his disciples, "Sit here while I pray." ³³He took Peter, James and John along with him, and he began to be deeply distressed and troubled. ³⁴"My soul is overwhelmed with sorrow to the point of death," he said to them. "Stay here and keep watch."

³⁵Going a little farther, he fell to the ground and prayed that if possible

---

ᵃ24 Some manuscripts *the new*   ᵇ27 Zech. 13:7   ᶜ30 Some early manuscripts do not have *twice.*

the hour might pass from him.
[36]"*Abba*,[a] Father," he said, "everything is possible for you. Take this
cup from me. Yet not what I will, but
what you will."

[37]Then he returned to his disciples
and found them sleeping. "Simon,"
he said to Peter, "are you asleep?
Could you not keep watch for one
hour? [38]Watch and pray so that you
will not fall into temptation. The spirit
is willing, but the body is weak."

[39]Once more he went away and
prayed the same thing. [40]When he
came back, he again found them
sleeping, because their eyes were
heavy. They did not know what to
say to him.

[41]Returning the third time, he said
to them, "Are you still sleeping and
resting? Enough! The hour has come.
Look, the Son of Man is betrayed into
the hands of sinners. [42]Rise! Let us go!
Here comes my betrayer!"

Jesus Arrested

[43]Just as he was speaking, Judas,
one of the Twelve, appeared. With
him was a crowd armed with swords
and clubs, sent from the chief priests,
the teachers of the law, and the elders. [44]Now the betrayer had arranged a
signal with them: "The one I kiss is
the man; arrest him and lead him
away under guard." [45]Going at once
to Jesus, Judas said, "Rabbi!" and
kissed him. [46]The men seized Jesus
and arrested him. [47]Then one of those
standing near drew his sword and
struck the servant of the high priest,
cutting off his ear.

[48]"Am I leading a rebellion," said
Jesus, "that you have come out with
swords and clubs to capture me? [49]Ev-
ery day I was with you, teaching in
the temple courts, and you did not arrest me. But the Scriptures must be
fulfilled." [50]Then everyone deserted
him and fled.

[51]A young man, wearing nothing
but a linen garment, was following

Jesus. When they seized him, [52]he fled
naked, leaving his garment behind.

Before the Sanhedrin

[53]They took Jesus to the high priest,
and all the chief priests, elders and
teachers of the law came together.
[54]Peter followed him at a distance,
right into the courtyard of the high
priest. There he sat with the guards
and warmed himself at the fire.

[55]The chief priests and the whole
Sanhedrin were looking for evidence
against Jesus so that they could put
him to death, but they did not find
any. [56]Many testified falsely against
him, but their statements did not
agree.

[57]Then some stood up and gave this
false testimony against him: [58]"We
heard him say, 'I will destroy this
man-made temple and in three days
will build another, not made by
man.'" [59]Yet even then their testimony did not agree.

[60]Then the high priest stood up before them and asked Jesus, "Are you
not going to answer? What is this testimony that these men are bringing
against you?" [61]But Jesus remained silent and gave no answer.

Again the high priest asked him,
"Are you the Christ,[b] the Son of the
Blessed One?"

[62]"I am," said Jesus. "And you will
see the Son of Man sitting at the right
hand of the Mighty One and coming
on the clouds of heaven."

[63]The high priest tore his clothes.
"Why do we need any more witnesses?" he asked. [64]"You have heard
the blasphemy. What do you think?"
They all condemned him as worthy
of death. [65]Then some began to spit at
him; they blindfolded him, struck him
with their fists, and said, "Prophesy!"
And the guards took him and beat
him.

Peter Disowns Jesus

[66]While Peter was below in the
courtyard, one of the servant girls of

a36 Aramaic for *Father*   *b61* Or *Messiah*

the high priest came by. 67When she saw Peter warming himself, she looked closely at him.

"You also were with that Nazarene, Jesus," she said.

68But he denied it. "I don't know or understand what you're talking about," he said, and went out into the entryway.*a*

69When the servant girl saw him there, she said again to those standing around, "This fellow is one of them." 70Again he denied it.

After a little while, those standing near said to Peter, "Surely you are one of them, for you are a Galilean."

71He began to call down curses on himself, and he swore to them, "I don't know this man you're talking about."

a68 Some early manuscripts entryway and the rooster crowed

VERSE:	AUTHOR:	PASSAGE:
Mark 14:42	Oswald Chambers	Mark 14:32–42

The Antidote to Despair

The disciples went to sleep when they should have kept awake, and when they realized what they had done it produced despair. If we imagine that this kind of despair is exceptional, we are mistaken; it is a very ordinary human experience. Whenever we realize that we have not done that which we had a magnificent opportunity of doing, then we are apt to sink into despair; and Jesus Christ comes and says — "Sleep on now, that opportunity is lost forever, you cannot alter it, but arise and go to the next thing." Let the past sleep, but let it sleep on the bosom of Christ, and go out into the irresistible future with him.

There are experiences like this in each of our lives. We are in despair, the despair that comes from actualities, and we cannot lift ourselves out of it. The disciples in this instance had done a downright unforgivable thing; they had gone to sleep instead of watching with Jesus, but he came with a spiritual initiative against their despair and said — "Rise and do the next thing."

ADDITIONAL SCRIPTURE READINGS
Luke 9:57–62; Philippians 3:12–16

Go to page 1274 for your next devotional reading.

72Immediately the rooster crowed the second time.a Then Peter remembered the word Jesus had spoken to him: "Before the rooster crows twiceb you will disown me three times." And he broke down and wept.

Jesus Before Pilate

15 Very early in the morning, the chief priests, with the elders, the teachers of the law and the whole Sanhedrin, reached a decision. They bound Jesus, led him away and handed him over to Pilate.

2"Are you the king of the Jews?" asked Pilate.

"Yes, it is as you say," Jesus replied.

3The chief priests accused him of many things. 4So again Pilate asked him, "Aren't you going to answer? See how many things they are accusing you of."

5But Jesus still made no reply, and Pilate was amazed.

6Now it was the custom at the Feast to release a prisoner whom the people requested. 7A man called Barabbas was in prison with the insurrectionists who had committed murder in the uprising. 8The crowd came up and asked Pilate to do for them what he usually did.

9"Do you want me to release to you the king of the Jews?" asked Pilate, 10knowing it was out of envy that the chief priests had handed Jesus over to him. 11But the chief priests stirred up the crowd to have Pilate release Barabbas instead.

12"What shall I do, then, with the one you call the king of the Jews?" Pilate asked them.

13"Crucify him!" they shouted.

14"Why? What crime has he committed?" asked Pilate.

But they shouted all the louder, "Crucify him!"

15Wanting to satisfy the crowd, Pilate released Barabbas to them. He had Jesus flogged, and handed him over to be crucified.

The Soldiers Mock Jesus

16The soldiers led Jesus away into the palace (that is, the Praetorium) and called together the whole company of soldiers. 17They put a purple robe on him, then twisted together a crown of thorns and set it on him. 18And they began to call out to him, "Hail, king of the Jews!" 19Again and again they struck him on the head with a staff and spit on him. Falling on their knees, they paid homage to him. 20And when they had mocked him, they took off the purple robe and put his own clothes on him. Then they led him out to crucify him.

The Crucifixion

21A certain man from Cyrene, Simon, the father of Alexander and Rufus, was passing by on his way in from the country, and they forced him to carry the cross. 22They brought Jesus to the place called Golgotha (which means The Place of the Skull). 23Then they offered him wine mixed with myrrh, but he did not take it. 24And they crucified him. Dividing up his clothes, they cast lots to see what each would get.

25It was the third hour when they crucified him. 26The written notice of the charge against him read: THE KING OF THE JEWS. 27They crucified two robbers with him, one on his right and one on his left.c 29Those who passed by hurled insults at him, shaking their heads and saying, "So! You who are going to destroy the temple and build it in three days, 30come down from the cross and save yourself!"

31In the same way the chief priests and the teachers of the law mocked him among themselves. "He saved others," they said, "but he can't save himself! 32Let this Christ,d this King of Israel, come down now from the cross, that we may see and believe."

a72 Some early manuscripts do not have the second time.   b72 Some early manuscripts do not have twice.   c27 Some manuscripts left, 28and the scripture was fulfilled which says, "He was counted with the lawless ones" (Isaiah 53:12)   d32 Or Messiah

Those crucified with him also heaped insults on him.

The Death of Jesus

³³At the sixth hour darkness came over the whole land until the ninth hour. ³⁴And at the ninth hour Jesus cried out in a loud voice, *"Eloi, Eloi, lama sabachthani?"*—which means, "My God, my God, why have you forsaken me?"*^a*

³⁵When some of those standing near heard this, they said, "Listen, he's calling Elijah."

³⁶One man ran, filled a sponge with wine vinegar, put it on a stick, and offered it to Jesus to drink. "Now leave him alone. Let's see if Elijah comes to take him down," he said.

³⁷With a loud cry, Jesus breathed his last.

³⁸The curtain of the temple was torn in two from top to bottom. ³⁹And when the centurion, who stood there in front of Jesus, heard his cry and*^b* saw how he died, he said, "Surely this man was the Son*^c* of God!"

⁴⁰Some women were watching from a distance. Among them were Mary Magdalene, Mary the mother of James the younger and of Joses, and Salome. ⁴¹In Galilee these women had followed him and cared for his needs. Many other women who had come up with him to Jerusalem were also there.

The Burial of Jesus

⁴²It was Preparation Day (that is, the day before the Sabbath). So as evening approached, ⁴³Joseph of Arimathea, a prominent member of the Council, who was himself waiting for the kingdom of God, went boldly to Pilate and asked for Jesus' body. ⁴⁴Pilate was surprised to hear that he was already dead. Summoning the centurion, he asked him if Jesus had already died. ⁴⁵When he learned from the centurion that it was so, he gave the body to Joseph. ⁴⁶So Joseph bought some linen cloth, took down the body, wrapped it in the linen, and placed it in a tomb cut out of rock. Then he rolled a stone against the entrance of the tomb. ⁴⁷Mary Magdalene and Mary the mother of Joses saw where he was laid.

The Resurrection

16 When the Sabbath was over, Mary Magdalene, Mary the mother of James, and Salome bought spices so that they might go to anoint Jesus' body. ²Very early on the first day of the week, just after sunrise, they were on their way to the tomb ³and they asked each other, "Who will roll the stone away from the entrance of the tomb?"

⁴But when they looked up, they saw that the stone, which was very large, had been rolled away. ⁵As they entered the tomb, they saw a young man dressed in a white robe sitting on the right side, and they were alarmed.

⁶"Don't be alarmed," he said. "You are looking for Jesus the Nazarene, who was crucified. He has risen! He is not here. See the place where they laid him. ⁷But go, tell his disciples and Peter, 'He is going ahead of you into Galilee. There you will see him, just as he told you.' "

⁸Trembling and bewildered, the women went out and fled from the tomb. They said nothing to anyone, because they were afraid.

[The earliest manuscripts and some other ancient witnesses do not have Mark 16:9–20.]

⁹When Jesus rose early on the first day of the week, he appeared first to Mary Magdalene, out of whom he had driven seven demons. ¹⁰She went and told those who had been with him and who were mourning and weeping. ¹¹When they heard that Jesus was alive and that she had seen him, they did not believe it.

¹²Afterward Jesus appeared in a

---

^a34 Psalm 22:1   *^b39* Some manuscripts do not have *heard his cry and*   *^c39* Or *a son*

PASSAGE: Mark 16:1–8; 1 Corinthians 15:35–57
AUTHOR: Charles Wesley

· ·

Christ Is Risen

Christ the Lord is ris'n today, Alleluia!
Sons of men and angels say: Alleluia!
Raise your joys and triumphs high, Alleluia!
Sing, ye heav'ns and earth reply: Alleluia!

Lives again our glorious King, Alleluia!
Where, O death, is now thy sting? Alleluia!
Dying once he all doth save, Alleluia!
Where thy victory, O grave? Alleluia!

Love's redeeming work is done, Alleluia!
Fought the fight, the battle won, Alleluia!
Death in vain forbids him rise, Alleluia!
Christ has opened paradise, Alleluia!

Soar we now where Christ has led, Alleluia!
Foll'wing our exalted head, Alleluia!
Made like him, like him we rise, Alleluia!
Ours the cross, the grave, the skies, Alleluia!

· ·

Go to page 1278 for your next devotional reading.

different form to two of them while they were walking in the country. ¹³These returned and reported it to the rest; but they did not believe them either.

¹⁴Later Jesus appeared to the Eleven as they were eating; he rebuked them for their lack of faith and their stubborn refusal to believe those who had seen him after he had risen.

¹⁵He said to them, "Go into all the world and preach the good news to all creation. ¹⁶Whoever believes and is baptized will be saved, but whoever does not believe will be condemned. ¹⁷And these signs will accompany those who believe: In my name they will drive out demons; they will speak in new tongues; ¹⁸they will pick up snakes with their hands; and when they drink deadly poison, it will not hurt them at all; they will place their hands on sick people, and they will get well."

¹⁹After the Lord Jesus had spoken to them, he was taken up into heaven and he sat at the right hand of God. ²⁰Then the disciples went out and preached everywhere, and the Lord worked with them and confirmed his word by the signs that accompanied it.

...**L**...uke writes the longest
and most comprehensive of the Gospels—
with the greatest variety of teachings, parables and events from Jesus' life. He presents
Jesus as a Savior for the entire human race.
He emphasizes Jesus' love and compassion
for the oppressed. As you read this book, reflect on your own experience of powerless-
ness, and rejoice that in Jesus the weak are
made strong.

LUKE

Introduction

1 Many have undertaken to draw up an account of the things that have been fulfilled[a] among us, ²just as they were handed down to us by those who from the first were eyewitnesses and servants of the word. ³Therefore, since I myself have carefully investigated everything from the beginning, it seemed good also to me to write an orderly account for you, most excellent Theophilus, ⁴so that you may know the certainty of the things you have been taught.

The Birth of John the Baptist Foretold

⁵In the time of Herod king of Judea there was a priest named Zechariah, who belonged to the priestly division of Abijah; his wife Elizabeth was also a descendant of Aaron. ⁶Both of them were upright in the sight of God, observing all the Lord's commandments and regulations blamelessly. ⁷But they had no children, because Elizabeth was barren; and they were both well along in years.

⁸Once when Zechariah's division was on duty and he was serving as priest before God, ⁹he was chosen by lot, according to the custom of the priesthood, to go into the temple of the Lord and burn incense. ¹⁰And when the time for the burning of incense came, all the assembled worshipers were praying outside.

¹¹Then an angel of the Lord appeared to him, standing at the right side of the altar of incense. ¹²When Zechariah saw him, he was startled and was gripped with fear. ¹³But the angel said to him: "Do not be afraid, Zechariah; your prayer has been heard. Your wife Elizabeth will bear

you a son, and you are to give him the name John. ¹⁴He will be a joy and delight to you, and many will rejoice because of his birth, ¹⁵for he will be great in the sight of the Lord. He is never to take wine or other fermented drink, and he will be filled with the Holy Spirit even from birth.ᵃ ¹⁶Many of the people of Israel will he bring back to the Lord their God. ¹⁷And he will go on before the Lord, in the spirit and power of Elijah, to turn the hearts of the fathers to their children and the disobedient to the wisdom of the righteous—to make ready a people prepared for the Lord."

¹⁸Zechariah asked the angel, "How can I be sure of this? I am an old man and my wife is well along in years."

¹⁹The angel answered, "I am Gabriel. I stand in the presence of God, and I have been sent to speak to you and to tell you this good news. ²⁰And now you will be silent and not able to speak until the day this happens, because you did not believe my words, which will come true at their proper time."

²¹Meanwhile, the people were waiting for Zechariah and wondering why he stayed so long in the temple. ²²When he came out, he could not speak to them. They realized he had seen a vision in the temple, for he kept making signs to them but remained unable to speak.

²³When his time of service was completed, he returned home. ²⁴After this his wife Elizabeth became pregnant and for five months remained in seclusion. ²⁵"The Lord has done this for me," she said. "In these days he has shown his favor and taken away my disgrace among the people."

The Birth of Jesus Foretold

²⁶In the sixth month, God sent the angel Gabriel to Nazareth, a town in Galilee, ²⁷to a virgin pledged to be married to a man named Joseph, a descendant of David. The virgin's name was Mary. ²⁸The angel went to her and said, "Greetings, you who are highly favored! The Lord is with you."

²⁹Mary was greatly troubled at his words and wondered what kind of greeting this might be. ³⁰But the angel said to her, "Do not be afraid, Mary, you have found favor with God. ³¹You will be with child and give birth to a son, and you are to give him the name Jesus. ³²He will be great and will be called the Son of the Most High. The Lord God will give him the throne of his father David, ³³and he will reign over the house of Jacob forever; his kingdom will never end."

³⁴"How will this be," Mary asked the angel, "since I am a virgin?"

³⁵The angel answered, "The Holy Spirit will come upon you, and the power of the Most High will overshadow you. So the holy one to be born will be calledᵇ the Son of God. ³⁶Even Elizabeth your relative is going to have a child in her old age, and she who was said to be barren is in her sixth month. ³⁷For nothing is impossible with God."

³⁸"I am the Lord's servant," Mary answered. "May it be to me as you have said." Then the angel left her.

Mary Visits Elizabeth

³⁹At that time Mary got ready and hurried to a town in the hill country of Judea, ⁴⁰where she entered Zechariah's home and greeted Elizabeth. ⁴¹When Elizabeth heard Mary's greeting, the baby leaped in her womb, and Elizabeth was filled with the Holy Spirit. ⁴²In a loud voice she exclaimed: "Blessed are you among women, and blessed is the child you will bear! ⁴³But why am I so favored, that the mother of my Lord should come to me? ⁴⁴As soon as the sound of your greeting reached my ears, the baby in my womb leaped for joy. ⁴⁵Blessed is she who has believed that what the Lord has said to her will be accomplished!"

Mary's Song

⁴⁶And Mary said:

ᵃ15 Or from his mother's womb   ᵇ35 Or So the child to be born will be called holy,

"My soul glorifies the Lord
47 and my spirit rejoices in God
      my Savior,
48for he has been mindful
    of the humble state of his
      servant.
  From now on all generations will
      call me blessed,

49 for the Mighty One has done
      great things for me—
    holy is his name.
50His mercy extends to those who
    fear him,
    from generation to generation.
51He has performed mighty deeds
      with his arm;

VERSE:	AUTHOR:	PASSAGE:
Luke 1:77	John Gilmore	Luke 1:67–79

An Indestructible Joy

Zechariah's poem was a reflection of his theology. He attributed salvation to the work of God. What sustained him through his various vexations in life was God's acceptance of him.

Life has its ups and downs, its crises and catastrophes, its gains and pains, its good and bad times. But life's tough spots become bearable when we have the confidence that all is right between us and God, that God has forgiven us of our sins. Troubles in life are hard to bear, but when our standing with God is on a secure basis, when we are accepted and loved by him, we can endure the slings and arrows of outrageous fortune . . .

One of the great blessings of trusting our lives to Christ is that though earthly frustrations surround us, the center of our existence is tranquil because we have been reconciled to God and count upon his righteousness alone as our salvation.

No matter what our age, we can enjoy a God-initiated and God-perpetuated standing. "The knowledge of salvation through the forgiveness of sins, because of the tender mercy of our God" is a joy that the worst disappointments of life cannot destroy.

ADDITIONAL SCRIPTURE READINGS
Romans 4:16–25; Romans 5:1–11

Go to page 1281 for your next devotional reading.

he has scattered those who are proud in their inmost thoughts.
⁵²He has brought down rulers from their thrones
but has lifted up the humble.
⁵³He has filled the hungry with good things
but has sent the rich away empty.
⁵⁴He has helped his servant Israel, remembering to be merciful
⁵⁵to Abraham and his descendants forever,
even as he said to our fathers."

⁵⁶Mary stayed with Elizabeth for about three months and then returned home.

The Birth of John the Baptist

⁵⁷When it was time for Elizabeth to have her baby, she gave birth to a son. ⁵⁸Her neighbors and relatives heard that the Lord had shown her great mercy, and they shared her joy.

⁵⁹On the eighth day they came to circumcise the child, and they were going to name him after his father Zechariah, ⁶⁰but his mother spoke up and said, "No! He is to be called John."

⁶¹They said to her, "There is no one among your relatives who has that name."

⁶²Then they made signs to his father, to find out what he would like to name the child. ⁶³He asked for a writing tablet, and to everyone's astonishment he wrote, "His name is John." ⁶⁴Immediately his mouth was opened and his tongue was loosed, and he began to speak, praising God. ⁶⁵The neighbors were all filled with awe, and throughout the hill country of Judea people were talking about all these things. ⁶⁶Everyone who heard this wondered about it, asking, "What then is this child going to be?" For the Lord's hand was with him.

Zechariah's Song

⁶⁷His father Zechariah was filled with the Holy Spirit and prophesied:

⁶⁸"Praise be to the Lord, the God of Israel,
because he has come and has redeemed his people.
⁶⁹He has raised up a horn^a of salvation for us
in the house of his servant David
⁷⁰(as he said through his holy prophets of long ago),
⁷¹salvation from our enemies
and from the hand of all who hate us—
⁷²to show mercy to our fathers
and to remember his holy covenant,
⁷³　the oath he swore to our father Abraham:
⁷⁴to rescue us from the hand of our enemies,
and to enable us to serve him without fear
⁷⁵　in holiness and righteousness before him all our days.

⁷⁶And you, my child, will be called a prophet of the Most High;
for you will go on before the Lord to prepare the way for him,
⁷⁷to give his people the knowledge of salvation
through the forgiveness of their sins,
⁷⁸because of the tender mercy of our God,
by which the rising sun will come to us from heaven
⁷⁹to shine on those living in darkness
and in the shadow of death,
to guide our feet into the path of peace."

⁸⁰And the child grew and became strong in spirit; and he lived in the desert until he appeared publicly to Israel.

---

^a69 Horn here symbolizes strength.

The Birth of Jesus

2 In those days Caesar Augustus is-sued a decree that a census should be taken of the entire Roman world. ²(This was the first census that took place while Quirinius was gover-nor of Syria.) ³And everyone went to his own town to register.

⁴So Joseph also went up from the town of Nazareth in Galilee to Judea, to Bethlehem the town of David, be-cause he belonged to the house and line of David. ⁵He went there to regis-ter with Mary, who was pledged to be married to him and was expecting a child. ⁶While they were there, the time came for the baby to be born, ⁷and she gave birth to her firstborn, a son. She wrapped him in cloths and placed him in a manger, because there was no room for them in the inn.

The Shepherds and the Angels

⁸And there were shepherds living out in the fields nearby, keeping watch over their flocks at night. ⁹An angel of the Lord appeared to them, and the glory of the Lord shone around them, and they were terrified. ¹⁰But the angel said to them, "Do not be afraid. I bring you good news of great joy that will be for all the peo-ple. ¹¹Today in the town of David a Savior has been born to you; he is Christ*ᵃ* the Lord. ¹²This will be a sign to you: You will find a baby wrapped in cloths and lying in a manger."

¹³Suddenly a great company of the heavenly host appeared with the an-gel, praising God and saying,

¹⁴"Glory to God in the highest,
    and on earth peace to men on
        whom his favor rests."

¹⁵When the angels had left them and gone into heaven, the shepherds said to one another, "Let's go to Beth-lehem and see this thing that has hap-pened, which the Lord has told us about."

¹⁶So they hurried off and found Mary and Joseph, and the baby, who was lying in the manger. ¹⁷When they had seen him, they spread the word concerning what had been told them about this child, ¹⁸and all who heard it were amazed at what the shepherds said to them. ¹⁹But Mary treasured up all these things and pondered them in her heart. ²⁰The shepherds returned, glorifying and praising God for all the things they had heard and seen, which were just as they had been told.

Jesus Presented in the Temple

²¹On the eighth day, when it was time to circumcise him, he was named Jesus, the name the angel had given him before he had been conceived.

²²When the time of their purifica-tion according to the Law of Moses had been completed, Joseph and Mary took him to Jerusalem to present him to the Lord ²³(as it is writ-ten in the Law of the Lord, "Every firstborn male is to be consecrated to the Lord"*ᵇ*), ²⁴and to offer a sacrifice in keeping with what is said in the Law of the Lord: "a pair of doves or two young pigeons."*ᶜ*

²⁵Now there was a man in Jerusa-lem called Simeon, who was righ-teous and devout. He was waiting for the consolation of Israel, and the Holy Spirit was upon him. ²⁶It had been re-vealed to him by the Holy Spirit that he would not die before he had seen the Lord's Christ. ²⁷Moved by the Spirit, he went into the temple courts. When the parents brought in the child Jesus to do for him what the custom of the Law required, ²⁸Simeon took him in his arms and praised God, say-ing:

²⁹"Sovereign Lord, as you have
        promised,
    you now dismiss*ᵈ* your servant
        in peace.
³⁰For my eyes have seen your
        salvation,

ᵃ11 Or *Messiah.* "The Christ" (Greek) and "the Messiah" (Hebrew) both mean "the Anointed One"; also in verse 26.   *ᵇ23* Exodus 13:2,12   *ᶜ24* Lev. 12:8   *ᵈ29* Or *promised, / now dismiss*

VERSE:	AUTHOR:	PASSAGE:
Luke 2:35	Bruce Larson	Luke 2:25–35

A Good and Faithful Servant

In the dark watches of the night, there is the disquieting thought that we have, in some invisible court, been weighed and found wanting, that we have fallen short of all we wanted to be and do in life.

If there is in each of us some ever-present fear, we must assume that we also have, however unformed, some goal we are working toward, some direction we want our life to take. We all have dreams, secret or confessed, modest or grandiose, and those dreams vary from person to person . . .

How, then, can we be sure that we will not miss out? Jesus outlines the way clearly. "Seek first his kingdom" (Matthew 6:33). The other things will come, those things that make for lasting joy. If we are seeking the kingdom second, or in addition to our personal ambitions, we are destined for disappointment . . .

Remember, a good many Biblical heroes died before they achieved their goals [but consider Simeon, who saw his dream realized]. Moses is a good example. He died on the edge of the promised land. Our only goal is to have the Lord of life say, "Well done, good and faithful servant." That's all we need. We don't need Mom to bless us, or our spouse, or our kids . . . Seek ye first the kingdom, and all else — all else — will be added to you.

ADDITIONAL SCRIPTURE READINGS
Matthew 6:31–34; Matthew 25:14–30

Go to page 1290 for your next devotional reading.

³¹which you have prepared in the
    sight of all people,
³²a light for revelation to the
    Gentiles
    and for glory to your people
    Israel."

³³The child's father and mother
marveled at what was said about him.
³⁴Then Simeon blessed them and said
to Mary, his mother: "This child is
destined to cause the falling and rising of many in Israel, and to be a sign
that will be spoken against, ³⁵so that
the thoughts of many hearts will be
revealed. And a sword will pierce
your own soul too."

³⁶There was also a prophetess,
Anna, the daughter of Phanuel, of the
tribe of Asher. She was very old; she
had lived with her husband seven
years after her marriage, ³⁷and then
was a widow until she was eighty-
four.ᵃ She never left the temple but
worshiped night and day, fasting and
praying. ³⁸Coming up to them at that
very moment, she gave thanks to God
and spoke about the child to all who
were looking forward to the redemption of Jerusalem.

³⁹When Joseph and Mary had done
everything required by the Law of the
Lord, they returned to Galilee to their
own town of Nazareth. ⁴⁰And the
child grew and became strong; he was
filled with wisdom, and the grace of
God was upon him.

The Boy Jesus at the Temple

⁴¹Every year his parents went to Jerusalem for the Feast of the Passover.
⁴²When he was twelve years old, they
went up to the Feast, according to the
custom. ⁴³After the Feast was over,
while his parents were returning
home, the boy Jesus stayed behind in
Jerusalem, but they were unaware of
it. ⁴⁴Thinking he was in their company, they traveled on for a day. Then
they began looking for him among
their relatives and friends. ⁴⁵When
they did not find him, they went back
to Jerusalem to look for him. ⁴⁶After

three days they found him in the temple courts, sitting among the teachers,
listening to them and asking them
questions. ⁴⁷Everyone who heard him
was amazed at his understanding and
his answers. ⁴⁸When his parents saw
him, they were astonished. His mother said to him, "Son, why have you
treated us like this? Your father and I
have been anxiously searching for
you."

⁴⁹"Why were you searching for
me?" he asked. "Didn't you know I
had to be in my Father's house?"
⁵⁰But they did not understand what
he was saying to them.

⁵¹Then he went down to Nazareth
with them and was obedient to them.
But his mother treasured all these
things in her heart. ⁵²And Jesus grew
in wisdom and stature, and in favor
with God and men.

John the Baptist Prepares the Way

3 In the fifteenth year of the reign of
Tiberius Caesar—when Pontius
Pilate was governor of Judea, Herod
tetrarch of Galilee, his brother Philip
tetrarch of Iturea and Traconitis, and
Lysanias tetrarch of Abilene— ²dur-
ing the high priesthood of Annas and
Caiaphas, the word of God came to
John son of Zechariah in the desert.
³He went into all the country around
the Jordan, preaching a baptism of repentance for the forgiveness of sins.
⁴As is written in the book of the
words of Isaiah the prophet:

"A voice of one calling in the
    desert,
'Prepare the way for the Lord,
    make straight paths for him.
⁵Every valley shall be filled in,
    every mountain and hill made
    low.
The crooked roads shall become
    straight,
    the rough ways smooth.
⁶And all mankind will see God's
    salvation.' "ᵇ

⁷John said to the crowds coming
out to be baptized by him, "You

brood of vipers! Who warned you to flee from the coming wrath? [8]Produce fruit in keeping with repentance. And do not begin to say to yourselves, 'We have Abraham as our father.' For I tell you that out of these stones God can raise up children for Abraham. [9]The ax is already at the root of the trees, and every tree that does not produce good fruit will be cut down and thrown into the fire."

[10]"What should we do then?" the crowd asked.

[11]John answered, "The man with two tunics should share with him who has none, and the one who has food should do the same."

[12]Tax collectors also came to be baptized. "Teacher," they asked, "what should we do?"

[13]"Don't collect any more than you are required to," he told them.

[14]Then some soldiers asked him, "And what should we do?"

He replied, "Don't extort money and don't accuse people falsely—be content with your pay."

[15]The people were waiting expectantly and were all wondering in their hearts if John might possibly be the Christ.[a] [16]John answered them all, "I baptize you with[b] water. But one more powerful than I will come, the thongs of whose sandals I am not worthy to untie. He will baptize you with the Holy Spirit and with fire. [17]His winnowing fork is in his hand to clear his threshing floor and to gather the wheat into his barn, but he will burn up the chaff with unquenchable fire." [18]And with many other words John exhorted the people and preached the good news to them.

[19]But when John rebuked Herod the tetrarch because of Herodias, his brother's wife, and all the other evil things he had done, [20]Herod added this to them all: He locked John up in prison.

The Baptism and Genealogy of Jesus

[21]When all the people were being baptized, Jesus was baptized too. And as he was praying, heaven was opened [22]and the Holy Spirit descended on him in bodily form like a dove. And a voice came from heaven: "You are my Son, whom I love; with you I am well pleased."

[23]Now Jesus himself was about thirty years old when he began his ministry. He was the son, so it was thought, of Joseph,

the son of Heli, [24]the son of Matthat,
the son of Levi, the son of Melki,
the son of Jannai, the son of Joseph,
[25]the son of Mattathias, the son of Amos,
the son of Nahum, the son of Esli,
the son of Naggai, [26]the son of Maath,
the son of Mattathias, the son of Semein,
the son of Josech, the son of Joda,
[27]the son of Joanan, the son of Rhesa,
the son of Zerubbabel, the son of Shealtiel,
the son of Neri, [28]the son of Melki,
the son of Addi, the son of Cosam,
the son of Elmadam, the son of Er,
[29]the son of Joshua, the son of Eliezer,
the son of Jorim, the son of Matthat,
the son of Levi, [30]the son of Simeon,
the son of Judah, the son of Joseph,
the son of Jonam, the son of Eliakim,
[31]the son of Melea, the son of Menna,
the son of Mattatha, the son of Nathan,
the son of David, [32]the son of Jesse,

the son of Obed, the son of
Boaz,
the son of Salmon,*a* the son of
Nahshon,
33the son of Amminadab, the son
of Ram,*b*
the son of Hezron, the son of Perez,
the son of Judah, 34the son of Jacob,
the son of Isaac, the son of Abraham,
the son of Terah, the son of Nahor,
35the son of Serug, the son of Reu,
the son of Peleg, the son of Eber,
the son of Shelah, 36the son of
Cainan,
the son of Arphaxad, the son of
Shem,
the son of Noah, the son of Lamech,
37the son of Methuselah, the son
of Enoch,
the son of Jared, the son of Mahalalel,
the son of Kenan, 38the son of
Enosh,
the son of Seth, the son of
Adam,
the son of God.

The Temptation of Jesus

4 Jesus, full of the Holy Spirit, returned from the Jordan and was
led by the Spirit in the desert, 2where
for forty days he was tempted by the
devil. He ate nothing during those
days, and at the end of them he was
hungry.
3The devil said to him, "If you are
the Son of God, tell this stone to become bread."
4Jesus answered, "It is written:
'Man does not live on bread
alone.'*c*"
5The devil led him up to a high
place and showed him in an instant
all the kingdoms of the world. 6And
he said to him, "I will give you all
their authority and splendor, for it

has been given to me, and I can give it
to anyone I want to. 7So if you worship me, it will all be yours."
8Jesus answered, "It is written:
'Worship the Lord your God and
serve him only.'*d*"
9The devil led him to Jerusalem and
had him stand on the highest point
of the temple. "If you are the Son of
God," he said, "throw yourself down
from here. 10For it is written:

" 'He will command his angels
concerning you
to guard you carefully;
11they will lift you up in their
hands,
so that you will not strike your
foot against a stone.'*e*"

12Jesus answered, "It says: 'Do not
put the Lord your God to the test.'*f*"
13When the devil had finished all
this tempting, he left him until an opportune time.

Jesus Rejected at Nazareth

14Jesus returned to Galilee in the
power of the Spirit, and news about
him spread through the whole countryside. 15He taught in their synagogues, and everyone praised him.
16He went to Nazareth, where he
had been brought up, and on the Sabbath day he went into the synagogue,
as was his custom. And he stood up
to read. 17The scroll of the prophet
Isaiah was handed to him. Unrolling
it, he found the place where it is written:

18"The Spirit of the Lord is on me,
because he has anointed me
to preach good news to the
poor.
He has sent me to proclaim
freedom for the prisoners
and recovery of sight for the
blind,
to release the oppressed,
19   to proclaim the year of the
Lord's favor."*g*

---

*a*32 Some early manuscripts *Sala*   *b*33 Some manuscripts *Amminadab, the son of Admin, the son
of Arni*; other manuscripts vary widely.   *c*4 Deut. 8:3   *d*8 Deut. 6:13   *e*11 Psalm 91:11,12
*f*12 Deut. 6:16   *g*19 Isaiah 61:1,2

20Then he rolled up the scroll, gave it back to the attendant and sat down. The eyes of everyone in the synagogue were fastened on him, 21and he began by saying to them, "Today this scripture is fulfilled in your hearing."

22All spoke well of him and were amazed at the gracious words that came from his lips. "Isn't this Joseph's son?" they asked.

23Jesus said to them, "Surely you will quote this proverb to me: 'Physician, heal yourself! Do here in your hometown what we have heard that you did in Capernaum.' "

24"I tell you the truth," he continued, "no prophet is accepted in his hometown. 25I assure you that there were many widows in Israel in Elijah's time, when the sky was shut for three and a half years and there was a severe famine throughout the land. 26Yet Elijah was not sent to any of them, but to a widow in Zarephath in the region of Sidon. 27And there were many in Israel with leprosy*a* in the time of Elisha the prophet, yet not one of them was cleansed—only Naaman the Syrian."

28All the people in the synagogue were furious when they heard this. 29They got up, drove him out of the town, and took him to the brow of the hill on which the town was built, in order to throw him down the cliff. 30But he walked right through the crowd and went on his way.

Jesus Drives Out an Evil Spirit

31Then he went down to Capernaum, a town in Galilee, and on the Sabbath began to teach the people. 32They were amazed at his teaching, because his message had authority.

33In the synagogue there was a man possessed by a demon, an evil*b* spirit. He cried out at the top of his voice, 34"Ha! What do you want with us, Jesus of Nazareth? Have you come to destroy us? I know who you are—the Holy One of God!"

35"Be quiet!" Jesus said sternly. "Come out of him!" Then the demon threw the man down before them all and came out without injuring him.

36All the people were amazed and said to each other, "What is this teaching? With authority and power he gives orders to evil spirits and they come out!" 37And the news about him spread throughout the surrounding area.

Jesus Heals Many

38Jesus left the synagogue and went to the home of Simon. Now Simon's mother-in-law was suffering from a high fever, and they asked Jesus to help her. 39So he bent over her and rebuked the fever, and it left her. She got up at once and began to wait on them.

40When the sun was setting, the people brought to Jesus all who had various kinds of sickness, and laying his hands on each one, he healed them. 41Moreover, demons came out of many people, shouting, "You are the Son of God!" But he rebuked them and would not allow them to speak, because they knew he was the Christ.*c*

42At daybreak Jesus went out to a solitary place. The people were looking for him and when they came to where he was, they tried to keep him from leaving them. 43But he said, "I must preach the good news of the kingdom of God to the other towns also, because that is why I was sent." 44And he kept on preaching in the synagogues of Judea.*d*

The Calling of the First Disciples

5 One day as Jesus was standing by the Lake of Gennesaret,*e* with the people crowding around him and listening to the word of God, 2he saw at the water's edge two boats, left there by the fishermen, who were washing their nets. 3He got into one of the boats, the one belonging to Si-

---

*a*27 The Greek word was used for various diseases affecting the skin—not necessarily leprosy.
*b*33 Greek *unclean*; also in verse 36   *c*41 Or *Messiah*   *d*44 Or *the land of the Jews*; some manuscripts *Galilee*   *e*1 That is, Sea of Galilee

mon, and asked him to put out a little from shore. Then he sat down and taught the people from the boat.

⁴When he had finished speaking, he said to Simon, "Put out into deep water, and let down*ᵃ* the nets for a catch."

⁵Simon answered, "Master, we've worked hard all night and haven't caught anything. But because you say so, I will let down the nets."

⁶When they had done so, they caught such a large number of fish that their nets began to break. ⁷So they signaled their partners in the other boat to come and help them, and they came and filled both boats so full that they began to sink.

⁸When Simon Peter saw this, he fell at Jesus' knees and said, "Go away from me, Lord; I am a sinful man!" ⁹For he and all his companions were astonished at the catch of fish they had taken, ¹⁰and so were James and John, the sons of Zebedee, Simon's partners.

Then Jesus said to Simon, "Don't be afraid; from now on you will catch men." ¹¹So they pulled their boats up on shore, left everything and followed him.

The Man With Leprosy

¹²While Jesus was in one of the towns, a man came along who was covered with leprosy.*ᵇ* When he saw Jesus, he fell with his face to the ground and begged him, "Lord, if you are willing, you can make me clean."

¹³Jesus reached out his hand and touched the man. "I am willing," he said. "Be clean!" And immediately the leprosy left him.

¹⁴Then Jesus ordered him, "Don't tell anyone, but go, show yourself to the priest and offer the sacrifices that Moses commanded for your cleansing, as a testimony to them."

¹⁵Yet the news about him spread all the more, so that crowds of people came to hear him and to be healed of their sicknesses. ¹⁶But Jesus often withdrew to lonely places and prayed.

Jesus Heals a Paralytic

¹⁷One day as he was teaching, Pharisees and teachers of the law, who had come from every village of Galilee and from Judea and Jerusalem, were sitting there. And the power of the Lord was present for him to heal the sick. ¹⁸Some men came carrying a paralytic on a mat and tried to take him into the house to lay him before Jesus. ¹⁹When they could not find a way to do this because of the crowd, they went up on the roof and lowered him on his mat through the tiles into the middle of the crowd, right in front of Jesus.

²⁰When Jesus saw their faith, he said, "Friend, your sins are forgiven."

²¹The Pharisees and the teachers of the law began thinking to themselves, "Who is this fellow who speaks blasphemy? Who can forgive sins but God alone?"

²²Jesus knew what they were thinking and asked, "Why are you thinking these things in your hearts? ²³Which is easier: to say, 'Your sins are forgiven,' or to say, 'Get up and walk'? ²⁴But that you may know that the Son of Man has authority on earth to forgive sins. . . ." He said to the paralyzed man, "I tell you, get up, take your mat and go home." ²⁵Immediately he stood up in front of them, took what he had been lying on and went home praising God. ²⁶Everyone was amazed and gave praise to God. They were filled with awe and said, "We have seen remarkable things today."

The Calling of Levi

²⁷After this, Jesus went out and saw a tax collector by the name of Levi sitting at his tax booth. "Follow me," Jesus said to him, ²⁸and Levi got up, left everything and followed him.

²⁹Then Levi held a great banquet for Jesus at his house, and a large

ᵃ4 The Greek verb is plural.   *ᵇ12* The Greek word was used for various diseases affecting the skin—not necessarily leprosy.

crowd of tax collectors and others were eating with them. ³⁰But the Pharisees and the teachers of the law who belonged to their sect complained to his disciples, "Why do you eat and drink with tax collectors and 'sinners'?"

³¹Jesus answered them, "It is not the healthy who need a doctor, but the sick. ³²I have not come to call the righteous, but sinners to repentance."

Jesus Questioned About Fasting

³³They said to him, "John's disciples often fast and pray, and so do the disciples of the Pharisees, but yours go on eating and drinking."

³⁴Jesus answered, "Can you make the guests of the bridegroom fast while he is with them? ³⁵But the time will come when the bridegroom will be taken from them; in those days they will fast."

³⁶He told them this parable: "No one tears a patch from a new garment and sews it on an old one. If he does, he will have torn the new garment, and the patch from the new will not match the old. ³⁷And no one pours new wine into old wineskins. If he does, the new wine will burst the skins, the wine will run out and the wineskins will be ruined. ³⁸No, new wine must be poured into new wineskins. ³⁹And no one after drinking old wine wants the new, for he says, 'The old is better.' "

Lord of the Sabbath

6 One Sabbath Jesus was going through the grainfields, and his disciples began to pick some heads of grain, rub them in their hands and eat the kernels. ²Some of the Pharisees asked, "Why are you doing what is unlawful on the Sabbath?"

³Jesus answered, "Have you never read what David did when he and his companions were hungry? ⁴He entered the house of God, and taking the consecrated bread, he ate what is lawful only for priests to eat. And he also gave some to his companions." ⁵Then Jesus said to them, "The Son of Man is Lord of the Sabbath."

⁶On another Sabbath he went into the synagogue and was teaching, and a man was there whose right hand was shriveled. ⁷The Pharisees and the teachers of the law were looking for a reason to accuse Jesus, so they watched him closely to see if he would heal on the Sabbath. ⁸But Jesus knew what they were thinking and said to the man with the shriveled hand, "Get up and stand in front of everyone." So he got up and stood there.

⁹Then Jesus said to them, "I ask you, which is lawful on the Sabbath: to do good or to do evil, to save life or to destroy it?"

¹⁰He looked around at them all, and then said to the man, "Stretch out your hand." He did so, and his hand was completely restored. ¹¹But they were furious and began to discuss with one another what they might do to Jesus.

The Twelve Apostles

¹²One of those days Jesus went out to a mountainside to pray, and spent the night praying to God. ¹³When morning came, he called his disciples to him and chose twelve of them, whom he also designated apostles: ¹⁴Simon (whom he named Peter), his brother Andrew, James, John, Philip, Bartholomew, ¹⁵Matthew, Thomas, James son of Alphaeus, Simon who was called the Zealot, ¹⁶Judas son of James, and Judas Iscariot, who became a traitor.

Blessings and Woes

¹⁷He went down with them and stood on a level place. A large crowd of his disciples was there and a great number of people from all over Judea, from Jerusalem, and from the coast of Tyre and Sidon, ¹⁸who had come to hear him and to be healed of their diseases. Those troubled by evil*a* spirits were cured, ¹⁹and the people all tried

a18 Greek unclean

to touch him, because power was coming from him and healing them all.

²⁰Looking at his disciples, he said:

"Blessed are you who are poor,
  for yours is the kingdom of
    God.
²¹Blessed are you who hunger now,
  for you will be satisfied.
Blessed are you who weep now,
  for you will laugh.
²²Blessed are you when men hate
    you,
  when they exclude you and
    insult you
  and reject your name as evil,
    because of the Son of Man.

²³"Rejoice in that day and leap for joy, because great is your reward in heaven. For that is how their fathers treated the prophets.

²⁴"But woe to you who are rich,
  for you have already received
    your comfort.
²⁵Woe to you who are well fed now,
  for you will go hungry.
Woe to you who laugh now,
  for you will mourn and weep.
²⁶Woe to you when all men speak
    well of you,
  for that is how their fathers
    treated the false prophets.

Love for Enemies

²⁷"But I tell you who hear me: Love your enemies, do good to those who hate you, ²⁸bless those who curse you, pray for those who mistreat you. ²⁹If someone strikes you on one cheek, turn to him the other also. If someone takes your cloak, do not stop him from taking your tunic. ³⁰Give to everyone who asks you, and if anyone takes what belongs to you, do not demand it back. ³¹Do to others as you would have them do to you.

³²"If you love those who love you, what credit is that to you? Even 'sinners' love those who love them. ³³And if you do good to those who are good to you, what credit is that to you? Even 'sinners' do that. ³⁴And if you lend to those from whom you expect repayment, what credit is that to you? Even 'sinners' lend to 'sinners,' expecting to be repaid in full. ³⁵But love your enemies, do good to them, and lend to them without expecting to get anything back. Then your reward will be great, and you will be sons of the Most High, because he is kind to the ungrateful and wicked. ³⁶Be merciful, just as your Father is merciful.

Judging Others

³⁷"Do not judge, and you will not be judged. Do not condemn, and you will not be condemned. Forgive, and you will be forgiven. ³⁸Give, and it will be given to you. A good measure, pressed down, shaken together and running over, will be poured into your lap. For with the measure you use, it will be measured to you."

³⁹He also told them this parable: "Can a blind man lead a blind man? Will they not both fall into a pit? ⁴⁰A student is not above his teacher, but everyone who is fully trained will be like his teacher.

⁴¹"Why do you look at the speck of sawdust in your brother's eye and pay no attention to the plank in your own eye? ⁴²How can you say to your brother, 'Brother, let me take the speck out of your eye,' when you yourself fail to see the plank in your own eye? You hypocrite, first take the plank out of your eye, and then you will see clearly to remove the speck from your brother's eye.

A Tree and Its Fruit

⁴³"No good tree bears bad fruit, nor does a bad tree bear good fruit. ⁴⁴Each tree is recognized by its own fruit. People do not pick figs from thornbushes, or grapes from briers. ⁴⁵The good man brings good things out of the good stored up in his heart, and the evil man brings evil things out of the evil stored up in his heart. For out of the overflow of his heart his mouth speaks.

The Wise and Foolish Builders

⁴⁶"Why do you call me, 'Lord, Lord,' and do not do what I say? ⁴⁷I

will show you what he is like who comes to me and hears my words and puts them into practice. ⁴⁸He is like a man building a house, who dug down deep and laid the foundation on rock. When a flood came, the torrent struck that house but could not shake it, because it was well built. ⁴⁹But the one who hears my words and does not put them into practice is like a man who built a house on the ground without a foundation. The moment the torrent struck that house, it collapsed and its destruction was complete."

The Faith of the Centurion

7 When Jesus had finished saying all this in the hearing of the people, he entered Capernaum. ²There a centurion's servant, whom his master valued highly, was sick and about to die. ³The centurion heard of Jesus and sent some elders of the Jews to him, asking him to come and heal his servant. ⁴When they came to Jesus, they pleaded earnestly with him, "This man deserves to have you do this, ⁵because he loves our nation and has built our synagogue." ⁶So Jesus went with them.

He was not far from the house when the centurion sent friends to say to him: "Lord, don't trouble yourself, for I do not deserve to have you come under my roof. ⁷That is why I did not even consider myself worthy to come to you. But say the word, and my servant will be healed. ⁸For I myself am a man under authority, with soldiers under me. I tell this one, 'Go,' and he goes; and that one, 'Come,' and he comes. I say to my servant, 'Do this,' and he does it."

⁹When Jesus heard this, he was amazed at him, and turning to the crowd following him, he said, "I tell you, I have not found such great faith even in Israel." ¹⁰Then the men who had been sent returned to the house and found the servant well.

Jesus Raises a Widow's Son

¹¹Soon afterward, Jesus went to a town called Nain, and his disciples and a large crowd went along with him. ¹²As he approached the town gate, a dead person was being carried out—the only son of his mother, and she was a widow. And a large crowd from the town was with her. ¹³When the Lord saw her, his heart went out to her and he said, "Don't cry."

¹⁴Then he went up and touched the coffin, and those carrying it stood still. He said, "Young man, I say to you, get up!" ¹⁵The dead man sat up and began to talk, and Jesus gave him back to his mother.

¹⁶They were all filled with awe and praised God. "A great prophet has appeared among us," they said. "God has come to help his people." ¹⁷This news about Jesus spread throughout Judea[a] and the surrounding country.

Jesus and John the Baptist

¹⁸John's disciples told him about all these things. Calling two of them, ¹⁹he sent them to the Lord to ask, "Are you the one who was to come, or should we expect someone else?"

²⁰When the men came to Jesus, they said, "John the Baptist sent us to you to ask, 'Are you the one who was to come, or should we expect someone else?' "

²¹At that very time Jesus cured many who had diseases, sicknesses and evil spirits, and gave sight to many who were blind. ²²So he replied to the messengers, "Go back and report to John what you have seen and heard: The blind receive sight, the lame walk, those who have leprosy[b] are cured, the deaf hear, the dead are raised, and the good news is preached to the poor. ²³Blessed is the man who does not fall away on account of me."

²⁴After John's messengers left, Jesus began to speak to the crowd about John: "What did you go out into the

---

a17 Or *the land of the Jews*   b22 The Greek word was used for various diseases affecting the skin—not necessarily leprosy.

desert to see? A reed swayed by the wind? 25If not, what did you go out to see? A man dressed in fine clothes? No, those who wear expensive clothes and indulge in luxury are in palaces. 26But what did you go out to see? A prophet? Yes, I tell you, and more than a prophet. 27This is the one about whom it is written:

" 'I will send my messenger ahead of you,

VERSE:
Luke 7:13

AUTHOR:
Ken Gire

PASSAGE:
Luke 7:11–17

A Deep Well of Compassion

Dear Lord,

Thank you for how deep the well of your compassion is . . . and how pure . . . and how sweet. Thank you for how freely and spontaneously that water is given.

Thank you that it is not great knowledge or great wealth or great power that moves you to draw from that well, but something as small and weak and tender as tears.

Thank you, O most merciful Savior, for that spring day when you gave back that son to his mother. What a beautiful picture of compassion. And what an enticing picture of the spring yet to come, when you will wipe every tear from our eyes and when there will no longer be any sickness or death.

Give me the heart you had for that bereaved mother, for those whose shoulders are stooped low under the weight of a loss too great for them to bear.

I pray for those who have lost a loved one, whether by sudden accident or by a slow, agonizing disease . . . Grant them grace to know that he who notices when a sparrow falls to the ground, took note of their loss with *his* tears.

ADDITIONAL SCRIPTURE READINGS
Psalm 56; 2 Corinthians 1:3–7

Go to page 1295 for your next devotional reading.

who will prepare your way
before you.'*a*

²⁸I tell you, among those born of women there is no one greater than John; yet the one who is least in the kingdom of God is greater than he."

²⁹(All the people, even the tax collectors, when they heard Jesus' words, acknowledged that God's way was right, because they had been baptized by John. ³⁰But the Pharisees and experts in the law rejected God's purpose for themselves, because they had not been baptized by John.)

³¹"To what, then, can I compare the people of this generation? What are they like? ³²They are like children sitting in the marketplace and calling out to each other:

" 'We played the flute for you,
    and you did not dance;
we sang a dirge,
    and you did not cry.'

³³For John the Baptist came neither eating bread nor drinking wine, and you say, 'He has a demon.' ³⁴The Son of Man came eating and drinking, and you say, 'Here is a glutton and a drunkard, a friend of tax collectors and "sinners." ' ³⁵But wisdom is proved right by all her children."

Jesus Anointed by a Sinful Woman

³⁶Now one of the Pharisees invited Jesus to have dinner with him, so he went to the Pharisee's house and reclined at the table. ³⁷When a woman who had lived a sinful life in that town learned that Jesus was eating at the Pharisee's house, she brought an alabaster jar of perfume, ³⁸and as she stood behind him at his feet weeping, she began to wet his feet with her tears. Then she wiped them with her hair, kissed them and poured perfume on them.

³⁹When the Pharisee who had invited him saw this, he said to himself, "If this man were a prophet, he would know who is touching him and what

kind of woman she is—that she is a sinner."

⁴⁰Jesus answered him, "Simon, I have something to tell you."

"Tell me, teacher," he said.

⁴¹"Two men owed money to a certain moneylender. One owed him five hundred denarii,*b* and the other fifty. ⁴²Neither of them had the money to pay him back, so he canceled the debts of both. Now which of them will love him more?"

⁴³Simon replied, "I suppose the one who had the bigger debt canceled."

"You have judged correctly," Jesus said.

⁴⁴Then he turned toward the woman and said to Simon, "Do you see this woman? I came into your house. You did not give me any water for my feet, but she wet my feet with her tears and wiped them with her hair. ⁴⁵You did not give me a kiss, but this woman, from the time I entered, has not stopped kissing my feet. ⁴⁶You did not put oil on my head, but she has poured perfume on my feet. ⁴⁷Therefore, I tell you, her many sins have been forgiven—for she loved much. But he who has been forgiven little loves little."

⁴⁸Then Jesus said to her, "Your sins are forgiven."

⁴⁹The other guests began to say among themselves, "Who is this who even forgives sins?"

⁵⁰Jesus said to the woman, "Your faith has saved you; go in peace."

The Parable of the Sower

8 After this, Jesus traveled about from one town and village to another, proclaiming the good news of the kingdom of God. The Twelve were with him, ²and also some women who had been cured of evil spirits and diseases: Mary (called Magdalene) from whom seven demons had come out; ³Joanna the wife of Cuza, the manager of Herod's household; Susanna; and many others. These women were helping to support them out of their own means.

---

a27 Mal. 3:1   *b41* A denarius was a coin worth about a day's wages.

4While a large crowd was gathering and people were coming to Jesus from town after town, he told this parable: 5"A farmer went out to sow his seed. As he was scattering the seed, some fell along the path; it was trampled on, and the birds of the air ate it up. 6Some fell on rock, and when it came up, the plants withered because they had no moisture. 7Other seed fell among thorns, which grew up with it and choked the plants. 8Still other seed fell on good soil. It came up and yielded a crop, a hundred times more than was sown."

When he said this, he called out, "He who has ears to hear, let him hear."

9His disciples asked him what this parable meant. 10He said, "The knowledge of the secrets of the kingdom of God has been given to you, but to others I speak in parables, so that,

" 'though seeing, they may not
    see;
  though hearing, they may not
    understand.'ᵃ

11"This is the meaning of the parable: The seed is the word of God. 12Those along the path are the ones who hear, and then the devil comes and takes away the word from their hearts, so that they may not believe and be saved. 13Those on the rock are the ones who receive the word with joy when they hear it, but they have no root. They believe for a while, but in the time of testing they fall away. 14The seed that fell among thorns stands for those who hear, but as they go on their way they are choked by life's worries, riches and pleasures, and they do not mature. 15But the seed on good soil stands for those with a noble and good heart, who hear the word, retain it, and by persevering produce a crop.

A Lamp on a Stand

16"No one lights a lamp and hides it in a jar or puts it under a bed. Instead, he puts it on a stand, so that those who come in can see the light. 17For there is nothing hidden that will not be disclosed, and nothing concealed that will not be known or brought out into the open. 18Therefore consider carefully how you listen. Whoever has will be given more; whoever does not have, even what he thinks he has will be taken from him."

Jesus' Mother and Brothers

19Now Jesus' mother and brothers came to see him, but they were not able to get near him because of the crowd. 20Someone told him, "Your mother and brothers are standing outside, wanting to see you."

21He replied, "My mother and brothers are those who hear God's word and put it into practice."

Jesus Calms the Storm

22One day Jesus said to his disciples, "Let's go over to the other side of the lake." So they got into a boat and set out. 23As they sailed, he fell asleep. A squall came down on the lake, so that the boat was being swamped, and they were in great danger.

24The disciples went and woke him, saying, "Master, Master, we're going to drown!"

He got up and rebuked the wind and the raging waters; the storm subsided, and all was calm. 25"Where is your faith?" he asked his disciples.

In fear and amazement they asked one another, "Who is this? He commands even the winds and the water, and they obey him."

The Healing of a Demon-possessed Man

26They sailed to the region of the Gerasenes,ᵇ which is across the lake from Galilee. 27When Jesus stepped ashore, he was met by a demon-possessed man from the town. For a long time this man had not worn clothes or lived in a house, but had lived in the

---

ᵃ10 Isaiah 6:9   ᵇ26 Some manuscripts Gadarenes; other manuscripts Gergesenes; also in verse 37

tombs. [28]When he saw Jesus, he cried out and fell at his feet, shouting at the top of his voice, "What do you want with me, Jesus, Son of the Most High God? I beg you, don't torture me!" [29]For Jesus had commanded the evil[a] spirit to come out of the man. Many times it had seized him, and though he was chained hand and foot and kept under guard, he had broken his chains and had been driven by the demon into solitary places.

[30]Jesus asked him, "What is your name?"

"Legion," he replied, because many demons had gone into him. [31]And they begged him repeatedly not to order them to go into the Abyss.

[32]A large herd of pigs was feeding there on the hillside. The demons begged Jesus to let them go into them, and he gave them permission. [33]When the demons came out of the man, they went into the pigs, and the herd rushed down the steep bank into the lake and was drowned.

[34]When those tending the pigs saw what had happened, they ran off and reported this in the town and countryside, [35]and the people went out to see what had happened. When they came to Jesus, they found the man from whom the demons had gone out, sitting at Jesus' feet, dressed and in his right mind; and they were afraid. [36]Those who had seen it told the people how the demon-possessed man had been cured. [37]Then all the people of the region of the Gerasenes asked Jesus to leave them, because they were overcome with fear. So he got into the boat and left.

[38]The man from whom the demons had gone out begged to go with him, but Jesus sent him away, saying, [39]"Return home and tell how much God has done for you." So the man went away and told all over town how much Jesus had done for him.

A Dead Girl and a Sick Woman

[40]Now when Jesus returned, a crowd welcomed him, for they were all expecting him. [41]Then a man named Jairus, a ruler of the synagogue, came and fell at Jesus' feet, pleading with him to come to his house [42]because his only daughter, a girl of about twelve, was dying.

As Jesus was on his way, the crowds almost crushed him. [43]And a woman was there who had been subject to bleeding for twelve years,[b] but no one could heal her. [44]She came up behind him and touched the edge of his cloak, and immediately her bleeding stopped.

[45]"Who touched me?" Jesus asked.

When they all denied it, Peter said, "Master, the people are crowding and pressing against you."

[46]But Jesus said, "Someone touched me; I know that power has gone out from me."

[47]Then the woman, seeing that she could not go unnoticed, came trembling and fell at his feet. In the presence of all the people, she told why she had touched him and how she had been instantly healed. [48]Then he said to her, "Daughter, your faith has healed you. Go in peace."

[49]While Jesus was still speaking, someone came from the house of Jairus, the synagogue ruler. "Your daughter is dead," he said. "Don't bother the teacher any more."

[50]Hearing this, Jesus said to Jairus, "Don't be afraid; just believe, and she will be healed."

[51]When he arrived at the house of Jairus, he did not let anyone go in with him except Peter, John and James, and the child's father and mother. [52]Meanwhile, all the people were wailing and mourning for her. "Stop wailing," Jesus said. "She is not dead but asleep."

[53]They laughed at him, knowing that she was dead. [54]But he took her by the hand and said, "My child, get up!" [55]Her spirit returned, and at once she stood up. Then Jesus told them to give her something to eat. [56]Her parents were astonished, but he ordered

---

[a]29 Greek unclean   [b]43 Many manuscripts years, and she had spent all she had on doctors

them not to tell anyone what had happened.

Jesus Sends Out the Twelve

9 When Jesus had called the Twelve together, he gave them power and authority to drive out all demons and to cure diseases, ²and he sent them out to preach the kingdom of God and to heal the sick. ³He told them: "Take nothing for the journey—no staff, no bag, no bread, no money, no extra tunic. ⁴Whatever house you enter, stay there until you leave that town. ⁵If people do not welcome you, shake the dust off your feet when you leave their town, as a testimony against them." ⁶So they set out and went from village to village, preaching the gospel and healing people everywhere.

⁷Now Herod the tetrarch heard about all that was going on. And he was perplexed, because some were saying that John had been raised from the dead, ⁸others that Elijah had appeared, and still others that one of the prophets of long ago had come back to life. ⁹But Herod said, "I beheaded John. Who, then, is this I hear such things about?" And he tried to see him.

Jesus Feeds the Five Thousand

¹⁰When the apostles returned, they reported to Jesus what they had done. Then he took them with him and they withdrew by themselves to a town called Bethsaida, ¹¹but the crowds learned about it and followed him. He welcomed them and spoke to them about the kingdom of God, and healed those who needed healing.

¹²Late in the afternoon the Twelve came to him and said, "Send the crowd away so they can go to the surrounding villages and countryside and find food and lodging, because we are in a remote place here."

¹³He replied, "You give them something to eat."

They answered, "We have only five loaves of bread and two fish—unless we go and buy food for all this crowd." ¹⁴(About five thousand men were there.)

But he said to his disciples, "Have them sit down in groups of about fifty each." ¹⁵The disciples did so, and everybody sat down. ¹⁶Taking the five loaves and the two fish and looking up to heaven, he gave thanks and broke them. Then he gave them to the disciples to set before the people. ¹⁷They all ate and were satisfied, and the disciples picked up twelve basketfuls of broken pieces that were left over.

Peter's Confession of Christ

¹⁸Once when Jesus was praying in private and his disciples were with him, he asked them, "Who do the crowds say I am?"

¹⁹They replied, "Some say John the Baptist; others say Elijah; and still others, that one of the prophets of long ago has come back to life."

²⁰"But what about you?" he asked. "Who do you say I am?"

Peter answered, "The Christ*a* of God."

²¹Jesus strictly warned them not to tell this to anyone. ²²And he said, "The Son of Man must suffer many things and be rejected by the elders, chief priests and teachers of the law, and he must be killed and on the third day be raised to life."

²³Then he said to them all: "If anyone would come after me, he must deny himself and take up his cross daily and follow me. ²⁴For whoever wants to save his life will lose it, but whoever loses his life for me will save it. ²⁵What good is it for a man to gain the whole world, and yet lose or forfeit his very self? ²⁶If anyone is ashamed of me and my words, the Son of Man will be ashamed of him when he comes in his glory and in the glory of the Father and of the holy angels. ²⁷I tell you the truth, some who are standing here will not taste death before they see the kingdom of God."

a20 Or *Messiah*

VERSE:	AUTHOR:	PASSAGE:
Luke 9:17	Mother Teresa	Luke 9:10–17

Daily Bread

We take God at his word. We depend solely on divine providence that comes through to us to the love of the people . . .

We deal with thousands of people and yet there has not been one occasion when we have had to say to somebody, "Very sorry, we don't have . . . "

In Calcutta, we cope with more than 20,000 people every day. (The day we don't cook, they don't eat.) I can remember, one day a sister came and told me, "Mother, there is no more rice for Friday and Saturday. We will have to tell the people that we don't have it." I was a little surprised because in all my years I had never heard that before. On Friday morning, at about 9:00, a truck full of bread—thousands of loaves of bread!—arrived. Nobody in Calcutta knew why the government closed the schools, but the schools were closed and all the bread was brought to us and for two days our people ate bread and bread and bread!

I knew why God closed the schools: He closed the schools because he wanted our people to know that they are more important than the grass, the birds and the flowers of the fields; they are special to him. Those thousands of people had to know he loved them, he cared for them. This is a repeated evidence of tender love, of the tender thoughtfulness of God himself for his people.

ADDITIONAL SCRIPTURE READINGS
Luke 1:46–55; Luke 12:22–34
Go to page 1299 for your next devotional reading.

The Transfiguration

²⁸About eight days after Jesus said this, he took Peter, John and James with him and went up onto a mountain to pray. ²⁹As he was praying, the appearance of his face changed, and his clothes became as bright as a flash of lightning. ³⁰Two men, Moses and Elijah, ³¹appeared in glorious splendor, talking with Jesus. They spoke about his departure, which he was about to bring to fulfillment at Jerusalem. ³²Peter and his companions were very sleepy, but when they became fully awake, they saw his glory and the two men standing with him. ³³As the men were leaving Jesus, Peter said to him, "Master, it is good for us to be here. Let us put up three shelters—one for you, one for Moses and one for Elijah." (He did not know what he was saying.)

³⁴While he was speaking, a cloud appeared and enveloped them, and they were afraid as they entered the cloud. ³⁵A voice came from the cloud, saying, "This is my Son, whom I have chosen; listen to him." ³⁶When the voice had spoken, they found that Jesus was alone. The disciples kept this to themselves, and told no one at that time what they had seen.

The Healing of a Boy With an Evil Spirit

³⁷The next day, when they came down from the mountain, a large crowd met him. ³⁸A man in the crowd called out, "Teacher, I beg you to look at my son, for he is my only child. ³⁹A spirit seizes him and he suddenly screams; it throws him into convulsions so that he foams at the mouth. It scarcely ever leaves him and is destroying him. ⁴⁰I begged your disciples to drive it out, but they could not."

⁴¹"O unbelieving and perverse generation," Jesus replied, "how long shall I stay with you and put up with you? Bring your son here."

⁴²Even while the boy was coming, the demon threw him to the ground in a convulsion. But Jesus rebuked the evilᵃ spirit, healed the boy and gave him back to his father. ⁴³And they were all amazed at the greatness of God.

While everyone was marveling at all that Jesus did, he said to his disciples, ⁴⁴"Listen carefully to what I am about to tell you: The Son of Man is going to be betrayed into the hands of men." ⁴⁵But they did not understand what this meant. It was hidden from them, so that they did not grasp it, and they were afraid to ask him about it.

Who Will Be the Greatest?

⁴⁶An argument started among the disciples as to which of them would be the greatest. ⁴⁷Jesus, knowing their thoughts, took a little child and had him stand beside him. ⁴⁸Then he said to them, "Whoever welcomes this little child in my name welcomes me; and whoever welcomes me welcomes the one who sent me. For he who is least among you all—he is the greatest."

⁴⁹"Master," said John, "we saw a man driving out demons in your name and we tried to stop him, because he is not one of us."

⁵⁰"Do not stop him," Jesus said, "for whoever is not against you is for you."

Samaritan Opposition

⁵¹As the time approached for him to be taken up to heaven, Jesus resolutely set out for Jerusalem. ⁵²And he sent messengers on ahead, who went into a Samaritan village to get things ready for him; ⁵³but the people there did not welcome him, because he was heading for Jerusalem. ⁵⁴When the disciples James and John saw this, they asked, "Lord, do you want us to call fire down from heaven to destroy themᵇ?" ⁵⁵But Jesus turned and re-

ᵃ42 Greek *unclean*   ᵇ54 Some manuscripts *them, even as Elijah did*

buked them, [56]and[a] they went to another village.

The Cost of Following Jesus

[57]As they were walking along the road, a man said to him, "I will follow you wherever you go."

[58]Jesus replied, "Foxes have holes and birds of the air have nests, but the Son of Man has no place to lay his head."

[59]He said to another man, "Follow me."

But the man replied, "Lord, first let me go and bury my father."

[60]Jesus said to him, "Let the dead bury their own dead, but you go and proclaim the kingdom of God."

[61]Still another said, "I will follow you, Lord; but first let me go back and say good-by to my family."

[62]Jesus replied, "No one who puts his hand to the plow and looks back is fit for service in the kingdom of God."

Jesus Sends Out the Seventy-two

10 After this the Lord appointed seventy-two[b] others and sent them two by two ahead of him to every town and place where he was about to go. [2]He told them, "The harvest is plentiful, but the workers are few. Ask the Lord of the harvest, therefore, to send out workers into his harvest field. [3]Go! I am sending you out like lambs among wolves. [4]Do not take a purse or bag or sandals; and do not greet anyone on the road.

[5]"When you enter a house, first say, 'Peace to this house.' [6]If a man of peace is there, your peace will rest on him; if not, it will return to you. [7]Stay in that house, eating and drinking whatever they give you, for the worker deserves his wages. Do not move around from house to house.

[8]"When you enter a town and are welcomed, eat what is set before you. [9]Heal the sick who are there and tell them, 'The kingdom of God is near you.' [10]But when you enter a town

and are not welcomed, go into its streets and say, [11]'Even the dust of your town that sticks to our feet we wipe off against you. Yet be sure of this: The kingdom of God is near.' [12]I tell you, it will be more bearable on that day for Sodom than for that town.

[13]"Woe to you, Korazin! Woe to you, Bethsaida! For if the miracles that were performed in you had been performed in Tyre and Sidon, they would have repented long ago, sitting in sackcloth and ashes. [14]But it will be more bearable for Tyre and Sidon at the judgment than for you. [15]And you, Capernaum, will you be lifted up to the skies? No, you will go down to the depths.[c]

[16]"He who listens to you listens to me; he who rejects you rejects me; but he who rejects me rejects him who sent me."

[17]The seventy-two returned with joy and said, "Lord, even the demons submit to us in your name."

[18]He replied, "I saw Satan fall like lightning from heaven. [19]I have given you authority to trample on snakes and scorpions and to overcome all the power of the enemy; nothing will harm you. [20]However, do not rejoice that the spirits submit to you, but rejoice that your names are written in heaven."

[21]At that time Jesus, full of joy through the Holy Spirit, said, "I praise you, Father, Lord of heaven and earth, because you have hidden these things from the wise and learned, and revealed them to little children. Yes, Father, for this was your good pleasure.

[22]"All things have been committed to me by my Father. No one knows who the Son is except the Father, and no one knows who the Father is except the Son and those to whom the Son chooses to reveal him."

[23]Then he turned to his disciples and said privately, "Blessed are the

---

[a]55,56 Some manuscripts them. And he said, "You do not know what kind of spirit you are of, for the Son of Man did not come to destroy men's lives, but to save them." [56]And   [b]1 Some manuscripts seventy; also in verse 17   [c]15 Greek Hades

eyes that see what you see. ²⁴For I tell you that many prophets and kings wanted to see what you see but did not see it, and to hear what you hear but did not hear it."

The Parable of the Good Samaritan

²⁵On one occasion an expert in the law stood up to test Jesus. "Teacher," he asked, "what must I do to inherit eternal life?"

²⁶"What is written in the Law?" he replied. "How do you read it?"

²⁷He answered: " 'Love the Lord your God with all your heart and with all your soul and with all your strength and with all your mind'ᵃ; and, 'Love your neighbor as yourself.'ᵇ "

²⁸"You have answered correctly," Jesus replied. "Do this and you will live."

²⁹But he wanted to justify himself, so he asked Jesus, "And who is my neighbor?"

³⁰In reply Jesus said: "A man was going down from Jerusalem to Jericho, when he fell into the hands of robbers. They stripped him of his clothes, beat him and went away, leaving him half dead. ³¹A priest happened to be going down the same road, and when he saw the man, he passed by on the other side. ³²So too, a Levite, when he came to the place and saw him, passed by on the other side. ³³But a Samaritan, as he traveled, came where the man was; and when he saw him, he took pity on him. ³⁴He went to him and bandaged his wounds, pouring on oil and wine. Then he put the man on his own donkey, took him to an inn and took care of him. ³⁵The next day he took out two silver coinsᶜ and gave them to the innkeeper. 'Look after him,' he said, 'and when I return, I will reimburse you for any extra expense you may have.'

³⁶"Which of these three do you think was a neighbor to the man who fell into the hands of robbers?"

³⁷The expert in the law replied, "The one who had mercy on him."

Jesus told him, "Go and do likewise."

At the Home of Martha and Mary

³⁸As Jesus and his disciples were on their way, he came to a village where a woman named Martha opened her home to him. ³⁹She had a sister called Mary, who sat at the Lord's feet listening to what he said. ⁴⁰But Martha was distracted by all the preparations that had to be made. She came to him and asked, "Lord, don't you care that my sister has left me to do the work by myself? Tell her to help me!"

⁴¹"Martha, Martha," the Lord answered, "you are worried and upset about many things, ⁴²but only one thing is needed.ᵈ Mary has chosen what is better, and it will not be taken away from her."

Jesus' Teaching on Prayer

11 One day Jesus was praying in a certain place. When he finished, one of his disciples said to him, "Lord, teach us to pray, just as John taught his disciples."

²He said to them, "When you pray, say:

" 'Father,ᵉ
hallowed be your name,
your kingdom come.ᶠ
³Give us each day our daily bread.
⁴Forgive us our sins,
    for we also forgive everyone
        who sins against us.ᵍ
And lead us not into
    temptation.ʰ' "

⁵Then he said to them, "Suppose one of you has a friend, and he goes to him at midnight and says, 'Friend, lend me three loaves of bread, ⁶because a friend of mine on a journey

---

ᵃ27 Deut. 6:5   ᵇ27 Lev. 19:18   ᶜ35 Greek *two denarii*   ᵈ42 Some manuscripts *but few things are needed—or only one*   ᵉ2 Some manuscripts *Our Father in heaven*   ᶠ2 Some manuscripts *come. May your will be done on earth as it is in heaven.*   ᵍ4 Greek *everyone who is indebted to us*   ʰ4 Some manuscripts *temptation but deliver us from the evil one*

VERSE:	AUTHOR:	PASSAGE:
Luke 10:42	Charlie W. Shedd	Luke 10:38–42

Only One Thing to Do

The story of Mary and Martha offers an interesting illustration of life's proper order . . .

Although there are several ways to interpret this story, we can improve our efficiency when we grasp what Jesus was trying to teach the two sisters and us. Martha wanted to be at her best for this meal. Jesus had been away for some time and this was an important homecoming. "Drop in for potluck anytime" was not the mood of this occasion. Most of us have little sympathy for Mary's sitting. It looks to us like idle shirking. But if there is time to do only one thing, then the "one thing" that "is needed" is the thing to do. And when there are countless items on our agenda, we do well to "center down in Christ" as the first business of the day.

The Christian life is the very reverse of spreading ourselves wide and thin. There will be time for all things, and all our living will be timely when our souls are inwardly concentrated on the inner presence. This is true Christian simplicity, and we move onto the soul's highway when we tell Christ that first of all we want to know him and let him live in us.

This is not some mystical abstraction reserved for visionaries and impractical saints. It is life's highest goal for ordinary servants of the Lord. This is the stuff of everyday assignment for modest men and women . . . All life for the Christian is for singling the eye to kingdom service.

ADDITIONAL SCRIPTURE READINGS
Jeremiah 9:23–25; Philippians 3:1–10

Go to page 1301 for your next devotional reading.

has come to me, and I have nothing to set before him.'

7"Then the one inside answers, 'Don't bother me. The door is already locked, and my children are with me in bed. I can't get up and give you anything.' 8I tell you, though he will not get up and give him the bread because he is his friend, yet because of the man's boldness[a] he will get up and give him as much as he needs.

9"So I say to you: Ask and it will be given to you; seek and you will find; knock and the door will be opened to you. 10For everyone who asks receives; he who seeks finds; and to him who knocks, the door will be opened.

11"Which of you fathers, if your son asks for[b] a fish, will give him a snake instead? 12Or if he asks for an egg, will give him a scorpion? 13If you then, though you are evil, know how to give good gifts to your children, how much more will your Father in heaven give the Holy Spirit to those who ask him!"

Jesus and Beelzebub

14Jesus was driving out a demon that was mute. When the demon left, the man who had been mute spoke, and the crowd was amazed. 15But some of them said, "By Beelzebub,[c] the prince of demons, he is driving out demons." 16Others tested him by asking for a sign from heaven.

17Jesus knew their thoughts and said to them: "Any kingdom divided against itself will be ruined, and a house divided against itself will fall. 18If Satan is divided against himself, how can his kingdom stand? I say this because you claim that I drive out demons by Beelzebub. 19Now if I drive out demons by Beelzebub, by whom do your followers drive them out? So then, they will be your judges. 20But if I drive out demons by the finger of God, then the kingdom of God has come to you.

21"When a strong man, fully armed, guards his own house, his possessions are safe. 22But when someone stronger attacks and overpowers him, he takes away the armor in which the man trusted and divides up the spoils.

23"He who is not with me is against me, and he who does not gather with me, scatters.

24"When an evil[d] spirit comes out of a man, it goes through arid places seeking rest and does not find it. Then it says, 'I will return to the house I left.' 25When it arrives, it finds the house swept clean and put in order. 26Then it goes and takes seven other spirits more wicked than itself, and they go in and live there. And the final condition of that man is worse than the first."

27As Jesus was saying these things, a woman in the crowd called out, "Blessed is the mother who gave you birth and nursed you."

28He replied, "Blessed rather are those who hear the word of God and obey it."

The Sign of Jonah

29As the crowds increased, Jesus said, "This is a wicked generation. It asks for a miraculous sign, but none will be given it except the sign of Jonah. 30For as Jonah was a sign to the Ninevites, so also will the Son of Man be to this generation. 31The Queen of the South will rise at the judgment with the men of this generation and condemn them; for she came from the ends of the earth to listen to Solomon's wisdom, and now one[e] greater than Solomon is here. 32The men of Nineveh will stand up at the judgment with this generation and condemn it; for they repented at the preaching of Jonah, and now one greater than Jonah is here.

The Lamp of the Body

33"No one lights a lamp and puts it in a place where it will be hidden, or

---

a8 Or persistence   b11 Some manuscripts for bread, will give him a stone; or if he asks for
c15 Greek Beezeboul or Beelzeboul; also in verses 18 and 19   d24 Greek unclean
e31 Or something; also in verse 32

Only by Your Faithfulness

Please, Lord,

Be with me when I am fearful
    to make me faithful.
Be with me when I am faithful
    to make me fruitful.
Be with me when I am fruitful
    to make me humble.

For it is only by your grace
    that I was chosen to serve you;
    only by your strength
    that I am even able to serve;
    only by *your* faithfulness
    that I am still serving you today . . .

Go to page 1304 for your next devotional reading.

under a bowl. Instead he puts it on its stand, so that those who come in may see the light. ³⁴Your eye is the lamp of your body. When your eyes are good, your whole body also is full of light. But when they are bad, your body also is full of darkness. ³⁵See to it, then, that the light within you is not darkness. ³⁶Therefore, if your whole body is full of light, and no part of it dark, it will be completely lighted, as when the light of a lamp shines on you."

Six Woes

³⁷When Jesus had finished speaking, a Pharisee invited him to eat with him; so he went in and reclined at the table. ³⁸But the Pharisee, noticing that Jesus did not first wash before the meal, was surprised.

³⁹Then the Lord said to him, "Now then, you Pharisees clean the outside of the cup and dish, but inside you are full of greed and wickedness. ⁴⁰You foolish people! Did not the one who made the outside make the inside also? ⁴¹But give what is inside ⌐the dish⌐ᵃ to the poor, and everything will be clean for you.

⁴²"Woe to you Pharisees, because you give God a tenth of your mint, rue and all other kinds of garden herbs, but you neglect justice and the love of God. You should have practiced the latter without leaving the former undone.

⁴³"Woe to you Pharisees, because you love the most important seats in the synagogues and greetings in the marketplaces.

⁴⁴"Woe to you, because you are like unmarked graves, which men walk over without knowing it."

⁴⁵One of the experts in the law answered him, "Teacher, when you say these things, you insult us also."

⁴⁶Jesus replied, "And you experts in the law, woe to you, because you load people down with burdens they can hardly carry, and you yourselves will not lift one finger to help them.

⁴⁷"Woe to you, because you build tombs for the prophets, and it was your forefathers who killed them. ⁴⁸So you testify that you approve of what your forefathers did; they killed the prophets, and you build their tombs. ⁴⁹Because of this, God in his wisdom said, 'I will send them prophets and apostles, some of whom they will kill and others they will persecute.' ⁵⁰Therefore this generation will be held responsible for the blood of all the prophets that has been shed since the beginning of the world, ⁵¹from the blood of Abel to the blood of Zechariah, who was killed between the altar and the sanctuary. Yes, I tell you, this generation will be held responsible for it all.

⁵²"Woe to you experts in the law, because you have taken away the key to knowledge. You yourselves have not entered, and you have hindered those who were entering."

⁵³When Jesus left there, the Pharisees and the teachers of the law began to oppose him fiercely and to besiege him with questions, ⁵⁴waiting to catch him in something he might say.

Warnings and Encouragements

12 Meanwhile, when a crowd of many thousands had gathered, so that they were trampling on one another, Jesus began to speak first to his disciples, saying: "Be on your guard against the yeast of the Pharisees, which is hypocrisy. ²There is nothing concealed that will not be disclosed, or hidden that will not be made known. ³What you have said in the dark will be heard in the daylight, and what you have whispered in the ear in the inner rooms will be proclaimed from the roofs.

⁴"I tell you, my friends, do not be afraid of those who kill the body and after that can do no more. ⁵But I will show you whom you should fear: Fear him who, after the killing of the body, has power to throw you into hell. Yes, I tell you, fear him. ⁶Are not five sparrows sold for two penniesᵇ? Yet not one of them is forgotten by

ᵃ41 Or *what you have*   ᵇ6 Greek *two assaria*

God. ⁷Indeed, the very hairs of your head are all numbered. Don't be afraid; you are worth more than many sparrows.

⁸"I tell you, whoever acknowledges me before men, the Son of Man will also acknowledge him before the angels of God. ⁹But he who disowns me before men will be disowned before the angels of God. ¹⁰And everyone who speaks a word against the Son of Man will be forgiven, but anyone who blasphemes against the Holy Spirit will not be forgiven.

¹¹"When you are brought before synagogues, rulers and authorities, do not worry about how you will defend yourselves or what you will say, ¹²for the Holy Spirit will teach you at that time what you should say."

The Parable of the Rich Fool

¹³Someone in the crowd said to him, "Teacher, tell my brother to divide the inheritance with me."

¹⁴Jesus replied, "Man, who appointed me a judge or an arbiter between you?" ¹⁵Then he said to them, "Watch out! Be on your guard against all kinds of greed; a man's life does not consist in the abundance of his possessions."

¹⁶And he told them this parable: "The ground of a certain rich man produced a good crop. ¹⁷He thought to himself, 'What shall I do? I have no place to store my crops.'

¹⁸"Then he said, 'This is what I'll do. I will tear down my barns and build bigger ones, and there I will store all my grain and my goods. ¹⁹And I'll say to myself, "You have plenty of good things laid up for many years. Take life easy; eat, drink and be merry." '

²⁰"But God said to him, 'You fool! This very night your life will be demanded from you. Then who will get what you have prepared for yourself?'

²¹"This is how it will be with anyone who stores up things for himself but is not rich toward God."

Do Not Worry

²²Then Jesus said to his disciples: "Therefore I tell you, do not worry about your life, what you will eat; or about your body, what you will wear. ²³Life is more than food, and the body more than clothes. ²⁴Consider the ravens: They do not sow or reap, they have no storeroom or barn; yet God feeds them. And how much more valuable you are than birds! ²⁵Who of you by worrying can add a single hour to his life*a*? ²⁶Since you cannot do this very little thing, why do you worry about the rest?

²⁷"Consider how the lilies grow. They do not labor or spin. Yet I tell you, not even Solomon in all his splendor was dressed like one of these. ²⁸If that is how God clothes the grass of the field, which is here today, and tomorrow is thrown into the fire, how much more will he clothe you, O you of little faith! ²⁹And do not set your heart on what you will eat or drink; do not worry about it. ³⁰For the pagan world runs after all such things, and your Father knows that you need them. ³¹But seek his kingdom, and these things will be given to you as well.

³²"Do not be afraid, little flock, for your Father has been pleased to give you the kingdom. ³³Sell your possessions and give to the poor. Provide purses for yourselves that will not wear out, a treasure in heaven that will not be exhausted, where no thief comes near and no moth destroys. ³⁴For where your treasure is, there your heart will be also.

Watchfulness

³⁵"Be dressed ready for service and keep your lamps burning, ³⁶like men waiting for their master to return from a wedding banquet, so that when he comes and knocks they can immediately open the door for him. ³⁷It will be good for those servants whose master finds them watching when he comes. I tell you the truth, he

*a*25 Or *single cubit to his height*

will dress himself to serve, will have them recline at the table and will come and wait on them. ³⁸It will be good for those servants whose master finds them ready, even if he comes in the second or third watch of the night. ³⁹But understand this: If the owner of the house had known at what hour the thief was coming, he would not have let his house be broken into. ⁴⁰You also must be ready, because the Son of Man will come at an hour when you do not expect him."

⁴¹Peter asked, "Lord, are you telling this parable to us, or to everyone?"

⁴²The Lord answered, "Who then is the faithful and wise manager, whom the master puts in charge of his servants to give them their food allowance at the proper time? ⁴³It will be good for that servant whom the master finds doing so when he returns. ⁴⁴I tell you the truth, he will put him in charge of all his possessions. ⁴⁵But suppose the servant says to himself, 'My master is taking a long time in coming,' and he then begins to beat the menservants and maidservants and to eat and drink and get drunk. ⁴⁶The master of that servant will come on a day when he does not expect him and at an hour he is not aware of. He

MONDAY

VERSE:
Luke 12:31

AUTHOR:
D. James Kennedy

PASSAGE:
Luke 12:22–34

Be An Overcomer

God is in the business of building character. What interests the Creator of the universe is not how much wealth or power you attain in this world. He is not interested in the size of your home, your car or your bank account. God does not keep his eye on you to see if you are a "winner" in this life; he is much more concerned with how you live each hour, how you love those around you, and how you prepare your heart for life in the kingdom of God. He cares most about your integrity, your conscience, your heart and your soul. God wants you to be filled with the love of Jesus Christ and the indwelling power of his Holy Spirit. He wants you to be an "overcomer," a follower of the Savior who confronts this sin-sick world with faith and conviction. He wants you to be one who helps to bring renewal and repentance.

ADDITIONAL SCRIPTURE READINGS
Romans 12:9–21; 1 John 5:1–4

Go to page 1309 for your next devotional reading.

will cut him to pieces and assign him a place with the unbelievers.

⁴⁷"That servant who knows his master's will and does not get ready or does not do what his master wants will be beaten with many blows. ⁴⁸But the one who does not know and does things deserving punishment will be beaten with few blows. From everyone who has been given much, much will be demanded; and from the one who has been entrusted with much, much more will be asked.

Not Peace but Division

⁴⁹"I have come to bring fire on the earth, and how I wish it were already kindled! ⁵⁰But I have a baptism to undergo, and how distressed I am until it is completed! ⁵¹Do you think I came to bring peace on earth? No, I tell you, but division. ⁵²From now on there will be five in one family divided against each other, three against two and two against three. ⁵³They will be divided, father against son and son against father, mother against daughter and daughter against mother, mother-in-law against daughter-in-law and daughter-in-law against mother-in-law."

Interpreting the Times

⁵⁴He said to the crowd: "When you see a cloud rising in the west, immediately you say, 'It's going to rain,' and it does. ⁵⁵And when the south wind blows, you say, 'It's going to be hot,' and it is. ⁵⁶Hypocrites! You know how to interpret the appearance of the earth and the sky. How is it that you don't know how to interpret this present time?

⁵⁷"Why don't you judge for yourselves what is right? ⁵⁸As you are going with your adversary to the magistrate, try hard to be reconciled to him on the way, or he may drag you off to the judge, and the judge turn you over to the officer, and the officer throw you into prison. ⁵⁹I tell you, you will not get out until you have paid the last penny.ᵃ"

ᵃ59 Greek lepton

Repent or Perish

13 Now there were some present at that time who told Jesus about the Galileans whose blood Pilate had mixed with their sacrifices. ²Jesus answered, "Do you think that these Galileans were worse sinners than all the other Galileans because they suffered this way? ³I tell you, no! But unless you repent, you too will all perish. ⁴Or those eighteen who died when the tower in Siloam fell on them—do you think they were more guilty than all the others living in Jerusalem? ⁵I tell you, no! But unless you repent, you too will all perish."

⁶Then he told this parable: "A man had a fig tree, planted in his vineyard, and he went to look for fruit on it, but did not find any. ⁷So he said to the man who took care of the vineyard, 'For three years now I've been coming to look for fruit on this fig tree and haven't found any. Cut it down! Why should it use up the soil?'

⁸"'Sir,' the man replied, 'leave it alone for one more year, and I'll dig around it and fertilize it. ⁹If it bears fruit next year, fine! If not, then cut it down.'"

A Crippled Woman Healed on the Sabbath

¹⁰On a Sabbath Jesus was teaching in one of the synagogues, ¹¹and a woman was there who had been crippled by a spirit for eighteen years. She was bent over and could not straighten up at all. ¹²When Jesus saw her, he called her forward and said to her, "Woman, you are set free from your infirmity." ¹³Then he put his hands on her, and immediately she straightened up and praised God.

¹⁴Indignant because Jesus had healed on the Sabbath, the synagogue ruler said to the people, "There are six days for work. So come and be healed on those days, not on the Sabbath."

¹⁵The Lord answered him, "You hypocrites! Doesn't each of you on the Sabbath untie his ox or donkey from

the stall and lead it out to give it water? [16]Then should not this woman, a daughter of Abraham, whom Satan has kept bound for eighteen long years, be set free on the Sabbath day from what bound her?"

[17]When he said this, all his opponents were humiliated, but the people were delighted with all the wonderful things he was doing.

The Parables of the Mustard Seed and the Yeast

[18]Then Jesus asked, "What is the kingdom of God like? What shall I compare it to? [19]It is like a mustard seed, which a man took and planted in his garden. It grew and became a tree, and the birds of the air perched in its branches."

[20]Again he asked, "What shall I compare the kingdom of God to? [21]It is like yeast that a woman took and mixed into a large amount[a] of flour until it worked all through the dough."

The Narrow Door

[22]Then Jesus went through the towns and villages, teaching as he made his way to Jerusalem. [23]Someone asked him, "Lord, are only a few people going to be saved?"

He said to them, [24]"Make every effort to enter through the narrow door, because many, I tell you, will try to enter and will not be able to. [25]Once the owner of the house gets up and closes the door, you will stand outside knocking and pleading, 'Sir, open the door for us.'

"But he will answer, 'I don't know you or where you come from.'

[26]"Then you will say, 'We ate and drank with you, and you taught in our streets.'

[27]"But he will reply, 'I don't know you or where you come from. Away from me, all you evildoers!'

[28]"There will be weeping there, and gnashing of teeth, when you see Abraham, Isaac and Jacob and all the prophets in the kingdom of God, but you yourselves thrown out. [29]People will come from east and west and north and south, and will take their places at the feast in the kingdom of God. [30]Indeed there are those who are last who will be first, and first who will be last."

Jesus' Sorrow for Jerusalem

[31]At that time some Pharisees came to Jesus and said to him, "Leave this place and go somewhere else. Herod wants to kill you."

[32]He replied, "Go tell that fox, 'I will drive out demons and heal people today and tomorrow, and on the third day I will reach my goal.' [33]In any case, I must keep going today and tomorrow and the next day—for surely no prophet can die outside Jerusalem!

[34]"O Jerusalem, Jerusalem, you who kill the prophets and stone those sent to you, how often I have longed to gather your children together, as a hen gathers her chicks under her wings, but you were not willing! [35]Look, your house is left to you desolate. I tell you, you will not see me again until you say, 'Blessed is he who comes in the name of the Lord.'[b]"

Jesus at a Pharisee's House

14 One Sabbath, when Jesus went to eat in the house of a prominent Pharisee, he was being carefully watched. [2]There in front of him was a man suffering from dropsy. [3]Jesus asked the Pharisees and experts in the law, "Is it lawful to heal on the Sabbath or not?" [4]But they remained silent. So taking hold of the man, he healed him and sent him away.

[5]Then he asked them, "If one of you has a son[c] or an ox that falls into a well on the Sabbath day, will you not immediately pull him out?" [6]And they had nothing to say.

[7]When he noticed how the guests picked the places of honor at the ta-

---

[a]21 Greek *three satas* (probably about 1/2 bushel or 22 liters)   [b]35 Psalm 118:26   [c]5 Some manuscripts *donkey*

ble, he told them this parable: 8"When someone invites you to a wedding feast, do not take the place of honor, for a person more distinguished than you may have been invited. 9If so, the host who invited both of you will come and say to you, 'Give this man your seat.' Then, humiliated, you will have to take the least important place. 10But when you are invited, take the lowest place, so that when your host comes, he will say to you, 'Friend, move up to a better place.' Then you will be honored in the presence of all your fellow guests. 11For everyone who exalts himself will be humbled, and he who humbles himself will be exalted."

12Then Jesus said to his host, "When you give a luncheon or dinner, do not invite your friends, your brothers or relatives, or your rich neighbors; if you do, they may invite you back and so you will be repaid. 13But when you give a banquet, invite the poor, the crippled, the lame, the blind, 14and you will be blessed. Although they cannot repay you, you will be repaid at the resurrection of the righteous."

The Parable of the Great Banquet

15When one of those at the table with him heard this, he said to Jesus, "Blessed is the man who will eat at the feast in the kingdom of God."

16Jesus replied: "A certain man was preparing a great banquet and invited many guests. 17At the time of the banquet he sent his servant to tell those who had been invited, 'Come, for everything is now ready.'

18"But they all alike began to make excuses. The first said, 'I have just bought a field, and I must go and see it. Please excuse me.'

19"Another said, 'I have just bought five yoke of oxen, and I'm on my way to try them out. Please excuse me.'

20"Still another said, 'I just got married, so I can't come.'

21"The servant came back and reported this to his master. Then the owner of the house became angry and ordered his servant, 'Go out quickly

into the streets and alleys of the town and bring in the poor, the crippled, the blind and the lame.'

22"'Sir,' the servant said, 'what you ordered has been done, but there is still room.'

23"Then the master told his servant, 'Go out to the roads and country lanes and make them come in, so that my house will be full. 24I tell you, not one of those men who were invited will get a taste of my banquet.'"

The Cost of Being a Disciple

25Large crowds were traveling with Jesus, and turning to them he said: 26"If anyone comes to me and does not hate his father and mother, his wife and children, his brothers and sisters—yes, even his own life—he cannot be my disciple. 27And anyone who does not carry his cross and follow me cannot be my disciple.

28"Suppose one of you wants to build a tower. Will he not first sit down and estimate the cost to see if he has enough money to complete it? 29For if he lays the foundation and is not able to finish it, everyone who sees it will ridicule him, 30saying, 'This fellow began to build and was not able to finish.'

31"Or suppose a king is about to go to war against another king. Will he not first sit down and consider whether he is able with ten thousand men to oppose the one coming against him with twenty thousand? 32If he is not able, he will send a delegation while the other is still a long way off and will ask for terms of peace. 33In the same way, any of you who does not give up everything he has cannot be my disciple.

34"Salt is good, but if it loses its saltiness, how can it be made salty again? 35It is fit neither for the soil nor for the manure pile; it is thrown out.

"He who has ears to hear, let him hear."

The Parable of the Lost Sheep

15 Now the tax collectors and "sinners" were all gathering around to hear him. 2But the Phari-

sees and the teachers of the law muttered, "This man welcomes sinners and eats with them."

3Then Jesus told them this parable: 4"Suppose one of you has a hundred sheep and loses one of them. Does he not leave the ninety-nine in the open country and go after the lost sheep until he finds it? 5And when he finds it, he joyfully puts it on his shoulders 6and goes home. Then he calls his friends and neighbors together and says, 'Rejoice with me; I have found my lost sheep.' 7I tell you that in the same way there will be more rejoicing in heaven over one sinner who repents than over ninety-nine righteous persons who do not need to repent.

The Parable of the Lost Coin

8"Or suppose a woman has ten silver coins[a] and loses one. Does she not light a lamp, sweep the house and search carefully until she finds it? 9And when she finds it, she calls her friends and neighbors together and says, 'Rejoice with me; I have found my lost coin.' 10In the same way, I tell you, there is rejoicing in the presence of the angels of God over one sinner who repents."

The Parable of the Lost Son

11Jesus continued: "There was a man who had two sons. 12The younger one said to his father, 'Father, give me my share of the estate.' So he divided his property between them.

13"Not long after that, the younger son got together all he had, set off for a distant country and there squandered his wealth in wild living. 14After he had spent everything, there was a severe famine in that whole country, and he began to be in need. 15So he went and hired himself out to a citizen of that country, who sent him to his fields to feed pigs. 16He longed to fill his stomach with the pods that the pigs were eating, but no one gave him anything.

17"When he came to his senses, he said, 'How many of my father's hired men have food to spare, and here I am starving to death! 18I will set out and go back to my father and say to him: Father, I have sinned against heaven and against you. 19I am no longer worthy to be called your son; make me like one of your hired men.' 20So he got up and went to his father.

"But while he was still a long way off, his father saw him and was filled with compassion for him; he ran to his son, threw his arms around him and kissed him.

21"The son said to him, 'Father, I have sinned against heaven and against you. I am no longer worthy to be called your son.[b]'

22"But the father said to his servants, 'Quick! Bring the best robe and put it on him. Put a ring on his finger and sandals on his feet. 23Bring the fattened calf and kill it. Let's have a feast and celebrate. 24For this son of mine was dead and is alive again; he was lost and is found.' So they began to celebrate.

25"Meanwhile, the older son was in the field. When he came near the house, he heard music and dancing. 26So he called one of the servants and asked him what was going on. 27'Your brother has come,' he replied, 'and your father has killed the fattened calf because he has him back safe and sound.'

28"The older brother became angry and refused to go in. So his father went out and pleaded with him. 29But he answered his father, 'Look! All these years I've been slaving for you and never disobeyed your orders. Yet you never gave me even a young goat so I could celebrate with my friends. 30But when this son of yours who has squandered your property with prostitutes comes home, you kill the fattened calf for him!'

31" 'My son,' the father said, 'you are always with me, and everything I have is yours. 32But we had to celebrate and be glad, because this broth-

---

a8 Greek *ten drachmas*, each worth about a day's wages   b21 Some early manuscripts *son.*
Make me like one of your hired men.

er of yours was dead and is alive again; he was lost and is found.' "

The Parable of the Shrewd Manager

16 Jesus told his disciples: "There was a rich man whose manager was accused of wasting his possessions. ²So he called him in and asked him, 'What is this I hear about you? Give an account of your management, because you cannot be manager any longer.'

³"The manager said to himself, 'What shall I do now? My master is taking away my job. I'm not strong enough to dig, and I'm ashamed to beg— ⁴I know what I'll do so that, when I lose my job here, people will welcome me into their houses.'

⁵"So he called in each one of his

TUESDAY

VERSE: AUTHOR: PASSAGE:
Luke 15:32   Ken Gire   Luke 15:11–32

Bring Us Home

Dear Beloved Son of the Father, how it must crush you when I turn my back on you and walk away. How you must weep when you see me disappear over a far horizon to squander my life in a distant country.

Thank you that although I have sometimes left home, I have never left your heart. Though I have forgotten about you, you have never forgotten about me . . .

Thank you for the forgiveness and the restoration you have lavished upon me — me, the one who needed them most but deserved them least.

I confess there is inside me not only a prodigal son but also a critical older brother.

How dutiful I have sometimes been, and yet so proud of the duties I have done. How generous I have been in my opinion of myself, and yet so judgmental in my opinion of others. How often I have entered into criticism, and yet how seldom I have entered into your joy.

Gather both the prodigal part of myself and the critical part of myself in your loving arms, O Lord. And bring them home . . .

ADDITIONAL SCRIPTURE READINGS
Matthew 18:10–14; Romans 6:1–14

Go to page 1311 for your next devotional reading.

master's debtors. He asked the first, 'How much do you owe my master?'

6" 'Eight hundred gallons*a* of olive oil,' he replied.

"The manager told him, 'Take your bill, sit down quickly, and make it four hundred.'

7"Then he asked the second, 'And how much do you owe?'

" 'A thousand bushels*b* of wheat,' he replied.

"He told him, 'Take your bill and make it eight hundred.'

8"The master commended the dishonest manager because he had acted shrewdly. For the people of this world are more shrewd in dealing with their own kind than are the people of the light. 9I tell you, use worldly wealth to gain friends for yourselves, so that when it is gone, you will be welcomed into eternal dwellings.

10"Whoever can be trusted with very little can also be trusted with much, and whoever is dishonest with very little will also be dishonest with much. 11So if you have not been trustworthy in handling worldly wealth, who will trust you with true riches? 12And if you have not been trustworthy with someone else's property, who will give you property of your own?

13"No servant can serve two masters. Either he will hate the one and love the other, or he will be devoted to the one and despise the other. You cannot serve both God and Money."

14The Pharisees, who loved money, heard all this and were sneering at Jesus. 15He said to them, "You are the ones who justify yourselves in the eyes of men, but God knows your hearts. What is highly valued among men is detestable in God's sight.

Additional Teachings

16"The Law and the Prophets were proclaimed until John. Since that time, the good news of the kingdom of God is being preached, and every-

one is forcing his way into it. 17It is easier for heaven and earth to disappear than for the least stroke of a pen to drop out of the Law.

18"Anyone who divorces his wife and marries another woman commits adultery, and the man who marries a divorced woman commits adultery.

The Rich Man and Lazarus

19"There was a rich man who was dressed in purple and fine linen and lived in luxury every day. 20At his gate was laid a beggar named Lazarus, covered with sores 21and longing to eat what fell from the rich man's table. Even the dogs came and licked his sores.

22"The time came when the beggar died and the angels carried him to Abraham's side. The rich man also died and was buried. 23In hell,*c* where he was in torment, he looked up and saw Abraham far away, with Lazarus by his side. 24So he called to him, 'Father Abraham, have pity on me and send Lazarus to dip the tip of his finger in water and cool my tongue, because I am in agony in this fire.'

25"But Abraham replied, 'Son, remember that in your lifetime you received your good things, while Lazarus received bad things, but now he is comforted here and you are in agony. 26And besides all this, between us and you a great chasm has been fixed, so that those who want to go from here to you cannot, nor can anyone cross over from there to us.'

27"He answered, 'Then I beg you, father, send Lazarus to my father's house, 28for I have five brothers. Let him warn them, so that they will not also come to this place of torment.'

29"Abraham replied, 'They have Moses and the Prophets; let them listen to them.'

30" 'No, father Abraham,' he said, 'but if someone from the dead goes to them, they will repent.'

31"He said to him, 'If they do not

---

a6 Greek *one hundred batous* (probably about 3 kiloliters) *b7* Greek *one hundred korous* (probably about 35 kiloliters) *c23* Greek *Hades*

VERSE:
Luke 16:15

AUTHOR:
Don Anderson

PASSAGE:
Luke 16:1–15

A Worthy Goal

People struggle with aging because they believe they will lose certain abilities as they grow older. They fear they will not be able to perform as effectively or efficiently as in younger days. A plaque belonging to my 85-year-old mom sums it up: "By the time you get to greener pastures, you can't climb the fence."

No matter what our age, we want to be able to do what we have always done. Much of our opinion of ourselves may depend on it. Performance counts in our culture. We can't escape it . . .

Seniors who are convinced they are less productive than before may feel discouraged by what they perceive to be a lack of ability to perform. But performance is clearly overrated in our society. The level of performance has nothing to do with the value of a person. Just because you can't do some things doesn't mean you can't do great things (see Luke 16:15).

Scripture reveals that it's not what you do that counts with God, it's what you are. The God of all creation and eternity is looking for a living, growing relationship with us, not some kind of power-packed performance!

He wants us to know him and his Son. In the context of that relationship, he wants to be our very best friend. What a goal with which to finish our years!

ADDITIONAL SCRIPTURE READINGS
2 Timothy 1:3–12; Titus 3:3–8
Go to page 1313 for your next devotional reading.

listen to Moses and the Prophets, they will not be convinced even if someone rises from the dead.' "

Sin, Faith, Duty

17 Jesus said to his disciples: "Things that cause people to sin are bound to come, but woe to that person through whom they come. ²It would be better for him to be thrown into the sea with a millstone tied around his neck than for him to cause one of these little ones to sin. ³So watch yourselves.

"If your brother sins, rebuke him, and if he repents, forgive him. ⁴If he sins against you seven times in a day, and seven times comes back to you and says, 'I repent,' forgive him."

⁵The apostles said to the Lord, "Increase our faith!"

⁶He replied, "If you have faith as small as a mustard seed, you can say to this mulberry tree, 'Be uprooted and planted in the sea,' and it will obey you.

⁷"Suppose one of you had a servant plowing or looking after the sheep. Would he say to the servant when he comes in from the field, 'Come along now and sit down to eat'? ⁸Would he not rather say, 'Prepare my supper, get yourself ready and wait on me while I eat and drink; after that you may eat and drink'? ⁹Would he thank the servant because he did what he was told to do? ¹⁰So you also, when you have done everything you were told to do, should say, 'We are unworthy servants; we have only done our duty.' "

Ten Healed of Leprosy

¹¹Now on his way to Jerusalem, Jesus traveled along the border between Samaria and Galilee. ¹²As he was going into a village, ten men who had leprosy*a* met him. They stood at a distance ¹³and called out in a loud voice, "Jesus, Master, have pity on us!"

¹⁴When he saw them, he said, "Go, show yourselves to the priests." And as they went, they were cleansed.

¹⁵One of them, when he saw he was healed, came back, praising God in a loud voice. ¹⁶He threw himself at Jesus' feet and thanked him—and he was a Samaritan.

¹⁷Jesus asked, "Were not all ten cleansed? Where are the other nine? ¹⁸Was no one found to return and give praise to God except this foreigner?" ¹⁹Then he said to him, "Rise and go; your faith has made you well."

The Coming of the Kingdom of God

²⁰Once, having been asked by the Pharisees when the kingdom of God would come, Jesus replied, "The kingdom of God does not come with your careful observation, ²¹nor will people say, 'Here it is,' or 'There it is,' because the kingdom of God is within*b* you."

²²Then he said to his disciples, "The time is coming when you will long to see one of the days of the Son of Man, but you will not see it. ²³Men will tell you, 'There he is!' or 'Here he is!' Do not go running off after them. ²⁴For the Son of Man in his day*c* will be like the lightning, which flashes and lights up the sky from one end to the other. ²⁵But first he must suffer many things and be rejected by this generation.

²⁶"Just as it was in the days of Noah, so also will it be in the days of the Son of Man. ²⁷People were eating, drinking, marrying and being given in marriage up to the day Noah entered the ark. Then the flood came and destroyed them all.

²⁸"It was the same in the days of Lot. People were eating and drinking, buying and selling, planting and building. ²⁹But the day Lot left Sodom, fire and sulfur rained down from heaven and destroyed them all.

³⁰"It will be just like this on the day the Son of Man is revealed. ³¹On that day no one who is on the roof of his house, with his goods inside, should

---

*a*12 The Greek word was used for various diseases affecting the skin—not necessarily leprosy.   *b*21 Or *among*   *c*24 Some manuscripts do not have *in his day*.

VERSE:	AUTHOR:	PASSAGE:
Luke 17:33	Max Lucado	Luke 17:20–37

The Voice of Adventure

The dawning of old age. The first pages of the final chapter. A golden speck appears on the green leaves of your life, and you are brought face to wrinkled face with the fact that you are getting older ...

Growing old can be dangerous. The trail is treacherous and the pitfalls are many. One is wise to be prepared. You know it's coming. It's not like God kept the process a secret. It's not like you are blazing a trail as you grow older. It's not as if no one has ever done it before. Look around you. You have ample opportunity to prepare and ample case studies to consider. If growing old catches you by surprise, don't blame God. He gave you plenty of warning. He also gave you plenty of advice ...

"Whoever tries to keep his life will lose it, and whoever loses his life will preserve it" (Luke 17:33). "There are two ways to view life," Jesus is saying, "those who protect it or those who pursue it. The wisest are not the ones with the most years in their lives, but the most life in their years" ...

There is a rawness and a wonder to life. Pursue it. Hunt for it ... Your goal is not to live long; it's to live. Jesus says the options are clear. On one side there is the voice of safety ... Or you can hear the voice of adventure — God's adventure ...

Your last chapters can be your best. Your final song can be your greatest. It could be that all of your life has prepared you for a grand exit. God's oldest have always been among his choicest.

ADDITIONAL SCRIPTURE READINGS
2 Timothy 1:3–12; Titus 3:3–8
Go to page 1319 for your next devotional reading.

go down to get them. Likewise, no one in the field should go back for anything. ³²Remember Lot's wife! ³³Whoever tries to keep his life will lose it, and whoever loses his life will preserve it. ³⁴I tell you, on that night two people will be in one bed; one will be taken and the other left. ³⁵Two women will be grinding grain together; one will be taken and the other left.ᵃ"

³⁷"Where, Lord?" they asked.

He replied, "Where there is a dead body, there the vultures will gather."

The Parable of the Persistent Widow

18 Then Jesus told his disciples a parable to show them that they should always pray and not give up. ²He said: "In a certain town there was a judge who neither feared God nor cared about men. ³And there was a widow in that town who kept coming to him with the plea, 'Grant me justice against my adversary.'

⁴"For some time he refused. But finally he said to himself, 'Even though I don't fear God or care about men, ⁵yet because this widow keeps bothering me, I will see that she gets justice, so that she won't eventually wear me out with her coming!' "

⁶And the Lord said, "Listen to what the unjust judge says. ⁷And will not God bring about justice for his chosen ones, who cry out to him day and night? Will he keep putting them off? ⁸I tell you, he will see that they get justice, and quickly. However, when the Son of Man comes, will he find faith on the earth?"

The Parable of the Pharisee and the Tax Collector

⁹To some who were confident of their own righteousness and looked down on everybody else, Jesus told this parable: ¹⁰"Two men went up to the temple to pray, one a Pharisee and the other a tax collector. ¹¹The Pharisee stood up and prayed aboutᵇ himself: 'God, I thank you that I am not like other men—robbers, evildoers, adulterers—or even like this tax collector. ¹²I fast twice a week and give a tenth of all I get.'

¹³"But the tax collector stood at a distance. He would not even look up to heaven, but beat his breast and said, 'God, have mercy on me, a sinner.'

¹⁴"I tell you that this man, rather than the other, went home justified before God. For everyone who exalts himself will be humbled, and he who humbles himself will be exalted."

The Little Children and Jesus

¹⁵People were also bringing babies to Jesus to have him touch them. When the disciples saw this, they rebuked them. ¹⁶But Jesus called the children to him and said, "Let the little children come to me, and do not hinder them, for the kingdom of God belongs to such as these. ¹⁷I tell you the truth, anyone who will not receive the kingdom of God like a little child will never enter it."

The Rich Ruler

¹⁸A certain ruler asked him, "Good teacher, what must I do to inherit eternal life?"

¹⁹"Why do you call me good?" Jesus answered. "No one is good—except God alone. ²⁰You know the commandments: 'Do not commit adultery, do not murder, do not steal, do not give false testimony, honor your father and mother.'ᶜ"

²¹"All these I have kept since I was a boy," he said.

²²When Jesus heard this, he said to him, "You still lack one thing. Sell everything you have and give to the poor, and you will have treasure in heaven. Then come, follow me."

²³When he heard this, he became very sad, because he was a man of great wealth. ²⁴Jesus looked at him and said, "How hard it is for the rich to enter the kingdom of God! ²⁵In-

---

ᵃ35 Some manuscripts left. ³⁶Two men will be in the field; one will be taken and the other left.
ᵇ11 Or to   ᶜ20 Exodus 20:12-16; Deut. 5:16-20

deed, it is easier for a camel to go through the eye of a needle than for a rich man to enter the kingdom of God."

²⁶Those who heard this asked, "Who then can be saved?"

²⁷Jesus replied, "What is impossible with men is possible with God."

²⁸Peter said to him, "We have left all we had to follow you!"

²⁹"I tell you the truth," Jesus said to them, "no one who has left home or wife or brothers or parents or children for the sake of the kingdom of God ³⁰will fail to receive many times as much in this age and, in the age to come, eternal life."

Jesus Again Predicts His Death

³¹Jesus took the Twelve aside and told them, "We are going up to Jerusalem, and everything that is written by the prophets about the Son of Man will be fulfilled. ³²He will be handed over to the Gentiles. They will mock him, insult him, spit on him, flog him and kill him. ³³On the third day he will rise again."

³⁴The disciples did not understand any of this. Its meaning was hidden from them, and they did not know what he was talking about.

A Blind Beggar Receives His Sight

³⁵As Jesus approached Jericho, a blind man was sitting by the roadside begging. ³⁶When he heard the crowd going by, he asked what was happening. ³⁷They told him, "Jesus of Nazareth is passing by."

³⁸He called out, "Jesus, Son of David, have mercy on me!"

³⁹Those who led the way rebuked him and told him to be quiet, but he shouted all the more, "Son of David, have mercy on me!"

⁴⁰Jesus stopped and ordered the man to be brought to him. When he came near, Jesus asked him, ⁴¹"What do you want me to do for you?"

"Lord, I want to see," he replied.

⁴²Jesus said to him, "Receive your sight; your faith has healed you."

⁴³Immediately he received his sight and followed Jesus, praising God. When all the people saw it, they also praised God.

Zacchaeus the Tax Collector

19 Jesus entered Jericho and was passing through. ²A man was there by the name of Zacchaeus; he was a chief tax collector and was wealthy. ³He wanted to see who Jesus was, but being a short man he could not, because of the crowd. ⁴So he ran ahead and climbed a sycamore-fig tree to see him, since Jesus was coming that way.

⁵When Jesus reached the spot, he looked up and said to him, "Zacchaeus, come down immediately. I must stay at your house today." ⁶So he came down at once and welcomed him gladly.

⁷All the people saw this and began to mutter, "He has gone to be the guest of a 'sinner.' "

⁸But Zacchaeus stood up and said to the Lord, "Look, Lord! Here and now I give half of my possessions to the poor, and if I have cheated anybody out of anything, I will pay back four times the amount."

⁹Jesus said to him, "Today salvation has come to this house, because this man, too, is a son of Abraham. ¹⁰For the Son of Man came to seek and to save what was lost."

The Parable of the Ten Minas

¹¹While they were listening to this, he went on to tell them a parable, because he was near Jerusalem and the people thought that the kingdom of God was going to appear at once. ¹²He said: "A man of noble birth went to a distant country to have himself appointed king and then to return. ¹³So he called ten of his servants and gave them ten minas.ᵃ 'Put this money to work,' he said, 'until I come back.'

¹⁴"But his subjects hated him and sent a delegation after him to say, 'We don't want this man to be our king.'

ᵃ13 A mina was about three months' wages.

<15>"He was made king, however, and returned home. Then he sent for the servants to whom he had given the money, in order to find out what they had gained with it.

<16>"The first one came and said, 'Sir, your mina has earned ten more.'

<17>"'Well done, my good servant!' his master replied. 'Because you have been trustworthy in a very small matter, take charge of ten cities.'

<18>"The second came and said, 'Sir, your mina has earned five more.'

<19>"His master answered, 'You take charge of five cities.'

<20>"Then another servant came and said, 'Sir, here is your mina; I have kept it laid away in a piece of cloth. <21>I was afraid of you, because you are a hard man. You take out what you did not put in and reap what you did not sow.'

<22>"His master replied, 'I will judge you by your own words, you wicked servant! You knew, did you, that I am a hard man, taking out what I did not put in, and reaping what I did not sow? <23>Why then didn't you put my money on deposit, so that when I came back, I could have collected it with interest?'

<24>"Then he said to those standing by, 'Take his mina away from him and give it to the one who has ten minas.'

<25>"'Sir,' they said, 'he already has ten!'

<26>"He replied, 'I tell you that to everyone who has, more will be given, but as for the one who has nothing, even what he has will be taken away. <27>But those enemies of mine who did not want me to be king over them—bring them here and kill them in front of me.'"

The Triumphal Entry

<28>After Jesus had said this, he went on ahead, going up to Jerusalem. <29>As he approached Bethphage and Bethany at the hill called the Mount of Olives, he sent two of his disciples, saying to them, <30>"Go to the village ahead of you, and as you enter it, you will find a colt tied there, which no one has ever ridden. Untie it and bring it here. <31>If anyone asks you, 'Why are you untying it?' tell him, 'The Lord needs it.'"

<32>Those who were sent ahead went and found it just as he had told them. <33>As they were untying the colt, its owners asked them, "Why are you untying the colt?"

<34>They replied, "The Lord needs it."

<35>They brought it to Jesus, threw their cloaks on the colt and put Jesus on it. <36>As he went along, people spread their cloaks on the road.

<37>When he came near the place where the road goes down the Mount of Olives, the whole crowd of disciples began joyfully to praise God in loud voices for all the miracles they had seen:

<38>"Blessed is the king who comes in the name of the Lord!"[a]

"Peace in heaven and glory in the highest!"

<39>Some of the Pharisees in the crowd said to Jesus, "Teacher, rebuke your disciples!"

<40>"I tell you," he replied, "if they keep quiet, the stones will cry out."

<41>As he approached Jerusalem and saw the city, he wept over it <42>and said, "If you, even you, had only known on this day what would bring you peace—but now it is hidden from your eyes. <43>The days will come upon you when your enemies will build an embankment against you and encircle you and hem you in on every side. <44>They will dash you to the ground, you and the children within your walls. They will not leave one stone on another, because you did not recognize the time of God's coming to you."

Jesus at the Temple

<45>Then he entered the temple area and began driving out those who

were selling. ⁴⁶"It is written," he said to them, " 'My house will be a house of prayer'ᵃ; but you have made it 'a den of robbers.'ᵇ"

⁴⁷Every day he was teaching at the temple. But the chief priests, the teachers of the law and the leaders among the people were trying to kill him. ⁴⁸Yet they could not find any way to do it, because all the people hung on his words.

The Authority of Jesus Questioned

20 One day as he was teaching the people in the temple courts and preaching the gospel, the chief priests and the teachers of the law, together with the elders, came up to him. ²"Tell us by what authority you are doing these things," they said. "Who gave you this authority?"

³He replied, "I will also ask you a question. Tell me, ⁴John's baptism—was it from heaven, or from men?"

⁵They discussed it among themselves and said, "If we say, 'From heaven,' he will ask, 'Why didn't you believe him?' ⁶But if we say, 'From men,' all the people will stone us, because they are persuaded that John was a prophet."

⁷So they answered, "We don't know where it was from."

⁸Jesus said, "Neither will I tell you by what authority I am doing these things."

The Parable of the Tenants

⁹He went on to tell the people this parable: "A man planted a vineyard, rented it to some farmers and went away for a long time. ¹⁰At harvest time he sent a servant to the tenants so they would give him some of the fruit of the vineyard. But the tenants beat him and sent him away empty-handed. ¹¹He sent another servant, but that one also they beat and treated shamefully and sent away empty-handed. ¹²He sent still a third, and they wounded him and threw him out.

¹³"Then the owner of the vineyard said, 'What shall I do? I will send my son, whom I love; perhaps they will respect him.'

¹⁴"But when the tenants saw him, they talked the matter over. 'This is the heir,' they said. 'Let's kill him, and the inheritance will be ours.' ¹⁵So they threw him out of the vineyard and killed him.

"What then will the owner of the vineyard do to them? ¹⁶He will come and kill those tenants and give the vineyard to others."

When the people heard this, they said, "May this never be!"

¹⁷Jesus looked directly at them and asked, "Then what is the meaning of that which is written:

" 'The stone the builders rejected
has become the capstoneᶜ'ᵈ?

¹⁸Everyone who falls on that stone will be broken to pieces, but he on whom it falls will be crushed."

¹⁹The teachers of the law and the chief priests looked for a way to arrest him immediately, because they knew he had spoken this parable against them. But they were afraid of the people.

Paying Taxes to Caesar

²⁰Keeping a close watch on him, they sent spies, who pretended to be honest. They hoped to catch Jesus in something he said so that they might hand him over to the power and authority of the governor. ²¹So the spies questioned him: "Teacher, we know that you speak and teach what is right, and that you do not show partiality but teach the way of God in accordance with the truth. ²²Is it right for us to pay taxes to Caesar or not?"

²³He saw through their duplicity and said to them, ²⁴"Show me a denarius. Whose portrait and inscription are on it?"

²⁵"Caesar's," they replied.

He said to them, "Then give to Caesar what is Caesar's, and to God what is God's."

²⁶They were unable to trap him in

ᵃ46 Isaiah 56:7   ᵇ46 Jer. 7:11   ᶜ17 Or cornerstone   ᵈ17 Psalm 118:22

what he had said there in public. And astonished by his answer, they became silent.

The Resurrection and Marriage

²⁷Some of the Sadducees, who say there is no resurrection, came to Jesus with a question. ²⁸"Teacher," they said, "Moses wrote for us that if a man's brother dies and leaves a wife but no children, the man must marry the widow and have children for his brother. ²⁹Now there were seven brothers. The first one married a woman and died childless. ³⁰The second ³¹and then the third married her, and in the same way the seven died, leaving no children. ³²Finally, the woman died too. ³³Now then, at the resurrection whose wife will she be, since the seven were married to her?"

³⁴Jesus replied, "The people of this age marry and are given in marriage. ³⁵But those who are considered worthy of taking part in that age and in the resurrection from the dead will neither marry nor be given in marriage, ³⁶and they can no longer die; for they are like the angels. They are God's children, since they are children of the resurrection. ³⁷But in the account of the bush, even Moses showed that the dead rise, for he calls the Lord 'the God of Abraham, and the God of Isaac, and the God of Jacob.'ᵃ ³⁸He is not the God of the dead, but of the living, for to him all are alive."

³⁹Some of the teachers of the law responded, "Well said, teacher!" ⁴⁰And no one dared to ask him any more questions.

Whose Son Is the Christ?

⁴¹Then Jesus said to them, "How is it that they say the Christᵇ is the Son of David? ⁴²David himself declares in the Book of Psalms:

" 'The Lord said to my Lord:
"Sit at my right hand
⁴³until I make your enemies
a footstool for your feet." 'ᶜ

⁴⁴David calls him 'Lord.' How then can he be his son?"

⁴⁵While all the people were listening, Jesus said to his disciples, ⁴⁶"Beware of the teachers of the law. They like to walk around in flowing robes and love to be greeted in the marketplaces and have the most important seats in the synagogues and the places of honor at banquets. ⁴⁷They devour widows' houses and for a show make lengthy prayers. Such men will be punished most severely."

The Widow's Offering

21 As he looked up, Jesus saw the rich putting their gifts into the temple treasury. ²He also saw a poor widow put in two very small copper coins.ᵈ ³"I tell you the truth," he said, "this poor widow has put in more than all the others. ⁴All these people gave their gifts out of their wealth; but she out of her poverty put in all she had to live on."

Signs of the End of the Age

⁵Some of his disciples were remarking about how the temple was adorned with beautiful stones and with gifts dedicated to God. But Jesus said, ⁶"As for what you see here, the time will come when not one stone will be left on another; every one of them will be thrown down."

⁷"Teacher," they asked, "when will these things happen? And what will be the sign that they are about to take place?"

⁸He replied: "Watch out that you are not deceived. For many will come in my name, claiming, 'I am he,' and, 'The time is near.' Do not follow them. ⁹When you hear of wars and revolutions, do not be frightened. These things must happen first, but the end will not come right away."

¹⁰Then he said to them: "Nation will rise against nation, and kingdom against kingdom. ¹¹There will be great earthquakes, famines and pestilences in various places, and fearful events and great signs from heaven.

ᵃ37 Exodus 3:6   ᵇ41 Or *Messiah*   ᶜ43 Psalm 110:1   ᵈ2 Greek *two lepta*

¹²"But before all this, they will lay hands on you and persecute you. They will deliver you to synagogues and prisons, and you will be brought before kings and governors, and all on account of my name. ¹³This will re-sult in your being witnesses to them. ¹⁴But make up your mind not to wor-ry beforehand how you will defend yourselves. ¹⁵For I will give you words and wisdom that none of your adversaries will be able to resist or

FRIDAY

VERSE:
Luke 21:4

AUTHOR:
Tim Stafford

PASSAGE:
Luke 21:4

What Love Requires

Love takes no competence. It does not require heroic en-deavor. It can be done by anyone in any condition, so long as they have stopped being wrapped up in them-selves. Someone who is paralyzed can love with her eyes. Someone who is blind can love with his voice and his touch. Only this is required: To love our neighbor or to love God, you must make the shift away from yourself as center of the universe. You must take God's (or your neighbor's) life story for your own.

You can find people in every nursing home who do this, making an impact through their love. They give their lives to others. They breathe out love. The contri-bution may seem puny. But Jesus intended to impress on his disciples that God judges our giving by percentage, not gross total. The widow's two cents weigh the scales more heavily than the piled-up gifts of the rich. This is one way in which the poor are blessed: they can much more easily give their all.

We are God's chosen, not to make us strong, but to confound the strong (1 Corinthians 1:27–29). Simply to be God's children is power and glory. You cannot wit-ness to his grace and love except as someone who re-mains weak.

ADDITIONAL SCRIPTURE READINGS
1 Corinthians 1:18–31; 2 Corinthians 12:1–10

Go to page 1322 for your next devotional reading.

contradict. [16]You will be betrayed even by parents, brothers, relatives and friends, and they will put some of you to death. [17]All men will hate you because of me. [18]But not a hair of your head will perish. [19]By standing firm you will gain life.

[20]"When you see Jerusalem being surrounded by armies, you will know that its desolation is near. [21]Then let those who are in Judea flee to the mountains, let those in the city get out, and let those in the country not enter the city. [22]For this is the time of punishment in fulfillment of all that has been written. [23]How dreadful it will be in those days for pregnant women and nursing mothers! There will be great distress in the land and wrath against this people. [24]They will fall by the sword and will be taken as prisoners to all the nations. Jerusalem will be trampled on by the Gentiles until the times of the Gentiles are fulfilled.

[25]"There will be signs in the sun, moon and stars. On the earth, nations will be in anguish and perplexity at the roaring and tossing of the sea. [26]Men will faint from terror, apprehensive of what is coming on the world, for the heavenly bodies will be shaken. [27]At that time they will see the Son of Man coming in a cloud with power and great glory. [28]When these things begin to take place, stand up and lift up your heads, because your redemption is drawing near."

[29]He told them this parable: "Look at the fig tree and all the trees. [30]When they sprout leaves, you can see for yourselves and know that summer is near. [31]Even so, when you see these things happening, you know that the kingdom of God is near.

[32]"I tell you the truth, this generation[a] will certainly not pass away until all these things have happened. [33]Heaven and earth will pass away, but my words will never pass away.

[34]"Be careful, or your hearts will be weighed down with dissipation, drunkenness and the anxieties of life,

and that day will close on you unexpectedly like a trap. [35]For it will come upon all those who live on the face of the whole earth. [36]Be always on the watch, and pray that you may be able to escape all that is about to happen, and that you may be able to stand before the Son of Man."

[37]Each day Jesus was teaching at the temple, and each evening he went out to spend the night on the hill called the Mount of Olives, [38]and all the people came early in the morning to hear him at the temple.

Judas Agrees to Betray Jesus

22 Now the Feast of Unleavened Bread, called the Passover, was approaching, [2]and the chief priests and the teachers of the law were looking for some way to get rid of Jesus, for they were afraid of the people. [3]Then Satan entered Judas, called Iscariot, one of the Twelve. [4]And Judas went to the chief priests and the officers of the temple guard and discussed with them how he might betray Jesus. [5]They were delighted and agreed to give him money. [6]He consented, and watched for an opportunity to hand Jesus over to them when no crowd was present.

The Last Supper

[7]Then came the day of Unleavened Bread on which the Passover lamb had to be sacrificed. [8]Jesus sent Peter and John, saying, "Go and make preparations for us to eat the Passover."

[9]"Where do you want us to prepare for it?" they asked.

[10]He replied, "As you enter the city, a man carrying a jar of water will meet you. Follow him to the house that he enters, [11]and say to the owner of the house, 'The Teacher asks: Where is the guest room, where I may eat the Passover with my disciples?' [12]He will show you a large upper room, all furnished. Make preparations there."

[13]They left and found things just as

Jesus had told them. So they prepared the Passover.

¹⁴When the hour came, Jesus and his apostles reclined at the table. ¹⁵And he said to them, "I have eagerly desired to eat this Passover with you before I suffer. ¹⁶For I tell you, I will not eat it again until it finds fulfillment in the kingdom of God."

¹⁷After taking the cup, he gave thanks and said, "Take this and divide it among you. ¹⁸For I tell you I will not drink again of the fruit of the vine until the kingdom of God comes."

¹⁹And he took bread, gave thanks and broke it, and gave it to them, saying, "This is my body given for you; do this in remembrance of me."

²⁰In the same way, after the supper he took the cup, saying, "This cup is the new covenant in my blood, which is poured out for you. ²¹But the hand of him who is going to betray me is with mine on the table. ²²The Son of Man will go as it has been decreed, but woe to that man who betrays him." ²³They began to question among themselves which of them it might be who would do this.

²⁴Also a dispute arose among them as to which of them was considered to be greatest. ²⁵Jesus said to them, "The kings of the Gentiles lord it over them; and those who exercise authority over them call themselves Benefactors. ²⁶But you are not to be like that. Instead, the greatest among you should be like the youngest, and the one who rules like the one who serves. ²⁷For who is greater, the one who is at the table or the one who serves? Is it not the one who is at the table? But I am among you as one who serves. ²⁸You are those who have stood by me in my trials. ²⁹And I confer on you a kingdom, just as my Father conferred one on me, ³⁰so that you may eat and drink at my table in my kingdom and sit on thrones, judging the twelve tribes of Israel.

³¹"Simon, Simon, Satan has asked to sift you*a* as wheat. ³²But I have prayed for you, Simon, that your faith may not fail. And when you have turned back, strengthen your brothers."

³³But he replied, "Lord, I am ready to go with you to prison and to death."

³⁴Jesus answered, "I tell you, Peter, before the rooster crows today, you will deny three times that you know me."

³⁵Then Jesus asked them, "When I sent you without purse, bag or sandals, did you lack anything?"

"Nothing," they answered.

³⁶He said to them, "But now if you have a purse, take it, and also a bag; and if you don't have a sword, sell your cloak and buy one. ³⁷It is written: 'And he was numbered with the transgressors'*b*; and I tell you that this must be fulfilled in me. Yes, what is written about me is reaching its fulfillment."

³⁸The disciples said, "See, Lord, here are two swords."

"That is enough," he replied.

Jesus Prays on the Mount of Olives

³⁹Jesus went out as usual to the Mount of Olives, and his disciples followed him. ⁴⁰On reaching the place, he said to them, "Pray that you will not fall into temptation." ⁴¹He withdrew about a stone's throw beyond them, knelt down and prayed, ⁴²"Father, if you are willing, take this cup from me; yet not my will, but yours be done." ⁴³An angel from heaven appeared to him and strengthened him. ⁴⁴And being in anguish, he prayed more earnestly, and his sweat was like drops of blood falling to the ground.*c*

⁴⁵When he rose from prayer and went back to the disciples, he found them asleep, exhausted from sorrow. ⁴⁶"Why are you sleeping?" he asked them. "Get up and pray so that you will not fall into temptation."

a31 The Greek is plural.   *b37* Isaiah 53:12   *c44* Some early manuscripts do not have verses 43 and 44.

PASSAGE: Luke 22:7–19; Luke 23:26–43
AUTHOR: James Montgomery

Lord, Remember Me

According to thy gracious word, in meek humility
This will I do, my loving Lord: I will remember
  thee.

Thy body given for my sake, my bread from
  heaven shall be;
Thy testamental cup I take, and thus remember
  thee.

When to the cross I turn mine eyes and rest on
  Calvary,
O Lamb of God, my sacrifice, I must remember
  thee.

And when these failing lips grow dumb, and mind
  and memory flee,
When thou shalt in thy kingdom come, then, Lord,
  remember me.

Go to page 1326 for your next devotional reading.

Jesus Arrested

47While he was still speaking a crowd came up, and the man who was called Judas, one of the Twelve, was leading them. He approached Jesus to kiss him, **48**but Jesus asked him, "Judas, are you betraying the Son of Man with a kiss?"

49When Jesus' followers saw what was going to happen, they said, "Lord, should we strike with our swords?" **50**And one of them struck the servant of the high priest, cutting off his right ear.

51But Jesus answered, "No more of this!" And he touched the man's ear and healed him.

52Then Jesus said to the chief priests, the officers of the temple guard, and the elders, who had come for him, "Am I leading a rebellion, that you have come with swords and clubs? **53**Every day I was with you in the temple courts, and you did not lay a hand on me. But this is your hour—when darkness reigns."

Peter Disowns Jesus

54Then seizing him, they led him away and took him into the house of the high priest. Peter followed at a distance. **55**But when they had kindled a fire in the middle of the courtyard and had sat down together, Peter sat down with them. **56**A servant girl saw him seated there in the firelight. She looked closely at him and said, "This man was with him."

57But he denied it. "Woman, I don't know him," he said.

58A little later someone else saw him and said, "You also are one of them."

"Man, I am not!" Peter replied.

59About an hour later another asserted, "Certainly this fellow was with him, for he is a Galilean."

60Peter replied, "Man, I don't know what you're talking about!" Just as he was speaking, the rooster crowed. **61**The Lord turned and looked straight at Peter. Then Peter remembered the word the Lord had spoken to him: "Before the rooster crows today, you will disown me three times." **62**And he went outside and wept bitterly.

The Guards Mock Jesus

63The men who were guarding Jesus began mocking and beating him. **64**They blindfolded him and demanded, "Prophesy! Who hit you?" **65**And they said many other insulting things to him.

Jesus Before Pilate and Herod

66At daybreak the council of the elders of the people, both the chief priests and teachers of the law, met together, and Jesus was led before them. **67**"If you are the Christ,*a*" they said, "tell us."

Jesus answered, "If I tell you, you will not believe me, **68**and if I asked you, you would not answer. **69**But from now on, the Son of Man will be seated at the right hand of the mighty God."

70They all asked, "Are you then the Son of God?"

He replied, "You are right in saying I am."

71Then they said, "Why do we need any more testimony? We have heard it from his own lips."

23 Then the whole assembly rose and led him off to Pilate. **2**And they began to accuse him, saying, "We have found this man subverting our nation. He opposes payment of taxes to Caesar and claims to be Christ,*b* a king."

3So Pilate asked Jesus, "Are you the king of the Jews?"

"Yes, it is as you say," Jesus replied.

4Then Pilate announced to the chief priests and the crowd, "I find no basis for a charge against this man."

5But they insisted, "He stirs up the people all over Judea*c* by his teaching. He started in Galilee and has come all the way here."

6On hearing this, Pilate asked if the man was a Galilean. **7**When he

*a*67 Or *Messiah*   *b*2 Or *Messiah; also in verses 35 and 39*   *c*5 Or *over the land of the Jews*

learned that Jesus was under Herod's jurisdiction, he sent him to Herod, who was also in Jerusalem at that time.

⁸When Herod saw Jesus, he was greatly pleased, because for a long time he had been wanting to see him. From what he had heard about him, he hoped to see him perform some miracle. ⁹He plied him with many questions, but Jesus gave him no answer. ¹⁰The chief priests and the teachers of the law were standing there, vehemently accusing him. ¹¹Then Herod and his soldiers ridiculed and mocked him. Dressing him in an elegant robe, they sent him back to Pilate. ¹²That day Herod and Pilate became friends—before this they had been enemies.

¹³Pilate called together the chief priests, the rulers and the people, ¹⁴and said to them, "You brought me this man as one who was inciting the people to rebellion. I have examined him in your presence and have found no basis for your charges against him. ¹⁵Neither has Herod, for he sent him back to us; as you can see, he has done nothing to deserve death. ¹⁶Therefore, I will punish him and then release him.ᵃ"

¹⁸With one voice they cried out, "Away with this man! Release Barabbas to us!" ¹⁹(Barabbas had been thrown into prison for an insurrection in the city, and for murder.)

²⁰Wanting to release Jesus, Pilate appealed to them again. ²¹But they kept shouting, "Crucify him! Crucify him!"

²²For the third time he spoke to them: "Why? What crime has this man committed? I have found in him no grounds for the death penalty. Therefore I will have him punished and then release him."

²³But with loud shouts they insistently demanded that he be crucified, and their shouts prevailed. ²⁴So Pilate decided to grant their demand. ²⁵He released the man who had been

thrown into prison for insurrection and murder, the one they asked for, and surrendered Jesus to their will.

The Crucifixion

²⁶As they led him away, they seized Simon from Cyrene, who was on his way in from the country, and put the cross on him and made him carry it behind Jesus. ²⁷A large number of people followed him, including women who mourned and wailed for him. ²⁸Jesus turned and said to them, "Daughters of Jerusalem, do not weep for me; weep for yourselves and for your children. ²⁹For the time will come when you will say, 'Blessed are the barren women, the wombs that never bore and the breasts that never nursed!' ³⁰Then

" 'they will say to the mountains,
  "Fall on us!"
and to the hills, "Cover us!" 'ᵇ

³¹For if men do these things when the tree is green, what will happen when it is dry?"

³²Two other men, both criminals, were also led out with him to be executed. ³³When they came to the place called the Skull, there they crucified him, along with the criminals—one on his right, the other on his left. ³⁴Jesus said, "Father, forgive them, for they do not know what they are doing."ᶜ And they divided up his clothes by casting lots.

³⁵The people stood watching, and the rulers even sneered at him. They said, "He saved others; let him save himself if he is the Christ of God, the Chosen One."

³⁶The soldiers also came up and mocked him. They offered him wine vinegar ³⁷and said, "If you are the king of the Jews, save yourself."

³⁸There was a written notice above him, which read: THIS IS THE KING OF THE JEWS.

³⁹One of the criminals who hung there hurled insults at him: "Aren't

---

ᵃ16 Some manuscripts him." 17Now he was obliged to release one man to them at the Feast.
ᵇ30 Hosea 10:8   ᶜ34 Some early manuscripts do not have this sentence.

you the Christ? Save yourself and us!"

⁴⁰But the other criminal rebuked him. "Don't you fear God," he said, "since you are under the same sentence? ⁴¹We are punished justly, for we are getting what our deeds deserve. But this man has done nothing wrong."

⁴²Then he said, "Jesus, remember me when you come into your kingdom.ᵃ"

⁴³Jesus answered him, "I tell you the truth, today you will be with me in paradise."

Jesus' Death

⁴⁴It was now about the sixth hour, and darkness came over the whole land until the ninth hour, ⁴⁵for the sun stopped shining. And the curtain of the temple was torn in two. ⁴⁶Jesus called out with a loud voice, "Father, into your hands I commit my spirit." When he had said this, he breathed his last.

⁴⁷The centurion, seeing what had happened, praised God and said, "Surely this was a righteous man." ⁴⁸When all the people who had gathered to witness this sight saw what took place, they beat their breasts and went away. ⁴⁹But all those who knew him, including the women who had followed him from Galilee, stood at a distance, watching these things.

Jesus' Burial

⁵⁰Now there was a man named Joseph, a member of the Council, a good and upright man, ⁵¹who had not consented to their decision and action. He came from the Judean town of Arimathea and he was waiting for the kingdom of God. ⁵²Going to Pilate, he asked for Jesus' body. ⁵³Then he took it down, wrapped it in linen cloth and placed it in a tomb cut in the rock, one in which no one had yet been laid. ⁵⁴It was Preparation Day, and the Sabbath was about to begin.

⁵⁵The women who had come with Jesus from Galilee followed Joseph and saw the tomb and how his body was laid in it. ⁵⁶Then they went home and prepared spices and perfumes. But they rested on the Sabbath in obedience to the commandment.

The Resurrection

24 On the first day of the week, very early in the morning, the women took the spices they had prepared and went to the tomb. ²They found the stone rolled away from the tomb, ³but when they entered, they did not find the body of the Lord Jesus. ⁴While they were wondering about this, suddenly two men in clothes that gleamed like lightning stood beside them. ⁵In their fright the women bowed down with their faces to the ground, but the men said to them, "Why do you look for the living among the dead? ⁶He is not here; he has risen! Remember how he told you, while he was still with you in Galilee: ⁷'The Son of Man must be delivered into the hands of sinful men, be crucified and on the third day be raised again.' " ⁸Then they remembered his words.

⁹When they came back from the tomb, they told all these things to the Eleven and to all the others. ¹⁰It was Mary Magdalene, Joanna, Mary the mother of James, and the others with them who told this to the apostles. ¹¹But they did not believe the women, because their words seemed to them like nonsense. ¹²Peter, however, got up and ran to the tomb. Bending over, he saw the strips of linen lying by themselves, and he went away, wondering to himself what had happened.

On the Road to Emmaus

¹³Now that same day two of them were going to a village called Emmaus, about seven milesᵇ from Jerusalem. ¹⁴They were talking with each other about everything that had happened. ¹⁵As they talked and discussed these things with each other, Jesus himself came up and walked along

ᵃ42 Some manuscripts *come with your kingly power*   ᵇ13 Greek *sixty stadia* (about 11 kilometers)

VERSE:	AUTHOR:	PASSAGE:
Luke 23:46	John White	Luke 23:44–49

As the Curtain Falls

As a Christian you must not be a passive, cringing victim of death. Your attitude must be what Christ's was and the core of his attitude is found in his final prayer ... There is a strong possibility that you will face death with your eyes open. What will you do? What attitude will you adopt?

We must confine ourselves to the heart of the matter, to what Christ prayed and how he prayed it. "Into your hands I commit my spirit!" The prayer is a prayer of faith. He did not say, "Into your hands I hope my spirit will eventually drift," but instead he made a declaration of firm trust. It was, in fact, more than a declaration. It was a commitment.

Death involves a choice. We cannot at the end choose whether we die, but we may choose how to do so. We may choose for instance whether we bear witness with joy to our faith in God or whether we are dragged off-stage.

For in life we are on a stage. The audience is both human and ghostly. Angels and demons watch as we enact the drama of our earthly existence, and it is important that the scene close properly. A brilliant opening act can be spoiled by a feeble ending. Christ has shown us how the lines should be uttered, as a cry of joyful triumph. "Father, into your hands I commit my spirit!"

ADDITIONAL SCRIPTURE READINGS
Psalm 31:1–16; 1 Peter 2:18–25

Go to page 1328 for your next devotional reading.

with them; ¹⁶but they were kept from recognizing him.

¹⁷He asked them, "What are you discussing together as you walk along?"

They stood still, their faces downcast. ¹⁸One of them, named Cleopas, asked him, "Are you only a visitor to Jerusalem and do not know the things that have happened there in these days?"

¹⁹"What things?" he asked.

"About Jesus of Nazareth," they replied. "He was a prophet, powerful in word and deed before God and all the people. ²⁰The chief priests and our rulers handed him over to be sentenced to death, and they crucified him; ²¹but we had hoped that he was the one who was going to redeem Israel. And what is more, it is the third day since all this took place. ²²In addition, some of our women amazed us. They went to the tomb early this morning ²³but didn't find his body. They came and told us that they had seen a vision of angels, who said he was alive. ²⁴Then some of our companions went to the tomb and found it just as the women had said, but him they did not see."

²⁵He said to them, "How foolish you are, and how slow of heart to believe all that the prophets have spoken! ²⁶Did not the Christ*a* have to suffer these things and then enter his glory?" ²⁷And beginning with Moses and all the Prophets, he explained to them what was said in all the Scriptures concerning himself.

²⁸As they approached the village to which they were going, Jesus acted as if he were going farther. ²⁹But they urged him strongly, "Stay with us, for it is nearly evening; the day is almost over." So he went in to stay with them.

³⁰When he was at the table with them, he took bread, gave thanks, broke it and began to give it to them. ³¹Then their eyes were opened and they recognized him, and he disap-

peared from their sight. ³²They asked each other, "Were not our hearts burning within us while he talked with us on the road and opened the Scriptures to us?"

³³They got up and returned at once to Jerusalem. There they found the Eleven and those with them, assembled together ³⁴and saying, "It is true! The Lord has risen and has appeared to Simon." ³⁵Then the two told what had happened on the way, and how Jesus was recognized by them when he broke the bread.

Jesus Appears to the Disciples

³⁶While they were still talking about this, Jesus himself stood among them and said to them, "Peace be with you."

³⁷They were startled and frightened, thinking they saw a ghost. ³⁸He said to them, "Why are you troubled, and why do doubts rise in your minds? ³⁹Look at my hands and my feet. It is I myself! Touch me and see; a ghost does not have flesh and bones, as you see I have."

⁴⁰When he had said this, he showed them his hands and feet. ⁴¹And while they still did not believe it because of joy and amazement, he asked them, "Do you have anything here to eat?" ⁴²They gave him a piece of broiled fish, ⁴³and he took it and ate it in their presence.

⁴⁴He said to them, "This is what I told you while I was still with you: Everything must be fulfilled that is written about me in the Law of Moses, the Prophets and the Psalms."

⁴⁵Then he opened their minds so they could understand the Scriptures. ⁴⁶He told them, "This is what is written: The Christ will suffer and rise from the dead on the third day, ⁴⁷and repentance and forgiveness of sins will be preached in his name to all nations, beginning at Jerusalem. ⁴⁸You are witnesses of these things. ⁴⁹I am going to send you what my Father has promised; but stay in the city un-

a26 Or Messiah; also in verse 46

VERSE:	AUTHOR:	PASSAGE:
Luke 24:31	Henri J.M. Nouwen	Luke 24:13–31

Under the Veil

Love is stronger than death. This sentence summarizes better than any other the meaning of the resurrection and therefore also the meaning of death ... The resurrection of Jesus Christ is the glorious manifestation of the victory of love over death. The same love that makes us mourn and protest against death will now free us to live in hope. Do you realize that Jesus appeared only to those who knew him, who had listened to his words and who had come to love him deeply [Luke 24:15]? It was that love that gave them the eyes to see his face and the ears to hear his voice when he appeared to them on the third day after his death. Once they had seen and heard him and believed, the rest of their lives became a continuing recognition of his presence in their midst. This is what life in the Spirit of the risen Christ is all about. It makes us see that under the veil of all that is visible to our bodily eyes, the risen Lord shows us his inexhaustible love and calls us to enter even more fully into that love ...

It is with this divine love in our hearts, a love stronger than death, that our lives can be lived as a promise. Because this great love promises us that what we have already begun to see and hear with the eyes and ears of the Spirit of Christ can never be destroyed, but rather is "the beginning" of eternal life.

ADDITIONAL SCRIPTURE READINGS
Song of Songs 8:6–7; Romans 6:1–14

Go to page 1334 for your next devotional reading.

til you have been clothed with power from on high."

The Ascension

50When he had led them out to the vicinity of Bethany, he lifted up his hands and blessed them. 51While he was blessing them, he left them and was taken up into heaven. 52Then they worshiped him and returned to Jerusalem with great joy. 53And they stayed continually at the temple, praising God.

*J*ohn writes his Gospel to present Jesus, the powerful Son of God who came to earth in human flesh—John's purpose was to convince people to believe in Jesus and receive eternal life. John spotlights the sacrificial love of Jesus, who gave his life on the cross for the forgiveness of our sins. As you read this book, look to Jesus as the One who can provide the joyful, purpose-filled life you desire.

JOHN

The Word Became Flesh

1 In the beginning was the Word, and the Word was with God, and the Word was God. ²He was with God in the beginning.

³Through him all things were made; without him nothing was made that has been made. ⁴In him was life, and that life was the light of men. ⁵The light shines in the darkness, but the darkness has not understood*ᵃ* it.

⁶There came a man who was sent from God; his name was John. ⁷He came as a witness to testify concerning that light, so that through him all men might believe. ⁸He himself was not the light; he came only as a witness to the light. ⁹The true light that gives light to every man was coming into the world.*ᵇ*

¹⁰He was in the world, and though the world was made through him, the world did not recognize him. ¹¹He came to that which was his own, but his own did not receive him. ¹²Yet to all who received him, to those who believed in his name, he gave the right to become children of God— ¹³children born not of natural descent,*ᶜ* nor of human decision or a husband's will, but born of God.

¹⁴The Word became flesh and made his dwelling among us. We have seen his glory, the glory of the One and Only,*ᵈ* who came from the Father, full of grace and truth.

¹⁵John testifies concerning him. He cries out, saying, "This was he of whom I said, 'He who comes after me has surpassed me because he was before me.' " ¹⁶From the fullness of his grace we have all received one blessing after another. ¹⁷For the law was

---

ᵃ5 Or *darkness, and the darkness has not overcome*   *ᵇ9* Or *This was the true light that gives light to*
every man who comes into the world   *ᶜ13* Greek *of bloods*   *ᵈ14* Or *the Only Begotten*

given through Moses; grace and truth came through Jesus Christ. ¹⁸No one has ever seen God, but God the One and Only,ᵃ,ᵇ who is at the Father's side, has made him known.

John the Baptist Denies Being the Christ

¹⁹Now this was John's testimony when the Jews of Jerusalem sent priests and Levites to ask him who he was. ²⁰He did not fail to confess, but confessed freely, "I am not the Christ.ᶜ"

²¹They asked him, "Then who are you? Are you Elijah?"

He said, "I am not."

"Are you the Prophet?"

He answered, "No."

²²Finally they said, "Who are you? Give us an answer to take back to those who sent us. What do you say about yourself?"

²³John replied in the words of Isaiah the prophet, "I am the voice of one calling in the desert, 'Make straight the way for the Lord.' "ᵈ

²⁴Now some Pharisees who had been sent ²⁵questioned him, "Why then do you baptize if you are not the Christ, nor Elijah, nor the Prophet?"

²⁶"I baptize withᵉ water," John replied, "but among you stands one you do not know. ²⁷He is the one who comes after me, the thongs of whose sandals I am not worthy to untie."

²⁸This all happened at Bethany on the other side of the Jordan, where John was baptizing.

Jesus the Lamb of God

²⁹The next day John saw Jesus coming toward him and said, "Look, the Lamb of God, who takes away the sin of the world! ³⁰This is the one I meant when I said, 'A man who comes after me has surpassed me because he was before me.' ³¹I myself did not know him, but the reason I came baptizing

with water was that he might be revealed to Israel."

³²Then John gave this testimony: "I saw the Spirit come down from heaven as a dove and remain on him. ³³I would not have known him, except that the one who sent me to baptize with water told me, 'The man on whom you see the Spirit come down and remain is he who will baptize with the Holy Spirit.' ³⁴I have seen and I testify that this is the Son of God."

Jesus' First Disciples

³⁵The next day John was there again with two of his disciples. ³⁶When he saw Jesus passing by, he said, "Look, the Lamb of God!"

³⁷When the two disciples heard him say this, they followed Jesus. ³⁸Turning around, Jesus saw them following and asked, "What do you want?"

They said, "Rabbi" (which means Teacher), "where are you staying?"

³⁹"Come," he replied, "and you will see."

So they went and saw where he was staying, and spent that day with him. It was about the tenth hour.

⁴⁰Andrew, Simon Peter's brother, was one of the two who heard what John had said and who had followed Jesus. ⁴¹The first thing Andrew did was to find his brother Simon and tell him, "We have found the Messiah" (that is, the Christ). ⁴²And he brought him to Jesus.

Jesus looked at him and said, "You are Simon son of John. You will be called Cephas" (which, when translated, is Peterᶠ).

Jesus Calls Philip and Nathanael

⁴³The next day Jesus decided to leave for Galilee. Finding Philip, he said to him, "Follow me."

⁴⁴Philip, like Andrew and Peter, was from the town of Bethsaida. ⁴⁵Philip found Nathanael and told

---

ᵃ18 Or the Only Begotten   ᵇ18 Some manuscripts but the only (or only begotten) Son   ᶜ20 Or Messiah. "The Christ" (Greek) and "the Messiah" (Hebrew) both mean "the Anointed One"; also in verse 25.   ᵈ23 Isaiah 40:3   ᵉ26 Or in; also in verses 31 and 33   ᶠ42 Both Cephas (Aramaic) and Peter (Greek) mean rock.

him, "We have found the one Moses wrote about in the Law, and about whom the prophets also wrote—Jesus of Nazareth, the son of Joseph."

⁴⁶"Nazareth! Can anything good come from there?" Nathanael asked.

"Come and see," said Philip.

⁴⁷When Jesus saw Nathanael approaching, he said of him, "Here is a true Israelite, in whom there is nothing false."

⁴⁸"How do you know me?" Nathanael asked.

Jesus answered, "I saw you while you were still under the fig tree before Philip called you."

⁴⁹Then Nathanael declared, "Rabbi, you are the Son of God; you are the King of Israel."

⁵⁰Jesus said, "You believe*a* because I told you I saw you under the fig tree. You shall see greater things than that." ⁵¹He then added, "I tell you*b* the truth, you*b* shall see heaven open, and the angels of God ascending and descending on the Son of Man."

Jesus Changes Water to Wine

2 On the third day a wedding took place at Cana in Galilee. Jesus' mother was there, ²and Jesus and his disciples had also been invited to the wedding. ³When the wine was gone, Jesus' mother said to him, "They have no more wine."

⁴"Dear woman, why do you involve me?" Jesus replied. "My time has not yet come."

⁵His mother said to the servants, "Do whatever he tells you."

⁶Nearby stood six stone water jars, the kind used by the Jews for ceremonial washing, each holding from twenty to thirty gallons.*c*

⁷Jesus said to the servants, "Fill the jars with water"; so they filled them to the brim.

⁸Then he told them, "Now draw some out and take it to the master of the banquet."

They did so, ⁹and the master of the banquet tasted the water that had been turned into wine. He did not realize where it had come from, though the servants who had drawn the water knew. Then he called the bridegroom aside ¹⁰and said, "Everyone brings out the choice wine first and then the cheaper wine after the guests have had too much to drink; but you have saved the best till now."

¹¹This, the first of his miraculous signs, Jesus performed at Cana in Galilee. He thus revealed his glory, and his disciples put their faith in him.

Jesus Clears the Temple

¹²After this he went down to Capernaum with his mother and brothers and his disciples. There they stayed for a few days.

¹³When it was almost time for the Jewish Passover, Jesus went up to Jerusalem. ¹⁴In the temple courts he found men selling cattle, sheep and doves, and others sitting at tables exchanging money. ¹⁵So he made a whip out of cords, and drove all from the temple area, both sheep and cattle; he scattered the coins of the money changers and overturned their tables. ¹⁶To those who sold doves he said, "Get these out of here! How dare you turn my Father's house into a market!"

¹⁷His disciples remembered that it is written: "Zeal for your house will consume me."*d*

¹⁸Then the Jews demanded of him, "What miraculous sign can you show us to prove your authority to do all this?"

¹⁹Jesus answered them, "Destroy this temple, and I will raise it again in three days."

²⁰The Jews replied, "It has taken forty-six years to build this temple, and you are going to raise it in three days?" ²¹But the temple he had spoken of was his body. ²²After he was raised from the dead, his disciples recalled what he had said. Then they

---

a50 Or *Do you believe . . . ?*   *b51* The Greek is plural.   *c6* Greek *two to three metretes*
(probably about 75 to 115 liters)   *d17* Psalm 69:9

believed the Scripture and the words that Jesus had spoken.

²³Now while he was in Jerusalem at the Passover Feast, many people saw the miraculous signs he was doing and believed in his name.ᵃ ²⁴But Jesus would not entrust himself to them, for he knew all men. ²⁵He did not need man's testimony about man, for he knew what was in a man.

Jesus Teaches Nicodemus

3 Now there was a man of the Pharisees named Nicodemus, a member of the Jewish ruling council. ²He came to Jesus at night and said, "Rabbi, we know you are a teacher who has come from God. For no one could perform the miraculous signs you are doing if God were not with him."

³In reply Jesus declared, "I tell you the truth, no one can see the kingdom of God unless he is born again.ᵇ"

⁴"How can a man be born when he is old?" Nicodemus asked. "Surely he cannot enter a second time into his mother's womb to be born!"

⁵Jesus answered, "I tell you the truth, no one can enter the kingdom of God unless he is born of water and the Spirit. ⁶Flesh gives birth to flesh, but the Spiritᶜ gives birth to spirit. ⁷You should not be surprised at my saying, 'Youᵈ must be born again.' ⁸The wind blows wherever it pleases. You hear its sound, but you cannot tell where it comes from or where it is going. So it is with everyone born of the Spirit."

⁹"How can this be?" Nicodemus asked.

¹⁰"You are Israel's teacher," said Jesus, "and do you not understand these things? ¹¹I tell you the truth, we speak of what we know, and we testify to what we have seen, but still you people do not accept our testimony. ¹²I have spoken to you of earthly things and you do not believe; how

then will you believe if I speak of heavenly things? ¹³No one has ever gone into heaven except the one who came from heaven—the Son of Man.ᵉ ¹⁴Just as Moses lifted up the snake in the desert, so the Son of Man must be lifted up, ¹⁵that everyone who believes in him may have eternal life.ᶠ

¹⁶"For God so loved the world that he gave his one and only Son,ᵍ that whoever believes in him shall not perish but have eternal life. ¹⁷For God did not send his Son into the world to condemn the world, but to save the world through him. ¹⁸Whoever believes in him is not condemned, but whoever does not believe stands condemned already because he has not believed in the name of God's one and only Son.ʰ ¹⁹This is the verdict: Light has come into the world, but men loved darkness instead of light because their deeds were evil. ²⁰Everyone who does evil hates the light, and will not come into the light for fear that his deeds will be exposed. ²¹But whoever lives by the truth comes into the light, so that it may be seen plainly that what he has done has been done through God."ⁱ

John the Baptist's Testimony About Jesus

²²After this, Jesus and his disciples went out into the Judean countryside, where he spent some time with them, and baptized. ²³Now John also was baptizing at Aenon near Salim, because there was plenty of water, and people were constantly coming to be baptized. ²⁴(This was before John was put in prison.) ²⁵An argument developed between some of John's disciples and a certain Jewʲ over the matter of ceremonial washing. ²⁶They came to John and said to him, "Rabbi, that man who was with you on the other side of the Jordan—the one you

---

ᵃ23 Or *and believed in him*   ᵇ3 Or *born from above*; also in verse 7   ᶜ6 Or *but spirit*
ᵈ7 The Greek is plural.   ᵉ13 Some manuscripts *Man, who is in heaven*   ᶠ15 Or *believes may have eternal life in him*   ᵍ16 Or *his only begotten Son*   ʰ18 Or *God's only begotten Son*
ⁱ21 Some interpreters end the quotation after verse 15.   ʲ25 Some manuscripts *and certain Jews*

testified about—well, he is baptizing, and everyone is going to him."

²⁷To this John replied, "A man can receive only what is given him from heaven. ²⁸You yourselves can testify

that I said, 'I am not the Christ^a but am sent ahead of him.' ²⁹The bride belongs to the bridegroom. The friend who attends the bridegroom waits and listens for him, and is full of joy

^a28 Or Messiah

VERSE:
John 3:16

AUTHOR:
Frederick Buechner

PASSAGE:
John 3:16–21

One Foot in Eternity

"For God so loved the world," John writes, "that he gave his one and only Son, that whoever believes in him shall not perish but have eternal life." That is to say that God so loved the world that he gave his only Son even to this obscene horror; so loved the world that in some ultimately indescribable way and at some ultimately immeasurable cost he gave the world himself. Out of this terrible death, John says, came eternal life not just in the sense of resurrection to life after death but in the sense of life so precious even this side of death that to live it is to stand with one foot already in eternity. To participate in the sacrificial life and death of Jesus Christ is to live already in his kingdom. This is the essence of the Christian message, the heart of the Good News, and it is why the cross has become the chief Christian symbol. A cross of all things—a guillotine, a gallows—but the cross at the same time as the crossroads of eternity and time, as the place where such a mighty heart was broken that the healing power of God himself could flow through it into a sick and broken world. It was for this reason that of all the possible words they could have used to describe the day of his death, the word they settled on was "good." *Good* Friday.

ADDITIONAL SCRIPTURE READINGS
John 12:20–36; 1 Timothy 1:12–17

Go to page 1342 for your next devotional reading.

when he hears the bridegroom's voice. That joy is mine, and it is now complete. [30]He must become greater; I must become less.

[31]"The one who comes from above is above all; the one who is from the earth belongs to the earth, and speaks as one from the earth. The one who comes from heaven is above all. [32]He testifies to what he has seen and heard, but no one accepts his testimony. [33]The man who has accepted it has certified that God is truthful. [34]For the one whom God has sent speaks the words of God, for God[a] gives the Spirit without limit. [35]The Father loves the Son and has placed everything in his hands. [36]Whoever believes in the Son has eternal life, but whoever rejects the Son will not see life, for God's wrath remains on him."[b]

Jesus Talks With a Samaritan Woman

4 The Pharisees heard that Jesus was gaining and baptizing more disciples than John, [2]although in fact it was not Jesus who baptized, but his disciples. [3]When the Lord learned of this, he left Judea and went back once more to Galilee.

[4]Now he had to go through Samaria. [5]So he came to a town in Samaria called Sychar, near the plot of ground Jacob had given to his son Joseph. [6]Jacob's well was there, and Jesus, tired as he was from the journey, sat down by the well. It was about the sixth hour.

[7]When a Samaritan woman came to draw water, Jesus said to her, "Will you give me a drink?" [8](His disciples had gone into the town to buy food.)

[9]The Samaritan woman said to him, "You are a Jew and I am a Samaritan woman. How can you ask me for a drink?" (For Jews do not associate with Samaritans.[c])

[10]Jesus answered her, "If you knew the gift of God and who it is that asks you for a drink, you would have

asked him and he would have given you living water."

[11]"Sir," the woman said, "you have nothing to draw with and the well is deep. Where can you get this living water? [12]Are you greater than our father Jacob, who gave us the well and drank from it himself, as did also his sons and his flocks and herds?"

[13]Jesus answered, "Everyone who drinks this water will be thirsty again, [14]but whoever drinks the water I give him will never thirst. Indeed, the water I give him will become in him a spring of water welling up to eternal life."

[15]The woman said to him, "Sir, give me this water so that I won't get thirsty and have to keep coming here to draw water."

[16]He told her, "Go, call your husband and come back."

[17]"I have no husband," she replied.

Jesus said to her, "You are right when you say you have no husband. [18]The fact is, you have had five husbands, and the man you now have is not your husband. What you have just said is quite true."

[19]"Sir," the woman said, "I can see that you are a prophet. [20]Our fathers worshiped on this mountain, but you Jews claim that the place where we must worship is in Jerusalem."

[21]Jesus declared, "Believe me, woman, a time is coming when you will worship the Father neither on this mountain nor in Jerusalem. [22]You Samaritans worship what you do not know; we worship what we do know, for salvation is from the Jews. [23]Yet a time is coming and has now come when the true worshipers will worship the Father in spirit and truth, for they are the kind of worshipers the Father seeks. [24]God is spirit, and his worshipers must worship in spirit and in truth."

[25]The woman said, "I know that Messiah" (called Christ) "is coming. When he comes, he will explain everything to us."

---

[a]34 Greek he   [b]36 Some interpreters end the quotation after verse 30.   [c]9 Or do not use dishes Samaritans have used

²⁶Then Jesus declared, "I who speak to you am he."

The Disciples Rejoin Jesus

²⁷Just then his disciples returned and were surprised to find him talking with a woman. But no one asked, "What do you want?" or "Why are you talking with her?"

²⁸Then, leaving her water jar, the woman went back to the town and said to the people, ²⁹"Come, see a man who told me everything I ever did. Could this be the Christ*ᵃ*?" ³⁰They came out of the town and made their way toward him.

³¹Meanwhile his disciples urged him, "Rabbi, eat something."

³²But he said to them, "I have food to eat that you know nothing about."

³³Then his disciples said to each other, "Could someone have brought him food?"

³⁴"My food," said Jesus, "is to do the will of him who sent me and to finish his work. ³⁵Do you not say, 'Four months more and then the harvest'? I tell you, open your eyes and look at the fields! They are ripe for harvest. ³⁶Even now the reaper draws his wages, even now he harvests the crop for eternal life, so that the sower and the reaper may be glad together. ³⁷Thus the saying 'One sows and another reaps' is true. ³⁸I sent you to reap what you have not worked for. Others have done the hard work, and you have reaped the benefits of their labor."

Many Samaritans Believe

³⁹Many of the Samaritans from that town believed in him because of the woman's testimony, "He told me everything I ever did." ⁴⁰So when the Samaritans came to him, they urged him to stay with them, and he stayed two days. ⁴¹And because of his words many more became believers.

⁴²They said to the woman, "We no longer believe just because of what you said; now we have heard for our-selves, and we know that this man really is the Savior of the world."

Jesus Heals the Official's Son

⁴³After the two days he left for Galilee. ⁴⁴(Now Jesus himself had pointed out that a prophet has no honor in his own country.) ⁴⁵When he arrived in Galilee, the Galileans welcomed him. They had seen all that he had done in Jerusalem at the Passover Feast, for they also had been there.

⁴⁶Once more he visited Cana in Galilee, where he had turned the water into wine. And there was a certain royal official whose son lay sick at Capernaum. ⁴⁷When this man heard that Jesus had arrived in Galilee from Judea, he went to him and begged him to come and heal his son, who was close to death.

⁴⁸"Unless you people see miraculous signs and wonders," Jesus told him, "you will never believe."

⁴⁹The royal official said, "Sir, come down before my child dies."

⁵⁰Jesus replied, "You may go. Your son will live."

The man took Jesus at his word and departed. ⁵¹While he was still on the way, his servants met him with the news that his boy was living. ⁵²When he inquired as to the time when his son got better, they said to him, "The fever left him yesterday at the seventh hour."

⁵³Then the father realized that this was the exact time at which Jesus had said to him, "Your son will live." So he and all his household believed.

⁵⁴This was the second miraculous sign that Jesus performed, having come from Judea to Galilee.

The Healing at the Pool

5 Some time later, Jesus went up to Jerusalem for a feast of the Jews. ²Now there is in Jerusalem near the Sheep Gate a pool, which in Aramaic is called Bethesda*ᵇ* and which is surrounded by five covered colonnades. ³Here a great number of disabled people used to lie—the blind, the lame,

---

*ᵃ*29 Or *Messiah*   *ᵇ*2 Some manuscripts *Bethzatha*; other manuscripts *Bethsaida*

the paralyzed.[a] [5]One who was there had been an invalid for thirty-eight years. [6]When Jesus saw him lying there and learned that he had been in this condition for a long time, he asked him, "Do you want to get well?"

[7]"Sir," the invalid replied, "I have no one to help me into the pool when the water is stirred. While I am trying to get in, someone else goes down ahead of me."

[8]Then Jesus said to him, "Get up! Pick up your mat and walk." [9]At once the man was cured; he picked up his mat and walked.

The day on which this took place was a Sabbath, [10]and so the Jews said to the man who had been healed, "It is the Sabbath; the law forbids you to carry your mat."

[11]But he replied, "The man who made me well said to me, 'Pick up your mat and walk.' "

[12]So they asked him, "Who is this fellow who told you to pick it up and walk?"

[13]The man who was healed had no idea who it was, for Jesus had slipped away into the crowd that was there.

[14]Later Jesus found him at the temple and said to him, "See, you are well again. Stop sinning or something worse may happen to you." [15]The man went away and told the Jews that it was Jesus who had made him well.

Life Through the Son

[16]So, because Jesus was doing these things on the Sabbath, the Jews persecuted him. [17]Jesus said to them, "My Father is always at his work to this very day, and I, too, am working." [18]For this reason the Jews tried all the harder to kill him; not only was he breaking the Sabbath, but he was even calling God his own Father, making himself equal with God.

[19]Jesus gave them this answer: "I tell you the truth, the Son can do nothing by himself; he can do only what he sees his Father doing, because whatever the Father does the Son also does. [20]For the Father loves the Son and shows him all he does. Yes, to your amazement he will show him even greater things than these. [21]For just as the Father raises the dead and gives them life, even so the Son gives life to whom he is pleased to give it. [22]Moreover, the Father judges no one, but has entrusted all judgment to the Son, [23]that all may honor the Son just as they honor the Father. He who does not honor the Son does not honor the Father, who sent him.

[24]"I tell you the truth, whoever hears my word and believes him who sent me has eternal life and will not be condemned; he has crossed over from death to life. [25]I tell you the truth, a time is coming and has now come when the dead will hear the voice of the Son of God and those who hear will live. [26]For as the Father has life in himself, so he has granted the Son to have life in himself. [27]And he has given him authority to judge because he is the Son of Man.

[28]"Do not be amazed at this, for a time is coming when all who are in their graves will hear his voice [29]and come out—those who have done good will rise to live, and those who have done evil will rise to be condemned. [30]By myself I can do nothing; I judge only as I hear, and my judgment is just, for I seek not to please myself but him who sent me.

Testimonies About Jesus

[31]"If I testify about myself, my testimony is not valid. [32]There is another who testifies in my favor, and I know that his testimony about me is valid.

[33]"You have sent to John and he has testified to the truth. [34]Not that I accept human testimony; but I mention it that you may be saved. [35]John was a lamp that burned and gave light, and you chose for a time to enjoy his light.

---

[a]3 Some less important manuscripts paralyzed—and they waited for the moving of the waters. [4]From time to time an angel of the Lord would come down and stir up the waters. The first one into the pool after each such disturbance would be cured of whatever disease he had.

³⁶"I have testimony weightier than that of John. For the very work that the Father has given me to finish, and which I am doing, testifies that the Father has sent me. ³⁷And the Father who sent me has himself testified concerning me. You have never heard his voice nor seen his form, ³⁸nor does his word dwell in you, for you do not believe the one he sent. ³⁹You diligently study*a* the Scriptures because you think that by them you possess eternal life. These are the Scriptures that testify about me, ⁴⁰yet you refuse to come to me to have life.

⁴¹"I do not accept praise from men, ⁴²but I know you. I know that you do not have the love of God in your hearts. ⁴³I have come in my Father's name, and you do not accept me; but if someone else comes in his own name, you will accept him. ⁴⁴How can you believe if you accept praise from one another, yet make no effort to obtain the praise that comes from the only God*b*?

⁴⁵"But do not think I will accuse you before the Father. Your accuser is Moses, on whom your hopes are set. ⁴⁶If you believed Moses, you would believe me, for he wrote about me. ⁴⁷But since you do not believe what he wrote, how are you going to believe what I say?"

Jesus Feeds the Five Thousand

6 Some time after this, Jesus crossed to the far shore of the Sea of Galilee (that is, the Sea of Tiberias), ²and a great crowd of people followed him because they saw the miraculous signs he had performed on the sick. ³Then Jesus went up on a mountainside and sat down with his disciples. ⁴The Jewish Passover Feast was near.

⁵When Jesus looked up and saw a great crowd coming toward him, he said to Philip, "Where shall we buy bread for these people to eat?" ⁶He asked this only to test him, for he already had in mind what he was going to do.

⁷Philip answered him, "Eight months' wages*c* would not buy enough bread for each one to have a bite!"

⁸Another of his disciples, Andrew, Simon Peter's brother, spoke up, ⁹"Here is a boy with five small barley loaves and two small fish, but how far will they go among so many?"

¹⁰Jesus said, "Have the people sit down." There was plenty of grass in that place, and the men sat down, about five thousand of them. ¹¹Jesus then took the loaves, gave thanks, and distributed to those who were seated as much as they wanted. He did the same with the fish.

¹²When they had all had enough to eat, he said to his disciples, "Gather the pieces that are left over. Let nothing be wasted." ¹³So they gathered them and filled twelve baskets with the pieces of the five barley loaves left over by those who had eaten.

¹⁴After the people saw the miraculous sign that Jesus did, they began to say, "Surely this is the Prophet who is to come into the world." ¹⁵Jesus, knowing that they intended to come and make him king by force, withdrew again to a mountain by himself.

Jesus Walks on the Water

¹⁶When evening came, his disciples went down to the lake, ¹⁷where they got into a boat and set off across the lake for Capernaum. By now it was dark, and Jesus had not yet joined them. ¹⁸A strong wind was blowing and the waters grew rough. ¹⁹When they had rowed three or three and a half miles,*d* they saw Jesus approaching the boat, walking on the water; and they were terrified. ²⁰But he said to them, "It is I; don't be afraid." ²¹Then they were willing to take him into the boat, and immedi-

---

*a*39 Or *Study diligently* (the imperative)   *b*44 Some early manuscripts *the Only One*
*c*7 Greek *two hundred denarii*   *d*19 Greek *rowed twenty-five or thirty stadia* (about 5 or 6 kilometers)

ately the boat reached the shore where they were heading.

²²The next day the crowd that had stayed on the opposite shore of the lake realized that only one boat had been there, and that Jesus had not entered it with his disciples, but that they had gone away alone. ²³Then some boats from Tiberias landed near the place where the people had eaten the bread after the Lord had given thanks. ²⁴Once the crowd realized that neither Jesus nor his disciples were there, they got into the boats and went to Capernaum in search of Jesus.

Jesus the Bread of Life

²⁵When they found him on the other side of the lake, they asked him, "Rabbi, when did you get here?"

²⁶Jesus answered, "I tell you the truth, you are looking for me, not because you saw miraculous signs but because you ate the loaves and had your fill. ²⁷Do not work for food that spoils, but for food that endures to eternal life, which the Son of Man will give you. On him God the Father has placed his seal of approval."

²⁸Then they asked him, "What must we do to do the works God requires?"

²⁹Jesus answered, "The work of God is this: to believe in the one he has sent."

³⁰So they asked him, "What miraculous sign then will you give that we may see it and believe you? What will you do? ³¹Our forefathers ate the manna in the desert; as it is written: 'He gave them bread from heaven to eat.'ᵃ"

³²Jesus said to them, "I tell you the truth, it is not Moses who has given you the bread from heaven, but it is my Father who gives you the true bread from heaven. ³³For the bread of God is he who comes down from heaven and gives life to the world."

³⁴"Sir," they said, "from now on give us this bread."

³⁵Then Jesus declared, "I am the bread of life. He who comes to me will never go hungry, and he who believes in me will never be thirsty. ³⁶But as I told you, you have seen me and still you do not believe. ³⁷All that the Father gives me will come to me, and whoever comes to me I will never drive away. ³⁸For I have come down from heaven not to do my will but to do the will of him who sent me. ³⁹And this is the will of him who sent me, that I shall lose none of all that he has given me, but raise them up at the last day. ⁴⁰For my Father's will is that everyone who looks to the Son and believes in him shall have eternal life, and I will raise him up at the last day."

⁴¹At this the Jews began to grumble about him because he said, "I am the bread that came down from heaven." ⁴²They said, "Is this not Jesus, the son of Joseph, whose father and mother we know? How can he now say, 'I came down from heaven'?"

⁴³"Stop grumbling among yourselves," Jesus answered. ⁴⁴"No one can come to me unless the Father who sent me draws him, and I will raise him up at the last day. ⁴⁵It is written in the Prophets: 'They will all be taught by God.'ᵇ Everyone who listens to the Father and learns from him comes to me. ⁴⁶No one has seen the Father except the one who is from God; only he has seen the Father. ⁴⁷I tell you the truth, he who believes has everlasting life. ⁴⁸I am the bread of life. ⁴⁹Your forefathers ate the manna in the desert, yet they died. ⁵⁰But here is the bread that comes down from heaven, which a man may eat and not die. ⁵¹I am the living bread that came down from heaven. If anyone eats of this bread, he will live forever. This bread is my flesh, which I will give for the life of the world."

⁵²Then the Jews began to argue sharply among themselves, "How can this man give us his flesh to eat?"

⁵³Jesus said to them, "I tell you the truth, unless you eat the flesh of the Son of Man and drink his blood, you

ᵃ31 Exodus 16:4; Neh. 9:15; Psalm 78:24,25   ᵇ45 Isaiah 54:13

have no life in you. 54Whoever eats my flesh and drinks my blood has eternal life, and I will raise him up at the last day. 55For my flesh is real food and my blood is real drink. 56Whoever eats my flesh and drinks my blood remains in me, and I in him. 57Just as the living Father sent me and I live because of the Father, so the one who feeds on me will live because of me. 58This is the bread that came down from heaven. Your forefathers ate manna and died, but he who feeds on this bread will live forever." 59He said this while teaching in the synagogue in Capernaum.

Many Disciples Desert Jesus

60On hearing it, many of his disciples said, "This is a hard teaching. Who can accept it?"

61Aware that his disciples were grumbling about this, Jesus said to them, "Does this offend you? 62What if you see the Son of Man ascend to where he was before! 63The Spirit gives life; the flesh counts for nothing. The words I have spoken to you are spirit*a* and they are life. 64Yet there are some of you who do not believe." For Jesus had known from the beginning which of them did not believe and who would betray him. 65He went on to say, "This is why I told you that no one can come to me unless the Father has enabled him."

66From this time many of his disciples turned back and no longer followed him.

67"You do not want to leave too, do you?" Jesus asked the Twelve.

68Simon Peter answered him, "Lord, to whom shall we go? You have the words of eternal life. 69We believe and know that you are the Holy One of God."

70Then Jesus replied, "Have I not chosen you, the Twelve? Yet one of you is a devil!" 71(He meant Judas, the son of Simon Iscariot, who, though one of the Twelve, was later to betray him.)

Jesus Goes to the Feast of Tabernacles

7 After this, Jesus went around in Galilee, purposely staying away from Judea because the Jews there were waiting to take his life. 2But when the Jewish Feast of Tabernacles was near, 3Jesus' brothers said to him, "You ought to leave here and go to Judea, so that your disciples may see the miracles you do. 4No one who wants to become a public figure acts in secret. Since you are doing these things, show yourself to the world." 5For even his own brothers did not believe in him.

6Therefore Jesus told them, "The right time for me has not yet come; for you any time is right. 7The world cannot hate you, but it hates me because I testify that what it does is evil. 8You go to the Feast. I am not yet*b* going up to this Feast, because for me the right time has not yet come." 9Having said this, he stayed in Galilee.

10However, after his brothers had left for the Feast, he went also, not publicly, but in secret. 11Now at the Feast the Jews were watching for him and asking, "Where is that man?"

12Among the crowds there was widespread whispering about him. Some said, "He is a good man."

Others replied, "No, he deceives the people." 13But no one would say anything publicly about him for fear of the Jews.

Jesus Teaches at the Feast

14Not until halfway through the Feast did Jesus go up to the temple courts and begin to teach. 15The Jews were amazed and asked, "How did this man get such learning without having studied?"

16Jesus answered, "My teaching is not my own. It comes from him who sent me. 17If anyone chooses to do God's will, he will find out whether my teaching comes from God or whether I speak on my own. 18He

*a*63 Or *Spirit*   *b*8 Some early manuscripts do not have *yet*.

who speaks on his own does so to gain honor for himself, but he who works for the honor of the one who sent him is a man of truth; there is nothing false about him. ¹⁹Has not Moses given you the law? Yet not one of you keeps the law. Why are you trying to kill me?"

²⁰"You are demon-possessed," the crowd answered. "Who is trying to kill you?"

²¹Jesus said to them, "I did one miracle, and you are all astonished. ²²Yet, because Moses gave you circumcision (though actually it did not come from Moses, but from the patriarchs), you circumcise a child on the Sabbath. ²³Now if a child can be circumcised on the Sabbath so that the law of Moses may not be broken, why are you angry with me for healing the whole man on the Sabbath? ²⁴Stop judging by mere appearances, and make a right judgment."

Is Jesus the Christ?

²⁵At that point some of the people of Jerusalem began to ask, "Isn't this the man they are trying to kill? ²⁶Here he is, speaking publicly, and they are not saying a word to him. Have the authorities really concluded that he is the Christ[a]? ²⁷But we know where this man is from; when the Christ comes, no one will know where he is from."

²⁸Then Jesus, still teaching in the temple courts, cried out, "Yes, you know me, and you know where I am from. I am not here on my own, but he who sent me is true. You do not know him, ²⁹but I know him because I am from him and he sent me."

³⁰At this they tried to seize him, but no one laid a hand on him, because his time had not yet come. ³¹Still, many in the crowd put their faith in him. They said, "When the Christ comes, will he do more miraculous signs than this man?"

³²The Pharisees heard the crowd whispering such things about him.

Then the chief priests and the Pharisees sent temple guards to arrest him. ³³Jesus said, "I am with you for only a short time, and then I go to the one who sent me. ³⁴You will look for me, but you will not find me; and where I am, you cannot come."

³⁵The Jews said to one another, "Where does this man intend to go that we cannot find him? Will he go where our people live scattered among the Greeks, and teach the Greeks? ³⁶What did he mean when he said, 'You will look for me, but you will not find me,' and 'Where I am, you cannot come'?"

³⁷On the last and greatest day of the Feast, Jesus stood and said in a loud voice, "If anyone is thirsty, let him come to me and drink. ³⁸Whoever believes in me, as[b] the Scripture has said, streams of living water will flow from within him." ³⁹By this he meant the Spirit, whom those who believed in him were later to receive. Up to that time the Spirit had not been given, since Jesus had not yet been glorified.

⁴⁰On hearing his words, some of the people said, "Surely this man is the Prophet."

⁴¹Others said, "He is the Christ."

Still others asked, "How can the Christ come from Galilee? ⁴²Does not the Scripture say that the Christ will come from David's family[c] and from Bethlehem, the town where David lived?" ⁴³Thus the people were divided because of Jesus. ⁴⁴Some wanted to seize him, but no one laid a hand on him.

Unbelief of the Jewish Leaders

⁴⁵Finally the temple guards went back to the chief priests and Pharisees, who asked them, "Why didn't you bring him in?"

⁴⁶"No one ever spoke the way this man does," the guards declared.

⁴⁷"You mean he has deceived you also?" the Pharisees retorted. ⁴⁸"Has any of the rulers or of the Pharisees

---

[a]26 Or Messiah; also in verses 27, 31, 41 and 42
[b]37,38 Or / If anyone is thirsty, let him come to me. / And let him drink, 38who believes in me. / As
[c]42 Greek seed

VERSE:	AUTHOR:	PASSAGE:
John 7:37	J. Oswald Sanders	John 7:37–44

Bubbling Streams

It is not without significance that Paul said, "*I have learned* to be content whatever the circumstances" (Philippians 4:11, italics added). He did not say, "I have always been content with any circumstances." For him, as it will be for us, it had been a painful learning process in the school of suffering. The point is that he graduated! It was in the same school that the Son of God learned obedience (Hebrews 5:8).

Our Lord likened the Christian life to a river that broadened, deepened and gathered volume as it flowed down to the sea—an encouraging picture for the aging Christian. There is no reason why our closing years should not be as enjoyable, stimulating and fruitful as in earlier life. A life of increasing instead of diminishing, a life of continual outflow, can be ours. Read again Christ's alluring picture: "If anyone is thirsty, let him come to me and drink. Whoever believes in me, as the Scripture has said, streams of living water will flow from within him."

Such people refuse to concede defeat to Father Time. They resolve to master old age, not to be defeated by it. They accept help from others, but only when it is absolutely necessary. They are grateful, thoughtful and cheerful in adversity. Their very resilience is a great encouragement to their contemporaries who are incited to discover their secret.

ADDITIONAL SCRIPTURE READINGS
Psalm 92; Philippians 4:10–13

Go to page 1347 for your next devotional reading.

believed in him? ⁴⁹No! But this mob that knows nothing of the law—there is a curse on them."

⁵⁰Nicodemus, who had gone to Jesus earlier and who was one of their own number, asked, ⁵¹"Does our law condemn anyone without first hearing him to find out what he is doing?"

⁵²They replied, "Are you from Galilee, too? Look into it, and you will find that a prophet*a* does not come out of Galilee."

_____

[The earliest manuscripts and many other ancient witnesses do not have John 7:53–8:11.]

⁵³Then each went to his own home.

8 But Jesus went to the Mount of Olives. ²At dawn he appeared again in the temple courts, where all the people gathered around him, and he sat down to teach them. ³The teachers of the law and the Pharisees brought in a woman caught in adultery. They made her stand before the group ⁴and said to Jesus, "Teacher, this woman was caught in the act of adultery. ⁵In the Law Moses commanded us to stone such women. Now what do you say?" ⁶They were using this question as a trap, in order to have a basis for accusing him.

But Jesus bent down and started to write on the ground with his finger. ⁷When they kept on questioning him, he straightened up and said to them, "If any one of you is without sin, let him be the first to throw a stone at her." ⁸Again he stooped down and wrote on the ground.

⁹At this, those who heard began to go away one at a time, the older ones first, until only Jesus was left, with the woman still standing there. ¹⁰Jesus straightened up and asked her, "Woman, where are they? Has no one condemned you?"

¹¹"No one, sir," she said.

"Then neither do I condemn you,"

Jesus declared. "Go now and leave your life of sin."

_____

The Validity of Jesus' Testimony

¹²When Jesus spoke again to the people, he said, "I am the light of the world. Whoever follows me will never walk in darkness, but will have the light of life."

¹³The Pharisees challenged him, "Here you are, appearing as your own witness; your testimony is not valid."

¹⁴Jesus answered, "Even if I testify on my own behalf, my testimony is valid, for I know where I came from and where I am going. But you have no idea where I come from or where I am going. ¹⁵You judge by human standards; I pass judgment on no one. ¹⁶But if I do judge, my decisions are right, because I am not alone. I stand with the Father, who sent me. ¹⁷In your own Law it is written that the testimony of two men is valid. ¹⁸I am one who testifies for myself; my other witness is the Father, who sent me."

¹⁹Then they asked him, "Where is your father?"

"You do not know me or my Father," Jesus replied. "If you knew me, you would know my Father also." ²⁰He spoke these words while teaching in the temple area near the place where the offerings were put. Yet no one seized him, because his time had not yet come.

²¹Once more Jesus said to them, "I am going away, and you will look for me, and you will die in your sin. Where I go, you cannot come."

²²This made the Jews ask, "Will he kill himself? Is that why he says, 'Where I go, you cannot come'?"

²³But he continued, "You are from below; I am from above. You are of this world; I am not of this world. ²⁴I told you that you would die in your sins; if you do not believe that I am

a52 Two early manuscripts the Prophet

ₗthe one I claim to be₌,ᵃ you will indeed die in your sins."

²⁵"Who are you?" they asked.

"Just what I have been claiming all along," Jesus replied. ²⁶"I have much to say in judgment of you. But he who sent me is reliable, and what I have heard from him I tell the world."

²⁷They did not understand that he was telling them about his Father. ²⁸So Jesus said, "When you have lifted up the Son of Man, then you will know that I am ₗthe one I claim to be₌ and that I do nothing on my own but speak just what the Father has taught me. ²⁹The one who sent me is with me; he has not left me alone, for I always do what pleases him." ³⁰Even as he spoke, many put their faith in him.

The Children of Abraham

³¹To the Jews who had believed him, Jesus said, "If you hold to my teaching, you are really my disciples. ³²Then you will know the truth, and the truth will set you free."

³³They answered him, "We are Abraham's descendantsᵇ and have never been slaves of anyone. How can you say that we shall be set free?"

³⁴Jesus replied, "I tell you the truth, everyone who sins is a slave to sin. ³⁵Now a slave has no permanent place in the family, but a son belongs to it forever. ³⁶So if the Son sets you free, you will be free indeed. ³⁷I know you are Abraham's descendants. Yet you are ready to kill me, because you have no room for my word. ³⁸I am telling you what I have seen in the Father's presence, and you do what you have heard from your father.ᶜ"

³⁹"Abraham is our father," they answered.

"If you were Abraham's children," said Jesus, "then you wouldᵈ do the things Abraham did. ⁴⁰As it is, you are determined to kill me, a man who has told you the truth that I heard from God. Abraham did not do such

things. ⁴¹You are doing the things your own father does."

"We are not illegitimate children," they protested. "The only Father we have is God himself."

The Children of the Devil

⁴²Jesus said to them, "If God were your Father, you would love me, for I came from God and now am here. I have not come on my own; but he sent me. ⁴³Why is my language not clear to you? Because you are unable to hear what I say. ⁴⁴You belong to your father, the devil, and you want to carry out your father's desire. He was a murderer from the beginning, not holding to the truth, for there is no truth in him. When he lies, he speaks his native language, for he is a liar and the father of lies. ⁴⁵Yet because I tell the truth, you do not believe me! ⁴⁶Can any of you prove me guilty of sin? If I am telling the truth, why don't you believe me? ⁴⁷He who belongs to God hears what God says. The reason you do not hear is that you do not belong to God."

The Claims of Jesus About Himself

⁴⁸The Jews answered him, "Aren't we right in saying that you are a Samaritan and demon-possessed?"

⁴⁹"I am not possessed by a demon," said Jesus, "but I honor my Father and you dishonor me. ⁵⁰I am not seeking glory for myself; but there is one who seeks it, and he is the judge. ⁵¹I tell you the truth, if anyone keeps my word, he will never see death."

⁵²At this the Jews exclaimed, "Now we know that you are demon-possessed! Abraham died and so did the prophets, yet you say that if anyone keeps your word, he will never taste death. ⁵³Are you greater than our father Abraham? He died, and so did the prophets. Who do you think you are?"

⁵⁴Jesus replied, "If I glorify myself, my glory means nothing. My Father,

---

ᵃ24 Or I am he; also in verse 28   ᵇ33 Greek seed; also in verse 37   ᶜ38 Or presence. Therefore do what you have heard from the Father.   ᵈ39 Some early manuscripts "If you are Abraham's children," said Jesus, "then

whom you claim as your God, is the one who glorifies me. ⁵⁵Though you do not know him, I know him. If I said I did not, I would be a liar like you, but I do know him and keep his word. ⁵⁶Your father Abraham rejoiced at the thought of seeing my day; he saw it and was glad."

⁵⁷"You are not yet fifty years old," the Jews said to him, "and you have seen Abraham!"

⁵⁸"I tell you the truth," Jesus answered, "before Abraham was born, I am!" ⁵⁹At this, they picked up stones to stone him, but Jesus hid himself, slipping away from the temple grounds.

Jesus Heals a Man Born Blind

9 As he went along, he saw a man blind from birth. ²His disciples asked him, "Rabbi, who sinned, this man or his parents, that he was born blind?"

³"Neither this man nor his parents sinned," said Jesus, "but this happened so that the work of God might be displayed in his life. ⁴As long as it is day, we must do the work of him who sent me. Night is coming, when no one can work. ⁵While I am in the world, I am the light of the world."

⁶Having said this, he spit on the ground, made some mud with the saliva, and put it on the man's eyes. ⁷"Go," he told him, "wash in the Pool of Siloam" (this word means Sent). So the man went and washed, and came home seeing.

⁸His neighbors and those who had formerly seen him begging asked, "Isn't this the same man who used to sit and beg?" ⁹Some claimed that he was.

Others said, "No, he only looks like him."

But he himself insisted, "I am the man."

¹⁰"How then were your eyes opened?" they demanded.

¹¹He replied, "The man they call Jesus made some mud and put it on my eyes. He told me to go to Siloam and wash. So I went and washed, and then I could see."

¹²"Where is this man?" they asked him.

"I don't know," he said.

The Pharisees Investigate the Healing

¹³They brought to the Pharisees the man who had been blind. ¹⁴Now the day on which Jesus had made the mud and opened the man's eyes was a Sabbath. ¹⁵Therefore the Pharisees also asked him how he had received his sight. "He put mud on my eyes," the man replied, "and I washed, and now I see."

¹⁶Some of the Pharisees said, "This man is not from God, for he does not keep the Sabbath."

But others asked, "How can a sinner do such miraculous signs?" So they were divided.

¹⁷Finally they turned again to the blind man, "What have you to say about him? It was your eyes he opened."

The man replied, "He is a prophet."

¹⁸The Jews still did not believe that he had been blind and had received his sight until they sent for the man's parents. ¹⁹"Is this your son?" they asked. "Is this the one you say was born blind? How is it that now he can see?"

²⁰"We know he is our son," the parents answered, "and we know he was born blind. ²¹But how he can see now, or who opened his eyes, we don't know. Ask him. He is of age; he will speak for himself." ²²His parents said this because they were afraid of the Jews, for already the Jews had decided that anyone who acknowledged that Jesus was the Christ[a] would be put out of the synagogue. ²³That was why his parents said, "He is of age; ask him."

²⁴A second time they summoned the man who had been blind. "Give

glory to God,*" they said. "We know this man is a sinner."

25He replied, "Whether he is a sinner or not, I don't know. One thing I do know. I was blind but now I see!"

26Then they asked him, "What did he do to you? How did he open your eyes?"

27He answered, "I have told you already and you did not listen. Why do you want to hear it again? Do you want to become his disciples, too?"

28Then they hurled insults at him and said, "You are this fellow's disciple! We are disciples of Moses! 29We know that God spoke to Moses, but as for this fellow, we don't even know where he comes from."

30The man answered, "Now that is remarkable! You don't know where he comes from, yet he opened my eyes. 31We know that God does not listen to sinners. He listens to the godly man who does his will. 32Nobody has ever heard of opening the eyes of a man born blind. 33If this man were not from God, he could do nothing."

34To this they replied, "You were steeped in sin at birth; how dare you lecture us!" And they threw him out.

Spiritual Blindness

35Jesus heard that they had thrown him out, and when he found him, he said, "Do you believe in the Son of Man?"

36"Who is he, sir?" the man asked. "Tell me so that I may believe in him."

37Jesus said, "You have now seen him; in fact, he is the one speaking with you."

38Then the man said, "Lord, I believe," and he worshiped him.

39Jesus said, "For judgment I have come into this world, so that the blind will see and those who see will become blind."

40Some Pharisees who were with him heard him say this and asked, "What? Are we blind too?"

41Jesus said, "If you were blind, you would not be guilty of sin; but now

that you claim you can see, your guilt remains.

The Shepherd and His Flock

10 "I tell you the truth, the man who does not enter the sheep pen by the gate, but climbs in by some other way, is a thief and a robber. 2The man who enters by the gate is the shepherd of his sheep. 3The watchman opens the gate for him, and the sheep listen to his voice. He calls his own sheep by name and leads them out. 4When he has brought out all his own, he goes on ahead of them, and his sheep follow him because they know his voice. 5But they will never follow a stranger; in fact, they will run away from him because they do not recognize a stranger's voice." 6Jesus used this figure of speech, but they did not understand what he was telling them.

7Therefore Jesus said again, "I tell you the truth, I am the gate for the sheep. 8All who ever came before me were thieves and robbers, but the sheep did not listen to them. 9I am the gate; whoever enters through me will be saved.b He will come in and go out, and find pasture. 10The thief comes only to steal and kill and destroy; I have come that they may have life, and have it to the full.

11"I am the good shepherd. The good shepherd lays down his life for the sheep. 12The hired hand is not the shepherd who owns the sheep. So when he sees the wolf coming, he abandons the sheep and runs away. Then the wolf attacks the flock and scatters it. 13The man runs away because he is a hired hand and cares nothing for the sheep.

14"I am the good shepherd; I know my sheep and my sheep know me— 15just as the Father knows me and I know the Father—and I lay down my life for the sheep. 16I have other sheep that are not of this sheep pen. I must bring them also. They too will listen to my voice, and there shall be one flock and one shepherd. 17The reason

---

*24 A solemn charge to tell the truth (see Joshua 7:19)   b9 Or kept safe

VERSE:	AUTHOR:	PASSAGE:
John 10:28	W. Phillip Keller	John 10:1–30

In His Hand—for Good

To know that God's hand is upon me for good is perhaps the most precious awareness a human being can savor in his earthly sojourn. To be acutely aware—"O my Shepherd, you are enfolding me in your great strong hand!" —is to sense a sweet serenity that nothing can disturb. To realize the intimacy of the Master's touch upon every minutiae of my affairs, to experience his hand guiding, leading, directing in every detail of each day, is to enter a delight words cannot describe.

My part is to be sensitive to his gentle Spirit. My part is to obey instantly his smallest wish. My part is to wait quietly for the unfolding of his best purposes and plans. In harmony, unity and mutual pleasure we commune together along the trails of life. He becomes my fondest friend and most intimate companion. More than that, he becomes my life.

This is the life of serene security. This is the relationship of quiet relaxation. This is the life of rest and repose; for the person willing to be led of the Lord there is endless enjoyment in his company . . .

It is ever he who holds us in his hand, if we will allow ourselves to be so owned and loved. We do not have to "hold on to him," as so many wrongly imagine. How much better to rest in the quiet assurance of knowing his hand is upon me rather than doubting my feeble efforts to hold on to him.

ADDITIONAL SCRIPTURE READINGS
Isaiah 40:9–11; Romans 8:28–39

Go to page 1350 for your next devotional reading.

my Father loves me is that I lay down my life—only to take it up again. ¹⁸No one takes it from me, but I lay it down of my own accord. I have authority to lay it down and authority to take it up again. This command I received from my Father."

¹⁹At these words the Jews were again divided. ²⁰Many of them said, "He is demon-possessed and raving mad. Why listen to him?"

²¹But others said, "These are not the sayings of a man possessed by a demon. Can a demon open the eyes of the blind?"

The Unbelief of the Jews

²²Then came the Feast of Dedication[a] at Jerusalem. It was winter, ²³and Jesus was in the temple area walking in Solomon's Colonnade. ²⁴The Jews gathered around him, saying, "How long will you keep us in suspense? If you are the Christ,[b] tell us plainly."

²⁵Jesus answered, "I did tell you, but you do not believe. The miracles I do in my Father's name speak for me, ²⁶but you do not believe because you are not my sheep. ²⁷My sheep listen to my voice; I know them, and they follow me. ²⁸I give them eternal life, and they shall never perish; no one can snatch them out of my hand. ²⁹My Father, who has given them to me, is greater than all[c]; no one can snatch them out of my Father's hand. ³⁰I and the Father are one."

³¹Again the Jews picked up stones to stone him, ³²but Jesus said to them, "I have shown you many great miracles from the Father. For which of these do you stone me?"

³³"We are not stoning you for any of these," replied the Jews, "but for blasphemy, because you, a mere man, claim to be God."

³⁴Jesus answered them, "Is it not written in your Law, 'I have said you are gods'[d]? ³⁵If he called them 'gods,' to whom the word of God came—and the Scripture cannot be broken— ³⁶what about the one whom the Father set apart as his very own and sent into the world? Why then do you accuse me of blasphemy because I said, 'I am God's Son'? ³⁷Do not believe me unless I do what my Father does. ³⁸But if I do it, even though you do not believe me, believe the miracles, that you may know and understand that the Father is in me, and I in the Father." ³⁹Again they tried to seize him, but he escaped their grasp.

⁴⁰Then Jesus went back across the Jordan to the place where John had been baptizing in the early days. Here he stayed ⁴¹and many people came to him. They said, "Though John never performed a miraculous sign, all that John said about this man was true." ⁴²And in that place many believed in Jesus.

The Death of Lazarus

11 Now a man named Lazarus was sick. He was from Bethany, the village of Mary and her sister Martha. ²This Mary, whose brother Lazarus now lay sick, was the same one who poured perfume on the Lord and wiped his feet with her hair. ³So the sisters sent word to Jesus, "Lord, the one you love is sick."

⁴When he heard this, Jesus said, "This sickness will not end in death. No, it is for God's glory so that God's Son may be glorified through it." ⁵Jesus loved Martha and her sister and Lazarus. ⁶Yet when he heard that Lazarus was sick, he stayed where he was two more days.

⁷Then he said to his disciples, "Let us go back to Judea."

⁸"But Rabbi," they said, "a short while ago the Jews tried to stone you, and yet you are going back there?"

⁹Jesus answered, "Are there not twelve hours of daylight? A man who walks by day will not stumble, for he sees by this world's light. ¹⁰It is when he walks by night that he stumbles, for he has no light."

¹¹After he had said this, he went on

---

a22 That is, Hanukkah   *b24* Or *Messiah*   *c29* Many early manuscripts *What my Father has given me is greater than all*   *d34* Psalm 82:6

to tell them, "Our friend Lazarus has fallen asleep; but I am going there to wake him up."

¹²His disciples replied, "Lord, if he sleeps, he will get better." ¹³Jesus had been speaking of his death, but his disciples thought he meant natural sleep.

¹⁴So then he told them plainly, "Lazarus is dead, ¹⁵and for your sake I am glad I was not there, so that you may believe. But let us go to him."

¹⁶Then Thomas (called Didymus) said to the rest of the disciples, "Let us also go, that we may die with him."

Jesus Comforts the Sisters

¹⁷On his arrival, Jesus found that Lazarus had already been in the tomb for four days. ¹⁸Bethany was less than two miles*a* from Jerusalem, ¹⁹and many Jews had come to Martha and Mary to comfort them in the loss of their brother. ²⁰When Martha heard that Jesus was coming, she went out to meet him, but Mary stayed at home.

²¹"Lord," Martha said to Jesus, "if you had been here, my brother would not have died. ²²But I know that even now God will give you whatever you ask."

²³Jesus said to her, "Your brother will rise again."

²⁴Martha answered, "I know he will rise again in the resurrection at the last day."

²⁵Jesus said to her, "I am the resurrection and the life. He who believes in me will live, even though he dies; ²⁶and whoever lives and believes in me will never die. Do you believe this?"

²⁷"Yes, Lord," she told him, "I believe that you are the Christ,*b* the Son of God, who was to come into the world."

²⁸And after she had said this, she went back and called her sister Mary aside. "The Teacher is here," she said, "and is asking for you." ²⁹When Mary heard this, she got up quickly and went to him. ³⁰Now Jesus had not yet entered the village, but was still at the place where Martha had met him. ³¹When the Jews who had been with Mary in the house, comforting her, noticed how quickly she got up and went out, they followed her, supposing she was going to the tomb to mourn there.

³²When Mary reached the place where Jesus was and saw him, she fell at his feet and said, "Lord, if you had been here, my brother would not have died."

³³When Jesus saw her weeping, and the Jews who had come along with her also weeping, he was deeply moved in spirit and troubled. ³⁴"Where have you laid him?" he asked.

"Come and see, Lord," they replied.

³⁵Jesus wept.

³⁶Then the Jews said, "See how he loved him!"

³⁷But some of them said, "Could not he who opened the eyes of the blind man have kept this man from dying?"

Jesus Raises Lazarus From the Dead

³⁸Jesus, once more deeply moved, came to the tomb. It was a cave with a stone laid across the entrance. ³⁹"Take away the stone," he said.

"But, Lord," said Martha, the sister of the dead man, "by this time there is a bad odor, for he has been there four days."

⁴⁰Then Jesus said, "Did I not tell you that if you believed, you would see the glory of God?"

⁴¹So they took away the stone. Then Jesus looked up and said, "Father, I thank you that you have heard me. ⁴²I knew that you always hear me, but I said this for the benefit of the people standing here, that they may believe that you sent me."

⁴³When he had said this, Jesus called in a loud voice, "Lazarus, come out!" ⁴⁴The dead man came out, his

a18 Greek *fifteen stadia* (about 3 kilometers)   *b27* Or *Messiah*

PASSAGE: Psalm 71; Romans 8:28–39
AUTHOR: Leslie Brandt

Good Lord, You Have Kept Me

Good Lord, You have kept me
    within the secure embrace of Your love
        these many years.
My life is one long list of divine deliverances.
I have come running to You again and again
    when the forces of evil
        set themselves against me . . .

Now, as I near
        the late afternoon and evening of my life
    I continue to seek out Your love and mercy.
Even while I shout Your praises
        and proclaim Your salvation,
    I reach for the assurance
        of your love and concern.

You have guided me
        through my precarious youth,
    now I need Your grace for my senior years.
Fill my heart with purpose
        and my mouth with praises
    that I may continue to proclaim
        Your name and salvation
        to all who will listen.

Go to page 1353 for your next devotional reading.

hands and feet wrapped with strips of linen, and a cloth around his face.

Jesus said to them, "Take off the grave clothes and let him go."

The Plot to Kill Jesus

⁴⁵Therefore many of the Jews who had come to visit Mary, and had seen what Jesus did, put their faith in him. ⁴⁶But some of them went to the Pharisees and told them what Jesus had done. ⁴⁷Then the chief priests and the Pharisees called a meeting of the Sanhedrin.

"What are we accomplishing?" they asked. "Here is this man performing many miraculous signs. ⁴⁸If we let him go on like this, everyone will believe in him, and then the Romans will come and take away both our place[a] and our nation."

⁴⁹Then one of them, named Caiaphas, who was high priest that year, spoke up, "You know nothing at all! ⁵⁰You do not realize that it is better for you that one man die for the people than that the whole nation perish."

⁵¹He did not say this on his own, but as high priest that year he prophesied that Jesus would die for the Jewish nation, ⁵²and not only for that nation but also for the scattered children of God, to bring them together and make them one. ⁵³So from that day on they plotted to take his life.

⁵⁴Therefore Jesus no longer moved about publicly among the Jews. Instead he withdrew to a region near the desert, to a village called Ephraim, where he stayed with his disciples.

⁵⁵When it was almost time for the Jewish Passover, many went up from the country to Jerusalem for their ceremonial cleansing before the Passover. ⁵⁶They kept looking for Jesus, and as they stood in the temple area they asked one another, "What do you think? Isn't he coming to the Feast at all?" ⁵⁷But the chief priests and Pharisees had given orders that if anyone found out where Jesus was,

he should report it so that they might arrest him.

Jesus Anointed at Bethany

12 Six days before the Passover, Jesus arrived at Bethany, where Lazarus lived, whom Jesus had raised from the dead. ²Here a dinner was given in Jesus' honor. Martha served, while Lazarus was among those reclining at the table with him. ³Then Mary took about a pint[b] of pure nard, an expensive perfume; she poured it on Jesus' feet and wiped his feet with her hair. And the house was filled with the fragrance of the perfume.

⁴But one of his disciples, Judas Iscariot, who was later to betray him, objected, ⁵"Why wasn't this perfume sold and the money given to the poor? It was worth a year's wages.[c]" ⁶He did not say this because he cared about the poor but because he was a thief; as keeper of the money bag, he used to help himself to what was put into it.

⁷"Leave her alone," Jesus replied. "⌐It was intended⌐ that she should save this perfume for the day of my burial. ⁸You will always have the poor among you, but you will not always have me."

⁹Meanwhile a large crowd of Jews found out that Jesus was there and came, not only because of him but also to see Lazarus, whom he had raised from the dead. ¹⁰So the chief priests made plans to kill Lazarus as well, ¹¹for on account of him many of the Jews were going over to Jesus and putting their faith in him.

The Triumphal Entry

¹²The next day the great crowd that had come for the Feast heard that Jesus was on his way to Jerusalem. ¹³They took palm branches and went out to meet him, shouting,

"Hosanna![d]"

---

a48 Or *temple*   *b3* Greek *a litra* (probably about 0.5 liter)   *c5* Greek *three hundred denarii*
d13 A Hebrew expression meaning "Save!" which became an exclamation of praise

"Blessed is he who comes in the name of the Lord!"[a]

"Blessed is the King of Israel!"

[14]Jesus found a young donkey and sat upon it, as it is written,

[15]"Do not be afraid, O Daughter of Zion;
see, your king is coming,
seated on a donkey's colt."[b]

[16]At first his disciples did not understand all this. Only after Jesus was glorified did they realize that these things had been written about him and that they had done these things to him. [17]Now the crowd that was with him when he called Lazarus from the tomb and raised him from the dead continued to spread the word. [18]Many people, because they had heard that he had given this miraculous sign, went out to meet him. [19]So the Pharisees said to one another, "See, this is getting us nowhere. Look how the whole world has gone after him!"

Jesus Predicts His Death

[20]Now there were some Greeks among those who went up to worship at the Feast. [21]They came to Philip, who was from Bethsaida in Galilee, with a request. "Sir," they said, "we would like to see Jesus." [22]Philip went to tell Andrew; Andrew and Philip in turn told Jesus.

[23]Jesus replied, "The hour has come for the Son of Man to be glorified. [24]I tell you the truth, unless a kernel of wheat falls to the ground and dies, it remains only a single seed. But if it dies, it produces many seeds. [25]The man who loves his life will lose it, while the man who hates his life in this world will keep it for eternal life. [26]Whoever serves me must follow me; and where I am, my servant also will be. My Father will honor the one who serves me.

[27]"Now my heart is troubled, and what shall I say? 'Father, save me from this hour'? No, it was for this very reason I came to this hour. [28]Father, glorify your name!"

Then a voice came from heaven, "I have glorified it, and will glorify it again." [29]The crowd that was there and heard it said it had thundered; others said an angel had spoken to him.

[30]Jesus said, "This voice was for your benefit, not mine. [31]Now is the time for judgment on this world; now the prince of this world will be driven out. [32]But I, when I am lifted up from the earth, will draw all men to myself." [33]He said this to show the kind of death he was going to die.

[34]The crowd spoke up, "We have heard from the Law that the Christ[c] will remain forever, so how can you say, 'The Son of Man must be lifted up'? Who is this 'Son of Man'?"

[35]Then Jesus told them, "You are going to have the light just a little while longer. Walk while you have the light, before darkness overtakes you. The man who walks in the dark does not know where he is going. [36]Put your trust in the light while you have it, so that you may become sons of light." When he had finished speaking, Jesus left and hid himself from them.

The Jews Continue in Their Unbelief

[37]Even after Jesus had done all these miraculous signs in their presence, they still would not believe in him. [38]This was to fulfill the word of Isaiah the prophet:

"Lord, who has believed our message
and to whom has the arm of the Lord been revealed?"[d]

[39]For this reason they could not believe, because, as Isaiah says elsewhere:

[40]"He has blinded their eyes
and deadened their hearts,
so they can neither see with their eyes,

---

[a]13 Psalm 118:25, 26   [b]15 Zech. 9:9   [c]34 Or *Messiah*   [d]38 Isaiah 53:1

nor understand with their
hearts,
nor turn—and I would heal
them."[a]

[41]Isaiah said this because he saw Jesus' glory and spoke about him.

[42]Yet at the same time many even among the leaders believed in him. But because of the Pharisees they would not confess their faith for fear they would be put out of the synagogue; [43]for they loved praise from men more than praise from God.

[44]Then Jesus cried out, "When a man believes in me, he does not believe in me only, but in the one who sent me. [45]When he looks at me, he sees the one who sent me. [46]I have come into the world as a light, so that

[a]40 Isaiah 6:10

VERSE:	AUTHOR:	PASSAGE:
John 12:24	Henri J.M. Nouwen	John 12:20–36

If It Dies, It Produces

Our death may be the end of our success, our productivity, our fame or our importance among people, but it is not the end of our fruitfulness. In fact, the opposite is true: the fruitfulness of our lives shows itself in its fullness only after we have died. We ourselves seldom see or experience our own fruitfulness. Often we remain preoccupied with our accomplishments and have no eye for the fruitfulness of what we live. But the beauty of life is that it bears fruit long after life itself has come to an end (John 12:24) . . .

The real question before our death, then, is not, How much can I still accomplish, or How much influence can I still exert? but, How can I live so that I can continue to be fruitful when I am no longer here among my family and friends? That question shifts our attention from doing to being. Our doing brings success, but our being bears fruit. The great paradox of our lives is that we are often concerned about what we do or still can do, but we are most likely to be remembered for who we were.

ADDITIONAL SCRIPTURE READINGS
Luke 9:18–27; John 16:5–16

Go to page 1355 for your next devotional reading.

no one who believes in me should stay in darkness.

⁴⁷"As for the person who hears my words but does not keep them, I do not judge him. For I did not come to judge the world, but to save it. ⁴⁸There is a judge for the one who rejects me and does not accept my words; that very word which I spoke will condemn him at the last day. ⁴⁹For I did not speak of my own accord, but the Father who sent me commanded me what to say and how to say it. ⁵⁰I know that his command leads to eternal life. So whatever I say is just what the Father has told me to say."

Jesus Washes His Disciples' Feet

13 It was just before the Passover Feast. Jesus knew that the time had come for him to leave this world and go to the Father. Having loved his own who were in the world, he now showed them the full extent of his love.ᵃ

²The evening meal was being served, and the devil had already prompted Judas Iscariot, son of Simon, to betray Jesus. ³Jesus knew that the Father had put all things under his power, and that he had come from God and was returning to God; ⁴so he got up from the meal, took off his outer clothing, and wrapped a towel around his waist. ⁵After that, he poured water into a basin and began to wash his disciples' feet, drying them with the towel that was wrapped around him.

⁶He came to Simon Peter, who said to him, "Lord, are you going to wash my feet?"

⁷Jesus replied, "You do not realize now what I am doing, but later you will understand."

⁸"No," said Peter, "you shall never wash my feet."

Jesus answered, "Unless I wash you, you have no part with me."

⁹"Then, Lord," Simon Peter replied, "not just my feet but my hands and my head as well!"

¹⁰Jesus answered, "A person who has had a bath needs only to wash his feet; his whole body is clean. And you are clean, though not every one of you." ¹¹For he knew who was going to betray him, and that was why he said not every one was clean.

¹²When he had finished washing their feet, he put on his clothes and returned to his place. "Do you understand what I have done for you?" he asked them. ¹³"You call me 'Teacher' and 'Lord,' and rightly so, for that is what I am. ¹⁴Now that I, your Lord and Teacher, have washed your feet, you also should wash one another's feet. ¹⁵I have set you an example that you should do as I have done for you. ¹⁶I tell you the truth, no servant is greater than his master, nor is a messenger greater than the one who sent him. ¹⁷Now that you know these things, you will be blessed if you do them.

Jesus Predicts His Betrayal

¹⁸"I am not referring to all of you; I know those I have chosen. But this is to fulfill the scripture: 'He who shares my bread has lifted up his heel against me.'ᵇ

¹⁹"I am telling you now before it happens, so that when it does happen you will believe that I am He. ²⁰I tell you the truth, whoever accepts anyone I send accepts me; and whoever accepts me accepts the one who sent me."

²¹After he had said this, Jesus was troubled in spirit and testified, "I tell you the truth, one of you is going to betray me."

²²His disciples stared at one another, at a loss to know which of them he meant. ²³One of them, the disciple whom Jesus loved, was reclining next to him. ²⁴Simon Peter motioned to this disciple and said, "Ask him which one he means."

²⁵Leaning back against Jesus, he asked him, "Lord, who is it?"

²⁶Jesus answered, "It is the one to whom I will give this piece of bread

---

ᵃ1 Or *he loved them to the last*   ᵇ18 Psalm 41:9

VERSE:
John 13:26

AUTHOR:
Ken Gire

PASSAGE:
John 13:18–38

Unmasking the Traitor

Dear Man of Sorrows, how painful that last supper must have been for you. How your heart must have broken. Thank you for offering yourself, O Lamb of God, as a sacrifice for sin. Thank you for sprinkling your blood on the beams of that cross so my iniquities might be passed over. And thank you for the exodus you brought about in my life, an exodus from the harsh Egypt where I was once a slave.

Lord, when I read of Judas, I can't help but see something of myself in him. Something that keeps my hands clutched to my purse strings. Something obsessively practical that keeps me from letting go and following you completely.

Thank you that you see the traitor in me, too, and yet still you love . . . still you wash the foot whose heel is set against you . . . still you offer bread to lips whose kiss would betray you.

I am unworthy of so great a love, dear Lord Jesus. Grant that love so pure would change my life. That it would loosen my grip on material things. That it would free me from serving two masters. That it would help me to serve — and love — only you . . .

Help me to be a friend who loves as you did at that last supper — a friend who loves to the end, even when that love is refused.

ADDITIONAL SCRIPTURE READINGS
Ephesians 2:1–10; 1 Peter 1:17–21

Go to page 1358 for your next devotional reading.

when I have dipped it in the dish." Then, dipping the piece of bread, he gave it to Judas Iscariot, son of Simon. [27]As soon as Judas took the bread, Satan entered into him.

"What you are about to do, do quickly," Jesus told him, [28]but no one at the meal understood why Jesus said this to him. [29]Since Judas had charge of the money, some thought Jesus was telling him to buy what was needed for the Feast, or to give something to the poor. [30]As soon as Judas had taken the bread, he went out. And it was night.

Jesus Predicts Peter's Denial

[31]When he was gone, Jesus said, "Now is the Son of Man glorified and God is glorified in him. [32]If God is glorified in him,[a] God will glorify the Son in himself, and will glorify him at once.

[33]"My children, I will be with you only a little longer. You will look for me, and just as I told the Jews, so I tell you now: Where I am going, you cannot come.

[34]"A new command I give you: Love one another. As I have loved you, so you must love one another. [35]By this all men will know that you are my disciples, if you love one another."

[36]Simon Peter asked him, "Lord, where are you going?"

Jesus replied, "Where I am going, you cannot follow now, but you will follow later."

[37]Peter asked, "Lord, why can't I follow you now? I will lay down my life for you."

[38]Then Jesus answered, "Will you really lay down your life for me? I tell you the truth, before the rooster crows, you will disown me three times!

Jesus Comforts His Disciples

14 "Do not let your hearts be troubled. Trust in God[b]; trust also in me. [2]In my Father's house are many rooms; if it were not so, I would have told you. I am going there to prepare a place for you. [3]And if I go and prepare a place for you, I will come back and take you to be with me that you also may be where I am. [4]You know the way to the place where I am going."

Jesus the Way to the Father

[5]Thomas said to him, "Lord, we don't know where you are going, so how can we know the way?"

[6]Jesus answered, "I am the way and the truth and the life. No one comes to the Father except through me. [7]If you really knew me, you would know[c] my Father as well. From now on, you do know him and have seen him."

[8]Philip said, "Lord, show us the Father and that will be enough for us."

[9]Jesus answered: "Don't you know me, Philip, even after I have been among you such a long time? Anyone who has seen me has seen the Father. How can you say, 'Show us the Father'? [10]Don't you believe that I am in the Father, and that the Father is in me? The words I say to you are not just my own. Rather, it is the Father, living in me, who is doing his work. [11]Believe me when I say that I am in the Father and the Father is in me; or at least believe on the evidence of the miracles themselves. [12]I tell you the truth, anyone who has faith in me will do what I have been doing. He will do even greater things than these, because I am going to the Father. [13]And I will do whatever you ask in my name, so that the Son may bring glory to the Father. [14]You may ask me for anything in my name, and I will do it.

Jesus Promises the Holy Spirit

[15]"If you love me, you will obey what I command. [16]And I will ask the Father, and he will give you another Counselor to be with you forever—

---

[a]32 Many early manuscripts do not have *If God is glorified in him.*   [b]1 Or *You trust in God*
[c]7 Some early manuscripts *If you really have known me, you will know*

17the Spirit of truth. The world cannot accept him, because it neither sees him nor knows him. But you know him, for he lives with you and will be[a] in you. 18I will not leave you as orphans; I will come to you. 19Before long, the world will not see me anymore, but you will see me. Because I live, you also will live. 20On that day you will realize that I am in my Father, and you are in me, and I am in you. 21Whoever has my commands and obeys them, he is the one who loves me. He who loves me will be loved by my Father, and I too will love him and show myself to him."

22Then Judas (not Judas Iscariot) said, "But, Lord, why do you intend to show yourself to us and not to the world?"

23Jesus replied, "If anyone loves me, he will obey my teaching. My Father will love him, and we will come to him and make our home with him. 24He who does not love me will not obey my teaching. These words you hear are not my own; they belong to the Father who sent me.

25"All this I have spoken while still with you. 26But the Counselor, the Holy Spirit, whom the Father will send in my name, will teach you all things and will remind you of everything I have said to you. 27Peace I leave with you; my peace I give you. I do not give to you as the world gives. Do not let your hearts be troubled and do not be afraid.

28"You heard me say, 'I am going away and I am coming back to you.' If you loved me, you would be glad that I am going to the Father, for the Father is greater than I. 29I have told you now before it happens, so that when it does happen you will believe. 30I will not speak with you much longer, for the prince of this world is coming. He has no hold on me, 31but the world must learn that I love the Father and that I do exactly what my Father has commanded me.

"Come now; let us leave.

The Vine and the Branches

15 "I am the true vine, and my Father is the gardener. 2He cuts off every branch in me that bears no fruit, while every branch that does bear fruit he prunes[b] so that it will be even more fruitful. 3You are already clean because of the word I have spoken to you. 4Remain in me, and I will remain in you. No branch can bear fruit by itself; it must remain in the vine. Neither can you bear fruit unless you remain in me.

5"I am the vine; you are the branches. If a man remains in me and I in him, he will bear much fruit; apart from me you can do nothing. 6If anyone does not remain in me, he is like a branch that is thrown away and withers; such branches are picked up, thrown into the fire and burned. 7If you remain in me and my words remain in you, ask whatever you wish, and it will be given you. 8This is to my Father's glory, that you bear much fruit, showing yourselves to be my disciples.

9"As the Father has loved me, so have I loved you. Now remain in my love. 10If you obey my commands, you will remain in my love, just as I have obeyed my Father's commands and remain in his love. 11I have told you this so that my joy may be in you and that your joy may be complete. 12My command is this: Love each other as I have loved you. 13Greater love has no one than this, that he lay down his life for his friends. 14You are my friends if you do what I command. 15I no longer call you servants, because a servant does not know his master's business. Instead, I have called you friends, for everything that I learned from my Father I have made known to you. 16You did not choose me, but I chose you and appointed you to go and bear fruit—fruit that will last. Then the Father will give you whatever you ask in my name. 17This is my command: Love each other.

---

a17 Some early manuscripts *and is*   b2 The Greek for *prunes* also means *cleans.*

VERSE:	AUTHOR:	PASSAGE:
John 15:8	Sherwood Eliot Wirt	John 15:1–17

Catch the Vision!

Vision! It comes from an understanding that life is intended for something, and that something is good. It is to be used. When we stop using it we begin to fall apart . . .

Having passed fourscore years, I find that the vision is what gives old age its splendor. It can turn wrinkles into beautiful smiles, senility into seniority, and slowness of speech into wisdom. It can change complaining spirits into prayer warriors. It can suffuse the gradual process of aging with dignity, and so attract the admiration and affection of younger people. Can you imagine what a thrill it is when someone says to you, "When I get old, I would like to be like you"? . . .

As the vision takes hold of you and gives you direction, God will write a new chapter in your biography—a chapter you never dreamed was possible. You will find that God is a Master Host: He serves dessert. He saves the sweets for the end of the banquet, the best for the last—the last for which the first was made . . .

Real inner joy . . . does not stem from dependence on relationships with other individuals, not even grandchildren. It comes from a vision of what life is for and the translation of that vision into reality . . . It derives from an acknowledgment that the Creator of the universe is our heavenly Father, that Jesus Christ is his Son, and that we belong to him forever.

ADDITIONAL SCRIPTURE READINGS
Psalm 92; Galatians 5:22–26

Go to page 1361 for your next devotional reading.

The World Hates the Disciples

[18]"If the world hates you, keep in mind that it hated me first. [19]If you belonged to the world, it would love you as its own. As it is, you do not belong to the world, but I have chosen you out of the world. That is why the world hates you. [20]Remember the words I spoke to you: 'No servant is greater than his master.'[a] If they persecuted me, they will persecute you also. If they obeyed my teaching, they will obey yours also. [21]They will treat you this way because of my name, for they do not know the One who sent me. [22]If I had not come and spoken to them, they would not be guilty of sin. Now, however, they have no excuse for their sin. [23]He who hates me hates my Father as well. [24]If I had not done among them what no one else did, they would not be guilty of sin. But now they have seen these miracles, and yet they have hated both me and my Father. [25]But this is to fulfill what is written in their Law: 'They hated me without reason.'[b]

[26]"When the Counselor comes, whom I will send to you from the Father, the Spirit of truth who goes out from the Father, he will testify about me. [27]And you also must testify, for you have been with me from the beginning.

16 "All this I have told you so that you will not go astray. [2]They will put you out of the synagogue; in fact, a time is coming when anyone who kills you will think he is offering a service to God. [3]They will do such things because they have not known the Father or me. [4]I have told you this, so that when the time comes you will remember that I warned you. I did not tell you this at first because I was with you.

The Work of the Holy Spirit

[5]"Now I am going to him who sent me, yet none of you asks me, 'Where are you going?' [6]Because I have said these things, you are filled with grief. [7]But I tell you the truth: It is for your good that I am going away. Unless I go away, the Counselor will not come to you; but if I go, I will send him to you. [8]When he comes, he will convict the world of guilt[c] in regard to sin and righteousness and judgment: [9]in regard to sin, because men do not believe in me; [10]in regard to righteousness, because I am going to the Father, where you can see me no longer; [11]and in regard to judgment, because the prince of this world now stands condemned.

[12]"I have much more to say to you, more than you can now bear. [13]But when he, the Spirit of truth, comes, he will guide you into all truth. He will not speak on his own; he will speak only what he hears, and he will tell you what is yet to come. [14]He will bring glory to me by taking from what is mine and making it known to you. [15]All that belongs to the Father is mine. That is why I said the Spirit will take from what is mine and make it known to you.

[16]"In a little while you will see me no more, and then after a little while you will see me."

The Disciples' Grief Will Turn to Joy

[17]Some of his disciples said to one another, "What does he mean by saying, 'In a little while you will see me no more, and then after a little while you will see me,' and 'Because I am going to the Father'?" [18]They kept asking, "What does he mean by 'a little while'? We don't understand what he is saying."

[19]Jesus saw that they wanted to ask him about this, so he said to them, "Are you asking one another what I meant when I said, 'In a little while you will see me no more, and then after a little while you will see me'? [20]I tell you the truth, you will weep and mourn while the world rejoices. You will grieve, but your grief will turn to joy. [21]A woman giving birth to a child

has pain because her time has come; but when her baby is born she forgets the anguish because of her joy that a child is born into the world. ²²So with you: Now is your time of grief, but I will see you again and you will rejoice, and no one will take away your joy. ²³In that day you will no longer ask me anything. I tell you the truth, my Father will give you whatever you ask in my name. ²⁴Until now you have not asked for anything in my name. Ask and you will receive, and your joy will be complete.

²⁵"Though I have been speaking figuratively, a time is coming when I will no longer use this kind of language but will tell you plainly about my Father. ²⁶In that day you will ask in my name. I am not saying that I will ask the Father on your behalf. ²⁷No, the Father himself loves you because you have loved me and have believed that I came from God. ²⁸I came from the Father and entered the world; now I am leaving the world and going back to the Father."

²⁹Then Jesus' disciples said, "Now you are speaking clearly and without figures of speech. ³⁰Now we can see that you know all things and that you do not even need to have anyone ask you questions. This makes us believe that you came from God."

³¹"You believe at last!"ᵃ Jesus answered. ³²"But a time is coming, and has come, when you will be scattered, each to his own home. You will leave me all alone. Yet I am not alone, for my Father is with me.

³³"I have told you these things, so that in me you may have peace. In this world you will have trouble. But take heart! I have overcome the world."

Jesus Prays for Himself

17 After Jesus said this, he looked toward heaven and prayed:

"Father, the time has come. Glorify your Son, that your Son may glorify you. ²For you grant-

ed him authority over all people that he might give eternal life to all those you have given him. ³Now this is eternal life: that they may know you, the only true God, and Jesus Christ, whom you have sent. ⁴I have brought you glory on earth by completing the work you gave me to do. ⁵And now, Father, glorify me in your presence with the glory I had with you before the world began.

Jesus Prays for His Disciples

⁶"I have revealed youᵇ to those whom you gave me out of the world. They were yours; you gave them to me and they have obeyed your word. ⁷Now they know that everything you have given me comes from you. ⁸For I gave them the words you gave me and they accepted them. They knew with certainty that I came from you, and they believed that you sent me. ⁹I pray for them. I am not praying for the world, but for those you have given me, for they are yours. ¹⁰All I have is yours, and all you have is mine. And glory has come to me through them. ¹¹I will remain in the world no longer, but they are still in the world, and I am coming to you. Holy Father, protect them by the power of your name—the name you gave me—so that they may be one as we are one. ¹²While I was with them, I protected them and kept them safe by that name you gave me. None has been lost except the one doomed to destruction so that Scripture would be fulfilled.

¹³"I am coming to you now, but I say these things while I am still in the world, so that they may have the full measure of my joy within them. ¹⁴I have given them your word and the world has hated them, for they are not

---

ᵃ31 Or "Do you now believe?"   ᵇ6 Greek your name; also in verse 26

VERSE:
John 17:11

AUTHOR:
Charles R. Swindoll

PASSAGE:
John 17:1–26

Standing on the Rock

Reality, though difficult, is dependable. It always keeps its word, though its word may be hard to bear.

I would much prefer to live my life on the sharp, cutting edge of reality than dreaming on the soft, phony mattress of fantasy. Reality is the tempered poker that keeps the fires alive ... the hard set of facts that refuses to let feeling overrule logic. It's reality that forces every Alice out of her Wonderland and into God's wonderful plan. Its undaunted determination has pulled many a wanderer, lost in the maze of meanderings, back to the real world of right and wrong, the false and the true ...

It was reality that enabled Jesus to perform spiritual heart surgery on the woman at the well (John 4), and to stand uncondemningly beside the adulteress (John 8), and to pray as he did the night of his arrest (John 17). Reality, in fact, was part of his motive in bearing the cross for you and me.

While our entire world is sinking in the quagmire of human opinions, theories, philosophies and dreams, our Lord invites us to stand firmly on the rock of reality. And what does the realistic mind-set include? Well, these are eternally etched in the granite of God's Book. They include such things as: Man is a depraved sinner, terribly in need. Our only hope is in Jesus Christ — his death and resurrection. Receiving him brings instant forgiveness and eternal grace ... We cannot escape standing before him. The time to prepare is NOW.

ADDITIONAL SCRIPTURE READINGS
Romans 5:1–11; 2 Corinthians 5:11 — 6:2

Go to page 1366 for your next devotional reading.

of the world any more than I am of the world. ¹⁵My prayer is not that you take them out of the world but that you protect them from the evil one. ¹⁶They are not of the world, even as I am not of it. ¹⁷Sanctify*ᵃ* them by the truth; your word is truth. ¹⁸As you sent me into the world, I have sent them into the world. ¹⁹For them I sanctify myself, that they too may be truly sanctified.

Jesus Prays for All Believers

²⁰"My prayer is not for them alone. I pray also for those who will believe in me through their message, ²¹that all of them may be one, Father, just as you are in me and I am in you. May they also be in us so that the world may believe that you have sent me. ²²I have given them the glory that you gave me, that they may be one as we are one: ²³I in them and you in me. May they be brought to complete unity to let the world know that you sent me and have loved them even as you have loved me.

²⁴"Father, I want those you have given me to be with me where I am, and to see my glory, the glory you have given me because you loved me before the creation of the world. ²⁵"Righteous Father, though the world does not know you, I know you, and they know that you have sent me. ²⁶I have made you known to them, and will continue to make you known in order that the love you have for me may be in them and that I myself may be in them."

Jesus Arrested

18 When he had finished praying, Jesus left with his disciples and crossed the Kidron Valley. On the other side there was an olive grove, and he and his disciples went into it.

²Now Judas, who betrayed him, knew the place, because Jesus had often met there with his disciples. ³So Judas came to the grove, guiding a detachment of soldiers and some officials from the chief priests and Pharisees. They were carrying torches, lanterns and weapons.

⁴Jesus, knowing all that was going to happen to him, went out and asked them, "Who is it you want?"

⁵"Jesus of Nazareth," they replied.

"I am he," Jesus said. (And Judas the traitor was standing there with them.) ⁶When Jesus said, "I am he," they drew back and fell to the ground.

⁷Again he asked them, "Who is it you want?"

And they said, "Jesus of Nazareth."

⁸"I told you that I am he," Jesus answered. "If you are looking for me, then let these men go." ⁹This happened so that the words he had spoken would be fulfilled: "I have not lost one of those you gave me."*ᵇ*

¹⁰Then Simon Peter, who had a sword, drew it and struck the high priest's servant, cutting off his right ear. (The servant's name was Malchus.)

¹¹Jesus commanded Peter, "Put your sword away! Shall I not drink the cup the Father has given me?"

Jesus Taken to Annas

¹²Then the detachment of soldiers with its commander and the Jewish officials arrested Jesus. They bound him ¹³and brought him first to Annas, who was the father-in-law of Caiaphas, the high priest that year. ¹⁴Caiaphas was the one who had advised the Jews that it would be good if one man died for the people.

Peter's First Denial

¹⁵Simon Peter and another disciple were following Jesus. Because this disciple was known to the high priest, he went with Jesus into the high priest's courtyard, ¹⁶but Peter had to wait outside at the door. The other disciple, who was known to the high

---

*ᵃ*17 Greek *hagiazo* (set apart for sacred use or make holy); also in verse 19   *ᵇ*9 John 6:39

priest, came back, spoke to the girl on duty there and brought Peter in.

¹⁷"You are not one of his disciples, are you?" the girl at the door asked Peter.

He replied, "I am not."

¹⁸It was cold, and the servants and officials stood around a fire they had made to keep warm. Peter also was standing with them, warming himself.

The High Priest Questions Jesus

¹⁹Meanwhile, the high priest questioned Jesus about his disciples and his teaching.

²⁰"I have spoken openly to the world," Jesus replied. "I always taught in synagogues or at the temple, where all the Jews come together. I said nothing in secret. ²¹Why question me? Ask those who heard me. Surely they know what I said."

²²When Jesus said this, one of the officials nearby struck him in the face. "Is this the way you answer the high priest?" he demanded.

²³"If I said something wrong," Jesus replied, "testify as to what is wrong. But if I spoke the truth, why did you strike me?" ²⁴Then Annas sent him, still bound, to Caiaphas the high priest.ᵃ

Peter's Second and Third Denials

²⁵As Simon Peter stood warming himself, he was asked, "You are not one of his disciples, are you?"

He denied it, saying, "I am not."

²⁶One of the high priest's servants, a relative of the man whose ear Peter had cut off, challenged him, "Didn't I see you with him in the olive grove?" ²⁷Again Peter denied it, and at that moment a rooster began to crow.

Jesus Before Pilate

²⁸Then the Jews led Jesus from Caiaphas to the palace of the Roman governor. By now it was early morning, and to avoid ceremonial uncleanness the Jews did not enter the palace; they wanted to be able to eat the Pass-

over. ²⁹So Pilate came out to them and asked, "What charges are you bringing against this man?"

³⁰"If he were not a criminal," they replied, "we would not have handed him over to you."

³¹Pilate said, "Take him yourselves and judge him by your own law."

"But we have no right to execute anyone," the Jews objected. ³²This happened so that the words Jesus had spoken indicating the kind of death he was going to die would be fulfilled.

³³Pilate then went back inside the palace, summoned Jesus and asked him, "Are you the king of the Jews?"

³⁴"Is that your own idea," Jesus asked, "or did others talk to you about me?"

³⁵"Am I a Jew?" Pilate replied. "It was your people and your chief priests who handed you over to me. What is it you have done?"

³⁶Jesus said, "My kingdom is not of this world. If it were, my servants would fight to prevent my arrest by the Jews. But now my kingdom is from another place."

³⁷"You are a king, then!" said Pilate.

Jesus answered, "You are right in saying I am a king. In fact, for this reason I was born, and for this I came into the world, to testify to the truth. Everyone on the side of truth listens to me."

³⁸"What is truth?" Pilate asked. With this he went out again to the Jews and said, "I find no basis for a charge against him. ³⁹But it is your custom for me to release to you one prisoner at the time of the Passover. Do you want me to release 'the king of the Jews'?"

⁴⁰They shouted back, "No, not him! Give us Barabbas!" Now Barabbas had taken part in a rebellion.

Jesus Sentenced to be Crucified

19 Then Pilate took Jesus and had him flogged. ²The soldiers twisted together a crown of thorns

ᵃ24 Or (Now Annas had sent him, still bound, to Caiaphas the high priest.)

and put it on his head. They clothed him in a purple robe ³and went up to him again and again, saying, "Hail, king of the Jews!" And they struck him in the face.

⁴Once more Pilate came out and said to the Jews, "Look, I am bringing him out to you to let you know that I find no basis for a charge against him." ⁵When Jesus came out wearing the crown of thorns and the purple robe, Pilate said to them, "Here is the man!"

⁶As soon as the chief priests and their officials saw him, they shouted, "Crucify! Crucify!"

But Pilate answered, "You take him and crucify him. As for me, I find no basis for a charge against him."

⁷The Jews insisted, "We have a law, and according to that law he must die, because he claimed to be the Son of God."

⁸When Pilate heard this, he was even more afraid, ⁹and he went back inside the palace. "Where do you come from?" he asked Jesus, but Jesus gave him no answer. ¹⁰"Do you refuse to speak to me?" Pilate said. "Don't you realize I have power either to free you or to crucify you?"

¹¹Jesus answered, "You would have no power over me if it were not given to you from above. Therefore the one who handed me over to you is guilty of a greater sin."

¹²From then on, Pilate tried to set Jesus free, but the Jews kept shouting, "If you let this man go, you are no friend of Caesar. Anyone who claims to be a king opposes Caesar."

¹³When Pilate heard this, he brought Jesus out and sat down on the judge's seat at a place known as the Stone Pavement (which in Aramaic is Gabbatha). ¹⁴It was the day of Preparation of Passover Week, about the sixth hour.

"Here is your king," Pilate said to the Jews.

¹⁵But they shouted, "Take him away! Take him away! Crucify him!"

"Shall I crucify your king?" Pilate asked.

"We have no king but Caesar," the chief priests answered.

¹⁶Finally Pilate handed him over to them to be crucified.

The Crucifixion

So the soldiers took charge of Jesus. ¹⁷Carrying his own cross, he went out to the place of the Skull (which in Aramaic is called Golgotha). ¹⁸Here they crucified him, and with him two others—one on each side and Jesus in the middle.

¹⁹Pilate had a notice prepared and fastened to the cross. It read: JESUS OF NAZARETH, THE KING OF THE JEWS. ²⁰Many of the Jews read this sign, for the place where Jesus was crucified was near the city, and the sign was written in Aramaic, Latin and Greek. ²¹The chief priests of the Jews protested to Pilate, "Do not write 'The King of the Jews,' but that this man claimed to be king of the Jews."

²²Pilate answered, "What I have written, I have written."

²³When the soldiers crucified Jesus, they took his clothes, dividing them into four shares, one for each of them, with the undergarment remaining. This garment was seamless, woven in one piece from top to bottom.

²⁴"Let's not tear it," they said to one another. "Let's decide by lot who will get it."

This happened that the scripture might be fulfilled which said,

"They divided my garments
        among them
    and cast lots for my clothing."ᵃ

So this is what the soldiers did.

²⁵Near the cross of Jesus stood his mother, his mother's sister, Mary the wife of Clopas, and Mary Magdalene. ²⁶When Jesus saw his mother there, and the disciple whom he loved standing nearby, he said to his mother, "Dear woman, here is your son," ²⁷and to the disciple, "Here is your

ᵃ24 Psalm 22:18

mother." From that time on, this disciple took her into his home.

The Death of Jesus

28Later, knowing that all was now completed, and so that the Scripture would be fulfilled, Jesus said, "I am thirsty." 29A jar of wine vinegar was there, so they soaked a sponge in it, put the sponge on a stalk of the hyssop plant, and lifted it to Jesus' lips. 30When he had received the drink, Jesus said, "It is finished." With that, he bowed his head and gave up his spirit.

31Now it was the day of Preparation, and the next day was to be a special Sabbath. Because the Jews did not want the bodies left on the crosses during the Sabbath, they asked Pilate to have the legs broken and the bodies taken down. 32The soldiers therefore came and broke the legs of the first man who had been crucified with Jesus, and then those of the other. 33But when they came to Jesus and found that he was already dead, they did not break his legs. 34Instead, one of the soldiers pierced Jesus' side with a spear, bringing a sudden flow of blood and water. 35The man who saw it has given testimony, and his testimony is true. He knows that he tells the truth, and he testifies so that you also may believe. 36These things happened so that the scripture would be fulfilled: "Not one of his bones will be broken,"a 37and, as another scripture says, "They will look on the one they have pierced."b

The Burial of Jesus

38Later, Joseph of Arimathea asked Pilate for the body of Jesus. Now Joseph was a disciple of Jesus, but secretly because he feared the Jews. With Pilate's permission, he came and took the body away. 39He was accompanied by Nicodemus, the man who earlier had visited Jesus at night. Nicodemus brought a mixture of myrrh and aloes, about seventy-five

pounds.c 40Taking Jesus' body, the two of them wrapped it, with the spices, in strips of linen. This was in accordance with Jewish burial customs. 41At the place where Jesus was crucified, there was a garden, and in the garden a new tomb, in which no one had ever been laid. 42Because it was the Jewish day of Preparation and since the tomb was nearby, they laid Jesus there.

The Empty Tomb

20 Early on the first day of the week, while it was still dark, Mary Magdalene went to the tomb and saw that the stone had been removed from the entrance. 2So she came running to Simon Peter and the other disciple, the one Jesus loved, and said, "They have taken the Lord out of the tomb, and we don't know where they have put him!"

3So Peter and the other disciple started for the tomb. 4Both were running, but the other disciple outran Peter and reached the tomb first. 5He bent over and looked in at the strips of linen lying there but did not go in. 6Then Simon Peter, who was behind him, arrived and went into the tomb. He saw the strips of linen lying there, 7as well as the burial cloth that had been around Jesus' head. The cloth was folded up by itself, separate from the linen. 8Finally the other disciple, who had reached the tomb first, also went inside. He saw and believed. 9(They still did not understand from Scripture that Jesus had to rise from the dead.)

Jesus Appears to Mary Magdalene

10Then the disciples went back to their homes, 11but Mary stood outside the tomb crying. As she wept, she bent over to look into the tomb 12and saw two angels in white, seated where Jesus' body had been, one at the head and the other at the foot.

13They asked her, "Woman, why are you crying?"

---

a36 Exodus 12:46; Num. 9:12; Psalm 34:20   b37 Zech. 12:10   c39 Greek a hundred litrai (about 34 kilograms)

FRIDAY

VERSE:
John 20:2

AUTHOR:
Philip Yancey

PASSAGE:
John 20:1–18

Love's Triumph

The apostles' faith, as they freely confessed, rested entirely on what happened on Easter Sunday, when God transformed that greatest tragedy in all history, the execution of his Son, into a day we now celebrate as Good Friday. Those disciples, who gazed at the cross from the shadows, soon learned what they had failed to learn in three years with their leader: When God seems absent, he may be closest of all. When God seems dead, he may be coming to life.

The three-day pattern—tragedy, darkness, triumph— became for New Testament writers a template that can be applied to all our times of testing. We can look back on Jesus, the proof of God's love, even though we may never get an answer to our "Why?" questions. Good Friday demonstrates that God has not abandoned us to our pain. The evils and sufferings that afflict our lives are so real and so significant to God that he willed to share them and endure them himself . . .

And Easter Sunday shows that, in the end, suffering will not triumph. Therefore . . . "In this you greatly rejoice, though now for a little while you may have had to suffer grief in all kinds of trials," writes Peter; and "we also rejoice in our sufferings," writes Paul . . .

Why rejoice? Not for the masochistic thrill of the trial itself, but because what God did Easter Sunday on large scale he can do on small scale for each of us . . . Just wait: God's miracle of transforming a dark, silent Friday into Easter Sunday will someday be enlarged to cosmic scale.

ADDITIONAL SCRIPTURE READINGS
James 1:2–12; 1 Peter 1:3–9

Go to page 1368 for your next devotional reading.

"They have taken my Lord away," she said, "and I don't know where they have put him." ¹⁴At this, she turned around and saw Jesus standing there, but she did not realize that it was Jesus.

¹⁵"Woman," he said, "why are you crying? Who is it you are looking for?"

Thinking he was the gardener, she said, "Sir, if you have carried him away, tell me where you have put him, and I will get him."

¹⁶Jesus said to her, "Mary."

She turned toward him and cried out in Aramaic, "Rabboni!" (which means Teacher).

¹⁷Jesus said, "Do not hold on to me, for I have not yet returned to the Father. Go instead to my brothers and tell them, 'I am returning to my Father and your Father, to my God and your God.' "

¹⁸Mary Magdalene went to the disciples with the news: "I have seen the Lord!" And she told them that he had said these things to her.

Jesus Appears to His Disciples

¹⁹On the evening of that first day of the week, when the disciples were together, with the doors locked for fear of the Jews, Jesus came and stood among them and said, "Peace be with you!" ²⁰After he said this, he showed them his hands and side. The disciples were overjoyed when they saw the Lord.

²¹Again Jesus said, "Peace be with you! As the Father has sent me, I am sending you." ²²And with that he breathed on them and said, "Receive the Holy Spirit. ²³If you forgive anyone his sins, they are forgiven; if you do not forgive them, they are not forgiven."

Jesus Appears to Thomas

²⁴Now Thomas (called Didymus), one of the Twelve, was not with the disciples when Jesus came. ²⁵So the other disciples told him, "We have seen the Lord!"

But he said to them, "Unless I see the nail marks in his hands and put my finger where the nails were, and put my hand into his side, I will not believe it."

²⁶A week later his disciples were in the house again, and Thomas was with them. Though the doors were locked, Jesus came and stood among them and said, "Peace be with you!" ²⁷Then he said to Thomas, "Put your finger here; see my hands. Reach out your hand and put it into my side. Stop doubting and believe."

²⁸Thomas said to him, "My Lord and my God!"

²⁹Then Jesus told him, "Because you have seen me, you have believed; blessed are those who have not seen and yet have believed."

³⁰Jesus did many other miraculous signs in the presence of his disciples, which are not recorded in this book. ³¹But these are written that you may[a] believe that Jesus is the Christ, the Son of God, and that by believing you may have life in his name.

Jesus and the Miraculous Catch of Fish

21 Afterward Jesus appeared again to his disciples, by the Sea of Tiberias.[b] It happened this way: ²Simon Peter, Thomas (called Didymus), Nathanael from Cana in Galilee, the sons of Zebedee, and two other disciples were together. ³"I'm going out to fish," Simon Peter told them, and they said, "We'll go with you." So they went out and got into the boat, but that night they caught nothing.

⁴Early in the morning, Jesus stood on the shore, but the disciples did not realize that it was Jesus.

⁵He called out to them, "Friends, haven't you any fish?"

"No," they answered.

⁶He said, "Throw your net on the right side of the boat and you will find some." When they did, they were

PASSAGE: 1 Corinthians 15:50–58; Ephesians 1:3–14
AUTHOR: Horatio Spafford

It Is Well

When peace like a river attendeth my way,
When sorrows like sea billows roll —
Whatever my lot, thou hast taught me to say,
It is well, it is well with my soul.

Though Satan should buffet, though trials should
     come,
Let this blest assurance control:
That Christ has regarded my helpless estate,
And has shed his own blood for my soul.

My sin — Oh, the bliss of this glorious thought! —
My sin, not in part, but the whole,
Is nailed to the cross, and I bear it no more:
Praise the Lord, praise the Lord, O my soul!

O Lord, haste the day when my faith shall be sight,
The clouds be rolled back as a scroll;
The trump shall resound and the Lord shall
     descend;
Even so, it is well with my soul.

Go to page 1371 for your next devotional reading.

unable to haul the net in because of the large number of fish.

⁷Then the disciple whom Jesus loved said to Peter, "It is the Lord!" As soon as Simon Peter heard him say, "It is the Lord," he wrapped his outer garment around him (for he had taken it off) and jumped into the water. ⁸The other disciples followed in the boat, towing the net full of fish, for they were not far from shore, about a hundred yards.ᵃ ⁹When they landed, they saw a fire of burning coals there with fish on it, and some bread.

¹⁰Jesus said to them, "Bring some of the fish you have just caught."

¹¹Simon Peter climbed aboard and dragged the net ashore. It was full of large fish, 153, but even with so many the net was not torn. ¹²Jesus said to them, "Come and have breakfast." None of the disciples dared ask him, "Who are you?" They knew it was the Lord. ¹³Jesus came, took the bread and gave it to them, and did the same with the fish. ¹⁴This was now the third time Jesus appeared to his disciples after he was raised from the dead.

Jesus Reinstates Peter

¹⁵When they had finished eating, Jesus said to Simon Peter, "Simon son of John, do you truly love me more than these?"

"Yes, Lord," he said, "you know that I love you."

Jesus said, "Feed my lambs."

¹⁶Again Jesus said, "Simon son of John, do you truly love me?"

He answered, "Yes, Lord, you know that I love you."

Jesus said, "Take care of my sheep."

¹⁷The third time he said to him, "Simon son of John, do you love me?"

Peter was hurt because Jesus asked him the third time, "Do you love me?" He said, "Lord, you know all things; you know that I love you."

Jesus said, "Feed my sheep. ¹⁸I tell you the truth, when you were younger you dressed yourself and went where you wanted; but when you are old you will stretch out your hands, and someone else will dress you and lead you where you do not want to go." ¹⁹Jesus said this to indicate the kind of death by which Peter would glorify God. Then he said to him, "Follow me!"

²⁰Peter turned and saw that the disciple whom Jesus loved was following them. (This was the one who had leaned back against Jesus at the supper and had said, "Lord, who is going to betray you?") ²¹When Peter saw him, he asked, "Lord, what about him?"

²²Jesus answered, "If I want him to remain alive until I return, what is that to you? You must follow me." ²³Because of this, the rumor spread among the brothers that this disciple would not die. But Jesus did not say that he would not die; he only said, "If I want him to remain alive until I return, what is that to you?"

²⁴This is the disciple who testifies to these things and who wrote them down. We know that his testimony is true.

²⁵Jesus did many other things as well. If every one of them were written down, I suppose that even the whole world would not have room for the books that would be written.

ᵃ8 Greek *about two hundred cubits* (about 90 meters)

Luke, in volume two of
his report, tells how Jesus' followers carried
his message of life and healing to others. It
wasn't an easy task, but the power of the
Holy Spirit gave them what they needed to
spread the message from Jerusalem to Rome.
As you read this book, remember that this
same divine power is available to help you
"walk the talk" and share the message with
those around you.

ACTS

Jesus Taken Up Into Heaven

1 In my former book, Theophilus, I wrote about all that Jesus began to do and to teach ²until the day he was taken up to heaven, after giving instructions through the Holy Spirit to the apostles he had chosen. ³After his suffering, he showed himself to these men and gave many convincing proofs that he was alive. He appeared to them over a period of forty days and spoke about the kingdom of God. ⁴On one occasion, while he was eating with them, he gave them this command: "Do not leave Jerusalem, but wait for the gift my Father promised, which you have heard me speak about. ⁵For John baptized with*ᵃ* water, but in a few days you will be baptized with the Holy Spirit."

⁶So when they met together, they asked him, "Lord, are you at this time going to restore the kingdom to Israel?"

⁷He said to them: "It is not for you to know the times or dates the Father has set by his own authority. ⁸But you will receive power when the Holy Spirit comes on you; and you will be my witnesses in Jerusalem, and in all Judea and Samaria, and to the ends of the earth."

⁹After he said this, he was taken up before their very eyes, and a cloud hid him from their sight.

¹⁰They were looking intently up into the sky as he was going, when suddenly two men dressed in white stood beside them. ¹¹"Men of Galilee," they said, "why do you stand here looking into the sky? This same Jesus, who has been taken from you into heaven, will come back in the same way you have seen him go into heaven."

Matthias Chosen to Replace Judas

¹²Then they returned to Jerusalem from the hill called the Mount of Olives, a Sabbath day's walk*ᵃ* from the city. ¹³When they arrived, they went upstairs to the room where they were staying. Those present were Peter, John, James and Andrew; Philip and Thomas, Bartholomew and Matthew; James son of Alphaeus and Simon the Zealot, and Judas son of James. ¹⁴They all joined together constantly in

ᵃ12 That is, about 3/4 mile (about 1,100 meters)

VERSE:	AUTHOR:	PASSAGE:
Acts 1:14	Cornelis Gilhuis	Acts 1:12–14

The Wide-angle View

When you have been shunted off the track of labor and production, ... it is understandable that your interests and your field of vision shrink a little ... When you are no longer directly involved with something, your interest wanes visibly. The field of vision becomes smaller.

You don't have to lose the wide-angle view, not even when your daily view is nothing more than four walls in a small room and one tree in front of a window: *if you only pray* — and pray profitably.

This means that you pray for the coming of God's kingdom, for the welfare of his church and similar matters of concern. By praying you travel the world. You visit the mission fields and the evangelism stations. You bring everything you come across to the Lord in prayer. This way it is impossible for your vision to become narrow or a feeling of purposelessness to overwhelm you. Isn't the praying home front of the greatest importance? When Moses' hands pointed prayerfully to heaven, Amalek lost and Israel won the battle (Exodus 17). Someone put it this way: God rules the world not from the conference centers of world powers, but from attic rooms and sickbeds in which prayers are offered.

ADDITIONAL SCRIPTURE READINGS
Ephesians 6:10–20; Colossians 4:2–6

Go to page 1379 for your next devotional reading.

prayer, along with the women and Mary the mother of Jesus, and with his brothers.

[15]In those days Peter stood up among the believers[a] (a group numbering about a hundred and twenty) [16]and said, "Brothers, the Scripture had to be fulfilled which the Holy Spirit spoke long ago through the mouth of David concerning Judas, who served as guide for those who arrested Jesus— [17]he was one of our number and shared in this ministry."

[18](With the reward he got for his wickedness, Judas bought a field; there he fell headlong, his body burst open and all his intestines spilled out. [19]Everyone in Jerusalem heard about this, so they called that field in their language Akeldama, that is, Field of Blood.)

[20]"For," said Peter, "it is written in the book of Psalms,

" 'May his place be deserted;
    let there be no one to dwell in
        it,'[b]

and,

" 'May another take his place of
    leadership.'[c]

[21]Therefore it is necessary to choose one of the men who have been with us the whole time the Lord Jesus went in and out among us, [22]beginning from John's baptism to the time when Jesus was taken up from us. For one of these must become a witness with us of his resurrection."

[23]So they proposed two men: Joseph called Barsabbas (also known as Justus) and Matthias. [24]Then they prayed, "Lord, you know everyone's heart. Show us which of these two you have chosen [25]to take over this apostolic ministry, which Judas left to go where he belongs." [26]Then they cast lots, and the lot fell to Matthias; so he was added to the eleven apostles.

The Holy Spirit Comes at Pentecost

2 When the day of Pentecost came, they were all together in one place. [2]Suddenly a sound like the blowing of a violent wind came from heaven and filled the whole house where they were sitting. [3]They saw what seemed to be tongues of fire that separated and came to rest on each of them. [4]All of them were filled with the Holy Spirit and began to speak in other tongues[d] as the Spirit enabled them.

[5]Now there were staying in Jerusalem God-fearing Jews from every nation under heaven. [6]When they heard this sound, a crowd came together in bewilderment, because each one heard them speaking in his own language. [7]Utterly amazed, they asked: "Are not all these men who are speaking Galileans? [8]Then how is it that each of us hears them in his own native language? [9]Parthians, Medes and Elamites; residents of Mesopotamia, Judea and Cappadocia, Pontus and Asia, [10]Phrygia and Pamphylia, Egypt and the parts of Libya near Cyrene; visitors from Rome [11](both Jews and converts to Judaism); Cretans and Arabs—we hear them declaring the wonders of God in our own tongues!" [12]Amazed and perplexed, they asked one another, "What does this mean?"

[13]Some, however, made fun of them and said, "They have had too much wine.[e]"

Peter Addresses the Crowd

[14]Then Peter stood up with the Eleven, raised his voice and addressed the crowd: "Fellow Jews and all of you who live in Jerusalem, let me explain this to you; listen carefully to what I say. [15]These men are not drunk, as you suppose. It's only nine in the morning! [16]No, this is what was spoken by the prophet Joel:

[17]" 'In the last days, God says,
    I will pour out my Spirit on all
        people.

---

[a]15 Greek brothers   [b]20 Psalm 69:25   [c]20 Psalm 109:8   [d]4 Or languages; also in verse 11
[e]13 Or sweet wine

Your sons and daughters will
  prophesy,
  your young men will see
    visions,
  your old men will dream
    dreams.
18Even on my servants, both men
    and women,
  I will pour out my Spirit in
    those days,
  and they will prophesy.
19I will show wonders in the heaven
    above
  and signs on the earth below,
  blood and fire and billows of
    smoke.
20The sun will be turned to
    darkness
  and the moon to blood
  before the coming of the great
    and glorious day of the
    Lord.
21And everyone who calls
  on the name of the Lord will be
    saved.'*a*

22"Men of Israel, listen to this: Jesus of Nazareth was a man accredited by God to you by miracles, wonders and signs, which God did among you through him, as you yourselves know. 23This man was handed over to you by God's set purpose and foreknowledge; and you, with the help of wicked men,*b* put him to death by nailing him to the cross. 24But God raised him from the dead, freeing him from the agony of death, because it was impossible for death to keep its hold on him. 25David said about him:

  " 'I saw the Lord always before
    me.
  Because he is at my right hand,
  I will not be shaken.
26Therefore my heart is glad and my
    tongue rejoices;
  my body also will live in hope,
27because you will not abandon me
    to the grave,
  nor will you let your Holy One
    see decay.

28You have made known to me the
    paths of life;
  you will fill me with joy in your
    presence.'*c*

29"Brothers, I can tell you confidently that the patriarch David died and was buried, and his tomb is here to this day. 30But he was a prophet and knew that God had promised him on oath that he would place one of his descendants on his throne. 31Seeing what was ahead, he spoke of the resurrection of the Christ,*d* that he was not abandoned to the grave, nor did his body see decay. 32God has raised this Jesus to life, and we are all witnesses of the fact. 33Exalted to the right hand of God, he has received from the Father the promised Holy Spirit and has poured out what you now see and hear. 34For David did not ascend to heaven, and yet he said,

  " 'The Lord said to my Lord:
    "Sit at my right hand
35until I make your enemies
  a footstool for your feet." '*e*

36"Therefore let all Israel be assured of this: God has made this Jesus, whom you crucified, both Lord and Christ."

37When the people heard this, they were cut to the heart and said to Peter and the other apostles, "Brothers, what shall we do?"

38Peter replied, "Repent and be baptized, every one of you, in the name of Jesus Christ for the forgiveness of your sins. And you will receive the gift of the Holy Spirit. 39The promise is for you and your children and for all who are far off—for all whom the Lord our God will call."

40With many other words he warned them; and he pleaded with them, "Save yourselves from this corrupt generation." 41Those who accepted his message were baptized, and about three thousand were added to their number that day.

*a*21 Joel 2:28-32   *b*23 Or *of those not having the law* (that is, Gentiles)   *c*28 Psalm 16:8-11
*d*31 Or *Messiah*. "The Christ" (Greek) and "the Messiah" (Hebrew) both mean "the Anointed One"; also in verse 36.   *e*35 Psalm 110:1

The Fellowship of the Believers

42They devoted themselves to the apostles' teaching and to the fellowship, to the breaking of bread and to prayer. 43Everyone was filled with awe, and many wonders and miraculous signs were done by the apostles. 44All the believers were together and had everything in common. 45Selling their possessions and goods, they gave to anyone as he had need. 46Every day they continued to meet together in the temple courts. They broke bread in their homes and ate together with glad and sincere hearts, 47praising God and enjoying the favor of all the people. And the Lord added to their number daily those who were being saved.

Peter Heals the Crippled Beggar

3 One day Peter and John were going up to the temple at the time of prayer—at three in the afternoon. 2Now a man crippled from birth was being carried to the temple gate called Beautiful, where he was put every day to beg from those going into the temple courts. 3When he saw Peter and John about to enter, he asked them for money. 4Peter looked straight at him, as did John. Then Peter said, "Look at us!" 5So the man gave them his attention, expecting to get something from them.

6Then Peter said, "Silver or gold I do not have, but what I have I give you. In the name of Jesus Christ of Nazareth, walk." 7Taking him by the right hand, he helped him up, and instantly the man's feet and ankles became strong. 8He jumped to his feet and began to walk. Then he went with them into the temple courts, walking and jumping, and praising God. 9When all the people saw him walking and praising God, 10they recognized him as the same man who used to sit begging at the temple gate called Beautiful, and they were filled with wonder and amazement at what had happened to him.

Peter Speaks to the Onlookers

11While the beggar held on to Peter and John, all the people were astonished and came running to them in the place called Solomon's Colonnade. 12When Peter saw this, he said to them: "Men of Israel, why does this surprise you? Why do you stare at us as if by our own power or godliness we had made this man walk? 13The God of Abraham, Isaac and Jacob, the God of our fathers, has glorified his servant Jesus. You handed him over to be killed, and you disowned him before Pilate, though he had decided to let him go. 14You disowned the Holy and Righteous One and asked that a murderer be released to you. 15You killed the author of life, but God raised him from the dead. We are witnesses of this. 16By faith in the name of Jesus, this man whom you see and know was made strong. It is Jesus' name and the faith that comes through him that has given this complete healing to him, as you can all see.

17"Now, brothers, I know that you acted in ignorance, as did your leaders. 18But this is how God fulfilled what he had foretold through all the prophets, saying that his Christ[a] would suffer. 19Repent, then, and turn to God, so that your sins may be wiped out, that times of refreshing may come from the Lord, 20and that he may send the Christ, who has been appointed for you—even Jesus. 21He must remain in heaven until the time comes for God to restore everything, as he promised long ago through his holy prophets. 22For Moses said, 'The Lord your God will raise up for you a prophet like me from among your own people; you must listen to everything he tells you. 23Anyone who does not listen to him will be completely cut off from among his people.'[b]

24"Indeed, all the prophets from Samuel on, as many as have spoken, have foretold these days. 25And you are heirs of the prophets and of the

---

a18 Or *Messiah*; also in verse 20   b23 Deut. 18:15,18,19

covenant God made with your fathers. He said to Abraham, 'Through your offspring all peoples on earth will be blessed.'[a] [26]When God raised up his servant, he sent him first to you to bless you by turning each of you from your wicked ways."

Peter and John Before the Sanhedrin

4 The priests and the captain of the temple guard and the Sadducees came up to Peter and John while they were speaking to the people. [2]They were greatly disturbed because the apostles were teaching the people and proclaiming in Jesus the resurrection of the dead. [3]They seized Peter and John, and because it was evening, they put them in jail until the next day. [4]But many who heard the message believed, and the number of men grew to about five thousand.

[5]The next day the rulers, elders and teachers of the law met in Jerusalem. [6]Annas the high priest was there, and so were Caiaphas, John, Alexander and the other men of the high priest's family. [7]They had Peter and John brought before them and began to question them: "By what power or what name did you do this?"

[8]Then Peter, filled with the Holy Spirit, said to them: "Rulers and elders of the people! [9]If we are being called to account today for an act of kindness shown to a cripple and are asked how he was healed, [10]then know this, you and all the people of Israel: It is by the name of Jesus Christ of Nazareth, whom you crucified but whom God raised from the dead, that this man stands before you healed. [11]He is

" 'the stone you builders rejected,
    which has become the
        capstone.'[b'c]

[12]Salvation is found in no one else, for there is no other name under heaven given to men by which we must be saved."

[13]When they saw the courage of Peter and John and realized that they were unschooled, ordinary men, they were astonished and they took note that these men had been with Jesus. [14]But since they could see the man who had been healed standing there with them, there was nothing they could say. [15]So they ordered them to withdraw from the Sanhedrin and then conferred together. [16]"What are we going to do with these men?" they asked. "Everybody living in Jerusalem knows they have done an outstanding miracle, and we cannot deny it. [17]But to stop this thing from spreading any further among the people, we must warn these men to speak no longer to anyone in this name."

[18]Then they called them in again and commanded them not to speak or teach at all in the name of Jesus. [19]But Peter and John replied, "Judge for yourselves whether it is right in God's sight to obey you rather than God. [20]For we cannot help speaking about what we have seen and heard."

[21]After further threats they let them go. They could not decide how to punish them, because all the people were praising God for what had happened. [22]For the man who was miraculously healed was over forty years old.

The Believers' Prayer

[23]On their release, Peter and John went back to their own people and reported all that the chief priests and elders had said to them. [24]When they heard this, they raised their voices together in prayer to God. "Sovereign Lord," they said, "you made the heaven and the earth and the sea, and everything in them. [25]You spoke by the Holy Spirit through the mouth of your servant, our father David:

" 'Why do the nations rage
    and the peoples plot in vain?
[26]The kings of the earth take their
        stand
    and the rulers gather together
        against the Lord

---

[a]25 Gen. 22:18; 26:4   [b]11 Or *cornerstone*   [c]11 Psalm 118:22

and against his Anointed
     One.[a][b]

[27]Indeed Herod and Pontius Pilate
met together with the Gentiles and
the people[c] of Israel in this city to
conspire against your holy servant
Jesus, whom you anointed. [28]They
did what your power and will had decided beforehand should happen.
[29]Now, Lord, consider their threats
and enable your servants to speak
your word with great boldness.
[30]Stretch out your hand to heal and
perform miraculous signs and wonders through the name of your holy
servant Jesus."

[31]After they prayed, the place
where they were meeting was shaken.
And they were all filled with the Holy
Spirit and spoke the word of God
boldly.

The Believers Share Their Possessions

[32]All the believers were one in heart
and mind. No one claimed that any of
his possessions was his own, but they
shared everything they had. [33]With
great power the apostles continued to
testify to the resurrection of the Lord
Jesus, and much grace was upon
them all. [34]There were no needy persons among them. For from time to
time those who owned lands or
houses sold them, brought the money
from the sales [35]and put it at the apostles' feet, and it was distributed to
anyone as he had need.

[36]Joseph, a Levite from Cyprus,
whom the apostles called Barnabas
(which means Son of Encouragement), [37]sold a field he owned and
brought the money and put it at the
apostles' feet.

Ananias and Sapphira

5 Now a man named Ananias, together with his wife Sapphira,
also sold a piece of property. [2]With
his wife's full knowledge he kept
back part of the money for himself,

but brought the rest and put it at the
apostles' feet.

[3]Then Peter said, "Ananias, how is
it that Satan has so filled your heart
that you have lied to the Holy Spirit
and have kept for yourself some of
the money you received for the land?
[4]Didn't it belong to you before it was
sold? And after it was sold, wasn't the
money at your disposal? What made
you think of doing such a thing? You
have not lied to men but to God."

[5]When Ananias heard this, he fell
down and died. And great fear seized
all who heard what had happened.
[6]Then the young men came forward,
wrapped up his body, and carried
him out and buried him.

[7]About three hours later his wife
came in, not knowing what had happened. [8]Peter asked her, "Tell me, is
this the price you and Ananias got for
the land?"

"Yes," she said, "that is the price."

[9]Peter said to her, "How could you
agree to test the Spirit of the Lord?
Look! The feet of the men who buried
your husband are at the door, and
they will carry you out also."

[10]At that moment she fell down at
his feet and died. Then the young
men came in and, finding her dead,
carried her out and buried her beside
her husband. [11]Great fear seized the
whole church and all who heard
about these events.

The Apostles Heal Many

[12]The apostles performed many miraculous signs and wonders among
the people. And all the believers used
to meet together in Solomon's Colonnade. [13]No one else dared join them,
even though they were highly regarded by the people. [14]Nevertheless,
more and more men and women believed in the Lord and were added to
their number. [15]As a result, people
brought the sick into the streets and
laid them on beds and mats so that
at least Peter's shadow might fall on
some of them as he passed by.
[16]Crowds gathered also from the

---

[a]26 That is, Christ or Messiah   [b]26 Psalm 2:1,2   [c]27 The Greek is plural.

towns around Jerusalem, bringing their sick and those tormented by evil[a] spirits, and all of them were healed.

The Apostles Persecuted

[17]Then the high priest and all his associates, who were members of the party of the Sadducees, were filled with jealousy. [18]They arrested the apostles and put them in the public jail. [19]But during the night an angel of the Lord opened the doors of the jail and brought them out. [20]"Go, stand in the temple courts," he said, "and tell the people the full message of this new life."

[21]At daybreak they entered the temple courts, as they had been told, and began to teach the people.

When the high priest and his associates arrived, they called together the Sanhedrin—the full assembly of the elders of Israel—and sent to the jail for the apostles. [22]But on arriving at the jail, the officers did not find them there. So they went back and reported, [23]"We found the jail securely locked, with the guards standing at the doors; but when we opened them, we found no one inside." [24]On hearing this report, the captain of the temple guard and the chief priests were puzzled, wondering what would come of this.

[25]Then someone came and said, "Look! The men you put in jail are standing in the temple courts teaching the people." [26]At that, the captain went with his officers and brought the apostles. They did not use force, because they feared that the people would stone them.

[27]Having brought the apostles, they made them appear before the Sanhedrin to be questioned by the high priest. [28]"We gave you strict orders not to teach in this name," he said. "Yet you have filled Jerusalem with your teaching and are determined to make us guilty of this man's blood."

[29]Peter and the other apostles replied: "We must obey God rather than men! [30]The God of our fathers raised Jesus from the dead—whom you had killed by hanging him on a tree. [31]God exalted him to his own right hand as Prince and Savior that he might give repentance and forgiveness of sins to Israel. [32]We are witnesses of these things, and so is the Holy Spirit, whom God has given to those who obey him."

[33]When they heard this, they were furious and wanted to put them to death. [34]But a Pharisee named Gamaliel, a teacher of the law, who was honored by all the people, stood up in the Sanhedrin and ordered that the men be put outside for a little while. [35]Then he addressed them: "Men of Israel, consider carefully what you intend to do to these men. [36]Some time ago Theudas appeared, claiming to be somebody, and about four hundred men rallied to him. He was killed, all his followers were dispersed, and it all came to nothing. [37]After him, Judas the Galilean appeared in the days of the census and led a band of people in revolt. He too was killed, and all his followers were scattered. [38]Therefore, in the present case I advise you: Leave these men alone! Let them go! For if their purpose or activity is of human origin, it will fail. [39]But if it is from God, you will not be able to stop these men; you will only find yourselves fighting against God."

[40]His speech persuaded them. They called the apostles in and had them flogged. Then they ordered them not to speak in the name of Jesus, and let them go.

[41]The apostles left the Sanhedrin, rejoicing because they had been counted worthy of suffering disgrace for the Name. [42]Day after day, in the temple courts and from house to house, they never stopped teaching and proclaiming the good news that Jesus is the Christ.[b]

The Choosing of the Seven

6 In those days when the number of disciples was increasing, the Gre-

---

[a]16 Greek *unclean*   [b]42 Or *Messiah*

cian Jews among them complained against the Hebraic Jews because their widows were being overlooked in the daily distribution of food. ²So the Twelve gathered all the disciples together and said, "It would not be right for us to neglect the ministry of the word of God in order to wait on tables. ³Brothers, choose seven men from among you who are known to be full of the Spirit and wisdom. We will turn this responsibility over to them ⁴and will give our attention to prayer and the ministry of the word."

⁵This proposal pleased the whole group. They chose Stephen, a man full of faith and of the Holy Spirit; also Philip, Procorus, Nicanor, Timon, Parmenas, and Nicolas from Antioch, a convert to Judaism. ⁶They presented these men to the apostles, who prayed and laid their hands on them.

⁷So the word of God spread. The number of disciples in Jerusalem increased rapidly, and a large number of priests became obedient to the faith.

Stephen Seized

⁸Now Stephen, a man full of God's grace and power, did great wonders and miraculous signs among the people. ⁹Opposition arose, however, from members of the Synagogue of the Freedmen (as it was called)—Jews of Cyrene and Alexandria as well as the provinces of Cilicia and Asia. These men began to argue with Stephen, ¹⁰but they could not stand up against his wisdom or the Spirit by whom he spoke.

¹¹Then they secretly persuaded some men to say, "We have heard Stephen speak words of blasphemy against Moses and against God."

¹²So they stirred up the people and the elders and the teachers of the law. They seized Stephen and brought him before the Sanhedrin. ¹³They produced false witnesses, who testified, "This fellow never stops speaking against this holy place and against the law. ¹⁴For we have heard him say that this Jesus of Nazareth will destroy this place and change the customs Moses handed down to us."

¹⁵All who were sitting in the Sanhedrin looked intently at Stephen, and they saw that his face was like the face of an angel.

Stephen's Speech to the Sanhedrin

7 Then the high priest asked him, "Are these charges true?"

²To this he replied: "Brothers and fathers, listen to me! The God of glory appeared to our father Abraham while he was still in Mesopotamia, before he lived in Haran. ³'Leave your country and your people,' God said, 'and go to the land I will show you.'ᵃ

⁴"So he left the land of the Chaldeans and settled in Haran. After the death of his father, God sent him to this land where you are now living. ⁵He gave him no inheritance here, not even a foot of ground. But God promised him that he and his descendants after him would possess the land, even though at that time Abraham had no child. ⁶God spoke to him in this way: 'Your descendants will be strangers in a country not their own, and they will be enslaved and mistreated four hundred years. ⁷But I will punish the nation they serve as slaves,' God said, 'and afterward they will come out of that country and worship me in this place.'ᵇ ⁸Then he gave Abraham the covenant of circumcision. And Abraham became the father of Isaac and circumcised him eight days after his birth. Later Isaac became the father of Jacob, and Jacob became the father of the twelve patriarchs.

⁹"Because the patriarchs were jealous of Joseph, they sold him as a slave into Egypt. But God was with him ¹⁰and rescued him from all his troubles. He gave Joseph wisdom and enabled him to gain the goodwill of Pharaoh king of Egypt; so he made him ruler over Egypt and all his palace. ¹¹"Then a famine struck all Egypt

VERSE:	AUTHOR:	PASSAGE:
Acts 6:3	Ted Engstrom	Acts 6:1–7

The Language of Love

During the worst days of World War II, a wounded G.I. sat up on his cot in a field hospital and watched a volunteer nurse dress the putrid wounds of a wounded soldier. The G.I. shook his head. "I wouldn't do that for a million dollars," he said. With a smile the nurse replied, "Neither would I."

Voluntarism today is not limited to mobilization for war. It extends to city streets, playgrounds, classrooms, churches, mission fields, camps, and even to such mundane venues as mailing rooms of service agencies. It began a long time ago in Jerusalem when twelve apostles appealed to Jewish Christians in the early church to make certain that Greek widows had enough food to eat and a place to live [Acts 6:1–7] . . .

Today people like us in the last third of life are signing on as volunteers in record numbers. We want to see and feel the need and work as partners with those on the scene looking for solutions. If national and international vision is to be extended, short-term service is the key.

With your extra time, how about taking a look at the options for volunteer work open to you? Instead of booking passage on a Caribbean cruise . . . sign on for a volunteer short-term mission. Call it a vacation with a purpose — a refreshing change for you and your spouse.

ADDITIONAL SCRIPTURE READINGS
Romans 12:3–16; 1 Peter 4:7–11

Go to page 1394 for your next devotional reading.

and Canaan, bringing great suffering, and our fathers could not find food. ¹²When Jacob heard that there was grain in Egypt, he sent our fathers on their first visit. ¹³On their second visit, Joseph told his brothers who he was, and Pharaoh learned about Joseph's family. ¹⁴After this, Joseph sent for his father Jacob and his whole family, seventy-five in all. ¹⁵Then Jacob went down to Egypt, where he and our fathers died. ¹⁶Their bodies were brought back to Shechem and placed in the tomb that Abraham had bought from the sons of Hamor at Shechem for a certain sum of money.

¹⁷"As the time drew near for God to fulfill his promise to Abraham, the number of our people in Egypt greatly increased. ¹⁸Then another king, who knew nothing about Joseph, became ruler of Egypt. ¹⁹He dealt treacherously with our people and oppressed our forefathers by forcing them to throw out their newborn babies so that they would die.

²⁰"At that time Moses was born, and he was no ordinary child.ᵃ For three months he was cared for in his father's house. ²¹When he was placed outside, Pharaoh's daughter took him and brought him up as her own son. ²²Moses was educated in all the wisdom of the Egyptians and was powerful in speech and action.

²³"When Moses was forty years old, he decided to visit his fellow Israelites. ²⁴He saw one of them being mistreated by an Egyptian, so he went to his defense and avenged him by killing the Egyptian. ²⁵Moses thought that his own people would realize that God was using him to rescue them, but they did not. ²⁶The next day Moses came upon two Israelites who were fighting. He tried to reconcile them by saying, 'Men, you are brothers; why do you want to hurt each other?'

²⁷"But the man who was mistreating the other pushed Moses aside and said, 'Who made you ruler and judge over us? ²⁸Do you want to kill me as you killed the Egyptian yesterday?'ᵇ ²⁹When Moses heard this, he fled to Midian, where he settled as a foreigner and had two sons.

³⁰"After forty years had passed, an angel appeared to Moses in the flames of a burning bush in the desert near Mount Sinai. ³¹When he saw this, he was amazed at the sight. As he went over to look more closely, he heard the Lord's voice: ³²'I am the God of your fathers, the God of Abraham, Isaac and Jacob.'ᶜ Moses trembled with fear and did not dare to look.

³³"Then the Lord said to him, 'Take off your sandals; the place where you are standing is holy ground. ³⁴I have indeed seen the oppression of my people in Egypt. I have heard their groaning and have come down to set them free. Now come, I will send you back to Egypt.'ᵈ

³⁵"This is the same Moses whom they had rejected with the words, 'Who made you ruler and judge?' He was sent to be their ruler and deliverer by God himself, through the angel who appeared to him in the bush. ³⁶He led them out of Egypt and did wonders and miraculous signs in Egypt, at the Red Seaᵉ and for forty years in the desert.

³⁷"This is that Moses who told the Israelites, 'God will send you a prophet like me from your own people.'ᶠ ³⁸He was in the assembly in the desert, with the angel who spoke to him on Mount Sinai, and with our fathers; and he received living words to pass on to us.

³⁹"But our fathers refused to obey him. Instead, they rejected him and in their hearts turned back to Egypt. ⁴⁰They told Aaron, 'Make us gods who will go before us. As for this fellow Moses who led us out of Egypt— we don't know what has happened to him!'ᵍ ⁴¹That was the time they made an idol in the form of a calf. They brought sacrifices to it and held a celebration in honor of what their

---

ᵃ20 Or *was fair in the sight of God*   ᵇ28 Exodus 2:14   ᶜ32 Exodus 3:6   ᵈ34 Exodus 3:5,7,8,10   ᵉ36 That is, Sea of Reeds   ᶠ37 Deut. 18:15   ᵍ40 Exodus 32:1

hands had made. ⁴²But God turned away and gave them over to the worship of the heavenly bodies. This agrees with what is written in the book of the prophets:

" 'Did you bring me sacrifices and
    offerings
forty years in the desert,
    O house of Israel?
⁴³You have lifted up the shrine of
    Molech
    and the star of your god
    Rephan,
    the idols you made to worship.
Therefore I will send you into
    exile'ᵃ beyond Babylon.

⁴⁴"Our forefathers had the tabernacle of the Testimony with them in the desert. It had been made as God directed Moses, according to the pattern he had seen. ⁴⁵Having received the tabernacle, our fathers under Joshua brought it with them when they took the land from the nations God drove out before them. It remained in the land until the time of David, ⁴⁶who enjoyed God's favor and asked that he might provide a dwelling place for the God of Jacob.ᵇ ⁴⁷But it was Solomon who built the house for him.

⁴⁸"However, the Most High does not live in houses made by men. As the prophet says:

⁴⁹" 'Heaven is my throne,
    and the earth is my footstool.
What kind of house will you build
    for me?
                        says the Lord.
Or where will my resting place
    be?
⁵⁰Has not my hand made all these
    things?'ᶜ

⁵¹"You stiff-necked people, with uncircumcised hearts and ears! You are just like your fathers: You always resist the Holy Spirit! ⁵²Was there ever a prophet your fathers did not persecute? They even killed those who predicted the coming of the Righteous One. And now you have betrayed and murdered him— ⁵³you who have received the law that was put into effect through angels but have not obeyed it."

The Stoning of Stephen

⁵⁴When they heard this, they were furious and gnashed their teeth at him. ⁵⁵But Stephen, full of the Holy Spirit, looked up to heaven and saw the glory of God, and Jesus standing at the right hand of God. ⁵⁶"Look," he said, "I see heaven open and the Son of Man standing at the right hand of God."

⁵⁷At this they covered their ears and, yelling at the top of their voices, they all rushed at him, ⁵⁸dragged him out of the city and began to stone him. Meanwhile, the witnesses laid their clothes at the feet of a young man named Saul.

⁵⁹While they were stoning him, Stephen prayed, "Lord Jesus, receive my spirit." ⁶⁰Then he fell on his knees and cried out, "Lord, do not hold this sin against them." When he had said this, he fell asleep.

8 And Saul was there, giving approval to his death.

The Church Persecuted and Scattered

On that day a great persecution broke out against the church at Jerusalem, and all except the apostles were scattered throughout Judea and Samaria. ²Godly men buried Stephen and mourned deeply for him. ³But Saul began to destroy the church. Going from house to house, he dragged off men and women and put them in prison.

Philip in Samaria

⁴Those who had been scattered preached the word wherever they went. ⁵Philip went down to a city in Samaria and proclaimed the Christᵈ there. ⁶When the crowds heard Philip and saw the miraculous signs he did,

ᵃ43 Amos 5:25-27   ᵇ46 Some early manuscripts *the house of Jacob*   ᶜ50 Isaiah 66:1,2
ᵈ5 Or *Messiah*

they all paid close attention to what he said. [7]With shrieks, evil[a] spirits came out of many, and many paralytics and cripples were healed. [8]So there was great joy in that city.

Simon the Sorcerer

[9]Now for some time a man named Simon had practiced sorcery in the city and amazed all the people of Samaria. He boasted that he was someone great, [10]and all the people, both high and low, gave him their attention and exclaimed, "This man is the divine power known as the Great Power." [11]They followed him because he had amazed them for a long time with his magic. [12]But when they believed Philip as he preached the good news of the kingdom of God and the name of Jesus Christ, they were baptized, both men and women. [13]Simon himself believed and was baptized. And he followed Philip everywhere, astonished by the great signs and miracles he saw.

[14]When the apostles in Jerusalem heard that Samaria had accepted the word of God, they sent Peter and John to them. [15]When they arrived, they prayed for them that they might receive the Holy Spirit, [16]because the Holy Spirit had not yet come upon any of them; they had simply been baptized into[b] the name of the Lord Jesus. [17]Then Peter and John placed their hands on them, and they received the Holy Spirit.

[18]When Simon saw that the Spirit was given at the laying on of the apostles' hands, he offered them money [19]and said, "Give me also this ability so that everyone on whom I lay my hands may receive the Holy Spirit."

[20]Peter answered: "May your money perish with you, because you thought you could buy the gift of God with money! [21]You have no part or share in this ministry, because your heart is not right before God. [22]Repent of this wickedness and pray to the Lord. Perhaps he will forgive you for having such a thought in your heart.

[23]For I see that you are full of bitterness and captive to sin."

[24]Then Simon answered, "Pray to the Lord for me so that nothing you have said may happen to me."

[25]When they had testified and proclaimed the word of the Lord, Peter and John returned to Jerusalem, preaching the gospel in many Samaritan villages.

Philip and the Ethiopian

[26]Now an angel of the Lord said to Philip, "Go south to the road—the desert road—that goes down from Jerusalem to Gaza." [27]So he started out, and on his way he met an Ethiopian[c] eunuch, an important official in charge of all the treasury of Candace, queen of the Ethiopians. This man had gone to Jerusalem to worship, [28]and on his way home was sitting in his chariot reading the book of Isaiah the prophet. [29]The Spirit told Philip, "Go to that chariot and stay near it."

[30]Then Philip ran up to the chariot and heard the man reading Isaiah the prophet. "Do you understand what you are reading?" Philip asked.

[31]"How can I," he said, "unless someone explains it to me?" So he invited Philip to come up and sit with him.

[32]The eunuch was reading this passage of Scripture:

"He was led like a sheep to the
    slaughter,
  and as a lamb before the
    shearer is silent,
  so he did not open his mouth.
[33]In his humiliation he was
    deprived of justice.
  Who can speak of his
    descendants?
  For his life was taken from the
    earth."[d]

[34]The eunuch asked Philip, "Tell me, please, who is the prophet talking about, himself or someone else?" [35]Then Philip began with that very passage of Scripture and told him the good news about Jesus.

---

[a]7 Greek unclean   [b]16 Or in   [c]27 That is, from the upper Nile region   [d]33 Isaiah 53:7,8

³⁶As they traveled along the road, they came to some water and the eunuch said, "Look, here is water. Why shouldn't I be baptized?"ᵃ ³⁸And he gave orders to stop the chariot. Then both Philip and the eunuch went down into the water and Philip baptized him. ³⁹When they came up out of the water, the Spirit of the Lord suddenly took Philip away, and the eunuch did not see him again, but went on his way rejoicing. ⁴⁰Philip, however, appeared at Azotus and traveled about, preaching the gospel in all the towns until he reached Caesarea.

Saul's Conversion

9 Meanwhile, Saul was still breathing out murderous threats against the Lord's disciples. He went to the high priest ²and asked him for letters to the synagogues in Damascus, so that if he found any there who belonged to the Way, whether men or women, he might take them as prisoners to Jerusalem. ³As he neared Damascus on his journey, suddenly a light from heaven flashed around him. ⁴He fell to the ground and heard a voice say to him, "Saul, Saul, why do you persecute me?"

⁵"Who are you, Lord?" Saul asked.
"I am Jesus, whom you are persecuting," he replied. ⁶"Now get up and go into the city, and you will be told what you must do."

⁷The men traveling with Saul stood there speechless; they heard the sound but did not see anyone. ⁸Saul got up from the ground, but when he opened his eyes he could see nothing. So they led him by the hand into Damascus. ⁹For three days he was blind, and did not eat or drink anything.

¹⁰In Damascus there was a disciple named Ananias. The Lord called to him in a vision, "Ananias!"

"Yes, Lord," he answered.

¹¹The Lord told him, "Go to the house of Judas on Straight Street and ask for a man from Tarsus named Saul, for he is praying. ¹²In a vision he has seen a man named Ananias come and place his hands on him to restore his sight."

¹³"Lord," Ananias answered, "I have heard many reports about this man and all the harm he has done to your saints in Jerusalem. ¹⁴And he has come here with authority from the chief priests to arrest all who call on your name."

¹⁵But the Lord said to Ananias, "Go! This man is my chosen instrument to carry my name before the Gentiles and their kings and before the people of Israel. ¹⁶I will show him how much he must suffer for my name."

¹⁷Then Ananias went to the house and entered it. Placing his hands on Saul, he said, "Brother Saul, the Lord—Jesus, who appeared to you on the road as you were coming here—has sent me so that you may see again and be filled with the Holy Spirit." ¹⁸Immediately, something like scales fell from Saul's eyes, and he could see again. He got up and was baptized, ¹⁹and after taking some food, he regained his strength.

Saul in Damascus and Jerusalem

Saul spent several days with the disciples in Damascus. ²⁰At once he began to preach in the synagogues that Jesus is the Son of God. ²¹All those who heard him were astonished and asked, "Isn't he the man who raised havoc in Jerusalem among those who call on this name? And hasn't he come here to take them as prisoners to the chief priests?" ²²Yet Saul grew more and more powerful and baffled the Jews living in Damascus by proving that Jesus is the Christ.ᵇ

²³After many days had gone by, the Jews conspired to kill him, ²⁴but Saul learned of their plan. Day and night they kept close watch on the city gates in order to kill him. ²⁵But his followers took him by night and lowered

---

ᵃ36 Some late manuscripts baptized?" ³⁷Philip said, "If you believe with all your heart, you may." The eunuch answered, "I believe that Jesus Christ is the Son of God."   ᵇ22 Or Messiah

him in a basket through an opening in the wall.

26When he came to Jerusalem, he tried to join the disciples, but they were all afraid of him, not believing that he really was a disciple. 27But Barnabas took him and brought him to the apostles. He told them how Saul on his journey had seen the Lord and that the Lord had spoken to him, and how in Damascus he had preached fearlessly in the name of Jesus. 28So Saul stayed with them and moved about freely in Jerusalem, speaking boldly in the name of the Lord. 29He talked and debated with the Grecian Jews, but they tried to kill him. 30When the brothers learned of this, they took him down to Caesarea and sent him off to Tarsus.

31Then the church throughout Judea, Galilee and Samaria enjoyed a time of peace. It was strengthened; and encouraged by the Holy Spirit, it grew in numbers, living in the fear of the Lord.

Aeneas and Dorcas

32As Peter traveled about the country, he went to visit the saints in Lydda. 33There he found a man named Aeneas, a paralytic who had been bedridden for eight years. 34"Aeneas," Peter said to him, "Jesus Christ heals you. Get up and take care of your mat." Immediately Aeneas got up. 35All those who lived in Lydda and Sharon saw him and turned to the Lord.

36In Joppa there was a disciple named Tabitha (which, when translated, is Dorcas[a]), who was always doing good and helping the poor. 37About that time she became sick and died, and her body was washed and placed in an upstairs room. 38Lydda was near Joppa; so when the disciples heard that Peter was in Lydda, they sent two men to him and urged him, "Please come at once!"

39Peter went with them, and when he arrived he was taken upstairs to the room. All the widows stood around him, crying and showing him the robes and other clothing that Dorcas had made while she was still with them.

40Peter sent them all out of the room; then he got down on his knees and prayed. Turning toward the dead woman, he said, "Tabitha, get up." She opened her eyes, and seeing Peter she sat up. 41He took her by the hand and helped her to her feet. Then he called the believers and the widows and presented her to them alive. 42This became known all over Joppa, and many people believed in the Lord. 43Peter stayed in Joppa for some time with a tanner named Simon.

Cornelius Calls for Peter

10 At Caesarea there was a man named Cornelius, a centurion in what was known as the Italian Regiment. 2He and all his family were devout and God-fearing; he gave generously to those in need and prayed to God regularly. 3One day at about three in the afternoon he had a vision. He distinctly saw an angel of God, who came to him and said, "Cornelius!"

4Cornelius stared at him in fear. "What is it, Lord?" he asked.

The angel answered, "Your prayers and gifts to the poor have come up as a memorial offering before God. 5Now send men to Joppa to bring back a man named Simon who is called Peter. 6He is staying with Simon the tanner, whose house is by the sea."

7When the angel who spoke to him had gone, Cornelius called two of his servants and a devout soldier who was one of his attendants. 8He told them everything that had happened and sent them to Joppa.

Peter's Vision

9About noon the following day as they were on their journey and approaching the city, Peter went up on the roof to pray. 10He became hungry and wanted something to eat, and

---

a36 Both *Tabitha* (Aramaic) and *Dorcas* (Greek) mean *gazelle*.

while the meal was being prepared, he fell into a trance. [11]He saw heaven opened and something like a large sheet being let down to earth by its four corners. [12]It contained all kinds of four-footed animals, as well as reptiles of the earth and birds of the air. [13]Then a voice told him, "Get up, Peter. Kill and eat."

[14]"Surely not, Lord!" Peter replied. "I have never eaten anything impure or unclean."

[15]The voice spoke to him a second time, "Do not call anything impure that God has made clean."

[16]This happened three times, and immediately the sheet was taken back to heaven.

[17]While Peter was wondering about the meaning of the vision, the men sent by Cornelius found out where Simon's house was and stopped at the gate. [18]They called out, asking if Simon who was known as Peter was staying there.

[19]While Peter was still thinking about the vision, the Spirit said to him, "Simon, three[a] men are looking for you. [20]So get up and go downstairs. Do not hesitate to go with them, for I have sent them."

[21]Peter went down and said to the men, "I'm the one you're looking for. Why have you come?"

[22]The men replied, "We have come from Cornelius the centurion. He is a righteous and God-fearing man, who is respected by all the Jewish people. A holy angel told him to have you come to his house so that he could hear what you have to say." [23]Then Peter invited the men into the house to be his guests.

Peter at Cornelius' House

The next day Peter started out with them, and some of the brothers from Joppa went along. [24]The following day he arrived in Caesarea. Cornelius was expecting them and had called together his relatives and close friends. [25]As Peter entered the house, Cornelius met him and fell at his feet

in reverence. [26]But Peter made him get up. "Stand up," he said, "I am only a man myself."

[27]Talking with him, Peter went inside and found a large gathering of people. [28]He said to them: "You are well aware that it is against our law for a Jew to associate with a Gentile or visit him. But God has shown me that I should not call any man impure or unclean. [29]So when I was sent for, I came without raising any objection. May I ask why you sent for me?"

[30]Cornelius answered: "Four days ago I was in my house praying at this hour, at three in the afternoon. Suddenly a man in shining clothes stood before me [31]and said, 'Cornelius, God has heard your prayer and remembered your gifts to the poor. [32]Send to Joppa for Simon who is called Peter. He is a guest in the home of Simon the tanner, who lives by the sea.' [33]So I sent for you immediately, and it was good of you to come. Now we are all here in the presence of God to listen to everything the Lord has commanded you to tell us."

[34]Then Peter began to speak: "I now realize how true it is that God does not show favoritism [35]but accepts men from every nation who fear him and do what is right. [36]You know the message God sent to the people of Israel, telling the good news of peace through Jesus Christ, who is Lord of all. [37]You know what has happened throughout Judea, beginning in Galilee after the baptism that John preached— [38]how God anointed Jesus of Nazareth with the Holy Spirit and power, and how he went around doing good and healing all who were under the power of the devil, because God was with him.

[39]"We are witnesses of everything he did in the country of the Jews and in Jerusalem. They killed him by hanging him on a tree, [40]but God raised him from the dead on the third day and caused him to be seen. [41]He was not seen by all the people, but by witnesses whom God had already

---

[a]19 One early manuscript *two*; other manuscripts do not have the number.

chosen—by us who ate and drank with him after he rose from the dead. [42]He commanded us to preach to the people and to testify that he is the one whom God appointed as judge of the living and the dead. [43]All the prophets testify about him that everyone who believes in him receives forgiveness of sins through his name."

[44]While Peter was still speaking these words, the Holy Spirit came on all who heard the message. [45]The circumcised believers who had come with Peter were astonished that the gift of the Holy Spirit had been poured out even on the Gentiles. [46]For they heard them speaking in tongues[a] and praising God.

Then Peter said, [47]"Can anyone keep these people from being baptized with water? They have received the Holy Spirit just as we have." [48]So he ordered that they be baptized in the name of Jesus Christ. Then they asked Peter to stay with them for a few days.

Peter Explains His Actions

11 The apostles and the brothers throughout Judea heard that the Gentiles also had received the word of God. [2]So when Peter went up to Jerusalem, the circumcised believers criticized him [3]and said, "You went into the house of uncircumcised men and ate with them."

[4]Peter began and explained everything to them precisely as it had happened: [5]"I was in the city of Joppa praying, and in a trance I saw a vision. I saw something like a large sheet being let down from heaven by its four corners, and it came down to where I was. [6]I looked into it and saw four-footed animals of the earth, wild beasts, reptiles, and birds of the air. [7]Then I heard a voice telling me, 'Get up, Peter. Kill and eat.'

[8]"I replied, 'Surely not, Lord! Nothing impure or unclean has ever entered my mouth.'

[9]"The voice spoke from heaven a second time, 'Do not call anything impure that God has made clean.' [10]This happened three times, and then it was all pulled up to heaven again.

[11]"Right then three men who had been sent to me from Caesarea stopped at the house where I was staying. [12]The Spirit told me to have no hesitation about going with them. These six brothers also went with me, and we entered the man's house. [13]He told us how he had seen an angel appear in his house and say, 'Send to Joppa for Simon who is called Peter. [14]He will bring you a message through which you and all your household will be saved.'

[15]"As I began to speak, the Holy Spirit came on them as he had come on us at the beginning. [16]Then I remembered what the Lord had said: 'John baptized with[b] water, but you will be baptized with the Holy Spirit.' [17]So if God gave them the same gift as he gave us, who believed in the Lord Jesus Christ, who was I to think that I could oppose God?"

[18]When they heard this, they had no further objections and praised God, saying, "So then, God has granted even the Gentiles repentance unto life."

The Church in Antioch

[19]Now those who had been scattered by the persecution in connection with Stephen traveled as far as Phoenicia, Cyprus and Antioch, telling the message only to Jews. [20]Some of them, however, men from Cyprus and Cyrene, went to Antioch and began to speak to Greeks also, telling them the good news about the Lord Jesus. [21]The Lord's hand was with them, and a great number of people believed and turned to the Lord.

[22]News of this reached the ears of the church at Jerusalem, and they sent Barnabas to Antioch. [23]When he arrived and saw the evidence of the grace of God, he was glad and encouraged them all to remain true to the Lord with all their hearts. [24]He was a good man, full of the Holy Spir-

---

[a]46 Or other languages   [b]16 Or in

it and faith, and a great number of people were brought to the Lord.

²⁵Then Barnabas went to Tarsus to look for Saul, ²⁶and when he found him, he brought him to Antioch. So for a whole year Barnabas and Saul met with the church and taught great numbers of people. The disciples were called Christians first at Antioch.

²⁷During this time some prophets came down from Jerusalem to Antioch. ²⁸One of them, named Agabus, stood up and through the Spirit predicted that a severe famine would spread over the entire Roman world. (This happened during the reign of Claudius.) ²⁹The disciples, each according to his ability, decided to provide help for the brothers living in Judea. ³⁰This they did, sending their gift to the elders by Barnabas and Saul.

Peter's Miraculous Escape From Prison

12 It was about this time that King Herod arrested some who belonged to the church, intending to persecute them. ²He had James, the brother of John, put to death with the sword. ³When he saw that this pleased the Jews, he proceeded to seize Peter also. This happened during the Feast of Unleavened Bread. ⁴After arresting him, he put him in prison, handing him over to be guarded by four squads of four soldiers each. Herod intended to bring him out for public trial after the Passover.

⁵So Peter was kept in prison, but the church was earnestly praying to God for him.

⁶The night before Herod was to bring him to trial, Peter was sleeping between two soldiers, bound with two chains, and sentries stood guard at the entrance. ⁷Suddenly an angel of the Lord appeared and a light shone in the cell. He struck Peter on the side and woke him up. "Quick, get up!" he said, and the chains fell off Peter's wrists.

⁸Then the angel said to him, "Put on your clothes and sandals." And Peter did so. "Wrap your cloak around you and follow me," the angel told him. ⁹Peter followed him out of the prison, but he had no idea that what the angel was doing was really happening; he thought he was seeing a vision. ¹⁰They passed the first and second guards and came to the iron gate leading to the city. It opened for them by itself, and they went through it. When they had walked the length of one street, suddenly the angel left him.

¹¹Then Peter came to himself and said, "Now I know without a doubt that the Lord sent his angel and rescued me from Herod's clutches and from everything the Jewish people were anticipating."

¹²When this had dawned on him, he went to the house of Mary the mother of John, also called Mark, where many people had gathered and were praying. ¹³Peter knocked at the outer entrance, and a servant girl named Rhoda came to answer the door. ¹⁴When she recognized Peter's voice, she was so overjoyed she ran back without opening it and exclaimed, "Peter is at the door!"

¹⁵"You're out of your mind," they told her. When she kept insisting that it was so, they said, "It must be his angel."

¹⁶But Peter kept on knocking, and when they opened the door and saw him, they were astonished. ¹⁷Peter motioned with his hand for them to be quiet and described how the Lord had brought him out of prison. "Tell James and the brothers about this," he said, and then he left for another place.

¹⁸In the morning, there was no small commotion among the soldiers as to what had become of Peter. ¹⁹After Herod had a thorough search made for him and did not find him, he cross-examined the guards and ordered that they be executed.

Herod's Death

Then Herod went from Judea to Caesarea and stayed there a while.

[20]He had been quarreling with the people of Tyre and Sidon; they now joined together and sought an audience with him. Having secured the support of Blastus, a trusted personal servant of the king, they asked for peace, because they depended on the king's country for their food supply. [21]On the appointed day Herod, wearing his royal robes, sat on his throne and delivered a public address to the people. [22]They shouted, "This is the voice of a god, not of a man." [23]Immediately, because Herod did not give praise to God, an angel of the Lord struck him down, and he was eaten by worms and died.

[24]But the word of God continued to increase and spread.

[25]When Barnabas and Saul had finished their mission, they returned from[a] Jerusalem, taking with them John, also called Mark.

Barnabas and Saul Sent Off

13 In the church at Antioch there were prophets and teachers: Barnabas, Simeon called Niger, Lucius of Cyrene, Manaen (who had been brought up with Herod the tetrarch) and Saul. [2]While they were worshiping the Lord and fasting, the Holy Spirit said, "Set apart for me Barnabas and Saul for the work to which I have called them." [3]So after they had fasted and prayed, they placed their hands on them and sent them off.

On Cyprus

[4]The two of them, sent on their way by the Holy Spirit, went down to Seleucia and sailed from there to Cyprus. [5]When they arrived at Salamis, they proclaimed the word of God in the Jewish synagogues. John was with them as their helper.

[6]They traveled through the whole island until they came to Paphos. There they met a Jewish sorcerer and false prophet named Bar-Jesus, [7]who was an attendant of the proconsul, Sergius Paulus. The proconsul, an intelligent man, sent for Barnabas and

Saul because he wanted to hear the word of God. [8]But Elymas the sorcerer (for that is what his name means) opposed them and tried to turn the proconsul from the faith. [9]Then Saul, who was also called Paul, filled with the Holy Spirit, looked straight at Elymas and said, [10]"You are a child of the devil and an enemy of everything that is right! You are full of all kinds of deceit and trickery. Will you never stop perverting the right ways of the Lord? [11]Now the hand of the Lord is against you. You are going to be blind, and for a time you will be unable to see the light of the sun."

Immediately mist and darkness came over him, and he groped about, seeking someone to lead him by the hand. [12]When the proconsul saw what had happened, he believed, for he was amazed at the teaching about the Lord.

In Pisidian Antioch

[13]From Paphos, Paul and his companions sailed to Perga in Pamphylia, where John left them to return to Jerusalem. [14]From Perga they went on to Pisidian Antioch. On the Sabbath they entered the synagogue and sat down. [15]After the reading from the Law and the Prophets, the synagogue rulers sent word to them, saying, "Brothers, if you have a message of encouragement for the people, please speak."

[16]Standing up, Paul motioned with his hand and said: "Men of Israel and you Gentiles who worship God, listen to me! [17]The God of the people of Israel chose our fathers; he made the people prosper during their stay in Egypt, with mighty power he led them out of that country, [18]he endured their conduct[b] for about forty years in the desert, [19]he overthrew seven nations in Canaan and gave their land to his people as their inheritance. [20]All this took about 450 years.

"After this, God gave them judges until the time of Samuel the prophet. [21]Then the people asked for a king, and he gave them Saul son of Kish, of

---

[a]25 Some manuscripts *to*   [b]18 Some manuscripts *and cared for them*

the tribe of Benjamin, who ruled forty years. ²²After removing Saul, he made David their king. He testified concerning him: 'I have found David son of Jesse a man after my own heart; he will do everything I want him to do.' ²³"From this man's descendants God has brought to Israel the Savior Jesus, as he promised. ²⁴Before the coming of Jesus, John preached repentance and baptism to all the people of Israel. ²⁵As John was completing his work, he said: 'Who do you think I am? I am not that one. No, but he is coming after me, whose sandals I am not worthy to untie.'

²⁶"Brothers, children of Abraham, and you God-fearing Gentiles, it is to us that this message of salvation has been sent. ²⁷The people of Jerusalem and their rulers did not recognize Jesus, yet in condemning him they fulfilled the words of the prophets that are read every Sabbath. ²⁸Though they found no proper ground for a death sentence, they asked Pilate to have him executed. ²⁹When they had carried out all that was written about him, they took him down from the tree and laid him in a tomb. ³⁰But God raised him from the dead, ³¹and for many days he was seen by those who had traveled with him from Galilee to Jerusalem. They are now his witnesses to our people.

³²"We tell you the good news: What God promised our fathers ³³he has fulfilled for us, their children, by raising up Jesus. As it is written in the second Psalm:

" 'You are my Son;
today I have become your
Father.'ᵃ′ᵇ

³⁴The fact that God raised him from the dead, never to decay, is stated in these words:

" 'I will give you the holy and
sure blessings promised to
David.'ᶜ

³⁵So it is stated elsewhere:

" 'You will not let your Holy One
see decay.'ᵈ

³⁶"For when David had served God's purpose in his own generation, he fell asleep; he was buried with his fathers and his body decayed. ³⁷But the one whom God raised from the dead did not see decay.

³⁸"Therefore, my brothers, I want you to know that through Jesus the forgiveness of sins is proclaimed to you. ³⁹Through him everyone who believes is justified from everything you could not be justified from by the law of Moses. ⁴⁰Take care that what the prophets have said does not happen to you:

⁴¹" 'Look, you scoffers,
wonder and perish,
for I am going to do something in
your days
that you would never believe,
even if someone told you.'ᵉ"

⁴²As Paul and Barnabas were leaving the synagogue, the people invited them to speak further about these things on the next Sabbath. ⁴³When the congregation was dismissed, many of the Jews and devout converts to Judaism followed Paul and Barnabas, who talked with them and urged them to continue in the grace of God.

⁴⁴On the next Sabbath almost the whole city gathered to hear the word of the Lord. ⁴⁵When the Jews saw the crowds, they were filled with jealousy and talked abusively against what Paul was saying.

⁴⁶Then Paul and Barnabas answered them boldly: "We had to speak the word of God to you first. Since you reject it and do not consider yourselves worthy of eternal life, we now turn to the Gentiles. ⁴⁷For this is what the Lord has commanded us:

" 'I have made youᶠ a light for
the Gentiles,

ᵃ33 Or *have begotten you*   ᵇ33 Psalm 2:7   ᶜ34 Isaiah 55:3   ᵈ35 Psalm 16:10
ᵉ41 Hab. 1:5   ᶠ47 The Greek is singular.

that you[a] may bring salvation
to the ends of the
earth.'[b]"

⁴⁸When the Gentiles heard this,
they were glad and honored the word
of the Lord; and all who were appointed for eternal life believed.

⁴⁹The word of the Lord spread
through the whole region. ⁵⁰But the
Jews incited the God-fearing women
of high standing and the leading men
of the city. They stirred up persecution against Paul and Barnabas, and
expelled them from their region. ⁵¹So
they shook the dust from their feet in
protest against them and went to Iconium. ⁵²And the disciples were filled
with joy and with the Holy Spirit.

In Iconium

14 At Iconium Paul and Barnabas
went as usual into the Jewish
synagogue. There they spoke so effectively that a great number of Jews and
Gentiles believed. ²But the Jews who
refused to believe stirred up the Gentiles and poisoned their minds against
the brothers. ³So Paul and Barnabas
spent considerable time there, speaking boldly for the Lord, who confirmed the message of his grace by en-
abling them to do miraculous signs
and wonders. ⁴The people of the city
were divided; some sided with the
Jews, others with the apostles. ⁵There
was a plot afoot among the Gentiles
and Jews, together with their leaders,
to mistreat them and stone them. ⁶But
they found out about it and fled to the
Lycaonian cities of Lystra and Derbe
and to the surrounding country,
⁷where they continued to preach the
good news.

In Lystra and Derbe

⁸In Lystra there sat a man crippled
in his feet, who was lame from birth
and had never walked. ⁹He listened to
Paul as he was speaking. Paul looked
directly at him, saw that he had faith
to be healed ¹⁰and called out, "Stand

up on your feet!" At that, the man
jumped up and began to walk.

¹¹When the crowd saw what Paul
had done, they shouted in the Lycaonian language, "The gods have come
down to us in human form!" ¹²Barna-
bas they called Zeus, and Paul they
called Hermes because he was the
chief speaker. ¹³The priest of Zeus,
whose temple was just outside the
city, brought bulls and wreaths to the
city gates because he and the crowd
wanted to offer sacrifices to them.

¹⁴But when the apostles Barnabas
and Paul heard of this, they tore their
clothes and rushed out into the
crowd, shouting: ¹⁵"Men, why are
you doing this? We too are only men,
human like you. We are bringing you
good news, telling you to turn from
these worthless things to the living
God, who made heaven and earth
and sea and everything in them. ¹⁶In
the past, he let all nations go their
own way. ¹⁷Yet he has not left himself
without testimony: He has shown
kindness by giving you rain from
heaven and crops in their seasons; he
provides you with plenty of food and
fills your hearts with joy." ¹⁸Even
with these words, they had difficulty
keeping the crowd from sacrificing to
them.

¹⁹Then some Jews came from Antioch and Iconium and won the crowd
over. They stoned Paul and dragged
him outside the city, thinking he was
dead. ²⁰But after the disciples had
gathered around him, he got up and
went back into the city. The next day
he and Barnabas left for Derbe.

The Return to Antioch in Syria

²¹They preached the good news in
that city and won a large number of
disciples. Then they returned to Lystra, Iconium and Antioch, ²²strength-
ening the disciples and encouraging
them to remain true to the faith. "We
must go through many hardships to
enter the kingdom of God," they said.
²³Paul and Barnabas appointed el-

---

[a]47 The Greek is singular.   [b]47 Isaiah 49:6

ders[a] for them in each church and, with prayer and fasting, committed them to the Lord, in whom they had put their trust. [24]After going through Pisidia, they came into Pamphylia, [25]and when they had preached the word in Perga, they went down to Attalia.

[26]From Attalia they sailed back to Antioch, where they had been committed to the grace of God for the work they had now completed. [27]On arriving there, they gathered the church together and reported all that God had done through them and how he had opened the door of faith to the Gentiles. [28]And they stayed there a long time with the disciples.

The Council at Jerusalem

15 Some men came down from Judea to Antioch and were teaching the brothers: "Unless you are circumcised, according to the custom taught by Moses, you cannot be saved." [2]This brought Paul and Barnabas into sharp dispute and debate with them. So Paul and Barnabas were appointed, along with some other believers, to go up to Jerusalem to see the apostles and elders about this question. [3]The church sent them on their way, and as they traveled through Phoenicia and Samaria, they told how the Gentiles had been converted. This news made all the brothers very glad. [4]When they came to Jerusalem, they were welcomed by the church and the apostles and elders, to whom they reported everything God had done through them.

[5]Then some of the believers who belonged to the party of the Pharisees stood up and said, "The Gentiles must be circumcised and required to obey the law of Moses."

[6]The apostles and elders met to consider this question. [7]After much discussion, Peter got up and addressed them: "Brothers, you know that some time ago God made a choice among you that the Gentiles might hear from my lips the message of the gospel and believe. [8]God, who knows the heart, showed that he accepted them by giving the Holy Spirit to them, just as he did to us. [9]He made no distinction between us and them, for he purified their hearts by faith. [10]Now then, why do you try to test God by putting on the necks of the disciples a yoke that neither we nor our fathers have been able to bear? [11]No! We believe it is through the grace of our Lord Jesus that we are saved, just as they are."

[12]The whole assembly became silent as they listened to Barnabas and Paul telling about the miraculous signs and wonders God had done among the Gentiles through them. [13]When they finished, James spoke up: "Brothers, listen to me. [14]Simon[b] has described to us how God at first showed his concern by taking from the Gentiles a people for himself. [15]The words of the prophets are in agreement with this, as it is written:

[16]" 'After this I will return
    and rebuild David's fallen tent.
  Its ruins I will rebuild,
    and I will restore it,
[17]that the remnant of men may seek
      the Lord,
    and all the Gentiles who bear
      my name,
  says the Lord, who does these
      things'[c]
[18] that have been known for
      ages.[d]

[19]"It is my judgment, therefore, that we should not make it difficult for the Gentiles who are turning to God. [20]Instead we should write to them, telling them to abstain from food polluted by idols, from sexual immorality, from the meat of strangled animals and from blood. [21]For Moses has been preached in every city from the earliest times and is read in the synagogues on every Sabbath."

a23 Or Barnabas ordained elders; or Barnabas had elders elected   b14 Greek Simeon, a variant of Simon; that is, Peter   c17 Amos 9:11,12   d17,18 Some manuscripts things'— / 18known to the Lord for ages is his work

The Council's Letter to Gentile Believers

22Then the apostles and elders, with the whole church, decided to choose some of their own men and send them to Antioch with Paul and Barnabas. They chose Judas (called Barsabbas) and Silas, two men who were leaders among the brothers. 23With them they sent the following letter:

The apostles and elders, your brothers,

To the Gentile believers in Antioch, Syria and Cilicia:

Greetings.

24We have heard that some went out from us without our authorization and disturbed you, troubling your minds by what they said. 25So we all agreed to choose some men and send them to you with our dear friends Barnabas and Paul— 26men who have risked their lives for the name of our Lord Jesus Christ. 27Therefore we are sending Judas and Silas to confirm by word of mouth what we are writing. 28It seemed good to the Holy Spirit and to us not to burden you with anything beyond the following requirements: 29You are to abstain from food sacrificed to idols, from blood, from the meat of strangled animals and from sexual immorality. You will do well to avoid these things.

Farewell.

30The men were sent off and went down to Antioch, where they gathered the church together and delivered the letter. 31The people read it and were glad for its encouraging message. 32Judas and Silas, who themselves were prophets, said much to encourage and strengthen the brothers. 33After spending some time there, they were sent off by the brothers with the blessing of peace to return to those who had sent them.[a] 35But Paul and Barnabas remained in Antioch, where they and many others taught and preached the word of the Lord.

Disagreement Between Paul and Barnabas

36Some time later Paul said to Barnabas, "Let us go back and visit the brothers in all the towns where we preached the word of the Lord and see how they are doing." 37Barnabas wanted to take John, also called Mark, with them, 38but Paul did not think it wise to take him, because he had deserted them in Pamphylia and had not continued with them in the work. 39They had such a sharp disagreement that they parted company. Barnabas took Mark and sailed for Cyprus, 40but Paul chose Silas and left, commended by the brothers to the grace of the Lord. 41He went through Syria and Cilicia, strengthening the churches.

Timothy Joins Paul and Silas

16 He came to Derbe and then to Lystra, where a disciple named Timothy lived, whose mother was a Jewess and a believer, but whose father was a Greek. 2The brothers at Lystra and Iconium spoke well of him. 3Paul wanted to take him along on the journey, so he circumcised him because of the Jews who lived in that area, for they all knew that his father was a Greek. 4As they traveled from town to town, they delivered the decisions reached by the apostles and elders in Jerusalem for the people to obey. 5So the churches were strengthened in the faith and grew daily in numbers.

Paul's Vision of the Man of Macedonia

6Paul and his companions traveled throughout the region of Phrygia and Galatia, having been kept by the Holy

Spirit from preaching the word in the province of Asia. [7]When they came to the border of Mysia, they tried to enter Bithynia, but the Spirit of Jesus would not allow them to. [8]So they passed by Mysia and went down to Troas. [9]During the night Paul had a vision of a man of Macedonia standing and begging him, "Come over to Macedonia and help us." [10]After Paul had seen the vision, we got ready at once to leave for Macedonia, concluding that God had called us to preach the gospel to them.

Lydia's Conversion in Philippi

[11]From Troas we put out to sea and sailed straight for Samothrace, and the next day on to Neapolis. [12]From there we traveled to Philippi, a Roman colony and the leading city of that district of Macedonia. And we stayed there several days.

[13]On the Sabbath we went outside the city gate to the river, where we expected to find a place of prayer. We sat down and began to speak to the women who had gathered there. [14]One of those listening was a woman named Lydia, a dealer in purple cloth from the city of Thyatira, who was a worshiper of God. The Lord opened her heart to respond to Paul's message. [15]When she and the members of her household were baptized, she invited us to her home. "If you consider me a believer in the Lord," she said, "come and stay at my house." And she persuaded us.

Paul and Silas in Prison

[16]Once when we were going to the place of prayer, we were met by a slave girl who had a spirit by which she predicted the future. She earned a great deal of money for her owners by fortune-telling. [17]This girl followed Paul and the rest of us, shouting, "These men are servants of the Most High God, who are telling you the way to be saved." [18]She kept this up for many days. Finally Paul became so troubled that he turned around and said to the spirit, "In the name of Jesus Christ I command you to come

out of her!" At that moment the spirit left her.

[19]When the owners of the slave girl realized that their hope of making money was gone, they seized Paul and Silas and dragged them into the marketplace to face the authorities. [20]They brought them before the magistrates and said, "These men are Jews, and are throwing our city into an uproar [21]by advocating customs unlawful for us Romans to accept or practice."

[22]The crowd joined in the attack against Paul and Silas, and the magistrates ordered them to be stripped and beaten. [23]After they had been severely flogged, they were thrown into prison, and the jailer was commanded to guard them carefully. [24]Upon receiving such orders, he put them in the inner cell and fastened their feet in the stocks.

[25]About midnight Paul and Silas were praying and singing hymns to God, and the other prisoners were listening to them. [26]Suddenly there was such a violent earthquake that the foundations of the prison were shaken. At once all the prison doors flew open, and everybody's chains came loose. [27]The jailer woke up, and when he saw the prison doors open, he drew his sword and was about to kill himself because he thought the prisoners had escaped. [28]But Paul shouted, "Don't harm yourself! We are all here!"

[29]The jailer called for lights, rushed in and fell trembling before Paul and Silas. [30]He then brought them out and asked, "Sirs, what must I do to be saved?"

[31]They replied, "Believe in the Lord Jesus, and you will be saved—you and your household." [32]Then they spoke the word of the Lord to him and to all the others in his house. [33]At that hour of the night the jailer took them and washed their wounds; then immediately he and all his family were baptized. [34]The jailer brought them into his house and set a meal before them; he was filled with joy be-

VERSE:	AUTHOR:	PASSAGE:
Acts 16:25	Paul B. Maves	Acts 16:16–36

Singing at Midnight

It is hard to deal with the fact that evil exists. It is even harder to explain why suffering is so unequally distributed among us. It is still more difficult to live with the suffering when it is visited on us or on those close to us. That is one side of the coin.

The other side of the coin is that in spite of suffering, many persons have learned how to endure suffering gracefully, to rise above the pain and to find joy in the midst of it.

If any person ever had occasion to rail against fate, it was the apostle Paul. Acts 16 describes how Paul and Silas ... were chained in the dungeons instead of being given an impartial trial. Most of us would have burned with anger, filled with apprehension if not despair. But when midnight came Paul and Silas were praying and singing hymns to God. As they sang, the prison doors were opened, their jailer was converted, and they were set free ...

My basic worth comes from the fact that I am one whom God loves so much that he sent his only Son so that I might be saved and given new life. In Christ we see God reaching across pain-filled gulfs, reconciling us to each other and all of us to him ... It is in the light of that knowledge that we can join with Paul and Silas in singing, even at midnight, in the darkest hour of our lives, while we wait for the doors of the prison to open and the daylight to dawn.

ADDITIONAL SCRIPTURE READINGS
2 Corinthians 4:7–18; Philippians 3:1–11

Go to page 1397 for your next devotional reading.

cause he had come to believe in God—he and his whole family.

35When it was daylight, the magistrates sent their officers to the jailer with the order: "Release those men." 36The jailer told Paul, "The magistrates have ordered that you and Silas be released. Now you can leave. Go in peace."

37But Paul said to the officers: "They beat us publicly without a trial, even though we are Roman citizens, and threw us into prison. And now do they want to get rid of us quietly? No! Let them come themselves and escort us out."

38The officers reported this to the magistrates, and when they heard that Paul and Silas were Roman citizens, they were alarmed. 39They came to appease them and escorted them from the prison, requesting them to leave the city. 40After Paul and Silas came out of the prison, they went to Lydia's house, where they met with the brothers and encouraged them. Then they left.

In Thessalonica

17 When they had passed through Amphipolis and Apollonia, they came to Thessalonica, where there was a Jewish synagogue. 2As his custom was, Paul went into the synagogue, and on three Sabbath days he reasoned with them from the Scriptures, 3explaining and proving that the Christ*a* had to suffer and rise from the dead. "This Jesus I am proclaiming to you is the Christ,*a*" he said. 4Some of the Jews were persuaded and joined Paul and Silas, as did a large number of God-fearing Greeks and not a few prominent women.

5But the Jews were jealous; so they rounded up some bad characters from the marketplace, formed a mob and started a riot in the city. They rushed to Jason's house in search of Paul and Silas in order to bring them out to the crowd.*b* 6But when they did not find them, they dragged Jason and some other brothers before the city officials,

shouting: "These men who have caused trouble all over the world have now come here, 7and Jason has welcomed them into his house. They are all defying Caesar's decrees, saying that there is another king, one called Jesus." 8When they heard this, the crowd and the city officials were thrown into turmoil. 9Then they made Jason and the others post bond and let them go.

In Berea

10As soon as it was night, the brothers sent Paul and Silas away to Berea. On arriving there, they went to the Jewish synagogue. 11Now the Bereans were of more noble character than the Thessalonians, for they received the message with great eagerness and examined the Scriptures every day to see if what Paul said was true. 12Many of the Jews believed, as did also a number of prominent Greek women and many Greek men.

13When the Jews in Thessalonica learned that Paul was preaching the word of God at Berea, they went there too, agitating the crowds and stirring them up. 14The brothers immediately sent Paul to the coast, but Silas and Timothy stayed at Berea. 15The men who escorted Paul brought him to Athens and then left with instructions for Silas and Timothy to join him as soon as possible.

In Athens

16While Paul was waiting for them in Athens, he was greatly distressed to see that the city was full of idols. 17So he reasoned in the synagogue with the Jews and the God-fearing Greeks, as well as in the marketplace day by day with those who happened to be there. 18A group of Epicurean and Stoic philosophers began to dispute with him. Some of them asked, "What is this babbler trying to say?" Others remarked, "He seems to be advocating foreign gods." They said this because Paul was preaching the good news about Jesus and the resurrec-

*a*3 Or *Messiah*   *b*5 Or *the assembly of the people*

tion. [19]Then they took him and brought him to a meeting of the Areopagus, where they said to him, "May we know what this new teaching is that you are presenting? [20]You are bringing some strange ideas to our ears, and we want to know what they mean." [21](All the Athenians and the foreigners who lived there spent their time doing nothing but talking about and listening to the latest ideas.)

[22]Paul then stood up in the meeting of the Areopagus and said: "Men of Athens! I see that in every way you are very religious. [23]For as I walked around and looked carefully at your objects of worship, I even found an altar with this inscription: TO AN UNKNOWN GOD. Now what you worship as something unknown I am going to proclaim to you.

[24]"The God who made the world and everything in it is the Lord of heaven and earth and does not live in temples built by hands. [25]And he is not served by human hands, as if he needed anything, because he himself gives all men life and breath and everything else. [26]From one man he made every nation of men, that they should inhabit the whole earth; and he determined the times set for them and the exact places where they should live. [27]God did this so that men would seek him and perhaps reach out for him and find him, though he is not far from each one of us. [28]'For in him we live and move and have our being.' As some of your own poets have said, 'We are his offspring.'

[29]"Therefore since we are God's offspring, we should not think that the divine being is like gold or silver or stone—an image made by man's design and skill. [30]In the past God overlooked such ignorance, but now he commands all people everywhere to repent. [31]For he has set a day when he will judge the world with justice by the man he has appointed. He has given proof of this to all men by raising him from the dead."

[32]When they heard about the resurrection of the dead, some of them sneered, but others said, "We want to hear you again on this subject." [33]At that, Paul left the Council. [34]A few men became followers of Paul and believed. Among them was Dionysius, a member of the Areopagus, also a woman named Damaris, and a number of others.

In Corinth

18 After this, Paul left Athens and went to Corinth. [2]There he met a Jew named Aquila, a native of Pontus, who had recently come from Italy with his wife Priscilla, because Claudius had ordered all the Jews to leave Rome. Paul went to see them, [3]and because he was a tentmaker as they were, he stayed and worked with them. [4]Every Sabbath he reasoned in the synagogue, trying to persuade Jews and Greeks.

[5]When Silas and Timothy came from Macedonia, Paul devoted himself exclusively to preaching, testifying to the Jews that Jesus was the Christ.[a] [6]But when the Jews opposed Paul and became abusive, he shook out his clothes in protest and said to them, "Your blood be on your own heads! I am clear of my responsibility. From now on I will go to the Gentiles."

[7]Then Paul left the synagogue and went next door to the house of Titius Justus, a worshiper of God. [8]Crispus, the synagogue ruler, and his entire household believed in the Lord; and many of the Corinthians who heard him believed and were baptized.

[9]One night the Lord spoke to Paul in a vision: "Do not be afraid; keep on speaking, do not be silent. [10]For I am with you, and no one is going to attack and harm you, because I have many people in this city." [11]So Paul stayed for a year and a half, teaching them the word of God.

[12]While Gallio was proconsul of Achaia, the Jews made a united attack on Paul and brought him into court.

---

[a]5 Or *Messiah*; also in verse 28

VERSE:	AUTHOR:	PASSAGE:
Acts 17:25	Tim Hansel	Acts 17:22–28

Life . . . and Everything Else

Many of us still have tragically limited understandings of grace. Unknowingly we still serve a God we think is stingy, who loves us only in proportion to how much we work for him, who is embarrassed by laughter and surprised by spontaneity. We have forgotten, or never realized, that each day is a gift—we did nothing to deserve it. We've forgotten, or refused out of arrogance to believe, that each breath is a gift, and all the work in the world won't give us more. We've forgotten, or never learned, that the mark of a believer is not only love but joy, wonder, appreciation, surprise, credibility, peace, tenacity, hope, simplicity, and even play.

When was the last time you saw something you've never seen before or smelled something you've never smelled before—in your own backyard? It's not so much the ability to sing but the desire to sing that counts.

Can you imagine the tragedy of having all that you desire at your fingertips and not appreciating it? Can you imagine the sadness of seeing someone squinting at the horizon desperately, while what he is looking for is right at his feet? . . .

May God open to us the little things in life—so that our hearts don't grow old. May he teach us to be supple and thirsty for the everyday wonders of being alive—so that our minds won't grow weary. May he help us not to have to be so useful that we become useless.

. . . .

ADDITIONAL SCRIPTURE READINGS
Matthew 18:1–4; 1 Timothy 6:17–19

Go to page 1401 for your next devotional reading.

[13]"This man," they charged, "is persuading the people to worship God in ways contrary to the law."

[14]Just as Paul was about to speak, Gallio said to the Jews, "If you Jews were making a complaint about some misdemeanor or serious crime, it would be reasonable for me to listen to you. [15]But since it involves questions about words and names and your own law—settle the matter yourselves. I will not be a judge of such things." [16]So he had them ejected from the court. [17]Then they all turned on Sosthenes the synagogue ruler and beat him in front of the court. But Gallio showed no concern whatever.

Priscilla, Aquila and Apollos

[18]Paul stayed on in Corinth for some time. Then he left the brothers and sailed for Syria, accompanied by Priscilla and Aquila. Before he sailed, he had his hair cut off at Cenchrea because of a vow he had taken. [19]They arrived at Ephesus, where Paul left Priscilla and Aquila. He himself went into the synagogue and reasoned with the Jews. [20]When they asked him to spend more time with them, he declined. [21]But as he left, he promised, "I will come back if it is God's will." Then he set sail from Ephesus. [22]When he landed at Caesarea, he went up and greeted the church and then went down to Antioch.

[23]After spending some time in Antioch, Paul set out from there and traveled from place to place throughout the region of Galatia and Phrygia, strengthening all the disciples.

[24]Meanwhile a Jew named Apollos, a native of Alexandria, came to Ephesus. He was a learned man, with a thorough knowledge of the Scriptures. [25]He had been instructed in the way of the Lord, and he spoke with great fervor[a] and taught about Jesus accurately, though he knew only the baptism of John. [26]He began to speak boldly in the synagogue. When Priscilla and Aquila heard him, they invited him to their home and explained to him the way of God more adequately.

[27]When Apollos wanted to go to Achaia, the brothers encouraged him and wrote to the disciples there to welcome him. On arriving, he was a great help to those who by grace had believed. [28]For he vigorously refuted the Jews in public debate, proving from the Scriptures that Jesus was the Christ.

Paul in Ephesus

19 While Apollos was at Corinth, Paul took the road through the interior and arrived at Ephesus. There he found some disciples [2]and asked them, "Did you receive the Holy Spirit when[b] you believed?"

They answered, "No, we have not even heard that there is a Holy Spirit."

[3]So Paul asked, "Then what baptism did you receive?"

"John's baptism," they replied.

[4]Paul said, "John's baptism was a baptism of repentance. He told the people to believe in the one coming after him, that is, in Jesus." [5]On hearing this, they were baptized into[c] the name of the Lord Jesus. [6]When Paul placed his hands on them, the Holy Spirit came on them, and they spoke in tongues[d] and prophesied. [7]There were about twelve men in all.

[8]Paul entered the synagogue and spoke boldly there for three months, arguing persuasively about the kingdom of God. [9]But some of them became obstinate; they refused to believe and publicly maligned the Way. So Paul left them. He took the disciples with him and had discussions daily in the lecture hall of Tyrannus. [10]This went on for two years, so that all the Jews and Greeks who lived in the province of Asia heard the word of the Lord.

[11]God did extraordinary miracles through Paul, [12]so that even handkerchiefs and aprons that had touched him were taken to the sick, and their

---

[a]25 Or *with fervor in the Spirit*   [b]2 Or *after*   [c]5 Or *in*   [d]6 Or *other languages*

illnesses were cured and the evil spirits left them.

¹³Some Jews who went around driving out evil spirits tried to invoke the name of the Lord Jesus over those who were demon-possessed. They would say, "In the name of Jesus, whom Paul preaches, I command you to come out." ¹⁴Seven sons of Sceva, a Jewish chief priest, were doing this. ¹⁵⌐One day⌐ the evil spirit answered them, "Jesus I know, and I know about Paul, but who are you?" ¹⁶Then the man who had the evil spirit jumped on them and overpowered them all. He gave them such a beating that they ran out of the house naked and bleeding.

¹⁷When this became known to the Jews and Greeks living in Ephesus, they were all seized with fear, and the name of the Lord Jesus was held in high honor. ¹⁸Many of those who believed now came and openly confessed their evil deeds. ¹⁹A number who had practiced sorcery brought their scrolls together and burned them publicly. When they calculated the value of the scrolls, the total came to fifty thousand drachmas.ᵃ ²⁰In this way the word of the Lord spread widely and grew in power.

²¹After all this had happened, Paul decided to go to Jerusalem, passing through Macedonia and Achaia. "After I have been there," he said, "I must visit Rome also." ²²He sent two of his helpers, Timothy and Erastus, to Macedonia, while he stayed in the province of Asia a little longer.

The Riot in Ephesus

²³About that time there arose a great disturbance about the Way. ²⁴A silversmith named Demetrius, who made silver shrines of Artemis, brought in no little business for the craftsmen. ²⁵He called them together, along with the workmen in related trades, and said: "Men, you know we receive a good income from this business. ²⁶And you see and hear how this fellow Paul has convinced and led astray large numbers of people here in Ephesus and in practically the whole province of Asia. He says that man-made gods are no gods at all. ²⁷There is danger not only that our trade will lose its good name, but also that the temple of the great goddess Artemis will be discredited, and the goddess herself, who is worshiped throughout the province of Asia and the world, will be robbed of her divine majesty."

²⁸When they heard this, they were furious and began shouting: "Great is Artemis of the Ephesians!" ²⁹Soon the whole city was in an uproar. The people seized Gaius and Aristarchus, Paul's traveling companions from Macedonia, and rushed as one man into the theater. ³⁰Paul wanted to appear before the crowd, but the disciples would not let him. ³¹Even some of the officials of the province, friends of Paul, sent him a message begging him not to venture into the theater.

³²The assembly was in confusion: Some were shouting one thing, some another. Most of the people did not even know why they were there. ³³The Jews pushed Alexander to the front, and some of the crowd shouted instructions to him. He motioned for silence in order to make a defense before the people. ³⁴But when they realized he was a Jew, they all shouted in unison for about two hours: "Great is Artemis of the Ephesians!"

³⁵The city clerk quieted the crowd and said: "Men of Ephesus, doesn't all the world know that the city of Ephesus is the guardian of the temple of the great Artemis and of her image, which fell from heaven? ³⁶Therefore, since these facts are undeniable, you ought to be quiet and not do anything rash. ³⁷You have brought these men here, though they have neither robbed temples nor blasphemed our goddess. ³⁸If, then, Demetrius and his fellow craftsmen have a grievance against anybody, the courts are open and there are proconsuls. They can press charges. ³⁹If there is anything

ᵃ19 A drachma was a silver coin worth about a day's wages.

further you want to bring up, it must be settled in a legal assembly. 40As it is, we are in danger of being charged with rioting because of today's events. In that case we would not be able to account for this commotion, since there is no reason for it." 41After he had said this, he dismissed the assembly.

Through Macedonia and Greece

20 When the uproar had ended, Paul sent for the disciples and, after encouraging them, said good-by and set out for Macedonia. 2He traveled through that area, speaking many words of encouragement to the people, and finally arrived in Greece, 3where he stayed three months. Because the Jews made a plot against him just as he was about to sail for Syria, he decided to go back through Macedonia. 4He was accompanied by Sopater son of Pyrrhus from Berea, Aristarchus and Secundus from Thessalonica, Gaius from Derbe, Timothy also, and Tychicus and Trophimus from the province of Asia. 5These men went on ahead and waited for us at Troas. 6But we sailed from Philippi after the Feast of Unleavened Bread, and five days later joined the others at Troas, where we stayed seven days.

Eutychus Raised From the Dead at Troas

7On the first day of the week we came together to break bread. Paul spoke to the people and, because he intended to leave the next day, kept on talking until midnight. 8There were many lamps in the upstairs room where we were meeting. 9Seated in a window was a young man named Eutychus, who was sinking into a deep sleep as Paul talked on and on. When he was sound asleep, he fell to the ground from the third story and was picked up dead. 10Paul went down, threw himself on the young man and put his arms around him. "Don't be alarmed," he said. "He's alive!" 11Then he went upstairs again and broke bread and ate. After talking until daylight, he left. 12The people took the young man home alive and were greatly comforted.

Paul's Farewell to the Ephesian Elders

13We went on ahead to the ship and sailed for Assos, where we were going to take Paul aboard. He had made this arrangement because he was going there on foot. 14When he met us at Assos, we took him aboard and went on to Mitylene. 15The next day we set sail from there and arrived off Kios. The day after that we crossed over to Samos, and on the following day arrived at Miletus. 16Paul had decided to sail past Ephesus to avoid spending time in the province of Asia, for he was in a hurry to reach Jerusalem, if possible, by the day of Pentecost.

17From Miletus, Paul sent to Ephesus for the elders of the church. 18When they arrived, he said to them: "You know how I lived the whole time I was with you, from the first day I came into the province of Asia. 19I served the Lord with great humility and with tears, although I was severely tested by the plots of the Jews. 20You know that I have not hesitated to preach anything that would be helpful to you but have taught you publicly and from house to house. 21I have declared to both Jews and Greeks that they must turn to God in repentance and have faith in our Lord Jesus.

22"And now, compelled by the Spirit, I am going to Jerusalem, not knowing what will happen to me there. 23I only know that in every city the Holy Spirit warns me that prison and hardships are facing me. 24However, I consider my life worth nothing to me, if only I may finish the race and complete the task the Lord Jesus has given me—the task of testifying to the gospel of God's grace.

25"Now I know that none of you among whom I have gone about preaching the kingdom will ever see me again. 26Therefore, I declare to you today that I am innocent of the blood

VERSE:
Acts 20:2

AUTHOR:
Charles Stanley

PASSAGE:
Acts 20:1–5

An Encouraging Word

Have you ever thought how influential the words you speak are? Do you know what kind of impact your speech can have on a person who desperately needs to hear an encouraging word? Solomon wrote, "Pleasant words are a honeycomb, sweet to the soul and healing to the bones" (Proverbs 16:24). What a wonderful way to describe our conversation. It can be medicine to a weary soul, healing to a bruised spirit. Kind words, spoken in due season, are God's bridges of love.

If you've been on the receiving end of gracious comments, you know the power of well-chosen words. Paul describes such speech as "full of grace, seasoned with salt" (Colossians 4:6). Our remarks, he says, are to be flavored with gentleness and loving-kindness, key ingredients of grace-filled speech.

The love of Christ can leap into the hearts of others through your words when you speak to them the way you want them to speak to you. Let words of cheer and praise be the order of the day, and you'll be amazed how you can change the atmosphere of your home ... The golden rule is never more effective than when it regulates our speech.

Ask God to make you aware of the needs of others. When we are completely absorbed in our problems or activities, complimentary words rarely grace our conversation. Accept others the way they are and allow God to change them through his Spirit. Your focus is on edification, not condemnation. Your speech is targeted for "building others up according to their needs, that it may benefit those who listen" (Ephesians 4:29). Let your tongue be God's instrument of love.

ADDITIONAL SCRIPTURE READINGS
Colossians 4:2–6; James 3:1–12

Go to page 1406 for your next devotional reading.

of all men. ²⁷For I have not hesitated to proclaim to you the whole will of God. ²⁸Keep watch over yourselves and all the flock of which the Holy Spirit has made you overseers.ᵃ Be shepherds of the church of God,ᵇ which he bought with his own blood. ²⁹I know that after I leave, savage wolves will come in among you and will not spare the flock. ³⁰Even from your own number men will arise and distort the truth in order to draw away disciples after them. ³¹So be on your guard! Remember that for three years I never stopped warning each of you night and day with tears.

³²"Now I commit you to God and to the word of his grace, which can build you up and give you an inheritance among all those who are sanctified. ³³I have not coveted anyone's silver or gold or clothing. ³⁴You yourselves know that these hands of mine have supplied my own needs and the needs of my companions. ³⁵In everything I did, I showed you that by this kind of hard work we must help the weak, remembering the words the Lord Jesus himself said: 'It is more blessed to give than to receive.'"

³⁶When he had said this, he knelt down with all of them and prayed. ³⁷They all wept as they embraced him and kissed him. ³⁸What grieved them most was his statement that they would never see his face again. Then they accompanied him to the ship.

On to Jerusalem

21 After we had torn ourselves away from them, we put out to sea and sailed straight to Cos. The next day we went to Rhodes and from there to Patara. ²We found a ship crossing over to Phoenicia, went on board and set sail. ³After sighting Cyprus and passing to the south of it, we sailed on to Syria. We landed at Tyre, where our ship was to unload its cargo. ⁴Finding the disciples there, we stayed with them seven days. Through the Spirit they urged Paul

not to go on to Jerusalem. ⁵But when our time was up, we left and continued on our way. All the disciples and their wives and children accompanied us out of the city, and there on the beach we knelt to pray. ⁶After saying good-by to each other, we went aboard the ship, and they returned home.

⁷We continued our voyage from Tyre and landed at Ptolemais, where we greeted the brothers and stayed with them for a day. ⁸Leaving the next day, we reached Caesarea and stayed at the house of Philip the evangelist, one of the Seven. ⁹He had four unmarried daughters who prophesied.

¹⁰After we had been there a number of days, a prophet named Agabus came down from Judea. ¹¹Coming over to us, he took Paul's belt, tied his own hands and feet with it and said, "The Holy Spirit says, 'In this way the Jews of Jerusalem will bind the owner of this belt and will hand him over to the Gentiles.'"

¹²When we heard this, we and the people there pleaded with Paul not to go up to Jerusalem. ¹³Then Paul answered, "Why are you weeping and breaking my heart? I am ready not only to be bound, but also to die in Jerusalem for the name of the Lord Jesus." ¹⁴When he would not be dissuaded, we gave up and said, "The Lord's will be done."

¹⁵After this, we got ready and went up to Jerusalem. ¹⁶Some of the disciples from Caesarea accompanied us and brought us to the home of Mnason, where we were to stay. He was a man from Cyprus and one of the early disciples.

Paul's Arrival at Jerusalem

¹⁷When we arrived at Jerusalem, the brothers received us warmly. ¹⁸The next day Paul and the rest of us went to see James, and all the elders were present. ¹⁹Paul greeted them and reported in detail what God had done

ᵃ28 Traditionally *bishops*   ᵇ28 Many manuscripts *of the Lord* among the Gentiles through his ministry. ²⁰When they heard this, they praised God. Then they said to Paul: "You see, brother, how many thousands of Jews have believed, and all of them are zealous for the law. ²¹They have been informed that you teach all the Jews who live among the Gentiles to turn away from Moses, telling them not to circumcise their children or live according to our customs. ²²What shall we do? They will certainly hear that you have come, ²³so do what we tell you. There are four men with us who have made a vow. ²⁴Take these men, join in their purification rites and pay their expenses, so that they can have their heads shaved. Then everybody will know there is no truth in these reports about you, but that you yourself are living in obedience to the law. ²⁵As for the Gentile believers, we have written to them our decision that they should abstain from food sacrificed to idols, from blood, from the meat of strangled animals and from sexual immorality."

²⁶The next day Paul took the men and purified himself along with them. Then he went to the temple to give notice of the date when the days of purification would end and the offering would be made for each of them.

Paul Arrested

²⁷When the seven days were nearly over, some Jews from the province of Asia saw Paul at the temple. They stirred up the whole crowd and seized him, ²⁸shouting, "Men of Israel, help us! This is the man who teaches all men everywhere against our people and our law and this place. And besides, he has brought Greeks into the temple area and defiled this holy place." ²⁹(They had previously seen Trophimus the Ephesian in the city with Paul and assumed that Paul had brought him into the temple area.)

³⁰The whole city was aroused, and the people came running from all directions. Seizing Paul, they dragged him from the temple, and immediately the gates were shut. ³¹While they were trying to kill him, news reached the commander of the Roman troops that the whole city of Jerusalem was in an uproar. ³²He at once took some officers and soldiers and ran down to the crowd. When the rioters saw the commander and his soldiers, they stopped beating Paul.

³³The commander came up and arrested him and ordered him to be bound with two chains. Then he asked who he was and what he had done. ³⁴Some in the crowd shouted one thing and some another, and since the commander could not get at the truth because of the uproar, he ordered that Paul be taken into the barracks. ³⁵When Paul reached the steps, the violence of the mob was so great he had to be carried by the soldiers. ³⁶The crowd that followed kept shouting, "Away with him!"

Paul Speaks to the Crowd

³⁷As the soldiers were about to take Paul into the barracks, he asked the commander, "May I say something to you?"

"Do you speak Greek?" he replied. ³⁸"Aren't you the Egyptian who started a revolt and led four thousand terrorists out into the desert some time ago?"

³⁹Paul answered, "I am a Jew, from Tarsus in Cilicia, a citizen of no ordinary city. Please let me speak to the people."

⁴⁰Having received the commander's permission, Paul stood on the steps and motioned to the crowd. When they were all silent, he said to them in Aramaic[a]: **22** ¹"Brothers and fathers, listen now to my defense."

²When they heard him speak to them in Aramaic, they became very quiet.

Then Paul said: ³"I am a Jew, born in Tarsus of Cilicia, but brought up in this city. Under Gamaliel I was thor-

[a]40 Or possibly *Hebrew*; also in 22:2

oughly trained in the law of our fathers and was just as zealous for God as any of you are today. ⁴I persecuted the followers of this Way to their death, arresting both men and women and throwing them into prison, ⁵as also the high priest and all the Council can testify. I even obtained letters from them to their brothers in Damascus, and went there to bring these people as prisoners to Jerusalem to be punished.

⁶"About noon as I came near Damascus, suddenly a bright light from heaven flashed around me. ⁷I fell to the ground and heard a voice say to me, 'Saul! Saul! Why do you persecute me?'

⁸" 'Who are you, Lord?' I asked.

" 'I am Jesus of Nazareth, whom you are persecuting,' he replied. ⁹My companions saw the light, but they did not understand the voice of him who was speaking to me.

¹⁰" 'What shall I do, Lord?' I asked.

" 'Get up,' the Lord said, 'and go into Damascus. There you will be told all that you have been assigned to do.' ¹¹My companions led me by the hand into Damascus, because the brilliance of the light had blinded me.

¹²"A man named Ananias came to see me. He was a devout observer of the law and highly respected by all the Jews living there. ¹³He stood beside me and said, 'Brother Saul, receive your sight!' And at that very moment I was able to see him.

¹⁴"Then he said: 'The God of our fathers has chosen you to know his will and to see the Righteous One and to hear words from his mouth. ¹⁵You will be his witness to all men of what you have seen and heard. ¹⁶And now what are you waiting for? Get up, be baptized and wash your sins away, calling on his name.'

¹⁷"When I returned to Jerusalem and was praying at the temple, I fell into a trance ¹⁸and saw the Lord speaking. 'Quick!' he said to me. 'Leave Jerusalem immediately, be-

cause they will not accept your testimony about me.'

¹⁹" 'Lord,' I replied, 'these men know that I went from one synagogue to another to imprison and beat those who believe in you. ²⁰And when the blood of your martyr*ᵃ* Stephen was shed, I stood there giving my approval and guarding the clothes of those who were killing him.'

²¹"Then the Lord said to me, 'Go; I will send you far away to the Gentiles.' "

Paul the Roman Citizen

²²The crowd listened to Paul until he said this. Then they raised their voices and shouted, "Rid the earth of him! He's not fit to live!"

²³As they were shouting and throwing off their cloaks and flinging dust into the air, ²⁴the commander ordered Paul to be taken into the barracks. He directed that he be flogged and questioned in order to find out why the people were shouting at him like this. ²⁵As they stretched him out to flog him, Paul said to the centurion standing there, "Is it legal for you to flog a Roman citizen who hasn't even been found guilty?"

²⁶When the centurion heard this, he went to the commander and reported it. "What are you going to do?" he asked. "This man is a Roman citizen."

²⁷The commander went to Paul and asked, "Tell me, are you a Roman citizen?"

"Yes, I am," he answered.

²⁸Then the commander said, "I had to pay a big price for my citizenship."

"But I was born a citizen," Paul replied.

²⁹Those who were about to question him withdrew immediately. The commander himself was alarmed when he realized that he had put Paul, a Roman citizen, in chains.

Before the Sanhedrin

³⁰The next day, since the commander wanted to find out exactly why Paul was being accused by the Jews,

he released him and ordered the chief priests and all the Sanhedrin to assemble. Then he brought Paul and had him stand before them.

23 Paul looked straight at the Sanhedrin and said, "My brothers, I have fulfilled my duty to God in all good conscience to this day." ²At this the high priest Ananias ordered those standing near Paul to strike him on the mouth. ³Then Paul said to him, "God will strike you, you whitewashed wall! You sit there to judge me according to the law, yet you yourself violate the law by commanding that I be struck!"

⁴Those who were standing near Paul said, "You dare to insult God's high priest?"

⁵Paul replied, "Brothers, I did not realize that he was the high priest; for it is written: 'Do not speak evil about the ruler of your people.'ᵃ"

⁶Then Paul, knowing that some of them were Sadducees and the others Pharisees, called out in the Sanhedrin, "My brothers, I am a Pharisee, the son of a Pharisee. I stand on trial because of my hope in the resurrection of the dead." ⁷When he said this, a dispute broke out between the Pharisees and the Sadducees, and the assembly was divided. ⁸(The Sadducees say that there is no resurrection, and that there are neither angels nor spirits, but the Pharisees acknowledge them all.)

⁹There was a great uproar, and some of the teachers of the law who were Pharisees stood up and argued vigorously. "We find nothing wrong with this man," they said. "What if a spirit or an angel has spoken to him?" ¹⁰The dispute became so violent that the commander was afraid Paul would be torn to pieces by them. He ordered the troops to go down and take him away from them by force and bring him into the barracks. ¹¹The following night the Lord stood near Paul and said, "Take courage! As you have testified about me in Jerusalem, so you must also testify in Rome."

The Plot to Kill Paul

¹²The next morning the Jews formed a conspiracy and bound themselves with an oath not to eat or drink until they had killed Paul. ¹³More than forty men were involved in this plot. ¹⁴They went to the chief priests and elders and said, "We have taken a solemn oath not to eat anything until we have killed Paul. ¹⁵Now then, you and the Sanhedrin petition the commander to bring him before you on the pretext of wanting more accurate information about his case. We are ready to kill him before he gets here."

¹⁶But when the son of Paul's sister heard of this plot, he went into the barracks and told Paul.

¹⁷Then Paul called one of the centurions and said, "Take this young man to the commander; he has something to tell him." ¹⁸So he took him to the commander.

The centurion said, "Paul, the prisoner, sent for me and asked me to bring this young man to you because he has something to tell you."

¹⁹The commander took the young man by the hand, drew him aside and asked, "What is it you want to tell me?"

²⁰He said: "The Jews have agreed to ask you to bring Paul before the Sanhedrin tomorrow on the pretext of wanting more accurate information about him. ²¹Don't give in to them, because more than forty of them are waiting in ambush for him. They have taken an oath not to eat or drink until they have killed him. They are ready now, waiting for your consent to their request."

²²The commander dismissed the young man and cautioned him, "Don't tell anyone that you have reported this to me."

Paul Transferred to Caesarea

²³Then he called two of his centuri-

ᵃ5 Exodus 22:28

PASSAGE: Psalm 56; Isaiah 65:17–25
AUTHOR: Joseph Bayly

A Psalm of Extremity

I cry tears
to you Lord
tears
because I cannot speak.
Words are lost
among my fears
pain
sorrows
losses
hurts
but tears
You understand
my wordless prayer
You hear.
Lord
wipe away my tears
all tears
not in distant day
but now
here.

Go to page 1412 for your next devotional reading.

ons and ordered them, "Get ready a detachment of two hundred soldiers, seventy horsemen and two hundred spearmen[a] to go to Caesarea at nine tonight. ²⁴Provide mounts for Paul so that he may be taken safely to Governor Felix."

²⁵He wrote a letter as follows:

²⁶Claudius Lysias,

To His Excellency, Governor Felix:

Greetings.

²⁷This man was seized by the Jews and they were about to kill him, but I came with my troops and rescued him, for I had learned that he is a Roman citizen. ²⁸I wanted to know why they were accusing him, so I brought him to their Sanhedrin. ²⁹I found that the accusation had to do with questions about their law, but there was no charge against him that deserved death or imprisonment. ³⁰When I was informed of a plot to be carried out against the man, I sent him to you at once. I also ordered his accusers to present to you their case against him.

³¹So the soldiers, carrying out their orders, took Paul with them during the night and brought him as far as Antipatris. ³²The next day they let the cavalry go on with him, while they returned to the barracks. ³³When the cavalry arrived in Caesarea, they delivered the letter to the governor and handed Paul over to him. ³⁴The governor read the letter and asked what province he was from. Learning that he was from Cilicia, ³⁵he said, "I will hear your case when your accusers get here." Then he ordered that Paul be kept under guard in Herod's palace.

The Trial Before Felix

24 Five days later the high priest Ananias went down to Caesarea with some of the elders and a lawyer named Tertullus, and they brought their charges against Paul before the governor. ²When Paul was called in, Tertullus presented his case before Felix: "We have enjoyed a long period of peace under you, and your foresight has brought about reforms in this nation. ³Everywhere and in every way, most excellent Felix, we acknowledge this with profound gratitude. ⁴But in order not to weary you further, I would request that you be kind enough to hear us briefly.

⁵"We have found this man to be a troublemaker, stirring up riots among the Jews all over the world. He is a ringleader of the Nazarene sect ⁶and even tried to desecrate the temple; so we seized him. ⁸By[b] examining him yourself you will be able to learn the truth about all these charges we are bringing against him."

⁹The Jews joined in the accusation, asserting that these things were true.

¹⁰When the governor motioned for him to speak, Paul replied: "I know that for a number of years you have been a judge over this nation; so I gladly make my defense. ¹¹You can easily verify that no more than twelve days ago I went up to Jerusalem to worship. ¹²My accusers did not find me arguing with anyone at the temple, or stirring up a crowd in the synagogues or anywhere else in the city. ¹³And they cannot prove to you the charges they are now making against me. ¹⁴However, I admit that I worship the God of our fathers as a follower of the Way, which they call a sect. I believe everything that agrees with the Law and that is written in the Prophets, ¹⁵and I have the same hope in God as these men, that there will be a resurrection of both the righteous and the wicked. ¹⁶So I strive always to

[a]23 The meaning of the Greek for this word is uncertain.   [b]6-8 Some manuscripts *him and wanted to judge him according to our law. ⁷But the commander, Lysias, came and with the use of much force snatched him from our hands ⁸and ordered his accusers to come before you. By*

keep my conscience clear before God and man.

17"After an absence of several years, I came to Jerusalem to bring my people gifts for the poor and to present offerings. 18I was ceremonially clean when they found me in the temple courts doing this. There was no crowd with me, nor was I involved in any disturbance. 19But there are some Jews from the province of Asia, who ought to be here before you and bring charges if they have anything against me. 20Or these who are here should state what crime they found in me when I stood before the Sanhedrin— 21unless it was this one thing I shouted as I stood in their presence: 'It is concerning the resurrection of the dead that I am on trial before you today.' "

22Then Felix, who was well acquainted with the Way, adjourned the proceedings. "When Lysias the commander comes," he said, "I will decide your case." 23He ordered the centurion to keep Paul under guard but to give him some freedom and permit his friends to take care of his needs.

24Several days later Felix came with his wife Drusilla, who was a Jewess. He sent for Paul and listened to him as he spoke about faith in Christ Jesus. 25As Paul discoursed on righteousness, self-control and the judgment to come, Felix was afraid and said, "That's enough for now! You may leave. When I find it convenient, I will send for you." 26At the same time he was hoping that Paul would offer him a bribe, so he sent for him frequently and talked with him.

27When two years had passed, Felix was succeeded by Porcius Festus, but because Felix wanted to grant a favor to the Jews, he left Paul in prison.

The Trial Before Festus

25 Three days after arriving in the province, Festus went up from Caesarea to Jerusalem, 2where the chief priests and Jewish leaders appeared before him and presented the charges against Paul. 3They urgently requested Festus, as a favor to them, to have Paul transferred to Jerusalem, for they were preparing an ambush to kill him along the way. 4Festus answered, "Paul is being held at Caesarea, and I myself am going there soon. 5Let some of your leaders come with me and press charges against the man there, if he has done anything wrong."

6After spending eight or ten days with them, he went down to Caesarea, and the next day he convened the court and ordered that Paul be brought before him. 7When Paul appeared, the Jews who had come down from Jerusalem stood around him, bringing many serious charges against him, which they could not prove.

8Then Paul made his defense: "I have done nothing wrong against the law of the Jews or against the temple or against Caesar."

9Festus, wishing to do the Jews a favor, said to Paul, "Are you willing to go up to Jerusalem and stand trial before me there on these charges?"

10Paul answered: "I am now standing before Caesar's court, where I ought to be tried. I have not done any wrong to the Jews, as you yourself know very well. 11If, however, I am guilty of doing anything deserving death, I do not refuse to die. But if the charges brought against me by these Jews are not true, no one has the right to hand me over to them. I appeal to Caesar!"

12After Festus had conferred with his council, he declared: "You have appealed to Caesar. To Caesar you will go!"

Festus Consults King Agrippa

13A few days later King Agrippa and Bernice arrived at Caesarea to pay their respects to Festus. 14Since they were spending many days there, Festus discussed Paul's case with the king. He said: "There is a man here whom Felix left as a prisoner. 15When I went to Jerusalem, the chief priests and elders of the Jews brought charges against him and asked that he be condemned.

16"I told them that it is not the Roman custom to hand over any man before he has faced his accusers and has had an opportunity to defend himself against their charges. 17When they came here with me, I did not delay the case, but convened the court the next day and ordered the man to be brought in. 18When his accusers got up to speak, they did not charge him with any of the crimes I had expected. 19Instead, they had some points of dispute with him about their own religion and about a dead man named Jesus who Paul claimed was alive. 20I was at a loss how to investigate such matters; so I asked if he would be willing to go to Jerusalem and stand trial there on these charges. 21When Paul made his appeal to be held over for the Emperor's decision, I ordered him held until I could send him to Caesar."

22Then Agrippa said to Festus, "I would like to hear this man myself."

He replied, "Tomorrow you will hear him."

Paul Before Agrippa

23The next day Agrippa and Bernice came with great pomp and entered the audience room with the high ranking officers and the leading men of the city. At the command of Festus, Paul was brought in. 24Festus said: "King Agrippa, and all who are present with us, you see this man! The whole Jewish community has petitioned me about him in Jerusalem and here in Caesarea, shouting that he ought not to live any longer. 25I found he had done nothing deserving of death, but because he made his appeal to the Emperor I decided to send him to Rome. 26But I have nothing definite to write to His Majesty about him. Therefore I have brought him before all of you, and especially before you, King Agrippa, so that as a result of this investigation I may have something to write. 27For I think it is

unreasonable to send on a prisoner without specifying the charges against him."

26 Then Agrippa said to Paul, "You have permission to speak for yourself."

So Paul motioned with his hand and began his defense: 2"King Agrippa, I consider myself fortunate to stand before you today as I make my defense against all the accusations of the Jews, 3and especially so because you are well acquainted with all the Jewish customs and controversies. Therefore, I beg you to listen to me patiently.

4"The Jews all know the way I have lived ever since I was a child, from the beginning of my life in my own country, and also in Jerusalem. 5They have known me for a long time and can testify, if they are willing, that according to the strictest sect of our religion, I lived as a Pharisee. 6And now it is because of my hope in what God has promised our fathers that I am on trial today. 7This is the promise our twelve tribes are hoping to see fulfilled as they earnestly serve God day and night. O king, it is because of this hope that the Jews are accusing me. 8Why should any of you consider it incredible that God raises the dead?

9"I too was convinced that I ought to do all that was possible to oppose the name of Jesus of Nazareth. 10And that is just what I did in Jerusalem. On the authority of the chief priests I put many of the saints in prison, and when they were put to death, I cast my vote against them. 11Many a time I went from one synagogue to another to have them punished, and I tried to force them to blaspheme. In my obsession against them, I even went to foreign cities to persecute them.

12"On one of these journeys I was going to Damascus with the authority and commission of the chief priests. 13About noon, O king, as I was on the road, I saw a light from heaven, brighter than the sun, blazing around me and my companions. 14We all fell to the ground, and I heard a voice saying to me in Aramaic,ᵃ 'Saul, Saul, why do you persecute me? It is hard for you to kick against the goads.'

¹⁵"Then I asked, 'Who are you, Lord?'

" 'I am Jesus, whom you are persecuting,' the Lord replied. ¹⁶'Now get up and stand on your feet. I have appeared to you to appoint you as a servant and as a witness of what you have seen of me and what I will show you. ¹⁷I will rescue you from your own people and from the Gentiles. I am sending you to them ¹⁸to open their eyes and turn them from darkness to light, and from the power of Satan to God, so that they may receive forgiveness of sins and a place among those who are sanctified by faith in me.'

¹⁹"So then, King Agrippa, I was not disobedient to the vision from heaven. ²⁰First to those in Damascus, then to those in Jerusalem and in all Judea, and to the Gentiles also, I preached that they should repent and turn to God and prove their repentance by their deeds. ²¹That is why the Jews seized me in the temple courts and tried to kill me. ²²But I have had God's help to this very day, and so I stand here and testify to small and great alike. I am saying nothing beyond what the prophets and Moses said would happen— ²³that the Christᵇ would suffer and, as the first to rise from the dead, would proclaim light to his own people and to the Gentiles."

²⁴At this point Festus interrupted Paul's defense. "You are out of your mind, Paul!" he shouted. "Your great learning is driving you insane."

²⁵"I am not insane, most excellent Festus," Paul replied. "What I am saying is true and reasonable. ²⁶The king is familiar with these things, and I can speak freely to him. I am convinced that none of this has escaped his notice, because it was not done in a corner. ²⁷King Agrippa, do you believe the prophets? I know you do."

²⁸Then Agrippa said to Paul, "Do you think that in such a short time you can persuade me to be a Christian?"

²⁹Paul replied, "Short time or long—I pray God that not only you but all who are listening to me today may become what I am, except for these chains."

³⁰The king rose, and with him the governor and Bernice and those sitting with them. ³¹They left the room, and while talking with one another, they said, "This man is not doing anything that deserves death or imprisonment."

³²Agrippa said to Festus, "This man could have been set free if he had not appealed to Caesar."

Paul Sails for Rome

27 When it was decided that we would sail for Italy, Paul and some other prisoners were handed over to a centurion named Julius, who belonged to the Imperial Regiment. ²We boarded a ship from Adramyttium about to sail for ports along the coast of the province of Asia, and we put out to sea. Aristarchus, a Macedonian from Thessalonica, was with us.

³The next day we landed at Sidon; and Julius, in kindness to Paul, allowed him to go to his friends so they might provide for his needs. ⁴From there we put out to sea again and passed to the lee of Cyprus because the winds were against us. ⁵When we had sailed across the open sea off the coast of Cilicia and Pamphylia, we landed at Myra in Lycia. ⁶There the centurion found an Alexandrian ship sailing for Italy and put us on board. ⁷We made slow headway for many days and had difficulty arriving off Cnidus. When the wind did not allow us to hold our course, we sailed to the lee of Crete, opposite Salmone. ⁸We moved along the coast with difficulty and came to a place called Fair Havens, near the town of Lasea.

⁹Much time had been lost, and sailing had already become dangerous

because by now it was after the Fast.[a] So Paul warned them, [10]"Men, I can see that our voyage is going to be disastrous and bring great loss to ship and cargo, and to our own lives also." [11]But the centurion, instead of listening to what Paul said, followed the advice of the pilot and of the owner of the ship. [12]Since the harbor was unsuitable to winter in, the majority decided that we should sail on, hoping to reach Phoenix and winter there. This was a harbor in Crete, facing both southwest and northwest.

The Storm

[13]When a gentle south wind began to blow, they thought they had obtained what they wanted; so they weighed anchor and sailed along the shore of Crete. [14]Before very long, a wind of hurricane force, called the "northeaster," swept down from the island. [15]The ship was caught by the storm and could not head into the wind; so we gave way to it and were driven along. [16]As we passed to the lee of a small island called Cauda, we were hardly able to make the lifeboat secure. [17]When the men had hoisted it aboard, they passed ropes under the ship itself to hold it together. Fearing that they would run aground on the sandbars of Syrtis, they lowered the sea anchor and let the ship be driven along. [18]We took such a violent battering from the storm that the next day they began to throw the cargo overboard. [19]On the third day, they threw the ship's tackle overboard with their own hands. [20]When neither sun nor stars appeared for many days and the storm continued raging, we finally gave up all hope of being saved.

[21]After the men had gone a long time without food, Paul stood up before them and said: "Men, you should have taken my advice not to sail from Crete; then you would have spared yourselves this damage and loss. [22]But now I urge you to keep up your courage, because not one of you will be lost; only the ship will be destroyed. [23]Last night an angel of the God whose I am and whom I serve stood beside me [24]and said, 'Do not be afraid, Paul. You must stand trial before Caesar; and God has graciously given you the lives of all who sail with you.' [25]So keep up your courage, men, for I have faith in God that it will happen just as he told me. [26]Nevertheless, we must run aground on some island."

The Shipwreck

[27]On the fourteenth night we were still being driven across the Adriatic[b] Sea, when about midnight the sailors sensed they were approaching land. [28]They took soundings and found that the water was a hundred and twenty feet[c] deep. A short time later they took soundings again and found it was ninety feet[d] deep. [29]Fearing that we would be dashed against the rocks, they dropped four anchors from the stern and prayed for daylight. [30]In an attempt to escape from the ship, the sailors let the lifeboat down into the sea, pretending they were going to lower some anchors from the bow. [31]Then Paul said to the centurion and the soldiers, "Unless these men stay with the ship, you cannot be saved." [32]So the soldiers cut the ropes that held the lifeboat and let it fall away.

[33]Just before dawn Paul urged them all to eat. "For the last fourteen days," he said, "you have been in constant suspense and have gone without food—you haven't eaten anything. [34]Now I urge you to take some food. You need it to survive. Not one of you will lose a single hair from his head." [35]After he said this, he took some bread and gave thanks to God in front of them all. Then he broke it and began to eat. [36]They were all encouraged and ate some food themselves. [37]Altogether there were 276 of us on board.

---

[a]9 That is, the Day of Atonement (Yom Kippur)   [b]27 In ancient times the name referred to an area extending well south of Italy.   [c]28 Greek *twenty orguias* (about 37 meters)   [d]28 Greek *fifteen orguias* (about 27 meters)

VERSE:	AUTHOR:	PASSAGE:
Acts 27:23	Millie Stamm	Acts 27:13–26

Spiritual Stabilizers

Paul was a champion survivor. On the way to Rome as a prisoner, he experienced a storm so severe that all hope vanished. But Paul had three stabilizers that carried him through.

His first stabilizer was his true *identity*, "whose I am." He discovered that neither his cultural nor religious background was sufficient. His personal relationship with Jesus gave him his identity. He said, "I consider everything a loss compared to the surpassing greatness of knowing Jesus Christ my Lord" (Philippians 3:8) . . .

His next stabilizer was his *trust in the Lord*. He said, "I know whom I have believed" (2 Timothy 1:12). His belief was not in some*thing* but in some*one*. It is easy to believe God when everything is going smoothly, but we can trust the Lord when hope is gone. We can say, "I have faith in God that it will happen just as he told me" (Acts 27:25).

The third stabilizer in his life was his *involvement*, "whom I serve." Serving the Lord brought purpose into his life. He said, "Forgetting what is behind and straining toward what is ahead, I press on toward the goal to win the prize" (Philippians 3:13–14) . . .

What do you do when a storm hits? What stabilizes your life? With our spiritual stabilizers at work, nothing can move us. Our stabilizers are: I am *his*! I believe *him*! I serve *him*! Nothing can move us, for our anchor in Jesus Christ stabilizes our lives.

ADDITIONAL SCRIPTURE READINGS
Philippians 3:1–14; 2 Timothy 1:8–12

Go to page 1416 for your next devotional reading.

³⁸When they had eaten as much as they wanted, they lightened the ship by throwing the grain into the sea.

³⁹When daylight came, they did not recognize the land, but they saw a bay with a sandy beach, where they decided to run the ship aground if they could. ⁴⁰Cutting loose the anchors, they left them in the sea and at the same time untied the ropes that held the rudders. Then they hoisted the foresail to the wind and made for the beach. ⁴¹But the ship struck a sandbar and ran aground. The bow stuck fast and would not move, and the stern was broken to pieces by the pounding of the surf.

⁴²The soldiers planned to kill the prisoners to prevent any of them from swimming away and escaping. ⁴³But the centurion wanted to spare Paul's life and kept them from carrying out their plan. He ordered those who could swim to jump overboard first and get to land. ⁴⁴The rest were to get there on planks or on pieces of the ship. In this way everyone reached land in safety.

Ashore on Malta

28 Once safely on shore, we found out that the island was called Malta. ²The islanders showed us unusual kindness. They built a fire and welcomed us all because it was raining and cold. ³Paul gathered a pile of brushwood and, as he put it on the fire, a viper, driven out by the heat, fastened itself on his hand. ⁴When the islanders saw the snake hanging from his hand, they said to each other, "This man must be a murderer; for though he escaped from the sea, Justice has not allowed him to live." ⁵But Paul shook the snake off into the fire and suffered no ill effects. ⁶The people expected him to swell up or suddenly fall dead, but after waiting a long time and seeing nothing unusual happen to him, they changed their minds and said he was a god.

⁷There was an estate nearby that belonged to Publius, the chief official of the island. He welcomed us to his home and for three days entertained us hospitably. ⁸His father was sick in bed, suffering from fever and dysentery. Paul went in to see him and, after prayer, placed his hands on him and healed him. ⁹When this had happened, the rest of the sick on the island came and were cured. ¹⁰They honored us in many ways and when we were ready to sail, they furnished us with the supplies we needed.

Arrival at Rome

¹¹After three months we put out to sea in a ship that had wintered in the island. It was an Alexandrian ship with the figurehead of the twin gods Castor and Pollux. ¹²We put in at Syracuse and stayed there three days. ¹³From there we set sail and arrived at Rhegium. The next day the south wind came up, and on the following day we reached Puteoli. ¹⁴There we found some brothers who invited us to spend a week with them. And so we came to Rome. ¹⁵The brothers there had heard that we were coming, and they traveled as far as the Forum of Appius and the Three Taverns to meet us. At the sight of these men Paul thanked God and was encouraged. ¹⁶When we got to Rome, Paul was allowed to live by himself, with a soldier to guard him.

Paul Preaches at Rome Under Guard

¹⁷Three days later he called together the leaders of the Jews. When they had assembled, Paul said to them: "My brothers, although I have done nothing against our people or against the customs of our ancestors, I was arrested in Jerusalem and handed over to the Romans. ¹⁸They examined me and wanted to release me, because I was not guilty of any crime deserving death. ¹⁹But when the Jews objected, I was compelled to appeal to Caesar—not that I had any charge to bring against my own people. ²⁰For this reason I have asked to see you and talk with you. It is because of the hope of Israel that I am bound with this chain."

²¹They replied, "We have not received any letters from Judea concerning you, and none of the brothers who have come from there has reported or said anything bad about you. ²²But we want to hear what your views are, for we know that people everywhere are talking against this sect."

²³They arranged to meet Paul on a certain day, and came in even larger numbers to the place where he was staying. From morning till evening he explained and declared to them the kingdom of God and tried to convince them about Jesus from the Law of Moses and from the Prophets. ²⁴Some were convinced by what he said, but others would not believe. ²⁵They disagreed among themselves and began to leave after Paul had made this final statement: "The Holy Spirit spoke the truth to your forefathers when he said through Isaiah the prophet:

²⁶" 'Go to this people and say,
"You will be ever hearing but
          never understanding;
    you will be ever seeing but
          never perceiving."
²⁷For this people's heart has become
          calloused;
    they hardly hear with their ears,
    and they have closed their eyes.
Otherwise they might see with
          their eyes,
    hear with their ears,
    understand with their hearts
    and turn, and I would heal
          them.'ᵃ

²⁸"Therefore I want you to know that God's salvation has been sent to the Gentiles, and they will listen!"ᵇ

³⁰For two whole years Paul stayed there in his own rented house and welcomed all who came to see him. ³¹Boldly and without hindrance he preached the kingdom of God and taught about the Lord Jesus Christ.

ᵃ27 Isaiah 6:9,10   ᵇ28 Some manuscripts listen!" ²⁹After he said this, the Jews left, arguing vigorously among themselves.

*...***W***...hile planning a
speaking trip to Spain, the apostle Paul
wrote this letter to introduce himself to the
church at Rome. In it he summarized all he
had been teaching about humanity's destructive way of living, people's desperate need for
God, and how they can be transformed when
they turn their lives over to Jesus. As you
read this book, rejoice in the great good news
of "no condemnation" for those who are in
Jesus.*

ROMANS

1 Paul, a servant of Christ Jesus, called to be an apostle and set apart for the gospel of God— ²the gospel he promised beforehand through his prophets in the Holy Scriptures ³regarding his Son, who as to his human nature was a descendant of David, ⁴and who through the Spirit*ᵃ* of holiness was declared with power to be the Son of God*ᵇ* by his resurrection from the dead: Jesus Christ our Lord. ⁵Through him and for his name's sake, we received grace and apostleship to call people from among all the Gentiles to the obedience that comes from faith. ⁶And you also are among those who are called to belong to Jesus Christ.

⁷To all in Rome who are loved by God and called to be saints:

Grace and peace to you from God our Father and from the Lord Jesus Christ.

Paul's Longing to Visit Rome

⁸First, I thank my God through Jesus Christ for all of you, because your faith is being reported all over the world. ⁹God, whom I serve with my whole heart in preaching the gospel of his Son, is my witness how constantly I remember you ¹⁰in my prayers at all times; and I pray that now at last by God's will the way may be opened for me to come to you.

¹¹I long to see you so that I may impart to you some spiritual gift to make you strong— ¹²that is, that you and I may be mutually encouraged by each other's faith. ¹³I do not want you

ᵃ4 Or *who as to his spirit*   *ᵇ4* Or *was appointed to be the Son of God with power*

VERSE:	AUTHOR:	PASSAGE:
Romans 1:5	Charles Colson	Romans 1:1–7

Mature Faith for the Mature

Maturing faith — faith which deepens and grows as we live our Christian life — is not just knowledge, but knowledge acted upon. It is not just belief, but belief lived out — practiced. James said we are to be doers of the word, not just hearers [James 1:22]. Dietrich Bonhoeffer, the German pastor martyred in a Nazi concentration camp, succinctly stated this crucial interrelationship: "Only he who believes is obedient; only he who is obedient believes."

This may sound like a circular proposition, but many things are — in truth and in practice. Think of learning how to swim. We are told what to do. We gingerly enter the water, launch out and promptly forget everything we've been told. We flail about, splashing frantically, gasping and sinking. Finally, usually at the point of utter despair, we capture for a moment the sensation of staying afloat. Realizing it is possible, we remember our instructions and begin to follow them. They work. Like learning to balance a bicycle or mastering a foreign language, faith is a state of mind that grows out of our actions, just as it also governs them.

So obedience is the key to real faith — the unshakable kind of faith so powerfully illustrated by Job's life ... Job confirmed his obedience with those classic words of faith: "Though he slay me, yet will I hope in him" (Job 13:15).

ADDITIONAL SCRIPTURE READINGS
Galatians 5:1–15; James 2:14–26
Go to page 1421 for your next devotional reading.

to be unaware, brothers, that I planned many times to come to you (but have been prevented from doing so until now) in order that I might have a harvest among you, just as I have had among the other Gentiles. ¹⁴I am obligated both to Greeks and non-Greeks, both to the wise and the foolish. ¹⁵That is why I am so eager to preach the gospel also to you who are at Rome.

¹⁶I am not ashamed of the gospel, because it is the power of God for the salvation of everyone who believes: first for the Jew, then for the Gentile. ¹⁷For in the gospel a righteousness from God is revealed, a righteousness that is by faith from first to last,*a* just as it is written: "The righteous will live by faith."*b*

God's Wrath Against Mankind

¹⁸The wrath of God is being revealed from heaven against all the godlessness and wickedness of men who suppress the truth by their wickedness, ¹⁹since what may be known about God is plain to them, because God has made it plain to them. ²⁰For since the creation of the world God's invisible qualities—his eternal power and divine nature—have been clearly seen, being understood from what has been made, so that men are without excuse.

²¹For although they knew God, they neither glorified him as God nor gave thanks to him, but their thinking became futile and their foolish hearts were darkened. ²²Although they claimed to be wise, they became fools ²³and exchanged the glory of the immortal God for images made to look like mortal man and birds and animals and reptiles.

²⁴Therefore God gave them over in the sinful desires of their hearts to sexual impurity for the degrading of their bodies with one another. ²⁵They exchanged the truth of God for a lie, and worshiped and served created things rather than the Creator—who is forever praised. Amen.

²⁶Because of this, God gave them over to shameful lusts. Even their women exchanged natural relations for unnatural ones. ²⁷In the same way the men also abandoned natural relations with women and were inflamed with lust for one another. Men committed indecent acts with other men, and received in themselves the due penalty for their perversion.

²⁸Furthermore, since they did not think it worthwhile to retain the knowledge of God, he gave them over to a depraved mind, to do what ought not to be done. ²⁹They have become filled with every kind of wickedness, evil, greed and depravity. They are full of envy, murder, strife, deceit and malice. They are gossips, ³⁰slanderers, God-haters, insolent, arrogant and boastful; they invent ways of doing evil; they disobey their parents; ³¹they are senseless, faithless, heartless, ruthless. ³²Although they know God's righteous decree that those who do such things deserve death, they not only continue to do these very things but also approve of those who practice them.

God's Righteous Judgment

2 You, therefore, have no excuse, you who pass judgment on someone else, for at whatever point you judge the other, you are condemning yourself, because you who pass judgment do the same things. ²Now we know that God's judgment against those who do such things is based on truth. ³So when you, a mere man, pass judgment on them and yet do the same things, do you think you will escape God's judgment? ⁴Or do you show contempt for the riches of his kindness, tolerance and patience, not realizing that God's kindness leads you toward repentance?

⁵But because of your stubbornness and your unrepentant heart, you are storing up wrath against yourself for the day of God's wrath, when his righteous judgment will be revealed. ⁶God "will give to each person ac-

a17 Or *is from faith to faith*   *b17* Hab. 2:4

cording to what he has done."[a] [7]To those who by persistence in doing good seek glory, honor and immortality, he will give eternal life. [8]But for those who are self-seeking and who reject the truth and follow evil, there will be wrath and anger. [9]There will be trouble and distress for every human being who does evil: first for the Jew, then for the Gentile; [10]but glory, honor and peace for everyone who does good: first for the Jew, then for the Gentile. [11]For God does not show favoritism.

[12]All who sin apart from the law will also perish apart from the law, and all who sin under the law will be judged by the law. [13]For it is not those who hear the law who are righteous in God's sight, but it is those who obey the law who will be declared righteous. [14](Indeed, when Gentiles, who do not have the law, do by nature things required by the law, they are a law for themselves, even though they do not have the law, [15]since they show that the requirements of the law are written on their hearts, their consciences also bearing witness, and their thoughts now accusing, now even defending them.) [16]This will take place on the day when God will judge men's secrets through Jesus Christ, as my gospel declares.

The Jews and the Law

[17]Now you, if you call yourself a Jew; if you rely on the law and brag about your relationship to God; [18]if you know his will and approve of what is superior because you are instructed by the law; [19]if you are convinced that you are a guide for the blind, a light for those who are in the dark, [20]an instructor of the foolish, a teacher of infants, because you have in the law the embodiment of knowledge and truth— [21]you, then, who teach others, do you not teach yourself? You who preach against stealing, do you steal? [22]You who say that people should not commit adultery, do you commit adultery? You who abhor idols, do you rob temples? [23]You who brag about the law, do you dishonor God by breaking the law? [24]As it is written: "God's name is blasphemed among the Gentiles because of you."[b]

[25]Circumcision has value if you observe the law, but if you break the law, you have become as though you had not been circumcised. [26]If those who are not circumcised keep the law's requirements, will they not be regarded as though they were circumcised? [27]The one who is not circumcised physically and yet obeys the law will condemn you who, even though you have the[c] written code and circumcision, are a lawbreaker.

[28]A man is not a Jew if he is only one outwardly, nor is circumcision merely outward and physical. [29]No, a man is a Jew if he is one inwardly; and circumcision is circumcision of the heart, by the Spirit, not by the written code. Such a man's praise is not from men, but from God.

God's Faithfulness

3 What advantage, then, is there in being a Jew, or what value is there in circumcision? [2]Much in every way! First of all, they have been entrusted with the very words of God.

[3]What if some did not have faith? Will their lack of faith nullify God's faithfulness? [4]Not at all! Let God be true, and every man a liar. As it is written:

"So that you may be proved right
　　when you speak
　　and prevail when you judge."[d]

[5]But if our unrighteousness brings out God's righteousness more clearly, what shall we say? That God is unjust in bringing his wrath on us? (I am using a human argument.) [6]Certainly not! If that were so, how could God judge the world? [7]Someone might argue, "If my falsehood enhances God's truthfulness and so increases his glo-

[a]6 Psalm 62:12; Prov. 24:12　　[b]24 Isaiah 52:5; Ezek. 36:22　　[c]27 Or *who, by means of a*
[d]4 Psalm 51:4

ry, why am I still condemned as a sinner?" ⁸Why not say—as we are being slanderously reported as saying and as some claim that we say—"Let us do evil that good may result"? Their condemnation is deserved.

No One Is Righteous

⁹What shall we conclude then? Are we any better*a*? Not at all! We have already made the charge that Jews and Gentiles alike are all under sin. ¹⁰As it is written:

"There is no one righteous, not
even one;
¹¹   there is no one who
understands,
no one who seeks God.
¹²All have turned away,
they have together become
worthless;
there is no one who does good,
not even one."*b*
¹³"Their throats are open graves;
their tongues practice deceit."*c*
"The poison of vipers is on their
lips."*d*
¹⁴   "Their mouths are full of
cursing and bitterness."*e*
¹⁵"Their feet are swift to shed blood;
¹⁶   ruin and misery mark their
ways,
¹⁷and the way of peace they do not
know."*f*
¹⁸   "There is no fear of God before
their eyes."*g*

¹⁹Now we know that whatever the law says, it says to those who are under the law, so that every mouth may be silenced and the whole world held accountable to God. ²⁰Therefore no one will be declared righteous in his sight by observing the law; rather, through the law we become conscious of sin.

Righteousness Through Faith

²¹But now a righteousness from God, apart from law, has been made known, to which the Law and the Prophets testify. ²²This righteousness from God comes through faith in Jesus Christ to all who believe. There is no difference, ²³for all have sinned and fall short of the glory of God, ²⁴and are justified freely by his grace through the redemption that came by Christ Jesus. ²⁵God presented him as a sacrifice of atonement,*h* through faith in his blood. He did this to demonstrate his justice, because in his forbearance he had left the sins committed beforehand unpunished— ²⁶he did it to demonstrate his justice at the present time, so as to be just and the one who justifies those who have faith in Jesus.

²⁷Where, then, is boasting? It is excluded. On what principle? On that of observing the law? No, but on that of faith. ²⁸For we maintain that a man is justified by faith apart from observing the law. ²⁹Is God the God of Jews only? Is he not the God of Gentiles too? Yes, of Gentiles too, ³⁰since there is only one God, who will justify the circumcised by faith and the uncircumcised through that same faith. ³¹Do we, then, nullify the law by this faith? Not at all! Rather, we uphold the law.

Abraham Justified by Faith

4 What then shall we say that Abraham, our forefather, discovered in this matter? ²If, in fact, Abraham was justified by works, he had something to boast about—but not before God. ³What does the Scripture say? "Abraham believed God, and it was credited to him as righteousness."*i*

⁴Now when a man works, his wages are not credited to him as a gift, but as an obligation. ⁵However, to the man who does not work but trusts God who justifies the wicked, his faith is credited as righteousness. ⁶David says the same thing when he speaks of the blessedness of the man to whom God credits righteousness apart from works:

---

*a*9 Or *worse*   *b*12 Psalms 14:1-3; 53:1-3; Eccles. 7:20   *c*13 Psalm 5:9   *d*13 Psalm 140:3
*e*14 Psalm 10:7   *f*17 Isaiah 59:7,8   *g*18 Psalm 36:1   *h*25 Or *as the one who would turn aside his wrath, taking away sin*   *i*3 Gen. 15:6; also in verse 22

[7]"Blessed are they
    whose transgressions are
      forgiven,
    whose sins are covered.
[8]Blessed is the man
    whose sin the Lord will never
      count against him."[a]

[9]Is this blessedness only for the circumcised, or also for the uncircumcised? We have been saying that Abraham's faith was credited to him as righteousness. [10]Under what circumstances was it credited? Was it after he was circumcised, or before? It was not after, but before! [11]And he received the sign of circumcision, a seal of the righteousness that he had by faith while he was still uncircumcised. So then, he is the father of all who believe but have not been circumcised, in order that righteousness might be credited to them. [12]And he is also the father of the circumcised who not only are circumcised but who also walk in the footsteps of the faith that our father Abraham had before he was circumcised.

[13]It was not through law that Abraham and his offspring received the promise that he would be heir of the world, but through the righteousness that comes by faith. [14]For if those who live by law are heirs, faith has no value and the promise is worthless, [15]because law brings wrath. And where there is no law there is no transgression.

[16]Therefore, the promise comes by faith, so that it may be by grace and may be guaranteed to all Abraham's offspring—not only to those who are of the law but also to those who are of the faith of Abraham. He is the father of us all. [17]As it is written: "I have made you a father of many nations."[b] He is our father in the sight of God, in whom he believed—the God who gives life to the dead and calls things that are not as though they were.

[18]Against all hope, Abraham in hope believed and so became the father of many nations, just as it had been said to him, "So shall your offspring be."[c] [19]Without weakening in his faith, he faced the fact that his body was as good as dead—since he was about a hundred years old—and that Sarah's womb was also dead. [20]Yet he did not waver through unbelief regarding the promise of God, but was strengthened in his faith and gave glory to God, [21]being fully persuaded that God had power to do what he had promised. [22]This is why "it was credited to him as righteousness." [23]The words "it was credited to him" were written not for him alone, [24]but also for us, to whom God will credit righteousness—for us who believe in him who raised Jesus our Lord from the dead. [25]He was delivered over to death for our sins and was raised to life for our justification.

Peace and Joy

5 Therefore, since we have been justified through faith, we[d] have peace with God through our Lord Jesus Christ, [2]through whom we have gained access by faith into this grace in which we now stand. And we[d] rejoice in the hope of the glory of God. [3]Not only so, but we[d] also rejoice in our sufferings, because we know that suffering produces perseverance; [4]perseverance, character; and character, hope. [5]And hope does not disappoint us, because God has poured out his love into our hearts by the Holy Spirit, whom he has given us.

[6]You see, at just the right time, when we were still powerless, Christ died for the ungodly. [7]Very rarely will anyone die for a righteous man, though for a good man someone might possibly dare to die. [8]But God demonstrates his own love for us in this: While we were still sinners, Christ died for us.

[9]Since we have now been justified by his blood, how much more shall we be saved from God's wrath through him! [10]For if, when we were God's enemies, we were reconciled to

---

[a]8 Psalm 32:1,2   [b]17 Gen. 17:5   [c]18 Gen. 15:5   [d]1,2,3 Or let us

VERSE:
Romans 5:5

AUTHOR:
Paul B. Maves

PASSAGE:
Romans 5:1–11

Hope Doesn't Disappoint

Suffering has been described by some as a pedagogue to teach us our limits and to prevent us from destroying ourselves. It is said to be a training ground on which we can develop strength of character, acquire patience, learn compassion and develop bonds of empathy with others. Paul says, "We also rejoice in our sufferings, because we know that suffering produces perseverance; perseverance, character; and character, hope. And hope does not disappoint us, because God has poured out his love into our hearts by the Holy Spirit, whom he has given us" (Romans 5:3–5).

We should note here, however, that it is not the suffering that is doing this, but the Holy Spirit, who enables Paul to make use of the suffering.

Paul is not talking about the suffering that comes from mistakes made out of ignorance or the negative consequences of his own sin, but of the evil encountered in the course of human existence . . .

The New Testament does not have an explanation for suffering. It only proclaims that God is in charge of his world and that a time will come when all suffering will cease, all tears will be dried, and all sorrow swallowed up in laughter. Then all things will be made clear, and the balances of justice will be redressed. God wills our salvation and our fulfillment, not our suffering or our destruction. God wills healing, not hurt. God wills eternal life, not death.

ADDITIONAL SCRIPTURE READINGS
Isaiah 55:8–13; 1 Peter 1:3–9

Go to page 1423 for your next devotional reading.

him through the death of his Son, how much more, having been reconciled, shall we be saved through his life! [11]Not only is this so, but we also rejoice in God through our Lord Jesus Christ, through whom we have now received reconciliation.

Death Through Adam, Life Through Christ

[12]Therefore, just as sin entered the world through one man, and death through sin, and in this way death came to all men, because all sinned— [13]for before the law was given, sin was in the world. But sin is not taken into account when there is no law. [14]Nevertheless, death reigned from the time of Adam to the time of Moses, even over those who did not sin by breaking a command, as did Adam, who was a pattern of the one to come.

[15]But the gift is not like the trespass. For if the many died by the trespass of the one man, how much more did God's grace and the gift that came by the grace of the one man, Jesus Christ, overflow to the many! [16]Again, the gift of God is not like the result of the one man's sin: The judgment followed one sin and brought condemnation, but the gift followed many trespasses and brought justification. [17]For if, by the trespass of the one man, death reigned through that one man, how much more will those who receive God's abundant provision of grace and of the gift of righteousness reign in life through the one man, Jesus Christ.

[18]Consequently, just as the result of one trespass was condemnation for all men, so also the result of one act of righteousness was justification that brings life for all men. [19]For just as through the disobedience of the one man the many were made sinners, so also through the obedience of the one man the many will be made righteous.

[20]The law was added so that the trespass might increase. But where sin increased, grace increased all the more, [21]so that, just as sin reigned in death, so also grace might reign through righteousness to bring eternal life through Jesus Christ our Lord.

Dead to Sin, Alive in Christ

6 What shall we say, then? Shall we go on sinning so that grace may increase? [2]By no means! We died to sin; how can we live in it any longer? [3]Or don't you know that all of us who were baptized into Christ Jesus were baptized into his death? [4]We were therefore buried with him through baptism into death in order that, just as Christ was raised from the dead through the glory of the Father, we too may live a new life.

[5]If we have been united with him like this in his death, we will certainly also be united with him in his resurrection. [6]For we know that our old self was crucified with him so that the body of sin might be done away with,[a] that we should no longer be slaves to sin— [7]because anyone who has died has been freed from sin.

[8]Now if we died with Christ, we believe that we will also live with him. [9]For we know that since Christ was raised from the dead, he cannot die again; death no longer has mastery over him. [10]The death he died, he died to sin once for all; but the life he lives, he lives to God.

[11]In the same way, count yourselves dead to sin but alive to God in Christ Jesus. [12]Therefore do not let sin reign in your mortal body so that you obey its evil desires. [13]Do not offer the parts of your body to sin, as instruments of wickedness, but rather offer yourselves to God, as those who have been brought from death to life; and offer the parts of your body to him as instruments of righteousness. [14]For sin shall not be your master, because you are not under law, but under grace.

---

[a]6 Or *be rendered powerless*

Slaves to Righteousness

¹⁵What then? Shall we sin because we are not under law but under grace? By no means! ¹⁶Don't you know that when you offer yourselves to someone to obey him as slaves, you are slaves to the one whom you obey—whether you are slaves to sin, which leads to death, or to obedience, which leads to righteousness? ¹⁷But thanks be to God that, though you used to be slaves to sin, you wholeheartedly obeyed the form of teaching to which you were entrusted. ¹⁸You have been set free from sin and have become slaves to righteousness.

¹⁹I put this in human terms because you are weak in your natural selves.

THURSDAY

VERSE: AUTHOR: PASSAGE:
Romans 6:5   Lloyd John Ogilvie   Romans 6:1–14

Resurrection Power

The power of the resurrection is the power of personal regeneration. Resurrection spells regeneration. The two things must always be kept together: the new world and the new person. Resurrection is not just a passport to heaven, but a power to change us now. It is a present gift, not a wistful longing. Paul says he wants to know Christ and the power of his resurrection [Philippians 3:10]. The two are the same. To know Christ today is to come under the influence of the same power that raised him from the dead. All life is meant to be an Eastertide full of perpetual renewal. Christ's mission is to change us and make us like himself. What a cruel thing an example is without the power to live it. Christ is the best of all examples, but more than that, he can come within us and give us his own Spirit to fulfill the example. The result is we actually become like him, we are able to do the things he did, and most of all, we are able to love as he loved. The Resurrection is the right angle where all the disillusionment, discouragement and disappointment with life, people and ourselves is met with power to change us and give us a new beginning.

ADDITIONAL SCRIPTURE READINGS
Ephesians 1:15–23; Ephesians 3:14–21

Go to page 1427 for your next devotional reading.

Just as you used to offer the parts of your body in slavery to impurity and to ever-increasing wickedness, so now offer them in slavery to righteousness leading to holiness. [20]When you were slaves to sin, you were free from the control of righteousness. [21]What benefit did you reap at that time from the things you are now ashamed of? Those things result in death! [22]But now that you have been set free from sin and have become slaves to God, the benefit you reap leads to holiness, and the result is eternal life. [23]For the wages of sin is death, but the gift of God is eternal life in[a] Christ Jesus our Lord.

An Illustration From Marriage

7 Do you not know, brothers—for I am speaking to men who know the law—that the law has authority over a man only as long as he lives? [2]For example, by law a married woman is bound to her husband as long as he is alive, but if her husband dies, she is released from the law of marriage. [3]So then, if she marries another man while her husband is still alive, she is called an adulteress. But if her husband dies, she is released from that law and is not an adulteress, even though she marries another man.

[4]So, my brothers, you also died to the law through the body of Christ, that you might belong to another, to him who was raised from the dead, in order that we might bear fruit to God. [5]For when we were controlled by the sinful nature,[b] the sinful passions aroused by the law were at work in our bodies, so that we bore fruit for death. [6]But now, by dying to what once bound us, we have been released from the law so that we serve in the new way of the Spirit, and not in the old way of the written code.

Struggling With Sin

[7]What shall we say, then? Is the law sin? Certainly not! Indeed I would not have known what sin was except through the law. For I would not have known what coveting really was if the law had not said, "Do not covet."[c] [8]But sin, seizing the opportunity afforded by the commandment, produced in me every kind of covetous desire. For apart from law, sin is dead. [9]Once I was alive apart from law; but when the commandment came, sin sprang to life and I died. [10]I found that the very commandment that was intended to bring life actually brought death. [11]For sin, seizing the opportunity afforded by the commandment, deceived me, and through the commandment put me to death. [12]So then, the law is holy, and the commandment is holy, righteous and good.

[13]Did that which is good, then, become death to me? By no means! But in order that sin might be recognized as sin, it produced death in me through what was good, so that through the commandment sin might become utterly sinful.

[14]We know that the law is spiritual; but I am unspiritual, sold as a slave to sin. [15]I do not understand what I do. For what I want to do I do not do, but what I hate I do. [16]And if I do what I do not want to do, I agree that the law is good. [17]As it is, it is no longer I myself who do it, but it is sin living in me. [18]I know that nothing good lives in me, that is, in my sinful nature.[d] For I have the desire to do what is good, but I cannot carry it out. [19]For what I do is not the good I want to do; no, the evil I do not want to do—this I keep on doing. [20]Now if I do what I do not want to do, it is no longer I who do it, but it is sin living in me that does it.

[21]So I find this law at work: When I want to do good, evil is right there with me. [22]For in my inner being I delight in God's law; [23]but I see another law at work in the members of my body, waging war against the law of my mind and making me a prisoner

---

[a]23 Or *through*   [b]5 Or *the flesh*; also in verse 25   [c]7 Exodus 20:17; Deut. 5:21
[d]18 Or *my flesh*

of the law of sin at work within my members. [24]What a wretched man I am! Who will rescue me from this body of death? [25]Thanks be to God— through Jesus Christ our Lord!

So then, I myself in my mind am a slave to God's law, but in the sinful nature a slave to the law of sin.

Life Through the Spirit

8 Therefore, there is now no condemnation for those who are in Christ Jesus,[a] [2]because through Christ Jesus the law of the Spirit of life set me free from the law of sin and death. [3]For what the law was powerless to do in that it was weakened by the sinful nature,[b] God did by sending his own Son in the likeness of sinful man to be a sin offering.[c] And so he condemned sin in sinful man,[d] [4]in order that the righteous requirements of the law might be fully met in us, who do not live according to the sinful nature but according to the Spirit.

[5]Those who live according to the sinful nature have their minds set on what that nature desires; but those who live in accordance with the Spirit have their minds set on what the Spirit desires. [6]The mind of sinful man[e] is death, but the mind controlled by the Spirit is life and peace; [7]the sinful mind[f] is hostile to God. It does not submit to God's law, nor can it do so. [8]Those controlled by the sinful nature cannot please God.

[9]You, however, are controlled not by the sinful nature but by the Spirit, if the Spirit of God lives in you. And if anyone does not have the Spirit of Christ, he does not belong to Christ. [10]But if Christ is in you, your body is dead because of sin, yet your spirit is alive because of righteousness. [11]And if the Spirit of him who raised Jesus from the dead is living in you, he who raised Christ from the dead will also give life to your mortal bodies through his Spirit, who lives in you.

[12]Therefore, brothers, we have an obligation—but it is not to the sinful nature, to live according to it. [13]For if you live according to the sinful nature, you will die; but if by the Spirit you put to death the misdeeds of the body, you will live, [14]because those who are led by the Spirit of God are sons of God. [15]For you did not receive a spirit that makes you a slave again to fear, but you received the Spirit of sonship.[g] And by him we cry, "Abba,[h] Father." [16]The Spirit himself testifies with our spirit that we are God's children. [17]Now if we are children, then we are heirs—heirs of God and co-heirs with Christ, if indeed we share in his sufferings in order that we may also share in his glory.

Future Glory

[18]I consider that our present sufferings are not worth comparing with the glory that will be revealed in us. [19]The creation waits in eager expectation for the sons of God to be revealed. [20]For the creation was subjected to frustration, not by its own choice, but by the will of the one who subjected it, in hope [21]that[i] the creation itself will be liberated from its bondage to decay and brought into the glorious freedom of the children of God.

[22]We know that the whole creation has been groaning as in the pains of childbirth right up to the present time. [23]Not only so, but we ourselves, who have the firstfruits of the Spirit, groan inwardly as we wait eagerly for our adoption as sons, the redemption of our bodies. [24]For in this hope we were saved. But hope that is seen is no hope at all. Who hopes for what he already has? [25]But if we hope for what we do not yet have, we wait for it patiently.

[26]In the same way, the Spirit helps us in our weakness. We do not know what we ought to pray for, but the

---

[a]1 Some later manuscripts Jesus, who do not live according to the sinful nature but according to the Spirit,   [b]3 Or the flesh; also in verses 4, 5, 8, 9, 12 and 13   [c]3 Or man, for sin   [d]3 Or in the flesh   [e]6 Or mind set on the flesh   [f]7 Or the mind set on the flesh   [g]15 Or adoption   [h]15 Aramaic for Father   [i]20,21 Or subjected it in hope. 21For

Spirit himself intercedes for us with groans that words cannot express. [27]And he who searches our hearts knows the mind of the Spirit, because the Spirit intercedes for the saints in accordance with God's will.

More Than Conquerors

[28]And we know that in all things God works for the good of those who love him,[a] who[b] have been called according to his purpose. [29]For those God foreknew he also predestined to be conformed to the likeness of his Son, that he might be the firstborn among many brothers. [30]And those he predestined, he also called; those he called, he also justified; those he justified, he also glorified.

[31]What, then, shall we say in response to this? If God is for us, who can be against us? [32]He who did not spare his own Son, but gave him up for us all—how will he not also, along with him, graciously give us all things? [33]Who will bring any charge against those whom God has chosen? It is God who justifies. [34]Who is he that condemns? Christ Jesus, who died—more than that, who was raised to life—is at the right hand of God and is also interceding for us. [35]Who shall separate us from the love of Christ? Shall trouble or hardship or persecution or famine or nakedness or danger or sword? [36]As it is written:

"For your sake we face death all
       day long;
   we are considered as sheep to
       be slaughtered."[c]

[37]No, in all these things we are more than conquerors through him who loved us. [38]For I am convinced that neither death nor life, neither angels nor demons,[d] neither the present nor the future, nor any powers, [39]neither height nor depth, nor anything else in all creation, will be able to separate us

from the love of God that is in Christ Jesus our Lord.

God's Sovereign Choice

9 I speak the truth in Christ—I am not lying, my conscience confirms it in the Holy Spirit— [2]I have great sorrow and unceasing anguish in my heart. [3]For I could wish that I myself were cursed and cut off from Christ for the sake of my brothers, those of my own race, [4]the people of Israel. Theirs is the adoption as sons; theirs the divine glory, the covenants, the receiving of the law, the temple worship and the promises. [5]Theirs are the patriarchs, and from them is traced the human ancestry of Christ, who is God over all, forever praised![e] Amen.

[6]It is not as though God's word had failed. For not all who are descended from Israel are Israel. [7]Nor because they are his descendants are they all Abraham's children. On the contrary, "It is through Isaac that your offspring will be reckoned."[f] [8]In other words, it is not the natural children who are God's children, but it is the children of the promise who are regarded as Abraham's offspring. [9]For this was how the promise was stated: "At the appointed time I will return, and Sarah will have a son."[g]

[10]Not only that, but Rebekah's children had one and the same father, our father Isaac. [11]Yet, before the twins were born or had done anything good or bad—in order that God's purpose in election might stand: [12]not by works but by him who calls—she was told, "The older will serve the younger."[h] [13]Just as it is written: "Jacob I loved, but Esau I hated."[i]

[14]What then shall we say? Is God unjust? Not at all! [15]For he says to Moses,

"I will have mercy on whom I
       have mercy,

---

a28 Some manuscripts *And we know that all things work together for good to those who love God*
b28 Or *works together with those who love him to bring about what is good—with those who*
c36 Psalm 44:22   d38 Or *nor heavenly rulers*   e5 Or *Christ, who is over all. God be forever praised! Or Christ. God who is over all be forever praised!*   f7 Gen. 21:12   g9 Gen. 18:10,14
h12 Gen. 25:23   i13 Mal. 1:2,3

VERSE: AUTHOR: PASSAGE:
Romans 8:31   Tim Stafford   Romans 8:31–39

If God Is for Us

Sometimes remembering is sad or bitter. It would be easier to drift in a nostalgic haze, avoiding some of the painful aspects of the past. But even melancholy thoughts are essential. An older person must come to grips with his losses and failures, and then come to grips with the larger fact of God's power, his understanding and his forgiveness. "If God is for us, who can be against us? He who did not spare his own Son, but gave him up for us all—how will he not also, along with him, graciously give us all things? Who will bring any charge against those whom God has chosen? It is God who justifies. Who is he that condemns?" (Romans 8:31–34).

An older person considering his past will certainly find reason for regret. Yet this exploration should carry him beyond regret, to the point of saying, with Christ, "Not guilty!" With that verdict on the past the future looks hopeful. "Will he not also ... graciously give us all things?"

Elders who accept Jesus' forgiveness may learn to echo Paul: "Whatever was to my profit I now consider loss for the sake of Christ. What is more, I consider everything a loss compared to the surpassing greatness of knowing Christ Jesus my Lord, for whose sake I have lost all things. I consider them rubbish, that I may gain Christ and be found in him" (Philippians 3:7–9).

ADDITIONAL SCRIPTURE READINGS
Psalm 103; Hebrews 8

Go to page 1429 for your next devotional reading.

and I will have compassion on whom I have compassion."[a]

¹⁶It does not, therefore, depend on man's desire or effort, but on God's mercy. ¹⁷For the Scripture says to Pharaoh: "I raised you up for this very purpose, that I might display my power in you and that my name might be proclaimed in all the earth."[b] ¹⁸Therefore God has mercy on whom he wants to have mercy, and he hardens whom he wants to harden.

¹⁹One of you will say to me: "Then why does God still blame us? For who resists his will?" ²⁰But who are you, O man, to talk back to God? "Shall what is formed say to him who formed it, 'Why did you make me like this?'"[c] ²¹Does not the potter have the right to make out of the same lump of clay some pottery for noble purposes and some for common use?

²²What if God, choosing to show his wrath and make his power known, bore with great patience the objects of his wrath—prepared for destruction? ²³What if he did this to make the riches of his glory known to the objects of his mercy, whom he prepared in advance for glory— ²⁴even us, whom he also called, not only from the Jews but also from the Gentiles? ²⁵As he says in Hosea:

"I will call them 'my people' who
     are not my people;
and I will call her 'my loved
     one' who is not my loved
     one,"[d]

²⁶and,

"It will happen that in the very
     place where it was said to
     them,
'You are not my people,'
they will be called 'sons of the
     living God.'"[e]

²⁷Isaiah cries out concerning Israel:

"Though the number of the
     Israelites be like the sand
     by the sea,
only the remnant will be saved.
²⁸For the Lord will carry out
     his sentence on earth with
     speed and finality."[f]

²⁹It is just as Isaiah said previously:

"Unless the Lord Almighty
     had left us descendants,
we would have become like
     Sodom,
we would have been like
     Gomorrah."[g]

Israel's Unbelief

³⁰What then shall we say? That the Gentiles, who did not pursue righteousness, have obtained it, a righteousness that is by faith; ³¹but Israel, who pursued a law of righteousness, has not attained it. ³²Why not? Because they pursued it not by faith but as if it were by works. They stumbled over the "stumbling stone." ³³As it is written:

"See, I lay in Zion a stone that
     causes men to stumble
     and a rock that makes them fall,
and the one who trusts in him
     will never be put to
     shame."[h]

10 Brothers, my heart's desire and prayer to God for the Israelites is that they may be saved. ²For I can testify about them that they are zealous for God, but their zeal is not based on knowledge. ³Since they did not know the righteousness that comes from God and sought to establish their own, they did not submit to God's righteousness. ⁴Christ is the end of the law so that there may be righteousness for everyone who believes.

⁵Moses describes in this way the righteousness that is by the law: "The man who does these things will live by them."[i] ⁶But the righteousness that is by faith says: "Do not say in

---

a15 Exodus 33:19   b17 Exodus 9:16   c20 Isaiah 29:16; 45:9   d25 Hosea 2:23
e26 Hosea 1:10   f28 Isaiah 10:22,23   g29 Isaiah 1:9   h33 Isaiah 8:14; 28:16   i5 Lev. 18:5

PASSAGE: Isaiah 54:1–10; Romans 8:28–39
AUTHOR: James Grindlay Small

I've Found a Friend

I've found a Friend, O such a Friend!
　　He loved me ere I knew Him;
He drew me with the cords of love,
　　And thus He bound me to Him;
And round my heart still closely twine
　　Those ties which nought can sever;
For I am His, and He is mine,
　　For ever and for ever.

I've found a Friend, O such a Friend!
　　All power to Him is given,
To guard me on my onward course,
　　And bring me safe to heaven.
The eternal glories gleam afar,
　　To nerve my faint endeavor;
So now to watch! to work! to war!
　　And then to rest for ever.

I've found a Friend, O such a Friend.
　　So kind, and true, and tender!
So wise a Counselor and Guide,
　　So mighty a Defender!
From Him who loves me now so well
　　What power my soul can sever?
Shall life or death, or earth or hell?
　　No! I am His for ever.

Go to page 1432 for your next devotional reading.

your heart, 'Who will ascend into heaven?'[a]" (that is, to bring Christ down) [7]"or 'Who will descend into the deep?'[b]" (that is, to bring Christ up from the dead). [8]But what does it say? "The word is near you; it is in your mouth and in your heart,"[c] that is, the word of faith we are proclaiming: [9]That if you confess with your mouth, "Jesus is Lord," and believe in your heart that God raised him from the dead, you will be saved. [10]For it is with your heart that you believe and are justified, and it is with your mouth that you confess and are saved. [11]As the Scripture says, "Anyone who trusts in him will never be put to shame."[d] [12]For there is no difference between Jew and Gentile—the same Lord is Lord of all and richly blesses all who call on him, [13]for, "Everyone who calls on the name of the Lord will be saved."[e]

[14]How, then, can they call on the one they have not believed in? And how can they believe in the one of whom they have not heard? And how can they hear without someone preaching to them? [15]And how can they preach unless they are sent? As it is written, "How beautiful are the feet of those who bring good news!"[f]

[16]But not all the Israelites accepted the good news. For Isaiah says, "Lord, who has believed our message?"[g] [17]Consequently, faith comes from hearing the message, and the message is heard through the word of Christ. [18]But I ask: Did they not hear? Of course they did:

"Their voice has gone out into all
    the earth,
  their words to the ends of the
    world."[h]

[19]Again I ask: Did Israel not understand? First, Moses says,

"I will make you envious by those
    who are not a nation;

I will make you angry by a
    nation that has no
    understanding."[i]

[20]And Isaiah boldly says,

"I was found by those who did
    not seek me;
  I revealed myself to those who
    did not ask for me."[j]

[21]But concerning Israel he says,

"All day long I have held out my
    hands
  to a disobedient and obstinate
    people."[k]

The Remnant of Israel

11 I ask then: Did God reject his people? By no means! I am an Israelite myself, a descendant of Abraham, from the tribe of Benjamin. [2]God did not reject his people, whom he foreknew. Don't you know what the Scripture says in the passage about Elijah—how he appealed to God against Israel: [3]"Lord, they have killed your prophets and torn down your altars; I am the only one left, and they are trying to kill me"[l]? [4]And what was God's answer to him? "I have reserved for myself seven thousand who have not bowed the knee to Baal."[m] [5]So too, at the present time there is a remnant chosen by grace. [6]And if by grace, then it is no longer by works; if it were, grace would no longer be grace.[n]

[7]What then? What Israel sought so earnestly it did not obtain, but the elect did. The others were hardened, [8]as it is written:

"God gave them a spirit of stupor,
  eyes so that they could not see
  and ears so that they could not
    hear,
to this very day."[o]

[9]And David says:

---

[a]6 Deut. 30:12   [b]7 Deut. 30:13   [c]8 Deut. 30:14   [d]11 Isaiah 28:16   [e]13 Joel 2:32   [f]15 Isaiah 52:7   [g]16 Isaiah 53:1   [h]18 Psalm 19:4   [i]19 Deut. 32:21 [j]20 Isaiah 65:1   [k]21 Isaiah 65:2   [l]3 1 Kings 19:10,14   [m]4 1 Kings 19:18   [n]6 Some manuscripts *by grace. But if by works, then it is no longer grace; if it were, work would no longer be work.*   [o]8 Deut. 29:4; Isaiah 29:10

"May their table become a snare
and a trap,
a stumbling block and a
retribution for them.
[10]May their eyes be darkened so
they cannot see,
and their backs be bent
forever." [a]

Ingrafted Branches

[11]Again I ask: Did they stumble so as to fall beyond recovery? Not at all! Rather, because of their transgression, salvation has come to the Gentiles to make Israel envious. [12]But if their transgression means riches for the world, and their loss means riches for the Gentiles, how much greater riches will their fullness bring!

[13]I am talking to you Gentiles. Inasmuch as I am the apostle to the Gentiles, I make much of my ministry [14]in the hope that I may somehow arouse my own people to envy and save some of them. [15]For if their rejection is the reconciliation of the world, what will their acceptance be but life from the dead? [16]If the part of the dough offered as firstfruits is holy, then the whole batch is holy; if the root is holy, so are the branches.

[17]If some of the branches have been broken off, and you, though a wild olive shoot, have been grafted in among the others and now share in the nourishing sap from the olive root, [18]do not boast over those branches. If you do, consider this: You do not support the root, but the root supports you. [19]You will say then, "Branches were broken off so that I could be grafted in." [20]Granted. But they were broken off because of unbelief, and you stand by faith. Do not be arrogant, but be afraid. [21]For if God did not spare the natural branches, he will not spare you either.

[22]Consider therefore the kindness and sternness of God: sternness to those who fell, but kindness to you, provided that you continue in his kindness. Otherwise, you also will be cut off. [23]And if they do not persist in unbelief, they will be grafted in, for God is able to graft them in again. [24]After all, if you were cut out of an olive tree that is wild by nature, and contrary to nature were grafted into a cultivated olive tree, how much more readily will these, the natural branches, be grafted into their own olive tree!

All Israel Will Be Saved

[25]I do not want you to be ignorant of this mystery, brothers, so that you may not be conceited: Israel has experienced a hardening in part until the full number of the Gentiles has come in. [26]And so all Israel will be saved, as it is written:

"The deliverer will come from
Zion;
he will turn godlessness away
from Jacob.
[27]And this is[b] my covenant with
them
when I take away their sins." [c]

[28]As far as the gospel is concerned, they are enemies on your account; but as far as election is concerned, they are loved on account of the patriarchs, [29]for God's gifts and his call are irrevocable. [30]Just as you who were at one time disobedient to God have now received mercy as a result of their disobedience, [31]so they too have now become disobedient in order that they too may now[d] receive mercy as a result of God's mercy to you. [32]For God has bound all men over to disobedience so that he may have mercy on them all.

Doxology

[33]Oh, the depth of the riches of the
wisdom and[e] knowledge
of God!
How unsearchable his
judgments,
and his paths beyond tracing
out!

---

[a]10 Psalm 69:22,23   [b]27 Or *will be*   [c]27 Isaiah 59:20,21; 27:9; Jer. 31:33,34   [d]31 Some manuscripts do not have *now*.   [e]33 Or *riches and the wisdom and the*

VERSE:	AUTHOR:	PASSAGE:
Romans 11:33	Charles R. Swindoll	Romans 11:33–36

Tomorrow

Tomorrow. It may bring sickness, sorrow or tragedy. It may announce an answer to your waiting prayer. It may introduce you to prosperity, the beginning of a friendship, a choice opportunity for sharing your Lord . . . or just another 24 hours of waiting, trusting and claiming his presence. It may not even come! God may choose this very day to intervene and take you home . . . We can speculate, we can dread, we can dream — but we do not know.

This sort of thinking leads to an inevitable question: Are you ready? "Ready for what?" you may ask. "Ready for *anything*" is my answer. Is your trust, your attitude of dependence, sufficiently stable to sustain you *regardless*? Remember Job's avalanche [Job 1–2]? Should your Lord be pleased to turn you into a Job, would he still be your Treasure and your Triumph? Don't let the answer slip off your tongue too easily. Think about the implications of that question to your own life, health, job and family. Should your Lord make you an Enoch, would you be reluctant to make that eternal journey?

Thank the Lord, it is his *love* that arranges our tomorrows . . . and we may be certain that whatever it brings, his love sent it our way. That is why I smile every time I read Romans 11:33. Let it bring a smile into your world. "Oh, the depth of the riches of the wisdom and knowledge of God! How unsearchable his judgments, and his paths beyond tracing out!"

ADDITIONAL SCRIPTURE READINGS
Philippians 4:10–20; 1 Peter 4:7–11

Go to page 1434 for your next devotional reading.

[34]"Who has known the mind of the
  Lord?
    Or who has been his
      counselor?"[a]
[35]"Who has ever given to God,
    that God should repay him?"[b]
[36]For from him and through him
    and to him are all things.
  To him be the glory forever!
    Amen.

Living Sacrifices

12 Therefore, I urge you, brothers, in view of God's mercy, to offer your bodies as living sacrifices, holy and pleasing to God—this is your spiritual[c] act of worship. [2]Do not conform any longer to the pattern of this world, but be transformed by the renewing of your mind. Then you will be able to test and approve what God's will is—his good, pleasing and perfect will.

[3]For by the grace given me I say to every one of you: Do not think of yourself more highly than you ought, but rather think of yourself with sober judgment, in accordance with the measure of faith God has given you. [4]Just as each of us has one body with many members, and these members do not all have the same function, [5]so in Christ we who are many form one body, and each member belongs to all the others. [6]We have different gifts, according to the grace given us. If a man's gift is prophesying, let him use it in proportion to his[d] faith. [7]If it is serving, let him serve; if it is teaching, let him teach; [8]if it is encouraging, let him encourage; if it is contributing to the needs of others, let him give generously; if it is leadership, let him govern diligently; if it is showing mercy, let him do it cheerfully.

Love

[9]Love must be sincere. Hate what is evil; cling to what is good. [10]Be devoted to one another in brotherly love. Honor one another above yourselves. [11]Never be lacking in zeal, but keep your spiritual fervor, serving the Lord. [12]Be joyful in hope, patient in affliction, faithful in prayer. [13]Share with God's people who are in need. Practice hospitality.

[14]Bless those who persecute you; bless and do not curse. [15]Rejoice with those who rejoice; mourn with those who mourn. [16]Live in harmony with one another. Do not be proud, but be willing to associate with people of low position.[e] Do not be conceited.

[17]Do not repay anyone evil for evil. Be careful to do what is right in the eyes of everybody. [18]If it is possible, as far as it depends on you, live at peace with everyone. [19]Do not take revenge, my friends, but leave room for God's wrath, for it is written: "It is mine to avenge; I will repay,"[f] says the Lord. [20]On the contrary:

  "If your enemy is hungry, feed
    him;
  if he is thirsty, give him
    something to drink.
  In doing this, you will heap
    burning coals on his
    head."[g]

[21]Do not be overcome by evil, but overcome evil with good.

Submission to the Authorities

13 Everyone must submit himself to the governing authorities, for there is no authority except that which God has established. The authorities that exist have been established by God. [2]Consequently, he who rebels against the authority is rebelling against what God has instituted, and those who do so will bring judgment on themselves. [3]For rulers hold no terror for those who do right, but for those who do wrong. Do you want to be free from fear of the one in authority? Then do what is right and he will commend you. [4]For he is God's servant to do you good. But if you do wrong, be afraid, for he does not bear the sword for nothing. He is God's servant, an agent of wrath to

---

[a]34 Isaiah 40:13   [b]35 Job 41:11   [c]1 Or *reasonable*   [d]6 Or *in agreement with the*   [e]16 Or *willing to do menial work*   [f]19 Deut. 32:35   [g]20 Prov. 25:21,22

TUESDAY

VERSE:	AUTHOR:	PASSAGE:
Romans 12:10	Jean Vanier	Romans 12:9–21

In Brotherly Love

Jesus calls his friends to community, where they live and share together. They are called in their unity and love for one another to be a sign of and a witness to something very special—the life of the Spirit, a rebirth, the good news.

We know that we need brothers and sisters if we are to grow in the Spirit. They help us by the way they live; they encourage and strengthen us ... Community is one of the most beautiful realities—brothers and sisters loving and being together. It is also one of the most difficult to accomplish ...

The road to community is the passage towards death to oneself and the rebirth of love, and that is a long road. It means the passage from our own interests to those of the community; the passage from my choice for me to my choice for others ...

As the barriers fall, you begin to get the feeling of unity, which is the reality of people growing together in love, sharing deeply and without fear ... But it is only, finally, by the Spirit coming into us that we can enter real community, whether this is a group of people who meet occasionally to pray or to share together, or people who live together. It is only when the Spirit changes our hearts that we can love all those of our community, whatever their age and background and character, because Jesus has called us to be together, because the other person is a gift of God to me today. This is the beauty of people when they live together, love together, when they are beginning to grow and share and be open in the Spirit together.

ADDITIONAL SCRIPTURE READINGS
John 13:31–38; John 17:20–26

Go to page 1437 for your next devotional reading.

bring punishment on the wrongdoer. [5]Therefore, it is necessary to submit to the authorities, not only because of possible punishment but also because of conscience.

[6]This is also why you pay taxes, for the authorities are God's servants, who give their full time to governing. [7]Give everyone what you owe him: If you owe taxes, pay taxes; if revenue, then revenue; if respect, then respect; if honor, then honor.

Love, for the Day Is Near

[8]Let no debt remain outstanding, except the continuing debt to love one another, for he who loves his fellowman has fulfilled the law. [9]The commandments, "Do not commit adultery," "Do not murder," "Do not steal," "Do not covet,"[a] and whatever other commandment there may be, are summed up in this one rule: "Love your neighbor as yourself."[b] [10]Love does no harm to its neighbor. Therefore love is the fulfillment of the law.

[11]And do this, understanding the present time. The hour has come for you to wake up from your slumber, because our salvation is nearer now than when we first believed. [12]The night is nearly over; the day is almost here. So let us put aside the deeds of darkness and put on the armor of light. [13]Let us behave decently, as in the daytime, not in orgies and drunkenness, not in sexual immorality and debauchery, not in dissension and jealousy. [14]Rather, clothe yourselves with the Lord Jesus Christ, and do not think about how to gratify the desires of the sinful nature.[c]

The Weak and the Strong

14 Accept him whose faith is weak, without passing judgment on disputable matters. [2]One man's faith allows him to eat everything, but another man, whose faith is weak, eats only vegetables. [3]The man who eats everything must not look down on him who does not, and the man who does not eat everything must not condemn the man who does, for God has accepted him. [4]Who are you to judge someone else's servant? To his own master he stands or falls. And he will stand, for the Lord is able to make him stand.

[5]One man considers one day more sacred than another; another man considers every day alike. Each one should be fully convinced in his own mind. [6]He who regards one day as special, does so to the Lord. He who eats meat, eats to the Lord, for he gives thanks to God; and he who abstains, does so to the Lord and gives thanks to God. [7]For none of us lives to himself alone and none of us dies to himself alone. [8]If we live, we live to the Lord; and if we die, we die to the Lord. So, whether we live or die, we belong to the Lord.

[9]For this very reason, Christ died and returned to life so that he might be the Lord of both the dead and the living. [10]You, then, why do you judge your brother? Or why do you look down on your brother? For we will all stand before God's judgment seat. [11]It is written:

> " 'As surely as I live,' says the
>   Lord,
> 'every knee will bow before me;
>   every tongue will confess to
>   God.' "[d]

[12]So then, each of us will give an account of himself to God.

[13]Therefore let us stop passing judgment on one another. Instead, make up your mind not to put any stumbling block or obstacle in your brother's way. [14]As one who is in the Lord Jesus, I am fully convinced that no food[e] is unclean in itself. But if anyone regards something as unclean, then for him it is unclean. [15]If your brother is distressed because of what you eat, you are no longer acting in love. Do not by your eating destroy your brother for whom Christ

---

[a]9 Exodus 20:13-15,17; Deut. 5:17-19,21   [b]9 Lev. 19:18   [c]14 Or *the flesh*   [d]11 Isaiah 45:23
[e]14 Or *that nothing*

died. ¹⁶Do not allow what you consider good to be spoken of as evil. ¹⁷For the kingdom of God is not a matter of eating and drinking, but of righteousness, peace and joy in the Holy Spirit, ¹⁸because anyone who serves Christ in this way is pleasing to God and approved by men.

¹⁹Let us therefore make every effort to do what leads to peace and to mutual edification. ²⁰Do not destroy the work of God for the sake of food. All food is clean, but it is wrong for a man to eat anything that causes someone else to stumble. ²¹It is better not to eat meat or drink wine or to do anything else that will cause your brother to fall.

²²So whatever you believe about these things keep between yourself and God. Blessed is the man who does not condemn himself by what he approves. ²³But the man who has doubts is condemned if he eats, because his eating is not from faith; and everything that does not come from faith is sin.

15 We who are strong ought to bear with the failings of the weak and not to please ourselves. ²Each of us should please his neighbor for his good, to build him up. ³For even Christ did not please himself but, as it is written: "The insults of those who insult you have fallen on me."ᵃ ⁴For everything that was written in the past was written to teach us, so that through endurance and the encouragement of the Scriptures we might have hope.

⁵May the God who gives endurance and encouragement give you a spirit of unity among yourselves as you follow Christ Jesus, ⁶so that with one heart and mouth you may glorify the God and Father of our Lord Jesus Christ.

⁷Accept one another, then, just as Christ accepted you, in order to bring praise to God. ⁸For I tell you that Christ has become a servant of the Jewsᵇ on behalf of God's truth, to confirm the promises made to the patriarchs ⁹so that the Gentiles may glorify God for his mercy, as it is written:

"Therefore I will praise you
    among the Gentiles;
I will sing hymns to your
    name."ᶜ

¹⁰Again, it says,

"Rejoice, O Gentiles, with his
    people."ᵈ

¹¹And again,

"Praise the Lord, all you Gentiles,
    and sing praises to him, all you
    peoples."ᵉ

¹²And again, Isaiah says,

"The Root of Jesse will spring up,
    one who will arise to rule over
    the nations;
the Gentiles will hope in him."ᶠ

¹³May the God of hope fill you with all joy and peace as you trust in him, so that you may overflow with hope by the power of the Holy Spirit.

Paul the Minister to the Gentiles

¹⁴I myself am convinced, my brothers, that you yourselves are full of goodness, complete in knowledge and competent to instruct one another. ¹⁵I have written you quite boldly on some points, as if to remind you of them again, because of the grace God gave me ¹⁶to be a minister of Christ Jesus to the Gentiles with the priestly duty of proclaiming the gospel of God, so that the Gentiles might become an offering acceptable to God, sanctified by the Holy Spirit.

¹⁷Therefore I glory in Christ Jesus in my service to God. ¹⁸I will not venture to speak of anything except what Christ has accomplished through me in leading the Gentiles to obey God by what I have said and done— ¹⁹by the power of signs and miracles,

ᵃ3 Psalm 69:9   ᵇ8 Greek circumcision   ᶜ9 2 Samuel 22:50; Psalm 18:49   ᵈ10 Deut. 32:43
ᵉ11 Psalm 117:1   ᶠ12 Isaiah 11:10

through the power of the Spirit. So from Jerusalem all the way around to Illyricum, I have fully proclaimed the gospel of Christ. ²⁰It has always been my ambition to preach the gospel where Christ was not known, so that I would not be building on someone else's foundation. ²¹Rather, as it is written:

"Those who were not told about
him will see,

VERSE:	AUTHOR:	PASSAGE:
Romans 14:8	Don Anderson	Romans 14:5–12

For Whom Am I Living?

As you approach senior adulthood, ask yourself, for whom and what am I living? Is it a marriage, a job, a house, a dream? Children or grandchildren? Leisure, recreation, sport? Television, church, music, food? Whatever you live for, will it last? . . .

Living for a pursuit, a career, an avocation, even a church are simply ways of living for ourselves. There is nothing wrong with recreation, relaxation and rest. There is nothing wrong with devoting ourselves to a hobby, sport or other avocation. But there is a problem when these activities become the sum total of our existence, our reason for being! Then life lacks deeper meaning and purpose. What really counts is missing.

Living for ourselves ultimately yields bitter fruit! We require a higher calling. C.T. Studd, a missionary to Africa who gave up fortune and family to spend himself for God, said, "If Christ be God and died for me, there is nothing too great that I can do for him."

As Christians we must ask ourselves, "For whom or what am I living?" The utter abandonment of ourselves to Jesus Christ is a vital step toward Christian maturity. It is never too late to begin living for the glory of God, no matter what.

ADDITIONAL SCRIPTURE READINGS
1 Corinthians 10:23 – 11:1; Philippians 1:12–30

Go to page 1442 for your next devotional reading.

and those who have not heard will understand."[a]

[22]This is why I have often been hindered from coming to you.

Paul's Plan to Visit Rome

[23]But now that there is no more place for me to work in these regions, and since I have been longing for many years to see you, [24]I plan to do so when I go to Spain. I hope to visit you while passing through and to have you assist me on my journey there, after I have enjoyed your company for a while. [25]Now, however, I am on my way to Jerusalem in the service of the saints there. [26]For Macedonia and Achaia were pleased to make a contribution for the poor among the saints in Jerusalem. [27]They were pleased to do it, and indeed they owe it to them. For if the Gentiles have shared in the Jews' spiritual blessings, they owe it to the Jews to share with them their material blessings. [28]So after I have completed this task and have made sure that they have received this fruit, I will go to Spain and visit you on the way. [29]I know that when I come to you, I will come in the full measure of the blessing of Christ.

[30]I urge you, brothers, by our Lord Jesus Christ and by the love of the Spirit, to join me in my struggle by praying to God for me. [31]Pray that I may be rescued from the unbelievers in Judea and that my service in Jerusalem may be acceptable to the saints there, [32]so that by God's will I may come to you with joy and together with you be refreshed. [33]The God of peace be with you all. Amen.

Personal Greetings

16 I commend to you our sister Phoebe, a servant[b] of the church in Cenchrea. [2]I ask you to receive her in the Lord in a way worthy of the saints and to give her any help she may need from you, for she has been a great help to many people, including me.

[3]Greet Priscilla[c] and Aquila, my fellow workers in Christ Jesus. [4]They risked their lives for me. Not only I but all the churches of the Gentiles are grateful to them. [5]Greet also the church that meets at their house.

Greet my dear friend Epenetus, who was the first convert to Christ in the province of Asia. [6]Greet Mary, who worked very hard for you. [7]Greet Andronicus and Junias, my relatives who have been in prison with me. They are outstanding among the apostles, and they were in Christ before I was. [8]Greet Ampliatus, whom I love in the Lord. [9]Greet Urbanus, our fellow worker in Christ, and my dear friend Stachys. [10]Greet Apelles, tested and approved in Christ.

Greet those who belong to the household of Aristobulus. [11]Greet Herodion, my relative.

Greet those in the household of Narcissus who are in the Lord. [12]Greet Tryphena and Tryphosa, those women who work hard in the Lord.

Greet my dear friend Persis, another woman who has worked very hard in the Lord. [13]Greet Rufus, chosen in the Lord, and his mother, who has been a mother to me, too. [14]Greet Asyncritus, Phlegon, Hermes, Patrobas, Hermas and the brothers with them. [15]Greet Philologus, Julia, Nereus and his sister, and Olympas and all the saints with them. [16]Greet one another with a holy kiss. All the churches of Christ send greetings.

[17]I urge you, brothers, to watch out

---

[a]21 Isaiah 52:15   [b]1 Or deaconess   [c]3 Greek Prisca, a variant of Priscilla

for those who cause divisions and put obstacles in your way that are contrary to the teaching you have learned. Keep away from them. [18]For such people are not serving our Lord Christ, but their own appetites. By smooth talk and flattery they deceive the minds of naive people. [19]Everyone has heard about your obedience, so I am full of joy over you; but I want you to be wise about what is good, and innocent about what is evil.

[20]The God of peace will soon crush Satan under your feet.

The grace of our Lord Jesus be with you.

[21]Timothy, my fellow worker, sends his greetings to you, as do Lucius, Jason and Sosipater, my relatives.

[22]I, Tertius, who wrote down this letter, greet you in the Lord.

[23]Gaius, whose hospitality I and the whole church here enjoy, sends you his greetings.

Erastus, who is the city's director of public works, and our brother Quartus send you their greetings.[a]

[25]Now to him who is able to establish you by my gospel and the proclamation of Jesus Christ, according to the revelation of the mystery hidden for long ages past, [26]but now revealed and made known through the prophetic writings by the command of the eternal God, so that all nations might believe and obey him— [27]to the only wise God be glory forever through Jesus Christ! Amen.

Paul the apostle wrote this letter to the church he started in Corinth (Acts 18:1–17). He addressed issues and questions on matters such as marriage, money, freedom, resolving conflict, using one's gifts, and death. As you read this letter, imagine Paul as your mentor, guiding you into a deeper understanding of God's will and encouraging you to live a life of love for God and for each other.

1 CORINTHIANS

1 Paul, called to be an apostle of Christ Jesus by the will of God, and our brother Sosthenes,

²To the church of God in Corinth, to those sanctified in Christ Jesus and called to be holy, together with all those everywhere who call on the name of our Lord Jesus Christ—their Lord and ours:

³Grace and peace to you from God our Father and the Lord Jesus Christ.

Thanksgiving

⁴I always thank God for you because of his grace given you in Christ Jesus. ⁵For in him you have been enriched in every way—in all your speaking and in all your knowledge— ⁶because our testimony about Christ was confirmed in you. ⁷Therefore you do not lack any spiritual gift as you eagerly wait for our Lord Jesus Christ to be revealed. ⁸He will keep you strong to the end, so that you will be blameless on the day of our Lord Jesus Christ. ⁹God, who has called you into fellowship with his Son Jesus Christ our Lord, is faithful.

Divisions in the Church

¹⁰I appeal to you, brothers, in the name of our Lord Jesus Christ, that all of you agree with one another so that there may be no divisions among you and that you may be perfectly united in mind and thought. ¹¹My brothers, some from Chloe's household have informed me that there are quarrels among you. ¹²What I mean is this: One of you says, "I follow Paul"; another, "I follow Apollos"; another, "I follow Cephas*a*"; still another, "I follow Christ."

¹³Is Christ divided? Was Paul crucified for you? Were you baptized

a12 That is, Peter

into[a] the name of Paul? [14]I am thankful that I did not baptize any of you except Crispus and Gaius, [15]so no one can say that you were baptized into my name. [16](Yes, I also baptized the household of Stephanas; beyond that, I don't remember if I baptized anyone else.) [17]For Christ did not send me to baptize, but to preach the gospel—not with words of human wisdom, lest the cross of Christ be emptied of its power.

Christ the Wisdom and Power of God

[18]For the message of the cross is foolishness to those who are perishing, but to us who are being saved it is the power of God. [19]For it is written:

"I will destroy the wisdom of the
    wise;
  the intelligence of the intelligent
    I will frustrate."[b]

[20]Where is the wise man? Where is the scholar? Where is the philosopher of this age? Has not God made foolish the wisdom of the world? [21]For since in the wisdom of God the world through its wisdom did not know him, God was pleased through the foolishness of what was preached to save those who believe. [22]Jews demand miraculous signs and Greeks look for wisdom, [23]but we preach Christ crucified: a stumbling block to Jews and foolishness to Gentiles, [24]but to those whom God has called, both Jews and Greeks, Christ the power of God and the wisdom of God. [25]For the foolishness of God is wiser than man's wisdom, and the weakness of God is stronger than man's strength.

[26]Brothers, think of what you were when you were called. Not many of you were wise by human standards; not many were influential; not many were of noble birth. [27]But God chose the foolish things of the world to shame the wise; God chose the weak things of the world to shame the

strong. [28]He chose the lowly things of this world and the despised things—and the things that are not—to nullify the things that are, [29]so that no one may boast before him. [30]It is because of him that you are in Christ Jesus, who has become for us wisdom from God—that is, our righteousness, holiness and redemption. [31]Therefore, as it is written: "Let him who boasts boast in the Lord."[c]

2 When I came to you, brothers, I did not come with eloquence or superior wisdom as I proclaimed to you the testimony about God.[d] [2]For I resolved to know nothing while I was with you except Jesus Christ and him crucified. [3]I came to you in weakness and fear, and with much trembling. [4]My message and my preaching were not with wise and persuasive words, but with a demonstration of the Spirit's power, [5]so that your faith might not rest on men's wisdom, but on God's power.

Wisdom From the Spirit

[6]We do, however, speak a message of wisdom among the mature, but not the wisdom of this age or of the rulers of this age, who are coming to nothing. [7]No, we speak of God's secret wisdom, a wisdom that has been hidden and that God destined for our glory before time began. [8]None of the rulers of this age understood it, for if they had, they would not have crucified the Lord of glory. [9]However, as it is written:

"No eye has seen,
  no ear has heard,
no mind has conceived
  what God has prepared for
    those who love him"[e]—

[10]but God has revealed it to us by his Spirit.

The Spirit searches all things, even the deep things of God. [11]For who among men knows the thoughts of a man except the man's spirit within him? In the same way no one knows

---

VERSE:
1 Corinthians
2:9

AUTHOR:
Elizabeth Skoglund

PASSAGE:
1 Corinthians
2:6–10

Preparing to Meet the King

Ultimately, the last fear of old age is death itself. For as much as we may long to see the face of our Savior, the process of getting there can be frightening. Even heaven is new, and new is always a little scary. We hear much today about people living on the street in filth, starvation and freezing weather. Yet many of these people refuse shelters, because the fear of the unknown, even though it may be infinitely better than the known, is still frightening since it is unknown. In the same way, when we enter heaven I am sure we will be amazed at the tenacious hold we had on earth, when there was all that glory awaiting us. For as beautiful as this earth can sometimes be — and I, for one, want to stay here as long as I can — "No eye has seen, no ear has heard, no mind has conceived what God has prepared for those who love him."

Not long ago I had the privilege of attending a dinner honoring the king and queen of Sweden. "What shall I wear?" was the question foremost in my mind. It was incredible how long it took to put all the right clothes, jewelry and accessories together. Then it took still more time to look up the protocol for meeting royalty. Dining with a king and queen was, in short, an event which required hours of preparation. As I looked back on the event, I could not help but conclude that if we put such pains into our preparation for meeting an earthly monarch, how much more should we prepare before going into the presence of our heavenly King!

ADDITIONAL SCRIPTURE READINGS
Matthew 25:1–13; 1 John 4:7–21

Go to page 1444 for your next devotional reading.

the thoughts of God except the Spirit of God. [12]We have not received the spirit of the world but the Spirit who is from God, that we may understand what God has freely given us. [13]This is what we speak, not in words taught us by human wisdom but in words taught by the Spirit, expressing spiritual truths in spiritual words.[a] [14]The man without the Spirit does not accept the things that come from the Spirit of God, for they are foolishness to him, and he cannot understand them, because they are spiritually discerned. [15]The spiritual man makes judgments about all things, but he himself is not subject to any man's judgment:

[16]"For who has known the mind of
     the Lord
   that he may instruct him?"[b]

But we have the mind of Christ.

On Divisions in the Church

3 Brothers, I could not address you as spiritual but as worldly—mere infants in Christ. [2]I gave you milk, not solid food, for you were not yet ready for it. Indeed, you are still not ready. [3]You are still worldly. For since there is jealousy and quarreling among you, are you not worldly? Are you not acting like mere men? [4]For when one says, "I follow Paul," and another, "I follow Apollos," are you not mere men?

[5]What, after all, is Apollos? And what is Paul? Only servants, through whom you came to believe—as the Lord has assigned to each his task. [6]I planted the seed, Apollos watered it, but God made it grow. [7]So neither he who plants nor he who waters is anything, but only God, who makes things grow. [8]The man who plants and the man who waters have one purpose, and each will be rewarded according to his own labor. [9]For we are God's fellow workers; you are God's field, God's building.

[10]By the grace God has given me, I laid a foundation as an expert builder, and someone else is building on it. But each one should be careful how he builds. [11]For no one can lay any foundation other than the one already laid, which is Jesus Christ. [12]If any man builds on this foundation using gold, silver, costly stones, wood, hay or straw, [13]his work will be shown for what it is, because the Day will bring it to light. It will be revealed with fire, and the fire will test the quality of each man's work. [14]If what he has built survives, he will receive his reward. [15]If it is burned up, he will suffer loss; he himself will be saved, but only as one escaping through the flames.

[16]Don't you know that you yourselves are God's temple and that God's Spirit lives in you? [17]If anyone destroys God's temple, God will destroy him; for God's temple is sacred, and you are that temple.

[18]Do not deceive yourselves. If any one of you thinks he is wise by the standards of this age, he should become a "fool" so that he may become wise. [19]For the wisdom of this world is foolishness in God's sight. As it is written: "He catches the wise in their craftiness"[c]; [20]and again, "The Lord knows that the thoughts of the wise are futile."[d] [21]So then, no more boasting about men! All things are yours, [22]whether Paul or Apollos or Cephas[e] or the world or life or death or the present or the future—all are yours, [23]and you are of Christ, and Christ is of God.

Apostles of Christ

4 So then, men ought to regard us as servants of Christ and as those entrusted with the secret things of God. [2]Now it is required that those who have been given a trust must prove faithful. [3]I care very little if I am judged by you or by any human court; indeed, I do not even judge myself. [4]My conscience is clear, but that does not make me innocent. It is the

VERSE:	AUTHOR:	PASSAGE:
1 Corinthians 4:4	Lewis B. Smedes	1 Corinthians 4:1–5

The Last Word Is Grace

"My judge is the Lord." Is this good news or bad news? Before it can be good news, it has to sound like very bad news. To run smack against a judge who never compromises and never makes a mistake could be terrifying . . .

It could be too much. With a critic like this, we need to come to terms. We certainly cannot stand up under his judgment; it will condemn us. We have two choices.

First, we can make believe he is not there. Lots of people do this . . . This is one option; live out the fantasy, act out our lives in the illusion that he is not really here. This may actually work for a while, but not forever, because sooner or later, the illusion will be shattered and the reality will be known, that God is alive.

There is only one other way we can live freely in the presence of our infallible critic. We can get to know him for what he is really like. This was Paul's secret; he knew his divine judge in a way that made him free. For he met him at the cross. The secret of what happened there was that our divine judge judged his own Son in our place. There, his accusing finger, once pointed at us, was changed to an open hand outstretched to us. His terrible swift sword was exchanged for his supporting arm. Our judge became our divine Savior. Our critic became our best friend. Now the last word is grace — the pardon, the power and the promise of grace. God is on *our* side.

ADDITIONAL SCRIPTURE READINGS
Psalm 139; Romans 8:1–4

Go to page 1446 for your next devotional reading.

Lord who judges me. [5]Therefore judge nothing before the appointed time; wait till the Lord comes. He will bring to light what is hidden in darkness and will expose the motives of men's hearts. At that time each will receive his praise from God.

[6]Now, brothers, I have applied these things to myself and Apollos for your benefit, so that you may learn from us the meaning of the saying, "Do not go beyond what is written." Then you will not take pride in one man over against another. [7]For who makes you different from anyone else? What do you have that you did not receive? And if you did receive it, why do you boast as though you did not?

[8]Already you have all you want! Already you have become rich! You have become kings—and that without us! How I wish that you really had become kings so that we might be kings with you! [9]For it seems to me that God has put us apostles on display at the end of the procession, like men condemned to die in the arena. We have been made a spectacle to the whole universe, to angels as well as to men. [10]We are fools for Christ, but you are so wise in Christ! We are weak, but you are strong! You are honored, we are dishonored! [11]To this very hour we go hungry and thirsty, we are in rags, we are brutally treated, we are homeless. [12]We work hard with our own hands. When we are cursed, we bless; when we are persecuted, we endure it; [13]when we are slandered, we answer kindly. Up to this moment we have become the scum of the earth, the refuse of the world.

[14]I am not writing this to shame you, but to warn you, as my dear children. [15]Even though you have ten thousand guardians in Christ, you do not have many fathers, for in Christ Jesus I became your father through the gospel. [16]Therefore I urge you to imitate me. [17]For this reason I am sending to you Timothy, my son whom I love, who is faithful in the Lord. He will remind you of my way of life in Christ Jesus, which agrees with what I teach everywhere in every church.

[18]Some of you have become arrogant, as if I were not coming to you. [19]But I will come to you very soon, if the Lord is willing, and then I will find out not only how these arrogant people are talking, but what power they have. [20]For the kingdom of God is not a matter of talk but of power. [21]What do you prefer? Shall I come to you with a whip, or in love and with a gentle spirit?

Expel the Immoral Brother!

5 It is actually reported that there is sexual immorality among you, and of a kind that does not occur even among pagans: A man has his father's wife. [2]And you are proud! Shouldn't you rather have been filled with grief and have put out of your fellowship the man who did this? [3]Even though I am not physically present, I am with you in spirit. And I have already passed judgment on the one who did this, just as if I were present. [4]When you are assembled in the name of our Lord Jesus and I am with you in spirit, and the power of our Lord Jesus is present, [5]hand this man over to Satan, so that the sinful nature[a] may be destroyed and his spirit saved on the day of the Lord.

[6]Your boasting is not good. Don't you know that a little yeast works through the whole batch of dough? [7]Get rid of the old yeast that you may be a new batch without yeast—as you really are. For Christ, our Passover lamb, has been sacrificed. [8]Therefore let us keep the Festival, not with the old yeast, the yeast of malice and wickedness, but with bread without yeast, the bread of sincerity and truth.

[9]I have written you in my letter not to associate with sexually immoral people— [10]not at all meaning the people of this world who are immoral, or the greedy and swindlers, or idola-

---

[a]5 Or *that his body*; or *that the flesh*

PASSAGE: Psalm 25; Hebrews 13:5–8
AUTHOR: Henry Francis Lyte

Abide With Me

Abide with me; fast falls the eventide;
The darkness deepens; Lord, with me abide:
When other helpers fail, and comforts flee,
Help of the helpless, oh abide with me.

Swift to its close ebbs out life's little day;
Earth's joys grow dim, its glories pass away;
Change and decay in all around I see;
O thou who changest not, abide with me.

I need thy presence every passing hour;
What but thy grace can foil the tempter's power?
Who like thyself my guide and stay can be?
Through cloud and sunshine, Lord, abide with me.

I fear no foe with thee at hand to bless;
Ills have no weight, and tears no bitterness;
Where is death's sting? where, grave, thy victory?
I triumph still, if thou abide with me.

Hold thou thy cross before my closing eyes;
Shine through the gloom, and point me to the
    skies;
Heaven's morning breaks, and earth's vain shadows
    flee;
In life, in death, O Lord, abide with me.

Go to page 1449 for your next devotional reading.

ters. In that case you would have to leave this world. [11]But now I am writing you that you must not associate with anyone who calls himself a brother but is sexually immoral or greedy, an idolater or a slanderer, a drunkard or a swindler. With such a man do not even eat.

[12]What business is it of mine to judge those outside the church? Are you not to judge those inside? [13]God will judge those outside. "Expel the wicked man from among you."[a]

Lawsuits Among Believers

6 If any of you has a dispute with another, dare he take it before the ungodly for judgment instead of before the saints? [2]Do you not know that the saints will judge the world? And if you are to judge the world, are you not competent to judge trivial cases? [3]Do you not know that we will judge angels? How much more the things of this life! [4]Therefore, if you have disputes about such matters, appoint as judges even men of little account in the church![b] [5]I say this to shame you. Is it possible that there is nobody among you wise enough to judge a dispute between believers? [6]But instead, one brother goes to law against another—and this in front of unbelievers!

[7]The very fact that you have lawsuits among you means you have been completely defeated already. Why not rather be wronged? Why not rather be cheated? [8]Instead, you yourselves cheat and do wrong, and you do this to your brothers.

[9]Do you not know that the wicked will not inherit the kingdom of God? Do not be deceived: Neither the sexually immoral nor idolaters nor adulterers nor male prostitutes nor homosexual offenders [10]nor thieves nor the greedy nor drunkards nor slanderers nor swindlers will inherit the kingdom of God. [11]And that is what some of you were. But you were washed, you were sanctified, you were justified in the name of the Lord Jesus Christ and by the Spirit of our God.

Sexual Immorality

[12]"Everything is permissible for me"—but not everything is beneficial. "Everything is permissible for me"—but I will not be mastered by anything. [13]"Food for the stomach and the stomach for food"—but God will destroy them both. The body is not meant for sexual immorality, but for the Lord, and the Lord for the body. [14]By his power God raised the Lord from the dead, and he will raise us also. [15]Do you not know that your bodies are members of Christ himself? Shall I then take the members of Christ and unite them with a prostitute? Never! [16]Do you not know that he who unites himself with a prostitute is one with her in body? For it is said, "The two will become one flesh."[c] [17]But he who unites himself with the Lord is one with him in spirit.

[18]Flee from sexual immorality. All other sins a man commits are outside his body, but he who sins sexually sins against his own body. [19]Do you not know that your body is a temple of the Holy Spirit, who is in you, whom you have received from God? You are not your own; [20]you were bought at a price. Therefore honor God with your body.

Marriage

7 Now for the matters you wrote about: It is good for a man not to marry.[d] [2]But since there is so much immorality, each man should have his own wife, and each woman her own husband. [3]The husband should fulfill his marital duty to his wife, and likewise the wife to her husband. [4]The wife's body does not belong to her alone but also to her husband. In the same way, the husband's body does not belong to him alone but also to his

---

[a]13 Deut. 17:7; 19:19; 21:21; 22:21,24; 24:7　　[b]4 Or matters, do you appoint as judges men of little account in the church?　　[c]16 Gen. 2:24　　[d]1 Or "It is good for a man not to have sexual relations with a woman."

wife. ⁵Do not deprive each other except by mutual consent and for a time, so that you may devote yourselves to prayer. Then come together again so that Satan will not tempt you because of your lack of self-control. ⁶I say this as a concession, not as a command. ⁷I wish that all men were as I am. But each man has his own gift from God; one has this gift, another has that.

⁸Now to the unmarried and the widows I say: It is good for them to stay unmarried, as I am. ⁹But if they cannot control themselves, they should marry, for it is better to marry than to burn with passion.

¹⁰To the married I give this command (not I, but the Lord): A wife must not separate from her husband. ¹¹But if she does, she must remain unmarried or else be reconciled to her husband. And a husband must not divorce his wife.

¹²To the rest I say this (I, not the Lord): If any brother has a wife who is not a believer and she is willing to live with him, he must not divorce her. ¹³And if a woman has a husband who is not a believer and he is willing to live with her, she must not divorce him. ¹⁴For the unbelieving husband has been sanctified through his wife, and the unbelieving wife has been sanctified through her believing husband. Otherwise your children would be unclean, but as it is, they are holy.

¹⁵But if the unbeliever leaves, let him do so. A believing man or woman is not bound in such circumstances; God has called us to live in peace. ¹⁶How do you know, wife, whether you will save your husband? Or, how do you know, husband, whether you will save your wife?

¹⁷Nevertheless, each one should retain the place in life that the Lord assigned to him and to which God has called him. This is the rule I lay down in all the churches. ¹⁸Was a man already circumcised when he was called? He should not become uncircumcised. Was a man uncircumcised when he was called? He should

not be circumcised. ¹⁹Circumcision is nothing and uncircumcision is nothing. Keeping God's commands is what counts. ²⁰Each one should remain in the situation which he was in when God called him. ²¹Were you a slave when you were called? Don't let it trouble you—although if you can gain your freedom, do so. ²²For he who was a slave when he was called by the Lord is the Lord's freedman; similarly, he who was a free man when he was called is Christ's slave. ²³You were bought at a price; do not become slaves of men. ²⁴Brothers, each man, as responsible to God, should remain in the situation God called him to.

²⁵Now about virgins: I have no command from the Lord, but I give a judgment as one who by the Lord's mercy is trustworthy. ²⁶Because of the present crisis, I think that it is good for you to remain as you are. ²⁷Are you married? Do not seek a divorce. Are you unmarried? Do not look for a wife. ²⁸But if you do marry, you have not sinned; and if a virgin marries, she has not sinned. But those who marry will face many troubles in this life, and I want to spare you this.

²⁹What I mean, brothers, is that the time is short. From now on those who have wives should live as if they had none; ³⁰those who mourn, as if they did not; those who are happy, as if they were not; those who buy something, as if it were not theirs to keep; ³¹those who use the things of the world, as if not engrossed in them. For this world in its present form is passing away.

³²I would like you to be free from concern. An unmarried man is concerned about the Lord's affairs—how he can please the Lord. ³³But a married man is concerned about the affairs of this world—how he can please his wife— ³⁴and his interests are divided. An unmarried woman or virgin is concerned about the Lord's affairs: Her aim is to be devoted to the Lord in both body and spirit. But a married woman is concerned about the affairs of this world—how she can

VERSE:	AUTHOR:	PASSAGE:
1 Corinthians 7:34	Tim Stafford	1 Corinthians 7:32–35

New Possibilities

A widow's life is not all sadness, for rising out of the depths of loss can be new growth. While the grieving continues, these possibilities seem remote; it would be cruel to mention them. Later, though, when the mourning has begun to spend itself, a widow begins to ask, "What next?"

A widow who has spent her life bending to the personality of a partner can now explore her own likes and dislikes. She is, as Paul indicates in Scripture, freer to develop her life with God (see 1 Corinthians 7:8,32–35; 1 Timothy 5:5). She is freer to strengthen friendships with her children and with others outside the family. She may be freer from responsibilities, freer to travel, freer to try new activities. One need not depreciate the marriage to believe that when the marriage is ended by death, new and positive possibilities arise. Sometimes family members and friends discover a man or woman whose character they barely knew before the death of the spouse ...

"With the time God gives me, and in these new circumstances of my life, what am I called to do and to be?" The answers will be as varied as those given to the same question after retirement. Some widows will volunteer for challenging new jobs. Some will concentrate on caring for grandchildren and children. Some will give themselves to friendships and Bible study.

ADDITIONAL SCRIPTURE READINGS
Psalm 86; 1 Timothy 5:1–10

Go to page 1453 for your next devotional reading.

please her husband. [35]I am saying this for your own good, not to restrict you, but that you may live in a right way in undivided devotion to the Lord.

[36]If anyone thinks he is acting improperly toward the virgin he is engaged to, and if she is getting along in years and he feels he ought to marry, he should do as he wants. He is not sinning. They should get married. [37]But the man who has settled the matter in his own mind, who is under no compulsion but has control over his own will, and who has made up his mind not to marry the virgin— this man also does the right thing. [38]So then, he who marries the virgin does right, but he who does not marry her does even better.[a]

[39]A woman is bound to her husband as long as he lives. But if her husband dies, she is free to marry anyone she wishes, but he must belong to the Lord. [40]In my judgment, she is happier if she stays as she is— and I think that I too have the Spirit of God.

Food Sacrificed to Idols

8 Now about food sacrificed to idols: We know that we all possess knowledge.[b] Knowledge puffs up, but love builds up. [2]The man who thinks he knows something does not yet know as he ought to know. [3]But the man who loves God is known by God.

[4]So then, about eating food sacrificed to idols: We know that an idol is nothing at all in the world and that there is no God but one. [5]For even if there are so-called gods, whether in heaven or on earth (as indeed there are many "gods" and many "lords"), [6]yet for us there is but one God, the Father, from whom all things came

and for whom we live; and there is but one Lord, Jesus Christ, through whom all things came and through whom we live.

[7]But not everyone knows this. Some people are still so accustomed to idols that when they eat such food they think of it as having been sacrificed to an idol, and since their conscience is weak, it is defiled. [8]But food does not bring us near to God; we are no worse if we do not eat, and no better if we do.

[9]Be careful, however, that the exercise of your freedom does not become a stumbling block to the weak. [10]For if anyone with a weak conscience sees you who have this knowledge eating in an idol's temple, won't he be emboldened to eat what has been sacrificed to idols? [11]So this weak brother, for whom Christ died, is destroyed by your knowledge. [12]When you sin against your brothers in this way and wound their weak conscience, you sin against Christ. [13]Therefore, if what I eat causes my brother to fall into sin, I will never eat meat again, so that I will not cause him to fall.

The Rights of an Apostle

9 Am I not free? Am I not an apostle? Have I not seen Jesus our Lord? Are you not the result of my work in the Lord? [2]Even though I may not be an apostle to others, surely I am to you! For you are the seal of my apostleship in the Lord.

[3]This is my defense to those who sit in judgment on me. [4]Don't we have the right to food and drink? [5]Don't we have the right to take a believing wife along with us, as do the other apostles and the Lord's brothers and Cephas[c]? [6]Or is it only I and Barnabas who must work for a living?

[7]Who serves as a soldier at his own

---

[a]36-38 Or [36]If anyone thinks he is not treating his daughter properly, and if she is getting along in years, and he feels she ought to marry, he should do as he wants. He is not sinning. He should let her get married. [37]But the man who has settled the matter in his own mind, who is under no compulsion but has control over his own will, and who has made up his mind to keep the virgin unmarried—this man also does the right thing. [38]So then, he who gives his virgin in marriage does right, but he who does not give her in marriage does even better.   [b]1 Or "We all possess knowledge," as you say   [c]5 That is, Peter

expense? Who plants a vineyard and does not eat of its grapes? Who tends a flock and does not drink of the milk? [8]Do I say this merely from a human point of view? Doesn't the Law say the same thing? [9]For it is written in the Law of Moses: "Do not muzzle an ox while it is treading out the grain."[a] Is it about oxen that God is concerned? [10]Surely he says this for us, doesn't he? Yes, this was written for us, because when the plowman plows and the thresher threshes, they ought to do so in the hope of sharing in the harvest. [11]If we have sown spiritual seed among you, is it too much if we reap a material harvest from you? [12]If others have this right of support from you, shouldn't we have it all the more?

But we did not use this right. On the contrary, we put up with anything rather than hinder the gospel of Christ. [13]Don't you know that those who work in the temple get their food from the temple, and those who serve at the altar share in what is offered on the altar? [14]In the same way, the Lord has commanded that those who preach the gospel should receive their living from the gospel.

[15]But I have not used any of these rights. And I am not writing this in the hope that you will do such things for me. I would rather die than have anyone deprive me of this boast. [16]Yet when I preach the gospel, I cannot boast, for I am compelled to preach. Woe to me if I do not preach the gospel! [17]If I preach voluntarily, I have a reward; if not voluntarily, I am simply discharging the trust committed to me. [18]What then is my reward? Just this: that in preaching the gospel I may offer it free of charge, and so not make use of my rights in preaching it.

[19]Though I am free and belong to no man, I make myself a slave to everyone, to win as many as possible. [20]To the Jews I became like a Jew, to win the Jews. To those under the law

I became like one under the law (though I myself am not under the law), so as to win those under the law. [21]To those not having the law I became like one not having the law (though I am not free from God's law but am under Christ's law), so as to win those not having the law. [22]To the weak I became weak, to win the weak. I have become all things to all men so that by all possible means I might save some. [23]I do all this for the sake of the gospel, that I may share in its blessings.

[24]Do you not know that in a race all the runners run, but only one gets the prize? Run in such a way as to get the prize. [25]Everyone who competes in the games goes into strict training. They do it to get a crown that will not last; but we do it to get a crown that will last forever. [26]Therefore I do not run like a man running aimlessly; I do not fight like a man beating the air. [27]No, I beat my body and make it my slave so that after I have preached to others, I myself will not be disqualified for the prize.

Warnings From Israel's History

10 For I do not want you to be ignorant of the fact, brothers, that our forefathers were all under the cloud and that they all passed through the sea. [2]They were all baptized into Moses in the cloud and in the sea. [3]They all ate the same spiritual food [4]and drank the same spiritual drink; for they drank from the spiritual rock that accompanied them, and that rock was Christ. [5]Nevertheless, God was not pleased with most of them; their bodies were scattered over the desert.

[6]Now these things occurred as examples[b] to keep us from setting our hearts on evil things as they did. [7]Do not be idolaters, as some of them were; as it is written: "The people sat down to eat and drink and got up to indulge in pagan revelry."[c] [8]We

---

[a]9 Deut. 25:4   [b]6 Or *types*; also in verse 11   [c]7 Exodus 32:6

should not commit sexual immorality, as some of them did—and in one day twenty-three thousand of them died. [9]We should not test the Lord, as some of them did—and were killed by snakes. [10]And do not grumble, as some of them did—and were killed by the destroying angel.

[11]These things happened to them as examples and were written down as warnings for us, on whom the fulfillment of the ages has come. [12]So, if you think you are standing firm, be careful that you don't fall! [13]No temptation has seized you except what is common to man. And God is faithful; he will not let you be tempted beyond what you can bear. But when you are tempted, he will also provide a way out so that you can stand up under it.

Idol Feasts and the Lord's Supper

[14]Therefore, my dear friends, flee from idolatry. [15]I speak to sensible people; judge for yourselves what I say. [16]Is not the cup of thanksgiving for which we give thanks a participation in the blood of Christ? And is not the bread that we break a participation in the body of Christ? [17]Because there is one loaf, we, who are many, are one body, for we all partake of the one loaf.

[18]Consider the people of Israel: Do not those who eat the sacrifices participate in the altar? [19]Do I mean then that a sacrifice offered to an idol is anything, or that an idol is anything? [20]No, but the sacrifices of pagans are offered to demons, not to God, and I do not want you to be participants with demons. [21]You cannot drink the cup of the Lord and the cup of demons too; you cannot have a part in both the Lord's table and the table of demons. [22]Are we trying to arouse the Lord's jealousy? Are we stronger than he?

The Believer's Freedom

[23]"Everything is permissible"—but not everything is beneficial. "Everything is permissible"—but not everything is constructive. [24]Nobody should seek his own good, but the good of others.

[25]Eat anything sold in the meat market without raising questions of conscience, [26]for, "The earth is the Lord's, and everything in it."[a]

[27]If some unbeliever invites you to a meal and you want to go, eat whatever is put before you without raising questions of conscience. [28]But if anyone says to you, "This has been offered in sacrifice," then do not eat it, both for the sake of the man who told you and for conscience' sake[b]— [29]the other man's conscience, I mean, not yours. For why should my freedom be judged by another's conscience? [30]If I take part in the meal with thankfulness, why am I denounced because of something I thank God for?

[31]So whether you eat or drink or whatever you do, do it all for the glory of God. [32]Do not cause anyone to stumble, whether Jews, Greeks or the church of God— [33]even as I try to please everybody in every way. For I am not seeking my own good but the good of many, so that they may be saved. [1]Follow my example, as I follow the example of Christ.

11

Propriety in Worship

[2]I praise you for remembering me in everything and for holding to the teachings,[c] just as I passed them on to you.

[3]Now I want you to realize that the head of every man is Christ, and the head of the woman is man, and the head of Christ is God. [4]Every man who prays or prophesies with his head covered dishonors his head. [5]And every woman who prays or prophesies with her head uncovered dishonors her head—it is just as though her head were shaved. [6]If a woman does not cover her head, she should have her hair cut off; and if it

---

[a]26 Psalm 24:1   [b]28 Some manuscripts *conscience' sake, for "the earth is the Lord's and everything in it"*   [c]2 Or *traditions*

is a disgrace for a woman to have her hair cut or shaved off, she should cover her head. [7]A man ought not to cover his head,[a] since he is the image and glory of God; but the woman is the glory of man. [8]For man did not come from woman, but woman from man; [9]neither was man created for woman, but woman for man. [10]For this reason, and because of the angels,

a4-7 Or [4]*Every man who prays or prophesies with long hair dishonors his head. [5]And every woman who prays or prophesies with no covering ⌞of hair⌟ on her head dishonors her head—she is just like one of the "shorn women." [6]If a woman has no covering, let her be for now with short hair, but since it is a disgrace for a woman to have her hair shorn or shaved, she should grow it again. [7]A man ought not to have long hair*

TUESDAY

VERSE:	AUTHOR:	PASSAGE:
1 Corinthians 11:1	Leslie E. Moser	1 Corinthians 10:31 — 11:1

Pioneers and Messengers

Somehow we must let people in their 30s know that life doesn't grow sour simply because the body grows old —but we can't convince the young until we convince ourselves. Also, we must realize that what we do now to enhance our mature life will impact our children and grandchildren. We must be role models because if we aren't, they won't know how to be productive during their golden years. We must be the pioneers in this new wilderness ... Those of us now in our late maturity must clear the way for those who will follow.

And why must we? Simply because there is no one else who can accomplish for God ... what we can accomplish ... We must make the world understand that active, meaningful, productive life does not necessarily end or even wane at age 50, 60, 70, or even 80. Most of all, we must be communicators of the good news that God has given us extra years on this planet. We are now spending a few more years of our everlasting life here on earth. Thanks be to God that our extra years on earth take nothing away from our time in heaven!

ADDITIONAL SCRIPTURE READINGS
1 Corinthians 4:14–17; 1 Thessalonians 1:2–10
Go to page 1456 for your next devotional reading.

the woman ought to have a sign of authority on her head. [11]In the Lord, however, woman is not independent of man, nor is man independent of woman. [12]For as woman came from man, so also man is born of woman. But everything comes from God. [13]Judge for yourselves: Is it proper for a woman to pray to God with her head uncovered? [14]Does not the very nature of things teach you that if a man has long hair, it is a disgrace to him, [15]but that if a woman has long hair, it is her glory? For long hair is given to her as a covering. [16]If anyone wants to be contentious about this, we have no other practice—nor do the churches of God.

The Lord's Supper

[17]In the following directives I have no praise for you, for your meetings do more harm than good. [18]In the first place, I hear that when you come together as a church, there are divisions among you, and to some extent I believe it. [19]No doubt there have to be differences among you to show which of you have God's approval. [20]When you come together, it is not the Lord's Supper you eat, [21]for as you eat, each of you goes ahead without waiting for anybody else. One remains hungry, another gets drunk. [22]Don't you have homes to eat and drink in? Or do you despise the church of God and humiliate those who have nothing? What shall I say to you? Shall I praise you for this? Certainly not!

[23]For I received from the Lord what I also passed on to you: The Lord Jesus, on the night he was betrayed, took bread, [24]and when he had given thanks, he broke it and said, "This is my body, which is for you; do this in remembrance of me." [25]In the same way, after supper he took the cup, saying, "This cup is the new covenant in my blood; do this, whenever you drink it, in remembrance of me." [26]For whenever you eat this bread and drink this cup, you proclaim the Lord's death until he comes.

[27]Therefore, whoever eats the bread or drinks the cup of the Lord in an unworthy manner will be guilty of sinning against the body and blood of the Lord. [28]A man ought to examine himself before he eats of the bread and drinks of the cup. [29]For anyone who eats and drinks without recognizing the body of the Lord eats and drinks judgment on himself. [30]That is why many among you are weak and sick, and a number of you have fallen asleep. [31]But if we judged ourselves, we would not come under judgment. [32]When we are judged by the Lord, we are being disciplined so that we will not be condemned with the world.

[33]So then, my brothers, when you come together to eat, wait for each other. [34]If anyone is hungry, he should eat at home, so that when you meet together it may not result in judgment.

And when I come I will give further directions.

Spiritual Gifts

12 Now about spiritual gifts, brothers, I do not want you to be ignorant. [2]You know that when you were pagans, somehow or other you were influenced and led astray to mute idols. [3]Therefore I tell you that no one who is speaking by the Spirit of God says, "Jesus be cursed," and no one can say, "Jesus is Lord," except by the Holy Spirit.

[4]There are different kinds of gifts, but the same Spirit. [5]There are different kinds of service, but the same Lord. [6]There are different kinds of working, but the same God works all of them in all men.

[7]Now to each one the manifestation of the Spirit is given for the common good. [8]To one there is given through the Spirit the message of wisdom, to another the message of knowledge by means of the same Spirit, [9]to another faith by the same Spirit, to another gifts of healing by that one Spirit, [10]to another miraculous powers, to another prophecy, to another distinguishing between spirits, to another speak-

ing in different kinds of tongues,[a] and to still another the interpretation of tongues.[a] [11]All these are the work of one and the same Spirit, and he gives them to each one, just as he determines.

One Body, Many Parts

[12]The body is a unit, though it is made up of many parts; and though all its parts are many, they form one body. So it is with Christ. [13]For we were all baptized by[b] one Spirit into one body—whether Jews or Greeks, slave or free—and we were all given the one Spirit to drink.

[14]Now the body is not made up of one part but of many. [15]If the foot should say, "Because I am not a hand, I do not belong to the body," it would not for that reason cease to be part of the body. [16]And if the ear should say, "Because I am not an eye, I do not belong to the body," it would not for that reason cease to be part of the body. [17]If the whole body were an eye, where would the sense of hearing be? If the whole body were an ear, where would the sense of smell be? [18]But in fact God has arranged the parts in the body, every one of them, just as he wanted them to be. [19]If they were all one part, where would the body be? [20]As it is, there are many parts, but one body.

[21]The eye cannot say to the hand, "I don't need you!" And the head cannot say to the feet, "I don't need you!" [22]On the contrary, those parts of the body that seem to be weaker are indispensable, [23]and the parts that we think are less honorable we treat with special honor. And the parts that are unpresentable are treated with special modesty, [24]while our presentable parts need no special treatment. But God has combined the members of the body and has given greater honor to the parts that lacked it, [25]so that there should be no division in the body, but that its parts should have equal concern for each other. [26]If one part suffers, every part suffers with it; if one part is honored, every part rejoices with it.

[27]Now you are the body of Christ, and each one of you is a part of it. [28]And in the church God has appointed first of all apostles, second prophets, third teachers, then workers of miracles, also those having gifts of healing, those able to help others, those with gifts of administration, and those speaking in different kinds of tongues. [29]Are all apostles? Are all prophets? Are all teachers? Do all work miracles? [30]Do all have gifts of healing? Do all speak in tongues[c]? Do all interpret? [31]But eagerly desire[d] the greater gifts.

Love

And now I will show you the most excellent way.

13 If I speak in the tongues[e] of men and of angels, but have not love, I am only a resounding gong or a clanging cymbal. [2]If I have the gift of prophecy and can fathom all mysteries and all knowledge, and if I have a faith that can move mountains, but have not love, I am nothing. [3]If I give all I possess to the poor and surrender my body to the flames,[f] but have not love, I gain nothing.

[4]Love is patient, love is kind. It does not envy, it does not boast, it is not proud. [5]It is not rude, it is not self-seeking, it is not easily angered, it keeps no record of wrongs. [6]Love does not delight in evil but rejoices with the truth. [7]It always protects, always trusts, always hopes, always perseveres.

[8]Love never fails. But where there are prophecies, they will cease; where there are tongues, they will be stilled; where there is knowledge, it will pass away. [9]For we know in part and we prophesy in part, [10]but when perfection comes, the imperfect disappears. [11]When I was a child, I talked like a child, I thought like a child, I reasoned like a child. When I became a

VERSE:
1 Corinthians 12:26

AUTHOR:
Tim Stafford

PASSAGE:
1 Corinthians 12:12–26

We're In It Together

How can we gain a view of old age that is positive, honorable, hopeful? Some of it comes just with looking at the facts. God loves older people, and he has created them with inherent dignity.

But another side of the dignity and worth of old age comes more specifically from a Christian understanding of the world ... Christians understand the existence of another world, the world of God's love, toward which or against which our lives are being shaped. If you believe in this other world, it is not very hard to see that old age is meant to prepare us for it. So much that will be valueless there becomes, already, valueless here—independence, pride, wealth. So much that the kingdom of love depends on becomes already vitally necessary—interdependence, kindness, humility.

These qualities are usually expressed in families. To a remarkable degree, children and other relatives do get involved. While other relationships may shrivel to almost nothing, family relationships often grow stronger ...

In that interlocking of parents and children, part of the goodness of the hardness of old age reveals itself. You see the solidarity of human beings of all ages, a solidarity expressed concretely by the family. We really are in this together, from birth to death. Though this togetherness is sometimes extremely wearing, it is fundamentally good. It is good that we learn to bear each other's burdens—that the young care for the old, and the old for the young, according to their different capacities.

ADDITIONAL SCRIPTURE READINGS
Galatians 6:1–4; 1 Peter 4:7–11

Go to page 1458 for your next devotional reading.

man, I put childish ways behind me. [12]Now we see but a poor reflection as in a mirror; then we shall see face to face. Now I know in part; then I shall know fully, even as I am fully known.

[13]And now these three remain: faith, hope and love. But the greatest of these is love.

Gifts of Prophecy and Tongues

14 Follow the way of love and eagerly desire spiritual gifts, especially the gift of prophecy. [2]For anyone who speaks in a tongue[a] does not speak to men but to God. Indeed, no one understands him; he utters mysteries with his spirit.[b] [3]But everyone who prophesies speaks to men for their strengthening, encouragement and comfort. [4]He who speaks in a tongue edifies himself, but he who prophesies edifies the church. [5]I would like every one of you to speak in tongues,[c] but I would rather have you prophesy. He who prophesies is greater than one who speaks in tongues,[c] unless he interprets, so that the church may be edified.

[6]Now, brothers, if I come to you and speak in tongues, what good will I be to you, unless I bring you some revelation or knowledge or prophecy or word of instruction? [7]Even in the case of lifeless things that make sounds, such as the flute or harp, how will anyone know what tune is being played unless there is a distinction in the notes? [8]Again, if the trumpet does not sound a clear call, who will get ready for battle? [9]So it is with you. Unless you speak intelligible words with your tongue, how will anyone know what you are saying? You will just be speaking into the air. [10]Undoubtedly there are all sorts of languages in the world, yet none of them is without meaning. [11]If then I do not grasp the meaning of what someone is saying, I am a foreigner to the speaker, and he is a foreigner to me. [12]So it is with you. Since you are eager to have spiritual gifts, try to excel in gifts that build up the church.

[13]For this reason anyone who speaks in a tongue should pray that he may interpret what he says. [14]For if I pray in a tongue, my spirit prays, but my mind is unfruitful. [15]So what shall I do? I will pray with my spirit, but I will also pray with my mind; I will sing with my spirit, but I will also sing with my mind. [16]If you are praising God with your spirit, how can one who finds himself among those who do not understand[d] say "Amen" to your thanksgiving, since he does not know what you are saying? [17]You may be giving thanks well enough, but the other man is not edified.

[18]I thank God that I speak in tongues more than all of you. [19]But in the church I would rather speak five intelligible words to instruct others than ten thousand words in a tongue.

[20]Brothers, stop thinking like children. In regard to evil be infants, but in your thinking be adults. [21]In the Law it is written:

"Through men of strange tongues
　　and through the lips of
　　　foreigners
I will speak to this people,
　　but even then they will not
　　　listen to me,"[e]
says the Lord.

[22]Tongues, then, are a sign, not for believers but for unbelievers; prophecy, however, is for believers, not for unbelievers. [23]So if the whole church comes together and everyone speaks in tongues, and some who do not understand[f] or some unbelievers come in, will they not say that you are out of your mind? [24]But if an unbeliever or someone who does not understand[g] comes in while everybody is prophesying, he will be convinced by all that he is a sinner and will be

---

[a]2 Or *another language*; also in verses 4, 13, 14, 19, 26 and 27　　[b]2 Or *by the Spirit*　　[c]5 Or *other languages*; also in verses 6, 18, 22, 23 and 39　　[d]16 Or *among the inquirers*　　[e]21 Isaiah 28:11,12　　[f]23 Or *some inquirers*　　[g]24 Or *or some inquirer*

VERSE: AUTHOR: PASSAGE:
1 Corinthians 13:4   Lewis B. Smedes   1 Corinthians 13:1–13

Love Is Patient

When we have the patience to accept ourselves, to accept our future in life, in the face of deep loss or persistent frustration, we are living in love's power. When we have learned to believe that our lives have meaning, when we have opened our hearts to some feelings of joy, when we have seen some rays of light that make us glad, we are long-suffering . . .

Love is the courage to love life and be glad for it. Love is the courage to discover that life is not completely tied to the precious goods we have lost or have not yet found. God's love song does not hammer at us with a demand to be more courageous. This would only defeat us. It says that, with God, there *is* the power. Its name is love.

The model of long-suffering love is God himself . . . God's love is his Yes to a lost world. It is a redemptive Yes, not merely an indifferent or indulgent one . . . So it is with the love that suffers indefinitely. It never suffers merely for the sake of suffering . . . Love is not cowardly. Love suffers long so that time can be created for redemptive powers to do their work, so that justice can be fought for without hasty and needless violence, so that healing and reconciliation may be possible. Love suffers long so that the evil suffered can be done *away*. Love suffers long so that suffering can finally cease.

And when love gives us the power to suffer long, love also gives us the power to see reasons for rejoicing while we suffer.

ADDITIONAL SCRIPTURE READINGS
Romans 5:1–8; 2 Peter 3:1–9

Go to page 1460 for your next devotional reading.

judged by all, [25]and the secrets of his heart will be laid bare. So he will fall down and worship God, exclaiming, "God is really among you!"

Orderly Worship

[26]What then shall we say, brothers? When you come together, everyone has a hymn, or a word of instruction, a revelation, a tongue or an interpretation. All of these must be done for the strengthening of the church. [27]If anyone speaks in a tongue, two—or at the most three—should speak, one at a time, and someone must interpret. [28]If there is no interpreter, the speaker should keep quiet in the church and speak to himself and God.

[29]Two or three prophets should speak, and the others should weigh carefully what is said. [30]And if a revelation comes to someone who is sitting down, the first speaker should stop. [31]For you can all prophesy in turn so that everyone may be instructed and encouraged. [32]The spirits of prophets are subject to the control of prophets. [33]For God is not a God of disorder but of peace.

As in all the congregations of the saints, [34]women should remain silent in the churches. They are not allowed to speak, but must be in submission, as the Law says. [35]If they want to inquire about something, they should ask their own husbands at home; for it is disgraceful for a woman to speak in the church.

[36]Did the word of God originate with you? Or are you the only people it has reached? [37]If anybody thinks he is a prophet or spiritually gifted, let him acknowledge that what I am writing to you is the Lord's command. [38]If he ignores this, he himself will be ignored.[a]

[39]Therefore, my brothers, be eager to prophesy, and do not forbid speaking in tongues. [40]But everything should be done in a fitting and orderly way.

The Resurrection of Christ

15 Now, brothers, I want to remind you of the gospel I preached to you, which you received and on which you have taken your stand. [2]By this gospel you are saved, if you hold firmly to the word I preached to you. Otherwise, you have believed in vain.

[3]For what I received I passed on to you as of first importance[b]: that Christ died for our sins according to the Scriptures, [4]that he was buried, that he was raised on the third day according to the Scriptures, [5]and that he appeared to Peter,[c] and then to the Twelve. [6]After that, he appeared to more than five hundred of the brothers at the same time, most of whom are still living, though some have fallen asleep. [7]Then he appeared to James, then to all the apostles, [8]and last of all he appeared to me also, as to one abnormally born.

[9]For I am the least of the apostles and do not even deserve to be called an apostle, because I persecuted the church of God. [10]But by the grace of God I am what I am, and his grace to me was not without effect. No, I worked harder than all of them—yet not I, but the grace of God that was with me. [11]Whether, then, it was I or they, this is what we preach, and this is what you believed.

The Resurrection of the Dead

[12]But if it is preached that Christ has been raised from the dead, how can some of you say that there is no resurrection of the dead? [13]If there is no resurrection of the dead, then not even Christ has been raised. [14]And if Christ has not been raised, our preaching is useless and so is your faith. [15]More than that, we are then found to be false witnesses about God, for we have testified about God that he raised Christ from the dead. But he did not raise him if in fact the dead are not raised. [16]For if the dead

---

[a]38 Some manuscripts *If he is ignorant of this, let him be ignorant*   [b]3 Or *you at the first*
[c]5 Greek *Cephas*

are not raised, then Christ has not been raised either. ¹⁷And if Christ has not been raised, your faith is futile; you are still in your sins. ¹⁸Then those also who have fallen asleep in Christ are lost. ¹⁹If only for this life we have hope in Christ, we are to be pitied more than all men.

²⁰But Christ has indeed been raised from the dead, the firstfruits of those who have fallen asleep. ²¹For since death came through a man, the resurrection of the dead comes also through a man. ²²For as in Adam all die, so in Christ all will be made alive. ²³But each in his own turn: Christ, the firstfruits; then, when he comes, those who belong to him. ²⁴Then the end will come, when he hands over the kingdom to God the Father after he

FRIDAY

VERSE:	AUTHOR:	PASSAGE:
1 Corinthians 15:19	Henri J.M. Nouwen	1 Corinthians 15:12–57

Love Is Stronger Than Death

The resurrection is the expression of God's faithfulness to Jesus and to all God's children. Through the resurrection God has said to Jesus, "You are indeed my beloved Son, and my love is everlasting," and to us God has said, "You indeed are my beloved children, and my love is everlasting." The resurrection is God's way of revealing to us that nothing that belongs to God will ever go to waste. What belongs to God will never get lost — not even our mortal bodies. The resurrection doesn't answer any of our curious questions about life after death, such as, How will it be? How will it look? But it does reveal to us that, indeed, love is stronger than death. After that revelation, we must remain silent, leave the whys, wheres, hows and whens behind, and simply trust . . .

As the father of the epileptic boy, who asked Jesus to heal his child, we will always have to say, "I do believe; help me overcome my unbelief!" (Mark 9:24). Still, when we keep our eyes fixed on the risen Lord, we may find not only that love is stronger than death, but also that our faith is stronger than our skepticism.

ADDITIONAL SCRIPTURE READINGS
Psalm 85; Romans 8:28–39

Go to page 1462 for your next devotional reading.

has destroyed all dominion, authority and power. ²⁵For he must reign until he has put all his enemies under his feet. ²⁶The last enemy to be destroyed is death. ²⁷For he "has put everything under his feet."[a] Now when it says that "everything" has been put under him, it is clear that this does not include God himself, who put everything under Christ. ²⁸When he has done this, then the Son himself will be made subject to him who put everything under him, so that God may be all in all.

²⁹Now if there is no resurrection, what will those do who are baptized for the dead? If the dead are not raised at all, why are people baptized for them? ³⁰And as for us, why do we endanger ourselves every hour? ³¹I die every day—I mean that, brothers—just as surely as I glory over you in Christ Jesus our Lord. ³²If I fought wild beasts in Ephesus for merely human reasons, what have I gained? If the dead are not raised,

"Let us eat and drink,
　for tomorrow we die."[b]

³³Do not be misled: "Bad company corrupts good character." ³⁴Come back to your senses as you ought, and stop sinning; for there are some who are ignorant of God—I say this to your shame.

The Resurrection Body

³⁵But someone may ask, "How are the dead raised? With what kind of body will they come?" ³⁶How foolish! What you sow does not come to life unless it dies. ³⁷When you sow, you do not plant the body that will be, but just a seed, perhaps of wheat or of something else. ³⁸But God gives it a body as he has determined, and to each kind of seed he gives its own body. ³⁹All flesh is not the same: Men have one kind of flesh, animals have another, birds another and fish another. ⁴⁰There are also heavenly bodies and there are earthly bodies; but the splendor of the heavenly bodies is one kind, and the splendor of the earthly bodies is another. ⁴¹The sun has one kind of splendor, the moon another and the stars another; and star differs from star in splendor.

⁴²So will it be with the resurrection of the dead. The body that is sown is perishable, it is raised imperishable; ⁴³it is sown in dishonor, it is raised in glory; it is sown in weakness, it is raised in power; ⁴⁴it is sown a natural body, it is raised a spiritual body.

If there is a natural body, there is also a spiritual body. ⁴⁵So it is written: "The first man Adam became a living being"[c]; the last Adam, a life-giving spirit. ⁴⁶The spiritual did not come first, but the natural, and after that the spiritual. ⁴⁷The first man was of the dust of the earth, the second man from heaven. ⁴⁸As was the earthly man, so are those who are of the earth; and as is the man from heaven, so also are those who are of heaven. ⁴⁹And just as we have borne the likeness of the earthly man, so shall we[d] bear the likeness of the man from heaven.

⁵⁰I declare to you, brothers, that flesh and blood cannot inherit the kingdom of God, nor does the perishable inherit the imperishable. ⁵¹Listen, I tell you a mystery: We will not all sleep, but we will all be changed—⁵²in a flash, in the twinkling of an eye, at the last trumpet. For the trumpet will sound, the dead will be raised imperishable, and we will be changed. ⁵³For the perishable must clothe itself with the imperishable, and the mortal with immortality. ⁵⁴When the perishable has been clothed with the imperishable, and the mortal with immortality, then the saying that is written will come true: "Death has been swallowed up in victory."[e]

⁵⁵"Where, O death, is your victory?
　Where, O death, is your
　　　　sting?"[f]

---

[a]27 Psalm 8:6   [b]32 Isaiah 22:13   [c]45 Gen. 2:7   [d]49 Some early manuscripts *so let us*
[e]54 Isaiah 25:8   [f]55 Hosea 13:14

PASSAGE: Isaiah 25:1–9; 1 Corinthians 15:50–58
AUTHOR: John Donne

Death, Be Not Proud

Death, be not proud, though some have called thee
Mighty and dreadful, for thou art not so;
For those whom thou think'st thou dost overthrow
Die not, poor Death; nor yet canst thou kill me.
From rest and sleep, which but thy picture be,
Much pleasure; then from thee much more must
    flow;
And soonest our best men with thee do go —
Rest of their bones and souls' delivery!
Thou'rt slave to fate, chance, kings, and desperate
    men,
And dost with poison, war, and sickness dwell;
And poppy or charms can make us sleep as well
And better than thy stroke. Why swell'st thou then?
    One short sleep past, we wake eternally,
    And Death shall be no more: Death, thou
        shalt die!

Go to page 1465 for your next devotional reading.

[56]The sting of death is sin, and the power of sin is the law. [57]But thanks be to God! He gives us the victory through our Lord Jesus Christ.

[58]Therefore, my dear brothers, stand firm. Let nothing move you. Always give yourselves fully to the work of the Lord, because you know that your labor in the Lord is not in vain.

The Collection for God's People

16 Now about the collection for God's people: Do what I told the Galatian churches to do. [2]On the first day of every week, each one of you should set aside a sum of money in keeping with his income, saving it up, so that when I come no collections will have to be made. [3]Then, when I arrive, I will give letters of introduction to the men you approve and send them with your gift to Jerusalem. [4]If it seems advisable for me to go also, they will accompany me.

Personal Requests

[5]After I go through Macedonia, I will come to you—for I will be going through Macedonia. [6]Perhaps I will stay with you awhile, or even spend the winter, so that you can help me on my journey, wherever I go. [7]I do not want to see you now and make only a passing visit; I hope to spend some time with you, if the Lord permits. [8]But I will stay on at Ephesus until Pentecost, [9]because a great door for effective work has opened to me, and there are many who oppose me.

[10]If Timothy comes, see to it that he has nothing to fear while he is with you, for he is carrying on the work of the Lord, just as I am. [11]No one, then, should refuse to accept him. Send him on his way in peace so that he may return to me. I am expecting him along with the brothers.

[12]Now about our brother Apollos: I strongly urged him to go to you with the brothers. He was quite unwilling to go now, but he will go when he has the opportunity.

[13]Be on your guard; stand firm in the faith; be men of courage; be strong. [14]Do everything in love.

[15]You know that the household of Stephanas were the first converts in Achaia, and they have devoted themselves to the service of the saints. I urge you, brothers, [16]to submit to such as these and to everyone who joins in the work, and labors at it. [17]I was glad when Stephanas, Fortunatus and Achaicus arrived, because they have supplied what was lacking from you. [18]For they refreshed my spirit and yours also. Such men deserve recognition.

Final Greetings

[19]The churches in the province of Asia send you greetings. Aquila and Priscilla[a] greet you warmly in the Lord, and so does the church that meets at their house. [20]All the brothers here send you greetings. Greet one another with a holy kiss.

[21]I, Paul, write this greeting in my own hand.

[22]If anyone does not love the Lord—a curse be on him. Come, O Lord[b]!

[23]The grace of the Lord Jesus be with you.

[24]My love to all of you in Christ Jesus. Amen.[c]

---

[a]19 Greek *Prisca*, a variant of *Priscilla*   [b]22 In Aramaic the expression *Come, O Lord* is *Marana tha.*   [c]24 Some manuscripts do not have *Amen.*

Paul sent this letter as he prepared to visit the church in Corinth (2 Corinthians 7:5; 13:1). The most personal of all his letters, it expresses both the excitement and the suffering Paul had experienced in his life. As you read this letter, look back on your life and acknowledge the good times and the bad times, and realize that through it all, God has been there, leading you toward growth and wholeness.

2 CORINTHIANS

1 Paul, an apostle of Christ Jesus by the will of God, and Timothy our brother,

To the church of God in Corinth, together with all the saints throughout Achaia:

²Grace and peace to you from God our Father and the Lord Jesus Christ.

The God of All Comfort

³Praise be to the God and Father of our Lord Jesus Christ, the Father of compassion and the God of all comfort, ⁴who comforts us in all our troubles, so that we can comfort those in any trouble with the comfort we ourselves have received from God. ⁵For just as the sufferings of Christ flow over into our lives, so also through Christ our comfort overflows. ⁶If we are distressed, it is for your comfort and salvation; if we are comforted, it is for your comfort, which produces in you patient endurance of the same sufferings we suffer. ⁷And our hope for you is firm, because we know that just as you share in our sufferings, so also you share in our comfort.

⁸We do not want you to be uninformed, brothers, about the hardships we suffered in the province of Asia. We were under great pressure, far beyond our ability to endure, so that we despaired even of life. ⁹Indeed, in our hearts we felt the sentence of death. But this happened that we might not rely on ourselves but on God, who raises the dead. ¹⁰He has delivered us from such a deadly peril, and he will deliver us. On him we have set our hope that he will continue to deliver us, ¹¹as you help us by your prayers. Then many will give thanks on our[a] behalf for the gracious favor granted us in answer to the prayers of many.

Paul's Change of Plans

¹²Now this is our boast: Our conscience testifies that we have conducted ourselves in the world, and especially in our relations with you, in the holiness and sincerity that are from God. We have done so not according to worldly wisdom but according to God's grace. ¹³For we do not write you anything you cannot read or understand. And I hope that, ¹⁴as you have understood us in part, you will come to understand fully that you can boast of us just as we will boast of you in the day of the Lord Jesus.

¹⁵Because I was confident of this, I planned to visit you first so that you might benefit twice. ¹⁶I planned to vis-

VERSE: AUTHOR: PASSAGE:
2 Corinthians 1:4   Billy Graham   2 Corinthians 1:3–11

The Best Comforters

Those who have suffered most are often able to comfort others best. Someone who has experienced the same sort of pain is the one who can minister best. However, to say "I know how you feel" is usually unnecessary and frequently unwelcome. No one knows exactly how another feels. Better to say, "I don't know how you feel, I can't really put myself in your shoes but this is how I was comforted . . . ." Our sufferings may be hard to bear; but they teach us lessons which enable us to help others.

Our attitude toward suffering should not be "grit your teeth and bear it," hoping it will pass as quickly as possible. We should learn all we can from our personal problems so that we can comfort others, just as Jesus did. "Because he himself suffered when he was tempted, he is able to help those who are being tempted" (Hebrews 2:18).

We are surrounded by hurting people. Some may wear a plastic mask, but beneath the mask is a scarred soul. Are we approachable and available? God does not comfort us to make us comfortable but to make us comforters.

ADDITIONAL SCRIPTURE READINGS
2 Corinthians 7:2–7; 1 Thessalonians 5:4–11

Go to page 1467 for your next devotional reading.

it you on my way to Macedonia and to come back to you from Macedonia, and then to have you send me on my way to Judea. ¹⁷When I planned this, did I do it lightly? Or do I make my plans in a worldly manner so that in the same breath I say, "Yes, yes" and "No, no"?

¹⁸But as surely as God is faithful, our message to you is not "Yes" and "No." ¹⁹For the Son of God, Jesus Christ, who was preached among you by us and Silas*a* and Timothy, was not "Yes" and "No," but in him it has always been "Yes." ²⁰For no matter how many promises God has made, they are "Yes" in Christ. And so through him the "Amen" is spoken by us to the glory of God. ²¹Now it is God who makes both us and you stand firm in Christ. He anointed us, ²²set his seal of ownership on us, and put his Spirit in our hearts as a deposit, guaranteeing what is to come.

²³I call God as my witness that it was in order to spare you that I did not return to Corinth. ²⁴Not that we lord it over your faith, but we work with you for your joy, because it is by faith you stand firm. ²¹So I made up my mind that I would not make another painful visit to you. ²For if I grieve you, who is left to make me glad but you whom I have grieved? ³I wrote as I did so that when I came I should not be distressed by those who ought to make me rejoice. I had confidence in all of you, that you would all share my joy. ⁴For I wrote you out of great distress and anguish of heart and with many tears, not to grieve you but to let you know the depth of my love for you.

Forgiveness for the Sinner

⁵If anyone has caused grief, he has not so much grieved me as he has grieved all of you, to some extent—not to put it too severely. ⁶The punishment inflicted on him by the majority is sufficient for him. ⁷Now instead, you ought to forgive and comfort him, so that he will not be overwhelmed by excessive sorrow. ⁸I urge you, therefore, to reaffirm your love for him. ⁹The reason I wrote you was to see if you would stand the test and be obedient in everything. ¹⁰If you forgive anyone, I also forgive him. And what I have forgiven—if there was anything to forgive—I have forgiven in the sight of Christ for your sake, ¹¹in order that Satan might not outwit us. For we are not unaware of his schemes.

Ministers of the New Covenant

¹²Now when I went to Troas to preach the gospel of Christ and found that the Lord had opened a door for me, ¹³I still had no peace of mind, because I did not find my brother Titus there. So I said good-by to them and went on to Macedonia.

¹⁴But thanks be to God, who always leads us in triumphal procession in Christ and through us spreads everywhere the fragrance of the knowledge of him. ¹⁵For we are to God the aroma of Christ among those who are being saved and those who are perishing. ¹⁶To the one we are the smell of death; to the other, the fragrance of life. And who is equal to such a task? ¹⁷Unlike so many, we do not peddle the word of God for profit. On the contrary, in Christ we speak before God with sincerity, like men sent from God.

³Are we beginning to commend ourselves again? Or do we need, like some people, letters of recommendation to you or from you? ²You yourselves are our letter, written on our hearts, known and read by everybody. ³You show that you are a letter from Christ, the result of our ministry, written not with ink but with the Spirit of the living God, not on tablets of stone but on tablets of human hearts.

⁴Such confidence as this is ours through Christ before God. ⁵Not that we are competent in ourselves to claim anything for ourselves, but our competence comes from God. ⁶He has

---

a19 Greek *Silvanus*, a variant of *Silas*

VERSE:	AUTHOR:	PASSAGE:
2 Corinthians 2:7	Jean Shaw	2 Corinthians 2:5–11

Take Out the Trash

Much that we keep stored in boxes is not valuable to anyone but us. Ticket stubs, blackened corsages, graduation programs are worthless . . . Yet we keep collecting, preserving memories of important occasions.

There are happy memories and sad ones. Perhaps some bitter ones. We remember angry words and hurt feelings. The relative who didn't come to our wedding. The daughter-in-law who told us to stop interfering. We keep these in our mental storage boxes, getting them out from time to time and reliving the experience.

In Isaiah 43:25 God says to his people, "I, even I, am he who blots out your transgressions, for my own sake, and remembers your sins no more." All those terrible things we have done — God cancels them, wipes them out. He doesn't stuff them away in a drawer just in case he wants to drag them out to jog his memory. He obliterates them. He can't remember them any more.

Has anyone sinned against us the way we have sinned against God? No, no one, regardless of how badly we think we were treated. Yet God forgives and forgets. And so should we. Why spend our final years hating? . . .

As we get older we can get careless about our spiritual housekeeping. Emotional trash can collect. This is a good day to confess it, make amends and enjoy life free from ugly clutter.

ADDITIONAL SCRIPTURE READINGS
Matthew 18:21–35; Colossians 3:12–17

Go to page 1469 for your next devotional reading.

made us competent as ministers of a new covenant—not of the letter but of the Spirit; for the letter kills, but the Spirit gives life.

The Glory of the New Covenant

7Now if the ministry that brought death, which was engraved in letters on stone, came with glory, so that the Israelites could not look steadily at the face of Moses because of its glory, fading though it was, 8will not the ministry of the Spirit be even more glorious? 9If the ministry that condemns men is glorious, how much more glorious is the ministry that brings righteousness! 10For what was glorious has no glory now in comparison with the surpassing glory. 11And if what was fading away came with glory, how much greater is the glory of that which lasts!

12Therefore, since we have such a hope, we are very bold. 13We are not like Moses, who would put a veil over his face to keep the Israelites from gazing at it while the radiance was fading away. 14But their minds were made dull, for to this day the same veil remains when the old covenant is read. It has not been removed, because only in Christ is it taken away. 15Even to this day when Moses is read, a veil covers their hearts. 16But whenever anyone turns to the Lord, the veil is taken away. 17Now the Lord is the Spirit, and where the Spirit of the Lord is, there is freedom. 18And we, who with unveiled faces all reflect[a] the Lord's glory, are being transformed into his likeness with ever-increasing glory, which comes from the Lord, who is the Spirit.

Treasures in Jars of Clay

4 Therefore, since through God's mercy we have this ministry, we do not lose heart. 2Rather, we have renounced secret and shameful ways; we do not use deception, nor do we distort the word of God. On the contrary, by setting forth the truth plainly we commend ourselves to every man's conscience in the sight of God. 3And even if our gospel is veiled, it is veiled to those who are perishing. 4The god of this age has blinded the minds of unbelievers, so that they cannot see the light of the gospel of the glory of Christ, who is the image of God. 5For we do not preach ourselves, but Jesus Christ as Lord, and ourselves as your servants for Jesus' sake. 6For God, who said, "Let light shine out of darkness,"[b] made his light shine in our hearts to give us the light of the knowledge of the glory of God in the face of Christ.

7But we have this treasure in jars of clay to show that this all-surpassing power is from God and not from us. 8We are hard pressed on every side, but not crushed; perplexed, but not in despair; 9persecuted, but not abandoned; struck down, but not destroyed. 10We always carry around in our body the death of Jesus, so that the life of Jesus may also be revealed in our body. 11For we who are alive are always being given over to death for Jesus' sake, so that his life may be revealed in our mortal body. 12So then, death is at work in us, but life is at work in you.

13It is written: "I believed; therefore I have spoken."[c] With that same spirit of faith we also believe and therefore speak, 14because we know that the one who raised the Lord Jesus from the dead will also raise us with Jesus and present us with you in his presence. 15All this is for your benefit, so that the grace that is reaching more and more people may cause thanksgiving to overflow to the glory of God.

16Therefore we do not lose heart. Though outwardly we are wasting away, yet inwardly we are being renewed day by day. 17For our light and momentary troubles are achieving for us an eternal glory that far outweighs them all. 18So we fix our eyes not on what is seen, but on what is unseen. For what is seen is temporary, but what is unseen is eternal.

---

a18 Or contemplate　　b6 Gen. 1:3　　c13 Psalm 116:10

VERSE: AUTHOR: PASSAGE:
2 Corinthians 4:17   Max Lucado   2 Corinthians 4:1–18

It's Worth It!

One line in the 2 Corinthians passage you just read makes me smile: "our light and momentary troubles." I wouldn't have called them that if I were Paul. Read what he called *light and momentary*, and I think you'll agree: imprisoned; beaten with a whip five times; faced death; beaten with rods three times; stoned once; shipwrecked three times . . . in constant danger; hungry and thirsty (see 2 Corinthians 11:23–27).

Long and trying ordeals, perhaps. *Arduous and deadly afflictions*, OK. But *light and momentary troubles*? How could Paul describe endless trials with that phrase?

He tells us. He could see "an eternal glory that far outweighs them all."

Can I speak candidly for a few lines? For some of you, the journey has been long. Very long and stormy. In no way do I wish to minimize the difficulties that you have had to face along the way. Some of you have shouldered burdens that few of us could ever carry. You have bid farewell to lifelong partners. You have been robbed of lifelong dreams. You have been given bodies that can't sustain your spirit. You have spouses who can't tolerate your faith . . . And you are tired.

It's hard for you to see the City in the midst of the storms . . . You want to go on, but some days the road seems so long. Let me encourage you: *It's worth it.*

God never said that the journey would be easy, but he did say that the arrival would be worthwhile. Remember this: God may not do what you want, but he will do what is right . . . and best. He's the Father of the forward motion. Trust him. He will get you home. And the trials of the trip will be lost in the joy of the feast.

ADDITIONAL SCRIPTURE READINGS
Psalm 30; 1 Peter 1:3–9

Go to page 1471 for your next devotional reading.

Our Heavenly Dwelling

5 Now we know that if the earthly tent we live in is destroyed, we have a building from God, an eternal house in heaven, not built by human hands. ²Meanwhile we groan, longing to be clothed with our heavenly dwelling, ³because when we are clothed, we will not be found naked. ⁴For while we are in this tent, we groan and are burdened, because we do not wish to be unclothed but to be clothed with our heavenly dwelling, so that what is mortal may be swallowed up by life. ⁵Now it is God who has made us for this very purpose and has given us the Spirit as a deposit, guaranteeing what is to come.

⁶Therefore we are always confident and know that as long as we are at home in the body we are away from the Lord. ⁷We live by faith, not by sight. ⁸We are confident, I say, and would prefer to be away from the body and at home with the Lord. ⁹So we make it our goal to please him, whether we are at home in the body or away from it. ¹⁰For we must all appear before the judgment seat of Christ, that each one may receive what is due him for the things done while in the body, whether good or bad.

The Ministry of Reconciliation

¹¹Since, then, we know what it is to fear the Lord, we try to persuade men. What we are is plain to God, and I hope it is also plain to your conscience. ¹²We are not trying to commend ourselves to you again, but are giving you an opportunity to take pride in us, so that you can answer those who take pride in what is seen rather than in what is in the heart. ¹³If we are out of our mind, it is for the sake of God; if we are in our right mind, it is for you. ¹⁴For Christ's love compels us, because we are convinced that one died for all, and therefore all died. ¹⁵And he died for all, that those who live should no longer live for themselves but for him who died for them and was raised again.

¹⁶So from now on we regard no one from a worldly point of view. Though we once regarded Christ in this way, we do so no longer. ¹⁷Therefore, if anyone is in Christ, he is a new creation; the old has gone, the new has come! ¹⁸All this is from God, who reconciled us to himself through Christ and gave us the ministry of reconciliation: ¹⁹that God was reconciling the world to himself in Christ, not counting men's sins against them. And he has committed to us the message of reconciliation. ²⁰We are therefore Christ's ambassadors, as though God were making his appeal through us. We implore you on Christ's behalf: Be reconciled to God. ²¹God made him who had no sin to be sin*a* for us, so that in him we might become the righteousness of God.

6 As God's fellow workers we urge you not to receive God's grace in vain. ²For he says,

"In the time of my favor I heard
you,
and in the day of salvation I
helped you."*b*

I tell you, now is the time of God's favor, now is the day of salvation.

Paul's Hardships

³We put no stumbling block in anyone's path, so that our ministry will not be discredited. ⁴Rather, as servants of God we commend ourselves in every way: in great endurance; in troubles, hardships and distresses; ⁵in beatings, imprisonments and riots; in hard work, sleepless nights and hunger; ⁶in purity, understanding, patience and kindness; in the Holy Spirit and in sincere love; ⁷in truthful speech and in the power of God; with weapons of righteousness in the right hand and in the left; ⁸through glory and dishonor, bad report and good report; genuine, yet regarded as impostors; ⁹known, yet regarded as unknown; dying, and yet we live on;

---

*a*21 Or *be a sin offering*   *b*2 Isaiah 49:8

VERSE:	AUTHOR:	PASSAGE:
2 Corinthians 5:1	Charles L. Allen	2 Corinthians 5:1–10

A Tottering Tent

In his book *The Meaning of Faith*, Harry Emerson Fosdick gave the account of John Quincy Adams, then 80 years old. He met a friend on a Boston street.

"Good morning," said the friend, "and how is John Quincy Adams today?"

"Thank you," the ex-president replied. "John Quincy Adams himself is well, quite well, thank you. But the house in which he lives at present is becoming dilapidated. It is tottering upon its foundation. Time and the seasons have nearly destroyed it. Its roof is pretty well worn out. The walls are much shattered, and it trembles with every wind. The old tenement is becoming almost uninhabitable, and I think John Quincy Adams will have to move out of it soon. But he himself is quite well, quite well."

This attitude has been called "body transcendence." It means you do not judge yourself solely on the state of your body. Aging does not automatically cause one to be less of a person. We can still maintain many of our abilities. As we grow older, we can continue to acquire wisdom, to love more deeply and to continue to contribute to the life of the world about us.

Remember these wise words: "There is a time for everything, and a season for every activity under heaven" (Ecclesiastes 3:1).

ADDITIONAL SCRIPTURE READINGS
Ecclesiastes 3:1–14; Philippians 1:18–30

Go to page 1473 for your next devotional reading.

beaten, and yet not killed; [10]sorrowful, yet always rejoicing; poor, yet making many rich; having nothing, and yet possessing everything.

[11]We have spoken freely to you, Corinthians, and opened wide our hearts to you. [12]We are not withholding our affection from you, but you are withholding yours from us. [13]As a fair exchange—I speak as to my children—open wide your hearts also.

Do Not Be Yoked With Unbelievers

[14]Do not be yoked together with unbelievers. For what do righteousness and wickedness have in common? Or what fellowship can light have with darkness? [15]What harmony is there between Christ and Belial[a]? What does a believer have in common with an unbeliever? [16]What agreement is there between the temple of God and idols? For we are the temple of the living God. As God has said: "I will live with them and walk among them, and I will be their God, and they will be my people."[b]

[17]"Therefore come out from them
    and be separate,
                    says the Lord.
  Touch no unclean thing,
    and I will receive you."[c]
[18]"I will be a Father to you,
    and you will be my sons and
      daughters,
        says the Lord Almighty."[d]

7 Since we have these promises, dear friends, let us purify ourselves from everything that contaminates body and spirit, perfecting holiness out of reverence for God.

Paul's Joy

[2]Make room for us in your hearts. We have wronged no one, we have corrupted no one, we have exploited no one. [3]I do not say this to condemn you; I have said before that you have such a place in our hearts that we would live or die with you. [4]I have great confidence in you; I take great pride in you. I am greatly encouraged; in all our troubles my joy knows no bounds.

[5]For when we came into Macedonia, this body of ours had no rest, but we were harassed at every turn—conflicts on the outside, fears within. [6]But God, who comforts the downcast, comforted us by the coming of Titus, [7]and not only by his coming but also by the comfort you had given him. He told us about your longing for me, your deep sorrow, your ardent concern for me, so that my joy was greater than ever.

[8]Even if I caused you sorrow by my letter, I do not regret it. Though I did regret it—I see that my letter hurt you, but only for a little while— [9]yet now I am happy, not because you were made sorry, but because your sorrow led you to repentance. For you became sorrowful as God intended and so were not harmed in any way by us. [10]Godly sorrow brings repentance that leads to salvation and leaves no regret, but worldly sorrow brings death. [11]See what this godly sorrow has produced in you: what earnestness, what eagerness to clear yourselves, what indignation, what alarm, what longing, what concern, what readiness to see justice done. At every point you have proved yourselves to be innocent in this matter. [12]So even though I wrote to you, it was not on account of the one who did the wrong or of the injured party, but rather that before God you could see for yourselves how devoted to us you are. [13]By all this we are encouraged.

In addition to our own encouragement, we were especially delighted to see how happy Titus was, because his spirit has been refreshed by all of you. [14]I had boasted to him about you, and you have not embarrassed me. But just as everything we said to you was true, so our boasting about you to Titus has proved to be true as well. [15]And his affection for you is all the

---

[a]15 Greek Beliar, a variant of Belial   [b]16 Lev. 26:12; Jer. 32:38; Ezek. 37:27   [c]17 Isaiah 52:11;
Ezek. 20:34,41   [d]18 2 Samuel 7:14; 7:8

VERSE: AUTHOR: PASSAGE:
2 Corinthians 7:4   Lewis B. Smedes   2 Corinthians 7:2–7

Joy Between the Clouds

Joy, not shame, is our destiny. We know, don't we, by a kind of intuition, what joy is. Is it not the ecstasy of gratitude? Not cheerfulness, not humor, not drugged highs, but plain and simple thankfulness, deeply felt, down to the bone: is this not what joy is? . . .

There is no right time for joy. The time our heart breaks may be the only time we have for it today. Joy does not repair the break; joy gets in between the splinters . . .

Every silver lining has a cloud. Cloudless joy comes when everything is right, when cancer never strikes and swords have become plowshares, when all children dance safely in their streets, and all tears are wiped away. When Shalom comes, then joy will have no clouds. But between now and then, joy comes between the clouds. If all must be right with the world before I may have a fling with joy, I shall be somber forever.

The truth is that if we refuse to feel joy until every problem of the world is solved, every stomach full, every person housed, all violence stopped, we will have no joy this side of the New Earth. Joy in a world that does not work right must be a generous joy. Joy is always, always in spite of the fact that the whole world is groaning while it waits for its redemption.

ADDITIONAL SCRIPTURE READINGS
John 15:1–17; Romans 8:18–27

Go to page 1475 for your next devotional reading.

greater when he remembers that you were all obedient, receiving him with fear and trembling. ¹⁶I am glad I can have complete confidence in you.

Generosity Encouraged

8 And now, brothers, we want you to know about the grace that God has given the Macedonian churches. ²Out of the most severe trial, their overflowing joy and their extreme poverty welled up in rich generosity. ³For I testify that they gave as much as they were able, and even beyond their ability. Entirely on their own, ⁴they urgently pleaded with us for the privilege of sharing in this service to the saints. ⁵And they did not do as we expected, but they gave themselves first to the Lord and then to us in keeping with God's will. ⁶So we urged Titus, since he had earlier made a beginning, to bring also to completion this act of grace on your part. ⁷But just as you excel in everything—in faith, in speech, in knowledge, in complete earnestness and in your love for us[a]—see that you also excel in this grace of giving.

⁸I am not commanding you, but I want to test the sincerity of your love by comparing it with the earnestness of others. ⁹For you know the grace of our Lord Jesus Christ, that though he was rich, yet for your sakes he became poor, so that you through his poverty might become rich.

¹⁰And here is my advice about what is best for you in this matter: Last year you were the first not only to give but also to have the desire to do so. ¹¹Now finish the work, so that your eager willingness to do it may be matched by your completion of it, according to your means. ¹²For if the willingness is there, the gift is acceptable according to what one has, not according to what he does not have.

¹³Our desire is not that others might be relieved while you are hard pressed, but that there might be equality. ¹⁴At the present time your plenty will supply what they need, so that in turn their plenty will supply what you need. Then there will be equality, ¹⁵as it is written: "He who gathered much did not have too much, and he who gathered little did not have too little."[b]

Titus Sent to Corinth

¹⁶I thank God, who put into the heart of Titus the same concern I have for you. ¹⁷For Titus not only welcomed our appeal, but he is coming to you with much enthusiasm and on his own initiative. ¹⁸And we are sending along with him the brother who is praised by all the churches for his service to the gospel. ¹⁹What is more, he was chosen by the churches to accompany us as we carry the offering, which we administer in order to honor the Lord himself and to show our eagerness to help. ²⁰We want to avoid any criticism of the way we administer this liberal gift. ²¹For we are taking pains to do what is right, not only in the eyes of the Lord but also in the eyes of men.

²²In addition, we are sending with them our brother who has often proved to us in many ways that he is zealous, and now even more so because of his great confidence in you. ²³As for Titus, he is my partner and fellow worker among you; as for our brothers, they are representatives of the churches and an honor to Christ. ²⁴Therefore show these men the proof of your love and the reason for our pride in you, so that the churches can see it.

9 There is no need for me to write to you about this service to the saints. ²For I know your eagerness to help, and I have been boasting about it to the Macedonians, telling them that since last year you in Achaia were ready to give; and your enthusiasm has stirred most of them to action. ³But I am sending the brothers in order that our boasting about you in this matter should not prove hollow, but that you may be ready, as I said you would be. ⁴For if any Macedoni-

PASSAGE: John 12:20–26; 2 Corinthians 8:1–15
AUTHOR: Francis of Assisi

. . . . ● ● . . . .

An Instrument for God

Lord, make me an instrument of your Peace!
Where there is hatred, let me sow love.
Where there is injury, pardon.
Where there is doubt, faith.
Where there is despair, hope.
Where there is darkness, light.
Where there is sadness, joy.
O divine Master, grant that I may not so much seek
To be consoled, as to console;
To be understood, as to understand;
To be loved, as to love;
For it is in giving that we receive.
It is in pardoning that we are pardoned.
It is in dying that we are born to eternal life.

. . . . ● ● . . . .

Go to page 1477 for your next devotional reading.

ans come with me and find you unprepared, we—not to say anything about you—would be ashamed of having been so confident. [5]So I thought it necessary to urge the brothers to visit you in advance and finish the arrangements for the generous gift you had promised. Then it will be ready as a generous gift, not as one grudgingly given.

Sowing Generously

[6]Remember this: Whoever sows sparingly will also reap sparingly, and whoever sows generously will also reap generously. [7]Each man should give what he has decided in his heart to give, not reluctantly or under compulsion, for God loves a cheerful giver. [8]And God is able to make all grace abound to you, so that in all things at all times, having all that you need, you will abound in every good work. [9]As it is written:

"He has scattered abroad his gifts
　　to the poor;
　his righteousness endures
　　forever."[a]

[10]Now he who supplies seed to the sower and bread for food will also supply and increase your store of seed and will enlarge the harvest of your righteousness. [11]You will be made rich in every way so that you can be generous on every occasion, and through us your generosity will result in thanksgiving to God.

[12]This service that you perform is not only supplying the needs of God's people but is also overflowing in many expressions of thanks to God. [13]Because of the service by which you have proved yourselves, men will praise God for the obedience that accompanies your confession of the gospel of Christ, and for your generosity in sharing with them and with everyone else. [14]And in their prayers for you their hearts will go out to you, because of the surpassing grace God has given you. [15]Thanks be to God for his indescribable gift!

Paul's Defense of His Ministry

10 By the meekness and gentleness of Christ, I appeal to you—I, Paul, who am "timid" when face to face with you, but "bold" when away! [2]I beg you that when I come I may not have to be as bold as I expect to be toward some people who think that we live by the standards of this world. [3]For though we live in the world, we do not wage war as the world does. [4]The weapons we fight with are not the weapons of the world. On the contrary, they have divine power to demolish strongholds. [5]We demolish arguments and every pretension that sets itself up against the knowledge of God, and we take captive every thought to make it obedient to Christ. [6]And we will be ready to punish every act of disobedience, once your obedience is complete.

[7]You are looking only on the surface of things.[b] If anyone is confident that he belongs to Christ, he should consider again that we belong to Christ just as much as he. [8]For even if I boast somewhat freely about the authority the Lord gave us for building you up rather than pulling you down, I will not be ashamed of it. [9]I do not want to seem to be trying to frighten you with my letters. [10]For some say, "His letters are weighty and forceful, but in person he is unimpressive and his speaking amounts to nothing." [11]Such people should realize that what we are in our letters when we are absent, we will be in our actions when we are present.

[12]We do not dare to classify or compare ourselves with some who commend themselves. When they measure themselves by themselves and compare themselves with themselves, they are not wise. [13]We, however, will not boast beyond proper limits, but will confine our boasting to the field God has assigned to us, a field that reaches even to you. [14]We are not going too far in our boasting, as would be the case if we had not come to you,

---

[a]9 Psalm 112:9　　[b]7 Or *Look at the obvious facts*

VERSE: AUTHOR: PASSAGE:
2 Corinthians 9:8   Dirk R. Buursma   2 Corinthians 9:6–15

The Grace of Giving

"Get yours!" Some would say it's the prevailing philosophy today, the formula for a happy life. Get your own needs met first—and then if any time or resources are left over, perhaps you can think about somebody else's needs. Make sure your own rights are respected—and then perhaps you can think about someone else's rights. Accumulate more and more wealth to ensure your own security—and then maybe, just maybe, you can give some of your leftovers to someone else.

"Entirely on their own, they urgently pleaded with us for the privilege of sharing in this service to the saints" (2 Corinthians 8:3–4). Wow! They begged to be given the privilege of giving. And as a sign of their faithfulness, they gave Jesus first place in their lives (2 Corinthians 8:5). Isn't it amazing what a difference God's grace can make in the lives and attitudes of people.

The grace of giving. It doesn't come easy. It goes against our selfish nature. But God is able! Yes, he's able to take hold of our insatiably greedy hearts—and transform us into generous people.

You too can grow in this grace of giving as your years increase. Look at the picture of the abundant harvest of generosity (2 Corinthians 9:10–14): People becoming more like Christ, giving freely from hearts of love; needs being met; God being praised; bonds of love being strengthened. And the motivation, the gracious motivation: "Thanks be to God for his indescribable gift!" Because he gave, we too must give.

ADDITIONAL SCRIPTURE READINGS
Acts 4:32–36; Romans 12:1–8

Go to page 1480 for your next devotional reading.

for we did get as far as you with the gospel of Christ. [15]Neither do we go beyond our limits by boasting of work done by others.[a] Our hope is that, as your faith continues to grow, our area of activity among you will greatly expand, [16]so that we can preach the gospel in the regions beyond you. For we do not want to boast about work already done in another man's territory. [17]But, "Let him who boasts boast in the Lord."[b] [18]For it is not the one who commends himself who is approved, but the one whom the Lord commends.

Paul and the False Apostles

11 I hope you will put up with a little of my foolishness; but you are already doing that. [2]I am jealous for you with a godly jealousy. I promised you to one husband, to Christ, so that I might present you as a pure virgin to him. [3]But I am afraid that just as Eve was deceived by the serpent's cunning, your minds may somehow be led astray from your sincere and pure devotion to Christ. [4]For if someone comes to you and preaches a Jesus other than the Jesus we preached, or if you receive a different spirit from the one you received, or a different gospel from the one you accepted, you put up with it easily enough. [5]But I do not think I am in the least inferior to those "super-apostles." [6]I may not be a trained speaker, but I do have knowledge. We have made this perfectly clear to you in every way.

[7]Was it a sin for me to lower myself in order to elevate you by preaching the gospel of God to you free of charge? [8]I robbed other churches by receiving support from them so as to serve you. [9]And when I was with you and needed something, I was not a burden to anyone, for the brothers who came from Macedonia supplied what I needed. I have kept myself from being a burden to you in any way, and will continue to do so. [10]As surely as the truth of Christ is in me, nobody in the regions of Achaia will stop this boasting of mine. [11]Why? Because I do not love you? God knows I do! [12]And I will keep on doing what I am doing in order to cut the ground from under those who want an opportunity to be considered equal with us in the things they boast about.

[13]For such men are false apostles, deceitful workmen, masquerading as apostles of Christ. [14]And no wonder, for Satan himself masquerades as an angel of light. [15]It is not surprising, then, if his servants masquerade as servants of righteousness. Their end will be what their actions deserve.

Paul Boasts About His Sufferings

[16]I repeat: Let no one take me for a fool. But if you do, then receive me just as you would a fool, so that I may do a little boasting. [17]In this self-confident boasting I am not talking as the Lord would, but as a fool. [18]Since many are boasting in the way the world does, I too will boast. [19]You gladly put up with fools since you are so wise! [20]In fact, you even put up with anyone who enslaves you or exploits you or takes advantage of you or pushes himself forward or slaps you in the face. [21]To my shame I admit that we were too weak for that!

What anyone else dares to boast about—I am speaking as a fool—I also dare to boast about. [22]Are they Hebrews? So am I. Are they Israelites? So am I. Are they Abraham's descendants? So am I. [23]Are they servants of Christ? (I am out of my mind to talk like this.) I am more. I have worked much harder, been in prison more frequently, been flogged more severely, and been exposed to death again and again. [24]Five times I received from the Jews the forty lashes minus one. [25]Three times I was beaten

---

[a]13-15 Or [13]We, however, will not boast about things that cannot be measured, but we will boast according to the standard of measurement that the God of measure has assigned us—a measurement that relates even to you. [14] .... [15]Neither do we boast about things that cannot be measured in regard to the work done by others.   [b]17 Jer. 9:24

with rods, once I was stoned, three times I was shipwrecked, I spent a night and a day in the open sea, ²⁶I have been constantly on the move. I have been in danger from rivers, in danger from bandits, in danger from my own countrymen, in danger from Gentiles; in danger in the city, in danger in the country, in danger at sea; and in danger from false brothers. ²⁷I have labored and toiled and have often gone without sleep; I have known hunger and thirst and have often gone without food; I have been cold and naked. ²⁸Besides everything else, I face daily the pressure of my concern for all the churches. ²⁹Who is weak, and I do not feel weak? Who is led into sin, and I do not inwardly burn?

³⁰If I must boast, I will boast of the things that show my weakness. ³¹The God and Father of the Lord Jesus, who is to be praised forever, knows that I am not lying. ³²In Damascus the governor under King Aretas had the city of the Damascenes guarded in order to arrest me. ³³But I was lowered in a basket from a window in the wall and slipped through his hands.

Paul's Vision and His Thorn

12 I must go on boasting. Although there is nothing to be gained, I will go on to visions and revelations from the Lord. ²I know a man in Christ who fourteen years ago was caught up to the third heaven. Whether it was in the body or out of the body I do not know—God knows. ³And I know that this man—whether in the body or apart from the body I do not know, but God knows— ⁴was caught up to paradise. He heard inexpressible things, things that man is not permitted to tell. ⁵I will boast about a man like that, but I will not boast about myself, except about my weaknesses. ⁶Even if I should choose to boast, I would not be a fool, because I would be speaking the truth. But I refrain, so no one will think more of me than is warranted by what I do or say.

⁷To keep me from becoming conceited because of these surpassingly great revelations, there was given me a thorn in my flesh, a messenger of Satan, to torment me. ⁸Three times I pleaded with the Lord to take it away from me. ⁹But he said to me, "My grace is sufficient for you, for my power is made perfect in weakness." Therefore I will boast all the more gladly about my weaknesses, so that Christ's power may rest on me. ¹⁰That is why, for Christ's sake, I delight in weaknesses, in insults, in hardships, in persecutions, in difficulties. For when I am weak, then I am strong.

Paul's Concern for the Corinthians

¹¹I have made a fool of myself, but you drove me to it. I ought to have been commended by you, for I am not in the least inferior to the "super-apostles," even though I am nothing. ¹²The things that mark an apostle—signs, wonders and miracles—were done among you with great perseverance. ¹³How were you inferior to the other churches, except that I was never a burden to you? Forgive me this wrong!

¹⁴Now I am ready to visit you for the third time, and I will not be a burden to you, because what I want is not your possessions but you. After all, children should not have to save up for their parents, but parents for their children. ¹⁵So I will very gladly spend for you everything I have and expend myself as well. If I love you more, will you love me less? ¹⁶Be that as it may, I have not been a burden to you. Yet, crafty fellow that I am, I caught you by trickery! ¹⁷Did I exploit you through any of the men I sent you? ¹⁸I urged Titus to go to you and I sent our brother with him. Titus did not exploit you, did he? Did we not act in the same spirit and follow the same course?

¹⁹Have you been thinking all along that we have been defending ourselves to you? We have been speaking in the sight of God as those in Christ; and everything we do, dear friends, is for your strengthening. ²⁰For I am afraid that when I come I may not

find you as I want you to be, and you may not find me as you want me to be. I fear that there may be quarreling, jealousy, outbursts of anger, factions, slander, gossip, arrogance and disorder. [21] I am afraid that when I come again my God will humble me before you, and I will be grieved over many who have sinned earlier and have not repented of the impurity, sexual sin and debauchery in which they have indulged.

Final Warnings

13 This will be my third visit to you. "Every matter must be es-

VERSE:
2 Corinthians
12:10

AUTHOR:
J. Oswald Sanders

PASSAGE:
2 Corinthians
12:1–10

I Am Weak, He Is Strong

Old age, with all its acknowledged handicaps and limitations, can, however, open up new horizons of joyous possibility to us. The very realization of our own finiteness that comes with the gradual waning of our powers affords us the opportunity of proving in our own experience the validity of Paul's paradoxical claim: "When I am weak, then I am strong" (2 Corinthians 12:10). We, too, can know the thrill of discovering that our inadequacy is complemented by God's sufficiency . . .

Here is an area of life in which the elderly can glorify God uniquely and find deep joy. Has he not caused it to be recorded that "God chose the weak things of the world to shame the strong" (1 Corinthians 1:27)? He can still achieve his purpose even in the absence of human strength and resource.

We may feel that we are too weak and insignificant to achieve much for God at our time of life, but Paul assures us that he has chosen "nonentities" to do battle for him. Our very weakness and dependence open the way for a greater display of his power and grace. Is it not a revolutionary thought that God is willing to use us, not *in spite of* our weakness, but actually *because* of it?

ADDITIONAL SCRIPTURE READINGS
1 Corinthians 1:18–31; 1 Timothy 1:12–17
Go to page 1484 for your next devotional reading.

tablished by the testimony of two or three witnesses."[a] [2]I already gave you a warning when I was with you the second time. I now repeat it while absent: On my return I will not spare those who sinned earlier or any of the others, [3]since you are demanding proof that Christ is speaking through me. He is not weak in dealing with you, but is powerful among you. [4]For to be sure, he was crucified in weakness, yet he lives by God's power. Likewise, we are weak in him, yet by God's power we will live with him to serve you.

[5]Examine yourselves to see whether you are in the faith; test yourselves. Do you not realize that Christ Jesus is in you—unless, of course, you fail the test? [6]And I trust that you will discover that we have not failed the test. [7]Now we pray to God that you will not do anything wrong. Not that people will see that we have stood the test but that you will do what is right even though we may seem to have failed. [8]For we cannot do anything against the truth, but only for the truth. [9]We are glad whenever we are weak but you are strong; and our prayer is for your perfection. [10]This is why I write these things when I am absent, that when I come I may not have to be harsh in my use of authority—the authority the Lord gave me for building you up, not for tearing you down.

Final Greetings

[11]Finally, brothers, good-by. Aim for perfection, listen to my appeal, be of one mind, live in peace. And the God of love and peace will be with you.

[12]Greet one another with a holy kiss. [13]All the saints send their greetings.

[14]May the grace of the Lord Jesus Christ, and the love of God, and the fellowship of the Holy Spirit be with you all.

[a]1 Deut. 19:15

Paul's letter to the

churches he founded in Galatia (Acts

13:13—14:28) is primarily about faith and

freedom. He warned against those who were

teaching salvation by performance, and in-

sisted that it comes by faith alone. As you

read this letter, review the basics and find

peace in knowing that nothing you do can

earn your salvation; as you are set free in

Jesus, you will bear much fruit—the fruit

of a Spirit-filled life.

GALATIANS

1 Paul, an apostle—sent not from men nor by man, but by Jesus Christ and God the Father, who raised him from the dead— ²and all the brothers with me,

To the churches in Galatia:

³Grace and peace to you from God our Father and the Lord Jesus Christ, ⁴who gave himself for our sins to rescue us from the present evil age, according to the will of our God and Father, ⁵to whom be glory for ever and ever. Amen.

No Other Gospel

⁶I am astonished that you are so quickly deserting the one who called you by the grace of Christ and are turning to a different gospel— ⁷which is really no gospel at all. Evidently some people are throwing you into confusion and are trying to pervert the gospel of Christ. ⁸But even if we or an angel from heaven should preach a gospel other than the one we preached to you, let him be eternally condemned! ⁹As we have already said, so now I say again: If anybody is preaching to you a gospel other than what you accepted, let him be eternally condemned!

¹⁰Am I now trying to win the approval of men, or of God? Or am I trying to please men? If I were still trying to please men, I would not be a servant of Christ.

Paul Called by God

¹¹I want you to know, brothers, that the gospel I preached is not something that man made up. ¹²I did not receive it from any man, nor was I taught it; rather, I received it by revelation from Jesus Christ.

¹³For you have heard of my previ-

ous way of life in Judaism, how intensely I persecuted the church of God and tried to destroy it. [14]I was advancing in Judaism beyond many Jews of my own age and was extremely zealous for the traditions of my fathers. [15]But when God, who set me apart from birth[a] and called me by his grace, was pleased [16]to reveal his Son in me so that I might preach him among the Gentiles, I did not consult any man, [17]nor did I go up to Jerusalem to see those who were apostles before I was, but I went immediately into Arabia and later returned to Damascus.

[18]Then after three years, I went up to Jerusalem to get acquainted with Peter[b] and stayed with him fifteen days. [19]I saw none of the other apostles—only James, the Lord's brother. [20]I assure you before God that what I am writing you is no lie. [21]Later I went to Syria and Cilicia. [22]I was personally unknown to the churches of Judea that are in Christ. [23]They only heard the report: "The man who formerly persecuted us is now preaching the faith he once tried to destroy." [24]And they praised God because of me.

Paul Accepted by the Apostles

2 Fourteen years later I went up again to Jerusalem, this time with Barnabas. I took Titus along also. [2]I went in response to a revelation and set before them the gospel that I preach among the Gentiles. But I did this privately to those who seemed to be leaders, for fear that I was running or had run my race in vain. [3]Yet not even Titus, who was with me, was compelled to be circumcised, even though he was a Greek. [4]⌊This matter arose⌋ because some false brothers had infiltrated our ranks to spy on the freedom we have in Christ Jesus and to make us slaves. [5]We did not give in to them for a moment, so that the truth of the gospel might remain with you.

[6]As for those who seemed to be important—whatever they were makes no difference to me; God does not judge by external appearance—those men added nothing to my message. [7]On the contrary, they saw that I had been entrusted with the task of preaching the gospel to the Gentiles,[c] just as Peter had been to the Jews.[d] [8]For God, who was at work in the ministry of Peter as an apostle to the Jews, was also at work in my ministry as an apostle to the Gentiles. [9]James, Peter[e] and John, those reputed to be pillars, gave me and Barnabas the right hand of fellowship when they recognized the grace given to me. They agreed that we should go to the Gentiles, and they to the Jews. [10]All they asked was that we should continue to remember the poor, the very thing I was eager to do.

Paul Opposes Peter

[11]When Peter came to Antioch, I opposed him to his face, because he was clearly in the wrong. [12]Before certain men came from James, he used to eat with the Gentiles. But when they arrived, he began to draw back and separate himself from the Gentiles because he was afraid of those who belonged to the circumcision group. [13]The other Jews joined him in his hypocrisy, so that by their hypocrisy even Barnabas was led astray.

[14]When I saw that they were not acting in line with the truth of the gospel, I said to Peter in front of them all, "You are a Jew, yet you live like a Gentile and not like a Jew. How is it, then, that you force Gentiles to follow Jewish customs?

[15]"We who are Jews by birth and not 'Gentile sinners' [16]know that a man is not justified by observing the law, but by faith in Jesus Christ. So we, too, have put our faith in Christ Jesus that we may be justified by faith in Christ and not by observing the law, because by observing the law no one will be justified.

---

[a]15 Or *from my mother's womb*   [b]18 Greek *Cephas*   [c]7 Greek *uncircumcised*   [d]7 Greek *circumcised*; also in verses 8 and 9   [e]9 Greek *Cephas*; also in verses 11 and 14

VERSE:	AUTHOR:	PASSAGE:
Galatians 2:20	F.B. Meyer	Galatians 2:15–21

Christ Lives in Us

The heart of true religion is to believe that Christ is literally within us. We must not simply look to him as our Mediator, Advocate and Example, but as being possessed by him. He is our life, the living fountain rising up in the well of our personality. The apostle Paul was never weary of reaffirming this great fact of his experience, and it would be well if each of us could say every day . . . "Christ is in me; let me make room for him to dwell."

We must say *No* to self, that the life of Christ may become manifest in and through us, and our standing become a reality in daily experience and conduct. When evil suggestions come to us, we must remember that we have entered a world where such things have no place. We are no longer in the realm of the god of this world, but have passed into the realm of the risen Christ. Let those who are tempted believe this, and assert it in the face of the tempter, counting upon the Holy Spirit to make their reckoning a living experience . . .

Our Master demands that we should always do and be what is right. When we fail in some sudden demand, it is because we have omitted to put on some trait of Christ, which was intended to be the complement of our need. Let us therefore day by day say, "Lord Jesus, wrap thyself around me, that I may go forth, adequately attired to meet life's demands." *In Christ* for standing; *Christ in us* for life; we *with him* for safety.

ADDITIONAL SCRIPTURE READINGS
Romans 8:9–17; Colossians 3:12–17

Go to page 1486 for your next devotional reading.

¹⁷"If, while we seek to be justified in Christ, it becomes evident that we ourselves are sinners, does that mean that Christ promotes sin? Absolutely not! ¹⁸If I rebuild what I destroyed, I prove that I am a lawbreaker. ¹⁹For through the law I died to the law so that I might live for God. ²⁰I have been crucified with Christ and I no longer live, but Christ lives in me. The life I live in the body, I live by faith in the Son of God, who loved me and gave himself for me. ²¹I do not set aside the grace of God, for if righteousness could be gained through the law, Christ died for nothing!"[a]

Faith or Observance of the Law

3 You foolish Galatians! Who has bewitched you? Before your very eyes Jesus Christ was clearly portrayed as crucified. ²I would like to learn just one thing from you: Did you receive the Spirit by observing the law, or by believing what you heard? ³Are you so foolish? After beginning with the Spirit, are you now trying to attain your goal by human effort? ⁴Have you suffered so much for nothing—if it really was for nothing? ⁵Does God give you his Spirit and work miracles among you because you observe the law, or because you believe what you heard?

⁶Consider Abraham: "He believed God, and it was credited to him as righteousness."[b] ⁷Understand, then, that those who believe are children of Abraham. ⁸The Scripture foresaw that God would justify the Gentiles by faith, and announced the gospel in advance to Abraham: "All nations will be blessed through you."[c] ⁹So those who have faith are blessed along with Abraham, the man of faith.

¹⁰All who rely on observing the law are under a curse, for it is written: "Cursed is everyone who does not continue to do everything written in the Book of the Law."[d] ¹¹Clearly no one is justified before God by the law, because, "The righteous will live by faith."[e] ¹²The law is not based on faith; on the contrary, "The man who does these things will live by them."[f] ¹³Christ redeemed us from the curse of the law by becoming a curse for us, for it is written: "Cursed is everyone who is hung on a tree."[g] ¹⁴He redeemed us in order that the blessing given to Abraham might come to the Gentiles through Christ Jesus, so that by faith we might receive the promise of the Spirit.

The Law and the Promise

¹⁵Brothers, let me take an example from everyday life. Just as no one can set aside or add to a human covenant that has been duly established, so it is in this case. ¹⁶The promises were spoken to Abraham and to his seed. The Scripture does not say "and to seeds," meaning many people, but "and to your seed,"[h] meaning one person, who is Christ. ¹⁷What I mean is this: The law, introduced 430 years later, does not set aside the covenant previously established by God and thus do away with the promise. ¹⁸For if the inheritance depends on the law, then it no longer depends on a promise; but God in his grace gave it to Abraham through a promise.

¹⁹What, then, was the purpose of the law? It was added because of transgressions until the Seed to whom the promise referred had come. The law was put into effect through angels by a mediator. ²⁰A mediator, however, does not represent just one party; but God is one.

²¹Is the law, therefore, opposed to the promises of God? Absolutely not! For if a law had been given that could impart life, then righteousness would certainly have come by the law. ²²But the Scripture declares that the whole world is a prisoner of sin, so that what was promised, being given

---

[a]21 Some interpreters end the quotation after verse 14.   [b]6 Gen. 15:6   [c]8 Gen. 12:3; 18:18; 22:18   [d]10 Deut. 27:26   [e]11 Hab. 2:4   [f]12 Lev. 18:5   [g]13 Deut. 21:23   [h]16 Gen. 12:7; 13:15; 24:7

VERSE: AUTHOR: PASSAGE:
Galatians 3:11   Reuel L. Howe   Galatians 3:1–14

A Faith to Live by

The faith we choose to live by is the one that will affect our aging, and the one by which we will die, since aging and dying are a part of life.

We can have at least two kinds of faith. One is the closed system set of beliefs once and for all accepted and within which one lives; the other is an open dynamic set of beliefs with which one lives dialogically as he deals with the issues of his world.

The closed system is not apt to change, nor is the person who lives within that system apt to change ... The God of this kind of system becomes the God whom I want to think he is, the God of whom I approve, who will okay what I like and want ...

The opposite kind of faith is the open, dynamic one. The believer in this instance is an inquiring, trusting person whose understanding of God grows. Such a person uses his faith as a basis for risking dialogue with God, man and events, as did the psalmist, Job and others ... An open faith was practiced by Abraham who departed for a country he knew not of, by Jesus who followed his course to its bitter and triumphant end ... and by any one of us who by faith risks all to maintain integrity and trust.

The question is: What kind of faith are you trying to live by? One that contains you and keeps you safe, or one that expands you and moves you into the most that your life can be? Have you created a God to serve you; or have you been grasped by the living God with whom you live in a relationship of trust? ...

ADDITIONAL SCRIPTURE READINGS
Romans 4; Hebrews 11:8–19

Go to page 1489 for your next devotional reading.

through faith in Jesus Christ, might be given to those who believe.

²³Before this faith came, we were held prisoners by the law, locked up until faith should be revealed. ²⁴So the law was put in charge to lead us to Christ[a] that we might be justified by faith. ²⁵Now that faith has come, we are no longer under the supervision of the law.

Sons of God

²⁶You are all sons of God through faith in Christ Jesus, ²⁷for all of you who were baptized into Christ have clothed yourselves with Christ. ²⁸There is neither Jew nor Greek, slave nor free, male nor female, for you are all one in Christ Jesus. ²⁹If you belong to Christ, then you are Abraham's seed, and heirs according to the promise.

4 What I am saying is that as long as the heir is a child, he is no different from a slave, although he owns the whole estate. ²He is subject to guardians and trustees until the time set by his father. ³So also, when we were children, we were in slavery under the basic principles of the world. ⁴But when the time had fully come, God sent his Son, born of a woman, born under law, ⁵to redeem those under law, that we might receive the full rights of sons. ⁶Because you are sons, God sent the Spirit of his Son into our hearts, the Spirit who calls out, "Abba,[b] Father." ⁷So you are no longer a slave, but a son; and since you are a son, God has made you also an heir.

Paul's Concern for the Galatians

⁸Formerly, when you did not know God, you were slaves to those who by nature are not gods. ⁹But now that you know God—or rather are known by God—how is it that you are turning back to those weak and miserable principles? Do you wish to be enslaved by them all over again? ¹⁰You are observing special days and months and seasons and years! ¹¹I fear for you, that somehow I have wasted my efforts on you.

¹²I plead with you, brothers, become like me, for I became like you. You have done me no wrong. ¹³As you know, it was because of an illness that I first preached the gospel to you. ¹⁴Even though my illness was a trial to you, you did not treat me with contempt or scorn. Instead, you welcomed me as if I were an angel of God, as if I were Christ Jesus himself. ¹⁵What has happened to all your joy? I can testify that, if you could have done so, you would have torn out your eyes and given them to me. ¹⁶Have I now become your enemy by telling you the truth?

¹⁷Those people are zealous to win you over, but for no good. What they want is to alienate you ⌊from us⌋, so that you may be zealous for them. ¹⁸It is fine to be zealous, provided the purpose is good, and to be so always and not just when I am with you. ¹⁹My dear children, for whom I am again in the pains of childbirth until Christ is formed in you, ²⁰how I wish I could be with you now and change my tone, because I am perplexed about you!

Hagar and Sarah

²¹Tell me, you who want to be under the law, are you not aware of what the law says? ²²For it is written that Abraham had two sons, one by the slave woman and the other by the free woman. ²³His son by the slave woman was born in the ordinary way; but his son by the free woman was born as the result of a promise. ²⁴These things may be taken figuratively, for the women represent two covenants. One covenant is from Mount Sinai and bears children who are to be slaves: This is Hagar. ²⁵Now Hagar stands for Mount Sinai in Arabia and corresponds to the present city of Jerusalem, because she is in slavery with her children. ²⁶But the Je-

---

[a]24 Or *charge until Christ came*   [b]6 Aramaic for *Father*

rusalem that is above is free, and she is our mother. ²⁷For it is written:

"Be glad, O barren woman,
    who bears no children;
break forth and cry aloud,
    you who have no labor pains;
because more are the children of
        the desolate woman
    than of her who has a
        husband."ᵃ

²⁸Now you, brothers, like Isaac, are children of promise. ²⁹At that time the son born in the ordinary way persecuted the son born by the power of the Spirit. It is the same now. ³⁰But what does the Scripture say? "Get rid of the slave woman and her son, for the slave woman's son will never share in the inheritance with the free woman's son."ᵇ ³¹Therefore, brothers, we are not children of the slave woman, but of the free woman.

Freedom in Christ

5 It is for freedom that Christ has set us free. Stand firm, then, and do not let yourselves be burdened again by a yoke of slavery.

²Mark my words! I, Paul, tell you that if you let yourselves be circumcised, Christ will be of no value to you at all. ³Again I declare to every man who lets himself be circumcised that he is obligated to obey the whole law. ⁴You who are trying to be justified by law have been alienated from Christ; you have fallen away from grace. ⁵But by faith we eagerly await through the Spirit the righteousness for which we hope. ⁶For in Christ Jesus neither circumcision nor uncircumcision has any value. The only thing that counts is faith expressing itself through love.

⁷You were running a good race. Who cut in on you and kept you from obeying the truth? ⁸That kind of persuasion does not come from the one who calls you. ⁹"A little yeast works through the whole batch of dough."

¹⁰I am confident in the Lord that you will take no other view. The one who is throwing you into confusion will pay the penalty, whoever he may be. ¹¹Brothers, if I am still preaching circumcision, why am I still being persecuted? In that case the offense of the cross has been abolished. ¹²As for those agitators, I wish they would go the whole way and emasculate themselves!

¹³You, my brothers, were called to be free. But do not use your freedom to indulge the sinful natureᶜ; rather, serve one another in love. ¹⁴The entire law is summed up in a single command: "Love your neighbor as yourself."ᵈ ¹⁵If you keep on biting and devouring each other, watch out or you will be destroyed by each other.

Life by the Spirit

¹⁶So I say, live by the Spirit, and you will not gratify the desires of the sinful nature. ¹⁷For the sinful nature desires what is contrary to the Spirit, and the Spirit what is contrary to the sinful nature. They are in conflict with each other, so that you do not do what you want. ¹⁸But if you are led by the Spirit, you are not under law.

¹⁹The acts of the sinful nature are obvious: sexual immorality, impurity and debauchery; ²⁰idolatry and witchcraft; hatred, discord, jealousy, fits of rage, selfish ambition, dissensions, factions ²¹and envy; drunkenness, orgies, and the like. I warn you, as I did before, that those who live like this will not inherit the kingdom of God.

²²But the fruit of the Spirit is love, joy, peace, patience, kindness, goodness, faithfulness, ²³gentleness and self-control. Against such things there is no law. ²⁴Those who belong to Christ Jesus have crucified the sinful nature with its passions and desires. ²⁵Since we live by the Spirit, let us keep in step with the Spirit. ²⁶Let us not become conceited, provoking and envying each other.

ᵃ27 Isaiah 54:1   ᵇ30 Gen. 21:10   ᶜ13 Or the flesh; also in verses 16, 17, 19 and 24
ᵈ14 Lev. 19:18

Doing Good to All

6 Brothers, if someone is caught in a sin, you who are spiritual should restore him gently. But watch yourself, or you also may be tempted. ²Carry each other's burdens, and in this way you will fulfill the law of Christ. ³If anyone thinks he is something when he is nothing, he deceives himself. ⁴Each one should test his own actions. Then he can take pride in himself, without comparing himself to somebody else, ⁵for each one should carry his own load.

⁶Anyone who receives instruction in the word must share all good things with his instructor.

⁷Do not be deceived: God cannot be mocked. A man reaps what he sows. ⁸The one who sows to please his sinful nature, from that nature*a* will reap destruction; the one who sows to please the Spirit, from the Spirit will reap eternal life. ⁹Let us not become weary in doing good, for at the proper time we will reap a harvest if we do not give up. ¹⁰Therefore, as we have opportunity, let us do good to all peo-

a8 Or his flesh, from the flesh

VERSE:	AUTHOR:	PASSAGE:
Galatians 6:10	Don Anderson	Galatians 6:1–10

Two-Minute Warning

Physical age is no sure indicator of spiritual maturity. Nor does it matter how much time has passed since conversion. Just because we are getting up there in years doesn't mean we have grown up to be like Jesus. Becoming more like Jesus means learning to love without conditions and to give freely of ourselves.

Daily we have the opportunity of allowing the love of Christ to flow through us. It should excite those of us who are approaching our 60s, 70s, 80s or beyond to realize that although we are playing in the fourth quarter, there is still time to grab the ball and make a positive contribution for the Lord. Games are often won or lost after the two-minute warning. There may not be *as much* time, but there is always *enough* time, for God's purposes to be accomplished through us.

ADDITIONAL SCRIPTURE READINGS
Ephesians 5:8–20; Hebrews 12:1–6

Go to page 1492 for your next devotional reading.

ple, especially to those who belong to the family of believers.

Not Circumcision but a New Creation

[11]See what large letters I use as I write to you with my own hand!

[12]Those who want to make a good impression outwardly are trying to compel you to be circumcised. The only reason they do this is to avoid being persecuted for the cross of Christ. [13]Not even those who are circumcised obey the law, yet they want you to be circumcised that they may boast about your flesh. [14]May I never boast except in the cross of our Lord Jesus Christ, through which[a] the world has been crucified to me, and I to the world. [15]Neither circumcision nor uncircumcision means anything; what counts is a new creation. [16]Peace and mercy to all who follow this rule, even to the Israel of God.

[17]Finally, let no one cause me trouble, for I bear on my body the marks of Jesus.

[18]The grace of our Lord Jesus Christ be with your spirit, brothers. Amen.

---

[a]14 Or whom

This letter, written to "the saints in Ephesus" while Paul was under house arrest for his faith, encourages believers to think of themselves in a whole new way—as those who are "in Christ." Paul describes the big picture of God's plan for redeeming the world through Christ and gives practical advice on how to live the Christian life. As you read this letter, rejoice that God gives you a purpose and a plan for living.

EPHESIANS

1 Paul, an apostle of Christ Jesus by the will of God,

To the saints in Ephesus,[a] the faithful[b] in Christ Jesus:

[2]Grace and peace to you from God our Father and the Lord Jesus Christ.

Spiritual Blessings in Christ

[3]Praise be to the God and Father of our Lord Jesus Christ, who has blessed us in the heavenly realms with every spiritual blessing in Christ. [4]For he chose us in him before the creation of the world to be holy and blameless in his sight. In love [5]he[c] predestined us to be adopted as his sons through Jesus Christ, in accordance with his pleasure and will— [6]to the praise of his glorious grace, which he has freely given us in the One he loves. [7]In him we have redemption through his blood, the forgiveness of sins, in accordance with the riches of God's grace [8]that he lavished on us with all wisdom and understanding. [9]And he[d] made known to us the mystery of his will according to his good pleasure, which he purposed in Christ, [10]to be put into effect when the times will have reached their fulfillment—to bring all things in heaven and on earth together under one head, even Christ.

[11]In him we were also chosen,[e] having been predestined according to the plan of him who works out everything in conformity with the purpose of his will, [12]in order that we, who were the first to hope in Christ, might

---

[a]1 Some early manuscripts do not have *in Ephesus*.   [b]1 Or *believers who are*   [c]4,5 Or *sight in love. 5He*   [d]8,9 Or *us. With all wisdom and understanding, 9he*   [e]11 Or *were made heirs*

PASSAGE: Ephesians 1:1–23; Philippians 1:12–30
AUTHOR: Christina Rossetti

If Only

If I might only love my God and die!
But now he bids me love him and live on,
Now when the bloom of all my life is gone,
The pleasant half of life has gone quite by.
My tree of hope is lopped that spread so high;
And I forget how summer glowed and shone,
While autumn grips me with its fingers wan,
And frets me with its fitful windy sigh.
When autumn passes then must winter numb,
And winter may not pass a weary while,
But when it passes spring shall flower again:
And in that spring who weepeth now shall smile,
Yea, they shall wax who now are on the wane,
Yea, they shall sing for love when Christ shall come.

Go to page 1494 for your next devotional reading.

be for the praise of his glory. ¹³And you also were included in Christ when you heard the word of truth, the gospel of your salvation. Having believed, you were marked in him with a seal, the promised Holy Spirit, ¹⁴who is a deposit guaranteeing our inheritance until the redemption of those who are God's possession—to the praise of his glory.

Thanksgiving and Prayer

¹⁵For this reason, ever since I heard about your faith in the Lord Jesus and your love for all the saints, ¹⁶I have not stopped giving thanks for you, remembering you in my prayers. ¹⁷I keep asking that the God of our Lord Jesus Christ, the glorious Father, may give you the Spirit^a of wisdom and revelation, so that you may know him better. ¹⁸I pray also that the eyes of your heart may be enlightened in order that you may know the hope to which he has called you, the riches of his glorious inheritance in the saints, ¹⁹and his incomparably great power for us who believe. That power is like the working of his mighty strength, ²⁰which he exerted in Christ when he raised him from the dead and seated him at his right hand in the heavenly realms, ²¹far above all rule and authority, power and dominion, and every title that can be given, not only in the present age but also in the one to come. ²²And God placed all things under his feet and appointed him to be head over everything for the church, ²³which is his body, the fullness of him who fills everything in every way.

Made Alive in Christ

2 As for you, you were dead in your transgressions and sins, ²in which you used to live when you followed the ways of this world and of the ruler of the kingdom of the air, the spirit who is now at work in those who are disobedient. ³All of us also lived among them at one time, gratifying the cravings of our sinful na-

ture^b and following its desires and thoughts. Like the rest, we were by nature objects of wrath. ⁴But because of his great love for us, God, who is rich in mercy, ⁵made us alive with Christ even when we were dead in transgressions—it is by grace you have been saved. ⁶And God raised us up with Christ and seated us with him in the heavenly realms in Christ Jesus, ⁷in order that in the coming ages he might show the incomparable riches of his grace, expressed in his kindness to us in Christ Jesus. ⁸For it is by grace you have been saved, through faith—and this not from yourselves, it is the gift of God— ⁹not by works, so that no one can boast. ¹⁰For we are God's workmanship, created in Christ Jesus to do good works, which God prepared in advance for us to do.

One in Christ

¹¹Therefore, remember that formerly you who are Gentiles by birth and called "uncircumcised" by those who call themselves "the circumcision" (that done in the body by the hands of men)— ¹²remember that at that time you were separate from Christ, excluded from citizenship in Israel and foreigners to the covenants of the promise, without hope and without God in the world. ¹³But now in Christ Jesus you who once were far away have been brought near through the blood of Christ.

¹⁴For he himself is our peace, who has made the two one and has destroyed the barrier, the dividing wall of hostility, ¹⁵by abolishing in his flesh the law with its commandments and regulations. His purpose was to create in himself one new man out of the two, thus making peace, ¹⁶and in this one body to reconcile both of them to God through the cross, by which he put to death their hostility. ¹⁷He came and preached peace to you who were far away and peace to those who were near. ¹⁸For through him we both have access to the Father by one Spirit.

---

^a17 Or *a spirit*   ^b3 Or *our flesh*

VERSE:	AUTHOR:	PASSAGE:
Ephesians 1:18	Brennan Manning	Ephesians 1:3 — 2:10

Facing Life, Facing Death

Suppose an eminent physician, well-informed of your medical history, told you that you have 24 hours to live . . .

When we hear the footsteps of the grim reaper, our perception of reality changes drastically. With precious time slipping away like sand in an hourglass, we quickly dismiss all that is petty and irrelevant and focus only on matters of ultimate concern . . .

The denial of death is not a healthy option for a disciple of Jesus. Nor is pessimism in the face of today's troubles. The significant shift in priorities that comes through living 24 hours at a time is not mere resignation to what we know cannot be changed. My life in the confrontation with trial and tribulations is not stoic passivity. My death-defying *no* to despair at the end of my life and my life-affirming *yes* to seemingly insurmountable problems in the midst of my life are both animated by hope in the invincible might of the risen Jesus and in *the immeasurable scope of his power in us who believe* (Ephesians 1:19).

We are not cowed into timidity by death and life. Were we forced to rely on our own shabby resources we would be pitiful people indeed. But the awareness of Christ's present risenness persuades us that we are buoyed up and carried on by a life greater than our own. Hope means that in Christ, by entrusting ourselves to him, we can courageously face evil, . . . our own need for further conversion, the lovelessness of others, and the whole legacy of sin in the world around us and in our own heritage. We can then face death just as we can face life.

ADDITIONAL SCRIPTURE READINGS
1 Corinthians 1:1–9; Colossians 3:1–17

Go to page 1496 for your next devotional reading.

[19]Consequently, you are no longer foreigners and aliens, but fellow citizens with God's people and members of God's household, [20]built on the foundation of the apostles and prophets, with Christ Jesus himself as the chief cornerstone. [21]In him the whole building is joined together and rises to become a holy temple in the Lord. [22]And in him you too are being built together to become a dwelling in which God lives by his Spirit.

Paul the Preacher to the Gentiles

3 For this reason I, Paul, the prisoner of Christ Jesus for the sake of you Gentiles—

[2]Surely you have heard about the administration of God's grace that was given to me for you, [3]that is, the mystery made known to me by revelation, as I have already written briefly. [4]In reading this, then, you will be able to understand my insight into the mystery of Christ, [5]which was not made known to men in other generations as it has now been revealed by the Spirit to God's holy apostles and prophets. [6]This mystery is that through the gospel the Gentiles are heirs together with Israel, members together of one body, and sharers together in the promise in Christ Jesus.

[7]I became a servant of this gospel by the gift of God's grace given me through the working of his power. [8]Although I am less than the least of all God's people, this grace was given me: to preach to the Gentiles the unsearchable riches of Christ, [9]and to make plain to everyone the administration of this mystery, which for ages past was kept hidden in God, who created all things. [10]His intent was that now, through the church, the manifold wisdom of God should be made known to the rulers and authorities in the heavenly realms, [11]according to his eternal purpose which he accomplished in Christ Jesus our Lord. [12]In him and through faith in him we may approach God with freedom and confidence. [13]I ask you,

therefore, not to be discouraged because of my sufferings for you, which are your glory.

A Prayer for the Ephesians

[14]For this reason I kneel before the Father, [15]from whom his whole family[a] in heaven and on earth derives its name. [16]I pray that out of his glorious riches he may strengthen you with power through his Spirit in your inner being, [17]so that Christ may dwell in your hearts through faith. And I pray that you, being rooted and established in love, [18]may have power, together with all the saints, to grasp how wide and long and high and deep is the love of Christ, [19]and to know this love that surpasses knowledge—that you may be filled to the measure of all the fullness of God.

[20]Now to him who is able to do immeasurably more than all we ask or imagine, according to his power that is at work within us, [21]to him be glory in the church and in Christ Jesus throughout all generations, for ever and ever! Amen.

Unity in the Body of Christ

4 As a prisoner for the Lord, then, I urge you to live a life worthy of the calling you have received. [2]Be completely humble and gentle; be patient, bearing with one another in love. [3]Make every effort to keep the unity of the Spirit through the bond of peace. [4]There is one body and one Spirit— just as you were called to one hope when you were called— [5]one Lord, one faith, one baptism; [6]one God and Father of all, who is over all and through all and in all.

[7]But to each one of us grace has been given as Christ apportioned it. [8]This is why it[b] says:

"When he ascended on high,
  he led captives in his train
  and gave gifts to men."[c]

[9](What does "he ascended" mean except that he also descended to the lower, earthly regions[d]? [10]He who

---

[a]15 Or *whom all fatherhood*   [b]8 Or *God*   [c]8 Psalm 68:18   [d]9 Or *the depths of the earth*

VERSE:	AUTHOR:	PASSAGE:
Ephesians 3:18	Brennan Manning	Ephesians 3:1–21

What a Love!

In reply to his haunting question "Who do you say that I am?" my own experience of Jesus Christ cries out: "You are the Son of God, the revealer of the Father's love." This astonishing truth, that Jesus embodies for us a Father who loves us even when we fail to love, is the Good News. The revelation that we are loved in an incomparable way empowers us to be fools for Christ, to celebrate the darkness under the signature of Jesus. "For Christ's love compels us" (2 Corinthians 5:14).

However, my past 25 years of pastoral experience indicate that the stunning disclosure that God is love has had negligible impact on the majority of Christians and minimal transforming power. The problem seems to be that either we don't know it, or know it but cannot accept it; or we accept it, but are not in touch with it; or we are in touch with it, but do not surrender to it . . .

Jesus revealed that God is a Father of incomparable tenderness, that if we take all the goodness, wisdom and compassion of the best mothers and fathers who have ever lived, they would only be a faint shadow of the love and mercy in the heart of the redeeming God.

Christianity moves in a climate completely penetrated by love, and we are called to a life of discipleship compatible with it . . . God is love. We are called by Jesus Christ into an intimate friendship in which one member is a human being and the other the eternal God. We are invited to personal dialogue with the holy One who is unreservedly involved with us. In his own person Jesus radically affirmed that God is not indifferent to human suffering. Jesus is God's Word to the world saying, "See how I love you."

ADDITIONAL SCRIPTURE READINGS
John 15:1–17; 1 John 4:7–21

Go to page 1497 for your next devotional reading.

descended is the very one who ascended higher than all the heavens, in order to fill the whole universe.) ¹¹It was he who gave some to be apostles, some to be prophets, some to be evangelists, and some to be pastors and teachers, ¹²to prepare God's people for works of service, so that the body of Christ may be built up ¹³until we all reach unity in the faith and in the knowledge of the Son of God and become mature, attaining to the

WEDNESDAY

VERSE: Ephesians 4:2	AUTHOR: Charles R. Swindoll	PASSAGE: Ephesians 4:1–13

Keep the Unity

Nobody is a whole chain. Each one is a link. But take away one link and the chain is broken.

Nobody is a whole team. Each one is a player. But take away one player and the game is forfeited.

Nobody is a whole orchestra. Each one is a musician. But take away one musician and the symphony is incomplete ...

You guessed it. We need each other. You need someone and someone needs you. Isolated islands we're not. To make this thing called life work, we gotta lean and support. And relate and respond. And give and take. And confess and forgive. And reach out and embrace. And release and rely.

Especially in God's family ... where working together is Plan A for survival. And since we're so different (thanks to the way God built us), love and acceptance are not optional luxuries. Neither is tolerance. Or understanding. Or patience. You know, all those things you need from others when your humanity crowds out your divinity. In other words, "Be devoted to one another in brotherly love" (Romans 12:10) ...

Why? Because each one of us is worth it. Even when we don't act like it or feel like it or deserve it.

ADDITIONAL SCRIPTURE READINGS
Romans 12:1–21; 1 Corinthians 12:12–26

Go to page 1499 for your next devotional reading.

whole measure of the fullness of Christ.

¹⁴Then we will no longer be infants, tossed back and forth by the waves, and blown here and there by every wind of teaching and by the cunning and craftiness of men in their deceitful scheming. ¹⁵Instead, speaking the truth in love, we will in all things grow up into him who is the Head, that is, Christ. ¹⁶From him the whole body, joined and held together by every supporting ligament, grows and builds itself up in love, as each part does its work.

Living as Children of Light

¹⁷So I tell you this, and insist on it in the Lord, that you must no longer live as the Gentiles do, in the futility of their thinking. ¹⁸They are darkened in their understanding and separated from the life of God because of the ignorance that is in them due to the hardening of their hearts. ¹⁹Having lost all sensitivity, they have given themselves over to sensuality so as to indulge in every kind of impurity, with a continual lust for more.

²⁰You, however, did not come to know Christ that way. ²¹Surely you heard of him and were taught in him in accordance with the truth that is in Jesus. ²²You were taught, with regard to your former way of life, to put off your old self, which is being corrupted by its deceitful desires; ²³to be made new in the attitude of your minds; ²⁴and to put on the new self, created to be like God in true righteousness and holiness.

²⁵Therefore each of you must put off falsehood and speak truthfully to his neighbor, for we are all members of one body. ²⁶"In your anger do not sin"ᵃ: Do not let the sun go down while you are still angry, ²⁷and do not give the devil a foothold. ²⁸He who has been stealing must steal no longer, but must work, doing something useful with his own hands, that he may have something to share with those in need.

²⁹Do not let any unwholesome talk come out of your mouths, but only what is helpful for building others up according to their needs, that it may benefit those who listen. ³⁰And do not grieve the Holy Spirit of God, with whom you were sealed for the day of redemption. ³¹Get rid of all bitterness, rage and anger, brawling and slander, along with every form of malice. ³²Be kind and compassionate to one another, forgiving each other, just as in Christ God forgave you.

5 Be imitators of God, therefore, as dearly loved children ²and live a life of love, just as Christ loved us and gave himself up for us as a fragrant offering and sacrifice to God.

³But among you there must not be even a hint of sexual immorality, or of any kind of impurity, or of greed, because these are improper for God's holy people. ⁴Nor should there be obscenity, foolish talk or coarse joking, which are out of place, but rather thanksgiving. ⁵For of this you can be sure: No immoral, impure or greedy person—such a man is an idolater— has any inheritance in the kingdom of Christ and of God.ᵇ ⁶Let no one deceive you with empty words, for because of such things God's wrath comes on those who are disobedient. ⁷Therefore do not be partners with them.

⁸For you were once darkness, but now you are light in the Lord. Live as children of light ⁹(for the fruit of the light consists in all goodness, righteousness and truth) ¹⁰and find out what pleases the Lord. ¹¹Have nothing to do with the fruitless deeds of darkness, but rather expose them. ¹²For it is shameful even to mention what the disobedient do in secret. ¹³But everything exposed by the light becomes visible, ¹⁴for it is light that makes everything visible. This is why it is said:

"Wake up, O sleeper,
    rise from the dead,
and Christ will shine on you."

ᵃ26 Psalm 4:4   ᵇ5 Or kingdom of the Christ and God

¹⁵Be very careful, then, how you live—not as unwise but as wise, ¹⁶making the most of every opportunity, because the days are evil. ¹⁷Therefore do not be foolish, but understand what the Lord's will is. ¹⁸Do not get drunk on wine, which leads to debauchery. Instead, be filled with the Spirit. ¹⁹Speak to one another with psalms, hymns and spiritual songs. Sing and make music in your heart to the Lord, ²⁰always giving thanks to

THURSDAY

VERSE:
Ephesians 4:24

AUTHOR:
Leslie E. Moser

PASSAGE:
Ephesians 4:17 — 5:21

Already and Not Yet

Let me tell you something that may change the way you think about heaven. I believe that this eternal life of which we speak and toward which we yearn has already begun. Today is the day of salvation, and now is the time to serve the Lord . . .

Think about it. Isn't it true that today, this day, is the first remaining day of your eternity? Eternity for you will not begin at death; it began the moment Christ entered your life. Christ came that we might have life. He does not teach us how to live in heaven. He teaches us to live on earth. His constant message is *hope* for the kingdom to come, but *help* for the kingdom at hand . . .

You and I must keep looking forward to heaven — that glorious place where we will be able to sit at the feet of Jesus, that place which is down the road just past the milestone of death. But as Christians, we look forward to the joys of heaven at the same time that we embrace the joys of this life. Although life is filled with frustrations, pain and misery, it is also a time for joy — joy not just because we shall soon be home with Christ, but joy that comes with living daily with and for him. Our Savior came that our joy might be full even before we get to heaven, and we are to appropriate that promise daily!

ADDITIONAL SCRIPTURE READINGS
1 Timothy 6:11–16; 1 John 1:1–4

Go to page 1501 for your next devotional reading.

God the Father for everything, in the name of our Lord Jesus Christ.

21Submit to one another out of reverence for Christ.

Wives and Husbands

22Wives, submit to your husbands as to the Lord. 23For the husband is the head of the wife as Christ is the head of the church, his body, of which he is the Savior. 24Now as the church submits to Christ, so also wives should submit to their husbands in everything.

25Husbands, love your wives, just as Christ loved the church and gave himself up for her 26to make her holy, cleansing*a* her by the washing with water through the word, 27and to present her to himself as a radiant church, without stain or wrinkle or any other blemish, but holy and blameless. 28In this same way, husbands ought to love their wives as their own bodies. He who loves his wife loves himself. 29After all, no one ever hated his own body, but he feeds and cares for it, just as Christ does the church— 30for we are members of his body. 31"For this reason a man will leave his father and mother and be united to his wife, and the two will become one flesh."*b* 32This is a profound mystery—but I am talking about Christ and the church. 33However, each one of you also must love his wife as he loves himself, and the wife must respect her husband.

Children and Parents

6 Children, obey your parents in the Lord, for this is right. 2"Honor your father and mother"—which is the first commandment with a promise— 3"that it may go well with you and that you may enjoy long life on the earth."*c*

4Fathers, do not exasperate your children; instead, bring them up in the training and instruction of the Lord.

Slaves and Masters

5Slaves, obey your earthly masters with respect and fear, and with sincerity of heart, just as you would obey Christ. 6Obey them not only to win their favor when their eye is on you, but like slaves of Christ, doing the will of God from your heart. 7Serve wholeheartedly, as if you were serving the Lord, not men, 8because you know that the Lord will reward everyone for whatever good he does, whether he is slave or free.

9And masters, treat your slaves in the same way. Do not threaten them, since you know that he who is both their Master and yours is in heaven, and there is no favoritism with him.

The Armor of God

10Finally, be strong in the Lord and in his mighty power. 11Put on the full armor of God so that you can take your stand against the devil's schemes. 12For our struggle is not against flesh and blood, but against the rulers, against the authorities, against the powers of this dark world and against the spiritual forces of evil in the heavenly realms. 13Therefore put on the full armor of God, so that when the day of evil comes, you may be able to stand your ground, and after you have done everything, to stand. 14Stand firm then, with the belt of truth buckled around your waist, with the breastplate of righteousness in place, 15and with your feet fitted with the readiness that comes from the gospel of peace. 16In addition to all this, take up the shield of faith, with which you can extinguish all the flaming arrows of the evil one. 17Take the helmet of salvation and the sword of the Spirit, which is the word of God. 18And pray in the Spirit on all occasions with all kinds of prayers and requests. With this in mind, be alert and always keep on praying for all the saints.

19Pray also for me, that whenever I open my mouth, words may be given

a26 Or *having cleansed*   *b31* Gen. 2:24   *c3* Deut. 5:16

me so that I will fearlessly make known the mystery of the gospel, [20]for which I am an ambassador in chains. Pray that I may declare it fearlessly, as I should.

Final Greetings

[21]Tychicus, the dear brother and faithful servant in the Lord, will tell you everything, so that you also may know how I am and what I am doing. [22]I am sending him to you for this very purpose, that you may know how we are, and that he may encourage you.

[23]Peace to the brothers, and love with faith from God the Father and the Lord Jesus Christ. [24]Grace to all who love our Lord Jesus Christ with an undying love.

VERSE:	AUTHOR:	PASSAGE:
Ephesians 6:13	Jean Shaw	Ephesians 6:10–18

Stand Firm to the End

We who love the Lord are to hate sin. Indeed, the Christian life is a battle against it. That's why we are equipped to be soldiers (Ephesians 6). Sometimes the veterans get tired and decide to leave warfare to the young recruits. Fighting for truth and justice is wearying . . .

Moses was past 80 when he led the Israelites out of Egypt. The next 40 years were full of fighting. Moses got weary . . . At 120 Moses was still warning the people about sin . . . In Hebrews 11, it says, "He regarded disgrace for the sake of Christ as of greater value than the treasures of Egypt, because he was looking ahead to his reward" (11:26). Looking ahead. Anticipating the day when he would be with the Lord.

When we feel like quitting—retiring or even going AWOL—let us remember Moses and look ahead. When we have fought the last battle, God stands ready to welcome us to eternal peace.

ADDITIONAL SCRIPTURE READINGS
Hebrews 11:23–29; James 5:7–12

Go to page 1503 for your next devotional reading.

*P*aul wrote this warm letter to the people of the church he started in Philippi (Acts 16:11–40). Although he was writing from prison, he expressed his joy at being connected to Jesus and having faithful friends to support him. As you read this letter, review the difficult experiences of your life and consider how God is using and has used those times to further his purposes in your life.

PHILIPPIANS

1 Paul and Timothy, servants of Christ Jesus,

To all the saints in Christ Jesus at Philippi, together with the overseers*a* and deacons:

²Grace and peace to you from God our Father and the Lord Jesus Christ.

Thanksgiving and Prayer

³I thank my God every time I remember you. ⁴In all my prayers for all of you, I always pray with joy ⁵because of your partnership in the gospel from the first day until now, ⁶being confident of this, that he who began a good work in you will carry it on to completion until the day of Christ Jesus.

⁷It is right for me to feel this way about all of you, since I have you in my heart; for whether I am in chains or defending and confirming the gospel, all of you share in God's grace with me. ⁸God can testify how I long for all of you with the affection of Christ Jesus.

⁹And this is my prayer: that your love may abound more and more in knowledge and depth of insight, ¹⁰so that you may be able to discern what is best and may be pure and blameless until the day of Christ, ¹¹filled with the fruit of righteousness that comes through Jesus Christ—to the glory and praise of God.

Paul's Chains Advance the Gospel

¹²Now I want you to know, brothers, that what has happened to me has really served to advance the gospel. ¹³As a result, it has become clear throughout the whole palace guard*b* and to everyone else that I am in chains for Christ. ¹⁴Because of my chains, most of the brothers in the

PASSAGE: Romans 15:1–13; Philippians 2:1–11
AUTHOR: Kate B. Wilkinson

Looking to Jesus

May the mind of Christ my Savior
live in me from day to day,
by his love and power controlling
all I do and say.

May the love of Jesus fill me
as the waters fill the sea.
Him exalting, self abasing:
this is victory.

May we run the race before us,
strong and brave to face the foe,
looking only unto Jesus
as we onward go.

Go to page 1505 for your next devotional reading.

Lord have been encouraged to speak the word of God more courageously and fearlessly.

¹⁵It is true that some preach Christ out of envy and rivalry, but others out of goodwill. ¹⁶The latter do so in love, knowing that I am put here for the defense of the gospel. ¹⁷The former preach Christ out of selfish ambition, not sincerely, supposing that they can stir up trouble for me while I am in chains.ᵃ ¹⁸But what does it matter? The important thing is that in every way, whether from false motives or true, Christ is preached. And because of this I rejoice.

Yes, and I will continue to rejoice, ¹⁹for I know that through your prayers and the help given by the Spirit of Jesus Christ, what has happened to me will turn out for my deliverance.ᵇ ²⁰I eagerly expect and hope that I will in no way be ashamed, but will have sufficient courage so that now as always Christ will be exalted in my body, whether by life or by death. ²¹For to me, to live is Christ and to die is gain. ²²If I am to go on living in the body, this will mean fruitful labor for me. Yet what shall I choose? I do not know! ²³I am torn between the two: I desire to depart and be with Christ, which is better by far; ²⁴but it is more necessary for you that I remain in the body. ²⁵Convinced of this, I know that I will remain, and I will continue with all of you for your progress and joy in the faith, ²⁶so that through my being with you again your joy in Christ Jesus will overflow on account of me.

²⁷Whatever happens, conduct yourselves in a manner worthy of the gospel of Christ. Then, whether I come and see you or only hear about you in my absence, I will know that you stand firm in one spirit, contending as one man for the faith of the gospel ²⁸without being frightened in any way by those who oppose you. This is a sign to them that they will be destroyed, but that you will be saved—

and that by God. ²⁹For it has been granted to you on behalf of Christ not only to believe on him, but also to suffer for him, ³⁰since you are going through the same struggle you saw I had, and now hear that I still have.

Imitating Christ's Humility

2 If you have any encouragement from being united with Christ, if any comfort from his love, if any fellowship with the Spirit, if any tenderness and compassion, ²then make my joy complete by being like-minded, having the same love, being one in spirit and purpose. ³Do nothing out of selfish ambition or vain conceit, but in humility consider others better than yourselves. ⁴Each of you should look not only to your own interests, but also to the interests of others.

⁵Your attitude should be the same as that of Christ Jesus:

⁶Who, being in very natureᶜ God,
　did not consider equality with
　　God something to be
　　grasped,
⁷but made himself nothing,
　taking the very natureᵈ of a
　　servant,
　being made in human likeness.
⁸And being found in appearance as
　　a man,
　he humbled himself
　and became obedient to death—
　　even death on a cross!
⁹Therefore God exalted him to the
　　highest place
　and gave him the name that is
　　above every name,
¹⁰that at the name of Jesus every
　　knee should bow,
　in heaven and on earth and
　　under the earth,
¹¹and every tongue confess that
　　Jesus Christ is Lord,
　to the glory of God the Father.

Shining as Stars

¹²Therefore, my dear friends, as you have always obeyed—not only in

---

ᵃ16,17 Some late manuscripts have verses 16 and 17 in reverse order.　　ᵇ19 Or *salvation*
ᶜ6 Or *in the form of*　　ᵈ7 Or *the form*

my presence, but now much more in my absence—continue to work out your salvation with fear and trembling, ¹³for it is God who works in you to will and to act according to his good purpose.

¹⁴Do everything without complaining or arguing, ¹⁵so that you may become blameless and pure, children of God without fault in a crooked and depraved generation, in which you shine like stars in the universe ¹⁶as

MONDAY

VERSE: AUTHOR: PASSAGE:
Philippians 2:2   W. Phillip Keller   Philippians 2:1–18

How to Be Like Christ

Jesus never made light of the cost involved in following him . . . It entailed a whole new set of attitudes . . . In brief, seven fresh attitudes have to be acquired . . .

1. Instead of loving myself most I am willing to love Christ best and others more than myself . . .

2. Instead of being one of the crowd I am willing to be singled out, set apart from the gang . . .

3. Instead of insisting on my rights I am willing to forego them in favor of others . . .

4. Instead of being "boss" I am willing to be at the bottom of the heap . . .

5. Instead of finding fault with life and always asking "Why?" I am willing to accept every circumstance of life in an attitude of gratitude . . .

6. Instead of exercising and asserting my will I learn to cooperate with his wishes and comply with his will . . .

7. Instead of choosing my own way I am willing to choose to follow in Christ's way . . .

God wants us all to move on with him . . . If we are in earnest about wanting to do his will, and to be led, *he makes this possible* by his own gracious Spirit. For it is he who works in us both to will and to act according to his good purpose (Philippians 2:13).

ADDITIONAL SCRIPTURE READINGS
Matthew 13:44–46; Galatians 5:16–26
Go to page 1507 for your next devotional reading.

you hold out*ᵃ* the word of life—in order that I may boast on the day of Christ that I did not run or labor for nothing. ¹⁷But even if I am being poured out like a drink offering on the sacrifice and service coming from your faith, I am glad and rejoice with all of you. ¹⁸So you too should be glad and rejoice with me.

Timothy and Epaphroditus

¹⁹I hope in the Lord Jesus to send Timothy to you soon, that I also may be cheered when I receive news about you. ²⁰I have no one else like him, who takes a genuine interest in your welfare. ²¹For everyone looks out for his own interests, not those of Jesus Christ. ²²But you know that Timothy has proved himself, because as a son with his father he has served with me in the work of the gospel. ²³I hope, therefore, to send him as soon as I see how things go with me. ²⁴And I am confident in the Lord that I myself will come soon.

²⁵But I think it is necessary to send back to you Epaphroditus, my brother, fellow worker and fellow soldier, who is also your messenger, whom you sent to take care of my needs. ²⁶For he longs for all of you and is distressed because you heard he was ill. ²⁷Indeed he was ill, and almost died. But God had mercy on him, and not on him only but also on me, to spare me sorrow upon sorrow. ²⁸Therefore I am all the more eager to send him, so that when you see him again you may be glad and I may have less anxiety. ²⁹Welcome him in the Lord with great joy, and honor men like him, ³⁰because he almost died for the work of Christ, risking his life to make up for the help you could not give me.

No Confidence in the Flesh

3 Finally, my brothers, rejoice in the Lord! It is no trouble for me to write the same things to you again, and it is a safeguard for you.

²Watch out for those dogs, those men who do evil, those mutilators of the flesh. ³For it is we who are the circumcision, we who worship by the Spirit of God, who glory in Christ Jesus, and who put no confidence in the flesh— ⁴though I myself have reasons for such confidence.

If anyone else thinks he has reasons to put confidence in the flesh, I have more: ⁵circumcised on the eighth day, of the people of Israel, of the tribe of Benjamin, a Hebrew of Hebrews; in regard to the law, a Pharisee; ⁶as for zeal, persecuting the church; as for legalistic righteousness, faultless.

⁷But whatever was to my profit I now consider loss for the sake of Christ. ⁸What is more, I consider everything a loss compared to the surpassing greatness of knowing Christ Jesus my Lord, for whose sake I have lost all things. I consider them rubbish, that I may gain Christ ⁹and be found in him, not having a righteousness of my own that comes from the law, but that which is through faith in Christ—the righteousness that comes from God and is by faith. ¹⁰I want to know Christ and the power of his resurrection and the fellowship of sharing in his sufferings, becoming like him in his death, ¹¹and so, somehow, to attain to the resurrection from the dead.

Pressing on Toward the Goal

¹²Not that I have already obtained all this, or have already been made perfect, but I press on to take hold of that for which Christ Jesus took hold of me. ¹³Brothers, I do not consider myself yet to have taken hold of it. But one thing I do: Forgetting what is behind and straining toward what is ahead, ¹⁴I press on toward the goal to win the prize for which God has called me heavenward in Christ Jesus.

¹⁵All of us who are mature should take such a view of things. And if on some point you think differently, that too God will make clear to you. ¹⁶Only let us live up to what we have already attained.

ᵃ16 Or hold on to

VERSE:	AUTHOR:	PASSAGE:
Philippians 3:13	Jacob D. Eppinga	Philippians 3:12 — 4:9

Press On Without Worry

How can we avoid worrying about the past or the future and concentrate on each day as it comes? We have discovered this is not easy. Yet we should observe the words of Matthew 6:34: "Do not worry about tomorrow, for tomorrow will worry about itself. Each day has enough trouble of its own." And we should live with, lean on and listen to the One who gives us these words ...

It is really not possible to keep ourselves from living yesterday or tomorrow today. Yesterday burdens us with regrets, tomorrow with fears. And yet by trusting in Jesus, we discover the only One who can release us from the guilt of the past, the only One who can relieve us from fear of the future, and the only One who can free us to live today today ...

On occasion I have had to wait a few hours at the big airport in Chicago ... I wondered how those pilots taxiing to the end of the runway dared to roar into the sky. The truth, of course, is none of them dare. There is a control tower, and someone is in it ... It is only when the pilot is told he can take off that he does.

So it is with us. Free of worry, we can take off in life, even at our age, because there is someone in the tower —our Lord in heaven. He tells us to lift our wings, free from fear, and soar. The only way we can do so is to trust ourselves wholly to him and to what he says ... He whispers, "Fear not." He says, "Don't worry." And so oldsters — in Christ, dare to live.

ADDITIONAL SCRIPTURE READINGS
Psalm 56; Matthew 6:25–34

Go to page 1509 for your next devotional reading.

[17]Join with others in following my example, brothers, and take note of those who live according to the pattern we gave you. [18]For, as I have often told you before and now say again even with tears, many live as enemies of the cross of Christ. [19]Their destiny is destruction, their god is their stomach, and their glory is in their shame. Their mind is on earthly things. [20]But our citizenship is in heaven. And we eagerly await a Savior from there, the Lord Jesus Christ, [21]who, by the power that enables him to bring everything under his control, will transform our lowly bodies so that they will be like his glorious body.

4 Therefore, my brothers, you whom I love and long for, my joy and crown, that is how you should stand firm in the Lord, dear friends!

Exhortations

[2]I plead with Euodia and I plead with Syntyche to agree with each other in the Lord. [3]Yes, and I ask you, loyal yokefellow,[a] help these women who have contended at my side in the cause of the gospel, along with Clement and the rest of my fellow workers, whose names are in the book of life.

[4]Rejoice in the Lord always. I will say it again: Rejoice! [5]Let your gentleness be evident to all. The Lord is near. [6]Do not be anxious about anything, but in everything, by prayer and petition, with thanksgiving, present your requests to God. [7]And the peace of God, which transcends all understanding, will guard your hearts and your minds in Christ Jesus.

[8]Finally, brothers, whatever is true, whatever is noble, whatever is right, whatever is pure, whatever is lovely, whatever is admirable—if anything is excellent or praiseworthy—think about such things. [9]Whatever you have learned or received or heard from me, or seen in me—put it into practice. And the God of peace will be with you.

Thanks for Their Gifts

[10]I rejoice greatly in the Lord that at last you have renewed your concern for me. Indeed, you have been concerned, but you had no opportunity to show it. [11]I am not saying this because I am in need, for I have learned to be content whatever the circumstances. [12]I know what it is to be in need, and I know what it is to have plenty. I have learned the secret of being content in any and every situation, whether well fed or hungry, whether living in plenty or in want. [13]I can do everything through him who gives me strength.

[14]Yet it was good of you to share in my troubles. [15]Moreover, as you Philippians know, in the early days of your acquaintance with the gospel, when I set out from Macedonia, not one church shared with me in the matter of giving and receiving, except you only; [16]for even when I was in Thessalonica, you sent me aid again and again when I was in need. [17]Not that I am looking for a gift, but I am looking for what may be credited to your account. [18]I have received full payment and even more; I am amply supplied, now that I have received from Epaphroditus the gifts you sent. They are a fragrant offering, an acceptable sacrifice, pleasing to God. [19]And my God will meet all your needs according to his glorious riches in Christ Jesus. [20]To our God and Father be glory for ever and ever. Amen.

Final Greetings

[21]Greet all the saints in Christ Jesus. The brothers who are with me send greetings. [22]All the saints send you greetings, especially those who belong to Caesar's household.

[23]The grace of the Lord Jesus Christ be with your spirit. Amen.[b]

---

[a]3 Or loyal Syzygus   [b]23 Some manuscripts do not have Amen.

VERSE:	AUTHOR:	PASSAGE:
Philippians 4:19	Charles R. Swindoll	Philippians 4:10–20

Growing Up

I like the question once asked by Satchel Paige, that venerable alumnus of baseball: "How old would you be if you didn't know how old you were?" An honest answer to that question depends on an honest admission of one's attitude. It has nothing to do with one's age . . .

The longer I live the more I become convinced that our major battle in life is not with age but with maturity. All of us are involuntary victims of the former. There is no choice involved in growing older. Our challenge is the choice of whether or not to grow up . . .

God is for us. God's goal is that we move toward maturity, all our past failures and faults and hang-ups notwithstanding . . . God's specialty is bringing renewal to our strength, not reminders of our weakness.

Let me leave you three bones to chew on:

1. *Look within . . . and release.* What is it down inside you that is stunting your growth? When you probe around and find something you are hanging onto too tightly, deliberately let go . . .

2. *Look around . . . and respond.* Don't wait for someone else. Act on your own, spontaneously . . . Is there some need you can help meet? Risk responding.

3. *Look up . . . and rejoice.* You are the recipient of his riches — enjoy them! Realize anew all he has done for you; then rejoice in the pleasure of getting involved with others . . . Stay involved! You will never regret it. Furthermore, it will help you grow up as you find yourself growing old. And the more involved you remain, the less concern you will have for how old you are. By the way, how old *would* you be if you didn't know how old you were?

ADDITIONAL SCRIPTURE READINGS
Ephesians 4:17 — 5:2; Hebrews 5:11 — 6:3

Go to page 1511 for your next devotional reading.

Paul wrote this letter to the church in Colosse at about the same time he wrote Ephesians. He urged the people not to listen to those who were spreading false teachings about Jesus. As you read this book, catch a fresh vision of the power and glory of Jesus and what that means for your everyday life. Look for ways to develop attitudes and actions that will honor him all the days of your life.

COLOSSIANS

1 Paul, an apostle of Christ Jesus by the will of God, and Timothy our brother,

²To the holy and faithful*a* brothers in Christ at Colosse:

Grace and peace to you from God our Father.*b*

Thanksgiving and Prayer

³We always thank God, the Father of our Lord Jesus Christ, when we pray for you, ⁴because we have heard of your faith in Christ Jesus and of the love you have for all the saints— ⁵the faith and love that spring from the hope that is stored up for you in heaven and that you have already heard about in the word of truth, the gospel ⁶that has come to you. All over the world this gospel is bearing fruit and growing, just as it has been doing among you since the day you heard it and understood God's grace in all its truth. ⁷You learned it from Epaphras, our dear fellow servant, who is a faithful minister of Christ on our*c* behalf, ⁸and who also told us of your love in the Spirit.

⁹For this reason, since the day we heard about you, we have not stopped praying for you and asking God to fill you with the knowledge of his will through all spiritual wisdom and understanding. ¹⁰And we pray this in order that you may live a life worthy of the Lord and may please him in every way: bearing fruit in every good work, growing in the knowledge of God, ¹¹being strengthened with all power according to his glorious might so that you may have great endurance and patience, and joyfully ¹²giving thanks to the Father, who has

---

*a*2 Or *believing*   *b*2 Some manuscripts *Father and the Lord Jesus Christ*   *c*7 Some manuscripts *your*

VERSE:
Colossians 1:11

AUTHOR:
Don Anderson

PASSAGE:
Colossians 1:3–14

His Glorious Might

You don't have the strength? Oh yes you do, if you know the Lord Jesus as Savior and if you are availing yourself of what he offers through his Spirit. "For God did not give us a spirit of timidity, but a spirit of power, of love and of self-discipline" (2 Timothy 1:7). Appropriating his strength should be a tangible goal of retirement. There is no better way to go out than by learning to lean on God . . .

We must not pray for life to be easier, but for God to make us stronger. We must not pray for tasks equal to our might, but for God-given might equal to our tasks. With Paul, we must learn that God's grace is sufficient, and his power is perfected in our weakness (2 Corinthians 12:10).

What a glorious realization to know that as we grow weaker and weaker, God's strength can be more radiantly displayed in us. He is there, he cares and he will supply us with what it takes to cope, that we might be "strengthened with all power according to his glorious might so that you may have great endurance and patience" (Colossians 1:11).

It is electrifying to understand that we have a source of strength outside ourselves to empower us to handle what lies ahead.

ADDITIONAL SCRIPTURE READINGS
Isaiah 40:25–31; 1 Corinthians 1:18 — 2:5

Go to page 1513 for your next devotional reading.

qualified you[a] to share in the inheritance of the saints in the kingdom of light. [13]For he has rescued us from the dominion of darkness and brought us into the kingdom of the Son he loves, [14]in whom we have redemption,[b] the forgiveness of sins.

The Supremacy of Christ

[15]He is the image of the invisible God, the firstborn over all creation. [16]For by him all things were created: things in heaven and on earth, visible and invisible, whether thrones or powers or rulers or authorities; all things were created by him and for him. [17]He is before all things, and in him all things hold together. [18]And he is the head of the body, the church; he is the beginning and the firstborn from among the dead, so that in everything he might have the supremacy. [19]For God was pleased to have all his fullness dwell in him, [20]and through him to reconcile to himself all things, whether things on earth or things in heaven, by making peace through his blood, shed on the cross.

[21]Once you were alienated from God and were enemies in your minds because of[c] your evil behavior. [22]But now he has reconciled you by Christ's physical body through death to present you holy in his sight, without blemish and free from accusation— [23]if you continue in your faith, established and firm, not moved from the hope held out in the gospel. This is the gospel that you heard and that has been proclaimed to every creature under heaven, and of which I, Paul, have become a servant.

Paul's Labor for the Church

[24]Now I rejoice in what was suffered for you, and I fill up in my flesh what is still lacking in regard to Christ's afflictions, for the sake of his body, which is the church. [25]I have become its servant by the commission God gave me to present to you the word of God in its fullness— [26]the mystery that has been kept hidden for ages and generations, but is now disclosed to the saints. [27]To them God has chosen to make known among the Gentiles the glorious riches of this mystery, which is Christ in you, the hope of glory.

[28]We proclaim him, admonishing and teaching everyone with all wisdom, so that we may present everyone perfect in Christ. [29]To this end I labor, struggling with all his energy, which so powerfully works in me.

2 I want you to know how much I am struggling for you and for those at Laodicea, and for all who have not met me personally. [2]My purpose is that they may be encouraged in heart and united in love, so that they may have the full riches of complete understanding, in order that they may know the mystery of God, namely, Christ, [3]in whom are hidden all the treasures of wisdom and knowledge. [4]I tell you this so that no one may deceive you by fine-sounding arguments. [5]For though I am absent from you in body, I am present with you in spirit and delight to see how orderly you are and how firm your faith in Christ is.

Freedom From Human Regulations Through Life With Christ

[6]So then, just as you received Christ Jesus as Lord, continue to live in him, [7]rooted and built up in him, strengthened in the faith as you were taught, and overflowing with thankfulness.

[8]See to it that no one takes you captive through hollow and deceptive philosophy, which depends on human tradition and the basic principles of this world rather than on Christ.

[9]For in Christ all the fullness of the Deity lives in bodily form, [10]and you have been given fullness in Christ, who is the head over every power and authority. [11]In him you were also

---

[a]12 Some manuscripts *us*   [b]14 A few late manuscripts *redemption through his blood*   [c]21 Or *minds, as shown by*

circumcised, in the putting off of the sinful nature,[a] not with a circumcision done by the hands of men but with the circumcision done by Christ, [12]having been buried with him in bap- tism and raised with him through your faith in the power of God, who raised him from the dead.

[13]When you were dead in your sins and in the uncircumcision of your sin-

[a]11 Or *the flesh*

VERSE:
Colossians 2:14

AUTHOR:
Alister E. McGrath

PASSAGE:
Colossians 2:6–15

A Symbol of Hope

The cross is a potent symbol of Christian realism. It declares that any outlook on life that cannot cope with the grim realities of suffering and death does not deserve to get a hearing. This symbol of suffering and death affirms that Christianity faces up to the grim, ultimate realities of life. It reminds us of something we must never be allowed to forget. God entered into our suffering and dying world in order to bring it newness of life. Those outside Christianity need to learn—need to be *told about*—its relevance and power for the tragic situation of humanity. It is a sign of a glory that is concealed. It confronts the worst that the world can offer and points to—and makes possible—a better way. It stands as a symbol of hope that transfigures, in a world that is too often tinged with sadness and tears.

So consider the cross. A symbol of death? No. A symbol of suffering? No. A symbol of a world of death and suffering? Not quite. A symbol of hope in the midst of a world of death and suffering? Yes! A symbol of a God who is with us in this dark world, and beyond? Yes! In short, the cross stands for a hope that is for real, in a world that is for real. But that world will pass away, while that hope will remain for eternity.

ADDITIONAL SCRIPTURE READINGS
1 Corinthians 1:18 — 2:5; Ephesians 2:11–22

Go to page 1515 for your next devotional reading.

ful nature,[a] God made you[b] alive with Christ. He forgave us all our sins, [14]having canceled the written code, with its regulations, that was against us and that stood opposed to us; he took it away, nailing it to the cross. [15]And having disarmed the powers and authorities, he made a public spectacle of them, triumphing over them by the cross.[c]

[16]Therefore do not let anyone judge you by what you eat or drink, or with regard to a religious festival, a New Moon celebration or a Sabbath day. [17]These are a shadow of the things that were to come; the reality, however, is found in Christ. [18]Do not let anyone who delights in false humility and the worship of angels disqualify you for the prize. Such a person goes into great detail about what he has seen, and his unspiritual mind puffs him up with idle notions. [19]He has lost connection with the Head, from whom the whole body, supported and held together by its ligaments and sinews, grows as God causes it to grow.

[20]Since you died with Christ to the basic principles of this world, why, as though you still belonged to it, do you submit to its rules: [21]"Do not handle! Do not taste! Do not touch!"? [22]These are all destined to perish with use, because they are based on human commands and teachings. [23]Such regulations indeed have an appearance of wisdom, with their self-imposed worship, their false humility and their harsh treatment of the body, but they lack any value in restraining sensual indulgence.

Rules for Holy Living

3 Since, then, you have been raised with Christ, set your hearts on things above, where Christ is seated at the right hand of God. [2]Set your minds on things above, not on earthly things. [3]For you died, and your life is now hidden with Christ in God. [4]When Christ, who is your[d] life, ap-

pears, then you also will appear with him in glory.

[5]Put to death, therefore, whatever belongs to your earthly nature: sexual immorality, impurity, lust, evil desires and greed, which is idolatry. [6]Because of these, the wrath of God is coming.[e] [7]You used to walk in these ways, in the life you once lived. [8]But now you must rid yourselves of all such things as these: anger, rage, malice, slander, and filthy language from your lips. [9]Do not lie to each other, since you have taken off your old self with its practices [10]and have put on the new self, which is being renewed in knowledge in the image of its Creator. [11]Here there is no Greek or Jew, circumcised or uncircumcised, barbarian, Scythian, slave or free, but Christ is all, and is in all.

[12]Therefore, as God's chosen people, holy and dearly loved, clothe yourselves with compassion, kindness, humility, gentleness and patience. [13]Bear with each other and forgive whatever grievances you may have against one another. Forgive as the Lord forgave you. [14]And over all these virtues put on love, which binds them all together in perfect unity.

[15]Let the peace of Christ rule in your hearts, since as members of one body you were called to peace. And be thankful. [16]Let the word of Christ dwell in you richly as you teach and admonish one another with all wisdom, and as you sing psalms, hymns and spiritual songs with gratitude in your hearts to God. [17]And whatever you do, whether in word or deed, do it all in the name of the Lord Jesus, giving thanks to God the Father through him.

Rules for Christian Households

[18]Wives, submit to your husbands, as is fitting in the Lord.

[19]Husbands, love your wives and do not be harsh with them.

[20]Children, obey your parents in everything, for this pleases the Lord.

---

[a]13 Or *your flesh*　[b]13 Some manuscripts *us*　[c]15 Or *them in him*　[d]4 Some manuscripts *our*　[e]6 Some early manuscripts *coming on those who are disobedient*

PASSAGE: Philippians 3:12–21; Colossians 1:9–14
AUTHOR: Ruth Bell Graham

Laughing, We Endure

We live a time
secure;
beloved and loving,
sure
it cannot last
for long,
then —
the goodbyes come
again — again —
like a small death,
the closing of a door.
One learns to live
with pain.
One looks ahead,
not back —
never back,
only before.
And joy will come again —
warm and secure,
if only for the now,
laughing,
we endure.

Go to page 1516 for your next devotional reading.

²¹Fathers, do not embitter your children, or they will become discouraged.

²²Slaves, obey your earthly masters in everything; and do it, not only when their eye is on you and to win their favor, but with sincerity of heart and reverence for the Lord. ²³Whatever you do, work at it with all your heart, as working for the Lord, not for men, ²⁴since you know that you will receive an inheritance from the Lord as a reward. It is the Lord Christ you are serving. ²⁵Anyone who does wrong will be repaid for his wrong, and there is no favoritism.

4 Masters, provide your slaves with what is right and fair, because you know that you also have a Master in heaven.

VERSE:	AUTHOR:	PASSAGE:
Colossians 4:6	F.B. Meyer	Colossians 4:2–6

Always Full of Grace

The ideal of Christian speech is given in the apostle's words to the Colossians. Our speech should be always gracious; and grace stands for mercifulness, charity, the willingness to put the best constructions upon the words and actions of another. It is a great help in dealing with envy, jealousy or unkind feeling to compel our lips to speak as Christ would have them. If you are jealous of another, the temptation is to say unkind or depreciating things, but if we live in the power of the Holy Spirit, he will enable us to check such words and replace them by those that suggest kindly consideration on the part of ourselves and others. Endeavor to say all the good that can be said, and none of the evil. It is remarkable that when we make the effort to speak kindly on behalf of those against whom we feel exasperated, the whole inward temper changes and takes on the tone of our voice.

Live in us, blessed Lord, by thy Holy Spirit, that our lives may be gospels of helpfulness and blessedness. May all foolish talking and covetousness, bitterness, wrath and anger be put away from us, with all malice. Amen.

ADDITIONAL SCRIPTURE READINGS
Matthew 12:33–37; Ephesians 4:25 — 5:2

Go to page 1519 for your next devotional reading.

Further Instructions

[2]Devote yourselves to prayer, being watchful and thankful. [3]And pray for us, too, that God may open a door for our message, so that we may proclaim the mystery of Christ, for which I am in chains. [4]Pray that I may proclaim it clearly, as I should. [5]Be wise in the way you act toward outsiders; make the most of every opportunity. [6]Let your conversation be always full of grace, seasoned with salt, so that you may know how to answer everyone.

Final Greetings

[7]Tychicus will tell you all the news about me. He is a dear brother, a faithful minister and fellow servant in the Lord. [8]I am sending him to you for the express purpose that you may know about our[a] circumstances and that he may encourage your hearts. [9]He is coming with Onesimus, our faithful and dear brother, who is one of you. They will tell you everything that is happening here.

[10]My fellow prisoner Aristarchus sends you his greetings, as does Mark, the cousin of Barnabas. (You have received instructions about him; if he comes to you, welcome him.) [11]Jesus, who is called Justus, also sends greetings. These are the only Jews among my fellow workers for the kingdom of God, and they have proved a comfort to me. [12]Epaphras, who is one of you and a servant of Christ Jesus, sends greetings. He is always wrestling in prayer for you, that you may stand firm in all the will of God, mature and fully assured. [13]I vouch for him that he is working hard for you and for those at Laodicea and Hierapolis. [14]Our dear friend Luke, the doctor, and Demas send greetings. [15]Give my greetings to the brothers at Laodicea, and to Nympha and the church in her house.

[16]After this letter has been read to you, see that it is also read in the church of the Laodiceans and that you in turn read the letter from Laodicea.

[17]Tell Archippus: "See to it that you complete the work you have received in the Lord."

[18]I, Paul, write this greeting in my own hand. Remember my chains. Grace be with you.

---

[a]8 Some manuscripts *that he may know about your*

...P...aul wrote this letter to the church he founded in Thessalonica (Acts 17:1–9), shortly after he had left them and discovered he would not be able to return. He commended the believers for growing in the Lord and urged them to correct some misunderstandings. As you read this book, take as your own the perspective on life that is shaped by eternity and seek God's help in living this day to the fullest.

1 THESSALONIANS

1 Paul, Silas*a* and Timothy,

To the church of the Thessalonians in God the Father and the Lord Jesus Christ:

Grace and peace to you.*b*

Thanksgiving for the Thessalonians' Faith

²We always thank God for all of you, mentioning you in our prayers. ³We continually remember before our God and Father your work produced by faith, your labor prompted by love, and your endurance inspired by hope in our Lord Jesus Christ.

⁴For we know, brothers loved by God, that he has chosen you, ⁵because our gospel came to you not simply with words, but also with power, with the Holy Spirit and with deep conviction. You know how we lived among you for your sake. ⁶You became imitators of us and of the Lord; in spite of severe suffering, you welcomed the message with the joy given by the Holy Spirit. ⁷And so you became a model to all the believers in Macedonia and Achaia. ⁸The Lord's message rang out from you not only in Macedonia and Achaia—your faith in God has become known everywhere. Therefore we do not need to say anything about it, ⁹for they themselves report what kind of reception you gave us. They tell how you turned to God from idols to serve the living and true God, ¹⁰and to wait for his Son from heaven, whom he raised from the dead—Jesus, who rescues us from the coming wrath.

*a*1 Greek *Silvanus*, a variant of *Silas*   *b*1 Some early manuscripts *you from God our Father and the Lord Jesus Christ*

Paul's Ministry in Thessalonica

2 You know, brothers, that our visit to you was not a failure. ²We had previously suffered and been insulted in Philippi, as you know, but with the help of our God we dared to tell you his gospel in spite of strong opposition. ³For the appeal we make does not spring from error or impure motives, nor are we trying to trick you. ⁴On the contrary, we speak as men approved by God to be entrusted with the gospel. We are not trying to please men but God, who tests our hearts. ⁵You know we never used flattery, nor did we put on a mask to cover up greed—God is our witness. ⁶We were not looking for praise from men, not from you or anyone else.

As apostles of Christ we could have been a burden to you, ⁷but we were gentle among you, like a mother car-

VERSE:
1 Thessalonians 1:7

AUTHOR:
Tim Stafford

PASSAGE:
1 Thessalonians 1:2–10

You Became a Model

Engraved on my memory is one of the last conversations my wife and I had with her mother, at that time 85, sitting in her room in a nursing home. Already her eyes had degenerated so that she could barely read on some days. And she, who had been a particularly intelligent and perceptive woman in earlier years, was plagued and embarrassed by the fact that it was sometimes impossible to remember the thought with which she had started a sentence. She felt she couldn't carry on a conversation, so the fabric of her relations with others was wearing very thin. In our conversation she kept asking both of us, "Why doesn't God take me? I'm just so useless here. There's nothing I can do anymore." How painful it was for her to recognize this, she who had done so much for so many all her life. "What's the purpose of my living now?" She pressed for an answer. Finally, my wife responded with, "Well, mother, you're the oldest one in our family, perhaps you can be an example for us of how to be old—and how to die."

ADDITIONAL SCRIPTURE READINGS
Philippians 4:4–9; James 5:7–12

Go to page 1521 for your next devotional reading.

ing for her little children. [8]We loved
you so much that we were delighted
to share with you not only the gospel
of God but our lives as well, because
you had become so dear to us. [9]Surely
you remember, brothers, our toil and
hardship; we worked night and day
in order not to be a burden to anyone
while we preached the gospel of God
to you.

[10]You are witnesses, and so is God,
of how holy, righteous and blameless
we were among you who believed.
[11]For you know that we dealt with
each of you as a father deals with his
own children, [12]encouraging, comforting and urging you to live lives worthy of God, who calls you into his
kingdom and glory.

[13]And we also thank God continually because, when you received the
word of God, which you heard from
us, you accepted it not as the word of
men, but as it actually is, the word of
God, which is at work in you who believe. [14]For you, brothers, became imitators of God's churches in Judea,
which are in Christ Jesus: You suffered from your own countrymen the
same things those churches suffered
from the Jews, [15]who killed the Lord
Jesus and the prophets and also drove
us out. They displease God and are
hostile to all men [16]in their effort to
keep us from speaking to the Gentiles
so that they may be saved. In this way
they always heap up their sins to the
limit. The wrath of God has come
upon them at last.[a]

Paul's Longing to See the Thessalonians

[17]But, brothers, when we were torn
away from you for a short time (in
person, not in thought), out of our intense longing we made every effort to
see you. [18]For we wanted to come to
you—certainly I, Paul, did, again and
again—but Satan stopped us. [19]For
what is our hope, our joy, or the
crown in which we will glory in the
presence of our Lord Jesus when he

comes? Is it not you? [20]Indeed, you
are our glory and joy.

3 So when we could stand it no
longer, we thought it best to be
left by ourselves in Athens. [2]We sent
Timothy, who is our brother and
God's fellow worker[b] in spreading
the gospel of Christ, to strengthen
and encourage you in your faith, [3]so
that no one would be unsettled by
these trials. You know quite well that
we were destined for them. [4]In fact,
when we were with you, we kept telling you that we would be persecuted.
And it turned out that way, as you
well know. [5]For this reason, when I
could stand it no longer, I sent to find
out about your faith. I was afraid that
in some way the tempter might have
tempted you and our efforts might
have been useless.

Timothy's Encouraging Report

[6]But Timothy has just now come to
us from you and has brought good
news about your faith and love. He
has told us that you always have
pleasant memories of us and that you
long to see us, just as we also long to
see you. [7]Therefore, brothers, in all
our distress and persecution we were
encouraged about you because of
your faith. [8]For now we really live,
since you are standing firm in the
Lord. [9]How can we thank God
enough for you in return for all the
joy we have in the presence of our
God because of you? [10]Night and day
we pray most earnestly that we may
see you again and supply what is
lacking in your faith.

[11]Now may our God and Father
himself and our Lord Jesus clear the
way for us to come to you. [12]May the
Lord make your love increase and
overflow for each other and for everyone else, just as ours does for you.
[13]May he strengthen your hearts so
that you will be blameless and holy in
the presence of our God and Father
when our Lord Jesus comes with all
his holy ones.

---

[a]16 Or *them fully*   [b]2 Some manuscripts *brother and fellow worker*; other manuscripts *brother and God's servant*

Living to Please God

4 Finally, brothers, we instructed you how to live in order to please God, as in fact you are living. Now we ask you and urge you in the Lord Jesus to do this more and more. ²For you know what instructions we gave you by the authority of the Lord Jesus.

³It is God's will that you should be sanctified: that you should avoid sexual immorality; ⁴that each of you should learn to control his own

VERSE:
1 Thessalonians
3:9

AUTHOR:
Max Lucado

PASSAGE:
1 Thessalonians
2:17 – 3:13

The Value of a Relationship

A nation's strength is measured by the premium it puts on its own people. When people value people, an impenetrable web is drawn, a web of vitality and security.

A relationship. The delicate fusion of two human beings. The intricate weaving of two lives; two sets of moods, mentalities and temperaments. Two intermingling hearts, both seeking solace and security.

A relationship. It has more power than any nuclear bomb and more potential than any promising seed . . . What matters most in life is not what ladders we climb or what ownings we accumulate. What matters most is a relationship.

What steps are you taking to protect your "possessions"? What measure are you using to ensure that your relationships are strong and healthy? What are you doing to solidify the bridges between you and those in your world? . . .

It's a wise man who values people above possessions. Many wealthy people have died paupers because they gave their lives to things and not to people. And many paupers have left this earth in contentment because they loved their neighbors.

ADDITIONAL SCRIPTURE READINGS
Philippians 1:3–11; 1 Peter 4:7–11
Go to page 1523 for your next devotional reading.

body[a] in a way that is holy and honorable, [5]not in passionate lust like the heathen, who do not know God; [6]and that in this matter no one should wrong his brother or take advantage of him. The Lord will punish men for all such sins, as we have already told you and warned you. [7]For God did not call us to be impure, but to live a holy life. [8]Therefore, he who rejects this instruction does not reject man but God, who gives you his Holy Spirit.

[9]Now about brotherly love we do not need to write to you, for you yourselves have been taught by God to love each other. [10]And in fact, you do love all the brothers throughout Macedonia. Yet we urge you, brothers, to do so more and more.

[11]Make it your ambition to lead a quiet life, to mind your own business and to work with your hands, just as we told you, [12]so that your daily life may win the respect of outsiders and so that you will not be dependent on anybody.

The Coming of the Lord

[13]Brothers, we do not want you to be ignorant about those who fall asleep, or to grieve like the rest of men, who have no hope. [14]We believe that Jesus died and rose again and so we believe that God will bring with Jesus those who have fallen asleep in him. [15]According to the Lord's own word, we tell you that we who are still alive, who are left till the coming of the Lord, will certainly not precede those who have fallen asleep. [16]For the Lord himself will come down from heaven, with a loud command, with the voice of the archangel and with the trumpet call of God, and the dead in Christ will rise first. [17]After that, we who are still alive and are left will be caught up together with them in the clouds to meet the Lord in the air. And so we will be with the Lord forever. [18]Therefore encourage each other with these words.

5 Now, brothers, about times and dates we do not need to write to you, [2]for you know very well that the day of the Lord will come like a thief in the night. [3]While people are saying, "Peace and safety," destruction will come on them suddenly, as labor pains on a pregnant woman, and they will not escape.

[4]But you, brothers, are not in darkness so that this day should surprise you like a thief. [5]You are all sons of the light and sons of the day. We do not belong to the night or to the darkness. [6]So then, let us not be like others, who are asleep, but let us be alert and self-controlled. [7]For those who sleep, sleep at night, and those who get drunk, get drunk at night. [8]But since we belong to the day, let us be self-controlled, putting on faith and love as a breastplate, and the hope of salvation as a helmet. [9]For God did not appoint us to suffer wrath but to receive salvation through our Lord Jesus Christ. [10]He died for us so that, whether we are awake or asleep, we may live together with him. [11]Therefore encourage one another and build each other up, just as in fact you are doing.

Final Instructions

[12]Now we ask you, brothers, to respect those who work hard among you, who are over you in the Lord and who admonish you. [13]Hold them in the highest regard in love because of their work. Live in peace with each other. [14]And we urge you, brothers, warn those who are idle, encourage the timid, help the weak, be patient with everyone. [15]Make sure that nobody pays back wrong for wrong, but always try to be kind to each other and to everyone else.

[16]Be joyful always; [17]pray continually; [18]give thanks in all circumstances, for this is God's will for you in Christ Jesus.

[19]Do not put out the Spirit's fire;

---

[a]4 Or *learn to live with his own wife;* or *learn to acquire a wife*

VERSE:	AUTHOR:	PASSAGE:
1 Thessalonians 5:18	Joni Eareckson Tada	1 Thessalonians 5:12–24

Finding God's Will

There's hardly a Christian who hasn't looked into the future and questioned, "What *is* God's will for my life?" Today's verse may be short and sweet, but it's all the answer you need. Be joyful. Pray continually. Give thanks. For *this* is God's will for you in Christ Jesus.

"But you don't know my circumstances," I hear you saying. "How can I be thankful for pain and heartache?" God is not asking you to *be* thankful but to *give* thanks. There's a big difference between feeling thankful and giving thanks. One response involves emotions, the other, your will. Trusting God has absolutely nothing to do with trustful feelings.

Also, God's not asking you to give thanks *for* the tough times—only that you give thanks *in* them. Give thanks that he is sovereign . . . that he is in control . . . giving you grace and peace . . . and planning it all for your good and his glory.

Today's verse became my anchor when I was first paralyzed. I gritted my teeth, pushed aside feelings of despair, and willfully gave thanks for everything from the hospital breakfast of cold cornmeal mush to the grueling hours of daily physical therapy. Many months later a miracle occurred. I began to *feel* thankful. My brighter attitude enabled me to give thanks for greater things. Later on another miracle happened: I was able to rejoice in suffering . . .

I want to find your will for my life, O Lord. In other words, I want to find your heart.

ADDITIONAL SCRIPTURE READINGS
Psalm 143; Romans 5:1–5
Go to page 1527 for your next devotional reading.

[20]do not treat prophecies with contempt. [21]Test everything. Hold on to the good. [22]Avoid every kind of evil.

[23]May God himself, the God of peace, sanctify you through and through. May your whole spirit, soul and body be kept blameless at the coming of our Lord Jesus Christ.

[24]The one who calls you is faithful and he will do it.

[25]Brothers, pray for us. [26]Greet all the brothers with a holy kiss. [27]I charge you before the Lord to have this letter read to all the brothers.

[28]The grace of our Lord Jesus Christ be with you.

Paul sent this second letter to the church in Thessalonica to clarify matters misunderstood in his first letter. As you read this letter, rejoice in what God has in store for your future and continue to look for ways to serve God in your present situation.

2 THESSALONIANS

1 Paul, Silas[a] and Timothy,

To the church of the Thessalonians in God our Father and the Lord Jesus Christ:

²Grace and peace to you from God the Father and the Lord Jesus Christ.

Thanksgiving and Prayer

³We ought always to thank God for you, brothers, and rightly so, because your faith is growing more and more, and the love every one of you has for each other is increasing. ⁴Therefore, among God's churches we boast about your perseverance and faith in all the persecutions and trials you are enduring.

⁵All this is evidence that God's judgment is right, and as a result you will be counted worthy of the kingdom of God, for which you are suffering. ⁶God is just: He will pay back trouble to those who trouble you ⁷and give relief to you who are troubled, and to us as well. This will happen when the Lord Jesus is revealed from heaven in blazing fire with his powerful angels. ⁸He will punish those who do not know God and do not obey the

gospel of our Lord Jesus. ⁹They will be punished with everlasting destruction and shut out from the presence of the Lord and from the majesty of his power ¹⁰on the day he comes to be glorified in his holy people and to be marveled at among all those who have believed. This includes you, because you believed our testimony to you.

¹¹With this in mind, we constantly pray for you, that our God may count you worthy of his calling, and that by his power he may fulfill every good purpose of yours and every act prompted by your faith. ¹²We pray this so that the name of our Lord Jesus may be glorified in you, and you in him, according to the grace of our God and the Lord Jesus Christ.[b]

The Man of Lawlessness

2 Concerning the coming of our Lord Jesus Christ and our being gathered to him, we ask you, brothers, ²not to become easily unsettled or alarmed by some prophecy, report or letter supposed to have come from us, saying that the day of the Lord has already come. ³Don't let anyone de-

ceive you in any way, for ⌊that day will not come⌋ until the rebellion occurs and the man of lawlessness[a] is revealed, the man doomed to destruction. [4]He will oppose and will exalt himself over everything that is called God or is worshiped, so that he sets himself up in God's temple, proclaiming himself to be God.

[5]Don't you remember that when I was with you I used to tell you these things? [6]And now you know what is holding him back, so that he may be revealed at the proper time. [7]For the secret power of lawlessness is already at work; but the one who now holds it back will continue to do so till he is taken out of the way. [8]And then the lawless one will be revealed, whom the Lord Jesus will overthrow with the breath of his mouth and destroy by the splendor of his coming. [9]The coming of the lawless one will be in accordance with the work of Satan displayed in all kinds of counterfeit miracles, signs and wonders, [10]and in every sort of evil that deceives those who are perishing. They perish because they refused to love the truth and so be saved. [11]For this reason God sends them a powerful delusion so that they will believe the lie [12]and so that all will be condemned who have not believed the truth but have delighted in wickedness.

Stand Firm

[13]But we ought always to thank God for you, brothers loved by the Lord, because from the beginning God chose you[b] to be saved through the sanctifying work of the Spirit and through belief in the truth. [14]He called you to this through our gospel, that you might share in the glory of our Lord Jesus Christ. [15]So then, brothers, stand firm and hold to the teachings[c] we passed on to you, whether by word of mouth or by letter.

[16]May our Lord Jesus Christ himself and God our Father, who loved us and by his grace gave us eternal encouragement and good hope, [17]encourage your hearts and strengthen you in every good deed and word.

Request for Prayer

3 Finally, brothers, pray for us that the message of the Lord may spread rapidly and be honored, just as it was with you. [2]And pray that we may be delivered from wicked and evil men, for not everyone has faith. [3]But the Lord is faithful, and he will strengthen and protect you from the evil one. [4]We have confidence in the Lord that you are doing and will continue to do the things we command. [5]May the Lord direct your hearts into God's love and Christ's perseverance.

Warning Against Idleness

[6]In the name of the Lord Jesus Christ, we command you, brothers, to keep away from every brother who is idle and does not live according to the teaching[d] you received from us. [7]For you yourselves know how you ought to follow our example. We were not idle when we were with you, [8]nor did we eat anyone's food without paying for it. On the contrary, we worked night and day, laboring and toiling so that we would not be a burden to any of you. [9]We did this, not because we do not have the right to such help, but in order to make ourselves a model for you to follow. [10]For even when we were with you, we gave you this rule: "If a man will not work, he shall not eat."

[11]We hear that some among you are idle. They are not busy; they are busybodies. [12]Such people we command and urge in the Lord Jesus Christ to settle down and earn the bread they eat. [13]And as for you, brothers, never tire of doing what is right.

[14]If anyone does not obey our instruction in this letter, take special note of him. Do not associate with him, in order that he may feel

---

[a]3 Some manuscripts *sin*   [b]13 Some manuscripts *because God chose you as his firstfruits*
[c]15 Or *traditions*   [d]6 Or *tradition*

VERSE:
2 Thessalonians
3:16

AUTHOR:
Billy Graham

PASSAGE:
2 Thessalonians
3:15–18

Peace at All Times

Everyone who knows the Lord Jesus Christ can go through any problem, and face death, and still have the peace of God in his heart. When your spouse dies, or your children get sick, or you lose your job, you can have a peace that you don't understand. You may have tears at a graveside, but you can have an abiding peace, a quietness . . .

Colossians 3:15 says, "Let the peace of Christ rule in your hearts." Some of you believe that you know Jesus Christ as your Savior, but you haven't really made him your Lord. You're missing the peace of God in your struggles and turmoils and trials and pressures of life. Is the peace of God in your heart?

We are all familiar with the transformation that took place in Saul on the road to Damascus . . . Many equally dramatic changes in human personalities are taking place today, and they are being brought about by the self-same means that transformed Saul into Paul — birth again in Jesus Christ!

There is no human philosophy that can achieve such changes or provide such strength. This mighty strength stands ready to be available at your beck and call at all times.

No man can bring peace to a troubled world because it is not his to give. Christ said, "My peace I give to you . . . " It is not the peace of man, but the peace of God. We cannot give what does not belong to us. Ask for God's peace and see what a transformation will take place in your life.

. . . .

ADDITIONAL SCRIPTURE READINGS
John 14:25–27; Philippians 4:2–9

Go to page 1530 for your next devotional reading.

ashamed. [15]Yet do not regard him as an enemy, but warn him as a brother.

Final Greetings

[16]Now may the Lord of peace himself give you peace at all times and in every way. The Lord be with all of you.

[17]I, Paul, write this greeting in my own hand, which is the distinguishing mark in all my letters. This is how I write.

[18]The grace of our Lord Jesus Christ be with you all.

...L...ater in life Paul served as a mentor to many new Christians. Here he corresponds with Timothy, a young pastor in Ephesus, giving him both affirmation and advice. As you read 1 Timothy, consider how you might be a role model to those who are younger, as you share your encouragement and wisdom.

1 TIMOTHY

1 Paul, an apostle of Christ Jesus by the command of God our Savior and of Christ Jesus our hope,

²To Timothy my true son in the faith:

Grace, mercy and peace from God the Father and Christ Jesus our Lord.

Warning Against False Teachers of the Law

³As I urged you when I went into Macedonia, stay there in Ephesus so that you may command certain men not to teach false doctrines any longer ⁴nor to devote themselves to myths and endless genealogies. These promote controversies rather than God's work—which is by faith. ⁵The goal of this command is love, which comes from a pure heart and a good conscience and a sincere faith. ⁶Some have wandered away from these and turned to meaningless talk. ⁷They want to be teachers of the law, but they do not know what they are talk-

ing about or what they so confidently affirm.

⁸We know that the law is good if one uses it properly. ⁹We also know that law*ᵃ* is made not for the righteous but for lawbreakers and rebels, the ungodly and sinful, the unholy and irreligious; for those who kill their fathers or mothers, for murderers, ¹⁰for adulterers and perverts, for slave traders and liars and perjurers—and for whatever else is contrary to the sound doctrine ¹¹that conforms to the glorious gospel of the blessed God, which he entrusted to me.

The Lord's Grace to Paul

¹²I thank Christ Jesus our Lord, who has given me strength, that he considered me faithful, appointing me to his service. ¹³Even though I was once a blasphemer and a persecutor and a violent man, I was shown mercy because I acted in ignorance and unbelief. ¹⁴The grace of our Lord was poured out on me abundantly, along

ᵃ9 Or that the law

PASSAGE: Psalm 42; Ephesians 3:14–21
AUTHOR: John Keble

Sun of My Soul

Sun of my soul! Thou Savior dear,
It is not night if Thou be near:
Oh, may no earth-born cloud arise
To hide Thee from Thy servant's eyes.

When with dear friends sweet talk I hold,
And all the flowers of life unfold:
Let not my heart within me burn,
Except in all I Thee discern.

When the soft dews of kindly sleep
My wearied eyelids gently steep,
Be my last thought, how sweet to rest
For ever on my Savior's breast.

Abide with me from morn till eve,
For without Thee I cannot live:
Abide with me when night is nigh,
For without Thee I dare not die.

Come near and bless us when we wake,
Ere through the world our way we take:
Till in the ocean of Thy love
We lose ourselves in heaven above.

Go to page 1533 for your next devotional reading.

with the faith and love that are in Christ Jesus.

¹⁵Here is a trustworthy saying that deserves full acceptance: Christ Jesus came into the world to save sinners—of whom I am the worst. ¹⁶But for that very reason I was shown mercy so that in me, the worst of sinners, Christ Jesus might display his unlimited patience as an example for those who would believe on him and receive eternal life. ¹⁷Now to the King eternal, immortal, invisible, the only God, be honor and glory for ever and ever. Amen.

¹⁸Timothy, my son, I give you this instruction in keeping with the prophecies once made about you, so that by following them you may fight the good fight, ¹⁹holding on to faith and a good conscience. Some have rejected these and so have shipwrecked their faith. ²⁰Among them are Hymenaeus and Alexander, whom I have handed over to Satan to be taught not to blaspheme.

Instructions on Worship

2 I urge, then, first of all, that requests, prayers, intercession and thanksgiving be made for everyone— ²for kings and all those in authority, that we may live peaceful and quiet lives in all godliness and holiness. ³This is good, and pleases God our Savior, ⁴who wants all men to be saved and to come to a knowledge of the truth. ⁵For there is one God and one mediator between God and men, the man Christ Jesus, ⁶who gave himself as a ransom for all men—the testimony given in its proper time. ⁷And for this purpose I was appointed a herald and an apostle—I am telling the truth, I am not lying—and a teacher of the true faith to the Gentiles.

⁸I want men everywhere to lift up holy hands in prayer, without anger or disputing.

⁹I also want women to dress modestly, with decency and propriety, not with braided hair or gold or pearls or expensive clothes, ¹⁰but with good deeds, appropriate for women who profess to worship God.

¹¹A woman should learn in quietness and full submission. ¹²I do not permit a woman to teach or to have authority over a man; she must be silent. ¹³For Adam was formed first, then Eve. ¹⁴And Adam was not the one deceived; it was the woman who was deceived and became a sinner. ¹⁵But women[a] will be saved[b] through childbearing—if they continue in faith, love and holiness with propriety.

Overseers and Deacons

3 Here is a trustworthy saying: If anyone sets his heart on being an overseer,[c] he desires a noble task. ²Now the overseer must be above reproach, the husband of but one wife, temperate, self-controlled, respectable, hospitable, able to teach, ³not given to drunkenness, not violent but gentle, not quarrelsome, not a lover of money. ⁴He must manage his own family well and see that his children obey him with proper respect. ⁵(If anyone does not know how to manage his own family, how can he take care of God's church?) ⁶He must not be a recent convert, or he may become conceited and fall under the same judgment as the devil. ⁷He must also have a good reputation with outsiders, so that he will not fall into disgrace and into the devil's trap.

⁸Deacons, likewise, are to be men worthy of respect, sincere, not indulging in much wine, and not pursuing dishonest gain. ⁹They must keep hold of the deep truths of the faith with a clear conscience. ¹⁰They must first be tested; and then if there is nothing against them, let them serve as deacons.

¹¹In the same way, their wives[d] are to be women worthy of respect, not malicious talkers but temperate and trustworthy in everything.

¹²A deacon must be the husband of but one wife and must manage his children and his household well. ¹³Those who have served well gain an excellent standing and great assurance in their faith in Christ Jesus.

¹⁴Although I hope to come to you soon, I am writing you these instructions so that, ¹⁵if I am delayed, you will know how people ought to conduct themselves in God's household, which is the church of the living God, the pillar and foundation of the truth. ¹⁶Beyond all question, the mystery of godliness is great:

> He[a] appeared in a body,[b]
>   was vindicated by the Spirit,
> was seen by angels,
>   was preached among the
>   nations,
> was believed on in the world,
>   was taken up in glory.

Instructions to Timothy

4 The Spirit clearly says that in later times some will abandon the faith and follow deceiving spirits and things taught by demons. ²Such teachings come through hypocritical liars, whose consciences have been seared as with a hot iron. ³They forbid people to marry and order them to abstain from certain foods, which God created to be received with thanksgiving by those who believe and who know the truth. ⁴For everything God created is good, and nothing is to be rejected if it is received with thanksgiving, ⁵because it is consecrated by the word of God and prayer.

⁶If you point these things out to the brothers, you will be a good minister of Christ Jesus, brought up in the truths of the faith and of the good teaching that you have followed. ⁷Have nothing to do with godless myths and old wives' tales; rather, train yourself to be godly. ⁸For physical training is of some value, but godliness has value for all things, holding promise for both the present life and the life to come.

⁹This is a trustworthy saying that deserves full acceptance ¹⁰(and for this we labor and strive), that we have put our hope in the living God, who is the Savior of all men, and especially of those who believe.

¹¹Command and teach these things. ¹²Don't let anyone look down on you because you are young, but set an example for the believers in speech, in life, in love, in faith and in purity. ¹³Until I come, devote yourself to the public reading of Scripture, to preaching and to teaching. ¹⁴Do not neglect your gift, which was given you through a prophetic message when the body of elders laid their hands on you.

¹⁵Be diligent in these matters; give yourself wholly to them, so that everyone may see your progress. ¹⁶Watch your life and doctrine closely. Persevere in them, because if you do, you will save both yourself and your hearers.

Advice About Widows, Elders and Slaves

5 Do not rebuke an older man harshly, but exhort him as if he were your father. Treat younger men as brothers, ²older women as mothers, and younger women as sisters, with absolute purity.

³Give proper recognition to those widows who are really in need. ⁴But if a widow has children or grandchildren, these should learn first of all to put their religion into practice by caring for their own family and so repaying their parents and grandparents, for this is pleasing to God. ⁵The widow who is really in need and left all alone puts her hope in God and continues night and day to pray and to ask God for help. ⁶But the widow who lives for pleasure is dead even while she lives. ⁷Give the people these instructions, too, so that no one may be open to blame. ⁸If anyone does not

---

[a]16 Some manuscripts *God*   [b]16 Or *in the flesh*

VERSE:	AUTHOR:	PASSAGE:
1 Timothy 4:4	John F. MacArthur, Jr.	1 Timothy 4:1–5

Received With Thanksgiving

God is the source of every good gift. God has given us everything good to enjoy, including rain to make things grow, minerals to make the soil fertile, animals for food and clothing, and energy for industry and transportation. Everything we have is from him, and we are to be thankful for it all.

Jesus said, "If you, then, though you are evil, know how to give good gifts to your children, how much more will your Father in heaven give good gifts to those who ask him!" (Matthew 7:11) ... Paul added, "For everything God created is good, and nothing is to be rejected if it is received with thanksgiving, because it is consecrated by the word of God and prayer" (1 Timothy 4:4–5).

Sadly, unbelievers don't acknowledge God's goodness, though they benefit from it every day. They attribute his providential care to luck or fate and his gracious provisions to nature or false gods. They do not honor him as God or give him thanks (Romans 1:21) ...

How sad to see such ingratitude, and yet how thrilling to know that the infinite God cares for us and supplies our every need. Don't ever take his provisions for granted! Look to him daily, and receive his gifts with a thankful heart.

ADDITIONAL SCRIPTURE READINGS
Psalm 24; James 1:12–18

Go to page 1535 for your next devotional reading.

provide for his relatives, and especially for his immediate family, he has denied the faith and is worse than an unbeliever.

⁹No widow may be put on the list of widows unless she is over sixty, has been faithful to her husband,ᵃ ¹⁰and is well known for her good deeds, such as bringing up children, showing hospitality, washing the feet of the saints, helping those in trouble and devoting herself to all kinds of good deeds.

¹¹As for younger widows, do not put them on such a list. For when their sensual desires overcome their dedication to Christ, they want to marry. ¹²Thus they bring judgment on themselves, because they have broken their first pledge. ¹³Besides, they get into the habit of being idle and going about from house to house. And not only do they become idlers, but also gossips and busybodies, saying things they ought not to. ¹⁴So I counsel younger widows to marry, to have children, to manage their homes and to give the enemy no opportunity for slander. ¹⁵Some have in fact already turned away to follow Satan.

¹⁶If any woman who is a believer has widows in her family, she should help them and not let the church be burdened with them, so that the church can help those widows who are really in need.

¹⁷The elders who direct the affairs of the church well are worthy of double honor, especially those whose work is preaching and teaching. ¹⁸For the Scripture says, "Do not muzzle the ox while it is treading out the grain,"ᵇ and "The worker deserves his wages."ᶜ ¹⁹Do not entertain an accusation against an elder unless it is brought by two or three witnesses. ²⁰Those who sin are to be rebuked publicly, so that the others may take warning.

²¹I charge you, in the sight of God and Christ Jesus and the elect angels, to keep these instructions without partiality, and to do nothing out of favoritism.

²²Do not be hasty in the laying on of hands, and do not share in the sins of others. Keep yourself pure.

²³Stop drinking only water, and use a little wine because of your stomach and your frequent illnesses.

²⁴The sins of some men are obvious, reaching the place of judgment ahead of them; the sins of others trail behind them. ²⁵In the same way, good deeds are obvious, and even those that are not cannot be hidden.

6 All who are under the yoke of slavery should consider their masters worthy of full respect, so that God's name and our teaching may not be slandered. ²Those who have believing masters are not to show less respect for them because they are brothers. Instead, they are to serve them even better, because those who benefit from their service are believers, and dear to them. These are the things you are to teach and urge on them.

Love of Money

³If anyone teaches false doctrines and does not agree to the sound instruction of our Lord Jesus Christ and to godly teaching, ⁴he is conceited and understands nothing. He has an unhealthy interest in controversies and quarrels about words that result in envy, strife, malicious talk, evil suspicions ⁵and constant friction between men of corrupt mind, who have been robbed of the truth and who think that godliness is a means to financial gain.

⁶But godliness with contentment is great gain. ⁷For we brought nothing into the world, and we can take nothing out of it. ⁸But if we have food and clothing, we will be content with that. ⁹People who want to get rich fall into temptation and a trap and into many foolish and harmful desires that plunge men into ruin and destruction. ¹⁰For the love of money is a root of all kinds of evil. Some people, eager for

---

ᵃ9 Or *has had but one husband*   ᵇ18 Deut. 25:4   ᶜ18 Luke 10:7

money, have wandered from the faith and pierced themselves with many griefs.

Paul's Charge to Timothy

¹¹But you, man of God, flee from all this, and pursue righteousness, godliness, faith, love, endurance and gentleness. ¹²Fight the good fight of the faith. Take hold of the eternal life to which you were called when you made your good confession in the presence of many witnesses. ¹³In the sight of God, who gives life to everything, and of Christ Jesus, who while testifying before Pontius Pilate made the good confession, I charge you ¹⁴to keep this command without spot or blame until the appearing of our Lord Jesus Christ, ¹⁵which God will bring about in his own time—God, the blessed and only Ruler, the King of kings and Lord of lords, ¹⁶who alone is immortal and who lives in unapproachable light, whom no one has

VERSE:	AUTHOR:	PASSAGE:
1 Timothy 6:12	Don Anderson	1 Timothy 6:11–16

Fight the Good Fight

The Christian life is a battle. Satan the enemy, suffering the great leveler, God the sustainer. Want to be a contender in the last lap of life? At the risk of sounding crude or callous, be prepared to learn from what happens to you.

Paul exhorted young Timothy, "Fight the good fight of the faith" (1 Timothy 6:12). Can we do less? When suffering strikes, I recommend the three A's to assist in fighting the good fight all the way home:

Acceptance. Realize suffering is coming. Accept it. Determine you'll take it no matter what, because you know your Father has allowed it for some reason.

Attitude. Know positively that because of the reputation and reliability of your heavenly Father, something good is going to result from your suffering.

Action. Anticipate the victory, but be sure to suit up. The coach always picks the best players to play the hardest quarters. This may be your finest hour.

ADDITIONAL SCRIPTURE READINGS
Psalm 119:65–72; 1 Peter 3:8–17

Go to page 1538 for your next devotional reading.

seen or can see. To him be honor and might forever. Amen.

[17]Command those who are rich in this present world not to be arrogant nor to put their hope in wealth, which is so uncertain, but to put their hope in God, who richly provides us with everything for our enjoyment. [18]Command them to do good, to be rich in good deeds, and to be generous and willing to share. [19]In this way they will lay up treasure for themselves as a firm foundation for the coming age, so that they may take hold of the life that is truly life.

[20]Timothy, guard what has been entrusted to your care. Turn away from godless chatter and the opposing ideas of what is falsely called knowledge, [21]which some have professed and in so doing have wandered from the faith.

Grace be with you.

Shortly before his death, Paul wrote a second letter to Timothy to encourage him to persevere in his Christian faith and life. As you read this letter, remember that these are Paul's final words. Reflect on what kind of testimony you would write at the end of your life; you might want to begin putting down on paper your reflections on the experiences of your life—words of encouragement and challenge for the next generation.

2 TIMOTHY

1 Paul, an apostle of Christ Jesus by the will of God, according to the promise of life that is in Christ Jesus,

²To Timothy, my dear son:

Grace, mercy and peace from God the Father and Christ Jesus our Lord.

Encouragement to Be Faithful

³I thank God, whom I serve, as my forefathers did, with a clear conscience, as night and day I constantly remember you in my prayers. ⁴Recalling your tears, I long to see you, so that I may be filled with joy. ⁵I have been reminded of your sincere faith, which first lived in your grandmother Lois and in your mother Eunice and, I am persuaded, now lives in you also. ⁶For this reason I remind you to fan into flame the gift of God, which is in you through the laying on of my hands. ⁷For God did not give us a spirit of timidity, but a spirit of power, of love and of self-discipline.

⁸So do not be ashamed to testify about our Lord, or ashamed of me his prisoner. But join with me in suffering for the gospel, by the power of God, ⁹who has saved us and called us to a holy life—not because of anything we have done but because of his own purpose and grace. This grace was given us in Christ Jesus before the beginning of time, ¹⁰but it has now been revealed through the appearing of our Savior, Christ Jesus, who has destroyed death and has brought life and immortality to light through the gospel. ¹¹And of this gospel I was appointed a herald and an apostle and a teacher. ¹²That is why I am suffering as I am. Yet I am not ashamed, because I know whom I have believed, and am convinced that he is able to

VERSE:	AUTHOR:	PASSAGE:
2 Timothy 1:2	J. Oswald Sanders	2 Timothy 1:1–7

Friends—Old and New

There is more than a grain of truth in the saying that you can tell a man by his friends. And friends are never so precious and appreciated as when we grow older. As the circle narrows, the close friends of earlier years who shared much of our own background and experience are especially valued. The best friends in old age are usually those whose friendship has been cultivated in earlier years.

Some, like Paul the apostle, have a genius for friendship, whereas others find it exceedingly difficult to establish and maintain a close and intimate relationship. But that need not always be so. Prayer, and a willingness to take the first step in making an approach, will often be richly rewarded. Of course, this is a problem that should have been faced and dealt with in earlier years, but better late than never.

As our older friends pass on before us, we should not rule out the possibility of forging new bonds of friendship and fellowship with younger people who will help to keep our viewpoint youthful. The lovely friendship of Paul the aged with young Timothy is a classic example of a satisfying friendship between old and young. How enriching it was for Timothy, and what a comfort he was to Paul the aged!

ADDITIONAL SCRIPTURE READINGS
Psalm 133; John 15:9–17

Go to page 1540 for your next devotional reading.

guard what I have entrusted to him for that day.

13What you heard from me, keep as the pattern of sound teaching, with faith and love in Christ Jesus. 14Guard the good deposit that was entrusted to you—guard it with the help of the Holy Spirit who lives in us.

15You know that everyone in the province of Asia has deserted me, including Phygelus and Hermogenes.

16May the Lord show mercy to the household of Onesiphorus, because he often refreshed me and was not ashamed of my chains. 17On the contrary, when he was in Rome, he searched hard for me until he found me. 18May the Lord grant that he will find mercy from the Lord on that day! You know very well in how many ways he helped me in Ephesus.

2 You then, my son, be strong in the grace that is in Christ Jesus. 2And the things you have heard me say in the presence of many witnesses entrust to reliable men who will also be qualified to teach others. 3Endure hardship with us like a good soldier of Christ Jesus. 4No one serving as a soldier gets involved in civilian affairs—he wants to please his commanding officer. 5Similarly, if anyone competes as an athlete, he does not receive the victor's crown unless he competes according to the rules. 6The hardworking farmer should be the first to receive a share of the crops. 7Reflect on what I am saying, for the Lord will give you insight into all this.

8Remember Jesus Christ, raised from the dead, descended from David. This is my gospel, 9for which I am suffering even to the point of being chained like a criminal. But God's word is not chained. 10Therefore I endure everything for the sake of the elect, that they too may obtain the salvation that is in Christ Jesus, with eternal glory.

11Here is a trustworthy saying:

If we died with him,

we will also live with him;
12if we endure,
we will also reign with him.
If we disown him,
he will also disown us;
13if we are faithless,
he will remain faithful,
for he cannot disown himself.

A Workman Approved by God

14Keep reminding them of these things. Warn them before God against quarreling about words; it is of no value, and only ruins those who listen. 15Do your best to present yourself to God as one approved, a workman who does not need to be ashamed and who correctly handles the word of truth. 16Avoid godless chatter, because those who indulge in it will become more and more ungodly. 17Their teaching will spread like gangrene. Among them are Hymenaeus and Philetus, 18who have wandered away from the truth. They say that the resurrection has already taken place, and they destroy the faith of some. 19Nevertheless, God's solid foundation stands firm, sealed with this inscription: "The Lord knows those who are his,"[a] and, "Everyone who confesses the name of the Lord must turn away from wickedness."

20In a large house there are articles not only of gold and silver, but also of wood and clay; some are for noble purposes and some for ignoble. 21If a man cleanses himself from the latter, he will be an instrument for noble purposes, made holy, useful to the Master and prepared to do any good work.

22Flee the evil desires of youth, and pursue righteousness, faith, love and peace, along with those who call on the Lord out of a pure heart. 23Don't have anything to do with foolish and stupid arguments, because you know they produce quarrels. 24And the Lord's servant must not quarrel; instead, he must be kind to everyone, able to teach, not resentful. 25Those

a19 Num. 16:5 (see Septuagint)

VERSE:	AUTHOR:	PASSAGE:
2 Timothy 2:8	Max Lucado	2 Timothy 2:1–13

Remember

Think about the first time you ever saw him. Think about your first encounter with the Christ. Robe yourself in that moment. Resurrect the relief. Recall the purity. Summon forth the passion. Can you remember? . . .

In what was perhaps the last letter Paul ever wrote, he begged Timothy not to forget. In a letter written within earshot of the sharpening of the blade that would sever his head, he urged Timothy to remember. "Remember Jesus Christ . . . " You can almost picture the old warrior smiling as he wrote the words. "Remember Jesus Christ, raised from the dead, descended from David. This is my gospel . . . "

When times get hard, remember Jesus. When people don't listen, remember Jesus. When tears come, remember Jesus . . . When death looms, when anger singes, when shame weighs heavily. Remember Jesus . . .

Can you still remember? Are you still in love with him? Remember, Paul begged, remember Jesus. Before you remember anything, remember him. If you forget anything, don't forget him . . .

Do yourself a favor. Stand before him again. Or, better, allow him to stand before you . . . Look into those eyes . . . Look at them as they look at you. You'll never be the same.

A man is never the same after he simultaneously sees his utter despair and Christ's unbending grace. To see the despair without the grace is suicidal. To see the grace without the despair is futility. But to see them both is conversion.

ADDITIONAL SCRIPTURE READINGS
John 20:19–31; Acts 2:22–37

Go to page 1541 for your next devotional reading.

who oppose him he must gently instruct, in the hope that God will grant them repentance leading them to a knowledge of the truth, ²⁶and that they will come to their senses and escape from the trap of the devil, who has taken them captive to do his will.

Godlessness in the Last Days

3 But mark this: There will be terrible times in the last days. ²People will be lovers of themselves, lovers of money, boastful, proud, abusive, disobedient to their parents, ungrateful,

VERSE:
2 Timothy 3:16,17

AUTHOR:
Millie Stamm

PASSAGE:
2 Timothy 3:10–17

Spiritual Food

As food is necessary for growth and development in our physical life, so God's Word is necessary for growth and maintenance of spiritual health. "When your words came, I ate them; they were my joy and my heart's delight" (Jeremiah 15:16).

Because the Bible is God-breathed, it is the direct revelation of the living God. It is his word of authority for our lives ... The Bible is more than a book to impart knowledge. It reveals our need of a Savior. It gives us nourishment, maturing us into well-balanced Christians.

Paul reminded Timothy of the importance of knowing the Word of God and appropriating it as a guideline for life. He outlined for Timothy a fourfold way in which the Bible is useful to life.

It is useful, first, for teaching. Secondly, it is useful for rebuking—showing us where we are wrong, where we have deviated from God's plan. Next, it is useful for correcting—setting and resetting the direction of our lives in the right way. It is also useful for training in righteousness—how to keep us right ...

The principles for everyday living and the answers to life's needs are in the Bible. What has the Bible done for your life? For mine? Is it your guide book?

ADDITIONAL SCRIPTURE READINGS
Psalm 119:57–72; Hebrews 4:12–13

Go to page 1543 for your next devotional reading.

unholy, [3]without love, unforgiving, slanderous, without self-control, brutal, not lovers of the good, [4]treacherous, rash, conceited, lovers of pleasure rather than lovers of God—[5]having a form of godliness but denying its power. Have nothing to do with them.

[6]They are the kind who worm their way into homes and gain control over weak-willed women, who are loaded down with sins and are swayed by all kinds of evil desires, [7]always learning but never able to acknowledge the truth. [8]Just as Jannes and Jambres opposed Moses, so also these men oppose the truth—men of depraved minds, who, as far as the faith is concerned, are rejected. [9]But they will not get very far because, as in the case of those men, their folly will be clear to everyone.

Paul's Charge to Timothy

[10]You, however, know all about my teaching, my way of life, my purpose, faith, patience, love, endurance, [11]persecutions, sufferings—what kinds of things happened to me in Antioch, Iconium and Lystra, the persecutions I endured. Yet the Lord rescued me from all of them. [12]In fact, everyone who wants to live a godly life in Christ Jesus will be persecuted, [13]while evil men and impostors will go from bad to worse, deceiving and being deceived. [14]But as for you, continue in what you have learned and have become convinced of, because you know those from whom you learned it, [15]and how from infancy you have known the holy Scriptures, which are able to make you wise for salvation through faith in Christ Jesus. [16]All Scripture is God-breathed and is useful for teaching, rebuking, correcting and training in righteousness, [17]so that the man of God may be thoroughly equipped for every good work.

4 In the presence of God and of Christ Jesus, who will judge the living and the dead, and in view of his appearing and his kingdom, I give you this charge: [2]Preach the Word; be prepared in season and out of season; correct, rebuke and encourage—with great patience and careful instruction. [3]For the time will come when men will not put up with sound doctrine. Instead, to suit their own desires, they will gather around them a great number of teachers to say what their itching ears want to hear. [4]They will turn their ears away from the truth and turn aside to myths. [5]But you, keep your head in all situations, endure hardship, do the work of an evangelist, discharge all the duties of your ministry.

[6]For I am already being poured out like a drink offering, and the time has come for my departure. [7]I have fought the good fight, I have finished the race, I have kept the faith. [8]Now there is in store for me the crown of righteousness, which the Lord, the righteous Judge, will award to me on that day—and not only to me, but also to all who have longed for his appearing.

Personal Remarks

[9]Do your best to come to me quickly, [10]for Demas, because he loved this world, has deserted me and has gone to Thessalonica. Crescens has gone to Galatia, and Titus to Dalmatia. [11]Only Luke is with me. Get Mark and bring him with you, because he is helpful to me in my ministry. [12]I sent Tychicus to Ephesus. [13]When you come, bring the cloak that I left with Carpus at Troas, and my scrolls, especially the parchments.

[14]Alexander the metalworker did me a great deal of harm. The Lord will repay him for what he has done. [15]You too should be on your guard against him, because he strongly opposed our message.

[16]At my first defense, no one came to my support, but everyone deserted me. May it not be held against them. [17]But the Lord stood at my side and gave me strength, so that through me the message might be fully proclaimed and all the Gentiles might hear it. And I was delivered from the lion's mouth. [18]The Lord will rescue

PASSAGE: Psalm 119:89–112; 1 Peter 1:22–25
AUTHOR: William W. How

O Word of God Incarnate

O Word of God incarnate,
O Wisdom from on high,
O Truth unchanged, unchanging,
O Light of our dark sky:
We praise you for the radiance
That from the Scripture's page,
A lantern to our footsteps,
Shines on from age to age.

The church from you, dear Master,
Received this gift divine;
And still that light is lifted
O'er all the earth to shine.
It is the chart and compass
That all life's voyage through,
Mid mists and rocks and quicksands,
Still guides, O Christ, to you.

Go to page 1546 for your next devotional reading.

me from every evil attack and will bring me safely to his heavenly kingdom. To him be glory for ever and ever. Amen.

Final Greetings

[19]Greet Priscilla[a] and Aquila and the household of Onesiphorus. [20]Erastus stayed in Corinth, and I left Trophimus sick in Miletus. [21]Do your best to get here before winter. Eubulus greets you, and so do Pudens, Linus, Claudia and all the brothers.

[22]The Lord be with your spirit. Grace be with you.

Paul wrote this letter to
Titus, a pastor serving in Crete, to advise
him on how to organize the local church and
what to teach. As you read this letter, think
about your relationships within the church
family, and look for ways in which, by your
words and actions, you can have a positive
influence on those who are younger.

TITUS

1 Paul, a servant of God and an apostle of Jesus Christ for the faith of God's elect and the knowledge of the truth that leads to godliness— ²a faith and knowledge resting on the hope of eternal life, which God, who does not lie, promised before the beginning of time, ³and at his appointed season he brought his word to light through the preaching entrusted to me by the command of God our Savior,

⁴To Titus, my true son in our common faith:

Grace and peace from God the Father and Christ Jesus our Savior.

Titus' Task on Crete

⁵The reason I left you in Crete was that you might straighten out what was left unfinished and appoint*a* elders in every town, as I directed you. ⁶An elder must be blameless, the husband of but one wife, a man whose children believe and are not open to the charge of being wild and disobedient. ⁷Since an overseer*b* is entrusted with God's work, he must be blameless—not overbearing, not quick-tempered, not given to drunkenness, not violent, not pursuing dishonest gain. ⁸Rather he must be hospitable, one who loves what is good, who is self-controlled, upright, holy and disciplined. ⁹He must hold firmly to the trustworthy message as it has been taught, so that he can encourage others by sound doctrine and refute those who oppose it.

¹⁰For there are many rebellious people, mere talkers and deceivers, especially those of the circumcision group. ¹¹They must be silenced, because they are ruining whole households by teaching things they ought not to teach—and that for the sake of dishonest gain. ¹²Even one of their own prophets has said, "Cretans are always liars, evil brutes, lazy gluttons." ¹³This testimony is true. Therefore, rebuke them sharply, so that

a5 Or *ordain*   *b7* Traditionally *bishop*

VERSE:	AUTHOR:	PASSAGE:
Titus 1:4	Gien Karssen	Titus 1:1–4

We Need Each Other

The life of the apostle Paul consisted of much traveling and a very irregular schedule. His body consequently received little rest. The emotional and spiritual tensions he had to deal with were worse than this lack of physical rest. Paul often encountered misunderstanding and suspicion. Some people even doubted his apostolic mission. It is easy to understand why Paul felt in danger of becoming disheartened.

God the Father, however, knew what his child needed. He comforted Paul through the person of Titus, who had been converted through Paul's preaching and later became his co-laborer [see 2 Corinthians 7:5–16].

Through a meeting with fellow Christians, Titus had recently received new courage and joy himself. Therefore he was in a cheerful mood when he visited Paul. Titus's friendship brought Paul rest. Their time together turned out to be spiritually and physically refreshing to Paul, and a stimulus to tackle his work again with renewed vigor.

The sense of rest that one person can convey to another can hardly be overestimated. People need one another, not only in important things such as functioning in society, church and the home, but also in small things such as when feeling discouraged or depressed. We cannot do without one another. We are privileged when we have friends who meet such needs ... Lord, thank you for like-minded friends who attend to my needs. Thank you for the encouragement and stimulus they present. Help me to detect this need in others and be humble enough to seek help myself. Amen.

ADDITIONAL SCRIPTURE READINGS
Romans 12; 1 Corinthians 12:12–30

Go to page 1548 for your next devotional reading.

they will be sound in the faith ¹⁴and will pay no attention to Jewish myths or to the commands of those who reject the truth. ¹⁵To the pure, all things are pure, but to those who are corrupted and do not believe, nothing is pure. In fact, both their minds and consciences are corrupted. ¹⁶They claim to know God, but by their actions they deny him. They are detestable, disobedient and unfit for doing anything good.

What Must Be Taught to Various Groups

2 You must teach what is in accord with sound doctrine. ²Teach the older men to be temperate, worthy of respect, self-controlled, and sound in faith, in love and in endurance.

³Likewise, teach the older women to be reverent in the way they live, not to be slanderers or addicted to much wine, but to teach what is good. ⁴Then they can train the younger women to love their husbands and children, ⁵to be self-controlled and pure, to be busy at home, to be kind, and to be subject to their husbands, so that no one will malign the word of God.

⁶Similarly, encourage the young men to be self-controlled. ⁷In everything set them an example by doing what is good. In your teaching show integrity, seriousness ⁸and soundness of speech that cannot be condemned, so that those who oppose you may be ashamed because they have nothing bad to say about us.

⁹Teach slaves to be subject to their masters in everything, to try to please them, not to talk back to them, ¹⁰and not to steal from them, but to show that they can be fully trusted, so that in every way they will make the teaching about God our Savior attractive.

¹¹For the grace of God that brings salvation has appeared to all men. ¹²It teaches us to say "No" to ungodliness and worldly passions, and to live self-controlled, upright and godly lives in this present age, ¹³while we wait for the blessed hope—the glorious appearing of our great God and Savior, Jesus Christ, ¹⁴who gave himself for us to redeem us from all wickedness and to purify for himself a people that are his very own, eager to do what is good.

¹⁵These, then, are the things you should teach. Encourage and rebuke with all authority. Do not let anyone despise you.

Doing What Is Good

3 Remind the people to be subject to rulers and authorities, to be obedient, to be ready to do whatever is good, ²to slander no one, to be peaceable and considerate, and to show true humility toward all men.

³At one time we too were foolish, disobedient, deceived and enslaved by all kinds of passions and pleasures. We lived in malice and envy, being hated and hating one another. ⁴But when the kindness and love of God our Savior appeared, ⁵he saved us, not because of righteous things we had done, but because of his mercy. He saved us through the washing of rebirth and renewal by the Holy Spirit, ⁶whom he poured out on us generously through Jesus Christ our Savior, ⁷so that, having been justified by his grace, we might become heirs having the hope of eternal life. ⁸This is a trustworthy saying. And I want you to stress these things, so that those who have trusted in God may be careful to devote themselves to doing what is good. These things are excellent and profitable for everyone.

⁹But avoid foolish controversies and genealogies and arguments and quarrels about the law, because these are unprofitable and useless. ¹⁰Warn a divisive person once, and then warn him a second time. After that, have nothing to do with him. ¹¹You may be sure that such a man is warped and sinful; he is self-condemned.

Final Remarks

¹²As soon as I send Artemas or Tychicus to you, do your best to come to me at Nicopolis, because I have de-

cided to winter there. [13]Do everything you can to help Zenas the lawyer and Apollos on their way and see that they have everything they need. [14]Our people must learn to devote themselves to doing what is good, in order that they may provide for daily necessities and not live unproductive lives.

[15]Everyone with me sends you greetings. Greet those who love us in the faith.

Grace be with you all.

VERSE:	AUTHOR:	PASSAGE:
Titus 2:2	Charles R. Swindoll	Titus 2:1–8

Drinking at God's Oasis

God's patriarchs have always been among his choicest possessions. Abraham was far more effective once he grew old and mellow. Moses wasn't used with any measure of success until he turned 80. Caleb was 85 when he began to enjoy God's best goals. Samuel was old, old when the God of Israel led him to establish the "school of the prophets," an institution that had a lasting influence for spirituality and godliness in the centuries to come. And who could deny the way God used Paul during his last days on his knees, writing words of encouragement in letters we cherish today!

No one fails to see that growing old has its difficulties and heartaches. It does, indeed. But to see only the hot sands of your desert experience and miss the lovely oasis here and there . . . is to turn the latter part of your journey through life into an arid, tasteless endurance which makes everyone miserable.

Please don't forget — God has decided to let you live this long. Your old age is not a mistake . . . nor an oversight . . . nor an afterthought. Isn't it about time you cooled your tongue and softened your smile with a refreshing drink from the water of God's oasis?

ADDITIONAL SCRIPTURE READINGS
Psalm 92; Isaiah 46

Go to page 1550 for your next devotional reading.

Paul *wrote this brief letter from prison to his friend Philemon, asking him to forgive Onesimus, a runaway slave. As you read this letter, take an honest look at your relationships and look for those situations in which you may need to forgive someone. Ask God for the courage to seek reconciliation with someone who has hurt you.*

PHILEMON

¹Paul, a prisoner of Christ Jesus, and Timothy our brother,

To Philemon our dear friend and fellow worker, ²to Apphia our sister, to Archippus our fellow soldier and to the church that meets in your home:

³Grace to you and peace from God our Father and the Lord Jesus Christ.

Thanksgiving and Prayer

⁴I always thank my God as I remember you in my prayers, ⁵because I hear about your faith in the Lord Jesus and your love for all the saints. ⁶I pray that you may be active in sharing your faith, so that you will have a full understanding of every good thing we have in Christ. ⁷Your love has given me great joy and encouragement, because you, brother, have refreshed the hearts of the saints.

Paul's Plea for Onesimus

⁸Therefore, although in Christ I could be bold and order you to do what you ought to do, ⁹yet I appeal to you on the basis of love. I then, as Paul—an old man and now also a prisoner of Christ Jesus— ¹⁰I appeal to you for my son Onesimus,ᵃ who became my son while I was in chains. ¹¹Formerly he was useless to you, but now he has become useful both to you and to me.

¹²I am sending him—who is my very heart—back to you. ¹³I would have liked to keep him with me so that he could take your place in helping me while I am in chains for the gospel. ¹⁴But I did not want to do anything without your consent, so that any favor you do will be spontaneous and not forced. ¹⁵Perhaps the reason he was separated from you for a little while was that you might have him back for good— ¹⁶no longer as a

ᵃ10 *Onesimus* means *useful.*

VERSE:	AUTHOR:	PASSAGE:
Philemon 17	Dirk R. Buursma	Philemon 4–22

Welcome Back!

Tears came to her eyes as she read the letter. It was from a friend of her son, yes, her son who had run out of her life so many years ago. Abandoned her. Left her. Without so much as a "fare thee well."

Her son's friend told the story of how her son had been pursued, and captured, by the Lord, the same Lord who had changed *her* life. He wanted to come back now, to make it right again. In fact, he's coming back today. Today! He's going to stop over any moment.

The pain he's put me through. I don't know. I just don't know if I can forgive him. I want him to hurt, to suffer, for all the pain he's caused. I want him to feel my pain and keep on feeling it all the days of his life. Why should I forgive him? He doesn't deserve it!

There was a knock at the door. Trembling with emotion, she opened it. The face—she had not seen the face for so long, but she knew who it was. The memories of rejection, pain, despair—all those memories came flooding back. Then she remembered the letter she had just read: "I appeal to you on the basis of love . . . welcome him."

Wow! "O Lord, I just don't know if I can forgive him. Please forgive me, Lord, forgive me." And at that moment, in the power of feeling forgiven, she reached out her arms—and welcomed him back.

ADDITIONAL SCRIPTURE READINGS
Matthew 18:21–35; 2 Corinthians 5:11–21

Go to page 1553 for your next devotional reading.

slave, but better than a slave, as a dear brother. He is very dear to me but even dearer to you, both as a man and as a brother in the Lord.

¹⁷So if you consider me a partner, welcome him as you would welcome me. ¹⁸If he has done you any wrong or owes you anything, charge it to me. ¹⁹I, Paul, am writing this with my own hand. I will pay it back—not to mention that you owe me your very self. ²⁰I do wish, brother, that I may have some benefit from you in the Lord; refresh my heart in Christ.

²¹Confident of your obedience, I write to you, knowing that you will do even more than I ask.

²²And one thing more: Prepare a guest room for me, because I hope to be restored to you in answer to your prayers.

²³Epaphras, my fellow prisoner in Christ Jesus, sends you greetings. ²⁴And so do Mark, Aristarchus, Demas and Luke, my fellow workers.

²⁵The grace of the Lord Jesus Christ be with your spirit.

The author of this letter encourages Christians who are being persecuted for their faith to rely on Jesus Christ, the Son of God, for strength. As you read this book, look for signs in your life of reliance on something other than on Jesus, and resolve anew to fix your eyes on Jesus; trust him to help you run with perseverance the race marked out for you.

HEBREWS

The Son Superior to Angels

1 In the past God spoke to our forefathers through the prophets at many times and in various ways, ²but in these last days he has spoken to us by his Son, whom he appointed heir of all things, and through whom he made the universe. ³The Son is the radiance of God's glory and the exact representation of his being, sustaining all things by his powerful word. After he had provided purification for sins, he sat down at the right hand of the Majesty in heaven. ⁴So he became as much superior to the angels as the name he has inherited is superior to theirs.

⁵For to which of the angels did God ever say,

"You are my Son;
today I have become your
Father*a*"*b*?

Or again,

"I will be his Father,
and he will be my Son"*c*?

⁶And again, when God brings his firstborn into the world, he says,

"Let all God's angels worship
him."*d*

⁷In speaking of the angels he says,

"He makes his angels winds,
his servants flames of fire."*e*

⁸But about the Son he says,

"Your throne, O God, will last for
ever and ever,
and righteousness will be the
scepter of your kingdom.
⁹You have loved righteousness and
hated wickedness;
therefore God, your God, has
set you above your
companions
by anointing you with the oil of
joy."*f*

---

*a*5 Or *have begotten you*   *b*5 Psalm 2:7   *c*5 2 Samuel 7:14; 1 Chron. 17:13   *d*6 Deut. 32:43
(see Dead Sea Scrolls and Septuagint)   *e*7 Psalm 104:4   *f*9 Psalm 45:6,7

VERSE:	AUTHOR:	PASSAGE:
Hebrews 1:2	Reuben Welch	Hebrews 1:1–14

God Has Spoken!

I don't know what you think about God, or what your attitude is toward him, but I wonder if you know and believe that he speaks and makes himself known. I think people come to God for many reasons and have many ways of expressing the quality of their relationship. But I think for me the richest thing about the gospel, at the practical life-level, is expressed in the words "fellowship" and "communication." To be able to pray, to be aware of God's presence, to know and believe he communicates with us — these are the most precious things in the world to me. I can't think of anything worse in all the whole universe than out of the depths of my humanness and individuality, out of the cosmic loneliness of my soul, to cry out, and have no answer back . . . What Hebrews tells us, oh, what the whole Bible tells us, is that God speaks. God has spoken!! Well what does he say? Jesus! . . .

Hebrews tells us, too, that this Jesus, through whom all things were created, is also the One who is heir of all things. Not only the creator, the beginner, the source, but he is the consummation! And the glory of the gospel is that it is all wrapped up in *who Jesus is*. He is the inheritor of all things. Before him "every knee should bow . . . and every tongue confess that Jesus Christ is Lord, to the glory of God the Father" (Philippians 2:10–11). That's why I can look out at the world, and so can you, in the midst of its evil, and sickness, and sin, and tragedy, and death — and know that underneath are the everlasting arms [Deuteronomy 33:27], and that the great purposes of God will finally be consummated.

ADDITIONAL SCRIPTURE READINGS
John 1:1–14; Philippians 2:1–11

Go to page 1556 for your next devotional reading.

¹⁰He also says,

"In the beginning, O Lord, you
        laid the foundations of the
        earth,
    and the heavens are the work of
        your hands.
¹¹They will perish, but you remain;
    they will all wear out like a
        garment.
¹²You will roll them up like a robe;
    like a garment they will be
        changed.
But you remain the same,
    and your years will never
        end."ᵃ

¹³To which of the angels did God ever
say,

"Sit at my right hand
until I make your enemies
    a footstool for your feet"ᵇ?

¹⁴Are not all angels ministering spirits
sent to serve those who will inherit
salvation?

Warning to Pay Attention

2 We must pay more careful atten-
    tion, therefore, to what we have
heard, so that we do not drift away.
²For if the message spoken by angels
was binding, and every violation and
disobedience received its just punishment, ³how shall we escape if we ignore such a great salvation? This salvation, which was first announced by
the Lord, was confirmed to us by
those who heard him. ⁴God also testified to it by signs, wonders and various miracles, and gifts of the Holy
Spirit distributed according to his
will.

Jesus Made Like His Brothers

⁵It is not to angels that he has subjected the world to come, about which
we are speaking. ⁶But there is a place
where someone has testified:

"What is man that you are
        mindful of him,
    the son of man that you care for
        him?
⁷You made him a littleᶜ lower
        than the angels;
    you crowned him with glory
        and honor
⁸   and put everything under his
        feet."ᵈ

In putting everything under him, God
left nothing that is not subject to him.
Yet at present we do not see everything subject to him. ⁹But we see
Jesus, who was made a little lower
than the angels, now crowned with
glory and honor because he suffered
death, so that by the grace of God he
might taste death for everyone.

¹⁰In bringing many sons to glory, it
was fitting that God, for whom and
through whom everything exists,
should make the author of their salvation perfect through suffering. ¹¹Both
the one who makes men holy and
those who are made holy are of the
same family. So Jesus is not ashamed
to call them brothers. ¹²He says,

"I will declare your name to my
        brothers;
    in the presence of the
        congregation I will sing
        your praises."ᵉ

¹³And again,

"I will put my trust in him."ᶠ

And again he says,

"Here am I, and the children God
        has given me."ᵍ

¹⁴Since the children have flesh and
blood, he too shared in their humanity so that by his death he might destroy him who holds the power of
death—that is, the devil— ¹⁵and free
those who all their lives were held in
slavery by their fear of death. ¹⁶For
surely it is not angels he helps, but
Abraham's descendants. ¹⁷For this
reason he had to be made like his

ᵃ12 Psalm 102:25-27   ᵇ13 Psalm 110:1   ᶜ7 Or *him for a little while*; also in verse 9
ᵈ8 Psalm 8:4-6   ᵉ12 Psalm 22:22   ᶠ13 Isaiah 8:17   ᵍ13 Isaiah 8:18

brothers in every way, in order that he might become a merciful and faithful high priest in service to God, and that he might make atonement for[a] the sins of the people. ¹⁸Because he himself suffered when he was tempted, he is able to help those who are being tempted.

Jesus Greater Than Moses

3 Therefore, holy brothers, who share in the heavenly calling, fix your thoughts on Jesus, the apostle and high priest whom we confess. ²He was faithful to the one who appointed him, just as Moses was faithful in all God's house. ³Jesus has been found worthy of greater honor than Moses, just as the builder of a house has greater honor than the house itself. ⁴For every house is built by someone, but God is the builder of everything. ⁵Moses was faithful as a servant in all God's house, testifying to what would be said in the future. ⁶But Christ is faithful as a son over God's house. And we are his house, if we hold on to our courage and the hope of which we boast.

Warning Against Unbelief

⁷So, as the Holy Spirit says:

"Today, if you hear his voice,
⁸   do not harden your hearts
  as you did in the rebellion,
      during the time of testing in the
        desert,
⁹where your fathers tested and
    tried me
  and for forty years saw what I
    did.
¹⁰That is why I was angry with that
    generation,
  and I said, 'Their hearts are
    always going astray,
  and they have not known my
    ways.'
¹¹So I declared on oath in my anger,
  'They shall never enter my
    rest.' "[b]

¹²See to it, brothers, that none of you has a sinful, unbelieving heart that turns away from the living God. ¹³But encourage one another daily, as long as it is called Today, so that none of you may be hardened by sin's deceitfulness. ¹⁴We have come to share in Christ if we hold firmly till the end the confidence we had at first. ¹⁵As has just been said:

"Today, if you hear his voice,
  do not harden your hearts
  as you did in the rebellion."[c]

¹⁶Who were they who heard and rebelled? Were they not all those Moses led out of Egypt? ¹⁷And with whom was he angry for forty years? Was it not with those who sinned, whose bodies fell in the desert? ¹⁸And to whom did God swear that they would never enter his rest if not to those who disobeyed[d]? ¹⁹So we see that they were not able to enter, because of their unbelief.

A Sabbath-Rest for the People of God

4 Therefore, since the promise of entering his rest still stands, let us be careful that none of you be found to have fallen short of it. ²For we also have had the gospel preached to us, just as they did; but the message they heard was of no value to them, because those who heard did not combine it with faith.[e] ³Now we who have believed enter that rest, just as God has said,

"So I declared on oath in my
    anger,
  'They shall never enter my
    rest.' "[f]

And yet his work has been finished since the creation of the world. ⁴For somewhere he has spoken about the seventh day in these words: "And on the seventh day God rested from all his work."[g] ⁵And again in the pas-

---

[a]17 Or *and that he might turn aside God's wrath, taking away*   [b]11 Psalm 95:7-11
[c]15 Psalm 95:7,8   [d]18 Or *disbelieved*   [e]2 Many manuscripts *because they did not share in the faith of those who obeyed*   [f]3 Psalm 95:11; also in verse 5   [g]4 Gen. 2:2

VERSE: AUTHOR: PASSAGE:
Hebrews 4:15   Dirk R. Buursma   Hebrews 4:14 — 5:10

Our Go-Between

Jesus. Lord. Master. Savior. Friend. Son of God. Priest. Priest?

Why in the world would we need a priest today? Rams, bulls, sacrifices, smoke, fire? That's Old Testament language, right?

Consider this. We need a mediator, a go-between. Someone to intercede between us and God, a middleman. Jesus. True God and truly human.

We're much too weak to handle our own relationship with God. We don't have the holiness to come into his presence. We don't have the ability to wipe out the past, to make amends for all we've done. But there *is* One who can!

Jesus Christ is that very person — appointed by his Father to be our Priest, to plead our case before God, to understand us totally, to *really* know and *really* feel where we are and where we've been and where we're going.

How about you? You who feel that your days of usefulness are over. You who are weary and burdened. You who have experienced a loss that has left a seemingly irreparable hole in your heart. Do you need a priest who really understands you, who can take all that you are to God?

Your loving God has appointed Jesus to act on your behalf. Trust him to take up your case. Let him then release you to live in the liberating power of his acceptance.

ADDITIONAL SCRIPTURE READINGS
Ephesians 3:1–13; Hebrews 2:5–18

Go to page 1558 for your next devotional reading.

sage above he says, "They shall never enter my rest."

⁶It still remains that some will enter that rest, and those who formerly had the gospel preached to them did not go in, because of their disobedience. ⁷Therefore God again set a certain day, calling it Today, when a long time later he spoke through David, as was said before:

"Today, if you hear his voice,
do not harden your hearts."ᵃ

⁸For if Joshua had given them rest, God would not have spoken later about another day. ⁹There remains, then, a Sabbath-rest for the people of God; ¹⁰for anyone who enters God's rest also rests from his own work, just as God did from his. ¹¹Let us, therefore, make every effort to enter that rest, so that no one will fall by following their example of disobedience.

¹²For the word of God is living and active. Sharper than any double-edged sword, it penetrates even to dividing soul and spirit, joints and marrow; it judges the thoughts and attitudes of the heart. ¹³Nothing in all creation is hidden from God's sight. Everything is uncovered and laid bare before the eyes of him to whom we must give account.

Jesus the Great High Priest

¹⁴Therefore, since we have a great high priest who has gone through the heavens,ᵇ Jesus the Son of God, let us hold firmly to the faith we profess. ¹⁵For we do not have a high priest who is unable to sympathize with our weaknesses, but we have one who has been tempted in every way, just as we are—yet was without sin. ¹⁶Let us then approach the throne of grace with confidence, so that we may receive mercy and find grace to help us in our time of need.

5 Every high priest is selected from among men and is appointed to represent them in matters related to God, to offer gifts and sacrifices for

sins. ²He is able to deal gently with those who are ignorant and are going astray, since he himself is subject to weakness. ³This is why he has to offer sacrifices for his own sins, as well as for the sins of the people.

⁴No one takes this honor upon himself; he must be called by God, just as Aaron was. ⁵So Christ also did not take upon himself the glory of becoming a high priest. But God said to him,

"You are my Son;
today I have become your
Father."ᶜ ᵈ

⁶And he says in another place,

"You are a priest forever,
in the order of Melchizedek."ᵉ

⁷During the days of Jesus' life on earth, he offered up prayers and petitions with loud cries and tears to the one who could save him from death, and he was heard because of his reverent submission. ⁸Although he was a son, he learned obedience from what he suffered ⁹and, once made perfect, he became the source of eternal salvation for all who obey him ¹⁰and was designated by God to be high priest in the order of Melchizedek.

Warning Against Falling Away

¹¹We have much to say about this, but it is hard to explain because you are slow to learn. ¹²In fact, though by this time you ought to be teachers, you need someone to teach you the elementary truths of God's word all over again. You need milk, not solid food! ¹³Anyone who lives on milk, being still an infant, is not acquainted with the teaching about righteousness. ¹⁴But solid food is for the mature, who by constant use have trained themselves to distinguish good from evil.

6 Therefore let us leave the elementary teachings about Christ and go on to maturity, not laying again the foundation of repentance from acts that lead to death,ᶠ and of faith

---

ᵃ7 Psalm 95:7,8   ᵇ14 Or gone into heaven   ᶜ5 Or have begotten you   ᵈ5 Psalm 2:7
ᵉ6 Psalm 110:4   ᶠ1 Or from useless rituals

PASSAGE: Matthew 11:25–30; Hebrews 4:1–13

AUTHOR: John Killinger

Eternal Rest

Life in all its hues
is beautiful, Lord, like the rainbow.
Forgive us if we have been
too busy to notice.
Help us to make time for you.
Teach us to see you everywhere.
And give us the eternal rest
that is promised to your servants.
Through Jesus Christ our Lord,
Amen.

Go to page 1560 for your next devotional reading.

in God, [2]instruction about baptisms, the laying on of hands, the resurrection of the dead, and eternal judgment. [3]And God permitting, we will do so.

[4]It is impossible for those who have once been enlightened, who have tasted the heavenly gift, who have shared in the Holy Spirit, [5]who have tasted the goodness of the word of God and the powers of the coming age, [6]if they fall away, to be brought back to repentance, because[a] to their loss they are crucifying the Son of God all over again and subjecting him to public disgrace.

[7]Land that drinks in the rain often falling on it and that produces a crop useful to those for whom it is farmed receives the blessing of God. [8]But land that produces thorns and thistles is worthless and is in danger of being cursed. In the end it will be burned.

[9]Even though we speak like this, dear friends, we are confident of better things in your case—things that accompany salvation. [10]God is not unjust; he will not forget your work and the love you have shown him as you have helped his people and continue to help them. [11]We want each of you to show this same diligence to the very end, in order to make your hope sure. [12]We do not want you to become lazy, but to imitate those who through faith and patience inherit what has been promised.

The Certainty of God's Promise

[13]When God made his promise to Abraham, since there was no one greater for him to swear by, he swore by himself, [14]saying, "I will surely bless you and give you many descendants."[b] [15]And so after waiting patiently, Abraham received what was promised.

[16]Men swear by someone greater than themselves, and the oath confirms what is said and puts an end to all argument. [17]Because God wanted to make the unchanging nature of his purpose very clear to the heirs of what was promised, he confirmed it with an oath. [18]God did this so that, by two unchangeable things in which it is impossible for God to lie, we who have fled to take hold of the hope offered to us may be greatly encouraged. [19]We have this hope as an anchor for the soul, firm and secure. It enters the inner sanctuary behind the curtain, [20]where Jesus, who went before us, has entered on our behalf. He has become a high priest forever, in the order of Melchizedek.

Melchizedek the Priest

7 This Melchizedek was king of Salem and priest of God Most High. He met Abraham returning from the defeat of the kings and blessed him, [2]and Abraham gave him a tenth of everything. First, his name means "king of righteousness"; then also, "king of Salem" means "king of peace." [3]Without father or mother, without genealogy, without beginning of days or end of life, like the Son of God he remains a priest forever.

[4]Just think how great he was: Even the patriarch Abraham gave him a tenth of the plunder! [5]Now the law requires the descendants of Levi who become priests to collect a tenth from the people—that is, their brothers—even though their brothers are descended from Abraham. [6]This man, however, did not trace his descent from Levi, yet he collected a tenth from Abraham and blessed him who had the promises. [7]And without doubt the lesser person is blessed by the greater. [8]In the one case, the tenth is collected by men who die; but in the other case, by him who is declared to be living. [9]One might even say that Levi, who collects the tenth, paid the tenth through Abraham, [10]because when Melchizedek met Abraham, Levi was still in the body of his ancestor.

Jesus Like Melchizedek

[11]If perfection could have been attained through the Levitical priest-

---

[a]6 Or *repentance while*   [b]14 Gen. 22:17

VERSE:	AUTHOR:	PASSAGE:
Hebrews 6:19	William L. Coleman	Hebrews 6:13–30

An Anchor for the Soul

"I don't get as excited as I used to get, but I do feel more content." That's how a 60-year-old explained her emotions.

We seem to move on a more even keel. The newest fads and trends may not set us off, but disappointment doesn't drag us down as far either. We've seen more of life. We've survived its great joys as well as its heartaches. We tend to be more stable, less flaky and more dependable.

When a television ad claims to offer the "immortal songs" of some singer, we know better. If a local furniture store advertises a "once in a lifetime offer," we no longer bolt out of our chairs and hustle across town. Politicians who say they will lower taxes and increase benefits don't give us goose pimples anymore.

Not that we have become cynical. But we aren't so easily excited about amazing offers or outlandish claims. We know Elvis is dead and we don't look for him at the local convenience store.

Even-handed. Calm. Cool. Steady. Faithful.

The only real security. While we look for financial security, millions at our age know there is only one source of real security. Pensions fall apart. Houses blow away. People die. Markets drop. Even governments fail and crumble. Only God offers us total security for eternity.

Our faith in God becomes the anchor for our souls. God is the anchor that will not be moved. "We have this hope as an anchor for the soul, firm and secure."

ADDITIONAL SCRIPTURE READINGS
Psalm 145; 2 Corinthians 3:7–18

Go to page 1565 for your next devotional reading.

hood (for on the basis of it the law was given to the people), why was there still need for another priest to come—one in the order of Melchizedek, not in the order of Aaron? ¹²For when there is a change of the priesthood, there must also be a change of the law. ¹³He of whom these things are said belonged to a different tribe, and no one from that tribe has ever served at the altar. ¹⁴For it is clear that our Lord descended from Judah, and in regard to that tribe Moses said nothing about priests. ¹⁵And what we have said is even more clear if another priest like Melchizedek appears, ¹⁶one who has become a priest not on the basis of a regulation as to his ancestry but on the basis of the power of an indestructible life. ¹⁷For it is declared:

"You are a priest forever,
    in the order of Melchizedek."[a]

¹⁸The former regulation is set aside because it was weak and useless ¹⁹(for the law made nothing perfect), and a better hope is introduced, by which we draw near to God.

²⁰And it was not without an oath! Others became priests without any oath, ²¹but he became a priest with an oath when God said to him:

"The Lord has sworn
    and will not change his mind:
'You are a priest forever.' "[a]

²²Because of this oath, Jesus has become the guarantee of a better covenant.

²³Now there have been many of those priests, since death prevented them from continuing in office; ²⁴but because Jesus lives forever, he has a permanent priesthood. ²⁵Therefore he is able to save completely[b] those who come to God through him, because he always lives to intercede for them.

²⁶Such a high priest meets our need—one who is holy, blameless, pure, set apart from sinners, exalted above the heavens. ²⁷Unlike the other high priests, he does not need to offer sacrifices day after day, first for his own sins, and then for the sins of the people. He sacrificed for their sins once for all when he offered himself. ²⁸For the law appoints as high priests men who are weak; but the oath, which came after the law, appointed the Son, who has been made perfect forever.

The High Priest of a New Covenant

8 The point of what we are saying is this: We do have such a high priest, who sat down at the right hand of the throne of the Majesty in heaven, ²and who serves in the sanctuary, the true tabernacle set up by the Lord, not by man.

³Every high priest is appointed to offer both gifts and sacrifices, and so it was necessary for this one also to have something to offer. ⁴If he were on earth, he would not be a priest, for there are already men who offer the gifts prescribed by the law. ⁵They serve at a sanctuary that is a copy and shadow of what is in heaven. This is why Moses was warned when he was about to build the tabernacle: "See to it that you make everything according to the pattern shown you on the mountain."[c] ⁶But the ministry Jesus has received is as superior to theirs as the covenant of which he is mediator is superior to the old one, and it is founded on better promises.

⁷For if there had been nothing wrong with that first covenant, no place would have been sought for another. ⁸But God found fault with the people and said[d]:

"The time is coming, declares the
        Lord,
    when I will make a new
        covenant
with the house of Israel
    and with the house of Judah.
⁹It will not be like the covenant
    I made with their forefathers

---

[a]17,21 Psalm 110:4   [b]25 Or *forever*   [c]5 Exodus 25:40   [d]8 Some manuscripts may be translated *fault and said to the people.*

when I took them by the hand
   to lead them out of Egypt,
because they did not remain
      faithful to my covenant,
  and I turned away from them,
        declares the Lord.
[10]This is the covenant I will make
    with the house of Israel
  after that time, declares the
    Lord.
I will put my laws in their minds
  and write them on their hearts.
I will be their God,
  and they will be my people.
[11]No longer will a man teach his
    neighbor,
  or a man his brother, saying,
    'Know the Lord,'
because they will all know me,
  from the least of them to the
    greatest.
[12]For I will forgive their wickedness
  and will remember their sins no
    more."[a]

[13]By calling this covenant "new," he has made the first one obsolete; and what is obsolete and aging will soon disappear.

Worship in the Earthly Tabernacle

9 Now the first covenant had regulations for worship and also an earthly sanctuary. [2]A tabernacle was set up. In its first room were the lampstand, the table and the consecrated bread; this was called the Holy Place. [3]Behind the second curtain was a room called the Most Holy Place, [4]which had the golden altar of incense and the gold-covered ark of the covenant. This ark contained the gold jar of manna, Aaron's staff that had budded, and the stone tablets of the covenant. [5]Above the ark were the cherubim of the Glory, overshadowing the atonement cover.[b] But we cannot discuss these things in detail now.

[6]When everything had been arranged like this, the priests entered regularly into the outer room to carry on their ministry. [7]But only the high priest entered the inner room, and that only once a year, and never without blood, which he offered for himself and for the sins the people had committed in ignorance. [8]The Holy Spirit was showing by this that the way into the Most Holy Place had not yet been disclosed as long as the first tabernacle was still standing. [9]This is an illustration for the present time, indicating that the gifts and sacrifices being offered were not able to clear the conscience of the worshiper. [10]They are only a matter of food and drink and various ceremonial washings—external regulations applying until the time of the new order.

The Blood of Christ

[11]When Christ came as high priest of the good things that are already here,[c] he went through the greater and more perfect tabernacle that is not man-made, that is to say, not a part of this creation. [12]He did not enter by means of the blood of goats and calves; but he entered the Most Holy Place once for all by his own blood, having obtained eternal redemption. [13]The blood of goats and bulls and the ashes of a heifer sprinkled on those who are ceremonially unclean sanctify them so that they are outwardly clean. [14]How much more, then, will the blood of Christ, who through the eternal Spirit offered himself unblemished to God, cleanse our consciences from acts that lead to death,[d] so that we may serve the living God!

[15]For this reason Christ is the mediator of a new covenant, that those who are called may receive the promised eternal inheritance—now that he has died as a ransom to set them free from the sins committed under the first covenant.

[16]In the case of a will,[e] it is necessary to prove the death of the one who made it, [17]because a will is in force only when somebody has died; it never takes effect while the one who made it is living. [18]This is why

---

[a]12 Jer. 31:31-34   [b]5 Traditionally *the mercy seat*   [c]11 Some early manuscripts *are to come*
[d]14 Or *from useless rituals*   [e]16 Same Greek word as *covenant*; also in verse 17

even the first covenant was not put into effect without blood. ¹⁹When Moses had proclaimed every commandment of the law to all the people, he took the blood of calves, together with water, scarlet wool and branches of hyssop, and sprinkled the scroll and all the people. ²⁰He said, "This is the blood of the covenant, which God has commanded you to keep."*a* ²¹In the same way, he sprinkled with the blood both the tabernacle and everything used in its ceremonies. ²²In fact, the law requires that nearly everything be cleansed with blood, and without the shedding of blood there is no forgiveness.

²³It was necessary, then, for the copies of the heavenly things to be purified with these sacrifices, but the heavenly things themselves with better sacrifices than these. ²⁴For Christ did not enter a man-made sanctuary that was only a copy of the true one; he entered heaven itself, now to appear for us in God's presence. ²⁵Nor did he enter heaven to offer himself again and again, the way the high priest enters the Most Holy Place every year with blood that is not his own. ²⁶Then Christ would have had to suffer many times since the creation of the world. But now he has appeared once for all at the end of the ages to do away with sin by the sacrifice of himself. ²⁷Just as man is destined to die once, and after that to face judgment, ²⁸so Christ was sacrificed once to take away the sins of many people; and he will appear a second time, not to bear sin, but to bring salvation to those who are waiting for him.

Christ's Sacrifice Once for All

10 The law is only a shadow of the good things that are coming—not the realities themselves. For this reason it can never, by the same sacrifices repeated endlessly year after year, make perfect those who draw near to worship. ²If it could, would they not have stopped being offered? For the worshipers would have been cleansed once for all, and would no longer have felt guilty for their sins. ³But those sacrifices are an annual reminder of sins, ⁴because it is impossible for the blood of bulls and goats to take away sins.

⁵Therefore, when Christ came into the world, he said:

"Sacrifice and offering you did not desire,
  but a body you prepared for me;
⁶with burnt offerings and sin offerings
  you were not pleased.
⁷Then I said, 'Here I am—it is written about me in the scroll—
  I have come to do your will, O God.' "*b*

⁸First he said, "Sacrifices and offerings, burnt offerings and sin offerings you did not desire, nor were you pleased with them" (although the law required them to be made). ⁹Then he said, "Here I am, I have come to do your will." He sets aside the first to establish the second. ¹⁰And by that will, we have been made holy through the sacrifice of the body of Jesus Christ once for all.

¹¹Day after day every priest stands and performs his religious duties; again and again he offers the same sacrifices, which can never take away sins. ¹²But when this priest had offered for all time one sacrifice for sins, he sat down at the right hand of God. ¹³Since that time he waits for his enemies to be made his footstool, ¹⁴because by one sacrifice he has made perfect forever those who are being made holy.

¹⁵The Holy Spirit also testifies to us about this. First he says:

¹⁶"This is the covenant I will make with them
  after that time, says the Lord.
I will put my laws in their hearts,

a20 Exodus 24:8   *b7* Psalm 40:6-8 (see Septuagint)

and I will write them on their minds."[a]

[17]Then he adds:

"Their sins and lawless acts
I will remember no more."[b]

[18]And where these have been forgiven, there is no longer any sacrifice for sin.

A Call to Persevere

[19]Therefore, brothers, since we have confidence to enter the Most Holy Place by the blood of Jesus, [20]by a new and living way opened for us through the curtain, that is, his body, [21]and since we have a great priest over the house of God, [22]let us draw near to God with a sincere heart in full assurance of faith, having our hearts sprinkled to cleanse us from a guilty conscience and having our bodies washed with pure water. [23]Let us hold unswervingly to the hope we profess, for he who promised is faithful. [24]And let us consider how we may spur one another on toward love and good deeds. [25]Let us not give up meeting together, as some are in the habit of doing, but let us encourage one another—and all the more as you see the Day approaching.

[26]If we deliberately keep on sinning after we have received the knowledge of the truth, no sacrifice for sins is left, [27]but only a fearful expectation of judgment and of raging fire that will consume the enemies of God. [28]Anyone who rejected the law of Moses died without mercy on the testimony of two or three witnesses. [29]How much more severely do you think a man deserves to be punished who has trampled the Son of God under foot, who has treated as an unholy thing the blood of the covenant that sanctified him, and who has insulted the Spirit of grace? [30]For we know him who said, "It is mine to avenge; I will repay,"[c] and again, "The Lord will judge his people."[d] [31]It is a dreadful thing to fall into the hands of the living God.

[32]Remember those earlier days after you had received the light, when you stood your ground in a great contest in the face of suffering. [33]Sometimes you were publicly exposed to insult and persecution; at other times you stood side by side with those who were so treated. [34]You sympathized with those in prison and joyfully accepted the confiscation of your property, because you knew that you yourselves had better and lasting possessions.

[35]So do not throw away your confidence; it will be richly rewarded. [36]You need to persevere so that when you have done the will of God, you will receive what he has promised. [37]For in just a very little while,

"He who is coming will come and
　　will not delay.
[38]　But my righteous one[e] will live
　　by faith.
And if he shrinks back,
　I will not be pleased with
　　him."[f]

[39]But we are not of those who shrink back and are destroyed, but of those who believe and are saved.

By Faith

11 Now faith is being sure of what we hope for and certain of what we do not see. [2]This is what the ancients were commended for.

[3]By faith we understand that the universe was formed at God's command, so that what is seen was not made out of what was visible.

[4]By faith Abel offered God a better sacrifice than Cain did. By faith he was commended as a righteous man, when God spoke well of his offerings. And by faith he still speaks, even though he is dead.

[5]By faith Enoch was taken from this life, so that he did not experience death; he could not be found, because God had taken him away. For before

---

[a]16 Jer. 31:33　　[b]17 Jer. 31:34　　[c]30 Deut. 32:35　　[d]30 Deut. 32:36; Psalm 135:14
[e]38 One early manuscript *But the righteous*　　[f]38 Hab. 2:3,4

VERSE:	AUTHOR:	PASSAGE:
Hebrews 11:10	Cornelis Gilhuis	Hebrews 11:1–12

How Time Flies!

How often do you say, "How time flies!"? The older one gets, the faster the weeks and years fly by. *Seem* to fly by, that is, because the clock in your room of course ticks at the same rate of speed as when you crawled on the floor as an infant.

When you were young, time often did not go fast enough for you. Young people don't say, "How time flies!" nearly as often as older persons do . . .

Young people live in expectation, and waiting always lasts long. To them, the hands of the clock move very slowly.

But what may people who have grown old still expect from this life? They are quite happy when everything remains as it was. The little life that is left and the years shrink visibly. And so they say, "How time flies!"

Here, too, everything becomes different when we do not only set our hopes on the things of this life — the things that are seen — but look forward to "the city with foundations, whose architect and builder is God" (Hebrews 11:10). Then even at an advanced age time does not go quite fast enough.

"It takes so long before the Savior comes." "I am yearning to see God in glory," I hear some witness. Then in the heart the poet's words resound: "Lord Jesus, why do you tarry still longer / every hour our yearning grows deeper and stronger."

ADDITIONAL SCRIPTURE READINGS
Matthew 25:1–13; Philippians 3:12–21

Go to page 1568 for your next devotional reading.

he was taken, he was commended as one who pleased God. ⁶And without faith it is impossible to please God, because anyone who comes to him must believe that he exists and that he rewards those who earnestly seek him.

⁷By faith Noah, when warned about things not yet seen, in holy fear built an ark to save his family. By his faith he condemned the world and became heir of the righteousness that comes by faith.

⁸By faith Abraham, when called to go to a place he would later receive as his inheritance, obeyed and went, even though he did not know where he was going. ⁹By faith he made his home in the promised land like a stranger in a foreign country; he lived in tents, as did Isaac and Jacob, who were heirs with him of the same promise. ¹⁰For he was looking forward to the city with foundations, whose architect and builder is God.

¹¹By faith Abraham, even though he was past age—and Sarah herself was barren—was enabled to become a father because he[a] considered him faithful who had made the promise. ¹²And so from this one man, and he as good as dead, came descendants as numerous as the stars in the sky and as countless as the sand on the seashore.

¹³All these people were still living by faith when they died. They did not receive the things promised; they only saw them and welcomed them from a distance. And they admitted that they were aliens and strangers on earth. ¹⁴People who say such things show that they are looking for a country of their own. ¹⁵If they had been thinking of the country they had left, they would have had opportunity to return. ¹⁶Instead, they were longing for a better country—a heavenly one. Therefore God is not ashamed to be called their God, for he has prepared a city for them.

¹⁷By faith Abraham, when God test-

ed him, offered Isaac as a sacrifice. He who had received the promises was about to sacrifice his one and only son, ¹⁸even though God had said to him, "It is through Isaac that your offspring[b] will be reckoned."[c] ¹⁹Abraham reasoned that God could raise the dead, and figuratively speaking, he did receive Isaac back from death.

²⁰By faith Isaac blessed Jacob and Esau in regard to their future.

²¹By faith Jacob, when he was dying, blessed each of Joseph's sons, and worshiped as he leaned on the top of his staff.

²²By faith Joseph, when his end was near, spoke about the exodus of the Israelites from Egypt and gave instructions about his bones.

²³By faith Moses' parents hid him for three months after he was born, because they saw he was no ordinary child, and they were not afraid of the king's edict.

²⁴By faith Moses, when he had grown up, refused to be known as the son of Pharaoh's daughter. ²⁵He chose to be mistreated along with the people of God rather than to enjoy the pleasures of sin for a short time. ²⁶He regarded disgrace for the sake of Christ as of greater value than the treasures of Egypt, because he was looking ahead to his reward. ²⁷By faith he left Egypt, not fearing the king's anger; he persevered because he saw him who is invisible. ²⁸By faith he kept the Passover and the sprinkling of blood, so that the destroyer of the firstborn would not touch the firstborn of Israel.

²⁹By faith the people passed through the Red Sea[d] as on dry land; but when the Egyptians tried to do so, they were drowned.

³⁰By faith the walls of Jericho fell, after the people had marched around them for seven days.

³¹By faith the prostitute Rahab, because she welcomed the spies, was not killed with those who were disobedient.[e]

---

a11 Or *By faith even Sarah, who was past age, was enabled to bear children because she*   b18 Greek *seed*   c18 Gen. 21:12   d29 That is, Sea of Reeds   e31 Or *unbelieving*

³²And what more shall I say? I do not have time to tell about Gideon, Barak, Samson, Jephthah, David, Samuel and the prophets, ³³who through faith conquered kingdoms, administered justice, and gained what was promised; who shut the mouths of lions, ³⁴quenched the fury of the flames, and escaped the edge of the sword; whose weakness was turned to strength; and who became powerful in battle and routed foreign armies. ³⁵Women received back their dead, raised to life again. Others were tortured and refused to be released, so that they might gain a better resurrection. ³⁶Some faced jeers and flogging, while still others were chained and put in prison. ³⁷They were stoned[a]; they were sawed in two; they were put to death by the sword. They went about in sheepskins and goatskins, destitute, persecuted and mistreated— ³⁸the world was not worthy of them. They wandered in deserts and mountains, and in caves and holes in the ground.

³⁹These were all commended for their faith, yet none of them received what had been promised. ⁴⁰God had planned something better for us so that only together with us would they be made perfect.

God Disciplines His Sons

12 Therefore, since we are surrounded by such a great cloud of witnesses, let us throw off everything that hinders and the sin that so easily entangles, and let us run with perseverance the race marked out for us. ²Let us fix our eyes on Jesus, the author and perfecter of our faith, who for the joy set before him endured the cross, scorning its shame, and sat down at the right hand of the throne of God. ³Consider him who endured such opposition from sinful men, so that you will not grow weary and lose heart.

⁴In your struggle against sin, you have not yet resisted to the point of shedding your blood. ⁵And you have forgotten that word of encouragement that addresses you as sons:

"My son, do not make light of the Lord's discipline,
and do not lose heart when he rebukes you,
⁶because the Lord disciplines those he loves,
and he punishes everyone he accepts as a son."[b]

⁷Endure hardship as discipline; God is treating you as sons. For what son is not disciplined by his father? ⁸If you are not disciplined (and everyone undergoes discipline), then you are illegitimate children and not true sons. ⁹Moreover, we have all had human fathers who disciplined us and we respected them for it. How much more should we submit to the Father of our spirits and live! ¹⁰Our fathers disciplined us for a little while as they thought best; but God disciplines us for our good, that we may share in his holiness. ¹¹No discipline seems pleasant at the time, but painful. Later on, however, it produces a harvest of righteousness and peace for those who have been trained by it.

¹²Therefore, strengthen your feeble arms and weak knees. ¹³"Make level paths for your feet,"[c] so that the lame may not be disabled, but rather healed.

Warning Against Refusing God

¹⁴Make every effort to live in peace with all men and to be holy; without holiness no one will see the Lord. ¹⁵See to it that no one misses the grace of God and that no bitter root grows up to cause trouble and defile many. ¹⁶See that no one is sexually immoral, or is godless like Esau, who for a single meal sold his inheritance rights as the oldest son. ¹⁷Afterward, as you know, when he wanted to inherit this blessing, he was rejected. He could bring about no change of mind, though he sought the blessing with tears.

¹⁸You have not come to a mountain

---

a37 Some early manuscripts *stoned; they were put to the test;*   *b6* Prov. 3:11,12   *c13* Prov. 4:26

VERSE:	AUTHOR:	PASSAGE:
Hebrews 12:2	Paul B. Maves	Hebrews 12:1–13

Run With Perseverance

Faith is sustained, courage is released, and hope is nourished by the knowledge that others have gone on before us and have made the transitions and have experienced the glory of achievement on the other side. So it is that the writer of the letter to the Hebrews reminds us to look to Jesus, whom he calls the "author and perfecter of our faith, who for the joy set before him endured the cross" (Hebrews 12:2).

The cross stands as a symbol for the destruction of that which we hold most dear and at the same time for the doorway to a new and better life. Without the crucifixion there would be no resurrection. Living is something like going up a ladder. We have to let go of one rung in order to get to the next. It is important to have a sturdy ladder well planted on a solid base, but there is no way to go up except by risking one step after another . . .

Since we have here no continuing city, we move out in faith, seeking a city with foundations, whose architect and builder is God. As we do so, we elect to face the terror of the unknown. We take the risk of falling. We endure the pain for the hope of the glory on the other side, knowing that we cannot go back. We go forward, knowing that we are not the first who has gone this way and that we are not alone.

We are a part of a long line of pioneers, carrying out our part of the mission assigned to the human race, until all of us make it to the mountaintop, and our journey here is ended, and we make the transition to that which lies beyond.

ADDITIONAL SCRIPTURE READINGS
Philippians 3:12 — 4:1; 2 Timothy 4:6–8

Go to page 1572 for your next devotional reading.

that can be touched and that is burning with fire; to darkness, gloom and storm; [19]to a trumpet blast or to such a voice speaking words that those who heard it begged that no further word be spoken to them, [20]because they could not bear what was commanded: "If even an animal touches the mountain, it must be stoned."[a] [21]The sight was so terrifying that Moses said, "I am trembling with fear."[b]

[22]But you have come to Mount Zion, to the heavenly Jerusalem, the city of the living God. You have come to thousands upon thousands of angels in joyful assembly, [23]to the church of the firstborn, whose names are written in heaven. You have come to God, the judge of all men, to the spirits of righteous men made perfect, [24]to Jesus the mediator of a new covenant, and to the sprinkled blood that speaks a better word than the blood of Abel.

[25]See to it that you do not refuse him who speaks. If they did not escape when they refused him who warned them on earth, how much less will we, if we turn away from him who warns us from heaven? [26]At that time his voice shook the earth, but now he has promised, "Once more I will shake not only the earth but also the heavens."[c] [27]The words "once more" indicate the removing of what can be shaken—that is, created things—so that what cannot be shaken may remain.

[28]Therefore, since we are receiving a kingdom that cannot be shaken, let us be thankful, and so worship God acceptably with reverence and awe, [29]for our "God is a consuming fire."[d]

Concluding Exhortations

13 Keep on loving each other as brothers. [2]Do not forget to entertain strangers, for by so doing some people have entertained angels without knowing it. [3]Remember those in prison as if you were their fellow prisoners, and those who are mis-treated as if you yourselves were suffering.

[4]Marriage should be honored by all, and the marriage bed kept pure, for God will judge the adulterer and all the sexually immoral. [5]Keep your lives free from the love of money and be content with what you have, because God has said,

"Never will I leave you;
    never will I forsake you."[e]

[6]So we say with confidence,

"The Lord is my helper; I will not
    be afraid.
What can man do to me?"[f]

[7]Remember your leaders, who spoke the word of God to you. Consider the outcome of their way of life and imitate their faith. [8]Jesus Christ is the same yesterday and today and forever.

[9]Do not be carried away by all kinds of strange teachings. It is good for our hearts to be strengthened by grace, not by ceremonial foods, which are of no value to those who eat them. [10]We have an altar from which those who minister at the tabernacle have no right to eat.

[11]The high priest carries the blood of animals into the Most Holy Place as a sin offering, but the bodies are burned outside the camp. [12]And so Jesus also suffered outside the city gate to make the people holy through his own blood. [13]Let us, then, go to him outside the camp, bearing the disgrace he bore. [14]For here we do not have an enduring city, but we are looking for the city that is to come. [15]Through Jesus, therefore, let us continually offer to God a sacrifice of praise—the fruit of lips that confess his name. [16]And do not forget to do good and to share with others, for with such sacrifices God is pleased.

[17]Obey your leaders and submit to their authority. They keep watch over you as men who must give an account. Obey them so that their work

---

[a]20 Exodus 19:12,13   [b]21 Deut. 9:19   [c]26 Haggai 2:6   [d]29 Deut. 4:24   [e]5 Deut. 31:6
[f]6 Psalm 118:6,7

will be a joy, not a burden, for that would be of no advantage to you.

[18]Pray for us. We are sure that we have a clear conscience and desire to live honorably in every way. [19]I particularly urge you to pray so that I may be restored to you soon.

[20]May the God of peace, who through the blood of the eternal covenant brought back from the dead our Lord Jesus, that great Shepherd of the sheep, [21]equip you with everything good for doing his will, and may he work in us what is pleasing to him, through Jesus Christ, to whom be glory for ever and ever. Amen.

[22]Brothers, I urge you to bear with my word of exhortation, for I have written you only a short letter. [23]I want you to know that our brother Timothy has been released. If he arrives soon, I will come with him to see you.

[24]Greet all your leaders and all God's people. Those from Italy send you their greetings.

[25]Grace be with you all.

*J*ames, *a brother of Jesus,*
wrote this letter to urge Christians to express
their faith through their daily lives. In fresh,
straightforward language, he reminded them
of some of Jesus' teachings, especially from
the Sermon on the Mount (Matthew 5–7).
As you read this book, ask yourself whether
you're demonstrating the kind of faith in
action about which James writes.

JAMES

1 James, a servant of God and of the Lord Jesus Christ,

To the twelve tribes scattered among the nations:

Greetings.

Trials and Temptations

²Consider it pure joy, my brothers, whenever you face trials of many kinds, ³because you know that the testing of your faith develops perseverance. ⁴Perseverance must finish its work so that you may be mature and complete, not lacking anything. ⁵If any of you lacks wisdom, he should ask God, who gives generously to all without finding fault, and it will be given to him. ⁶But when he asks, he must believe and not doubt, because he who doubts is like a wave of the sea, blown and tossed by the wind. ⁷That man should not think he will receive anything from the Lord; ⁸he is a double-minded man, unstable in all he does.

⁹The brother in humble circumstances ought to take pride in his high position. ¹⁰But the one who is rich should take pride in his low position, because he will pass away like a wild flower. ¹¹For the sun rises with scorching heat and withers the plant; its blossom falls and its beauty is destroyed. In the same way, the rich man will fade away even while he goes about his business.

¹²Blessed is the man who perseveres under trial, because when he has stood the test, he will receive the crown of life that God has promised to those who love him.

¹³When tempted, no one should say, "God is tempting me." For God cannot be tempted by evil, nor does he tempt anyone; ¹⁴but each one is tempted when, by his own evil desire, he is dragged away and enticed. ¹⁵Then, after desire has conceived, it gives birth to sin; and sin, when it is full-grown, gives birth to death.

¹⁶Don't be deceived, my dear broth-

VERSE: AUTHOR: PASSAGE:
James 1:22   Jerry Bridges   James 1:19–25

Obeying the Word

The practice of meditation on the Word of God — simply thinking about it and its application to life — is a practice we develop through discipline. Most of us think we don't have time for this, but there are blocks of minutes during the day when we can meditate if we develop the habit . . .

The objective of our meditation is application — obedience to the Scriptures. This too requires discipline. Obeying the Scriptures usually requires change in our patterns of life. Because we are sinful by nature, we have developed sinful patterns, which we call habits. Discipline is required to break any habit . . .

Our patterns of disobedience to God have been developed over a number of years and are not broken easily or without discipline. Discipline does not mean gritting your teeth and saying, "I'll not do that anymore." Rather, discipline means structured, planned training. Just as you need a plan for regular Bible reading or study, so you need a plan for applying the Word to your life.

As you read or study the Scriptures and meditate on them during the day, ask yourself these three questions: 1. What does this passage teach concerning God's will for a holy life? 2. How does my life measure up to that Scripture; specifically where and how do I fall short? (Be specific; don't generalize.) 3. What definite steps of action do I need to take to obey?

ADDITIONAL SCRIPTURE READINGS
Psalm 119:97–104; Matthew 7:15–29

Go to page 1574 for your next devotional reading.

ers. [17]Every good and perfect gift is from above, coming down from the Father of the heavenly lights, who does not change like shifting shadows. [18]He chose to give us birth through the word of truth, that we might be a kind of firstfruits of all he created.

Listening and Doing

[19]My dear brothers, take note of this: Everyone should be quick to listen, slow to speak and slow to become angry, [20]for man's anger does not bring about the righteous life that God desires. [21]Therefore, get rid of all moral filth and the evil that is so prevalent and humbly accept the word planted in you, which can save you.

[22]Do not merely listen to the word, and so deceive yourselves. Do what it says. [23]Anyone who listens to the word but does not do what it says is like a man who looks at his face in a mirror [24]and, after looking at himself, goes away and immediately forgets what he looks like. [25]But the man who looks intently into the perfect law that gives freedom, and continues to do this, not forgetting what he has heard, but doing it—he will be blessed in what he does.

[26]If anyone considers himself religious and yet does not keep a tight rein on his tongue, he deceives himself and his religion is worthless. [27]Religion that God our Father accepts as pure and faultless is this: to look after orphans and widows in their distress and to keep oneself from being polluted by the world.

Favoritism Forbidden

2 My brothers, as believers in our glorious Lord Jesus Christ, don't show favoritism. [2]Suppose a man comes into your meeting wearing a gold ring and fine clothes, and a poor man in shabby clothes also comes in. [3]If you show special attention to the man wearing fine clothes and say, "Here's a good seat for you," but say to the poor man, "You stand there" or "Sit on the floor by my feet," [4]have you not discriminated among yourselves and become judges with evil thoughts?

[5]Listen, my dear brothers: Has not God chosen those who are poor in the eyes of the world to be rich in faith and to inherit the kingdom he promised those who love him? [6]But you have insulted the poor. Is it not the rich who are exploiting you? Are they not the ones who are dragging you into court? [7]Are they not the ones who are slandering the noble name of him to whom you belong?

[8]If you really keep the royal law found in Scripture, "Love your neighbor as yourself,"[a] you are doing right. [9]But if you show favoritism, you sin and are convicted by the law as lawbreakers. [10]For whoever keeps the whole law and yet stumbles at just one point is guilty of breaking all of it. [11]For he who said, "Do not commit adultery,"[b] also said, "Do not murder."[c] If you do not commit adultery but do commit murder, you have become a lawbreaker.

[12]Speak and act as those who are going to be judged by the law that gives freedom, [13]because judgment without mercy will be shown to anyone who has not been merciful. Mercy triumphs over judgment!

Faith and Deeds

[14]What good is it, my brothers, if a man claims to have faith but has no deeds? Can such faith save him? [15]Suppose a brother or sister is without clothes and daily food. [16]If one of you says to him, "Go, I wish you well; keep warm and well fed," but does nothing about his physical needs, what good is it? [17]In the same way, faith by itself, if it is not accompanied by action, is dead.

[18]But someone will say, "You have faith; I have deeds."

Show me your faith without deeds, and I will show you my faith by what I do. [19]You believe that there is one

[a]8 Lev. 19:18   [b]11 Exodus 20:14; Deut. 5:18   [c]11 Exodus 20:13; Deut. 5:17

VERSE:	AUTHOR:	PASSAGE:
James 2:8	Don Anderson	James 2:1–13

Learning to Love

Loving the unlovely doesn't come naturally. It is a learned response. James has shown us that growing Christians are those who are responding to tests, resisting temptations and absorbing the word. An equally valid signpost of spiritual growth is that we are learning to love even those who are tough to love.

We grow as God's love grows in us, and we become his channels to show his love to others. We are spurred on to tell the unsaved world about the Lord Jesus Christ. We begin to want the best for other people, no matter who they are, how they dress or what they do, because God's is a love without partiality . . .

No matter who we are, we are one in our need of the Savior. God is no respecter of persons. "For God does not show favoritism" (Romans 2:11). God longs for fellowship with *everyone* — the ugly and the beautiful, the cultured and the crude, the wealthy socialite and the welfare mother. We are all the same in significance to him . . .

I was a Christian for many years before I discovered that I could grow spiritually through expressing my love to others. I can manifest God's love to other people by my willingness to be involved in their lives, in order to help them to grow. I've found I never give my time, talents, knowledge or skills without coming away a richer person myself. Love in action is a means of maturing in the faith.

ADDITIONAL SCRIPTURE READINGS
Matthew 25:31–46; Acts 10:34–43

Go to page 1576 for your next devotional reading.

God. Good! Even the demons believe that—and shudder.

²⁰You foolish man, do you want evidence that faith without deeds is useless*? ²¹Was not our ancestor Abraham considered righteous for what he did when he offered his son Isaac on the altar? ²²You see that his faith and his actions were working together, and his faith was made complete by what he did. ²³And the scripture was fulfilled that says, "Abraham believed God, and it was credited to him as righteousness,"* and he was called God's friend. ²⁴You see that a person is justified by what he does and not by faith alone.

²⁵In the same way, was not even Rahab the prostitute considered righteous for what she did when she gave lodging to the spies and sent them off in a different direction? ²⁶As the body without the spirit is dead, so faith without deeds is dead.

Taming the Tongue

3 Not many of you should presume to be teachers, my brothers, because you know that we who teach will be judged more strictly. ²We all stumble in many ways. If anyone is never at fault in what he says, he is a perfect man, able to keep his whole body in check.

³When we put bits into the mouths of horses to make them obey us, we can turn the whole animal. ⁴Or take ships as an example. Although they are so large and are driven by strong winds, they are steered by a very small rudder wherever the pilot wants to go. ⁵Likewise the tongue is a small part of the body, but it makes great boasts. Consider what a great forest is set on fire by a small spark. ⁶The tongue also is a fire, a world of evil among the parts of the body. It corrupts the whole person, sets the whole course of his life on fire, and is itself set on fire by hell.

⁷All kinds of animals, birds, reptiles and creatures of the sea are being tamed and have been tamed by man,

⁸but no man can tame the tongue. It is a restless evil, full of deadly poison.

⁹With the tongue we praise our Lord and Father, and with it we curse men, who have been made in God's likeness. ¹⁰Out of the same mouth come praise and cursing. My brothers, this should not be. ¹¹Can both fresh water and salt* water flow from the same spring? ¹²My brothers, can a fig tree bear olives, or a grapevine bear figs? Neither can a salt spring produce fresh water.

Two Kinds of Wisdom

¹³Who is wise and understanding among you? Let him show it by his good life, by deeds done in the humility that comes from wisdom. ¹⁴But if you harbor bitter envy and selfish ambition in your hearts, do not boast about it or deny the truth. ¹⁵Such "wisdom" does not come down from heaven but is earthly, unspiritual, of the devil. ¹⁶For where you have envy and selfish ambition, there you find disorder and every evil practice.

¹⁷But the wisdom that comes from heaven is first of all pure; then peace-loving, considerate, submissive, full of mercy and good fruit, impartial and sincere. ¹⁸Peacemakers who sow in peace raise a harvest of righteousness.

Submit Yourselves to God

4 What causes fights and quarrels among you? Don't they come from your desires that battle within you? ²You want something but don't get it. You kill and covet, but you cannot have what you want. You quarrel and fight. You do not have, because you do not ask God. ³When you ask, you do not receive, because you ask with wrong motives, that you may spend what you get on your pleasures.

⁴You adulterous people, don't you know that friendship with the world is hatred toward God? Anyone who chooses to be a friend of the world becomes an enemy of God. ⁵Or do

*20 Some early manuscripts *dead*   *23 Gen. 15:6   *11 Greek *bitter* (see also verse 14)

PASSAGE: Isaiah 40:28–31; Matthew 11:25–30

AUTHOR: Christina Rossetti

In Weariness

O Lord, Jesus Christ,
    who art as the shadow of a great rock in a weary
        land,
who beholdest thy weak creatures
weary of labour, weary of pleasure,
weary of hope deferred, weary of self;
in thine abundant compassion,
and fellow feeling with us,
and unutterable tenderness,
bring us, we pray thee,
unto thy rest.

Go to page 1577 for your next devotional reading.

you think Scripture says without reason that the spirit he caused to live in
us envies intensely?[a] [6]But he gives
us more grace. That is why Scripture
says:

"God opposes the proud
　　but gives grace to the
　　humble."[b]

[7]Submit yourselves, then, to God.

[a]5 Or *that God jealously longs for the spirit that he made to live in us*; or *that the Spirit he caused to
live in us longs jealously*　　[b]6 Prov. 3:34

VERSE:	AUTHOR:	PASSAGE:
James 4:2	Billy Graham	James 4:1–10

Prayer Changes Us!

How many times have you heard someone say, "All I can
do is pray"?

All I can do is pray?!! You might as well say to a starving man, "All I can do is offer you food" . . .

Praying unlocks the doors of heaven and releases the
power of God. James 4:2 says, "You do not have, because you do not ask God." And Jesus said, "If you believe, you will receive whatever you ask for in prayer"
(Matthew 21:22).

Many of us want to do a work *for* God, but few of us
want to spend hours in prayer *to* God. It goes against
our natural inclinations to pray, which is precisely why
prayer counts so much with God. It is unnatural. It is, in
fact, supernatural! And it always gets God's attention.

I am sometimes amused when people tell me, "God answered my prayer." What they mean is that God gave
them what they asked for. But if he had not granted
their request, he would still have answered their prayer.
We forget that "No" and "Wait" are also answers, as is
"Yes" . . .

And remember, whether prayer changes our situation
or not, one thing is certain: Prayer *will* change us!

ADDITIONAL SCRIPTURE READINGS
Matthew 7:7–12; Philippians 4:4–7

Go to page 1579 for your next devotional reading.

Resist the devil, and he will flee from you. [8]Come near to God and he will come near to you. Wash your hands, you sinners, and purify your hearts, you double-minded. [9]Grieve, mourn and wail. Change your laughter to mourning and your joy to gloom. [10]Humble yourselves before the Lord, and he will lift you up.

[11]Brothers, do not slander one another. Anyone who speaks against his brother or judges him speaks against the law and judges it. When you judge the law, you are not keeping it, but sitting in judgment on it. [12]There is only one Lawgiver and Judge, the one who is able to save and destroy. But you—who are you to judge your neighbor?

Boasting About Tomorrow

[13]Now listen, you who say, "Today or tomorrow we will go to this or that city, spend a year there, carry on business and make money." [14]Why, you do not even know what will happen tomorrow. What is your life? You are a mist that appears for a little while and then vanishes. [15]Instead, you ought to say, "If it is the Lord's will, we will live and do this or that." [16]As it is, you boast and brag. All such boasting is evil. [17]Anyone, then, who knows the good he ought to do and doesn't do it, sins.

Warning to Rich Oppressors

5 Now listen, you rich people, weep and wail because of the misery that is coming upon you. [2]Your wealth has rotted, and moths have eaten your clothes. [3]Your gold and silver are corroded. Their corrosion will testify against you and eat your flesh like fire. You have hoarded wealth in the last days. [4]Look! The wages you failed to pay the workmen who mowed your fields are crying out against you. The cries of the harvesters have reached the ears of the Lord Almighty. [5]You have lived on earth in luxury and self-indulgence. You have

fattened yourselves in the day of slaughter.[a] [6]You have condemned and murdered innocent men, who were not opposing you.

Patience in Suffering

[7]Be patient, then, brothers, until the Lord's coming. See how the farmer waits for the land to yield its valuable crop and how patient he is for the autumn and spring rains. [8]You too, be patient and stand firm, because the Lord's coming is near. [9]Don't grumble against each other, brothers, or you will be judged. The Judge is standing at the door!

[10]Brothers, as an example of patience in the face of suffering, take the prophets who spoke in the name of the Lord. [11]As you know, we consider blessed those who have persevered. You have heard of Job's perseverance and have seen what the Lord finally brought about. The Lord is full of compassion and mercy.

[12]Above all, my brothers, do not swear—not by heaven or by earth or by anything else. Let your "Yes" be yes, and your "No," no, or you will be condemned.

The Prayer of Faith

[13]Is any one of you in trouble? He should pray. Is anyone happy? Let him sing songs of praise. [14]Is any one of you sick? He should call the elders of the church to pray over him and anoint him with oil in the name of the Lord. [15]And the prayer offered in faith will make the sick person well; the Lord will raise him up. If he has sinned, he will be forgiven. [16]Therefore confess your sins to each other and pray for each other so that you may be healed. The prayer of a righteous man is powerful and effective.

[17]Elijah was a man just like us. He prayed earnestly that it would not rain, and it did not rain on the land for three and a half years. [18]Again he prayed, and the heavens gave

[a]5 Or *yourselves as in a day of feasting*

rain, and the earth produced its crops.

¹⁹My brothers, if one of you should wander from the truth and someone should bring him back, ²⁰remember this: Whoever turns a sinner from the error of his way will save him from death and cover over a multitude of sins.

VERSE:	AUTHOR:	PASSAGE:
James 5:7	Don Anderson	James 5:7–12

Broken Hearts, Firm Foundations

Often I've seen that before the Lord can use people, he has to break them. When we pray for patience, we can almost count on the Lord's sending us some trouble so that patience might be produced in us. When we pray to be more loving, the Lord will try us so that the fragrance of his love can flow through us. We pray for joy, and there will probably come tears as we learn the true meaning of his joy in the midst of difficult circumstances. God is sovereign. He knows how to produce the qualities we pray for . . .

One woman whom God has enabled to grow better through brokenness is my mother. Mom is over 80 now. Dad has been gone for a couple of years, his loss still a difficult reality for her . . . Mom has undergone cancer surgery herself and suffers from arthritis. Despite it all, she just keeps on, ministering to others, attending her church, sharing her meager funds with people in need. She inspires all of us because she refuses to feel sorry for herself. She has chosen to fix her primary focus on the Lord and on the needs of others. I pray I grow old just like her.

ADDITIONAL SCRIPTURE READINGS
1 Thessalonians 1:2–10; Hebrews 12:1–13

Go to page 1581 for your next devotional reading.

*P*eter wrote to a group of
Christians who were suffering because of
their faith, counseling them to look to Jesus
for courage. As you read this letter, remember that God can use difficulties to
strengthen you; take comfort in knowing that
Jesus is coming again, and you will receive
the "crown of glory that will never fade
away."

1 PETER

1 Peter, an apostle of Jesus Christ,

To God's elect, strangers in the world, scattered throughout Pontus, Galatia, Cappadocia, Asia and Bithynia, [2]who have been chosen according to the foreknowledge of God the Father, through the sanctifying work of the Spirit, for obedience to Jesus Christ and sprinkling by his blood:

Grace and peace be yours in abundance.

Praise to God for a Living Hope

[3]Praise be to the God and Father of our Lord Jesus Christ! In his great mercy he has given us new birth into a living hope through the resurrection of Jesus Christ from the dead, [4]and into an inheritance that can never perish, spoil or fade—kept in heaven for you, [5]who through faith are shielded by God's power until the coming of the salvation that is ready to be re-vealed in the last time. [6]In this you greatly rejoice, though now for a little while you may have had to suffer grief in all kinds of trials. [7]These have come so that your faith—of greater worth than gold, which perishes even though refined by fire—may be proved genuine and may result in praise, glory and honor when Jesus Christ is revealed. [8]Though you have not seen him, you love him; and even though you do not see him now, you believe in him and are filled with an inexpressible and glorious joy, [9]for you are receiving the goal of your faith, the salvation of your souls.

[10]Concerning this salvation, the prophets, who spoke of the grace that was to come to you, searched intently and with the greatest care, [11]trying to find out the time and circumstances to which the Spirit of Christ in them was pointing when he predicted the sufferings of Christ and the glories that would follow. [12]It was revealed to them that they were not serving

themselves but you, when they spoke of the things that have now been told you by those who have preached the gospel to you by the Holy Spirit sent from heaven. Even angels long to look into these things.

Be Holy

¹³Therefore, prepare your minds for action; be self-controlled; set your hope fully on the grace to be given you when Jesus Christ is revealed. ¹⁴As obedient children, do not con-

VERSE:	AUTHOR:	PASSAGE:
1 Peter 1:7	A.B. Simpson	1 Peter 1:3–12

Treasures of the King's Palace

Our trials are great opportunities. Too often we look on them as great obstacles.

It would be an inspiration of unspeakable power if each of us would recognize every difficult situation as one of God's chosen ways of proving his love and power to us; and if, instead of expecting defeat, we should begin to look around for the messages of his glorious manifestations. Then indeed every mountain would become a path of ascension and a scene of transfiguration.

If we will look upon the past, many of us will find that the very time our heavenly Father has given us the richest blessings has been the time when we were strained and shut in on every side. God's jewels are often sent to us in unexpected packages and by dark servants, but within we find the very treasures of the King's palace.

The brilliance of gold twice refined, then crafted into exquisite jewelry, is breathtaking indeed. But from the comfort of the jewelry store, no one recalls the heat and pressure, stamping and shaping at the hand of the goldsmith that made it possible.

Are you living in the crucible? Then take heart! Something beautiful is about to happen at the hands of your Creator.

ADDITIONAL SCRIPTURE READINGS
Romans 5:1–5; James 1:2–4

Go to page 1583 for your next devotional reading.

form to the evil desires you had when you lived in ignorance. [15]But just as he who called you is holy, so be holy in all you do; [16]for it is written: "Be holy, because I am holy."[a]

[17]Since you call on a Father who judges each man's work impartially, live your lives as strangers here in reverent fear. [18]For you know that it was not with perishable things such as silver or gold that you were redeemed from the empty way of life handed down to you from your forefathers, [19]but with the precious blood of Christ, a lamb without blemish or defect. [20]He was chosen before the creation of the world, but was revealed in these last times for your sake. [21]Through him you believe in God, who raised him from the dead and glorified him, and so your faith and hope are in God.

[22]Now that you have purified yourselves by obeying the truth so that you have sincere love for your brothers, love one another deeply, from the heart.[b] [23]For you have been born again, not of perishable seed, but of imperishable, through the living and enduring word of God. [24]For,

"All men are like grass,
    and all their glory is like the
        flowers of the field;
the grass withers and the flowers
        fall,
[25] but the word of the Lord stands
        forever."[c]

And this is the word that was preached to you.

2 Therefore, rid yourselves of all malice and all deceit, hypocrisy, envy, and slander of every kind. [2]Like newborn babies, crave pure spiritual milk, so that by it you may grow up in your salvation, [3]now that you have tasted that the Lord is good.

The Living Stone and a Chosen People

[4]As you come to him, the living Stone—rejected by men but chosen

by God and precious to him— [5]you also, like living stones, are being built into a spiritual house to be a holy priesthood, offering spiritual sacrifices acceptable to God through Jesus Christ. [6]For in Scripture it says:

"See, I lay a stone in Zion,
    a chosen and precious
        cornerstone,
and the one who trusts in him
    will never be put to shame."[d]

[7]Now to you who believe, this stone is precious. But to those who do not believe,

"The stone the builders rejected
    has become the capstone,[e]"[f]

[8]and,

"A stone that causes men to
        stumble
    and a rock that makes them
        fall."[g]

They stumble because they disobey the message—which is also what they were destined for.

[9]But you are a chosen people, a royal priesthood, a holy nation, a people belonging to God, that you may declare the praises of him who called you out of darkness into his wonderful light. [10]Once you were not a people, but now you are the people of God; once you had not received mercy, but now you have received mercy.

[11]Dear friends, I urge you, as aliens and strangers in the world, to abstain from sinful desires, which war against your soul. [12]Live such good lives among the pagans that, though they accuse you of doing wrong, they may see your good deeds and glorify God on the day he visits us.

Submission to Rulers and Masters

[13]Submit yourselves for the Lord's sake to every authority instituted among men: whether to the king, as the supreme authority, [14]or to governors, who are sent by him to punish those who do wrong and to commend

---

[a]16 Lev. 11:44,45; 19:2; 20:7   [b]22 Some early manuscripts *from a pure heart*   [c]25 Isaiah 40:6-8
[d]6 Isaiah 28:16   [e]7 Or *cornerstone*   [f]7 Psalm 118:22   [g]8 Isaiah 8:14

VERSE:	AUTHOR:	PASSAGE:
1 Peter 1:18	Dwight L. Moody	1 Peter 1:13 — 2:3

The Precious Blood

Peter was an old man when he wrote these words. I suppose the blood of Jesus grew more precious to him as the years went by.

Now, why is it precious? Because it *redeems us*. Not only from the hands of the devil, but from the hands of the law. It redeems me from the curse of the law. The law condemns me, but Christ has satisfied the claims of the law. He tasted death for every man, and he has made it possible for every man to be saved. Paul says that God gave him up freely for us all [Romans 8:32], and what we want to do is to take him.

Silver and gold could not redeem our souls. Our life had been forfeited. Death had come into the world by sin, and nothing but blood could atone for the soul. If gold and silver could have redeemed us, do you not think that God would have created millions of worlds full of gold? It would have been an easy matter for him. But we are not redeemed by such corruptible things, but by the precious blood of Christ. Redemption means "buying back"; we had sold ourselves for naught, and Christ redeemed us and bought us back ... This is what redemption is — buying back and setting free. Christ came to break the fetters of sin, to open the prison doors and set the sinner free.

ADDITIONAL SCRIPTURE READINGS
Galatians 3:1–14; Titus 2:11–14

Go to page 1585 for your next devotional reading.

those who do right. [15]For it is God's will that by doing good you should silence the ignorant talk of foolish men. [16]Live as free men, but do not use your freedom as a cover-up for evil; live as servants of God. [17]Show proper respect to everyone: Love the brotherhood of believers, fear God, honor the king.

[18]Slaves, submit yourselves to your masters with all respect, not only to those who are good and considerate, but also to those who are harsh. [19]For it is commendable if a man bears up under the pain of unjust suffering because he is conscious of God. [20]But how is it to your credit if you receive a beating for doing wrong and endure it? But if you suffer for doing good and you endure it, this is commendable before God. [21]To this you were called, because Christ suffered for you, leaving you an example, that you should follow in his steps.

[22]"He committed no sin,
    and no deceit was found in his
        mouth."[a]

[23]When they hurled their insults at him, he did not retaliate; when he suffered, he made no threats. Instead, he entrusted himself to him who judges justly. [24]He himself bore our sins in his body on the tree, so that we might die to sins and live for righteousness; by his wounds you have been healed. [25]For you were like sheep going astray, but now you have returned to the Shepherd and Overseer of your souls.

Wives and Husbands

3 Wives, in the same way be submissive to your husbands so that, if any of them do not believe the word, they may be won over without words by the behavior of their wives, [2]when they see the purity and reverence of your lives. [3]Your beauty should not come from outward adornment, such as braided hair and the wearing of gold jewelry and fine clothes. [4]Instead, it should be that of

your inner self, the unfading beauty of a gentle and quiet spirit, which is of great worth in God's sight. [5]For this is the way the holy women of the past who put their hope in God used to make themselves beautiful. They were submissive to their own husbands, [6]like Sarah, who obeyed Abraham and called him her master. You are her daughters if you do what is right and do not give way to fear.

[7]Husbands, in the same way be considerate as you live with your wives, and treat them with respect as the weaker partner and as heirs with you of the gracious gift of life, so that nothing will hinder your prayers.

Suffering for Doing Good

[8]Finally, all of you, live in harmony with one another; be sympathetic, love as brothers, be compassionate and humble. [9]Do not repay evil with evil or insult with insult, but with blessing, because to this you were called so that you may inherit a blessing. [10]For,

"Whoever would love life
    and see good days
must keep his tongue from evil
    and his lips from deceitful
        speech.
[11]He must turn from evil and do
        good;
    he must seek peace and pursue
        it.
[12]For the eyes of the Lord are on
        the righteous
    and his ears are attentive to
        their prayer,
but the face of the Lord is against
        those who do evil."[b]

[13]Who is going to harm you if you are eager to do good? [14]But even if you should suffer for what is right, you are blessed. "Do not fear what they fear[c]; do not be frightened."[d] [15]But in your hearts set apart Christ as Lord. Always be prepared to give an answer to everyone who asks you to give the reason for the hope that you have. But do this with gentleness and

---

VERSE:	AUTHOR:	PASSAGE:
1 Peter 3:15	Louis M. Tamminga	1 Peter 3:8–17

The Reason for Your Hope

Most Christians find it hard to talk about their faith. One reason, perhaps, is this: our faith is not really part of our daily life.

The apostle Peter sums up our commitment to Christ in one word — *hope*. Hope is the vision that whatever happens, Christ is in control. Hope goes very deep; it is in the marrow of our bones.

Now what do you do with this hope? You give the reason for it! That's what Peter says.

Easier said than done. Peter wrote to Christians who were hated in the community because of their faith. That faith excluded emperor worship and the Roman way of life. Christians were dragged before judges who demanded an account of their loyalties. That was the situation Peter was talking about. And he tells these Christians to answer the judges' questions with a full account of their hope.

That took a lot of courage. It takes a lot of courage today. Only when your whole life is bound to Jesus Christ by hope can you do it. It means that your own life must be placed on a new Christian footing.

Now that would be the best thing that ever happened to you. A heart full of hope would be better than a safe full of gold. You would be an inspiring person, you would be drawn to people and you wouldn't find it hard to make conversation with them. May our prayer be: Lord, fill us with hope and remove barriers among us. Bless the account we will give of our hope. Amen.

ADDITIONAL SCRIPTURE READINGS
Galatians 3:1–14; Titus 2:11–14

Go to page 1587 for your next devotional reading.

respect, ¹⁶keeping a clear conscience, so that those who speak maliciously against your good behavior in Christ may be ashamed of their slander. ¹⁷It is better, if it is God's will, to suffer for doing good than for doing evil. ¹⁸For Christ died for sins once for all, the righteous for the unrighteous, to bring you to God. He was put to death in the body but made alive by the Spirit, ¹⁹through whomᵃ also he went and preached to the spirits in prison ²⁰who disobeyed long ago when God waited patiently in the days of Noah while the ark was being built. In it only a few people, eight in all, were saved through water, ²¹and this water symbolizes baptism that now saves you also—not the removal of dirt from the body but the pledgeᵇ of a good conscience toward God. It saves you by the resurrection of Jesus Christ, ²²who has gone into heaven and is at God's right hand—with angels, authorities and powers in submission to him.

Living for God

4 Therefore, since Christ suffered in his body, arm yourselves also with the same attitude, because he who has suffered in his body is done with sin. ²As a result, he does not live the rest of his earthly life for evil human desires, but rather for the will of God. ³For you have spent enough time in the past doing what pagans choose to do—living in debauchery, lust, drunkenness, orgies, carousing and detestable idolatry. ⁴They think it strange that you do not plunge with them into the same flood of dissipation, and they heap abuse on you. ⁵But they will have to give account to him who is ready to judge the living and the dead. ⁶For this is the reason the gospel was preached even to those who are now dead, so that they might be judged according to men in regard to the body, but live according to God in regard to the spirit.

⁷The end of all things is near. Therefore be clear minded and self-controlled so that you can pray. ⁸Above all, love each other deeply, because love covers over a multitude of sins. ⁹Offer hospitality to one another without grumbling. ¹⁰Each one should use whatever gift he has received to serve others, faithfully administering God's grace in its various forms. ¹¹If anyone speaks, he should do it as one speaking the very words of God. If anyone serves, he should do it with the strength God provides, so that in all things God may be praised through Jesus Christ. To him be the glory and the power for ever and ever. Amen.

Suffering for Being a Christian

¹²Dear friends, do not be surprised at the painful trial you are suffering, as though something strange were happening to you. ¹³But rejoice that you participate in the sufferings of Christ, so that you may be overjoyed when his glory is revealed. ¹⁴If you are insulted because of the name of Christ, you are blessed, for the Spirit of glory and of God rests on you. ¹⁵If you suffer, it should not be as a murderer or thief or any other kind of criminal, or even as a meddler. ¹⁶However, if you suffer as a Christian, do not be ashamed, but praise God that you bear that name. ¹⁷For it is time for judgment to begin with the family of God; and if it begins with us, what will the outcome be for those who do not obey the gospel of God? ¹⁸And,

"If it is hard for the righteous to
    be saved,
  what will become of the
      ungodly and the sinner?"ᶜ

¹⁹So then, those who suffer according to God's will should commit themselves to their faithful Creator and continue to do good.

To Elders and Young Men

5 To the elders among you, I appeal as a fellow elder, a witness of Christ's sufferings and one who also

PASSAGE: Ephesians 3:1–13; Hebrews 4:14–16
AUTHOR: Joseph M. Scriven

What a Friend!

What a Friend we have in Jesus
    All our sins and griefs to bear;
What a privilege to carry
    Everything to God in prayer.
O what peace we often forfeit,
    O what needless pain we bear;
All because we do not carry
    Everything to God in prayer.

Have we trials and temptations?
    Is there trouble anywhere?
We should never be discouraged;
    Take it to the Lord in prayer.
Can we find a friend so faithful
    Who will all our sorrows share?
Jesus knows our every weakness;
    Take it to the Lord in prayer.

Are we weak and heavy-laden,
    Cumbered with a load of care?
Precious Savior, still our refuge —
    Take it to the Lord in prayer.
Do thy friends despise, forsake thee?
    Take it to the Lord in prayer;
In his arms he'll take and shield thee,
    Thou wilt find a solace there.

Go to page 1590 for your next devotional reading.

will share in the glory to be revealed: ²Be shepherds of God's flock that is under your care, serving as overseers—not because you must, but because you are willing, as God wants you to be; not greedy for money, but eager to serve; ³not lording it over those entrusted to you, but being examples to the flock. ⁴And when the Chief Shepherd appears, you will receive the crown of glory that will never fade away.

⁵Young men, in the same way be submissive to those who are older. All of you, clothe yourselves with humility toward one another, because,

> "God opposes the proud
>   but gives grace to the
>   humble."ᵃ

⁶Humble yourselves, therefore, under God's mighty hand, that he may lift you up in due time. ⁷Cast all your anxiety on him because he cares for you.

⁸Be self-controlled and alert. Your enemy the devil prowls around like a roaring lion looking for someone to devour. ⁹Resist him, standing firm in the faith, because you know that your brothers throughout the world are undergoing the same kind of sufferings.

¹⁰And the God of all grace, who called you to his eternal glory in Christ, after you have suffered a little while, will himself restore you and make you strong, firm and steadfast. ¹¹To him be the power for ever and ever. Amen.

Final Greetings

¹²With the help of Silas,ᵇ whom I regard as a faithful brother, I have written to you briefly, encouraging you and testifying that this is the true grace of God. Stand fast in it.

¹³She who is in Babylon, chosen together with you, sends you her greetings, and so does my son Mark. ¹⁴Greet one another with a kiss of love.

Peace to all of you who are in Christ.

ᵃ5 Prov. 3:34   ᵇ12 Greek *Silvanus*, a variant of *Silas*

*P*eter *followed up his first letter with a second because of false teachers who were disrupting the church. He urged his readers to become firmly grounded in their faith and character. As you read this letter, reflect on your commitment to becoming mature in your faith, and take encouragement as you live in the hope of Jesus' certain return.*

2 PETER

1 Simon Peter, a servant and apostle of Jesus Christ,

To those who through the righteousness of our God and Savior Jesus Christ have received a faith as precious as ours:

²Grace and peace be yours in abundance through the knowledge of God and of Jesus our Lord.

Making One's Calling and Election Sure

³His divine power has given us everything we need for life and godliness through our knowledge of him who called us by his own glory and goodness. ⁴Through these he has given us his very great and precious promises, so that through them you may participate in the divine nature and escape the corruption in the world caused by evil desires. ⁵For this very reason, make every effort to add to your faith goodness; and to goodness, knowledge; ⁶and to

knowledge, self-control; and to self-control, perseverance; and to perseverance, godliness; ⁷and to godliness, brotherly kindness; and to brotherly kindness, love. ⁸For if you possess these qualities in increasing measure, they will keep you from being ineffective and unproductive in your knowledge of our Lord Jesus Christ. ⁹But if anyone does not have them, he is nearsighted and blind, and has forgotten that he has been cleansed from his past sins.

¹⁰Therefore, my brothers, be all the more eager to make your calling and election sure. For if you do these things, you will never fall, ¹¹and you will receive a rich welcome into the eternal kingdom of our Lord and Savior Jesus Christ.

Prophecy of Scripture

¹²So I will always remind you of these things, even though you know them and are firmly established in the truth you now have. ¹³I think it is

VERSE:	AUTHOR:	PASSAGE:
2 Peter 1:4	Charles Stanley	2 Peter 1:1–11

Standing on a Promise

You can rely on the promises of God's Word. The Bible is a book of promises as well as principles. It is freighted with sparkling verses that declare God's intention to graciously bestow good gifts. Some promises are conditional; God will act in a certain way if you obey certain criteria, as in "Give, and it will be given to you" (Luke 6:38). But there are thousands of Scriptures that wait only for a ready faith and a willing spirit to claim them.

Bible promises are assertions of God's love for you. God has assumed full responsibility for meeting your needs and provides nourishing promises as one means of his supply. Claim a promise from God that applies to your particular need. If anxiety has become a part of your lifestyle, Philippians 4:6–7 and Psalm 46:10 are God's answers. You can be certain that God will fulfill his promise when the context of Scripture is not violated, when the answer to the promise glorifies God and demonstrates his character, and when the Holy Spirit quietly impresses on your heart that he is speaking to you through the specific promise . . .

Don't lose heart or be discouraged in the process. It may take days, months, even years for the promise to ripen, but God will keep his word . . .

God's promises are anchors for your soul. They keep you grounded in his love and faithfulness, reminding you of your dependence on him. What God promises, he will fulfill.

ADDITIONAL SCRIPTURE READINGS
Psalm 46; 2 Corinthians 1:18–22

Go to page 1593 for your next devotional reading.

right to refresh your memory as long as I live in the tent of this body, ¹⁴because I know that I will soon put it aside, as our Lord Jesus Christ has made clear to me. ¹⁵And I will make every effort to see that after my departure you will always be able to remember these things.

¹⁶We did not follow cleverly invented stories when we told you about the power and coming of our Lord Jesus Christ, but we were eyewitnesses of his majesty. ¹⁷For he received honor and glory from God the Father when the voice came to him from the Majestic Glory, saying, "This is my Son, whom I love; with him I am well pleased."ᵃ ¹⁸We ourselves heard this voice that came from heaven when we were with him on the sacred mountain.

¹⁹And we have the word of the prophets made more certain, and you will do well to pay attention to it, as to a light shining in a dark place, until the day dawns and the morning star rises in your hearts. ²⁰Above all, you must understand that no prophecy of Scripture came about by the prophet's own interpretation. ²¹For prophecy never had its origin in the will of man, but men spoke from God as they were carried along by the Holy Spirit.

False Teachers and Their Destruction

2 But there were also false prophets among the people, just as there will be false teachers among you. They will secretly introduce destructive heresies, even denying the sovereign Lord who bought them—bringing swift destruction on themselves. ²Many will follow their shameful ways and will bring the way of truth into disrepute. ³In their greed these teachers will exploit you with stories they have made up. Their condemnation has long been hanging over them, and their destruction has not been sleeping.

⁴For if God did not spare angels when they sinned, but sent them to hell,ᵇ putting them into gloomy dungeonsᶜ to be held for judgment; ⁵if he did not spare the ancient world when he brought the flood on its ungodly people, but protected Noah, a preacher of righteousness, and seven others; ⁶if he condemned the cities of Sodom and Gomorrah by burning them to ashes, and made them an example of what is going to happen to the ungodly; ⁷and if he rescued Lot, a righteous man, who was distressed by the filthy lives of lawless men ⁸(for that righteous man, living among them day after day, was tormented in his righteous soul by the lawless deeds he saw and heard)— ⁹if this is so, then the Lord knows how to rescue godly men from trials and to hold the unrighteous for the day of judgment, while continuing their punishment.ᵈ ¹⁰This is especially true of those who follow the corrupt desire of the sinful natureᵉ and despise authority.

Bold and arrogant, these men are not afraid to slander celestial beings; ¹¹yet even angels, although they are stronger and more powerful, do not bring slanderous accusations against such beings in the presence of the Lord. ¹²But these men blaspheme in matters they do not understand. They are like brute beasts, creatures of instinct, born only to be caught and destroyed, and like beasts they too will perish.

¹³They will be paid back with harm for the harm they have done. Their idea of pleasure is to carouse in broad daylight. They are blots and blemishes, reveling in their pleasures while they feast with you.ᶠ ¹⁴With eyes full of adultery, they never stop sinning; they seduce the unstable; they are experts in greed—an accursed brood! ¹⁵They have left the straight way and wandered off to follow the way of Balaam son of Beor,

ᵃ17 Matt. 17:5; Mark 9:7; Luke 9:35   ᵇ4 Greek *Tartarus*   ᶜ4 Some manuscripts *into chains of darkness*   ᵈ9 Or *unrighteous for punishment until the day of judgment*   ᵉ10 Or *the flesh*   ᶠ13 Some manuscripts *in their love feasts*

who loved the wages of wickedness. [16]But he was rebuked for his wrongdoing by a donkey—a beast without speech—who spoke with a man's voice and restrained the prophet's madness.

[17]These men are springs without water and mists driven by a storm. Blackest darkness is reserved for them. [18]For they mouth empty, boastful words and, by appealing to the lustful desires of sinful human nature, they entice people who are just escaping from those who live in error. [19]They promise them freedom, while they themselves are slaves of depravity—for a man is a slave to whatever has mastered him. [20]If they have escaped the corruption of the world by knowing our Lord and Savior Jesus Christ and are again entangled in it and overcome, they are worse off at the end than they were at the beginning. [21]It would have been better for them not to have known the way of righteousness, than to have known it and then to turn their backs on the sacred command that was passed on to them. [22]Of them the proverbs are true: "A dog returns to its vomit,"[a] and, "A sow that is washed goes back to her wallowing in the mud."

The Day of the Lord

3 Dear friends, this is now my second letter to you. I have written both of them as reminders to stimulate you to wholesome thinking. [2]I want you to recall the words spoken in the past by the holy prophets and the command given by our Lord and Savior through your apostles.

[3]First of all, you must understand that in the last days scoffers will come, scoffing and following their own evil desires. [4]They will say, "Where is this 'coming' he promised? Ever since our fathers died, everything goes on as it has since the beginning of creation." [5]But they deliberately forget that long ago by God's word the heavens existed and the earth was formed out of water and by water. [6]By these waters also the world of that time was deluged and destroyed. [7]By the same word the present heavens and earth are reserved for fire, being kept for the day of judgment and destruction of ungodly men.

[8]But do not forget this one thing, dear friends: With the Lord a day is like a thousand years, and a thousand years are like a day. [9]The Lord is not slow in keeping his promise, as some understand slowness. He is patient with you, not wanting anyone to perish, but everyone to come to repentance.

[10]But the day of the Lord will come like a thief. The heavens will disappear with a roar; the elements will be destroyed by fire, and the earth and everything in it will be laid bare.[b]

[11]Since everything will be destroyed in this way, what kind of people ought you to be? You ought to live holy and godly lives [12]as you look forward to the day of God and speed its coming.[c] That day will bring about the destruction of the heavens by fire, and the elements will melt in the heat. [13]But in keeping with his promise we are looking forward to a new heaven and a new earth, the home of righteousness.

[14]So then, dear friends, since you are looking forward to this, make every effort to be found spotless, blameless and at peace with him. [15]Bear in mind that our Lord's patience means salvation, just as our dear brother Paul also wrote you with the wisdom that God gave him. [16]He writes the same way in all his letters, speaking in them of these matters. His letters contain some things that are hard to understand, which ignorant and unstable people distort, as they do the other Scriptures, to their own destruction.

[17]Therefore, dear friends, since you

already know this, be on your guard so that you may not be carried away by the error of lawless men and fall from your secure position. ¹⁸But grow in the grace and knowledge of our Lord and Savior Jesus Christ. To him be glory both now and forever! Amen.

VERSE:	AUTHOR:	PASSAGE:
2 Peter 3:13	Dirk R. Buursma	2 Peter 3:8–18

Lord of Hopes and Dreams

"I sure hope she feels better soon." "I hope to make it out there tomorrow." "I hope my children love the Lord." "I hope I stay healthy this winter."

Lots and lots of hopes. Some come true. Others don't. Some are vitally important. Others are trivial.

What would life be without hopes and dreams? We need hope to live. We need hope to survive. We need hope to keep going — to find healing from the failures, hurts and sins of the past, to face new mornings, to face uncertain futures.

Lord, will you help me abandon today the false hopes in which I have too long trusted? Money. A bigger home. Knowledge. Myself. Friends. Hoping against hope that they — or someone or something else — will provide me with meaning, purpose, happiness.

Will you give me the power to hear your promise that a bright new world is coming? A world where righteousness lives, where love reigns, where peace and justice rule. And knowing that my future hopes and dreams are safe with you, I can live with contentment and joy, Lord of my past, my present and my future.

ADDITIONAL SCRIPTURE READINGS
Romans 8:18–25; Revelation 21:1–5

Go to page 1595 for your next devotional reading.

Using many of the same images he highlighted in his Gospel (walking in the truth, knowing the truth, loving one another), John wrote this first letter to set the record straight about who Jesus was. As you read this letter, take to heart John's words about God's love as an example for you to follow in your relationships with others. Rejoice, too, that God gives you assurance of eternal life if you believe in Jesus.

1 JOHN

The Word of Life

1 That which was from the beginning, which we have heard, which we have seen with our eyes, which we have looked at and our hands have touched—this we proclaim concerning the Word of life. ²The life appeared; we have seen it and testify to it, and we proclaim to you the eternal life, which was with the Father and has appeared to us. ³We proclaim to you what we have seen and heard, so that you also may have fellowship with us. And our fellowship is with the Father and with his Son, Jesus Christ. ⁴We write this to make our*ᵃ* joy complete.

Walking in the Light

⁵This is the message we have heard from him and declare to you: God is light; in him there is no darkness at all. ⁶If we claim to have fellowship with him yet walk in the darkness, we lie and do not live by the truth. ⁷But if we walk in the light, as he is in the light, we have fellowship with one another, and the blood of Jesus, his Son, purifies us from all*ᵇ* sin.

⁸If we claim to be without sin, we deceive ourselves and the truth is not in us. ⁹If we confess our sins, he is faithful and just and will forgive us our sins and purify us from all unrighteousness. ¹⁰If we claim we have not sinned, we make him out to be a liar and his word has no place in our lives.

2 My dear children, I write this to you so that you will not sin. But if anybody does sin, we have one who speaks to the Father in our defense—Jesus Christ, the Righteous One. ²He

ᵃ4 Some manuscripts *your*   ᵇ7 Or *every*

is the atoning sacrifice for our sins, and not only for ours but also for[a] the sins of the whole world.

³We know that we have come to know him if we obey his commands. ⁴The man who says, "I know him," but does not do what he commands is a liar, and the truth is not in him. ⁵But if anyone obeys his word, God's love[b] is truly made complete in him. This is how we know we are in him:

⁶Whoever claims to live in him must walk as Jesus did.

⁷Dear friends, I am not writing you a new command but an old one, which you have had since the beginning. This old command is the message you have heard. ⁸Yet I am writing you a new command; its truth is seen in him and you, because the darkness is passing and the true light is already shining.

[a]2 Or *He is the one who turns aside God's wrath, taking away our sins, and not only ours but also*
[b]5 Or *word, love for God*

VERSE: AUTHOR: PASSAGE:
1 John 1:9   Walter Wangerin, Jr.   1 John 1:5 — 2:14

Seeing Sin

The sins we see easiest in others we learned first in ourselves; we know their behavior and their signs from the inside. Though they deny the personal fault, gossips spot gossips a mile away, as wolves know wolves by a familial scent. Is he neglectful? Impatient? Judgmental? Self-indulgent? Jealous? Scornful? Abusive? So, sometime and somewhere, were you—

Recall: that if you did not commit the sin against your spouse, yet you did, once, against your parents, your adolescent classmates, your friends, your colleagues at work, the teller in the bank, another race, another class of people, the poor. Or you did in your heart what you didn't have the temerity to do openly with your hands.

But recall these sins not to torment yourself, rather to rejoice in the forgiveness God has given you—you personally—since God was always at the other end of your sin, and did not return judgment for iniquity, but mercy.

ADDITIONAL SCRIPTURE READINGS
Psalm 32; Hebrews 10:15–23

Go to page 1596 for your next devotional reading.

VERSE: AUTHOR: PASSAGE:
1 John 3:2   Don Anderson   1 John 2:20 – 3:6

To Become Like Christ

It is the Father's purpose, when we come to know Jesus
Christ as Savior, to begin a work in our lives using every
means possible to make us more like his Son (2 Corinthians 3:18; 1 John 3:2). The believer's ultimate goal?
Simple: to cooperate with the Father's purpose of making us more like his Son. Cooperation with the Father is
a lifelong process that does not end with retirement. Our
pursuit of the spiritual disciplines should never stop.

Think about it. As we near the finish line, we have the
opportunity to cooperate even more fully with God than
earlier in our lives when other demands weighed heavily
upon us. We've got the time! Yesterday's priorities no
longer distract us. Earning a living no longer consumes
us. Retirement can be a marvelous occasion for God to
put the finishing touches on our lives so that the world
will see Christ in us . . .

In his intimate letter to the Philippians, Paul outlined
ten goals for godly living to help us demonstrate authen-
tic Christlikeness: loving with the love of Jesus; living
for the glory of God; confronting life one day at a time;
remaining stable in the storm of suffering; being a servant; knowing Christ intimately; keeping the joy; maintaining an effective prayer life; planning financially for a
Christlike finish; depending upon the adequacy of Christ
all the way home.

ADDITIONAL SCRIPTURE READINGS
Philippians 1; Philippians 3

Go to page 1598 for your next devotional reading.

⁹Anyone who claims to be in the light but hates his brother is still in the darkness. ¹⁰Whoever loves his brother lives in the light, and there is nothing in him*ᵃ* to make him stumble. ¹¹But whoever hates his brother is in the darkness and walks around in the darkness; he does not know where he is going, because the darkness has blinded him.

¹²I write to you, dear children,
    because your sins have been
        forgiven on account of his
        name.
¹³I write to you, fathers,
    because you have known him
        who is from the beginning.
I write to you, young men,
    because you have overcome the
        evil one.
I write to you, dear children,
    because you have known the
        Father.
¹⁴I write to you, fathers,
    because you have known him
        who is from the beginning.
I write to you, young men,
    because you are strong,
    and the word of God lives in
        you,
    and you have overcome the evil
        one.

Do Not Love the World

¹⁵Do not love the world or anything in the world. If anyone loves the world, the love of the Father is not in him. ¹⁶For everything in the world—the cravings of sinful man, the lust of his eyes and the boasting of what he has and does—comes not from the Father but from the world. ¹⁷The world and its desires pass away, but the man who does the will of God lives forever.

Warning Against Antichrists

¹⁸Dear children, this is the last hour; and as you have heard that the antichrist is coming, even now many antichrists have come. This is how we know it is the last hour. ¹⁹They went out from us, but they did not really belong to us. For if they had belonged to us, they would have remained with us; but their going showed that none of them belonged to us.

²⁰But you have an anointing from the Holy One, and all of you know the truth.*ᵇ* ²¹I do not write to you because you do not know the truth, but because you do know it and because no lie comes from the truth. ²²Who is the liar? It is the man who denies that Jesus is the Christ. Such a man is the antichrist—he denies the Father and the Son. ²³No one who denies the Son has the Father; whoever acknowledges the Son has the Father also.

²⁴See that what you have heard from the beginning remains in you. If it does, you also will remain in the Son and in the Father. ²⁵And this is what he promised us—even eternal life.

²⁶I am writing these things to you about those who are trying to lead you astray. ²⁷As for you, the anointing you received from him remains in you, and you do not need anyone to teach you. But as his anointing teaches you about all things and as that anointing is real, not counterfeit—just as it has taught you, remain in him.

Children of God

²⁸And now, dear children, continue in him, so that when he appears we may be confident and unashamed before him at his coming.

²⁹If you know that he is righteous, you know that everyone who does what is right has been born of him.

3 How great is the love the Father has lavished on us, that we should be called children of God! And that is what we are! The reason the world does not know us is that it did not know him. ²Dear friends, now we are children of God, and what we will be has not yet been made known. But we know that when he appears,*ᶜ* we shall be like him, for we shall see him as he is. ³Everyone who has this hope

---

*ᵃ*10 Or *it*   *ᵇ*20 Some manuscripts *and you know all things*   *ᶜ*2 Or *when it is made known*

VERSE:	AUTHORS:	PASSAGE:
1 John 3:18	Jerry Schreur & Jack Schreur	1 John 3:11–24

An Unflagging Commitment

Grandparents cannot express their love too much, too often, or in too many ways to their wonder-years grandchildren. We are not spoiling them when we give them constant reassurances of our love. On the contrary, we will find it easier to say no to them because they already know that we love them.

Creative grandparents make an unflagging commitment to finding new ways to say "I love you." We accept this Biblical principle as our mandate: "Dear children, let us not love with words or tongue but with actions and in truth" (1 John 3:18).

One way we can do it is by mail. When grandparents are on a vacation, take the time to send a postcard to each of your grandchildren. Make sure to mail them separately. Preschool children seldom receive personal mail, and they are thrilled when Mom or Dad reads a card sent personally to them . . .

Another way creative grandparents show their love is by reading to their grandchildren. In a world of, "Hurry up . . . Come on, we're late," grandparents can slow down to be with their grandchildren. We have the time to read them their favorite story — again, and again, and again.

We can also converse with them and listen to them. Children have a profound need to be spoken to and heard. We build trust and self-acceptance in our grandchildren simply by listening as they chatter on about anything and everything that pops into their active little brains.

ADDITIONAL SCRIPTURE READINGS
John 15:1–17; Romans 12:9–13

Go to page 1600 for your next devotional reading.

in him purifies himself, just as he is pure. ⁴Everyone who sins breaks the law; in fact, sin is lawlessness. ⁵But you know that he appeared so that he might take away our sins. And in him is no sin. ⁶No one who lives in him keeps on sinning. No one who continues to sin has either seen him or known him.

⁷Dear children, do not let anyone lead you astray. He who does what is right is righteous, just as he is righteous. ⁸He who does what is sinful is of the devil, because the devil has been sinning from the beginning. The reason the Son of God appeared was to destroy the devil's work. ⁹No one who is born of God will continue to sin, because God's seed remains in him; he cannot go on sinning, because he has been born of God. ¹⁰This is how we know who the children of God are and who the children of the devil are: Anyone who does not do what is right is not a child of God; nor is anyone who does not love his brother.

Love One Another

¹¹This is the message you heard from the beginning: We should love one another. ¹²Do not be like Cain, who belonged to the evil one and murdered his brother. And why did he murder him? Because his own actions were evil and his brother's were righteous. ¹³Do not be surprised, my brothers, if the world hates you. ¹⁴We know that we have passed from death to life, because we love our brothers. Anyone who does not love remains in death. ¹⁵Anyone who hates his brother is a murderer, and you know that no murderer has eternal life in him.

¹⁶This is how we know what love is: Jesus Christ laid down his life for us. And we ought to lay down our lives for our brothers. ¹⁷If anyone has material possessions and sees his brother in need but has no pity on him, how can the love of God be in him? ¹⁸Dear children, let us not love with words or tongue but with actions and in truth. ¹⁹This then is how we know that we belong to the truth, and how we set our hearts at rest in his presence ²⁰whenever our hearts condemn us. For God is greater than our hearts, and he knows everything.

²¹Dear friends, if our hearts do not condemn us, we have confidence before God ²²and receive from him anything we ask, because we obey his commands and do what pleases him. ²³And this is his command: to believe in the name of his Son, Jesus Christ, and to love one another as he commanded us. ²⁴Those who obey his commands live in him, and he in them. And this is how we know that he lives in us: We know it by the Spirit he gave us.

Test the Spirits

4 Dear friends, do not believe every spirit, but test the spirits to see whether they are from God, because many false prophets have gone out into the world. ²This is how you can recognize the Spirit of God: Every spirit that acknowledges that Jesus Christ has come in the flesh is from God, ³but every spirit that does not acknowledge Jesus is not from God. This is the spirit of the antichrist, which you have heard is coming and even now is already in the world.

⁴You, dear children, are from God and have overcome them, because the one who is in you is greater than the one who is in the world. ⁵They are from the world and therefore speak from the viewpoint of the world, and the world listens to them. ⁶We are from God, and whoever knows God listens to us; but whoever is not from God does not listen to us. This is how we recognize the Spirit[a] of truth and the spirit of falsehood.

God's Love and Ours

⁷Dear friends, let us love one another, for love comes from God. Everyone who loves has been born of God and knows God. ⁸Whoever does not

---

a6 Or spirit

PASSAGE: Ephesians 3:14–21; 1 John 4:7–21

AUTHOR: Horatius Bonar

O Love of God

O love of God, how strong and true,
Eternal and yet ever new,
Uncomprehended and unbought,
Beyond all knowledge and all thought.

O heavenly love, how precious still!
In days of weariness and ill,
In nights of pain and helplessness,
To heal, to comfort, and to bless.

O love of God, our shield and stay
Through all the perils of our way;
Eternal love, in thee we rest,
Forever safe, forever blest.

Go to page 1604 for your next devotional reading.

love does not know God, because God is love. ⁹This is how God showed his love among us: He sent his one and only Son*a* into the world that we might live through him. ¹⁰This is love: not that we loved God, but that he loved us and sent his Son as an atoning sacrifice for*b* our sins. ¹¹Dear friends, since God so loved us, we also ought to love one another. ¹²No one has ever seen God; but if we love one another, God lives in us and his love is made complete in us.

¹³We know that we live in him and he in us, because he has given us of his Spirit. ¹⁴And we have seen and testify that the Father has sent his Son to be the Savior of the world. ¹⁵If anyone acknowledges that Jesus is the Son of God, God lives in him and he in God. ¹⁶And so we know and rely on the love God has for us.

God is love. Whoever lives in love lives in God, and God in him. ¹⁷In this way, love is made complete among us so that we will have confidence on the day of judgment, because in this world we are like him. ¹⁸There is no fear in love. But perfect love drives out fear, because fear has to do with punishment. The one who fears is not made perfect in love.

¹⁹We love because he first loved us. ²⁰If anyone says, "I love God," yet hates his brother, he is a liar. For anyone who does not love his brother, whom he has seen, cannot love God, whom he has not seen. ²¹And he has given us this command: Whoever loves God must also love his brother.

Faith in the Son of God

5 Everyone who believes that Jesus is the Christ is born of God, and everyone who loves the father loves his child as well. ²This is how we know that we love the children of God: by loving God and carrying out his commands. ³This is love for God: to obey his commands. And his commands are not burdensome, ⁴for everyone born of God overcomes the world. This is the victory that has overcome the world, even our faith. ⁵Who is it that overcomes the world? Only he who believes that Jesus is the Son of God.

⁶This is the one who came by water and blood—Jesus Christ. He did not come by water only, but by water and blood. And it is the Spirit who testifies, because the Spirit is the truth. ⁷For there are three that testify: ⁸the*c* Spirit, the water and the blood; and the three are in agreement. ⁹We accept man's testimony, but God's testimony is greater because it is the testimony of God, which he has given about his Son. ¹⁰Anyone who believes in the Son of God has this testimony in his heart. Anyone who does not believe God has made him out to be a liar, because he has not believed the testimony God has given about his Son. ¹¹And this is the testimony: God has given us eternal life, and this life is in his Son. ¹²He who has the Son has life; he who does not have the Son of God does not have life.

Concluding Remarks

¹³I write these things to you who believe in the name of the Son of God so that you may know that you have eternal life. ¹⁴This is the confidence we have in approaching God: that if we ask anything according to his will, he hears us. ¹⁵And if we know that he hears us—whatever we ask—we know that we have what we asked of him.

¹⁶If anyone sees his brother commit a sin that does not lead to death, he should pray and God will give him life. I refer to those whose sin does not lead to death. There is a sin that leads to death. I am not saying that he

a9 Or his only begotten Son   *b10 Or as the one who would turn aside his wrath, taking away*
c7,8 Late manuscripts of the Vulgate testify in heaven: the Father, the Word and the Holy Spirit, and these three are one. ⁸And there are three that testify on earth: the (not found in any Greek manuscript before the sixteenth century)

should pray about that. ¹⁷All wrongdoing is sin, and there is sin that does not lead to death.

¹⁸We know that anyone born of God does not continue to sin; the one who was born of God keeps him safe, and the evil one cannot harm him. ¹⁹We know that we are children of God, and that the whole world is under the control of the evil one. ²⁰We know also that the Son of God has come and has given us understanding, so that we may know him who is true. And we are in him who is true—even in his Son Jesus Christ. He is the true God and eternal life.

²¹Dear children, keep yourselves from idols.

*J*ohn wrote this second letter to warn Christians to stand firm and not allow false teachers to shake their faith. As you read this book, make a commitment to hold on to the essentials of the Christian faith, no matter how many other voices beckon you to follow their way of life.

2 JOHN

¹The elder,

To the chosen lady and her children, whom I love in the truth—and not I only, but also all who know the truth— ²because of the truth, which lives in us and will be with us forever:

³Grace, mercy and peace from God the Father and from Jesus Christ, the Father's Son, will be with us in truth and love.

⁴It has given me great joy to find some of your children walking in the truth, just as the Father commanded us. ⁵And now, dear lady, I am not writing you a new command but one we have had from the beginning. I ask that we love one another. ⁶And this is love: that we walk in obedience to his commands. As you have heard from the beginning, his command is that you walk in love.

⁷Many deceivers, who do not ac-knowledge Jesus Christ as coming in the flesh, have gone out into the world. Any such person is the deceiver and the antichrist. ⁸Watch out that you do not lose what you have worked for, but that you may be rewarded fully. ⁹Anyone who runs ahead and does not continue in the teaching of Christ does not have God; whoever continues in the teaching has both the Father and the Son. ¹⁰If anyone comes to you and does not bring this teaching, do not take him into your house or welcome him. ¹¹Anyone who welcomes him shares in his wicked work.

¹²I have much to write to you, but I do not want to use paper and ink. Instead, I hope to visit you and talk with you face to face, so that our joy may be complete.

¹³The children of your chosen sister send their greetings.

VERSE:	AUTHOR:	PASSAGE:
2 John 1	Louis M. Tamminga	2 John 1–13

The Chosen Lady

Christians know the joy of warm personal relationships. They meet one another, get to know each other, appreciate each other, are introduced to other believers, perform tasks together and later treasure the good memories of it all.

Every once in a while the Bible affords us a glimpse of such practical Christian living. Read the second letter of John carefully. One day John met some visitors in church whose mother, it turned out, he had known well in another place (verse 4) . . . There was a lot of news to be exchanged and memories of the past were discussed with relish. John was happy with the good tidings, but especially with the fact that her children had turned out to be fine Christians. And so he decided to write the mother of his visitors a letter for old times' sake, but above all for the Lord's sake. Though the letter is brief, it is full of solid substance. He urged the chosen lady to remain vigorous in faith, to be alert against false teachings and to stay close to Christ . . . He put his pen down and felt happy that their friendship in the Lord had been strengthened again.

Thus we are reminded that our faith is not only a matter of conviction of the heart but that it flourishes in actual situations, in common tasks, in circles of people with names, in relationships of love, appreciation, understanding and concern. They are the strands that form the fabric of life. And as the years go by, we treasure it all as God's gift to us. In his letter to the chosen lady, John gives the honor to Christ, in whose grace all life is sacred.

ADDITIONAL SCRIPTURE READINGS
Romans 16; 1 Corinthians 13

Go to page 1606 for your next devotional reading.

*J*ohn wrote this third letter to commend a church leader for his hospitality and to warn against another leader who was strong-willed and cruel. As you read this letter, ask God to fill you with a spirit of hospitality and gentleness toward others, so that others may speak well of you and be drawn to your loving Lord.

3 JOHN

¹The elder,

To my dear friend Gaius, whom I love in the truth.

²Dear friend, I pray that you may enjoy good health and that all may go well with you, even as your soul is getting along well. ³It gave me great joy to have some brothers come and tell about your faithfulness to the truth and how you continue to walk in the truth. ⁴I have no greater joy than to hear that my children are walking in the truth.

⁵Dear friend, you are faithful in what you are doing for the brothers, even though they are strangers to you. ⁶They have told the church about your love. You will do well to send them on their way in a manner worthy of God. ⁷It was for the sake of the Name that they went out, receiving no help from the pagans. ⁸We ought therefore to show hospitality to such men so that we may work together for the truth.

⁹I wrote to the church, but Diotrephes, who loves to be first, will have nothing to do with us. ¹⁰So if I come, I will call attention to what he is doing, gossiping maliciously about us. Not satisfied with that, he refuses to welcome the brothers. He also stops those who want to do so and puts them out of the church.

¹¹Dear friend, do not imitate what is evil but what is good. Anyone who does what is good is from God. Anyone who does what is evil has not seen God. ¹²Demetrius is well spoken of by everyone—and even by the truth itself. We also speak well of him, and you know that our testimony is true.

¹³I have much to write you, but I do not want to do so with pen and ink. ¹⁴I hope to see you soon, and we will talk face to face.

Peace to you. The friends here send their greetings. Greet the friends there by name.

VERSE:	AUTHOR:	PASSAGE:
3 John 12	Gigi Graham Tchividjian	3 John 1–14

The Example

My grandfather never disappointed me as a man or as a Christian. Until the day he died, he set an example of balanced, fun-loving, disciplined, godly living.

When I examine my own life, I wonder what my children see. Do they see a concern for others, or do they see criticism, cynicism and compromise? Do the things of eternal and spiritual value have priority in my life, or am I too preoccupied with the material and temporal things? . . . Do they discern a sense of peace and serenity in our home, or strife and tension? Do I walk my talk? Is there a noticeable difference in my life? Do they perceive acceptance, love and understanding? Do they experience the results of my prayers? Is the fruit of the Spirit exemplified in my life?

Lord, "I will be careful to lead a blameless life — when will you come to me? I will walk in my house with blameless heart" (Psalm 101:2).

ADDITIONAL SCRIPTURE READINGS
Galatians 5:22–26; 1 Peter 5:1–11
Go to page 1608 for your next devotional reading.

*J*ude, a brother of Jesus and James, wrote this letter to warn against subversive teaching that lured Christians into immoral living. As you read this book, dedicate yourself to resting in God's love for you, as you hold to the truth, and be comforted to know that God will so keep you that one day you will stand in his presence without fault and with great joy.

JUDE

¹Jude, a servant of Jesus Christ and a brother of James,

To those who have been called, who are loved by God the Father and kept by*a* Jesus Christ:

²Mercy, peace and love be yours in abundance.

The Sin and Doom of Godless Men

³Dear friends, although I was very eager to write to you about the salvation we share, I felt I had to write and urge you to contend for the faith that was once for all entrusted to the saints. ⁴For certain men whose condemnation was written about*b* long ago have secretly slipped in among you. They are godless men, who change the grace of our God into a license for immorality and deny Jesus Christ our only Sovereign and Lord.

⁵Though you already know all this, I want to remind you that the Lord*c* delivered his people out of Egypt, but later destroyed those who did not believe. ⁶And the angels who did not keep their positions of authority but abandoned their own home—these he has kept in darkness, bound with everlasting chains for judgment on the great Day. ⁷In a similar way, Sodom and Gomorrah and the surrounding towns gave themselves up to sexual immorality and perversion. They serve as an example of those who suffer the punishment of eternal fire.

⁸In the very same way, these dreamers pollute their own bodies, reject authority and slander celestial beings. ⁹But even the archangel Michael, when he was disputing with the devil about the body of Moses, did not dare to bring a slanderous accusation against him, but said, "The Lord rebuke you!" ¹⁰Yet these men speak abusively against whatever they do not understand; and what

---

*a*1 Or *for; or in*   *b*4 Or *men who were marked out for condemnation*   *c*5 Some early manuscripts *Jesus*

VERSE:	AUTHOR:	PASSAGE:
Jude 24	Millie Stamm	Jude 17–25

To Him Who Is Able

We begin our Christian walk with faltering steps. We encounter obstacles that cause us to stumble. Burdens become so heavy, we almost go down under their weight. Our paths are often rough and our enemy strong. We need help.

We have a Guide who is able to keep us from falling. A key word in this verse is *keep*. It means to protect, guide, watch over. The Bible says, "For I am the LORD your God, who takes hold of your right hand and says to you, Do not fear. I will help you" (Isaiah 41:13). We can be thankful that he holds our hand. If we had to hold onto his, we might lose our grip and fall.

At times, our paths may take us up rocky mountains. Mountain climbers often rope themselves together, so that if an inexperienced climber should slip, the skilled climber could hold him steady and break his fall. In our Christian climb, we are *tied* to our Guide, the One who never misses a step. With him, we can scale the dangerous mountain cliffs before us in safety. The Bible says, "He makes my feet like the feet of a deer; he enables me to stand on the heights" (Psalm 18:33).

If we stumble or fall, he is there to lift us up and put us back on our feet. "The LORD upholds all those who fall and lifts up all who are bowed down" (Psalm 145:14).

And one day Christ will present us *without fault* to his heavenly Father ... Through our position in Christ, we can stand before him perfect and complete. What a day!

ADDITIONAL SCRIPTURE READINGS
Psalm 18:25–36; Isaiah 41:11–16

Go to page 1611 for your next devotional reading.

things they do understand by instinct, like unreasoning animals—these are the very things that destroy them.

¹¹Woe to them! They have taken the way of Cain; they have rushed for profit into Balaam's error; they have been destroyed in Korah's rebellion.

¹²These men are blemishes at your love feasts, eating with you without the slightest qualm—shepherds who feed only themselves. They are clouds without rain, blown along by the wind; autumn trees, without fruit and uprooted—twice dead. ¹³They are wild waves of the sea, foaming up their shame; wandering stars, for whom blackest darkness has been reserved forever.

¹⁴Enoch, the seventh from Adam, prophesied about these men: "See, the Lord is coming with thousands upon thousands of his holy ones ¹⁵to judge everyone, and to convict all the ungodly of all the ungodly acts they have done in the ungodly way, and of all the harsh words ungodly sinners have spoken against him." ¹⁶These men are grumblers and faultfinders; they follow their own evil desires; they boast about themselves and flatter others for their own advantage.

A Call to Persevere

¹⁷But, dear friends, remember what the apostles of our Lord Jesus Christ foretold. ¹⁸They said to you, "In the last times there will be scoffers who will follow their own ungodly desires." ¹⁹These are the men who divide you, who follow mere natural instincts and do not have the Spirit.

²⁰But you, dear friends, build yourselves up in your most holy faith and pray in the Holy Spirit. ²¹Keep yourselves in God's love as you wait for the mercy of our Lord Jesus Christ to bring you to eternal life.

²²Be merciful to those who doubt; ²³snatch others from the fire and save them; to others show mercy, mixed with fear—hating even the clothing stained by corrupted flesh.

Doxology

²⁴To him who is able to keep you from falling and to present you before his glorious presence without fault and with great joy— ²⁵to the only God our Savior be glory, majesty, power and authority, through Jesus Christ our Lord, before all ages, now and forevermore! Amen.

...T... *he apostle John wrote this book while on the island of Patmos. In it he records a graphic and ultimately glorious vision of Jesus' victory over sin, evil and death and a wonderful description of the joy and freedom we will experience in heaven. As you read this book, let its message of hope penetrate your heart: God and good will win over evil. Rejoice in the promise of life with Jesus that will never end.*

REVELATION

Prologue

1 The revelation of Jesus Christ, which God gave him to show his servants what must soon take place. He made it known by sending his angel to his servant John, ²who testifies to everything he saw—that is, the word of God and the testimony of Jesus Christ. ³Blessed is the one who reads the words of this prophecy, and blessed are those who hear it and take to heart what is written in it, because the time is near.

Greetings and Doxology

⁴John,

To the seven churches in the province of Asia:

Grace and peace to you from him who is, and who was, and who is to come, and from the seven spirits*a* be-
fore his throne, ⁵and from Jesus Christ, who is the faithful witness, the firstborn from the dead, and the ruler of the kings of the earth.

To him who loves us and has freed us from our sins by his blood, ⁶and has made us to be a kingdom and priests to serve his God and Father— to him be glory and power for ever and ever! Amen.

⁷Look, he is coming with the
        clouds,
    and every eye will see him,
    even those who pierced him;
    and all the peoples of the earth
        will mourn because of him.
            So shall it be! Amen.

⁸"I am the Alpha and the Omega," says the Lord God, "who is, and who was, and who is to come, the Almighty."

a4 Or the sevenfold Spirit

One Like a Son of Man

⁹I, John, your brother and companion in the suffering and kingdom and patient endurance that are ours in Jesus, was on the island of Patmos because of the word of God and the testimony of Jesus. ¹⁰On the Lord's Day I was in the Spirit, and I heard behind me a loud voice like a trumpet, ¹¹which said: "Write on a scroll what you see and send it to the seven churches: to Ephesus, Smyrna, Pergamum, Thyatira, Sardis, Philadelphia and Laodicea."

¹²I turned around to see the voice that was speaking to me. And when I turned I saw seven golden lampstands, ¹³and among the lampstands

VERSE:	AUTHOR:	PASSAGE:
Revelation 1:6	Ben Patterson	Revelation 1:1–8

He Has Made Us to Serve

We live in a society that worships retirement. How odd that we should spend all our lives doing something so we don't have to do it anymore. That is not to say that we should not retire, but we should be cautious about retirement. We should look critically at the notion that the good life is to be rewarded for long years of labor with an extended season of recreation and play in our twilight years. We should see retirement instead as perhaps a time to slow down, but not to stop what we are doing, if health permits — or perhaps a time to embark on a brand new field of endeavor altogether!

I love what my father- and mother-in-law have done with their retirement. Everything they did before, they continue to do in retirement. The only change is that they now do these things at their own pace and in the proportions they desire. They are having a lot of fun doing everything they always did before retirement. The only difference is that now they don't have to get up and go to work every day . . . Now they do all they did before because they want to be of service.

ADDITIONAL SCRIPTURE READINGS
Galatians 5:1–15; 1 Peter 4:7–11
Go to page 1613 for your next devotional reading.

was someone "like a son of man,"[a] dressed in a robe reaching down to his feet and with a golden sash around his chest. [14]His head and hair were white like wool, as white as snow, and his eyes were like blazing fire. [15]His feet were like bronze glowing in a furnace, and his voice was like the sound of rushing waters. [16]In his right hand he held seven stars, and out of his mouth came a sharp double-edged sword. His face was like the sun shining in all its brilliance.

[17]When I saw him, I fell at his feet as though dead. Then he placed his right hand on me and said: "Do not be afraid. I am the First and the Last. [18]I am the Living One; I was dead, and behold I am alive for ever and ever! And I hold the keys of death and Hades.

[19]"Write, therefore, what you have seen, what is now and what will take place later. [20]The mystery of the seven stars that you saw in my right hand and of the seven golden lampstands is this: The seven stars are the angels[b] of the seven churches, and the seven lampstands are the seven churches.

To the Church in Ephesus

2 "To the angel[c] of the church in Ephesus write:

These are the words of him who holds the seven stars in his right hand and walks among the seven golden lampstands: [2]I know your deeds, your hard work and your perseverance. I know that you cannot tolerate wicked men, that you have tested those who claim to be apostles but are not, and have found them false. [3]You have persevered and have endured hardships for my name, and have not grown weary.

[4]Yet I hold this against you: You have forsaken your first love. [5]Remember the height from which you have fallen! Repent and do the things you did at first. If you do not repent, I will come to you and remove your lampstand from its place. [6]But you have this in your favor: You hate the practices of the Nicolaitans, which I also hate.

[7]He who has an ear, let him hear what the Spirit says to the churches. To him who overcomes, I will give the right to eat from the tree of life, which is in the paradise of God.

To the Church in Smyrna

[8]"To the angel of the church in Smyrna write:

These are the words of him who is the First and the Last, who died and came to life again. [9]I know your afflictions and your poverty—yet you are rich! I know the slander of those who say they are Jews and are not, but are a synagogue of Satan. [10]Do not be afraid of what you are about to suffer. I tell you, the devil will put some of you in prison to test you, and you will suffer persecution for ten days. Be faithful, even to the point of death, and I will give you the crown of life.

[11]He who has an ear, let him hear what the Spirit says to the churches. He who overcomes will not be hurt at all by the second death.

To the Church in Pergamum

[12]"To the angel of the church in Pergamum write:

These are the words of him who has the sharp, double-edged sword. [13]I know where you live—where Satan has his throne. Yet you remain true to my name. You did not renounce your faith in me, even in the days of Antipas, my faithful witness, who was put to death in your city—where Satan lives.

---

[a]13 Daniel 7:13   [b]20 Or *messengers*   [c]1 Or *messenger*; also in verses 8, 12 and 18

¹⁴Nevertheless, I have a few things against you: You have people there who hold to the teaching of Balaam, who taught Balak to entice the Israelites to sin by eating food sacrificed to idols and by committing sexual immorality. ¹⁵Likewise you also have those who hold to the teaching of the Nicolaitans. ¹⁶Repent therefore! Otherwise, I will soon come to you and will fight

VERSE: AUTHOR: PASSAGE:
Revelation 2:17   Peter J. Kreeft   Revelation 2:12–17

Heaven Is Home

Alienation is the opposite of being at home. If the Bible is not wrong when it calls us "aliens and strangers" (1 Peter 2:11), then that's why we feel alienation: We feel what *is* . . . We have a homing instinct, a "home detector," and it doesn't ring for earth. That's why nearly every society in history except our own instinctively believes in life after death . . . Earth just doesn't smell like home. However good a road it is, however good a motel it is, however good a training camp it is, it is not home. Heaven is.

Play with that thought for a minute: Heaven is *home*. Experiment with the thought; feel the gem; look at the picture; explore the house before deciding whether to buy. Heaven means not just a pleasant place but *our* place, not just a good place but a good place for us. We fit there . . .

It is our home because we receive there our true identity. We don't know who we are, remember; we are alienated not only from our home but from ourselves. This is beautifully symbolized in Revelation 2:17: "To him who overcomes I will give some of the hidden manna. I will also give him a white stone with a new name written on it, known only to him who receives it."

ADDITIONAL SCRIPTURE READINGS
Isaiah 62:1–5; Isaiah 65:13–25

Go to page 1615 for your next devotional reading.

against them with the sword of my mouth.

17He who has an ear, let him hear what the Spirit says to the churches. To him who overcomes, I will give some of the hidden manna. I will also give him a white stone with a new name written on it, known only to him who receives it.

To the Church in Thyatira

18"To the angel of the church in Thyatira write:

These are the words of the Son of God, whose eyes are like blazing fire and whose feet are like burnished bronze. 19I know your deeds, your love and faith, your service and perseverance, and that you are now doing more than you did at first.

20Nevertheless, I have this against you: You tolerate that woman Jezebel, who calls herself a prophetess. By her teaching she misleads my servants into sexual immorality and the eating of food sacrificed to idols. 21I have given her time to repent of her immorality, but she is unwilling. 22So I will cast her on a bed of suffering, and I will make those who commit adultery with her suffer intensely, unless they repent of her ways. 23I will strike her children dead. Then all the churches will know that I am he who searches hearts and minds, and I will repay each of you according to your deeds. 24Now I say to the rest of you in Thyatira, to you who do not hold to her teaching and have not learned Satan's so-called deep secrets (I will not impose any other burden on you): 25Only hold on to what you have until I come.

26To him who overcomes and does my will to the end, I will give authority over the nations—

27'He will rule them with an iron scepter; he will dash them to pieces like pottery'ᵃ—

just as I have received authority from my Father. 28I will also give him the morning star. 29He who has an ear, let him hear what the Spirit says to the churches.

To the Church in Sardis

3 "To the angelᵇ of the church in Sardis write:

These are the words of him who holds the seven spiritsᶜ of God and the seven stars. I know your deeds; you have a reputation of being alive, but you are dead. 2Wake up! Strengthen what remains and is about to die, for I have not found your deeds complete in the sight of my God. 3Remember, therefore, what you have received and heard; obey it, and repent. But if you do not wake up, I will come like a thief, and you will not know at what time I will come to you.

4Yet you have a few people in Sardis who have not soiled their clothes. They will walk with me, dressed in white, for they are worthy. 5He who overcomes will, like them, be dressed in white. I will never blot out his name from the book of life, but will acknowledge his name before my Father and his angels. 6He who has an ear, let him hear what the Spirit says to the churches.

To the Church in Philadelphia

7"To the angel of the church in Philadelphia write:

These are the words of him who is holy and true, who holds the key of David. What he opens no one can shut, and what he shuts no one can open. 8I know

ᵃ27 Psalm 2:9   ᵇ1 Or messenger; also in verses 7 and 14   ᶜ1 Or the sevenfold Spirit

PASSAGE: Revelation 7:9–17; Revelation 19:1–10
AUTHOR: Charles Wesley

With Thanks Never Ceasing

You servants of God, your Master proclaim,
And publish abroad his wonderful name;
The name all-victorious of Jesus extol;
His kingdom is glorious and rules over all.

"Salvation to God who sits on the throne!"
Let all cry aloud, and honor the Son;
The praises of Jesus, the angels proclaim,
Fall down on their faces and worship the Lamb.

Then let us adore and give him his right:
All glory and power, all wisdom and might,
All honor and blessing—with angels above—
And thanks never ceasing for infinite love.

Go to page 1617 for your next devotional reading.

your deeds. See, I have placed
before you an open door that no
one can shut. I know that you
have little strength, yet you have
kept my word and have not denied my name. 9I will make those
who are of the synagogue of Satan, who claim to be Jews though
they are not, but are liars—I will
make them come and fall down
at your feet and acknowledge
that I have loved you. 10Since
you have kept my command to
endure patiently, I will also keep
you from the hour of trial that is
going to come upon the whole
world to test those who live on
the earth.

11I am coming soon. Hold on
to what you have, so that no one
will take your crown. 12Him who
overcomes I will make a pillar in
the temple of my God. Never
again will he leave it. I will write
on him the name of my God and
the name of the city of my God,
the new Jerusalem, which is
coming down out of heaven
from my God; and I will also
write on him my new name. 13He
who has an ear, let him hear
what the Spirit says to the
churches.

To the Church in Laodicea

14"To the angel of the church in Laodicea write:

These are the words of the
Amen, the faithful and true witness, the ruler of God's creation.
15I know your deeds, that you
are neither cold nor hot. I wish
you were either one or the other!
16So, because you are luke-
warm—neither hot nor cold—I
am about to spit you out of my
mouth. 17You say, 'I am rich; I
have acquired wealth and do not
need a thing.' But you do not realize that you are wretched, pitiful, poor, blind and naked. 18I
counsel you to buy from me gold
refined in the fire, so you can become rich; and white clothes to
wear, so you can cover your
shameful nakedness; and salve
to put on your eyes, so you can
see.

19Those whom I love I rebuke
and discipline. So be earnest, and
repent. 20Here I am! I stand at the
door and knock. If anyone hears
my voice and opens the door, I
will come in and eat with him,
and he with me.

21To him who overcomes, I
will give the right to sit with me
on my throne, just as I overcame
and sat down with my Father on
his throne. 22He who has an ear,
let him hear what the Spirit says
to the churches."

The Throne in Heaven

4 After this I looked, and there before me was a door standing open
in heaven. And the voice I had first
heard speaking to me like a trumpet
said, "Come up here, and I will show
you what must take place after this."
2At once I was in the Spirit, and there
before me was a throne in heaven
with someone sitting on it. 3And the
one who sat there had the appearance
of jasper and carnelian. A rainbow,
resembling an emerald, encircled the
throne. 4Surrounding the throne were
twenty-four other thrones, and seated
on them were twenty-four elders.
They were dressed in white and had
crowns of gold on their heads. 5From
the throne came flashes of lightning,
rumblings and peals of thunder. Before the throne, seven lamps were
blazing. These are the seven spirits[a]
of God. 6Also before the throne there
was what looked like a sea of glass,
clear as crystal.

In the center, around the throne,
were four living creatures, and they
were covered with eyes, in front and
in back. 7The first living creature was
like a lion, the second was like an ox,
the third had a face like a man, the
fourth was like a flying eagle. 8Each

[a]5 Or *the sevenfold Spirit*

VERSE: AUTHOR: PASSAGE:
Revelation 4:3   Cornelis Gilhuis   Revelation 4:1–11

To See God, and Live

John, the old visionary, was allowed to have a brief view
through the door to eternity. In the last book of the Bible
he presents what he saw, but he does not do so in a logical discourse. He paints a picture for us. He *shows* us
through his eyes. What does he see?

He sees many things, but one thing stands out: the
throne of God. That throne is the center around which
everything is concentrated. That throne draws all of
John's attention. The splendor that goes forth from it is
so overwhelming, and the glitter of something like a
glass sea around the throne so blinding, that John actually cannot see God. He sees only the shining reflection,
which reminds him of diamonds. Even John's sanctified,
inspired eye could not see God in a vision. So great is
God's glory that no eye has ever seen it.

That is the heart of what heaven will be like: *we shall see
God.* Before that reality we can only be still in amazement: to see God and not to be lost; to see God and *live.*

We shall never be weary of looking at him; for we shall
never see everything. We shall fall from one ecstasy into
the next. We forget time and place. We *live,* in the deepest, most intense sense of the word . . .

To enter heaven and to see Jesus; to enjoy the company of the Redeemer. When I think of that, a strong desire to be there gets hold of me.

ADDITIONAL SCRIPTURE READINGS
John 1:1–18; 1 Timothy 6:11–16
Go to page 1621 for your next devotional reading.

of the four living creatures had six wings and was covered with eyes all around, even under his wings. Day and night they never stop saying:

"Holy, holy, holy
is the Lord God Almighty,
who was, and is, and is to come."

⁹Whenever the living creatures give glory, honor and thanks to him who sits on the throne and who lives for ever and ever, ¹⁰the twenty-four elders fall down before him who sits on the throne, and worship him who lives for ever and ever. They lay their crowns before the throne and say:

¹¹"You are worthy, our Lord and God,
to receive glory and honor and power,
for you created all things,
and by your will they were created
and have their being."

The Scroll and the Lamb

5 Then I saw in the right hand of him who sat on the throne a scroll with writing on both sides and sealed with seven seals. ²And I saw a mighty angel proclaiming in a loud voice, "Who is worthy to break the seals and open the scroll?" ³But no one in heaven or on earth or under the earth could open the scroll or even look inside it. ⁴I wept and wept because no one was found who was worthy to open the scroll or look inside. ⁵Then one of the elders said to me, "Do not weep! See, the Lion of the tribe of Judah, the Root of David, has triumphed. He is able to open the scroll and its seven seals."

⁶Then I saw a Lamb, looking as if it had been slain, standing in the center of the throne, encircled by the four living creatures and the elders. He had seven horns and seven eyes, which are the seven spirits[a] of God sent out into all the earth. ⁷He came and took the scroll from the right hand of him who sat on the throne. ⁸And when he had taken it, the four living creatures and the twenty-four elders fell down before the Lamb. Each one had a harp and they were holding golden bowls full of incense, which are the prayers of the saints. ⁹And they sang a new song:

"You are worthy to take the scroll
and to open its seals,
because you were slain,
and with your blood you
purchased men for God
from every tribe and language
and people and nation.
¹⁰You have made them to be a
kingdom and priests to
serve our God,
and they will reign on the
earth."

¹¹Then I looked and heard the voice of many angels, numbering thousands upon thousands, and ten thousand times ten thousand. They encircled the throne and the living creatures and the elders. ¹²In a loud voice they sang:

"Worthy is the Lamb, who was
slain,
to receive power and wealth and
wisdom and strength
and honor and glory and praise!"

¹³Then I heard every creature in heaven and on earth and under the earth and on the sea, and all that is in them, singing:

"To him who sits on the throne
and to the Lamb
be praise and honor and glory and
power,
for ever and ever!"

¹⁴The four living creatures said, "Amen," and the elders fell down and worshiped.

The Seals

6 I watched as the Lamb opened the first of the seven seals. Then I heard one of the four living creatures say in a voice like thunder, "Come!" ²I

---

a6 Or *the sevenfold Spirit*

looked, and there before me was a white horse! Its rider held a bow, and he was given a crown, and he rode out as a conqueror bent on conquest.

³When the Lamb opened the second seal, I heard the second living creature say, "Come!" ⁴Then another horse came out, a fiery red one. Its rider was given power to take peace from the earth and to make men slay each other. To him was given a large sword.

⁵When the Lamb opened the third seal, I heard the third living creature say, "Come!" I looked, and there before me was a black horse! Its rider was holding a pair of scales in his hand. ⁶Then I heard what sounded like a voice among the four living creatures, saying, "A quart*ᵃ* of wheat for a day's wages,*ᵇ* and three quarts of barley for a day's wages,*ᵇ* and do not damage the oil and the wine!"

⁷When the Lamb opened the fourth seal, I heard the voice of the fourth living creature say, "Come!" ⁸I looked, and there before me was a pale horse! Its rider was named Death, and Hades was following close behind him. They were given power over a fourth of the earth to kill by sword, famine and plague, and by the wild beasts of the earth.

⁹When he opened the fifth seal, I saw under the altar the souls of those who had been slain because of the word of God and the testimony they had maintained. ¹⁰They called out in a loud voice, "How long, Sovereign Lord, holy and true, until you judge the inhabitants of the earth and avenge our blood?" ¹¹Then each of them was given a white robe, and they were told to wait a little longer, until the number of their fellow servants and brothers who were to be killed as they had been was completed.

¹²I watched as he opened the sixth seal. There was a great earthquake. The sun turned black like sackcloth made of goat hair, the whole moon turned blood red, ¹³and the stars in the sky fell to earth, as late figs drop from a fig tree when shaken by a strong wind. ¹⁴The sky receded like a scroll, rolling up, and every mountain and island was removed from its place.

¹⁵Then the kings of the earth, the princes, the generals, the rich, the mighty, and every slave and every free man hid in caves and among the rocks of the mountains. ¹⁶They called to the mountains and the rocks, "Fall on us and hide us from the face of him who sits on the throne and from the wrath of the Lamb! ¹⁷For the great day of their wrath has come, and who can stand?"

144,000 Sealed

7 After this I saw four angels standing at the four corners of the earth, holding back the four winds of the earth to prevent any wind from blowing on the land or on the sea or on any tree. ²Then I saw another angel coming up from the east, having the seal of the living God. He called out in a loud voice to the four angels who had been given power to harm the land and the sea: ³"Do not harm the land or the sea or the trees until we put a seal on the foreheads of the servants of our God." ⁴Then I heard the number of those who were sealed: 144,000 from all the tribes of Israel.

⁵From the tribe of Judah 12,000
  were sealed,
from the tribe of Reuben 12,000,
from the tribe of Gad 12,000,
⁶from the tribe of Asher 12,000,
from the tribe of Naphtali
  12,000,
from the tribe of Manasseh
  12,000,
⁷from the tribe of Simeon 12,000,
from the tribe of Levi 12,000,
from the tribe of Issachar 12,000,
⁸from the tribe of Zebulun
  12,000,
from the tribe of Joseph 12,000,
from the tribe of Benjamin
  12,000.

ᵃ6 Greek *a choinix* (probably about a liter)   *ᵇ6* Greek *a denarius*

The Great Multitude in White Robes

⁹After this I looked and there before me was a great multitude that no one could count, from every nation, tribe, people and language, standing before the throne and in front of the Lamb. They were wearing white robes and were holding palm branches in their hands. ¹⁰And they cried out in a loud voice:

"Salvation belongs to our God,
who sits on the throne,
and to the Lamb."

¹¹All the angels were standing around the throne and around the elders and the four living creatures. They fell down on their faces before the throne and worshiped God, ¹²saying:

"Amen!
Praise and glory
and wisdom and thanks and
honor
and power and strength
be to our God for ever and ever.
Amen!"

¹³Then one of the elders asked me, "These in white robes—who are they, and where did they come from?"

¹⁴I answered, "Sir, you know."

And he said, "These are they who have come out of the great tribulation; they have washed their robes and made them white in the blood of the Lamb. ¹⁵Therefore,

"they are before the throne of God
and serve him day and night in
his temple;
and he who sits on the throne will
spread his tent over them.
¹⁶Never again will they hunger;
never again will they thirst.
The sun will not beat upon them,
nor any scorching heat.
¹⁷For the Lamb at the center of the
throne will be their
shepherd;
he will lead them to springs of
living water.

And God will wipe away every
tear from their eyes."

The Seventh Seal and the Golden Censer

8 When he opened the seventh seal, there was silence in heaven for about half an hour.

²And I saw the seven angels who stand before God, and to them were given seven trumpets.

³Another angel, who had a golden censer, came and stood at the altar. He was given much incense to offer, with the prayers of all the saints, on the golden altar before the throne. ⁴The smoke of the incense, together with the prayers of the saints, went up before God from the angel's hand. ⁵Then the angel took the censer, filled it with fire from the altar, and hurled it on the earth; and there came peals of thunder, rumblings, flashes of lightning and an earthquake.

The Trumpets

⁶Then the seven angels who had the seven trumpets prepared to sound them.

⁷The first angel sounded his trumpet, and there came hail and fire mixed with blood, and it was hurled down upon the earth. A third of the earth was burned up, a third of the trees were burned up, and all the green grass was burned up.

⁸The second angel sounded his trumpet, and something like a huge mountain, all ablaze, was thrown into the sea. A third of the sea turned into blood, ⁹a third of the living creatures in the sea died, and a third of the ships were destroyed.

¹⁰The third angel sounded his trumpet, and a great star, blazing like a torch, fell from the sky on a third of the rivers and on the springs of water— ¹¹the name of the star is Wormwood.[a] A third of the waters turned bitter, and many people died from the waters that had become bitter.

¹²The fourth angel sounded his

a11 That is, Bitterness

VERSE:	AUTHOR:	PASSAGE:
Revelation 7:17	James Dobson	Revelation 7:9–17

No More Tears

"And God will wipe away every tear from their eyes" (Revelation 7:17). This is the hope of the ages that burns within my breast. It is the ultimate answer to those who suffer and struggle today. It is the only solace for those who have said good-bye to a loved one. Though the pain is indescribable now, we must never forget that our separation is temporary. We will be reunited forever on that glad resurrection morning. As the Scripture promises, our tears will be banished forever! . . .

Your loved ones who died in Christ will also be in that great throng, singing and shouting the praises of the Redeemer. What a celebration it will be!

This is the reward for the faithful—for those who break through the betrayal barrier and persevere to the end. This is the crown of righteousness prepared for those who have fought a good fight, finished the race and kept the faith (2 Timothy 4:7). Throughout our remaining days in this life, therefore, let me urge you not to be discouraged by temporal cares. Accept the circumstances as they are presented to you. Expect periods of hardship to occur, and don't be dismayed when they arrive. "Lean into the pain" when your time to suffer comes around, knowing that God will use the difficulty for his purposes—and, indeed, for our own good. The Lord is very near, and he has promised that your temptation will not be greater than you can bear.

ADDITIONAL SCRIPTURE READINGS
2 Timothy 4:6–8; Hebrews 12:1–13

Go to page 1626 for your next devotional reading.

trumpet, and a third of the sun was struck, a third of the moon, and a third of the stars, so that a third of them turned dark. A third of the day was without light, and also a third of the night.

¹³As I watched, I heard an eagle that was flying in midair call out in a loud voice: "Woe! Woe! Woe to the inhabitants of the earth, because of the trumpet blasts about to be sounded by the other three angels!"

9 The fifth angel sounded his trumpet, and I saw a star that had fallen from the sky to the earth. The star was given the key to the shaft of the Abyss. ²When he opened the Abyss, smoke rose from it like the smoke from a gigantic furnace. The sun and sky were darkened by the smoke from the Abyss. ³And out of the smoke locusts came down upon the earth and were given power like that of scorpions of the earth. ⁴They were told not to harm the grass of the earth or any plant or tree, but only those people who did not have the seal of God on their foreheads. ⁵They were not given power to kill them, but only to torture them for five months. And the agony they suffered was like that of the sting of a scorpion when it strikes a man. ⁶During those days men will seek death, but will not find it; they will long to die, but death will elude them.

⁷The locusts looked like horses prepared for battle. On their heads they wore something like crowns of gold, and their faces resembled human faces. ⁸Their hair was like women's hair, and their teeth were like lions' teeth. ⁹They had breastplates like breastplates of iron, and the sound of their wings was like the thundering of many horses and chariots rushing into battle. ¹⁰They had tails and stings like scorpions, and in their tails they had power to torment people for five months. ¹¹They had as king over them the angel of the Abyss, whose name in Hebrew is Abaddon, and in Greek, Apollyon.ᵃ

¹²The first woe is past; two other woes are yet to come.

¹³The sixth angel sounded his trumpet, and I heard a voice coming from the hornsᵇ of the golden altar that is before God. ¹⁴It said to the sixth angel who had the trumpet, "Release the four angels who are bound at the great river Euphrates." ¹⁵And the four angels who had been kept ready for this very hour and day and month and year were released to kill a third of mankind. ¹⁶The number of the mounted troops was two hundred million. I heard their number.

¹⁷The horses and riders I saw in my vision looked like this: Their breastplates were fiery red, dark blue, and yellow as sulfur. The heads of the horses resembled the heads of lions, and out of their mouths came fire, smoke and sulfur. ¹⁸A third of mankind was killed by the three plagues of fire, smoke and sulfur that came out of their mouths. ¹⁹The power of the horses was in their mouths and in their tails; for their tails were like snakes, having heads with which they inflict injury.

²⁰The rest of mankind that were not killed by these plagues still did not repent of the work of their hands; they did not stop worshiping demons, and idols of gold, silver, bronze, stone and wood—idols that cannot see or hear or walk. ²¹Nor did they repent of their murders, their magic arts, their sexual immorality or their thefts.

The Angel and the Little Scroll

10 Then I saw another mighty angel coming down from heaven. He was robed in a cloud, with a rainbow above his head; his face was like the sun, and his legs were like fiery pillars. ²He was holding a little scroll, which lay open in his hand. He planted his right foot on the sea and his left foot on the land, ³and he gave a loud shout like the roar of a lion. When he shouted, the voices of the seven thunders spoke. ⁴And when the seven

---

ᵃ11 *Abaddon* and *Apollyon* mean *Destroyer*.   ᵇ13 That is, projections

thunders spoke, I was about to write; but I heard a voice from heaven say, "Seal up what the seven thunders have said and do not write it down."

⁵Then the angel I had seen standing on the sea and on the land raised his right hand to heaven. ⁶And he swore by him who lives for ever and ever, who created the heavens and all that is in them, the earth and all that is in it, and the sea and all that is in it, and said, "There will be no more delay! ⁷But in the days when the seventh angel is about to sound his trumpet, the mystery of God will be accomplished, just as he announced to his servants the prophets."

⁸Then the voice that I had heard from heaven spoke to me once more: "Go, take the scroll that lies open in the hand of the angel who is standing on the sea and on the land."

⁹So I went to the angel and asked him to give me the little scroll. He said to me, "Take it and eat it. It will turn your stomach sour, but in your mouth it will be as sweet as honey." ¹⁰I took the little scroll from the angel's hand and ate it. It tasted as sweet as honey in my mouth, but when I had eaten it, my stomach turned sour. ¹¹Then I was told, "You must prophesy again about many peoples, nations, languages and kings."

The Two Witnesses

11 I was given a reed like a measuring rod and was told, "Go and measure the temple of God and the altar, and count the worshipers there. ²But exclude the outer court; do not measure it, because it has been given to the Gentiles. They will trample on the holy city for 42 months. ³And I will give power to my two witnesses, and they will prophesy for 1,260 days, clothed in sackcloth." ⁴These are the two olive trees and the two lampstands that stand before the Lord of the earth. ⁵If anyone tries to harm them, fire comes from their mouths and devours their enemies. This is how anyone who wants to harm them must die. ⁶These men

have power to shut up the sky so that it will not rain during the time they are prophesying; and they have power to turn the waters into blood and to strike the earth with every kind of plague as often as they want.

⁷Now when they have finished their testimony, the beast that comes up from the Abyss will attack them, and overpower and kill them. ⁸Their bodies will lie in the street of the great city, which is figuratively called Sodom and Egypt, where also their Lord was crucified. ⁹For three and a half days men from every people, tribe, language and nation will gaze on their bodies and refuse them burial. ¹⁰The inhabitants of the earth will gloat over them and will celebrate by sending each other gifts, because these two prophets had tormented those who live on the earth.

¹¹But after the three and a half days a breath of life from God entered them, and they stood on their feet, and terror struck those who saw them. ¹²Then they heard a loud voice from heaven saying to them, "Come up here." And they went up to heaven in a cloud, while their enemies looked on.

¹³At that very hour there was a severe earthquake and a tenth of the city collapsed. Seven thousand people were killed in the earthquake, and the survivors were terrified and gave glory to the God of heaven.

¹⁴The second woe has passed; the third woe is coming soon.

The Seventh Trumpet

¹⁵The seventh angel sounded his trumpet, and there were loud voices in heaven, which said:

"The kingdom of the world has
   become the kingdom of our
   Lord and of his Christ,
and he will reign for ever and
   ever."

¹⁶And the twenty-four elders, who were seated on their thrones before God, fell on their faces and worshiped God, ¹⁷saying:

"We give thanks to you, Lord God
    Almighty,
  the One who is and who was,
because you have taken your great
    power
  and have begun to reign.
[18]The nations were angry;
  and your wrath has come.
The time has come for judging the
    dead,
  and for rewarding your servants
    the prophets
and your saints and those who
    reverence your name,
  both small and great—
and for destroying those who
    destroy the earth."

[19]Then God's temple in heaven was opened, and within his temple was seen the ark of his covenant. And there came flashes of lightning, rumblings, peals of thunder, an earthquake and a great hailstorm.

The Woman and the Dragon

12 A great and wondrous sign appeared in heaven: a woman clothed with the sun, with the moon under her feet and a crown of twelve stars on her head. [2]She was pregnant and cried out in pain as she was about to give birth. [3]Then another sign appeared in heaven: an enormous red dragon with seven heads and ten horns and seven crowns on his heads. [4]His tail swept a third of the stars out of the sky and flung them to the earth. The dragon stood in front of the woman who was about to give birth, so that he might devour her child the moment it was born. [5]She gave birth to a son, a male child, who will rule all the nations with an iron scepter. And her child was snatched up to God and to his throne. [6]The woman fled into the desert to a place prepared for her by God, where she might be taken care of for 1,260 days.

[7]And there was war in heaven. Michael and his angels fought against the dragon, and the dragon and his angels fought back. [8]But he was not strong enough, and they lost their place in heaven. [9]The great dragon was hurled down—that ancient serpent called the devil, or Satan, who leads the whole world astray. He was hurled to the earth, and his angels with him.

[10]Then I heard a loud voice in heaven say:

"Now have come the salvation
  and the power and the
    kingdom of our God,
  and the authority of his Christ.
For the accuser of our brothers,
  who accuses them before our
    God day and night,
  has been hurled down.
[11]They overcame him
  by the blood of the Lamb
  and by the word of their
    testimony;
they did not love their lives so
    much
  as to shrink from death.
[12]Therefore rejoice, you heavens
  and you who dwell in them!
But woe to the earth and the sea,
  because the devil has gone
    down to you!
He is filled with fury,
  because he knows that his time
    is short."

[13]When the dragon saw that he had been hurled to the earth, he pursued the woman who had given birth to the male child. [14]The woman was given the two wings of a great eagle, so that she might fly to the place prepared for her in the desert, where she would be taken care of for a time, times and half a time, out of the serpent's reach. [15]Then from his mouth the serpent spewed water like a river, to overtake the woman and sweep her away with the torrent. [16]But the earth helped the woman by opening its mouth and swallowing the river that the dragon had spewed out of his mouth. [17]Then the dragon was enraged at the woman and went off to make war against the rest of her offspring—those who obey God's commandments and hold to the testimony

13
of Jesus. [1]And the dragon[a] stood on the shore of the sea.

The Beast out of the Sea

And I saw a beast coming out of the sea. He had ten horns and seven heads, with ten crowns on his horns, and on each head a blasphemous name. [2]The beast I saw resembled a leopard, but had feet like those of a bear and a mouth like that of a lion. The dragon gave the beast his power and his throne and great authority. [3]One of the heads of the beast seemed to have had a fatal wound, but the fatal wound had been healed. The whole world was astonished and followed the beast. [4]Men worshiped the dragon because he had given authority to the beast, and they also worshiped the beast and asked, "Who is like the beast? Who can make war against him?"

[5]The beast was given a mouth to utter proud words and blasphemies and to exercise his authority for forty-two months. [6]He opened his mouth to blaspheme God, and to slander his name and his dwelling place and those who live in heaven. [7]He was given power to make war against the saints and to conquer them. And he was given authority over every tribe, people, language and nation. [8]All inhabitants of the earth will worship the beast—all whose names have not been written in the book of life belonging to the Lamb that was slain from the creation of the world.[b]

[9]He who has an ear, let him hear.

[10]If anyone is to go into captivity,
   into captivity he will go.
If anyone is to be killed[c] with the
      sword,
   with the sword he will be
      killed.

This calls for patient endurance and faithfulness on the part of the saints.

The Beast out of the Earth

[11]Then I saw another beast, coming out of the earth. He had two horns like a lamb, but he spoke like a dragon. [12]He exercised all the authority of the first beast on his behalf, and made the earth and its inhabitants worship the first beast, whose fatal wound had been healed. [13]And he performed great and miraculous signs, even causing fire to come down from heaven to earth in full view of men. [14]Because of the signs he was given power to do on behalf of the first beast, he deceived the inhabitants of the earth. He ordered them to set up an image in honor of the beast who was wounded by the sword and yet lived. [15]He was given power to give breath to the image of the first beast, so that it could speak and cause all who refused to worship the image to be killed. [16]He also forced everyone, small and great, rich and poor, free and slave, to receive a mark on his right hand or on his forehead, [17]so that no one could buy or sell unless he had the mark, which is the name of the beast or the number of his name.

[18]This calls for wisdom. If anyone has insight, let him calculate the number of the beast, for it is man's number. His number is 666.

The Lamb and the 144,000

14
Then I looked, and there before me was the Lamb, standing on Mount Zion, and with him 144,000 who had his name and his Father's name written on their foreheads. [2]And I heard a sound from heaven like the roar of rushing waters and like a loud peal of thunder. The sound I heard was like that of harpists playing their harps. [3]And they sang a new song before the throne and before the four living creatures and the elders. No one could learn the song except the 144,000 who had been redeemed from the earth. [4]These are those who did not defile themselves with women, for they kept themselves pure. They follow the Lamb wherever he goes. They were purchased from

---

[a]1 Some late manuscripts *And I belonging to the Lamb that was slain*   [b]8 Or *written from the creation of the world in the book of life*   [c]10 Some manuscripts *anyone kills*

VERSE:	AUTHOR:	PASSAGE:
Revelation 14:13	Gien Karssen	Revelation 14:9–13

The Best Is Still to Come!

The Bible leaves no doubt that there is life after death. Man is created for eternity. The earthly life is but an overture, a prelude, of the reality to come.

Blessed — happy, to be envied — are the dead "who die in the Lord." They are people who during their earthly life believed in Jesus Christ as their Savior and Lord. When they exchange the temporal for the eternal, their work is done forever. They finally have rest. All the troubles and tensions of their earthly existence are behind them. They have arrived at their eternal destination. They are HOME! . . .

The dead who die in the Lord not only enjoy eternally the absence of unrest, pain and sorrow, but they also are rewarded. "Their deeds will follow them."

Man is free to live his life according to his own choices. But he has to keep in mind that there will be a future settling of accounts. Every individual will — justly — be rewarded according to his deeds. The measuring staff will be administered according to his attitude towards the Lord Jesus Christ.

Lord, thank you for eternal rest to come for those who believe in Jesus Christ. Thank you for the reality of future life with you. Certainly the best is still to come! Amen.

ADDITIONAL SCRIPTURE READINGS
1 Corinthians 3:1–15; Hebrews 4:1–13
Go to page 1632 for your next devotional reading.

among men and offered as firstfruits to God and the Lamb. ⁵No lie was found in their mouths; they are blameless.

The Three Angels

⁶Then I saw another angel flying in midair, and he had the eternal gospel to proclaim to those who live on the earth—to every nation, tribe, language and people. ⁷He said in a loud voice, "Fear God and give him glory, because the hour of his judgment has come. Worship him who made the heavens, the earth, the sea and the springs of water."

⁸A second angel followed and said, "Fallen! Fallen is Babylon the Great, which made all the nations drink the maddening wine of her adulteries."

⁹A third angel followed them and said in a loud voice: "If anyone worships the beast and his image and receives his mark on the forehead or on the hand, ¹⁰he, too, will drink of the wine of God's fury, which has been poured full strength into the cup of his wrath. He will be tormented with burning sulfur in the presence of the holy angels and of the Lamb. ¹¹And the smoke of their torment rises for ever and ever. There is no rest day or night for those who worship the beast and his image, or for anyone who receives the mark of his name." ¹²This calls for patient endurance on the part of the saints who obey God's commandments and remain faithful to Jesus.

¹³Then I heard a voice from heaven say, "Write: Blessed are the dead who die in the Lord from now on."

"Yes," says the Spirit, "they will rest from their labor, for their deeds will follow them."

The Harvest of the Earth

¹⁴I looked, and there before me was a white cloud, and seated on the cloud was one "like a son of man"ᵃ with a crown of gold on his head and a sharp sickle in his hand. ¹⁵Then another angel came out of the temple and called in a loud voice to him who was sitting on the cloud, "Take your sickle and reap, because the time to reap has come, for the harvest of the earth is ripe." ¹⁶So he who was seated on the cloud swung his sickle over the earth, and the earth was harvested.

¹⁷Another angel came out of the temple in heaven, and he too had a sharp sickle. ¹⁸Still another angel, who had charge of the fire, came from the altar and called in a loud voice to him who had the sharp sickle, "Take your sharp sickle and gather the clusters of grapes from the earth's vine, because its grapes are ripe." ¹⁹The angel swung his sickle on the earth, gathered its grapes and threw them into the great winepress of God's wrath. ²⁰They were trampled in the winepress outside the city, and blood flowed out of the press, rising as high as the horses' bridles for a distance of 1,600 stadia.ᵇ

Seven Angels With Seven Plagues

15 I saw in heaven another great and marvelous sign: seven angels with the seven last plagues—last, because with them God's wrath is completed. ²And I saw what looked like a sea of glass mixed with fire and, standing beside the sea, those who had been victorious over the beast and his image and over the number of his name. They held harps given them by God ³and sang the song of Moses the servant of God and the song of the Lamb:

"Great and marvelous are your
        deeds,
    Lord God Almighty.
Just and true are your ways,
    King of the ages.
⁴Who will not fear you, O Lord,
    and bring glory to your name?
For you alone are holy.
All nations will come
    and worship before you,
for your righteous acts have been
        revealed."

⁵After this I looked and in heaven

ᵃ14 Daniel 7:13   ᵇ20 That is, about 180 miles (about 300 kilometers) the temple, that is, the tabernacle of the Testimony, was opened. [6]Out of the temple came the seven angels with the seven plagues. They were dressed in clean, shining linen and wore golden sashes around their chests. [7]Then one of the four living creatures gave to the seven angels seven golden bowls filled with the wrath of God, who lives for ever and ever. [8]And the temple was filled with smoke from the glory of God and from his power, and no one could enter the temple until the seven plagues of the seven angels were completed.

The Seven Bowls of God's Wrath

16 Then I heard a loud voice from the temple saying to the seven angels, "Go, pour out the seven bowls of God's wrath on the earth."

[2]The first angel went and poured out his bowl on the land, and ugly and painful sores broke out on the people who had the mark of the beast and worshiped his image.

[3]The second angel poured out his bowl on the sea, and it turned into blood like that of a dead man, and every living thing in the sea died.

[4]The third angel poured out his bowl on the rivers and springs of water, and they became blood. [5]Then I heard the angel in charge of the waters say:

"You are just in these judgments,
   you who are and who were, the
      Holy One,
   because you have so judged;
[6]for they have shed the blood of
      your saints and prophets,
   and you have given them blood
      to drink as they deserve."

[7]And I heard the altar respond:

"Yes, Lord God Almighty,
   true and just are your
      judgments."

[8]The fourth angel poured out his bowl on the sun, and the sun was given power to scorch people with fire. [9]They were seared by the intense heat and they cursed the name of God, who had control over these plagues, but they refused to repent and glorify him.

[10]The fifth angel poured out his bowl on the throne of the beast, and his kingdom was plunged into darkness. Men gnawed their tongues in agony [11]and cursed the God of heaven because of their pains and their sores, but they refused to repent of what they had done.

[12]The sixth angel poured out his bowl on the great river Euphrates, and its water was dried up to prepare the way for the kings from the East. [13]Then I saw three evil[a] spirits that looked like frogs; they came out of the mouth of the dragon, out of the mouth of the beast and out of the mouth of the false prophet. [14]They are spirits of demons performing miraculous signs, and they go out to the kings of the whole world, to gather them for the battle on the great day of God Almighty.

[15]"Behold, I come like a thief! Blessed is he who stays awake and keeps his clothes with him, so that he may not go naked and be shamefully exposed."

[16]Then they gathered the kings together to the place that in Hebrew is called Armageddon.

[17]The seventh angel poured out his bowl into the air, and out of the temple came a loud voice from the throne, saying, "It is done!" [18]Then there came flashes of lightning, rumblings, peals of thunder and a severe earthquake. No earthquake like it has ever occurred since man has been on earth, so tremendous was the quake. [19]The great city split into three parts, and the cities of the nations collapsed. God remembered Babylon the Great and gave her the cup filled with the wine of the fury of his wrath. [20]Every island fled away and the mountains could not be found. [21]From the sky huge hailstones of about a hundred pounds each fell upon men. And they cursed God on account of the plague

---

[a]13 Greek *unclean*

of hail, because the plague was so terrible.

The Woman on the Beast

17 One of the seven angels who had the seven bowls came and said to me, "Come, I will show you the punishment of the great prostitute, who sits on many waters. ²With her the kings of the earth committed adultery and the inhabitants of the earth were intoxicated with the wine of her adulteries."

³Then the angel carried me away in the Spirit into a desert. There I saw a woman sitting on a scarlet beast that was covered with blasphemous names and had seven heads and ten horns. ⁴The woman was dressed in purple and scarlet, and was glittering with gold, precious stones and pearls. She held a golden cup in her hand, filled with abominable things and the filth of her adulteries. ⁵This title was written on her forehead:

MYSTERY
BABYLON THE GREAT
THE MOTHER OF PROSTITUTES
AND OF THE ABOMINATIONS OF THE EARTH.

⁶I saw that the woman was drunk with the blood of the saints, the blood of those who bore testimony to Jesus.

When I saw her, I was greatly astonished. ⁷Then the angel said to me: "Why are you astonished? I will explain to you the mystery of the woman and of the beast she rides, which has the seven heads and ten horns. ⁸The beast, which you saw, once was, now is not, and will come up out of the Abyss and go to his destruction. The inhabitants of the earth whose names have not been written in the book of life from the creation of the world will be astonished when they see the beast, because he once was, now is not, and yet will come.

⁹"This calls for a mind with wisdom. The seven heads are seven hills on which the woman sits. ¹⁰They are also seven kings. Five have fallen, one is, the other has not yet come; but

when he does come, he must remain for a little while. ¹¹The beast who once was, and now is not, is an eighth king. He belongs to the seven and is going to his destruction.

¹²"The ten horns you saw are ten kings who have not yet received a kingdom, but who for one hour will receive authority as kings along with the beast. ¹³They have one purpose and will give their power and authority to the beast. ¹⁴They will make war against the Lamb, but the Lamb will overcome them because he is Lord of lords and King of kings—and with him will be his called, chosen and faithful followers."

¹⁵Then the angel said to me, "The waters you saw, where the prostitute sits, are peoples, multitudes, nations and languages. ¹⁶The beast and the ten horns you saw will hate the prostitute. They will bring her to ruin and leave her naked; they will eat her flesh and burn her with fire. ¹⁷For God has put it into their hearts to accomplish his purpose by agreeing to give the beast their power to rule, until God's words are fulfilled. ¹⁸The woman you saw is the great city that rules over the kings of the earth."

The Fall of Babylon

18 After this I saw another angel coming down from heaven. He had great authority, and the earth was illuminated by his splendor. ²With a mighty voice he shouted:

"Fallen! Fallen is Babylon the
   Great!
She has become a home for
   demons
and a haunt for every evil*ª* spirit,
   a haunt for every unclean and
   detestable bird.
³For all the nations have drunk
   the maddening wine of her
   adulteries.
The kings of the earth committed
   adultery with her,

ª2 Greek *unclean*

and the merchants of the earth
   grew rich from her
   excessive luxuries."

4Then I heard another voice from
heaven say:

"Come out of her, my people,
   so that you will not share in her
      sins,
   so that you will not receive any
      of her plagues;
5for her sins are piled up to
      heaven,
   and God has remembered her
      crimes.
6Give back to her as she has given;
   pay her back double for what
      she has done.
   Mix her a double portion from
      her own cup.
7Give her as much torture and grief
   as the glory and luxury she
      gave herself.
In her heart she boasts,
   'I sit as queen; I am not a
      widow,
   and I will never mourn.'
8Therefore in one day her plagues
      will overtake her:
   death, mourning and famine.
She will be consumed by fire,
   for mighty is the Lord God who
      judges her.

9"When the kings of the earth who
committed adultery with her and
shared her luxury see the smoke of
her burning, they will weep and
mourn over her. 10Terrified at her torment, they will stand far off and cry:

" 'Woe! Woe, O great city,
   O Babylon, city of power!
In one hour your doom has come!'

11"The merchants of the earth will
weep and mourn over her because no
one buys their cargoes any more—
12cargoes of gold, silver, precious
stones and pearls; fine linen, purple,
silk and scarlet cloth; every sort of cit-
ron wood, and articles of every kind
made of ivory, costly wood, bronze,
iron and marble; 13cargoes of cinnamon and spice, of incense, myrrh and
frankincense, of wine and olive oil, of

fine flour and wheat; cattle and sheep;
horses and carriages; and bodies and
souls of men.

14"They will say, 'The fruit you
longed for is gone from you. All your
riches and splendor have vanished,
never to be recovered.' 15The merchants who sold these things and
gained their wealth from her will
stand far off, terrified at her torment.
They will weep and mourn 16and cry
out:

" 'Woe! Woe, O great city,
   dressed in fine linen, purple
      and scarlet,
   and glittering with gold,
      precious stones and pearls!
17In one hour such great wealth has
      been brought to ruin!'

"Every sea captain, and all who
travel by ship, the sailors, and all who
earn their living from the sea, will
stand far off. 18When they see the
smoke of her burning, they will exclaim, 'Was there ever a city like this
great city?' 19They will throw dust on
their heads, and with weeping and
mourning cry out:

" 'Woe! Woe, O great city,
   where all who had ships on the
      sea
   became rich through her wealth!
In one hour she has been brought
      to ruin!
20Rejoice over her, O heaven!
   Rejoice, saints and apostles and
      prophets!
God has judged her for the way
      she treated you.' "

21Then a mighty angel picked up a
boulder the size of a large millstone
and threw it into the sea, and said:

"With such violence
   the great city of Babylon will be
      thrown down,
   never to be found again.
22The music of harpists and
      musicians, flute players
      and trumpeters,
   will never be heard in you
      again.
No workman of any trade

will ever be found in you again.
The sound of a millstone
   will never be heard in you
      again.
23The light of a lamp
   will never shine in you again.
The voice of bridegroom and bride
   will never be heard in you
      again.
Your merchants were the world's
   great men.
By your magic spell all the
   nations were led astray.
24In her was found the blood of
      prophets and of the saints,
   and of all who have been killed
      on the earth."

Hallelujah!

19 After this I heard what sounded like the roar of a great multitude in heaven shouting:

"Hallelujah!
Salvation and glory and power
   belong to our God,
2   for true and just are his
      judgments.
He has condemned the great
      prostitute
   who corrupted the earth by her
      adulteries.
He has avenged on her the blood
   of his servants."

3And again they shouted:

"Hallelujah!
The smoke from her goes up for
   ever and ever."

4The twenty-four elders and the
four living creatures fell down and
worshiped God, who was seated on
the throne. And they cried:

"Amen, Hallelujah!"

5Then a voice came from the
throne, saying:

"Praise our God,
   all you his servants,
you who fear him,
   both small and great!"

6Then I heard what sounded like a
great multitude, like the roar of rushing waters and like loud peals of
thunder, shouting:

"Hallelujah!
   For our Lord God Almighty
      reigns.
7Let us rejoice and be glad
   and give him glory!
For the wedding of the Lamb has
      come,
   and his bride has made herself
      ready.
8Fine linen, bright and clean,
   was given her to wear."
(Fine linen stands for the righteous
acts of the saints.)

9Then the angel said to me, "Write:
'Blessed are those who are invited to
the wedding supper of the Lamb!' "
And he added, "These are the true
words of God."
10At this I fell at his feet to worship
him. But he said to me, "Do not do it!
I am a fellow servant with you and
with your brothers who hold to the
testimony of Jesus. Worship God! For
the testimony of Jesus is the spirit of
prophecy."

The Rider on the White Horse

11I saw heaven standing open and
there before me was a white horse,
whose rider is called Faithful and
True. With justice he judges and
makes war. 12His eyes are like blazing
fire, and on his head are many
crowns. He has a name written on
him that no one knows but he himself. 13He is dressed in a robe dipped
in blood, and his name is the Word of
God. 14The armies of heaven were following him, riding on white horses
and dressed in fine linen, white and
clean. 15Out of his mouth comes a
sharp sword with which to strike
down the nations. "He will rule them
with an iron scepter."[a] He treads the
winepress of the fury of the wrath of
God Almighty. 16On his robe and on
his thigh he has this name written:

KING OF KINGS AND LORD OF LORDS.

a15 Psalm 2:9

VERSE: AUTHOR: PASSAGE:
Revelation 19:7   Jacob D. Eppinga   Revelation 19:1–10

The End of the Beginning

For the Christian, old age, the beginning of the end, is really just the end of the beginning. After all, much more is to follow . . .

In a New England cemetery is a gravestone that reads, "Death has overcome." Next to it is another, "Death is overcome." Because it is overcome, the Christian has life on both sides of the grave . . .

The world sees old people as being over the hill or at the end of their ropes. We are on a downward course. Aristotle equated age with degeneration on all fronts. If we were physical beings and nothing more, there might be something to say for this worldly view. But we are soul and body, made in God's image. Because we are up in years does not mean we are down on the graph of life. Instead of being on the far side of a bell curve, we are ever rising, rising, rising. And so, at evening, it will be light [Zechariah 14:7].

This is not the order of nature. In the natural ordering of the day, evening is dark. It is then that the shadows lengthen, and the darkness deepens. But the order of grace is the reverse. The sun never stops climbing. At evening the light is brighter than ever. God saves the best for last . . .

For the Christian, full of years, it will be light at evening. As Paul wrote to the Thessalonians, "You are all sons of the light and sons of the day. We do not belong to the night or to the darkness" (1 Thessalonians 5:5).

We are not at the beginning of the end. We are only at the end of the beginning. There is much more to come.

ADDITIONAL SCRIPTURE READINGS
1 Thessalonians 4:13 – 5:11; Revelation 21:22 – 22:6

Go to page 1634 for your next devotional reading.

17And I saw an angel standing in the sun, who cried in a loud voice to all the birds flying in midair, "Come, gather together for the great supper of God, 18so that you may eat the flesh of kings, generals, and mighty men, of horses and their riders, and the flesh of all people, free and slave, small and great."

19Then I saw the beast and the kings of the earth and their armies gathered together to make war against the rider on the horse and his army. 20But the beast was captured, and with him the false prophet who had performed the miraculous signs on his behalf. With these signs he had deluded those who had received the mark of the beast and worshiped his image. The two of them were thrown alive into the fiery lake of burning sulfur. 21The rest of them were killed with the sword that came out of the mouth of the rider on the horse, and all the birds gorged themselves on their flesh.

The Thousand Years

20 And I saw an angel coming down out of heaven, having the key to the Abyss and holding in his hand a great chain. 2He seized the dragon, that ancient serpent, who is the devil, or Satan, and bound him for a thousand years. 3He threw him into the Abyss, and locked and sealed it over him, to keep him from deceiving the nations anymore until the thousand years were ended. After that, he must be set free for a short time.

4I saw thrones on which were seated those who had been given authority to judge. And I saw the souls of those who had been beheaded because of their testimony for Jesus and because of the word of God. They had not worshiped the beast or his image and had not received his mark on their foreheads or their hands. They came to life and reigned with Christ a thousand years. 5(The rest of the dead did not come to life until the thousand years were ended.) This is the first resurrection. 6Blessed and holy are those who have part in the first resurrection. The second death has no power over them, but they will be priests of God and of Christ and will reign with him for a thousand years.

Satan's Doom

7When the thousand years are over, Satan will be released from his prison 8and will go out to deceive the nations in the four corners of the earth—Gog and Magog—to gather them for battle. In number they are like the sand on the seashore. 9They marched across the breadth of the earth and surrounded the camp of God's people, the city he loves. But fire came down from heaven and devoured them. 10And the devil, who deceived them, was thrown into the lake of burning sulfur, where the beast and the false prophet had been thrown. They will be tormented day and night for ever and ever.

The Dead Are Judged

11Then I saw a great white throne and him who was seated on it. Earth and sky fled from his presence, and there was no place for them. 12And I saw the dead, great and small, standing before the throne, and books were opened. Another book was opened, which is the book of life. The dead were judged according to what they had done as recorded in the books. 13The sea gave up the dead that were in it, and death and Hades gave up the dead that were in them, and each person was judged according to what he had done. 14Then death and Hades were thrown into the lake of fire. The lake of fire is the second death. 15If anyone's name was not found written in the book of life, he was thrown into the lake of fire.

The New Jerusalem

21 Then I saw a new heaven and a new earth, for the first heaven and the first earth had passed away, and there was no longer any sea. 2I saw the Holy City, the new Jerusalem, coming down out of heaven from God, prepared as a bride beautifully dressed for her husband. 3And I

heard a loud voice from the throne saying, "Now the dwelling of God is with men, and he will live with them. They will be his people, and God himself will be with them and be their God. ⁴He will wipe every tear from their eyes. There will be no more death or mourning or crying or pain, for the old order of things has passed away."

⁵He who was seated on the throne said, "I am making everything new!"

VERSE:	AUTHOR:	PASSAGE:
Revelation 21:3	John Gilmore	Revelation 21:1–4

Going Home

Solomon referred to life after death as going home: "man goes to his eternal home" (Ecclesiastes 12:5) ... The God-oriented believer can be assured of a home with God in the future. "Now the dwelling of God is with men, and he will live with them" (Revelation 21:3).

Christians do not need to panic when their bodies fall apart. We will not be homeless. Our powers may dwindle, our frames droop and shrink, our appetites wane, our movements cease and our hearts stop. But though the outward body perishes, the inward person is being readied for a new place, a reserved home. Jesus has gone ahead to prepare us a place, ready for occupancy. We will not be spiritually homeless at death, for God has given forethought to our eternal dwelling.

The human body is a wonderful home and we hate to vacate it. We would prefer to stay with our family and friends where the fellowship has been good. But there is an expanded version of God's goodness ahead. "To die is gain," said Saint Paul (Philippians 1:21). No matter how well we have managed the property God has loaned to us, we must eventually move on to a new home. We will not be locked out of heaven, for Jesus Christ is the key to our eternal residence.

ADDITIONAL SCRIPTURE READINGS
John 14:1–14; 2 Corinthians 5:1–10

Go to page 1636 for your next devotional reading.

Then he said, "Write this down, for these words are trustworthy and true."

[6]He said to me: "It is done. I am the Alpha and the Omega, the Beginning and the End. To him who is thirsty I will give to drink without cost from the spring of the water of life. [7]He who overcomes will inherit all this, and I will be his God and he will be my son. [8]But the cowardly, the unbelieving, the vile, the murderers, the sexually immoral, those who practice magic arts, the idolaters and all liars—their place will be in the fiery lake of burning sulfur. This is the second death."

[9]One of the seven angels who had the seven bowls full of the seven last plagues came and said to me, "Come, I will show you the bride, the wife of the Lamb." [10]And he carried me away in the Spirit to a mountain great and high, and showed me the Holy City, Jerusalem, coming down out of heaven from God. [11]It shone with the glory of God, and its brilliance was like that of a very precious jewel, like a jasper, clear as crystal. [12]It had a great, high wall with twelve gates, and with twelve angels at the gates. On the gates were written the names of the twelve tribes of Israel. [13]There were three gates on the east, three on the north, three on the south and three on the west. [14]The wall of the city had twelve foundations, and on them were the names of the twelve apostles of the Lamb.

[15]The angel who talked with me had a measuring rod of gold to measure the city, its gates and its walls. [16]The city was laid out like a square, as long as it was wide. He measured the city with the rod and found it to be 12,000 stadia[a] in length, and as wide and high as it is long. [17]He measured its wall and it was 144 cubits[b] thick,[c] by man's measurement, which the angel was using. [18]The wall was made of jasper, and the city of pure gold, as pure as glass. [19]The foundations of the city walls were decorated with every kind of precious stone. The first foundation was jasper, the second sapphire, the third chalcedony, the fourth emerald, [20]the fifth sardonyx, the sixth carnelian, the seventh chrysolite, the eighth beryl, the ninth topaz, the tenth chrysoprase, the eleventh jacinth, and the twelfth amethyst.[d] [21]The twelve gates were twelve pearls, each gate made of a single pearl. The great street of the city was of pure gold, like transparent glass.

[22]I did not see a temple in the city, because the Lord God Almighty and the Lamb are its temple. [23]The city does not need the sun or the moon to shine on it, for the glory of God gives it light, and the Lamb is its lamp. [24]The nations will walk by its light, and the kings of the earth will bring their splendor into it. [25]On no day will its gates ever be shut, for there will be no night there. [26]The glory and honor of the nations will be brought into it. [27]Nothing impure will ever enter it, nor will anyone who does what is shameful or deceitful, but only those whose names are written in the Lamb's book of life.

The River of Life

22 Then the angel showed me the river of the water of life, as clear as crystal, flowing from the throne of God and of the Lamb [2]down the middle of the great street of the city. On each side of the river stood the tree of life, bearing twelve crops of fruit, yielding its fruit every month. And the leaves of the tree are for the healing of the nations. [3]No longer will there be any curse. The throne of God and of the Lamb will be in the city, and his servants will serve him. [4]They will see his face, and his name will be on their foreheads. [5]There will be no more night. They will not need the light of a lamp or the light of the sun,

[a]16 That is, about 1,400 miles (about 2,200 kilometers)   [b]17 That is, about 200 feet (about 65 meters)   [c]17 Or high   [d]20 The precise identification of some of these precious stones is uncertain.

PASSAGE: Jude 24; Revelation 5
AUTHOR: Egyptian Doxology

To God, the Giver of Grace

May none of God's wonderful works
  keep silence, night or morning.
Bright stars, high mountains, the depths of the seas,
  sources of rushing rivers:
may all these break into song as we sing
  to Father, Son and Holy Spirit.
May all the angels in the heavens reply:
  Amen! Amen! Amen!
Power, praise, honor, eternal glory
  to God the only Giver of grace.
  Amen! Amen! Amen!

Go to page 2 for your next devotional reading.

for the Lord God will give them light. And they will reign for ever and ever.

⁶The angel said to me, "These words are trustworthy and true. The Lord, the God of the spirits of the prophets, sent his angel to show his servants the things that must soon take place."

Jesus Is Coming

⁷"Behold, I am coming soon! Blessed is he who keeps the words of the prophecy in this book."

⁸I, John, am the one who heard and saw these things. And when I had heard and seen them, I fell down to worship at the feet of the angel who had been showing them to me. ⁹But he said to me, "Do not do it! I am a fellow servant with you and with your brothers the prophets and of all who keep the words of this book. Worship God!"

¹⁰Then he told me, "Do not seal up the words of the prophecy of this book, because the time is near. ¹¹Let him who does wrong continue to do wrong; let him who is vile continue to be vile; let him who does right continue to do right; and let him who is holy continue to be holy."

¹²"Behold, I am coming soon! My reward is with me, and I will give to everyone according to what he has done. ¹³I am the Alpha and the Omega, the First and the Last, the Beginning and the End.

¹⁴"Blessed are those who wash their robes, that they may have the right to the tree of life and may go through the gates into the city. ¹⁵Outside are the dogs, those who practice magic arts, the sexually immoral, the murderers, the idolaters and everyone who loves and practices falsehood.

¹⁶"I, Jesus, have sent my angel to give you*a* this testimony for the churches. I am the Root and the Offspring of David, and the bright Morning Star."

¹⁷The Spirit and the bride say, "Come!" And let him who hears say, "Come!" Whoever is thirsty, let him come; and whoever wishes, let him take the free gift of the water of life.

¹⁸I warn everyone who hears the words of the prophecy of this book: If anyone adds anything to them, God will add to him the plagues described in this book. ¹⁹And if anyone takes words away from this book of prophecy, God will take away from him his share in the tree of life and in the holy city, which are described in this book.

²⁰He who testifies to these things says, "Yes, I am coming soon."

Amen. Come, Lord Jesus.

²¹The grace of the Lord Jesus be with God's people. Amen.

---

a16 The Greek is plural.

WEIGHTS AND MEASURES

· ·

The figures of the table are calculated on the basis of a shekel equaling 11.5 grams, a cubit equaling 18 inches and an ephah equaling 22 liters. The quart referred to is either a dry quart (slightly larger than a liter) or a liquid quart (slightly smaller than a liter), whichever is applicable. The ton referred to in the footnotes is the American ton of 2,000 pounds.

This table is based upon the best available information, but it is not intended to be mathematically precise; like the measurement equivalents in the footnotes, it merely gives approximate amounts and distances. Weights and measures differed somewhat at various times and places in the ancient world. There is uncertainty particularly about the ephah and the bath; further discoveries may give more light on these units of capacity.

		BIBLICAL UNIT	APPROXIMATE AMERICAN EQUIVALENT	APPROXIMATE METRIC EQUIVALENT
WEIGHTS	talent	(60 minas)	75 pounds	34 kilograms
	mina	(50 shekels)	1 1/4 pounds	0.6 kilogram
	shekel	(2 bekas)	2/5 ounce	11.5 grams
	pim	(2/3 shekel)	1/3 ounce	7.6 grams
	beka	(10 gerahs)	1/5 ounce	5.5 grams
	gerah		1/50 ounce	0.6 gram
LENGTH	cubit		18 inches	0.5 meter
	span		9 inches	23 centimeters
	handbreadth		3 inches	8 centimeters
CAPACITY				
Dry Measure	cor [homer]	(10 ephahs)	6 bushels	220 liters
	lethek	(5 ephahs)	3 bushels	110 liters
	ephah	(10 omers)	3/5 bushel	22 liters
	seah	(1/3 ephah)	7 quarts	7.3 liters
	omer	(1/10 ephah)	2 quarts	2 liters
	cab	(1/18 ephah)	1 quart	1 liter
Liquid Measure	bath	(1 ephah)	6 gallons	22 liters
	hin	(1/6 bath)	4 quarts	4 liters
	log	(1/72 bath)	1/3 quart	0.3 liter

ACKNOWLEDGMENTS INDEX

Page 2:   Taken from THE KNOWLEDGE OF THE HOLY by A.W. Tozer. Copyright © 1961 by Aiden Wilson Tozer. Used by permission of HarperCollins Publishers.

Page 5:   Taken from TWILIGHT by Andrew Kuyvenhoven. Copyright © 1994 by CRC Publications, Grand Rapids, MI 49560. Used by permission.

Page 15:   Taken from GOD OF WEAKNESS by John Timmer. Copyright © 1988 by John Timmer. Used by permission of Zondervan Publishing House.

Page 18:   Taken from ON ASKING GOD WHY by Elisabeth Elliot. Copyright © 1989 by Fleming H. Revell, a division of Baker Book House Company. Used by permission.

Page 22:   Taken from TOO YOUNG TO BE OLD by John Gilmore. Copyright © 1992 by John Gilmore. Used by permission of Harold Shaw Publishers, Wheaton, IL.

Page 25:   Taken from WEATHER OF THE HEART by Gigi Graham Tchividjian. Copyright © 1991 by Gigi Graham Tchividjian. Published by Multnomah Books, Questar Publishers. Used by permission.

Page 28:   Taken from MY UTMOST FOR HIS HIGHEST by Oswald Chambers. Copyright © 1935 by Dodd, Mead and Company, Inc. Copyright renewed 1963 by Oswald Chambers Publications Assn., Ltd. Used by permission of Discovery House Publishers, Box 3566, Grand Rapids, MI 49501. All rights reserved.

Page 61:   Taken from LET GO by François Fénelon. Copyright © 1973 by Banner Publishing. Used by permission of Whitaker House, 580 Pittsburgh St., Springdale, PA 15144.

Page 66:   Taken from A TOUCH OF HIS FREEDOM by Charles Stanley. Copyright © 1991 by Charles Stanley. Used by permission of Zondervan Publishing House.

Page 71:   Taken from OUR DAILY WALK by F.B. Meyer. Published by Zondervan Publishing House.

Page 84:   Taken from DIAMONDS IN THE DUST by Joni Eareckson Tada. Copyright © 1993 by Joni Eareckson Tada. Used by permission of Zondervan Publishing House.

Page 87:   Public Domain. Reprinted in MASTERPIECES OF RELIGIOUS VERSE, edited by James Dalton Morrison. Published by Harper & Brothers.

Page 90:   Taken from ENJOYING YOUR BEST YEARS by J. Oswald Sanders. Copyright © 1993. Used by permission of Discovery House Publishers, Box 3566, Grand Rapids, MI 49501. All rights reserved.

Page 108:   Taken from THE KNOWLEDGE OF THE HOLY by A.W. Tozer. Copyright © 1961 by Aiden Wilson Tozer. Used by permission of HarperCollins Publishers.

Page 137:   Taken from DRAWING NEAR by John F. MacArthur, Jr. Copyright © 1993 by John F. MacArthur, Jr. Used by permission of Good News Publishers/Crossway Books, Wheaton, IL 60187.

Page 141:   Taken from FROM FULL HOUSE TO EMPTY NEST by William L. Coleman. Copyright © 1994. Used by permission of Discovery House Publishers, Box 3566, Grand Rapids, MI 49501. All rights reserved.

Page 152:   Taken from CHARACTER AND DESTINY by D. James Kennedy. Copyright © 1994 by D. James Kennedy with Jim Nelson Black. Used by permission of Zondervan Publishing House.

Page 160:   Public Domain. Reprinted in PSALTER HYMNAL. Published by CRC Publications.

Page 169:   Taken from NO WRINKLES ON THE SOUL by Richard L. Morgan. Copyright © 1990. Published by The Upper Room, PO Box 189, Nashville, TN 37202. Used by permission.

Page 176:   Taken from PROMISED LAND LIVING by J. Oswald Sanders. Copyright © 1984 by the Moody Bible Institute of Chicago. Moody Press. Used by permission.

Page 185:   Taken from DAYLIGHT DEVOTIONAL BIBLE. Copyright © 1988 by The Zondervan Corporation. Used by permission.

Page 211:   Taken from KEEP THE FIRE by Don Anderson. Copyright © 1994 by Donald E. Anderson. Published by Multnomah Books, Questar Publishers. Used by permission.

Page 215:   Taken from PERSONAL FINANCES by Larry Burkett. Copyright © 1991 by Christian Financial Concepts. Moody Press. Used by permission.

Page 216:   Public Domain. Reprinted in CHAPTERS INTO VERSE (Volume I) assembled and edited by Robert Atwan & Laurance Wieder. Published by Oxford University Press.

Page 217:   Taken from SEPTEMBER SONG by Leslie E. Moser. Copyright © 1991 by Leslie E. Moser. Published by Star Song Publishing Group, a division of Jubilee Communications, Inc. Used by permission.

Page 220:   Public Domain. Reprinted as "The Review of Life" (anonymous) in NEARING HOME, by William Schenk. Published by Presbyterian Board of Publications.

Page 236:   Taken from WISE AND WONDERFUL by Charles L. Allen. Copyright © 1994 by Charles L. Allen. Published by Fleming H. Revell, a division of Baker Book House Company. Used by permission.

Page 245:   Taken from SEPTEMBER SONG by Leslie E. Moser. Copyright © 1991 by Leslie E. Moser. Published by Star Song Publishing Group, a division of Jubilee Communications, Inc. Used by permission.

Page 249:   Taken from A DIVINE BLESSING by Elizabeth Skoglund. Copyright © 1988 by Elizabeth R. Skoglund. Used by permission of World Wide Publications.

Page 252:   Public Domain. Reprinted in YOU CAN SAY THAT AGAIN, compiled by R.E.O. White. Published by Zondervan Publishing House.

Page 254:   Taken from BELOVED by Kay Arthur. Copyright © 1994 by Kay Arthur. Used by permission.

Page 260:   Taken from DAYLIGHT DEVOTIONAL BIBLE. Copyright © 1988 by The Zondervan Corporation. Used by permission.

Page 271:   Taken from GROWING STRONG IN THE SEASONS OF LIFE by Charles R. Swindoll. Copyright © 1983 by Charles R. Swindoll, Inc. Used by permission of Zondervan Publishing House.

Page 281:   Taken from "I DON'T KNOW WHAT OLD IS, BUT OLD IS OLDER THAN ME" by Sherwood Eliot Wirt. Copyright © 1992 by Sherwood Eliot Wirt. Used by permission.

Page 283:   Taken from FAITH FOR THE OLDER YEARS by Paul B. Maves. Copyright © 1986 by Augsburg Publishing House. Used by permission of Augsburg Fortress.

Page 289:   Public Domain. Reprinted in THE ENGLISH SPIRIT. Published by Abingdon Press.

Page 294: Taken from SILENT STRENGTH FOR MY LIFE by Lloyd John Ogilvie. Copyright © 1990 by Harvest House Publishers, Eugene, Oregon. Used by permission.

Page 298: Taken from A DIVINE BLESSING by Elizabeth Skoglund. Copyright © 1988 by Elizabeth R. Skoglund. Used by permission of World Wide Publications.

Page 318: Taken from NO WRINKLES ON THE SOUL by Richard L. Morgan. Copyright © 1990. Published by The Upper Room, PO Box 189, Nashville, TN, 37202. Used by permission.

Page 323: Taken from WINTER: A TIME FOR PEACE by Debra Klingsporn. Copyright © 1994 by Thomas Nelson Publishers. Used by permission.

Page 331: Taken from FROM FULL HOUSE TO EMPTY NEST by William L. Coleman. Copyright © 1994. Used by permission of Discovery House Publishers, Box 3566, Grand Rapids, MI. All rights reserved.

Page 336: Public Domain. Reprinted in THE ENGLISH SPIRIT. Published by Abingdon Press.

Page 340: Taken from A TESTAMENT OF DEVOTION by Thomas R. Kelly. Copyright © 1941 by Harper & Brothers. Copyright renewed © 1969 by Lois Lael Kelly Statler. Used by permission of HarperCollins Publishers.

Page 342: Taken from A TOUCH OF HIS LOVE by Charles Stanley. Copyright © 1994 by Charles F. Stanley. Used by permission of Zondervan Publishing House.

Page 362: Taken from THE BETTER HALF OF LIFE by Jean Shaw. Copyright © 1983 by The Zondervan Corporation. Used by permission.

Page 384: Taken from GRIEVING THE LOSS OF SOMEONE YOU LOVE. Copyright © 1993 by Raymond R. Mitsch and Lynn Brookside. Published by Servant Publications, Box 8617, Ann Arbor, MI 48107. Used by permission.

Page 386: Taken from TOO YOUNG TO BE OLD by John Gilmore. Copyright © 1992 by John Gilmore. Used by permission of Harold Shaw Publishers, Wheaton, IL.

Page 390: Public Domain. Reprinted as an excerpt in THE MEANING OF PRAYER by Harry Emerson Fosdick. Published by American Baptist Publications Society.

Page 393: Taken from DIAMONDS IN THE DUST by Joni Eareckson Tada. Copyright © 1993 by Joni Eareckson Tada. Used by permission of Zondervan Publishing House.

Page 411: Taken from MINISTRY WITH OLDER PERSONS by Arthur H. Becker. Copyright © 1986 Augsburg Publishing House. Used by permission of Augsburg Fortress.

Page 425: Taken from MORNING AND EVENING by Charles H. Spurgeon. Copyright © 1980 by the Zondervan Corporation. Used by permission.

Page 429: Taken from HE IS REAL by Millie Stamm. Copyright © 1991 by Millie Stamm. Used by permission of Zondervan Publishing House.

Page 437: Taken from TWILIGHT by Andrew Kuyvenhoven. Copyright © 1994 by CRC Publications, Grand Rapids, MI 49560. Used by permission.

Page 441: Taken from PSALMS OF MY LIFE by Joseph Bayly, available through your local Christian bookstore. Copyright © 1987 by the estate of Joseph Bayly. Used by permission of Chariot FAMILY Publishing.

Page 446: Taken from HE IS REAL by Millie Stamm. Copyright © 1991 by Millie Stamm. Used by permission of Zondervan Publishing House.

Page 462: Taken from CHRIST IN THE SEASONS OF MINISTRY by John Killinger. Copyright © 1981 by Word, Inc. Used by permission.

Page 499: Taken from SILENT STRENGTH FOR MY LIFE by Lloyd John Ogilvie. Copyright © 1990 by Harvest House Publishers, Eugene, Oregon. Used by permission.

Page 505: Taken from LIVING POWERFULLY ONE DAY AT A TIME by Robert H. Schuller. Copyright © 1982 by Robert H. Schuller. Published by Fleming H. Revell, a division of Baker Book House Company. Used by permission.

Page 509: Taken from STREAMS IN THE DESERT by Mrs. Charles E. Cowman. Published by Zondervan Publishing House.

Page 512: Taken from WRITING THE RIVER by Luci Shaw. Copyright © 1994 by Luci Shaw. Published by Piñon Press. Used by permission of NavPress, Colorado Springs, CO. All rights reserved.

Page 515: Taken from TOO YOUNG TO BE OLD by John Gilmore. Copyright © 1992 by John Gilmore. Used by permission of Harold Shaw Publishers, Wheaton, IL.

Page 522: Taken from DAYLIGHT DEVOTIONAL BIBLE. Copyright © 1988 by The Zondervan Corporation. Used by permission.

Page 538: Taken from STREAMS IN THE DESERT by Mrs. Charles E. Cowman. Published by Zondervan Publishing House.

Page 549: Taken from SILENT STRENGTH FOR MY LIFE by Lloyd John Ogilvie. Copyright © 1990 by Harvest House Publishers, Eugene, Oregon. Used by permission.

Page 563: Taken from SEPTEMBER SONG by Leslie E. Moser. Copyright © 1991 by Leslie E. Moser. Published by Star Song Publishing Group, a division of Jubilee Communications, Inc. Used by permission.

Page 571: Public Domain. Reprinted in WAITING by Ben Patterson. Published by InterVarsity Press.

Page 579: Taken from FIGHT FOR THE FAMILY by Jill Briscoe. Copyright © 1981 by The Zondervan Corporation. Used by permission.

Page 581: Taken from CONVERSATIONS ON GROWING OLDER by Cornelis Gilhuis, translated from the Dutch by Cor Barendrecht. Copyright © 1977 by Wm. B. Eerdmans Publishing Co. Used by permission.

Page 585: Taken from MORNING AND EVENING by Charles H. Spurgeon. Copyright © 1980 by the Zondervan Corporation. Used by permission of Zondervan Publishing House.

Page 599: Taken from PRIME RIB & APPLE by Jill Briscoe. Copyright © 1976 by The Zondervan Corporation. Used by permission.

Page 601: Taken from GETTING READY FOR A GREAT RETIREMENT by Barbara Deane. Copyright © 1992 by Barbara Deane. Used by permission of NavPress, Colorado Springs, CO. All rights reserved.

Page 603: Public Domain. Reprinted in TOO YOUNG TO BE OLD by John Gilmore. Copyright © 1992 by John Gilmore. Published by Harold Shaw Publishers.

Page 607: Taken from MORNING AND EVENING by Charles H. Spurgeon. Copyright © 1980 by the Zondervan Corporation. Used by permission of Zondervan Publishing House.

Page 609: Taken from THE LAST THING WE TALK ABOUT by Joseph Bayly, available through your local Christian bookstore. Copyright © 1969 by David C. Cook Publishing Co. Used by permission of Chariot FAMILY Publishing.

Page 620: Taken from ENJOYING YOUR BEST YEARS by J. Oswald Sanders. Copyright © 1993. Used by permission of Discovery House Publishers, Box 3566, Grand Rapids, MI. All rights reserved.

ACKNOWLEDGMENTS INDEX 1645

Page 1456: Taken from AS OUR YEARS INCREASE by Tim Stafford. Copyright © 1989 by Tim Stafford. Used by permission of Zondervan Publishing House.

Page 1458: Taken from LOVE WITHIN LIMITS by Lewis B. Smedes. Copyright © 1978 by Wm. B. Eerdmans Publishing Co. Used by permission.

Page 1460: Taken from OUR GREATEST GIFT by Henri J.M. Nouwen. Copyright © 1994 by Henri J.M. Nouwen. Used by permission of HarperCollins Publishers.

Page 1462: Public Domain. Reprinted in YOU CAN SAY THAT AGAIN, compiled by R.E.O. White. Published by Zondervan Publishing House.

Page 1465: Taken from HOPE FOR THE TROUBLED HEART by Billy Graham. Copyright © 1991 by Billy Graham. Used by permission of Word, Inc., Dallas. All rights reserved.

Page 1467: Taken from THE BETTER HALF OF LIFE by Jean Shaw. Copyright © 1983 by The Zondervan Corporation. Used by permission.

Page 1469: Taken from IN THE EYE OF THE STORM by Max Lucado. Copyright © 1991 by Max Lucado. Used by permission of Word, Inc., Dallas. All rights reserved.

Page 1471: Taken from WISE AND WONDERFUL by Charles L. Allen. Copyright © 1994 by Charles L. Allen. Published by Fleming H. Revell, a division of Baker Book House Company. Used by permission.

Page 1473: Taken from SHAME AND GRACE by Lewis B. Smedes. Copyright © 1993 by Lewis B. Smedes. Used by permission of HarperCollins Publishers.

Page 1475: Public Domain. Reprinted in FAMOUS PRAYERS. Published by Lion Publishing.

Page 1477: Taken from DAYLIGHT DEVOTIONAL BIBLE. Copyright © 1988 by The Zondervan Corporation. Used by permission.

Page 1480: Taken from ENJOYING YOUR BEST YEARS by J. Oswald Sanders. Copyright © 1993. Used by permission of Discovery House Publishers, Box 3566, Grand Rapids, MI. All rights reserved.

Page 1484: Taken from OUR DAILY WALK by F.B. Meyer. Published by Zondervan Publishing House.

Page 1486: Taken from LIVE ALL YOUR LIFE by Reuel L. Howe. Copyright © 1974. Used by permission of Word, Inc., Dallas. All rights reserved.

Page 1489: Taken from KEEP THE FIRE by Don Anderson. Copyright © 1994 by Donald E. Anderson. Published by Multnomah Books, Questar Publishers. Used by permission.

Page 1492: Public Domain. Reprinted in CHRISTIAN POETRY. Published by Lion Publishing.

Page 1494: Taken from ABBA'S CHILD by Brennan Manning. Copyright © 1994 by Brennan Manning. Used by permission of NavPress, Colorado Springs, CO. All rights reserved.

Page 1496: Taken from THE SIGNATURE OF JESUS by Brennan Manning. Copyright © 1992 by Brennan Manning. Published by Multnomah Press, Questar Publishers. Used by permission.

Page 1497: Taken from COME BEFORE WINTER AND SHARE MY HOPE by Charles R. Swindoll. Copyright © 1985 by Charles R. Swindoll, Inc. Used by permission of Zondervan Publishing House.

Page 1499: Taken from SEPTEMBER SONG by Leslie E. Moser. Copyright © 1991 by Leslie E. Moser. Published by Star Song Publishing Group, a division of Jubilee Communications, Inc. Used by permission.

Page 1501: Taken from THE BETTER HALF OF LIFE by Jean Shaw. Copyright © 1983 by The Zondervan Corporation. Used by permission.

Page 1503: Public Domain. Reprinted in PSALTER HYMNAL. Published by CRC Publications.

Page 1505: Taken from A SHEPHERD LOOKS AT PSALM 23 by W. Phillip Keller. Copyright © 1970 by W. Phillip Keller. Used by permission of Zondervan Publishing House.

Page 1507: Taken from AS LONG AS I LIVE by Jacob D. Eppinga. Copyright © 1993 by CRC Publications, Grand Rapids, MI 49560. Used by permission.

Page 1509: Taken from LAUGH AGAIN by Charles R. Swindoll. Copyright © 1992 by Charles R. Swindoll. Used by permission of Word, Inc., Dallas. All rights reserved.

Page 1511: Taken from KEEP THE FIRE by Don Anderson. Copyright © 1994 by Donald E. Anderson. Published by Multnomah Books, Questar Publishers. Used by permission.

Page 1513: Taken from WHAT WAS GOD DOING ON THE CROSS? by Alister E. McGrath. Copyright © 1993 by Alister E. McGrath. Used by permission of Zondervan Publishing House.

Page 1515: Taken from WEATHER OF THE HEART by Gigi Graham Tchividjian. Copyright © 1991 by Gigi Graham Tchividjian. Published by Multnomah Books, Questar Publishers. Used by permission.

Page 1516: Taken from OUR DAILY WALK by F.B. Meyer. Published by Zondervan Publishing House.

Page 1519: Taken from AS OUR YEARS INCREASE by Tim Stafford. Copyright © 1989 by Tim Stafford. Used by permission of Zondervan Publishing House.

Page 1521: Taken from ON THE ANVIL, pp. 69–70, by Max Lucado. Copyright © 1985 by Max Lucado. Used by permission of Tyndale House Publishers, Inc. All rights reserved.

Page 1523: Taken from DIAMONDS IN THE DUST by Joni Eareckson Tada. Copyright © 1993 by Joni Eareckson Tada. Used by permission of Zondervan Publishing House.

Page 1527: Taken from UNTO THE HILLS by Billy Graham. Copyright © 1986 by Billy Graham. Used by permission of Word, Inc., Dallas. All rights reserved.

Page 1530: Public Domain. Reprinted in MASTERPIECES OF RELIGIOUS VERSE, edited by James Dalton Morrison. Published by Harper & Brothers.

Page 1533: Taken from DRAWING NEAR by John F. MacArthur, Jr. Copyright © 1993 by John F. MacArthur, Jr. Used by permission of Good News Publishers/Crossway Books, Wheaton, IL 60187.

Page 1535: Taken from KEEP THE FIRE by Don Anderson. Copyright © 1994 by Donald E. Anderson. Published by Multnomah Books, Questar Publishers. Used by permission.

Page 1538: Taken from ENJOYING YOUR BEST YEARS by J. Oswald Sanders. Copyright © 1993. Used by permission of Discovery House Publishers, Box 3566, Grand Rapids, MI. All rights reserved.

Page 1540: Taken from SIX HOURS ONE FRIDAY by Max Lucado. Copyright © 1989 by Max Lucado. Published by Multnomah Press, Questar Publishers. Used by permission.

Page 1541: Taken from BE STILL AND KNOW by Millie Stamm. Copyright © 1978 by Millie Stamm. Used by permission of Zondervan Publishing House.

Page 1543: Public Domain. Reprinted in PSALTER HYMNAL. Published by CRC Publications.

Page 1546: Taken from BESIDE STILL WATERS by Gien Karssen. Copyright © 1985 by Gien Karssen. Used by permission of NavPress, Colorado Springs, CO. All rights reserved.

Page 1548: Taken from GROWING STRONG IN THE SEASONS OF LIFE by Charles R. Swindoll. Copyright © 1983 by Charles R. Swindoll, Inc. Used by permission of Zondervan Publishing House.

Page 1550: Taken from DAYLIGHT DEVOTIONAL BIBLE. Copyright © 1988 by The Zondervan Corporation. Used by permission.

Page 1553: Taken from NO SUBSTITUTE FOR PERSEVERING by Reuben Welch. Copyright © 1976 by Impact Books, a div. of John T. Benson Pub. Co. Reassigned to Zondervan Publishing House. Used by permission.

Page 1556: Taken from DAYLIGHT DEVOTIONAL BIBLE. Copyright © 1988 by The Zondervan Corporation. Used by permission.

Page 1558: Taken from CHRIST IN THE SEASONS OF MINISTRY by John Killinger. Copyright © 1981 by Word, Inc. Used by permission.

Page 1560: Taken from FROM FULL HOUSE TO EMPTY NEST by William L. Coleman. Copyright © 1994. Used by permission of Discovery House Publishers, Box 3566, Grand Rapids, MI. All rights reserved.

Page 1565: Taken from CONVERSATIONS ON GROWING OLDER by Cornelis Gilhuis, translated from the Dutch by Cor Barendrecht. Copyright © 1977 by Wm. B. Eerdmans Publishing Co. Used by permission.

Page 1568: Taken from FAITH FOR THE OLDER YEARS by Paul B. Maves. Copyright © 1986 by Augsburg Publishing House. Used by permission of Augsburg Fortress.

Page 1572: Taken from THE PURSUIT OF HOLINESS by Jerry Bridges. Copyright © 1978 by Jerry Bridges. Used by permission of NavPress, Colorado Springs, CO. All rights reserved.

Page 1574: Taken from JAMES: RUNNING UPHILL INTO THE WIND by Don Anderson. Copyright © 1990 by Don Anderson. Used by permission of Don Anderson Ministries, PO Box 6611, Tyler, TX 75711.

Page 1576: Public Domain. Reprinted in FAMOUS PRAYERS. Published by Lion Publishing.

Page 1577: Taken from UNTO THE HILLS by Billy Graham. Copyright © 1986 by Billy Graham. Used by permission of Word, Inc., Dallas. All rights reserved.

Page 1579: Taken from JAMES: RUNNING UPHILL INTO THE WIND by Don Anderson. Copyright © 1990 by Don Anderson. Used by permission of Don Anderson Ministries, PO Box 6611, Tyler, TX 75711.

Page 1581: Taken from DAYS OF HEAVEN ON EARTH by A.B. Simpson. Copyright © 1984 by Christian Publications, Inc. Used by permission.

Page 1583: Taken from THE BEST OF D.L. MOODY by D.L. Moody. Published by Baker Book House.

Page 1585: Taken from ON YOUR WAY REJOICING by Louis M. Tamminga. Published by Paideia Press. Used by permission of author.

Page 1587: Public Domain. Reprinted in PSALTER HYMNAL. Published by CRC Publications.

Page 1590: Taken from A TOUCH OF HIS LOVE by Charles Stanley. Copyright © 1994 by Charles F. Stanley. Used by permission of Zondervan Publishing House.

Page 1593: Taken from DAYLIGHT DEVOTIONAL BIBLE. Copyright © 1988 by The Zondervan Corporation. Used by permission.

Page 1595: Taken from MEASURING THE DAYS by Walter Wangerin, Jr. Copyright © 1993 by Walter Wangerin, Jr. Used by permission.

Page 1596: Taken from KEEP THE FIRE by Don Anderson. Copyright © 1994 by Donald E. Anderson. Published by Multnomah Books, Questar Publishers. Used by permission.

Page 1598: Taken from CREATIVE GRANDPARENTING by Jerry and Jack Schreur. Copyright © 1992. Used by permission of Discovery House Publishers, Box 3566, Grand Rapids, MI. All rights reserved.

Page 1600: Public Domain. Reprinted in PSALTER HYMNAL. Published by CRC Publications.

Page 1604: Taken from ON YOUR WAY REJOICING by Louis M. Tamminga. Published by Paideia Press. Used by permission of author.

Page 1606: Taken from WEATHER OF THE HEART by Gigi Graham Tchividjian. Copyright © 1991 by Gigi Graham Tchividjian. Published by Multnomah Books, Questar Publishers. Used by permission.

Page 1608: Taken from HE IS REAL by Millie Stamm. Copyright © 1991 by Millie Stamm. Used by permission of Zondervan Publishing House.

Page 1611: Taken from SERVING GOD by Ben Patterson. Copyright © 1994 by Ben Patterson. Used by permission of InterVarsity Press, P.O. Box 1400, Downers Grove, IL 60515.

Page 1613: Taken from HEAVEN by Peter J. Kreeft. Copyright © 1980 by Peter J. Kreeft. Used by permission.

Page 1615: Public Domain. Reprinted in PSALTER HYMNAL. Published by CRC Publications.

Page 1617: Taken from CONVERSATIONS ON GROWING OLDER by Cornelis Gilhuis, translated from the Dutch by Cor Barendrecht. Copyright © 1977 by Wm. B. Eerdmans Publishing Co. Used by permission.

Page 1621: Taken from WHEN GOD DOESN'T MAKE SENSE by James Dobson. Copyright © 1993 by Tyndale House Publishers, Inc. Used by permission. All rights reserved.

Page 1626: Taken from BESIDE STILL WATERS by Gien Karssen. Copyright © 1985 by Gien Karssen. Used by permission of NavPress, Colorado Springs, CO. All rights reserved.

Page 1632: Taken from AS LONG AS I LIVE by Jacob D. Eppinga. Copyright © 1993 by CRC Publications, Grand Rapids, MI 49560. Used by permission.

Page 1634: Taken from TOO YOUNG TO BE OLD by John Gilmore. Copyright © 1992 by John Gilmore. Used by permission of Harold Shaw Publishers, Wheaton, IL.

Page 1636: Public Domain. Reprinted in FAMOUS PRAYERS. Published by Lion Publishing.

AUTHOR BIOGRAPHIES

Charles L. Allen was pastor for 23 years at the First United Methodist Church in Houston, Texas. He has written more than 45 books. *Devotions are found on pages 236, 673, 1471.*

Don Anderson holds a doctorate in marriage and family counseling. For the past 20 years he has been working with senior adults. *Devotions are found on pages 211, 846, 1311, 1437, 1489, 1511, 1535, 1574, 1579, 1596.*

Lancelot Andrewes (1555–1626) was among those who produced the King James Version of the Bible. *A devotion is found on page 289.*

Anselm (1033–1109), one of the most enlightened thinkers of his time, served as Archbishop of Canterbury. *A devotion is found on page 336.*

Charles Arn is an instructional designer, researcher and seminar leader. He is president of Church Growth, Inc. *A devotion is found on page 688.*

Winfield Arn is an international spokesperson on church growth, founder of a ministry that helps churches organize ministries to senior adults, and author of 12 books. *A devotion is found on page 688.*

Kay Arthur is the founder, along with her husband, Jack, of Precept Ministries, which reaches people internationally through inductive Bible studies. *A devotion is found on page 254.*

Augustine (354–430), who became a bishop after a spiritual struggle that brought him back to the Christian faith, is best known for his *Confessions* and his theological work *The City of God. A devotion is found on page 1145.*

Joseph Bayly, first director of InterVarsity Press, later held several key positions at David C. Cook Publishing. He died in 1986, joining three sons who preceded him in death. *Devotions are found on pages 441, 609, 741, 1406.*

Arthur H. Becker has served as a pastor, hospital chaplain and professor of pastoral care. He wrote *Ministry With Older Persons. A devotion is found on page 411.*

Horatius Bonar (1808–1889) was a Scottish clergyman and hymn writer known for his hymns n*IT/I Heard the Voice of Jesus Say and *O Love of God, How Strong and True. A devotion is found on page 1600.*

Dietrich Bonhoeffer (1906–1945), a German Lutheran pastor and theologian, was arrested for his involvement in anti-Nazi activities in Germany and hanged in a concentration camp in 1945. *A devotion is found on page 675.*

Leslie Brandt has had a powerful ministry through his work as an evangelist, retreat leader and author. *A devotion is found on page 1350.*

Jerry Bridges has served on staff at The Navigators since 1955, most recently as a vice-president. He has written several books. *Devotions are found on pages 815, 1572.*

Jill Briscoe is the editor of *Just Between Us,* a magazine for ministry wives and women in the ministry. She and her husband Stuart are well-known Bible teachers. *Devotions are found on pages 579, 599.*

Stuart Briscoe has written many books and has preached and taught all over the world. The Briscoes moved from England in 1970 to join the staff of Elmbrook Church in Waukesha, Wisconsin. *Devotions are found on pages 1029, 1037.*

Lynn Brookside is a free-lance writer and counselor. *A devotion is found on page 384.*

Robert Browning (1812–1889) was the most-loved poet of the late Victorians and the Edwardians. *A devotion is found on page 651.*

Frederick Buechner is a critically acclaimed author of more than 20 novels and nonfiction works, including *The Book of Bebb* and *Wishful Thinking. A devotion is found on page 1334.*

Larry Burkett is founder and president of Financial Concepts, Inc., a ministry that teaches God's principles of finances. He is the author of several books, including *Investing for the Future. A devotion is found on page 215.*

Dirk R. Buursma is senior theological editor at Zondervan Publishing House. He has served as editor on such Bible editions as *The New Student Bible* and the *Men's Devotional Bible. Devotions are found on pages 185, 260, 1023, 1128, 1138, 1477, 1550, 1556, 1593.*

Oswald Chambers (1874–1917) was a Bible teacher, conference leader and YMCA chaplain. After his death his widow compiled his writings in *My Utmost for His Highest* and other devotional books. *Devotions are found on pages 28, 669, 1156, 1271.*

Margaret Clarkson is the author of many hymns, songs and poems as well as several books. *A devotion is found on page 961.*

William L. Coleman, author of more than 30 books, has combined his vast experience as a pastor, researcher and speaker to write devotionals dealing with family relationships. *Devotions are found on pages 141, 331, 757, 1560.*

Charles W. Colson served as Special Counsel to President Richard Nixon from 1969 to 1973. He is founder of Prison Fellowship Ministries, an international prison outreach. His books include *Loving God. Devotions are found on pages 1224, 1416.*

Mrs. Charles E. Cowman (1870–1960) served along with her husband as missionaries in Japan and China from 1901 to 1917. Mrs. Cowman's devotional books have been popular for many years. *Devotions are found on pages 509, 538.*

Ralph Spaulding Cushman served as bishop of the St. Paul Area of The Methodist Church from 1939 until 1952. His books of meditations and original poetry have been warmly received. *A devotion is found on page 791.*

Barbara Deane is a writer, lecturer and workshop leader on issues of caregiving and aging. *Devotions are found on pages 601, 777.*

James Dobson is founder and president of Focus on the Family, a nonprofit organization that produces his nationally syndicated radio program. He is the author of *Dare to Discipline. A devotion is found on page 1621.*

John Donne (1571–1631) was the greatest of the "metaphysical" poets of the 17th century. An Anglican priest, his sermons, like his poems, won him fame for their powerful imagery. *Devotions are found on pages 1054, 1462.*

Elisabeth Elliot was a young missionary wife and mother when her husband was killed while bringing the gospel to the Auca Indians. She is the author of several books. *Devotions are found on pages 18, 934.*

Ted Engstrom is president emeritus of World Vision International. He has written 40 books. *Devotions are found on pages 699, 1379.*

Jacob D. Eppinga is a retired Christian Reformed minister who served three churches during his ministry. He is the author of *Cabbages & Kings*, a column in *The Banner*. *Devotions are found on pages 759, 805, 824, 837, 889, 1507, 1632.*

François Fénelon (1651–1715) was a member of the court of Louis XIV and was later appointed to a local church where he was described as an ideal pastor. *A devotion is found on page 61.*

Annie Johnson Flint (1862–1932) was an American writer of religious verse. *A devotion is found on page 810.*

Richard Foster is Distinguished Professor of Spiritual Formation at Azusa Pacific University and the founder of Renovaré, a movement committed to church renewal. He is the author of *Celebration of Discipline* and *Prayer*. *A devotion is found on page 827.*

Francis of Assisi (1182–1226) was the most beloved of saints of the Middle Ages and founder of the Franciscan religious order. *A devotion is found on page 1475.*

Ronald Geschwendt is a pastor in the Reformed Church of America (RCA) and editor of the *Sunday School Guide*. *A devotion is found on page 727.*

Cornelis Gilhuis was a pastor in the Netherlands. A popular lecturer and speaker, he wrote *Conversations on Growing Older*. *Devotions are found on pages 581, 1371, 1565, 1617.*

John Gilmore is the pastor of Madisonville Baptist Church in Cincinnati, Ohio and a frequent speaker on senior life. He has written several books. *Devotions are found on pages 22, 386, 515, 725, 1278, 1634.*

Ken Gire is a writer living in Fullerton, California. He is the award-winning author of the "Moments with the Savior" devotional series. *Devotions are found on pages 1290, 1301, 1309, 1355.*

Billy Graham has perhaps reached more people with the gospel than any other person alive today. In addition to being an international evangelist, he is an accomplished author. *Devotions are found on pages 622, 656, 1465, 1527, 1577.*

Ruth Bell Graham is the daughter of missionaries to China, the wife of evangelist Billy Graham, the mother of five, a grandmother to 18, and now a great-grandmother. She wrote *One Wintry Night* and *Sitting by My Laughing Fire*. *Devotions are found on pages 25, 1515.*

Lady Jane Grey (1537–1554) was an English noblewoman beheaded as a possible rival for the throne of Mary I. *A devotion is found on page 390.*

Tim Hansel is founder of Summit Expeditions. He has written several books, including *What Kids Need Most in a Dad*. *A devotion is found on page 1397.*

Kevin Harney is pastor of the Reformed Church of Corinth, located in the metropolitan Grand Rapids, Michigan, area. *A devotion is found on page 1142.*

Frances R. Havergal (1836–1879) was a writer of religious verse known for such hymns as *Take My Life, and Let It Be* and *Who Is on the Lord's Side?* *A devotion is found on page 160.*

George Herbert (1593–1633) was one of England's foremost Christian poets. A classical scholar and musician, he served for much of his career as a well-loved parish priest. *A devotion is found on page 216.*

Kathryn Hillen retired from her profession as an executive secretary to pursue a degree in Biblical literature. *A devotion is found on page 761.*

William How (1823–1897) was an English clergyman and hymn writer known for his hymns *For All the Saints* and *We Give Thee But Thine Own*. *A devotion is found on page 1543.*

Reuel L. Howe was a clergyman, pastoral counselor and educator. He wrote numerous books, including *The Creative Years*. *A devotion is found on page 1486.*

Martin A. Janis has served as a member of the Ohio House of Representatives. A popular speaker on issues relating to aging, he has been active in establishing programs that benefit older adults. *A devotion is found on page 795.*

Gien Karssen served on the Navigators' staff in the Netherlands. She is the author of several books, including *Beside Still Waters*. *Devotions are found on pages 1104, 1546, 1626.*

John Keble (1792–1866) was a professor of poetry at Oxford University and later an Anglican minister. He published a collection of poems titled *The Christian Year*. *A devotion is found on page 1530.*

W. Phillip Keller is the author of over 35 books, including the popular *A Shepherd Looks at Psalm 23*. *Devotions are found on pages 667, 1347, 1505.*

Thomas R. Kelly (1893–1941) was born into a Quaker family in Ohio. A pastor and teacher, he was known as a man of genuine devotion. *A devotion is found on page 340.*

D. James Kennedy is one of the most respected Christian communicators in America and the pastor of Coral Ridge Presbyterian Church in Ft. Lauderdale, Florida. *Devotions are found on pages 152, 1304.*

John Killinger is Distinguished Professor of Religion and Culture at Samford University in Birmingham, Alabama. He is an internationally recognized author, preacher and retreat leader. *Devotions are found on pages 462, 1192, 1558.*

Debra Klingsporn is a free-lance writer and publicist and the author of *Winter: A Time for Peace* in the *Seasons of Life* series. *A devotion is found on page 323.*

John Knox served as Baldwin Professor of Sacred Literature at Union Theological Seminary. His many books include *Never Far From Home*. *Devotions are found on pages 692, 1226.*

Peter Kreeft is professor of philosophy at Boston College and the author of many books, including *Heaven*. *A devotion is found on page 1613.*

Andrew Kuyvenhoven is a retired pastor in the Christian Reformed Church. He served as editor of *The Banner*, director of the Education Department for CRC Publications, and pastor of several churches. *Devotions are found on pages 5, 437.*

Bruce Larson is co-pastor, along with Robert Schuller, of the Crystal Cathedral. He is the author of more than 20 books. *Devotions are found on pages 1245, 1281*

Henry Wadsworth Longfellow (1807–1882) was Professor of Modern Languages at Harvard University. A popular poet, among his best-known poems are *Hiawatha* and *The Village Blacksmith*. *A devotion is found on page 252.*

Max Lucado is a pastor, author and speaker whose books regularly become best-sellers. *Devotions are found on pages 905, 1202, 1221, 1313, 1469, 1521, 1540.*

Henry Francis Lyte (1793–1847) was an Anglican pastor, poet and writer of 80 hymn texts, best known for hymns such as *Abide With Me* and *Jesus, I My Cross Have Taken*. *A devotion is found on page 1446.*

John MacArthur, Jr., is the pastor-teacher of Grace Community Church, Sun Valley, California, and the author of several books. *Devotions are found on pages 137, 1533.*

Brennan Manning spends six months each year directing spiritual retreats. His books include *Abba's Child* and *The Ragamuffin Gospel*. *Devotions are found on pages 902, 1494, 1496.*

George Matheson (1842–1902) was an esteemed Scottish minister and hymn writer who was blind. His most popular hymn was titled *O Love That Wilt Not Let Me Go*. *A devotion is found on page 990.*

Paul B. Maves has studied aging since 1949 when he coauthored *Old People and the Church*. *Devotions are found on pages 283, 1394, 1421, 1568.*

Carole Mayhall, author of several books, speaks regularly at conferences around the world on the subjects of discipleship, marriage and family relationships. *A devotion is found on page 781.*

Alister E. McGrath teaches theology at Oxford University and is research professor of systematic theology at Regent College, Vancouver, B.C. *A devotion is found on page 1513.*

F.B. Meyer (1847–1929) held Baptist pastorates in Liverpool, Leicester, London and Lambeth, England. A gifted expositor, he wrote more than 70 books, including *Our Daily Walk*. *Devotions are found on pages 71, 878, 955, 1110, 1484, 1516.*

Raymond R. Mitsch is founder and executive director of Cornerstone Counseling Center. He has coauthored three devotional books. *A devotion is found on page 384.*

James Montgomery (1771–1854) was a Scottish poet and hymn writer who worked as a newspaper editor. He wrote more than 400 hymns, including *Angels From the Realms of Glory*. *A devotion is found on page 1322.*

Dwight L. Moody (1837–1899) began full-time Sunday school and youth work in 1860 and later established a non-denominational church and a Bible Institute. *A devotion is found on page 1583.*

Richard L. Morgan is an ordained Presbyterian minister. He conducts seminars on aging and related issues. *Devotions are found on pages 169, 318, 1238.*

Leslie E. Moser has been professor of the Psychology of Aging at the Baylor University Institute of Gerontology. He spent over 10 years teaching about the hopes and needs of aging persons. *Devotions are found on pages 218, 245, 563, 1453, 1499.*

Mother Teresa founded her own order, the Sisters of Charity, to work with the poorest of the poor. *A devotion is found on page 1295.*

John Henry Newman (1801–1890) was a leader in the Oxford Movement, a group that sought to help the Church of England return to its historic roots. He eventually joined the Roman Catholic Church. *A devotion is found on page 87.*

John Newton (1725–1807) was renowned as a slave trader turned clergyman. He became well known through his letters and his hymns, most notably *Amazing Grace*. *Devotions are found on pages 603, 1164.*

Henri J.M. Nouwen is a renowned speaker and the author of many books. A native of Holland, he shares his life with people with mental disabilities at the L'Arche Daybreak Community in Toronto. *Devotions are found on pages 707, 1207, 1328, 1353, 1460.*

Lloyd John Ogilvie, author of over 20 books, is chaplain of the United States Senate and former pastor of Hollywood Presbyterian Church in Hollywood, California. *Devotions are found on pages 294, 499, 549, 1172, 1423.*

Thomas Olivers (1725–1799) was one of John Wesley's evangelists. He traveled extensively throughout England and Ireland, preaching the gospel. *A devotion is found on page 1194.*

Ben Patterson serves as dean of the chapel at Hope College in Holland, Michigan. He is a contributing editor for *Christianity Today*. *Devotions are found on pages 1228, 1611.*

Eugene Peterson, a seasoned pastor, is on the faculty at Regent College in Vancouver, B.C. He is the author of *The Message*. *A devotion is found on page 995.*

Frances J. Roberts is an author and poet known for such books as *Come Away, My Beloved* and *On the Highroad of Surrender*. *A devotion is found on page 764.*

Christina Rossetti (1830–1894) was one of England's foremost women poets. A woman of devout faith, her poetry and prose has spiritual longing as its recurring theme. *Devotions are found on pages 1115, 1492, 1576.*

J. Oswald Sanders was a Christian leader for nearly 70 years and the author of over 40 books on spiritual living. *Devotions are found on pages 90, 176, 620, 965, 1124, 1260, 1342, 1480, 1538.*

Jack Schreur is director of Face to Face Ministries and a popular youth speaker. *A devotion is found on page 1598.*

Jerry Schreur is the pastor of family ministries at Calvary Church in Grand Rapids, Michigan. *A devotion is found on page 1598.*

Robert H. Schuller is founder and senior pastor of the Crystal Cathedral in Garden Grove, California. *Devotions are found on pages 505, 841, 863.*

Joseph Scriven (1819–1886) emigrated from Ireland to Canada, where he spent his life helping the physically handicapped. The words of his famous hymn *What a Friend We Have in Jesus* were sent to his mother when she was in distress. *A devotion is found on page 1587.*

Jean Shaw is the author of several books. A seminary graduate, she speaks to groups on the subject of the Christian life. *Devotions are found on pages 362, 678, 732, 880, 1467, 1501.*

Luci Shaw is the critically acclaimed author of several collections of poetry, including *Writing the River*. She is writer-in-residence at Regent College, a teacher, an editor and a frequent speaker. *A devotion is found on page 512.*

Charlie W. Shedd, a popular minister and father of five, wrote many books, including *Letters to Karen. A devotion is found on page 1299.*

A.B. Simpson (1844–1919), an author, hymn writer and speaker, was an evangelist to the urban masses of New York City. He was the founder of The Christian and Missionary Alliance. *A devotion is found on page 1581.*

Elizabeth Skoglund is a marriage, family and child counselor. She is the author of several books, including *More Than Coping. Devotions are found on pages 249, 298, 1442.*

James Grindlay Small (1817–1888), a writer of religious verse, was best known for his hymn *I've Found a Friend, O Such a Friend. A devotion is found on page 1429.*

Lewis B. Smedes is professor-emeritus, Fuller Theological Seminary, in Pasadena, California. He has written several books, including *Forgive and Forget. Devotions are found on pages 749, 1149, 1205, 1444, 1458, 1473.*

Hannah Whitall Smith was an American Quaker philanthropist. A well-known speaker in the late 1800s, she wrote hundreds of religious tracts and many books. *Devotions are found on pages 1214, 1242.*

Betty Southard is minister of caring for the Hour of Power International and also leads seminars on choices, changes and challenges. A grandmother of eight, she coauthored *The Grandmother Book. A devotion is found on page 787.*

Horatio Spafford (1828–1888) was best known for his song *It Is Well With My Soul*, written after his four daughters died in a tragic collision of ships at sea that left 226 people dead. *A devotion is found on page 1368.*

Charles H. Spurgeon (1834–1892) was pastor of New Park Street Baptist Church in London, England, for 38 years and founder of the Pastor's College. *Devotions are found on pages 425, 585, 607, 1069, 1201.*

Tim Stafford, senior writer for *Christianity Today* magazine, is the author of several books, including *Knowing the Face of God. Devotions are found on pages 1119, 1319, 1427, 1449, 1456, 1519.*

Millie Stamm, author of several books, has worked for many years directing Meditation Moments, a prayer ministry to Christian women. *Devotions are found on pages 429, 446, 1160, 1412, 1541, 1608.*

Charles Stanley is senior pastor of First Baptist Church in Atlanta, Georgia. His popular radio and TV program "In Touch" is broadcast nationwide. He has written many books. *Devotions are found on pages 66, 342, 665, 1401, 1590.*

Jan Stoop is a counselor with the Minirth-Meier-Stoop Clinic and leads seminars on marriage and family issues. A grandmother of two, she coauthored *The Grandmother Book. A devotion is found on page 787.*

Charles R. Swindoll, a well-known author and speaker, is president of Dallas Theological Seminary. A prolific writer, he has written numerous books, including *Laugh Again. Devotions are found on pages 271, 648, 714, 803, 835, 887, 1019, 1361, 1432, 1497, 1509, 1548.*

Joni Eareckson Tada is a successful artist, writer of several books and articles, speaker, wife, and founder of a ministry to persons with disabilities. She became a quadriplegic in a diving accident in 1967. *Devotions are found on pages 84, 393, 767, 911, 941, 1093, 1147, 1523.*

Louis M. Tamminga is a retired pastor who has served the Christian Reformed Church as pastor of five churches and as director of Pastor-Church Relations. *Devotions are found on pages 1585, 1604.*

Gigi Graham Tchividjian, the wife of psychologist Stephan Tchividjian and oldest daughter of Billy and Ruth Bell Graham, is an accomplished author and popular speaker. *Devotions are found on pages 754, 853, 1606.*

Alfred Tennyson (1809–1892) was an English poet laureate known for such works as *In Memoriam. A devotion is found on page 833.*

John Timmer has served the Christian Reformed Church as a missionary in Japan and as a pastor in two different churches in the United States. *Devotions are found on pages 15, 898.*

R.A. Torrey (1856–1928) was a Congregational evangelist, teacher and author of 40 books. He was president of Moody Bible Institute from 1899–1908. *Devotions are found on pages 920, 979.*

A.W. Tozer (1897–1963) was a pastor of The Christian and Missionary Alliance from 1919 until his death. His books include *The Pursuit of God* and *The Knowledge of the Holy. Devotions are found on pages 2, 108, 736, 778.*

Herbert VanderLugt served for many years on the staff of Radio Bible Class in Grand Rapids, Michigan. *A devotion is found on page 1262.*

Jean Vanier has devoted his life to caring for the wounded members of society, the poor, those with disabilities, and the elderly. He founded L'Arche, a community for mentally disabled persons in France. L'Arche communities are now found in many parts of the world. *Devotions are found on pages 1180, 1250, 1434.*

Verlyn D. Verbrugge is senior editor of academic and reference books at Zondervan Publishing House. *Devotions are found on pages 522, 799.*

Walter Wangerin, Jr., is a columnist, author and lecturer, and professor of English at Valparaiso University. He has published numerous volumes of short stories, novels and nonfiction works. *Devotions are found on pages 828, 1595.*

Reuben Welch, author and popular conference speaker, has served as professor of religion at Point Loma Nazarene College in San Diego. *A devotion is found on page 1553.*

Charles Wesley (1707–1788) wrote more than 6,500 hymns, including the well-loved favorites *Jesus, Lover of My Soul* and *Christ the Lord Is Risen Today. Devotions are found on pages 1274, 1615.*

John White, former professor of psychiatry, is a writer and speaker with a worldwide ministry. *A devotion is found on page 1326.*

Warren W. Wiersbe is general director and Bible teacher of Back to the Bible and the author of more than 80 books. *Devotions are found on pages 1158, 1167.*

Kate B. Wilkinson (1829–1928), a member of the Church of England, wrote the well-known hymn *May the Mind of Christ, My Savior. A devotion is found on page 1503.*

Sherwood Eliot Wirt, editor emeritus of *Decision* magazine, author of 24 books, world traveler and mountain climber, is an active visionary who enjoys life. *Devotions are found on pages 281, 830, 1090, 1175, 1358.*

Philip Yancey, editor-at-large for *Christianity Today* magazine, has written many books, including *Disappointment With God*. He was general editor of *The Student Bible. A devotion is found on page 1366.*

SUBJECT INDEX

(continued in the back)

Risk Management and Insurance

The McGraw-Hill/Irwin Series in Finance, Insurance and Real Estate

Stephen A. Ross
*Franco Modigliani Professor of Financial Economics
Sloan School of Management
Massachusetts Institute of Technology
Consulting Editor*

FINANCIAL MANAGEMENT

Benninga and Sarig
Corporate Finance: A Valuation Approach

Block and Hirt
Foundations of Financial Management
Tenth Edition

Brealey and Myers
Principles of Corporate Finance
Seventh Edition

Brealey, Myers, and Marcus
Fundamentals of Corporate Finance
Fourth Edition

Brooks
FinGame Online 4.0

Bruner
Case Studies in Finance: Managing for Corporate Value Creation
Fourth Edition

Chew
The New Corporate Finance: Where Theory Meets Practice
Third Edition

Crabb
Finance and Investments Using *The Wall Street Journal*

DeMello
Cases in Finance

Grinblatt and Titman
Financial Markets and Corporate Strategy
Second Edition

Helfert
Techniques of Financial Analysis: A Guide to Value Creation
Eleventh Edition

Higgins
Analysis for Financial Management
Seventh Edition

Kester, Fruhan, Piper, and Ruback
Case Problems in Finance
Eleventh Edition

Ross, Westerfield, and Jaffe
Corporate Finance
Sixth Edition

Ross, Westerfield, and Jordan
Essentials of Corporate Finance
Fourth Edition

Ross, Westerfield, and Jordan
Fundamentals of Corporate Finance
Sixth Edition

Smith
The Modern Theory of Corporate Finance
Second Edition

White
Financial Analysis with an Electronic Calculator
Fifth Edition

INVESTMENTS

Bodie, Kane, and Marcus
Essentials of Investments
Fifth Edition

Bodie, Kane, and Marcus
Investments
Fifth Edition

Cohen, Zinbarg, and Zeikel
Investment Analysis and Portfolio Management
Fifth Edition

Corrado and Jordan
Fundamentals of Investments: Valuation and Management
Second Edition

Crabb
Finance and Investments Using *The Wall Street Journal*

Farrell
Portfolio Management: Theory and Applications
Second Edition

Hirt and Block
Fundamentals of Investment Management
Seventh Edition

FINANCIAL INSTITUTIONS AND MARKETS

Cornett and Saunders
Fundamentals of Financial Institutions Management

Rose
Commercial Bank Management
Sixth Edition

Rose
Money and Capital Markets: Financial Institutions and Instruments in a Global Marketplace
Eighth Edition

Santomero and Babbel
Financial Markets, Instruments, and Institutions
Second Edition

Saunders and Cornett
Financial Institutions Management: A Risk Management Approach
Fourth Edition

Saunders and Cornett
Financial Markets and Institutions: A Modern Perspective
Second Edition

INTERNATIONAL FINANCE

Beim and Calomiris
Emerging Financial Markets

Eun and Resnick
International Financial Management
Third Edition

Levich
International Financial Markets: Prices and Policies
Second Edition

REAL ESTATE

Brueggeman and Fisher
Real Estate Finance and Investments
Eleventh Edition

Corgel, Ling, and Smith
Real Estate Perspectives: An Introduction to Real Estate
Fourth Edition

FINANCIAL PLANNING AND INSURANCE

Allen, Melone, Rosenbloom, and Mahoney
Pension Planning: Pension, Profit-Sharing, and Other Deferred Compensation Plans
Ninth Edition

Crawford
Life and Health Insurance Law
Eighth Edition (LOMA)

Harrington and Niehaus
Risk Management and Insurance
Second Edition

Hirsch
Casualty Claim Practice
Sixth Edition

Kapoor, Dlabay, and Hughes
Personal Finance
Seventh Edition

Williams, Smith, and Young
Risk Management and Insurance
Eighth Edition

Risk
Management
and Insurance

Second Edition

Scott E. Harrington
University of South Carolina

Gregory R. Niehaus
University of South Carolina

Boston   Burr Ridge, IL   Dubuque, IA   Madison, WI   New York   San Francisco   St. Louis
Bangkok   Bogotá   Caracas   Kuala Lumpur   Lisbon   London   Madrid   Mexico City
Milan   Montreal   New Delhi   Santiago   Seoul   Singapore   Sydney   Taipei   Toronto

 Irwin

RISK MANAGEMENT AND INSURANCE

Published by McGraw-Hill/Irwin, a business unit of The McGraw-Hill Companies, Inc., 1221 Avenue of the
Americas, New York, NY, 10020. Copyright © 2004, 1999 by The McGraw-Hill Companies, Inc. All rights
reserved. No part of this publication may be reproduced or distributed in any form or by any means, or stored in
a database or retrieval system, without the prior written consent of The McGraw-Hill Companies, Inc.,
including, but not limited to, in any network or other electronic storage or transmission, or broadcast for
distance learning.

Some ancillaries, including electronic and print components, may not be available to customers outside the
United States.

This book is printed on acid-free paper.

3 4 5 6 7 8 9 0 DOC/DOC 0 9 8 7 6 5

ISBN 0-07-233970-5

Publisher: *Stephen M. Patterson*
Sponsoring editor: *Michele Janicek*
Editorial coordinator: *Barbara Hari*
Executive marketing manager: *Rhonda Seelinger*
Producer, media technology: *Chet Smith*
Senior project manager: *Lori Koetters*
Senior production supervisor: *Michael R. McCormick*
Designer: *Kami Carter*
Supplement producer: *Betty Hadala*
Senior digital content specialist: *Brian Nacik*
Cover image: © Photodisc
Typeface: *10/12 Times New Roman*
Compositor: *Carlisle Communications, Ltd.*
Printer: *R. R. Donnelley, Crawfordsville*

Library of Congress Cataloging-in-Publication Data

Harrington, Scott E.
    Risk management and insurance / Scott E. Harrington, Gregory R. Niehaus. -- 2nd e.d.
        p. cm. -- (McGraw-Hill/Irwin series in finance, insurance, and real estate)
    Includes index.
    ISBN 0-07-233970-5
    1. Risk (Insurance) 2. Risk management   I. Niehaus, Gregg   II. Title.   III. Series.
HG8054.5.H37 2004
    368—dc21   2003044900

www.mhhe.com

For Marcia, Liz, and our parents

About the Authors

Scott E. Harrington
University of South Carolina
Scott Harrington is W. Frank Hipp Professor of Insurance and Professor of Finance in the Moore School of Business at the University of South Carolina. He received his Ph.D. in Finance from the University of Illinois in 1979 and was on the faculty of the Wharton School at the University of Pennsylvania during 1978–88. Dr. Harrington has authored and edited many books and published numerous articles in academic and professional journals. A frequent speaker on insurance markets and regulation, he has consulted for many leading insurance organizations and is former president of both the American Risk and Insurance Association and the Risk Theory Society. He was named the 1990 Insurance Educator of the Year by the Professional Insurance Agents Foundation.

Gregory R. Niehaus
University of South Carolina
Greg Niehaus is Professor of Insurance and Finance in the Moore School of Business at the University of South Carolina. He received his Ph.D. in Economics from Washington University in 1985. From 1985 to 1990, he was on the finance faculty at the University of Michigan and from 1996 to 1997, he held the A. J. Pasant Chair of Life Insurance and Financial Services at Michigan State University. He has published articles in the *Journal of Risk and Insurance,* the *Journal of Finance,* the *Journal of Financial Economics,* the *Journal of Business,* the *Journal of Banking and Finance, Financial Management, The Accounting Review,* and the *Journal of Insurance Regulation.* He has won several teaching awards in the Moore School. In 2000, he became Chair of the Banking, Finance, Insurance, and Real Estate Department.

Preace

BACKGDUND

The vast majority of business students do not plan to enter the insurance field. They are being trained to be general managers or specialists in other fields. Business students therefore need a general framework for thinking about the effects of risk and a broad knowledge of risk management and insurance. In addition, they need to be aware of the many important public policy issues related to risk, including legal liability and economic security issues. Students who seek careers in risk management and insurance also need a strong conceptual foundation for understanding institutional details. Because institutional details are constantly changing, it is very important for students to learn general concepts that can be applied to new sets of problems, new types of risk, and new institutional structures. In addition, introductory courses in risk management and insurance should stimulate critical thinking and promote the development of problem-solving skills to better prepare students for meaningful careers in an information-intensive global economy.

PHILOSOPIY AND OBJECTIVES

As was true for the first edition of this book, we have sought to achieve four major objectives:

1. Provide students with a broad perspective of risk management that, while emphasizing traditional risk management and insurance, introduces other types of risk management and stresses that the same general framework can be used to manage all types of risk.

2. Provide students with a conceptual framework for (*a*) making risk management and insurance decisions to increase business value and individual welfare; (*b*) understanding insurance contracts and institutional features of the insurance industry, including their relationship to contracts used to manage other types of risks; and (*c*) understanding the effects of and the rationale for public policies that affect risk and the allocation of risk among businesses and individuals.

3. Acquaint students with the essential details of insurance contracts and insurance markts without providing extensive descriptions of numerous types of insurance contracts, emphasizing how and why insurance contracts are designed as they are and how insurance markets function.

4. Enhance the ability of students to think critically and analytically and solve problems in order to better prepare them to confront the myriad opportunities and problems that confront business managers and individuals.

Examples of questions and issues that are examined in this book and receive much less coverage or no coverage in other texts include: (1) What are the economic functions of particular features of insurance contracts and insurer operations? (2) How does risk management affect the value of businesses with diversified shareholders, and why do these firms buy substantial amounts of insurance and use hedging instruments to reduce risk? (3) What decision rules are appropriate for loss control and the choice among loss financing methods, and how can these methods be applied? (4) Why are some types of risk insured, while other types of risk are hedged with financial contracts, such as futures and options contra? (5) What are the causes and consequences of government policies to protect citizens from risk?

The objective of providing a broader perspective than other risk management and insurance texts reflects several influences. Because most contracts allocate risk among the contracting parties, many of the concepts and tools that we discuss are drawfrom and apply to a wide variety of contracts, not just insurance contracts. In addition, t'e obviously are many important types of risk besides the risks covered in traditional rishanagement and insurance courses. These risks often can be successfully hedged using to that are in many respects similar to insurance. We introduce these risks and associated hedging methods, again emphasizing that the same general framework is applicable to all 1es of risk. Given the increased importance of overall risk management in business magement in recent years, this broader perspective is important for students who are beinrained as general managers or specialists in other fields. It also has become increasinglmportant for specialists in traditional risk management and insurance to be familiar witther types of business risk and the tools used to manage these risks.

Finally, we believe that the issues associated with the allocation of ;k in society are of fundamental importance and are inherently interesting. Without losi; sight of our main task of studying risk management and insurance, we have tried to covey our enthusiasm for the topics and the wide applicability of the concepts and tools.

INTENDED AUDIENCE

This book is designed for use in introductory risk management and inirance courses at the undergraduate and MBA levels and in second level risk managemenourses. We have designed the book to be as flexible as possible. In particular, the strucre and content allow instructors who do not wish to emphasize corporate risk manageme: and financial issues in an introductory class to omit selected chapters or parts of chapterwithout loss of continuity. The main sections of each chapter are numbered to facilite selective coverage. Moreover, while we frequently relate the material to concepts to wlch most business students will be exposed in basic economics, finance, and statistics clases, we have developed all of the key ideas assuming little or no student background in thes subjects. Appendices to several chapters provide more in-depth treatment of selected svjects. Instructors who feel that their students could profit from more discussion can assig these appendices.

CHANGES FROM THE FIRST EDITION

Although the basic philosophy and objectives of the book are unchnged from the first edition, we have made numerous improvements. Most important,

- We broadened the introductory chapters to include more disussion of personal risk management and placed the material on personal insurance (aub, homeowners, and life) earlier in the book to enhance the book's usefulness in classesthat emphasize personal risk management.
- We incorporated new chapters on loss control (Chapter 11), business risk retention decisions (Chapter 22), commercial insurance contracts (Chapter 23), and enterprise risk management (Chapter 27) to enhance the book's usefulness in courses with a strong emphasis on corporate risk management.
- We placed some of the more difficult material in appendices.
- Examples, exhibits, and current events boxes have all been updated as needed.

The second edition is more flexible than the first edition. Thus, it is likely to fit the needs of more instructors teaching introductory courses with a personal insurance emphasis, while also expanding the treatment of corporate risk management for instructors that seek additional depth on those issues.

PEDAGOGY

To further support the objectives of this text—that is, to present a broad perspective of risk management, provide a conceptual framework, and enhance critical and analytical thinking—the following features are included:

Chapter Objectives.   Each chapter begins with a list of key objectives, which provide students with an overview of the material they will learn in reading the chapter.

Concept Checks.   Strategically placed throughout most chapters, these self-test questions enable students to determine whether they have understood the preceding material and enhance critical thinking skills. Answers to these questions are found at the end of chapters.

Key Terms.   Key terms are found in bold throughout the text and are listed at the end of chapters with page references for easy review.

Examples. The examples in the narrative of the text emphasize real-world applications of the material being covered. Students will recognize the context of the examples and therefore will be able to more easily apply concepts learned from this text to future situations.

Current Events and Concepts Boxes.   Boxes containing business press and journal articles are included in various chapters to provide an additional view of current risk management issues. Also, concepts and issues that are more specialized or advanced are set off in a separate boxed feature. This enables the discussion to be easily skipped if it is not integral to the course, but it also provides a good summary if the instructor chooses to cover it.

Exhibits.   Tables, figures, and diagrams are included to help illustrate the topics in each chapter.

Summaries.   This bulleted feature expands on the learning objectives by revisiting the important points in the chapter, providing an extra study aid for students at the end of the chapter.

Questions and Problems.   This section includes both numerical problems and conceptual questions that build on the material learned in the chapter. Solutions are included in the Instructor's Manual.

References. Key articles are included at the end of chapters, along with one-sentence descriptions.

SUPPLEMENTS

Instructor Resource CD.   This CD contains the following assets:

Instructor's Manual.   Prepared by the authors, this teaching tool includes lecture outlines for each chapter, transparency masters, and solutions to the end-of-chapter questions and problems.

PowerPoint Presentation Software.   Also prepared by the authors, the PowerPoint slides include the transparency masters in an electronic format. Instructors with

PowerPoint have the ability to edit, print, or rearrange the complete presentation to meet their needs.

Test Bank.   Prepared by Joe Haley, Herberger College of Business, St. Cloud State University, the Test Bank includes multiple-choice questions, fill-ins, problems, and short answers. Each question is coded as a knowledge-based or an application-based question. There are 15–20 questions per chapter.

ACKNOWLEDGMENTS

We wish to thank the reviewers and class testers for their valuable comments, many of whom had a material impact on the finished product. They include:

Tom Aiuppa, *University of Wisconsin—La Crosse*

Vickie Bajtelsmit, *Colorado State University*

Norm Baglini, *Temple University*

Mark Browne, *University of Wisconsin—Madison*

Ann Butler, *University of Illinois at Urbana-Champaign*

James Carson, *Illinois State University*

David Cather, *University of Pennsylvania, The Wharton School of Business*

Lisa Gardner, *Bradley University*

Jim Garven, *Baylor University*

Martin F. Grace, *Georgia State University*

Joe Haley, *St. Cloud State University*

Dan Jones, *University of Houston*

Anne Kleffner, *University of Calgary*

Robert Klein, *Georgia State University*

Joan Lamm-Tennant, *Villanova University,* and *vice president, General Reinsurance Corporation*

Pierre Lemaire, *University of Pennsylvania*

Weili Lu, *California State University—Fullerton*

Fred McKenna, *University of South Alabama*

Joseph Meador, *Northeastern University*

Craig Merrill, *Brigham Young University*

Tom Morehart, *New Mexico State University*

Laureen Regan, *Temple University*

Allen Seward, *Baylor University*

David Shaheen, *Michigan State University*

David Sommer, *University of Georgia*

Sharon Tennyson, *Cornell University*

Hedi Zereri, *Northeastern University*

Special thanks are due to David Cather and Sharon Tennyson for taking the time and trouble to survey their Wharton students concerning the effectiveness of the first edition of the book. Additional thanks are due to Sharon for her suggestions throughout our development process. Two of our doctoral students, Karen Epermanis and Tong Yu, also provided useful input on the first edition.

The editorial and production staff at McGraw-Hill were a delight to work with. Special thanks are due to Lori Koetters, project manager; Rhonda Seelinger, marketing manager; and especially Michele Janicek, sponsoring editor, and Barbara Hari, editorial coordinator.

The concepts and ideas developed in this book reflect our years of reading, thinking, and teaching about these subjects. Because this is a textbook and not a treatise, we did not attempt to cite a material fraction of the dozens of articles that have influenced us, apart from including a small number of end-of-chapter references that are likely to be appropriate for our target audience. Our intellectual debt is nonetheless very large.

Scott Harrington and Greg Niehaus

Columbia, South Carolina

June 2003

Brief Contents

Contents

Risk
Management
and Insurance

Chapter 1

Risk and Its Management

Chapter Objectives

- Discuss different meanings of the term *risk*.
- Describe major types of business risk and personal risk.
- Explain and compare pure risk to other types of risk.
- Outline the risk management process and describe major risk management methods.
- Discuss organization of the risk management function within business.

1.1 Risk

Different Meanings of Risk

The term *risk* has a variety of meanings in business and everyday life. At its most general level, risk is used to describe any situation where there is uncertainty about what outcome will occur. Life is obviously very risky. Even the short-term future is often highly uncertain. In probability and statistics, financial management, and investment management, risk is often used in a more specific sense to indicate possible variability in outcomes around some expected value.

We will develop the ideas of expected value and risk as reflecting variability around the expected value in Chapter 3. For now it is sufficient for you to think of the expected value as the outcome that would occur on average if a person or business were repeatedly exposed to the same type of risk. If you have not yet encountered these concepts in statistics or finance classes, the following example from the sports world might help. Allen Iverson has averaged about 30 points per game in his career in the National Basketball Association. As we write this, he shows little sign of slowing down. It is therefore reasonable to assume that the expected value of his total points in any given game is about 30 points. Risk, in the sense of variability around the expected value, is clearly present. He might score 50 points or even higher in a particular game, or he might score as few as 10 points.

In other situations, the term risk may refer to the expected losses associated with a situation. In insurance markets, for example, it is common to refer to high-risk policyholders. The meaning of risk in this context is that the expected value of losses to be paid by the insurer (the expected loss) is high. As another example, California often is described as having a high risk of earthquake. While this statement might encompass the notion of variability around the expected value, it usually simply means that California's expected loss from earthquakes is high relative to other states.

In summary, (see Figure 1.1) risk is sometimes used in a specific sense to describe variability around the expected value and other times to describe the expected losses. We employ each of these meanings in this book because it is customary to do so in certain types of risk management and in the insurance business. The particular meaning usually will be obvious from the context.

Risk Is Costly

Regardless of the specific meaning of risk being used, greater risk usually implies greater cost. To illustrate the cost of risk we use a simple example: Suppose that two identical homes are in different but equally attractive locations. The structures have the same value, say $100,000, and initially there is no risk of damage to either house. Then scientists announce that a meteor might hit the earth in the coming week and that one house is in the potential impact area. We would naturally say that one house now has greater risk than the other.

Let's assume that everyone agrees that the probability of one house being hit by the meteor is 0.1 and that the probability of the other house being hit is zero. Also assume that the house would be completely destroyed if it were hit (all $100,000 would be lost). Then the expected property loss at one house is greater by an amount equal to 0.1 times $100,000, or $10,000. If the owner were to sell the house immediately following the release of news about the meteor, potential buyers would naturally pay less than $100,000 for the house. Rational people would pay at least $10,000 less, because that is the expected loss from the meteor. Thus, greater risk—in the sense of higher expected losses—is costly to the original homeowner. The value of the house would drop by at least the expected loss.

In addition to greater expected losses, one homeowner has greater uncertainty in the sense that potential outcomes have greater variation. At the end of the week, one house will be worth $100,000 with certainty, but the other house could be worth zero or $100,000. This greater uncertainty about the value of the house also is likely to impose costs on the owner. Because of the greater uncertainty, potential buyers might require a price decrease in excess of the expected loss ($10,000). Let's say the additional price drop is $5,000. Thus, greater risk—in the sense of greater uncertainty—is also costly to the original homeowner.

FIGURE 1.1
Two meanings of risk.

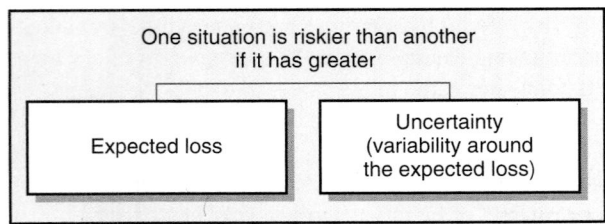

One situation is riskier than another if it has greater

Expected loss

Uncertainty (variability around the expected loss)

To summarize, this example illustrates that both meanings of risk depicted in Figure 1.1 are costly. In this example, the value of the house declined by the expected loss (the first meaning of risk) plus an additional amount due to increased uncertainty (the second meaning of risk). As you will see throughout this book, risk management is concerned with decreasing the cost of risk.

Direct versus Indirect Expected Losses

When considering the potential losses from a risky situation, you must consider indirect losses that arise in addition to direct losses. In the previous example, if the meteor destroyed the house, the direct loss would be $100,000. Indirect losses arise as a consequence of direct losses. If the house were destroyed, the owner would likely have additional expenses, such as hotel and restaurant costs; these additional expenses would be indirect losses. As another example, when a person's car is damaged, the time spent getting it repaired is an indirect loss.

For businesses, indirect losses are extremely important. Indeed, as we discuss in later chapters, the possibility of indirect losses is one of the main reasons that businesses try to reduce risk. Figure 1.2 summarizes the major types of indirect losses that can arise from the risks faced by businesses. For example, damage to productive assets can produce an indirect loss by reducing or eliminating the normal profit (net cash flow) that the asset would have generated if the damage had not occurred. Large direct losses also can lead to indirect losses if they threaten the viability of the business and thereby reduce the willingness of customers and suppliers to deal with the business or change the terms (prices) at which they transact.

Moreover, if sales or production are reduced in response to direct losses, certain types of normal operating expenses (known as continuing expenses) may not decline in proportion to the reduction in revenues, thus increasing indirect losses. If a long interruption in production would cause many customers to switch suppliers, or if a firm has binding contractual commitments to supply products, it also may be desirable for the firm to increase operating costs above normal levels following direct losses. For example, some businesses might find it desirable to maintain production by leasing replacement equipment at a higher cost so as to avoid loss of sales. The increased operating cost would create an indirect loss. Similarly, a business that decides to recall defective products that have produced liability claims will incur product recall expenses and perhaps increased advertising costs to reduce damage to the firm's reputation.

FIGURE 1.2
Types of indirect losses.

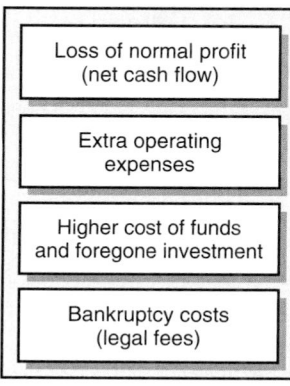

Other forms of indirect losses include the possibility that the business will face a higher cost of obtaining funds from lenders or from new equity issues following large direct losses. In some cases, the higher costs of raising capital will cause the firm to forgo making otherwise profitable investments. Finally, in the case of severe direct and indirect losses, the firm might have to reorganize or be liquidated through costly legal proceedings under bankruptcy law.

1.2   Types of Risk Facing Businesses and Individuals

Business Risk

Broadly defined, business risk management is concerned with possible reductions in business value from any source. Business value to shareholders, as reflected in the value of the firm's common stock, depends fundamentally on the expected size, timing, and risk (variability) associated with the firm's future net cash flows (cash inflows less cash outflows). Unexpected changes in expected future net cash flows are a major source of fluctuations in business value. In particular, unexpected reductions in cash inflows or increases in cash outflows can significantly reduce business value. The major business risks that give rise to variation in cash flows and business value are price risk, credit risk, and pure risk (see Figure 1.3).

Price Risk

Price risk refers to uncertainty over the magnitude of cash flows due to possible changes in output and input prices. Output price risk refers to the risk of changes in the prices that a firm can demand for its goods and services. Input price risk refers to the risk of changes in the prices that a firm must pay for labor, materials, and other inputs to its production process. Analysis of price risk associated with the sale and production of existing and future products and services plays a central role in strategic management.[1]

FIGURE 1.3
Major types of business risk.

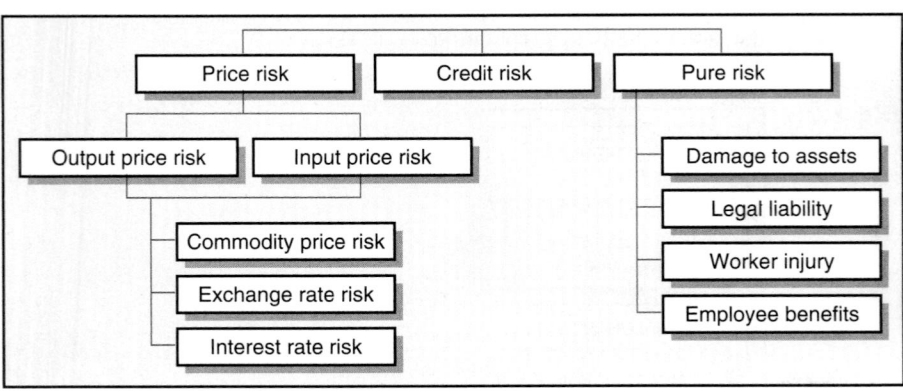

[1]Thus, most strategic risks and operational risks can be viewed as particular examples of price risk.

Three specific types of price risk are *commodity price risk, exchange rate risk,* and *interest rate risk.* Commodity price risk arises from fluctuations in the prices of commodities, such as coal, copper, oil, gas, and electricity, that are inputs for some firms and outputs for others. Given the globalization of economic activity, output and input prices for many firms also are affected by fluctuations in foreign exchange rates. Output and input prices also can fluctuate due to changes in interest rates. For example, increases in interest rates may alter a firm's revenues by affecting both the terms of credit allowed and the speed with which customers pay for products purchased on credit. Changes in interest rates also affect the firm's cost of borrowing funds to finance its operations.[2]

Credit Risk

The risk that a firm's customers and the parties to which it has lent money will delay or fail to make promised payments is known as **credit risk.** Most firms face some credit risk for account receivables. The exposure to credit risk is particularly large for financial institutions, such as commercial banks, that routinely make loans that are subject to risk of default by the borrower. When firms borrow money, they in turn expose lenders to credit risk (i.e., the risk that the firm will default on its promised payments). As a consequence, borrowing exposes the firm's owners to the risk that the firm will be unable to pay its debts and thus be forced into bankruptcy, and the firm generally will have to pay more to borrow money as credit risk increases.

Pure Risk

The risk management function in medium-to-large corporations (and the term *risk management*) has traditionally focused on the management of what is known as **pure risk.** As summarized in Figure 1.3, the major types of pure risk that affect businesses include:

1. The risk of reduction in value of business assets due to physical damage, theft, and expropriation (i.e., seizure of assets by foreign governments).

2. The risk of legal liability for damages for harm to customers, suppliers, shareholders, and other parties.

3. The risk associated with paying benefits to injured workers under workers' compensation laws and the risk of legal liability for injuries or other harms to employees that are not governed by workers' compensation laws.

4. The risk of death, illness, and disability to employees (and sometimes family members) for which businesses have agreed to make payments under employee benefit plans, including obligations to employees under pension and other retirement savings plans.

Personal Risk

The risks faced by individuals and families can be classified in a variety of ways. In Figure 1.4, we classify personal risk into six categories: earnings risk, medical expense risk, liability risk, physical asset risk, financial asset risk, and longevity risk. Earnings risk refers to the potential fluctuation in a family's earnings, which can occur as a result of a decline in the value of an income earner's productivity due to death, disability, aging, or a change in technology. A

---

[2]More generally, changes in interest rates affect value through their effect on the present value of the firm's net cash flows, as reflected in the value of the firm's assets and liabilities.

FIGURE 1.4   **Major types of personal risk.**

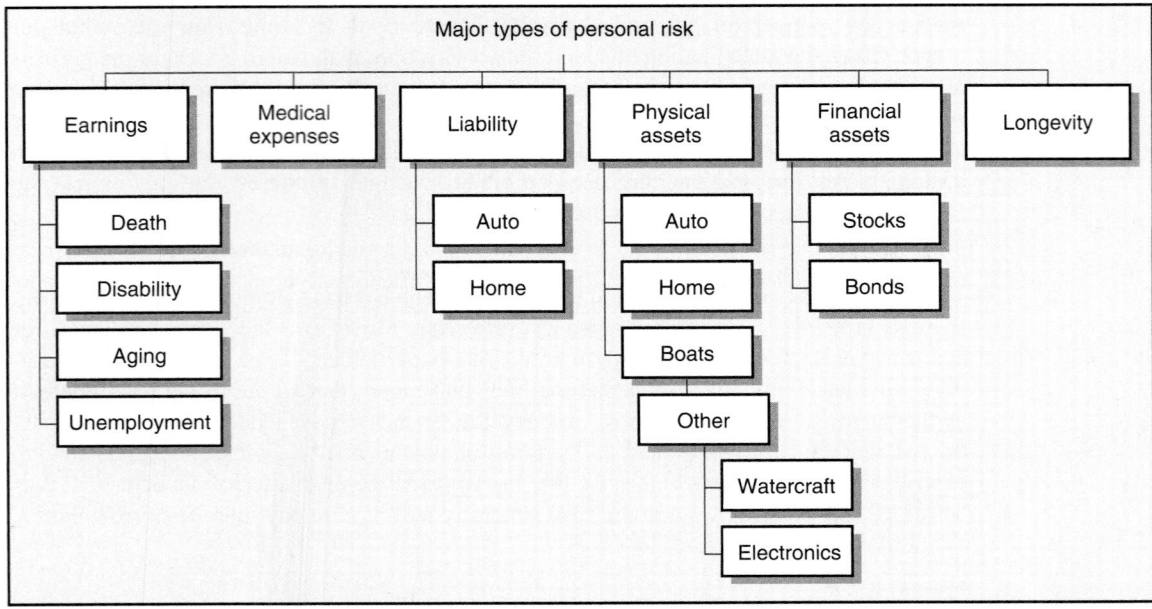

family's expenses also are uncertain. Health care costs and liability suits, in particular, can cause large unexpected expenses. A family also faces the risk of a loss in the value of the physical assets that it owns. Automobiles, homes, boats, and computers can be lost, stolen, or damaged. Financial assets' values also are subject to fluctuation due to changes in inflation and changes in the real values of stocks and bonds. Finally, longevity risk refers to the possibility that retired people will outlive their financial resources. Often individuals obtain advice about personal risk management from professionals, such as insurance agents, accountants, lawyers, and financial planners.

Comparison of Pure Risk and Its Management with Other Types of Risk

Much of this book focuses on pure risk and its management, including the use of insurance as a tool to reduce risk and finance losses for businesses and individuals. The framework that we present for managing risk, however, is very general. It can be applied with little or no modification to other types of risk. In addition, our detailed discussion of insurance markets and comparison of insurance contracts to the tools used to reduce other types of business risk will help you understand the rich variety of risk reduction methods available in modern risk management.

Common (but not necessarily distinctive) features of pure risk include the following.

1. Losses from destruction of property, legal liability, and employee injuries or illness often have the potential to be very large relative to a business's resources. While business value can increase if losses from pure risk turn out to be lower than expected, the maximum

possible gain in these cases is usually relatively small. In contrast, the potential reduction in business value from losses greater than the expected value can be very large and even threaten the firm's viability.[3]

2. The underlying causes of losses associated with pure risk, such as the destruction of a plant by the explosion of a steam boiler or product liability suits from consumers injured by a particular product, are often largely specific to a particular firm and depend on the firm's actions. As a result, the underlying causes of these losses are often subject to a significant degree of control by businesses; that is, firms can reduce the frequency and severity of losses through actions that alter the underlying causes (e.g., by taking steps to reduce the probability of fire or lawsuit). In comparison, while firms can take a variety of steps to reduce their exposure or vulnerability to price risk, the underlying causes of some important types of price changes are largely beyond the control of individual firms (e.g., economic factors that cause changes in foreign exchange rates, marketwide changes in interest rates, or aggregate consumer demand).

3. Businesses commonly reduce uncertainty and finance losses associated with pure risk by purchasing contracts from insurance companies that specialize in evaluating and bearing pure risk. The prevalence of insurance in part reflects the firm-specific nature of losses caused by pure risk. The fact that events that cause large losses to a given firm commonly have little effect on losses experienced by other firms facilitates risk reduction by diversification, which is accomplished with insurance contracts (see Chapters 5 and 6). Insurance contracts generally are not used to reduce uncertainty and finance losses associated with price risk (and many types of credit risk). Price risks that can simultaneously produce gains for many firms and losses for many others are commonly reduced with *financial derivatives,* such as forward and futures contracts, option contracts, and swaps. With these contracts, much of the risk of loss is often shifted to parties that have an opposite exposure to the particular risk.

4. Losses from pure risk usually are not associated with offsetting gains for other parties. In contrast, losses to businesses that arise from other types of risk often are associated with gains to other parties. For example, an increase in input prices harms the purchaser of the inputs but benefits the seller. Likewise, a decline in the dollar's value against foreign currencies can harm domestic importers but benefit domestic exporters and foreign importers of U. S. goods.[4] One implication of this difference between pure risk and price risk is that losses from pure risk reduce the total wealth in society, whereas fluctuations in output and input prices need not reduce total wealth. In addition, and as we hinted above, the fact that price changes often produce losses for some firms and gains for others in many cases allows these firms to reduce risk by taking opposite positions in derivative contracts.

[3]Pure risk sometimes is defined as risk where the random outcome can only result in loss (produce a cash outflow); that is, no outcome involving a gain (cash inflow) is possible. But this is also true for other uncertain cash outflows faced by firms (e.g., the cost of raw materials). This definition also ignores the fact that businesses or individuals gain financially whenever losses from pure risk are less than expected. The gain is no different in substance from the gain that would occur if the price of raw materials dropped so that the firm could buy them more cheaply.

[4]With respect to credit risk, one party's loss also is often associated with the other party's gain in the sense that the party that defaults on its obligation does not make payment.

While many of the details concerning pure risk and its management differ from other types of risk, it is nonetheless important for you to understand that pure risk and its management are conceptually similar, if not identical, to other types of risk and their management. To make this concrete, consider the case of a manufacturer that uses oil in the production of consumer products. Such a firm faces the risk of large losses from product liability lawsuits if its products harm consumers, but it also faces the risk of potentially large losses from oil price increases. The business can manage the expected cost of product liability settlements or judgments by making the product's design safer or by providing safety instructions and warnings. While the business might not be able to do anything to reduce the likelihood or size of increases in oil prices, it might be able to reduce its exposure to losses from oil price increases by adopting a flexible technology that allows low cost conversion to other sources of energy. The business might purchase product liability insurance to reduce its liability risk; it might hedge its risk of loss from oil price increases using oil futures contracts.

While the concepts and broad risk management strategies are the same for pure risk and other types of business risk, the specific characteristics of pure risk and the significant reliance on insurance contracts as a method of managing these risks generally lead to their management by personnel with specialized expertise. Major areas of expertise needed for pure risk management include risk analysis, safety management, insurance contracts, and other methods of reducing pure risk, as well as broad financial and managerial skills. The insurance business, with its principal function of reducing pure risk for businesses and individuals, employs millions of people and is one of the largest industries in the United States (and other developed countries). In addition, pure risk management and insurance have a major effect on many other sectors of the economy, such as the legal sector, medical care, real estate lending, and consumer credit.

Increases in business risk of all types and dramatic growth in the use of financial derivatives for hedging price risks in recent years have stimulated substantial growth in the scope and efforts devoted to overall business risk management. It has become increasingly important for managers that focus on pure risk to understand the management of other types of business risk. Similarly, general managers and managers of other types of risk need to understand how pure risk affects specific areas of activity and the business as a whole.

1.3   Risk Management

The Risk Management Process

Regardless of the type of risk being considered, the risk management process involves several key steps:

1. Identify all significant risks.
2. Evaluate the potential frequency and severity of losses.[5]
3. Develop and select methods for managing risk.

---

[5]If possible, this includes an estimation of the maximum loss that can reasonably be expected to occur in a given period with a relatively high level of confidence. This value is known in pure risk management as the *maximum probable loss* and in financial risk management as *value at risk*.

4. Implement the risk management methods chosen.
5. Monitor the performance and suitability of the risk management methods and strategies on an ongoing basis.

The same general framework applies to business and individual risk management. You will learn more about major exposures to losses from pure risk, risk evaluation, and the selection and implementation of risk management methods in subsequent chapters. Chapter 2 discusses risk management objectives for businesses and individuals. It is useful in this introductory chapter to further acquaint you with basic aspects of risk management by summarizing the major methods used to manage risk.

Risk Management Methods

Figure 1.5 summarizes the major methods of managing risk. These methods, which are not mutually exclusive, can be broadly classified as (1) loss control, (2) loss financing, and (3) internal risk reduction. Loss control and internal risk reduction commonly involve decisions to invest (or forgo investing) resources to reduce expected losses. They are conceptually equivalent to other investment decisions, such as a firm's decision to buy a new plant or an individual's decision to buy a computer. Loss financing decisions refer to decisions about how to pay for losses if they do occur.

Loss Control

Actions that reduce the expected cost of losses by reducing the frequency of losses and/or the severity (size) of losses that occur are known as **loss control.** Loss control also is sometimes known as risk control.[6] Actions that primarily affect the frequency of losses are commonly called *loss prevention* methods. Actions that primarily influence the severity of losses that do occur are often called *loss reduction* methods. An example of loss prevention

FIGURE 1.5
Major risk management methods.

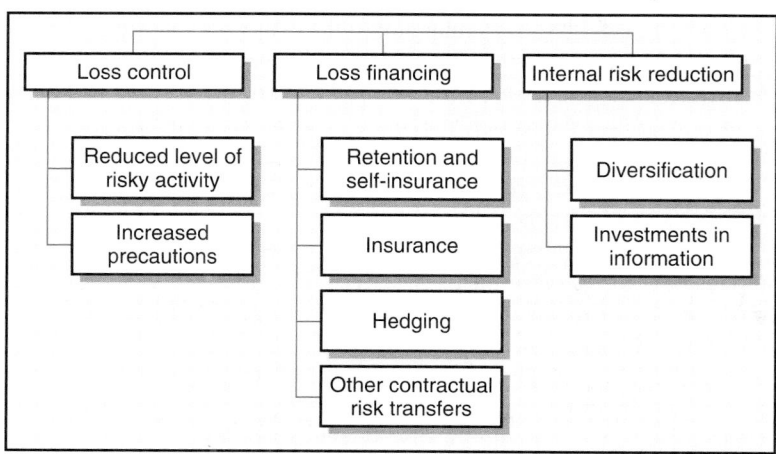

[6] Use of the term *loss control* as opposed to *risk control* helps avoid confusion between activities that reduce the expected cost of losses and activities that reduce risk (variability), such as internal risk reduction. Terminology aside, the most important thing for you to understand is how these activities work and can be used to increase business value.

would be routine inspection of aircraft for mechanical problems. These inspections help reduce the frequency of crashes; they have little impact on the magnitude of losses for crashes that occur. An example of loss reduction is the installation of heat- or smoke-activated sprinkler systems that are designed to minimize fire damage in the event of a fire.

Many types of loss control influence both the frequency and severity of losses and cannot be readily classified as either loss prevention or loss reduction. For example, thorough safety testing of consumer products will likely reduce the number of injuries, but it also could affect the severity of injuries. Similarly, equipping automobiles with airbags in most cases should reduce the severity of injuries, but airbags also might influence the frequency of injuries. Whether injuries increase or decrease depends on whether the number of injuries that are completely prevented for accidents that occur exceeds the number of injuries that might be caused by airbags inflating at the wrong time or too forcefully, as well as any increase in accidents and injuries that could occur if protection by airbags causes some drivers to drive less safely.

Viewed from another perspective, there are two general approaches to loss control: (1) reducing the level of risky activity, and (2) increasing precautions against loss for activities that are undertaken. First, exposure to loss can be reduced by reducing the level of risky activities, for example, by cutting back production of risky products or shifting attention to less risky product lines. Limiting the level of risky activity primarily affects the frequency of losses. The main cost of this strategy is that it forgoes any benefits of the risky activity that would have been achieved apart from the risk involved. In the limit, exposure to losses can be completely eliminated by reducing the level of activity to zero; that is, by not engaging in the activity at all. This strategy is called *risk avoidance.*

As a specific example of limiting the level of risky activity, consider a trucking firm that hauls toxic chemicals that might harm people or the environment in the case of an accident and thereby produce claims for damages. This firm could reduce the frequency of liability claims by cutting back on the number of shipments that it hauls. Alternatively, it could avoid the risk completely by not hauling toxic chemicals and instead hauling nontoxic substances (such as clothing or, apart from cholesterol, cheese). An example from personal risk management would be a person who flies less frequently to reduce the probability of dying in a plane crash. This risk could be completely avoided by never flying. Of course, alternative transportation methods might be much riskier (e.g., driving down Interstate 95 from New York to Miami the day before Thanksgiving—along with many long-haul trucks, including those transporting toxic chemicals).

The second major approach to loss control is to increase the amount of precautions (level of care) for a given level of risky activity. The goal here is to make the activity safer and thus reduce the frequency and/or severity of losses. Thorough testing for safety and installation of safety equipment are examples of increased precautions. The trucking firm in the example above could give its drivers extensive training in safety, limit the number of hours driven by a driver in a day, and reinforce containers to reduce the likelihood of leakage. Increased precautions usually involve direct expenditures or other costs (e.g., the increased time and attention required to drive an automobile more safely).

Concept Checks

1. Explain how the two major approaches to loss control (reducing risky activity and increasing precautions) could be used to reduce the risk of injury to construction firm employees.

2. How could these two approaches be used to reduce the risk of contracting a sexually transmitted disease?

Loss Financing

Methods used to obtain funds to pay for or offset losses that occur are known as **loss financing** (sometimes called risk financing). There are four broad methods of financing losses: (1) retention, (2) insurance, (3) hedging, and (4) other contractual risk transfers. These approaches are not mutually exclusive; that is, they often are used in combination.

With **retention,** a business or individual retains the obligation to pay for part or all of the losses. For example, a trucking company might decide to retain the risk that cash flows will drop due to oil price increases. When coupled with a formal plan to fund losses for medium-to-large businesses, retention often is called *self-insurance.*

Firms can pay retained losses using either internal or external funds. Internal funds include cash flows from ongoing activities and investments in liquid assets that are dedicated to financing losses. External sources of funds include borrowing and issuing new stock, but these approaches may be very costly following large losses. Note that these approaches still involve retention even though they employ external sources of funds. For example, the firm must pay back any funds borrowed to finance losses. When new stock is issued, the firm must share future profits with new stockholders.

The second major method of financing losses is the purchase of insurance contracts. As you most likely already know, the typical insurance contract requires the insurer to provide funds to pay for specified losses (thus financing these losses) in exchange for receiving a premium from the purchaser at the inception of the contract. Insurance contracts reduce risk for the buyer by transferring some of the risk of loss to the insurer. Insurers in turn reduce risk through diversification. For example, they sell large numbers of contracts that provide coverages for a variety of different losses (see Chapter 4).

The third broad method of loss financing is **hedging.** As noted above, financial derivatives, such as forwards, futures, options, and swaps are used extensively to manage various types of risk, most notably price risk. These contracts can be used to hedge risk; that is, they may be used to offset losses that can occur from changes in interest rates, commodity prices, foreign exchange rates, and the like. Some derivatives have begun to be used in the management of pure risk, and it is possible that their use in pure risk management will expand in the future.

Individuals and small businesses do relatively little hedging with derivatives. We discuss derivatives, their use in hedging risk, and how they compare to insurance in Chapter 24. At this point, it is useful to illustrate hedging with a very simple example (which we elaborate in Chapter 24). Firms that use oil in the production process are subject to loss from unexpected increases in oil prices; oil producers are subject to loss from unexpected decreases in oil prices. Both types of firms can hedge their risk by entering into a *forward contract* that requires the oil producer to provide the oil user with a specified amount of oil on a specified future delivery date at a predetermined price (known as the *forward price*), regardless of the market price of oil on that date. Because the forward price is agreed upon when the contract is written, the oil user and the oil producer both reduce their price risk.

The fourth major method of loss financing is to use one or more of a variety of **other contractual risk transfers** that allow businesses to transfer risk to another party. Like insurance contracts and derivatives, the use of these contracts also is pervasive in risk management.

For example, businesses that engage independent contractors to perform some task routinely enter into contracts, commonly known as *hold harmless* and *indemnity agreements,* that require the contractor to protect the business from losing money from lawsuits that might arise if persons are injured by the contractor.

Internal Risk Reduction

In addition to loss financing methods that allow businesses and individuals to reduce risk by transferring it to another entity, businesses can reduce risk internally. There are two major forms of **internal risk reduction:** (1) *diversification,* and (2) *investment in information.* Regarding the first of these, firms can reduce risk internally by diversifying their activities (i.e., not putting all of their eggs in one basket). You will learn the basics of how diversification reduces risk in Chapter 4. Individuals also routinely diversify risk by investing their savings in many different stocks. The ability of shareholders to reduce risk through portfolio diversification is an important factor affecting insurance and hedging decisions of firms (see Chapters 9 and 20).

The second major method of reducing risk internally is to invest in information to obtain superior forecasts of expected losses. Investing in information can produce more accurate estimates or forecasts of future cash flows, thus reducing variability of cash flows around the predicted value. Examples abound, including estimates of the frequency and severity of losses from pure risk, marketing research on the potential demand for different products to reduce output price risk, and forecasting future commodity prices or interest rates. One way that insurance companies reduce risk is by specializing in the analysis of data to obtain accurate forecasts of losses. Medium-to-large businesses often find it advantageous to reduce pure risk in this manner as well. Given the large demand for accurate forecasts of key variables that affect business value and determine the price of contracts that can be used to reduce risk (such as insurance and derivatives), many firms specialize in providing information and forecasts to other firms and parties.

1.4   Business Risk Management Organization

Where does the risk management function fit within the overall organizational structure of businesses? In general, the views of senior management concerning the need for, scope, and importance of risk management and possible administrative efficiencies determine how the risk management function is structured and the exact responsibilities of units devoted to risk management. Most large companies have a specific department responsible for managing pure risk that is headed by the *risk manager* (or director of risk management). However, given that losses can arise from numerous sources, the overall risk management process ideally reflects a coordinated effort between all of the corporation's major departments and business units, including production, marketing, finance, and human resources.

Depending on a company's size, a typical risk management department includes various staff specializing in areas such as property–liability insurance, workers' compensation, safety and environmental hazards, claims management, and, in many cases, employee benefits. Given the complexity of modern risk management, most firms with significant exposure to price risk related to the cost of raw materials, interest rate changes, or changes in foreign exchange rates have separate departments or staff members that deal with these risks. Whether there will be more movement in the future toward combining the management of these risks with pure risk management within a unified risk management department is uncertain.

In most firms, the risk management function is subordinate to and thus reports to the finance (treasury) department. This is because of the close relationships between protecting assets from loss, financing losses, and the finance function. However, some firms with substantial liability exposures have the risk management department report to the legal department. A smaller proportion of firms have the risk management unit report to the human resources department.

Firms also vary in the extent to which the risk management function is centralized, as opposed to having responsibility spread among the operating units. Centralization may achieve possible economies of scale in arranging loss financing. Moreover, many risk management decisions are strategic in nature, and centralization facilitates effective interaction between the risk manager and senior management.

A possible limitation of a centralized risk management function is that it can reduce concern for risk management among the managers and employees of a firm's various operating units. However, allocating the cost of risk or losses to particular units often can improve incentives for unit managers to control costs even if the overall risk management function is centralized. On the other hand, there are advantages to decentralizing certain risk management activities, such as routine safety and environmental issues. In these cases, operating managers are close to the risk and can deal effectively and directly with many issues.

1.5 Summary

- The term *risk* broadly refers to situations where outcomes are uncertain. Risk often refers specifically to variability in outcomes around the expected value. In other cases, it refers to the expected value (e.g., the expected value of losses). Regardless of the specific notion of risk being used, risk is costly.

- Major types of business risk that produce fluctuations in business value include price risk, credit risk, and pure risk.

- Pure risk encompasses risk of loss from (1) damage to and theft or expropriation of business assets, (2) legal liability for injuries to customers and other parties, (3) workplace injuries to employees, and (4) obligations assumed by businesses under employee benefit plans. Pure risk frequently is managed in part by the purchase of insurance to finance losses and reduce risk.

- Risk management involves (1) identification of potential direct and indirect losses, (2) evaluation of their potential frequency and severity, (3) de-

velopment and selection of methods for managing risk to maximize business value, (4) implementation of these methods, and (5) ongoing monitoring.

- Major risk management methods include loss control, loss financing, and internal risk reduction.

- Loss control reduces expected losses by lowering the level of risky activity and/or increasing precautions against loss for any given level of risky activity.

- Loss financing methods include retention (self-insurance), insurance, hedging, and other contractual risk transfers.

- Many businesses achieve internal risk reduction through diversification and through investments in information to improve forecasts of expected cash flows.

- Most large corporations have a specific department, headed by the risk manager, that is devoted to the management of pure risk and, in some cases, other types of risk.

Key Terms

price risk 4	loss control 9	hedging 11
credit risk 5	loss financing 11	other contractual risk transfers 11
pure risk 5	retention 11	internal risk reduction 12

Questions and Problems

1. Describe possible direct and indirect losses to a business from: (*a*) an explosion that produces major damage to a manufacturing plant, and (*b*) lawsuits arising from the business's release of toxic chemicals that damage the environment.

2. Explain how a business could reduce the risk of loss from lawsuits by consumers injured by the business's products.

3. Describe loss control measures that you could take to reduce your risk of being injured in an automobile accident.

4. What major methods are used to finance losses? How does loss financing differ from internal risk reduction?

Answers to Concept Checks

1. Taking on less hazardous projects and/or reducing the total number of projects would reduce the level of risky activity. Examples of increasing precautions for a given level of risky activity include giving employees safety instruction and making them wear protective devices (such as hard hats).

2. The level of risky activity could be reduced by abstinence (complete or partial). An example of increasing precautions for a given level of risk activity (number of contacts) would be the regular use of protective devices (such as condoms).

Chapter 2

Objective of Risk Management

Chapter Objectives

- Define and explain the overall objective of risk management.
- Explain the cost of risk concept.
- Explain how minimizing the cost of risk maximizes business value.
- Discuss possible conflicts between business and societal objectives.

2.1   The Need for a Risk Management Objective

In the first chapter you learned that risk refers to either variability around the expected value or, in other contexts, the expected value of losses. Holding all else equal, both types of risk—variability and expected losses—are costly (i.e., they generally reduce the value of engaging in various activities). At a broad level, risk management seeks to mitigate this reduction in value and thus increase welfare. We begin this chapter with two simple examples to illustrate how risk management can increase value: (1) the risk of product liability claims against a pharmaceutical company, and (2) the risk to individuals associated with automobile accidents.

Consider first a pharmaceutical company that is developing a new prescription drug for the treatment of rheumatoid arthritis, a crippling disease of the joints. The risk of adverse health reactions to the drug and thus legal liability claims by injured users could be substantial. The possibility of injuries, which cause the firm (and/or its liability insurer) to defend lawsuits and pay damages, will increase the business's expected costs. Loss control, such as expenditures on product development and safety testing that reduce expected legal defense costs and expected damage payments, also will be costly.

If the firm purchases liability insurance to finance part of the potential losses, the premium paid will include a "loading" to cover the insurer's administrative costs and provide a reasonable expected return on the insurer's capital (see Chapter 8). The possibility of uninsured damage claims (self-insured losses or losses in excess of liability insurance coverage limits) will create uncertainty about the amount of costs that will be incurred in any given period.

Most and perhaps all of these factors can increase the price that the firm will need to charge for the drug, thus reducing demand. For a given price, the risk of injury also might discourage some doctors from prescribing the drug. The risk of injury also might cause the firm and the medical profession to distribute the drug only to the most severe cases of the disease, or the firm might even decide not to introduce the drug. As a result, from the company's perspective, the risk of consumer injury could have a significant effect on the value of introducing the drug.

Now consider the risk that you will be involved in an auto accident, which could cause physical harm to you and your vehicle, as well as exposing you to the risk of a lawsuit for harming someone else. The possibility of being involved in an accident reduces the value of driving. Other things being equal, people obviously would prefer to have a lower likelihood of accident. But other things are not equal. Safety equipment included in vehicles usually increases their price. Attempting to reduce the likelihood of injury by driving less also can be costly. You either must stay home or take alternative transportation that may not be as attractive as driving (apart from the risk of accident). Driving more safely usually means taking more time to get places, or it requires greater concentration, which means you cannot think as much about other things while you are behind the wheel.

In addition to the component needed to pay losses, auto and health insurance premiums must again include a loading for the insurer's administrative costs and provide a reasonable expected return on the insurer's capital. Even with insurance, you face some uncertainty about the cost of losses that are less than your deductible (or for liability losses greater than policy limits). You also are exposed to uninsured indirect losses that arise from accidents, such as the time lost in getting your car repaired and submitting a claim to your insurer.

Along with the discussion in Chapter 1, you should be convinced by now that risk is costly and so is the management of risk. We therefore need some guiding principles to determine how much and what types of risk management should be pursued. That is, we need to identify the underlying objective of risk management.

The guiding principle or fundamental objective of risk management is to minimize the cost of risk. When we consider business risk management decisions, the objective is to minimize the firm's cost of risk. When we consider individual risk management, the objective is to minimize the individual's cost of risk. And, if we consider public policy risk management decisions, the objective is to minimize society's cost of risk.

After explaining the cost of risk concept in more detail in the next section, we show how minimizing a firm's cost of risk is the same as maximizing the firm's value (section 2.3). Then we introduce the concept of risk aversion and explain how individuals' cost of risk depends on their degree of risk aversion (section 2.4). Finally, we show how actions that minimize society's cost of risk may differ from actions that minimize the cost of risk for an individual or business (section 2.5).

2.2 Understanding the Cost of Risk

Recall from Chapter 1 that most risk management decisions must be made before losses are known. The magnitude of actual losses during a given time period can be determined after the fact (i.e., after the number and severity of accidents are known). Before losses occur, the cost of direct and indirect losses reflects the predicted or expected value of losses during an upcoming time period. Thus, the cost of losses can be determined ex post (after the fact) and estimated ex ante (before the fact). Most risk management decisions must be based on ex ante estimates of the cost of losses and thus the cost of risk.

Components of the Cost of Risk

Regardless of the type of risk being considered, the **cost of risk** has five main components. For concreteness, we discuss these components from a business perspective for the case of pure risk. Using the ex ante perspective, the cost of pure risk includes: (1) expected losses, (2) the cost of loss control, (3) the cost of loss financing, (4) the cost of internal risk reduction, and (5) the cost of any residual uncertainty that remains after loss control, loss financing, and internal risk reduction methods have been implemented. Figure 2.1 summarizes these five components.

Expected Cost of Losses

The **expected cost of losses** includes the expected cost of both direct and indirect losses. As you learned in the last chapter, major types of direct losses include the cost of repairing or replacing damaged assets, the cost of paying workers' compensation claims to injured workers, and the cost of defending against and settling liability claims. Indirect losses include reductions in net profits that occur as a consequence of direct losses, such as the loss of normal profits and continuing and extra expense when production is curtailed or stopped due to direct damage to physical assets. In the case of large losses, indirect losses can include loss of profits from forgone investment and, in the event of bankruptcy, legal expenses and other costs associated with reorganizing or liquidating a business.

In the case of the pharmaceutical company discussed earlier, the expected cost of direct losses would include the expected cost of liability settlements and defense. The expected cost of indirect losses would include items such as (1) the expected cost of lost profit if sales had to be reduced due to adverse liability experience, (2) the expected cost of product recall

FIGURE 2.1 **Components of the cost of risk.**

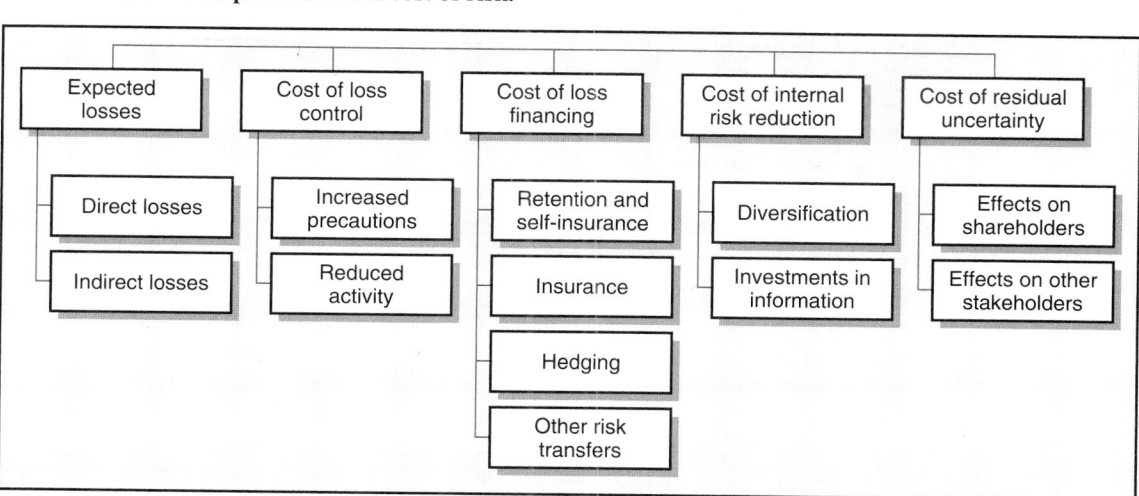

expenses, and (3) the expected loss in profit on any investments that would not be undertaken if large liability losses were to deplete the firm's internal funds available for investment and increase the cost of borrowing or raising new equity.

Cost of Loss Control

The **cost of loss control** reflects the cost of increased precautions and limits on risky activity designed to reduce the frequency and severity of accidents. For example, the cost of loss control for the pharmaceutical company would include the cost of testing the product for safety prior to its introduction and any lost profit from limiting distribution of the product in order to reduce exposure to lawsuits.

Cost of Loss Financing

The **cost of loss financing** includes the cost of self-insurance, the loading in insurance premiums, and the transaction costs in arranging, negotiating, and enforcing hedging arrangements and other contractual risk transfers. The cost of self-insurance includes the cost of maintaining reserve funds to pay losses. This cost in turn includes taxes on income from investing these funds, as well as the possible opportunity cost that can occur if maintaining reserve funds reduces the ability of a business to undertake profitable investment opportunities.

Note that when losses are insured, the cost of loss financing through insurance only reflects the loading in the policy's premium for the insurer's administrative expenses and required expected profit. The amount of premium required for the expected value of insured losses is included in the firm's expected cost of losses.

Cost of Internal Risk Reduction Methods

Insurance, hedging, other contractual risk transfers, and certain types of loss control can reduce the uncertainty associated with losses; that is, these risk management methods can make the cost of losses more predictable. You learned in Chapter 1 that uncertainty also can be reduced through diversification and investing in information to obtain better forecasts of losses. The **cost of internal risk reduction** includes transaction costs associated with achieving diversification and the cost associated with managing a diversified set of activities. It also includes the cost of obtaining and analyzing data and other types of information to obtain more accurate cost forecasts. In some cases this may involve paying another firm for this information; for example, the pharmaceutical company may pay a risk management consultant to estimate the firm's expected liability costs.

Cost of Residual Uncertainty

Uncertainty about the magnitude of losses seldom will be completely eliminated through loss control, insurance, hedging, other contractual risk transfers, and internal risk reduction. The cost of uncertainty that remains (that is "left over") once the firm has selected and implemented loss control, loss financing, and internal risk reduction is called the **cost of residual uncertainty.** This cost arises because uncertainty generally is costly to risk-averse individuals and investors. For example, residual uncertainty can affect the amount of compensation that investors require to hold a firm's stock.

Residual uncertainty also can reduce value through its effects on expected net cash flows. For example, residual uncertainty might reduce the price that customers are willing to pay for the firm's products or cause managers or employees to require higher wages (e.g., the top managers of the pharmaceutical company could require higher pay to compensate them for uncertainty associated with product liability claims).[1] We provide detailed discussion of how residual uncertainty affects individuals and shareholders of large corporations in Chapters 9 and 20.

Cost Tradeoffs

A number of tradeoffs exist among the components of the cost of risk. The three most important cost tradeoffs are those between: (1) the expected cost of direct/indirect losses and loss control costs, (2) the cost of loss financing/internal risk reduction and the expected cost of indirect losses, and (3) the cost of loss financing/internal risk reduction and the cost of residual uncertainty.

First, recall from Chapter 1 that a tradeoff normally exists between expected losses (both direct and indirect) and loss control costs. Increasing loss control costs should reduce expected losses. In the case of the pharmaceutical company, for example, expenditures on developing a safer drug will reduce the expected cost of liability suits. Ignoring for simplicity the possible effects of loss control on other components of the cost of risk (such as the cost of residual uncertainty), minimizing the cost of risk requires the firm to invest in loss control until the marginal benefit—in the form of lower expected costs resulting from direct and indirect losses—equals the marginal cost of loss control (see Chapter 11).

The amount of loss control that minimizes the cost of risk generally will not involve eliminating the risk of loss.[2] (We touched on this point in Chapter 1.) It will not produce a world in which buildings never burn, workers are never hurt, and products never harm customers because *reducing the probability of loss to zero would be too costly.* Beyond some point, the cost of additional loss control exceeds the reduction in the expected cost of losses (that is, the marginal cost exceeds the marginal benefit) so that additional loss control will increase the cost of risk. Eliminating the risk of loss will not minimize the cost of risk for either businesses or society.

Even if it were technologically feasible to eliminate the risk of harm, people would not want to live in such a world. It simply would be too expensive. To use an absurd example to prove this point, injuries from automobile accidents might be virtually eliminated if automobiles were simply tanks without weapons. But very few people could afford to drive a tank, and those who could would rather risk injury and get to their destination more quickly with a pickup or luxury sports sedan. Because loss control is costly, a point is reached where people prefer some risk of harm to paying more for goods and services or incurring other costs to reduce risk.

The second major tradeoff among the components of the cost of risk is the tradeoff between the costs of loss financing/internal risk reduction and the expected cost of indirect

---

[1]Note that these managers also may require higher pay because of the expected cost of indirect losses to them from, for example, lost pay and the costs of seeking new employment if large losses cause them to lose their jobs. The cost of residual uncertainty in this case reflects the increase in pay above the amount needed to compensate managers for the expected cost of these indirect losses. That is, the cost of residual uncertainty arises because of the uncertainty about whether these costs will be incurred.

[2]For a couple of days following 9/11/01, the entire U.S. airline industry was shut down to reduce the probability of a crash to zero. After a few days of no air travel, however, the cost of eliminating the risk of loss was deemed to be too high and commercial flights resumed.

losses. As more money is spent on loss financing/internal risk reduction, variability in the firm's cash flows declines. Lower variability reduces the probability of costly bankruptcy and the probability that the firm will forgo profitable investments as a result of large uninsured losses. As a result, the expected cost of these indirect losses declines. This tradeoff between the costs of loss financing/internal risk reduction and the expected cost of indirect losses is of central importance in understanding when firms with diversified shareholders will purchase insurance or hedge (see Chapters 7 and 9).

The third major tradeoff is that which often occurs between the costs of loss financing/internal risk reduction and the cost of residual uncertainty. For example, if the firm incurs higher loss financing costs by purchasing insurance, residual uncertainty declines. Greater and more costly internal risk reduction also reduces residual uncertainty.

Concept Checks

1. For an airline, describe the most important components of the cost of risk that arise from the risk of plane crashes.
2. How might the risk of crashes be eliminated by the airline, if at all?
3. Assume that you want to fly across the country and that for a price of $400 the probability of a fatal crash is one in a million trips. To reduce this probability to one in 1.5 million trips, the price of a ticket would increase to $800. Would you be willing to pay the extra $400?

Cost of Other Types of Risk

We illustrated the cost of risk concept using a business perspective and analyzing pure risk. However, the cost of risk is a general concept. With some modification, our discussion of the cost of pure risk is applicable to other types of risk. To illustrate, we will briefly discuss the risk of input price changes, using the specific example of a manufacturer that uses oil in its production process. In this case, the prices charged for the firm's products generally will not immediately adjust to reflect changes in the price of oil so that the firm's profits will be affected by oil price changes. Oil price increases will cause the firm's profits (or net cash flows) to decline in the short run, and oil price decreases will lead to a short-run increase in profits.

From an ex ante perspective, the expected cost of oil is analogous to the expected cost of direct losses from pure risk, such as those associated with product liability claims against the pharmaceutical company. Ex post, the actual cost of oil price changes can differ from what was expected, just as the actual costs from product liability claims can differ from those expected. If costs are greater than expected, then profits will be lower than expected in both cases. However, because oil is an integral input to the production process for which ongoing expenditures are routinely expected, the expected cost of oil normally would not be considered as part of the cost of risk. (Similarly, while wages paid to employees can differ from what is expected, the expected cost of wages normally would not be considered as part of the cost of risk.)

Large increases in the price of oil could cause indirect costs if, for example, production is reduced, alternative sources of energy need to be arranged, or profitable investment is curtailed. The possibility of indirect costs increases the expected cost of using oil in the production process. Expenditures on loss control, such as redesigning the production process to allow for the substitution of other sources of energy, would decrease the expected cost of oil use and indirect losses.

With regard to loss financing, the manufacturer might choose to reduce its exposure to the risk of oil price changes with futures contracts. As we explain in Chapter 24, the appropriate use of futures will produce a profit if oil prices increase, thus offsetting all or part of the loss to the firm. (If oil prices drop, all or part of the gain that the firm otherwise would experience will be offset by a loss on its futures contracts.) However, the use of futures contracts involves transaction costs that are analogous to the loading in insurance premiums. The firm also might engage in internal risk reduction by diversifying its activities to reduce the sensitivity of its profits to oil price changes or by investing in information to obtain better forecasts of oil prices.

You can see from this simple example that the cost of risk concept illustrated in Figure 2.1 is quite general. This concept provides a useful way of thinking about and evaluating all types of risk management decisions.

2.3   Firm Value Maximization and the Cost of Risk

Determinants of Value

As we noted in Chapter 1, a business's value to shareholders depends fundamentally on the expected magnitude, timing, and risk (variability) associated with future net cash flows (cash inflows minus cash outflows) that will be available to provide shareholders with a return on their investment.

Business value and the effects of risk on value reflect an ex ante perspective: Value depends on expected future net cash flows and risk associated with these cash flows. Cash inflows primarily result from sales of goods and services. Cash outflows primarily arise from the production of goods and services (e.g., wages and salaries, the cost of raw materials, interest on borrowed funds, and liability losses). Increases in the expected size of net cash flows increase business value; decreases in expected net cash flows reduce value. The timing of cash flows affects value because a dollar received today is worth more than a dollar received in the future.

Because most investors are risk averse, the risk of cash flows reduces the price that they are willing to pay for the firm's stock and thus its value (provided that this risk cannot be eliminated by investors holding a diversified portfolio of investments, which we discuss in more detail in Chapter 9). For a given level of expected net cash flows, this reduction in the firm's stock price due to risk increases the expected return from buying the stock. In other words, the variation in net cash flows causes investors to pay less for the rights to future cash flows, which increases the expected return on the amount that they invest. Thus, a fundamental principle of business valuation is that risk reduces value and increases the expected return required by investors. The actual return to investors in any given period will depend on realizations of net cash flows during the period and new information about the expected future net cash flows and risk.

Maximizing Value by Minimizing the Cost of Risk

Unexpected increases in losses that are not offset by cash inflows from insurance contracts, hedging arrangements, or other contractual risk transfers (see Chapter 1) increase cash outflows and often reduce cash inflows, thus reducing the value of a firm's stock. The effects of risk and risk management on firm value before losses are known reflect their influence on (1) the expected value of net cash flows and (2) the compensation required by shareholders to bear risk. Much of basic financial theory deals with the kind of risk for which investors demand compensation and the amount of compensation required. We will have more to say about how risk affects expected cash flows, risk, and required compensation in later chapters. For now, it is sufficient for you to understand that making risk management decisions to maximize business value requires an understanding of how risk and risk management methods affect (1) expected net cash flows and (2) the compensation for risk that is required by shareholders.

If the firm's cost of risk is defined to include all risk-related costs from the perspective of shareholders, *a business can maximize its value to shareholders by minimizing the cost of risk.* To see this more clearly, we define:

$$\text{Cost of risk} = \text{Value without risk} - \text{Value with risk} \qquad \textbf{(2.1)}$$

Writing this expression in terms of the firm's value to shareholders in the presence of risk gives:

$$\text{Value with risk} = \text{Value without risk} - \text{Cost of risk} \qquad \textbf{(2.2)}$$

The value of the firm without risk is a hypothetical and abstract concept that is nonetheless very useful. It equals the hypothetical value of the business in a world in which uncertainty associated with net cash flows could be eliminated at zero cost. This hypothetical value reflects the magnitude and timing of future net cash flows that would occur without risk and risk-related costs. We emphasize that this value is entirely hypothetical because risk is inherent in real-world business activities.

To illustrate the cost of risk, consider the product liability example introduced earlier. For the pharmaceutical company, the value of the firm without risk is the hypothetical value that would arise if (1) it were impossible for the drug to hurt consumers and thus produce lawsuits and (2) the firm did not have to incur any cost to achieve this state of riskless bliss. The reality of injury risk and the costs of loss control give rise to risk-related costs, thus reducing the value of the business.

Equation 2.2 implies that if the firm seeks to maximize value, it can do so by minimizing the cost of risk. It accomplishes this by making the reduction in value due to risk as small as possible. Thus, *as long as costs are defined to include all the effects on value of risk and risk management,* minimizing the cost of risk is the same thing as maximizing value.

Why bother introducing the cost of risk instead of just talking about **value maximization?** First, the cost of risk concept helps focus attention on and facilitates categorization of the major ways that risk reduces value. Second, the concept is used extensively in practice (although its breadth is sometimes narrower, as is noted below).

Measuring the Cost of Risk

In order to maximize business value by minimizing the cost of risk, businesses ideally will estimate the size of the various components of the cost of risk and consider how these costs will be affected by the firm's operating and risk management decisions. However, in practice, the necessary analysis is costly. Moreover, some of the components are particularly difficult to measure. Examples include the estimated cost of forgone activity (e.g., profits that would have been achieved but for risk and the reduction in activity), the impact of decisions on customers or suppliers, and the cost of residual uncertainty.

As a result of these practical limitations, businesses often will not attempt to quantify all of their costs precisely. Small businesses especially are unlikely to measure costs with much precision because the cost of analysis is usually large compared to the potential benefit in the form of improved decisions. However, even when quantifying the various components of the cost of risk is not cost-effective, managers need to understand these components and the general ways in which their magnitude will be affected by risk management. This understanding is necessary for making informed decisions using intuitive and subjective assessments of the effects of decisions on costs.[3]

Subsidiary Goals

While the overall objective of risk management is to maximize business value to shareholders by minimizing the cost of risk, a variety of subsidiary goals is used to guide day-to-day decision making. Examples of these subsidiary goals include making insurance decisions to keep the realized cost of uninsured losses below a specified percent of revenues, purchasing insurance against any loss that could be large enough to seriously disrupt operations, making decisions to comply with stipulations in loan contracts on the types and amounts of insurance that must be purchased, and spending money on loss control when the savings on insurance premiums are sufficient to outweigh the costs. These types of rules generally can be viewed as a means to an end (i.e., as practical guides to increasing business value). However, in each case, there should be a reasonably clear link between the particular goal and the increase in value.

Objectives for Nonprofit Firms

How does the overall objective of risk management differ for nonprofit or government entities that do not have shareholders? Nonprofit firms can be viewed as attempting to maximize the value of products or services provided to various customers and constituents (e.g., taxpayers or persons that donate money to finance the firm's operations), where value depends on the preferences of these parties. If the cost of risk is defined as the reduction in value of the nonprofit firm's activities due to risk, the appropriate goal of risk management remains minimization of the cost of risk to those constituents.

Minimizing the cost of risk for a nonprofit firm may involve giving greater weight to certain factors than would be true for a for-profit firm. A nonprofit hospital, for example, might place greater emphasis on the adverse effects of large losses on its customers than would a for-profit firm.

---

[3] Some survey evidence exists on the magnitude of the cost of pure risk for large corporations (see *Cost of Risk Survey,* Risk and Insurance Management Society, New York, NY). Corporate respondents provide estimates of amounts spent on property–liability insurance, uninsured losses, and loss control and loss financing programs. While still valuable to managers, these estimates of the total cost of risk will underestimate the true cost (perhaps substantially in many cases) because information on the cost of loss control that arises from reducing the level of risky activity and many indirect costs of losses are not included, presumably due to the difficulty of estimating these costs.

However, while the details may differ, the overall objective of risk management and the key decisions that must be made by nonprofit firms are similar to those for for-profit firms. Nonprofit firms need to identify how risk reduces the net value of services provided and make decisions with the goal of minimizing the cost of risk. They have to consider the same basic components of the cost of risk as for-profit firms. It is not clear whether the absence of shareholders and the possibly fewer penalties for failing to minimize costs make agency costs (see Box 2.1) greater for nonprofit firms than for for-profit firms, or, if so, whether this affects risk management.

Will Managers Maximize Value?   2.1

Owner-managers (e.g., sole proprietors, managing partners, and owner-managers of corporations without publicly traded common stock) have a clear incentive to operate their businesses to achieve their own interests. This generally will involve value maximization provided that value is appropriately defined to reflect the owners' attitude toward risk and their ability to diversify their risk of ownership.

One of the longest and most thoroughly debated subjects in business economics and finance is whether managers of large corporations with widely held common stock (i.e., with large numbers of shareholders that are not involved in management) will diligently strive to maximize value to shareholders. The ownership and management functions are separated in businesses with widely held common stock. Managers can be viewed as agents of shareholders. Managers may have incentives to take actions that benefit themselves at a cost to shareholders, thus failing to maximize shareholder wealth. The costs associated with these actions, including the costs incurred by shareholders in monitoring managerial behavior, are broadly referred to as *agency costs*.

Agency costs reduce business value. In the context of risk management, agency costs might be manifested by managers being excessively cautious. Because managers could be seriously harmed by financial distress of the firm, they might spend more money than is needed on insurance, loss control, or other methods of reducing the likelihood of financial distress.

From a normative perspective (i.e., from the perspective of how people or businesses *should* behave), managers are agents of shareholders and therefore should seek to maximize value. As a practical matter, a number of factors give managers strong incentives not

to deviate too much from value maximization, thus reducing agency costs:

1. Managers often are compensated in part with bonuses linked to the firm's profitability (and thus indirectly to its stock price), or with stock or stock options that directly increase managers' personal wealth when the firm's stock price increases. These performance-based compensation systems provide a direct incentive for value maximization. Poor performance by managers also can reduce their prospects for achieving employment with other firms (it can reduce their value in the managerial labor market).

2. Failing to maximize the value of the firm's stock makes it more likely that the firm will be acquired by another firm or parties that can then replace current top management with managers that will take actions to increase firm value.

3. If failure by managers to control costs, including the cost of risk, increases the price or reduces the quality of the firm's products, the firm will lose sales to firms with managers who are more inclined to control costs and increase value. This outcome makes it more likely that managers will be replaced and/or that the managers' salaries will be lower than if they maximized value.

4. Many firms have stockholders with large stakes and other stakeholders (such as lenders) that routinely monitor managerial performance.

5. State laws and the legal liability system impose fiduciary duties on managers. Failing to act in the interest of shareholders can give rise to lawsuits against managers and potential legal liability.

2.4 Individual Risk Management and the Cost of Risk

The cost of risk concept also applies to individual risk management decisions. For example, when choosing how to manage the risk of automobile accidents, an individual would consider the expected losses (both direct and indirect) from accidents, possible loss control activities (such as driving less at night) and the cost of these activities, loss financing alternatives (amount of insurance coverage) and the cost of these alternatives, and the cost and benefits of gathering information (e.g., about the weather and road conditions). In addition, an individual would consider the cost of any residual uncertainty, which depends on that person's attitude toward risk (uncertainty).[4]

The amount of risk management undertaken by individuals depends in part on their degree of risk aversion. A person is **risk averse** if when having to decide between two risky alternatives that have the same expected outcome, the person chooses the alternative whose outcomes have less variability. This example illustrates the concept of risk aversion: Suppose that you must choose between the following alternatives. With alternative A, you have a 50 percent chance of winning $100 and a 50 percent chance of losing $100. With alternative B, you have a 50 percent chance of winning $10,000 and a 50 percent chance of losing $10,000. Both gambles have an expected value equal to zero, but alternative A's outcomes have less variability (i.e., they are closer to the expected outcome).[5] Stated more simply, most would agree that alternative B is riskier than A. Thus, if you choose alternative A, you are risk averse. If you choose alternative B, you would be called risk loving; and if you are indifferent between the two, you are risk neutral.

As mentioned earlier, most people are averse to risk. Risk-averse people generally are willing to pay to reduce risk, or must be compensated for taking on risk. For example, risk-averse people buy insurance to reduce risk. Also, risk-averse people require higher expected returns to invest in riskier securities. The degree of risk aversion can vary across people. If Mary is more risk averse than David, then Mary would likely purchase more insurance than David, all else being equal.

2.5 Risk Management and Societal Welfare

From a societal perspective, the key question is how risky activities and risk management by individuals and businesses can best be arranged to minimize the total cost of risk for society. This cost is the aggregate—for all members of society—of the costs of losses, loss control, loss financing, internal risk reduction, and residual uncertainty. Minimizing the total cost of risk in society would maximize the value of societal resources.

Minimizing the total cost of risk for society produces an **efficient level of risk.** Efficiency requires individuals and businesses to pursue activities until the marginal benefit equals the marginal cost, including risk-related costs. Expressed in terms of the cost of pure risk, *efficiency requires that loss control, loss financing, and internal risk reduction be pursued until the marginal reduction in the expected cost of losses and residual uncertainty equals the marginal cost of these risk management methods.* As was discussed

[4]For some types of risk (e.g. automobile liability), regulations constrain choices.

[5]These ideas will be presented with more precision in later chapters.

earlier, however, achieving the efficiency goal does not eliminate losses because it is simply too costly to do so.

While the efficiency concept is abstract and the benefits and costs of risk management are often difficult to measure, the efficiency goal is nonetheless viewed as appropriate by many people (especially economists). The main reason for this is that maximizing the value of resources by minimizing the cost of risk makes the total size of the economic "pie" as large as possible. Other things being equal, this permits the greatest number of economic needs to be met.

Greater total wealth allows greater opportunity for governments to transfer income from parties that are able to pay taxes to parties that need assistance. A fundamental problem that affects these transfers, however, is that the size of the economic pie is not invariant to how it is sliced (i.e., divided among the population). High marginal tax rates, for example, discourage work effort beyond some point, thus tending to reduce the size of the economic pie. Thus, attempts to produce a more equal distribution of income generally involve some reduction in economic value. The goal is to achieve the right balance between the amount of total wealth and how it is distributed.

Similar issues arise within the context of risk. An important example (discussed in Chapter 8) is the effect of government regulations that cause insurance premium rates for some buyers to differ from the expected costs of providing them coverage. By changing how the total cost of risk is divided (or how the total cost pie is sliced), these regulations can alter incentives in ways that increase the total cost of risk (e.g., by encouraging too much risky activity by individuals whose insurance premiums are subsidized). While many persons might argue that these regulations produce a fairer distribution of costs, they nonetheless involve some increase in cost.

It is reasonable to assume that individuals, acting privately, will make risk management decisions that minimize their own cost of risk. Similarly, businesses that seek to maximize value to shareholders will make risk management decisions to minimize the cost of risk to the business. The question arises: Will minimizing the cost of risk to the business or individual minimize the cost of risk to society?

Note first that maximizing business value by minimizing the cost of risk generally will involve some consideration of the effects of risk management decisions on other major stakeholders in the firm. As suggested above and explained in detail in later chapters, the firm's value to shareholders and the reduction in value due to the cost of risk will depend in part on how risk and risk management affect employees, customers, suppliers, and lenders. The basic reason is that risk and its management affect the terms at which these parties are willing to contract with the business. For example, other things being equal, businesses that expose employees to obvious safety hazards will have to pay higher wages to attract employees. This provides some incentive for the firm to improve safety conditions in order to save on wages (apart from any legal requirement for the firm to pay for injuries).

Unfortunately, because we do not live in a perfect world, the goal of making money for shareholders can lead to risk management decisions that may not necessarily minimize the total cost of risk to society. In order for business value maximization to minimize the total cost of risk to society, the business must consider all societal costs in its decisions. In other words, all social costs should be internalized by the business so that its private costs equal social costs. If the **private cost of risk** (the cost to the business) differs from the **social cost**

of risk (the total cost to society), business value maximization generally will not minimize the total cost of risk to society.

A few simple examples should help to illustrate the increase in the social cost of risk that can arise when the private cost is less than the social cost. To illustrate the point simply, assume that there is no government regulation of safety, no workers' compensation law, and no legal liability system that allows persons to recover damages from businesses that cause them harm. Under this assumption, businesses that seek to maximize value to shareholders may not consider possible harm to persons from risky activity. It would be very likely that many businesses would make decisions without fully reflecting upon their possible harm to "strangers" (persons with no connection to the business).

In addition, businesses would tend to produce products that are too risky and expose workers to an excessive risk of workplace injury given the social cost if consumers and workers underestimate the risk of injury. Note in contrast that if consumers and workers can accurately assess the risk of injury, they can influence the business to consider the risk of harm by reducing the price they are willing to pay for products and increasing the wages demanded in view of the risk of injury.

You will learn more about these issues in chapters that address the legal liability system and workers' compensation law. For now, it is sufficient to note that a major function of liability and workplace injury law is to get businesses to reflect more upon the risk of harm to consumers, workers, and other parties in making their decisions. If legal rules are designed so that private costs are approximately equal to social costs, then value maximizing decisions by businesses will help to minimize the total cost of risk in society. Efficient legal rules are those that achieve this goal.[6]

2.6 Summary

- The overall objective of risk management is to minimize the cost of risk.

- Components of the cost of risk include: (1) the expected cost of losses, (2) the cost of loss control, (3) the cost of loss financing, (4) the cost of internal risk reduction, and (5) the cost of any residual uncertainty that remains after loss control, loss financing, and internal risk reduction methods have been implemented.

- In the context of business risk management, maximizing firm value is equivalent to minimizing the cost of risk.

- Loss control reduces the expected cost of losses. Beyond some point, the cost of additional loss control will exceed the reduction in the expected cost of losses. As a result, minimizing the cost of risk will not eliminate completely the risk of loss. If it were feasible, eliminating the risk of loss would be excessively costly to businesses and consumers alike.

- Loss financing and internal risk reduction reduce risk and therefore can reduce both the expected cost of indirect losses and the cost of residual uncertainty.

---

[6]In concluding this chapter, we note that some of this material might seem fairly abstract to you at this point. If so, these ideas will become clearer to you as you progress further along in the course. It also might be helpful for you to reread parts of this chapter after covering the related material that comes later.

- The overall objective of risk management for nonprofit firms also should be to minimize the cost of risk, provided that the special objectives and circumstances of these firms are incorporated into the cost of risk.

- The overall objective of risk management for individuals can be viewed as minimizing the cost of risk and thus maximizing the welfare of individuals.

- If businesses do not bear the full costs of their risky activities (that is, if the private cost of risk is less than the social cost), the total cost of risk in society will not be minimized when businesses maximize value. A major function of business liability and workplace injury law is to align private costs with social costs so that business value maximization will minimize the social cost of risk.

Key Terms

cost of risk 17	cost of internal risk reduction 18	efficient level of risk 25
expected cost of losses 17	cost of residual uncertainty 18	private cost of risk 26
cost of loss control 18	value maximization 22	social cost of risk 26
cost of loss financing 18	risk averse 25	

Questions and Problems

1. Some people argue that *any* risk of injury from toxic chemicals and environmental pollutants is too high. Explain why this "zero risk" goal would not lead to an efficient level of risk in society.

2. Describe specific factors included in the cost of risk for: (*a*) the risk that workers in a manufacturing plant will be injured by machines and equipment, (*b*) the risk that an international business will suffer loss from the expropriation of its investments by a foreign government, and (*c*) the risk that the price that a beer manufacturer can charge will decline due to a change in consumer preferences toward wine and soda.

3. Ignoring incentives from the legal system, what incentives do businesses have to: (*a*) make safe products, (*b*) reduce worker injury risk, and (*c*) avoid polluting the environment?

4. Mr. Fatcat manages a large corporation. Given his preferences, he would like to take expensive and frivolous trips in the company jet, receive a large salary, decorate his office with ancient artifacts, and throw cor-

porate money at projects with borderline prospects for making any significant returns. What motivating influences can help Mr. Fatcat resist these temptations and maximize firm value?

5. We-Dump-It is in the business of disposing of toxic chemicals. Explain why a legal system might be necessary to increase the private cost of risk for We-Dump-It in order to better align its goal of maximizing firm value with the goal of achieving an efficient level of risk in society.

6. Describe how the risk of injury to consumers and "bystanders" could affect the design, production, distribution, and pricing of jet skis if the manufacturer seeks to maximize firm value (assuming no safety regulations and that the producer cannot be held liable for harm to consumers or bystanders). Will value maximization cause the manufacturer to consider the effects of noise on the tranquillity of beaches and inland waterways?

7. Air travel can be made safer by increasing the security efforts. Identify the trade-offs

associated with increasing security checks of individual passengers and their luggage. Be sure to consider the effect on the demand for air travel and the resulting effects on automobile travel that statistically has greater risk of injury and death per mile than air travel.

Answers to Concept Checks

1. The most important components of the cost of risk for the airline are: (*a*) the expected cost of damage to aircraft and liability claims and defense costs for injured people; (*b*) the expected cost of indirect losses, such as a reduction in profits and continuing and extra expenses if a major crash harms the airline's reputation for safety; and (*c*) the costs of retention and of premium loadings for aircraft property and liability insurance.

2. While enormous sums of money could be spent on precautions such as design changes that improve safety and more comprehensive maintenance between flights, it almost certainly would be impossible to eliminate the risk of crashes completely without shutting down the airline ("stuff happens").

3. Your answer will be no unless you are extremely risk averse or suffer from a pathological fear of flying, in which case we encourage you to take the bus. You also might answer yes if you are extremely rich.

References

Mishan, E. J. *What Political Economy Is All About.* New York, NY: Cambridge University Press, 1982. (*Part One provides a very readable introduction to the nature and rationale of the efficiency criterion used by economists. Reading this material will help you understand economic efficiency and the efficient level of risk in society.*)

Risk and Insurance Management Society. *Cost of Risk Survey.* New York, NY: Risk and Insurance Management Society. (*Annual report on the cost of insurance, uninsured losses, and loss control based on a survey of medium-to-large corporations.*)

Chapter 3

Risk Identification and Measurement

Chapter Objectives

- Discuss frameworks for identifying business and individual risk exposures.
- Review concepts from probability and statistics.
- Apply mathematical concepts to understand the frequency and severity of losses.
- Explain the concepts of maximum probable loss and value at risk.

3.1 Risk Identification

As introduced in Chapter 1, the five major steps in the risk management decision-making process are: (1) identify all significant risks that can cause loss; (2) evaluate the potential frequency and severity of losses; (3) develop and select methods for managing risk; (4) implement the risk management methods chosen; and (5) monitor the suitability and performance of the chosen risk management methods and strategies on an ongoing basis. This chapter focuses on the first two steps of this process.

Identifying Business Risk Exposures

The first step in the risk management process is **risk identification:** the identification of loss exposures. Unidentified loss exposures most likely will result in an implicit retention decision, which may not be optimal. There are various methods of identifying exposures. For example, comprehensive checklists of common business exposures can be obtained from risk management consultants and other sources. Loss exposures also can be identified through analysis of the firm's financial statements, discussions with managers throughout the firm, surveys of employees, and discussions with insurance agents and risk management consultants. Regardless of the specific methods used, risk identification requires an overall understanding of the business and the specific economic, legal, and regulatory factors that affect the business.

Property Loss Exposures

Some of the major practical questions asked when identifying property loss exposures for businesses are listed in Table 3.1. In addition to identifying what property is exposed to loss and the potential causes of loss, the firm must consider how property should be valued for the purpose of making risk management decisions. Several valuation methods are available. **Book value**—the purchase price minus accounting depreciation—is the method commonly used for financial reporting purposes. However, since book value does not

Table 3.1
Some practical questions in identifying business property and liability loss exposures.

Type of Loss	Property Losses	Liability Losses
Direct Losses	1. What types of property are subject to damage or disappearance? 2. What factors (perils) can lead to loss? 3. What is the value of property exposed to loss? 4. Will the property be replaced if it is lost?	1. What parties might be harmed by the firm (customers, suppliers, and other parties)? 2. How might these parties be harmed? 3. What is the potential magnitude of damages? 4. What is the potential magnitude of defense costs?

Indirect Losses	1. Will the firm have to raise external funds to replace uninsured property?
	2. Assuming replacement, will the firm suspend or cut back operations following a direct loss?
	3. If the firm suspends or cuts back its operations:
	  (a) What is the potential duration and how much normal profit could be lost?
	  (b) What operating expenses would continue despite the suspension or slowdown?
	  (c) Will revenue losses continue after normal levels of production are resumed, and, if so, what actions might reduce these losses and at what cost?
	4. If the firm continues operating at preloss levels:
	  (a) What facilities or resources will be needed?
	  (b) What will be the additional cost from using alternative facilities or resources?
		1. Will revenues decline in response to possible damage to the firm's reputation?
		  (a) What is the potential magnitude of this loss?
		  (b) What actions might reduce the resulting indirect losses and at what cost?
		2. Will products and services likely be abandoned or products recalled in the event of large uninsured losses?
		3. Will the firm have to raise additional capital in the event that cash flows decline?
		4. Could large uninsured losses push the firm into financial distress?

necessarily correspond to economic value, it generally is not relevant for risk management purposes (except for the tax reasons discussed in Chapter 21). **Market value** is the value that the next-highest-valued user would pay for the property. **Firm-specific value** is the value of the property to the current owner. If the property does not provide firm-specific benefits, then firm-specific value will equal market value. Otherwise, firm-specific value will exceed market value. **Replacement cost new** is the cost of replacing the damaged property with new property. Due to economic depreciation and improvements in quality, replacement cost new often will exceed the market value of the property.[1]

Indirect losses also can arise from damage to property that will be repaired or replaced. For example, if a fire shuts down a plant for four months, the firm not only incurs the cost of replacing the damaged property, it also loses the profits from not being able to produce. In addition, some operating expenses might continue despite the shutdown (e.g., salaries for certain managers and employees and advertising expenses). These exposures are known as **business income exposures** (or, sometimes, business interruption exposures), and they frequently are insured with *business interruption insurance.* Note that business interruption losses also might result from property losses to a firm's major customers or suppliers that prevent them from transacting with the firm. This exposure can be insured with "contingent" business interruption insurance.

Firms also may suffer losses after they resume operations if previous customers that have switched to other sources of supply do not return. In the event that a long-term loss of customers would occur and/or a shutdown temporarily would impose large costs on customers or suppliers, it might be optimal for the firm to keep operating following a loss by arranging for the immediate use of alternative facilities at higher operating costs. The resulting exposure to higher costs is known as the **extra expense exposure.** Insurance purchased to reimburse the firm for these higher costs is known as *extra expense coverage.*

Liability Losses

As we analyze in detail in later chapters, firms face potential legal liability losses as a result of relationships with many parties, including suppliers, customers, employees, shareholders, and members of the public. The settlements, judgments, and legal costs associated with liability suits can impose substantial losses on firms. Lawsuits also may harm firms by damaging their reputation, and they may require expenditures to minimize the costs of this damage. For example, in the case of liability to customers for injuries arising out of the firm's products, the firm might incur product recall expenses and higher marketing costs to rehabilitate a product.

Losses to Human Resources

Losses in firm value due to worker injuries, disabilities, death, retirement, and turnover can be grouped into two categories. First, as a result of contractual commitments and compulsory benefits, firms often compensate employees (or their beneficiaries) for injuries, dis-

---

[1]As noted in Chapter 10 property insurance policies can cover either the replacement cost or the *actual cash value* of the property. Actual cash value commonly is defined as replacement cost new less depreciation. A substantial number of court cases deal with disagreements over what this means. In many cases, actual cash value is treated as equivalent to market value. However, some court decisions might allow a corporation to argue that actual cash value equals firm-specific value if this is greater than the market value.

abilities, death, and retirement. Second, worker injuries, disabilities, death, retirement, and turnover can cause indirect losses when production is interrupted and employees cannot be replaced at zero cost with other employees of the same quality. In some cases, firms purchase life insurance to compensate for the death or disability of important employees. Also, as the discussion of pension benefits in Chapter 18 will show, employment contracts can be designed to reduce employee turnover.

Losses from External Economic Forces

The final category of losses arises from factors that are outside of the firm. Losses can arise because of changes in the prices of inputs and outputs. For example, increases in the price of oil can cause large losses to firms that use oil in the production process. Large changes in the exchange rate between currencies can increase a multinational firm's costs or decrease its revenues. As another example, an important supplier or purchaser can go bankrupt, thus increasing costs or decreasing revenues. We discuss how some of these types of losses can be managed using derivative contracts in later chapters.

Identifying Individual Exposures

One method of identifying individual/family exposures is to analyze the sources and uses of funds in the present and planned for the future. Potential events that cause decreases in the availability of funds or increases in uses of funds represent risk exposures (see Box 3.1). Because both physical and financial assets represent potential future sources of funds, potential losses in asset values also represent risk exposures. Just as business risk management consultants can aid in the identification of business risks, individual/family financial planners can help identify and then manage personal risks.

An important risk for most families is a drop in earnings prior to retirement due to the death or disability of a breadwinner. The magnitude of this risk depends, among other factors, on the number and age of dependents and on alternative sources of income (e.g., a spouse's income or investment income). The losses due to death or disability can be managed with life and disability insurance. The risk of a drop in earnings prior to retirement due to external economic factors is also an important risk facing households. Private methods for dealing with this risk, except for perhaps investments in education, are limited. Some public support often is available in the form of compulsory social insurance and unemployment insurance programs.

One of the most important sources of risk for most individuals and families is from medical expenses. The methods of dealing with this risk vary across countries. Some countries, like the United States, rely largely on the private medical and insurance industry to provide or pay for services and insurance to deal with medical expense risk. Other countries, such as Canada and the United Kingdom, rely more on government provision of medical services and insurance.

Another major source of expense risk is from personal liability exposures. Individuals can be sued and held liable for damages inflicted on others. The main sources of personal liability arise from driving an automobile and owning property with potential hazards. These risks are typically managed by using loss control and purchasing liability insurance.

Retirement often implies a large drop in earnings. To continue to pay living expenses during retirement, an individual needs to have saved substantial funds prior to retirement and/or rely on public programs, such as social security. The risk associated with pre-retirement

Consider some of the risks that you face during a semester as a student. The obvious risks are that you could become ill or injured, you could have an automobile accident, your residence could burn down, your vehicle could be stolen, and so on. A common aspect of these risks is that insurance contracts generally exist to help you manage the risk. In addition, you could reduce your exposure to the risk by taking additional precautions or by avoiding the activity that gives rise to the risk.

Consider some other risks that you face: You could buy food that is contaminated, you could purchase a product that causes an accident, or your bank could fail. A common aspect of these risks is that some type of government or social policy exists to help you deal with the consequences. Notice that the existence of these social policies lessens the extent to which you will deal with them privately, either by purchasing insurance or by taking additional precautions.

You also are exposed to many other risks where neither insurance contracts nor public programs exist to help you. For example, a sibling could die, causing you emotional distress. Your teacher could give a very diffi-cult exam, or you could forget a fundamental concept—so that in either case you bomb the exam, causing your grade point average to suffer. Alternatively, your best friend could decide to avoid you forever. Generally, the only way to deal with these risks is to engage in some loss control activity (e.g., studying more often) that will reduce either the chance of the loss occurring or the size of the loss if it does occur.

The pervasiveness of risk is apparent. The optimal response to risk from a business's or an individual's perspective is one of the central issues addressed in this book. In addition, we will provide answers to other interesting and important questions, such as: Why do insurance contracts exist for some, but not all risks? Why do we have government programs to lessen some types of risk? What are the effects of these programs on individual behavior? Answers to these questions and many others require a framework in which to analyze risky situations. The framework we use is based on some fundamental concepts from probability and statistics, which are presented in the subsequent sections of this chapter.

savings and thus the risk of not having sufficient assets during retirement to fund expenses depends on how the assets are invested. The choice of assets, (for example, between stocks, bonds, and real estate) is an important risk management decision for all individuals and households. Even after someone has retired with substantial assets, the person faces the risk of living so long all savings are depleted prior to death. This longevity risk can be managed using annuities, including government mandated annuities, such as those provided in the U.S. social security system.

3.2   Basic Concepts from Probability and Statistics

Risk assessment and measurement require a basic understanding of several concepts from probability and statistics. We review these concepts in this section. These concepts also are needed to understand much of the material in subsequent chapters.

Random Variables and Probability Distributions

A **random variable** is a variable whose outcome is uncertain. For example, suppose a coin is to be flipped and the variable X is defined to be equal to $1 if heads appears and $-$1 if tails appears. Then prior to the coin flip, the value of X is unknown; that is, X is a random variable. Once the coin has been flipped and the outcome revealed, the uncertainty about X is resolved, because the value of X is then known.

Information about a random variable is summarized by the random variable's probability distribution. In particular, a **probability distribution** identifies all the possible outcomes for the random variable and the probability of the outcomes. For the coin flipping example, Table 3.2 gives the probability distribution for *X*.

In addition to describing a probability distribution by listing the outcomes and probabilities, we also can describe probability distributions graphically. Figure 3.1 illustrates the probability distribution for the coin flipping example. On the horizontal axis, we graph the possible outcomes. On the vertical axis, we graph the probability of a particular outcome. There are only two possible outcomes in this very simple example: $1 and −$1, and the probability of each is 0.5. When discussing random variables, we use the term *actual* or *observed* outcome (or, sometimes *realized* outcome) to refer to the outcome observed (realized) in a particular case, as opposed to the *possible* outcomes that could have occurred. In the coin flipping example, once the coin has been tossed we can observe the actual outcome, which either must be $1 or −$1.

As emphasized in the first two chapters, risk management decisions need to be made prior to knowing what the actual (realized) outcomes of key variables will be. Managers do not know beforehand which outcomes of the random variables affecting the firm's profits will occur. Nevertheless, they must make decisions. Once the outcomes are observed, it usually is easy to say what would have been the best decision. However, we cannot evaluate decisions from this perspective, which is why probability distributions are so important. Probability distributions tell us all of the possible outcomes and the probability of those outcomes. Information about probability distributions is needed to make good risk management decisions.

As a second example of a probability distribution, we can approximate the probability distribution for the dollar amount of damages to your car during the coming year. For simplicity, our approximation will assume only five possible levels of damages: $0; $500;

TABLE 3.2
Probability distribution for coin flipping example.

Possible Outcomes for X	Probability
$1	0.5 or 50%
−$1	0.5 or 50%

FIGURE 3.1
Probability distribution for coin flipping example.

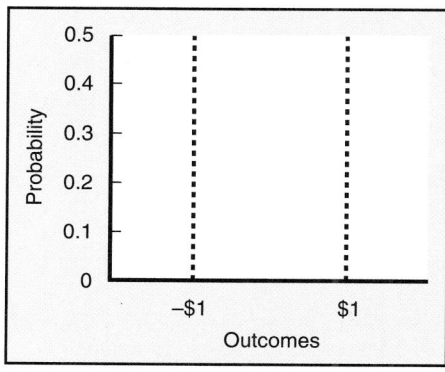

$1,000; $5,000; and $10,000. The probabilities of each of these outcomes are listed in Table 3.3. The most likely outcome is zero damages, and the least likely outcome is that damages equal $10,000. Note that the sum of the probabilities equals 1; this must always be the case. An alternative way of describing the probability distribution is provided by Figure 3.2, where the height of each dotted line gives the probability of each possible outcome.

As a final example, consider an automaker. Two of the many reasons why the automaker's profits are uncertain are steel price changes and labor conditions. In the language just introduced, the automaker's profits are a random variable. There are numerous possible outcomes for the automaker's profits. For example, steel prices could increase so much that profits could be negative. On the other hand, favorable outcomes for steel prices and the economy could cause very high profits.

What is the probability distribution for the automaker's profits? Recall that a probability distribution identifies all of the possible outcomes and associates a probability with each outcome. The coin flipping example had only two possible outcomes and so listing the probabilities was simple. In the automaker example, however, we could spend hours listing all the possible outcomes for profits and still not be finished, due to the large number of possible outcomes. In these situations, it is useful to assume that the possible outcomes can be *any* number between two extremes (the minimum possible outcome and the maximum possible outcome) and that the probability of the outcomes between the extremes is represented by a specific mathematical function.[2] For example, assume that profits for the automaker

Table 3.3
Probability distribution for automobile damages.

Possible Outcomes for Damages	Probability
$ 0	0.50
$ 500	0.30
$ 1,000	0.10
$ 5,000	0.06
$10,000	0.04

FIGURE 3.2   **Probability distribution for automobile damages.**

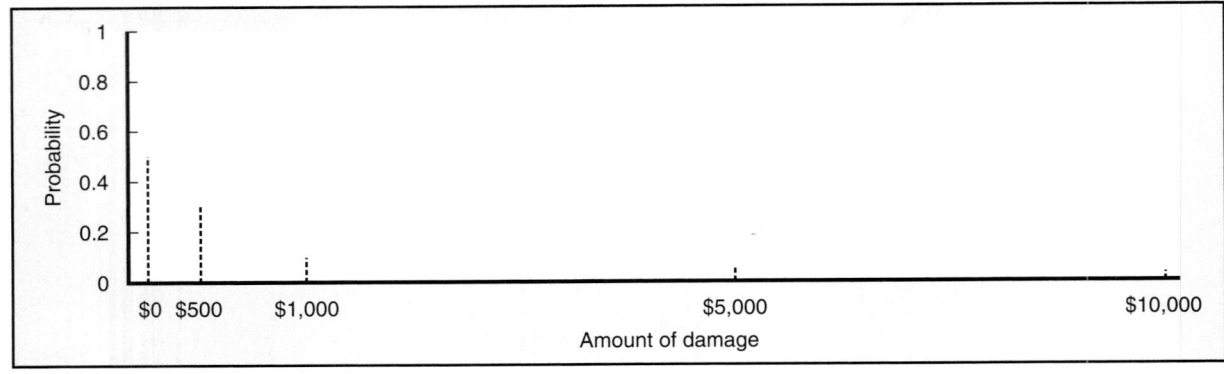

[2]This is equivalent to assuming that the probability of outcomes below the assumed minimum or above the assumed maximum is so small that these outcomes can be ignored.

could be any number between −$20 million and $50 million. Just as with the earlier graphs, we can identify the possible outcomes for profits between these amounts on the horizontal axis of Figure 3.3, which illustrates the probability distribution for the automaker's profits. Analogous to the earlier graphs, the vertical axis will measure the probability of the possible outcomes.[3] The probabilities of the outcomes are illustrated in Figure 3.3 by a bell-shaped curve, which might appear familiar to you.

Recall that the sum of the probabilities of all the possible outcomes must equal 1 (some outcome must occur). In the coin flipping example and the automobile damage example, this property is easy to verify because the number of possible outcomes is small. Stating that the probabilities sum to 1 in these examples is equivalent to stating that the heights of the dotted lines in Figures 3.1 and 3.2 sum to 1. This is a useful observation because it helps to illustrate the analogous property in the automaker example, where any outcome between −$20 million and $50 million is possible. You can think of the curve in Figure 3.3 as a curve that connects the tops of many thousands of bars that have very small widths, and the sum of the heights of all these bars is equivalent to the area under the curve.[4] Thus, stating that the probabilities must sum to 1 is equivalent to stating that the area under the curve must equal 1.

Since the area under the curve in Figure 3.3 equals 1, we can graphically identify the probability that profits are within a certain interval. For example, the probability that profits are greater than $40 million is the area under the curve to the right of $40 million. The probability that profits are less than $0 is the area under the curve to the left of $0. The probability that profits are between $10 and $30 million is the area under the curve between $10 and $30 million. Thus, the bell-shaped curve in Figure 3.3 tells us that for the automaker, there is a relatively high probability that profits will be between $10 and $30 million. In contrast, while very low profits and very high profits are possible, they do not have a high probability of happening.

FIGURE 3.3
Probability distribution for automaker's profits.

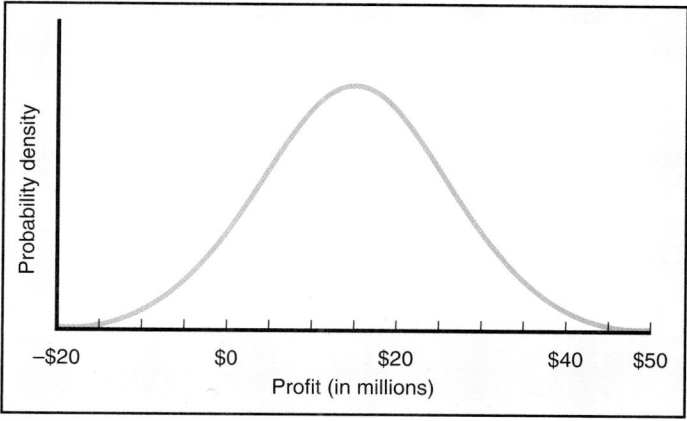

[3]Given that any outcome is possible between −$20 million and $50 million, the vertical axis measures what technically is known as the "probability density," rather than the probability. However, the basic idea is the same, and you can think of it as the probability in order to understand the essential ideas of this book.

[4]Adding up the heights of these bars is a problem in calculus, which is not needed for understanding the material in this book.

Concept Checks

1. What information is given by a probability distribution? What are the two ways of describing a probability distribution?

2. Earthquakes are rare, but the property damage can be very large when they occur. Illustrate these features by drawing a probability distribution for property losses due to an earthquake for a business that has property valued at $50 million. Identify on your graph the probability that losses will exceed $30 million.

Characteristics of Probability Distributions

In many applications, it is necessary to compare probability distributions of different random variables. Indeed, most of the material in this book is concerned with how decisions (e.g., whether to purchase insurance) change probability distributions. Understanding how decisions affect probability distributions will lead to better decisions. The problem is that most probability distributions have many different outcomes and are difficult to compare. It is therefore common to compare certain key characteristics of probability distributions: the expected value, variance or standard deviation, skewness, and correlation.

Expected Value

The **expected value** of a probability distribution provides information about where the outcomes tend to occur, on average. For example, if the expected value of the automaker's profits is $10 million, then profits should average about $10 million. Thus, a distribution with a higher expected value will tend to have a higher outcome, on average.

To calculate the expected value, you multiply each possible outcome by its probability and then add up the results. In the coin flipping example there are two possible outcomes for X, either $1 or –$1. The probability of each outcome is 0.5. Therefore, the expected value of X is $0:

$$\text{Expected value of } X = (0.5)(\$1) + (0.5)(-\$1) = \$0$$

If one were to play the coin flipping game *many* times, the *average* outcome would be approximately $0. This does not imply that the actual value of X on any single toss will be $0; indeed, the actual outcome for one toss is never $0.

To define expected value in general terms, let the possible outcomes of a random variable, X, be denoted by $x_1, x_2, x_3, \ldots, x_M$ (these correspond to $-\$1$ and $\$1$ in the coin flipping example) and let the probability of the respective outcomes be denoted by $p_1, p_2, p_3, \ldots, p_M$ (these correspond to the 0.5's in the coin flipping example). Then, the expected value is defined mathematically as:

$$\text{Expected value} = x_1 p_1 + x_2 p_2 + \ldots + x_M p_M = \sum_{i=1}^{M} x_i p_i \qquad (3.1)$$

If we examine a probability distribution graphically, we often can learn something about the expected value of the distribution. For example, Figure 3.4 illustrates two probability distributions. Since the distribution for A is shifted to the right compared with B, distribution A has a higher expected value than distribution B.

When distributions are symmetric, as in Figure 3.4, identifying the expected value is relatively easy; it is the midpoint in the range of possible outcomes. When the probability distri-

FIGURE 3.4
Comparing the expected values of two distributions (distribution A has a higher expected value than distribution B).

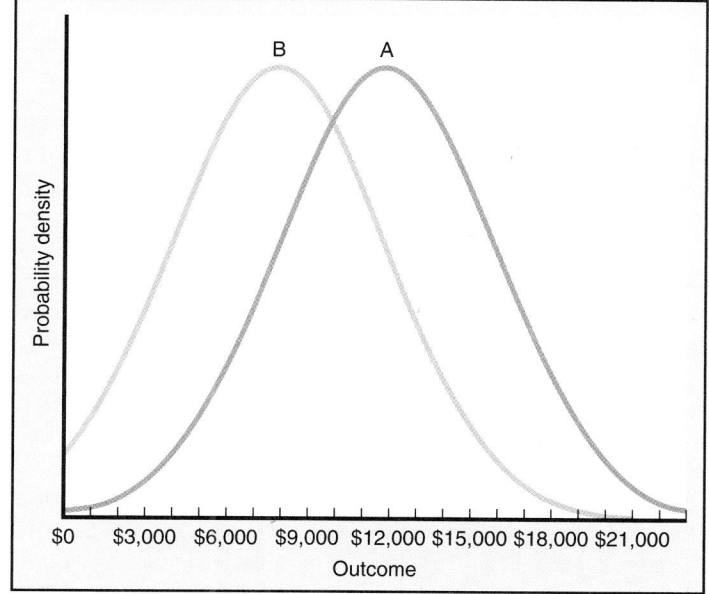

butions are not symmetric, identifying the expected value by examining a diagram sometimes can be difficult. Nevertheless, you often can compare the expected values of different distributions visually. Consider, for example, the two distributions illustrated in Figure 3.5. Distribution C has a higher expected value than distribution D. Intuitively, the high outcomes are more likely with distribution C than with D, and the low outcomes are less likely with C than with D.

Many risk management decisions depend on the probability distribution of losses that can arise from lawsuits, worker injuries, damage to property, and the like. When a probability distribution is for possible losses that can occur, the distribution is called a **loss distribution.** The expected value of the distribution is called the **expected loss.**

FIGURE 3.5
Comparing expected values of distributions (distribution C has a higher expected value than distribution D).

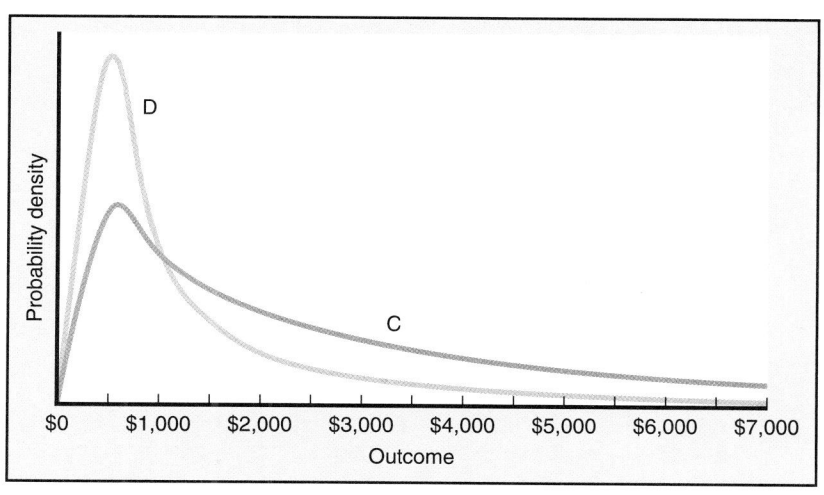

Concept Check

3. What is the expected value of damages for the distribution listed in Table 3.3?

Variance and Standard Deviation

The **variance** of a probability distribution provides information about the likelihood and magnitude by which a particular outcome from the distribution will differ from the expected value. In other words, variance measures the probable variation in outcomes around the expected value. If a distribution has low variance, then the actual outcome is likely to be close to the expected value. Conversely, if the distribution has high variance, then it is more likely that the actual (realized) outcome from the distribution will be far from the expected value. A high variance therefore implies that outcomes are difficult to predict. For this reason, variance is a commonly used measure of risk. In some instances, however, it is more convenient to work with the square root of the variance, which is known as the **standard deviation.**

To illustrate variance and standard deviation, consider three possible probability distributions for accident losses. Each distribution has three possible outcomes, but the outcomes and the probabilities differ. The three probability distributions are shown in Table 3.4.

For each of the loss distributions in Table 3.4, the expected value is $500 (you should verify this for yourself), but the variances of the three distributions differ. Loss distribution 2 has a larger variance than distribution 1, because the extreme outcomes for distribution 2 are farther from the expected value than they are for distribution 1. Distribution 3 has a larger variance than distribution 2, because even though the outcomes are the same for distributions 2 and 3, the extreme outcomes are more likely with distribution 3 than with distribution 2. That is, the probability of having a loss far from the expected value ($500) is greater with distribution 3 than with distribution 2. The comparison of distributions 2 and 3 illustrates that the variance depends not only on the dispersion of the possible outcomes but also on the probability of the possible outcomes.

The mathematical definitions of variance and standard deviation show precisely how the probabilities of the different outcomes and the deviation of each outcome from the expected value affect these measures of risk. The definitions are:

$$\text{Variance} = \sum_{i=1}^{N} p_i (x_i - \mu)^2 \tag{3.2}$$

and

$$\text{Standard deviation} = \sqrt{\sum_{i=1}^{N} p_i (x_i - \mu)^2} \tag{3.3}$$

Table 3.4   **Comparing standard deviations of three distributions (distribution 1 has the lowest standard deviation and distribution 3 has the highest).**

Distribution 1		Distribution 2		Distribution 3	
Loss Outcome	Probability	Loss Outcome	Probability	Loss Outcome	Probability
$250	0.33	$ 0	0.33	$ 0	0.4
$500	0.34	$ 500	0.34	$ 500	0.2
$750	0.33	$1,000	0.33	$1,000	0.4

where

μ(mu) = the expected value;

x_i = the possible outcome; and

p_i = the probability of the outcome.

Notice that the quantity in parentheses measures the deviation of each outcome from the expected value. This difference is squared so that positive differences do not offset negative differences. Each squared difference is then multiplied by the probability of the particular outcome so those outcomes that are more likely to occur receive greater weight in the final sum than those outcomes that have a low probability of occurrence.

Additional insights about these measures of risk can be gained by going step-by-step through the calculations for distribution 1 introduced above. Table 3.5 provides this analysis. It indicates that distribution 1 has a standard deviation equal to $204. Similar calculations for distributions 2 and 3 (not shown) indicate that their standard deviations equal $408 and $447, respectively.

As noted earlier, variance and standard deviation measure the likelihood that and magnitude by which an outcome from the probability distribution will deviate from the expected value. They thus measure the predictability of the outcomes. As a consequence, when referring to risk as variability around the expected value, *we generally will measure risk using variance or standard deviation.*[5]

Like expected values, standard deviations of distributions often can be compared by visually inspecting the probability distributions. For example, Figure 3.6 illustrates two distributions for accident losses. Both have an expected value of $1,000, but they differ in their standard deviations. There is a greater chance that an outcome from distribution A will be close to the expected value of $1,000 than with distribution B.

Table 3.5
Calculating variance and standard deviation for distribution 1 from Table 3.4.

Step 1: Take difference between each outcome and the expected value ($500).	Step 2: Square the results of step 1.	Step 3: Multiply the results of step 2 by the respective probabilities.
$250 − $500 = −$250	(−$250)² = $62,500	0.33 ($62,500) = $20,833
$500 − $500 = $0	($0)² = $0	0.34 ($0) = $0
$750 − $500 = $250	($250)² = $62,500	0.33 ($62,500) = $20,833

Step 4: Sum the results of step 3 to find the variance. $41,666
Step 5: Calculate the square root of the result of step 4 to find the standard deviation. $204

[5]Other measures of risk sometimes are used. For example, in some situations it is useful to measure risk as the probability of an extreme outcome (e.g., a large loss). Another commonly used measure of risk is the maximum probable loss or value at risk, both of which identify the loss amount that will not be exceeded with some confidence, say 95 percent of the time. We define these risk concepts later in this chapter.

FIGURE 3.6
Comparing the standard deviations of two distributions (distribution B has a larger standard deviation).

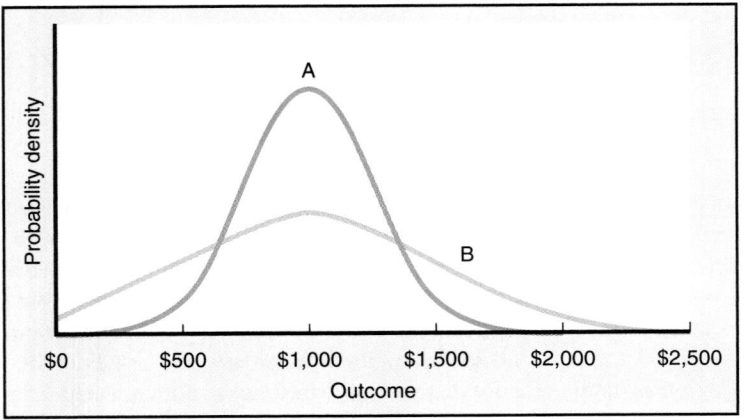

Concept Checks

4. Explain why variance and standard deviation are useful measures of risk.
5. Without doing any calculations, can you compare the standard deviations of the following distributions?

Distribution 1		Distribution 2		Distribution 3	
Loss Outcome	Probability	Loss Outcome	Probability	Loss Outcome	Probability
$ 5,000	0.33	$ 5,000	0.00	$ 0	0.2
$10,000	0.34	$10,000	1.00	$10,000	0.6
$15,000	0.33	$15,000	0.00	$20,000	0.2

6. Compare the expected values and standard deviations of distributions A and B illustrated in the following figure:

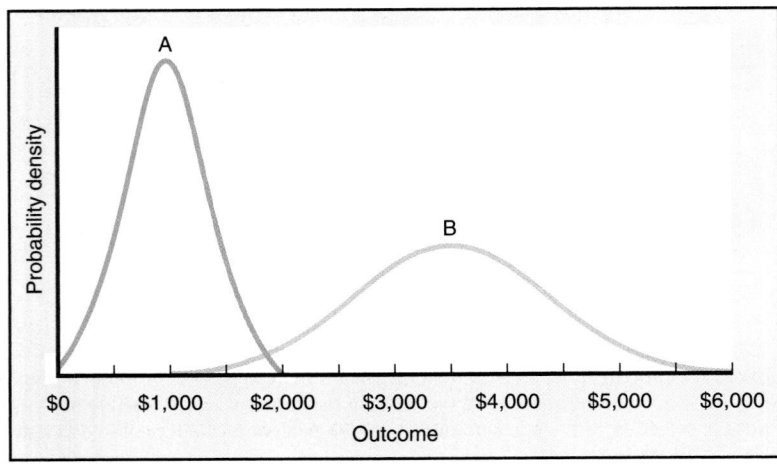

Sample Mean and Sample Standard Deviation

Sometimes the expected value is called the *mean of the distribution.* We avoid using this term because it leads to confusion with another concept: the average value from a sample of outcomes from a distribution, which also is known as the **sample mean.** A simple illustration will help you understand the difference between the average outcome from a sample (the sample mean) and the expected value of the probability distribution. Assume that there is a 0.5 probability that the fertilization of an egg will produce a female, and there is a 0.5 probability that the fertilization will produce a male.[6] The group of babies born this month in the town where you live can be viewed as a sample from this distribution. The sample mean proportion of females is the number of females in the sample divided by the total number of newborns in the sample. The sample mean proportion generally will differ from the expected value of 0.5 due to random fluctuations (unless there are lots and lots of babies in the sample). Similarly, if the expected loss from accidents for a large group of people is $500, the sample mean loss or **average loss** during a given time period for a sample of these people will differ from the expected value due to random fluctuations.

The **sample standard deviation** (or, similarly, the sample variance) reflects the variation in outcomes of a particular sample from a distribution. It is calculated with the same formula that we used above for the standard deviation but with three differences. First, only the outcomes that occur in the sample are used. Second, the sample mean is used instead of the expected value, which usually is not known. Third, the squared deviations between the outcomes and the sample mean are multiplied by the proportion of times that the particular outcome actually occurs in the sample—rather than by the proportion of times that the outcome is likely to occur, according to the probability distribution.[7]

It is useful to introduce the sample mean and sample standard deviation at this point for several reasons. First, the probability distributions for random variables that concern managers generally are not known. The sample mean and sample standard deviation sometimes can be used to estimate the unknown expected value and standard deviation of a probability distribution. Thus, estimation of the expected value and standard deviation of losses is often very important in risk management. In addition, the concept of the average loss for a group of people that pools its risk (i.e., the sample mean loss for the group) and the standard deviation of the average loss for the group (i.e., the sample standard deviation) are used in Chapter 4 to explain how pooling can reduce risk. Finally, you will no doubt calculate sample means and sample standard deviations if you take a statistics course. We don't want you to confuse the expected value and standard deviation of the underlying probability distribution with the sample mean and sample standard deviation for a particular sample.

Concept Check

7. Recall the coin flipping game discussed earlier in the chapter where you win $1 if heads appears and lose $1 if tails appears. What is the expected value of the outcome from the

[6]Actually, evidence suggests that the probability that a female will be conceived is very slightly greater than 0.5.

[7]This calculation is equivalent to adding the squared deviations, dividing by the sample size, and then taking the square root. (In many cases, statisticians divide by the sample size minus one instead. This adjustment causes the sample standard deviation to be a better [unbiased] estimator of the true standard deviation.)

game if it is played only one time? Calculate the sample mean and sample standard deviation if the game is played five times with the following results: T, T, H, T, H.

Skewness

Another statistical concept that is important in the practice of risk management is the **skewness** of a probability distribution. Skewness measures the symmetry of the distribution. If the distribution is symmetric, it has no skewness. For example, consider the two distributions for accident losses illustrated in Figure 3.7. The distribution at the top of Figure 3.7 is symmetric; it has zero skewness. However, the distribution at the bottom is not symmetric; it has positive skewness. Many of the loss distributions that are relevant to risk management are skewed.

Note how the skewed distribution has a higher probability of very low losses and a higher probability of very high losses when compared to the symmetric distribution. Recognizing this characteristic of skewed distributions is important when assessing the likelihood of large losses. If you incorrectly assume that the loss distribution is symmetric (you

FIGURE 3.7
Skewness in probability distributions (top distribution is symmetric; bottom distribution is skewed).

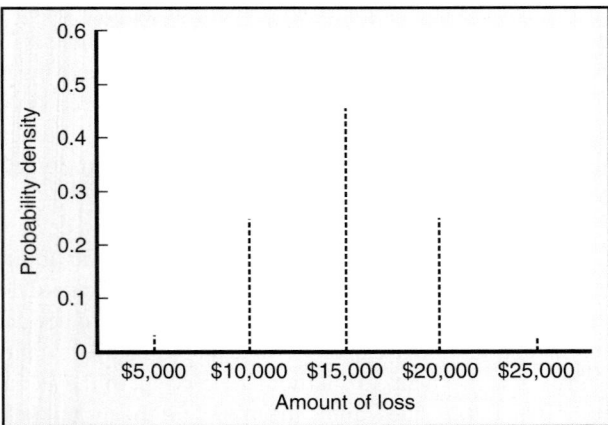

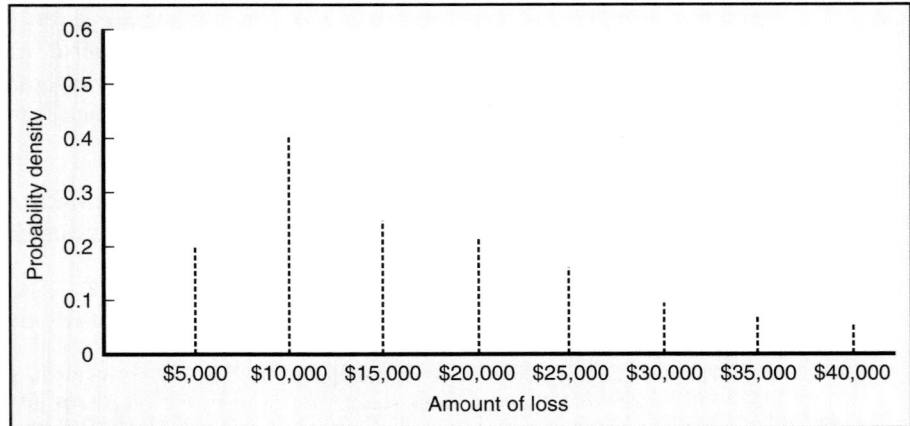

think that losses have distribution 1 when they really have distribution 2 in Figure 3.7), you will underestimate the likelihood of very large losses. As you will see in later chapters, large losses usually are the most harmful.

Concept Check

8. Draw a distribution that might describe your automobile liability losses for the coming year (i.e., the losses that you could cause to other people for which you could be sued and held liable).

Maximum Probable Loss and Value-at-Risk

A frequently used measure of risk is maximum probable loss or value-at-risk, Although used in different contexts, these terms essentially mean the same thing. **Maximum probable loss** usually describes a loss distribution, whereas **value-at-risk** describes the probability distribution for the value of a portfolio or the value of a firm subject to loss. These concepts are easily illustrated with simple examples.

Suppose that the probability distribution for annual liability losses is described by the probability density function in Figure 3.8. Since the random variable being described is losses, high values are bad and low values are good. If $20 million is the maximum probable loss (MPL) at the 5 percent level, the probability that losses will be greater than $20 million is 5 percent. (That is, the area under the probability density function to the right of $20 million is 0.05.) If $30 million is the MPL at the 1 percent level, the probability that losses will be greater than $30 million is 0.01.

To illustrate value-at-risk, consider the probability distribution for the change in the value of an investment portfolio over a month depicted in Figure 3.9. Since the random variable being described is portfolio value changes, high values are good and low values are bad. If $5 million is the monthly value-at-risk for this portfolio at the 5 percent level, the probability that the portfolio will lose more than $5 million over the month is 5 percent. (The area under the density function to the left of −$5 million is 0.05.) If $7.5 million is the monthly value-at-risk at the 1 percent level, the probability that the portfolio will lose more than $7.5 million over the month is 0.01.

FIGURE 3.8
Maximum probable loss.

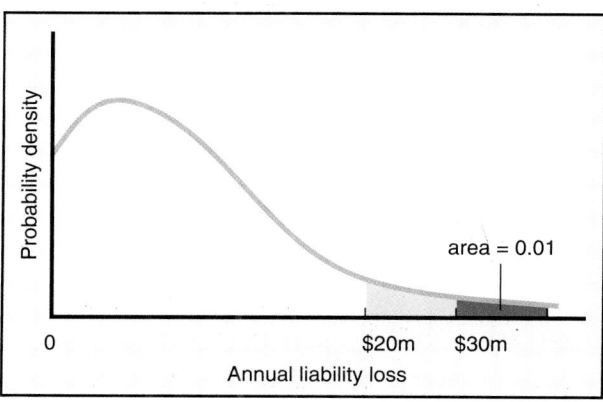

FIGURE 3.9
Value-at-risk.

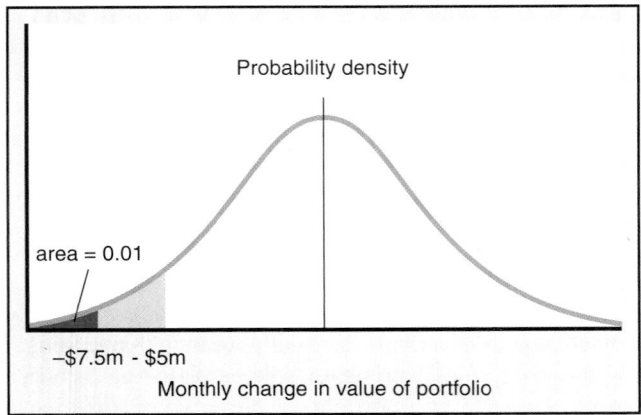

Probability density

area = 0.01

−$7.5m - $5m

Monthly change in value of portfolio

Many large corporations estimate maximum probable losses from different exposures to evaluate risk. Most large financial institutions calculate a daily measure of value-at-risk.[8] To illustrate this concept, suppose that Mr. David, the risk manager at First Babbel Corp., receives a report that the firm's daily value-at-risk at the 5 percent level is $50 million. This number tells Mr. David that the firm has a 5 percent chance of losing more than $50 million over the coming day. If Mr. David determines that the firm should not take this much risk, he might take actions to reduce the firm's value-at-risk, such as hedging or selling some risky assets. After taking these risk management actions, presumably the firm's value at risk would drop to an acceptable level. See Box 3.2.

Correlation

To this point, we have limited our discussion to probability distributions of a single random variable. Because businesses and individuals are exposed to many types of risk, it is important to identify the relationships among random variables. The **correlation** between random variables measures how random variables are related.

If the correlation between two random variables is zero, then the random variables are not related. Intuitively, if two random variables have zero correlation, then knowing the outcome of one random variable will not give you information about the outcome of the other random variable. For example, an automaker has risk due to an uncertain number of product liability claims for autos previously sold and also due to uncertain steel prices. There is no reason to believe that these two variables will be related. Knowing that steel prices are high will not imply anything about the frequency or severity of liability claims for autos already sold. Similarly, knowing that a large liability claim for damages has occurred will not imply anything about steel prices. Thus, the correlation between steel prices and product liability costs (for past sales) is zero. When the correlation between random variables is zero, we will say that the random variables are *independent* or *uncorrelated.* These terms are used because they suggest that the outcome observed for one distribution is unrelated to the outcome observed for the other distribution.

[8]We illustrate some of the tools for estimating maximum probable loss and value-at-risk, such as Monte Carlo simulation, later in the book.

One of the most frequently used probability distributions is the normal distribution. The probability density function of the normal distribution is the familiar symmetric, bell-shaped curve illustrated in Figure 3.10. The normal distribution is frequently used to describe the returns on financial assets and, as you will see in later chapters, it is used to describe the average loss from many individual, uncorrelated exposures.

The following properties of the normal distribution are useful for calculating value-at-risk (maximum probable loss) if changes in value (losses) are assumed to be normally distributed. If X is normally distributed with an expected value of μ and standard deviation of σ, then

$$\text{Probability } (X > \mu + 2.33\sigma) = 0.01$$
$$\text{and}$$
$$\text{Probability } (X < \mu - 2.33\sigma) = 0.01$$
$$\text{Probability } (X > \mu + 1.645\sigma) = 0.05$$
$$\text{and}$$
$$\text{Probability } (X < \mu - 1.645\sigma) = 0.05$$

Figure 3.10 illustrates the relationship. If, for example, the changes in a portfolio's value over the coming day are normally distributed with mean of $0 and standard deviation of $10 million, then,

Probability [change in value < $0 − 2.33 ($10 million)]
= 0.01.

That is, the probability that the portfolio will drop in value by more than $23.3 million is 1 percent.

FIGURE 3.10   **Characteristics of the normal distribution.**

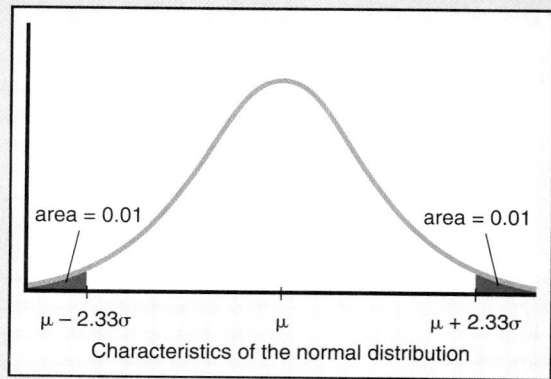

area = 0.01   area = 0.01

$\mu - 2.33\sigma$ μ $\mu + 2.33\sigma$

Characteristics of the normal distribution

In many cases random variables will be correlated. For example, a recession may decrease the demand for new cars and also decrease steel prices. Thus, the demand for new cars and steel prices both are affected by general economic conditions, and as a result, the demand for new cars and steel prices are correlated. When demand for new cars is high, steel prices also tend to be high.[9]

Positive correlation implies that the random variables tend to move in the same direction. For example, the returns on common stocks of different companies are positively correlated—the return on one stock tends to be high when the returns on other stocks are high. Random variables can be negatively correlated as well. Negative correlation implies that the random variables tend to move in opposite directions. For example, sales of sunglasses and sales of umbrellas on any given day in a given city are likely to be negatively correlated.

You should keep in mind that positive (negative) correlation does not imply that the random variables will always move in the same (opposite) direction. Positive correlation simply implies that when the outcome of one random variable—for example, the demand for cars—is above (below) its expected value, the other random variable—for example, steel

[9]Note also that lower sales of new cars could produce fewer product liability claims in the future. Thus, while steel prices and the number of liability claims for autos previously sold will likely be uncorrelated, liability claims arising from new sales and steel prices will likely be correlated.

costs—tends to be above (below) its expected value. Similarly, negative correlation implies that when one random variable—for example, sales of sunglasses—is above (below) its expected value, the other random variable—for example, umbrella sales—tends to be below (above) its expected value.

Concept Check

9. For each scenario below, explain whether the correlation between random variable 1 and random variable 2 is likely to be zero (the random variables are uncorrelated), positive, or negative.

   (*a*) Random variable 1: Your automobile accident costs for the coming year.
   Random variable 2: The automobile accident costs of a student in another country for the coming year.

   (*b*) Random variable 1: The property damage due to hurricanes in Miami, Florida, in September.
   Random variable 2: The property damage due to hurricanes in Ft. Lauderdale, Florida, in September.

   (*c*) Random variable 1: The property damage due to hurricanes in Miami, Florida, in September 2003.
   Random variable 2: The property damage due to hurricanes in Miami, Florida, in September 2008.

   (*d*) Random variable 1: The number of people in New York who die from AIDS in the year 2008.
   Random variable 2: The number of people in London who die from AIDS in the year 2008.

3.3   Evaluating the Frequency and Severity of Losses

After identifying loss exposures, a risk manager ideally would obtain information about the entire probability distribution of losses and how different risk management methods affect this distribution. We illustrate how larger firms might estimate the relevant loss distributions in Chapter 26. Frequently, risk managers use summary measures of probability distributions, such as frequency and severity measures, as well as expected losses and the standard deviation of losses during a given period. These measures help a risk manager assess the costs and benefits of loss control and retention versus insurance. We therefore illustrate how these summary measures can be obtained in practice.

Frequency

The **frequency** of loss measures the number of losses in a given period of time. If historical data exist on a large number of exposures, then the probability of a loss per exposure (or the expected frequency per exposure) can be estimated by the number of losses divided by the number of exposures. For example, if Sharon Steel Corp. had 10,000 employees in each of the past five years and over the five-year period there were 1,500 workers injured, then an estimate of the probability of a particular worker becoming injured would be 0.03 per year (1,500 injuries/50,000 employee-years). When historical data do not exist for a firm, frequency of losses can be difficult to quantify. In this case, industry data might be used, or an informed judgment would need to be made about the frequency of losses.

Severity

The **severity** of loss measures the magnitude of loss per occurrence. One way to estimate expected severity is to use the average severity of loss per occurrence during a historical period. If the 1,500 worker injuries for Sharon Steel cost $3 million in total (adjusted for inflation), then the expected severity of worker injuries would be estimated at $2,000 ($3,000,000/1,500). That is, on average, each worker injury imposed a $2,000 loss on the firm. Again due to the lack of historical data and the infrequency of losses, adequate data may not be available to estimate precisely the expected severity per occurrence. With a little effort, however, risk managers can estimate the range of possible loss severity (minimum and maximum loss) for a given exposure.

Expected Loss and Standard Deviation

When the frequency of losses is uncorrelated with the severity of losses, the expected loss is simply the product of frequency and severity. Thus, the expected loss per exposure in our example can be estimated by taking expected loss severity per occurrence times the expected frequency per exposure. Expected loss obviously is an important element that affects business value and insurance pricing. Thus, accurate estimates of expected losses can help a manager determine whether insurance will increase firm value. Continuing with the Sharon Steel example, the annual expected loss per employee from worker injury is 0.03 × $2,000 = $60. With 10,000 employees, the annual expected loss is $600,000. Ideally, many firms also will estimate the standard deviation of losses for the total loss distribution or for losses in different size ranges.

One way to summarize information about potential losses is to create a table for various types of exposures (property, liability, etc.) that provides characteristics of the probability distribution of losses for the particular type of exposure. An example for Sharon Steel's property exposures is provided in Table 3.6.

To create an accurate categorization of a firm's loss exposures (like Table 3.6), considerable information, time, and expertise are needed. For most companies, especially smaller ones and new ones, detailed data on loss exposures do not exist. Nevertheless, the framework of Table 3.6 still can be used. For example, each type of exposure can be classified as having low, medium, or high frequency and severity. Table 3.7 provides an example for Penn Steel Corp., a firm that is engaged in the same activities and is of the same size as Sharon Steel Corp.

Tables 3.6 and 3.7 both show that the standard deviation of losses for high frequency, low severity losses is low, while the standard deviation is high for low frequency losses with

Table 3.6
Categorization
of Sharon
Steel's
property losses.

Property Exposures	Frequency of Losses per Year	Severity Range	Average Severity	Expected Loss	Standard Deviation
Damage to automobiles	100	$0–$20,000	$5,000	$500,000	$100,000
Stolen property	200	0–2,000	500	100,000	20,000
Small fires	1	100,000–500,000	125,000	125,000	400,000
Major fires	.05	500,000–10,000,000	2,000,000	100,000	800,000

Table 3.7
Categorization of Penn Steel Corp.'s property losses.

Property Exposures	Frequency	Severity Range	Average Severity	Expected Loss	Standard Deviation
Damage to automobiles	Medium	$0–$20,000	Low	Medium	Medium
Stolen property	High	0–2,000	Low	Low	Low
Small fires	Low	100,000–500,000	Medium	Low	High
Major fires	Low	500,000–10,000,000	High	Low	High

high potential severity. This relationship is fairly general: Infrequent but potentially large losses are less predictable and pose greater risk than more frequent, smaller losses. Using the type of information illustrated in these tables, firms pay particular attention to exposures that can produce potentially large, disruptive losses, either from a single event or from the accumulation of a number of smaller but still significant losses during a given period.

3.4 Summary

- The risk management process begins with risk identification.
- Businesses typically identify their major property risks, liability risks, human resource risks, and risks arising from external economic events.
- Individuals typically identify their major earnings risks, expense risks, asset risks, and longevity risks.
- A probability distribution describes the possible outcomes and the probabilities of those outcomes for a random variable.

- The expected value of a probability distribution is the weighted average of the possible outcomes, where the weights are the probabilities.
- Standard deviation or variance is a measure of probable variation around the expected value of a probability distribution for a random variable and, thus, of the risk (unpredictability) of the variable.
- Skewness measures symmetry of a distribution. Many loss exposures have skewed probability distributions.

Key Terms

risk identification 30
book value 31
market value 32
firm-specific value 32
replacement cost new 32
business income exposures 32
extra expense exposure 32
random variable 34

probability distribution 35
expected value 38
loss distribution 39
expected loss 39
variance 40
standard deviation 40
sample mean 43
average loss 43

sample standard deviation 43
skewness 44
maximum probable loss 45
value-at-risk 45
correlation 46
frequency 48
severity 49

Questions and Problems

1. Suppose that L is a random variable equal to property losses from a hurricane and that L has the following probability distribution:

   $L =$
   - $90,000 with probability 0.02
   - $10,000 with probability 0.06
   - $ 0 with probability 0.92

   What is the expected value of hurricane losses (i.e., the expected loss)?

2. Suppose that P is a random variable equal to profits from an ice cream stand at the beach and that P has the following probability distribution:

   $P =$
   - $70,000 with probability 0.05
   - $50,000 with probability 0.25
   - $30,000 with probability 0.35
   - $10,000 with probability 0.20
   - −$10,000 with probability 0.15

   What is the expected value of profits?

3. Assume that property losses for Buckeye Brewery have the following distribution:

   Loss =
   - $3,000,000 with probability 0.004
   - $1,500,000 with probability 0.010
   - $ 800,000 with probability 0.026
   - $ 0 with probability 0.96

   What is the expected value of property losses (i.e., the expected loss)?

4. Assume that Buckeye Brewery determines that its liability losses have the following distribution:

   Loss =
   - $5,000,000 with probability 0.004
   - $1,500,000 with probability 0.025
   - $ 500,000 with probability 0.030
   - $ 0 with probability 0.941

   What is the expected value of liability losses?

5. Do you think that Buckeye Brewery's property losses are independent, positively correlated, or negatively correlated with its liability losses?

6. Company Blue is located in Toronto and has property valued at $5 million. Sketch a reasonable probability distribution of Company Blue's property losses.

7. Company Red is located in Cincinnati, Ohio, and has property valued at $5 million. Sketch a reasonable probability distribution for Company Red's property losses.

8. Suppose that Company Blue buys Company Red and the new firm is called Big Red (not to be confused with Big Blue). Sketch a reasonable probability distribution for Big Red's property losses.

9. Bell Curve, Inc., estimates the expected value and standard deviation of its total liability losses for the forthcoming year as $10 million and $3 million, respectively. If Bell Curve assumes that total losses have the normal distribution, what is the predicted maximum probable loss at the 95 percent level? At the 99 percent level?

Answers to Concept Checks

1. A probability distribution identifies all the possible outcomes and the probabilities of those outcomes for a particular random variable. Simple probability distributions can be described by listing the possible outcomes and the corresponding probabilities.

Probability distributions also can be described graphically, with the possible outcomes listed on the horizontal axis and the probabilities of these outcomes measured on the vertical axis.

2. The following probability distribution indicates that the probability of low losses is relatively high, but that the probability of very high losses is relatively low. The maximum loss (ignoring indirect losses) is $50 million. The shaded area is the probability that losses exceed $30 million.

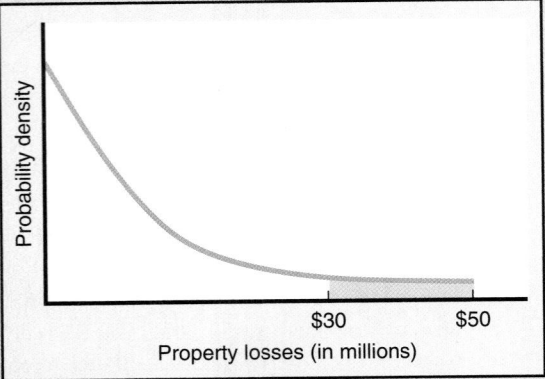

3. Expected loss = ($0 × 0.5) + (500 × 0.3) + ($1,000 × 0.1) + ($5,000 × 0.06) + ($10,000 × 0.04) = $0 + $150 + $100 + $300 + $400 = $950

4. Variance (standard deviation) is a measure of risk, because variance measures the predictability of outcomes. The greater the variance, the more likely it is that a realization from the distribution will deviate materially from the expected value.

5. First, note that the expected value of each distribution is $10,000. Distribution 2 has zero standard deviation; the $10,000 outcome occurs all the time. Thus, there is no variation around the expected value. The standard deviation of distribution 1 is difficult to compare to that of distribution 3 without doing the calculations, because the

probability of an outcome other than $10,000 is greater with distribution 1, but the deviation of the outcomes from the expected value is greater with distribution 3.

6. Distribution A has a lower expected value and a lower standard deviation than distribution B.

7. The expected value of the game is $0, as our earlier calculation demonstrated $((0.5)(\$1) + (0.5)(-\$1) = \$0)$. The sample mean equals $(2/5)(\$1) + (3/5)(-\$1) = -\$0.20$. The point is that the sample mean can and usually will differ from the expected value. The sample standard deviation equals $[(2/5)(\$1 + 0.20)^2 + (3/5)(-\$1 + \$0.20)^2]^{1/2} = [(2/5)(6/5)^2 + (-4/5)^2]^{1/2} = [(72 + 48)/125]^{1/2} = (120/125)^{1/2} = (24/25)^{1/2} = \$0.98$.

8. The distribution would be expected to be highly skewed (i.e., you most likely would have a relatively high probability of no liability losses and a very low probability of extremely high liability losses). The following distribution is consistent with this description.

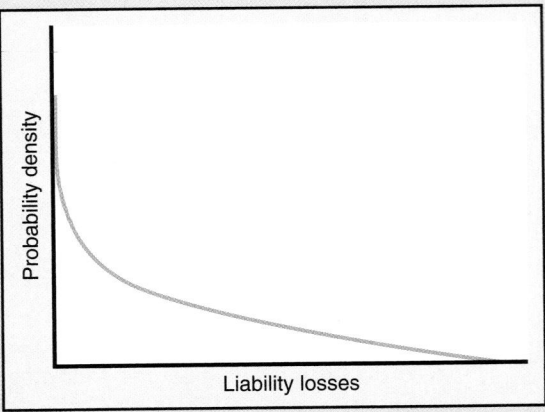

9. a. Uncorrelated.

    b. Given the proximity of Miami and Ft. Lauderdale, if Miami experiences hurricane losses greater than the expected value, then Ft. Lauderdale also is likely to experience hurricane losses greater than the expected value. Thus, these random variables would be positively correlated.

c. Given that the weather in one year is likely to be independent of the weather in the subsequent year, hurricane losses in one year are likely to be independent of the hurricane losses in the same location in another year.

d. Since the number of people who die from AIDS in a given year (regardless of where they live) will be affected by the development of drugs to treat or possibly cure AIDs, these random variables would likely be positively correlated.

4

Pooling Arrangements and Diversification of Risk

Chapter Objectives

- Show how pooling of independent loss exposures reduces risk.
- Show how correlation in losses affects the amount of risk that is reduced in a pooling arrangement.
- Discuss how pooling arrangements provide the foundation for insurance transactions and how insurers are efficient managers of pooling arrangements.
- Discuss other examples of diversification including stock markets.

4.1   Risk Reduction through Pooling Independent Losses

The most important risk management concept may be the diversification of risk. Diversification is an essential aspect of insurance and financial markets. We analyze diversification in this chapter, highlighting the factors influencing the extent to which risk can be and is diversified. We illustrate diversification in several different contexts, beginning with a simple pooling arrangement between two people and ending with diversification among thousands of people or businesses through insurance and financial markets.

Using the probability and statistics concepts reviewed in the previous chapter, we can now explain how pooling arrangements reduce risk when losses are independent (uncorrelated).

Two Person Pooling Arrangement

Suppose that Emily and Samantha each are exposed to the possibility of an accident in the coming year. In particular, assume that each person has a 20 percent chance of an accident that will cause a loss of $2,500 and an 80 percent chance of no accident. The probability distribution for accident losses for each woman is summarized in Table 4.1. Note that the distribution is very skewed; that is, there is a high probability of zero loss and a much smaller probability of a large loss. Also assume that Emily's and Samantha's accident losses are uncorrelated.

We want to examine what will happen if Emily and Samantha agree to *split evenly any accident costs that the two might incur.* That is, they agree to share losses equally, each paying the average loss. This arrangement often is called a **pooling arrangement** (or risk pooling arrangement), because Emily and Samantha are pooling their resources to pay the accident costs that may occur.

Because Emily and Samantha each have a 20 percent chance of having an accident that causes $2,500 in losses, the expected costs and the standard deviation for each person without a pooling arrangement are as follows:

$$\text{Expected cost} = (0.80)\ (\$0) + (0.20)\ (\$2,500) = \$500$$

$$\text{Standard deviation} = \sqrt{0.8\ (\$0 - \$500)^2 + 0.2(\$2,500 - \$500)^2} = \$1,000$$

Our goal is to determine how the pooling arrangement will affect the expected cost and standard deviation for each person.

Note that the pooling arrangement changes the distribution of costs paid by each person in Table 4.1; this is because the costs paid by Emily now depend on the accident losses incurred by Samantha, and vice versa. Specifically, with pooling, the cost paid by each person is the average loss of the two people.

The first column of Table 4.2 lists the possible outcomes for Emily and Samantha with pooling. If neither woman has an accident, total accident costs are zero and each woman pays zero. If either of the women has an accident, total accident costs are $2,500 and each woman pays $1,250. If both women have an accident, total accident costs equal $5,000 and each pays $2,500.

Now let's find the probabilities of each of these outcomes (the last column of Table 4.2). Since the losses incurred by Emily are independent of the losses incurred by Samantha, the probability that neither woman has an accident is simply the probability that Emily does not have an accident times the probability that Samantha does not have an accident. Thus, the probability of the first outcome is (0.8)(0.8) = 0.64. An analogy might help reinforce this result. Consider flipping a coin twice. The result of the second coin flip is independent of the result of the first coin flip. The probability of obtaining two heads is the probability of heads on the first coin flip times the probability of heads on the second coin flip, or (0.5)(0.5) = 0.25. You can convince yourself that this is true by noting that there are four

Table 4.1   **Probability distribution of accident losses for each person (Emily and Samantha) without pooling.**

Outcomes	Probability
$ 0	0.80
$2.500	0.20

Table 4.2
Probability distribution of accident costs paid by each woman with pooling.

Possible Outcomes	Total Cost	Cost Paid by Each Woman (Average Loss)	Probability
1. Neither Samantha nor Emily has an accident	$ 0	$ 0	(0.8)(0.8) = 0.64
2. Samantha has an accident, but Emily does not	$2,500	$1,250	(0.2)(0.8) = 0.16
3. Emily has an accident, but Samantha does not	$2,500	$1,250	(0.2)(0.8) = 0.16
4. Both Samantha and Emily have an accident	$5,000	$2,500	(0.2)(0.2) = 0.04

possible outcomes: heads–heads, heads–tails, tails–heads, and tails–tails. Each of these outcomes has a 0.25 probability of occurring.

Returning to the accident costs example, let's find the probability of the second and third outcomes shown in Table 4.2 (in which only one of the two women has an accident). The probability that Samantha has an accident, but Emily does not equals (0.2)(0.8) = 0.16. The probability that Emily has an accident, but Samantha does not is also 0.16. Thus, the probability that only one of the women has an accident equals 0.16 + 0.16 = 0.32. The probability of the fourth outcome (both Emily and Samantha have an accident) is (0.2)(0.2) = 0.04.[1]

As can be seen clearly from this example, *the pooling arrangement changes the probability distribution of accident costs facing each person.* The probability that Emily will have accident costs equal to $2,500 is reduced from 0.20 to 0.04. This is because in order for Emily to pay $2,500, both Emily and Samantha must experience an accident. Given that accidents are independent, the probability that both Emily and Samantha will have an accident is lower than the probability that only Emily (or only Samantha) will have an accident.

Because the pooling arrangement reduces the probabilities of the extreme outcomes, the standard deviation (risk) of accident costs paid by both Emily and Samantha is reduced. Recall that, without pooling, the standard deviation of accident costs in this example is $1,000. With pooling, the standard deviation of accident costs declines to $707:

Standard deviation =

$$\sqrt{0.64 \times (\$0 - \$500)^2 + 0.32 \times (\$1,250 - \$500)^2 + 0.04 \times (\$2,500 - \$500)^2} = \$707$$

While both Samantha's and Emily's risk is reduced by pooling, each person's expected accident cost is unchanged by pooling. It still equals $500:

$$\text{Expected cost} = (0.64)(\$0) + (0.32)(\$1,250) + (0.04)(\$2,500) = \$500$$

[1]As another example, suppose that the probability that Allen Iverson makes a free throw is 0.8. Then, assuming that the outcome of each free throw is independent of the other free throws, the probability that Iverson will make two in a row is (0.8)(0.8) = 0.64, the probability that he will make one of two is (0.8)(0.2) + (0.2)(0.8) = 0.32, and the probability that he will make neither is (0.2)(0.2) = 0.04.

In summary, the pooling arrangement does not change either person's expected cost, but it reduces the standard deviation of costs from $1,000 to $707. Accident costs have become more predictable. The pooling arrangement reduces risk (uncertainty) for each individual.

Pooling arrangements provide a major example of how risk is reduced through diversification. Simply stated, diversification means that you do not "put all your eggs in one basket." By entering into a pooling arrangement, Emily and Samantha made their accident costs for the year equal the average loss for the participants. If they had not entered into the pooling arrangement, their accident costs would equal their own losses. The key point is that the average loss is much more predictable than each individual's loss. Applying the egg analogy to the pooling arrangement, (1) each woman puts half of her eggs into one basket and half into another basket, and (2) Emily carries one basket and Samantha carries the other. After reaching their destination, they divide the surviving eggs equally.

Pooling Arrangement with Many People or Businesses

Additional risk reduction can be obtained from pooling by adding people (or businesses) to the arrangement. To illustrate, suppose that Anne, who has the same probability distribution for accident costs as Samantha and Emily, joins the pooling arrangement. At the end of the year, each woman will pay one-third of the total losses (the average loss). The addition of a third person whose losses are independent of the other two causes an additional reduction in the probability of the extreme outcomes. For example, in order for Samantha to pay $2,500 in accident costs, all three individuals must experience a $2,500 loss. The probability of this occurring is $(0.02)(0.02)(0.02) = 0.008$. As a consequence, the standard deviation for each individual decreases with the addition of another participant. While risk (standard deviation) decreases, each individual's expected accident cost again remains constant at $500.

The probability distribution of each person's accident cost will continue to change as more people are added. Figure 4.1 compares the probability distribution for average accident costs when there are 4 and 20 participants in the pooling arrangement. Note that as the number of participants in the pooling arrangement increases the probability of the extreme outcomes (very high average losses and very low average losses) goes down. Stated differently, the probability that average losses (the amount paid by each participant) will be close to $500, the expected loss, increases. Also, as the number of participants increases, the probability distribution of each person's cost (the average loss) becomes more bell shaped, that is, less skewed. In summary, pooling makes the amount of accident losses that each person must pay less risky (more predictable), because pooling reduces the standard deviation of the average loss for all the participants and thus the standard deviation of the payment by each participant. The pooling arrangement therefore reduces risk for each participant.[2] As even more participants are added, the probability distribution would become more and more bell shaped (less skewed).

---

[2]Note that in the simple example shown in Figure 4.1, where there are only two discrete outcomes for each individual, the height of the bars generally decreases as the number of participants increases. This is because additional outcomes become possible as the number of participants increases. This feature would not carry over to more realistic examples, where each individual's loss lies on a continuum. That is, when individual losses can assume any value within a range, the probability of outcomes near the expected value generally increases as participants are added.

FIGURE 4.1

Probabity distribution of average losses with 4 and 20 participants in a pooling arrangement when each individual has a 0.2 probability of incurring a loss of $2,500 (pooling with 20 participants results in a lower probability of extreme losses and a lower standard deviation of losses).

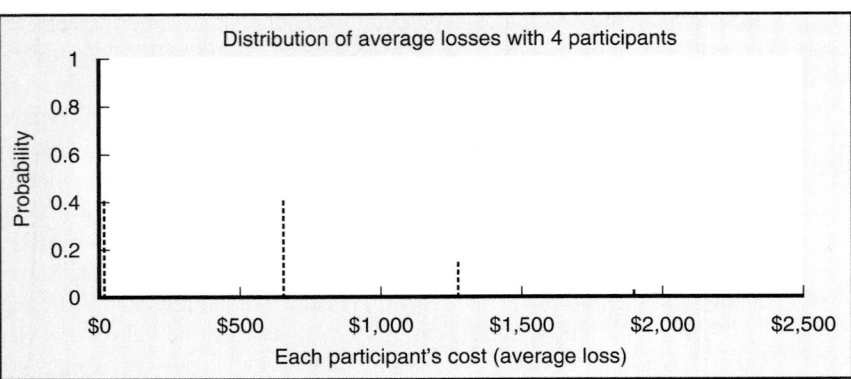

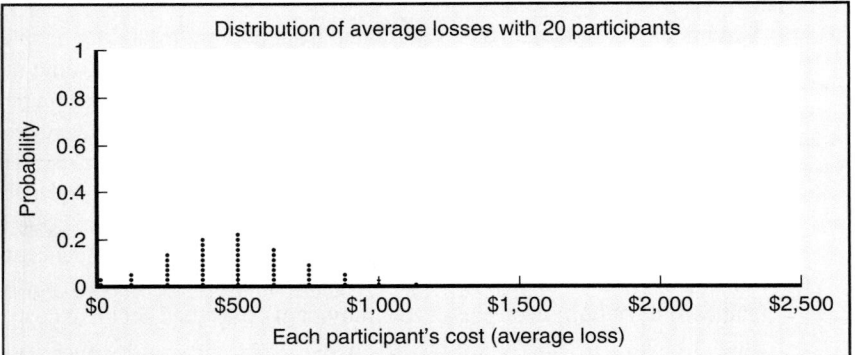

As a more realistic illustration, consider the case of a large number of small businesses. The solid line in Figure 4.2 presents the probability distribution for each business's property losses without a pooling arrangement. Each business's property losses could be any number between $0 and $100,000, and, although not obvious from the graph, the expected loss is $20,000. Without pooling, the distribution for each business is skewed and has a relatively high standard deviation. By entering into a pooling arrangement, the distribution of property losses for each business changes to that shown by the dashed line in Figure 4.2. The diagram highlights the two important effects of pooling arrangements on the probability distributions facing each participant. First, the standard deviation of property losses is lower. Second, the distribution of property losses becomes less skewed and more bell shaped around the expected loss.

Notice in all of these examples that each participant is *not* simply transferring risk to someone else. Instead, there is a reduction in risk for each individual. This is the beauty of risk pooling arrangements: *Risk can be reduced substantially for the participants.* This point is extremely important and often is not fully appreciated by students. Pooling arrangements reduce the amount of risk that *each* participant has to bear.[3]

---

[3]While the standard deviation of average loss declines as the number of participants grows, the standard deviation of the sum of losses for the group grows. The latter result does not alter the fact that each participant's risk is lower.

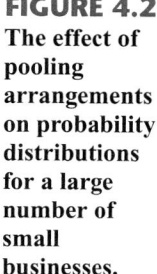

FIGURE 4.2
The effect of pooling arrangements on probability distributions for a large number of small businesses.

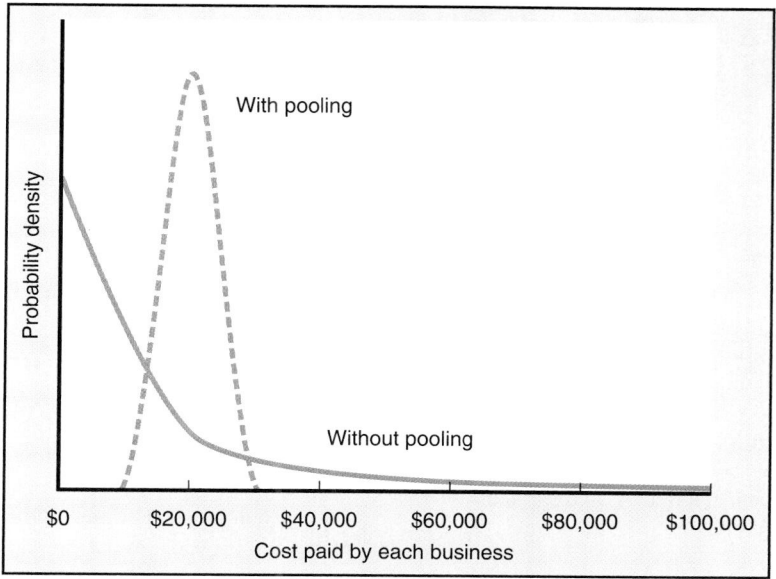

To summarize, when losses are independent, pooling arrangements have two important effects on the probability distribution of the accident cost paid by each participant. First, the standard deviation of the average loss is reduced. As a consequence, the probability of extreme outcomes for participants—both high and low—is reduced. Second, the distribution of average losses becomes more bell shaped.

In the extreme (i.e., as the number of people in the pooling arrangement becomes very large), the standard deviation of each participant's cost becomes very close to zero and the risk thus becomes negligible for each participant. This result reflects what is known as the **law of large numbers** (see Box 4.1). In addition, as the number of participants grows, the probability distribution of the average loss (each participant's cost) becomes more and more bell shaped until it eventually equals the **normal distribution,** the most famous distribution in all of statistics. This result reflects what is known as the **central limit theorem** (which we also discuss in Box 4.1).

Finally, our examples of risk reduction through pooling arrangements have assumed that all participants have the same probability distribution. This assumption is not essential. The standard deviation of average loss also tends to decline when more and more participants with different loss distributions are added to a pooling arrangement.[4] Furthermore, risk in principle still becomes negligible as the number of participants becomes infinitely large.

---

[4]An exception can occur if a participant with a very high standard deviation of losses is added to the pool. Also, participants with different expected losses may be unwilling to share losses equally in a pooling arrangement (e.g., would Emily and Samantha want to share losses with someone whose probability of an accident is twice the size of theirs?). For related reasons, insurers charge people with different expected losses different premiums (see Chapter 8).

The effects of pooling arrangements on probability distributions are derived from two important theorems from probability theory: the law of large numbers and the central limit theorem.

THE LAW OF LARGE NUMBERS

Let X_i equal a random variable (the loss for one participant in a pooling arrangement), where $i = 1, \ldots, N$ (where N equals the number of participants—not the number of possible outcomes for each participant's loss). Assume that the expected value of $X_i = \mu$ and that the standard deviation of $X_i = \sigma$ for all i (each participant has the same expected loss and standard deviation). Then, for any small number $\epsilon > 0$

$$\text{Prob}\left(\left| \frac{\sum_{i=1}^{N} X_i}{N} - \mu \right| > \varepsilon \right) \to 0 \text{ as } N \to \infty$$

The quantity within the straight brackets is the absolute value of the average loss for the pool minus the expected loss for each participant. In words, this formula states that the probability that the average outcome (the loss each participant in the pooling arrangement must pay) differs from the expected value by more than a small number Σ approaches zero as N approaches infinity. Simply stated, as N gets large, the average outcome is likely to get very close to the expected value.

THE CENTRAL LIMIT THEOREM

Given the same assumptions and notation as the law of large numbers, according to the central limit theorem the distribution of the average outcome approaches a normal distribution with mean μ and standard deviation $\sigma / \sqrt{N}$ as N gets very large. Thus, as N gets large, the distribution of the average outcome becomes more symmetric and bell shaped. Since the distribution of the average outcome will be approximately normal for large N, it also is possible to use probability values from the normal distribution to estimate the probability that the average outcome will exceed any given value. Note that, consistent with the law of large numbers, the standard deviation decreases as N increases. For example, if the standard deviation of losses for each participant in a pooling arrangement is initially $5,000 and there are 10,000 participants, then the standard deviation of losses after entering the pooling arrangement equals $5,000/100 = $50. See the appendix at the end of this chapter for further discussion.

Concept Checks

1. Explain how a pooling arrangement reduces risk for each participant when losses are uncorrelated. Does pooling reduce the expected cost paid by each participant? Explain.

2. Suppose that each participant in a pooling arrangement has potential losses ranging from $0 to $4,000 and that each participant's expected loss is $1,000. Using Figure 4.2 as a guide, sketch the probability distribution of average losses if the losses across participants are independent and if:

   (a) there is one participant (i.e., no pooling)
   (b) there are 100 participants
   (c) there are 1,000 participants

4.2   Pooling Arrangements with Correlated Losses

Since in many instances losses will be positively correlated, we need to examine risk reduction through pooling in this case. We will demonstrate that the essential point—that pooling arrangements reduce risk for each participant—continues to hold provided losses are not perfectly positively correlated. However, *the magnitude of risk reduction is lower when losses are positively correlated than when they are independent (uncorrelated).*

Losses across many different businesses or individuals may be positively correlated for a number of reasons. The occurrence of a loss is often due to events that are common to many people. Catastrophes, such as hurricanes and earthquakes, are examples of events that cause property losses to increase for many individuals at the same time. Consequently, losses in certain geographical regions during a given time period are positively correlated. Similarly, since epidemics can cause medical costs to increase for many people during a given time period, the medical costs across people can be positively correlated.

The severity or magnitude of losses also is often influenced by common factors. For example, unexpected inflation can cause everyone who needs health care to pay more than expected. The probability of receiving medical care may be independent across people (in contrast to the epidemic example), but the magnitude of the medical costs incurred by different people is related to a common underlying factor—inflation.

How do positively correlated losses affect pooling arrangements? Intuitively, positively correlated losses imply that when one person (or business) has a loss that is greater than the expected loss, then other people (or businesses) also will tend to have losses that are above the expected loss. Similarly, when one person has a loss that is less than the expected loss (e.g., no loss), then other people also will tend to have losses below the expected value. Thus, when losses are positively correlated, there is a greater chance that lots of people will have high losses and a greater chance that lots of people will have low losses, relative to the case of uncorrelated losses. Consequently, pooling arrangements do not decrease the standard deviation of average losses as much when losses are positively correlated. Stated differently, average losses are more difficult to predict when losses are positively correlated.

To reinforce this idea, with uncorrelated losses, there is a relatively high probability that unexpectedly high losses experienced by one person will be offset by the unexpectedly low losses of other participants. Thus, the average loss becomes very predictable. When losses are positively correlated, similar losses are incurred by more participants, and one person's unexpectedly high losses are less likely to be offset by another person's unexpectedly low losses.

To illustrate, consider the effect of introducing positive correlation between Emily's and Samantha's losses. Positive correlation does not change Emily's or Samantha's initial probability distribution for accident costs. We start the year knowing that the probability of an accident is 0.2 for both Emily and Samantha. Now suppose you hear later that Emily has had an accident, but you do not know whether Samantha has had an accident. What is your assessment of the probability that Samantha will have an accident? If the accidents are assumed to be independent, then your assessment will not change; the probability of Samantha having an accident still will be 0.2. However, if the accidents are assumed to be positively correlated, then knowing Emily has had an accident will raise your assessment of Samantha's accident probability above 0.2.

Positive correlation between Emily's and Samantha's accident costs implies that the probability of both women having an accident is greater than 0.04. Similarly, positive correlation implies that the probability of neither woman having an accident is greater than 0.64. Unless we make more assumptions, we cannot specify the exact probabilities of the various outcomes. The critical point, however, is that positive correlation between Emily's and Samantha's accident costs implies that the probability of the extreme outcomes (i.e., that either both or neither will have an accident) is higher than if accident costs were independent.

The maximum degree of positive correlation is *perfect positive correlation.* In this case, if Emily has an accident, so will Samantha, and if Emily does not have an accident, neither will Samantha. Perfect positive correlation implies that whatever happens to Emily also happens to Samantha. As a result, the probability of both women having an accident is the same as the probability that either one of them will have an accident (0.2), and the probability that neither woman will have an accident is the same as the probability that one of them will not have an accident (0.8).

The effect of positively correlated losses on the distribution of average losses is summarized in Figure 4.3. Two cases are presented. In both cases, there are 1,000 participants in the pooling arrangement and each participant has an expected loss of $500. In one case, the losses of each participant are uncorrelated; in the other case, they are positively correlated. As illustrated, when losses are positively correlated, the distribution of average losses has a higher standard deviation so that average losses are less predictable.

Figure 4.4 further illustrates the effect of correlated losses on pooling arrangements by examining how the standard deviation of average losses changes as the number of participants increases. The vertical axis measures the standard deviation of average losses. The horizontal axis measures the number of participants in the sharing arrangement. When losses are uncorrelated, the standard deviation approaches zero as the number of participants gets large (recall the law of large numbers). When losses are perfectly positively correlated, the standard deviation of average losses does not change as the number of participants increases. Intuitively, when losses are perfectly positively correlated, there can be no risk reduction from pooling, because whatever happens to one participant happens to all other participants.

Figure 4.4 also illustrates the intermediate case, where losses are characterized by less than perfect positive correlation. As can be seen, the standard deviation of average losses decreases as the number of participants increases, but the standard deviation does not approach zero. The amount of risk (standard deviation) cannot be reduced as much by adding participants when losses are positively correlated; the greater the degree of correlation, the less is the reduction in risk.

FIGURE 4.3
Distribution of average losses with and without positive correlation (positive correlation increases the standard deviation).

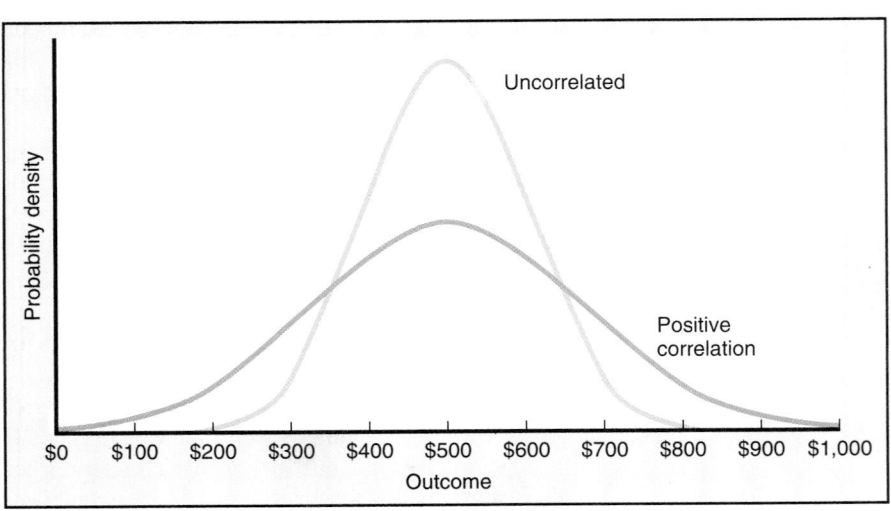

FIGURE 4.4

Effect of positive correlation in losses on risk reduction in pooling arrangements (risk is not reduced when losses are perfectly positively correlated; risk is reduced when there is less than perfect positive correlation, but not as much as when losses are uncorrelated).

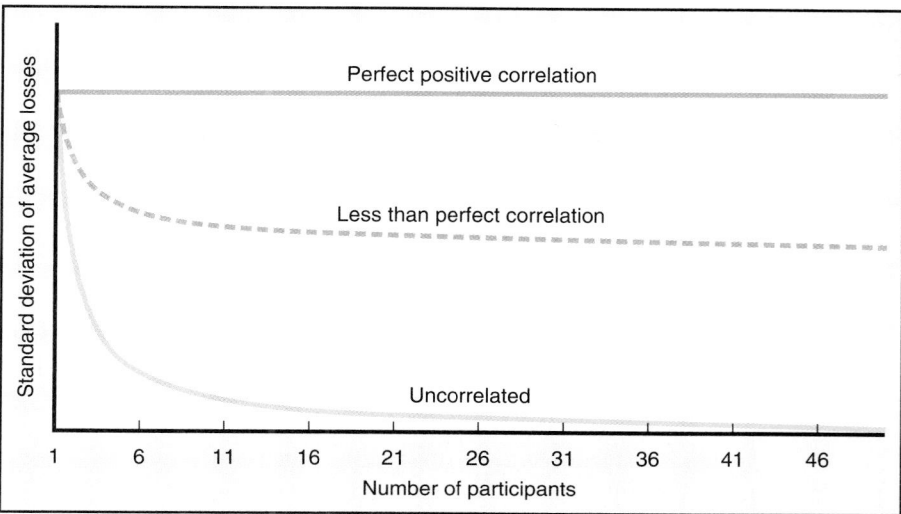

Later chapters will show that correlation in losses has very important implications for risk management and insurance. You will learn, for example, how positive correlation in losses affects business risk, insurance pricing, the types of provisions included in insurance contracts, and insurer operations (e.g., reinsurance transactions and insurer capital structure).

Concept Check

3. Sketch the probability distribution for average losses in a pooling arrangement in each of the following cases. The appearance of any one distribution is not important; instead, the relative appearance of the distribution matters.
   (*a*) The expected loss for each participant is $500, and losses for the 100 participants are independent.
   (*b*) The expected loss for each participant is $500, and losses for the 100 participants are positively correlated.
   (*c*) The expected loss for each participant is $1,500, and losses for the 100 participants are independent.
   (*d*) The expected loss for each participant is $1,500, and losses for the 100 participants are positively correlated.

4.3   Insurers as Managers of Risk Pooling Arrangements

As we just learned, individuals or businesses can reduce their risk by forming a pooling arrangement. As a result, risk-averse individuals and businesses that value lower risk would have strong incentives to participate in pooling arrangements if they could be organized at zero cost. However, risk pooling arrangements obviously are not costless to operate. Indeed, the cost of organizing and operating pooling arrangements is the main reason why insurance companies exist and why most pooling arrangements take place indirectly through insurance contracts. In essence, insurance contracts are a way of lowering the costs of operating pooling arrangements.

Types of Contracting Costs

Consider a risk pooling arrangement like the one introduced earlier, in which Emily and Samantha agree to share losses equally. We showed how this type of pooling arrangement reduces each participant's risk, as measured by the standard deviation of his or her payment, provided that losses are not perfectly positively correlated. The greater the number of people who participate in a pooling arrangement, the greater is the reduction in risk. There are, however, several important costs associated with writing and enforcing contracts among participants, which in general are referred to as contracting costs. To illustrate how insurance companies economize on these costs, this section describes the major types of contracting costs associated with pooling arrangements.

Consider first the costs associated with adding participants to risk pools. In practice, risk pooling arrangements incur substantial costs in marketing and in specifying the terms of agreement. These costs often are called **distribution costs.** As discussed in Box 4.2, insurers employ a variety of distribution systems, including exclusive agents and independent agents and brokers. Once a potential participant in a pooling arrangement has been identified, it must be decided whether to allow the individual to participate. For example, suppose that existing participants in a pooling arrangement all have expected losses of $200. Then those participants will be reluctant to allow a person with an expected loss of $400 to join on the same terms. Thus, the pool members will want to evaluate each potential participant's expected loss. The process of identifying (estimating) a potential participant's expected loss is known as **underwriting,** and the costs of doing so are called *underwriting expenses.*[5]

When a participant in a pooling arrangement experiences a loss, the person must inform and seek payment from the other members. To prevent people from fraudulently claiming that a loss has occurred or exaggerating loss amounts, the pooling arrangement must monitor claims. The costs associated with this process usually are called **loss adjustment expenses** (or *claims settlement expenses*). Pooling arrangements also involve collection costs. If, for example, a particular member has a valid claim of $10,000, each participant will ultimately have to be assessed the specified share of the $10,000 loss (e.g., $10 each if there are 1,000 members that agree to share losses equally). Alternatively, each member will have to be billed periodically for his or her share of total claim costs since the last payment. In either case, the collection of funds will involve costs in sending a bill to each member and attempting to ensure that each member pays his or her assessment.

You can think of insurance companies as organizations that have emerged to reduce the costs of operating pooling arrangements. For example, without a central organization to recruit new members and distribute contracts (marketing and distribution), screen applicants (underwriting), monitor claims (loss adjustment), and collect assessments, each member of a pooling arrangement would need to contract with each of the other members. With 1,000 members, 499,500 separate contracts would be needed (1,000 members × 999 contracts per member ÷ 2, since only one contract per pair is needed). With a central organization, only 1,000 contracts between the organization and the members are needed.

---

[5]In practice, the term *underwriting expenses* often encompasses both underwriting expenses and distribution costs or even all costs apart from claim and capital costs.

In addition, without a central organization, each member would have to (1) become involved in underwriting each of the other members, (2) investigate each claim, and (3) individually collect assessments. These activities involve expertise that most people do not have and require considerable amounts of time. The existence of insurance companies that specialize in these activities typically is efficient (i.e., it lowers costs).[6]

Ex Ante Premium Payments versus Ex Post Assessments

In contrast to pure pooling arrangements, insurance companies usually do not have the legal right to assess members of the pooling arrangement (policyholders) for losses that have occurred. Instead, policyholders pay an ex ante premium—that is, prior to knowing the magnitude of losses—without giving the insurer the right of assessment if more money is ultimately needed to pay claims (ex post). One explanation for having fixed ex ante premiums as opposed to ex post assessments is that collecting assessments from people who do not have losses is costly. Some people will attempt to delay and in some cases avoid paying assessments.

Moreover, with a pure assessment system, funds might not be available to pay losses quickly. The resulting delay in claim payments would be costly to those participants that have experienced losses. Finally, assessments impose risk on participants: They do not know in advance how much they will have to contribute (although the risk still is lower than if they were not members). For these reasons, insurers commonly charge policyholders a fixed, advance premium without having the right to assess policyholders for losses during the coverage period if realized losses for the insured group turn out to be higher than expected.[7]

Fixed ex ante premiums imply that the insurer obtains revenue (premium payments) prior to paying claims. As we elaborate in the next chapter, insurers typically invest these funds in a variety of financial assets. The resulting investment earnings can be used to help pay claims when they come due. As you will see in Chapter 8, the insurer's expected investment earnings reduce the premium that needs to be charged to cover the insurer's expected costs, all else being equal.

4.4   Other Examples of Diversification: Stock Markets

There are many ways that people and businesses diversify risk in addition to pooling arrangements through insurance contracts. Stock markets, for example, provide a mechanism for entrepreneurs to share risk associated with new business ventures with other people.[8] A share of stock entitles the owner of the share to a portion of a company's dividends. If the company does well, then dividends and/or stock prices will increase, and the owner

---

[6]Some pooling arrangements are organized without the involvement of insurance companies. As you would expect given the previous discussion, these pooling arrangements typically involve relatively small numbers of business participants with similar exposures to loss, which helps to reduce underwriting and collection costs. Also, many mutual life insurers began as "assessable" mutuals, which are organizations that operate very similarly to a "pure" pooling arrangement.

[7]Commercial insurance contracts with retrospective experience rating make the premium payment depend on the insured's loss experience during the contract period. The reasons for these types of contracts are discussed in Chapter 25.

[8]Prior to organized insurance and financial markets, people participated in informal pooling arrangements simply by being members of families and communities, and people continue to participate in these pooling arrangements, albeit to a lesser extent in most areas.

The three principal means of distributing insurance are (1) independent agents and brokers, (2) exclusive (captive) agents and/or insurance company employees, and (3) direct response methods, such as telemarketing, mail order systems, and on-line marketing. A large majority of insurance contracts are sold through the first two methods. On-line marketing is in its infancy; it is not clear how significant it may become. Insurers that rely on exclusive agents, employees, or direct response methods are known as *direct writers*.

Independent agencies and brokerages are independent organizations that have agency and/or brokerage relationships with multiple insurers. Technically, a *broker* represents the insurance buyer for the purpose of arranging insurance coverage with one or more insurers, while an *agent* represents the insurer for the purpose of selling coverage to buyers. This distinction can be important in the event of disputes between the buyer, agent or broker, and insurer.

These firms range in size from those with only a few personnel specializing in personal lines and small business insurance, up to the large international insurance brokerage firms that employ thousands of people in order to provide a wide range of risk management, insurance, and employee benefit services, primarily to medium-to-large businesses. Many businesses enter into a brokerage arrangement with a specific firm (the *broker of record*), but it also is common for larger firms to utilize more than one broker.

Insurers that use independent agents/brokers traditionally have been dominant in property-liability insurance sold to businesses (commercial lines). However, the market share of these insurers has been declining, largely due to the growth of direct writers in the small business market. According to the A.M. Best Company, insurers that use independent agents and brokers wrote 72 percent of U.S. commercial lines premiums in 1996. The remainder was written by direct writers (most commonly through exclusive agents). The large commercial lines market share of insurers that use independent agents and brokers reflects their important function of matching business buyers with widely varying risk characteristics to insurers with different areas of specialization. In contrast, direct writers wrote 68 percent of personal lines premiums (auto and homeowners insurance). Direct writers generally emphasize careful underwriting and achieve a large volume of sales per agent by targeting consumers with well-defined risk characteristics and coverage needs. For both commercial and personal lines, direct writers have lower distribution/underwriting expenses as a proportion of premiums than insurers that use independent agents and brokers.

Direct writers and insurers that use independent agents and brokers both have a major presence in the market for employee benefit plan services (group life-health insurance and retirement plans). Direct writers dominate the market for individual life-health insurance, where the most common distribution method is through exclusive agents (known as career agents). However, the amount of individual life and health insurance and annuity products purchased through independent agents and brokers increased significantly in the 1980s and 1990s. A significant proportion of annuities is marketed by life-health insurers through banks and securities firms (especially banks). The market penetration of banks and other noninsurance firms into insurance distribution (and possibly underwriting) is likely to expand significantly in coming years as a result of the Financial Modernizatio Act of 1999, which substantially reduced the complex set of government regulations that have historically discouraged the distribution and underwriting of insurance by banks.

will gain accordingly. If the company does poorly, then dividends and/or stock prices will decline, and the owner of the share will lose accordingly. Thus, the owner of a share of stock shares in the risk of the venture.

Most investors (including entrepreneurs) do not invest all of their wealth into one company's stock; instead, they invest relatively small amounts of their wealth in many different stocks. This can be accomplished at low costs using a mutual fund. In this way, their wealth at the end of their investment horizon does not totally depend on the fortunes of just one company. Investing in a number of different stocks is an example of portfolio diversification, and it is recommended by almost all financial advisors. Portfolio diversification reduces the investor's risk without necessarily sacrificing expected return.

The main message from the discussion of pooling arrangements with correlated losses is that positive correlation limits the amount of risk that can be eliminated through pooling arrangements. An analogous result holds for stock portfolio (investment) diversification. Returns on different stocks are positively correlated, because all firms are affected to some degree by common factors, such as general economic conditions and interest rates. Consequently, some of the risk associated with holding stocks cannot be diversified away. That is, the positive correlation in stock returns limits the amount of risk that can be eliminated through portfolio diversification. The risk that cannot be eliminated usually is called systematic risk or sometimes nondiversifiable or market risk.

4.5 Summary

- Pooling arrangements reduce risk (standard deviation) for each participant, provided losses are not perfectly positively correlated.
- The amount of risk that can be reduced through pooling arrangements increases as the number of participants increases, all other factors being held constant.
- In the special case where losses are uncorrelated across participants, risk can be virtually eliminated with a very large number of participants in a pooling arrangement.
- The amount of risk that can be reduced through pooling arrangements decreases as the correlation in losses across participants increases, all other factors being held constant.
- Insurance companies are institutions that economize on the contracting costs associated with pooling arrangements, including distribution, underwriting, and loss adjustment.

Key Terms

pooling arrangement 55
law of large numbers 59
normal distribution 59

central limit theorem 59
distribution costs 64

underwriting 64
loss adjustment expenses 64

Questions and Problems

1. Suppose that Kate and Anne enter into a pooling arrangement. Assume that both women have the following loss distributions and that losses are independent.

   $50,000 with probability 0.005

   $20,000 with probability 0.01

   Loss = $10,000 with probability 0.02

   $ 0 with probability 0.965

   a. Write out the possible outcomes and the probability of each outcome for Kate and Anne after they enter into a pooling arrangement. That is, write out the probability distribution for each of the women after they enter into a pooling arrangement.

   b. Calculate the expected loss to each person prior to and subsequent to entering into a pooling arrangement.

c. What happens to the standard deviation of the distribution of losses to each individual subsequent to the pooling arrangement?

2. Suppose that Nancy enters into a pooling arrangement with 1,000 people all of whom have the same loss distribution as Nancy. Assume that the losses of the participants in the pooling arrangement are uncorrelated. Draw a reasonable probability distribution for Nancy's payment in the pooling arrangement.

    Now assume that the 1,000 people in the pooling arrangement have losses that are positively correlated, but not perfectly positively correlated. On the same graph, draw a reasonable probability distribution for Nancy's payment in this pooling arrangement.

    Which scenario would have the highest maximum probable loss? Briefly explain.

3. Suppose that Marsha enters into a pooling arrangement with 1,000 people, all of whom have the same loss distribution as Marsha. Assume that the losses of the participants in the pooling arrangement are uncorrelated. Draw a reasonable probability distribution for Marsha's payment in the pooling arrangement.

Now assume that there are 10,000 people in the pooling arrangement, that all the people have the same loss distributions, and that losses are uncorrelated. On the same graph, draw a reasonable probability distribution for Nancy's payment in this pooling arrangement.

4. Consider the following descriptions of pooling arrangements;

    a. The expected loss for each participant is $50,000 and losses for the 50 participants are uncorrelated.

    b. The expected loss for each participant is $50,000 and the losses for the 100 participants are uncorrelated.

    c. The expected loss for each participant is $50,000 and the losses for the 100 participants are positively correlated.

    Sketch the probability distribution for average losses for the pooling arrangement (*a*) and the pooling arrangement (*b*). Label your graphs.

    Sketch the probability distribution for average losses for the pooling arrangement (*b*) and the pooling arrangement (*c*). Label your graphs.

Answers to Concept Checks

1. By entering a pooling arrangement, a person pays the average loss of the members of the group as opposed to his or her own loss. The average loss is more predictable (that is, has a lower standard deviation) than an individual's loss. The pooling arrangement, however, does not change the expected loss of the participants.

2.

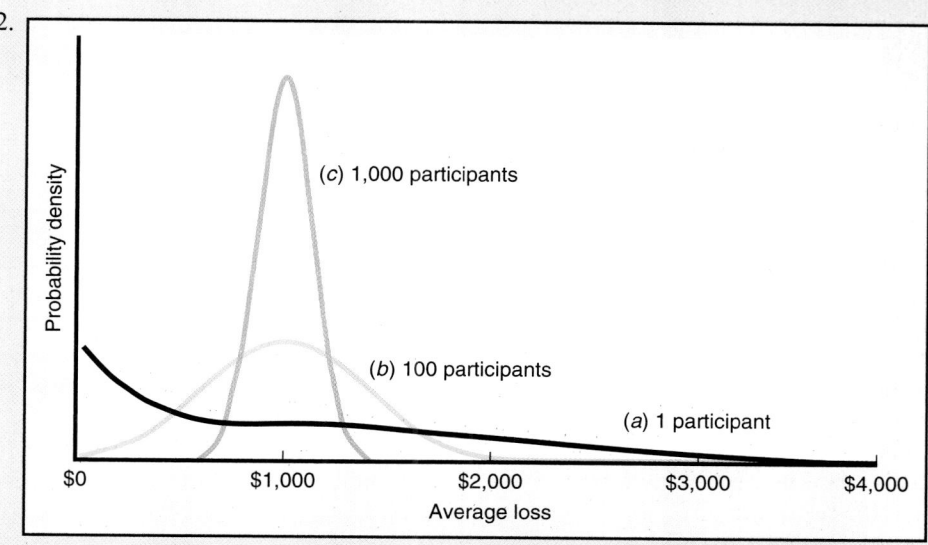

3.

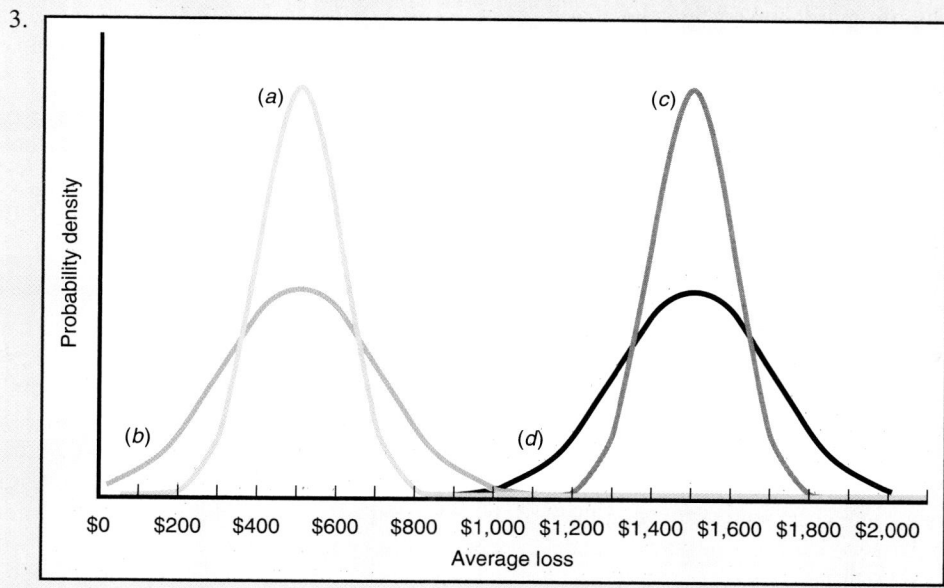

References

Cummins, J. David. "Statistical and Financial Models of Insurance Pricing and the Insurance Firm." *Journal of Risk and Insurance,* June 1991, pp. 261–302. (*The first part of this article provides a more advanced treatment of the material presented in this chapter.*)

Appendix 4A

More on Risk Measurement and Risk Reduction

4A.1 The Concept of Covariance and More about Correlation

Although none of the problems or analyses in this book will require you to measure or calculate the correlation between random variables, additional insight into the meaning of correlation and its effect on risk reduction in pooling arrangements can be obtained by explaining how correlation is measured. To begin, it helps to introduce a related measure of the relationship between two random variables, known as the **covariance.**

To illustrate the meaning of covariance, consider how macroeconomic conditions might affect the revenue and costs of an automaker. Suppose that there are three types of economic conditions: strong growth, weak growth, or no growth. For simplicity, assume that each outcome is equally likely (the probability is one-third) and that the outcomes for revenue and costs under each economic outcome are those presented in Table 4A.1. Under these assumptions, the expected values of revenue and costs equal $717 and $650, respectively.

We want to find the covariance between the random variables: revenue and costs. First, notice that when revenue is above its expected value (as in the strong and weak growth conditions), costs are either above or equal to their expected value, and when revenue is below its expected value (as in the no growth condition), costs are below their expected value. Thus, revenue and costs tend to move in the same direction, relative to their respective expected values. Based on our earlier discussion of correla-

tion, we therefore know that revenue and costs are positively correlated.

The mathematical definition of covariance is:

$$Cov\,(X,Y) = \sum_{i=1}^{N} p_i(x_i - \mu_x)(y_i - \mu_y) \quad (3A.1)$$

where

N = the number of possible outcomes ($N = 3$ in the example);

X = one random variable (revenue) with possible outcomes $x_1, \ldots, x_N$;

Y = the other random variable (costs) with possible outcomes $y_1, \ldots, y_N$;

$p_1, \ldots, p_N$ = the probabilities of each joint outcome (one-third in the example);

μ_x = the expected value of X ($717); and

μ_y = the expected value of Y ($650).

Note that this formula implies that if X has outcomes that are greater than its expected value when Y has outcomes that are greater than its expected value, then the terms in parentheses will both be positive and their product also will be positive. Similarly, if X has outcomes that are less than its expected value when Y has outcomes that are less than its expected value, then the terms in parentheses both will be negative and again their product will be positive. Thus, when X and Y tend to move in the

Table 4A.1

Economic Condition	Probability	Revenue	Costs
Strong growth	1/3	$850	$700
Weak growth	1/3	800	650
No growth	1/3	500	600
Expected value		$717	$650

same direction, the terms being summed in the formula will be positive, so that the covariance between X and Y will be positive.

In contrast, if X and Y tend to move in opposite directions (high outcomes for X occur when Y has low outcomes), then the terms in parentheses will have opposite signs and their product will be negative. Consequently, the terms being summed will be negative, and the covariance will be negative. Notice that this discussion of covariance sounds very much like our discussion of correlation. In fact, covariance has the same sign as correlation. Returning to the revenue and costs example, if revenue is high when costs are high, then revenue and costs have positive covariance and positive correlation.[1]

Applying the formula for covariance to the automaker's revenue and costs, we find

$$
\begin{aligned}
\text{Cov(Revenue, Costs)} = \ & 1/3\,[(\$850 - \$717)(\$700 \\
& - \$650) + (\$800 \\
& - \$717)(\$650 - \$650) \\
& + (\$500 - \$717)(\$600 \\
& - \$650)] = 1/3\,[(\$133)(\$50) \\
& + (\$83)(\$0) + (-\$217)(-\$50)] \\
= \ & \$3{,}617
\end{aligned}
$$

While the sign of covariance tells us whether the two random variables tend to move together, the magnitude of the covariance measure has little intuitive meaning by itself. For this reason, the covariance often is scaled to obtain the **correlation coefficient.** The correlation coefficient, usually denoted by the Greek letter ρ (rho), equals the covariance divided by the product of the standard deviations. Mathematically, the correlation coefficient between X and Y is defined as:

$$
p(X,Y) = \frac{\text{Cov}(X,\,Y)}{\text{Std}(X)\,\text{Std}(Y)} \qquad \text{(3A.2)}
$$

where

$\text{Std}(X) =$ the standard deviation of X, and
$\text{Std}(Y) =$ the standard deviation of Y.

A nice feature of the correlation coefficient is that it is always between -1 and 1. The greater the correlation coefficient in absolute value, the more strongly related are the two random variables. If the correlation coefficient is 1, then the two random variables are perfectly positively correlated. If the correlation coefficient is -1, then the two random variables are perfectly negatively correlated. Perfect correlation implies that if you were to plot the outcomes of X and Y on a two-dimensional graph, the outcomes would lie along a straight line (i.e., X and Y would be perfectly linearly related). If the correlation coefficient is 0 between two random variables, then they are uncorrelated or independent.[2] Intuitively, a correlation coefficient of 0 implies that the outcomes for X are unrelated to the outcomes for Y.

To calculate the correlation coefficient in our example, we must find the standard deviations of revenue and costs:

$$
\begin{aligned}
\text{Std(Revenue)} = \ & \{\tfrac{1}{3}[(\$850 - \$717)^2 + (\$800 - \$717)^2 \\
& + (\$500 - \$717)^2\,]\}^{\frac{1}{2}} = \$154.6
\end{aligned}
$$

$$
\begin{aligned}
\text{Std(Costs)} = \ & \{\tfrac{1}{3}[(\$700 - \$650)^2 + (\$650 - \$650)^2 \\
& + (\$550 - \$650)^2\,]\}^{\frac{1}{2}} = \$40.8
\end{aligned}
$$

Dividing the covariance by the product of the standard deviations gives:

$$
\begin{aligned}
p(\text{Revenue, Costs}) = \ & \$8{,}333/(\$154.6)(\$40.8) \\
= \ & \$3{,}617/\$6{,}306 = 0.57
\end{aligned}
$$

That is, the correlation coefficient between revenue and costs is positive, but the two random variables are not perfectly correlated.

---

[1]You may have noticed that the formula for covariance is very similar to the formula for variance presented in the previous chapter. Indeed, you can view them as the same formula, because the variance of a random variable is the covariance of that random variable with itself. You can see this by substituting X and its expected value for Y and its expected value in the covariance formula.

[2]There is actually a subtle distinction between random variables that are uncorrelated and random variables that are independent. Independent random variables always are uncorrelated, but some uncorrelated random variables do not satisfy the technical definition of independence. It is not important for you to know the distinction to understand the ideas in this book.

4A.2 Expected Value and Standard Deviation of Combinations of Random Variables

We now can illustrate how distributions of random variables change when they are combined in certain ways. These results are important in measuring the amount of risk (standard deviation) that is eliminated by pooling arrangements.

EXPECTED VALUE OF A CONSTANT TIMES A RANDOM VARIABLE

Suppose that X is a random variable equal to Samantha's auto accident costs for the coming year and that X equals $2,500 with probability 0.8 and $0 with probability 0.2 (as in our earlier example). The expected value of X is:

$$E(X) = (0.2)(\$2,500) + (0.8)(\$0) = \$500$$

Now suppose that Samantha's father, because he is so nice, agrees to pay one-half of her accident losses. Thus, there is a difference between Samantha's accident losses and the costs she must pay. Samantha's accident costs for the year will equal $\frac{1}{2}X$, which is a constant (one-half) times the original random variable. The expected value of the new random variable is simply the constant times the expected value of the original random variable:

$$E(\tfrac{1}{2}X) = \tfrac{1}{2}E(X) = \tfrac{1}{2}(\$500) = \$250$$

In general, the expected value of a constant times a random variable equals the constant times the expected value of the random variable.

STANDARD DEVIATION AND VARIANCE OF A CONSTANT TIMES A RANDOM VARIABLE

What is the standard deviation of Samantha's accident costs after her father agrees to pay one-half of her accident costs? Once again, the standard deviation of a constant times a random variable equals the constant ($\frac{1}{2}$) times the standard deviation of the random variable. That is

$$\text{Std}(\tfrac{1}{2}X) = \tfrac{1}{2}\,\text{Std}(X)$$

Samantha's total accident costs (without the subsidy from her father) have a standard deviation equal to

$$\text{Std}(X) =$$
$$\sqrt{0.8\,(\$0 - \$500)^2 + 0.2\,(\$2.500 - \$500)^2} = \$1,000$$

Therefore, the standard deviation of Samantha's accident costs after her father agrees to pay 50 percent is $\frac{1}{2}(\$1,000) = \$500$. (This result can be shown to hold by plugging in one-half of the accident costs and one-half of the original expected value in the standard deviation formula; that is, by calculating the standard deviation of $1/2X$ directly.)

Recall that the variance of a random variable is the square of the standard deviation. Therefore, the variance of a constant times a random variable is the *constant squared* times the variance of the random variable. Algebraically

$$\text{Var}(\tfrac{1}{2}X) = [\text{Std}(\tfrac{1}{2}X)]^2 = [\tfrac{1}{2}\text{Std}(X)]^2 = (\tfrac{1}{2})^2\text{Var}(X)$$

In Samantha's case, the variance of accident costs was originally $1,000^2$. After her father agreed to pay one-half of her accident costs, the variance decreased to $(\frac{1}{4})(\$1,000)^2$.

EXPECTED VALUE OF A SUM OF RANDOM VARIABLES

The expected value of a sum of random variables is the sum of the expected values. To illustrate this result, consider the Emily–Samantha example. Both Emily and Samantha have expected accident costs equal to $500. The expected value of Emily's costs plus Samantha's costs is therefore $500 + $500 = $1,000. This is true no matter what the correlation coefficient is between Emily's and Samantha's costs. In general

$$E(X + Y) = E(X) + E(Y)$$

One combination of random variables that plays a particularly important role in statistics, insurance, and investments is the average of random variables. Remember the pooling arrangement between Emily and Samantha. By entering the pooling arrangement, each woman basically trades her personal loss for the average loss. That is, if X = Emily's personal loss and Y = Samantha's personal loss, then by entering the pooling arrangement Emily pays $(X + Y)/2$ instead of X and Samantha pays $(X + Y)/2$ instead of Y. Applying the results just derived (that the expected value of a sum equals the sum of the expected values and that the expected value of a constant times a random variable is the constant times the expected value), we find that the expected cost to Emily and Samantha after entering the pooling arrangement is:

$$E[(X + Y)/2] = \tfrac{1}{2} E(X) + \tfrac{1}{2} E(Y) = \$250 + \$250 = \$500$$

That is, the pooling arrangement does not change either woman's expected cost.

VARIANCE AND STANDARD DEVIATION OF A SUM OF RANDOM VARIABLES

Algebraically, the variance of a sum of random variables X and Y is given by the following equation:

$$\text{Var}(X + Y) = \text{Var}(X) + \text{Var}(Y) + 2\text{Cov}(X, Y)$$

If the covariance is 0, the variance of the sum equals the sum of the variances.

The standard deviation of the sum is:

$$\text{Std}(X + Y) = \sqrt{\text{Var}(X) + \text{Var}(Y) + 2\text{Cov}(X,Y)}$$

Often it is more convenient to use this formula by first substituting the relation between the covariance and the correlation coefficient. Recall $\rho(X,Y) = \text{Cov}(X,Y)/[\text{Std}(X)\,\text{Std}(Y)]$. Therefore

$$\text{Std}(X + Y) =$$

$$\sqrt{\text{Var}(X) + \text{Var}(Y) + 2\rho(X,Y)\text{Std}(X)\text{Std}(Y)}$$

The standard deviation of a sum of random variables is the sum of the standard deviations in one special case—perfect positive correlation. (To see this, set $\rho = 1$ and note that the expression under the square root sign equals $\text{Std}(X)$ plus $\text{Std}(Y)$ squared.) In all other cases, the standard deviation of a sum of random variables is less than the sum of the standard deviations.

VARIANCE AND STANDARD DEVIATION OF THE AVERAGE OF HOMOGENEOUS RANDOM VARIABLES

Recall that the average of random variables plays a particularly important role in insurance because participants in pooling arrangements pay the average loss of the group. Using the results already presented, the variance of an average of random variables is:

$$\text{Var}\left[\frac{X + Y}{2}\right] =$$

$$\text{Var}\left[\frac{X}{2}\right] + \text{Var}\left[\frac{Y}{2}\right] + 2\rho(X,Y)\text{Std}\left[\frac{X}{2}\right]\text{Std}\left[\frac{Y}{2}\right]$$

If the random variables X and Y have the same variance (standard deviation), then the formula can be simplified as follows (recalling that

$$\text{Var}\left[\frac{X}{2}\right] = \frac{1}{4}\text{Var}(X)$$

$$\text{Var}\left[\frac{X + Y}{2}\right] =$$

$$\frac{1}{4}\text{Var}(X) + \frac{1}{4}\text{Var}(X) + 2\rho(X,Y)\frac{1}{4}\text{Var}(X)$$

Combining terms yields the following equation:

$$\text{Var}\left[\frac{X + Y}{2}\right] = \frac{1}{2}\text{Var}(X)[1 + \rho(X,Y)]$$

If the correlation coefficient is 0 (X and Y are uncorrelated), then the variance of the average loss is one-half of the original variance. This indicates that averaging uncorrelated losses reduces variance (risk). This is the fundamental result that was presented, in less technical terms, in the text.

In general, if losses are uncorrelated and have the same variance, then the variance of the average loss is the original variance divided by the number of participants in the pooling arrangement. Thus, if N people each having a variance of losses equal to Var decide to create a pooling arrangement, then the variance of losses paid by each individual changes from Var to Var/N (assuming losses are uncorrelated). As N gets large, the variance approaches 0.

The effect of pooling arrangements on the standard deviation of losses paid by each participant is found by taking the square root of the variances. If each participant has a variance of losses equal to Var and a standard deviation of losses equal to Std ($= \sqrt{\text{Var}}$), then a pooling arrangement with N participants and uncorrelated losses changes the standard deviation of the amount paid by each person to Std/$\sqrt{N}$.

To apply these results to the accident costs paid by Emily and Samantha after they enter the pooling arrangement, let X equal Samantha's accident costs and Y equal Emily's accident costs. Recall that the standard deviations of Emily's and Samantha's accident costs are $1,000, since $\text{Std}(X) = \text{Std}(Y) = 1,000$. What is the standard deviation of accident costs for each woman after entering the pooling arrangement?

If Emily's and Samantha's accident costs are uncorrelated ($\rho = 0$), then the standard deviation after entering the pooling arrangement (using the above expression for the variance of $(X + Y)/2$ with $\rho = 0$) equals:

$$\text{Std}\left(\frac{X + Y}{2}\right) = \frac{\text{Std}(X)}{\sqrt{2}} = \frac{\$1,000}{\sqrt{2}} = \$707$$

The standard deviation is reduced from $1,000 to $707, indicating that losses for Emily and Samantha are more predictable.

If Emily's and Samantha's accident costs are perfectly positively correlated ($\rho = 1$), then the standard deviation after entering the pooling arrangement (using the expression for the variance of $(X + Y)2$ with $\rho = 1$) equals the average standard deviation of the random variables:

$$\text{Std}\left(\frac{X + Y}{2}\right) = \frac{1}{\sqrt{2}}(\$1,000)\sqrt{1 + 1} = \$1,000$$

The standard deviation is unchanged by the pooling arrangement when losses are perfectly positively correlated. These results highlight that the effect of a pooling arrangement on the standard deviation depends on the correlation between losses. The greater the correlation, the less that risk is reduced by the pooling arrangement.

Key Terms   covariance 70
correlation coefficient 71

5

Insurer Ownership, Financial, and Operational Structure

Chapter Objectives

- Describe different types of insurance company ownership.
- Discuss the role of insurer capital and factors that affect insurer capital decisions.
- Describe how insurers reduce insolvency risk through diversification of underwriting risk, reinsurance, and investment choices.

5.1 Insurer Capital

With a typical insurance policy, the policyholder pays a fixed premium to the insurer and the insurer promises to pay losses or benefits as provided under the terms of the policy. This arrangement raises the question: If the premiums and investment income are insufficient to pay administrative costs and claim costs, who (if anyone) is obligated to pay the shortfall? Conversely, if premium revenue and investment income exceed the insurer's costs, who receives the excess? The short (and incomplete) answer to these questions is that the owners of the insurer are responsible for any shortfall and the owners have rights to any excess. Actually, owners of most insurers are responsible for shortfalls up to the amount of capital that the insurer holds. To understand this point, we must define what we mean by capital.

Economic capital is defined as the difference between the market value of assets and the market value of liabilities. The market value of assets reflects the market value of the insurer's stocks, bonds, real estate, cash, and the like. The market value of liabilities equals the present value of the payments the insurer has promised to make in the future for policies already sold. Note that the economic value of assets, liabilities, and capital does not correspond to the way accountants measure these items. We will briefly comment on some of these accounting issues later.

To clarify these concepts using a simple example, suppose that Drennan Capital Corporation (DCC) sells policies to 10,000 homogeneous policyholders at the beginning of the year. DCC will cease operations after the claims on the policies have been paid at the end of the year. The expected claim cost for each policyholder is $500. The actual claim cost for any given policyholder, of course, could be much different from $500. Suppose that DCC charges each policyholder a premium of $525. To keep things simple, we will ignore the distribution, underwriting, and claims processing costs and the investment income from investing premiums and capital.

Immediately after receiving the premium payments, DCC has assets of $525 × 10,000 = $5.25 million. DCC's (economic) liabilities equal the expected value of its obligations to pay policyholders' claims, which equals $5 million (10,000 policyholders × $500 expected cost per policyholder). Thus, immediately after selling the policies, DCC has $5.25 million in assets and $5 million in liabilities, giving it $0.25 million in (economic) capital.

Now let's look at DCC's capital after paying losses at the end of the year. Suppose that policyholders had fewer losses than were expected, so that the average loss was $450. Then, DCC would pay claims of $450 × 10,000 = $4.5 million. Assets would be diminished by $4.5 million and liabilities would be eliminated. At this point, DCC would have assets of $0.75 million and no liabilities, and its capital would be $0.75 million. This capital belongs to the owners of DCC.

Suppose, however, that claim costs at the end of the year exceeded the amount expected so that the average loss was $550. In this case, DCC's assets of $5.25 million would be insufficient to pay all of the $5.5 million in claim costs (10,000 policyholders × $550 average claim cost). We could say that the insurer in this case has negative capital, or, more commonly, that the insurer is *insolvent*—it cannot meet all of its obligations.

As discussed in Chapter 7, the frequency of insurer insolvencies generally is relatively low and, historically, most insolvent insurers have been relatively small companies. One reason the insolvency probability is very small for most insurers is that they hold enough capital to cover unexpectedly high claim costs. We will discuss the incentives for insurers to hold capital after describing who owns insurance companies.

Concept Check

1. Why might insurer capital sometimes be referred to as a cushion?

5.2   Ownership and Sources of Capital

Who owns insurance company capital? That is, (1) who commits the capital to provide a cushion from which unexpectedly high claims costs are paid, and (2) who has rights to excess funds when claim costs are lower than expected? There are two broad approaches to insurance company ownership. One approach is to make the policyholders the owners; the other is to make investors the owners. Each approach has several variations.

Mutual Insurers

The most common form of policyholder-owned insurer is called a **mutual insurer.** Mutual insurers are incorporated insurance companies that usually charge fixed, advance premiums to policyholders. Because policyholders usually cannot be assessed to pay unexpectedly high claim costs, their liability for the insurer's claim costs is limited to what they originally paid in premiums.

The capital needed to start a mutual insurer and to provide an initial cushion from which unexpectedly high claim costs could be paid usually is obtained by borrowing money from investors. The loan then is repaid from operating profits over time.[1] In addition, when a mutual insurer retains operating profits (earnings), it accumulates additional assets, which are used as a cushion (capital) for future liabilities. If the managers of a mutual insurer determine that all the additional capital is not needed, they can pay out profits to policyholders as policyholder dividends. Policyholder dividends are low in property-liability insurance compared to life insurance. One explanation is that many life insurance products bundle insurance with investment products, and a portion of the investment return is paid as dividends. A fuller discussion of life insurance contracts and policy dividends is provided in Chapter 15.

Another type of insurer with policyholder ownership is called a **reciprocal.** In practice, mutuals and reciprocals operate similarly. One technical difference is that a reciprocal is not incorporated but is instead managed by an entity known as an *attorney in fact,* which is in essence a management company.

Stock Insurers

Stock insurers are incorporated insurance companies that are owned by investors who have purchased the stock (equity) of the company. At its inception, a stock insurer issues shares of stock. Thereafter, capital is accumulated through retained earnings and through additional stock or bond issues.[2] Stockholders can suffer losses from unexpectedly high claim costs (or low returns on the insurer's assets). However, as is true for stockholders of corporations in general, their maximum loss is limited to the amount of money that they have invested in the stock, according to the legal doctrine of *limited liability.* Stockholders have the right to any profits that the insurer earns. If managers decide that the firm has accumulated enough capital, dividends can be paid to the stockholders (or stock can be repurchased). Like mutual insurers, stock insurers sometimes pay dividends to policyholders although the amount of dividends paid by stock insurers is typically lower than that paid by mutual insurers.

There are large numbers of both mutual and stock insurers in the property–liability and life–health insurance industries. In order to achieve greater access to capital (i.e., by issuing stock), a number of mutual insurers have converted to stock insurers and hybrid stock-mutual structures in recent years. Figure 5.1 provides information on the 2000 premiums written by all stock and mutual insurance groups in the United States for both the property–liability and life–health insurance industries. Mutual insurers wrote 24 percent of property–liability insurance premiums in 2000; stock insurers wrote 69 percent. Reciprocals accounted for approximately 6 percent of premiums.

---

[1]The securities that mutual insurers issue to obtain capital generally are called *surplus notes.* They are similar to corporate bonds, but the repayment of principal usually must be approved by state insurance regulators.

[2]From the policyholder's perspective, debt obligations of the insurer provide additional capital because policyholders' claims generally must be paid prior to interest and principal on debt contracts. Shareholders, however, would not view funds provided by debt as additional capital, because shareholders have the residual claim; that is, they only get paid after policyholders and debtholders.

FIGURE 5.1
Property–
liability and
life–health
insurance
industry
premiums
written for
mutual
insurers, stock
insurers, and
total industry
in 2000.

Source: Data obtained from *Best's Aggregates and Averages 2001.* Property–Liability and Life–Health editions.

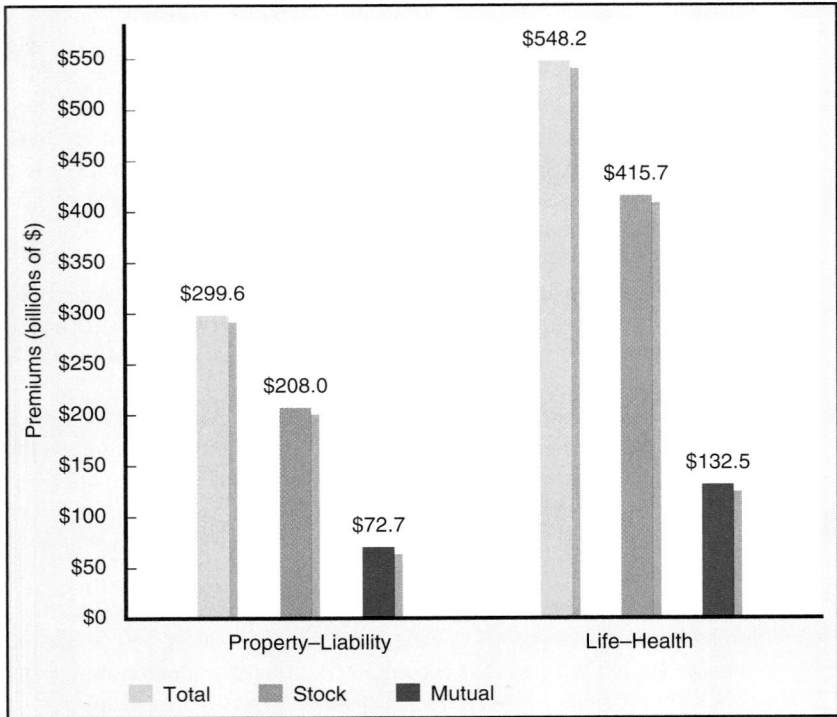

Table 5.1 illustrates that some of the largest property–liability and life–health insurers are mutuals. It lists the 2000 premium volume and ownership form for the 10 largest US insurance organizations in each industry based on 2000 premiums. Note that some groups rank in the top 10 for both industries.

Lloyd's of London

Lloyd's of London provides another example of investor ownership of insurers. Strictly speaking, Lloyd's of London is not an insurance company; it is an organization that provides a location and, more importantly, a set of rules and procedures under which insurance business is transacted. Also, contrary to what many people often think, Lloyd's of London does not provide unusual insurance coverage alone. Instead, the vast majority of business conducted at Lloyd's of London is commercial insurance, reinsurance, and auto insurance,

The owners of the insurance organizations that conduct business at Lloyd's are called **names.** Until the early 1990s, all names were individuals with relatively large amounts of wealth. At Lloyd's, insurance policies are sold through syndicates (groups) of names. Each syndicate has a lead underwriter who usually specializes in a particular type of business (e.g., aviation risks) and who makes decisions about what policies to sell and the terms of those policies. When joining Lloyd's and each year thereafter, a name decides which syndicates to participate in and the extent of participation. For example, a name with $150,000 of capital to commit to Lloyd's may allocate $50,000 each to three different syndicates. Essentially, the name has invested in three different insurance companies.

Table 5.1
Ownership form and premium volume for the 10 largest writers of US property–liability and life–health insurance in 2000.

	Ownership	Net Premiums Written ($ millions)
Property–Liability		
State Farm Insurance Group	Mutual	$33,294
Allstate Insurance Group	Stock	21,622
Zurich/Farmers Group	Stock	16,754
American International Group	Stock	12,248
Berkshire Hathaway Ins. Group	Stock	10,404
Travelers/Citigroup Cos.	Stock	9,880
Nationwide Group	Mutual	9,464
Liberty Mutual Ins. Cos.	Mutual	8,675
CNA Ins. Cos.	Stock	8,115
Hartford Ins. Group	Stock	6,872
Life–Health		
Metropolitan LFA Affiliates	Stock	$30,571
ING Group	Stock	23,999
American Int'l. Group	Stock	23,497
AEGON USA Inc.	Stock	23,044
Hartford Life	Stock	18,554
Nationwide Group	Stock	18,191
CIGNA Group	Stock	17,467
Prudential of Am. Group	Stock	16,957
Principal Life Ins.	Stock	15,653
New York Life	Mutual	14,377

Note: Rankings based on 2000 premiums. Data are for insurer groups, which include affiliated companies under common ownership. Data obtained from *Best's Aggregates and Averages,* 2001. Property-Liability and Life-Health editions.

The investment by an individual name, however, differs from investment in a stock insurance company, because an individual name has **unlimited liability.** If the syndicate does not have sufficient funds to pay all the claims on its policies from its premium revenue, its investment income, and the capital contributed by the names, then the names can be assessed for the shortfall. As noted earlier, an investor in a stock insurance company cannot be assessed; the investor's loss is limited to the amount invested in the stock.

While the unlimited liability feature of Lloyd's of London would appear to enhance its ability to pay claims, this organizational form was severely tested during the 1990s. Large losses from catastrophes, environmental liability claims, and asbestos liability claims forced a number of syndicates to assess names. As we discussed in general terms earlier, the collection of assessments turned out to be difficult and very costly for Lloyd's. Many names refused to pay their assessments, alleging that they were misled about the risks involved and that the agents they hired to allocate their capital to various syndicates breached their duty. At one time, more than 19,000 names were involved in lawsuits related to these circumstances (the number of names reached its peak in 1989, when there were approximately 30,000 names). The failure of names to pay assessments pushed Lloyd's to the brink of financial distress and forced it to reorganize—a process that included the introduction of corporate names, with limited liability, in the early 1990s. Lloyd's now operates with both

Many expected the merger of Travelers and Citicorp in 1998 to herald a wave of cross-industry consolidations between the US insurance and banking industries. In 1999 Congress responded to the transaction swiftly by passing the Gramm–Leach–Bliley Act, which created a legal structure for affiliations among companies in the insurance, securities, and commercial banking industries. The table was set for other major US companies to join Citigroup as one-stop financial services providers.

In 1999 and early 2000, many experts predicted convergence within the financial services industry. The European model of integrated financial services firms that provides insurance and reinsurance, commercial and consumer banking, and investment banking and securities services was widely touted as the future for the United States. Contrary to these predictions, more than three years after the formation of Citigroup and two years after adoption of Gramm–Leach–Bliley, there have been no additional combinations of major US insurance and banking firms. In fact, Citigroup announced in December 2001 that it planned to spin off the Travelers property/casualty business to its stockholders, taking a step back from its strategy of being able to offer its customers a full range of financial products under the Citigroup umbrella.

Consolidation has continued in the US insurance industry. For example, AIG's acquisition of Hartford Steam Boiler gave it access to a brand name dominant in certain niche markets. The big banks have also gotten bigger. Some examples are Chase's acquisition of J.P. Morgan and First Union's victory in the bruising battle with Sun Trust for Wachovia. Certainly, many insurance companies are offering a broader range of financial products. Major insurers such as MetLife have chartered start-up banks to market banking products to customers. The last three years have seen national and regional commercial banking firms go on a binge, buying insurance agencies to market a full range of insurance products to their customers.

Since the formation of Citigroup and the adoption of Gramm–Leach–Bliley, there has been a clear trend toward convergence in the delivery of banking and insurance products. Major financial services companies are following Citigroup's lead and have positioned or plan to position themselves to make all types of financial products available. J.P. Morgan Chase and others are actively marketing a full range of insurance products to business and retail customers, yet bankers have not rushed to underwrite or reinsure insurance risks. Similarly, insurance companies are using their capital to write more insurance; provide reinsurance; or acquire insurers, reinsurers, agencies, and firms providing financial planning and management services. However, AIG and other large US insurance companies have been conspicuous in not pursuing opportunities to acquire or affiliate with large full-service commercial or retail banks, although many are marketing a variety of banking products.

Internationally, particularly in Europe, consolidation among the integrated financial services companies has continued, but the expected major push of these large, well-capitalized institutions into US commercial banking has not occurred, with the exception of Deutsche Bank's acquisition of Bankers Trust. The lack of cross-industry consolidation in the United States is caused by many factors. Some are specific to individual companies, but others have a more general impact. For example, with few exceptions, US insurers with national franchises lack the capital necessary to acquire national or super-regional bank holding companies.

Mergers of equals between the largest insurers and commercial banks are, therefore, hard to engineer. Accordingly, insurance and reinsurance companies have the option of either buying regional institutions that don't have brand recognition or creating their own banking operations using their own brands. The large market capitalizations of the national bank holding companies resulted—at least in part—for the recent success of the US economy making it difficult for large foreign financial services firms to think about swallowing US firms.

Successful integration of a regional banking institution into a national insurance firm may cost more than starting a bank from scratch. While establishing a new bank takes time and requires the creation of a management team, insurance companies have sufficient capital to charter relatively large banks that can immediately generate significant levels of business activity. In addition, a new bank provides a clean slate that allows an insurance company to focus specifically on the products that are most attractive to its existing customers. In fact, ING is pursuing a strategy much like this in attempting to create a new branded bank online.

On the other hand, the commercial banking industry has been more interested in building the scope of commercial banking franchises. Firms such as Bank of America and J.P. Morgan Chase have grown dramatically, and so-called super-regionals such as FleetBoston and First Union have toiled to expand their geographic footprints and commercial banking product offerings, rather than invest in underwriters of insurance and reinsurance.

There are significant differences in the business models traditionally followed by insurance companies and commercial banks in the United States; these pose barriers to convergence because they make integration of the insurance and banking businesses more difficult. Examples are the roles of agents in the sale of insurance and reinsurance brokers and intermediaries in reinsurance cessions. Banks traditionally have not relied on third parties to sell their products, and some banking concerns have sometimes stumbled in trying to institutionalize insurance agency forces or investment bankers that are often quite entrepreneurial and do not mesh well with commercial bank cultures.

Many successful mergers and acquisitions among financial services firms are dependent upon cost savings, which are often the primary justification provided to the investment community for such deals. It is much harder to identify duplicative expenses in cross-industry combinations. When Citicorp and Travelers combined to create Citigroup, the management of the commercial banking and insurance lines remained split.

Returns on equity also drive merger considerations. The property/casualty industry, in particular, does not generate the returns on equity that many stockholders of bank holding companies expect. Citigroup acknowledged this was at least one reason for its planned divestiture of the Travelers property/casualty business. As noted earlier, though, a great deal of capital has recently been allocated to the property/casualty business, and major industry players clearly expect significant opportunities for investment returns.

Another underlying barrier to the convergence of the banking and insurance industries in the United States is a fundamental difference in the way firms manage their balance sheets and operate their businesses. While insurance and reinsurance companies generate significant pools of capital through premiums and often achieve excellent returns on investing that capital, their fundamental focus is on managing liabilities through reinsurance, reserving, and underwriting to maximize underwriting returns.

Banking firms, on the other hand, while focused on credit risk, manage assets to generate returns. US financial executives at the highest levels typically have not worked on both sides of the fence, and it takes an unusual individual to combine the qualities and skills necessary to manage both businesses.

While the expected convergence has not occurred to date in the US financial services industries, the trend is clearly toward larger, more sophisticated companies. As insurance companies become more comfortable with consumer and commercial banking and bank holding companies learn more about the business of insurance, industry executives will develop the expertise to make cross-industry mergers work.

Source: *Business Insurance*. Chicago, March 18, 2002. Geoffrey Etherington III and Theodore P. Augustinos, "Bank/Insurer Consolidation Faces Barriers to Success,"

individual names (with unlimited liability) and corporate names. Corporate names have begun to dominate, and unlimited liability for individual names may be eliminated.

Convergence of Financial Service Providers

During the latter part of the 1990s, a number of analysts predicted that many insurance companies would be combined with banking and investment companies. One of the first examples of this convergence in the provision of financial services was the formation of Citigroup in 1998, which combined the banking giant Citicorp and the insurance giant Travelers. Congress then passed the Gramm–Leach–Bliley Act in 1999, which broke down regulatory barriers to ownership of insurance operations by banks and vice versa. As Box 5.1 indicates, the efficiencies associated with having one financial institution provide insurance, banking, and investment services have been questioned in recent years.

5.3   Factors Affecting Insurer Capital Decisions

An important decision facing all insurers is how much capital to hold, given underwriting and investment decisions. This section analyzes the key factors that affect this decision in the absence of regulation. Capital regulation is discussed in Chapters 6 and 7. To make the ideas in this chapter concrete, we consider a hypothetical stock insurer, Tennant-Lamm Corporation (TLC). TLC came into existence when it issued stock to investors for $5 million. Some of this start-up capital was used to develop a corporate plan, conduct marketing research, and train employees. The remainder was used to acquire office facilities, computer equipment, and the like. TLC intends to write automobile liability insurance policies during its first year, with total expected claim costs equal to $20 million. For simplicity, it is assumed that all claim costs will be paid at the end of the year. While expected claim costs equal $20 million, actual claim costs could be higher or lower than $20 million. Figure 5.2 presents the probability distribution for TLC's claim costs.

The issue to be addressed is: How much more capital, if any, should TLC raise by issuing additional stock before it begins operations? The additional capital that TLC raises, along with the premium revenue remaining after paying underwriting and distribution costs, will be invested in risk-free bonds until year-end.[3] The accumulated funds from the new capital and premium revenue then will be available to pay claim costs. Assuming that TLC sells its policies at prices that cover its expected costs, any new capital that TLC raises should provide an extra cushion from which unexpectedly high claim costs could be paid. Our objective is to identify the main factors that influence the capital decision rather than to provide a numerical answer for the amount of new capital to raise.

Benefits of Increasing Capital

The most important effect of issuing more stock is that the additional capital obtained will decrease the likelihood that claim costs will exceed TLC's assets at the end of the year; in other words, additional capital reduces the likelihood of insolvency. The more money that TLC raises from issuing stock, the more money it will have to pay claim costs

FIGURE 5.2
Probability distribution for TLC's claim costs.

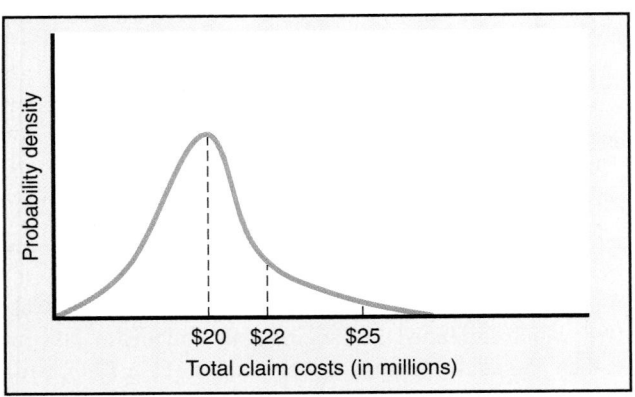

[3]The assumption that the assets are invested in risk-free bonds is used to simplify the analysis.

at year-end (holding all other factors constant). This effect of new capital can be illustrated using Figure 5.2.

Assume that if TLC issues no stock, year-end assets from investing the premiums received (less the underwriting and distribution costs paid) will equal $22 million. Thus, the probability that claim costs will exceed the value of assets (the probability of insolvency) is the area under the probability distribution (see Chapter 3) to the right of $22 million. If TLC raises additional capital, then the assets available at year-end to pay claim costs will increase beyond $22 million, and the probability of insolvency will decrease accordingly. For example, if TLC issues enough additional stock so that the value of assets at year-end is $25 million, the probability of insolvency decreases to the area under the curve to the right of $25 million.

Why would the stockholders of TLC care about decreasing the probability of insolvency? There are two main answers: (1) to achieve higher premium revenues, and (2) to protect against the loss of the insurer's specific assets, known as its franchise value.

Higher Premium Revenue

If policyholders are well-informed about the risk of insolvency, they will be reluctant to purchase insurance from TLC if it does not issue additional stock because the insurer will have a relatively high probability of insolvency.[4] The more stock that TLC issues, the greater the likelihood that policyholders will receive what they are promised. Since informed policyholders generally are willing to pay higher prices for policies from insurers that are more likely to fulfill their promises, TLC can increase its premium revenue by raising additional capital.

You may question the importance of this effect if you have purchased auto insurance without giving any thought to your insurer's probability of insolvency. In fact, your behavior may not be that unusual. One explanation is that insurance solvency regulation helps to ensure that most insurers hold sufficient capital so that some people feel that they do not need to go to the trouble of monitoring insurer solvency. Also, all states in the United States have guaranty funds that pay much (and for many policyholders all) of the claim costs of policyholders should their insurer become insolvent. These guaranty funds can reduce incentives for people to monitor insurer insolvency risk and to pay a higher premium to obtain coverage from an insurer with lower insolvency risk, as we discuss in Chapter 7.

In contrast, business risk managers who buy commercial insurance usually are very concerned about the ability of their insurers to pay claims as promised. The magnitude of potential claim costs for businesses is often much larger than for individuals, and guaranty funds typically provide relatively less protection to businesses against insurer insolvencies. Consequently, risk managers (or their brokers) investigate the probability of insurer insolvency and generally are willing to pay higher prices for insurance from companies that have more capital. Also, independent agents who recommend insurers to individuals and businesses are concerned about the insolvency risk of insurers, in part because independent agents are subject to lawsuits if the recommended insurer fails. We will discuss the insurer

---

[4]An exception to this includes policyholders who are forced to buy compulsory liability insurance, but who have little or no wealth that could be lost from lawsuits by persons they might harm.

solvency ratings routinely used by many business insurance buyers (and independent agents and some personal insurance buyers) in Chapter 7.[5]

In summary, consumers of insurance, especially commercial customers, generally are willing to pay higher premiums to insurers that have a lower probability of insolvency. As a result, insurers are motivated to hold capital. The magnitude by which additional capital will increase premium revenue will likely decline as more and more capital is added (i.e., there are likely to be diminishing returns to additional capital).

Protect the Value of Specific Assets (Franchise Value)

Recall that the stockholders of TLC have already invested $5 million to set up operations. Some of these funds were used for activities such as training employees and obtaining market research, which have zero salvage value—that is, they cannot be sold to someone else. TLC made these investments with the expectation that they would help generate returns (profits) over time. Thus, the return on this investment occurs only if TLC continues to operate. If TLC becomes insolvent, then the future returns on the investment are lost. TLC also invested in physical property like land, buildings, and computer equipment. These assets would have positive salvage value. However, if TLC experiences financial difficulty in paying claims, it may lose some or even most of the value of these assets if it cannot readily find buyers. Finally, over the course of its operations, TLC will make considerable investments to develop a "book of business"—a pool of policyholders likely to renew policies year after year. The value of an insurer's book of business is an important asset that is created by investments in sales forces, marketing, and high quality service. While its book of business could be sold to another insurer if TLC were to experience financial difficulty, part of its value again could be lost.

In summary, TLC (as is true with most insurers) has assets whose entire value cannot be recouped if TLC experiences financial difficulties. That is, TLC has assets whose value is greater to TLC as an ongoing enterprise than if TLC ceases operations. When assets have greater value to one firm than to other firms, the assets are said to be **specific assets.** A major reason for an insurer to hold capital is to protect the value of its specific assets, which commonly is called the insurer's **franchise value.** The key point is that an insurer could lose its franchise value if it were to experience financial distress due to unexpectedly high claim costs or a reduction in the value of its investment portfolio. Holding more capital reduces the likelihood that franchise value will be lost.

Costs of Increasing Capital

Given the benefits of raising additional capital, why doesn't TLC necessarily increase its capital to the point where the probability of insolvency is infinitesimal (or virtually zero)? The reason is that there are also costs of holding more capital. Investors who contribute capital to TLC (buy stock) forgo the opportunity to invest their money in other ventures. Thus, there is an *opportunity cost* associated with investing in TLC. This opportunity cost depends on the differences between an investment in TLC and an alternative investment.

---

[5]Just as consumers of insurance will pay higher premiums to insurers that have a lower likelihood of insolvency, insurer employees and other suppliers may demand lower compensation from insurers that are more likely to remain in business. Thus, reducing the probability of insolvency by holding more capital can reduce the costs of contracting with employees and other suppliers. We discuss this issue as applied to corporate risk management in general in later chapters.

To identify these opportunity costs, it is helpful to compare an investment in TLC with an investment in a mutual fund. When investing in a mutual fund, an individual gives the mutual fund some money and the mutual fund managers invest that money in financial assets such as stocks and bonds. Notice that this is similar to investing in TLC. Someone who buys stock in TLC gives the managers of TLC some money, and the managers invest that money in financial assets. Moreover, an individual could find a mutual fund (or a portfolio of mutual funds) that invests in the same mix of securities as TLC. Thus, the relevant benchmark to assess the opportunity cost of investing in TLC is an investment in a mutual fund with the same portfolio of securities as TLC. What are the differences between an investment in an insurer like TLC and an investment in such a mutual fund?

One difference between a mutual fund investment and an investment in an insurer like TLC is that the mutual fund investor does not face the possibility that part of his or her investment could be used to pay unexpectedly high insurance claims costs. At first, this might seem like a disadvantage to investing in TLC. However, insurance claim costs are a two-edged sword. An investment in TLC also creates the possibility that the return from investing in an insurer will be higher than the return on the mutual fund investment, because insurance claim costs could be lower than expected. It can be shown that an insurer's potential claim costs (liabilities) do not create a net advantage or disadvantage for an investor relative to an investment in a mutual fund if the claim costs are uncorrelated with the rest of the investor's wealth and if there are no greater tax, agency, or issuance costs for investing with insurers.[6] Thus, the opportunity costs of investing in an insurer like TLC arise because of potential correlation between insurer claim costs and investors' other assets and because of potentially greater tax, agency, and issuance costs compared to investing in a mutual fund with the same asset portfolio.

Correlation of Insurer Liabilities with Investors' Other Assets

Suppose that TLC's claim costs tend to be high when the value of investors' other wealth tends to be low (i.e., there is negative correlation between the insurer's liabilities and the value of investors' other assets). This negative correlation implies that TLC's profits will tend to be low when the returns on other assets are low. Thus, investors will tend to receive low returns from investing in TLC when they would want low returns the least—when other assets have performed poorly. Conversely, negative correlation implies that TLC's profits will tend to be high when the returns on other assets are high. But again, investors would be receiving high returns from investing in TLC when they would want them the least—when other assets have performed well. As a result, investors will require additional compensation to invest in TLC because of the correlation of its stock return with their other assets. The additional expected return required by investors if there is a negative correlation between insurer liabilities and the value of investors' other assets is a cost of raising additional capital for insurers.

If, on the other hand, insurer claim costs are positively correlated with the value of investors' other assets (i.e., claim costs tend to be high when the returns on other assets are high and claim costs tend to be low when the returns on other assets are low), then investors

---

[6]An insurer's liabilities (claim costs) create what is called *financial leverage*. For students with a finance background, the irrelevance of financial leverage in the absence of tax, agency, and issuance costs is an application of the famous Modigliani and Miller theorem, which was noted by the Nobel committee when both Franco Modigliani and Merton Miller were awarded their Nobel prizes.

would view an investment in TLC as a partial hedge for the uncertainty associated with the investors' other assets. That is, when other assets have low returns, TLC will tend to have high returns because its claim costs will tend to be low. In this case (positive correlation between claim costs and the value of other assets), investors would require less expected return for investing in TLC than from a mutual fund that held the same asset portfolio as TLC.

In summary, uncertain claim costs increase (decrease) the expected return required by investors in an insurer, compared to an investment in a mutual fund with the same assets, if claim costs are negatively (positively) correlated with the value of investors' other assets. Although studies have been conducted to examine the correlation between insurer claim costs and the value of other assets, the evidence generally is inconclusive regarding the sign and magnitude of the correlation. Thus, subsequent discussions of insurer capital costs usually will focus on the tax, agency, and issuance costs of capital, to which we now turn.

Double Taxation of Investment Returns

The US tax code presents another important difference between investing in TLC and investing in a mutual fund with the same portfolio of stocks and bonds. When an individual invests directly in a mutual fund, the fund managers invest the money in financial assets. The returns on these securities then are distributed to the individual through dividends and capital gains. The investor has to pay tax on the returns, but the mutual fund does not. In contrast, when an individual buys stock in an insurance company, the managers invest the money in financial assets, but the insurer has to pay corporate income tax on the investment returns. When the insurer pays dividends to the stockholders or they sell their stock and realize a capital gain, the stockholders have to pay tax on the investment returns again. Thus, by investing in an insurance company's stock, investment returns are taxed first at the corporate level and then again at the personal level. This double taxation of investment returns imposes a cost on insurer capital.

Because of the double taxation of investment returns, an insurer must earn a higher before-tax rate of return on its capital in order to give investors the same after-tax return they could receive by investing in a mutual fund. This higher before-tax return must be generated from selling insurance policies at a price that exceeds expected claim costs and administrative costs. That is, insurance premiums must be large enough to compensate investors for the double taxation of investment returns on capital.[7]

Agency Costs

When investors buy stock, they give some discretion to managers as to how to use those funds. In essence, stockholders make managers their agents. As discussed in Chapter 2, managers sometimes use the firm's assets to further their own interests as opposed to the interests of the stockholders. The reduction in firm value due to managers not acting in the stockholders' interest is called an **agency cost.** Likewise, any costs incurred in monitoring and motivating managers to act in the stockholders' interest are additional agency costs. If agency costs are greater for an insurance company than for a mutual fund company, then investors will view agency costs as a disadvantage of investing in the insurance company.

---

[7]Note that the focus here is on the double taxation of investment returns on capital. Any taxes on investment returns of assets backing liabilities and any profits from underwriting exclusive of investment returns also will increase insurance prices. However, these taxes do not increase the cost of holding capital as a cushion, and they are reduced substantially by the tax deductibility of claim costs.

Thus, agency costs represent another cost of holding capital in an insurer. With agency costs, the insurer must sell insurance at prices above expected claim costs and administrative costs in order to give investors a return which, net of agency costs, is equal to the return investors can receive by investing in a mutual fund.

Issuance and Underpricing Costs

Insurers also may limit the amount of capital that they raise through equity issues because of equity issuance and underpricing costs. When an insurer issues new stock, it usually employs investment bankers to help sell the new stock. The fees charged by investment bankers are a cost associated with raising additional capital.

In addition, whenever a firm issues new stock, it faces the possibility that the price received for the new shares will be less than the true value of the shares. This problem is worse when investors are not as well informed about the firm's prospects as the firm's managers and when investors know that they are not as well informed. Before purchasing the new stock, these investors will ask themselves: Why do the better-informed managers want to sell additional shares? If the investors decide it is because the stock is worth less than what the managers say it is, then the investors may lower the price that they are willing to pay below the true value of the stock. In other words, the stock may then be underpriced. This underpricing limits the extent to which insurers will raise new capital and leads to greater reliance on retained earnings to accumulate capital.

Summary and Relationship to Business Risk Management

Additional capital reduces the probability of insolvency, which can both increase the price consumers will pay for insurance and protect the insurer's franchise value that could be lost in the event of insolvency. Additional capital, however, is costly. Investors require compensation for (1) any additional risk arising from the negative correlation between insurer liabilities and investors' other assets, (2) the double taxation of investment returns, (3) agency costs, and (4) issuance and underpricing costs.

In later chapters, where we discuss business risk management, many of these arguments will be revisited. In essence, insurer capital decisions are business risk management decisions. Therefore, the factors affecting insurer capital decisions are similar to the factors affecting business risk management in general.

Amount of Capital Held by Insurers

The amount of capital held by insurers varies across companies and across lines of business. Figure 5.3 gives the total industry assets, liabilities, and capital for property–liability insurers compared to life–health insurers for 2000. The numbers reported in Figure 5.3 reflect accounting numbers from financial statements filed with insurance regulators, not economic (market) values. (Accounting values equal market values for common and preferred stock but not for most other investments and liabilities.)

Property–liability insurers had 2000 year-end assets of $931 billion, liabilities of $610 billion, and capital (assets minus liabilities) of $321 billion, producing an aggregate ratio of capital to assets of about 35 percent. The capital-to-asset ratio varies considerably across individual insurers, depending on product mix, assets, and reinsurance (see below). The principal assets of property–liability insurers are described later in this chapter. The principal liabilities are: (1) the *loss reserve,* which equals the liability for claims that have

FIGURE 5.3
Insurer assets, liabilities, and capital in 2000.

Source: Data obtained from *Best's Aggregates and Averages, 2001,* Property–Liability and Life–Health editions.

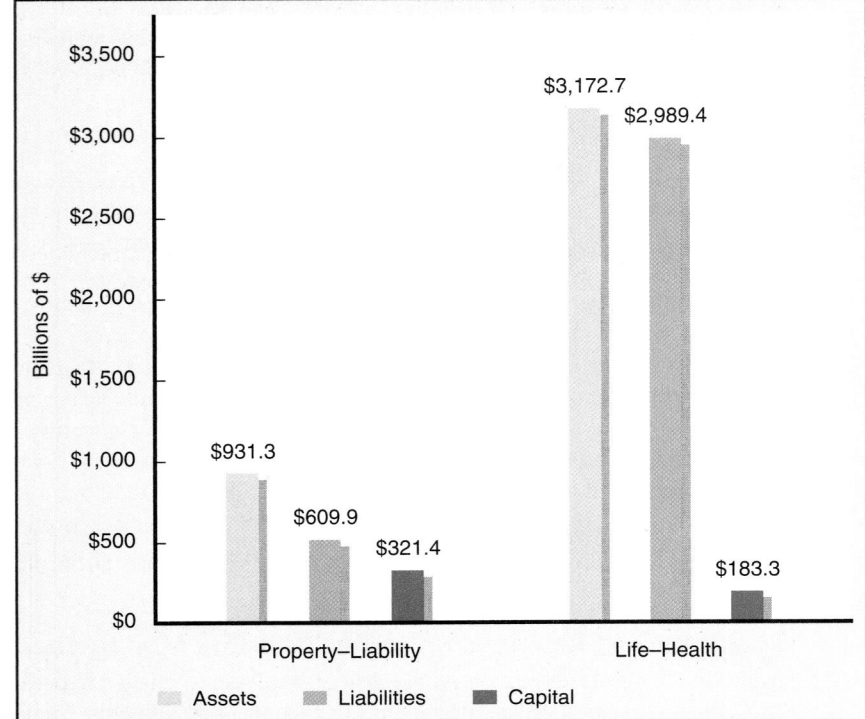

occurred but have not yet been paid, and (2) the *unearned premium reserve,* which equals the liability for premiums that have been paid but not yet earned by insurers because the entire coverage period has not elapsed.

Life–health insurers' assets totaled $3,173 billion at year-end 2000, which is much greater than property–liability insurers. This difference reflects, in part, that many of the products sold by life–health insurers are investment products bundled with insurance products. Life–health insurance liabilities, which primarily reflect insurer obligations for policyholder savings under life insurance and annuity contracts (known as *policy reserves*), were $2,989 billion, resulting in total capital of $183 billion and an aggregate capital-to-as set ratio of 6 percent.[8]

The much lower aggregate capital-to-asset ratio for life-health insurers as compared to property-liability insurers (6 percent versus 35 percent) in part reflects differences in risk for the products that the groups sell. Variability of claim costs generally is lower for life and health insurance than for property–liability insurance, with life insurance generally

[8] The life–health insurance data in Figure 5.3 include "separate account" assets and liabilities associated with some pension and other retirement plans. The risk of separate account asset returns is borne by the retirement plan rather than the insurer. Separate account assets and liabilities equaled $141.6 and $1,138.4 billion, respectively, in 2000. Excluding separate account assets and liabilities, the ratio of capital to assets for life–health insurers was 8.9 percent. Also, the data reported in this chapter for life–health insurers do not include data from Blue Cross/Blue Shield organizations and health maintenance organizations (HMOs).

having the lowest variability in claim costs. In addition, some of the variability in the value of life insurer investment products usually is borne by policyholders. As a result, a smaller cushion (or amount of capital per dollar of assets) is needed to achieve a given probability of insolvency.

Concept Check

2. Which of the following statements is true? Explain.
    (*a*) The US tax code decreases the amount of capital that insurers hold.
    (*b*) If policyholders are uninformed or don't care about insolvency, then owners of insurers do not care about reducing the probability of insolvency.

5.4   Insurer Operations, Reinsurance, and Insolvency Risk

Diversification of Underwriting Risk

You learned in Chapter 4 that the standard deviation of average claim costs in a risk pooling arrangement declines as the number of participants increases, provided that claim costs are not perfectly correlated across participants. The standard deviation also decreases as the correlation between claim costs across participants declines. As a result, insurers generally can reduce **underwriting risk**—the risk that average claim costs will differ from the amount expected when policies are sold—by selling large numbers of policies across different types of insurance coverage in different areas. Lower underwriting risk reduces the amount of capital needed for a given level of insolvency risk.

To elaborate, many insurers routinely reduce underwriting risk by selling policies in different geographic regions. Geographic diversification reduces the correlation in claim costs across policies that arises from factors such as catastrophes and other weather-related claims (as well as from state legislation, court decisions, and regulations that affect claim costs). Insurers also reduce underwriting risk by selling multiple types of policies, for example, by selling a variety of commercial and personal lines coverages, and sometimes both property–liability and life–health insurance. Other things equal, risk reduction through geographic and product line diversification reduces the amount of capital that the insurer must hold in relation to its liabilities to achieve a given level of insolvency risk. A potential disadvantage of diversification is less focus on "core" coverages or geographic regions. Moreover, insurers that specialize more narrowly can often achieve the benefits of diversification indirectly by transferring underwriting risk to other insurers by buying reinsurance.

Reinsurance

Primary Function of Reinsurance

Just as businesses and individuals purchase insurance, insurers also purchase insurance. **Reinsurance** is the purchase of insurance by an insurer. In addition to reducing underwriting risk (and the amount of capital needed to achieve a given level of insolvency risk) by diversifying across geographic areas and lines of business, insurers can reduce underwriting risk by purchasing reinsurance. As a result, the purchase of reinsurance can substitute for capital and allow an insurer to hold less capital without increasing its insolvency probability.

To illustrate this major function of reinsurance, suppose that Southeast Property & Transportation Insurance Company (SEPTIC) has written property insurance on the coast of Florida with expected claim costs equal to $100 million. The probability distribution of claim costs is shown in Figure 5.4. Midwest Insurance Company (MIC) also has written property insurance in the Midwest with expected claim costs equal to $100 million and a probability distribution of claim costs that is identical to SEPTIC's. Since specific events that cause variability in claim costs in the Southeast are different from those in the Midwest, the claim costs of the two insurers are assumed to be independent (which also simplifies the example).

Suppose that the two insurers agree to pay one-half of each other's claim costs; that is, they enter into a pooling arrangement similar to the one formed by Emily and Samantha in Chapter 4. This pooling arrangement will reduce risk (the standard deviation of claim costs for each insurer). As depicted in Figure 5.4, the new distribution of claim costs facing each insurer will become tighter around the expected value of $100 million. The lower standard deviation implies that each insurer reduces its probability of insolvency for a given amount of capital. For example, if each insurer initially had assets equal to $125 million and hence capital equal to $25 million, then the pooling arrangement would change the probability of insolvency from the area under the "without reinsurance" curve in Figure 5.4 to the area under the "with reinsurance" curve.

In this example, reinsurance allows SEPTIC and MIC to diversify without marketing their policies and establishing sales and claims facilities in another geographic area. In addition, reinsurance can allow insurers specializing in particular lines of business to diversify across lines. For example, SEPTIC could enter into a reinsurance arrangement with an environmental liability insurer. In this way, both SEPTIC and the liability insurer could change their books of business from a single line to two lines of insurance.

This discussion illustrates the primary benefit of reinsurance: It allows greater diversification of claim costs, which in turn reduces the probability of insurer insolvency for a given amount of total capital held by all insurers/reinsurers or, equivalently, reduces the total capital needed for a given insolvency probability. Of course, reinsurance also involves costs. The distribution, underwriting, and loss adjustment costs associated with primary insurance also apply to reinsurance contracts. Reinsurers also must hold capital (which is costly) to make their promises to insurers credible (recall our earlier discussion of the costs

FIGURE 5.4
Probability distribution for SEPTIC's and MIC's claim costs with and without reinsurance.

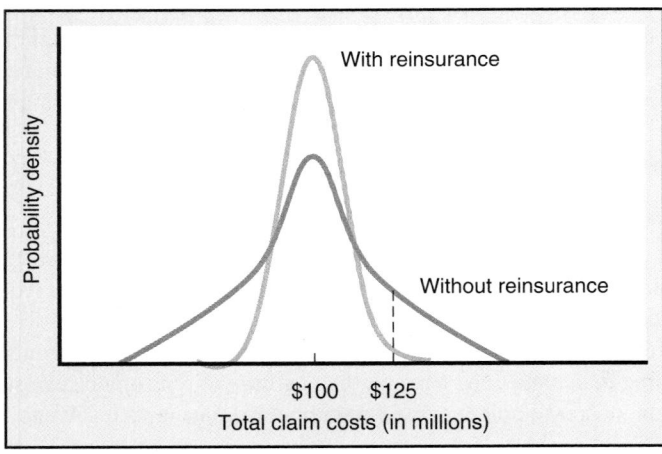

of insurer capital). The key point is that reinsurance reduces the total amount of capital that must be held by all insurers and reinsurers combined in order to achieve a given level of insolvency risk in the industry.

Types of Reinsurance

While reinsurance transactions sometimes take the form of the simple pooling arrangement described between SEPTIC and MIC, most reinsurance transactions are more like typical insurance transactions. The reinsurance contract specifies the conditions under which the reinsurer will pay some of the buyer's claim costs and the amount that the reinsurer will pay. In exchange, the buyer, known as the **ceding insurer** or **primary insurer,** pays the reinsurer a premium.

With respect to the way in which risk is shared, property–liability reinsurance arrangements can be categorized broadly as either *proportional contracts* (also called pro-rata reinsurance) and *nonproportional contracts* (also called excess-of-loss reinsurance). Similar risk-sharing arrangements between ceding insurers and reinsurers are used in life-health insurance. With proportional reinsurance, the ceding company pays a proportion of its premium on a pool of policies to a reinsurer. In exchange, the reinsurer pays the same proportion of the claim costs on those policies. The contract also requires the reinsurer to pay a commission to the ceding insurer as compensation for the ceding insurer's distribution, underwriting, and loss adjustment expenses.[9]

With nonproportional contracts, the reinsurer pays part of the ceding insurer's claims only if a particular threshold (or attachment point) is reached. The attachment point is analogous to a deductible amount in many insurance contracts. While reinsurance contracts can be tailored to the needs of the two insurers, several types of thresholds are common. Often the threshold will be based on the claim costs from a single policy written by the ceding insurer (known as *per risk excess reinsurance*). For example, a property insurer may reinsure claim costs in excess of $25 million arising from a policy that the ceding insurer sold to a large manufacturer covering its plant and equipment (either during a year or from a single event). Another common type of nonproportional contract, known as *catastrophe reinsurance,* specifies that the reinsurer will start paying claim costs on a pool of policies written by the ceding insurer if total claims costs arising from a single event, such as a hurricane, exceed some dollar amount (the attachment point). Other nonproportional reinsurance contracts require the reinsurer to pay claim costs in excess of a specified threshold if total claim costs on a pool of policies exceed the threshold during a specified time period, such as one year.

Reinsurance is also classified by the nature of the transaction. A **reinsurance treaty** covers multiple policies written by the ceding insurer. For example, at the beginning of the year, a workers' compensation insurer may engage in a reinsurance treaty whereby the reinsurer agrees to accept, without the right to refuse, a portion of each policy that the primary insurer wishes to cede during the year. In contrast, with *facultative reinsurance,* the reinsurer evaluates each risk (policy) that the primary insurer would like to cede and decides whether

---

[9] The pooling arrangement described between SEPTIC and MIC could be replicated by two proportional reinsurance contracts. For example, suppose (1) SEPTIC buys proportional reinsurance from MIC that requires MIC to pay 50 percent of the claim costs on the policies SEPTIC has written, and (2) SEPTIC sells proportional reinsurance to MIC that requires SEPTIC to pay 50 percent of the claim costs on the policies MIC has written. If the premiums on the two reinsurance contracts are equal, then the two transactions have the same effect as the pooling arrangement.

to accept it on a case-by-case basis. Both treaty reinsurance and facultative reinsurance can use either pro rata or excess contracts.

The reinsurance market is global in scope. Some organizations that sell reinsurance (known as "professional" reinsurers) specialize exclusively in reinsurance and do not offer primary insurance. Some insurers that sell primary insurance have subsidiaries or divisions that sell reinsurance. The international flavor of the reinsurance market is illustrated by the largest reinsurers in the world listed in Table 5.2. The table does not list Lloyd's of London. However, when considered as a group, the syndicates at Lloyd's represent one of the largest writers of reinsurance.

Many property insurers have traditionally purchased catastrophe reinsurance to reduce the likelihood that a catastrophe, such as a hurricane or earthquake, would cause huge claim costs and thereby threaten the insurer's solvency. In 1996 USAA (a large national insurer) became the first insurer to use an interesting alternative to traditional catastrophe reinsurance, called a **catastrophe bond.** As explained in Box 5.2, catastrophe bonds allow insurers to share catastrophe risk with institutional investors who are not reinsurance companies.

Just as individuals and businesses are concerned about the insolvency risk of the insurance company from which they purchase insurance, primary insurers are concerned about the insolvency risk of the reinsurers from which they purchase reinsurance. If a reinsurer fails to pay the claims under a reinsurance contract, the primary insurer becomes responsible for paying the claims.

Asset Choice and Investment Risk

The asset choices made by insurers also have a major effect on insurer risk and the need to hold capital. In order to maximize insurer value and compete successfully with other insurers, insurer investment decisions need to balance higher expected returns from holding riskier investments against the increased **investment risk** and need for capital. Insurer investment decisions also are strongly influenced by the tax treatment of investment returns.

Figure 5.5 shows the percentage distribution of invested assets at year-end 2000 for both property–liability and life–health insurers (as reported in financial statements filed with regulators).[10] As a group, insurers invest heavily in medium- to long-term fixed income se-

Table 5.2
Five largest reinsurers in terms of 2000 premiums.

Reinsurer	Location	Net Premiums Written ($ millions)
Munich Reinsurance Company	Germany	$14,975
Swiss Re Group	Switzerland	13,790
Berkshire Hathaway/General Cologne Re	US	13,540
Employers Reinsurance Group	US	8,342
Hannover Re Group	Germany	4,896

Source: *Business Insurance,* September 3, 2001.

[10] The life–health data exclude investments in separate accounts because the necessary breakdown by type of investments was not available. Separate account assets are invested much more heavily in common stocks than are insurer "general account" assets. Figure 5.5 also understates the extent to which life–health insurers (and, to a lesser extent, property–liability insurers) invest in assets with returns that depend on mortgages because mortgage and other asset-backed securities (including collateralized mortgage obligations) are included in the corporate and municipal bond categories.

Following 1992's Hurricane Andrew that caused about $16 billion of insured losses and 1994's Northridge earthquake that caused about $13 billion of insured losses, the financial markets developed some interesting and innovative approaches for helping insurers deal with catastrophe risk. Perhaps the most important development was the use of so-called catastrophe bonds.

To illustrate how a catastrophe bond might work, suppose that FLCoast has written a substantial amount of property insurance along the coast of Florida, and as a consequence, FLCoast is concerned about hurricane losses. To reduce this catastrophe risk, suppose that on January 1 FLCoast issues a one-year catastrophe bond with a value of $300 million and a promised annual interest rate of 8 percent. As a result of this transaction, FLCoast receives $300 million at the beginning of the year from a group of institutional investors (e.g., hedge funds), and promises to pay investors $324 million ($300 million of principal plus 8 percent of $300 million in interest) at the end of the year if a major hurricane does not occur. (The meaning of the word *major* would be clearly defined in the contract.) If a major hurricane does occur, then investors agree to receive nothing back at the end of the year, and FLCoast can use the $300 million (plus some interest) to pay hurricane losses. Essentially, FLCoast has shifted some of its hurricane risk to the institutional investors who buy the catastrophe bonds.

Obviously, potential investors will want some assurance that FLCoast will pay what it has promised ($324 million) if a major hurricane does not occur. To provide this assurance, FLCoast can put the money received from investors at the beginning of the year ($300 million) into a trust and invest the money in one-year government bonds, which we assume are paying 5 percent annual interest. However, investing $300 million at a 5 percent interest rate will provide only $315 million at the end of the year, $9 million short of what is promised investors. Therefore, FLCoast will also have to make a payment of $8.57 million to the trust at the beginning of the year so that when this money is invested at 5 percent, it will make up the $9 million shortfall. In essence, the $8.57 million payment by FLCoast is the upfront cost of shifting the risk to the investors who buy the catastrophe bonds.

More than 50 catastrophe bonds were issued during the latter part of the 1990s. Most of the issuers were insurers and reinsurers. However, a few non-insurance companies also issued catastrophe bonds. For example, Walt Disney Company issued a catastrophe bond to help it pay potential earthquake losses on its Tokyo park.

curities, such as US government bonds, municipal bonds, corporate bonds, and mortgages. The average risk of default on the specific securities held is very low. Life–health insurers invest more heavily in corporate bonds and mortgages (largely on commercial properties) than do property–liability insurers, in part due to the long-term nature of many life insurance and annuity products. Property–liability insurers invest more heavily in tax exempt municipal bonds than do life–health insurers, in large part to reduce taxes on investment income associated with their larger amount of capital in relation to assets and liabilities. The comparatively greater investment in common stocks by property–liability insurers also is due in part to taxes (since dividends received by corporate owners of common stock are largely exempt from income tax).

Asset choices by insurers also affect their vulnerability to *interest rate risk* (i.e., changes in the economic or market value of capital due to changes in interest rates). A majority of both property–liability and life–health insurers are exposed to reductions in the value of assets when interest rates increase. The reason is that they invest heavily in long-term fixed income securities that decline in value when interest rates increase. The economic value of insurer liabilities also declines when interest rates increase, because the present value of

FIGURE 5.5
Insurer invested assets in 2000.

Source: Data obtained from *Best's Aggregates and Averages, 2001,* Property–Liability and Life–Health editions.

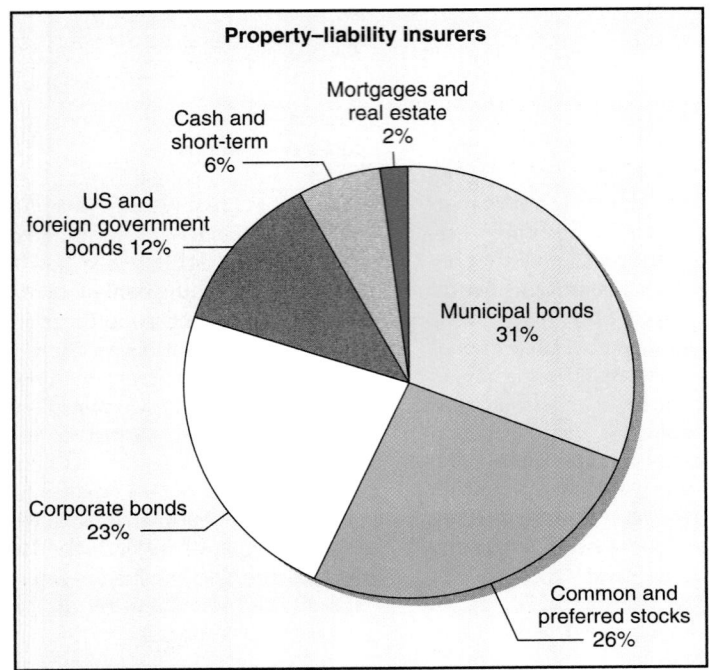

Property–liability insurers

Mortgages and real estate 2%

Cash and short-term 6%

US and foreign government bonds 12%

Municipal bonds 31%

Corporate bonds 23%

Common and preferred stocks 26%

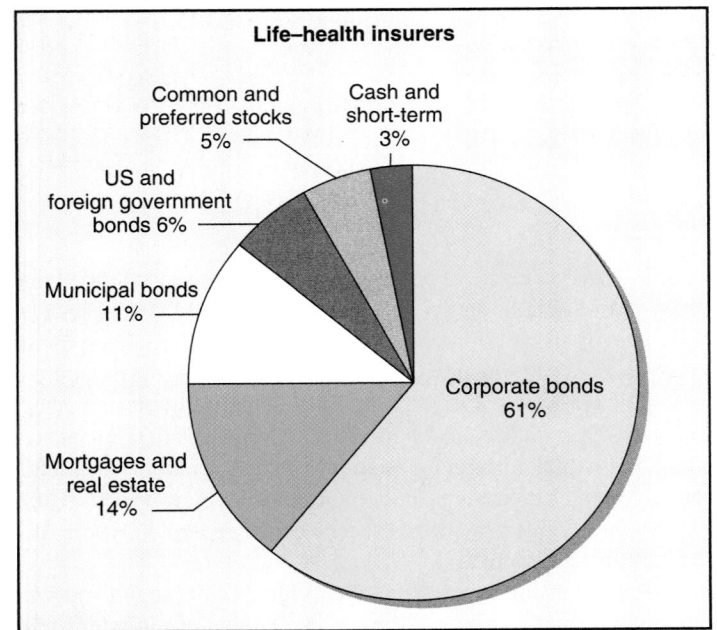

Life–health insurers

Common and preferred stocks 5%

Cash and short-term 3%

US and foreign government bonds 6%

Municipal bonds 11%

Corporate bonds 61%

Mortgages and real estate 14%

cash outflows for contracts sold declines, other factors being held constant. However, the decline in the value of liabilities for a majority of insurers does not completely offset the decline in asset values, so that the value of capital declines when interest rates rise.

Many insurers could reduce their exposure to interest rate risk by investing in shorter-term fixed income securities, which are less sensitive to interest rate changes. This strategy might allow insurers to hold less capital to achieve a given level of insolvency risk. On average, however, it would reduce investment yields because long-term fixed income securities have higher yields on average than short-term investments. Many insurers reduce their interest rate risk by hedging with a variety of financial derivatives that increase in value when interest rates rise. However, insurers often do not fully hedge interest rate risk because hedging involves transaction costs and can reduce expected yields.

5.5 Summary

- Insurance companies are institutions that economize on the contracting costs associated with pooling arrangements, including distribution, underwriting, and loss adjustment expenses.

- Because few insurers have the right to access policyholders for losses during the coverage period (in addition to the premium paid), they must hold capital to serve as a cushion in the event of adverse experience.

- With respect to who owns insurer capital, insurers are commonly organized as either stock insurers, which are owned by stockholders, or as mutual insurers, which are owned by policyholders.

- Benefits that encourage insurers to hold more capital to reduce insolvency risk include the ability to (1) obtain higher premiums from policyholders and (2) better protect against loss of the insurer's franchise value. Costs to insurers of increasing capital include the double taxation of investment returns on capital, agency costs, and issuance and underpricing costs.

- Insurers commonly reduce insolvency risk and/or the amount of capital needed to achieve a given level of insolvency risk by (1) diversifying underwriting risk across geographic regions and different types of coverage, (2) entering into reinsurance contracts that help achieve better diversification of risk among insurers, and (3) investing heavily in fixed income securities with low default risk.

Key Terms

economic capital 75	unlimited liability 79	ceding or primary insurer 91
mutual insurer 76	specific assets 84	reinsurance treaty 91
reciprocal 77	franchise value 84	catastrophe bond 92
stock insurer 77	agency costs 86	investment risk 92
Lloyd's of London 78	underwriting risk 89	
names 78	reinsurance 89	

Questions and Problems

1. What is economic capital for an insurer with assets of $200 million and liabilities of $175 million?

2. Is your (or your family's) automobile insurer a mutual, stock, or reciprocal insurer?

3. How do mutual insurers accumulate capital? How does this differ for stock insurers?

4. Draw a graph of an insurer's probability distribution for total claim costs, assuming that it has expected claim costs of $500 million. Identify the probability of insolvency if the insurer has assets equal to $750 million.

5. Explain the principal ways in which insurance companies can reduce risk through diversification.

6. Identify on your graph how the probability of insolvency for the insurer described in question 4 changes if:
   a. The insurer raises $100 million of new capital.
   b. The insurer cedes a proportion of its liabilities to a reinsurer and simultaneously reinsures a similar amount of business from another insurer with a similar, but uncorrelated book of business.

7. Describe the major investments held by property–liability insurers and life–health insurers.

Answers to Concept Checks

1. Insurer capital is referred to as a cushion because it is the amount of funds available to pay unexpected claim costs. If economic capital equals $50 million, then the insurer can withstand $50 million of unexpected claim costs without becoming insolvent.

2. a. This is true, because the US tax code creates a disincentive to hold capital.
   b. This is false, because owners still will want to protect the firm's franchise value.

References

Brockett, Patrick; Robert Witt; and Paul Aird. "An Overview of Reinsurance and the Reinsurance Markets." *Journal of Insurance Regulation* 9, no. 3 (March 1991), pp. 432–54. (*Provides additional discussion of reinsurance.*)

Hansmann, Henry. "The Organization of Insurance Companies: Mutual versus Stock." *Journal of Law, Economics, and Organization* 1 (1985), pp. 125–53. (*Discusses the evolution and functions of mutual insurers compared to stock insurers.*)

Chapter 6

Insurance Regulation

Chapter Objectives

- Briefly describe state insurance regulation and summarize major activities that are regulated.
- Explain the historical evolution of state regulation and arguments for and against state regulation compared with federal regulation.
- Discuss the normative view that regulation should serve the public interest by mitigating market imperfections and illustrate the application of this view to the problem of costly and imperfect information concerning the quality of insurance coverage.
- Discuss how political pressure may cause the practice of regulation to deviate from the public interest view.

6.1   Scope and Operation of State Insurance Regulation

The insurance business is heavily regulated in the United States and most other developed countries. In significant part this regulation reflects the goal of promoting safety and soundness, given that unregulated market incentives and conditions might not produce an efficient level of solvency risk.

Each state has a **state insurance department** (or commission) that implements state legislation governing the purchase and sale of insurance that is set forth in the state's *state insurance code*. In addition to mandates specified in the state insurance code, the insurance department has the authority to establish rules and procedures in order to implement legislative directives. The head of the state insurance department usually is called the **state insurance commissioner.** In most states the governors appoint the insurance commissioners but in about one-quarter of the states the voters elect the commissioners.

Regulated Activities

When viewed broadly, insurance regulation includes the state insurance code, its implementation by the state insurance department, and other legislation related to insurance (such as compulsory insurance requirements) governing the purchase, sale, or enforcement of insurance contracts. In addition to regulation, the courts have a significant effect on contractual relations between insurers and policyholders through the interpretation and enforcement of contract provisions. The major activities that are regulated are discussed briefly below and summarized in Table 6.1. This table also shows the chapter, if any, in which additional discussion is provided for a particular form of regulation.

• Licensing of insurers and agents/brokers: State insurance departments grant and renew licenses to conduct business in the state to insurers, agents, and brokers, and they have the power to revoke licenses. Regulation also stipulates conditions under which unlicensed insurers may conduct business through the nonadmitted market.

• Solvency: State solvency regulation includes solvency monitoring by state insurance departments, risk-based capital requirements, financial reporting requirements, direct controls on behavior (e.g., investment regulations), and the establishment of guaranty funds to pay claims against insolvent insurers.

• Rates: Many states require insurers to obtain prior regulatory approval of rate changes and rate differentials for different consumers from the state insurance department for certain types of voluntary market coverage. Rate regulation is most prevalent for workers' compensation insurance, automobile insurance, homeowners insurance, and individual health insurance.

• Residual markets: State law requires insurers to supply certain types of coverage through a residual market mechanism, such as an assigned risk plan, at a regulated rate to applicants who have difficulty obtaining coverage voluntarily. Residual markets are most prevalent for workers' compensation insurance, automobile insurance, urban and coastal property insurance, and individual health insurance.

• Content of policy forms: All state insurance departments regulate most contract language, except for large commercial policyholders (in about half the states), by requiring certain contract provisions and prohibiting other provisions, including regulation of insurance policy language that restricts the ability of insurers to cancel policies within the coverage period or to deny renewal at the end of a coverage period. Prior regulatory approval of policy forms usually is required.

• Contract interpretation and enforcement: State insurance departments enforce legislation dealing with market conduct and unfair trade practices, such as provisions related to unfair claim settlement practices. Insurance contract provisions also are interpreted and enforced by the courts through resolution of litigation between insurers and customers.

• Insurer sales practices and information disclosure: State insurance departments regulate potentially deceptive sales practices by insurers and agents through enforcement of market conduct and unfair trade practices legislation. Allegations of deceptive or misleading sales practices also are subject to litigation and resolution by the courts. Most states require the disclosure of specified price information in the sale of life insurance. Some states produce summary information on personal insurance rates charged by different insurers and/or the frequency of consumer complaints against different insurers. This information usually is available on insurance department websites or is provided to consumers on request.

TABLE 6.1 Overview of regulated activities.

Activity	Description	Principal Types of Coverage and Prevalence across States
Licensing of insurers and agents/brokers	Granting, renewal, and revocation of license to conduct business by state insurance departments (see Chapter 21)	All types of coverage and states
Insurer solvency	Solvency monitoring by state insurance departments, capital and financial reporting requirements, investment regulations, and guaranty funds (see Chapter 7)	All types of coverage and states
Rates	Prior approval of rate changes and regulation of rate differentials across consumers by state insurance departments for the voluntary market (see Chapters 8, 13, and 17)	• Workers compensation rates in about 2/3 of the states • Personal auto, homeowners, and other business property-liability insurance rates in about half of the states • Individual health insurance in some states • Credit life and health insurance in some states
Residual markets	Industry must supply coverage through residual market at a regulated rate to applicants who have difficulty obtaining it voluntarily, such as through an assigned risk plan or joint underwriting association (see Chapters 8, 13, 14, and 17)	• Personal automobile in all states • Workers' compensation in all states • Urban and coastal property insurance in some states • Individual health insurance in some states
Content of policy forms	Regulation of contract language (including provisions governing cancellation and nonrenewal, see Chapter 13) and approval of forms by state insurance departments	Most types of coverage in all states, except for large commercial policyholders in about half the states
Contract interpretation and enforcement	State insurance department enforcement of legislation dealing with market conduct/unfair trade practices (see Chapter 10)	Most types of coverage in all states
Insurer sales practices and information disclosure	Regulation of sales practices through state insurance department enforcement of market conduct/unfair trade practices legislation; required disclosure of price information; production and dissemination of information about prices and quality by regulators	Mainly for personal insurance in most states
Compulsory purchase of coverage	Compulsory insurance laws and their enforcement by the states (see Chapters 13 and 17)	• Personal auto liability in almost all states • Automobile personal injury protection coverage in most no-fault states • Workers' compensation insurance • Some types of professional liability insurance (e.g., medical malpractice insurance) and environmental liability insurance in most states

• Compulsory purchase of coverage: State law generally mandates the purchase of certain types of coverage (e.g., auto liability and workers' compensation insurance). A variety of methods and state agencies are used to enforce these laws.

National Association of Insurance Commissioners

Insurance regulation is complex because of the scope of activities that are regulated and differences in regulation across states. However, a number of major activities are regulated in most or all states using the same broad type of regulation, such as solvency regulation and regulation of policy forms. These similarities are not surprising given that the problems that give rise to these regulations (see below) exist in all states.

Additional uniformity, cooperation, and coordination of state insurance regulation are achieved by the activities of the **National Association of Insurance Commissioners (NAIC).** The NAIC is a voluntary organization of all state insurance commissioners that holds regular meetings to discuss insurance regulatory issues and develop **model laws.** These model laws, or laws that are very similar to the model, often are adopted by many states. In addition to state insurance commissioners and insurance department staff, NAIC meetings are widely attended by representatives of the insurance industry and consumer groups. Industry and consumer group representatives provide input to the NAIC committees that develop model laws.[1]

An important example of efforts to coordinate state regulation exists in the area of solvency regulation (see Chapter 7). Some coordination of state solvency regulation has been achieved by having the state insurance department in which the insurer is domiciled (chartered) play a leading role in certain aspects of solvency oversight, such as conducting and preparing reports based on on-site financial examinations. The NAIC plays a major role in promoting uniform financial reporting and risk-based capital requirements across states. In addition, the NAIC oversees the coordination of financial examinations of insurance companies by state regulators.

Changes in solvency regulation in the early 1990s in response to earlier increases in the frequency and severity of insurance company insolvencies provide an important illustration of the coordination and cooperation of state regulators through the NAIC. Risk-based capital requirements (see Chapter 7), for example, were developed by the NAIC. In addition, the NAIC established a solvency regulation accreditation program in 1991 that specifies minimum standards for state solvency regulation. States that adopt specified model laws related to solvency regulation and meet minimum standards for solvency monitoring are accredited by the NAIC. States that are not accredited face some risk of increased monitoring or regulation of their home (i.e., domestic) insurers by other states' insurance departments and of being known for weak regulation. Most states have been accredited; many states adopted or amended their laws and procedures to qualify for accreditation.

6.2   History and Efficacy of State Regulation

This section deals with two related issues: (1) how state regulation came about, and (2) the pros and cons of state regulation versus federal regulation. The description of how state regulation came about provides insight into rate regulation, the activities of insurance advisory

---

[1]The NAIC has a central office in Kansas City, Missouri.

organizations, and the insurance industry's limited exemption from federal antitrust law.[2] While we have our own opinions, we make no attempt to resolve the debate about state versus federal regulation. Instead, we have the more modest objective of summarizing the main arguments that favor state regulation and those that favor the replacement of much or even most state regulation with federal regulation.

History of State Regulation

State regulation of insurance companies and agents began to develop in the early part of the nineteenth century. The primary sources of regulation were restrictions and limitations concerning insurer operations contained in state charters issued to insurers and allowing them to conduct business. Domestic insurers were required to file annual reports as early as 1818, beginning in Massachusetts. The first state insurance department (commission) was established in New Hampshire in 1851, and other states soon followed.

Bills that would have created a federal agency to regulate insurance were introduced in the US Congress in 1866 and 1868, but they were not enacted. The Commerce Clause of the United States Constitution gives the federal government explicit authority to regulate *interstate commerce*. In addition, Article 10 of the Constitution states that powers not expressly given to the federal government are reserved for the states. In the twentieth century the US Supreme Court has interpreted Article 10 and other provisions to allow federal legislation and regulation to go beyond specific powers stated in the Constitution. However, this broad interpretation of federal powers was not the case during the formative years of insurance regulation. Thus, to the extent that the insurance business was considered to be "local" in nature (i.e., conducted within a state) rather than interstate commerce, it could be argued that the Constitution permitted state regulation and prohibited federal regulation.

Paul v. Virginia

The question of whether states had the power to regulate insurance was addressed in 1868 by the United States Supreme Court in the celebrated case of *Paul v. Virginia*. Mr. Paul was an agent for a group of New York fire insurers. Virginia law required out-of-state insurers and their agents to be licensed by the state. Mr. Paul refused to pay the security deposit that was required to obtain a license, kept selling policies, and subsequently was arrested, fined, and hanged (just kidding). Actually, he was fined $50, which was a lot of money back then. Mr. Paul and the New York insurers challenged the conviction, arguing in part that the sale of insurance across borders was interstate commerce and thus that the Virginia law was unconstitutional because it interfered with interstate commerce. The US Supreme Court reached an interesting conclusion concerning this issue. It held that insurance was not commerce and therefore was not subject to laws affecting interstate commerce. Since insurance was not commerce, Virginia's law was not unconstitutional (see Box 6.1). Thus, *Paul v. Virginia* implied that states had the power to regulate insurance and that the federal government did not. This decision was upheld for approximately 75 years in many other cases that argued that insurance constituted interstate commerce.

[2]Much of our discussion of state regulation's history is based on Robert I. Mehr and Emerson Cammack, *Principles of Insurance,* 6th ed. (Homewood, IL: Richard D. Irwin, 1976), chapter 28, "Regulation of the Insurance Business: Objectives, Methods, and History."

In *Paul v. Virginia*, 75 US 168 (1868), the United States Supreme Court concluded that insurance was not commerce in the sense used by the Constitution and thus that the interstate commerce clause could not be used to prohibit state laws regulating insurance. The Court's reasoning is reproduced in part below:

> Issuing a policy of insurance is not a transaction of commerce. The contracts are simple contracts of indemnity against loss by fire, entered into between the corporations and the insured, for a consideration paid by the latter. These contracts are not articles of commerce in any proper meaning of the word. They are not subjects of trade or barter offered in the market as something having an existence and value independent of the parties to them. They are not commodities to be shipped or forwarded from one state to another and then put up for sale. They are like other personal contracts between parties, which are completed by their signature and the transfer of consideration. Such transactions are not interstate transactions, though the parties may be domiciled in different states. The policies do not take effect—are not executed contracts—until delivered by the agent in Virginia. They are, then, local transactions, and are governed by local law. They do not constitute a part of the commerce between States any more than a contract for the purchase and sale of goods in Virginia by a citizen of New York whilst in Virginia would constitute a portion of such commerce.

This ruling was overturned in *United States v. Southeastern Underwriters Association et al.,* 51 F. Supp. 712 (1943). The majority opinion stated:

> Our basic responsibility in interpreting the Commerce Clause is to make certain that the power to govern intercourse among the states remains where the Constitution placed it . . . No commercial enterprise of any kind which conducts its activities across state lines has been held to be wholly beyond the regulatory power of the Congress under the Commerce Clause. We cannot make an exception for the business of insurance.

The court went on to say, however, that the opinion only affected state regulation that was inconsistent with federal law. The power of the states to regulate insurance was not overturned by this decision.

Southeastern Underwriters Association Case

During the 1870s, numerous insurance companies became insolvent as a result of major fires in Boston and Chicago. These events helped spur the development of *insurance rating bureaus,* precursor organizations to modern insurance *advisory organizations* (such as the Insurance Services Office). The rating bureaus set property insurance rates that would be charged by most companies, in principle to ensure adequate prices and therefore reduce insolvency risk. Many states either permitted or encouraged the development of rating bureaus, and some states began to regulate their activities. Regulators in a few states determined the rates that had to be charged by all insurance companies.

In response to a request from the Missouri attorney general in 1942, the antitrust division of the US Department of Justice began an investigation into the activities of a large rating bureau known as the Southeastern Underwriters Association. This association was subsequently indicted by the US attorney general for alleged violations of the federal Sherman Antitrust Act (which prohibits price fixing and related noncompetitive activities). The charges included restraining and monopolizing commerce, fixing prices and agents' commissions, attempting to force buyers to buy from member insurers, denying nonmember insurers access to reinsurance from member insurers, and refusing to do business with agents who represented nonmember insurers.

The Southeastern Underwriters Association suggested that many of these practices were beneficial given the nature of insurance. But its defense against this legal action was that the Sherman Antitrust Act did not apply to insurance because insurance was not commerce according to *Paul v. Virginia*. A federal district court upheld this view and dismissed the case. The US attorney general appealed to the Supreme Court.

The Supreme Court did not decide on the merit of the charges, but in the **Southeastern Underwriters Association decision** in 1943 it overturned *Paul v. Virginia* (by a four to three vote with two justices not voting). The court basically ruled that insurance is commerce, that it is interstate commerce when it takes place across state lines, that Congress therefore could regulate insurance, and that the Sherman Antitrust Act applied to insurance (see Box 6.1). The decision did not prohibit state regulation, but it held that state laws that were contrary to federal law were invalid. Nonetheless, the decision led to considerable uncertainty about the allowable scope of state regulation and the taxation of insurers. It also created considerable uncertainty about the legality of industry operating procedures, especially the use of rating bureaus.

The McCarran-Ferguson Act

Given the uncertainty created by the Southeastern Underwriters Association decision, representatives of both the insurance industry and state insurance regulation sought legislation to clarify regulatory and taxation issues related to insurance. In response, the Congress enacted the **McCarran-Ferguson Act** in 1945.[3] This law states (1) that the continued regulation and taxation of insurance by the states is in the public interest, and (2) that the insurance business is exempt from federal antitrust law, provided that the relevant activities are subject to state regulation and do not involve "any agreement to boycott, coerce, or intimidate, or act of boycott, coercion, or intimidation." The implications of this legislation were clear. First, states would continue to have primary authority for insurance regulation, although the federal government could enact legislation regulating insurance if state regulation were found to be deficient. Second, many of the activities of rating bureaus would not be subject to federal antitrust law provided that they were regulated by the states and did not involve boycott, coercion, or intimidation.

Following the enactment of the McCarran-Ferguson Act, many states revised their regulatory systems to provide greater oversight of rating bureau activities. The most common approach was to make property-liability insurance rates developed by rating bureaus subject to regulatory prior approval. The laws generally either required or strongly encouraged all insurers to use bureau rates. Beginning in the late 1950s, most states began to permit or make it easier for insurers to charge rates that differed from bureau rates, and the large direct writers generally obtained approval to charge lower rates. Beginning in the mid-1960s, a significant number of states ultimately eliminated prior approval regulation, replacing their prior approval laws with competitive rating laws. During 1998 through 2001, about 20 states eliminated rate regulation for large commercial policyholders. As discussed more in

[3]This act is named after the two principal senators who sponsored the legislation. After attending a number of staff and insurance industry meetings where the McCarran-Ferguson Act was mentioned, a newly appointed insurance commissioner (in a state that will remain anonymous) is reported to have asked one of his staff, "Who is this Karen Ferguson, anyway?"

later chapters, insurance advisory organizations now commonly file prospective loss costs with state regulators (as opposed to final rates) that can be used by insurers in their own rate filings. State oversight of these activities has been sufficient to keep them from being subject to federal antitrust law.

Challenges to McCarran-Ferguson

During the mid-1980s and early 1990s, significant support for modifying or eliminating the McCarran-Ferguson Act arose in conjunction with rapid increases in property-liability insurance rates. Although that pressure for significant change waned, some observers argue that the insurance industry's limited exemption from antitrust law facilitates collusion among insurers to increase prices. There are two main counterarguments. First, unless prevented by price regulation, property-liability insurance markets are characterized by substantial heterogeneity in prices and underwriting standards. This heterogeneity is inconsistent with price fixing. Second, advisory organizations in principle can help promote healthy competition and thereby benefit consumers by providing insurers with valuable, low-cost information concerning projected loss costs. Specifically, the availability of loss forecasts based on aggregate industry data at low cost, when combined with an insurer's own data analysis, helps insurers obtain more accurate forecasts, thus reducing insurer risk and the need for capital. It also reduces the cost of rate-making and entry into a particular market or line of business.

A second challenge to state regulation and to the endorsement of state regulation contained in the McCarran-Ferguson Act occurred in the early 1990s in response to increases in the frequency and severity of insurance company insolvencies. Legislation was introduced in the Congress that would have allowed insurers to choose federal solvency regulation instead of state solvency regulation. This bill would have created a new federal agency with broad powers to regulate insurer activities that could affect solvency. Support for this proposal declined in conjunction with improved insolvency experience and changes in state solvency regulation following the early 1990s, such as the development of risk-based capital requirements and the NAIC's solvency regulation accreditation program. However, legislation that would allow optional federal chartering and regulation of insurers was proposed again in 2002, in conjunction with pressure by some insurers that hoped to escape the shackles of state regulation of rates and policy forms.

As a practical matter, the US Congress can put substantial pressure on state regulators to change regulatory practices by threatening to adopt some form of federal regulation. While it is sometimes difficult to determine the extent to which changes in state regulation are undertaken to deter federal regulation, many observers believe that state regulators are influenced materially by the threat of federal intervention.

Concept Check

1. What is the economic rationale for allowing the activities of rating bureaus (advisory organizations) to have a limited exemption from federal antitrust law? In what ways is the exemption limited?

State versus Federal Regulation

The preceding discussion illustrates the long debate over whether the primary responsibility for insurance regulation should lie with the states or the federal government. This debate is one example of the general debate in political philosophy and economics over the advantages and disadvantages of centralization of government power versus decentralization. As a result, people that favor decentralization of power tend to view state regulation more kindly than do those who favor greater centralization of power in Washington.

Economists generally focus on the comparative efficiency of state versus federal regulation, but uncertainty about the magnitude of the costs and benefits associated with each system leads to diversity of opinion. The subject can become quite complicated given that the arguments for and against either type of regulation can vary across specific types of regulation (e.g., solvency regulation versus price regulation). The optimal system of regulation in theory also might involve some combination of state and federal regulation. As a practical matter, the enactment of any significant form of federal insurance regulation probably would leave some material role for state regulation. Thus, some form of *dual regulation* would be likely as opposed to the complete replacement of state regulation by federal regulation. We do not attempt to resolve the debate concerning state versus federal regulation. Instead, we simply summarize the most common arguments.

Arguments in favor of optional federal regulation or of replacing a large part of or most state regulation with federal regulation can be summarized as follows:

• The lack of uniformity in state regulation across states increases costs to insurers (and therefore to consumers) of complying with regulation, and it is confusing and undesirable to consumers in view of the large mobility of the population.

• Federal regulation could achieve possible economies of scale and avoid costly duplication of regulatory activities.

• Cost savings from efficiencies in federal regulation would free up funds to improve regulation, for example, for attracting a greater number of talented people (or people with greater talent) to careers in insurance regulation.

• The quality of state regulation varies significantly across states and is inadequate in some states.

• Weak regulation in a given state can adversely affect people and insurers in other states. For example, inadequate solvency monitoring by regulators in an insurer's state of domicile might harm the insurer's policyholders in other states.

• State regulators may have an incentive to "free-ride" on the regulatory efforts of other states, which might reduce the average quality of regulation.

• Optional federal regulation would allow insurers relief from outmoded rate and policy form regulation that exists in many states.

• Optional federal regulation would create healthy competition between state and federal regulation.

Arguments in favor of state regulation include:

• State regulation is tailored to reflect local needs, which vary across states in relation to state law, average income, and other characteristics of a state's population.

• State regulation facilitates regional experimentation to determine what works and what fails, and the consequences of regulatory mistakes are localized.

• The NAIC reduces costly duplication, encourages desirable uniformity, and reduces free-rider problems.

• Significant federal regulation probably will duplicate some state regulation.

• The state system is known, whereas federal regulation would involve substantial start-up costs and uncertainty. ("The devil you know is better than the one that you don't know.")

• Federal regulators could face substantial pressure to adopt economically inefficient rate regulation, as has occurred in some states (see Chapter 8).

• The track record of federal regulation of depository institutions does not inspire confidence. Federal regulation did not prevent and probably aggravated massive insolvency problems in the savings and loan industry due to congressional pressure for regulatory forbearance (i.e., for allowing weak or insolvent institutions to continue operating).

Until recently, the insurance industry traditionally has favored state regulation. Smaller insurers have been especially supportive, perhaps because they often have to deal with fewer state insurance departments. They also might fear that federal regulation would be accompanied by repeal of the industry's limited antitrust exemption, which in turn might have a greater adverse effect on small insurers if the activities of rating bureaus are curtailed. However, state rate regulation, which has constrained rate increases in the presence of rising claim costs and produced large residual markets in some states in recent years, has reduced insurer support for state regulation. As noted previously, it has caused some insurers to explore whether some form of federal regulation might allow them a partial or complete exemption from price regulation.

6.3   Objectives of Regulation: The Public Interest View

Serving the Public Interest by Mitigating Market Imperfections

The classical, normative (i.e., how it *should* work) view of economic regulation is that its objective should be to mitigate the impact of significant market imperfections (or market "failures") compared to the ideal of a perfectly competitive market. According to this view, which is commonly known as the **public interest view of regulation,** the decision to regulate is based on whether characteristics of the market differ significantly from those of a competitive market characterized by: (1) large numbers of sellers with relatively low market shares and low cost entry by new firms; (2) low cost information to firms concerning the cost of production and to consumers concerning prices and quality; and (3) an absence of spillovers (i.e., all costs are internalized to sellers or buyers).[4]

Desirable conduct and performance will characterize markets with these structural characteristics. Markets that significantly deviate from these characteristics and also exhibit conduct and performance that differ significantly from a competitive market are candidates for regulation to mitigate these imperfections and move the market's structure, conduct, and performance toward the competitive ideal. A well-known example, which most business students learn about at some point in their studies, is that firms may be able to exercise market power and raise prices above marginal costs if the market has only a few firms and large entry barriers. If so, the consequences include reduced output, excess profits, and an over-

---

[4]The public interest view of regulation also is sometimes called the *consumer protection view*. This description is potentially misleading. Some "consumer protection" groups argue for regulation that goes well beyond mitigation of market failure.

all reduction in welfare. As a result, markets with these characteristics may be candidates for antitrust enforcement, to increase the number and limit the size of firms, or for rate of return regulation (e.g., in the case of a so-called natural monopoly).[5]

According to the public interest view, the costs and limitations of regulation should be considered when deciding when and how to regulate. Regulatory tools are necessarily imperfect. Regulation always involves costs, and it entails the risk of unintended consequences. These problems suggest a two-pronged test before regulating a given market. First, there should be demonstrable market imperfections that lead to a significant deviation between market performance and the competitive market ideal. Second, there should be substantial evidence that the benefits from using the regulatory tool being contemplated will exceed the costs of regulation. Otherwise, regulation that is intended to mitigate market failure will make matters worse rather than better (i.e., the cure will be worse than the disease).[6]

The view that regulation should be used cautiously, while perhaps the most widely held view among informed, objective, and dispassionate observers (like us), is not held by everyone. Opinions vary substantially concerning how well particular markets perform and whether regulation is likely to be effective in any given case. At one extreme (even ignoring socialists), some people believe that very few markets work well without regulation, and they are confident in the ability of government experts to improve on market outcomes. At the other extreme, some people think that almost all markets work reasonably well in conjunction with contract enforcement by the courts, and they doubt that regulation will improve markets that do not.

An Example of the Public Interest View: Dealing with Costly and Imperfect Information

Although it does not imply that insurance regulation by and large minimizes the cost of risk in practice (see below), many of the regulatory tools summarized in Table 6.1 are related to imperfections in insurance markets. In particular, insurance markets often are characterized by imperfect and costly information. Consumers are not fully informed about product quality and becoming better informed is costly. Much insurance regulation is related to these information problems, including, for example, licensing of insurers and agents, solvency regulation, regulation of contract language, regulation of deceptive sales and unfair claims practices, and information disclosure rules.[7]

---

[5]As one example of using antitrust policy, United Airlines and US Airways dropped their plans for merger after the antitrust division of the US Department of Justice fought the merger. Critics of antitrust enforcement often argue that it sometimes prevents economically efficient mergers that would benefit both producers and consumers. Electric utilities have traditionally been subject to rate regulation that is designed to limit their rates of return to fair levels.

[6]In general, insurance regulation that focuses on cost-effective mitigation of insurance market imperfections can help reduce the cost of risk. Thus, the public interest view of insurance regulation might be restated as: *Regulation should be designed and implemented to minimize the total cost of risk.* At an abstract level, achieving this goal requires that the benefits from regulation (moving market conduct/performance closer to the competitive ideal) be weighed against the costs of regulation.

[7]Residual market mechanisms might be justified based on the rationale that adverse selection might prevent viable markets for some customers. As we discuss in Chapter 13, compulsory insurance laws may reduce spillovers that arise when persons with few assets at risk drive without insurance.

The court system can address some problems related to imperfect information, such as litigation that alleges misrepresentation by an insurer in its sales practices or improper refusals to settle claims. However, reliance on the courts to settle disputes ex post often will not be an effective or efficient means of mitigating information-based problems, so that regulation may be desirable. If, for example, costly and imperfect information causes people to inadvertently buy coverage from a financially weak insurer that later fails, litigation following insolvency will be unable to compensate policyholders for their losses because the defendant will be insolvent. Moreover, the threat of such litigation obviously will not deter excessively risky behavior by insurers prior to failure. Costly and imperfect information also may lead to comparatively small harms to many people that might be more efficiently addressed by regulation than litigation.

Why Some Unregulated Markets May Not Provide Adequate Information

Obtaining information about the quality of insurance is costly to consumers (it requires time and effort). Information that is available to consumers usually will be imperfect, which increases the risk that some consumers will inadvertently buy coverage from a company with lower quality than the consumer is willing to pay for. Incentives for insurers or other parties to provide useful information are reduced by the cost of producing the information and several additional factors, including:

• In an unregulated environment with imperfect information, it may be difficult or impossible for high-quality insurers to develop accurate measures to demonstrate their quality that can be readily understood by most consumers.

• If high-quality insurers advertise their quality, in some cases it might reduce overall consumer confidence in the industry by highlighting that quality might be low for other companies.

• Low-quality insurers might be able to provide false or misleading information and thus fool some unsophisticated consumers and perhaps some sophisticated consumers, at least for a time.

• Incentives for outside parties, such as the A. M. Best Company (see Chapter 7), to invest in the development and marketing of information about insurer quality are reduced (1) by the cost and difficulty of obtaining useful and accurate measures of quality, and (2) because the information produced might be obtained by many buyers without their paying for it.

Insurers might be able to cooperate to provide information about quality. For example, insurers with prompt and fair claim settlement, or with very low insolvency risk, might form an association that establishes minimum standards for membership and then advertises membership to the public. One limitation of this approach, in addition to the direct costs of forming the association and monitoring compliance, is that an insurer's proprietary information might have to be revealed to competitors. In addition, insurers who are denied membership might argue that the standards are too high and that the organization represents a noncompetitive restraint of trade that might involve "boycott, threat, or intimidation" and thus not be exempt from antitrust law.

The Potential Role for Regulation

As a result of the limitations of private actions to reduce information problems, some degree of regulation to mitigate information problems may improve market performance and reduce the cost of risk. Moreover, most insurers will likely support some degree of regulation to prevent harm to the reputation of the entire industry. For example, many if not most insurers have an incentive to support solvency regulation and regulatory monitoring and oversight of unfair trade practices. Most insurers also have an incentive to support regulation of contract language to prevent industrywide reputation damage that would be likely if some insurers sold excessively restrictive coverage to unwitting consumers. While some standardization of contract language can be achieved from voluntary arrangements among insurers, regulation can facilitate this process by making it more costly or illegal for insurers to deviate from suitable contract terms. As suggested above, voluntary arrangements also might be challenged as noncompetitive agreements that harm firms that do not comply.

This discussion also suggests, however, that regulation can create a type of moral hazard problem. If people are protected by regulation, they may expend less effort in locating a high-quality insurer (e.g., guaranty funds reduce the incentive to purchase coverage from a financially strong insurer; see Chapter 7). In addition, insurers, agents, and other parties have less incentive to provide consumers with information about quality. If regulation does not effectively replace or substitute for these reduced incentives, it might increase the number of people that buy products from insurers that they would have avoided with less regulation, thus reducing the advantages (increasing the costs) of regulation.

Information Disclosure and Minimum Standards

Assuming that information problems are severe enough to justify government action, there are two broad approaches to regulation: (1) information disclosure, and (2) establishing minimum standards and monitoring compliance with these standards. These approaches are not mutually exclusive.

Information disclosure, either in the form of mandatory disclosure of information by insurers or regulatory dissemination of information, has the appeal of going to the heart of the problem. The idea is this: If imperfect and costly information creates significant problems, then let's provide consumers with better information and let the market work! Unfortunately, as we suggested above, it is often difficult or impossible to develop accurate and easily understood measures of quality that will not be misleading or subject to misuse by many consumers (or insurers). If regulators disseminate insolvency risk ratings, for example, two types of mistakes will be common. Some insurers will be rated too high compared to the true but unobservable risk; others will be rated too low. The over-rated companies will tend to be rewarded by increased sales and profits; the under-rated companies will be punished and perhaps pushed toward insolvency. If regulators instead disseminate complex but more accurate information, the information will be unintelligible to many consumers, especially those who might need the most help.

As another illustration of practical problems that arise with disclosure, consider the case of regulators making available information about complaints against insurers. Many states publish complaint ratios, that is, the number of consumer complaints against an insurer divided by its premium volume or number of customers. For a given level of quality, such as promptness and fairness of claims settlement, complaint ratios will tend to be higher for companies with higher risk policyholders. The reason is that high-risk insureds generate more claims. Holding average quality per claim constant, a greater number of claims will tend to produce more complaints.[8] In addition, complaint ratios could vary substantially across

---

[8]To illustrate, if two auto insurers both have a 0.01 probability that a claim will result in a complaint, an auto insurer with policyholders with an average accident rate of 0.06 per year will on average have a 50 percent larger ratio of complaints to policyholders than an auto insurer for which the average accident rate is 0.04 per year.

smaller companies and over time due to random variation in claim frequency, thus reducing the information's accuracy with potentially undesirable distortions in consumer decisions.

Problems with the disclosure approach to dealing with costly and imperfect information encourage greater use of minimum quality standards, whether through formal rules or informal benchmarks, and monitoring of compliance with standards by regulatory experts. This approach is used in solvency regulation and in regulation of unfair claims practices and deceptive sales practices. As suggested above, a limitation of minimum standards is that those standards might not be accurate. They might misclassify and unfairly penalize and/or increase costs for some high-quality firms and fail to catch low-quality firms. These limitations bring us back to an earlier point: Because regulation will be costly and imperfect, it probably should be used only when people are fairly confident that the benefits will exceed the costs.

6.4   Regulation and Political Pressure

Regulators as Agents of the Public

You may be convinced that regulation *should* serve the public interest by attempting to minimize the cost of risk through the cost-effective mitigation of significant market imperfections. Then the question arises: Will regulation generally attempt to achieve this goal?

While many of the types of regulation summarized in Table 6.1 are plausibly related to material imperfections in insurance markets, some regulations are more difficult to reconcile with the classical goal of mitigating market imperfections. As we explain further in later chapters, for example, regulation of voluntary market rates, restrictions on rate classification, and residual market rate regulation have produced large residual markets and cross-subsidies for some types of business in some states. These policies arguably create distortions beyond any that previously existed. Given that many sellers with comparatively small market shares and low entry barriers generally characterize insurance markets, competition can be expected to prevent excessive prices and profits. Until the 1960s, some observers argued that rate regulation was needed to prevent inadequate prices and too many insolvencies. Even if this argument had merit at the time, it cannot explain the focus of modern price regulation on restraining rates.[9]

Instead of asking how regulation *should* be designed and implemented to achieve some normative goal, such as the mitigation of market failure, much economic analysis of regulation instead focuses on how regulation *will* be designed and implemented if legislators and regulators seek their own interest. Analogous to our discussion in Chapter 2 of whether managers seek to maximize firm value, regulators (and legislators) can be viewed as agents of the "public." As with all principal-agent relations, agents may seek their own interests to the detriment of the principal. Thus, regulators might attempt to minimize conflict, ensure generous campaign contributions to the governor (or, if elected, to their own campaigns), and/or obtain high-paying positions in the regulated industry after they leave office (see Box 6.2).

---

[9]It might be argued that some forms of price regulation (e.g., restrictions on rate classification) increase fairness, as opposed to being a rational response to some form of traditional market failure (see Chapter 8). In principle, the traditional view could be expanded to include fairness; then, benefits of possible increased fairness from regulatory policies designed to deviate from the results that would arise with competition could be weighed against the costs.

The governor appoints the insurance commissioner in a majority of states. The commissioner is elected in most other states. Whether one approach is more efficient than the other is uncertain in theory and practice.

An argument for having the governor appoint the insurance commissioner is that it helps insulate the commissioner from political pressure in support of inefficient market intervention (such as price controls). Short-sighted and uninformed consumers might press for lower rates even if rate reductions will produce an inefficient reduction in the supply and quality of coverage. Self-interested groups of consumers might press for lower rates even if other consumers have to pay more in order to finance the subsidy. Many of these people, however, will not be exclusively influenced by insurance regulatory policy when voting in gubernatorial and legislative elections; that is, they are unlikely to be "single issue" voters with respect to insurance. As a result, governors and their appointed commissioners may be less vulnerable to pressure of this sort. The counterargument is that appointed commissioners might favor the industry to the detriment of consumers because they are less "accountable to the public" and therefore more readily influenced by insurance companies and agents.

A related issue concerns the background and qualifications of commissioners. People with prior experience in the insurance industry often are appointed, and many insurance commissioners accept employment in the industry following their tenure in office. Critics argue that this "revolving door" constitutes obvious evidence of capture by the industry. They argue that electing rather than appointing the insurance commissioner will make this outcome less likely. If people without substantial background in insurance are appointed, the process is criticized for leading to the appointment of incompetent, political hacks.

Although these criticisms often play well and are not implausible, an alternative perspective is that extensive background in insurance makes for more knowledgeable and effective commissioners. In addition, the expertise developed by regulating competitive insurance markets efficiently makes talented commissioners attractive employees in the industry when they leave office, especially in government affairs. As a result, the best regulators, from the perspective of both the industry and the average consumer, will be most likely to obtain attractive industry positions following their tenure as commissioner. If serving as an effective regulator enhances future employment prospects, agency costs will decline because commissioners will have more incentive to regulate efficiently. If so, the labor market for former commissioners may reduce the agency problem in insurance regulation, just as the managerial labor market helps reduce agency costs associated with possible conflicts between managers and shareholders.

As a result, regulation generally involves agency costs: Regulators need to be monitored, and they sometimes deviate from seeking the public interest. Also, the agency problem that arises with regulation may be especially severe because the principal (the public) consists of a large number of people with heterogeneous objectives and goals. In contrast, stockholders usually share the objective of wanting the stock price to be as high as possible.

The Economic Theory of Regulation

A major alternative to the public interest view posits that regulators seek their own interest by maximizing political support (or, equivalently, minimizing opposition).[10] Known as the

[10]Political support is broadly defined to include contributions of time and money, intensity of support, and the like. Several University of Chicago economists have played leading roles in the development of this theory, including George Stigler, Gary Becker, and Sam Peltzman. Stigler and Becker are both recipients of the Nobel Prize in economics. Stigler's prize was based in part on his work on the theory of economic regulation.

theory of economic regulation, this analysis predicts that the maximization of political support often will lead regulators to redistribute income between producers and consumers or between different groups of consumers, as opposed to pursuing the public interest by efficiently mitigating market failures. Groups that can more effectively generate political support (or pressure) will likely be favored by regulation at the expense of groups that are less effective in generating support.

One prediction from this theory is that relatively small groups that have large stakes per member in the outcome of regulation have a significant incentive to become informed about regulation and organize to influence regulation. As a result, these groups are likely to benefit at the expense of larger groups for which the stakes per member are small. This possible comparative advantage in generating political support for small groups with large stakes per member might frequently cause regulators to be captured by the regulated industry. In other words, regulators will adopt policies that increase profits for the regulated industry at the expense of the public interest (large numbers of uninformed consumers with low per member stakes in the regulatory outcome). The prediction that regulation often will benefit the regulated industry at the expense of consumers is accordingly known as the **capture theory,** or perhaps more accurately, the *capture hypothesis* or *producer protection hypothesis.*

Some observers suggest that strict prior approval regulation of property-liability insurance rates up until the late 1950s and 1960s, which made it difficult for insurers to charge rates lower than those developed by insurance rating bureaus, is consistent with the capture hypothesis (also see Box 6.2). Regardless of the extent to which this is historically accurate, the capture of regulators is inconsistent with the modern emphasis of rate regulation in many states on limiting rate increases to make coverage more affordable or on promoting large cross-subsidies between groups of insurance buyers (see Chapter 8). It appears instead that rapidly rising costs produce effective political pressure for policies that slow the growth in premiums, even if this reduces the supply and quality of coverage and causes insurers to suffer losses—the opposite of what would be expected if regulators are captured by insurers.

Cross-subsidies that have occurred from lower to higher risk consumers (e.g., in some auto and workers' compensation insurance markets, see Chapter 13 and 17) also might suggest that higher risk buyers may be able to exert more pressure for lower rates than lower risk buyers. This might occur, for example, if high-risk buyers have greater incentive to become informed about and influence regulation, to be single issue voters, or simply to complain to the insurance department or legislators. In addition to diffuse pressure by relatively large groups of consumers, some organized consumer groups actively fight insurance rate increases and support regulatory policies that produce cross-subsidies and large residual markets.

6.5 Summary

- State insurance codes and insurance departments regulate (1) the licensing of insurers, agents, and brokers; (2) solvency; (3) premium rates in many lines and states; (4) residual markets; (5) the content of policy forms; and (6) insurer sales practices and information disclosure. The National Association of Insurance Commissioners helps to coordinate state regulation.

- The McCarran-Ferguson Act of 1945 endorses state regulation of insurance and provides the insurance industry with a limited exemption from federal antitrust law. This exemption allows insurers to cooperate in ways that otherwise would be illegal. In particular, the exemption facilitates joint analysis of data, including the development of claim cost forecasts using industrywide data.

• State regulation is criticized for its lack of uniformity, unnecessary duplication, differences in quality across states and the persistence in many states of outmoded rate and policy form regulation. On the other hand, state regulation is more readily tailored to local needs, it facilitates cautious experimentation, and the effects of regulatory mistakes are localized.

• The public interest view of regulation holds that regulation should be designed to alleviate significant market imperfections, such as problems that arise due to costly and imperfect information in insurance markets. In practice, political pressure sometimes causes regulatory policies to deviate from this objective, responding instead in ways that benefit particular groups at the expense of others.

Key Terms

state insurance department 97
state insurance commissioner 97
National Association of Insurance
    Commissioners (NAIC) 100
model laws 100
Southeastern Underwriters Association
    decision 103

Paul v. Virginia 103
McCarran-Ferguson Act 103
public interest view of regulation 106
theory of economic regulation 112
capture theory 112

Questions and Problems

1. Briefly describe the historical evolution of state insurance regulation including the effects of *Paul v. Virginia,* the Southeastern Underwriters Association decision, and the McCarran-Ferguson Act.

2. Summarize the main arguments that favor federal insurance regulation and the main arguments that favor state regulation. Based on the discussion in the text and your own views concerning centralization versus decentralization of government power, which type of insurance regulation do you believe is better?

3. Contrast the public interest view of regulation with the economic theory of regulation.

4. Are problems associated with costly and imperfect information concerning product quality likely to be more severe in insurance markets than for: (*a*) commercial banking, (*b*) the market for personal computers, and (*c*) the market for stereo equipment? Explain. (Note: We did not address this specific ques-

tion in the chapter. You should be able to come up with a reasonable response given your knowledge of insurance and your knowledge and experience with these other markets.)

5. Why might establishing and monitoring compliance with minimum quality standards be preferable in some cases to disclosure of more information as a method of addressing the problem of costly and imperfect information?

6. Some state insurance departments develop summaries of auto insurance rates charged by different insurers for a benchmark set of coverages and driver characteristics and make this available to consumers on request. Briefly describe the possible benefits and costs of this form of disclosure, including the usefulness of the information. (Hint: Also consider the possible impact of differences in standards for accepting or rejecting applicants across insurers on the information's utility to buyers.)

7. The Internet makes the transmission of information to large numbers of people much cheaper than in the past. Does this reduce the case for using regulation to deal with costly and imperfect information in insurance markets?

8. Suppose that insurance price regulation suppresses rates below the cost of providing coverage. Explain why this outcome is inconsistent with the public interest view of regulation.

9. What is the NAIC and what is its role?

Answer to Concept Check

1. The limited antitrust exemption increases the accuracy of claim cost forecasts, thus reducing the amount of capital that many insurers need to hold to achieve a high probability of solvency and a potential barrier to entry. It also lowers insurers' costs of rate-making. The exemption is limited in two main ways: (1) an activity must be subject to state regulatory oversight in order to be exempt, and (2) any activity involving boycott, coercion, or intimidation is not exempt.

References

Breyer, Stephen. *Regulation and Its Reform.* Cambridge, MA: Harvard University Press, 1982. (*Detailed discussion of the public interest view of regulation, the limitations of regulation, and major types of economic regulation that have been used in the United States for a variety of industries.*)

Danzon, Patricia. "The McCarran-Ferguson Act: Anticompetitive or Procompetitive?" *Regulation: Cato Review of Business and Government* 15 (1992), pp. 38–47. (*Detailed discussion of the effects of the limited antitrust exemption.*)

Harrington, Scott. "An Historical Overview of Federal Involvement in Insurance Regulation." *Optional Federal Chartering for Insurance Companies,* Peter Wallison, ed. Washington, D.C.: AEI Press, 2000. (*Detailed discussion of Federal threats to state insurance regulation.*)

Harrington, Scott; and Helen Doerpinghaus. "The Economics and Politics of Automobile Insurance Rate Classification." *Journal of Risk and Insurance* 60 (1993). (*Discussion of how interest group pressure may affect auto insurance rate classification.*)

Joskow, Paul. "Cartels, Competition, and Regulation in the US Property-Liability Insurance Industry." *Bell Journal of Economics and Management Science* 4 (1973), pp. 375–427. (*A classic economic analysis of property-liability insurance market structure, conduct, and regulation.*)

Mehr, Robert I.; and Emerson Cammack. *Principles of Insurance.* 6th ed. Chapter 28. Homewood, IL: Richard D. Irwin, 1976. (*Discusses the history of insurance regulation.*)

Stigler, George. "The Theory of Economic Regulation." *Bell Journal of Economics and Management Science* 2 (1971), pp. 3–21. (*A classic article on the economic theory of regulation and capture theory by a Nobel Prize–winning economist.*)

Chapter 7

Insolvencies, Solvency Ratings, and Solvency Regulation

Chapter Objectives

- Summarize the historical record of insurance company insolvencies.
- Describe the insurance company solvency ratings provided by financial rating agencies and how they are used.
- Introduce the main features and functions of solvency regulation, including solvency monitoring, capital requirements, and insurance guaranty funds.

7.1   Insurer Insolvencies

In order for insurance contracts and other loss financing devices to be effective in reducing risk, the party that agrees to provide funds following a loss must honor its promise. As a result, an important issue in risk management is the credit risk associated with loss financing arrangements such as insurance and hedging. In Chapter 5 we discussed how insurer capital, diversification of underwriting risk, reinsurance, and investment decisions affect insolvency risk. We also discussed the major factors influencing the amount of capital held by an insurer to reduce insolvency risk given its underwriting and investment decisions.

In this chapter we review the historical record of insurer insolvencies to acquaint you with the magnitude of insolvency risk and the reasons why insurers become insolvent. We describe solvency ratings of insurers that are provided by several financial rating agencies and used widely by business risk managers, insurance agents and brokers, and many individuals. We then introduce the objectives and major features of solvency regulation.

Frequency and Severity of Insurance Company Insolvencies

Figure 7.1 shows the number of property–liability insurers and life–health insurers declared insolvent each year during the period 1981–2001. It also shows assessments by state insurance guaranty funds against surviving insurers during 1981–1999 (in constant 1999 dollar amounts) to pay some of the claims against insolvent insurers. (We discuss guaranty funds in section 7.5.) We noted in the last chapter that insolvency rates for insurers generally have been low and that most insolvent companies have been small. Nonetheless, beginning in the mid-1980s and continuing through the early 1990s, the number of insurer insolvencies increased significantly compared to historical norms. During this period, approximately 1 percent of both property–liability insurers and life–health insurers have failed on average each year. The increase in the number of insolvencies and an increase in the average size of insolvent insurers have substantially increased guaranty fund assessments.

The largest property–liability insurer insolvency to date was the Reliance Insurance Group in 2000. It is estimated that this insolvency will require $1.1 billion of assessments. The insolvency of Mission Insurance Group in 1987 required guaranty fund assessments of nearly $500 million. Several other insolvent property–liability insurers have required assessments of $250 million or more. Several relatively large life insurers failed in 1991, including two insurer groups that ranked in the top 25 in terms of assets (Executive Life and Mutual Benefit Life). Executive Life invested heavily in high yield (junk) bonds that later experienced sharp declines in value. Guaranty fund assessments for Executive Life totaled $2.1 billion, over five times greater than for any other life–health insurer insolvency. Assessments for Mutual Benefit Life totaled $81 million.

The increase in the frequency and severity of insurer insolvencies during the 1980s and early 1990s generated concern about the quality of state solvency regulation and the performance of financial rating agencies. It also led to proposals for federal solvency regulation and to the adoption of significant changes in state solvency regulation, such as risk-based capital requirements (see section 7.3). When considering insurer insolvency experience, you should keep in perspective that preventing insolvencies is costly, whether by insurers voluntarily reducing risk or increasing capital or through solvency regulation. Recall from Chapter 5, for example, that holding additional capital increases insurer tax costs and thus the amount of premiums needed to provide a given amount of coverage. Like our earlier discussion of loss control in general, beyond some point, the marginal costs of reducing insolvency risk will exceed the benefits. As a result, the total costs of an "insolvency proof" insurance system would be unattractive to consumers.

Causes of Insolvencies

Many factors contribute to insurer insolvencies, including inadequate prices, excessive growth in business written compared to capital, excessive investment risk, catastrophe losses, and declines in asset values. Management fraud sometimes has played a role, and many insolvent insurers appear to have deliberately understated claim liabilities and overstated asset values prior to insolvency. Unless there is clear evidence of fraud, however, it usually is difficult to distinguish whether an insolvency has been caused primarily by inadequate capitalization or risk management prior to the adverse events, as opposed to large, unpredictable reductions in capital.

FIGURE 7.1 Number of insurer insolvencies (1981–2001) and guaranty fund assessments (1981–1999, in constant 1999 dollar amounts).

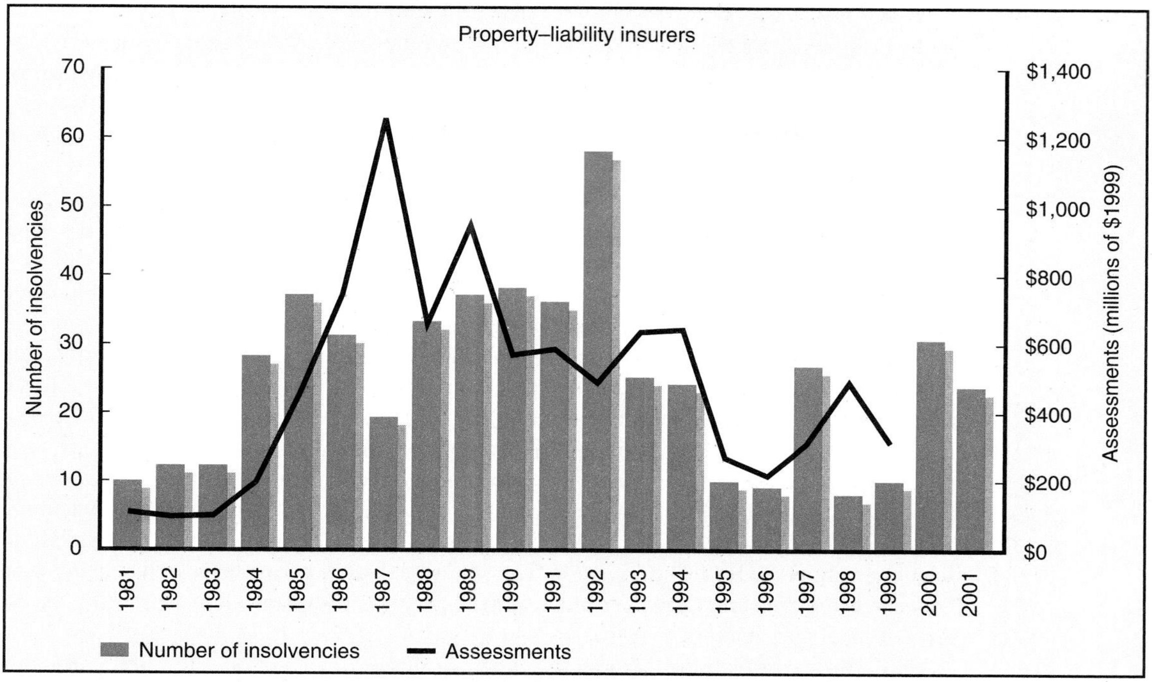

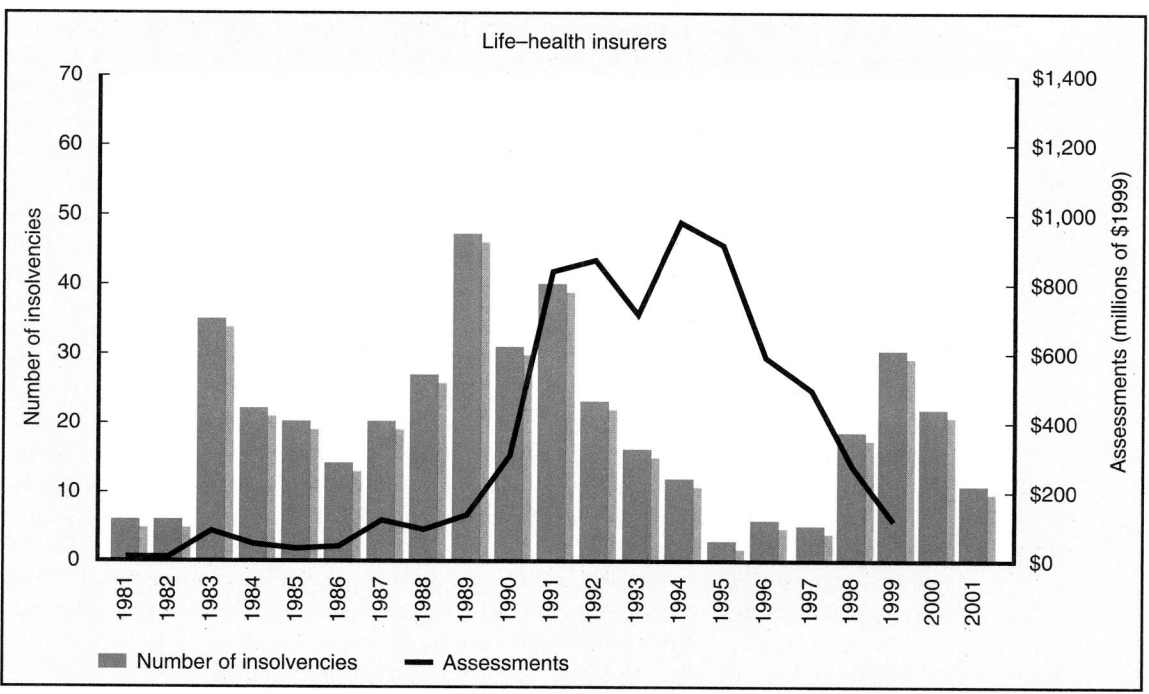

Note: Number of insolvencies obtained from the National Association of Insurance Commissioners and Standard & Poor's. Property–liability assessments obtained from the National Conference of Insurance Guaranty Funds; life–health assessments obtained from the National Organization of Life and Health Insurance Guaranty Association. Constant 1999 dollar amounts calculated by the authors using the US consumer price index.

Property–Liability Insurer Insolvencies

Many property–liability insurers that failed during the 1980s wrote large amounts of business liability insurance, including products liability, environmental liability, and professional liability insurance (e.g., for physicians, architects, and engineers). These insolvencies were associated with much higher claim costs than the insurers originally reported on their financial statements. Evidence suggests that a large component of the increase in claim costs was probably unexpected in many cases; in other words, the actual costs were significantly higher than could reasonably have been expected when the insurers wrote the business and initially reported estimates of claim costs.

Conversely, it has been argued that some of these insurers deliberately wrote large amounts of business at prices that they knew to be too low in comparison to expected claim costs, either because they had inadequate incentives to be safe or in an attempt to generate cash and buy time after they began to experience difficulty. These insurers also are alleged to have hidden their inadequate prices and capital by deliberately understating their estimated liabilities and using questionable (if not completely phony) reinsurance arrangements. Whether fraudulent or not, the reinsurance mechanism often broke down. Many reinsurers failed to pay because they became insolvent. Other reinsurers denied payment, alleging that the now insolvent primary insurer had deliberately failed to report material information about the business reinsured. The resulting disputes produced extensive litigation between some reinsurers and the state insurance departments responsible for settling the estates of insolvent insurers.[1]

Some property–liability insurer insolvencies during the mid- to late 1980s probably were influenced by low prices during the "soft market" for business liability insurance during the early 1980s (see Chapter 8). A large increase in market interest rates in the late 1970s and early 1980s also may have contributed to some of those insolvencies. Higher interest rates substantially reduced the market value of bonds held by many insurers. Some companies might have been weakened to the point that they engaged in excessively risky behavior in the hope of getting lucky and avoiding insolvency. (This behavior sometimes is known as "going-for-broke" or "gambling for resurrection.") The prolonged soft market (period of low insurance prices) in the 1990s contributed to the insolvency of Reliance Insurance Group and the increased number of insolvencies that occurred in the late 1990s and early 2000s.

Life–Health Insurer Insolvencies

The increase in the frequency of life–health insurer insolvencies that began in the mid-1980s (see Figure 7.1) was due in large part to small health insurers that experienced large claim costs in relation to premiums and the claim liabilities that they originally reported. Similar problems contributed to the increased number of insolvencies that began in the late 1990s. The insolvency of several large life insurance companies in 1991 accounted for much of the increase in guaranty fund assessments shown in Figure 7.1. The large life insurer insolvencies primarily reflected reductions in the value of assets held; these insolvencies received enormous attention in the national media. The most highly publicized insolvencies were those of a few insurers, such as Executive Life, that invested heavily in high yield bonds.

---

[1] As was true for a number of large insolvencies in the savings and loan industry, insurance departments sometimes sued and obtained settlements from the accounting firms responsible for auditing the books of the insolvent insurer.

More widespread financial problems were caused by depressed commercial real estate values, which reduced the value of real estate and mortgage holdings for hundreds of life insurers. Problem real estate precipitated the insolvency of Mutual Benefit Life.

The insolvencies of Executive Life, Mutual Benefit Life, and a few other insurers were preceded by substantial cash withdrawals by life insurance and annuity policyholders who had accumulated savings with these insurers and who had become concerned with the safety of their funds. Following concerns expressed by some state regulators about its financial condition, Mutual Benefit Life asked to be taken over by New Jersey insurance regulators when confronted with massive demands for funds by its policyholders.

There was significant concern during the spring and summer of 1991 that large numbers of life insurance and annuity policyholders might panic and attempt to withdraw funds from other insurers that were not experiencing significant financial problems. If this had happened, it could have created severe stress for many companies, forcing them to sell assets at a time when asset values were already depressed. These sales would have created additional downward pressure on asset prices in the short run, further weakening the life-health insurance industry and possibly causing more insurers to fail.

No other large insurer failed in 1991, however, and asset values subsequently rebounded in many cases, which significantly strengthened the capital of the industry. Some evidence suggests that because of the rebound in high yield bond prices that occurred in 1991, Executive Life might have remained solvent if it could have survived until year-end. In addition, the corporation that succeeded Mutual Benefit Life and was supervised by New Jersey regulators was in good enough financial shape to be offered for sale to the private sector in 1997 (see Box 7.1). Whether some regulators took action against some insurers prematurely or made statements that unduly frightened policyholders and contributed to the insolvency of others is subject to debate.

Following the events of 1991, many life insurers raised new capital and improved the quality of their assets. Evidence suggests that policyholder withdrawals of funds during 1990 and 1991 primarily occurred for weak companies, as opposed to reflecting irrational panic and contagion that adversely affected all insurers. Many policyholders appear to have become more concerned with insurer safety during this time. The resulting *flight to quality* provided additional incentives for insurers to increase their capital and reduce risk.

7.2 Solvency Ratings

A number of financial **rating agencies** provide **solvency ratings** of insurance companies. The leading rating agencies include the A. M. Best Company, Moody's, Standard and Poor's, and Duff and Phelps. Solvency ratings are used extensively by corporate risk managers and independent insurance agents and brokers when deciding on an insurer. Many corporate risk managers restrict their attention to highly rated insurers. In addition, risk managers routinely enter into hold harmless and indemnity agreements that require another entity to protect their firm against loss under specified circumstances (see Chapter 28). In order to reduce the credit risk of these agreements, the party required to respond in the event of loss commonly backs its promise with an insurance contract from a highly rated insurer. Given the widespread uses of solvency ratings, an insurer could experience a significant reduction in sales to business policyholders if it were to lose a high rating. Insurer solvency ratings also are used, albeit to a lesser extent, by individual insurance buyers.

Old Mutual Benefit Is Putting Itself Up for Sale as Financial Shape Improves

The Old Mutual Benefit Life Insurance Company, an insurer once largely given up for dead as the nation's biggest life insurance failure, is putting itself up for sale in better financial shape than ever expected.

With the blessing of the New Jersey insurance regulators who are still its overseers, the Newark, NJ, company will announce today that it has hired Goldman, Sachs & Company to identify potential bidders, Alan J. Bowers, its president and chief executive officer, said in an interview Friday. Since its seizure in 1991, the company now known as MBL Life Assurance Corporation, has continued to pay policyholders and annuitants under terms of its contracts but hasn't made new sales.

Analysts said the company could well fetch its book value, or net worth, of approximately $600 million, and may possibly bring more given feverish insurance industry merger and acquisition activity.

Mutual Benefit, which was a mutual owned by policyholders rather than shareholders, collapsed under a mountain of poorly performing real estate holdings, including ill-fated Florida luxury condominium developments. The company was one of several high profile insurance failures in the early 1990s.

REAL ESTATE ASSETS

MBL's improved financial condition—an eightfold increase in book value since 1994—stems largely from a rebound in the market that caused its biggest problems. Over the past two years, the company has sold more than $1 billion of real estate assets at higher than anticipated prices.

The insurer's board opted to explore a sale after concluding the company had "created a lot of value," while trying to become a sales operation again would be "risky" given competitive industry conditions, said Mr. Bowers, a former Coopers & Lybrand managing partner who joined MBL in 1995. He noted that an important factor in MBL's decision is the current frenzied consolidation activity.

"We thought we should at least explore the opportunity to take advantage of what's happening" in that arena, he said.

Any proceeds would be split between the insurer's 450,000 remaining customers, who have received below-market interest rates on their investments since the seizure, among other penalties, and a group of creditors, including numerous big banks, with claims totaling $625 million, according to Mr. Bowers. For creditors, a sale represents their only source of payment. A steep sales price could make them whole, while a book value one wouldn't.

The takeover of Mutual Benefit, whose $14 billion in assets made it one of the nation's 25 biggest life insurers, came after the company searched unsuccessfully for a merger partner or investors to boost its capital. In the weeks leading up to the seizure, redemptions by Mutual Benefit policyholders tallied $1 billion. The insurer then had about 400,000 policy-holders and 200,000 workers whose pension plans had bought annuities from it.

Rating agencies provide valuable summary information about insurer financial strength at a relatively low cost. These firms are compensated by sales of publications that include ratings and updates of rating changes and by fees from rated insurers. The willingness of insurers to pay to be rated indicates the importance of receiving a financial rating by one or more rating agencies.

The A. M. Best Company is the oldest and largest insurance rating agency. It reviews a large majority of US insurers and many international insurers. Companies are placed in two broad categories: (1) some insurers receive an A. M. Best "letter" rating based on a statistical and qualitative analysis of financial information and management interviews, and

Table 7.1
A. M. Best Company rating categories and associated letter ratings.

Major Category	Subcategory	Letter Ratings
Secure	Superior	A++, A+
	Excellent	A, A−
	Very good	B++, B+
Vulnerable	Fair	B, B−
	Marginal	C++, C+
	Weak	C, C−
	Poor	D
	Regulatory supervision	E
	Liquidation	F
	Rating Suspended	S

Source: http://www.ambest.com/ratings/guide.htm/#definitions

(2) other insurers are placed in the "rating not assigned" category. Table 7.1 provides a description of A.M. Best letter ratings as of 2002. Roughly 75 percent of insurers with over 90 percent of insurer assets receive letter ratings. The remaining companies are included in the "rating not assigned" category because, for example, the insurer is very small, has too little data or experience, or buys extensive reinsurance from an unrated reinsurer. Insurers also can request that a rating not be assigned. Best's provides a numerical "financial performance rating" for many insurers that are not assigned a letter rating. The financial performance rating is based on a less extensive analysis than the letter ratings.

Apart from using "++" grades and basing ratings on current and future prospects as opposed to past performance only, Best ratings look a lot like the grades you receive in school. Most insurers rated by Best and most other rating agencies receive high marks. (Different agencies have different rating definitions and do not rank insurers the same.) Approximately 85–90 percent of rated property–liability insurance companies have an A. M. Best of A− or better. About one-third of rated insurers (with about one-half of total industry assets) received grades of A+ or, much less frequently, A++. Less than 5 percent of insurers received ratings lower than B+. Very few insurers received ratings below B−. To keep these numbers in perspective, however, recall that roughly 25 percent of insurers do not receive a letter rating. The main reason that ratings are high on average is that the majority of insurers with the bulk of total industry assets are reasonably secure.

Statistical analysis indicates that solvency ratings help predict insurer insolvencies. Lower rated or unrated insurers are more likely to become insolvent than higher rated insurers. However, the ability of ratings to distinguish between weak and strong insurers on average does not mean that a high rating ensures solvency. Some of the larger insurers that failed in the late 1980s and early 1990s received high solvency ratings until a year or two before they were declared insolvent.

Some people argue that insurer solvency ratings are of questionable accuracy and could be biased upward due to pressure from insurers, which are a significant source of revenue for rating agencies. Evaluating these criticisms is problematic because of the difficulty in determining whether many insolvencies are caused by severe but unpredictable adverse events, as opposed to poor ex ante capitalization and risk management. Demand for accurate ratings by risk managers, insurance agents and brokers, and financially strong insurers should provide a substantial incentive for accuracy.

7.3 Overview of Solvency Regulation

Solvency regulation has three main parts: (1) regulatory monitoring of insurer insolvency risk (including regulatory intervention against troubled insurers), (2) restrictions on insurers' capital and assets, and (3) state guaranty systems, which pay some of the claims of insolvent insurers. Primary responsibility for regulating a specific insurer's solvency lies with the insurance department in the state where the insurer is domiciled (where it has its corporate charter). Nevertheless, most state insurance departments provide some level of monitoring for all insurers that write business in their states. As explained in the last chapter, regulation by the different states is loosely coordinated by the National Association of Insurance Commissioners (NAIC).[2]

Objectives of Solvency Regulation

Consumers generally desire two things from solvency regulation: (1) the reduction of insolvency risk, through monitoring and controls, and (2) protection against loss if insurers fail. Because reducing risk and providing protection against loss are costly, solvency regulation must examine both the benefits and the costs of each approach if it is to minimize the total cost of risk in society.

To elaborate, recall that a tradeoff exists between the benefits of lower insolvency risk and the price of insurance because increasing insurer capital to reduce insolvency risk is costly. In addition, regulatory monitoring and controls to reduce insolvency risk involve direct costs, such as the salaries of regulators and the cost of data collection and processing. Moreover, regulatory monitoring and controls might produce indirect costs, for example, if they distort the decisions of some financially sound insurers in ways that increase their costs.

A tradeoff also exists between protecting people against loss when insurers fail and incentives for insurers to be safe.[3] The reason is that protection against loss reduces consumers' demand for lower insolvency risk and the incentive to seek a safe insurer, thus dulling one of the major influences that encourages insurers to hold more capital. The tradeoff between protection against loss and incentives to reduce loss is a general phenomenon, known as the *moral hazard* problem, which we discuss in detail in Chapter 10.

Minimizing the total cost of risk basically requires that the sum of the expected cost of insolvencies, the cost of solvency regulation, and the cost of residual uncertainty concerning insolvencies be made as small as possible. The optimal mix of monitoring, controls, and protection is not known with precision. It is clear, however, that neither zero insolvency risk nor complete protection of all policyholders against loss when insurers fail is optimal, given the costs that either solution would impose on consumers. It also is clear that regulation should try to (1) target those insurers that have little incentive to be safe without regulation (e.g., insurers with little franchise value or with a majority of policyholders fully protected

---

[2] Recall that the NAIC established an accreditation program for state solvency regulation in the early 1990s. This program allows states that meet minimum standards for solvency regulation to become accredited by the NAIC. Most states passed legislation and took other actions to meet the minimum standards and become accredited.

[3] A large degree of protection against bank insolvencies often is justified by the need to avoid financial panics and bank runs that could have a large effect on the economy. As suggested earlier, these concerns might have some relevance to providers of savings-oriented life insurance and annuity products.

by guaranty funds), and (2) avoid distorting the decisions of insurers that have strong safety incentives without regulation.

Concept Checks

1. Why would complete protection of consumers against loss from insurer insolvency tend to increase the frequency of insolvencies?

2. Assuming that complete elimination of insolvency risk through regulation is feasible, why would achieving this goal increase the total cost of risk in society?

Regulatory Monitoring of Insurer Insolvency Risk

In effect, consumers that would find it very costly to evaluate and monitor insurer insolvency risk (or who might have little incentive to do so) delegate the major responsibility for such monitoring to state solvency regulators. Regulatory monitoring of insolvency risk, including the early detection of financially weak insurers, thus can be viewed as a form of **delegated monitoring.** Regulatory monitoring sometimes can detect insurer financial problems early enough to prevent insolvency. In other cases, monitoring can help regulators intervene before the deficit between an insolvent insurer's assets and liabilities gets any larger. Regulatory intervention against troubled insurers is an important part of solvency regulations.

The practice of solvency monitoring focuses on financial ratios and other insurer characteristics that presumably are correlated with factors that affect insurer incentives for safety (e.g., policyholder desires for safety, insurer franchise value, and capital costs). Some states have their own systems for screening insurers that may need more in-depth scrutiny by regulators, but most states rely to some extent on screening or "early warning" systems developed through the NAIC. These systems rely heavily on regulatory financial statements that must be filed by every insurer. Early warning system results are used to prioritize insurers for in-depth analysis and on-site examinations by regulators. Otherwise, each insurer normally receives a detailed financial examination every three to five years.

IRIS

The NAIC's Insurance Regulatory Information System (**IRIS**) is a basic solvency screening system that has been used by the NAIC and state regulators since the mid-1970s. Separate but similar systems are used for property–liability insurers and life–health insurers. IRIS involves calculating 11 financial ratios for each insurer with subsequent review and analysis by a team of examiners. A "usual range" is established for each IRIS ratio based on historical comparisons of ratio values for insurers that later failed to insurers that remained solvent. Insurers are initially selected for more in-depth review by the examiner team based on several criteria, including having four or more unusual ratio values (values that fall outside the usual ranges). The examiners then conduct a more in-depth review of the financial statements of these insurers to determine whether further analysis by their domiciliary (home-state) regulators is warranted. Insurers are placed into priority categories for further analysis and/or action by regulators. Several of the IRIS ratios for property–liability insurers and their usual ranges are shown in Table 7.2.

FAST

The NAIC developed another solvency screening system for nationally significant insurers in the early 1990s. Known as **FAST** (short for Financial Analysis Solvency Tools), this

Table 7.2

Examples of IRIS and FAST variables for property–liability insurers.

Variable	System	Rationale for Variable	IRIS Usual Range
Net premiums written ÷ surplus (capital)	IRIS & FAST	Higher values increase vulnerability to underwriting risk.	Less than 300%
Percent change in net premiums written	IRIS & FAST	High premium growth could indicate inadequate prices; low values could indicate constrained resources.	Between −25% and +25%
Loss and unearned premium reserves ÷ surplus	FAST	Higher values increase vulnerability to underwriting risk.	Not applicable
Reinsurance recoverable on unpaid losses ÷ surplus	FAST	Large amounts due from reinsurers increase vulnerability to credit risk.	Not applicable

system employs separate screening models for property–liability, life, and health insurers. FAST employs an expanded set of financial ratios compared to IRIS (two examples for property–liability insurers are shown in Table 7.2). In contrast to IRIS, FAST assigns different point values for different ranges of ratio results, and the point values are summed to produce a total *FAST score* for each insurer. The FAST score is used by an NAIC committee to classify companies for regulatory scrutiny. The point values and total FAST score are not released to the public.

Statistical analysis indicates that both IRIS and FAST help predict insurer insolvencies and that the FAST score is a better predictor of insolvencies than the IRIS ratios. However, the effectiveness of these systems has been debated (especially for IRIS, which has been around a lot longer than FAST). Some persons argue that better systems could be developed to identify a greater proportion of "weak" insurers without incorrectly classifying any more "strong" insurers. This argument usually is based on a finding that one or more financial ratios not used in the existing systems could have predicted more insolvencies based on historical data. Whether these additional ratios are correlated with insolvency risk for insurers that have yet to fail is more difficult to establish.

Similar to the criticisms of the rating agencies we discussed earlier, some people argue that regulators often wait too long to take action against weak companies. Unjustified *regulatory forbearance* generally is regarded as a major contributor to the large insolvency costs for the savings and loan industry during the 1980s and early 1990s. Factors that might lead to unjustified forbearance against troubled insurers include: (1) weak insurers might exert substantial pressure for forbearance; (2) insolvencies might make regulators appear incompetent, so that they delay taking action with the hope that the insurer's condition will improve; or (3) some regulators might indeed be incompetent.

On the other hand, regulators have to be concerned about premature intervention. Premature action against a weak but still solvent insurer might cause it to become insolvent. This result could occur if the news of intervention spreads and inappropriately damages the insurer's ability to operate and take steps to improve its condition. As stated earlier, some observers suggest that regulatory action may have been premature against one or more of the large life insurers that failed in the early 1990s. Balancing the risks of acting too soon (premature intervention) and waiting too long (excessive forbearance) can be difficult in practice.

Restrictions on Insurers' Capital and Assets

Regulations also limit an insurer's ability to take on risk. Most states have complex investment regulations that constrain an insurer's ability to invest in risky assets. For example, regulation often limits total investments in "risky" investments (such as common stocks and, since the early 1990s, high yield bonds) and investments in a single issuer's securities to specified percentages of either the insurer's capital or assets.

Historically, insurers also have had to meet **fixed minimum capital requirements** to establish and continue operations in a state. These requirements, which usually vary depending on the type of insurer (stock or mutual) and the broad type of business written (e.g., property–liability versus life–health insurance), average around $2 million, varying from $100,000 in a few states up to $5 million or more in a few others. Fixed minimum capital requirements are more appropriate for start-up operations than for established insurers with significant liabilities and premiums. Because insurers vary substantially in size, underwriting risk, and investment risk, fixed minimum capital requirements are of little relevance for many insurers.

In a major development in insurance solvency regulation during 1991–1995, which paralleled developments in bank solvency regulation, the NAIC developed **risk-based capital requirements** for adoption by the states. In contrast to the historical system of fixed minimum capital requirements, risk-based capital (RBC) requirements vary in relation to the specific amounts and types of an insurer's assets, liabilities, and premiums. The basic idea is that insurers with riskier activities need to hold more capital to meet the minimum RBC requirements.[4]

The NAIC's property–liability RBC formula encompasses four major risk categories: (1) asset risk (the risk of issuer default and market value declines); (2) credit risk (e.g., the risk that reinsurance and other receivables will prove to be uncollectible); (3) underwriting risk (the risk that prices and reported claim liabilities will be inadequate compared to realized claim costs); and (4) miscellaneous "off-balance sheet" risks, such as the risk associated with rapid premium growth. The life insurer formula (and a separate formula for health insurers) also include four major risk categories: (1) asset risk; (2) insurance risk (underwriting risk associated with sickness and mortality); (3) interest rate risk (which focuses on the risk that policyholders will withdraw funds and invest them elsewhere if market interest rates increase); and (4) miscellaneous business risks, such as the risk of guaranty fund assessments.

The specific RBC formulas and calculations are complicated. The appendix to this chapter provides a simple example that illustrates the basic procedure. The important point is that in states that have adopted the NAIC's model RBC law, each insurer must calculate a dollar figure called its RBC. This figure is higher for insurers that take on more risk. An insurer's actual capital is then compared to its RBC. If the insurer's actual capital falls below specified percentages of its RBC, regulators can take the actions shown in Table 7.3.

---

[4]The European Union uses a much simpler system of required capital known as the solvency margin to evaluate an insurer's premiums or losses. Japan, Canada, and Australia have US style risk-based capital systems, although the specifics vary considerably.

Table 7.3
Required actions if insurer capital falls below specified RBC thresholds.

Insurer Capital Level	Action
Between 150 and 200% of formula RBC	Company must file plan with insurance commissioner explaining cause of deficiency and how it will be corrected.
Between 100 and 150% of formula RBC	Commissioner must examine insurer and take corrective action as necessary.
Between 70 and 100% of formula RBC	Commissioner has legal grounds to rehabilitate or liquidate the company.
Less than 70% of formula RBC	Commissioner must take over the company.

Most insurers were able to easily meet the RBC requirements when they were adopted by the NAIC in the mid 1990s. In the property–liability insurance industry, for example, the median property-liability insurer had actual capital equal to 400–500 percent of its RBC. The RBC requirements nevertheless may significantly affect the insurance industry and solvency regulation. Specifically, they should (1) encourage some weak insurers to limit their risk or increase their capital; (2) encourage faster corrective action by regulators in some cases and thus discourage unjustified forbearance; and (3) perhaps help regulators and other parties identify insurers with too little capital to produce a reasonably low level of insolvency risk.[5]

State Guaranty Systems

All states have guaranty systems, known as **guaranty funds** or **guaranty associations,** that provide substantial protection to consumers that have coverage with an insolvent insurer. The basic function of these systems is to pay part of the claims that exceed the assets of insolvent insurers. While only a few states had guaranty funds in 1970, most states had guaranty funds for both property–liability and life–health insurance by 1980. All states had funds for both industries by the early 1990s.[6]

Coverage
Each state's property–liability insurance guaranty fund covers all of the major types of coverage sold by the primary insurers licensed in the state (reinsurance is excluded). Coverage limits vary across states. Claims in excess of a small deductible, typically $100, commonly

---

[5]The NAIC's RBC requirements have been criticized for a variety of reasons, including the crudity of some of the risk factors and omission of some types of risk (e.g., the property–liability formula does not consider interest rate risk or fully reflect the risk of catastrophe losses). Some people have argued that the relatively low levels of total RBC compared to total industry capital indicate that the formulas on average do not require enough capital to keep many insurers from operating with excessive insolvency risk. However, given that a substantial proportion of insurers has strong incentives to be reasonably safe without risk-based capital requirements, this conclusion does not necessarily follow. Moreover, a drawback to increasing the overall level of RBC relative to actual capital is that more decisions of sound insurers probably would be distorted, which could lead to a reduced willingness among these insurers to provide coverage, less efficient investment strategies, and/or higher prices.

[6]Several European Union countries have guaranty systems that like the US involve expost funding (see below). Japan and Canada have prefunded systems.

are covered up to a maximum limit of $300,000 per claim (or, if lower, the limit in the policyholder's insurance contract). A significant majority of guaranty funds do not have a maximum limit for workers' compensation insurance claims. Most states also provide some protection against the loss of premiums paid for unexpired coverage at the time of insolvency. Some states exclude or further limit coverage for large business insurance buyers in order to encourage them to search for coverage from safe insurers.

Like the property–liability systems, life–health guaranty funds exclude reinsurance. They also exclude coverage for savings accumulations in contracts where the investment risk is borne by the policyholder (e.g., variable life insurance and annuities, which are discussed in Chapter 15, and certain pension plans). They commonly pay up to $300,000 for death and illness claims and $100,000 for life insurance policyholder savings and annuity accumulations (see Chapter 15 for descriptions of these products). Some states provide coverage from $1 million to $5 million for group annuity contracts (e.g., for groups of employees) where accumulations are not allocated to individual participants. Other states exclude coverage for these "unallocated" annuities.

Most states have interest rate adjustment clauses ("haircut" provisions), which limit coverage of investment income for policies that involve savings accumulation. The typical guaranty fund guarantees a rate of interest that is 2 percentage points less than the average yield for the Moody's corporate bond index during a three- to four-year period prior to the insurer's insolvency. To prevent undue hardship that would occur to some policyholders if their contracts were terminated at insolvency (for example, if a life insurance policyholder had become uninsurable since purchasing the policy), policyholders generally are allowed to keep their contracts in force by continuing to pay premiums to a successor insurer established or chosen by state regulators and the guaranty association. However, the future rate of interest credited for savings accumulations will be relatively low (e.g., 2–3 percent less than the Moody's corporate bond yield).

Funding

State guaranty funds (associations), which are composed of all licensed insurers in a state, obtain money to pay claims by levying **post-insolvency assessments** on surviving insurers. (An exception is New York, which assesses insurers before insolvencies occur to build up a fund to pay covered claims.) Following an insolvency, the representatives of the state guaranty association estimate how much money is needed to pay covered claims in excess of the assets of the insolvent insurer. Each surviving member insurer that writes business in the state is then assessed a pro rata share of the total assessment based on its market share of premiums in the state.[7] In order to reduce the risk of a domino effect from large assessments (i.e., large assessments that could push other insurers into insolvency), annual assessments typically are capped at 1 or 2 percent of premiums in a state. If the cap is hit, which is uncommon, the guaranty association usually can borrow funds. Insurers then are assessed in subsequent years to pay back the loan.

---

[7]Again, separate systems are used for property–liability insurance and life–health insurance. For both property–liability and life–health insurance, many states have two or three separate guaranty fund accounts for broad classes of coverage. Separate assessments are made for each account (e.g., the auto insurance account) based on the insurer's share of total premiums for each account. If the amounts originally assessed turn out to exceed the amount needed to pay claims, the excess is refunded to insurers.

The countrywide guaranty fund assessments shown in Figure 7.1 might seem large to you in absolute terms. However, assessments have averaged a very small percentage of premiums. For example, in 1987, the worst year for assessments (in 1999 dollars) for either the property–liability or life–health insurance industries, countrywide property–liability insurer assessments were less than one-half of 1 percent of countrywide property–liability insurance premiums.

Depending on the state, the cost of assessments generally is shared by policyholders, insurers, and the government (taxpayers). Some states allow insurers to offset 50 to 100 percent of assessments against future state premium taxes over a 5 to 10 year period. (State premium taxes commonly equal about 2 percent of premiums.) An offset against premium taxes is more prevalent for life–health insurance guaranty systems. Assessments also are deductible when calculating insurer state and federal taxable income. Most states specify that insurers can increase premiums to reflect the cost of assessments. In a competitive market, however, premiums generally will reflect the expected cost of assessments for the period of coverage as opposed to being continually adjusted to reflect assessments in the prior year. (The next chapter discusses how insurance prices usually reflect expected costs rather than past experience.) As a result, the risk of year-to-year changes in the after-tax cost of assessments is borne primarily by insurance company owners.

Design Issues

The design of state guaranty systems has sometimes been the subject of considerable controversy. This controversy will resume if one or more large insurers fails in the future (or if proposals for optional federal chartering and regulation pick up steam). Three of the most important issues are: (1) the level of coverage, (2) pre-insolvency versus post-insolvency assessments, and (3) the potential advantages of risk-based assessments.

Level of Coverage   Some people argue that guaranty fund limits are too low, especially in the few states that cover only $100,000 per claim. As discussed in section 7.3, however, a problem with increasing protection for policyholders is that the resulting reduction in policyholder concern with safety weakens incentives for insurers to be safe.[8] Because of this problem, other observers believe instead that guaranty fund protection is too generous and suggest that it should be restricted. They support adoption by more states of limits on protection for large commercial property–liability insurance buyers with safeguards to protect injured employees and third-party liability claimants against these businesses. The argument is that large businesses are better able to monitor and bear insolvency risk than personal insurance buyers and that restricting their guaranty fund protection will provide greater incentives for insurer safety.

Risk managers of large firms generally have opposed the elimination of guaranty fund protection for commercial insurance, in large part because premiums for large businesses reflect guaranty fund assessments. They argue that their firms should not be excluded from guaranty fund coverage as long as they have to pay more for insurance over time to cover at least part of the cost of assessments.

---

[8]This effect is probably less severe for life insurance and annuity products that provide savings accumulation because policyholders may still be very concerned about access to their funds and haircut provisions may reduce the insured yield on savings below what the insurer had promised.

Pre-Insolvency versus Post-Insolvency Funding It has frequently been argued that the system of post-insolvency assessments provides inadequate capacity to handle potentially large insolvencies. Pre-insolvency funding could increase capacity by creating a large pool of assets that would be available to finance covered claims. Counterarguments include: (1) by reducing risk to insurers, pre-insolvency assessments might reduce incentives for safe insurers to press for effective regulatory solvency monitoring and for state governments to monitor effectively; (2) pre-insolvency assessments might tempt state legislatures to use the accumulated funds for other purposes; (3) pre-insolvency assessments are not needed to enhance capacity in view of the guaranty funds' ability to borrow money if assessment caps are reached in a given year; and (4) procedures that allow early access of guaranty funds to an insolvent insurers' assets produce reasonably timely payments to policyholders.

The question of pre- versus post-insolvency assessments also is related to the discussion of risk pooling arrangements in Chapter 5, which pointed out the disadvantages of assessing policyholders after losses. Collection and enforcement costs are relatively low for guaranty funds, however, because the entities that are assessed are insurers subject to state insurance law. Other things being equal, this weakens the case for pre-insolvency assessments.

Risk-based Assessments Another issue is whether better incentives for safety could be achieved with risk-based assessments, whether on a post-insolvency or a pre-insolvency basis. Similar to risk-based capital requirements, either pre- or post-insolvency assessments could be varied across insurers in relation to measures of insolvency risk. In principle, risk-based assessments could help deter excessive insolvency risk, because higher risk behavior would require an insurer to pay higher assessments. In practice, however, risk-based assessments might reflect only a few broad risk categories (as is true in banking), which would reduce any beneficial effect on incentives. Risk-based assessments also are at least partially redundant in principle as a means to reduce insolvency risk given the existence of risk-based capital requirements.

The risk-based assessment issue is related to pre- versus post-insolvency funding. Post-insolvency risk-based assessments, which would allocate a greater share of total post-insolvency assessments to higher risk insurers than to lower risk insurers, would probably have less effect on incentives for safety than pre-insolvency risk-based assessments. The reason is that higher risk insurers are more likely to become insolvent and thus less likely to have to pay post-insolvency risk-based assessments following an increase in insolvencies. In contrast, pre-insolvency risk-based assessments require insurers to pay in advance in order to operate with higher risk (i.e., they have to pay in order to play). Post-insolvency risk-based assessments also could further harm companies that have been weakened by an industry shock, such as a major catastrophe, thus increasing their likelihood of insolvency.

As a result of these influences, risk-based guaranty fund assessments might need to be prefunded. As noted above, risk associated with unexpected changes in pro rata (nonrisk-based) post-insolvency assessments gives safe insurers more incentive to exert pressure for effective regulation that will reduce the likelihood of large assessments. A combination of some pre-insolvency funding with risk-based assessments that vary over time in relation to the average cost of paying claims of insolvent insurers might provide safe insurers with similar incentives to press for effective regulation. The reason is that insurers still would be exposed to increased assessments in the event of adverse insolvency experience.

7.4 Summary

- The frequency and severity of insurer insolvencies increased beginning in the mid-1980s in conjunction with unexpected increases in claim costs and reductions in asset values. It is difficult to determine the extent to which the increase in insolvencies reflected inadequate ex ante capitalization and risk management by some insurers, as opposed to large, unexpected shocks that reduced insurer capital.

- A number of financial rating agencies rate insurer insolvency risk. These solvency ratings are widely used by business insurance buyers, insurance agents and brokers, and some personal insurance buyers.

- State regulation of insurer solvency includes: (1) regulatory monitoring of insurer insolvency risk, (2) controls on insurer assets and capital, and (3) guaranty funds that pay part of the claims of insolvent insurers.

- Solvency screening systems, such as IRIS and FAST, are used by regulators to help identify insurers that have high insolvency risk.

- Risk-based capital requirements link required capital to an insurer's exposure to risk, including asset risk and the risk that claims will be higher than expected. If an insurer's ratio of capital to its risk-based capital requirement falls below one or more specified thresholds, the insurer is subject to specific regulatory actions.

- Insurance guaranty funds provide substantial protection against loss to consumers when insurers fail. Guaranty fund payments generally are financed by post-insolvency assessments on surviving insurers.

- Guaranty fund protection of consumers against losses from insurer insolvency reduces the incentive for consumers to seek coverage from safe insurers. As a result, increases in guaranty fund protection can increase insurer insolvency risk.

Key Terms

rating agencies 119	fixed minimum capital requirements 125
solvency ratings 119	risk-based capital requirements 125
delegated monitoring 123	guaranty funds or associations 126
IRIS 123	post-insolvency assessments 127
FAST 123	

Questions and Problems

1. Does the insolvency of an insurance company necessarily imply that the insurer had too little capital before insolvency, thus leading to a high risk of insolvency?

2. Does the insolvency of an insurance company necessarily imply that solvency regulators either engaged in unjustified forbearance or were asleep at the switch and thereby failed to intervene in time to prevent insolvency?

3. Why are solvency ratings more likely to be used by business insurance buyers than by personal insurance buyers?

4. Would risk-based capital be desirable in a world in which each insurer's insolvency risk was known to consumers? Would guaranty funds be desirable in such a world?

5. Explain why (*a*) and (*b*) might be related: (*a*) Insolvency problems have been much worse in the banking and savings and loan

industries than in the insurance industry. (*b*) Federal deposit insurance and other guarantees of banks and savings and loan obligations provide broader and more comprehensive protection to bank depositors than guaranty funds provide to insurance consumers.

6. Why might some insurers be reluctant to reduce their capital if guaranty fund coverage was increased and the incentives of insurance buyers to deal with safe insurers were therefore reduced?

Answers to Concept Checks

1. Complete guaranty fund protection would substantially eliminate consumers' incentive to buy coverage from safe insurers. As a result, insurers would have less incentive to hold capital and take other actions to reduce insolvency risk, thus increasing the probability of insolvency for many insurers.

2. The large amount of capital required and the regulatory costs of making every insurer hold enough capital would exceed what most consumers would be willing to pay to eliminate insolvency risk. (Note the similarity of this question and response to concept checks 2 and 3 in Chapter 2, on the willingness of consumers to pay more for airline safety.)

References

Best's Insolvency Study—Life/Health Insurers, 1976–1991. Oldwick, NJ: A. M. Best Company, 1991. (*Comprehensive discussion of the frequency, severity, and causes of life-health insurer insolvencies.*)

Best's Insolvency Study—Property/Casualty Insurers, 1969–1990. Oldwick, NJ: A. M. Best Company, 1991. (*Comprehensive discussion of the frequency, severity, and causes of property–liability insurer insolvencies.*)

Cummins, J. David; Scott Harrington; and Greg Niehaus. "Risk-Based Capital Requirements for Property-Liability Insurers: A Financial Analysis." In *The Financial Dynamics of the Insurance Industry,* eds. Edward I. Altman and Irwin T. Vanderhoof. New York: New York University Salomon Center, 1995. (*Analyzes risk-based capital, including the NAIC system.*)

Harrington, Scott. "Policyholder Runs, Life Insurance Company Failures, and Insurance Solvency Regulation." *Regulation: Cato Review of Business and Government,* Spring 1992. (*Reviews insolvency problems in the life insurance industry and discusses guaranty funds and possible changes in regulation.*)

Klein, Robert W. "Solvency Monitoring of Insurance Companies: Regulators' Role and Future Direction." In *The Financial Dynamics of the Insurance Industry,* eds. Edward I. Altman and Irwin T. Vanderhoof. New York: New York University Salomon Center, 1995. (*Detailed introduction to regulatory solvency monitoring and screening systems.*)

Appendix 7A

Illustration of Risk-Based Capital

Given the complexity of insurer operations and the RBC formulas, our purpose here is not to provide a detailed description of the property–liability and life–health insurer RBC formulas. We will, however, illustrate the main ideas underlying RBC for a property–liability insurer using an expanded version of the TLC Insurance Company example introduced in Chapter 5.

Assume that:

1. TLC wrote personal auto liability policies during the year with expected claim costs equal to $20 million.

2. TLC received premiums of $30 million, of which $15 million was earned during the year for accounting purposes with the remaining $15 million reported as its year-end liability for unearned premiums (known as the *unearned premium reserve*).[9]

3. TLC paid underwriting and distribution expenses of $10 million.

4. TLC estimated that claim costs (including loss adjustment expenses) for accidents that had occurred by year-end equaled $10 million, of which $5 million had been paid by year-end and $5 million was unpaid and reported as its year-end liability for unpaid claim costs (known as the *loss reserve*).

5. TLC had assets at year-end of $25 million, with $7.5 million invested in US government bonds, $15 million in municipal and corporate bonds in the highest NAIC quality category (i.e., with the lowest default risk), and $2.5 million in common stocks.

Under the RBC system, TLC's accounting capital (known as *surplus*) is compared to its RBC. (To focus on the main ideas, this discussion ignores a number of adjustments to capital required by the RBC system before conducting this comparison.) TLC's accounting capital equals its assets minus its accounting liabilities for unearned premiums and unpaid claims. That is, its accounting capital equals assets ($25 million) minus the unearned premium reserve ($15 million) minus the loss reserve ($5 million), so that its capital equals $5 million.

Ignoring (again for simplicity) credit risk and off–balance sheet risk, TLC's required RBC will reflect its asset risk and underwriting risk. The asset and underwriting risk factors and charges for TLC as of 1996 are shown in Table 7.A1. The risk factors for asset risk are the same for each insurer, and they will not vary over time unless changed by the NAIC. The calculations of the underwriting risk factors depend on several variables, including (in part) an average of industry and individual company experience using the worst underwriting profit (loss) experience during the preceding decade. The underwriting risk factors vary across insurers and over time.

The total RBC for TLC is obtained using the charges by (1) summing the squares of each charge, (2) taking the square root of this sum, and (3) multiplying the result by 0.5. Taking the square root of the sum of squared charges adjusts for the less than perfect correlation across risk categories.[10] The purpose of multiplying by 0.5 is to reduce the amount of RBC produced by the formula so as not to produce an excessive level of

---

[9]Accounting rules require insurers to recognize premiums as earned evenly over the coverage period. For example, for a one-year policy sold on July 1, one-half of the annual premium would be earned by December 31. The remaining one-half would be unearned and thus included in the unearned premium reserve liability. The term *reserve* is potentially confusing. Keep in mind that the unearned premium reserve and loss reserve are liabilities, not earmarked asset accounts as might be implied by the term *reserve*.

[10]This procedure is theoretically appropriate if the risks associated with each item are uncorrelated.

Table 7A.1 RBC Charges for TLC at year-end (in thousands).

Risk Category	Description	Amount for TLC (a)	RBC Factor (b)	RBC Charge (a) × (b)
Assets	US government bonds	$ 7,500	0.0	$ 0
	Highest quality bonds	15,000	0.003	45
	Common stocks	2,500	0.15	375
Underwriting	Loss reserve	5,000	0.155	775
	Premiums written during year	30,000	0.172	5,160

RBC in relation to industry capital when the formula was adopted.

This calculation produces total RBC for TLC equal to $2,615,764. The ratio of TLC's accounting capital ($5 million) to its total RBC is 191.1 percent. How would TLC look to regulators and other parties interested in whether its capital was adequate? The answer would be, not very good, even though TLC's $5 million in capital would exceed the fixed minimum capital requirement in almost all states. Specifically, TLC's ratio of capital to RBC would require the insurer to file a plan with regulators explaining why its ratio of capital to RBC was less than 200 percent and describing its plan to correct the deficiency (see Table 7.3).

TLC could increase its ratio of capital to RBC by raising more capital or by altering its investment policy. However, if TLC sold its common stock investments and invested the proceeds in US government bonds, its total RBC would only decline from $2,615,764 to $2,609,035. Its ratio of capital to RBC would only increase from 191.1 percent to 191.6 percent. The increase is negligible because (1) TLC has

written a relatively large amount of premiums in relation to its capital, and (2) the property–liability insurer RBC formula gives more weight to under-writing risk than asset risk. The greater weight for underwriting risk in the property–liability insurer RBC formula is based on the historical evidence that underwriting risk generally plays a greater role than asset risk in property–liability insurer insolvencies. The life–health insurer RBC formula gives more weight to asset risk, given that changes in asset values have led to more insolvencies for life–health insurers.

TLC's basic problem is that it has too little capital compared to the amount of business it has written. (The typical insurer with this amount of business would have two to three times as much capital.) In order for TLC to reduce its ratio of capital to RBC significantly, it would have to raise more capital, write less coverage, and/or reinsure more of its business. If TLC did this, its ratio of RBC to capital would be dominated less by the RBC charge for underwriting risk; the ratio thus would become more sensitive to changes in TLC's investment mix.

Chapter 8

Insurance Pricing

Chapter Objectives

- Explain the fundamental determinants of insurance premiums.
- Explain why and how insurers classify buyers into different groups based on estimates of expected claim cost, and describe the effects of this classification on societal welfare.
- Explain how insurance premiums may be affected by shocks to insurer capital.
- Summarize the evidence and explanations for the insurance underwriting cycle.
- Discuss reasons for and consequences of government regulation of insurance prices.

8.1   Insurance Costs and Fair Premiums

This chapter provides a general introduction to insurance pricing. Later chapters contain more details on pricing particular types of coverage, such as workers' compensation insurance, automobile insurance, and life insurance. A fundamental principle of insurance pricing is that if insurers are to sell coverage willingly, they must receive premiums that (1) are sufficient to fund their expected claim costs and administrative costs and (2) provide an expected profit to compensate for the cost of obtaining the capital necessary to support the sale of coverage. The premium level that is just sufficient to fund the insurer's expected costs and provide insurance company owners with a fair return on their invested capital is known as the **fair premium.** The fair premium is the premium that would be charged in a perfectly competitive insurance market; its major determinants are summarized in Figure 8.1.

FIGUR
Major
determi
of fair
insurance
premiums.

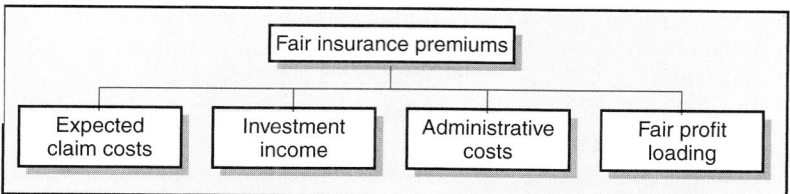

8.2   Expected Claim Costs

In this section we ignore investment income, administrative costs, and any required profit and focus on the expected cost of claims—known as the **expected claim cost**—that must be paid by the insurer for a contract or group of contracts. The expected claim cost represents the largest component of the fair premium for most types of insurance.

Homogeneous Buyers

Suppose that within a large group of insurance buyers each has the following loss distribution: Each buyer has a 0.15 probability of suffering a loss of $1,000 and a 0.85 probability of having no loss. Since each buyer has the same loss distribution, the buyers are said to be *homogenous*. Also assume that each buyer's loss is independent of (uncorrelated with) the loss of other buyers.

How much would an insurer need to charge each buyer to cover its claim costs if it insures a large group of these buyers, agreeing to pay the amount of each buyer's loss if a loss occurs? Since the policy pays the full loss of the buyer, the expected claim cost for each buyer equals the buyer's expected loss, which equals $150 (that is, 0.15[$1,000] + 0.85[$0]).[1] The actual claim cost could differ from the expected claim cost. Nevertheless, from the law of large numbers, the insurer knows that the distribution of average losses will be tightly concentrated around the expected value of $150, because losses are uncorrelated and there are large numbers of policyholders. In practice, an insurer will always have some uncertainty about its claim costs. For now we will ignore this complexity and assume that there are enough policyholders so that average claim costs will equal $150. (The effects of uncertainty in claim costs are introduced in section 8.5.)

Thus, if the insurer charges each buyer $150, it will collect enough money to pay claim costs given that the expected claim cost for each buyer is $150 and average claim costs are assumed to equal expected claim costs. If the probability of loss for each buyer increased from 0.15 to 0.20, then the average claim cost would increase to $200, and the insurer would need to increase premiums from $150 to $200 in order to pay its claim costs.

As can be seen in this simple example of a large number of independent homogeneous insurance buyers, an insurer can charge a premium equal to the expected claim cost and be able to cover all of its claim costs. Thus, a fundamental determinant of insurance premiums

---

[1]If insurance contracts do not cover the entire loss (see Chapter 10), using the term expected claim cost helps distinguish expected claim costs to be paid by the insurer from the policyholder's full expected loss. Other terms that are used to indicate the expected claim cost in the insurance business are *pure premium* and *actuarially fair premium*.

is the expected claim cost. If the insurer charged less than the expected claim cost, average claim costs would exceed average revenues. On the other hand, competition keeps the insurer from charging more than the expected claim cost.

Heterogeneous Buyers

Consider next what happens when there are two groups of consumers—bookworms and skateboarders—with different loss distributions as described in Table 8.1. The expected loss equals $100 for each buyer classified as a bookworm and equals $200 for each buyer classified as a skateboarder. Assume for simplicity that there are equal numbers of buyers in each group and that the number of buyers is large enough for the law of large numbers to imply that the average loss is equal to the expected loss for each group.

Now let's examine how the insurance market might operate when faced with this situation. Suppose Equal Treatment Insurance Company charged $150 to consumers in both groups and sold equal numbers of policies to both groups. It would expect to lose $50 on policies sold to skateboarders, but it would expect to make a profit of $50 on policies sold to bookworms. On average, it would break even.

Consider what would happen, however, if Careful Selection Insurance Company discovered how to identify the bookworms at zero cost. Careful Selection could then charge the bookworms a premium less than $150 and not offer any coverage to the skateboarders (or offer coverage at $200 or higher) and make a large profit. For example, suppose Careful Selection sold policies only to bookworms at a price of $130. Careful Selection's claim costs would be very close to $100 per policyholder, but it would receive $130 in revenue from each policyholder. The expected profit therefore would be $30 on each policy sold.

What will happen to Equal Treatment Insurance Company? When Careful Selection charges a lower premium to bookworms, Equal Treatment will lose the bookworms as policyholders and end up only with skateboarders. As a result, Equal Treatment will experience **adverse selection,** which is defined as the tendency of buyers with high expected losses to buy more coverage than buyers with low expected losses when charged the same premium. The term *adverse selection* is derived from the fact that, from the insurer's perspective (that is, from Equal Treatment's perspective), it receives an adverse selection of policyholders. The adverse selection is caused by the bookworms being attracted to Careful Selection Company.

As a result of the adverse selection, Equal Treatment Company will lose money if it continues to charge $150 to all policyholders because the only policyholders that it will attract are the policyholders with an expected claim cost of $200 (the skateboarders). Thus, Equal Treatment Company either has to increase premiums or classify policyholders in the same way as Careful Selection Company.

The story of Equal Treatment and Careful Selection illustrates the following points:

Table 8.1 Loss distributions for bookworms and skateboarders.	**Group**	**Probability of Loss**	**Probability of No Loss**	**Size of Loss**	**Expected Loss**
	Bookworms	0.10	0.90	$1,000	$100
	Skateboarders	0.20	0.80	$1,000	$200

1. Identifying low and high risk buyers has the potential to produce large profits (at least in the short run) for an insurer.
2. An insurer that fails to base premiums on information that is known to explain differences in expected claim cost across buyers will lose money due to adverse selection.

These points lead to a fundamental principle of insurance pricing: In a competitive market, differences in expected claim cost across consumers will produce differences in premiums across consumers as long as three conditions hold:

1. Insurance companies want to make money or at least avoid losing money.
2. Insurance buyers generally look for policies with low premiums for a given amount and quality of coverage.
3. One or more insurers can predict differences in expected claim costs across consumers at a sufficiently low cost.

By now you should be convinced that when differences in expected claim costs are known, competition, profit-seeking, and consumer desire for low premiums give rise to **cost-based prices**—that is, premiums that are commensurate with the expected claim cost of each buyer. In practice, insurers incur costs gathering and processing information in order to estimate differences in expected claim costs across buyers. These information costs and intrinsic uncertainty about the expected claim cost for different buyers make it infeasible in practice to have each buyer pay a premium based on the buyer's true but unknown expected claim cost. Instead, insurers estimate buyers' expected claim costs using all of the information that can help predict differences in expected claim costs as long as the information can be obtained at reasonable cost. The process by which insurers estimate the expected claim cost for different buyers and charge premiums that vary according to expected claim costs is known as **risk classification** (or *categorization*). Note that in the classification context, a "high risk" policyholder has high expected claim costs.[2]

Concept Checks

1. Innovative Collision Insurance Company has discovered that the weight of cars and "light" trucks helps to predict collision claim costs for its policyholders (heavier vehicles have lower collision claim costs). Explain how Innovative can maximize profits with this information and the likely effect of this on the firm's competitors.
2. Will Innovative's customers be happy that it has discovered this new factor that predicts claim costs?

Competition, Risk Classification, and Societal Welfare

The previous section demonstrated that risk classification naturally results from competition among insurers. In this section, we consider an important and often controversial issue: Is risk classification good for society? We will discuss this issue by considering a situation in which risk classification is not allowed and then examine the effects of introducing risk classification. In the context of the previous example, we start with the bookworms and the skateboarders all being charged the same price ($150) and examine the

---

[2]As we explained in Chapter 1, the term *risk* refers to expected claim costs in some contexts and variability around the expected value in other contexts.

effects of allowing bookworms to be charged a different price than skateboarders. We will see that there are three general effects of allowing classification: (1) a redistribution of wealth (bookworms will benefit from lower premiums and skateboarders will have to pay higher premiums); (2) a change in behavior (more people might become bookworms); and (3) the introduction of classification costs (insurers' efforts to identify bookworms might be costly). When deciding whether classification is "good for society," all three factors must be considered.

Redistributive Effects of Classification

When low risk (low expected claim cost) and high risk (high expected claim cost) buyers are forced to pay the same rate, a **cross-subsidy** takes place in that low risk buyers pay more than their expected claim cost and high risk buyers pay less. The high risk buyers typically like this cross-subsidy and the low risk buyers do not. If risk classification is then introduced, the price paid by the high risk buyers will increase and the price paid by the low risk buyers will decrease, thereby reducing cross-subsidies. In our previous example, classification caused a premium reduction for each bookworm and a premium increase for each skateboarder and thereby reduced the cross-subsidy from bookworms to skateboarders. Thus, one effect of classification is to redistribute wealth: bookworms benefit and skateboarders lose.

As noted earlier, it would be too costly and ultimately impossible to have each buyer pay a rate based on the buyer's true but unknown expected cost. Thus, introducing risk classification is not likely to eliminate cross-subsidies completely. Nevertheless, allowing classification will shift or redistribute wealth from high risk to low risk buyers. Viewed from the opposite perspective, if insurers are prevented by regulation from using certain types of information to classify buyers that helps predict claim costs, wealth is shifted from low risk buyers to high risk buyers. As we discuss later in this chapter and in the chapters that follow, this sometimes has occurred in auto, workers' compensation, health, and other insurance markets.

Note that by itself the redistribution effect from classification does not provide much guidance concerning whether classification is good or bad for society. This is because some buyers will benefit from classification and others will not. A value judgment must be made as to which buyers should receive greater weight when making the public policy decision. If the skateboarders were in charge of public policy, they would most likely say that classification should not be allowed, but the bookworms would likely disagree.

We showed in the last section that allowing insurers to compete based on price would lead bookworms to be charged less and skateboarders to be charged more if bookworms could be identified at low cost. Thus, allowing insurers to compete in this way would reflect a value judgment that buyers with higher estimated expected claim cost should pay more for coverage. Such a value judgment often is based on the notion that buyers with higher expected claim costs should pay more because they are expected to receive more money in claim payments from the insurer. On the other hand, some people feel that they should not have to pay more when their higher expected claim costs are due to circumstances largely outside of their control (e.g., due to their genes or the location of their residence). In contrast to the redistributive effects of classification, the next two effects to be discussed—behavioral changes and classification costs—in principle provide a more objective basis on which to decide whether classification is good for society.

Behavioral Effects of Classification

If changes in insurance prices affect behavior, classification can increase societal wealth by reducing the cost of risk. Before explaining this idea in general terms, we can convey some basic intuition using the skateboarders as an example. Note first that being a skateboarder results in an additional $100 in expected claim costs. That is, each person who decides to be a skateboarder, as opposed to a bookworm, increases the expected claim costs in society by $100. With classification, skateboarders have to pay all these additional costs, because their insurance premiums reflect the fact that they are skateboarders. Consequently, the only people who will choose to be skateboarders are those that value that activity more than the costs associated with the activity. Without classification (when everyone pays $150), however, part of the cost associated with being a skateboarder is paid by the bookworms. Since skateboarders do not pay all the costs associated with their activity, *too many people may choose to be skateboarders*. As a consequence, there may be too much skateboarding in society without classification and the cost of risk may increase.

These points can be stated in general terms. Recall from Chapter 2 that individuals and businesses generally make economic decisions based on the *private* benefits and costs that will accrue to the individual or business. Activities are undertaken until the marginal private cost equals the marginal private benefit. This type of decision making minimizes the cost of risk in society provided that decision makers pay all the costs associated with their actions and receive all the benefits. Thus, charging higher premiums to insurance buyers with higher expected claim costs provides higher risk individuals and businesses with more incentive to take actions to reduce the cost of risk through increased precautions and reduced levels of risky activity. Lowering their premiums below expected costs would reduce their incentive to reduce the cost of risk.

The magnitude of the reduction in the cost of risk due to the incentive effects of cost-based insurance pricing depends on how much behavior is affected by insurance prices. For example, charging higher premiums for workers' compensation insurance to businesses that have more frequent or severe worker injuries has been shown to reduce the number of injuries. Charging higher premiums for life and health insurance to people with genetic conditions that cause a higher incidence of sickness or illness may have much less, if any, effect on behavior.

Behavioral responses to insurance prices are complex and often cannot be measured accurately. In many cases, however, intuition suggests that cost-based prices can have a significant effect on risky behavior. In addition, cost-based insurance prices also affect the amount of insurance purchased, which in turn can affect incentives to avoid loss.[3] If, for example, the price of insurance is reduced (increased) to high (low) risk people or businesses because of government restrictions on classification (see section 8.7), then high (low) risk people or businesses will buy more (less) insurance coverage. This change in the amount of insurance coverage can increase the cost of risk by (1) increasing the cost of residual uncertainty for low risk people or businesses that purchase less coverage in response to the restrictions, and by (2) further reducing incentives for high risk people or businesses to undertake loss control.

[3]We discuss how increases in the amount of coverage can reduce incentives to engage in loss control in detail when we explain the concept of moral hazard in Chapter 10.

Concept Check

3. Other things being equal, 20-year-old males in most states face significantly higher rates for auto insurance than 20-year-old females because young males are involved in more accidents and have greater average loss costs. Explain how charging 20-year-old males and females an equal rate based on their average expected loss might affect behavior. Would total losses from accidents increase for males?

Classification Costs

Consider next the effects of classification costs; that is, the money spent by insurers on the collection and evaluation of information to classify applicants based on estimates of their expected claim costs. These costs obviously reduce the economic advantages of classification. In some cases, classification costs might cause classification to increase the total cost of risk because classification costs are greater than any savings due to changes in behavior. To see why, let's modify the Careful Selection Insurance Company example. Recall that Equal Treatment is charging everyone $150. Now Careful Selection enters the market and is able to identify bookworms by spending $25 for each policy sold to a bookworm (e.g., they administer a test on literature, history, and insurance). Careful Selection charges $135 for applicants classified as bookworms and $200 to applicants classified as skateboarders. Since skateboarders can buy coverage from Equal Treatment at a price of $150, only bookworms will buy Careful Selection's policies. At a premium of $135, Careful Selection has an expected profit of $10 per policy ($135 in revenue, $100 in expected claim costs, and $25 in classification costs).

Other insurers eventually will copy Careful Selection and also classify policyholders. Competition will cause the price for bookworms to fall to $125 and skateboarders eventually will have to pay $200. If behavior is not affected, the $50 loss to high risk persons from classification ($200 − $150) will substantially exceed the $25 gain to low risk persons ($150 − $125), and this type of classification will increase total costs, including classification costs. If classification costs money, but if it does not affect behavior, there is no reduction in the cost of losses (and the cost of loss control, including the value of forgone activity) that would offset the cost of classification. The total cost of risk is more likely to decline from classification when classification costs are small or the effects of premiums on behavior (in the way of precautions, a reduced amount of risky activity, or a greater amount of insurance purchased) are large.

When considering the possibility that classification might increase the total cost of risk, you should consider at least two other issues. First, disincentives for insurers to spend money on classification sometimes might lead to too little classification. For example, if competing insurers can quickly discover and copy new methods that better predict claim costs and lead to significant reductions in the cost of risk, insurers will have less incentive to develop these methods. This is one major advantage of insurers making underwriting decisions (decisions to accept or reject an applicant in a given rate class, which we discuss below) using information that is not disclosed to competitors. Second, any attempt to prevent classification by regulating insurance company classification processes will involve some cost. Regulation also will be less than completely effective, and it could have unexpected and unintended effects. You will learn about the types of regulations that restrict the use of information and their consequences later in this chapter and in subsequent chapters on automobile and workers' compensation insurance.

Risk Classification Practices

When allowed by law, insurers generally use elaborate risk classification systems. This section describes some of the common classification methods used by insurers. Subsequent chapters provide more detail on the classification methods used in specific lines of business.

Classification involves grouping together consumers with similar characteristics and charging them a premium or *rate* that differs from consumers with different characteristics. The term *rate* often is used synonymously with "premium" in the insurance business. In other cases, it refers to the price per unit of coverage (e.g., $1,000 of life insurance), with the total premium equal to the rate per unit of coverage times the amount of coverage purchased. These risk classes and the rates charged to each risk class are based on analysis performed by actuaries who examine historical data and estimate expected claim costs. They also are affected by competition and, in many states, regulation. Each insurer then employs selection standards to determine whether an applicant in a given class will be offered coverage at the insurer's **class rate.**

As was introduced in Chapter 5, the overall process of assessing the expected claim costs for buyers, determining the applicable rate, and deciding whether to offer coverage is known as **underwriting.** Class rates and associated underwriting standards generally differ across insurers. Insurers with more stringent standards generally offer lower premiums in any given class. For many types of business insurance, the underwriter also has substantial flexibility to modify the class rate to reflect the underwriter's evaluation of additional characteristics of the business applicant, such as the condition of business premises or property, the existence of safety programs, and so on. This procedure is commonly known as *schedule rating.*

Class rates and underwriting standards are based on a variety of characteristics of the buyer. For many types of insurance, class rates are modified to reflect the prior loss experience of the applicant. These modifications are known as **experience rating,** or *merit rating.* A special form of experience rating is known as a **bonus-malus** or *no-claims discount* system (see Box 8.1). Medium-to-large businesses also may have their premiums for a given coverage period modified based on loss experience during the same period. This is known as *retrospective experience rating.*

For example, workers' compensation insurance rates are routinely based on the buyer's prior loss experience, except for very small businesses where the prior loss experience has little ability to predict future claim costs (see below). Rates for larger firms also often reflect their claims experience during the coverage period. Personal auto insurance rates generally will be increased for drivers involved in an accident, at least when the driver is at fault. The simple reason is that the driver's past auto accident experience helps to predict future claim costs. People that cause accidents in a given year on average have more accidents during the next three to five years than people who do not.

However, a fundamental feature of insurance pricing for individuals and small- and medium-sized businesses is that factors besides prior loss experience of the buyer (or other direct evidence of risky activity, such as traffic citations for automobile insurance or safety regulation violations for a business) have a major effect on prices. The reason for this is that the use of nonexperience factors leads to substantially improved estimates of future loss experience. As noted above for the case of workers' compensation insurance for very small businesses, experience rating sometimes is not used at all because a buyer's prior loss experience does not reliably predict future claim costs. In the language of actuaries, the loss experience has insufficient *credibility* for use in rating.

European auto insurers generally use a special form of experience rating, known as the bonus-malus system. Similar systems are expanding in the United States where permitted by regulation and are beginning to be used in some medical insurance plans. The systems usually are called no-claim discount programs in the United States. With bonus-malus (no-claim discount) experience rating, the insured receives a percentage premium discount that increases with the number of years of claim free experience up to some maximum discount (such as 65 percent). If the insured files a claim, either part or the entire discount is lost, depending on the number of prior years of claim free driving. European insurers generally compete vigorously on the terms of their bonus-malus systems, and prior years' claim free experience is often portable if the insured changes insurers.

Bonus-malus systems may produce greater accuracy in pricing and therefore help reduce adverse selection and moral hazard. Like surcharges for accidents under more traditional merit rating programs, they also discourage the filing of small claims above and beyond the effects of any deductible. Some US consumer advocates argue that bonus-malus systems unfairly penalize a policyholder who files a claim for an accident that wasn't the policyholder's fault.

Many US insurers employ—and some states require—good driver discounts that give insured drivers a flat percentage reduction in premium, such as 20 percent, unless they have an at-fault accident or commit specified traffic violations. In contrast to true bonus-malus systems, the amount of discount is not directly linked (or linked less closely) to the number of years of claim free experience and the discount often is not lost in the event of a claim for an accident unless the insured was at fault.

8.3   Investment Income and the Timing of Claim Payments

The timing of claim payments and the ability of the insurer to earn investment income before claims are paid also affect the fair premium. In the simplest insurance contracts, the full premium is paid in a lump sum when the policy is issued, whereas claim payments are made over time. In some contracts, such as business liability insurance, a significant proportion of total claim costs are paid over a period of years after the coverage period has ended. Payments occur slowly over time as the insurer negotiates and settles known claims against its policyholders and is notified of additional injuries that occurred during the period of coverage. The lag between the time that coverage is sold and claims are paid is known as the *claims tail*.

Liability and workers' compensation insurance are "long-tailed" lines; that is, a large proportion of claims are paid a number of years after the coverage period. Property insurance coverage and coverage for employee medical costs under group health insurance contracts are examples of "short-tailed" lines; that is, most claims are paid during the year of coverage or the year after. Figure 8.2 illustrates the claims tail for several types of property–liability insurance. (In this figure, "other liability" insurance consists of business liability insurance other than auto liability, product liability, and medical malpractice liability.)

The fair premium reflects the ability of the insurer to invest premium dollars and earn interest until claims are paid. As interest rates rise, the amount of premium that needs to be charged to fund claim payments declines because the insurer can earn more interest. Similarly, as the claims tail gets longer (i.e., as a given total value of claims is paid over a longer period of time), the amount of money that the insurer needs to fund claims payments declines be-

FIGURE 8.2
Cumulative
percentage of
total losses
paid over time
for accidents
in year *t*.

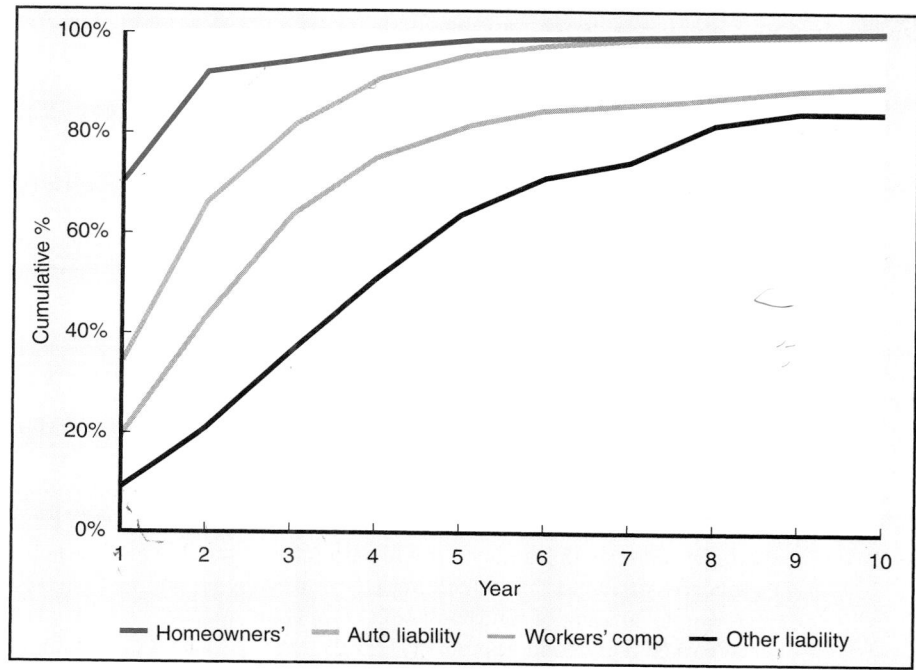

cause more investment income will be earned before claims are paid. Thus, a fundamental principle of insurance pricing is that *fair premiums reflect the ability of the insurer to earn interest on premium dollars before it has to pay claims*. In other words, the fair premium reflects the time value of money. The fair premium is negatively related to both the level of interest rates and the length of the claims tail. The following two examples will help you understand the relationship between premiums, interest rates, and the speed with which claims are paid.

All Claims Paid at the End of One Year

An insurer sells a policy that will produce $100 in claim payments at the end of one year. The timing of premium and claim payments is illustrated below:

Ignoring administrative costs and the fair profit loading, how much money does the insurer need to collect at the beginning of the year to pay the $100? Let P denote this amount of money and let r denote the annual interest rate. The interest earned by investing P for one year equals rP (i.e., it equals the interest rate times the amount invested). At the end of the year, the insurer will have $P + rP = P(1 + r)$. This sum must equal $100, the amount of claims to be paid at the end of the year. Thus,

$$P(1 + r) = 100$$

Solving this expression for P by dividing both sides by $(1 + r)$ gives:

$$P = 100/(1 + r)$$

If $r = 0.10$ (10%), then $P = \$90.91$. If $r = 0.05$ (5%), then $P = \$95.24$. Note that P is lower for the higher interest rate.

All Claims Paid at the End of Two Years

Let's go one step further and consider what happens if the $100 is paid in a lump sum at the end of two years rather than at the end of one year. The timing of premium and claim payments is illustrated below.

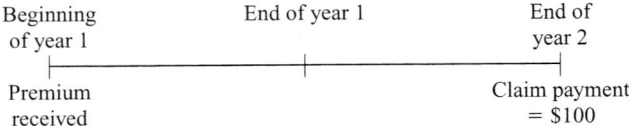

Beginning of year 1	End of year 1	End of year 2
Premium received		Claim payment = $100

Again we will let P indicate the money collected at the time the contract is sold and r denote the interest rate. As we explained above, the insurer will have $P(1 + r)$ at the end of one year. If it reinvests this amount, it will earn interest equal to $rP(1 + r)$ the second year (i.e., the interest rate times the amount invested during the second year). At the end of the second year, its total amount of funds will equal P, plus the interest earned the first year, plus the interest earned the second year, or $P(1 + r) + rP(1 + r)$. This amount must equal $100:

$$P(1 + r) + rP(1 + r) = 100$$

Dividing both sides by $(1 + r)$ gives:

$$P + rP = 100/(1 + r)$$

Solving for P (by dividing by $[1 + r]$ again) gives:

$$P = 100/(1 + r)^2$$

If $r = 0.10$, then $P = \$82.64$. If $r = 0.05$, then $P = \$90.71$. Note that these values are lower than when claims are paid at the end of one year.

The amount of money needed to fund expected claim costs taking into consideration the insurer's ability to earn investment income is called the **discounted expected claim cost;** that is, the expected claim cost times a discount factor (or *present value* factor) to reflect the time value of money. The discount factors in the preceding examples were $1/(1 + r)$ for the one-year case and $1/(1 + r)^2$ for the two-year case. When claims are paid gradually over time, the discount factors are more complicated.

Figure 8.3 shows the discounted expected claim cost for $100 of undiscounted expected claim cost for several different types of coverage (based on historic claim cost payment patterns) and two interest rates. As can be seen, the discounted expected claim cost is materially lower using the 10 percent interest rate than the 5 percent interest rate for each type of coverage. In addition, the discounted expected claim cost declines with the length of the claims tail (compare Figure 8.2). For example, $87 would be needed to fund the payment of $100 of expected claim cost for homeowners coverage when the interest rate is 10 percent; only $65 would be needed for other liability coverage due to its much longer claims tail.

FIGURE 8.3
Discounted expected claim cost per $100 of undiscounted expected claim cost using 5 percent and 10 percent interest rates.

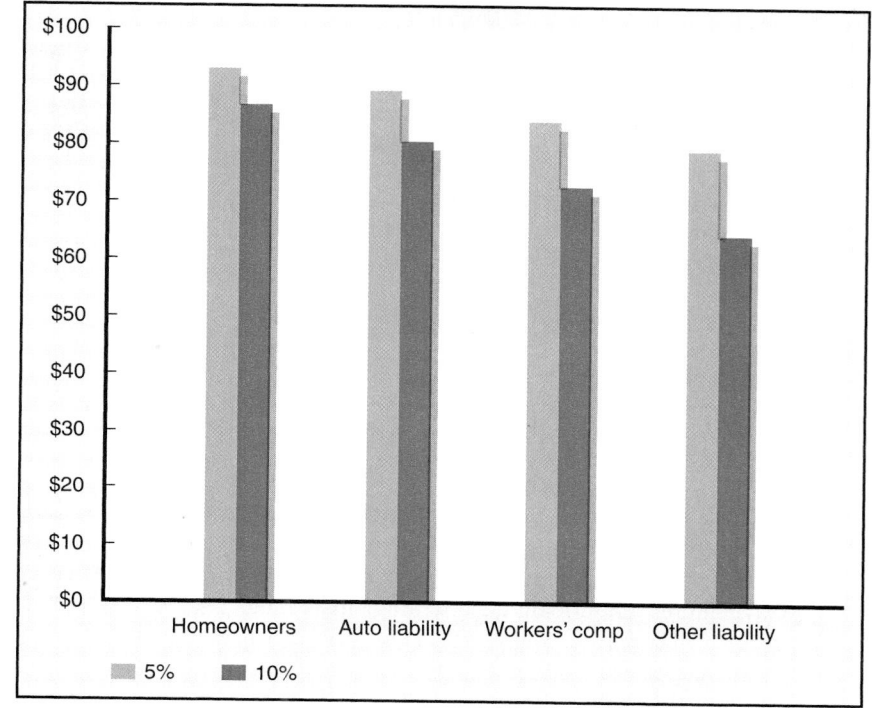

In more complicated cases, premiums for coverage during a given period are made in installments (e.g., quarterly premiums for a one-year homeowners policy), or coverage lasts for multiple years with premiums due annually, quarterly, or monthly (e.g., most types of life insurance). In these cases, the sum of the periodic premium must be higher than when the premium is paid in a single sum at the beginning of the coverage period because the insurer will earn less investment income.

Concept Checks

4. Other factors being held constant, why do long-tailed lines of insurance have lower fair premiums than short-tailed lines?

5. An insurer sells a policy for which it expects to pay $500 at the end of one year. It can invest funds at 6 percent per year. What is the expected claim cost? What is the discounted expected claim cost? What is the discounted expected claim cost if the $500 is expected to be paid after two years rather than one?

8.4 Administrative Costs

Insurers incur significant administrative costs for pricing/underwriting and distributing policies. As noted in Chapter 5, these costs commonly are called underwriting expenses. You also have learned about insurer costs associated with processing claims, known as loss adjustment expenses. The fair premium must include an **expense loading** to cover both underwriting and loss adjustment expenses.

Table 8.2
Underwriting
expenses and
loss adjustment
expenses as a
percent of
premiums for
selected types
of insurance:
1991–2000.

	Underwriting Expenses			
Type of Insurance	Commissions	General Expenses	Total Underwriting Expenses	Loss Adjustment Expenses
Homeowners	14.6%	16.1%	30.7%	12.1%
Personal auto liability	8.5	14.5	23.0	13.5
Personal auto physical damage	8.4	14.5	22.9	9.6
Workers' compensation	6.3	17.0	23.3	13.6
Other liability	10.9	17.2	28.1	27.5

Source: Data obtained from *Best's Aggregates & Averages, Property–Casualty,* 2001 edition.

Table 8.2 illustrates the magnitude of total underwriting expenses and the two major categories of underwriting expenses—commissions to agents and general expenses—as a percent of premiums for four types of property–liability insurance. General expenses include expenditures for pricing/underwriting, marketing, and issuing policies not written by agents. Table 8.2 also shows loss adjustment expenses as a percent of premiums. Loss adjustment expenses for liability insurance coverage are greater than for property coverage because of defense costs (e.g., attorney fees) involved in negotiating settlement or taking a case to trial.

The total expense loading for underwriting and loss adjustment expenses ranges from about 30 percent for personal auto physical damage insurance to about 50 percent for other liability coverage. It should be kept in perspective that some of these expenses are incurred to provide valuable ancillary services to insurance buyers (e.g., defense costs for liability coverage, much of the cost of settling workers' compensation claims, and general expenses that are incurred to provide business insurance buyers with advice on loss control).

Many types of insurance require significantly higher underwriting expenses when an insurer first sells coverage to a particular buyer than when the coverage is renewed. In these cases, only part of the first year's expense usually will be recovered in the first year's premium. The remainder of the expense is expected to be recovered over the duration of the relationship with the policyholder. Other factors held constant, this implies that fair premium rates will be lower the longer the buyer is expected to renew coverage, because the insurer then needs a lower periodic charge to recover its initial expenditure. The amount of renewal premiums that is available to recover first-year expenses constitutes a significant source of franchise value for many insurers and thus provides additional incentive for these insurers to hold capital to reduce the probability of insolvency (see Chapter 5).

8.5   Profit Loading

We now eliminate the unrealistic assumption made at the beginning of the chapter that an insurer's average claim costs equal its expected claim costs. You learned in Chapter 5 that when claim costs are uncertain, fixed premium insurance contracts make it necessary for the insurer to hold capital—that is, to hold assets in excess of expected claim costs—in order to increase the likelihood that it can pay all claims. In order to obtain capital, an insurer must offer investors an expected after-tax return equal to what they could earn elsewhere on an investment of similar risk.

We also explained in Chapter 5 that a disadvantage of investing in an insurance company is the double taxation on the investment income earned on the financial capital held by the insurer.[4] To offset this disadvantage, an insurer must find an additional source of income for capital providers; otherwise, investors will not provide capital. The additional income is obtained by charging premiums in excess of the discounted value of expected claim costs and administrative costs. Stated differently, policyholders must compensate investors for the disadvantages of investing in an insurance company. The extra amount that policyholders must pay to compensate investors for providing capital is called the fair **profit loading.** Since the underlying reason that the profit loading exists is uncertainty in claim costs, the profit loading also is sometimes called the *risk loading.*

As we explained in Chapter 5, the greater the risk that claim costs could be substantially higher than expected, the more capital an insurer needs to achieve a given probability of solvency. As a result, when claim costs are more variable (less predictable), greater amounts of capital will be required and thus a higher profit loading will be needed by insurers. Recall from Chapter 4 that variability in average claim costs increases as the correlation in claim costs across policyholders increases. Thus, other things being equal, the fair profit loading typically will be higher in lines of insurance that cover correlated losses (such as homeowners insurance, which covers windstorm damage).[5]

Concept Check

6. Assume that (*a*) the discounted expected claim cost for windstorm (hurricane) insurance is $100, (*b*) the discounted expected claim cost for fire insurance is $100, and (*c*) administrative costs are the same for both types of insurance. Which type of coverage will have the higher fair premium? Why?

To summarize the material on the determinants of fair premiums, we will work through a simple numerical example that will incorporate each of the four determinants. Suppose that you wanted to find the fair premium for a group of insurance policies each having the following loss distribution:

$$\text{Loss} = \begin{array}{ll} \$\ 10{,}000 & \text{with probability } 0.1 \\ \$\ \ \ \ \ \ \ 0 & \text{with probability } 0.9 \end{array}$$

---

[4]If the insurer invests in tax-exempt bonds to reduce this cost, there is still a cost due to lower returns on these bonds. In addition to the tax disadvantage, Chapter 5 also identified that an investment in an insurance company might suffer from greater agency costs and greater risk compared to an investment in a mutual fund that holds the same portfolio of assets as the insurer.

[5]Note that this discussion has focused on a basic economic model of insurance pricing that emphasizes the need to achieve profits to compensate insurers for the cost of holding capital to back their policies. Actuarial models of insurance prices usually describe the profit loading as a risk loading that is necessary due to the unpredictability of claim costs, with less predictability (higher standard deviation) leading to a higher risk charge. The economic model instead focuses on how higher standard deviation increases the capital required, which in turn increases the required profit loading necessary to cover tax and other costs of holding capital. While the details vary, both approaches have the same implication: Greater variability in claim costs increases the premium needed to sell coverage.

Assume that all claim payments will be made at the end of one year, the interest rate is 10 percent, and administrative expenses, which are paid immediately, equal 20 percent of the expected claim cost. Some administrative costs in practice are proportional to premiums rather than proportional to expected claim costs (e.g., commissions to agents). In addition, some administrative costs are fixed (i.e., they are approximately the same for each policy of a given type). We ignore these complications, which are readily handled, to focus on the main ideas. Finally, assume that this type of policy requires a profit loading (due when policies are sold) equal to 5 percent of the expected claim cost.

To calculate the fair premium, we separately measure each of the four factors affecting fair premiums and then add them together.

Step 1 (Expected claim cost): The expected claim cost equals $(0.1)(\$10{,}000) = \$1{,}000$.

Step 2 (Discounted expected claim cost): The discounted expected claim cost equals $\$1{,}000/1.1 = \$909.09$.

Step 3 (Expense loading): Administrative expenses equal $(0.20)(\$1{,}000) = \$200$.

Step 4 (Profit loading): The required profit loading is $(0.05)(\$1{,}000) = \$50$.

Step 5 (Fair premium): The fair premium therefore must equal $\$909.09 + \$200 + \$50 = \$1{,}159.09$.

Now, let's see what happens if policies are sold at the fair premium and actual claim payments average $1,000 per policy. Each policyholder pays a premium of $1,159.09, from which administrative expenses of $200 are paid immediately. After deducting this amount and the amount of premium necessary to provide the desired profit loading ($50), the insurer will have $909.09 to invest for one year at a 10 percent interest rate in order to pay claims. At the end of the year, the insurer will have $1,000, which equals the actual claim cost per policy. Thus, the fair premium is just sufficient to pay claim costs and administrative costs and produce the required profit loading.

8.6   Capital Shocks and Underwriting Cycles

Two related phenomena have been difficult to explain with the basic theory of fair premiums. First, some insurance markets have experienced dramatic increases in premiums following large industrywide reductions in capital caused by adverse loss or investment experience. We refer to these large reductions in capital as **capital shocks.** The magnitude of the premium increases cannot readily be explained by probable changes in fair premiums (i.e., by changes in the discounted value of expected claim costs, expenses, and normal profits). Instead, it appears that the adverse experience and the corresponding decrease in capital causes actual premiums to rise above fair premiums. Second, most analysts of the property–liability insurance industry believe that historically many lines of business have been characterized by a cycle in premium rates and profits. These cyclical price movements also suggest that actual premiums depend on past profitability. Before discussing these two influences on premiums, it is first important to review a basic implication of fair premiums.

Fair Premiums Are Forward Looking

As you learned earlier in this chapter, fair premiums depend on expected future claim costs and underwriting expenses, as opposed to depending on whether the insurer made more or less money than expected last year. Thus, *fair premiums are forward looking.* This point sometimes is subject to some confusion. Our goal is to help you clearly understand what "forward looking" means.

Consider an insurer that has completed operations in year one and that is writing policies in year two. Year one's results are presented in Table 8.3, along with the expected claim cost and fair premium for year two. The example ignores investment income and expense and profit loadings to keep things simple.

Because the actual claim cost for year one exceeds the expected claim cost, the insurer experiences an operating loss (negative profit). The expected claim cost for year two grows to $115, so the fair premium also increases to $115. The higher expected claim cost perhaps is partially due to the information that the insurer received from year one's results. That is, because claim costs were higher than expected in year one, the insurer's estimate of expected claim costs for year two may have increased. The actual claim cost and profit for year two is not known at the beginning of the year, but the expected profit is $0.

A common belief is that an insurer will routinely increase prices in order to make up for any bad experience in the prior year. However, this example illustrates that a price increase following a bad year need not indicate that an insurer is increasing rates to make up for unexpectedly high prior claim costs. The fair premium generally will increase following unexpected growth in claim costs because this often leads to upward revisions in insurer estimates of future expected claim costs.

Competition normally should keep an insurer from raising its rates in order to replenish its capital after a bad year. If an insurer with the experience shown for year one tried to raise the premium to $125 to cover the $115 expected claim cost for year two and recover the $10 loss for year one, other insurers could attract some of its customers by charging less than $125 and still have enough premium to cover the expected cost of selling the coverage. More generally, since insurance buyers usually prefer greater price stability, insurers that insulate buyers from fluctuations in premium rates due to random fluctuations in losses will tend to dominate those who do not (as is implied by our discussion of the advantages of fixed premium insurance in Chapter 5). Given this background, you are ready to examine situations in which insurance prices may depend on past underwriting profitability or investment performance.

Large Losses and Capital Shocks

Extensions to the theory of insurance prices and some empirical evidence suggest that insurance premiums sometimes increase by more than the discounted value of expected claim costs, expenses, and normal profits if *most insurers in a given market simultaneously experience very*

Table 8.3
Insurer operating results in years one and two.

Year	Expected Claim Cost	Fair Premium	Actual Claim Cost	Profit
One (past)	$100	$100	$110	$ −10
Two (future)	$115	$115	$?	$?

large losses on insurance contracts or investments. Many observers, for example, believe that this happened following large unexpected growth in business liability insurance claim costs in the mid-1980s and the destruction of the World Trade Center in 2001.

Large unexpected losses that affect most insurers at once substantially reduce industry capital. Thus, there is a depletion in the funds insurers hold to make sure that claims will be paid. In order for insurers to renew policies without increasing the likelihood of insolvency following large losses on previously issued policies, they would need to raise large amounts of capital in a short time period. However, the cost of raising capital is likely to be especially high following large losses due to uncertainty about the magnitude of losses and insurers' financial conditions. If capital cannot be obtained quickly at a reasonable cost, insurers have the choice of either increasing the probability of insolvency or reducing the amount of coverage they are willing to sell at a given price. To the extent that insurers reduce the amount of coverage they are willing to sell at a given price, there will be a reduction in the supply of coverage. As in any market, if industry supply is reduced, prices will increase (holding demand fixed).

The possible effects of capital shocks are illustrated in Figure 8.4 using the simplifying assumption that the demand curve for coverage does not change over time. The demand curve slopes downward: As price falls, more coverage is demanded. The industry (short-run) supply curves slope upward: A higher price increases supply. Now consider what happens if large losses occur in year zero. Two effects are illustrated in Figure 8.4.

First, the large loss may increase the expected claim cost for new policies. For example, following the destruction of the World Trade Center, insurers and reinsurers revised their expectations of losses on new business that covered losses from terrorist activity. In the case of earthquake/hurricanes, the magnitude of losses incurred might indicate that property is more vulnerable to damage than previously believed. In either case, the higher expected claim cost on new business causes the industry supply curve to shift back (up) because a higher price is needed to cover the higher expected claim cost. This effect on prices is consistent with the basic theory of fair premiums: Higher expected claim costs imply higher insurance premiums.

FIGURE 8.4
Effect of large losses on industry supply.

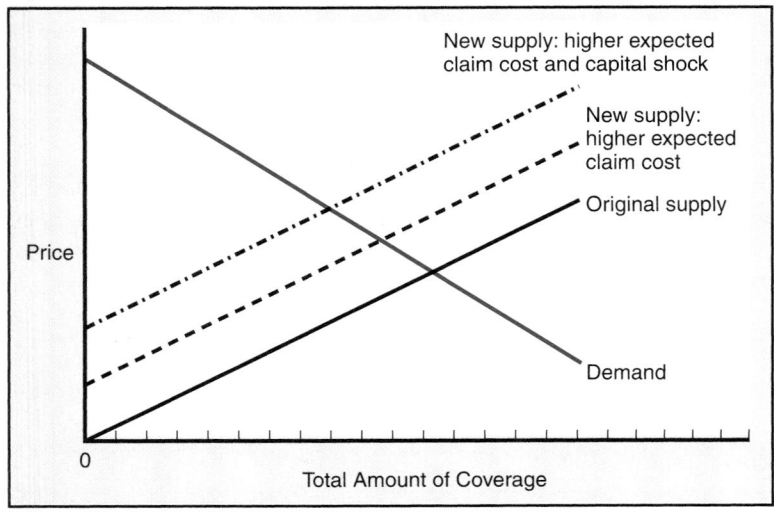

Second, the large loss in year zero depletes insurer capital, and, given the costs of raising new capital quickly and the reluctance to substantially increase the likelihood of insolvency, insurers reduce the amount of coverage they are willing to sell. Thus, there is an additional shift in supply, leading to an additional increase in price (and an additional reduction in total quantity of coverage sold). This second effect appears inconsistent with the theory of fair premiums, because premiums are increasing by more than the discounted value of expected claim costs, expenses, and normal profits.

The higher premiums imply that short-run profits will exceed the long-run fair return to suppliers of capital. This high return is not due to a lack of competition among insurers. Instead, the explanation is that large losses deplete capital and, given that capital is costly to replenish, existing insurer capital becomes a scarce factor of production. Given its scarcity, it is not surprising that it will earn higher returns. However, this situation is not likely to last long. Prices higher than implied by changes in expected claim costs will help restore insurer capital. In addition, over time, the sale of new stock and borrowing by insurers will restore capital. As capital accumulates, insurers will expand supply (the supply curve will shift out), thus putting downward pressure on price. Note that if price increases help replenish insurer capital, then policyholders are sharing the risk of very large, industrywide losses with insurers.

The Underwriting Cycle

Many lines of property–liability insurance, especially business insurance, historically have exhibited a cycle in premiums and insurer operating profits known as the **underwriting cycle.** The underwriting cycle can be described in terms of periodic soft and hard markets. Soft markets are characterized by numerous insurers seeking to write new coverage and by stable or even falling prices. Hard markets consist of reductions in the supply of coverage and sharp price increases. Many observers believe and some evidence suggests that the underwriting cycle causes actual premiums to fluctuate in a cyclical fashion around fair premium levels. Figure 8.5 illustrates a hypothetical cycle in the ratio of actual premiums to fair premiums.

FIGURE 8.5
Illustration of cycle in ratio of actual premiums to fair premiums.

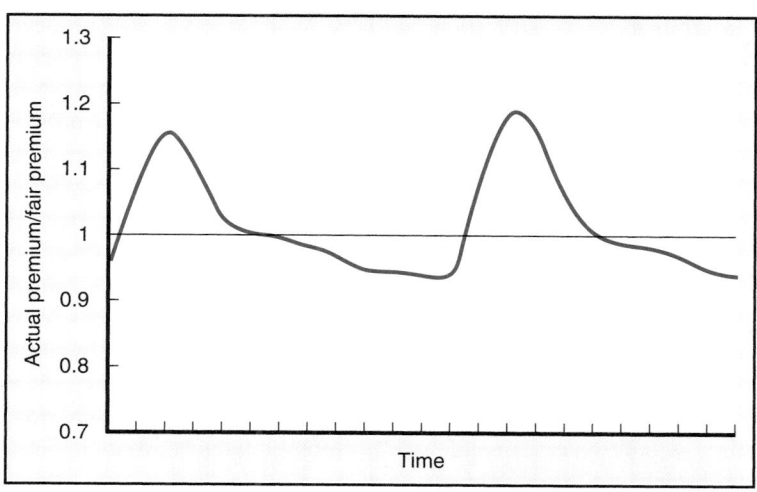

Uncertainty associated with cyclical movements in insurance prices is a major concern to insurance consumers, especially business risk managers. We will discuss the ramifications and response to this uncertainty in Chapter 24. For now, we simply will describe the basic evidence on the underwriting cycle and discuss some possible explanations.

The underwriting cycle does not appear to be strongly related to the general business cycle. Until the 1980s, the insurance cycle appeared to regularly last about six years between hard markets. However, the last three hard markets began in 1974, 1984, and 2000. Until the year 2000, some "cycle watchers" had started to proclaim that the underwriting cycle was dead.

One explanation for the underwriting cycle begins with the capital shock theory presented above. Large losses might cause capital to be depleted, which in turn causes premiums to rise above fair premiums and coverage to be reduced (the hard market). Subsequently, high prices during the hard market help to restore capital and new capital is raised. Both sources of capital increase industry supply and lower premiums (the soft market). If competition among insurers causes premiums to decline below fair premium levels, operating losses and reductions in capital will occur again, thus contributing to price increases and another hard market.

This explanation, however, does not make clear why competition would produce a persistent tendency for premiums to fall below fair premium levels (discounted expected claim costs, expenses, and normal profit levels) in soft markets. Some observers suggest that prices repeatedly tend to fall too low because of the difficulty in accurately forecasting claim costs for some types of insurance and strong pressure on insurers to retain clients (market share). One possible explanation is that some insurers charge inadequate prices due to overly optimistic forecasts of expected claim costs. Difficulty in accurately forecasting claim costs and thus in knowing whether an insurer's prices are adequate also makes it difficult for buyers and regulators to identify financially weak insurers. Some weak insurers could offer coverage at inadequate prices to generate cash to pay claims on previously sold policies and thereby delay being discovered and shut down by regulators. In either of these cases, inadequate prices by some companies could contribute to price cuts by other companies that wish to avoid losing their customers and the return on their investments in building a customer base.

In summary, there are various explanations for the underwriting cycle, but there is no consensus regarding why it has occurred or whether it still exists. Regardless of its explanation, corporate risk managers generally view the underwriting cycle as a disadvantage of purchasing insurance. The reason is that the cycle causes undesirable fluctuations in the availability and price of coverage from year to year.

8.7   Price Regulation

Government regulation of insurance prices assumes two major forms. First, many state governments regulate the size of changes in premium rates. Second, some state governments significantly restrict the type of information that can be used in risk classification. The first form of regulation governs changes in rate levels over time; the second form affects the magnitude of differences in rates across buyers within a given time period. There is a long history of both types of regulation in property–liability insurance. More recently, many states have begun to regulate rate changes and risk classification for health insurance sold to individuals and small businesses. The remainder of this chapter provides a broad overview of these types of regulation. Additional details are provided in later chapters that deal with particular types of insurance.

Regulation of Rate Changes

As explained in Chapter 6, until the 1960s most property–liability insurers were essentially required to charge rates developed by insurer-controlled rating organizations (formerly known as rating bureaus). These rates were subject to **prior approval laws,** which require regulators to approve rate changes proposed by the industry before new rates can be used. Beginning in the late 1960s, many states began to replace their prior approval laws with **competitive rating laws.** These laws generally require insurers to file rate changes with state insurance departments, but they do not require rate changes to be approved by regulators. Today, about one-half of the states have competitive rating laws for most types of property–liability insurance. Moreover, between 1998 and 2001, about 20 states even have eliminated requirements that rates for large commercial policyholders be filed with regulators. An exception is workers' compensation insurance, for which a significant majority of states continue to make rate changes subject to prior approval. A number of states also require prior approval of some health insurance rates.

Why Regulate Rate Changes?

While it might surprise some of you, economists generally agree that the economic case for prior approval regulation of insurance rate changes is very weak. Most insurance markets have many insurers, the market shares of the major firms are relatively low compared to many major industries, and there has been ongoing entry by new firms in many states. These features and other evidence suggest substantial price competition and no danger of excessive profits due to monopoly power (even though some insurance industry critics argue otherwise. As we explained in Chapter 6, the persistence of restrictive rate regulation in some states has increased pressure by some insurers for optional federal chartering and regulation.

Most insurers supported the regulation of property–liability insurance rates (and rate classes) into the 1960s, ostensibly to foster stability and availability of coverage. Consumer pressure for rate regulation was modest at that time. Today, most insurers oppose rate regulation—at least when it creates a significant risk of inadequate rates. Periods of rapid growth in claim costs and associated increases in premiums for auto, workers' compensation, and health insurance since the 1960s often created strong consumer pressure for rate regulation to reduce and delay rate increases (also see Box 8.2). Rapid growth in both costs and premiums appears to make relying on market competition to keep rates in line with costs politically untenable.

Because insurance markets are competitive, efforts to lower overall rates through price regulation in response to consumer pressure are ultimately self-defeating. Unless prices would be higher than costs in the absence of regulation, the only way in which regulation can persistently lower rates without causing insurers to leave a market is by inducing insurers to restrict supply or to reduce quality in ways that lower the cost of providing coverage. Temporary suppression of rates with rate regulation can cause insurers to (1) suffer operating losses, (2) reduce supply, and (3) curtail investments that are necessary to support the sale of quality coverage. In addition, a significant risk that prior approval regulation might produce inadequate rates can increase the price needed by insurers to make investments in building their operations and meeting demand for coverage in a given state.

King Canute's Revenge? California's Proposition 103

8.2

The mythical King Canute commanded the tides to go back—without much success. A slight majority of California voters commanded property–liability insurance rates to be rolled back by enacting Proposition 103 in 1988, following a period of rapid growth in business liability and personal auto insurance claim costs and premiums. Among other features, Proposition 103 called for a mandatory 20 percent reduction in property–liability insurance rates and prior approval of subsequent rate increases. The California Supreme Court later held that the 20 percent rate cut was unconstitutional to the extent that it would deprive insurers of a fair rate of return on capital.

Were California voters more successful than King Canute? Following extensive hearings, court rulings, California Department of Insurance rulings, and more hearings, a few insurers agreed to make refunds in the mid-1990s, based on insurance department rulings that their rates of return in 1988 exceeded the level deemed as fair by the department. Other insurers fought the rollback orders for nearly a decade, arguing that the insurance department's methodology overstated their rates of return and understated fair rates of return.

In 1997, a California consumer group that had advocated Proposition 103 and that was involved in much of the subsequent litigation filed suit against leading California auto insurers, alleging that the insurers had achieved profits in the 1990s in excess of the amounts permitted by Proposition 103. Although the saga continues in California, the rate rollback movement never really caught on in other states.

Effects of Regulating Rate Changes

With the exception of workers' compensation, proposals for changes in business property–liability rates commonly are approved without modification. In contrast, regulators in a number of states frequently have not approved proposed rate increases for personal auto insurance, workers' compensation, and, to a lesser extent, homeowners insurance. When their requests are not approved, insurers often will submit a subsequent request for a lower increase that will be approved. In cases where agreement with regulators is not reached, insurers sometimes have challenged state regulators in court.

Numerous studies have estimated the effect of rate regulation on rate levels. This research suggests wide variation in its effect across states, types of insurance, and over time. Focusing on the last two decades, rate regulation appears to have had little effect on rate levels in some states and lines of insurance. In other states, regulation of auto and workers' compensation insurance rates has reduced, at least temporarily, the margin between premiums and claim costs. A few states (e.g., Massachusetts and New Jersey for auto insurance and Maine and Massachusetts for workers' compensation) were characterized by chronic suppression of rate increases relative to growth in claim costs during much of the 1970s and 1980s. Significant numbers of insurers stopped selling auto or workers' compensation insurance in these states during this time.

Regulation of Rating Factors

Earlier in this chapter we discussed the effects of risk classification and noted that classification is often a controversial issue. We now discuss in more detail the debate over whether insurers should be allowed to charge higher premiums to those buyers perceived as having high expected claim costs. This debate has focused primarily on personal auto insurance and, in recent years, workers' compensation and personal and small business health insurance. Current issues include whether auto and health insurers should be able to base rates on age, sex, geographic region, health status or diagnostic tests for conditions such as AIDs (for health insurance), and credit history (for auto insurance). Some states have restricted either the types of information that personal auto insurers can use, or the right of insurers to reject applicants, or both. For example, a number of states do not allow personal auto insurers to base rates on the sex of the driver, and many states have imposed some limits on the use of credit ratings in auto and homeowners insurance pricing and underwriting. A few states require each insurer to accept almost all auto insurance applicants for coverage. Several states have adopted community rating programs for health insurance that require insurers to offer coverage using risk classification plans that significantly limit differences in rates based on the applicant's age, sex, or health status. Some states restrict genetic testing and use of genetic factors in pricing life and health insurance. Some of the pressure for restricting risk classification undoubtedly arises because classification often produces high premiums that create significant affordability problems for some buyers.

The participants in the debate over insurance risk classification find it difficult to agree on much of anything, including whether competitive risk classification actually produces cost-based prices. It is nonetheless possible to provide an overview of the key issues.

Incentives for Risk Control

As you learned earlier, charging higher premiums to insurance buyers with higher expected claim costs often helps reduce the cost of risk by providing higher risk individuals and businesses with a greater incentive to reduce losses. Lowering their premiums below expected costs would reduce this incentive and thereby increase the cost of risk. While it is generally difficult to measure how much the cost of risk changes due to cost-based insurance pricing, an important argument for allowing classification is that it does provide incentives to reduce the cost of risk.

Fairness, Imperfect Classification, and Control/Causality Issues

Many people regard cost-based insurance prices as fundamentally fair; people with higher expected claim costs on average should pay higher premiums. Other people argue that the imperfections in cost-based pricing justify government intervention to improve fairness.

You learned earlier that, due to the costs associated with classifying policyholders, classification systems will not be perfect; that is, policyholders with different expected claim costs will be placed in the same risk class. Consequently, low risk buyers in a given rating class who cannot be identified at reasonable cost pay premiums that are too large given their unobservable but lower expected claim costs. High risk buyers in a given rating class who cannot be identified get subsidized. For example, the very safest teenage drivers must pay high rates because most teenage drivers have high expected claim costs even if they have clean driving records to date. The problem is that the safe teenage drivers cannot be distinguished (at low cost) from other teenagers and consequently these safe teenage drivers subsidize the other teenage drivers.

Some persons argue that it would be fairer to prevent classification based on age and instead spread the burden of the subsidy to high risk teenage drivers broadly across all age groups, rather than making the safe teenage drivers bear the entire burden. For example, suppose that the expected claim cost for teenage drivers with clean driving records as a group is $500, but that 20 percent of the individuals in this group (who cannot be identified) have an expected claim cost of $100 and 80 percent have an expected claim cost of $600 (0.2 × $100 + 0.8 × $600 = $500). The argument against using age as a classification factor is that it is unfair to the teenagers with expected claim costs of $100 to pay $500 and thereby fully subsidize the high risk teenage drivers. Note that similar arguments can be used for other rating factors and types of insurance.

The counterargument is that preventing the use of a rating characteristic can increase the total subsidy to high risk buyers. Continuing with the example, suppose that the expected claim cost for drivers of other ages with clean driving records is $100 and that 10 percent of all drivers with clean records are teenage drivers. Then, if age cannot be used as a rating factor, all drivers with clean driving records would be charged $140, the average expected claim cost of all such drivers ($140 = 0.10 × $500 + 0.9 × $100). As a result, safe teenage drivers pay a much smaller subsidy to high risk teenage drivers, and drivers of other ages now pay an equal subsidy ($40). Notice, however, that the subsidy to high risk teenage drivers increases. Instead of being subsidized by only $100 ($600 − $500) with age as a rating factor, high risk teenage drivers receive a subsidy of $460 ($600 − $140) without age as a rating factor. Any adverse consequences on the behavior of high risk teenage drivers (see above) from not paying the premiums commensurate with their expected claim costs are likely to worsen.

Some people also argue that it is unfair to base rates on factors that are largely or completely beyond the control of the individual, such as age and sex, or, as sometimes is argued, where a person lives. Moreover, they object to these variables as only being proxies for higher expected claim costs, as opposed to measuring risky behavior directly. In addition, the use of uncontrollable factors in pricing often will have less impact on safety than basing rates on controllable factors. For example, auto insurance experience rating surcharges for accidents and tickets will likely do more to motivate young drivers to slow down than will basing premiums on age and sex. On the other hand, basing rates on uncontrollable factors still may help to significantly reduce the cost of risk by providing incentives to alter the level of risky activity or to reduce the value of property exposed to damage. For example, when young males pay higher rates in conjunction with their greater likelihood of accident involvement, fewer young males may buy cars, and those that do might on average buy less expensive vehicles. Both responses reduce the cost of risk.

Excessive Classification and Use of Subjective Assessments

The possibility that classification costs could cause some forms of risk classification to increase the cost of risk implies that government restrictions on classification could improve societal welfare in some cases. However, much of the debate over rating factors has focused on factors that can be observed at low cost (e.g., age, sex, geographic region, and credit history). Classification using low cost information is likely to reduce the cost of risk.

A related issue is whether insurers use too much subjective judgment in underwriting and, if so, whether this use should be prohibited. No consensus exists as to what constitutes subjective judgment. Some people feel that basing rates on geographic region is subjective. Others would not go this far, but they would argue that employing information about factors such as a person's credit history or personal life (e.g., a recent divorce) is subjective and undesirable. The basic theory of competitive risk classification suggests that use of subjective judgment by an insurer will not be rewarded and could easily cause an insurer to lose money—unless the judgment helps predict future losses, administrative costs, or the expected length of time that the policyholder will renew. Thus, insurers have no economic incentive to use information that does not improve predictions. There is substantial evidence that the major classification factors used by insurers help predict expected claim costs.

Concept Check

7. Subjective Life Insurance Company has a hunch that brown-eyed 25-year-
   less likely to die young than blue-eyed 25-year-old males. The compar
   (*a*) lower rates to the brown-eyed buyers by an amount that will attract mor
   still produce a profit, and (*b*) raise rates to the blue-eyed group to cover the higher number of expected death claims. What will happen to Subjective Life if its hunch is wrong (i.e., if there is no difference in expected death rates based on eye color)?

Ensuring Availability When Regulation Depresses Rates

When the regulation of rate changes or risk classification lowers rates for some buyers below the levels needed to cover expected costs and produce a reasonable profit, insurers will not voluntarily sell coverage. Severe supply shortages under these circumstances are prevented by state **residual market** systems. These systems force insurers that write a given type of coverage in a state to collectively supply coverage to most if not all applicants. An insurer must participate in the residual market if it wants to sell coverage in the voluntary market.

All states have residual markets for auto insurance and workers' compensation insurance. Some states also have residual markets for other types of insurance, such as homeowners and health insurance. While residual market policies usually are issued and serviced by private insurers, the prices for these policies are regulated by the state. The prices often are regulated to be below the cost of supplying the coverage (i.e., below the fair premium). As a consequence, residual market business generally produces operating losses. Residual markets usually are designed so that these operating losses are divided among insurers writing the given coverage in proportion to their market share in the voluntary insurance market.

Residual markets originally developed as a market of last resort; that is, to make coverage available to small numbers of high risk applicants that otherwise would be uninsurable or face prohibitively high premiums. However, residual markets for auto and workers' compensation insurance periodically have become very large in some states during the past three decades. The major reason is that regulation of rate changes or risk classification has caused rates for many buyers to fall below levels needed by insurers to provide coverage voluntarily. You will learn more about residual markets for different types of insurance in later chapters.

8.8 Summary

- The fair premium is the premium that is just sufficient to fund an insurer's expected costs and provide insurance company owners with a fair return on their invested capital. The fair premium depends on (1) expected claim costs; (2) investment income that can be earned on premiums prior to the payment of claims and administrative costs; (3) administrative costs; and (4) the fair profit loading.

- Risk classification by insurers involves grouping together buyers with similar expected claim costs and charging them the same premium rate. Buyers in risk classes with higher expected claim costs are charged higher rates. Insurers have strong incentives to classify buyers based on all information that helps predict differences in claim costs across buyers, provided that the information can be obtained at a sufficiently low cost.

- Risk classification generally helps reduce the total cost of risk by providing insurance buyers with incentives to alter their behavior (in terms of precautions, amount of risky activity, and amount of insurance purchased) in ways that reduce the cost of risk.
- Given the ability of insurers to earn investment income on premiums prior to the payment of claims, the fair premium reflects the discounted value of expected claim costs. As a result, the fair premium is inversely related to the level of interest rates and to the length of the claims tail (i.e., the average lag between the time that coverage is sold and the time that claims are paid).
- The fair premium includes an expense loading to cover the insurer's administrative costs, including both underwriting expenses and loss adjustment expenses.
- The fair premium includes a profit loading to compensate investors for the disadvantages (e.g., double taxation of investment returns) of investing in an insurance company. Other things being equal, the fair profit loading is higher for lines of insurance with more uncertainty concerning future claim costs because the insurer needs to hold more capital to achieve a given probability of insolvency.
- Fair premiums are forward looking: They depend on expected future claim costs and administrative costs, as opposed to depending on whether the insurer made more or less money than expected in the past.
- If most insurers in a given market simultaneously experience very large capital shocks in the form of either losses on insurance contracts or investments, insurance premiums may increase temporarily by more than any increase in the discounted value of expected claim costs, administrative costs, and the normal fair profit loading. To the extent that this occurs, policyholders share the risk of very large, industrywide losses with insurers.
- Many lines of property–liability insurance have historically exhibited a cycle in premiums and insurer operating profits known as the underwriting cycle. Coverage is readily available and prices are stable and falling during soft market periods; coverage is comparatively scarce and prices increase sharply during hard market periods.
- Some states have prior approval laws that require insurers to obtain prior regulatory approval of rate changes for one or more lines of insurance; other states have competitive rating laws that allow insurers to change rates without prior approval. Some states have restricted the types of information that insurers can use in rate classification based on arguments that use of the information would either be unfair or make coverage unaffordable for some buyers.
- If regulation of rate changes or risk classification lowers the premium that can be charged to some buyers below the fair premium, state residual markets for some types of coverage prevent supply shortages by requiring insurers to collectively supply coverage to most if not all applicants.

Key Terms

fair premium 134	class rate 141	profit loading 147
expected claim cost 135	underwriting 141	capital shocks 148
adverse selection 136	experience rating 141	underwriting cycle 151
cost-based prices 137	bonus-malus system 141	prior approval laws 153
risk classification 137	discounted expected claim cost 144	competitive rating laws 153
cross-subsidy 138	expense loading 145	residual market 157

Questions and Problems

1. An insurer sells a very large number of policies to people with the following loss distribution:

$$\text{Loss} = \begin{cases} \$100,000 & \text{with probability } 0.005 \\ \$\ 60,000 & \text{with probability } 0.010 \\ \$\ 20,000 & \text{with probability } 0.020 \\ \$\ 10,000 & \text{with probability } 0.05 \\ \$\ \ \ \ \ \ \ \ 0 & \text{with probability } 0.915 \end{cases}$$

   a. Calculate the expected claim cost per policy.
   b. Assume claims are paid one year after premiums are received and that the interest rate is 6 percent. Calculate the discounted expected claim cost per policy.
   c. Assume that the only administrative cost is the cost of processing an application, which equals $100 per policy, and that the fair profit loading is $50. What is the fair premium?

2. Redo problem 1, but include the expected cost of loss adjustment expenses (the cost of processing claims), assuming that loss adjustment expenses equal 12 percent of losses and are paid at the same time that claims are paid.

3. Redo problem 1 with the following loss distribution:

$$\text{Loss} = \begin{cases} \$2,000,000 & \text{with probability } 0.001 \\ \$1,000,000 & \text{with probability } 0.005 \\ \$\ \ 200,000 & \text{with probability } 0.010 \\ \$\ \ 100,000 & \text{with probability } 0.020 \\ \$\ \ \ \ \ \ \ \ \ \ 0 & \text{with probability } 0.964 \end{cases}$$

4. Suppose an insurer estimates that an exposure has the following loss distribution:

$$\text{Loss} = \begin{cases} \$600,000 & \text{with probability } 0.01 \\ \$100,000 & \text{with probability } 0.02 \\ \$\ 30,000 & \text{with probability } 0.03 \\ \$\ \ \ \ \ \ \ 0 & \text{with probability } 0.94 \end{cases}$$

   Claim payments are not expected to be paid until one year after the premium is received. If the interest rate is 5 percent, what is the discounted expected claim cost?

5. Redo problem 4 assuming a 8 percent interest rate.

6. Redo problem 4 assuming claim payments are not made until two years after the premium is received.

7. Based on your answers to problems 4 through 6, make general statements about the effect of interest rates and the claims tail on insurance premiums.

8. You have been hired to prepare a report examining whether gender should be outlawed as a rating factor for all insurance. Summarize your main arguments for and against.

9. Chapter 5 explained how fixed premium insurance contracts cause insurers to bear the risk that losses will be greater than expected. Explain why this might not be true if capital shocks affect insurance prices.

10. Given the existence of an underwriting cycle, when is the best time for individuals or businesses to have to buy insurance? When is the worst time?

Answers to Concept Checks

1. Innovative could profit by reducing collision premiums for owners of heavier vehicles below levels offered by competitors in order to attract more of these owners and provide a substantial profit to the insurer. Innovative probably would increase premiums for own- ers of other types of vehicles to reflect their higher expected claim costs. Some of these other owners would switch to other insurers. Other insurers would experience a reduction in the proportion of their customers that own heavier vehicles and experience losses from

adverse selection. (Note: Some data indicate that heavier vehicles cause more harm to drivers of other vehicles than do lighter vehicles. As a result, some insurers charge higher *liability insurance* rates for owners of heavier vehicles and lower liability insurance rates for owners of other vehicles. Thus, owners of heavier vehicles may pay lower collision insurance rates but higher liability insurance rates than owners of other vehicles.)

2. Innovative's customers that own heavier vehicles will be pleased; those that own other vehicles will not be happy if their rates are increased. Some of them will switch to other insurers unless other insurers also begin to base collision insurance premiums on vehicle weight.

3. Because their rates would decline, some 20-year-old males would be more likely to (a) buy a car, (b) buy a more expensive car, (c) buy an auto insurance policy with a lower deductible, and (d) reduce precautions while driving if they have lower deductibles. Total accident losses would increase because of (a), (b), and (d).

4. Other factors held constant, long-tailed lines will have lower premiums than short-tailed lines because the insurer will have more time to invest premiums before claims are paid (the discounted expected value of claim costs is lower).

5. The expected claim cost is $500. The discounted expected claim cost if claims are paid at the end of one year is $471.70 = $500/1.06. The discounted expected claim cost if claims are paid at the end of two years is $445 = $500/1.06^2.

6. Higher correlation for windstorm insurance claim costs across policyholders—as opposed to fire insurance claim costs—will require the insurer to hold more capital to achieve a given probability of solvency. Thus, the fair premium for windstorm insurance will be higher to compensate the insurer's investors for providing the higher amount of capital needed for windstorm coverage. (Note: In practice most property insurance policies that cover fire losses also cover windstorm losses. Fair premiums for policies that cover both fire and windstorm losses will be higher in geographic areas that are more prone to large windstorm losses because of (a) the higher expected claim costs from windstorms, and (b) the higher amount of capital needed to sell coverage in these areas.)

7. If the hunch that brown-eyed males are less likely to die young is wrong, Subjective Life will lose money. The insurer will attract brown-eyed males at premium rates that are inadequate to cover costs given that the insurer's hunch is incorrect; it will insure fewer blue-eyed males because of the higher premium rates charged to these buyers. As a result, Subjective Life's customer base will consist of a disproportionate number of brown-eyed males with inadequate premiums. Any profits on its blue-eyed customers will be insufficient to offset losses on its brown-eyed customers.

References

Abraham, Kenneth. "Efficiency and Fairness in Insurance Risk Classification." *Virginia Law Review* 71 (1985), pp. 403–51. (*Provides a clear summary of fairness issues.*)

Harrington, Scott; and Greg Niehaus. "Volatility and Underwriting Cycles," in George Dionne, ed., *Handbook of Insurance.* Boston, MA: Kluwer Academic, 2000. (*Summarizes theory and empirical evidence on capital shocks and the underwriting cycle.*)

D'Arcy, Stephen; and Neil Doherty. *The Financial Theory of Pricing Property–Liability*

Insurance Contracts. S. S. Huebner
Foundation Monograph No. 15. Homewood,
IL: Richard D. Irwin, 1988. (*Provides an in-
depth treatment of the theory of fair
premiums.*)

Harrington, Scott; and Helen Doerpinghaus. "The
Economics and Politics of Automobile
Insurance Rate Classification." *Journal of
Risk and Insurance* 60 (March 1993),
pp. 59–84. (*Discusses possible effects on
behavior, political pressure for restrictions on
classification, and consequences of
restrictions.*)

Chapter 9

Risk Aversion and Risk Management by Individuals and Corporations

Chapter Objectives

- Describe what it means to be risk averse and why risk-averse individuals buy insurance.
- Explain the main factors affecting individuals' demand for insurance.
- Explain how business risk management differs from individual risk management.
- Explain how business risk reduction can benefit shareholders even when shareholders hold diversified portfolios of investments.

9.1 Risk Aversion and Demand for Insurance by Individuals

One objective of this section is to explain why individuals take actions to reduce risk, where risk is defined as uncertainty in the outcomes facing an individual. This objective may sound trivial. You may be thinking: People reduce risk because they do not like risk; that is, they are risk averse—end of discussion! While this reasoning is essentially correct, this section provides additional insight into risk aversion and explains why individuals may purchase insurance in some circumstances and not others. Many of these insights about individual demand for insurance are important in later chapters where we discuss public policy issues related to insurance.

The Effects of Insurance on Wealth

To show why people often take actions to reduce risk (e.g., by buying insurance), we first describe an insurance transaction from an individual's point of view. This perspective probably will differ from the way that you have previously thought about insurance (assuming you have thought about it at all). Suppose that Mr. Grace is faced with the possibility of being sued and held liable for damages this coming year as a result of a car accident. Assume that the probability of being sued successfully by a plaintiff is 0.5. (Mr. Grace probably is a more reckless driver than you are.) For simplicity, assume that the payment to a successful plaintiff is $20,000 and ignore defense costs. Finally, assume that Mr. Grace will have $100,000 at the end of the year if he is not sued.

Without insurance, Mr. Grace's wealth at the end of the year is uncertain: It either will be $100,000 or $80,000, depending on whether he loses a lawsuit. Using different terminology, Mr. Grace is faced with two possible outcomes for his wealth, and he does not know which outcome will occur. Given that the probability of a loss is 0.5, Mr. Grace's expected level of wealth at the end of the year is $90,000 ($100,000 × 0.5 + $80,000 × 0.5). His actual wealth will be either $10,000 above the expected outcome or $10,000 below the expected outcome. Thus, there is variability around the expected value.

Consider what happens if Mr. Grace purchases $10,000 of liability insurance coverage at a price of $5,000, where the premium is paid at the end of the year so that we can ignore the time value of money and thereby simplify the calculations. Note that the premium is equal to the insurer's expected claim costs ($5,000 = 0.5 × $10,000). Thus, we also are ignoring for simplicity the other factors (administrative costs and capital costs) discussed in Chapter 8 that affect the fair premium.

With insurance, if Mr. Grace does not have a loss, his wealth will be $95,000 ($100,000 minus the premium). On the other hand, if Mr. Grace has a loss, his wealth will be $85,000 ($80,000 minus the premium of $5,000 plus the $10,000 reimbursement from the insurer). Figure 9.1 illustrates the key point that the purchase of insurance reduces wealth when no losses occur, but increases wealth when losses do occur. By purchasing this insurance contract, Mr. Grace narrows the range of possible wealth outcomes; he reduces the variability (standard deviation) of wealth around the expected level of wealth.

Suppose instead that Mr. Grace purchases $20,000 of coverage, which is full insurance coverage since the severity of the loss equals $20,000. As before, we assume that the premium equals expected claim costs, or $10,000. With this higher level of coverage and higher premium, if a loss does not occur, Mr. Grace has wealth of $90,000 ($100,000 minus the $10,000 premium). If a loss does occur, he also has wealth of $90,000 ($80,000 minus the insurance premium of $10,000 plus the reimbursement from the insurer of $20,000). Full coverage implies that wealth is the same regardless of whether the loss occurs. Assuming that there are no uncompensated losses associated with the lawsuit, such

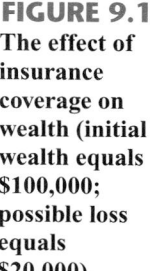

FIGURE 9.1
The effect of insurance coverage on wealth (initial wealth equals $100,000; possible loss equals $20,000).

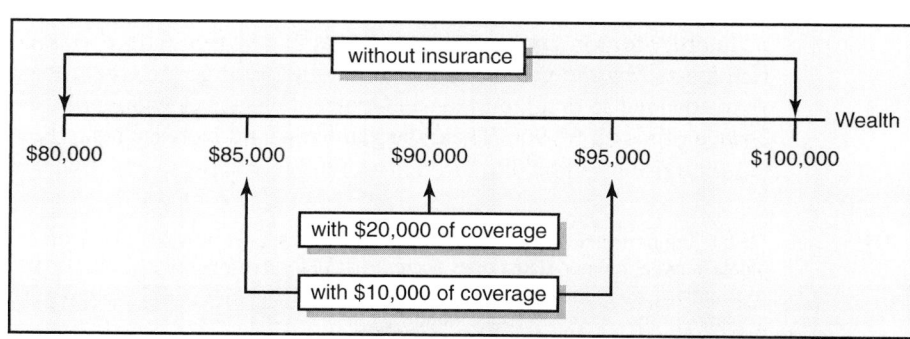

as time away from work or aggravation, Mr. Grace would not care whether he is sued or not. His risk has been eliminated.

In summary, this example demonstrates that by purchasing insurance Mr. Grace increases his wealth if a loss occurs and reduces his wealth if a loss does not occur. The increase in wealth if a loss occurs can be viewed as the *benefit* of insurance and the reduction in wealth if a loss does not occur can be viewed as the *cost* of insurance. This perspective is a useful way to think about insurance decisions. By purchasing auto insurance, for example, you reduce your wealth if you do not have an accident over the policy period, but you increase your wealth if you do have a serious accident. If a parent purchases life insurance on a child's life, the parent reduces the amount of money available when the child is alive but increases the amount of money available if the child dies.[1]

While the amount of insurance coverage that people purchase depends on several factors to be discussed below (e.g., the price of coverage and the buyer's income), this discussion indicates that one of the factors affecting insurance purchases is a person's preference for when he or she would rather have more money. Does a person prefer more money following a loss, or does a person prefer to have more money when the loss does not occur? Although people would prefer more money in both cases, this is not possible. To receive additional money following a loss, a person must decrease wealth when a loss does not occur. Most people are willing to give up some money when a loss does not occur (pay an insurance premium) in order to receive additional money from the insurer after a financial loss. In essence, the payment of the premium when a loss does not occur hurts individuals less than the benefit that individuals receive from having the insurer pay part of the loss. The reason is that money is more valuable to a person when the person has less of it and a monetary loss causes people to have less money.

Risk Aversion

The issue of when money is more valuable to a person is related to the concept of risk aversion. Technically, a person who is **risk averse** prefers a certain amount of wealth to a risky situation that yields the same expected wealth. For example, suppose that Mr. Grace is asked whether he would accept a 50–50 chance of winning $1,000 and losing $1,000. The expected value of the gamble is $0 ($0.5 \times \$1,000 + 0.5 \times -\$1,000$); thus, the gamble does not change his expected wealth. If Mr. Grace were risk averse he would not accept the gamble, because the risk (uncertainty) created by the gamble makes him worse off. Note that Mr. Grace's aversion to risk implies that the possible loss of $1,000 hurts him more than the possible gain of $1,000 benefits him. This is the essence of risk aversion. People are averse to risk because a loss of $X hurts them more than a gain of $X benefits them.

In order for Mr. Grace to accept the gamble he would need to be compensated for the risk created by the gamble. Suppose that he would only accept the gamble if the odds were changed so that there was a 60 percent chance of winning $1,000 and a 40 percent chance of losing $1,000. Then, the gamble would increase his expected wealth by $200 ($\$1,000 \times 0.6 - \$1,000 \times 0.4$). The $200 in additional expected wealth is the *risk pre-*

---

[1] While the perspective that purchasing insurance reduces wealth when a loss does not occur and increases wealth when a loss does occur is useful for many purposes, this perspective does not apply to situations when insurance covers losses that can be less than the premium, because it is then possible for insurance to reduce wealth if there is a small loss.

mium required to induce Mr. Grace to accept the gamble. All else being equal, people who are more risk averse will require a higher risk premium to induce them to accept risk.

In contrast, if Mr. Grace were risk neutral, he would be indifferent between accepting the original gamble and rejecting the gamble. The reason is that the gamble does not change his expected wealth and the uncertainty created by the gamble does not bother him. In other words, a person who is **risk neutral** cares only about expected wealth. A risk-neutral person therefore would not require a risk premium to accept risk.

These examples illustrate that risk-averse people require a risk premium to accept risk. Similarly, risk-averse people are willing to pay a risk premium to reduce risk. Suppose for example that Mr. Phillips has a 2 percent chance of losing $10,000. Then his expected loss is $200 (0.02 × $10,000). If Mr. Phillips were risk averse, he would be willing to pay more than $200 to eliminate the risk. However, if Mr. Phillips is risk neutral, the most he would pay to eliminate the risk is $200.

Risk aversion appears to be a characteristic of most people as evidenced by their behavior when faced with risky scenarios. Most people are willing to pay insurance premiums in excess of expected claim costs for insurance; that is, they are willing to pay a risk premium. Also, most people require additional compensation to induce them to accept or take on risk. For example, people require higher expected returns to induce them to invest in common stocks rather than government bonds, because stocks have greater risk. The appendix to this chapter provides additional analysis relating to risk aversion.

Other Factors Affecting an Individual's Demand for Insurance

The previous section showed that risk aversion is the fundamental force that induces people to purchase insurance. This section expands on the analysis of individual demand for insurance by explaining some of the other factors that influence people's decisions about insurance purchases.

Premium Loading

Although risk-averse people generally desire insurance, the extent to which they will purchase insurance depends on the policy's premium loading. Recall from Chapter 8 that the premium on an insurance policy equals expected claim costs plus a loading for administrative and capital costs.[2] If the loading is zero, then purchasing insurance does not change a person's expected wealth, because the premium equals the expected payments from the insurer. Since insurance with a zero loading does not change expected wealth but reduces the variability of wealth, a risk-averse person will purchase full insurance coverage if the policy has a zero loading.

Unfortunately, the premium loading is rarely zero because insurers must be compensated for their costs. A positive loading implies that the policyholder pays a premium in excess of the expected payments from the insurer. As discussed in the previous section, a risk-averse person may be willing to pay this additional amount (the positive loading) because insurance reduces risk. However, the amount of coverage that risk-averse people will purchase generally will decline as the loading on the policy increases. That is, the demand for insurance follows the fundamental economic principle that the quantity demanded decreases as

[2] For simplicity, we ignore the time value of money in this discussion—that is, that the premium depends on the discounted value of expected costs.

the price increases. (Price in this context refers to the policy's loading.) In the extreme, if the loading on an insurance policy is too high, then people will not purchase insurance.

Income and Wealth

Income and wealth can influence a person's demand for insurance for at least four reasons. First, having more wealth usually is associated with having more assets subject to loss, which typically will increase the total amount of insurance purchased. Second, some people simply do not have sufficient income to afford large amounts of insurance coverage. The necessities of life (food and shelter) may exhaust a person's income. Consequently, very poor people are likely to bear more risk (insure less). Third, the degree of risk aversion may decline as a person's wealth increases. For example, a person with $20,000 of wealth is likely to be more willing to insure against the possibility of losing $10,000 than a person with $1 million in wealth. Fourth, limited liability often induces people with little wealth to purchase relatively little insurance against liability risk. Most legal systems give individuals the ability to declare bankruptcy and thus be shielded from debts that cannot be paid from their existing wealth. This feature, known as limited liability, can reduce the demand for liability insurance by people with low levels of wealth, because it limits the loss a person can suffer from a liability suit.

An example helps illustrate the effect of limited liability. Suppose that Ms. Ambrose has wealth of $5,000 and a 0.005 probability of causing $100,000 of damages to another person as a result of driving an automobile. If Ms. Ambrose purchased insurance to cover the entire loss to potential victims, she would need to purchase $100,000 of coverage. Ignoring any loading and investment income, the fair premium would be $500 (0.005 × $100,000). The benefit received by Ms. Ambrose from this policy is the protection of her wealth. Since she has only $5,000, she perceives the expected benefit as $5,000 × 0.005, which is only $25. From Ms. Ambrose's perspective, this insurance policy is extremely high priced; she has to pay $500 to cover an expected loss of $25, which she is unlikely to do voluntarily. The failure of individuals to buy auto liability coverage has influenced the adoption of compulsory insurance laws in most states. You will learn more about this issue in Chapter 13. We discuss the implications of limited liability for business risk management in detail in Chapter 29.

Information

The demand for insurance will depend on the information that the individual has about the loss distribution. For example, if an individual does not perceive that a loss is possible, the person will not purchase insurance unless forced to do so. More generally, if an individual perceives that the expected loss is lower than the amount perceived by the insurer, the individual will demand less insurance than a person who has the same probability assessment as the insurer. The reason is simple. As you learned in previous chapters, the insurer will price the policy based on its expectation of claim costs. If an individual has a lower estimate of expected claim costs than the insurer, the policy will appear to have a high loading, and the individual will demand less insurance. The opposite situation also can occur. Overestimation of expected claim costs compared to the insurer will induce the individual to purchase more coverage.

This discussion of the effect of information on the demand for insurance assumes that both the policyholder and the insurer view their information as correct and place no weight on the other party's information. The implications of different information are more complicated when one party (e.g., the policyholder) is better informed about expected losses than the other party (the insurer) and the other party knows that its information is inferior. These situations lead to adverse selection problems, which were discussed in Chapter 8 and will play an important role in subsequent chapters.

Other Sources of Indemnity

When deciding whether to purchase insurance, a person will consider whether there are other sources of payment (indemnity). Consider the decision to purchase property insurance that will cover windstorm damage from hurricanes. An individual may expect that if a catastrophe occurs the government (society) will provide some compensation for losses that are suffered (e.g., through disaster relief). The availability of these payments in essence constitutes implicit insurance, which can reduce the demand for explicit coverage. The individual is not charged directly for this implicit insurance (taxpayers will foot the bill), but the person has to pay the premium for explicit insurance. A similar situation can arise with respect to the purchase of health insurance—if a person thinks that society will pay some of his or her medical costs, then the demand for health insurance will be reduced. We discuss these issues in more detail in Chapters 14 and 16.

Nonmonetary Losses

Most of our discussion has been concerned with situations where people suffer monetary losses. However, people can experience **nonmonetary losses** as well as monetary losses (e.g., pain and suffering from physical injuries and grief when a loved one dies). People generally do not purchase insurance against nonmonetary losses for reasons discussed below. However, insurance against nonmonetary losses often is provided implicitly by the court system (and by liability insurance) when injured parties receive compensation for pain and suffering. For example, by forcing lawnmower manufacturers to compensate people who are injured using their products, the court system essentially makes lawnmower manufacturers provide insurance to their customers. Customers pay for this insurance in the form of higher lawnmower prices. If the court system makes lawnmower manufacturers compensate customers for pain and suffering, then the court system makes customers purchase this type of insurance. Thus, it is useful to consider whether people really would want to purchase insurance against nonmonetary losses, such as pain and suffering.

The demand for insurance coverage against nonmonetary losses differs fundamentally from the demand for insurance against monetary losses. To provide some intuition for why this is true, recall why people buy insurance against monetary losses: They demand insurance against monetary losses because the payment from the insurer following a loss benefits them more than they are hurt by the forgone income from paying the insurance premium when a loss does not occur. This is because money is more valuable to risk-averse people when they have less of it. In contrast, a purely nonmonetary loss (e.g., pain) does not lower a person's wealth. Thus, the fundamental reason why people buy insurance to cover monetary losses—money means more to them when they have less of it—does not apply to purely nonmonetary losses.

Since wealth is not lower when a purely nonmonetary loss occurs, the demand for insurance against nonmonetary losses depends on different factors, such as whether the person values money more following a purely nonmonetary loss than without such a loss. The key point is that many people probably would not be willing to pay even the expected claim cost for insurance against some types nonmonetary losses, even though they would be willing to pay a risk premium to insure against monetary losses.[3] Thus, it would be incorrect to assume that people automatically would want to insure against nonmonetary losses.

One example of when private insurance could be purchased against nonmonetary losses is life insurance on a child. Ignoring the cost of funerals, the loss of a child typically does not cause a monetary loss, but it does cause a huge nonmonetary loss for most parents. Ignoring tax reasons for purchasing life insurance on children, most parents do not voluntarily purchase insurance to compensate them for nonmonetary loss if a child would die. This is because the parents prefer not to give up money when their children are alive to receive additional money if they should die. Note, however, that even if people do not purchase insurance against nonmonetary losses, they often will engage in loss control to reduce expected nonmonetary losses. For example, parents who do not purchase life insurance on their children often will spend considerable resources to reduce the probability of them dying (e.g., putting a fence in the backyard to prevent them from falling into a neighbor's unfenced swimming pool, and buying safer cars).

Concept Checks

1. Using the following scenario, describe why a risk-averse person would purchase insurance.

   Loss = $5,000 with probability 0.1 and $0 with probability 0.9.
   Premium for full coverage = $500

2. Why might we observe wealthier people purchasing more insurance?

3. Why might we observe wealthier people purchasing less insurance?

9.2   Business Risk Management and Demand for Insurance

Even though businesses are owned by individuals, business risk management may differ in fundamental ways from individual risk management. The reason is that businesses often are organized in a way that allows business owners to diversify business risk on their own. This section explains when and why this distinction between individual and business risk management is relevant.

Shareholder Diversification

Recall from Chapter 4 how diversification reduces risk to individuals. Because risk reduction through diversification is desirable to risk-averse individuals, many institutions have developed to reduce the cost of diversification. Chapter 4 explained how insurance companies allow individuals to diversify risk at low cost. The stock market is another institution that allows individuals to diversify risk.

To see how stock markets can diversify risk, consider the risk that Ms. Butler would bear if she started her own business, called Butler Incorporated. Suppose that $100,000 is

---

[3] Specifically, the basic theory of insurance demand predicts that a purely nonmonetary loss only will be insured if the person values money more following a purely nonmonetary loss. In this case, insuring the loss produces an increase in income when money is more valuable and decreases income (because of the premium) when money is less valuable. In contrast, many persons argue and some evidence suggests that money often is less valuable after a purely nonmonetary loss so that these losses will not be insured. We return to this issue in Chapter 12.

needed to begin operations and that Ms. Butler has just enough savings to pay the start-up costs. The problem with Ms. Butler using all of her savings for this new business is that she bears substantial risk. She might make a lot of money, or she could lose her entire wealth. Specifically, assume for simplicity that at the end of the year there is a 95 percent chance that Ms. Butler's business will be worth $150,000 and a 5 percent chance that it will be worth $0, where the latter outcome would occur if her facility blows up.

An alternative way for Ms. Butler to pay the start-up costs would be to issue stock to investors. By issuing stock, many individuals could contribute small amounts of money to start the business. Ms. Butler also could contribute a small portion of her wealth to the new business. For example, if 20 investors (including Ms. Butler) each contributed $5,000, then sufficient funds would be generated to start the business. Ms. Butler would have to share the returns from the business with the other investors. Each investor (including Ms. Butler) would receive 1/20th of the firm's profits.[4] The benefit of issuing stock, however, is that Ms. Butler shares the risk associated with her business with the other 19 investors. If the plant blows up, then all 20 investors share in the loss.

By issuing the stock, Ms. Butler can take the $95,000 not invested in her company and invest it in other companies, which will reduce her risk relative to the case where she invested all her wealth in Butler Inc. To illustrate how Ms. Butler reduces her risk by investing her wealth in a number of different companies, suppose 20 new businesses are going to be created and that each one requires an initial investment of $100,000. Also assume that each business has the same probability distribution for value as Butler Inc. Further assume that the outcome for each business is independent of the outcomes for the other businesses.

If Ms. Butler (and the other entrepreneurs) invest $5,000 in each of the 20 businesses, then each one will own 1/20th of the stock of each business. In essence, each entrepreneur has entered into a pooling arrangement with the other entrepreneurs that involves equal sharing of profits and losses. This pooling arrangement is similar to the pooling arrangements discussed in Chapter 4 between Emily, Samantha, and their friends, where each person had the potential for a loss and all members of the pooling arrangement agreed to pay an equal share of the total losses. Recall that because losses were independent, risk was reduced for each member of the pooling arrangement relative to the situation where each paid his or her own loss. Similarly, each entrepreneur's risk is reduced by holding 1/20th of the stock of each company, as opposed to being a sole owner.

This example illustrates that stock markets allow business risk to be pooled, just as insurance companies allow certain types of risk to be pooled. Corporate insurance contracts and shareholder diversification are alternative mechanisms for diversifying pure risk for shareholders. That is, both mechanisms reduce the variability (risk) in shareholders' returns that arises because of pure risk.[5] More generally, any corporate activities that reduce the

---

[4] Not being the sole owner, we would expect Ms. Butler also to receive a salary as manager of the business.

[5] The effect of stock portfolio diversification on risk is just like the effect of pooling arrangements. As discussed in Chapter 5, fixed premium insurance contracts can reduce risk more than pooling arrangements. Similarly, fixed premium corporate insurance purchases can reduce risk more than investors can achieve through portfolio diversification. This technical point does not diminish the importance of portfolio diversification as a means of reducing the risk borne by the owners of corporations.

variability of corporate cash flows will not necessarily reduce shareholders' risk, because shareholders already may have diversified away the risk.

Since individual portfolio diversification and corporate insurance purchases are close substitutes for the purpose of reducing shareholders' risk, it is necessary to consider which mechanism has lower expected cost. The cost of diversifying through the stock market is the cost to shareholders of obtaining a diversified portfolio. With mutual funds, it is easy for an individual to spread even a modest amount of money across many stocks. The cost of buying into a mutual fund typically is not higher than the transaction cost of buying just one stock. In other words, the marginal cost to hold a diversified portfolio typically is close to zero.[6]

Recall that insurance contracts must be priced to include a loading for insurers' administrative and capital costs. Typical loadings range from about 10 percent to 50 percent of the premium, depending on the line of insurance and the amount of coverage. Why would diversified owners be willing to pay a positive loading for insurance (pay more than expected claim costs) when the insurance does not materially reduce their risk? We will answer this question shortly; for now simply note that corporate purchases of insurance often will increase a firm's value even when shareholders are diversified.

Concept Checks

4. True or false: Business insurance purchases do not reduce shareholders' risk significantly if shareholders hold diversified portfolios.

5. True or false: Shareholder diversification implies that business insurance purchases are contrary to shareholders' interests.

Closely Held Businesses

Even though stock markets allow business risk to be diversified, it is important to emphasize that the risk borne by a particular individual investing in the stock market depends on the proportion of his or her wealth that is invested in each stock. As we discussed above, if Ms. Butler invests all of her wealth ($100,000) in Butler Incorporated, she bears significant risk. On the other hand, she could invest $5,000 in Butler Incorporated and $95,000 in other businesses, thus spreading her wealth across many firms and creating a diversified portfolio. By holding a diversified portfolio, she reduces her risk without necessarily sacrificing expected return.

If the owners of a business are not well diversified, business insurance purchases will reduce the owners' risk. This reduction in risk is potentially an important benefit of business insurance. Just as our discussion of individual risk management indicated that individual insurance is beneficial to risk-averse people, business insurance is beneficial to risk-averse owners that are not diversified. Thus, most small businesses and most privately held businesses will find that business insurance is beneficial because it reduces the owners' risk.

---

[6] There are, however, other potential costs of diversifying through the stock market. For example, if Ms. Butler diversifies, then she has less incentive to operate her business to the best of her ability. Similarly, she will be concerned that the managers of the other businesses in which she invested will not manage efficiently. These moral hazard problems are an additional cost of diversification through stock markets. Note, however, that insurance markets also have moral hazard problems, the implications of which will be discussed in Chapter 10.

Why Purchase Insurance When Shareholders Are Diversified?[7]

The previous sections highlighted the fact that corporate activities that reduce the variability of the firm's cash flows (such as purchasing insurance) do not necessarily reduce shareholders' risk, because shareholders already may have diversified away the risk by holding a diversified portfolio. We noted, however, that corporate insurance purchases can nonetheless be beneficial to shareholders. These benefits arise because insurance has indirect effects that cause a firm's expected cash flows to increase. In particular, this section briefly and intuitively explains how business insurance purchases can (1) provide an efficient method of purchasing claims processing and loss control services; (2) reduce the expected cost of financing losses; (3) reduce the likelihood that the firm will have to raise costly external capital for new investment projects and thereby increase the likelihood that it will adopt good investment projects; (4) reduce the likelihood of financial distress and thereby improve the terms at which the firm will be able to contract with other claimants, such as employees, suppliers, lenders, and customers; and (5) reduce expected tax payments. Chapter 20 provides a more in-depth analysis of these effects.

Insurer Services

A portion of an insurance policy's loading covers the insurer's cost of providing services to policyholders, such as claims processing and loss control, that a firm would have to undertake or purchase elsewhere if it did not purchase insurance. If the loading were less than the firm's cost of obtaining comparable services, then purchasing insurance would benefit shareholders even if they were diversified. In this case, however, the firm would not be purchasing insurance to reduce risk for shareholders but to obtain claims processing and loss control services at the lowest cost.[8]

Reducing the Expected Cost of Financing Losses

The failure to reduce risk implies that there is a greater likelihood of large losses that must be paid either from the firm's internal funds or, if internal funds are not available, by raising new funds through borrowing or issuing new securities. Significant costs can be incurred if new securities have to be issued.[9] Thus, firms that are not likely to have the internal

---

[7] Although this section focuses on corporate insurance, the arguments generally apply to other corporate activities that reduce risk, with the exception of the services provided by insurers.

[8] In some cases it may be more efficient (lower cost) to bundle claims processing and loss control services with the financial responsibility of paying losses, because by doing so, the service provider has greater incentive to provide high quality service. For example, a firm that provides loss control services that also must pay losses has an additional incentive to identify and undertake cost-effective loss control measures. A firm that provides claims processing services that also must pay losses has an additional incentive to identify fraudulent claims. If the service and financial responsibility are not bundled, then a firm must expend some resources monitoring the service providers or alternatively design a contract that provides proper incentives. When monitoring is too costly and contract design efforts ineffective, bundling the services with financial responsibility for paying losses can be the least costly method of obtaining services.

[9] Raising capital by issuing new securities is costly for several reasons. First, there are explicit costs, such as investment banker fees, associated with issuing new securities. Second, there are legal and regulatory costs associated with filing appropriate documents. Finally, there are implicit costs associated with selling new securities if the new securities are priced below their true value. Underpricing is more likely to occur if investors view themselves as having less information about the true value of the new securities than managers have. To protect themselves from paying too high a price, investors may lower the price they are willing to pay for new issues.

funds to finance losses might prefer to purchase insurance to reduce the likelihood of incurring the costs associated with issuing new securities to pay for losses.

Reducing Financing Costs for New Investment Opportunities

Another reason for reducing risk by purchasing insurance is to increase the likelihood that the firm will have sufficient internal funds to adopt new investment projects. Without insurance, the firm's internal funds could be used to pay losses that occur, in which case the firm will have to raise new funds to pay for new investment projects. But since external funds generally are more costly than internal funds (see footnote 9), their use reduces the profitability of new investment projects net of financing costs. In some cases, the additional costs from raising external funds can cause the firm to pass up new investment projects that would have been profitable had the firm had the internal resources to pay for the project. By purchasing insurance to cover losses, a firm can reduce the likelihood that costly external capital will be needed for new investment opportunities and thereby increase the profitability of new projects (net of financing costs).

Reducing the Likelihood of Financial Distress and Improving Contractual Terms

If a firm does not have the internal funds to pay losses that occur and cannot convince banks or investors to provide new funds, then it will be forced into bankruptcy. When this occurs, the firm either must liquidate or reorganize so that it can continue to operate. Reorganization can take place under Chapter 11 of the federal bankruptcy code or outside of bankruptcy in what commonly is called a "workout." Substantial legal costs can be incurred when a firm liquidates or reorganizes. By reducing the probability of bankruptcy, a firm reduces the likelihood of incurring these costs. Thus, risk reduction that protects a firm from large losses and therefore reduces the likelihood of bankruptcy can benefit shareholders by reducing the likelihood of incurring these bankruptcy costs.

When a firm is in financial distress (either in bankruptcy or close to bankruptcy), other claimants besides shareholders typically are harmed. To illustrate, consider the plight of banks and investors who have lent money to a firm that now finds itself in financial distress. In an effort to receive the money that they were promised, these lenders will incur legal costs.[10] As a result of these costs, lenders will demand compensation for investing in a firm with a high probability of financial distress. Consequently, if a firm can reduce its risk, say through insurance, lenders will be willing to contract with the firm at better terms. One benefit of risk reduction from the shareholders' perspective therefore is that it can improve the terms at which the firm can borrow money.

Employees, suppliers, and customers also incur costs when their relationships with a firm are interrupted due to financial distress. For example, employees who are laid off incur costs while being out of work and customers incur costs if their products are not serviced. In addition, risk-averse individuals and closely held suppliers will require compensation (a risk premium) for the uncertainty associated with receiving their promised payments. As a result, employees, suppliers, and customers will demand compensation when contracting with a firm with a high probability of financial distress. Employees, for example, will demand

---

[10] Also, if managers are acting in the shareholders' interests, managers will have incentives either to adopt bad investment projects or fail to adopt some good investment projects, which would reduce the expected payments to lenders (see Chapter 20).

higher compensation from a firm that has a greater likelihood of distress. Similarly, customers will pay lower prices to a firm with a higher probability of not being around to service its products. When product prices and input prices reflect the expected costs imposed by financial distress, then the firm's shareholders can benefit by reducing the probability of distress because doing so increases product prices and decreases input prices.

Reducing Expected Tax Payments

Another reason risk reduction can benefit diversified shareholders is that it can reduce expected tax payments when corporate tax rates are progressive. Progressivity in tax rates implies that tax rates increase as a firm makes higher profits. For example, if profits up to $100,000 were taxed at a 20 percent tax rate and profits above $100,000 were taxed at a 30 percent tax rate, then tax rates would be progressive. Although the details of the corporate tax code in practice are complex, corporate taxes are in effect progressive. Operating profits generally are taxed at a 34 percent rate; operating losses (negative profits) may not be fully deductible against past and future profits. It can be shown that with progressivity in tax rates firms can lower the expected value of taxes paid by reducing variability in their profits (see Chapter 21). The advantage of insurance when taxes are progressive is analogous to our earlier discussion of insurance demand by risk-averse individuals. Insurance allows risk-averse individuals to obtain money following a loss, when money is more valuable because they have less of it. Likewise, insurance allows businesses to obtain money following a loss, when money is more valuable (in part) because it is subject to a lower effective tax rate.

Insurance purchases also can reduce expected tax payments for three other reasons, which are analyzed in some detail in Chapter 21. One tax benefit arises because insurance companies are taxed differently than noninsurance companies. The difference allows insurers to deduct loss payments earlier than noninsurance firms, which lowers the present value of expected tax payments. Assuming that part of the value of this benefit is passed on to the policyholder, firms will have an incentive to purchase insurance. Another tax benefit arises from the tax treatment of depreciated property. Finally, reducing risk through insurance can allow a firm to borrow more than otherwise would be optimal, which increases the tax shield from interest payments.

9.3 Summary

- Risk aversion is the major underlying force that motivates most individuals to purchase insurance even though insurance premiums exceed expected claim costs.

- Individuals' demand for insurance depends on (1) the premium loading; (2) a person's income and wealth; (3) an individual's information about expected losses relative to the insurer's information; (4) the availability of other sources of indemnity, such as government assistance; and (5) the nature of losses (monetary versus nonmonetary).

- One of the fundamental functions of the stock market is to allow investors in corporations to diversify risk.

- When shareholders are well diversified, corporate activities to reduce the variability in cash flows due to pure risk are largely redundant from the perspective of the shareholders, who already have reduced their risk by diversification.

- When shareholders are well diversified, corporate insurance still can benefit shareholders by (1) reducing the costs of purchasing claims processing and loss control services; (2) reducing the expected cost of financing losses; (3) reducing the likelihood that the firm will have to raise costly external capital for new investment projects and thereby increasing the likelihood that it will adopt good investment projects; (4) reducing the likelihood of incurring bankruptcy costs and thereby improving the terms at which the firm contracts with other claimants, such as employees, suppliers, lenders, and customers; and (5) reducing expected tax payments.

Key Terms

risk averse 164   risk neutral 165   nonmonetary losses 167

Questions and Problems

1. What are the possible wealth outcomes for a person with $10,000 in wealth who faces a 10 percent chance of losing $5,000 under each of the following insurance policies?

   a. $2,500 of coverage; premium = $250.
   b. $2,500 of coverage; premium = $280.
   c. $5,000 of coverage; premium = $500.
   d. $5,000 of coverage; premium = $550.

2. Would a risk-averse person necessarily purchase policy (c) in the previous question? Would a risk-averse person necessarily purchase policy (d)?

3. Poor people often do not purchase liability insurance. What are some of the explanations?

4. Suppose that a liability insurance policy with a coverage limit of $100,000 (i.e., the insurer will pay liability claims up to $100,000) has a premium of $600. For each of the following people, what is the premium per dollar of personal wealth protected if the policy were purchased?

Person	Person's Wealth
Mary	$ 5,000
Curly	$ 50,000
Moe	$100,000
Alice	$150,000
Nancy	$200,000

5. Suppose that Skipper's insurer views him as having the following distribution for the present value of losses:

$$\text{Loss} = \begin{cases} \$20,000 & \text{with probability } 0.02 \\ \$ 5,000 & \text{with probability } 0.04 \\ \$ 1,000 & \text{with probability } 0.10 \\ \$ \quad 0 & \text{with probability } 0.84 \end{cases}$$

   a. What is the fair premium for full coverage if the competitive loading (administrative costs and capital costs) equals 15 percent of expected claim costs?

   b. Suppose that Skipper believes his probabilities of losses are one-half of what the insurer believes. What is the loading on the policy from Skipper's perspective?

6. Intuitively explain why corporate actions to reduce variability in cash flows may be redundant from the perspective of diversified shareholders.

7. Intuitively explain how the absence of insurance can cause a firm to forgo good investment projects.

8. Suppose that a business expects to have profits of $100,000 if it is not sued over the coming year. The probability of a suit is 0.04 and the loss if a suit occurs is $250,000. The firm's tax rate if it earns positive profits is 30 percent. If it makes negative profits, it pays a 0 percent rate.

   a. What is the firm's before-tax expected profit without insurance? What is its after-tax expected profit without insurance?

b. Suppose the firm can purchase a liability insurance policy with full coverage for a premium of $11,000. From the insurer's point of view, does this policy have a positive loading?

c. What is the firm's expected before- and after-tax profit if it purchases the insurance policy (assume that the premium is a tax-deductible expense)?

d. Compare the expected after-tax profits with and without insurance. Explain.

Answers to Concept Checks

1. A risk-averse person would purchase full insurance coverage because the premium equals the expected claim cost. This would eliminate risk without reducing the person's expected wealth.

2. Wealthier people are likely to purchase higher property and liability insurance coverage limits because the values of assets owned are likely to be higher. Wealthier people are likely to purchase more life insurance coverage in order to maintain a high standard of living for their dependents after their death. Also, very poor people might purchase very little insurance coverage because their resources are used for more basic necessities.

3. Wealthier people might purchase less insurance in some cases (e.g.,they may buy policies with higher deductibles) because risk aversion might decrease as wealth increases.

4. True. The type of risk that business insurance eliminates generally can be eliminated by investors through holding a diversified portfolio.

5. False. Business insurance purchases still can increase shareholder wealth even when shareholders are diversified.

Appendix 9A

Expected Utility

9A.1   Risk Aversion and Utility

Additional insights about what it means to be risk averse can be gained by introducing the concept of *utility,* which is a measure of a person's well-being associated with different amounts of wealth. Suppose that people prefer more wealth to less. Then a person's utility increases with wealth. This relationship is illustrated in Figure 9A.1, where utility is measured on the vertical axis and wealth is measured on the horizontal axis. Since people prefer more wealth to less, the function relating utility to wealth is positively sloped. In Figure 9A.1, the utility associated with $80,000 of wealth is given by the point labeled $U(80,000)$, and the utility of $100,000 is given by the point labeled $U(100,000)$. The units of utility are not important for our purposes.

Risk aversion implies that utility does not increase linearly with wealth; instead, utility increases at a decreasing rate as wealth increases (the utility function is thus concave in shape). This feature is called *diminishing marginal utility,* because the additional utility received from an increment in wealth (the marginal utility) diminishes as wealth increases. An increment to wealth of $1,000 raises utility more

when a person has $80,000 than when the same person has $100,000. Since the curve relating utility to wealth in Figure 9A.1 is concave, the utility function is for a risk-averse person.

Using Figure 9A.1, we can gain additional insight into a person's decision to purchase insurance. Recall the example used in the text where Mr. Grace has wealth of $100,000 and a 0.5 chance of losing $20,000. Assuming that Mr. Grace's utility is given by Figure 9A.1, let's analyze the effect on his utility of purchasing full insurance coverage for a premium of $10,000. If the loss occurs, the insurance policy will increase his wealth from $80,000 to $90,000. Using utility as a measure of his well-being, the gain in utility from having insurance is

$$U(90,000) - U(80,000) \qquad \textbf{(9A.1)}$$

which is depicted on the vertical axis in Figure 9A.1. If the loss does not occur, the insurance policy reduces his wealth from $100,000 to $90,000. The cost in terms of utility is

$$U(100,000) - U(90,000) \qquad \textbf{(9A.2)}$$

which also is depicted in Figure 9A.1.

FIGURE 9A.1
Relationship between utility and wealth.

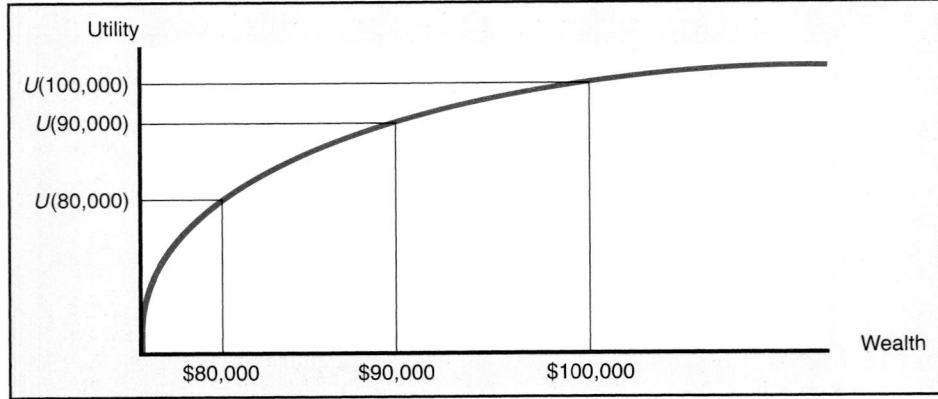

Of course, Mr. Grace has to make a decision about whether to purchase insurance before he knows whether a loss will occur. That is, he does not know whether insurance will increase utility by the amount given by expression 9A.1 or decrease utility by the amount given by expression 9A.2. Therefore, he has to weigh the benefit of insurance (expression 9A.1) and the cost of insurance (expression 9A.2) by their respective probabilities. In this example, the two outcomes are equally likely; therefore, both possible outcomes receive equal weight and the decision to purchase insurance entails comparing expression 9A.1 to expression 9A.2.

Figure 9A.1 indicates that expression 9A.1 is greater than 9A.2. The reason is the concavity of the utility function. Diminishing marginal utility implies that the loss in utility of having less wealth when a loss does not occur is less than the gain in utility of having more wealth when a loss does occur. Therefore, anyone who has diminishing marginal utility will want to purchase this insurance policy. This example illustrates that diminishing marginal utility implies that a person is risk averse. A loss of $X hurts Mr. Grace more than a gain of $X benefits him.

The assumptions of equal probabilities and only two possible outcomes in the previous example are used to simplify the discussion; the results do not depend on these simplifying assumptions. Intuitively, the purchase of insurance implies that an individual gives up wealth if a loss does not occur (when wealth is relatively high) so that additional wealth may be received if a loss occurs (when wealth is relatively low). Diminishing marginal utility (risk aversion) implies that an increment to wealth means more to individuals when they have less of it. Therefore, a person with diminishing marginal utility will be willing to give up wealth if a loss does not occur so that additional wealth can be received if a loss does occur.

9A.2 Cost of Uncertainty and the Total Cost of Risk

The utility function introduced in the previous section can be used to identify conceptually the cost of uncertainty and the total cost of risk for an uninsured individual. Consider, for example, Mr. Grace's situation when he is uninsured. He has a 50 percent chance of having wealth equal to $100,000 and a 50 percent chance of losing the lawsuit and having wealth equal to $80,000. Figure 9A.2 illustrates the utility levels associated with these possible outcomes.

Now consider the question: How much would Mr. Grace be willing to pay for full insurance coverage? To answer this question, we must calculate Mr. Grace's expected utility without insurance. Without insurance, Mr. Grace has a 50 percent chance of receiving utility of $U(100,000)$ and a 50 percent chance of receiving $U(80,000)$. Because the probability of each outcome is 0.5, Mr. Grace's expected utility without insurance is equal to $[0.5 \times U(100,000) + 0.5 \times U(80,000)]$. This number is illustrated on the vertical axis in Figure 9A.2 as the midpoint between $U(100,000)$ and $U(80,000)$.

FIGURE 9A.2
Relationship between the utility function, the cost of uncertainty, and the total cost of risk.

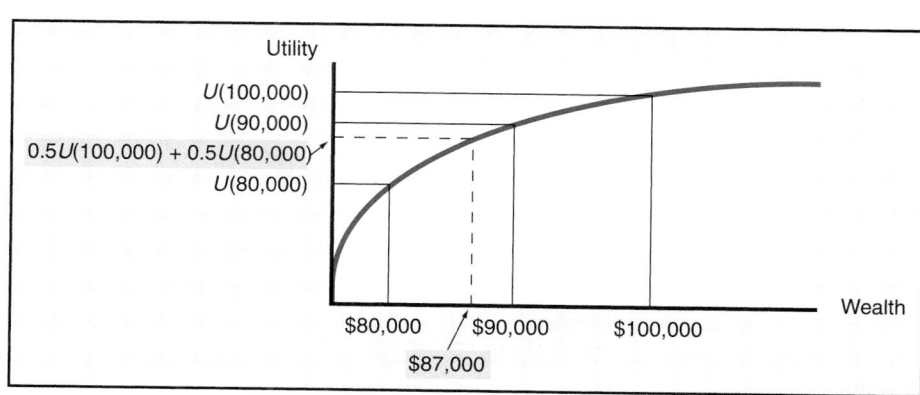

Now we can find the amount of wealth that Mr. Grace would accept if he could eliminate the uncertainty. By following the horizontal dotted line from the expected utility level until it reaches the utility curve and then following the vertical dotted line down to the wealth axis, we find $87,000. If Mr. Grace had wealth of $87,000 for certain, then he would have the same expected utility as he has without insurance. In other words, Mr. Grace is indifferent between having $87,000 for certain and having a 50–50 chance of either $80,000 or $100,000. Thus, Mr. Grace would be willing to pay $13,000 ($100,000 minus $87,000) for full insurance coverage.

Notice that the amount that Mr. Grace would be willing to pay exceeds the expected claim cost, which is $10,000 (0.5 × $20,000). That is, when faced with expected losses of $10,000, Mr. Grace is willing to spend more than $10,000 to eliminate the uncertainty as to whether the losses will occur. The amount that Mr. Grace is willing to spend in excess of the expected loss ($3,000) measures Mr. Grace's cost of uncertainty due to his risk aversion. In total, Mr. Grace is willing to spend $13,000 to eliminate risk—$10,000 of which would be spent by a risk–neutral person (this is the expected loss) and $3,000 because Mr. Grace is risk averse. Thus, $13,000 is the total cost of risk for Mr. Grace if he is uninsured or if he insures for a premium equal to $13,000.

In this chapter, we intuitively argued that if the loading on insurance contracts is too high, then consumers will not purchase insurance. This analysis provides some justification. If the loading for a full coverage policy exceeded $3,000 (e.g., if the total

premium equaled $13,500), then Mr. Grace would not purchase the policy. His cost of risk would be greater with insurance than without. On the other hand, if the loading were less than $3,000, Mr. Grace could reduce his cost of risk by buying insurance.

Utility functions are not commonly used to help make risk management decisions. Nevertheless, the conceptual framework provided by utility functions helps us understand individual decision making. That is, utility functions provide a model to help us understand and predict individual decisions. We do not suggest that individuals actually use utility functions or calculate expected utility, rather we are simply pointing out that individuals often behave *as if* they calculate expected utility.

Questions and Problems

1. A person who is risk neutral has a linear utility function, as opposed to a risk-averse person, who has a concave utility function. Redraw Figure 9A.1 assuming Mr. Grace is risk neutral.

2. Redraw Figure 9A.2 and calculate the cost of uncertainty and the total cost of risk for a risk-neutral person who is uninsured.

3. Suppose that an individual has wealth of $20,000 and utility function $U(W) = ln(W)$, where $ln(W)$ indicates the natural logarithm of wealth. What is the maximum amount this individual would pay for full insurance to cover a loss of $5,000 with probability 0.10?

Chapter 10

Insurability of Risk, Contractual Provisions, and Legal Doctrines

Chapter Objectives

- Identify and explain factors that can limit the insurability of risk.
- Describe and explain the major provisions that limit coverage in insurance contracts.
- Explain the fundamental legal doctrines underlying insurance contracts.

10.1 Factors that Limit the Insurability of Risk

Previous chapters explained how insurance reduces risk and that risk averse people prefer to have less risk. It might seem to follow therefore that insurance would be provided against most risks. This conclusion, however, is incorrect because it ignores the costs of providing insurance. These costs cause people to demand less than full coverage against most risks and no insurance against some risks.

The first part of this chapter summarizes the three major factors that increase costs and thereby limit the insurability of risk in private insurance markets. As highlighted in Figure 10.1, the three factors are: (1) premium loadings, which reflect insurer administrative and capital costs; (2) moral hazard that arises because insurance changes a person's incentive to take precautions; and (3) adverse selection that arises when policyholders are better informed about expected claim costs than insurers. While these factors can lead to no insurance coverage for some types of risk, more typically these factors lead to partial, rather than full, insurance coverage. The second part of the chapter therefore describes contractual provisions in insurance contracts, such as deductibles and coinsurance, which limit insurance coverage. The third part discusses legal doctrines that affect insurance coverage. A major function of these contractual provisions and legal doctrines is to reduce the contracting costs associated with insurance and thus facilitate the insurability of risk.

**FIGURE
10.1**
Factors
limiting the
insurability of
risk.

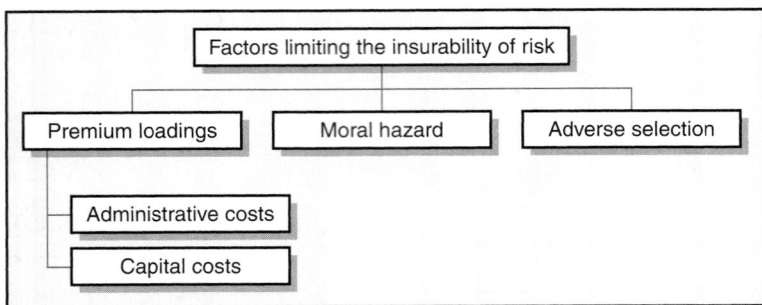

Premium Loadings

As discussed in Chapter 9, if an insurance contract's premium equals the present value of expected claim costs, a risk-averse person will likely demand full insurance coverage for monetary losses that otherwise would be paid by the person. Because premiums almost always have a positive loading, however, risk-averse people will demand less than full coverage. As the loading increases, the quantity of coverage demanded is likely to decrease. Thus, any factor that increases administrative or capital costs (and thus the loading on a policy) will limit the amount of private market insurance coverage. Simply stated, higher premium loadings generally imply less coverage.

In addition, insurance coverage for some risk exposures is likely to be extremely limited or even nonexistent because of administrative and capital costs. As we now explain, limited insurance coverage is more likely to occur for exposures with low severity, high frequency, correlated losses across people or businesses, and unknown loss distributions (parameter uncertainty). Box 10.1 illustrates some of these problems in the context of losses from terrorism.

Exposures with Low Severity

Exposures with low severity of losses are not likely to be insured on an individual basis because the fixed costs associated with underwriting and distributing a policy make the loading very high compared to expected losses. For example, the paperwork involved in processing an application is essentially the same whether the applicant is trying to obtain coverage for a diamond-studded, gold Rolex watch (high expected claim costs) or an inexpensive Casio watch (low expected claim costs). These fixed administrative costs imply that exposures with very small severity will have a high loading relative to expected claim costs, making the cost of insuring small losses on an individual basis unattractive to most people.

To illustrate, consider two bicycles: one worth $200 and the other worth $6,000. Assume that the probability of each bike being stolen is 0.05. Then the expected claim costs for full insurance would be $10 ($200 $\times$ 0.05) and $300 ($6,000 $\times$ 0.05), respectively. Assume that the fixed costs of paying employees to market, underwrite, and process an application for bike insurance are $100, that these are the only administrative costs, and that capital costs are $0. Then, ignoring investment income, the fair premiums would be $110 for the $200 bike and $400 for the $6,000 bike. The loading as a proportion of expected claim costs would be $100/$10 = 1,000 percent for the policy on the $200 bike and $100/$300 = 33.3 percent for the policy on the $6,000 bike. Very few people, if any, would be sufficiently risk averse

The September 11, 2001, destruction of the World Trade Center in New York City is estimated to have produced roughly $40–$50 billion of insured losses that are being paid by insurers and reinsurers around the world. Following the attack representatives of many reinsurers announced that they would be unwilling to reinsure losses from terrorism when contracts were renewed. Representatives of many US primary insurers argued that they could not cover terror risk without reinsurance. The US House of Representatives passed a bill in November 2001 that would provide a government backstop of loans to insurers to cover large losses from future terrorist attacks. In June 2002 the US Senate debated an alternative bill that would provide direct federal government payments for 80 to 90 percent of any losses above specified insurer retentions. Other countries that enacted some type of government backstop for private sector coverage of losses from terrorist attacks either before or after September 11, 2001, include Great Britain, France, Germany, Israel, and South Africa.

In early 2002, primary insurers received regulatory approval in most states to exclude coverage for terrorist losses except for workers' compensation and, in many states, fire damage. However, coverage remained available for most properties on a limited basis and at a high price. New and existing insurers had raised $15–$20 billion of new capital (frequently offshore) to back the sale of property coverage, but it was unclear how much of that capital was available to support the sale of coverage for losses from terrorism.

The most common argument made by insurer and reinsurer representatives who sought help from the US government was that the risk of loss from terrorist attacks was unpredictable (i.e., it was subject to large parameter uncertainty). Other factors that raise the price and reduce the availability of such coverage are the possibility of correlated losses and the large loss potential from a single loss. Adverse selection is not a significant issue. Moral hazard would not appear to be any worse than for other property coverages.

to be willing to pay a 1,000 percent loading (the $110 premium) to insure a $200 bike. More people would be willing to pay the 33.3 percent loading (the $400 premium) to insure the $6,000 bike.

Items with small value and thus low severity are more likely to be insured if they are bundled together with other exposures. For example, a homeowners policy routinely covers most types of property with low values. By bundling, the fixed administrative costs are spread over many items and consequently the cost per item falls.

Exposures with High Frequency

When the probability of a loss is high, insurance is less likely to be observed. With a high probability of loss, expected claim costs are high, which in turn causes administrative costs, which are proportional to expected claim costs, to be high.[1] Consequently, the fair premium is close to the potential loss and, in some cases, can exceed the potential loss. The demand for insurance in such a situation is low, because the high insurance premium reduces a person's wealth almost as much as the contingency being insured. For example, suppose that

---

[1]While some of an insurer's administrative costs are fixed, most administrative costs increase at a proportional or approximately proportional rate with expected claim costs. For example, underwriters are likely to spend more time learning about an exposure when expected claim costs are high. Sales commissions typically are a percentage of premiums, which increase with expected claim costs. Finally, the extent to which claims are investigated and litigated increases with the size of the claim. For all these reasons and others, the bulk of an insurer's administrative costs associated with a particular policy are likely to increase at a roughly proportional rate as expected claim costs increase.

the probability of a $10,000 loss is 0.75 and administrative costs equal 20 percent of expected losses. Then the fair premium would equal $9,000, or $(0.75 \times \$10,000) + (0.20 \times 0.75 \times \$10,000)$.

Correlated Exposures

When losses are highly correlated across potential policyholders, the variance of the distribution of average losses also will be high (see Chapter 4). Examples of highly correlated losses are losses from major earthquakes, hurricanes, and other storms, war, and contagious diseases. The problem with insuring highly correlated losses is that insurers need to hold a large amount of capital to keep the probability of insolvency low. The costs of raising and holding this capital imply that insurance against highly correlated losses will have a high premium loading. As a result, the amount of coverage purchased is likely to be limited and in some cases private insurance coverage will not exist.[2]

Exposures with Parameter Uncertainty (Uncertain Expected Losses)

When insurers are uncertain about the true expected losses of insureds, **parameter uncertainty** is said to exist.[3] From the insurer's perspective, parameter uncertainty has an effect that is similar to positively correlated losses. A high level of parameter uncertainty about expected losses can limit the insurability of losses.

The effect of parameter uncertainty can be illustrated using a simple example. Suppose that losses are uncorrelated across policyholders and that there are a huge number of policyholders, each having the same probability of losing $50,000. The law of large numbers would then imply that the insurer could predict average losses very accurately if the insurer knew the probability of a loss. Suppose, however, that nobody (including the insurer) knows the true probability of a loss (there is parameter uncertainty), but that everyone knows that the true loss probability for all policyholders is either 0.02 or 0.04. Since all the consumers have a probability of 0.02 or all the consumers have a probability of 0.04, the average loss either will be very close to $1,000 ($50,000 loss $\times$ 0.02) or very close to $2,000 ($50,000 $\times$ 0.04). If we assume that the insurer believes that the two possible probabilities are equally likely, then the insurer's prediction of expected claim costs per policyholder is $1,500. However, average losses are likely to differ from $1,500, because average losses are likely to be either very close to $1,000 or very close to $2,000, depending on whether the true probability is 0.02 or 0.04. The insurer therefore perceives that there is a large variance in the distribution of average losses around the expected value of $1,500.

---

[2]In situations where losses are highly correlated across insureds for a particular type of exposure, an insurer can diversify across exposures by selling insurance in different lines of business or through reinsurance. Also, when losses are highly correlated across insureds during a given time period, losses tend to be uncorrelated over time. For example, the occurrence of a major earthquake in one year is likely to be uncorrelated with major earthquakes in subsequent years. This observation suggests the possibility that risk pooling could work through time. That is, an insurer could pool correlated exposures over many time periods. As a result of pooling through time, the variance of average losses over the many time periods would be reduced relative to the variance of average losses during one time period. Note, however, that to pool over time, long-term contracts are needed as well as financing arrangements to pay unexpected losses should they occur early during the contractual period. Enforcement costs often make private insurance contracts ineffective in these situations. The ability of government to tax may overcome some of these enforcement problems, although possibly at the expense of introducing other problems associated with government allocation of resources.

[3]Some authors also refer to this situation as *ambiguity*.

Thus, parameter uncertainty causes the distribution of average losses around the insurer's estimate of expected loss per policyholder to have greater variance, which is the same effect as having high correlation in losses. The analogy to a high correlation in losses is reinforced by noting that parameter uncertainty implies that the insurer's estimate of expected loss could be wrong. In the example above, the insurer's estimate is $1,500, and the true expected loss is either $1,000 or $2,000. Any error in the estimate of expected loss will apply to all policyholders. Thus, there is correlation in the insurer's estimation errors across policyholders.

Some parameter uncertainty always exists; insurers simply cannot know the true expected losses of a group of insureds. Just as when losses are highly correlated, an insurer faced with a high level of parameter uncertainty must hold large amounts of capital to achieve a low probability of insolvency. In our example where the insurer's estimate of expected loss is $1,500 but the true expected loss could be $2,000, the insurer would have to hold more than $500 of capital per policyholder to have a low insolvency probability. The costs of holding larger amounts of capital imply that when it is more difficult to estimate expected losses (i.e., when there is a high level of parameter uncertainty), insurance coverage will be limited.

Moral Hazard

Moral hazard refers to the effect of insurance on the insured's incentives to reduce expected losses. For example, once Bob Puelz purchases theft insurance, his incentive to take precautions to reduce the likelihood of theft is reduced. This is because, once insured, Bob bears all the cost of additional precautions, but he does not receive all the benefits of additional precautions. Since losses are insured, a portion of the benefits accrues to the insurer in the form of lower expected claim costs.

To illustrate in more detail, suppose that Bob is at home and ready to go to bed when he realizes that he forgot to lock the door to his office, which is five miles away, and that he has left his personal computer in the office. He must decide whether to go to his office to reduce the likelihood that his computer is stolen. Bob incurs all the costs (the hassle) associated with reducing the probability of his computer being stolen. However, if his insurer pays for theft losses, then some of the benefits of going to his office do not accrue to Bob. Instead, the insurer receives the benefits. In contrast, if he were not insured, the entire benefit from protecting his computer would accrue to him in the form of lower expected theft losses. Consequently, Bob is less likely to go to his office if he is insured.

Insurers understand that insurance reduces policyholders' incentive to prevent losses. The insurance market responds to this moral hazard problem in several ways, which we elaborate below. A central point is that, as a result of moral hazard, insurance contracts are not likely to offer full coverage. Instead, part of the losses will have to be paid by the insured. Thus, moral hazard implies that policyholders will have to bear risk (i.e., moral hazard limits the insurability of risk). In addition, because moral hazard is seldom if ever completely eliminated, moral hazard increases the cost of coverage that is provided by increasing expected claim costs.

Conditions for Moral Hazard

Two conditions are required for moral hazard to arise. First, expected losses must depend on the insured's behavior after having obtained insurance. Second, it must be costly for the insurer to observe precautions by policyholders and measure their impact on expected claim costs.

Examples where expected losses depend on the insured's behavior are numerous. With automobile insurance, expected claim costs depend on the speed at which the car is driven, when the car is driven, and where the car is parked. With life insurance, the expected claim cost (the probability of death) depends on the insured's eating and drinking habits, leisure activities, and exercise routine. Expected claim costs for workers' compensation insurance depend on the implementation of safety programs and the treatment of employees following an injury. Medical insurance losses depend on how much medical care the policyholder seeks and the doctor prescribes (e.g., the number of tests or the number of office visits).

In all of these situations, expected losses depend on the insured's behavior after being insured. Since insurance pays losses, insurance can affect the incentive to take precautions. As noted above, the basic problem is that once someone is insured, some of the benefits of additional precautions accrue to the insurer rather than the policyholder and therefore the insured does not take these benefits into account when deciding whether to take additional precautions.

One potential solution to the moral hazard problem is to make the premium or coverage contingent on the insured's behavior during the policy period. For example, if a driver increases expected claim costs by driving fast, then the premium could be increased immediately or coverage reduced. This solution requires that the insurer monitor quite closely the insured's behavior, which is costly and sometimes impossible. This gives rise to the second condition that is required for moral hazard problems to arise: that it is costly to observe and measure the impact of people's behavior on expected claim costs.

To illustrate these points, consider an automobile insurance policy for Dave Appel, who enjoys driving fast. Holding other factors constant, expected claim costs increase with driving speed, but the relationship between driving speed and expected claim costs also depends on other factors, such as traffic congestion and road conditions. Suppose that the insurer could put a device in Dave's car that (1) accurately measures driving speed, road conditions, and traffic congestion, as well as their effects on expected claim costs, and (2) instantly incorporates that information into a visual display telling Dave how much additional premium he must pay if he decides to go faster. If this device were costless, there would be no moral hazard problem. Even though Dave's driving speed affects expected claim costs (a necessary condition for moral hazard), Dave would take the appropriate level of precautions, because his premiums would decline if additional precautions were taken (or would increase if fewer precautions were taken). In other words, if the measuring device were both perfectly accurate and costless, Dave would consider the effect of driving speed on expected claim costs when making decisions about how fast to drive and consequently there would be no moral hazard problem.

Monitoring insureds' behavior and incorporating this behavior into the premium obviously is costly. Consequently, monitoring will be used only if it is cost-effective (i.e., if the reduction in expected claim costs from monitoring exceeds the monitoring costs). Monitoring is common after a claim is filed. Insurers routinely investigate claims to identify if the insured has purposely caused the loss or if the claim has been exaggerated. In recent years, insurance fraud (an extreme form of moral hazard) has increased, which in turn has led to additional investigation of claims by insurers. Note as well that since insurance fraud is usually a violation of criminal law, governments also expend resources investigating and punishing insurance fraud, which helps to control extreme forms of moral hazard.

When it is not cost-effective to eliminate moral hazard by monitoring, it may appear that Dave does not pay for the expected cost of his driving behavior. However, an insurer usually will incorporate a person's expected behavior when setting the premium. In our example, the premium would not vary with Dave's *actual* driving speed, but the premium in effect would incorporate Dave's *expected* driving speed. Since the premium Dave pays reflects the insurer's expectations about Dave's behavior after being insured, Dave has an incentive to accept contracts that give him incentives to take precautions. It is better for Dave to have a contract that induces him to take cost-justified precautions and therefore have a lower premium than to have a contract that does not induce him to take cost-justified precautions and therefore have a higher premium.

Reducing Moral Hazard

Experience rating and limited coverage are the two major methods of reducing moral hazard. Both approaches provide incentives for insureds to take precautions after policies are issued by placing some risk on the insured.[4]

Experience rating makes the premium charged contingent on the claims in prior periods. As described in Chapter 8, one reason for experience rating is to incorporate new information about future expected claim costs into the premium. Another reason for experience rating is to reduce moral hazard. An insured, knowing that future premiums depend on his or her behavior, is more likely to take precautions.

Limiting the amount of insurance coverage through deductibles and other provisions that require the insured to bear part of any loss (see below) also reduces moral hazard. The general point is that, when moral hazard problems exist (which to some extent is always the case), insurance contracts will likely offer incomplete coverage. The intuition is simple: Since insurance creates moral hazard, providing less of it reduces moral hazard.

Moral Hazard in Other Contexts

Our discussion of moral hazard illustrates a very important concept. A tradeoff exists between risk shifting (e.g., insurance coverage) and incentives: More risk shifting implies less incentive to reduce expected costs. The application of this concept is not limited to insurance contracts. The tradeoff between risk shifting and incentives in contracts is pervasive because most contracts shift risk in some way, and whenever risk is shifted, incentives are altered. For example, you probably do not like having uncertainty associated with your grade in this course. Your instructor could "insure" you by guaranteeing a B in the course. The problem with this response and the reason that your instructor will not offer such insurance (we hope) is that your incentive to learn the material would be greatly reduced. That is, eliminating your risk of a low grade creates a moral hazard problem.

Employment contracts provide a more important example. An employer could eliminate risk for employees by offering guaranteed employment for life at a fixed wage that is indexed to inflation (assuming that the employer could credibly make this promise). This type of contract is rare. One reason is moral hazard. Once this contract is offered, the employee's incentive to be productive is greatly reduced. Thus, employment contracts almost always impose some risk on employees. As another example, once society guarantees a certain standard of living for everyone through social programs, some people will have less incentive to work. Again this is a moral hazard problem—reducing risk causes some people to work less. As noted above, moral hazard is mitigated by limiting the extent of insurance coverage. Politicians and public policymakers constantly debate what the optimal

---

[4]Note that premium credits for safety devices (e.g., airbags, antilock brakes, and antitheft devices) encourage precautions before coverage begins.

balance is between social insurance and providing incentives for people to work hard and be productive.

In summary, moral hazard implies that there is a tradeoff between risk shifting and incentives. Since people designing contracts typically understand this tradeoff, private contracts (insurance contracts being one example) usually will involve incomplete risk shifting so that moral hazard limits the insurability of risk.

A potential impression from this discussion is that the changes in behavior induced by insurance are necessarily undesirable because insurance encourages people to take fewer precautions. However, one of the primary benefits of insurance is that it encourages risk-averse people to engage in productive, yet risky, activities. Without insurance, risk-averse people would take excessive precautions by avoiding certain risky activities, thus increasing the total cost of risk. For example, without the ability to purchase liability insurance, people with considerable wealth would likely take excessive precautions to avoid being sued. The key point is that a balance is needed. A complete lack of insurance coverage is likely to lead to too many precautions and full insurance is likely to lead to too few precautions. Consequently, the optimal level of insurance coverage typically is partial coverage, which takes both effects into account.

Adverse Selection

Another factor that limits the insurability of risk is adverse selection. Recall from Chapter 8 that **adverse selection** refers to situations in which consumers have different expected losses (e.g., bookworms versus skateboarders), but the insurer is unable to distinguish between the two types of consumers and charge them different premiums. If an insurer offers insurance at the same price to heterogeneous consumers and consumers know their expected losses, then the higher expected loss consumers (skateboarders) will tend to purchase more insurance coverage relative to the case where insureds are charged premiums based on their expected losses. Conversely, the lower expected loss consumers (bookworms) will tend to purchase less insurance coverage. When this scenario occurs, adverse selection takes place.

As described in Chapter 8, classification (basing premiums on expected claim costs) reduces adverse selection. Thus, adverse selection arises because it is too costly to classify insureds perfectly. Indeed, if each consumer's expected claim costs could be observed costlessly, then insurance premiums (barring government restrictions) would vary exactly with expected claim costs and there would be no adverse selection.

Classification is costly in practice and thus insurers will only classify to the extent that it is cost-effective to do so. When consumers know more about their expected losses than insurers, adverse selection occurs. Insurers understand adverse selection, and they design and price policies taking it into account. For example, if insurers believed there would be adverse selection with a particular policy, then premiums would be increased to reflect the expected adverse selection. The net result of adverse selection is that consumers with low expected losses (bookworms) purchase less coverage than they would if classification were costless. Thus, adverse selection limits the insurability of risk for consumers with low expected losses.

Example of Adverse Selection

For the sake of argument, suppose that it is prohibitively costly for insurers to classify bookworms and skateboarders. Suppose also that (1) there are an equal number of bookworms and skateboarders; (2) both bookworms and skateboarders can lose $1,000 in an accident; and (3) bookworms have an accident probability equal to 0.1 and skateboarders have an accident probability of 0.2. Ignoring administrative/capital costs and the time value of money, insurers need to charge rates (premiums per dollar of coverage) that are sufficient to cover expected claim costs. Assume that insurers consider charging a rate equal to the average accident probability for bookworms and skateboarders (i.e., premiums equal 0.15 times the amount of coverage). At this rate, skateboarders would view the insurance as having a negative loading (the expected claim cost for skateboarders equals 0.2 times the amount of coverage) and bookworms would view the insurance as having a high loading (the expected claim cost for bookworms equals 0.1 times the amount of coverage). Consequently, skateboarders would be likely to purchase more insurance coverage than bookworms; that is, adverse selection would occur.

Assume specifically that each bookworm purchases $500 of coverage and each skateboarder purchases $1,000 of coverage. Then, the insurer's premium revenue per policyholder equals

$$[\$500 \ (0.15) + \$1,000 \ (0.15)]/2 = \$112.50$$

However, the expected claim cost per policyholder equals

$$[\$500 \ (0.1) + \$1,000 \ (0.2)]/2 = \$125.00$$

Thus, the insurer cannot charge $0.15 per dollar of coverage and expect to break even.

Understanding this adverse selection problem, insurers will not charge $0.15 per dollar of coverage, but instead will charge a higher rate that reflects the fact that they are providing more coverage to skateboarders than bookworms. Assume, for example, that insurers charge $0.18 per dollar of coverage. At this higher rate, bookworms will purchase even less coverage. If bookworms purchase $250 of coverage and skateboarders continue to purchase $1,000 of coverage, the insurer's premium revenue per policyholder equals

$$[\$250 \ (0.18) + \$1,000 \ (0.18)]/2 = \$112.50$$

The expected claim cost per policyholder equals

$$[\$250 \ (0.1) + \$1,000 \ (0.2)]/2 = \$112.50$$

In this example, a rate of $0.18 per dollar of coverage allows the insurer to break even, and both bookworms and skateboarders purchase some insurance. Nevertheless, the inability to classify implies that bookworms are not fully insured (i.e., costly classification limits the insurability of their risk).

Another possibility is that an insurer will not be able to find a price that allows it to break even and induces bookworms to purchase insurance. In this extreme case, the insurer will have to charge such a high price that all bookworms will stop buying insurance and only skateboarders will purchase insurance.[5] Examples of this extreme outcome are difficult to find in practice. One possible reason is that insurers can design policies to help sort out the high expected loss consumers (skateboarders) from the low expected loss consumers

---

[5]Furthermore, if skateboarders were for some reason unwilling to buy coverage at a premium that reflects their expected claim costs (e.g., due to the possible effects of limited liability on the demand for liability insurance discussed in the last chapter), the market for coverage would break down completely.

(bookworms). We will discuss how deductibles and coinsurance can serve this purpose in the next section.

Concept Check

1. What are the major reasons that insurance contracts rarely provide full coverage?

10.2   Contractual Provisions that Limit Coverage

The central theme of the previous section is that a number of factors (administrative and capital costs, correlated losses, parameter uncertainty, moral hazard, and adverse selection) limit the extent to which risk exposures are insured. In extreme cases, these factors can eliminate the market for insurance coverage. In most cases, however, the amount of coverage is limited by contractual provisions that are discussed in this section.

Deductibles

A common way to limit the amount of coverage is through **deductibles,** which eliminate coverage for relatively small losses. To illustrate, suppose that Annie buys a six-month automobile insurance policy that covers damage to her car from events other than collisions (for more details on this type of coverage, see Chapter 13) and that her policy has a $250 deductible per occurrence. Then Annie will pay up to $250 of the loss each time her car is damaged. If the loss is less than $250, then Annie will pay the entire loss. If the loss is $1,000, Annie will pay $250 and the insurer will pay $750.

As discussed earlier, risk-averse people are likely to desire less than full coverage when policies have a positive loading. Thus, deductibles chosen by policyholders are likely to increase in size as premium loadings increase. There are other important effects of deductibles that also help to explain why they are so prevalent in insurance contracts. In particular, deductibles reduce claims processing costs, reduce moral hazard problems, and mitigate adverse selection.

Deductibles and Claims Processing Costs

One reason that policies have deductibles is to reduce the costs of processing small claims that occur relatively frequently. Some claims processing costs are unrelated to the size of the claim. For example, regardless of the claim severity, the insurer must pay a claims adjuster to process the claim and issue a check. These fixed claim processing costs make insuring small claims that occur relatively frequently very expensive (i.e., they have a high loading). To illustrate, if there is a 0.1 probability of a $50 loss and the fixed cost of processing a claim is $100, the required loading to cover the expected fixed cost associated with insuring the $50 loss is $10 ($0.1 \times 100), which is twice as large as the expected claim cost ($0.1 \times 50). This is one reason that consumers prefer not to purchase insurance for small losses; that is, they prefer to bear a modest amount of risk with a deductible, as opposed to paying a relatively large loading.

Deductibles and Moral Hazard

As noted earlier, another important function of deductibles is to reduce moral hazard. For example, with the $250 deductible, Annie has greater incentive to park her car in safe places where the likelihood of damage is lower. Without the deductible, the insurer would be forced to charge Annie a higher price, not only because a larger amount of coverage is being offered (coverage of losses below $250) and higher transaction costs but also because the expected loss for a given amount of coverage would be greater due to the higher likelihood of a claim. In other words, deductibles change people's behavior in a way that reduces the likelihood and severity of losses, which in turn lowers premiums.

Deductibles and Adverse Selection

Recall that adverse selection arises when it is too costly for insurers to classify perfectly and when consumers have superior information about their expected losses. In our previous discussion of this situation, we assumed that the insurer simply charged all consumers the same rate per unit of coverage. This resulted in the low expected loss consumers in our example (the bookworms) purchasing less coverage than the high expected loss consumers (the skateboarders).

However, insurers also may be able to use deductibles to induce (1) high expected loss consumers to choose a policy that is priced to reflect their expected claim costs, and (2) low expected loss consumers to choose a policy with a larger deductible that is priced to reflect their lower expected claim costs. Thus, even though insurers cannot distinguish skateboarders from bookworms, in theory, contracts might be designed to induce consumers to reveal their expected loss by their choice of deductible so that the bookworms and the skateboarders are separated into two classes and charged different prices.

The key to understanding how deductibles might separate consumers is to recognize that people with a higher probability of a loss (skateboarders) usually will be willing to pay more for a given amount of coverage than will people with a lower probability of a loss (bookworms). With this in mind, consider what happens if an insurer offers the following two contracts to skateboarders and bookworms, where each has a potential loss of $1,000.

Contract 1:   Deductible = $500   →   Coverage = $500
              Premium = $50   Premium per $ of coverage (rate) = $50/$500
                                      = $0.10

Contract 2:   Deductible = $250   →   Coverage = $750
              Premium = $150   Premium per $ of coverage (rate) = $150/$750
                                      = $0.20

Notice that to obtain an additional $250 of coverage (move from the $500 deductible to the $250 deductible), the consumer must pay $100 more in premiums. Also notice that the premium per dollar of coverage (the rate) for the higher amount of coverage is 20 cents, compared to 10 cents for the lower amount of coverage. Because of their higher loss probability, skateboarders will be more willing to pay the higher rate to obtain the additional coverage. Thus, it is possible that the skateboarders will choose contract 2 and that the bookworms will choose contract 1. If so, the two types have separated themselves, and they are being charged different prices per unit of coverage to reflect their different accident probabilities. The separation of bookworms and skateboarders is not costless, however. Bookworms have to accept less insurance—a higher deductible—in order to separate themselves from skateboarders. In essence, bookworms reveal themselves by their willingness to bear more risk.

The extent to which insurers actually are able to design policies to induce consumers to separate themselves into distinct risk classes is uncertain. We suspect that some degree of separation is achieved in practice. To the extent that separation occurs, the degree to which low expected loss buyers subsidize high expected loss buyers is reduced.

Coinsurance

A **coinsurance** provision requires an insured to pay a specified proportion of the loss (e.g., 20 percent).[6] Medical expense insurance policies often have a coinsurance requirement. Coinsurance reduces coverage below full coverage, just as risk-averse consumers would demand when policies have a positive loading. Coinsurance also reduces moral hazard. Since the insured pays part of any loss with a coinsurance provision, the insured has a greater incentive to reduce losses with the coinsurance provision.[7]

The following anecdote helps illustrate how coinsurance can reduce moral hazard. When Liz had a new baby in 1996, her medical insurance paid all the costs of doctor visits; that is, there was no coinsurance and no deductible. Whenever the infant was grouchy, Liz thought that the baby might have an ear infection and therefore took the baby to the doctor, who was only a short distance away. These happy days were short-lived. When the baby was six months old, Liz's medical insurance plan changed. She had to pay a coinsurance charge every time she visited the doctor's office. Although the baby's disposition remained the same, Liz seldom visited the doctor.

Policy Limits

Insurance policies often limit the amount of coverage by placing an upper limit, known as a **policy limit,** on the amount that the insurer will pay for any loss. Policy limits always are used in liability insurance policies. For example, an automobile liability insurance policy may state that the insurer will pay up to $20,000 in physical damage to another person's car and up to $100,000 in bodily injury damages to a driver or passenger of another car. As discussed in Chapter 9, the demand for liability insurance depends on a person's wealth. Thus, one explanation for liability policy limits below the level of potential damages is that people have a limited amount of wealth that they want to protect from liability suits. They therefore have little incentive to purchase insurance for the entire amount of damage that they potentially can cause other people.

Policy limits in property insurance keep people from paying for coverage in excess of the amount of loss that they could sustain. Policy limits also can reduce classification costs when consumers have information that is relevant for classification but which is costly for insurers to obtain. Suppose, for example, that the vast majority of homeowners have jewelry that has value less than $2,500, but that some homeowners have jewelry that has value greater than $2,500. The loss severity of the latter group obviously is higher than that of the former group. The problem is that insurers cannot distinguish people with expensive jewelry from those without expensive jewelry without incurring some costs (by evaluating each homeowner's jewelry prior to selling a policy). However, individuals are likely to know whether they have expensive jewelry. By limiting coverage for jewelry losses to $2,500 and offering special coverage for jewelry valued greater than $2,500 (through what is called an *endorsement* to the policy or with a separate policy), the insurer induces the homeowners with valuable jewelry to reveal themselves.

---

[6]Insurance-to-value provisions in property insurance contracts, which also are known as coinsurance clauses, differ in their operation and purpose.

[7]Coinsurance also can be used to reduce adverse selection in a manner similar to that described for deductibles.

Coordination of Benefits (Pro Rata and Excess Coverage Clauses)

Insureds sometimes will have multiple insurance policies that apply to the same loss. Coverage of a loss under multiple policies potentially could allow an insured to receive more from insurance than the loss suffered, which would require the insured to pay more for coverage and also increase moral hazard. For these reasons, insurers commonly prevent recovery in excess of the amount of the loss by including a clause, known as a **pro rata clause,** that specifies that each policy will pay a proportion of the loss. Alternatively, the policy may include an **excess clause** that specifies that the insurer will pay only losses in excess of the coverage provided by another policy.

Exclusions

You no doubt already are aware that insurance policies often contain **exclusions**—that is, they exclude coverage for specific types of losses. For example, homeowners policies exclude coverage for losses arising from flood, normal wear and tear, war, and a variety of other causes. Life insurance policies usually have exclusions for suicide within two years of policy purchase. Other examples of exclusions are presented in later chapters that deal with specific types of insurance. There are several reasons for exclusions. One reason is that the capital costs of insuring some types of losses are high due to the correlation in losses. This explains why losses from war, nuclear accidents, and perhaps flood often are excluded. Moral hazard also helps to explain why losses from some events, such as suicide in the case of life insurance, are excluded. Nonfortuitous losses, such as losses from normal wear and tear, are excluded because they involve little or no risk.

Another function of exclusions is similar to that described above for coverage limits for particular types of coverage. Exclusions often are designed to eliminate coverage that is not needed by the typical buyer. Policyholders thus do not have to pay for coverage that they do not need, and persons or businesses that need the coverage are induced to reveal themselves through purchasing an endorsement or a separate policy. In fact, many exclusions can in effect be removed for a price, especially in business insurance policies.

Indemnity versus Valued Contracts

Insurance policies can be classified into two types: indemnity contracts and valued contracts. With an **indemnity contract,** the amount that the insurer pays is determined after a loss, and the amount paid equals the value of the loss (as defined in the policy and subject to deductibles, coinsurance, limits, and exclusions). Depending on the policy, the insurer agrees to pay the cost of replacing the property (e.g., in homeowners insurance), the actual cash value (replacement cost minus depreciation), or repair cost up to the actual cash value (e.g., in auto insurance). We discuss these policy terms further in the chapters on auto and homeowners insurance. In any case, the amount that the insurer pays under an indemnity contract depends on the amount of damage. In contrast to indemnity contracts, **valued contracts** establish the amount that the insurer pays at the time the contract is initiated without regard to the amount of loss caused by the insured event. For example, the life insurance benefit paid following someone's death is fixed in the contract. The insurer does not determine the death benefit based on the circumstances of the beneficiaries at the time of death.

The choice between indemnity and valued contracts can be explained largely by the costs of assessing value and moral hazard. In many situations, the size of the loss can be determined at low cost after a loss has occurred; for example, an auto mechanic can estimate repair costs following a car accident. In these circumstances, indemnity contracts have the advantage that the amount paid by the insurer is related to the size of the loss and does not exceed the loss suffered, thus reducing moral hazard. The policyholder does not have an incentive to cause a loss (or to take fewer precautions), because the indemnity payment from the insurer will not exceed the value of the loss.

In other situations, however, the occurrence of a loss can make it costly (if not impossible) to determine the size of the loss. If expensive artwork is stolen, for example, its value cannot be readily assessed. This can lead to a moral hazard problem: Policyholders may overstate the value of the property, and, if they think they can do so with impunity, even might have an incentive to arrange for the property to be stolen. In these circumstances, contracts which assess the value and establish the insured value of the property when the contract is initiated are more likely.

Other losses can be costly or impossible to value either before a loss or after a loss. For example, the value of a person's life, including the present value of future earnings, is costly to estimate and subject to considerable uncertainty regardless of whether the person is alive or dead. In order to avoid costly haggling following a loss in these circumstances, insurance contracts are likely to be valued contracts. Moral hazard problems associated with valued contracts in life insurance are reduced by insurer underwriting standards that limit the amount of coverage in relation to the buyer's income, by suicide clauses (discussed earlier), and by the inherent value people place on their life. People purchasing life insurance also usually choose beneficiaries carefully, and criminal penalties for murder help deter murder for profit by beneficiaries.[8]

Insurance-to-Value (Coinsurance) in Property Insurance

Property insurance contracts for homeowners and business owners often have an insurance-to-value clause. This clause commonly is called a *coinsurance provision,* although it differs from the coinsurance requirement discussed above. The **insurance-to-value (coinsurance) clause** in property contracts specifies the percentage of the property's value that the insurer requires the insured to purchase to receive full reimbursement (above any deductible and up to the policy limit) following a loss. A typical coinsurance percentage is 80 percent, with percentages for commercial property insurance varying from 50 to 100 percent. These clauses are much less important than they used to be, especially in residential property insurance, given that many insurers have underwriting standards that essentially require a policy limit that is approximately equal to the value of the property. It is nonetheless useful to briefly describe the basic operation and purpose of these clauses.[9]

If the policy limit is less than the coinsurance percentage times the value of the property at the time of a loss, then the insurer will reduce the reimbursement for losses using the following formula:

$$\begin{array}{l}\text{Maximum}\\\text{proportion of}\\\text{loss paid by}\\\text{insurer}\end{array} = \left[\dfrac{\text{Amount of insurance purchased}}{\text{Value of property at time of loss}}\right]\dfrac{1}{\text{Coinsurance percentage}}$$

[8]As we discuss later, insurable interest requirements also reduce moral hazard.

[9]The specific coinsurance clause in homeowners insurance is described briefly in Chapter 14.

If the ratio in brackets is less than the coinsurance percentage, then the maximum proportion of the loss paid by the insurer is less than one. For example, if the policy limit is $150,000, the property's value is $200,000, and the coinsurance percentage is 80 percent, then the maximum proportion of the loss paid by the insurer is

$$\left[\frac{\$150,000}{\$200,000}\right]\frac{1}{0.80} = \frac{0.75}{0.80} = 93.75\%$$

Regardless of whether the insured purchased the required amount of coverage, the insurer will neither pay more than the amount of insurance purchased nor more than the actual loss. Thus, the amount paid by the insurer is the lesser of (1) the maximum proportion of loss paid by the insurer (given by the formula above) times the actual loss, (2) the amount of insurance coverage purchased, and (3) the actual loss.

Why did insurers develop a formula to impose a penalty on insureds who fail to maintain coverage equal to the coinsurance percentage? The explanation lies, in part, on industry practice that establishes premiums by multiplying the policy limit (the amount of coverage purchased) times a rate that does not vary with the policy limit. Thus, the premium charged is proportional to the limit chosen by the policyholder. The straight line in Figure 10.2 illustrates this relationship. However, the probability that a small proportion of the property is damaged is higher than the probability that a large proportion of the property is damaged (small fires are more likely than large fires). This implies that the fair premium for a policy without a coinsurance clause would be higher than the premium with a coinsurance clause (except if the policyholder chose a 100% policy limit). This relationship is depicted by the curve in Figure 10.2. Thus, without a coinsurance penalty, policyholders who insure property for less than the coinsurance percentage assumed in the flat rate premium structure would pay less than the fair premium. The coinsurance penalty reduces the amount of coverage so that the premium charged in these cases is closer to the fair premium.

Instead of the existing practice of charging a constant rate regardless of the amount of coverage, insurers could alter the rate based on the amount of coverage purchased relative to the market value of the property. This would be more complicated, and there would be a greater need for insurers to assess the value of property accurately every time a policy is written or renewed to determine more precisely how much coverage is being purchased relative to the

FIGURE 10.2
Explanation for coinsurance provision in property contracts (industry practice is to charge premiums that are proportional to coverage, but fair premiums are not proportional to coverage).

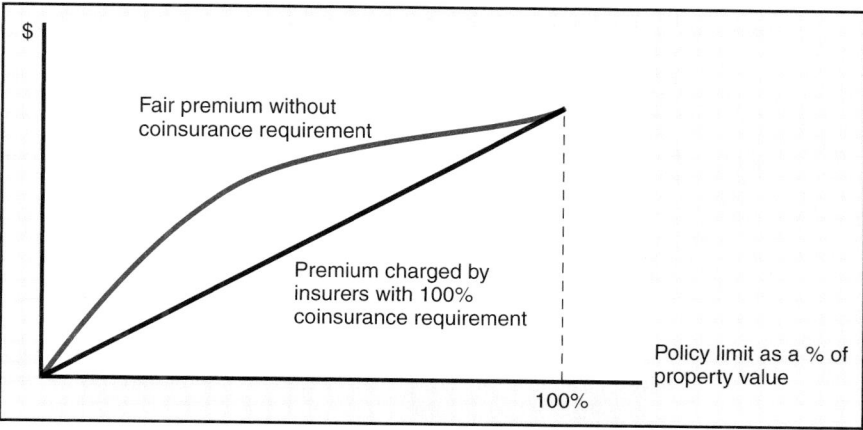

market value of the property. Because in some cases the property owner is likely to incur lower costs obtaining information about the market value of the property, it can be less costly to place the ultimate burden on the owner by including a coinsurance provision. As noted earlier, however, modern underwriting criteria and property valuation methods used by insurers often require property insurance policyholders to insure property for at least 80 percent of its estimated value, so that the coinsurance clause is much less important than in the past. This in part reflects the development of lower cost methods of estimating the approximate value of property when coverage is issued. It also reflects increasing insurer concern that imposing coinsurance penalties could lead to litigation by policyholders against insurers and agents.

10.3 Legal Doctrines

Before discussing legal doctrines affecting insurance contracts, it is useful to discuss briefly how the legal system potentially can improve private insurance contracts. The issue is: Why not let people contract with each other without the legal system imposing restrictions on the nature of contracts? One role of the legal system is to reduce contracting costs by establishing legal rules or fundamental doctrines that apply to all insurance contracts. With fundamental legal doctrines, participants in the insurance market begin with a mutual understanding of how insurance contracts will be interpreted under some unforeseen circumstances. This mutual understanding can reduce contracting costs. A second role of the legal system is to enforce private contracts and to resolve disputes at a lower cost than could be achieved through private contracts.

Reducing Contracting Costs through Fundamental Legal Doctrines

As discussed earlier in this chapter, one problem with insurance is moral hazard—once someone is insured, the incentive to take precautions and to lower claim costs is reduced. Another problem is information disclosure; that is, consumers often have information that is relevant to the pricing of insurance. As we discussed earlier, it is mutually beneficial for the insurer and the insured to have contracts that mitigate moral hazard and that induce people to reveal information truthfully that otherwise would be costly for insurers to gather. As a result, legal principles that mitigate moral hazard and promote information disclosure have developed over time.

Mitigating Moral Hazard

Moral hazard problems become particularly severe if a policyholder can benefit from the occurrence of an insured event. For example, if an event causes $10,000 of damage, but a policyholder can collect $20,000 from the insurer, then the policyholder has some incentive to see that the insured event occurs. The **indemnity principle** states that an insurance policy cannot pay more than the financial loss suffered. Most property and liability insurance policies are indemnity contracts. The financial loss is measured after the loss has occurred and payment is limited to the amount of the loss as defined in the contract (e.g., replacement cost or actual cash value).[10] As we discussed earlier, when it is costly or impossible to

[10]Note that the indemnity principle could be seriously violated with replacement cost coverage if the property's replacement cost greatly exceeds its market value. As we discuss in Chapter 14, some homeowners policies limit payment to the actual cash value or market value for this reason.

measure the loss subsequent to its occurrence, valued policies are used. The indemnity principle does not apply to valued contracts.

Another legal doctrine related to the indemnity principle is the requirement that the insurance policyholder have an **insurable interest.** This generally means that the policyholder must suffer adverse financial consequences if the event that causes the insurance company to pay a claim occurs. A policy can be voided if insurable interest is found to be nonexistent. To illustrate the moral hazard problems that could arise without an insurable interest rule, suppose that Anne and Carol are not related and that Anne can buy an insurance policy that pays her 80 percent of Carol's medical expenses over the coming year. Then Anne would have an incentive to see that Carol needs medical care.

For property and liability insurance, an insurable interest must exist at the time of the loss, and a person cannot receive more than his or her insurable interest from the insurer. In this case, the insurable interest rule is essentially the same as the indemnity principle. With life insurance contracts, the owner of the policy must have an insurable interest in the subject (the person whose death triggers payment) at the time the policy is purchased. The insurable interest rule is not applied to immediate family members. In addition, a person can insure his or her own life and name a beneficiary who does not have an insurable interest in the person's life. As noted earlier, several other factors help mitigate moral hazard in life insurance. For example, social norms and criminal penalties reduce the likelihood of murder, and a policyholder whose life is insured usually chooses the beneficiary with care.[11]

Moral hazard problems also would arise if people could collect compensation from multiple sources following an event that causes a loss. Earlier we discussed how pro rata and excess clauses prevent an insured from recovering more than the loss from multiple insurance policies. People also might potentially collect twice for the same loss when their insurance covers the loss and another party is legally liable. For example, if a neighbor's negligence destroys Joe's property, he might seek compensation by suing his neighbor. In these circumstances, if Joe files a claim with his insurer, then the insurer receives the legal right to obtain compensation from the party who caused the loss. The transfer of Joe's right to seek compensation through the courts to his insurer is called **subrogation;** it prevents Joe from recovering twice for his loss and thus mitigates moral hazard.[12]

Information Disclosure

Insurance contracts require that both the policyholder and the insurer disclose all relevant information; that is, the two parties must negotiate with **utmost good faith.** This doctrine implies that policyholders must respond truthfully to questions that the insurer asks. For example, if an insurer asks whether you smoke, your answer is called a *representation,* and it must be truthful. If incorrect, it is known as a **misrepresentation.** The doctrine also applies to any information that the policyholder knows to be relevant to the decision to insure, but about which the insurer does not directly ask. For example, seeking property insurance

---

[11]As an additional safeguard against moral hazard, the person on whose life the policy is written typically must also sign the application if the policy is purchased by someone else.

[12]Subrogation also allows a victim to receive compensation immediately from his or her insurer, who may then receive reimbursement from the other party at a later date. Subrogation also reduces the price of property insurance; people do not have to pay for the right of double recovery. Insurance policies often include subrogation clauses (even though it is a legal doctrine) to clarify the conditions of subrogation.

without telling the agent that a forest fire is raging one-half mile from your business would be considered **concealment** of relevant information.

Although the specific rules vary across states and types of insurance, the legal remedy for misrepresentation or concealment of a material fact is that the insurer can void the contract. *Material* means that the information is relevant to the insurer's decision to sell or price the policy. The contract usually can be voided even if the nondisclosed or incorrect information is unrelated to the cause of the accident. For example, if a life insurance policyholder lies about smoking and later dies in an automobile accident (unrelated to smoking) within two years of buying the policy, then the life insurer may be able to void the contract. After two years, life insurance policies (but not property–liability insurance contracts) are generally *incontestable*. This means that the insurer cannot deny coverage for misrepresentation or concealment.

Voiding the contract for misrepresentation and/or concealment can be justified by the importance of information for risk classification (underwriting) and the fact that the policyholder often is the lowest cost provider of information. If the courts instead pursued the less stringent resolution of simply making the beneficiary reimburse the insurer for the higher premium that should have been paid, policyholders would have stronger incentives to misrepresent and conceal information.[13] If caught, which usually occurs when a claim is filed, the policyholder simply could pay the higher premiums that should have been paid initially. Thus, there would be little or no cost to misrepresentation or concealment and people would misrepresent and conceal information more often. Insurers also would expend greater resources trying to gather information. To the extent that such efforts are unsuccessful, other policyholders who have lower expected claim costs would be charged higher prices in order to cover those who have higher expected claim costs but who fail to truthfully reveal the information.

Resolving Coverage Disputes

When coverage disputes arise between a policyholder and an insurer, the courts generally apply several legal principles in interpreting insurance contracts. Insurance contracts generally are **contracts of adhesion,** which means that the insurer has written and offered the contract to the policyholder for acceptance or rejection. Since the insurer writes the contract and has expertise in anticipating conditions that could cause disputes, the courts generally interpret any ambiguous policy language in favor of the policyholder. However, this practice is not followed for some large business insurance policies where the terms are mutually negotiated between the insurer and the insured.

In addition, some courts have adopted the **doctrine of reasonable expectations.** This doctrine holds that policies will be interpreted according to the expectations of a reasonable person who is not trained in the law. For example, if a reasonable person would expect a policy to cover a certain loss, the courts might require the insurer to pay even if the contract language clearly excludes coverage. To illustrate, in one instance a liability claim was brought against a tavern owner for negligently serving alcohol to a person who later caused an auto accident. The tavern owner had been sold a standard business liability insurance

---

[13]In fact, life insurance policies usually contain a provision that specifies this less stringent remedy (paying the extra premium) in the event of misrepresentation of a person's age or sex. In these cases, the insurer should be able to obtain the information at low cost.

contract that clearly excluded coverage for all claims arising out of the sale of alcoholic beverages. The insurer claimed that the policyholder knowingly chose this policy to receive a lower premium. However, the courts ruled that the insurer had to pay the liability claim because a tavern owner would reasonably expect that the claim would be covered.

The general point is that the courts usually place the burden of anticipating events and writing explicit contracts to handle events on insurers. The placement of this burden on insurers usually makes sense given the information, experience, and expertise that insurers develop as a result of dealing with many contracts. On the other hand, it sometimes is argued that some courts have gone too far in ignoring contract language in order to compensate policyholders or the victims of policyholders' actions, because insurers are viewed as having "deep pockets." A controversial example involves environmental liability insurance coverage. As discussed in more detail in Chapter 28, over the past 30 years, some courts' interpretation of business liability insurance policies has expanded coverage for environmental damage beyond the circumstances originally envisioned by insurers. The insurance market has responded with policies that contain more explicit and more restrictive exclusions.

A related issue concerns the general legal duty of the insurer to negotiate in good faith with claimants. Based on the rationale that market incentives and normal judicial remedies for breach of contract may be insufficient to prevent some insurers from behaving opportunistically by refusing to pay claim costs or by offering to pay too little for claims, some courts have allowed policyholders (or third-party claimants) to sue an insurer for bad faith. These **bad-faith suits** allege that insurers have acted in a manner inconsistent with what a reasonable policyholder would have expected and therefore have failed to act in good faith. In some cases, courts have awarded damages to claimants many times over the disputed amount. These cases sometimes have been quite controversial, with some observers suggesting that courts often have found bad faith on the part of insurers even when their dispute with claimants over the existence or amount of coverage was reasonable. To the extent that courts find insurers liable in bad-faith suits when the disputes are reasonable, premium rates for all policyholders must increase.

10.4 Summary

- Because of administrative costs, capital costs, moral hazard, and adverse selection, individuals and businesses generally do not demand full insurance coverage for their loss exposures.

- Low severity losses generally are not insured on a stand-alone basis (i.e., unless bundled with other losses) because of fixed administrative costs.

- High frequency losses generally are not insured because the fair premium is close to or exceeds the potential loss.

- Insurance for highly correlated losses generally is limited due to the costs of holding the capital needed to achieve a low probability of insolvency.

- Insurance for losses with high parameter uncertainty (uncertain loss distributions) generally is limited because of the costs of holding the capital needed to achieve a low probability of insolvency.

- Moral hazard limits the extent to which risk is insured.

- Adverse selection limits the insurance coverage purchased by low expected loss consumers who are pooled with higher expected loss consumers.

- Insurance coverage is limited through contractual provisions like deductibles, coinsurance, policy limits, exclusions, and pro rata and excess coverage provisions.

- Legal doctrines have been developed that reduce the cost of coverage by (1) mitigating moral hazard, (2) providing incentives for insureds to disclose relevant information to insurers, and (3) reducing the costs of resolving disputes.
- The indemnity principle and insurable interest rule help to reduce moral hazard.
- Voiding insurance contracts when policyholders make misrepresentations or conceal material information helps to promote low cost information disclosure.
- When resolving contract disputes, courts generally interpret any ambiguous policy terms in favor of the insured. Some courts go further and interpret the policy in terms of the insured's reasonable expectations even if contract language clearly specifies a different outcome.

Key Terms

parameter uncertainty 182	insurance-to-value (coinsurance) clause 192
moral hazard 183	indemnity principle 194
adverse selection 186	insurable interest 195
deductibles 188	subrogation 195
coinsurance 190	utmost good faith 195
policy limit 190	misrepresentation 195
pro rata clause 191	concealment 196
excess clause 191	contracts of adhesion 196
exclusions 191	doctrine of reasonable expectations 196
indemnity contract 191	bad-faith suits 197
valued contracts 191	

Questions and Problems

1. Explain how the amount of insurance coverage purchased by a risk-averse person is likely to change in response to each of the following:

   a. The legal costs associated with processing claims increase.

   b. Regulatory compliance costs decrease.

   c. The tax on insurer investment earnings increases.

   d. The variability of claim costs increases.

   e. The criminal penalties for fraud increase.

2. Explain why a business property insurance policy may have an exclusion for damages due to a nuclear accident.

3. A friend says "Insurance policies are a ripoff; they always have provisions that limit how much you can be compensated." You enlighten your friend by saying . . .

4. For each of the following risk exposures, explain why the amount of private market insurance coverage may be significantly limited through contractual provisions (exclusions, limits, coinsurance, and deductibles) or in extreme cases nonexistent:

   a. A pet's life

   b. Pain from injuries

   c. Earthquakes

   d. Unemployment

5. Suppose that Annie's loss distribution is as follows:

$$\text{Loss} = \begin{cases} \$5,000 & \text{with probability } 0.004 \\ \$1,000 & \text{with probability } 0.006 \\ \$\ 250 & \text{with probability } 0.055 \\ \$\ \ \ 0 & \text{with probability } 0.935 \end{cases}$$

Assume that the only administrative cost is the cost of processing a claim, which equals

$500 regardless of the claim size. Ignoring moral hazard, adverse selection, the time value of money, and capital costs, the cost of providing insurance is the sum of expected claim costs and expected claim processing costs. Fill in the table below for a policy with a $250 deductible and a policy without a deductible. What does the table illustrate about the marginal cost of insuring small losses and the desirability of deductibles?

		Policy with Full Coverage (1)	Policy with a $250 Deductible (2)	Implicit Cost of Coverage for $250 Loss (1) – (2)
(a)	Expected claim costs			
(b)	Expected claim processing costs			
(a) + (b)	Fair premium			
(b)/(a)	Percent loading			

6. A lawnmower manufacturer has the following loss distribution for its annual products liability costs:

$$\text{Loss} = \begin{cases} \$ \ \ \ \ \ \ 0 & \text{with probability } 0.984 \\ \$ \ 50{,}000 & \text{with probability } 0.010 \\ \$250{,}000 & \text{with probability } 0.004 \\ \$750{,}000 & \text{with probability } 0.002 \end{cases}$$

Determine the expected claim costs for each of the following policies:

a. Full insurance.
b. $50,000 deductible and a $500,000 limit.
c. No deductible and a $700,000 limit.

7. Captain Mack's, a seafood restaurant, offers medical cost coverage for its employees. Its probability distribution for medical costs for the coming year is as follows:

$$\text{Medical costs} = \begin{cases} \$ \ \ \ \ \ \ 0 & \text{with probability } 0.9335 \\ \$ \ \ 2{,}000 & \text{with probability } 0.0500 \\ \$ \ \ 5{,}000 & \text{with probability } 0.0100 \\ \$ \ 10{,}000 & \text{with probability } 0.0050 \\ \$ \ 50{,}000 & \text{with probability } 0.0010 \\ \$500{,}000 & \text{with probability } 0.0005 \end{cases}$$

Calculate Captain Mack's expected claim costs for each of the following policies:

a. Full insurance.
b. $5,000 deductible and a $200,000 limit.
c. 20 percent coinsurance and a $200,000 limit.
d. $5,000 deductible, 20 percent coinsurance, and a $200,000 limit.

8. Lawrence lives in California but buys his automobile insurance from a Colorado insurer, which violates California law. He says he lives in Colorado and uses a friend's Colorado address when filling out the application in order to pay the lower Colorado premium rates. What could happen if Lawrence is involved in an accident?

9. Mary buys a woodburning stove for her cabin in the mountains. She remembers that when she originally purchased homeowners insurance for the cabin, the insurance agent asked if she had a woodburning stove, because woodburning stoves increase the risk of fire. At that time, she correctly answered no. Now, she must decide whether to inform her insurance agent about the new stove. Would you advise her to inform the insurance agent? Explain.

Answer to Concept Check

1. Insurance contracts rarely provide full coverage because (*a*) people prefer less than full coverage when premiums exceed expected claim costs (i.e., have positive premium loadings) due to administrative and capital costs; (*b*) less than full coverage reduces moral hazard; and (*c*) adverse selection causes low expected loss consumers to have less than full coverage.

References

Arrow, Kenneth. "Insurance, Risk, and Resource Allocation." In *Essays in the Theory of Risk Bearing.* Chicago: Marham Press, 1971. (*Explains how moral hazard and adverse selection limit the insurability of risk.*)

Mayers, David; and Clifford Smith. *Toward a Positive Theory of Insurance.* New York, NY: Salomon Center, New York University, 1982. (*Explains many insurance contract provisions as well as other institutional arrangements in insurance.*)

Rea, Samuel A., Jr. "The Economics of Insurance Law." *International Review of Law and Economics* 13 (1993), pp. 145–62. (*Provides historical and economic background on the important doctrines in insurance law.*)

Chapter 11

Loss Control

Chapter Objectives

- Define loss control.
- Describe the various types of loss control.
- Derive the optimal amount of loss control using information on the costs and benefits.
- Discuss the rationale for government safety programs.

11.1 Types of Loss Control

Loss control refers to efforts that reduce expected losses. For example, persons who drive slowly and cautiously reduce their expected accident losses. Because loss control usually involves investments of resources (funds, effort, or time), finding the optimal level of loss control requires consideration of both the benefits (lower expected losses) and the costs of additional loss control activities. An important dimension of this problem is the identification and assessment of the types and amounts of losses that particular activities can produce. We begin this chapter by illustrating the different types of loss control with individual and business examples. This discussion also highlights that loss control decisions involve trade-offs, sometimes difficult, between the benefits of loss control and the costs of loss control.

Recall from Chapter 3 that expected losses can be calculated by multiplying the frequency of losses times the severity of losses. Consequently, a useful way of categorizing loss control activities is to distinguish activities that alter the frequency of losses from those that alter the severity of losses. Of course, some activities influence both the frequency and severity of losses.

Loss Prevention

Numerous activities reduce expected losses by reducing the frequency of losses **(loss prevention)**. For instance, a family that builds a fence around their yard reduces the probability of their child being hit by a car or drowning in a neighbor's pool. The cost of the loss prevention is the cost of the materials for the fence, the time spent installing the fence, and any reduction in the beauty of the landscaping. The benefit is the reduction in the probability of a child being injured or killed. If families make decisions on whether to build a fence based on the costs and benefits, then families with smaller children, families with more income, families with neighbors who have pools, and families that live on busy streets are more likely to build fences.

Businesses reduce the probability of being sued under products liability law by designing, manufacturing, and marketing safe products. Safe products, however, generally are more costly because more careful design and more extensive testing takes time and money. Reducing the likelihood of a manufacturing defect increases manufacturing costs. Informing potential consumers about the safe use of a product increases marketing costs. The benefits of reducing the probability of a lawsuit include a reduction in expected legal costs, a reduction in expected injuries and thus judgments for those injuries, and a reduction in the expected damage to the firm's reputation, which influences demand for the firm's products. If legal costs increase or monetary judgments increase, then firms can be expected to increase their investment in loss prevention.

An extreme example of loss prevention is to avoid completely the activity that potentially gives rise to the loss. This form of loss prevention, which reduces the probability of loss to zero, is sometimes called **loss avoidance.** The cost of loss avoidance is the sacrifice of the benefits from the activity that gave rise to the potential loss. For example, if a firm avoids the possibility of being sued by shutting down its operations, then the owners forgo the potential profits from the business. Presumably, loss avoidance would imply that the benefits from the risky activity are less than the costs of the risky activity.

An example of loss avoidance is provided by the small airplane industry. During the mid-1980s, the damages from product liability suits increased substantially for small airplane manufacturers and consequently so did liability insurance premiums. From a public policy perspective, a potential justification for the increase in damages was that the increase would induce airplane manufacturers to make safer planes. However, some manufacturers decided to avoid the potential product liability losses by going out of business—the expected revenues from selling small airplanes presumably were lower than the expected costs, including the expected product liability costs. An ironic consequence was that with fewer new airplanes being produced, people used older, less-safe planes.

Loss Reduction

Activities that reduce expected losses by decreasing the size of the loss conditional on a loss occurring are called **loss reduction;** they can occur before or after a loss. **Pre-loss activities** occur before a loss; they decrease the magnitude of a loss if one occurs. For example, investment in fire-fighting equipment, such as fire extinguishers, reduces the magnitude of a loss from a fire but this investment does not prevent a fire from occurring. **Post-loss activities** occur subsequent to an event that causes a loss. For example, placing plywood over windows that were broken in a storm can reduce subsequent water damage and theft losses.

An important type of pre-loss loss reduction activity is catastrophe planning. To reduce the magnitude of losses from both natural catastrophes (hurricanes, earthquakes, etc.) and man-made catastrophes (nuclear accidents, plant explosions, chemical spills, or terrorist attacks), local, state, and federal governments, as well as many companies, have detailed plans for evacuation, medical treatment, power restoration, and cleanup. This planning can significantly reduce the magnitude of losses from catastrophes.

Diversification and Expected Indirect Losses

Recall from Chapter 4 that diversification of risk changes the probability distribution of losses in a way that keeps expected *direct* losses constant, but reduces the variance of losses. In addition, diversification reduces the probability of very high losses, which can be measured by the maximum probable loss. Because diversification does not change expected direct losses, it generally would not be considered an example of direct loss control. However, diversification can reduce expected *indirect* losses. We illustrate this point with an example in which a firm diversifies risk by segregating loss exposures into smaller exposure units. This type of diversification is commonly called **segregation (or separation) of exposure units.**

Suppose that a firm has the choice of doubling the size of its existing plant or building a replica of the existing plant at another location. Assume that the value of each individual plant would be $50 million and the value of one plant if it were doubled in size is $100 million. Further suppose that both locations are exposed to losses from hurricanes. More specifically, assume that the probability of a hurricane at each location is 0.05, that the outcomes at the separate locations are independent, and that a hurricane at either location would result in a complete loss.

If the firm doubles the size of its existing plant, it has a 0.05 chance of losing $100 million, and its expected direct loss is $5 million. If the firm builds separate plants, the hurricane loss distribution is

$$\text{Direct Loss} = \begin{cases} \$100 \text{ million} & \text{with probability } 0.05 \times 0.05 = 0.0025 \\ 50 \text{ million} & \text{with probability } 2 \times 0.05 \times 0.95 = 0.095 \\ 0 & \text{with probability } 0.95 \times 0.95 = 0.9025 \end{cases}$$

Segregation of the exposure units increases the expected frequency of losses from 0.05 to 0.0975 (0.0025 + 0.095), but it reduces the expected severity of losses. The latter point can be seen intuitively by noting that if a loss occurs, it equals $100 million without segregation, but generally equals only $50 million with segregation.[1] The higher frequency and lower expected severity counteract each other in this example, resulting in no change in expected direct losses ($5 million).[2]

Thus, in this example the segregation of assets did not alter expected direct losses. But, if there are indirect losses associated with a large direct loss, segregation of assets (and other

[1]The expected severity falls from $100 million to $51.282 million. The expected severity with segregation can be calculated using conditional probabilities. Conditional on a loss occurring, the probability of $100 million loss is 0.0256 (0.0025/0.0975) and the probability of a $50 million loss is 0.9744 (0.095/0.0975). Thus, the expected severity is $51.282 (0.0256 × 100 + 0.9744 × 50).

[2]The expected direct loss with segregation equals $100 × 0.0025 + $50 × 0.095 = $5 million. Alternatively, you can calculate expected direct loss using expected frequency and expected severity as follows: 0.0975 × $51.282 million = $5 million.

methods of diversification) nonetheless represents a form of indirect loss control. For example, if a $100 million property loss (but not $50 million loss) causes the firm to incur financial distress costs (an indirect loss), then expected indirect losses are reduced by the segregation of assets. Note that segregation of assets is not always optimal, because of the associated costs. Separating the plants could decrease labor productivity, increase transportation costs, and increase overhead costs above any reduction in expected losses.

Effects of Insurance on Loss Control

Since purchasing insurance coverage and loss control are alternative risk management tools, it is natural to wonder how insurance coverage affects loss control incentives. This is an issue that we have addressed on several occasions in prior chapters under the heading of *moral hazard.* The important point to remember is that provided insurance premiums are adjusted to accurately reflect the effects of loss control activities on expected insured losses, insurance coverage will not reduce incentives for loss control (i.e., insurance coverage will not cause moral hazard). For example, a restaurant will have greater incentive to install flooring material that reduces slips and falls if its insurance premiums are reduced following installation of the new flooring. However, in situations where premiums do not accurately reflect loss control activities, insurance coverage can cause moral hazard. If the restaurant gets little or no premium reduction, it may have too little incentive to modify the floors.

11.2   Optimal Loss Control When Costs and Benefits Are Known

Loss control typically involves an expenditure of effort, money, and/or time. The optimal amount of loss control ideally weighs the costs and benefits (the reduction in expected losses). It is very important to reflect all the important benefits and costs in the analysis. This often creates difficult measurement issues, some of which we briefly discuss later in the chapter. The failure to do so will lead to suboptimal decisions and perhaps to too many injuries with severe consequences to victims. To illustrate the main ideas of comparing costs and benefits associated with loss control decisions, we present two simplified hypothetical examples in which all the information necessary to calculate the potential costs and benefits is known. In practice, the magnitude of the potential costs and benefits would have to be estimated, which in some cases can be very difficult and often requires subjective judgment. We describe later how firms can estimate some of the costs and benefits of loss control. Remember that these hypothetical examples illustrate conceptual points related to cost-benefit analysis; they do not incorporate all of the factors that would need to be considered in an actual situation.

A Simple Example of Safety Expenditures

Suppose that a firm is deciding how much to spend to make its workplace safer. The first two columns of Table 11.1 provide a simple example of the effect of various levels of safety expenditures on the annual frequency of accidents per employee. For simplicity, we ignore insurance and assume that the firm's safety expenditures can be made only in increments of $500,000. If the firm spends nothing on safety, then the annual frequency is 10 percent. If the firm spends $1 million, then the annual frequency falls to 7 percent. If the firm spends $2 million, then the annual frequency falls to 6.3 percent. Note the diminishing returns to

TABLE 11.1
Cost/benefit analysis for loss control decisions.

	Average Loss Severity = $20,000 Total employees = 5,000				
Safety Expenditure	Accident Frequency per Employee	Expected Accident Cost per Employee	Total Expected Accident Costs	Marginal Costs	Marginal Benefits
0	0.100	$2,000	$10,000,000	—	—
$ 500,000	0.080	1,600	8,000,000	$500,000	$2,000,000
1,000,000	0.070	1,400	7,000,000	500,000	1,000,000
1,500,000	0.066	1,320	6,600,000	500,000	400,000
2,000,000	0.063	1,260	6,300,000	500,000	300,000

safety expenditures; that is, each additional safety expenditure increment reduces the accident frequency by a smaller amount.

Assuming that the average severity of accidents is $20,000 (and that this properly measures the value of harm to employees), the third column gives the expected accident cost per employee. For example, when the firm spends nothing on safety, the expected accident cost per employee equals $2,000 (0.1 frequency times $20,000 in severity). Assuming that the firm employs 5,000 workers, the fourth column gives the total expected accident costs associated with each level of safety expenditures. How much should the firm spend on safety, assuming that the safety expenditures listed in column one are the only costs and that the reduction in expected accident costs is the only benefit?

Consider the first expenditure increment (from zero dollars to $500,000). By spending $500,000, the firm reduces the accident frequency to 8 percent, which in turn lowers total expected accident costs by $2 million. Obviously, the firm would be willing to spend $500,000 to reduce its expected accident costs by $2 million. By spending another $500,000, accident frequency falls from 0.08 to 0.07, and total expected accident costs drop from $8 million to $7 million. Again, the firm would be willing to spend the additional $500,000 to reduce its expected accident costs by $1 million. With the next $500,000 expenditure, the firm reduces its accident frequency from 0.07 to 0.066 and its total expected accident costs from $7 million to $6.6 million. If, as we are assuming, the only benefit of additional safety is the reduction in expected accident costs, the firm would not want to make the additional expenditure, because the additional cost ($500,000) exceeds the additional benefit (a reduction in expected accident cost of $400,000). Thus, the firm would spend only $1 million on safety in this example.[3]

The analysis just presented illustrates that the firm should spend money on loss control until the additional (marginal) costs exceed the additional (marginal) benefits. To highlight the calculation of marginal costs and marginal benefits, the last two columns of Table 11.1 give the marginal costs and marginal benefits in this example. The marginal costs equal the change in the loss control expenditures and the marginal benefits equal the reduction in total expected accident costs. At $1 million expenditure, the marginal cost is $500,000, but the marginal benefit is $1 million; therefore, the firm should spend at least $1 million. For

[3]If safety expenditures represent part of the cost of employment, then workers as a group would likely support that expenditure if they understood and agreed with the technical details. We return to this issue in Chapter 18.

a $1.5 million safety expenditure, the marginal cost is again $500,000, but the marginal benefit is only $400,000; therefore, the firm should not spend up to $1.5 million.

You may object to some of the assumptions in this highly simplified example. In practice, there might be additional benefits of making the workplace safe, such as increased productivity. The example, nevertheless, illustrates three points: First, individuals, firms, and governments should weight the costs and benefits of loss control expenditures, even if they are difficult to quantify in practice. Second, the optimal level of expenditures on loss control is determined by the marginal costs and marginal benefits. Loss control expenditures should be made until the marginal cost exceeds the marginal benefits. Third, an important implication of cost/benefit analysis is that minimizing expected losses in almost all cases is too costly. At some point, the cost of additional safety exceeds the benefits.

Incorporating the Timing of Benefits and Costs

If the benefits (costs) of loss control accrue (are incurred) over time, a comparison of the costs and benefits should take into account the time value of money by calculating present values. To illustrate, suppose that a firm is considering spending $15 million this year to enhance the safety of its manufacturing facilities. It estimates that the annual frequency of accidents per employee will fall from 5 percent to 4 percent and that the average severity of accidents will fall from $20,000 to $15,000 per year as a result of the renovation in each of the next 10 years. Assuming a constant workforce of 5,000 employees over this time period, each year expected losses will decrease from $5 million ($0.05 \times 5,000 \times \$20,000$) to $3 million ($0.04 \times 5,000 \times \$15,000$). Should the firm spend the $15 million?

The cash flows (in millions) are illustrated in the first row of Table 11.2. The firm will invest $15 million today and expects to save $2 million in accident costs each year for 10 years. To determine whether it should spend the $15 million, the firm must find the present value of the future expected cash flows by discounting them back to the present using the appropriate cost of capital. A detailed discussion of the appropriate cost of capital is not necessary at this point; we will simply assume that the cost of capital equals 8 percent. The present value of the expected cash flow in year 1 is $2/1.08 = $1.852 million, the present value of the cash flow in year 2 is $2/1.08^2 = $1.715 million, and so on as illustrated in rows two and three of Table 11.2. The net present value of the project is simply the sum of the present values of all the cash flows (or equivalently, the present value of the future cash flows minus the initial investment). In this case, the net present value equals $-$1.58 million. Assuming all the relevant cost and benefits have been incorporated in the analysis, this investment would reduce the firm's value and should not be undertaken.

TABLE 11.2
Cash flows from hypothetical loss control decisions.

Cost of capital = 8%, all numbers in millions of dollars				
	Today	Year 1	Year 2 $\cdots$	Year 10
Expected cash flows	$-$15	$2.000	$2.000 $\cdots$	$2.000
Present value of individual expected cash flows	$-$15	$\dfrac{\$2.000}{(1+.08)}$	$\dfrac{\$2.000}{(1+.08)^2}$ $\cdots$	$\dfrac{\$2.000}{(1+.08)^{10}}$
Present value of individual expected cash flows	$-$15	$1.852	$1.715 $\cdots$	$0.926
Net present value	$-$1.58			

11.3   Examples of Identification of Benefits and Costs

In order to make loss control decisions to increase firm value, firms must estimate the expected benefits and costs. Our focus in this section is on illustrating the major types of benefits and costs by discussing three specific examples of loss control. We also will point out some of the problems in measuring benefits and costs. Each example deals with voluntary decisions by firms.

Installation of Automatic Sprinkler System

Safety Supply stores large volumes of its products in a warehouse prior to shipment to distributors. Safety is considering the installation of heat- and smoke-activated sprinklers that will reduce property damage in the event of a fire. The principal benefits from installing the sprinklers include reductions in expected cash outflows or increases in expected cash inflows that would arise from reducing expected fire damage. For simplicity we will assume that no risk of harm to employees or other people is involved and focus only on the benefits and costs associated with property damage.

The principal benefits from installing the sprinklers include: (1) reduced fire insurance premiums for direct damage to property and business interruption losses, and (2) reduced expected losses retained under per occurrence deductibles in Safety's fire insurance and for possible business interruption losses in excess of Safety's coverage limits. Safety probably can obtain reasonably accurate estimates of percentage savings in insurance premiums from insurance brokers, and it can assume a likely growth rate in premiums over time to estimate dollar premium savings. Safety might be able to estimate savings in uninsured losses from a historical analysis of its own or industry loss experience or by analyzing premium increases that would be needed if the firm were to buy more complete insurance coverage. Safety also might rely heavily on judgment to estimate reductions in uninsured losses.

The decision to install sprinklers involves two major costs. First, Safety will have to pay for the equipment and installation. Second, the sprinklers will involve routine maintenance and upkeep. The direct cost of purchase and installation will be known. The ongoing costs of maintenance and upkeep can be reasonably estimated based on discussions with sprinkler vendors, and they will be known for the duration of any maintenance agreement that Safety buys from the vendor.

As is true in many loss control decisions and, more generally, many other types of business investment decisions, the installation of sprinklers involves a comparatively large up-front investment in equipment and installation. The benefits in the form of lower insurance premiums and uninsured losses, as well as the costs of maintenance and upkeep, will be realized over the useful life of the sprinklers. Deciding whether to invest in sprinklers to increase firm value requires that Safety weigh the expected benefits and costs by discounting expected net cash flows to present value using an appropriate cost of capital.

Installation of Safety Guards

Presto Manufacturing uses drill presses in the manufacture of its products. Employees of Presto are exposed to serious injuries to their hands and arms from using the presses. Presto can retool its presses to include guards that will reduce the frequency and severity of injury to employees.

Like the sprinkler example, installation of the safety guards involves a comparatively large, up-front cost for Presto, as well as a minor increase in machine maintenance costs over time. Presto also believes, based on industry information and its own technical analysis, that the guards will reduce the normal output per employee by making it more difficult for employees to perform their tasks. As a result, holding wages fixed (see below), this effect will tend to increase Presto's labor costs per unit of output.

The benefits to Presto of installing the safety guards include lower workers' compensation insurance premiums in the form of possible up-front premium rate reductions for safer equipment and lower experience rating surcharges for poor experience (or greater rate reductions from experience rating due to better than average claims experience) if injuries are reduced. These benefits can be estimated with reasonable accuracy using insurance market data. Installation of the safety guards also will produce expected savings in Presto's retained workers' compensation costs (i.e., costs under its per occurrence deductible), which might be estimated with its own data, insurance market data, or managerial judgment. Another important benefit to Presto from installing the guards is that fewer accidents will mean fewer interruptions in production and lower costs of hiring/retraining either temporary or permanent replacement employees. These savings might be estimated using the firm's own data, industry data, and/or judgment.

A final potential benefit that Presto should consider when deciding whether to install the guards is the possible impact of greater safety on wages. Workers value safety, and safety is one dimension that affects job choice by workers. Numerous studies indicate that a tradeoff exists between wages and the risk of on-the-job injury: Higher risk jobs pay higher wages, other factors held constant. Thus, if Presto increases safety, then it should be able to attract and retain workers at lower wages over time. Presto may be able to estimate these savings from the evidence reported in these studies, or it may rely heavily on managerial judgment.

You should note that if workers are unable to assess safety accurately and underestimate the effect of the guards on safety, Presto's incentive to install the guards will be reduced. You will learn more about the tradeoff between wages and risk and its relation to workers' compensation laws and job safety legislation in Chapter 18.

Child-Resistant Packaging of Nonprescription Drugs

No-More-Pain Drug Company markets a nonprescription pain medication that can provide relief for routine aches and pains in the head, neck, back, joints, and other body parts. No-More-Pain is considering modifying its packaging to make it more difficult for small children to open the bottle and swallow the contents. (The drug is toxic in large quantities.) Making this change requires large, up-front costs to retool No-More-Pain's packaging process. It also will require an ongoing increase in the cost of materials per unit sold.

A major benefit to No-More-Pain of increasing safety for children is that its premiums for product liability insurance will decline. The company can obtain an estimate of the potential savings by consulting with its insurance brokers. It can estimate savings in uninsured liability claims and defense costs using its own data, insurance market data, and judgment. Another potential benefit of changing the packaging is that it will reduce the likelihood of damage to No-More-Pain's reputation that could occur if one or more children were seriously hurt or killed from ingesting its product. The new packaging also makes it less likely that the company will have to undertake a costly product recall in the event of adverse loss experience. No-More-Pain can develop several scenarios for the probability and severity of these costs based on judgment and anecdotal evidence from prior injuries by its products and related products.

No-More-Pain also needs to consider the effect of the change in packaging on the price and demand for its product. To the extent that customers value the increased safety, No-More-Pain may be able to increase the price of its product without any loss of sales. Sales even may increase despite the price increase. On the other hand, based on some preliminary market research and trade publications, No-More-Pain is concerned that many of its customers will find it a hassle to open child-resistant caps on bottles. These customers might switch to cheaper "no-name" brands with easy-to-open bottles if No-More-Pain makes its bottles harder to open. The company also is concerned that some customers with small children might leave the bottle open in order to avoid taking off the cap. To the extent that this occurs, the benefits in the form of liability claims could be reduced if the courts continue to hold No-More-Pain liable for any injuries.

Qualitative versus Quantitative Decision Making

In general, these examples make it clear that some of the important benefits and costs of loss control may be difficult to quantify. In many cases, the best that firms can do is to make educated guesses about the magnitude of benefits and costs. Chapter 26 provides more detail on quantitative analysis in risk management decision making. While the tools that we cover there are important in practice, you should keep in mind that many important decisions in risk management necessarily involve reasonable judgment based on limited information and data.

11.4   Government Safety Programs

Governments have established safety regulations for many activities. For example, the Consumer Product Safety Commission imposes safety requirements on products, the Environmental Protection Agency regulates activities that potentially can cause damage to the environment, and the Occupational Safety and Health Administration (OSHA) regulates workplace safety.

One justification for government safety programs is that businesses may not have sufficient incentives to undertake the right level of loss control. This argument can be illustrated using the workplace safety example presented earlier. Suppose that the firm did not have to pay all the accident costs associated with workplace injuries. This might occur, for example, if the employer does not fully compensate employees for the losses they suffer as a result of workplace injuries (and if workers did not have to be paid more because of the higher risk of injury). In this case, a profit-maximizing firm might view the benefits of additional safety expenditures to be less than the true benefits. That is, the reduction in the firm's expected costs from additional safety expenditures is less than the reduction in total expected losses for society (employees and the firm's owners). Consequently, the firm might spend too little on workplace safety relative to what should be spent if it had considered all the costs and benefits. Conceptually, this problem can be reduced by government regulations that require firms to engage in particular loss control activities.

Note, however, that government regulation does not automatically improve the situation. First, government regulation is costly. People must be hired to administer and enforce regulations. These costs can exceed the costs associated with no regulations. Second, government officials do not necessarily have the appropriate incentives to promulgate and enforce regulations to achieve the optimal level of safety. Instead, optimal safety levels might be compromised (in either direction) to achieve other objectives, such as gaining more power, managing a larger organization, or job security.

Another justification for government safety regulations is that it might be more efficient to have the research and information gathering necessary to make good safety decisions conducted by one government agency as opposed to a multitude of companies or individuals, because centralization of the research can avoid costly duplication. Centralization of safety research and then promulgation of safety regulations, however, can result in rules that might work in many situations, but not all. The imposition of regulations that are designed for a typical firm may not be optimal for many firms. Thus, as with everything else, government safety regulation involves trade-offs.

11.5   Valuing Loss of Life and Cost-Benefit Analysis of Safety Regulation

Many situations involving accidents require that compensation be paid for the loss of a person's life. Similarly when assessing the benefits of safety regulation, regulators must value life because many safety regulations affect the probability of death. While a discussion of how to value life can be troubling for some, it is necessary in many situations. Indeed, individuals implicitly make decisions on a daily basis that affect the probability of dying and thus they implicitly make tradeoffs about the value of their own life. For example, deciding to drive a small car versus a large car usually increases the probability of dying in a car accident. Thus, the choice of what car to buy often involves a choice between a lower car price and a lower probability of dying. The necessity of valuing life is highlighted by Box 11.1.

While the courts and regulators use a variety of methods to value life, we present an approach that attempts to measure the value that people implicitly place on their own life. The idea is to infer the value of people's lives based on the compensation that they are willing to accept for an increased probability of dying. The typical setting in which this analysis is conducted is the labor market.

Suppose, for example, that a construction firm has two job openings. Assume that both jobs require the same skill and have the same working conditions, except that one job has a higher probability that the worker will be killed on the job. For simplicity, assume that one job has a zero chance of death and that the other job has a 0.0005 chance of death per year. Finally, assume that the firm must pay additional annual wages of $2,000 to attract an employee to accept the riskier job. The wage premium ($2,000) for the riskier job reflects the value that employees place on the increased probability of losing their lives. Implicitly, employees are acting as if $2,000 is equivalent to a 0.0005 chance of dying. Accordingly, the value employees place on their life is found by solving the following equation:

$$\$2,000 = 0.0005 \times (\text{Value of life})$$

Solving this equation yields a value for life equal to $4 million ($2.000/0.0005). Implicitly, an employee is valuing his or her life at $4 million when he or she is willing to accept this riskier job for a $2,000 wage premium.

Human life is precious, of course. But is it priceless?

That weighty question ought to be reserved for advanced philosophy seminars. Instead it is being debated in a setting—John Grisham-land—where the answers are practically guaranteed to be simple minded.

Here's the setting: In 1991, an errant trailer broke off a pickup truck and careened straight into an Oldsmobile Cutlass station wagon parked at a Virginia tollbooth. The trailer punctured the car's gas tank, located behind the rear axle, and the car caught fire, killing a 13-year-old-boy. His parents sued General Motors, contending the station wagon's design was defective.

At the trial, now going on in Hollywood, Florida, the plaintiffs' lawyers introduced a "smoking gun" document found in GM's own files. Written in 1973 by a GM engineer named Edward Ivey, the memo calculates that there are a "maximum of 500 fatalities per year in accidents with fuel-fed fires where the bodies were burnt. Each fatality has a value of $200,000." Based on those assumptions, the memo calculates that each fatality costs GM "$2.40 per automobile in current operation."

A plaintiffs' witness who used to work for GM testified that an executive told him that, since it would cost $4.50 per vehicle to remedy this defect, GM had decided not to make the change. Naderite Clarence Ditlow gleefully went on television to conclude: "Hundreds of Americans have burned to death because of GM's callous disregard for human life."

GM's reaction has been predictable. The company angrily denies that it relied on the Ivey memo and indignantly declares. "General Motors believes that a dollar value *cannot* be placed on human life." If the company genuinely believes that, its shareholders should sue for mismanagement. More likely, the company simply believes that it cannot share some hard truths with an American jury.

In this case, the hard truth is that it's almost impossible *not* to put a value on human life when conducting any cost-benefit analysis, whether of a consumer product or a government regulation. Say the EPA is considering a new clean air rule. It figures the regulation will cost industry $100 million and save 200 lives. To figure out whether the regulation makes sense the EPA must calculate how much saving those lives is worth. Saying that we'll spend an infinite amount to save even one life isn't an option, since studies reveal

that anything that reduces national wealth causes deaths in its own right.

For this reason, all federal regulatory agencies are required to conduct cost-benefit studies, many of which involve putting a price tag on human life. Courts do the same thing. In an airplane crash lawsuit, the relatives of Victim A—a 30-year-old investment banker with plenty of high-income years ahead of him—stand to win more than the family of Victim B—a 70-year-old retired factory worker. That is not to say that the banker's life is worth more in the kingdom of heaven, only that these kinds of distasteful calculations are inescapable in our material realm.

Courts do it. Governments do it. And it's perfectly OK. But when corporations engage in cost-benefit analysis, it's a scandal. Why? How can auto engineers avoid using cost-benefit analysis?

Imagine if car designers sat down and decided to make safety their only criterion in designing a car. The product they designed would probably resemble a Bradley Fighting Vehicle and have a price tag to match. In every car certain tradeoffs have to be made. Typically, the heavier a vehicle, the safer. Thus, it's hardly surprising that a recent study found that sport utility vehicles are more crashworthy than passenger cars.

Does that mean we should get rid of less-safe vehicles? Only if you don't want poor people (or daring people) to drive. The better alternative would be simply to publicize the risks of cars like the Ford Pinto, so buyers could make their own decisions about how much safety is worth to them.

But can you imagine what would happen if a manufacturer announced: "Our car is a great buy! It's cheaper than the standard midsize sedan and gets better gas mileage. Oh, and by the way: You're much more likely to be burned to a crisp while driving it."

Human psychology being what it is, nobody would buy the car—even though the ad is only making explicit a tradeoff that everyone makes anyway. And, of course, every tort lawyer in America would rush to the local courthouse to sue the automaker. This kind of honesty is *verboten* in public discussions. So GM is forced to go to great lengths to explain away an innocent document like the Ivey memo.

The courts, in theory, are supposed to be better equipped to balance these types of issues. Judge

Learned Hand's famous formula holds that a defendant should be held liable for negligence only if the probability of an accident multiplied by the gravity of the resulting injury is greater than the burden of adequate preparations.

In GM's Florida case, the gravity of the injury is great, but its probability is pretty remote. To be exact, fatal rear-impact collisions with fire damage occur at a rate of one for every 23 billion miles traveled by owners of the station wagon in question. (That's almost a million trips around the Earth—if you could find a route) So perhaps it's not so callous to avoid spending an extra $4.50 per vehicle for a redesigned fuel tank.

After all, even if GM were to move the fuel tank from the rear, it would just be opening up a new area of potential injury—and liability. Lots of lawyers have filed suits over GM trucks with side mounted fuel tanks; in those cases, the lawyers no doubt argue the fuel tanks should be located in the rear.

The reality is that certain activities are inherently dangerous. Driving is one of them. We simply have to accept the risks and not blame some big company every time fate is cruel to us. But try telling that to a jury.

Source: Max Boot, "Your Money or Your Life? That Depends," *The Wall Street Journal,* March 4, 1998, p. A18.

This example was simplified to illustrate the approach to valuing life. Actual studies that use labor market data are more complex than the example suggests. For example, these studies attempt to control for the many factors that affect wages and apply the analysis to situations where the differential risks of dying generally are known. While it is important to recognize that valuing life in this manner depends on a number of assumptions and that the analysis does not yield a magical number on the value of a person's life, the approach yields a range of values that are useful for many purposes. For example, from a safety regulation perspective, regulators must decide whether to impose costly regulations that reduce the probability of death for a portion of the population. The costs of the regulation need to be compared to the benefits. The benefits can be measured by multiplying an estimate of the value of a life by an estimate of the number of lives saved due to the regulation. The value of life implicit in wage differentials between jobs of different risks is particularly appropriate for evaluating safety regulation, because safety regulation usually involves changes in probabilities of dying of similar magnitude to the differences in probabilities of dying in a labor market setting.

Congress now requires that most regulatory agencies undertake a cost-benefit analysis of proposed regulations. Earlier safety regulations, however, were not subject to such a requirement. One study that has looked at the costs and benefits of earlier regulations has found that the government's record on safety regulations is varied. Using estimates of regulatory costs and the reduced probability of dying as a result of the regulation, Table 11.3 summarizes the estimated costs per life saved of various regulations. The estimates suggest that some regulations clearly were beneficial from a cost per life saved perspective. For example, the cost per life saved due to the regulation of unvented space heaters was estimated to be $100,000. On the other hand, a number of regulations appear to be unjustified from a cost per life saved perspective. For example, the estimated cost per life saved due to EPA asbestos regulations is estimated to be $104 million; the cost per life saved from arsenic regulation is estimated to be $764 million.

TABLE 11.3
Costs per
estimated life
saved of
various safety
regulations.

Regulation	Year Passed	Agency	Cost per Life Saved (in millions of $1984)
Unvented space heaters	1980	Consumer Product Safety Commission	$ 0.10
Passive restraints/ belts	1984	National Highway and Traffic Safety Administration	0.30
Crane suspended personnel platform	1988	Occupational Safety and Health Administration	1.20
Grain dust	1987	Occupational Safety and Health Administration	5.30
Uranium mill tailings (inactive)	1983	Environmental Protection Agency	27.60
Asbestos	1989	Environmental Protection Agency	104.20
Arsenic/low-arsenic copper	1986	Environmental Protection Agency	764.00
Formaldehyde	1987	Occupational Safety and Health Administration	72,000.00

Source: W. Kip Viscusi, *Pricing Environmental Risks,* Center for the Study of American Business, Policy No. 112, June 1992.

11.6 Summary

- Loss control refers to expenditures of time, effort, and money to reduce expected losses.
- Loss prevention is a type of loss control that reduces the frequency of losses.
- Loss reduction is a type of loss control that reduces the severity of losses.
- Segregating assets is a method of diversifying risk. Therefore, segregating assets reduces the variance of direct losses and the maximum probable direct loss. Although segregation of assets does not reduce expected direct losses, it can reduce expected indirect losses.
- Optimal loss control decisions require that loss control expenditures be made up to the point that the marginal benefits no longer exceed the marginal costs, provided that all the important benefits and costs are suitably considered in the analysis.
- The costs and benefits of loss control often can be quantified, but qualitative assessment also is usually necessary.
- There are numerous government safety programs that influence loss control decisions of individuals and businesses.
- Loss control decisions often need to assess the value of human life. One method of valuing human life is to infer the values that individuals place on their own lives when they choose to take on greater risk (e.g., accept a job with a higher probability of death).

Key Terms

loss control 201
loss prevention 202
loss avoidance 202

loss reduction 202
pre-loss activities 202

post-loss activities 202
segregation of exposure units 203

Questions and Problems

1. Sommer Inc. is trying to determine how much to spend on safety equipment for its plant. The first column in the following table gives values for possible expenditures. The second column gives the expected number of worker injuries and the third column gives the expected severity per injury (cost to Sommer per injury) associated with each expenditure level. How much should Sommer spend on safety if it is trying to maximize firm value? Ignore the time value of money.

Expenditure	Expected Injuries	Severity
0	10	$10,000
$15,000	7	8,000
30,000	5	7,000
45,000	4	5,000
60,000	3	5,000
75,000	2	5,000

2. Mayers & Smith Corp. has a fertilizer plant. The probability of an explosion at the plant depends on how much the firm spends on safety as given by the table. If an explosion occurs, the loss to society (damaged equipment, death of employees, etc.) is expected to be $250 million. Find the optimal level of safety from a societal perspective.

Safety Expenditure (millions of $)	Probability of Loss
$0.0	0.030
0.5	0.020
1.0	0.016
1.5	0.013
2.0	0.011
2.5	0.010

Suppose that Mayers & Smith has to pay only one-half of the losses that occur. How much would Mayers & Smith spend on safety?

3. Pottier Transportation is trying to decide whether to require its drivers to take a driver safety course. The firm has 100 drivers and the cost of the course per driver is $1,500, which includes the cost to the firm of people not working. If all 100 drivers take the course immediately, the insurance company will reduce the firm's auto insurance premiums by $80,000 immediately, and by $45,000 in each of the next two years. In the managers' view, the only benefit of the course is a reduction in insurance premiums. The firm's chief financial officer says that the appropriate cost of capital is 7 percent. Should the firm require its drivers to take the course?

4. Lawn-Girl Inc. sells self-propelled lawn-mowers. Lawn-Girl's mowers currently include a device that shuts down the mower when both of the operator's hands are removed from the handle. It is contemplating installing a device that will shut down the mower if the operator removes either hand from the handle. Identify the main benefits and costs to Lawn-Girl of installing the new device.

5. "We should spend whatever it takes to eliminate the possibility that a death could occur at this construction site." Comment briefly on whether you agree or disagree with the idea conveyed in this quote.

References

Essentials of Risk Control, vol. 1 and 2. Ed. George Head, Insurance Institute of America. *(Provides an in-depth analysis of loss control decisions in a variety of settings.)*

Viscusi, W. Kip. *Pricing Environmental Risks.* Center for the Study of American Business,

Policy No. 112, June 1992. *(Analyzes the government's record of regulating environmental risk.)*

Internet search on loss control. *(Provides a number of private companies that specialize in providing loss control services.)*

Chapter 12

Legal Liability for Injuries

Chapter Objectives

- Provide background on the general structure of US law.
- Describe basic legal liability rules and procedures, including negligence law.
- Describe the economic functions of the legal liability system.
- Explain the circumstances in which the assignment of legal liability affects safety incentives.
- Discuss the relationship between liability law and safety regulation.
- Briefly introduce various proposals for tort reform.

12.1   Some Background on the Law

The variety and potential magnitude of personal and business liability exposures have increased tremendously in the past 30 years. Firms now are subject to liability risk in almost every aspect of their operations. For example, liability can arise from (1) employment practices (in addition to employer responsibility for paying workers' compensation benefits to injured workers), (2) products sold to consumers, (3) the disposal of waste or use of toxic chemicals, and (4) the actions of corporate boards of directors. The evolution of the US liability system has been subject to substantial controversy and debate. This chapter provides an introduction to the legal liability system that is necessary to understand issues related to legal liability risk. Many of the subsequent chapters require some understanding of the legal liability system.

Table 12.1 summarizes the two main types of law: (1) common law, and (2) statutory law. **Common law** refers to the law that has evolved over time as a result of previous court

TABLE 12.1
Sources and branches of law.

Source of Law	
Common law	Evolved over time through court decisions.
Statutory law	Enacted by government bodies.
Branches of Law	
Criminal law	Applies to acts against the state.
Civil law	Applies to acts against other individuals or entities.
Contract law	Applies when a contract governs the relationship between the parties in the dispute.
Tort law	Applies when a contract does not govern the relationship between the parties in the dispute.

decisions; it has not been enacted by a legislative body. The rule of precedent, which states that a court generally should follow the logic and rulings of prior court decisions, is the source of common law. In contrast, **statutory law** refers to laws that have been passed by a legislative body, such as a state legislature or the US Congress, and then signed into law by the executive branch (a governor or president). Although there are important exceptions, much legal liability is based on common law.

As shown in Table 12.1, law also can be categorized as either criminal or civil. **Criminal law,** which is usually the result of statutes, covers acts against the state (an individual state or local government, or the federal government). For example, since murder is contrary to the public interest, it is considered to be an act against the state and is therefore a violation of criminal law. In contrast, **civil law** deals with acts that cause losses to another individual, but for which the state (the public at large) has a less direct interest. There are in turn two branches of civil law: contract law and tort law. **Contract law** interprets contractual provisions and resolves disputes between contractual parties, such as when one party is harmed as a result of another party's failure to fulfill its contractual obligations. Parties found liable for breach of contract must pay monetary damages and, in some instances, perform their obligations under the contract. **Tort law** deals with wrongs done to someone where a contract does not govern the interaction that caused the harm. Parties held liable for injuries under tort law must pay the injured party monetary damages. For example, if an automobile hits and harms a pedestrian, the driver and the pedestrian do not have a contract to help them determine how the interaction will be handled; therefore, tort law handles the issue of who is responsible for the damages. In contrast, if an automobile dealer fails to deliver a car to a buyer at an agreed upon date and as a result the buyer suffers monetary losses, the issue of who is responsible for the damages is handled under contract law. The focus of this chapter is tort law. Unless otherwise noted, the term *liability* refers to tort liability.

12.2   Overview of Tort Liability Rules and Procedures

There are various ways of assigning liability for losses that arise from the interaction among parties who do not have contractual relations. As an example, consider the losses (medical costs) suffered by a pedestrian who has been hit by an automobile. The law could make the pedestrian responsible for his or her own losses regardless of the circumstances of an accident. Alternatively, the law could make the driver responsible for the pedestrian's losses regardless of the circumstances of the accident. Or an intermediate approach could be taken where the law examines the circumstances of the accident and decides who should be responsible for the pedestrian's medical expenses. The law also must allocate responsibility for the other potential losses suffered by the pedestrian, such as lost wages, mental anguish, and the like, as well as decide who is responsible for the driver's losses (if any were suffered).

When the law assigns liability for a general type of loss, the law is essentially allocating risk. For example, a rule that always makes the driver liable for all losses suffered in pedestrian accidents places the risk of such accidents on drivers and removes this risk from pedestrians. Drivers, in essence, are forced to insure all pedestrians. (The driver could in turn transfer this risk to an insurance company.) Thus, many of the tools and concepts that have been discussed earlier in this book are relevant for understanding the effects of alternative liability rules.

Basic Tort Liability Rules

Liability for harm to another person varies depending on the context. For example, liability arising from automobile accidents generally differs from liability arising from product injuries. This section provides an overview of the alternative methods of assigning liability. Section 12.3 elaborates on liability arising from negligence. As summarized in Table 12.2, liability of the party who caused the accident, who is known as the *tortfeasor,* can range from immunity from liability to always being held liable.[1]

No Liability

While its incidence has decreased substantially over time, some institutions and some professions are immune from liability for certain types of actions. For example, charitable institutions and government entities sometimes are at least partially immune from being liable for losses suffered by people who use the institution's services. Another example would be the immunity from liability of foreign diplomats who harm US citizens while in the United

TABLE 12.2
The range of alternative tort liability rules.

	Description	Example
No liability	Defendant cannot be held liable.	Charitable institutions in some cases.
Negligence	Defendant is liable if found negligent, but might be able to avoid liability using certain defenses.	Liability for damages caused by automobile accidents.
Strict liability	Defendant is liable even if not negligent, but might be able to avoid liability using certain defenses.	Liability of firms for damages resulting from defective products.
Absolute liability	Defendant is always liable; no defenses are available if the defendant caused the injury.	Liability for damages caused by the use of dynamite.

[1]This description of tort liability omits intentional torts, such as libel and slander, invasion of privacy, copyright or trademark infringement, assault, and false imprisonment, where the action by the tortfeasor is intentional. The legal rules generally are different for each type of intentional tort. Liability for intentional torts that do not involve intentional harm or damage often is insurable.

States. When one party is immune from liability, the law implicitly makes other parties who interact with the immune party liable for their own losses. Perhaps more important for our purposes, the concept of no liability for harm is useful in explaining the rationale for alternative liability rules and the safety effects of these rules (see section 12.4).

Liability for Negligence

A common way of assigning liability is to make one party liable for someone else's losses if the former party is negligent. The burden of proof under a **negligence rule** usually is on the plaintiff; that is, the plaintiff must prove that the defendant was negligent. (The conditions to prove negligence are discussed in the next section of this chapter.) An exception is the *res ipsa loquitor* rule ("the thing speaks for itself"), which switches the burden of proof to the defendant when the nature of the injury makes it highly improbable that the injury could have occurred without the defendant's negligence (e.g., a surgeon leaves a scalpel in the patient). A negligence standard is used to some degree in all states for determining liability for losses suffered from automobile accidents, and it is the standard used for medical malpractice. A negligence standard also is used in many business liability cases, including many product injury cases. As you will learn in more detail in Chapter 28, persons injured by products commonly bring suits under the doctrine of strict liability as well, which we briefly explain in this chapter, and sometimes they can sue for breach of contract.

Strict Liability

Under a **strict liability** standard, the defendant does not have to be negligent to be liable for the plaintiff's losses. As noted, strict liability often is applied in products liability cases. In these cases, the plaintiff generally has to show that the design, production, or warnings associated with the product were defective and unreasonably dangerous and that the defect caused the injury (see Chapter 28). But the plaintiff does not need to show that the product's defect was due to the manufacturer's negligence.

Absolute Liability

According to the doctrine of **absolute liability,** the defendant is liable for the plaintiff's losses as long as the plaintiff can establish that the defendant's action caused the loss. The defendant does not have to be negligent, and the defendant has no defenses. Absolute liability traditionally has been limited to tort cases involving ultradangerous activities. For example, the common law applies absolute liability for injuries arising out of blasting operations and the use of explosives. Thus, if your parents' favorite and very expensive glass figurine topples from a shelf and crumbles when a road construction company blasts through rock three miles away, your parents can recover damages under the doctrine of absolute liability. They need only prove that the blast caused the loss, as opposed to mischievous behavior by the family cat. Similarly, someone who harbors a wild animal faces absolute liability for any injuries the animal may cause. Of considerably greater importance and seriousness, the concept of absolute liability (with restrictions on the types of damages that must be paid) provides the basis for workers' compensation laws governing workplace injuries, which we discuss in Chapter 18.

Damages

Tort liability law allows injured parties to recover damages for losses caused by tortfeasors. Courts can award two broad types of damages: compensatory damages and punitive damages.

Compensatory Damages

As the name implies, **compensatory damages** are designed to compensate injured parties for loss. There are in turn two main types of compensatory damages: (1) special damages, and (2) general damages. **Special damages** refer to compensation to the plaintiff for monetary losses, such as medical expenses, lost wages, and the value of lost services from bodily injury, and repair/replacement costs and loss of use for property damage. Estimation of special damages can be complex; for example, it often is necessary to estimate the present value of future wage losses and medical expenses over many years.

General damages refer to compensation for nonmonetary losses, such as pain and suffering and loss of consortium with an injured or deceased spouse, and emotional distress from the death of a spouse or family member. These types of losses are very difficult to measure accurately. The courts and out-of-court settlements often rely on rules of thumb that relate general damages to special damages for certain types of injuries. For example, a rule of thumb for auto accidents might be to set general damages equal to two times special damages. These informal benchmarks can then be modified in view of the particular or unique circumstances in a case. Depending on the type of case, empirical studies of damages suggest that general damages commonly represent between one-half and three-fourths of total compensatory damages. The ultimate authority for determining general damages rests with the judge or with the jury in a jury trial. The amount of general damages that juries can be expected to award if a case goes to trial has a major effect on out-of-court settlements.

Punitive Damages

Damages paid to the plaintiff that are not designed to compensate for the plaintiff's losses but are meant to punish the defendant for the actions that led to the injury and to deter future actions are known as **punitive damages.** Punitive damages in principle are reserved for situations where the defendant recklessly or willfully disregarded the risk of harm to the plaintiff. While punitive damages are awarded in a small fraction of cases, punitive damage awards can be very large and sometimes vastly exceed the plaintiff's losses and compensatory damages.

In principle, the amount of punitive damages awarded reflects the goal of punishing the defendant and thus depends on the nature of the defendant's conduct and the severity of the risk of harm to the plaintiff. As we discuss in section 12.7, punitive damages have been highly controversial in recent years. Some observers argue that decisions to award punitive damages and the amounts awarded often reflect arbitrary and capricious behavior by juries. A number of cases brought before the US Supreme Court have invited the court to impose meaningful guidelines for punitive damages. To date these efforts have not been successful.

Joint and Several Liability

Often situations arise in which the actions of multiple parties combine to cause loss. For example, the family of a teenager who purchased computer cleaner at a store, sniffed it and got high, and then drove his car into a lake and drowned could name the producer of the computer cleaner, the store that sold the cleaner, and the contractor who designed the road as defendants (a situation similar to this actually happened in 1996—also see Box 12.1). Under the doctrine of **joint and several liability,** each defendant can be held responsible for the entire damage.

While the name of the driver has been changed, the following scenario is true. It happened in the Northeast during the early 1970s. Cases with similar results and implications have occurred elsewhere.

Jones noticed that the brakes on his old car were not working properly. He took the car to a service station about 5:30 P.M. One of the rear brakes was defective. The mechanic did not have the part needed to make an immediate and permanent repair. He made a temporary repair and cautioned Jones to take the car home (Jones lived nearby) and bring the car back first thing in the morning. Jones drove 15 miles to a cookout where he apparently drank one or more beers. After leaving the cookout, Jones was spotted making an illegal pass by a state trooper. A high-speed chase ensued. Evidence later suggested that one of the brakes on Jones's car was not working properly, but it also appeared that Jones had no interest in stopping. Jones eventually approached a railroad crossing at the bottom of a long grade on a curve in the road. A train was entering the crossing at a speed of two miles per hour. Jones's car collided with the train and caromed into a phone booth located nearby, severely injuring a person making a call (who lost both legs). Jones, who was uninsured, was not seriously hurt. The phone booth, which had been there for many years, was nine feet from the road and six feet from the railroad tracks.

The injured party sued Jones, the mechanic, the railroad, and the phone company. The jury, which visited the scene of the accident, held Jones and the phone company jointly and severally liable for negligence. The decision was upheld on appeal. The phone company argued that Jones's conduct and the other events should constitute a superseding cause and prevent the company from being held liable for negligence as a result of its placement of the phone booth. The court disagreed, holding that the phone company should have reasonably foreseen that its placement of the phone booth created a significant risk of injury to occupants (a question of fact for the jury to decide) and that the specific circumstances of the accident should not prevent liability. The phone company, which was self-insured, paid several hundred thousand dollars to the injured party, an amount that might seem low by today's standards.

You should note, however, that the plaintiff nevertheless can only recover damages once. If multiple parties are held liable under the doctrine of joint and several liability, the court might instruct one party to pay the plaintiff the entire amount of damages. The division of damages among the liable parties is then determined in subsequent negotiations or litigation between the liable parties. Similarly, if the plaintiff only sues and recovers from one defendant, this defendant may be able to seek recovery from other parties that were involved in causing the loss. The legal rules used in proceedings for determining the ultimate division of the cost of damages among multiple parties that cause a loss are extremely complex.

An important feature of joint and several liability is that if some parties are unable to pay; the full burden of paying damages will fall on other parties. As we discuss in Chapter 28, an important example is joint and several liability for environmental damages, which sometimes can make firms that contributed little to environmental damage responsible for the entire cleanup costs. Joint and several liability also provides incentives for plaintiffs to seek defendants with deep pockets (i.e., to name as defendants parties that have substantial assets or insurance to pay damages even if the party's role in causing the injury was minor compared to other parties with less ability to pay).

12.3   Liability from Negligence

Elements of Negligence

In most circumstances, four conditions must be satisfied to prove negligence: (1) legal duty by the defendant, (2) breach of duty, (3) proximate cause, and (4) injury to plaintiff.

Legal Duty

In order to be held liable for negligence, the defendant must have had a duty to behave so as to protect other parties from harm. For example, a driver has a duty to stop at a stop sign and otherwise drive in a reasonably safe manner. In general, people and businesses have a duty to protect from injury those parties with whom they reasonably can be expected to come into contact. The law, however, usually does not impose a positive duty to come to the assistance of people who may be harmed by others or who may already be hurt.

Breach of Duty

Assuming a legal duty, the defendant must have breached this duty by failing to exercise the required standard of care for the protection of the other party. In many nonbusiness liability cases, such as automobile accidents, the required standard of care to avoid a **breach of duty** usually is what a "reasonably prudent person" would have done in similar circumstances. In the case of professional liability, such as liability of a physician for alleged malpractice, the standard often is what a reasonable, adequately trained professional with the same area of expertise would have done in the same circumstances.

In many business liability cases (beginning with a US Supreme Court decision, *US v. Carroll Towing, 1944*), the courts often apply a specific economic standard for negligence in which the defendant is held to have exercised inadequate care if the business has failed to take **cost-justified precautions** to prevent harm. As discussed in the previous chapter, a precaution is cost-justified if the cost of taking the precaution is less than the expected reduction in harm that occurs if the precaution is taken.

To illustrate this economic standard, assume that a trucking company could reduce the expected harm to other people and property from truck accidents by $1 million if it limits the number of hours that each trucker can drive in a week, but that this action would increase the firm's costs by $800,000 because it has to hire more drivers. Then, under the economic standard for negligence, the trucking firm would be liable for the injuries caused by its failure to limit driving time because the expected benefit of the precaution ($1 million reduction in expected injury costs) exceeds the cost of the precautions ($800,000). If, on the other hand, limiting driving hours would cost $2 million, the business would not be found negligent for failing to spend $2 million to reduce expected injury costs by $1 million.

Application of the economic criterion for negligence requires the legal system to estimate the expected benefits and costs of additional precautions that could have been undertaken by the defendant. This process can be quite complicated in practice. We will discuss further the safety incentives of liability law in section 12.4. For now it is sufficient to note that the economic criterion for negligence provides incentives for firms to take cost-justified precautions in cases where other incentives for doing so might be insufficient.

Proximate Cause

The third requirement for showing negligence is that the defendant's behavior is the **proximate cause** of the plaintiff's injury. In most cases, proximate cause is readily established. For example, if failure to stop at a stop sign results in a collision with another car or pedestrian and the injury would not have occurred but for the driver's failure to stop, this failure would be the proximate cause of the injury. Conversely, a defendant's action will not be considered the proximate cause of injury if the injury would have occurred regardless of whether the defendant failed to satisfy the standard of care required for protection of the other party. These results reflect what is known as the *sine qua non* or "but for" rule: If the injury would not have occurred but for the defendant's action, then the defendant's action is the proximate cause of the injury. An example that clearly illustrates this rule was provided many years ago by the Supreme Court of Minnesota when it refused to hold a railroad company liable for injuries to a driver who collided with a train after the train had failed to sound the legally required warning bell while approaching an intersection (*Sullivan v. Boone*). The court reasoned astutely that since the driver collided with the 68th car of the train, the accident would have occurred even if the bell had been sounded.

Complications sometimes arise in determining proximate cause when there are intervening events between the defendant's action and the ultimate injury. For example, assume that Fred leaves his keys in the car on the way to the door to pick up his date and that his car is stolen and crashes into a neighbor's car in the thief's haste to depart from the crime scene. The question arises as to whether Fred's failure to remove the keys could be considered the proximate cause of the damage to the neighbor's car so that the neighbor could successfully sue Fred. (Such a suit is likely since the thief is unlikely to have much money or liability insurance.) Or should the theft of the car constitute a superseding cause that prevents Fred from being liable? When dealing with these issues, many courts apply a *foreseeability test*. If a defendant should have reasonably foreseen that his or her action could create a significant risk of injury, then the defendant's action will be deemed the proximate cause of the injury even if there are unusual intervening events. A more elaborate and interesting case involving a complicated series of intervening events is described in Box 12.1.

Injury to Plaintiff

The fourth condition for negligence is that the plaintiff has suffered loss, which essentially prevents people from bringing suits unless someone has been harmed. You learned earlier about the types of losses that are eligible for compensatory damages.

Defenses to Negligence

If all four conditions are established and the defendant is therefore negligent, the defendant may nonetheless be able to escape liability for the plaintiff's losses if the defendant can successfully use one of the defenses described below. A key aspect of a negligence rule is that the defendant's negligence is a necessary condition for the defendant to be liable, but not a sufficient condition. In many jurisdictions, defendants can avoid or at least reduce liability under a negligence rule (and sometimes under a strict liability rule) in two main ways: (1) prove that the plaintiff assumed the risk of injury, or (2) prove that the plaintiff also was negligent.

Assumption of Risk

In some cases the defendant can avoid liability for damages using the **assumption of risk defense.** This requires the defendant to prove that the plaintiff voluntarily assumed a known risk. The logic underlying the assumption of risk defense is that if the plaintiff understood the risk involved in the activity and chose to participate in the activity anyway (e.g., downhill skiing or driving a vehicle that is known to have defective tires at a high rate of speed), then the plaintiff presumably was compensated for the risk in the form of a price concession or in any case valued the activity enough to undertake it despite the risk. Establishing the assumption of risk defense requires that the defendant prove that the plaintiff had knowledge of the particular risk and voluntarily assumed the risk. In modern times the courts have applied strict standards for proving that the plaintiff was aware of the risk, thus limiting the use of this defense.

Contributory and Comparative Negligence

The second major type of defense that often may be available to the defendant is to establish that the plaintiff also was negligent. Under a **contributory negligence** standard, if the plaintiff also is shown to be negligent, then the defendant is not liable for any of the plaintiff's losses. For example, if a contributory negligence standard is applied to auto accidents with pedestrians and a pedestrian crosses the intersection against the light, then the driver might escape liability. Note that under a strict interpretation of the contributory negligence rule, any degree of negligence by the plaintiff prevents recovery.

Under a **comparative negligence** standard, the defendant can be found partially liable for the plaintiff's losses if the court finds that both the defendant's and the plaintiff's negligence contributed to the losses. Virtually all states have replaced the contributory negligence rule for auto accidents with a comparative negligence rule. While several types of comparative negligence rules exist, a typical rule would allow a person who is less than (or in some states less than or equal to) 50 percent responsible for the loss to recover damages from the other party. The damages, however, are reduced in proportion to the person's responsibility. For example, if a court finds that the defendant was 60 percent responsible, then the defendant will pay 60 percent of the plaintiff's losses. Compared to contributory negligence, comparative negligence rules tend to increase the number of losses that are compensated through the tort system.

12.4   Economic Objectives of the Tort Liability System

From an economic perspective, the tort system has two fundamental objectives: (1) to provide the right incentives for safety, and (2) to provide the right amount of compensation for accident victims. When trying to achieve these objectives, one must consider the transaction costs of operating the tort system and the costs of alternative methods of achieving these objectives. The following subsections explain each of the objectives in more detail. Before doing so, however, it is important to realize that the objectives often cannot be achieved simultaneously. The right amount of compensation for victims may yield the wrong incentives for safety and vice versa. Similarly, the transaction costs that would have to be incurred to achieve these objectives may imply that society should accept less than optimal safety incentives and less than optimal compensation for victims compared to a hypothetical world without transaction costs.

The objectives of the tort system should be familiar to you. The first goal—optimal safety incentives—means that we want the tort system to provide incentives for individuals and firms to optimally invest in loss control. The second goal—optimal compensation for victims—means that we want the tort system to provide the optimal amount of protection (insurance coverage) to people. The pursuit of these goals, however, must take into consideration the costs of loss control and the costs of insuring victims through the court system. Thus, the objective of the tort system can be succinctly stated as follows: The tort system should attempt to minimize the cost of risk to society, where the cost of risk includes expected accident losses, the cost of loss control, the cost of compensating victims (loss financing), and the cost of residual uncertainty (see Chapter 2).

By focusing on how the tort system affects loss control and victim compensation, our analysis ignores what some legal scholars view as important issues. For example, the distribution of wealth sometimes is affected by liability rules, and some people may view the reallocation of wealth as an objective of the tort system.[2] While the influence of liability rules on the distribution of wealth will be identified, we do not treat the redistribution of wealth as a fundamental objective. Also, some legal scholars focus on philosophical issues like social justice. We ignore these issues, apart from noting that some of the basic principles of tort law, such as the principle that persons who cause harm to others through negligence should compensate for injuries, have strong historical roots in both ancient secular and religious philosophy.

Optimal Safety (Optimal Loss Control)

As we have emphasized earlier in the book, it is rarely optimal to minimize the probability of loss or expected losses suffered by injured parties. Rather than attempting to achieve a "zero-risk" society, the tort system should provide incentives for people to invest in additional safety only if the additional benefits (marginal benefits) exceed the additional costs (marginal costs). The following example helps illustrate this point.

Suppose that Nielson Inc. produces riding lawnmowers that have the potential of causing an injury to the consumer and that the loss suffered is $10,000. Thus, the expected loss to a consumer is simply the probability of an accident times $10,000. To simplify the analysis, assume that consumers are either risk neutral or that they can purchase full insurance at premiums equal to expected claim costs (zero premium loading). Under either of these assumptions, consumers only care about the expected loss from an accident and do not care about the uncertainty associated with losses.

If Nielson Inc. spends nothing on safety features, then the probability of an accident is 0.07. Nielson, however, can reduce the probability of an accident below 0.07 by incurring some costs. Table 12.3 lists the costs and the associated accident probabilities. To reduce the probability of an accident to 0.06, Nielson must spend $45 per mower; to reduce the probability of an accident to 0.05, Nielson must spend $130 per mower, and so on. Our objective is to identify the amount of money that Nielson should spend on making its mowers safer. We answer this question from society's perspective, not from the profit maximizing perspective of Nielson. Thus, we answer the hypothetical question: How much would fully informed consumers be willing to pay for safer mowers?

[2]From an ex post perspective, the tort system obviously redistributes wealth from persons that cause loss (or their liability insurance companies) to persons that are harmed. The discussion here refers to long-run effects of the tort system and the distribution of wealth and income in society.

TABLE 12.3
Analysis of
Nielson's safety
expenditures
when the
severity of a
loss is $10,000.

Safety Expenditure	Probability of Loss	Expected Loss to Consumer	Marginal Benefit to Consumer	Marginal Cost to Consumer
$ 0	0.07	$700	$ 0	$ 0
45	0.06	600	100	45
130	0.05	500	100	85
225	0.04	400	100	95
400	0.03	300	100	175
590	0.02	200	100	190
900	0.01	100	100	310

Similar to our analysis in the previous chapter, we answer this hypothetical question by starting at the point where safety expenditures equal zero and the probability of an accident equals 0.07 and ask: Would a consumer who has to pay the cost of increased safety be willing to pay $45 to reduce the accident probability to 0.06? The answer is yes, because the benefit of the reduction in the accident probability is the reduction in expected loss, which equals $100 ($700 – $600). Stated differently, the marginal social cost to reduce the accident probability to 0.06 equals $45 and the marginal social benefit equals $100. Next, consider whether a consumer would be willing to spend an additional $85 on safety (for a total of $130) and thereby reduce the accident probability to 0.05. Again the answer is yes, because the additional $85 expenditure lowers expected losses by $100 (from $600 to $500). Thus, from society's perspective, Nielson should spend at least $130 on safety. Continuing, a consumer also would be willing to spend an additional $95 ($225 – $130) to reduce the accident probability to 0.04, because the additional benefit is $100 (expected losses are reduced from $500 to $400). A consumer, however, would not want to reduce the accident probability below 0.04, because the marginal cost of lowering the probability to 0.03 equals $175 and the marginal benefit of doing so is only $100.

Thus, the optimal amount of money that Nielson should spend on making each mower safer is $225, which would reduce the accident probability to 0.04. This amount minimizes the cost of risk. Spending less than $225 yields too little safety and spending more than $225 yields too much safety from the perspective of the consumer. The notion that a firm can spend too much on safety sometimes bothers students. It should be clear, however, that in a world of scarcity the costs of additional resources to make one activity safer implies that these resources cannot be spent on other activities (including other safety activities). Thus, at some point, the costs of additional safety expenditures exceed the benefits.

The point of this example is to clarify one of the objectives of tort law. In the context of this example, we would want the tort system to provide incentives for Nielson Inc. to spend $225 on safety. If the tort system provides incentives to spend less than $225 or more than $225, then the system has not achieved one of its objectives.

The main point of this section also can be illustrated graphically. In Figure 12.1, the level of safety as measured by the probability of *no* accident is listed on the horizontal axis and the marginal costs and marginal benefits of safety are measured by dollars on the vertical axis. Instead of discrete increments in safety, the graph assumes a continuum of possible safety levels (i.e., the probability of a loss can assume any value). As was true in the numerical example above, the marginal benefit of safety is assumed to be constant at $100 and the marginal cost of additional safety is assumed to increase with additional safety. The optimal level of safety is where the marginal cost and marginal benefit curves intersect.

FIGURE 12.1

Optimal level of safety is where the marginal benefit and marginal cost of safety are equal.

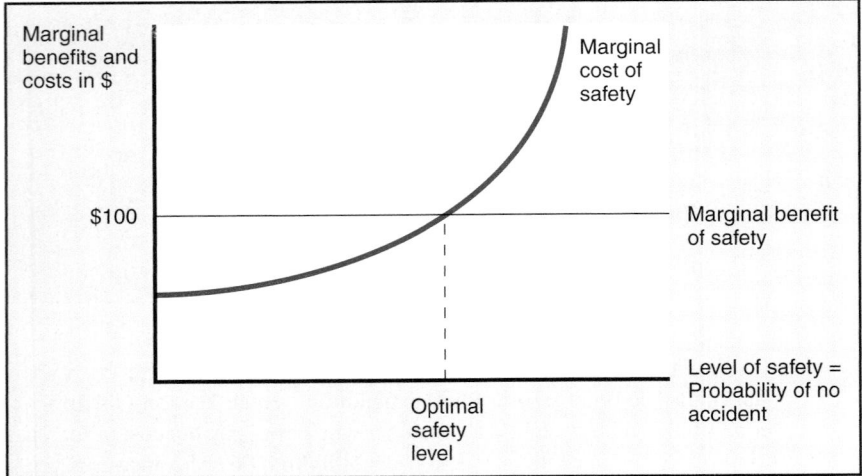

Optimal Compensation to Victims

The other objective of the tort system is to optimally compensate victims of accidents. Note that compensation awarded by the tort liability system is in many ways analogous to an insurance mechanism. Just as an insurance company compensates policyholders under certain conditions following a loss, the tort system compensates accident victims under certain conditions following a loss. Just as policyholders pay for insurance in the form of premiums, people pay higher prices for goods and services for the implicit insurance they obtain from the tort system. If the tort liability system systematically awards accident victims higher compensation for product-related injuries, then the prices of products will increase. In situations such as automobile accidents where a person can both cause harm to others and be harmed, the cost of liability insurance reflects the expected compensation awarded to victims of automobile accidents. If the tort liability system systematically awards greater compensation to automobile accident victims, then liability insurance premiums will increase. Thus, individuals implicitly pay for the insurance that is provided by the tort system.

Recognizing that the compensation aspect of the tort system is essentially an insurance mechanism has an important implication. When viewed solely from a compensation perspective (i.e., ignoring safety effects), the tort system should award compensation to a victim by answering the following hypothetical question: How much insurance coverage would the victim have wanted to purchase prior to knowing whether he or she would be involved in an accident if (1) the victim were fully informed about the risk of an accident, and (2) the terms of the insurance reflected the transaction costs, moral hazard, and adverse selection problems associated with offering insurance through the tort system?

Several aspects of this hypothetical question need elaboration. First, it is important to evaluate the amount of compensation from a *potential* victim's perspective, prior to knowing whether the person will be involved in an accident. Once losses have been incurred, the victim generally will want as much compensation as possible. The critical question, however, is how much compensation (insurance coverage) the victim would have been willing to pay for prior to knowing whether he or she would be involved in an accident. If compensation from the tort liability system exceeds the amount of insurance coverage that people are willing to pay for, then the legal system in effect forces people to buy too much insurance; people would prefer to spend their money in other ways. Similarly, if the compensation awarded by the tort system were less than the amount of coverage people are willing to pay for, then additional compensation would make people better off.

Second, the hypothetical question asks how much compensation from the tort system would people want if the terms of the insurance reflected the transactions costs, moral hazard, and adverse selection problems inherent in providing insurance through the tort system. The transaction costs include attorney fees and court costs. Moral hazard problems arise, in part, because some types of losses such as pain and suffering are difficult to measure. Adverse selection problems arise because the price paid for compensation provided by the tort system (e.g., which is embedded in product prices) typically is not differentiated across consumers, even though the expected losses of potential victims vary. As discussed in Chapter 10, transaction costs, moral hazard, and adverse selection lead people to want less than full insurance in most cases. A similar result holds for the insurance provided by the tort system: The transaction costs, moral hazard, and adverse selection problems associated with providing insurance through the tort system imply that most people will not be willing to pay for full insurance coverage (full compensation).

The US tort system generally attempts to compensate victims fully for their losses. In addition, there is widespread use of the **collateral source rule,** which precludes courts from reducing damages awarded by the amount of coverage provided by a plaintiff's first-party life, health, or property insurance. The use of the collateral source rule can imply that victims receive aggregate compensation from first-party insurance and damage payments in excess of losses, which is inconsistent with the result that people typically would not want to purchase full insurance. Thus, it appears that the US tort system forces many people to pay for more insurance than they probably desire.

One possible justification for this emphasis is that less than full compensation for damages (or reducing damages by the amount of the plaintiff's own insurance protection) could yield insufficient safety incentives (e.g., lowering victim compensation will reduce a manufacturer's incentive to make safe products or reduce a driver's incentive to take proper precautions) and that the US tort system places greater weight on optimal safety than optimal compensation. As an important example, we will explain in Chapter 28 that from a compensation perspective it might be better *not* to have pain and suffering compensation for product-related injuries. From a safety perspective, however, it might be better to have pain and suffering compensation.

In summary, the economic goal of the tort system is to minimize the cost of risk to society. That is, the tort system should provide optimal safety incentives (loss control) and optimal compensation to victims (insurance coverage), taking into account the costs of achieving these objectives. Unfortunately, these objectives probably conflict so that public policy must reflect a choice as to which objective to emphasize. The safety and compensation objectives will be central to the discussion of a number of liability issues in subsequent chapters.[3]

---

[3]This section tacitly assumed that a tort liability system might be needed to improve safety and compensation. The appendix to this chapter examines the validity of this assumption. That is, the appendix examines when the tort system can improve safety incentives and victim compensation compared to an economy without a tort system.

Concept Check

Suppose that Joe is injured using a stepladder and he sues the manufacturer to recover damages for all of his costs, which consist of medical bills equal to $50,000 and lost wages equal to $40,000.

1. If the court were trying to provide optimal incentives for the manufacturer to produce safe ladders (and the court assumes that all injured consumers would seek compensation through the tort system), what would be the damage award to Joe?
2. If the court were trying to provide optimal compensation (insurance coverage) to accident victims, what would be the damage award to Joe?

12.5   Limited Wealth and Limited Liability

The safety and compensation objectives of the tort system may be undermined if the party who is liable for losses can escape liability for damages. People can avoid paying damages either because they do not have sufficient wealth or because their wealth is protected by limited liability (bankruptcy) rules. If the victim does not receive the optimal amount of compensation because of the defendant's limited wealth or limited liability, then the compensation objective is undermined. Similarly, if limited wealth or limited liability allow some people to avoid paying damages, then these people may invest too little in safety. Intuitively a person who knows that he or she will not be forced to pay all the costs imposed on others might have insufficient safety incentives. After describing situations in which people do not have to pay full damages, we discuss how compulsory insurance in some cases may help solve the problems caused by limited wealth and limited liability.

Situations in Which Injurers Can Escape Liability

Suppose that Mrs. Smith, a retiree who has $10,000 in assets, is physically and mentally unable to work (i.e., she has no human capital). If the courts rule that Mrs. Smith must pay $500,000 in damages to a pedestrian she hit with her car, then Mrs. Smith will be unable to pay the entire damage. The court may force Mrs. Smith to pay $10,000, but that is the limit of her liability. Since she has insufficient wealth to pay the entire judgment, Mrs. Smith is **judgment proof** for damages in excess of her wealth (or in excess of the assets she would be allowed to keep if she filed bankruptcy).[4]

Suppose that the same situation occurs for Mrs. Smith's son, Jules, a capable employee who has many years left to work. Jules has liquid assets of only $10,000, but he has human capital that is worth $2 million; that is, the present value of his future earnings equals $2 million. While Jules has sufficient resources to pay the entire $500,000 judgment over time, he does not have the liquid assets to pay the judgment immediately. The courts could force Jules to pay the entire judgment by making him pay a portion of his future earnings to the victim over time (i.e., the court could *garnish* future wages). However, because of the costs of collecting future earnings and the adverse effect such an action could have on

---

[4]Complex federal and state laws determine how much wealth a person can retain after filing bankruptcy.

Jules's incentives to produce in the future, the law usually does not garnish future wages (an exception sometimes occurs if a defendant engages in willful and reckless conduct). Thus, like his mother, Jules would likely be judgment proof for liability in excess of his liquid assets.

Owners of corporations also can escape liability (are judgment proof) for judgments made against the corporation that exceed the amount that the owners have contributed to the corporation. For example, if Mrs. Cagle pays $5,000 for shares of common stock of a corporation, then the most that Mrs. Cagle can lose from her investment is $5,000. If a judgment is made against the corporation that the corporation cannot pay, the individual owners (like Mrs. Cagle) will not have to pay the shortfall from their personal assets. Chapter 29 explores in more detail situations involving the use of corporate boundaries to limit liability.

Compulsory Liability Insurance and the Judgment Proof Problem

As discussed in Chapter 13, all states have laws that either encourage or require the purchase of auto liability insurance. In most states, auto liability insurance is compulsory. States also either mandate the purchase of workers' compensation insurance by businesses or require firms to meet detailed financial responsibility rules to qualify as a self-insurer (see Chapter 18), and some states make medical malpractice insurance coverage compulsory for physicians. Both the compensation and safety objectives of the tort system may be better achieved in some cases when parties with limited wealth and limited liability are required to purchase liability insurance.

In the example above, if Mrs. Smith had liability insurance with a limit of $500,000, then the victim would have been fully compensated. And, to the extent that liability insurance premiums reflect the safety precautions taken by Mrs. Smith with perfect accuracy, she will have the right safety incentives. For example, the premium reduction from taking a driver's training course may induce Mrs. Smith to take a course that she would not have taken without insurance. Thus, accurately priced liability insurance can help restore the compensation and safety objectives of the tort system in situations in which limited wealth and limited liability undermine these objectives.

Compulsory liability insurance also might discourage people and businesses from engaging in risky activities that are valued less than the full cost of the activity. For example, compulsory auto liability insurance might cause some persons to give up driving who do not value driving enough to pay the premium for compulsory coverage. (Of course, other persons might instead decide to break the law and drive without coverage.) We discuss these issues further in Chapters 13 and 18.

In practice, liability insurance prices cannot reflect the expected loss with perfect accuracy, and the purchase of liability insurance can create a moral hazard problem that counteracts the positive safety effects of the insurance. For example, some drivers might drive less safely once they have purchased compulsory liability insurance because there is less likelihood that they will lose part of their limited wealth from a lawsuit. Intuitively, a poor uninsured person may act more cautiously in an effort to protect his or her limited wealth than would the same person with significant liability insurance. This possibility makes the effects of compulsory liability insurance on safety precautions theoretically ambiguous in some cases.

12.6   Tort Liability and Safety Regulation

The tort system is not the only mechanism available to create safety incentives or to provide compensation to accident victims. Government regulation and the use of taxes and subsidies to encourage and discourage certain activities also can be used to deal with these issues. For example, if the government knew that lawnmower manufacturers should spend $225 per mower on safety, the government could simply mandate that manufacturers spend $225. In this section, we discuss the trade-offs between using the liability system and government regulation as a means of correcting the problems that the private marketplace does not optimally solve.

Determining the optimal level of safety expenditures requires (1) information about the causes of accidents, (2) an understanding of the methods and technology that can be used to reduce the frequency and severity of accidents, (3) an understanding of the costs of implementing safety measures, and (4) the willingness of people to pay for additional safety. All of this information is costly to obtain. Effective safety regulation requires that regulators obtain this information, whereas providing effective safety incentives through the tort system requires that private entities (firms and individuals) have this information. Thus, in some cases, economies of scale in obtaining and using safety information may exist and thus provide a justification for a greater emphasis on safety regulation versus tort liability. A related argument in favor of centralized safety regulation (over safety incentives via tort liability) is that regulation can reduce costly duplication of investments in safety research. On the other hand, when it would be too costly for the government to obtain the information available to private parties, or when it is important to keep information about the sources of risk and optimal loss control methods private (perhaps because this information is inseparable from valuable proprietary information about product design), tort liability is more likely to be an efficient method of obtaining optimal safety incentives (also see Box 12.2).

Additional trade-offs between liability and safety regulation become more apparent by recognizing that safety regulation is essentially an ex ante approach and liability is an ex post approach. That is, safety regulation imposes restrictions or guidelines before an accident occurs to prevent accidents. The liability system waits until after an accident occurs and then makes one party pay for the victim's losses. (Of course, ex post liability affects ex ante safety decisions.) In some cases, the occurrence of a loss is so devastating that safety regulation has an advantage over the liability system, other factors being held constant. For example, it may make sense to rely more on safety regulation to deal with potential nuclear accidents than to use the liability system.

A potential disadvantage of the liability system is that the party who is responsible for the loss might be judgment proof. As we discussed above, if the party who causes the loss does not have to pay the full amount of the loss, then there may be too little safety. Thus, in situations where the judgment proof problem undermines safety incentives, safety regulation has an advantage over tort liability, all else being equal. Given the different strengths and weaknesses of tort law and safety regulation, it is not surprising that both tools often are used to promote safety. When these tools are used jointly, compliance with a government safety standard generally does not necessarily prevent a defendant from being held liable for injuries (see Box 12.2).

For many types of risk, both regulation and liability co-exist. An interesting question often arises in these circumstances: If a firm satisfies the safety regulations can it nevertheless be held liable for damages? The answer is yes. Critics of the tort system often contend that this is an unfair aspect of the tort system.

One justification for holding a firm liable even though it has met all safety regulations is that government standards must focus on typical or average risks of loss associated with many activities. While there may be economies of scale in risk assessment by the gov-ernment in these cases, legal rules should provide firms with an incentive to use any additional or specific information that they may have concerning a particular risk. In some cases, the benefits (reduction in expected harm) of additional precautions beyond those implied in government standards may exceed the costs. Allowing injured parties to recover damages in these cases, despite the fact the firm has met the regulatory standard, provides the firm with the incentive to undertake cost-justified precautions.

12.7 Proposals for Tort Reform

When liability costs for many businesses and professions increase substantially, these businesses and professional organizations often lobby state legislatures and the US Congress to pass tort reform legislation to reduce the magnitude of liability costs. This section provides an overview of the major types of tort reform proposals and the problems they are meant to address.[5]

Modifying Incentives to Bring Suits

Most plaintiffs in the United States hire their attorneys on a contingency fee basis; that is, the attorney receives a percentage of the damages awarded by the court or in a settlement, but if the plaintiff loses, then the attorney receives nothing. The use of contingency fees is much more frequent in the United States than in other countries. One advantage of contingency fees is that they allow access to the courts to people who otherwise could not afford to pay an attorney. In essence, the attorney finances the lawsuit for the plaintiff. Also, contingency fees can provide incentives for plaintiff attorneys to screen out cases that are not likely to succeed. However, critics of contingency fees argue that they lead plaintiff attorneys to take cases with a low probability of winning, but with potentially high damages. These speculative lawsuits, the critics contend, impose substantial costs on defendants. As a result, proposals often are made to place **limits on contingency fees.**[6]

[5]Considerable research exists on the effects of each of these proposals. Some references are provided at the end of the chapter.

[6]The United Kingdom has experimented with one approach to limiting contingency fees. It allows a conditional fee where the plaintiff attorney receives up to twice the compensation he/she would normally receive on an hourly basis if the plaintiff wins, but zero otherwise. Theoretically, this conditional fee induces plaintiff attorneys to turn down any case in which the probability of winning is less than 50 percent.

Unlike the systems in most countries, the US tort system generally does not require that losing plaintiffs pay any of the legal costs of a winning defendant. A common proposal for reforming the US system is the adoption of a **loser pays rule,** where the loser pays at least part of the winning side's legal costs. Proponents of a loser pays rule argue that it would reduce litigation in cases where the plaintiff has little chance of winning. A potential concern is that the adoption of a loser pays rule will reduce access to the justice system because plaintiffs will be averse to incurring the risk of paying the potentially large legal costs of the defendant. However, to the extent that plaintiff law firms can diversify this risk across many cases and have expertise in judging the merits of a case, plaintiff law firms would likely bear the risk of paying the defendant's legal costs under a loser pay system. Whether a loser pays rule nevertheless would have an excessively chilling effect on litigation and safety is hotly contested.

Reducing Damages

The United States also differs from most other countries in that tort cases are heard more frequently by juries, as opposed to judges. The reason for the frequent use of jury trials is that the US Constitution and most state constitutions generally require a jury trial if either side requests one. Nevertheless, jury trials for personal injury cases have received considerable criticism from legal scholars for several reasons. Unlike judges, juries do not have to explain the reasoning for their decisions and juries are not bound by decisions in similar cases. Consequently, a jury adds uncertainty about the outcome, which in turn induces plaintiff attorneys to pursue speculative lawsuits. An additional criticism of juries is that they often are not capable of evaluating the expert testimony presented. Although it would be difficult to eliminate jury trials given the constitutional barriers, jury discretion in setting damages can be limited by legislation. For example, judges could be granted authority to set damages.

A number of state legislatures have enacted laws that limit or place **caps on pain and suffering awards.** Proponents of these reforms argue that because pain and suffering is difficult to measure, awards for pain and suffering have high variance, bear little relation to the loss actually suffered, and are not the type of compensation for which most consumers would be willing to pay. Proponents of reform further contend that the difficulty in predicting pain and suffering awards provides incentives for plaintiff attorneys to pursue speculative litigation with the threat of having an emotional and sympathetic jury ultimately determine the outcome. On the other hand, critics of caps on pain and suffering awards argue that caps reduce safety incentives.

Some critics of the tort system argue that juries often award excessive punitive damages and therefore advocate **limits on punitive damages.** One argument for punitive damages from a safety perspective is that because all victims of harm do not bring legal actions against the wrongdoer, damages in the cases that are brought need to exceed the losses that the specific victim suffered. Otherwise, the wrongdoer's expected total liability will be less than the expected total losses imposed on victims, and the wrongdoer will have too little incentive for safety. Punitive damages also could reflect society's desire to seek retribution against parties that inflict egregious harm on others.

Attempts to restrict punitive damages have met with limited success thus far. In 1991, the US Supreme Court refused to consider a case on punitive damages, *Pacific Mutual Life v. Haslip,* in which a life insurer was found to have defrauded a woman (Haslip) for $4,000. An Alabama court awarded the plaintiff the $4,000 and also assessed $1 million in punitive damages. Many observers interpret the Supreme Court's decision as implying that existing methods of limiting jury discretion on punitive damages are sufficient. The Supreme Court, however, did highlight that judges should instruct juries on the purposes of punitive damages and review jury awards. The court later overturned several punitive damage awards as excessive, but it has yet to impose clear guidelines for setting the appropriate amount of punitive damages.

A third proposal that would reduce damages is to alter the collateral source rule. Often accident victims receive compensation from sources other than the tort system. For example, private insurance, social insurance benefits, and charity help pay the losses suffered by accident victims and are therefore called collateral benefits. The basic issue is whether courts should take these other benefits into account when setting damages. From a safety perspective, the answer is no. If the sole purpose is to provide incentives for safety, then subtracting collateral benefits from total losses when setting damages would cause damages to be less than losses. If the damages that the defendant must pay are less than the losses imposed on the victims, then there will be too little incentive for safety. However, from a compensation perspective, the subtraction of collateral benefits makes sense; otherwise, victims would be overcompensated for their losses. During the latter part of the 1980s, several states enacted laws that restricted the application of the collateral source rule under certain conditions.

Limiting the Application of Joint and Several Liability

Recall that when defendants are jointly and severally liable, each individual defendant can be held responsible for the entire damages. While the doctrine of joint and several liability can be defended on the grounds that it provides compensation to victims, its justification from a safety perspective is more suspect. The reason is that joint and several liability can cause a party to pay more than the costs its actions have imposed on other parties. As explained in the appendix to this chapter (see case 5), imposing liability in excess of the losses actually imposed can provide too much incentive for safety.

During the latter part of the 1980s, the majority of the states enacted legislation on the use of joint and several liability. A few states completely eliminated the use of joint and several liability, but most states restricted its use, for example, by disallowing its use for noneconomic damages (pain and suffering). Other states disallowed its use when the plaintiff was more than 50 percent responsible for the damages.

12.8 Summary

- Liability rules allocate accident risk to various members of society and thereby affect incentives to engage in loss control (incentives to undertake risky activities and to take precautions). Also, by forcing some parties to compensate other parties (accident victims) for their losses, the tort liability system essentially forces the former party to provide insurance to victims.

- Liability rules range from (1) immunity from liability (e.g., charitable organizations in some circumstances), to (2) a negligence rule that holds people liable if they fail to exercise the required standard of care to prevent injury to another party, to (3) strict liability that holds manufacturers of defective products liable even if the manufacturer was not negligent, to (4) absolute liability.

- Compensatory damages in tort liability cases compensate victims for monetary losses (e.g., medical expenses, lost wages) and nonmonetary losses (e.g., pain and suffering). Punitive damages are damages in excess of the losses suffered by the victim.

- To recover damages under a negligence rule, a plaintiff generally must establish (1) the existence of a legal duty by the defendant to prevent harm to the plaintiff, (2) a breach of this legal duty by failing to exercise the required standard of care, (3) that the breach was the proximate cause of the plaintiff's harm, and (4) that an injury was suffered. Under a negligence rule (and sometimes under strict liability), a defendant in some cases may be able to avoid or reduce liability by showing that the plaintiff assumed the risk or that the plaintiff's negligence or actions contributed to the accident.

- The main objectives of the tort liability system from an economic perspective are to provide incentives for parties to engage in the optimal level of loss control and to provide optimal compensation (insurance coverage) to accident victims.

- Limited wealth and limited liability can cause some people to be judgment proof for damages imposed on others. In this case, victims may not receive optimal compensation and incentives for loss control may be insufficient. Compulsory liability insurance—forcing judgment proof people to purchase liability insurance—in some cases can improve victim compensation and loss control incentives.

- Government safety regulation and taxes also can be used to address the loss control and victim compensation problems that arise when people are uninformed or when transaction costs prevent these problems from being solved privately.

Key Terms

common law 215	compensatory damages 219	contributory negligence 223
statutory law 216	special damages 219	comparative negligence 223
criminal law 216	general damages 219	collateral source rule 227
civil law 216	punitive damages 219	judgment proof 228
contract law 216	joint and several liability 219	limits on contingency fees 231
tort law 216	breach of duty 221	loser pays rule 232
negligence rule 218	cost-justified precautions 221	caps on pain and suffering
strict liability 218	proximate cause 222	awards 232
absolute liability 218	assumption of risk defense 223	limits on punitive damages 232

Questions and Problems

1. Ms. Schmit, a famous marathon runner and legal scholar, was out for a long run one day. While thinking about the arguments for and against joint and several liability, she crossed a street between intersections without looking for oncoming traffic. A speeding car hit her; luckily only her leg was injured. Medical expenses came to $750, but she was unable to run in the Boston marathon that year, something for which she had been training for the previous 10 years. Assume that the noneconomic loss (e.g., emotional distress and disappointment) of not being able to run in Boston is worth $100,000. Under each of the following liability standards, identify who is responsible for paying Ms. Schmit's medical expenses and her noneconomic losses.

   a. Negligence rule with no defenses.
   b. Negligence rule with a contributory negligence defense.
   c. Negligence rule with a comparative negligence defense.
   d. Absolute liability for drivers of vehicles involved in pedestrian accidents.

2. The liability standard for medical malpractice generally is a negligence rule. Compare the negligence rule to a liability standard where physicians are always liable for losses

suffered as a result of a medical procedure on each of the following dimensions:

a.   Physicians' incentives to provide care.
b.   Victim compensation.
c.   Legal costs.

3. Find the optimal level of safety (probability of an accident) from a societal perspective using the data on the costs of safety given in the table below. Assume that an accident imposes costs on a victim equal to $500,000.

Probability of Loss	Safety Expenditures
0.030	$ 0
0.020	1,000
0.015	2,000
0.012	3,000
0.0095	4,000
0.009	5,000

4. Graphically illustrate the solution to the problem in question 3.

5. Using the data in question 3, how much would a profit-maximizing producer spend on safety if the tort liability system would award each victim $150,000?

6. Using the data in question 3, how much would a profit-maximizing producer spend on safety if the tort liability system would award $500,000 to each victim?

7. Using the data in question 3, how much would a profit-maximizing producer spend on safety if the tort liability system would award $500,000 to one-half of the accident victims?

8. Using the data in question 3, how much would a profit-maximizing producer spend on safety if the tort liability system would award $500,000 to each victim, but the producer only had $250,000 to pay liability awards and therefore the producer's liability was limited to $250,000?

9. Consider the same scenario as described in problem 8, but suppose that the producer is required to purchase liability insurance with a $500,000 limit. Assume that the insurance premium equals expected liability costs and that the insurer can costlessly observe the producer's safety expenditures. How much will the producer spend on safety?

Answers to Concept Check

1. The court would award $90,000, because by forcing the manufacturer to pay all of the costs incurred by accident victims, the manufacturer will consider all of the expected costs of unsafe products when designing, manufacturing, and marketing products.

2. The court would award less than $90,000, because consumers would not voluntarily purchase full insurance coverage when there are positive loadings (transaction costs) or moral hazard problems associated with providing such insurance.

References

Bernstein, David E. "Procedural Tort Reform: Lessons from Other Nations." *Regulation— Cato Review of Business and Government* 19 (1996). (*Discusses various tort reforms and their likely effects on litigation outcomes.*)

Demsetz, Harold. "When Does the Rule of Liability Matter?" *Journal of Legal Studies.* (*Classic article on how transaction costs cause the liability rule to affect resource allocation.*)

Lee, Han-Duck; Mark Browne; and Joan Schmit.

"How Does Joint and Several Tort Reform Affect the Rate of Tort Filing? Evidence from State Courts." *Journal of Risk and Insurance* 61 (1994), pp. 295–316. (*Empirically examines the effect of tort joint and several tort reform on litigation.*)

Shavell, Steven. *Economic Analysis of Accident Law.* Cambridge, MA: Harvard University Press, 1987. (*Comprehensive economic analysis of tort law.*)

Why Have a Tort System?—A Closer Look

When will the private marketplace fail to yield the optimal incentives for safety and the optimal amount of compensation to victims? We focus on two factors that can cause the private marketplace to yield nonoptimal safety: (1) imperfect information about the risk of harm, and (2) transaction costs that prevent people from achieving efficient outcomes without well-defined tort liability rules. We then note that similar results hold for the issue of whether the private marketplace will provide optimal compensation without a tort system.[7]

The Role of Information

Consider the Nielson Inc. example discussed earlier, where the optimal amount of safety expenditures from society's perspective equals $225. Instead of considering what is best for society, we now consider how much Nielson will spend on safety in various situations. The specific issue is whether the tort system is needed to induce Nielson Inc. to spend $225 on safety. We will show that the tort system is not needed if consumers are fully informed about the product's risk, because fully informed consumers are willing to pay more for safer products, which in turn gives manufacturers incentives to spend the optimal amount on product safety. However, if consumers underestimate product risk, then the tort system may be needed to induce Nielson to spend the right amount on safety.

CASE 1: FULL INFORMATION IMPLIES OPTIMAL SAFETY

Consider first the case where consumers are fully informed and manufacturers are not liable for losses suffered by consumers who are injured using the

manufacturer's products. If Nielson spent nothing on safety, then expected losses to consumers would be $700. Fully informed risk-neutral consumers (or fully insured consumers with no premium loading) would know that if they purchased a mower from Nielson they could expect losses (or have to pay a premium) equal to $700. Consequently, consumers would be willing to pay $700 less for a Nielson mower than for an otherwise equivalent mower that had no risk. If Nielson spent $45 on safety and thereby reduced the accident probability from 0.07 to 0.06, then consumers would increase the price that they would pay for the mower by $100. Nielson obviously would find the $45 safety expenditure a profitable move.

Now consider the next increment in safety. Consumers will pay an additional $100 per mower if Nielson lowers the accident probability to 0.05. Since the cost of doing this is an additional $85 (a total expenditure on safety equal to $130), it is in Nielson's own interest to lower the probability of an accident to 0.05. Continuing, since the cost of lowering the probability to 0.04 is $95 and since consumers will pay an additional $100 per mower for this change in the accident probability, Nielson will spend the additional $95 and lower the probability to 0.04. However, Nielson will not increase safety beyond this point, because the next increment in safety (lowering the probability to 0.03) will cost an additional $175 but will yield only an additional $100 in the mower's price. Thus, Nielson will spend $225 on safety, exactly what is optimal from society's perspective.

This example illustrates that *if consumers are fully informed about product risk, then the tort system is not needed to induce optimal safety*. The private marketplace provides manufacturers with the right incentives for safety. Informed consumers induce Nielson to consider appropriately the potential accident costs associated with risky products.

---

[7]Some people might argue that less than full information is due to transaction costs; it is more straightforward to analyze the information and transaction costs separately.

CASE 2: UNINFORMED PEOPLE AND NO LIABILITY IMPLIES TOO LITTLE SAFETY

Now suppose that consumers are completely uninformed about product safety. How much would Nielson spend on safety if it is trying to maximize profits and if it is not liable for consumers' losses? The answer is zero. Nielson has no incentive to invest in safety, because consumers will not pay a higher price for a safer product. The private marketplace does not provide the right incentives to invest in safety. Although risky products impose accident costs on consumers, Nielson is not motivated to consider these costs because (1) consumers are unaware of them at the time they purchase products, and (2) Nielson is not liable for subsequent losses.

CASE 3: UNINFORMED PEOPLE AND FULL LIABILITY IMPLIES OPTIMAL SAFETY

To see how the tort system can improve safety incentives when consumers are completely uninformed, assume that Nielson is held liable for losses suffered by consumers who are injured using Nielson's mowers. In particular, suppose that every accident victim sues Nielson and each victim is fully compensated. Nielson therefore will view each additional safety expenditure as reducing the probability of losing a lawsuit. Since the tort system forces Nielson to pay all accident losses, Nielson will spend $225 per mower on safety, which is the optimal amount.[8]

Combining the results of cases 2 and 3, it is clear that one justification for making producers liable for all consumer losses is that consumers are uninformed. With no liability, Nielson has too little incentive to produce safe products when consumers are uninformed (case 2). By making Nielson liable for all consumer accident losses, Nielson has incentives to invest the optimal amount in safety (case 3). The next two cases expand this analysis by considering two other situations where Nielson is liable, but not to the optimal extent.

CASE 4: UNINFORMED PEOPLE AND LESS THAN FULL LIABILITY IMPLIES TOO LITTLE SAFETY

Suppose that the legal liability system only compensates accident victims for their monetary losses, instead of all losses. In our example, expected accident severity is $10,000. Suppose that one-half of this loss is nonmonetary (pain and suffering losses) and one-half is monetary (medical expenses and lost wages). If courts only award compensation for monetary losses, then victims will receive only $5,000 from Nielson. In this case, Nielson will spend less than the optimal amount on safety. From Nielson's perspective, the benefit of making mowers safer is one-half of the societal benefit. That is, there is a divergence between the societal benefits of making products safer and the private benefits to Nielson. Consequently, when deciding how much to spend on safety, Nielson will spend too little on safety.

Using Table 12.3 we can calculate specifically how much Nielson will choose to spend. Starting from zero expenditure and an accident probability equal to 0.07, Nielson can reduce the probability of an accident to 0.06 by spending $45; thus, the marginal cost is $45. The marginal benefit to Nielson of reducing the probability to 0.06 is the reduction in expected liability costs, which equals the reduction in the probability of being sued, 0.01 (0.07 minus 0.06) times the amount of damages, which equals $5,000. Thus, the expected benefit is $50. Thus, Nielson will spend $45 to improve mower safety because doing so reduces its expected liability cost by $50. However, Nielson will not spend any additional amount on safety because the marginal cost will exceed the marginal benefit. This example illustrates that if the tort system undercompensates victims, then there will be too little

---

[8]Note that if the economic criterion for negligence, discussed in section 12.3, is used to determine whether Nielson is liable, then Nielson also would have incentives to spend $225. That is, holding Nielson liable for failure to undertake cost-justified precautions would induce Nielson to spend the $225. If Nielson spent less than $225, its expected liability for damages would exceed the savings in safety expenditures.

incentive to invest in safety (provided people are completely uninformed).

This example also highlights a point made earlier about the possible tradeoffs between optimal safety and optimal compensation. As discussed in Chapter 9, many people will not want to purchase insurance for nonmonetary losses such as pain and suffering. In addition, moral hazard problems associated with insuring nonmonetary losses imply that insurance typically will not be provided for such losses. This example illustrates that the tort system faces a potential conflict: If the tort system does not provide compensation for pain and suffering, which is likely to be optimal from a compensation perspective, then it may provide too little incentive for safety. As mentioned earlier, US courts typically attempt to compensate victims for nonmonetary losses. One explanation for this approach is that the US tort system places greater weight on optimal safety than optimal compensation in situations where a conflict between the safety and compensation objectives exists. Another interpretation is that the procedural process of personal injury cases, particularly the use of jury trials, causes awards to be influenced by sympathy for victims and not just optimal safety and compensation goals.

CASE 5: UNINFORMED PEOPLE AND MORE THAN FULL LIABILITY IMPLIES TOO MUCH SAFETY

As a final example, suppose that the tort system overcompensates each accident victim. For example, suppose that each accident victim receives twice the losses that are actually suffered. In this case, Nielson will spend more than what is socially optimal on safety. From Nielson's perspective, the benefit of making products safer is the reduction in expected liability costs, which exceed the true expected cost of unsafe products.

From Table 12.3, the benefit to Nielson of each increment in safety is a reduction in the probability of being sued (0.01) times the amount of damages ($20,000). Thus, the expected benefit to Nielson from each safety increment is $200, which is twice the social marginal benefit. Thus, there is a diver-

gence between private and social benefits: Nielson's private marginal benefit of additional safety exceeds the social marginal benefit. Consequently, Nielson will spend too much on safety. Nielson will decrease the accident probability until its private marginal cost exceeds its private marginal benefit, which occurs when the probability of an accident equals 0.02. Thus, Nielson will spend $590 per mower on safety. This example illustrates that if the tort system overcompensates victims, then firms will be given an incentive to invest in safety to the point where the cost of additional safety exceeds the benefit. In this case, buyers get very safe lawnmowers, but the mowers are too safe in that the additional safety is not worth the increase in price to the buyers. The buyers would prefer to have cheaper (less safe) mowers.

Transaction Costs and Assignment of Legal Rights

In some respects, the Nielson example is simpler than other scenarios where tort liability applies because the potential accident occurs in the context of a transaction between consumers and Nielson. The price at which the parties transact reflects the perceived risk involved in the exchange. If the parties are well informed, the private marketplace effectively deals with the risky situation. Other scenarios involving tort liability are complicated by the lack of a transaction prior to the potential accident. For example, pedestrians do not transact with all the drivers that could potentially hit them. In these scenarios, the private marketplace would require additional transactions to deal effectively with the risk. Due to the costs of arranging these additional transactions, the tort system may be a better mechanism for achieving the goals of optimal safety incentives and optimal compensation than the private marketplace.

To illustrate these concepts, consider the harm that can potentially arise from a factory that disposes waste in a river that people use for fishing. Assume that the waste has a 50 percent chance of damaging the fish in the river. Also assume that everyone knows that the cost of damaged fish equals $400 (in present value terms). Thus, the fol-

TABLE 12A.1

Analysis of factory polluting river (benefit of waste treatment equals $200).

		Cost of Treatment	
		$150	**$250**
Panel A	Socially optimal outcome	No pollution	Pollution
Panel B	Outcomes with zero transaction costs		
	Outcome if factory is liable	No pollution	Pollution
	Outcome if factory is not liable	No pollution	Pollution
Panel C	Outcomes if transaction costs equal $55		
	Outcome if factory is liable	No pollution	Pollution
	Outcome if factory is not liable	Pollution	Pollution

lowing probability distribution summarizes the loss from the waste that the factory places in the river.

$$\text{Cost to anglers} = \begin{array}{l} \text{\$400 with probability 0.5} \\ \text{\$0 with probability 0.5} \end{array}$$

Assume that everyone is risk neutral or that full insurance can be purchased at a premium equal to expected claim costs. This assumption implies that we can ignore residual uncertainty and the cost of loss financing, so that the cost of risk associated with water pollution is simply the expected loss plus the cost of loss control (if any is undertaken).

Suppose that the factory can treat the waste prior to disposing of it in the river, which would eliminate the risk of loss to the anglers. We consider two scenarios for the magnitude of the waste treatment cost: (1) the treatment of waste costs $150, or (2) the treatment of waste costs $250. We first examine whether it is optimal from society's perspective to treat the waste before dumping it in the river. Then we examine whether the liability rule (whether the factory or the anglers are liable) affects whether the factory will treat the waste.

OPTIMAL LEVEL OF LOSS CONTROL

If the treatment cost is $150, it is optimal to treat the waste because the $200 benefit from treatment (anglers are spared a cost of $400 with probability 0.5) exceeds the treatment cost. If the treatment cost is $250, however, it is optimal not to treat the waste because the benefit ($200) is less than the cost ($250). Stated differently, the cost of risk is minimized by treating the waste if the cost of treatment is $150, but the cost of risk is minimized by allow-

ing pollution if the cost of treatment is $250. Panel A of Table 12A.1 summarizes these results.

An important implication of this analysis is that it is not always optimal to eliminate pollution or other risks of harm. The costs of eliminating the pollution must be compared to the benefits. Because reasonable people can disagree about the magnitudes of the costs and benefits (unreasonable people are sure to disagree), arguments concerning the optimal amount of pollution are common. These issues are ignored in this example by assuming that everyone agrees on the costs and benefits.

DOES THE LIABILITY RULE MATTER

We now will demonstrate that in the absence of transaction costs, it does not matter whether the factory is liable: The factory will treat the waste if the treatment cost is $150; it will not treat the waste if the treatment cost is $250. Stated differently, with zero transaction costs, the factory will invest the optimal amount in preventing pollution regardless of whether it is liable for the losses imposed on anglers.[9]

Consider first the case where the cost of treating the waste is $150, so that it is optimal from society's perspective to treat the waste. Will the factory do what is optimal from society's perspective? If the factory is liable for the losses suffered by the anglers, then the factory obviously will consider the costs imposed on the anglers. Since the cost of

[9]This analysis originated in the work of Ronald Coase, who was awarded the Nobel Prize in economics in part for his work on these types of problems.

treating the waste ($150) is less than the expected cost of compensating anglers for their losses ($200), the factory will treat the waste. Thus, if the factory is liable, we get the optimal outcome: The waste is treated.

Now suppose that the factory cannot be held liable, so that the anglers must bear the costs of pollution. In this case, it may at first appear that the factory will not consider the costs imposed on the anglers and therefore will not treat the waste. However, this conclusion is incorrect. If the cost of treating the waste is $150, then without transaction costs the anglers will join together and pay the factory to treat the waste. The cost to the anglers of paying the factory ($150) is less than the expected cost of pollution ($200); consequently, there will be no pollution even though the factory is not liable. Thus, when the cost of treating the waste is $150 and anglers can costlessly agree to pay the factory to treat the waste, the waste will be treated regardless of whether the factory is liable. Like the earlier discussion of product injuries when consumers are fully informed about the risk of harm, the key to this finding is that a contractual solution to the pollution issue exists. The tort system is not needed to solve the problem; the private marketplace handles it optimally.

Now suppose instead that the cost of treating the waste is $250 so that the waste should not be treated because the cost of doing so exceeds the benefits. If the factory is not liable, the anglers will not pay the factory to treat the waste, because the cost of treating the waste ($250) exceeds the expected cost to the anglers with no treatment ($200). If the factory is liable, then the factory is better off paying the losses to the anglers if they occur than treating the waste, because the expected cost of compensating the anglers ($200) is less than the cost of treating the waste ($250). Thus, regardless of whether the factory is liable, the waste is not treated.

As summarized in Panel B of Table 12A.1, when the factory and the anglers can costlessly negotiate a solution to the pollution issue, it does not matter who is liable for the losses that occur. When it is optimal to avoid pollution (when the cost of treatment is less than the harm prevented), no pollution will occur. When it is optimal to have pollution (when the cost of treatment exceeds the harm prevented), pollution will occur.

ASSIGNMENT OF LIABILITY AND THE DISTRIBUTION OF WEALTH

You may object to the conclusion that the assignment of liability does not matter, because when the factory is not liable, the anglers have to pay the costs of preventing the pollution, but when the factory is liable the anglers do not have to pay. This point is valid: The assignment of liability can affect the distribution of wealth; anglers are better off if the factory is liable (factory owners are worse off). Nonetheless, in order to achieve the optimal level of safety, it does not matter whether the factory is liable or not—optimal safety takes place regardless of the liability rule.

The focus on safety may bother you. You might think that it is only fair that the factory should be liable for the losses imposed on the anglers. You should keep in perspective, however, that this notion of fairness is not universal. One could just as easily view the interaction between the factory and the anglers as one in which the anglers' decision to fish on that river created the risk and thus that the anglers should pay the cost of treating the waste. The key point is that fairness is a subjective notion. While fairness issues should not affect whether the waste should be treated, people's notions of fairness will affect who they think should pay for the treatment (if the waste should be treated). As a result, notions of fairness may well affect the assignment of liability in the real world.

THE ZERO TRANSACTION COSTS ASSUMPTION

Zero transaction costs is a critical assumption underlying the conclusion that the assignment of liability does not affect whether the waste will be treated. To highlight the importance of this assumption, we now redo the analysis assuming that the anglers must incur $55 to organize themselves and negotiate a contract with the factory. Let's begin by assuming that the cost of treating the waste is $150, so that the optimal outcome is to treat the waste. If the factory is liable, then the factory will treat the waste, because the cost of treatment ($150) is less than the expected cost of compensating the anglers ($200). If, however, the factory is not liable, then the factory will not treat the waste, contrary to what the previous analysis showed and contrary to what is optimal. When transaction costs were zero, the anglers organized themselves and paid the factory the money needed to treat the waste. Now, however, the cost of organizing the anglers ($55) plus the cost of treatment ($150) exceeds the expected cost of pollution to the anglers ($200). Consequently, pollution will result even though it is optimal not to have pollution. This conclusion is illustrated in Panel C of Table 12A.1.

This example illustrates that the liability rule can affect optimal safety incentives if there are positive transaction costs. In this case, transaction costs prevented a contractual solution to the pollution problem when the factory was not liable. Consequently, the liability rule should make the factory liable, because the factory invests optimally in pollution prevention only when it is made liable. (Thus, transaction costs in this example favor the same outcome that many people believe to be fair: The factory should be held liable.)

The key point is that liability rules can improve safety incentives when transaction costs prevent private contracting from providing the right safety incentives. For example, it would be too costly for every driver to privately contract with each other driver to determine how automobile accidents will be handled. Instead of private contracts, society is better off having the tort system govern these interactions. This reasoning suggests that, in addition to the case of underestimation of the risk of harm considered earlier, society should use tort liability when (1) interactions between people can cause harm, and (2) transaction costs prevent these people from entering into optimal contracts to deal with the potential harm.

Summary

This analysis illustrates that uninformed people and transaction costs provide a justification for assigning liability to certain parties. That is, uninformed people and transaction costs sometimes cause the private marketplace to handle the problems associated with accident risks suboptimally. You should not conclude, however, that tort liability is always the best solution to the problems that arise in the private marketplace. Other methods exist for dealing with safety and compensation issues. For example, government regulation with fines for noncompliance or taxes can help provide proper safety incentives, and social insurance programs can provide compensation to those who have been harmed. All of these methods of dealing with safety and compensation issues, however, are costly, which implies that the inefficiencies of the private marketplace must be compared to the inefficiencies (costs) of the methods used to deal with the shortcomings of the private marketplace.

While our discussion in this appendix has focused on safety incentives, similar points apply to the compensation (implicit insurance coverage) objectives of the tort system. If people are fully informed, private contracting generally will provide the implicit insurance coverage that people desire. However, if people underestimate some risks or if transaction costs prevent optimal contracts, then people may obtain too little insurance. In principle, the tort system can improve compensation in these situations.

Chapter 13

Automobile Insurance

Chapter Objectives

- Describe personal exposures to loss arising out of automobile ownership and use, and personal auto insurance coverage for these losses.
- Explain major features of personal auto insurance pricing and underwriting.
- Explain compulsory auto insurance laws and the rationale and effects of these laws.
- Explain no-fault auto insurance laws and the rationale and effects of these laws.

13.1 Overview of Auto Loss Exposures and Insurance

Over 35 million auto accidents occur annually in the United States, killing more than 40,000 people and producing well over $100 billion in economic loss. Personal auto insurance, which protects against many losses associated with auto accidents, is the largest line of property-liability insurance in terms of premium volume, with year 2000 written premiums of $120 billion. Commercial auto insurance premiums totaled another $18 billion. The largest four personal auto insurers, with national premium market shares shown in parentheses, were: State Farm Insurance (19 percent), Allstate Insurance (13 percent), Zurich/Farmers Insurance (6 percent), and Berkshire Hathaway (GEICO, 5 percent). All of these insurers are direct writers that primarily rely on exclusive agents to market coverage, and 68 percent of the personal auto insurance market is written by direct writers as opposed to insurers that primarily rely on independent agents and brokers.

The major loss exposures arising out of automobile accidents are: (1) legal liability for harm that you may cause others as a result of your negligence, (2) bodily injury to you and members of your family, and (3) property damage to and/or theft of your vehicle(s). Table 13.1 summarizes these exposures and indicates insurance coverage that is available to cover part or all of these losses. It shows auto insurance coverages that are available with the **personal auto policy.** This contract, along with very similar versions offered by many insurers, is the largest selling type of auto policy and is the focus of this section. Table 13.1 also shows other (i.e., nonauto) insurance that may be available to pay for losses from auto accidents. In a majority of states, these nonauto coverages, which include individual and group medical expense coverage, disability insurance, life insurance, and Social Security, represent major sources of payment for auto-related losses.

The personal auto policy includes four main types of coverage: (1) "third-party" liability coverage for liability to third parties harmed by negligence of an insured person; (2) "first-party" medical payments coverage for the insured, or in states with no-fault or related laws, personal injury protection coverage for the insured's medical expenses *and* loss of income; (3) uninsured and underinsured motorists coverage for losses caused to an

TABLE 13.1   Automobile loss exposures and insurance for losses.

Type of Loss	Auto Insurance Coverage	Other Insurance That May Apply
Your legal liability for negligently causing (1) bodily injury to others, including economic losses and pain and suffering; (2) property damage to others, including loss of use; and (3) defense costs	• Your liability coverage	• Your personal "umbrella" liability insurance coverage (see Chapter 14)
Your economic losses from bodily injury	• An at-fault driver's liability coverage • Your "first-party" medical payments coverage or personal injury protection coverage • Your uninsured or underinsured motorists coverage if other driver is at fault (and uninsured or underinsured)	• Your group or individual medical/disability/life insurance • Workers' compensation insurance if work-related injury • Social Security disability, survivor benefits, or Medicare
Your pain and suffering	• An at-fault driver's liability insurance • Your uninsured or underinsured motorists coverage if other driver is at fault	• None
Collision damage to your vehicle	• An at-fault driver's liability coverage • Your collision coverage • Your uninsured or underinsured motorists coverage if other driver is at fault	• None
Other damage to and theft of your vehicle	• Your "other than collision" (comprehensive) coverage	• None

insured by drivers without liability insurance and drivers with comparatively low liability insurance limits; and (4) coverage for physical damage to or theft of insured autos. This section provides a brief overview of these coverages. We emphasize that while personal auto policies are written in language that most buyers can understand, these contracts nonetheless are reasonably complex with numerous clauses and definitions. Our purpose is to acquaint you with key provisions rather than provide a comprehensive restatement of coverage terms and conditions.

Liability Coverage

The **auto liability coverage** in the personal auto policy provides broad coverage for liability for bodily injury and property damage to other parties arising out of the use of an automobile by an insured person. As is customary with liability insurance, the insurer also agrees to defend the insured and bear the defense costs and is responsible for negotiating and settling claims.

Personal auto liability coverage may be sold with a "single limit" that specifies the maximum amount that the insurer will pay for all damages from a single accident. (The policy does not include an aggregate annual limit.) For example, a policy with a single limit of $300,000 will pay up to $300,000 for liability for bodily injury and property damage, regardless of how many persons or autos are damaged by the insured. Alternatively, the policy can include separate limits ("split limits") that specify the maximum that the insurer will pay per accident (1) to each injured person for bodily injury, (2) in total to all injured persons for bodily injury, and (3) for total property damage. For example, split limits equal to $100,000 per person for bodily injury, $300,000 per accident for bodily injury, and $50,000 per accident for property damage would pay: (1) up to $100,000 for bodily injury to each person injured by the driver in an accident, (2) no more than $300,000 in total if more than one person is hurt, and (3) up to $50,000 for total property damage regardless of how many vehicles are damaged by the insured.

As of 2001, 45 states and the District of Columbia had **compulsory liability insurance laws** that mandate the purchase of a minimum amount of auto liability coverage by auto owners. The minimum amounts generally are specified as split limits with the per person minimum for bodily injury generally ranging from $10,000 to $50,000 (see Table 13.2.) All states also had **financial responsibility laws** that penalize drivers with fines and possible loss of driving privileges under certain conditions if they negligently cause accidents and are unable to pay specified minimum amounts of damages. Financial responsibility laws predate compulsory insurance laws. Purchasing liability insurance with limits equal to or greater than the minimums specified in a state's financial responsibility law satisfies both the financial responsibility law and any compulsory liability insurance law.

The minimum liability coverage available in a personal auto policy from most insurers equals the "basic limits" that are required under the state's financial responsibility law/compulsory liability insurance law. Most insurers also offer higher limits for higher premiums. When you travel out of state, the liability limits under the personal auto policy automatically adjust to provide the limits required by law if they are higher than in your home state.

The policy covers the liability of the "named insured," which includes a resident spouse and other family members residing in the same household (including college students temporarily away from home while attending school). These persons are covered for liability arising out of use of a "covered auto" and any other auto with reasonable belief that they

TABLE 13.2 Compulsory auto insurance coverages and minimum liability limits (in $ thousands).

State	Compulsory Coverages	Minimum Liability Limits	State	Compulsory Coverages	Minimum Liability Limits
Alabama	Liability	20/40/10	Montana	Liability	25/50/10
Alaska	Liability	50/100/25	Nebraska	Liability	25/50/25
Arizona	Liability	15/30/10	Nevada	Liability	15/30/10
Arkansas	Liability	25/50/25	New Hampshire	FR, UM	25/50/25
California	Liability	15/30/5	New Jersey	Liability, PIP, UM	15/30/5
Colorado	Liability, PIP	25/50/15	New Mexico	Liability	25/50/10
Connecticut	Liability, UM, UIM	20/40/10	New York	Liability, PIP, UM	25/50/10
Delaware	Liability, PIP	15/30/5	North Carolina	Liability	30/60/25
DC	Liability, UM	25/50/10	North Dakota	Liability, PIP, UM	25/50/25
Florida	PDL, PIP	10/20/10	Ohio	Liability	12.5/25/7.5
Georgia	Liability	25/50/25	Oklahoma	Liability	10/20/10
Hawaii	Liability, PIP	20/40/10	Oregon	Liability, PIP, UM	25/50/10
Idaho	Liability	25/50/15	Pennsylvania	Liability, PIP	15/30/5
Illinois	Liability, UM	20/40/15	Rhode Island	BIL, UM	25/50/25
Indiana	Liability	25/50/10	South Carolina	FR, UM	15/30/10
Iowa	Liability	20/40/15	South Dakota	Liability, UM	25/50/25
Kansas	Liability, PIP, UM	25/50/10	Tennessee	FR only	20/50/10
Kentucky	Liability, PIP	25/50/10	Texas	Liability	20/40/15
Louisiana	Liability	10/20/10	Utah	Liability, PIP	25/50/15
Maine	Liability, UM	50/100/25	Vermont	Liability, UM, UIM	25/50/10
Maryland	Liability, PIP, UM	20/40/15	Virginia	FR, UM	25/50/20
Massachusetts	Liability, PIP, UM	20/40/5	Washington	Liability	25/50/10
Michigan	Liability, PIP	20/40/10	West Virginia	Liability, UM	20/40/10
Minnesota	Liability, PIP, UM, UIM	30/60/10	Wisconsin	FR, UM	25/50/10
Mississippi	Liability	10/20/05	Wyoming	Liability	25/50/20
Missouri	Liability, UM	25/50/10			

Note: Minimum liability limits are per person/per accident for all persons injured/property damage liability limits. Liability = property damage and bodily injury liability; PDL = property damage liability only; BIL = bodily injury liability only; PIP = personal injury protection; UM = uninsured motorists; UIM = underinsured motorists; and FR = financial responsibility law.

Source: Minimum Levels of Required Auto Insurance, *Insure.com.*

have the permission of the owner (subject to a number of exclusions, several of which we note below). The policy also covers liability of any person using the insured's covered auto(s), again with a reasonable belief that they have permission to do so. Covered autos are defined to include vehicles specifically listed in the policy, newly acquired vehicles, trailers owned by the insured, and temporary substitute autos, such as an auto used while a listed auto is being repaired.

Thus, you are insured under your personal auto policy for use of any auto with the permission of the owner, and people whom you permit to use your covered auto(s) also are insured under your policy. In addition, if you borrow another person's car with permission, you will be covered under the car owner's personal auto policy, if any, and if you lend your car to someone else, the driver will be covered under his or her own policy, if any. If a person is covered under more than one policy, the general rule (there are exceptions) is that insurance on a covered auto is primary and other coverage is excess. For example, if you borrow your friend's car, your friend's insurance is primary and yours is excess.[1]

Liability coverage under the personal auto policy contains many exclusions. Several of the major ones include (but are not limited to): (1) intentional injury or damage; (2) losses to property owned by, transported by, rented to, or in the insured's care, which often are covered under homeowners insurance; (3) bodily injury to an employee covered by workers' compensation; (4) coverage for a vehicle that is being hired out to the general public, such as using your car as a taxi; (5) certain types of business vehicles, for example, those used in the automobile business and large trucks; (6) vehicles used without a reasonable belief that the owner has given permission; and (7) vehicles with less than four wheels, such as motorcycles, which generally can be covered by adding an endorsement to the policy. Note that business use of an auto by an insured person is covered unless subject to a specific exclusion.

Medical Payments Coverage

By purchasing optional first-party **auto medical payments coverage,** the auto owner can receive payment for medical expenses arising out of an accident. Coverage is for medical expenses for the named insured and family members hurt in any auto and other persons that are hurt while occupying a covered auto. Coverage limits generally are comparatively low, such as $1,000 to $10,000 per injured person, with many persons purchasing amounts in the $1,000 to $2,500 range. In part this reflects that many persons have individual or group medical insurance that pays much of the cost of medical expenses associated with auto accidents. Payments under auto medical payments coverage are not contingent on fault and generally are not coordinated with other medical insurance that the person may have. Thus, the insured usually can recover from both policies. Exclusions to auto medical payments coverage are largely similar to those for liability coverage.

In states with no-fault or related laws, the personal auto policy includes **personal injury protection coverage** for the named insured, family members, and parties hurt while occupying a covered auto instead of medical payments coverage. In contrast to medical payments coverage, personal injury protection coverage generally provides limited coverage for loss of income in addition to medical expenses. In some states, purchase of personal injury protection coverage is optional. Other states make purchase compulsory with benefit amounts specified by law (see Table 13.2), in contrast to optional medical payments coverage. States with no-fault laws also limit tort liability. You will learn more about personal injury protection coverage and no-fault laws in section 13.4.

Uninsured and Underinsured Motorists Coverage

If an insured person is legally entitled to recover damages from the owner or operator of a motor vehicle who has not purchased auto liability insurance, whose insurer is insolvent or denies coverage, or who is a hit-and-run driver, **uninsured motorists coverage** allows the insured to recover damages *from his or her own insurer* up to the policy limit. Coverage for

---

[1]The policy also covers the liability of any other person or organization arising out of an insured person's use of a covered auto (or other auto not owned by this other person or organization) on behalf of the person or organization. For example, if you used your car for your employer, your employer would be protected under your policy (and have excess coverage under its own policy).

bodily injury includes all amounts that the insured presumably would have been able to recover if the driver had collectible liability insurance, including medical expenses, loss of income, and pain and suffering. Insured persons include the named insured and resident family members, any other person occupying a covered auto, and any person legally entitled to recover damages, such as surviving dependents of an insured person that is killed.

While uninsured motorists coverage is first-party coverage between the insurer and the insured, roughly half of insured persons with uninsured motorists claims hire an attorney to negotiate settlements with their insurers. Disagreements are subject to arbitration, but the result is not binding; that is, the parties can continue to litigate if the award exceeds the minimum policy limits under the state's compulsory liability/financial responsibility laws. Some exclusions to uninsured motorists coverage are similar to those for liability coverage (for example, using a vehicle without a reasonable belief of permission), while others are unique.

A related type of coverage that is available as an option in the personal auto policy is **underinsured motorists coverage.** As is true for uninsured motorists coverage, underinsured motorists coverage allows an insured person to recover damages from his or her own insurer that in principle could have been obtained from an insured, at-fault driver, including damages for pain and suffering. The difference is that underinsured motorists coverage applies when the at-fault driver has liability insurance with limits that are less than the insured's underinsured motorists limits. The maximum amount payable under underinsured motorists coverage is the difference between the underinsured motorists coverage limit and the at-fault driver's liability insurance limit.

Assume, for example, that you purchased underinsured motorists coverage with split bodily injury limits of $50,000 per person/$100,000 per accident and were harmed by a negligent driver with liability limits of $25,000 per person/$50,000 per accident. If your total damages were $75,000, you would recover $25,000 from the driver's liability coverage and $25,000 ($50,000 − $25,000) from your underinsured motorists coverage. Thus, you would need an underinsured motorists coverage limit of $75,000 to have all of your damages covered. An exception arises for people with multiple cars in states that allow "stacking" of uninsured motorists coverage limits, in which case the courts may allow the limits to be multiplied by the number of cars insured under a policy or may add up the limits in separate policies. Because the limits are effectively higher in these situations, stacking increases the costs of uninsured motorists coverage.

Students often have two questions regarding these coverages. First, you might wonder why uninsured motorists coverage exists if all drivers are required to have liability insurance. The answer is simple: As we elaborate later in the chapter, many people break the law and drive without required liability insurance. The second question is: Why is there separate coverage for uninsured and underinsured motorists instead of having combined coverage that, along with the at-fault driver's liability coverage (if any), would provide the policyholder with a specified level of protection (such as $100,000 per person/$300,000 per accident)? Note that if the coverages were combined, then purchasing coverage equal to the state's basic liability limits would be equivalent to having uninsured motorists coverage equal to these limits and no underinsured motorists coverage.

The economic rationale for separating the two coverages is not obvious. As a practical matter, uninsured motorists coverage was developed first. Underinsured coverage then was added as an option later, which may have been simpler than doing away with the existing uninsured motorists coverage and substituting new, combined coverage. It also might be easier to explain separate coverages in a way that most people can understand.

In any case, many states mandate the purchase of a minimum amount of *uninsured motorists* coverage equal to the minimum amount of liability coverage specified by the state's compulsory liability/financial responsibility law (see Table 13.2). Coverage for property damage caused by uninsured motorists varies widely among the states. Some states mandate property damage coverage under uninsured motorists coverage; others make it optional, sometimes by automatically including property damage coverage with bodily injury coverage unless the insured rejects coverage in writing. The purchase of *underinsured motorists* coverage usually is not mandatory. However, some states encourage people to buy both uninsured and underinsured motorists coverage limits equal to their liability insurance limits by requiring insurers to provide equal limits automatically unless the insured signs a form rejecting higher limits.

One interesting feature of uninsured and underinsured motorists coverage is that they provide first-party compensation for pain and suffering. We are aware of no other first-party insurance that does this. This coverage of pain and suffering does not necessarily imply that many or most people who buy these coverages are revealing a desire to insure pain and suffering losses. You just learned that purchase of these coverages often is either required or encouraged by law, and state law requires that both uninsured and underinsured motorists coverage include coverage for pain and suffering. Thus, the purchase of pain and suffering compensation through uninsured and underinsured motorists coverage may in part reflect the interests of politically influential groups that might benefit from such coverage, such as attorneys who represent policyholders seeking recovery under these coverages.

Damage and Other Losses to Autos

The personal auto policy provides two optional coverages for damage and theft to vehicles: **collision coverage** and **other-than-collision coverage.** These coverages apply to autos listed in the policy and newly acquired autos if requested by the owner within 30 days. Nonowned autos, such as an auto that you have permission to use but do not own or use on a regular basis, including a temporary substitute auto, also are covered on an excess basis over the owner's insurance. Coverage of nonowned autos includes car rentals, at least for personal use as car rental firms generally do not automatically provide physical damage coverage (see Box 13.1). Many insurers exclude liability and physical damage coverage for autos rented for business use unless an endorsement to the policy is purchased.

Collision coverage covers the upset (rollover) of a covered auto or impact with another object. Other-than-collision coverage covers theft of the vehicle and damage from "missiles" or falling objects, explosion, earthquake, windstorm, hail, water, flood, vandalism, riot, glass breakage, and contact with a bird or animal. Other-than-collision coverage in auto policies used to be called "comprehensive coverage," and this terminology is still commonly used on an informal basis. One might guess that the newer, awkward name reflects the desire of insurers to avoid litigation from policyholders that might argue that a "comprehensive" policy should pay for everything without exclusion! Exclusions under collision and other-than-collision coverage include but are not limited to damage from wear and tear, freezing, and mechanical breakdown; loss to custom furnishings and equipment; and loss to campers or trailers not listed in the policy unless newly acquired and the damage occurs within 30 days of acquisition; as well as several exclusions similar to those under liability coverage.

Losses under these coverages are covered above a deductible. The size of the deductible may differ between the coverages. Losses are paid on a repair cost basis up to the actual

So you just landed for your dream vacation and are picking up your rental car. How is the insurance handled? In most states, car rental companies provide liability insurance limits equal to the minimum required by the state with the cost built into the daily rental fee. If your personal policy has higher limits, it generally will serve as excess coverage. Alternatively, you can shell out a daily fee to get higher limits from the car rental company. In a few states car rental firms provide excess coverage over your policy if you pay a daily fee. In at least one state (California), they provide no liability coverage without a fee. If you do not have an auto and personal auto liability coverage, you may then need to pay for the coverage from the rental company to comply with the state's compulsory insurance and financial responsibility laws.

With respect to physical damage and theft coverage, your personal auto coverages (if you have them) generally will cover a rental, but it's a good idea to check with your agent to make sure that you have coverage. Losses will be paid above any deductible. Some people (about one out of five renters) nonetheless decide to shell out $7 to $25 a day to buy collision coverage available from the car rental company. While this coverage is comparatively expensive, there is no deductible, and it substantially eliminates the likelihood that a rental agent will discover a slight scratch or crack in the windshield when you return the car, thus requiring you to fill out papers and perhaps miss your flight home. Some credit cards provide cardholders with automatic collision coverage for car rentals up to a specified limit.

As noted in the text, some personal auto insurers no longer provide liability or collision coverage for rentals used for business purposes unless the insured purchases an endorsement to coverage. (Some employers have contracts with rental companies to provide coverage.) You also should be aware that the personal auto policy only provides coverage for the United States, its territories and possessions, Puerto Rico, and Canada. Thus, if you vacation in Mexico or England you will not be covered for any car rental (or if you take your own car). You will be offered and sometimes required to buy medical coverage, physical damage coverage, and theft coverage from the rental company (although again some credit card companies offer collision coverage for foreign travel that might be accepted by the rental company). If you cannot afford the coverage or cannot stand the thought of buying the required coverage, you probably should either take the train or vacation in areas where your personal auto policy provides coverage. Finally, if you take your own car to Mexico, some people suggest that it is a good idea to obtain liability coverage from a Mexican insurer in order to be protected against loss and to avoid potential hassle by the police if you are involved in an accident.

cash value of the vehicle for a total loss. There also is limited coverage of additional transportation expenses until a vehicle is repaired or a new auto is obtained. The insurer has the option to declare the auto a total loss and pay the actual cash value. In this case, the insurer has the right to take the vehicle; that is, it has the right of *salvage.* While this sometimes annoys people, it helps lower premiums, and the insurer usually has a comparative advantage in disposing of the auto, selling parts, and so on, compared to most policyholders. (We know this to be true in our case.)

Whether the loss is total or partial, if a dispute arises concerning the amount of settlement, the policy includes an appraisal provision, which allows either party to demand an appraisal. Each party then selects and pays an appraiser, and these two appraisers select and split the cost of an umpire. If the appraisers do not agree, the difference is submitted to the umpire, who decides which party to agree with or works out an agreeable compromise, thus determining the settlement. The appraisal provision reduces litigation but, in a few cases, policyholders still may sue the insurer, alleging bias or fraud by the umpire.

13.2   Auto Insurance Pricing and Underwriting

The pricing and the underwriting of automobile insurance have long been a source of controversy to many consumers, regulators, and insurers. During the 1980s and early 1990s the average price of auto insurance nationally grew much faster than the overall rate of inflation, as is illustrated using the auto insurance and overall consumer price in Figure 13.1. The auto insurance CPI increased 206 percent during 1981–1997, an average annual (geometric) percentage increase of 6.8 percent. The overall CPI increased by 95 percent during this period, an average annual increase of 4 percent. During 1998–2001, the average increase for auto insurance was very low, but it picked up again in 2001. Preliminary estimates indicate a 9–10 percent growth in the auto insurance CPI for 2002.

The average premium per car insured varies widely across states and drivers. Table 13.3 and Figure 13.2 illustrate the variation across states in combined expenditures for auto liability, medical payments/personal injury protection, collision, and comprehensive coverage per vehicle with liability insurance in 1999 (the last year of available data). As you know and as we discuss further below, many drivers, such as young drivers and those who live in higher cost urban areas, face premium rates that are substantially greater than average.

FIGURE 13.1   **Auto insurance and all items consumer price indexes.**

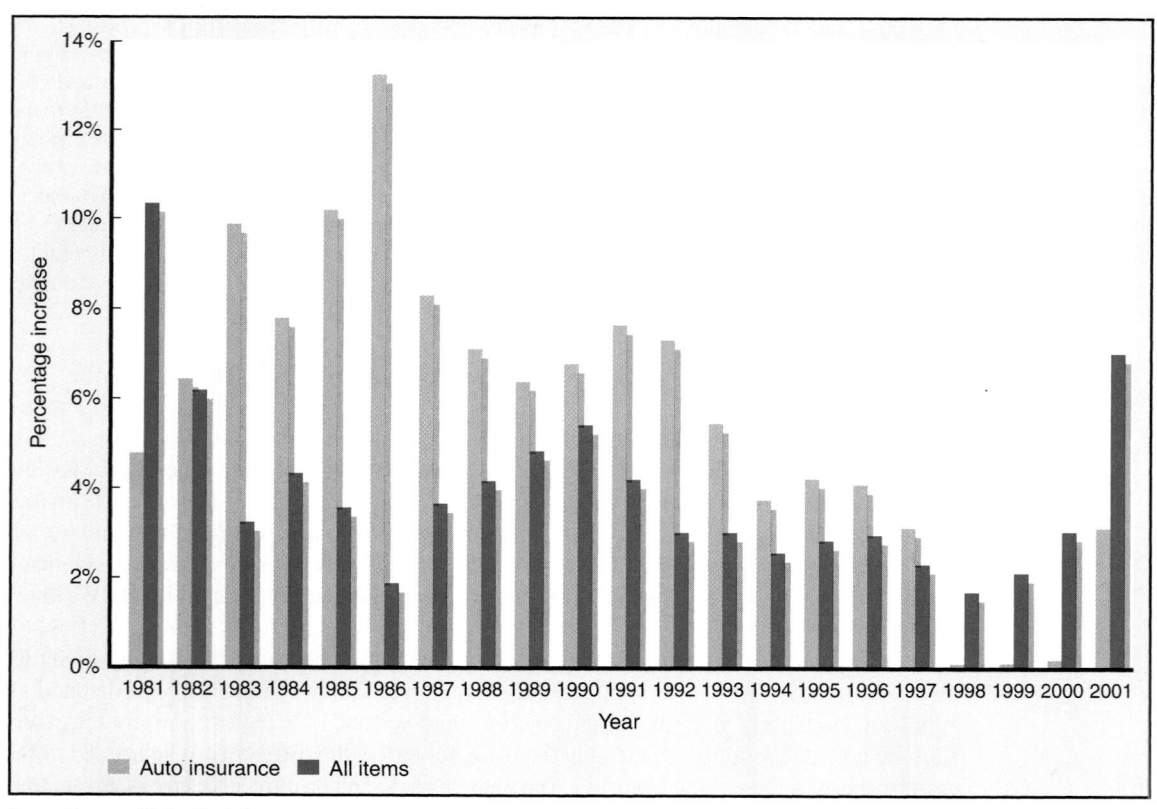

Source: Bureau of Labor Statistics.

TABLE 13.3   Average auto insurance expenditure per vehicle with liability coverage.

State	Average Expenditure per Auto and Rank 1999		Rank*	Average Expenditure	State	Average Expenditure per Auto and Rank 1999		Rank*	Average Expenditure
Alabama	$578	33	34	$704.99	Montana	$ 479	44	40	$653.11
Alaska	751	16	10	$896.23	Nebraska	475	45	44	$636.19
Arizona	785	12	11	$876.12	Nevada	803	9	7	$938.97
Arkansas	558	34	28	$721.15	New Hampshire	621	26	26	$737.57
California	791	11	23	$773.26	New Jersey	1,099	1	1	$1,200.40
Colorado	751	15	12	$866.85	New Mexico	660	22	16	$816.64
Connecticut	899	5	9	$927.89	New York	960	3	3	$1,107.96
Delaware	806	8	8	$936.79	North Carolina	518	41	39	$656.95
DC	993	2	2	$1,139.58	North Dakota	402	51	49	$595.94
Florida	783	13	19	$800.90	Ohio	553	36	41	$646.34
Georgia	627	25	18	$804.85	Oklahoma	545	39	31	$712.84
Hawaii	959	4	13	$857.43	Oregon	585	30	33	$705.32
Idaho	465	47	48	$596.81	Pennsylvania	687	19	21	$781.93
Illinois	638	24	30	$713.79	Rhode Island	870	6	4	$981.24
Indiana	548	38	38	$659.99	South Carolina	602	28	35	$692.36
Iowa	445	50	51	$543.44	South Dakota	448	49	46	$617.84
Kansas	495	43	37	$671.34	Tennessee	557	35	36	$675.53
Kentucky	581	31	27	$731.22	Texas	726	17	22	$778.01
Louisiana	802	10	6	$944.40	Utah	581	32	29	$716.31
Maine	470	46	50	$591.40	Vermont	514	42	43	$640.74
Maryland	759	14	15	$830.33	Virginia	550	37	45	$634.92
Massachusetts	833	7	5	$976.32	Washington	666	21	20	$784.56
Michigan	697	18	14	$837.46	West Virginia	671	20	17	$813.81
Minnesota	654	23	25	$752.57	Wisconsin	533	40	47	$604.82
Mississippi	604	27	24	$763.86	Wyoming	452	48	42	$642.24
Missouri	599	29	32	$706.67	Total US	685			$783.14

Note: Average expenditure includes premiums for liability, medical payments/personal injury protection, collision, and comprehensive coverage.
Sources: National Association of Insurance Commissioners, as reported by *Insure.com*.

You learned about the basic economics of insurance pricing in Chapter 8. The key idea is that there are strong incentives for insurers to base prices on the discounted expected costs of providing coverage, where costs include expected claim costs, administrative costs, and the cost of holding capital to increase the likelihood that the insurer will have sufficient funds to pay claims. In this section you will learn about the major rating factors used in personal auto insurance pricing, about auto insurance underwriting, and about government regulation that affects auto insurance pricing and underwriting.

Rating Factors

Auto insurance rates charged to different consumers reflect differences in the discounted expected costs of providing coverage. In order to classify different persons into homogeneous groups with respect to expected claim costs, insurers generally use rate classification

FIGURE 13.2 Average auto insurance expenditures by state in 1999.

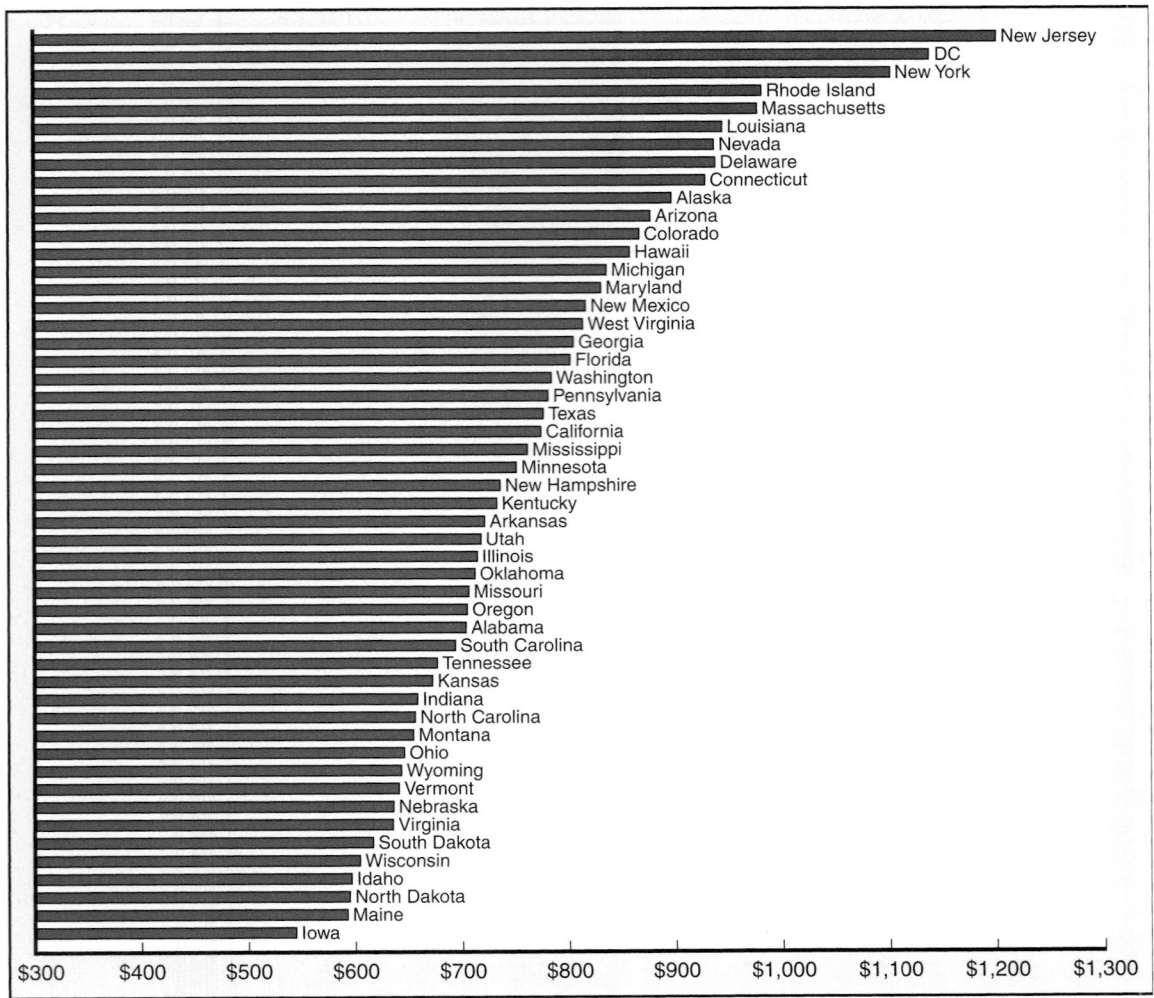

Source: National Association of Insurance Commissioners, as reported by *Insure.com.*

systems that include (1) driver classes that reflect the characteristics of individual insureds, and (2) **territorial rating** to reflect expected differences in claim costs for people who live in different geographical areas (holding individual characteristics constant). Of course, physical damage rates also depend on the value and type of vehicle. Liability insurance rates sometimes also depend on the type of vehicle, given evidence that certain vehicles, such as red cars (not really) and high performance cars, are more likely to be involved in at-fault accidents. We will briefly explain the major factors considered in establishing driver classes and the use of territorial rating factors.

Driver Classes

Insurers generally assign an applicant to a driver class based on a number of primary characteristics, including the person's (or household's) driving record. Major factors that commonly are used besides driving record are summarized first before turning to the use of driving record.

• Age: Other factors held constant, claim costs generally are higher for persons up to approximately age 30 than for older drivers. There also is evidence that people aged about 55–65 have lower claim costs than people aged 30–55 but that average claim costs are higher at advanced ages. Thus, other things being equal, rates generally start out high for young drivers, decline with age until approximately age 30, and then level off. Many insurers then provide discounts for older drivers until they reach an advanced age, at which point some insurers charge a higher rate than for drivers aged 30–55.

• Gender: Young males (up to approximately age 30) have higher average claim costs than young females and thus generally pay higher rates than females at these ages.

• Marital status: Up to age 25–30, married males and females generally have lower average claim costs (per vehicle) than unmarried males and females. As a result, many insurers offer a discount to young married persons.

• Use of the automobile: Average claim costs vary according to whether vehicles are driven to work or are used for business or farm work. A typical rating plan will have higher rates for autos driven to work than for those that are not. It is common to have two classes for cars driven to work based on approximate commuting mileage. For example, an insurer might have one rate for autos driven to work less than 20 miles per day (e.g., 10 miles one way) and a higher rate for autos driven more than this amount. Autos customarily used for business will pay a higher rate due to higher expected claims costs; automobiles primarily used on farms typically have lower costs and thus are charged a lower rate.

• Number of automobiles and accompanying homeowners coverage: Many insurers provide a multiple car discount to reflect possibly lower expected claim costs per auto in multiple car households and, more importantly, savings in administration costs. Some insurers also provide a discount if the person buys both auto and homeowners coverage from the same insurer to reflect reduced administrative expense loadings that are possible in these cases.

• Miscellaneous factors: Many companies (sometimes due to state law requirements) include discounts for youthful drivers who have completed an approved driver education program and for good students. There is evidence that driver education helps reduce accident costs for young drivers, at least during the first year or two following completion of the course. The evidence that good students have lower claim costs is somewhat weaker (although "bookworms" may study more and drive less). Some factors of this sort might be used to help an insurer target and keep customers with high renewal rates and opportunities for selling multiple types of coverage (see below).

Driving Record

Another very important factor that affects rates is the driving record of insured persons in the household. Students often want to know whether their rates will increase if they have had an accident or traffic violation. Because practices vary across insurers (and across states in large part due to differences in regulation), instructors often cannot give a precise answer. However, your agent/insurer will know and can provide you with the rules that apply to you. The theory is simple: In principle, rate increases for past accidents and traffic violations will reflect the predicted effect on expected costs during the next policy period. That is, if past accident involvement or tickets affect predicted claim costs, rates will be adjusted to reflect the effect of this information.

In practice and unless constrained by regulation, accidents that produce a specified minimum amount of damage often will lead to a percentage rate increase under traditional experience rating systems due to the loss of a "safe driver" discount. Additional accidents and/or certain types of violations can produce additional charges as the person accumulates accident and violation "points" and associated surcharges. At-fault accidents generally will lead to some rate increase for a negligent driver. Accidents between two people where neither party is at fault often produce rate increases for both people given evidence that these accidents are associated with higher accident frequency in the future. Accidents between an at-fault party and a party that is not at fault sometimes will not produce a rate increase, or only a small increase, for the party that is not at fault. You might ask: Why should my rate go up if I'm not at fault? The answer is that evidence often suggests that persons involved in accidents that are not at fault nonetheless are more likely to have subsequent accidents. Insurers that ignore this information in order to be fair will face adverse selection. Many insurers will not increase rates if an insured's car is damaged while parked. Similarly, other-than-collision claims often do not produce rate increases.

As discussed in Chapter 8, many non-US auto insurers and a growing number of US companies use bonus-malus (no claims discount systems) that provide increasing percentage discounts based on the number of years without a claim, up to some maximum discount. Whether those systems will become the norm in the United States is uncertain, in part because of regulation of rates and experience ratings in many states.

Recall again the key idea that insurers have strong incentives to use information as long as it helps predict costs. Sometimes the results do not seem fair to people who have their rates go up. In these situations, they might shop around to see whether another insurer provides a better deal. Some states have detailed regulations governing surcharges for accidents and violations. In a few states, the government specifies what insurers must do. In these cases, when people get upset and blame their insurer, at least part of the blame may be misplaced.

Territorial Rating

Other things being equal, claim costs vary significantly across states and areas within states. In general, large cities have the highest average claim costs, followed by suburban areas, smaller cities, and small towns or rural areas. Figure 13.3 illustrates these differences using data on liability claim frequency in a number of large cities compared to claim frequency in the remainder of the state in which each city is located.

Insurers develop rating territories to reflect these differences. Buyers pay a rate that is based on where they live (where the vehicle is garaged). An exception often is made for college students who take a car to school while temporarily residing at a different location. In this case, the car usually is rated based on the student's permanent residence (i.e., where mom and/or dad live). Unless constrained by regulation, different insurers often use different territorial boundaries and have different price differences across territories. This provides additional motivation for buyers to compare prices across insurers.

FIGURE 13.3
Claim costs and coverage territory: Bodily injury liability claim frequency in selected large cities as a percentage of claim frequency in remainder of state (five-year aggregates in the 1980s).

Source: *Factors Affecting Urban Auto Insurance Costs* (Insurance Services Office and National Association of Independent Insurers, 1988).

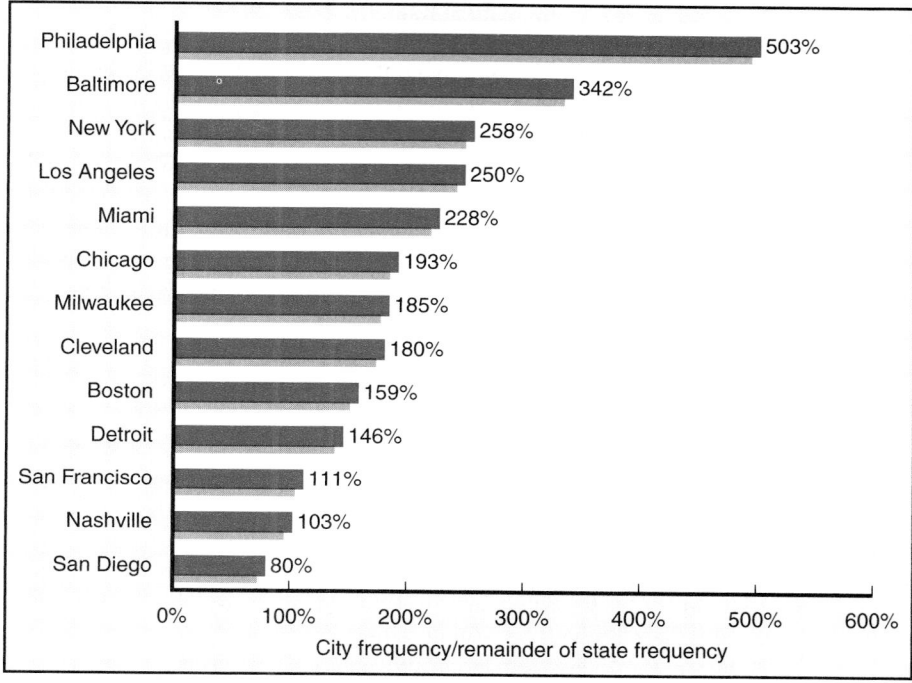

Government Restrictions on Rating Factors

As we discussed briefly in Chapters 6 and 8, some state governments have prohibited the use of certain rating factors in automobile insurance. For example, several states have prohibited the use of gender and/or marital status. At least one state (Massachusetts) has prohibited the use of age, substituting years of driving experience. A number of states have restricted territorial rating, either by mandating the use of certain territories or limiting rate differences that can be charged between adjacent territories. When these restrictions prevent insurers from charging rates commensurate with differences in predicted costs, insurers have a clear incentive to avoid sales to people for whom rates are less than predicted costs. As we discuss more below, this tends to increase the size of the state's auto insurance residual market. In some cases, insurers may at least in part be able to work around these restrictions by target marketing to particular types of drivers or territories. You learned about possible behavioral effects of restrictions that could increase the cost of risk and fairness issues associated with restrictions in Chapter 8.

Underwriting

An insurer's rating plan produces different rates for numerous driver classes and territories. These plans are complex and produce a large number of rating classes, each with a distinct rate. For example, ignoring differences associated with the type and value of an auto, an insurer in a large state might have 300–400 driver classes and 30–40 territories. Assuming 300 driver classes and 30 territories would produce 9,000 (300 × 30) driver class/territory combinations.

However, this complexity in rating classes is not the end of the story. Most states do not require insurers to offer coverage to all applicants. Insurers establish **underwriting criteria** that determine whether a given applicant will be sold coverage. An insurer's rates depend on these criteria. The underwriting criteria might be designed to reflect information about the applicant that is not included in the insurer's rating plan, but which is related to expected claim costs and administrative costs. For example, an insurer without a bonus-malus system might nonetheless consider the number of years that a policyholder or prospective policyholder has been claim free. Similarly, the criteria might relate to the expected length of time that the person will be likely to renew coverage, which determines how long the insurer will have on average to recover up-front underwriting and policy issue costs that are not fully recovered in the first period's premium. Moreover, the criteria might be designed to attract customers that will be likely to buy multiple types of insurance from the insurer, thus allowing the company to spread certain types of fixed underwriting and distribution costs across a larger policy base.

In general, insurers with more "stringent" criteria for coverage sell policies to people who have lower expected claim costs and/or require a lower expense loading. Prospective buyers who do not meet the insurer's criteria generally will have higher expected claim costs and/or require a higher expense loading than contemplated in the insurer's rate structure. They therefore may not be eligible to obtain coverage from this particular insurer. However, they almost always will be able to find an auto insurer that does not employ the same criteria and therefore will be willing to insure them at a higher rate that reflects the higher expected costs, unless regulation prevents insurers from charging adequate rates to these buyers. In this way, variation across insurers with respect to underwriting criteria produces variation in rates across insurers for similar driver classes and territories. The result is that policyholders are sorted into more homogeneous groups with respect to expected claim costs and required expense loadings.

A few examples of underwriting criteria might help illustrate this process and its effects. A few auto insurers only offer coverage to people who totally abstain from alcohol. If these people on average have lower expected claim costs than other people, the insurer might be able to attract them with a lower premium and make a nice profit in the bargain (at least until other companies enter the nondrinker market). In addition, teetotalers won't have to subsidize social drinkers. Another insurer may have information that people in certain types of occupations have higher expected claim costs on average. It might then deny coverage to people in these occupations who apply for coverage, charge lower rates to people in other occupations, and again make a nice profit if the insurer's information is accurate and other companies do not quickly adopt similar strategies.

Similarly, substantial evidence suggests that people with poor credit histories (e.g., a bad credit rating or bankruptcy in the past few years) have higher auto insurance claim costs on average than people with good credit histories. People with poor credit histories on average also might require a higher expense loading because of the greater likelihood of nonpayment of premiums and a lower expected renewal frequency. As a result, many insurers now use credit history as an underwriting criterion (or as a rating factor). A few states have placed some restrictions on those practices. As a final example that was suggested earlier, many insurers, including many of the larger direct writers, have designed their marketing strategies and underwriting criteria to attract buyers who are likely to have good loss experience, renew coverage for a long period, and buy multiple policies.

Should the Government Restrict Underwriting?

Some people get annoyed by insurer underwriting practices and argue that the ability of insurers to underwrite should be heavily restricted by the government.[2] A handful of states have substantially constrained the ability of insurers to underwrite, in some cases by requiring each insurer to accept virtually all applicants. There generally is a close connection between regulatory prohibitions on rating factors and restrictions on underwriting. For example, if the government prohibits the use of a person's gender as a rating factor, then it may need to restrict insurer underwriting. Otherwise, some insurers may readily circumvent the prohibition by offering rates commensurate with the expected cost of insuring young females and then denying coverage to most young males.

When thinking about whether underwriting is socially beneficial, you should keep in mind that if restrictions prevent rates from being closely related to expected costs, they can distort behavior in ways that increase the cost of risk. In addition, we noted above that insurer underwriting practices do not prevent significant numbers of drivers from finding an insurer that is willing to accept them given their cost characteristics. Underwriting does not force large numbers of drivers into the residual market unless price regulation keeps the rate that can be charged below expected costs (see below). In most states that do not substantially restrict underwriting, an active specialty insurance market, known as the **nonstandard insurance market,** exists to serve drivers with characteristics that suggest significantly above-average expected claim and/or administrative costs.

Given the preceding discussion and the discussion in Chapter 8, you also should recognize that the use of underwriting criteria that do not separate buyers into more homogeneous groups would not be rewarded in the marketplace. Instead, the use of criteria that do not predict costs often will cause insurers to lose money due to adverse selection. It also is usually very difficult and costly to enforce constraints on underwriting given strong market incentives for insurers to charge prices commensurate with expected claim costs.

You might be wondering why insurers don't simply develop more rating classes with different prices that reflect their underwriting criteria and then accept all applicants at a price that reflects expected costs. (If you are, you are to be commended because this indicates that you are thinking about what you are reading.) One reason is that a single insurer seldom will have or find it cost-efficient to develop the expertise needed to prosper in all market segments. In other words, there are gains from specialization in different cost segments and underwriting helps achieve specialization. For example, it might not be efficient for an insurer to develop, market, and price to serve customers at all income levels due to income-related differences in the value of cars and homes, the amount of assets at risk from a lawsuit, the need for life insurance, the expected length of time that policies will be renewed, and so on.

In addition, to a certain extent, an insurer's underwriting criteria are proprietary. As a result, if an insurer obtains or develops information that helps it to more accurately classify drivers, it can use the information to establish underwriting criteria and thereby benefit its customers and make money without having its competitors immediately catch on. In contrast, rating plans almost always are filed with regulators and are therefore public informa-

---

[2]Recall also from Chapter 8 that theory suggests the possibility that insurers may engage in excessive risk classification (and thus underwriting) in some instances.

tion. Thus, rating plans can be quickly copied by competitors. If insurers had to announce all of their new ideas and analysis to the world, they would have less profit potential from investing resources to develop more accurate classifications. This would reduce their incentive to develop more accurate rating/underwriting systems that reduce cross-subsidies among buyers.

Cancellation and Nonrenewal

Insurers usually give agents authority to issue policies (or "bind" coverage) before underwriting is completed. If additional investigation discovers new information indicating that the applicant does not meet the insurer's underwriting criteria, the insurer may be able to cancel the policy. This most commonly occurs when the applicant has failed to provide full and accurate information on the application for coverage. Similarly, events may occur during the coverage period, such as serious at-fault accidents or traffic violations, that cause the applicant to no longer meet the insurer's criteria. In these cases, the insurer may notify the customer that his or her coverage will not be renewed.

The personal auto policy allows the policyholder to cancel at any time, by giving the insurer advance written notice, and to receive a premium refund specified in the company's rate manual. If the policy has been in force for less than 60 days, the insurer can cancel by providing 10 days written notice for nonpayment of a premium and 20 days notice in other cases. Thus, this contractual provision allows the insurer to issue a policy before fully investigating whether a policyholder is acceptable and then cancel coverage if it is determined that the applicant does not meet its criteria. After 60 days (or after renewal), the policy only allows the insurer to cancel for nonpayment of a premium, suspension or revocation of a driver's license, or material misrepresentation. However, at the end of a policy period (generally six months or in some cases one year), the contract allows the insurer to deny renewal for any reason with 20 days written notice.

Many states have further limited the right of insurers to cancel coverage within a policy period. For example, cancellation within 60 days of issue also may be restricted to nonpayment of a premium, suspension or revocation of the owner's driver's license, or material misrepresentation or fraud. While much less common than restrictions on cancellation, some states only allow insurers to deny renewal for reasons specified by state law. In a few states, for example, insurers are required to renew coverage unless an owner or other insured is at fault in a serious accident or is convicted of a serious violation (e.g., driving under the influence).

Residual Markets

All states have automobile insurance residual markets that enable drivers who might otherwise find it difficult to obtain coverage to obtain coverage at a regulated price. As is illustrated in Figure 13.4, the share of personal autos covered by liability insurance that is insured in the residual market varies widely across states. A large majority of states have very small residual markets. In 1999, for example, the residual market for auto liability coverage insured less than 1 percent of insured cars in 42 states. On the other hand, a handful of states have large residual markets.

The most important factor that explains differences in residual market share across states is regulation of prices and underwriting that prevents insurers from charging rates high

**FIGURE
13.4**
**States with
auto liability
insurance
residual
market shares
of at least 0.5
percent in
1999.**

Source: Automobile
Insurance Plans
Service Office,
AIPSOFACTS
2001/2002. Data not
reported for Texas.

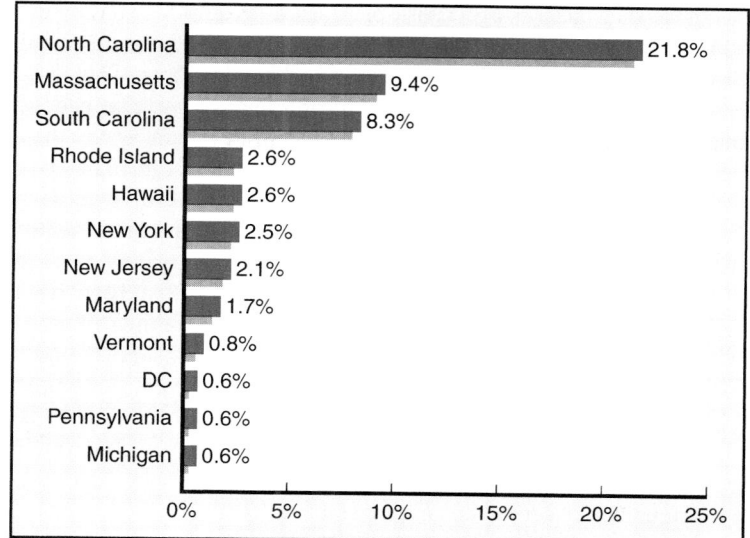

enough to cover expected costs for some drivers. States with large residual markets restrict insurer rate classification (i.e., driver classes or territories) and/or in effect set a maximum permissible rate that is inadequate for insurers to cover their costs of insuring many drivers voluntarily. One method of limiting maximum rates is simply to establish residual market rates below expected costs for some drivers, which then in effect prevents insurers from charging higher rates to many of these drivers.

Another factor that can cause a state's residual market to become larger is prior approval regulation of rate changes. About half the states have prior approval regulation for auto insurance. If regulators in these states do not approve rate increases commensurate with growth in expected claim costs, insurers will be less willing to take on new customers and more likely to deny renewal to some existing customers. Regulatory restrictions on rate increases are especially likely when costs are growing rapidly because of political pressure exerted by consumers against large rate increases. If cost growth slows and regulators are more willing to approve higher rates, the residual market will tend to decline in size, as insurers become more willing to write coverage voluntarily. Thus, to some extent, prior approval regulation will have temporary effects on residual market size. Restrictions on rate classification and maximum prices that can be charged to some consumers have a more permanent effect on residual market size.

There are four types of auto insurance residual markets. The common features are (1) guaranteed access to coverage at a regulated rate, and (2) any residual market deficit (excess of losses and expenses over premiums) is spread broadly across auto insurers and/or auto insurance policyholders.

Over 40 states use an **assigned risk plan.** (These plans are officially called "automobile insurance plans." We use the traditional name because it conveys useful information about how these plans work.) Applicants who have difficulty obtaining coverage can apply (using an agent) to the state's assigned risk plan, which is administered by insurers. The plan assigns applicants to individual insurers at rates that have been approved by regulators. Assignments are made in proportion to an insurer's total volume of auto insurance that it writes voluntarily in the state. For example, an insurer that writes 10 percent of the total voluntary business will get 10 percent of the assignments. The insurer issues the assigned policy, receives the premium, and is responsible for paying claims. Assigned risk plan rates in most states are significantly higher than rates charged by the leading voluntary insurers.

A few states with large residual markets use a **reinsurance facility** instead of an assigned risk plan. Under this approach, *each insurer is required to issue coverage to virtually anyone who applies to the insurer* using rates that have been approved by the government. Thus, underwriting is prohibited. Insurers are then allowed to reinsure policies for which they believe the rates are too low in a state reinsurance pool, known as the reinsurance facility. Because the rates are too low on business that is reinsured, the facility chronically loses money. Two different approaches have been used to deal with reinsurance facility deficits: (1) charge the deficit to all insurers in proportion to their total share of business that is not reinsured, and (2) charge the deficit directly to all insured drivers in the form of a recoupment fee set by the government.[3]

Another type of residual market used in several states is a **joint underwriting association.** In this system, agents can submit applications to a number of insurers under contract with the state to issue residual market policies. These insurers receive fees with the net financial results (usually a deficit) for the residual market divided among all auto insurers in the state in proportion to their share of the voluntary auto insurance market. Maryland uses a **state insurer** as the residual market, with any deficits of its state insurer divided among auto insurers in proportion to their share of the voluntary auto insurance market.

Because large residual markets are caused by rate inadequacy, large residual markets produce large operating deficits. With a reinsurance facility and recoupment fees, other drivers directly subsidize the residual market deficit. In other cases, policyholders insured in the voluntary market also usually end up paying higher rates to subsidize the residual market. In fact, rates must eventually go up for the voluntary market if insurers are to cover their total expected costs of providing coverage. (We will explain the effects of expected residual market deficits on voluntary market prices in some detail when we discuss workers' compensation insurance residual markets in Chapter 18.) Thus, large residual markets and deficits produce a system of cross-subsidies where some policyholders are in essence taxed through higher charges to offset, at least in part, inadequate residual market rates.

Concept Checks

1. Distinguish the use of underwriting criteria from the use of rating factors by insurers.

2. Can auto insurers underwrite in states that have assigned risk plans? In states with reinsurance facilities? In states with joint underwriting associations?

---

[3]Recoupment fees were used, for example, in South Carolina, the state with the largest residual market until it reformed its insurance system in the late 1990s. While the fee for a given insured did not depend on whether his or her policy had been reinsured in the facility, it did depend on the person's driving record, with hefty charges for a poor record (e.g., about $1,000 over three years for one ticket for speeding more than 10 miles per hour over the limit). This system substantially annoyed a majority of drivers and was phased out, along with elimination of most of the restrictions on underwriting and rating that led to a large residual market.

13.3   Should Auto Insurance Be Compulsory?

Many people fail to buy auto liability insurance voluntarily. Many other drivers are uninsured for medical expenses/loss of income that could result from an accident. To some extent, this lack of coverage might simply reflect that some people might not have the money to pay for insurance, or that they possibly might underestimate the risk of loss so that insurance looks like a bad deal (see Chapter 9). But a major reason people fail to buy these coverages is that part or most of the costs of accidents will fall on other parties. For example, a driver with few assets is essentially judgment proof and thus has limited economic incentive to buy auto liability coverage. Similarly, if an uninsured person will receive medical care if injured in an automobile accident with the costs paid by other parties, the person will have much less incentive to buy insurance.

Economic arguments for compulsory insurance laws in these cases focus on the possibility that compulsory insurance can reduce the cost of risk by getting people to consider more of the costs of their actions when deciding whether to drive, what kind of car to buy, how safely to drive, and so on. However, many observers have criticized compulsory insurance laws in theory and in practice on a number of dimensions. We will first briefly review the economic rationale for compulsory insurance and then turn to some of these criticisms. We also will point out the effects of the laws on the revenues and costs of various parties and briefly introduce you to the issue of whether these laws are fair.

Economic Rationale

Effect on Decisions to Drive

We begin by ignoring the issue of how safely people might drive if they are not insured for liability or their own economic losses and instead focus exclusively on the effects of compulsory insurance on the decision to drive. The key idea is as follows: Without compulsory insurance, some people will drive even though the full costs that arise when they drive exceed their benefits from driving. Compulsory insurance will make some of these people give up driving, thus reducing the cost of risk.

Assume for example that the cost to Jack of having a car and driving compared to relying on alternative transportation is $150 per month. This amount includes the cost of the car, gas, and the expected costs of uninsured accidents that would be borne by Jack or any insurance that Jack has purchased against these losses. Also assume that the expected cost of harm to others when Jack drives without auto liability and medical coverage is $50 per month. This would include the expected damage to others from Jack's negligence and any expected medical expenses for Jack that would be borne by other parties. Thus, the total expected costs when Jack drives are $200 per month.

If Jack places a value on driving (compared to not driving) of at least $200, then the benefits of driving to Jack outweigh the total costs. However, if Jack only values driving at $175, then the total costs on all parties exceed the benefits to Jack by $25 ($200 − $175). But Jack will nonetheless drive (unless forced to buy insurance) because his benefits exceed the costs borne by him. In this case the cost of risk is not minimized when Jack drives, because the cost of driving ($200) exceeds the benefit of driving ($175).

Assume now for simplicity that Jack can buy auto liability and medical insurance coverage at a premium equal to the expected cost ($50). If a compulsory insurance law forces

Jack to buy this coverage if he drives, then he will face a total cost of driving (including premiums) of $200. With the compulsory insurance law, Jack's benefits from driving ($175) are less than Jack's costs ($200). Therefore, in principle, he will give up driving. In this way, compulsory insurance reduces the cost of risk by getting people not to drive unless they value driving by an amount more than the costs associated with their driving.

We will call this argument for compulsory insurance the "pay or take the bus" rationale. You either pay for coverage and drive, or you give up driving and take the bus, walk, and so on. We think that this type of argument represents one reason that economists often puzzle people. Our guess is that if 10,000 randomly chosen adults were asked why auto liability insurance is compulsory, only a handful would say that it is important to have people give up driving who do not value driving more than the total costs. Many people might strongly support "getting uninsured drivers off the road," but this really is not the same point.

We conclude this brief discussion of the effect of compulsory insurance on the decision to drive with two observations. First, the fact that an argument seems obscure to many people does not mean it is a poor one. The "pay or take the bus" rationale is sound in principle. Second, if most people in America value driving a lot, then compulsory insurance will cause comparatively few people to give up driving: Most people will pay rather than take the bus.

Safety Effects

A related rationale for compulsory insurance is that it might encourage people to drive more safely. This too can reduce the cost of risk. For example, a judgment proof driver without liability insurance will often have too little incentive to take precautions to reduce harm to other drivers. Forcing the person to buy auto liability insurance with premiums based on the person's driving record can encourage greater safety.

This argument also is relevant for compulsory auto medical coverage—even for people with group medical coverage. Making drivers buy auto medical coverage with premiums tied to their driving record will provide greater safety incentives than when group insurance is used because the cost of group coverage to the employee is unlikely to depend on the person's driving habits. On the other hand, the lower expense loading and other advantages of group insurance would have to be considered before concluding that the cost of risk could be reduced by making people buy auto medical coverage that would pay for losses up to the limit, with group medical serving as excess coverage. As we discuss in the next section, this issue also arises in the context of auto no-fault laws.

Criticisms and Limitations of Compulsory Insurance

Compulsory auto liability insurance laws have been criticized for a number of reasons and have several limitations in practice. Some of these criticisms and limitations also apply to compulsory auto medical or loss of income coverage.

Regressive Impact on the Distribution of Income/Pressure for Subsidies

To the extent that compulsory insurance laws get people to buy coverage, they tend to shift income from low-income people with few assets to higher-income people with more assets. The reason is simple: Low-income people are the ones most likely to be affected by compulsory insurance laws, and they will be forced to pay more of the costs of losses that previously fell on other people who, on average, have higher incomes and assets. For example, with compulsory liability insurance, previously insured drivers should see some reduction in the cost of uninsured motorists insurance as more low-income drivers pay for liability cov-

Like Ishmael and Queequeg in Melville's *Moby Dick*, opponents of compulsory auto liability laws sometimes make for strange bedfellows. For example, some liberals oppose the laws because they harm many low-income people. The regressive impact of the laws is difficult to reconcile with accepted liberal philosophies of fairness/justice, such as the "maximin" criterion for justice enunciated by John Rawls in his book, *The Theory of Justice*. The maximin criterion holds that differences in wealth across people are fair only if they maximize the welfare of the least well-off people in society. Rawls argues that people would rationally support this criterion if they had to decide on how to organize society without knowing what their talents or circumstances would be—for example, if people had to decide on the rules of the game without knowing anything about whether they would be good at it compared to other people. Some people say that compulsory liability laws are at best very difficult to reconcile with this notion of justice.

On the opposite end of the spectrum, libertarians are not very excited about compulsory liability insurance, either. The late Robert Nozick's classic exposition of libertarian philosophy in his book, *Anarchy, State, and Utopia*, specifically rejects compulsory liability insurance as representing an unjust intrusion of the state on private decisions. The reason is that it forces people to incur large costs just because they *might* behave in a

way that is harmful to others. (We suspect that Nozick might support tough financial responsibility laws that do not force people to pay for expensive coverage before they harm others.)

On the other hand, compulsory auto liability insurance laws might be consistent with what can be called the "Do the Right Thing" argument. (We don't know whether Spike Lee has ever thought about this—or whether you remember him.) The idea is that responsible people will buy liability insurance to make sure that they can pay for at least part of the harm that they may cause others and that it is ethical for people to behave responsibly. This idea has its roots in ancient Greek philosophy and the Old Testament. For example, while silent about insurance companies and trial lawyers, Aristotle's concept of "corrective justice" and the discussion of responsibility for harm in Chapters 20–21 in the book of Exodus both more or less support the idea that people should bear responsibility for the harm that they cause.

The extent to which a majority of people hold "Do the Right Thing" views and whether this materially influences their support for compulsory liability laws is not clear. It is possible that a majority of people support these laws just because they think that they will save money when other people are compelled to buy coverage, regardless of whether this savings actually is achieved to any significant extent in practice.

erage. Similarly, group medical coverage is more prevalent for middle-income and upper-income workers than for low-wage workers or the unemployed. The cost of group coverage might decline if compulsory medical coverage reduces the cost of hospital bad debts that might in part be shifted to group medical expense plans.

Some people are uneasy about whether compulsory coverage is fair given its regressive impact on the distribution of income (see Box 13.2). The regressive effects can be reduced if the cost of coverage is subsidized. This could be achieved, for example, by using price regulation to limit the price of auto coverage in low-income urban areas where the unregulated price would be high. As a practical matter, low-income people who are forced to buy expensive liability coverage also might exert meaningful political pressure for subsidies that outweighs pressure against subsidies, even though low-income people may not generally be known for having substantial political power.

While any rate subsidies in response to compulsory insurance reduce the burden of compulsory insurance on low-income persons, they also reduce the ability of these laws to reduce the cost of risk by making low-income persons bear the costs of their actions. Previously insured drivers might now pay lower premiums for uninsured motorists coverage but have to pay higher premiums for other coverage to finance subsidies to low-income persons. Under these conditions, the effects on different people and the cost of risk can become quite murky. In addition, rate subsidies often lead to other distortions, such as large residual markets and decreased incentives to take care.

Weak Enforcement

While detailed data on uninsured drivers are not available, it is estimated that 15–20 percent of drivers violate compulsory insurance laws nationwide. Allowable penalties for a first-time violation usually include a fine, such as $100–$250, and possible suspension or revocation of the driver's license or vehicle registration, with harsher penalties for subsequent violations. However, the penalty for first-time violators is not mandatory in many states and often is not imposed. Some states have recently increased penalties and improved enforcement. (Several states also have adopted laws that prevent uninsured drivers from suing other drivers for pain and suffering damages.) Nonetheless, some people suggest that relatively weak penalties and enforcement lead to a perverse result: low-income, honest people "pay through the nose" for liability insurance that benefits other people, while low-income, dishonest people break the law.

While weak enforcement reduces the political pressure that arises when low-income people with little wealth are told that they have to buy expensive insurance that benefits other parties in order to drive a car, this argument for weak enforcement comes close to saying that strictly enforced compulsory insurance is not politically viable. This raises the question: Then why bother to have the laws? An answer is that some people will comply with the law, thus helping to reduce the cost of risk. In addition, people who break the law might drive more safely in order to avoid getting caught and having to pay a fine and demonstrate that they have purchased coverage in the future. In this regard, compulsory insurance laws may be like speed limits. They are not very threatening, but they get people to slow down, at least a little.

Alternatives to Compulsory Insurance

It might surprise you that most insurance company trade organizations have traditionally opposed compulsory auto liability insurance. At least in part, this reflects the belief that forcing people to buy products that do not benefit them much will likely lead to other problems, such as efforts by regulators to regulate the price of coverage to make it affordable. Insurers and other opponents of compulsory liability laws often recommend returning to financial responsibility laws with tougher sanctions. People would not have to buy coverage, but if they cause an accident and do not have coverage they will face significant fines and a possible loss of driving privileges.

Instead of compulsory liability insurance, two states (Virginia and South Carolina) require drivers who do not want to buy coverage to pay an annual fee to the state that is less than the cost of liability coverage for some buyers (e.g., $400–$500). The funds are used to reduce the cost of uninsured motorists insurance. At last count almost no one did this in South Carolina, perhaps because they could still be sued, or, in many cases, preferred to take their chances by illegally driving uninsured without paying the fee. The future of compulsory liability coverage appears to be secure (at least for the time being!). A majority of voters appear to support compulsory liability insurance laws (see Box 13.2). Politically powerful trial lawyer groups also generally support the laws.

Concept Check

3. What effect will compulsory auto liability insurance laws have on the demand for personal injury lawyers? (This question is not as easy as it seems if you consider the impact of compulsory liability on the number of uninsured motorist claims.)

13.4   Should Tort Liability Be Limited with No-fault Laws?

No-fault Compared to Tort Liability

Under tort liability systems for auto accidents, drivers who cause accidents can be sued for damages by injured parties under a negligence standard. For the reasons discussed in the previous section, most drivers are required to pay at least part of the costs they impose on others. Under a **pure no-fault** approach to compensating auto accident victims, tort liability for auto accidents would be eliminated. Instead, drivers would bear their own losses. For the same types of reasons given for compulsory liability insurance under a tort system, a no-fault system usually requires drivers to purchase first-party personal injury protection (PIP) insurance that will pay their own losses (or be covered for these losses by other types of health insurance). Without some medical cost and loss-of-income insurance, some drivers could shift the cost of accidents to others in society. Thus, first-party health coverage for losses from auto accidents would be required under a pure no-fault approach, but liability insurance would not be needed because drivers could neither sue nor be sued for damages.

Table 13.4 lists the 24 states as of early 2001 with either compulsory or optional PIP coverage and shows which states limit tort liability. No state has adopted a pure no-fault system.[4] However, during the 1970s, 15 states (Colorado, Connecticut, Florida, Georgia, Hawaii, Kansas, Massachusetts, Michigan, Minnesota, Nevada, New Jersey, New York, North Dakota, Pennsylvania, and Utah) adopted **compulsory no-fault laws** for automobile insurance with two main features. First, the purchase of first-party PIP coverage with specified benefits for medical expenses and loss of income was made compulsory for auto owners. Second, tort liability for bodily injury arising from auto accidents was limited but not eliminated.[5] These laws often are called modified no-fault to contrast them with pure no-fault. We will resist this temptation because we feel that this naming convention conveys little information (compared to "limited" or "partial" or even "half-a-loaf" no-fault) and therefore should itself be "modified."

Kentucky enacted what is appropriately known as a **choice no-fault law** during this period, which allows auto owners to choose whether to buy PIP coverage and limit their tort liability. In addition, several states enacted so-called "add-on laws" that mandated purchase of PIP coverage without limiting tort liability, and several others made insurers offer optional PIP coverage without making people buy it, again without restricting tort liability. Three states (Connecticut, Georgia, and Nevada) subsequently repealed their compulsory no-fault laws, and two states (New Jersey and Pennsylvania) converted to choice no-fault, largely in response to rapid claim cost growth under their compulsory no-fault laws.

[4]Pure no-fault is used in New Zealand.

[5]Most no-fault statutes apply only to personal autos and exclude motorcycles. Only Michigan limits tort liability for property damage.

TABLE 13.4
Personal injury coverage and limits on tort liability.

State	PIP Coverage	Tort Limitation	Threshold
Arkansas	Optional		
Colorado	Compulsory	Yes	Dollar
Delaware	Compulsory		
DC	Optional		
Florida	Compulsory	Yes	Verbal
Hawaii	Compulsory	Yes	Dollar
Kansas	Compulsory	Yes	Dollar
Kentucky	Optional	Choice	Dollar
Maryland	Compulsory		
Massachusetts	Compulsory	Yes	Dollar
Michigan	Compulsory	Yes	Verbal
Minnesota	Compulsory	Yes	Dollar
New Hampshire	Optional		
New Jersey	Optional	Choice	Verbal
New York	Compulsory	Yes	Verbal
North Dakota	Compulsory	Yes	Dollar
Oregon	Compulsory		
Pennsylvania	Optional	Choice	Verbal
South Carolina	Optional		
South Dakota	Optional		
Texas	Optional		
Utah	Compulsory	Yes	Dollar
Virginia	Optional		
Wisconsin	Optional		

Sources: Minimum Levels of Required Auto Insurance, *Insure.com* and Information Institute.

You should note that compulsory no-fault laws are similar to workers' compensation laws in that they specify mandatory insurance benefits for injuries and limit (although in the case of no-fault they do not eliminate) tort liability (see Chapter 18). No-fault laws thus might be viewed as state-mandated covenants among drivers to limit tort liability (the right to sue and be sued) coupled with mandatory first-party insurance. We will now (1) describe PIP coverage and tort limitations, (2) discuss the rationale for and against no-fault, including its possible effects on safety, and (3) explain the effects of no-fault on premiums for auto insurance and group medical insurance. This discussion focuses first on compulsory no-fault; we then discuss choice no-fault and alternative no-fault proposals.

PIP Benefits and Limitations on Tort Liability with Compulsory No-fault

PIP Benefits

The magnitude of required PIP benefits for medical expenses and loss of income varies widely across states with compulsory no-fault laws. For example, the minimum amount of total benefits for medical expenses and loss of income is less than $10,000 in Massachusetts, approximately $50,000 in New York, over $100,000 in Colorado, and unlimited (due to unlimited medical coverage) in Michigan. Like first-party medical payments coverage in states without no-fault laws, drivers and occupants of the vehicle are paid these benefits for injuries without regard to fault, and the policyholder must pay a premium that reflects the cost of providing these benefits. PIP benefits generally are primary and group/individual medical expense coverage is excess.[6] As a result, mandatory PIP benefits produce a reduction in the costs of group/individual medical insurance. (Our later discussion for simplicity focuses on the possible effects on group medical costs.)

Limitations on Tort Liability

Compulsory no-fault laws limit tort liability in two ways. First, an injured party who receives PIP benefits generally cannot sue another driver for losses covered by PIP coverage. Second, and very important, an injured party cannot sue for pain and suffering unless the magnitude of the injury satisfies a **threshold** specified in the no-fault law. Some states (see Table 13.4) specify a "dollar threshold" that requires economic losses (usually medical expenses) to exceed a specified dollar amount. In recent years the dollar thresholds used in different states generally have ranged from $2,000 to $4,000. Other states use a "verbal threshold" that generally eliminates suits for pain and suffering unless there is "significant permanent injury." The ultimate effect of a verbal threshold depends on how its specific wording is interpreted by the state's court system. Michigan's verbal threshold generally is regarded as having the strongest limitation on suits for pain and suffering compared to other states' verbal and dollar thresholds. It has eliminated suits for pain and suffering in a large majority of at-fault accidents.

We emphasize that no real world no-fault law eliminates tort liability. There is no "pure" no-fault, and most laws still allow large numbers of lawsuits. As a result, persons with assets to protect or who wish to comply with state compulsory liability/financial responsibility laws still need to buy auto liability insurance, and it often won't be cheap.

The Rationales for and against No-fault

Does no-fault have the potential to reduce the cost of risk? Academics, legislators, and other parties have debated the pros and cons of no-fault for 35 years. Recent debate has focused on choice no-fault, and a federal choice no-fault bill has periodically been introduced in Congress. The advantages of no-fault primarily relate to its ability to improve compensation compared to the tort liability system. The disadvantages relate to its possible effects on safety. However, the key issue that many consumers focus on is how no-fault will affect the cost of insurance, especially the cost of auto insurance.

More Efficient Compensation with No-fault

In Chapter 12 you learned about a number of disadvantages of the tort liability system when viewed solely as a compensation (insurance) system. Compared to traditional tort liability systems, all no-fault laws to some extent increase compensation for economic loss through first-party insurance and reduce compensation for economic loss and pain and suffering through third-party liability insurance. From the perspective of optimal compensation, this has several advantages:

• The reduction in coverage for pain and suffering is potentially beneficial from the perspective of optimal compensation if consumers generally would not be willing to purchase coverage for pain and suffering voluntarily.

---

[6]Drivers in Michigan can make PIP coverage excess over group or individual medical insurance coverage and receive a premium reduction.

• More economic losses are covered by insurance because, among other reasons, more people will have first-party coverage that pays even when no other driver is at fault.

• Payment for loss generally is faster with PIP coverage than with a tort liability suit.

• There is less duplication of coverage because PIP benefits and group medical benefits are coordinated. With tort liability the injured party's medical insurance does not reduce the person's tort claim for damages (see Chapter 12), and group medical insurers sometimes do not have or exercise the right of subrogation against negligent drivers.

• Dispute resolution costs are lower with no-fault because there are fewer tort liability suits. Bodily injury liability suits almost always involve attorney representation for the injured party, and they often produce significant defense costs for the liability insurer. While some policyholders hire an attorney to represent them when seeking recovery for losses covered by their PIP coverage, a majority of PIP claims are settled without attorney representation for the claimant and without significant dispute resolution costs for insurers.

Effect on Safety and the Decision to Drive

A major argument that has been used against no-fault is that limitations on tort liability will lead to less safety and more accidents. This key idea follows directly from the main rationale for tort liability in the first place: Tort liability often is necessary to get people to consider the expected cost of harm to others when making decisions about risky activities and precautions. In principle, limits on tort liability will cause more costs of driver negligence to fall on other parties, thus reducing incentives not to be negligent. Limits on tort liability also will encourage some people to drive who value driving less than its full cost, including expected harm to others (recall "pay or take the bus").

These predictions hold when tort liability is restricted, other things being equal. But it also is important to consider that other things will not be equal if no-fault is adopted. In particular, under the traditional tort system, many drivers buy only small amounts of medical payments coverage, are covered by group medical insurance, or are basically uninsured for most medical expenses that would arise from an auto accident. Other things being equal, requiring these drivers to buy primary PIP coverage will increase incentives for safety and perhaps encourage some drivers who value driving less than the full cost to give up driving. This is because medical expense/loss-of-income insurance premiums are more closely tied to precautions and the decision to drive under no-fault.[7]

In principle, premiums for PIP coverage will depend on accident involvement, traffic safety violations, and whether the driver was "at-fault" as long as these factors help predict future accident involvement. Thus, reduced safety incentives under experience-rated liability insurance when tort liability is limited will at least in part be offset by improved safety incentives associated with experience-rated PIP coverage. In addition, persons will have to consider the cost of PIP coverage when they decide whether to drive. As a result, the overall effects of no-fault on safety and the decision to drive are uncertain in theory. If no-fault were to reduce safety and increase accidents in practice, the state might be able to increase penalties for traffic violations or even levy fines for at-fault accidents in a way that would limit any adverse effects on safety.

Have no-fault laws affected accident rates? Quite a few studies have examined this issue, mostly by comparing motor vehicle fatality rates between states with and without no-fault

---

[7]Limitations on compensation for pain and suffering also might cause drivers to drive more safely to avoid being injured.

and, less commonly, before and after the adoption of no-fault. The results of these studies do not demonstrate any consistent effect of no-fault. This in part may reflect that tort limitations and PIP benefits under many no-fault laws are modest so that it is hard to estimate their effects on accident rates.

Retribution and Fairness

A common argument against no-fault with strong limitations on tort liability is that it would be unfair to allow a drunk and/or grossly reckless driver not to be sued for causing a severe injury. There are at least two responses to this argument: (1) do not limit tort liability in these specific cases, and/or (2) increase fines and other legal penalties for these cases, which might achieve more punishment/retribution than simply having the person's liability insurance premium go up. However, the more that people like to sue or derive psychological or emotional satisfaction from recovering from another driver's liability insurer, the more advantageous is traditional tort liability compared to no-fault.

How Does No-fault Affect Premiums?

Now, for the issue that some of you have been waiting for: Will no-fault reduce my auto insurance premium? We first discuss the possible effects in principle and then discuss the evidence concerning existing laws. We also address the effects on group medical insurance costs. Our discussion of the theory will not consider possible effects on safety and the decision to drive. Compared to the main effects discussed, these effects generally would be expected to be small.

Effect on Auto Insurance Premiums

The overall effect of a no-fault law on average auto insurance premiums depends on the effects on liability premiums and PIP premiums:

1. Liability insurance premiums will decline for three reasons: (*a*) injured parties who have losses paid by PIP coverage will not be able to sue the at-fault driver for these losses; (*b*) suits for pain and suffering will be reduced by the state's threshold for such suits; and (*c*) auto liability insurers' defense costs will decline accordingly. The greater the amount of PIP benefits and the stronger the state's threshold for pain and suffering suits, the greater will be the reduction in liability insurance premiums.

2. Premiums for PIP coverage increase directly with the magnitude of required benefits. PIP premiums will reflect the expected cost of benefits paid to persons injured by at-fault drivers that previously would have been paid by at-fault drivers' liability insurance. PIP premiums also will reflect the expected cost of losses to persons who are not injured by at-fault drivers with liability insurance and thus who would not be compensated by auto insurance without mandatory PIP coverage (apart from small amounts of auto medical payments coverage that might be purchased voluntarily).

In general, large mandatory PIP benefits with little restriction on lawsuits for pain and suffering will cause average premiums to go up. There is evidence that this occurred in some states that originally adopted no-fault laws with large PIP benefits and low dollar thresholds ($250–$1,000) for pain and suffering suits (e.g., Nevada, New Jersey, and Pennsylvania). In contrast, if the threshold for pain and suffering suits is strong enough, the reduction in liability insurance premiums can exceed the magnitude of required PIP premiums so that total auto premiums will decline.

It is difficult to measure these effects with existing laws. However, simulated analysis of hypothetical PIP benefit amounts and tort thresholds using data on injury losses suggests that material limitations on suits for pain and suffering coupled with moderate PIP benefits could produce total liability and PIP premiums 25–40 percent lower than liability insurance premiums without no-fault (see the Carroll et al. study listed at the end of the chapter). The reason is that reduced payments for pain and suffering and lower dispute resolution costs are more than sufficient to pay PIP benefit costs for persons that are not injured by at-fault drivers and thus who would have received on average little compensation through voluntary auto medical payments coverage.

Figure 13.5 illustrates these effects graphically for laws with low and high thresholds for pain and suffering (P&S) suits. If PIP benefits are less than L, the restriction of pain and suffering suits by the low threshold cuts liability costs enough to produce an average premium for combined liability and PIP coverage that is lower than the average liability premium without no-fault. With the high tort threshold, PIP benefits will produce a lower average combined premium than the average liability premium without no-fault as long as PIP benefits do not exceed H. A stronger threshold might permit even higher PIP benefits before no-fault would increase average premiums.

Effect on Premiums for Group Medical Coverage

The focus of many consumers and much of the political debate about how no-fault affects auto insurance premiums, while perhaps understandable, is a bit shortsighted. To the extent that PIP benefits are primary and group medical benefits are excess, group medical insurance costs will decline as mandatory PIP benefits are increased. Other things being equal, this will allow employers to pay higher wages or reduce employee contributions to group medical insurance costs without increasing the employer's total cost of labor (see Chapter 16). To be sure, this benefit to employees is likely to be much less visible than the effects of no-fault on auto insurance premiums.

As we noted earlier, a possible disadvantage of having PIP coverage primary compared to group medical insurance is that the expense loading for auto PIP coverage sold to indi-

**FIGURE
13.5
Effect of no-
fault on auto
insurance
premiums.**

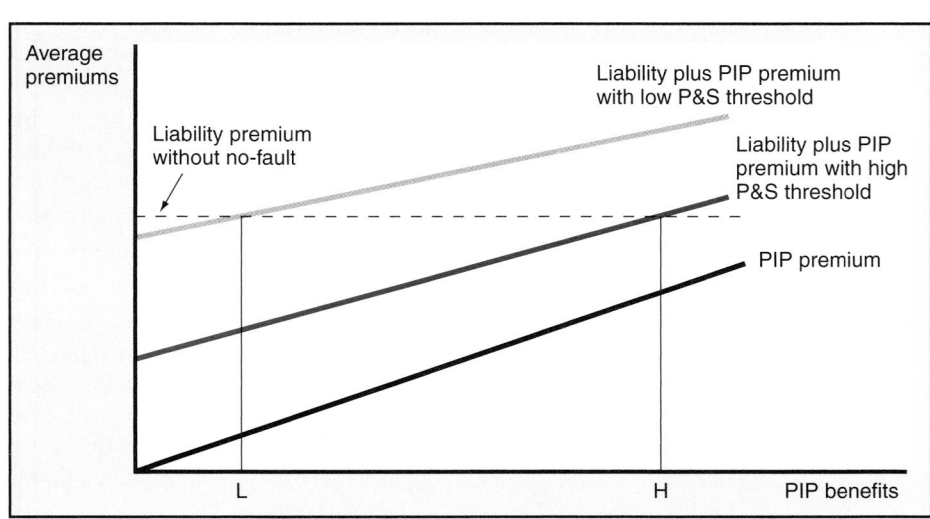

viduals generally is higher than for group insurance (or administrative costs for group self-insurance). In addition, auto PIP premiums are not income-tax deductible, whereas the costs for group coverage usually are not taxed as income to the employee. These factors suggest that it might be advantageous (to people who prefer lower taxes) to make auto PIP coverage excess, as is done in a few states. However, making PIP coverage excess can create administrative problems associated with verifying other insurance and providing a suitable premium reduction for PIP coverage given that the amount of group medical coverage differs across drivers. Moreover, making auto coverage excess will reduce safety incentives by reducing the extent to which premiums for medical/loss-of-income coverage for auto accidents will depend on a person's driving record, and less of the expected costs of accidents will be considered by people when deciding whether to drive.

Choice No-fault

Auto insurance company trade associations historically have supported no-fault. Physician and hospital groups generally have supported mandatory PIP benefits because these laws make it more likely that people injured in auto accidents will have medical insurance. Trial lawyers have strongly resisted no-fault and have fought to prevent increases in thresholds in existing laws. In a few states the outcome of political battles over no-fault has been the adoption of choice no-fault.

As the name implies, choice no-fault allows drivers to decide whether to purchase PIP coverage and accept some modification in tort rights. Under current choice no-fault laws, drivers who opt for no-fault generally cannot sue other drivers for losses covered by PIP coverage and cannot sue for pain and suffering unless losses exceed a specified threshold. In exchange, drivers who choose no-fault receive a mandatory reduction in their liability insurance premiums. However, drivers who do not choose no-fault still can sue them.[8]

Two other types of choice no-fault laws have been proposed. One proposal would allow people who do not choose no-fault to sue each other without limitation. People who choose no-fault would have their exposure to tort liability and their rights to sue others limited. If person A did not choose no-fault and was harmed by person B who did, A could recover damages from his or her own insurer from coverage similar to uninsured motorists coverage. Thus, compared to people who chose no-fault, people who rejected no-fault would have to pay more for liability insurance and pay for the right to recover damages from their own insurer if they were hurt by an at-fault driver that had chosen no-fault. An alternative proposal would allow persons who rejected no-fault to sue everybody, but drivers who had chosen no-fault could sue them in turn.

We noted earlier that compulsory no-fault laws might be viewed as agreements among drivers to limit tort liability (the right to sue and be sued) coupled with mandatory first-party insurance. Viewed within this framework, choice no-fault laws make participation in the agreement to limit tort liability voluntary. However, you can see that choice no-fault

---

[8]The premium reductions that must be given are designed to reflect the total savings in liability claim costs. The savings in liability claim costs for a given insurer need not equal the reduction in premiums. For example, while most of a given insurer's customers might accept no-fault, many of them may harm drivers who have not chosen no-fault, and the insurer will have to defend them and pay claims without any restriction on tort liability. Insurers and regulators have developed "risk exchanges" to deal with this problem by, in essence, requiring insurers that have cost savings greater than the reduction in premiums to compensate insurers whose costs savings are less than the reduction in liability insurance premiums.

laws and proposals are not necessarily simple. This complexity reduces the attractiveness of some of these proposals. But if you like the idea of limiting your rights to sue in exchange for limits on your exposure to liability, choice no-fault may be better than no no-fault.

Other Proposals to Limit Tort Liability

Another type of no-fault proposal that has been suggested in some states would restrict recovery for pain and suffering in lawsuits without making the purchase of PIP coverage compulsory. People could still sue for economic loss and perhaps recover attorney fees. They also could choose to buy some PIP coverage or simply rely on individual/group health insurance to cover their losses.

A more radical proposal would restrict lawsuits for both economic loss and pain and suffering without mandating PIP coverage, as is done in a few states for uninsured drivers. How would people be compensated for economic losses if they could not sue? The same way that they are now compensated if they are hurt in an auto accident and no one else is at fault. They could rely on group or individual health insurance or buy auto medical coverage or optional PIP coverage. As is now the case, low-income uninsured persons generally would receive "free" medical care with the costs falling on other parties.

The possibility of restricting tort liability for economic loss and pain and suffering without requiring PIP coverage has received little discussion. Perhaps this is because it would exacerbate the uninsured problem and reduce incentives for safety. This lack of discussion also may reflect the notion (enunciated in early court decisions on the constitutionality of no-fault laws) that if people give up tort rights they have to be given some other "remedy" (such as the *obligation* to buy first-party coverage). But this linkage is not very tight. A person who "gives up some rights" when tort liability is restricted automatically receives something in return—reduced exposure to lawsuits from other people.

Concept Check

4. Assume that restrictions on recovery of damages for pain and suffering in lawsuits are adopted without mandating purchase of PIP coverage. Describe the possible effects on safety and the decision to drive compared to: (*a*) the traditional tort liability system, and (*b*) a compulsory no-fault law (restrictions on tort liability with compulsory PIP coverage).

13.5 Summary

- The personal auto policy includes four main coverages: (1) coverage for liability to third parties harmed by the negligence of an insured person; (2) coverage for medical payments or, in some states, personal injury protection coverage for medical expenses and loss of income; (3) coverage for losses caused by uninsured or underinsured motorists; and (4) coverage for physical damage to and theft of insured autos.

- Personal auto insurers generally use rate classification systems that reflect driver characteristics such as age, sex, marital status, whether the car is driven to work or for business, driving record, and the geographic territory in which the auto is located. Rates are lower for insurers with more stringent underwriting criteria.

- All states have auto insurance residual markets that allow drivers to obtain coverage who would not be insured voluntarily due to rate inadequacy. Most states use an assigned risk plan. The residual market is very small in a majority of states because insurers are allowed to charge rates commensurate with the expected costs of insuring different people. A few states require each insurer to accept almost all applicants but they then may reinsure applicants for which rates are perceived as inadequate in a state reinsurance facility.

- Almost all states make the purchase of auto liability insurance compulsory; a number of states mandate the purchase of personal injury protection coverage. Economic arguments for compulsory insurance focus on the possible benefits of getting people to reflect more upon the costs of their actions when deciding whether to drive, what kind of car to buy, and how safely to drive—as opposed to having these costs fall on others. Compulsory insurance laws are criticized for weak enforcement in many states and for having a regressive impact on the distribution of income, which increases pressure to subsidize rates for certain groups through price regulation.

- Some states have compulsory no-fault laws that require drivers to purchase specified personal injury protection coverage and restrict tort liability. A few states have choice no-fault laws that allow drivers to elect whether to buy personal injury protection coverage and have restricted tort liability rights. No-fault laws with moderate personal injury protection coverage limits and material restrictions on tort liability have the potential both to improve the efficiency of compensation and to reduce auto insurance premiums. One argument against no-fault is that restricting tort liability might lead to more accidents; another criticism is that some no-fault laws have not reduced premiums.

Key Terms

personal auto policy 243
auto liability coverage 244
compulsory liability insurance laws 244
financial responsibility laws 244
auto medical payments coverage 246
personal injury protection coverage 246
uninsured motorists coverage 246
underinsured motorists coverage 247
collision coverage 248
other-than-collision coverage 248
territorial rating 252

underwriting criteria 256
nonstandard insurance market 257
assigned risk plan 259
reinsurance facility 260
joint underwriting association 260
state insurer 260
pure no-fault 265
compulsory no-fault laws 265
choice no-fault law 265
threshold 267

Questions and Problems

1. Why might a person rationally buy liability insurance with limits greater than his or her limits on underinsured motorists coverage?

2. Develop an argument for how uninsured motorists and underinsured motorists insurance might be improved from the perspective of optimal compensation.

3. Describe the major rating factors used in automobile insurance.

4. In view of moral hazard, explain why it might be optimal for a person to have a lower deductible for other-than-collision coverage than for collision coverage.

5. Consider an auto insurance policy that for a period of five years would guarantee annual renewal to the policyholder at the same premium rate the insurer charges to drivers that have not had accidents or tickets. In other words, the contract would guarantee the policyholder against rate increases that otherwise would occur from a poor driving record. (Thus, to some extent it would be

similar to guaranteed renewable health insurance discussed in Chapter 16.) Do you think that people would be willing to pay enough for this contract to allow the insurer to cover expected costs over the life of the contract? Explain.

6. Explain why insurers have the incentive to sell coverage voluntarily to a driver as long as the price that can be charged is greater than or equal to the expected costs of providing coverage (i.e., the fair premium). Why does this imply that residual markets usually will lose money?

7. Explain how compulsory insurance laws might lead to fewer accidents for people who disobey the law and drive without coverage.

8. Explain what might happen to accident rates if compulsory auto liability insurance laws were repealed and tort liability were restricted without mandating the purchase of PIP coverage. How could the government promote greater driving safety if these changes were made?

9. Argue (a) the case for compulsory auto liability insurance laws, and (b) the case against these laws. Do the same thing for compulsory PIP coverage assuming no restriction on tort liability.

10. Who would benefit most from restrictions on tort liability for auto accidents, a high-risk driver or a low-risk driver? Answer the same question if restrictions on tort liability are combined with mandatory PIP coverage in a no-fault system.

11. Many state legislators are personal injury lawyers. How might this affect the likelihood that no-fault is adopted and the main features of no-fault laws that are adopted? Do you think that voting on no-fault legislation represents a conflict of interest for these lawyers/legislators? Why or why not?

Answers to Concept Checks

1. Rating factors are used to place drivers in a specific rate class. Insurers then employ underwriting criteria to determine whether to offer coverage to the applicant at the class rate.

2. Auto insurers can underwrite in states with assigned risk plans and joint underwriting associations. An insurer can deny coverage to an applicant, who then can apply for coverage through the assigned risk plan or through a servicing insurer for the joint underwriting association. In states with reinsurance facilities, each insurer is required to offer coverage to most applicants, but the insurer can use some underwriting criteria to determine whether to retain the risk or reinsure the coverage in the state reinsurance facility.

3. Because more people will have liability insurance to pay tort liability settlements, compulsory liability laws tend to increase the number of lawsuits and thus the demand for personal injury lawyers. However, because compulsory liability will reduce the number of uninsured motorists, the increase in demand will be offset in part by reductions in the number of uninsured motorist claimants who would have hired an attorney.

4. a.   Unless greater penalties for unsafe driving are adopted or enforcement of motor vehicle codes is increased, incentives for safety will likely decline, and more people will drive compared to the traditional tort system because liability insurance costs will decline and thus have less effect on safety and the decision to drive.

   b.   Incentives for safety will likely decline and more people will drive compared to a compulsory no-fault law because experience-rated compulsory PIP coverage raises the cost of driving and provides increased incentives for safety.

References

Carroll, Stephen, et al. *No-Fault Approaches to Compensating People Injured in Automobile Accidents.* Rand Institute for Civil Justice Report R-4019-ICJ. Santa Monica, CA: Rand, 1991. (*Discussion and analysis of the effects of no-fault on compensation and premiums.*)

Cummins, J. David; and Sharon Tennyson. "Controlling Automobile Insurance Costs." *The Journal of Economic Perspectives* 6 (1992), pp. 95–115. (*Discusses how claim cost increases are the major cause of premium increases and possible approaches to controlling costs, including no-fault.*)

Harrington, Scott. "Taxing Low Income Households in Search of the Public Interest: The Case of Compulsory Automobile Insurance." In *Insurance, Risk Management, and Public Policy: Essays in Honor of Robert I. Mehr,* eds. Scott Harrington and Sandra Gustavson. Boston: Kluwer Academic, 1994. (*Detailed discussion of the economics, fairness, and politics of compulsory auto insurance laws.*)

O'Connell, Jeffrey; and Robert H. Joost. "Giving Motorists a Choice between Fault and No-Fault." *Virginia Law Review* 72 (1986). (*Detailed analysis of choice no-fault.*)

Chapter 14

Homeowners Insurance

Chapter Objectives

- Describe homeowners insurance and personal umbrella liability insurance policies.
- Describe property insurance arrangements for catastrophic perils, including FAIR plans, the National Flood Insurance Program, and beach and windstorm plans.
- Analyze the impact of catastrophes on property insurance and the market's response to large catastrophes.

14.1   Homeowners Insurance

Homeowners insurance is the second largest line of personal insurance for property–liability insurers, behind auto insurance. Most insurers writing homeowners policies are multiline insurers who also sell personal auto and life insurance. Over 500 companies sell homeowners insurance across the United States, and the market shares of the leading insurers within each state generally are not large. The largest five writers of homeowners insurance in the United States (with 2000 national market shares in parentheses) were State Farm (22.1 percent), Allstate (13.7 percent), Zurich/Farmers Insurance Group (8.8 percent), Nationwide (4.3 percent), and Travelers/Citigroup (4.0 percent). The top four insurers are direct writers.

Types of Policies

Homeowners policies are multiple-line, multiple-peril policies. They provide first-party property, third-party liability, and third-party medical expense coverage. Property is covered from losses due to multiple perils (e.g., fire, windstorms, and theft). In some cases, the policy lists the perils that are covered (a **named peril policy**). In other cases, the policy covers all perils except those specifically excluded (known as an **open peril policy** or **all risk policy**).

Homeowners policies are standardized to a large extent. That is, the policy structure and language, as well as the types of coverages, the exclusions, and so on, generally are similar across insurers. Most insurers sell policies that are very similar if not identical to the standard policy forms that have been developed by the Insurance Services Office (ISO), a private organization that provides rating and policy form services to the insurance industry. There are seven basic types of policy forms: HO1 (basic form), HO2 (broad form), HO3 (special form), HO4 (contents broad form), HO5 (comprehensive form), HO6 (condominium unit owners form), and HO8 (modified coverage form).[1] The different forms generally apply to different types of situations; forms HO1, HO2, HO3, HO5, and HO8 are for homeowners, HO4 is for renters, and HO6, as is obvious from its name, is for condominium owners. As we describe below, the policies for homeowners differ in the amount of coverage provided. The most common homeowners policy is the **HO3 policy.**

Description of Major Coverages

Policies for homeowners typically provide six basic coverages. These coverages, which are listed in Table 14.1, are labeled A through F. The first three coverages provide reimbursement for property damage, and the other three provide reimbursement for loss of use, liability losses, and medical expenses, respectively. Next to the name of each type of coverage in Table 14.1 is a brief description of how the amount of coverage is determined under the HO3 form. Homeowners policies also provide a number of other coverages, such as coverage for debris removal and fire department service charges.

The amount of dwelling coverage (A) chosen by the policyholder determines the amount of coverage for other structures (B), personal property (C), and additional living expenses (D). For example, if the policyholder chooses $100,000 of dwelling coverage, then the HO3 policy provides $10,000 for other structures, $50,000 for personal property, and $20,000 for additional living expenses. The limits for liability and medical coverage for others (i.e., persons injured other than the insured or family members) are not contingent on the amount of dwelling coverage chosen. The basic limit for personal liability coverage is $100,000 and the limit for medical coverage for others is $1,000 per person, although these limits can be increased.

Table 14.2 summarizes the differences between the main HO policy forms with respect to property coverage. The five policies for homeowners (excluding renters and condominium

TABLE 14.1 Homeowners insurance coverages.

Type of Coverage	Amount of Coverage in HO3 Policy
A. Dwelling	Chosen by policyholder
B. Other structures	10% of dwelling coverage
C. Unscheduled personal property	50% of dwelling coverage
D. Loss of use (e.g., additional living expenses if dwelling cannot be occupied)	20% of dwelling coverage
E. Personal liability	$100,000*
F. Medical payments to others	$1,000 per person*
	$25,000 aggregate limit*

*These limits can be increased.

[1] The HO7 policy form has been discontinued.

TABLE 14.2   Overview of property coverage under different homeowners policy forms.

Policy Form (user)	Perils Covered A, B, & D Dwelling Coverage, Other Structures, and Loss of Use	C Coverage for Personal Property	Additional Coverages	Percent of Homeowners Policies 1977	1995
HO8 (Homeowner)	Basic list, except coverage for theft is subject to $1,000 limit and does not extend "off the residence premises"	Basic list, except coverage for theft is subject to $1,000 limit and does not extend "off the residence premises"	Basic List minus "collapse"	0%	< 1%
HO1 (Homeowner)	Basic list	Basic list	Basic List minus "collapse"	14%	< 1%
HO2 (Homeowner)	Expanded list	Expanded list	Basic List plus "ordinance and law"	41%	6%
HO3 (Homeowner)	Open peril	Expanded list, but can be changed to an open peril policy through an endorsement	Basic List plus "ordinance and law"	45%	93%
HO5 (Homeowner)	Open peril	Open peril	Expanded List	NA	NA
HO4 (Renter)	NA	Expanded list	Basic List plus "building additions and alterations"	NA	NA
HO6* (Condominium owner)	Expanded, but coverage for plumbing discharge and freezing differs; also can be changed to open peril policy through an endorsement	Expanded, but coverage for plumbing discharge and freezing differs; open peril coverage available through an endorsement	Basic List plus "ordinance and law"	NA	NA

Note: NA means not applicable.

*Dwelling and other structures coverage are combined.

Basic list perils covered: Fire, lightning, windstorm, hail, explosion, riot, civil commotion, vehicles, aircraft, smoke, vandalism, malicious mischief, theft, and volcanic eruption.

Expanded list perils covered: Basic perils plus falling objects, weight of ice, snow, sleet, plumbing discharge, rupture of hot water and air conditioning systems, freezing of plumbing, and artificially generated electricity.

Basic list of additional coverages: Debris removal, reasonable repairs, plants and trees, fire department service charge, property removed, fund transfer and credit cards, loss assessment, glass or safety glazing material, and collapse.

Expanded list of additional coverages: Basic list plus building and contents replacement cost, lock replacement, and others.

Source: Percent of policies obtained from *Homeowners Insurance: Threats from Without, Weakness Within,* Insurance Services Office, 1996.

owners) are listed in order of the comprehensiveness of coverage provided by the form; that is, HO8 offers the least comprehensive coverage, followed by HO1, HO2, HO3, and HO5. Coverage differences are evident by comparing the entries in the columns titled "Perils Covered" and "Additional Coverages." A third dimension on which the coverage of the policy forms differs is the method of loss settlement, which is discussed below.

Table 14.2 also provides estimates of the percentage of all policies purchased by homeowners (excluding renters and condominium owners) represented by the different policy forms in 1977 and 1995. Ignoring HO8, which did not exist in 1977, the sale of more comprehensive coverage has expanded as indicated by the shift of HO1 and HO2 policies to HO3 policies over time. In 1995, 93 percent of homeowners policies were HO3 policies. The HO5 form, which was introduced in 2000, is expected to reduce the market share of the HO3 form.

Homeowners insurance **dwelling coverage** (coverage A) covers the policyholder's main residence and attached structures. The property insured by a homeowners policy must be primarily used as a place of residence and not for business purposes. While limited amounts of business activity can be conducted at a residence without jeopardizing coverage under a homeowners policy, if a person's main residence also is where a significant amount of business is transacted, a separate business property policy may be needed.

Other structures coverage (coverage B) covers structures not attached to the main residence, such as detached garages, garden sheds, swimming pools (above and in-ground), and fences. As stated above, the amount of coverage for other structures is limited to 10 percent of the dwelling coverage. This limit is an aggregate limit; that is, it applies across all other structures, not separately for each structure. Additional coverage can be purchased through an endorsement.

Unscheduled personal property coverage (coverage C) covers items that are owned or used by the insured regardless of whether they are lost or damaged at the insured's home or away from home. The limit for coverage C under HO3 equals 50 percent of the dwelling coverage, but the limit can be increased through an endorsement. The typical homeowners policy, however, excludes or limits coverage for specific items. For example, motor vehicles are excluded, as are animals and sound equipment in a car. Coverage sublimits apply to many items that could potentially be very valuable, such as silverware, jewelry, and guns. As explained in Chapter 9, coverage limits for these items help make the coverage more suitable for the typical buyer and thereby reduce classification costs. Additional coverage for items with sublimits can be purchased using an endorsement to the policy or with a separate contract, called a *personal articles floater.*

Loss of use coverage (coverage D) provides reimbursement for additional living expenses if the dwelling cannot be used because it is damaged or because civil authorities prevent its use. As an example of the latter situation, authorities could prevent people from living in a neighborhood because of potentially dangerous pollution. Loss of use coverage also provides coverage for lost rental income if a portion of the residence can no longer be rented.

Personal liability coverage pays for judgments, settlements, and defense costs for bodily injury and property damage liability that arise from accidents at the residence or may result from certain actions of the insured away from the residence. For example, damages to a visitor or neighbor from a dog bite would typically be covered. **Coverage for medical payments to others** pays the medical expenses of nonresidents who are injured while on

Following the Oakland Hills fire in California in 1993 and Hurricane Andrew in Florida in 1992, many people found themselves to be underinsured because of the ordinance and law exclusion in their HO policies. As a result of this exclusion, losses that occur as a result of laws or ordinances (e.g., building codes) are not covered.

Many of the homes damaged by the Oakland Hills fire were built prior to the enactment of building codes designed to reduce losses from earthquakes. The difference between the cost of rebuilding according to code and the cost of rebuilding using the original type of construction materials and building techniques often was not covered because of the ordinance and law exclusion in the HO policy.

Similarly, many coastal areas, including those in Florida, require that new homes and homes that are more than 50 percent destroyed be built a certain number of feet above ground level. Following Hurricane Andrew, the additional cost of rebuilding according to this requirement was not covered under some people's homeowners policies because of the ordinance and law exclusion.

the premises. This coverage is provided without regard to fault or negligence of the insured. For example, if a visiting child falls off of a swing and breaks an arm, the homeowners policy will cover medical expenses up to $1,000.

Excluded Perils

Homeowners policies exclude coverage for a number of perils. One way this is done is through a named-peril policy, which excludes coverage for all perils not named. In addition, named-peril policies have specific exclusions to reduce ambiguity about what is not covered under the policy. Open peril policies, like the HO3 and HO5 forms, specifically name perils that will not be insured.

Examples of exclusions include property losses caused by intentional acts, normal wear and tear, smog, and animals owned or kept by the insured.[2] These exclusions can be explained using the principles presented in earlier chapters (especially see Chapter 9). Some exclusions (e.g., excluding losses caused by pets) reduce the insurer's exposure to events that depend largely on the homeowner's actions and therefore are subject to moral hazard. Other exclusions eliminate coverage for events that have a high probability of occurrence and little uncertainty (normal wear and tear) and therefore would be too costly to insure once claims processing costs are considered. Homeowners policies also have exclusions that reduce an insurer's exposure to correlated losses. For example, losses from changes in laws, earthquakes, floods, nuclear accidents, and war are excluded. Box 14.1 illustrates how the exclusion for losses arising from laws can in some circumstances cause people to be significantly underinsured. Consumers can purchase coverage for some of these excluded perils through endorsements or separate coverage (e.g., earthquake coverage) or through special government programs (e.g., flood coverage). We describe some of these coverages later in the chapter.

[2]Note, however, that liability for bodily injury or property damage caused by pets is covered under personal liability coverage.

There are over 100,000 types of molds, but only a small fraction of them are toxic to humans. The most common health concerns according to the Center for Disease Control are hay-fever like symptoms. However, the list of alleged illnesses that have been caused by mold include nose bleeds, cognitive disorders, liver damage, brain damage, and cancer. Even though toxic mold lawsuits have been brought against builders, former homeowners, and homeowners' associations, the majority of toxic mold suits have been brought against insurers alleging bad faith. One highly publicized toxic mold case involved the Ballard family of Texas. They claimed that their insurer failed to cover promptly and adequately the repairs needed following a water leak, which in turn caused mold to ruin their 22-room estate. In June 2001, a jury awarded the family $32 million ($6.2 million for replacement of the home and contents, $5 million for mental anguish, $12 million in punitive damages, and $8.9 million for legal fees).

An exclusion that has received considerable attention in recent years is the exclusion for mold damage. Most homeowners' policies exclude damage from mold, just as they exclude coverage for losses from rust and rot. One explanation for these exclusions is moral hazard. Moisture, which is needed for mold to grow, is likely to be observable and preventable at low cost by normal maintenance on the part of the homeowner. If an insurer provided coverage for such losses, then incentives for homeowners to take low-cost loss prevention measures would be reduced.

Despite the exclusion, mold coverage can be subject to dispute, in part, because mold can arise from perils that are covered under most homeowners' policies, such as an unexpected water discharge from a pipe. The number of mold claims increased dramatically in the early 2000s, especially in Texas. Not surprisingly, insurers denied coverage for many of these claims, which in turn prompted some policyholders to sue insurers. In some highly publicized cases, the plaintiffs sought damages not only for property losses but also for health problems alleged to have been caused by toxic molds. A few plaintiffs won very large awards (see Box 14.2), which led many insurers to clarify the policy language regarding mold coverage. A number of insurers explicitly excluded coverage for mold damage (although some of these insurers then allowed consumers to add mold coverage through an endorsement). Some insurers also changed their underwriting criteria and would no longer renew policies that had previous water claims, under the reasoning that water damage increases the likelihood of future mold claims.

Property Loss Settlement

Property losses under homeowners insurance are covered above a per occurrence deductible. A common deductible would be $250. Higher and lower deductibles usually are available for an adjustment in the premium. The actual amount of coverage provided above the deductible is complicated because different types of property are valued in different ways for the purpose of settling losses and because policies differ in their valuation methods. In addition, the co-insurance (insurance-to-value) provision limits coverage in some instances (see Chapter 9 for a general discussion of the co-insurance provision). Table 14.3 summarizes the different loss settlement provisions.

TABLE 14.3
Typical methods for loss settlement for different coverages.

Policy Form	A and B Dwelling and Other Structures Coverage	C Personal Property Coverage
HO8	Functional replacement cost or actual cash value	Actual cash value
HO1	Like-kind replacement cost*	Actual cash value
HO2	Like-kind replacement cost*	Actual cash value or like-kind replacement cost
HO3	Like-kind replacement cost* or guaranteed replacement cost	Actual cash value or like-kind replacement cost
HO5	Guaranteed replacement cost	Like-kind replacement cost
HO4 (Renter)	NA	Actual cash value or like-kind replacement cost with an endorsement
HO6 (Condominium owner)	Actual cash value $1,000 limit (can be increased)	Actual cash value or like-kind replacement cost

*Provided coverage exceeds 80 percent of replacement cost; if not, then settlement equals maximum of actual cash value and x percent of the loss, where x = (actual coverage/replacement cost)/0.8. Also, endorsements for guaranteed replacement cost coverage are available.

Dwellings and Other Structures

Under most homeowners policies, dwellings and other structures are insured up to their **like-kind replacement cost,** which means that the insurer will pay the cost for "like construction," provided the coverage chosen by the policyholder exceeds 80 percent of the building's full replacement cost prior to the loss (i.e., provided the co-insurance provision is met). Thus, if the minimum insurance requirement is met and the policy limit is adequate, replacement cost coverage will allow the insured to replace damaged property with new property: There is no deduction for depreciation of the damaged property prior to the loss. Exceptions are made for certain types of property covered under dwelling coverage, such as outdoor antennas, which are insured up to their actual cash value. The **actual cash value** generally is defined as the replacement cost minus depreciation. As discussed further below, personal property also is sometimes insured for its actual cash value.

In most cases, homeowners policies are issued only if the property is insured for at least 80 percent of the replacement cost, which implies that the co-insurance provision usually is satisfied. However, situations sometimes arise where the property is not insured up to 80 percent of the full replacement cost, in which case the insurer will pay less than the replacement cost even if the replacement cost is less than the amount of coverage. In particular, if coverage equals x percent of the full replacement cost, then the insurer will pay $(x/80)$ percent of the loss or the actual cash value, whichever is greater. In no case, however, will the insurer pay more than the coverage limits chosen by the policyholder.

Instead of like-kind replacement cost coverage with a co-insurance provision, homeowners can purchase **guaranteed replacement cost** coverage for the dwelling and other structures. This coverage will pay the like-kind replacement cost even if it turns out to exceed the policy limit. Some insurers, however, cap reimbursement at 125 or 150 percent of the limit under guaranteed replacement cost coverage. In addition to paying a higher premium for this type of coverage, most guaranteed replacement cost policies require that the insured purchase coverage equal to 100 percent of the originally estimated replacement cost and to increase the coverage with inflation and improvements in the property.

An alternative method of loss settlement that is used for dwellings and other structures under the HO8 policy and variations sold by some insurers is to pay the **functional replacement cost,** which is the cost of replacement of damaged property using materials that serve the same function as the original materials but are not necessarily the same. (In some states, HO8 or similar policies are required to pay actual cash value.) For example, with functional replacement cost coverage, the replacement cost could be calculated assuming that repairs/replacements are made with carpeting over plywood instead of hardwood, sheetrock instead of plaster, and linoleum instead of marble. To illustrate one common situation where functional replacement cost is likely to be used, consider an older home with unique features (e.g., wood floors, marble bathrooms, crown moldings) but a relatively low market value because of its location. The replacement cost of the home could greatly exceed the market value of the home, because of the cost of the materials and the craftspeople that would be needed for their installation. Another situation where either functional replacement cost or actual cash value coverage is sometimes used is for old, lower valued homes that have experienced substantial depreciation over time so that the market value or actual cash value is small compared to the like-kind replacement cost.

Insuring these types of homes for 80 percent or more of their like-kind replacement cost generally would cause the policy limit to exceed the market value of the home. This outcome might require a higher premium than many owners of such property would be willing to pay. Like-kind replacement cost coverage with a limit substantially in excess of the home's market value also could increase moral hazard because the homeowner could be better off financially after a loss (e.g., he or she could replace the home with a new home that would be worth substantially more than the existing home prior to the loss). By settling losses using functional replacement cost or actual cash value instead of using replacement cost with like-kind materials, the homeowner can purchase lower limits and the moral hazard problem can be reduced. Thus, the use of either functional replacement cost or actual cash value coverage instead of "like-kind" replacement cost can increase the availability and the affordability of coverage in depressed neighborhoods with older homes.[3]

Personal Property

The standard homeowners forms generally cover personal property on an actual cash value basis (above the deductible).[4] However, like-kind replacement cost coverage is available through an endorsement to the leading forms for an additional premium. A majority of homeowners purchase this replacement cost endorsement, thus avoiding a reduction in the indemnity paid to reflect depreciation. The HO5 policy automatically includes replacement cost coverage.

---

[3]If the policyholder does not replace the home following a loss, the HO8 policy will pay the minimum of the market value, actual cash value, or functional replacement cost. This provision also helps reduce moral hazard. Some insurers offer a hybrid coverage on homes with low market value compared to replacement cost that pays functional replacement cost up to the market value of the home.

[4]Note that if dwellings and personal property are damaged in one occurrence, the deductible is applied only once.

TABLE 14.4
Characteristics of homes commonly used by insurers to estimate replacement costs.

Ground Floor Square Footage	Dwelling Type	Construction Grade and Quality	Construction Materials
Less than 1,000	Ranch	Economy	Frame
1,000–1,200	Cape Cod	Standard	Masonry
1,200–1,300	Colonial	Custom	Masonry
.	Victorian	Luxury	Veneer
.	Town house		
.	Contemporary		
Greater than 3,500	Split level		

Pricing Homeowners Policies

Homeowners insurance premiums are set using two basic components. One component is the insured value of the property (e.g., the replacement cost) and the other is the rate per dollar of insured value. The premium is found by multiplying the two components. For example, if a home with a replacement cost of $220,000 is insured for this amount and the insurer charges a rate equal to 0.003, then the annual premium would equal $660 (plus the charge for liability and medical expense coverage).

Policies generally are initially issued with a dwelling limit equal to 100 percent of the dwelling's estimated replacement cost. Insurers use various methods to estimate replacement cost. One method can be explained with the aid of Table 14.4, which lists the characteristics used by some insurers to estimate a dwelling's replacement cost. Insurers use tables that provide an estimate of the replacement cost per square foot for each combination of the factors listed in the table—ground floor square footage, dwelling type, construction grade, and construction materials. The replacement cost per square foot is multiplied by the home's square footage to find a base *replacement cost,* which is then multiplied by a location modifier to arrive at the replacement cost used for establishing premiums. The *location modifier* adjusts the base replacement cost for the variation across locations in construction costs.

To illustrate the estimation of replacement cost, suppose that an all-brick, custom ranch has 2,300 square feet and the insurer's table of replacement costs indicates that the cost per square foot to replace the home is $75. Then the base replacement cost equals 2,300 × $75 = $172,500. Assuming that the location modifier equals 1.1, the replacement cost is estimated to be $189,750 ($172,500 × 1.1). Although this procedure for calculating replacement costs is reasonably accurate for standard homes, it can result in considerable errors for high-priced, custom-built homes, which are becoming more common. Consequently, some insurers have moved to more sophisticated methods of calculating replacement costs, especially for pricing guaranteed replacement cost coverage.

The rates per dollar of replacement cost charged for homeowners insurance can vary with a number of factors (see Box 14.3). The home's location is one important factor, because it determines the home's exposure to weather-related perils (hurricanes, earthquakes, tornadoes, hail, etc.), its exposure to crime, and its proximity to fire protection. Rates also depend on the construction materials, such as wood versus brick.

Some insurers employ the controversial practice of underwriting and basing rates for homeowners policies on the homeowner's credit history. There is statistical evidence that without higher rates the profitability of homeowners policies is lower, on average, for homeowners that have low credit ratings. This relationship might be explained by the reasoning that people with low credit ratings are (1) less likely to pay premiums on time, (2) more likely to fail to renew policies, (3) more likely to have claims, and (4) more likely to submit fraudulent claims. Critics of the practice of using credit information for insurance underwriting and pricing decisions sometimes allege that the practice predominantly affects lower-income individuals who disproportionately are minorities and therefore that the practice amounts to racial discrimination.

The specific allegation that insurers use credit histories to racially discriminate is an example of a more general allegation that insurers engage in the racially discriminatory practice of **redlining**. The term *redlining* refers to a practice of drawing red lines on a map to indicate areas that insurers (or other financial institu-

tions) will not serve. While explicit drawing of lines on a map is unlikely today, insurers nevertheless are alleged to practice redlining by providing lower quality service (e.g., fewer offices) and charging higher prices in areas predominately populated by minorities. Insurers respond that they do not base business decisions on a person's race and that any differences in average quality and prices reflect cost differences, not racial discrimination.

Statistical analyses of the profitability of homeowners (and auto) insurance in different regions generally do not provide evidence of a relationship with percent minority population. While a detailed examination of this evidence is beyond the scope of this book, this evidence is inconsistent with discrimination at the market level. It also is worth noting that racial discrimination that had a substantive effect on the price charged or the service quality provided by insurers would imply unexploited profitable investment opportunities. It would thus require pervasive prejudice and significant entry barriers for potential nonprejudiced entrants.

14.2   Personal Umbrella Policies

Wealthier individuals often find the liability coverage limits available with their homeowners policy to be inadequate given their potential exposure. A common way to insure against large liability losses is through a personal umbrella policy, which usually provides excess coverage of at least $1 million for liability losses that could arise from multiple sources. The umbrella policy usually requires that the consumer have other liability coverage, such as homeowners and automobile liability. If losses exceed the limits on these other "primary" coverages, then the umbrella policy will pay losses up to its limit. Most umbrella policies also provide some coverage for liability exposures not covered under the insured's primary policies (e.g., libel or slander) subject to a self-insured retention that operates like a deductible.

To illustrate the basic coverage provided by an umbrella policy, suppose that a homeowner has the following liability coverages and limits:

Auto liability	$ 300,000
Homeowners	$ 100,000
Umbrella	$1,000,000

If the homeowner has a liability claim of $500,000 as a result of an automobile accident, then the auto insurer will pay $300,000 and the umbrella insurer will pay $200,000.

The premium required for $1 million of umbrella coverage commonly falls within the $150 to $250 range. The additional premium required for an additional $1 million (producing total coverage of $2 million) is smaller than the amount for the first $1 million. As a result, people with significant assets to protect against liability claims generally can purchase substantial coverage at a relatively modest cost.

14.3   Coverage of High Risk/Catastrophic Perils

This section provides an overview of insurance arrangements for high risk/catastrophic perils, including (1) private market earthquake coverage, (2) the National Flood Insurance Program, and (3) state residual market plans for urban property insurance and windstorm exposures. Section 14.4 then provides a discussion of the impact of catastrophes on the private market and public sector programs.

Earthquake Coverage

Although earthquake coverage is excluded from the basic homeowners policy, most insurers offer earthquake coverage as an endorsement (or sometimes as a separate policy). Losses generally are covered above a deductible that is expressed as a percentage of the property's pre-loss value (e.g., 15 percent). California is the only state that requires homeowner insurers to offer earthquake coverage along with homeowners coverage. This requirement has been in effect since 1985. As we discuss in section 14.4, the inability of California insurers to deny earthquake coverage to homeowners policyholders led some insurers to stop selling homeowners policies in the state and thus, ironically, reduced the availability of coverage from the private market in general.

National Flood Insurance

As mentioned earlier, homeowners policies exclude coverage for damage caused by floods. Flood risk generally is viewed as being uninsurable privately because of the high correlation in losses and potential adverse selection and moral hazard. Homeowners who live in areas that have adopted zoning and building codes to reduce losses from floods can purchase coverage against flood losses through the **National Flood Insurance Program (NFIP).** The flood insurance program, however, excludes some coastal areas that Congress has sought to protect from development for environmental reasons. Flood insurance from the NFIP can be purchased through many private insurance companies. Although these companies service the policy, the risk is borne by the federal government. The program does not receive general tax revenue, but it has an ability to borrow from the Treasury if premiums are insufficient to pay claims in a particular year.

Structures that were built prior to 1978, which was when flood hazard areas were officially identified by the NFIP, are insured by the NFIP using a flat rate, regardless of construction and location. Structures that were built subsequent to 1978, however, pay premiums that reflect differences in expected claim costs. People with pre-1978 built structures, however, can receive the post-1978 built rate. These features of the NFIP imply that many NFIP policyholders (mostly owners of structures built prior to 1978) pay rates that are below fair premiums; many policies are subsidized.

Subsidized rates often are criticized because they encourage people to develop property in some flood plains beyond the point that is justified if one were trying to minimize the cost of risk. That is, because of subsidized flood insurance, people who develop property in flood plain areas do not pay the full costs associated with their development. Consequently, an ex ante moral hazard problem develops—too much of the risky activity (building in flood plains) takes place. Since the subsidy mostly applies to properties built prior to 1978, the moral hazard problem associated with excessive development might not be severe. However, the subsidy still might encourage excessive redevelopment of properties damaged by floods. The designers of the NFIP have recognized the moral hazard problem and in recent years have increased efforts to discourage excessive development. For example, to be eligible to participate in the NFIP, a community must satisfy certain loss control requirements. In effect, the insurance is only available to residents of communities that have taken appropriate safety precautions that help to reduce expected losses.

One justification for subsidized flood insurance is that there are many low-income people who would not purchase flood insurance if it were fairly priced. These people, however, would obtain disaster relief following a flood and thus they ultimately might in effect obtain insurance at no cost. Taxpayers, in general, would pay the full cost of the insurance (disaster relief). Thus, it might be better to subsidize the insurance so that less disaster relief would be needed and, more importantly, so that people would incorporate at least part of the expected cost of floods when making decisions about where to live. This justification for the subsidy does not imply, however, that the subsidy would be based on when the structure was built; instead, it would imply that the subsidy would be based on income or wealth.

The pricing of NFIP policies also is criticized for not taking into consideration the differences in expected claim costs across potential policyholders. Consequently, adverse selection results—the people with the highest expected losses are more likely to purchase flood insurance. In an effort to reduce an extreme form of adverse selection, Congress passed a bill in 1994 (The National Flood Insurance Reform Act) that extends the waiting period for an NFIP policy to become effective from 5 days to 30 days. This change reduces the likelihood that people will buy flood insurance when they think a flood is imminent (e.g., when the house of their friend who lives upstream floats by).

Despite often being priced below fair premium levels, many eligible residents fail to purchase insurance from the NFIP. One explanation is that they underestimate the expected losses from floods and therefore view the price as excessive despite the subsidy. Many low-income people simply may be unable to afford flood insurance even though it is subsidized. Also, as mentioned above, the incentive to purchase flood insurance may be reduced because of the disaster relief that often is available following major floods. In 1994, however, Congress passed legislation that limited disaster relief for people who do not participate in the NFIP.

Residual Market Plans

Insurers may view some areas as having high expected losses and high correlation in losses apart from the risk of earthquakes and floods. Insurers therefore will either not offer coverage or offer coverage only at very high premiums in these areas. States have responded to problems associated with insuring these other high risk or catastrophic perils by creating insurance arrangements for people who cannot obtain coverage in the private market at "affordable" prices. The basic structure and consequences of these plans are similar to the residual market plans used for automobile insurance that were discussed in the previous chapter.

FAIR Plans

Following large losses caused by urban riots in 1967 and 1968, many insurers either withdrew or raised premiums substantially for property coverage in some urban areas. A number of states created **FAIR plans** to provide coverage for urban residents and businesses. (FAIR stands for "fair access to insurance requirements.") FAIR plans provide insurance coverage typically at rates below what private insurers would charge. It is not surprising therefore that FAIR plans typically receive less in premiums than they pay out in claim and administrative costs. Assessing property insurers operating in the state in proportion to their premium revenue makes up the shortfall. Thus, FAIR plans typically cause a subsidy from policyholders who purchase coverage in the private market to participants in FAIR plans. In 2002, 28 states, Puerto Rico, and the District of Columbia had FAIR plans.

Some states have expanded their FAIR plans beyond the original purpose of ensuring availability in the presence of potentially large (and correlated) losses from civil unrest, crime, and the like. California's experience in this regard is noteworthy, because it illustrates the problems that can develop when a state attempts to make insurance coverage available at below-market prices (below fair premiums) for all or a large part of its residents. Prior to May of 1996, the California FAIR plan was open to residents in nonurban areas under the reasoning that all consumers in California needed access to earthquake insurance. Following the Northridge earthquake in 1994, however, some insurers refused to write earthquake coverage and many insurers raised premiums for earthquake coverage (see section 14.4). As a result, a number of homeowners applied for insurance through the FAIR plan. The number of policies in the California FAIR plan tripled. Given that premiums in the FAIR plan typically were less than a fair market price, there was a high likelihood that the FAIR plan would not be able to pay all of its claims if a major earthquake occurred. In May of 1996, the commissioner limited access to the FAIR plan to property in areas exposed to brush fires and in "underserved" (i.e., urban) zip codes, thus returning the FAIR plan to the more narrowly defined market segment for which it was originally intended.

Beach and Windstorm Plans

Seven states on the East and Gulf coasts of the United States have special insurance programs called **beach and windstorm insurance plans.**[5] These plans cover property owners who live in specified coastal regions that may find coverage "unavailable" in the private market due to the risk of large losses from hurricanes. Like other residual market plans, the underwriting results of beach and windstorm plans are shared across all property insurers in the state in proportion to market share, and there generally is some subsidy from policyholders in the private market to those in the beach and windstorm plan. Figure 14.1 provides information about the number of policies in the beach and windstorm plans for each of the seven states for 1999. The large number of policies in Florida will be explained in section 14.4.

Concept Check

1. What would you expect to happen to the number of policies in residual market plans (such as FAIR and beach and windstorm plans) if state insurance commissioners froze property insurance rates for five years?

---

[5]In 2002 Florida combined its windstorm plan with its residential residual market plan. See the discussion in section 14.4.

FIGURE 14.1

Number of policies for beach and windstorm plans in 1999.

Source: 2001 *Fact Book on Property and Casualty Insurance,* Insurance Information Institute.

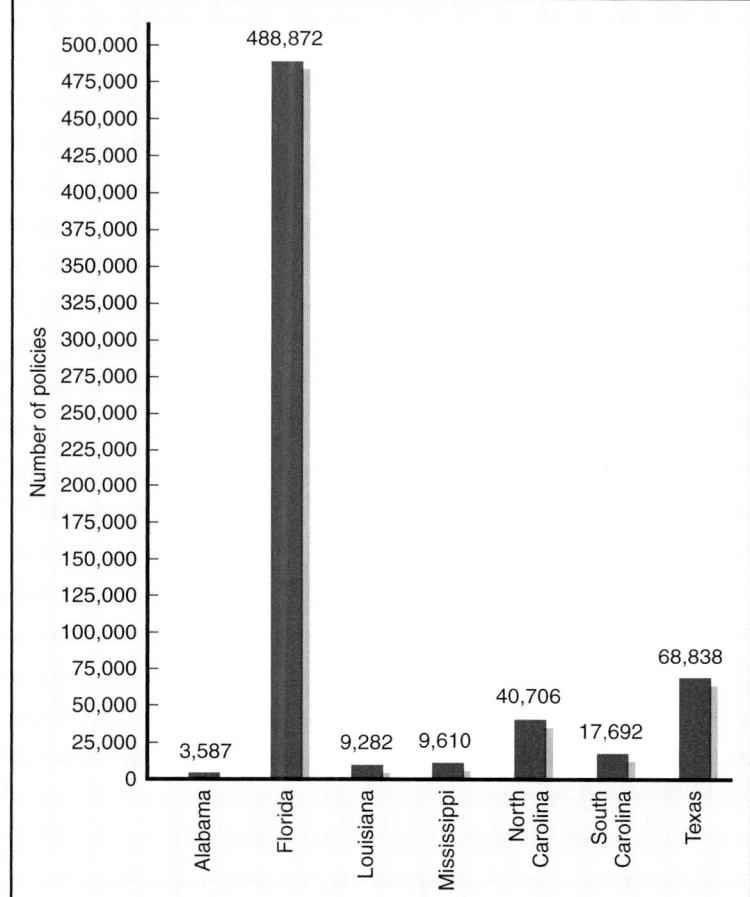

14.4 Impact of Catastrophes on Property Insurance

During the 1990s, US homeowners insurers experienced extremely poor operating results. One factor that caused the low profitability for many insurers was the frequency and severity of losses from catastrophes. Hurricane Andrew in 1992 ($16.3 billion in insured losses), the Northridge earthquake in 1994 ($12.5 billion), Hurricane Hugo in 1989 ($4.9 billion), and the Oakland Hills fire in 1991 ($1.8 billion) caused unusually high losses for homeowners insurers.

We begin our discussion of the impact of catastrophes by describing how two states, Florida and California, have responded to large catastrophe losses. These are interesting stories in their own right but, more importantly, they illustrate (1) the problems that arise from insuring losses with a large correlated component, (2) private market responses to large catastrophe losses, and (3) additional government efforts to satisfy residents' demand for affordable property insurance. We then briefly discuss two phenomena that have emerged in the wake of the large catastrophe losses to help finance future catastrophe losses. The first method is the creation of government-sponsored reinsurance programs; the second method is an expanded menu of capital market instruments to enable insurers to write coverage at a lower total cost.

Florida and Hurricane Andrew

The majority of the $16 billion of insured damage caused by Hurricane Andrew occurred in southern Dade County. The losses from Andrew could have been much worse. If, instead of hitting south of Miami, Andrew had gone through the heart of Miami, losses likely would have been over $50 billion. As it was, the losses caused seven small insurers to become insolvent and disrupted the Florida property insurance market for a number of years as insurers tried to reduce their exposure to future hurricanes and raise rates. Also, the state of Florida attempted to ensure that its citizens could purchase affordable property insurance.

Before describing the events following Hurricane Andrew, it is worth considering why Andrew would have caused as much disruption as it did. After all, could insurers have failed to anticipate that such a large hurricane was possible? Why was the risk associated with hurricanes not reinsured more fully so that the impact of such an event would have been spread relatively thinly across many people/insurers all over the world? The costs of capital and reinsurance provide at least a partial answer, if not the full answer to these questions. It is possible that the events following Andrew were not surprising. That is, some smaller insurers may have knowingly accepted the risk (given the cost of reducing the risk) that they would become insolvent if a large hurricane hit. Other insurers may have figured they could withstand one major hurricane, but after one hit they would reduce their future exposure. Alternatively, the magnitude of the losses from Andrew, especially the severity of losses per damaged home, may have taken some insurers by surprise, which caused them to increase their forecasts of expected future claim costs and to reevaluate how to deal with catastrophe exposures.

As noted above, a number of insurers decided to reduce their exposure in Florida following Hurricane Andrew and seek rate increases on future business. For example, Allstate, the largest homeowners insurer in Florida, announced that it would drop about one-third (300,000) of its Florida homeowners policies and that it would seek a 41 percent rate increase.[6] The Florida legislature responded to possible reductions in the supply of coverage by restricting insurers' ability to stop selling policies for three years. Insurers were not permitted to cancel or fail to renew more than 5 percent of their residential policies in one year or 10 percent in a single county. (These restrictions were extended in 1996.) In addition, the law required insurers that were expanding in Florida to write at least 20 percent of their new policies in Dade, Broward, and Palm Beach counties. While the Florida insurance commissioner granted rate increases, the increases were less than the amounts sought by insurers.

Despite the restrictions on insurers, a large number of homeowners found that their policies were canceled or not renewed. In response to the demand for homeowners insurance, Florida created the Residential Property and Casualty Joint Underwriting Association (JUA) in 1993 as an insurer of last resort. By 1996, the JUA had become the second largest homeowners insurer in the state. Annually, the JUA operated at a loss and imposed assessments on private insurers to make up its shortfall.

---

[6]Allstate also announced plans to reorganize its Florida business by establishing new subsidiaries that would serve Florida policyholders. In essence, the reorganization would "wall off" Florida losses from the rest of the company's assets (see Chapter 29).

**FIGURE
14.2**
**Number of
homeowners'
policies in
florida
residual
markets.**

Source: "The History
of the FRPCJUA,"
October 2001
Florida RPCJUA,
Tallahassee, FL and
various reports avail-
able at the FWUA
website.

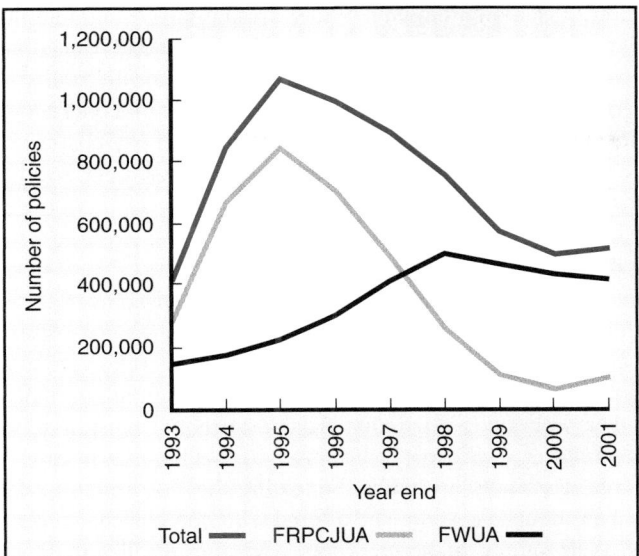

Florida already had in place a residual market mechanism for providing insurance against windstorm and hail losses. In particular, the Florida Windstorm Underwriting Association (FWUA) is one of the beach and windstorm plans discussed earlier. Its purpose is to sell windstorm and hail insurance policies in counties that may not be adequately served by the voluntary market. It originally wrote in one county, but by 1996, it wrote in 27 of 35 coastal counties. The FWUA's exposure increased significantly following Hurricane Andrew (see Figure 14.2).

FWUA and JUA rates generally are lower than private insurers' rates for similar coverage, which in large part explains the FWUA's and JUA's relatively high market share. If it were not for restrictions on cancellations and nonrenewals, the market shares of the FWUA and JUA would have been even greater following Andrew. By 1996, the state took steps to provide incentives for the voluntary market to take out policies from the FWUA and JUA. For example, insurers who sold policies to people who previously were insured by the JUA were granted an exemption from JUA assessments. In addition, bonuses up to $100 were paid for each policy that was removed from the JUA.

The incentives to depopulate the residual market plans (the JUA and FWUA) have been somewhat successful. By 1999 the number of policies in the JUA dropped below 200,000, after reaching a peak in 1996. In 2002, the JUA and FWUA were merged into one plan called the Citizens Property Insurance Company (CPIC). The new plan received special tax-exempt status, allowing it to avoid taxes on income earned and to issue tax-exempt bonds following a major hurricane.

In 1993, Florida took another step to deal with its property insurance problems when it created the Hurricane Catastrophe Fund (CAT Fund) to reinsure private insurance companies operating in the state. A controversial aspect of the CAT Fund is that all insurers operating in the state are required to purchase its reinsurance. In addition to receiving premiums from insurers, the CAT Fund has the authority to borrow by issuing tax-exempt bonds and to assess insurers based on premiums written from property and liability policies (excluding workers' compensation). The IRS granted the CAT Fund special tax status, which allows it to avoid paying tax on investment earnings. Recall from Chapter 5 and other discussions throughout the book that the tax on investment income is one of the costs to insurers of holding the capital that makes their promises to pay claims credible when losses are positively correlated. Thus, the special tax status of the CAT Fund has the potential to reduce the cost of reinsurance to Florida insurers.

California and the Northridge Earthquake

Following the Northridge earthquake in 1994, which caused over $12.5 billion in insured losses, the California homeowners insurance market experienced problems similar to those of the Florida market following Hurricane Andrew.[7] A few relatively small insurers became insolvent, many others tried to reduce their exposure to future earthquake losses, and the state developed a program to provide affordable earthquake insurance to its residents.

As discussed earlier, California is the only state that requires insurers to offer earthquake coverage with homeowners insurance. Following the Northridge quake, however, the requirement that earthquake coverage be offered with homeowners coverage led some insurers to reduce their supply of homeowners coverage. Similar to Florida, the California legislature responded in two ways. First, it limited the ability of insurers to cancel or fail to renew homeowners policies. Second, it created the California Earthquake Authority (CEA) to reduce insurers' exposure to earthquake risk.

The CEA is a state-run, privately financed plan for insuring earthquake risk. An insurer can satisfy its requirement to offer earthquake insurance with homeowners insurance by offering a basic CEA earthquake policy, which covers the primary residence with a 15 percent deductible, $5,000 of contents coverage, and $1,500 of living expense coverage, as well as supplemental coverages. Each participating insurer can write CEA earthquake policies, keep a portion of the premium for administrative expenses, and have the risk borne by the CEA. The rates for a CEA policy vary depending on a variety of factors, including construction method, age of construction, and location. The CEA is financed from policyholder premiums, assessments on participating insurers, reinsurance, and borrowing capacity.

Rationale for Government-sponsored Reinsurance Arrangements

As discussed above, both Florida and California have adopted reinsurance arrangements to finance future catastrophe losses. Hawaii also has adopted a program to finance hurricane losses, and there have been proposals for a federal catastrophe reinsurance program. These reinsurance arrangements provide two potential advantages relative to private catastrophe reinsurance arrangements. First, assuming that they obtain preferential tax treatment on investment earnings, they reduce the cost of maintaining a pool of capital to pay future catastrophe losses compared with private reinsurance arrangements. Of course, the government could alter the tax treatment to private insurers and reinsurers and obtain a similar effect.

Second, the arrangements can facilitate risk pooling over time. Both the Florida CAT Fund and the CEA have the authority to borrow money to pay current catastrophe losses.

---

[7]Potential earthquake losses in California could be much greater than those inflicted by the Northridge quake. Loss estimates from an earthquake of the same intensity as the 1906 San Francisco quake are higher than $50 billion.

The participants in the reinsurance arrangement have to pay back the funds that are borrowed so, in essence, the ability to borrow allows the participating insurers to pool catastrophe risk across years. To the extent that catastrophe risk cannot be diversified across insurers within a given time period because of the high correlation in losses, pooling over time is the only feasible method of pooling.

The question remains: Why does a government entity have an advantage relative to private contracts in pooling risk over time? The answer may be that governments can mitigate problems associated with enforcing intertemporal pooling contracts. To illustrate, suppose that a $20 billion catastrophe will occur sometime over the next 20 years, but nobody knows which year. Ignoring the time value of money, an arrangement could be established whereby insurers privately agree to contribute $1 billion each year for 20 years to pay the losses. One problem with this arrangement is that the catastrophe could occur early on, when insufficient funds have been accumulated to pay all the losses. The insurers as a group would have to borrow the funds, but there is a chance that some insurers would not fulfill their promise to repay their portion of the loan. As a result, private borrowing would entail monitoring costs as well as the payment of risk premiums to the lenders. A government, however, may largely avoid these costs because its ability to tax people in the future reduces the default risk to the lenders.

While government reinsurance arrangements could potentially lower the cost of dealing with catastrophe risk, they have several problems that could undermine their effectiveness. One problem relates to inadequate pricing. If a program like the California Earthquake Authority charges premiums that are less than expected losses, then the program will discourage the private supply of insurance and promote the development of catastrophe-prone areas beyond the level that would minimize society's cost of risk. Another potential problem is political in nature. If large amounts of funds are built up over time for the purpose of paying catastrophe losses, political pressure may emerge to use those funds for other purposes.

New Capital Market Instruments for Financing Catastrophe Losses

In recent years, some interesting and innovative approaches for helping insurers finance catastrophe losses have been introduced by the private capital market. Recall again that insurers bond their promises to pay claims by holding capital. When claim costs are highly correlated due to the possibility of a catastrophe, insurers need to hold relatively large amounts of capital to make their promises to pay claims credible. The costs of holding capital, such as taxes and agency costs, cause insurers to charge high premiums for coverage or to not offer coverage at all. The new capital market instruments provide an alternative method of bonding promises to pay claims. Instead of the insurer holding equity capital until a catastrophe occurs, these instruments arrange for investors to provide funds to the insurer only if the insurer needs the funds to pay claims (i.e., following a catastrophe).

An example of one these new capital market instruments is *contingent equity,* whereby investors precommit to purchasing new common stock from an insurer at agreed upon prices if a certain contingency occurs, such as an earthquake. Also, several insurers have issued *cat bonds* (catastrophe-linked bonds) to raise capital to pay potential catastrophe losses. With these transactions, an insurer issues bonds for which the required payments of interest and principal are contingent on the occurrence of a catastrophe. For example, if a catastrophe occurs, the insurer may not have to pay interest (coupons) on the bonds, or the insurer may be able to delay the repayment of principal for many years.

Only time will tell whether these new capital market instruments will ultimately be successful. Their success depends on whether they provide a lower cost method than holding capital for insurers to bond their promises to pay claims. One potential advantage of the instruments is that since insurers do not hold as much capital, the tax costs associated with insurers bonding promises to pay claims is reduced. Another potential advantage is that investors do not have to incur the agency costs associated with giving insurance company managers access to funds that are not immediately needed. While these new mechanisms for providing capital to insurers after a loss also may involve both tax and agency costs, these costs could be lower than with traditional capital arrangements.

14.5 Summary

- Homeowners policies generally are standardized policies that provide property and liability coverage against a broad range of perils.
- Loss settlement for homeowners policies varies depending on the type of policy and whether the loss is part of a structure or personal property. The most common types of loss settlement methods are like-kind replacement cost, guaranteed replacement cost, and actual cash value.
- Rates for homeowners policies are based on the type of construction, the size of the home, and the location of the home.
- Personal umbrella policies provide liability coverage with high limits (typically $1 million or higher) above liability coverage provided by

homeowners and automobile liability coverage.
- Losses arising from earthquakes and floods are excluded in the homeowners policy. Earthquake coverage can be purchased from private insurers as an endorsement to an HO policy or as a separate policy. Coverage for floods is available from the National Flood Insurance Program.
- Residual market plans for urban property (FAIR plans) and for coastal property (beach and windstorm plans) exist in a number of states.
- Catastrophes have disrupted property insurance markets and led to government provision of reinsurance as well as innovative private capital market instruments for financing catastrophe losses.

Key Terms

named peril policy 276
open peril policy 276
all risk policy 276
HO3 policy 277
dwelling coverage 279
other structures coverage 279
unscheduled personal property
  coverage 279
loss of use coverage 279
personal liability coverage 279

coverage for medical payments to others 279
like-kind replacement cost 282
actual cash value 282
guaranteed replacement cost 282
functional replacement cost 283
redlining 285
National Flood Insurance Program
  (NFIP) 286
FAIR plans 288
  beach and windstorm insurance plans 288

Questions and Problems

1. Assuming that the loss is covered, how much would be paid for the following losses under a standard HO3 policy with dwelling coverage of $50,000? Assume no endorsements have been purchased.

   a. The homeowner's dog bites a child and $5,000 of medical expenses are needed.

   b. A fire in the yard causes the following damage: $2,000 to a picket fence, $10,000 to an in-ground swimming pool, and $2,500 to a tool shed.

   c. A social guest trips over a tricycle, smashes her head, and obtains a judgment of $75,000.

2. Suppose a policy provides like-kind replacement cost coverage for the dwelling and that $80,000 of coverage is purchased. How much will the insurer pay under each of the following scenarios (ignoring any deductible):

Loss	Replacement Cost for the Dwelling at Time of Loss
$20,000	$100,000
80,000	100,000
20,000	130,000
80,000	130,000

3. If the base replacement cost equals $200,000, the location modifier equals 1.1, and the rate per dollar of replacement cost equals $0.005, what is the homeowner's premium for property insurance coverage?

4. While homeowners policies generally cover personal property losses (contents) only up to their actual cash value but cover dwellings up to their replacement cost, a majority of policies are endorsed to provide replacement cost coverage on contents. Explain how replacement cost coverage on contents will lead to moral hazard. Given this problem, why is such replacement cost coverage provided?

5. If you were a manager of an insurance company and evidence came to your attention that other insurers operating in a particular urban area with a large proportion of minorities were charging premiums well above fair premiums because of their bigotry, what would you do if you were trying to maximize firm value?

6. Describe a proposal for changing the NFIP to eliminate subsidized policies. What are the advantages and disadvantages of your proposal?

7. Subsidized coverage under state beach and windstorm plans sometimes is justified as desirable to promote the tourist industry, which can then be taxed to benefit citizens who live outside of the subsidized areas. What is a counterargument to these subsidies?

8. Develop arguments for and against eliminating income taxes on insurer investment income on capital as a method of enhancing the availability and affordability of catastrophe coverage.

Answers to Concept Check

1. Freezing homeowners insurance rates would not allow premiums to increase with the value of property being insured, which would lead insurers to reduce the amount of coverage that they would voluntarily sell to homeowners. This would likely lead to an enormous increase in the number of policies in residual markets.

References

earthquakeauthority.com *(Describes the California Earthquake Authority.)*

Harrington, Scott; Steven Mann; and Greg Niehaus. "Insurer Capital Structure Decisions and the Viability of Insurance Derivatives." *Journal of Risk and Insurance,* September 1995. *(Analyzes alternative ways that insurers can finance catastrophe losses, including catastrophe options.)*

Hartwig, Robert P. "Mold and the Insurance Industry: Truth and Consequences," Insurance Information Institute, May 20, 2002. *(Provides information on mold and insurance.)*

Homeowners Insurance: Threats from Without, Weakness Within. Insurance Services Office, 1996. *(Analyzes a number of issues facing homeowners insurers, including a brief discussion of new capital market instruments.)*

Marlett, David C. "The Expansion of the Public Sector's Involvement in Florida's Residential Property Insurance Market," *CPCU Journal,* Summer 1999. *(Discusses the Florida homeowners market during the 1990s.)*

Richardson, Diane. *Insuring to Value.* Cincinnati, OH: The National Underwriter, 1996. *(Provides a detailed description of homeowners policies and issues associated with fully insuring a home.)*

Chapter 15

Life Insurance and Annuities

Chapter Objectives

- Provide a brief overview of major life insurance and annuity products.
- Describe the key features and uses of term, endowment, and whole life insurance policies.
- Describe the key features and uses of universal and variable life insurance policies and how these contracts compare to traditional whole life.
- Describe the key features and uses of annuity products.
- Discuss the tax benefits of life insurance and annuity products.
- Analyze the pricing of basic life insurance policies and annuities.
- Describe methods for comparing the cost of life insurance policies across insurers.

15.1   Life Insurance Product Overview

Table 15.1 summarizes the major types of individual life insurance. There are two broad types of life insurance: term and cash value policies. **Term insurance** simply provides death protection: If the insured dies during the policy period, the beneficiaries receive the amount of coverage purchased. In contrast, **cash value policies** bundle death protection and savings accumulation. When purchasing a cash value life insurance policy, a person essentially is both purchasing death protection and saving money with the insurance company. The amount of savings accumulated is called the policy's **cash value.** As discussed further below, policyholders can withdraw or alter the savings accumulations from cash value life insurance policies in various ways.

TABLE 15.1 Overview of types of life insurance policies.

	Term Insurance	Whole Life	Cash Value Life Insurance		Variable Life
			Whole Life	Universal Life	Variable Life
Death benefit	Level death benefit equal to face amount over fixed number of years; decreasing term has a declining schedule of death benefits	Death benefit is equal to the face amount and is usually level over entire life; if policyholder survives to age 100, then receives death benefit; can purchase more coverage using policyholder dividends	Policyholder chooses between a level death benefit that equals face amount or a death benefit that equals face amount plus cash value	Guaranteed minimum death benefit plus a death benefit that varies with cash value
Typical premium schedules	Annual or five-year level	Single premium; level premium over fixed number of years or until death or surrender	First year required premium but flexible thereafter; sometimes subject to minimum and maximum	Same as whole life
Lapse or surrender	Fail to make premium payment	Fail to make scheduled premium payment, or cash value minus loan value equals zero	Cash value is less than cost of coverage for the period	Fail to make scheduled premium payment or cash value minus loan value equals zero
Cash value	None	Yes, follows a fixed schedule	Yes, varies over time depending on premium payments, charges, and credited interest	Yes, varies over time depending on investment returns
Return on savings accumulation	Not applicable	Implicit in fixed cash value schedule	Varies with interest rates, usually short term rates	Varies with returns on investments chosen by policyholder
Flexibility	Little; most have option to convert to cash value coverage	Limited flexibility; can borrow against cash value	Flexible premium and death benefits; often can borrow against cash value	Same as whole life
Risk borne by policyholder	Amount of dividends with participating policies; insurer insolvency risk	Amount of dividends with participating policies; insurer insolvency risk	Credited interest rate charges; mortality charges; insurer insolvency risk	Investment returns; insurer insolvency risk
Percentage of face amount of coverage sold in US in 2000	41.8%	22.8%	19.9%	0.9%
Percentage of policies sold in US in 2000	21.9%	58.9%	13.0%	0.6%

Note: Variable-universal life, which combines the flexible features of universal life and those of variable life, accounted for 14.4 percent of the face amount of coverage and 4.6 percent of the policies sold in

The most common types of cash value policies are whole life, universal life, and variable life. With whole life policies, the schedule of cash values over time is fixed at the time the policy is purchased. Implicit in this schedule of cash values are returns earned on the savings that are accumulated within the policy. The implicit returns on a whole life policy generally are not reported to the policyholder, and no attempt is made to unbundle the death protection from the savings accumulation. Under modern variations of cash value life insurance (universal life and variable life), however, the separation of the death protection and savings accumulation are made more transparent to the policyholder. Also, instead of having a fixed schedule of cash values, the cash values can vary (depending on the type of policy) with current interest rates, the return earned on the insurer's entire asset portfolio, or the return on specific portfolios of investments, such as stock mutual funds. As a result, universal and variable life often are called investment sensitive contracts.

Policyholders are entitled to at least a portion of a policy's cash value if they **surrender** (terminate) the policy. Early policy surrenders are called **lapses.** With universal life and variable life policies, a surrender charge often is applied, which causes the amount of money that the policyholder can withdraw—the **cash surrender value**—to be less than the cash value. The surrender charges typically decrease with the number of years that the policy is in force. With whole life, explicit surrender charges are not used, and (assuming that no policy loan has been taken, see below) the policy's cash surrender value each year equals the predetermined cash value. However, the predetermined schedule of cash values reflects implicit surrender charges during the early years of the policy, which makes the implicit return earned on the policy's savings low if the policy is surrendered after only several years.

Why would a person wish to bundle death protection coverage with savings accumulation in a life insurance contract? One reason is that people desire permanent (i.e., lifelong) life insurance protection and, for budgeting purposes, they prefer to pay for this protection using a level premium over time. As will become clearer later, paying for permanent death protection with a level premium automatically gives rise to a cash value that increases over time. In other words, the savings accumulation is a byproduct of a fundamental desire for permanent life insurance and level premiums. Perhaps a more important reason for bundling death protection and savings accumulation is that there are tax advantages of saving with a life insurance policy, which we will analyze below. One disadvantage of saving through life insurance for some persons is that death protection also must be purchased to achieve these tax advantages. In addition, the transactions costs (including surrender charges) included in cash value policies often are comparatively large. These costs can offset the tax benefits from cash value policies, especially if the savings are withdrawn early. In some cases, tax penalties also can be applied if the policy is surrendered early.

When discussing life insurance policies, several terms can cause confusion. The **death benefit** is the amount of money that the beneficiaries receive from the insurer when the insured dies. As previously described, the cash value is the amount of savings accumulation from the policy. For term insurance, whole life insurance, and some types of universal life insurance, the death benefit equals the policy's **face amount,** which is the stated amount of coverage purchased by the policyholder. However, for some types of universal life policies, the death benefit equals the face amount plus the cash value. **Death protection** is the amount of pure death protection coverage provided by the policy. The amount of death protection equals the death benefit minus the cash value (i.e., death protection equals the total amount the policy would pay upon death of the insured compared to the amount that the insured could receive if the policy was surrendered).

15.2   Traditional Products: Term, Endowment, and Whole Life

Term Insurance

About 20 percent of the life insurance policies sold in the United States in 2000 were term policies, but these policies represented 42 percent of the amount of death protection purchased (*2001 Life Insurance Fact Book*). A term policy provides a death benefit over a fixed term, usually one year or five years. Term insurance typically provides pure death protection; there is no savings feature and therefore no cash surrender value.

Almost all term policies are **guaranteed renewable,** which means that the policy can be renewed at a predetermined premium at the end of the term without proving insurability (e.g., by taking a physical exam) up to an advanced age, such as 65 or 70. To illustrate, suppose that you purchase a one-year renewable term policy with a $100,000 death benefit. At the end of the year, you can renew the policy for another year with a $100,000 death benefit at a predetermined premium without proving insurability. Also, again without showing proof of insurability, many term policies can be converted to a cash value policy.

The premium for yearly renewable term policies typically increases at the end of each year. For policies that extend over several years, such as a five-year renewable term policy, premiums can increase annually or they can be constant for the term (e.g., five years) and then increased upon renewal. Term insurance premiums increase as the policyholder ages because the probability of a person dying generally increases with age (see section 15.6). Compared to cash value life insurance (see below), the initial premium per $1,000 of face amount is much lower for term insurance, thus allowing a person to buy substantially more coverage for a given premium outlay.

Endowment Insurance

Although the market for endowment insurance in the United States is very small, endowment insurance is common in other countries. A basic understanding of endowment policies also will help you understand more common types of policies. For example, the whole life policy described next is just an endowment policy with a very long term. An **endowment policy** pays the face amount of the policy if the insured dies, but it also pays the face amount of the policy if the insured survives the policy term. For example, if Mr. Cox purchases a five-year endowment policy with a face amount equal to $100,000, the insurer will pay $100,000 to the beneficiaries if he dies in the subsequent five years. If he survives the five-year period, he would be paid the $100,000 at the end of this period. As you might expect, this policy would require a relatively large premium because the insurer will have to pay $100,000 regardless of whether Mr. Cox dies. The main source of uncertainty with an endowment policy is when the benefit payment will occur. Since either Mr. Cox or his beneficiaries will receive $100,000 sometime in the future, an endowment policy has similarities to a savings account.

The insight that endowment policies are largely savings vehicles helps to explain why endowment insurance has declined in importance in the United States but not in other countries. At one time, savings accumulation through endowment policies in the United States received tax advantages. People could save through endowment policies and not pay tax on part of the implicit returns that they earned. Unlike some other countries, the United States no longer grants this favorable tax treatment to endowment policies unless they have a very long duration, such as whole life insurance.

Whole Life Insurance

As the name suggests, the contract length of a **whole life policy** is, in effect, the policyholder's entire life. The death benefit equals the policy's face amount, which generally is fixed for the insured's entire life. For example, a $100,000 face amount whole life policy will pay the beneficiaries $100,000 regardless of when the policyholder dies. If the policyholder survives to age 100 and has paid all the required premiums, the policyholder is paid the $100,000 face amount at that time. Thus, most whole life policies are endowment policies to age 100.

Some whole life policies allow death benefits to be reduced over the course of the contract, and some policies have death benefits that are indexed to inflation. Some whole life contracts are sold with an option, known as the *guaranteed insurability option,* for the policyholder to purchase additional amounts of coverage at specified times and premium rates without proving insurability. Limits on the additional amounts of coverage and the times at which additional coverage can be purchased help reduce adverse selection.

Premium Payment

Whole life insurance policies commonly use a level premium schedule over a fixed number of years. With a *single premium whole life* policy, the buyer pays the entire premium in a lump sum when the policy is issued. Alternatively, a level premium may be payable for a 10-year or 20-year period; these policies are called *limited pay whole life* (e.g., 10-pay life). However, a substantial majority of whole life policies sold in the United States have level premiums that continue until the policyholder dies, surrenders the policy, or reaches the age of 100—whichever comes first. These contracts are known as *continuous premium whole life.*

The key feature of the premium payment methods for whole life policies is that the premium generally does not increase over time in conjunction with the increased probability of dying. This feature contrasts with most term insurance policies, where the premium generally increases over time to reflect the higher probability of dying. Comparing premiums for yearly renewable term insurance and level premium whole life insurance issued at a given age, the term premium starts off much lower than the level whole life premium, but the term premium eventually exceeds the whole life premium. In the early years of a whole life contract, the level whole life insurance premium must exceed the term insurance premium for an insured at the same age in order to fund benefits in the future when the level premium is less than the annual cost of coverage.

Savings Accumulation

In essence, when purchasing a whole life contract, you prepay part of the costs of life insurance for future years. That is, you pay more than the true cost of death protection in the early years of the contract and, assuming that you survive, you pay less than the true cost of death protection in the later years. As a result, with whole life and other cash value policies, policyholders are entitled to a return of their prepayments if they decide to surrender the policy. Policyholders can surrender the policy and, in effect, receive at least a portion of their prepayments back—in the form of the policy's cash surrender value. As mentioned above, the cash surrender value is the amount of money that the policyholder can receive if the policy is surrendered. Thus, the savings accumulate under whole life insurance policies because the premium payment schedule requires the policyholder to prepay the expected costs of future death protection. If the policy stays in force, the insurer needs these funds to cover future expected mortality costs (claim costs) when future premiums are insufficient to cover these costs. If the policy is surrendered, the insurer no longer needs these funds to cover future mortality costs associated with the policy. Therefore, the insurer refunds the cash value to the policyholder.

Note that with whole life policies the beneficiaries do not receive the cash value in addition to the face amount if the insured dies. The beneficiaries receive the face amount only (which generally is fixed). If the policy has a face amount of $100,000, for example, the beneficiaries receive $100,000 regardless of the cash value. This $100,000 payment, however, can be viewed as consisting of a return of cash value plus an amount of pure death protection. If, at the time the insured dies, the cash value is $25,000, then the beneficiaries *in effect* receive the $25,000 cash value plus $75,000 in death protection for a total death benefit of $100,000 (the face amount). From this perspective, the effective or "net" amount of death protection with a whole life policy is less than the policy's face amount (death benefit) whenever the cash value is greater than zero. Stated differently, the amount of death protection varies inversely with the policy's cash value. We can summarize this fundamental aspect of a whole life policy as follows:

$$\text{Death protection}_t = \text{Death benefit} - \text{Cash value}_t = \text{Face amount} - \text{Cash value}_t$$

where the subscript t indicates a particular point in time.

Traditional whole life policies are structured so that the policy's cash value grows each year and the amount of death protection declines. Figure 15.1 illustrates this pattern for a level-premium whole life policy with a level death benefit (face amount equal to $100,000). It is important to note, however, that the division of the face amount of the policy into death protection and cash value is not explicit in a whole life policy. That is, the death protection and the savings accumulation aspects of the policy are not unbundled. The contract simply promises payment of the face amount upon death or payment of the cash surrender value upon surrender.[1]

FIGURE 15.1
Pattern of cash value and death protection for a $100,000 whole life policy issued at age 30.

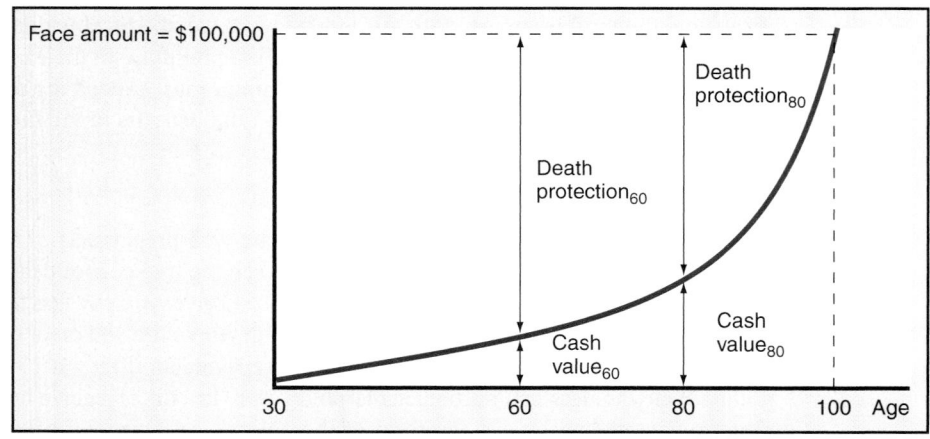

[1]Additional details on the relationship between cash values and death protection are presented in the chapter appendix.

Participating Whole Life and Policy Dividends

Most whole life policies (and many term policies) are **participating policies,** which means that the policy can and usually does pay annual dividends. All whole life and term policies sold by mutual insurers are participating policies. Some stock insurers also sell participating policies. Participating whole life insurance policy premiums are based on conservative assumptions. Because the insurer's actual operating experience is expected to result in lower costs or higher rates of return on assets than are assumed in the premium calculation, the insurer generally pays a portion of the profits to policyholders in the form of policyholder dividends. These dividends are treated as a return of premiums and therefore are not taxable to the policyholder. Insurers generally do not vary dividends with year-to-year fluctuations in operating experience; instead, policyholder dividend formulas are changed periodically based on long-term changes in interest rates, expenses, and mortality costs.

Thus, when pricing participating whole life policies, insurers typically use conservative assumptions with the anticipation that dividends will be positive. If insurers instead determined premiums using assumptions that were closer to what was actually expected, premiums and expected dividends would be lower. Why do insurers follow the conservative approach? One answer relates to our discussion of correlated risk in the earlier chapters. The main factors affecting policyholder dividends are changes in interest rates and aggregate mortality experience. Because these factors cause profits on individual policies to be highly correlated, the uncertainty associated with these factors is costly, if not impossible, to diversify away. The use of conservative assumptions along with paying policyholder dividends shifts some of this correlated risk to policyholders. For example, if a highly contagious and deadly disease occurred or if returns on insurer investments declined substantially and remained at low levels over long periods, insurers could reduce policyholder dividends. The alternative would be for insurers to bear more of this correlated risk. The problem is that insurers then would need to hold much more capital to achieve the same level of insolvency risk. The costs of holding this capital would increase expected prices for life insurance. In summary, policyholder dividends are one method of allowing insurers and policyholders to share correlated risk.

Policies usually provide several options for the use of dividends. For example, whole life policyholders often have a choice as to whether dividends are used to increase the policy's face amount (known as paid-up additions) or pay part of the next premium due. When selling whole life insurance policies, agents present a table of illustrated dividends, net premiums (premiums minus illustrated dividends) if the policyholder uses the dividends to reduce future premiums, and illustrated death benefits if dividends are used to increase the policy's face amount. **Illustrated dividends** usually reflect what the insurer is currently paying on comparable policies. It is important to note, however, that these illustrations are not guaranteed (see Box 15.1). Illustrated dividends typically increase over time. The main reason for this increase is that most insurer dividend formulas reflect a credit for greater than assumed investment returns that is approximately proportional to the policy's cash value. As the guaranteed cash value grows over time, so does the illustrated dividend.

Surrender Options

As mentioned above, a whole life policy can be surrendered for its cash surrender value. Most whole life policies provide two other surrender options (technically known as nonforfeiture options): paid-up insurance and extended term insurance. With **paid-up insurance,**

Universal life policies were introduced in 1979 when interest rates were at a very high level. Insurers marketed these policies by advertising that the cash value of the policy would vary directly with interest rates. Policy illustrations based on current interest rates at the time created the impression that the cash values of universal life policies would grow to enormous sums. Because interest rates fell in the late 1980s and early 1990s, many illustrations did not materialize. As a result, a number of policyholders filed suit against and obtained settlements from insurers, alleging that the insurers and their agents misled policyholders. Some participating whole life insurers similarly were sued by their policyholders when they reduced dividends below illustrated levels due to declining interest rates.

the cash surrender value is used as a single premium to purchase a paid-up whole life policy. For example, suppose that a 55-year-old person has a policy with face amount of $100,000 and cash surrender value of $30,000. The policy can be surrendered and the cash value can be used as a single premium to purchase life insurance for the remainder of the insured's life. If $30,000 is the single premium for a $75,000 face amount policy, then $75,000 is the amount of paid-up insurance. With **extended term insurance,** the cash value is used as a single premium to purchase a paid-up term policy with the same face amount as the original policy (e.g., $100,000). For example, if $30,000 is the single premium for a 15-year term policy with a $100,000 face amount, the policyholder could surrender the policy and receive the 15-year term policy. Whole life policy illustrations generally include a schedule of paid-up insurance and extended term insurance amounts available at various ages in addition to the schedule of cash values.

Policy Loans

Most whole life policies also allow the policyholder to obtain a large portion of the cash value of the policy without surrendering the policy by borrowing against the cash value in the form of a **policy loan.** To illustrate how a policy loan works, suppose that a $100,000 face amount policy has cash value of $30,000 and the policyholder borrows $10,000. Premiums still need to be paid after the loan is taken (unless more loans are used to pay the premium, see below), and the policy's cash value grows as originally scheduled. However, the policyholder owes the principal and interest on the loan. If the insured dies prior to paying back the loan, the loan balance reduces the death benefit. If the insured in this example died immediately after taking out the loan, the death benefit would be reduced to $90,000 ($100,000 face amount minus $10,000 loan amount). Similarly, the cash value available upon surrender would only be $20,000 ($30,000 cash value minus $10,000 loan amount). Some whole life policies have provisions whereby if a policyholder fails to make a premium payment, a loan against the cash value is automatically taken out in an amount equal to the missed premium (assuming that the cash value exceeds the premium).

Until the late 1970s and early 1980s, the interest rate on policy loans usually was fixed in the contract at the time the policy was issued. Periods of high interest rates during the 1970s and early 1980s led many policyholders to take loans in order to invest the loan principal in higher yielding securities. The resulting larger than expected cash withdrawals, known as disintermediation, caused insurers to reduce dividends on participating policies. As a result of their experience during these periods, many insurers moved to variable loan rates on whole life policies, and some insurers began paying lower dividends on policies that have loans outstanding.

Expense Loadings

Life insurance premiums must cover the insurer's underwriting, marketing, and claims processing costs, as well as other administrative costs (see Chapter 8 for a general discussion of these costs). The issue of how and when to recover these expenses is particularly important for life insurers because of the long-term nature of the policies and because a large part of the insurer's expenses are incurred at the time the policy is issued, such as expenses for marketing, underwriting, and sales commissions.

Whole life (and term) insurers generally front-end load expense charges. With a whole life policy, the front-end loading of expenses is accomplished by having a relatively low accumulation of cash value in the early years of the policy. Even with this front-end loading, insurers generally experience a net loss on policies that lapse within a few years of issue. The alternative of spreading expense charges more evenly over the life of the contract would imply that the insurer would recover even less of its costs from policies that were surrendered early.

The front-end loading of expense charges causes the implicit return earned on the savings accumulation portion of the policy to be relatively low until the contract has been in force for a number of years. In addition, insurers with higher early lapse rates need to charge higher rates, holding other factors constant, to recover all of their costs over time. The higher rates further reduce the implicit return available on their policies. Thus, there are two implications that you should be aware of: (1) Implicit returns on savings accumulated through life insurance will be low or even negative if the policy is dropped early, and (2) insurers with lower lapse rates can offer policies with higher returns.

Concept Checks

1. Assume that the face amount of a whole life policy equals $100,000 and that the cash value equals $20,000. What is the death benefit (total amount paid upon death)? What is the amount of death protection?
2. Show graphically how the cash value and death benefit change over time for a nonparticipating whole life policy with a face amount of $50,000.

15.3 Product Innovation: Universal and Variable Life

Universal Life

The period of high interest rates in the late 1970s led to the introduction in 1979 of **universal life policies** (see Box 15.1). Like traditional whole life policies, these policies provide permanent death protection and savings accumulation. However, universal life policies differ in that (1) they offer greater flexibility with respect to premium payments, and (2) the cash value varies explicitly over time based on premium payments, expense and mortality charges, and credited interest.

Premium Flexibility

A fixed premium schedule is not used with universal life. The policyholder instead has flexibility in the payment of premiums, sometimes subject to annual minimum and maximum amounts. A scheduled premium payment generally can be skipped without surrendering the policy or taking a policy loan. Premium flexibility is one reason that the cash value of a universal life policy is not fixed in advance like a whole life policy. If the policy-holder exercises the option to pay more or less in premiums, then the cash value of the policy will be adjusted accordingly. Lower premium payments imply lower cash values, all else being equal.

Cash Value Accumulation

The cash value for a universal life policy varies over time, depending on the interest rate the insurer uses to credit the policy's cash value and on the explicit expense and mortality cost charges used to debit the policy's cash value. Implicit in a whole life policy is a predetermined interest rate credited to the policy's cash value, which, along with predetermined mortality and expense charges, determines the schedule of cash values. With universal life policies, the interest rate credits to the policy's cash value can vary monthly, depending on current market interest rates. For example, if market interest rates increase, the insurer will likely increase the interest rate credited to cash values, and then cash values will grow at a faster rate.

Given these explicit credits and charges (debits), the death protection and the savings accumulation portions of the policy are essentially unbundled with a universal life policy. The policyholder is given an explicit statement showing how the policy's cash value changes from period to period, depending on premium payments, interest rates, and expense and mortality charges. Figure 15.2 shows the important relationships.

Additional premium payments or higher interest credits cause the cash value to increase, holding mortality and expense charges constant. The annual mortality charge generally reflects the insurer's expected claim costs for death protection. The insurer can modify the mortality charge per $1,000 of death protection for a given age, but this charge cannot exceed a maximum amount for each age that is specified in the contract. Expense charges commonly equal a percent of premiums, with a higher percent charge for the initial premium. This front-end loading of expense charges will cause the cash value to grow at a lower rate in the early years of the policy, all else being equal. The same is true for whole life policies, but the relationships are not made explicit. Most universal life policies also include a stipulated schedule of surrender charges.

The formula in Figure 15.2 makes it clear that the savings accumulation with a universal life policy explicitly depends on the insurer's charges, which can be expected to change over time in relation to its operating experience. The policyholder explicitly bears the risk associated with credited interest rates and mortality charges. In contrast, with nonparticipating whole life policies, the insurer's operating experience does not affect the policyholder (ignoring the risk of insolvency); that is, the schedule of cash values is guaranteed at the time the policy is purchased. With participating whole life policies, the effect of the insurer's operating experience on a policyholder is less immediate and direct than with universal life policies, because dividends generally change only slowly compared to those illustrated at the time of purchase. That is, dividends on whole life policies are based on longer term trends in interest rates, mortality charges, and other expenses, whereas cash

FIGURE 15.2

Main factors affecting cash value of a universal life policy.

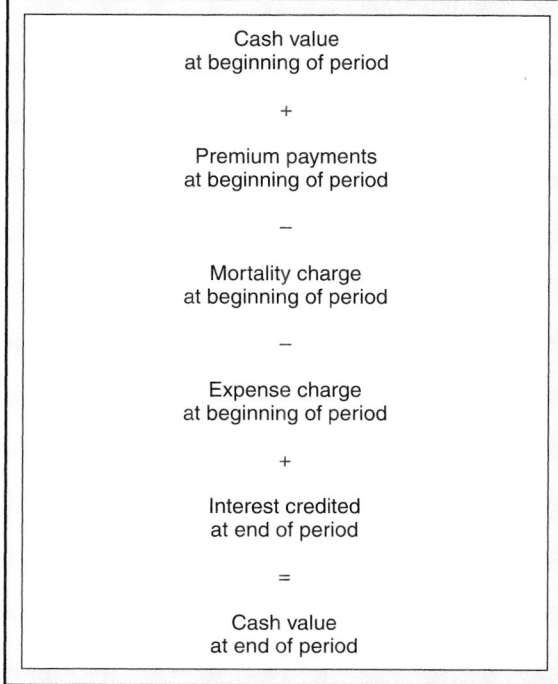

Cash value
at beginning of period

+

Premium payments
at beginning of period

−

Mortality charge
at beginning of period

−

Expense charge
at beginning of period

+

Interest credited
at end of period

=

Cash value
at end of period

value changes with universal life generally depend on short-term changes in interest rates (and sometimes mortality).

Universal life policies usually guarantee a minimum interest rate that will be credited to the cash value. Interest credits above the guaranteed rate are determined in various ways. One method is to explicitly link the interest credited to a short-term interest rate (e.g., the rate paid on specified US Treasury securities). Another method is for the insurer to choose a crediting rate for the coming year in view of the interest it can earn on new investments or on the expected return it will earn on its entire portfolio of investments.

When selling universal life policies, agents present projections of future premiums and cash values. The projections, by definition, are based on assumptions about crediting interest rates, mortality charges, expense charges, and other factors. Agents often have made projections using a current market interest rate as the crediting rate over the course of the entire policy. When interest rates were at historically high levels, projections based on current interest rate levels assumed that high interest rates would continue to prevail into the foreseeable future. The use of a high crediting interest rate will imply that the policy's cash value will grow at a fast rate and can suggest that premiums will vanish (no longer need to be paid) at some date, because the cash value will grow to a level that is sufficient to cover future charges.[2] If, however, interest rates do not stay at the high level that was assumed in the projections, cash values will not grow as rapidly and premiums will not vanish as projected.

[2]This also can (and did) occur for participating whole life policies during prolonged periods of high long-term interest rates.

Box 15.1 describes the legal problems some insurers experienced after universal life policies did not meet projections, in part because of falling interest rates.

Death Benefit Options

With a universal life policy, the policyholder generally has a choice between two death benefit options. One option is to have the total death benefit (the amount paid upon the insured's death) equal to a level amount over time, as is true for a whole life policy. The other option is to have the death benefit increase as the cash value of the policy increases. That is, unlike whole life, the total death benefit at a point in time equals the initial face amount plus the cash value at that time. With the second option, the amount of death protection equals the face amount of the policy at all times (i.e., Death protection = Total death benefit − Cash value).

Under the level death benefit option, the amount of death protection decreases as the cash value increases, just as in a whole life policy. However, because the cash value is uncertain under a universal life policy, it is possible under the level death benefit option that the cash value could increase above the face amount of the policy. If this occurred, there would be no death protection and the policy's savings accumulation would not qualify for preferential tax treatment because the policy would not satisfy the IRS's definition of insurance. For this reason, if the level death benefit option is chosen, the death benefit is automatically increased if the cash value approaches the policy's face amount so that a gap is always maintained between the death benefit and the cash value. This gap allows the policy to meet the complex rules (concerning the minimum amount of death protection in relation to savings accumulation) required to qualify for tax treatment as life insurance. Figure 15.3 illustrates how the death benefit and death protection vary if the cash value increases over time under each of the death benefit options.

Loans and Partial Surrenders

As with traditional whole life policies, policyholders can take out loans on some universal life policies. Any unpaid interest on the loan is automatically deducted from the policy's cash value. In some cases, a lower interest rate is credited to the portion of the policy's cash

FIGURE 15.3   Death benefit options for a universal life policy

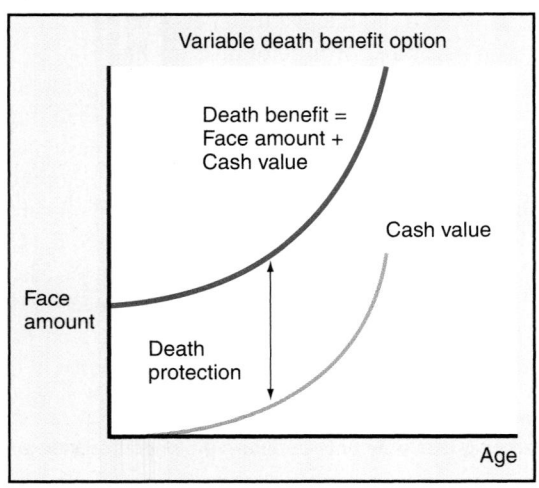
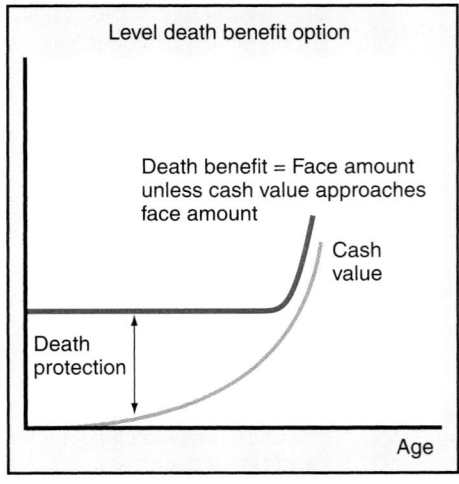

value that is borrowed. For example, an insurer might credit 8 percent on unborrowed cash values and 6 percent on any amount borrowed. One reason for this provision is that if the loan rate (the interest rate paid by the policyholder) is fixed up front (e.g., at 6 percent), then the lower rate paid on the cash value helps prevent disintermediation by policyholders. That is, it reduces the extent to which policyholders take out loans at lower than market rates and still receive interest credited at market rates. Instead of loan provisions, some universal life policies allow partial surrenders. The policyholder can simply remove a portion of the cash value without terminating the policy. In these cases, no interest is credited (or no loan interest is due) on the portion of the cash value that is surrendered.

Concept Check

3. Other things being equal, explain how each of the following would be likely to affect the growth of a universal life policy's cash value.
   (*a*) The policyholder reduces the annual premium payment by 50 percent after five years.
   (*b*) Market interest rates are stable for five years and then decline sharply and remain at the lower level.
   (*c*) Researchers discover a cure for cancer five years after the policy is issued.

Variable Life

With a **variable life policy,** the growth in the cash value of a policy depends directly on the return earned on a portfolio of assets chosen by the policyholder. Recall that with universal life, credited interest rates are expected to vary in relation to current yields available to the insurer on new investments, its overall portfolio, or, in some cases, market interest rates. For variable life policies, however, the growth in cash value varies directly with the return earned on a portfolio of stocks and bonds that is chosen by the policyholder. If the return on the portfolio is negative, the cash value can decline with variable life. This contrasts with universal life policies, which specify a minimum rate of return that will be credited to cash values. Since the purchaser of a variable life policy is in effect investing in a mutual fund with an insurance wrapper, agents selling variable life policies are required to have a securities license. The policyholder also must be given a prospectus, as is required for sales of other securities.

The death benefit on a variable life policy varies with the policy's cash value, but a minimum death benefit is guaranteed. Thus, one can view the death benefit on a variable life policy as consisting of a level guaranteed death benefit plus an additional death benefit if the rates of return on the investments selected by the policyholder exceed some minimum threshold. In the latter case, the additional funds generated from the high returns are automatically used to purchase additional death benefits. If the rates of return on the investments selected by the policyholder fall short of the threshold, then previously purchased additional death benefits are surrendered.

Variable life policies, like whole life policies, generally have fixed and level premiums. Policy loans can be taken, with some policies offering a fixed loan rate and others offering a variable loan rate. Some policies have automatic loans to pay missed premiums. Absent this provision, failure to pay a premium due will produce a lapse or surrender. Not surprisingly, insurers have merged the variable life idea, where the rate of return on the policy's cash value varies with rates of return on portfolios of stocks and bonds chosen by the policy-holder, with the universal life idea of flexibility in premium payments and death benefits. The result commonly is called **variable-universal life.**

15.4   Tax Benefits from Life Insurance Policies

Cash value life insurance policies are an income tax–advantaged method of saving. The tax advantages arise from the interaction of the following aspects of the tax code:

1. Death benefits are not taxable as income. (They may be subject to estate taxes.)
2. No income tax is paid on the annual increase in cash value while the policy is in force.
3. If the policy is surrendered, the policyholder pays income tax on the difference between the cash surrender value and the sum of all premiums less policyholder dividends.

The first and second features of the tax code in effect imply that the implicit returns on life insurance policy savings accumulation escape income taxation if the insured dies. In contrast, if an equivalent amount of funds were saved for the insured's beneficiaries in a nontax-advantaged account, then the nontax-exempt interest and dividends on those funds would have been taxed as they were paid and the capital gains would have been taxed as they were realized.

If the insured does not die, the second and third features imply that returns earned on life insurance policy savings are tax deferred until the policy is surrendered and are only partially taxed upon surrender. In some countries, the premiums paid for life insurance also are tax deductible. The combination of premium deductibility and tax deferment of investment earnings causes the tax benefits from life insurance in these countries to be equivalent to the tax benefits of qualified retirement plans in the United States (discussed in Chapter 17). Life insurance premiums are not tax deductible in the United States.[3] Thus, the tax benefits are similar to retirement accounts with tax deferral of investment income, but no deductibility of contributions.

Since Chapter 17 provides a detailed analysis of the benefits of tax-deferred savings plans, we provide only a simple example here to illustrate this tax benefit. Suppose that the annual before-tax rate of return on taxable securities is 10 percent. Then an investor with a 28 percent marginal tax rate would earn 7.2 percent in a nontax-deferred account. Saving $1 in this way would yield $1.072 after one year and $1.072^{20} = \$4.02$ after 20 years. If, instead, the investor earned 10 percent on $1 for 20 years through a tax-deferred account (as cash value life insurance policies are), the investor would have $1.1^{20} = \$6.73$ before paying tax and $6.73 - 0.28 \times (\$6.73 - \$1.00) = \$5.13$ after paying tax at the end of 20 years. The difference between $5.13 and $4.02 is the benefit of tax-deferred savings in this example.

The actual benefit from tax deferral of investment earnings from life insurance is greater than what we just calculated, because the third feature of the tax code listed above overstates the "tax basis" (the amount deducted from the gross amount received to determine taxable income) compared to a nonlife insurance tax-deferred savings account. A higher tax basis implies that less tax is paid when the policy is surrendered. To illustrate,

---

[3]An exception is that the premiums on the first $50,000 of employer-provided life insurance are not taxable to the employee.

recall that the premium payments on a cash value policy can be viewed as consisting of two parts: (1) an amount needed to cover the cost of death protection (face amount minus the cash value in the case of whole life), and (2) an amount saved through the insurer. By allowing the total premium to be used as the tax basis, the tax basis allows a deduction for the cost of death protection in addition to the implicit savings contributions by the policyholder. Consequently, the tax paid once the policy is surrendered is less than what would be paid on an otherwise identical tax deferred savings account.

In summary, life insurance policies with cash values allow investors to (1) escape income taxes on the returns earned on the savings invested with the insurer if the insured dies, (2) defer income taxes on the returns earned on the savings invested with the insurer if the policy is surrendered, and (3) pay lower taxes when the policy is surrendered, compared to other tax-deferred savings accounts that allow tax deferral of investment income but no up-front deductibility of contributions. This tax treatment significantly increases the demand for cash value life insurance.

15.5   Annuity Contracts

Annuity contracts are an important and growing source of business for life insurers and tax-deferred savings for annuity policyholders. In 2000, US life insurers received $303 billion in annuity premiums, which was 56 percent of their total premiums for life insurance, health insurance, and annuities. Moreover, the percentage of premiums from annuities increased dramatically over the past 30 years. Annuity premiums represented only 17 percent of all life insurance company premiums in 1975 and 48 percent in 1990.

A useful starting point for understanding annuities is to recognize that two periods are associated with any annuity: (1) the period when the policyholder pays premiums to the insurer, known as the **accumulation period,** and (2) the period when the insurer makes payments to the policyholder, known as the **payout period.** The nature of payments during both the accumulation period and the payout period can take many forms. Table 15.2 summarizes the most common variations.

TABLE 15.2
Overview of annuity contracts.

Characteristic	Variations
Premium payments	(a) Single premium (b) Fixed period, level premium up to an advanced age (c) Flexible premium over time
Annuity benefits begin	(a) Immediately (b) Deferred
Annuity benefits end	(a) Fixed number of years (b) Death of one or more individuals (c) Combination of (a) and (b)
Insurer payments	(a) Fixed (b) Vary with interest rates, with guaranteed minimum (c) Vary with returns on stock and bond funds chosen by policyholder

During the payout period, annuities pay a specified amount of money at given time intervals (e.g., monthly) over a specified length of time.[4] An annuity that only pays until the annuitant dies is called a **straight life annuity.** An annuity that pays over a fixed period of time regardless of death is called an *annuity certain.* These basic types of annuities can be combined, as well. For example, a life annuity, period-certain pays for a fixed number of years regardless of death, after which payments end when one or more people die. Joint and last survivor annuities are structured so that the insurer's payments end only after the death of two people (e.g., a husband and wife). Annuity contracts also can be purchased where payments are reduced, but not eliminated, when one person dies, but not the other.

Uses of Annuities

From a risk management perspective, the primary role of annuities during the payout period is to protect a person or persons from outliving their financial resources. For example, a retiree can pay an insurer a fixed amount of money (a portion of preretirement savings) and in exchange receive a monthly payment from the insurer for as long as the person lives. This would be an example of a single-premium life annuity with immediate payments. In contrast, a person who attempts to spread retirement savings over his or her remaining life without an annuity faces the risk that the savings fund will be exhausted prior to death (the person lives longer than expected). Alternatively, the person might die sooner than expected with money left in the bank (to the benefit of strangers or obnoxious heirs). Thus, annuities can be used to reduce the risk that savings are exhausted before the annuitant dies or vice versa. In effect, the funds of annuitants that die earlier are used by the insurer to fund payments for annuitants that die later.

As the previous example illustrated, a retiree can use a portion of preretirement savings to purchase a single premium annuity at retirement. In essence, the person accumulates funds while working and then spreads the funds over retirement using the annuity contract. An alternative approach is to purchase, prior to retirement, annuity contracts with deferred payments. **Deferred annuities,** which represent about 95 percent of all annuity purchases, essentially combine the preretirement accumulation of savings and the postretirement distribution of savings in one contract. The main reason for combining these two steps is the tax advantages of saving through deferred annuities: The returns implicitly earned from these contracts are not taxed until the insurer distributes them. Thus, like cash value life insurance policies, deferred annuity contracts are a tax-deferred savings vehicle.

While deferred annuities and cash value life insurance policies serve a similar purpose with respect to deferring tax on investment income, expense charges typically are lower with an annuity contract. Consequently, annuities often are the preferred method of savings. If death protection (pure insurance) and/or greater liquidity (see below) also are desired, there may be advantages of purchasing cash value life insurance rather than or in addition to annuities.

Specific Savings Features

The accumulation of savings through an annuity contract follows a pattern similar to other savings plans. Premium payments (contributions) and the return credited on past accumu-

---

[4]Annuities are discussed in Chapter 17 in the context of defined benefit pension plans that pay monthly benefits until death.

lations cause the savings accumulation to grow and expense charges reduce the growth rate. With **fixed annuities,** the return credited to an annuity contract in a given period usually varies with current interest rates, but the insurer guarantees a minimum rate of return (often 3 or 4 percent). With **variable annuities,** the return credited to the contract varies with the return on stock and bond funds that the policyholder chooses; there is no minimum rate of return. Thus, variable annuities are very similar to mutual fund investments. As is true for variable life insurance contracts, the agent selling variable annuities must be licensed to sell securities. Expense charges typically are a percentage (e.g., 2 percent) of the value of the accumulated funds. Some annuities have higher expense charges in the initial year than in later years; that is, there is a front-end load.

Deferred annuities have two basic types of premium payment methods. Single premium deferred annuities (SPDAs) are purchased with a single premium. Of course, multiple SPDAs can be purchased over time and in varying amounts. A flexible premium deferred annuity (FPDA) gives the purchaser flexibility as to the timing and amount of premium payments. A natural question is, Why distinguish SPDAs and FPDAs when both products allow the purchaser to make the same sequence of payments? One difference between the two contracts is in the nature of the guarantee provided by the insurer with respect to the rates of interest credited on the savings accumulations. SPDAs often will guarantee that interest will be credited on the savings accumulations using the current specified interest rate for several years. FPDAs typically do not provide such a guarantee.

When evaluating a deferred annuity it is important not only to consider the rate at which savings accumulate, but also the rate that is used to annuitize the savings accumulations. The benefit of a comparatively high interest rate used for crediting savings during the accumulation phase might be mitigated by a comparatively low interest rate used for distributing the savings accumulations over the payout phase.

Deferred annuities, however, do not have to be and often are not annuitized; that is, the purchaser can withdraw the accumulated funds prior to the payout period by surrendering the policy. Depending on the length of time that the contract has been in force, surrender charges may be applied. Insurers typically recover a large portion of their expenses associated with selling and administering annuity contracts that are surrendered early through surrender charges (i.e., most annuities have backend loads). Surrender charges generally are a percentage of the funds accumulated and decline over time. As a result, the return on these annuity contracts is higher, all else being equal, the longer that the contract is held prior to surrender.

There also are tax penalties if people withdraw their savings from annuity contracts prior to retirement. For example, if a person withdraws savings from an annuity contract prior to age 59½, then a 10 percent penalty on the returns from the savings generally is applied unless the funds are rolled into another annuity contract. Thus, although there is a tax advantage of saving through annuity contracts, the savings are illiquid in that they cannot be used for purposes other than retirement without paying a significant penalty. In contrast, loan provisions in most cash value life insurance policies allow access to savings without surrender charges or tax penalties.

Concept Checks

4. Explain how annuities are a form of insurance against living too long.
5. Explain how annuities are a tax-advantaged savings vehicle.

15.6   Life Insurance Pricing

A greater understanding of how life insurance works can be obtained by studying basic aspects of pricing. In this section, we start by pricing a sequence of one-year term life insurance policies. We then consider the pricing of a two-year term policy under two assumptions about the payment of premiums. A comparison of a two-year term policy with a sequence of one-year term policies provides many of the insights necessary for understanding whole life insurance policies. We then move on to the pricing of basic annuities and whole life insurance. Our discussion of pricing focuses on mortality costs and ignores expense loadings; that is, we examine what normally are called **net premiums.**

One-year Term Insurance

To price life insurance and annuity products, an insurer needs to estimate the probability of a person dying at different ages. For example, suppose that Mr. Babbel, a 40-year-old, purchases a one-year term life insurance policy with a face amount of $100,000. This policy will pay the beneficiaries of the policy (Mr. Babbel's family) $100,000 if Mr. Babbel dies. Assume that the insurer uses an estimate of the probability that Mr. Babbel will die during the coming year from a **mortality table** like Table 15.3 (also see Box 15.2). The column labeled "Probability of Dying" in the mortality table gives the probability of a male dying at the age of x given that he has lived x years. The other columns of the mortality table will be discussed as we proceed.

Table 15.3 indicates that the probability of a male who has lived to his 40th birthday dying at the age of 40 (before his 41st birthday) is 0.00302. Thus, the claim cost distribution for this one-year term policy is:

$$\text{Loss} = \begin{array}{ll} \$0 & \text{with probability } 0.99698 \\ \$100,000 & \text{with probability } 0.00302 \end{array}$$

Mortality Tables   15.2

According to the mortality table (Table 15.3), the probability of a 99-year-old person dying during the coming year equals 1. Of course, not all 99-year-olds will die by their 100th birthday. The assumption that everyone dies before the age of 100 is not restrictive for two reasons. First, term insurance is rarely sold to people beyond the age of 70, so that the probabilities during the older ages are not relevant to most term insurance policies. Second, most whole life policies are equivalent to endowment policies to age 100; that is, if the policyholder survives to be 100, he or she receives the face amount of the policy.

Many mortality tables exist; Table 15.3 is simply one example. Since the mortality risk of females and males differs, insurers typically use different mortality tables for males and females (if the law allows it). Insurers also use different mortality tables for smokers and non-smokers. As discussed in Chapter 8, competition among insurers would be expected to lead insurers to identify and use low-cost information that helps predict the probability of a person dying.

Although we will not do so in this chapter, insurers use different mortality tables for life insurance products than for annuities. One reason is that the selection of people who purchase life insurance policies differs from the selection of people who typically buy annuities. Other things being equal, people who have a lower than average probability of dying are more likely to buy life annuities and less likely to buy life insurance.

TABLE 15.3 1980 standard mortality table for males.

Age	Probability of Dying	Number of People	Number of Deaths	Age	Probability of Dying	Number of People	Number of Deaths
0	0.00418	1000000	4180				
1	0.00107	995820	1066	51	0.00730	890645	6502
2	0.00099	994754	985	52	0.00796	884144	7038
3	0.00098	993770	974	53	0.00871	877106	7640
4	0.00095	992796	943	54	0.00956	869466	8312
5	0.00090	991853	893	55	0.01047	861154	9016
6	0.00086	990960	852	56	0.01146	852138	9766
7	0.00080	990108	792	57	0.01249	842372	10521
8	0.00076	989316	752	58	0.01359	831851	11305
9	0.00074	988564	732	59	0.01477	820546	12119
10	0.00073	987832	721	60	0.01608	808427	13000
11	0.00077	987111	760	61	0.01754	795427	13952
12	0.00085	986351	838	62	0.01919	781476	14997
13	0.00099	985513	976	63	0.02106	766479	16142
14	0.00115	984537	1132	64	0.02314	750337	17363
15	0.00133	983405	1308	65	0.02542	732974	18632
16	0.00151	982097	1483	66	0.02785	714342	19894
17	0.00167	980614	1638	67	0.03044	694448	21139
18	0.00178	978976	1743	68	0.03319	673309	22347
19	0.00186	977234	1818	69	0.03617	650962	23545
20	0.00190	975416	1853	70	0.03951	627416	24789
21	0.00191	973563	1860	71	0.04330	602627	26094
22	0.00189	971703	1837	72	0.04765	576533	27472
23	0.00186	969867	1804	73	0.05264	549061	28903
24	0.00182	968063	1762	74	0.05819	520159	30268
25	0.00177	966301	1710	75	0.06419	489891	31446
26	0.00173	964591	1669	76	0.07053	458445	32334
27	0.00171	962922	1647	77	0.07712	426111	32862
28	0.00170	961275	1634	78	0.08390	393249	32994
29	0.00171	959641	1641	79	0.09105	360255	32801
30	0.00173	958000	1657	80	0.09884	327454	32366
31	0.00178	956343	1702	81	0.10748	295089	31716
32	0.00183	954640	1747	82	0.11725	263372	30880
33	0.00191	952893	1820	83	0.12826	232492	29819
34	0.00200	951073	1902	84	0.14025	202673	28425
35	0.00211	949171	2003	85	0.15295	174248	26651
36	0.00224	947168	2122	86	0.16609	147597	24514
37	0.00240	945047	2268	87	0.17955	123082	22099
38	0.00258	942779	2432	88	0.19327	100983	19517
39	0.00279	940346	2624	89	0.20729	81466	16887
40	0.00302	937723	2832	90	0.22177	64579	14322
41	0.00329	934891	3076	91	0.23698	50257	11910
42	0.00356	931815	3317	92	0.25345	38347	9719
43	0.00387	928498	3593	93	0.27211	28628	7790
44	0.00419	924905	3875	94	0.29590	20838	6166
45	0.00455	921029	4191	95	0.32996	14672	4841
46	0.00492	916838	4511	96	0.38455	9831	3780
47	0.00532	912328	4854	97	0.48020	6050	2905
48	0.00574	907474	5209	98	0.65798	3145	2069
49	0.00621	902265	5603	99	1.00000	1076	1076
50	0.00671	896662	6017	100		0	

The expected claim cost equals $302. From Chapter 8, you know that the expected claim cost is one of the fundamental factors affecting fair insurance premiums.

Another factor affecting fair premiums is the time value of money. Therefore, we must consider the time between the receipt of premiums and the payment of claims, as well as the interest rate. To focus on the main points, we will assume that people purchase life insurance on the insured's birthday and that if they die during the year, the insurer pays the beneficiaries of the policy on the eve of what would have been the insured's next birthday. The other factors affecting fair premiums—expense loadings and profit loadings—will be ignored for simplicity.

To find the present value of expected claim costs on Mr. Babbel's one-year term policy, assume that the one-year interest rate equals 10 percent. Then the present value of expected claim costs equals $302/1.1 = $275; that is, the insurer would need to charge Mr. Babbel $275 in order to cover its expected claim costs. Ignoring insurer nonclaim costs, the fair premium for this one-year term policy would be $275.

Suppose that Mr. Babbel is lucky enough to survive his 40th year and decides to purchase another one-year term policy with a $100,000 death benefit for his 41st year. What is the fair premium (ignoring expense and profit loadings)? From the mortality table, the probability that Mr. Babbel dies in his 41st year is 0.00329, slightly higher than the previous year. The undiscounted expected claim costs therefore equal $329. Assuming the interest rate is still 10 percent, the present value of expected claim costs equals $299 ($329/1.1). The important point to notice is that the premium for one-year term insurance is higher than in the previous year. This premium increase is simply a reflection of the higher probability of dying as Mr. Babbel ages, as all other factors (e.g., interest rates, expense loadings) have been held constant.[5] If Mr. Babbel continued to purchase one-year term policies, the premium per $1,000 of coverage would continue to rise as depicted in Figure 15.4.

Concept Check

6. Assuming an interest rate of 8 percent, and using Table 15.3, calculate the present value of expected claim costs for a one-year term policy with a $1,000 death benefit for (*a*) a 50-year-old, and (*b*) a 95-year-old.

FIGURE 15.4
Expected claim costs on a one-year term policy with a $1,000 death benefit from age 35 to 99.

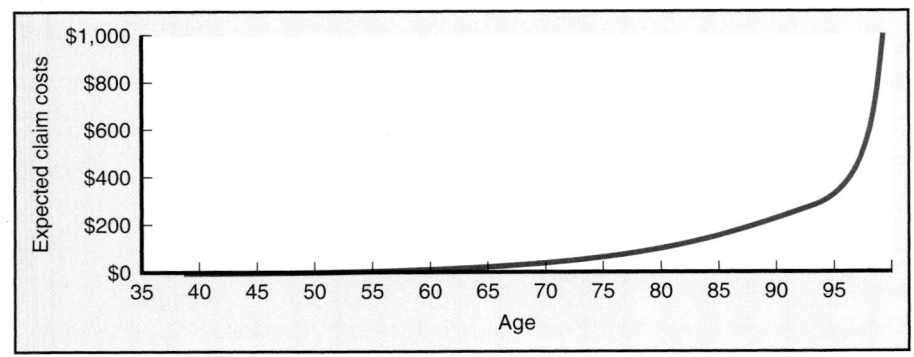

[5]Over a brief period in a person's twenties, the probability of dying declines with age, because of fewer accidental deaths (largely due to drunk driving) and suicides. After this period, the probability of dying increases with age.

Two-year Term Insurance

Now let's return to the situation where Mr. Babbel is 40 years old and suppose that, instead of purchasing a one-year term policy, he decides to purchase a two-year $100,000 term insurance policy. We will find the premium (ignoring expense and profit loadings) for this policy under two alternative methods of payment: a single premium and a level premium.

Single Premium

A single premium policy requires Mr. Babbel to pay one premium at the initiation of the policy and no premiums thereafter. Since we are ignoring expense and profit loadings, the fair single premium equals the present value of expected claim costs. As in any present value problem, the best way to proceed is to identify all the expected cash flows and the timing of these cash flows. Table 15.4 summarizes the timing of possible claim costs and their expected values.

If Mr. Babbel dies in the first year, then the insurer will pay $100,000 one year after the contract is initiated. The probability that this will occur is 0.00302. Thus, the expected claim cost at the end of one year is $302. Assuming an interest rate of 10 percent, the present value of this expected cash outflow equals $275 = $302/1.1. This calculation is the same as was done earlier for the one-year term policy at age 40.

Now comes the more difficult part. If Mr. Babbel does not die in the first year of the policy, it is possible that he will die in the second year. The probability of dying at age 41 that is listed in the mortality table is the probability of dying conditional on the person living up to his 41st birthday. To find the expected claim costs, however, the insurer needs to know a different probability. Since the insurer is pricing the policy when Mr. Babbel is 40 years old, the insurer needs to know the probability that a person who just turned 40 will die at age 41 (in his 42nd year). For a 40-year-old male to die in his 42nd year, he must first live through his 41st year and then die in his 42nd year.

To calculate the relevant probability, we will use columns labeled "Number of People" and "Number of Deaths" in the mortality table. The mortality table starts with an arbitrary number of people at age zero; in Table 15.3, the initial number of people is 1,000,000. This imaginary group of people is then followed through time, assuming that the listed probabilities of death occur. Since the probability of death in a person's first year is 0.00418, then 4,180 of the 1,000,000 people who started the year are expected to be dead after one year. This leaves 995,820 people alive after one year. The table continues to track the expected deaths each year. At age 99, there are only 1,076 people left alive and by assumption they all depart before they reach the age of 100.

These columns can be used to calculate the probability of a 40-year-old male dying in his 42nd year. The table indicates that there are 937,723 people who will be expected to

TABLE 15.4
Insurer's expected claim costs for a two-year $100,000 term policy for a 40-year-old male.

Time	Claim Cost	Probability of Dying Given Alive at Contract Initiation	Expected Claim Cost	Present Value of Expected Claim Cost
End of year 1	$100,000	0.00302	$302	$302/1.1 = $275
End of year 2	100,000	0.00328	328	$328/1.1^2 = 271$
Total				546

reach the age of 40. Of those people, 3,076 are expected to die in their 42nd year. Thus, the probability that a 40-year-old male dies in his 42nd year equals 3,076/937,723 = 0.00328. In general, the probability of an x-year-old person dying when he or she is $x + y$ years old equals the number of people dying in year $x + y$ divided by the number of people alive at year x.

Returning to the calculation of the single premium for the two-year term policy, since the probability of Mr. Babbel dying in his 42nd year is 0.00328, expected claim costs at the end of the second year equal $328 (see Table 15.4). Adding the present values of expected claim costs for each year, we find that the single premium is $546 = $275 + $271.

A useful exercise for gaining insight into the pricing of multiple year life insurance policies is to track the cash flows received and paid by the insurer through time under the assumption that everything happens as expected. With Mr. Babbel's two-year, single premium term policy, the insurer would receive $546 when the contract is initiated. This money would be invested and after earning 10 percent interest for one year would grow to $546 × 1.1 = $600.60. However, at the end of the year, the insurer would expect claim costs of $302 (see Table 15.4), leaving $298.60. This amount would again be invested and after earning 10 percent interest for another year would grow to $298.60 × 1.1 = $328.46, which is the expected claim cost in the second year (plus some change due to rounding).

Concept Checks

7. Calculate the probability that a 35-year-old male dies when he is 55 years old.

8. Calculate the single premium for a two-year $100,000 term policy issued to a 50-year-old if the interest rate is 8 percent.

Level Premiums

With a level premium payment schedule, the policyholder pays the same premium for a fixed number of years. In our two-year example, the level premium will be paid once at the initiation of the policy and then again at the beginning of the second year (or equivalently at the end of the first year) if the person survives to pay the second year's premium. The cash flows to the insurer from the two-year term policy with level premiums are summarized as follows:

	Contract Initiation	End of Year 1	End of Year 2
Inflows:	Premium payment	Possible premium payment	$0
Outflows:	$0	Possible claim payment	Possible claim payment

Notice that in the description of the cash flows, we wrote "possible premium payment" at the end of year 1, because the premium payment at the end of year 1 will occur only if the policyholder survives the first year (we are ignoring lapses).

The level premium is the amount that equates the present value of expected cash inflows to the present value of expected cash outflows. The present value of cash outflows is the same as with the single premium policy—$546; indeed, the single premium equals the present value of expected cash outflows at the time the policy is sold. Table 15.5 summarizes the cash inflows. Since we do not yet know the value of the premium (it is what we are trying to find), we denote the premium as P in Table 15.5. The insurer will receive a premium payment at the initiation of the policy with probability 1 (otherwise, the insurer would not issue the policy). If Mr. Babbel lives through the first year, the insurer will receive another premium payment, P, at the beginning of the second year. The probability that the insurer

TABLE 15.5

Insurer's cash inflows with a level premium schedule for a two-year term policy for a 40-year-old.

Time	Premium Payments	Probability	Expected Premium	Present Value of Expected Premium
Contract initiation	P	1	P	P
End of year 1	P	0.99698	0.99698P	$\dfrac{0.99698P}{1.1} = 0.906345P$
End of year 2	0	0	0	0

receives the second payment equals 0.99698, the probability of Mr. Babbel's survival $(1 -$ Probability of death $= 1 - 0.00302)$. The expected cash inflow at the beginning of the second year is therefore $0.99698 \times P$. The present value of expected cash inflows for the life insurer therefore equals

$$P + \frac{0.99698 \times P}{1.1} = P\left[1 + \frac{0.99698}{1.1}\right] = 1.906P$$

Setting the present value of expected cash inflows equal to the present value of expected cash outflows yields the following equation:

$$1.906\,P = \$546$$

Solving for P, we find that the level premium equals $286.41. Note that the level premium is not simply one-half of the single premium. This is because (1) there is a chance that the second premium payment will not be made, and (2) if the second premium payment is made, it occurs one year later, which reduces its present value.

Comparison

One of the important insights needed for understanding cash value life insurance can be obtained by comparing the three payment methods that Mr. Babbel can use to obtain life insurance coverage over his 41st and 42nd years. The first method is to purchase successive one-year term policies, paying $275 at the beginning of his 41st year and paying $299 at the beginning of his 42nd year if he survives. The second method is to purchase a single premium two-year term policy for a premium of $546. The third method is to purchase a two-year term policy using level premiums of $286 per year. The present value of expected premium payments is the same for all three methods, but the timing of cash flows differs. Table 15.6 summarizes these differences.[6]

Before comparing the three payment methods, it is important to note that the annual premiums for successive one-year term insurance policies reflect the annual costs of insuring someone over each successive year for a fixed amount of coverage. The premiums for successive one-year term policies—$275 and $298, respectively—therefore give the cost of insuring Mr. Babbel over time. With both the single premium and the level premium, the policyholder thus pays more in the first year than the cost of providing the insurance for the first year and pays less in the second year than the cost of providing insurance in the second year. The single premium of $546 greatly exceeds the cost of providing insurance in the first year ($275) and there are no future premium payments. With the level premium

---

[6]You can verify that the present values are the same using the cash flows in this table.

TABLE 15.6
Timing differences in expected premium payments for alternative payment methods (Mr. Babbel buys coverage for his 41st and 42nd years; interest rate = 10 percent).

	Beginning of 1st Year	Beginning of 2nd Year	Present Value
Successive one-year term policies	$275	$299 × 0.99698 = $298	$546
Level premium two-year term policy	286	$286 × 0.99698 = $285	546
Single premium two-year term policy	546	$0	546

payment plan, the difference between the payments and the cost of providing the insurance is comparatively small ($286 versus $275). Of course, this does not imply that the policyholder is worse off by buying the two-year policy with a single or level premium. As we mentioned above, the present value of expected premium payments is the same for all three payment methods.

In summary, the cost of providing insurance increases over time because the probability of dying increases over time. Whenever premium payments are leveled over time or pushed toward the beginning of the contract period, the policyholder pays more than the cost of coverage in the early part of the coverage period and less than the cost of coverage during the latter part of the coverage period. This point is central to an understanding of cash value life insurance, where the magnitude of timing differences between premium payments and cost of coverage is much greater than in the two-year example.

Pricing Immediate Annuities

Before analyzing the pricing of whole life insurance policies, we first will consider the pricing of simple immediate annuity contracts. Annuity pricing is of interest in its own right, and the method used also plays a role in the derivation of level premiums for whole life insurance. Recall that a straight life annuity pays a given amount of money every year until the person dies. To price a life annuity with a constant annual payment by the insurer, we will use the standard mortality table given in Table 15.3 that assumes a person dies by the age of 100. Recall, however, that mortality experience is lower for annuity purchasers than for life insurance purchasers (see Box 15.2).

Assume that the annuity purchaser is a 96-year-old male. The annuity will pay $5,000 at the end of each year, unless the person dies during the year. (In practice, most annuities make monthly payments.) Table 15.7 summarizes the expected cash outflows for the insurer. At the end of the first year, the insurer will pay $5,000 if the person survives, which occurs with probability 0.61545 (6,050/9,831). The expected cash flow therefore is $3,077, which has a present value of $2,797. The insurer will make another $5,000 payment at the end of the second year, provided the person survives the first two years. From the mortality table (Table 15.3), the probability of a 96-year-old male surviving two years equals the number of people at the beginning of year 98 divided by the number of people at the beginning of year 96. This ratio is 3,145/9,831, which equals 0.31991. The insurer will make a third payment with probability 0.10941, which is the number of people at year 99 divided by the number of people at year 96 (1,076/9,831). Since the probability of a 99-year-old male surviving one year is assumed to be zero, the insurer will not have to make a fourth payment. The present value of the insurer's expected cash outflows equals $4,530. Thus, ignoring expense loadings, the 96-year-old would have to pay $4,530 for a $5,000 life annuity.

TABLE 15.7
Insurer's annuity payments for a $5,000 life Annuity for a 96-year-old male (the first payment occurs at the end of the person's 96th year).

Age	Probability of 96-year-old Male Living to Specified Age	Expected Annuity Payment ($5,000 × Probability)	Present Value of Expected Annuity Payment
97	6,050/9,831 = 0.61545	$3,077	$3,077/1.1 = $2,797
98	3,145/9,831 = 0.31991	1,600	$1,600/1.1^2 = 1,322
99	1,076/9,831 = 0.10941	547	$547/1.1^3 = 411
100	0/9,831 = 0	0	0
Total			$4,530

Pricing Whole Life Insurance

The basic procedure for pricing whole life insurance is the same as for pricing term insurance. The only difference is that we must forecast cash flows until the policyholder reaches the age of 100.

Single Premium

Suppose that at the age of 40 Mr. Babbel decides to purchase a whole life policy with a face amount of $100,000. Table 15.8 summarizes the calculation of expected claim costs using a 5 percent interest rate. The first step is to find the probability that a 40-year-old dies at each age between 40 and 99. This is done using the mortality table by taking the number of deaths at each age divided by the number of people at age 40. For example, the probability that Mr. Babbel dies at age 44 is 3,875/937,723 = 0.00413, and the probability that he dies at age 98 is 2,069/937,723 = 0.002207. By multiplying the probability of death at each age times $100,000, we find the expected claim cost at the end of each year. We then discount the expected claim cost to the present using the 5 percent rate of return. The sum

TABLE 15.8
Calculation of expected claim costs for a whole life policy for a 40-year-old.

Age	Probability of 40-Year-Old Dying at Specified Age	Expected Claim Costs	Present Value of Expected Claim Costs
40	0.003020	$302.00	$302.00/1.05 = $288
41	0.003280	328.00	$328.00/1.05^2 = 298
42	0.003538	353.80	$353.80/1.05^3 = 306
43	0.003832	383.20	$383.20/1.05^4 = 315
44	0.004133	413.30	$413.30/1.05^5 = 324
.	.	.	.
.	.	.	.
.	.	.	.
96	0.004032	403.20	$403.20/1.05^{57} = 25
97	0.003098	309.80	$309.80/1.05^{58} = 18
98	0.002207	220.70	$220.70/1.05^{59} = 12
99	0.001147	114.70	$114.7/1.05^{60} = 6
Total			$22,373

of the individual present value calculations is the present value of expected claim costs. In this case, the present value of Mr. Babbel's expected claim costs equals $22,373. Ignoring expense and profit loadings, the present value of expected claim costs is the *single premium* (or net single premium).

Continuous Level Premium

Now let's find the *continuous level premium* for this policy, which is the amount that Mr. Babbel would have to pay each year that he is alive. Notice that the continuous level premium is a life annuity (Mr. Babbel makes a payment each year until his death). Applying the general principle that the present value of expected premium payments must equal the single premium (which in turn equals the present value of expected claim costs), we need to find the life annuity payment amount that has a present value of $22,373 for a 40-year-old.

The first step in finding the life annuity payment amount is to find the probability that Mr. Babbel will be alive at each age between 41 and 99, because these probabilities determine the likelihood that Mr. Babbel will make a particular premium payment. The probability that Mr. Babbel is alive on his 41st birthday and thus makes the second premium payment is calculated from the mortality table by dividing the number of people alive at age 41 by the number of people alive at age 40, which equals 934,891/937,723 = 0.99698. The probability that he is alive on his 42nd birthday and thus makes the third premium payment is the number of people alive at age 42 divided by the number of people alive at age 40, which is 931,815/937,723 = 0.99370. Table 15.9 shows similar calculations for several of the years. Each of the probabilities is multiplied by the variable P, the symbol for the level premium that we are trying to calculate.

The next step is to calculate the present value of the expected premium payments assuming a 5 percent interest rate. The last column lists the present value of each expected premium payment. The final step is to sum the individual present value calculations to find the present value of all the expected premium payments. The last row of Table 15.9 indicates that the present value of paying P until he dies equals $16.30 \times P$. We want to find

TABLE 15.9 Calculation of the level premium for a whole life policy for a 40-year-old.

Age	Probability of 40-Year-Old Living until Specified Age	Expected Premium Payment	Present Value of Expected Claim Costs
40	1	$1 \times P$	P
41	0.996980	$0.996980 \times P$	$(0.996980 \times P)/1.05 = \$0.9524P$
42	0.993700	$0.993700 \times P$	$(0.993700 \times P)/1.05^2 = 0.9013P$
43	0.990162	$0.990162 \times P$	$(0.990162 \times P)/1.05^3 = 0.8553P$
44	0.986330	$0.986330 \times P$	$(0.986330 \times P)/1.05^4 = 0.8115P$
.	.	.	.
.	.	.	.
.	.	.	.
96	0.010484	$0.010484 \times P$	$(0.010484 \times P)/1.05^{56} = 0.0007P$
97	0.006452	$0.006452 \times P$	$(0.006452 \times P)/1.05^{57} = 0.0004P$
98	0.003354	$0.003354 \times P$	$(0.003354 \times P)/1.05^{58} = 0.0002P$
99	0.001147	$0.001147 \times P$	$(0.001147 \times P)/1.05^{59} = 0.0001P$
Total			$\$16.30P$

the value of P that makes paying $\$P$ until Mr. Babbel dies equal to the present value of expected claim costs. Thus, we solve the following equation for P:

$$\$16.30 \times P = \$22,373$$

This calculation produces a level premium for this whole life policy of $P = \$1,372.58$. Mr. Babbel could either pay $\$22,373$ at the time the policy is initiated or pay $\$1,373.58$ each year until he dies (again we are ignoring surrenders).

Limited Payment Whole Life Premiums

Another premium schedule for whole life insurance is *limited payment,* whereby the policyholder pays a level premium for a fixed (limited) number of years, such as 20 years, provided that he or she is still alive. To find the 20-year level premium, we calculate the value of P such that the present value of receiving $\$P$ each year for 20 years if Mr. Babbel is alive equals the present value of expected claim costs ($\$22,373$). As before, we have to take into consideration that Mr. Babbel might die before making all of his premium payments. Following the same procedure as above, we solve the following equation for P (12.58 is the present value of paying $\$1$ each year for 20 years or until death):

$$12.58 \times P = \$22,373$$

so that $P = \$1,778.45$.

To summarize, we analyzed three possible payment schedules for Mr. Babbel's whole life policy:

Pay $\$22,373$ up front for a single premium whole life policy.

Pay $\$1,778$ each year for 20 years for a 20-pay whole life policy.

Pay $\$1,373$ each year for life for a continuous premium whole life policy.

With each payment schedule, Mr. Babbel pays more in the first years of the contract than the cost of death protection under annual term insurance. For example, not until Mr. Babbel reaches the age of 59 does the cost of $\$100,000$ of term insurance under these assumptions exceed the level payment of $\$1,373$. Conversely, in the later years of the contract period, Mr. Babbel pays less than what $\$100,000$ of term insurance would cost. Thus, each of these premium schedules involves prepayment of Mr. Babbel's future expected claim costs and thus each causes the accumulation of cash values. The growth in cash values with a whole life policy depends on the premium payment pattern (e.g., single premium, continuous premium, etc.). Figure 15.5 illustrates how cash values will grow under the three options analyzed here.

15.7 How Much Life Insurance Coverage Should Be Purchased?

Many different models and approaches are available for helping someone choose an amount of life insurance coverage. Indeed, numerous life insurance calculators are available on the Internet. Some models are nothing more than a simple rule of thumb—for example, coverage should equal 6 to 10 times annual income. Accordingly, if a person earns $\$100,000$ a year, then the recommended amount of life insurance coverage would be $\$600,000$ to $\$1$ million.

FIGURE 15.5

Accumulation of cash value on a traditional whole life policy under three premium payment methods.

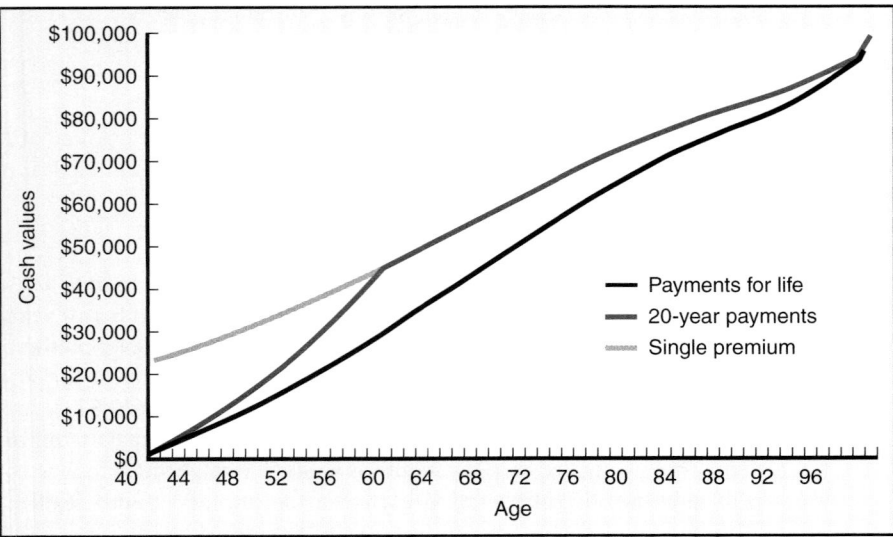

Other models require the purchaser to forecast the consumption needs of the policy's beneficiaries and then suggests purchasing enough life insurance coverage to meet those needs. To use a very simple example (which ignores taxes and many other complications), suppose that Rasheed is considering how much life insurance coverage to purchase to cover his family's consumption needs if he dies. Rasheed has a one-year-old child and a wife whom he would like to support at their current standard of living so she does not have to work outside the home for pay, until the child reaches the age of 21. (Thereafter, he reasons the child and wife can support themselves.) Rasheed could then calculate how much the family currently spends on food, shelter, insurance, school, and so on. Suppose that this amount is $50,000 above what Rasheed's family would expect to receive from social security (see Chapter 19) and that he expects this amount to remain constant over time (an un-realistic, simplifying assumption).[7] Since Rasheed has no savings, he needs to purchase enough life insurance coverage so that it will finance $50,000 of consumption (in today's dollars) annually for 20 years. In other words, Rasheed needs to find the present value of a 20-year simple annuity that would pay $50,000 a year in real terms. The appropriate dis-count rate for this present value calculation would be the risk-free, real rate of return, which we will assume equals 2 percent. The present value is $817,572 ($50,000 × (1/0.02)[1 − 1/(1.02)^{20}]), which is the amount of life insurance coverage Rasheed would need to pur-chase according to this consumption needs approach.[8]

---

[7] For example, social security survivor benefits generally would cease when the child reaches age 18.

[8] In recent years, another approach for choosing the amount of life insurance coverage has emerged, which is based on the life-cycle economic model of individual behavior. The main implication of this model is that people typically want to "smooth" their standard of living over time; they do not want extremely high consumption one year followed by very low consumption the next year. The main difference between the life cycle model and the "consumption needs" approach is that the life cycle model simultaneously chooses consumption and life insurance coverage to optimally smooth a person's standard of living, whereas, the consumption needs approach identifies the amount of life insurance coverage to meet the forecasted consumption needs of the beneficiaries.

15.8   Life Insurance Cost Comparisons

Background

Buying life insurance involves choosing a type of policy and an insurer. While buyers should consider insolvency risk and service when selecting an insurer, a particularly important issue for many buyers is how to compare the cost (or value) of different life insurance policies across insurers. Substantial evidence indicates significant variation in the cost of comparable policies among insurers due to differences in expense loadings, lapse and surrender rates, and other factors. Cost comparisons are complicated because life insurance policy cash flows occur over many years and are subject to uncertainty from various sources, such as whether the person dies, the effect of changes in interest rates on participating life policy cash values and universal life credited interest rates, and so on.

Commonly used cost comparison methods attempt to produce a single measure or index that can be used to compare policies of the same general type (e.g., two term policies offered by different insurers) with the same face amount. Given fundamental differences in contract design and risk to policyholders, these methods usually are less applicable, if at all, for comparing different types of policies (e.g., whole life to universal life or term insurance). While some cost comparison methods can provide broad guidance as to whether the buyer might prefer either cash value insurance or term insurance with noninsurance savings, it usually is preferable for a buyer to decide on a broad type of contract before conducting detailed comparisons of costs across insurers.

When making decisions about which type of coverage to buy, it is important to recognize that a given initial premium outlay will allow the purchase of a much larger face amount of term insurance than whole life or some other form of cash value insurance. As discussed earlier, although the term premium will increase over time, for many years it will remain lower than the level premium that would have to be paid if whole life were purchased. As a result, persons or families with a large need for death protection and limited funds for premiums often are advised (e.g., by consumer advisory organizations) to buy term insurance. In general, people need to consider several questions when deciding which type of policy to buy: (1) Am I able to afford to save through cash value insurance and still meet my need for death protection? (2) If so, do I want to save through cash value insurance as opposed to buying term insurance and investing elsewhere? (3) Among the different types of cash value insurance policies, which is most attractive given my goals and attitude toward risk? Given this background, we now briefly describe major cost comparison methods for different types of life insurance products.

Term Insurance

The most common method of comparing the cost of term insurance across insurers is to use the **interest adjusted cost index.** Almost all states require insurers to disclose this index in their sales solicitations, and a number of publications contain interest adjusted costs for policies issued by many insurers. The interest adjusted cost per $1,000 of face amount commonly is calculated assuming that the policy will be held for 20 years and assuming a 5 percent interest rate. The cost index is derived in two steps. In the first step, the accumulated value or cost of scheduled premiums less any illustrated dividends for participating insurance over the 20-year period is calculated. The second step annualizes this accumulated cost.

The 20-year accumulated cost (AC_{20}) from the first step (assuming annual premiums and that all values are per $1,000 of face amount) is given by

$$AC_{20} = \sum_{t=1}^{20} P_t (1.05)^{20-t+1} - \sum_{t=1}^{20} D_t (1.05)^{20-t}$$

where P_t equals the annual premium payable at the *beginning of year t* and D_t equals the illustrated annual dividend to be paid at the *end of year t*. This amount (AC_{20}) has a simple interpretation. It represents the amount of money that the person could have accumulated at a 5 percent interest rate (after-tax) after 20 years if, instead of buying the policy, the person had invested an amount equal to the required premium less any dividend at the beginning of each year. It thus provides a simple measure of cost that considers the magnitude and timing of cash flows assuming that (1) the person survives to pay premiums and receive dividends for 20 years, and (2) dividends are paid as illustrated.

The interest adjusted cost index (IAC_{20}) is obtained in the second step as follows:

$$IAC_{20} = AC_{20} / \sum_{t=1}^{20} 1.05^t$$

The denominator is the accumulated value of $1 paid at the beginning of each year for 20 years at 5 percent interest. This value equals 34.7. The interest adjusted cost index is the level annual payment that would accumulate to AC_{20} over 20 years at 5 percent. It equals the accumulated difference between premiums and illustrated dividends divided by 34.7. While dividing the accumulated difference by 34.7 annualizes the cost measure, it does not affect the ranking of policies. That is, policies will be ranked identically using AC_{20} or IAC_{20}. In addition, the same ranking would be obtained if the policies were ranked based on the difference between the present value of future premiums and illustrated dividends.

The interest adjusted cost index does not consider the probability of surviving to pay premiums. Studies suggest, however, that incorporating this refinement produces a cost measure that is highly correlated with the interest adjusted cost index. Comparison of the interest adjusted cost index for a shorter assumed holding period, such as 10 years, can provide insight into whether cost rankings are sensitive to the assumed holding period of the policy. However, 10- and 20-year interest adjusted cost indexes generally are highly correlated across insurers.

Whole Life Insurance

The interest adjusted cost index also is commonly used to compare whole life insurance policy costs across insurers, and its disclosure by insurers to buyers again is usually required by law. For whole life insurance, one important change is made in the calculation of the index: The policy's cash value at the end of 20 years (CV_{20}) is deducted in the first step. Thus, the formula for the 20-year interest adjusted cost index becomes:

$$IAC_{20} = (AC_{20} - CV_{20}) / \sum_{t=1}^{20} 1.05^t$$

The numerator of this formula again has a simple interpretation. It represents the difference between (1) the funds that would be available at 5 percent interest (after-tax) after 20 years if, instead of buying the policy, the person invested an amount equal to the required premium less the illustrated dividend at the beginning of each year (AC_{20}), and (2) the cash available from purchasing the policy and surrendering it for the cash value after 20 years (CV_{20}). (The formula ignores possible taxes that could be due upon surrender.) Comparison of interest adjusted cost indexes for a shorter horizon, such as 10 years, can give some insight into how cost rankings are affected by earlier surrender due to the impact of differences in expenses and lapse experience across insurers on premiums, dividends, and the cash value schedule.

Whole life insurance policy costs also can be compared using the estimated **implicit rate of return** on the portion of premiums that can be viewed as a contribution to a savings fund. The calculation of implicit returns is complicated, and there is no standard set of assumptions used. In addition, insurers are not required to disclose implicit rates of return.

The calculation of the implicit rate of return on a whole life policy involves dividing the whole life premium, net of any illustrated dividend, into two parts: (1) a contribution to savings, and (2) a term insurance premium to pay for death protection in a given year (defined as the policy's face amount less the value of the calculated savings accumulation to date). A computer program is then used to solve for the annual investment return needed on the savings fund to duplicate the policy's guaranteed cash value at a given point in time. This return is the estimated implicit rate of return on savings for the policy. Varying the assumed holding period produces implicit rates of return for different holding periods.

Although some insurers provide prospective buyers with an estimated implicit rate of return, the lack of standard assumptions suggests caution in using these figures. In particular, a critical input into the calculation is the assumed cost per $1,000 of death protection each year (that is, the assumed one-year term rates). A high assumed cost of term insurance reduces the assumed contribution to savings and drives up the calculated rate of return needed for the savings fund to equal the policy's cash value. The outcome is that a particular policy—or whole life insurance in general—may look artificially attractive.

Some organizations, such as Consumers Union (publisher of the magazine *Consumer Reports*), periodically calculate implicit rates of return for many policies using uniform assumptions. Assuming at least a 20-year holding period, the results generally indicate that insurers with higher return (lower cost) policies have attractive implicit rates of return compared to returns available on government and high-grade corporate bonds, especially in view of the tax deferral available with life insurance. Implicit returns generally decline substantially for holding periods of 10 years or less (and often are negative for holding periods under 5 years) due to the adverse effects of front-end expense loadings and early lapses on policy values.

Universal Life Insurance and Other Investment-Sensitive Products

Possible variation in future interest rates that will be credited to universal life insurance policy cash values considerably complicates the process of cost comparison. One approach is to calculate an interest adjusted cost index (or, less commonly, an implicit rate of return) using the cash value that would arise under an assumed premium payment pattern and the interest rate that currently is being credited by the insurer. However, in addition to uncertainty about future credited interest rates, differences in investment strategy and associated risk-related differences in credited rates reduce the comparability of policies issued by different companies. This problem is more pronounced for universal life comparisons than for participating whole life policy comparisons given the greater sensitivity of universal life policy values to short-term changes in interest rates and investment performance. A similar problem complicates cost comparisons for variable life and variable-universal life policies.

An alternative approach to comparing costs and values for these investment-sensitive products is to compare similar policy types across insurers on two dimensions: (1) the cost of expense, mortality, and surrender charges, and (2) investment strategy and credited investment rates. One method of comparing expense, mortality, and surrender charges is to assume a fixed premium schedule and then compare the cash values (after any surrender charges) that would be available for different insurers' policies (assuming comparable death benefit options) after a period such as 20 years at one or more assumed interest rates.[9] Policies with higher and/or earlier expense charges, higher mortality charges, and higher surrender charges will produce lower cash values. Thus, this method isolates differences in investment strategy and interest credits and allows policies to be ranked instead on the basis of other factors that affect cost or value. This information can then be used, along with information about the insurer's investment strategy and policy for crediting interest rates, to make an informed choice among insurers. A number of more elaborate methods also have been suggested for comparing costs for these contracts. There is no consensus, however, on which of these methods is likely to be most useful.

15.9 Summary

- There are two broad types of life insurance policies: term insurance and cash value policies. Term insurance provides pure death protection coverage. Cash value policies bundle death protection and savings accumulation. The main types of cash value policies are whole life, universal life, variable life, and variable-universal life.

- With a typical whole life insurance policy, level premiums are paid over a fixed number of years or until death. The policy provides a level death benefit and the sequence of cash values grows according to a fixed schedule over time. Most whole life policies are participating; that is, they pay annual policy dividends.

- With a typical universal life policy, the policyholder has considerable flexibility in the payment of premiums. The policy provides either a level death benefit or one that increases with the cash value of the policy. The cash value of the policy grows at an uncertain rate that depends on premium payments, expense and mortality charges,

and interest rates credited over the course of the policy period.

- With a typical variable life policy, the policyholder pays premiums according to a fixed schedule. The policy provides a death benefit equal to a minimum amount plus the cash value of the policy. The cash value grows at an uncertain rate that depends on the rate of return earned on a pool of assets (mutual funds) chosen by the policyholder.

- Cash value policies provide a tax-advantaged method of saving, including income tax deferral on savings accumulations.

- Annuity contracts provide insurance coverage against living beyond a person's financial resources as well as a tax-deferred savings vehicle.

- A common method of comparing the cost of alternative life insurance policies of the same type is the interest adjusted cost method. In addition, implicit rates of return can be compared for whole life policies.

[9]For a given interest rate, the same ranking would be produced by calculating the present value of expense and mortality charges.

Key Terms

Questions and Problems

1. Jane is divorced with two small children. Her salary is $40,000 per year, and she has no group life insurance. Should Jane buy any life insurance? If so, should she buy term or whole life? Explain.

2. Suppose the following graph depicts the cash value of a universal life policy over the future years if all variables affecting the cash value take their expected value.

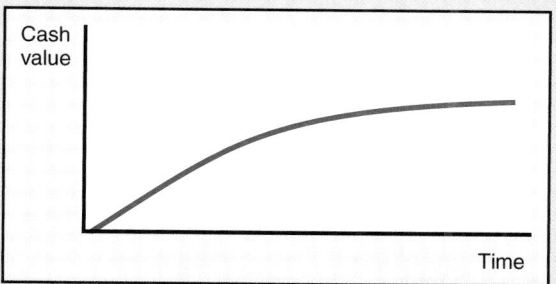

How would the cash value change if interest rates turned out to be lower than expected?

3. The following table provides information about a universal life policy. Fill in the table.

	Year 1	Year 2	Year 3
Cash value at beginning of year	$10,000		
Premium payments made at beginning of year	1,000	1,000	1,500
Mortality cost	550	600	675
Expense cost	100	50	50
Interest rate used for crediting cash value	6.0%	5.0%	5.0%
Credited interest			
Cash value at end of year			

4. Explain why death rates for life insurance buyers generally are higher than for people who buy annuities.

5. What is the sequence of net premiums for one-year term policies with face amounts equal to $1,000 for a male for the ages 60 through 62, assuming an interest rate of 6 percent? Assume premiums are paid at the

beginning of the year and claims are paid at the end of the year.

6. What is the net single premium for a $1,000 face amount three-year term policy for a 50-year-old male, assuming an interest rate of 5 percent?

7. What is the net level premium for a $1,000 face amount three-year term policy for a 50-year-old male, assuming an interest rate of 5 percent?

8. Using Table 15.3, calculate the net level premium for a two-year endowment policy for a 50-year-old with an interest rate of 5 percent. Show that this premium is just sufficient to fund benefits over the two years at the assumed interest and mortality rates. Ignoring expenses, what would the policy's cash value equal after one year? If the policyholder surrendered the policy for this cash value after one year, would the insurer still have enough funds (given assumed interest and mortality) to pay off the other policyholders at the end of the second year?

9. Should the interest adjusted cost method be used to compare the cost of a term policy to the cost of a whole life policy? Explain.

10. Insurer testing for HIV provides a good example of how the cost of gathering information about mortality risk can sometimes cause insurers not to gather information. Insurers commonly use blood tests to identify HIV (if permitted by law). However, since blood tests are not free, insurers only use blood tests if the expected costs of misclassification exceed the cost of the test. Suppose that the cost of the blood test is $100 and the probabilities of death for HIV-infected males is 20 times the probability listed in Table 15.3.

  a. What are the expected claim costs for a 30-year-old male applying for $100,000 of one-year term insurance if he is HIV negative? HIV positive?

  b. Suppose that 1,000 30-year-old males apply for insurance. The insurer knows that 2 percent of them are HIV positive but needs the blood test to identify those specific applicants. Should the insurer give all applicants a blood test?

Answers to Concept Checks

1. The death benefit would equal $100,000 and the amount of death protection would equal $80,000.

2.

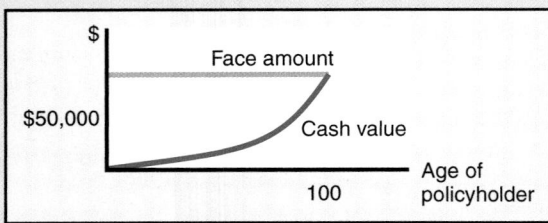

3. a. The cash value would grow more slowly or decline if the policyholder reduced premium payments.

  b. The cash value would grow more slowly or decline if interest rates declined.
  c. The cash value would grow more rapidly if the cure for cancer caused mortality charges to decline.

4. A retiree with a fixed amount of retirement savings faces the risk that the savings will be depleted before the person dies. Annuities provide insurance against this risk; that is, annuities provide insurance coverage against the risk of outliving a person's resources.

5. With deferred annuities, a person pays an annuity premium to an insurer, who in turn invests this premium (net of expenses) until the payout period begins. The returns earned

on the annuity are not taxed as they are earned. Consequently, annuities provide a tax-advantaged method of savings.

6. a. Using Table 15.3, the expected claim costs = $1,000 \times 0.00671$ = $6.71. The present value of expected claim costs = $6.71/1.08 = $6.21.

   b. The expected claim costs = $1,000 \times 0.32996$ = $329.96. The present value of expected claim costs = $329.96/1.08 = $305.52.

7. The probability that a 35-year-old dies when he is 55 = 9,016/949,171 = 0.00949.

8. The expected claim costs in the first year = $100,000 (0.00671) = $6.71. The expected claim costs in the second year = $100,000 (6,502/896,662) = $7.25. The present value of expected claim costs = $6.71/1.08 + $7.25/1.08^2$ = $6.21 + $6.22 = $12.43.

References

Black, Kenneth; and Harold Skipper. *Life Insurance.* 12th ed. Englewood Cliffs, NJ: Prentice-Hall, 1994. (*Provides additional detail on the topics covered in this chapter.*)

Gokhale, Jagadeesh; and Laurence Kotlikoff. *The Adequacy of Life Insurance,* Research Dialogue No. 72, TIAA-CREF Institute, July 2002.

Gustavson, Sandra; and Robert I. Mehr. *Life Insurance: Theory and Practice.* 4th ed. Plano, TX: Business Publications, 1987. (*Provides additional detail on the topics covered in this chapter.*)

Life Insurance Fact Book. Washington DC: American Council of Life Insurance. (*Provides data and other information on the life insurance industry.*)

Appendix 15A

Retrospective Analysis of Cash Value Accumulation

One of the most difficult concepts associated with cash value life insurance contracts is how the cash values accumulate over time. This appendix provides a framework for understanding the factors affecting cash value accumulation. While the actual calculations of cash values differ from the approach presented here, our objective is to provide some insight as to how cash values change over time within a framework that is capable of explaining many of the variations of cash value life insurance.[10] For simplicity, we continue to ignore nonclaim costs in this discussion.

[10]We focus exclusively on a retrospective view of cash value accumulation as opposed to the mathematically equivalent (for given assumptions) prospective view that derives the cash value as the present value of expected future benefits minus the present value of expected future premiums. The retrospective approach to cash values is easier to follow and more useful for our purpose.

As previously discussed, cash value life insurance involves prepayments of expected future claim costs. While neither technically nor legally accurate, a useful way of thinking about cash value life insurance is to view the insurer as placing the policyholder's prepayments into a fund. Each year, the fund grows as a result of additional premium payments made by the policyholder and interest earned on these additional premiums and the previous period's fund balance, and each year the insurer removes a portion of the fund to "pay" the policyholder's expected claim costs (and expenses). You can think of this fund as the policy's cash value. From this retrospective perspective, the policy's cash value moves over time according to the following formula:

Cash value$_t$

= Cash value$_{t-1}$ + Premium$_t$ − Mortality cost$_t$ + Interest credited to cash value$_t$

The interest credited to the cash value over a given period can be viewed as some rate of return for the period times the amount of funds at the beginning of the period. Assuming premiums are paid at the beginning of the period and mortality costs are paid at the end of the period, the amount of funds at the beginning of the period equals the initial cash value plus any additional premium payments. Therefore, the interest credited to the cash value during the period equals

Interest credited to cash value$_t$

= Rate of return$_t$ × (Cash value$_{t-1}$ + Premium$_t$)

Each period's mortality cost equals the expected claim cost, which equals the probability of dying times the amount of death protection for the period:

Mortality cost$_t$

= Probability of dying$_t$ × Amount of death protection$_t$

The equation for mortality cost illustrates that the mortality cost may vary over time for two reasons: (1) the probability of dying increases as a person ages, and (2) the amount of death protection may vary over time (depending on the policy). For example, with a whole life policy the death benefit equals the face amount minus the cash value. Consequently, the amount of death protection is less than the face amount of the policy; in particular,

Amount of death protection$_t$

= Policy's face amount$_t$ − Cash value$_t$

The last two equations help answer a question about whole life policies that often is asked by students: How can the cash value grow over time when we know that the cost per dollar of death protection increases over time? The answer is that the increased cost per dollar of death protection as a person ages is offset in a whole life policy by a declining amount of death protection over time.

The equations above can be used to find how the cash value of a policy accumulates over time for a given set of assumptions. In particular, you would need to know (1) the expected cost per dollar of death protection from a mortality table; (2) a sequence of annual rates of return; (3) a schedule of premium payments; and (4) how the death benefit changes over time (i.e., whether it is fixed or varies directly with cash values). Given this information, you could find the sequence of cash values and the amount of death protection at each point in time by plugging into the above equations.[11] Figure 15A–1 summarizes these relationships.

With whole life, the dynamics described above are hidden from the policyholder. That is, no attempt is made to explicitly partition the change in the cash value from one period to the next into premium payments, interest credits, and mortality cost components. Nevertheless, the equations are a useful way of thinking about how whole life policies work. In particular, the mortality costs, premium payments, interest credits, and death benefits are all fixed for the entire contract based on assumptions at the time the policy is issued. As a result, the schedule of cash values (and decline in death protection) over time is completely predetermined. Absent in-

---

[11]You may notice that the amount of death protection at time *t* depends on the cash value at time *t* and vice versa. Therefore, the sequence of cash values must be solved simultaneously with the sequence of insurance coverage.

Figure 15A.1

Summary of variables affecting cash values.

Inputs	Outputs
Expected cost per dollar of death protection Rates of return each period Premium payment each period Is death benefit level or does it vary with cash value?	→ Amount of death protection each period Cash value each period

surer insolvency and ignoring policyholder dividends, all the benefits from a whole life policy are guaranteed in advance, so that the policyholder bears no risk. In addition, because the cash value accumulates based on the same assumptions used to calculate the premiums, the cash value automatically grows to equal the face amount at age 100. The premium calculation produces a cash value, which, along with future premiums, is sufficient to fund future benefits at any point in time. Except for the ability to take out loans against cash values, whole life policyholders have limited flexibility with regard to premium payments or adjustments in death benefits.

The key point is that with a whole life policy the factors affecting cash values (the "inputs") generally are preset and equivalent to the assumptions used to calculate the premium. The modern variations of cash value life insurance, however, allow one or more of the inputs to vary over the course of the contract from the assumptions used in premium calculation. The precise variation is unknown at the time the contract is initiated. In some cases, policyholders have the flexibility to change the inputs over time; that is, policyholders can change the amount of premium paid and death benefits. In other cases, mortality costs and credited rates of return are varied in view of current experience or market conditions. Consequently, more of the risk of unexpected changes in mortality costs or rates of return is placed on the policyholder.

Specifically, with a universal life insurance policy, the mortality costs and credited rates of return can vary from year to year, depending on the insurer's experience and competitive pressure. The main risk borne by policyholders with universal life policies is that the credited return can vary over time depending on interest rates. Flexibility with respect to premium payments implies that cash values can grow or decline over time depending upon the amount of premiums paid. Universal life policies also provide the flexibility to increase death benefits as cash values grow. In contrast, premium payments on a variable life policy are fixed in advanced like a whole life policy. The credited return on savings, however, varies directly with the return earned on a portfolio of stocks and bonds chosen by the policyholder, and the amount of death protection varies with cash values.

16

Employee Benefits: Overview and Group Medical Coverage

Chapter Objectives

- Explain the major types of employee benefits and why firms provide employee benefits.
- Describe and analyze group medical expense coverage, including traditional fee-for-service arrangements, health maintenance organizations, and other forms of managed care.
- Summarize key group medical expense plan coverage provisions and pricing issues.
- Discuss causes of high health care costs and why many people are not insured for medical expenses.
- Briefly describe alternative proposals for reforming the US health care system to control costs and increase the number of insured people.

16.1   Major Types of Employee Benefits

Employers usually voluntarily offer a variety of benefits to employees in addition to cash wages. The most common types of benefits are insurance programs (medical insurance, life insurance, disability insurance, and dental insurance) and retirement plans. Other examples of employee benefits are paid vacations and maternity/paternity leave. This chapter and Chapter 17 discuss benefit plans that are voluntarily offered by employers. Chapter 18 discusses compulsory state workers' compensation systems. The compulsory federal social security program, which pays benefits to retired and disabled workers and survivors of deceased workers and medical expenses for the elderly population, is discussed in Chapter 19.

e benefits represent a substantial proportion of total employee compensation

c   ny employers. Table 16.1 provides the percentages of US employees who par-
ti   various types of benefits by type and size of employer during the mid-to late-
1   ger employers are more likely to provide benefits than smaller employers, and
government employees are more likely to receive benefits than employees of private enterprises. For private employers, estimates indicate that aggregate employee benefit plan costs
represent between 20 and 25 percent of total compensation costs. For some firms, employee
benefit costs represent over one-half of total compensation.

Table 16.1

Percentage of US employees participating in various types of benefit plans.

Type of Benefit	Description	Medium and Large Private Businesses (1997)	Small Private Businesses (1996)	State and Local Government (1998)
Medical insurance	Covers eligible medical expenses for employee and covered dependents through fee-for-service arrangement or health maintenance organization	76%	64%	86%
Retirement plan	Defined contribution or defined benefit pensions and related retirement savings plans	79	46	98
Life insurance	Typically term life insurance with death benefit equal to a multiple of salary (e.g., 1–2 times salary)	87	62	89
Short-term disability insurance	Replaces a percentage of lost wages for short-term disability (e.g., up to six months)	55	29	20
Long-term disability insurance	Replaces a percentage of lost wages for long-term disability (e.g., up to age 65) with offset for any disability benefits paid by social security	43	22	34
Dental insurance	Covers eligible dental expenses for employee and covered dependents	59	31	60

Source: Data obtained from Bureau of Labor Statistics, Bulletins 2507, 2517, and 2531.

[1]More recent data are not yet available in a comparable format due to changes in the Bureau of Labor Statistics methods of data collection and reporting.

Who Pays the Cost of Benefits?

Employee benefit plans that do not require workers to contribute directly toward the cost of benefits through payroll deductions are *noncontributory plans.* Plans that require workers to contribute part of their wages or salary are *contributory plans.* In both contributory and noncontributory plans, an implicit trade-off between employer contributions and wages is likely to exist, at least in the long run. That is, higher employer contributions will result in lower wages, all else equal. Similarly, in order to attract equally qualified employees, an employer that does not pay for any benefits will have to pay higher wages than an employer that pays part or all of the cost of benefits.

While in the long run employees are likely to pay the full cost of their benefits via higher payroll deductions and lower wages, short-run increases in employee benefit costs are likely to reduce employer profits. For example, employers are likely to experience lower short-run profits if the cost of medical expense insurance or self-insured medical expense benefits suddenly increases. The fact that employers bear the risk of employee benefit costs in the short run helps explain why employee benefit plans often fall under the topic of risk management. The other reason employee benefit plans fall under risk management is that many employee benefits provide insurance protection for employees. Consequently, the tools and institutional knowledge needed for corporate risk management also are needed to manage employee benefits plans.

Flexibility in Choice of Benefits

In some cases employees have no choice regarding their benefits; the employer offers a particular benefit package for all employees. Usually, however, employees have some choice as to the benefits they receive, especially in contributory plans. Employee choice is maximized with **cafeteria benefit plans** (often known as flexible benefit plans and, more formally, **Section 125 plans** after the Internal Revenue Code section that addresses them), in which employees typically receive a core (minimum) package of required benefits and credits to select from a menu of optional benefits. If employees are offered the option of receiving cash instead of benefits, the entire value of the credits is taxable as income (and the trade-off between wages and benefit costs becomes explicit). The primary advantage of cafeteria plans is that employees are able to choose benefits that better meet their needs. Disadvantages include increased adverse selection (discussed later in the chapter) and administrative costs for record keeping, providing employees with information about options, and so on.

A related method of providing employees with some choice regarding benefits and of utilizing the tax advantages of benefits is through a **flexible spending account.** With a flexible spending account, the employee chooses to reduce salary by some amount, such as $1,000. This amount can be used to pay for a variety of benefits, including uninsured medical and dental expenses and dependent child care. The advantage of a flexible spending account is that the employee is not taxed on the amount of salary that is used for this purpose (e.g., the $1,000).[2] However, to qualify for favorable tax treatment (see below), the employee must incur the expenses and request reimbursement within a specified period. The fact that unused amounts of the salary reduction are forfeited is known as "use it or lose it."

---

[2] For contributory plans, a similar mechanism commonly is used for employee contributions toward the cost of medical expense coverage in order to exclude the amount contributed from the employee's taxable income.

16.2   Why Firms Provide Employee Benefits

If employees pay for their benefits in the long run, a natural question is: Why are benefits provided through an employer as opposed to workers purchasing them individually? Instead of providing employee benefits, businesses could pay higher cash wages and allow employees to contract for benefits on their own. The explanations for why employers provide employee benefits fall into three main categories. One important reason for employer provided benefits is that taxes paid by the employer and employee generally are lower if the employer provides the benefits as opposed to paying higher cash wages and having the employee purchase the benefits individually. A second reason for employer provided benefits is that percentage loadings for administrative expenses in group insurance premiums are lower than for individual insurance. Finally, employers sometimes find that employer provided benefits promote employee productivity. We now examine each of these explanations in more detail.

Income Tax Advantages of Employee Benefits

Employee benefit plans that receive preferential income tax treatment are called **qualified plans.** As discussed in Chapter 21, the tax benefits of a particular transaction can be assessed only by examining the tax payments of all parties involved. In the case of employee benefits, it is necessary to examine the tax treatment from both the employer's and the employee's perspective.

   The federal income tax treatment of employee benefits generally is the same as the tax treatment of cash wages from the employer's perspective. Both benefits and wages are deductible expenses. Consequently, the income tax effects to an employer of paying an additional $100 in cash wages are the same as paying an additional $100 in employee benefits. The major tax advantage of employee benefits therefore arises from the personal income tax treatment of employee benefits versus cash wages.[3] Specifically, the tax advantage exists because: (1) the cost of qualified employee benefit plans either is not taxed or is tax deferred at the personal level, whereas salary and wages are taxed in the year earned, and (2) employees generally are not able to obtain the same tax treatment if benefits are purchased individually.

   To illustrate the main tax benefit, suppose that the annual cost of medical insurance for Helen is $4,000 regardless of whether it is purchased through the employer or individually by Helen. Consider two potential compensation packages for Helen:

   Package 1: Salary = $50,000 and no medical insurance
   Package 2: Salary = $46,000 plus medical insurance

---

[3]State income tax rules generally are similar. For most workers, the social security system provides additional tax incentives to substitute employee benefits for cash wages. The social security system is financed mainly through payroll taxes equal to specified percentages of payroll paid by both the employer and the employee (see Chapter 19). Since the value of many employee benefits is not subject to payroll taxes, employees can save on payroll taxes by taking a greater portion of their total compensation in the form of employee benefits as opposed to cash wages. However, since social security benefits are tied to the taxes paid by a particular employee, the substitution of employee benefits for cash wages might reduce social security benefits as well. Thus, the net effect of social security on employee benefits is complex.

The after-tax cost to the employer is the same for both packages; however, the tax treatment of the two packages differs for Helen. Assume, for example, that Helen has a 20 percent income tax rate and that she cannot deduct any of the cost of individual medical insurance from her taxable income.[4] With package 1, Helen then has after-tax income of $40,000 [$50,000 × (1 − 0.20)], from which she purchases health insurance at a cost of $4,000, leaving $36,000 to spend on other goods and services. With package 2, she has after-tax income of $36,800 [$46,000 × (1 − 0.20)] to spend on other goods and services. The difference of $800 is the tax savings on the cost of medical insurance (0.20 × $4,000).

While the initial cost of qualified employee benefits is not taxable, the benefits from some plans, such as retirement plans and disability insurance, may be taxed if and when they are received. For example, retirement income is taxed when it is received. Thus, there is a deferral of taxes on the contributions to retirement plans. Qualified retirement plans also have the feature that taxes on investment income are deferred until funds are withdrawn. Tax deferral is beneficial because it reduces the present value of tax payments. Tax deferral also can be beneficial if the tax rate applied in the future is expected to be lower than the current tax rate. Chapter 17 examines the tax benefits of qualified retirement plans in more detail.

Cost Savings with Group Insurance

Group insurance purchased by an employer (implicitly purchased by employees in the form of lower wages) can be less costly than having each employee individually purchase the same amount of insurance. One reason for the lower cost is that the insurer's administrative costs of marketing, underwriting, billing, and premium collection are lower with group insurance than with selling separate policies to each individual employee. Thus, group insurance through an employer has a lower percentage expense loading than individual insurance. Another cost savings associated with employer provided benefits is that the total costs of designing benefits and selecting an appropriate insurer are lower than if each individual were to arrange for their own benefits.

Group insurance also can reduce adverse selection problems relative to providing insurance on an individual basis. Because of the heterogeneity in individuals applying for medical insurance and life insurance, insurers typically find it cost effective to gather information that will help them predict expected claim costs and thus classify applicants. Without classification (charging all applicants the same price), insurers could experience severe adverse selection problems (see Chapter 8). That is, individuals with higher (lower) expected claim costs could purchase higher (lower) amounts of coverage than with classification. Classification is never perfect, however; therefore, some adverse selection is likely to occur despite insurers' efforts to classify individuals.

With group insurance, individual members of the group typically have limited opportunities to choose their level of coverage. Consequently, group insurers need to worry less about adverse selection even though they generally do not classify individual members. Group insurance therefore can reduce classification costs and adverse selection if individual members of the group have limited choices.[5] The mitigation of adverse selection helps

---

[4]Individual medical insurance premiums are deductible if the premiums and other deductible medical costs exceed 7.5 percent of the person's (adjusted) gross income. Self-employed persons can deduct only part of the cost of coverage.

[5]Insurers still are likely to classify groups to prevent adverse selection at the group level.

to explain why group insurance often is mandatory or why coverage options are limited for a particular firm.

Productivity and Employee Benefits

Another reason for including benefits in an employee compensation package is that suitably defined benefit plans can increase productivity. As discussed in more detail in Chapter 17, deferred compensation (such as retirement benefits) can be structured to induce employees to work harder and to reduce employee turnover. Other types of benefits also can enhance labor productivity by improving morale and the retention of key employees. In addition, productivity can be enhanced by employee benefits such as medical insurance if the benefits improve the health of employees, reduce time away from work, and reduce turnover.

Regulatory Restrictions on Employee Benefits

The regulatory restrictions on employee benefits are numerous and complex. We have no intention of trying to learn or memorize them fully ourselves, much less pretend that you should do so. (Of course, if your career plans are in the employee benefit area, then you will have to learn many of the regulations and keep track of how they change every year.) Nevertheless, you should be aware that employee benefits can be subject to restrictions from a number of sources, including federal laws dealing with labor contracts and labor relations, antidiscrimination laws, the tax code, and state laws dealing with insurance contracts. Minimum employee participation requirements represent one important source of restrictions. Those regulations require qualified plans to be formed to benefit broad groups of employees, not some small subset, like top executives. We discuss some of the specific regulations dealing with group medical insurance later in the chapter and with retirement plans in the next chapter.

Concept Check

1. Explain why the income tax treatment of qualified employee benefits will likely cause higher paid employees to demand a greater proportion of their total compensation in the form of benefits than lower paid employees.

16.3   Overview of Group Medical Expense Coverage

One of the most common and important types of employee benefits is **group medical expense coverage,** whereby the employer provides employees with insurance coverage to pay eligible medical expenses. Almost 90 percent of people with private (i.e., nongovernmental) medical expense insurance in the United States are enrolled in employer-based group plans.

Traditional Fee-for-Service Insurance Arrangements

From the 1940s through the 1980s, the predominant form of employer-based group medical expense insurance was a fee-for-service arrangement. These arrangements have become much less common since that time, especially in their pure form. Knowledge of these arrangements is nonetheless important for understanding the development of health maintenance organizations and other managed care alternatives to traditional fee-for-service plans.

Traditional fee-for-service arrangements have several main features:

- Employers provide coverage for specified medical expenses, either self-insuring or purchasing insurance to cover all or part of the costs.
- Employees and covered dependents have substantial discretion (choice) over what doctor or hospital to use when care is needed.
- When an employee or covered dependent receives medical care, the health care provider charges a fee to the employee and/or insurer for the services provided (thus the name "fee-for-service"). Depending on the plan, the provider either bills the employee, who is then reimbursed by the insurer, subject to deductibles and coinsurance, or the provider bills the insurer directly. In the latter case, the employee either pays the provider for any charge not covered by the plan or reimburses the insurer.

Large employers generally self-insure most or all of the benefits under these plans, in many cases using an insurer or third-party administrator to administer the insurance benefits. Small- to medium-sized employers commonly purchase group medical insurance to pay benefits from either a commercial insurance company or Blue Cross–Blue Shield organization (see Box 16.1). In noncontributory plans, employers provide medical expense coverage without an explicit premium contribution from employees. Contributory plans require employees to pay a part of the cost as an explicit payroll deduction. Most plans that provide coverage for an employee's dependents are contributory.

There are two main methods of arranging insurance protection for employees under fee-for-service plans: (1) provide basic coverage with "supplementary" major medical insurance, and (2) provide "comprehensive" major medical insurance without separate benefits under basic coverage.

Under the first approach, employees generally receive **basic benefits** in the form of coverage for hospitalization, surgery, physician services apart from surgery (for example, while hospitalized or following a period of hospitalization), and specified diagnostic tests. These benefits often are subject to small deductibles and the benefit is limited (e.g., 60 days of hospitalization per illness, or a specified maximum number of physician visits). The costs of routine care, such as periodic physical examinations or physician visits for minor illnesses (e.g., visits for colds and infections) usually are limited or in many cases excluded from the basic benefits package. Coverage generally is provided for "usual, customary, and reasonable" charges and/or based on a fee schedule. If the hospital or physician charges more than what is defined as reasonable or specified in the schedule, then the employee has to pay the excess.

In addition to basic benefits, the employee typically receives additional protection in the form of supplementary **major medical coverage.** The major medical coverage pays eligible expenses not covered by the basic benefits package, subject to an annual deductible (for each family member or less often for the family as a whole) and a co-insurance clause that requires the employee to pay a specified percentage (e.g., 15–25 percent) of expenses in excess of the deductible. Major medical coverage usually provides a large lifetime limit on total benefits, such as $500,000 to $1 million; some plans have no upper limit. Common exclusions include elective cosmetic surgery, vision and dental care, and medical expenses payable under workers' compensation.

Many major medical plans cap the employee's maximum out-of-pocket cost for eligible expenses during the year using a **stop loss clause** or "out-of-pocket maximum," which

Blue Cross–Blue Shield (BC–BS) organizations originally were formed during the 1930s and 1940s as non-profit (and therefore income tax-exempt) associations of health care providers who offered services to covered workers and other consumers for annual premiums. Although there was little material difference, these plans differed from indemnity insurance policies in that groups of hospitals and doctors agreed to provide specified health care services in exchange for premiums, as opposed to having an unrelated insurer pay hospitals and physicians for services rendered. Blue Cross plans provided hospital services; Blue Shield plans provided physician services. Most separate Blue Cross and Blue Shield plans later merged to provide both hospital and physician services.

Modern BC–BS organizations operate as separate entities in almost all states; a few states have more than one BC–BS organization. Most of these organizations operate in the same general manner as other medical expense insurers. BC–BS organizations have a large share (e.g., up to 50 percent or more) of the group medical expense coverage market in many states. The Congress repealed the federal income tax exemption for BC–BS plans in 1986. Some states exempt the plans from state premium taxes. In part due to loss of their income tax-exempt status, some BC–BS entities converted to mutual insurance companies during the mid-1980s. Beginning in the mid-1990s, a number of BC–BS organizations have converted to stock insurance companies. Many BC–BS organizations have diversified their operations by creating HMOs, by expanding into lines of insurance beyond medical insurance, and by providing claims processing services for self-insured employer medical plans.

specifies that the major medical coverage will pay 100 percent of eligible expenses (usually including some services not covered by the basic plan) once the employee has paid a specified amount under the co-insurance clause (or under both the deductible and co-insurance clause). For example, the stop loss clause might limit the employee's maximum out-of-pocket cost from the application of co-insurance to $1,500 in a year. This limit could apply to all costs for the employee and covered dependents, or it could only apply to the employee's expenses with a higher stop loss amount, such as $3,000, to cap total co-insurance costs (or in some plans total deductible and co-insurance costs) for the family. Note that major medical coverage and the stop loss clause apply only to eligible expenses. Medical expenses that are not eligible are paid in full by the employee. In many plans, ineligible expenses include amounts charged by physicians in excess of the amount that the plan is willing to pay for specified services. Thus, in some cases employees may have material out-of-pocket costs in addition to the maximum amounts specified by the stop loss clause.

To illustrate the basic operation of these provisions, consider an employee-only major medical plan with a $300 annual deductible, 20 percent coinsurance, and an $1,800 annual stop loss. If the employee incurred $1,300 of eligible major medical expenses during a year, the plan would pay $800 = (1 − .2) × ($1,300 − $300) of the expenses (i.e., 80 percent of the expenses above the deductible). If the employee incurred $15,300 in eligible expenses, the stop loss would apply because $300 plus 20 percent of the loss above the deductible exceeds $1,800. The plan would pay $15,300 − $1,800 = $13,500.

The splitting of coverage into basic benefits and major medical benefits reflects to some extent the historical development of employer provided group medical coverage and associated insurance products. When group medical coverage first became common, employers often started with hospitalization coverage and later added coverage for surgery and other physicians' services. Major medical coverage eventually was developed to protect against large losses not covered by the basic benefits package.

The second approach to providing benefits under a fee-for-service arrangement is simply to use stand-alone major medical insurance, sometimes known as "comprehensive major medical coverage." There is no separate package of basic benefits. Eligible expenses simply are covered subject to a lifetime limit on costs, if any, and subject to a deductible, co-insurance, and, if included, a stop loss provision.

Fee-for-Service and Utilization of Health Care Services

The health care system has three major players: (1) health care providers, such as physicians, nurses, and hospitals; (2) employees/individuals who seek and consume health care; and (3) employers/insurers who provide insurance to pay the unexpected health care costs of individuals. The main point of this section is to show how the incentives of these parties under traditional fee-for-service arrangements can increase overall medical expenses.

An important characteristic of health care is that providers typically know more about the services needed than do consumers. For example, if a physician recommends a particular test or procedure, most consumers are not qualified to question the physician and many consumers are reluctant (or find it costly) to obtain second opinions except for major treatments. As a consequence, providers in many cases have considerable influence over the demand for the product that they provide. In the extreme, providers can create demand for their services. The influence of providers on the demand for their services is strengthened to the extent that someone other than the consumer, such as an insurer, pays most of the costs of services recommended by the provider.

Moral Hazard with Fee-for-Service

Group medical coverage in general and fee-for-service coverage in particular leads to moral hazard, which increases the cost of medical care. There are two aspects of the moral hazard problem associated with group medical coverage. First, the group nature of coverage implies that any premium contributions of employees and forgone wages to pay for the employer's contribution generally are not closely related to the individual employee's expected claim costs. As a result, before they are hurt or become ill, employees (and covered dependents) might behave in ways that are riskier than would be true if the employee's cost of insurance was more closely related to the employee's risk. For example, employees might be more likely to smoke or maintain lifestyles that are more conducive to illness or injury. This type of "ex ante" (before injury or illness) moral hazard is not unique to fee-for-service coverage; it also occurs with alternatives to fee-for-service, such as health maintenance organizations.

Second, moral hazard associated with group medical coverage can lead to excessive utilization of health care once a person develops an ailment. This "ex post" (after injury or illness) moral hazard is especially pronounced for fee-for-service coverage that allows ready access to medical specialists and that includes comparatively small deductibles and co-insurance percentages. Under a fee-for-service arrangement, the provision of health care services is separate and distinct from the provision of insurance. This separation of the provision of insurance from the provision of care aggravates moral hazard because insureds and providers have limited incentives to economize on costly medical care when most of the costs are paid or reimbursed by insurers and employers.

Understanding Excessive Utilization

To elaborate, medical insurance benefits under fee-for-service arrangements imply that patients typically bear only a small part of the cost of care. Consequently, patients tend to demand too much care, or they are at least willing to accept care that is recommended by providers without paying significant attention to costs. Since providers' revenues increase as more services are provided, providers have an incentive to provide care that has any real prospect of benefiting the patient, given that much of the provider's costs are paid by insurance rather than the patient. Providers also might have an incentive to provide extra care to reduce the likelihood of a malpractice suit. In some cases, providers might even have an incentive to provide unnecessary care.

It is important for you to get a firm handle on what we mean by the term *excessive utilization*. While most people have an intuitive understanding of this idea, it can be a little hard to pin down precisely. We define **excessive utilization** as occurring when a patient receives care for which the cost of providing the care exceeds the expected benefit to the patient, where the expected benefit to the patient depends on the value that a typical person would place on the expected improvement in health status (including any lessening of risk that the condition will worsen). We define the idea in terms of the value to a typical person to avoid subtle issues dealing with how a person's income might affect his or her valuation of care (e.g., a high income person might be willing or able to pay more for health care and thus place a higher monetary value on the care than a low income person).

To illustrate how excessive utilization can arise with fee-for-service arrangements, assume that the cost of providing a particular service to a patient is $100 but that the expected benefit to the patient of receiving the care is only $50. Thus, the cost exceeds the benefit, and the total cost of risk will be lower if the care is not provided. If the patient had to pay the full cost of the care and knew the expected benefit, he or she would choose not to receive the care, thus reducing the cost of risk.

Now consider what happens if the patient has to pay only $20 (20 percent) of the cost with the person's medical insurance paying the other $80. Then the patient will demand the care (and/or the physician or other health care provider will encourage the care) because the marginal cost to the patient is $20 and the marginal benefit is $50. The provider will provide the care because it benefits the patient and because the full $100 cost is covered by the patient and the insurer. However, because the care is provided even though the cost exceeds the benefit, the cost of risk goes up by $50.

The moral hazard problem associated with providing care to a given patient is illustrated further in Figure 16.1 under the plausible assumption that as additional care is provided, the marginal benefit to the patient declines and the marginal cost of providing care increases. The optimal amount of care is Q*, the point at which the marginal cost equals the marginal benefit. Up to Q*, the marginal benefit from an additional unit of care exceeds the marginal cost; beyond this point the marginal cost exceeds the marginal benefit. Because the patient has to pay only part of the cost of additional care (e.g., a co-insurance percentage), the marginal cost to the patient is less than the full marginal cost of providing the additional care. As a result, care will be provided until the marginal benefit to the patient equals the marginal cost to the patient, so that with insurance Q^I units of care are provided. The difference between Q^I and Q* represents excessive utilization of care.

Note that employees as a group will have to pay for excessive utilization over time in the form of lower wages and/or higher explicit contributions toward the cost of coverage. Also note that excessive utilization implies that employees receive excessive quality of health

FIGURE 16.1
Excessive utilization due to moral hazard.

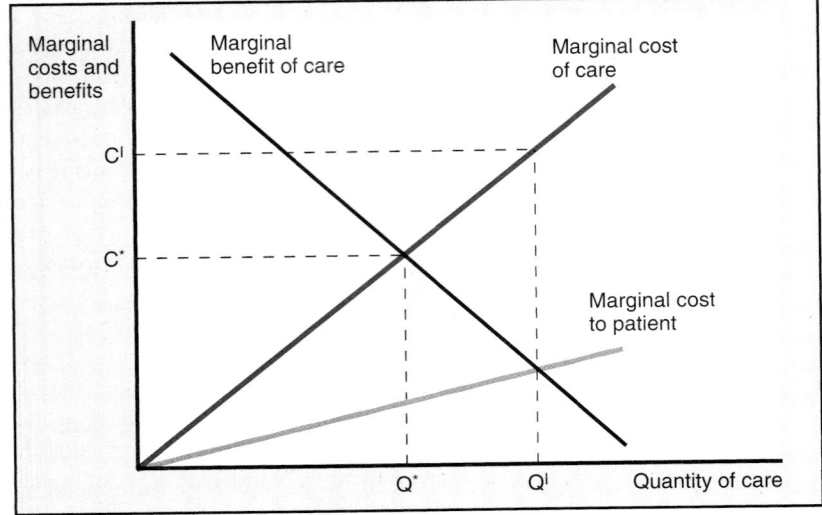

care (i.e., more care than a fully informed employee would choose to have if covered under an optimal insurance arrangement that only provided care for which the expected benefits exceeded the costs; see below). While in some cases care may be provided that has no expected benefit to the patient, the more fundamental problem concerns the provision of care with positive expected benefits that do not exceed the costs. Thus, the incentives provided by fee-for-service coverage lead to higher quality of health care than employees in general are willing to pay for. In practice, this problem is manifested in many ways, including excessive visits to the doctor and specialists, excessive days in the hospital, excessive investment in diagnostic testing devices and other medical technology, and so on. The good news is that people will be healthier; the bad news is that they would prefer a little less health and a little more money for other things.

If employees have to pay the full cost of insurance in the form of either lower wages or higher contributions toward the cost of coverage, they have an incentive to demand insurance coverage that helps reduce the moral hazard problem. In an ideal world where the expected benefits of care and the costs of care could be measured without cost by the insurer, insurance contracts could be written that would exclude coverage of any care with a cost higher than the expected benefit. However, the optimal amount of care (i.e., where the marginal expected benefit equals the marginal cost) is not observable. It generally cannot be determined or verified by the insurer without incurring a cost. As a result, the moral hazard problem cannot be eliminated by simply excluding payment for excessively costly care.

To highlight how uncertainty concerning the optimal amount of care is the underlying cause of excessive utilization in traditional fee-for-service arrangements, compare the medical insurance example to auto physical damage insurance. When a person wrecks his or her car, there are a variety of reasonably accurate and low cost sources of information to determine how much it will cost to repair the car so that it is in roughly the same condition as it was before the wreck (i.e., to "make the car well"). Thus, physical damage insurance is written on a repair cost basis (see Chapter 13) without producing inordinately large verification costs for insurers or pervasive excessive utilization of the services of body shops. The insured might like to get some scratches repaired that are unrelated to the wreck or get an expensive, custom paint job, but the insurer simply can refuse to pay for this type of excessive quality. In contrast, because of uncertainty about the optimal amount of medical care, it is much more difficult/costly for insurers to intervene in physician-patient relationships.[6]

Reducing Moral Hazard under Fee-for-Service Arrangements

Rapid growth in health care costs during the 1980s and early 1990s led many employers to modify traditional fee-for-service arrangements to help control costs. This section briefly describes some of these changes before turning to the subject of health maintenance organizations and how they address the moral hazard problem. Recall first that in Chapter 10 you learned about several means of reducing moral hazard in insurance contracts, including having the policyholder pay part of the loss, experience rating, and claims investigation and monitoring by insurers. Apart from the growth of health maintenance organizations, many employers have modified traditional fee-for-service arrangements in several ways in order to limit moral hazard.

Numerous employers have changed benefits and employee contribution rules to encourage cost control. For example, deductibles and other forms of copayments by patients have been increased.[7] You should note that increased cost-sharing by patients can reduce excessive utilization even though patients are not knowledgeable about medical care. The reason is that with increased cost-sharing, consumers will demand more information from physicians about the expected benefits of costly treatments. In addition, consumers will choose physicians based, in part, on their reputations for providing cost-effective care (at least in theory). Consequently, in an effort to develop a reputation for providing high-quality, cost-effective care, physicians will be less likely to suggest treatments with small expected benefits relative to the costs.

In addition to increased cost-sharing, many employers now offer employees a choice of cost-sharing arrangements and require them to contribute more toward the cost if a more expensive plan is chosen. This approach, which often is used in conjunction with the employer providing a choice between fee-for-service coverage and coverage under a health maintenance organization, provides employees with a financial incentive to take less complete insurance coverage that is less subject to moral hazard.

Another major and very important approach to cost control under fee-for-service type arrangements has been the adoption of a variety of methods that incorporate some form of **managed care,** where the insurer becomes more active in monitoring/managing the provision of health care services, often in conjunction with less flexibility for employees to choose providers. For example, most fee-for-service plans now have requirements for review by the insurer before certain types of procedures, tests, or hospital admissions are approved for coverage. In effect, traditional fee-for-service arrangements—where decisions on care were made almost exclusively by the physician and patient—have largely disappeared. The growth of managed care has required insurers and other plan administrators to develop additional expertise in evaluating care.

---

[6]We do not mean to imply that the problem of excessive quality does not arise in automobile physical damage insurance, but simply that the problem is much worse for medical expense coverage.

[7]This includes reducing maximum fees that the plan will pay for services. Note also that moral hazard is mitigated by nonmonetary costs borne by patients, such as the time and hassle involved in seeing physicians, receiving medical tests, and so on.

In an attempt to reduce costs further, some employers/insurers also have contracted with providers to provide treatment at discounted prices. Under these **preferred provider organizations,** employees that go to a provider that is not included in the agreement have to pay more of the cost of care. This saves the plan money and encourages the employee to go to a preferred provider. Providers are willing to enter into these arrangements with large employers or insurers in order to obtain a large volume of business from covered workers.

Health Maintenance Organizations

Another form of managed care that addresses the moral hazard problem is the health maintenance organization. **Health maintenance organizations** (HMOs) either merge the provision of care and insurance functions into one entity or involve contracts between the HMO and physicians that reduce the moral hazard problem. The proportion of employees covered by HMOs grew very rapidly in the 1990s. Many of the earliest and largest HMOs have been corporations that are unrelated to traditional health insurers. In recent years most of the largest health insurers and Blue Cross–Blue Shield organizations have established HMOs to supplement their fee-for-service insurance operations.

The distinction between HMOs and fee-for-service arrangements has become blurred as fee-for-service arrangements have adopted the various forms of managed care described earlier. A key difference, however, is that workers covered by an HMO generally must receive care from physicians that are associated with the HMO (see below), whereas fee-for-service plans generally allow greater choice of physicians, including access to specialists. In addition, HMOs usually have more influence on the types of care that will be provided compared to fee-for-service plans with some form of managed care.

HMOs generally charge employers a fixed annual fee, called a capitation fee, in exchange for providing a wide range of medical care services to employees. The benefits provided are usually comprehensive, including some coverage for routine care. HMO coverage may involve small copayments for some services, but it usually does not involve annual deductibles and co-insurance.

There are several types of HMOs. Under an *individual practice association,* the HMO contracts with physicians to provide covered services on a fee-for-service basis. However, the compensation contract with physicians provides incentives for cost control (e.g., a reduction in fees or possible termination of the agreement if utilization of care exceeds certain levels or a bonus if utilization is below certain levels) and/or provisions that allow close monitoring of the physician by the HMO. Under a second type of HMO, sometimes known as a *group practice plan,* groups of physicians contract with the HMO, agreeing to provide covered services for a per capita fee. Under both of these approaches, the physicians often treat non-HMO patients as well as HMO patients. Under a third type of HMO, services are provided by a group of physicians that are employed by the HMO, which may also own one or more hospitals.

Incentives for Cost Control

An HMO has a strong incentive to control costs in order to increase profits and allow it to compete more effectively with other HMOs and fee-for-service plans. Compared with fee-for-service plans with some form of managed care and especially compared with traditional fee-for-service plans, the HMO is able to exert more control over physicians and/or provide physicians with greater incentives to control costs, thus reducing moral hazard. Note that linking physicians' compensation to their success at controlling costs can provide greater incentives for cost control in the same way that experience rating can provide greater incentives for cost control in other insurance arrangements.

Under an HMO, employees usually choose a primary care physician from the group of physicians that have contracts with (or are employed by) the HMO. Employees (and covered dependents) usually must see this physician when they are ill, and the primary care physician largely determines whether the patient will have access to care by a specialist. (Special provisions govern payment of emergency care by non-HMO physicians or hospitals.) As a result, primary care physicians commonly serve a **gatekeeper function:** They control access to specialists and other forms of costly care. A number of HMOs have recently modified this approach by using what are known as *point of service plans*. With these plans, an HMO primary care physician manages the employee's care. However, employees can seek care from non-HMO physicians if they are willing to pay a higher proportion of the cost of treatment.

Evidence suggests that HMOs experience higher utilization of certain types of "walk-in care" than fee-for-service arrangements, which probably is attributable to lower copayments for these types of care. However, HMOs experience lower utilization of more costly types of care. For example, HMOs on average have fewer days of hospitalization per covered employee, fewer surgeries, and fewer consultations with specialists. In view of the fact that some employers give employees a choice between fee-for-service coverage and one or more HMOs, this result in part reflects the tendency for less healthy employees to choose fee-for-service coverage even though they usually have to pay a higher contribution toward the cost of coverage than if they were to choose an HMO. The reason is that people with health problems or that are concerned that problems might be imminent want more freedom of access to specialist care. However, evidence suggests that HMOs have fewer hospitalizations, surgeries, and specialist visits even after controlling for the tendency for HMO enrollees to be healthier than people covered by fee-for-service plans.

HMOs and the Quality of Care

HMOs reduce incentives for excessive care and thereby control costs relative to traditional fee-for-service plans. However, HMOs often are criticized for providing too little care or poor quality care. While other forms of managed care have been similarly criticized, much of the attention has focused on HMOs. Many enrollees have complained about limited access to specialists and other forms of care. Some states have passed laws that have limited the discretion of HMOs and other managed care plans to control costs (see Box 16.2).

While HMOs have strong incentives to control costs, a number of factors in principle reduce the risk that HMOs on average will tend to provide inadequate quality (i.e., that they will have *too little* utilization of care). First, if an HMO provides too little initial care for a problem, it may have to pay for more expensive care if the problem worsens. Second, although federal law prevents many HMOs from being sued and held vicariously liable under tort law for malpractice by HMO physicians and hospitals, individual physicians and hospitals that are part of HMO networks nonetheless can be sued for malpractice by HMO patients.

Third, HMOs compete with other HMOs and fee-for-service plans for enrollees based on a combination of price and quality. The resulting market discipline should help control any tendency for HMOs to provide inadequate quality over time. To be sure, if workers are uninformed about differences in coverage and quality among HMOs and fee-for-service plans, the possibility exists that many workers might mistakenly prefer coverage with too

As HMOs and other forms of managed care expanded rapidly in the 1990s, limitations on choice of physician and types of care were subject to increased criticism. Many states have enacted legislation restricting HMOs and, in some instances, other forms of managed care; other state legislatures are considering such legislation. In some states, legislation has been proposed that basically would ban HMOs by requiring group medical plans to allow workers to choose a physician and have access to specialists. Other restrictions adopted in many states and debated in others include:

- Requiring HMOs (or other managed care plans) to provide broader coverage of emergency care by non-network physicians.

- Requiring plans to provide direct access to specialists under certain conditions.
- Requiring plans to allow treatment by non-HMO or non-network physicians for an additional charge to the patient (i.e., requiring point of service plans).
- Requiring larger insured employers to offer workers a fee-for-service plan as an alternative to an HMO (subject to a higher contribution from the worker).
- Establishing specified procedures for patients to appeal denials of certain types of care by HMOs.
- Prohibiting "gag rules" in which HMOs may attempt to keep physicians from discussing certain types of care with patients.

many restrictions in order to reduce their contributions toward a plan's cost or increase cash wages. If so, market discipline will provide less incentive for HMOs to provide good quality, and many workers might be disappointed by the types and quality of care that ultimately are provided. However, many workers might be expected to learn more over time, especially given publicity associated with the HMO/managed care backlash, so that fewer mistakes will be made.

When considering the question of whether HMOs are likely to provide (or have provided) inadequate quality and possible government restrictions on HMOs, you also should be aware of how the incentives and desires of patients may change once they become ill or hurt. Prior to illness or injury, employees may be willing to accept limitations on the quality of care that they will receive if they need medical treatment in order to save money on the cost of coverage. However, once a person is hurt or becomes ill, he or she has a strong incentive to seek the highest quality care possible when the costs are spread among the insured pool. Even if employees are fully informed about how HMOs work and the quality of care compared with fee-for-service plans, they might rationally choose an HMO but then turn around and complain about the quality of care and seek to expand their options for receiving care once they need treatment. This behavior could produce substantial political pressure for restrictions that might be too severe from the perspective of fully informed workers who do not know what their future medical needs will be but who have to pay the cost of care through lower wages or contributions. In any case, to the extent that any such efforts by HMO patients are successful, the treatment and cost differences between HMOs and fee-for-service plans will narrow.

Concept Checks

2. Assume that an employee has a choice between (*a*) comprehensive major medical coverage with a $250 annual deductible, 20 percent co-insurance, and a $1,750 stop loss limit on co-insurance charges, and (*b*) HMO coverage with no deductibles and no co-insurance. The required employee contribution for employee coverage is $20

per month lower for HMO coverage. Other things being equal, which plan would most likely be chosen by a 22-year-old person just entering the labor force? By a 45-year-old with a chronic back problem?

3. Suppose that the comprehensive major medical coverage described above is chosen. If the employee incurs $750 of eligible medical expenses during a year, how much of this expense will be paid by the employee and how much will be paid by the insurer?

16.4   Group Medical Plan Provisions and Pricing Issues

In this section you will learn about a number of coverage provisions and pricing issues for group medical coverage including: (1) coverage for dependents, (2) cross-subsidies among employees that are inherent in group coverage, (3) government mandated benefits that must be included in group plans, (4) portability of coverage when employees change jobs, and (5) renewability of group health insurance.

Dependent Coverage

Most group health care plans offer coverage for the employee and the employee's eligible dependents. Plans usually require a small employee contribution or sometimes no contribution for employee coverage and a significantly higher contribution for dependent coverage. The contribution for dependents may be a flat charge per pay period regardless of how many dependents are covered or there may be a higher charge for coverage of children than for spouse-only coverage.

When both a husband and wife without children work for employers with group health plans, they often will minimize their contributions to the cost of coverage by each receiving coverage from their own employer. An exception would be when one plan does not require an additional contribution for spouse coverage and the spouse's coverage requires a contribution. In this case, the spouse working for the employer that requires a contribution may decide to be covered under the other spouse's plan. A possible limitation of this strategy is that if this spouse later wants to be covered under his or her own employer's plan, he or she may have to provide evidence of insurability. When parents with children both work for firms with medical plans, the choice of dependent coverage commonly will be made based on a comparison of the coverage terms and required contributions for the two plans.

In the event that a person is covered by more than one plan, the plans will coordinate payments for covered expenses. While this sometimes can be complicated, a standard coordination of benefits provision holds that the employee's plan is primary for the employee and excess for a covered spouse with children covered by the plan of the parent whose birthday falls earliest in the year.

Cross-Subsidies in Group Medical Coverage

Apart from differences in required employee contributions for different types of plans (e.g., HMO versus fee-for-service) or depending on whether dependents are covered, employee contributions for group medical coverage usually do not vary across workers for a given firm. That is, employees choosing the same plan typically make the same contribution even though their expected claim costs may vary. Since it is unlikely that wages typically vary to reflect these differences in risk, some employees are subsidized by others. For example, an employee who smokes and has five dependent children is likely to be subsidized by a nonsmoking employee without dependents. However, as suggested by our earlier discussion of why firms provide benefits, lower risk employees still might prefer the group medical plan over individual coverage because of the tax and administrative cost advantages of group insurance. Recall that the administrative cost savings for group plans are in substantial part due to the absence of risk classification for individual workers.

Mandated Benefits

We explained earlier that employees have limited flexibility to choose types of benefits under group medical coverage. Limitations on choice are necessary to help control adverse selection, especially since the cost of coverage to individual employees is not closely related to differences in expected claim costs among employees. The coverage provisions of group medical plans agreed upon by employers and employees generally will provide benefits that the typical employee desires given the cost of providing benefits. Because employees are heterogeneous, some employees might prefer alternative benefits.

Many states have mandated that employer group medical plans (and sometimes individual plans) provide certain types of benefits, such as minimum benefits for alcohol/drug use treatment and mental health services, and payment for a specified minimum period of hospitalization for childbearing. Similarly, in 1996 the US Congress enacted legislation requiring that medical plans for firms with 50 or more employees provide minimum coverage of 48 hours hospitalization for normal childbirth and 96 hours for cesarean births. This law also included some restrictions on the ability of group medical plans to limit coverage for mental health services.

An argument often used to justify certain types of government **mandated benefits** is that private decision making by employers and employees might fail to provide desirable coverage to employees with special needs, thus creating hardship for these employees and perhaps having part of the costs of uninsured treatment fall on other parties. Opponents argue that mandated benefits increase the cost of coverage without benefiting many employees and increase cross-subsidies among employees. They also argue that much of the political pressure for mandates comes from those health care providers who gain business if certain types of coverage are required or expanded.

Portability of Coverage

An important issue that received substantial attention during the 1990s is the portability (or lack of portability) of group medical coverage when employees are terminated or change jobs. One reason employees may lose coverage when they change jobs is that fee-for-service group medical plans usually contain a **pre-existing conditions clause,** which excludes coverage for new employees for any ailment for which the person received medical treatment in the prior 12 months. Pre-existing condition clauses are relatively uncommon for HMOs. HMOs that were established under federal legislation enacted in the early 1970s to spur the growth of HMOs cannot exclude coverage for pre-existing conditions, and competition has led many other HMOs to forgo using these clauses.

The rationale for a pre-existing conditions clause is that it controls costs by reducing the adverse selection that otherwise could occur. For example, some persons might seek employment to obtain coverage for known medical problems. A problem with the pre-existing conditions clause is that it might discourage some employees from making desirable job changes, if, for example, the new job does not provide HMO coverage without a pre-existing conditions clause. Under the provisions of some insured group health plans, employees are allowed to convert their group coverage to individual coverage with the insurer without proving insurability. However, the individual coverage sometimes is less comprehensive and commonly requires a higher premium.

In 1985, the US Congress enacted the Consolidated Omnibus Reconciliation Act of 1985 (COBRA), which required group health plans for firms with 20 or more employees to offer continued coverage to employees (and covered dependents) for a period of up to 18 months following the date that the employee is terminated or quits. (Coverage must be offered for three years if the employee dies and to dependents in the event of a divorce.) Persons who wish to continue coverage must pay a premium for coverage that cannot exceed 102 percent of the employer's cost of providing coverage.

The Federal Health Insurance Portability and Accountability Act of 1996 (HIPAA) further enhanced the portability of group medical coverage for many employees. The law permits plans to exclude coverage for pre-existing conditions for 12 months, but previous coverage under another employer's plan can be used to satisfy the 12-month period as long as the employee has not gone without coverage for 63 days or longer between jobs. Thus, a person who has been covered for a year under a prior plan who obtains a new job within approximately two months will not have a gap in coverage due to the pre-existing conditions clause in the new employer's plan.

Renewability of Small Group Health Insurance

With **guaranteed renewable health insurance,** the insurer must renew coverage regardless of the health of the insured (or members of the insured group). While the premium can increase to reflect the expected experience for the policyholder's rating class, the premium cannot be increased on an individual basis to reflect possible deterioration in health. In effect, the contract does not allow individual experience rating and thus provides insurance against a rate increase due to deterioration in a person's or group's health. To emphasize, the policyholder is exposed to the risk of rate increases based on changes in the average expected claim cost for the policyholder's rating class, but there can be no surcharge based on the policyholder's own experience.

You learned above that small employers commonly insure their obligations to pay medical expenses under their group medical plan. An interesting feature of small group medical insurance contracts is that (prior to legislative mandates, see below) these contracts often were not offered on a guaranteed renewable basis. As a result, if the health of one or more employees deteriorates, the employer may have faced a large rate increase at renewal or, in some cases, be denied renewal. The inability of small employers to be protected against rate increases when one or a few employees become seriously ill reduced the incentive for small employers to offer group medical coverage.

Why were small group policies often not guaranteed renewable (until required by law) when individual policies with this feature were routinely available? If an insurer offers a guaranteed renewable contract, it has to charge a higher price at renewal to employers with good experience in order to cover the insurer's total expected costs because it cannot selectively increase the price for employers with poor experience to reflect their higher expected claim costs. The underlying problem in the small group market appeared to be the ability of small employers with good health experience to readily qualify for a lower rate with a new insurer. Thus, if an insurer offered guaranteed renewable coverage, it would lose many of the employers with good experience to other insurers who could charge them a lower premium based on their good experience. As a result, the insurer would have to increase the rate substantially for the employers that it renewed, which primarily would have poor experience, thus defeating the purpose of the guaranteed renewal feature.

Why does the ability of individual insureds that remain healthy to qualify for new, low rate coverage not prevent guaranteed renewable individual health insurance without a government mandate? The answer to this question appears to be that the direct costs, inconvenience, and hassle of qualifying for new coverage are proportionally larger for individuals than for small employer groups. These higher costs deter the "best risks" from leaving the insurance pool if the insurer charges the same rate to them and to people that have experienced a deterioration in health compared to the average person in the rating class.

By the mid-1990s, most states had enacted legislation to address the lack of guaranteed renewability in the small group health insurance market. While the details vary and the laws are complex, they generally required each insurer to offer coverage at a rate that does not consider the health of individual employees, and the laws often restricted the magnitude of rate increases at renewal. The Federal Health Insurance Portability and Accountability Act of 1996 then required insurers to guarantee the issue of all their small-group health plans to small employers and required all individual and group coverage to be guaranteed renewable. As a result, state and federal law has made it much more difficult for a new insurer to price its products or design coverage in a way that would allow small employers with good health experience to obtain significantly lower rates than employers with poor experience.

Concept Check

4. (*a*) Explain why a majority of employees might prefer group medical insurance that provides very limited benefits for mental illness/psychological problems. How will these employees be affected if the state mandates large benefits of this type? (*b*) Answer the same question with respect to hospitalization coverage for childbirth.

16.5   Health Care Cost Inflation and the Uninsured Problem

Two recurring issues have been subject to intense debate in the United States during the past two decades: rising costs of health care and the number of persons without health insurance. As illustrated in Figure 16.2, the rate of increase in the cost of medical care exceeded the general inflation rate by a sizable margin in the 1980s and early 1990s. Cost growth slowed substantially in the mid-1990s due in large part to greater use of HMOs, other forms of managed care, and increased cost-sharing under fee-for-service plans. However, inflation and cost growth have recently picked up speed again. The medical care consumer price index (CPI) increased 268 percent during the period 1981–2001, an average (geometric) annual increase of 6.4 percent. The overall CPI increased by 106 percent during this period, a 3.5 percent average annual increase. Health care expenditures per capita increased at an average annual rate of approximately 8 percent. The total cost of health care represented approximately 13.2 percent of the US gross domestic product (GDP) in 1997, compared with 8.8 percent of GDP in 1980.

FIGURE 16.2   **Annual percentage changes in medical care CPI and overall CPI: 1981–2001.**

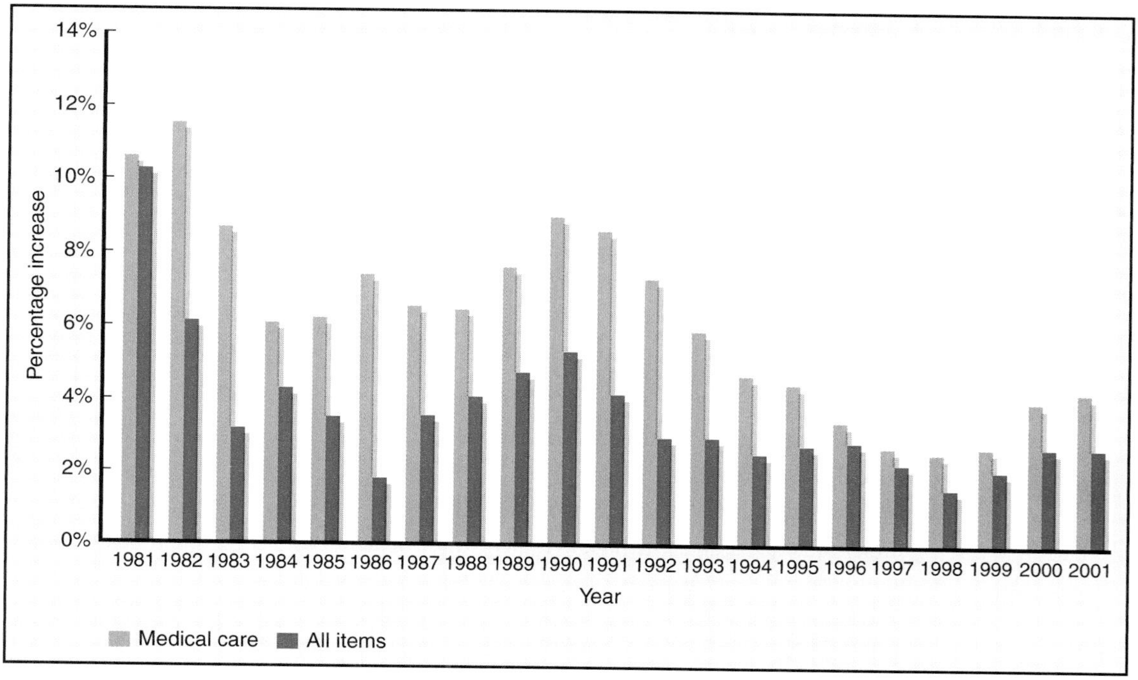

Source: Data obtained from Bureau of Labor Statistics, www.bls.govSearch

The average cost of US employment-based health benefits rose by about 15 percent in 2002. Depending on the plan type (fee-for-service, HMO, etc.), the average medical plan cost per employee ranged from about $4,800 to $5,600.[8]

In year 2000, 14 percent of the US population (39 million people) did not have private or government medical insurance (see Figure 16.3). Many of these uninsured persons were employed or were dependents of employees. Thus, although most people obtain their medical expense insurance from employer-based group plans, a large number of employees do not have such coverage. It is estimated that between 4 and 5 million employees that are uninsured have rejected employer coverage, presumably to avoid paying a contribution toward the cost.

In this section, we discuss some of the factors that have led to high medical costs and inflation in medical costs, characteristics of uninsured people, and the reasons that large numbers of people are uninsured. Our purpose is to provide you with perspective to help you understand the nature and scope of these problems. Broad proposals for dealing with these issues are discussed in the following section.

[8]Cost data from Mercer Human Resource Consulting, as reported in the *Wall Street Journal,* December 12, 2002, p. D6.

FIGURE 16.3
Percent of Americans with health insurance by type: 2000.

Source: U.S. Census Bureau, "Health Insurance Coverage: 2000," *Current Population Reports,* P60–215.

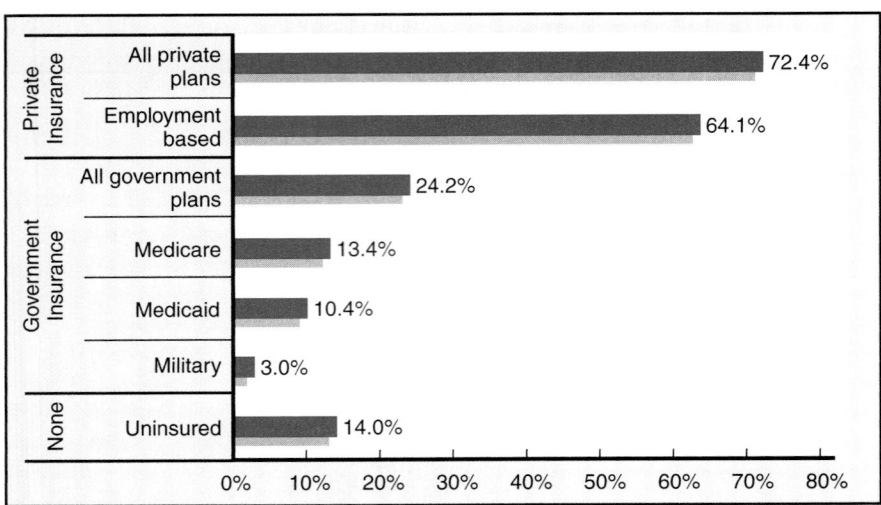

Why Does Health Care Cost So Much?

A number of factors can contribute to rapid growth in health care costs, including: (1) moral hazard and resultant excessive utilization, (2) increased demand for high quality care and technological advances, and (3) aging of the population. Increased costs associated with uninsured persons and medical malpractice litigation also has led to higher costs.

Moral Hazard/Excessive Utilization

One factor that contributed to rapid growth in health care costs up to the mid-1980s was growth in the amount of insurance coverage for medical expenses under fee-for-service plans that required relatively little cost-sharing by employees. In particular, many insurance plans up through the mid-1980s basically offered first dollar coverage (i.e., there were few or no deductibles or little co-insurance). As discussed above, this type of coverage provides little incentive for consumers and providers to keep health care costs low. In an effort to control costs, many of these plans increased deductibles and co-insurance provisions in the 1980s and early 1990s.

Demand for Increased Quality of Care and Technological Advances

The demand for high quality health care increases with income. Thus, substantial income growth for many persons in the United States over time would be expected to increase the quality of care and the cost of health care as a proportion of GDP apart from any moral hazard. Higher quality of care often has been achieved through expensive technological advances. For example, technological advances have been especially prominent in keeping premature babies alive and in extending the life of the elderly. It is often very difficult to determine the extent to which these improvements in quality are excessive due to moral hazard or efficient due to changes in income and technological capability.

Increased Elderly Population

An important factor leading to higher aggregate health care costs is simply that the proportion of the US population that is elderly has increased substantially during the past several decades (see Chapter 19). Other things being equal, increased age of the population will lead to a higher proportion of GDP going toward the cost of health care. The increased proportion of elderly individuals in part reflects declining birthrates over time and in part reflects greater quality of health care, which can keep people alive longer.

Other Factors

While we have pointed out that too much insurance causes higher health care costs, too little insurance also can increase costs. Even though uninsured poor people may not be able to pay for their health care, they typically are not denied health care. The costs tend to be shifted to other parties or entities, including group medical expense plans, thus increasing the costs of these plans. Another problem is that the uninsured often receive health care in inefficient (high cost) ways. For example, instead of seeing a physician who can treat an illness in its early stages at relatively low costs, poor uninsured people may wait to obtain medical care in the hope that the illness will subside. If the illness continues and/or gets worse, they may finally seek care in an emergency room, which is a high cost method of providing care. In addition, the amount of treatment needed may be greater than otherwise would have been needed if the illness had been treated earlier or if diagnostic tests had been performed.

Another factor that many people argue has led to higher health care costs is the increased frequency and severity of medical malpractice suits. During the mid-1970s and again in the mid-1980s and early 2000s, malpractice liability insurance premiums increased dramatically, at least in part because of a higher frequency of suits and increases in damages awarded by the courts. In addition to producing higher malpractice insurance premiums, increased frequency and severity of medical malpractice liability suits is likely to increase health care costs because providers will be more likely to practice defensive medicine—that is, providers are more likely to require extensive tests and treatment to reduce the likelihood of a malpractice suit. (As suggested above, the growth of HMO coverage and other forms of managed care in the 1990s has shifted the debate toward whether too little care might sometimes be provided under these plans.)

The Uninsured: Who, Why, and Effects on Others

As noted above, 14 percent of the current US population is not covered by any public or private medical expense insurance. In most cases, uninsured persons with acute illnesses or injuries receive emergency and follow-up care at hospitals and/or clinics. Much of the cost of unpaid bills for these persons is shifted to other parties in the form of higher charges for physicians and hospital services. Some uninsured persons with severe medical problems who cannot work will be eligible for public medical insurance under the Medicaid program, which is financed by state and federal income taxes. As a result, much of the cost of medical treatment for the uninsured is shifted to insured people and taxpayers.

When thinking about the scope of the uninsured problem, you should be aware that a large majority of uninsured people is uninsured for a relatively short period of time. For example, it is estimated that about one-half of the uninsured persons remain uninsured for less than four months and that almost three-quarters are uninsured for nine months or less. Many of these people are young, comparatively healthy, and/or between jobs. Some have not taken advantage of the ability to extend coverage under COBRA; others have rejected employer provided coverage (see above). It is estimated that 15 to 20 percent of the uninsured are uninsured for a period of two years or longer. Many of these long-term uninsured people are employed without group medical coverage or have turned down coverage. Many are younger and healthier than the general population.

There are a variety of factors that contribute to large numbers of persons being uninsured for medical expenses.[9] High medical costs naturally will lead to uninsured individuals, because as medical costs increase, medical insurance coverage becomes less affordable. Another factor that affects the demand for insurance is whether the person has other sources of indemnity for medical expenses (see Chapter 9). To the extent that poor people can shift the cost of their health care to other people in ways described above, the incentive to purchase insurance is reduced further as its price increases.

Many people have the misperception that the employer pays the cost of medical expense insurance and thus employers are to blame for the large numbers of working people without insurance. This view, however, fails to recognize that, at least in the long run, employees pay for their employee benefits. The fact that large numbers of working people are uninsured therefore implies that many employees are unwilling (or cannot afford) to give up enough wages to receive medical expense coverage through employer-provided group medical plans, especially given that large numbers of uninsured workers have declined coverage.

16.6 Health Care Reform

Trade-offs Involving Cost, Quality, and the Scope of Insurance

The twin problems of the high cost of health care and significant numbers of uninsured people create a serious dilemma for policymakers because of two unavoidable trade-offs. First, increasing access to health insurance (reducing the number of uninsured people) tends to increase health care costs. The reason is that other things being equal, extending health insurance to more people will lead to more health care being provided and higher total costs (even if some care is then provided more efficiently). Second, attempts to reduce costs for the insured population generally will lead to some reduction in the overall quality of care. The goal in principle is to reduce excessive utilization, that is, to cut back on quality for which people are unwilling to pay. In practice, however, it will likely be difficult to reform the US system in ways that achieve this goal accurately. In addition, it is important for you to realize that there will be little or no "free lunch" (lower cost without lower quality) under any reform proposal.

These policy trade-offs are highlighted in Figure 16.4, which illustrates the relationship between the best achievable average health per person and expenditures on health care per person. Thus, the figure illustrates the level of health that could be achieved at each level of expenditure if the health care system were fully efficient. As more money is spent, the best achievable level of average health increases, but plausibly at a decreasing rate.

Different groups of people would be located at different points on the graph. For example, suppose that the point I_1 represents the (hypothetical, of course!) position of persons that currently have medical expense insurance. The fact that this point is below the best achievable health-expenditure curve indicates that there is some waste in the system. In

---

[9]About 1 percent of the population is chronically uninsurable due to adverse health conditions, but many of these persons are insured in high risk health insurance pools that many states have created to make coverage available at subsidized rates.

**FIGURE
16.4**
**Maximum
achievable
health versus
expenditures
per person.**

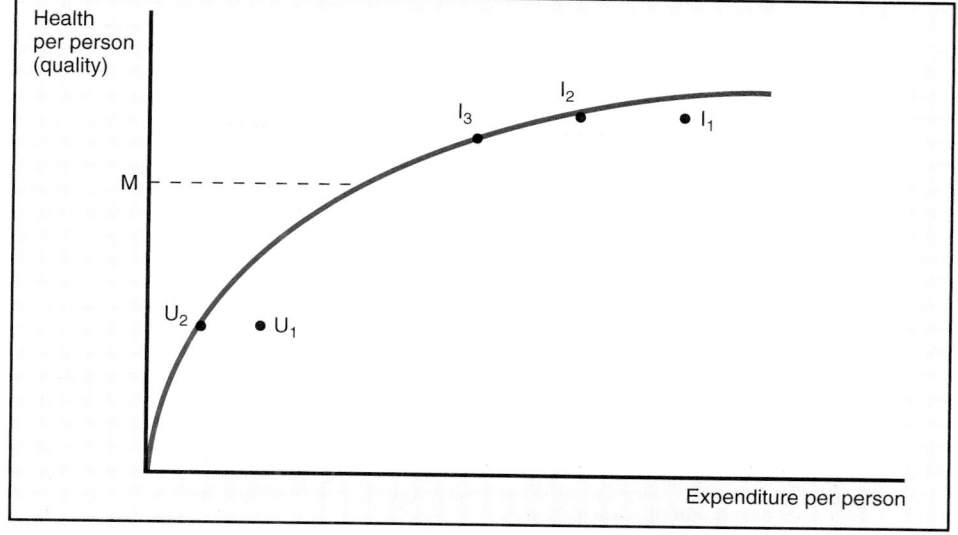

principle, either greater health could be achieved with the same expenditure or the same level of health could be achieved by a lower expenditure. For example, the point I_2 would give the same level of health as I_1 but at a lower cost.

With the exception of health care providers or other parties that might benefit when useless care (care which has no effect on health) is provided, people generally agree that we should make changes that cut costs without reducing health. However, although some might disagree, most people appear to believe that large sums are not spent on useless care. This means that most proposals that would cut expenditures on health care would lead to some reduction in quality. For example, a proposal might primarily involve a movement down the curve for the insured group (e.g., from point I_1 to point I_3). Such a reduction in expenditures and a reduction in quality would be desirable to this group if it eliminated excessive quality (i.e., if these people preferred to spend those resources on other goods and services).

Now consider the point U_1, which represents the hypothetical position of people that are currently working but uninsured. The point could plausibly fall below the best achievable health level for the given expenditure for reasons mentioned earlier (e.g., some uninsured people might receive expensive care in emergency rooms or fail to obtain routine care, which might lead to more costly problems later). In general, most people can agree that it would be better to be at point U_2 than U_1: It provides the same level of health at a lower cost. Alternatively, people agree that it would be better to have the same level of expenditure as U_1 but attain the best achievable level of health (i.e., get more health for the buck).

Now suppose that society feels that the minimum health status for any group of people should be no less than M. This minimum might be achieved in part by actions that provide all people with health insurance. Of course, the expansion of insurance coverage might increase excessive utilization due to moral hazard. More important, it is clear from Figure 16.4 that this minimum level of health can be achieved for the uninsured only if their expenditures increase. The question then arises: Who should pay the increase in cost?

Compelling currently uninsured people to pay might be problematic, given that they generally have lower than average income. However, the alternative of requiring currently insured people to pay more to help pay for expanded coverage for currently uninsured people is inconsistent with the goal of reducing their costs. A third alternative is to force currently insured people to sacrifice some quality but keep their expenditures (payments) constant. The resulting excess of expenditures over costs for the currently insured group could then be used to increase the quality of the uninsured group. None of these alternatives appear to be very attractive to a majority of people.

In summary, health care reform proposals to control costs will lead to some reduction in health (quality), and they entail the risk of an excessive reduction in quality. Proposals to increase the number of insured people generally will increase total health care expenditures, and someone will have to pay for this increase.

Possible Approaches to Reform

Given this background, we now turn to some of the major approaches that have been suggested for reforming the US health care system in order to deal with the problem of high costs and to increase the number of insured people. We emphasize that there are numerous complicated proposals. Our purpose is simply to acquaint you with several broad approaches to reform.

Nationalization or Quasi-nationalization of Medical Care and Insurance

One approach to reforming the health care system would be for the government to nationalize the provision of medical care and medical expense insurance, as has essentially been done in Canada and the United Kingdom. The government basically could specify what insurance would be provided to all people and how the insurance would be paid for. In order to control the total cost of care, the government could assume ownership of hospitals and health care facilities, employ all physicians, and set expenditure limits in ways that restrict (ration) the amount of care provided. A less intrusive but still comprehensive version of this approach would be for the government to allow private entities to provide specified insurance and medical care, with prices for insurance and medical care and expenditure limits set by the government.

Under this approach, the government in effect would attempt to specify one or more points on the health-expenditure curve for different groups of people and achieve the desired points by central planning or extensive regulation. The key point is that the government would determine how much is spent on what types of services and thus the quality of care. A large majority of American voters presently have little appetite for this sort of radical change (which some pundits call the "US Postal Service approach" to health care reform), perhaps because of the potential for lower quality care and waiting lists (rationing) for costly treatments.

Universal Private Sector Insurance

Another approach would require most people (except the very poor and the elderly) to be insured by private insurance that provides a minimum level of benefits. This expansion of coverage typically would be achieved by: (1) requiring employers either to provide coverage to employees or to pay an earmarked tax that would be used to subsidize the cost of coverage for people not covered at work (known as the "play-or-pay" approach), and (2) requiring the self-employed and any workers who do not obtain coverage at work to buy a minimum level of individual medical insurance, perhaps at subsidized rates for lower wage workers.

Because this approach would expand coverage, it would tend to aggravate the moral hazard problem, depending on the extent to which newly insured persons were covered by HMOs or other forms of managed care. For this reason, proposals for universal coverage sometimes also include proposals for government regulation of the prices of health care services or government-established limits on expenditures. The more comprehensive the proposals for government regulation of prices and services, the more this approach resembles quasi-nationalization of the medical care system and medical insurance.

Play-or-pay proposals that would mandate all employers to provide minimum levels of group medical coverage or pay additional taxes have received extensive debate. Proponents of this approach argue that it would: (1) alleviate hardship for uninsured workers and their dependents, (2) reduce the extent to which the cost of care for these persons is shifted to other employers and other parties, and (3) reduce the use of inefficient and expensive care by uninsured persons. As we suggested above, a possible problem is an increase in excessive utilization of health care services, especially if the additional insurance coverage is not accompanied by managed care and employee cost-sharing. In addition, this proposal would reduce wages and reduce employment of lower paid workers. Subsidizing the cost of coverage to alleviate these effects would require that other employees and other taxpayers pay the subsidies.

Selective and Limited Intervention

A more cautious approach to reform focuses on specific problems related to the cost and availability of health care and addresses these problems with targeted, limited intervention. To a great extent this approach has been followed in many states, such as through the enactment of legislation addressing the lack of guaranteed renewability in small employer group insurance, or legislation creating state-mandated insurance pools for individuals with chronic and expensive-to-insure health problems. This approach also is reflected in some federal legislation, such as COBRA, and the Health Insurance Portability and Accountability Act of 1996, which allows prior coverage to count toward meeting the requirements of a pre-existing conditions clause when a person changes jobs and mandates guaranteed renewability of private sector coverage. The selective and limited intervention approach often is criticized for not doing enough to control costs and to reduce the number of uninsured persons.

Providing Incentives through Changes in Tax Law

The last broad approach to reform that we will introduce would modify the income tax treatment of medical expense insurance to provide increased incentives for cost control. One major proposal that has been extensively debated would eliminate (or significantly limit) the current tax subsidy to group medical coverage by requiring employees to pay tax on employer contributions toward the cost of coverage and eliminating the tax deductibility of employee contributions.

The key idea underlying this proposal is that the current tax treatment leads employees to demand and employers to provide too much insurance coverage (relatively low deductibles and co-insurance) for small losses, which exacerbates the moral hazard problem. If the "tax subsidy" to medical expense insurance is eliminated, it is predicted that employees will demand less costly insurance arrangements that are less prone to moral hazard. The predicted result is less utilization of care for which the expected benefits do not exceed the costs and substantial savings in costs over time (and perhaps more complaints about quality, an increased HMO backlash, and so on).

The proposal to eliminate the tax subsidy to group medical coverage has been criticized on a number of dimensions. Some people question whether employees will be wise or informed enough to make intelligent decisions about what coverage to demand and what care to receive if they have to pay a greater share of the cost. Another criticism is that this change would further discourage some employees from receiving any group medical coverage and would therefore exacerbate the uninsured problem. Finally, some people are concerned that this change would substantially increase income taxes and are therefore opposed. Although a reduction in other income taxes could accompany the change, some people are understandably skeptical that there would be a dollar-for-dollar reduction.

Another type of proposal that has received extensive attention would in effect expand tax breaks associated with medical care by allowing employees (and the self-employed) to establish tax sheltered **medical savings accounts (MSAs).** The Health Insurance Accountability and Portability Act of 1996 permitted MSAs on an experimental basis for a four-year period for self-employed workers and employers with fewer than 50 employees. Relatively few accounts were formed during the next 4 years, and the Congress extended the program in 2000. Under an MSA, the person buys or receives insurance protection that provides protection against "catastrophic" losses but which contains a substantial deductible (e.g., $2,000 per year for individual coverage and $4,000 for family coverage). An amount equal to 65 percent of the deductible for individual coverage and 75 percent of the deductible for family coverage can then be contributed to the MSA on a tax-sheltered basis. Money can be withdrawn from the account to reimburse the person for annual medical expenses less than the deductible. Money that is not withdrawn accumulates toward retirement on a tax-deferred basis (i.e., no current income taxes are paid on the money deposited or on investment income on these funds). Funds may be withdrawn for any purpose prior to retirement subject to normal income tax and a penalty tax.

Like proposals to eliminate the tax subsidy to medical expense coverage, MSAs encourage participants to economize on the cost of care because receiving additional care reduces their MSA balance. The MSA concept has been controversial, however. Opponents of MSAs have expressed fear that severe adverse selection will result if employees are allowed to choose between MSAs and more traditional coverage. It is argued that many younger, healthier employees will opt for MSAs, thus increasing the cost of more comprehensive coverage arrangements for older employees or employees with health problems and undermining traditional notions of risk-sharing in employer-provided group medical plans.

16.7 Summary

- Many employees receive a material amount of their total compensation in the form of employment-related retirement plans and group life and health insurance. Obtaining benefits through work often is advantageous compared to employees purchasing individual coverage because: (1) qualified employment-related benefits reduce income taxes for employees, and (2) administrative expense loadings in group insurance premiums are lower than for individual insurance. Employer provided

benefits also can promote greater productivity among employees.
- Traditional fee-for-service arrangements for medical expense coverage pay specified medical expenses through basic and/or major medical coverage that include deductibles and co-insurance requirements. Employees receive treatment from the physicians and hospitals that they choose; physicians and hospitals are compensated by fees for services rendered. These arrangements can lead

to excessive utilization of health care due to moral hazard.

- In order to control costs and reduce excessive utilization, many fee-for-service plans have been modified to incorporate some form of managed care in which the types and amounts of medical care are subject to considerable monitoring by the insurer or employer. Health maintenance organizations, which merge the provision of health care and insurance and therefore provide the HMO with substantial incentives to control costs, grew rapidly in the 1990s. Whether HMOs sometimes provide inadequate care has been hotly debated. Many states have adopted regulations that limit the ability of HMOs to control costs.

- The federal government and many states have mandated that employer-provided group medical plans provide certain types of benefits. Federal law also has been changed to enhance portability of coverage by lessening the extent to which coverage can be denied for pre-existing conditions. Many states and the federal government have adopted laws to encourage or mandate guaranteed renewability of group medical expense coverage for small employers.

- The problems of rapid increases in health care costs and the relatively large number of uninsured persons have produced numerous proposals for health care reform. The main approa nationalization of medical care and surance, universal private sector ins better incentives for appropriate utilization of care through changes in the tax law. Key unresolved dilemmas include how to reduce the number of uninsured persons without increasing total costs and how to weed out excessive utilization without producing inadequate quality.

Key Terms

cafeteria benefit plans 336	excessive utilization 343
Section 125 plans 336	managed care 345
flexible spending account 336	preferred provider organizations 346
qualified plans 337	health maintenance organizations 346
group medical expense coverage 339	gatekeeper function 347
traditional fee-for-service arrangements 340	mandated benefits 350
basic benefits 340	pre-existing conditions clause 350
major medical coverage 340	guaranteed renewable health insurance 351
stop loss clause 340	medical savings accounts (MSAs) 360

Questions and Problems

1. Suppose that Helen's marginal income tax rate is 28 percent. Compare her after-tax income and her group medical costs under three scenarios: (*a*) She receives $45,000 in salary and pays $2,500 for individual medical coverage, (*b*) she receives $43,000 in salary and group medical coverage on a noncontributory basis with the employer's contribution to the cost of coverage equal to $2,500, and (*c*) she receives $46,000 in salary and group medical coverage on a contributory basis with the employer's contribution equal to $1,250 and her required (tax deductible) contribution equal to $1,250. What would the difference be between (*a*) and the other two scenarios if individual insurance costs Helen $2,700 due to a higher expense loading?

2. Given the rationale for why firms provide benefits, why do you think firms seldom provide personal auto insurance to employees as an employee benefit?

3. Alonzo has basic coverage and supplementary major medical with a $200 deductible, 20 percent co-insurance, and a $2,000 stop loss on co-insurance payments. How much will the major medical coverage pay if Alonzo incurs $1,500 in expenses during the year that are not covered by basic coverage but that are eligible for major medical? If he incurs $6,000 in eligible expenses? At what level of eligible expenses will major medical coverage begin to pay 100 percent of additional expenses?

4. A patient pays $200 for a test that costs $500 to provide. How large must the expected benefit to the patient be to avoid excessive utilization?

5. Explain how each of the following would affect the degree of excessive utilization of medical care in a fee-for-service plan: (*a*) the time, hassle, and inconvenience of seeing a doctor and receiving tests and treatment, and (*b*) the number of primary care physicians and specialists in a community.

6. Compare incentives for reducing excessive utilization under: (*a*) a group practice HMO where the group receives a capitation fee per enrollee, and (*b*) an individual practice association HMO where physicians' fees do not depend on utilization.

7. How does a preferred provider organization differ from a health maintenance organization?

8. Explain how requiring employees to contribute toward the cost of dependent coverage for medical care will reduce cross-subsidies among employees. What disadvantages might exist in varying employee contributions for employee coverage in relation to each employee's expected claim costs in order to further reduce cross-subsidies?

9. Individual life insurance policies are guaranteed renewable with the additional feature that the maximum premium rate that can be charged in any year is specified in the contract. Individual medical expense insurance policies often are guaranteed renewable, but there is no limit on the maximum premium rate that can be charged for the class at renewal. Given what you learned about the determinants of insurance prices in Chapter 8, what do you think might account for this difference? (Hint: Consider possible differences in risk to insurers between life insurance and medical expense insurance.)

10. Explain how the federal income tax subsidy to employer provided medical expense coverage might contribute to excessive utilization of medical care and how limiting or eliminating the subsidy could reduce excessive care.

11. Explain why limiting or eliminating the tax subsidy for group medical coverage may increase the number of people that are uninsured for medical expenses. If the tax subsidy were eliminated, would the fact that most uninsured workers are paid relatively low wages affect the size of any increase in the number of uninsured?

Answers to Concept Checks

1. Higher paid employees will have a higher income tax rate while working and therefore will prefer to receive a greater proportion of their compensation in benefits that either are not taxed or are tax deferred. The deferral of tax decreases the present value of tax payments, plus the employee's tax rate might be lower during retirement, which would lower the nominal amount of tax paid. Note that the demand for insurance protection and retirement plans also is likely to increase with income apart from tax considerations.

2. A 22-year-old person just entering the labor force is more likely to choose the HMO option. The HMO has lower monthly costs, and it has no deductibles or co-insurance. The main disadvantage of the HMO is that the employee will have limited flexibility in the choice of physicians. Since this person is likely to be healthy and therefore not require major medical attention from specialists, he or she will not find this disadvantage to be very costly. In contrast, the 45-year-old person with a chronic back problem will be more willing to pay the higher costs (both in premiums and expected deductible and co-insurance payments) associated with the comprehensive major medical coverage so that he or she can retain the option of seeing specialists in case that extensive care or surgery becomes desirable.

3. Total expenditure = $750
Amount paid by employee =
$250 + 0.20 ($750 − $250) = $350
Amount paid by insurer =
0.80 ($750 − $250) = $400

4. (*a*) Because most employees perceive that they have little (if any) chance of becoming mentally ill (Los Angeles residents excluded), they often will be unwilling to pay for extensive insurance coverage for the costs associated with such treatment, especially given the possibility of excessive utilization. Given that employees pay for their benefits, at least in the long run, by forgoing other forms of compensation (e.g., cash wages), if the state mandates more extensive benefits for mental illness, then many employees will be forced to purchase insurance that they prefer not to have. (*b*) The same points apply for mandated hospitalization coverage for childbirth, except that a much larger proportion of the working population is likely to view these benefits as being valuable.

References

Pauly, Mark. "Taxation, Health Insurance, and Market Failure in the Medical Economy." *Journal of Economic Literature* 14 (1986), pp. 629–75. (*Comprehensive survey of the economics of medical care and medical care coverage.*)

Pollite, Karen; Nicole Tapay; Elizabeth Hadley; and Jalena Specht. "Early Experience with 'New Federalism' in Health Insurance Regulatioin." *Health Affairs* 19 (2002), pp. 7–22. (*Detailed discussion of HIPAA and its enforcement.*)

Rottenberg, Simon. "Unintended Consequences: The Probable Effects of Mandated Medical Insurance." *Regulation: Cato Review of Business & Government,* Summer 1990, pp. 21–28. (*Discusses possible adverse effects of requiring employers to provide health insurance.*)

Chapter 17

Retirement Plans

Chapter Objectives

- Describe the major types and features of employment-related retirement plans, including defined benefit and defined contribution plans.
- Explain the tax and incentive effects of retirement plans.
- Explain the growing use of defined contribution plans.
- Introduce self-employed plans and individual retirement accounts (IRAs), including Roth IRAs.
- Discuss government regulations and government insurance affecting defined benefit plans.

17.1   Overview of Retirement Plans

One risk faced by every individual is that their human capital (ability to earn a living) will decline. Productivity, especially physical productivity, generally declines after some age, which in part explains why people choose to stop working and retire. There are three ways that people provide for retirement income. In this chapter, we focus on private employment-related retirement plans. Another important source of retirement income comes from the mandatory federal government program, commonly called social security, which we will discuss in Chapter 19. In addition, many people save additional money for retirement outside of private pension plans.

Saving through employment-related retirement plans differs from private saving in several important respects, which are emphasized throughout the chapter. First, employment-

related retiren   receive special tax treatment that generally makes them a preferred
method of sa   :tirement. A second advantage of employer-sponsored retirement
plans is that th   ect employee incentives; in particular, these plans can improve employee produc   reduce employee turnover. Offsetting some of the tax and incentive
benefits is the disadvantage that retirement plans are subject to numerous government regulations. Some of the regulations limit the extent to which people can save through retirement plans. Other regulations, such as those that restrict one's ability to use savings in
retirement plans prior to retirement, reduce the desirability of saving through such plans.

Employer-sponsored retirement plans can be divided into two general categories: defined benefit plans and defined contribution plans. A majority of employees in the United
States are covered by defined benefit plans, but a majority of plans are defined contribution plans. In the past two decades, there has been a gradual shift away from defined benefit plans and toward defined contribution coverage. After describing the two types of plans,
we will discuss some of the reasons for the shift toward defined contribution plans.

Defined Benefit Plans

In a **defined benefit plan,** an employer promises employees a monthly retirement benefit
that is defined by a benefit formula. Hourly workers often have a benefit formula that
equals a flat amount times the employee's number of years of service. For example, employees might be promised $50 a month times years of service. A worker with 20 years of
service would receive $1,000 a month during retirement. This type of benefit formula is not
indexed to inflation during the employees' preretirement years; consequently, the benefit
formula typically is adjusted periodically to correct for the effects of inflation.

The benefit formula for salaried employees typically is based on the number of years
of service and the employee's salary during the final years of service. For example, a
salaried employee's monthly benefit might equal 2 percent times the number of years of
service times the employee's average monthly salary during the last five years of service.
As an illustration, suppose an employee worked 20 years and during the last five years of
employment earned $3,000 a month. Then, the monthly retirement benefit would be
$1,200 ($0.02 \times 20 \times \$3,000$). An important feature of a benefit formula that is based on
the employee's final salary (or average of salaries during the final years of service) is that
retirement benefits are automatically indexed to preretirement inflation, assuming that
wages increase with inflation.

The retirement benefit as a percentage of the employee's final salary is called the **replacement rate.** For the previous example, the monthly retirement benefit was $1,200 and
the final salary was $3,000; thus the replacement rate was 40 percent ($1,200/$3,000). An
employee who worked 30 years with the same salary history would have a monthly benefit
of $1,800 or a 60 percent replacement rate ($1,800/$3,000). Few defined benefit plans have
explicit indexing of benefits to postretirement inflation. Thus, the replacement rate can
overstate the actual purchasing power of retirees if inflation occurs following retirement.
During the high inflation period of the 1970s, some employers increased retirees' pension
benefits to make up, at least in part, for the effects of inflation even though the employer
had no contractual requirement to do so.

When benefit formulas depend on the employee's final salary, the retirement benefit
can be greatly reduced if the employee switches employers. To illustrate, suppose that Mr.
Sherris worked for two employers over the course of his career and that both employers

sponsored a defined benefit plan that provided a monthly retirement benefit equal to 2 percent times final salary times years of service. If Mr. Sherris's service with the first employer was 15 years and his final monthly salary was $4,000 and his service with the second employer was 10 years and his final monthly salary was $6,000, then his retirement benefit would equal

$$(0.02 \times 15 \times \$4,000 + 0.02 \times 10 \times \$6,000) = (\$1,200 + \$1,200) = \$2,400$$

which gives a replacement rate of 40 percent ($2,400/$6,000). In contrast, if Mr. Sherris had worked for just one employer for all 25 years, then his retirement benefit would be $3,000 (0.02 × 25 × $6,000) for a replacement rate of 50 percent. Thus, changing employers will result in a lower retirement benefit, assuming that salaries and benefit formulas remain the same.

Since sponsors of defined benefit plans promise to pay employees a retirement benefit in the future, a potential issue is whether the employer will fulfill its promise. For example, the employer may not exist when some employees retire or the employer may not have sufficient funds to pay the promised benefits. The concern about employers defaulting on pension promises is reduced by requiring that employers make contributions to a fund, called a pension fund, based on the present value of the new benefits that have been accrued by employees during the year. Some defined benefit plans also require employees to contribute to the pension fund. We will return to the potential problem of the employer not fulfilling its promises later in the chapter when regulation and government insurance for defined benefit plans are discussed.

For now, we will assume that employer default on pension promises is not a problem. Also, although it ignores some practical complications (which will be discussed later), assume that if the pension fund has excess assets, then the employer can remove the excess funds and use them for purposes other than compensating employees. Under these assumptions, the employer bears all the investment risk associated with the pension fund; that is, higher than expected investment earnings on the pension assets benefit the employer and lower than expected investment earnings hurt the employer by requiring additional contributions to the pension fund.

In summary, the essential aspects of a defined benefit plan are that (1) the employer promises employees a retirement benefit defined by a formula, (2) the employer, and sometimes employees, contribute to a pension fund each year so that sufficient funds accumulate to pay the promised benefits, and (3) the employer bears most of the risk associated with investment performance.

Defined Contribution Plans

With a **defined contribution plan,** the employer—and often the employee—makes a specific (defined) contribution to a fund. The contributions are invested on behalf of the employee, and the employee's retirement benefit depends on the investment returns. The greater the investment returns, the greater the employee's retirement benefit. Thus, the employee bears the investment risk in a defined contribution plan.

To illustrate, suppose that Vickie's salary is $50,000 and that her employer will contribute 10 percent of her salary if she contributes 5 percent to a defined contribution plan. Then, the annual contribution equals $7,500 (Vickie contributes $2,500 and the employer contributes $5,000). The contributions are invested on behalf of Vickie until she retires.

Employees usually have a choice as to how the funds are invested; for example, Vickie might be able to choose among stock funds, bond funds, real estate funds, and money market funds. Each year of service, Vickie and her employer would make additional contributions, which also would be invested. At retirement, Vickie would receive the accumulated value of the contributions and the earnings on the contributions. These funds could be taken as a lump sum or they could be used to purchase an annuity that would provide Vickie with a fixed monthly income until death. Employees, however, cannot obtain the use of defined contribution funds prior to retirement unless a particular hardship, such as a permanent disability, death, or high family medical expenses, strikes the employee.

While defined benefit plans fix the benefit employees receive during retirement, defined contribution plans fix the employer's contribution to the plan. The benefit that the employee receives and thus the employee's replacement rate depends on the return earned on the contributed funds until retirement. As a result, an important distinction between defined benefit and defined contribution plans is that the employee bears the risk associated with investment earnings under a defined contribution plan. The uncertainty about the return in a defined contribution plan can make retirement planning with these plans more difficult for the employee than with defined benefit plans.

Concept Check

1. A treasurer of a major corporation states: "The pension fund assets had a negative return this year. Therefore, we will have to contribute more money to the fund over future years than was expected." Does this corporation sponsor a defined contribution or a defined benefit plan?

Cash Balance Plans

During the 1990s, interesting hybrids of defined benefit and defined contribution plans became more popular. The most common hybrid plan is called a **cash balance plan.** These plans operate like defined benefit plans from a sponsor's perspective and are classified as defined benefit plans for regulatory purposes, but cash balance plans are similar to defined contribution plans from an employee's perspective.

With a cash balance plan, retirement benefits are determined by the size of an employee's hypothetical account balance when leaving the firm. While employed, the account balance grows based on salary credits and interest credits. Salary credits typically are stated as a percentage of earnings with the percentage often varying with years of service. As an illustration, suppose that Tong Corporation's cash balance plan credits an employee's account balance with 3 percent of salary for employees with less than 20 years of service and 9 percent of salary for employees with 20 years of service, and that interest is credited at a guaranteed rate of 5 percent a year. Then for an employee with a salary of $50,000 a year, 10 years of service, and an account balance at the beginning of the year of $10,000, the account balance would increase to $12,000 at the end of the year (salary credit of $0.03 \times $50,000 = $1,500$ plus interest credit of $0.05 \times $10,000 = 500). For an employee with the same characteristics, except 25 years of service, the account balance would increase to $15,000 at the end of the year (salary credit of $0.09 \times $50,000 = $4,500$ plus interest credit of $0.05 \times $10,000 = 500).

Although each participant has an account balance, the funds are managed like a traditional defined benefit plan. Contributions and investment earnings are not actually allocated to individual accounts; instead, contributions are made to a common trust fund for all participants and benefits are paid from the fund. Participants do not choose how their account balance is invested. The plan's trustee invests the assets and the sponsor is liable for any shortfall that might occur. If the return on the plan's assets exceeds the guaranteed interest credit, then the extra investment earnings are used to build up the plan assets and thereby reduce future sponsor contributions. Thus, from the sponsor's perspective a cash balance plan operates like a traditional defined benefit plan, and it is subject to the same regulations as a defined benefit plan.

From employees' perspective, however, a cash balance plan more closely resembles a defined contribution plan with employer contributions and a guaranteed rate of return. At any time, employees can identify their account balance, and prior to retirement the account balance is portable (they can roll their accounts into other retirement plans).

17.2   Tax Advantages of Retirement Plans

An important factor leading to the widespread use of employment-related retirement plans is the preferential tax treatment granted these plans. To explain these tax advantages, we will compare the after-tax amounts that can be accumulated via saving through a **qualified retirement plan** (one that qualifies for favorable tax treatment) versus saving outside of a qualified retirement plan. Two important aspects of the US tax code influence the tax advantage of retirement plan savings. First, contributions to qualified defined benefit and defined contribution plans are not subject to personal income taxes until retirement benefits are received. Second, earnings on assets in qualified retirement plans are not taxed until they are received. As we will show, the deferral of tax on both contributions and investment earnings implies that saving through a qualified retirement plan allows an employee to earn the before-tax rate of return, whereas saving outside of a qualified plan gives an employee the after-tax rate of return. This difference can be substantial.

Saving Outside of a Qualified Retirement Plan

Suppose that Vickie's employer is considering whether to make a $1,000 contribution to a defined contribution plan on her behalf. The alternative is for the employer to pay the $1,000 to Vickie in the form of cash wages, which Vickie would then invest for retirement. (For simplicity, we ignore social security taxes that are payable on wages.) Assume that, in either case, the savings will earn a 10 percent annual before-tax rate of return over two years, which is when Vickie will retire. Also assume that Vickie has a constant 28 percent income tax rate.

If the $1,000 is paid to Vickie in the form of cash wages, then she would have to pay income tax on the $1,000, which implies that she could invest $720 [$100 $\times$ (1 − 0.28)]. This amount would earn a before-tax rate of return of 10 percent per year. However, the investment earnings would be taxed each year, which implies that Vickie's after-tax return is 7.2 percent [10% $\times$ (1 − 0.28)] per year.[1] Thus, if Vickie were to save the $1,000 in before-tax wages (or $720 in after-tax wages), she would accumulate $827.41 ($720 $\times$ 1.072^2) for retirement.

---

[1] We briefly discuss the effects of investing in stocks and tax-exempt securities below.

In general, each dollar of before-tax wages that is invested for T years outside of a retirement plan would yield

$$(1 - \tau)[1 + r(1 - \tau)]^T \tag{17.1}$$

where τ is the individual's tax rate (assumed constant over time) and r is the annual before-tax rate of return. This amount will be compared in the next two sections to the amount that would be available if the individual could either defer tax on investment earnings or defer tax on both investment earnings and contributions to a retirement plan.

Effect of Deferral of Tax on Investment Earnings

Now suppose that Vickie can invest in an account in which tax on investment earnings is deferred until retirement. We examine this tax feature in isolation because, while qualified retirement plans have this tax advantage as well as the advantage of deferring tax on contributions to retirement plans, other financial products, such as some forms of life insurance and annuities, allow for tax deferment of only investment earnings. In addition, income taxes on contributions to some individual retirement accounts (IRAs) and 401(k) plans (discussed later) are not deferred but investment earnings are tax deferred.

If Vickie receives $1,000 in before-tax wages, then after paying income tax she will have $720 to save for retirement. These savings would earn 10 percent a year and, since the investment earnings are not taxed as they are earned, she would accumulate $871.20 ($720 \times 1.1^2$) prior to paying tax on the investment earnings. The difference between the accumulated savings and the initial investment equals the investment earnings. Therefore, she must pay tax on $151.20 ($871.20 - $720). Given her 28 percent tax rate, she would have to pay tax of $42.34, leaving $828.86 after taxes. Note that this amount exceeds what she would have if she were unable to defer tax on the investment earnings, which from the previous section we know equals $827.41. While this difference is small, in examples using longer time periods the tax advantage of deferring tax on investment earnings can be substantial.

In general, each dollar in before-tax wages would allow an individual to invest $(1 - \tau)$ in an account that defers tax on investment earnings. Assuming an annual before-tax rate of return of r, this $(1 - \tau)$ would grow to the following amount after paying taxes at the end of T years:

$$\$(1 - \tau)\{\underbrace{(1 + r)^T}_{\substack{\text{Accumulated saving} \\ \text{from \$1 prior to paying} \\ \text{tax on investment earnings}}} - \underbrace{\tau[(1 + r)^T - 1]}_{\substack{\text{Investment} \\ \text{earnings on \$1}}}\} \tag{17.2}$$

The second term in the bracketed expression is the tax rate, τ, times the investment earnings, where the investment earnings is the difference between the ending value of the fund and the initial amount contributed.

Effect of Deferring Tax on Both Investment Earnings and Contributions

We now consider the tax treatment of qualified retirement plans, which in addition to the deferral of investment earnings allows an investor to defer tax on contributions to the retirement plan. Continuing with our example, if $1,000 is contributed to a qualified plan on behalf of Vickie, then she will not have to pay tax on the $1,000 until she retires in two years. Moreover, since taxes on the earnings in the retirement plan also are deferred, Vickie will accumulate $1,210 ($1,000 × 1.1²) prior to paying taxes when she retires in two years. She will have to pay tax on the entire amount, which means that after taxes, she will have $871.20 [$1,210 × (1 − 0.28)]. This amount exceeds the amount she would have if she saved outside of the retirement plan ($827.41) and the amount she would have if she saved in an account where only the investment earnings are tax deferred ($828.86).

In general, tax deferral of contributions and earnings implies that each dollar of before-tax wages that is invested in a qualified retirement account for T years will grow to

$$(1 + r)^T (1 - \tau) \tag{17.3}$$

Comparing this expression to the amount that $1 will earn after taxes outside of a pension plan (equation 17.1), $[1 + r(1 - \tau)]^T (1 - \tau)$, indicates that the essential difference between saving in a qualified retirement plan and saving outside of a qualified retirement plan is the difference between earning the before-tax rate of return and the after-tax rate of return. That is, saving $1,000 through a qualified plan is the same as receiving $1,000, paying tax on this amount, and then earning the before-tax rate of return, r, until retirement. Saving outside of a qualified plan is the same as receiving $1,000, paying tax on this amount, and then earning the after-tax rate of return, $r(1 - \tau)$, until retirement.

Figure 17.1 illustrates the difference between the accumulated amounts under the three

FIGURE 17.1
Comparison of accumulated value of $2,000 in before-tax wages under different tax treatments (assumptions: 10 percent rate of return, 30 percent tax rate).

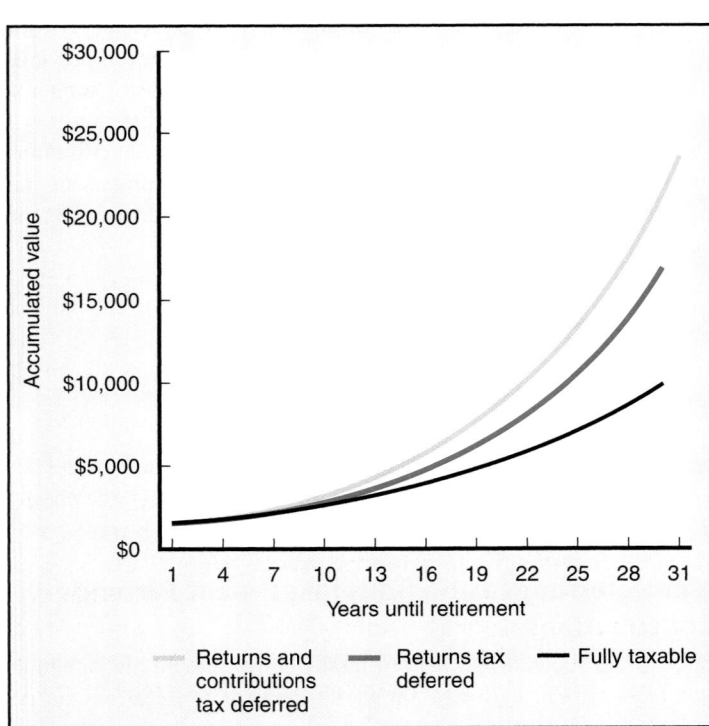

different tax scenarios analyzed here assuming a 10 percent annual before-tax rate of return and a 30 percent tax rate for various times until retirement. As you can see, there is a substantial difference between the accumulated value of savings available in a nonqualified account versus an account in which investment earnings are tax deferred and versus a qualified retirement account (investment earnings and contributions are tax deferred).

Since the essential tax advantage of a qualified retirement plan is that savings accumulate at the before-tax rate of return (i.e., you avoid paying tax on investment earnings), it is important to compare returns from investing in retirement plans to other tax-advantaged ways of investing, such as the returns from investing in municipal bonds or low dividend paying stocks. Municipal bonds are tax advantaged because the investor does not have to pay federal income tax on the interest received. Low dividend paying stocks are tax advantaged because capital gains, which would be expected to be higher if dividends were lower, are taxed at a lower rate than dividend income if they are realized. In addition, unrealized capital gains can be deferred until death and then passed on to heirs without having to pay tax on the capital gains in some cases.

Securities that are tax advantaged generally offer lower before-tax expected returns than other securities with the same risk. To illustrate this conceptual point, suppose that a US government bond and a municipal bond have the same risk and that the US government bond is paying a 10 percent rate of return. The interest on the US government bond is taxed, but the interest on the municipal bond is not. If the municipal bond also provided a 10 percent return, then investors with a positive tax rate would never buy US government bonds. Consequently, the municipal bond would be expected to provide a return less than 10 percent. If all investors had a 28 percent tax rate, then the municipal bond would be expected to pay 7.2 percent. If the municipal bond paid more than 7.2 percent, then all investors would prefer municipal bonds because they would offer a higher after-tax return than US government bonds. Similarly, if the municipal bond pays less than 7.2 percent, then all investors would prefer US government bonds.

Since the returns on tax-advantaged securities (e.g., municipal bonds) are reduced relative to the returns on tax-disadvantaged securities of the same risk (e.g., US government bonds), a higher return can be earned by investing in tax-disadvantaged securities in a qualified retirement plan than can be earned by investing in tax-advantaged securities (either within or outside of a qualified account). To illustrate using the previous example, investing in US government bonds through a qualified plan will yield a 10 percent annual return, but investing in municipal bonds (either within a qualified account or a nonqualified account) will yield a return of only 7.2 percent. Thus, all else equal, the most tax-disadvantaged securities are the best investments within a qualified plan.

Lower Tax Rates during Retirement

The previous examples assume that people's tax rates are constant over time. To the extent that people are expected to have a lower tax rate during retirement, then the tax advantages of retirement plans increase. For example, suppose that an employee has a 36 percent tax rate while working and expects a 28 percent tax rate during retirement. Then, deferring tax on contributions and investment earnings provides a greater tax benefit than previously described because, in addition to deferring taxes (and thus decreasing the present value of tax payments), the absolute amount of taxes paid is lower due to the lower tax rate during retirement.

372 Chapter 17 *Retirement Plans*

Tax Advantages of Defined Benefit Plans

The previous example illustrated the tax advantage of saving through a qualified retirement account versus saving through a nonqualified account by comparing a defined contribution plan to a nonqualified private investment account. In both cases, a sum of money was invested in an account until retirement; the only difference in the two methods of savings was in the tax treatment. Since defined benefit plans operate differently than defined contribution plans, the tax benefits of defined benefit plans may not be apparent. However, the tax benefits from a defined benefit plan are the same as a defined contribution plan that provides equivalent retirement benefits.

Perhaps the easiest way to see that the tax benefits from a defined contribution and defined benefit plan are the same from an individual's perspective is to recognize that with defined benefit plans employers and sometimes employees must make contributions to a pension fund so that promised benefits can be paid from the fund. These contributions are then invested until employees retire. Thus, the retirement benefits that employees receive from a defined benefit plan are equivalent to a series of employer and employee contributions to a pension fund and the accumulation of the earnings on those contributions. In this sense, defined benefit plans are similar to defined contribution plans—employees receive retirement benefits as a result of employer and employee contributions and the earnings on those contributions. These contributions are not taxable to the employee when the contributions are made, and the earnings on the pension assets are not taxed as they are earned. However, since the retirement benefits are taxable, the contributions and investment earnings that are used to pay the defined benefit are tax deferred. Thus, a defined benefit plan provides the same tax benefits as a defined contribution plan with equivalent benefits.

Concept Check

2. Consider the following three investment options:
   (*a*) A $1,000 investment in Treasury bonds in a qualified retirement plan.
   (*b*) A $1,000 investment in municipal bonds in a qualified retirement plan.
   (*c*) A $1,000 investment in municipal bonds outside of a qualified retirement plan.

Assume that the Treasury bonds and the municipal bonds have the same risk. Compare the after-tax retirement income that would be available from (*a*) versus (*b*), (*a*) versus (*c*), and (*b*) versus (*c*).

17.3   Incentive Effects of Employer-sponsored Pension Plans

The first employer-sponsored retirement plan in the United States was created by American Express in 1875, and a number of large firms introduced retirement plans prior to the introduction of federal income taxes in 1913. Although taxes are a major factor in explaining the growth of employer-sponsored retirement plans, the fact that employers established plans prior to the existence of tax benefits strongly suggests that there are important incentive effects of retirement plans. In this section, we explain how retirement plans can be used (1) to increase employee productivity by inducing greater employee effort and by reducing turnover, and (2) to promote retirement at an age when employee productivity often declines.

Increasing Productivity

One way to induce employees to put forth greater effort is to defer part of their compensation and make the receipt of their deferred compensation contingent upon their performance. Retirement plans, of course, provide deferred compensation. These plans therefore can induce employees to work harder—provided that workers lose part of their retirement benefits if they are fired. As we discuss below, participation and vesting schedules and the backend loading of retirement benefits can induce employees to put forth greater effort early in their careers because these features cause them to lose part of their benefits if they leave the firm.

Employers often provide training to workers that increases the employees' human capital and therefore their productivity. If this training is transferable to other employers, then the employer providing the training is confronted with the potential problem that the worker will quit, in which case, the original employer will have paid the training cost but will not have received the anticipated benefit of the training. Employers who provide training therefore need some method of compensating employees so that the employees forfeit some of their compensation if they leave. Again, retirement plans with participation and vesting schedules and with backend loading of benefits can provide the answer. Without these mechanisms, employers would be less likely to provide the training that increases employee productivity.

Participation and Vesting Requirements

Many retirement plans do not allow employees to participate until they have worked at the firm for some period of time, for example, two years. Prior to satisfying the participation requirements, an employee is not entitled to retirement benefits. Therefore, once the employee satisfies the participation requirement, his or her total compensation is bumped up. As a result, participation requirements provide incentives for employees to not quit and to work harder so as not to be fired.

In addition to participation requirements, plans typically have **vesting requirements,** which cause participants to forfeit part or all of their retirement benefits due to employer contributions if they leave prior to being fully vested. (Employees always are entitled to benefits based on their own contributions to the plan.) An employee's retirement benefits are vested if he or she receives the irrevocable right to those benefits. In other words, the benefits cannot be taken away. A commonly used vesting schedule is **cliff vesting** after three years, whereby an employee receives full retirement benefits after three years of service. Another commonly used vesting schedule is **graded vesting,** whereby an employee's retirement benefits are vested gradually over time (e.g., 20 percent vested after two years, 40 percent vested after three years, 60 percent vested after four years, 80 percent vested after five years, and 100 percent vested after six years). We will discuss the regulations on vesting schedules later in the chapter. The important point for this discussion is that plans that do not provide immediate vesting provide employees with some incentive to work hard and to stay with the firm. Both defined benefit and defined contribution plans have vesting schedules.

Backend Loading of Benefits

Defined benefit plans offer another way of structuring benefits so that employees will lose part of their benefits if they leave the firm. With most defined benefit formulas, benefits are backend-loaded, which means that relatively larger retirement benefits are accrued late in a person's service with the company. To see how benefits are backend-loaded, consider the following defined benefit formula:

Annual retirement benefit
$$= 2.0\% \times \text{Years of service} \times \text{Annual salary during last year of service}$$

Now examine the benefits that Jack would accrue each year if he started working for VanDerhei Inc. at the age of 30. Assume that his initial salary is $25,000 and that his salary grows 4.0 percent each year. For simplicity, we will assume that there are no participation requirements and that he is immediately vested.

After working one year, Jack's accrued benefits would equal $0.02 \times 1 \times \$25,000 = \$500$/year. That is, if Jack left VanDerhei Inc. after one year, his annual retirement benefit from VanDerhei Inc. would be $500. In his second year, Jack receives a 4.0 percent raise so his salary increases to $26,000 and his accrued annual benefit equals $0.02 \times 2 \times \$26,000 = \$1,040$. If Jack leaves after two years, he will receive $1,040 annually during retirement. Thus, his additional accrued retirement benefit as a result of his second year of service is $540 ($1,040 − $500). An important point to notice is that the higher salary in the second year is, in essence, applied to the first year of service under this type of benefit formula since the accrued benefit is determined by multiplying the final salary by the number of years of service. Indeed, each year that Jack's salary increases, his accrued benefit increases for previous years of service because that higher salary is applied to all previous years of service. If we continued to calculate Jack's additional accrued benefit for each additional year of service, we would find that, assuming that his salary grows at a 4 percent rate over time, the additional accrued benefit increases at an increasing rate over time, as depicted in Figure 17.2.

To highlight the difference in the additional accrued benefit at different service levels, we will calculate the accrued benefit in Jack's final year of service. Jack's annual salary in

FIGURE 17.2
Jack's additional accrued annual retirement benefit under a defined benefit plan with initial salary = $25,000 and salary growth = 4.0%.

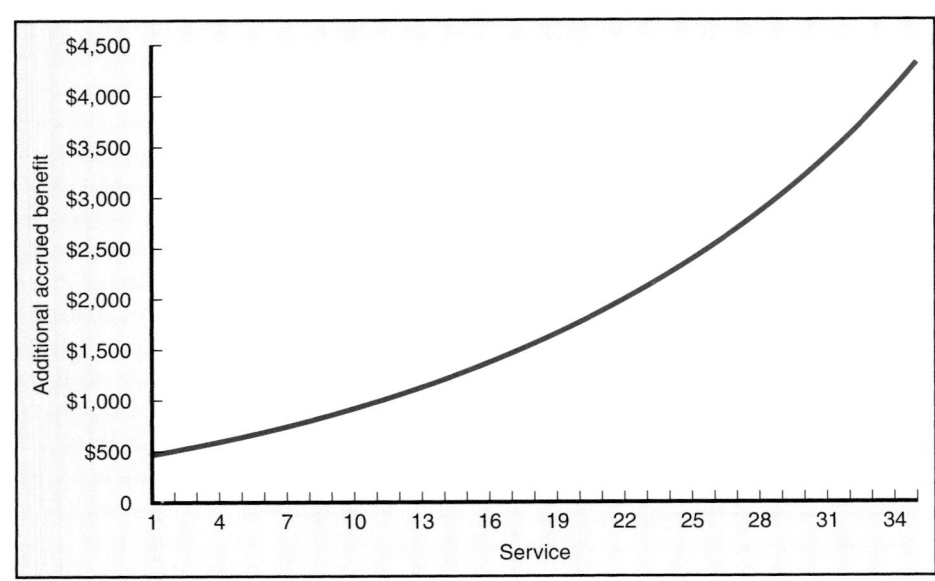

his 34th year will equal $91,210 [$25,000 $\times$ (1.04)^{34}], and his salary in his 35th (and last) year will equal $94,858 [$25,000 $\times$ (1.04)^{35}]. If Jack left the firm after 34 years of service, his annual retirement benefit would equal $62,023 (0.02 $\times$ 34 $\times$ $91,210). If instead he worked an additional year, his retirement benefit would increase to $66,401 (0.02 $\times$ 35 $\times$ $94,858). Thus, by working his 35th year with the firm, Jack would accrue an additional annual benefit of $4,378 ($66,401 − $62,023). In comparison, Jack accrued an additional retirement benefit of only $500 in his first year of service. Thus, the majority of Jack's retirement benefits are accrued late in his career.

Since accrued benefits are heavily backend-loaded with most defined benefit plans, these plans provide employees with incentives not to be fired and thus to work harder. In addition, these plans encourage workers not to quit. To illustrate the magnitude of the losses an employee can suffer from leaving a firm with a defined benefit plan, suppose that Dick has been working for Ippolito Inc. for the past 15 years and that he expects to work an additional 15 years. The issue is whether he will work the last 15 years with Ippolito Inc. or with another firm, Bulow Corp. Both firms have the same defined benefit formula: 2 percent times years of service times final salary. Dick's current salary is $50,000 and he expects it to grow at a 5 percent rate until he retires—regardless of his employer. Thus, Dick's final salary is expected to be $103,947 [$50,000 (1.05)^{15}]. If he stays with Ippolito Inc. then he expects that his annual retirement benefit will be 2 percent times 30 years of service times $103,947, which equals $62,368 for a 60 percent replacement rate. If instead he switches employers, then he will receive a retirement benefit from Ippolito Inc. equal to 2 percent times 15 years of service times $50,000, which equals $15,000, plus a retirement benefit from Bulow Corp. equal to 2 percent times 15 years of service times $103,947, which equals $31,184. Thus, Dick's total retirement benefit is $46,184 for a replacement rate of 44.4 percent. Switching employers in this case reduces annual retirement income by $16,184 ($46,184 − $31,184). This example illustrates that defined benefit plans can provide powerful incentives to stay with one firm.

Inducing Retirement

The backend loading of retirement benefits can create a problem for employers—since additional service results in higher benefits, employees may delay retirement well beyond the point where their productivity warrants their continued employment. Simply stated, some people will work too long. Under current law, most employers cannot force employees to retire at a certain age. Most defined benefit plans therefore deal with this problem by structuring benefits to provide incentives for employees to retire at certain ages.

A plan's **normal retirement age** determines the age at which a retiree receives full retirement benefits. The normal retirement age can be defined using the employee's age and/or the employee's years of service with the company. Since 1986, defined benefit plans must change the retirement benefit to reflect salary increases and additional years of service beyond the normal retirement age. Nevertheless, working beyond the normal retirement age can reduce the present value of retirement benefits if, as is commonly done, the plan does change the retirement benefit to reflect that the employee is expected to receive the retirement benefit for a shorter period of time. Reducing the present value of the expected benefits if the employee works beyond the normal retirement age provides a strong incentive for workers to retire no later than the normal retirement age.

Benefits often are structured to induce early retirement. Under many defined benefit plans, employees can retire earlier than the normal retirement age. When an employee retires early, benefits usually are reduced relative to normal retirement benefits, but they may not be reduced as much as would be projected given the fewer years of service and a greater number of years for which benefits would be expected to be received. In essence, plans can be structured so that employees receive a "retirement bonus" if they retire early.

17.4   Types of Defined Contribution Plans

Money Purchase and Profit Sharing Plans

One of the most common types of defined contribution plans is a **money purchase plan,** in which the employer makes contributions on behalf of the employee regardless of the firm's profits. The contribution usually equals a percentage of the employee's salary but can be a flat amount. In some instances employers require that employees also make contributions to the plan. A profit sharing plan is another common type of defined contribution plan. As the name suggests, the employer's contribution to a **profit sharing plan** depends on the firm's profits. With some profit sharing plans, contributions are based on an explicit formula (e.g., 5 percent of pretax profit) and in other plans the contributions are at the discretion of the corporation's board of directors. Profit sharing contributions usually are allocated across employees based on the proportion of the employee's salary as a percentage of total payroll costs.

401(k) Plans

Section 401(k) of the Revenue Act of 1978 allowed a new form of defined contribution plan that has become known as a 401(k) plan. The distinguishing feature of a **401(k) plan** compared to other defined contribution plans is that employees can elect (subject to limitations) to make tax-deferred contributions, in addition to the employer's tax-deferred contributions. Recall that a tax-deferred contribution implies that the employee does not pay tax on the contribution until the money is withdrawn from the plan (usually at retirement). The use of 401(k) plans has grown tremendously in the past two decades.

Many firms have adopted 401(k) plans in addition to their other defined benefit or defined contribution plans. Employee participation in 401(k) plans typically is voluntary and the level of employee contributions if they do participate is voluntary. Employees also typically have more discretion in how the funds of their 401(k) plan are invested compared to other defined contribution plans.

An interesting feature of many 401(k) plans is that employers often match employee contributions. For example, an employer may match employee contributions dollar-for-dollar. Whereas employee contributions are immediately vested, employer contributions can be subject to vesting requirements. Box 17.1 provides four potential explanations for employer matching of 401(k) contributions. The matching feature increases the administrative costs of 401(k) plans compared to money purchase or profit sharing plans.

Employees can withdraw (or borrow funds) funds from their 401(k) plans prior to retirement under certain hardship conditions. For example, funds possibly could be withdrawn to pay family medical expenses, to pay for college tuition, or to purchase a principal residence. The funds withdrawn are subject to tax in the year they are withdrawn.

NONDISCRIMINATION RULES

One explanation for employer matching is that regulation requires that employer-sponsored plans follow nondiscrimination rules, which do not allow highly compensated employees to make contributions that far exceed the contributions of lower paid employees. The details of nondiscrimination rules are not important for our purposes (but are extremely important to benefit plan managers). The important point is that nondiscrimination rules induce employers to provide an incentive for lower paid employees to contribute to 401(k) plans, which in turn allows highly compensated employees to make larger contributions. Employer matching of contributions is a method of inducing lower paid employees to make contributions.

INCENTIVES

A second explanation for employer matching relates to incentives. Since the matching contribution can be subject to vesting rules, employees have incentives to remain with the firm to get its matching contributions. Thus, employer matching can increase productivity and reduce turnover, just like other retirement plans.

ALIGNING COMPENSATION AND PRODUCTIVITY

A third reason an employer may match employee contributions is that it more closely aligns compensation with employee productivity when employees have different skills and/or willingness to work. For example, suppose that there are two types of workers; one type is more productive than the other is, but the employer cannot identify the more productive workers until they have worked a long time period (or alternatively that for legal considerations the firm finds it costly to fire workers once they have been found to be of the low productivity type). Also assume that the more productive workers tend to be people that are more concerned about the future than less productive workers and therefore that the more productive workers will tend to save more than the less productive workers do, all else being equal. Under these conditions, the more productive workers would be the people who would make larger contributions to their 401(k) plan. If the employer matches employee contributions, then the employer pays the more productive workers more than the less productive workers, which helps reduce turnover of the more productive workers.

TAXES

A final explanation for employer matching has to do with taxes. Payroll taxes (e.g., social security taxes) apply to employee contributions, but they do not apply to employer contributions. Thus, from a tax management perspective, total tax payments are reduced if employees accept lower wages in exchange for an employer match of the employees' 401(k) contributions.

Employee Stock Ownership Plans

With all defined contribution plans, contributions are allocated to individual employee accounts and the money is invested in various assets on behalf of employees. In all of the defined contribution plans discussed so far, the proportion of the funds in an employee's account that can be invested in the sponsoring firm's stock is limited by regulation to 10 percent. The purpose of this regulation is to force employees to hold somewhat diversified portfolios. One type of retirement plan, however, is not subject to this regulation. An **employee stock ownership plan (ESOP)** is a defined contribution plan that is required to hold at least 50 percent of its assets in the sponsoring firm's stock. ESOPs have another distinguishing feature relative to other retirement plans—they can be leveraged. That is, an ESOP plan can borrow money to purchase stock for employees. ESOP loans are repaid using the sponsoring firm's contributions.

The unique features of ESOPs have made them an important financing tool for some corporations and a means of placing stock in friendly hands to prevent takeovers. ESOPs also have been promoted as a means of (1) improving employee productivity by tying employee compensation to the firm's stock price, and (2) improving labor relations, although there is limited evidence consistent with these effects. ESOPs also have received tax advantages beyond other retirement plans. An important disadvantage of ESOPs as retirement plans is that they force employees to hold poorly diversified portfolios. Employees enrolled in an ESOP have both their employment income and their retirement income tied to the fortunes of the firm. For this reason, ESOPs are required by regulation to allow employees reaching the age of 55 to diversify the funds in their ESOP accounts.

Simplified Employee Pensions (SEP) and SIMPLE Plans

Employers without other qualified retirement plans can with minimal paperwork establish retirement plans called **simplified employee pension (SEP) accounts** for each of their employees. The employer then can make tax-deductible contributions up to 15 percent of employee compensation, or $35,000 whichever is less in 2002. These SEP accounts must be established for each employee over the age of 21 who has worked for three of the last five years. Small employers can also create, with minimal paperwork a SIMPLE plan (Savings Incentive Match Plan for Employees). With these plans, the owner can match employees contributions up to three percent, or $7,000 whichever is less in 2002. From the employee's perspective, the contributions and investment earnings are tax deferred as in other qualified retirement plans.

Growth in Defined Contribution Plans

Enrollment in defined contribution plans has grown dramatically in the past 20 years. The growth in defined contribution plans primarily reflects the growth in 401(k) plans. The growth in defined contribution plans in general also can be attributed in part to the effects of increased regulation of defined benefit plans. First, the regulatory burden and administrative costs of operating defined benefit plans have increased. Second, there are economies of scale in the administration of defined benefit plans, which makes smaller firms more likely to choose defined contribution plans. A shift in the US economy toward smaller firms therefore also helps explain the increased use of defined contribution plans. Third, the increased regulations on vesting and early retirement provisions in defined benefit plans make their use as an incentive mechanism less effective. A fourth potential explanation is that the economy has changed in a way that has increased the benefits and decreased the costs of greater labor mobility; as a result, firms are less likely to adopt defined benefit plans, which reduce labor mobility. Finally, regulatory restrictions on a firm's ability to remove excess pension assets from defined benefit plans (see below) reduce some of the advantages of these plans from a corporate financing perspective, as well as from a labor contracting perspective.

17.5   Self-employed (Keogh) and Individual Retirement Accounts (IRAs)

Keogh Plans

Self-employed individuals can establish retirement plans called **Keogh plans** for themselves and all full-time employees. These plans can be either defined benefit or defined contribution plans. From a regulatory and tax perspective, they are treated very similarly to corporate-sponsored retirement plans.

Individual Retirement Plans (IRAs)

An important source of retirement income for many people, especially those who are not participants in employer-sponsored plans, is an **individual retirement account (IRA).** In addition, participants in employer-sponsored plans can in some circumstances augment their retirement savings through IRAs. There are two basic types of IRAs: traditional IRAs and Roth IRAs. The latter type was introduced in 1998. Regardless of the type of IRA, contributions are limited to $3,000 a year in 2002, $4,000 in 2005, and $5,000 in 2008. Withdrawals made prior to age 59½ can trigger an excise tax of 10 percent, unless death or permanent disability occurs.

Traditional IRAs

People who are not participating in an employer-sponsored retirement plan can make tax-deductible contributions to a traditional IRA. The earnings on these funds are tax deferred. All withdrawals from a traditional IRA are taxed as income. The combination of tax-deductible contributions and tax-deferred investment earnings make traditional IRAs similar to corporate sponsored retirement plans from an individual tax perspective. To illustrate, a $3,000 IRA contribution that earns a before-tax rate of return of r for T years will grow to $3,000 $(1 + r)^T$. If the individual's tax rate at retirement is 30 percent, the amount accumulated after-tax will be $0.7 \times \$3,000 (1 + r)^T = \$2,100 (1 + r)^T$. In effect, the IRA allows the individual to earn the before-tax rate of return on $2,100. As we will see, an advantage of a Roth IRA is that the individual can in effect earn the before-tax rate of return on a larger amount (the entire $3,000).

Individuals who are participants in employer-sponsored plans also can make tax-deductible contributions to an IRA if they earn less than a certain amount ($43,000 for individuals and $63,000 for couples filing jointly in 2001). After these cutoffs, the ability to make contributions is phased out as income increases. Starting in 1998, individuals who cannot make tax-deductible contributions to an IRA still can contribute to an IRA up to $2,000 a year. While the contributions are not tax deductible, the investment earnings on the IRA funds are tax deferred until the funds are withdrawn during retirement.

Roth IRAs

Roth IRAs differ from traditional IRAs in that (1) contributions to a Roth IRA are not tax deductible, and (2) withdrawals during retirement from a Roth IRA are not taxed. (Traditional IRAs have the opposite treatment—contributions are tax deductible and withdrawals are taxed.) Thus, once money is placed in a Roth IRA, it is no longer taxed (assuming it is not withdrawn early), which implies that investment earnings on the entire contribution to a Roth IRA escape taxation. A contribution of $3,000 to a Roth IRA that earns a before-tax rate of return of r for T years will yield $3,000 $(1 + r)^T$ in retirement income. Eligibility rules for Roth IRAs also differ from traditional IRAs. Maximum contributions can be made if earnings are less than $95,000 for individuals and $110,000 for couples filing jointly in 2001.

An important difference between a Roth IRA and a traditional IRA is that the Roth IRA effectively relaxes the constraint on the amount of money on which an individual can earn the before-tax rate of return. With a traditional IRA, a contribution of $3,000 by an individual with a 30 percent tax rate effectively allows the individual to avoid tax on the investment earnings generated from $2,100 [$3,000(1 − 0.3)]. With a Roth IRA, a contribution of

$3,000 by an individual with a 30 percent tax rate effectively allows the individual to avoid tax on the investment earnings generated from $3,000. For individuals who do not find the traditional IRA constraint binding (those who wish to contribute less than $2,100 of after-tax earnings in our example), the Roth IRA would not dominate a traditional IRA.

A potential disadvantage of the Roth IRA compared to the traditional IRA arises when investors expect to have a lower tax rate during retirement. Since the traditional IRA gives a tax deduction when the contribution is made and then taxes withdrawals during retirement, investors with lower tax rates during retirement under some circumstances can achieve higher retirement income with a traditional IRA.

17.6   Retirement Plan Provisions and Regulations

There are numerous contractual provisions in any retirement plan, and many of the provisions are influenced by detailed and complex regulations. In this section we provide a broad overview of some of the more important provisions and regulations. The regulatory restrictions on retirement plans greatly expanded with the passage of the **Employee Retirement Income Security Act (ERISA)** of 1974 by the US Congress. ERISA has been changed numerous times since 1974.

Nondiscrimination and Vesting Rules

To qualify for preferential tax treatment, employer-sponsored retirement plans must satisfy certain rules. As noted in Box 17.1, qualified plans must meet complex **nondiscrimination rules** that allow a broad range of employees to participate and that ensure that benefits do not disproportionately favor highly compensated employees. Qualified plans also must be operated solely for the benefit of the plan's beneficiaries, and funds contributed to retirement plans cannot be diverted for other corporate purposes.

As mentioned earlier, an important provision in retirement plans is the vesting schedule, which determines when employees receive the right to the benefits resulting from the employer's contributions. Recall that cliff vesting means that benefits are not vested at all until a certain number of years of service have been completed and then benefits are fully vested. ERISA sets the maximum length of service for cliff vesting at five years. Graded vesting means that benefits are vested gradually over time. If graded vesting is chosen, regulation requires that benefits be vested at least 20 percent after three years, 40 percent after four years, 60 percent after five years, 80 percent after six years, and 100 percent after seven years.

Funding Requirements

The risk that the employer might not fulfill its promises to pay benefits to employees under a defined benefit plan is handled in a number of ways, including required funding rules and mandatory pension insurance. With respect to funding, sponsors must make periodic contributions to a pension fund from which the promised benefit will be paid. Although sponsors have some discretion over their contributions, ERISA imposes minimum funding requirements on sponsors of defined benefit plans. For example, new benefit accruals must be funded immediately and shortfalls in funding must be amortized over time.

To assess funding adequacy for defined benefit pension plans, it is useful to examine the firm's pension plan balance sheet. A comparison of the value of the pension assets and the

Measuring pension liabilities can be complex. To calculate pension liabilities, one must make assumptions about numerous factors, such as employee turnover rates, death rates, and discount rates. In addition, the calculation of pension liabilities requires an assumption about the nature of the firm's pension contract with employees. To illustrate the latter point, consider the plan described earlier in which Jack's salary is initially $25,000, his salary grows 4.0 percent each year, he retires in 35 years, and he is immediately vested. The benefit formula is 2.0 percent times years of service times final salary. After one year of service, Jack's accrued benefit is $500 (0.02 × 1 × $25,000). What is the firm's pension liability after one year? One approach is to calculate the pension liability assuming that Jack's participation in the plan ends after one year. Under this assumption, the firm would have to pay Jack an annual benefit of $500 when he retires. Thus, the pension liability would equal the present value (discounted over 34 years) of the value of a $500 annual retirement annuity. This method of calculating the pension liability is called the *accumulated benefit obligation (ABO)* and is based on the view that the labor contract is a one-year contract.

An alternative approach is to calculate the pension liability assuming that Jack's participation in the plan will continue until his retirement. According to this approach, this first year of service is expected to create a benefit equal to 2 percent of his projected final salary. Assuming Jack works for 35 years, his projected final salary is $94,858 [25,000 × $(1.04)^{35}$]. Thus, the pension liability is the present value of the value of a $1,897 (0.02 × 1 × $94,858) retirement annuity, nearly four times the value of the ABO in this case. This method of calculating the pension liability is called the *projected benefit obligation (PBO)*.

The difference between the accumulated benefit obligation and the projected benefit obligation depends on a number of factors, including the age of the participants, the benefit formula, and the expected salary growth. In general, the pension liability will grow at a faster rate over time if ABO is used. Stated differently, if a firm funded its plans so that pension assets always equaled ABO, then pension contributions initially would be low but would increase rapidly over time. Funding so that the value of pension assets always equaled PBO would result in a more uniform pattern of contributions. Most pension economists would view the PBO measure as the better way of measuring an ongoing firm's pension liability because its more uniform growth pattern more accurately reflects how employees pay for their pension benefits through forgone wages.

value of the pension liabilities provides a snapshot of the plan's funding status. The value of **pension assets** is the market value of the assets held in the pension fund; the value of **pension liabilities** is the present value of the promised benefits to employees. As discussed in Box 17.2, there are various ways of calculating the value of a plan's pension liabilities. When pension assets exceed pension liabilities, the plan is *overfunded*. When pension assets are less than pension liabilities, the plan is *underfunded*. For example, General Motors had some pension plans in 2001 that were underfunded and some plans that were overfunded. The underfunded plans had assets equal to $48.2 billion and liabilities equal to $58.8 billion; the overfunded plans had assets equal to $19.1 billion and liabilities equal to $17.6 billion.

Pension Insurance

Despite most firms' attempts to adequately fund their pension plans and despite regulations on funding, pension plans can become underfunded for a variety of reasons. For example, the return on the plan's assets could be less than expected, or interest rates could decline, thus increasing the present value of pension liabilities, or any one of a number of assumptions needed to calculate promised pension benefits (e.g., employee turnover, employee wage growth, death rates) could differ from expectations.

ERISA created the **Pension Benefit Guaranty Corporation (PBGC)** to insure employees' promised benefits in defined benefit pension plans against the contingency that a firm terminates an underfunded plan. Under the PBGC insurance program, the PBGC will pay promised benefits (valued at the time of termination, see below) up to a maximum amount if a pension plan is terminated with insufficient funds to pay promised benefits. Employers sponsoring defined benefit plans are charged an annual premium for the compulsory insurance. The history of the PBGC insurance program illustrates some of the problems associated with insurance programs that are not structured to take into account moral hazard problems.

When the PBGC was first created, each firm sponsoring a defined benefit plan was charged an annual premium equal to $1 per participant. Because the premium was independent of the funding of a firm's plans, some employers probably paid more than their expected claim costs and other employers certainly paid less than their expected claim costs. Insurance arrangements that charge all insureds the same premium despite differences in expected claim costs normally would suffer from adverse selection—the high-risk (high-expected claim cost) sponsors would buy the insurance and the low risk would not. The compulsory nature of the program mitigated such adverse selection, although in the long run some firms might have selected out of the insurance program by switching to defined contribution plans.

The more important problem with the premium schedule was that it reduced the incentive of some firms to contribute sufficient funds to pay all their promised benefits (i.e., it created a moral hazard problem). Essentially, a firm could shift part of the expected cost of compensating its employees to the PBGC by promising employees pension benefits and then not fully funding those benefits. Although the source of this moral hazard problem was the fixed premium schedule, the insurance program incorporated several factors that, at least in principle, could have helped reduce the moral hazard problem. For example, funding requirements could have prevented firms from not fully funding the promised benefits. However, the rules gave firms sufficient discretion over funding so that some plans still became significantly underfunded. In recent years, though, the funding requirements have been tightened.

One factor that helped reduce the moral hazard problem associated with the PBGC insurance was that, when an underfunded plan was terminated, the PBGC could claim up to 30 percent of the sponsoring employer's net worth. That is, if a firm wanted to make the PBGC pay the unfunded pension liabilities, then the firm had to give the PBGC 30 percent of the firm's equity value. This restriction effectively prevented financially strong firms from making the PBGC pay unfunded pension liabilities. It did not, however, eliminate the moral hazard problem for financially distressed firms whose net worth was close to zero. It also provided incentives for firms to spin off divisions that had underfunded pension plans in an effort to protect the rest of the corporation's assets from being claimed by the PBGC.

Another factor that mitigated moral hazard is that the PBGC does not guarantee all promised pension benefits. In addition to the limit on the level of benefits guaranteed, the PBGC's guarantee applies only to benefits based on employees' salaries at the time the underfunded plan is terminated, not benefits based on projected salaries. As a result, an underfunded plan termination is likely to impose losses on employees whose benefits are backend loaded. Since employees are not fully insured, they have an incentive to stop firms from terminating underfunded plans. Stated differently, the PBGC insurance has an important co-insurance provision (employees are not fully insured) that helps to reduce moral hazard.

Employers, however, have a way of circumventing the co-insurance aspect of the insurance. After terminating an underfunded plan, employers can compensate employees for their losses by establishing a follow-on plan that gives employees the difference between their promised benefits and the PBGC guaranteed benefits. With such a follow-on plan, employees will not try to block the termination of an underfunded plan. Since follow-on plans eliminate the co-insurance associated with the PBGC insurance, the PBGC has actively sought to prevent follow-on plans. One of the more important cases involving follow-on plans was the LTV case, in which the PBGC was successful in stopping LTV from establishing a follow-on plan (see Box 17.3).

Two laws enacted in the 1980s gave the PBGC the means to reduce "abuses" of the insurance program. Both the Single Employer Pension Protection Act of 1986 (SEPPA) and the Pension Protection Act of 1987 (PPA) restrict the ability of a firm to use the PBGC insurance to walk away from its pension promises. In particular, firms seeking to make the PBGC pay unfunded pension liabilities must demonstrate that the pension plan termination is necessary for the continued existence of the firm. In addition, these laws have expanded the PBGC's claims against a firm's assets when an underfunded plan is terminated beyond the 30 percent net worth claim.

In part because of the moral hazard and in part because the initial premium level ($1 per employee) was too low given the PBGC's exposure even in the absence of moral hazard, the PBGC was forced to increase the premium several times. In 1987, a variable premium schedule was adopted. All employers now pay a base annual premium of $19 per employee, but employers with underfunded plans pay an additional premium that increases with the amount of underfunding (0.9 percent of unfunded vested liabilities).

Excess Assets in Defined Benefit Plans

Just as plans can become underfunded, plans can accumulate pension assets in excess of pension liabilities (i.e., they can become overfunded). An important issue for the financial management of defined benefit plans and for participants in these plans is who owns the excess assets. The answer to this question depends on the ability of firms to remove excess assets from the plan. A firm can remove excess assets either gradually, by reducing future contributions, or all at once, by terminating the plan and taking the excess through a **pension asset reversion.**

During the 1980s, a large number of firms removed excess assets through reversions. These reversions were criticized because reversions require that the plan be terminated, which potentially can impose losses on employees because, as discussed earlier, retirement benefits for a terminated plan are based on employees' salaries at the time of the termination. Even if a new plan with the same benefit formula were established, employees could suffer losses, because the service under the new plan would not include the service under the old plan. Just as the earlier example showed how Dick would lose pension benefits if he changed employers, employees of a firm that terminates a plan could experience losses.

In an effort to discourage pension asset reversions, Congress imposed an excise tax (in addition to the normal income tax) on the value of excess pension assets claimed in reversions. Currently, the excise tax is 20 percent, provided that 25 percent of pension surplus is used as a cushion for a replacement plan or that employee benefits are increased by 25 percent; otherwise, the excise tax is 50 percent. These rules reduce firms' incentives to fund their defined benefit plans because, once the money has been placed in the fund, only a small portion can be recovered all at once through a reversion.[2]

17.7 Summary

- The primary reasons that employers offer retirement plans are to reduce taxes for employees and to improve labor productivity.

- With a defined contribution plan, the employer and usually the employee contribute to a fund, according to a defined schedule (e.g., 5 percent of salary). These contributions are invested on behalf of the employee, and the employee receives retirement benefits equal to the accumulated value of all contributions and the associated investment earnings. Thus, employees bear most of the investment risk in defined contribution plans.

- With a defined benefit plan, an employer promises employees a benefit during retirement that is defined by a formula. The employer (and sometimes the employees) contribute to a fund, and the defined benefits are paid from the assets in the fund. If the assets have a lower than expected re-

turn, then the employer has to make additional contributions to pay the promised benefits. Consequently, the employer bears most of the investment risk associated with pension assets.

- Qualified retirement plans satisfy the regulations necessary to receive preferential tax treatment. In a qualified plan, contributions and earnings on the pension assets are tax deferred to the employee. The combination of tax deferral of contributions and tax deferral of investment earnings implies that employees essentially earn the before-tax rate of return on money contributed to a qualified plan. The returns that can be earned by saving for retirement through a qualified plan can materially exceed those that can be earned outside of a qualified plan.

- Often the benefit formula in a defined benefit plan is structured so that benefits are strongly

[2]In 1987, Congress denied firms the ability to make tax-deductible contributions to plans that have pension assets equal to 150 percent of the accumulated benefit obligation (ABO). Critics of the excise tax and the funding limitations argue that these initiatives could lead to underfunded plans and more claims against the PBGC.

backend loaded. The backend loading of benefits implies that employees can suffer large losses in the value of their retirement benefits if they leave the firm or if the firm terminates the plan prior to retirement. Consequently, the backend loading discourages turnover, which provides greater incentives for employers to make investments in training employees and provides employees with incentives to put forth greater effort.

- Section 401(k) plans have grown dramatically in the past two decades. These plans are defined contribution plans that allow employees to make discretionary tax-deferred contributions subject to some limitations. Employers often match employee contributions.

- Individual retirement accounts (IRAs) allow people who are not participants in employer-sponsored plans to save for retirement and receive the same tax benefits as qualified plans. Participants in employer-sponsored plans also can contribute to IRAs under some circumstances. Annual contributions to IRAs, however, were limited to $3,000, in 2002. Roth IRAs were introduced in 1998. The tax treatment of Roth IRAs and traditional IRAs differs.

- ERISA, which was introduced in 1974, regulates private pension plans. It imposes participation, vesting, and nondiscrimination rules that plans must satisfy. It also mandates minimum funding of defined benefit plans.

- Defined benefit plans can be over~~funded~~ ~~or~~ ~~un~~derfunded (i.e., the value of pensi~~on~~ exceed or fall short of the present v~~alue of prom-~~ ised benefits). ERISA established~~ an agency to~~ insure the promised benefits of employees who participate in underfunded plans that terminate.

Key Terms

defined benefit plan 365	simplified employee pension (SEP)
replacement rate 365	accounts 378
defined contribution plan 366	Keogh plans 378
cash balance plan 367	individual retirement account (IRA) 379
qualified retirement plan 368	Employee Retirement Income Security
vesting requirements 373	Act (ERISA) 380
cliff vesting 373	nondiscrimination rules 380
graded vesting 373	pension assets 381
normal retirement age 375	pension liabilities 381
money purchase plan 376	Pension Benefit Guaranty Corporation
profit sharing plan 376	(PBGC) 382
401(k) plan 376	pension asset reversion 384
employee stock ownership plan (ESOP) 377	

Questions and Problems

1. If saving through a retirement plan allows an individual to reduce tax payments relative to saving outside of a retirement plan, then why would anyone save outside of a retirement plan?

2. Determine the replacement rate in the following scenarios if an employee is enrolled in a defined benefit plan with the following benefit formula: 2.5% × Years of service × Final salary

   a. Service = 10 years; final salary = $40,000

   b. Service = 10 years; final salary = $60,000

   c. Service = 20 years; final salary = $60,000

3. Determine the replacement rate (as a percentage of final salary) for an employee who is enrolled in a defined contribution plan in which the employer annually contributes 10 percent of salary and the before-tax rate of return each year equals 8 percent under each of the scenarios listed below. Assume that the cost of a $100 life annuity at retirement equals $900. That is, by giving an insurance company $900 at retirement, the insurer will give the retiree $100 every year until he or she dies.

   a. Five years of service; constant salary = $75,000

   b. Five years of service; salary in years 1–3 equals $50,000; salary in years 4–5 equals $100,000

4. Suppose that Ken is enrolled in a defined contribution plan in which the employer contributes 10 percent of his salary each year. Ken is earning $80,000 this year and his tax rate is 30 percent (which is not expected to change). Assume that the before-tax rate of return is 8 percent.

   a. What is the additional amount of funds that Ken will have when he reaches retirement in 10 years as a result of this year's service?

   b. Suppose that Ken's employer is planning to stop contributing to the defined contribution plan. Assume that Ken would like to keep his retirement funds the same as they would have been with the defined contribution plan. If Ken's only opportunity to save for retirement is in a nonqualified savings plan (no tax benefits), how much would Ken need to receive in additional salary (which he would then save) to achieve his objective?

5. What is the accumulated value of a $1,000 contribution to a qualified defined contribution plan under each of the circumstances described in the table below?

Tax Rate	Before-tax Rate of Return	Investment Period
10%	8%	5 years
30	8	5 years
30	4	5 years
30	4	10 years

Suppose instead that the $1,000 is paid to an employee who then invests the funds in a nonqualified account. What is the accumulated value under each of the circumstances in the table? Compare the results.

6. A complicating feature of the tax code is that interest and dividends are taxed at a higher rate than capital gains for individuals. A lower capital gains tax rate reduces the desirability of investing in assets with high expected capital gains within a tax-eferred account. The reason is that in a tax-deferred account investment earnings are taxed at the ordinary income tax rate even if some of the earnings are from capital gains. Thus, when decid-ing to save through an account with tax-deferred earnings, one must compare the advantage of deferring tax versus the disadvantage of potentially paying a higher tax rate on some of the earnings. To illustrate, suppose that Travis is going to retire in 10 years, the annual before-tax rate of return is 10 percent, one-half of this return is from capital gains, his income tax rate is 30 percent, and his capital gains tax rate is 20 percent. Will Travis have more money at retirement by saving $1,000 of before-tax wages in a qualified account or will he have more money by saving in an account with no tax benefits?

7. Would an employee want to invest his or her defined contribution plan funds in municipal bonds? Explain.

8. Describe how the tax advantages of qualified employer-sponsored retirement plans would change under each of the following conditions:

a. The employee is expected to have a lower tax rate during retirement than while working.

b. The employer is expected to have a higher tax rate in the future than currently.

9. Predict some of the likely consequences from Congress passing a law requiring that all defined benefit plans be fully portable (i.e., when an employee switches employers, the new employer will have to provide a pension based on service with prior employers).

References

Allen, Everett; Joseph Melone; Jerry Rosenbloom; and Jack VanDerhei. *Pension Planning.* 8th ed. Burr Ridge, IL: McGraw-Hill Professional Book Group, 1997. (*Comprehensive discussion of the institutional characteristics of retirement plans.*)

Ippolito, Richard. *Pensions, Economics, and Public Policy.* Homewood, IL: Pension Research Council, 1986. (*Analyzes public policy issues related to pensions.*)

Ippolito, Richard. *The Economics of Pension Insurance.* Homewood, IL: Pension Research Council, 1989. (*Examines the economic reasons for having government insurance of private pensions and the economic effects of PBGC insurance.*)

Ippolito, Richard. *An Economic Appraisal of Pension Tax Policy in the United States.* Homewood, IL: Pension Research Council, 1990. (*Examines US tax policy toward pensions.*)

Ippolito, Richard. *Pension Plans and Employee Performance.* Chicago: The University of Chicago Press, 1997. (*Focuses on the incentive effects of pensions—especially defined contribution plans.*)

Answers to Concept Checks

1. The corporation sponsors a defined benefit plan.

2. a. would provide a higher retirement income than b.

   a. would provide a higher retirement income than c.

   b. would provide the same retirement income as c.

Chapter 18

Workers' Compensation and Employee Injuries

Chapter Objectives

- Describe the history and basic features of workers' compensation laws.
- Explain the economic rationale for workers' compensation laws.
- Explain the major features of workers' compensation and employers' liability insurance.
- Review problems in workers' compensation related to cost growth and insurance price regulation and related reform legislation.
- Introduce workplace safety regulation and other sources of employer liability for harm to employees, including violations of the Americans with Disabilities Act.

18.1 Overview of Workers' Compensation Laws

All states have workers' compensation laws that govern employer responsibility for workplace injuries to employees. Certain types of federal employees (e.g., railroad and maritime workers) are governed by comparable federal legislation, while other federal employees are governed by state laws. Many countries besides the United States have similar laws. As we describe in more detail below, **workers' compensation laws** have two important features: (1) employers are required to pay specified benefits for economic loss to injured employees without regard to employer fault or negligence, and (2) employees are not allowed to sue employers for injuries under tort law.

Prior to the enactment of state workers' compensation laws beginning in the second decade of the 1900s, employer responsibility for workplace injuries to employees was governed by tort liability law. Employers were legally responsible for employee injuries only if the employee could prove that the injury was caused by the employer's negligence. Prior to the 1880s three main defenses were available to employers even if the employee could prove negligence.

First, employers sometimes could avoid liability using an assumption of risk defense, arguing that for obviously hazardous jobs the employee assumed the risk of injury in return for a higher wage. Second, employers were not held liable if they could prove contributory negligence by the employee. Third, according to the fellow servant rule, employers were not held liable if they could establish that the employee's injury was caused by the negligence of a fellow employee. While some employers voluntarily provided compensation to injured employees, these defenses, along with the requirement of proving employer negligence, resulted in many employees not receiving any compensation from the employer for workplace injuries. In addition, very few employees had individual insurance to provide compensation for such injuries.

Starting in the 1880s, many states enacted **employer liability laws.** These laws generally prohibited employers from using one or more and typically all three of their traditional common law defenses. Employer liability laws still apply today in cases where a workplace injury is not governed by workers' compensation legislation. In these cases, the worker must prove employer negligence in order to recover damages in a lawsuit, but the employer's defenses are limited by the state's employer liability law.

As noted, workers' compensation laws in the United States began to be adopted by the states during the early twentieth century. All states had enacted workers' compensation laws by 1948. These laws require most employers to pay specified economic losses of injured employees without regard to fault or negligence. Thus, they make employers absolutely liable for specified losses from work-related injuries and essentially mandate that employers insure workers against those losses. We provide an overview of workers' compensation benefits in the next section of this chapter.

Injured employees subject to workers' compensation laws do not have the right to sue their employers for injury under tort liability. Employer immunity from tort liability claims by injured employees is known as the **exclusive remedy** rule; that is, the employee's only remedy against the employer is to obtain benefits under the workers' compensation law. While employers are required to pay specified benefits for economic loss, the laws do not require the employer to compensate employees for pain and suffering. Note, however, that if some party besides the employer contributed to the injury, the worker may be able to sue that party for pain and suffering and any monetary losses not covered by workers' compensation (see Box 18.1).

Although the enactment of workers' compensation laws prevented injured employees from suing to recover economic losses not covered by workers' compensation and damages for pain and suffering, the laws were supported by employees and unions because they ensured that employees would receive specified compensation for economic loss without having to prove negligence by the employer. Employers generally favored the laws because they eliminated the employer's exposure to tort liability claims for employee injuries, which could involve significant defense costs and potentially large awards for pain and suffering. Employer support for workers' compensation strengthened following an increase in the frequency of tort liability suits by injured employees that accompanied the enactment of employer liability laws. In addition, many employers already had begun to provide limited

The exclusive remedy rule only applies to the employer. Thousands of tort liability suits for workplace injuries are filed each year against other parties that contributed to the injury. A major example is when a worker is injured by a machine that was manufactured by another business. In these cases employees often recover damages in a product liability suit against the machine manufacturer for pain and suffering and any monetary losses not covered by workers' compensation. The employer's workers' compensation insurer (or the employer if it is self-insured) is subrogated (see Chapter 10) to the employee's tort rights to the extent of any workers' compensation benefits paid and generally will seek to recover these costs from the product manufacturer. Another common situation where a worker could sue under tort liability is when the worker is hurt from an on-the-job automobile accident caused by another driver. Again, the workers' compensation insurer or the self-insured employer is subrogated to the employee's tort rights against any at-fault driver to the extent of any workers' compensation benefits paid.

Because of these tort liability cases, for a given type of injury and amount of loss, an employee will receive more money if some other party is at fault than if the injury only involves the employer. Some people suggest that this is inequitable, proposing either that workers be allowed to sue their employers or that employee/employer suits against other parties be restricted. We discuss the disadvantages of extending tort liability rights (and allowable employee suits against employers under the so-called *dual capacity doctrine,* see Box 18.3) later in this chapter. A disadvantage of restricting suits against nonemployers that contributes to workplace injuries is that safety incentives could be reduced for these firms or parties.

benefits for economic loss to injured employees without regard to negligence. We discuss the economic rationale for workers' compensation laws in detail in section 18.3.

Coverage under workers' compensation is compulsory for specified types of employment in all but one state—Texas. Some states do not apply workers' compensation laws to employers with fewer than two or sometimes three or four employees. Some states exclude certain categories of employment, such as domestic services, from their workers' compensation laws. In these cases, employers can and typically do voluntarily choose to be governed by the workers' compensation law; a few of these states require the employee's consent. In order to be governed by a workers' compensation law, an employee's injury must be work-related in that it must arise out of and during the course of employment. Whether an injury satisfies this test is sometimes difficult to determine (see Box 18.2).

Workers' compensation laws require employers to either purchase workers' compensation insurance or meet specified eligibility standards in order to qualify to self-insure workers' compensation benefits. Workers' compensation insurance prices traditionally have been subject to comprehensive regulation. In addition, five states (Ohio, North Dakota, Washington, West Virginia, and Wyoming) require workers' compensation insurance to be purchased from a state government insurer.[1] These government monopolies are known as **monopolistic state funds.** About one-third of the states have state insurers, known as **competitive state funds,** that compete with private insurers and/or serve as the residual market.

Concept Check

1. How does a workers' compensation law differ from an employers' liability law?

---

[1] Nevada also had that requirement until the year 2000.

Workers' compensation benefits are payable for injuries and occupational disease that *arise out of and during the course of employment*. In some cases it is not clear whether this requirement is met. If a dispute arises between the employer/workers' compensation insurer and the employee about whether an injury is covered, in most states the issue is settled by the state's workers' compensation commission. (A few states rely on the court system.) Examples of injuries and illnesses that may involve uncertainty about whether they are compensable by workers' compensation and how they are typically treated are shown below:

- On-the-job heart attack: May be compensable if conditions of employment gave rise to unusual risk of heart attack.
- Stress-related illness: Often compensable only if the employment involved stressful conditions above and beyond the ordinary conditions for that particular type of employment.
- Injuries while traveling to and from work: Generally not compensable, even if the employee has regular use of a company car; injuries incurred while using a vehicle for work (e.g., sales calls) are compensable, but not while using a vehicle for personal errands.
- Out-of-town travel within the United States: Injuries en route generally are compensable; injuries while off duty (e.g., in the hotel) may be compensable if the employer selects the accommodations.
- Foreign travel: Off-duty injuries are likely to be compensable if the location involves unusual risk compared to the United States.

18.2 Workers' Compensation Benefits

Workers' compensation benefits are paid for work-related bodily injuries and occupational disease. The specific types and amounts of benefits vary widely across states, and the details are complicated. Our purpose here is to acquaint you with the major types of benefits (and hint at some of the complexity). Understanding the basic structure of benefits is important for understanding the operation of the system, the economic rationale for workers' compensation, and the problems that have arisen with workers' compensation in many states.

There are three main types of workers' compensation benefits: (1) payment of medical expenses; (2) payments for lost income associated with total or partial disability, whether temporary or permanent (i.e., the disability is expected to continue until normal retirement age or death, whichever comes first); and (3) death benefits in the form of payments to survivors of workers that are killed on the job.[2] Medical expenses represent 40–50 percent of total workers' compensation benefit payments in the typical state. A large majority of benefits for loss of income are for permanent partial disabilities. Benefit payments for permanent total disability and death represent a very small fraction of total payments.

Medical Benefits

Most jurisdictions provide for payment of all medical expenses associated with covered injuries and diseases without limitation during the lifetime of the employee. Medical benefits usually are paid without any deductible or co-insurance for the employee. Consistent with

[2] A majority of states also pay specified benefits for vocational rehabilitation (e.g., compensation during a period of retraining, transportation expenses, prostheses, etc.). Comparable benefits usually are provided in other states even if they are not specifically enumerated in the workers' compensation law.

full insurance coverage for losses aggravating moral hazard (see Chapter 10), there is evidence that utilization of medical care for injuries covered by workers' compensation is greater than for nonoccupational injuries where medical expense insurance coverage often is subject to deductibles and co-insurance.

About half the states allow employers to (1) specify the physicians who shall initially treat the employee and (2) approve treatment by other physicians. This can reduce moral hazard because physicians then have an incentive to control costs in order to maintain their relationships with employers and workers' compensation insurers. In addition, increases in workers' compensation medical expenses during the 1980s led many states to adopt fee schedules for workplace injuries. These schedules specify the level of fees that physicians can receive for treating injured workers. In an effort to control costs, some states also have allowed employers to implement various types of managed care that provide employers and workers' compensation insurers with a greater ability to control costs (see Chapter 16).

Disability Benefits

Total Disability Benefits

Injured workers who are unable to work commonly receive benefits equal to two-thirds of their pre-injury wage. The maximum weekly benefit usually is capped at an amount equal to 100 percent of the state's average weekly wage. Many states also specify a minimum weekly benefit. To illustrate typical benefits, suppose that the state's average weekly wage is $500. Then an employee with a pre-injury wage of $400 would receive a weekly benefit of $267 while disabled (two-thirds of $400). If instead the employee's pre-injury wage was $800, the employee would be paid the maximum benefit of $500 (since two-thirds of $800 exceeds the maximum benefit amount of $500). These benefit maximums, along with benefit minimums in many states, produce a higher wage replacement rate for lower paid workers than for higher paid workers. Workers' compensation benefits are not subject to federal and state income taxes, which increase the wage replacement rate compared to pre-injury wages on an after-tax basis. Some—but not all—states index benefits payable following an injury to increases in the state's average weekly wage.

Many states have a three-to-seven-day waiting period following the onset of the disability before benefits are paid. These waiting periods help to control costs and reduce the moral hazard (see below) associated with less serious injuries. If the duration of the disability exceeds a specified number of days (e.g., 21), then benefits usually are paid retroactively for the waiting period.

A **temporary total disability** ends when the worker can return to work. Total disability that is expected to continue until death or retirement age is known as **permanent total disability.** Almost all states pay permanent total disability benefits based on the amount of time from the onset of injury until a specified retirement age (e.g., age 65). Some states specify a maximum limit on the total amount of benefits paid (e.g., $200,000) or cap the duration of benefits at a lower amount (e.g., 500 weeks). In many permanent total disability cases, the injured worker and the workers' compensation insurer (or self-insured employer) agree to a lump sum settlement equal to the present value of future benefits instead of having benefits paid over time.

Like most insurance benefits, workers' compensation disability benefits (and other types of disability insurance benefits) are subject to a moral hazard problem. This problem has two dimensions. First, some injured workers may fake or exaggerate injuries to avoid working and become eligible for benefits. Second, some injured workers may delay returning to work following an injury because the marginal benefit of working may be small compared to not working and collecting workers' compensation benefits.

To illustrate the moral hazard problem, consider a worker with pre-injury wages of $500 per week before taxes and after-tax wages of $380. If the worker becomes eligible for temporary total disability payments, assume that he or she will receive $333 per week, which equals two-thirds of $500 (and is less than the maximum weekly benefit in the state). Compared to collecting workers' compensation benefits of $333 per week, the worker would gain only $47 per week after taxes ($380 − $333) by working. Thus, in this example, a worker who returns to work following an injury and temporary disability would make roughly $1 per hour from working ($47 per week more for a 40-hour work week) compared to receiving workers' compensation benefits.

Because the proportion of after-tax wages that is replaced by workers' compensation benefits is higher for lower paid workers than for higher paid workers (and perhaps because lower paid jobs are less attractive/stimulating than higher paid jobs), the moral hazard problem is more severe for lower paid jobs. For example, for the worker who makes a much higher wage, such as $1,500 per week, the moral hazard problem is lower because the worker only receives the maximum weekly benefit (for example, $500) while disabled. Employers and workers' compensation insurers often attempt to mitigate moral hazard by monitoring and investigating claims and by using physician reports that certify whether the worker is able to work.

Permanent Partial Disability Benefits

Payments for **permanent partial disability** are made to workers who experience permanent injuries that partially reduce the worker's earnings capacity. For example, if a person whose job routinely involves lifting heavy objects herniates a disk in his or her back, the injury may permanently prevent the worker from working in this capacity. If the worker can work only in jobs that pay less following the injury (for example, in lower paying service jobs), he or she has suffered a loss of earnings capacity that is compensable under workers' compensation laws. Payments for permanent partial disability usually follow a period of temporary total disability. As noted above, permanent partial disability payments generally represent a large proportion of total disability payments.

Most states combine two methods of determining permanent partial disability payments: (1) scheduled payments, and (2) payments based on an estimated reduction in earnings capacity. With the first approach, scheduled injuries will be compensated at amounts listed on a benefit schedule. Fixed benefit amounts will be scheduled for well-defined injuries, such as the loss of one or both limbs, fingers, eyes, hearing, and so on. For example, a state might have a benefit amount of $50,000 for loss of a thumb and $75,000 for loss of an eye. Scheduled amounts vary widely across the states.

A large proportion of permanent partial injuries are not amenable to using the simple schedule method. Examples include most injuries to shoulders, necks, backs, and other joints; these injuries reduce earnings capacity but do not prevent gainful employment. Although the rules and procedures for determining amounts of compensation in these cases are complex, the typical approach is to base compensation on the estimated percentage reduction in earnings capacity.[3] For example, assume that the worker with the herniated disk is estimated to have experienced a permanent reduction of earnings capacity of 50 percent (compared to 100 percent for total disability) and that the worker's predisability weekly wage was $600. Then the worker's weekly earnings loss would be estimated at $300 (0.5 $\times$ $600) and the weekly permanent partial disability benefits would be estimated at $200 (2/3 $\times$ $300). (This amount would be capped if it were greater than the statewide average weekly wage.) The $200 then would be multiplied by the number of weeks that benefits would be payable, which might be a fixed number of weeks (e.g., 300), or, if shorter, until retirement age. Assuming a 300-week period, the total benefit in this example would be $60,000 ($200 $\times$ 300). This benefit often would be discounted to present value (subject to state rules on the discount rate) and paid as a lump sum to the worker.

Because an injured employee's true reduction in earnings capacity must be estimated for permanent partial disability cases, disputes between the employee and the employer and/or workers' compensation insurer are common. Injured employees often retain an attorney to negotiate settlements with the employer and/or the workers' compensation insurer. Many states provide that the employee's attorney fees are paid by the employer/insurer. If the employee and the employer/insurer cannot agree on a settlement, most states have a workers' compensation commission that will resolve the dispute (parties may be able to appeal the commission's decision to the courts). A few states allow direct access to the court system.

As an alternative to negotiated settlements for permanent partial disability based on the estimated reduction in earnings capacity, a few states have experimented with paying employees an amount equal to their actual wage loss over time. These experiments have met with little success due to two main problems. First, it is administratively costly to keep track of employees and their current wages. Second, actual wage-loss systems are subject to the moral hazard problem described above for total disability payments. They reduce the incentive for the employee to return to work and to obtain a higher paying job. This effect increases the costs of a wage-loss system.

Survivor Benefits

In addition to payment of a flat amount toward burial costs (e.g., $1,000–$5,000), all states pay workers' compensation benefits to surviving spouses and eligible children of workers that are killed on the job. The total weekly benefit usually is similar in magnitude to payments for total disability (two-thirds of the pre-injury wage). Some states pay a lower percentage of the pre-injury wage, such as 50 percent, if there are no children or if there is only one child and no surviving spouse. Depending on the jurisdiction, the duration of benefits often is limited by a number of factors, such as the remarriage of a spouse or a child's 18th birthday.

Concept Check

2. A state requires workers' compensation weekly disability benefits equal to 60 percent of pre-injury weekly wages but no more than the statewide average weekly wage of $540. How large must a worker's weekly wage be before his or her benefit will be less than 60 percent of the pre-injury wage?

---

[3]The fact that several states refer to some of these injuries as scheduled injuries even though flat payment amounts cannot be specified adds to possible confusion.

18.3   Why Have Workers' Compensation?

You might wonder why we ask this question. Many students find the rationale for workers' compensation to be self-evident. The reasoning is: If workers are hurt on the job, then the employer should pay—end of story! However, life is seldom so simple. The economic rationale for workers' compensation rests on whether it can minimize the cost of risk by maximizing the welfare of workers compared to alternative systems that might be used.

Recall that workers' compensation laws combine mandatory provision of insurance coverage by employers with employer immunity from tort liability (exclusive remedy). Possible alternatives to the current system of workers' compensation include: (1) no mandatory workers' compensation benefits and no tort liability for employers; (2) no mandatory benefits but employees can recover from employers under tort law if the employer is negligent (no exclusive remedy); and (3) mandatory benefits but employees also can sue negligent employers for damages under tort law, thus allowing workers to receive workers' compensation benefits and seek compensation for the types of losses that are not covered under workers' compensation (e.g., pain and suffering and any lost wages in excess of allowed benefit maximums).

Note that there are many possible variations. For example, employers might be held strictly liable under a system that allows employees to sue, as opposed to requiring the employee to prove negligence on the part of the employer. Our discussion assumes that employees would have to prove negligence to keep things simple and because employees must currently prove employer negligence to recover for injuries that are not governed by workers' compensation.

As was true of our discussion of the rationale for tort liability in Chapter 12, the economic rationale for workers' compensation rests on its effects on safety, compensation for injury (including the extent to which persons uninsured for injuries might impose costs on other parties), and administrative/dispute resolution costs. Given the background provided in Chapter 12, our discussion in this section is comparatively brief.

Who Pays for Injury Costs?

To understand the rationale for workers' compensation compared to alternative methods, as well as issues associated with the design of workers' compensation benefits, you need to recognize that laws or contracts that require employers to pay part or all of the cost of employee injuries will tend to reduce wages over time by the amount necessary for employers to recover these costs. Indeed, economic theory and evidence both suggest that this is the case. The intuition is that the demand for labor by employers depends on the marginal value added by workers (worker productivity) and the *full marginal cost* of labor to the employer, which includes the cost of worker injuries that the employer must pay, as well as the cost of employee benefits (see Chapters 16 and 17) and wage-based taxes paid by employers, such as social security taxes. In the context of workers' compensation, this means that employers primarily care about the total cost of employing a given worker, not how it is divided between wages and workers' compensation costs.[4]

---

[4]In Chapters 16 and 17 we discussed how the division of total compensation between employee benefits and cash compensation is relevant to employers to the extent that it affects factors such as employee productivity and turnover, as well as income taxes paid by employees.

Because employees as a group ultimately bear injury costs, there is no free lunch. Other things being equal, worker injury compensation systems that increase what employers have to pay eventually will reduce wages, and if wages cannot be reduced, fewer workers will be employed.[5] Note that we are referring to a long-run, aggregate tendency. In the short run, employers are affected by changes in injury costs and those better at controlling costs can profit compared to other firms. Nonetheless, as a result of this long-run, aggregate tendency, the relevant question for employees to ask before they know whether they will be injured is: *What is the best method of providing compensation for workplace injuries given that we have to bear the costs?*

Some groups dispute this view. Leaders of organized labor groups, for example, often argue that the cost of greater payments by employers for injuries (and benefits) simply will reduce employer profits. However, if profits are at competitive levels, any increase in the cost of employer obligations for workplace injuries that cannot be offset by savings in wage payments will cause employers to hire fewer workers. Alternatively, it may lead to some increase in the prices of products, which also will tend to reduce employment due to reduced demand for goods and services following the price increase.

Benefits and Costs of Different Arrangements

Given the preceding background, you now are ready for an overview of the benefits and costs of traditional workers' compensation (mandatory benefits without tort liability) compared with three alternatives: (1) no mandatory benefits and no tort liability, (2) no mandatory benefits with tort liability, and (3) mandatory benefits with tort liability. Table 18.1 highlights the main differences in the systems.

TABLE 18.1
Theoretical comparison of alternative systems for dealing with workplace injuries.

Mandatory Benefits	Tort Liability	Safety Incentives	Compensation	Administrative/ Dispute Resolution Costs
No	No	Inadequate if employees underestimate risk	Inadequate	Low
No	Yes	Adequate	Excessive if employer is negligent; otherwise inadequate	High
Yes	No	Adequate with labor market incentives and safety regulation	About right	Moderate
Yes	Yes	Adequate or possibly excessive	Excessive if employer is negligent	Highest

[5]Some increase in the prices of goods and services also is possible (see below), but employees as a group then will have to pay higher prices and thus have lower real wages.

No Mandatory Benefits and No Tort Liability

Consider the case where employers are not required to provide compensation for workplace injuries and cannot be sued by employees. This "no remedy" case is analogous to the case of no liability for harm discussed in Chapter 12. In essence, we are analyzing safety and compensation in an unregulated market with no employer liability.

With neither mandatory workers' compensation benefits nor tort liability, employer safety decisions will reflect the benefits and costs to employers. It may at first appear that employers will invest virtually nothing on workplace safety. However, if employees are well informed about the risk of injury, increases in safety will allow employers to pay lower wages to the extent that the increased safety is valued by employees. With well-informed employees, this system will produce the right amount of safety: Employees will get the level of safety that they desire given that they have to pay for greater safety through lower wages.

Evidence indicates that higher risk jobs require higher wages, which is consistent with employee demand for safety providing significant incentives for employers to increase safety. Potential adverse publicity following major workplace accidents provides additional safety incentives for employers. Thus, even in an unregulated market with no tort liability, employers have substantial incentives to reduce workplace injuries. Given the complexity of many workplace environments and possible causes of injuries, however, many employees may not be sufficiently informed for safety to be adequate under a "no remedy" system.

Specifically, if employees underestimate the risk of injury, they will demand too little safety, and the no remedy system will produce too little safety. The employers' savings in wages from increasing safety will be insufficient to induce the employer to provide the level of safety that would be demanded by workers if they were better informed (and other influences, such as potential adverse publicity, may not fully offset this problem). As a result, one rationale for either workers' compensation or tort liability is to prevent suboptimal safety.

A second problem with no workers' compensation and no tort liability for workplace injuries is that many workers probably would fail to buy insurance coverage for workplace injuries or to negotiate employee benefit packages that would pay medical expenses and loss of income for their injuries. Many workers, especially lower paid workers, currently are uninsured for medical expenses for injuries and illnesses that are not work-related (see Chapter 16). In addition to possible hardship to uninsured people, a significant proportion of medical costs for the uninsured ends up being borne by other parties (insured persons and taxpayers). Thus, uninsured workers commonly impose costs on other parties. Workers' compensation reduces this problem for on-the-job injuries. Tort liability for employers would provide implicit insurance for injuries caused by employer negligence.

No Mandatory Benefits with Tort Liability

We now examine workplace safety, compensation for injury, and administrative costs if employers can be held liable for workplace injury under a negligence standard. In this case, tort liability for employers would have the potential to provide proper safety incentives to employers without mandatory workers' compensation benefits, provided that employers have liability insurance or sufficient assets to pay damages. Compulsory liability insurance or requiring proof of adequate assets might be necessary to prevent some employers from being judgment proof (avoiding liability) and therefore having excessively risky workplaces and inadequate compensation for injured employees. However, even ignoring the problem of judgment-proof employers, a number of problems arise with the tort liability/no workers' compensation benefits approach.

First, as was discussed in Chapter 12, in order to provide parties with proper incentives to consider the full cost of harm they might cause to other parties, tort liability violates the principle of optimal compensation by requiring damages for pain and suffering and by providing payments that duplicate other sources of recovery to the injured party. Second, the tort liability system produces large costs for dispute resolution, as well as substantial uncertainty associated with the possibility of punitive damages. Both of these factors would increase injury costs and thereby reduce wages and/or employment. Third, unlike a workers' compensation system that compensates monetary accident losses regardless of whether the employer is negligent, a tort liability system would leave some employees uninsured for these losses.

Workers' Compensation: Mandatory Benefits without Tort Liability
Consider next the effect of the traditional workers' compensation system on safety, compensation, and administrative costs. To the extent that workers underestimate the risk of workplace injury, mandatory workers' compensation benefits provide greater incentives for safety than would exist with neither mandatory workers' compensation benefits nor tort liability for injuries. Because employers must pay for injury costs as defined by law, increased safety has the potential to lower employer costs by reducing self-insured claim costs or workers' compensation insurance premiums (see below). While in the long run such savings will tend to benefit employees through increased wages and employment, in the short run, employers that can lower these costs can expand output, compete more effectively for labor, and increase profits compared to other employers.

The failure of mandatory workers' compensation benefits to encompass all economic losses and nonmonetary losses (pain and suffering) in principle could lead to suboptimal safety compared to tort liability. However, the design of workers' compensation benefits is more consistent with principles of optimal compensation and generally involves significantly lower dispute resolution costs than tort liability. In addition, government regulation of workplace safety can be and is used to supplement private incentives for safety, which in principle further reduces the potential advantage of tort liability as a means to promote safety.

You need to be aware, however, of at least one caveat to this favorable view of workers' compensation. If a workers' compensation system provides benefits greater than what employees are willing to pay for, has few cost controls, and is plagued by fraud and comparatively high dispute resolution costs in determining whether the injury is work-related and the magnitude of disability, a point might be reached where employees can be made better off by providing them with a nonworkers' compensation benefit package and allowing employees to sue employers for negligence. In fact, many employers in Texas that have opted out of workers' compensation, and insurers that sell specialized benefit packages and liability insurance to these employers, argue that this solution is preferable to workers' compensation for many employers and workers.

Mandatory Benefits with Tort Liability
Now consider the possibility of adding tort liability to mandatory workers' compensation benefits (i.e., eliminating employer immunity from tort liability and thus ending exclusive remedy). Some people advocate this change, including a number of lawyers and law professors. Under this system, workers would receive workers' compensation benefits and

also be allowed to sue employers for uncovered economic losses and pain and suffering if the injury is alleged to be caused by employer negligence. Punitive damages also could be sought in some cases (in principle if the employer engaged in willful disregard of worker safety). Advocates argue that this change is necessary to increase workplace safety and hold employers accountable for the full costs of their actions.

Until the costs are considered, combining tort liability with workers' compensation might seem like the best of both worlds. It would combine the advantages of workers' compensation with improved safety incentives from the tort system. However, the additional compensation would violate principles of optimal compensation and result in large dispute resolution costs and substantial uncertainty for employers. The likely result would be lower wages and less employment. The current consensus is that the additional safety that might arise from such a system would not be worth the costs, which would largely be borne by employees over time.

Not knowing whether you will be injured and assuming that you would have to accept lower wages to cover the increased costs (thus preventing any subsidy), ask yourself whether you would like to be covered by workers' compensation *and* have the right to sue your employer for uncovered economic losses, pain and suffering, and punitive damages. If you understand the material in this section and in Chapter 12, we suspect that your answer will be no.

Concept Check

3. If a worker knew for certain that he or she was going to be hurt on the job (and the employer did not know this), which of the four systems described in this section would the employee most likely prefer? Explain how this employee's preference might be different if he or she did not have this prior knowledge.

18.4 Workers' Compensation Insurance and Self-insurance

The private workers' compensation insurance market, with 2001 premium volume of $26.0 billion, is the largest business property-liability insurance market in the United States and the third largest market overall behind personal auto insurance and homeowners insurance.[6] The four largest private workers' compensation insurers in the United States in 2001 were (1) Liberty Mutual Group with 8.9 percent of countrywide premiums; (2) American International Group (6.8 percent); (3) Zurich/Farmers Group (5.5 percent); and (4) Hartford Insurance Group (4.3 percent). While comprehensive data on self-insurance are not readily available, rough estimates suggest that approximately 40 percent of workers' compensation claim costs are self-insured. Workers' compensation insurance prices traditionally have been subject to comprehensive price regulation, and this remains true today in a majority of states.

Description of Insurance Coverage

In most states insurers are required to issue a policy developed by the National Council on Compensation Insurance (NCCI), the leading insurance industry advisory organization that specializes in workers' compensation insurance, or a policy that is substantially similar to

[6]Premium data obtained from *Best's Aggregates & Averages, Property-Casualty, United States,* 2002 edition (Oldwick, NJ: A. M. Best Co.).

Some tort liability suits have allowed injured employees to recover damages for pain and suffering and any monetary losses not covered by workers' compensation based on the argument that the injury occurred while the employer was acting in a second, distinct capacity from its primary capacity, as employer. This has occurred when the employer has provided negligent medical care to an employee. Another example would be if an employer-owned and -operated cafeteria served contaminated food that harmed employees.

The basic idea behind the dual capacity doctrine is that when employers assume functions that are not integral to the employment relationship, exclusive remedy should not apply. Thus far the courts have refused to extend the dual capacity doctrine broadly. For example, employers that manufacture their own equipment that in turn injures a worker have not been successfully sued for products liability based on the argument that the employer acted in a dual capacity as product manufacturer.

this contract. The policy has two main coverage parts: (1) workers' compensation insurance and (2) employers' liability insurance.

The **workers' compensation insurance coverage** part of the workers' compensation and employers' liability insurance policy simply requires the insurer to pay all benefits required by the state's workers' compensation law for work-related bodily injury or disease without limitation. There are no exclusions, but insurers are allowed to seek reimbursement from the employer in some circumstances (e.g., if the injury results from willful misconduct by the employer). For accidental bodily injury, the insurer whose policy is in effect on the date of the accident pays the claim. For occupational disease, the claim is paid by the insurer whose policy is in effect on the last day of exposure to the hazard that caused the disease. (The latter provision has helped reduce disputes over which insurer should pay compared to the case of occurrence-based liability coverage discussed in Chapters 23 and 28.)

The second part of the workers' compensation and employers' liability insurance policy is the **employers' liability insurance coverage** part. This coverage provides employers with specified limits of coverage for tort liability suits by employees (or family members) for bodily injuries or disease that are not governed by workers' compensation. Examples of suits for which the insurer agrees to defend the employer and pay damages include, where permitted by common law or statute: (1) suits by a spouse of an injured employee for the value of lost services due to the injury; (2) suits by a family member who is injured in conjunction with injury to the employee; and (3) **dual capacity suits,** which allege that the injury resulted from the employer acting in a dual capacity, such as a suit for medical malpractice if the employer negligently provides emergency medical care (see Box 18.3). Exclusions include but are not limited to losses covered by workers' compensation benefits (they are paid by the workers' compensation coverage), injuries to employees that are knowingly employed in violation of the law (e.g., minors), and injuries that are intentionally caused by the employer (such as an employer striking an employee).

Insurance Pricing, Residual Markets, and State Funds

Pricing

Insured employers generally pay premiums equal to a **class rate** per $100 of payroll times the amount of the firm's payroll (in $100s) in different occupational (industry) classifications. The NCCI (or other rating advisory organization) begins by projecting the loss cost per $100 of payroll for each of approximately 500 occupational classifications in each state. This projection, which is known as the **prospective loss cost,** thus varies across states and occupational classifications. A total rate then is determined by adding a loading for expenses and profit (which reflects anticipated investment income) to the prospective loss cost. In recent years many states have required each insurer to determine this loading, as opposed to the prior practice (still followed in some states) of having the loading determined by the rating advisory organization and added to the prospective loss cost to produce an **advisory rate.** A majority of states require prior regulatory approval of prospective loss costs and expense/profit loadings.

To illustrate these concepts, consider three employment classes used in most states: (1) wholesale beer or ale dealers, (2) tree pruning/spraying, and (3) attorneys and other law firm employees. The prospective loss costs for these three classes per $100 of payroll for a given state and year might be, for example, $4, $15, and $0.50, respectively. Consistent with historical loss experience, these numbers indicate large differences in expected claim costs for these classes.[7]

If the advisory organization or individual insurer loading for expenses and profit (including an offset for expected investment income) equaled 20 percent of the class rate, then the class rates per $100 of payroll would be $5, $18.75, and $0.63, respectively, for the three classes. (These class rates equal the prospective loss costs divided by 0.8, which produces the 20 percent loading for expenses and profits.) Thus, the total premium for tree pruning employees with a total payroll of $100,000 using this class rate would be $18,750 ($18.75 × 1,000). Similarly, the total premium for a law firm with payroll of $1 million using the class rate would be $6,300.

Depending on the state and the characteristics of the employer, the class rate for each job classification then is modified by one or more of the following factors to produce the final rate that a particular employer is charged for each class:

• Many states permit individual insurers to file (subject to regulatory approval) a percentage deviation from prospective loss costs (or advisory rates) developed by the advisory organization to reflect better or worse than average expected experience in the insurer's target markets. The percentage deviation usually must be the same for all classes. For example, an insurer might file for a 10 percent reduction compared to advisory organization prospective loss costs and file its own expense and profit loading. (Some states permit independent rate filings that do not use advisory organization prospective loss costs.)

• All states mandate that an **experience rating** system be used except for small employers. These systems generally modify the employer's rate for the coming year either up or down depending on whether the employer's loss costs have been greater or lower than the expected average experience for the class during the preceding three years. This system produces a rate that reflects a weighted average of the expected average experience for all employers in the class and the particular employer's own loss experience during the experience period. The weight given to the employer's own experience increases with its payroll to reflect greater credibility of loss experience (less random variation) for larger employers.

• Additional charges and discounts may be added because loss costs and expenses (e.g., commissions to agents) per $100 of payroll decline with firm size. The effect of these

[7]These numbers are consistent with historical loss data in one state.

modifications is to produce rates per $100 of payroll that decline commensurately with expected costs.

- Most states permit **schedule rating,** whereby insurers can modify the rate for a particular employer within allowable percentage ranges (e.g., up to plus or minus 25 percent) to reflect the underwriter's evaluation of the employer's expected claim costs based on analysis of factors such as safety programs.
- Large employers may have the final rate paid for a given year adjusted over time based on loss experience during the same year under retrospective experience rating systems (see Chapter 24).
- Many insurers pay dividends to employers whose historical loss experience has been better than expected.

If regulators approve class rates that are high enough to cover the expected costs of most employers in each class, then rate deviations, schedule rating, and dividend plans can be used by insurers to lower prices for those employers in each class that are predicted to have better loss experience than implied by the class rate. The outcome from using these procedures in many states is a refined pricing system in which rates are closely related to expected claim costs for different employers. As we discuss further below, however, significant distortions in supply can occur if regulators refuse to approve class rates that are large enough to cover the expected costs of insuring most employers.

Residual Markets and State Funds

You learned earlier that five states mandate the purchase of workers' compensation insurance from a monopolistic government insurer known as a monopolistic state fund. These government monopolies offer coverage to all employers at rates determined by the state. States that allow private insurance do not require each insurer to offer coverage to each employer that applies for coverage. If an employer is unable to readily find an insurer that is willing to provide coverage voluntarily because, for example, price regulation prevents insurers from charging a high enough price, the employer is able to obtain coverage in the **residual market.**

About one-fourth of the states use a competitive state fund as the residual market. As the name implies, competitive state funds sometimes also compete with private insurers in the voluntary market. The remaining states with private insurance generally provide that employers that cannot readily obtain voluntary coverage will be charged a regulated price and randomly assigned to insurers in proportion to each insurer's premiums for workers' compensation insurance written voluntarily.[8] In most of these states, workers' compensation insurers have developed reinsurance pools in lieu of these assignments. Most of the pools are administered by rating advisory organizations (most often the NCCI).

Under the pooling system, insurers contract with a number of servicing insurance carriers who issue residual market policies, collect premiums, and settle claims in exchange for a fee paid by the pool. The net financial results of the residual market pool then are split among all insurers that participate in the pooling arrangement in proportion to the amount of premiums that an insurer received in a given year for policies that it wrote voluntarily. This system therefore involves insurer specialization in administering residual market poli-

---

[8]Self-insurers are excluded from the system; they do not participate in the residual market.

cies and reduces the risk that individual insurers otherwise might face from highly uncertain cash flows if they were randomly assigned individual employers with varying degrees of price inadequacy due to regulation.[9]

As we will discuss further below, residual markets in many states became very large during the 1980s and produced large deficits and cross-subsidies from the voluntary market to the residual market due to inadequate residual market premium rates through the early 1990s. As a result, regulators in many of these states began to approve significantly higher rates for employers insured in the residual market compared to employers insured voluntarily.

Self-insurance and Large Deductible Policies

As noted at the beginning of the chapter, employers are required to purchase workers' compensation insurance unless they meet minimum financial requirements for qualifying as a self-insurer. These requirements generally prevent small- to medium-sized employers from self-insuring workers' compensation claims on an individual basis. However, since the early 1980s, many states have passed laws permitting **group self-insurance** for these employers, which enables a group of companies to combine together to jointly self-insure benefits. Group self-insurance has contributed to growth in self-insurance in recent years. It also is commonly believed that self-insurance has grown in many states as commercial insurance in the voluntary insurance market became less attractive to many employers because voluntary market rates in effect were increased to make up for inadequate residual market rates (see above).

Self-insurers often use outside firms known as **third-party administrators** to settle workers' compensation claims, and this practice is customary for group self-insurance. Otherwise, the employer must settle its own claims. Workers' compensation self-insurers and self-insurance groups often purchase excess insurance to protect against large losses from a single claim and/or in total for a given year.

Until the early 1990s regulation generally only permitted comparatively small deductibles under workers' compensation insurance policies. Thus, employers basically had two choices: (1) self-insurance (if they could qualify) with excess insurance above a large retention, and (2) workers' compensation insurance with low deductibles. At this time many states began to permit the sale of **large deductible policies** in the voluntary market (generally defined as policies with per injury deductibles of $100,000 or more). Under these policies, the insurer has to settle and pay the full amount of the claim to the injured employee, but the insurer then seeks reimbursement from the employer for the amount of the claim below the deductible.

Like traditional workers' compensation policies with little or no deductible, the payment of mandatory workers' compensation benefits under large deductible policies is guaranteed by the insurer, thus mitigating the potential judgment proof problem (see Chapter 12), but the employer does not have to pay for full (or nearly full) coverage. Thus, these policies offer employers an intermediate risk-sharing option compared to traditional

---

[9]During the decade a number of insurers in some states have withdrawn from these pooling arrangements, opting instead to receive direct assignments and in many cases then entering into a separate contract with one or more insurers to service the business.

policies and self-insurance.[10] The market for large deductible policies grew rapidly in many states beginning in the early 1990s, which contributed in part to a 16 percent reduction in countrywide workers' compensation insurance premium volume during 1992–1996.

Second Injury Funds

Virtually all states have a **second injury fund** that allows insurers and self-insured employers to be reimbursed for the estimated increase in benefit costs when a subsequent ("second") injury occurs to an employee that was previously injured. The cost of the combined reimbursements then is spread among insurers and self-insurers in proportion to their total claim costs. The original rationale for second injury funds was to increase employment opportunities for workers with an earlier injury. The concern was that employers would be reluctant to hire an employee that had previously lost the use of an arm because injury to another arm or leg might produce a total disability, which would require larger workers' compensation benefits than if the worker had not been hurt previously. With the second injury fund, this increased cost is spread among all employers, thus reducing the disincentive to hire the worker.

In modern times, second injury funds in some states have been plagued by high costs. Injuries in some states are eligible for reimbursement even if the employer did not know of the prior injury at the time of hire. This tends to increase second injury fund assessments and associated administrative costs. It is not clear that the ability to be reimbursed for these "undiscovered" injuries will have much if any effect on hiring. A disadvantage of second injury funds is that they might reduce the incentive of an insurer or self-insurer to dispute questionable claims. The reason is that any increase in investigation or dispute costs will be borne by the insurer or self-insurer but any reduction in the amount of payment also will reduce reimbursement from the second injury fund (and thus benefit other employers/insurers).

Another problem is that it is very difficult to estimate the incremental effects of second injuries to backs and other soft tissues. This measurement problem might induce insurers/employers to go out of their way to argue that the injury was aggravated by a prior injury. Finally, some observers question the need for these funds in modern times, especially in view of federal legislation designed to increase employment opportunities for disabled persons (see below).

18.5   Problems and Reforms in Workers' Compensation

The workers' compensation system and insurance market experienced considerable turmoil in the 1980s and early 1990s, and currently there are signs some of that turmoil may be returning. Workers' compensation claim costs grew rapidly in many states during the 1980s. For example, benefit costs per $100 of payroll increased approximately 5 percent per year during this time, and increases in the average indemnity and medical cost per injury involving lost wages averaged 10 percent per year or more in many states before leveling off

[10]Because they have much lower premiums than traditional policies, large deductible policies also reduce any implicit taxes that the employer might have to pay to subsidize the residual market (see below). That advantage was a major cause of the growth of large deductible policies in the early 1990s.

in the 1990s and picking up speed again in the past few years. The causes of cost growth include: (1) increases in medical care costs in excess of wage and general medical care cost inflation; (2) growth in benefit levels in many states; (3) compensation for new types of injuries, including cumulative injuries, due to repetitive motion and expansion (in some states) of the ability to receive benefits for job-related stress; (4) increased dispute resolution costs and greater settlements for difficult to measure, permanent partial disabilities; and (5) increased claims fraud (e.g., faked or exaggerated injuries, or seeking compensation for injuries that occurred away from work).

The rapid growth in workers' compensation costs and insurance premiums during the 1980s was accompanied by deteriorating financial results for workers' compensation insurance. Insurers commonly argued that state regulators failed to allow rate increases commensurate with cost increases. These arguments are plausible. Regulators often approved rate increases much smaller than requested, and they were subject to substantial pressure from many employers to deny or at least delay rate increases that were necessary to keep pace with rapid growth in expected claim costs. Consistent with regulatory constraints on rate increases in the presence of rising costs, the nationwide workers' compensation insurance residual market increased sharply during the 1980s (see Figure 18.1). By 1992, the peak of the workers' compensation insurance crisis, the residual market share of premiums had grown to over 50 percent in a number of states (see Figure 18.2).

FIGURE 18.1 **Workers' compensation insurance residual market premiums as a percent of total workers' compensation insurance premiums: 1980–2001 (countrywide aggregates for NCCI states; data reported in *NCCI Management Summary,* annual editions).**

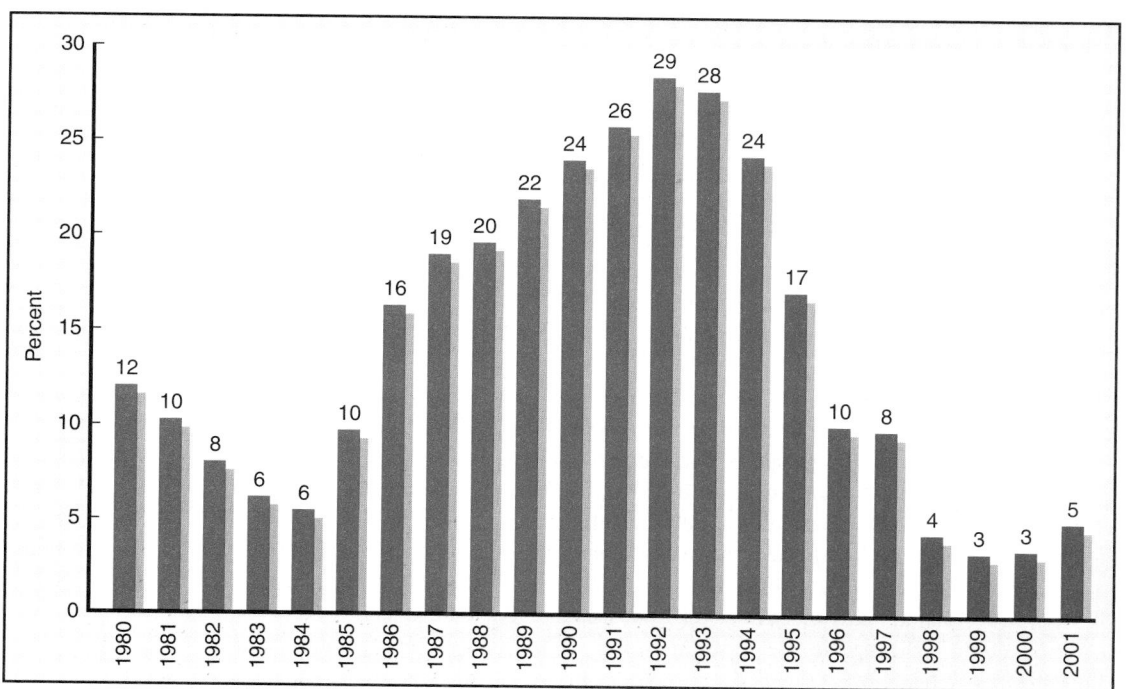

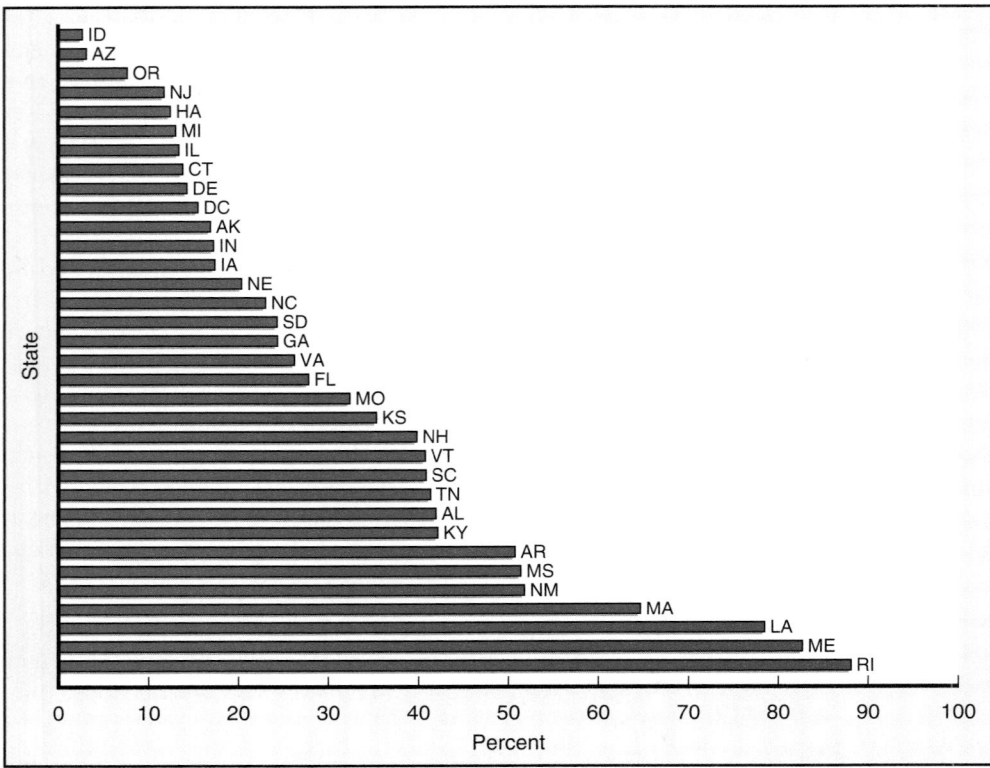

Recall that insurers generally are responsible for residual market deficits in proportion to their voluntary market premiums. As a result, if residual market rates are too low to cover expected costs, insurers know that they will have to contribute to the resulting deficit in proportion to their voluntary market premiums. When they write a policy voluntarily, their charge for the residual market deficit therefore will increase. This effectively increases the cost of selling a policy voluntarily. In order to cover the total expected costs of selling a policy voluntarily, the insurer needs to charge a high enough premium to cover the expected costs for the particular employer plus the cost of higher assessments for the residual market deficit.

For example, assume that an insurer estimates that it needs a premium of $20,000 to provide coverage to an employer without any residual market deficit, but if the insurer writes the policy, it estimates that the present value of its future assessments for the residual market deficit will increase by $2,000. Then the insurer will require a premium of at least $22,000 to write the policy. The required premium might be higher than $22,000 because of substantial uncertainty associated with the size of assessments, as well as uncertainty concerning whether regulators will approve future rate increases for the voluntary market that are sufficient to cover increases in expected costs.

During the late 1980s and early 1990s, many state regulators approved higher voluntary market rates to help make up for residual market rate inadequacy, and insurers often had the flexibility to lower dividends and schedule rating discounts that previously had been provided to many employers insured voluntarily, thus increasing the net price charged to many employers insured in the voluntary market in order to offset expected deficits for the residual market. As a result, these actions produced a large cross-subsidy from the voluntary to the residual market. Employers insured in the voluntary market were charged more than their expected costs in order to offset all or part of the cost of expected deficits for the residual market. In many states this enabled private insurers to cover more of their total costs and reduced pressure for them to exit the market.

As suggested earlier, higher rates in the voluntary market to finance residual market deficits might cause more businesses to self-insure, thus avoiding subsidies to other employers. To the extent that this occurs, the size of the voluntary market is further reduced. Escalating growth in the residual market and an inability to shift residual market deficits to a shrinking voluntary market led to insurance company exits and the virtual collapse of the voluntary workers' compensation insurance market in a few states (such as Maine; see Figure 18.2).

There also is evidence that inadequate residual market rates for higher risk employers aggravated claim cost growth. This result is predicted to the extent that regulatory caps reduce modifications in class rates from experience rating and/or allow higher risk employers to grow more rapidly by reducing their workers' compensation insurance costs.

The 1980s claims cost surge and regulatory responses threatened to undermine the historical basis of workers' compensation legislation. Many observers viewed legislation to control claim costs as essential to preserve the system and maintain substantial private sector involvement in the provision of workers' compensation insurance. Others disputed that regulation produced inadequate rates and argued that cost-benefit control measures deprived injured workers of needed compensation.

Beginning in the late 1980s, numerous states adopted workers' compensation reform legislation designed to reduce the growth in claim costs. Examples of changes include: (1) adoption of medical expense fee schedules and permission for employers to adopt managed care practices to help control workers' compensation medical costs; (2) changes in disability benefit administration designed to encourage employees to return to work after injury and to clarify calculation of permanent partial disability benefits; (3) restrictions on the compensability of stress-related claims; and (4) actions to increase detection of, prosecution of, and penalties for workers' compensation claims fraud.

Many states also made changes in their systems of voluntary and residual market price regulation to reduce residual market deficits and cross-subsidies from the voluntary market to the residual market, including (1) regulatory approval of significantly higher class rates for the residual market compared to the voluntary market; (2) elimination of premium discounts for larger employers insured in the residual market; and (3) increases in experience rating surcharges (discounts) for worse (better) than average loss experience for employers insured in the residual market. These changes in price regulation and in benefit design and administration were associated with slower claim cost growth, improved insurer financial results, and declining residual markets and residual market deficits during the mid-1990s. However, cost growth has recently increased in many states, and residual markets have begun to grow again.

18.6 Government Safety Regulation and Other Sources of Liability

The Occupational Safety and Health Act

The federal **Occupational Safety and Health Act** (OSHA) became effective in 1971. This act, which applies to all private sector businesses engaged in commerce with employees, provides for the promulgation and enforcement of comprehensive safety standards by the Occupational Safety and Health Administration or, if approved by the US Department of Labor, by state administrators. About one-half of the states have received approval to administer and enforce their own standards and laws. Under OSHA, businesses are subject to unannounced safety inspections and can be cited and fined for safety violations. Severe violations also can result in criminal penalties for managers. The law also requires detailed record-keeping and reporting of occupational injuries by employers.

OSHA has been criticized by many businesses and academics for imposing costs on businesses without having a major, demonstrable effect on safety. Many of the voluminous standards are alleged to represent attempts at micromanagement of safety by government bureaucrats. It is argued that the additional incentives for safety provided by OSHA are small and that they are not necessary given the strong incentives provided by workers' compensation laws, employee demand for safety, and the adverse effects of occupational injuries on business productivity. In addition, the enforcement of the law has been criticized for failing to target higher risk employers.

Studies of the effects of OSHA have failed to demonstrate a consistent negative effect on serious injury rates, but this in part may reflect difficulty in disentangling the possible effects of OSHA from the downward trend in serious injuries and fatalities that began prior to the enactment of OSHA. In recent years, the Occupational Safety and Health Administration and some of its state counterparts have experimented with ways of simplifying standards and improving the cost-effectiveness of standards and inspections.

Americans with Disabilities Act

The federal **Americans with Disabilities Act** (ADA) was enacted in 1990 and became effective in 1992. The ADA applies to businesses engaged in interstate commerce with 15 or more employees. The law makes it illegal to discriminate against qualified workers with disabilities. In particular, the law makes it illegal to deny employment or a particular type of job to a disabled person unless the individual is unable to perform the job. The law also requires businesses to reasonably accommodate disabled workers by, for example, providing ready access to facilities (e.g., ramps for wheelchairs) or redesigning jobs and equipment. Employers are relieved from the accommodation requirements if they would create "undue hardship" (substantial difficulty or expense).

Disabled persons can sue employers under tort liability for violating the ADA. At the time of its adoption, many business groups predicted large compliance costs and an explosion in litigation due in part to the vague and somewhat open-ended nature of the requirements. Early experience suggests a significant increase in litigation, but defenders of the ADA argue that litigation is relatively infrequent and that it generally has focused on egregious cases of discrimination. As suggested earlier, some observers argue that the ADA has largely eliminated the need for second injury funds as a means of promoting employment of previously injured workers. However, it currently appears unlikely that a political consensus will emerge for doing away with second injury funds.

Other Sources of Liability

Apart from responsibility for worker injuries under workers' compensation laws and potential liability to disabled persons under the ADA, businesses in recent years have faced increased frequency of lawsuits from current, prospective, and former employees that allege harm from a number of causes. The most important sources of liability include: (1) suits by employees alleging that they were wrongfully terminated or discharged; (2) suits by employees claiming that they were negligently subjected to extreme stress (if the injury is not covered by workers' compensation) or verbal harassment; (3) suits against employers alleging that the employer engaged in or failed to take reasonable actions to prevent sexual harassment; (4) suits claiming age, sex, or racial discrimination in hiring, promotion, or firing; and (5) suits alleging damages due to unfavorable or inaccurate written or oral comments made by the employer to a prospective employer of a former employee.

These suits commonly seek damages for alleged harm due to lost income, damage to a person's reputation, or mental distress. Many of these exposures generally can be insured with **employment practices liability insurance,** subject to a variety of exclusions, including intentional harm. The provisions of this insurance vary significantly across insurers. Expected claim costs from these liability exposures often can be reduced substantially with risk identification and loss control. For example, many employers have reduced their exposure to suits alleging inaccurate or prejudicial remarks to prospective employers of former employees by indicating only whether and how long the person was employed.

18.7   Summary

- State workers' compensation laws have two main features: (1) employers are required to pay specified benefits for monetary loss to injured employees without regard to employer fault or negligence, and (2) employees are not allowed to sue employers for injuries under tort law (i.e., workers' compensation is the employee's exclusive remedy).

- Workers' compensation benefits include medical benefits, benefits for total disability, benefits for permanent partial disability, and survivor benefits. For permanent partial disability payments, which represent a large proportion of the total cost of disability benefits, the amount of benefits for some injuries generally is specified in a schedule. For nonscheduled injuries, benefit amounts generally are based on the worker's estimated loss of earnings capacity.

- Alternative approaches to workers' compensation include (1) no mandatory employer-provided benefits and no tort liability of employers; (2) no mandatory benefits with employer tort liability for injuries; and (3) mandatory benefits with tort liability for employers. Compared to these alternatives, workers' compensation systems provide reasonable safety incentives and compensation for monetary loss. They also produce lower dispute resolution costs than would be the case with tort liability. Many workers are likely to find the broad structure of workers' compensation laws attractive compared to alternative systems given that workers bear the cost of whatever system is chosen.

- Employers subject to workers' compensation laws are required to purchase workers' compensation insurance or to meet state rules to qualify as a self-insurer. Five states have government monopoly workers' compensation insurers known as monopolistic state funds. Some states have state insurers, known as competitive state funds, that either compete with private insurers or serve as the residual market.

- Workers' compensation insurance policies cover workers' compensation benefits and employer tort liability for certain work-related injuries not governed by workers' compensation. Workers' compensation rates vary across numerous occupational classes in each state. A variety of methods, including experience rating, are used to modify the rate to reflect differences in expected claim costs across employers within an occupational class.

- From the mid-1980s through the early 1990s, workers' compensation claim costs grew rapidly, insurance company financial results deteriorated, and state residual markets mushroomed. Large residual markets in some states produced large operating deficits and cross-subsidies from the voluntary to the residual market. Residual market shares and deficits then declined in conjunction with residual and voluntary market rate increases and with slower growth in claims due in part to state legislation enacted to reduce cost growth. Cost and resid-

ual market growth have recently returned.

- Extensive government regulation of safety exists at both the federal and state level. Whether safety regulation has a material effect and is cost-effective have been subject to considerable debate.
- Many businesses are exposed to tort liability claims for employment practices that cause injuries apart from bodily injury and disease governed by workers' compensation law. Major tort liability exposures include allegations of illegal discrimination based on factors such as age, sex, race, and disability, and allegations of wrongful termination. Many of these liability exposures can be insured with employment practices liability insurance.

Key Terms

workers' compensation laws 388	prospective loss cost 401
employer liability laws 389	advisory rate 401
exclusive remedy 389	experience rating 401
monopolistic state funds 390	schedule rating 402
competitive state funds 390	residual market 403
temporary total disability 392	group self-insurance 403
permanent total disability 392	third-party administrators 403
permanent partial disability 393	large deductible policies 403
workers' compensation insurance coverage 400	second injury fund 404
employers' liability insurance coverage 400	Occupational Safety and Health Act 408
dual capacity suits 400	Americans with Disabilities Act 408
class rate 400	employment practices liability insurance 409

Questions and Problems

1. Assume a statewide average wage of $600 and a workers' compensation weekly disability benefit equal to two-thirds of the pre-injury wage but no more than 100 percent of the statewide average weekly wage. What percentage of pre-injury weekly wages would be replaced by workers' compensation benefits for (*a*) a worker with pre-injury weekly wages of $700? (*b*) a worker with pre-injury weekly wages of $2,500? Graph the relationship between the workers' compensation wage re-

placement rate and pre-injury wages. How would the graph change if the replacement rate were calculated after income taxes?

2. Compare and contrast permanent partial disability claims under workers' compensation with a tort liability claim for a comparable injury arising out of an off-the-job auto accident.

3. Assume that there is no workers' compensation law but that employers can be sued by employees for on-the-job injuries. Assum-

ing that the government would not prohibit such a contract, describe a contract between an employer and its employees that would have the same effect as a workers' compensation law. Would it be mutually beneficial for the employer and employees to negotiate this contract? Explain.

4. Imagine that you are on a spaceship and must decide between landing and living for five years on one of two planets. All you know about the two planets is that (*a*) one requires employers to pay workers' compensation benefits but also allows employees to sue their employer for negligence, and (*b*) the other has a traditional workers' compensation system (mandatory benefits are the employee's exclusive remedy). Which planet would you pick and why? Would your answer differ if you knew that you would suffer an on-the-job injury within two months of landing but that overall injury rates were the same for the two planets? Explain.

5. In which case will the argument for government regulation of safety be stronger? (*a*) Workers are well informed about injury risk versus workers underestimate injury risk.

(*b*) There is workers' compensation with exclusive remedy versus there is a workers' compensation system without exclusive remedy.

6. A business with a high risk of injury to employees that faces correspondingly high workers' compensation premiums argues that its workers' compensation insurance rate should be lowered by regulation to make coverage more affordable and reduce the adverse effects of high workers' compensation premiums on its ability to hire more workers and pay them higher wages. Explain why you agree or disagree with this firm's argument.

7. Which is likely to have a greater variance for the typical firm: (*a*) the average claim cost per $100 of payroll for workers' compensation claims, or (*b*) the average cost of damages, awards, and defense costs per $100 of payroll for tort liability suits alleging racial discrimination, sexual harassment, excessive stress, and so on?

8. Self-insurers do not have to contribute toward workers' compensation insurance residual market deficits. Explain how this might affect the demand for workers' compensation insurance.

Answers to Concept Checks

1. An employers' liability law restricts defenses available to employers in defending tort liability suits brought by injured employees. A workers' compensation law requires the employer to pay specified benefits to injured workers and eliminates tort liability claims against the employer.

2. If the worker's weekly wage exceeds $900 ($540/0.60), the worker's benefit will be less than 60 percent of wages because the benefit is capped at $540. If, for example, the worker's weekly wage was $1,000, the weekly benefit would equal 54 percent of the worker's pre-injury wage ($540/$1,000).

3. The worker who knew that he or she would be hurt probably would prefer to receive mandatory benefits without regard to negligence by the employer and also have the right to allege negligence and sue under tort liability for pain and suffering and any uncovered monetary losses. If the worker did not know that he or she would be hurt and realized that wages would have to be lowered to cover the cost of the system in place, the worker probably would prefer workers' compensation with its exclusive remedy rule.

References

Danzon, Patricia; and Scott Harrington. *Rate Regulation and Cost Growth in Workers' Compensation Insurance.* Washington, DC: American Enterprise Institute, 1998. (*Detailed discussion of price regulation, the resulting cross-subsidies, and the effects on growth in claim costs.*)

Hood, John. "OSHA's Trivial Pursuit." *Policy Review,* Summer 1995, pp. 59–64. (*Argues that federal safety regulations have achieved little compared to private incentives for workplace safety.*)

Rejda, George. *Social Insurance and Economic Security.* New York: Prentice-Hall, 1999. (*Provides detailed discussion of the history and features of workers' compensation.*)

United States Chamber of Commerce. *Analysis of Workers' Compensation Laws,* annual. (*Detailed statistics on workers' compensation benefit and coverage provisions across states.*)

Chapter 19

Social Security

Chapter Objectives

- Describe social security retirement, survivor, and disability benefits and the financing of these benefits.
- Explain the major factors that determine the implicit rate of return on contributions to pay-as-you-go retirement programs, such as social security.
- Discuss possible rationales for the social security retirement program versus alternatives to social security and proposed modifications to the social security retirement program.
- Describe the social security Medicare program and its financing.

19.1 Overview of Social Security

The US social security program, which was first enacted in 1935, is known more formally as the **Old-Age, Survivors, Disability, and Health Insurance (OASDHI)** program. This giant federal program has two broad components: (1) the **Old-Age, Survivors, and Disability Insurance (OASDI)** program, which provides monthly retirement benefits, benefits to dependents of deceased workers, and disability benefits; and (2) the federal **Medicare** program, which provides medical insurance to retirees and nonretirees aged 65 and over and to certain disabled persons under age 65. Coverage under OASDI is work-related: People become eligible for coverage by working and paying social security payroll tax. Coverage is compulsory for most workers. Primary exceptions include federal government employees hired before 1984 and some state and local government employees covered by alternative programs. Part A of Medicare coverage (see section 19.7) also is compulsory for almost all workers.

The social security program is a social insurance program that provides a floor of protection that many workers supplement with private pensions, savings, and insurance coverage. As you will learn in this chapter, social security has some features that are similar to private pensions and insurance arrangements and some features that are not. Similar to private pensions and insurance, the program is (1) largely self-supporting, in that OASDI benefits are largely financed through OASDI payroll taxes; (2) the amount of OASDI benefits payable to a worker increases with the amount of payroll taxes paid by the worker and by the employer on the worker's behalf; and (3) the payment of benefits is based on specified events (e.g., retirement, death, and disability) and is not conditional on meeting a means test (i.e., demonstrating financial need).

The absence of a means test distinguishes the OASDI program from pure welfare programs. Unlike private pensions and insurance, however, OASDI benefit formulas provide comparatively higher benefits in relation to taxes paid for lower paid workers than for higher paid workers. In addition, earned (accrued) benefits are not funded in advance. Instead, although there is currently some temporary partial funding, over the long run benefits for retirees and other beneficiaries are paid largely from payroll taxes on current workers on a pay-as-you-go basis.

In 2001, nearly 46 million Americans were receiving monthly OASDI benefit payments totaling $432 billion. The Medicare program had total expenditures of $244 billion.[1] OASDHI expenditures represented approximately 20 percent of total expenditures by the federal government, exceeding any other program, including national defense. OASDHI payroll taxes represented about 25 percent of total tax revenues.

19.2 Old-Age, Survivors, and Disability Insurance (OASDI) Benefits

Eligibility

Workers and specified dependents become eligible to receive OASDI benefits by paying compulsory OASDI payroll taxes (which are described in detail in section 19.3). The types of coverage for which a worker is eligible depend on the amount of wages that have been earned and the length of time that the worker has been in the workforce. The unit of measurement for determining coverage is known as a *quarter of coverage.* In 2002, for example, a worker would be credited with one quarter of coverage for each $870 in annual earnings (up to a maximum of four per year). The amount of earnings required for a quarter of coverage is increased each year to reflect growth in national average wages. Eligibility for specific benefits depends on the number of quarters of coverage.

Types of OASDI Benefits

Retirement Benefits

Table 19.1 summarizes the major types of OASDI benefits. Workers with either 40 quarters of coverage or an average of at least 1 quarter of coverage per year from age 21 until age 62 or the age of death or disability (whichever comes first) are said to be *fully insured*

[1]Information on expenditures and most other statistics reported in this chapter were obtained from the *2002 Annual Report of the Board of Trustees of the Federal Old-Age and Survivors Insurance and Disability Trust Funds* and *Status of the Social Security and Medicare Programs—A Summary of the 2002 Annual Reports,* Social Security and Medicare Boards of Trustees, Washington, DC.

TABLE 19.1 Summary of old-age, survivor, and disability insurance (OASDI) benefits.

Type of Benefit	Benefit Payable	Cessation of Benefits	Required Insured Status	Amount of Benefit
Retirement	Retired worker aged 62 or older	Death	Fully insured	100% of PIA at age 65
	Spouse aged 62 or older (or unmarried divorced spouse if married at least 10 years)	Death (or divorce if married less than 10 years)	Fully insured	50% of worker's PIA at age 65 (or 100% of working spouse's own PIA, if greater)
	Spouse under age 62 with dependent child under age 16 or disabled child	Nondisabled dependent child reaches age 16	Fully insured	50% of worker's PIA
	Unmarried dependent children	Age 18 (19 if full-time elementary or high school student; no age limit if disabled before age 22)	Fully insured	50% of worker's PIA
Survivors	Spouse under age 60 with dependent child under age 16 or disabled child	Nondisabled child reaches age 16	Fully or currently insured	75% of worker's PIA
	Spouse aged 60 or older (or divorced spouse if married at least 10 years)	Death	Fully insured	100% of PIA at age 65
	Disabled spouse aged 50–59	Age 60 or cessation of disability	Fully insured	71.5% of worker's PIA
	Unmarried dependent children	Age 18 (19 if full-time elementary or high school student; no age limit if disabled before age 22)	Fully or currently insured	75% of worker's PIA
	Deceased worker with dependent parents aged 62 and older	Death; remarriage subject to certain limitations	Fully insured	82.5% of worker's PIA at age 62 (150% total for two parents)
Disability	Disabled worker	Death, cessation of disability, or age 65 (when retirement benefits begin)	Disability insured	100% of worker's PIA
	Dependents (similar categories to retirement benefits)	Limits generally similar to retirement benefits	Disability insured	Similar to retirement benefits

Note: PIA equals primary insurance amount. Maximum benefits payable to a family generally range from 50 to 188 percent of the eligible worker's PIA (150 percent for disability). Normal retirement age gradually increased from age 65 to age 67 for people that reached age 62 during the period 2000 to 2022. Retirement benefits are adjusted downward for retirement prior to normal retirement age and adjusted upward for retirement after normal retirement age.

and qualify for monthly **retirement benefits** (which sometimes are called old-age benefits, after the program's name). Retirement benefits represented about 60 percent of annual OASDI benefits paid in 2001.

Covered workers become eligible to receive retirement benefits at age 62. The *normal retirement age* for workers that reached age 62 before the year 2000 was 65. Beginning in 2003, the normal retirement age is gradually increasing until it reaches a maximum of 67 for workers that reach age 62 in the year 2022 or later. Workers that retire and request benefits prior to the normal retirement age receive reduced benefits; workers that delay retirement receive higher benefits. Retirement benefits also are payable to eligible dependents, such as spouses and dependent children (see Table 19.1).

Survivor Benefits

Eligible beneficiaries of fully insured workers who die prior to retirement age receive monthly **survivor benefits.** These survivor benefits represent about 16 percent of total OASDI benefits paid in 2001. For workers who are fully insured at the time of death, monthly benefits are payable to spouses with dependent children, dependent children under age 16 or disabled before age 22, dependent children under age 18 (or 19 if still in high school or elementary school) or disabled before age 22, and spouses age 60 and above (or age 50 and above if the spouse is disabled) without dependent children. A deceased worker's spouse and dependent children also qualify for survivor benefits if the worker is *currently insured,* which requires the worker to have had at least 6 quarters of coverage during the 13 quarters ending in death (or, if earlier, the quarter of any disability or when the person reached age 62). A single, lump sum death benefit of $255 also is paid under certain conditions when a fully or currently insured worker dies.

An important limitation on survivor benefits is that a spouse's benefit will cease when the youngest child reaches age 16 unless the spouse has reached age 60 (age 50 if disabled). Thus, if a covered male worker dies and has a 30-year-old wife and a 4-year-old child at the time of death, the spouse's benefit would cease when the wife reaches age 42 (the child reaches age 16). The child's benefit would continue until age 18 (age 19 if the child is still in high school or elementary school or disabled before age 22). The wife again would qualify for benefits at age 60 (age 50 if disabled at the time of the worker's death or within seven years of the worker's death). The resulting gap in survivor benefits for many spouses is known as the social security blackout period.

Disability Benefits

Workers who are fully insured with at least 20 quarters of coverage during the 40 quarters ending with the onset of disability are said to be *disability insured* and qualify for monthly **disability benefits;** less restrictive eligibility rules apply to younger workers. Disability benefits represent about 18 percent of total OASDI benefits paid in 2001. Benefits are paid to disabled workers and dependents, including dependent children and the worker's spouse if there are dependent children.

In addition to meeting the quarters of coverage requirement to qualify for disability benefits, workers must meet the definition of disability. The worker must have "a mental or physical impairment that prevents the worker from engaging in any substantial gainful employment," and the disability must be expected to last for at least 12 months or result in death. This definition of disability is more stringent than the definition found in many individual and group disability plans. A five-month waiting period is required following the month of onset of disability before benefits are paid.

OASDI Benefit Amounts

Primary Insurance Amount

The social security retirement program is a special form of a defined benefit retirement plan (see Chapter 18). The basic monthly benefit payable to a worker who retires at normal retirement age is known as the **primary insurance amount (PIA),** which depends on the worker's earnings history. As shown in Table 19.1, survivor and disability benefits also depend on the worker's PIA, and benefits payable to eligible dependents are expressed as a percent of the worker's PIA.[2] In addition, the total of all benefits payable to a worker and eligible dependents is subject to a family maximum that generally varies from 150 to 188 percent of an eligible worker's PIA. The maximum is 150 percent for disability benefits.

A retired worker's PIA is calculated in two steps. (An analogous procedure is used for survivor and disability benefits.) In the first step, the worker's **average indexed monthly earnings (AIME)** is calculated. While the precise procedure is complicated, the basic idea is to first adjust or index the retired worker's annual earnings that were subject to OASDI tax (see below) up through the second year prior to age 62 (the index year) for growth in national average wages since the time the wages were earned. (The second year prior to death or disability is used for survivor and disability benefits.) For example, if the worker became 62 in 1998, his or her annual wages earned in 1980 would be multiplied by the ratio of average annual wages in 1998 to average annual wages in 1980. The highest 35 years of indexed wages and any wages earned following the index year are then summed and divided by the number of months during this period to produce the AIME.[3]

In the second step, the worker's PIA is obtained by applying a formula to the worker's AIME. In 2002, the PIA would equal: (1) 0.9 times the first $592 of AIME; (2) 0.32 times the amount of AIME, if any, between $592 and $3,567; and (3) 0.15 times the amount of AIME, if any, in excess of $3,567. For example, the PIA for a worker with an AIME of $4,000 would be

$$[0.9 \times \$592 + 0.32 \times (\$3,567 - \$592) + 0.15 \times (\$4,000 - \$3,567)] = \$1,549.50$$

The values $592 and $3,567, which are known as "bend points," increase each year in conjunction with growth in national average wages.

Figure 19.1 illustrates how the PIA varies as a function of a worker's AIME. As earnings increase, so does the PIA. The maximum PIA is achieved by workers who earned at least the maximum amount of earnings subject to OASDI taxes each year during the earnings measurement period. However, given the bend points in the formula, the increase in the PIA as the AIME increases is not linear up to this maximum. Instead, the PIA formula gives greater weight to lower earnings than higher earnings.

Figure 19.1 also shows the ratio of the PIA to a worker's AIME. This ratio provides one

---

[2]Note that while the benefit payable to a 65-year-old spouse on behalf of a retired worker equals 50 percent of the worker's PIA, a spouse who also worked and is fully insured is entitled to 100 percent of his or her own PIA at age 65 if it exceeds 50 percent of the spouse's PIA.

[3]Different rules for choosing the number of years are used for workers that became 62 prior to 1991.

FIGURE 19.1 **Primary insurance amount (PIA) versus average indexed monthly earnings (AIME) for workers retiring at age 65 in 2002.**

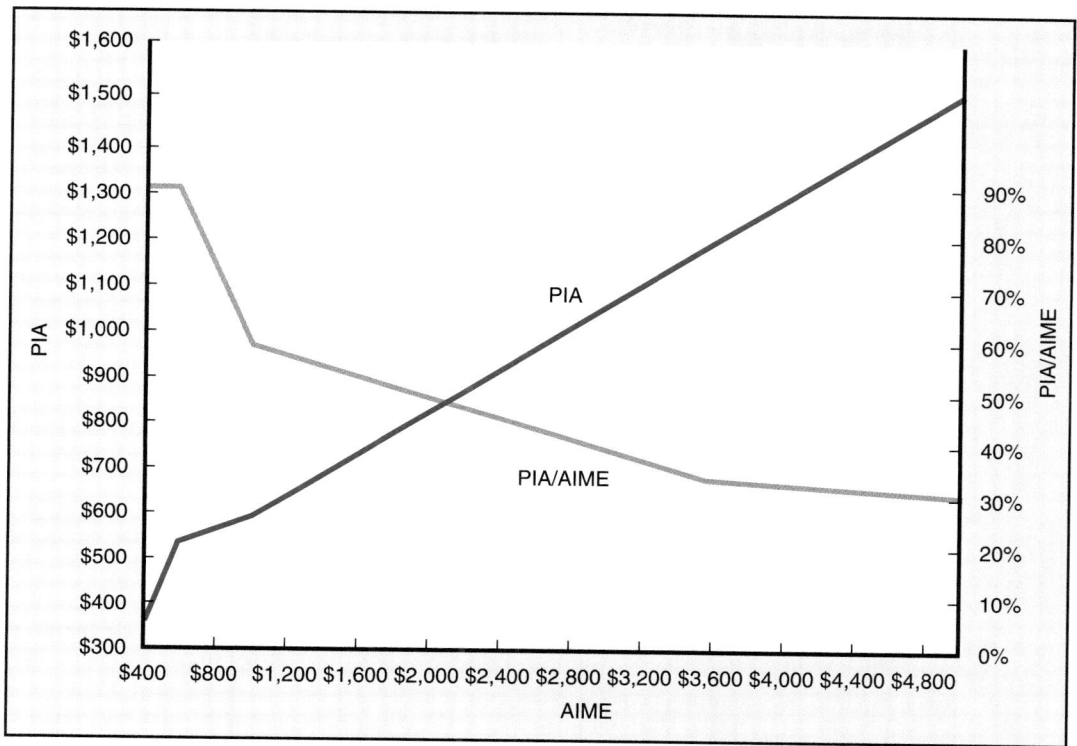

measure of the OASDI earnings replacement rate (i.e., the extent to which OASDI benefits replace a worker's prior earnings). Note that the greater weighting of lower wages produces a replacement rate that declines as wages increase. Another, and from a retiring worker's perspective, better method of calculating the replacement rate is to divide a worker's PIA by the worker's average monthly earnings in the year immediately before retirement (or the date at which other benefits begin). Table 19.2 shows replacement rates relative to earnings in the year before retirement for workers with several different levels of preretirement wages (assuming that each worker's wages grew by the national growth rate in average taxable wages each year prior to retirement).

Cost-of-living Adjustment

Monthly OASDI benefits are subject to a yearly **automatic cost-of-living adjustment (COLA)** based on the percentage change in the consumer price index (CPI). Thus, these benefits are protected against reductions in purchasing power due to general price inflation.

During the mid-1990s it often was argued that indexing social security benefits to the CPI inflated expenditures unnecessarily because technical issues with the CPI overstated increases in living costs for the average American and that correcting the price index used to adjust benefits would reduce future expenditures substantially. Whether the CPI adjustment

TABLE 19.2

Old-age benefits and replacement rates compared to earnings in prior year for workers retiring at age 65 in 2002.

Preretirement Earnings Level	2001 Annual Earnings	2002 Annual Benefits	2002 Benefits/ 2001 Earnings
Low earnings (45% of national average)	$15,263	$ 8,181	53.6%
Average earnings	33,900	13,526	39.9
High earnings (160% of national average)	54,262	17,635	32.5
Maximum earnings (earned maximum taxable wage base or more each year)	80,400	19,942	24.8

Source: Benefits and replacement rates obtained from *2002 Annual Report of the Board of Trustees of the Federal OASDI Trust Funds,* Table VI.E11. Preretirement earnings are assumed to grow by the annual growth rate in national average taxable earnings. We calculated 2001 earnings for low, average, and high earnings categories by dividing the reported annual benefit by the replacement rate.

might overstate inflation for retirees is uncertain. A number of technical corrections to the CPI formula appear to have reduced concern with this issue, at least for the time being.

Earnings Test

As noted earlier, social security benefits are not subject to a **means test;** that is, people do not have to show that they have little or no income/wealth from any source to qualify for benefits. Instead, benefits are payable for specified contingencies (retirement, disability, or death of a covered worker). Social security benefits, however, are subject to an **earnings test,** which reduces benefits if earnings exceed specified thresholds under certain conditions. In 2002, for example, persons under age 65 receiving retirement benefits would have benefits reduced by $1 for each $2 in annual earnings above $11,280 in 2002. The distinction between a means test and the social security earnings test is not a distinction without a difference. In contrast to a means test, the earnings test does not apply to nonwage/salary income, such as investment income and payments from private pension plans.

Income Taxation of Benefits

OASDI benefits for higher income recipients became subject to federal income tax in 1984. While the details are complicated, 50 percent of social security benefits is taxable as income once the sum of adjusted gross income, tax-exempt interest, and one-half of annual social security benefits exceeds specified thresholds ($25,000 for individual returns or $32,000 for joint returns; these thresholds are not indexed to wage growth or inflation). Up to 85 percent of benefits is taxable for persons with total income that exceeds higher thresholds ($34,000 for individual returns or $44,000 for joint returns). The income taxes on 50 percent of benefits to higher income beneficiaries used to help finance benefit payments, thus tilting after-tax benefits even more toward social adequacy versus individual equity.[4]

[4]Although taxing benefits annoys many higher income beneficiaries, the receipt of benefits substantially in excess of contributions by many higher income retirees that retired prior to the early 1990s (see below) annoys many baby boomers who pay higher social security taxes to support these benefits.

19.3 OASDI Financing

OASDI and HI Payroll Tax

With the exception of the use of income taxes on OASDI benefits paid by higher income beneficiaries and interest income on assets in the OASDI trust funds, OASDI benefits are financed almost exclusively from **payroll taxes.** (These taxes are known more formally as Federal Insurance Contribution Act taxes and usually are shown as FICA on your pay stub.) Both the employer and the employee pay an OASDI tax rate of 6.2 percent on the employee's annual wages up to a specified **maximum taxable wage base.** The maximum taxable wage base, $87,000 in 2003, increases each year according to growth in national average wages.

In addition to the OASDI tax, both the employee and the employer pay a tax for Medicare Part A Hospital Insurance (see section 19.7) equal to 1.45 percent of all wages; there is no maximum wage base. Thus, the combined OASDHI tax rate payable by both the employee and employer on wages up to the maximum taxable wage base is 7.65 percent (6.2 percent for OASDI plus 1.45 percent for HI). This tax rate has increased substantially since the inception of social security (see Figure 19.2).[5]

To illustrate the amount of OASDHI taxes paid, an employee making $40,000 in 2003 would pay $3,060 [$40,000 × (0.062 + 0.0145)]. The employer also would pay this

FIGURE 19.2
History of social security payroll tax rates.

Source: Data obtained from 2002 *Annual Report of the Board of Trustees of the Federal OASDI Trust Funds.*

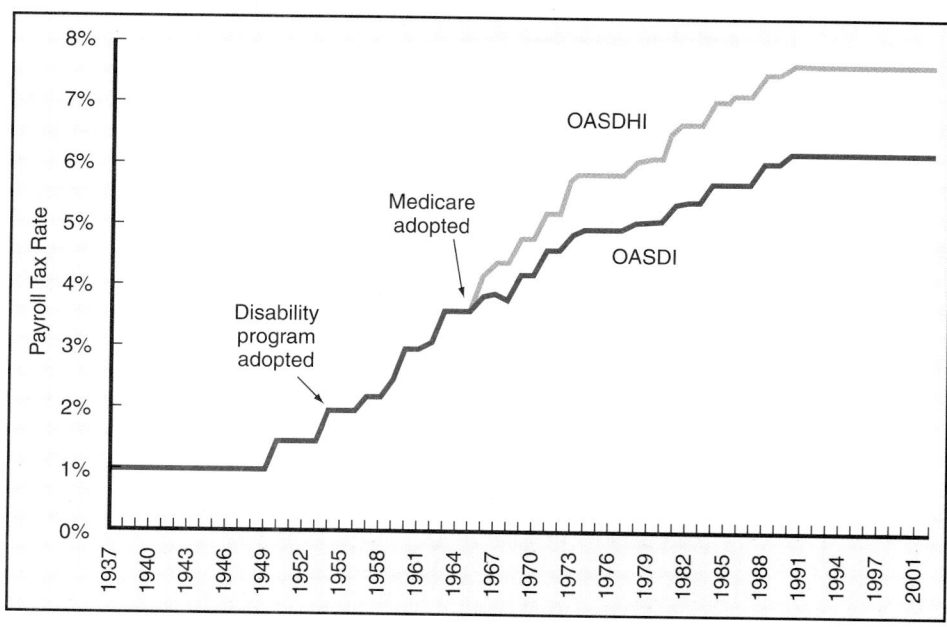

[5]Self-employed persons pay OASDI taxes equal to 12.4 percent of wages up to the maximum taxable wage base. This rate equals the combined employer-employee rate (2 × 0.062). Similarly, they pay 2.9 percent (2 × 0.145) of all wages to finance Medicare Part A. Self-employed persons are allowed to deduct one-half of their OASDHI taxes from their income subject to federal income tax, which places the income tax treatment on a par with employees who cannot deduct their share of payroll taxes but are not taxed on the employer's share (see below).

amount, producing a total tax of $6,120. An employee with wages of $100,000 in 2003 would pay $6,844 which equals 0.0765 (the combined OASDHI rate, 0.062 + 0.0145) times the maximum taxable wage base of $87,000, plus 0.0145 (the Medicare Part A rate) times $13,000 (the excess of wages over $87,000). The employer would match this amount, producing a total tax of $13,688. The employee earning $40,000 effectively pays a 15.3 percent payroll tax, and the employee earning $100,000 effectively pays an 13.7 percent payroll tax. Thus, total social security taxes effectively increase at a decreasing rate, just as social security benefits increase at a decreasing rate as wages increase. Whether social security is on average a progressive system (i.e., a system that transfers wealth from higher income persons to lower income persons) is not immediately obvious, but studies examining this issue generally conclude that the system is progressive (at least looking toward the future; see below).

Payroll taxes for social security significantly decrease the after-tax income of workers. Indeed, almost half of all employees pay more in social security taxes (combining employer and employee payments) than in income taxes. At least part of the employer's share of social security taxes generally is believed to be borne largely by workers in the form of lower wages. That is, long-run wages are lower by an amount that reflects a significant proportion of the employer tax. Moreover, at least part of any payroll tax paid by employers that is not offset by lower wages might be expected over time to produce higher prices for goods and services, as opposed to lower business profits (returns to capital).

When viewed as an employee benefit, the income tax treatment of social security payroll taxes is less favorable than the treatment of contributions to qualified retirement plans (discussed in the last chapter). Like employer contributions to a qualified retirement plan, the amount of OASDHI tax paid by the employer is not taxable as income to the employee. However, the worker's share of total OASDHI taxes is not deductible from his or her income subject to federal and state income taxes. Thus, workers' OASDHI taxes come out of after-tax wages, in contrast to tax-deductible employee contributions to a qualified retirement plan. On the other hand, only part of social security benefits is taxable as income to beneficiaries, and then only for higher income beneficiaries; whereas all benefits received from qualified plans are taxable as income.[6]

Concept Check

1. (a) How much OASDI tax and HI tax would be paid by an employee with wages of $50,000 in 2003? By an employee with wages of $120,000? (b) What would the employer pay in each case?

Pay-as-you-go Financing

As is true for social insurance programs in most western developed countries, apart from some temporary partial funding, social security benefits are largely financed using what is commonly called **pay-as-you-go financing.** In contrast to contributions to private pensions and individual deferred annuities, most payroll taxes are not invested when collected to fund the payment of accrued benefits (i.e., benefits earned to date, see Chapter 18) for participants in the program. Instead, apart from some temporary partial funding, payroll taxes on

[6]Note also that because the cost of providing employees with employee benefits as opposed to higher cash benefits is not subject to social security payroll tax, this increases the incentive for employees to take compensation in the form of employee benefits (see Chapter 16).

current wages are largely used to pay benefits to current beneficiaries. Any short-term excess of current taxes over expenditures is credited to social security trust funds. (There are separate funds for old-age/survivor benefits, disability insurance, and the hospital insurance program.)

In 1983 Congress enacted scheduled increases in OASDI payroll tax rates to build a temporary surplus to help finance increased retirement benefit costs after the turn of the century. As a result of these tax rate increases and economic growth, the OASDI trust funds had assets of $1.2 trillion at year-end 2001. Despite the size of the trust funds, however, benefits accrued to date are largely unfunded. As we explain more fully below, combined OASDI trust funds are expected to grow for another 15 years or so and then be exhausted rapidly during the third and fourth decades of this century.

Social security "surpluses" (excesses of current tax revenues over benefit payments) are used to purchase special issue, US government bonds. The interest earned is credited to the trust funds. The purchase of government securities with any positive cash flow from social security reduces the amount that the federal government otherwise would have to borrow to finance any nonsocial security expenditures in excess of general tax revenues (assuming that positive cash flow from social security does not encourage Congress to spend more or discourage cuts in spending for other programs). You should note that this process is largely equivalent to the US Treasury spending positive social security cash flow on other government programs and issuing an IOU with interest to the social security trust funds.

Projected OASDI Deficits

Each year the board of trustees of the social security program prepares 75-year projections of program expenditures, tax revenues, and trust fund balances under a variety of assumptions. Based on the "intermediate" assumptions concerning wage and employment growth, the OASDI program faces a substantial long-term deficit (see Figure 19.3). Annual payroll taxes are projected to exceed expenditures until approximately 2017 but then projected expenditures increase above projected tax revenues. The OASDI trust funds will begin to decline once credited interest on securities held is insufficient to cover the shortfall. Under these assumptions, the OASDI trust funds are projected to be exhausted around the year 2041. The total projected funding deficit over 75 years represents 1.87 percent of projected taxable payroll. As we elaborate later on, a variety of changes to the system are being discussed for reducing or eliminating the projected deficit.

Long-range social security projections are subject to considerable error. However, assuming that these projections are reasonably accurate, the question arises as to how this state of affairs came about. The simple answer is that, during the 1960s and 1970s, Congress repeatedly expanded the program and increased benefits based on favorable economic and demographic projections that were not realized. While payroll tax rates also increased substantially during this period, low real wage growth during parts of the 1970s and 1980s and unexpected (or at least unprojected) increases in the number of retirees compared to the size of the workforce due to declining birthrates have led to the projected deficit. The ratio of workers paying taxes to OASDI beneficiaries is projected (based on the board of trustees' intermediate assumptions) to be 2.1 in the year 2030, compared to the current value of 3.4, and a value of 5.1 in 1960 (see Figure 19.4). Under a pay-as-you-go system, a significant decrease in the ratio of workers to beneficiaries over time means that the tax per worker has to be significantly higher to finance a given level of benefits.

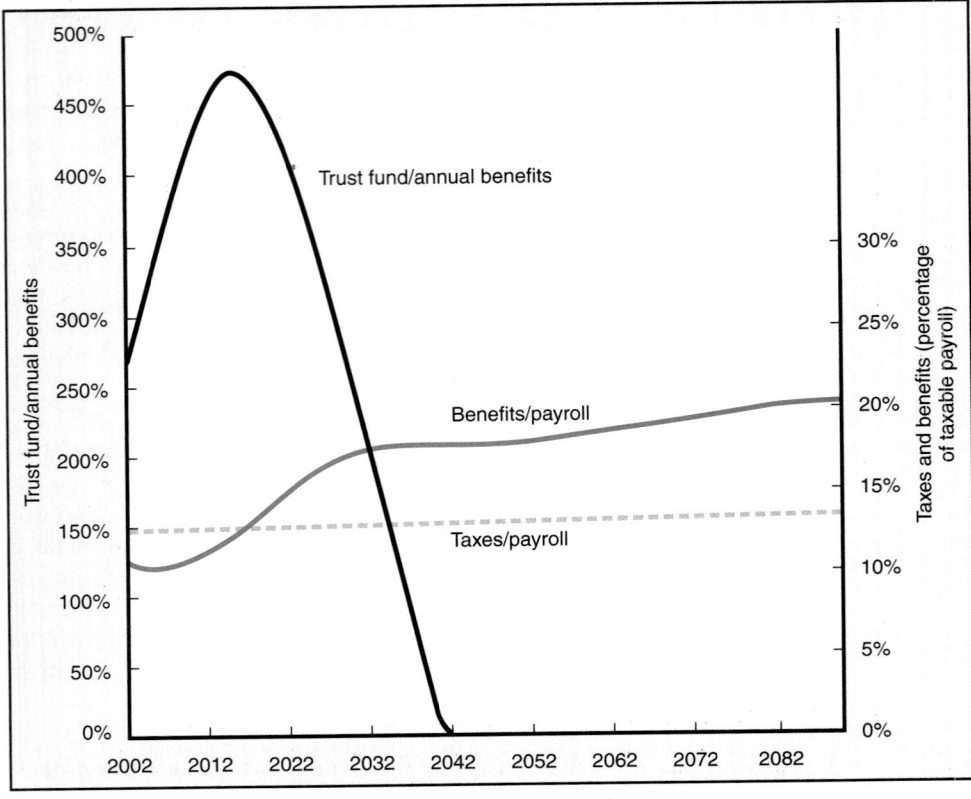

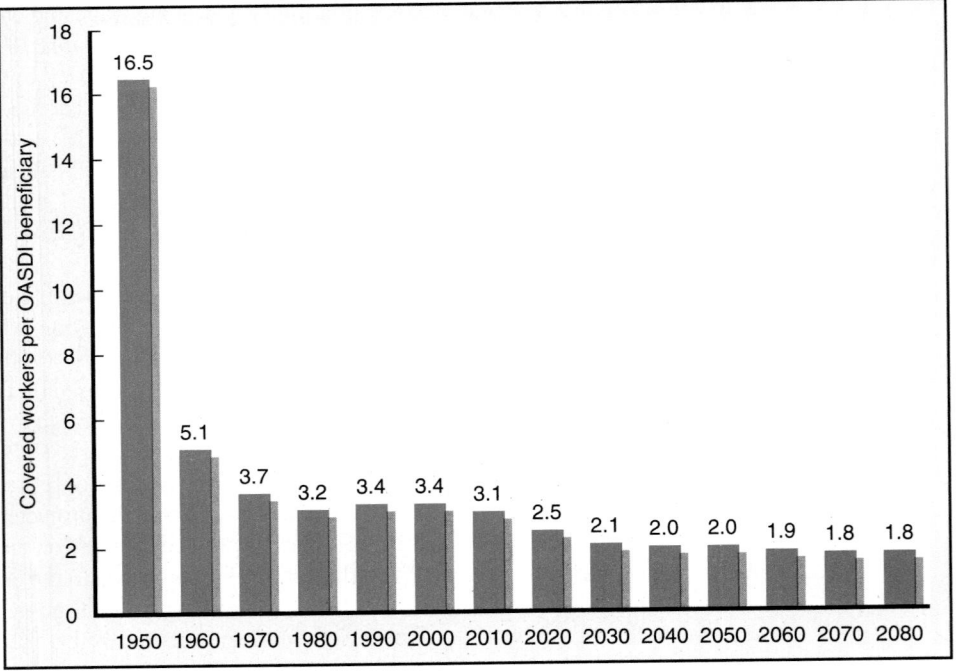

19.4 Understanding Pay-as-you-go Systems

Economic and Demographic Factors Affecting Benefits and Taxes

To help you understand the effects of wage and population (employment) growth on social security financing and the value of social security to workers who pay for the system, it is useful to examine the average benefit per recipient that can be paid in a year assuming that all taxes are used to pay benefits. This assumption highlights the essence of pay-as-you-go systems. If all taxes are used to pay benefits in a given year, the average benefit equals total tax revenues divided by the number of beneficiaries. Total tax revenues equal the product of the (combined employee-employer) payroll tax rate, the average annual taxable wage per worker, and the number of workers. As a result, the average benefit can be expressed as:

Average benefit = Tax rate × Average taxable wage × Ratio of workers to beneficiaries

This expression makes it clear that, for a given tax rate, the average benefit that can be paid under a pay-as-you-go system increases with the ratio of workers to beneficiaries, which in turn depends largely on population (employment) growth. The average benefit also increases with the level of wages, which depends on productivity growth. Conversely, the payroll tax rate that is needed to pay a given average benefit decreases as wage rates increase and as the ratio of workers to beneficiaries increases, as is seen by rearranging the terms in the above expression as follows:

$$\text{Tax rate} = \frac{\text{Average benefit}}{(\text{Average taxable wage} \times \text{Ratio of workers to beneficiaries})}$$

For example, a combined employer-employee payroll tax rate of 11.2 percent was needed to pay OASDI benefits in 1997 given that the ratio of covered workers to beneficiaries was 3.4. If the ratio had been 5.1 (the 1960 value; see Figure 19.4), a tax rate of only 7.4 percent would have been necessary to pay the same average benefit. If the ratio of covered workers to beneficiaries was 2.0 (as projected for the year 2030), a tax rate of 18.9 percent would be required to pay the same average benefit.

More generally, these expressions for the average benefit and tax rate make it clear that slow wage and population growth will produce either smaller benefits or higher tax rates if a pay-as-you go system is to be self-financing.[7] These expressions also illustrate how the long-range projected deficit for the OASDI program might be substantially reduced or eliminated without changes in benefits or taxes: Real wage growth could increase more rapidly than projected, or people, including you and your classmates, could surprise the social security forecasters by having more children. This increased birthrate would increase the number of workers compared to the number of retirees (and thus compared to the total number of beneficiaries).

Historical and Projected Implicit Rates of Return with Pay-as-you-go Financing

Has the social security program been a good deal for retirees to date? Will it provide a good deal to future retirees? While a worker's payroll taxes are not invested to fund his or her

---

[7]Increases in the maximum taxable wage base, which increase the average taxable wage, also permit higher benefits and/or a lower payroll tax rate for a given level of wages and ratio of workers to beneficiaries.

future benefits, an **implicit rate of return on payroll taxes** paid by a worker can nonetheless be calculated. While the details of the calculation generally are complicated, the basic idea is to solve for the rate of return that would be needed *if the tax payments had been (or were to be) invested* in order to accumulate a fund equal to the present value of the worker's expected monthly benefits at retirement. A similar approach is to compare the present value of expected benefits at retirement to the accumulated value of assets that could have been generated by investing payroll taxes in specified securities, such as government bonds. If the present value of expected benefits exceeds (is less than) the accumulated value of taxes, then the implicit rate of return from social security exceeds (is less than) the average return that could have been earned if the payroll taxes for the worker had been invested in the specified securities.

Historical Returns

Analyses of implicit returns under the social security retirement program indicate that the program was attractive for most workers who retired up until the early 1990s. Implicit returns were especially high for persons who retired prior to the 1980s due to legislated benefit increases prior to that time and because earlier retirees were awarded significant benefits even though they had paid taxes during only a fraction of their working years.[8] Implicit rates of return were very high (and highest) for lower paid workers due to the weighted benefit formula, but they also were very good for higher paid workers. In addition, the absolute increase in wealth from participating in the program (which can be measured as the difference between the present value of a worker's expected social security benefits at retirement and the accumulated value of the worker's taxes at reasonable interest rate assumptions) was larger for higher paid workers than for lower paid workers.

Future Returns

As suggested by our earlier discussion of the projected long-range OASDI deficit, the days of attractive implicit returns on payroll taxes are over for many if not most workers. Going forward, projections indicate comparatively low implicit returns on average and especially low and even negative implicit returns for higher paid workers, at least if both employee and employer taxes are considered. As a result, if social security were not compulsory for young and middle-aged workers, many of these workers would withdraw from the program. These withdrawals would greatly reduce the ability of the program to subsidize returns to lower paid workers.

We discussed earlier how wage growth and the ratio of workers to retirees, which depends on population growth, primarily determine the level of benefits that can be paid at a given payroll tax rate. The same framework can be used to analyze the implicit rate of return on payroll taxes for the average worker under a mature, pay-as-you-go system (i.e., a system with stable payroll tax rates and where all retirees have paid taxes over their entire work life). Under a mature, pay-as-you-go system, the implicit rate of return depends primarily on wage and population (employment) growth. Intuitively, larger wage growth over time means that retired workers who paid taxes when wages were lower can be paid higher benefits from higher national wage levels during retirement, thus increasing their implicit

[8]An analogous result occurs when new private defined pension benefit plans are created that give significant credits to workers for service prior to plan adoption.

returns. Higher population growth means that relatively more workers can be taxed to provide benefits to retired workers, again increasing the implicit rate of return.

With constant growth rates in wages and population and a number of other simplifying assumptions, it can be shown that *the long-run implicit rate of return on payroll taxes under a mature, pay-as-you-go retirement program equals the growth rate in wages plus the growth rate in population.* Thus, for example, if the (long-run) annual growth rate in wages is 4 percent and the population growth rate is 1 percent, the long-run implicit return would be 5 percent. If the population growth rate were 3 percent instead of 1 percent, the implicit return would be 7 percent. (The appendix to this chapter develops this relationship between implicit returns, wage growth, and population growth for a pay-as-you-go retirement program under simple assumptions.) Similarly, the long-run real (after-inflation) implicit rate of return, as opposed to the nominal return, on payroll taxes with a pay-as-you-go program depends on the real (after-inflation) growth rate in wages and the population growth rate. Under simplifying assumptions, *the long-run implicit real rate of return on payroll taxes equals the real growth rate in wages plus the population growth rate.*

If the population growth rate is small, a real rate of return equal to the growth rate in real wages plus the population growth rate might not be attractive to many workers. Real growth in wages on average equals the growth rate in worker productivity, which generally has been in the 1–2 percent per year range in recent decades. Small population growth rates are the norm in Western developed economies. The current birth rate in the United States, for example, will produce little population growth over the long run. With a productivity growth rate of 2 percent and zero population growth, the long-run implicit real rate of return on payroll taxes would be 2 percent, which is approximately equal to the average real rate of return on riskless government bonds in recent decades.

Whether the rate of return available under a mature pay-as-you-go system compares favorably with long-run returns that would be available on savings is complicated because it depends on factors such as the relationship between real wage growth and the long-run real rate of interest on riskless bonds, the expected return available on risky investments, risk associated with implicit rates of return on social security, and the risk tolerance of investors. However, it is reasonably safe to conclude that average implicit real rates of return in the 2–3 percent range are significantly lower than the average real returns that have historically been realized in the past and presumably can be expected in the future on a balanced portfolio of corporate stocks and bonds. As noted above, due to the social adequacy aspect of the benefit formula, higher paid workers can anticipate implicit returns that are lower than this average level and could easily be negative for the highest paid workers.

Illustration

Table 19.3 provides evidence consistent with the preceding discussion of historical and future implicit returns. It compares the present value of expected benefits to the accumulated value of payroll taxes for hypothetical male workers who retire at normal retirement age during various years based on calculations from a 1992 study by Robert Myers and Bruce Schobel. This study compares the present value of expected retirement benefits to the accumulated values of taxes based on numerous assumptions for workers at two different wage levels: (1) workers earning the national average wage each year prior to retirement, and (2) workers earning the maximum wage subject to OASDI tax each year.

TABLE 19.3

Estimated present value of expected retirement benefits compared to accumulated value of taxes for male workers who retire at normal retirement age.

Year of Retirement	Earnings Level	Accumulated Taxes (3)	Present Value of Expected Benefits (4)	Absolute Gain or Loss (4) − (3)	Relative Gain or Loss (4) / (3)
1960	Average	$ 1,974	$ 13,986	$ 12,012	709%
	Maximum	2,756	15,731	12,975	571
1970	Average	7,020	23,376	16,356	333
	Maximum	9,040	26,347	17,307	291
1980	Average	24,502	66,531	42,029	272
	Maximum	34,258	84,400	50,142	246
1991	Average	101,084	117,409	16,325	116
	Maximum	166,722	159,896	−6,826	96
2002	Average	237,232	202,760	−34,472	85
	Maximum	439,554	298,295	−141,259	68
2009	Average	369,762	280,228	−89,534	76
	Maximum	735,118	431,644	−303,474	59
2020	Average	653,034	496,001	−157,033	76
	Maximum	1,481,788	787,309	−694,479	53
2027	Average	889,310	683,981	−205,329	77
	Maximum	2,197,030	1,084,443	−1,112,587	49

Source: Data obtained from Robert Myers and Bruce Schobel, "An Updated Money's-Worth Analysis of Social Security Retirement Benefits," *Transactions* (Society of Actuaries) 44 (1992), pp. 247–70. We adjusted the reported figures to reflect combined employer-employee taxes. Average earner earned the national average wages each year from age 21 until the year prior to retirement; maximum earner earned wages equal to the maximum earnings subject to OASDI taxes.

While the study's results are based on the employee's share of payroll taxes only, we converted these estimates to reflect combined employer-employee taxes.[9]

The results shown in Table 19.3 indicate that prior to 1991 the present value of expected benefits at retirement age exceeded the accumulated value of taxes for both average and maximum earners. The ratio of the present value of expected benefits to accumulated taxes is larger for the average earner than for the maximum earner, which reflects the social adequacy feature of the weighted-benefit formula. The absolute difference between the present value of expected benefits and accumulated taxes prior to 1991, however, is greater for the maximum earner than for the average earner. In other words, the total gain compared to the accumulated value of taxes was higher for higher paid workers. This makes it very difficult to argue that higher paid workers subsidized lower paid workers during the first 50 years of the program.

[9]Myers and Schobel note that "conversion from one to the other is a trivial calculation." The specific assumptions used by these authors that provide the basis for Table 19.3 include: (1) workers survive until normal retirement age and then receive benefits; (2) investment returns used to accumulate taxes for years prior to 1991 equal 2.25 percent for 1937–1950, the returns paid on the special-purpose US government bonds acquired by the social security trust funds for 1951–1990, and the projected interest rates (intermediate assumptions) for 1991and later years reported in the *1991 OASDI Trustees Report*; (3) expected retirement benefits are discounted using a 2 percent real interest rate and for mortality using historical and projected postretirement mortality rates for different age cohorts from the *1991 OASDI Trustees Report*. Thus, the present value of expected benefits at retirement reflects the probabilities of survival after reaching age 65, but the accumulated tax estimates assume that the worker survives until retirement. The accumulated tax calculations reflect taxes used to pay survivor benefits, as well as taxes for retirement benefits. While this overstates the accumulated value of taxes needed to pay retirement benefits only, assuming that workers survive until retirement overstates the present value of expected benefits for the typical worker who participates in the program.

The results for later years present a different picture. For maximum earners retiring in 1991 and later years, accumulated taxes exceed the present value of expected benefits. The ratio of the present value of expected benefits to accumulated taxes for maximum earners retiring in 2027 is 49 percent. In effect these workers receive no benefit from employer taxes paid on their behalf (recall that employers pay half of the combined tax). For average earners, the accumulated taxes exceed the present value of expected benefits for workers who retire in 2002 and later years. Although Myers and Schobel do not analyze lower paid workers, the present value of expected benefits presumably would still exceed the accumulated taxes for many workers with less than average earnings.

Based on the findings of this and other studies, there is little doubt that workers who retired up until the late 1980s generally received favorable implicit returns and that average returns will be low in the future and negative for many higher paid workers. Specific calculations, however, must be based on numerous assumptions, and realized results over time for different groups of workers will reflect changes in economic and demographic factors compared to the values projected at any point in time. For example, stronger real growth in wages and higher than projected birthrates will increase implicit returns to all workers.

In addition, specific workers may receive returns much different from the average worker. For example, females generally have higher implicit returns than males due to their longer life expectancy at retirement. (The results of the Myers and Schobel study indicate that the present value of expected retirement benefits for average earner females who retired in 1991 was 141 percent of the accumulated value of combined employer-employee taxes, compared to the 116 percent value for males shown in Table 19.3.) Moreover, all else being equal, married couples with one spouse who does not work outside the home for pay and thus who is not a covered worker are entitled to a retirement benefit equal to 150 percent of the worker's PIA (see Table 19.1). The 50 percent spouse's benefit significantly increases the implicit return on payroll taxes paid for these workers.

Concept Checks

2. Other things being equal and assuming that total taxes equal total benefits, how would each of the following affect the average benefit that can be paid over time to retirees under a pay-as-you-go plan?
   (*a*) An increase in the payroll tax rate.
   (*b*) A decrease in population growth.
   (*c*) A long-run increase in the unemployment rate.
3. Other things being equal, how would each of the following affect the long-run implicit rate of return available with a pay-as-you-go retirement program?
   (*a*) An increase in the birthrate.
   (*b*) A decrease in real productivity growth.
   (*c*) A cure for cancer (assuming no increase in the retirement age).

19.5   Why Have Social Security?

Why have the social security retirement program or, alternatively, should there be some other type of compulsory retirement income program or no program at all? Arguments for government insurance in general often suggest that problems associated with private insurance, such as moral hazard, adverse selection, and correlated losses, limit the amount of private insurance that is sold and sometimes provide a rationale for government insurance. For example, it sometimes is argued that mandatory government insurance can mitigate adverse selection by forcing lower risk persons or businesses to buy coverage or that government insurance possibly might produce economies of scale in administrative costs. A counterargument is that governments generally will not be able to design insurance arrangements that are better able to mitigate these problems than private insurance arrangements. In addition, it often is suggested that government insurance arrangements in practice may have fewer incentives for controlling moral hazard, thus driving up costs, and that political pressure may cause prices for government insurance to be substantially inadequate, at least for some buyers.

With respect to the social security retirement program, the discussion in the previous section suggests that it may be difficult to make a compelling case for the program given the low implicit rates of return that are likely to be available in a mature, pay-as-you-go system. Opinions concerning the efficacy of the OASDI program vary widely, even among people who have carefully studied the program. At one end of the spectrum, some observers regard the OASDI program as an ingenious method of providing a floor of inflation-protected income with an appropriate emphasis on social adequacy. At the other extreme, some people regard the program's history as one in which several generations of workers essentially voted themselves large wealth transfers at the expense of future generations—with a significant reduction in both private savings and economic growth as by-products. Going forward, they regard the program as a sneaky form of redistribution that leads subsidized beneficiaries to believe that they are not the recipients of government handouts financed by taxes on other people.

We obviously will not resolve this debate. We can, however, increase your understanding of the program and help you to develop an informed opinion by discussing three additional aspects of pay-as-you-go systems that affect their attractiveness (or lack thereof) over the long run: (1) the ability to finance automatic cost-of-living adjustments; (2) the possible advantages of a compulsory retirement program with a social adequacy component (i.e., with what basically amounts to cross-subsidies from higher to lower paid workers); and (3) the possible effects of social security on savings, capital formation, and economic growth. While the discussion focuses on retirement benefits, much of what we say also applies to the social security survivor and disability benefit programs.

Self-financing COLAs

One argument for a public, pay-as-you-go retirement plan is that it might provide an efficient, self-financing means of indexing retirement benefits to postretirement inflation. Moreover, private annuity contracts that provide inflation-indexed benefits for a fixed, advance premium are not available. One explanation for the lack of privately provided inflation-indexed benefits is that changes in indexed benefits due to inflation will be very highly correlated across pension plan participants or annuitants. As a result, providing indexed benefits would expose pension plan sponsors and insurance companies to substantial risk that cannot be reduced by selling large numbers of contracts or other types of insurance. The resulting need to hold a large amount of capital to guarantee indexed benefits drives up the cost of providing these contracts and makes them unattractive. Retirees therefore face the risk that unexpected inflation during retirement could significantly erode the purchasing power of any fixed monthly benefits financed through preretirement savings.

A pay-as-you-go mandatory retirement system potentially can solve the correlated risk problem that impedes inflation-linked private benefits. To illustrate, recall that for a given payroll tax rate and ratio of workers to retirees, the average benefit that can be paid from current taxes depends on average wages. As a result, as long as increases in wages on average keep pace with inflation, tax revenues will tend to grow automatically with inflation. As a result, indexing benefits to inflation is essentially self-financing under a pay-as-you-go system. Inflation leads to higher wages and thus taxes, which in turn can be used to pay higher benefits. Thus, a pay-as-you-go program might be desirable given that correlated risk generally prevents inflation-indexed retirement benefits from being offered in the private marketplace.

To be sure, retirees can partially hedge reductions in retirement income purchasing power without a government program by investing retirement funds in assets with returns that are positively correlated with inflation (e.g., by investing in real estate). However, this strategy is imperfect and exposes retirees to significant risk. In 1997 the US Treasury began selling bonds with returns indexed to inflation. Investing retirement savings in these bonds could allow retirees to be protected against inflation, but the expected yields on these bonds are significantly lower than on traditional government bonds (risk reduction is not free). Thus, despite the introduction of inflation-indexed government bonds, one advantage of pay-as-you-go social security benefits is the ability to readily finance inflation-indexed benefits.

Compulsion and Social Adequacy

The decades of high or reasonably attractive average implicit returns under social security are over (absent much higher economic growth and birthrates than are currently projected). The difficult question therefore arises as to whether there is anything inherently desirable about forcing people to participate in a social security retirement program that provides higher implicit returns to workers with low wages and relatively low or negative returns to average and higher paid workers.

Subsidizing Low Wage Workers May Be Inevitable

In a world without a social security retirement program or alternative government program, many lower paid workers might save little for retirement so that many elderly persons would have very low income without any government program. This outcome probably would not be politically viable for a variety of reasons. For one, workers who fail to save can vote for politicians that support transfer payments. In addition, due to compassion or altruism, many workers who would save for their own retirement may support policies that require them to finance payments to workers who save little or nothing. Some form of income transfer program also might be supported because it would reduce the need for younger people to provide direct support to elderly parents, and because it would reduce possible spillover effects from large numbers of poor, elderly people (e.g., higher crime rates if grandma becomes a burglar).

The adoption of some program that provides some subsidy to people who save little for retirement therefore appears inevitable. Workers who view the social security program as a "bad deal" and who would like to pull out need to recognize that taxes on middle- and higher-wage workers will likely be used to transfer income to retirees with low preretirement wages with or without social security. One advantage of the compulsory social security retirement program in this regard is that it requires workers to pay something in order to receive subsidized benefits. While payroll taxes are not saved and invested, workers in essence are required to contribute something toward the cost of their benefits.

"Earned" rather than Means-tested Benefits

There also are several potential advantages of paying "socially adequate" benefits without regard to need (i.e., to not having a means test). The costs of administering a means test are avoided, and any means test will likely involve some evasion (e.g., hiding wealth). Making benefits contingent on a means test also can significantly reduce the incentive for some people to save. Moreover, it sometimes is argued that the absence of a means test and the (admittedly erroneous) belief by many lower paid workers that they have paid the full cost of their benefits enhance self-esteem. Holding income constant, many elderly parents and their working children might be happier if the parents receive social security benefits instead of means-tested benefits or increased support from their children.

Effect on Savings, Capital Formation, and Economic Growth

The effects of social security on savings, capital formation, and economic growth also should be considered when deciding whether it is desirable to have such a system. The effect of social security on aggregate savings has been debated for many years. Recall that pay-as-you-go financing does not produce any significant amount of savings. If the promise of future social security benefits reduces incentives for many workers to save for retirement and aggregate savings therefore decline, less capital will be available for investment, thus raising the cost of capital and reducing investment and economic growth. Downward pressure on savings also may arise because social security payroll taxes reduce disposable income. And, to the extent that payroll taxes increase the cost of labor, social security taxes will reduce employment and aggregate output. Less savings will tend to occur if fewer people work and if people on average work fewer hours.

The extent to which social security reduces savings is uncertain in theory and practice. Some economists argue that because favorable implicit rates of return on taxes throughout most of the program's history have increased the total wealth of covered workers, at least part of this additional wealth probably has been saved. It also has been argued (we are not making this up) that social security might encourage workers to save money to help their children pay higher payroll taxes in the future. A more important practical issue is how much additional savings would be generated if social security were substantially modified to promote savings. This issue plays an important role in a number of social security reform proposals that we describe briefly in the next section.

19.6   Proposed Changes and Alternatives to Social Security

Policymakers currently are debating a variety of changes or alternatives to the social security retirement program, in large part because projected future deficits very likely will necessitate some action. A number of proposals attempt to eliminate projected deficits without fundamentally altering the system; other proposals would fundamentally alter the system. In general, unless the government modifies benefits that have been accrued to date by covered workers, the projected OASDI deficits imply that substantially higher taxes of some kind will be needed.[10]

Changes That Would Maintain the Basic Structure of OASDI

Changes in Benefits and Payroll Taxes

One approach to eliminating the projected OASDI deficit without fundamentally altering the system is to enact benefit reductions and/or payroll tax increases. Proposals for reducing benefits include reducing the cost-of-living adjustment or omitting the adjustment in one or more years, increasing the normal retirement age above currently scheduled amounts (perhaps by linking it to changes in average life expectancy), and reducing after-tax benefits by making more benefits taxable as income. Proposals for raising payroll taxes include raising the payroll tax rate and raising or eliminating the limit on the amount of wages subject to OASDI tax. Benefit reductions will cause current and future retirees who have already paid substantial taxes to bear a significant part of the cost of eliminating the deficit. Payroll tax increases will shift more of the cost of the deficits to younger and future workers.

Investing Trust Fund Assets in Common Stocks

Another proposal would maintain the basic program but require that all or part of the projected excess of tax revenues over expenditures for the next 15 years or so be invested in common stocks. The main rationale would be the hope of achieving higher returns for the OASDI trust fund. Positive social security cash flow probably would be invested in stock index funds to help resolve the thorny issue of which stocks to pick (but an index would have to be specified). Unanswered questions concerning this proposal include its effect on stock prices and on any overall federal deficit if these funds are no longer used to buy government bonds, as well as the possible adverse ramifications if stock returns are significantly lower than expected. Indeed, the significant stock market declines during 2000–2002 have probably eliminated the possibility that this change will be adopted any time soon.

Crediting the Trust Funds with Any Operating Budget Surplus

It has sometimes been proposed that any surpluses from the federal operating budget (i.e., from programs other than social security) be credited to the social security trust funds to reduce the social security deficit, as opposed to reducing income taxes or reducing the national debt. It is currently uncertain whether material operating surpluses will arise and, if so, whether they will be credited to social security. However, the use of any surplus of general revenues over general operating costs to shore up the OASDI program would move the system away from its historical self-supporting basis.

Changes That Would Modify the Basic Structure of OASDI

Privatization Proposals

Other proposals for dealing with the long-range OASDI deficit would modify the basic

---

[10]While estimates vary considerably, the unfunded liability for OASDI benefits accrued by workers to date (including persons currently receiving benefits and current workers who are eligible for future benefits based on payment of taxes to date) has been estimated to exceed $5 trillion. Note that the unfunded liability is not a hard figure. It could be eliminated by legislation that changed benefits or taxes.

structure of the program. Perhaps most important, **privatization proposals** would require workers to invest either part of the current OASDI tax or an additional percentage of wages in tax-deferred accounts similar to individual retirement accounts (see Chapter 18). One approach would offset part of the retirement income from these accounts against promised benefits. An alternative approach would gradually replace the social security retirement program with compulsory individual retirement savings accounts, perhaps with a subsidy for lower income workers. One potential advantage of these approaches is that they might yield higher overall returns to workers than with a purely pay-as-you-go system. A second potential advantage is that they could increase savings and economic growth.

Note that privatization proposals for replacing the pay-as-you-go retirement plan with individual accounts (with or without any subsidy to low wage workers) most likely would not eliminate the need for benefit reductions for current or future retirees or higher taxes on workers. Unless benefits are reduced, partial or full privatization of social security still would likely require many workers to pay significant taxes to pay unfunded benefits in addition to contributing to their individual accounts. Privatization proposals also would entail sizable administrative costs for employers and program administrators, especially in relation to earnings for low-paid workers.

Converting Social Security to Welfare

Another alternative to social security would be a means-tested retirement benefit financed perhaps all or in part with general revenues as opposed to payroll taxes. Retirees with income or wealth lower than specified minimums would eventually receive payments analogous to welfare. Other workers eventually would rely exclusively on private pension plans and other private savings; they would not qualify for benefits. Higher overall taxes on workers still would be needed to pay social security benefits accrued prior to adoption of a means test unless the government reduced benefits payable without a means test.

Rapid adoption and implementation of a means test would produce large negative implicit returns for workers in their 40s, 50s, and 60s who have already paid large amounts in OASDI taxes (although this in part might be offset by their possibly paying lower taxes in the future compared to alternative approaches). As noted previously, means tests also are imperfect, costly to administer, and possibly degrading to recipients.

The welfare approach also would have to address a difficult trade-off between adequacy of means-tested benefits and incentives for saving. Any level of means-tested benefits deemed reasonably adequate might discourage large numbers of workers from saving anything for retirement, thus increasing the costs of the program, which would have to be borne by taxpayers. This incentive (moral hazard) problem helps explain why most proposals for fundamentally modifying social security involve some form of compulsory, individual savings.

19.7   Medicare

Medicare Benefits

Medicare benefits for specified medical expenses are available to most persons aged 65 and above and to certain disabled people under age 65. There are two main parts of Medicare: (1) Medicare Part A Hospital Insurance and (2) Medicare Part B Supplementary Medical Insurance.

Medicare Part A Hospital Insurance (HI) provides coverage for up to 90 days of in-patient hospitalization for each "spell of illness," subject to a deductible for each spell and co-insurance for the 61st through the 90th days. There also is a lifetime reserve of an additional 60 days. Part A also provides up to 100 days of coverage in a skilled nursing facility, as well as coverage of certain home health care services and hospice care.

Hospitals have been reimbursed under Medicare since the late 1980s according to a schedule of payments for different *diagnostic related groups* (DRGs). Under this system, which is intended to control costs and reduce excessive utilization, hospitals are paid scheduled amounts (which vary by geographic location and whether the hospital is urban or rural) for different ailments (diagnoses), as opposed to being paid for charges on a fee-for-service basis.

Medicare Part B Supplementary Medical Insurance (SMI) pays 80 percent of expenses above a $100 annual deductible for physicians' services, outpatient hospital services, home health care visits not covered by HI coverage, and a wide variety of other medical services. Most prescription drugs are not covered (unless the person is hospitalized), although that limitation may change soon in view of the rising costs and usage of such drugs by seniors. As is discussed further below, a monthly premium is required for SMI coverage. All persons covered by the HI program are covered unless they reject coverage.

Physicians are reimbursed under the SMI program based on a fee scale (known as the *resource-based relative-value scale*), as opposed to charges. The fee scale is designed to reflect the time, skill, and intensity of the service provided, as well as geographical differences. Physicians who accept "assignment" of Medicare claims agree to accept these fees as payment in full. They bill Medicare directly for fees above the annual deductible and 20 percent co-insurance paid by the patient. Medicare pays 95 percent of the fee schedule for services provided by physicians who do not accept assignment of claims, and the maximum amounts that these physicians can charge their patients is limited. The patient pays the physician and then is reimbursed by Medicare subject to the annual deductible and co-insurance. In an effort to control rapidly rising Medicare costs (see below), the program has been modified in recent years to encourage Medicare beneficiaries to be covered by a health maintenance organization (HMO) type program (known as the Medicare + Choice program) instead of the traditional program.

Medicare Financing

Recall from Section 19.3 that the Medicare HI program is financed with a payroll tax equal to 1.45 percent of all wages. This amount is paid by both the employee and the employer (self-employed workers pay 2.9 percent). Like OASDI, the HI program faces significant projected deficits. The HI Trust Fund is projected to be depleted by the year 2030. At year-end 2001, the long-range (75-year) projected deficit was 2 percent of payroll based on the Medicare Board of Trustees' intermediate assumptions.

The SMI program is not financed by payroll taxes. Beneficiaries pay monthly premiums ($54 in 2002) that are modified each year to cover approximately 25 percent of the total cost of the program. The remaining 75 percent of costs for the SMI program is financed in large part with general Treasury revenues (i.e., individual and corporate income taxes and so on) and in small part by interest on assets in the SMI Trust Fund.

Like the HI program, the amount of general revenue financing needed for SMI coverage is projected to continue to grow rapidly in the future, thus putting upward pressure on any federal budget deficit. Proposals for addressing this problem include measures to help control medical expenditures, such as more managed care, and increasing premiums to pay a larger share of SMI costs, perhaps by raising premiums for higher income retirees.

Private Coverage to Supplement Medicare

Because Medicare contains deductibles, co-insurance, and other limitations on coverage, many persons purchase private medical insurance to supplement Medicare, which commonly is known as medigap coverage. To reduce the likelihood that some financially unsophisticated, elderly people will be duped by unscrupulous insurers and agents (e.g., in extreme cases by selling them multiple high-priced, low-benefit policies), most states have legislation providing some standardization of medigap coverage and regulating the marketing of these policies. Federal legislation concerning the coverage and marketing of medigap policies applies absent state legislation. In addition to nonemployment related supplementary coverage, many employers provide some amount of post-retirement health benefits.

19.8   Summary

- The federal Old-Age, Survivors, Disability, and Health Insurance (OASDHI) program provides monthly benefits (known as OASDI benefits) to retired workers, eligible dependents of deceased workers, and disabled workers. The health insurance program (Medicare) provides limited coverage for hospitalization and other specified medical expenses for persons aged 65 and older and for certain disabled persons under age 65.

- OASDI benefit amounts are based on the worker's average earnings subject to OASDI payroll taxes prior to receiving benefits, with past earnings adjusted for subsequent wage growth. Eligible beneficiaries do not have to satisfy a means test to receive benefits. The benefit formula provides relatively greater benefits compared to payroll taxes paid for lower paid workers, thus stressing social adequacy of benefits. Benefits are automatically adjusted each year to reflect changes in the consumer price index.

- Employees pay a payroll tax equal to 6.2 percent of wages up to the maximum taxable wage base in a year ($87,000 in 2003) to finance OASDI benefits. The employer matches this amount. In addition, the employee and employer each pay 1.45 percent of the employee's entire wage to finance Medicare Part A Hospital Insurance (HI). Medicare Part B Supplementary Medical Insurance (SMI) is financed with monthly premiums from covered persons and with general tax revenues.

- OASDHI benefits are largely financed on a pay-as-you-go basis. Current payroll taxes are largely used to pay current benefits without advance funding of the projected cost of accrued benefits. Although the OASDI trust funds are expected to grow substantially for another decade, significant long-run deficits are projected for both OASDI and the Medicare HI program.

- Until around 1990, the social security retirement program on average provided attractive implicit rates of return on payroll taxes paid by workers and employers prior to retirement. The average implicit rate of return for subsequent retirees is projected to be relatively low and negative for many higher paid workers. As is true concerning projected OASDI deficits, low implicit rates of return are due in large part to increases in the number of beneficiaries compared to the number of workers paying taxes.

- Important characteristics of the pay-as-you-go social security system include: (*a*) the ability of the pay-as-you-go approach to provide cost-of-living adjustments on a self-financing basis, since inflation generally increases wages and thus payroll tax revenues; (*b*) the requirement that workers who otherwise might save little for retirement pay something in exchange for future support by other persons; (*c*) the absence of a means test, thus avoiding the disadvantages of means testing; and (*d*) the potential adverse effects of the program on savings and economic growth.

- Proposals for reducing or eliminating projected OASDHI deficits and otherwise modifying social security include: (*a*) raise payroll taxes; (*b*) re-

duce future benefits; (*c*) replace all or part of the retirement program with compulsory individual savings; and (*d*) make workers satisfy a means test to receive benefits. Regardless of the approach or approaches used, current and future workers almost surely will have to pay higher taxes unless the government reduces benefits accrued as of the date of any change in the system.

Key Terms

Questions and Problems

1. Briefly describe the major categories of OASDI and Medicare benefits.

2. Using the payroll tax rates discussed in the text and the maximum taxable wage base for 2003 of $87,000, calculate the payroll tax (OASDI and HI combined) that would be paid by the employee and the employer for each of the following amounts of annual wages: (*a*) $20,000; (*b*) $35,000; (*c*) $50,000; (*d*) $100,000; and (*e*) $150,000.

3. Graph the ratio of the payroll tax paid by an employee to wages for the amounts of wages in question 2.

4. How do each of the following affect the social adequacy of social security benefits compared to individual equity?

(*a*) The formula used to derive the primary insurance amount.

(*b*) Limiting the maximum amount of wages subject to payroll tax.

(*c*) Making higher income beneficiaries pay income tax on part of their social security benefits.

5. A regressive tax is a tax that represents a greater proportion of income or earnings for lower income people than for higher income people. Is the financing of social security with payroll taxes regressive? Does the way in which benefits are designed to promote social adequacy affect your answer?

6. Contrast pay-as-you-go financing with financing of private pension plan benefits.

7. Other factors held constant, explain how each of the following factors would affect the average amount of benefits that could be paid under a pay-as-you-go retirement plan:

    (*a*) A decrease in the payroll tax rate.

    (*b*) Removal of the maximum limit on annual wages subject to OASDI tax without increasing the maximum benefit payable.

    (*c*) A long-run increase in productivity growth.

    (*d*) A long-run increase in the birthrate.

8. How does the social security earnings test differ from a means test?

9. The following changes would reduce social security expenditures for and/or increase tax revenues from higher paid workers and thus help eliminate the projected long-range OASDI deficits: (*a*) remove the maximum limit on wages subject to OASDI tax without increasing the maximum benefit amount; (*b*) subject all social security benefits for higher income beneficiaries to income tax; and (*c*) eliminate benefits for high income beneficiaries. Why might these changes undermine support for social security and ultimately lead to more radical changes?

10. Why is it likely to be very costly for private pension plan sponsors and insurance companies to provide guaranteed automatic cost-of-living adjustments to pension and annuity benefits? How does pay-as-you-go financing of retirement benefits facilitate the provision of automatic cost-of-living adjustments to benefits?

11. Briefly explain the possible effects of the social security retirement program on private savings and economic growth.

Answers to Concept Checks

1. (*a*) The worker with $50,000 in wages would pay $3,100 (0.062 × $50,000) in OASDI taxes and $725 (0.0145 × $50,000) in HI taxes. The worker with $120,000 in wages would pay $5,394 (0.062 × $87,000, the 2003 OASDI maximum taxable wage base) in OASDI taxes and $1,740 (0.0145 × $120,000) in HI taxes (there is no maximum wage base).

    (*b*) The employer would match the amounts calculated above.

2. (*a*) An increase in the payroll tax increases the average benefit that can be paid because more tax revenues are available to pay benefits.

    (*b*) A decrease in population growth decreases the average benefit that can be paid because there will be relatively fewer workers compared to beneficiaries at any point in time.

    (*c*) A long-run increase in the unemployment rate decreases the average benefit that can be paid because there will be fewer workers paying taxes.

3. (*a*) An increase in the birthrate increases population growth and the number of future workers paying taxes compared to the number of retirees at any point in time, thus increasing the long-run implicit rate of return.

    (*b*) A decrease in real productivity growth reduces real wage growth, which in turn will reduce payroll tax revenues available to pay beneficiaries and thus reduce the implicit rate of return.

    (*c*) A cure for cancer would reduce the long-run implicit rate of return because it would increase the number of beneficiaries compared to the number of workers.

References

2002 Annual Report of the Board of Trustees of the Federal Old-Age and Survivors Insurance and Disability Insurance Trust Funds. Washington, DC: US Government Printing Office, 2002. (*Comprehensive discussion of OASDI financing, including projected benefits, taxes, and trust fund balances. Available at Social Security Administration's website: http://www.ssa.gov.*)

Boadway, Robin W.; and David E. Wildasin. *Public Sector Economics.* 2nd ed. New York: Little, Brown, 1984. (*Chapter 14 contains an informative introduction to the economics of social security and welfare, including redistributive aspects and effects on savings.*)

Myers, Robert J.; and Bruce Schobel. "An Updated Money's-Worth Analysis of Social Security Retirement Benefits." *Transactions* (Society of Actuaries) 44 (1992), pp. 242–70. (*Detailed comparisons of the present value of expected social security retirement benefits to accumulated payroll taxes.*)

Rejda, George E. *Social Insurance and Economic Security.* 5th ed. Englewood Cliffs, NJ: Prentice Hall, 1994. (*Comprehensive treatment of social security and other social insurance programs.*)

Status of the Social Security and Medicare Programs—A Summary of the 2002 Annual Reports. Washington, DC: US Government Printing Office, 2002. (*Summary information on OASDI and Medicare financing. Available at http://www.ssa.gov.*)

Appendix 19A

Implicit Rate of Return on Payroll Taxes with Pay-As-You-Go Financing

The effects of wage and population growth on implicit returns under a pay-as-you-go retirement program can be illustrated easily using the simple assumption that people live for two periods. In the first period, they are born, work, and pay taxes. In the second period, they retire, receive benefits, and then die. We also will assume that all people have the same wages in a given period and that retirees in a given period all receive the same benefit. We emphasize that the key implications of this analysis also hold for more realistic assumptions.

Assuming that all taxes in a given year are used to pay benefits, it is first useful to write the expression for average benefits that was used in the text in a slightly different way:

$$\text{Benefit}_t = \tau \times \text{Wage}_t \times \text{Workers}_t/\text{Retirees}_t$$

where, for period t, Benefit_t is the average benefit, Wage_t equals wages earned by each worker, Workers_t is the number of workers, Retirees_t is the number of retirees, and τ is the payroll tax rate. If wages then are assumed to grow at a rate of g per period, wages during period t equal $1 + g$ times wages in period $t - 1$ [i.e., $\text{Wage}_t = (1 + g)\text{Wage}_{t-1}$]. Likewise, if the population grows at a rate of s per period, the number of workers that pay taxes in period t equals $1 + s$ times the number of retirees in period t [i.e., $\text{Workers}_t = (1 + s)\text{Retirees}_t$]. (Note that $\text{Retirees}_t = \text{Workers}_{t-1}$; workers in period $t - 1$ become retirees in period t.) Substituting these relations into the above expression, the benefit paid to retirees in period t can be written:

$$\text{Benefit}_t = \tau \times (1 + g)\text{Wage}_{t-1} \times (1 + s)$$

Period t retirees had to pay taxes on their wages prior to retirement to receive this benefit. The amount of tax paid was $\tau \times \text{Wage}_{t-1}$ (the payroll tax rate times the wages while they worked).

Armed with these results, we now can get to the punch line. The implicit rate of return in this simple case can be calculated directly by comparing the retirement benefit to the tax paid by the retiree. The rate of return equals the excess of the benefit over the tax paid divided by the tax paid. Given that the tax paid is $\tau \times \text{Wage}_{t-1}$, the rate of return equals:

$$\text{Rate of return}_t = (\text{Benefit}_t - \tau \times \text{Wage}_{t-1})/(\tau \times \text{Wage}_{t-1})$$

Substituting the earlier expression for the benefit in period t, the expression for the rate of return for period t retirees reduces to:

$$\text{Rate of return}_t = (1 + g)(1 + s) - 1 \approx g + s$$

where $\approx$ indicates "is approximately equal to." In words, the implicit rate of return on taxes paid equals the growth rate in wages plus the population growth rate.

Thus far we have considered the nominal rate of return, as opposed to the real (after-inflation) rate of return. As noted in the text, it can be readily shown that *the real implicit rate of return on taxes paid equals the real growth rate in wages plus the population growth rate.* Because real wage growth will be approximately equal to productivity growth, this result implies that the real implicit rate of return will approximately equal the productivity growth rate plus the population growth rate. As we mentioned above, this result holds for more realistic assumptions. For example, the same simple result arises when workers work and are retired for multiple periods when the growth rate in wages and the population growth rate are constant over time.

20

Risk Management and Shareholder Wealth

Chapter Objectives

- Analyze corporate risk management using the concepts and tools of modern financial management.
- Explain the fundamental determinants of firm value: (1) expected cash flows and (2) the cost of capital.
- Describe how investor diversification affects the cost of capital.
- Explain why corporate risk reduction often does not affect the cost of capital.
- Analyze how corporate risk reduction affects expected cash flows.

20.1 Principles of Business Valuation

In Chapter 2 we stated that the objective of business risk management is to increase the value of the business to its owners. In this chapter, we first explain the fundamental determinants of business value and then analyze how corporate risk management affects value.

Valuation Formula

A business's value is defined as the present (discounted) value of its expected net cash flows, where net cash flows equal cash inflows minus cash outflows. Thus, to calculate firm value you must first estimate the firm's expected cash flows and then discount the expected cash flows using the appropriate discount rate.

A simple example will illustrate how to calculate a firm's value. Schmit Enterprises is a corporation that will exist for one year. It has no outstanding debt, and the net cash flows

TABLE 20.1
Probability
distribution of
cash flows per
share for
Schmit
Enterprises.

Outcome	Probability	End-of-Year Cash Flow per Share
No lawsuit	0.9	$100
Lawsuit	0.1	$100 − $30 = $70

Expected cash flow = (0.9 × $100) + (0.1 × $70) = $97

per share of its common stock at the end of the year are forecasted to be $100 if it does not lose a lawsuit. However, there is a 10 percent chance that it will lose a lawsuit that will cost $30 per share. We ignore taxes for simplicity. These assumptions imply that the probability distribution for the firm's cash flows is as given in Table 20.1.

The expected cash flow per share at the end of the year is $97 (see Table 20.1). To find the value of Schmit Enterprises today, we discount the end-of-year expected cash flow back to the present. Assuming that the appropriate discount rate is 13.5 percent, the value of one share of stock in Schmit Enterprises today is

$$\text{Value} = \frac{\$97}{1 + 0.135} = \$85.46 \qquad (20.1)$$

This is the value of Schmit Enterprises without undertaking any risk management activities. In the subsequent sections we will examine how various risk management activities might affect the probability distribution of cash flows, the discount rate, and thus the stock value of Schmit Enterprises.

It is important to emphasize that we are interested in the value of Schmit Enterprises *today*—that is, prior to knowing what the actual cash flows at the end of the year will be. If you bought one share of Schmit Enterprises today, it would likely cost $85.46. At the end of the year, you would expect the value of your share to be greater than $85.46. Specifically, you would expect it to be worth 13.5 percent more than $85.46, since 13.5 percent is the discount rate used to value the firm. Your actual return for the year, however, would depend on the firm's actual cash flows at the end of the year. If the firm's actual cash flows equal $100 (no lawsuit), then each share of stock will be worth $100 at the end of the year. This will produce a rate of return on your investment equal to 17.01 percent [(100 − 85.46)/85.46]. If Schmit Enterprises's cash flow per share at the end of the year is $70, then each share of stock will be worth $70 at the end of the year, and your realized rate of return will be −18.09 percent [(70 − 85.46)/85.46]. Thus, your realized rate of return will be either 17.01 percent or −18.09 percent, which implies an expected rate of return equal to 13.5 percent [(17.01 × 0.9) − (18.09 × 0.1)].

This example illustrates the two fundamental determinants of value: (1) the level and timing of expected cash flows, and (2) the interest rate used to discount each cash flow. More complicated examples that increase the number of years considered or that have more complicated cash flow distributions do not change these basic determinants of value. When examining the effects of risk management on value, we must examine how risk management affects each of these fundamental determinants.

In general, the value of a firm can be written as follows:

$$\text{Value} = \sum_{t=1}^{\infty} \frac{\text{Expected net cash flow in year } t}{(1 + r)^t} \qquad (20.2)$$

where r is the appropriate discount rate. The appropriate discount rate is the rate of return an investor could expect to earn on an alternative investment with the same risk as the firm's cash flows. It is important to emphasize that the appropriate discount rate depends on the risk of the cash flows. Because investors generally are risk averse, cash flows that are more uncertain should have a higher discount rate. The appropriate discount rate is called the **opportunity cost of capital,** because it is the expected return an investor could have received had the person invested in a similar risk investment.

Concept Checks

1. Assume Schmit Enterprises's end-of-year cash flow is as described by Table 20.1, but suppose that the price of a share of stock is $90 today.
   (*a*) What are the possible rates of return for the coming year?
   (*b*) What is the expected rate of return?
2. Compare your answer to part (*b*) of question 1 to the example in the text where the stock price today is $85.46 and the expected rate of return is 13.5 percent. What does this example illustrate about the relationship between the expected rate of return on a share of stock and its price, holding the expected cash flows constant?

Components of the Opportunity Cost of Capital

The opportunity cost of capital has two basic components. The first component is the return needed to compensate investors for the time value of money. The second component is the expected return needed to compensate investors for risk. Since the first component only reflects the time value of money and does not consider risk, it is equal to the return an investor could earn on a risk free asset, such as US government bonds. This return usually is called the **risk-free rate** of return. The second component is the additional compensation (premium) over the risk-free rate that is needed to compensate investors for risk. This additional expected return is called the **risk premium.** As mentioned earlier, risk aversion suggests that as the cash flows become riskier, the risk premium increases. As we will see shortly, this intuition is correct, provided that risk is appropriately defined from the perspective of the investor.

As an example, assume that the rate of return on government bonds (the risk-free rate) is 7.0 percent. If the uncertainty associated with the cash flows of Schmit Enterprises causes investors to require a 6.5 percent expected return as compensation for risk, then the risk premium is 6.5 percent. Adding the risk-free rate and the risk premium yields a 13.5 percent opportunity cost of capital for Schmit Enterprises. This is the discount rate that should be used when finding the present value of Schmit Enterprises's expected cash flows. If another firm, Browne Brothers Inc., had riskier cash flows than Schmit Enterprises, the risk premium for Browne Brothers would be higher than 6.5 percent, and the discount rate used to find the value of Browne Brothers would be higher. The important point is that the opportunity cost of capital for a particular expected cash flow should reflect the uncertainty about the expected cash flow. Thus, the valuation formula (equation 20.2) incorporates the expected value of cash flows (in the numerator) and the risk of cash flows (in the denominator).

Compensation for Risk

The risk premium for Schmit Enterprises in the previous example was assumed to be 6.5 percent. We now discuss determinants of the risk premium. Intuitively, as the risk of the cash flows increases, one would expect the risk premium to increase because investors require compensation for bearing more risk. We must recognize, however, that some risk can be eliminated by investors at virtually zero cost by holding well-diversified portfolios. If investors can diversify away some risk at zero cost, then they will not need to be compensated for this risk. Obviously, any security that provides compensation for risk that can be eliminated at zero cost will be highly desirable to well-diversified investors. However, competition among these investors will bid up the price of such securities (which lowers the expected return) until the investors receive compensation only for that risk that they cannot eliminate through diversification.[1]

To make these ideas more concrete, suppose that the stock of Schmit Enterprises is priced so that investors receive compensation for *all* risk, including risk that investors can eliminate through diversification. In particular, assume that 6.5 percent is the appropriate risk premium for risk that cannot be diversified away by investors, but that the stock is currently priced using 8.0 percent as the risk premium. Assuming a risk-free rate of 7.0 percent, the stock is therefore priced using a discount rate equal to 15.0 percent (when it should be priced using 13.5 percent) so that:

$$\text{Price} = \frac{\$97}{1 + 0.15} = \$84.35 \tag{20.3}$$

An investor buying a share of stock at $84.35 would expect a return of 15.0 percent—the expected value of each share at the end of the year equals $97, which is 15.0 percent higher than the purchase price of $84.35. If the investor were well-diversified, this would be viewed as a good investment because the expected return is greater than the amount needed, 13.5 percent, to compensate the investor for that risk that cannot be eliminated through diversification. Other well-diversified investors also would view the stock of Schmit Enterprises as an attractive investment—that is, they would expect a return greater than what is needed to compensate them for risk that they could not diversify away. Stated differently, the price of the stock is too low because it reflects risk that investors can diversify away on their own. Well-diversified investors would start buying the stock, which would increase the price. As the price increased, the expected return would decrease. Investors would continue to buy the stock and bid up its price until the stock price reached $85.46, which produces the appropriate expected return of 13.5 percent. Thus, in equilibrium Schmit Enterprises's stock would be priced to provide compensation only for risk that could not be eliminated by investors holding diversified portfolios.

This discussion highlights that there are two types of risk.[2] Risk that can be eliminated by investors by holding diversified portfolios is called **diversifiable risk.** Risk that cannot be eliminated by diversification is called **nondiversifiable risk.** Recall from Chapter 4 the intuition for why risk can be eliminated by diversification: When holding a diversified portfolio, the good outcomes (high returns) of some firms tend to offset the bad outcomes of other firms. This "offsetting" effect will work when the events that affect one firm are uncorrelated with the events that affect other firms. Thus, the type of risk that can be

---

[1]Students who have studied finance will notice that this is the logic underlying the capital asset pricing model (CAPM).

[2]Various models are used to calculate the opportunity cost of capital for firms in practice and controversy exists regarding the appropriate measure of risk. However, almost all models adopt the fundamental principle that some risk can be diversified away by investors and therefore only nondiversifiable risk affects the opportunity cost of capital.

FIGURE 20.1
The components of a firm's total risk and their influence on the opportunity cost of capital.

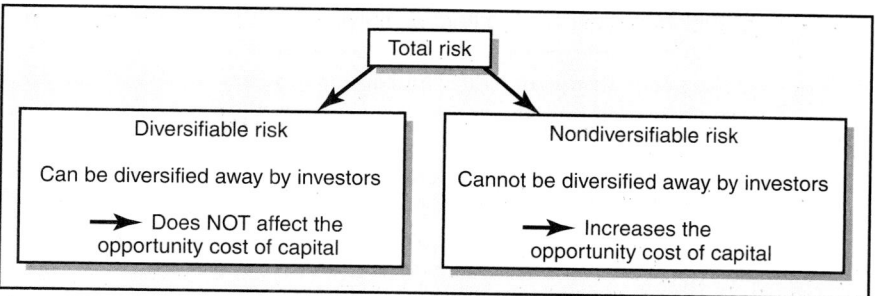

diversified away is the risk due to events that are "firm specific," such as an explosion at a plant, theft, a decision by the government to award a company a new contract, and so on. Because the risk that can be diversified away is the risk of events that are specific or idiosyncratic to a particular firm, diversifiable risk often is called *firm-specific risk, idiosyncratic risk,* or *nonsystematic risk.*

In contrast, the risk due to events that affect all firms cannot be diversified away. For example, changes in general economic activity, as reflected in interest rate changes or the growth in gross national product (GNP), affect most firms. Consequently, risk associated with general economic activity cannot be diversified away by investors. Intuitively, when all firms are affected by an event, there are no good outcomes to offset bad outcomes in a portfolio of many stocks. Since risk that cannot be diversified away arises from common, marketwide events, nondiversifiable risk often is called *market risk* or *systematic risk.*

Figure 20.1 summarizes this discussion. The total risk of a firm can be divided into two categories: diversifiable risk and nondiversifiable risk. The appropriate discount rate (the required return) is unaffected by diversifiable risk. The intuition again is that investors can eliminate diversifiable risk on their own at no cost so that investors do not require compensation for this type of risk. Nondiversifiable risk, however, affects the opportunity cost of capital because investors require compensation for risk that they cannot diversify away on their own.

20.2   Risk Management and the Opportunity Cost of Capital

We now examine how risk management affects the discount rate (opportunity cost of capital) that should be used when valuing a firm. From the previous discussion we know that the discount rate equals the risk-free rate plus a risk premium. The risk-free rate is the rate of return on government bonds and cannot be influenced by firm decisions. Thus, if risk management is to affect the discount rate it must affect the risk premium. Recall that the risk premium depends only on the amount of nondiversifiable risk. As a result, if risk management decreases diversifiable risk only (the risk that investors can eliminate by holding diversified portfolios), the risk premium will be unaffected and so the opportunity cost of capital will be unaffected.

Risk management activities like insurance purchases and loss control expenditures typically only reduce a firm's diversifiable risk. The types of risk that insurance companies tend to insure also are risks that the insurance company can largely diversify by selling insurance to many different policyholders. If insurance companies can diversify the risk, then so can shareholders by holding well-diversified portfolios, and thus insurance purchases generally do not reduce a firm's opportunity cost of capital. The risk that is reduced through loss control also tends to be firm-specific risk. For example, the frequency and severity of workplace accidents and product failures are likely to be uncorrelated across firms. These firm-specific risks can be diversified by shareholders and so loss control activities usually will not decrease a firm's opportunity cost of capital.

Recall that nondiversifiable risk exists because there are unexpected events that affect the value of most firms. For example, an unexpected change in aggregate consumer demand is likely to change the value of all companies. Obviously, individual firm actions cannot influence the occurrence of these systematic events, but individual firm actions can reduce the sensitivity of the firm's cash flows to these events. For example, a firm could hedge against nondiversifiable risk, which would decrease the firm's opportunity cost of capital. Even when this occurs, however, one must be careful before concluding that firm's value has been increased. The reason is that, while a decrease in nondiversifiable risk will decrease the opportunity cost of capital, it also is likely to decrease the firm's expected cash flows. To see this, note that when a firm hedges nondiversifiable risk, it is shifting this risk to someone else who cannot eliminate it through diversification. The party who accepts nondiversifiable risk will require compensation for taking on this risk, and the cost of compensating the other party will decrease the firm's cash flows. As a consequence, reducing nondiversifiable risk has an ambiguous effect on value. The cost of shifting nondiversifiable risk to someone else (as reflected in lower expected cash flows) often will offset the benefit of reducing the discount rate. Provided everyone prices nondiversifiable risk in the same way, the two effects will offset each other perfectly. The amount that the firm must pay the other party for accepting the nondiversifiable risk would equal the amount by which the value of the firm would otherwise have increased from the lower discount rate.[3]

In summary, risk management is unlikely to decrease the opportunity cost of capital for firms with well-diversified shareholders because risk management activities generally decrease the type of risk (diversifiable risk) that shareholders can eliminate on their own by holding diversified portfolios. If risk management does decrease nondiversifiable risk and therefore the opportunity cost of capital, the cost of doing so is likely to negate the benefits of reducing the discount rate.

Concept Check

3. Identify whether each of the following loss exposures is likely to involve nondiversifiable risk or diversifiable risk: (*a*) revenue losses for an automaker due to higher interest rates, and (*b*) property losses due to theft.

20.3   Risk Management and Expected Cash Flows

The previous section explained that corporate risk reduction is unlikely to affect the firm's opportunity cost of capital (the denominators in equation 20.2). Therefore, if corporate risk

---

[3]Similarly, insurers will demand compensation (in the form of a higher premium) for insuring nondiversifiable risk. Therefore, the effect of such insurance on a firm's opportunity cost of capital will be offset by lower expected cash flows because the firm must pay a higher premium loading.

reduction is to increase shareholder wealth, risk reduction must increase expected cash flows to shareholders (the numerators in equation 20.2). We show how this can occur in this section. For concreteness, our discussion focuses on corporate insurance purchases. The main points, however, generally apply to other corporate activities, such as hedging and loss control, that reduce the variability of cash flows.

Table 20.2 provides an overview of the effects of corporate insurance purchases on a firm's expected cash flows to shareholders. The main disadvantage of purchasing insurance is that the firm must pay the loading on the insurance premium, which—holding all other factors constant—decreases expected cash flows. As introduced in Chapter 9, there are four main advantages of purchasing insurance:

1. By bundling insurance coverage with claim processing and loss control services, a firm may be able to lower the costs of obtaining these services.

2. Insurance reduces the likelihood that the firm will have to raise new funds to finance losses or to finance new investment projects. Since raising new funds, either by borrowing from a bank or issuing new debt or equity securities, can be costly, insurance can be beneficial because it reduces the likelihood of having to incur these costs and of forgoing otherwise profitable investments because of these costs.

3. Insurance reduces the likelihood that a firm will experience financial distress, which lowers expected bankruptcy costs. Financial distress also can impose costs on other parties who contract with the firm, such as employees, suppliers, lenders, and customers. Firms with a higher likelihood of financial distress find that these other parties offer less attractive contractual terms—for example, employees may require additional compensation to work for a firm with a higher likelihood of financial distress. By reducing the likelihood of financial distress, insurance therefore increases the firm's expected cash flows.

TABLE 20.2
Main effects of purchasing insurance on expected cash flows.

Description	Effect on Expected Cash Flows
Pay loading on insurance premiums	Decrease
Decrease cost of services from insurers	Increase
• Claims processing services	
• Loss control services	
Decrease likelihood of having to raise new funds	Increase
• To pay for losses	
• To finance new projects	
Decrease likelihood of financial distress	Increase
• Decreases expected bankruptcy costs	
• Improves contractual terms with other claimants (i.e., lenders, suppliers, employees, customers)	
Reduce expected tax payments	Increase
• Tax benefits of insurance	
• Ability to increase debt-related tax shields	

4. Insurance can reduce a firm's expected tax payments. The direct tax effects of insurance are discussed in detail in Chapter 21. Risk reduction also can indirectly reduce expected tax payments by allowing a firm to increase its use of debt financing, which increases interest tax deductions.

Notice that many of the advantages of purchasing insurance result from decreasing the likelihood that either shareholders or other claimants will incur some additional cost, beyond the loss that is being insured. For example, insurance reduces both the probability that the firm will have to raise costly external capital and the probability that other claimants will incur costs due to financial distress. Thus, many of the benefits of insurance arise because insurance reduces the probability that some cost beyond the insured loss will be incurred. In this respect, insurance can be viewed as a loss control device: The purchase of insurance reduces the expected cost of indirect losses.

The remainder of this chapter illustrates the main cash flow effects of purchasing insurance with a series of examples. To present the ideas as simply as possible, we do not use an elaborate example that simultaneously incorporates all of the main effects; instead, each effect is examined in isolation. In practice, however, these effects are not mutually exclusive; they all are potentially relevant for a firm deciding how much insurance to purchase.

Insurance Premium Loadings

We begin by considering how the purchase of insurance would affect the share price of Schmit Enterprises if none of the benefits shown in Table 20.2 were present. Recall from section 20.1 that with no insurance Schmit's end-of-year per share cash flows will be $100 with probability 0.9 and $70 with probability 0.1 and that an opportunity cost of capital of 13.5 percent implies that the share price is $85.46. Note in this example that there are no taxes. And since Schmit Enterprises only exists for one year and its end-of-year cash flows are always positive, the firm will not have to raise new funds in the future, and it has no chance of financial distress. Finally, we will assume that if insurance is purchased, the insurer provides no services other than reimbursing the losses that the firm incurs. Under all these assumptions, none of the potential benefits of insurance listed in Table 20.2 exist.

Insurance with No Loading

Suppose that Schmit Enterprises purchases a liability insurance policy with coverage equal to $30 per share of stock and a premium of $3 per share of stock. For simplicity we assume that the insurance premium is paid at the end of the year. Because the premium is equal to expected claim costs (0.1 is the probability of a claim and the size of a claim is $30 per share), the premium has no loading. In this case, the purchase of insurance will not change Schmit's expected cash flows and therefore will not change its share price.

To verify this, Table 20.3 summarizes how the insurance policy changes the firm's cash flows. If a lawsuit does not occur, then the cash flow per share equals $100 minus the per share insurance premium of $3, which equals $97. If the firm loses the lawsuit, then the firm's cash flow per share equals $100 minus the loss of $30, plus the reimbursement from the insurance company of $30, minus the insurance premium of $3. Thus, insurance causes the cash flow to equal $97 regardless of whether a lawsuit occurs. Referring to Table 20.1, $97 also is the value of expected cash flows without the insurance policy.

TABLE 20.3   **Probability distribution for Schmit Enterprises's cash flow per share with $30 of insurance coverage per share and a premium of $3 per share.**

Outcome	Probability	End-of-Year Cash Flow
No lawsuit	0.9	$100 − $3 = $97
Lawsuit	0.1	$100 − $30 + $30 − $3 = $97
Expected cash flow = (0.9 × $97) + (0.1 × $97) = $97		

In this case, the insurance policy does not change the firm's expected cash flows; it just makes cash flows more predictable. But from section 20.2 we know that the shareholders can diversify away the cash flow risk on their own so that insurance will not change the discount rate (13.5 percent). Consequently, the share price is unchanged by the insurance policy.

Insurance with a Loading

Insurance premiums of course usually will exceed expected claim costs because of the insurer's administrative and capital costs. Suppose that the markup over claim costs is 40 percent, so that the insurance premium is $3(1.40) = $4.20 per share, which again for simplicity is paid at the end of the year. Under these conditions, the firm's cash flows are given by Table 20.4. If a lawsuit does not occur, then the firm's cash flow equals $95.80 ($100 per share minus the insurance premium of $4.20). If the firm loses the lawsuit, then the firm's cash flow also equals $95.80 ($100 minus the loss of $30, plus the $30 reimbursement from the insurance company, minus the insurance premium of $4.20). Comparing this scenario to Table 20.1 indicates that purchasing insurance at a premium of $4.20 causes Schmit's expected cash flow to be less than the expected cash flow without insurance ($95.80 versus $97). The difference is due to the loading of $1.20 on the insurance policy. The price per share with insurance equals $95.80/1.135 = $84.41, which is less than the share price if no insurance is purchased ($85.46). The lower price is due to the present value of the costs of the insurance policy's loading ($1.20/1.135). Intuitively, the firm can save the cost of the loading by not purchasing insurance.

These examples illustrate that by purchasing insurance a firm shifts its expected losses to an insurer. However, since the insurance premium exceeds the value of expected losses, purchasing the insurance policy reduces the firm's expected cash flows.

TABLE 20.4   **Probability distribution for Schmit Enterprises's cash flow per share with $30 of insurance coverage per share and a premium of $4.20 per share.**

Outcome	Probability	End-of-Year Cash Flow
No lawsuit	0.9	$100 − $4.20 = $95.80
Lawsuit	0.1	$100 − $30 + $30 − $4.20 = $95.80
Expected cash flow = (0.9 × $95.80) + (0.1 × $95.80) = $95.80		

Services Provided by Insurers

The previous example assumed that the insurer reimbursed losses but provided no other services. In practice, insurers frequently provide loss control services and almost always provide claims processing services; these services are bundled with the promise to pay claims. A firm, however, also can hire its own employees to provide these services or purchase them from noninsurance companies. In addition, many insurers sell these services without bundling them with insurance.

The key issue is whether bundling loss control and claims processing services with an insurer's promise to pay claims is the least-cost way of purchasing the services demanded by the firm. For a given level of quality, if the firm can obtain these services at the lowest cost through an insurance policy, then the firm would have an incentive to purchase insurance apart from any value obtained from the insurer's promise to pay claims.

To illustrate, assume that the cash flows in the Schmit Enterprises example are prior to the purchase of the loss control and claims processing services and that the cost for Schmit Enterprises to purchase these services in the absence of insurance is $1.50 per share. Then, without insurance, its cash flows will be either $98.50 ($100 − $1.50) or $68.50 ($100 − $30 − $1.50), and its expected cash flows will equal $95.50. As illustrated in Table 20.4, its expected cash flow with insurance is $95.80, which is $0.30 per share higher than without insurance. Assuming the insurer provides the same level and quality of services as Schmit Enterprises desires, the firm has higher expected cash flow by purchasing insurance. The reason is that the cost of purchasing these services when they are bundled with insurance is lower than the cost of purchasing these services elsewhere. Specifically, the implicit cost of the services bundled with insurance is the loading on the policy ($1.20 per share), whereas the cost of purchasing the services elsewhere is $1.50 per share.

Why would bundling services with the promise to pay claims result in lower costs? One reason is that with bundling the service provider has greater incentive to provide high quality service. For example, a firm that both provides loss control services and pays losses has an additional incentive to identify and undertake cost-effective loss control measures. A firm that both provides claims processing services and pays losses has an additional incentive to identify fraudulent claims. If the service and financial responsibility for claims are not bundled, additional resources must be expended in order to monitor the service provider and design contracts that provide proper incentives. When monitoring is too costly and contract design efforts ineffective, bundling the services with the financial responsibility for paying losses can be the least-cost method of obtaining services.

Insurance and the Likelihood of Having to Raise Costly External Funds

Raising New Funds to Pay for Losses

In the Schmit Enterprises example, the firm had enough internal funds to pay the losses from a lawsuit. Sometimes, however, a firm will not have sufficient internal funds to pay all uninsured losses. When this occurs, the firm must find a way to pay losses from future cash flows or else declare bankruptcy. Well-functioning financial markets provide a way of using future cash flows. For example, by borrowing money from a bank or issuing new debt or equity securities, a firm can raise the funds needed to pay losses and then use future cash flows to pay back the bank or the new investors. The use of bank borrowings or new security issues to pay losses does not imply that the loss is borne by the bank or the new investors. The loss is borne by the owners of the firm at the time of the loss because a portion of the firm's future cash flows will be used to repay the bank or the new investors.

Although firms can pay losses by issuing new securities or borrowing, it is important to recognize that raising external funds to pay losses can be costly. In addition to the transaction costs paid to commercial and investment bankers, newly issued securities might be underpriced (i.e., new investors pay less than the securities' real worth). When a firm issues underpriced securities, the existing owners essentially give part of the firm's value to the new investors. The decision facing risk managers and financial managers is whether the firm should pay losses by raising new funds following the loss or purchase insurance prior to the loss. This decision involves a comparison of the expected cost of raising new funds versus the premium loading on the insurance. Appendix 20A provides an example to highlight these issues.

Increased Likelihood of Raising New Funds for New Investment Projects

Even if a firm has sufficient internal funds to pay losses, the use of these funds can create an opportunity cost that was ignored in the previous example. The use of internal funds to pay uninsured losses implies that fewer internal funds will be available to finance new projects. Consequently, firms that use internal funds to pay uninsured losses are more likely to have to issue costly new securities to finance new projects. The costs of raising new funds reduce the value of new projects. In some cases, issuance and underpricing costs can be so high that a firm will forgo what otherwise would have been value-increasing investment projects. In addition to savings on the costs of issuing securities, insurance can improve investment decisions in these cases.

To illustrate, assume Sommers Corp. will have a valuable investment opportunity available at the end of the year (e.g., building a new plant). In particular, if Sommers invests $25 million, the project will generate additional cash flows that have a present value of $27 million. Using the language of finance, this project is a positive net present value project, where **net present value (NPV)** is defined as the present value of the project's net cash flows. This particular project has NPV equal to $2 million ($27 − $25). Sommers Corp. has several alternative methods of financing the $25 million investment, including issuing new equity or new debt at the end of the year. Issuing securities, however, is costly because of security underwriting costs paid to investment bankers and because the new securities may be underpriced. The costs of issuing securities reduce the **adjusted net present value** of the project; that is, the net present value minus the costs associated with financing the project.[4] For example, if the costs of issuing securities were equal to $1 million, then the adjusted net present value would be only $1 million ($2 − $1). If the costs of issuing securities were equal to $2.5 million, then the adjusted net present value would be negative ($2 − $2.5) and Sommers would not adopt the project.

As noted earlier, security issuance costs can be avoided if the new project is financed with internal funds. Consistent with this idea, most projects are financed with internal funds in practice. The problem is that Sommers may not have sufficient internal funds available. Assume, for example, that there is a 5 percent chance that Sommers will lose a lawsuit and be forced to pay damages of $30 million. If this occurs, Sommers will have insufficient internal funds to finance the new project and, without insurance, it will either have to issue

---

[4]The costs of financing the project could be negative due to the interest tax shields on debt, in which case the adjusted net present value would exceed the net present value.

new securities or forgo the project. Alternatively, Sommers can ensure that sufficient funds will be available to finance the new project by purchasing liability insurance.

Suppose that a liability insurance policy with a $25 million limit has a premium equal to $1.34 million. Since the expected claim costs equal $1.25 million ($25 million × 0.05), the loading on the policy is $90,000 ($1.34 million minus $1.25 million).[5] Sommers must compare the premium loading to the expected cost of not having sufficient internal funds to finance the project. As described above, without insurance, Sommers will pass up the investment project if it loses the lawsuit and the cost of issuing securities equals $2.5 million. Since the probability of losing a lawsuit is 0.05, the expected cost of not having sufficient internal funds to finance the investment project is the net present value of the project ($2 million) times 0.05, which equals $100,000. Because the premium loading of $90,000 is less than the expected cost of forgoing the project ($100,000), Sommers should purchase the insurance.

In summary, because of the costs of issuing new securities, the lower cost method of financing new investment often is to use internal funds. The amount of internal funds available, however, is uncertain due to events such as liability suits. An uninsured firm sometimes will find that it has insufficient internal funds to adopt positive net present value projects. When this occurs, the firm will either have to forgo the project or incur the costs associated with issuing new securities. Insurance can ensure that the firm will have sufficient internal funds to adopt positive net present value projects without having to incur the costs of issuing new securities.

Concept Checks

4. If Sommers were uninsured, would it adopt the new project following a $25 million liability loss if the security issuance costs were $1.5 million instead of $2.5 million?

5. Would Sommers purchase the insurance policy described in the text if the premium were $1.5 million (instead of $1.34 million) and security issuance costs were $2.5 million?

Insurance and Financial Distress

A firm is bankrupt when it does not have sufficient funds to pay what it owes other parties (creditors) and therefore either must be legally reorganized to restructure the terms of its obligations or liquidated with the proceeds paid to creditors. The process of reorganizing or liquidating is costly—attorneys and accountants must be hired. Thus, actions that reduce the probability of bankruptcy can be beneficial because they reduce the probability of incurring these direct bankruptcy costs.

In addition to bankruptcy, a firm also can experience **financial distress** when it has difficulty meeting its obligations and therefore has a relatively high probability of bankruptcy. Financially distressed firms sometimes become bankrupt, but not always. Since bankruptcy and financial distress short of bankruptcy can impose costs on parties who have contractual relationships with the firm (such as employees, lenders, suppliers, and customers), the

---

[5]The loading in this example is less than 10 percent, which is small compared to what would be observed in practice for liability insurance. The example nevertheless illustrates that risk reduction helps to preserve internal funds for investment purposes, which can increase value if raising external funds is costly. The premium loading on actual policies also reflects the expected cost of loss control and claim processing services, which are not considered in this example. Sommers presumably would need to purchase these services separately if the insurance policy were not purchased.

terms at which these parties will contract with the firm reflect the firm's probability of financial distress. Insurance can decrease the likelihood that a firm will experience financial distress and thereby improve the terms at which these other claimants are willing to contract with the firm. This in turn increases the firm's expected cash flows. To illustrate these effects, we will first focus on how the probability of bankruptcy affects contractual terms and then expand on the problems created by financial distress short of bankruptcy.

Manager Compensation Example

Consider a simple example in which insurance changes the terms at which a manager will work for a firm because insurance decreases the probability of bankruptcy. J. R., the manager of Garven Corp., knows that he will not receive the compensation that he was promised if the firm goes bankrupt and that he will be forced to incur the costs of finding a new job. Since insurance reduces the probability that the firm will go bankrupt, insurance reduces the expected amount of compensation demanded by J. R. Consequently, the firm's expected costs decrease and its expected cash flows increase.

Specifically, assume that Garven's end-of-year cash flows prior to paying J. R. equal $1 million if the firm is not sued and $0 if it is sued. The probability of a suit is 0.05. Also assume that J. R. would work for $100,000 if he were certain to receive his promised compensation. The problem is that if Garven Corp. loses a lawsuit, the firm will not have any money to pay J. R. Since J. R. views working for this firm as risky, he will do so only if the firm promises to pay him $125,000. The additional $25,000 is demanded as compensation for the risk of not being paid what was promised and the hassle of finding another job. Because of the possibility of a lawsuit, J. R. knows that he will receive $125,000 with probability 0.95 and $0 with probability 0.05. His expected compensation therefore is $118,750.

Table 20.5 summarizes the cash flows of Garven Corp. without insurance. With probability 0.95, equityholders will receive $875,000 ($1 million minus the $125,000 in managerial compensation), and with probability 0.05, the firm will be bankrupt and equityholders will receive $0, in which case J. R. also will receive $0.

Now suppose that Garven Corp. purchases $400,000 of liability insurance coverage at a premium of $30,000. Since the expected claim cost equals $20,000 ($400,000 × 0.05), the premium loading is $10,000. The purchase of insurance, however, will keep the firm from going bankrupt if a lawsuit occurs, which implies that the managerial compensation contract can be changed if the firm insures.

Let's work through the effects of insurance on the firm's cash flows. If the lawsuit does not occur, cash flow before managerial compensation equals $1 million minus the $30,000

TABLE 20.5

Cash flows of Garven Corp. without insurance (manager is promised $125,000 but receives it only if a lawsuit does not occur).

Outcome	Probability	Cash Flow before Managerial Compensation	Managerial Compensation	Net Cash Flow to Stockholders
No lawsuit	0.95	$1,000,000	$125,000	$875,000
Lawsuit	0.05	$ 0	$ 0	$ 0

Expected cash flow = (0.95 × $875,000) + (0.05 × $0) = $831,250

TABLE 20.6

Cash flows for Garven Corp. with $400,000 of liability coverage (premium equals $25,000 and the manager is promised $100,000).

Outcome	Probability	Cash Flow before Managerial Compensation	Managerial Compensation	Net Cash Flow to Stockholders
No lawsuit	0.95	$1,000,000 − $30,000	$100,000	$870,000
Lawsuit	0.05	$0 + $400,000 − $30,000	$100,000	$270,000
Expected cash flow = (0.95 × $870,000) + (0.05 × $270,000) = $840,000				

insurance premium. If a lawsuit does occur, cash flow before managerial compensation equals $0, plus the $400,000 of insurance proceeds, minus the $30,000 premium for a total of $370,000. Thus, with insurance the firm always has enough money to pay the manager, so that J. R. can be promised $100,000 with certainty. Table 20.6 summarizes the cash flows if Garven Corp. purchases insurance and the manager's compensation equals $100,000.

A comparison of Tables 20.5 and 20.6 indicates that the expected cash flows are higher with insurance in this example. Thus, insurance increases Garven's stock price because it reduces Garven's expected cost of managerial compensation. Without insurance expected managerial compensation is $118,750 (0.95 × $125,000). With insurance expected managerial compensation is $100,000. The savings in expected managerial compensation amounts to $18,750, while the premium loading is only $10,000. The increase in expected cash flows therefore is $8,750. The reason that insurance decreases the cost of compensating the manager is that it reduces the expected cost to the manager from possibly having to find a new job. In addition, the manager is risk averse and cannot diversify away the risk associated with being employed in the firm. In effect, the firm purchases insurance for its risk-averse manager (i.e., it guarantees that he will be paid), who in turn pays for the insurance by accepting lower compensation.

Implications for Other Claimants

Insurance can alter the terms at which claimants other than managers contract with the firm as well. Suppliers, for example, are likely to contract with the firm at lower prices if the firm decreases the probability that it will become bankrupt. In many cases, suppliers will simply refuse to do business with firms that are insufficiently insured. Indeed, firms often have to present certificates of insurance prior to the consummation of a transaction or contract (see Chapter 29). The effect of insurance on supplier contracts is likely to be greater when the supplier has to make specific investments in order to supply the firm. For example, if Regan's Parts needed to make or acquire specialized machinery to supply Garven Corp., Regan's Parts would require compensation for the risk that the specific value of its investment would be lost. Similarly, customers will be willing to pay higher prices if they know the firm is likely to be around in the future and able to service its products. The effect on product prices is likely to be greater when the firm sells products that will be used over time and for which the manufacturer has expertise in servicing.[6] A firm's lenders also are con-

---

[6]Another scenario in which customers are likely to be concerned with the possibility that a firm will go bankrupt is when the product or service imposes the possibility of personal injury on the consumer. For example, air travelers may not be willing to purchase tickets (or will only purchase tickets at a lower price) from an airline that is financially weak because of fear that the airline will invest less in safety.

cerned with a firm's probability of bankruptcy. The interest rate that lenders charge will increase as the probability of bankruptcy increases because of the costs associated with collecting promised payments. As a result, lenders (and debtholders) often require that a firm be insured.

Financial Distress Prior to Bankruptcy

The Garven Corp. example assumed that the firm could experience a large loss that would bankrupt the firm. You might have the wrong impression that only those losses that cause bankruptcy need to be insured to increase firm value. As we now explain, the issues just discussed also are relevant to situations where losses cause a firm to experience financial distress without actually going bankrupt. This is because financial distress can create incentives that cause the firm's managers to make decisions that increase the likelihood of bankruptcy. Consequently, insurance that reduces the likelihood that a firm will experience financial distress apart from bankruptcy can be beneficial because it enables the firm to improve contractual terms with other claimants.

A general characteristic of the claims of bondholders, employees, customers, and suppliers is that these parties must be paid before the shareholders of the firm receive any funds. This characteristic can distort the investment choices of shareholders following a major loss in two ways. First, shareholders sometimes will have an incentive to forgo good investment projects (positive net present value projects) following a loss that causes a firm to experience financial distress. Second, shareholders may have an incentive to invest in some negative net present value projects with high risk.

Some positive net present value projects may not be undertaken following a major loss that causes financial distress because the returns from the new investment will mostly accrue to other claimants who must be paid before shareholders. For example, suppose that if Mayers Inc. experiences a major flood that destroys its plant, Mayers Inc. will be unable to pay its lenders what they were promised unless the firm replaces the plant. The shareholders of Mayers Inc., however, may be reluctant to pay for replacement after the flood even if the cost of replacement is less than the total returns from replacement. The reason is that the returns from replacement following the flood will mostly accrue to the lenders. That is, replacement bails out the lenders (pun intended).

Flood insurance would provide the funds necessary to replace the equipment and therefore commit Mayers Inc. to replacement following a flood. Since insurance commits the firm to replacement, it alleviates lenders' concerns about being paid following a loss. Lenders therefore are willing to lend money at lower rates when the firm is insured. Stated differently, if the firm does not have insurance, lenders will raise the interest rate that will be charged, because they know that the firm sometimes will pass up good investment projects that would have increased lenders' payoffs. Consequently, this cost of not being insured is borne by shareholders in the form of a higher interest rate paid on the firm's debt. Appendix 20B provides a more detailed example of how insurance can solve the *underinvestment problem* that can arise following a major loss.

As noted, investment decisions also can be distorted in that financial distress may cause shareholders to have an incentive to invest in negative net present value projects with high risk. Intuitively, if a firm is close to bankruptcy, shareholders have little to lose if a high-risk project turns out bad. However, if the high-risk project turns out well, shareholders can earn a high return. Investors will price a firm's debt securities taking into account the likelihood that the firm will go into financial distress and invest in negative net present value projects. Corporate actions that reduce the likelihood of financial distress—like purchasing insurance—will therefore induce investors to pay higher prices for the firm's debt, because the likelihood that the firm will adopt risky projects with negative net present value has been reduced.

20.4 Summary

- The value of an asset equals the present value of its expected cash flows using the opportunity cost of capital as the discount rate.
- The opportunity cost of capital equals the risk-free rate of return plus a risk premium. The risk premium depends upon the amount of nondiversifiable risk associated with the cash flows.
- Risk management activities, such as purchasing insurance and engaging in loss control, typically do not affect nondiversifiable risk and therefore do not decrease the opportunity cost of capital.
- Corporate insurance purchases can affect expected cash flows in five key ways:
  1. Insurance premium loadings decrease expected cash flows.

2. Services provided by insurers increase expected cash flows if the necessary premium loading is less than the cost of obtaining these services elsewhere.
3. The reduction in the likelihood of having to raise new funds to pay losses or to finance new investment projects increases expected cash flows.
4. The reduction in the likelihood of financial distress, including costly bankruptcy, improves contractual terms with nonowner claimants and therefore increases expected cash flows.
5. The reduction in expected tax payments increases expected cash flows (see Chapter 21).

Key Terms

opportunity cost of capital 443	diversifiable risk 444	adjusted net present value 451
risk-free rate 443	nondiversifiable risk 444	financial distress 452
risk premium 443	net present value (NPV) 451	

Questions and Problems

1. An analyst knows with certainty that Skipper Inc. will exist for two years and have the following cash flows per share:

	Year 1	Year 2
Revenue	$100	$100
Costs	$ 80	$ 80
Net cash flow	$ 20	$ 20

What is the stock price of Skipper Inc. if the opportunity cost of capital is 8 percent?

2. The analyst in problem 1 realizes that Skipper Inc.'s costs may not be $80 per share with certainty. Instead, each year there is a 10 percent chance that a worker will be seriously injured and that Skipper will have to pay the employee's medical expenses and lost wages. If an injury does occur, Skipper's costs equal $85 per share. If an injury does not occur (which has a probability of 0.9), then Skipper's costs equal $79.445 per share.

   (a) What is Skipper's expected net cash flow in each year?
   (b) If the opportunity cost of capital is 8 percent, what is the stock price?
   (c) Provide an argument for why the opportunity cost of capital should not change because of the risk of worker injury.

3. Suppose that Skipper Inc. (from problem 2) purchases workers' compensation insurance to cover the costs of medical expenses and lost wages. The premium for full coverage is $0.555 per share. What is the stock price? Compare your answer to that obtained in 2(*b*) and intuitively explain the relationship.

4. Redo problem 3 using a premium of $0.75 per share. Compare your answer to that obtained in problem 3 and intuitively explain the relationship.

5. If the risk-free rate equals 7 percent and the risk premium for Thistle Corp. is 5 percent, what is the opportunity cost of capital for Thistle? Suppose Thistle purchases insurance to cover property damage. What is likely to happen to its opportunity cost of capital?

6. Ambrose Motor Corp. has expected earnings before interest payments for the next year equal to $100 million if it does not lose a product liability lawsuit. Interest and principal payments on its debt equal $60 million, leaving $40 million for shareholders if it does not lose a product liability suit.

The probability of losing a product liability suit is 0.02, and the expected damage if a suit is lost equals $50 million. If the suit is lost, the firm will be unable to make its promised payments to debtholders and it will have to renegotiate its debt payments. The legal and administrative costs of renegotiations (including the cost of managers' time) equal $5 million. Should Ambrose Motor purchase a liability insurance policy with a $50 million limit for a premium of $1.2 million? Explain.

7. Because of its relatively high probability of going bankrupt, Snow Corp.'s consumers are concerned about its ability to fulfill warranties, employees are de~~manding greater~~ compensation for the risk ~~of losing their~~ jobs, and suppliers are de~~manding higher~~ prices for the risk of losing ~~their firm-~~ specific investments. Assume that Snow's high probability of bankruptcy can be reduced by purchasing additional insurance coverage. What factors should Snow's managers examine when deciding whether to purchase additional coverage? Explain.

Answers to Concept Checks

1. (*a*) The possible rates of return are 11.1 percent [(100 − 90)/90] and −22.2 percent [(70 − 90)/90].

   (*b*) The expected rate of return equals 7.8 percent [(11.1 × 0.9) − (22.2 × 0.1)].

2. There is an inverse relationship between expected return on a stock and the stock price, holding the expected cash flows constant.

3. (*a*) Since the level of interest rates affects the present value of most firms, the risk due to changes in interest rates is likely to be nondiversifiable risk.

   (*b*) Since a firm's property loss due to theft is largely the result of firm-specific

   events, the risk due to theft is likely to be largely diversifiable risk.

4. If the costs of issuing securities were $1.5 million, Sommers would still adopt the project since its net present value is $2 million. In this case, the cost of being uninsured is the lost net present value due to the cost of issuing securities (i.e., the $1.5 million).

5. Sommers would not purchase insurance because the premium loading would be $250,000 ($1.5 million minus $1.25 million), which exceeds the expected cost of forgoing the project ($100,000).

References

Froot, Ken; David Scharfstein; and Jeremy Stein. "A Framework for Risk Management." *Harvard Business Review,* December 1994. (*Provides examples of how risk reduction can avoid financing costs and improve investment decisions.*)

Mayers, David; and Clifford Smith. "On the Corporate Demand for Insurance." *Journal of Business* 22 (1982), pp. 281–96. (*Analyzes the demand for insurance by corporations using modern financial theory.*)

Appendix 20A

Issuing Securities versus Purchasing Insurance

We develop a simple example to illustrate the trade-offs between issuing new securities to pay for losses versus purchasing insurance. Consider Cather Inc., which, in contrast to Schmit Enterprises, is expected to operate over a two-year period. The first year's cash flows are uncertain because of the possibility of a lawsuit. Specifically, the firm will have cash flows equal to $15 per share with probability 0.9 and −$5 per share with probability 0.1. In essence, the firm has a 10 percent chance of suffering a $20 per share loss relative to its normal cash flow. If the loss occurs and the firm is uninsured, it must raise new funds or else go bankrupt. Fortunately for Cather, its second year cash flows are known to be $25 a share. If the uninsured loss occurs, Cather therefore can pay for the loss by borrowing money or issuing new stock and using the second year's cash flows to pay back the loan or the

new investors. We will assume that Cather issues new stock, although borrowing the funds would yield the same conclusions.

We will initially assume that issuing new stock is costless in the sense that the firm only has to offer the new stockholders a rate of return equal to the opportunity cost of capital, which is assumed to equal 10 percent. In other words, there are no transaction costs, such as investment banker fees, and securities are properly priced so that investors do not receive more than the opportunity cost of capital. Under these conditions, if Cather raises $20 per share to pay for the loss (if it occurs), it must pay the new investors $22 ($20 × 1.1) at the end of the second year.

Table 20A.1 compares the cash flows available for the original investors under two alternative methods of paying losses: (1) Cather purchases $20

TABLE 20A.1
Cash flow comparison: purchasing insurance versus issuing new stock to pay for losses.

Loss Financing Approach	Outcome	Cash Flows at End of Year 1	Cash Flows at End of Year 2 Available for Original Shareholders
Purchase $20 of insurance coverage for a premium of $2 at the beginning of year 1	No loss	$13	$25
	Loss	$13	$25
Issue equity worth $20 at end of year 1 if loss occurs	No loss	$15	$25
	Loss	$15	$ 3

of insurance coverage at the beginning of the first year and pays a premium of $2 per share (the expected claim cost) at the end of the first year, and (2) Cather issues $20 of new stock at the end of the first year if the loss occurs. If Cather purchases insurance, then its cash flows at the end of the first year are $13 ($15 minus the $2 premium) and $25 at the end of the second year, regardless of whether the loss occurs. If instead Cather issues new stock if the loss occurs, then cash flows depend on whether the loss occurs. If the loss does not occur, then shareholders receive $15 at the end of the first year and $25 at the end of the second year. If the loss occurs, then Cather raises $20 from new investors to pay for the loss; this leaves $15 for the original shareholders at the end of the first year. But at the end of the second year, the original shareholders receive only $3 because $22 must go to the new investors.

While issuing new stock to pay for the loss results in different cash flows for the firm compared to buying insurance, it does not result in a different stock price at the beginning of the first year. As illustrated in Table 20A.2, the stock price if insurance is purchased equals the present value of the $13 first year cash flow plus the present value of the $25 second year cash flow, for a total $32.48. When the firm issues equity to pay for the loss, the stock price equals the present value of the $15 first year cash flow plus the present value of the expected second year cash flow (90 percent chance of $25 and 10 percent chance of $3), which again totals $32.48. Thus, in this example with no insurance premium loading and no transaction costs associated with issuing new securities, the shareholders would be indifferent between the two alternatives.

Although Table 20A.2 illustrates that the stock price at the beginning of the first year is unaffected by whether the firm purchases insurance or issues equity if it is needed, the two loss financing strategies differ regarding stock price uncertainty in the future. If insurance is purchased, the stock price at the end of the first year will be certain since cash flows in this example are certain with full insurance. The end of the first year stock price with insurance will be $13 + $25/1.1 = $35.73, regardless of whether the loss occurs. If instead the firm issues equity if the loss occurs, then the end of year 1 stock price will depend on whether the loss occurs. Without a loss the stock price will be $15 + $25/1.1 = $37.73, and with a loss the stock price will be $15 + $3/1.1 = $17.73. Thus, the stock price drops by $20 (the size of the loss) if the loss occurs. This illustrates that by issuing equity to finance the loss payment, the original equityholders bear the cost of the loss.

Issuing securities can be costly in practice because of investment banking fees and security registration costs. New securities also may be underpriced by the market, which implies that existing owners are selling securities for less than their true value. This underpricing is a cost imposed on existing owners— they are not fully paid for the part of the firm given to new investors. When choosing how to finance losses, a firm must compare the expected costs of issuing securities to the premium loading for insurance.

Suppose, for example, that the premium loading is 20 percent of expected claim costs or $0.40 per share (0.20 × 0.1 × $20), while the total costs of issuing securities equals 25 percent of the funds raised or $5 per share (0.25 × $20). Since the probability

TABLE 20A.2 Stock price comparison: purchasing insurance versus issuing new stock to pay for losses.	Loss Financing Approach	Stock Price at Beginning of Year 1
	Purchase $20 of insurance coverage for a premium of $2 at the beginning of year 1	$\dfrac{\$13}{1.1} + \dfrac{\$25}{1.1^2} = \$32.48$
	Issue equity worth $20 at end of year 1 if loss occurs	$\dfrac{\$15}{1.1} + \dfrac{(0.9)(\$25) + (0.1)(\$3)}{1.1^2} = \$32.48$

that securities will be issued equals 0.1, the expected cost of issuing securities is $0.50 per share. Because the premium loading is less than the expected cost of issuing securities, the cost of financing losses is less with insurance.

In summary, this example illustrates three important points. First, if the firm has insufficient internal funds to pay uninsured losses, the firm must raise new funds by either borrowing or issuing new securities (assuming bankruptcy is not the best option). Second, when new funds are raised to pay for uninsured losses, the firm's owners at the time of the loss still bear the cost of the uninsured losses, because the value of their shares declines by the value of the loss. Third, when deciding how much insurance to purchase, the insurance premium loading must be compared to the expected cost of raising new funds following a loss.

Appendix 20B

How Insurance Can Mitigate the Underinvestment Problem

Mr. Mayers is planning to build a new plant to produce airplane parts. He has great ideas regarding how to build a more efficient plant than his competitors. After building the plant and operating for one year, he will sell the operation and retire to Hilton Head. The project requires a $30 million investment. Although he is quite wealthy, Mr. Mayers does not have $30 million sitting around and he therefore decides to borrow some money. He asks a bank how much he can borrow if he promises to repay $28 million at the end of the year. For simplicity, assume that the time value of money is zero and that the risk premium is zero. As a result, when calculating present values, the discount rate is zero.

The bank investigates what Mr. Mayers is planning to do with the borrowed funds (it wants to know whether he will be able to repay the $28 million). The investigation uncovers the following information. At the end of the year, the assets of the plant will be worth $35 million with probability 0.95. However, with probability 0.05, an explosion will damage the plant and the assets will be worth $20 million. If the explosion does occur, Mr. Mayers could invest an additional $10 million and restore the assets to $35 million. Notice that the $10 million investment following an explosion is a positive net present value project: A $10 million investment increases the value of assets by $15 million ($35 − $20). Figure 20B.1 summarizes this information.

The amount that the bank will be repaid at the end of the year depends on whether an explosion occurs and, if so, whether Mr. Mayers will invest the additional $10 million. If Mr. Mayers will commit to reinvesting, the bank will be repaid what was promised, $28 million, regardless of whether the explosion oc-

FIGURE 20B.1
Asset values for Mr. Mayers's project.

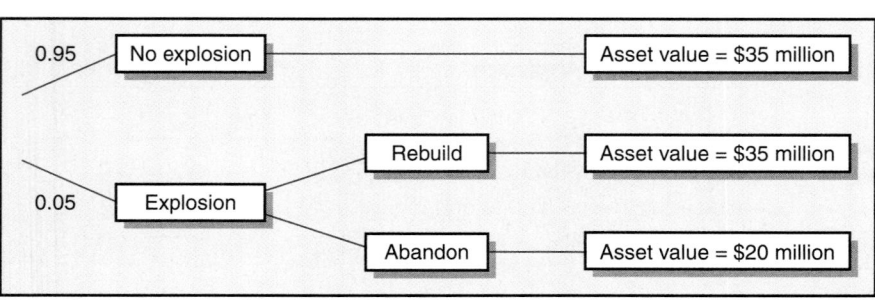

curs. However, if Mr. Mayers cannot commit to reinvesting, the bank may not receive the promised payment of $28 million. With probability 0.95, the bank will receive $28 million, but with probability 0.05 the bank will receive only what the assets are worth following an explosion—$20 million. Figure 20B.2 summarizes the payoffs to the bank.

As Figure 20B.2 indicates, the amount that the bank is willing to lend Mr. Mayers depends on whether Mr. Mayers can commit to reinvesting. If he can commit, the bank will lend $28 million, because the bank is certain that it will be repaid (recall that the discount rate is zero). If Mr. Mayers cannot commit to reinvesting, the bank will lend less than $28 million because, with probability 0.05, the bank will receive only $20 million. Without a reinvestment commitment, the bank will be willing to lend the expected value of the amount repaid, which equals $27.6 million [(0.95 × $28) + (0.05 × $20)]. In summary, the amount that Mr. Mayers can borrow if he *can* commit to reinvesting is $28.0 million, and the amount that Mr. Mayers can borrow if he *cannot* commit to reinvesting is $27.6 million.

To see whether Mr. Mayers would like to commit to reinvesting following an explosion, we must compare the payoffs to Mr. Mayers if he commits to reinvesting to the payoffs if he does not commit to reinvesting following an explosion. This comparison will demonstrate whether Mr. Mayers would like to commit to reinvesting. (After doing this, we will consider whether Mr. Mayers can commit to reinvesting.)

If Mr. Mayers commits to reinvesting, he will receive $28 million from the bank, which implies that he will have to invest $2 million of his own money up front. With probability 0.95, the assets will be

worth $35 million, of which $28 million will go to repay the loan, leaving $7 million for Mr. Mayers. Subtracting the initial investment of $2 million yields $5 million with probability 0.95. With probability 0.05, an explosion will occur and Mr. Mayers will have to invest an additional $10 million. By doing so, the assets again will be worth $35 million; the bank will receive $28 million, leaving $7 million for Mr. Mayers. However, once he takes into account the additional investment of $10 million and the initial investment of $2 million, he loses $5 million by reinvesting. The expected value of Mr. Mayers's cash flows if he can commit to reinvesting is {[0.95 × ($5)] + [0.05 × (−$5)]} = $4.5 million. That is, by building the plant and committing to reinvesting, Mr. Mayers expects to earn $4.5 million.

How much would Mr. Mayers earn if he builds the plant but does not commit to reinvesting? In this case, the bank will loan him $27.6 million, which implies that he has to invest $2.4 million of his own money. (This is a critical difference between committing and not committing.) With probability 0.95, the assets will be worth $35 million, the bank will receive $28 million, and Mr. Mayers will receive $7 million. After subtracting his initial investment, Mr. Mayers earns $4.6 million with probability 0.95. With probability 0.05, an explosion occurs, in which case Mr. Mayers gives the $20 million in assets to the bank and receives nothing. Thus, with probability 0.05, he loses his initial investment of $2.4 million. The expected value of his earnings equals [(0.95 × $4.6) + (0.05 × −$2.4)] = $4.25 million. Thus, by building the plant and not committing to reinvesting, Mr. Mayers expects to earn $4.25 million.

FIGURE 20B.2
Payoffs to the bank that lends Mr. Mayers money.

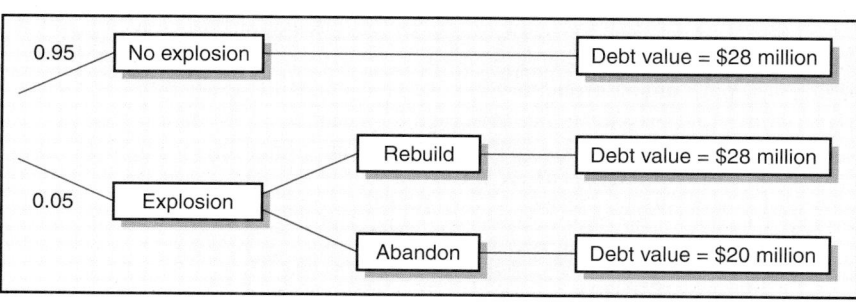

As a result, Mr. Mayers expects to earn more if he can commit to reinvesting ($4.5 million versus $4.25 million). The difference in value results because a positive net present value project is forgone if an explosion occurs and Mr. Mayers does not commit to reinvesting. Reinvestment of $10 million increases the asset value by $15 million, yielding a net present value of $5 million. An explosion occurs with probability 0.05; therefore the expected value that is lost by not committing is $0.25 million (0.05 × $5 million). This is the difference in expected payoffs to Mr. Mayers ($4.5 million minus $4.25 million).

Can Mr. Mayers simply tell the bank that he will reinvest if an explosion occurs? Mr. Mayers would like to commit to reinvesting, but the issue is whether the bank will believe him if he simply says, "Trust me—I will reinvest if an explosion occurs." The answer is no. The reason is that even though Mr. Mayers would like to commit to reinvesting, he will have no incentive to reinvest if an explosion actually occurs. In other words, his promise to reinvest is not credible. If an explosion occurs, Mr. Mayers realizes that he has to invest $10 million but will only get $7 million back. Therefore, he will not invest the additional money needed to restore the assets to their original value. The problem is that most of the returns from the investment will accrue to the bank.

Given the length of this example, it is worth recapping the analysis to this point. Mr. Mayers would like to commit to reinvesting, because by doing so he will receive more funds from the bank and consequently earn more money. But the promise to reinvest following an explosion is not credible. Once an explosion occurs, he has no incentive to invest because the returns from investment accrue to the bank. The bank therefore will assume that Mr. Mayers will not reinvest and will structure the loan accordingly.

Consider now how insurance can potentially solve Mr. Mayers's commitment problem. Suppose that Mr. Mayers buys property insurance coverage that will pay to repair the damage caused by an ex-

plosion for a premium of $600,000. Since the expected claim cost equals $500,000 (0.05 × $10 million), the premium loading is $100,000. With the insurance company paying the reinvestment costs, the assets of the firm always will be $35 million. The bank will be certain to receive what has been promised ($28 million), and Mr. Mayers will receive the remainder ($7 million). Since the bank's claims are risk free, it lends $28 million. Mr. Mayers then has to invest $2 million of his own money plus pay the $600,000 insurance premium. He therefore earns $7 million minus $2 million minus $600,000, which equals $4.4 million. This amount is greater than what he earns if he does not purchase insurance ($4.25 million). By contracting with an insurer to provide the funds necessary for reinvestment following an explosion, Mr. Mayers commits to reinvestment. This increases the amount of money that the bank will lend him and therefore increases his return.

The important points are more general than this example may suggest. Whenever a firm borrows money, lenders will be concerned about the firm forgoing good investment projects when the firm is performing poorly. The reason is that most of the returns from these projects will accrue to lenders but will not benefit shareholders. Insurance helps ensure that the firm will reinvest following large losses.

An astute reader may notice that the underinvestment problem also can be solved by having the bank take over the firm and provide the funds for the reinvestment if an explosion occurs. Note, however, that the process of taking over the firm in financial distress also is costly. First, the bank has to monitor the firm's activities to see whether it is in financial distress and if the underinvestment problem has arisen. Second, attorney and accountant fees will have to be paid to take control of a financially distressed firm. The important point is that insurance may be the lower cost way of solving the underinvestment problem.

Chapter 21

Tax, Regulatory, and Accounting Factors Affecting Corporate Risk Management

Chapter Objectives

- Show how progressive tax rates induce firms to reduce risk.
- Explain how the different tax treatment of insurers and noninsurance companies provides a tax benefit to insurance.
- Illustrate that the tax treatment of depreciated property provides a tax benefit to property insurance.
- Show that risk reduction can increase a firm's use of debt financing and thereby create tax benefits.
- Describe insurance premium taxes and excise taxes that increase premium loadings.
- Describe government regulations that require businesses to buy insurance and influence the choice of an insurer.
- Identify and analyze how accounting rules affect risk management.

21.1 Tax Benefits Defined

A major portion of this chapter examines how tax issues affect corporate risk management. The chapter identifies the most important implications of the tax system; some of the more complicated details are omitted. Before describing specific tax effects, it is important to define the term *tax benefit*. A transaction provides a **tax benefit** if it lowers the aggregate present value of expected tax payments for all parties involved in the transaction. For example, the purchase of property insurance by Cox Corp. provides a tax benefit if the present value of expected tax payments for Cox Corp. and the insurer are lower than the present value of Cox Corp.'s expected tax payments if it uses internal funds to finance property losses.

Several points about this definition of a tax benefit are important to emphasize. First, tax benefits are defined in terms of *expected* tax payments, not actual tax payments. Thus, the magnitude of tax benefits must be evaluated at the time loss financing decisions are made, not after losses have been realized. For example, tax benefits might exist if Cox Corp. purchases insurance, but unexpected events also might occur that would cause realized tax payments to be higher with insurance than with retention. Second, tax benefits are defined in present value terms, which highlights the fact that tax benefits may arise from shifting tax payments to later time periods.[1]

The third point is that the party that nominally receives a tax break may differ from the party that actually obtains the tax benefit. To illustrate, suppose that Bermuda insurers do not have to pay taxes on interest income that has been earned on funds set aside to pay future losses, but that US corporations are required to pay taxes on such interest income. Then the purchase of insurance by a US corporation from a Bermuda insurer could provide a tax benefit. The Bermuda insurer would nominally receive the tax break, but the actual benefit of the tax break could accrue to the US corporation. If Bermuda insurers compete with each other, then most or even all of the tax benefit would likely be passed through to US corporations in the form of lower insurance premiums. Because the party that receives the tax benefit can differ from the party that nominally receives the break, it is important to look at the effects on all the parties involved in a transaction.

Note finally that the definition of a tax benefit ignores any cost of obtaining the benefit. Thus, a transaction that provides a tax benefit does not necessarily increase shareholders' wealth. According to the definition, a tax benefit exists if a firm with a 34 percent tax rate makes a tax-deductible contribution of $1,000 to a charity. While the charitable contribution lowers the firm's taxes by $340 (34 percent of $1,000) and thus provides a tax benefit, the contribution will increase shareholders' wealth only if the contribution causes other cash flows to increase by more than $660 (the after-tax cost of the contribution). Thus, tax minimization is not the same as shareholder wealth maximization. (A firm could usually minimize tax payments by giving away all of its profits.)

In the next four sections of this chapter, we analyze the main tax benefits of insurance versus retention. These tax benefits arise because (1) effective corporate income tax rates sometimes are progressive; (2) the tax treatment of losses is different for insurers than for noninsurance companies; (3) the tax treatment of losses to depreciated property depends on whether the property is insured; and (4) the risk reduction provided by insurance may allow a corporation to increase its use of debt with tax-deductible interest payments. The first and fourth tax benefits apply to most risk-reducing activities (including hedging); the second and third are specific to insurance.

---

[1]The risk associated with tax payments would be reflected in the discount rate used to calculate the present value of expected tax payments.

21.2 Progressivity in Corporate Income Tax Rates

Overview

Tax rate progressivity means that tax rates increase as taxable income increases. When tax rates are progressive a firm can lower its expected tax payments by reducing the variability of its before-tax income (e.g., by purchasing insurance). The intuition for this result is easily conveyed by considering how insurance affects a firm's tax payments when taxable income is volatile from year to year because of unexpected losses in some years. In years when losses are low and taxable income is high, the government takes a larger percentage of the firm's profits than in years when losses are high and taxable income is low. By purchasing insurance, a firm essentially lowers its taxable income in years when losses are low and increases taxable income in years when losses are high. This transfer of taxable income is beneficial because it lowers tax payments in years when losses are low by more than it increases tax payments in years when losses are high.

The curve in Figure 21.1 illustrates the relationship between taxable income and after-tax income when tax rates are progressive. When tax rates increase with taxable income, after-tax income increases at a decreasing rate as taxable income increases. (Note that this is the same relationship between wealth and utility for a risk-averse person.) The figure also illustrates the effect of insurance on after-tax income in a simple example where a firm has a 50 percent chance of experiencing a $10 million loss each year. Without insurance, the firm has $12 million of taxable income in years without a loss and $2 million of taxable income in years when a loss occurs. By purchasing full insurance at a premium of $6 million, the firm's taxable income is always $6 million. As a result of progressive tax rates, the reduction in after-tax income in the years without a loss (distance between A and B) is less than the increase in after-tax income in the years with a loss (distance between B and C). Because the two outcomes are equally likely in this simple example, the firm would prefer to give up $(A–B) with probability 0.5 to receive $(B–C) with probability 0.5.

FIGURE 21.1
Effect of insurance on after-tax income when tax rates are progressive (in $ millions).

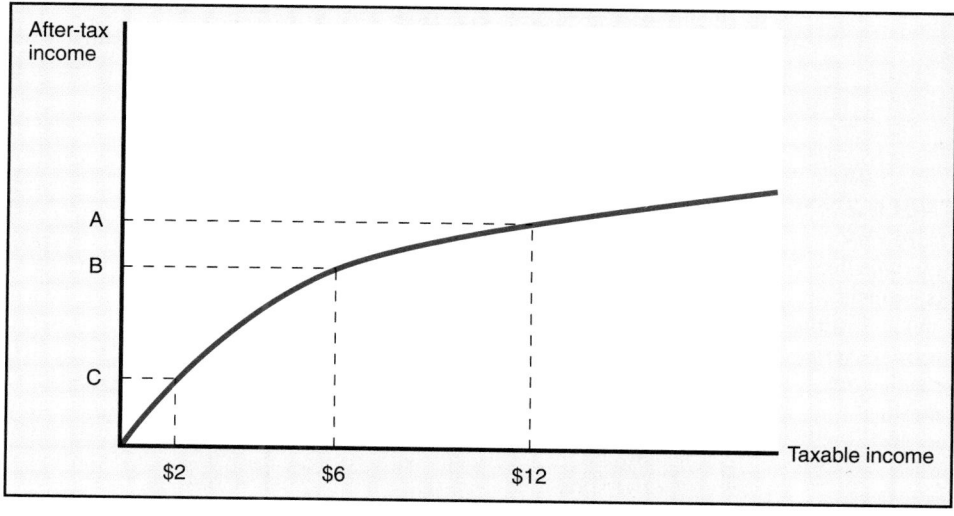

Numerical Example and Additional Insights

Suppose that DARCY Corp. has a tax rate of 34 percent if it has positive taxable earnings and a zero tax rate if it has negative taxable earnings, which is an extreme form of progressivity in tax rates. DARCY Corp. has a 0.02 probability that it will lose a lawsuit that will cost $30 million. Without a lawsuit, DARCY's taxable earnings equal $10 million. As illustrated in Table 21.1, DARCY's taxable earnings are either $10 million or −$20 million. Without insurance, DARCY's after-tax earnings equal either $6.6 million ($10 − $10 × 0.34) or −$20 million, implying that its expected after-tax earnings equal $6.068 million ($6.6 × 0.98 − $20 × 0.02).

Now suppose that DARCY purchases liability insurance with a $30 million limit for a premium of $600,000. This policy has a zero premium loading because expected claim costs equal $600,000 (0.02 × $30 million). Since the insurer pays the entire loss if it occurs, DARCY's taxable earnings will be $9.4 million with certainty ($10 million minus the insurance premium of $600,000). DARCY's expected after-tax earnings therefore equal $6.204 million ($9.4 − $9.4 × 0.34), which is $136,000 greater than without insurance.

Comparing DARCY's situation to another firm will help explain further how insurance lowers expected taxes for DARCY. Suppose that Barrese Inc. is faced with the same liability exposure as DARCY but that Barrese Inc. has taxable earnings of $50 million if it is not sued. The higher taxable earnings for Barrese ($50 million) than DARCY ($10 million) imply that Barrese Inc. will have positive earnings even if it loses the lawsuit ($50 million − $30 million). Thus, the tax rates facing Barrese Inc. are not progressive. As is illustrated in Table 21.2, this difference eliminates the tax benefit from insurance. Without insurance, Barrese's after-tax earnings equal $33 million ($50 − $50 × 0.34) with probability 0.98 and $13.2 million ($20 − $20 × 0.34) with probability of 0.02. Expected after-tax earnings without insurance therefore equal $32.604 million ($0.98 × $33 + 0.02 × $13.2). If Barrese purchases $30 million of liability insurance coverage for $600,000, its taxable earnings equal $49.4 million regardless of whether it loses a lawsuit. Its after-tax earnings with insurance therefore equal $32.604 million ($49.4 − $49.4 × 0.34), which is the same as without insurance.

The important difference between DARCY and Barrese is that without insurance Barrese is able to fully deduct the entire $30 million liability loss to lower its taxable earnings. DARCY, on the other hand, can only use $10 million of the $30 million loss to offset

TABLE 21.1 DARCY's expected after-tax earnings (in $ millions) with insurance versus retention (tax rate when income is positive = 34%; tax rate when income is negative = 0%).	**No Lawsuit (probability = 0.98)**	**Loses a Lawsuit (probability = 0.02)**
No Insurance		
Taxable earnings	$10.0	−$20
After-tax earnings	$ 6.6	−$20
Expected after-tax earnings = $6.6 × 0.98 − $20 × 0.02 = $6.068		
Full Insurance (with a $0.6 premium)		
Taxable earnings	$ 9.4	$9.4
After-tax earnings	$ 6.204	$6.204
Expected after-tax earnings = $9.4 − $9.4 × 0.34 = $6.204		

TABLE 21.2
Barrese's expected after-tax earnings (in $ millions) with Insurance versus retention (tax rate when income is positive = 34%; tax rate when income is negative = 0%).

	No Lawsuit (probability = 0.98)	Loses a Lawsuit (probability = 0.02)
No Insurance		
Taxable earnings	$50.0	$20.0
After-tax earnings	$33.0	$13.2
Expected after-tax earnings = $33 × 0.98 + $13.2 × 0.02 = $32.604		
Full Insurance (with a $0.6 premium)		
Taxable earnings	$49.400	$49.400
After-tax earnings	$32.604	$32.604
Expected after-tax earnings = $49.4 − $49.4 × 0.34 = $32.604		

taxable earnings; the other $20 million in liability losses does not reduce its taxes. Of course, losses are not desirable, but if they occur a firm would like to fully utilize them to reduce taxable income. When uninsured, DARCY has a 0.02 probability that it will not be able to take a $20 million tax deduction that could be taken by a firm with higher taxable income (e.g., Barrese). The value of this deduction to such a firm equals the probability of the loss, 0.02, times the amount of tax that would be avoided by deducting the loss, $20 million, times the 34 percent tax rate. Multiplying these quantities yields $136,000, which is the amount by which insurance increases DARCY's after-tax income ($6.204 million − 6.068 million; see Table 21.1). By purchasing insurance, DARCY in effect is able to deduct the entire expected loss, thus reducing its expected tax payments and increasing expected after-tax earnings.[2]

Progressivity of US Corporate Income Tax Rates

The nominal tax rates on US corporations have limited progressivity. Taxable income between $0 and $50,000 is taxed at a 15 percent rate, between $50,000 and $75,000 at a 25 percent rate, and all taxable income above $100,000 is taxed at least at a 34 percent rate. In addition, firms can carry losses forward 20 years and backward 2 years to offset future or past profits. Thus, if a firm has negative taxable income in a given year, in effect it can obtain a refund based on taxes paid in the prior two years, or it can reduce the taxes it pays in future years.

The ability to carry losses forward and backward reduces—but does not eliminate—the progressivity of the tax system for two reasons. First, when carrying losses backward or forward, a firm loses interest on the value of the tax deductions (i.e., the present value of the tax deductions declines). Second, when carrying losses forward, a firm is uncertain whether it will be able to fully deduct the losses in the future. The firm may go bankrupt prior to deducting all of the losses (or reach the 20-year limit before the full loss has been deducted).

A recent study quantified the extent to which US corporations have incentives to reduce risk as a result of progressive tax rates.[3] They found that in approximately 50 percent of the

---

[2]Premium loadings, which this example ignores, reduce the benefits of insurance.

[3]See John Graham and Clifford Smith, "Tax Incentives to Hedge," *Journal of Finance* 54 (1999), 2241–62.

cases analyzed, corporations effectively faced progressive tax rates, and that in approximately 25 percent of these cases, expected tax liabilities could have been materially reduced if the firms hedged some of their risk. Thus, although not universally true, many corporations could reduce expected tax payments by reducing risk.

21.3   Tax Treatment of Insurers versus Noninsurance Companies

Overview

When calculating its taxable income, a noninsurance company can deduct only losses that were paid during the year. In contrast, an insurer can deduct the discounted value of **incurred losses,** which equals losses paid during the year plus the change during the year in the discounted value of its liability for unpaid claims (the loss reserve). This distinction essentially allows insurers to deduct losses earlier than noninsurance companies, which all else equal increases the present value of expected tax deductions if a loss exposure is insured. Although the tax break is granted to insurers, competition among insurers for business will cause most or even the entire tax break to be given to policyholders through lower premiums.

Example and Additional Insights

To illustrate the distinction between paid losses and incurred losses, suppose that Crocker Snowblowers is subject to the risk that it will be sued as a result of its operations in year 1. The expected value and timing of loss payments are as follows:

	Year 1	Year 2
Expected loss payments due to events occurring in year 1	$2 million	$2 million

Even though expected losses arise from events that occur in year 1, half of the losses are not expected to be paid until year 2 because of delays in the reporting of claims and delays in the liability system.

   If Crocker Snowblowers retains the risk of liability suits (e.g., pays liability losses from its cash flow), it can deduct damage payments in the year they are paid. Thus, the decision to retain the liability risk would generate expected tax deductions of $2 million in both years 1 and 2.[4] With a 34 percent tax rate, each dollar of tax deductions reduces the firm's tax payments by 34 cents, or, stated differently, each dollar of tax deductions creates a tax shield of 34 cents. A **tax shield** is the amount by which tax payments are reduced as a result of the ability to deduct an expense when calculating taxable income. Therefore, $2 million of expected loss payments creates an expected tax shield equal to $0.68 million ($0.34 \times$ $2 million). Assuming that the appropriate opportunity cost of capital equals 8 percent, the present value (as of the beginning of year 1) of expected tax shields if Crocker retains the risk associated with its liability exposure is:

$$\frac{(\$2)(0.34)}{1.08} + \frac{(\$2)(0.34)}{1.08^2} = \frac{\$0.68}{1.08} + \frac{\$0.68}{1.08^2} = \$1.213 \text{ million}$$

---

[4]As a follow-up to the discussion in section 21.2, note that in this example we are ignoring the possibility that Crocker faces a progressive tax system. In other words, Crocker is able to fully deduct any loss payments in the year they occur.

Suppose instead that Crocker Snowblowers purchases full insurance from Tennyson Insurance, which has the same forecast of expected loss payments as Crocker Snowblowers (i.e., $2 million in year 1 and $2 million in year 2). Also assume that for tax purposes Tennyson anticipates recording losses in an unbiased manner (see below). As we will explain shortly, the different tax treatment implies that at the time the policy is written, Tennyson expects deductions for losses in year 1 and year 2 of $3.85 million and $0.15 million, respectively. The sum of expected loss deductions for Tennyson is the same as for Crocker Snowblowers, but the timing is different. Tennyson is able to deduct losses earlier. This timing difference increases the present value of expected tax shields.

With the aid of Table 21.3, we can explain how Tennyson calculates its expected loss deductions for its policy with Crocker Snowblowers. After one year, Tennyson expects to pay losses equal to $2 million and expects to have unpaid losses of $2 million. The loss reserve (liability for unpaid losses) for the policy at the end of year 1 therefore equals $2 million. Note as well that the associated change in Tennyson's total loss reserve during year 1 from selling this policy equals $2 million. The undiscounted value of incurred losses equals paid losses ($2 million) plus the change in the loss reserve ($2 million), or $4 million. Using an 8 percent discount rate, the present value of unpaid losses (and the change in the present value of the loss reserve) at the end of year 1 is $2/1.08 = $1.852 million. The discounted value of incurred losses therefore equals paid losses ($2 million) plus $1.852 million, or $3.852 million.

At the end of year 2, the remaining $2 million in expected losses is expected to be paid. Since no additional losses are expected to be paid after year 2, the loss reserve and the present value of the loss reserve are expected to be zero. Consequently, the expected change in the present value of the loss reserve is $-$1.852 = ($0 - $2)/1.08$. The discounted value of incurred losses therefore equals $2 million in paid losses plus $-$1.852 million in the change in the loss reserve, for a total of $0.148 million.

In summary, by selling the liability policy to Crocker Snowblowers, Tennyson expects to be able to reduce its taxable income by $3.852 million at the end of year 1 and by $0.148 million at the end of year 2. The expected tax shield equals 34 percent of incurred losses for tax purposes, which in year 1 equals $1.309 million (0.34 × $3.852 million) and in year 2 equals $0.050 million (0.34 × $0.148 million). The present value of the expected tax shields therefore equals

$$\frac{1.309}{1.08} + \frac{0.050}{1.08^2} = \$1.256 \text{ million}$$

TABLE 21.3 Effect of Crocker Snowblowers purchasing insurance from Tennyson Insurance (in $ millions).

Expected values of:	Beginning of Year 1	End of Year 1	End of Year 2
1. Paid losses		$2.000	$2.000
2. Loss reserve	$0.00	$2.000	$0.000
3. Change in loss reserve		$2.000	-$2.000
4. Undiscounted incurred losses (1) + (3)		$4.000	$0.000
5. Present value of loss reserve (discounted value of 2)	$0.00	$1.852	$0.000
6. Change in present value of loss reserve		$1.852	-$1.852
7. Incurred losses for tax purposes (1) + (6)		$3.852	$0.148

The present value of the expected tax shield from insuring the loss exposure ($1.256 million) exceeds Crocker's present value of expected tax shields from retention ($1.213 million), which was calculated earlier. Thus, there is a tax advantage to insurance as a means of financing losses. The tax advantage in this case equals $43,184 ($1.256 million − $1.213 million).

The tax benefit arises because insurers are able to shield a greater amount of their income (in present value terms) from taxes than are noninsurance companies. This observation leads to a useful way of viewing this tax benefit. The additional income that an insurer can shield equals the income generated from investing the funds needed to pay expected future losses. In this example, $1.852 million ($2/1.08) is needed after year 1 to fund expected future loss payments, and the interest earned on these funds between years 1 and 2 equals $148,148 (0.08 × $1.85 million). This interest essentially escapes taxation under the insurer's tax treatment, but not under the noninsurance company's tax treatment. To confirm this, note that by avoiding tax on $148,148 of interest, an insurer would save $50,370 (0.34 × $148,148) in taxes at the end of year 2. The present value of these tax savings equals $43,184 ($50,370/1.08^2), which is the tax advantage derived earlier. Thus, the different tax treatment of insurers and noninsurance companies implies that insurers can avoid tax on the interest earned on the funds needed to pay future losses; noninsurance companies cannot.[5]

The magnitude of this tax benefit can be very large, especially for lines of insurance such as liability insurance, where claims are paid many years after losses are incurred (i.e., there is a long claims tail). In many situations the tax advantage arising from the differential treatment of losses for insurers and noninsurance companies is the most important tax benefit of insurance.[6]

Tax Benefit with Overstated Loss Reserves

The tax benefit from the different tax treatment of insurers and noninsurance companies increases if insurers overstate loss reserves. While any overstatement of loss reserves eventually must be corrected in later years on a dollar-for-dollar basis, overstatement brings tax deductions earlier in time, thus increasing the present value of tax shields. We illustrate this effect in Appendix 21A.

You might conclude that the greater value of tax shields from overstating loss reserves leads some insurers to overstate loss reserves and thus charge a lower price to better compete for business. One factor that helps mitigate this incentive is that the overstatement of loss reserves decreases reported insurer capital. Insurers therefore must balance the tax benefits from overstating loss reserves against the costs that arise if any market participants infer that the insurer has higher insolvency risk as well as the regulatory costs from lower reported capital.

[5]To eliminate the tax advantage, the IRS would have to eliminate Tennyson's deduction of $0.15 million in the second year. This could be done by forcing the present value of the loss reserve to be increased each year to reflect the implicit interest earned over the year. To illustrate, when calculating the change in the present value of the loss reserve in year 2, if Tennyson had to use the present value of the loss reserve in year 1 plus implicit interest, then the prior year present value of the loss reserve would be $2 million ($1.85 × 1.08), which would imply that the discounted value of incurred losses in year 2 would be zero and the present value of expected tax shields with insurance would be the same as with retention.

[6]The tax benefit arising from the different tax treatment of insurers and noninsurance corporations was greater prior to 1986, because insurers did not have to discount incurred losses when calculating taxes.

Concept Check

1. Suppose that Phillips Inc. has a products liability exposure where accidents this year are expected to cause loss payments equal to $3 million at the end of this year and $4 million at the end of next year. What is the present value of expected tax shields from this products liability exposure if Phillips retains its risk? Assume that the opportunity cost of capital is 10 percent and that the tax rate is 34 percent. What is the present value of expected tax shields that an insurer would have from deducting losses if it insured the same exposure?

21.4   Insuring Depreciated Property

Overview

Corporations also can obtain tax benefits from insuring depreciated property. The simplest way to explain this tax benefit is to assume that: (1) the value of existing property has been depreciated to zero (its book value is zero); (2) future depreciation expenses resulting from replacement of damaged property are the same whether the firm is insured or uninsured; and (3) the premium loading is zero (the premium equals the expected indemnity payment from the insurer). Under these assumptions, the purchase of property insurance has two tax effects. First, the firm is able to deduct the insurance premium when calculating taxable earnings, regardless of whether a loss occurs. Second, if a loss occurs, the firm will have to recognize a capital gain equal to the insurance indemnity payment. If the income tax rate exceeds the capital gains tax rate, the income tax savings from deducting the premium exceeds the expected capital gains tax payment.

As the following example illustrates, the actual tax treatment of depreciated property usually is more complex than this simple explanation might suggest. One reason is that property is not always depreciated to zero (assumption 1). Another reason is that when insurance proceeds are used to replace damaged property, firms have a choice of whether to recognize or defer the capital gain. If the gain is deferred, depreciation expenses following an uninsured loss differ from those following an insured loss. Although insurance still provides a tax benefit when the capital gain is deferred, it is more difficult to illustrate the result.

Example and Additional Insights

Suppose that Gaunt Corp. has a tax rate equal to 34 percent and the following property loss exposure:

$$\text{Property loss} = \begin{cases} \$0 & \text{with probability } 0.95 \\ \$4 \text{ million} & \text{with probability } 0.05 \end{cases}$$

Also assume that the property originally was purchased three years earlier, that the property's original cost was $4 million, and that the replacement cost of the property also is $4 million. Although the firm probably would use an accelerated depreciation method, assume for simplicity that Gaunt has used the straight-line method for tax purposes and that it is depreciating the asset over a four-year period. Since the property was purchased for $4 million three years ago, the property has been depreciated to $1 million; that is, its current tax basis equals $1 million. Finally, assume that if a loss occurs this year (year 1), the property will be immediately replaced, implying that the firm is able to begin taking a depreciation deduction for the new property this year.

To focus on the tax effects of insurance versus retention, assume that the insurance premium does not include a loading so that the premium for full replacement cost coverage equals $200,000 (expected claim costs equal 0.05 × $4 million). We also will ignore possible nontax reasons for purchasing insurance discussed in previous chapters (e.g., improvements in contracts with employees and customers, avoidance of the cost of issuing new securities, and so on) and any tax benefits not associated with depreciated property.

Retention

Table 21.4 summarizes the tax consequences if Gaunt retains the risk. If a loss does not occur, Gaunt will depreciate the asset from $1 million to $0, thus generating a depreciation tax shield of $0.34 million. If a loss occurs, Gaunt can deduct the lesser of the fair market value of the property or the tax basis. In this example, the tax basis ($1 million) is less than the fair market value. Thus, the loss generates a tax shield of $1 million times 0.34, which equals $0.34 million. Since Gaunt immediately replaces the property by purchasing another capital asset with a cost of $4 million, the new asset also generates a depreciation tax shield in year 1. Assuming that Gaunt uses a four-year straight-line depreciation schedule for the new property, the depreciation tax shield in year 1 is $0.34 million. The new property is further depreciated by $1 million in years 2 through 4, generating depreciation tax shields in each of those years equal to $0.34 million. The key points to notice are: (1) the loss eliminates the remaining depreciation tax shields on the book value of the lost property, but the firm receives a tax shield equal to the book value of the loss; and (2) the replacement of the property gives rise to additional depreciation tax shields on the new property.

Insurance and Recognition of a Capital Gain

If insured, Gaunt can deduct the insurance premium, which gives it a tax shield equal to 0.34 × $200,000 = $68,000, regardless of whether a loss occurs. If a loss occurs, Gaunt can either (1) recognize a capital gain of $3 million, pay capital gains taxes, and then depreciate the new asset over time; or (2) defer the gain from the insurance proceeds, keep the tax basis on the new property at the old tax basis ($1 million), and limit its depreciation tax shields to the same level as if the property were not lost. We analyze the first option in Table 21.5.

By replacing the asset with the insurance proceeds and recognizing the capital gain, Gaunt obtains depreciated tax shields on the entire value of the new property ($4 million).

TABLE 21.4
Tax consequences of retention for Gaunt Corp. (in $ millions; income tax rate = 34%).

Tax Shield	If No Loss Occurs (probability = 0.95)		If a Loss Occurs in Year 1 (probability = 0.05)	
	Year 1	Year 2–Year 4	Year 1	Year 2–Year 4
Uninsured loss	$0	$0	$0.34	$0
Depreciation	0.34	0	0.34	0.34
Insurance premium	0	0	0	0
Capital gains	0	0	0	0
Total tax shields	$0.34	0	$0.68	$0.34

Expected tax shields in year 1 = 0.95 × $34 + 0.05 × $68 = $0.357
Expected tax shields in years 2 through 4 = 0.95 × $0 + 0.05 × $0.34 = $0.017

TABLE 21.5
Tax consequences of full insurance and recognition of capital gain for Gaunt Corp. (in $ millions; income tax rate = 34%; capital gains tax rate = 20%).

Tax Shield	If No Loss Occurs (probability = 0.95)		If a Loss Occurs in Year 1 (probability = 0.05)	
	Year 1	Year 2–Year 4	Year 1	Year 2–Year 4
Uninsured loss	$0	$0	$0	$0
Depreciation	0.340	0	0.340	0.34
Insurance premium	0.068	0	0.068	0
Capital gains	0	0	−0.600	0
Total tax shield	$0.408	$0	−$0.192	$0.34

Expected tax shields in year 1 = 0.95 × $0.408 − 0.05 × $0.192 = $0.378
Expected tax shields in years 2 through 4 = 0.95 × 0 + 0.05 × $0.34 = $0.017

In particular, $1 million of the new property is depreciated in the year of the loss and the remaining $3 million is depreciated in equal increments in years 2 through 4. Thus, Gaunt's depreciation tax shields if an insured loss occurs are the same as when it is uninsured (see Table 21.4).

The tax differences between insurance and retention in this case arise because Gaunt generates a tax shield on the insurance premium and it must pay a capital gains tax. The insurance premium tax shield equals 0.34 times $200,000, or $68,000, regardless of whether the loss occurs. The capital gains tax arises if a loss occurs. Following a loss, the firm must pay tax on the difference between the new tax basis ($4 million) and the old tax basis ($1 million). Assuming a 20 percent capital gains rate, the capital gains tax equals $0.6 million (0.2 × $3 million).

Table 21.5 summarizes the results. Notice that the expected tax shields in years 2 through 4 are the same with insurance as with retention (see Table 21.4). Insurance, however, raises the expected tax shields in year 1 from $0.357 million (without insurance) to $0.378 million. The difference equals $21,000. This benefit from insurance arises because the capital gains tax rate (20 percent) is lower than the income tax rate (34 percent). In this example, a capital gain of $3 million occurs with probability 0.05. Thus, insurance allows the firm to reduce its expected tax payments by $3 million (the capital gain) times 0.05 (the probability of the gain) times 0.14 (the difference in tax rates), which equals $21,000. In summary, insurance and recognition of the capital gain provide a tax benefit if the capital gains rate is less than the income tax rate.

Insurance and Deferral of the Capital Gain

The second method of treating the insurance proceeds is to defer the capital gain; that is, keep the tax basis on the new property at the same level as the old property. In this example, the insurance proceeds would be used to purchase a new asset but the tax basis of the new property would be $1 million. The tax shields arising from this approach are presented in Table 21.6. Since a capital gain is not realized, there are no depreciation tax shields in years 2 through 4. Instead, the asset is replaced and then fully depreciated in year 1. Thus, regardless of whether a loss occurs, the firm receives a depreciation tax shield equal to $340,000 (0.34 times $1 million) plus the tax shield on the insurance premium, which equals $68,000. The total tax shield in year 1 therefore equals $408,000.

Comparing expected tax shields from insurance (see Table 21.6) to expected tax shields from retention (see Table 21.4) indicates that insurance increases the expected tax shield in

TABLE 21.6
Tax consequences of full insurance and deferral of the capital gain (in $ millions)

Tax Shield	If No Loss Occurs (probability = 0.95)		If a Loss Occurs in Year 1 (probability = 0.05)	
	Year 1	Year 2–Year 4	Year 1	Year 2–Year 4
Uninsured loss	$0	$0	$0	$0
Depreciation	0.34	0	0.34	0
Insurance premium	0.068	0	0.068	0
Capital gains	0	0	0	0
Total tax shield	$0.408	$0	$0.408	$0

Expected tax shields in year 1 = 0.95 × $408 + 0.05 × $0.408 = $0.408

Expected tax shields in years 2 through 4 = $0

year 1 by $51,000 ($408,000 − $357,000) and insurance reduces expected tax shields in years 2 through 4 by $17,000 per year. Notice, however, that $17,000 times three (the number of years) equals $51,000. Thus, the effect of insurance is to bring the tax shields forward in time, thereby increasing their present value.

In summary, regardless of whether the firm defers or recognizes the capital gain from using the insurance proceeds to purchase new assets, a tax benefit exists from insurance relative to retention. Comparing the deferral method to the recognition method, the tax benefit from deferral is more likely to dominate the tax benefit from recognition of the capital gain as (1) the difference between the income tax rate and the capital gains rate becomes smaller, and (2) the length of time required to depreciate the asset increases.

21.5   Insurance and Interest Tax Shields on Debt

A firm's **capital structure** refers to the way that it has raised capital to finance its assets. At a general level, a firm's capital structure often is described by the value of its debt (i.e., the amount that it has borrowed) divided by the value of its equity (assets minus liabilities). For example, if a firm has $50 million in outstanding debt and the value of equity equals $50 million, then the debt-to-equity ratio is 1. Although the optimal capital structure for a particular firm is subject to debate, financial analysts generally agree that the principal advantage of using debt financing is that debt creates **interest tax shields;** that is, the interest payments on debt are deductible when calculating taxable income. In contrast, the firm cannot deduct dividend payments to equityholders. Thus, for a firm with a 34 percent tax rate, each dollar of interest paid to debtholders generates a tax shield of 34 cents, assuming the firm has sufficient earnings before interest and taxes to deduct the entire interest payment.

Debt financing, however, has some disadvantages, which generally stem from the possibility that the firm could experience financial distress. As discussed in Chapter 20, debtholders will be concerned about bankruptcy costs and whether the firm will adopt risky, negative net present value projects or fail to adopt positive net present value projects. Consequently, debtholders require additional compensation (higher promised interest payments) as the probability of financial distress increases. At some point, debtholders simply may refuse to lend any more money to the firm because the probability of financial distress is too high.

In Chapter 20 we discussed how risk reduction (e.g., purchasing insurance) lowers the probability of financial distress and therefore allows the firm to borrow funds at lower costs. Here, we make a related point. By reducing risk, firms might find it optimal to use more debt financing. The additional debt financing generates additional interest tax shields, which can increase firm value. Focusing purely on the effect of risk reduction on the amount of debt financing used, firms can be expected to decrease risk until the marginal cost of doing so equals the value of the additional interest tax shields generated by the additional debt.

Note that risk management affects a firm's capital structure and that a firm's capital structure affects its decision regarding how much risk to reduce. Thus, a firm's capital structure and risk management policy are interrelated so that these decisions should not be made independently.

21.6 Insurance Premiums and Excise Taxes

Insurance premiums are subject to two other forms of taxation that can influence loss financing decisions. All states impose **premium taxes** on insurance transactions. Although there is some variation, premium taxes commonly equal about 2 percent of the premium. Premium taxes can differ depending on whether or not the insurer is domiciled (incorporated) in the state.[7] For example, some states impose higher premium taxes on insurers that are domiciled in other states. In response, other states have passed retaliatory taxes on insurers that are domiciled in states that impose higher premium taxes on nondomiciled insurers. The important point is that premium taxes increase the insurer's cost of providing insurance and thus can potentially influence the decision to purchase insurance or the choice of a particular insurer.

The federal government also imposes **excise taxes** if insurance is purchased from an insurer that is domiciled outside of the United States (i.e., an alien insurer). The excise tax is 1 percent on reinsurance transactions and 4 percent on primary insurance transactions. Unlike premium taxes, the insurance buyer, not the insurer, nominally pays the excise tax on primary insurance. Similarly, the insurer, not the reinsurer, nominally pays the excise tax on reinsurance. The higher excise tax rate on primary insurance can influence the loss financing decisions of corporations, which we discuss in the next section.

21.7 Regulatory Effects on Loss Financing

Government regulation can influence loss financing decisions in two main ways.[8] First, the government may require companies to purchase insurance. Second, the government may restrict the pool of insurers from whom businesses may purchase insurance.

[7]From the perspective of a particular state, a domestic insurer is an insurer that is domiciled in the state, a foreign insurer is an insurer that is domiciled in another state in the United States, and an alien insurer is an insurer that is domiciled outside of the United States.

[8]Price regulation also can affect loss financing decisions by affecting the premium loading (see Chapter 8). For example, if regulated premiums are less than competitive market levels, then a business will view insurance as having a low premium loading, which will increase the desirability of insurance, all else equal. Also see the discussion of this issue in Chapter 18.

Compulsory Insurance

The main reason why the government sometimes makes business insurance compulsory is to reduce the likelihood that firms will be unable to fulfill their legal obligations to individuals or other firms. For example, as we discussed in more detail in Chapter 18, firms are obligated to pay workers' compensation benefits to workers who become injured or ill as a result of their jobs. To ensure that firms are financially capable of paying workers' compensation benefits, firms must either purchase insurance or qualify as self-insurers (which usually is difficult for small firms). Similarly, automobile liability and truck liability insurance coverage often is compulsory if the firm that owns the cars and trucks does not qualify as a self-insurer. When insurance is mandatory, firms have no choice between retention and insurance.

Restriction on the Choice of Insurers

As we have mentioned in earlier chapters, insurance is regulated at the state level in the United States. Insurers can become licensed to sell insurance to cover risk exposures that are located in a particular state by meeting the state's licensing requirements. A licensed insurer in a particular state is called an **admitted insurer** for that particular state.[9]

An unlicensed or **nonadmitted insurer** also can sell insurance that covers a risk located in a state in which it is not licensed. However, the nonadmitted insurer must be licensed in at least one state and must sell nonadmitted insurance through an agent who has met the state's regulations for placing insurance with a nonadmitted insurer. Typically, agents placing insurance with a nonadmitted insurer face stricter regulations than agents placing insurance with an admitted insurer. Regulation of agents in principle substitutes for the lack of regulation of nonadmitted insurers.

While the specific regulatory provisions and their enforcement vary across states, a company (or individual) technically can buy insurance from a nonadmitted insurer only if it cannot obtain insurance from an admitted insurer. In some states, proof of being denied coverage from one or more admitted insurers is required. Thus, nonadmitted insurers typically provide coverage for exposures that are unusual or require very high limits. Because nonadmitted insurance coverage often is excess coverage (coverage in excess of some limit), the market for nonadmitted insurance also is called the **excess and surplus (E&S) lines market.** In 2001, direct premiums written by E&S insurers totaled approximately $15.7 billion (*Best's Review,* October 2002). This was about an 11 percent share of the commercial insurance market.

Due to the requirement that firms purchase insurance from an admitted insurer if it is available, admitted insurers sometimes serve as an intermediary between a firm that wishes to purchase insurance from a nonadmitted insurer. For example, Weiss Corp. may purchase insurance from ADM Insurance Company (an admitted insurer), who will then reinsure most or all of the exposure with NONADM Insurance Company (a nonadmitted insurer). This arrangement is called **fronting,** and the fronting insurer (ADM in this example) will charge a fee for providing the fronting service.[10]

[9]In footnote 7, we described three types of insurers from the perspective of a particular state: domestic, foreign, and alien. All three types of insurers can be licensed by a state and thus all three can be admitted insurers.

[10]As discussed in Chapter 25 fronting often is used in offshore captive insurance transactions to satisfy state laws requiring that insurance be purchased from an admitted insurer or to satisfy third-party requirements of a certificate of insurance from a rated insurer.

Excise taxes provide another reason for using a fronting insurer. Recall that excise taxes on reinsurance transactions are 1 percent of the premium, while excise taxes on primary insurance transactions are 4 percent of the premium. As a result, paying insurance premiums to a primary carrier who then reinsures the bulk of the exposure with a non-US insurer may lower total tax payments. The primary insurer would have to pay premium taxes on the primary insurance, but as long as the state's premium tax rate is less than 3 percent, the sum of the premium taxes on the primary insurance plus the excise taxes on the reinsurance will be less than the excise tax that otherwise would have been paid on primary insurance with a non-US insurer.

Another reason for a firm to purchase insurance through a fronting insurer is that a contractual party may require a certificate of insurance from a particular set of insurers (e.g., insurers with a high A. M. Best rating, as discussed in Chapter 7), although an alternative insurer is preferred by the insurance purchaser. For example, suppose that Thornton Corp. requires that its suppliers have liability insurance from an insurer that is A-rated from Best's, but that one of the suppliers prefers to have insurance from an unrated insurer (such as a captive insurer, which we discuss in Chapter 25). Then, the supplier can purchase insurance from an A-rated insurer, which in turn will reinsure the entire exposure with the supplier's preferred insurer.

Some of the reasons for using fronting insurers might suggest that a fronting arrangement is a sham transaction without economic substance. The fronting insurer, however, is liable for claims costs if the reinsurer becomes insolvent. Consequently, the fronting insurer has an incentive to monitor the solvency of the reinsurer prior to engaging in a fronting transaction, and the fee charged by the fronting insurer will reflect the insolvency risk of the reinsurer. The fact that a fronting insurer will cede the entire exposure for a relatively low fee indicates that the reinsurer has low insolvency risk. In essence, a fronting insurer acts as a guarantor that the reinsurer has low insolvency risk.

Fronting for nonadmitted insurers sometimes comes under regulatory scrutiny. Regulators' concern with fronting arrangements arises for two reasons. As mentioned, fronting insurers must assume the liabilities that were originally ceded to a nonadmitted reinsurer if the reinsurer becomes insolvent. Regulators' concern is that nonadmitted reinsurers may be poorly capitalized, which in turn jeopardizes the solvency of the ceding insurer. The second reason is that regulators may experience difficulty or high costs collecting payments from nonadmitted reinsurers if the fronting insurer becomes insolvent. As a result, either guarantee funds end up paying a greater share of the insolvent fronting insurer's liabilities or policyholders are uncompensated for some of their losses.

21.8 Financial Accounting Influences on Loss Financing

The decision to finance losses using internal funds as opposed to using insurance also influences financial accounting income statements and balance sheets. It is important at the outset to distinguish financial reporting from tax accounting. The Financial Accounting Standards Board (FASB) promulgates rules (called generally accepted accounting principles, or GAAP) that firms should follow in reporting information to investors. These rules can and often do differ from tax accounting rules. This section is concerned with financial reporting rather than taxes.

Generally, reported accounting numbers, in and of themselves, do not influence firm valuation (although exceptions will be noted below). Value depends on expected cash flows, the timing of these cash flows, and the risk of the cash flows. To the extent that reported accounting numbers provide information about cash flows, then they will appear to influence valuation. Thus, if Frickel Corp. announces unexpected positive accounting earnings and the announcement increases investors' expectations of cash flows, its stock price will likely increase. However, the valuation effect arises not from the accounting numbers per se but from the expectation of higher cash flows.

Consider another scenario. Suppose that Frickel Corp. alters its reported accounting earnings without changing its cash flows. In particular, assume that Frickel Corp. defers the recognition of some of its expenses to a later year, thus allowing it to report higher earnings this year. Will the stock price increase as a result of the higher reported earnings? The answer is probably not. Since value depends on cash flows, informed investors will likely "see through" the accounting manipulation and realize that cash flows have not been changed.

This discussion of accounting may suggest that, from a valuation perspective, the accounting effects of loss financing decisions are irrelevant. This conclusion, however, is too hasty, because there are potential indirect cash flow effects of accounting numbers. In the remainder of this section we describe the main accounting differences between insurance and retention and then describe the potential cash flow effects of financial accounting numbers.

Financial Accounting for Insurance Premiums and Uninsured Losses

Insurance premiums are reported as an expense in the year in which coverage is provided. Since insurance premiums reflect expected insured losses (not actual losses), an insured firm reduces its reported income by an amount that is directly related to the value of expected insured losses. With multiple year policies, the premium expense is allocated proportionately. If, for example, Frickel Corp. pays $20,000 for an insurance policy that provides coverage over a two-year period, a $10,000 expense will be recognized in each of the two years.

Uninsured losses are reported as an expense in the year in which they occur. For example, if Frickel Corp. experiences a $10 million uninsured loss in 1998, it would recognize the entire $10 million as an expense in 1998. Thus, an uninsured firm reduces its income by an amount that reflects actual losses (not expected losses). An uninsured firm cannot deduct contingency reserves that reflect the expected value of losses each year; instead, it must deduct actual losses when they occur.

Note that the financial reporting of uninsured losses differs from the tax reporting of uninsured losses. For financial reporting purposes, a firm should deduct losses in the year in which the losses occur, not when they are paid. In contrast, for tax purposes, a noninsurance firm can deduct losses only in the year the losses are paid. To illustrate this difference, suppose that Frickel Corp. knows that a liability suit has been filed alleging that an accident occurred because one of the firm's products was defective. Also assume that the suit is likely to take several years to be resolved. Once the company realizes that a loss from the liability suit is probable and can be reasonably estimated, then it should recognize an expense for the likely amount of the loss even if the loss may not be paid and deducted for tax purposes until some time in the future. Thus, reported income and shareholders' equity should be lowered in the year the loss becomes probable (Financial Accounting Standard SFAS 5).

Regardless of whether insurance premiums or uninsured losses occur, a firm's balance sheet will reflect the reported after-tax expense as a decrease in shareholders' equity. If the loss is paid in the same year that the expense is recognized, then the firm's reported assets will decrease by the same amount that shareholders' equity decreases. However, if the loss is not paid until some time in the future, then the firm's reported liabilities will increase by the amount of the after-tax expense. In the latter case, in the year the loss is finally paid, the liability for the unpaid loss will be removed and assets will decrease by the amount of the expense.

When comparing the effects of insurance versus retention on accounting earnings, the main difference is that insurance generally will result in smoother or less variable earnings. Stated differently, accounting earnings are less likely to experience large jumps when a firm is insured. To provide a simple illustration, suppose that Frickel Corp. is subject to the risk of a product liability suit. Assume that the probability of a suit is 0.05 and that damages equal $10 million. Ignoring administrative costs, capital costs, and the time value of money, the fair premium equals $500,000. The purchase of liability insurance for a $500,000 premium will decrease before-tax earnings by $500,000 regardless of whether a loss occurs. With retention (the payment of liability losses from internal funds), before-tax earnings depend on whether a loss occurs. If a loss occurs, then reported before-tax earnings will be reduced by $10 million. If a loss does not occur, before-tax earnings will be unaffected by the retention decision. Thus, retention results in greater variance in reported earnings. In this case, the greater variability in accounting earnings from retention mirrors the greater variability in cash flows from retention that was discussed in earlier chapters.

When considering the effects of insurance versus retention on a firm's accounting (as opposed to economic) balance sheet, insurance again will result in less volatile numbers. A simple example will illustrate the different effects. Suppose that if Frickel Corp. uses retention and a loss does not occur, it will have assets equal to $100 million, liabilities equal to $50 million, and shareholders' equity equal to $50 million. This scenario is summarized by the balance sheet on the top left of Table 21.7. If a $10 million loss occurs and is paid from the firm's internal funds, then Frickel's assets will fall by $10 million and its shareholders' equity also will fall by $10 million. The top right side of Table 21.7 gives Frickel's balance sheet if a loss occurs. The important point is that the firm's liability-to-equity ratio is subject to considerable variability depending on whether a loss occurs. In contrast, if Frickel Corp. purchases insurance for $0.5 million, then its assets and shareholders' equity will fall by $0.5 million regardless of whether a loss occurs. The bottom of Table 21.7 summarizes the firm's balance sheet with insurance.

Impact of Financial Accounting Numbers on Cash Flow

Suppose that Mr. Eastman, the risk manager of Seminole Corporation, has analyzed the advantages and disadvantages of insurance versus retention discussed in this chapter and in Chapter 20 and has concluded that the present value of expected cash flows will be the same with insurance as with retention. After reporting his results at a meeting, Ms. Petroni, the company's accountant, tells Mr. Eastman that insurance is better than retention because it results in smoother (less variable) reported earnings. Mr. Eastman replies, "Financial accounting numbers are irrelevant to firm valuation; investors care about cash flows." Ms. Petroni goes back to her office and writes a brief report outlining how less volatile accounting numbers can influence the magnitude or variability of cash flows.

Her first argument is that less volatile earnings allow investors to predict earnings and thus cash flows more accurately, which means that investors will view the firm's cash flows as having lower risk and thus will pay a higher price for the firm's stock. (Mr. Eastman prob-

TABLE 21.7
Frickel Corp.'s
balance sheet
with retention
and with
insurance
(in $ millions).

Balance Sheet with Retention and No Loss	Balance Sheet with Retention and a $10 Million Loss
Assets = $100 Liabilities = $50 Shareholders' equity = $50 Liability/Equity ratio = 100%	Assets = $90 Liability = $50 Shareholders' equity = $40 Liability/Equity ratio = 125%

**Frickel Corp.'s Balance Sheet with Full Insurance
(regardless of whether a loss occurs)**

Assets = $99.5   Liabilities = $50
Shareholders' equity = $49.5
Liability/Equity ratio = 101%

ably will not be very sympathetic to this argument because he believes that the only risk that matters for valuation is nondiversifiable risk and that the risk Ms. Petroni is talking about is firm-specific risk and therefore diversifiable.)

Ms. Petroni's second argument is that the firm's debt contracts state that the firm is technically in default if reported earnings fall below a certain level or the firm's liabilities-to-assets ratio increases above a certain level. The purchase of insurance implies that the firm is less likely to trigger default and therefore less likely to incur the costs of renegotiating its debt contracts. (Mr. Eastman is likely to find this argument persuasive.)

Ms. Petroni's third argument is that managers' bonuses (including Mr. Eastman's) are based on reported earnings. Less volatile earnings imply that earnings are more likely to be above the minimum level necessary for managers to receive a bonus. Thus, managers should purchase insurance. (Mr. Eastman probably will find this argument persuasive.)

Ms. Petroni's final argument is that insurance reduces earnings volatility, which in turn allows the firm's shareholders to monitor managers more effectively (at a lower cost). Her reasoning is that insurance reduces the extent to which factors that are outside of the control of managers influence earnings. Consequently, reported earnings are a more accurate representation of managers' performance. (Mr. Eastman, being a superior manager, will like this argument because it increases the likelihood that the board of directors will notice his efforts and skills.)

In summary, loss financing choices influence reported accounting numbers. While accounting numbers, in and of themselves, usually are not the most important consideration when making loss financing decisions, the accounting effects sometimes are relevant, especially when contracts (e.g., debt covenants and management compensation contracts) are written based on accounting numbers.

21.9   Summary

- A transaction provides a tax benefit if it lowers the aggregate present value of expected tax payments for the parties involved.

- When effective tax rates are progressive, reducing the variability of cash flows will lower expected tax payments.

- Insurers can deduct estimates of unpaid losses when calculating their taxable income, but noninsurance companies cannot. This difference provides a tax benefit to insurance. Essentially, insurers can earn the before-tax rate of return on funds set aside to pay future losses.

- The tax treatment of losses on depreciated property provides a tax benefit to property insurance.

- By lowering the variability in cash flows, firms might be able to borrow more funds than otherwise. The additional borrowing creates interest tax shields, which can increase firm value.

- Premium taxes and excise taxes increase the premium loading on insurance, thus reducing its attractiveness.

- Government regulation makes some insurance compulsory and restricts firms' choices of insurers.

- Fronting refers to the practice of purchasing primary insurance from one insurer that immediately reinsures most of the exposure with another insurer. Fronting is used to: (1) comply with regulations that restrict the choice of insurers; (2) reduce excise taxes; and (3) satisfy third-party demands that insurance be provided by a particular set of insurers.

- In contrast to the tax treatment of uninsured losses, the financial reporting of uninsured losses requires firms to recognize losses when they become probable and can be reasonably estimated.

- Insurance generally reduces the variability of reported income and balance sheet numbers. Since contracts often are based on accounting numbers, accounting effects can be important when considering loss financing alternatives.

Key Terms

tax benefit 464
tax rate progressivity 465
incurred losses 468
tax shield 468
capital structure 474

interest tax shields 474
premium taxes 475
excise taxes 475
admitted insurer 476

nonadmitted i
excess and sur
 lines market
fronting 476

Questions and Problems

1. True or false: "This transaction will reduce expected tax payments; therefore, we should do it!" Briefly explain your answer.

2. True or false: "This insurance transaction does not provide a tax benefit, because the tax law gives the favorable tax treatment to the insurer." Briefly explain your answer.

3. Suppose that the Lai Jean Co. expects before-tax earnings of $5 million this coming year, assuming no liability losses. However, there is a 2 percent chance that Lai will lose a $10 million lawsuit during the year. Profits are taxed at a rate of 34 percent. Assume that Lai cannot carry losses forward or backward (e.g., it has had no profits in the past and it expects to close down next year). Would lia-

bility insurance with a $10 million limit for a premium of $225,000 increase expected after-tax earnings for this coming year? (Assume that negative earnings are taxed at a rate of zero percent.)

4. Suppose that Neilson's Restaurants has a liability exposure with expected loss payments equal to $3 million this year, $3 million next year, and $1 million in two years. Assume that Neilson's can fully deduct all losses when calculating its taxable income, that it has a 34 percent tax rate, and that the interest rate equals 10 percent.

a. What is the present value of the expected tax shield arising from Neilson's liability exposure if retention is chosen?

b. What is the present value of the expected tax shield arising from Neilson's
liability exposure if its liability exposure
is insured through the Tennyson Insurance Company? That is, what would
Tennyson's expected tax shield equal?

5. Suppose that Gardner Manufacturing has
assets that are worth $50 million. If these
assets are destroyed, Gardner plans to replace them at a cost of $50 million. Gard-
ner uses the straight-line depreciation
method and the nature of the assets requires that they be depreciated over a two-
year period. For tax purposes, the assets
already have been depreciated to zero. Assume that the probability that the assets
will be destroyed during the coming year
equals 0.05, the income tax rate is 34 percent, and the capital gains tax rate is 28
percent. Calculate the expected tax shield
generated from the property in the coming
year and in future years if:

a. Gardner plans to use internal funds to fi-

nance replacement of the property if it is
destroyed.

b. Gardner purchases replacement cost insurance for a premium of $2.5 million
and plans to recognize a capital gain if
the insurance proceeds are used to replace the property.

c. Gardner purchases replacement cost insurance for a premium of $2.5 million
and plans to defer the capital gain if the
insurance proceeds are used to replace
the property.

6. Explain the practice of fronting. Does a
fronting insurer provide a service other than
allowing a business to circumvent unpleasant regulations? Explain.

7. Describe how tax accounting and financial
reporting differ with regard to losses that
occur in a given year.

8. Explain how (a) reported income, (b) reported balance sheet assets and liabilities,
and (c) the variability of reported income
each might affect a firm's cash flows.

Answers to Concept Check

1. The tax shields generated by the exposure
without insurance:

	End of Year 1	End of Year 2
Expected tax shields	0.34 × $3= $1.02	0.34 × $4= $1.36

Present value of tax shields = $2.05

The tax shields generated by the exposure
with insurance:

	End of Year 1	End of Year 2
Expected tax shields	0.34 × ($3 +4/1.1) = $2.051	0.34 × ($4 − 4/1.1) = $0.102

Present value of tax shields = $2.153

References

Aird, Paul; Robert Witt; and Patrick Brockett. "Economic Overview of the Market for Excess & Surplus Lines Insurance." *Journal of Insurance Regulation* 9 (December 1990), pp. 234–58. (*Provides an overview of the excess and surplus lines market.*)

Mayers, David; and Clifford Smith. "On the Corporate Demand for Insurance." *Journal of Business* 55 (1982), pp. 281–96. (*Provides an overview of why corporations with diversified shareholders purchase insurance, including the tax reasons for purchasing insurance.*)

Appendix 21A

Tax Benefits when Insurers Overstate Loss Reserves

Table 21A.1 illustrates the additional tax benefit from overstatement of loss reserves by insurers. Instead of reporting loss reserves in year 1 of $2 million, suppose that Tennyson plans to report loss reserves of $3 million (for comparison, see Table 21.3 in the chapter). The present value of the loss reserve is $3/1.08 = $2.778 million, which, when added to paid losses, gives a value of $4.778 million for the discounted value of incurred losses. In year 2, Tennyson plans to correct the overstatement in the prior year by reporting $0 for the loss reserve. The change in the present value of the loss reserve is therefore −$2.778 million, which, when added to paid losses, gives a value of −$0.778 million for incurred losses in year 2. The negative value for incurred losses implies that Tennyson reports higher taxable earnings in year 2.

The expected tax shield equals 34 percent of incurred losses for tax purposes, which for year 1 equals $1.624 million (0.34 × $4.778 million) and for year 2 equals −$0.265 million (0.34 × −$0.778 million). The present value of the expected tax shields therefore equals

$$\frac{1.624}{1.08} + \frac{-0.265}{1.08^2} = \$1.277 \text{ million}$$

This value exceeds the present value of expected tax shields that was calculated in section 21.3 with unbiased reporting ($1.256 million) by $21,600. The difference arises because Tennyson is able to bring some of its tax shields earlier in time by overstating loss reserves. In particular, by overstating loss reserves by $1 million, the discounted value of incurred losses is increased by $0.926 million in year 1. This overstatement generates an additional tax shield of $0.315 million (0.34 × $0.926) in year 1. The tax shield is reversed in year 2; that is, Tennyson has $0.315 million in higher taxes in year 2, but by pushing the tax shield forward, Tennyson essentially earns interest on the tax shield equal to $0.025 million (0.08 × $0.315 million). The present value of this interest is $0.025/1.08² = $21,600.

TABLE 21A.1 Effect of Crocker Snowblowers purchasing insurance from Tennyson Insurance when Tennyson overstates loss reserves in year 1 (in $ millions).

	Beginning of Year 1	End of Year 1	End of Year 2
1. Paid losses		$2.000	$2.000
2. Loss reserve	$0.000	$3.000	$0.000
3. Change in loss reserve		$3.000	−$3.000
4. Undiscounted incurred losses (1) + (3)		$5.000	−$1.000
5. Present value of loss reserve (discounted value of 2)	$0.000	$2.778	$0.000
6. Change in present value of loss reserve		$2.778	−$2.778
7. Incurred losses for tax purposes (1) + (6)		$4.778	−$0.778

Chapter 22

Risk Retention/ Reduction Decisions

Chapter Objectives

- Identify firm characteristics that influence firm decisions about risk retention/reduction.
- Summarize evidence indicating which types of firms are more likely to reduce risk.
- Identify the variables on which a firm should focus its risk reduction activities.
- Explain the advantages and disadvantages of following a disaggregated approach to risk reduction.

22.1 Firm Characteristics Affecting Risk Retention (Reduction) Decisions

The previous two chapters outlined conceptual reasons why firms might find it advantageous to reduce risk even when the firm's owners can reduce risk on their own through portfolio diversification. In short, the reasons given in Chapter 20 are that firm-level risk affects the likelihood that a firm not only will have to raise costly external capital but also will encounter financial distress, which in turn affects the terms at which a firm contracts with lenders, employees, suppliers, and customers. In Chapter 21, we explained that firms might reduce risk because risk reduction is required by regulation or reduces expected tax payments. In this section, we use the conceptual arguments from the previous two chapters to derive implications about specific firm characteristics that are likely to influence risk reduction decisions.

Risk retention refers to the decision to accept the uncertainty (variability) associated with a particular risk exposure. Conversely, **risk reduction** refers to the decision to reduce uncertainty (variability). Our discussion of the retention decision assumes that the alternative to retention is to reduce risk using an insurance contract. However, the points generalize to other risk reduction methods that are discussed in subsequent chapters, such as risk reduction using derivative contracts.

Benefits of Increased Retention

Potential savings to a firm from increasing retention include: (1) savings on premium loadings, (2) reducing exposure to insurance market volatility, (3) reducing moral hazard, (4) avoiding high premiums that may accompany asymmetric information, and (5) avoiding implicit taxes that arise from insurance price regulation.

Savings on Premium Loadings

A key factor motivating additional retention is the ability to save on some of the administrative expense and profit loadings in insurance premiums, thus reducing the expected cash outflows for these loadings. Specific sources of savings include lower commissions to insurance brokers, possible savings in underwriting expenses and administrative costs of claim settlement, and savings in state premium taxes (typically 2 percent of the premium) and implicit taxes for expected guaranty fund assessments. Recall, however, that part of an insurer's administrative costs are due to the provision of services to the insured. Thus, the savings on premium loadings depend on the insurer's cost of providing these services relative to the firm's own costs. The savings on premium loadings also depend on the amount of profit loading that the firm can avoid paying by retaining more risk, which in turn depends on the insurer's capital costs and ability to reduce risk through diversification and reinsurance, relative to the firm's capital costs and ability to diversify risk.

Potential savings in profit loadings also can depend on the degree of competition in insurance markets. While most insurance markets are competitively structured, the market for very large limits of business insurance often involves negotiation between the corporate buyer and a group of insurers that share the risk. In these instances, it has been suggested that insurers may achieve higher expected profits than is the case where many independent insurers are competing to sell coverage (see Box 22.1 later in this chapter).

Reducing Exposure to Insurance Market Volatility

Another motivation for some corporations to increase risk retention has been the desire to reduce their vulnerability to annual swings in insurance prices due to the effects of shocks to insurer capital on the supply of insurance and/or the insurance underwriting cycle. Loss financing decisions often are part of a long-term business strategy or plan. Once a firm decides to insure a particular exposure, it may be costly to change its strategy in response to an insurance price increase. This is because an immediate large increase in the amount of risk retained can increase the probability of financial distress, increase the likelihood that the firm will not have sufficient internal funds to adopt positive net present value projects, and damage relationships with customers, suppliers, or lenders. Arranging alternative loss financing, such as accumulating internal funds or establishing a captive (see Chapter 25), also can take time.

As a result of these influences, the demand for insurance by individual firms often is inelastic in the short run (i.e., comparatively unresponsive to a change in price in the short run). As a consequence, the purchase of insurance can lead to the perverse result: Even though a major purpose of purchasing insurance generally is to reduce uncertainty in cash flows, the volatility in insurance prices exposes the firm to uncertainty. When making long-term loss financing decisions, therefore, the volatility in insurance prices often is viewed by risk managers as a negative aspect of insurance, which leads them to increase retention.

Reducing Moral Hazard

You learned in Chapter 10 that deductibles and other copayments reduce moral hazard. Without these contractual provisions, expected claim costs would be higher and therefore so would insurance premiums. Consequently, when moral hazard is more of a potential problem, firms tend to retain more risk.

Avoiding High Premiums Caused by Asymmetric Information

The inability of insurers to estimate claim costs precisely for all potential buyers causes some buyers to face prices that are relatively high compared to their true, unobservable expected claim costs. These buyers have an incentive to retain more risk (see the discussion of adverse selection in Chapter 10). Higher risk buyers would have the opposite incentive (i.e., they would retain less risk to the extent that they face a lower price for insurance because they are pooled with lower risk firms). Note, however, that the reasoning "We have lower expected claim costs than what the insurer thinks" might be seductive and somewhat dangerous. Recall that insurers have substantial incentives to forecast costs accurately. Firms also can provide insurers with any available evidence that their expected claim costs might be lower than predicted by the insurer.

Avoiding Implicit Taxes Due to Insurance Price Regulation

In the case of workers' compensation insurance, some states periodically have had large residual markets characterized by significant cross-subsidies from the voluntary market to the residual market (see Chapter 18). To the extent that this occurs in workers' compensation or other lines of business insurance that have residual markets (e.g., commercial auto liability and some other types of liability coverage), any higher premiums needed to subsidize the residual market increase the incentives for firms that would be insured in the voluntary market to self-insure or otherwise increase their retention. Firms that can obtain subsidized coverage in the residual market will tend to purchase more coverage (retain less risk).

Maintaining Use of Funds

It often is argued that another advantage of retention is that the firm gets to maintain use of the funds that otherwise would be paid in premiums until claim costs are paid. Given that competitive insurance premiums will reflect the present value of expected claim costs, it is not obvious that this argument is valid. The reason is that discounting expected claim costs to present value implicitly provides insurance buyers with a return on funds paid in premiums until claims are paid. As explained in Chapter 21, income tax rules for insurance versus self-insurance might even allow insurers to provide greater implicit after-tax returns to insurance buyers than could be obtained if buyers held the same amount of funds in similar assets to finance retained losses.

It sometimes is argued that a firm should view its opportunity cost of paying premiums as equal to its opportunity cost of capital for general investment decisions, which will exceed the risk-free rate of interest due to the presence of nondiversifiable risk, whereas insurers will discount expected claim costs at the risk-free rate (or something close to the risk-free rate). However, this argument is problematic because theory generally suggests that the rate used to discount losses should depend on the risk of losses rather than whether the firm or the insurer pays the losses. As a result, the appropriate discount rate for losses is the same for the firm and the insurer (apart from any tax considerations). At a minimum, it is important for you to recognize that premiums in competitive insurance markets will provide some implicit return for the expected average time lag between the payment of premiums and claim costs.

Costs of Increased Retention

Increased retention obviously exposes the firm to greater risk. As you learned in Chapter 20, increased risk can be costly for a number of reasons. For example, the greater risk from increased retention increases the probability of costly financial distress with associated adverse effects on lenders, employees, suppliers, and customers, which causes them to contract with the firm at less favorable terms. Increased retention also may require the firm to raise costly external funds and forgo some profitable investment opportunities. Moreover, increased retention may reduce expected tax shields and sacrifice possible advantages to insurance from bundling responsibility for claims payment with claims settlement. Other things being equal, the costs associated with increased retention will vary across firms depending on the nature of their ownership and operations.

Closely Held versus Publicly Traded Firms with Widely Held Stock

The owners of closely held firms typically have a significant proportion of their wealth invested in the firm and thus are undiversified compared to shareholders of publicly traded firms with widely traded stock. Because the owners of closely held firms are not diversified, they have an incentive to retain less risk (purchase more insurance) than publicly traded firms with widely held stock. Similarly, firms that have managers who own a large amount of stock and therefore are undiversified are more likely to reduce risk.

Firm Size and Correlation among Losses

If a firm has a large number of independent exposures, then the law of large numbers operates at the firm level, allowing the firm to predict its average loss per exposure more accurately. Consequently, one major benefit of insurance—the reduction in the variability of the average loss per exposure—can also be achieved by firms with a large number of uncorrelated loss exposures. Positive correlation among losses within a firm reduces the extent to which firms can diversify risk internally. Consequently, other things being equal, positive correlation increases the demand for insurance (provided that insurers are able to achieve superior diversification). Larger firms with their generally larger cash flows also are better able to readily finance losses of any given size out of cash flow than are smaller firms, and they often are able to raise external funds at lower cost. Each of these influences reduces the demand for insurance by large firms.

Investment Opportunities

Firms that are likely to have good investment opportunities will need funds to finance those investment opportunities. These firms will be more likely to reduce risk because an unexpected drop in cash flow can force the firm to either forgo the investment project or raise costly external capital in order to undertake the investment project. Firms that operate in growth industries and firms that require continual investment in research and development are likely to benefit from risk reduction, all else equal.

Product Characteristics When consumers expect future services from the provider of products and services, then the demand for those products and services will depend on consumers' perceptions about the likelihood that the provider will be able to provide the future services. Of course, the likelihood that a firm will be able to provide futures services is inversely related to the likelihood of bankruptcy. Consumer durables, such as electronic equipment and cars, and financial services, such as insurance, are examples of products and services for which consumer demand is likely to be especially vulnerable to consumers' perceptions about the provider's probability of bankruptcy. Thus, firms in industries such as these tend to benefit more from risk reduction than firms in industries that produce products for which future services are not expected.

Correlation of Losses with Other Cash Flows and with Investment Opportunities
Firms whose losses are positively correlated with other cash inflows will have a lower standard deviation of total cash flows, other things being equal, and thus will tend to retain more risk. In these cases, firms have a natural hedge: When losses tend to be high, other cash flows also tend to be high, thus reducing the likelihood of financial distress and the need for external funds. For example, if a firm has more workplace injuries when demand for its products is unexpectedly high, the increased profits due to the increase in demand will at least partially offset the increase in worker injury costs.

A related result is that a positive (negative) correlation between losses and the rate of return on new investment will reduce (increase) the ability of the firm to pursue profitable investments without raising external funds, thus increasing (decreasing) the demand for insurance. The reason is that the demand for funds for new investment will tend to be high when losses are high and available internal funds are low. This case often is more applicable to hedging than insurance. For example, a reduction in oil prices is likely to reduce the rate of return on new investment in the exploration for oil. Firms in the oil industry will desire to invest less money in exploration following an oil price decline, and they will therefore have less incentive to hedge the risk of lower oil prices (see Chapter 24).

Financial Leverage
Firms with higher financial leverage (ratio of debt to equity) will have a higher likelihood of financial distress, holding the probability distribution of future asset values constant. Consequently, firms with higher leverage are likely to find risk reduction more advantageous (and vice versa; see Chapter 20).

Concept Check

1. Other factors held constant, which type of firm would be more likely to fully retain (self-insure) its workers' compensation losses?
(*a*) A firm with an individual shareholder who owns 50 percent of the stock versus a firm in which no shareholder owns more than 1 percent of the stock.
(*b*) A trucking firm with 5,000 drivers versus a manufacturing firm with 5,000 workers at a single plant.
(*c*) A firm with operating profits positively correlated with claim costs versus a firm with operating profits uncorrelated with claim costs.
(*d*) A firm with a large amount of debt in its capital structure versus a firm with no debt.

A Basic Guideline for Optimal Retention

The previous section highlights the basic trade-off between the benefits of increased retention through savings on explicit and implicit loadings in insurance premiums and the costs of increased uncertainty. A basic guideline for optimal retention decisions in view of this trade-off is: *Retain reasonably predictable losses and insure potentially large, disruptive losses.*

As noted above, potentially large losses that can cause financial distress and interrupt planned investment can arise from a single event, or they can arise from a series of smaller events during a given period. For example, a company that transports chemicals may face the possibility of very large liability claims from a single accident (e.g., several hundred million dollars). It also may face large aggregate claims in a given year if it has an unexpectedly large number of smaller claims (e.g., 50 claims averaging $3 million each). These two possibilities help explain the demand for per occurrence deductibles (or self-insured retentions) and stop loss provisions, which are discussed in Chapter 23.

For individual firms, application of the guideline that firms should retain predictable losses but insure potentially large, unpredictable, and disruptive losses depends on the specific magnitude of the benefits and costs of increased retention, including managerial judgment about the magnitude of losses that can be tolerated without producing significant costs. For example, the point or points at which losses cease to be "reasonably predictable" and become "potentially disruptive" depends on many factors, including firm size, the cost of raising external funds, and the expected value and variability of cash flows apart from any losses. Due to special circumstances (e.g., compulsory insurance rules), retention strategies adopted by particular firms may vary substantially from this basic guideline. Box 22.1 provides an example of retention policy for a very large corporation, British Petroleum, which deviates to some extent from this guideline.

You also should recognize that while the underlying motives for buying insurance differ, this guideline also is applicable to risk management decisions by individuals and closely held businesses. For example, auto owners routinely choose per occurrence deductibles for automobile collision coverage by considering the trade-off between increased risk and lower premiums for policies with larger deductibles. Moreover, risk management decisions by small, closely held businesses often reflect this trade-off.

22.2 Evidence on Business Risk Reduction Decisions

A number of studies have examined whether various firms's decisions regarding risk reduction correspond to the factors that have been outlined above. This type of research is difficult because most firms do not disclose details of their risk reduction decisions. For example, relatively few firms disclose the types and amounts of insurance they purchase. An interesting exception comes from the insurance industry. For regulatory reasons, US insurers disclose information about their use of reinsurance. One study examined reinsurance purchases by insurers and found that insurers with owners that were not well diversified purchase more reinsurance.[1] It also found that smaller insurers, which tend to have greater financial distress costs and greater costs of raising external capital, purchase more reinsurance. Thus, evidence on reinsurance is consistent with several of the reasons given in the previous chapters for why firms should reduce risk.

[1] See Mayers and Smith (1990).

Retention Policy for a Giant Corporation: The Case of British Petroleum

The insurance purchasing strategy of British Petroleum (BP), a large oil company involved in the exploration, extraction, refinement, and distribution of oil and gas, provides an interesting example of risk management at a giant corporation. BP's strategy has been analyzed by Professor Neil Doherty of Wharton and Professor Clifford W. Smith, Jr., of the University of Rochester (see the references at the end of this chapter). During the five-year period preceding the Doherty-Smith analysis (1987–91), BP's accounting profits averaged about $2 billion per year with a standard deviation of approximately $1 billion. BP had over $50 billion of assets in 1991. In conjunction with a review of its insurance purchasing by Professors Doherty and Smith, BP revamped its strategy to purchase less coverage against large losses.

Local managers are allowed the discretion to purchase coverage for losses up to $10 million. In many cases, economies in having insurers administer claims, local rules governing the purchase of liability insurance, and local tax considerations favor insuring against losses of this magnitude. Losses in the $10 to $500 million range generally are not insured, in contrast to BP's previous policy. Doherty and Smith state that this strategy change was motivated by several factors: (1) BP had paid over $1.15 billion in premiums for coverage of these losses during the prior decade and had received only $250 million in claim payments; (2) coverage disputes with insurers were more likely for losses of this magnitude; (3) the impact of losses of this size on firm value was small, given BP's size; and (4) insurers have no advantage compared to BP in providing safety and loss control services.

Doherty and Smith attribute the first two factors to less competition in the market for very large limits of insurance coverage than for smaller limits and the fact that insurers have a greater incentive to dispute coverage for large complicated events. We note, however, that there is some uncertainty as to whether the low level of claim payments compared to premiums was due to chance as opposed to high prices at the time coverage was sold. Large shocks to liability insurer capital and subsequent price increases (see Chapter 8) also could have contributed to high prices.

For losses above $500 million, BP also does not purchase insurance. Doherty and Smith note that (1) insurance market capacity to provide coverage for losses this large is limited, (2) the ability to deduct losses from taxable income reduces demand for coverage, and (3) a loss of this size due, for example, to destruction of a major oil rig could increase the price of oil, thus mitigating the loss.

Is BP's strategy of allowing managers to insure small losses but generally retaining larger losses inconsistent with the basic guideline of retaining relatively predictable losses and insuring large, potentially disruptive losses? When considering this issue, you should recall the rationale for BP's strategy. First, small losses are insured only when it is advantageous to do so for reasons other than risk transfer (e.g., service, regulatory, and tax reasons). Second, a major reason that BP stopped insuring losses in the $10 to $500 million range was that losses of this size were not likely to seriously disrupt BP's operations and investment given the size of its profits and assets. For losses above $500 million, insurance capacity often is limited. Limited capacity can make retention desirable or the only feasible option for insuring very large losses, regardless of the basic guideline.

Source: Neil Doherty and Clifford Smith. "Corporate Insurance Strategy: The Case of British Petroleum." *Journal of Applied Corporate Finance*, Fall, 1993, pp. 4–15.

Although firms rarely disclose specific information about their insurance purchases, they are required to disclose specific information about their use of derivative contracts, which are generally used to hedge price risk (see Chapter 24). Thus, a number of studies have examined whether the use of derivative contracts corresponds to the factors outlined above. These studies generally find that larger firms are more likely to use derivatives. The most likely explanation relates to the relatively large investment in computers and knowl-

Risk Reduction at Merck and R&D Expenditures 22.2

Merck & Company, Inc., the large multinational pharmaceutical company, estimated that between 1980 and 1985, the company lost more than $900 million in sales as a result of currency fluctuations. The underlying reason was that a majority of Merck's sales was denominated in foreign currencies, but a majority of its costs was denominated in US dollars. When the value of the dollar increased relative to other currencies during the early 1980s, Merck's sales that were denominated in foreign currencies converted into fewer dollars—$900 million over a five-year period!

A potential problem with this volatility was that Merck needed to continue to make substantial investments in research and development to be a leader in the pharmaceutical industry. The volatility in cash flow resulting from volatility in the value of the dollar threatened Merck's ability to fund research and development from internal funds. After an extensive analysis of its currency exposure, Merck eventually decided to hedge its currency exposure using currency options (see Chapter 24).

Source: Judy Lewent and A. John Kearney. "Identifying, Measuring, and Hedging Currency Risk at Merck." *Journal of Applied Corporate Finance,* 9 (Winter 1990), pp. 19–28.

edgeable personnel that is necessary to have a derivatives trading operation. Smaller firms are likely to find that the fixed cost of setting up an internal hedging operation exceed the benefits of reducing price risk.

Some studies have found that firms with relatively greater research and development expenses are more likely to use derivatives.[2] This finding is consistent with one of the reasons for reducing risk (hedging) discussed earlier. Firms that make large investments in research and development need funds on a consistent basis. If internal funds are not available, then these firms will have to either raise costly external capital or forgo some research and development expenditures. To ensure that internal funds are available, firms with greater research and development are more likely to hedge. As Box 22.2 indicates, Merck, the large pharmaceutical company, provides a good illustration of this motivation for hedging. Merck engaged in a currency hedging program in the 1990s, in part, to ensure that it had sufficient internally generated funds to continue its investments in research and development of new pharmaceuticals.

Other research provides interesting findings about the hedging practices of gold mining companies operating in the United States and Canada.[3] The primary risk faced by gold mining companies is the price of gold. When the price of gold increases, gold mining companies can sell their output for higher prices and thus make greater profits. Conversely, a drop in gold prices can reduce cash flows substantially and even threaten the viability of a company. This gold price risk can be hedged using derivative contracts. There is wide variation in the degree to which gold mining companies actually hedge gold price risk. Some companies hedge a large proportion of their risk and others do not hedge at all. Interestingly, gold mining companies are more likely to hedge gold price risk as the managers'

[2]See Geszky, Minton, and Shrand (1997) and Nance, Smith, and Smithson (1993).

[3]See Tufano (1996).

stock ownership of the company increases. One interpretation is that managers with large undiversified ownership interests are more likely to hedge than managers with more diversified portfolios.[4]

There is also evidence that firms are more likely to hedge as their financial leverage increases.[5] One study examined the hedging practices of oil and gas producers. The output of these firms is subject to oil and gas price risk. If the price of gas decreases, then all else equal, revenues decrease. Fortunately, this risk can be hedged with derivative contracts. Among oil and gas producers that use derivatives, the extent of hedging (the proportion of expected output) increases as the firm's financial leverage ratio increases.

22.3   Aggregated or Disaggregated Risk Management?

Assuming risk reduction is appropriate, firms must decide where to focus their risk reduction activities. Should firms take a disaggregated or micro approach and hedge (insure) each individual risk exposure separately? Or, should firms hedge (insure) some aggregate or macro measure of performance, such as earnings, which depends on each separate risk exposure, as well as the relationships between the various risk exposures? Traditionally, risk management has taken a disaggregated approach. Pure risk managers focused their attention on individual sources of risk, such property losses, liability losses, and workers' compensation losses. Financial risk managers focused their attention on other sources of risk, such as exchange rate risk or commodity price risk. The respective managers would attempt to reduce risk from individual exposures, without considering the interactions among the various sources of risk.

Many of the arguments for why firms should reduce risk suggest a more aggregate focus. For example, the progressive tax rate argument implies that firms should focus on taxable income, which depends on many sources of risk, including property losses, exchange rates, and so on. If a more aggregate approach is adopted, then firms need to consider interactions between the various sources of risk.[6] This section has two objectives: First, we highlight the level at which risk reduction would take place under each of the arguments we outlined in the previous chapters for why firms should reduce risk. Second, we discuss the advantages and disadvantages of the disaggregated versus aggregated approach to risk reduction.

Linking Theory with Practice

The left column in Table 22.1 lists the reasons value-maximizing firms would try to reduce risk and the right column identifies the variables that the argument in column one suggests should be the focus of risk reduction. In other words, a firm reducing risk for a reason in the first column would generally seek contracts (e.g., insurance contracts or derivative contracts) to influence the variable in the second column.

---

[4]Knopf, Nam, and Thornton (2002) provide additional evidence that managers are more likely to hedge as the sensitivity of their compensation to stock price increases.

[5]See Graham and Rogers (2002) and Haushalter (2000).

[6]Chapter 26 illustrates how Monte Carlo simulation can be used to consider interactions among the various sources of risk.

TABLE 22.1

Reasons for risk reduction and variables to hedge/insure.

Reason	What to Hedge/Insure
Shareholders are not diversified.	Equity value
Lower probability of financial distress to improve contractual terms with other claimants (debtholders, employees, suppliers, customers).	Earnings or cash flow
Lower probability of raising external capital reduced.	Cash flow
Expected taxes reduced because of progressive tax rates.	Taxable income
Expected taxes reduced because of different tax treatment of insurers and noninsurers.	Any potential loss on which insurers could write a policy, especially losses with a long claims tail
Expected taxes reduced because of tax treatment of depreciated property.	Property losses
Regulation requires insurance.	Workers compensation losses, environmental exposures, and auto liability losses

Advantages and Disadvantages of Disaggregation

Even though many of the arguments for business risk reduction imply that the uncertainty associated with some aggregate financial variable, such as earnings, cash flow, or equity value, is ultimately what matters, uncertainty associated with these aggregate variables could be reduced by reducing the risk associated with one or more of the disaggregated variables that comprise the aggregate variable. For example, earnings uncertainty might be decreased by reducing the risk associated with any or all of the individual components of earnings (sales, raw material costs, interest, taxes, property losses, workers' compensation losses, etc.). The issue addressed in this subsection is whether there are advantages of hedging the aggregate variable versus a disaggregated approach; that is, hedging all the individual components of the aggregate variable.

A Disaggregated Approach Can Increase Transaction Costs

The main disadvantage of insuring/hedging each individual risk exposure separately is that the use of separate contracts can increase transactions costs. Negotiating, writing, and purchasing insurance and derivative contracts involve transaction costs for both the supplier and the purchaser. Because there are fixed costs associated with this process, using a single contract that covers multiple sources of risk can reduce transaction costs.

Bundling exposures for risk transfer purposes also can reduce proportional transaction costs, although the argument is slightly more complex than the previous argument. Suppose that a firm's cash flows are subject to two sources of variability—liability risk and property risk—which are uncorrelated. The distribution for liability losses is

$$\text{Liability Loss} = \begin{array}{ll} \$50 \text{ million} & \text{with probability } 0.02 \\ \$25 \text{ million} & \text{with probability } 0.04 \\ 0 \text{ million} & \text{with probability } 0.94 \end{array}$$

For simplicity, assume that property losses have the same distribution:

$$\text{Property loss} = \begin{array}{ll} \$50 \text{ million} & \text{with probability } 0.02 \\ \$25 \text{ million} & \text{with probability } 0.04 \\ 0 \text{ million} & \text{with probability } 0.94 \end{array}$$

To capture the idea that firms often want to avoid large losses, assume that the managers do not want total retained losses to exceed some critical value, say $40 million (perhaps because the firm would then be forced to raise costly external capital or violate a debt covenant). The firm can insure each loss exposure to achieve its objective, but assume that contracts are priced so that the firm must pay 120 percent of the contract's expected payout, implying a 20 percent loading or transaction cost. As you will see below, this proportional transaction cost can make the cost of managing each exposure separately greater than the cost of managing the bundled exposure.

If the firm hedges each exposure separately, it can achieve its objective (total retained losses less than $40 million) by retaining $20 million of each exposure. In other words, the firm could purchase a liability insurance policy under which it would be reimbursed for liability losses in excess of $20 million and a property insurance policy under which it would be reimbursed for property losses in excess of $20 million.[7] The expected claim cost on each policy equals

$$(\$30 \text{ million} \times 0.02) + (\$5 \text{ million} \times 0.04) = \$600{,}000 + \$200{,}000 = \$800{,}000$$

With a 20 percent loading, the premium on each policy would equal $800,000 in expected claim costs plus $160,000 ($800,000 × 0.2) in loading. Because two policies are purchased, the total loading paid by the firm would equal $320,000.

Panel A of Table 22.2 summarizes the results of purchasing separate policies on each exposure. The first four columns list all the possible outcomes and the associated probabilities. For example, row two indicates that one possible outcome is that the liability loss equals $25 million and the property loss equals zero; this outcome occurs with probability 0.0376 (0.94 × 0.04). The later columns indicate the coverage provided by the separate contracts. For example, row two indicates that the insurer would pay $5 million of the liability loss and the insured would pay $20 million.

Recall that the firm was willing to retain losses up to $40 million. The important point to notice is that in some cases the coverage provided by the separate contracts results in a payout from the insurer even though retained losses are less than $40 million. In these cases, the firm has purchased coverage that, ex post, it did not really need. We refer to this extra coverage as unnecessary coverage, and report it in the final column. The problem with purchasing unnecessary coverage under these assumptions is that there is a positive loading associated with purchasing coverage. Thus, the unnecessary coverage is costly for the firm's owners.

Now suppose that the firm was able to purchase an insurance policy that would indemnify the firm based on total losses. To achieve its objective of not having retained losses exceed $40 million, the firm could use one policy under which the insurer would pay aggregate (sum of property and liability) losses in excess of $40 million. We refer to a policy like this that bundles multiple exposures as a **bundled policy.** The outcomes with the

---

[7]Other combinations of contracts would also achieve the stated objective, but the main implication of the example would be unchanged.

TABLE 22.2 Outcomes from insuring two exposures.

Panel A: With separate policies, the insurer pays all losses in excess of $20 million for each

Liability Loss	Property Loss	Total Loss	Probability	Liability Coverage	Property Coverage	Total Coverage	Total Retention	Unnecessary Coverage
0	0	0	0.8836	0	0	0	0	0
25	0	25	0.0376	5	0	5	20	5
50	0	50	0.0188	30	0	30	20	20
0	25	25	0.0376	0	5	5	20	5
25	25	50	0.0016	5	5	10	40	0
50	25	75	0.0008	30	5	35	40	0
0	50	50	0.0188	0	30	30	20	20
25	50	75	0.0008	5	30	35	40	0
50	50	100	0.0004	30	30	60	40	0
			Expected Value = 0.8	0.8	1.6		2.4	1.128

Panel B: With a bundled policy the insurer pays aggregate losses in excess of $40 million

Liability Loss	Property Loss	Total Loss	Probability	Combined Coverage	Total Retention	Unnecessary Coverage
0	0	0	0.8836	0	0	0
25	0	25	0.0376	0	25	0
50	0	50	0.0188	10	40	0
0	25	25	0.0376	0	25	0
25	25	50	0.0016	10	40	0
50	25	75	0.0008	35	40	0
0	50	50	0.0188	10	40	0
25	50	75	0.0008	35	40	0
50	50	100	0.0004	60	40	0
			Expected Value =	0.472	3.528	0

bundled policy are summarized in Panel B of Table 22.2. The important point is that with the bundled policy, there is no unnecessary coverage.

As indicated in the final row of Panel B, the expected claim cost for the bundled policy is $472,000, which implies a loading cost equal to $94,400 (0.2 × $472,000). This policy achieves the firm's objective of not having retained losses above $40 million, but at a lower loading cost ($94,400 versus $320,000) compared to purchasing separate policies.

The advantage of bundling can be illustrated using Figure 22.1. The horizontal axis indicates the property loss and the vertical axis indicates the liability loss. Using the same assumptions as the numerical example, suppose that the firm can retain losses up to $40 million, but would like coverage for aggregate losses in excess of $40 million. One way to achieve this objective is to purchase separate property and liability insurance policies, with each policy having a $20 million self-insured retention. The property policy would pay losses whenever property losses exceed $20 million, which is illustrated in Figure 22.1A as the shaded area to the right of the vertical line labeled "P". The liability policy would pay losses whenever losses exceed $20 million, which is illustrated in Figure 22.1A as the shaded area above the horizontal line labeled "L".

**FIGURE
22.1
Illustration of
unnecessary
coverage.**
(shaded areas
indicate
coverage.)

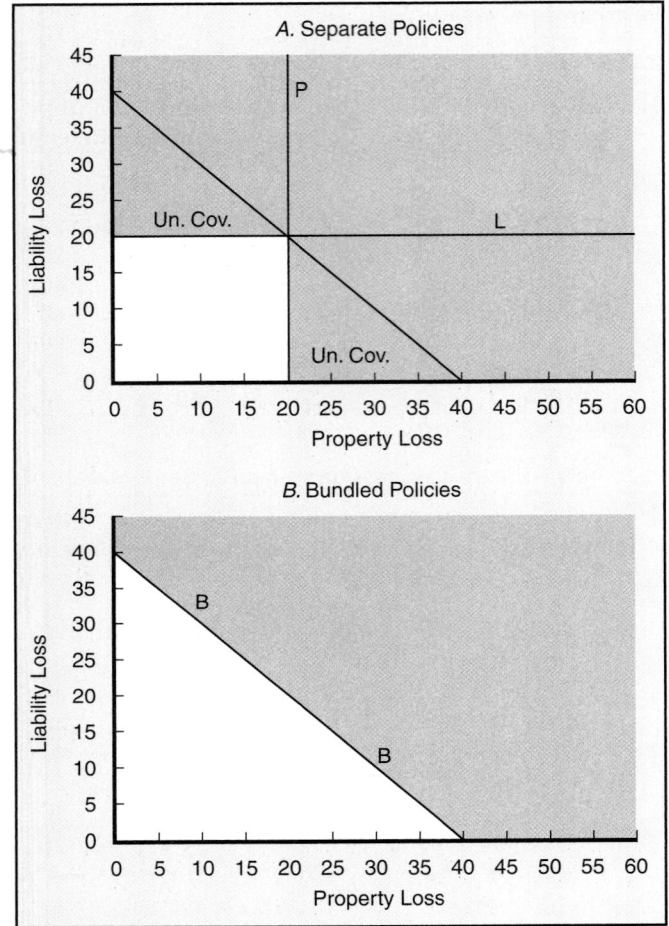

A bundled policy that would achieve the firm's objective would pay losses whenever the sum of property and liability losses exceeds $40 million, which is illustrated in Figure 22.1B as the area above the line labeled B. The important point to notice is that the losses paid by the bundled policy (the shaded area in Figure 22.1B) are a subset of the losses paid by the separate policies (the shaded areas in Figure 22.1A). The difference in the shaded areas is the sum of the triangles labeled "Un. Cov." (for unnecessary coverage) in Figure 22.1A. Because of proportional loading costs, the purchase of unnecessary insurance coverage is costly to the firm's owners. Box 22.3 discusses unnecessary coverage in the context of the US federal crop insurance program.

Moral Hazard

A completely bundled policy would only have an aggregate retention level and an aggregate limit; consequently, the source of a loss would not matter for the contract's payoff. The problem with such a policy is that once a firm's aggregate retention level was reached, any additional loss (up to the aggregate limit) would be covered. Such a policy therefore would greatly reduce the insured's incentive to reduce additional losses once the retention level

Farmers's revenue and thus income can decline for two main reasons: (1) lower than expected crop yields, which reduce revenues for any given crop price, and (2) lower than expected crop prices at harvest, which reduce revenues for any given yield. Because lower (higher) than expected yields for a given crop often are associated with higher (lower) than expected prices, these two risks are negatively correlated, and farmers' revenue risk is often lower than if yields and prices were uncorrelated. Thus, many farmers have a partial natural hedge against revenue losses, which reduces their demand for insurance/hedging that protects them from lower than expected crop yields and from lower than expected prices.

Traditionally, farmers who sought to reduce revenue risk did so on a disaggregated basis. They would insure against reductions in yields by buying *crop yield insurance* offered by the US federal government (at taxpayer subsidized rates), and they would commonly hedge the risk of low crop prices at harvest by selling crops forward at a guaranteed price or by selling crop futures contracts (see Chapter 24). Like the numerical example in the text, the disaggregated approach can cause farmers to pay for unnecessary coverage. For example, a farmer may be indemnified for yield reductions even when crop prices turn out to be quite high and revenue losses are less than the amount of loss that the farmer could reasonably retain. In the mid-1990s the US government introduced a number of *crop revenue insurance* programs that allow farmers to reduce their aggregate revenue risk. The programs pay farmers only if revenues fall below specified thresholds. The concept of crop revenue insurance is theoretically sound. However, the advantage of aggregation—paying lower premium loadings for unnecessary coverage—is less transparent in this case because of taxpayer subsidized premium loadings. Some observers questioned whether the introduction and popularity of crop revenue insurance may in significant part reflect an expansion of taxpayers's subsidies.

was reached.[8] To mitigate this moral hazard problem, per occurrence deductibles for each type of loss exposure would likely be included in any bundled policy.

Costs Associated with a More Complex Contract

A disadvantage of bundling multiple exposures into one contract is that the parties need to have an understanding of all of the risk exposures and their correlations. The cost associated with performing this analysis can increase the transaction costs relative to those that would be incurred on separate contracts for each type of exposure. In the example above, we assumed a 20 percent loading regardless of whether each exposure was insured separately or bundled together under one insurance contract. If the proportional transaction costs were higher for the bundled policy, then the benefit of bundling illustrated above would be reduced (or even eliminated).

Since the number of counterparties that will have the expertise to price a complicated bundled contract might be limited, the market for such policies could be relatively thin and less liquid. Also, those institutions that possess the modeling expertise needed to price a complicated bundled policy may not have expertise in other areas, such as loss control and claims processing, that are demanded by firms. A bundled policy therefore could result in lower quality of services. Finally, a large body of insurance contract law exists, which lowers the transaction cost of settling coverage disputes and claims for standard policies. Until a similar body of law is developed for bundled policies, these transaction costs could be higher for bundled policies.

---

[8]This moral hazard problem is not unique to bundled insurance contracts; it would also apply to contracts with an aggregate deductible.

22.4 Summary

- Optimal risk retention/reduction decisions would consider the costs and benefits of reducing risk.
- Some of the firm characteristics that influence the benefits of reducing risk include firm size, the correlation among loss exposures, investment opportunities, whether future services are expected from the product or services produced, the correlation between losses and cash flows, and financial leverage.
- A basic rule of thumb for retention decisions is to retain relatively small, predictable loss exposures and insure against large losses that could cause financial distress or cause the firm to raise costly external capital.
- Several of the reasons for reducing risk imply that a firm should focus its risk reduction activities on an aggregate financial variable, such as earnings, cash flow, or taxable income.
- The risk of an aggregate financial variable can be reduced either by focusing risk reduction activities on the aggregate variable or by focusing on the risk of each individual component of the aggregate financial variable.

Key Terms

Risk retention 484   Risk reduction 484   Bundled policy 494

Questions and Problems

1. The risk manager of Cagle Corporation argues that retention should be increased to allow the firm to maintain the use of funds that otherwise would go for premiums until claims are paid. If you were either the risk manager's supervisor or on the board of directors, which questions would you ask?

2. Suppose that Company A and Company B are identical in all respects, except that Company A is twice the size of Company B. Which firm would you expect to purchase more insurance? Briefly explain.

3. Suppose that Company A and Company B are identical in all respects, except that Company A has greater financial leverage than Company B. Which firm would you expect to purchase more insurance? Briefly explain.

4. Suppose that Company A and Company B are identical in all respects, except that Company A is in declining industry and Company B is in a growing industry. Which firm would you expect to purchase more insurance? Briefly explain.

5. List the advantages and disadvantages of purchasing an insurance policy on aggregate property and liability losses versus purchasing a separate property insurance policy and a separate liability insurance policy.

Answer to Concept Check

1. (*a*) The firm in which no shareholder owns more than 1 percent of the stock is more likely to retain risk because the owners are more likely to be diversified.

(*b*) The trucking company is more likely to retain the risk because the injury losses of different workers are likely to have low correlation and, therefore, the firm can achieve greater diversification than the manufacturing firm.

(*c*) The firm with operating profits positively correlated with claim costs is more likely to retain the risk because of

its natural hedge—claim costs are high when its operating profits are high.

(*d*) The firm with no debt is more likely to retain the risk because, all else equal, it has a lower probability of financial distress.

References

Doherty, Neil; and Clifford Smith. "Corporate Insurance Strategy: The Case of British Petroleum." *Journal of Applied Corporate Finance* 6 (Fall 1993), pp. 4–15.

Froot, Kenneth A.; David Scharfstein; and Jeremy C. Stein. "A Framework for Risk Management." *Journal of Applied Corporate Finance* 7 (Fall 1994), pp. 22–31.

Geszky, Christopher; Bernadette A. Minton; and Catherine Schrand. "Why Firms Use Currency Derivatives." *Journal of Finance* 52 (1997) pp. 1323–54.

Graham, John R.; and Daniel A. Rogers. "Do Firms Hedge in Response to Tax Incentives?" *Journal of Finance* 57 (2002), pp. 815–40.

Haushalter, David G. "Financing Policy, Basis Risk, and Corporate Hedging: Evidence from Oil and Gas Producers." *Journal of Finance* 55 (2000), pp. 107–52.

Knopf, John D.; Jouahn Nam; and John H. Thornton, Jr. "The Volatility and Price Sensitivities of Managerial Stock Option Portfolios and Corporate Hedging." *Journal of Finance* 57 (2002), pp. 801–14.

Lewent, Judy C; and A. John Kearney. "Identifying, Measuring, and Hedging Currency Risk at Merck." *Journal of Applied Corporate Finance* 9 (Winter 1990), pp. 19–28.

Mayers, David; and Clifford W. Smith, Jr. "On the Corporate Demand for Insurance: Evidence from the Reinsurance Market." *Journal of Business* 63 (1990), pp. 19–40.

Nance, Deana R.; Clifford W. Smith, Jr.; and Charles W. Smithson. "On the Determinants of Corporate Hedging." *Journal of Finance* 48 (1993), pp. 267–84.

Stulz, Rene. "Rethinking Risk Management." *Journal of Applied Corporate Finance* 9 (Fall 1996), pp. 8–24.

Tufano, Peter. "Who Manages Risk? An Empirical Examination of Risk Management Practices in the Gold Mining Industry." *Journal of Finance* 51 (1996), pp. 1097–137.

Chapter 23

Commercial Insurance Contracts

Chapter Objectives

- Identify major types of property–casualty insurance contracts purchased by businesses and describe the negotiation of commercial insurance programs.
- Explain the operation of deductibles and self-insured retentions in commercial insurance programs.
- Explain the operation of policy limits, primary coverage, excess coverage, and umbrella liability coverage.
- Describe key provisions of insurance coverage for damage to business property, including associated loss of income and extraordinary operating expenses.
- Describe key provisions of commercial general liability insurance, including occurrence and claims-made coverage.
- Highlight differences between commercial and personal insurance pricing and underwriting.

23.1 Overview of Contracts and Markets

Commercial insurance contracts are broadly classified as either property–casualty or life-health-retirement contracts. The latter classification includes group life, medical, disability, annuity, and related pension contracts associated with employee benefit plans, as well as corporate-owned life insurance on key personnel and other employees. We focus on commercial property-casualty insurance contracts in this chapter.

Major Types of Commercial Property–Casualty Insurance

Table 23.1 summarizes the major types of property–casualty insurance sold to business buyers. There are four main types of contracts: (1) first-party coverage for policyholders' losses from property damage and associated loss of income, (2) liability and related coverages for injury to third-parties, (3) multiple-peril contracts, which, analogous to homeowners insurance (Chapter 14) cover both property and liability losses in a single contract, and (4) surety bonds and financial guarantees (see Box 23.1).

TABLE 23.1   **Major property–casualty insurance products.**

Property	Liability or Casualty	Multiple-Peril	Fidelity, Surety, and Guaranty
First-party coverage of buildings, contents, and associated loss of use or income	Covers awards, settlement, and defense costs for injuries to third parties	Covers both property and liability risks in a single policy	Protects against loss caused by other parties; insurer usually can subrogate
1. *Fire and allied:* covers property exposures at fixed locations on named peril or all-risk basis; includes stand-alone earthquake coverage and private flood insurance	1. *General liability:* covers liability arising out of premises, products, and completed operations, contracts	1. *Commercial multiperil:* covers property and general liability	1. *Surety bonds:* guarantees performance, for example, of contractors
2. *Marine:* specialized mobile equipment and goods in transit over land and inland waterways (inland marine) and oceans (ocean marine); includes coverage for damage to hulls	2. *Workers' compensation and employers' liability:* (Ch. 18)	2. *Commercial automobile:* covers automobile and truck physical damage, theft, and liability	2. *Fidelity bonds:* covers specified acts of employee dishonesty
3. *Crime:* stand-alone coverage for robbery, burglary, or theft	3. *Medical malpractice professional liability:* covers liability of hospitals, physicians, dentists	3. *Boiler and machinery:* covers damage to and liability for injury from steam boilers and related heavy machinery	3. *Financial guarantees:* mortgage guarantees, credit enhancement
	4. *Other professional liability:* directors and officers (see Ch. 28), errors and omissions of advisors, consultants, agents	4. *Aircraft:* covers damage to hulls and liability for injuries	
	5. *Environmental liability:* (Ch. 28)		
	6. *Employment practices liability:* (Ch. 18)		

Many insurers sell surety bonds, known as performance bonds, that guarantee the performance of another party, such as a contractor. Some insurers offer other types of guarantees with features similar to surety bonds, such as mortgage guarantees, municipal bond insurance, and related forms of credit enhancement. The main differences between insurance contracts and surety bonds (and most other financial guarantees provided by insurers) are

Surety Bonds	Insurance
Contracts involve three parties: the party that owes performance (the principal), the party to which performance is owed (the obligee), and the surety.	Contracts involve two parties: the insurer and the insured. (Third-party liability coverage makes payments to injured parties that are not a party to the contract.)
The surety is required to respond to the obligee if the principal defaults.	The insurer is required to respond to the policyholder.
The surety usually has subrogration rights or other legal recourse against the principal.	The insurer generally cannot subrogate against its policyholders.

The third point (subrogation and legal resource against the principal) is the most important difference. It is sometimes argued that the surety expects no loss (it underwrites to prevent loss and can reduce its loss through actions against the principal), whereas the insurer does expect a loss. That distinction is quantitative rather than qualitative. The probability of loss is rarely zero for either a surety bond or an insurance contract.

Figure 23.1 shows countrywide US net premiums written (premiums written for direct business plus premiums from assumed reinsurance less premiums for reinsurance ceded) by major lines of property-casualty insurance during 2001. Premiums for commercial lines totaled about $159 billion compared with about $165 billion for personal lines (personal auto and homeowners/farmowners). To put these figures in perspective, keep in mind that businesses often retain substantial amounts of loss and/or rely on alternative risk transfer devices where the costs are not reflected in commercial lines insurance premiums. The largest three commercial lines of business are workers' compensation; general liability, which covers liability arising out of common business hazards; and commercial multiperil, which covers business property and liability risks in a single policy rather than with separate stand-alone contracts.

US commercial property-casualty insurance markets generally are highly competitive with numerous insurers offering coverage in each line of business and state. The market share of the top four and top eight insurers in each line and state is usually small (less than 50 percent). Markets for more specialized coverage, such as directors and officers liability, environmental liability, and medical malpractice are more concentrated, as are markets for businesses more difficult to insure. However, the cost for insurers to enter new markets and submarkets is relatively low. The US commercial insurance market is international in scope: many foreign owned or controlled insurers are active in the primary US market (and vice versa). In addition, many US insurers routinely purchase reinsurance from non-US insurers.

The major types of commercial property-casualty insurance contracts are subject to a large degree of standardization through insurance advisory organizations. As explained in Chapter 18, the *National Council of Compensation Insurance* (NCCI) develops standard

FIGURE 23.1 **US property–casualty insurance net premiums written by line of business in 2001.**

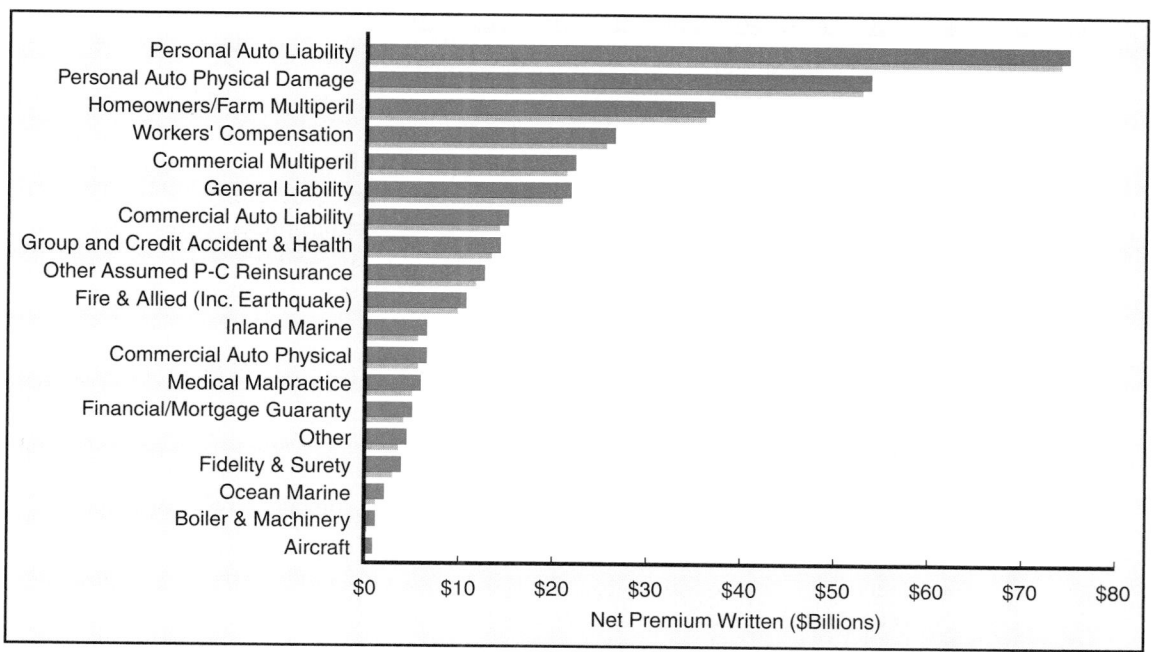

Note: General liability includes all liability coverage not included in another category.

Source: *Best's Aggregates & Averages, Property-Casualty Edition,* 2002.

forms for workers' compensation insurance. Most insurers use policy forms for other coverages that are prepared and promulgated by the *Insurance Services Office* (ISO) or that are based on the ISO forms. ISO (or NCCI) staff develops standardized contracts with substantial input from industry representatives, brokers, risk managers, and sometimes insurance regulators. Standard policies are designed to meet the main needs of a broad class of buyers. Separate policies and hundreds of endorsements are available to customize contracts, either by adding coverage for a higher premium, or deleting coverage for a premium reduction. Some insurers develop their own commercial policies, but they usually are very similar to the ISO contracts (known as policy forms or simply forms). Larger business buyers often negotiate customized terms of coverage to meet special needs. Highly customized contracts often are called manuscript policies.

Policy standardization facilitates price and service comparisons among insurers by risk managers, brokers, and other commercial insurance buyers. It also facilitates the aggregation of loss and premium data across insurers for use in summarizing costs and estimating prospective loss costs for different types of business and regions (see Chapter 8). Property-casualty insurance policy forms in the United States generally are subject to prior approval by state regulators, with the exception that about half the states do not require regulatory approval or filing with regulators of policy forms sold to large businesses.

Designing and Negotiating Commercial Insurance Programs

Many medium-to-large businesses are relatively sophisticated in insurance matters. Many have employees or consultants devoted to risk management and insurance and/or are represented by knowledgeable brokers. Brokers are instrumental in designing and negotiating coverage that meets the needs of their business clients.

Arranging a commercial insurance program typically begins with preliminary program specifications that outline the firm's willingness to retain risk and general preferences for coverages and terms. The broker then provides the specifications to insurers and solicits coverage proposals. Insurance company underwriters develop the proposals based on an analysis of the specifications and the insurer's cost of providing coverage. Review of insurers' proposals by the buyer and broker often leads to a revised set of specifications and subsequent revisions to one or more of the insurers' proposals. The buyer and broker then negotiate with one or more insurers to finalize a deal. Insurers generally are willing to negotiate price, coverage, and service concessions provided that the overall arrangement is expected to allow the insurer to cover its costs and achieve a reasonable expected profit.

Negotiating and selecting the best commercial property–casualty insurance program generally involves quantitative and subjective analysis by the buyer based on consultation with its broker. The major criteria used to choose among competing proposals include:

1. The program's expected cost, on a present value basis, which reflects the total amount of expected premium payments, the timing of those payments, and the possibility of dividends if the firm has favorable loss experience.
2. Possible variation in the firm's cost that arises because the firm retains ultimate responsibility for paying some losses through deductibles, self-insured retentions, policy limits, or loss sensitive price adjustments (sections 23.2 and 23.6; Chapter 25).
3. The availability and scope of specialized coverages and endorsements.
4. The types and quality of loss control, claim settlement, and other services provided by the insurer, and the insurer's willingness and ability to accommodate special needs of the buyer with respect to the timing of premium payments, loss control, and claim settlement.
5. Any prior experience of the buyer with the insurer (or insurers).
6. The insurer's reputation and financial strength.

Business buyers and their brokers usually devote substantial effort to evaluating alternative proposals based on these criteria. Because several proposals often reflect the buyer's tolerance for risk, contain similar coverage features, and are made by financially strong insurers with solid support services, the most important criterion in many cases is the expected cost of the program. To negotiate the best possible program with the lowest possible cost, business buyers and their brokers often prefer proposals that include substantial detail about specific charges, coverage limits, the timing of premium payments, collateral requirements, and other relevant factors. Those details facilitate negotiation, for example, by giving the buyer a clearer picture of the insurer's costs and expected profit, and they often provide useful information that may influence the firm's loss financing or loss control decisions.

23.2   Deductibles and Self-insured Retentions

As discussed in Chapter 10, insurance contracts typically do not provide full coverage. Instead, policies almost always require the policyholder to bear some risk. Through the use of policy provisions like deductibles and limits, some element of retention exists even when a firm purchases a policy with a guaranteed (fixed) premium that does not depend on the policyholder's loss experience during the coverage period.

A useful method of describing the coverage provided by a particular policy is to use an **exposure diagram,** which visually displays how the contract apportions losses between the insurer and the insured. To illustrate, Figure 23.2 graphs the exposure of a firm that buys no insurance (i.e., the firm retains all the risk associated with a particular loss exposure). The horizontal axis identifies the possible losses from the exposure, and the vertical axis identifies the amount of loss paid by the firm. When a firm retains all of its risk, it pays the entire loss. For example, if the loss is $10,000, then the firm pays $10,000; if the loss is $50,000, the firm pays $50,000. Consequently, if a firm buys no insurance, the 45-degree line from the graph's origin describes the firm's exposure to losses.

Whenever the line describing a firm's exposure to a loss has a positive slope, then the firm is retaining some of the risk. When interpreting exposure diagrams like Figure 23.2, it is important to keep in perspective that the losses measured on the horizontal axis are uncertain and that the graph identifies how much the insured will pay under any possible loss that may occur. Only one point on the graph will actually occur.

An insurance policy with a *deductible* of $2 million implies that the firm pays losses up to $2 million and that the insurer pays losses above $2 million. Deductibles can be per occurrence (claim) or aggregate. With a **per occurrence deductible,** the firm pays up to the deductible amount on each loss that is covered. For example, if Sharon Steel has a policy with a $2 million per occurrence deductible and it experiences five losses during the policy period with each loss equal to $1.5 million, then Sharon Steel would pay all losses. With an

FIGURE 23.2
Losses paid by a firm that purchases no insurance.

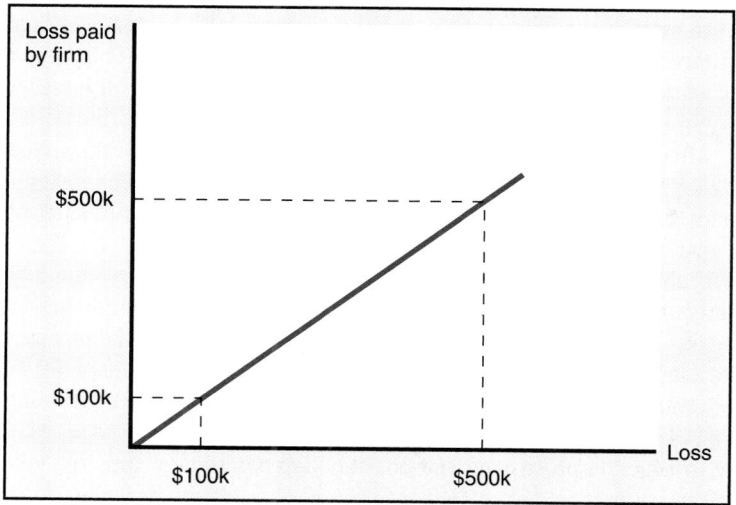

aggregate deductible, the firm pays all losses during the policy period until the aggregate amount paid equals the aggregate deductible. If Sharon Steel has a $2 million aggregate deductible in the example above, it would pay $2 million in total and the insurer would pay $5.5 million (assuming sufficient policy limits, see below).

While aggregate deductibles have the advantage of allowing the policyholder to place a cap on its loss payments for the policy period, they have the disadvantage of possibly promoting moral hazard, because once the aggregate deductible has been reached, the marginal cost of additional claims to the policyholder is zero (apart from any possible effect on future premiums). Thus, when the policyholder is likely to have considerable influence over the occurrence or severity of additional claims, aggregate deductibles are less likely to be used, all else equal.

Firms with a per occurrence deductible policy sometimes purchase a *stop loss provision,* which essentially combines an aggregate deductible with a per occurrence deductible. It caps the amount that the insured will pay during the policy period as a result of the accumulation of per occurrence deductibles. Thus, if Sharon Steel has a $2 million per occurrence deductible and a $4 million stop loss provision, then five losses of $1.5 million each would imply that Sharon Steel will pay $4 million and the stop loss insurer will pay $3.5 million.

The lower line in the top diagram in Figure 23.3 illustrates the amount of loss that the firm would retain with an aggregate deductible policy. The positive slope in the range of losses between $0 and $2 million indicates that the firm retains risk in this range. The lower line does not take into account the premium paid for the insurance policy. A fixed premium is easily incorporated by shifting the entire exposure line up by the amount of the premium. For example, if the premium for the aggregate deductible policy were $500,000, then the upper line illustrates the sum of the premium and the amount of loss paid by Sharon Steel. We will not incorporate the premium in most of the diagrams. The bottom diagram in Figure 23.3 illustrates the loss paid by the insurer. If you added the amounts of loss paid by each party, you would obtain a 45° line, which simply indicates that the firm and insurer pay all the losses.

Often the deductible amount ($2 million in the previous example) is called a **self-insured retention (SIR)** to indicate that losses below that point are self-insured or retained. A distinction often is made between a deductible and a self-insured retention in the commercial insurance market. The term "deductible" (especially in reference to large deductible policies, see Chapter 25) often indicates that the insurer will first pay all losses and then bill the insured for the amount of losses up to the deductible. In contrast, the term "self-insured retention" often indicates that the insurer will only pay losses once they exceed the self-insured retention level. When the insurer pays losses and then bills the insured for the deductible amount, the insurer usually will require that the insured provide a letter of credit from a bank that guarantees that the insured will pay losses as promised.

The choice between having the insurer pay losses up to the deductible amount and then bill the insured or having the insured pay the self-insured retention depends in part on which party has a comparative advantage in processing claims. If the insurer has an expertise in processing claims relative to the insured, then having the insurer bill the policyholder can be advantageous. In addition, inefficiencies can occur in the processing of a high severity claim if a self-insured retention is used, because both the insured and the insurer might have to be involved in processing and possibly defending the claim. To avoid some duplication of effort, it might be more efficient (lower cost) to simply have the insurer process the claim and then bill the policyholder for the deductible. Another reason to have the insurer pay the

FIGURE 23.3
Losses paid by the firm and insurer under a $2 million aggregate deductible policy.

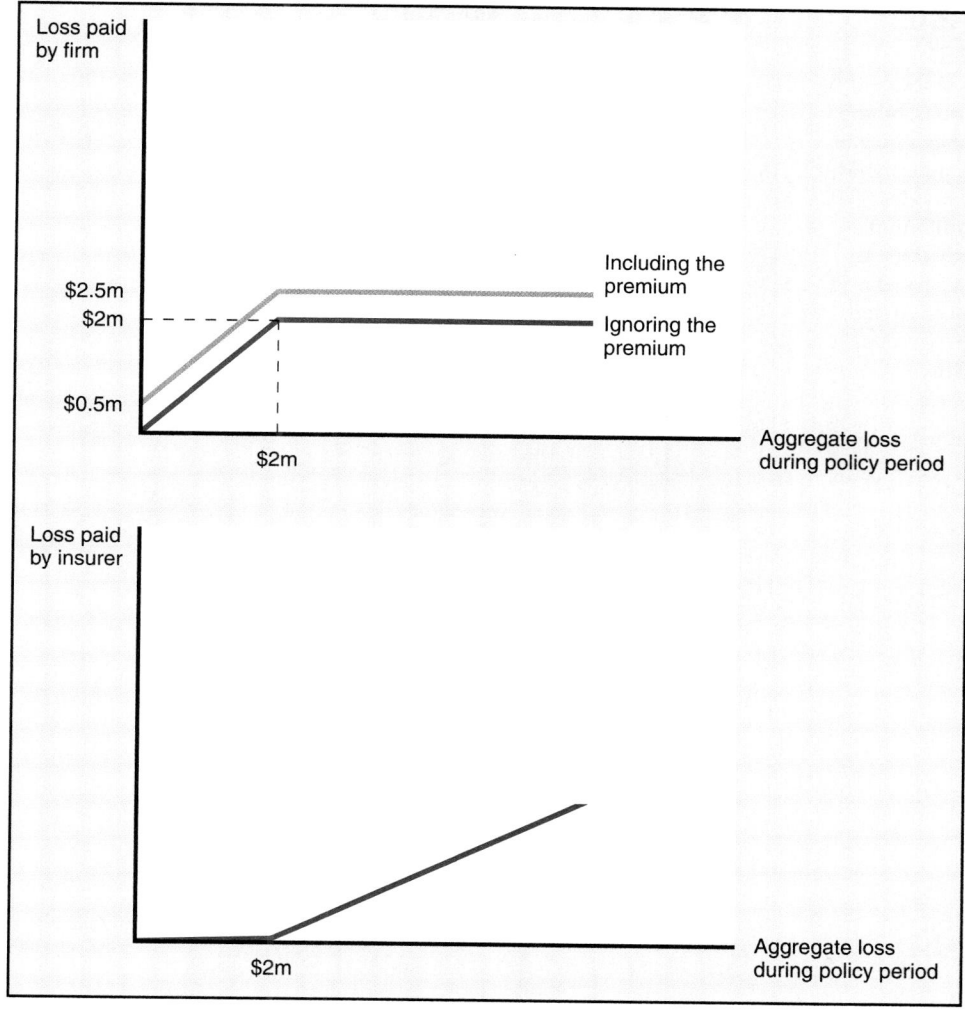

loss and then bill the insured is to provide additional security to a third-party claimant (e.g., an injured worker under workers' compensation insurance).

23.3   Policy Limits and Primary/Excess/Umbrella Policies

The previous examples for deductibles and self-insured retentions ignored that insurance policies usually cap the amount that the insurer pays at some *policy limit.* Both property and liability policies typically have **per occurrence limits.** (Claims-made liability policies have per claim limits.) Liability policies also usually have an **annual aggregate limit.**

A policy limit establishes the maximum amount paid by the insurer. For example, a policy that provides $3 million of coverage per occurrence above a $1 million self-insured retention would require: (1) the policyholder to pay the first $1 million of losses, (2) the

FIGURE 23.4
Losses paid by the firm and insurer under a policy that provides $3 million of coverage in excess of a $1 million per occurrence SIR.

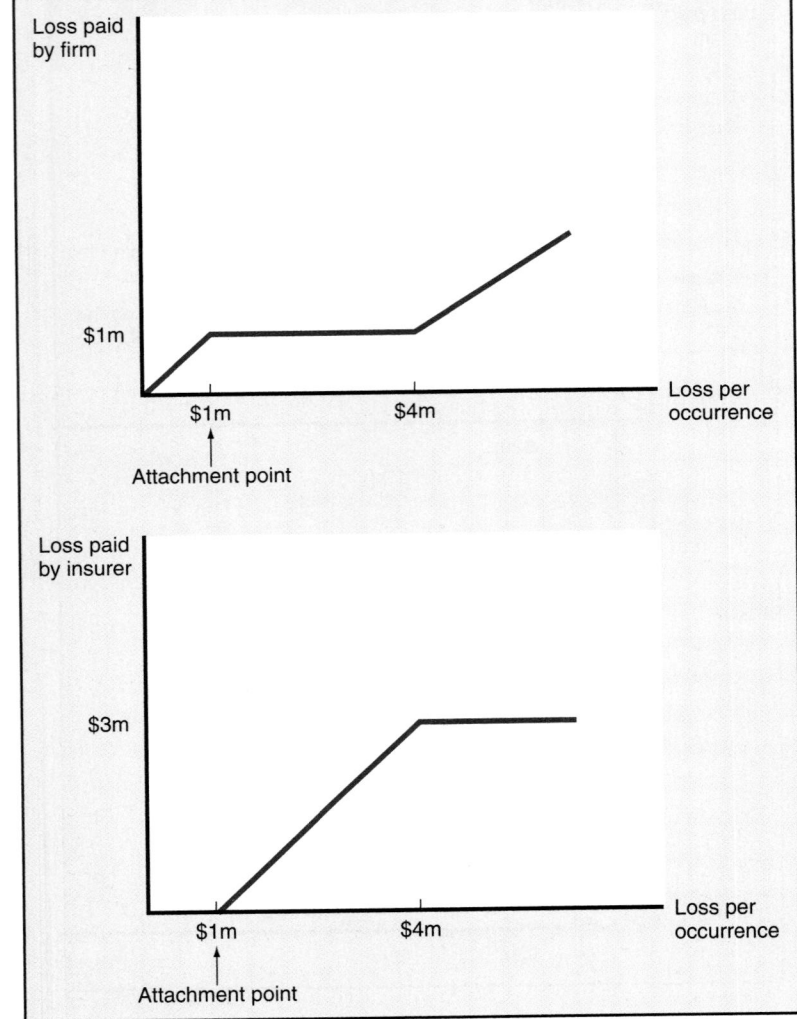

insurer to pay the next $3 million of losses, and (3) the policyholder to pay losses beyond $4 million on each occurrence. Figure 23.4 illustrates the amounts paid by the insured firm and the insurer for this policy. Policies like this often are called **excess policies,** because they provide coverage if losses are in excess of some relatively large threshold, called the **attachment point.** Thus, the policy in our example provides $3 million of coverage with an attachment point of $1 million or, equivalently, $3 million of coverage in excess of $1 million. Excess policies can be structured to provide coverage above a self-insured retention or above the limit on another policy. A policy that attaches immediately above the firm's retention is commonly referred to as **primary coverage,** even though the

FIGURE 23.5

Losses paid by a firm that purchases two policies in layers (first policy provides $3 million of coverage in excess of $1 million per occurrence; the other policy provides $2 million of coverage in excess of $4 million on the same occurrence).

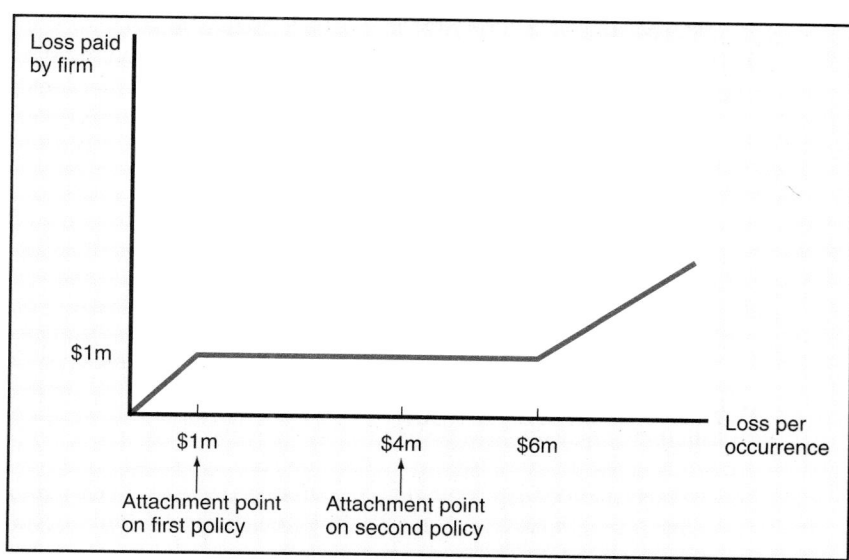

policy is excess over a relatively large SIR. This distinction is important for liability coverage, where the primary insurer usually has the lead responsibility for providing, paying for, and controlling the defense (see section 23.5).

Firms often purchase coverage in layers from different insurers, referred to as **layering coverage.** To illustrate, suppose that a firm purchases (1) a policy from insurer A that provides $3 million of coverage in excess of a $1 million self-insured retention (SIR), and (2) an excess policy from insurer B that provides $2 million of coverage in excess of $4 million. In combination, the two policies provide coverage over the range of losses from $1 million to $6 million. The firm's exposure to losses is shown in Figure 23.5. Large firms often have several layers of coverage and multiple insurers may participate in each layer, on a pro rota basis in relation to their limits, especially at the higher layers. For example, the property insurance program for the World Trade Center at the time of its destruction is reported to have consisted of 11 layers of coverage with multiple insurers on each layer.

Layering helps to limit a particular insurer's exposure to a single loss and to distribute losses across insurers, thereby providing greater diversification. This explanation for layering is incomplete, however, because the same diversification can be achieved if one insurer writes the entire coverage and then cedes the higher layer of coverage to a reinsurer. In the example above, instead of purchasing two policies from separate insurers, the firm could purchase one policy providing $5 million of coverage in excess of $1 million. The insurer selling that policy could then cede part of the coverage to a reinsurer. Greater diversification of risk occurs regardless of whether the insured or the primary insurer layers the coverage.

Why is it often more desirable to layer coverage as opposed to having a single insurer provide coverage and buy reinsurance? The answer depends on a number of factors, including the insured firm's costs of arranging the transactions versus the primary insurer's cost of transacting in the reinsurance market. The reinsurance scenario tends to involve some duplication in pricing and underwriting by the insurer and reinsurer for the same coverage. In addition, because of the possibility of insurer insolvency and thus the failure to pay claims, the insured firm may find it desirable to be involved in the selection of those insurers that will ultimately provide the coverage. The firm would have a direct claim against each insurer. With the reinsurance scenario, the firm would not have a direct claim to any reinsurance if the primary insurer failed unless it negotiated special contract language that was enforceable by the courts. Finally, policies from multiple insurers can yield greater coverage protection from state guaranty funds should any of the insurers become insolvent, in part because guaranty funds do not cover reinsurance.

Umbrella liability coverage is similar to excess coverage in that the policy provides excess coverage over other policies or self-insured retentions. The difference is that an **umbrella policy** covers liability losses from multiple exposures or perils. To illustrate, suppose that Lilly Inc. purchases the following set of policies: (1) an auto liability policy providing $1 million excess coverage above a $100,000 self-insured retention (SIR) per occurrence; (2) a products liability policy providing $10 million excess coverage above a $1 million SIR per occurrence; and (3) an umbrella policy providing $20 million of coverage per occurrence, excess of liability limits on the other two policies. Table 23.2 shows how these policies would apportion the losses between Lilly and the three insurers if Lilly incurs a $10.1 million auto liability loss and a $15 million products liability loss during the coverage period. In addition to providing coverage in excess of other policies' limits, umbrella policies often cover some losses not covered by another policy above a self-insured retention.

Structuring commercial insurance programs in layers of primary, excess, and umbrella policies often results in complex programs. Over time the layers and participating insurers often are summarized in a **coverage chart.** Figure 23.6 illustrates a relatively simple coverage chart for a liability insurance program. To help you understand the chart, note that it includes multiple years of coverage. That approach is typical practice for liability insurance because policies in effect during the year the injury occurred often cover a particular claim for damages, even though the claim in many cases is made in a later year. (Section 23.5 provides details.)

Now let's consider the coverage for 2003 shown in Figure 23.6. There is $4 million of primary coverage per occurrence above a $1 million SIR (or deductible); $20 million of excess coverage above $5 million, shared pro rata by insurers A, C, and D in relation to their pol-

TABLE 23.2 Illustration of coverage provided by an umbrella insurer (umbrella coverage = $20 million per occurrence above limits on auto and products liability policies; auto policy coverage = $1 million above $100,000 SIR per occurrence; products liability coverage = $10 million above $1 million SIR per occurrence).

		Loss Paid by (in $ millions)			
	Amount of Loss	Insured Firm	Auto Liability Insurer	Products Liability Insurer	Umbrella Insurer
Auto liability loss	$10.1	$0.1	$1	$ 0	$ 9
Products liability loss	$15.0	$1.0	$0	$10	$ 4
Total loss	$25.1	$1.1	$1	$10	$13

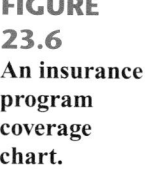

FIGURE 23.6
An insurance program coverage chart.

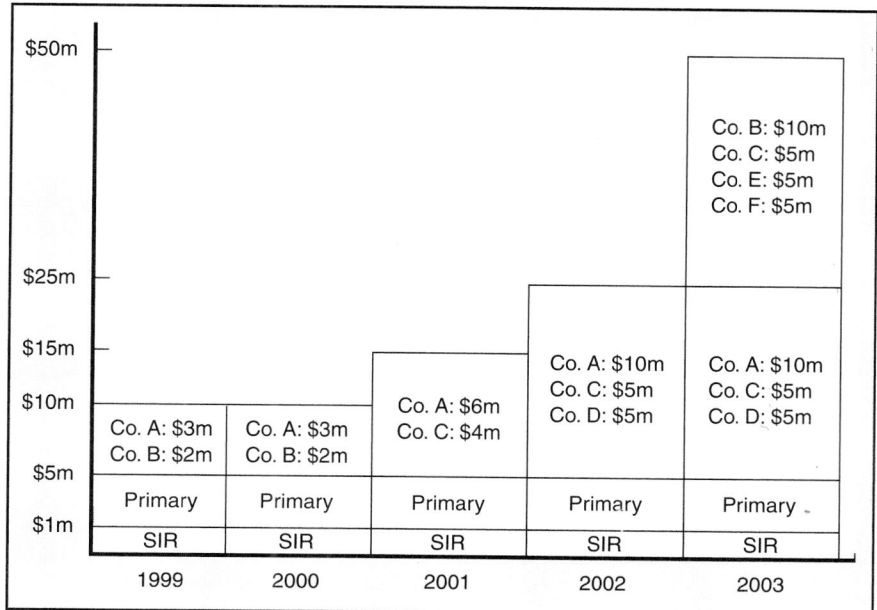

icy limits; and $25 million of excess coverage above $25 million, shared pro rata by insurers B, C, E, and F in relation to their limits. (Note that insurer C participates in two layers.) In the event of a $30 million loss, the policyholder would pay $1 million, the primary insurer would pay $4 million (and provide the defense). The $20 million excess layer above $5 million would "exhaust": each insurer in that layer would pay its limit. The $5 million of loss above $25 million would be split among insurers B, C, E, F, which provide the $25 million excess layer above $25 million, in proportion to their policy limits. Insurer B would pay $2 million of the excess loss (10/25 × $5 million). Insurers C, E, and F would each pay $1 million (5/25 × $5 million).

23.4   Property Insurance

This section describes key types and features of commercial property insurance, focusing on the coverage provided by ISO forms. Commercial property coverage is very often packaged with other coverages, such as general liability, auto, crime, boiler and machinery, and inland marine coverage in either the *ISO commercial package policy* or individual insurer variants of that policy. Commercial property coverage generally has five components: (1) *policy declarations,* which summarize the types and locations of covered property, policy limits, and premium rates; (2) *coverage forms,* which describe the types of property and/or associated loss of income that is insured; (3) *causes of loss forms,* which enumerate the causes of loss that are covered by the contract; (4) *policy conditions,* which outline various duties and responsibilities of the insurer and insurers; and (5) *endorsements,* which tailor the coverage to a particular buyer.

Covered Losses

The main losses that can be covered with one or more commercial property insurance forms are (1) damage to buildings and contents, (2) loss of business income following physical damage, (3) extra expenses to maintain operations following damage, and (4) damage or disappearance of goods in transit.

Damage to Buildings and Contents

Commercial property insurance forms usually allow the buyer to select one or more of the following coverages for physical damage to business property on either a replacement cost or actual cash value basis:[1]

- Coverage for damage to buildings.
- Coverage for damage to business property within buildings or on the business's premises (known as "personal property of the insured" in the ISO form).
- Coverage for damage to property on the business's premises that is not owned by the business (known as "personal property of others" in the ISO form).

To illustrate, a business that owns a building and property within the building would generally insure both the building and its contents. A lessor that retains responsibility for damage to a leased building according to the terms of the lease might insure the building but not the contents, and the lessee might buy coverage for its property within the leased building.

Coverage forms for personal property of the insured usually include a small amount of coverage for property not owned by the business, such as personal effects of employees on business premises. Businesses with a major exposure to loss from damage to property of others, such as warehouses, dry cleaners, and so on, often purchase specific coverage for property of others with higher limits. All property insurance coverage forms exclude losses to certain types of property, such as money, motor vehicles, aircraft, watercraft, trees and landscaping, and valuable papers and records. In most instances, these types of property can be insured by endorsement or under a separate policy.

Loss of Business Income Arising from Physical Damage to Property

Loss of income associated with a curtailment or cessation of operations following physical damage to property can be insured with **business interruption coverage** (e.g., with the ISO Business Income Form). Basic business interruption coverage covers the loss of normal income and continuing business expenses that result from direct physical damage to business property from an insured cause of loss. For example, if a building is destroyed by fire and the business's operations are interrupted, the insurer would pay the estimated reduction in profit and continuing expenses such as some salaries, interest on borrowing, and electric power, during the time reasonably needed to restore the facilities to their preloss condition (known as the period of restoration). It also pays expenses incurred by the firm that reduce the overall amount of loss (but not expenses that exceed any reduction in loss from the expenditure). Basic business interruption coverage does not protect against the possibility that revenues will remain relatively low for a period after the damage has been repaired. Firms

---

[1]As explained in Chapter 10, actual cash value equals replacement cost new less depreciation prior to the loss. Replacement cost coverage is more common.

that desire that protection need to purchase an endorsement or special coverage form that extends the period of recovery.

A special type of business income coverage, known as *contingent business interruption coverage,* covers losses of normal income and continuing expenses that arise indirectly from damage to some other business or businesses identified in the contract, such as a major customer, supplier, or business that attracts customers to the policyholder. For example, a relatively small retailer in a shopping center might use this type of coverage to insure losses that might arise if a lead property were damaged, reducing the flow of customers to the center.

The destruction of the World Trade Center in 2001 highlights the underlying risk of loss from damage to another business's property and the possible need for contingent business interruption coverage (as well as for coverage against losses caused by interruption of power and government services). Following the attacks, many New York businesses experienced substantial revenue losses. Many of these businesses had no contingent interruption coverage, and in many other cases the coverage was not broad enough to encompass losses that arose indirectly from the physical damage to World Trade Center and surrounding properties.

Extra Expenses Following Physical Damage to Property

Extraordinary expenses that a firm may incur to maintain its operations following damage to facilities can be insured with **extra expense coverage** through a separate coverage form or combined with business interruption coverage. For some businesses, a temporary cessation or reduction in certain types of operations could lead to large long-term losses due to a loss of customers that will not return and contracts that will not be renewed once the firm resumes operations. A printing company, for example, could lose a substantial proportion of its customers if it ceased operation for several months following damage to its facilities. In such cases, the firm may reduce the present value of its total loss by incurring extraordinarily high costs to keep operating following physical damage to its property. That could involve, for example, renting facilities and equipment, perhaps from competitors, at a much higher cost. Extra expense coverage can be used to fund the increase in costs.

Damage or Disappearance of Goods in Transit

Common coverage forms for business property restrict coverage to losses that occur at business premises. Losses from damage or disappearance of goods in transit (or specialized transportation equipment) on roads or inland waterways can be insured with *inland marine* coverage. *Ocean marine* insurance can be purchased to protect against losses to goods at sea. The ocean marine insurance market also encompasses coverage for damage or disappearance of oceangoing vessels. Damage to business autos and trucks that transport goods can be insured with commercial automobile/truck coverage.

Covered Causes of Loss

A **causes of loss form** is used to specify the insured causes of loss (perils) in business property insurance contracts. For example, and analogous to homeowners insurance (see Chapter 14), the ISO commercial property program offers three main causes of loss forms: (1) the basic form, (2) the broad form, and (3) the special form. The basic and broad forms are named-peril contracts; this means to be covered, the cause of a loss must be listed in the contract. The special form covers all causes of loss unless specifically excluded.

To illustrate the common causes of losses covered by commercial property insurance, the ISO Basic Causes of Loss Form covers the following causes of loss to insured property:

- Fire, lightning, explosion, and smoke
- Windstorm and hail
- Aircraft and vehicles (i.e., that cause loss to insured property)
- Vandalism, riot, and civil commotion
- Sinkhole collapse and volcanic action
- Sprinkler leakage

Additional causes of loss covered under the ISO Broad Form include certain types of water damage, weight of ice and snow, and damage from falling objects. Both the basic and broad forms contain a variety of exclusions and limitations that sometimes can restrict or exclude coverage caused by a listed peril. The special (all-risk) form contains many similar restrictions and exclusions, including losses due to earthquake, flood, war, normal wear and tear, interruption of utility services if the failure occurs away from the described premises unless direct physical damage occurs. Separate, stand-alone coverage is often available for some of the excluded risks under special conditions and prices.

23.5   Commercial General Liability Insurance

The major product lines for commercial casualty insurance (see Table 23.1) include auto liability, workers' compensation and employers' liability, medical professional liability, other professional liability, and general liability (sometimes called other liability). General liability covers liability for losses that do not fall within the other product lines that arise from injuries on business premises, from the sale of products and performing services, and from various types of liability that a firm may assume under contract (such as hold harmless or indemnity agreements, see Chapter 29).

The ISO Commercial General Liability Insurance Policy, known as **CGL coverage,** is the dominant coverage policy form used, and customized forms often incorporate much of its language. The CGL form covers all sources of liability unless they are specifically excluded in the contract. The coverage is therefore analogous to all-risk property insurance coverage. In effect the number and scope of exclusions limit coverage to certain types of losses from premises and operations, products and completed operations, and contractual liability. Coverage for the excluded hazards can often be purchased by endorsement or in a separate form or policy.

CGL Covered Losses

The CGL policy covers court awards, litigation settlements, and defense for third-party bodily injury and property damage (including loss of use) claims. Optional coverage can be added to cover: (1) losses arising from personal injury (e.g., for defamation) and advertising injury (e.g., for copyright or trademark infringement), and (2) medical payments to injured parties on a no-fault basis. CGL coverage includes a limit on the insurer's aggregate liability per occurrence of loss (or claim) and aggregate annual limits (section 23.3).

The defense provisions are central to CGL coverage. The standard CGL policy places a **duty to defend** the policyholder and pay defense costs on the insurer. Defense costs are paid in addition to the insurer's limit of liability for damages (i.e., they do not apply toward the policy limits). The standard policy gives the insurer the right to *control* the defense, including deciding when and for how much to settle a claim and whether to go to trial.

An exception to the insurer's right to control the defense arises if there is a clear conflict of interest between the insurer and the policyholder. An example might be where the lawsuit against the insured alleges that the injury was intentional. Because CGL coverage excludes intentional loss, the insurer's financial interest could conflict with its duty to defend. When there is a bona fide conflict of interest, the courts usually have held that the policyholder has the right to retain its own counsel to be paid by the insurer. Absent such a conflict, however, the insurer controls defense and settlement. As a result, business buyers who wish to be involved in defense and settlement decisions for marketing, customer relations, or reputation purposes need to negotiate customized contract language or side agreements that modify the basic policy.

Courts have interpreted the insurer's duty to defend broadly. The general rule is that the insurer has to provide a defense if *any* claim within the lawsuit is *potentially* covered by the CGL policy. An insurer that refuses to defend because it believes that the claim is not covered by the policy runs the risk of being forced by court order to defend the claim or of being held liable for breach of contract. If the insurer doubts that a claim is covered, or believes that it is not covered but is not sure the courts would agree, it is therefore customary for the insurer to provide the defense subject to a *reservation of rights* to later deny indemnity. Without a formal reservation of rights, providing a defense may be construed as a waiver of the insurer's ability to deny the claim later on. We discuss these and related claim settlement issues further in Chapter 29.

CGL Exclusions

Because the CGL policy covers any claim for bodily injury and property damage unless it is specifically excluded under the policy, the policy exclusions are fundamental to coverage. In most cases, buyers with significant exposure to loss from excluded events can purchase separate coverage or an endorsement to the CGL to provide protection, but they have to negotiate and pay for the extra coverage.

The standard CGL contract excludes coverage for bodily injury or property damage caused by or arising out of the following:

- Injury that is expected or intended by the insured
- Injury to an employee of the insured, including workers' compensation claims
- Sale or distribution of alcohol
- Most pollution (damage to the environment; see Chapter 28)
- Aircraft, automobiles, watercraft, and certain types of mobile equipment
- War
- Damage to property owned; rented; or in the care, custody, or control of the insured
- Damage to the insured's product, work, or property
- Damage arising from impairment of property caused by the insured's product or work, unless the impaired property is physically injured or the impairment arises out of sudden and accidental physical injury to the insured's product or work
- Product recalls

- Certain types of contracts
- Personal injury or advertising injury (recall, however, that standard CGL coverage offers such coverage as an option)

The reasons for some of these exclusions are obvious. For example, worker injuries are covered by workers' compensation/employers' liability insurance or are often insurable under specialized employment practices liability insurance (Chapter 18). Commercial auto liability coverage covers automobile liability risk. Damage to property owned, rented, or in an insured's care, custody, and control can be covered by the owner's or user's property insurance. Most firms are not involved in the sale or distribution of alcoholic beverages, and those that are face special risks better insured separately or by endorsement to the CGL contract.

The exclusions of liability for damage to the insured's product, work, and impaired property are sometimes known as the **business risk exclusions.** While the application of these exclusions can be complex in practice, they essentially keep CGL coverage from becoming a guaranty of the insured's product or work. If, for example, a heating and air conditioning contractor installs equipment improperly, resulting in its failure to perform and the need for repair or replacement, the contractor's CGL insurer is not responsible for the harm to the buyer of the equipment, including any loss of use of the building until the equipment is repaired. If, on the other hand, the equipment catches fire and damages the building, the CGL policy would provide coverage for the property damage, including loss of use (and any bodily injury).

Occurrence Coverage

CGL buyers can choose coverage that is triggered by an occurrence of injury or coverage that is triggered by a claim being made. The former type of coverage is called **occurrence coverage**; the latter type of coverage is known as **claims-made coverage.** In either case, triggered policies usually are responsible for all direct and consequential loss from the injury, subject to deductibles or self-insured retentions and policy limits. Occurrence coverage dominates the CGL market except for certain types of exceptionally risky businesses (e.g., chemical companies). Medical malpractice liability coverage, directors and officers liability coverage, and environmental liability coverage are often insured on a claims-made basis.

CGL coverage written on an occurrence basis covers bodily injury and property damage that arises from an occurrence during the policy period. The relevant language is generally identical or similar to the following language from the ISO CGL policy (1997 version):

> *This insurance applies to "bodily injury" and "property damage" only if: (1) The "bodily injury" or "property damage" is caused by an "occurrence" . . . ; and (2) The "bodily injury" or "property damage" occurs during the policy period. . . .*
> *"Occurrence" means an accident, including continuous or repeated exposure to substantially the same general harmful conditions.*

The meaning of this language and similar language in earlier versions of the CGL policy has been extensively debated and litigated for several decades. However, the key ideas are:

1. The bodily injury or property damage must occur during the policy period.
2. Because the policy does not specify when the claim must be made, the claim does not have to be made within the policy period. Thus, an occurrence policy provides coverage

for injuries that occur during the policy period no matter how long it takes for a claim to be made.

3. The injury should be accidental (recall also that expected or intended injury is specifically excluded), but it need not be sudden in time. Gradual, accidental damage is covered unless it is excluded by one of the CGL exclusions described above.

The following sequence of events for the typical liability claim should help you understand occurrence coverage, the problems that sometimes arise with such coverage, and the solution provided by claims-made coverage:

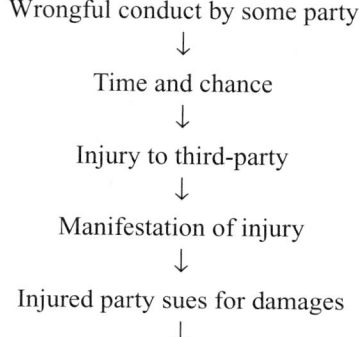

Wrongful conduct by some party
↓
Time and chance
↓
Injury to third-party
↓
Manifestation of injury
↓
Injured party sues for damages
↓
Policyholder makes a claim (notifies insurer and requests coverage and defense)

Consistent with the first key idea presented above, states generally hold that the date of injury to the plaintiff triggers CGL occurrence coverage. Thus, the trigger of occurrence coverage is the date of injury, not the date of wrongful conduct by a policyholder or the date that the claim is made. To illustrate, assume that a brake manufacturer sells defective brakes that are installed in a vehicle assembled and sold in 1999. In 2002, the owner of the vehicle is injured in an accident when the brakes malfunction. The owner sues the manufacturer for damages in 2003. With occurrence coverage, the date of the driver's injury, 2002, triggers the manufacturer's coverage in effect on that date. An occurrence policy in effect in 1999 would not be triggered; nor would a subsequent occurrence be triggered when the claim is made in 2003.

Problems with Gradual Injuries and Determining When Injury Occurred

Many injuries involve little or no uncertainty about the date of injury. Accidents produce sudden injury, the injury is quickly apparent, and lawsuits are filed relatively soon following the injury. However, gradual injuries and uncertainty as to when certain types of injuries occurred and thus which CGL policies are triggered has produced an enormous volume of CGL coverage litigation during the past several decades, especially for claims involving bodily injury and property damage from pollutants and toxic substances, which were commonly insured on an occurrence basis until the late 1970s and 1980s (see Chapter 28). Box 23.2 illustrates the difficulty that can arise in identifying the date of certain types of injuries with some real-world examples. Because coverage limits, exclusions, deductibles, or self-insured retentions, and insurers involved in commercial liability insurance programs change over time, the trigger determination can have a major impact on how much loss insurers indemnify and which insurers have to pay.

- A worker for a shipbuilder during World War II is repeatedly exposed to asbestos dust. The worker is diagnosed with asbestosis in 1999 and brings suit against several asbestos manufacturers.
- A fertility drug is associated with increased frequency of cervical cancer in the adult children of women who took the drug. The drug manufacturers are sued.
- Troops exposed to Agent Orange in Vietnam later develop a variety of ailments. The manufacturers of the defoliant are sued.
- California farmers apply agricultural chemicals to kill pests. The chemicals eventually contaminate the groundwater, migrate over years to the wells for a number of cities, and exceed the maximum allowable concentration under California law, thus requiring the cities to remediate the contamination. The cities sue the chemical manufacturer.
- A defective mortar additive slowly leads to widespread cracking in the facades of buildings where it is applied. The owners sue the manufacturer.
- Defective application of synthetic stucco leads to extensive moisture and termite damage to residential properties. The owners sue the manufacturer and installers.
- Petroleum products are spilled on a business's premises, migrate slowly to property owned by another party, and eventually cause a fire. The owner of the site where the products were spilled is sued.
- A building contractor drives pilings into the ceiling of a tunnel under the Chicago River. The tunnel floods the following year. The city sues the contractor.
- An excavator damages tree roots. The tree eventually falls causing bodily injury and property damage. The victims sue the excavator.

The issues are complex, and the courts have been divided in their interpretation of the date of occurrence in these types of situations. Some early decisions for bodily injury from exposure to asbestos held that the time of exposure to the toxic substance triggered coverage. The most common doctrines now, especially for property damage, are the **manifestation trigger** and the **injury-in-fact trigger.** Under the manifestation trigger, if the date of injury cannot be reasonably determined, the date that the injury manifests itself to the plaintiff triggers coverage. Under the injury-in-fact trigger, the court (fact-finder) attempts to estimate when the injury actually occurred based on expert testimony and other evidence.

Allocation Among Triggered Years of Coverage

If more than one year of coverage is triggered, damages often are allocated to the triggered years equally over time (i.e., based on time on the risk). If, for example, a business had $15 million of coverage each year above a $1 million retention, damages are $10 million, and five years of coverage are triggered, each years' policies would be allocated $2 million of damage ($10 million/5 years). The insured business would therefore bear $1 million of damage and receive $1 million in indemnity for each year.

The specific coverage trigger used can have a major effect on the division of loss among the insured, primary insurers, and excess insurers. The manifestation trigger generally allocates more damages to a single year, which pushes damage payments to higher layers of coverage and is more likely to exhaust the policyholder's limits of coverage. If, for example, the manifestation trigger caused the $10 million of damages in the previous example to be allocated to one year, the policyholder would only bear $1 million of loss. The insurers on the risk in that year would bear $9 million. If the damages were $19 million, the insurance would exhaust. The policyholder would have to pay $4 million (the $1 million retention plus the remaining $3 million of loss above the $15 million of coverage).

An alternative to allocating damages based on time on the risk that is used in some states holds each year of triggered coverage jointly liable for the entire amount of damages. The policyholder can choose the year of coverage for defense and indemnity, and it is the insurers' problem to allocate the losses among the covered years and policies, usually according the policies' "other insurance" provisions (see Chapter 10). In practice this approach provides more indemnity because the insured will choose a year with higher limits and/or lower self-insured retentions.

Single versus Multiple Occurrences

Whether a loss constitutes a single occurrence or multiple occurrences is another thorny issue that sometimes affects the interpretation of occurrence coverage and leads to litigation between insurers and policyholders over the meaning of the phrase "including continuous or repeated exposure to substantially the same general harmful conditions" or similar language in the definition of occurrence. Because of per occurrence limits and per occurrence deductibles/self-insured retentions, whether damage is viewed as arising from a single occurrence, as opposed to multiple occurrences, can sometimes have a major impact on the allocation of loss between the insurer and policyholder.

Until the late 1960s and early 1970s, for example, it was not uncommon for CGL policies to include per occurrence limits without any aggregate annual limit. If a series of injuries from the same basic cause (e.g., application of defective mortar to numerous buildings) constituted multiple occurrences rather than a single occurrence, the insurer would have to pay up to the per occurrence limit for each injury (occurrence). Alternatively, if the loss per injury were relatively small and the policyholder had a relatively large per occurrence deductible, treating the injuries as arising from multiple occurrences might cause the policyholder to get relatively little indemnity compared with summing the damages and treating them as arising from a single occurrence.

The majority rule in the United States (known as the cause test) is that all injuries arising out of the same basic cause constitute a single occurrence. A significant minority of states, however, treats each event leading to injury as a separate occurrence (known as the event test). Risk managers, brokers, and insurance company underwriters need to be familiar with these distinctions when negotiating deductibles and limits.

In contrast to liability insurance, the number of occurrences is rarely an issue in property insurance, because the property damage is clearly attributable to a single event, and policy limits are usually reinstated following the event to provide the same amount of coverage for any subsequent events. The destruction of the World Trade Center in 2001, however, represents an interesting exception (see Box 23.3).

Claims-Made Coverage

Uncertainty over when injury occurs and possibly long lags between the onset of injury and the manifestation of injury and claim for damages make certain types of exposures very expensive to insure or even uninsurable on an occurrence basis. The uncertainty and long claims tail increase insurers' risk of large forecast errors when pricing coverage, increasing the amount of capital needed to support the sale of coverage and the premium needed to cover the tax and agency costs of capital (Chapter 8). They also aggravate moral hazard and

The property insurance program in place for the World Trade Center on September 11, 2001, is reported to have consisted of 11 layers of coverage with numerous insurers and reinsurers involved in each layer. The towers were insured for a total of $3.55 billion for damage from a single event. As this book went to press, a number of insurers and WTC leaseholder Larry Silverstein were litigating whether the destruction of the second tower constituted a separate event. Silverstein claimed that it was and wanted the insurers to pay $7.1 billion. The insurers argued otherwise and offered to pay $3.55 billion. The property insurance program had recently been renewed. As is not unusual, all of the coverage documents had not been finalized and issued at the time of the attack. According to press reports, the language in some of the policies defined an occurrence as "all losses or damages that are attributable directly or indirectly to one cause or to one series of similar causes." While that language implies a single occurrence, whether many of the insurers had adopted that language, as opposed to binding coverage that did not define occurrence, was being disputed.

adverse selection. For these reasons, and as noted above, a variety of risky hazards, such as environmental liability, medical malpractice liability, and directors' and officers' liability, are commonly insured on a claims-made basis rather than an occurrence basis.

Basic Concept of Claims-Made Coverage

While the details are often complex, the basic concept of claims-made coverage is simple: *The insurer agrees to cover and provide a defense only for claims made during the policy period or within a relatively short, specified time period after the policy period.* Compared with occurrence coverage, claims-made coverage reduces ambiguity or uncertainty about what claims are covered by a particular policy, and it shortens the time between the pricing and underwriting of coverage and the date that all claims covered by the policy will be paid. As a result, the claims-made trigger reduces insurers' risk, the amount of capital they need to hold, and moral hazard and adverse selection.

As we elaborate later, other things being equal, business buyers generally would prefer occurrence coverage because they bear less risk than with claims-made coverage. But other things are not equal, at least for businesses with risky, long-tail exposures. The main reason that those exposures are insured on a claims-made basis is that businesses are unwilling to pay a high enough premium to obtain occurrence coverage.[2]

ISO Claims-Made Form

Let's add some real-world complexity to the preceding simple description of claims-made coverage. The ISO claims-made CGL form provides coverage for a claim if two conditions are met:

1. The injury occurred after a **retroactive date** specified in the contract.

---

[2]At the risk of oversimplifying, the reason that occurrence coverage for certain hazards may at times be completely unavailable is that too few buyers would be willing to pay the high price insurers would need to offer the coverage.

2. The claim is made during the policy period, or, under the form's automatic *Basic Extended Reporting Period,* within five years after the end of the policy period, provided that the claim arises out of an occurrence reported to the insurer within 60 days after the end of the policy period. This provision does not increase the coverage limits or require any additional premium payment at the end of the policy period.

In addition, the ISO claims-made form includes an option for the policyholder to buy a *Supplemental Extended Reporting Period* endorsement by notifying the insurer within 60 days after the end of the policy period. The endorsement provides coverage for future claims for injuries that occurred during the policy period with new coverage limits equal to the policy's original limits. The insurer must offer the endorsement at a price no greater than 200 percent of the original annual premium. By exercising this option, the insured can essentially convert the claims-made policy to occurrence coverage within 60 days after the policy period by paying an additional premium.

The ISO claims-made form was developed during the mid-1980s liability insurance crisis (Chapter 8) amid considerable controversy, with substantial input from risk managers, brokers, and insurance regulators. Coverage under this form differs significantly from the simple concept of claims-made coverage explained above. The ISO form is a claims-made policy with an embedded option for the policyholder to convert the policy to occurrence coverage by paying an additional premium.

Nonstandard Claims-Made Forms

In contrast to the ISO form, many claims-made policies written on nonstandard basis come closer to the simple concept that underlies claims-made coverage. The policies cover claims made during the policy period or within a specified and relatively short time after the policy period without including an option for the policyholder to convert to occurrence coverage. However, nonstandard claims-made policies generally require covered claims to result from injuries that commenced following a retroactive date specified in the policy.

Purpose of the Retroactive Date

Restricting coverage to injuries that commenced after a specified date helps coordinate coverage when a business switches from occurrence to claims-made coverage. Injuries that occurred prior to the retroactive date trigger occurrence coverage in effect at the time of injury. Injuries that occur after the retroactive date that produce claims within the policy period or any extended reporting periods trigger the claims-made policy, but they are not covered by the preceding occurrence policy (or policies). Moreover, without a retroactive date, claims-made coverage could be prohibitively expensive for firms with a prior history of injuries and thus high expected claim costs and because of possible adverse selection.

Whether the retroactive date is moved forward or kept the same when a claims-made policy is renewed is subject to negotiation between the insurer and insured. Figure 23.7 illustrates the key distinction between occurrence and claims-made coverage assuming that claims-made contract has a retroactive date equal to policy's date of inception and has no extended reporting period. If the retroactive date is moved forward each year, claims-made coverage essentially eliminates coverage for long-tailed claims. If, on the other hand, the retroactive date remains the same each year, the insurer can base renewal premiums on expected claim costs for new occurrences that give rise to claims during the coverage period *and* expected claim costs for injuries that occurred after the retroactive date but prior to the

FIGURE 23.7

Occurrence coverage (top) requires that the injury occur during the policy period (*t* through *t* + 1); the claim can be made during or after the policy period. Pure claims-made coverage (bottom) with a retroactive date at time *t* requires that the injury both occur and produce a claim during the policy period.

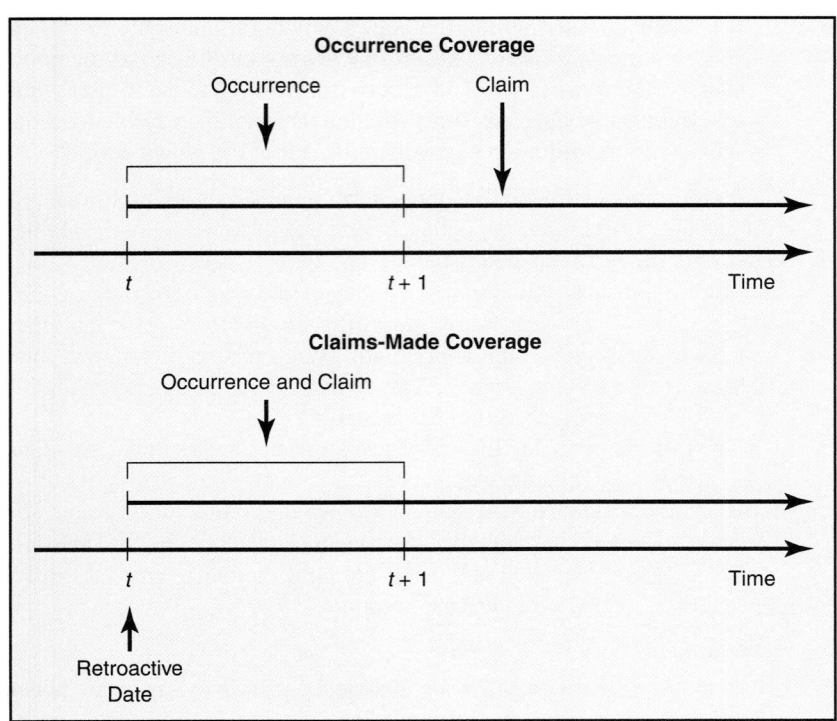

renewal date. With occurrence coverage, competition will allow insurers to base premiums on only expected claim costs for injuries during the policy period. Thus, while the amount of additional risk borne by a claims-made policyholder compared to occurrence coverage depends on whether the retroactive date is advanced or not, in either case claims-made coverage shifts more risk to the insured.

Concept Check

1. Claims-made coverage first began to be used on a widespread basis in the mid-1970s for medical malpractice insurance and environmental liability insurance. Why would these types of insurance be particularly good candidates for claims-made coverage?

23.6   Pricing and Underwriting: Commercial versus Personal Coverage

As described briefly in Chapter 8, the pricing and underwriting of insurance sold to medium-to-large businesses differs from that for personal and small business insurance in three important ways:

First, insurance underwriters of coverage for medium-to-large businesses often have substantial discretion based on their expert judgment to negotiate: (*a*) the premium rate and other pricing terms, and (*b*) special coverage features and services. Personal lines underwriters have much less, if any, discretion on these dimensions.

Second, pricing plans for medium-to-large businesses often make charges to policyholders a function of the policyholders' loss experience *during the coverage period.* These pricing plans, known broadly as *loss sensitive rating plans,* generally are not used for personal and small business coverage. The most common loss sensitive plans used in commercial insurance are (*a*) retrospective rating plans, which make the policyholder's ultimate premium for the period depend on its losses for the period up to a specified maximum premium, and (*b*) dividend plans, where the amount of dividend paid to the policyholder primarily depends on the policyholder's own loss experience during the coverage period. We describe retrospective rating and a number of other loss sensitive plans in detail in Chapter 25.

Third, although the distinction is sometimes not sharp, especially for workers' compensation insurance, insurance sold to medium-to-large businesses often is subject to less (or less intense) rate and policy form regulation than is personal insurance. One reason for this difference is that medium-to-large businesses often are relatively sophisticated in insurance and financial matters. A second reason is that many medium-to-large businesses have greater options in the face of rising insurance prices, such as significantly increasing retention levels, modifying operations to reduce the risk of loss, and access to alternative risk transfer mechanisms (Chapter 25), which reduce their incentives to press for regulatory constraints on rate increases. Third, medium-to-large business buyers exhibit more heterogeneity in coverage needs and risk of loss than personal and small-business insurance buyers, which makes tight regulatory controls on rates and policy forms much more difficult to implement.

23.7 Summary

• Standardized policy forms or contract language provide the basis for many commercial property–casualty insurance programs. Prices, specific coverage features, and services, however, are often heavily negotiated between insurers and medium-to-large sized business policyholders and their brokers.

• Medium-to-large business insurance policies often include relatively large deductibles or self-insured retentions. Coverage limits are commonly structured in layers, with multiple insurers participating in excess (or umbrella) layers above primary coverage.

• The major types of commercial property insurance include (1) coverage for property damage to business buildings and contents, (2) business interruption coverage for reduced income and continuing expenses following physical damage to property, (3) coverage for extra expenses that some businesses may incur to maintain operations and avoid a significant loss of customers following physical damage to business property,

and (4) coverage for loss to goods in transit.

• Commercial general liability (CGL) insurance covers bodily and property damage to third-parties that occurs on business premises or arises from business operations, from the sale of products, and from liability that the business assumes under many contracts. The insurer has the duty to defend the policyholder and, absent special coverage terms or a conflict of interest, the right to control the defense and settlement. The standard CGL insurance form excludes coverage for damage claims arising out of hazards that are better insured under an endorsement or separate coverage, that are insurable only under special conditions, or that may be uninsurable.

• CGL coverage written on an occurrence basis covers bodily injury and property damage that occurs during the policy period, regardless of when the claim is made.

• CGL occurrence coverage can be prohibitively expensive for risks where the date of injury may be difficult or impossible to identify and/or where there may be long lags between the occurrence (or commencement) of injury and the manifestation of injury and filing of a claim for damages. Those risks commonly are insured on a claims-made basis. Claims-made contracts pay claims that (1) are made within or shortly after the end of the policy period or made within an extended reporting period, and (2) arise from injuries that oc-

curred after a date specified in the policy, known as the retroactive date.

• Compared with personal and small-business insurance, underwriters for medium-to-large business accounts often have substantial discretion to negotiate the price and terms of coverage. Loss sensitive rating plans, which make the cost of insurance depend on the policyholder's loss experience during the coverage period, are commonly used.

Key Terms

exposure diagram 505
per occurrence deductible 505
aggregate deductible 506
self-insured retention 508
per occurrence limits 508
annual aggregate limit 508
excess policies 508
attachment point 508
primary coverage 508
layering coverage 509
umbrella policy 510
coverage chart 510

business interruption coverage 512
extra expense coverage 513
causes of loss form 513
CGL coverage 514
duty to defend 514
business risk exclusions 516
occurrence coverage 516
claims-made coverage 516
manifestation trigger 518
injury-in-fact trigger 518
retroactive date 520

Questions and Problems

1. Distinguish surety bonds from insurance contracts.

2. A business with business interruption coverage suffers damage to a plant and loses $400,000 in profits and continuing expenses during the period the plant is restored to its preloss condition. After the period of restoration, it loses another $200,000 in profits due to lower sales than would have been generated had the damage not occurred. Assuming adequate coverage limits and no deductible, how much will the firm recover from its business interruption insurer?

3. A Web server company faces the risk of fire or other damage to its premises and servers. Should the company consider buying extra expense coverage?

4. A building is insured under the ISO Basic Causes of Loss Form. After a severe winter storm, the weight of ice and snow causes the roof to collapse. Will the policy cover the damage?

5. Explain the scope of a CGL insurer's duty to defend and its rights to control the defense.

6. Explain why it might benefit insurance buyers to allow the insurer the right to control the defense of a liability claim. (Hint: we discuss related issues in Chapter 29.)

7. A person injured in an auto accident by a patron who drank too much sues a tavern owner. The tavern owner has standard ISO CGL occurrence coverage. Is the claim covered? If not, what might the tavern owner argue in litigation that attempts to compel the insurer to provide a defense and cover dam-

ages? (Hint: see Chapter 10 for help in answering the latter question.)

8. Distinguish the injury-in-fact trigger under CGL occurrence coverage from the manifestation trigger. Which trigger is more consistent with the contract language? Which trigger would likely be less costly to implement and produce fewer disputes between insurers and policyholders?

9. Explain the key differences between occurrence and claims-made liability coverage.

10. Explain why claims-made coverage is relatively uncommon for products liability but very common for environmental liability.

11. A product manufactured by Kaufman, Inc., in 1998 injures Peter Wallison on June 1, 2001. Kaufman had annual claims-made coverage during 1995–2003, with coverage renewing on January 1 each year. The policy's retroactive date was advanced each year to coincide with the renewal date. Which year's policy provides coverage if Wallison sues Kaufman for damages in 2003?

12. Assume the same circumstances as in question 11, but now assume that Kaufman has occurrence coverage. Which year's policy provides coverage?

13. Now assume that Kaufman has occurrence coverage with a self-insured retention of $100,000 per occurrence, primary per occurrence limits of $400,000, a first excess layer with $2 million per occurrence limits excess of $500,000, and a second excess layer with $5 million per occurrence limits excess of $2,500,000. The primary insurer settles the claim in consultation with the excess insurers for $3 million. How much of the $3 million will the second layer excess insurers be required to pay?

14. Illustrate Kaufman's insurance program described in the preceding question with a coverage chart. Also illustrate Kaufman's general exposure to liability loss with an exposure diagram like Figure 23.5.

15. Why might it make good sense for insurers to allow underwriters for medium-to-large commercial accounts to have substantial discretion in negotiating price terms but not allow such discretion to personal lines and small business underwriters?

Answer to Concept Check

1. Both medical malpractice liability and environmental liability were particularly good candidates for claims-made coverage given the difficulty in accurately identifying when certain injuries occur and the possibility of long lags between the onset of injury and the manifestation of injury and lawsuit for damages. For malpractice, injuries from negligently performed medical procedures may take a number of years to evolve until they are recognized and diagnosed. The long lag problem is even worse for many types of pollution damage, which can go undiscovered for years.

References

Commercial Insurance. American Institute for Property-Casualty Insurance, Malvern, PA: Flitner, Arthur L., 2002. *(Chartered Property–Casualty Underwriter program text with details on commercial insurance contracts.)*
The Insurance Professionals' Policy Kit, 2000 ed.

Alliance of American Insurers, Downers Grove, IL. *(A collection of sample policies and forms for personal and commercial lines. Updated periodically.)*

Chapter 24

Hedging with Derivative Contracts

Chapter Objectives

- Explain the basic derivative contracts (options, forwards, futures, and swaps) commonly used for hedging.
- Discuss similarities and differences between insurance contracts and derivative contracts.
- Explain differences between exchange-traded and over-the-counter derivative markets.
- Describe the major types of risk that are typically hedged using derivatives.

24.1 Introduction to Derivatives and Hedging

The traditional use of the term *risk management* suggests activities such as purchasing insurance and loss control that are used to manage pure risk. Currently, risk management increasingly is used to indicate financial risk management: the hedging of financial price risk using derivative contracts like futures, swaps, and options. Perhaps because of the need for specialization, the two types of risk management often are performed by different people within the same corporation without consideration of the possible interrelationships. Ideally, both types of activities should be analyzed using the firm value maximization framework (see Chapter 2), taking into consideration that the optimal management of one type of risk (e.g., pure risk) depends on how other types of risk (e.g., price risk) are being managed. Indeed, some corporations are adopting such an approach under the name enterprise risk management (see Chapter 27).

This chapter introduces some of the basic tools, terminology, and concepts used in financial risk management. Armed with this background, a major objective is to identify and discuss similarities and differences between financial risk management and traditional risk management.

Exposure Diagrams Revisited

To introduce some of the basic ideas of hedging with derivatives, we use a simple example of a firm called NeedOil that uses oil in its production process. If the price of oil increases, then the firm's costs will increase. On the other hand, if the price of oil decreases, the firm's costs will decrease. The important point is that the firm's costs are uncertain due to the price of oil being uncertain. We assume that NeedOil cannot pass on all incremental costs to customers and therefore that cost increases produce lower profits.

NeedOil's risk from uncertain oil prices can be illustrated using exposure diagrams similar to those introduced in Chapter 23. Figure 24.1 indicates that, holding other factors constant, NeedOil's profits are negatively related to the price of oil over the coming year. In particular, the horizontal axis gives the possible prices for the particular grade of oil that NeedOil will purchase in New Orleans in six months. If the price equals $15 a barrel, then NeedOil's profits will equal $1 million. However, if the price of oil is $16 a barrel, then NeedOil's profits will be only $750,000. The negatively sloped line in Figure 24.1 gives NeedOil's profits for each possible oil price.

Recall that the horizontal axis in an exposure diagram gives the possible outcomes for some random variable.[1] Only one of these outcomes will actually be realized. In this example, NeedOil does not know the price that it must pay for oil in six months. The horizontal axis gives possible oil prices and the vertical axis gives NeedOil's profits under these alternative outcomes. Only one point on the graph will occur. As with the exposure diagrams in Chapter 23, if the exposure diagram is not flat (horizontal), then the firm is exposed to risk.

Before showing how NeedOil can reduce its risk (flatten the line in Figure 24.1), two points are worth noting about the relation between NeedOil's profits and oil prices depicted in Figure 24.1. First, the relationship between oil prices and profits would not be known with certainty. Instead the relationship depicted in Figure 24.1 would be viewed as

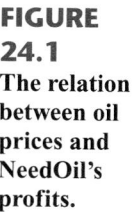

FIGURE 24.1
The relation between oil prices and NeedOil's profits.

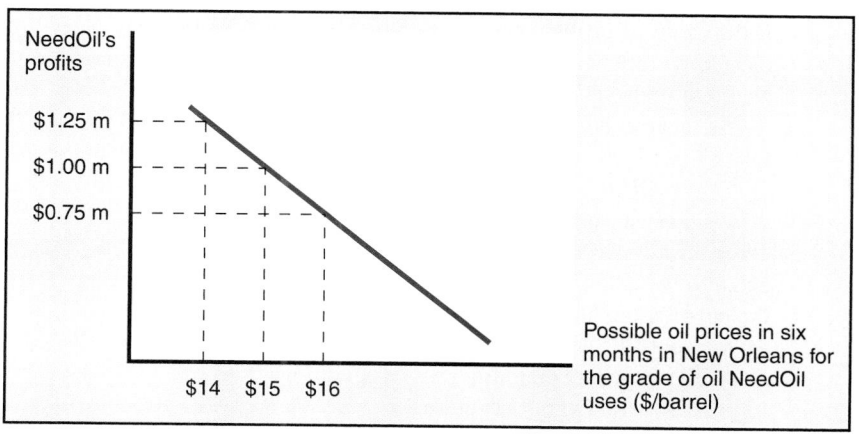

[1]The exposure diagrams presented in this chapter differ from those in Chapter 23 in that profits are graphed on the vertical axis here and costs were graphed on the vertical axis in Chapter 23.

the relationship between oil prices and the expected value of profits, but generally there would be random variation in profits around the expected value. Second, considerable analysis (which is beyond the scope of this chapter) would be needed to determine the relationship between expected profits and possible oil prices. For example, the downward sloping line in Figure 24.1 could have been estimated using historical data on how NeedOil's profits varied with oil prices.

Concept Checks

1. Golddigger Inc. is a gold mining company. Draw a graph that identifies the likely relationship between gold prices and the value of Golddigger.

2. Zeiser Inc. is a construction company. Draw a graph that identifies the likely relationship between interest rates and the value of Zeiser Inc. Also draw a graph that identifies the likely relationship between government bond prices and the value of Zeiser Inc. (Hint: Higher interest rates reduce bond prices and the demand for new construction.)

Hedging with Call Option Contracts

The negatively sloped line in Figure 24.1 indicates that NeedOil is exposed to oil price risk. To reduce this risk, NeedOil must do something to flatten the line depicting the relationship between its profits and oil prices. If it could make the line horizontal over some range of oil prices, then it would eliminate its oil price risk over that range of prices (profits would be the same under different oil prices).

Suppose that NeedOil decides that it does not want to bear the risk that it will have to pay more than $15 a barrel for oil. That is, NeedOil wants to engage in some transaction that changes its profit line in Figure 24.1 from being negatively sloped when oil prices are above $15 to one that is flat when oil prices are above $15. NeedOil can do this by contracting with another party who will give NeedOil money when the price of oil rises above $15. For example, suppose that NeedOil signs a contract with OPTCO that requires OPTCO to pay NeedOil 250,000 times the difference between the actual price of oil in six months and $15, provided that the actual price exceeds $15. Under this contract, if the price of oil in six months turns out to be $16, then OPTCO will pay NeedOil $250,000; if the price of oil turns out to be $17, then OPTCO will pay NeedOil $500,000, and so on. On the other hand, if the price of oil ends up being less than $15, OPTCO will pay NeedOil nothing.

So far, the description of the contract between NeedOil and OPTCO indicates that OPTCO will pay NeedOil money in six months if oil prices are higher than $15. Obviously, OPTCO will require compensation for agreeing to do this. In a sense, OPTCO can be viewed as insuring NeedOil against high costs due to high oil prices. OPTCO will demand compensation for selling this insurance. Let's assume that OPTCO requires a premium equal to $100,000. Taking into account this premium, but ignoring the time value of money, the payoff from NeedOil's contract with OPTCO is illustrated in Figure 24.2.

To identify NeedOil's exposure to oil prices after arranging this contract, we must add NeedOil's exposure diagram from its operations (Figure 24.1) to the exposure diagram from its contract with OPTCO (Figure 24.2). That is, for each possible oil price, we add the profits from operations to the payoffs from the contract with OPTCO. The following calculations indicate how this is done for three prices.

If oil price = $14 → Profits from operations (Figure 24.1)   = $1,250,000
                      Profits from OPTCO contract (Figure 24.2)   = −$100,000
                      Total profits   = $1,150,000

If oil price = $15 → Profits from operations (Figure 24.1)   = $1,000,000
                      Profits from OPTCO contract (Figure 24.2)   = −$100,000
                      Total profits   = $900,000

If oil price = $16 → Profits from operations (Figure 24.1)   = $750,000
                      Profits from OPTCO contract (Figure 24.2)   = $150,000
                      Total profits   = $900,000

Figure 24.3 illustrates the total profits to NeedOil after engaging in the contract with OPTCO. No matter what happens to the price of oil, expected profits never fall below $900,000, which is the level of profits NeedOil would have if the price of oil were $15 minus the premium paid to OPTCO.

FIGURE 24.2
The relation between oil prices and NeedOil's payoff from its contract with OPTCO.

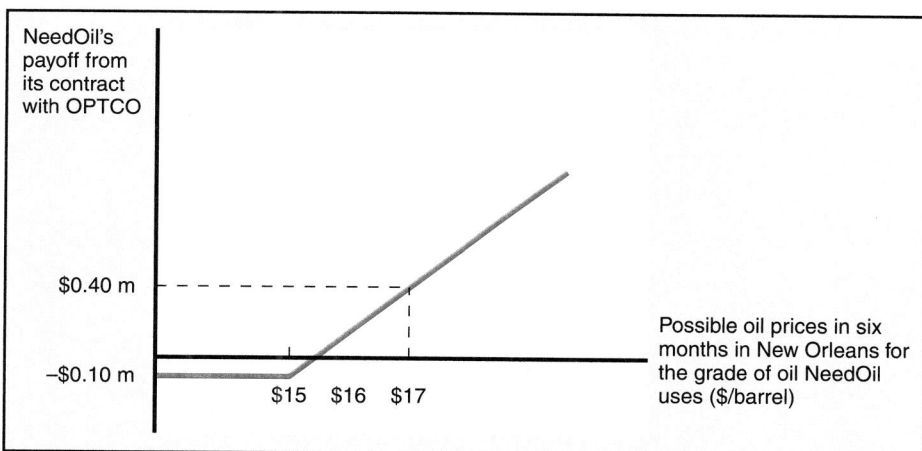

FIGURE 24.3
The relation between oil prices and NeedOil's profits from operations plus profits from contract with OPTCO.

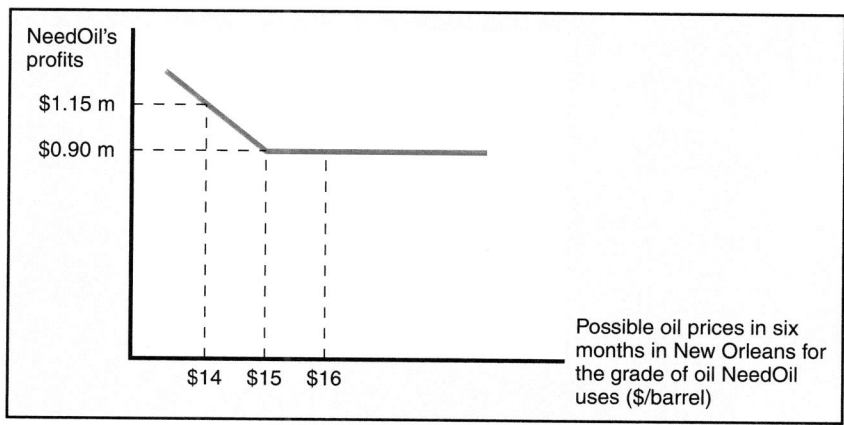

The transaction between NeedOil and OPTCO is an example of a derivative contract. A **derivative contract** is a contract whose payoff or value is derived from the value of something else, most commonly some other asset, but sometimes an index or other item. The asset on which a derivative contract is based is called the **underlying asset** of the derivative contract. In the example with NeedOil, the underlying asset is the market value (price) of a particular grade of oil six months hence in New Orleans. Derivative contracts exist with underlying assets ranging from financial assets like bonds and stocks to commodities like orange juice, pork bellies, and lumber. The underlying asset of a derivative contract also could be an index that measures the level or rate of change in some economic variable. For example, derivatives could be based on a consumer price index or an index measuring the magnitude of insured losses from hurricanes in Florida.

The derivative contract purchased by NeedOil from OPTCO was an example of a call option contract. The buyer of a **call option contract** receives a positive payoff only if the value of the underlying asset exceeds some threshold, called the **exercise price** (or *strike price*). NeedOil's call option contract had an exercise price of $15. The price paid for a call option (the premium) is called the **option price;** NeedOil paid $100,000 for its call option, so the option price was $100,000.

An important feature of a call option is that the payoff is asymmetric: A buyer of a call option receives a payoff that increases linearly with the value of the underlying asset when the value of the underlying asset is above the exercise price, but the payoff is flat when the value of the underlying asset is below the exercise price. The asymmetric payoff to a buyer of a call option is illustrated in Figure 24.2.

We have discussed call options from the perspective of the buyer of the call option, NeedOil. Now consider the payoff to the seller of the call option—OPTCO. Graphically, OPTCO's payoff can be found by reflecting the mirror image of NeedOil's payoff on the other side of the horizontal axis. This payoff is illustrated in Figure 24.4. If the price of oil is high, OPTCO loses money on the contract, but if the price of oil is less than $15, OPTCO makes a profit on the contract. The possible gain from selling the option is limited to the price of the option, but the possible loss can be very large (a large increase in the price of oil will cause the seller to make a large payment). Notice that the payoffs to the option buyer (NeedOil) are opposite of the payoffs to the option seller (OPTCO) and therefore that the sum of the payments is always zero.

FIGURE 24.4
Payoff to a seller of a call option on oil with an exercise price of $15.

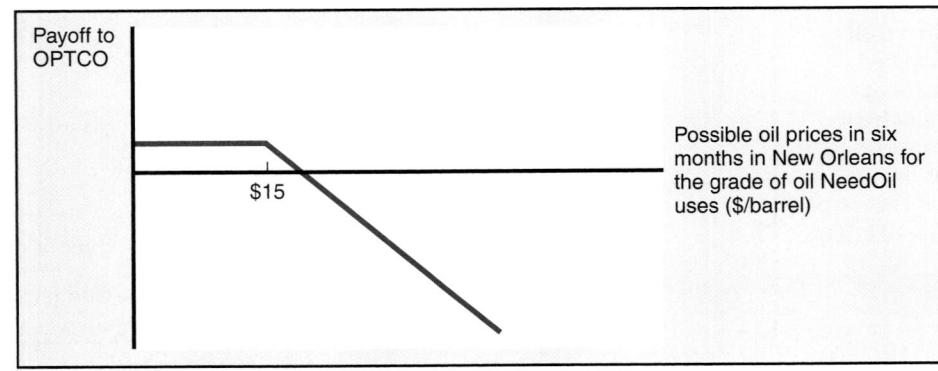

Payoff to OPTCO

$15

Possible oil prices in six months in New Orleans for the grade of oil NeedOil uses ($/barrel)

FIGURE 24.5
Payoff from put options on oil with an exercise price of $15.

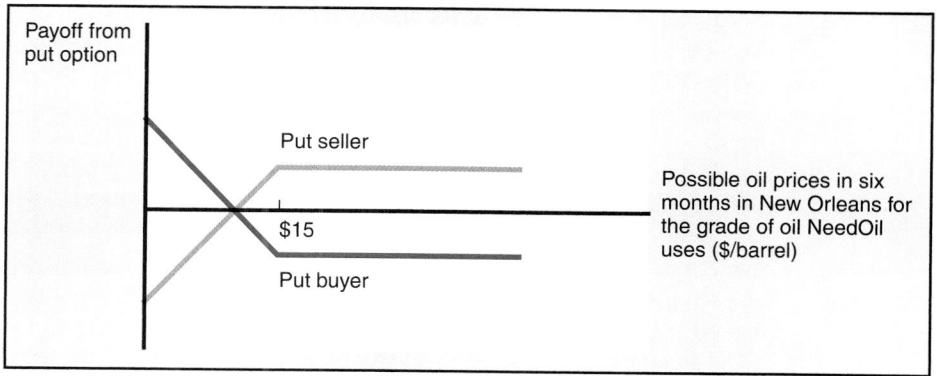

Hedging with Put Options

The other basic type of option contract is a put option contract. The buyer of a **put option contract** receives a positive payoff only if the value of the underlying asset falls below the exercise price. The payoff from a put option on oil with an exercise price of $15 is given by the kinked line labeled "put buyer" in Figure 24.5. Since the put buyer's payoff increases as oil prices fall, an oil producer could use a put option contract to hedge the risk of low oil prices.

For every put buyer, there is also a put seller. The payoff to the seller of a put option is the mirror image of the buyer's payoff reflected across the horizontal axis. This is illustrated in Figure 24.5 by the kinked line labeled "put seller." Notice that the seller's payoff is just the opposite of the buyer's payoff.

In summary, both call and put option contracts are derivative contracts that can be used to protect firm value from price changes that otherwise would decrease firm value. For firms whose value decreases when the value of the underlying asset increases, call options can protect firm value. For firms whose value decreases when the value of the underlying asset decreases, put options can protect firm value. Thus, option contracts have features like insurance contracts: Both option and insurance contracts can be used to generate cash when events occur that otherwise would have caused a loss in value. Just as a firm pays a premium for insurance, a firm pays a premium for an option contract.

Concept Checks

3. Golddigger Inc.'s value increases as gold prices increase. If Golddigger wanted to protect firm value against a possible decrease in the price of gold, would it use a call option or a put option? What would be the underlying asset?

4. Suppose that Zeiser Construction Co.'s value decreases as interest rates increase. If Zeiser wanted to protect firm value against an increase in interest rates, would it use a call option or a put option? What would be the underlying asset?

Cash Settlement versus Physical Delivery

Our presentation of call and put options has emphasized their similarity to insurance contracts. Specifically, the call option purchased by NeedOil provides cash to NeedOil if oil prices turn out to be high. This cash can then be used to offset the high cost of oil that

NeedOil needs to purchase for its operations. Consequently, the call option "insures" NeedOil from losses resulting from high oil prices. Many derivative contracts are structured similar to NeedOil's call option; that is, they are settled in cash at the expiration of the contract. **Cash settled derivative contracts** are purely financial transactions with cash payments based on (derived from) the value of some other commodity, security, or index; the underlying asset of the derivative contract (oil in our example) is not physically delivered.

Many derivative contracts, however, are based on the **physical delivery** of the underlying asset.[2] Indeed, the description of physical delivery contracts helps to explain some of the terminology used to describe options. With physical delivery, a call option on oil with an exercise price of $15/barrel gives the call option buyer the right (not the obligation) to buy oil at $15/barrel. For example, if the price of oil were $17/barrel, then the option buyer could force the option seller to deliver oil at $15/barrel. Thus, the term *call option* comes from the ability of the call option buyer to "call" the underlying asset away from the option seller for less than it is worth at the time of delivery.

A put option gives the put buyer the right (not the obligation) to make the put seller purchase the underlying asset at the exercise price. If the value of the underlying asset is less than the exercise price, then the put buyer will exercise the option and make the put seller purchase the underlying asset for more than the asset is worth. Thus, the term *put option* comes from the ability of the put buyer to "put" the underlying asset to the put seller for more than it is worth at the time of delivery. (Box 24.1 summarizes some other terminology used to describe option contracts.)

The distinction between physical delivery and cash settled derivative contracts is inconsequential for our purposes. The essential point is that call options can be used to generate cash if the price of some commodity, index, or security turns out to be high. And put options can be used to generate cash if the price of some commodity, index, or security turns out to be low.

Basis Risk

The above examples illustrating how NeedOil might use options (and in later examples, forward contracts and other derivatives) to hedge its oil price risk are simplified by the assumption that the underlying asset of the derivative contracts also is the type of oil that NeedOil purchases for its operations. As a result, a perfect hedge can be constructed. In the option example, if oil prices increase beyond $15, then the lost operating profits can be exactly offset by increased profits from the option contract.

In reality, "the only perfect hedge is in a Japanese garden" (source unknown). The risk from an imperfect hedge is called **basis risk.** The *basis* for a hedge is the difference between the value of what's being hedged and the value of the hedging instrument. Thus, the basis for NeedOil is the difference between its oil costs and the payoff from the call option. If an increase in its oil costs is always offset by an equal increase in the payoff from the call option, then the hedge is perfect and there is no basis risk. However, if changes in NeedOil's

[2]Even with physical delivery contracts, most traders do not actually take physical delivery. Instead, they unwind their positions by taking the opposite position prior to the contract's expiration. For example, NeedOil could purchase a call option on oil today and prior to the option's expiration sell the call option to someone else. If the price of oil increased during the intervening period, then the call option price would increase (see the next subsection) and NeedOil could use the gain to offset the higher price of oil that it must purchase for its operations.

European options can be exercised only at the expiration of the contract. If a call option contract is for six months, then the call buyer can only exercise the option at the end of six months. Thus, the ultimate payoff on European options is determined by the difference between the exercise price and the price of the underlying asset at expiration.

American options can be exercised any time prior to expiration. Thus, the ultimate payoff on American options can depend on the difference between the exer-cise price and the price of the underlying asset at any time prior to expiration.

The payoff on *Asian options* depends on the differ-ence between the exercise price and the average of the prices of the underlying asset prior to exercise. Some Asian options can be exercised only at the contract ex-piration (like European options) and some Asian op-tions can be exercised prior to the contract's expiration (like American options).

oil costs are not always offset perfectly by the option's payoff, then there is basis risk. With basis risk, there is uncertainty in how good the hedge will actually work.

There are a number of sources of basis risk. For example, NeedOil may purchase a cer-tain grade (sulfur content) of oil, but the derivative contract may be based on a different grade. NeedOil may purchase oil the last day of every month, but the derivative contract may mature during the middle of every three months. NeedOil may take delivery of its oil in New Orleans, but the derivative contract may be based on the price of oil delivered in New York. As a result of the differences in the factors affecting the value of its oil costs (and thus profits) and the factors affecting the value of a derivative contract, NeedOil is unlikely to find a perfect hedge for its oil costs.

24.2   Option Pricing

In the NeedOil example, we simply assumed that the price of the option equaled $100,000. We now examine the factors that affect the price of an option contract. Ultimately, the forces of supply and demand determine option prices. For example, suppose that the price of a par-ticular option equals $100. If the number of option contracts that people want to purchase at a price of $100 exceeds the number of option contracts that people are willing to sell, then the option's price will increase.

Financial economists have developed a method, which is widely used by practitioners, for determining the price where supply and demand for options generally will coincide.[3] The key result of option pricing theory is that, for traders who can trade both the option contract and the underlying asset at relatively low costs, there is a critical price (called the no-arbitrage price) above which traders can profit from selling call options and below which traders can profit from buying call options. Using finance terminology, traders can make arbitrage profits (riskless profits without investing any money) if the price is above or below the no-arbitrage price and there are no transaction costs. As a consequence,

[3]Financial economists Fischer Black, Robert Merton, and Myron Scholes developed the fundamental option pricing models during the early 1970s. Merton and Scholes were awarded the 1997 Nobel Prize in economics in large part for their work on option pricing. Black's death prevented him from receiving the award; Nobel Prizes are not awarded posthumously.

traders always supply option contracts if the price is above the no-arbitrage price (which in turn depresses the price) and traders always demand call option contracts if the price is below the no-arbitrage price (which in turn increases the price). Option prices therefore should always be close to the no-arbitrage price.

Influence of Underlying Asset, Contract, and Market Characteristics

Although option pricing theory is based on mathematical models beyond the scope of this book, some of the most important implications of these models can be explained intuitively. The basic option pricing model implies that the price of a call option at time t depends on five factors:

1. The price of the underlying asset at time t.
2. The volatility (standard deviation) of the return on the underlying asset per unit of time.
3. The exercise price.
4. The option's time to maturity (time to expiration).
5. The interest rate on government bonds.

The first two factors are characteristics of the underlying asset. The third and fourth factors are contract characteristics, and the final factor is a characteristic of the economic environment.

Price of the Underlying Asset

If the price of the underlying asset increases and the other four factors remain constant, then the call option price will increase. The intuition is that an increase in the current price of the underlying asset implies a higher expected value for the price of the underlying asset when the call option contract expires, which increases the expected payoff from buying the call option. Since the expected payoff increases as the price of the underlying asset increases, so does the option's price.

Volatility

Greater *volatility* in the price of the underlying asset increases the price of the call option. At first, this result may seem strange—greater risk increases the price of the option. The reason for this result is that the payoff from an option is asymmetric. Increases in the price of the underlying asset beyond the exercise price continue to increase the payoff from a call option, but decreases in the price of the underlying asset below the exercise price do not cause additional losses. This asymmetry implies that more variability in the price of the underlying asset increases the expected payoff from the option.

A simple example, which is summarized in Table 24.1, illustrates the effect of increased volatility in the underlying asset on the payoffs from a call option with an exercise price of $100. Compare two scenarios for the price of the underlying asset at the option's maturity. In the low volatility scenario, the underlying asset has a 50 percent chance of being $110 and a 50 percent chance of being $90. Consequently, the payoff from the call option is either $10 or $0, yielding an expected payoff of $5. In the high volatility scenario, the underlying asset has a 50 percent chance of being $130 and a 50 percent chance of being $70. Note that the expected value of the underlying asset is $100 in both scenarios, but that the variance of the underlying asset's price is greater in the second scenario. The greater variance causes the expected payoff from the call option in the second scenario to be greater

TABLE 24.1

Illustration of how greater volatility in the underlying asset increases the price of a call option (exercise price = $100; each outcome is equally likely).

	Possible Outcomes for the Value of the Underlying Asset at Expiration	Possible Outcomes for the Payoff from the Call Option
Low volatility	$ 90	$ 0
	110	10
High volatility	$ 70	$ 0
	130	30

than the first scenario. In particular, the call option has a payoff of either $30 or $0, yielding an expected payoff of $15. Thus, even though the expected price of the underlying asset under each scenario is the same, the greater volatility in the return on the underlying asset in the second scenario implies that the expected payoff from the call option is greater. Thus, greater volatility implies higher option prices, holding all other factors constant.

Exercise Price

Compared to a call option contract with an exercise price of $20, an otherwise identical option contract with a lower exercise price will have a higher option price. The intuition is similar to that given above for why the call option price increases as the price of the underlying asset increases. A call option with a lower exercise price has a higher expected payoff to the purchaser of the call option. Consequently, a call option's price will be higher for option contracts with lower exercise prices, holding the other factors constant.

Time to Expiration

Holding the other factors constant, an option's price is higher the longer the time to expiration. An option that expires in one year will have a higher price than an otherwise equivalent option that matures in six months. There are two reasons for this result. To see the first reason, assume that the price of the underlying asset at expiration will exceed the exercise price with certainty so that the call option will have a positive payoff with certainty. Then, as summarized in the first row of Table 24.2, the expected payoff at expiration will equal the expected value of the underlying asset at expiration minus the exercise price. Today's option price will depend on the present value of these cash flows, which equals the present value of the underlying asset minus the present value of the exercise price (see the second row of Table 24.2). We already have discussed how the option price depends on the current value of the underlying asset and the exercise price. However, as the second row of Table 24.2 indicates, the option's price depends not just on the exercise price, but on the present value of the exercise price. Thus, the longer the time until the option expires, the lower will be the present value of the exercise price and thus the greater will be the option's price today given the current value of the underlying asset.

TABLE 24.2 **Payoff at expiration and call option price assuming a positive payoff.**

Call option payoff at expiration	= Value of the underlying asset at expiration	− Exercise price
Call option price today	= Value of the underlying asset today	− Present value of exercise price

TABLE 24.3
Determinants of the price of european call and put options.

Determinants (holding other factors fixed)	Call Option Price	Put Option Price
As the price of the underlying asset increases	Increases	Decreases
As the exercise price increases	Decreases	Increases
As the volatility in the return of the underlying asset increases	Increases	Increases
As the time to maturity increases	Increases	Increases
As interest rates increase	Increases	Decreases

The second reason that the price of a call option increases with the time to expiration follows directly from the discussion of volatility. Holding the volatility per unit of time constant, the greater the time to maturity, the greater the total volatility and, consequently, the greater the price of the option. Intuitively, the longer the maturity, the greater the chance that the price of the underlying asset will increase by a large amount. Of course, there also is a greater chance that the price of the underlying asset will decrease by a large amount. Because of the asymmetric payoff from the call option, however, the greater total volatility arising from the greater time to maturity increases the price of the option, holding the other factors fixed.

Interest Rate

The higher the level of interest rates, the higher is the price of the option, all else being equal. The intuition is similar to that given for the time to maturity. A higher interest rate lowers the present value of the exercise price, and thus the greater is the price of the option, holding the other factors constant.

This discussion has focused on the determinants of call options. These same factors affect the price of a put option. However, since the payoffs from a put option differ from the payoffs from a call option, some of the determinants of the price have the opposite effect for put options. Table 24.3 summarizes how each factor influences call and put option prices.

24.3   Hedging with Forward/Futures Contracts

Illustration

Let's return to our example of NeedOil. Recall that NeedOil's profits from operations are negatively related to the price of oil as indicated by Figure 24.1. Assume that NeedOil has decided to protect itself against increases in the price of oil. In the previous example, it purchased a call option contract to provide this protection, paying an option premium of $100,000. We now consider another way for NeedOil to obtain protection against increases in the price of oil above $15.

Suppose that a company called F-CO will provide protection against increases in oil prices, but that F-CO differs from OPTCO in that it does not make NeedOil pay a fixed premium. NeedOil, instead, only pays F-CO if the price of oil at the expiration of the contract falls below $15, and the more the price falls below $15, the more NeedOil must pay F-CO. Figure 24.6 illustrates the payoffs to NeedOil under its contract with F-CO for alternative oil prices at contract expiration. Just like NeedOil's option contract with OPTCO, if the

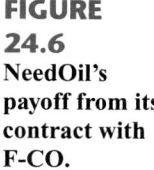

FIGURE 24.6
NeedOil's payoff from its contract with F-CO.

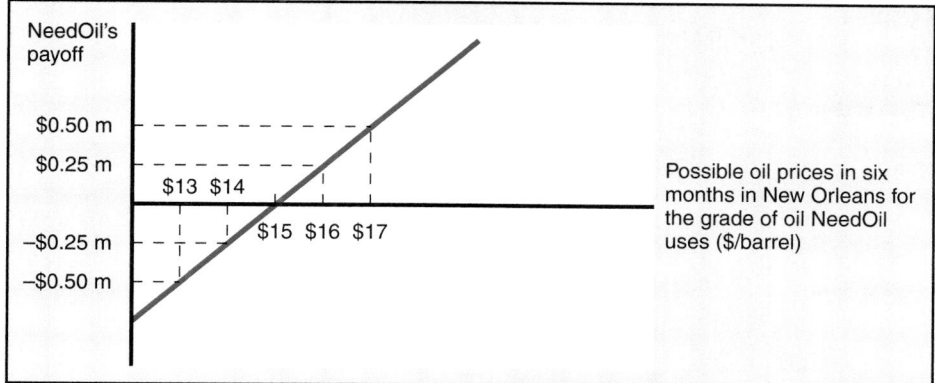

price of oil exceeds $15, then F-CO pays NeedOil some money: If the price of oil equals $16, then F-CO will pay NeedOil $250,000; if the price of oil equals $17, F-CO will pay NeedOil $500,000. However, if the price of oil falls below $15, then NeedOil pays F-CO some money: If the price of oil falls to $14, then NeedOil must pay F-CO $250,000; if the price of oil equals $13, NeedOil must pay F-CO $500,000. Thus, the payoffs on this contact are symmetric around the $15 price.

Since the payoffs from the contract between F-CO and NeedOil are derived from the price of oil, the contract is another example of a derivative contract. There are two types of derivative contracts that have payoff structures like this contract: forward contracts and futures contracts. We will describe the differences between forward and futures contracts later. The important point for now is that a **forward contract** or a **futures contract** gives the buyer (NeedOil) a symmetric payoff that is equal to the difference between the actual price of the underlying asset and some predetermined price called the **forward price** or the **futures price.** In our example, the forward price is $15. Again, the important feature of forward and futures contracts is that the payoff is symmetric: If the price rises above the forward price, the buyer of the contract receives a positive payoff and if the price falls below the forward price, then the buyer receives a negative payoff.

Notice that the payoff to the buyer, NeedOil, from a forward contract is positively related to the price of oil. The payoff to the seller, F-CO, is just the opposite: The greater the price of oil, the more that F-CO has to pay. The lower the price of oil, the more that F-CO receives. Figure 24.7 illustrates the payoff to the seller of a forward contract.

We have described forward (futures) contracts assuming that the contracts are settled in cash. Some of the terminology, however, is derived from forward (futures) contracts based on physical delivery of the underlying asset. For example, by buying (taking a long position) in a forward contract, NeedOil essentially is agreeing to buy oil in six months (the expiration of the contract) at $15 a barrel (the forward price). Conversely, by selling (taking a short position) in a forward contract, F-CO is agreeing to sell oil in six months at $15 a barrel. Thus, the terms *forward* and *futures* are derived from the parties agreeing to transact at a fixed price (the forward or futures price) in the future. If the actual price of oil at contract expiration differs from the forward price, then one party gains and the other party loses. For example, if the actual price of oil in six months exceeds $15, then NeedOil is able to buy and F-CO must sell oil for less than it is worth.

FIGURE 24.7
Payoff to F-CO, the seller of a forward contract.

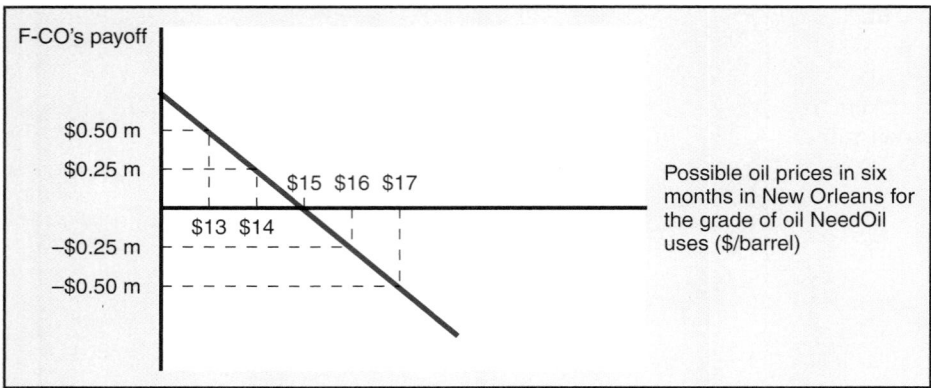

Forward Prices

When a firm buys an option contract, it pays the seller a premium up front. In contrast, when a firm buys a forward contract, no cash exchanges hands. Instead, the payoffs all occur when the contract expires. Demand and supply in forward contracts are not adjusted by changes in an up-front price. Instead, demand and supply are adjusted by changes in the forward price. For example, if the forward price equals $15 and at that price the demand for forward contracts exceeds the supply of forward contracts, then the forward price will increase. Thus, you cannot choose a forward contract with a particular forward price; the forward price is determined by the marketplace.

The theory of forward (futures) prices has similarities to the theory of option pricing. As we discussed with options, if people can trade both the forward (futures) contracts and the underlying asset at relatively low costs, there is a critical price (called the no-arbitrage price). If the forward (futures) price is above the critical price, traders will be willing to sell forward (futures) contracts, thus putting downward pressure on the price. If the price is below the critical price, then traders will be willing to buy forward (futures) contracts, thus putting upward pressure on the price. The no-arbitrage forward (futures) price at time t for a contract that expires at time $t + T$ (T is the amount of time until the futures contract expires) satisfies what is called the **cost of carry relationship:**

$$\text{Forward (futures) price} = \text{Spot price at time } t + \text{Cost of carry}$$

where the cost of carry equals the sum of (1) the interest paid from t to $t + T$ on a loan that could finance the purchase of the underlying asset, (2) the cost of storing the underlying asset from t to $t + T$, and (3) the cost of insuring the underlying asset from t to $t + T$. Intuitively, the price paid in the future for the underlying asset (the forward or futures price) must be equal to the price paid today plus the cost of carrying the asset to the future.

As an example, suppose that the current spot price of oil is $16 a barrel, the interest rate equals 9 percent, and the cost of storing and insuring oil for one year is 1 percent of the value of the oil. Then the forward (futures) price on a contract that expires in one year would be expected to equal $16 + $16 × (0.09 + 0.01) per barrel, or $17.60.

Suppose that instead of being $17.60, the one-year forward price was equal to $18 a barrel. Then, a trader could sell (take a short position in) the forward contract at the $18 price, which is equivalent to agreeing to sell oil in one year at $18. Simultaneously, the trader could buy oil today and store and insure the oil for one year for a total cost of $17.60 a barrel. At the end of the year, the trader could use the oil it has stored to deliver on its promise to sell oil for $18. The trader would make $0.40 a barrel. If 1 million barrels were purchased initially and if the forward contract was for 1 million barrels, then the trader would make $400,000. If traders faced a situation like this, they would continue to sell forward contracts, which would eventually depress the forward price until it reached the $17.60 a barrel price implied by the cost of carry relationship.

24.4   Other Derivative Contracts

Constructing Other Derivatives

We have introduced call options, put options, and forward contracts. Futures contracts are essentially the same as forward contracts at this introductory level of analysis. Call and put options give asymmetric payoffs and forward and futures contracts give symmetric payoffs. While there are many other types of derivative contracts, they generally can be constructed from the basic contracts we have already described. For this reason, many practitioners and academics find it useful to view options and forwards as building blocks that can be used to construct other derivative contracts. The building block approach starts with the basic payoffs summarized in Figure 24.8.[4]

To illustrate the usefulness of the building block approach, suppose that NeedOil decides that it wants protection from high oil prices, but that it does not believe oil prices will rise above $18 a barrel. If NeedOil hedged by buying a call option with an exercise price of $15 (as was described earlier), it would be buying protection against any increase in oil prices

FIGURE 24.8
Derivative building blocks.

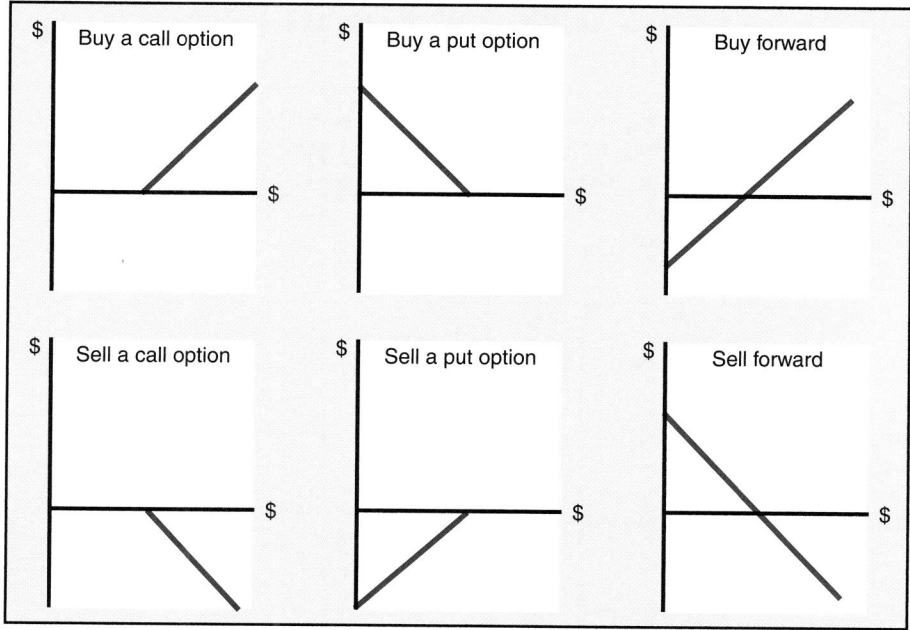

[4]Notice that even the blocks in the figure are redundant in that a forward contract can be constructed with options. In particular, the same payoff can be obtained by buying a forward contract or by buying a call option and simultaneously selling a put option.

above $15, including protection against oil prices above $18. Since it does not believe oil prices will rise above $18, it is buying protection that it deems as having little or no value. NeedOil therefore would like to have a derivative contract with a payoff that increases with prices between $15 and $18, but that does not increase when oil prices are above $18. The solid line in Figure 24.9 illustrates the payoff NeedOil wants (ignoring the cost of obtaining protection).

NeedOil can obtain its desired payoff by buying a call option with an exercise price of $15 and selling a call option with an exercise price of $18. To see this, you simply need to graph the payoff on each option separately and then vertically add the payoffs. Figure 24.9 illustrates the payoffs from the two options with dashed lines.

Swap Contracts

The final type of derivative contract that we will highlight is called a swap contract. **Swap contracts** have payoffs like a series of forward contracts. That is, instead of having just one payoff at the contract's expiration (or when the option is exercised), a swap contract has a series of payoffs over time. Each payoff depends on the difference between the market price of the underlying asset and a predetermined price, called the swap price.

To illustrate a swap contract, we will again use the example of NeedOil. In this example, NeedOil plans to purchase oil every six months for the next two years and it wants protection against high oil prices at each date. It therefore purchases a swap contract from SWAPCO with the payoffs described in Table 24.4. Notice that at each date, the payoff to NeedOil is just like the payoff from buying a forward contract. Thus, swap contracts can be viewed as a series of forward contracts.

The term *swap* is used because these transactions allow parties to reduce risk by swapping payments. Without hedging, NeedOil's payments for oil every six months would be uncertain; the payment would equal 250,000 times the price of oil at that time (P_t). By transacting with SWAPCO, NeedOil swaps its uncertain payment for oil for a certain oil payment. Specifically, SWAPCO gives NeedOil the funds needed to make its uncertain oil payment (250,000 times P_t) and NeedOil gives SWAPCO $15 times 250,000. By swapping its uncertain payments for certain payments, NeedOil reduces its risk.

In this example, the difference between the price of oil at a given date and $15 is always multiplied by 250,000. This is a common feature of swap contracts (and many other deriv-

FIGURE 24.9
NeedOil's desired payoff from a derivative contract given its belief that oil prices will not rise above $18.

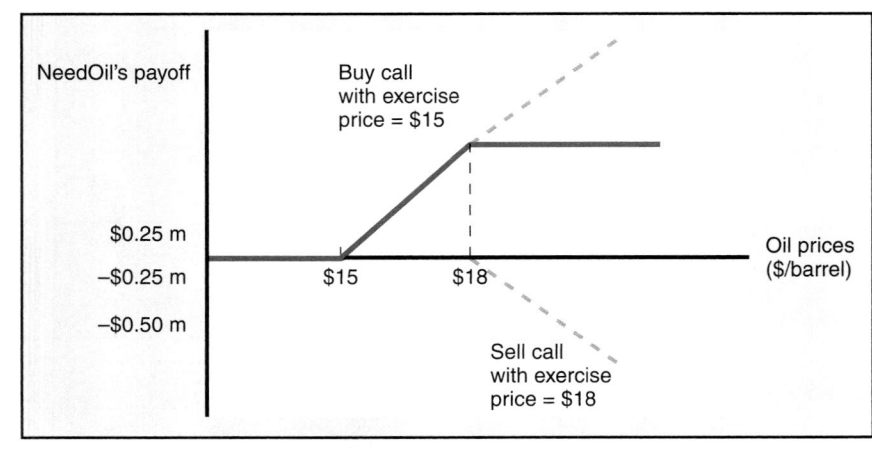

TABLE 24.4 Description of an oil swap contract between NeedOil and SWAPCO (P_t = Price of oil at time t).

	6 Months	12 Months	18 Months	24 Months
Payoff to NeedOil	$(P_{6\ months} - \$15) \times$ 250,000	$(P_{1\ year} - \$15) \times$ 250,000	$(P_{18\ months} - \$15) \times$ 250,000	$(P_{2\ years} - \$15) \times$ 250,000
Payoff to SWAPCO	$(\$15 - P_{6\ months}) \times$ 250,000	$(\$15 - P_{1\ year}) \times$ 250,000	$(\$15 - P_{18\ months}) \times$ 250,000	$(\$15 - P_{2\ years}) \times$ 250,000

TABLE 24.5 Description of an interest rate swap contract between NeedOil and SWAPCO (r_t = One-year T-bill rate at time t).

	6 Months	12 Months	18 Months	24 Months
Payoff to NeedOil	$(r_{6\ months} - 5\%) \times$ \$1 million	$(r_{1\ year} - 5\%) \times$ \$1 million	$(r_{18\ months} - 5\%) \times$ \$1 million	$(r_{2\ years} - 5\%) \times$ \$1 million
Payoff to SWAPCO	$(5\% - r_{6\ months}) \times$ \$1 million	$(5\% - r_{1\ year}) \times$ \$1 million	$(5\% - r_{18\ months}) \times$ \$1 million	$(5\% - r_{2\ years}) \times$ \$1 million

ative contracts)—the difference between two prices is multiplied by some number, called the *notional principal* (in this case 250,000), to determine the dollar payoff.

While notional principal often is used to measure the value of outstanding swap contracts, notional principal usually is a flawed measure of how much money the parties could potentially gain or lose because potential swap payments depend on the units used for quoting prices and the volatility of prices, as well as the notional principal. For example, if oil prices could vary between $13 and $17 during the time period covered by NeedOil's swap contract, then the payments made by NeedOil could vary between −$500,000 and $500,000. In this particular case, the notional principal understates the potential gain or loss in any given six-month period.

For other types of swaps, like interest rate swaps, the notional principal greatly overstates the amount of money at risk. Table 24.5 gives an example of an interest rate swap. Here, the notional principal is $1 million and SWAPCO pays NeedOil the prevailing one-year T-bill rate minus 5 percent. For example, if the one-year T-bill rate in 12 months equals 6 percent, then SWAPCO pays NeedOil 1 percent times $1 million, or $10,000. If the one-year T-bill rate in two years equals 4.5 percent, then NeedOil pays SWAPCO 0.5 percent times $1 million, or $5,000. Even though the notional principal is $1 million, the likely payments are only a fraction of the notional principal. Thus, for interest rate swaps, the notional principal greatly overstates the amount of money at risk.

24.5 Comparison of Derivative and Insurance Contracts

We hope that you noticed that the payoff diagrams illustrated in the previous section have similarities to the diagrams in Chapter 23 describing features of insurance contracts.[5] Indeed, an insurance contract can be viewed as a derivative contract where the underlying asset is the

[5] As noted earlier, the exposure diagrams in this chapter have profits on the vertical axis, but the exposure diagrams describing insurance contracts in Chapter 23 have costs on the vertical axis.

value of losses experienced by the insured. While there are similarities between derivatives and insurance contracts, there are also important differences. In particular, the types of risk that tend to be hedged using derivative contracts have different characteristics from the risks that tend to be hedged using insurance contracts. As a consequence, insurance and derivative contracts generally differ with regard to transaction costs, basis risk, and liquidity.

Market Prices versus Specific Losses

Derivative contracts usually are used to hedge risk arising from unexpected changes in market prices; on the other hand, insurance contracts tend to hedge risk arising from losses specific to the insured. Contracts based on market prices are likely to be useful to many firms. For example, an option on oil prices or a forward contract on oil prices could be of interest to hundreds of companies that use or produce oil. In contrast, a contract derived from the liability or property losses of NeedOil often will be of interest to only one firm—NeedOil.

Basis Risk and Extent of Risk Reduction

An advantage of contracts based on firm-specific factors as opposed to market prices is less basis risk. Recall that basis risk can be viewed as uncertainty about the effectiveness of a hedge. When an insurance contract is based on a firm's liability losses, there is little uncertainty about the quality of the hedge—that is, if the firm experiences $10 million in insured losses, then it will be reimbursed for $10 million from the insurer (ignoring insurer insolvency). In contrast, with a derivative contract, a firm may experience a drop in profits of $3 million due to higher oil prices and the derivative contract used to hedge this risk may have a payoff of only $2 million because of basis risk. In short, since derivative contracts are not based on firm-specific outcomes, there is greater basis risk than with insurance contracts.[6]

Contracting Costs

The contracting costs for insurance tend to be higher than those for derivatives. This difference arises in part because of greater moral hazard and adverse selection problems with insurance and because of greater capital costs.

Moral Hazard and Adverse Selection

When the underlying asset is a market price or an aggregate index (as is true with most derivative contracts), individual firms generally cannot influence the payoffs on the derivative contracts. For most insurance contracts, however, the value of the underlying asset is the loss experienced by the insured firm, which often is influenced indirectly, if not directly, by the actions of the insured party. Consequently, moral hazard problems tend to be more severe with insurance contracts. In addition, firms often have private information about expected losses, which creates adverse selection problems from the insurer's perspective. The moral hazard and adverse selection problems associated with contracts based on individual firm losses imply that considerable investigation and monitoring costs must be incurred

---

[6]Note, however, that more complete coverage and thus lower risk with insurance increase moral hazard. For this reason and others (administrative costs and adverse selection) insurance contracts almost always provide less-than-complete coverage (see Chapter 10), reducing the effectiveness of risk reduction.

when selling such contracts. In contrast, when contracts are based on market prices, which are outside of the influence of individual firms, fewer investigative and monitoring costs need to be incurred.

Capital Costs

When market prices change, there tend to be winners and losers: Some firms increase in value and other firms decrease in value. Stated differently, situations often arise where firm values are negatively correlated. In this case, two firms can construct a derivative contract that will neutralize the effect of a price change on each firm's value. For example, an oil user can hedge by buying an oil forward contract and an oil producer can hedge by selling the same oil forward contract. Derivative markets therefore can bring the oil user and the oil producer together and create a contract that reduces price risk for both, without the two parties having to physically trade oil.

In contrast, the property and liability losses experienced by one firm typically do not trigger a simultaneous gain by another firm. That is, these types of losses tend to be independent (or even positively correlated) across firms. Consequently, substantial reduction in property and liability risks is achieved through diversification (i.e., by selling policies to many different policyholders). The marketing and underwriting costs associated with achieving diversification tend to be higher than the costs of matching two parties with negatively correlated exposures.

Moreover, because insurers hold capital to ensure that they will be able to perform their contractual promises (pay claims) to policyholders, the cost of holding this capital is an additional cost of insurance contracts. In contrast, once two parties with negatively correlated exposures have been identified, a comparatively small amount of capital is needed to ensure contractual performance on a derivative contract that hedges the risk of both parties. The reason is that the derivative contract will require a payment only when the firm's cash flows otherwise would be high. For example, an oil user who has purchased an oil forward contract will have to pay the seller of the forward contract (the oil producer) when oil prices are low, which is when the oil user has relatively high cash flows from operations. Conversely, the oil producer will have to pay the oil user when oil prices are high, which is when the oil producer has relatively high cash flows. Provided derivative contracts are used to hedge, the contractual parties should need comparatively little capital to bond their performance under the derivative contract. Insurers, on the other hand, typically hold considerable capital to bond their performance to policyholders.

Liquidity

Because of the greater number of parties who are potentially affected by market prices and because of lower transaction costs, derivative contracts tend to have greater liquidity than insurance contracts. In a **liquid market,** someone can sell or buy an asset quickly with little price concession. In contrast, in an illiquid market, someone trying to sell an asset may either have to wait to find a buyer who will pay the asking price or accept a much lower price in order to sell the asset quickly. The greater liquidity of derivative contracts implies that a firm can quickly establish a hedge using derivatives and also quickly remove a hedge at relatively lower cost. In contrast, modifying insurance contracts to provide more or less coverage can take a considerable amount of time and expense.

TABLE 24.6

Differences between insurance and derivative contracts.

Characteristics	Derivative Contracts	Insurance Contracts
Type of risk hedged	Market-price risk	Firm-specific risk
Number of firms potentially interested in a specific contract	Many	One (or few)
Basis risk	High	Low
Contracting costs (due to moral hazard, adverse selection, and bonding contractual performance)	Low	High
Liquidity (due to greater number of firms potentially interested in a particular contract and contracting costs)	High	Low

Summary

Table 24.6 summarizes the generalizations made in this section concerning the differences between derivative and insurance contracts. Of course, there are exceptions to each of the generalizations listed in the table. Also, in recent years, there have been attempts to introduce derivative contracts on risks that traditionally have been handled through insurance and reinsurance contracts.

24.6   Markets for Derivatives

Over-the-counter versus Exchange-traded Derivatives

Earlier we mentioned that the payoffs from forward and futures contracts are similar. One difference in the two contracts is that forward contracts are traded in the over-the-counter (OTC) market and futures contracts are traded at exchanges like the Chicago Board of Trade. Call and put option contracts trade on exchanges as well as in the over-the-counter market. Swap contracts are traded over-the-counter.

An **over-the-counter (OTC) derivative** contract resembles a privately negotiated contract between two firms. For example, if NeedOil wanted to purchase an option contract to hedge its oil price risk, NeedOil could contact a financial institution in the OTC market, which could then tailor a contract to NeedOil's hedging needs. **Exchange-traded derivatives** are standardized contracts with the terms established by the exchanges. Since specific details are not subject to negotiation, contracting costs tend to be lower with exchange-traded derivatives than with OTC derivatives. While exchanges try to create standardized contracts that appeal to many participants, the standardization often implies that exchange-traded derivatives have greater basis risk than OTC derivatives.[7] As Box 24.2 illustrates, OTC derivatives and exchange-traded derivatives actively compete with each other. This competition has led exchanges to introduce more flexible derivative terms.

Initially, financial institutions operating in the OTC market acted as *brokers* who would identify another firm that would transact with a party such as NeedOil. Today, fi-

---

[7]The ability to tailor contracts to individual hedging needs makes OTC derivatives similar to insurance and reinsurance contracts.

Options exchanges are battling for a bigger share of the market.

Their competitor: the privately negotiated, or over-the-counter derivative market.

Last month, the Chicago Board Options Exchange and the American Stock Exchange began offering custom-tailored options on a number of widely held and heavily traded stocks. Yesterday, the Philadelphia Stock Exchange announced it is awaiting Securities and Exchange Commission approval for a similar move. These "flex" options are like other options in that they give the investor, in return for a small premium payment, the right to buy or sell the underlying stock at a specified price at or before a certain date in the future.

But unlike other, standardized, exchange-traded stock options, the new flex products give the holders the freedom to pick a specific expiration date as well as offering them some leeway in setting the strike price. Until now, the pension funds and mutual funds that are the natural customers for these products would have had to turn to dealers to structure customized, over-the-counter derivatives to obtain a similar degree of flexibility.

"They're declaring war on the structured derivatives market," says Michael Schwartz, chief options strategist at Oppenheimer & Co. in New York. "There's a big effort under way to bring back to the exchange floor the kind of products that are now being done by the over-the-counter equity derivatives dealers."

Source: Suzanne McGee, "Exchanges Try to Win More of Options Pie," *The Wall Street Journal,* November 20, 1996.

nancial institutions operate more like *dealers,* taking positions directly with each firm. Thus, NeedOil could buy the option directly from the financial institution. Having sold a call option, the dealer would be exposed to oil price risk and thus the dealer probably would try to hedge this risk either by engaging in an offsetting transaction with someone else in the OTC market or by using exchange-traded options and futures contracts.

In addition to the ability to tailor contracts, there are other differences between the OTC and exchange markets. One difference is liquidity, the ability to buy or sell without making a large price concession. When the OTC market creates a contract that is tailored to one participant's needs, this contract tends to be illiquid. In contrast, if the contract were a standardized exchange-traded futures contract, there would likely be more liquidity. The greater liquidity arises in part because the standardized exchange contracts attract many traders.

The greater liquidity also is due in part to the method of ensuring that the parties who trade derivatives uphold their agreements. OTC contracts are bilateral contracts. That is, a buyer and seller are specified on the contract and if one party cannot fulfill its part of the contract, the other party becomes a creditor. As a result, when trading OTC contracts, firms assess the default risk (or credit risk) of the parties with whom they transact. In addition, if a firm wishes to reverse its position, the firm must negotiate with the specific counterparty to the contract. These features make OTC contracts less liquid.

Default risk is handled differently with exchange-traded contracts. When taking a futures position, a trader must post a performance bond, called a **margin.** The bond equals some percentage of the value of the contracts and must be posted either in the form of cash, letters of credit, or government bonds. The purpose of the bond is to ensure the solvency of the trader over the coming day of trading. Thus, at the end of each day, the margin account is monitored to see if there are sufficient funds to ensure solvency over the subsequent day.

As an example, suppose that the required margin is always 20 percent of the value of the contract and that Ms. Weiss takes a long position in (buys) one contract when the futures price equals $1,000. Then, Ms. Weiss must post margin equal to $200. Now suppose that over the course of the following day, the futures price falls to $900. Ms. Weiss has lost $100 ($1,000 − $900), which is subtracted from her margin account, leaving only $100. Since Ms. Weiss's position now is worth $900, she needs to have margin equal to $180 (20% of $900). Consequently, Ms. Weiss must add $80 to the margin account. If she does not add this amount, then her position will be closed; that is, she will have to take an offsetting short position in (sell) one contract.

The other important difference between OTC markets and exchange markets is that exchanges have a clearinghouse that acts as an intermediary in every transaction. As stated above, with an OTC contract, the buyer knows the identity of the seller. With exchange-traded contracts, a buyer is not matched with a particular seller. Instead, each transaction is with the clearinghouse. The number of contracts purchased by the clearinghouse must always equal the number that it has sold, but buyers and sellers are not explicitly matched. Thus, if a trader wants to reverse a position (sell the derivative the trader had previously purchased or buy the derivative contract the trader had previously sold), a specific counterparty does not have to be notified. Any counterparty willing to take the other side of the transaction may be used. The clearinghouse, along with the daily settlement and margin system for ensuring performance, helps create a liquid market.

Common Risks That Are Hedged with Derivatives

Although OTC contracts can be tailored to meet the specific hedging needs of individual firms, the types of risk that are most often hedged with derivatives are: (1) foreign exchange rates, (2) interest rates, (3) commodity prices, and (4) equity prices.

Foreign Exchange Derivatives

With the increasing amount of trade among foreign countries and the increased volatility in exchange rates due to the breakdown in 1973 of the previous system of fixed foreign exchange rates, firms have become more interested in hedging against changes in foreign exchange rates. Most multinational companies utilize derivatives to manage their foreign exchange exposures. The most commonly used currency derivatives are swap and forward contracts, which had notional principal of over $1.46 trillion in 2002.

Interest Rate Derivatives

Several factors have contributed to the use of interest rate derivatives to hedge against changes in value due to interest rate changes. One factor is the high level and volatility of interest rates in the 1970s and 1980s, which resulted from high levels of expected inflation as well as changes in expected inflation. Also, in 1979 the Federal Reserve changed its policy of trying to stabilize interest rates directly and instead started targeting monetary aggregates. The consequence of this change in policy was to increase interest rate volatility substantially. Interest rate futures, options, and swaps are frequently used to hedge interest rate risk. The notional principal in 2002 of interest rate derivatives was close to $90 trillion.

Commodity Derivatives

Derivative contracts on agricultural commodities have existed for a long time. For example, the Chicago Board of Trade has traded futures contracts since 1865, and forwards and options on agricultural products date back several centuries. Users and producers of commodities such as metals and oil also frequently trade both OTC and exchange-traded derivatives. The use of electricity derivatives also has grown significantly in recent years due in part to deregulation of the industry.

Equity Derivatives

Equity derivatives are contracts derived from stock market indexes like the Standard & Poor's 500. Futures contracts exist that are based on US stock market indexes and on foreign stock market indexes, such as the Nikkei index for the Japanese stock market. In addition, options have traded on individual stocks for some time. The notional principal on futures and options in 2002 equaled about $2.2 trillion.

24.7 Summary

- Derivative contracts are contracts with payoffs derived from the value of some other asset or index, called the underlying asset. The basic types of derivative contracts are: call options, put options, and forward (futures) contracts. Option contracts have asymmetric payoffs and forward (futures) contracts have symmetric payoffs as a function of the underlying asset. Swap contracts are equivalent to a series of forward contracts.

- By purchasing a call option on an underlying asset that is positively correlated with a firm's costs (and thus negatively correlated with profits, such as oil in the NeedOil example), a firm can hedge against losses from higher-than-expected costs. That is, the call option provides cash when the costs otherwise would be high (profits would be low). The purchase of the call option requires the firm to pay an up-front premium to the seller of the call option (similar to an insurance premium). Alternatively, a firm can "purchase" a forward (futures) contract on the underlying asset, in which case no up-front premium is required. Instead, the firm agrees to pay the seller of the forward contract if the underlying asset's price is below the forward (futures) price.

- By purchasing a put option on an underlying asset that is positively correlated with a firm's revenue (and thus positively correlated with profits), a firm can hedge against losses from lower-than-expected revenue. That is, the put option provides cash when the firm's revenue and profits otherwise would be low. Alternatively, a firm can "sell" a forward (futures) contract on the underlying as-

set, in which case the firm agrees to pay the buyer of the forward contract if the underlying asset's price is higher than the forward (futures) price.

- The determinants of call and put option prices are (1) the current price of the underlying asset, (2) the exercise price of the option, (3) the time to expiration, (4) the volatility of the rate of return of the underlying asset, and (5) the risk-free rate of interest.

- The determinants of forward (futures) prices include: (1) the current price of the underlying asset, (2) the time to expiration, (3) the risk-free rate of interest, and (4) the cost of storing and insuring the underlying asset.

- Basis risk refers to the uncertainty associated with whether a particular derivative contract will be an effective hedge. In practice, most derivative contracts expose hedgers to some basis risk (i.e., the hedge does not work perfectly).

- The payoffs of derivative contracts are based on (derived from) the market prices of assets and indexes. Consequently, derivative contracts tend to be more liquid and subject to less moral hazard and adverse selection problems compared to insurance contracts. Capital costs associated with ensuring contractual performance tend to be lower with derivative contracts because the contracting parties' cash flows often are negatively correlated.

- The types of risk most commonly hedged with derivatives are (1) foreign exchange risk, (2) interest rate risk, (3) commodity price risk, and (4) equity value risk.

Key Terms

derivative contract 530
underlying asset 530
call option contract 530
exercise price 530
option price 530
put option contract 531
cash settled derivative
　contracts 532

physical delivery 532
basis risk 532
forward contract 537
futures contract 537
forward price 537
futures price 537
cost of carry relationship 538

swap contracts 540
liquid market 543
over-the-counter (OTC)
　derivative 544
exchange-traded
　derivatives 544
margin 545

Questions and Problems

1. Draw an exposure diagram to illustrate a firm's exposure to interest rate risk if the firm is going to borrow $10 million six months from today. Assume the loan will be a one-year loan with all interest paid at the end of the year. Graph the relation between the firm's interest costs and interest rates. Also graph the relation between the firm's profit and interest rates assuming that higher interest costs cannot be passed on to consumers.

2. Draw an exposure diagram to illustrate the relationship between a firm's costs and the exchange rate between US dollars and British pounds if the firm plans to purchase goods from a British firm one year from to-day. Assume that the transaction is denominated in pounds, but that the firm is concerned about its costs in dollars. Also draw an exposure diagram to illustrate the relationship between a firm's profit and the exchange rate between US dollars and British pounds.

3. Draw an exposure diagram to illustrate the relationship between a gold mining firm's profit and the price of gold in three months.

4. Would a call option or a put option hedge the exposure of the firms described in problems 1, 2, and 3?

5. Would a long (buy) or a short (sell) forward position hedge the exposure of the firms described in problems 1, 2, and 3?

6. What is the difference between a forward contract and a swap contract?

7. Fill in the table below describing the payoffs on an interest rate swap contract under each of the scenarios for interest rates. Assume that under the terms of the swap, Strickler Inc. agrees to pay the swap dealer the six-month T-bill rate minus 4 percent at the end of each of the next three six-month periods and that the notional principal equals $2 million.

	6 Months	12 Months	18 Months
Six-month T-bill rate	3%	4%	4.5%
Payoff to Strickler			
Payoff to swap dealer			

8. What combination of derivatives would yield the following payoff (ignore the premiums paid for the options)?

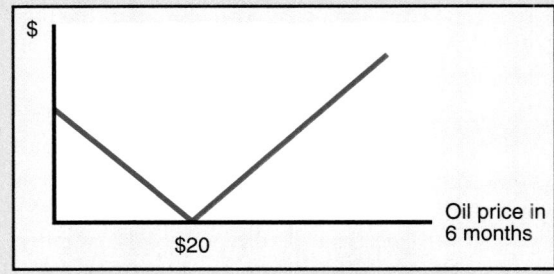

9. What combination of derivatives would yield the following payoff (ignore the premiums paid for the options)?

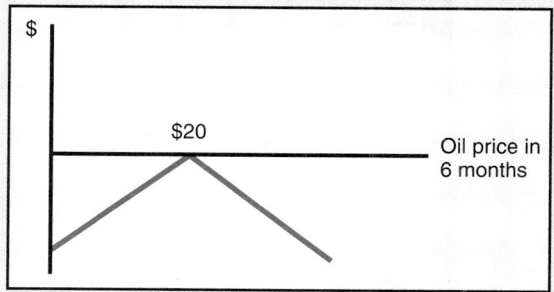

10. What combination of derivatives would yield the following payoff (ignore the premiums paid for the options)?

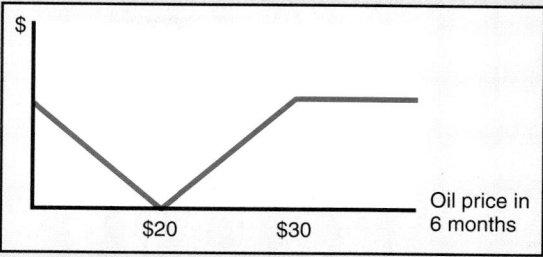

Answers to Concept Checks

1.

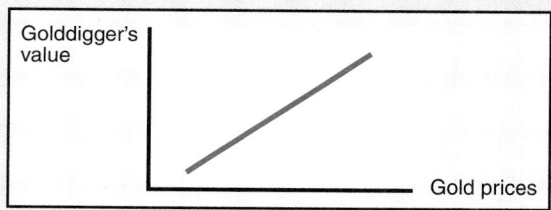

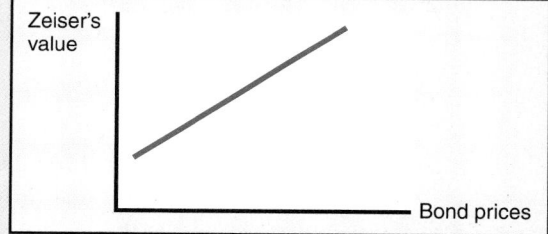

2.

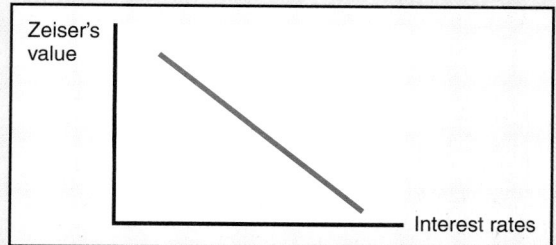

3. Golddigger would purchase a put option with the underlying asset being gold.

4. Zeiser would purchase a call option with the underlying asset being interest rates. Alternatively, because bond prices and interest rates are inversely related, Zeiser could purchase a put option with the underlying asset being bonds (e.g., US Treasury bonds).

References

Smith, Clifford W., Jr.; and Charles Smithson. *Managing Financial Price Risk: A Guide to Derivative Products, Financial Engineering, and Value Maximization.* Burr Ridge, IL: Irwin Professional Publishing, 1995. (*Describes and analyzes how derivatives are used for hedging and also provides details on pricing models for options, forwards, futures, and swap contracts.*)

Stoll, Hans; and Robert Whaley. *Futures and Options: Theory and Applications.* Cincinnati, OH: South-Western College Publishing, 1993. (*Describes and analyzes how derivatives are used for hedging and also provides details on derivative pricing models.*)

Chapter 25

Alternative Risk Transfer

Chapter Objectives

- Describe what is meant by alternative risk transfer.
- Describe examples of specific types of alternative risk transfer products, such as finite risk plans and captive insurance companies.
- Explain why alternative risk transfer products are used.

25.1   Description of Alternative Risk Transfer (ART)

A generally accepted definition of alternative risk transfer does not exist. One approach is to call any alternative to a traditional insurance contract alternative risk transfer. Of course, that approach leads to the problem of defining a traditional insurance contract. Ignoring the cosmic question of how to define alternative risk transfer, we provide a list of the characteristics that **alternative risk transfer** transactions typically have one or more of:

- They involve a high level of retention
- They span multiple years
- They include multiple sources of risk
- They cover sources of risk that are not normally covered by insurance contracts
- They involve capital market institutions and securities

The motivation for using alternative risk transfer arrangements comes from a variety of factors. In most cases, a firm would like to retain a large portion of its potential losses and only transfer the risk of extremely high losses to another party. The underlying reasons for retention include savings in premium loadings, reducing moral hazard, and avoiding being pooled with higher risk policyholders (see Chapter 22). The alternative risk transfer arrangement allows a firm to retain most of its risk while simultaneously obtaining the tax benefits associated with insurance, purchasing services from the insurer, satisfying compulsory insurance regulations, or third-party requirements for insurance, or providing a preferred accounting treatment of losses.

The types of alternative risk transfer arrangements discussed in this chapter include loss sensitive insurance contracts (some with features that often accompany traditional insurance), finite risk contracts, captives, multiline and multitrigger policies, contingent debt and equity, and structured debt instruments. Swiss Re Group estimates that worldwide premium volume in 2000 for the alternative risk transfer market was about $83 billion, compared to $370 billion in traditional commercial insurance premiums. They estimate that about 60 percent of the alternative risk transfer premium volume is from the largest 2,500 companies in the world, whereas, these companies account for only about 13 percent of traditional insurance premiums (Swiss Re New Markets 2003). Thus, large companies are the primary users of alternative risk transfer.

25.2   Loss Sensitive Contracts

With **loss sensitive insurance contracts,** the premiums ultimately paid by the insured depend on the losses that occur (or are paid) *during the policy period.* Consequently, loss sensitive contracts typically shift less risk to the insurer compared with traditional fixed premium insurance contracts. Stated differently, loss sensitive contracts typically involve greater retention than traditional, fixed-premium policies.

The ultimate amount paid by the policyholder under a loss sensitive contract is determined only after some time period has elapsed. To the extent that the insurer initially pays (or is legally bound to pay) losses for the coverage period that eventually will be reimbursed by the policyholder, the insurer essentially provides a loan to the policyholder. Consequently, loss sensitive plans often require the policyholder to provide a letter of credit from a major bank to guarantee that the policyholder will fulfill its obligation to make the agreed upon future payments.

Experience-rated Policies

As discussed in Chapter 8, experience-rated policies base the premium for the coming period on the individual insured's past loss experience. In contrast to the contracts described later in this section, experience-rated policies typically are not designed for the purpose of having the policyholder pay a large portion of unexpected losses during the coverage period. Instead, experience rating usually is used because (1) it reduces moral hazard, and (2) it formalizes how insurers will update their predictions of expected future losses based on the insured firm's past losses. Nevertheless, to the extent that past losses are given considerable weight in the determination of future premiums, experience-rated policies can be viewed as loss sensitive contracts.

Large Deductible Policies and Retrospectively Rated Policies

Policies with deductibles often are structured so that the insurer pays all losses and then is reimbursed by the policyholder for the losses up to the deductible amount. When the deductible

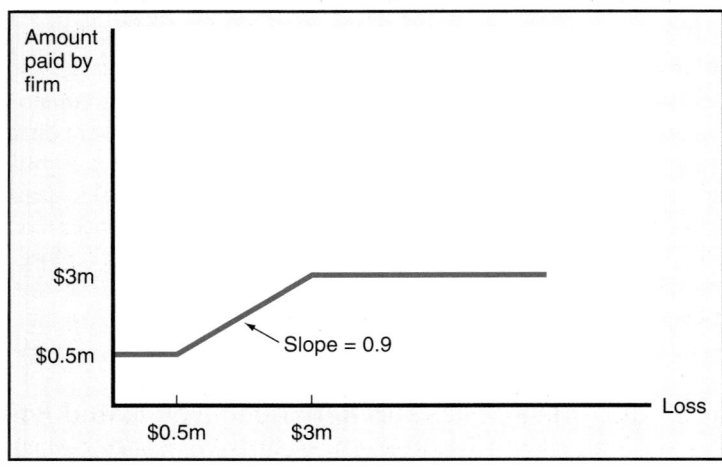

amount is set at such a high level that the policyholder expects to reimburse the insurer for substantial losses (e.g., $100,000 per injury in workers' compensation insurance), policies often are called **large deductible policies.** With these policies, the policyholder essentially retains a large amount of the risk, but the insurer temporarily finances the losses.

A related type of loss sensitive contract is called a **retrospectively rated policy,** or a retro. With these plans, an up-front premium usually is paid. However, the size of the total premium ultimately paid by the policyholder, known as the retro premium, depends on the magnitude of losses during the policy period. The policyholder must make an additional payment if the retro premium is greater than the up-front premium; the policyholder can receive a refund if the retro premium is lower than the up-front premium. Like large deductible policies, the insurer settles all the claims.

The retro premium is subject to both a minimum and a maximum amount, both of which are defined when the policy is initiated. For example, the following formula could be used: The retro premium (to be paid at a specified time after the policy period ends) will equal 90 percent of losses (including a loading for the insurer's loss adjustment expenses), with a minimum premium equal to $500,000 and a maximum premium equal to $3 million. As depicted in Figure 25.1, the minimum premium, the maximum premium, and the percentage of losses paid between the maximum and minimum determines the amount of retained losses under a retro policy. The greater the maximum premium and the greater the sensitivity of premiums to losses (90 percent in this example, although 100 percent is common), the more risk retained by the policyholder. One essential aspect of both retros and large deductible policies is that the insured retains a large portion of its risk; only the risk of very high losses is typically shifted to the insurer.

Retrospectively rated policies must specify the timing of retro premium payments. With a *paid loss retro,* the policyholder agrees to make payments that correspond to the insurer's payments for losses. Since losses that occur during the policy period may not be paid for several years, the paid loss retro policy often requires the insured to make periodic payments to the insurer over future years. The other possibility is to base the retrospective premium on incurred losses (the insurer's estimate of losses that eventually will be paid due to

FIGURE 25.1

Exposure diagram for a firm that purchases a retrospectively rated policy (the minimum premium equals $0.5 million and the maximum premium equals $3 million).

events that occur during the year). With an *incurred loss retro* policy, the retro premium payment at the end of the first year (or specified later date) will be based on losses paid as of this date plus the insurer's estimate of future loss payments for losses that occur during the coverage period. Thus, all else equal, the premium will be higher in the first year under an incurred loss retro policy than under a paid loss retro policy. Nevertheless, since insurers receive information over time concerning the value of loss payments for losses that occur during the policy period, incurred loss retros also can require periodic premium payments or reimbursements. For example, if subsequent to the policy period an insurer learns that its initial estimate of unpaid losses was too low, then it will recognize incurred losses, causing the insured to make a premium payment (provided the maximum premium has not been reached).

Why do businesses use large deductible and retro policies, instead of just purchasing an excess policy with a high attachment point? Tax reasons help explain why firms purchase policies based on incurred losses. As discussed in the previous chapter, when calculating its taxable income, a noninsurance business can deduct retained losses only when the losses are paid. Since insurance premiums are deductible, however, an incurred loss retro policy or a large deductible policy based on incurred losses may allow the business to deduct the value of losses incurred and thereby move its tax deductions for losses earlier.[1] Another reason for using a retro policy is that it might be an efficient way for the business to contract with the insurer to process claims, but at the same time, the business is able to retain risk. Finally, firms often purchase large deductible and retro policies to satisfy compulsory insurance requirements for workers' compensation and automobile liability insurance. In this way, the firm retains most of the risk of losses but satisfies regulatory requirements. The insurer serves the function of certifying that the business can pay its retained losses.

Related Loss Sensitive Plans

With large deductible and retro policies, the insured pays the insurer after the losses have occurred or have been paid. Consequently, the insured retains, at least temporarily, the use of the funds that eventually will be used to pay losses. As a result, these and other plans with this characteristic sometimes are called cash flow plans, because the buyer has greater initial cash flow than if insurance is purchased. While this can be advantageous if the funds are needed for other projects, it can have several disadvantages. If the business invests the funds that eventually will be needed to pay the insurer, then the business will have to pay a tax on the investment earnings of these funds. In addition, the insurer typically will require that the policyholder provide a letter of credit, which is costly to arrange and requires the policyholder to pay a fee to the bank.

Several approaches have been used to reduce the need for letters of credit but which continue to require the insured to pay most of the losses that occur. These plans require that the policyholder make up-front payments to the insurer (i.e., the policyholder essentially prefunds losses). However, the plans allow the insured to receive explicit investment income on the funds before losses are paid. If structured appropriately, these plans will be treated

---

[1]At one time paid loss retros were used to reduce taxes by having the insured pay a large advance premium, which would be tax deductible when paid, with the expectation of receiving a refund at the end of the retro period. Congress eliminated this potential advantage in 1986.

as insurance for tax purposes, which will allow the insured firm to deduct premium payments (prefunding payments) and allow the insurer to deduct incurred losses. Assuming the tax benefits are passed on to the insured firm via lower premium payments, these tax features essentially allow the insured firm to avoid tax on the investment income generated on funds used to pay losses that have been incurred but not yet paid.

With an **investment credit program,** the insured pays the insurer an amount to cover loss payments up to the desired deductible amount and the insurer, after subtracting some of the money for expenses, places the funds in a trust account. This account is used to pay losses and accrues interest at an agreed upon rate. Any funds that remain in the account after a certain length of time (depending on the length of the claims tail) are returned to the policyholder. If the account does not have sufficient resources to pay all the claims, then the insured will have to make additional premium payments. Provided maximum premium payments are set so that the insurer bears significant risk, these plans will qualify as insurance, thus providing tax benefits.

As discussed in Chapter 21, an insightful way of viewing the tax benefit arising from the different tax treatment of insurers and noninsurance companies is that the insurer is able to avoid paying tax on investment income that is generated from funds that are set aside to pay losses than have been incurred but not yet paid.[2] This way of viewing the tax benefit helps to explain why policyholders will sometimes combine an investment credit type plan with a **premium financing arrangement,** whereby it borrows the funds that are deposited with the insurer. In this way, the policyholder is able to deduct interest payments on the loan but avoid tax on the investment income that is generated to fund incurred losses that have not yet been paid. This arrangement can be viewed as a tax-arbitrage scheme—the policyholder's after-tax cost of paying off interest on the loan is less than the after-tax interest received on part of the borrowed funds, thus generating a certain profit.

Loss Portfolio Transfers

Insurance sometimes is purchased to cover losses that have already been incurred, but for which the timing and/or ultimate size of loss payments is uncertain. Thus, the premium depends on the present value of expected payments for the incurred losses. Suppose, for example, that as a result of a manufacturing defect a firm expects that it will incur product liability claims of $200 million over the next five years. The exact dollar amount of losses is subject to some uncertainty, as is the timing of the payments. The firm can transfer the entire loss to an insurer, called a **loss portfolio transfer,** by paying the present value of expected (predicted) claim payments in one lump sum (or possibly in installments). In this situation, the insurer accepts some underwriting risk (the risk associated with the variability in the dollar amount of payments) and timing risk (the risk due to the uncertainty of when payments will be paid). Provided that the insurer accepts considerable risk, the payment made by the insured firm is deductible and the insurer can deduct the present value of incurred losses, thus providing a tax benefit. In addition, for financial accounting reporting purposes, the insured firm can report the entire amounts paid to the insurer (the present value of expected losses) as an expense in the year they are paid. This can help smooth reported earnings.

[2]Note that insurers are taxed on investment income on capital, however.

25.3   Finite Risk Contracts

Insurers (and reinsurers) also offer multiple year loss sensitive plans that commonly are called **finite risk insurance** or **financial insurance.** The term *finite risk* is used to indicate that there is relatively little risk transferred to the insurer. In other words, the insured firm usually pays most of the losses. The contract period for finite risk contracts often is three to five years. The insured firm pays premiums each year to the insurer who places the premiums in a fund (after taking out a fee). The fund accumulates interest at an agreed upon rate of return, and losses are paid from the fund. If the fund is insufficient to pay all the losses in a given year, then the insurer will pay losses up to a stated limit. However, the policyholder's future premium payments are used to reimburse the insurer. Any surplus remaining in the fund at the end of the policy period is returned to the insured firm. Together, these features imply that the policyholder pays most losses, but that the payments are smoothed over time. Thus, finite risk plans provide protection against the timing of loss payments but offer limited protection against unexpected loss payments over the course of the policy period.

An example will help illustrate the essential aspects of finite risk contracts. Suppose that a three-year contract is signed that (1) requires the insured firm to pay premiums of $4 million a year, (2) credits interest at 6.0 percent annually on the year's beginning balance, (3) provides the insurer with a fee equal to 10 percent of each premium, and (4) has an aggregate limit of $20 million for the three years. Table 25.1 illustrates the cash flows that would occur if paid losses in the three years equal $2 million, $4 million, and $5 million, respectively. We assume for simplicity that these loss amounts are paid at the end of each year. In the first year, the policyholder pays the premium of $4 million, the insurer takes its fee, and interest is earned on the balance. Since claim payments at the end of the first year equal $2 million, all claims are paid from the policyholder's fund. The ending balance in the fund after the first year equals $1,816,000. The premium payment in the second year increases the size of the fund, so that even though claim payments equal $4 million at the end of year 2, the policyholder's fund again is sufficient to pay all claims. The same scenario occurs in year 3; the policyholder's fund has enough money to pay all claims, leaving a surplus of $661,418. In this example, the $661,418 remaining in the fund

TABLE 25.1
Cash Flows (in $ thousands) from a three-year finite risk contract (premium = $4 million; interest = 6% of beginning balance; $20 million aggregate limit).

	Year 1	Year 2	Year 3
At Beginning of Year:			
Balance from previous year	$ 0	$ 1,816	$ 1,741
Premium	4,000	4,000	4,000
Insurer's fee	−400	−400	−400
Beginning balance	3,600	5,416	5,341
At End of Year:			
Claim payments	−2,000	−4,000	−5,000
Interest on beginning balance	216	325	320
Ending balance	$ 1,816	$ 1,741	$ 661

at the end of the policy period would be returned to the policyholder. Alternatively, if another finite risk plan were established for the subsequent three-year period, the surplus at the end of the first three-year period could be used to reduce the premiums for the second three-year period.

Notice that in the example presented in Table 25.1, the insured firm has essentially paid all losses because claims were always below the amount in the fund. If losses were to exceed the amount in the fund, then the insurer would have to pay the losses up to the limit of $20 million. Thus, finite risk insurance is similar to a multiyear policy with a high deductible.

Table 25.2 illustrates the same policy as before, but with higher overall loss payments. In particular, claim payments equal $1 million, $12 million, and $1 million, respectively, at the end of years one through three. The large claim payment at the end of the second year depletes the policyholder's fund, so the insurer makes up the shortfall by paying $5,199,040. As a consequence, the policyholder's fund has a deficit after two years. In this example, the deficit is larger than the premium payment in the third and final year, which implies that the insurer will pay some of the insured's losses (up to the $20 million aggregate limit).

Finite risk contracts also can have provisions that make the policyholder pay a large percentage (e.g., 80 or 90 percent) of any deficit in the fund at the end of the policy period. The payment of the deficit usually can be paid in installments, thus allowing the policyholder to spread the cost over time. For example, in the previous example, a $2.695 million deficit existed at the end of the policy period. The contract could require that the policyholder pay 80 percent of this amount in equal installments over the subsequent three years. This $898,327 payment (0.80 × $2,695,000 ÷ 3) also could be added to the premium for another finite risk contract over the subsequent three-year time period.

This example illustrates that while the policyholder bears most of the risk of unexpected losses with finite risk plans, these plans allow firms to smooth their payments for losses over time. To highlight this feature, Figure 25.2 graphs the annual premium payments and loss payments under two successive three-year finite risk contracts. The premiums and losses for the first three-year period are the same as those used in Table 25.2. The premium payments for the second three-year period assume that the deficit in the first period is added to the premium payments for the second three-year period.

As discussed in Chapter 21, the smoothing of loss payments can be beneficial from a tax standpoint. However, to obtain these tax benefits, the finite risk contract must be classified

TABLE 25.2
Cash flows (in $ thousands) from a three-year finite risk contract (premium = $4 million; interest = 6% of beginning balance; $20 million aggregate limit).

	Year 1	Year 2	Year 3
At Beginning of Year:			
Balance from previous year	$ 0	$ 2816	−$5,199
Premium	4,000	4,000	4,000
Insurer's fee	−400	−400	−400
Beginning balance	3,600	6,416	−1,599
At End of Year:			
Claim payments	−1,000	−12,000	−1,000
Interest on beginning balance	216	385	−96
Ending balance	$ 2,816	−$ 5,199	−2,695

FIGURE 25.2

Illustration of how finite risk contracts smooth loss costs.

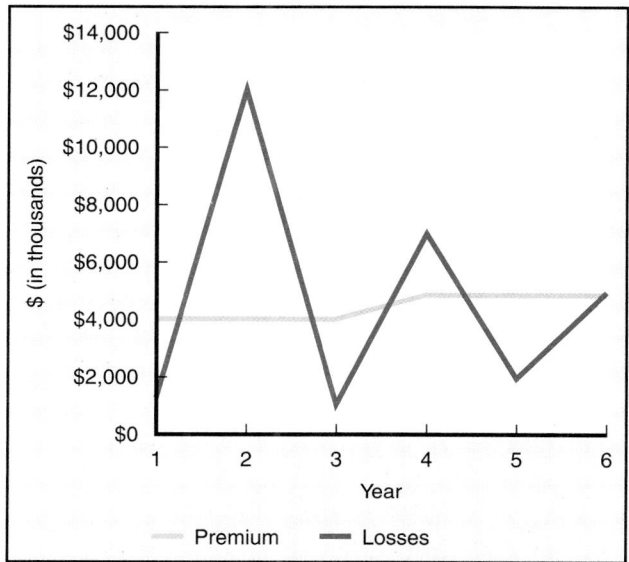

as insurance, which requires that a material amount of the risk associated with unexpected loss payments be shifted to the insurer. Having the insurer bear risk above a reasonable threshold (attachment point) usually can satisfy this requirement. The smoothing of loss payments over time also can have advantages because it reduces the variability of reported earnings. While financial analysis should in general focus on the present value of cash flows as opposed to accounting earnings, we discussed in Chapter 21 how reported accounting numbers can influence expected cash flows and therefore be relevant when making financial decisions.

Concept Check

1. Briefly summarize the main reasons for purchasing a loss sensitive insurance policy.

25.4   Captive Insurers

An important method of financing losses for many large corporations is to make payments to a wholly owned subsidiary, called a **captive insurer,** which then pays losses. For reasons discussed below, captive insurers usually have insurance transactions with corporations other than the parent corporation, including the purchase of reinsurance to transfer risk of large losses. The typical relationships are illustrated in Figure 25.3, where solid lines indicate ownership relationships and dashed lines indicate possible insurance/reinsurance transactions with the captive insurer. If the captive only insures its single parent corporation and/or subsidiaries owned by the parent, it is called a **pure captive.** Often when captives insure other wholly owned subsidiaries of the parent, the transactions are called **brother-sister transactions** to indicate that the transactions are between corporations that have the same parent. Many captives have **unrelated business;** that is, the captive sells insurance to noninsurance corporations that are not owned by the captive's parent. In addition, many captives engage in

FIGURE 25.3
Ownership relationship (solid lines) and insurance transactions (dashed lines) involving captive insurers.

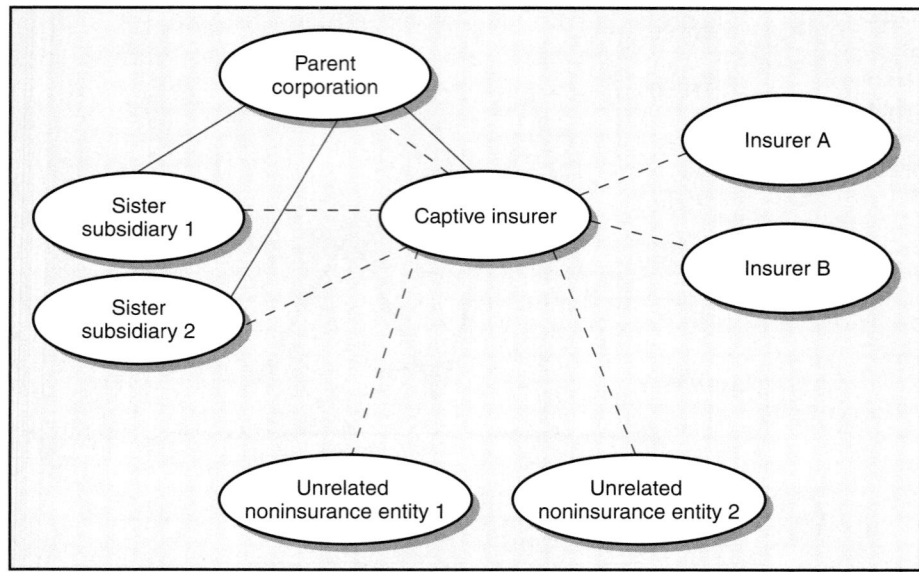

reinsurance transactions with other insurers (including other captives). Finally, some captives have multiple parents (this relationship is not illustrated in Figure 25.3); these captives are called **group captives.**

Many US companies establish captive insurers offshore in places like Bermuda, Barbados, and the Cayman Islands. These locations impose few regulatory restrictions and offer favorable tax treatment relative to domestic captive insurance companies. However, several US states, such as Vermont, Colorado, and South Carolina have offered favorable regulatory environments for captives in recent years. Regardless of where captives are established, few, if any, employees usually work where the captive is domiciled. Instead, management companies are hired or the parent's risk management department manages the captive's operations. Table 25.3 provides information on the number of captive insurers in various locations.

Many small- and medium-sized companies have insufficient exposures to justify the fixed costs of establishing and operating a captive. To provide some of the benefits of captives to these smaller businesses, existing captives and captive management companies

Table 25.3
Locations of captive insurers in 2000.

Location	Number of Captives
Bermuda	1,405
Cayman Islands	535
Vermont	381
Guernsey	370
Luxembourg	273
Barbados	237
British Virgin Islands	184

Source: David Pilla, "Captivating Growth," *Best's Review,* May 2001.

have offered firms the ability to "rent-a-captive." In essence, an existing captive segregates the business of the renter from the other business of the captive and returns the renter's underwriting profit and investment income to the renter, after subtracting a fee.

Motivations for Forming Captive Insurers

Tax and Regulatory Factors

Loss financing through pure captives (single parent captives with no unrelated business) is, in essence, a form of retention (self-insurance). Several tax and regulatory factors help explain why a firm would go to the trouble and expense of forming a pure captive. Historically, an important motivation for creating a captive was to reduce expected tax payments. As discussed in Chapter 21, the different tax treatment of insurers versus noninsurance corporations gives rise to a tax advantage for insurance compared with retention. This tax advantage provides an incentive for firms to arrange loss financing transactions that will be treated as insurance for tax purposes. Thus, to the extent that captive transactions are treated as insurance transactions, firms can reduce expected tax payments relative to retention. We discuss the specific tax treatment of captives below.

Additional tax benefits can be obtained by locating captives offshore, in locations such as Bermuda and the Cayman Islands. These tax benefits arise if the captive's income does not have to be recognized by the parent as taxable income in the year it is earned. In this case, the taxes paid on the captive are subject to the tax treatment afforded insurers in the country in which the captive is domiciled. Since many offshore locations have lower tax rates on investment and underwriting income, the offshore location reduces expected tax payments relative to domestic captives. The issue of whether the parent must recognize the income of the captive as taxable income is complex. Prior to 1987, corporations could defer recognition of the underwriting income from an offshore captive indefinitely. If the country in which the captive was domiciled did not impose taxes on underwriting income, then corporations essentially could avoid taxation on the profits of their captive insurer. The Tax Reform Act of 1986, however, makes parents of most captives pay tax on their captive's profits in the year the profits are earned under Subpart F of the Internal Revenue Code.

Another potential motivation for establishing a captive is to allow the business to purchase excess insurance coverage directly from reinsurers. Since reinsurance transactions typically are subject to less stringent regulation, having a transaction classified as reinsurance (by first insuring through a captive, which then purchases reinsurance) can reduce regulatory constraints on the transaction. Excise taxes also create an incentive to have transactions with foreign insurers treated as reinsurance as opposed to insurance. Recall that excise taxes on foreign transactions equal 4 percent of insurance premiums, but only 1 percent of reinsurance premiums.[3]

A captive also allows a firm to retain a large portion of its risk and still satisfy compulsory insurance requirements, comply with restrictions on the selection of insurers, and meet third-party demands for certificates of insurance from rated insurers, provided that the firm uses a fronting insurer. Specifically, a firm can purchase insurance through a fronting insurer that meets the necessary requirements (i.e., is an admitted insurer or satisfies the

---

[3]These savings also can be obtained by using a domestic insurer as a front. See Chapter 21.

rating requirement of the party who demands a certificate of insurance). The fronting insurer then reinsures with the captive.

Risk Reduction

Captives also can be used to reduce risk. When a captive sells insurance or reinsurance to unrelated entities, then the parent's exposures (and the parent's wholly owned subsidiaries' exposures) are pooled with the unrelated entities' exposures. Consequently, risk (the variance of average losses) is reduced as a result of the captive's transactions (see Chapter 4). Similarly, group captives reduce risk—the loss exposures of each owner are pooled together and each owner shares in the aggregate results of the group. Group captives often are formed to serve firms in a specific industry. Thus, provided that a captive has either multiple parents or unrelated business, captive transactions are not pure retention but instead are a form of insurance that reduces risk.

The Tax Treatment of Captive Transactions

General Legal Principles

The tax courts have two sometimes conflicting principles that guide their decisions regarding the tax treatment of captive insurers. One principle is that risk reduction is important. That is, the courts will view with suspicion captive insurance transactions that do not reduce risk. The basis for this principle is a 1941 Supreme Court opinion (*Helvering v. LeGierse*) which states that insurance transactions entail "risk shifting" and "risk distribution."[4] Although experts differ in interpretation of the terms *risk shifting* and *risk distribution*, the courts have generally adopted a view that is consistent with the discussion in Chapter 4 on risk pooling. If a captive transaction results in a pooling of risk and therefore a reduction in the variance of average losses, then risk shifting and risk distribution exist, and the transaction is treated as insurance.

The courts also use the principle that the legal separateness of corporations should be respected (*Moline Properties v. Commissioner, 1943*). Using this principle, the tax courts will view transactions between a corporation and a separately incorporated captive as transactions between separate corporations that *could* constitute insurance. As discussed below, the use of this principle has led courts to view brother-sister captive transactions as insurance, even though these transactions result in little if any risk reduction.

Captives That Only "Insure" a Single Parent

Captives that only insure a single parent do not reduce risk for the parent corporation. This follows from the observation that the parent is the sole residual claimant to the captive's profits and the captive only transacts with the parent. Thus, any of the profits or losses of the captive are the direct result of the parent's payments to the captive and the parent's losses. From a risk-bearing perspective, pure captives are equivalent to self-insurance. Consistent with the risk-bearing effects, the tax law views these transactions as retention (*Carnation v. Commissioner, 1981*). The purchase of reinsurance, however, by the captive from an unrelated reinsurer is treated as insurance.

---

[4]In addition, the courts often look to see if the transactions with the captive resemble insurance transactions in the "commonly accepted sense."

Captives with Unrelated Business

When a captive insures or reinsures unrelated entities in addition to its parent corporation, the parent's loss exposures are pooled with the exposures of other entities. Consequently, captives that insure unrelated entities are essentially pooling arrangements that reduce the variance of the average losses of those parties transacting with the captive. Thus, the tax law treats transactions with captives that have unrelated business as insurance transactions.[5] Tax rulings on this issue have induced many captives to write unrelated business in an effort to achieve favorable tax status.

The question of how much unrelated business is needed for the transaction to be treated as insurance (for risk shifting and risk distribution to be material) is not settled. Of the cases addressing unrelated business (see footnote 5), the Harper case had the least proportion of unrelated business—approximately 30 percent. It is uncertain how the courts would rule if the percentage of unrelated business were less than 30 percent.

Captives That Only Insure a Single Parent and Sister Corporations

As discussed earlier, in addition to insuring the parent corporation, some captives also insure other wholly owned subsidiaries of the parent corporation without providing insurance or reinsurance to any unrelated businesses. Before discussing the tax treatment of these brother-sister transactions, it is useful to discuss two approaches that have not been adopted by the courts and taxing authorities.

One approach would be to treat the brother-sister transactions as unrelated business. Since the sister corporations are separate corporations from both the captive and the captive's parent, some experts have argued that the transactions between the captive and its sister corporations are just like unrelated business and, consequently, that both the parent's and the sister subsidiaries' transactions with the captive should be treated as insurance. Others, however, argue that since the parent wholly owns the sister corporations and the captive, the transactions between the sister corporations and the captive do not reduce the risk for the consolidated entity. An owner of the parent, for example, would not view the transactions with the captive as reducing his or her risk because the owner bears the cost of unexpected losses whether or not the captive exists. The captive simply changes the name of the legal entity that pays losses. This view leads to the recommendation that the brother-sister transactions should be treated as retention. That is, neither the parent's nor the brother-sister transactions should be treated as insurance.

In contrast to either of the views presented, the tax courts have adopted the following approach when the captive only insures its parent and its sister corporations: Transactions between the parent and the captive are not treated as insurance, but transactions between the sister subsidiaries and the captive (the brother-sister transactions) are treated as insurance (see *Humana Inc. v. Commissioner, 1989*). This approach was upheld in two 1997 cases, *Hospital Corporation of America v. Commissioner* and *Kidde Industries, Inc. v. The United States*. The logic given is that the parent's captive transactions do not reduce risk (and therefore are not insurance) because the parent owns all the corporations that the captive insures. The sister subsidiaries' transactions with the captive reduce risk because the

---

[5]See *Harper v. Commissioner, 1991; AMERCO v. Commissioner, 1991; Ocean Drilling & Exploration Co. v. United States, 1991;* and *Sears, Roebuck and Co. v. Commissioner, 1991.*

sister corporation's exposures are being pooled with the exposures of entities that they do not own (i.e., sister corporations or the parent corporation).[6] In June 2001, the I.R.S. issued ruling 2001–31 essentially stating that the I.R.S. accepts the Court's decisions regarding brother-sister transactions.

Risk Retention Groups

Although technically not captive insurers, risk retention groups have most of the characteristics of group captives. We therefore discuss them here. Prior to 1981, the formation of pooling arrangements among firms was hindered by the requirement that pooling arrangements generally had to satisfy state insurance regulations in order to legally provide primary insurance. Congress passed a law in 1981 that allows firms to bypass some state regulations and form groups to pool risk arising from products liability exposures. These groups, which are very similar to group captives, are called **risk retention groups.** In 1986, the law was expanded to allow risk retention groups for all liability exposures, except employers' liability and workers' compensation. In 1997, about 70 risk retention groups existed.

25.5   Multiline/Multitrigger Insurance Policies

Multiline insurance policies provide coverage against an aggregate measure of losses from different risk exposures. For example, instead of having separate policies providing coverage for property, liability, and workers' compensation losses, a firm could purchase one multiline policy that has indemnity payments and limits based on total losses from all three exposures. These policies also are called integrated, basket, or bundled policies.

The development of multiline policies is consistent with many of the explanations of why corporations purchase insurance in the first place. As summarized in Chapter 22, for corporations with diversified shareholders, insurance is most useful as a device to reduce exposure to large disruptive losses that either push a firm into financial distress or force it to raise costly external capital. From this perspective, the firms would like to avoid large aggregate losses regardless of whether they result from one type of exposure or from an accumulation of losses from multiple exposures. A firm can avoid large disruptive losses by either purchasing separate policies on each exposure or by purchasing a multiline policy that bundles the exposures together. Provided the additional modeling costs associated with pricing a multiline policy are not too large, a multiline policy can save on the transaction costs associated with negotiating multiple policies. In addition, a multiline policy can save on proportion loading costs by avoiding the purchase of unnecessary coverage (see Chapter 22). Although some multiline policies have been adopted (see Box 25.1 for two examples), they have not been used frequently.

Multitrigger insurance policies specify that the insurer will not make payments to the insured unless multiple conditions or contingencies occur. A traditional insurance policy has a single trigger—the loss must exceed the deductible (or self-insured retention). That is, the event that triggers a payment from the insurer is a loss that exceeds the deductible or

[6]One potential problem with the courts' rulings on this issue is that it creates an incentive for a parent simply to be a shell and place the vast majority of its loss exposures in wholly owned subsidiaries, which then insure through the captive. From the perspective of the primary risk bearer of corporate activities, the shareholders, these transactions do not reduce risk (i.e., the firm has essentially self-insured). However, brother-sister captive transactions might reduce risk for nonshareholder claimants of the subsidiaries.

COCA-COLA

In 1997, the Coca-Cola Company terminated its array of traditional insurance contracts and adopted an integrated risk program that combines most of its loss exposures in a single contract. The new policy provides an aggregate amount of coverage above a self-insured retention for each type of loss exposure covered.

Source: "All-in-One Insurance," *Financial Executive,* May/June 1997.

HONEYWELL COVERS PURE RISK AND PRICE RISK IN ONE POLICY

In July 1997, Honeywell Inc. initiated a program to finance losses from four different exposures: property, liability, directors and officers' liability, and currency fluctuations. By including coverage for currency risk exposures in the contracts. Honeywell was one of the first companies to combine pure and price risk into one policy. The loss financing program provides an aggregate limit and lasts two and one-half years.

Source: "Integrated Financing of Risk Gains Ground," *Business Insurance,* October 20, 1997.

Follow-up: Honeywell did not renew the policy.

---

self-insured retention. In contrast, a multitrigger policy would specify that the insurer will pay the insured once the loss exceeds the deductible and when some other variable hits a specified threshold. For example, suppose that sales are highly correlated with gross national product (GNP) growth. Then the second trigger could be that GNP growth is less than 1 percent for the year. In this case, the insurer pays only when losses are high and sales are low.

The motivation for multitrigger policies is the same as that for multiline policies. The second trigger gives a firm coverage when it needs it the most—that is, when earnings are low because of some other risk—and thus avoids the purchase of costly unnecessary coverage. As with multiline policies, multitrigger policies have not been used frequently.

25.6   Contingent Financing Arrangements

With a contingent financing arrangement, a firm arranges with a financial institution or investor to borrow money or issue new stock at prearranged terms, contingent on some event occurring. To introduce how contingent financing arrangements can be used, suppose that Hoyt Company is considering alternative ways of financing potential property losses over the coming year to its manufacturing facility that is valued at $5 million. Hoyt is able to pay up to $1 million of losses from cash flow, but no more, and therefore is seeking ways of paying for property losses above $1 million.

Contingent Debt

As an example of **contingent debt** (contingent borrowing), suppose that on January 2 Hoyt obtains an option from Bank Two to borrow up to $4 million at an 8 percent rate at any time during the coming year if the manufacturing facility incurs more than $1 million in damage. Bank Two requires a fee of $20,000 paid up-front for granting Hoyt this option. In essence, Hoyt plans to finance any property losses above $1 million by borrowing money, but instead of borrowing ex post (after the loss occurs, if it does occur), Hoyt arranges the terms of the loan ex ante. In this case, the interest rate on the loan is guaranteed to not exceed 8 percent.

Since the loan must be repaid, the owners of Hoyt bear most of the property risk: that is, the existing owners end up paying most of the losses (if they occur). However, some risk is shifted to Bank Two, because Bank Two fixes the interest rate on the loan ex ante. If Hoyt exercises its option to borrow from Bank Two at the 8 percent rate, then Bank Two will bear part of the property loss. Hoyt will exercise this option whenever property damage exceeds $1 million and the interest rate that Hoyt would have paid without this arrangement would have exceeded 8 percent. The $20,000 fee is the price that Bank Two charges for taking on this risk.

Contingent Equity

Instead of agreeing to borrow money at prearranged terms, Hoyt could arrange to issue new stock (equity) at a prearranged price if property damage occurs. As an example of a **contingent equity** arrangement, suppose that Hoyt arranges to issue up to 100,000 shares of stock at a price of $40 a share if property damage in excess of $1 million occurs. In this case, Hoyt finances the loss with funds raised from issuing new equity. The investors who agree to buy the new equity bear some risk because they agree to purchase shares at a price of $40 a share. If property losses in excess of $1 million occur and the price of the stock falls below $40 a share, then the new stockholders pay more for the shares than they are worth. In exchange for taking on this risk, the contingent equity providers would likely require an up-front fee.

Advantages and Disadvantages

Contingent debt and equity arrangements are not common, but they are being used. Box 25.2 briefly describes arrangements used by the Royal Bank of Canada and Compagnie Financiere Michelin. Contingent debt or equity capital can be advantageous relative to borrowing money or issuing new equity ex ante and holding that capital until it is needed because the firm avoids the costs associated with holding capital over time. As explained in Chapter 5, holding capital can be costly because of the taxes that have to be paid on the earnings generated from the capital and because managers might be tempted to use the capital for other purposes. Contingent debt or equity capital can be advantageous relative to insurance when the firm does not need the services provided by insurers and when the cost of the contingent capital facility is less than the loading on the insurance.

Lines of Credit

Most large businesses have an arrangement with a bank, called a **line of credit,** whereby the bank agrees to lend money to the firm over some future period (often a year) if the firm decides it needs to borrow. Lines of credit differ from the contingent financing arrangements described above in that the borrowing is not triggered by a prespecified event (the property loss in the example above). Instead, the firm can draw on the line of credit whenever it finds it advantageous.

A line of credit specifies the maximum amount that can be borrowed over the period and often requires that the firm keep a compensating balance with the bank; that is, the firm must have deposits earning a low interest rate. The compensating balance is usually stated as some percentage (e.g., 5 percent) of the maximum amount that can be borrowed. For ex-

In 2000, Royal Bank of Canada and the French tire maker Compagnie Financiere Michelin sought access to capital for future contingencies—in the bank's case, to absorb severe credit losses, and in Michelin's, to fund future acquisitions or expansions. Rather than access capital from the debt or equity markets, they opted for a new insurance strategy called committed long-term capital solutions, or CLOCS. According to Peter Currie, CFO and a vice chairman of the Toronto-based bank, the move allows the institution "to tap capital in those times when it normally would be difficult and costly to raise it traditionally."

The policies, marketed by Swiss Re New Markets, a division of Zurich-based Swiss Re Group, are triggered by economic metrics—a fall in a country's gross domestic product in Michelin's case, or a reduction in reserves in the Royal Bank of Canada's. And because CLOCS is insurance, it neatly sidesteps the Catch 22 of customary capital-raising—when you need it most is usually when it's most expensive. "Unfortunately, you can never guess what the cost of capital will be when the right investment opportunity arises," says Jacques Tierny, deputy CFO of the € 15 billion Michelin Group, based in Clermont Ferrand, France, and Fribourg, Switzerland. "At the same time, you don't want to raise equity and have it sitting around on your balance sheet." "Nor," he adds, "do you always want to issue debt during a recession for acquisition or expansion purposes, since it would increase your risk profile."

Together, the two CLOCS deals, which are both off-balance-sheet, represent an entirely new way of accessing contingent capital. "Essentially, you're given standby access to money if a certain adverse event happens," says Carl Groth, managing director of enterprise risk strategies at Willis Risk Solutions, a New York-based alternative risk transfer specialist. "If the economy is doing well and you want to make an acquisition, you can go out and raise capital in the normal way. If it is doing poorly, you can trigger the insurance. And pursuing both strategies [allows] you to diversify your sources of capital."

The deals also represent the first significant incursion by insurers into a market heretofore owned by the investment banks. In much the same way that banks are offering capital market alternatives to insurance policies, insurers are now offering insurance alternatives to traditional banking strategies. More important, says Currie, is that "CLOCS was a much less expensive option than other insurance structures or more-traditional balance-sheet-mitigation strategies."

Source: Russ Banham. "Just-in-Case Capital: How Companies Are Tapping into Contingent Capital through, of all Things, an Insurance Policy." *CFO Magazine,* June 1, 2001.

ample, if the line of credit is for $3 million and a compensating balance of 5 percent is required, then the firm must deposit $150,000 (0.05 × $3,000,000) with the bank.

There are two basic ways that lines of credit can be arranged. A committed line of credit is a formal agreement that specifies the interest rate at which the bank will lend money. The bank charges a fee (e.g., 0.25 to 1.00 percent of the funds that can be borrowed) for committing to an interest rate. Committed lines of credit often include a material adverse change (MAC) in financial condition clause, which allows the bank to deny a loan to the firm if it experiences a material change in financial condition. A noncommitted line of credit is an informal agreement whereby the bank agrees to lend money to the firm during the contract period, but the bank is free to quote any interest rate on the loan.

25.7   Structured Debt Instruments

When a firm borrows money and agrees to pay a fixed rate of interest over the course of the loan, it takes on the risk that earnings will not be sufficient to pay the interest due each period. Thus, all else equal, greater financial leverage (more borrowing) increases the likelihood of financial distress. Firms can reduce the risk of financial distress by having the interest payments (and even the principal payments) contingent on some variable that is highly correlated with the firm's earnings. Debt securities that link payments to some other variable often are called **structured debt instruments.**

Price or Index-Linked Debt

Consider the Devereux gold mining company that needs to raise capital to develop a new mine. One possibility would be for Devereux to issue new debt. An advantage of issuing new debt, versus new equity, is that the interest payments to debtholders are treated as a deductible expense when calculating income taxes (but dividends paid to equityholders are not). A potential disadvantage is that the additional debt will increase the risk of financial distress. Specifically, if Devereux issues fixed rate debt (promised interest payments are constant over time), and the price of gold at some point in the future drops, then Devereux's cash flows might be insufficient to pay the promised interest payments. Thus, the risk of gold price declines combined with fixed rate debt increases Devereux's risk of financial distress.

An alternative would be for Devereux to issue debt with interest payments that are explicitly linked to the price of gold. If gold prices drop, then the promised interest payments drop; if gold prices increase, then promised interest payments increase. By issuing debt with interest payments linked to the price of gold, Devereux can obtain the interest tax deductions, without increasing the risk of financial distress too much.[7]

Catastrophe Bonds

Another interesting example of structured debt is called a catastrophe bond. Although the details can be complex, firms issuing catastrophe bonds promise the bondholders that they will repay the principal plus interest, unless a catastrophe, such as an earthquake, occurs. If the catastrophe occurs, the issuer is relieved of its obligation of paying some of the promised interest and principal without defaulting on the debt. Since 1997, more than 60 catastrophe bonds have been issued. Although most of the issuers have been insurers or reinsurers, some noninsurers, such as Walt Disney Company, have issued catastrophe bonds. Box 25.3 describes the first catastrophe bond issued by United States Automobile Association (USAA), a large insurer.

25.8   Trends in Loss Financing

During the past three decades, many large firms have increased their retention levels and their use of alternative risk transfer. The trend toward greater retention and reliance on alternative risk transfer has several explanations, including, at least in part, growth in understanding by managers and investors that risk reduction for diversified shareholders is beneficial only if it has positive effects on expected cash flows (see Chapter 20).

One economic factor that helps explain these trends is that, beginning in the late 1960s and continuing until the 1980s, larger fluctuations in the price of business insurance associated with the cycle of hard and soft markets (wherein periods of high insurance prices and low availabil-

---

[7]Of course, another approach would be for Devereux to issue fixed rate debt and hedge the risk of a reduction in gold prices with gold forwards, futures, or options. In some instances, however, price or indexed link debt can involve lower contracting costs.

In July 1997, United Services Automobile Association (USAA), a large property and automobile insurer, raised capital by issuing bonds with the interest and principal payments on the bonds contingent on whether USAA experienced a hurricane catastrophe. More specifically, USAA established a wholly owned reinsurance subsidiary in the Cayman Islands, which then issued bonds worth $477 million. Using the proceeds from the bond issue as capital, the reinsurance subsidiary issued a one-year catastrophe reinsurance contract to USAA that covered 80 percent of insured losses between $1 billion and $1.5 billion from a single hurricane on the Gulf or the East coasts. Thus, the maximum loss paid by the reinsurer was $400 million (80 percent of $0.5 billion).

The bond issue had two tranches. The first tranch was worth $163.8 million and the other was worth $313.2 million. Investors who purchased the first tranch could only lose their promised interest payments. That is, if a catastrophe occurred, then the investors would receive less interest on their bonds than they were promised. Investors in the first tranch could not lose their promised principal payment, although if a catastrophe occurred the principal would not be paid for 10 years. Investors who purchased the second tranch could lose both their interest and principal if a sufficiently large catastrophe occurred. To guarantee that the $163.8 principal payment for the first tranch would be paid after 10 years, $77 million of the $477 million was invested in 10-year government bonds that guaranteed a dollar return of $163.8 million in 10 years. The remaining $400 million from the bond issue backed the reinsurance contract issued to USAA. In return for taking the risk of losing their interest and/or principal, investors received a higher promised interest payment than most corporate bonds, with investors of the second tranch receiving a higher promised interest payment than investors in the first tranch.

Source: Rodd Zolkos. "Catastrophe Bonds Take Risk Financing by Storm," *Business Insurance,* December 22, 1997.

ity of coverage follow periods of low prices and readily available coverage) led businesses to look for alternative mechanisms for financing losses. This was especially true during the liability crisis in the mid-1980s, when premiums increased dramatically and coverage was restricted for some types of liability insurance. Increased volatility in insurance prices and reduced availability generally discourages corporations from purchasing insurance. The increase in the number of insurer and reinsurer insolvencies in the late 1980s and early 1990s also may have reduced confidence in traditional commercial insurance by some risk managers.

The commercial insurance market has responded to the reduced corporate demand for traditional insurance by designing new products that offer corporations larger retentions, such as paid-loss retro plans, large deductible policies, and loss portfolio transfers. Commercial insurers also have increased their risk management services, including claims processing and loss control services.

25.9   Summary

- With loss sensitive insurance contracts, premiums depend on losses that occur during the contract period. Retrospectively rated policies and large deductible policies are examples of loss sensitive contracts.

- A finite risk contract is a special type of multiyear loss sensitive contract that allows loss payments to be smoothed over time. Finite risk contracts may provide some of the tax advantages of traditional insurance if they involve material risk shifting.

- Large businesses often form captives (subsidiaries) to pay losses of the captive's parent and sister corporations. In part because of tax rulings, many captives also sell insurance to unrelated entities, including reinsurance to other insurers.

- Captives may provide tax advantages and allow corporations to purchase excess insurance in the reinsurance market. In combination with a fronting insurer, captives also allow corporations to self-insure but at the same time (1) satisfy compulsory insurance laws, (2) comply with restrictions on the purchase of insurance from admitted insurers, and (3) meet third-party requirements for certificates of insurance from rated insurers.
- Risk retention groups and group captives are pooling arrangements that reduce risk for their participants.

- Multiline and multitrigger policies have loss payments contingent on the outcome of multiple variables. Multiline policies base loss payments on aggregate losses from multiple exposures.
- Contingent financing arrangements allow a firm to set the terms at which it will raise capital if some contingency, such as a large loss, occurs.
- Structured debt instruments make the payment of interest and principal contingent on some variable that is correlated with the firm's earnings.

Key Terms

Questions and Problems

1. Using the finite risk contract described in the text, how much would the policyholder get back at the end of three years if loss payments at year-end were

    (a) $3 million in year 1; $3 million in year 2; and $3 million in year 3?

    (b) $8 million in year 1; $1 million in year 2; and $1 million in year 3?

2. Suppose Porat Power Company establishes a captive insurer in Bermuda to "insure" its workers' compensation costs. Explain the various alternative ownership and operational characteristics that could describe the captive. What are the advantages of these alternatives?

3. ACQ Inc. is considering the acquisition of TRG Corporation. However, TRG has product liability claims that have been reported but not yet paid; the claims are estimated to be equal to $300 million in present value terms. These product liability claims are expected to be paid over the course of the next 10 years, but the exact amounts due each year are subject to some uncertainty. ACQ does not want to deal with this exposure. Suggest a method by which ACQ could acquire TRG, but not deal with TRG's product liability claims.

4. Describe the advantages of a contingent equity arrangement for dealing with the risk that a natural catastrophe would cause sub-

stantial property losses compared to (*a*) issuing new equity immediately and holding the funds until a loss occurs, and (*b*) purchasing property insurance.

5. Pottier Corporation is a textile manufacturer. Analysis indicates that Pottier's lowest cost method of dealing with its property exposure is to pay any losses from operating cash flows. The problem is that its operating cash flows are dependent on the price of oil, because it purchases large quantities of oil to power its facilities. If the price of oil rises above $30 a barrel, then there is too high of a probability that it will not have sufficient cash flows to pay for all of its property losses. Describe an insurance contract that might be of interest to Pottier.

Answer to Concept Check

1. The main reasons for purchasing a loss sensitive insurance policy are (1) to obtain the tax benefits from insurance, (2) to purchase claims processing services from the insurer, and (3) to satisfy compulsory insurance laws.

References

Banham, Russ. "Shopping the Market for Finite Risk Products." *Risk Management,* September 1994, pp. 34–43. (*Practical overview of the variety of finite risk products, their uses, and tax and accounting issues.*)

Culp, Christopher L. *The Art of Risk Management.* John Wiley & Sons, New York: 2002.

Hein, Eric P.; and Michael J. O'Malley. "Two Birds with One Stone: How to Reduce Dependence on Letters of Credit and Accelerate Tax Deductibility." *Risk Management,* April 1996, pp. 59–71. (*Discusses retros, investment credit, and related loss sensitive plans.*)

Huebner, S. S.; Kenneth Black, Jr.; and Bernard C. Webb. *Property and Liability Insurance.* 4th ed. Upper Saddle River, NJ: Prentice-Hall, 1996. (*Comprehensive treatment of traditional commercial property–liability insurance contracts for a wide variety of risk exposures.*)

Larkins, Ernest. "Taxation and the Future of Offshore Insurers." *Risk Management,* September 1, 1991, pp. 42–45. (*Provides detailed treatment of the taxation of captive insurers.*)

May, David. "All-in-One-Insurance." *Financial Executive,* May/June 1997. (*Provides a discussion and examples of integrated risk programs.*)

Modern ART Practice. Gerling Global Financial Products, Inc. New York: 2000.

Shimpi, Prakesh. "Multi-Line and Multi-Trigger Products." New York: Swiss Re New Markets, 1999.

"The Picture of ART." Swiss Re New Markets *Sigma No. 1/2003.* New York: 2003.

26

Analysis Tools Used in Corporate Risk Management

Chapter Objectives

- Show how to use historical loss data to calculate the characteristics of a probability distribution of future losses.
- Illustrate how to use regression analysis in risk management problems and how to interpret regression results.
- Show how to calculate and use correlation coefficients.
- Illustrate how to use Monte Carlo simulation to assess the desirability of alternative risk management policies.
- Show how to calculate incremental cash flows and their present values.

26.1 Risk Management Tools

In Chapter 3, you learned about probability distributions and the characteristics of probability distributions (expected values, standard deviations, correlations). In this chapter, we extend the analysis of Chapter 3 by presenting some tools used by corporate risk managers to analyze their risks and improve decision making. We note at the outset that the tools discussed in this chapter are primarily used by large firms. Generally it is not worthwhile for small businesses (and individuals) to spend resources conducting the analysis described in this chapter. The information generated from the analysis would have little impact on determining how much risk they can reasonably retain. For small businesses and individuals, risk management decisions depend largely on judgment, and commonly they are influenced by the advice of insurance agents and brokers. For large firms, the value of information provided by statistical analysis is much more likely to exceed the cost of undertaking the analysis (the cost of data collection, analysis, and interpretation). The information provided is likely to be more meaningful and reliable, and large firms can spread the fixed costs of analysis over a larger number of exposures.

26.2 Calculating Frequency and Severity of Losses from Historical Data

Table 26.1 presents data on medical payments resulting from workplace accidents at two restaurants owned by Klare Corporation. The restaurants are of similar size and design, employ the same number of people, conduct similar amounts of business (revenue), and are located in areas with similar health care costs. The table provides the date of the accident and the amount of the loss for the year 2002. In this particular case, the loss payments are matched to the date of the accident, not when the payments were actually made. Sandeep, the risk manager for Klare Corporation, would like to examine the frequency and severity

TABLE 26.1
Data on loss payments for Klare Corporation for 2002.

Restaurant A		Restaurant B	
Accident Date	**Medical Payments**	**Accident Date**	**Medical Payments**
01/24	$ 3,000	01/25	$ 2,000
02/08	12,000	02/12	92,000
02/11	800	02/22	1,800
03/23	7,500	02/23	1,500
04/01	4,000	04/28	14,000
04/07	15,000	04/29	2,000
05/16	105,000	05/01	12,000
06/07	1,800	05/08	500
06/21	500	06/23	7,500
07/21	9,000	06/30	4,000
08/01	45,000	07/03	12,000
08/16	12,000	07/15	77,000
09/26	500	07/21	900
10/15	5,500	08/23	10,500
10/25	8,000	09/08	34,000
11/24	1,000	10/24	42,000
11/30	10,000	10/28	12,000
12/07	400	11/01	800
12/23	7,000	11/13	18,500
12/28	2,000	11/28	25,000
12/29	2,000	12/01	22,000
		12/06	6,000
		12/18	2,000
		12/27	32,000
		12/29	18,000
Total losses	$252,000		$450,000
Frequency of accidents	21		25
Average severity	$ 12,000		$ 18,000

of losses during the year at the two restaurants. Using the data in the top panel, total loss payments for the year, the frequency (number) of losses per year, and the average severity (the total loss payments divided by the frequency) are calculated and reported in the bottom panel. The data indicate that restaurant B had greater frequency and severity of losses in 2002 than restaurant A.

Because one year of data is insufficient to conclude that restaurant B has a worse safety record, Sandeep collects loss data for the two restaurants for the past eight years. Before comparing these data, he adjusts the historical data to take into account health care cost inflation. More specifically, he multiplies each loss payment by one plus the rate of inflation from the year of the loss to 2002. For example, if health care costs increased by 4 percent from 2000 to 2001 and by 5 percent from 2001 to 2002, then Sandeep multiplies the 2001 losses by 1.05 to put them in 2002 dollars. He multiplies the 2000 losses by $(1.04)(1.05) =$ 1.092 to put them in 2002 dollars.

The results of Sandeep's analysis are reported in Table 26.2. On average, restaurant A has about 20 losses per year compared to about 22 for restaurant B. This is a relatively large difference.[1] In contrast to the 2002 results, the average severity of accidents at restaurant B are slightly lower than those at A. The difference in average severity, however, is not very large. Thus, Sandeep concludes that restaurant B appears to have an accident frequency problem relative to A.

After examining the frequency numbers in more detail, Sandeep suspects that restaurant B's frequency of loss has shown an increasing trend over time. To visually inspect the data, he plots the loss frequency in each year for both restaurants as in Figure 26.1. The figure strongly suggests an increasing trend in loss frequency for restaurant B. Sandeep could use this information to justify expending some resources on trying to identify the reasons for the increasing frequency and thereby identify some potential ways of reducing loss frequency.

Now suppose that Sandeep would like to forecast expected losses for the year 2003 at each restaurant. If Sandeep makes the reasonable assumption that the probability distributions for loss frequency and loss severity have been and will continue to be stable over time for restaurant A, then he can use the historical averages to calculate expected frequency and expected severity for 2003. That is, he can expect about 19.6 accidents in 2003 with an av-

TABLE 26.2
Frequency and severity data (adjusted for inflation).

	Restaurant A		Restaurant B	
Year	Frequency	Average Severity	Frequency	Average Severity
1995	20	$13,000	18	$11,000
1996	18	11,000	20	14,000
1997	18	9,000	21	8,000
1998	21	10,500	21	11,500
1999	19	19,000	23	13,000
2000	21	18,500	25	12,500
2001	19	13,000	24	12,000
2002	21	12,000	25	18,000
Average	19.6	$13,250	22.1	$12,500

[1]A t-test indicates that the difference in means is statistically significant at the 0.03 level using a two-tailed test.

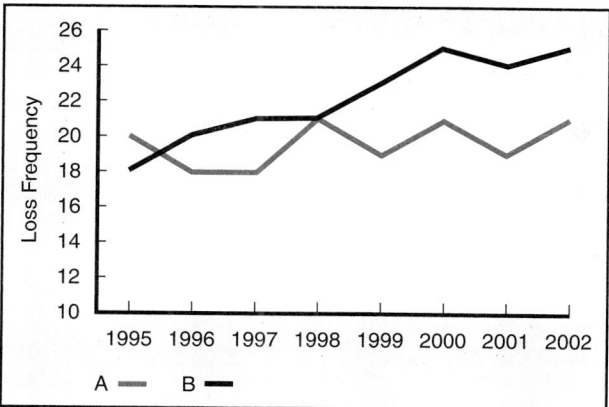

FIGURE 26.1
Loss frequency for Klare Corporation over time.

erage loss of about $13,250 per accident. Multiplying expected frequency and severity, he finds the expected total loss for restaurant A to be about $260,000 (in 2002 dollars).

The same type of analysis, however, is problematic for restaurant B, because the assumption that the frequency distribution is stable over time for restaurant B is not likely to be appropriate. The data suggest an upward trend in accident frequency for restaurant B; this means the historical average accident frequency will underestimate the true expected frequency in 2003. Essentially, Sandeep must find a way to extrapolate from the trend the expected frequency in 2003. The easiest way to do this is to estimate a linear regression line for restaurant B's frequency, where the explanatory variable is the number of years since 1994, denoted as TIME TREND. While the details of regression analysis are beyond the scope of this book, essential ideas of linear regression are conveyed in Box 26.1. In this example, Sandeep is using the variable TIME TREND (equal to the number of years since 1994) to explain restaurant B's accident frequency.

Sandeep's estimated regression line for the loss frequency and year data for restaurant B is

$$\text{FREQUENCY} = 17.7 + 0.99 \,(\text{TIME TREND})$$

$$(28.3)\ (7.9)$$

The equation indicates that accident frequency increases by about 1 (0.99) each additional year. In Figure 26.2 we plot the actual frequency data for restaurant B versus YEAR, as well as the estimated regression line. As you can see, the regression line fits the data well.

Returning now to the problem of estimating expected losses for restaurant B for 2003, Sandeep can use the estimated regression line to forecast accident frequency (assuming no changes are made at the restaurant). By plugging 9 for the variable TIME TREND variable (year equals 2003) into the estimated regression line equation, frequency is forecasted to be 26.6 ($17.7 + 0.99 \times 9$). Assuming that the probability distribution for severity is stable over time, Sandeep can use the historical average of $12,500 as the expected severity of losses in 2003. Multiplying expected frequency by expected severity gives $332,500 as an estimate of expected losses for restaurant B in 2003. Note that if Sandeep had simply used the historical average frequency (22.1), he would have predicted a much lower level of expected losses.

Consider the scatter plot depicting data points for the variables X and Y.

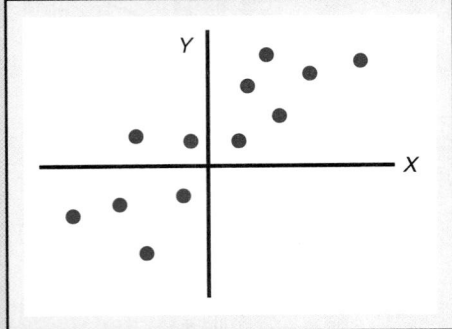

A simple **linear regression line** is the equation of a line that best approximates the actual data for X and Y. Recall from your high school algebra classes that the equation of a line can be written as $Y = \alpha + \beta X$, where α (alpha) is the y-intercept and β (beta) is the slope. When a computer estimates a linear regression line, it finds the intercept and the slope that best approximates the actual data. In essence, the computer chooses α and β so that the errors between the actual data and the line are minimized.*

A multiple linear regression equation extends the idea of a simple regression line by including more than one variable on the right side of the equation. Suppose that the variable Y is thought to be related to the variables X and Z. Then a multiple linear regression equation would be written as $Y = \alpha + \beta_1 X + \beta_2 Z$. In this case, the computer finds the y-intercept, α, and the slope coefficients, β_1 and β_2, to best fit the actual data.

The output of most computer packages that estimate regression models includes statistical tests for whether the slope coefficients are significantly different from zero. The most common method of testing for statistical significance is to use a t-statistic. A coefficient estimate that has a t-statistic greater than two is generally considered to be reliably different from zero. For example, suppose that we obtain the following estimated multiple regression equation, where the t-statistics are reported in parentheses below the estimated slope coefficients.

$$Y = 2.5 + 1.2 X + 0.6 Z$$

$$(3.5) \quad (2.7) \quad (1.1)$$

In this case, the slope coefficient for X, 1.2, is reliably different from zero, because the t-statistic is 2.7. Thus, there is a statistically significant relationship between Y and X. However, the slope coefficient for Z, 0.6, is not significantly different from zero, indicating that there is not a significant linear relationship between Y and Z.

* More formally, regression analysis finds the intercept and slope that minimizes the sum of squared deviations from each point and the regression line.

FIGURE 26.2
Frequency data for restaurant B and a linear regression line.

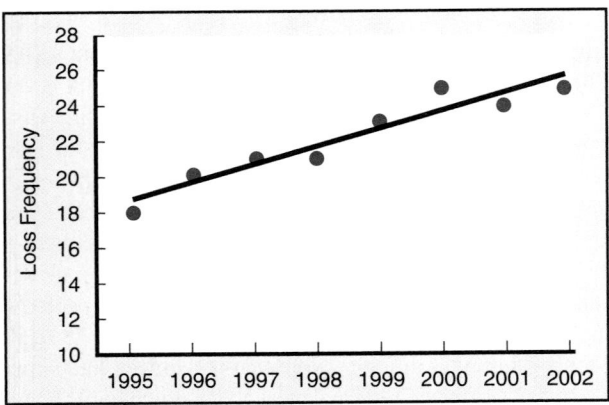

26.3   Using Entire Probability Distributions

In the previous analysis, we focused on the expected values of the frequency and severity of losses. In some situations, analysts would like to know the entire probability distribution for important variables (e.g., property losses, taxable earnings, after-tax cash flows) under alternative risk management policies. For example, to determine the optimal liability property insurance coverage, a risk manager ideally would like to know each possible loss amount during the year and their associated probabilities under alternative policy provisions (deductibles and limits). While this ideal is seldom achieved in practice, a variety of approaches can be used as a means to improve decision making. These approaches usually involve approximating the total loss distribution, or at least estimating the expected value, standard deviation, and maximum probable loss of total losses or costs.

The remainder of this section focuses on two common approaches to estimating loss distributions or key summary measures of these distributions: (1) relying on large sample probability distribution theory (i.e., assuming that the loss distribution can be approximated by the normal distribution), and (2) using computer simulation.

Approximating Loss Distributions with the Normal Distribution

You learned in Chapters 3 and 4 that if losses are independent across exposures, then the probability distribution of the average loss per exposure approaches the normal probability distribution, with its familiar bell shape, as the number of exposures increases. This result is known as the *central limit theorem.* Thus, if a firm has a large number of exposures with zero or very low correlation in losses across exposures, the distribution of its average loss will be approximately normal. The distribution of the total loss for all exposures also will be approximately normal.

A nice feature of the normal distribution is that knowledge of the expected value and standard deviation is sufficient to obtain the entire probability distribution. Consequently, if we can find the expected value and standard deviation of total losses, then we know the entire probability distribution for total losses (provided the total loss distribution is normal, which is the same as assuming a large number of uncorrelated exposure units). Fortunately, the expected value and standard deviation of total losses can be calculated given information about the expected value and standard deviation of loss *per exposure.* The expected value of the total loss distribution will equal the number of exposures times the expected loss per exposure. The standard deviation of total losses will equal the square root of the number of exposures times the standard deviation of loss for each exposure (see the appendix to Chapter 3).

Illustration

To illustrate how the firm might rely on the assumption that losses have the normal distribution, consider the case of Stallone Steel. Stallone has obtained data on workers' compensation losses for each of its workers for the last five years and has adjusted the historical data to current values based on inflation (and possible changes in workers' compensation benefits). The sample mean loss per worker (total losses during the sample period/number of workers) is $300 and the sample standard deviation (see Chapter 3) is $20,000. Because Stallone has 10,000 workers, it is willing to assume that the total losses for the upcoming year will be normally distributed with expected total loss of $3,000,000 (10,000 × $300) and a standard deviation of total losses of $2,000,000 (100 [the square root of 10,000] × $20,000).

Using the properties of the normal distribution, Stallone can estimate both the probability that losses are less than any given amount during the year and the maximum probable loss at any desired level of confidence. For example, there is a 0.95 probability that any normally distributed random variable is less than its expected value plus 1.645 standard deviations. Thus, Stallone's maximum probable loss at the 95 percent level is approximately $6,300,000 ($3,000,000 + 1.645 × $2,000,000). Similarly, there is a 0.99 probability that any normally distributed random variable is less than its expected value plus 2.33 standard deviations, which implies that Stallone's maximum probable loss at the 99 percent level is $7,660,000 ($3,000,000 + 2.33 × $2,000,000).

While the formulas are too complicated for us to cover here, the expected value and standard deviation of a normally distributed random variable that is "truncated" at particular points also can be readily calculated (using the right formula). This means, for example, that if Stallone decided to purchase excess insurance with a $5 million annual aggregate retention, it could calculate the expected value and standard deviation of retained losses (losses less than the $5 million retention limit).

Problems and Limitations

The principal limitation of assuming that losses are normally distributed is that the assumption often will be inappropriate in practice. First, the assumption is based on the central limit theorem, which simply describes a tendency as the number of exposures becomes infinitely large. Unless firms have very large numbers of exposures, the true distribution of total losses will likely exhibit positive skewness, and the difference from the normal distribution could be substantial. Compared to the true, positively skewed distribution, the normal distribution will tend to understate the probability of large losses. (We illustrate this result in the next section.) As a consequence, the firm will underestimate the likelihood of large, potentially disruptive losses.[2] This is not the type of mistake that firms wish to make.

Second, in many cases losses will not be independent across exposures. In the case of worker injuries, for example, many workers might be hurt in a single accident. Positive correlation in losses across exposures increases the standard deviation of total losses. Again, the result is that the procedure illustrated above will tend to underestimate the probability of large losses. In addition, the central limit theorem assumes independence so that assuming the normal distribution may produce significant errors even if a firm is very large.

A third limitation of the procedure illustrated above is that it does not facilitate analysis of per occurrence deductibles and policy limits. The reason is that the procedure provides estimates of the aggregate loss distribution only; it does not provide evidence about the loss distribution for individual losses (occurrences). As a consequence, while the method might help some firms make decisions about aggregate annual retention limits without per occurrence deductibles, it is not useful in the many cases where firms wish to consider limiting their exposure to losses from a single occurrence.

Computer Simulation of Loss Distributions

In many cases, realistic probability distributions for loss frequency and severity cannot be combined mathematically to derive the distribution of total losses. If, however, a firm is

---

[2]Actuaries and statisticians have developed several approximation methods to allow estimation of the maximum probable loss at specified confidence levels that incorporate information about skewness in the distribution of losses.

willing to estimate or make assumptions concerning the shape of the loss frequency and severity distributions, **computer simulation of loss distributions** using one of several software packages can be employed to estimate the probability distribution of total losses, as well as the effects of per occurrence deductibles and policy limits. Computer simulation also can be used to obtain this type of information on loss frequency and severity and expected losses. In general, computer simulation of loss distributions often provides a versatile and valuable method of providing insight into the distribution of losses and the effects of alternative risk management strategies. It does not rely on the assumption that total losses are normally distributed. While more difficult to do accurately, it also is possible to incorporate in the simulation assumptions concerning possible correlation in losses across exposures.

Illustration

We illustrate the method of computer simulation for the product liability exposure of Get-Well Pharmaceutical Company. Based on an analysis of its own data as well as industry data on product liability claims, Get-Well assumes that the frequency of lawsuits by consumers claiming damages for adverse reactions to drugs that it has manufactured can be reasonably approximated by a **Poisson distribution.** This probability distribution often is used to describe accident probabilities. The Poisson distribution assumes that the probability that an event will occur (such as an accident) is constant in any small time period. However, you do not need to worry about the technical details of this distribution. All that you need to recognize is that this distribution often provides a reasonable description of reality and that it gives the probability that there will be zero claims, one claim, two claims, and so on during a given year (or other specified time period).

Get-Well believes that the expected number of lawsuits during the year is 30, but it also wishes to allow for parameter uncertainty (see Chapter 10) that arises due, among other factors, to uncertainty associated with legal standards that will be applied to product-related injuries. Get-Well decides to allow for this uncertainty by making the assumptions shown in Table 26.3. In this way, Get-Well builds assumptions about uncertainty in the legal system into its analysis. In effect, it allows for increased risk due to dependence in claim frequency across exposures that can arise from changes in legal standards.

Based on analysis of historical data and published research on distributions for the severity of the costs of liability claims, Get-Well assumes that the loss severity will have the **lognormal distribution,** a distribution that is commonly used to describe the severity of property and liability losses.[3] For a random variable with a lognormal distribution, the natural logarithm of the variable's value has the normal distribution—thus the name *lognormal.* The lognormal distribution is characterized by positive skewness, as is true for most

TABLE 26.3
Get-Well's assumptions about expected claim frequency.

Legal Environment	Probability of Environment	Expected Annual Claim Frequency
Current standards applied	1/3	30
Stricter standards applied	1/3	20
More lenient standards applied	1/3	40

[3]For simplicity we assume that claim costs include defense costs and that all costs are discounted to present value.

severity distributions. Get-Well estimates that the expected value of the severity distribution is $100,000 and that the standard deviation is $300,000. If desirable, Get-Well also could allow for uncertainty in these parameters, but we assume that you will get the main idea without us going to any more trouble.

The loss frequency and severity distributions for Get-Well are illustrated in Figure 26.3. The first panel shows the claim frequency distribution assuming a Poisson distribution with an expected value of 30. Note that the distribution is bell shaped for an expected number of losses this large. For lower expected numbers of claims per period, such as 0.1, which might describe the frequency of your having an auto accident, the distribution would be highly skewed (large probability of no loss, increasingly small probabilities for one, two, three losses, etc.). The second panel shows the sample frequency distribution obtained by randomly drawing 1,000 outcomes (i.e., from 1,000 "trials" of a simulation) from a Poisson distribution where the expected value varies according to the assumptions shown in Table 26.3. As can be seen, allowing for uncertainty in the expected value increases the variability of claim frequency compared to the first panel. The third panel shows the sample distribution of 1,000 trials from a lognormal distribution with expected value equal to $100,000 and standard deviation equal to $300,000. Note that most claims are less than $600,000, but some are much larger.

Given these assumed distributions, Get-Well can use computer simulation to generate many years of hypothetical losses in order to estimate its probability distribution of losses and the effects of different insurance arrangements. The simulation proceeds as follows for each trial (year):

1. In the first step, an expected claim frequency is randomly sampled from the distribution shown in Table 26.3. The outcome of this step is either 20, 30, or 40.

2. In the second step, the number of claims is randomly sampled from a Poisson distribution with expected value determined by the first step. That is, if the first step produces an expected value of 20, then the sampled frequency distribution has an expected value of 20, and so on. The specific value drawn might be 4, 9, 19, 32, and so on.

3. In the third step, a claim severity amount for each claim is randomly sampled from a lognormal distribution with expected value of $100,000 and standard deviation of $300,000. For example, if the second step produces a claim frequency of 35, then 35 claim amounts are sampled in this step. The specific severities drawn might range from a very small loss to a loss in the millions of dollars.

4. Summing the claim severities sampled in step 3 yields the total loss for the given trial (year).

5. The effects of alternative insurance arrangements on the distribution of retained losses can be estimated using the output of the simulation by applying coverage limits and deductibles to the loss amounts generated in steps 3 and/or 4. For example, with a $500,000 per occurrence retention, Get-Well will retain the amount of each loss sampled in step 3 up to a maximum of $500,000.

6. Repeating steps 1 through 5 over many trials provides an estimate of the probability distribution of annual total losses and the probability distribution of annual retained losses for any arrangements considered in step 5.

We summarize the results of a 1,000 trial simulation of Get-Well's loss distribution and its retained losses for the three alternative insurance policies summarized in Table 26.4. The

FIGURE 26.3

Loss frequency and severity distributions for Get-Well.

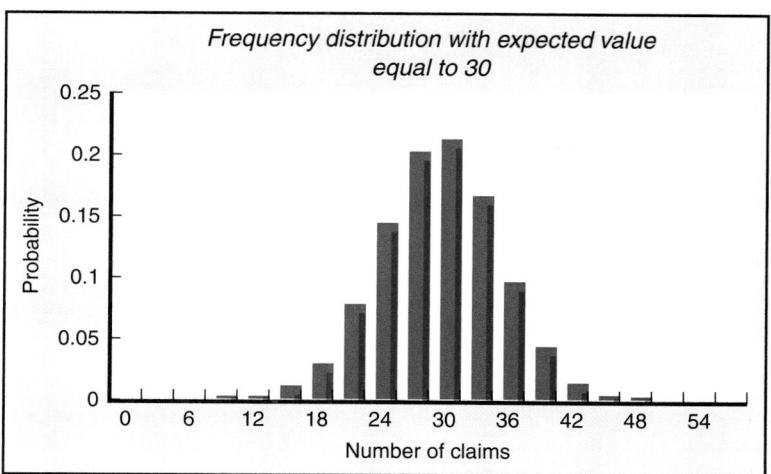

Frequency distribution with expected value equal to 30

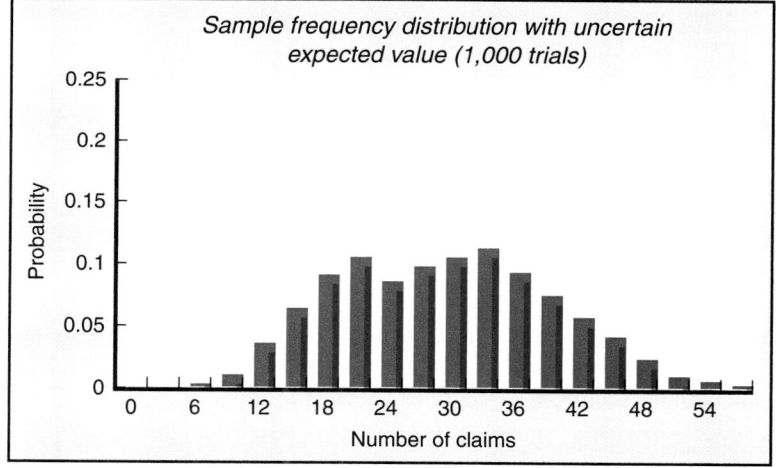

Sample frequency distribution with uncertain expected value (1,000 trials)

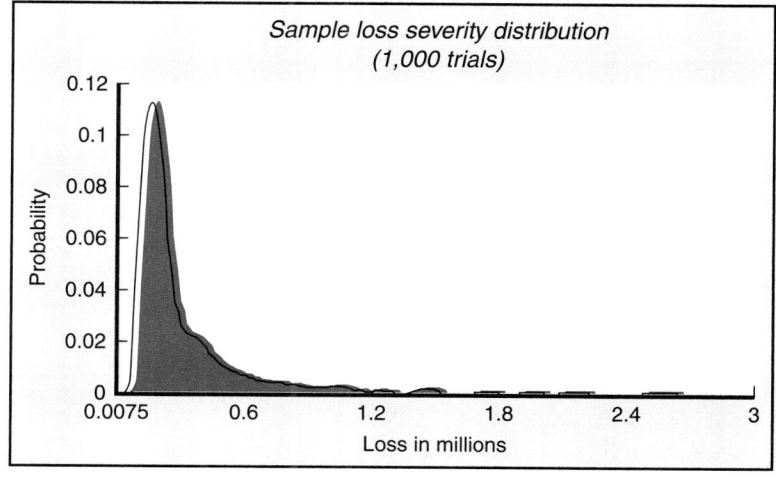

Sample loss severity distribution (1,000 trials)

TABLE 26.4
**Alternative
insurance
policies for
Get-Well.**

Policy	Per Occurrence Deductible	Per Occurrence Policy Limit	Aggregate Deductible	Aggregate Policy Limit	Premium
1	$ 500,000	$5,000,000	None	None	$780,000
2	$1,000,000	$5,000,000	None	None	$415,000
3	None	None	$6,000,000	$10,000,000	$165,000

first policy provides $5 million of coverage per occurrence above a $500,000 per occurrence retention (deductible) for a premium of $780,000.[4] Get-Well pays the first $500,000 of any loss. The insurer pays any amount above $500,000 up to its limit of $5 million (a total loss of $5.5 million). There is no aggregate annual policy limit. The second policy provides $5 million of coverage per occurrence above a $1 million per occurrence retention for a premium of $415,000, again with no aggregate annual policy limit. The third policy provides an aggregate annual limit of $10 million in excess of a $6 million aggregate annual retention. There is no per occurrence limit or deductible. Get-Well pays the first $6 million of losses during the year; the insurer pays the next $10 million. Get-Well has to pay any losses above $16 million. The premium is $165,000.

Figure 26.4 shows the simulated distribution of total losses and retained losses for the alternative retention/insurance plans. Using the simulated distribution, Table 26.5 shows the mean, standard deviation, and maximum probable value of retained losses at the 95 percent level for each alternative. It also shows the maximum value of retained losses, the probability that total losses will exceed the insurance coverage limits, and the probability that retained losses will be less than or equal to $6 million. Since retained losses are only one component of the cost of risk, Table 26.5 also shows the mean total cost, defined as the mean value of retained losses plus the insurance premium, and the maximum probable total cost at the 95 percent level.

Based on the maximum probable total cost at the 95 percent level and the standard deviation of retained losses, the least risky strategy for Get-Well is the policy with the $500,000 per occurrence retention, followed in order of increasing risk by the $1 million per occurrence retention policy, the $6 million aggregate annual retention policy, and no insurance.[5] (Note, however, that this order does not hold for the maximum value of retained losses obtained in the 1,000 trials because more of a very large loss in one year was paid by the $10 million aggregate limit policy than by the $5 million per occurrence limit policies.) Due to savings on insurance premium loadings from increased retention, the ranking in terms of the mean total cost (premium plus mean retained loss) is reversed. The $500,000 per occurrence retention policy is the most expensive strategy, followed by the $1 million retention policy, the $6 million aggregate annual retention policy, and no insurance.

Based on this information, Get-Well can make an informed decision about which strategy to pursue. For example, it can decide whether the additional risk reduction made possible by the $500,000 per occurrence retention policy compared to the $6 million aggregate

---

[4] The premiums used in the example equals estimates of the expected value of insured claim costs obtained from the simulation, plus a loading charge equal to $25,000, plus 20 percent of expected claim costs, rounded to the nearest $5,000.

[5] Because the premium is not random, the standard deviation of the total cost equals the standard deviation of retained losses.

FIGURE 26.4 **Simulated distributions of retained losses for alternative retention arrangements (1,000 trials).**

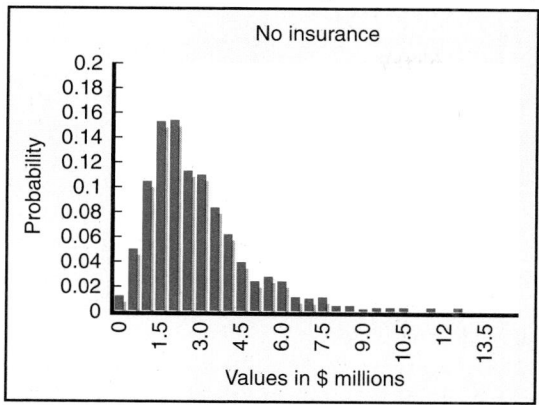

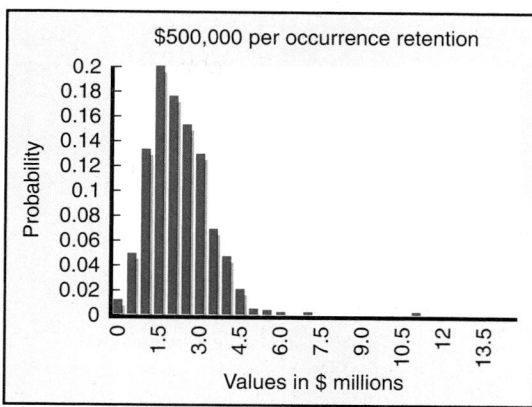

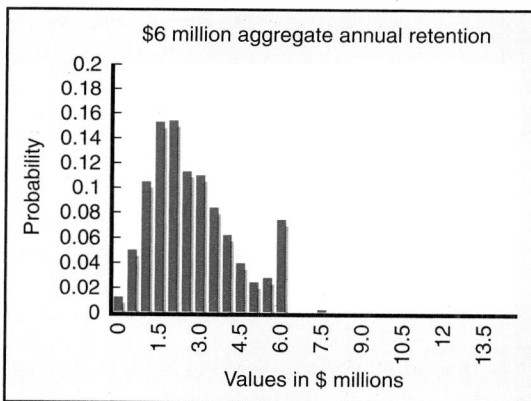

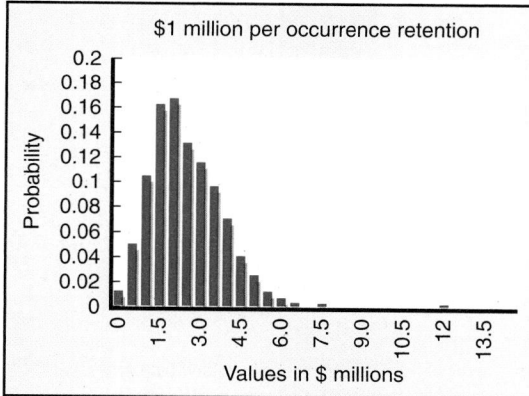

retention policy is worth the additional expected cost of $104,000 ($3,194,000 − $3,090,000).

Comparison of Results to Assuming the Normal Distribution

We noted earlier that assuming that losses have the normal distribution can cause a firm to underestimate its maximum probable loss (at a given percentage level) if the true loss distribution is positively skewed. As can be seen in Figure 26.4, the simulated distribution of total losses for Get-Well is positively skewed. Consider what would happen if Get-Well assumed that total losses had the normal distribution with the expected value and standard deviation equal to the mean and standard deviation for the simulated distribution of total losses shown in the "no insurance" column of Table 26.5. The predicted maximum probable total loss at the 95 percent level assuming the normal distribution equals $6,067,000 (the mean value of $3,042,000 plus 1.645 times the standard deviation of $1,839,000). This amount is 6 percent lower than $6,462,000, the simulated value of the maximum probable loss at the 95 percent level. You also should recall that assuming the normal distribution for

TABLE 26.5
Simulation results for alternative insurance/retention plans (1,000 trials in the simulation; all dollar values in $1,000s).

Statistic	Policy 1 ($5 million excess $500,000 per occurrence retention)	Policy 2 ($5 million excess $1 million per occurrence retention)	Policy 3 ($10 million excess $6 million aggregate retention)	No Insurance
Mean value of retained losses	$2,414	$2,716	$2,925	$3,042
Standard deviation of retained losses	1,065	1,293	1,494	1,839
Maximum probable retained loss at 95% level	4,254	5,003	6,000	6,462
Maximum value of retained losses	11,325	12,125	7,899	18,898
Probability that losses exceed policy limits	1.1%	0.7%	0.1%	n.a.
Probability that retained losses ≤ $6 million	99.7%	98.7%	99.9%	92.7%
Premium	$780	$415	$165	$0
Mean total cost	3,194	3,131	3,090	3,042
Maximum probable total cost at 95% level	5,034	5,418	6,165	6,462

total losses would not allow Get-Well to evaluate the effects of per occurrence retention and coverage limits.

Limitations of Computer Simulation

Computer simulation can be a valuable tool in guiding decision making to the extent that reasonable assumptions or estimates of the shape and parameters (e.g., the expected value and standard deviation) of loss frequency and severity distributions can be obtained. The principal limitation of the method arises from parameter uncertainty: At best, the inputs to the simulation are only estimates of the true parameters and distributions. It might be especially difficult to incorporate accurate information about dependence in losses across exposures. Note, however, that parameter uncertainty can be incorporated in the analysis, as was illustrated for Get-Well in the case of claim frequency. In addition, different simulations can be run to examine the sensitivity of the results to different assumptions concerning the type and parameters of the assumed frequency and severity distributions. For example, Get-Well might examine the results assuming that claim frequency is described by one of the commonly used alternatives to the Poisson distribution.

26.4 Correlation Analysis

In Chapter 3, we discussed correlation between two random variables. Recall that two random variables can be positively correlated, negatively correlated, or uncorrelated. In this section, we describe how to calculate correlation coefficients and present an application.

The **correlation coefficient,** which is typically denoted by the Greek letter rho (ρ), between two random variables, X and Y, is defined as the covariance between X and Y divided by the product of the standard deviations of X and Y:

$$\rho = \frac{\text{Cov}(X,Y)}{\text{Std}(X)\,\text{Std}(Y)}$$

The correlation coefficient is always within the range -1 through 1.

A correlation coefficient of -1 indicates perfect negative correlation; that is, X and Y move in opposite directions and by equal amounts in units of standard deviation relative to their expected values. For example, if the realization of X is above its expected value by one standard deviation, then Y will be below its expected value by one standard deviation. To give a numerical example, suppose that X has an expected value of 5 and a standard deviation of 10, and Y has an expected value of 6 and a standard deviation of 3. Then, if the correlation coefficient between X and Y is -1, and we observe an X value of 15 (one standard deviation above its expected value), then Y will take on the value of 3 (one standard deviation below its expected value).

A correlation coefficient of 1 indicates perfect positive correlation, that is, X and Y move in the same direction and by equal amounts relative to their expected values in units of standard deviation. Using the numerical example above, but changing the correlation coefficient to 1, if we observe X taking a value of 15, then we observe Y taking a value of 9.

A correlation coefficient of zero indicates that the random variables are uncorrelated; that is, the outcome of one variable does not provide information about the likely outcome of the other variable. A value of ρ between -1 and 0 indicates that the variables are negatively correlated (but not perfectly). Negatively correlated variables tend to move in opposite directions, but they do not always move in opposite directions. The closer ρ is to -1, the greater the likelihood that the variables will move in opposite directions. A value of ρ between 0 and 1 indicates that the variables are positively correlated and therefore tend to move in same direction. Again, the closer ρ is to 1, the greater the likelihood that the variables will move together.

The typical method of calculating the correlation coefficient between two variables is to gather historical data on each variable and then calculate the sample covariance between the two variables and divide by the sample standard deviations. The sample covariance can be calculated as follows:

$$\text{sample covariance between } X \text{ and } Y = \frac{\sum_{t=1}^{T}(x_t - \bar{x})(y_t - \bar{y})}{T - 1}$$

where T is the number of observations, x_t and y_t are observations for X and Y during period t, $\bar{x}$ and $\bar{y}$ are the sample means for X and Y. The sample standard deviation is given by the formula:

$$\text{sample standard deviation for } X = \sqrt{\frac{\sum_{t=1}^{T}(x_t - \bar{x})^2}{T - 1}}$$

TABLE 26.6
Correlation between McMinn's fuel costs and the price of oil.

Month	Barrels of Fuel Purchased	Fuel Cost per Barrel	Total Fuel Costs	Price of Oil
1	9,915	$23.26	$230,646	$24.80
2	10,372	28.51	295,751	28.95
3	9,737	29.58	288,018	29.29
4	9,354	25.69	240,351	27.49
5	9,041	28.95	261,729	28.13
6	9,738	23.07	224,692	22.90
7	12,309	26.48	325,962	27.24
8	10,618	26.45	280,857	26.85
9	9,337	22.34	208,585	21.41
10	8,313	27.30	226,941	28.47
11	9,961	17.89	178,179	18.55
12	9,278	24.47	227,045	25.16
13	11,650	24.96	290,768	25.14
14	10,223	20.37	208,251	22.75
15	10,084	28.17	284,020	27.59
16	9,975	25.51	254,451	27.01
17	10,532	25.52	268,733	25.02
18	11,337	23.74	269,158	24.40
19	11,738	19.66	230,752	20.25
20	10,609	27.78	294,699	28.71
21	8,427	23.92	201,610	24.92
22	10,258	29.55	303,126	27.84
23	10,063	26.16	263,265	26.17
24	9,807	20.35	199,570	21.96
Correlation Coefficient with Price of Oil		0.95	0.73	1.00

One application of correlation coefficients is for assessing basis risk associated with a hedging instrument (Chapter 25). Table 26.6 gives data for fuel purchased (in barrels), fuel cost per barrel, and total fuel costs for McMinn Trucking Company during a 24-month period, as well as the price of oil on which a futures contract is based. McMinn would like to know whether the futures contract is likely to provide a good hedge for its fuel costs. McMinn therefore calculates the correlation coefficient between its per barrel fuel costs and the price of oil and the correlation coefficient between its total fuel costs and the price of oil. As indicated at the bottom of the table, the correlation between the per barrel fuel cost is 0.95, indicating that the price of oil and McMinn fuel costs per barrel are highly correlated. However, the correlation between McMinn's *total* fuel costs and the price of oil is only 0.73. The reason for the lower correlation with total fuel costs is because of the variation over time in the amount of fuel purchased by McMinn. Thus, the futures contract would have relatively little basis risk with McMinn's per unit fuel costs, but considerable basis risk with McMinn's total fuel costs.

26.5   Use of Discounted Cash Flow Analysis

The Net Present Value Criterion

To analyze the effects of risk management decisions that involve cash flows over multiple periods, it is necessary to discount the expected net cash flows to present value. Discounting cash flows was employed to determine the fair price of insurance in Chapter 8, to illustrate the effects of risk management on firm value in Chapter 20, and to illustrate the tax consequences of insurance versus retention in Chapter 21. In this section we review the key concept and illustrate its application.

Assuming that cash flows occur initially (beginning of year 1) and then at the end of each year for n years, the discounted value of expected net cash flows equals:

$$\sum_{t=0}^{n} \frac{E(NCF_t)}{(1+r)^t} \tag{26.1}$$

where $E(NCF_t)$ is the expected value of the net cash flow in year t and r is the opportunity cost of capital. It is important that the numerators in equation 26.1 reflect cash flows, not accounting earnings.

Many risk management decisions involve a comparatively large up-front investment of funds that produces positive expected net cash flows in future years. For example, the earlier example of the decision to install sprinklers was of this type. In these cases, the expression for the discounted value of expected net cash flows is known as the **net present value** of the investment. The net present value often is written in a slightly different way to emphasize the initial cash outflow for the investment (which we denote as I_0):

$$\sum_{t=0}^{t=n} \frac{E(NCF_t)}{(1+r)^t} - I_0 \tag{26.2}$$

Calculating Incremental Expected Cash Flows

When using discounted cash flow analysis, it is important to properly calculate expected cash flows. Always remember that only incremental cash flows are relevant; that is, the cash flows that change as a result of the decision being considered. To illustrate how to calculate expected cash flows, suppose that Zoe Building Supply is considering building a fence around its premises to reduce theft losses. For simplicity, we assume that the firm will only exist for three years, the fence will cost $150,000, and it will be depreciated using straight-line depreciation over three years. The fence will reduce theft losses by $55,000 each year and, therefore, increase net sales revenue (sales revenue less theft losses) by that amount. Security expenses also will be reduced each year by $15,000.

Table 26.6 shows how Zoe could calculate the expected incremental cash flows from the fence project. The only cash flow immediately is the capital investment of $150,000. For years 1 through 3, the reduction in theft losses increases expected cash flows by $55,000, security costs decrease by $15,000, and depreciation expense increases by $50,000 ($150,000 divided by three), resulting in an increase in earnings before interest and taxes of $20,000. Using a 34 percent tax rate, taxes increase by $6,800, yielding an increase in

TABLE 26.6   Incremental expected cash flows from Zoe's fence project.

	This Year	Year 1	Year 2	Year 3
Capital investment	−$150,000			
Reduction in theft losses		$55,000	$55,000	$55,000
Reduction in security		15,000	15,000	15,000
Depreciation		50,000	50,000	50,000
Earnings before interest and taxes		20,000	20,000	20,000
Taxes (34%)		6,800	6,800	6,800
After-tax earnings		13,200	13,200	13,200
Cash flow adjustments				
Add depreciation		50,000	50,000	50,000
Expected net cash flow		63,200	63,200	63,200
PV of cash flow				
(10% discount rate)	−$150,000	57,454	52,231	47,483
NPV =	$ 7,169			

after-tax earnings of $13,200. Earnings, however, are not cash flows. Depreciation expenses need to be added back because depreciation is not a cash flow.[6] After making the cash flow adjustments to after-tax earnings, the expected cash flows from the project can be calculated: $63,200 in years one through three. Assuming that the appropriate discount rate is 10 percent, the present value of the expected cash flows can be calculated. Summing the present values of the individual expected cash flows, we find that the net present value of the project is $7,169. Assuming Zoe is confident in all of the assumptions, the fence project should be undertaken.

Example: Forming a Captive Insurer

To provide another illustration of the use of discounted cash flow analysis, consider the case of Long-Haul Trucking. Long-Haul currently has an annual self-insured retention of $500,000 per occurrence for both workers' compensation and auto liability insurance. The combined premium for its excess workers' compensation insurance, which pays losses without a per occurrence limit, and for excess auto liability coverage, with a $3 million per occurrence limit, is $2.15 million. Long-Haul is considering establishing a captive in Vermont to fund its retained losses. If it forms the captive, it will incur start-up costs in the amount of $140,000 for licensing the captive and one-time administrative costs. This expenditure can be regarded as the initial investment required to establish the captive.

    If Long-Haul forms the captive, it will be able to obtain comparable excess coverage in the reinsurance market for an annual premium of $2 million, for a savings of $150,000. (Thus, in this example, other cash flows also occur at the time that the investment is made.) Long-Haul also plans to use a captive management firm to administer the captive on an ongoing basis. The fees paid to this firm will increase its total administrative costs by $30,000 per year. If it establishes the captive, Long-Haul also will use a fronting arrangement with

[6]Similarly, any change in working capital (inventory, accounts receivable, accounts payable) resulting from the project would be cash flows.

an insurance company to meet state requirements concerning the purchase of coverage from an admitted insurer (see Chapter 21). The fronting insurer then will reinsure the coverage with the captive, which in turn will purchase the excess reinsurance coverage. The fee for this fronting arrangement is $80,000 per year.

Long-Haul plans to pay the same amount to the captive to fund its retained losses as it maintains under its current program, and it will not change the way in which funds are invested. In addition, it does not plan to write outside business in the captive or to seek to have the transactions with the captive treated as insurance for federal income tax purposes. As a result, neither its investment income on assets dedicated to fund retained losses nor its income taxes will be affected by the establishment of the captive.

Table 26.7 shows the *change in expected cash flows* for Long-Haul from forming the captive assuming that premium payments and other expenses are paid at the beginning of each year and that all costs are tax deductible when paid. For simplicity, the example assumes a five-year time horizon and that the fees and premium savings do not change during this period. Under these assumptions, Long-Haul will incur a net after-tax cash outflow of $66,000 upon establishing the captive (beginning of year 1) and a net cash inflow of $26,400 at the end of years 1 through 4.

Given these data and assuming an opportunity cost of capital equal to 10 percent, the net present value of establishing the captive is:

$$\text{NPV} = -66,000 + \frac{26,400}{1.1} + \frac{26,400}{1.1^2} + \frac{26,400}{1.1^3} + \frac{26,400}{1.1^4} = \$17,685 \quad (26.3)$$

Because the net present value is positive, the managers of Long-Haul can increase the firm's value by establishing the captive. The reason is that the savings in premiums from direct access to the reinsurance market outweigh the start-up costs and increased administrative costs.

Other applications of discounted cash flow analysis in risk management include choosing from a larger number of loss financing alternatives and making decisions concerning investments in loss control. With multiple loss financing options, it is customary to estimate the discounted value of expected net cash outflows for retained losses, insurance premiums, and other costs and choose the method with the lowest discounted cost. Since only two options were considered in the captive example, it was simpler to calculate the discounted value of the change in expected net cash flows from forming the captive compared to the current self-insurance arrangement. Investments in loss control commonly apply the net present value criterion once the size and timing of expected net cash flows have been estimated.

TABLE 26.7
Change in Long-Haul's expected net cash flows from establishing a captive.

Type of Cash Flow	Time Period	
	Beginning of First Year	End of Years 1, 2, 3, 4
Captive start-up costs	−$140,000	$ 0
Captive administration fee	−30,000	−30,000
Fronting fee	−80,000	−80,000
Reduction in excess insurance premium	150,000	150,000
Total before-tax cash flow	−100,000	40,000
Income tax (34%)	34,000	−13,600
Total after-tax cash flow	−66,000	26,400

The Appropriate Cost of Capital

Basic financial theory suggests that the cost of capital used in discounting the expected net cash flows for a particular investment (or cost) should reflect the nondiversifiable risk associated with that particular investment. The key idea is that the rate of return required to compensate shareholders for risk will depend on the riskiness of the cash flows of the particular project from the shareholders' perspective. Since shareholders generally are assumed to be diversified, the appropriate way to measure the riskiness of the cash flows is by the amount of nondiversifiable risk.

In practice, risk managers sometimes must choose between two alternative (mutually exclusive) methods of financing losses that have different patterns of expenditures but do not materially affect the variability of *any of the firm's cash flows* (e.g., insurance premiums, losses, or other cash flows). In these cases, the appropriate cost of capital for discounting these expenditures is the rate that the firm would use to discount riskless cash flows. For example, Long-Haul's decision to form a captive versus paying losses from internal funds does not change the expected value or the risk associated with retained losses. Consequently, the decision to form a captive depends critically on the present value of the costs of forming a captive (the fronting fees, administrative costs, etc.). Since these cash flows generally are certain or their risk is diversifiable, the cash flows associated with captive formation (or other retention methods that do not affect the level of retained losses) should be treated as riskless.

26.6   Summary

- Larger firms often conduct a detailed statistical analysis to estimate the probability distribution of retained losses/costs for different types of losses and loss financing arrangements, or to estimate key features of these loss distributions, such as the expected value, standard deviation, and maximum probable loss.

- Historical loss data can be used to identify areas within a firm that might have unusually high frequency or severity of losses.

- Regression analysis can be used to forecast loss distribution characteristics.

- While loss distributions sometimes can be approximated with the normal distribution, problems and limitations of assuming the normal distribution often favor more elaborate and accurate estimation methods. In particular, computer simulation can be used in many cases to obtain more accurate estimates of losses and costs for different loss financing arrangements.

- Discounted cash flow analysis often is used by firms to compare the net present value of various loss control and loss financing decisions. This procedure requires an estimation of the expected value and timing of cash flows for each alternative and the choice of an appropriate discount rate in view of the risk of the cash flows.

Key Terms

linear regression line 574
computer simulation of loss distributions 577
Poisson distribution 577

lognormal distribution 577
correlation coefficient 583
net present value 585

Questions and Problems

1. Use the following data to calculate expected total losses for 2003 assuming that the probability distributions of frequency and severity have been and will continue to be stable.

Year	Frequency of Accidents	Average Accident Severity	Inflation Rate during Year
1996	33	$1,800	2.0%
1997	25	2,100	1.5
1998	35	3,000	2.5
1999	31	2,800	1.5
2000	29	3,100	2.0
2001	27	3,200	1.8
2002	34	3,500	1.5

(handwritten: 109, 11000, 1500, 3400)

2. What is the correlation coefficient between Irwin's sales and costs and between sales and GNP growth?

Year	GNP growth	Sales	Costs
1990	2.0%	$105,400	$71,000
1991	1.5	101,900	72,200
1992	−2.0	100,400	72,300
1993	−1.0	102,200	72,500
1994	0.5	104,000	72,000
1995	−1.0	99,950	71,300
1996	1.0	103,300	72,300
1997	2.0	102,800	72,100
1998	2.5	104,900	72,300
1999	0.0	100,100	72,500
2000	2.0	104,600	71,200
2001	1.5	102,000	71,730
2002	3.0	103,300	70,600

3. Describe the major steps involved in a computer simulation of loss distributions. Also describe the advantages of computer simulation (compared to assuming that losses have the normal distribution) and the limitations of computer simulation.

4. Wood Warehousing has property insurance on a replacement cost basis with a $5,000 per occurrence deductible. It can install automatic sprinklers in its warehouse for an initial cost of $10,000. The sprinklers will last five years (they would last much longer in real life). Annual upkeep of the sprinklers will be $1,000, payable at the end of each of the first four years from the time of installation. If Wood installs the sprinklers, it will deduct one-fifth of the installation price at the end of each year for five years as depreciation (a noncash expense) for tax purposes. Without the sprinklers, the firm believes that its expected cash outflow for losses less than the deductible will be $1,000 per year and that its insurance premium will be $10,000 per year. With the sprinklers, it believes that its expected cash outflow for losses less than the deductible will be $500 per year and that its insurance premium will be $7,000 per year. Wood's opportunity cost of capital for this decision is 10 percent. Retained losses are paid and deductible for tax purposes at the end of each year. Insurance premiums are paid at the beginning of the year and are deductible for tax purposes when paid. The tax rate is 34 percent. Should Wood install the sprinklers? Support your answer by calculating the net present value of installing the sprinklers.

5. Seward Go-Carts has annual sales of $150 million with an expected profit of $5 million. It currently has a retention limit for annual liability losses equal to $5 million. The premium for excess insurance coverage above the $5 million retention is $50,000. With the $5 million retention, its expected retained losses (including claims settlement costs) for accidents during the year equal $1 million. Half of all retained losses for accidents during the year will be paid at the end of the year; the remaining half will be paid at the end of the next year. If Seward changes its retention level to $2 million, the premium for excess coverage will be $170,000. Its expected retained losses for accidents during the year will drop to $900,000. Again, half of retained losses for accidents during the year will be paid at the end of the year; the remaining half will be

paid at the end of the second year. Premiums are paid at the beginning of the year. Seward's opportunity cost of capital for this decision is 10 percent. The tax rate is 34 percent. The decision horizon is one year of coverage because the firm can change its retention level again the following year. (Note, however, that cash flows associated with the decision occur over two years.)

(*a*) Calculate the present value of the after-tax *change in expected net cash flows* from reducing Seward's retention level from $5 million to $2 million.

(*b*) Calculate the present value of the after-tax change in net cash flows from reducing Seward's retention level *assuming that actual retained losses equal the retention limits* rather than the expected values.

(*c*) Which approach do you think the firm should take? Why? What factors (other than the present values that you calculated) would be likely to influence its decision?

References

Holler, Keith D. "The Confidence Game: Using Confidence Levels to Estimate Losses." *Risk Management,* August 1995, pp. 53–57.

(Practitioner-oriented introduction to estimation of losses, including the use of computer simulation.)

Chapter 27

Enterprise Risk Management: A Case Study

Chapter Objectives

- Describe enterprise risk management.
- Illustrate enterprise risk management as well as many of the concepts and tools presented in previous chapters with a real-world case.

27.1 Enterprise Risk Management

For many corporate risk managers, risk management refers to the management of pure risks; for example, losses arising from property damage, liability suits, and worker injuries.[1] These risks typically are managed individually through a combination of loss control and loss financing. To many financial managers, however, risk management refers to the management of price risks (e.g., exchange rate risk, interest rate risk, commodity price risks, and credit risk). These risks usually are managed through derivative contracts, such as options, forwards, futures, and swaps (see Chapter 24). Most corporations manage financial risks separately from pure risks, often within separate departments, and the terminology and methods used by financial risk managers often differ from those used by pure risk managers.

This silo approach to risk management was seriously questioned during the latter part of the 1990s by many consultants and risk management professionals. They argued that a firm should identify and measure (when possible) all of its risk exposures and manage them within a unified framework. This idea came to be known as **enterprise risk management (ERM).** To facilitate ERM, some corporations established a new position—the chief risk officer.[2]

---

[1]Much of the material in this chapter is taken from Harrington, Niehaus, and Risko (2002).

[2]Examples include St. Paul, Duke Energy, Credit Agricole Indusuez (Lam, 2001).

Proponents of enterprise risk management suggest that the exercise of identifying and measuring all of a firm's risk exposures is valuable in and of itself, because the process provides managers with a better understanding of their business and the events that can potentially hinder the firm's strategic objectives. Thus, a potential benefit of ERM is that managers will make better decisions as a result of having a better understanding of the firm's risk. Consistent with this logic, several organizations concerned with corporate governance have recommended that firms engage in a comprehensive risk assessment process and adopt appropriate risk management policies. For example, the 1994 Dey Report issued by the Toronto Stock Exchange and the 1999 Turnbull Report issued by the London Stock Exchange recommend that boards of directors of listed corporations be responsible for making sure that a corporation identify its principal risks and implement appropriate systems to manage those risks.

As discussed previously in Chapter 22, several of the reasons why firms should reduce risk (e.g., to avoid costly financial distress) suggest that firms should be concerned about the risk associated with some aggregate financial variable, such as earnings or cash flows, which depends on a number of underlying risk exposures. Thus, the idea that all of an enterprise's risk exposures should be identified and managed in a unified framework is consistent with several of the theories for why firms should reduce risk.

The remainder of the chapter discusses how United Grain Growers (UGG) implemented an enterprise risk management process during the late 1990s. As the case discusses, UGG followed the risk management process described in this book: After they identified their exposures, they quantified them (using statistical methods and Monte Carlo simulation). This process illustrated that weather was the main source of unmanaged risk. They then considered alternative methods of dealing with weather risk, including retention, shifting the risk using a weather derivative contract, or shifting it using an insurance contract. The chapter does not reveal the choice that UGG eventually made, but leaves the solution for students to answer in the end-of-chapter questions.

27.2   Enterprise Risk Management at United Grain Growers

Background on UGG

Based in Winnipeg, Manitoba, United Grain Growers (UGG) provides commercial services to farmers and markets agricultural products worldwide.[1] It was founded in 1906 as a farmer-owned cooperative and became a publicly traded company on the Toronto and Winnipeg stock exchanges in 1993. Although UGG is a public company, it retains some of its farmer cooperative roots. The company has both members and shareholders. An individual can be both a member and a shareholder. Although a member is not entitled to share in any profit or distribution by the company (unless the member is also a shareholder), members have control rights. Of the 15 people on UGG's board of directors, 12 must be members who are elected by delegates representing various geographical regions.

UGG is comprised of four main business segments: Grain Handling Services, Crop Production Services, Livestock Services, and Business Communications. As illustrated in Figure 27.1 and discussed below, UGG's four business units help farmers plan, produce, and market their products.

Western Canada is a major producer and exporter of wheat, barley, canola, and other grains and oilseeds. The role of UGG's Grain Handling Services unit is to identify sources

---

[1] Some of the information has changed due to UGG's merger with another company in 2002.

FIGURE 27.1 United Grain Growers main business.

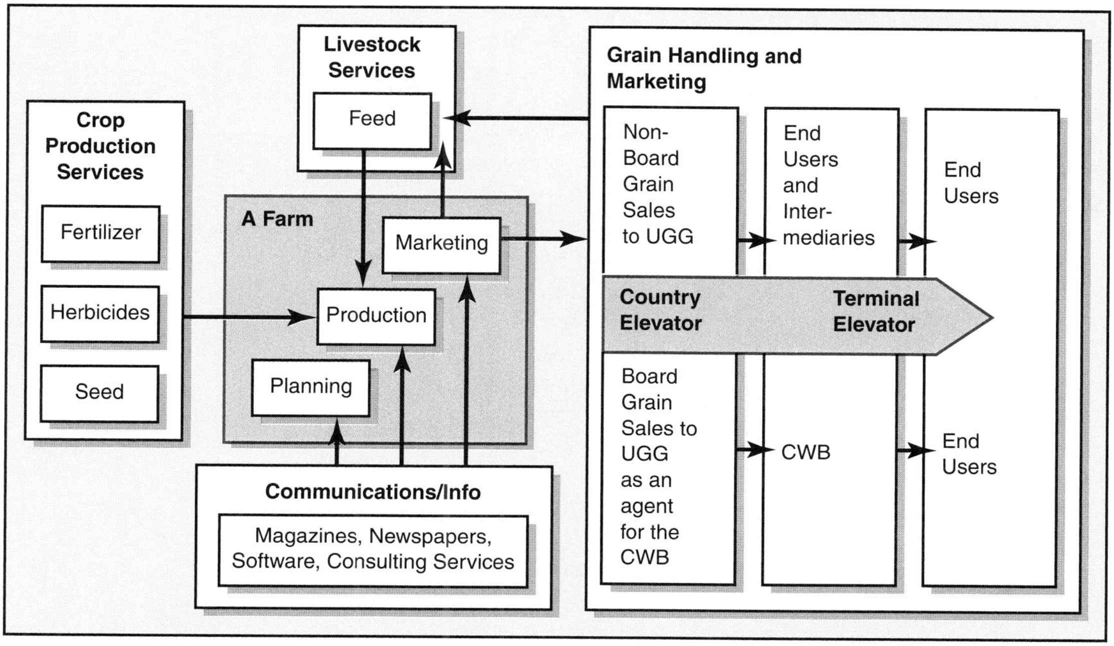

Source: United Grain Growers.

of grain and oilseeds and deliver them to exporters and to domestic end users, such as food processors. A farmer's production of grain and oilseeds usually is transported to a country elevator, where the product is weighed, graded, blended, purchased, and stored. From the elevator, the product is shipped to a domestic consumer (e.g., a mill) or to an export terminal. UGG historically owned hundreds of relatively small country elevators, which the firm has been replacing with a smaller number of large, more efficient elevators with high-throughput.

The farming industry in Canada is regulated by several government agencies. The Canadian Wheat Board (CWB) markets grains for human consumption on behalf of farmers. About 85 percent of the wheat and 45 percent of the barley produced in Canada is sold through the CWB. The CWB must ensure that the sales it has arranged are available to customers at the agreed-upon site and date. Thus, the CWB contracts with companies like UGG to collect, store, and deliver grains. About 60 percent of UGG's grain handling unit's business is on behalf of the CWB. The CWB determines the prices paid to farmers and the prices for storage and transportation of their grains.

The Canadian Grain Commission regulates grain handling and maintains quality standards for Canadian grain. Firms like UGG must obtain an operating license from the commission. The commission also maintains extensive records of the grain that is shipped from country elevators and from export terminals. Table 27.1 provides data on grain shipments and deliveries for the industry and for UGG from 1981 through 1999. UGG has a market share of approximately 15 percent, which makes it the third largest provider of grain handling services in western Canada. Table 27.2 provides information on the volume of grain

TABLE 27.1
Data on industry grain volume and UGG's grain volume (in tonnes) and the weighted average crop yields (bushels per acre).

| | Tonnes | | Weighted Average Crop Yields in Previous Year* |
	Industry Shipments	UGG Shipments	
1981	26,871	4,298	30.9
1982	30,392	4,842	34.7
1983	33,142	5,367	37.4
1984	33,905	5,320	33.3
1985	27,183	4,020	28.6
1986	27,443	4,394	32.5
1987	33,322	5,368	40.0
1988	33,435	5,072	36.3
1989	23,364	3,928	26.3
1990	29,682	4,954	31.3
1991	33,376	5,498	38.4
1992	34,374	5,720	37.3
1993	30,989	5,125	37.0
1994	33,489	5,503	
1995	35,898	6,059	
1996	29,877	4,937	
1997	35,663	5,591	
1998	33,921	5,170	
1999	29,729	4,328	

* Data for 1994–1999 are not available.

shipped by UGG, as well as UGG's gross margin and earnings on grain shipments. The table also provides information on gross margin and earnings per tonne of grain shipments.

The Crop Production Services unit provides inputs (e.g., seed, fertilizer, and crop protection products) to farmers. In addition, through its Farm Sales and Services division, it provides a range of consulting, agronomic, and financial services to farmers. UGG tries to differentiate itself from its competitors by developing distinctive products sold under brand names and by providing superior services to farmers.

TABLE 27.2
Earnings for grain handling segment.

| | For years ended July 31 | | |
	1997	1998	1999
Grain shipments (tonnes)	5,591	5,170	4,328
Gross margin (thousands of C$)	113,013	112,459	93,542
Expenses excluding depreciation	73,108	72,886	69,140
Depreciation	11,502	9,763	10,082
Earnings before interest and taxes	28,403	29,810	14,320
Per Tonne of Grain Shipped			
Gross margin	20.2	21.8	21.6
Earnings before interest and taxes	5.1	5.8	3.3

UGG's third largest unit, Livestock Services, provides inputs to producers of cattle, hogs, and poultry. This unit also faces competition from a number of other grain and feed companies. UGG's smallest business unit, Farm Business Communications, provides information needed to run a profitable agribusiness. In addition to publishing periodicals (*Farm Investor Newsletter* and *Disease, Weeds & Insects*), this unit has developed Web-based information on weather, market prices, and agribusiness news.

Figure 27.2 illustrates earnings before interest and taxes (EBIT) for each of UGG's business units over time. The two largest lines of business, Grain Handling Services and Crop Production Services, account for more than 80 percent of UGG's earnings in most years. The figure also illustrates the substantial earnings volatility in these main business segments.

Table 27.3 contains information from UGG's balance sheet, income, and cash flow statements. Earnings before interest, taxes, depreciation, and amortization (EBITDA) declined substantially in 1999 relative to the prior years. UGG increased capital expenditures substantially in 1998 and then again in 1999. Most of these expenditures were for large grain elevators with high throughput. As a result of the low EBITDA in 1999, UGG's return on equity (defined as net earnings to book value of equity) was just 1.17 percent. Note as well that in 1999, the percentage of the firm's total assets financed with debt increased to 36.76 percent with the issuance of another $50 million in long-term debt.

UGG's Analysis

UGG started its enterprise risk management process by forming a risk management committee, consisting of the CEO, CFO, risk manager, treasurer, compliance manager (for commodity trading), and manager of corporate audit services. This committee, along with a number of UGG employees, then met with a representative from Willis Group Ltd., a major insurance broker, for a brainstorming session to identify and qualitatively rank the firm's major risks. This process identified 47 exposure areas, from which the top 6 were chosen

FIGURE 27.2
Earnings before interest and taxes over time for UGG's business segments.

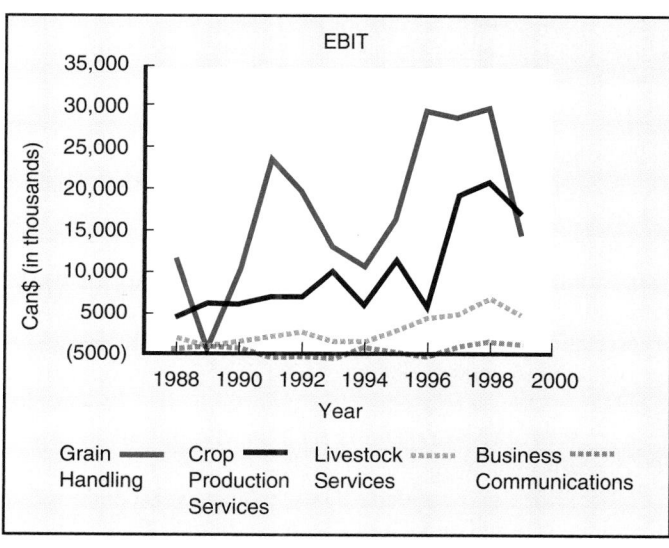

TABLE 27.3 Consolidated financial highlights.

For the years ended July 31 (In thousands except per share amounts)	Restated 1994	1995	1996	1997	1998	1999
Operating						
Gross profit and revenue from services	$156,030	$185,637	$198,749	$216,260	$224,953	**$209,227**
Earnings before interest, taxes, and depreciation	25,538	30,573	40,198	54,788	60,577	**42,423**
Operating income	12,612	15,151	24,090	38,452	43,335	**21,636**
Earnings before income taxes and unusual items	3,772	282	8,065	24,744	31,926	**8,067**
Net earnings	153	−7,385	5,851	9,059	16,332	**3,575**
Cash flow provided by operations	12,533	16,177	21,322	32,770	35,871	**29,853**
Capital expenditures and business acquisitions	27,725	43,894	26,826	21,904	53,760	**91,002**
Financial						
Working capital	$ 75,028	$ 44,573	$ 71,557	$101,790	$136,155	**$119,249**
Net investment in capital assets	153,228	182,079	190,308	193,323	226,304	**287,442**
Total assets	564,043	544,284	531,416	489,214	515,209	**554,322**
Shareholders' equity	140,516	130,620	133,694	161,290	234,611	**233,182**
Ratios						
Total debt to net assets	59.11%	57.72%	55.36%	36.01%	26.24%	**36.76%**
Return on average common equity, before unusual items	0.06%	−2.20%	4.30%	8.51%	8.69%	**1.17%**
Per Share						
Earnings (loss), before unusual items (net of taxes)	$ 0.01	−$ 0.24	$ 0.45	$ 0.89	$ 0.91	**$ 0.15**
Cash flow from operations	1.30	1.47	1.94	2.66	2.08	**1.72**

for further investigation and quantification. The six risks were (1) environmental liability, (2) the effect of weather on grain volume, (3) counterparty risk (suppliers or customers not fulfilling contracts), (4) credit risk, (5) commodity price and basis risk, and (6) inventory risk (damage to products in inventory).

Willis Risk Solutions, a unit of the Willis Group Ltd., took on the task of gathering data and estimating the probability distribution of losses from each of the six risk exposures and associated correlations. Willis used these probability distributions to quantify the impact of each source of risk on several measures of UGG's performance, including return on equity and earnings before interest and taxes (EBIT). In addition, Willis used the correlations between the six sources of risk to quantify the impact of the six sources of risk in combination on UGG's performance.

Figure 27.3 provides an example of the type of analysis conducted by Willis Risk Solutions. The example is based on UGG's counterparty risk. Based on data provided by UGG

**FIGURE
27.3**

**Analysis of
counterparty
risk.**

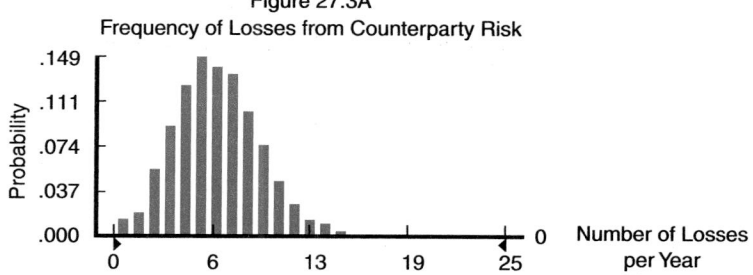

Figure 27.3A
Frequency of Losses from Counterparty Risk

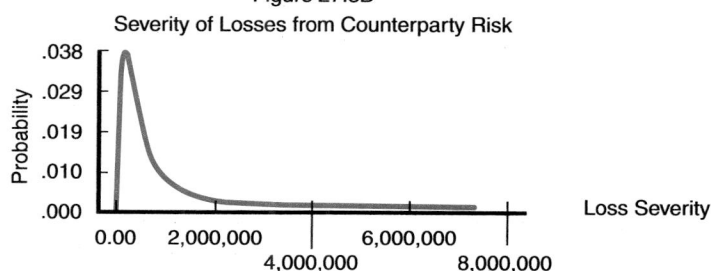

Figure 27.3B
Severity of Losses from Counterparty Risk

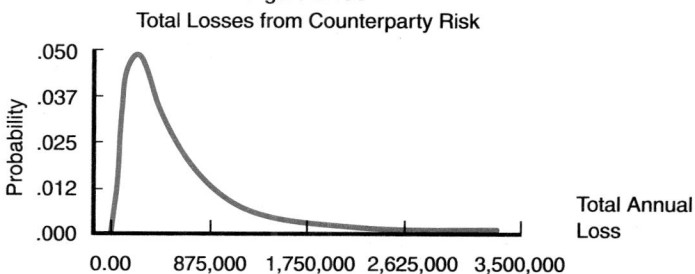

Figure 27.3C
Total Losses from Counterparty Risk

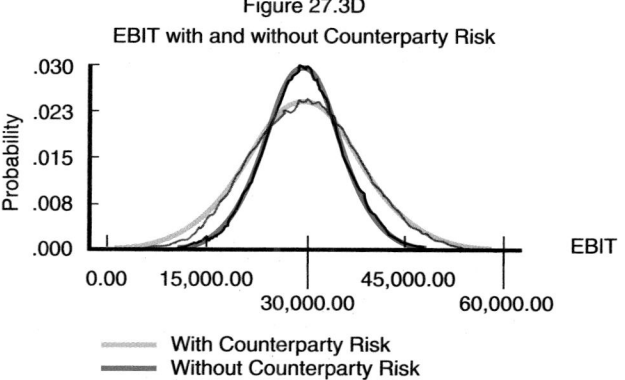

Figure 27.3D
EBIT with and without Counterparty Risk

and discussions with UGG employees, Willis estimated that the number of counterparty losses per year could be described by a Poisson distribution (see Figure 27.3A) and that the loss severity on any given loss could be described by a lognormal distribution (see Figure 27.3B). Given the probability distributions for the number of losses and for the loss per event, an annual loss distribution from counterparty risk could be estimated (see Figure 27.3C). Finally, the impact of counterparty risk on the probability distributions of various performance measures (e.g., EBIT) could be estimated under the assumption that all other risk factors took on a specific value (see Figure 27.3D).

The analysis conducted by Willis Risk Solutions led to the conclusion that, of the six risks originally identified, UGG's main source of unmanaged risk was from the weather. The parties therefore focused their energies on understanding how weather affected UGG's performance. Willis Risk Solutions' statistician Ken Risko and actuary Michelle Bradley conducted an in-depth regression analysis of how crop yields in each province of western Canada were influenced by temperature and precipitation.

Examples of the regression analysis Ken and Michelle conducted are presented in Table 27.4. The table provides the results of estimating a regression equation where the dependent variable is the crop yield (bushels per acre) for either wheat or oats, and the explanatory variables are a time trend (to capture productivity increases over time), the average June temperature, and the average July precipitation. The analysis was conducted using data from 1960 to 1992 for the provinces of Alberta, Manitoba, and Saskatchewan. They also conducted a similar analysis for other grains and seeds.

TABLE 27.4   **Results of regression analysis of crop yields (bushel per acre) and weather conditions in two Canadian provinces using data from 1960 to 1992.** Temperature is measured in degrees Fahrenheit and precipitation in inches. The time trend variable equals (year -1960); thus, for the year 2000 the time trend equals 40.

Dependent Variable			Explanatory Variables				
Province	Crop		Intercept	Time Trend	Average June Temperature	Average July Precipitation	R-Squared
Alberta	Wheat	Coef:	59.88	0.33	−0.76	2.70	0.68
		t-stat:	4.49	6.19	−3.19	2.63	
Manitoba	Wheat	Coef:	79.34	0.42	−0.98	1.00	0.65
		t-stat:	5.70	5.94	−4.38	0.95	
Saskat-chewan	Wheat	Coef:	55.6	0.19	−0.69	4.80	0.61
		t-stat:	4.02	2.65	−3.01	4.44	
Alberta	Oats	Coef:	43.53	0.69	−0.17	4.70	0.72
		t-stat:	1.89	7.59	−0.41	2.71	
Manitoba	Oats	Coef:	121.02	0.65	−1.50	5.30	0.64
		t-stat:	4.89	5.16	−3.77	2.96	
Saskat-chewan	Oats	Coef:	74.07	0.24	−0.76	9.30	0.56
		t-stat:	2.93	1.91	−1.82	4.70	

To illustrate the results, consider the first row of Table 27.4. The positive coefficient (0.33) on the time trend variable indicates that Alberta's wheat yields have increased over time. On average, wheat yields have increased about 0.33 bushels/acre each year since 1960. The negative coefficient (-0.76) on the average June temperature variable indicates that wheat yields in Alberta are negatively related to the average June temperature. Finally, the positive coefficient (2.7) on the average July precipitation variable indicates that crop yields increase on average with rainfall in July. The r-squared indicates that about 68 percent of the annual variation in Alberta wheat yields is explained by these three variables.

The remainder of Table 27.4 indicates that, in general, crop yields for wheat and oats have increased over time, are negatively related to average June temperature, and are positively related to average July precipitation. There are, however, some exceptions to these generalizations. Note that the three variables in the regression equation explain a substantial proportion of the variability in yields in all of the provinces; that is, the r-squareds generally are high.

The regression results can be used to assess how expected crop yields would be affected by deviations from normal weather conditions. For example, if temperature and precipitation were expected to take on their historical average values (presented in Table 27.5), then the predicted wheat crop yield for 2000 would be

$$\text{Yield} = 59.88 + .33\,(40) - 0.76\,(56.6) + 2.7\,(2.06) = 35.6 \text{ bushels per acre}$$

If instead the average June temperature was higher than the mean value by one standard deviation (2.2 degrees from Table 27.5), the Alberta wheat crop yield would be predicted to be

$$\text{Yield} = 59.88 + .33\,(40) - 0.76\,(58.8) + 2.7\,(2.06) = 34.0 \text{ bushels per acre}$$

Thus, an increase of 2.2 degrees from normal reduces crop yields on average by about 1.6 bushels per acre.

TABLE 27.5 Descriptive statistics for variables used in regression analysis.

	1960–1992 Average June Temperature		Average July Precipitation	
	Mean Value	Standard Deviation	Mean Value	Standard Deviation
Alberta	56.6°F	2.2°F	2.06 inches	0.51 inches
Manitoba	61.7	3.0	1.83	0.67
Saskatchewan	60.4	2.8	1.55	0.61

	Correlation Coefficients for Average June Temperature			Correlation Coefficients for Average July Precipitation		
	Alberta	Manitoba	Saskatchewan	Alberta	Manitoba	Saskatchewan
Alberta	1.00	0.41	0.69	1.00	0.51	0.74
Manitoba		1.00	0.87		1.00	0.55
Saskatchewan			1.00			1.00

Having established a relationship between crop yields and weather, Ken and Michelle then estimated the relationship between crop yields and UGG's grain volume. They first calculated a weighted average crop yield for western Canada using crop yields by grain/seed and by province and the proportions of total production of each grain/seed in each province. The values for this weighted average crop yield are reported in Table 27.1. They found that UGG's grain volume in year t was highly correlated with overall crop yields in year $t-1$.

The next step in Ken and Michelle's analysis was to relate UGG's grain volume to UGG's financial results using the information in Table 27.2. For each tonne of shipments, UGG had gross profit of 21.2 Canadian dollars on average during the 1997–1999 period. Thus, if shipments dropped by 100 tonnes, gross profit would drop by about Can $2,120.

To summarize, Ken and Michelle established a relationship between weather and UGG's gross profit using the following steps and information:

$$\text{Weather} \;\rightarrow\; \text{Crop Yields} \rightarrow \text{UGG's Grain Volume} \;\rightarrow\; \text{UGG's Profit}$$

↑	↑	↑
Table 27.4	Table 27.1	Table 27.2

The results of this analysis are summarized in Figure 27.4, which illlustrates how weather influences UGG's gross profits. The relatively volatile curve indicates UGG's actual gross profit during the 1980–1992 period and the less volatile curve indicates what UGG's gross profit would have been if weather would have been constant over the period.

Choices Faced by UGG's Managers

Having quantified their exposure to weather risk, UGG managers explored several options: retention, weather derivatives, and an insurance contract.

Retention

The retention approach meant continuing operating as they had been and not trying to reduce their weather exposure. As previously discussed, retention exposed their profitability to large swings due to weather variation. There were three disadvantages of such volatility.

FIGURE 27.4
Actual gross profit compared to gross profit if weather risk were removed.

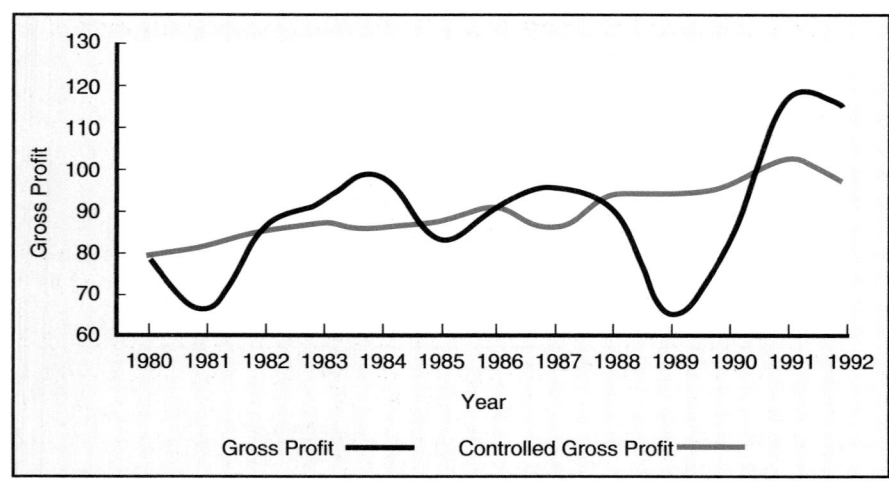

First, UGG had been and planned to continue making large investments in storage facilities (grain elevators). The ability to finance these capital expenditures from internally generated funds would allow the firm to avoid the costs associated with raising external capital. And, to the extent external capital would be needed, the rate that the firm would have to pay on borrowed funds would likely be higher if they retained the weather risk.

Second, the variability in its cash flows caused UGG to hold extra equity capital as a cushion against unexpected low cash flows in any given year. If the firm could reduce its weather risk, it could increase the proportion of the firm financed with debt without paying higher yields, which in turn would allow it to gain additional interest tax shields.

Third, although much of UGG's current business could be characterized as a commodity business, UGG tried to distinguish itself from competitors by creating products with brand names and by providing ongoing services to customers. Stability in the firm's cash flows would help the firm characterize itself as a company that suppliers and customers could rely on for service and high-quality products for many years. Moreover, the importance of supplier and customer relationships was likely to increase in the coming years as the marketplace for agricultural products adjusted to scientific advances. Analysts predicted that over the next decade, food producers would demand specific genetically engineered crops, which in turn would require farmers to plant specific seeds. The coordination of these activities between farmers and food producers would require an information, storage, and transportation network. UGG saw itself as a provider of these intermediary services.

The main advantage of retaining the weather risk was the cost associated with shifting it to someone else. In addition, UGG managers were not sure that the capital markets really would reward the firm for eliminating weather risk, given that this was a risk most investors could easily diversify on their own.

Weather Derivatives

In the late 1990s, weather derivatives were a relatively new risk management tool. These contracts were sold in the over-the-counter (OTC) market by firms such as Enron, Duke Energy, and Goldman Sachs. A contract could be tailored on a number of dimensions to meet the specific needs of the buyer. For example, the underlying variable determining the payoffs could be one or a combination of weather variables, such as average temperature, rainfall, snowfall, a heat index, or the number of heating or cooling degree days. The payoff structure could resemble a put option, a call option, a swap, or combinations of these structures.

Figure 27.5 provides an example of how UGG could potentially use a weather derivative. Suppose that based on Willis' analysis of the sensitivity of crop yields to weather and the sensitivity of gross profit to crop yields, UGG's expected gross profit exhibited the pattern depicted in Figure 27.5A. The vertical axis measures expected gross profit, and the horizontal axis measures a weather index that equals a weighted average of various temperature and precipitation measures in western Canada. As the index increases, expected gross profit increases (because crop yields increase, which in turn increases UGG's shipments of grains and seeds). For simplicity, the illustration assumes that the relationship between gross profit and the weather index is linear. Since low values of the weather index correspond to low expected profits for UGG, a derivative contract that would pay UGG money when the index is low would provide a hedge. For example, the put option structure illustrated in Figure 27.5B would help to hedge UGG's risk. When the put option payoff from Figure 27.5B is added to expected gross profit from Figure 27.5A, UGG's expected profit would vary with the weather index as depicted in Figure 27.5C.

**FIGURE
27.5**
**A weather
derivative.**

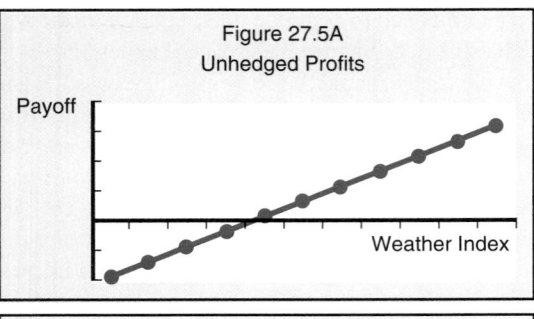

Figure 27.5A
Unhedged Profits

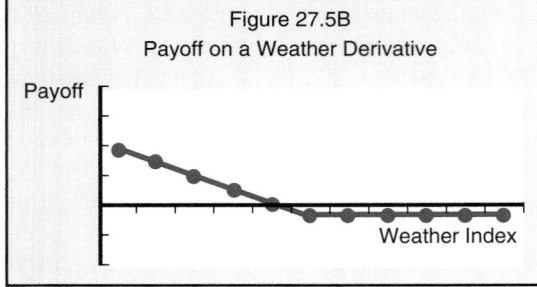

Figure 27.5B
Payoff on a Weather Derivative

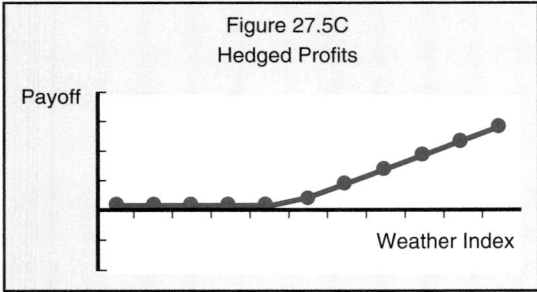

Figure 27.5C
Hedged Profits

Hedging their weather risk with derivatives was feasible, but it entailed several difficulties. Although Willis Risk Solutions had performed a sophisticated analysis of the effect of weather on UGG's gross profit, the results of this analysis had to be converted into a desired contract structure. That is, the underlying weather index that determined the derivative contract's payoff would need to be specified. Next, the effectiveness of the derivative contract in hedging UGG's risk would have to be assessed. UGG then would have to obtain price quotes in a marketplace that had relatively few participants.

Insurance Contract

When discussing the weather analysis, UGG's managers thought of an alternative way of dealing with the firm's weather risk. They knew that the primary reason weather was important was because weather affected UGG's grain shipments. They therefore wondered whether they could construct an insurance contract that would pay UGG when its grain shipments were abnormally low. The problem with such a contract is moral hazard—UGG's pricing and service also influences its grain shipments. One solution to this problem was to use industry-wide grain shipments as the variable that would trigger payments to UGG. Industry shipments would likely be highly correlated with UGG's shipments, which would imply that the basis risk would be minimal. In addition, because of its relatively low market share, UGG would have minimal effect on the value of industry-wide shipments, which would significantly reduce the moral hazard problem.

UGG also considered the possibility of integrating grain volume coverage with UGG's other insurance coverage. Currently, UGG purchased a number of different insurance policies for various traditional risk exposures. For example, it purchased a variety of policies to cover its property exposures (e.g., a boiler and machinery policy to cover losses on machinery and equipment) and liability policies to cover its exposure to tort liability (e.g, environmental impairment liability). Each policy had its own retention level and its own coverage limit. By integrating various coverages under one policy, UGG could replace the individual deductibles and limits with an overall annual aggregate deductible and limit that would apply to all or a subset of losses, including grain volume losses.

UGG asked Willis to investigate the possibility of structuring an insurance contract on industry grain shipments. Willis then contacted several major commercial insurers, including a division of the large reinsurer Swiss Re, called Swiss Re New Markets. Located in New York City, this group structures innovative risk financing deals for commercial entities.

27.3   Summary

- Enterprise risk management refers to the management of all of an enterprise's risk in a consistent unified manner.

- A number of firms have adopted an enterprise risk management approach, including United Grain Growers.

Key Term

Enterprise risk management (ERM) 591

Questions and Problems

1. Use the data in Table 27.1 to calculate the correlation coefficient between industry grain shipments and UGG's grain shipments.

2. Use the data in Table 27.1 to calculate the correlation coefficient between crop yields and UGG's grain shipments.

3. Given that any method of reducing the weather risk exposure will be costly, what are the benefits to UGG's diversified owners from reducing the weather risk? In other words, what characteristics of UGG's operations and strategy would make risk reduction potentially beneficial to UGG's owners who hold well-diversified portfolios?

4. Should UGG's rather unique ownership structure influence the decision to reduce the weather risk exposure?

5. How could the parties structure a weather derivative to cover the exposure? More specifically, what would be the underlying index? Would the contract be a put, call, or forward? Would they buy or sell? Would a separate contract for each province and/or each crop be needed?

6. How could the parties structure an insurance contract to cover the grain volume exposure? More specifically, how would a loss be defined? What would be the payment to

UGG conditional on a loss? (Hint: Use information in Table 27.1 and Table 27.2.)

7. What are the advantages and disadvantages of integrating the grain volume coverage with the firm's other insurance coverages? That is, instead of having separate policies with separate deductibles and limits for the various exposures (including the grain volume exposure), what are the advantages and disadvantages of bundling all of the firm's exposures in one policy with one deductible and one limit? (Hint: review Chapter 22).

8. Ignoring cost differences, are there any advantages of the insurance contract approach versus the use of weather derivatives? (Hint: Think about basis risk—see Chapter 25.)

References

Harrington, Scott; Greg Niehaus; and Ken Risko. "Enterprise Risk Management: The Case of United Grain Growers." *Journal of Applied Corporate Finance,* Winter 2002.

Lam, James. "The CRO Is Here to Stay." *Risk Management,* April 2001, pp. 16–22.

Chapter 28

Corporate Liability to Customers, Third Parties, and Shareholders

Chapter Objective

• Describe legal liability rules, insurance coverage, and public policy issues relating to products liability, environmental liability, and directors and officers' liability.

This chapter provides more in-depth treatment of three important types of legal liability for businesses: (1) liability for product injuries, (2) liability for environmental damage, and (3) liability for actions of corporate officers and directors. We emphasize at the outset that the law concerning these subjects is complex and varies across states. Our purpose is to provide an introduction to key aspects of the relevant law, explain and analyze the insurance market's response to changes in liability rules, and discuss key public policy issues that arise from these liability rules.

28.1 Products Liability

Legal Background

Evolution of Tort Liability

Products liability law has an interesting history that provides important insights about the evolving tort liability system. Prior to 1916, most injuries and illnesses resulting from products were covered under contract law, not tort law. A manufacturer could not be held liable unless the victim and the manufacturer had a direct contractual relationship. For example, if a manufacturer sold a product to a retailer who in turn sold the product to a consumer, then the manufacturer generally could not be held liable for the consumer's losses. Because of the contractual requirement (known as the *privity limitation*), manufacturers seldom were held liable for damages to injured consumers.

An important 1916 case, *MacPherson v. Buick,* established that consumers injured by defective products can recover damages under tort law. MacPherson was thrown out of his Buick and injured when one of the wooden spokes on a wheel collapsed. Even though Buick subcontracted the production of the wheel to another firm and Buick sold the car to a retailer, who in turn sold it to MacPherson, the court found that Buick was liable for damages. Importantly, the *MacPherson v. Buick* case determined that a contractual relationship is not needed for the injured party to recover damages from the manufacturer. As a result, manufacturers could be held liable for losses suffered by the ultimate consumers of their products. However, the case also made clear that a consumer could not recover damages unless the manufacturer had been negligent. While the negligence rule was generally used in products liability tort cases during the first half of the 1900s, courts eventually started to hold manufacturers liable even when they were not negligent; that is, the courts moved toward a strict liability standard.

An important case that helped establish the strict liability standard for certain kinds of product-related injuries was *Escola v. Coca-Cola Bottling Company* in 1944. Escola was loading Coke bottles into a refrigerator when one of the bottles exploded, injuring her hand. The California Supreme Court ruled that Coca-Cola was liable for the losses even though it was not found to be negligent. Judge Traynor's opinion in the case clearly states that the negligence rule should be replaced by a standard that makes manufacturers liable whenever their products are defective.

> I believe the manufacturer's negligence should no longer be singled out as the basis of a plaintiff's right to recover in cases like the present one. In my opinion it should now be recognized that a manufacturer incurs an absolute liability when an article that he has placed on the market, knowing that it is to be used without inspection, proves to have a defect that causes injury to human beings.

Judge Traynor's opinion also clearly states that the reason for moving from negligence to strict liability is that manufacturers are best suited to provide consumers with insurance against losses from product injuries:

> Those who suffer injury from defective products are unprepared to meet its consequences. The cost of an injury and the loss of time or health may be an overwhelming misfortune to the person injured and a needless one, for the risk of injury can be insured by the manufacturer and distributed among the public as a cost of doing business . . . Against such a risk there should be general and constant protection and the manufacturer is best suited to afford such protection.

The *Escola v. Coca-Cola* case helped establish victim compensation (insurance) as an important objective of products liability law.

The *Second Restatement of Torts,* published in 1965, outlined legal doctrines that should be applied in tort law. Regarding products liability, it stated that manufacturers are liable if consumers are harmed as a result of using a product that is "unreasonably dangerous" and "defective" (see section 402A). The important point is that, under this doctrine, courts do not focus on the manufacturer's actions (as they would under a negligence rule) to determine whether the manufacturer is liable; instead, courts focus on whether the product is unreasonably dangerous and defective. However, determining in some cases when a product is unreasonably dangerous or defective may involve an analysis very similar to that used in assessing negligence, as we explain below. The *Second Restatement* also stated that contributory negligence is not an allowable defense by manufacturers. The doctrines in the *Second Restatement* were adopted by almost all states in the subsequent decade.[1]

There are three general types of product defects: (1) manufacturing defects, (2) design defects, and (3) warning defects. Depending upon the alleged defect (and the jurisdiction), manufacturers can defend themselves by arguing that the consumers (1) assumed the risk, or (2) engaged in the unforeseeable misuse of the product, in which case the defendant's liability may be reduced in a manner similar to a comparative negligence standard.[2]

A **manufacturing defect** exists if a particular product deviates from what the manufacturer intended. In most jurisdictions, if a product differs from the normal production run and a consumer is harmed as a result of the defect, then the manufacturer is liable; the manufacturer has no defense and the courts give no consideration to the costs and benefits of eliminating the manufacturing defect. The example of the exploding Coke bottle in the *Escola v. Coca-Cola* case illustrates a manufacturing defect. The manufacturer did not intend for the bottle to explode under normal conditions; thus, the explosion of one bottle suggests that that particular bottle was different from the normal production run and thus defective.

A **design defect** exists if foreseeable risks of harm presented by the product could have been reduced by the adoption of a reasonably safer design (or discovered and corrected through more exhaustive testing of the product). To determine whether a product is unreasonably dangerous, most jurisdictions use some form of a cost-benefit analysis. A manufacturer's liability depends on the court's answers to questions such as: Could the defect have been corrected at a reasonable cost? To answer this question, both the plaintiffs and the defendant usually employ engineering experts to testify on issues related to the feasibility and costs of alternative safer designs. Thus, when deciding whether a design defect exists, courts consider issues similar to those considered under a negligence standard. Since a finding that a product has a design defect implies that all the products of that particular design are defective, the costs associated with losing a design defect case usually are greater than the damages in that particular case. Box 28.1 provides a few examples of design defects that have led to large liability awards.

A **warning defect** exists if the product has not been properly labeled or the risks associated with using the product have not been properly explained. In most jurisdictions, courts will hold manufacturers liable if the danger was foreseeable and the manufacturer failed to provide a warning that could have reduced the risks of harm. The foreseeability requirement essentially implies that courts consider issues similar to those under a negligence standard. Some jurisdictions, however, do not require that the danger was foreseeable and instead hold manufacturers liable if a warning would have prevented the harm that was caused by the product (under the assumption that if the warning had existed, then the consumer would have heeded the warning and prevented the harm). Manufacturers' liability based on warning defects explains, in large part, the proliferation of warning labels and pamphlets that are

---

[1]The *Second Restatement* has since been replaced by the *Third Restatement*.

[2]Recall from Chapter 12 that contributory negligence, which prevailed until the 1970s, precludes recovery altogether if the plaintiff is at all negligent. Comparative negligence, which has replaced the previous rule in most jurisdictions, reduces the amount of the plaintiff's recovery to reflect his or her relative negligence.

Examples of design defects that have led to large liability awards include:

- Liability of a manufacturer of three-wheel, all-terrain vehicles for injuries to children harmed when the vehicles overturn.

- Liability of an auto manufacturer for failing to install a rollbar to minimize injury if the vehicle overturns.
- Liability of a pick-up truck manufacturer for injuries caused by the explosion of a side-mounted fuel tank.

attached to many products. Box 28.2 provides examples of warning defects that have led to large liability awards.

In summary, since producers are strictly liable for product defects, the important issue is whether a product is defective. Deviation from the normal production run is taken as evidence of a manufacturing defect and thus manufacturers effectively are strictly liable for injuries resulting from such a defect. When determining whether a product has a defective design or warning, courts generally examine the manufacturer's knowledge and behavior. In this sense, the liability rule is somewhat analogous to negligence for design and warning defects.

Contractual Liability

In addition to tort liability, firms also are subject to liability under contract law as a result of warranties that are made when products and services are sold to consumers. An **express warranty** is an explicit statement (promise) that a product or service will perform according to some standard. An **implied warranty** is an implicit performance guarantee that usually accompanies the sale of any product or service (e.g., that the product will be reasonably fit for its intended use). Consumers who are injured as a result of products not performing according to implied or express warranties can sue the seller for damages.

As an example of a breach of an express warranty, suppose that Mr. Madden buys a stepladder that has a sticker stating that it will safely support a person weighing up to 300 pounds. If Mr. Madden is injured when the ladder breaks under his weight (which is less than 300 pounds), he can sue the manufacturer on the grounds that the ladder did not perform as the company expressly said it would. As an example of an implied warranty, suppose that Mr. O'Neal purchases a basketball. While playing a game at the local YMCA, he goes up for a rebound. While his head is above the rim, the ball bursts when it hits the rim and inflicts damage to Mr. O'Neal's face. In this scenario, the ball was not fit for ordinary use, and Mr. O'Neal therefore can sue the ball manufacturer for the damages suffered.

Insurance Coverage

As explained in Chapter 23, insurance coverage for products liability generally is provided by a firm's Commercial General Liability (CGL) insurance policy.[3] As the name suggests, the CGL policy provides liability insurance coverage for property damage and bodily injuries for a wide range of liability exposures. The CGL policy, however, excludes some specific types of exposures that are insured by separate policies, such as auto liability and

---

[3] Prior to 1986, the policy was called Comprehensive General Liability, also referred to as the CGL.

Examples of warning defects that have led to large liability awards include:

- Liability of a crane manufacturer for an inadequate warning that the operator could be harmed if the crane contacted electrical wires.

- Liability of a refinishing fluid manufacturer for injuries caused by combustion of the fluid when used too close to an open flame.

- Liability of a manufacturer of a nonstick cooking spray for deaths to teenagers who deliberately inhaled the substance.

---

workers' compensation, or that are uninsurable for other reasons, such as war (see Chapter 23). As we will elaborate later in this chapter, there are important exclusions for environmental hazards. Recall that the CGL policy also provides that the insurer has a duty to defend the firm in the case of a lawsuit and the insurer pays the defense costs.

In 1986, the CGL policy was changed to allow liability coverage to be written on either an occurrence basis or a claims-made basis, as opposed to an occurrence basis only. Recall from Chapter 23 that under an occurrence policy the insurer pays claims if the loss occurred during the policy period, regardless of when the claim is filed. Under a claims-made policy, the insurer pays claims if the claim is filed during the policy period, provided that the loss occurred after the retroactive date of the policy. Claims-made coverage usually is only purchased for hazards that involve a large risk of unexpected increases in claim costs for the insurer, such as environmental liability, directors and officers' liability, and some product and professional liability exposures.

Issues

Critics of the products liability system contend that the scope and scale of products liability has expanded to the point that both the safety and compensation objectives of the liability system have been undermined. In response to these criticisms, a number of state legislatures have passed product liability reforms, and federal legislation has been proposed. After discussing whether the current system meets its safety and compensation objectives, we discuss some product liability reform measures.

Product Safety

As discussed several times earlier in the book, safety can be increased by (1) taking more precautions (e.g., greater product safety features or warnings), and (2) decreasing the level of the risky activity (e.g., selling fewer products that might cause harm). From a public policy perspective, there are two main safety issues: (1) Do producers and consumers have incentives to take proper precautions to prevent accidents? and (2) Do consumers purchase too many (or too few) risky products? Arguments can be made that strict products liability is justified because it provides incentives for manufacturers to take the right amount of safety precautions when designing, manufacturing, and selling their products and because it induces consumers to purchase the right amount of risky products. As we will see shortly, however, counterarguments also can be made.

Regarding the issue of manufacturers' safety incentives, strict liability for all consumer losses provides strong incentives for manufacturers to make safe products. If consumers are uninformed about product risk, then manufacturers have too little incentive to produce safe products in the absence of liability. Thus, strict liability for all accident losses provides incentives for manufacturers to invest in more safety.

Another potential problem remedied by making manufacturers strictly liable is that consumers who are uninformed about product risk might otherwise consume too many risky products. To illustrate, suppose that consumers are uninformed and producers are not liable for damages. Then, the product's price will reflect only the manufacturing and distribution costs; the price will not reflect the expected losses that consumers could suffer. Consequently, the product's price is less than the true cost of consuming the product. Uninformed consumers therefore may buy too much of the risky product relative to what they would consume if they were informed about the product's risk. Making the manufacturer liable for damages can help correct this problem, because the product's price will reflect the producer's expected liability costs and thus consumers' expected losses. Since the price reflects consumers' expected losses, even uninformed consumers will make consumption choices based on the true cost of consuming the product. Making producers strictly liable for all consumer losses therefore helps correct the problem of overconsumption of risky products by uninformed consumers.

The weight given to these arguments for strict liability depends, in part, on your view of how well the marketplace works to give manufacturers incentives to make safe products in the absence of liability (or under a negligence standard) and whether consumers would make the right consumption choices regarding risky products in the absence of liability (or under a negligence standard). If consumers properly evaluate product risks, then manufacturers will have the right safety incentives without liability. Similarly, if consumers properly evaluate product risks, then consumers will not consume an excessive amount of risky products. Thus, the safety justification for the existing products liability system is premised on consumers underestimating product risk. While some would argue that consumers do not understand product risks, it is worth noting two points. First, the extent to which people become informed about product risks depends in part on whether manufacturers are liable for damages. To the extent that consumers view themselves as being insured by the products liability system, their incentive to gather information about product risks declines. Second, consumers' lack of information could cause them to overestimate product risk, which undermines the argument that manufacturers need to be held liable for safety reasons.

Regarding manufacturers' safety incentives, strict liability and a negligence rule are likely to have similar effects. In particular, a negligence standard that examines the costs and benefits of additional safety measures is likely to give manufacturers the right incentives to make safe products. If a manufacturer fails to undertake cost-effective safety measures, the courts will find it liable. Thus, from the perspective of manufacturers' safety incentives, there is little advantage of a strict liability standard over a negligence standard, if the negligence standard is appropriately used. On the other hand, because product prices will not reflect the expected costs of non-negligent injuries under a negligence rule, too many risky products might be purchased compared to strict liability if consumers underestimate the risk of injury.

Problems with strict liability from a safety perspective may arise when other firms in the chain of supply (for example, retailers) and consumers can influence the frequency and severity of accidents. For example, strict liability for defective products may give consumers too little incentive to use defective products safely. This problem is an example of the moral hazard problem discussed numerous times earlier in the book; if consumers are fully insured, then their incentives to take precautions are reduced. The effect of strict liability on consumer safety is uncertain. Some people argue that consumers are unlikely to increase their risk of injury because of the potential for a large damage award if injured. On the other hand, the observation that people increase their level of precautions in response to an increase in the probability of incurring small fines (e.g., driving slower when more police are patrolling) suggests that people also might decrease their level of precautions in response to an increase in the probability of receiving large damage awards. Indeed, some people have staged accidents in order to possibly receive a large award or settlement.

Whether the current products liability system provides the right safety incentives depends on a number of factors, including the damages awarded by courts, their assessment of the costs and benefits of additional safety efforts by manufacturers and consumers, and the implementation of procedures and standards of proof. These factors are likely to vary across jurisdictions as well as across individual cases within a jurisdiction. Some commentators argue that courts make systematic errors by holding manufacturers liable when the manufacturer could not have foreseen the danger or when the danger was created by the consumer's misuse of the product, and by awarding excessive damages, especially for pain and suffering. To the extent that these charges are true, manufacturers are likely to have excessive incentives to make products safe. While it is unlikely that courts award excessive damages in all cases, at a minimum there is little doubt that the courts have introduced considerable uncertainty into products liability.

In response to the high expected value and variance of product liability costs, many manufacturers claim that they have withdrawn products from the marketplace. In some cases, withdrawing dangerous products is beneficial. In other cases, however, the products withdrawn actually may have reduced risk relative to other products. For example, some analysts have argued that certain pharmaceuticals have been withdrawn as a result of products liability even though the evidence is that the vast majority of people would experience a reduction in risk through their use. Small airplanes provide another example. Products liability has increased the cost of new airplanes, so pilots are induced to fly older planes, which often are more risky.

Compensation for Injury

Even though one of the main justifications of the current products liability system is as an insurance system (see the quote of Justice Traynor earlier in the chapter), the current system nonetheless can be criticized on the grounds that it provides excessive compensation (insurance coverage) to victims. Under the existing system, courts generally try to compensate victims fully for medical expenses, lost wages, and pain and suffering. As discussed in Chapters 10 and 12, full insurance coverage rarely is desired by consumers because of transaction costs and moral hazard. The legal fees and court costs associated with providing insurance through the tort system are akin to the transaction costs associated with private insurance contracts. Also, to the extent that consumers' behavior affects the likelihood and severity of product injuries, the insurance provided by the tort system is subject to moral hazard. Moral hazard problems are especially severe for noneconomic losses. The transaction costs and moral hazard problems suggest that consumers would demand less than full coverage (compensation) for product-related injuries.

Moreover, many consumers are unlikely to demand insurance coverage for noneconomic losses, such as pain and suffering, even if the insurance had no loading and was not subject to moral hazard. To the extent that compensation for noneconomic losses is awarded, the courts force consumers to purchase insurance coverage that many of them do not want. That is, most consumers would prefer to have lower pain and suffering compensation if injured (lower insurance coverage) and lower product prices.

As discussed in Chapter 12, one interpretation of why the courts award full compensation to accident victims is that the courts are concerned with giving manufacturers the right incentives to produce safe products, which may require full compensation to victims. Other explanations for the courts' attempts to provide full compensation are that (1) courts do not understand or they reject the insurance theory underlying the argument for less than full compensation, and (2) other factors, such as jury sympathy, play a role in determining victim compensation.

Regressivity of Current System

The wealth redistribution effects of the products liability system are interesting because they violate many people's notions of fairness. In particular, lower income people, on average, tend to be hurt by having insurance bundled with products.

To illustrate this point, note first that product prices reflect producers' expected liability costs, which in turn reflect the average level of damages awarded in products liability suits. Second, all consumers typically pay the same price for the same type of product (poor people pay the same price for a stepladder as do rich people). The problem is that the expected liability awards vary across people in predictable ways so that poor people typically receive lower awards. This occurs because courts typically award damages for lost wages, which vary with income. Also, evidence indicates that pain and suffering awards are greater for people with higher incomes (perhaps because pain and suffering awards are linked to monetary losses). Thus, the insurance coverage that is bundled with products is greater for higher income consumers. To the extent that higher income people buy the same risky products and pay the same prices as lower income people, the products liability system is therefore like a regressive tax: Lower income people pay the same price but receive less insurance coverage for the insurance implicitly bundled with products. (Of course, rich people might be less likely than poor people to use some risky products—like ladders.)

Products Liability Reform Proposals

A number of products liability reform measures have been adopted by individual states and proposed at the federal level. These reforms include measures that would (1) reduce the potential liability of producers (e.g., by curtailing joint and several liability, capping pain and suffering awards, imposing limitations on punitive damages, and altering the collateral source rule so that plaintiffs cannot be compensated twice for the same losses); and (2) reduce the incentive of plaintiffs' attorneys to file marginal cases (e.g., by adopting a loser pays rule and reducing contingency fees for plaintiffs' attorneys).

A reform proposal that is unique to products is the adoption of a **statute of repose,** which states that products liability suits must be brought within a certain number of years (e.g., 20 years) after the product has been purchased. One justification for a statute of repose is that product safety deteriorates over time with or without proper consumer care. Given a strict liability standard, a statute of repose is a way of limiting manufacturer liability for product deterioration that would be excessively costly to prevent or when consumers are likely to have a significant influence on the product's safety.

Concept Check

1. Which liability standard would generally make it most difficult for a person injured by a product to recover from the manufacturer: negligence or strict liability?

28.2 Environmental Liability

Legal Background

With increasing frequency, individuals exposed to toxic chemicals in the water, air, or soil are suing the firms that have contributed to the contaminants. The recent history of both common and statutory environmental law helps indicate how the scope of a firm's liability for environmental hazards has expanded dramatically during the past 35 years.[4]

Common Law

For many years, diffuse environmental hazards, such as loud noise and gradual pollution, were handled under nuisance law, which requires that the plaintiff demonstrate that the hazard is "serious, continuing, and unreasonable," and that the plaintiff is not hypersensitive to the hazard. Strict liability was reserved for situations where the environmental damage was caused by sudden events that occurred because someone brought something unnatural to the area and when losses were easily linked to a particular event (i.e., cause and effect were easily identified). The application of strict liability usually was based on an 1868 English case, *Rylands v. Fletcher,* in which the defendant's dam broke and flooded the plaintiff's mine. Although the defendant was not negligent, the court ruled that he was liable for the plaintiff's losses, because the losses clearly were the result of the defendant bringing something unnatural to the area (water), which had subsequently escaped.

Scientific advances have altered common law in two ways. First, we have improved our ability to measure small amounts of contaminants in the air, water, and soil over the past 50 years. Second, scientists have demonstrated that some illnesses may be linked to our exposure to certain contaminants. These advances have led some courts to interpret gradual leaks of potentially toxic substances into the environment as being equivalent to sudden events that directly lead to illness or death. To illustrate how gradual releases of potentially toxic substances might be equated to a sudden event that directly causes damage, consider the case of an underground storage tank that develops a hole and then gradually releases into the groundwater a substance that, when given in high doses to laboratory animals, causes cancer. The emergence of the hole in the tank is the sudden event, analogous to the dam breaking in the *Rylands v. Fletcher* case. The evidence from laboratory animals provides a way of arguing that the cancer that some residents of the area have developed is a direct effect of the hole. Using this line of reasoning, courts began to apply a strict liability standard in cases involving low-level, gradual releases of potentially toxic substances.

Statutory Liability

An important source of statutory liability is the Comprehensive Environmental Response, Compensation, and Liability Act of 1980 **(CERCLA),** usually known as the **Superfund**

---

[4]This section benefitted substantially from an article written by Peter Huber, titled "Environmental Hazards and Liability Law."

Famous Cases of Environmental Contamination

LOVE CANAL

Between 1942 and 1953, the Hooker Chemical Company dumped 21,000 tons of hazardous waste into a landfill in the Love Canal area of Niagara Falls, New York. The dumpsite was selected because of the sparse population and because the clay soil would contain the potentially toxic substances. Despite Hooker's warnings to local officials of the potential danger, local officials pressured Hooker into selling the land to the city so that it could be developed. The city subsequently sold some of the land for further development. The development damaged the safety measures undertaken by Hooker (linings and layers of clay) and the potentially toxic substances eventually leaked. In 1980, the level of contaminants in the groundwater and soil were deemed to be so high that 700 residents of the area were forced to move. Despite an explicit provision in the original sales contract absolving Hooker of any liability, 1,300 current and former residents of Love Canal sued Hooker Chemical and the city of Niagara Falls. The suit was settled in 1984 for $20 million. According to numerous studies, Love Canal residents have not experienced a higher rate of disease than the general population.

THREE-MILE ISLAND

Following the nuclear accident at Three-Mile Island, Pennsylvania, in 1979, 280 residents of the area sued the operator of the nuclear power plant, General Public Utilities Corporation. The plaintiffs sought damages for economic losses associated with relocating and medical expenses, as well as damages for emotional distress. The suit was settled in 1982 for $20 million in economic damages and $5 million for creation of a public health fund.

TIMES BEACH

Waste oil, containing the potentially toxic substance dioxin, was sprayed near the town of Times Beach, Missouri, during the 1970s. In 1983, the EPA, under the authority of the Superfund law, bought the land in the town and began to clean up the site. A few former residents of the area successfully sued the parties responsible for spraying the waste oil, alleging they had an increased risk of cancer. More recent evidence has questioned the toxicity of dioxin.

AGENT ORANGE

As a result of exposure to agent orange in Vietnam, 2.4 million veterans and relatives of veterans sued Dow Chemical Company as well as other firms. The plaintiffs received $180 million in 1985.

---

law.[5] The Superfund law was passed, in part, because of the Love Canal incident described in Box 28.3. The stated purpose of Superfund is to provide the funds needed to clean up waste dumps and accidental spills of toxic substances. The funds are obtained from taxes on petroleum and chemical companies and from recoveries from those who have dumped waste in the cleanup sites. Most courts interpret the Superfund law as imposing strict, retroactive, and joint and several liability on owners, former owners, and anyone who has dumped waste at the site, including transporters of that waste.

An example will illustrate the scope of liability. Suppose that the EPA determines that a waste site needs to be cleaned up. The EPA then identifies the parties who have dumped waste at the site. The retroactive part of the liability standard implies that the EPA can hold someone liable who dumped at the site many years earlier. The strict liability standard implies that a party can be held liable even though it took all the cost-effective safety precau-

[5]In addition to the federal Superfund law, many states have environmental laws governing cleanup and victim compensation.

tions known at the time that the waste was dumped. The joint and several liability standard implies that each party who dumped at the site could be held liable for the entire cleanup costs regardless of how little they contributed to the contamination. The liability of firms linked to the waste site does not end with the strict, retroactive, and joint and several liability associated with EPA cleanup suits. Often, common law cases, seeking damages for bodily injury and property damages, follow EPA lawsuits.

Initially, CERCLA was expected to last five years and clean up about 400 sites (at least one from each state). Each time the program's life has ended, however, Congress has voted to continue its activities. Over 30,000 potential cleanup sites have been identified, with about 1,500 classified as priority sites. From 1980 through 1995, the EPA spent about $20 billion to clean up about 300 sites and to partially clean up about 500 sites. A large percentage of these costs were used to pay attorneys, consultants, and overhead expenditures.

Insurance Coverage

The history of private market insurance coverage for environmental hazards reflects an opposite trend to the scope of liability: As the common law and statutory liability for environmental hazards have expanded, insurers have curtailed coverage, especially in basic liability policies. Large environmental liability claims, in many cases for policies written many years earlier, have contributed to significant financial problems at numerous insurance companies.

Prior to 1970, most CGL policies did not specifically address the issue of environmental hazards, but being *general* liability insurance policies, they covered environmental damages that were neither expected nor intended by the insured business. As environmental liability increased during the 1960s, insurers began to alter policies to exclude coverage arising from pollution by endorsement to the standard CGL policy, except if the event causing the pollution was "sudden and accidental." In 1973, the **sudden and accidental clause** was incorporated in the standard CGL contract. Some insurers offered a separate policy, called an environmental impairment liability (EIL) policy, to cover gradual pollution.

As discussed earlier, courts increasingly found firms liable for low-level, gradual releases of potentially toxic substances during the 1970s and 1980s under the logic of the *Rylands* case (that such releases were equivalent to sudden releases with a clear cause and effect). In addition, the introduction of the Superfund law in 1980 increased firms' liability for environmental hazards. Naturally, when firms experience environmental liability losses, they look to their liability insurers to pay the losses. Since pollution usually occurs over many years, multiple policies can potentially provide coverage. Complicating matters further, many of the policies have an exclusion for all but sudden and accidental pollution. The result has been enormous litigation between insurers and policyholders over whether policies cover environmental losses.

Coverage of Cleanup Costs

One of the issues that frequently arose in insurance policy disputes during the 1980s was whether the policy would cover the costs arising from Superfund actions. The standard CGL policy provides coverage for liability payable "as damages." Thus, the issue was whether Superfund costs should be viewed as damages. Insurers made two arguments to deny coverage for Superfund costs. First, some of Superfund's actions can be classified as preventative and thus insurers argue that the costs of these actions are not damages, but instead are loss-control expenditures. Second, in some instances, the EPA requires that a firm clean up a site, as opposed to the EPA undertaking the cleanup and then holding the firm liable for the cleanup costs. Insurers argued that when the policyholder cleans up a site, the cleanup costs are not damages and therefore are not covered. Most state courts settled these disputes in favor of the policyholder.

Coverage Trigger

One of the main sources of dispute over environmental claims relates to the **trigger of coverage** (see Chapter 23). That is, disputes arise over what policies are triggered by a claim and, if more than one policy is triggered, how claim costs are to be divided among the various policies. The answer seems straightforward: Occurrence policies cover damage for injury that occurs during the policy period and claims-made policies cover damage for injury that has occurred since the retroactive date and for which a claim is filed during the policy period (or any extended reporting period). However, environmental contamination is especially likely to create situations where it is difficult to identify when the injury occurred and produce a long-claims tail under occurrence coverage. To illustrate, consider the case of a plaintiff who is awarded damages as a result of a chemical leak that started in 1971. The plaintiff was exposed between 1971 and 1975, he first learned of the disease in 1980, and he filed a claim in 1982.

As we explained in Chapter 23, depending on the case and jurisdiction, the courts have adopted several alternative triggers of coverage. An *exposure trigger* rule would trigger all polices that were in place while the plaintiff was exposed to the substance (1971 through 1975). A *manifestation trigger* rule states that the policy that provided coverage when the injury was first manifested (1980) provides coverage, which often implies that only one policy is triggered. More recently, many courts have adopted an *injury-in-fact trigger,* which bases the trigger on specific facts (evidence) concerning when the substance actually harmed the plaintiff.[6]

Gradual Pollution and Broader Pollution Exclusions

Another important issue relating to insurance coverage disputes is whether claims related to gradual pollution are covered under the policies that contain an exclusion for all but sudden and accidental losses. Some courts have found that these policies provided coverage even when the pollution was gradual and occurred over many years. The courts' decisions in these cases have been based on one of several arguments. For example, policyholders sometimes argue that the exclusion is ambiguous. As discussed in Chapter 10, contract ambiguities often are settled in favor of the policyholder. Policyholders also have argued that, even though the pollution has occurred over several years, they were unaware that it was occurring. The revelation that the pollution occurred was sudden and the consequences of the pollution were unintended. Thus, they argue, the exclusion for all but sudden and accidental pollution does not apply. In 1986, insurers responded to some courts' tendency to provide coverage by changing the exclusion in the standard CGL contract for all but sudden and accidental pollution to an **absolute pollution exclusion** that excludes coverage for most pollution, except environmental damage due to sale and use of the insured's product. In the

---

[6]Some courts have adopted another trigger rule, known as a continuous trigger. A continuous trigger rule states that all policies that provided coverage between the date of first exposure (1971 in our example) to the date the damage was first manifested (1980), or in some decisions the date the claim was filed (1982), provide coverage.

After studying the genesis of pollution exclusions in general liability insurance policies, two state supreme courts late last year ruled in favor of policyholders by narrowing the scope of the absolute pollution exclusion.

The Illinois and Massachusetts high courts ruled the exclusion does not bar coverage for carbon monoxide-related bodily injury claims that do not involve "traditional environmental pollution." After all, the courts found, cleanup costs resulting from gradually and abruptly occurring pollution were the only insurable, contaminant-related risks that insurers sought to exclude when the industry introduced the 1970 and 1985 pollution exclusions.

As the decisions demonstrate, the nearly 30-year battle over the scope of the pollution exclusion is far from over. Policyholders and insurers remain sharply divided—even when interpreting the same evidence—over the intentions of the insurance industry.

Insurers, not surprisingly, protest that the Illinois and Massachusetts courts awarded policyholders coverage that insurers had specifically barred in the absolute pollution exclusions.

Source: Dave Lenckus, "Drafting History Debated: Policyholders, Insurers Spar over Intentions behind Pollution Exclusion," *Business Insurance*, January 5, 1998.

case of products, however, firms with significant exposure to environmental damage usually are insured on a claims-made basis, which significantly reduces insurability problems for the environmental hazard. Thus, as courts expanded liability and broadened their interpretation of insurance coverage (arguably beyond what insurers originally intended), insurers responded by explicitly restricting coverage.

The law and insurance coverage for environmental hazards continues to evolve. The absolute exclusion for environmental liability in the CGL policy has increased demand for EIL coverage, and this market experienced dramatic growth during the 1990s. On the legal front, some courts have found, despite its name, that the absolute pollution exclusion is not absolute. For example, a Louisiana Supreme Court in 1994 found that the absolute pollution exclusion is ambiguous and does not bar coverage for some types of environmental claims. A number of other states also have ruled that the absolute pollution exclusion does not necessarily bar coverage (see Box 28.4). The CGL policy was subsequently modified to include a stronger exclusion, often known as the *total pollution exclusion.*

Issues

Safety

There is little doubt the increased liability from common and statutory law (e.g., Superfund) has increased incentives for firms to take more precautions when handling or disposing of potentially hazardous substances. Some analysts, however, argue that the law has provided excessive safety incentives in some instances. For example, joint and several liability and the tendency of some courts to find liability when only a tenuous link exists between a firm's actions and losses suffered by victims might lead a firm with substantial net worth to take excessive precautions with respect to environmental issues.

Critics of the Superfund law also argue that the EPA spends excessive resources (obtained from businesses and insurers) on cleaning up sites that have little chance of posing harm to area residents. Many studies indicate that the incidence of disease for people living near cleanup sites is not significantly higher than elsewhere. So why does the EPA spend resources cleaning up sites? Critics contend that the EPA overstates health risks because the EPA's risk assessment is based on worst case scenarios for each of multiple contributing factors. The probability that one of the factors will take on its worst value is remote and the probability that all the factors will take on their worst values is next to impossible. Even in situations where sites are potentially hazardous, the EPA is criticized for its selection of remedies. The EPA usually attempts to remedy the situation by cleaning up the site for any potential future use. Thus, even if a site is unoccupied, the EPA attempts to make it safe for a residential community. Alternatives, like limiting future use of the site and paying the relocation costs of existing residents, could be more cost-effective and preferred by many residents. In a few specific cases, the EPA has been criticized for increasing risk of exposure to toxic substances because its cleanup efforts have freed some of these substances into the environment when they were previously encased.

Compensation

People generally would like to have insurance coverage against diseases and property damage caused by environmental hazards. To a large extent, private insurance for medical expenses, disability, and life insurance provides the types of coverage people are most likely to desire. Thus, the compensation for medical expenses, disability, and loss of life provided by the tort system for environmental hazards is likely to be redundant, at least in part, for many people. Private insurance coverage is not available, however, for the loss in property value or the pain and suffering and emotional distress associated with environmental hazards.

Legal Costs

A large amount of legal costs has been incurred as a result of environmental liability (estimated at up to one-half of total costs). Considerable litigation has occurred determining whether a firm is liable for cleanup costs and for personal losses suffered by individuals. In addition, as noted earlier, insurers and policyholders have litigated extensively over policy coverage. Part of the reason for the high litigation costs is that state courts vary in their interpretation of the liability rules and insurance coverage. The question is whether an alternative method exists that would compensate victims and pay cleanup costs and yet involve lower legal costs. For example, instead of using the liability system, additional taxes could be assessed on manufacturers and insurers to pay cleanup costs and compensate victims.

Incentives to Develop Former Industrial Sites

Critics of Superfund also argue that it has deterred the development of former industrial sites because of the possibility that new owners may be held liable for cleanup costs in the future. This problem is likely to be especially severe in older cities, where manufacturing was once the major industry. An advantage of locating in suburban areas is the avoidance of potential environmental liability. This problem likely has contributed to the urban decline in many cities and has had a disproportionate effect on lower income people.

28.3   Directors and Officers' Liability

Legal Background

As with other types of legal liability, directors and officers' liability has expanded during the last two decades. Directors and officers of corporations have a legal duty to act in the interest of shareholders. If they breach this duty, they can be held personally liable for the losses suffered by shareholders.[7] Directors and officers' liability is one method of providing incentives for managers to act in shareholders' interests. As discussed in Chapter 2, the managerial labor market, the market for corporate control, compensation contracts, and monitoring by shareholders also help to ensure that managers act in shareholders' interests.

State incorporation law holds that directors and officers have a duty of care and a duty of loyalty to shareholders. The **duty of care** generally is interpreted as requiring directors and officers to make informed decisions. That is, directors and officers must seek information and consider the pros and cons of a decision. Generally, the burden of proof is on the plaintiff when a duty of care violation is alleged. Also, the courts typically use the principle, called the **business judgment rule,** that they will not question informed decisions. Thus, even if a business decision turns out to have produced poor results (e.g., it decreased shareholder wealth), the courts will not hold directors and officers liable, provided that the decision was an informed decision. If the courts did not follow the business judgment rule, then the courts would be overseers of all major corporate decisions and in essence become corporate managers.

The **duty of loyalty** applies when a corporate decision involves a potentially material conflict of interest between shareholders and officers and directors. Consider, for example, a decision by the directors to accept a management buyout offer when some of the directors are part of the management team that is proposing the buyout. As part of the buyout team, the directors want as low a price as possible, but as agents for shareholders, the directors want as high a price as possible. When faced with such situations, directors and officers are required to act in the interests of shareholders, and courts hold them to a much higher standard than in duty of care cases. Not only must directors and officers become informed (as the duty of care requires), they also must take whatever steps are necessary to ensure that decisions are in shareholders' best interests.

In addition, officers and directors can be held liable for violating federal securities laws. The Securities Act of 1993 and the Securities Exchange Act of 1934 impose a number of requirements on a firm and its officers and directors. For example, firms are required to disclose information that is relevant to investors in a timely manner. If the firm fails to do so, then officers and directors, as well as the firm, can be sued by shareholders.

Shareholder suits can be classified as either derivative or direct. **Derivative suits** are brought by shareholders on behalf of the corporation. Any court-awarded damages or settlements are received by the corporation. In contrast, in **direct actions suits,** plaintiffs bringing the suit (and their attorneys) receive the damages and settlements. Direct actions against officers and directors can be either individual actions or class actions. *Class actions* are suits brought on behalf of a group of plaintiffs that are alleged to have been harmed.

Shareholder suits alleging that officers and directors violated their duty of care or duty of loyalty often are related to corporate activities like acquisitions and bankruptcies. It is not surprising, therefore, that the number of shareholder suits increased during the 1980s with the increased takeover activity and bankruptcies of financial institutions during that period. Shareholder suits alleging violation of securities laws often are associated with the process of going public through the initial public offering of equity securities and with seasoned equity offerings. In these cases, the purchasers of the new securities claim that officers and directors failed to disclose material information. Also, as we discuss in more detail below, a large number of shareholder class actions have been filed in recent years against

[7]Directors and officers also can be sued by nonshareholder claimants.

the officers and directors of publicly traded companies alleging that managers failed to disclose information in a timely manner, or, as in the cases of Enron and World Com deliberately misled investors by bogus accounting and other deceptive practices.

Indemnification and Insurance Coverage

Before describing directors and officers' insurance policies, we must describe corporate **indemnification** of officers and directors, which refers to the reimbursement by the corporation for officers and directors' legal costs and losses from settlements, judgments, and fines. As summarized in Table 28.1, many states limit the extent to which officers and directors can be indemnified based on the type of suit that is filed. For derivative actions, indemnification can cover only litigation expenses. However, for direct actions, indemnification can cover judgments, settlements, and fines, as well as litigation expenses. The logic for limiting indemnification for derivative suits lies in the observation that if indemnification also covered judgments and settlements, then the corporation would be paying damages to itself.

Prior to the mid-1980s, almost all states had indemnification laws as described in Table 28.1. Around that time, courts began to hold officers and directors liable in circumstances where they previously had not. As a result, insurance premiums increased, which caused firms to look for new ways of compensating officers and directors for damages awarded in derivative suits. In response to corporate lobbying efforts, a number of state legislatures passed laws expanding the ability of firms to indemnify officers and directors for judgments and settlement amounts in derivative actions.

Directors and officers' (D&O) insurance generally has two parts. One part provides coverage for officers and directors for losses that are not indemnified by the corporation. The other part provides coverage to the corporation for indemnification costs. Many policies include per director deductibles as well as aggregate deductibles. In addition, many policies have a coinsurance provision that requires officers and directors to pay some percentage of losses above a limit. D&O insurance policies generally are claims-made policies. Unlike CGL policies, D&O insurance policies do not permit the insurer to take over the defense of the claim. An explanation for this difference is that the reputation of the officers and directors often is at stake in a shareholder suit and therefore that officers and directors often would want to be involved in their defense and in settlement decisions.

D&O insurance policies typically have a number of exclusions, which are important for understanding the incentives of officers and directors to settle cases (see below). A common provision excludes coverage for claims that arise as a result of an officer or director gaining illegal personal profit. Thus, insurers may deny coverage for damages resulting from a director's violation of his or her duty of loyalty (i.e., where a conflict of interest with

TABLE 28.1
Summary of the types of officers and directors' losses that can be indemnified by corporations in many states.

Type of Action	Corporation Can Indemnify
Derivative actions	Litigation expenses
Direct actions	Litigation expenses and judgments, fines, and settlement amounts

shareholders exists). Another important provision excludes coverage for damages that are "uninsurable under the law." A fundamental legal principle states that as a matter of public policy, people should not be insured for liability damages that arise from their willful misconduct. This exclusion can be used to deny coverage for known violations of security laws.

The Enron collapse in 2001 has produced numerous suits against its former directors and officers by shareholders (and employees whose retirement savings were heavily invested in Enron stock). Along with other firms' problems, such as World Com, this collapse also has roiled D&O insurance markets. Enron had $350 million of D&O coverage in 11 layers. Some of the insurers are seeking to have their coverage declared null and void, alleging material misrepresentation by Enron to their underwriters.

Issues

Incentives to Settle Securities Class Actions

A controversial issue related to directors and officers' liability in the 1990s was the number of class actions alleging that public firms failed to disclose material information in a timely manner. The following circumstances are typical of these suits. Suppose that Posey Inc. announces that its annual earnings are substantially less than expected and that its stock price immediately falls 20 percent. A day or two later, an attorney files a class action alleging that directors and officers had the negative information long before it was released and therefore that the managers committed fraud and misrepresentation by failing to release the information for a period of time, called the *class period*. Because the firm's stock price did not reflect the negative information during the class period, investors who purchased shares during the class period and held their shares through the end of the class period suffered losses and are eligible for compensation.

Many analysts believed that a large proportion of securities class actions were **strike suits** (i.e., they have little or no merit but they are filed to coerce management into a settlement). Managers often have compelling reasons to settle, in part because of their directors and officers' insurance contracts. As noted above, defendant managers who are found guilty of fraud and misrepresentation can be held personally liable for alleged plaintiff shareholders' losses. In most instances, the magnitude of alleged damages easily exceeds managers' wealth. D&O insurance and corporate indemnification typically will pay settlement amounts, but exclusions in the D&O insurance policies allow the insurer to deny coverage if managers are found by the court to have committed fraud and misrepresentation. Thus, managers face a decision of fighting the class action in court (which carries a small probability of incurring very large personal losses) or settling out of court (which ensures that their immediate personal financial losses will be relatively small).[8]

---

[8]A natural question is why D&O insurers go along with a settlement if a case has no merit. The insurer would appear to be better off fighting the case in court, because, even though insurers may lose a few cases at trial, the fact that there are large numbers of cases suggests that most of the risk of large average losses is diversified away. One answer is that the settlement costs are lower than the expected legal fees from fighting the case. A second possibility is that insurers typically are not given control of the officers and directors' defense. Finally, insurers may be fearful of bad-faith suits (see Chapter 10). If the insurer convinces directors and officers to fight the case in court and they lose, then the officers and directors might sue the insurer for bad faith. Thus, insurers usually acquiesce to the desire of officers and directors to settle cases.

The Merit of Securities Class Actions

As noted, considerable controversy exists regarding the merit of a large proportion of class actions alleging violations of securities laws. Critics of these suits claim that (1) the suits typically have little merit; (2) they are brought solely to coerce a settlement, which mainly benefits attorneys; (3) large costs are imposed on corporations defending these suits; and (4) the effect of these suits on corporate disclosure is the opposite of what the securities laws were originally intended to accomplish. With respect to the last criticism, it is argued that instead of promoting information disclosure, firms are reluctant to provide forward-looking information that may not be realized due to chance. For example, statements that the managers expect sales to increase significantly over the next year could be used in a shareholder suit alleging the statement was misleading if the forecast turns out to be inaccurate ex post, no matter how accurate the prediction ex ante (i.e., given information available at the time the prediction was made). Whether rightly or wrongly, Enron and other highly publicized financial collapses have undermined these criticisms.

Plaintiffs' attorneys counter that class actions compensate victims of corporate fraud and misrepresentation. In addition, plaintiffs' attorneys argue that by imposing personal costs on fraudulent managers, these suits encourage the timely release of accurate information, which reduces information asymmetries in the stock market and thus lowers the cost of capital in the United States. They also point out that since plaintiff attorneys have incentives to identify disclosure violations, taxpayers are not burdened with enforcement costs.

Congress passed the Securities Litigation Reform Act in 1995. One aspect of the law was intended to deter plaintiffs' attorneys from filing suits with little or no evidence that fraud had occurred except for the fact that the firm's stock price has dropped by a large percentage. The law also gives firms a safe-harbor provision intended to reduce the likelihood that firms will have to pay damages for forward-looking statements. Lately this act has been criticized for perhaps having gone too far. Congress enacted legislation in 2002 that beefed up criminal penalties for corporate wrongdoing.

28.4   Summary

- Products liability law has evolved from contract law to negligence to strict liability for product defects. Product manufacturers can be held liable under strict liability for design, manufacturing, or warning defects.

- Making manufacturers strictly liable for all consumer losses can improve safety incentives when consumers are uninformed about product risk, because strict liability gives manufacturers proper incentives to make safe products and reduce the likelihood that consumers will purchase too many risky products. However, it also is argued that the application of strict liability in practice may lead to excessive safety and higher prices, discourage innovation, and encourage continued use of older,

less safe products. Strict liability for all consumer losses is likely to force consumers to purchase more implicit insurance coverage than they desire.

- Liability for environmental damage under common law expanded greatly during the last half of the 20th century, and Superfund legislation expanded liability for the cleanup of waste sites. As liability expanded, insurers first attempted to restrict coverage in CGL policies to only sudden and accidental pollution; subsequently, they introduced an absolute pollution exclusion in these policies. Pollution coverage now is available through customized environmental impairment liability (EIL) policies, which usually are sold on a claims-made basis.

- Directors and officers of corporations have a duty of care and a duty of loyalty to shareholders. If they breach these duties, they can be sued by shareholders. Directors and officers also can be sued by shareholders for violations of securities laws that require firms to disclose material information in a timely manner. Depending on the state and corporate charter, directors and officers are indemnified by their corporations for legal defense costs and/or settlements and awards. D&O insurance coverage often is purchased to cover (1) some nonindemnified losses to directors and officers, and (2) some corporate costs of indemnification.

Key Terms

manufacturing defect 607	absolute pollution exclusion 616
design defect 607	duty of care 619
warning defect 607	business judgment rule 619
express warranty 608	duty of loyalty 619
implied warranty 608	derivative suits 619
statute of repose 612	direct action suits 619
CERCLA or Superfund law 613	indemnification 620
sudden and accidental clause 615	strike suits 621
trigger of coverage 616	

Questions and Problems

1. Compare the incentives of manufacturers to design safe products under the following scenarios for products liability:

   a. Consumers cannot sue manufacturers for injuries.

   b. Manufacturers have strict liability for defective products.

2. Critically evaluate the following statement: "Strict liability for products is socially beneficial because it provides correct safety incentives for manufacturers and consumers."

3. Provide an argument that the US products liability system results in excessive compensation to victims.

4. Provide an argument that strict liability lowers legal costs compared to a negligence rule.

5. Chapter 12 summarized the advantages and disadvantages of government regulation versus legal liability. Apply those arguments to critically evaluate the following statement: "As a society, we should place more reliance on government regulation than on personal injury suits to influence firms' disposal of potentially toxic substances into the air, water, and soil."

6. Outline a procedure for assessing whether the benefits of Superfund cleanup operations are worth the costs.

7. Explain how increased uncertainty concerning products liability risk and possibly large punitive damages will affect the fair premium for products liability insurance.

8. Using the factors that influence the willingness of insurers to supply insurance coverage and consumers' willingness to pay for coverage (i.e., the insurability of risk, see Chapter 10), provide an explanation for why insurers have restricted coverage as the courts have expanded liability for environmental damage.

9. Suppose that an officer of a corporation has been sued for $55 million, where the suit alleges that the officer knowingly failed to disclose relevant information to investors. The officer believes the case has no merit, but because of the uncertainties of court

cases, the officer estimates that the probability of losing the suit at a trial is 0.01. The
expected legal fees from going to trial equal
$200,000. The plaintiff attorney has made a
settlement offer of $1 million.

a. Assuming that the officer is uninsured,
what is the officer's expected cost of going to trial?

b. Assuming that the officer is uninsured,
explain why the officer may accept the
settlement offer.

Answer to Concept Check

1. Negligence, because the injured party has to
prove that the manufacturer did not use reasonable care (cost-justified precautions).
Strict liability requires proof that the product
was defective and unreasonably dangerous,
although this sometimes involves standards
similar to negligence. With absolute liability,
the injured party would need to prove only
that the product caused the injury.

References

Abraham, Kenneth. "Cleaning Up the
Environmental Liability Insurance Mess."
Valparaiso Law Review 27 (1993),
pp. 601–36. (*Analyzes insurance policy
disputes related to environmental claims.*)

Epstein, Richard. *Modern Products Liability Law.*
Westport, CT: Quorum Books, 1980.
(*Provides a detailed discussion of the history
and effects of products liability law.*)

Huber, Peter. "Environmental Hazards and
Liability Law." In *Liability: Perspectives and
Policy,* eds. R. Litan and C. Winston.
Washington, DC: The Brookings Institution,
1988. (*Provides background and discussion of
the problems in environmental liability.*)

Priest, George. "The Insurance Crisis and Modern
Tort Law." *Yale Law Journal* 96 (1987),
pp. 1521–90. (*General discussion of the
effects of expanding liability and uncertain
legal costs on liability insurance markets and
the insurability of liability risk.*)

Romano, Roberta. "Corporate Governance in the
Aftermath of the Insurance Crisis." In *Tort
Law and the Public Interest: Competition,
Innovation, and Consumer Welfare,* ed. Peter
Schuck. New York: W. W. Norton, 1991.
(*Analyzes shareholder suits and their effect on
insurance prices and coverage during the
1980s.*)

Chapter 29

Issues in Liability Risk and Its Management

Chapter Objectives

- Explain how the doctrine of limited liability allows businesses to reduce tort liability risk and describe the rationale and limitations of this doctrine.
- Discuss how businesses are liable for the actions of agents, employees, and independent contractors and describe the effects of applicable legal doctrines on incentives for loss control and the cost of risk.
- Explain how businesses manage liability risk through hold harmless and indemnity agreements and the effects of these agreements on the cost of risk.
- Provide an overview of key strategic and operational issues in the management and administration of liability and workers' compensation claims.

29.1   Risk Shifting through Limited Liability

Chapter 12 briefly discussed the doctrine of limited liability, the resulting judgment proof problem, and the possible effects of this doctrine on safety. For corporations, the limited liability doctrine holds (except in unusual circumstances discussed below) that shareholders cannot be held liable for claims against the corporation that exceed the value of the corporation's assets. As a result, the liability of shareholders is limited to their ownership interest in the corporation: Claimants against the corporation generally cannot reach the personal assets of individual shareholders or other business assets of corporate shareholders (e.g., other assets of a parent corporation). In this section you will learn more about (1) limited liability for corporations and its relation to tort liability risk and its management, including how limited liability sometimes can lead to excessive risk of injury; (2) the rationale for limited liability despite this problem; and (3) exceptions to the doctrine.

Limited Liability as Insurance against Loss

We begin by explaining a fundamental point: Compared to a system of unlimited liability, limited liability essentially provides shareholders with insurance against losses that exceed corporate assets. Consider a corporation with assets of $10 million, and initially assume that the corporation has no debt. What happens if the business causes injuries that produce tort liability awards against the corporation equal to $12 million? The doctrine of limited liability holds that the claimants can obtain only the value of the corporation's assets. Therefore, only $10 million will be available to claimants; $2 million will be unpaid.

If, contrary to actual legal rules, unlimited liability existed, then the tort claimants could obtain the remaining $2 million from the personal wealth of individual shareholders or other business assets of corporate shareholders. Thus, compared to the doctrine of unlimited liability, in this example, limited liability reduces the loss to shareholders by $2 million. The effect of limited liability is directly analogous to insurance against losses in excess of $10 million. The limited liability rule is equivalent to giving shareholders an insurance contract that pays losses above an aggregate deductible equal to the value of the corporation's assets.

Figure 29.1 illustrates the payoff to shareholders with a limited liability rule when the corporation has no debt in its capital structure. Up to the value of assets, shareholders bear the full cost of tort claims (i.e., tort claims reduce shareholder wealth dollar for dollar). However, because of limited liability, the loss to shareholders is capped at an amount equal to the value of assets. This figure looks just like Figure 25.2, which showed the amount of loss borne by a business that buys an insurance policy for losses in excess of an aggregate deductible.

If the business has issued debt to finance investment, the situation becomes a little more complicated, but the same basic result holds. To illustrate, assume that the firm has $15 million in assets but that it owes $5 million to lenders (i.e., one-third of its assets are financed with debt and two-thirds with equity). Now what happens if $12 million in tort claims arise? In this case, the firm's assets are less than its total liabilities (debt plus tort claims). The value of the firm's stock is zero. Because tort claimants have legal priority over lenders (i.e., tort claims are satisfied before the claims of lenders), tort claimants will receive $12 million. Lenders will receive the remaining assets of $3 million, but lenders do not receive the other $2 million that they are owed.

FIGURE 29.1

How limited liability limits losses with no debt claims.

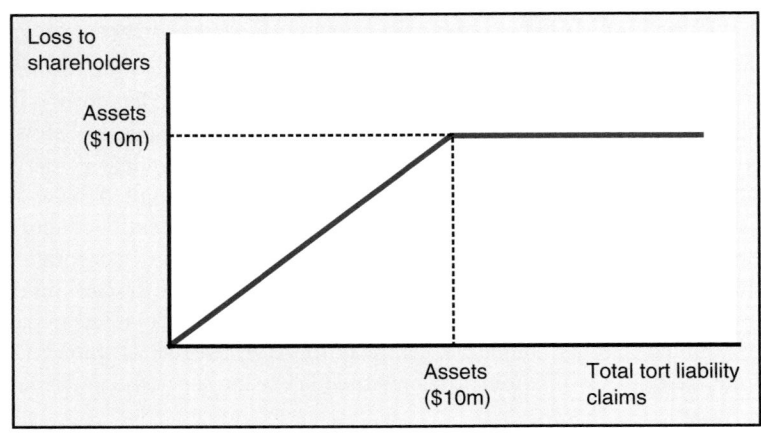

Note that with debt the loss to shareholders from tort liability claims in this example is still limited to $10 million by the doctrine of limited liability. Shareholders can lose only the excess of assets over the amount owed to lenders ($15 million – $5 million). In this case, the lenders can be viewed as having provided the shareholders with $5 million of insurance coverage against losses above $10 million. If tort liability claims exceed the $10 million, lenders in effect pay the excess up to the total value of assets. If tort claims exceed the total value of assets ($15 million), tort claimants will be paid $15 million and lenders will receive nothing.

These simple examples should convince you that limited liability allows risk shifting that is analogous to insurance. Without borrowing by the firm, the risk of losses in excess of assets is shifted from shareholders to tort claimants. With borrowing, the risk of losses in excess of the firm's equity value is shifted first to lenders and, if claims exceed the value of assets, to tort claimants. An important implication is that the financing decisions of corporations (how much debt and equity are used) affect who bears risk in the economy.

The Case of Parents and Subsidiaries

The organization of a corporation—whether subsidiary corporations or operating divisions are used—also affects who bears risk. To see this, consider a parent that has two subsidiaries (A and B), no debt, and no assets besides the stock of the subsidiaries. Each subsidiary has assets of $25 million, so the parent has consolidated assets of $50 million. Each subsidiary has a 0.01 probability of a $50 million tort liability claim and a 0.99 probability of no claim. Also assume for simplicity that the probability that both subsidiaries have a tort claim is zero. Finally, if a tort claim occurs, assume that the parent will use the subsidiary's assets of $25 million to pay the claimants and declare the subsidiary insolvent, thus limiting the reduction in the parent's assets to $25 million. (We discuss later why the parent sometimes might decide to use its remaining assets, in effect the assets of the other subsidiary, to pay all claims.)

How does limited liability affect the risk to the parent and thus its shareholders under these assumptions? Table 29.1 shows the probability distribution, expected value, and standard deviation of (1) losses to the parent (or corporate group) when the parent has limited liability for claims against its subsidiaries, and (2) losses to the parent if the parent does not have limited liability so that the parent will have to use assets from the other subsidiary to pay the full claim. In this example, the probability distribution with unlimited liability for the parent equals the probability distribution of total damage claims because tort claims cannot exceed the parent's assets. The table also shows the expected value of unpaid tort

TABLE 29.1
Illustration of risk reduction with limited liability of parent for claims against subsidiaries.

	Parent Loss Distribution (values in $ millions)	
	Limited Liability for Parent	Unlimited Liability for Parent
Probability:		
0.98 (no claim)	$ 0.0	$ 0.0
0.01 (claim against A)	25.0	50.0
0.01 (claim against B)	25.0	50.0
Expected value	0.5	1.0
Standard deviation	3.5	7.0
Expected value of unpaid claims	0.5	0.0

claims in each case. We also have assumed that the limited liability rule does not affect the probability of a tort claim. As you will learn below, this assumption is not as innocent as it might first appear. It is nonetheless useful at this point to highlight the risk reduction associated with limited liability.

As illustrated in Table 29.1, compared to unlimited liability for the parent, limited liability (1) reduces the expected loss to the parent by $0.5 million, (2) increases the expected value of unpaid claims by $0.5 million, and (3) reduces the standard deviation of losses to the parent by 50 percent (from $7 million to $3.5 million). The risk reduction indicated by the lower standard deviation is directly analogous to the risk reduction that would occur with a liability insurance policy that pays claims in excess of a per occurrence deductible (retention limit) equal to $25 million. In essence, the parent is insured for claims above a $25 million deductible (the value of assets) for each subsidiary.

This example suggests that the judicious use of subsidiary corporations can allow a parent corporation to limit its exposure to large tort liability claims that otherwise might seriously weaken or even threaten the viability of the parent and other subsidiaries. This does not mean, however, that parents automatically will declare subsidiaries bankrupt and walk away from tort claims or other obligations that exceed a subsidiary's assets. In many cases parents will have an incentive to pay claims in excess of a subsidiary's assets in order to avoid adverse effects on the reputation of the parent and other subsidiaries.[1] Limited liability nonetheless provides a valuable risk-reducing option for the parent: It gives the parent the option to walk away and thereby preserve other assets, including valuable investment opportunities, if the cost of paying the claims exceeds the adverse reputation effects from not paying claims.

Who Pays for the Implicit Insurance?

You may be wondering whether firms have to pay for the implicit insurance protection provided by limited liability. The answer depends on the situation. For example, when firms borrow money, lenders routinely consider the likelihood that they will not be repaid in full because of limited liability, and they require the borrower to pay more for credit because of this risk. This increase in the promised interest rate on the loan can be viewed as a charge (premium) for the implicit insurance provided by the lender due to the limited liability of the borrower. Similarly, and related to the discussion in earlier chapters, consumers (including business customers) who might be harmed by a firm's products and not have their damages fully paid because of limited liability might therefore reduce the price that they are willing to pay for the firm's products. The price reduction could be viewed as a premium for the implicit insurance provided by product users as a result of limited liability for product manufacturers.

The Moral Hazard Problem

As discussed in Chapter 12, limited liability reduces the ability of the tort liability system to provide optimal safety incentives, which in some cases can lead to an excessive risk of harm. To elaborate, limited liability implies that firms may not bear all of the costs of tort liability claims. Thus, when making decisions about which activities to pursue, firms may not consider all of the costs that they impose on others. Consequently, some firms will en-

---

[1] As an example, State Farm Mutual provided about $3 billion to its major subsidiary insurer to pay its claims from Hurricane Andrew in 1992.

gage in excessively risky activities. If the parties that may be harmed are able to charge a price (an implicit premium) to the firm that perfectly reflects the expected value of unpaid claims from the firm's activities, then the moral hazard problem disappears.[2] Of course, due to costly and imperfect information, perfect pricing of this sort is infeasible in the real world. In some cases the risk may not be priced at all. This outcome might occur, for example, for the risk of environmental damage to persons that have no relation to the firm.

Our earlier example assumed no moral hazard; that is, we assumed that the probability and severity of tort claims did not depend on the limited liability rule. However, because the parent would not have to pay the amount of the claim above $25 million with limited liability, its incentive to invest in precautions to reduce the probability of a claim or the amount of claim could be lower than if the parent did not have limited liability. As a result, the expected amount of damages could be higher with limited liability, and the social cost of risk would not be minimized. Similarly, because firms may not have to bear all of the costs of tort liability claims, their investments might be tilted toward projects that create greater risk of harm than would be the case with unlimited liability.

The moral hazard problem associated with limited liability is reduced by a number of factors in addition to the possible ability of potential claimants to charge some price for the implicit insurance protection. Just as deductibles reduce moral hazard with conventional insurance, the fact that valuable assets must be lost before liability for tort claims is capped by limited liability reduces the moral hazard problem. For this reason alone, the moral hazard problem is likely to be negligible for firms with substantial assets. In addition, all of the factors that encourage firms to reduce risk by hedging or insurance (e.g., the effect of risk on expected bankruptcy costs, possible loss of profitable investment opportunities, and so on) will mitigate the tendency to take on excessive risk. Finally, as we discuss below, the courts may not enforce limited liability in cases of severe moral hazard.

Why Have Limited Liability?

Why have limited liability for tort claims given the potential for moral hazard? Entire books have been written on the rationale for limited liability for debt, tort, and other claims. The simple answer is that it commonly is believed that limited liability increases productive investment compared to unlimited liability and that the value of this increased investment outweighs the costs of excessive risk taking.

Again, an insurance analogy may be helpful. Without insurance against property and liability losses, risk aversion might greatly reduce the amount of risky but productive investment. Insurance is socially valuable because it reduces risk and facilitates productive activity. But insurance is not perfect—it generally is characterized by moral hazard and a variety of other problems that reduce its value and increase the cost of risk. Imperfect and costly information make it infeasible for insurance pricing to eliminate moral hazard. As a result, it often is optimal to reduce insurance protection through the use of deductibles and other forms of partial insurance (see Chapter 10). Similarly, it can be argued that limited liability is socially valuable despite the moral hazard problem. As noted above, moral hazard from limited liability is mitigated by the partial nature of the insurance protection: The firm's equity must be lost before the insurance kicks in.

---

[2]This situation is conceptually identical to that described for moral hazard in general in Chapter 10. If insurance premiums reflect all of the effects of the insured on expected claim costs with perfect accuracy, there is no moral hazard.

Individual Shareholders

One specific advantage of limited liability for individual shareholders is that it facilitates separation of the management and risk-bearing functions in a firm. That is, without the protection of limited liability, individuals often would be much less willing to invest without engaging in more costly monitoring of managers or becoming managers themselves. Since the people who are more efficient at bearing risk (people with money) are not necessarily the people who are good managers, the absence of limited liability would yield an economy with less effective managers and, more important, less investment in risky yet productive activities. Another argument for limited liability is that without limited liability the risk of owning a firm's stock would depend on the total wealth of all of its shareholders, because the amount of damages that one shareholder might have to pay would depend on the wealth of all shareholders. At a minimum, this would complicate stock valuation and individual decisions about which stocks to own. In addition, each investor would likely incur costs monitoring every other investor's wealth, which would increase the total cost of investing in stocks and of holding a diversified portfolio.

Limited Liability for Parent Corporations

The preceding arguments are less applicable to limited liability for parents of subsidiary corporations. Some people believe that the rationale for limited liability is much weaker in this case, especially for tort claims. A few lawyers and law professors even have suggested elimination of limited liability for parent corporations. While the issues are complicated, you should be aware of two related points. First, elimination of limited liability for parent corporations in many cases would not reduce and sometimes even might increase moral hazard and the expected value of unpaid liability claims. The reason is that if limited liability for parent corporations were eliminated, fewer firms would combine under common ownership and some existing corporate groups would split up to reduce the risk of having to use assets in one subsidiary to pay claims against another subsidiary.

To illustrate using our earlier example, without limited liability the parent simply could divest one of the subsidiaries. The relationship between subsidiaries A and B would end. The assets of either firm therefore would never be available to pay tort claims against the other. The expected value of unpaid liability claims would not decrease. For each firm there still would be a 0.01 probability of an unpaid tort claim in the amount of $25 million (the $50 million claim minus $25 million in assets). There also is little or no reason to expect that firms A and B would have more incentive to invest in loss control. In addition, if corporate groups were to split into unaffiliated entities, the possibility that a parent might pay tort claims in excess of the value of a subsidiary's assets in order to avoid damage to the group's reputation would disappear.

The second and related problem that would arise if limited liability for parent corporations were eliminated is that any resulting division of corporate groups into unaffiliated entities would sacrifice any valuable synergies that otherwise might occur from affiliation, such as possible cost savings in raising capital. While valuable synergies might provide incentives for continued affiliation (or new affiliations), if limited liability for parents were eliminated, the reduction in value from splitups that did occur and future affiliations that would not take place still would weaken any case for eliminating limited liability. Our own view is that eliminating limited liability for parent corporations might primarily encourage large numbers of costly lawsuits and possibly create a severe recession.

One of the most important areas of debate regarding limited liability of parents for subsidiaries has involved environmental liability under Superfund (see Chapter 28). In a key case decided in 1989 that has been followed in other cases, Kayser-Roth Corporation, an apparel manufacturer, was held liable for damages and cleanup costs associated with the activities of its wholly-owned subsidiary Stamina Mills, a textile mill that had been dissolved in 1979. The government brought action against Kayser-Roth, arguing that the corporate veil should be pierced. The court agreed because Kayser-Roth had exercised practical control of the subsidiary's decision making and had appointed its board of directors.

Exceptions to Limited Liability

In some cases courts have refused to uphold limited liability and instead have forced shareholders to pay claims in excess of corporate assets or equity. This outcome is colorfully known as **piercing the corporate veil** or simply veil piercing. The possibility of veil piercing reduces the ability of shareholders to rely on limited liability as a risk-shifting device, and it is another factor that reduces moral hazard associated with limited liability. We stress, however, that veil piercing is not common. Courts do not routinely hold shareholders liable for claims in excess of corporate assets or equity.

While the law is fairly complex in this area, veil piercing has occurred in two main types of tort liability situations. The first is where the corporation is closely held with the primary shareholders directly involved with the firm's decisions or actually responsible for operations (e.g., they are owner/managers) and the firm engages in obviously risky activity with limited assets and insurance. You should note that moral hazard would appear to be severe in this case. One advantage of limited liability, the separation of management and risk bearing, also is not present. Thus, the benefits of limited liability are comparatively small, and the moral hazard problem is comparatively large.

The second main situation in which veil piercing has occurred for tort liability claims is for parent-subsidiary relationships where the parent has strong control over or common management with the subsidiary and the subsidiary has engaged in obviously risky activity with relatively little capital. Again, it can be argued in this situation that the benefits of limited liability are low compared to the costs. Box 29.1 discusses an example of veil piercing in a parent-subsidiary relationship involving liability for environmental damages and cleanup.

Another situation in which a parent might be held liable for claims against a subsidiary is where the parent makes statements or behaves in a way that causes potential claimants to assume that the parent guarantees the obligations of the subsidiary. A variant would involve misrepresentation of material facts to potential claimants. These situations have been more common for debt or other financial obligations as opposed to tort liability claims for bodily injury or property damage.

Concept Check

1. Explain intuitively why limited liability might cause a firm to take on excessive risk of tort liability.

29.2   Liability for Actions of Employees and Other Parties

Vicarious Liability Doctrine

A fundamental legal doctrine in tort law is that in relationships between principals and agents, the principal is liable for the negligence and related torts (e.g., any strict liability) of the agent in performing his or her duties for the principal. This doctrine is known as **vicarious liability** and is sometimes called *imputed negligence.* In this context, "agent" is a general legal/economic term to indicate any party that is acting on behalf of another party known as the principal. The most important principal-agent relationship governed by the vicarious liability doctrine is the relationship between an employer (the principal) and an employee (the agent). But the doctrine is much broader than this. If, for example, you agree to run an errand for a friend using your car and negligently run down a pedestrian, your friend (the principal) conceivably could be sued and held liable because you would be acting as your friend's agent.[3]

The injured party in these situations can sue both the agent and the principal but can only recover the amount of the loss. In some cases, the principal might subsequently sue the agent to recover money that the principal had to pay because of the agent's negligence. However, suits by employers against employees in this context are rare for several reasons. First, because employees are risk averse, it usually is advantageous for employers to guaranty employees either implicitly or explicitly with liability insurance that they will not suffer loss of personal assets for ordinary negligence. General business liability insurance policies, for example, usually explicitly include employees as insureds under the policy. Second, without either explicitly insuring the employee or an implicit guaranty that the employer will not sue the employee, suits by the employer would in many cases recover little money because many employees have comparatively little wealth and will not have liability insurance coverage for business torts.

The rationale for vicarious liability is that it provides the principal, the party that is directing and managing the activity, with incentives to train, supervise, and monitor agents in order to reduce the risk of harm to other parties. The doctrine also prevents principals from using financially weak, uninsured, and thus judgment proof agents as a method of avoiding responsibility for harm. As a result, holding principals liable for the torts of agents increases safety and reduces the judgment proof problem that arises because agents have limited liability (due to their limited personal wealth).

Liability of Businesses for Actions of Independent Contractors

Does vicarious liability apply to the actions of independent contractors who are hired by businesses to perform some task (e.g., to construct a building)? Before turning to this question, you need to learn a little about the difference between an independent contractor and an employee (agent). The common law distinguishes independent contractors from employees on a variety of dimensions, including (1) whether the business actively supervises and directs the other party (i.e., dictates how the work should be done as opposed to what result is expected), and (2) whether the business establishes hours of work, provides tools

---

[3]Your friend would be protected by your auto liability insurance, however (see Chapter 13).

and equipment, and so on.[4] If a business does either or both of these things, the other party will be considered an employee (or agent). If not, the party is an independent contractor. (You should be aware that the terminology can be a little confusing here. For example, some insurance agents are legally considered to be independent contractors.)

The original common law rule was that businesses (or individuals) that hired independent contractors could not be held vicariously liable for the torts of the contractor. While this rule still is applied in some narrow instances, there are so many exceptions that for most intents and purposes a business faces substantial risk of liability if the contractor injures some other party. There are three main situations where the firm can be held liable.

First, we hinted above that sometimes there is ambiguity or disagreement over whether a party is an employee or an independent contractor. If the court determines that the party is acting as an employee, which has occurred in many cases, the business that hired the party can be held vicariously liable. Second, many states have held that protecting the public safety constitutes a **nondelegable duty.** This means that the business cannot delegate the duty to keep the public safe to an independent contractor. As a result, if the contractor injures a member of the public, the business that hired the contractor can be held vicariously liable. The third situation does not involve vicarious liability, but it has substantially the same effect: The business must pay damages. Many cases have held businesses liable for negligence in failing to take reasonable precautions to select a safe contractor. In these instances, the business is sued for damages directly by the injured party.

As a result of these exceptions, businesses have limited ability to shift legal responsibility for harm by using independent contractors. Some people suggest a deep pockets rationale for these exceptions: The primary purpose is to allow the injured party access to the business's assets or insurance coverage, which often might be larger than for the independent contractor. In a sense this may be true, but the pejorative context of the term *deep pockets* would appear to be inappropriate for describing the general legal rules. (How they are applied in some cases may be another matter.)

The economic rationale for significant limitations on shifting legal liability risk through the use of independent contractors is that these limitations help reduce the cost of risk. Limited liability might cause contractors with few assets and little or no liability insurance to have too little incentive for safety if the parties that might be harmed by the contractor (such as members of the public) cannot force the contractor to bear the expected costs of its actions. If contractors with few assets and little or no liability insurance do not have to bear the full cost of their actions, they also might be able to charge a lower price than firms with substantial assets at risk and/or liability insurance. Note that the issue here is not one of desirable variation in price and quality. The key point is that limited liability may allow some firms to have levels of safety and prices that are too low to minimize the cost of risk, and these low prices might tempt firms to hire such contractors if the firms cannot be held liable for the contractors' actions.

In short, if firms could routinely avoid the risk of legal liability for injury by using independent contractors, they would have less incentive to seek and pay the higher price required to cover the costs of contractors that bear more of the expected cost of harm to other

---

[4]Whether a party is an employee or independent contractor also has important tax implications which, fortunately for you and us, are beyond the scope of this book.

parties. As a result, an unlimited ability of businesses to shift legal liability risk to independent contractors would result in lower than optimal safety in society.

One drawback to legal rules that hold firms liable for the actions of independent contractors is that they might reduce the incentives of contractors to be safe if the contractor has more of an effect on safety than the principal but the rules allow the costs of injuries to be shared with the principal. However, as we elaborate in the next section, these situations can be handled by agreements between the firm and the contractor that reallocate the ultimate financial responsibility for harm.

Concept Check

2. Other things being equal, compare the expected cost of liability claims from a lawsuit for a small construction business with no liability insurance or assets at risk to a comparable business that buys substantial liability insurance.

29.3   Hold Harmless and Indemnity Agreements

Businesses routinely use two closely related types of contracts to manage their liability risk in view of the legal rules described in the preceding section. A **hold harmless agreement** is a contract between (in the simplest case) two parties in which one party agrees to hold the other party harmless for losses that arise out of some activity. This means that if the party that is to be held harmless (party B) is ordered to pay or agrees to settle damages under circumstances covered by the agreement, then the other party (party A) will pay the injured party on behalf of party B. An **indemnity agreement** is similar except that party B (known as the indemnitee) pays the injured party and is then reimbursed by party A (known as the indemnitor).

In some principal-agent relationships, agents agree to hold harmless or indemnify principals for injuries caused by the negligence of the agent. For example, independent contractors routinely agree to hold harmless or indemnify businesses that hire their services for liability due to negligence of the contractor. Manufacturers often agree to hold harmless or indemnify product retailers for possible liability of the retailer for injuries caused by manufacturing defects. Similarly, retailers that modify products prior to sale may agree to hold harmless or indemnify the manufacturer if the modifications contribute to consumer injury. These contracts often are also used in lessor-lessee relationships. For example, the lessee may agree to hold harmless or indemnify the lessor for injuries on the premises that result from the lessee's negligence.

Effect on the Cost of Risk

Hold harmless/indemnity agreements help minimize the cost of risk by allowing the contracting parties to reallocate financial responsibility for harm away from what might occur from application of the underlying legal doctrines governing liability.[5] To understand the key idea, first recall that limitations on the ability of businesses to shift legal liability for harm to independent contractors are desirable because they encourage businesses to deal with safe and financially responsible contractors. However, given these legal limitations, it often will be advantageous for the parties to use a hold harmless or indemnity agreement

---

[5]To some extent this reallocation is similar to the reallocation of liability in the example of the factory polluting the river in Chapter 12.

to ensure that financial responsibility for injuries caused by the independent contractor will be borne fully by the contractor.

Making the contractor bear full responsibility for the contractor's negligence gives the contractor proper incentives to invest in loss control. Without the hold harmless or indemnity agreement, part of the cost of injuries might be borne by the business that hired the contractor, which would reduce the contractor's incentives to take precautions. While this point is closely related to what you learned about the incentives provided by the tort liability system in Chapter 12, it is useful to provide a simple numerical example to make sure that you understand it.

Table 29.2 shows expected injury costs for different levels of precautions under two scenarios. Under the first scenario, the contractor bears the full cost of injuries and will minimize costs by spending $9,000 on precautions, producing expected injury costs of $6,000 and total expected costs of $15,000. The second scenario assumes that the contractor only bears 50 percent of injury costs, with the remainder borne by the firm that hires the contractor. In this case, the contractor will spend only $5,000 on precautions to minimize the contractor's costs. For the contractor this produces expected injury costs of $6,000 and expected total costs of $11,000. Expected total injury costs and expected total costs for both parties, however, will be $12,000 and $17,000, respectively. Thus, sharing responsibility between the contractor and the business that hires the contractor increases expected total costs by $2,000 ($17,000 − $15,000).

The business and the contractor can reduce expected total costs by $2,000 if the contractor spends $9,000 on precautions instead of $5,000. If the contractor agrees to hold harmless or indemnify the business, it will bear 100 percent of injury costs and spend the $9,000, thus minimizing total expected costs for the activity and allowing the business and the contractor to share the increased expected profit. The division of gains between the two parties will be affected by their negotiating skills and/or competitive conditions in the market for independent contractor services. However, the key point is that the parties have an incentive to enter into a hold harmless or indemnity agreement to provide incentives for cost minimization. This generally will be achieved by allocating responsibility to the party that is best able to control the risk.[6]

TABLE 29.2
Investment in loss control by a contractor (all costs in $1,000's).

	Contractor Bears Full Injury Cost			Contractor Bears 50% of Injury Cost	
Cost of Precautions	Expected Injury Cost	Expected Total Cost		Expected Injury Cost	Expected Total Cost
2	20	22		10	12
5	12	17		6	11
9	6	15		3	12
14	4	18		2	16

[6]It sometimes is argued that one of the parties might be better able to bear risk (e.g., by having access to insurance at more favorable terms), and that this might influence who holds whom harmless. While this possibly might have some effect in some cases, it still generally will be preferable to have the party best able to control the risk hold harmless or indemnify the other party. If the other party can buy insurance with a lower loading, then it could buy the insurance and charge the contractor for the protection.

Hold harmless and indemnity agreements typically require party A to hold harmless or indemnify party B only in the case that the injury is due to the *sole negligence of party A*. Enforcement of these contracts sometimes is challenged by party A. For example, party A may argue that it was coerced into signing the agreement, or that it did not agree to bear a particular type of risk. Some courts have held in these situations that the contract is enforceable only if there is a "clear and unequivocal evidence of the parties' intent" to shift risk. These types of disputes, which should be less common when valid liability insurance is in force to back the agreement, make it important for risk managers to draw up the agreements as clearly as possible, to be knowledgeable about applicable case law in different states, and to consider the likelihood that the other party might renege on its promise.

Many states will not enforce a contract where party A agrees to hold harmless or indemnify party B for injuries caused by the *sole negligence of party B* as against public policy, and there is little economic rationale for such agreements. Some hold harmless or indemnity agreements require party A to hold harmless or indemnify party B for injuries caused by the *joint negligence of A and B*. Some states will not enforce these agreements, which again indicates that many risk managers need to be familiar with differences in state practices.

A second motive for entering into hold harmless and indemnity agreements is to reduce dispute resolution costs in the event that an injury occurs. Absent this type of agreement, both parties may be held liable by the court, with one party ordered to pay. This party then will seek to recover all or part of the damages from the other party, thus producing significant dispute resolution costs (attorney fees and so forth). By helping to clarify who is responsible in advance, hold harmless and indemnity agreements make post-injury disputes between the parties less common. The process is not perfect; disputes sometimes arise despite the agreement. In addition, some types of hold harmless and indemnity agreements may not be enforceable in court (see Box 29.2).

The Role of Insurance

The party that agrees to hold harmless or indemnify the other party commonly is required to bond (back up) its promise to pay by purchasing liability insurance and providing evidence of insurance to the other party. The required purchase of liability insurance (or in some cases some other form of security, such as a bank letter of credit) further reduces the judgment proof problem. Moreover, the fact that liability insurance premiums are based on factors related to the contractor's expected claim costs, including information on prior claims experience, further enhances incentives for safety.

An important practical issue for risk managers is the type of evidence to require. Two main methods are used. First, the insurer may issue a **certificate of insurance** to the party that is to be held harmless or indemnified that indicates that the other party has insurance and the amount of coverage purchased. Second, the insurance policy may be endorsed to list the business that is to be held harmless or indemnified as an "additional named insured," thus making the business an insured party under the contract. Being named as an additional insured provides greater legal rights, and the business is more likely to be notified of changes in limits or cancellation of coverage on a timely basis than with a certificate of insurance.

In addition to liability insurance, independent contractors also are routinely required to provide evidence of workers' compensation insurance or qualified self-insurance for their employees. If the firm uses a contractor with employees who are not covered by workers' compensation (if, for example, the contractor has only one or two employees and is not required to be covered by workers' compensation in a given state), or if the contractor has violated the rules requiring insurance or qualified self-insurance, exclusive remedy may not apply in some jurisdictions. The business that hires the contractor then may be sued in tort for injuries to the contractor's employees. In other jurisdictions exclusive remedy may apply, but the firm that hires the contractor may be required to pay workers' compensation benefits to injured employees of the contractor.

Summary of Incentive Effects

Assuming that insurance is purchased in the business/independent contractor example, the role of legal rules and hold harmless and indemnity agreements backed by insurance in helping to minimize the cost of risk can be summarized briefly as follows. First, limits on the ability of businesses to shift legal liability risk to independent contractors encourage businesses to hire safe and financially sound contractors. Second, hold harmless and indemnity agreements are used to reallocate or clarify responsibility for damages in order to provide proper incentives for safety and reduce costly disputes between the parties. Third, the required purchase of insurance by the contractor helps guarantee that the contractor will honor the commitment, reduces the judgment proof problem, and further enhances incentives for safety by giving an advantage to safe contractors with good safety records.

Concept Check

3. Using the information in Table 29.2, how much would the contractor spend on safety without a hold harmless or indemnity agreement if it had to pay only 25 percent of injury costs? How much would the expected total cost of precautions and injuries increase compared to the case where the contractor has to hold harmless or indemnify the firm that hired it?

29.4   Claims Management and Administration

Liability and workers' compensation claims management and administration have a significant effect on the firm's cost of risk. In this section, we briefly address three issues: (1) general strategy, (2) monitoring the performance of insurers and third-party administrators, and (3) claim cost allocation to operating divisions or subsidiaries. Box 29.3 contains a number of practical tips for investigating and dealing with product liability claims.

General Claims Strategy

The overall strategic objective of liability and workers' compensation claims management is to minimize the expected sum of (1) claim costs, (2) claim settlement and dispute resolution costs, and (3) indirect costs such as adverse effects on the firm's reputation that could increase its cost of contracting with various parties. When insurance is purchased, the insurer bears defense costs and takes primary responsibility for negotiating and settling

What should a firm do when it gets the news that its product has injured someone? According to the *Journal of American Insurance*, there are a number of dos and don'ts, including:

- Act promptly, create a case file, and gather relevant information about the injury, who was involved, when the accident occurred, whether the product was used properly, and so on.

- Obtain and keep the product involved because it might be valuable as evidence.

- Do not make negative statements about the product, including comments about any prior com-plaints or problems with the product; instead, make positive statements about the product and the firm's concern with the customer.

- Try to be helpful and cooperative with the injured party, telling the person that the firm wants to be of assistance in dealing with the problem.

- Contact the firm's product liability insurer as soon as it becomes apparent that a material incident has oc-curred and definitely after the firm receives a sum-mons or complaint.

Source: "A Product Liability Guide for Manufacturers," *Journal of American Insurance*, Third Quarter, 1988.

claims. As we discuss further below, it is therefore important for the firm to pick an insurer that has a claims settlement strategy that is compatible with the firm's overall objective. Workers' compensation self-insurers that use a third-party administrator also need to choose an administrator with compatible objectives.

While many strategic issues are similar for liability and workers' compensation claims, the fact that employers are required to pay valid claims without regard to fault or negligence and the closer, ongoing relationship between employers and employees than between em-ployers and tort liability claimants, such as customers, can give rise to differences in strat-egy. Employers usually have strong economic incentives to pay legitimate workers' compensation claims promptly without having the employee retain legal counsel with as-sociated increases in dispute resolution costs. In addition, in the long run, both employers and employees have an interest in controlling the cost of claims. Nonetheless, problems can arise for injuries that are difficult to verify and measure with the result that settlement of these claims often is more similar to liability claims. We comment further on these and other differences between liability and workers' compensation claims where appropriate.

Incentives to Settle

Over 90 percent of tort liability cases settle without trial, and a similarly large proportion of workers' compensation claims are settled without a hearing before either a workers' com-pensation insurance commissioner or judge. Defendants and plaintiffs in liability cases both have strong incentives to settle before trial, because avoiding trial reduces legal costs for both parties. In addition, the parties usually are risk averse (or, in the case of businesses, have incentives to behave as though they were risk averse). Settling before trial avoids the uncer-tainty associated with the outcome of a trial. Cases that go to trial usually involve either mu-tual optimism by the parties (i.e., they both expect a good result from a trial) or have much larger stakes due to reputation effects or effects on the settlement of other suits (see below).

Workers' compensation claims commonly settle before formal dispute resolution be-cause the injury is clearly work-related and there are no factual disputes about the required benefit payment. For cases where it is not clear that the injury is work-related or where the extent of disability is unclear, settlement before formal dispute resolution again reduces legal costs and avoids the uncertainty associated with a hearing.

Reputation Effects

In some cases, defendants have an additional incentive to resist claims and avoid settlement when admitting liability may damage their reputation for safety with an adverse effect on their future ability to sell goods and services. For example, before medical malpractice suits became commonplace beginning in the 1970s, physicians were reluctant to settle claims because it would be construed as an admission of malpractice that might lead to significant damage to the physician's ability to practice, including the ability to obtain referrals from other physicians. For this reason, older malpractice policies did not give malpractice insurers the right to settle. This aversion to settlement declined as malpractice suits became more widespread (and thus less scandalous and less indicative of poor practice). Malpractice insurance now often gives insurers the right to settle just as is the case for most other types of liability insurance.

In other cases, refusing to settle or perceived excessive toughness in negotiations might damage a business's reputation. For example, if these actions receive extensive negative publicity that makes the business look stingy (e.g., they are the subject of a "60 Minutes" episode), there may be significant damage to the firm's general reputation that adversely affects sales. With respect to injured employees, an aggressive posture in trying to settle permanent partial disability claims for the lowest possible amount and/or to get workers back to work early might damage the firm's relations with other workers and make it more costly for the firm to attract and retain employees.

Effects of Multiple Suits

If a defendant in a liability case or an employer in certain types of difficult-to-value workers' compensation cases will likely face many similar claims over time, the incentive to spend more resources to achieve a favorable outcome increases if this outcome will establish a precedent for other cases. For example, the defendant business or employer may attempt to establish a reputation for toughness in negotiation that will lower costs for other claims. Some observers suggest that this incentive stacks the deck in favor of corporate defendants or employers against individual plaintiffs or employees. The counterargument is that liability plaintiffs' attorneys and attorneys that represent injured workers will in many cases also have greater incentives to achieve a favorable outcome that could influence other cases.

A related issue is when one or both parties desire to keep the details of a settlement private in order to not have the settlement influence other litigation. In these cases, the party that desires privacy (in a liability case usually the defendant who does not want the details to increase demands by plaintiffs in other cases) may be willing to offer a more generous settlement in order to keep the details private in what is known as a "sealed settlement." A number of states have recently enacted laws to prohibit this practice.

Nuisance Suits and Fraud

A nuisance suit is a suit where the plaintiff's case is known to be very weak by both parties. In these cases, the defendant often will nonetheless minimize the sum of defense and claim costs by offering to settle the case for an amount that essentially buys off the plaintiff to save on defense costs. A limitation of this strategy is that it may increase the frequency of similar suits. As a result, a key strategic decision is whether to invest significant amounts of money fighting these low-value suits in an attempt to establish a reputation for toughness and thereby deter these types of suits.

Fraudulent or exaggerated workers' compensation claims raise similar issues. The employer has to decide whether to incur greater costs fighting these claims in the short run with the hope of reducing the present value of total costs over time. This decision must consider the possible adverse effects on legitimate claimants. While fraud might be suspected, in some cases the claim may be legitimate. Fighting the claim will harm the employee with possible adverse effects on relations with other employees.

Releases and Advance Payments

Payments are not made to most plaintiffs in liability cases unless the plaintiff signs a contract known as a **release,** which releases the defendant from any obligation to make additional payments. **Advance payments** are payments made by the defendant (or insurer) to the plaintiff prior to receiving a release. Possible advantages to advance payments are: (1) they might sometimes reduce harm to the plaintiff and thus damages in some instances (e.g., paying the plaintiff's expenses to get necessary medical treatment), and (2) they might ultimately encourage a more favorable settlement if the plaintiff has a cooperative attitude and/or is uncomfortable with litigation.

Advance payments generally will be disadvantageous in cases where it is not clear that the defendant is liable as they may be construed as an admission of liability. A serious drawback to advance payments in many other instances is that they can significantly reduce the incentive for a noncooperative plaintiff to settle the case. A major factor that creates pressure for plaintiffs to settle is that they do not want to wait for the money.

Lump Sum versus Structured Settlements

The vast majority of liability suits are settled with a lump sum payment. Large settlements sometimes are paid over time, however, in what is called a **structured settlement.** The typical practice is for the defendant or the defendant's insurer to purchase an annuity contract to make periodic payments to the plaintiff instead of a lump sum settlement. In some cases these deals have been arranged to provide the annuity payment at a lower after-tax cost than would be the case if the plaintiff were paid a lump sum and then to purchase an annuity on their own from the proceeds. This cost savings has allowed the structured settlement to be advantageous to both the plaintiff and the defendant.

As noted in Chapter 18, most workers' compensation claims for permanent disability are settled in a lump sum rather than paid over time. Workers (and any legal counsel) usually prefer lump sum payments. Lump sum awards also avoid the disincentive for work that can arise with periodic benefit payments given that these benefits normally cease if the recipient returns to work.

Monitoring Performance of Insurers and Outside Contractors

Bundling responsibility for settling and paying claims in liability insurance contracts generally provides strong incentives for the insurer to minimize the sum of claim payments and claim settlement costs. This result also generally holds for insured workers' compensation claims. There are a number of issues that firms need to consider when selecting an insurer and evaluating insurer performance.

Recall that insurers usually are legally responsible for defending and settling claims and that they have the legal authority to settle claims. In the case of potentially large liability claims that could have significant adverse reputation effects or could affect other claims in the future that might not be insured by the same insurer, risk managers will need to select insurers that will be willing to work closely with the firm to meet its objectives in view of these issues. However, advance agreement on strategy and an appropriate price may be difficult when there is substantial uncertainty about the types of losses that could occur and the possible effects of different settlement strategies. In some cases it may be possible for insurers and their policyholders to agree on a strategy for dealing with such claims after they occur, perhaps including price concessions or adjustments to achieve a mutually beneficial result. In other cases, disagreements over settlement strategy may arise that result in a termination of the relationship or litigation between the firm and its insurer.

A related issue is the possible incentive conflict that can arise between a liability insurer and a policyholder in cases where it may be fairly obvious that the claim will ultimately settle for an amount equal to or greater than the policy limit. The insurer might then be tempted to delay paying the claim as long as possible to maintain use of the funds. If this behavior occurs, it may expose the policyholder to risk that the amount ultimately needed to settle the claim will increase (i.e., forcing the plaintiff to wait can increase the amount demanded to settle the case). Because the increase in the settlement amount is in excess of the policy limit, the policyholder will be responsible for the increased cost.

Insurer incentives to engage in this type of behavior are mitigated by: (1) an interest in having a long-term relationship with the policyholder, (2) possible adverse effects on the insurer's reputation and thus the insurer's ability to sell or renew coverage to other parties, and (3) the possibility that the policyholder or injured party might successfully sue the insurer for failing to negotiate in good faith. In addition, risk managers can reduce this risk by carefully selecting an insurer and monitoring the insurer's settlement efforts after the claim.

When liability claims are not insured, firms sometimes will have to employ outside attorneys. For self-insured workers' compensation claims, firms often find it desirable to use outside administrators (third-party administrators or TPAs) given the specialized expertise of these firms and the possible advantage of having a third party intervene in potentially adversarial situations between the employer and the employee.[7] In these situations, the outside attorneys and claims administrators are paid by fees. In contrast to insurers, they are not responsible for paying the cost of claims. As a result, they may have less incentive to pursue strategies that reduce claim costs and thus total costs for firms that use their services. Risk managers need to select these parties carefully, based on their reputations for quality, and monitor their performance over time.

A problem that often arises in practice is how to determine whether a TPA has done a good job in controlling costs. In some cases, data may be available to compare the average claim costs (or other variables such as the average time needed to settle a claim) for a particular TPA to other TPAs or to workers' compensation insurers. Risk managers also can review and compare factors such as the TPA's pursuit of subrogation rights and second injury fund recoveries to gather additional information about performance.

---

[7]TPAs also are often used for self-insured medical insurance claims.

Claim Cost Allocation

An important practical issue associated with administering liability and workers' compensation claims is how to best allocate costs to operating divisions (or subsidiaries). The method used to allocate costs can have a material impact on (1) managers' incentives to control costs, (2) performance measures for the divisions, and thus (3) managerial compensation, to the extent that it is linked to these performance measures. A general principle is that if division managers have information and authority to make decisions to control certain types of costs, then it is desirable to allocate these costs to the division to increase incentives for cost control.

When claims are insured, cost allocations often can be made by allocating relevant premiums for liability or workers' compensation coverage. For uninsured claims, the firm needs to decide how to allocate claim costs in view of the fact that realized costs in a given period may be highly variable due to random fluctuations. If claim costs turn out to be very high in a given period due to chance (bad luck), allocating the entire cost will give a distorted picture of performance, and it may expose managers to excessive risk if their compensation is directly linked to a performance measure that reflects the entire cost of claims.

For this reason it often will be desirable to smooth cost allocations over time. For example, the division might be charged an amount based on a moving average of costs in the current and prior years. Sometimes this process is taken one step further by attempting to estimate and charge for expected costs using methods similar to those that would be used by insurers, including the use of experience-rating charges. Although use of a captive is not essential, these approaches often are formalized when the firm has a captive insurer. Premiums paid by divisions to the captive allocate the cost of claims across divisions.

Concept Check

4. Reinterpret the example in Table 29.2 to explain how allocating all relevant expected injury costs to a division manager can provide the manager with incentives to invest in loss control to minimize the cost of risk.

29.5 Summary

- The doctrine of limited liability limits the liability of corporate shareholders to the value of their equity investment. The protection provided by limited liability is analogous to insurance protection against large tort liability claims for both individual shareholders of a corporation and a parent corporation with multiple subsidiaries.

- Like insurance in general, limited liability can lead to moral hazard and excessive risk of injury because corporations might not have to pay for all of the harm they might cause from risky activities.

- Courts sometimes allow tort claimants to recover from corporate parents for torts of subsidiary corporations if the subsidiary's assets are insufficient

to pay damages. Known as piercing the corporate veil, allowing recovery from parent corporations is most likely when moral hazard is severe and the social benefits of limited liability are negligible.

- Principals generally are liable for the torts of their agents, which include liability of employers for torts of employees in the course of their employment. Firms that use independent contractors often can be held liable for torts of the contractor in order to mitigate the judgment proof problem and encourage safety.

- Hold harmless/indemnity agreements backed by liability insurance help reduce the cost of risk by allocating the ultimate responsibility for harm to the party best able to reduce injury costs and by reducing costly disputes between the parties.

- Risk aversion and savings on dispute resolution costs motivate plaintiffs and defendants to settle most cases before trial. The general overall goal of defense and claims settlement for businesses that face tort liability claims is to minimize the expected total costs of damages and defense.

Factors that influence strategy in specific instances include potential adverse effects of fighting claims on a firm's reputation and the effects of settlement on the frequency and severity of other suits.

- Appropriate procedures for allocating injury costs to divisions or subsidiaries can improve incentives to control costs and thus reduce the cost of risk.

Key Terms

piercing the corporate veil 631
vicarious liability 632
nondelegable duty 633
hold harmless agreement 634
indemnity agreement 634

certificate of insurance 636
release 640
advance payments 640
structured settlement 640

Questions and Problems

1. A corporation has assets of $200 million and owes $80 million to a bank. Given limited liability, what is the maximum amount of loss to the corporation's shareholders from tort claims? What is the maximum loss to the bank from tort claims against the corporation? Explain how the bank is providing implicit liability insurance to the corporation's shareholders. Also explain how the bank can charge a premium for this insurance.

2. Rework the example in Table 29.1 assuming that each subsidiary has assets of $40 million. Then rework the example assuming that each subsidiary has assets of $50 million and that the probability of a tort liability suit increases to 0.02 for each subsidiary. Does limited liability of the parent for torts of the subsidiaries reduce risk for the parent in the latter case? Why or why not?

3. Other things being equal, is the moral hazard problem associated with limited liability likely to be worse for firms with substantial profitable future investment opportunities or firms that have few if any such opportunities? Explain.

4. Other things being equal, is the moral hazard problem associated with limited liability likely to be worse for the risk of product-related injuries to consumers or for the risk of environmental damage to the public? Explain.

5. You have just inherited $10 million. Rather than kicking back and avoiding all work, you are contemplating starting and operating a landscaping business with a friend that would require each of you to invest $5,000 for equipment. Your friend suggests that the business be formed as a corporation so that you won't have to buy a lot of expensive liability insurance to protect your inheritance from tort claims from people that you conceivably might injure. Given your knowledge of veil piercing, what do you tell your friend?

6. Argue the case for eliminating the limited liability of parent corporations for tort liability claims from parties that do not have a contractual relationship with the firm. Then argue the case for keeping limited liability in these situations.

7. Firms A and B form a joint venture to produce and service machines used by tire manufacturers. Firm A will build the machines; firm B will set up the machines and perform maintenance. What type of hold harmless or indemnity contracts should the firms enter into in order to minimize the cost of risk associated with possible tort liability claims from workers who are injured by the machines?

8. A business faces a nuisance suit that demands \$5,000 in damages. The business and the plaintiff both know that no damages will be awarded if the case goes to court. It will cost the business \$3,000 to fight the case and win in court. Ignoring the timing of payments, the time value of money, and the possible effect of settlement on other cases, what is the maximum settlement offer that the firm will make?

9. Consider the same scenario in question 8 and assume that the firm can settle the case for \$2,000. Also assume that if the firm settles the case, it will face nine identical cases in the future. If the firm refuses to settle, it will discourage some of these suits. Again ignoring the time value of money, how many suits would have to be deterred in order for the firm to minimize its costs by refusing to settle any suits versus settling each suit for \$2,000?

10. Liability insurance contracts generally require the insurer to defend policyholders (and incur the cost of defense) and give the insurer the right to settle suits. Explain why these provisions in the contract are normally desirable from the standpoint of policyholders who must pay for the cost of coverage. Also describe circumstances where conflicts over defense/settlement strategy might arise between the liability insurer and the policyholder.

Answers to Concept Checks

1. Because of limited liability, a firm may not have to pay the entire cost of harm that it causes to other parties. Unless these parties can induce the firm to consider the full cost of potential harm by somehow charging the firm an appropriate price, the firm has less incentive to avoid activities that may give rise to large injury costs, especially since any profits from the risky activities will accrue to the firm.

2. Because of limited liability, the expected cost of liability claims for a small construction firm with no liability insurance or assets at risk will be smaller than the expected cost of injuries to other parties because the firm will be judgment proof, at least for sizable losses. In contrast, a comparable business that buys liability insurance will bear the expected cost of liability claims up to the limit of the policy because the insurance premium will reflect these expected costs. (Liability insurance will not eliminate moral hazard, however, because of imperfect experience rating and the fact that the magnitude of harm to other parties could exceed the limit of insurance.)

3. A revised version of Table 29.2 follows for the case where the contractor has to pay only 25 percent of injury costs:

Investment in Loss Control by Contractor ($1,000s)

Cost of Precautions	Contractor Bears Full Injury Cost		Contractor Bears 25% of Injury Cost	
	Expected Injury Cost	Expected Total Cost	Expected Injury Cost	Expected Total Cost
2	20	22	5	7
5	12	17	3	8
9	6	15	1.5	10.5
14	4	18	1	15

The contractor would minimize its expected total cost by spending $2,000, which would produce expected total costs of $7,000 to the contractor. The expected injury cost if $2,000 is spent on precautions is $20,000, producing total expected costs of $22,000. If the contractor has to indemnify or hold harmless the firm that hired it, it would spend $9,000 on precautions, producing total expected costs of $15,000. Thus, the total expected cost increases by $7,000 (from $15,000 to $22,000) if the contractor has to pay only 25 percent of injury costs.

4. Apart from other influences (e.g., monitoring by senior managers), a division manager that is only charged with a portion of expected injury costs might have incentives comparable to a contractor that has to bear only part of injury costs. Thus, the division manager might spend too little on precautions (e.g., less than $9,000) in order to increase the expected income of the division. Allocating all relevant expected injury costs to the manager would increase his or her incentives to spend the optimal amount on precautions ($9,000).

References

Cooter, Robert D.; and Daniel L. Rubinfield. "Economic Analysis of Legal Disputes and Their Resolution." *Journal of Economic Literature* 27 (1989), pp. 1067–97. (*Detailed discussion of the economics of negotiating and settling liability claims.*)

Easterbrook, Frank; and Daniel Fischel. "Limited Liability and the Corporation." *University of Chicago Law Review* 52 (1989), pp. 89–117. (*Detailed discussion of the rationale for limited liability and its incentive effects.*)

Sykes, Alan O. "The Economics of Vicarious Liability." *Yak Law Journal* 93 (1984), pp. 1231–1280. (*In-depth treatment of the economics of vicarious liability.*)

Index

CHAPTERS 16-18 focus on risk management and insurance issues arising in the employee-employer relationship.

CHAPTERS 20-29 focus on business risk management.

CHAPTERS 20-22 provide a detailed explanation of the theory of why firms seek to reduce risk even when their owners are well-diversified and provide examples and evidence on how the theory can be and is applied in practice.